Conrad Poulsen
3271 WEAVER RD
L2E 6S6

DEDICATED TO

THE AMERICAN INSTITUTE OF ARCHITECTS

"The objects of the Institute are to organize and unite in fellowship the architects of the United States of America; to combine their efforts so as to promote the aesthetic, scientific, and practical efficiency of the profession; to advance the science and art of planning and building by advancing the standards of architectural education, training, and practice; to coordinate the building industry and the profession of architecture to insure the advancement of the living standards of our people through their improved environment; and to make the profession of increasing service to society."

ARCHITECTURAL

for Architects, Engineers, Decorators, Builders, Draftsmen and Students

FIFTH EDITION

GRAPHIC STANDARDS

CHARLES GEORGE RAMSEY, A.I.A.

The Late HAROLD REEVE SLEEPER, F.A.I.A.

JOHN WILEY & SONS, INC.

NEW YORK • LONDON • SYDNEY

23 22 21 20 19 18 17

Printed in the United States of America

FOREWORD

I am honored to write a foreword to the Fifth Edition of *Architectural Graphic Standards.* I can do no better than to add my endorsement to the opinions of the late Frederick Ackerman, who wrote the foreword to the first three Editions, and Ralph Walker, who performed this service for the Fourth Edition.

Both of them pointed out that such an encyclopedic handbook as this is an essential part of architectural practice. It gathers into one well-organized source the vast and important factual references which are necessary to the architect, draftsman and builder but which are too complex to be memorized and too scattered to be available in the files of any office.

The value of such a book depends basically on two things. One is the judgment as well as the thoroughness of its editors—and thus its worth is a reflection of the experience and enlightenment of Harold R. Sleeper and Charles G. Ramsey. The other is its contemporaneity. The Fifth Edition—revised, increased, including information on problems not even dreamed of at the time of the First Edition in 1932—brings the book up to date.

Just as Vitruvius gives us understanding of the vocabulary of Renaissance architects, so *Architectural Graphic Standards* will show the future the dizzy speed and expanding horizons of architectural developments and practice in our time.

EERO SAARINEN

May 1956

PREFACE

Since the publication of the Fourth Edition of *Architectural Graphic Standards* five years ago, the building industry has made great strides, new techniques have been developed, new standards have been made and others have been changed.

Our goal for the Fifth Edition was to include all these new developments as well as to bring standards up to date and to include such data, previously omitted, as now appears useful.

What this would entail was unknown until our staff had spent two and a half years of necessary research and work.

However, we do feel our goal has been achieved and the Fifth Edition of *Architectural Graphic Standards* is complete and ready for your use.

Every page of the Fourth Edition was first analyzed, then checked and reviewed. If no great change was indicated, pages were sent out for comments and criticisms. Many pages were scrapped and new ones substituted. New pages were developed for added subjects with the help of various associations, manufacturers or individuals. When completed, every page was finally reviewed by the best qualified organization or person.

We have been greatly benefited in securing data, technical material and advice from persons and organizations for this edition because of the present wide acceptance of the book by the building industry.

The problem "how to keep the volume within bounds of usefulness in weight and size" was alleviated greatly by the publication late last year of *Building Planning and Design Standards* by Harold R. Sleeper. Pages relevant to specific types of building were revised and published in that book. These books may be used as companion volumes. Which volume to consult may be decided by asking:

Is it a question or item of a general nature that may occur in a variety of buildings? If so, consult *Architectural Graphic Standards.*

Is it a question pertaining to a specific type of building? Then use *Building Planning and Design Standards.*

In all, some 38 pages from the Fourth Edition were omitted, thus making room for new material. Our desire to limit the size and weight of this

Edition has been further assisted by cutting the weight of paper. So, in spite of the additions of 161 pages of drawings, no noticeable increase in weight or size has occurred.

Although standards or data no longer currently used have generally been omitted, a few such pages have been retained; for instance, on the advice of our mechanical engineers, a page on an obsolete type of radiator has been retained for alteration work.

The entire order and make-up of the Fifth Edition have been rearranged. The contents have been grouped into twenty-three sections, each with its own table of contents. These groups are shown on the inside of the front and back covers for those who are interested in one entire subject rather than a specific item.

The index has been modified and clarified by a change in format that makes it more readily useful.

Besides adding new pages relative to new subjects, many old subjects have been redrawn in toto. For instance, the entire section on furring, lathing and plastering was deleted and re-created with many added pages.

The hundreds of companies, associations, consultants and advisors are given acknowledgment on the pages to which they contributed. We wish to thank them for their generous aid.

Special thanks are due the following consultants for their contribution and excellent advice:

Anthony J. Amendola, A.I.A. (Food Service Equipment)
Prentice Bradley, A.I.A. (Modular Coordination)
Ralph Eberlin, Consulting Engineer (Site Engineering)
Andre Halasz, A.I.A.
Leo Novick, Landscape Architect
Mongitore & Moesel, Consulting Engineers (Mechanical Work)
Daniel Schwartzman, A.I.A.
Elwyn E. Seelye, Consulting Engineer (Structural Work)
Frederic N. Whitley, P.E., Consulting Fireplace Engineer

We are grateful to the many architects who have suggested subject matter for inclusion in this Edition. The authors' most irksome duty, that of selection, was guided by such thoughtful advice. There is no limit to what might have been included except that of the size of the volume. We hope that our choice will prove useful and adequate.

The revision of this book, an immense task, has been possible because of a devoted task force working for two and a half years. This work could not have been done by the authors alone, as it was in the earlier Editions.

Our grateful thanks are due:

John D. Chase, for his excellent direction of this work, and to Laurel Anderson, Joanna Arfman, Warren E. Bendixon, Marian Dorr-Dorynek, Paul Hertgen, Robert J. Jacuruso, Edwin T. Kehrle, George Klett, Jane F. Patton, Fred Y. Senftleber, Francis J. Sheridan, Paula J. Treder.

CHARLES G. RAMSEY
HAROLD R. SLEEPER

June 1956

CONTENTS

FOOTINGS, FOUNDATIONS and RETAINING WALLS

TABLE OF CONTENTS

SOIL BEARING TEST

TESTING PROCEDURE

1. Make test on leveled but otherwise undisturbed portions of bearing material.
2. When tests are sufficiently below ground level, remove material immediately adjoining test location.
3. Test assembly consists of a vertical timber or post, with or without braced timber footing, resting upon soil to be tested and supporting a platform on which test loads are to be placed.
4. Exact area resting on soil may be not less than 1 sq. ft. for bearing materials of classes 1 thru 4 (see table "Soil Bearing Values") and not less than 4 sq. ft. for other bearing materials.
5. Platform to be symmetrical in respect to post and as close to soil as practicable.
6. Maintain post vertically by guys or wedges.
7. Load may be any convenient material which can be applied in required increments. EX: cement or sand in bags, pig iron or steel in bars.
8. Take all possible precautions to prevent jarring or moving post while applying load.
9. Take settlement readings at least once every 24 hours at a point which remains undisturbed during test.
10. Plot settlement against time.
11. Apply proposed allowable load per sq. ft. and allow to remain undisturbed until there has been no settlement for 24 hours.

NOTES FOR THE TEST ASSEMBLY SHOWN:

1. Load per sq. ft. on soil equals ¼ of load on platform times Y/Z, plus approximately 500 lbs. for the test assembly.
2. Establish bench mark before steel plate and 6"x8"s are in place, in order to include the weight of the test assembly.

SOIL BEARING VALUES*

CLASS	MATERIAL	Allowable bearing tons/sq. ft.	
1	Massive crystalline bed rocks (granite, gneiss, trap rock, etc.) in sound condition.	100	
2	Foliated rocks (bedded limestones; schist, slate) sound cond'n.	40	
3	Sedimentary rocks (hard shales, siltstones, sandstones, soft limestones), sound condition.	15	
4	Hard pan; gravel, sands, exceptionally compacted.	10	
5	Gravel, sand-gravel mixtures; compact.	6	
6	Gravel, loose; coarse sand, compact.	4	
7	Coarse sand, loose; sand-gravel mixtures, loose; fine sand, compact; coarse sand, wet, confined.	3	
8	Fine sand, loose; fine sand, wet, confined.	2	
9	Stiff clay.	4	
10	Medium stiff clay.	2	2.5**
11	Soft clay.	1	1.5**

*Based on data in N.Y. State Illustrated Code Manual (1953) and Nat'l Bldg Code (1949)

**Nat'l Bldg. Code recommendations

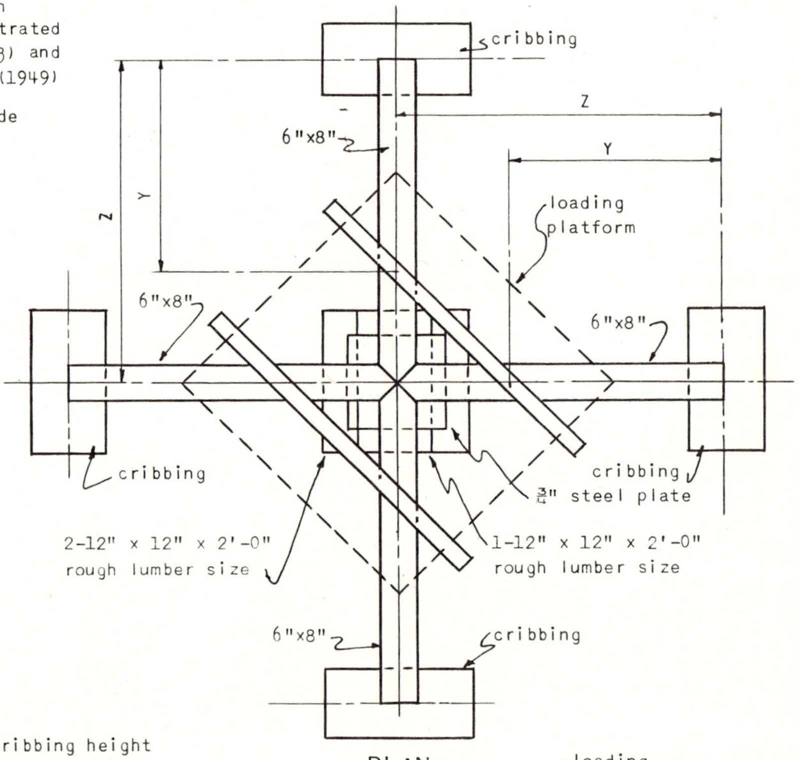
cribbing
6"x8"
Z
Y
loading platform
6"x8"
6"x8"
cribbing
cribbing
¾" steel plate
2-12" x 12" x 2'-0" rough lumber size
1-12" x 12" x 2'-0" rough lumber size
6"x8"
cribbing

PLAN

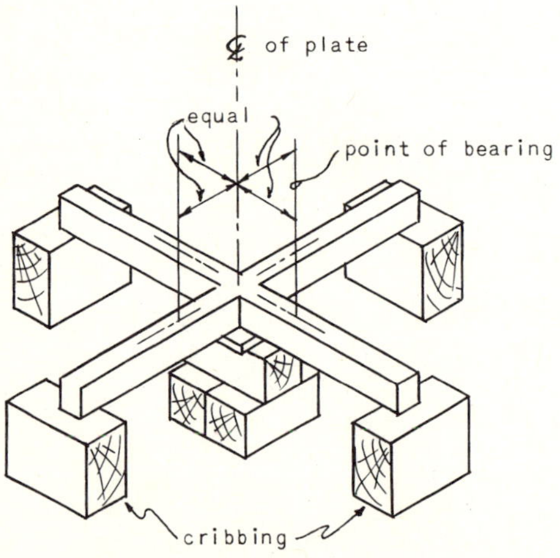
℄ of plate
equal
point of bearing
cribbing

BEARING OF LOADING PLATFORM

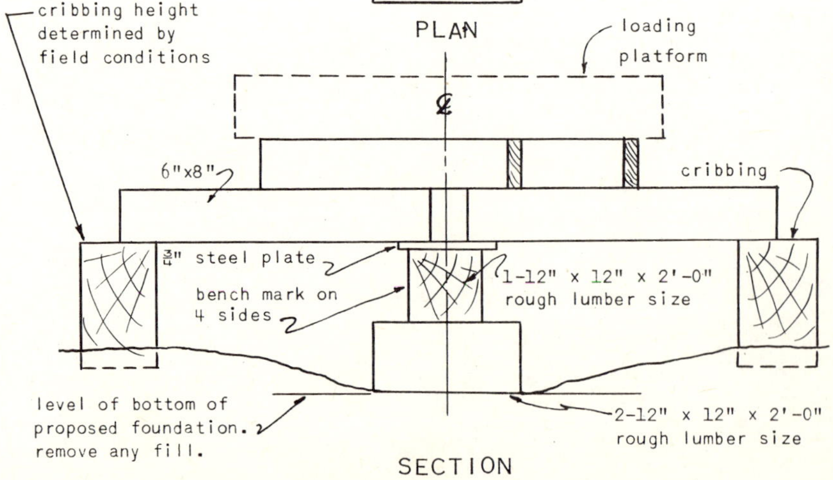
cribbing height determined by field conditions
loading platform
℄
6"x8"
cribbing
¾" steel plate
bench mark on 4 sides
1-12" x 12" x 2'-0" rough lumber size
level of bottom of proposed foundation. remove any fill.
2-12" x 12" x 2'-0" rough lumber size

SECTION

PILES

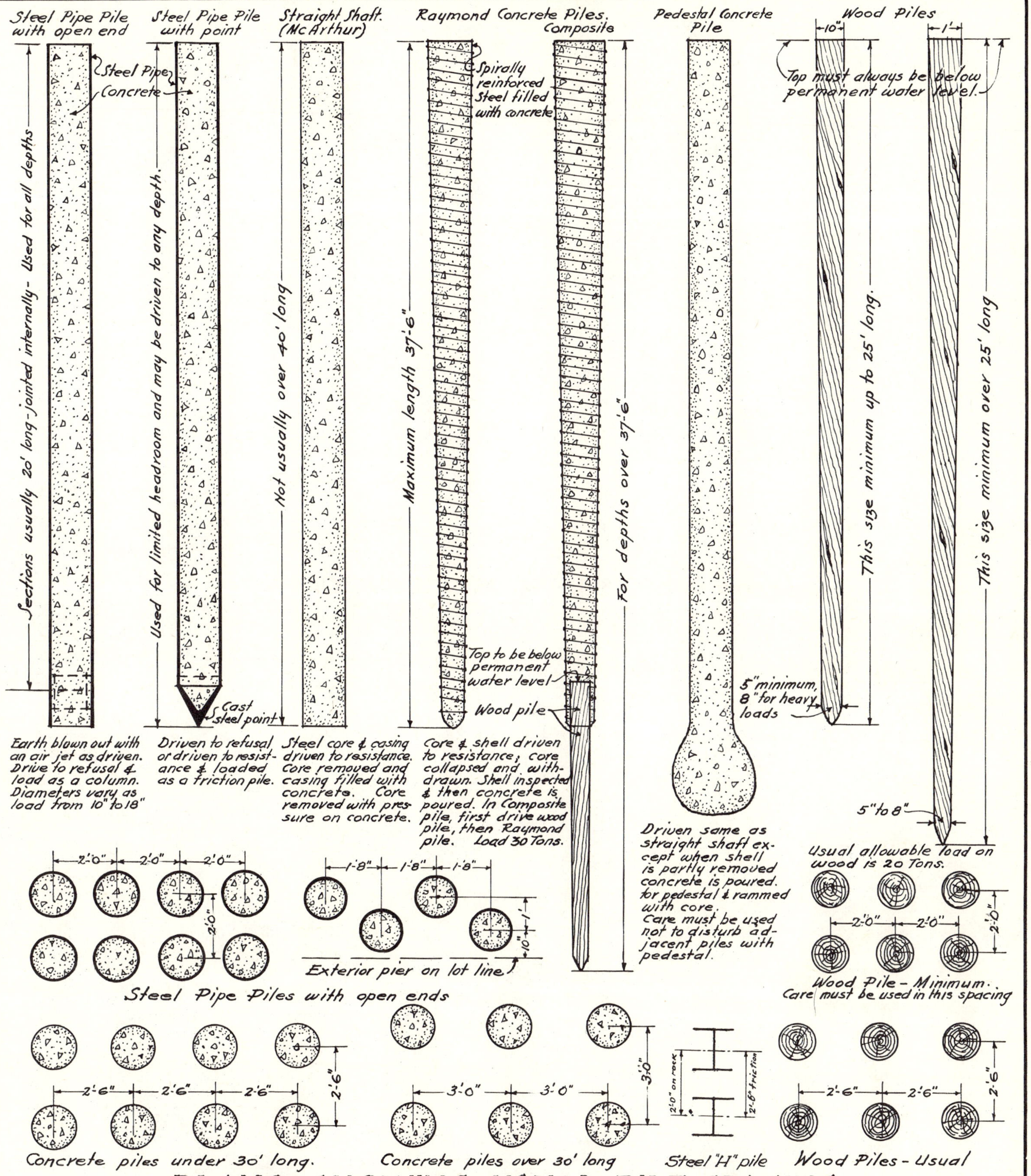
Steel Pipe Pile with open end
Steel Pipe Pile with point
Straight Shaft. (McArthur)
Raymond Concrete Piles.
Composite
Pedestal Concrete Pile
Wood Piles
Steel Pipe
Concrete
Sections usually 20' long-jointed internally- Used for all depths
Used for limited headroom and may be driven to any depth.
Cast steel point
Not usually over 40' long
Spirally reinforced Steel filled with concrete
Maximum length 37'-6"
For depths over 37'-6"
Top to be below permanent water level
Wood pile
10"
1'
Top must always be below permanent water level.
This size minimum up to 25' long.
This size minimum over 25' long
5" minimum, 8" for heavy loads
5" to 8"
Earth blown out with an air jet as driven. Drive to refusal & load as a column. Diameters vary as load from 10" to 18"
Driven to refusal or driven to resistance & loaded as a friction pile.
Steel core & casing driven to resistance. Core removed and casing filled with concrete. Core removed with pressure on concrete.
Core & shell driven to resistance; core collapsed and withdrawn. Shell inspected & then concrete is poured. In Composite pile, first drive wood pile, then Raymond pile. Load 30 Tons.
Driven same as straight shaft except when shell is partly removed concrete is poured. for pedestal & rammed with core. Care must be used not to disturb adjacent piles with pedestal.
Usual allowable load on wood is 20 Tons.
2'-0"
1'-8"
1'
10"
Exterior pier on lot line
Steel Pipe Piles with open ends
Wood Pile - Minimum. Care must be used in this spacing
2'-6"
3'-0"
2'-0" on rock
2'-6" friction
Concrete piles under 30' long.
Concrete piles over 30' long
Steel "H" pile
Wood Piles - Usual

PLANS SHOWING USUAL PILE SPACING

Pre-cast Piles of Concrete are made in a variety of sizes & used largely in Marine work.
The Engineering News Formula is usually used in figuring resistance to penetration - it is :-

$L = \frac{2WH}{S+0.1}$ L = load. W = Weight in pounds of falling part. H = drop in feet of falling part. S = penetration per blow in."

A #1 Steamhammer has weight of 5000 lbs falling 36". A #2 steamhammer has weight of 3000 lbs falling 30"

1/4" = 1'-0"

Data checked by: Elwyn E. Seelye, Consulting Engineer.

BUILDING LAYOUT - FOOTINGS

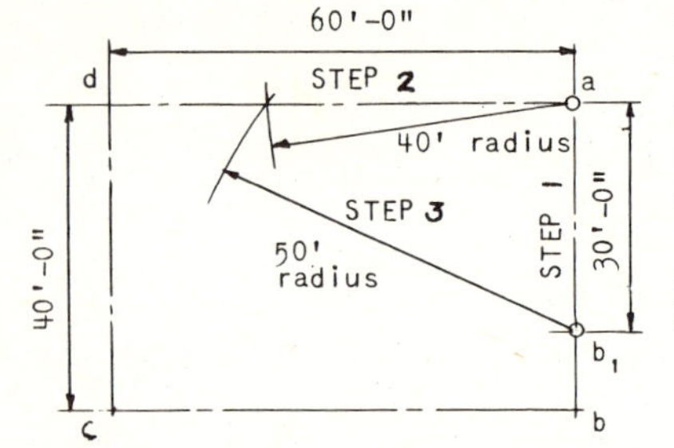
60'-0"
d
a
STEP 2
40' radius
STEP 3
50' radius
STEP 1
30'-0"
40'-0"
b1
c
b

DIAGRAM NO. 1: SQUARING BUILDING LINES WITH TAPE

STEPS 1, 2 & 3 are shown above.

"a" may be any corner of bldg. "ab" may be taken along any side of bldg.

STEP 4: Extend lines to actual length of walls (lengths shown are assumed, to complete STEPS 1, 2, 3) and drive stakes in all other corners of bldg.

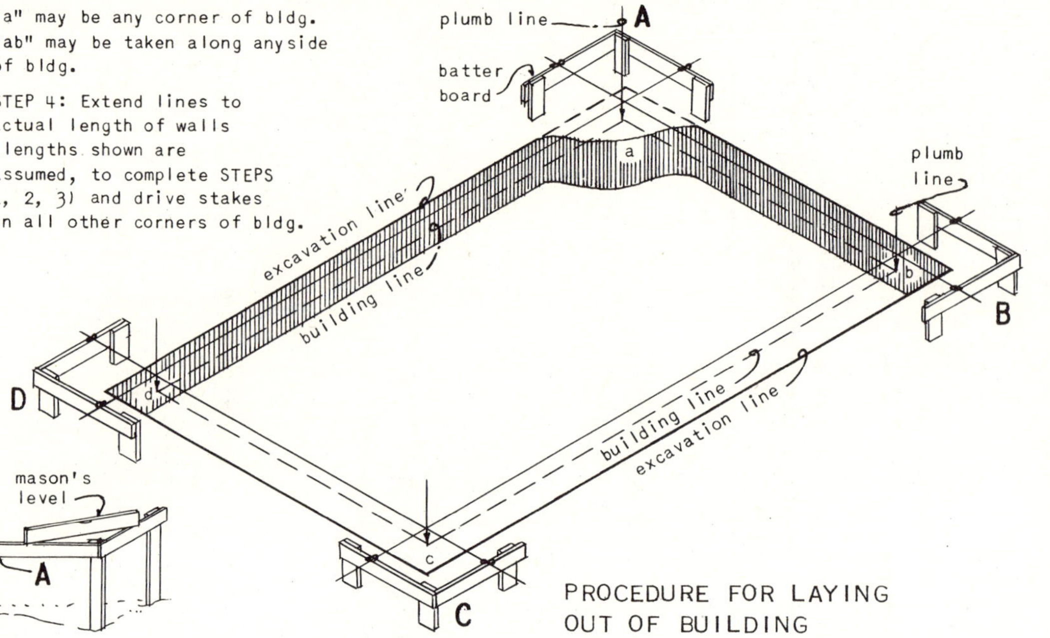
plumb line
A
batter board
a
plumb line
excavation line
building line
b
B
D
d
building line
excavation line
c
C

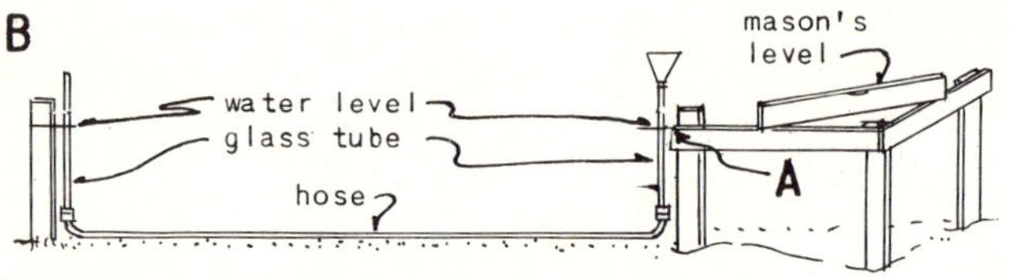
B
mason's level
water level
glass tube
hose
A

DIAGRAM NO. 2: LEVELING BATTER BOARDS WITHOUT TRANSIT.

1. Fill hose until water reaches top of batter board (A)
2. Mark off level on stake (B).
3. Place top of batter board at B.

PROCEDURE FOR LAYING OUT OF BUILDING

1. Square corners of building lines (Diagram 1).
2. Drive stakes A, B, C, D 4' to 10' from a, b, c, d respectively.
3. Erect batter boards to A, B, C, D. Use hosed funnel to get same elevation for all batter boards (Diagram 2).
4. String building lines to pass directly over a, b, c, d (Use plumb line) and tie to batter boards.
5. Establish foundation and excavation lines from building line.

LAYING OUT OF BUILDING AND FOUNDATION LINES

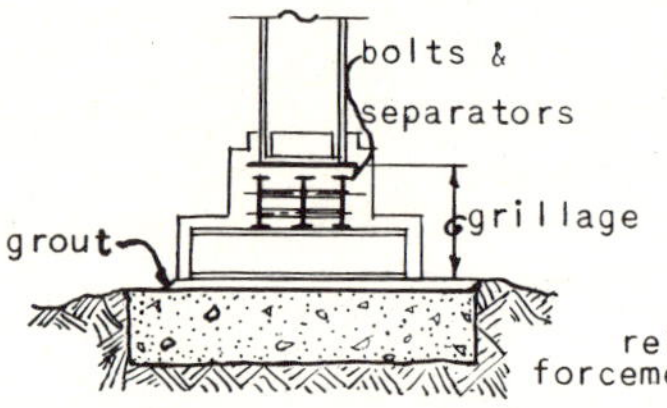
bolts & separators
grillage
grout

STEEL GRILLAGE FOUNDATION

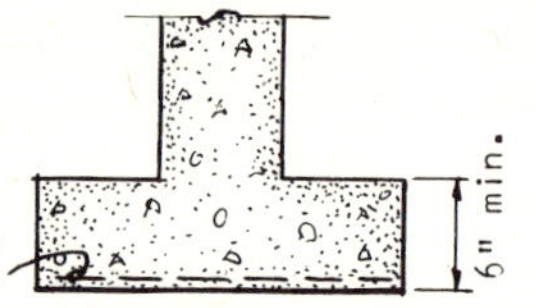
A
rein-forcement
6" min.

FOOTING FOR HEAVY WALL
Cantilever Span type

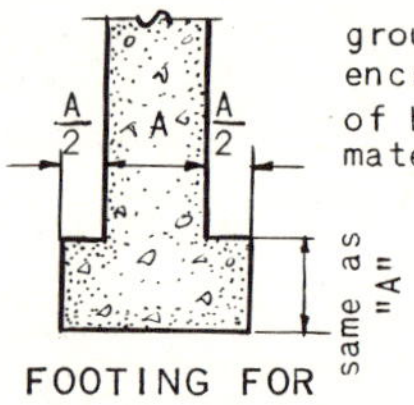
A/2
A
A/2
same as "A"

FOOTING FOR LIGHT WALL

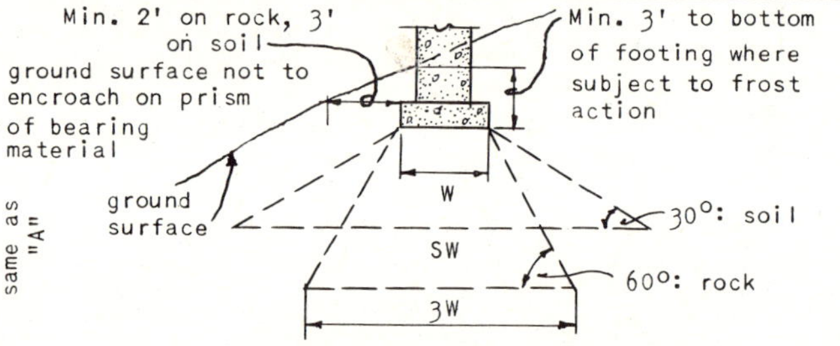
Min. 2' on rock, 3' on soil
ground surface not to encroach on prism of bearing material
Min. 3' to bottom of footing where subject to frost action
ground surface
W
30°: soil
SW
60°: rock
3W

FOOTINGS IN OR ADJACENT TO SLOPING GROUND

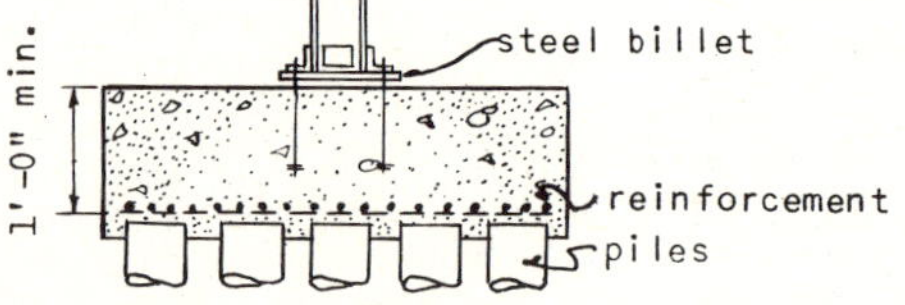
steel billet
1'-0" min.
reinforcement
piles

PILE FOUNDATION

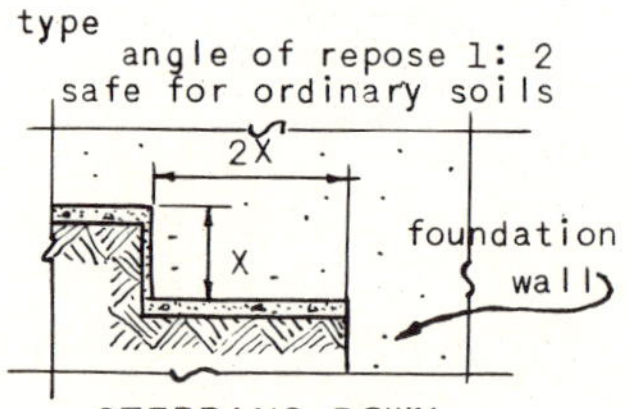
angle of repose 1: 2
safe for ordinary soils
2X
X
foundation wall

STEPPING DOWN A FOOTING

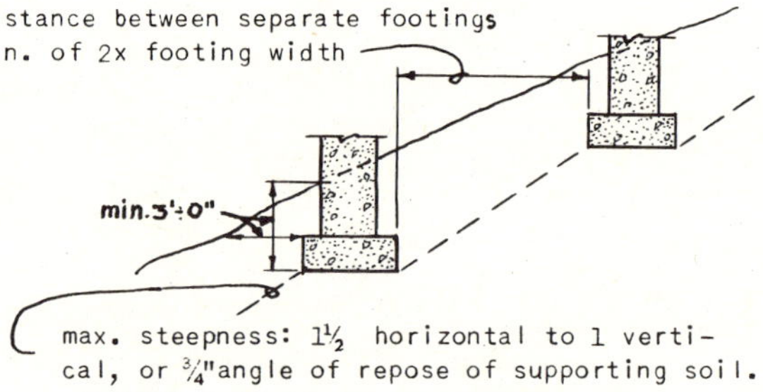
distance between separate footings min. of 2x footing width
min.3'-0"
max. steepness: 1½ horizontal to 1 vertical, or ¾"angle of repose of supporting soil.

STEPPING OF ADJACENT FOOTINGS

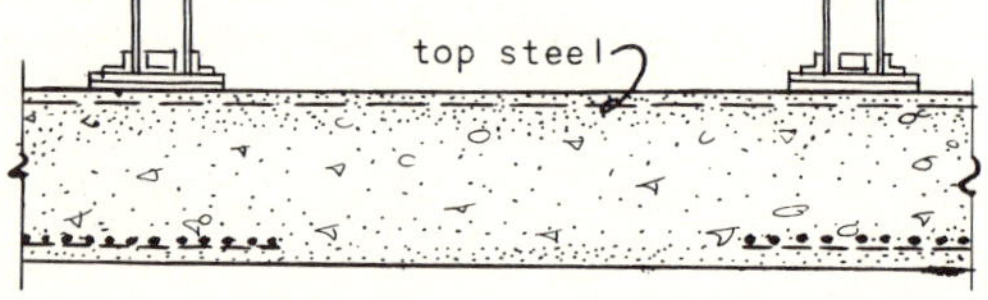
top steel

COMBINED FOUNDATION

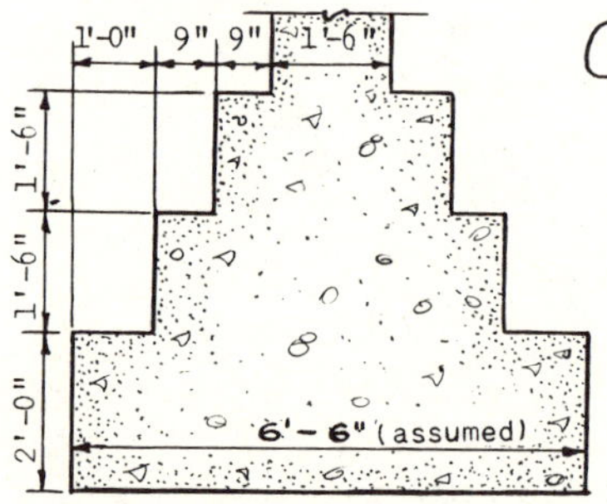
1'-0"
9"
9"
1'-6"
1'-6"
1'-6"
2'-0"
6'-6" (assumed)

Depth of steps to be twice their projection

MASS CONCRETE FOOTING FOR HEAVY WALL OR CHIMNEY

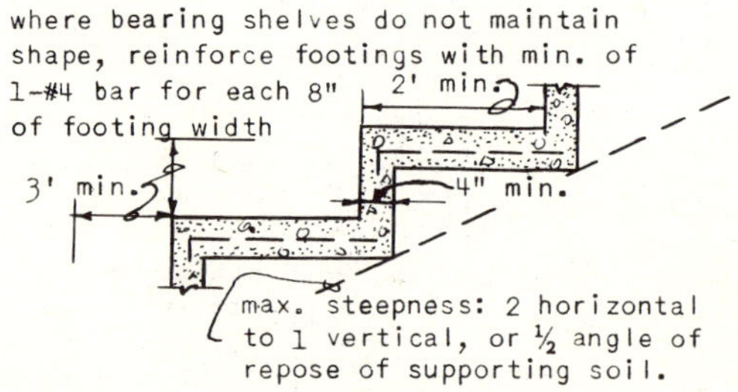
where bearing shelves do not maintain shape, reinforce footings with min. of 1-#4 bar for each 8" of footing width
2' min.
3' min.
4" min.
max. steepness: 2 horizontal to 1 vertical, or ½ angle of repose of supporting soil.

STEPPING OF CONTINUOUS FOOTINGS

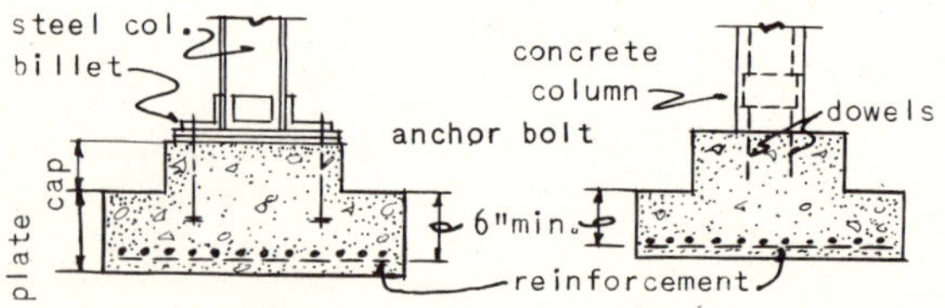
steel col.
billet
anchor bolt
cap
plate
6"min.
reinforcement
concrete column
dowels

STEEL COLUMN   REINFORCED CONCRETE

COLUMNS ON SPREAD FOOTINGS

Data checked by Elwyn E. Seelye, Consulting Engineer

FOUNDATION WALLS and SLABS on GRADE

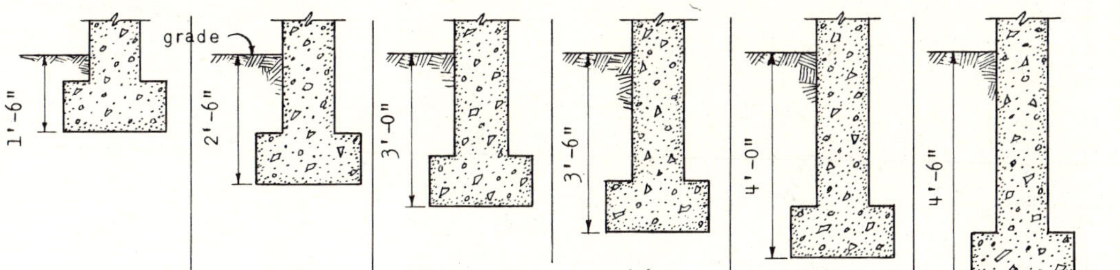
grade
1'-6"
2'-6"
3'-0"
3'-6"
4'-0"
4'-6"

FOUNDATION WALLS

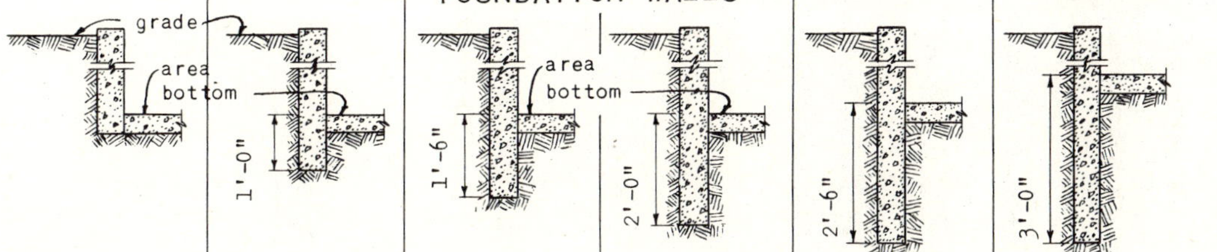
grade
area
bottom
1'-0"
1'-6"
2'-0"
2'-6"
3'-0"

No freezing weather. (Southern Florida, Southern Calif., Southern Texas)	Where minimum temperature is +20°.	Where minimum temperature is +10°.	Where minimum temperature is 0°. (New York, Central States.)	Where minimum temperature is -10°. (Northern Atlantic States.)	Where temperature goes below -20°. (Montana, N. Dakota, Canada.)

AREA WALLS

Scale: $\frac{1}{4}$" = 1'-0"

NOTE: Same dimensions apply with brick or stone walls.

"Minimum temperature" (Fahrenheit): temperatures sustained for a period of days, not just for a few hours. Minimum temperatures are 10°-15° above lowest recorded; are those used for calculating heating requirements.

DEPTHS OF FOUNDATION WALLS

Data checked by Elwyn E. Seelye, Consulting Engineer

DEPTHS REQUIRED BY BUILDING CODES

Atlanta, Ga.	below grade
Baltimore, Md.	3'-0"
Boston, Mass.	4'-0"
Butte, Mont.	3'-0"
Chicago, Ill.	4'-0"
Denver, Colo.	1'-6"
Detroit, Mich.	3'-6"
El Paso, Texas	No Mention
Halifax, Canada	4'-0"
Jacksonville, Fla.	1'-0"
Kansas City, Mo.	3'-0"
Louisville, Ky.	2'-6"
Milwaukee, Wisc.	5'-0"
Minneapolis, Minn.	No Mention
New Orleans, La.	No Mention
New York, N.Y.	4'-0"
Omaha, Neb.	3'-0"
Portland, Ore.	No Mention
Philadelphia, Pa.	3'-0"
St. Louis, Mo.	2'-6"
St. Paul, Minn.	4'-0"
Salt Lake City, Utah	No Mention
Seattle, Wash.	1'-6"
Washington, D.C.	No Mention
Winnepeg, Canada	No Mention

NOTE: National Building Code requires a minimum of 1'-0" below frost line. Consult local building code for requirements.

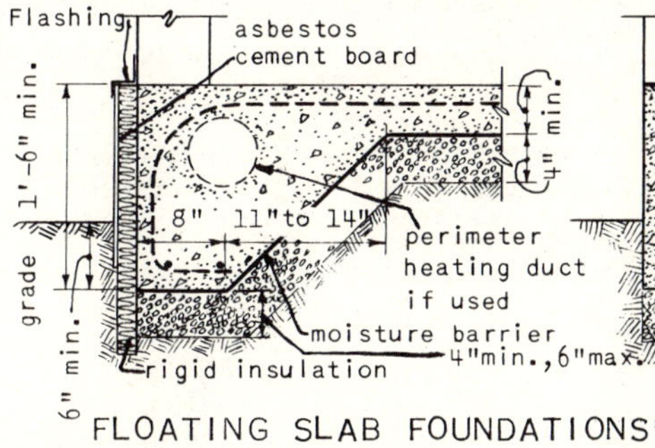
Flashing
asbestos cement board
1'-6" min.
4" min.
8"
11" to 14"
perimeter heating duct if used
grade
6" min.
moisture barrier
rigid insulation
4"min., 6"max.
moisture barrier
4"min.
6"max.
6"min.

FLOATING SLAB FOUNDATIONS*

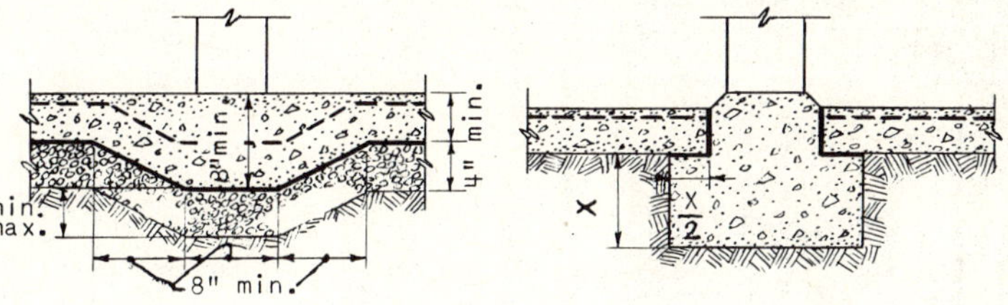
8" min.
4" min.
8" min.
X
X/2

INTERIOR BEARING PARTITIONS

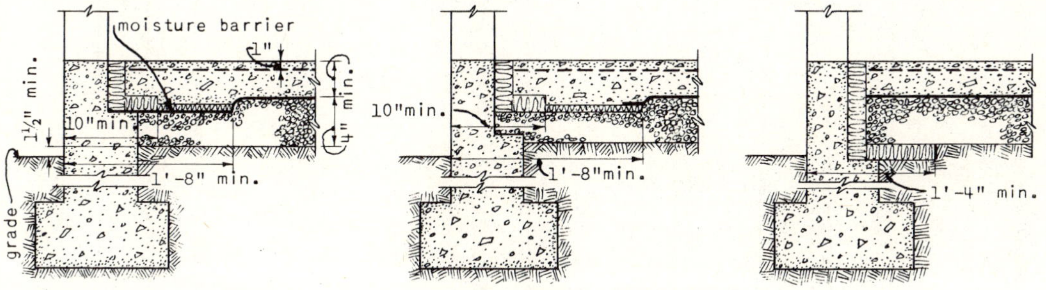
moisture barrier
1"
1½" min.
10" min
4" min.
1'-8" min.
grade
10"min.
1'-8"min.
1'-4" min.

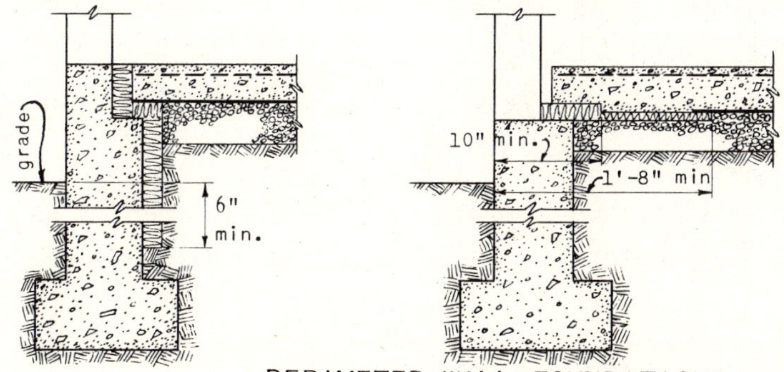
grade
6" min.
10" min.
1'-8" min

PERIMETER WALL FOUNDATIONS

*Floating slab foundations shown are for wood frame buildings with heights of 12'-0" max. from floor to eave and 20'-0" max. from floor to gable.

NOTE:

Apply coating of mastic to top of footing to stop capillary action.

NOTE:

The following are recommendations from the New York State Illustrated Code Manual, 1953 ed.

1. Moisture barrier, to be either membrane water-proofing or 35-lb. roofing felt, lapped 6" all edges.
2. For footing drains see pages on waterproofing and dampproofing.
3. Protection against frost action:
   a. adjoining ground to slope away from foundation in all directions and underlying soil to be preferably sand or gravel to reduce to a minimum heaving due to frost action.
   b. for perimeter wall foundations, bottom of footing to be below frost line. See local code for requirements

——— moisture barrier
– – – – reinforcement

FOUNDATIONS FOR SLABS ON GRADE

Scale: $\frac{1}{2}$" = 1'-0"

RETAINING WALLS

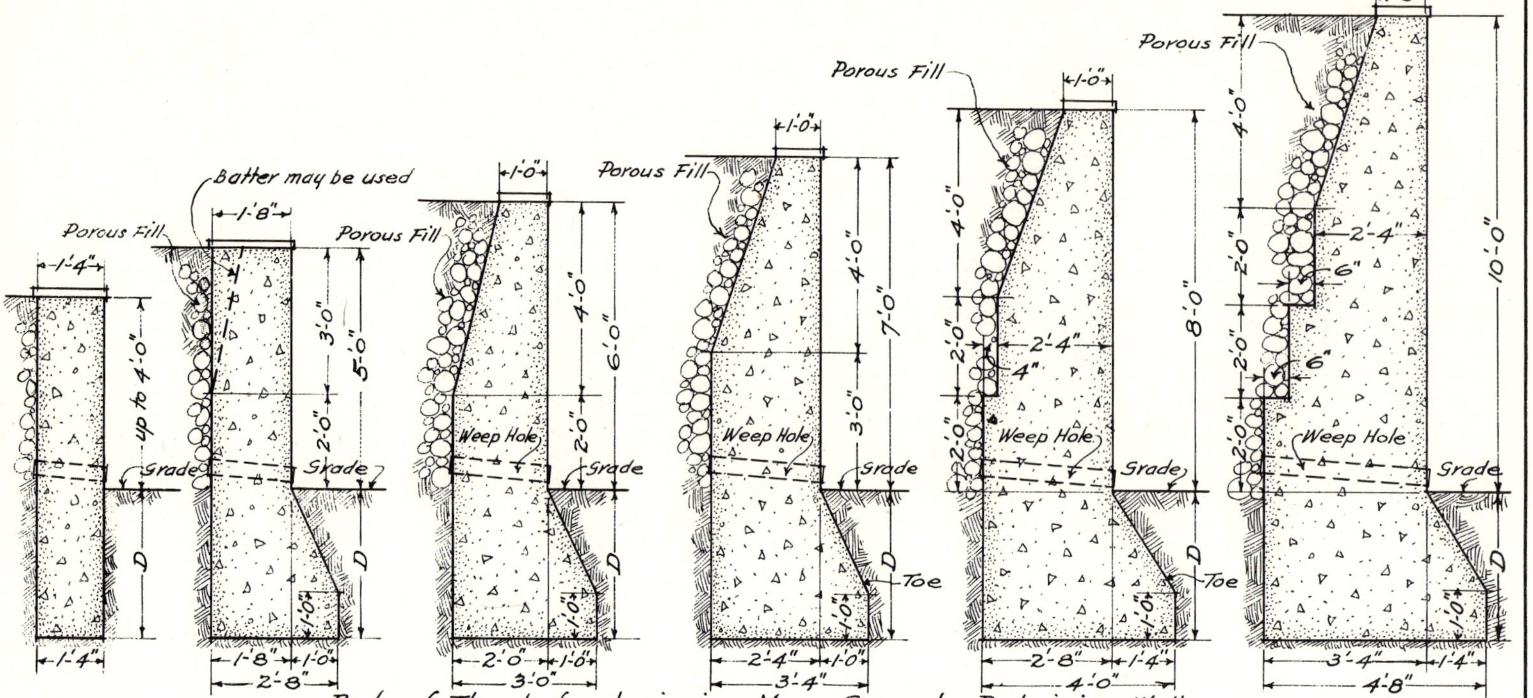
Porous Fill
Batter may be used
1'-4"
up to 4'-0"
1'-8"
3'-0"
5'-0"
2'-0"
1'-0"
4'-0"
6'-0"
7'-0"
8'-0"
10'-0"
3'-0"
2'-4"
4"
6"
Weep Hole
Grade
D
Toe
1'-0"
2'-8"
2'-0"
3'-0"
2'-4"
3'-4"
1'-4"
4'-0"
3'-4"
4'-8"

Rule of Thumb for designing Mass Concrete Retaining Walls.

Assume earth level with top of wall. Minimum width at top of wall 1'-0". Width of wall at each step must be 1/3 of distance from this point to the top of wall. No increase in width required below grade except for toe. For wall without steps minimum width is 1/3 distance from grade to top. Use same rule for Brick or Rubble retaining walls, except minimum width to be 2'-0", and use 2/5 in place of 1/3. Assumed adequate bearing cap. of soil & 33° ∠ of repose. To avoid surface cracks in concrete walls place 3/8" bars 2'-0" o.c. both ways and 2" from the exposed face of the wall. These walls are designed for typical soil conditions with grade not above top of wall. Weep holes of 4" Tile or 2" Brass pipe 10'-0" o.c. Construction joints to be 30'-0" apart.

MASS CONCRETE RETAINING WALLS.

"D" indicates depth to frost line - see "Foundation Walls and Slabs on Grade".

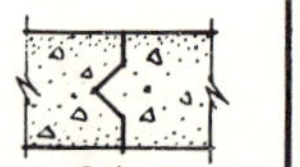

Plan
CONSTRUCTION JOINT

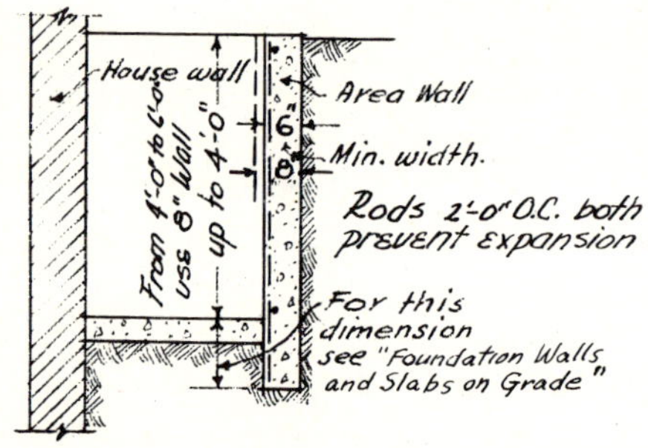
House wall
Area Wall
6"
8"
Min. width.
From 4'-0" to 6'-0" use 8" Wall
up to 4'-0"
Rods 2'-0" O.C. both ways prevent expansion cracks.
For this dimension see "Foundation Walls and Slabs on Grade"

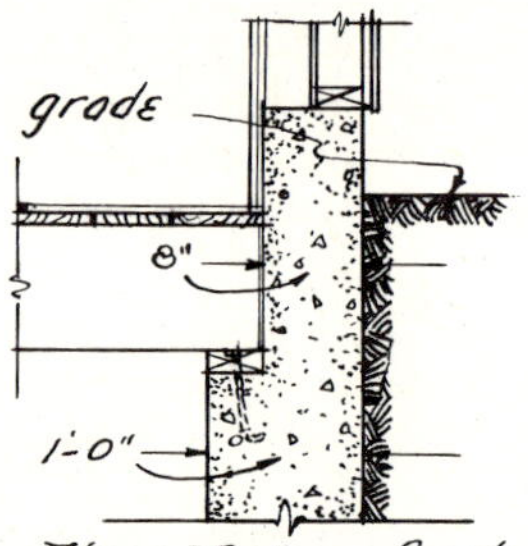
grade
8"
1'-0"

Floor Below Grade

Reinforced Walls are usually more economical than mass walls. No surcharge has been figured in the design of the walls.

Walls shown are for areas not over 6'-0" long, for each additional 1'-0" in length up to 10'-0" increase wall 1", if over 10'-0" long brace areas with cross walls.

AREA WALLS.

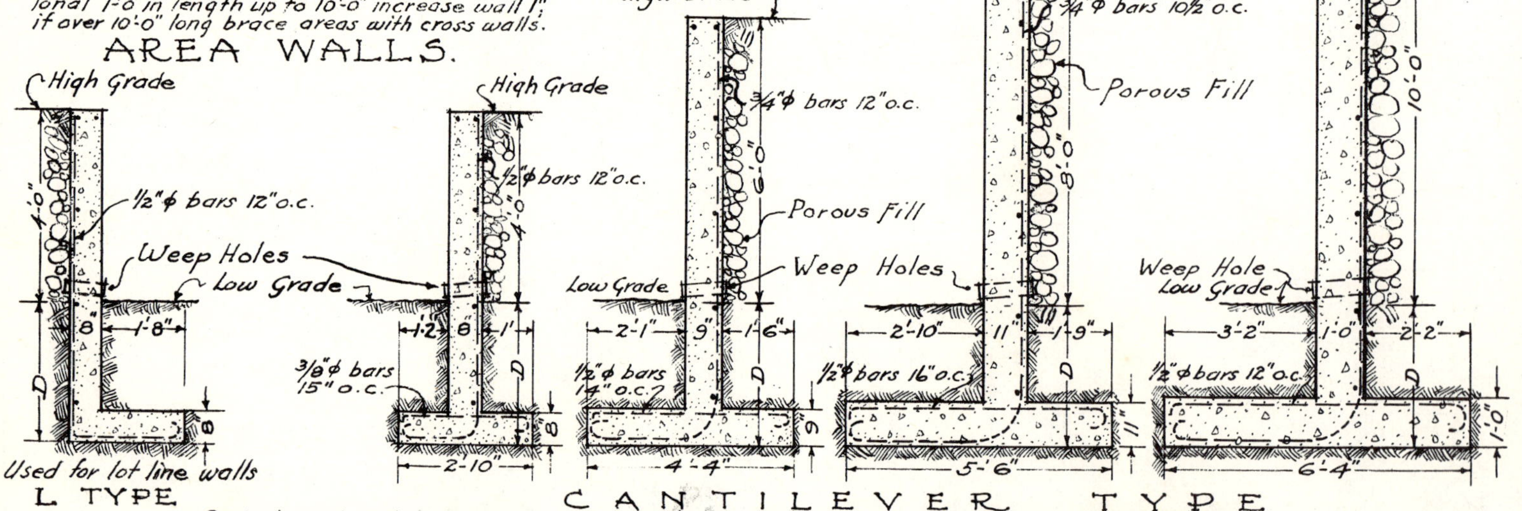
High Grade
4'-0"
1/2"φ bars 12" o.c.
Weep Holes
Low Grade
8"
1'-8"
D
Used for lot line walls
L TYPE
3/8"φ bars 15" o.c.
1'-2"
1'
2'-10"
3/4"φ bars 12" o.c.
6'-0"
Porous Fill
2'-1"
9"
1'-6"
1/2"φ bars 14" o.c.
9
4'-4"
3/4"φ bars 10 1/2" o.c.
8'-0"
2'-10"
11"
1'-9"
1/2"φ bars 16" o.c.
5'-6"
1"φ Bars 13" o.c.
10'-0"
Weep Hole
3'-2"
1'-0"
2'-2"
1/2"φ bars 12" o.c.
6'-4"

CANTILEVER TYPE

Designs are based on adequate soil to resist toe pressure and an angle of repose of 33°, which is average soil. Horizontal bars to prevent cracking to be No. 3 rods, 2'-0" o.c., with construction joints 30'-0" apart. If construction joints are omitted, heavier bars must be used. For greater heights and special conditions, walls to be designed individually.

REINFORCED CONCRETE RETAINING WALLS.

All calculations made by Elwyn E. Seelye, Consulting Engineer.

1/4" = 1'-0"

REINFORCED CONCRETE BLOCK RETAINING WALLS

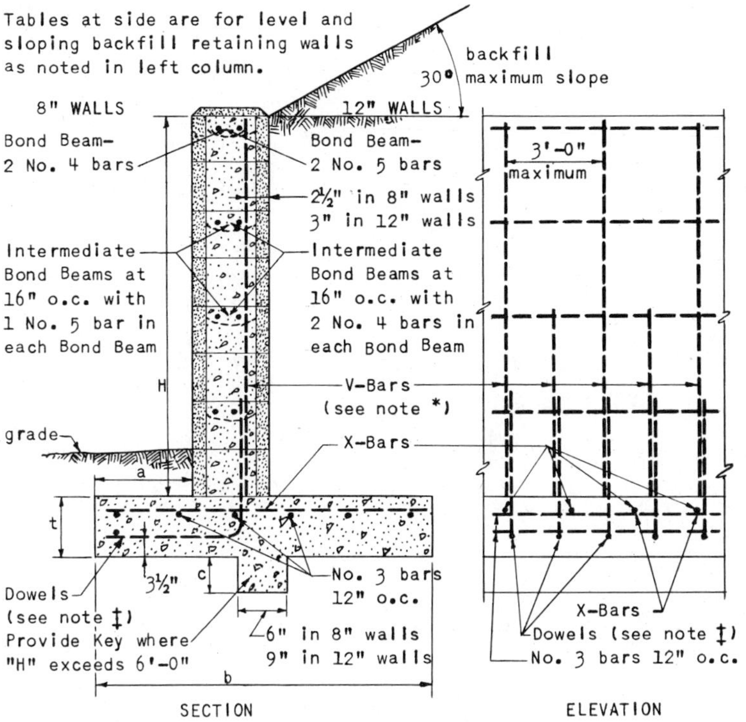
Tables at side are for level and sloping backfill retaining walls as noted in left column.
backfill
30° maximum slope
8" WALLS
12" WALLS
Bond Beam–
2 No. 4 bars
Bond Beam–
2 No. 5 bars
2½" in 8" walls
3" in 12" walls
3'-0"
maximum
Intermediate Bond Beams at 16" o.c. with 1 No. 5 bar in each Bond Beam
Intermediate Bond Beams at 16" o.c. with 2 No. 4 bars in each Bond Beam
V-Bars
(see note *)
H
grade
X-Bars
a
t
3½"
c
No. 3 bars 12" o.c.
Dowels (see note ‡)
Provide Key where "H" exceeds 6'-0"
6" in 8" walls
9" in 12" walls
b
X-Bars
Dowels (see note ‡)
No. 3 bars 12" o.c.
SECTION
ELEVATION

TYPICAL DETAIL FOR LEVEL AND SLOPING BACKFILL
CANTILEVER RETAINING WALLS

	SOIL	H	a	b	c	t	V-Bars*		X-Bars	
		ft-in	in	ft-in	in	in	Bar No.	Spacing o.c.	Bar No.	Spacing o.c.
LEVEL BACKFILL	TYPE "A"	3'-4"	4"	2'-0"	-	9"	3	2'-8"	3	2'-3"
		4'-0"	5"	2'-4"	-	9"	3	2'-8"	3	2'-3"
		4'-8"	6"	2'-8"	-	9"	4	2'-8"	3	2'-3"
		5'-4"	8"	3'-0"	-	10"	4	2'-0"	3	2'-0"
		6'-0"	9"	3'-4"	-	10"	4	1'-4"	4	2'-4"
		6'-8"	12"	3'-8"	-	12"	6	2'-0"	4	2'-4"
	TYPE "B"	3'-4"	8"	2'-4"	-	9"	3	2'-8"	3	2'-3"
		4'-0"	10"	2'-9"	-	9"	4	2'-8"	3	2'-3"
		4'-8"	12"	3'-3"	-	10"	5	2'-8"	3	2'-3"
		5'-4"	14"	3'-8"	-	10"	4	1'-4"	4	2'-6"
		6'-0"	15"	4'-2"	-	12"	6	2'-0"	4	2'-1"
SLOPING BACKFILL	TYPE "A"	3'-4"	6"	2'-6"	-	9"	3	2'-8"	3	2'-3"
		4'-0"	8"	3'-0"	-	9"	4	2'-8"	4	2'-3"
		4'-8"	10"	3'-4"	-	9"	4	2'-0"	4	1'-7"
		5'-4"	12"	4'-0"	-	10"	5	2'-0"	5	1'-10"
		6'-0"	14"	4'-6"	-	10"	5	1'-4"	6	1'-10"
		6'-8"	16"	4'-10"	-	12"	7	1'-4"	6	1'-8"
	TYPE "B"	3'-4"	10"	3'-0"	-	9"	3	2'-0"	4	2'-3"
		4'-0"	12"	3'-8"	-	9"	4	2'-0"	5	2'-3"
		4'-8"	14"	4'-4"	-	10"	5	2'-0"	6	2'-1"
		5'-4"	16"	4'-10"	-	10"	6	1'-4"	8	1'-5"
LEVEL BACKFILL	TYPE "A"	3'-4"	4"	2'-0"	-	9"	3	2'-8"	3	2'-3"
		4'-0"	5"	2'-4"	-	9"	3	2'-8"	3	2'-3"
		4'-8"	6"	2'-8"	-	9"	3	2'-8"	3	2'-3"
		5'-4"	8"	3'-0"	-	10"	4	2'-8"	3	2'-3"
		6'-0"	9"	3'-4"	-	10"	3	1'-4"	3	1'-10"
		6'-8"	12"	3'-8"	-	12"	5	2'-8"	3	1'-10"
		7'-4"	13"	4'-0"	-	12"	4	1'-4"	4	2'-2"
		8'-0"	15"	4'-4"	-	12"	6	2'-0"	4	1'-10"
		8'-8"	16"	4'-8"	-	12"	7	2'-0"	5	2'-2"
		9'-4"	18"	5'-0"	-	12"	6	1'-4"	5	1'-8"
		10'-0"	20"	5'-4"	-	12"	8	1'-4"	6	2'-0"
	TYPE "B"	3'-4"	8"	2'-4"	-	9"	3	2'-8"	3	2'-3"
		4'-0"	10"	2'-9"	-	9"	3	2'-8"	3	2'-3"
		4'-8"	12"	3'-3"	-	10"	4	2'-8"	3	2'-3"
		5'-4"	14"	3'-8"	-	10"	4	2'-0"	3	2'-1"
		6'-0"	15"	4'-2"	-	12"	4	1'-4"	4	2'-6"
		6'-8"	16"	4'-6"	-	12"	6	2'-0"	4	1'-10"
		7'-4"	18"	4'-10"	-	12"	7	2'-8"	5	2'-2"
		8'-0"	20"	5'-4"	-	12"	7	2'-0"	5	1'-9"
		8'-8"	22"	5'-10"	-	14"	7	1'-4"	6	2'-2"
		9'-4"	24"	6'-4"	-	14"	8	8"	6	1'-9"
SLOPING BACKFILL	TYPE "A"	3'-4"	6"	2'-4"	6"	9"	3	2'-8"	3	2'-3"
		4'-0"	8"	2'-10"	6"	9"	3	2'-8"	3	2'-3"
		4'-8"	10"	3'-2"	6"	9"	3	2'-0"	3	1'-8"
		5'-4"	12"	3'-8"	6"	10"	3	1'-4"	4	2'-0"
		6'-0"	14"	4'-0"	6"	10"	4	1'-4"	5	2'-0"
		6'-8"	16"	4'-6"	6"	12"	6	2'-0"	6	2'-6"
		7'-4"	18"	5'-0"	6"	12"	5	1'-4"	6	1'-10"
		8'-0"	20"	5'-6"	6"	14"	7	2'-0"	7	2'-2"
		8'-8"	22"	6'-0"	6"	14"	5	8"	7	1'-8"
		9'-4"	24"	6'-6"	6"	14"	8	8"	8	1'-9"
	TYPE "B"	3'-4"	9"	2'-10"	6"	9"	3	2'-8"	3	2'-3"
		4'-0"	11"	3'-6"	6"	9"	3	2'-0"	4	2'-2"
		4'-8"	13"	4'-0"	6"	10"	4	2'-0"	5	2'-2"
		5'-4"	15"	4'-6"	6"	10"	4	1'-4"	6	2'-1"
		6'-0"	17"	5'-0"	8"	12"	6	2'-0"	6	1'-8"
		6'-8"	19"	5'-8"	8"	12"	7	2'-0"	8	2'-0"
		7'-4"	21"	6'-4"	10"	14"	8	2'-0"	8	1'-8"
		8'-0"	24"	7'-0"	10"	14"	7	8"	8	1'-4"

NOTE:

TYPE "A" SOIL – Very permeable coarse-grained material such as clean sand and gravel.

TYPE "B" SOIL – Granular material with a conspicuous clay content such as fine silty sand.

NOTES:

* Alternate V-Bars may be stopped at the midheight of the wall if the spacing of the bars continued to the top does not exceed 3'-0".

‡ Dowels shall be at least equal in size and spacing to V-Bars and shall project a minimum of thirty (30) bar diameters into concrete filled block cores and shall extend to the toe of the footing.

Reinforcement of a size and spacing not given in the tables may be used, providing such other reinforcement furnishes an area of steel at least equal to that indicated in the tables.

Deformed steel bars, Grade "A" Hollow Load-Bearing units (ASTM C) (90-52), Type M (A-1) Mortar attaining a strength of 2500 pounds per square inch within 28 days, and concrete with an ultimate compressive strength of 3000 pounds per square inch within 28 days are assumed in the design.

GENERAL NOTES:

Retaining walls exceeding fifty (50) feet in length should have vertical expansion joints at 20 to 30 foot intervals to prevent occurrence of unsightly cracks due to volume changes in the masonry. Such joints should be of the tongue and groove type, or designed with a key to prevent faulting at the joint, but still allow for longitudinal movement. In walls exceeding 100 feet in length, consideration should be given to the need for expansion joints extending continuously from the top of the footing to the top of the wall. Under some conditions it may be advisable to extend expansion joints thru the footing. Horizontal reinforcement should not be continued across expansion or contraction joints.

DATA SUPPLIED BY NATIONAL CONCRETE MASONRY ASSOCIATION

WOOD CONSTRUCTION

TABLE OF CONTENTS

PLANK and BEAM FRAMING for RESIDENCES

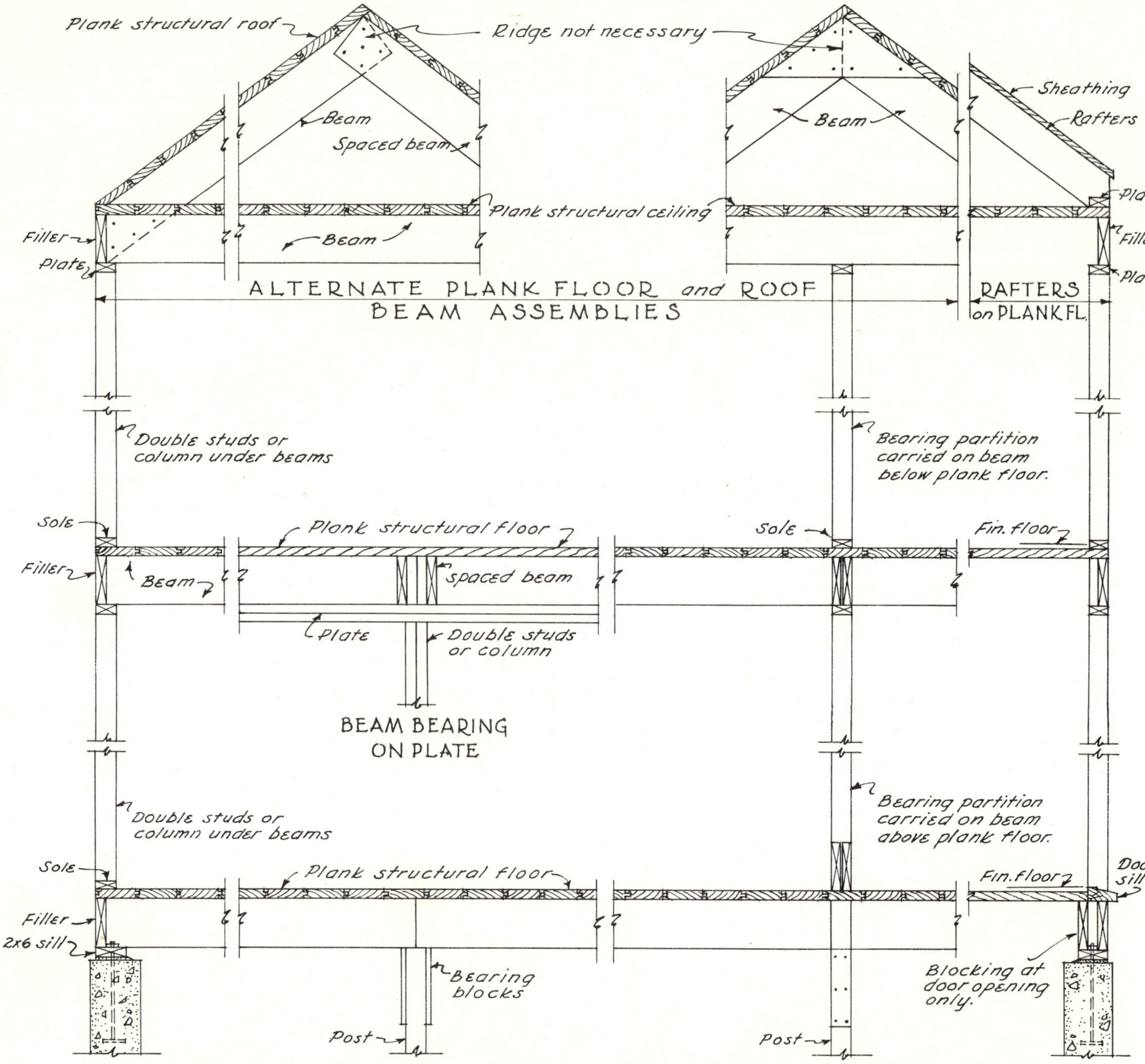
Plank structural roof
Ridge not necessary
Sheathing
Rafters
Beam
Spaced beam
Beam
Plate
Plank structural ceiling
Filler
Beam
Filler
Plate
Plate
ALTERNATE PLANK FLOOR and ROOF BEAM ASSEMBLIES
RAFTERS on PLANK FL.
Double studs or column under beams
Bearing partition carried on beam below plank floor.
Sole
Plank structural floor
Sole
Fin. floor
Filler
Beam
Spaced beam
Plate
Double studs or column
BEAM BEARING ON PLATE
Double studs or column under beams
Bearing partition carried on beam above plank floor.
Sole
Plank structural floor
Fin. floor
Door sill
Filler
2x6 sill
Bearing blocks
Blocking at door opening only.
Post
Post

SECTIONS *showing* VARIOUS DETAILS *and* ALTERNATIVES
(For exterior studs, bracing and sheathing, see page on "Western Framing")

Plank and beam structural floor and/or roof system is the use of a plank sub-floor or roof decking with supporting beams spaced up to 7 feet apart, instead of the usual boards for sub-floor or roof decking with joists or rafters spaced 12 to 24 inches. It may be employed in a building having joist construction for other floors or for the roof and it is possible to utilize the advantageous features of both types by selecting that which is the more suitable for each part of the structure. Its adaptation to small house construction is a relatively new development. Compared with 2x8 joists spaced 16" o. c., 2" plank continuous over two 7'-0" spans gives the same stiffness as 2x8 joists with an 11'-4" span and the same strength as 2x8 joists with a 10'-4" span. 2x6 or 2x8 well-seasoned plank should be used; and, if serving as exposed ceiling of rooms below, No. 1 Common or other tight-knotted material, selected for good appearance, should be used. Finish flooring should be laid at right angles with the plank of sub-floor. When a 25/32" thickness of flooring is used, and the underside of plank exposed as finish ceiling, finish floor nails should not be longer than 1 3/4".

Properly designed plank spans up to 7'-0" are practical for the fulfilling of the requirements of the Federal Housing Administration for residences.

Scale: 3/8" = 1'-0"

Adapted from data by the National Lumber Manufacturers Association

PLANK and BEAM CONSTRUCTION

PLANK-AND-BEAM FRAMING

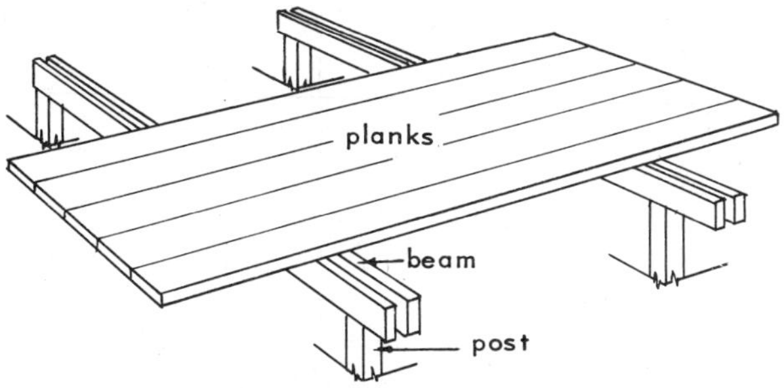
planks
beam
post

PLANK-AND-BEAM FRAMING

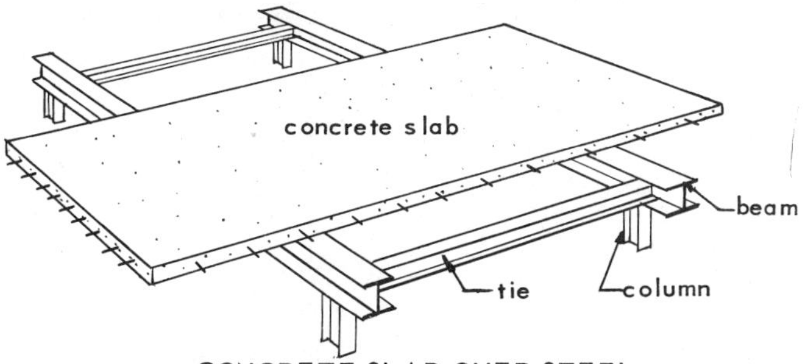
concrete slab
beam
tie
column

CONCRETE SLAB OVER STEEL

To show its characteristics more clearly, plank-and-beam wood framing can be compared to standard steel framing, which is very similar in principle.

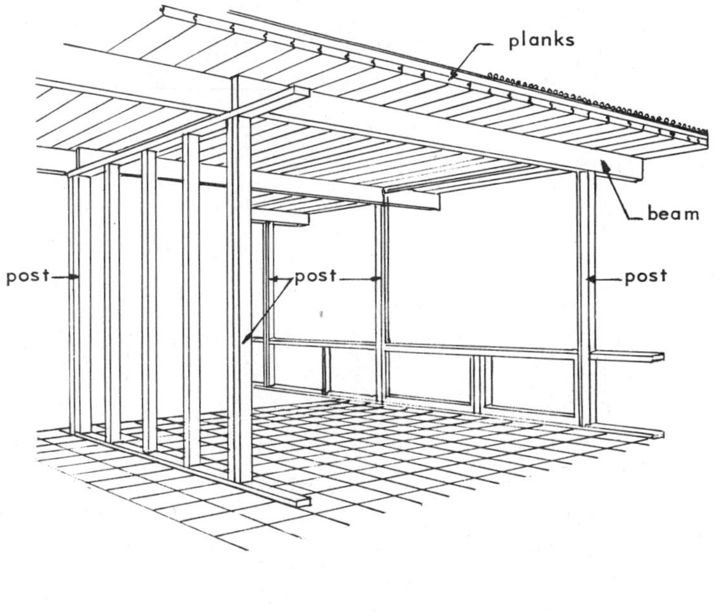
planks
beam
post
post
post

PLANK-AND-BEAM FRAMING

Full benefit of this system is obtained in residential work with an open plan and a modular panel treatment such as 4'-0" dry-wall units and large glass areas.

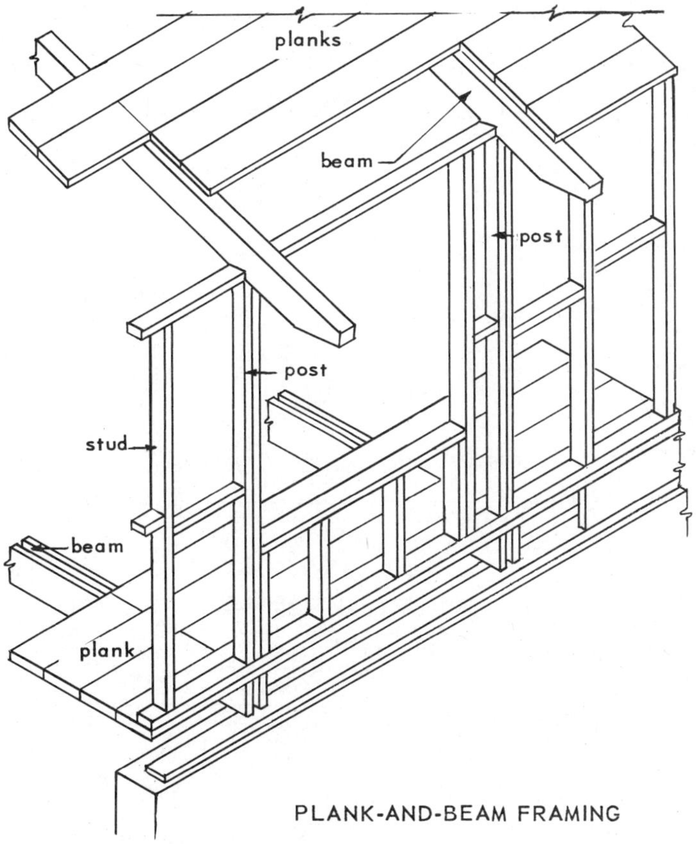
planks
beam
post
post
stud
beam
plank

PLANK-AND-BEAM FRAMING

In this construction, a few large members replace the many small members used in typical wood framing. This results in a saving in the number of members, and, due to rapid site assembly, makes possible a saving in erection labor costs.

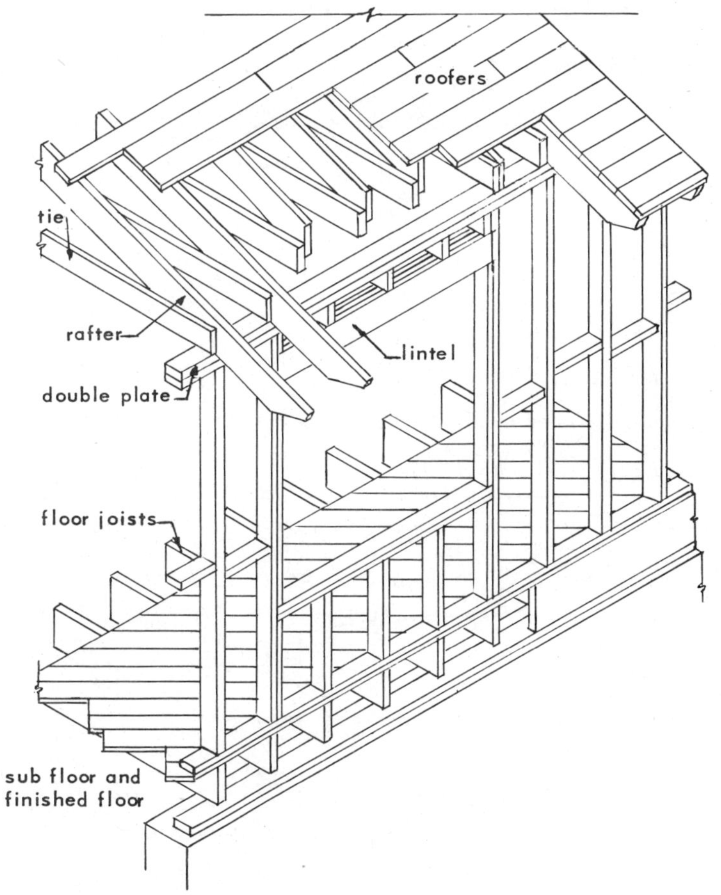
roofers
tie
rafter
lintel
double plate
floor joists
sub floor and finished floor

CONVENTIONAL WOOD FRAMING

Compiled from "Plank-and-Beam Systems for Residential Construction" — Housing and Home Finance Agency.

PLANK and BEAM CONSTRUCTION

ADVANTAGES OF THE PLANK-AND-BEAM FRAMING SYSTEM

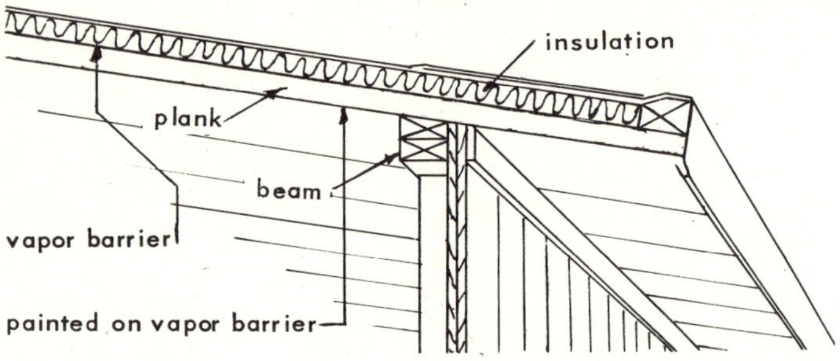
insulation
plank
beam
vapor barrier
painted on vapor barrier

PLANK-AND-BEAM

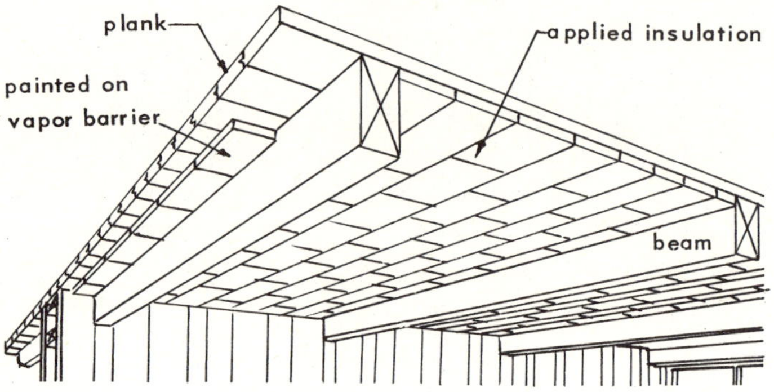
plank
applied insulation
painted on
vapor barrier
beam

PLANK-AND-BEAM

Lath and plaster may be eliminated by placing the insulation on top of the planks and finishing their undersides or by affixing exposed insulation to the lower side of the plank members.

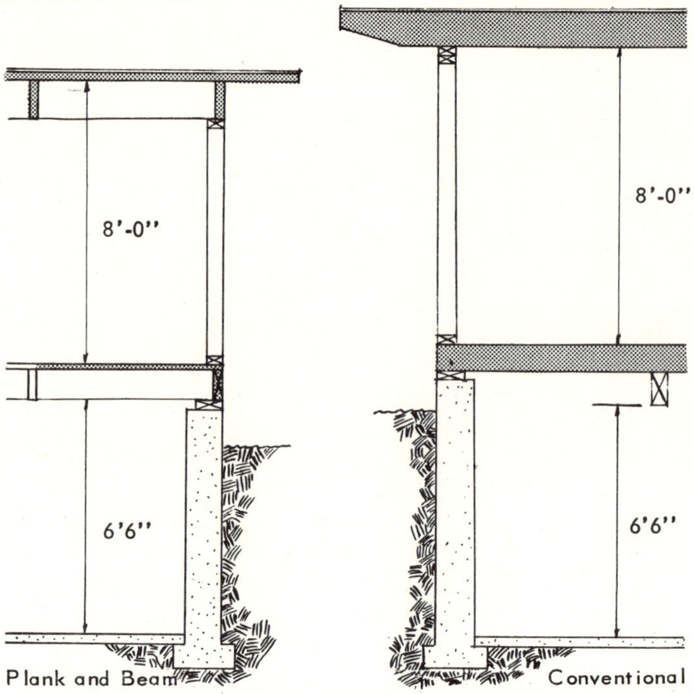
8'-0"
6'6"
Plank and Beam
8'-0"
6'6"
Conventional

HEIGHT SAVING OF PLANK-AND-BEAM CONSTRUCTION

Plank-and-beam framing saves on building height, making it possible to use shorter wall studs and shallower basement foundation walls.

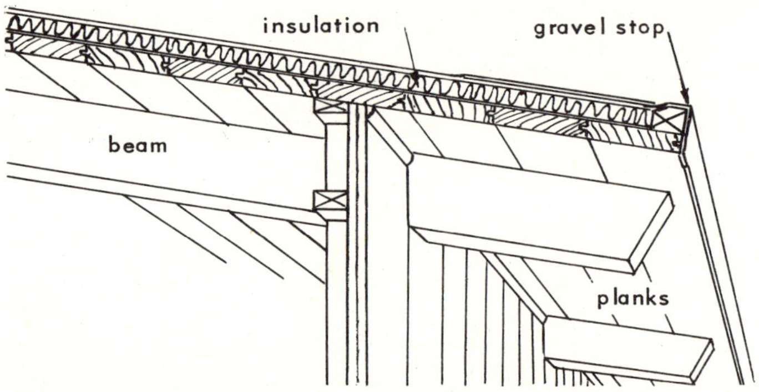
insulation
gravel stop
beam
planks

PLANK-AND-BEAM – EXPOSED OVERHANG

Overhang planks can be left exposed without marring the exterior appearance of the building, saving special soffit treatment, fascia and molds.

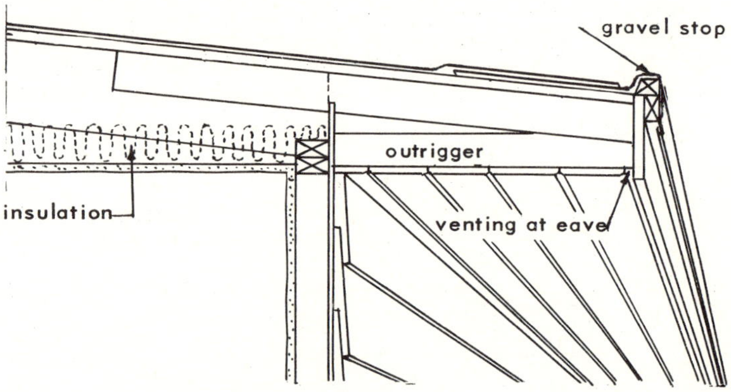
gravel stop
outrigger
insulation
venting at eave

CONVENTIONAL BOXED OVERHANG

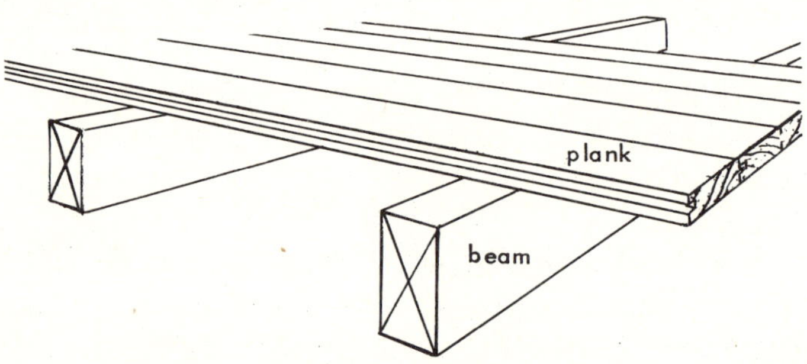
plank
beam

PLANK-AND-BEAM – ROOF OR FLOOR

One thickness of heavy planks, finished on both sides and supported on beams, may form the entire floor construction, replacing the usual finished flooring, subflooring, paper, framing, bridging, and plaster ceiling.

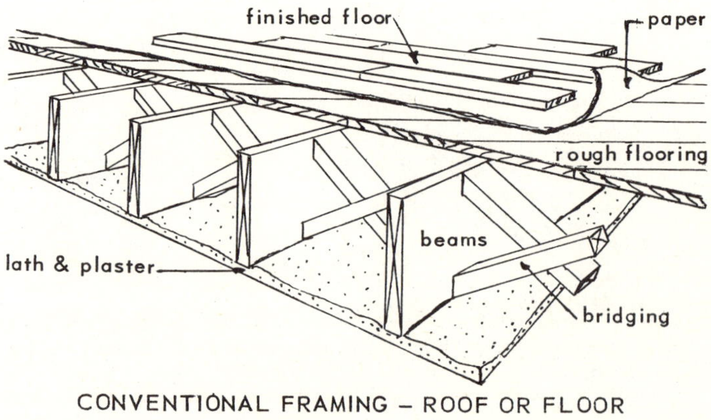
finished floor
paper
rough flooring
beams
lath & plaster
bridging

CONVENTIONAL FRAMING – ROOF OR FLOOR

Compiled from "Plank-and-Beam Systems for Residential Construction" – Housing and Home Finance Agency

PLANK and BEAM CONSTRUCTION

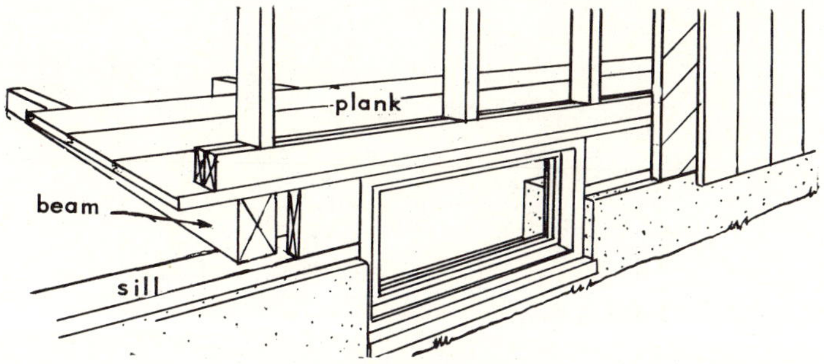
plank
beam
sill

PLANK-AND-BEAM

Basement windows may be placed higher, making it unnecessary to use areaways.

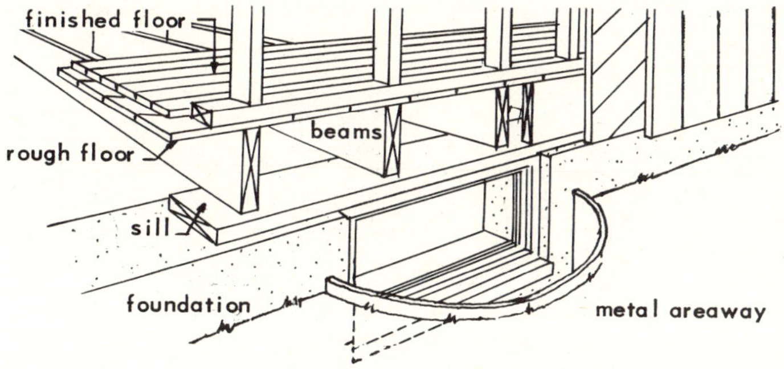
finished floor
rough floor
beams
sill
foundation
metal areaway

CONVENTIONAL

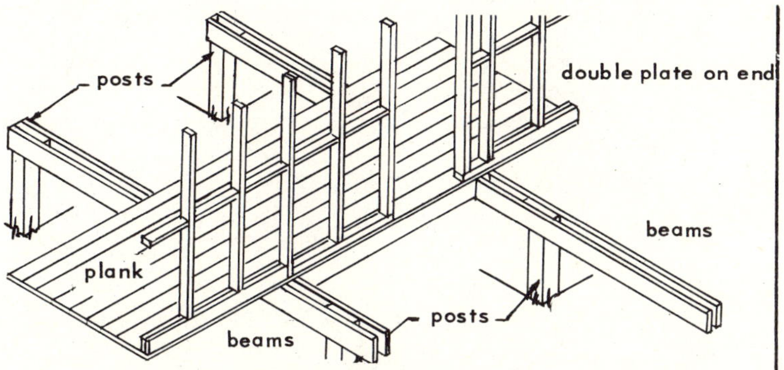
posts
double plate on end
beams
plank
posts
beams

PLANK-AND-BEAM

Additional framing is necessary under concentrated loads such as partitions and bathtubs. Cross beams or double plates can be used to take care of these conditions.

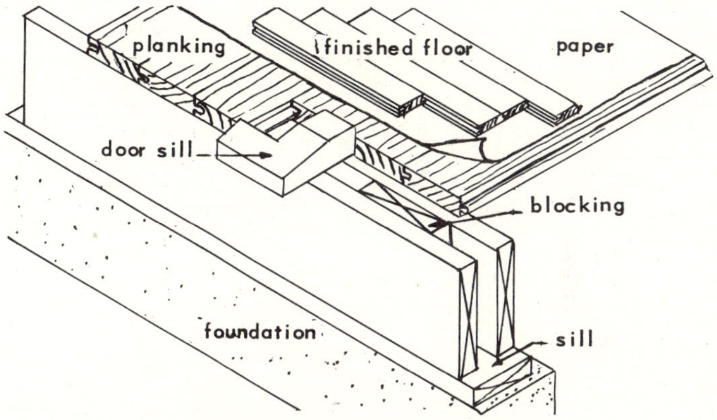
planking
finished floor
paper
door sill
blocking
foundation
sill

DETAIL OF DOOR SILL

PLANK AND BEAM FRAMING

MECHANICAL AND ELECTRICAL CONSIDERATIONS OF PLANK-AND-BEAM FRAMING.

Furring may be used to conceal pipes, exposed for basement or unfinished areas

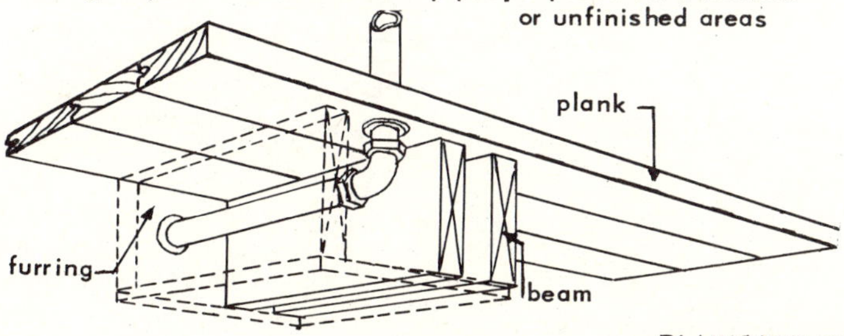
plank
furring
beam

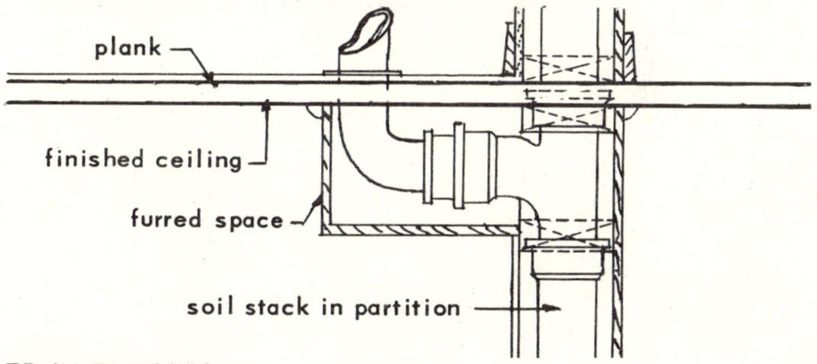
plank
finished ceiling
furred space
soil stack in partition

PLUMBING CONCEALED IN FURRING

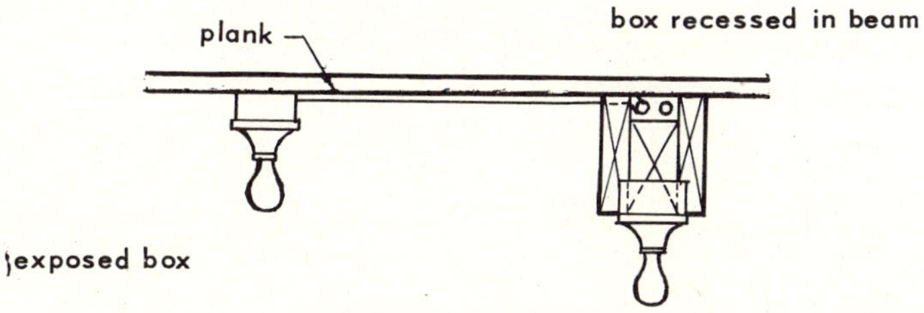
plank
box recessed in beam
exposed box

CEILING FIXTURES

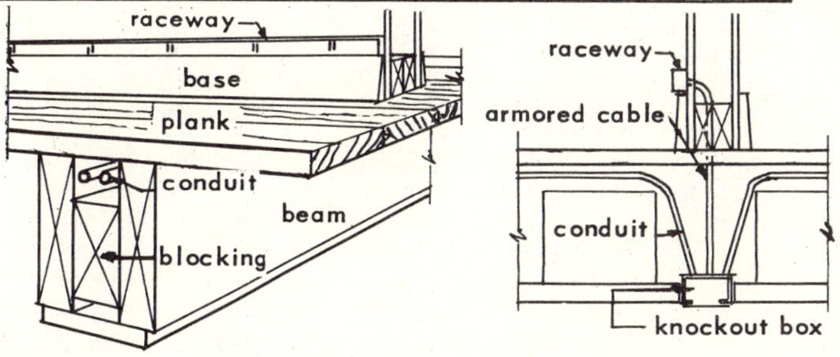
raceway
base
plank
conduit
beam
blocking
raceway
armored cable
conduit
knockout box

SURFACE MOUNTED RACEWAY

Electrical layouts for plank-and-beam framing should indicate actual locations of runs and details of installation. Conduits left exposed on the ceiling become less conspicuous if they are run along the top side of beams or along the joints of the planking. In some cases the conduit may be concealed in a built-up beam.

Elimination of ceiling lighting fixtures simplifies this problem. However, when desired, they may be left exposed or they may be recessed in the beam.

Surface mounted plug-in strips may be used in place of base receptacles and over kitchen counters to reduce wiring costs.

Compiled from "Plank-and-Beam System for Residential Construction" – Housing and Home Finance Agency

PLANK and BEAM CONSTRUCTION

Plank-and-beam framing may produce economy in construction if its design is carefully studied. In all cases local building codes must be consulted.

Following is a summary of possible economies in this construction.

1. Fewer different lengths and sizes of lumber are handled and placed.
2. Such items as bridging, subflooring, plastered ceilings, fascias, moldings, etc., can be completely eliminated.
3. Increased insulation is provided without extra cost.
4. Shorter wall studs and shallower basement foundation walls are required.
5. Areaways can be eliminated.

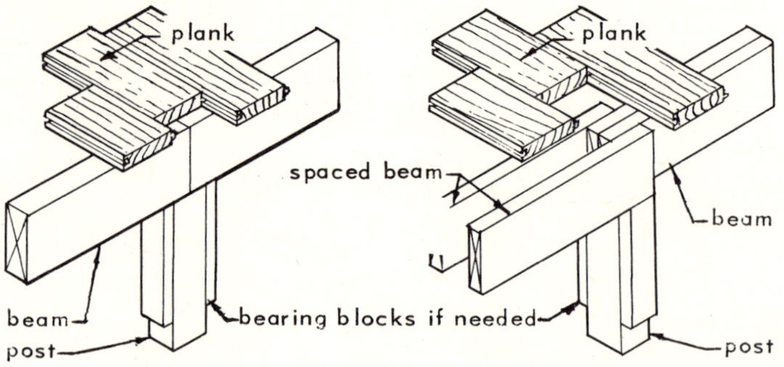
plank
beam
post
bearing blocks if needed
plank
spaced beam
beam
post

SOLID BEAM SPACED BEAM

BEARING OVER BASEMENT POST

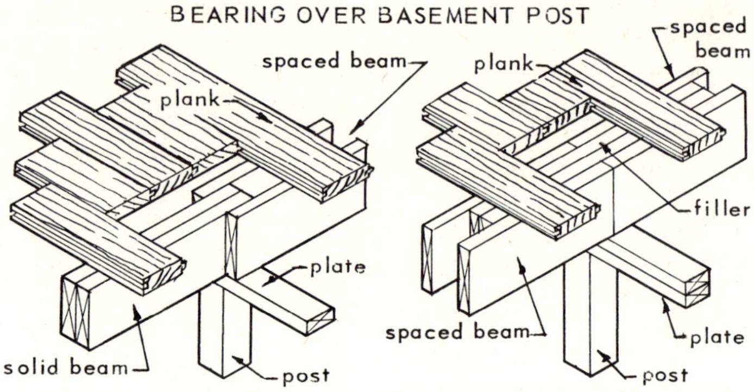
spaced beam
plank
plate
solid beam
post
plank
spaced beam
filler
spaced beam
plate
post

SOLID SPACED BEAMS SPACED BEAMS

BEARING AT SECOND FLOOR INTERIOR

Adopted from data by the National Lumber Manufactures' Assoc.

CONSTRUCTION DETAILS AND FASTENINGS

The members of built-up beams should be securely spiked together from both outside faces. When beam members are spaced, they should be blocked at frequent intervals, and each member should be securely nailed to the blocking.

Where planks butt over a single member beam, a nominal beam width of three or more inches is necessary to provide a suitable bearing and nailing surface for the planks. Planks should be both blind and face-nailed to the beam.

Beams should not be notched unless additional section is added.

At the first floor exterior, a sill may be used, or the beam may bear directly on the foundation wall.

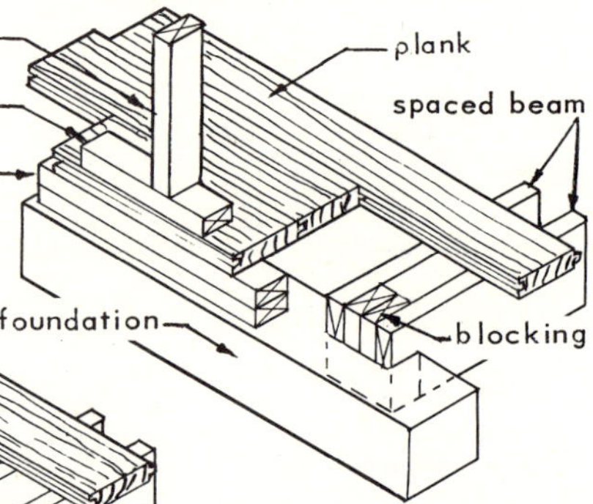
stud
sole
sill
plank
spaced beam
foundation
blocking

BEAM BEARING ON WALL

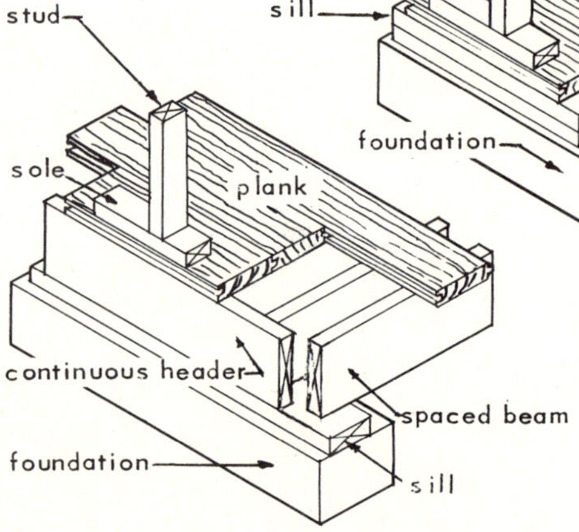
stud
sole
plank
continuous header
spaced beam
foundation
sill

BEAM BEARING ON SILL

Adopted from data by the National Lumber Manufacturers Assoc.

At the exterior wall, solid blocking (box plate) should be provided between beams and between members of built-up beams. The plank flooring should extend over the blocking and studs should rest on a plate placed on top of the planking. The beams should bear on solid or built-up posts which are adequate to support the load.

In this construction posts (rather than studs) carry the loads, which are concentrated; therefore they must be individually designed for each condition. Column ends should be squared to provide uniform bearing for the beams. Posts, either free-standing or in a partition, should not be smaller than 4 x 4 in section, and when they are built up, the members should be securely spiked together.

When solid beams butt at a column, a nominal column dimension of 6 or more inches parallel to the direction of the beams is recommended to provide suitable bearing for the beams. It may be necessary to spike bearing blocks to the column to increase the bearing surface. Columns should not be notched unless extra section is provided.

In two story plank-and-beam construction it is best to cut the studs at the second floor and cap them with a plate to provide bearing for the second-floor beams.

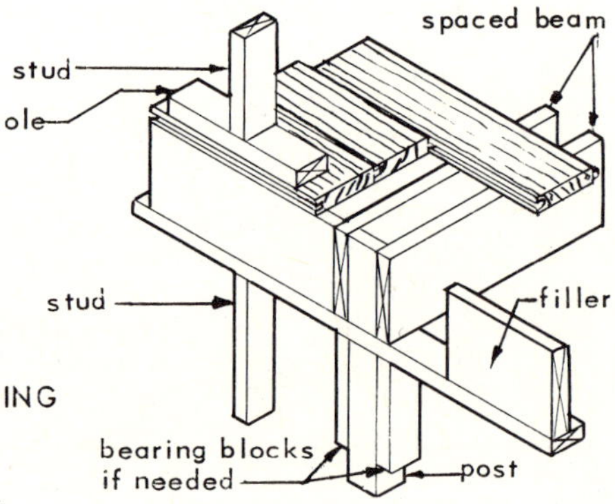
spaced beam
stud
sole
stud
filler
bearing blocks if needed
post

SPACED BEAM BEARING AT SECOND FLOOR EXTERIOR

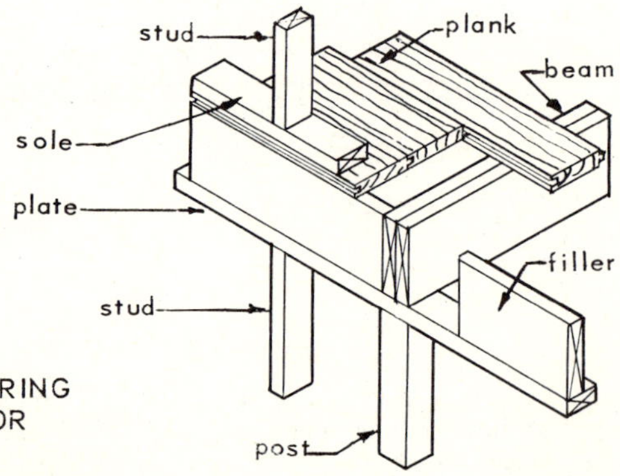
stud
plank
beam
sole
plate
filler
stud
post

SOLID BEAM BEARING AT SECOND FLOOR EXTERIOR

Adopted from data by the National Lumber Manufacturers' Assoc.

Compiled from "Plank-and-Beam System for Residential Construction" — Housing and Home Finance Agency

PLANK and BEAM CONSTRUCTION

It is necessary to have secure connections between the roof beams (or rafters) and the ceiling beams where they converge at the exterior wall.

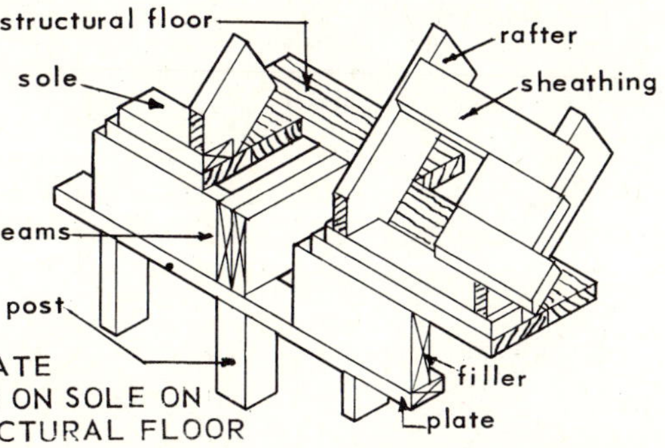
plank structural floor
rafter
sole
sheathing
beams
post
filler
plate

BEAM ON PLATE
AND RAFTER ON SOLE ON
PLANK STRUCTURAL FLOOR

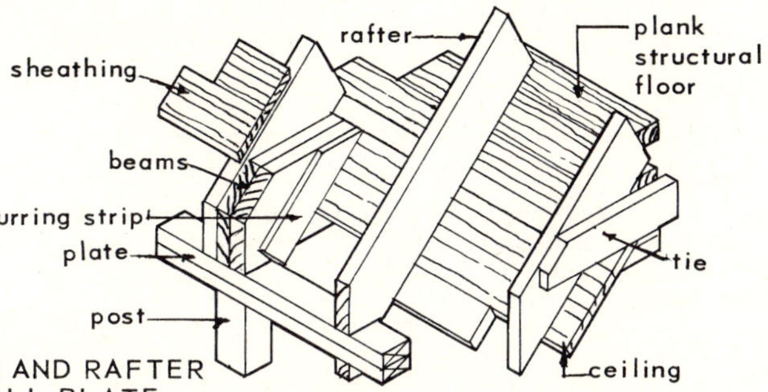
rafter
plank
structural
floor
sheathing
beams
furring strip
plate
tie
post
ceiling

BEAM AND RAFTER
ON WALL PLATE

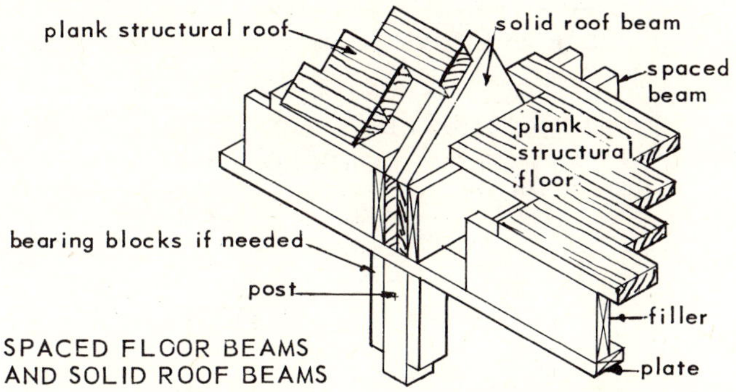
plank structural roof
solid roof beam
spaced
beam
plank
structural
floor
bearing blocks if needed
post
filler
plate

SPACED FLOOR BEAMS
AND SOLID ROOF BEAMS

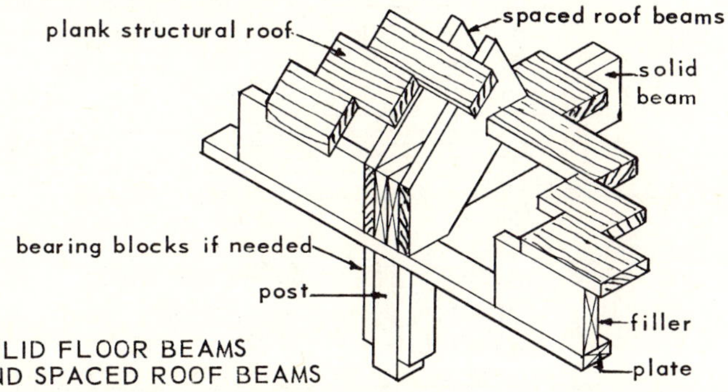
plank structural roof
spaced roof beams
solid
beam
bearing blocks if needed
post
filler
plate

SOLID FLOOR BEAMS
AND SPACED ROOF BEAMS

Adopted from data by the National Lumber Manufacturers. Assoc.

Where the ceiling beam serves as a tie, it must be considered as a continuous member in tension. Where these tie beams butt together, they should lap or be spliced together and spiked securely.

Because plank-and-beam framing utilizes larger members, each carrying larger and more highly concentrated loads than members in conventional frame construction, it is absolutely necessary that the connections and fastenings between these larger members be designed accordingly. Structural members must be securely nailed to each other to provide a well integrated structure. It is advised that all connections in a plank-and-beam framing system be thoroughly checked for strength.

INSULATION AND CONDENSATION

Much more study is necessary to select the proper amount and type of insulation and vapor barriers which are to be used in plank-and-beam framing than would be necessary for conventional framing where the insulation is concealed between joists or rafters. In plank-and-beam framing the insulation is either exposed to view on the ceiling, or installed over the planks and under the roofing.

Insulation used on roofs should be sturdy enough to support the weight of men working on it. Since small leaks will develop in any roof, it is best to use an insulation which will not rot, deteriorate, or fall apart when slightly wet, and one whose resistance to the flow of heat is not appreciably lowered by slight wetting.

Condensation on walls and ceilings is caused when moisture-laden warm air comes in contact with a cold surface. This generally occurs in the winter months when there is a great temperature difference between outside and inside.

Warm air can hold more moisture, by weight, than cold air. When warm moist air hits cold air or a cold surface the warm air is cooled to a dew point where it can no longer hold all of its moisture and thus drops particles of its moisture in the form of droplets called condensation.

Therefore, if the moisture in a house is kept to a minimum by exhausting moist air created from such activities as cooking, bathing, laundering, etc. through the use of exhaust fans, this condensation is much less apt to take place since the warm air in the house will contain less moisture.

A dwelling vented in this manner need not have an inside relative humidity of more than 40 or 45 percent at a design temperature of 70 degrees F. If such a condition is achieved vapor barriers may be omitted.

Uncontrolled condensation in a plank-and-beam roof may cause paint to peel, planks to rot, or a blistered and leaky roof.

Insulation installed above roof planks should be thick enough to keep the vapor barrier between the insulation and the roof planks warm enough so that the dew point is reached at the point of the barrier.

If the temperature of the roof planks can be kept close to the air temperature in the room, condensation will not occur. As an additional safeguard it is recommended that a vapor barrier be placed between the roof planks and the insulation to keep the moisture in the warm air from penetrating the insulation.

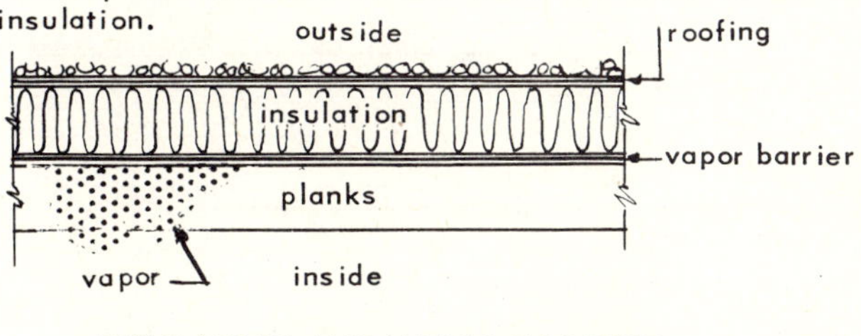
outside
roofing
insulation
vapor barrier
planks
vapor
inside

INSULATION AND VAPOR BARRIER

An additional vapor barrier on the underside of the ceiling will prevent the moisture-laden air from penetrating the wood. This additional protection can be provided by applying various finishing materials to the planks. Several types of paint and "natural" wood finishes are to a high degree impervious to vapor. However, ruptures in this protection may occur from the expansion and contraction of the planks.

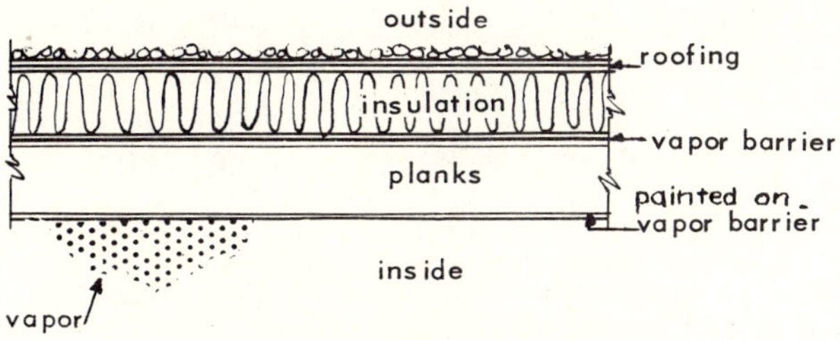
outside
roofing
insulation
vapor barrier
planks
painted on
vapor barrier
inside
vapor

INSULATION AND VAPOR BARRIER

Compiled from "Plank-and-Beam System for Residential Construction" – Housing and Home Finance Agency.

PLANK and BEAM FRAMING

THEORY FOR DESIGN OF PLANKING

All planking computations are based on the use of 2x6 or 2x8 members, tongue-and-grooved or splined, laid flat, and blind and face-nailed. Four jointing types are shown below.
For a good job, well-milled, well-seasoned, straight planks with a moisture content of not more than 14 to 19 percent should be used. Planks should be primed as soon as they are on the job with whatever finish is to be used. After installation of the planking, insulation and roofing should be applied as soon as possible.

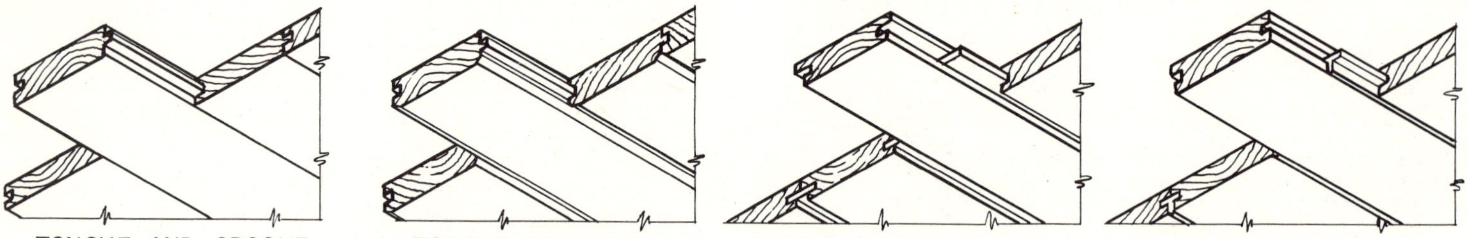

TONGUE-AND-GROOVE | TONGUE-AND-GROOVE WITH V-JOINT | GROOVED AND SPLINED WITH EXPOSED SPLINE | GROOVED PLANK WITH MOLDED SPLINE INSERT

PLANK JOINTING TYPES

Design factors to consider are:
1. Strength of the planks to carry an evenly distributed live load plus an allowance of 10 lbs. per sq. ft. dead load, or weight of the materials.
2. Stiffness to overcome objectionable deflections.

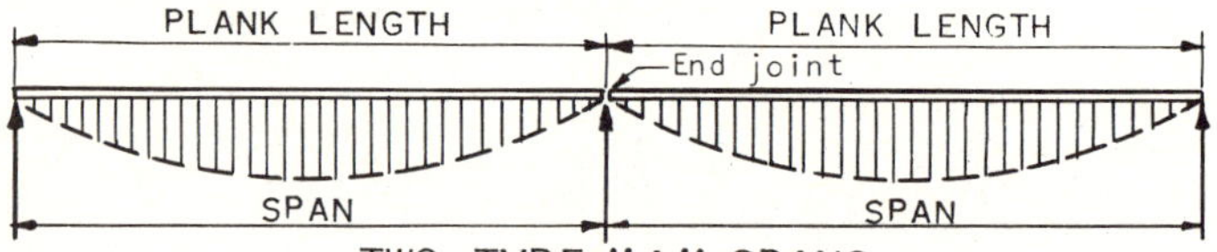

PLANK LENGTH
PLANK LENGTH
End joint
SPAN
SPAN

TWO TYPE "A" SPANS

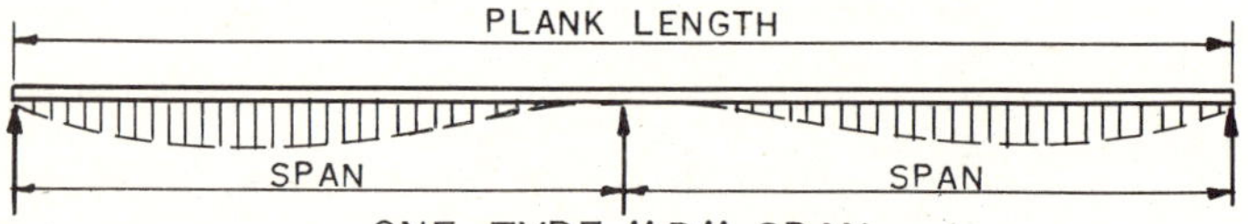

PLANK LENGTH
SPAN
SPAN

ONE TYPE "B" SPAN

DEFLECTION DIAGRAMS FOR EVENLY DISTRIBUTED LOADS

Plank-and-beam framing becomes structurally more efficient when continuous spans are used to develop extra strength.

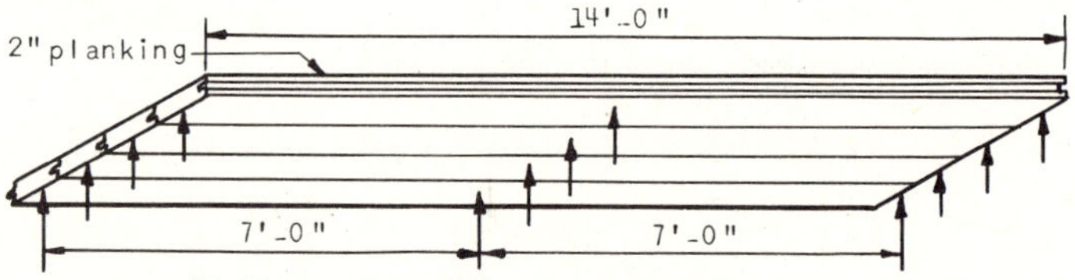

14'-0"
2" planking
7'-0"
7'-0"

PLANK-AND-BEAM FRAMING

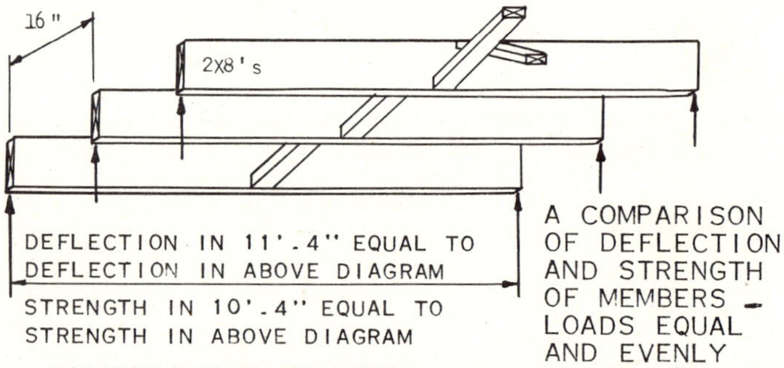

16"
2X8's
DEFLECTION IN 11'-4" EQUAL TO DEFLECTION IN ABOVE DIAGRAM
STRENGTH IN 10'-4" EQUAL TO STRENGTH IN ABOVE DIAGRAM

CONVENTIONAL FRAMING

A COMPARISON OF DEFLECTION AND STRENGTH OF MEMBERS — LOADS EQUAL AND EVENLY DISTRIBUTED

Beams designed as continuous must be built as such or serious failure of members will result. It is recommended that careful inspection of construction be made in all cases where plank-and-beam framing is used.

For any number of spans desired the planking can be laid out in one of the following ways.

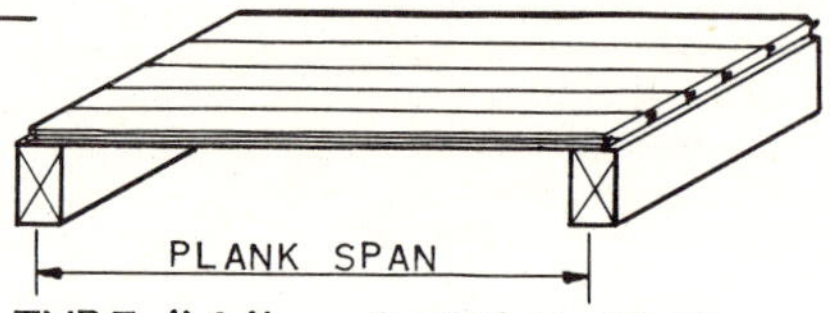

PLANK SPAN

TYPE "A" - SINGLE SPAN

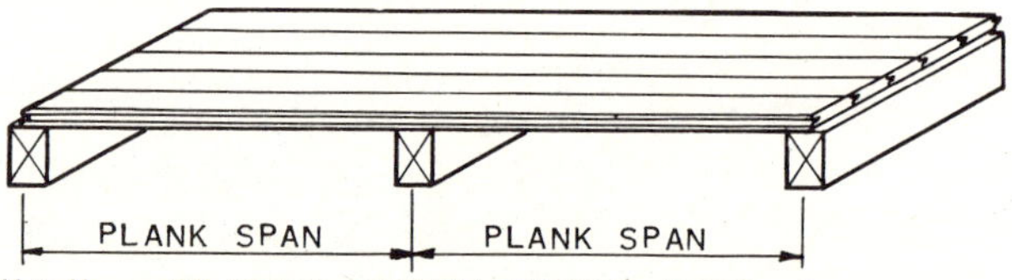

PLANK SPAN
PLANK SPAN

TYPE "B" - PLANKS CONTINUOUS OVER 2 EQUAL SPANS (Nearly 2½ times as stiff as Type "A")

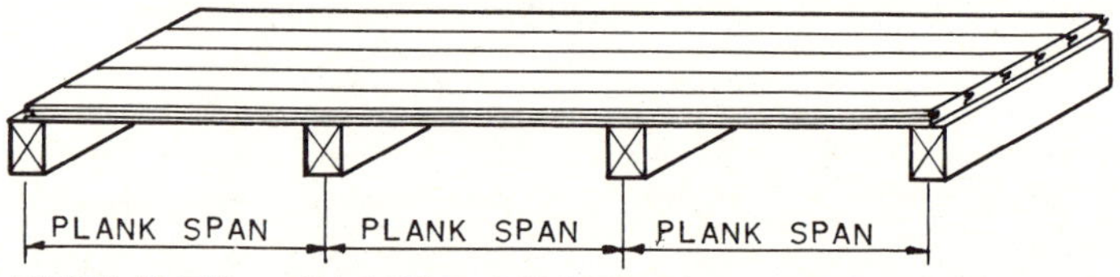

PLANK SPAN
PLANK SPAN
PLANK SPAN

TYPE "C" - PLANKS CONTINUOUS OVER 3 EQUAL SPANS

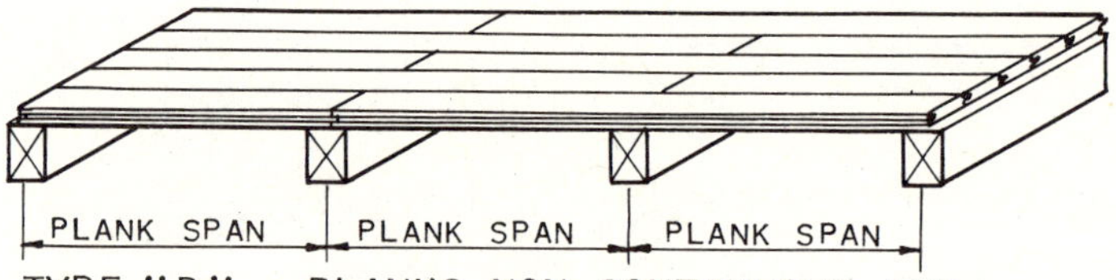

PLANK SPAN
PLANK SPAN
PLANK SPAN

TYPE "D" - PLANKS NON-CONTINUOUS AND STAGGERED OVER 3 EQUAL SPANS

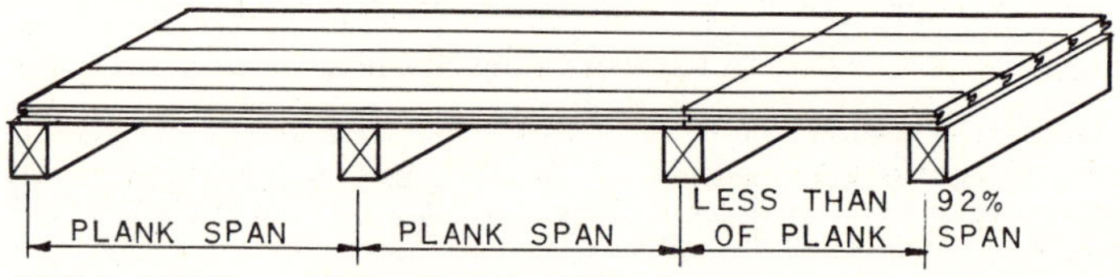

PLANK SPAN
PLANK SPAN
LESS THAN 92% OF PLANK SPAN

TYPE "E" END SPAN NOT EQUAL TO OTHER SPANS

PLANK SPANNING TYPES

If the end span is less than 92% of other plank spans, TYPE E should be used. If the end span is greater than 92%, TYPE D should be used.

Compiled from "Plank-and-Beam System for Residential Construction" — Housing and Home Finance Agency

PLANK and BEAM FRAMING

ROOF AND FLOOR PLANK SELECTION

TABLES ARE BASED ON THE FOLLOWING:

1. All planks are 2 x 6 or 2 x 8 tongue-and-grooved or splined members.
2. Loads are uniformly distributed in pounds per square foot (PSF) on planking.
3. Deflections of 1/240 of span for roof planking and 1/360 of span for floor planking have been arbitrarily used and have been set to avoid deflections which might be objectionable.

TABLES SHOULD BE USED AS FOLLOWS:

1. Select the plank spanning type desired (type A, B, C, D, or E, as previously illustrated).
2. Assume the length of span desired.
3. Determine the total roof or floor load, in pounds per square feet, (which will exist).
4. Refer to TABLE 1 - ROOF AND FLOOR PLANKING to find a group number. Each group number represents a group of species and grades of wood which have a similar modulus of elasticity.
5. Refer to TABLE II - ACCEPTABLE SPECIES AND GRADES OF LUMBER. Under each group number are listed the names and grades of lumber suitable for use under the conditions previously determined.
6. A selection may be made from any group as long as it has a higher modulus of elasticity than the group designated in the tables on roof or floor planking.

TABLE I . ROOF AND FLOOR PLANKING

TO DETERMINE THE GROUP NUMBER (SEE TABLE II) OF THE SPECIES AND GRADES OF WOOD HAVING A SATISFACTORY MODULUS OF ELASTICITY FOR A GIVEN CONDITION

TOTAL LOAD=	ROOF PLANKING-DEFLECTION=1/240 OF SPAN												FLOOR PLANKING DEFLECTION= 1/360 OF SPAN			
	30 PSF				40 PSF				50 PSF				50 PSF			
LENGTH OF PLANK	PLANK TYPE				PLANK TYPE				PLANK TYPE				PLANK TYPE			
	A	B	C	D	A	B	C	D	A	B	C	D	A	B	C	D
6'.0"	1	1	1	1	1	1	1	1	1	1	1	1	3	1	1	1
6'.6"	1	1	1	1	1	1	1	1	2	1	1	1		1	1	3
7'.0"	1	1	1	1	1	1	1	1	4	1	1	1		1	2	5
7'.6"	1	1	1	1	3	1	1	1		1	1	3		2	3	
8'.0"	1	1	1	1		1	1	2		1		5		2		
8'.6"	3	1		1		1		3		1						
9'.0"	5	1		1		1				3						
9'.6"		1		3		1				4						
10'.0"		1		4		3										

NOTE: Numbers refer to group numbers in TABLE II

TABLE II . ACCEPTABLE SPECIES AND GRADES OF LUMBER FOR ROOF AND FLOOR PLANKING

ABBREVIATIONS:

MAS = maximum allowable stress
j & p = joists and plank
PSI = pounds per square inch
f = extreme fiber stress in bending in PSI

GROUP I – MODULUS OF ELASTICITY = 1,100,000 PSI

MAS	COMMERCIAL GRADE NAME	SPECIES
f=1,300	Select structural j & p	Hemlock, eastern
f=1,200	Prime structural j & p	
f=1,100	Common structural j & p	
f= 950	Utility structural j & p	

GROUP 2 – MODULUS OF ELASTICITY = 1,200,000 PSI

MAS	COMMERCIAL GRADE NAME	SPECIES
f=1,250	No. 1 common	Cypress, southern coast type (tidewater red) and inland type
f=1,700	1,700f – grade j & p	
f=1,300	1,300f – grade j & p	
f=1,200	Prime structural j & p	Pine, Norway
f=1,100	Common structural j & p	
f= 950	Utility structural j & p	
f=1,700	Dense structural j & p	Redwood (California)
f=1,300	Heart, structural j & p	
f=1,450	1,450f – structural grade j & p	Spruce, eastern
f=1,300	1,300f – structural grade j & p	
f=1,200	1,200f – structural grade j & p	

GROUP 3 – MODULUS OF ELASTICITY = 1,400,000 PSI

MAS	COMMERCIAL GRADE NAME	SPECIES
f=1,600	1,600f select struct. framing j & p	Hemlock, west coast
f=1,450	1,450f – No. 1 j & p	
f=1,100	1,100f – No. 2 j & p	

GROUP 4 – MODULUS OF ELASTICITY = 1,500,000 PSI

MAS	COMMERCIAL GRADE NAME	SPECIES
f=1,900	Structural j & p	Douglas fir, inland region
f=1,450	Common structural j & p	
f=2,150	Select structural j & p	Larch
f=1,900	Structural j & p	
f=1,450	Common structural j & p	

GROUP 5 – MODULUS OF ELASTICITY = 1,600,000 PSI

MAS	COMMERCIAL GRADE NAME	SPECIES
f=2,150	Dense select structural j & p	Douglas fir, coast region
f=1,900	Select structural j & p	
f=1,700	1,700f – Dense No. 1 j & p	
f=1,450	1,450f – No. 1 j & p	
f=1,100	1,100f – No. 2 j & p	
f=2,150	Select structural j & p	Douglas fir, inland region
f=2,400	Dense select structural j & p	Pine, southern
f=2,000	Dense structural j & p	
f=1,800	Dense struct. sq. edge & sound j & p	
f=1,600	Dense No. 1 structural j & p	
f=1,400	No. 1 dense 1,400f j & p	
f=1,200	No. 1 1,200f j & p	
f=1,700	No. 1 dense j & p	
f=1,450	No. 1 j & p	
f=1,250	No. 2 dense j & p	
f=1,100	No. 2 j & p	
f=2,400	Select structural longleaf j & p	Pine, southern longleaf
f=2,000	Prime structural longleaf j & p	
f=1,800	Merchantable struct. longleaf j & p	
f=1,800	Struct. sq. edge & sound longleaf j&p	
f=1,600	No. 1 structural longleaf j & p	
f=1,400	No. 1 longleaf 1,400f j & p	
f=1,700	No. 1 longleaf j & p	
f=1,250	No. 2 longleaf j & p	

Compiled from "Plank-and-Beam System for Residential Construction" – Housing and Home Finance Agency

PLANK and BEAM FRAMING

STRUCTURAL DESIGN OF BEAMS

The following graphs are to aid in the selection of wood species and sizes for roof and floor beams. For roof beams the maximum deflection is limited to 1/240 of the beam span and the graphs cover 20, 30, and 40 PSF (pounds per square foot) uniformly distributed live loads, each with a 10 PSF dead load. For floor beams the maximum deflection is limited to 1/360 of the beam span, and the graphs cover a 40 PSF uniformly distributed live load with a 10 PSF dead load. The species and grades of lumber suitable for the beam sizes and spans indicated are listed below each graph.

The graphs are set up to cover bending, and selections made from them must be checked to determine whether or not horizontal shear will govern the size of the beam. If the beam has an L/h (L = beam length in feet and h = beam depth in inches) equal to or greater than the L/h for the species and grade of lumber desired, the horizontal shear does not govern, and therefore the selection made from the graph is valid.

ROOF BEAMS

MAXIMUM DEFLECTION LIMITED TO 1/240 OF THE BEAM SPAN

GRAPHS NO. 1, 2 AND 3 ARE FOR A 20 PSF UNIFORMLY DISTRIBUTED LIVE LOAD AND A 10 PSF DEAD LOAD EQUALING A TOTAL LOAD OF 30 PSF

GRAPHS NO. 4, 5 AND 6 ARE FOR A 30 PSF UNIFORMLY DISTRIBUTED LIVE LOAD AND A 10 PSF DEAD LOAD EQUALING A TOTAL LOAD OF 40 PSF

GRAPHS NO. 7, 8 AND 9 ARE FOR A 40 PSF UNIFORMLY DISTRIBUTED LIVE LOAD AND A 10 PSF DEAD LOAD EQUALING A TOTAL LOAD OF 50 PSF

GRAPH #1 TOTAL LOAD= 30 PSF

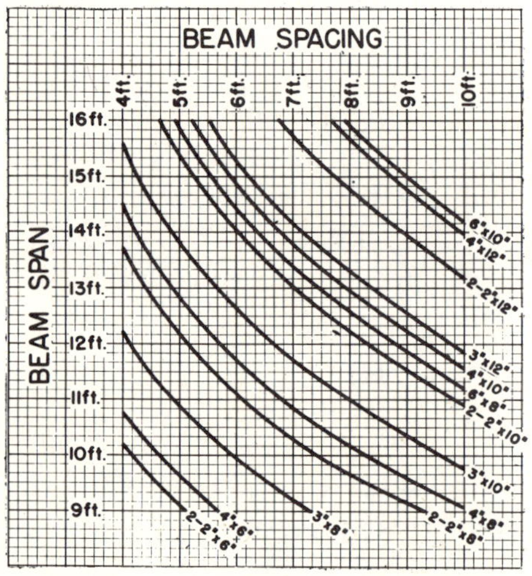
BEAM SPACING
4ft.
5ft.
6ft.
7ft.
8ft.
9ft.
10ft.
BEAM SPAN
16ft.
15ft.
14ft.
13ft.
12ft.
11ft.
10ft.
9ft.

SPECIES	GRADE	MIN L/h
Douglas fir, coast region	1,000f - No 2 joists & plank	0.83
Hemlock, eastern	Common structural joists & plank	1.53
Hemlock, west coast	1,000f - No. 2 joists & plank	1.02
Pine, Norway	Common structural joists & plank	1.22
Pine, southern	No. 2 joists & plank	1.08

GRAPH #2 TOTAL LOAD= 30 PSF

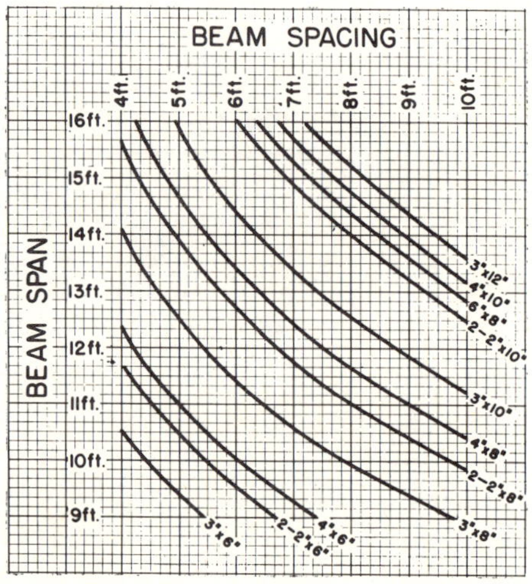
BEAM SPACING
4ft.
5ft.
6ft.
7ft.
8ft.
9ft.
10ft.
BEAM SPAN
16ft.
15ft.
14ft.
13ft.
12ft.
11ft.
10ft.
9ft.

SPECIES	GRADE	MIN L/h
Douglas fir, coast region	1,450f - No. 1 joists & plank	1.01
Douglas fir, inland region	Common structural joists & plank	1.27
Hemlock, west coast	1,450f - No. 1 joists & plank	1.21
Larch	Common structural joists & plank	1.01
Pine, southern	No. 1 joists & plank	0.97
Spruce, eastern	1,450f structural grade joists & plank	1.10

GRAPH #3 TOTAL LOAD= 30 PSF

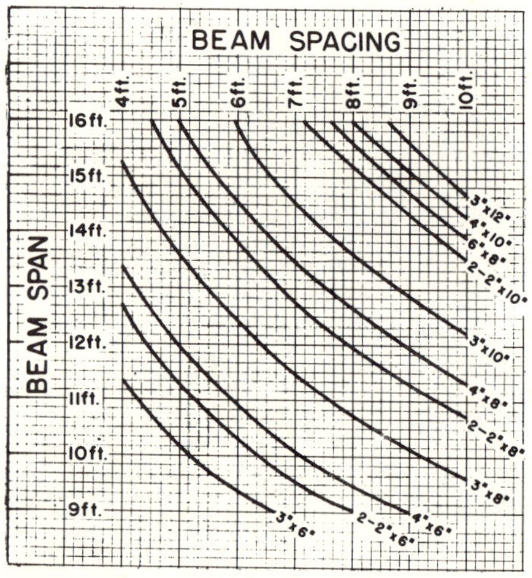
BEAM SPACING
4ft.
5ft.
6ft.
7ft.
8ft.
9ft.
10ft.
BEAM SPAN
16ft.
15ft.
14ft.
13ft.
12ft.
11ft.
10ft.
9ft.

SPECIES	GRADE	MIN L/h
Pine, southern	No. 1 dense joists & plank	0.94
Pine, southern longleaf	No. 1 longleaf joists & plank	0.94

Compiled from "Plank-and-Beam System for Residential Construction" – Housing and Home Finance Agency

PLANK and BEAM FRAMING

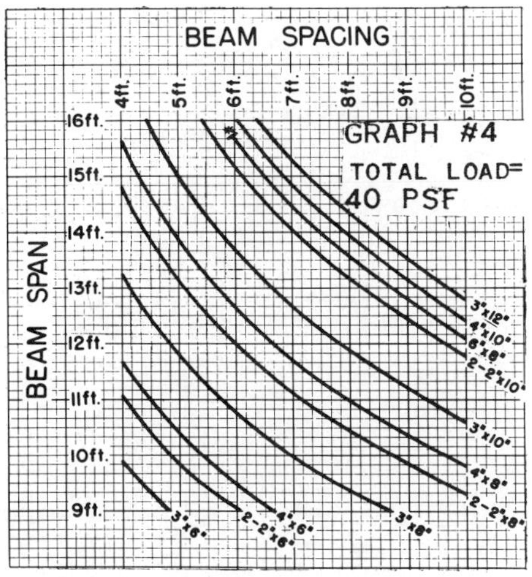
BEAM SPACING
4ft. 5ft. 6ft. 7ft. 8ft. 9ft. 10ft.
BEAM SPAN
16ft. 15ft. 14ft. 13ft. 12ft. 11ft. 10ft. 9ft.
GRAPH #4
TOTAL LOAD= 40 PSF
3"x12"
4"x10"
6"x8"
2-2"x10"
3"x10"
4"x8"
2-2"x8"
3"x8"
4"x6"
2-2"x6"
3"x6"

SPECIES	GRADE	MIN L/h
Pine, southern	No. 1 dense joists & plank	0.94
Pine, southern longleaf	No. 1 longleaf joists & plank	0.94

* On graph indicates the beam span beyond which the deflection will exceed 1/240 of the span.

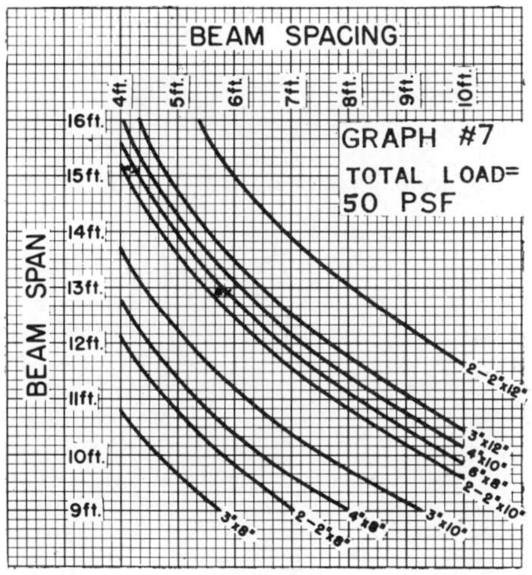
BEAM SPACING
4ft. 5ft. 6ft. 7ft. 8ft. 9ft. 10ft.
BEAM SPAN
16ft. 15ft. 14ft. 13ft. 12ft. 11ft. 10ft. 9ft.
GRAPH #7
TOTAL LOAD= 50 PSF
2-2"x12"
3"x12"
4"x10"
6"x8"
2-2"x10"
3"x8"
2-2"x8"
4"x8"
3"x10"

SPECIES	GRADE	MIN L/h
Douglas fir, coast region	1,450f - No.1 joists & plank	1.01
Douglas fir, inland region	Common structural joists & plank	1.27
Hemlock, west coast	1,450f - No. 1 joists& plank	1.21
Larch	Common structural joists & plank	1.01
Pine, southern	No.1 joists & plank	0.97
Spruce, eastern	1,450 f structural grade joists & plank	1.10

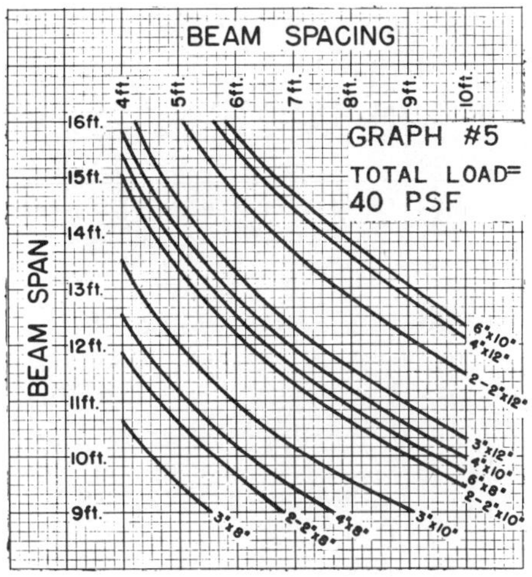
BEAM SPACING
4ft. 5ft. 6ft. 7ft. 8ft. 9ft. 10ft.
BEAM SPAN
16ft. 15ft. 14ft. 13ft. 12ft. 11ft. 10ft. 9ft.
GRAPH #5
TOTAL LOAD= 40 PSF
6"x10"
4"x12"
2-2"x12"
3"x12"
4"x10"
6"x8"
2-2"x10"
3"x8"
2-2"x8"
4"x8"
3"x10"

SPECIES	GRADE	MIN L/h
Douglas fir, coast region	1,100f - No. 2 joists & plank	0.83
Hemlock, eastern	Common structural joists & plank	1.53
Hemlock, west coast	1,100f - No. 2 joists & plank	1.02
Pine, Norway	Common structural joists & plank	1.22
Pine, southern	No. 2 joists & plank	1.08

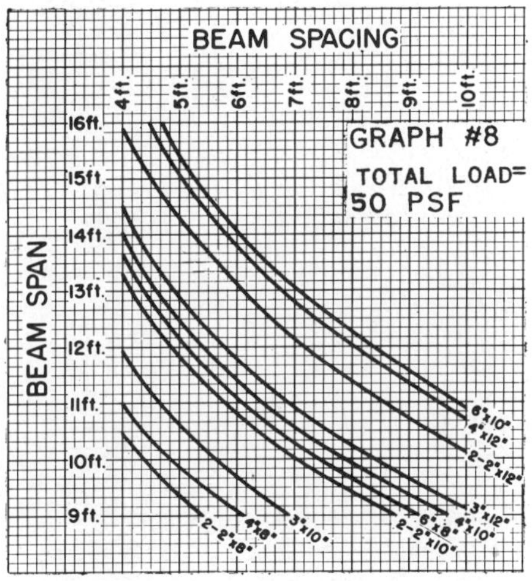
BEAM SPACING
4ft. 5ft. 6ft. 7ft. 8ft. 9ft. 10ft.
BEAM SPAN
16ft. 15ft. 14ft. 13ft. 12ft. 11ft. 10ft. 9ft.
GRAPH #8
TOTAL LOAD= 50 PSF
6"x10"
4"x12"
2-2"x12"
3"x12"
4"x10"
6"x8"
2-2"x10"
2-2"x8"
4"x8"
3"x10"

SPECIES	GRADE	MIN L/h
Douglas fir, coast region	1,100f - No. 2 joists & plank	0.83
Hemlock, eastern	Common structural joists & plank	1.53
Hemlock, west coast	1,100f - No. 2 joists & plank	1.02
Pine, Norway	Common structural joists & plank	1.22
Pine, southern	No. 2 joists & plank	1.08

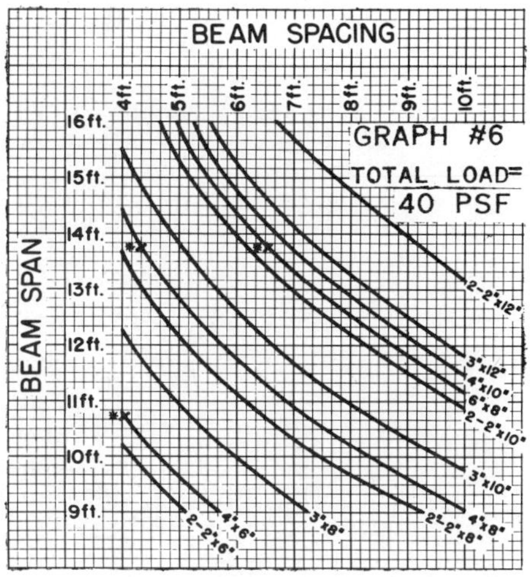
BEAM SPACING
4ft. 5ft. 6ft. 7ft. 8ft. 9ft. 10ft.
BEAM SPAN
16ft. 15ft. 14ft. 13ft. 12ft. 11ft. 10ft. 9ft.
GRAPH #6
TOTAL LOAD= 40 PSF
2-2"x12"
3"x12"
4"x10"
6"x8"
2-2"x10"
3"x10"
4"x8"
2-2"x8"
3"x8"
4"x6"
2-2"x6"

SPECIES	GRADE	MIN L/h
Douglas fir, coast region	1,450f - No. 1 joists & plank	1.01
Douglas fir, inland region	Common structural joists & plank	1.27
Hemlock, west coast	1,450f - No. 1 joists & plank	1.21
Larch	Common structural joists & plank	1.01
Pine, southern	No.1 joists & plank	0.97
Spruce, eastern	1,450f structural grade joists & plank	1.10

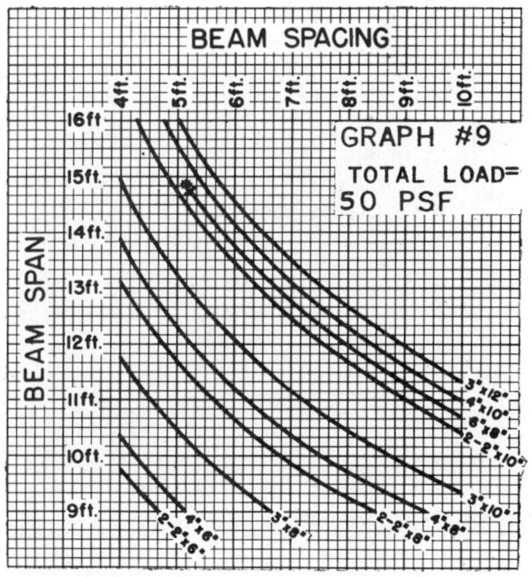
BEAM SPACING
4ft. 5ft. 6ft. 7ft. 8ft. 9ft. 10ft.
BEAM SPAN
16ft 15ft. 14ft. 13ft. 12ft. 11ft. 10ft. 9ft.
GRAPH #9
TOTAL LOAD= 50 PSF
3"x12"
4"x10"
6"x8"
2-2"x10"
3"x10"
4"x8"
2-2"x8"
3"x8"
4"x6"
2-2"x6"

SPECIES	GRADE	MIN L/h
Pine, southern	No. 1 dense joists & plank	0.94
Pine southern longleaf	No. 1 longleaf joists & plank	0.94

* On graph indicates the beam span beyond which the deflection will exceed 1/240 of the span.

Compiled from "Plank-and-Beam System for Residential Construction" – Housing and Home Finance Agency

FLOOR BEAMS

MAXIMUM DEFLECTION LIMITED TO 1/360 OF THE BEAM SPAN

THE FOLLOWING GRAPHS ARE FOR A 40 PSF UNIFORMLY DISTRIBUTED LIVE LOAD AND A 10 PSF DEAD LOAD, EQUALING A TOTAL LOAD OF 50 PSF

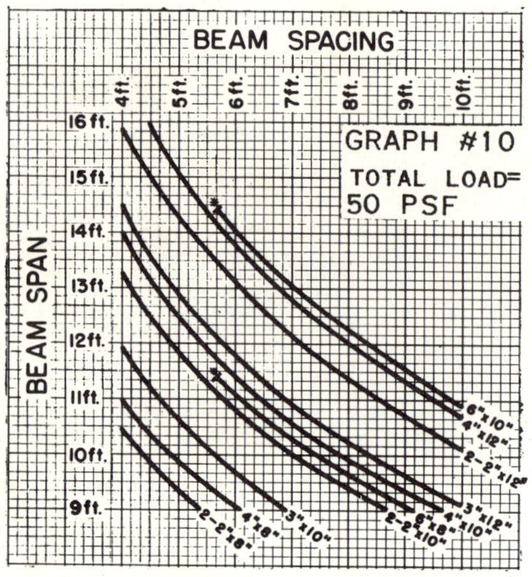
BEAM SPACING
4ft. 5ft. 6ft. 7ft. 8ft. 9ft. 10ft.
GRAPH #10
TOTAL LOAD= 50 PSF
BEAM SPAN
16ft. 15ft. 14ft. 13ft. 12ft. 11ft. 10ft. 9ft.
6"x10"
4"x12"
2-2"x12"
3"x12"
4"x10"
6"x8"
2-2"x10"
3"x10"
4"x8"
2-2"x8"

SPECIES	GRADE	MIN L/h
Pine, Norway	Common structural joists & plank	1.22

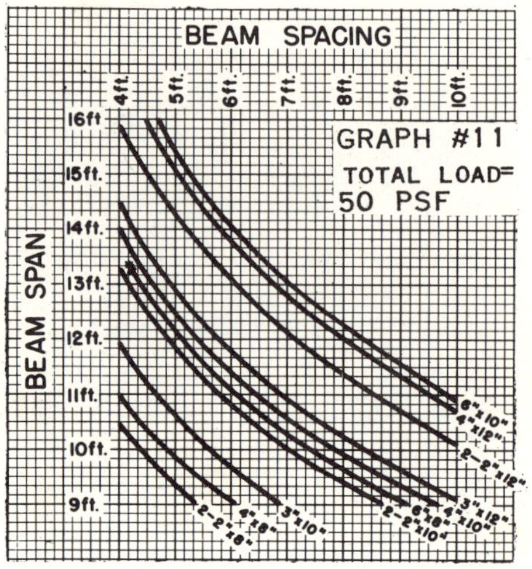
BEAM SPACING
4ft. 5ft. 6ft. 7ft. 8ft. 9ft. 10ft.
GRAPH #11
TOTAL LOAD= 50 PSF
BEAM SPAN
16ft 15ft. 14ft. 13ft. 12ft. 11ft. 10ft. 9ft.
6"x10"
4"x12"
2-2"x12"
3"x12"
4"x10"
6"x8"
2-2"x10"
3"x10"
4"x8"
2-2"x8"

SPECIES	GRADE	MIN L/h
Hemlock, west coast	1,000 f - No. 2 joists & plank	1.02

* On graph indicates the beam span beyond which the deflection will exceed 1/360 of the span.

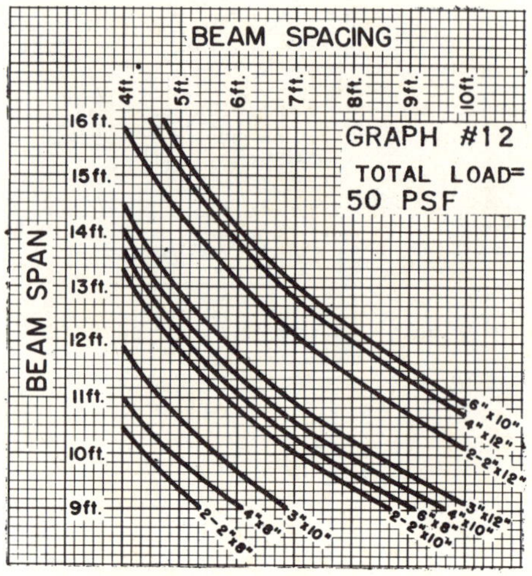
BEAM SPACING
4ft. 5ft. 6ft. 7ft. 8ft. 9ft. 10ft.
GRAPH #12
TOTAL LOAD= 50 PSF
BEAM SPAN
16ft. 15ft. 14ft. 13ft. 12ft. 11ft. 10ft. 9ft.
6"x10"
4"x12"
2-2"x12"
3"x12"
4"x10"
6"x8"
2-2"x10"
3"x10"
4"x8"
2-2"x8"

SPECIES	GRADE	MIN L/h
Douglas fir, coast region	1,100 f - No. 2 joists & plank	0.83
Pine, southern	No. 2 joists & plank	1.08

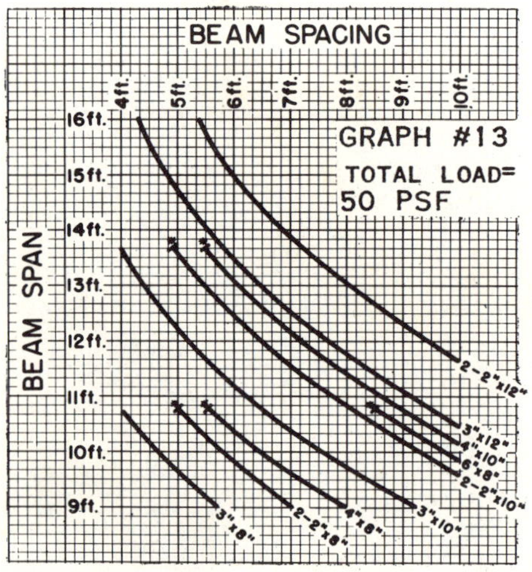
BEAM SPACING
4ft. 5ft. 6ft. 7ft. 8ft. 9ft. 10ft.
GRAPH #13
TOTAL LOAD= 50 PSF
BEAM SPAN
16ft. 15ft. 14ft. 13ft. 12ft. 11ft. 10ft. 9ft.
2-2"x12"
3"x12"
4"x10"
6"x8"
2-2"x10"
3"x10"
4"x8"
2-2"x8"
3"x8"

SPECIES	GRADE	MIN L/h
Douglas fir, Inland region	Common structural joists & plank	0.96
Larch	Common structural joists & plank	1.01

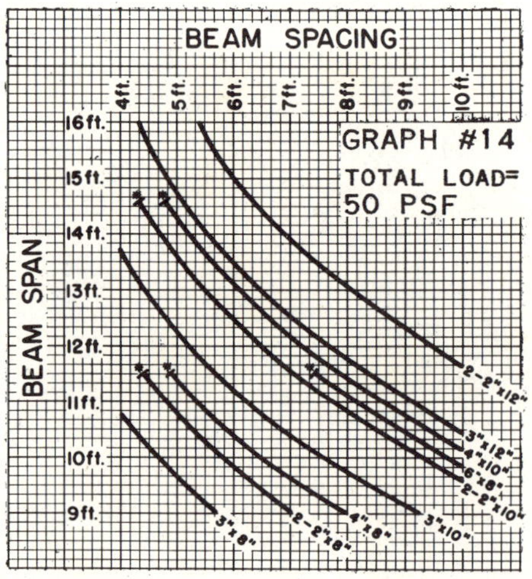
BEAM SPACING
4ft. 5ft. 6ft. 7ft. 8ft. 9ft. 10ft.
GRAPH #14
TOTAL LOAD= 50 PSF
BEAM SPAN
16ft. 15ft. 14ft. 13ft. 12ft. 11ft. 10ft. 9ft.
2-2"x12"
3"x12"
4"x10"
6"x8"
2-2"x10"
3"x10"
4"x8"
2-2"x8"
3"x8"

SPECIES	GRADE	MIN L/h
Douglas fir, coast region	1,450 f - No. 1 joists & plank	1.01
Pine, southern	No. 1 joists & plank	0.97

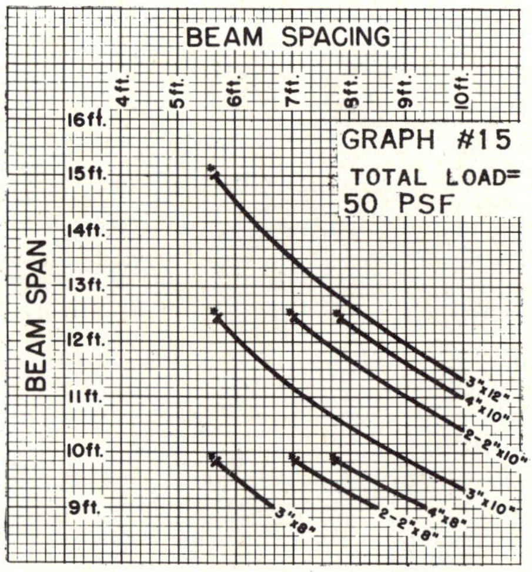
BEAM SPACING
4ft. 5ft. 6ft. 7ft. 8ft. 9ft. 10ft.
GRAPH #15
TOTAL LOAD= 50 PSF
BEAM SPAN
16ft. 15ft. 14ft. 13ft. 12ft. 11ft. 10ft. 9ft.
3"x12"
4"x10"
2-2"x10"
3"x10"
4"x8"
2-2"x8"
3"x8"

SPECIES	GRADE	MIN L/h
Pine, southern	No. 1 dense joists & plank	0.94
Pine, southern longleaf	No. 1 longleaf joists & plank	0.94

* On graph indicates the beam span beyond which the deflection will exceed 1/360 of the span.

Compiled from "Plank-and-Beam System for Residential Construction" – Housing and Home Finance Agency

LUMBER GRADING and SIZES

YARD LUMBER - GRADE STANDARDS

Yard Lumber: Lumber which is manufactured and classified, on a quality basis, into those sizes, shapes, and qualities required for ordinary construction and general-purpose uses.

Total products of a typical log arranged in a series according to quality as determined by appearance and use.

- SELECT — Lumber of good appearance & finishing qualities
  - Suitable for natural finishes.
    - Grade A: Practically clear
    - Grade B: Of high quality-generally clear.
  - Suitable for paint finishes.
    - Grade C: Adapted to high quality paint finish.
    - Grade D: Intermediate between higher finishing grades and common grades & partaking somewhat, the nature of both.
- COMMON — Lumber which is suitable for general utility & construction purposes. Not of fin. quality.
  - Suitable for use without waste.
    - #1 Common: Sound & tight-knotted. May be considered water-tight lumber.
    - #2 Common: Less restricted in quality than #1 but of the same general quality.
  - For use permitting some waste.
    - #3 Common: Prevailing grade characteristics larger than in #2
    - #4 Common: Low quality.
    - #5 Common: Lowest recognized grade, but must be usable.

YARD LUMBER - SIZE STANDARDS

The minimum thicknesses & widths of finished lumber, surfaced either 1 side, 2 sides, 1 edge, 2 edges, or any combination thereof, are as follows:(Widths apply to all thick. & vice versa, except as modified).*

PRODUCT All sizes in inches	SIZE Board Measure Thickness	 Width	DRESSED DIMENSIONS Thickness	 Width
FINISH: COMMON OR SELECT	3/8	3	5/16	2 5/8
	1/2	4	7/16	3 1/2
	5/8	5	9/16	4 1/2
	3/4	6	11/16	5 1/2
	1	7	25/32	6 1/2
	1 1/4	8	1 1/16	7 1/4
	1 1/2	9	1 5/16	8 1/4
	1 3/4	10	1 7/16	9 1/4
	2	11	1 5/8	10 1/4
	2 1/2	12	2 1/8	11 1/4
	3	14	2 5/8	13
DIMENSION, PLANK & JOISTS	.	2	.	1 5/8
	.	3	.	2 5/8
	2	4	1 5/8	3 5/8
	2 1/2	6	2 1/8	5 1/2
	3	8	2 5/8	7 1/2
	3 1/2	10	3 1/8	9 1/2
	4	12	3 5/8	11 1/2
	.	14	.	13 1/2
	.	16	.	15 1/2
	.	18	.	17 1/2
STEPPING	.	.	.	.
	1	.	25/32	.
	1 1/4	8	1 1/16	7 1/4
	1 1/2	10	1 5/16	9 1/4
	2	12	1 5/8	11 1/4
	.	.	.	.
BEVEL SIDING	.	4	7/16 x 3/16	3 1/2
	.	5	15/32 x 3/16	4 1/2
	.	6	.	5 1/2
WIDE BEVEL SIDING	.	8	7/16 x 3/16	7 1/4
	.	10	9/16 x 3/16	9 1/4
	.	12	11/16 x 3/16	11 1/4
RUSTIC & DROP SIDING shiplapped	.	4	9/16	3 1/8
	.	5	3/4	4 1/8
	.	6	.	5 1/16
	.	8	.	6 7/8
RUSTIC & DROP SIDING dressed & matched	.	4	9/16	3 1/4
	.	5	3/4	4 1/4
	.	6	.	5 3/16
	.	8	.	6 11/16

PRODUCT All sizes in inches	SIZE Board Measure Thickness	 Width	DRESSED DIMENSIONS Thickness	 Width
FLOORING (excluding hardwoods)	3/8	2	5/16 *	1 1/2 *
	1/2	3	7/16 *	2 3/8 *
	5/8	4	9/16 *	3 1/4
	1	5	25/32	4 1/4
	1 1/4	6	1 1/16	5 3/16
	1 1/2	.	1 5/16	.
CEILING	3/8	3	5/16 *	2 3/8 *
	1/2	4	7/16 *	3 1/4 *
	5/8	5	9/16 *	4 1/4 *
	3/4	6	11/16	5 3/16
PARTITION	1	3	23/32	2 3/8
	.	4	.	3 1/4
	.	5	.	4 1/4
	.	6	.	5 3/16
SHIPLAP 3/8" or 1/2" lap	1	4	25/32	3 1/8
	.	6	.	5 1/8
	.	8	.	7 1/8
	.	10	.	9 1/8
	.	12	.	11 1/8
CENTER MATCHED	1	4	25/32	3 1/4
	1 1/4	6	1 1/16	5 3/16
	1 1/2	8	1 5/16	7
	.	10	.	9
	.	12	.	11

PRODUCT	SIZE Board Measure Thickness	 Width	DRESSED DIMENSION Thickness	FACE WIDTH D & M	 Shiplapped	 Grooved for Splines
† FACTORY FLOORING HEAVY ROOFING, DECKING & SHEET PILING	2	4	1 5/8	3 1/8	3	3 1/2
	2 1/2	6	2 1/8	5 1/8	5	5 1/2
	3	8	2 5/8	7	7	7 1/2
	4	10	3 5/8	9	9	9 1/2
	5	12	4 5/8	11	11	11 1/2

† In patterned lumber 2" or more thick, board measure, the tongue (in T & G) shall be 3/8" wide, the lap (in shiplapped) 1/2" wide, with overall widths 3/8" and 1/2" wider respectively than face widths above.

* Tongue (in T & G) or lap (in shiplap) 3/16" wide with overall width 3/16" wider than shown above. In all other patterned lumber, the tongue shall be 1/4" wide, the lap 3/8" wide, with overall widths 1/4" and 3/8" wider respectively.

American Lumber Standard - Simplified Practice Recommendation R16-53

WOOD JOIST and RAFTER SIZES

NOTES APPLICABLE TO FOLLOWING PAGES ON JOIST AND RAFTER SIZES*

SPANS LIMITED BY DEFLECTION *were computed for the assumed loads to cause a deflection not exceeding 1/360 of the span. This limit usually chosen to prevent cracking of plastered ceilings. The weight of plaster itself was ignored in the assumed loads for the deflection computations as the initial deflection from the dead load occurs before plaster sets. The influence of live loads, rather than dead loads, when the ratio of live to dead loads is relatively high, is the principal factor to be considered. Also with joisted floors, flooring and bridging serve to distribute moving or concentrated loads to adjoining members. The omission of the plaster weight in load assumptions applies to deflection computations only; the full dead and live load is considered when computing for strength.*

SPANS LIMITED BY BENDING STRENGTH OF PIECE *may be used where ceilings are not plastered and deflection is not objectionable.*

SPANS LIMITED BY HORIZONTAL SHEAR. *For the heavier loads where horizontal shear may be a factor, the tables give the horizontal shear "H" induced by the load for each beam for the spans shown. If the horizontal shear "H" shown is greater than permitted for the material used, select another size joist or spacing within the proper shear limit.*

E - *modulus of elasticity.*
f - *extreme fiber stress in bending.*
H - *horizontal shear.*
L - *span length between supports.*

DEAD LOAD ASSUMPTIONS. *The following average weights of various materials were used as the basis for dead loads in computing the span lengths. All in lbs. per sq. ft.*

Finished floor 2.5
Rough floor 2.5
Roof sheathing 2.5
Plaster and lath 10.0
Roof Coverings
Group 1 Assumed as 2.5 lbs. per sq. ft. including:
Shingles 2.5
Copper sheets 1.5
Copper tile 1.75
Three-ply ready roofing 1.00
Group 2 Assumed as 8 lbs. per sq. ft. including:
Five-ply felt and gravel. 7
Slate, 3/16" 7-¼
Roman tile 8
Spanish tile. 8
Ludowici tile 8
Joists based on average weight of wood of 40 lbs. per cu. ft.

LIVE LOAD ASSUMPTIONS. *Uniformly distributed.*

PARTITIONS. *Spans shown are computed for the given live load plus the dead load and do not provide for additional loads such as partitions. Where concentrated loads are imposed the spans should be re-computed to provide for them.*

"Maximum Spans for Joists and Rafters", Supplement No. 3, National Lumber Manufacturers Association.

MAXIMUM ALLOWABLE LENGTHS BETWEEN SUPPORTS

CEILING JOISTS

SIZE NOMINAL	C TO C INCHES		SPAN LIMITED BY DEFLECTION			
		E=	1000000	1200000	1400000	1600000
			Ft In	Ft In	Ft In	Ft In
2 X 4	12	L	9- 4	10- 0	10- 6	11- 0
	16	L	8- 7	9- 2	9- 8	10- 1
	24	L	7- 7	8- 1	8- 6	8-11
2 X 6	12	L	14- 2	15- 1	15-10	16- 7
	16	L	13- 1	13-11	14- 8	15- 4
	24	L	11- 8	12- 5	13- 1	13- 8
2 X 8	12	L	18- 6	19- 8	20- 8	21- 7
	16	L	17- 2	18- 3	19- 3	20- 1
	24	L	15- 4	16- 4	17- 2	17-11
2 X 10	12	L	22-11	24- 4	25- 7	26- 9
	16	L	21- 5	22- 9	23-11	25- 0
	24	L	19- 2	20- 5	21- 6	22- 5
2 X 12	12	L	27- 2	28-11	30- 5	
	16	L	25- 5	27- 1	28- 6	29- 9
	24	L	23- 0	24- 5	25- 8	26-10

NOTE: – The span lengths are based on:
Ceiling joists –
Maximum allowable deflection of 1/360 of the span length.
Dead load –* Weight of joists plus plaster ceiling (10# sq. ft.)
Live load – None.

* Weight of joist assumed to be 40 lbs. per cu. ft.

ATTIC FLOOR JOISTS

SIZE NOMINAL	C TO C INCHES		SPAN LIMITED BY DEFLECTION			
		E=	1000000	1200000	1400000	1600000
			Ft In	Ft In	Ft In	Ft In
2 X 4	12	L	6- 6	6-11	7- 4	7- 8
	16	L	6- 0	6- 4	6- 8	7- 0
	24	L	5- 3	5- 7	5-10	6- 1
2 X 6	12	L	10- 1	10- 8	11- 3	11- 9
	16	L	9- 2	9- 9	10- 4	10- 9
	24	L	8- 1	8- 7	9- 1	9- 6
2 X 8	12	L	13- 4	14- 2	14-11	15- 7
	16	L	12- 2	13- 0	13- 8	14- 3
	24	L	10- 9	11- 5	12- 0	12- 7
2 X 10	12	L	16- 9	17- 9	18- 8	19- 7
	16	L	15- 4	16- 4	17- 2	17-11
	24	L	13- 6	14- 5	15- 2	15-10
2 X 12	12	L	20- 1	21- 4	22- 5	23- 6
	16	L	18- 6	19- 7	20- 8	21- 7
	24	L	16- 4	17- 4	18- 3	19- 1

NOTE: – The span lengths are based on:
Attic Floor joists –
Maximum allowable deflection of 1/360 of the span length.
Dead load –* Weight of joist, plus:
Weight of lath and plaster ceiling (10# sq. ft.)
Single thickness of flooring (2.5 to 3 lbs. sq. ft)
Live load – 20 lbs. per sq. ft. of floor area.

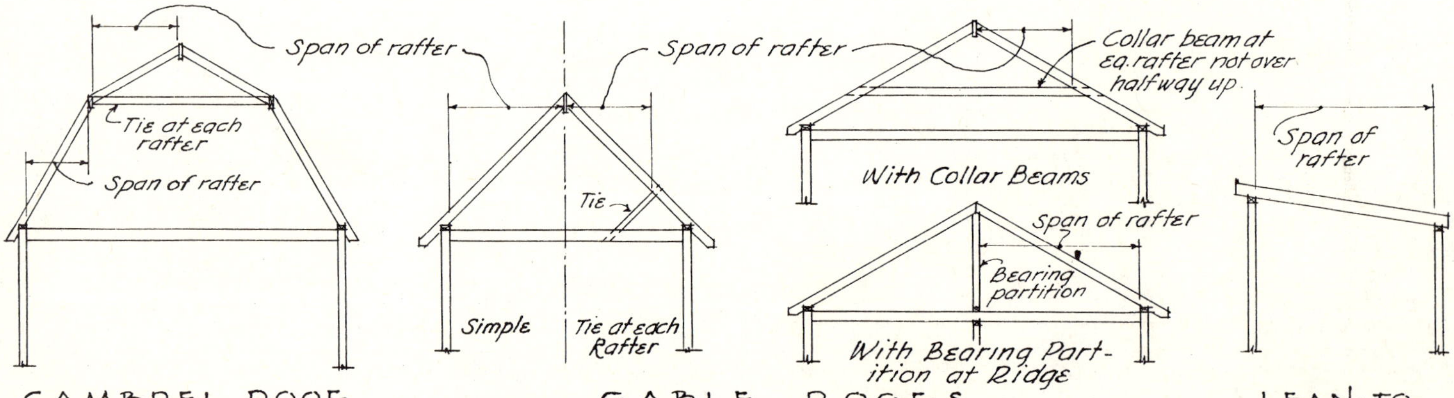
Span of rafter
Tie at each rafter
Span of rafter
Span of rafter
Tie
Simple
Tie at each Rafter
Collar beam at ea. rafter not over halfway up
With Collar Beams
Span of rafter
Bearing partition
With Bearing Partition at Ridge
Span of rafter

GAMBREL ROOF　　GABLE ROOFS　　LEAN-TO or SHED

RAFTER SPANS

WOOD JOIST *and* RAFTER SIZES

RAFTERS and ROOF JOISTS - 20 POUND LIVE LOAD - GROUP I ROOF COVERING

MAXIMUM ALLOWABLE LENGTHS BETWEEN SUPPORTS

From building code or other authority determine the allowable modulus of elasticity "E" (if span is to be limited by deflection) or the allowable extreme fiber stress in bending "f" (if span is to be determined by bending) for the species and grade of lumber used. Refer to the column below with corresponding value to determine the safe span for size and spacing of rafter and roof joist desired. Check span selected for deflection with spans for bending to see it does not exceed length permitted for bending stress "f" of material used.

SECTION MODULUS $S = \frac{bd^2}{6}$

2 x 4 = 3.56 in.^{3}	
2 x 6 = 8.57	3 x 6 = 13.84 in.^{3}
2 x 8 = 15.32	3 x 8 = 24.60
2 x 10 = 24.44	3 x 10 = 39.48
2 x 12 = 35.82	3 x 12 = 57.86
2 x 14 = 49.36	3 x 14 = 79.73

SIZE (NOM.) IN INCHES	SPAC'G C to C IN INCHES	SPAN LIMITED BY DEFLECTION					SPAN DETERMINED BY BENDING										
		E=	1000000	1200000	1400000	1600000	f=	900	1000	1100	1200	1300	1400	1500	1600	1700	1800
			Ft In	Ft In	Ft In	Ft In		Ft In	Ft In	Ft In	Ft In	Ft In	Ft In	Ft In	Ft In	Ft In	Ft In
2 X 4	12	L	7- 1	7- 7	7-11	8- 4	L	9- 0	9- 5	9-11	10- 4	10- 9	11- 2	11- 7	11-11	12- 4	12- 8
	16	L	6- 6	6-11	7- 3	7- 7	L	7-10	8- 3	8- 8	9- 0	9- 5	9- 9	10- 1	10- 5	10- 9	11- 1
2 X 6	12	L	10-11	11- 7	12- 2	12- 9	L	13- 8	14- 5	15- 1	15- 9	16- 5	17- 1	17- 8	18- 3	18- 9	19- 4
	16	L	10- 0	10- 7	11- 2	11- 8	L	12- 0	12- 8	13- 3	13-10	14- 5	14-11	15- 6	16- 0	16- 6	16-11
2 X 8	12	L	14- 5	15- 3	16- 1	16-10	L	17-11	18-11	19-10	20- 9	21- 7	22- 4	23- 2	23-11	24- 8	25- 4
	16	L	13- 3	14- 0	14- 9	15- 5	L	15- 9	16- 8	17- 5	18- 3	19- 0	19- 8	20- 4	21- 0	21- 8	22- 4
2 X 10	12	L	18- 0	19- 2	20- 2	21- 1	L	22- 4	23- 7	24- 9	25-10	26-11	27-11	28-11	29-10	30- 9	
	16	L	16- 7	17- 8	18- 7	19- 5	L	19- 9	20-10	21-10	22-10	23- 9	24- 8	25- 6	26- 4	27- 2	27-11
2 X 12	12	L	21- 7	23- 0	24- 2	25- 3	L	26- 8	28- 1	29- 6	30-10						
	16	L	19-11	21- 2	22- 3	23- 4	L	23- 8	24-11	26- 1	27- 3	28- 5	29- 6	30- 6			
2 X 14	12	L	25- 2	26- 8	28- 1	29- 5	L	30-10									
	16	L	23- 3	24- 8	26- 0	27- 2	L	27- 5	28-11	30- 4							
3 X 6	12	L	12- 7	13- 4	14- 1	14- 8	L	16-11	17-10	18- 8	19- 6	20- 4	21- 1	21-10	22- 6	23- 3	23-11
	16	L	11- 7	12- 3	12-11	13- 6	L	14-11	15- 9	16- 6	17- 3	17-11	18- 7	19- 3	19-10	20- 6	21- 1
3 X 8	12	L	16- 6	17- 6	18- 5	19- 3	L	22- 0	23- 2	24- 4	25- 5	26- 5	27- 5	28- 5	29- 4	30- 3	
	16	L	15- 3	16- 2	17- 0	17-10	L	19- 6	20- 7	21- 7	22- 6	23- 5	24- 4	25- 2	26- 0	26-10	27- 7
3 X 10	12	L	20- 7	21-10	23- 0	24- 1	L	27- 3	28- 9	30- 2							
	16	L	19- 1	20- 3	21- 4	22- 3	L	24- 3	25- 7	26-10	28- 0	29- 2	30- 3				

Live load - 20 lbs. per sq. ft. of roof surface acting normal to surface.

See notes on first page of tables for data on which spans are based.

RAFTERS and ROOF JOISTS - 20 POUND LIVE LOAD - GROUP 2 ROOF COVERING

SIZE	SPC'G	SPAN LIMITED BY DEFLECTION					SPAN DETERMINED BY BENDING										
		E=	1000000	1200000	1400000	1600000	f=	900	1000	1100	1200	1300	1400	1500	1600	1700	1800
			Ft In	Ft In	Ft In	Ft In		Ft In	Ft In	Ft In	Ft In	Ft In	Ft In	Ft In	Ft In	Ft In	Ft In
2 X 4	12	L	6- 8	7- 1	7- 6	7-10	L	8- 2	8- 7	9- 0	9- 5	9-10	10- 2	10- 6	10-11	11- 3	11- 6
	16	L	6- 1	6- 6	6-10	7- 1	L	7- 1	7- 6	7-10	8- 3	8- 6	8-10	9- 2	9- 6	9- 9	10- 1
2 X 6	12	L	10- 3	10-11	11- 6	12- 0	L	12- 6	13- 2	13-10	14- 5	15- 0	15- 7	16- 1	16- 8	17- 2	17- 8
	16	L	9- 5	10- 0	10- 6	11- 0	L	10-11	11- 6	12- 1	12- 7	13- 1	13- 7	14- 1	14- 6	15- 0	15- 5
2 X 8	12	L	13- 7	14- 5	15- 2	15-10	L	16- 5	17- 4	18- 2	19- 0	19- 9	20- 6	21- 2	21-11	22- 7	23- 3
	16	L	12- 5	13- 3	13-11	14- 6	L	14- 5	15- 2	15-11	16- 7	17- 4	17-11	18- 7	19- 2	19- 9	20- 4
2 X 10	12	L	17- 0	18- 1	19- 1	19-11	L	20- 6	21- 8	22- 8	23- 8	24- 8	25- 7	26- 6	27- 4	28- 3	29- 0
	16	L	15- 8	16- 7	17- 6	18- 3	L	18- 1	19- 0	20- 0	20-10	21- 8	22- 6	23- 4	24- 1	24-10	25- 6
2 X 12	12	L	20- 5	21- 9	22-10	23-11	L	24- 6	25-10	27- 2	28- 4	29- 6	30- 7				
	16	L	18-10	20- 0	21- 0	22- 0	L	21- 8	22-10	23-11	25- 0	26- 0	27- 0	27-11	28-10	29- 9	30- 7
2 X 14	12	L	23-10	25- 3	26- 7	27-10	L	28- 5	30- 0								
	16	L	21-11	23- 4	24- 6	25- 8	L	25- 2	26- 6	27-10	29- 1	30- 3					
3 X 6	12	L	11-10	12- 7	13- 3	13-10	L	15- 6	16- 4	17- 2	17-11	18- 7	19- 4	20- 0	20- 8	21- 3	21-11
	16	L	10-11	11- 7	12- 2	12- 9	L	13- 7	14- 4	15- 1	15- 9	16- 4	17- 0	17- 7	18- 2	18- 9	19- 3
3 X 8	12	L	15- 7	16- 7	17- 5	18- 3	L	20- 3	21- 4	22- 5	23- 5	24- 4	25- 3	26- 2	27- 0	27-10	28- 8
	16	L	14- 4	15- 3	16- 1	16- 9	L	17-11	18-10	19- 9	20- 8	21- 6	22- 4	23- 1	23-10	24- 7	25- 3
3 X 10	12	L	19- 6	20- 9	21-10	22-10	L	25- 2	26- 6	27-10	29- 1	30- 3					
	16	L	18- 0	19- 2	20- 2	21- 1	L	22- 4	23- 6	24- 8	25- 9	26-10	27-10	28-10	29- 9	30- 8	
3 X 12	12	L	23- 4	24- 9	26- 1	27- 3	L	29-10	31- 6								
	16	L	21- 7	22-11	24- 2	25- 3	L	26- 7	28- 0	29- 5	30- 8						

Live load - 20 lbs. per sq. ft. of roof surface acting normal to surface.

See notes on first page of tables for data on which spans are based.

WOOD JOIST and RAFTER SIZES

RAFTERS and ROOF JOISTS - 30 POUND LIVE LOAD - GROUP I ROOF COVERING

MAXIMUM ALLOWABLE LENGTHS BETWEEN SUPPORTS

From building code or other authority determine the allowable modulus of elasticity ''E'' (if span is to be limited by deflection) or the allowable extreme fiber stress in bending ''f'' (if span is to be determined by bending) for the species and grade of lumber used. Refer to the column below with corresponding value to determine the safe span for size and spacing of rafter and roof joist desired. Check span selected for deflection with spans for bending to see it does not exceed length permitted for bending stress ''f'' of material used.

SIZE (NOM.) IN INCHES	SPAC'G C to C IN INCHES	SPAN LIMITED BY DEFLECTION					SPAN DETERMINED BY BENDING										
		E=	1000000	1200000	1400000	1600000	f=	900	1000	1100	1200	1300	1400	1500	1600	1700	1800
			Ft In	Ft In	Ft In	Ft In		Ft In	Ft In	Ft In	Ft In	Ft In	Ft In	Ft In	Ft In	Ft In	Ft In
2 X 4	12	L	6- 5	6- 9	7- 2	7- 6	L	7- 8	8- 1	8- 5	8-10	9- 2	9- 6	9-10	10- 2	10- 6	10-10
	16	L	5-10	6- 2	6- 6	6-10	L	6- 8	7- 0	7- 4	7- 8	8- 0	8- 3	8- 7	8-10	9- 2	9- 5
2 X 6	12	L	9-10	10- 5	11- 0	11- 6	L	11- 9	12- 4	12-11	13- 6	14- 1	14- 7	15- 1	15- 7	16- 1	16- 7
	16	L	9- 0	9- 7	10- 1	10- 6	L	10- 3	10- 9	11- 4	11-10	12- 3	12- 9	13- 2	13- 8	14- 1	14- 6
2 X 8	12	L	13- 0	13-10	14- 7	15- 3	L	15- 5	16- 3	17- 1	17-10	18- 6	19- 3	19-11	20- 7	21- 2	21-10
	16	L	11-11	12- 8	13- 4	13-11	L	13- 6	14- 3	14-11	15- 7	16- 3	16-10	17- 5	18- 0	18- 7	19- 1
2 X 10	12	L	16- 4	17- 5	18- 4	19- 2	L	19- 4	20- 4	21- 4	22- 4	23- 3	24- 1	24-11	25- 9	26- 7	27- 4
	16	L	15- 0	15-11	16- 9	17- 6	L	17- 0	17-10	18- 9	19- 7	20- 5	21- 2	21-11	22- 7	23- 4	24- 0
2 X 12	12	L	19- 8	20-11	22- 0	23- 0	L	23- 1	24- 4	25- 7	26- 8	27- 9	28-10	29-10	30-10		
	16	L	18- 1	19- 2	20- 2	21- 1	L	20- 4	21- 5	22- 6	23- 6	24- 6	25- 5	26- 3	27- 2	28- 0	28- 9
2 X 14	12	L	22-11	24- 4	25- 7	26- 9	L	26-10	28- 4	29- 8	31- 0						
	16	L	21- 1	22- 5	23- 7	24- 8	L	23- 8	25- 0	26- 2	27- 4	28- 6	29- 6	30- 7			
3 X 6	12	L	11- 5	12- 1	12- 9	13- 4	L	14- 7	15- 4	16- 1	16-10	17- 6	18- 2	18-10	19- 5	20- 0	20- 7
	16	L	10- 5	11- 1	11- 8	12- 2	L	12- 9	13- 6	14- 2	14- 9	15- 4	15-11	16- 6	17- 1	17- 7	18- 1
3 X 8	12	L	15- 0	15-11	16- 9	17- 7	L	19- 1	20- 2	21- 1	22- 1	22-11	23-10	24- 8	25- 6	26- 3	27- 0
	16	L	13- 9	14- 8	15- 5	16- 1	L	16-10	17- 9	18- 7	19- 5	20- 3	21- 0	21- 9	22- 5	23- 1	23- 9
3 X 10	12	L	18- 9	20- 0	21- 0	22- 0	L	23- 9	25- 1	26- 3	27- 6	28- 7	29- 8	30- 8			
	16	L	17- 4	18- 5	19- 4	20- 3	L	21- 0	22- 2	23- 3	24- 3	25- 3	26- 3	27- 2	28- 0	28-11	29- 9

Live load - 30 lbs. per sq. ft. of roof surface acting normal to surface.

See notes on first page of tables for data on which spans are based.

RAFTERS and ROOF JOISTS - 30 POUND LIVE LOAD - GROUP 2 ROOF COVERING

SIZE	SPAC'G	SPAN LIMITED BY DEFLECTION					SPAN DETERMINED BY BENDING										
		E=	1000000	1200000	1400000	1600000	f=	900	1000	1100	1200	1300	1400	1500	1600	1700	1800
			Ft In	Ft In	Ft In	Ft In		Ft In	Ft In	Ft In	Ft In	Ft In	Ft In	Ft In	Ft In	Ft In	Ft In
2 X 4	12	L	6- 1	6- 6	6-10	7- 2	L	7- 1	7- 6	7-10	8- 3	8- 7	8-11	9- 2	9- 6	9- 9	10- 1
	16	L	5- 7	5-11	6- 3	6- 6	L	6- 2	6- 6	6-10	7- 2	7- 5	7- 9	8- 0	8- 3	8- 6	8- 9
2 X 6	12	L	9- 5	10- 0	10- 6	11- 0	L	10-11	11- 6	12- 1	12- 8	13- 2	13- 8	14- 1	14- 7	15- 0	15- 6
	16	L	8- 7	9- 1	9- 7	10- 0	L	9- 6	10- 1	10- 7	11- 0	11- 6	11-11	12- 4	12- 9	13- 1	13- 6
2 X 8	12	L	12- 5	13- 3	13-11	14- 7	L	14- 5	15- 3	15-11	16- 8	17- 4	18- 0	18- 8	19- 3	19-10	20- 5
	16	L	11- 5	12- 1	12- 9	13- 4	L	12- 7	13- 4	13-11	14- 7	15- 2	15- 9	16- 3	16-10	17- 4	17-10
2 X 10	12	L	15- 8	16- 8	17- 6	18- 4	L	18- 1	19- 1	20- 0	20-11	21- 9	22- 7	23- 4	24- 1	24-10	25- 7
	16	L	14- 4	15- 3	16- 0	16- 9	L	15-10	16- 9	17- 6	18- 4	19- 1	19- 9	20- 6	21- 2	21-10	22- 5
2 X 12	12	L	18-10	20- 0	21- 1	22- 0	L	21- 8	22-10	24- 0	25- 0	26- 1	27- 1	28- 0	28-11	29-10	30- 8
	16	L	17- 3	18- 4	19- 4	20- 2	L	19- 1	20- 1	21- 1	22- 0	22-11	23- 9	24- 7	25- 5	26- 2	26-11
2 X 14	12	L	22- 0	23- 4	24- 7	25- 8	L	25- 2	26- 7	27-10	29- 1	30- 4					
	16	L	20- 2	21- 5	22- 7	23- 7	L	22- 2	23- 5	24- 6	25- 8	26- 8	27- 8	28- 8	29- 7	30- 6	
3 X 6	12	L	10-11	11- 7	12- 2	12- 9	L	13- 8	14- 5	15- 1	15- 9	16- 5	17- 0	17- 7	18- 2	18- 9	19- 4
	16	L	10- 0	10- 7	11- 2	11- 8	L	12- 0	12- 7	13- 3	13-10	14- 4	14-11	15- 5	15-11	16- 5	16-11
3 X 8	12	L	14- 5	15- 3	16- 1	16-10	L	17-11	18-11	19-10	20- 8	21- 6	22- 4	23- 2	23-11	24- 8	25- 4
	16	L	13- 2	14- 0	14- 9	15- 5	L	15- 9	16- 7	17- 5	18- 2	18-11	19- 8	20- 4	21- 0	21- 8	22- 3
3 X 10	12	L	18- 0	19- 2	20- 2	21- 1	L	22- 4	23- 7	24- 9	25-10	26-10	27-11	28-10	29-10	30- 9	
	16	L	16- 7	17- 7	18- 6	19- 5	L	19- 9	20- 9	21-10	22- 9	23- 8	24- 7	25- 6	26- 3	27- 1	27-11
3 X 12	12	L	21- 7	22-11	24- 2	25- 3	L	26- 8	28- 1	29- 6	30- 9						
	16	L	19-11	21- 2	22- 3	23- 3	L	23- 7	24-10	26- 1	27- 3	28- 4	29- 5	30- 5			
3 X 14	12	L	25- 1	26- 8	28- 1	29- 4	L	30-10									
	16	L	23- 2	24- 8	26- 0	27- 2	L	27- 5	28-10	30- 3							

Live load - 30 lbs. per sq. ft. of roof surface acting normal to surface.

See notes on first page of tables for data on which spans are based.

WOOD JOIST and RAFTER SIZES

RAFTERS and ROOF JOISTS - 40 POUND LIVE LOAD - GROUP I ROOF COVERING

MAXIMUM ALLOWABLE LENGTHS BETWEEN SUPPORTS

From building code or other authority determine the allowable modulus of elasticity ''E'' (if span is to be limited by deflection) or the allowable extreme fiber stress in bending ''f'' (if span is to be determined by bending) for the species and grade of lumber used. Refer to the column below with corresponding value to determine the safe span for size and spacing of rafter and roof joist desired. Check span selected for deflection with spans for bending to see it does not exceed length permitted for bending stress ''f'' of material used.

SIZE (NOM.) IN INCHES	SPAC'G C to C IN INCHES	SPAN LIMITED BY DEFLECTION					SPAN DETERMINED BY BENDING										
		E=	1000000	1200000	1400000	1600000	f=	900	1000	1100	1200	1300	1400	1500	1600	1700	1800
			Ft In	Ft In	Ft In	Ft In		Ft In	Ft In	Ft In	Ft In	Ft In	Ft In	Ft In	Ft In	Ft In	Ft In
2 X 4	12	L	5-11	6-3	6-7	6-11	L	6-9	7-2	7-6	7-10	8-2	8-5	8-9	9-0	9-4	9-7
	16	L	5-4	5-9	6-0	6-3	L	5-11	6-3	6-6	6-10	7-1	7-4	7-7	7-10	8-1	8-4
2 X 6	12	L	9-1	9-8	10-2	10-8	L	10-5	11-0	11-6	12-0	12-6	13-0	13-5	13-10	14-4	14-9
	16	L	8-4	8-10	9-3	9-8	L	9-1	9-7	10-0	10-6	10-11	11-4	11-9	12-1	12-6	12-10
2 X 8	12	L	12-1	12-10	13-6	14-1	L	13-9	14-6	15-2	15-10	16-6	17-2	17-9	18-4	18-11	19-5
	16	L	11-0	11-8	12-4	12-11	L	12-0	12-8	13-3	13-10	14-5	15-0	15-6	16-0	16-6	17-0
2 X 10	12	L	15-2	16-1	17-0	17-9	L	17-3	18-2	19-1	19-11	20-9	21-6	22-3	23-0	23-8	24-6
	16	L	13-11	14-9	15-6	16-3	L	15-1	15-11	16-8	17-5	18-2	18-10	19-6	20-2	20-9	21-4
2 X 12	12	L	18-4	19-5	20-5	21-4	L	20-8	21-10	22-11	23-11	24-10	25-10	26-9	27-7	28-5	29-3
	16	L	16-9	17-9	18-9	19-7	L	18-2	19-2	20-1	21-0	21-10	22-8	23-5	24-3	24-11	25-8
2 X 14	12	L	21-4	22-7	23-10	24-11	L	24-1	25-5	26-7	27-10	28-11	30-0				
	16	L	19-7	20-9	21-10	22-10	L	21-2	22-4	23-5	24-5	25-5	26-5	27-4	28-3	29-1	29-11
3 X 6	12	L	10-7	11-3	11-10	12-4	L	13-0	13-9	14-5	15-0	15-8	16-3	16-9	17-4	17-10	18-5
	16	L	9-8	10-3	10-10	11-3	L	11-5	12-0	12-7	13-2	13-8	14-2	14-8	15-2	15-8	16-1
3 X 8	12	L	13-11	14-10	15-7	16-4	L	17-1	18-0	18-11	19-9	20-7	21-4	22-1	22-10	23-6	24-2
	16	L	12-9	13-7	14-4	14-11	L	15-0	15-10	16-7	17-4	18-0	18-9	19-5	20-0	20-8	21-3
3 X 10	12	L	17-5	18-7	19-7	20-6	L	21-4	22-6	23-7	24-8	25-8	26-8	27-7	28-6	29-4	30-3
	16	L	16-1	17-1	18-0	18-10	L	18-10	19-10	20-10	21-9	22-7	23-6	24-3	25-1	25-10	26-7
3 X 12	12	L	21-0	22-3	23-6	24-6	L	25-6	26-11	28-2	29-5	30-8					
	16	L	19-4	20-6	21-7	22-7	L	22-6	23-9	24-11	26-0	27-1	28-1	29-1	30-3		
3 X 14	12	L	24-5	25-11	27-4	28-7	L	29-7	31-2								
	16	L	22-6	23-11	25-2	26-4	L	26-2	27-7	28-11	30-3						

Live loads - 40 lbs. per sq. ft. of roof surface acting normal to surface.

See notes on first page of tables for data on which spans are based.

RAFTERS and ROOF JOISTS - 40 POUND LIVE LOAD - GROUP 2 ROOF COVERING

SIZE	SPAC'G	SPAN LIMITED BY DEFLECTION					SPAN DETERMINED BY BENDING										
		E=	1000000	1200000	1400000	1600000	f=	900	1000	1100	1200	1300	1400	1500	1600	1700	1800
			Ft In	Ft In	Ft In	Ft In		Ft In	Ft In	Ft In	Ft In	Ft In	Ft In	Ft In	Ft In	Ft In	Ft In
2 X 6	12	L	8-9	9-4	9-10	10-3	L	9-10	10-5	10-11	11-4	11-10	12-3	12-9	13-2	13-6	13-11
	16	L	8-0	8-6	8-11	9-4	L	8-7	9-1	9-6	9-11	10-4	10-8	11-1	11-5	11-9	12-2
2 X 8	12	L	11-7	12-4	13-0	13-7	L	13-0	13-9	14-5	15-0	15-8	16-3	16-10	17-4	17-11	18-5
	16	L	10-7	11-3	11-11	12-5	L	11-4	12-0	12-7	13-2	13-8	14-2	14-8	15-2	15-7	16-1
2 X 10	12	L	14-8	15-7	16-5	17-1	L	16-4	17-3	18-1	18-11	19-8	20-5	21-1	21-10	22-6	23-2
	16	L	13-5	14-3	15-0	15-8	L	14-4	15-1	15-10	16-6	17-2	17-10	18-6	19-1	19-8	20-3
2 X 12	12	L	17-8	18-9	19-9	20-7	L	19-8	20-9	21-9	22-8	23-7	24-6	25-4	26-2	27-0	27-9
	16	L	16-2	17-2	18-1	18-11	L	17-3	18-2	19-0	19-11	20-8	21-6	22-3	23-0	23-8	24-4
2 X 14	12	L	20-7	21-10	23-0	24-1	L	22-10	24-1	25-3	26-5	27-6	28-6	29-6	30-6		
	16	L	18-10	20-1	21-1	22-1	L	20-1	21-2	22-3	23-2	24-2	25-1	25-11	26-9	27-7	28-5
3 X 6	12	L	10-2	10-10	11-5	11-11	L	12-4	13-0	13-8	14-3	14-10	15-5	15-11	16-5	16-11	17-5
	16	L	9-4	9-11	10-5	10-11	L	10-9	11-4	11-11	12-5	13-0	13-5	13-11	14-5	14-10	15-3
3 X 8	12	L	13-6	14-4	15-1	15-9	L	16-3	17-1	17-11	18-9	19-6	20-3	21-0	21-8	22-4	23-0
	16	L	12-4	13-1	13-10	14-5	L	14-3	15-0	15-9	16-5	17-1	17-9	18-5	19-0	19-7	20-2
3 X 10	12	L	16-11	18-0	18-11	19-9	L	20-4	21-5	22-6	23-6	24-5	25-4	26-3	27-1	27-11	28-9
	16	L	15-6	16-6	17-4	18-2	L	17-10	18-10	19-9	20-8	21-6	22-3	23-1	23-10	24-7	25-3
3 X 12	12	L	20-4	21-7	22-8	23-9	L	24-3	25-7	26-10	28-0	29-2	30-3				
	16	L	18-8	19-10	20-11	21-10	L	21-5	22-7	23-8	24-9	25-9	26-9	27-8	28-7	29-5	30-3
3 X 14	12	L	23-8	25-1	26-5	27-8	L	28-2	29-8	31-2							
	16	L	21-9	23-2	24-4	25-6	L	24-11	26-3	27-6	28-9	29-11	31-1				

Live load - 40 lbs. per sq. ft. of roof surface acting normal to surface.

See notes on first page of tables for data on which spans are based.

WOOD JOIST SIZES

FLOOR JOISTS - LIVE LOAD 40 POUNDS PER SQUARE FOOT

MAXIMUM ALLOWABLE LENGTHS BETWEEN SUPPORTS

From building code or other authority determine the allowable modulus of elasticity ''E'' (if span is to be limited by deflection) or the allowable extreme fiber stress in bending ''f'' (if span is to be determined by bending) for the species and grade of lumber used. Refer to the column below with corresponding value to determine the safe span for size and spacing of rafter and roof joist desired. Check span selected for deflection with spans for bending to see it does not exceed length permitted for bending stress ''f'' of material used.

SIZE (NOM.) IN INCHES	SPAC'G C to C IN INCHES	SPAN LIMITED BY DEFLECTION					SPAN DETERMINED BY BENDING										
		E=	1000000	1200000	1400000	1600000	f=	900	1000	1100	1200	1300	1400	1500	1600	1700	1800
			Ft In	Ft In	Ft In	Ft In		Ft In	Ft In	Ft In	Ft In	Ft In	Ft In	Ft In	Ft In	Ft In	Ft In
2 X 6	12	L	9- 1	9- 8	10- 2	10- 8	L	9- 6	10- 0	10- 5	10-11	11- 4	11- 9	12- 3	12- 7	13- 0	13- 4
	16	L	8- 4	8-10	9- 3	9- 8	L	8- 3	8- 8	9- 1	9- 6	9-11	10- 3	10- 8	11- 0	11- 4	11- 8
2 X 8	12	L	12- 1	12-10	13- 6	14- 1	L	12- 6	13- 2	13-10	14- 5	15- 0	15- 7	16- 2	16- 8	17- 2	17- 8
	16	L	11- 0	11- 8	12- 4	12-11	L	10-11	11- 6	12- 1	12- 7	13- 1	13- 7	14- 1	14- 7	15- 0	15- 5
2 X 10	12	L	15- 2	16- 1	17- 0	17- 9	L	15- 9	16- 7	17- 5	18- 2	18-11	19- 7	20- 4	21- 0	21- 7	22- 3
	16	L	13-11	14- 9	15- 6	16- 3	L	13- 9	14- 6	15- 2	15-10	16- 6	17- 2	17- 9	18- 4	18-11	19- 5
2 X 12	12	L	18- 4	19- 5	20- 5	21- 4	L	18-11	19-11	20-11	21-10	22- 9	23- 7	24- 5	25- 2	26- 0	26- 9
	16	L	16- 9	17- 9	18- 9	19- 7	L	16- 7	17- 5	18- 3	19- 1	19-11	20- 8	21- 4	22- 1	22- 9	23- 5
2 X 14	12	L	21- 4	22- 7	23-10	24-11	L	22- 0	23- 3	24- 4	25- 5	26- 6	27- 6	28- 5	29- 4	30- 3	
	16	L	19- 7	20- 9	21-10	22-10	L	19- 4	20- 4	21- 4	22- 4	23- 3	24- 1	24-11	25- 9	26- 6	27- 4
3 X 6	12	L	10- 7	11- 3	11-10	12- 4	L	11-10	12- 6	13- 1	13- 8	14- 3	14- 9	15- 4	15-10	16- 3	16- 9
	16	L	9- 8	10- 3	10-10	11- 3	L	10- 4	10-11	11- 5	12- 0	12- 5	12-11	13- 4	13-10	14- 3	14- 8
3 X 8	12	L	13-11	14-10	15- 7	16- 4	L	15- 7	16- 6	17- 3	18- 0	18- 9	19- 6	20- 2	20-10	21- 6	22- 1
	16	L	12- 9	13- 7	14- 4	14-11	L	13- 8	14- 5	15- 2	15-10	16- 5	17- 1	17- 8	18- 3	18-10	19- 4
3 X 10	12	L	17- 5	18- 7	19- 7	20- 6	L	19- 7	20- 7	21- 8	22- 7	23- 6	24- 5	25- 3	26- 1	26-11	27- 8
	16	L	16- 1	17- 1	18- 0	18-10	L	17- 2	18- 1	19- 0	19-10	20- 8	21- 5	22- 2	22-11	23- 7	24- 4
3 X 12	12	L	21- 0	22- 3	23- 6	24- 6	L	23- 5	24- 8	25-10	27- 0	28- 1	29- 2	30- 2			
	16	L	19- 4	20- 6	21- 7	22- 7	L	20- 7	21- 9	22- 9	23-10	24- 9	25- 9	26- 7	27- 6	28- 4	29- 2
3 X 14	12	L	24- 5	25-11	27- 4	28- 7	L	27- 2	28- 8	30- 0							
	16	L	22- 6	23-11	25- 2	26- 4	L	24- 0	25- 3	26- 6	27- 8	28-10	29-11	31- 0			

Live load - 40 lbs. per sq. ft. with plastered ceiling.

Live load - 40 lbs. per sq. ft. with plastered ceiling, and 50 lbs. per sq. ft. with unplastered ceiling.

FLOOR JOISTS - LIVE LOAD 50 POUNDS PER SQUARE FOOT

SIZE	SPAC'G	SPAN LIMITED BY DEFLECTION					SPAN DETERMINED BY BENDING										
		E=	1000000	1200000	1400000	1600000	f=	900	1000	1100	1200	1300	1400	1500	1600	1700	1800
			Ft In	Ft In	Ft In	Ft In		Ft In	Ft In	Ft In	Ft In	Ft In	Ft In	Ft In	Ft In	Ft In	Ft In
2 X 6	12	L	8- 6	9- 1	9- 6	10- 0	L	8- 9	9- 2	9- 8	10- 1	10- 6	10-11	11- 3	11- 8	12- 0	12- 4
	16	L	7- 9	8- 3	8- 8	9- 1	L	7- 7	8- 0	8- 5	8- 9	9- 2	9- 6	9-10	10- 1	10- 5	10- 9
2 X 8	12	L	11- 4	12- 0	12- 8	13- 3	L	11- 7	12- 2	12- 9	13- 4	13-11	14- 5	14-11	15- 5	15-11	16- 4
	16	L	10- 4	11- 0	11- 7	12- 1	L	10- 1	10- 7	11- 2	11- 8	12- 1	12- 7	13- 0	13- 5	13-10	14- 3
2 X 10	12	L	14- 3	15- 2	15-11	16- 8	L	14- 7	15- 4	16- 1	16-10	17- 6	18- 2	18- 9	19- 5	20- 0	20- 7
	16	L	13- 0	13-10	14- 7	15- 3	L	12- 8	13- 5	14- 0	14- 8	15- 3	15-10	16- 5	16-11	17- 5	17-11
2 X 12	12	L	17- 2	18- 3	19- 3	20- 1	L	17- 6	18- 5	19- 4	20- 2	21- 0	21-10	22- 7	23- 4	24- 1	24- 9
	16	L	15- 9	16- 9	17- 7	18- 5	L	15- 3	16- 1	16-11	17- 8	18- 5	19- 1	19- 9	20- 5	21- 0	21- 8
2 X 14	12	L	20- 1	21- 4	22- 5	23- 6	L	20- 5	21- 6	22- 7	23- 7	24- 6	25- 5	26- 4	27- 3	28- 1	28-10
	16	L	18- 5	19- 6	20- 7	21- 6	L	17-10	18-10	19- 9	20- 8	21- 6	22- 3	23- 1	23-10	24- 7	25- 3
3 X 6	12	L	9-11	10- 6	11- 1	11- 7	L	11- 0	11- 7	12- 1	12- 8	13- 2	13- 8	14- 2	14- 7	15- 1	15- 6
	16	L	9- 1	9- 8	10- 2	10- 7	L	9- 7	10- 1	10- 7	11- 0	11- 6	11-11	12- 4	12- 9	13- 2	13- 6
3 X 8	12	L	13- 1	13-11	14- 8	15- 4	L	14- 6	15- 3	16- 0	16- 9	17- 5	18- 1	18- 8	19- 4	19-11	20- 6
	16	L	12- 0	12- 9	13- 5	14- 1	L	12- 8	13- 4	14- 0	14- 7	15- 3	15- 9	16- 4	16-10	17- 5	17-11
3 X 10	12	L	16- 6	17- 6	18- 5	19- 3	L	18- 2	19- 2	20- 1	21- 0	21-10	22- 8	23- 5	24- 2	24-11	25- 8
	16	L	15- 2	16- 1	16-11	17- 8	L	15-11	16- 9	17- 7	18- 4	19- 1	19-10	20- 6	21- 3	21-10	22- 6
3 X 12	12	L	19-10	21- 1	22- 2	23- 2	L	21- 9	22-11	24- 0	25- 1	26- 2	27- 1	28- 1	29- 0	29-11	30- 9
	16	L	18- 2	19- 4	20- 4	21- 3	L	19- 1	20- 2	21- 1	22- 1	23- 0	23-10	24- 8	25- 6	26- 3	27- 0
3 X 14	12	L	23- 1	24- 6	25-10	27- 0	L	25- 3	26- 8	28- 0	29- 2	30- 5					
	16	L	21- 3	22- 7	23- 9	24-10	L	22- 3	23- 6	24- 7	25- 9	26- 9	27- 9	28- 9	29- 8	30- 7	

Live load - 50 lbs. per sq. ft. with plastered ceiling

Live load - 50 lbs. per sq. ft. with plastered ceiling, and 60 lbs. per sq. ft. with unplastered ceiling.

NOTE: The above span lengths are based on:

When limited by deflection -
Maximum allowable deflection of 1/360 of the span length.
Modulus of elasticity as noted for ''E''.
Dead load - Weight of joist.
Double thickness of flooring (5#).
Weight of plaster ceiling ignored.

When limited by bending strength of piece -
Allowable stress in extreme fiber in bending as noted for "f".
Dead Load - Weight of joist
Double thickness of flooring (5#).
Plastered ceiling (10#).

WOOD JOIST SIZES

FLOOR JOISTS - LIVE LOAD 60 POUNDS PER SQUARE FOOT

MAXIMUM ALLOWABLE LENGTHS BETWEEN SUPPORTS

From building code or other authority determine the allowable modulus of elasticity ''E'' (if span is to be limited by deflection) or the allowable extreme fiber stress in bending ''f'' (if span is to be determined by bending) for the species and grade of lumber used. Refer to the column below with corresponding value to determine the safe span for size and spacing of rafter and roof joist desired. Check span selected for deflection with spans for bending to see it does not exceed length permitted for bending stress ''f'' of material used. If horizontal shear ''H'' induced by load is greater than permitted for the material used, another size joist or spacing should be selected within the proper horizontal shear (''H'') limit. Horizontal shear "H" is in lbs. per sq. in

SIZE (NOM.) IN INCHES	SPAC'G C to C IN INCHES	SPAN LIMITED BY DEFLECTION					SPAN DETERMINED BY BENDING										
		E=	1000000	1200000	1400000	1600000	f=	900	1000	1100	1200	1300	1400	1500	1600	1700	1800
			Ft In	Ft In	Ft In	Ft In		Ft In	Ft In	Ft In	Ft In	Ft In	Ft In	Ft In	Ft In	Ft In	Ft In
2 X 6	12	L	8- 1	8- 7	9—1	9- 6	L	8- 2	8- 7	9- 0	9- 5	9- 9	10- 2	10- 6	10-10	11- 2	11- 6
		H	45	49	52	54	H	46	49	51	54	56	59	61	63	65	67
	16	L	7- 4	7-10	8- 3	8- 7	L	7- 1	7- 6	7-10	8- 2	8- 6	8-10	9- 2	9- 5	9- 9	10- 0
		H	54	58	61	64	H	52	55	58	61	64	66	69	71	74	76
2 X 8	12	L	10- 9	11- 5	12- 0	12- 7	L	10-10	11- 5	11-11	12- 6	13- 0	13- 6	13-11	14- 5	14-10	15- 3
		H	46	49	52	55	H	46	49	52	54	57	59	61	63	66	68
	16	L	9- 9	10- 5	11- 0	11- 5	L	9- 5	9-11	10- 5	10-10	11- 4	11- 9	12- 2	12- 6	12-11	13- 3
		H	54	58	62	65	H	52	55	58	61	64	67	69	72	74	77
2 X 10	12	L	13- 6	14- 5	15- 2	15-10	L	13- 7	14- 4	15- 0	15- 8	16- 4	17- 0	17- 7	18- 2	18- 8	19- 3
		H	46	49	52	55	H	46	49	52	54	57	59	62	64	66	68
	16	L	12- 4	13- 2	13-10	14- 6	L	11-10	12- 6	13- 1	13- 8	14- 3	14- 9	15- 4	15-10	16- 4	16- 9
		H	55	59	62	65	H	52	55	58	61	64	67	70	72	75	77
2 X 12	12	L	16- 4	17- 4	18- 3	19- 1	L	16- 4	17- 3	18- 1	18-11	19- 8	20- 5	21- 2	21-10	22- 6	23- 2
		H	47	50	53	55	H	47	50	52	55	57	60	62	64	66	69
	16	L	14-11	15-10	16- 8	17- 5	L	14- 3	15- 1	15-10	16- 6	17- 2	17-10	18- 5	19- 1	19- 8	20- 3
		H	55	59	62	66	H	52	56	59	62	65	67	70	72	75	77
2 X 14	12	L	19- 1	20- 3	21- 4	22- 4	L	19- 1	20- 2	21- 2	22- 1	23- 0	23-10	24- 8	25- 6	26- 3	27- 0
		H	47	50	53	56	H	47	50	53	55	58	60	62	65	67	69
	16	L	17- 6	18- 7	19- 6	20- 5	L	16- 9	17- 7	18- 6	19- 3	20- 1	20-10	21- 7	22- 3	23- 0	23- 8
		H	55	59	63	66	H	53	56	59	62	65	68	70	73	75	78
3 X 6	12	L	9- 5	10- 0	10- 6	11- 0	L	10- 3	10-10	11- 4	11-10	12- 4	12- 9	13- 3	13- 8	14- 1	14- 6
		H	34	36	38	40	H	37	39	42	44	45	47	49	51	53	54
	16	L	8- 7	9- 2	9- 7	10- 1	L	8-11	9- 5	9-10	10- 4	10- 9	11- 2	11- 6	11-11	12- 3	12- 8
		H	40	43	46	48	H	42	45	47	50	52	54	56	58	60	62
3 X 8	12	L	12- 6	13- 3	13-11	14- 7	L	13- 6	14- 3	15- 0	15- 8	16- 3	16-11	17- 6	18- 1	18- 7	19- 2
		H	34	37	39	41	H	38	40	42	44	46	48	50	51	53	55
	16	L	11- 5	12- 1	12- 9	13- 4	L	11-10	12- 6	13- 1	13- 8	14- 3	14- 9	15- 3	15- 9	16- 3	16- 9
		H	41	44	46	49	H	43	45	48	50	52	54	56	58	60	62
3 X 10	12	L	15- 8	16- 8	17- 7	18- 4	L	17- 0	17-11	18-10	19- 8	20- 5	21- 3	22- 0	22- 8	23- 4	24- 1
		H	35	37	39	41	H	38	40	42	44	46	48	50	52	54	55
	16	L	14- 4	15- 3	16- 1	16-10	L	14-11	15- 8	16- 6	17- 2	17-11	18- 7	19- 3	19-10	20- 6	21- 1
		H	41	44	47	49	H	43	45	48	50	53	55	57	59	61	63
3 X 12	12	L	18-10	20- 1	21- 1	22- 1	L	20- 5	21- 6	22- 7	23- 7	24- 6	25- 5	26- 4	27- 2	28- 0	28-10
		H	35	38	40	42	H	38	41	43	45	47	49	51	52	54	56
	16	L	17- 4	18- 5	19- 4	20- 3	L	17-11	18-10	19- 9	20- 8	21- 6	22- 4	23- 1	23-10	24- 7	25- 4
		H	42	45	47	50	H	43	46	48	51	53	55	57	59	61	63
3 X 14	12	L	22- 0	23- 5	24- 7	25- 9	L	23- 9	25- 0	26- 3	27- 5	28- 7	29- 7	30- 8			
		H	36	38	40	42	H	39	41	43	45	47	49	51			
	16	L	20- 3	21- 6	22- 7	23- 8	L	20-10	22- 0	23- 1	24- 1	25- 1	26- 0	26-11	27-10	28- 8	29- 6
		H	42	45	48	50	H	43	46	49	51	53	55	58	60	62	64
4 X 8	12	L	13- 9	14- 7	15- 5	16- 1	L	15- 9	16- 7	17- 4	18- 2	18-11	19- 7	20- 3	20-11	21- 7	22- 3
		H	28	30	32	34	H	33	35	37	38	40	42	43	45	46	48
	16	L	12- 7	13- 5	14- 1	14- 9	L	13- 9	14- 6	15- 3	15-11	16- 6	17- 2	17- 9	18- 4	18-11	19- 6
		H	33	36	38	40	H	37	39	41	43	45	47	49	50	52	54
4 X 10	12	L	17- 3	18- 4	19- 4	20- 2	L	19- 8	20- 9	21- 9	22- 9	23- 8	24- 6	25- 5	26- 3	27- 0	27-10
		H	29	31	33	34	H	33	35	37	39	41	42	44	45	47	48
	16	L	15-10	16-10	17- 9	18- 6	L	17- 3	18- 3	19- 1	19-11	20- 9	21- 7	22- 4	23- 0	23- 9	24- 5
		H	34	36	38	40	H	37	39	42	44	46	47	49	51	53	54

NOTE: - The above span lengths are based on:

When limited by deflection -
Maximum allowable deflection of 1/360 of the span length.
Modulus of elasticity as noted for "E".
Dead load - Weight of joist.
Double thickness of flooring (5#).
Weight of plaster ceiling ignored.
Live load - 60 pounds per square foot with plastered ceiling.
Weight of plaster ceiling was included in computing horizontal shear "H" induced by load.

When limited by bending strength of piece -
Allowable stress in extreme fiber in bending as noted for "f".
Dead load - Weight of joist.
Double thickness of flooring (5#).
Plastered ceiling (10#).
Live load - 60 pounds per square foot with plastered ceiling, and
70 pounds per square foot with unplastered ceiling.
Total load was considered in computing the horizontal shear "H" induced by load.

WOOD LINTELS and BEAMS

STRESSES of VARIOUS GRADES of WOOD

TYPE of WOOD	GRADE	f Unit Stress (#/□")	V Horizontal Shear (#/□")	E Modulus of Elast. (#/□")
Douglas Fir, Coast Region	Dense Select Structural	2150	145	1,600,000
	Select Structural	1900	120	
	1700f Dense #1	1700	145	
	1450f - #1	1450	120	
	1100f - #2	1100	110	
Douglas Fir, Inland Region	Select Structural	2150	145	1,600,000
	Structural	1900	100	1,500,000
	Common Structural	1450	95	
Hemlock, Eastern	Select Structural	1300	85	1,100,000
	Prime Structural	1200	60	
	Common Structural	1100		
Hemlock, West Coast	1600f - Select Structural	1600	100	1,400,000
	1450f #1	1450		
	1100f - #2	1100	90	
Pine, Southern	Dense Select Structural	2400	120	1,600,000
	Dense Structural	2000		
	Dense Structural S. E. & S.	1800		
	Dense #1 Structural –	1600		
	#1 Dense	1700	150	
	#1	1450	125	
	#2 Dense	1250	100	
	#2	1100	85	
Pine, Southern Long Leaf	Select Structural Long Leaf	2400	120	1,600,000
	Prime Structural Long Leaf	2000		
	Merchantable Structural Long Leaf	1800		
	Structural S.E.&S. Long Leaf			
	#1 Structural Long Leaf	1600		
	#1 Long Leaf	1700	150	
	#2 Long Leaf	1250	100	
Redwood	Dense Structural	1700	110	1,200,000
	Heart Structural	1300	95	
Spruce, Eastern	1450f - Structural Grade	1450	110	1,200,000
	1300f - Structural Grade	1300	95	
	1200f - Structural Grade	1200		

WOOD LINTELS & BEAMS – MAX LOAD in lbs.

SPAN (c.c. of supports)		NOMINAL DEPTH of MEMBER 6"	8"	10"	12"	14"
6'-0"	M	561	1310	1667	2450	3400
	D	568	1800	2910	5200	8400
7'-0"	M	482	1060	1425	2090	2900
	D	417	1320	2140	3800	6160
8'-0"	M	422	985	1250	1840	2540
	D	318	1020	1680	3000	4850
9'-0"	M	375	870	1111	1630	2260
	D	252	805	1310	2340	3780
10'-0"	M	337	784	1000	1462	2030
	D	204	650	1050	1870	3040
11'-0"	M	307	710	910	1340	1850
	D	168	536	870	1550	2503
12'-0"	**M**	280	651	833	**1220**	1690
	D	141	458	745	**1330**	2150
13'-0"	M	260	600	770	1130	1562
	D	120	383	620	1051	1700
14'-0"	M	241	560	715	1050	1450
	D	103	330	535	955	1550
15'-0"	M	225	521	667	980	1355
	D	90	289	470	840	1360
16'-0"	M	210	490	625	920	1272
	D	80	254	410	730	1180
Horizontal Shear	V	880	1200	1520	**1840**	2080

Loads given are uniform loads per inch of finished width of member & are based on f = 1000 #/□"
M = total safe load in bending measured in # (lbs)
V = total safe load in shear (120 #/□")
D = total safe load in deflection (1/360)
E = 1,000,000 #/□"

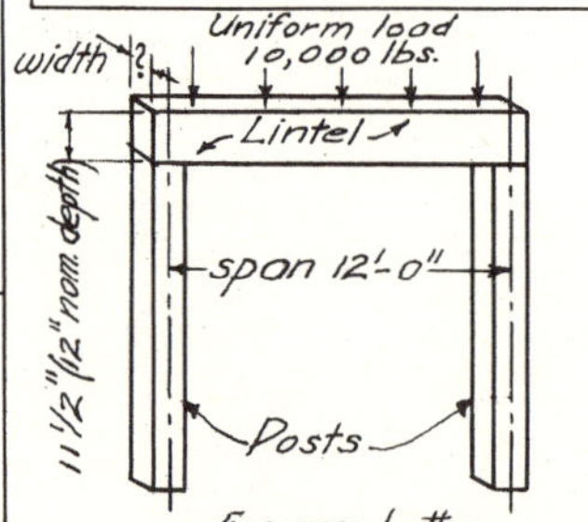

Uniform load 10,000 lbs.
width
?
Lintel
span 12'-0"
11 1/2" (12" nom. depth)
Posts

Example #1

USING THE ABOVE TABLE

Given: Conditions of example #1
Find: Required width of lintel

Solution

In table above, loads M = 1220, D = 1330 and V = 1840

$$\frac{\text{Uniform load}}{\text{Lowest of 3 loads}} = \frac{10{,}000}{1220} = 8.2''$$

Answer: 8.2" is width required. Lintel can be made up of two 2 x 12's & two 3 x 12's which gives a total width of 8 3/8", closest above that required. See "Lumber Grading & Sizes" for finished dimensions (2 x 12's etc.)

USING THE TABLE FOR STRONGER WOODS

The following formulae are used with the above table to determine new values for the three loads M, D & V in case a wood of greater strength than that which the table is based on is used. For example #1 Southern Pine (see "Stresses of Various Grades of Woods" table on left): f = 1450, E = 1,600,000 and V = 125.

$$\text{New M Load} = \frac{\text{new } f \times \text{M load in table}}{f \text{ of table}} = \frac{1450 \times 1220}{1000} = 1769$$

$$\text{New D Load} = \frac{\text{new } E \times \text{D load in table}}{E \text{ of table}} = \frac{1{,}600{,}000 \times 1330}{1{,}000{,}000} = 2128$$

$$\text{New V Load} = \frac{\text{new } V \times \text{V load in table}}{V \text{ of table}} = \frac{125 \times 1840}{120} = 1917$$

The three new values replace those in table for Example #1 and the width of lintel required is then obtained similarly. (The width required would be 5.6")

Data by Elwyn E. Seelye, Consulting Engineer

WOOD COLUMNS or POSTS

WOOD COLUMNS for LIGHT CONSTRUCTION – MAX. LOAD IN LBS.

SECTION	SIZE	COMPRESSIVE STRENGTH in lbs/sq.in.	VARIOUS HEIGHT OF WOOD COLUMNS						
			6'-0"	7'-0"	8'-0"	9'-0"	10'-0"	11'-0"	12'-0"
3⅝" × 3⅝"	4×4	1150 to 1400	13,460	12,170					
	*A = 13.1	1400 to 1750	15,370	13,060	10,280	7,700	5,670	4,340	
		1750	17,000	13,130					
5⅝" × 5⅝"	6×6	1150 to 1400	33,800		32,800	31,500	27,800		
	*A = 30.3	1400 to 1750	40,800		38,700	35,300	30,000	23,500	
		1750	49,700		45,850	39,000	30,500		
7½" × 7½"	8×8	1150 to 1400	64,740		63,000	60,910			57,420
	*A = 56.3	1400 to 1750	78,820		75,670	71,950			65,590
		1750	98,520		92,330	84,960			72,510
9½" × 9½"	10×10	1150 to 1400	103,840				101,050		97,700
	*A = 90.3	1400 to 1750	126,420				121,360		115,450
		1750	158,020				148,090		136,250
11½" × 11½"	12×12	1150 to 1400	152,140					148,040	
	*A = 132	1400 to 1750	185,220					177,810	
		1750	231,520					217,970	

*Area of Sections

COMPRESSIVE STRENGTHS of VARIOUS TYPES of WOOD used for COLUMNS

COMPRESSIVE STRENGTH in lbs./sq. in.	WOOD	TYPE	GRADE
1150	Pine	Southern Long Leaf	#1 Structural Long Leaf
		Southern	Dense #1 Structural
1200	Douglas Fir	Coast Region	#1
	Oak	Red & White	1200 C - Grade
1250	Douglas Fir	Inland Region	Common Structural
1300	Pine	Southern	Dense Structural S.E. & S.
		Southern Long Leaf	Merchantable Structural Long Leaf
			Structural S.E. & S. Long Leaf
1325	Oak	Red & White	1325 C - Grade
1400	Douglas Fir	Coast Region	Dense #1
		Inland Region	Structural
	Pine	Southern	Dense Structural
		Southern Long Leaf	Prime Structural Long Leaf
1450	Douglas Fir	Coast Region	Select Structural
	Redwood		Dense Structural
1550	Douglas Fir	Coast Region	Dense Select Structural
1750	Douglas Fir	Inland Region	Select Structural
	Pine	Southern	Select Structural
		Southern Long Leaf	Select Structural Long Leaf

Data by: Elwyn E. Seelye, Consulting Engineer.

WOOD TRUSSED RAFTERS for HOUSES

FOR DRY WALL CONSTRUCTION

Dead Load 12#/□'
Live Load 33#/□'
Total Load 45#/□'
Trussed Rafter Spaced 2'-0" o.c.

FOR PLASTER FINISH

Dead Load 17#/□'
Live Load 28#/□'
Total Load 45#/□'
Trussed Rafters Spaced 2'-0" o.c.

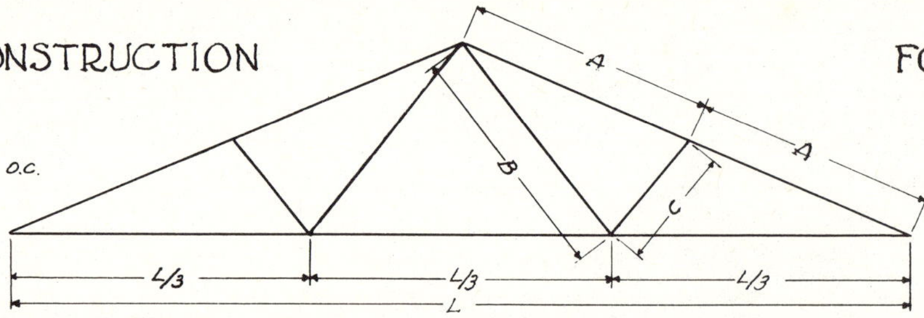
A
A
B
C
L/3
L/3
L/3
L

SLOPE	SPAN "L"	A	B	C	SLOPE	SPAN "L"	A	B	C
4 on 12	20'-0"	5' - 3 1/4"	4' - 8 3/16"	2' - 3 15/16"	6 on 12	20'-0"	5' - 7 1/16"	5' - 11 11/16"	2' - 11 5/8"
	22'-0"	5' - 9 9/16"	5' - 1 7/8"	2' - 6 3/4"		22'-0"	6' - 1 13/16"	6' - 6 7/8"	3' - 3 1/4"
	24'-0"	6' - 3 7/8"	5' - 7 1/2"	2' - 9 9/16"		24'-0"	6' - 8 1/2"	7' - 2 1/8"	3' - 6 7/8"
	26'-0"	6' - 10 3/16"	6' - 1 9/16"	3' - 0 7/16"		26'-0"	7' - 3 3/16"	7' - 9 5/16"	3' - 10 7/16"
	28'-0"	7' - 4 9/16"	6' - 6 13/16"	3' - 3 1/4"		28'-0"	7' - 9 15/16"	8' - 4 9/16"	4' - 2 1/16"
	30'-0"	7' - 10 7/8"	7' - 0 1/2"	3' - 6 1/16"		30'-0"	8' - 4 5/8"	8' - 11 3/4"	4' - 5 11/16"
	32'-0"	8' - 5 3/16"	7' - 6 3/16"	3' - 8 7/8"		32'-0"	8' - 11 5/16"	9' - 6 15/16"	4' - 9 1/4"
5 on 12	20'-0"	5' - 5"	5' - 3 5/8"	2' - 7 5/8"	7 on 12	20'-0"	5' - 9 7/16"	6' - 8 3/16"	3' - 3 7/8"
	22'-0"	5' - 11 1/2"	5' - 10 1/16"	2' - 10 13/16"		22'-0"	6' - 4 7/16"	7' - 4 1/4"	3' - 7 15/16"
	24'-0"	6' - 6"	6' - 4 7/16"	3' - 2"		24'-0"	6' - 11 3/8"	8' - 0 5/16"	3' - 11 15/16"
	26'-0"	7' - 0 1/2"	6' - 10 7/8"	3' - 5 1/4"		26'-0"	7' - 6 5/16"	9' - 8 3/8"	4' - 4"
	28'-0"	7' - 7"	7' - 5 1/4"	3' - 8 7/16"		28'-0"	8' - 1 1/4"	9' - 4 7/16"	4' - 8"
	30'-0"	8' - 1 1/2"	7' - 11 11/16"	3' - 11 5/8"		30'-0"	8' - 8 3/16"	10' - 0 1/2"	5' - 0 1/16"
	32'-0"	8' - 8"	8' - 6 1/16"	4' - 2 13/16"		32'-0"	9' - 3 1/8"	10' - 8 9/16"	5' - 4 1/16"

Dimensions shown will provide approximately 1/2" camber at bottom chord panel points. Utilize full uncut length of bottom chord pieces by increasing the spacing of the connectors in the splice.

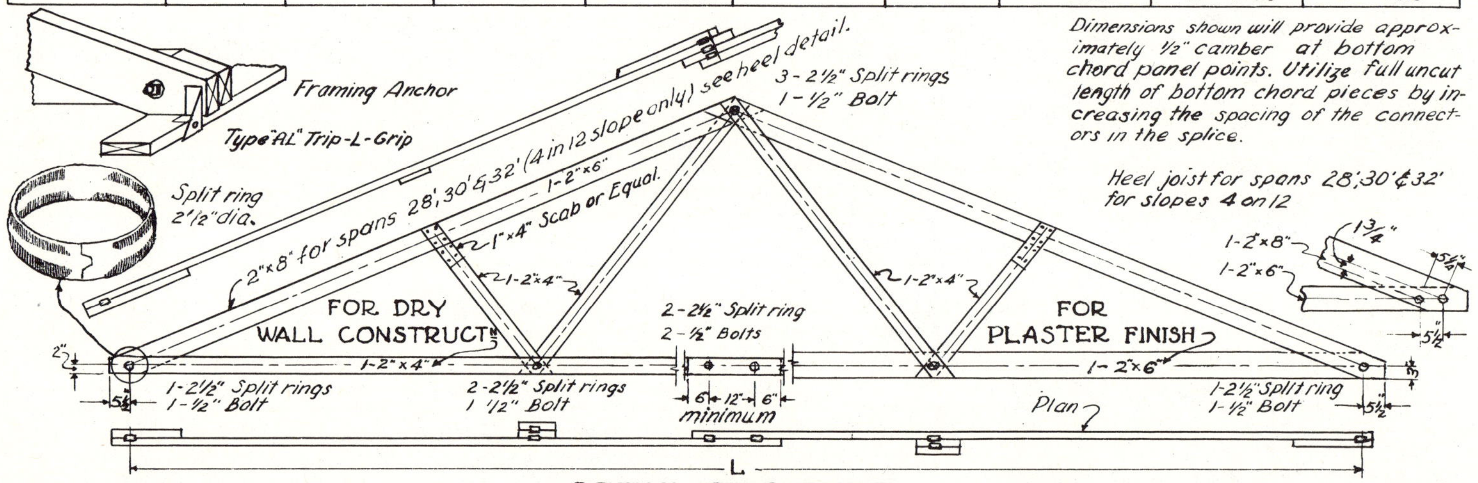
Framing Anchor
Type "AL" Trip-L-Grip
Split ring
2 1/2" dia.
2"x8" for spans 28', 30' & 32' (4 in 12 slope only) see heel detail.
3 - 2 1/2" Split rings
1 - 1/2" Bolt
1-2"x6"
1"x4" Scab or Equal.
1-2"x4"
1-2"x4"
FOR DRY WALL CONSTRUCT'N
FOR PLASTER FINISH
2-2 1/2" Split ring
2 - 1/2" Bolts
1-2"x4"
1- 2"x6"
1-2 1/2" Split rings
1 - 1/2" Bolt
2-2 1/2" Split rings
1 1/2" Bolt
6 12" 6"
minimum
1-2 1/2" Split ring
1- 1/2" Bolt
Plan
L
Heel joist for spans 28', 30' & 32' for slopes 4 on 12
1-2"x8"
1-2"x6"
1 3/4"
5 1/4"
5 1/2"

DETAIL OF RAFTER

Lumber
Compression parallel to grain .... 900 psi
Extreme fiber in bending .... 900 psi
Modulus of Elasticity .... 1,760,000 psi

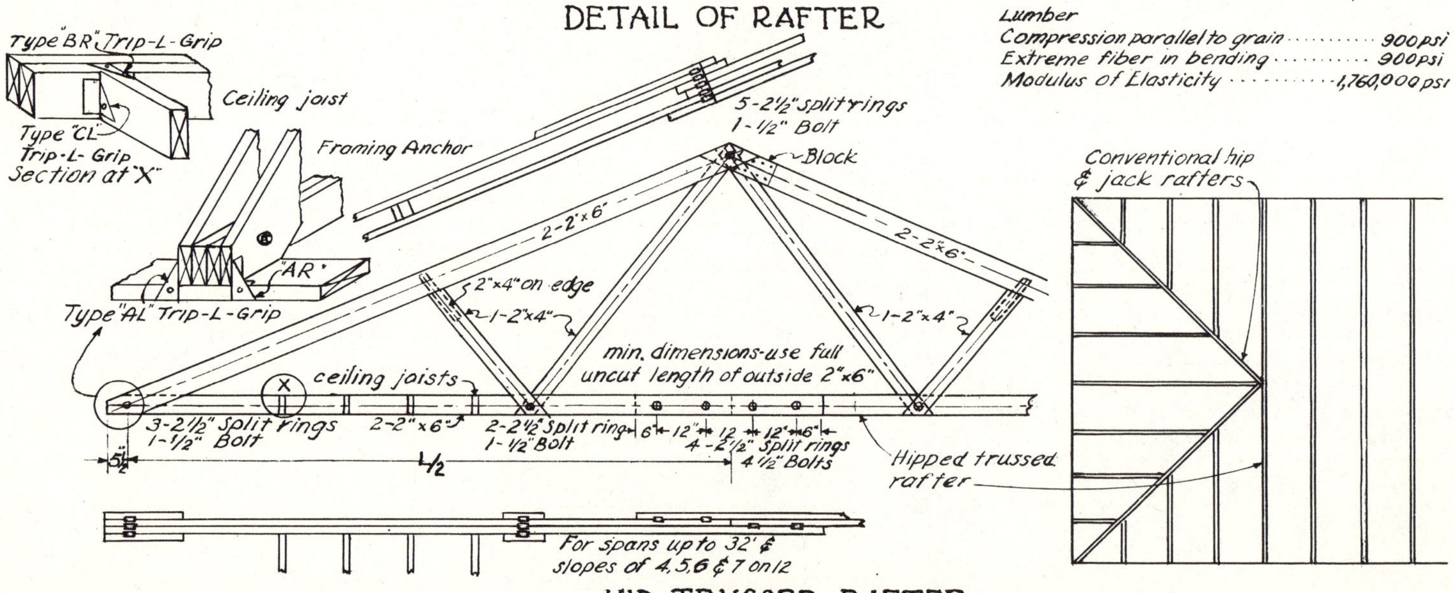
Type "BR" Trip-L-Grip
Ceiling joist
Type "CL" Trip-L-Grip
Section at "X"
Framing Anchor
"AR"
Type "AL" Trip-L-Grip
5-2 1/2" split rings
1- 1/2" Bolt
Block
2-2"x6"
2-2"x6"
2"x4" on edge
1-2"x4"
1-2"x4"
min. dimensions-use full uncut length of outside 2"x6"
ceiling joists
X
3-2 1/2" Split rings
1-1/2" Bolt
2-2"x6"
2-2 1/2" Split ring
1- 1/2" Bolt
6" 12" 12 12" 6"
4-2 1/2" Split rings
4 1/2" Bolts
L/2
Hipped trussed rafter
Conventional hip & jack rafters
For spans up to 32' & slopes of 4, 5, 6 & 7 on 12

HIP TRUSSED RAFTER

Courtesy of Timber Engineering Company, Washington, D.C.

GLUED LAMINATED BEAMS and PURLINS

DESIGN OF GLUED LAMINATED BEAMS

(for horizontal straight beam)

STEP 1. Required / Assume
- Span 28 ft.
- Length 63 ft.
- Spacing 9 ft. o.c. 7 spaces: 6 beams required. End walls with sill plates support purlins at end bays.

STEP 2. Assume size of beam. Try: width b = 5", depth h = 17"

STEP 3. Find total load per beam.

Load	Lbs. per Sq. Ft.	
Live	30.0	
Beam	2.5	
2" T.&G.	4.4	
5 ply roofig, gravel	6.5	
Total:	43.4	Use: 45 psf

Total load per beam = W

W = Span x Spacing x 45 psf
= 28 x 9 x 45 = 11,340 lbs.

STEP 4. Find bending moment M at center of span.

M = 1.5 x W x Span
= 1.5 x 11,340 x 28 = 476,000 in.-lbs.

STEP 5. Find bending stress "f" (actual).

$$f = \frac{6M}{bh^2} = \frac{6 \times 476{,}000}{5 \times 17^2} = 1980 \text{ psi.}$$

f (allowable) = 2400 psi.*

Therefore 5" x 17" beam O.K.

STEP 6. To find deflection, use the formula:

$$D = \frac{5WL^3}{32Ebh^3} = \frac{5 \times 11340 \times 336^3}{32 \times 1800000 \times 5 \times 17^3} = 1.52'' \ (1/220 \text{ of span})$$

where: W = load: 11340 lbs.
L = length: 28x12 = 336"
E = modulus of elasticity: 1,800,000 psi.
b = (width) 5";
h = (depth) 17"

(Allowable deflection varies from 1/180 to 1/360 of span; is normally used at 1/240).

*See "Nat'l Design Spec. for Stress-Grade Lumber", pub. by Nat'l Lumber Mfrs. Assn., or see preceding page.

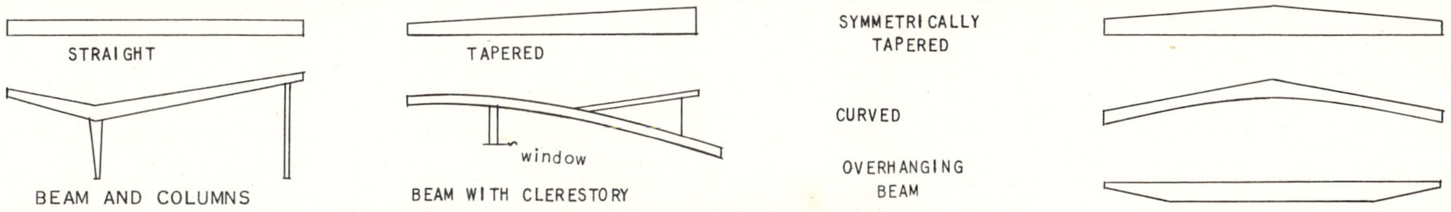
STRAIGHT
TAPERED
SYMMETRICALLY TAPERED
BEAM AND COLUMNS
window
BEAM WITH CLERESTORY
CURVED
OVERHANGING BEAM

TYPICAL BEAM SHAPES

PURLIN SELECTION

SECTION SIZE inches ‡	SECTION MODULUS $= \frac{bd^2}{6}$	TOTAL SAFE UNIFORM LOAD, LBS. — SPAN IN FEET: 8	10	12	14	16	18	20
3¼ x 6½	22.9	4576	2980	2067	1521	1163	919	741
5 x 6½	35.2	7040	4585	3180	2340	1790	1415	1140
3¼ x 8⅛	35.8	6250	5720	4039	2970	2271	1794	1500
5 x 7¼	43.8	8755	6360	4415	3245	2485	1960	1585
3¼ x 9¾	51.5	8450	8238	6860	5131	3926	3100	2509
5 x 8⅛	55.0	10800	8800	6215	4570	3495	2760	2230
5 x 8⅞	65.6	11825	10500	8105	5955	4555	3600	2910
3¼ x 11⅜	70.0	9850	9850	9337	8004	6236	4923	3984
7 x 8⅛	77.0	15160	12320	8700	6398	4893	3864	3112
5 x 9¾	79.2	13100	12675	10555	7898	6040	4770	3860
3¼ x 13	91.5	11260	11500	11500	10455	9155	7351	5947
5 x 10½	91.8	14000	14000	12240	9860	7545	5960	4820
5 x 11⅜	107.8	15200	15200	14365	12315	9595	7575	6130
7 x 9¾	110.9	18200	17745	14777	11053	8456	6678	5404
5 x 12⅛	122.5	16200	16200	16200	13995	11620	9180	7420
5 x 13	140.8	17400	17400	17400	16085	14085	11310	9150
7 x 11⅜	151.0	21200	21200	20111	17241	13433	10605	8582
7 x 13	197.2	24200	24200	24200	22519	19719	15834	12810
7 x 14⅝	249.5	27300	27300	27300	27300	24955	22155	18235

‡Based on 1⅝" laminations. For intermediate sizes, a ¾" lamination may be included with the 1⅝" ones.

DESIGN: **

Purlins given are designed for maximum bending stress "f" of 2400 psi, or maximum deflection of 1/240 of span, or 200 psi shear.

USE OF TABLE:

Example: What purlin size is required for span 16', 7' o.c. spacing, and roof load of 40 psf?

Total uniform load = span x spacing x load
= 16 x 7 x 40 = 4480 lbs.

In column under 16' span a 3¼" x 11-3/8" is adequate for 6236 lbs.; a 5" x 8-7/8" is adequate for 4555 lbs.

SELECTION:

Table gives minimum adequate sizes. Final selection should be based on roof pitch and architectural appearance. On flat or low-pitched roofs (less than 30°), deep and narrow purlins will be most economical. On steeply pitched roofs (over 30°), wider purlins will give more lateral strength.

**See So. Pine Specs. for Structural Glued Laminated Southern Pine.

Standard plate available for each size of arch. Consult mfr.

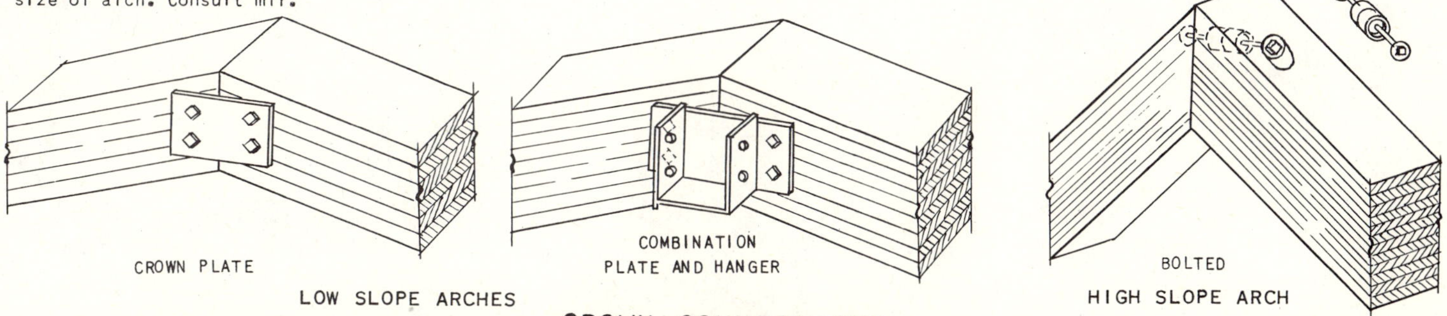
CROWN PLATE
COMBINATION PLATE AND HANGER
LOW SLOPE ARCHES
BOLTED
HIGH SLOPE ARCH

CROWN CONNECTIONS

Data checked by Unit Structures Inc.

FRAME WALLS

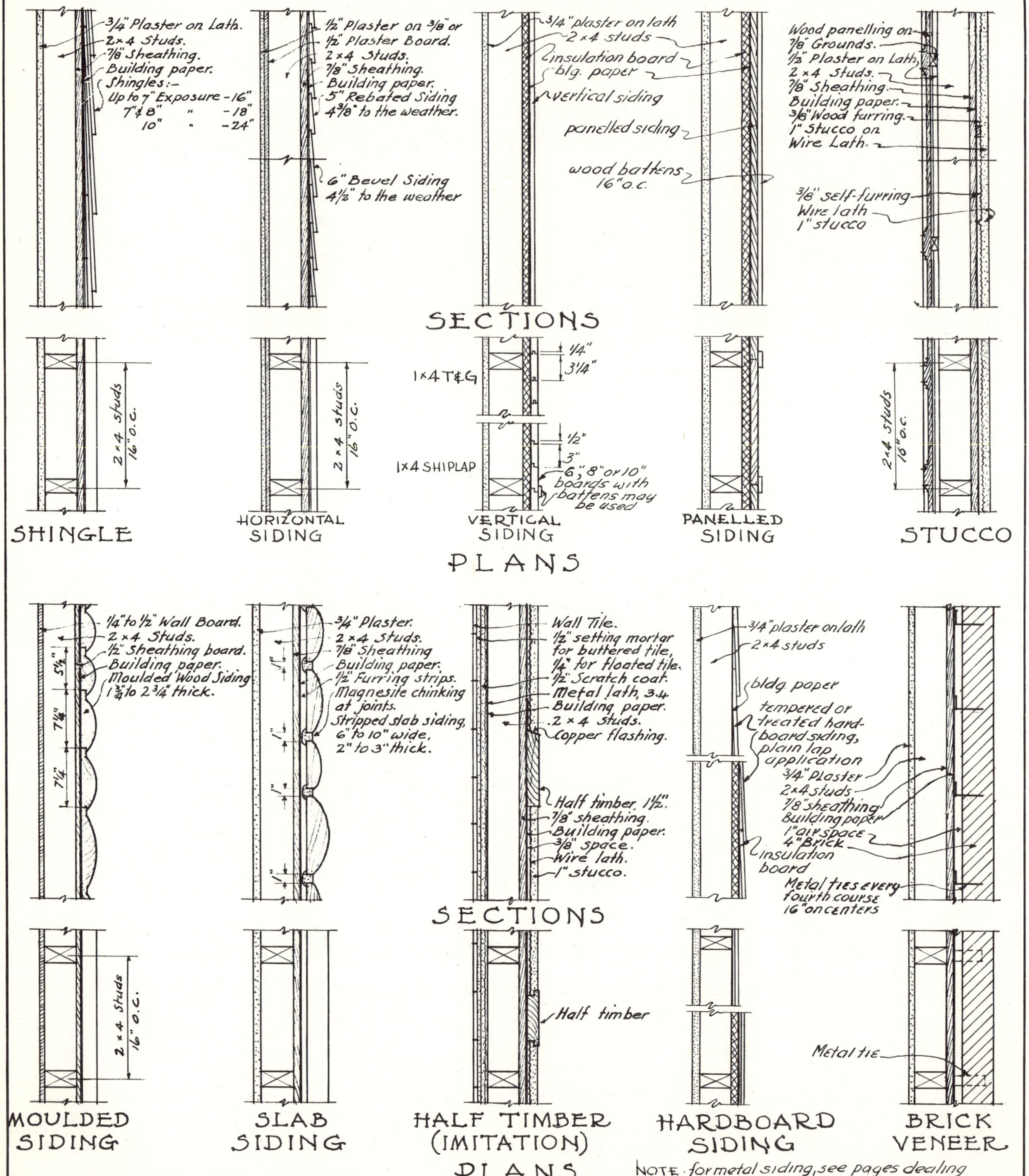

3/4" Plaster on Lath.
2×4 Studs.
7/8" Sheathing.
Building paper.
Shingles:–
Up to 7" Exposure – 16"
7" & 8" " – 18"
10" " – 24"
1/2" Plaster on 3/8" or
1/2" Plaster Board.
2×4 Studs.
7/8" Sheathing.
Building paper.
5" Rebated Siding
4 3/8" to the weather.
6" Bevel Siding
4 1/2" to the weather
3/4" plaster on lath
2×4 studs
insulation board
blg. paper
vertical siding
panelled siding
wood battens
16" o.c.
Wood panelling on
7/8" Grounds.
1/2" Plaster on Lath,
2×4 Studs.
7/8" Sheathing.
Building paper.
3/8" Wood furring.
1" Stucco on
Wire Lath.
3/8" self-furring
Wire lath
1" stucco
SECTIONS
2×4 studs 16" o.c.
1/4"
3 1/4"
1×4 T&G
1/2"
3"
1×4 SHIPLAP
6", 8" or 10" boards with battens may be used
SHINGLE
HORIZONTAL SIDING
VERTICAL SIDING
PANELLED SIDING
STUCCO
PLANS
1/4" to 1/2" Wall Board.
2×4 Studs.
1/2" Sheathing board.
Building paper.
Moulded Wood Siding
1 3/4" to 2 3/4" thick.
5 1/2"
7 1/4"
7 1/4"
3/4" Plaster.
2×4 Studs.
7/8" Sheathing
Building paper.
1/2" Furring strips.
Magnesite chinking at joints.
Stripped slab siding,
6" to 10" wide,
2" to 3" thick.
1"
Wall Tile.
1/2" setting mortar for buttered tile,
1/4" for floated tile.
1/2" Scratch coat.
Metal lath, 3.4
Building paper.
2×4 Studs.
Copper flashing.
Half timber, 1 1/2".
7/8" sheathing.
Building paper.
3/8" space.
Wire lath.
1" stucco.
3/4" plaster on lath
2×4 studs
bldg. paper
tempered or treated hard-board siding, plain lap application
3/4" Plaster
2×4 studs
7/8" sheathing
Building paper
1" air space
4" Brick
insulation board
Metal ties every fourth course 16" on centers
SECTIONS
2×4 studs 16" o.c.
Half timber
Metal tie
MOULDED SIDING
SLAB SIDING
HALF TIMBER (IMITATION)
HARDBOARD SIDING
BRICK VENEER
PLANS

NOTE – for metal siding, see pages dealing with specific material

Various interior finishes shown.

TYPICAL FRAME WALLS

Scale 3/4" = 1'-0"

WOOD SIDING PATTERNS

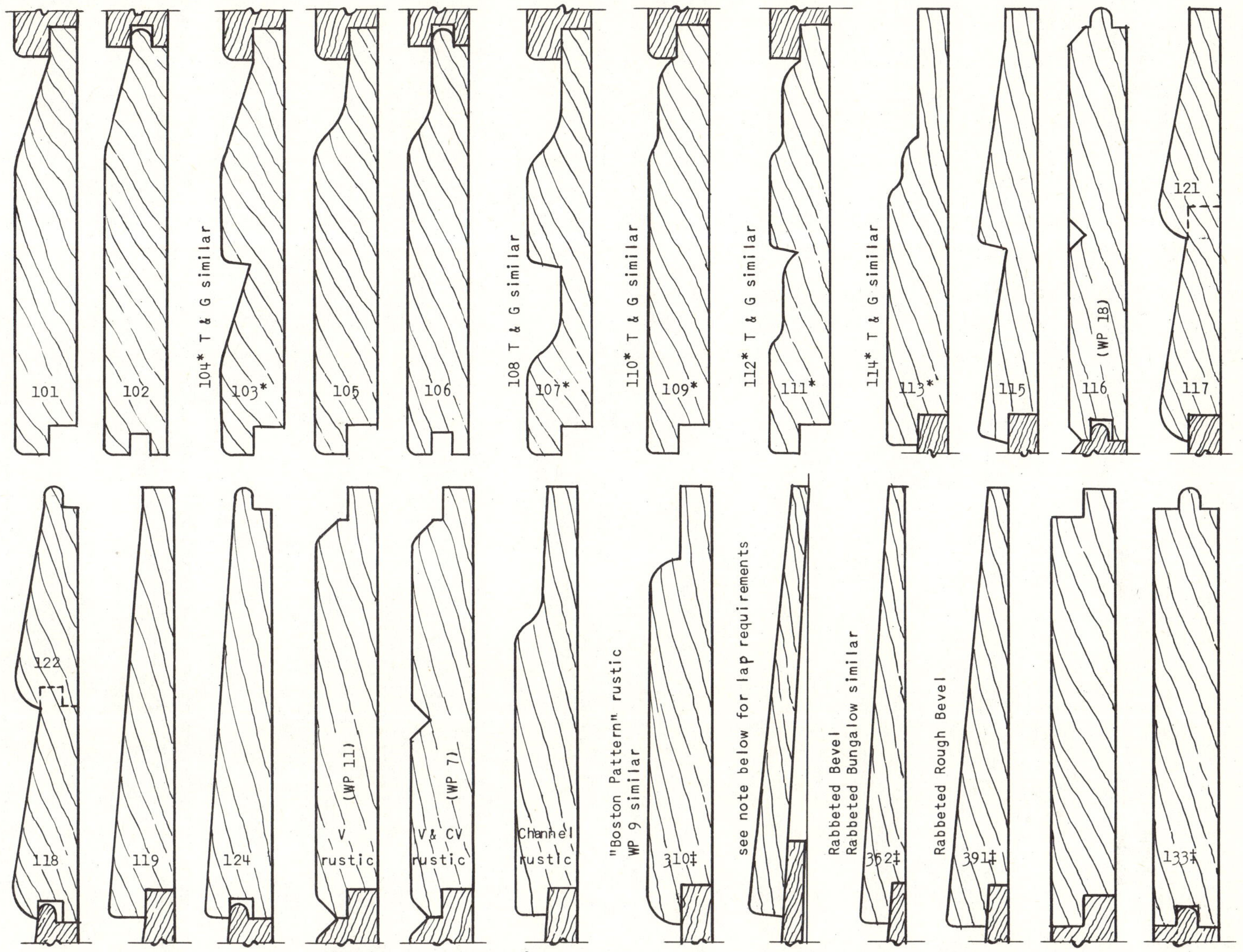
101
102
104* T & G similar
103*
105
106
108 T & G similar
107*
110* T & G similar
109*
112* T & G similar
111*
114* T & G similar
113*
115
(WP 18)
116
121
117
122
118
119
124
(WP 11)
V rustic
(WP 7)
V & CV rustic
Channel rustic
"Boston Pattern" rustic
WP 9 similar
310‡
see note below for lap requirements
Rabbeted Bevel
Rabbeted Bungalow similar
362‡
Rabbeted Rough Bevel
391‡
133‡

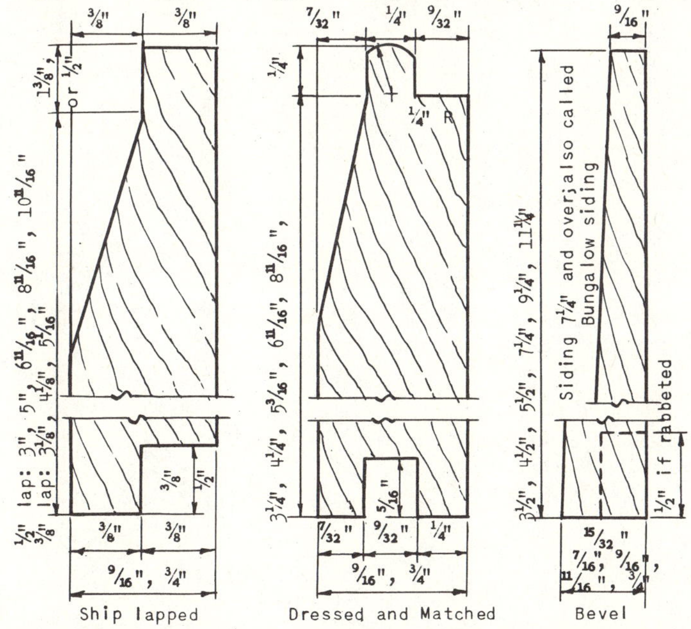
3/8"
3/8"
1 3/8", or 1/2"
lap: 3", 5", 6 11/16", 8 11/16", 10 11/16"
lap: 3 1/8", 4 7/8", 5 1/16"
1/2"
3/8"
3/8"
3/8"
1/2"
9/16", 3/4"
Ship lapped
7/32"
1/4"
9/32"
1/4"
1/4" R
3 1/4", 4 1/4", 5 3/16", 6 11/16", 8 11/16",
5/16"
7/32"
9/32"
1/4"
9/16", 3/4"
Dressed and Matched
9/16"
Siding 7 1/4" and over also called Bungalow siding
3 1/2", 4 1/2", 5 1/2", 7 1/4", 9 1/4", 11 1/4"
1/2" if rabbeted
15/32"
7/16", 9/16",
11/16", 3/4"
Bevel

STANDARD SIDING, MINIMUM DRESSED DIMENSIONS**

FULL SIZE

Patterns are shown at ½ full size except as noted

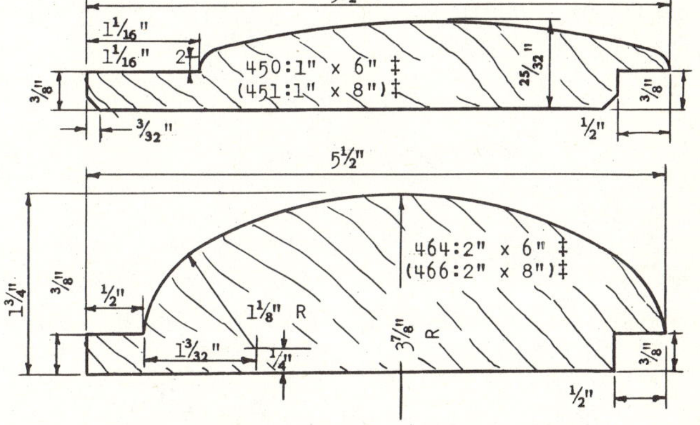
5 1/2"
1 1/16"
1 1/16"
2"
450:1" x 6" ‡
(451:1" x 8")‡
25/32
3/8
3/32"
1/2"
3/8
5 1/2"
464:2" x 6" ‡
(466:2" x 8")‡
1 3/4"
3/8
1/2"
1 1/8" R
3 7/8" R
1 3/32"
1/4"
3/8
1/2"

LOG CABIN SIDING - SHIP LAP

WP: Western Pine pattern number.
* Indicates pattern is not generally available
**From American Lumber Standards, Simplified practice Recommendation 16-53. Manufacturer may exceed these minimum dimensions.
‡ Indicates California Redwood Association.
Bevel siding laps: 4" width, ¾" lap; 6" width, 1"; 8" & over 1½".
Data checked by: Arkansas Soft Pine Bureau; Calif. Redwood Assn.; North'n Hardwood & Hemlock Mfrs. Assn.; Southern Pine Inspection Bureau; Western Pine Assn.

BALLOON FRAMING

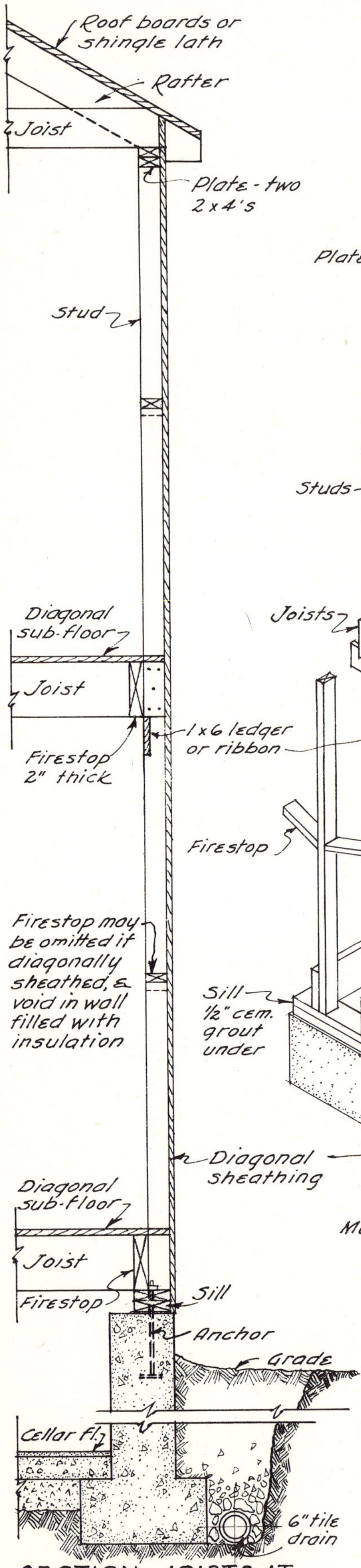
Roof boards or shingle lath
Rafter
Joist
Plate - two 2 x 4's
Stud
Diagonal sub-floor
Joist
1 x 6 ledger or ribbon
Firestop 2" thick
Firestop may be omitted if diagonally sheathed, & void in wall filled with insulation
Diagonal sheathing
Diagonal sub-floor
Joist
Firestop
Sill
Anchor
Grade
Cellar Fl.
6" tile drain

SECTION - JOISTS AT RT. ANGLES TO EXT. WALL with EXCAV. CELLAR
3/8" = 1'- 0"

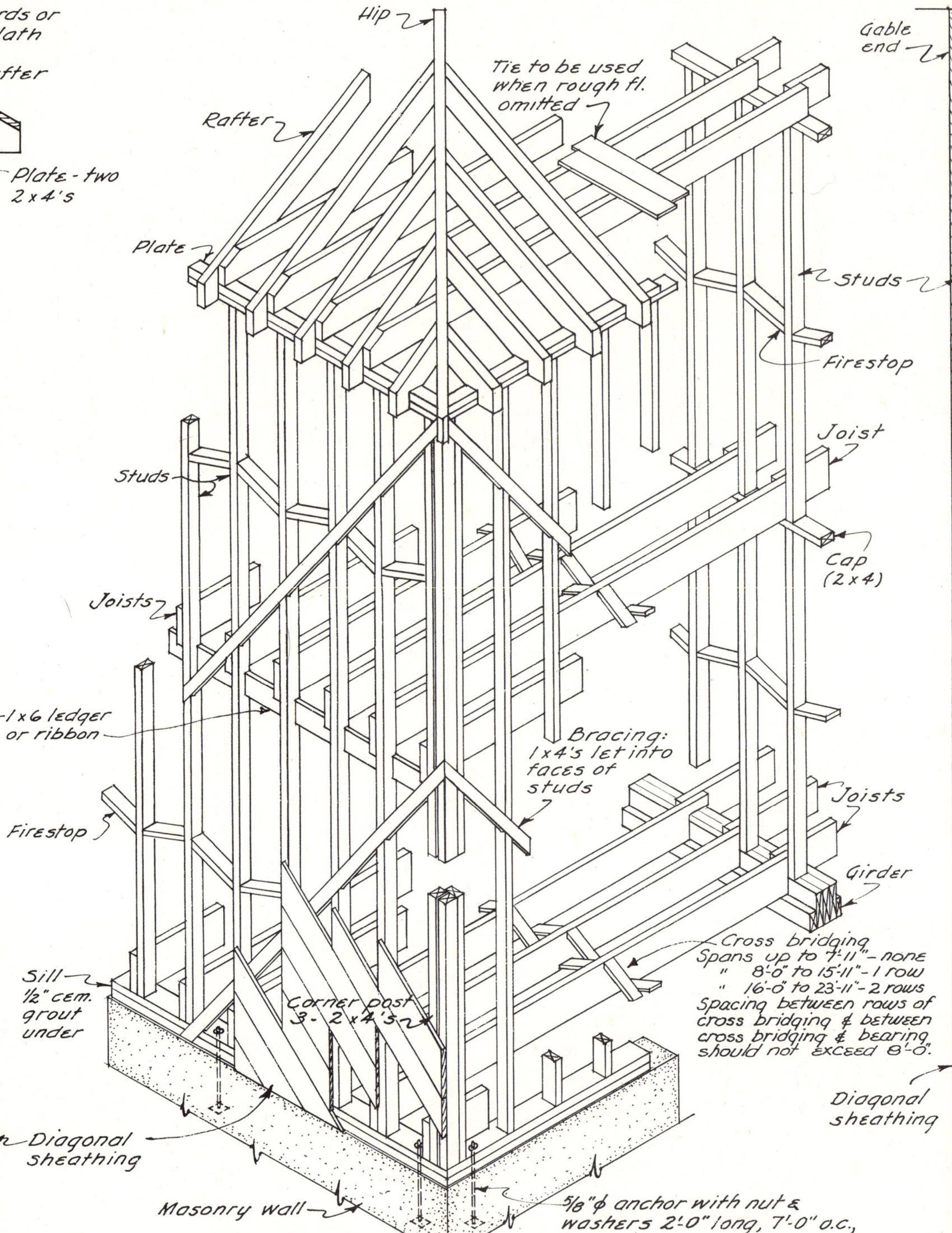
Hip
Tie to be used when rough fl. omitted
Rafter
Plate
Studs
Firestop
Joist
Studs
Cap (2 x 4)
Joists
Bracing: 1 x 4's let into faces of studs
Firestop
Joists
Girder
Cross bridging
Spans up to 7'-11" - none
" 8'-0" to 15'-11" - 1 row
" 16'-0" to 23'-11" - 2 rows
Spacing between rows of cross bridging & between cross bridging & bearing should not exceed 8'-0".
Sill
1/2" cem. grout under
Corner post 3 - 2 x 4's
Masonry wall
5/8" ϕ anchor with nut & washers 2'-0" long, 7'-0" o.c., two near each corner.

Scale 1/4" = 1'-0"

Standard spacing of studs is 16" c. to c. to receive lath. Rough floor when laid diagonally gives added strength. Laid horizontally, it is more economical. Diagonal sheathing is preferable to horizontal for the same reason. Change its direction at corners. If diagonal rough flooring is used, reverse direction at each floor. Hips, ridges and valleys should not be less than full depth of rafters. Ridges and hips thickness not less than 2", valleys 3" min. Sizes are nominal. When sheathing is horizontal, exterior walls should be diagonally braced at corners for the purpose of stiffening. Unequal shrinkage exists between ext. & int. walls unless steel is used for int. girder. Best for stucco or brick veneer construction. Usually cheaper for 2 story bldgs. Less overall shrinkage.

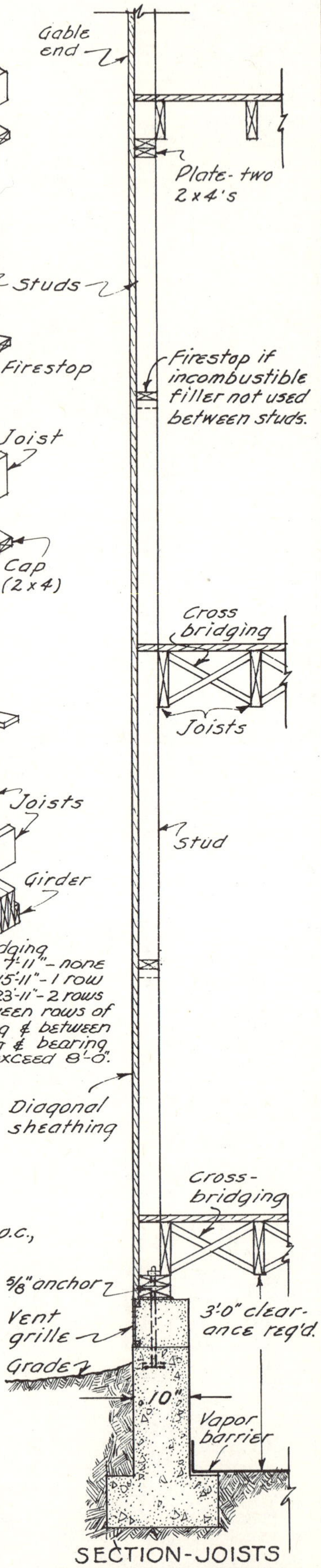
Gable end
Plate - two 2 x 4's
Studs
Firestop if incombustible filler not used between studs.
Cross bridging
Joists
Stud
Diagonal sheathing
Cross-bridging
5/8" anchor
Vent grille
Grade
3'-0" clearance req'd.
10"
Vapor barrier

SECTION - JOISTS PARALLEL to EXT. WALL with CRAWL SPACE
3/8" = 1'- 0"

Adapted from data by the National Lumber Manufacturers Association

BRACED FRAMING

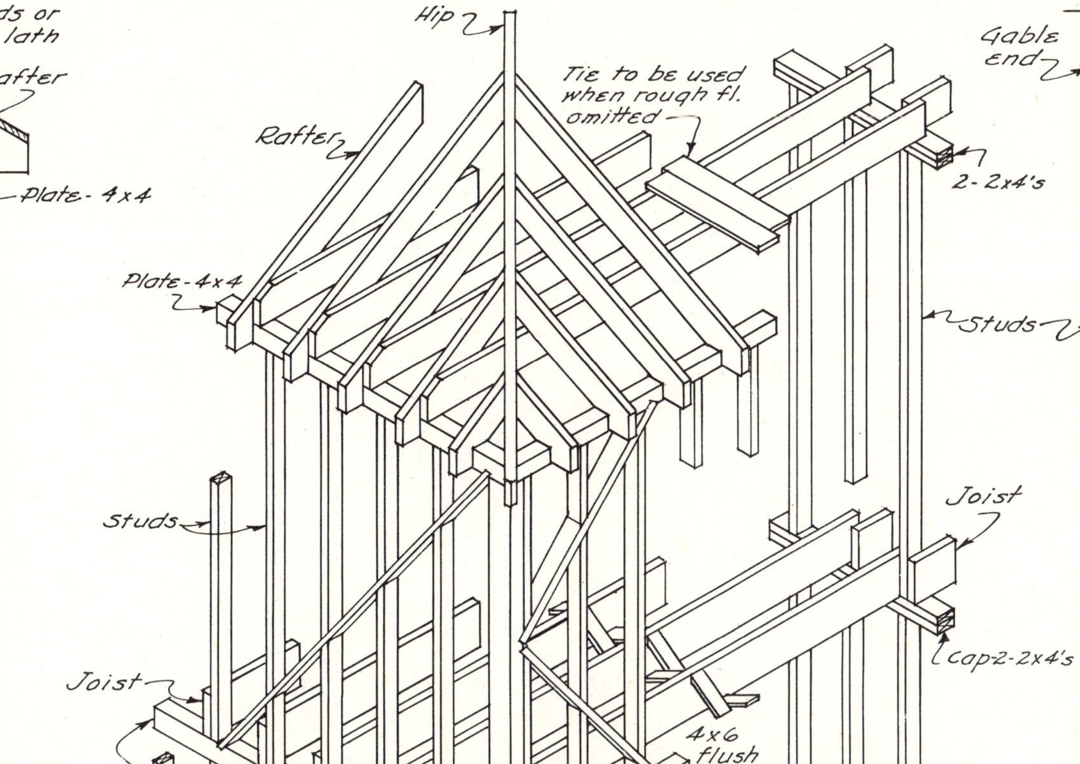
Hip
Tie to be used when rough fl. omitted
Rafter
2-2x4's
Plate-4x4
Studs
Studs
Joist
Cap-2-2x4's
Joist
4x6 flush girt
Knee brace 2x4
45°
Joists
2x4 diagonal brace
Solid girder
Cross bridging
Spans up to 7'-11" – none
" 8'-0" to 15'-11" – 1 row
" 16'-0" to 23'-11" – 2 rows
Spacing between rows of cross bridging & between cross bridging & bearing should not exceed 8'-0".
Sill
1/2" cem. grout under
Corner post 4x6
Diagonal sheathing
Diagonal sheathing
Masonry wall
5/8"ϕ anchor with nut & washers 2'-0" long 7'-0" o.c., 2 near each corner.

Scale 1/4" = 1'-0"

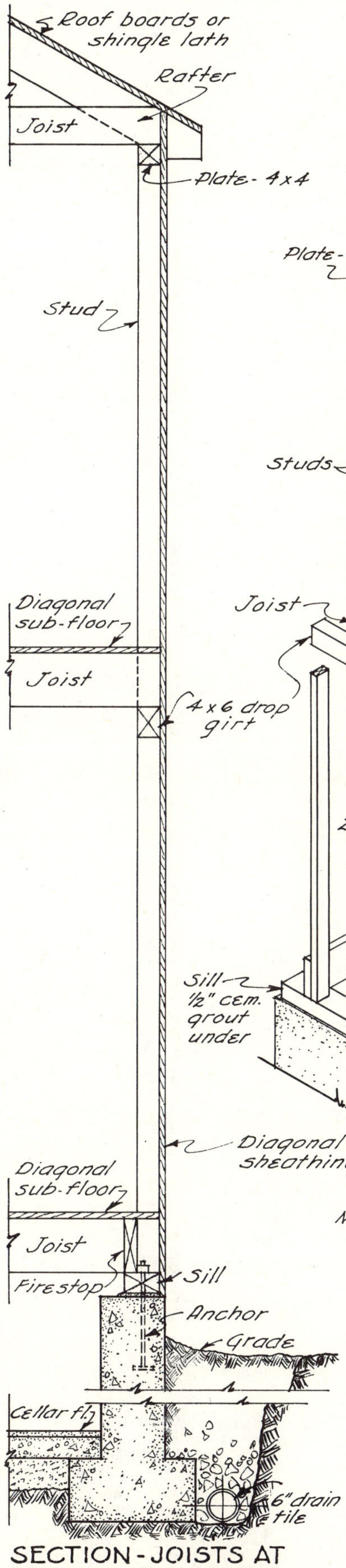
Roof boards or shingle lath
Rafter
Joist
Plate-4x4
Stud
Diagonal sub-floor
Joist
4x6 drop girt
Diagonal sub-floor
Joist
Firestop
Sill
Anchor
Grade
Cellar fl.
6" drain tile

SECTION-JOISTS AT RT. ANGLES to EXT. WALL with EXCAV. CELLAR
3/8" = 1'-0"

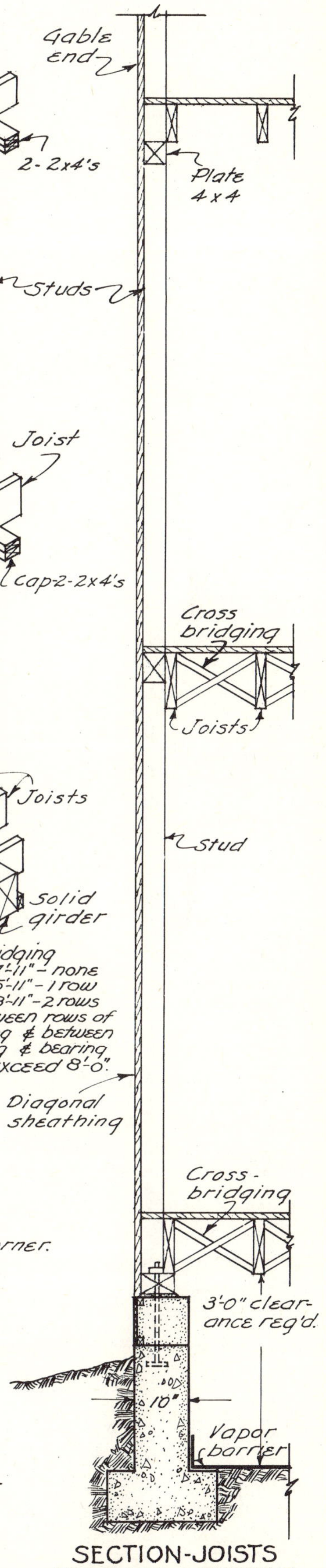
Gable end
Plate 4x4
Cross bridging
Joists
Stud
Cross-bridging
3'-0" clearance req'd.
10"
Vapor barrier

SECTION-JOISTS PARALLEL to EXT. WALL with CRAWL SPACE
3/8" = 1'-0"

Standard spacing of studs is 16" c. to c. to receive lath. Rough floor when laid diagonally gives added strength. Laid horizontally, it is more economical. Diagonal sheathing is preferable to horizontal for the same reason. Change direction of diagonal sheathing at each corner; change direction of diagonal rough flooring at each floor. Hips, ridges, & valleys should not be less than full depth of rafters. Ridge & hip thickness not less than 2"; valleys 3" min. Knee braces are resorted to when windows are too close to corner for full bracing. Sizes shown are nominal. Unequal shrinkage exists between exterior and interior walls, and total shrinkage is very great. This is the oldest & strongest type of framing. Not suitable for either stucco or brick veneer construction. It is difficult to run pipes up walls.

Adapted from data by National Lumber Manufacturers Association

WESTERN (or PLATFORM) FRAMING

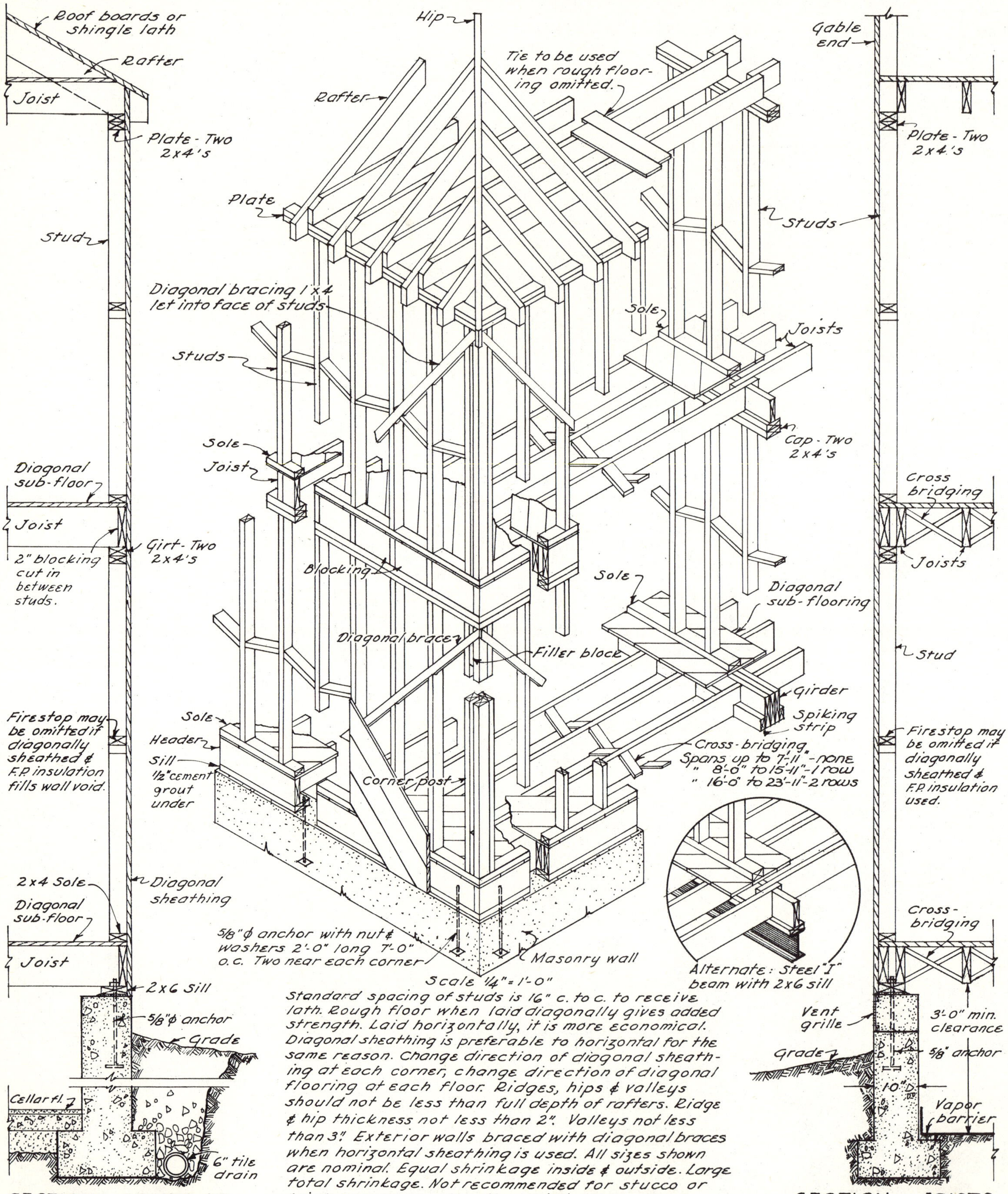
Roof boards or shingle lath
Rafter
Joist
Plate - Two 2x4's
Stud
Diagonal sub-floor
Joist
Girt - Two 2x4's
2" blocking cut in between studs.
Firestop may be omitted if diagonally sheathed & F.P. insulation fills wall void.
2x4 Sole
Diagonal sheathing
Diagonal sub-floor
Joist
2x6 Sill
5/8"ϕ anchor
Grade
Cellar fl.
6" tile drain
Hip
Tie to be used when rough flooring omitted.
Rafter
Plate
Studs
Diagonal bracing 1x4 let into face of studs
Studs
Sole
Joists
Sole
Joist
Cap - Two 2x4's
Blocking
Sole
Diagonal sub-flooring
Diagonal brace
Filler block
Girder
Spiking strip
Sole
Header
Sill
1/2" cement grout under
Corner post
Cross-bridging
Spans up to 7'-11" - none
" 8'-0" to 15'-11" - 1 row
" 16'-0" to 23'-11" - 2 rows
5/8"ϕ anchor with nut & washers 2'-0" long 7'-0" o.c. Two near each corner
Masonry wall
Scale 1/4" = 1'-0"
Alternate: Steel "I" beam with 2x6 sill
Gable end
Plate - Two 2x4's
Studs
Cross bridging
Joists
Stud
Firestop may be omitted if diagonally sheathed & F.P. insulation used.
Cross-bridging
Vent grille
3'-0" min. clearance
Grade
5/8" anchor
10"
Vapor barrier

Standard spacing of studs is 16" c. to c. to receive lath. Rough floor when laid diagonally gives added strength. Laid horizontally, it is more economical. Diagonal sheathing is preferable to horizontal for the same reason. Change direction of diagonal sheathing at each corner, change direction of diagonal flooring at each floor. Ridges, hips & valleys should not be less than full depth of rafters. Ridge & hip thickness not less than 2". Valleys not less than 3". Exterior walls braced with diagonal braces when horizontal sheathing is used. All sizes shown are nominal. Equal shrinkage inside & outside. Large total shrinkage. Not recommended for stucco or brick veneer construction. Difficult to run pipes up walls. Good for 1 story buildings.

SECTION - JOISTS AT RT. ANGLES to EXT. WALL with EXCAV. CELLAR
3/8" = 1'-0"

SECTION - JOISTS PARALLEL to EXT. WALL with CRAWL SPACE
3/8" = 1'-0"

Adapted from data by National Lumber Manufacturers Association

MODERN BRACED FRAMING

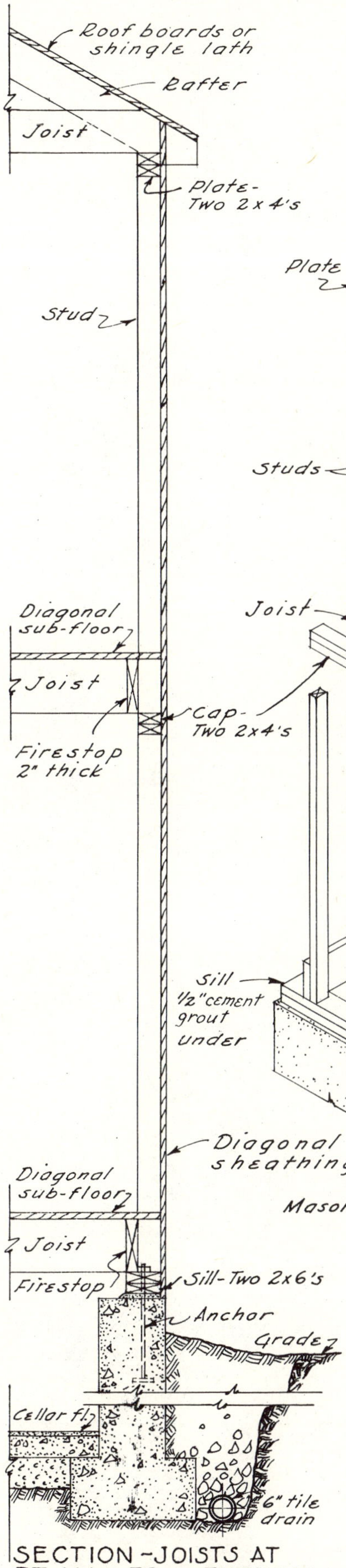

Roof boards or shingle lath
Rafter
Joist
Plate- Two 2x4's
Stud
Diagonal sub-floor
Joist
Cap- Two 2x4's
Firestop 2" thick
Diagonal sheathing
Diagonal sub-floor
Joist
Firestop
Sill- Two 2x6's
Anchor
Grade
Cellar fl.
6" tile drain

SECTION–JOISTS AT RT. ANGLES to EXT. WALL with EXCAV. CELLAR

3/8" = 1'- 0"

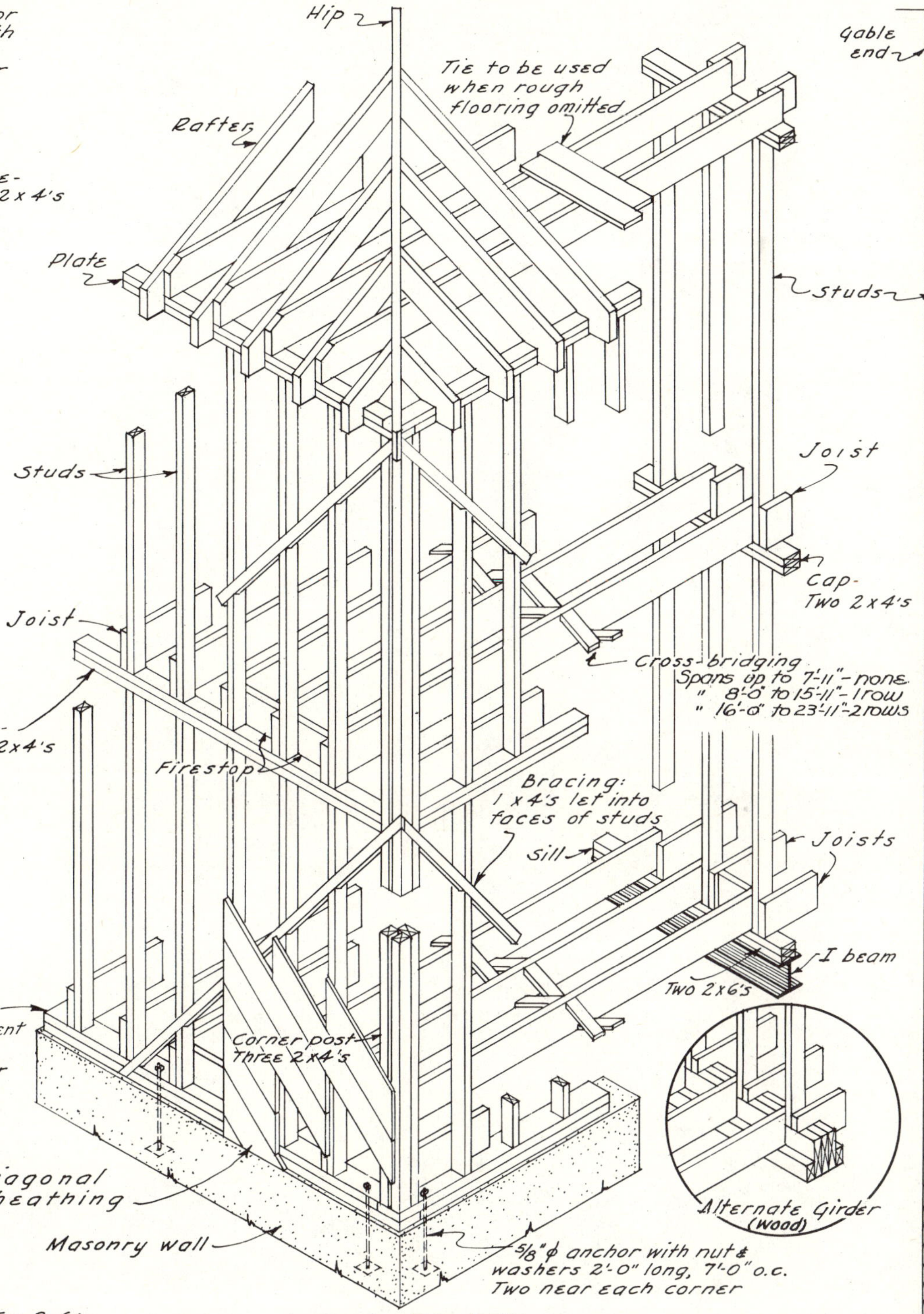

Hip
Tie to be used when rough flooring omitted
Rafter
Plate
Studs
Studs
Joist
Cap- Two 2x4's
Joist
Cross-bridging
Spans up to 7'-11" - none
" 8'-0" to 15'-11" - 1 row
" 16'-0" to 23'-11" - 2 rows
Firestop
Bracing: 1 x 4's let into faces of studs
Sill
Joists
I beam
Two 2x6's
Sill
1/2" cement grout under
Corner post- Three 2x4's
Diagonal sheathing
Masonry wall
5/8" ϕ anchor with nut & washers 2'-0" long, 7'-0" o.c. Two near each corner
Alternate Girder (wood)

Scale: 1/4" = 1'- 0"

This type is a combination of balloon (at sill) and braced (at cap) & is cheaper than braced framing. Shrinkage moderate, equal both inside & out if steel beam is used. May be used for any type construction. Standard spacing for studs is 16" center to center to receive lath. Rough floor when laid diagonally gives added strength. Laid horizontally, it is more economical. Diagonal sheathing is preferable to horizontal for the same reason. Change its direction at corners. If diagonal rough flooring is used, reverse direction at each floor. Hips, ridges and valleys should not be less than full depth of rafters. Ridge & hip thickness not less than 2", valleys 3" min. Sizes shown are nominal.

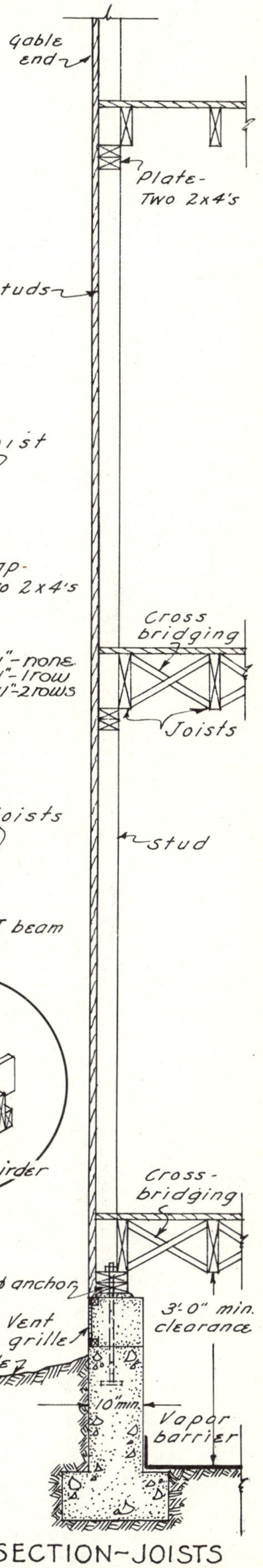

Gable end
Plate- Two 2x4's
Studs
Cross bridging
Joists
Stud
Cross- bridging
5/8" ϕ anchor
Vent grille
3'-0" min. clearance
Grade
10" min.
Vapor barrier

SECTION–JOISTS PARALLEL to EXT. WALL with CRAWL SPACE

3/8" = 1'- 0"

Adapted from data by National Lumber Manufacturers Association

LIGHT WOOD FRAMING DETAILS

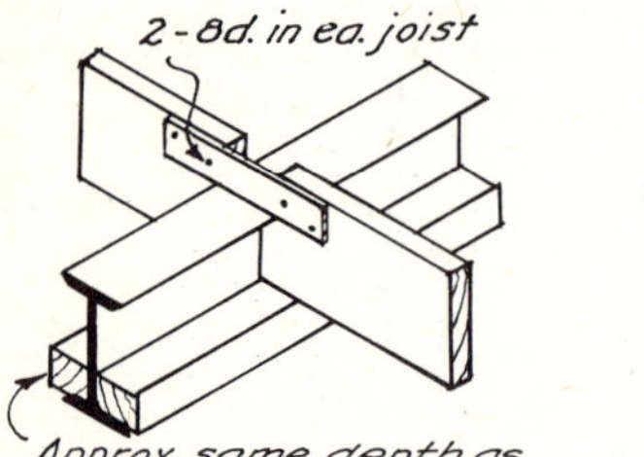
2-8d. in ea. joist
Approx. same depth as
ext. sill to equalize shrinkage.
ON WOOD BLOCKING

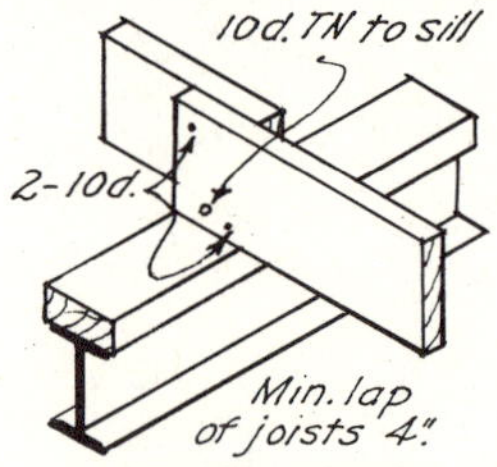
10d. TN to sill
2-10d.
Min. lap
of joists 4".
LAPPED OVER WOOD SILL

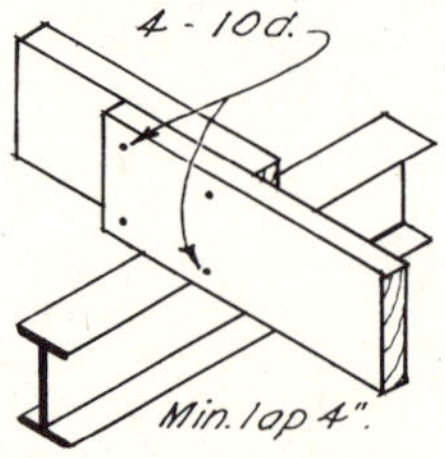
4 - 10d.
Min. lap 4".
LAPPED OVER GIRDER

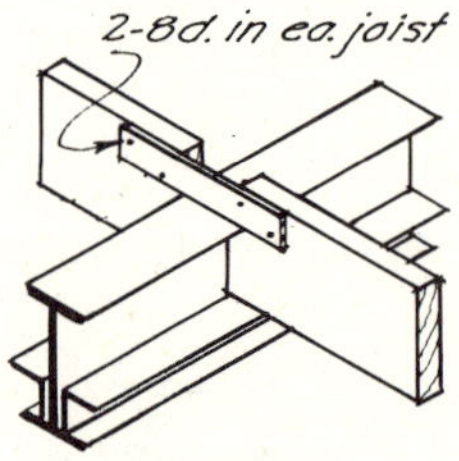
2-8d. in ea. joist
ON STEEL ANGLES

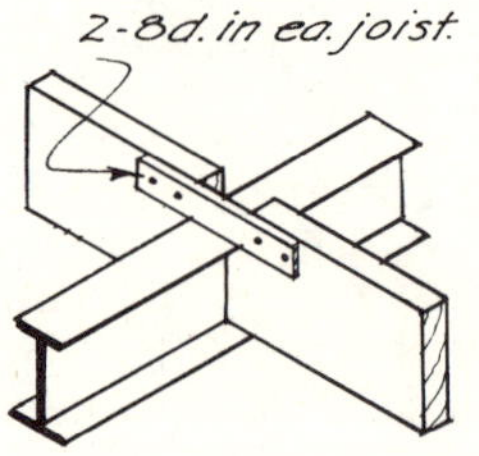
2-8d. in ea. joist.
ON LOWER FLANGE

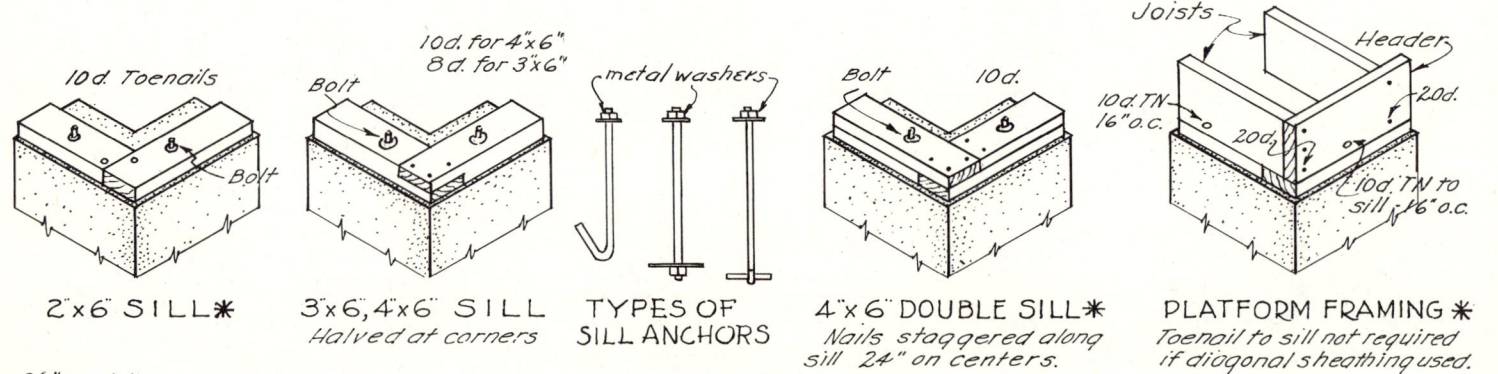

WOOD JOISTS SUPPORTED on STEEL GIRDERS

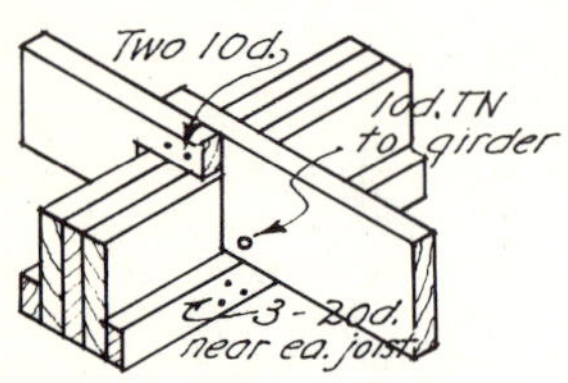
Two 10d.
10d. TN
to girder
3-20d.
near ea. joist
OVERLAPPING JOISTS NOTCHED over GIRDER *
Bearing only on ledger, not on top of girder.

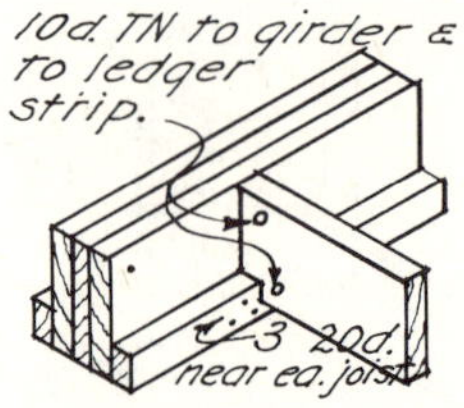
10d. TN to girder &
to ledger
strip.
3-20d.
near ea. joist
JOIST NOTCHED OVER LEDGER STRIP *
Notching over bearing not recommen'd.

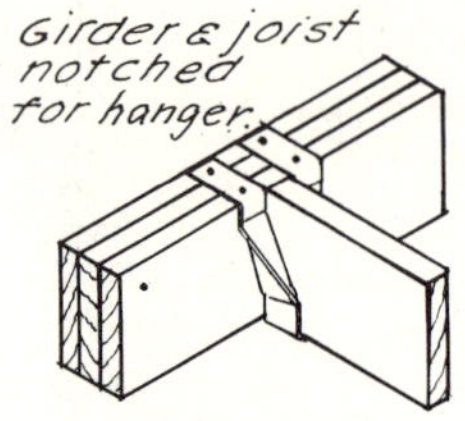
Girder & joist
notched
for hanger.
JOIST IN BRIDLE IRON
Also called joist hanger or stirrup

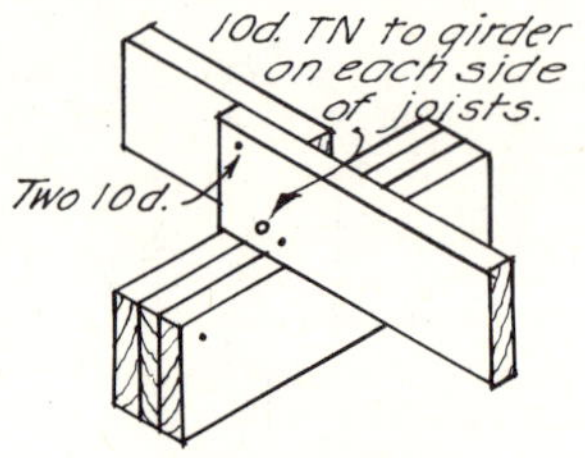
10d. TN to girder
on each side
of joists.
Two 10d.
JOISTS BEARING on GIRDER *
Min. lap 4" inches

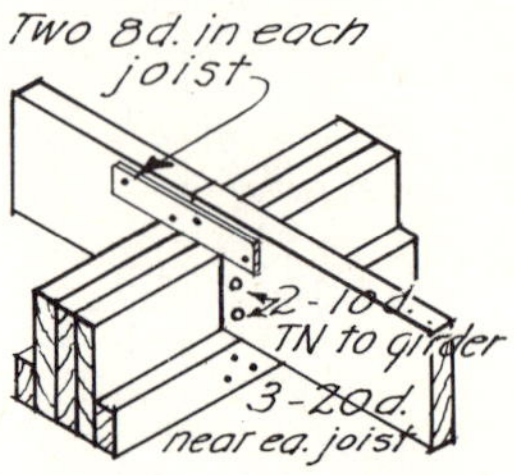
Two 8d. in each
joist
2-10d.
TN to girder
3-20d.
near ea. joist
JOISTS NOTCHED OVER GIRDER *
Bearing only on ledger, not on top of girdr.

WOOD JOISTS SUPPORTED on WOOD GIRDERS

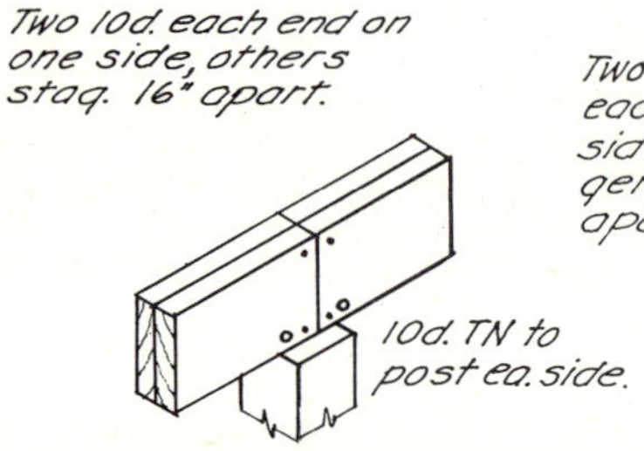
Two 10d. each end on
one side, others
stag. 16" apart.
10d. TN to
post ea. side.
TWO PIECE GIRDER *
Girder joints only at supports.

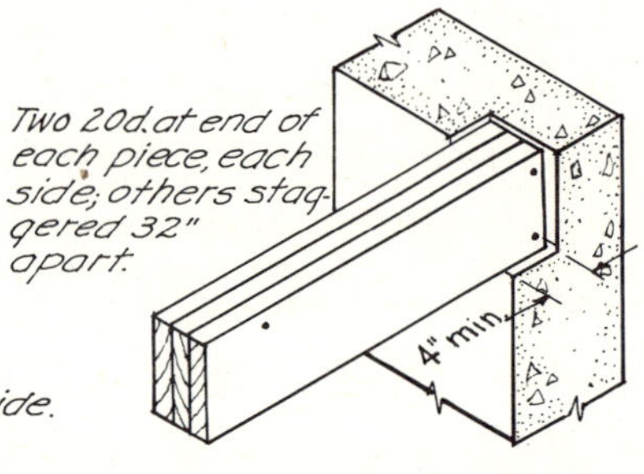
Two 20d. at end of
each piece, each
side; others stag-
gered 32"
apart.
4" min.
THREE PIECE GIRDER *
Four piece girder: add 1 pc. nailed with 20d. to three pc.

GIRDERS

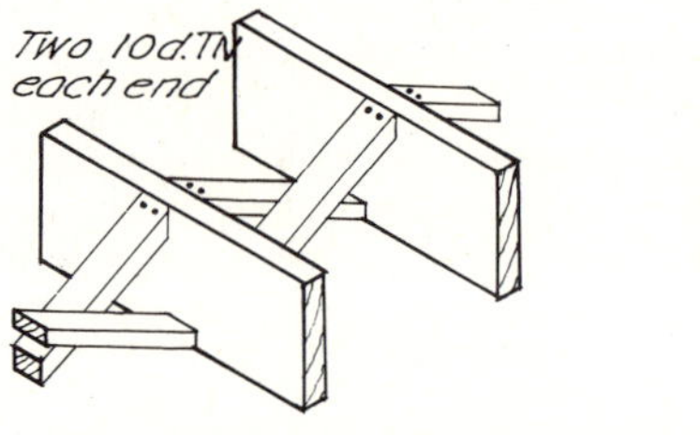
Two 10d. TN
each end
1"x3" CROSS BR'G. 2"x3" REC'D. *
Lower ends not nailed until flooring is layed.

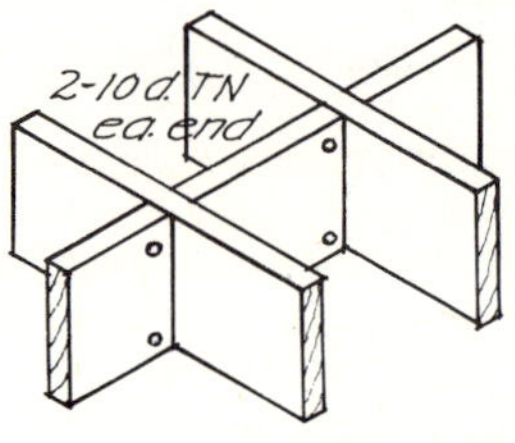
2-10d. TN
ea. end
SOLID BRIDGING
Used for heavy loading; under partitions

BRIDGING

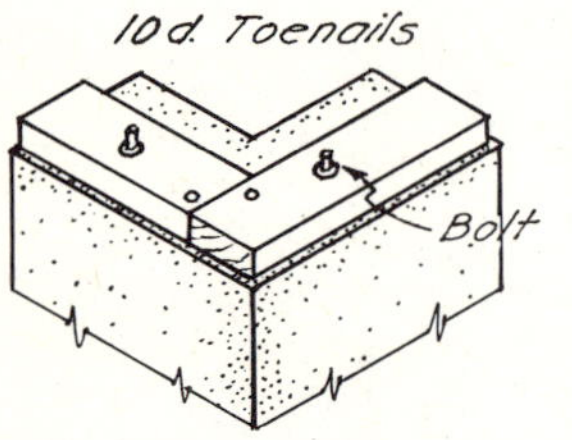
10d. Toenails
Bolt
2"x6" SILL *

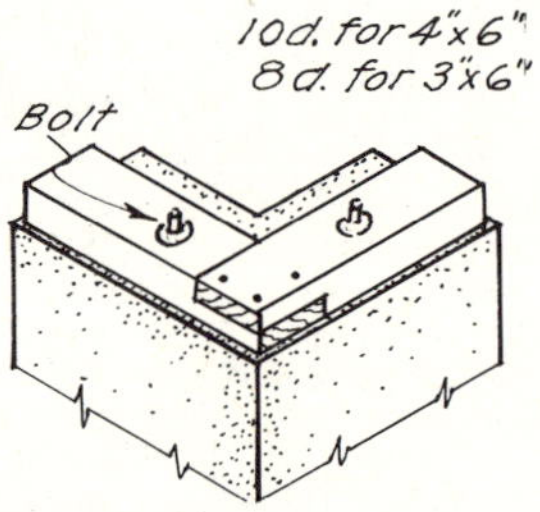
10d. for 4"x6"
8d. for 3"x6"
Bolt
3"x6", 4"x6" SILL
Halved at corners

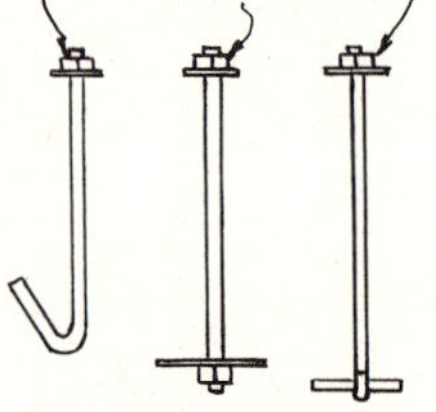
metal washers
TYPES OF SILL ANCHORS

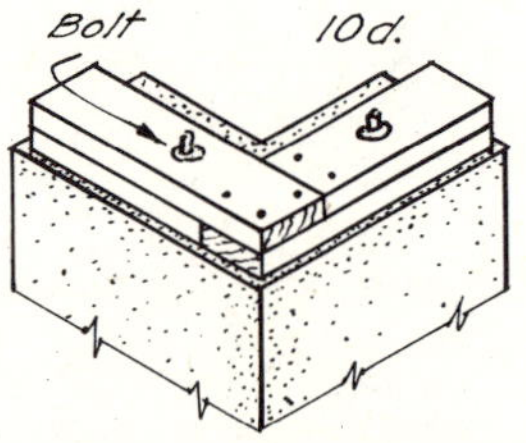
Bolt
10d.
4"x6" DOUBLE SILL *
Nails staggered along sill 24" on centers.

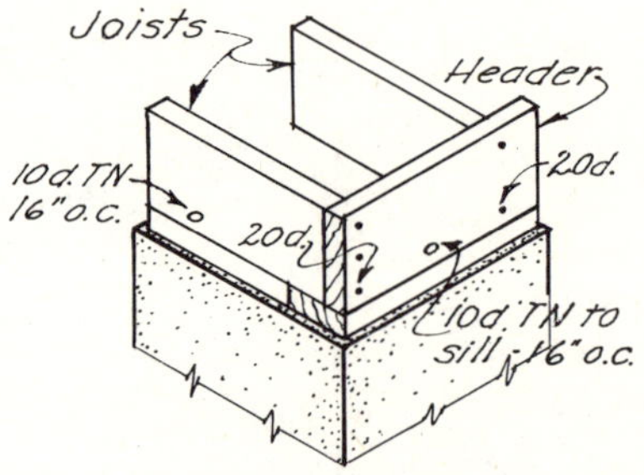
Joists
Header
10d. TN
16" o.c.
20d.
20d.
10d. TN to
sill 16" o.c.
PLATFORM FRAMING *
Toenail to sill not required if diagonal sheathing used.

3/8" = 1'-0"

SILL DETAILS

SHRINKAGE

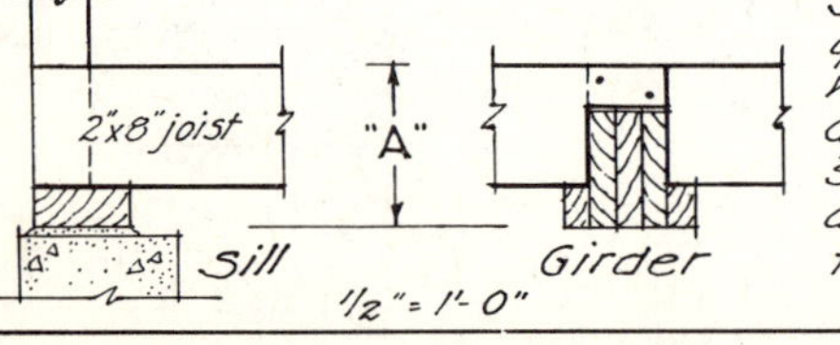
2"x8" joist
"A"
Sill
Girder
1/2" = 1'-0"

Select joist-girder detail which has the approx. same shrinkage "A" as the sill detail used.

Steel Girders: Provide steel bearing plate on outside wall.
Anchor Bolts: 1/2" to 3/4" dia. 1'-6" to 2'-0" long, 6' to 8' o.c. Two at each corner (see Sill Details), two at each joint.
Sills: 3" thickness or more affords more nailing surface for sheathing & a better lap splice. Impregnate or creosote for long life. Lay on 1/2" cement mortar grout.
Wood Posts: Rest on C.I. plates or cement footing & keep at least 3" above floor to prevent rotting & termites.
All dimensions nominal.

* *Data developed from "Technique of House Nailing," Nov. 1947, Housing & Home Finance Agency, Washington, D.C.*

LIGHT WOOD FRAMING DETAILS

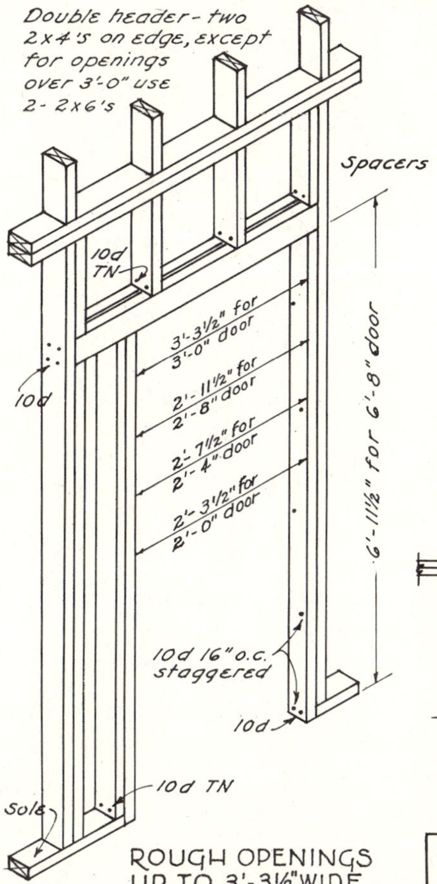
Double header - two
2x4's on edge, except
for openings
over 3'-0" use
2 - 2x6's
Spacers
10d
TN
10d
3'-3½" for
3'-0" door
2'-11½" for
2'-8" door
2'-7½" for
2'-4" door
2'-3½" for
2'-0" door
6'-11½" for 6'-8" door
10d 16" o.c.
staggered
10d
10d TN
Sole

ROUGH OPENINGS
UP TO 3'-3½" WIDE

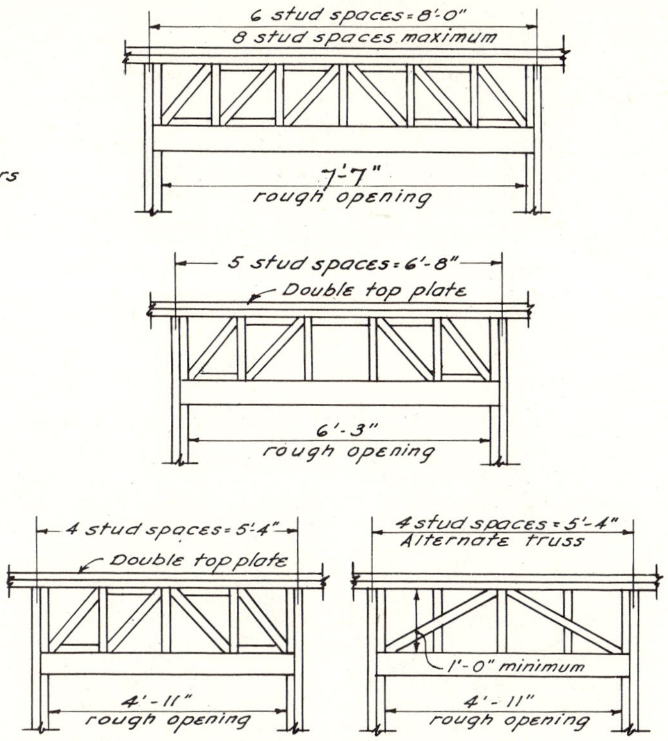
6 stud spaces = 8'-0"
8 stud spaces maximum
7'-7"
rough opening
5 stud spaces = 6'-8"
Double top plate
6'-3"
rough opening
4 stud spaces = 5'-4"
Double top plate
4'-11"
rough opening
4 stud spaces = 5'-4"
Alternate truss
1'-0" minimum
4'-11"
rough opening

TRUSSES for VARIOUS
WIDTHS of OPENINGS

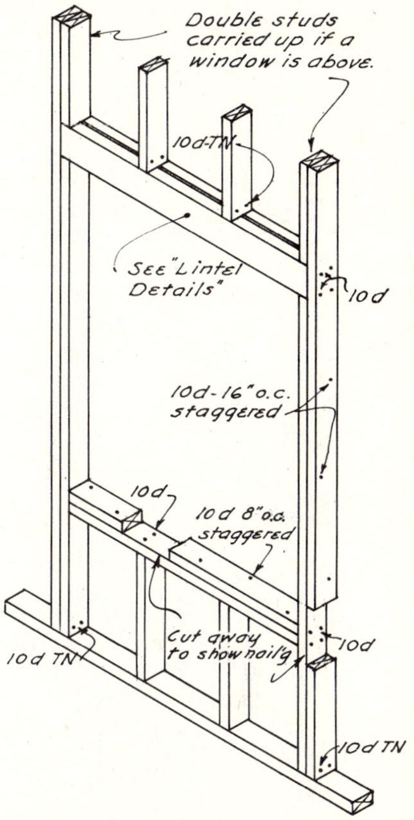
Double studs
carried up if a
window is above.
10d-TN
See "Lintel
Details"
10d
10d - 16" o.c.
staggered
10d
10d 8" o.c.
staggered
Cut away
to show nailg
10d
10d TN
10d TN

WINDOW OPENING

MAX. JOIST SPACING for PLYWOOD SUBFL'RS	
thickness	max. spacing c. to c.
½"	16"
⅝"	20"
¾"	24"

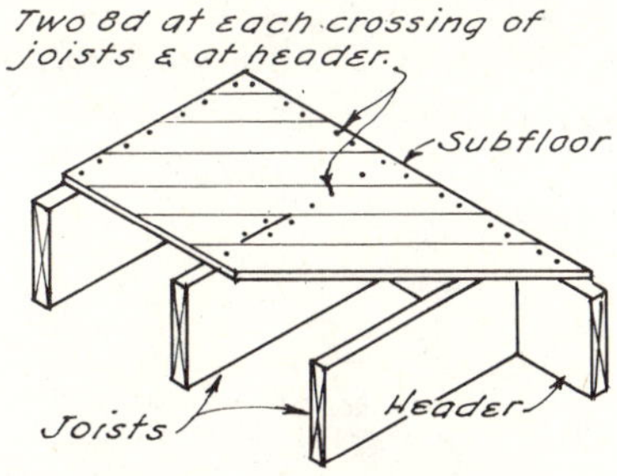
Two 8d at each crossing of
joists & at header.
Subfloor
Joists
Header

Three 8d at each crossing if
boards are wider than 6"

WOOD SUBFLOOR
or ATTIC FLOOR*

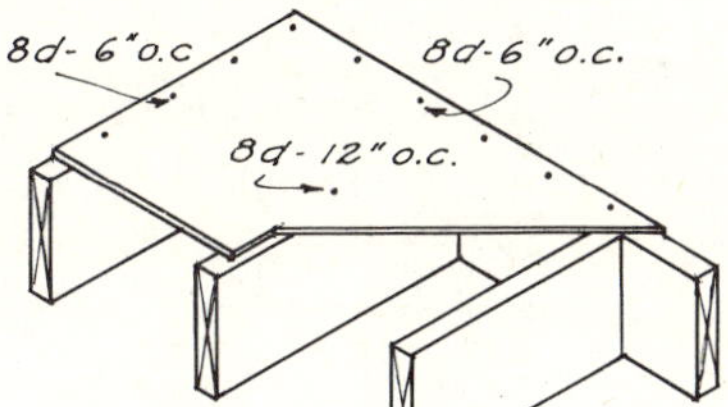
8d - 6" o.c.
8d - 6" o.c.
8d - 12" o.c.

Plywood placed with grain
at right angles to joists.

PLYWOOD SUBFLOORS

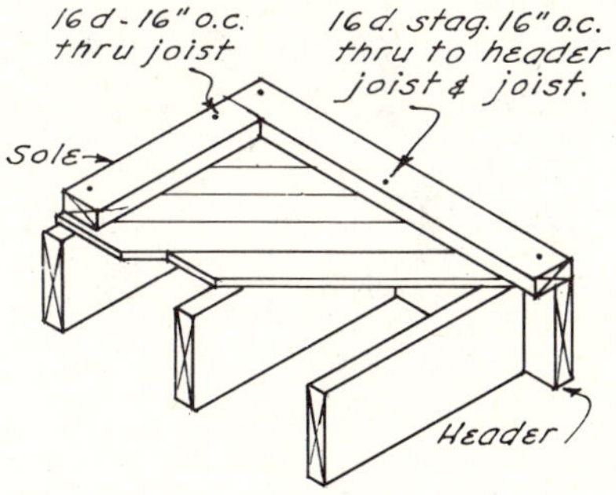
16d - 16" o.c.
thru joist
16d. stag. 16" o.c.
thru to header
joist & joist.
Sole
Header

For Western (platform) framing - 1 or 2 floors.

WOOD SUBFLOOR
& SOLE*

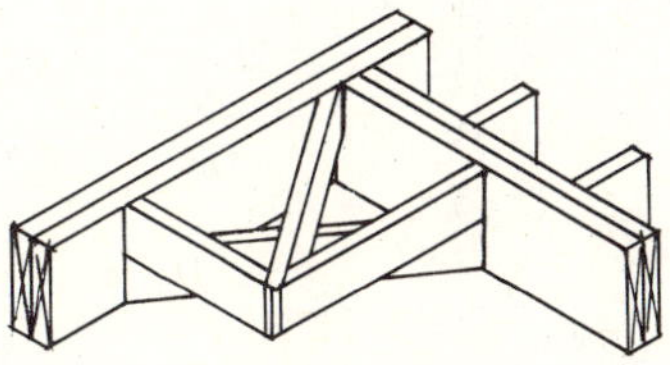

SMALL
CANTILEVER PLATFORM
(such as hearths)

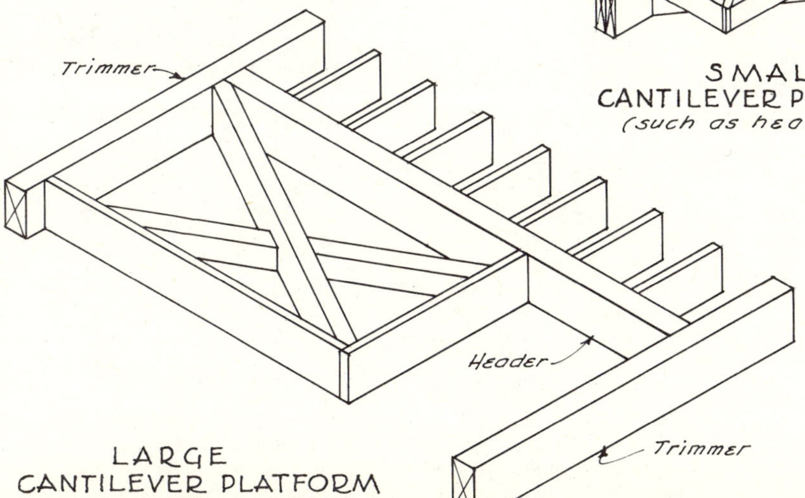
Trimmer
Header
Trimmer

LARGE
CANTILEVER PLATFORM
(such as stair landing)

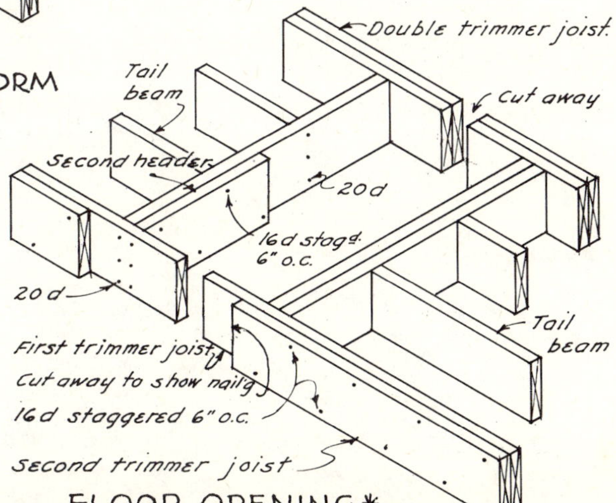
Double trimmer joist.
Tail
beam
Cut away
Second header
20d
16d stagd.
6" o.c.
20d
Tail
beam
First trimmer joist
Cut away to show nailg
16d staggered 6" o.c.
Second trimmer joist

FLOOR OPENING*

* Data developed from "Technique of House Nailing," Nov. 1947, Housing & Home Finance Agency, Washington, D.C.

LIGHT WOOD FRAMING DETAILS

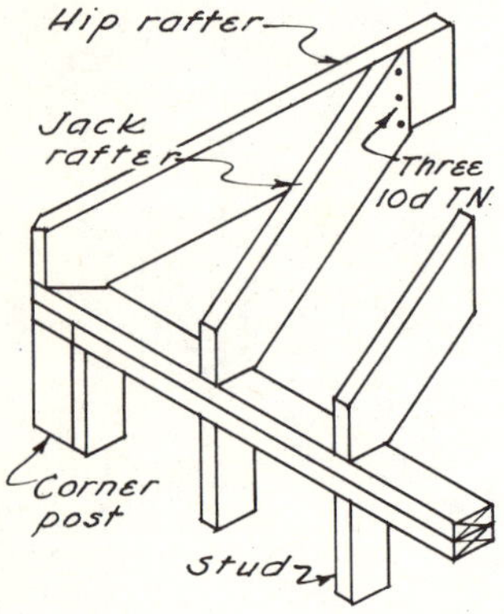
Hip rafter
Jack rafter
Three 10d TN.
Corner post
Stud

JACK RAFTERS *

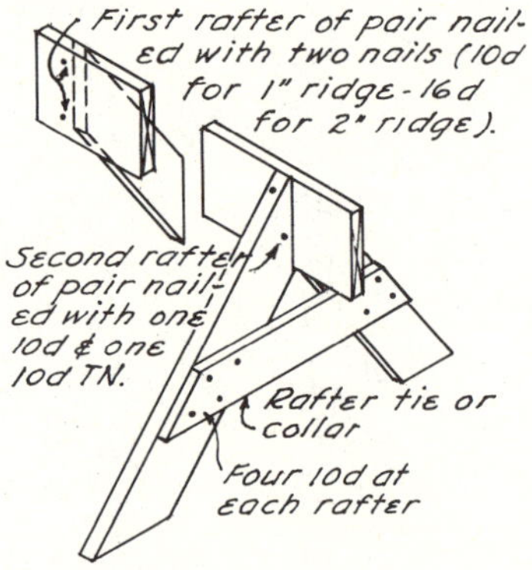
First rafter of pair nailed with two nails (10d for 1" ridge - 16d for 2" ridge).
Second rafter of pair nailed with one 10d & one 10d TN.
Rafter tie or collar
Four 10d at each rafter

ROOF PEAK *

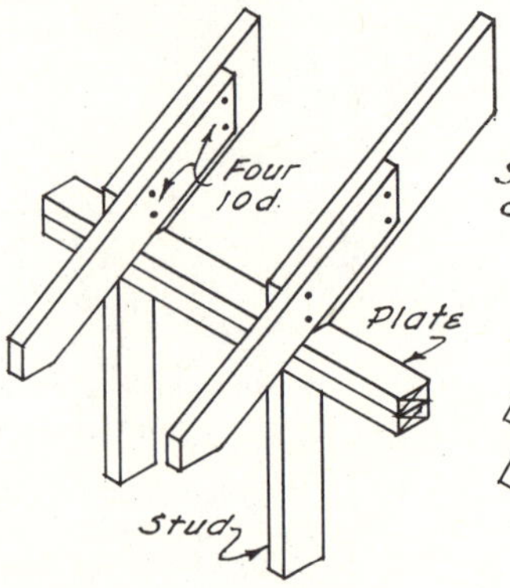
Four 10d.
Plate
Stud

RAFTER ENDS *

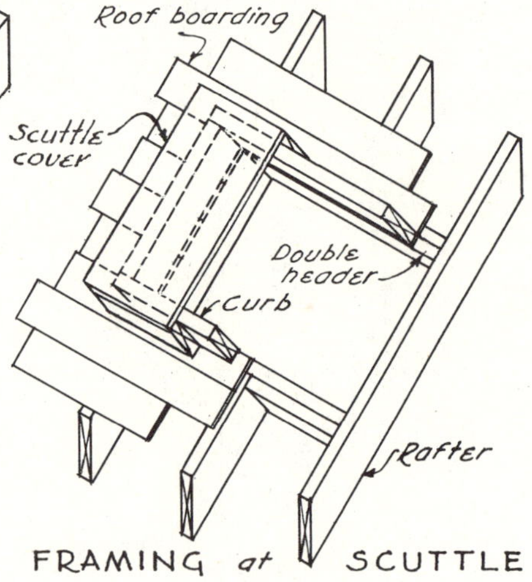
Roof boarding
Scuttle cover
Double header
Curb
Rafter

FRAMING at SCUTTLE

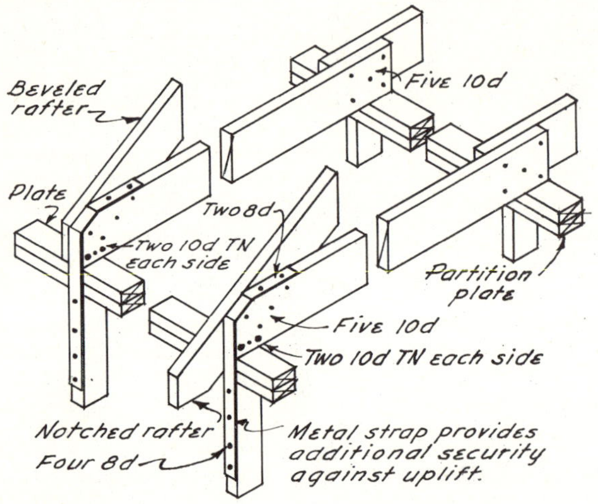
Beveled rafter
Five 10d
Plate
Two 8d
Two 10d TN each side
Partition plate
Five 10d
Two 10d TN each side
Notched rafter
Four 8d
Metal strap provides additional security against uplift.

RAFTERS and CEILING JOISTS RESTING on WALL PLATES *

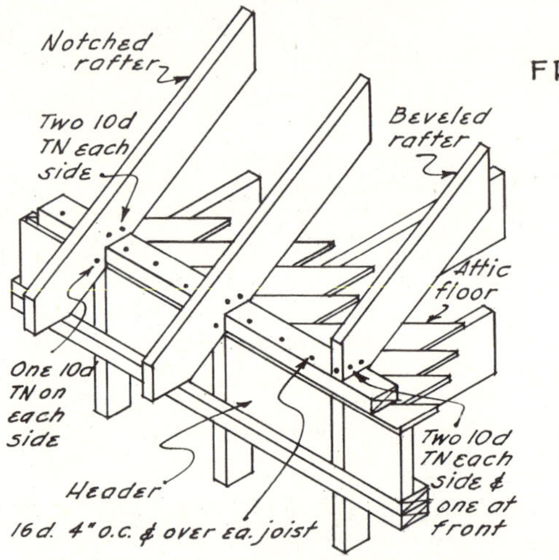
Notched rafter
Two 10d TN each side
Beveled rafter
Attic floor
One 10d TN on each side
Header
Two 10d TN each side & one at front
16d. 4" o.c. & over ea. joist

NOTCHED or BEVELED RAFTERS RESTING on PLATE *

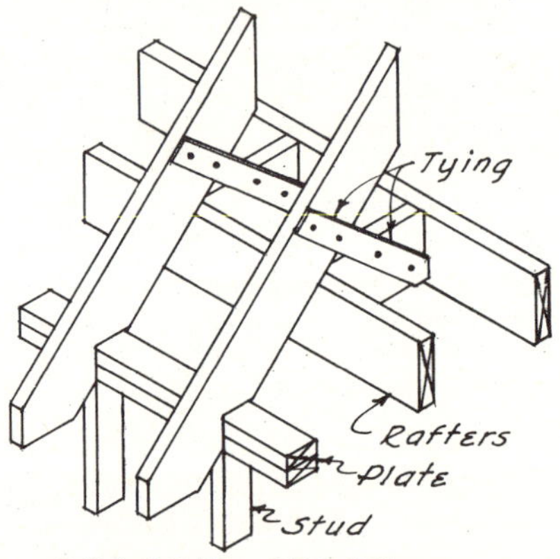
Tying
Rafters
Plate
Stud

BRACING of ROOF where RAFTERS are at rt. angles to joists

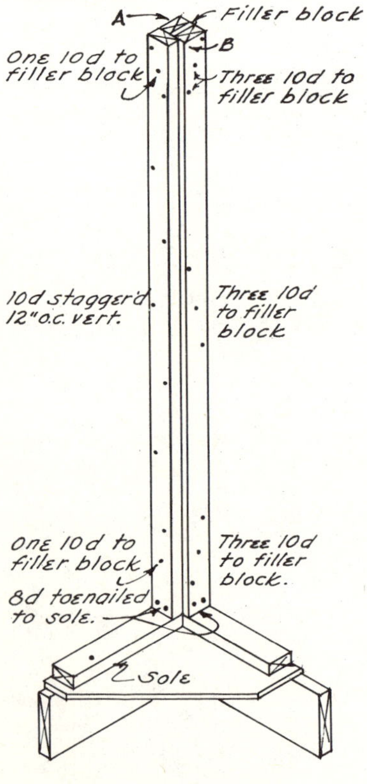
A
Filler block
B
One 10d to filler block
Three 10d to filler block
10d stagger'd 12" o.c. vert.
Three 10d to filler block
One 10d to filler block
Three 10d to filler block.
8d toenailed to sole.
Sole

CORNER POST *

Stud "A" to have same nailing to filler block as stud "B".

Scale: 3/8" = 1'-0"

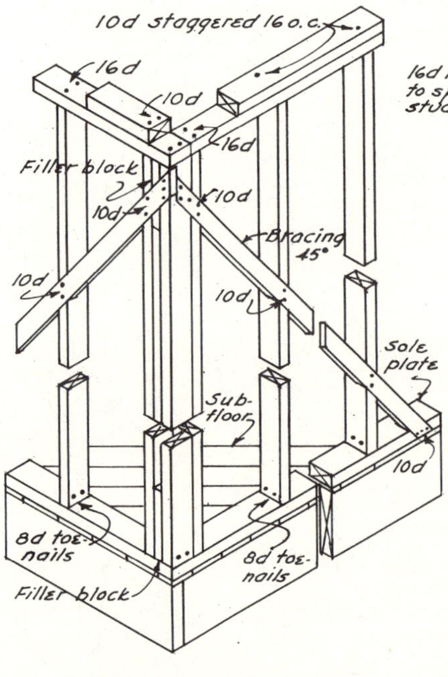
10d staggered 16 o.c.
16d
10d
16d
Filler block
10d
10d
Bracing 45°
10d
10d
Sole plate
Sub-floor
10d
8d toe-nails
8d toe-nails
Filler block

TOP PLATE and LET-IN BRACING *

One toenail thro studs to sole plate sufficient if diagonal sheathing used.

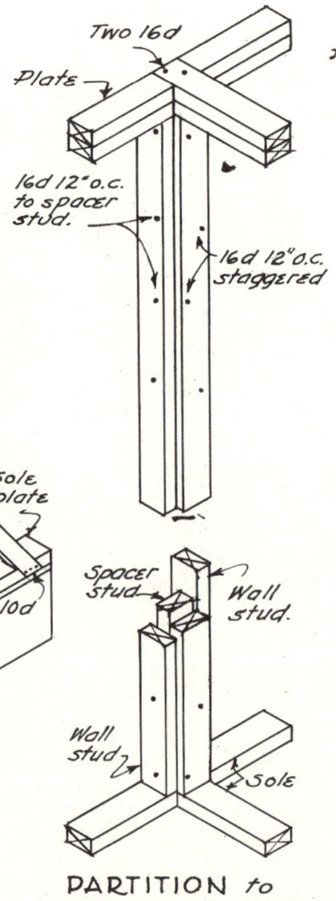
Two 16d
Plate
16d 12" o.c. to spacer stud.
16d 12" o.c. staggered
Spacer stud
Wall stud.
Wall stud
Sole

PARTITION to WALL CONNECTION *

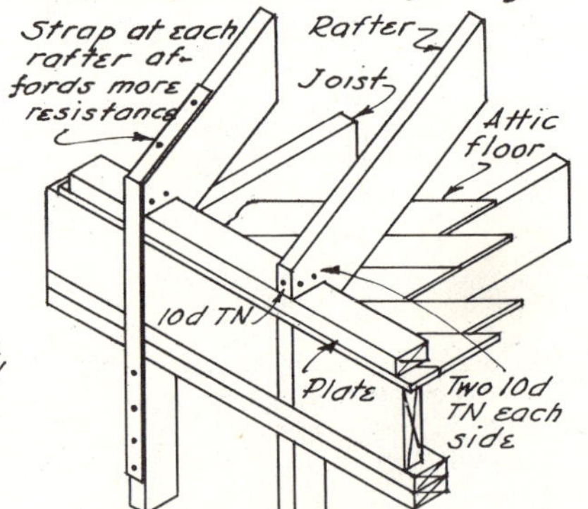
Strap at each rafter affords more resistance
Rafter
Joist
Attic floor
10d TN
Plate
Two 10d TN each side

BEVELED RAFTERS BACK-NOTCHED over PLATE *

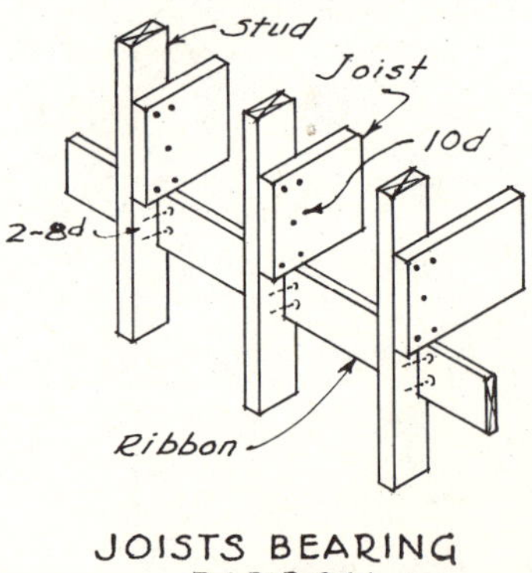
Stud
Joist
10d
2-8d
Ribbon

JOISTS BEARING on RIBBON *

Two nails in each joist are sufficient if full story above ribbon.

* Data developed from "Technique of House Nailing", Nov. 1947, Housing & Home Finance Agency, Washington, D.C.

LIGHT WOOD FRAMING DETAILS

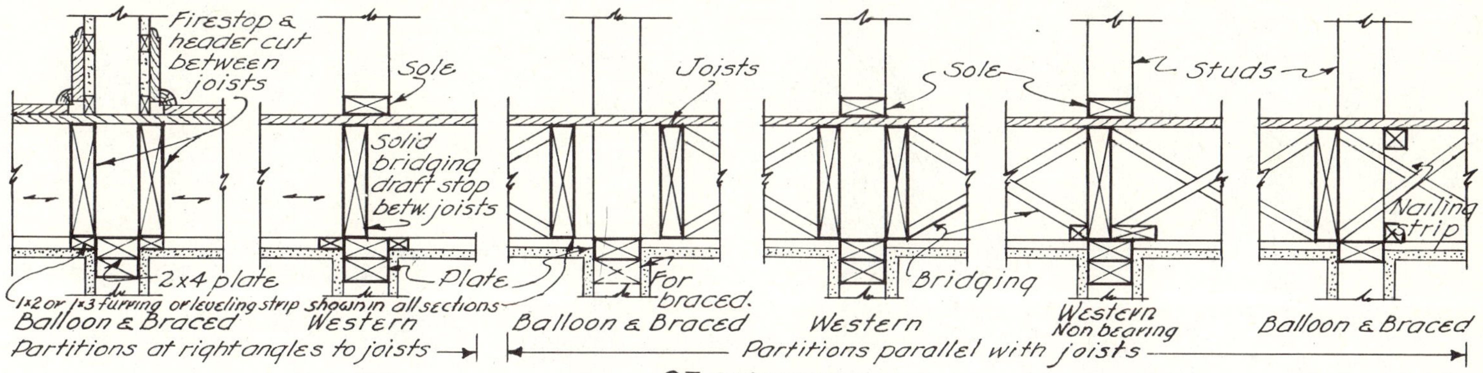
Firestop & header cut between joists
Sole
Joists
Sole
Studs
Solid bridging draft stop betw. joists
Nailing strip
2x4 plate
Plate
For braced.
Bridging
1x2 or 1x3 furring or leveling strip shown in all sections
Balloon & Braced
Western
Balloon & Braced
Western
Western Non bearing
Balloon & Braced
Partitions at right angles to joists
Partitions parallel with joists

SECTIONS
BEARING PARTITIONS (Except as noted)

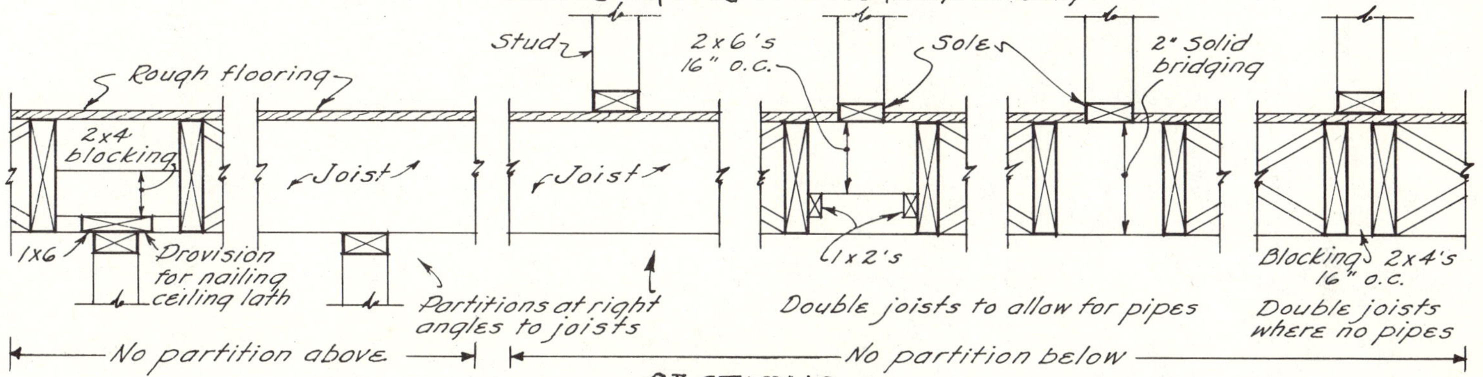
Stud
2x6's 16" o.c.
Sole
2" Solid bridging
Rough flooring
2x4 blocking
Joist
Joist
1x6
Provision for nailing ceiling lath
Partitions at right angles to joists
1x2's
Double joists to allow for pipes
Blocking
2x4's 16" o.c.
Double joists where no pipes
No partition above
No partition below

SECTIONS
NON-BEARING PARTITIONS

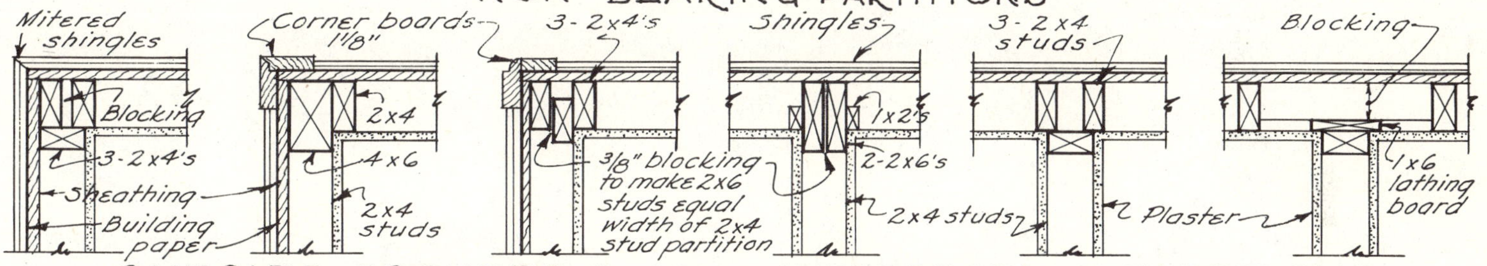
Mitered shingles
Corner boards 1 1/8"
3-2x4's
Shingles
3-2x4 studs
Blocking
Blocking
2x4
1x2's
3-2x4's
4x6
3/8" blocking to make 2x6 studs equal width of 2x4 stud partition
2-2x6's
Sheathing
Building paper
2x4 studs
2x4 studs
Plaster
1x6 lathing board

OUTSIDE CORNERS-PLANS-INTERSECTING PARTITIONS

Scale: 3/4"=1'-0"

WALL FRAMING

Anchors are 18 ga. zinc-coated sheet steel.
Same size anchors hold joists from 2"x4" to 2"x12"

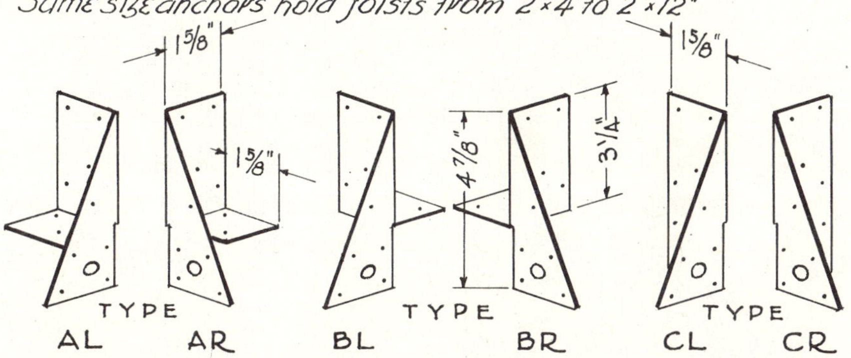
1 5/8"
1 5/8"
1 5/8"
4 7/8"
3 1/4"
TYPE
AL
AR
TYPE
BL
BR
TYPE
CL
CR

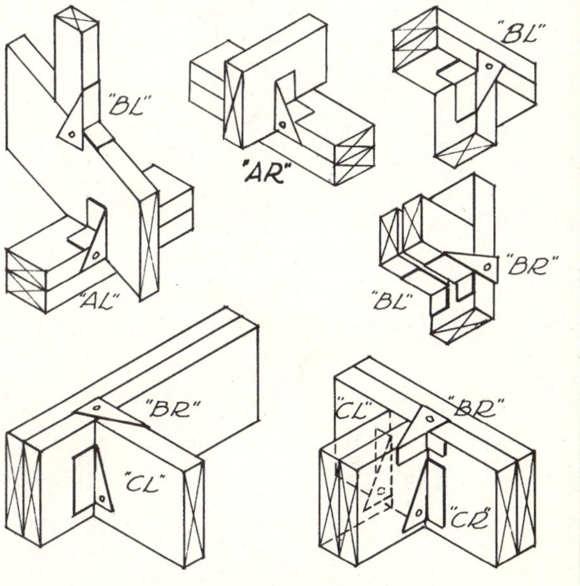
"BL"
"AR"
"BL"
"AL"
"BR"
"BL"
"BR"
"CL"
"CL"
"BR"
"CR"

MAXIMUM SPANS for ANCHORS as NOTED - 40# LIVE LOAD			
Joists	1 Type C	1 Type C & 1 Type B	2 Type C
16" o.c.	12'-2"	16'-10"	27'-4"
20" o.c.	9'-8"	13'-4"	12'-9"
24" o.c.	8'-1"	11'-2"	18'-2"

TECO TRIP-L-GRIP FRAMING ANCHORS

Data checked by Timber Engineering Co., Washington, D.C.

LIGHT WOOD FRAMING DETAILS

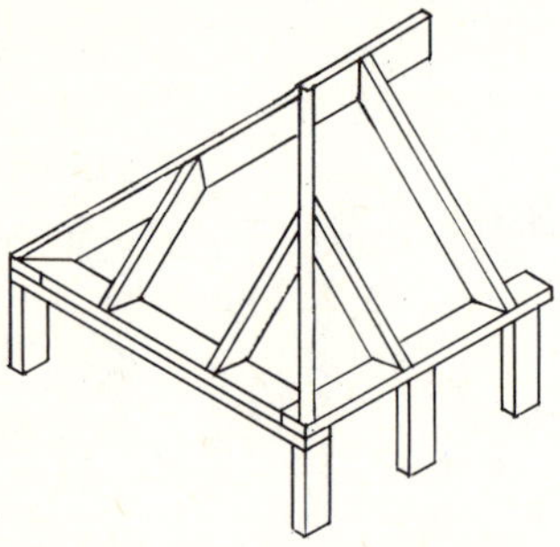

HIP ROOF DORMER

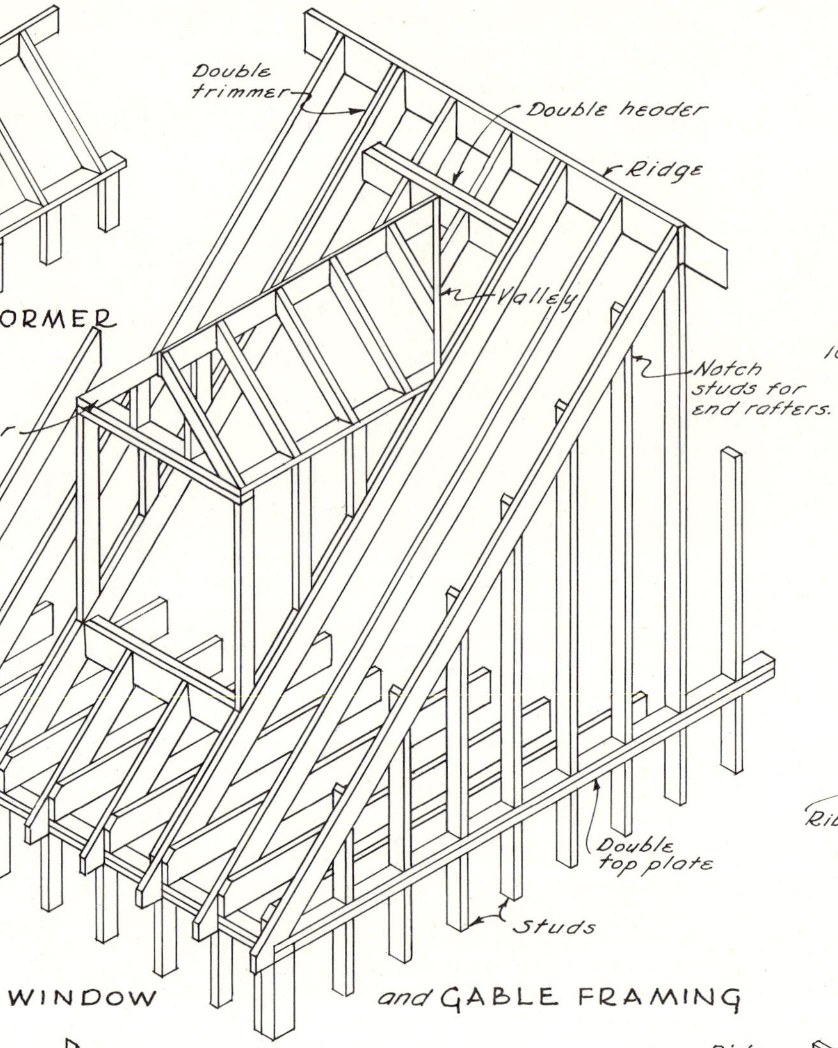
Double trimmer
Double header
Ridge
Valley
Notch studs for end rafters.
Gable roof dormer
Double top plate
Studs

DORMER WINDOW and GABLE FRAMING

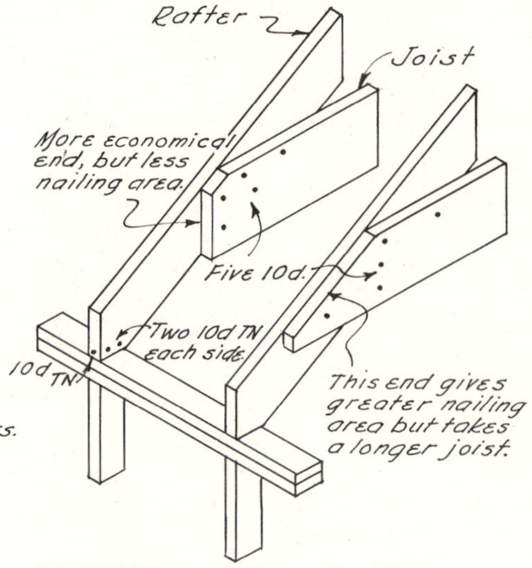
Rafter
Joist
More economical end, but less nailing area.
Five 10d.
Two 10d TN each side.
10d TN
This end gives greater nailing area but takes a longer joist.

RAFTERS on WALL PLATE with CEILING JOISTS HIGHER

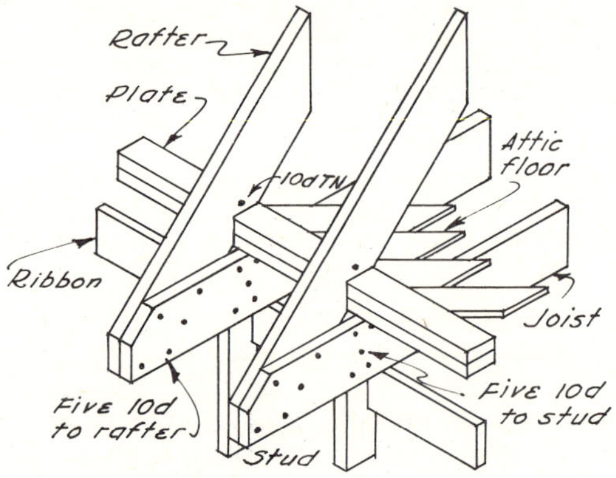
Rafter
Plate
10d TN
Attic floor
Ribbon
Joist
Five 10d to rafter
Five 10d to stud
Stud

SUPERIOR RAFTER NAIL'G

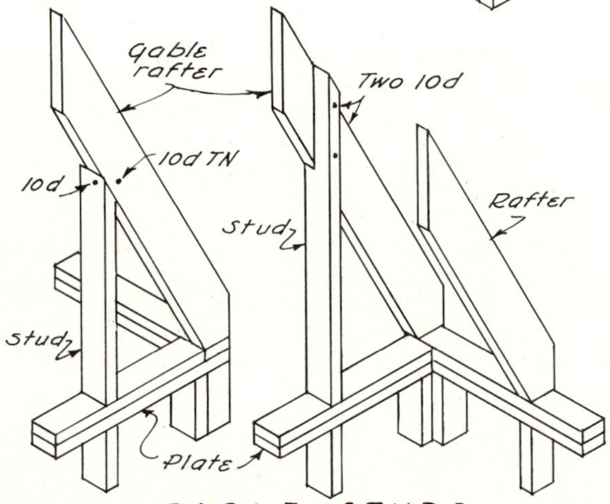
Gable rafter
Two 10d
10d TN
10d
Stud
Rafter
Stud
Plate

GABLE STUDS

BEVELED NOTCHED

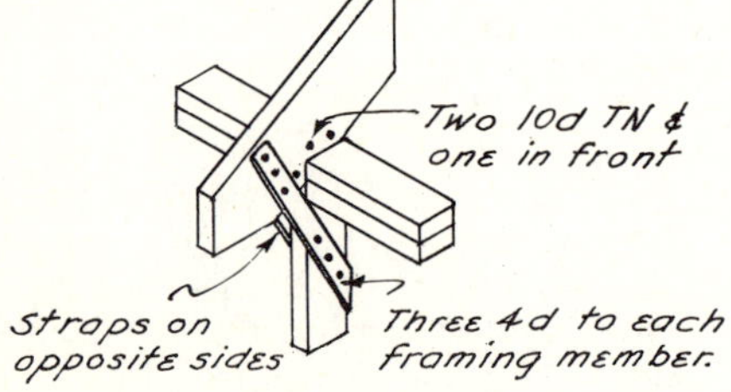
Two 10d TN & one in front
Straps on opposite sides
Three 4d to each framing member.

NOTCHED RAFTER STRAPS
(to resist uplift)

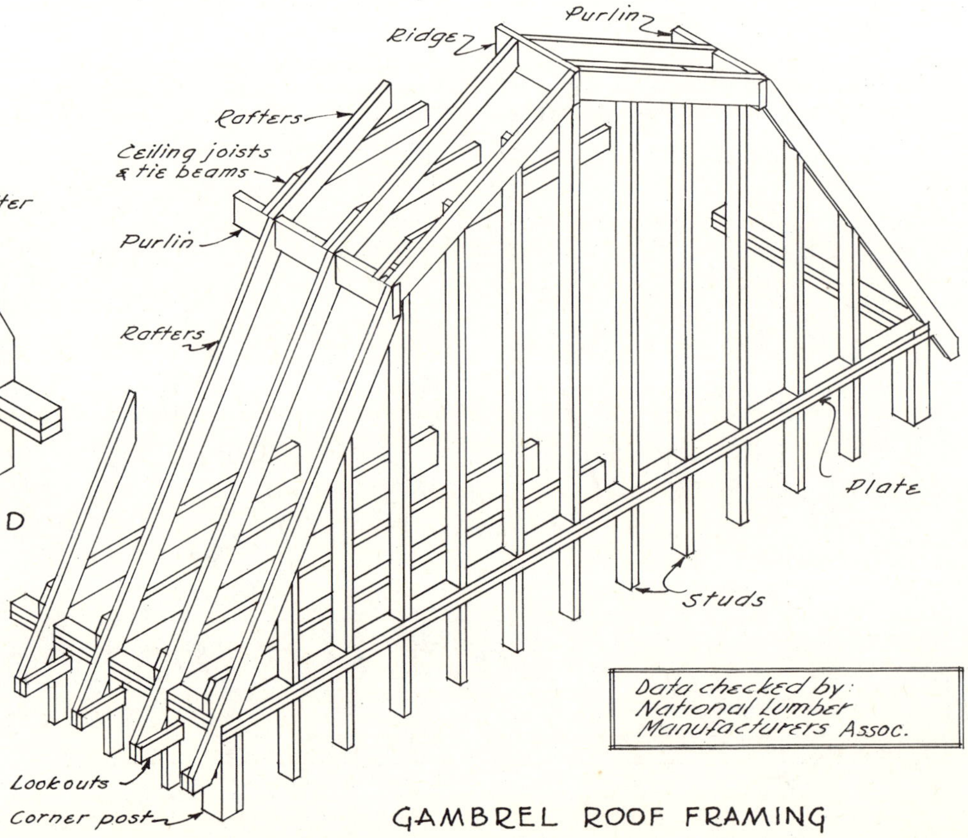
Ridge
Purlin
Rafters
Ceiling joists & tie beams
Purlin
Rafters
Plate
Studs
Lookouts
Corner post

GAMBREL ROOF FRAMING

Data checked by:
National Lumber
Manufacturers Assoc.

STAIR FRAMING

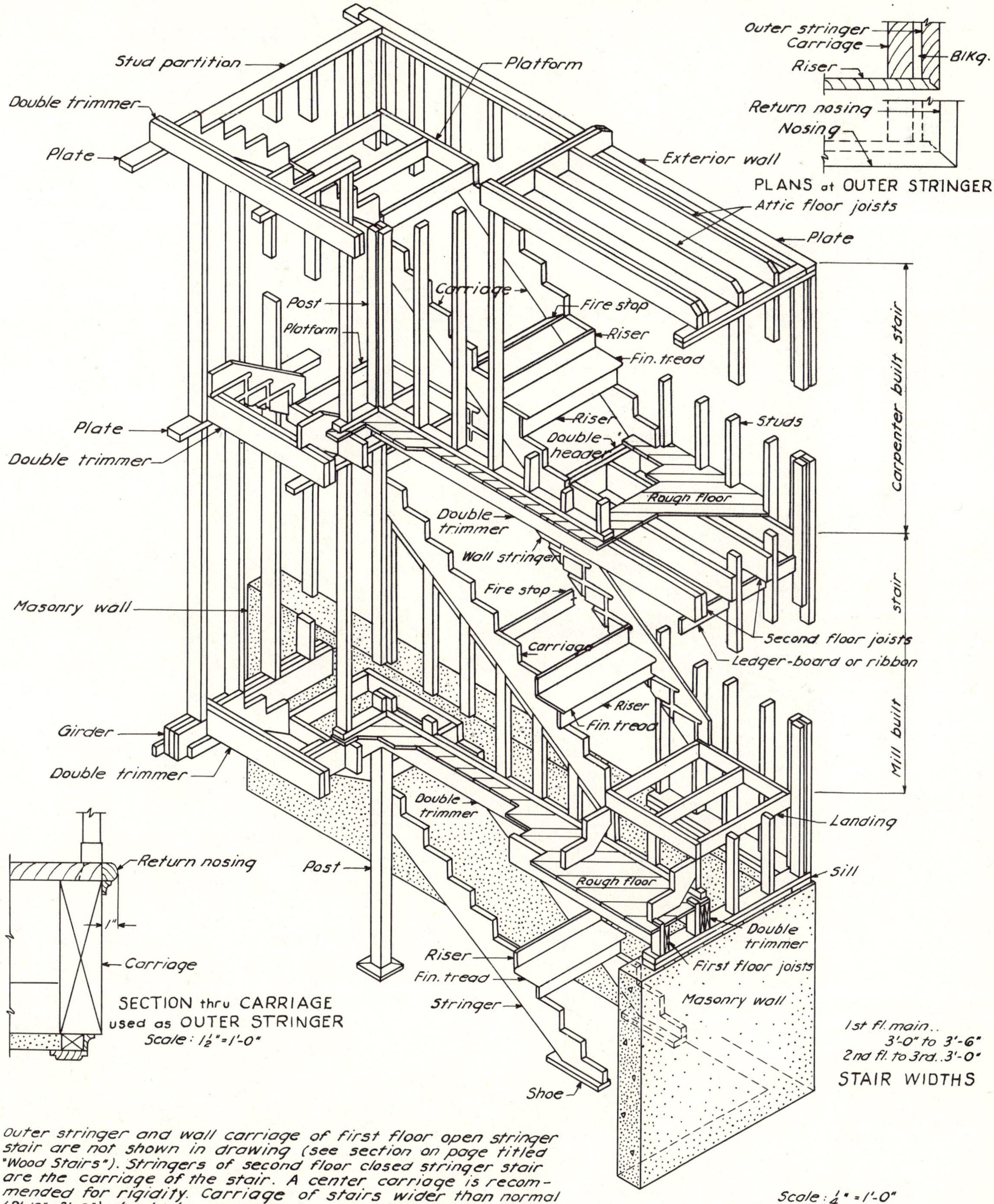
Stud partition
Platform
Double trimmer
Plate
Exterior wall
Attic floor joists
Plate
Carriage
Post
Fire stop
Platform
Riser
Fin. tread
Plate
Riser
Studs
Double trimmer
Double header
Rough floor
carpenter built stair
Double trimmer
Wall stringer
Masonry wall
Fire stop
stair
Carriage
Second floor joists
Ledger-board or ribbon
Riser
Fin. tread
Girder
Mill built
Double trimmer
Double trimmer
Landing
Post
Rough floor
Sill
Double trimmer
Riser
First floor joists
Fin. tread
Masonry wall
Stringer
Shoe
Outer stringer
Carriage
Blkg.
Riser
Return nosing
Nosing
Return nosing
1"
Carriage

PLANS at OUTER STRINGER

SECTION thru CARRIAGE used as OUTER STRINGER
Scale: 1½" = 1'-0"

1st fl. main.. 3'-0" to 3'-6"
2nd fl. to 3rd.. 3'-0"

STAIR WIDTHS

Outer stringer and wall carriage of first floor open stringer stair are not shown in drawing (see section on page titled "Wood Stairs"). Stringers of second floor closed stringer stair are the carriage of the stair. A center carriage is recommended for rigidity. Carriage of stairs wider than normal (2'-10", 3'-0") should be spaced not more than 2'-0" o.c. For open stringer stairs, 3" thick carriage is recommended.

Scale: ¼" = 1'-0"

Adapted from Data by National Lumber Manufacturers Association

SHEATHING on WOOD FRAMING

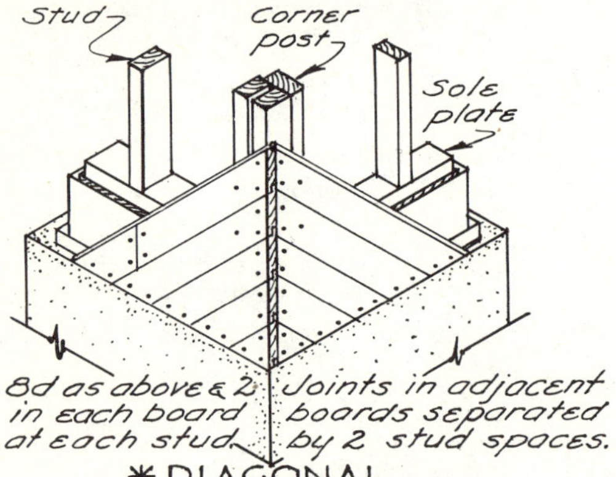
Stud
Corner post
Sole plate
8d as above & 2 in each board at each stud.
Joints in adjacent boards separated by 2 stud spaces.

✱ DIAGONAL

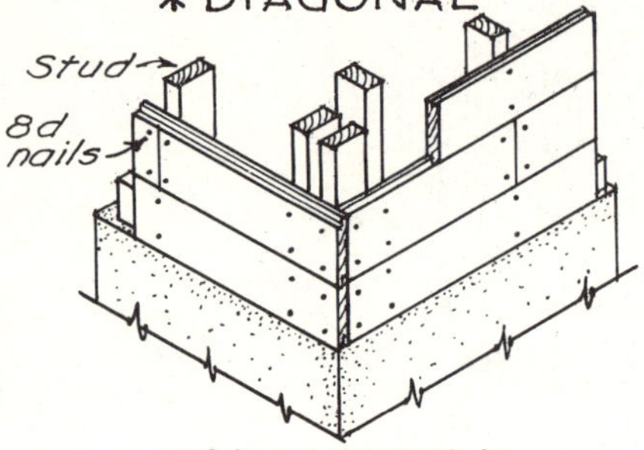
Stud
8d. nails

HORIZONTAL

✱ WOOD WALL-SHEATHING

For boards wider than 8" use three nails in place of two.

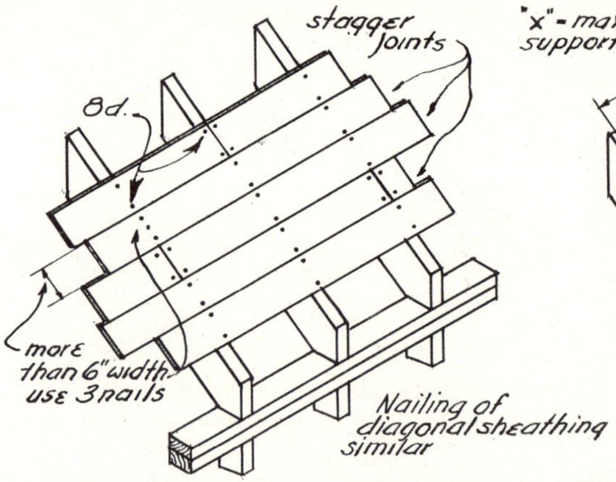
stagger joints
8d.
more than 6" width use 3 nails
Nailing of diagonal sheathing similar

✱ WOOD ROOF-SHEATHING

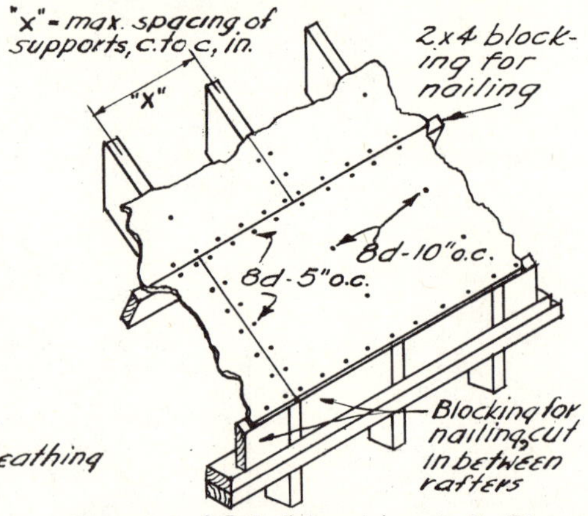
"x" = max. spacing of supports, c. to c, in.
"x"
2x4 blocking for nailing
8d-10" o.c.
8d-5" o.c.
Blocking for nailing cut in between rafters

Plywood thickness	"x" for dead loads 20 psf	30 psf	40 psf
5/16" rough	20"	20"	20"
3/8" rough	24"	24"	24"
1/2" rough	32"	32"	30"
5/8" rough	42"	42"	39"
3/4"	48"	47"	42"

Plywood continuous over 2 spans. Deflection 1/240 of span

PLYWOOD ROOF-SHEATHING

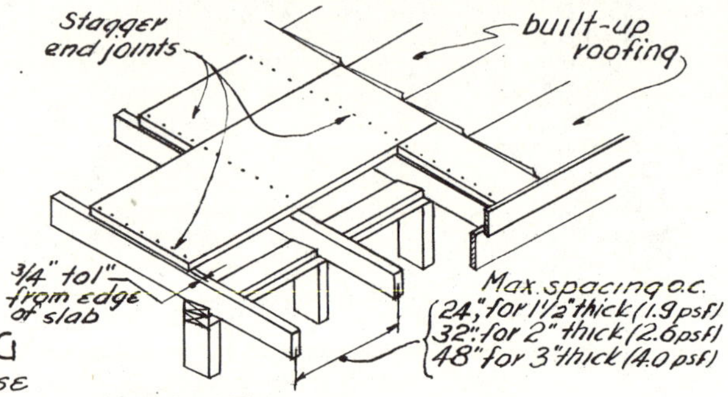
Stagger end joints
built-up roofing
3/4" tol" from edge of slab
Max. spacing o.c.
24" for 1 1/2" thick (1.9 psf)
32" for 2" thick (2.6 psf)
48" for 3" thick (4.0 psf)

INSULATING ROOF DECK

Scale: 1/4" = 1'-0"

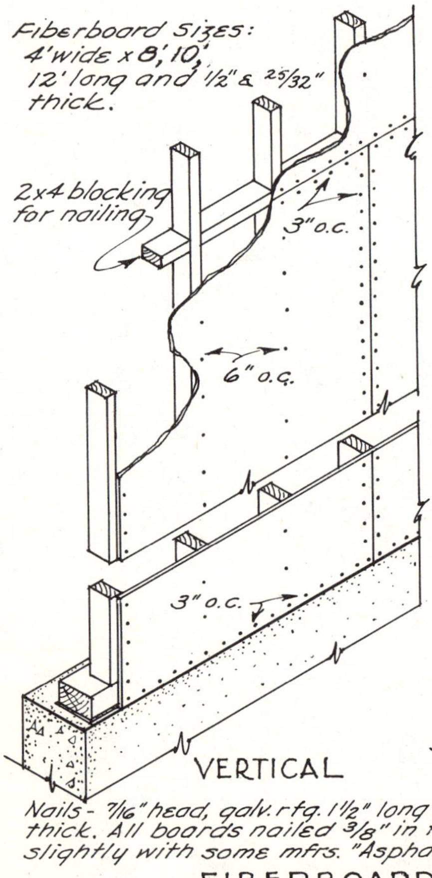
Fiberboard sizes:
4' wide x 8', 10', 12' long and 1/2" & 25/32" thick.
2x4 blocking for nailing
3" o.c.
6" o.c.
3" o.c.

VERTICAL

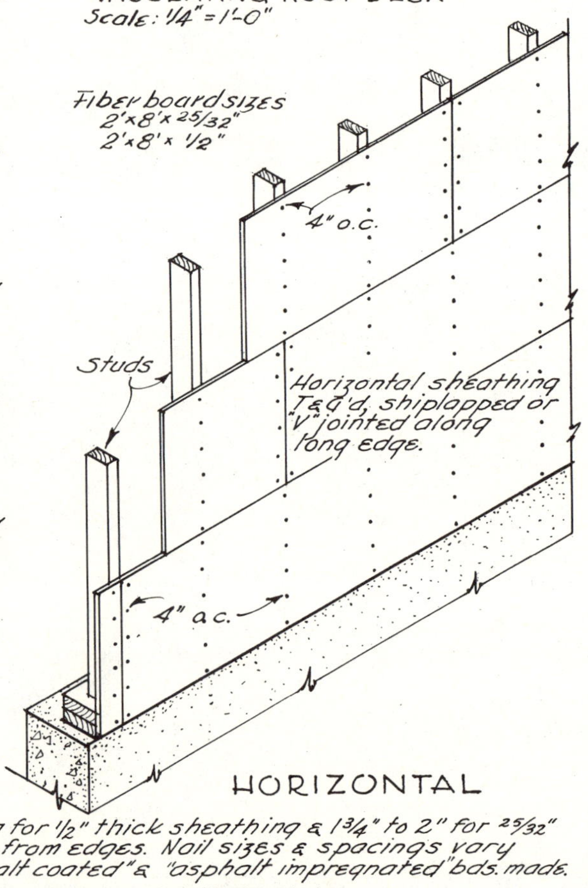
Fiber board sizes
2'x8'x 25/32"
2'x8'x 1/2"
4" o.c.
Studs
Horizontal sheathing T&G'd, shiplapped or "V" jointed along long edge.
4" o.c.

HORIZONTAL

Nails - 7/16" head, galv. rfg. 1 1/2" long for 1/2" thick sheathing & 1 3/4" to 2" for 25/32" thick. All boards nailed 3/8" in from edges. Nail sizes & spacings vary slightly with some mfrs. "Asphalt coated" & "asphalt impregnated" bds. made.

FIBERBOARD WALL-SHEATHING

Recommendations of Insulation Board Institute

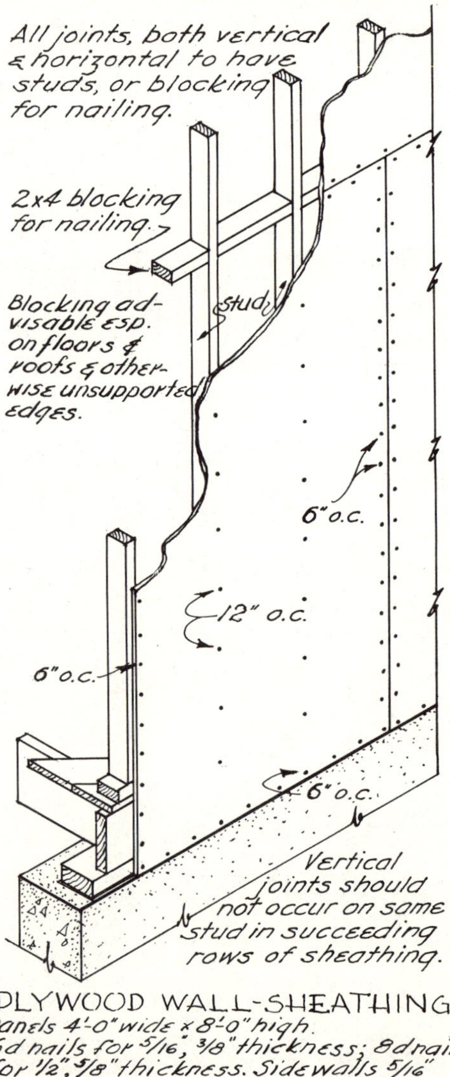
All joints, both vertical & horizontal to have studs, or blocking for nailing.
2x4 blocking for nailing.
Blocking advisable esp. on floors & roofs & otherwise unsupported edges.
Stud
6" o.c.
12" o.c.
6" o.c.
6" o.c.
Vertical joints should not occur on same stud in succeeding rows of sheathing.

PLYWOOD WALL-SHEATHING

Panels 4'-0" wide x 8'-0" high.
6d nails for 5/16", 3/8" thickness; 8d nails for 1/2", 5/8" thickness. Sidewalls 5/16" thickness for stud spac'g 16" o.c. Subflooring 1/2" thickness for joists 16" o.c. Western softwood Plywood Commercial Standard 122-49; Douglas Fir Plywood Commercial Standard CS 45-48.

GYPSUM BOARD WALL-SHEATHING

Board 2'x8'x 1/2" thick laid hor. (similar to above dwg.). Nailing 4" o.c. at all bearings & 3/8" from edges. Nails 1 3/4" galv. rfg. #11 gauge - 7/16" head.

Data checked by Insulation Board Institute - Scale 3/8" = 1'-0" except as noted.
✱ Data developed from "Technique of House Nailing," Nov. 1947, Housing & Home Finance Agency, Washington, D.C.

EAVES and WATERTABLES

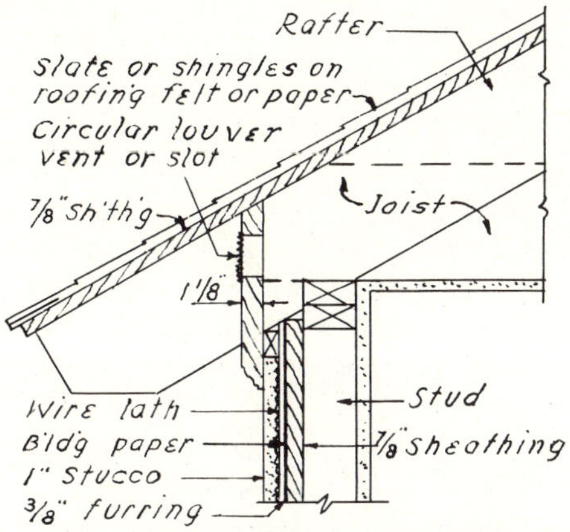
Rafter
Slate or shingles on roofing felt or paper
Circular louver vent or slot
7/8" Sh'th'g
Joist
1 1/8"
Wire lath
Bldg paper
1" Stucco
3/8" furring
Stud
7/8 Sheathing

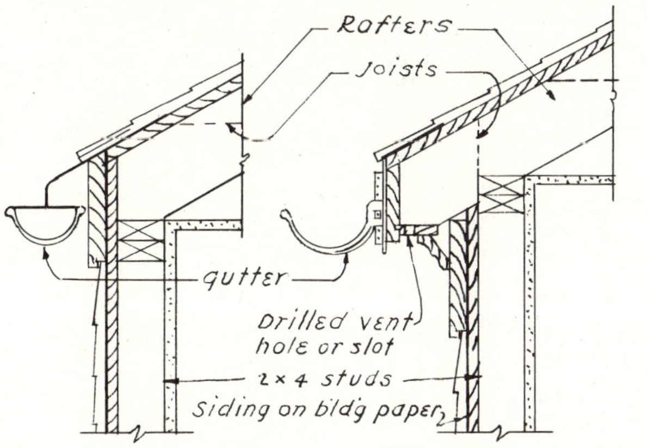
Rafters
Joists
gutter
Drilled vent hole or slot
2×4 studs
Siding on bldg paper

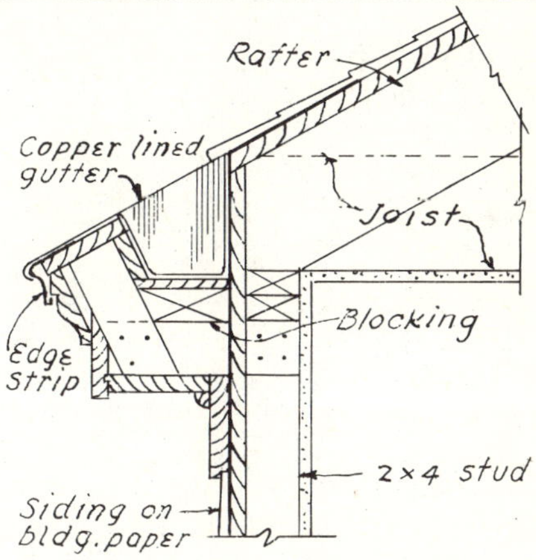
Rafter
Copper lined gutter
Joist
Blocking
Edge strip
2×4 stud
Siding on bldg. paper

EXPOSED RAFTER ENDS
See "Attic Ventilation" page for vent types & requirements.

HANGING GUTTER　　ADJUSTABLE GUTTER
See pages on gutter types stock sizes in metal & wood. leaders and accessories.

BUILT-IN GUTTER
See "Built-in Gutters" page for copper lining data, etc.

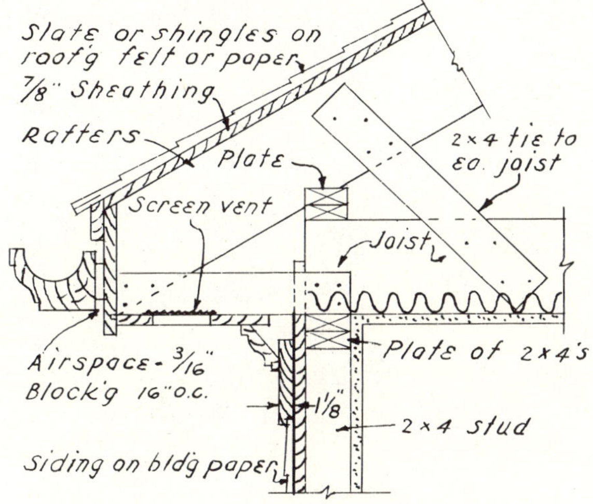
Slate or shingles on roof'g felt or paper
7/8" Sheathing
Rafters
Plate
2×4 tie to ea. joist
Screen vent
Joist
Airspace - 3/16"
Block'g 16" o.c.
Plate of 2×4's
1 1/8
2×4 stud
Siding on bldg paper

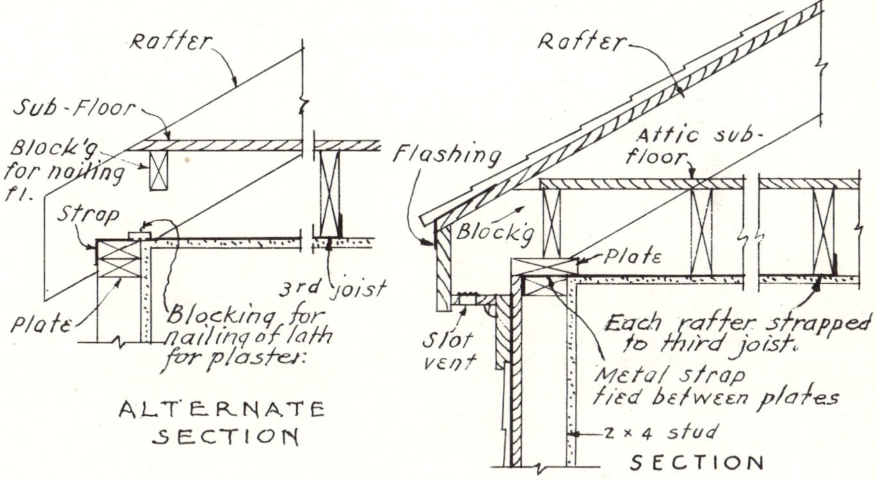
Rafter
Sub-Floor
Block'g for nailing fl.
Strap
Plate
3rd joist
Blocking for nailing of lath for plaster.
ALTERNATE SECTION
Rafter
Flashing
Attic sub-floor
Block'g
Plate
Slot vent
Each rafter strapped to third joist.
Metal strap tied between plates
2×4 stud
SECTION

WOOD GUTTER on PROJECTED EAVE
Used to keep windows at normal elevation when overhang is large.

RAFTERS at RIGHT ANGLES to CEILING JOISTS
Means used to anchor roof where design necessitates construction of this type. (Infrequently encountered).

EAVE DETAILS for PITCHED ROOFS

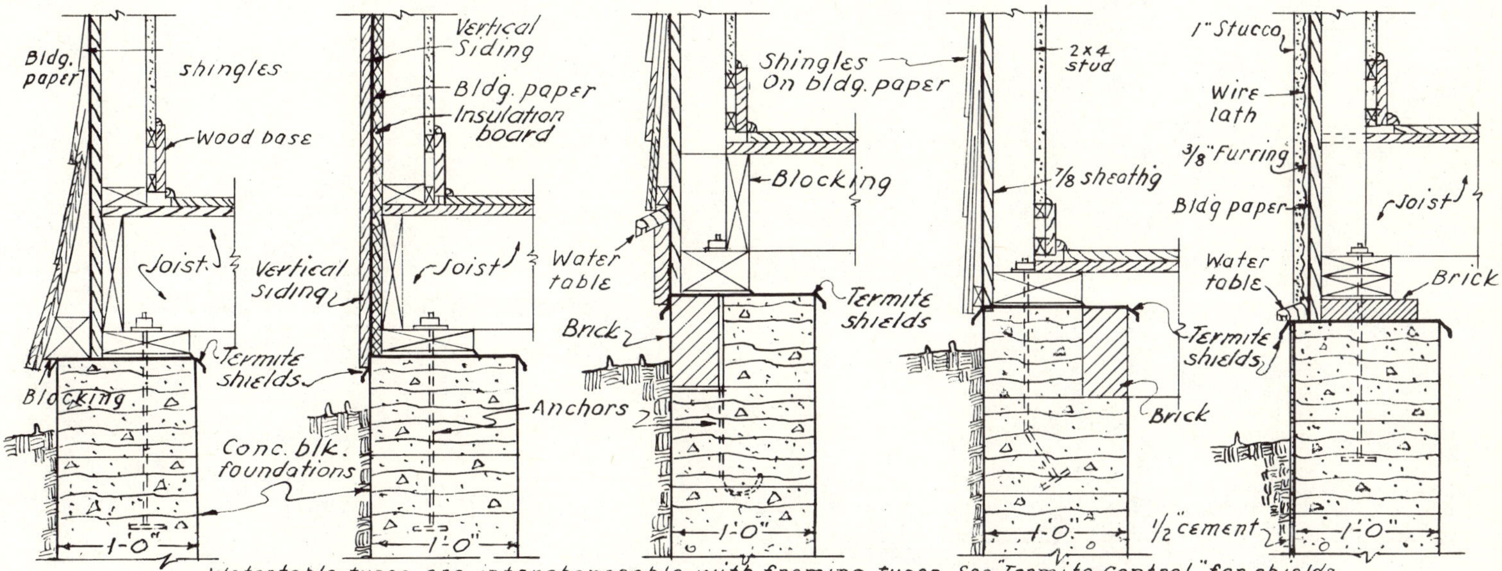
Bldg. paper
shingles
Wood base
Joist
Blocking
Vertical Siding
Bldg. paper
Insulation board
Vertical siding
Joist
Termite shields
Anchors
Conc. blk. foundations
1'-0"
Shingles on bldg. paper
Blocking
Water table
Termite shields
Brick
2×4 stud
7/8 sheath'g
Termite shields
Brick
1" Stucco
Wire lath
3/8" Furring
Bldg paper
Joist
Water table
Brick
1/2" cement

Watertable types are interchangeable with framing types. See "Termite control" for shields.
Top block solid or concrete filled. If poured concrete wall may be 10" thick.

PLATFORM or WESTERN FRAMING　　**BALLOON or BRACED**　　**WITH JOISTS BELOW GRADE**　　**STUCCO FINISH**

SILLS and WATERTABLES

Scale 3/4" = 1'-0"

EAVES and OVERHANGS

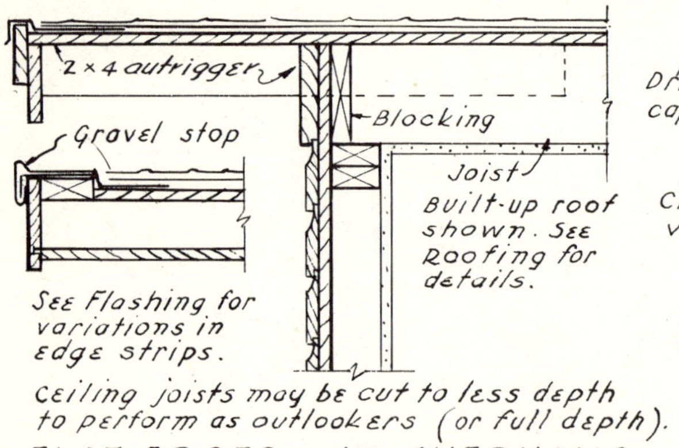
2×4 outrigger
Blocking
Gravel stop
Joist
Built-up roof shown. See Roofing for details.
See Flashing for variations in edge strips.
Ceiling joists may be cut to less depth to perform as outlookers (or full depth).

FLAT ROOFS with OVERHANG

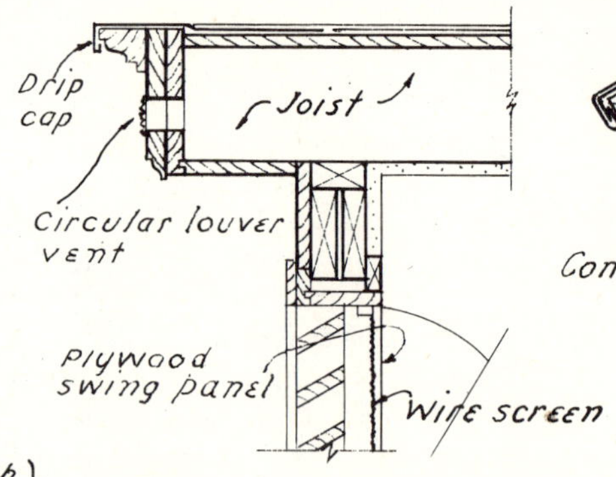
Drip cap
Joist
Circular louver vent
Plywood swing panel
Wire screen

EAVE with LOUVER

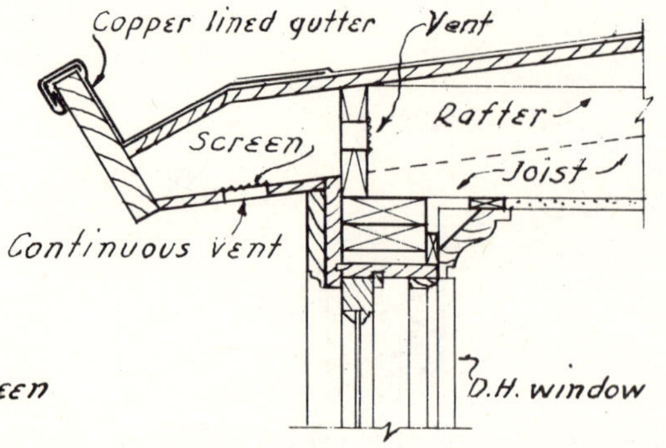
Copper lined gutter
Vent
Rafter
Screen
Joist
Continuous vent
D.H. window

BUILT-IN GUTTER

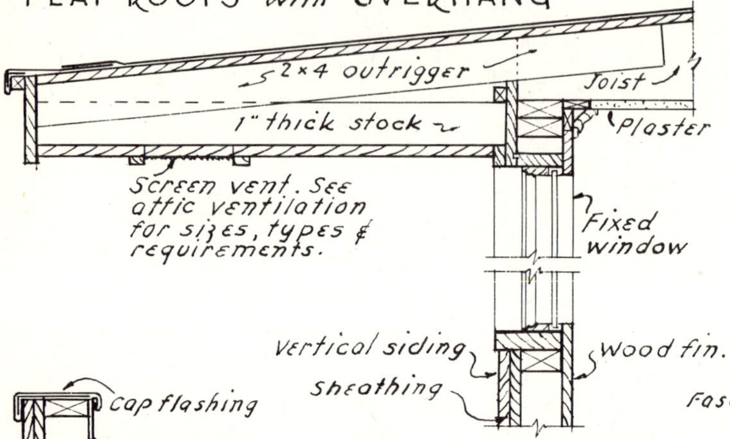
2×4 outrigger
Joist
1" thick stock
Plaster
Screen vent. See attic ventilation for sizes, types & requirements.
Fixed window
Vertical siding
Sheathing
Wood fin.

WIDE OVERHANG

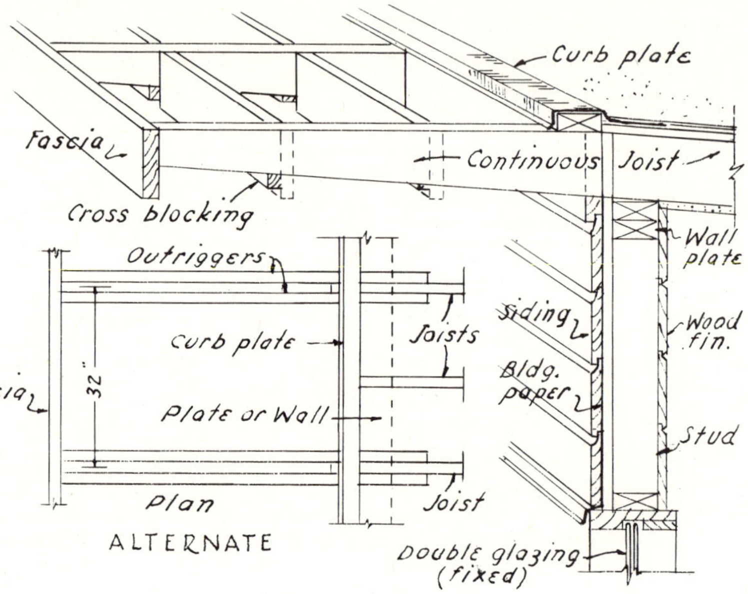
Curb plate
Fascia
Continuous Joist
Cross blocking
Wall plate
Outriggers
Curb plate
Joists
32"
Fascia
Plate or Wall
Siding
Bldg. paper
Wood fin.
Stud
Plan
Joist
ALTERNATE
Double glazing (fixed)

OPEN OVERHANG

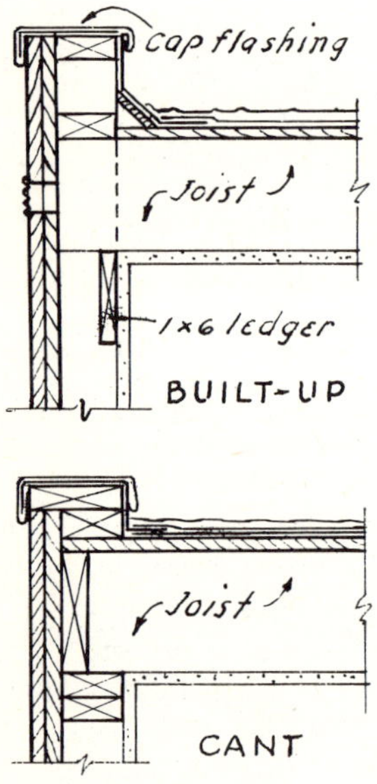
Cap flashing
Joist
1×6 ledger
BUILT-UP
Joist
CANT

CURBS

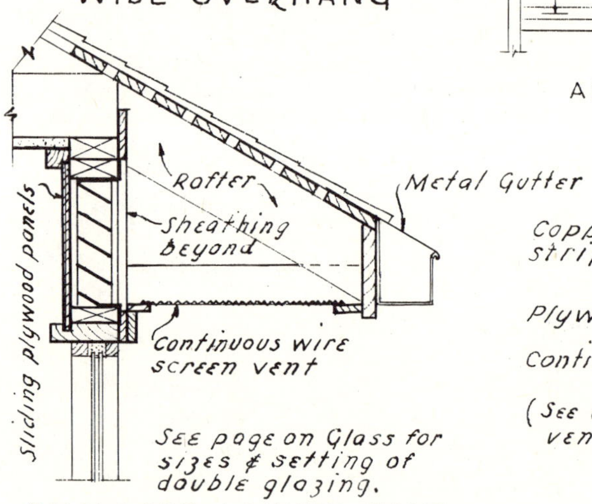
Rafter
Metal Gutter
Sheathing beyond
Sliding plywood panels
Continuous wire screen vent
See page on Glass for sizes & setting of double glazing.

ENCLOSED LOUVER EAVE

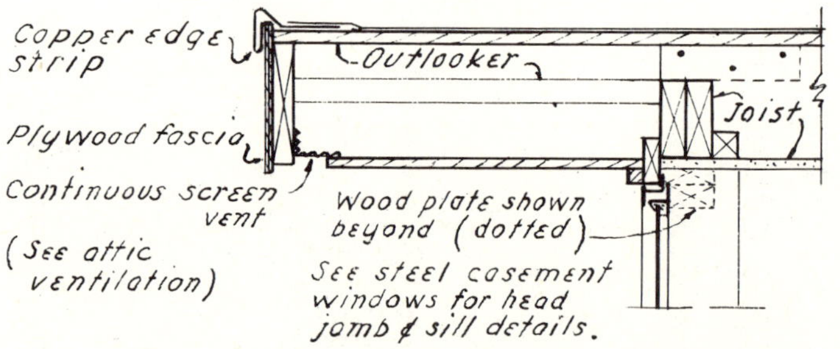
Copper edge strip
Outlooker
Joist
Plywood fascia
Continuous screen vent
(See attic ventilation)
Wood plate shown beyond (dotted)
See steel casement windows for head jamb & sill details.

BOXED FLAT ROOF OVERHANG

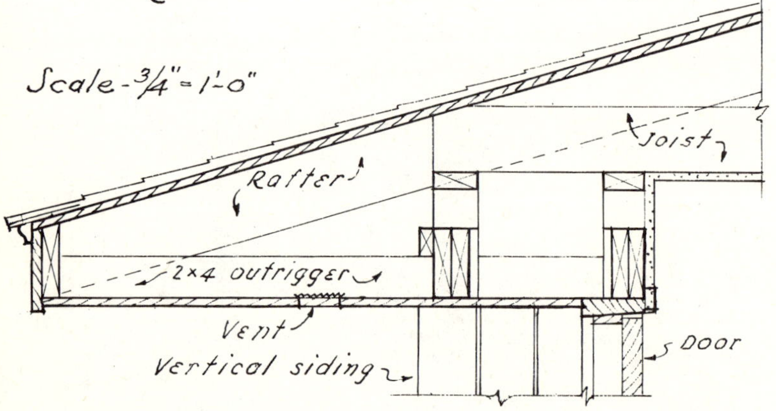
Scale-3/4"=1'-0"
Joist
Rafter
2×4 outrigger
Vent
Vertical siding
Door

SET BACK ENTRY with WIDE OVERHANG

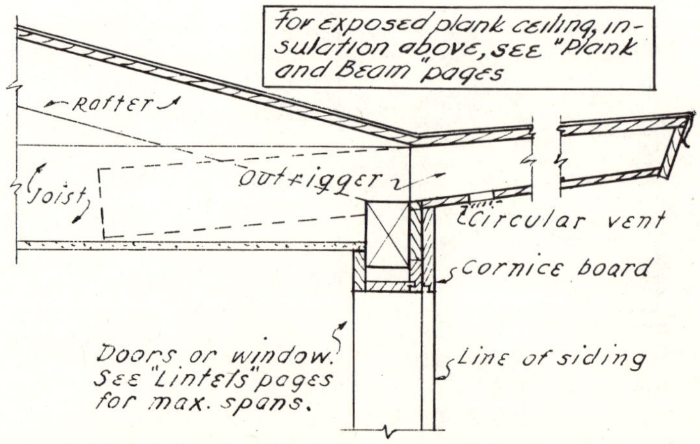
For exposed plank ceiling, insulation above, see "Plank and Beam" pages
Rafter
Joist
Outrigger
Circular vent
Cornice board
Doors or window. See "Lintels" pages for max. spans.
Line of siding

REVERSE SLOPE OVERHANG

STANDARD MILL CONSTRUCTION

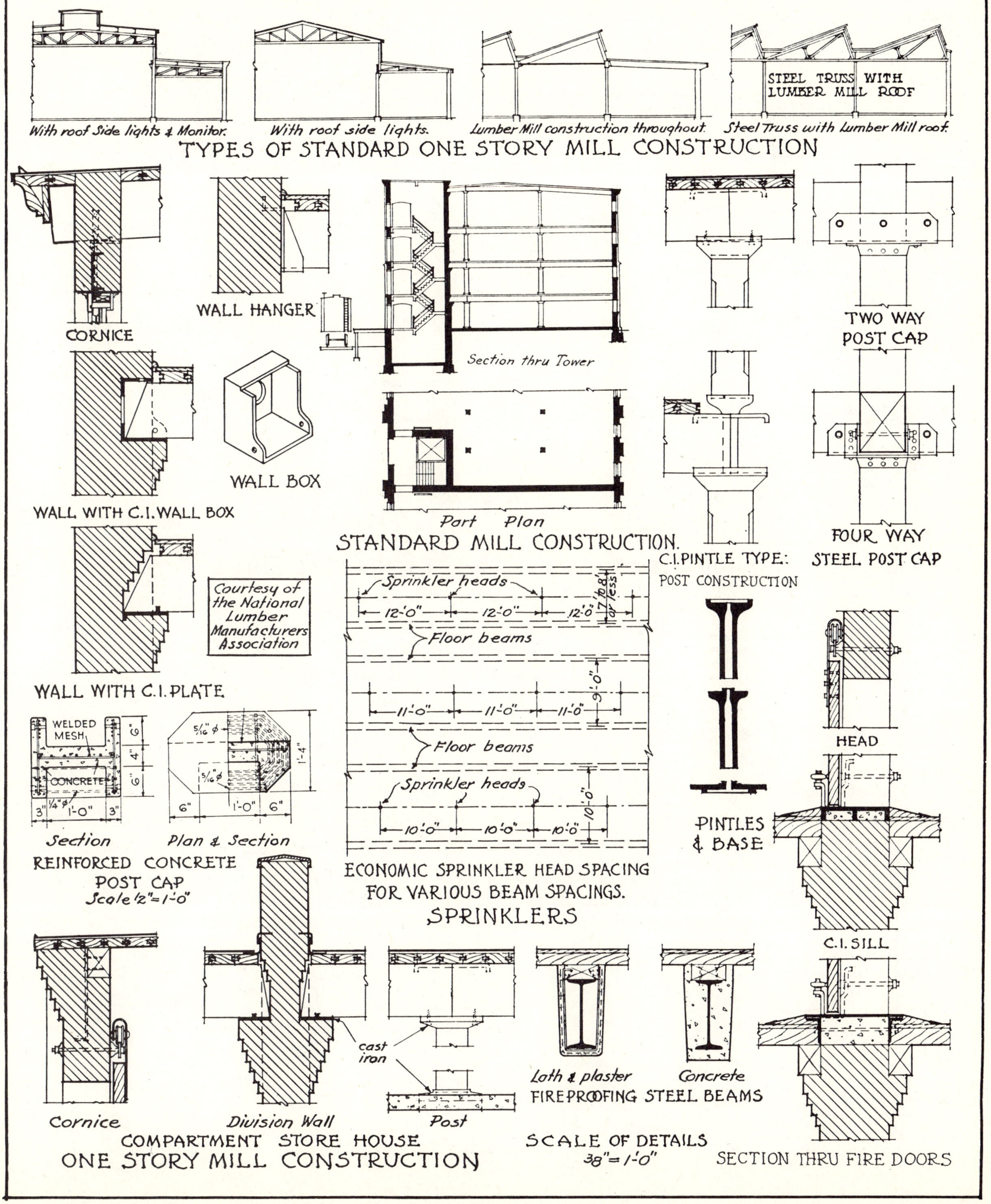
STEEL TRUSS WITH LUMBER MILL ROOF
With roof Side lights & Monitor.
With roof side lights.
Lumber Mill construction throughout.
Steel Truss with Lumber Mill roof.
TYPES OF STANDARD ONE STORY MILL CONSTRUCTION
CORNICE
WALL HANGER
Section thru Tower
TWO WAY POST CAP
WALL BOX
WALL WITH C.I. WALL BOX
Part Plan
STANDARD MILL CONSTRUCTION.
C.I. PINTLE TYPE: POST CONSTRUCTION
FOUR WAY STEEL POST CAP
WALL WITH C.I. PLATE
Courtesy of the National Lumber Manufacturers Association
Sprinkler heads
12'-0"
7'10 8' or less
Floor beams
11'-0"
9'-0"
10'-0"
HEAD
WELDED MESH
CONCRETE
6"
4"
1'-4"
5/16" ø
1/4" ø
3"
1'-0"
Section
Plan & Section
REINFORCED CONCRETE POST CAP
Scale 1/2"=1'-0"
PINTLES & BASE
ECONOMIC SPRINKLER HEAD SPACING FOR VARIOUS BEAM SPACINGS.
SPRINKLERS
C.I. SILL
cast iron
Lath & plaster
Concrete
FIREPROOFING STEEL BEAMS
Cornice
Division Wall
Post
COMPARTMENT STORE HOUSE
ONE STORY MILL CONSTRUCTION
SCALE OF DETAILS 3/8"=1'-0"
SECTION THRU FIRE DOORS

STANDARD MILL CONSTRUCTION

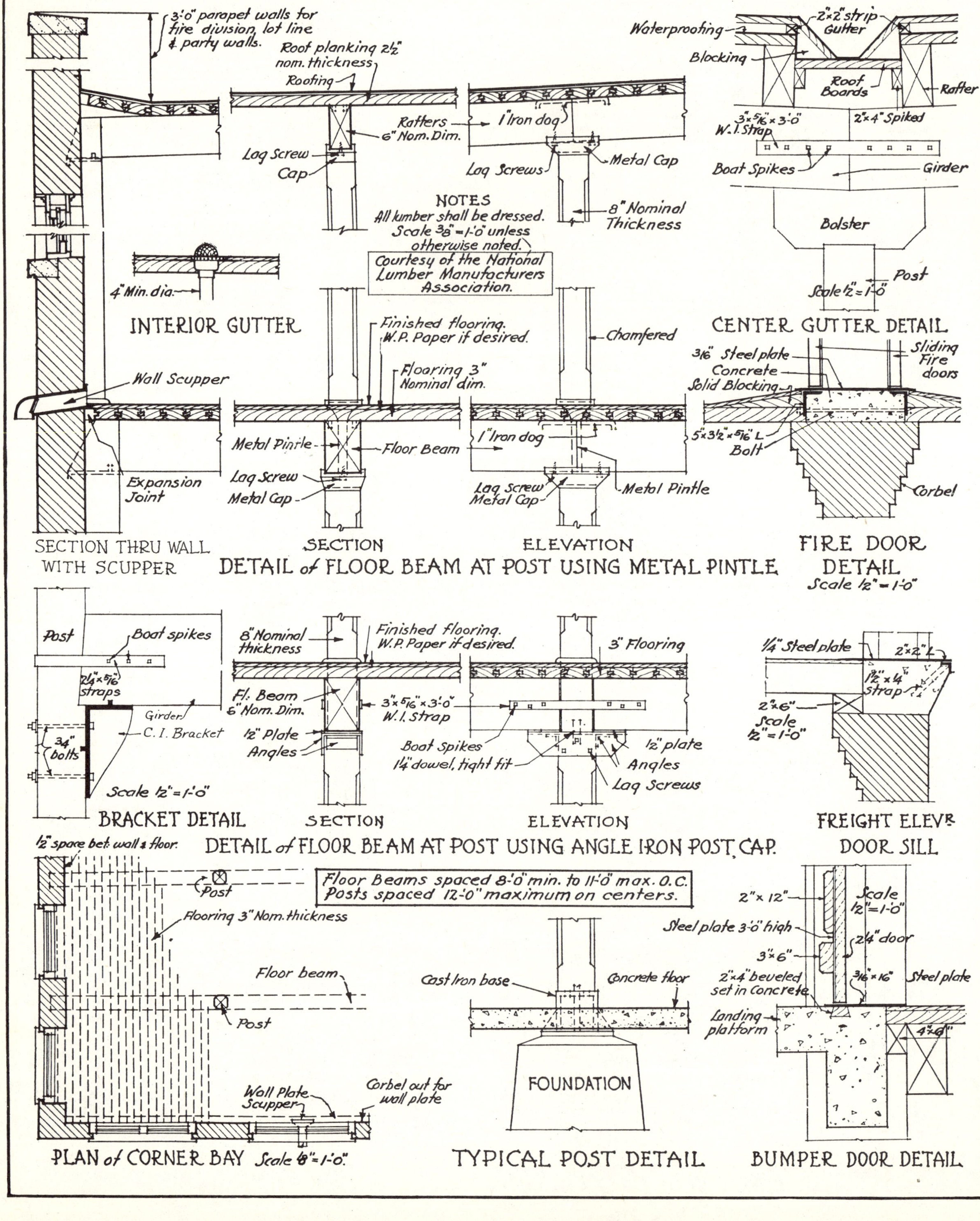
3'-0" parapet walls for fire division, lot line & party walls.
Roof planking 2½" nom. thickness
Roofing
Rafters
6" Nom. Dim.
Lag Screw
Cap
1" Iron dog
Lag Screws
Metal Cap
8" Nominal Thickness
NOTES
All lumber shall be dressed.
Scale ⅜"=1'-0" unless otherwise noted.
Courtesy of the National Lumber Manufacturers Association.
Waterproofing
2"×2" strip
Gutter
Blocking
Roof Boards
Rafter
3"×5/16"×3'-0" W.I. Strap
2"×4" Spiked
Boat Spikes
Girder
Bolster
Post
Scale ½"=1'-0"
4" Min. dia.
INTERIOR GUTTER
CENTER GUTTER DETAIL
Finished flooring. W.P. Paper if desired.
Flooring 3" Nominal dim.
Chamfered
Wall Scupper
Metal Pintle
Floor Beam
1" Iron dog
Lag Screw
Metal Cap
Expansion Joint
Lag Screw
Metal Cap
Metal Pintle
3/16" Steel plate
Concrete
Solid Blocking
Sliding Fire doors
5×3½×5/16" L
Bolt
Corbel
SECTION THRU WALL WITH SCUPPER
SECTION
ELEVATION
DETAIL of FLOOR BEAM AT POST USING METAL PINTLE
FIRE DOOR DETAIL
Scale ½"=1'-0"
Post
Boat spikes
2¼×5/16 straps
Girder
C. I. Bracket
¾" bolts
Scale ½"=1'-0"
8" Nominal thickness
Finished flooring. W.P. Paper if desired.
Fl. Beam 6" Nom. Dim.
½" Plate
Angles
3"×5/16"×3'-0" W.I. Strap
3" Flooring
Boat Spikes
1¼" dowel, tight fit
½" plate
Angles
Lag Screws
¼" Steel plate
2"×2" L
1½"×¼" Strap
2"×6"
Scale ½"=1'-0"
BRACKET DETAIL
SECTION
ELEVATION
DETAIL of FLOOR BEAM AT POST USING ANGLE IRON POST CAP.
FREIGHT ELEVR DOOR SILL
½" space bet. wall & floor.
Post
Floor Beams spaced 8'-0" min. to 11'-0" max. O.C.
Posts spaced 12'-0" maximum on centers.
Flooring 3" Nom. thickness
Floor beam
Post
Wall Plate Scupper
Corbel out for wall plate
Cast Iron base
Concrete floor
FOUNDATION
2"×12"
Scale ½"=1'-0"
Steel plate 3'-0" high
2¼" door
3"×6"
2"×4" beveled set in Concrete
3/16×16" Steel plate
Landing platform
4"×6"
PLAN of CORNER BAY Scale ⅛"=1'-0"
TYPICAL POST DETAIL
BUMPER DOOR DETAIL

SEMI-MILL CONSTRUCTION

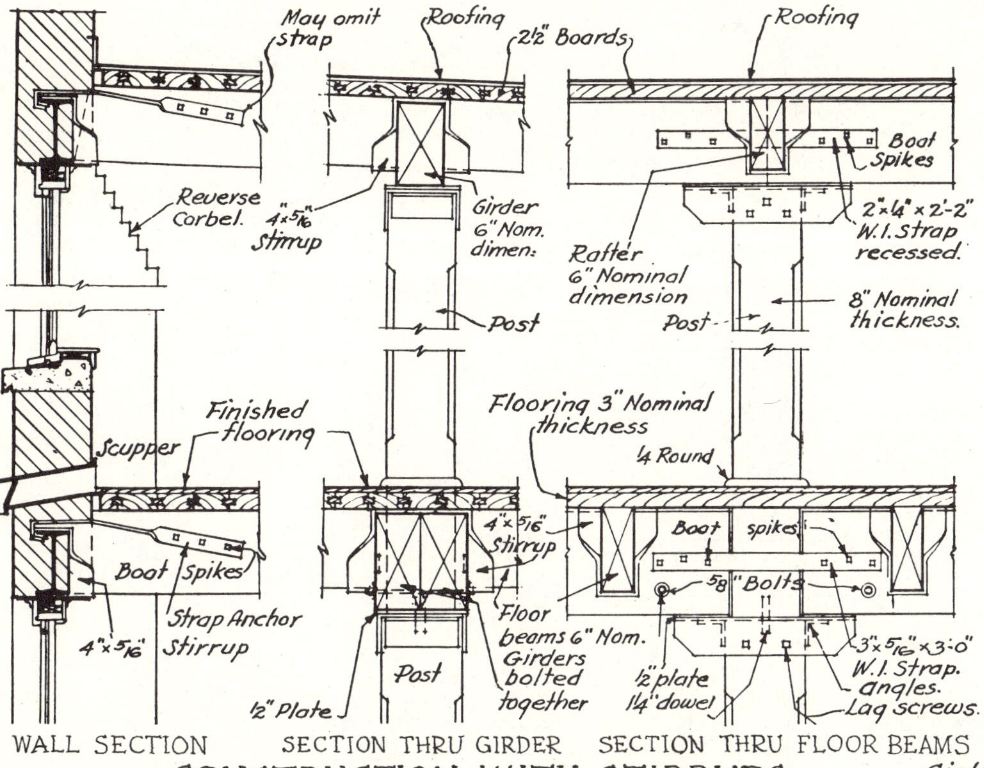
May omit strap
Roofing
2½" Boards
Roofing
Reverse Corbel.
4"×5/16" Stirrup
Girder 6" Nom. dimen:
Boat Spikes
2"×¼"×2'-2" W.I. Strap recessed.
Rafter 6" Nominal dimension
Post
8" Nominal thickness.
Finished flooring
Scupper
Flooring 3" Nominal thickness
¼ Round
4"×5/16" Stirrup
Boat spikes
5/8" Bolts
Boat Spikes
Strap Anchor Stirrup
4"×5/16"
Floor beams 6" Nom. Girders bolted together
3"×5/16"×3'-0" W.I. Strap.
Angles.
½" plate
1¼" dowel
Lag screws.
Post
½" Plate
WALL SECTION
SECTION THRU GIRDER
SECTION THRU FLOOR BEAMS

CONSTRUCTION WITH STIRRUPS

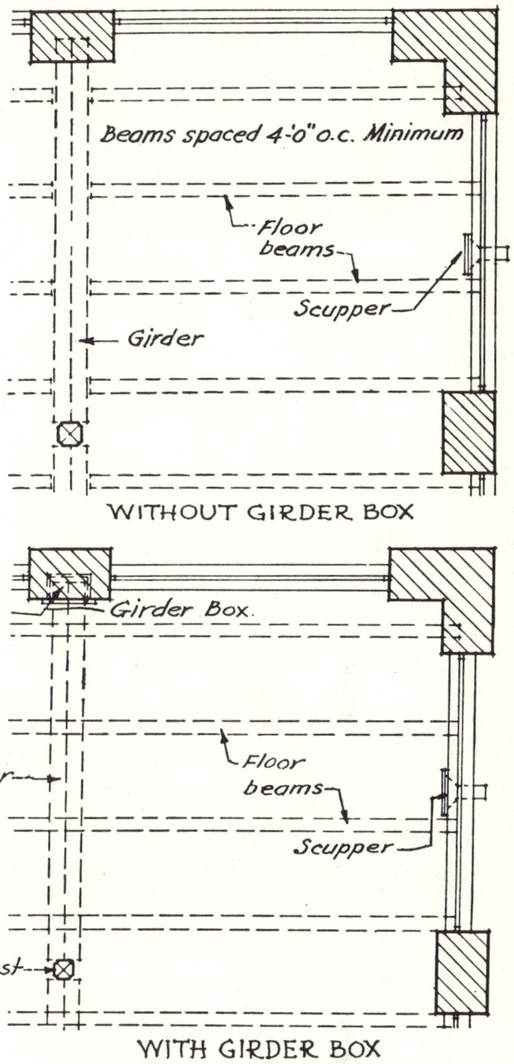
Beams spaced 4'-0" o.c. Minimum
Floor beams
Scupper
Girder
WITHOUT GIRDER BOX
Girder Box.
Girder
Floor beams
Scupper
Post
WITH GIRDER BOX

CORNER BAY PLANS

NOTES
All lumber shall be dressed.
Scale 3/8" = 1 Foot.
Courtesy of the National Lumber Manufacturers Assocn

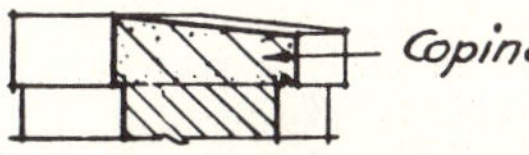
Coping

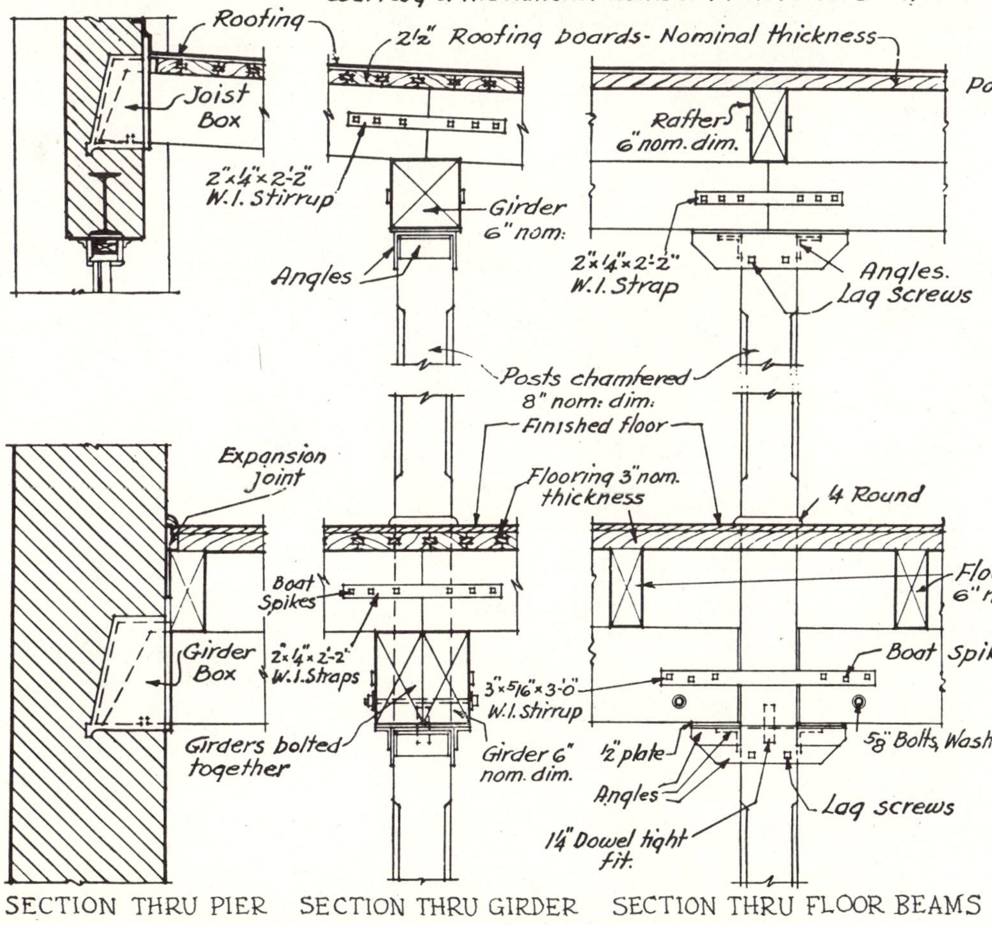
Roofing
2½" Roofing boards - Nominal thickness
Joist Box
Rafter 6" nom. dim.
2"×¼"×2'-2" W.I. Stirrup
Girder 6" nom.
2"×¼"×2'-2" W.I. Strap
Angles.
Lag Screws
Angles
Posts chamfered 8" nom. dim.
Finished floor
Expansion joint
Flooring 3" nom. thickness
¼ Round
Boat Spikes
Floor beams 6" nom. dim.
Girder Box
2"×¼"×2'-2" W.I. Straps
Boat Spikes
3"×5/16"×3'-0" W.I. Stirrup
Girders bolted together
Girder 6" nom. dim.
½" plate
5/8" Bolts, Washer, etc.
Angles
Lag screws
1¼" Dowel tight fit.
SECTION THRU PIER
SECTION THRU GIRDER
SECTION THRU FLOOR BEAMS

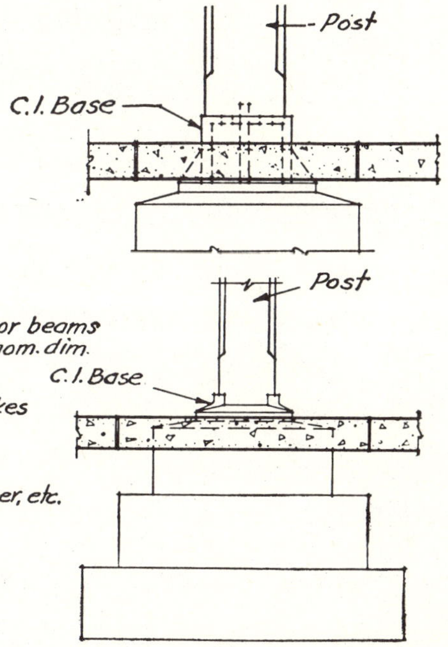
Post
C.I. Base
Post
C.I. Base

CONSTRUCTION WITHOUT STIRRUPS

TYPICAL POST DETAILS

LAMINATED MILL CONSTRUCTION

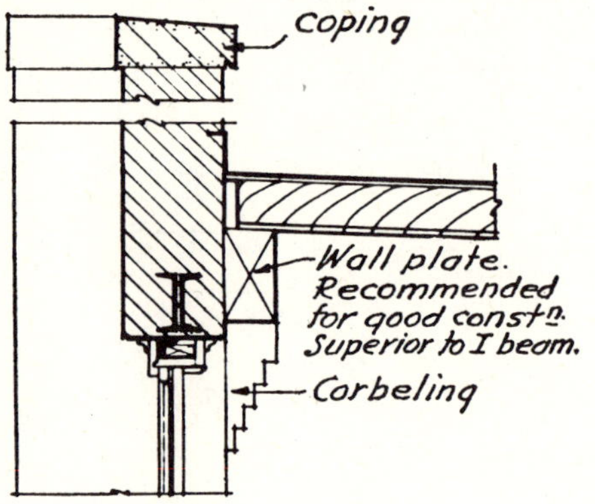
Coping
Wall plate. Recommended for good constn. Superior to I beam.
Corbeling

SECTION THRU WINDOW

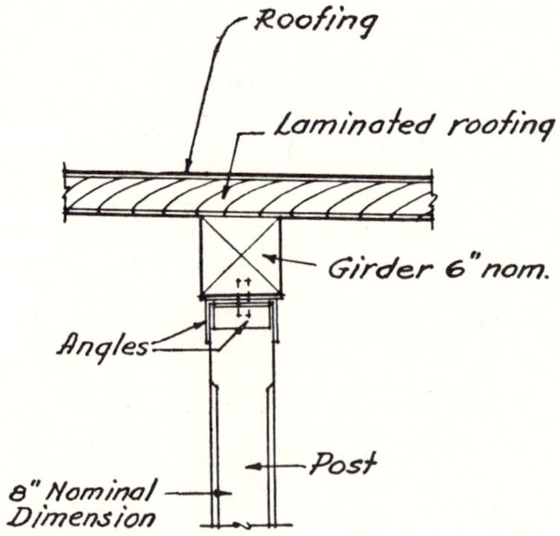
Roofing
Laminated roofing
Girder 6" nom.
Angles
Post
8" Nominal Dimension

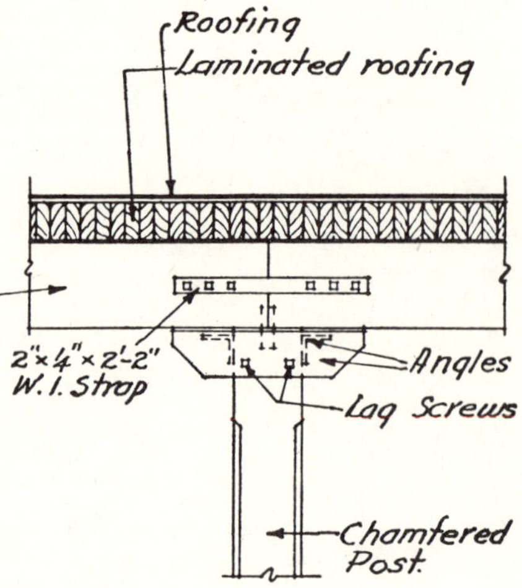
Roofing
Laminated roofing
2"×4"×2'-2" W.I. Strap
Angles
Lag Screws
Chamfered Post.

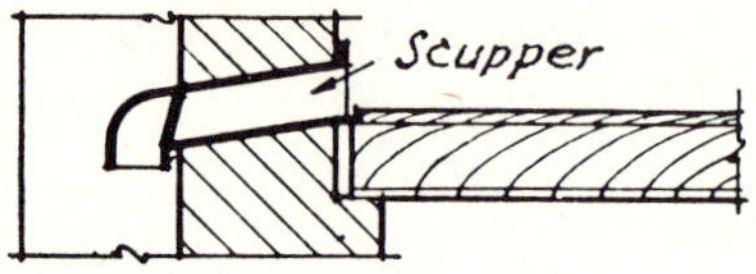
Scupper

SCUPPER DETAIL

Girders spaced 12'-0" minimum to 18'-0" maximum on centers
Posts spaced preferably 16'-0" on centers

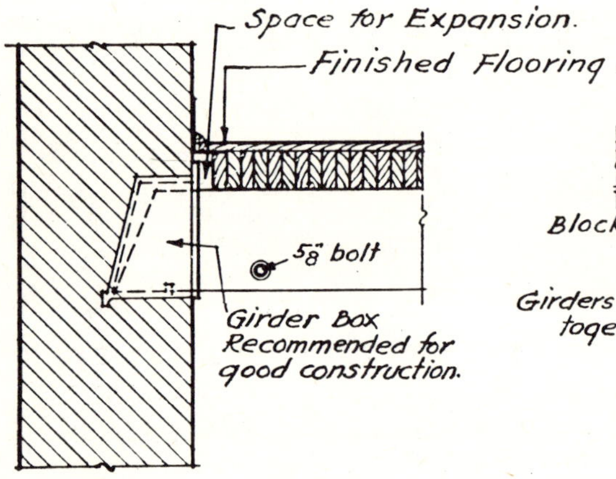
Space for Expansion.
Finished Flooring
5/8" bolt
Girder Box Recommended for good construction.

SECTION THRU PIER

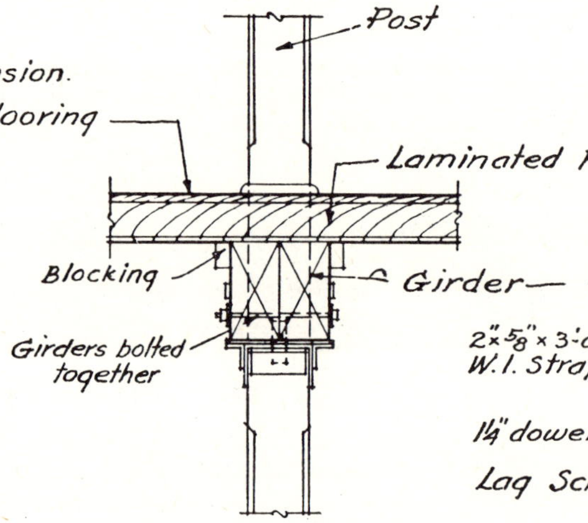
Post
Laminated Flooring
Blocking
Girder
Girders bolted together

SECTION THRU GIRDER

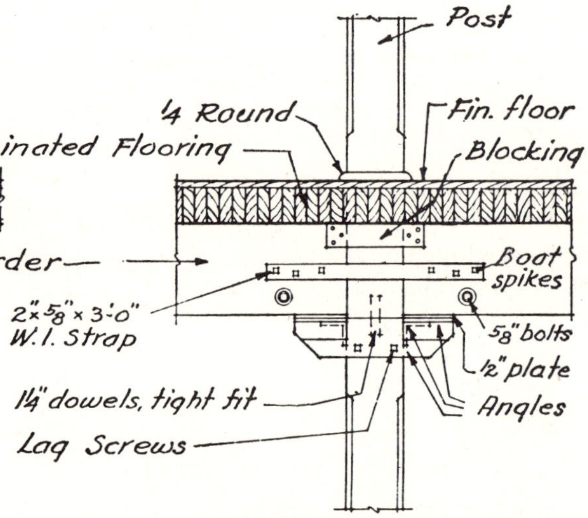
Post
1/4 Round
Fin. floor
Blocking
Boat spikes
2"×5/8"×3'-0" W.I. Strap
5/8" bolts
1/2" plate
1 1/4" dowels, tight fit
Angles
Lag Screws

SECTION THRU LAMINATED FLOORING

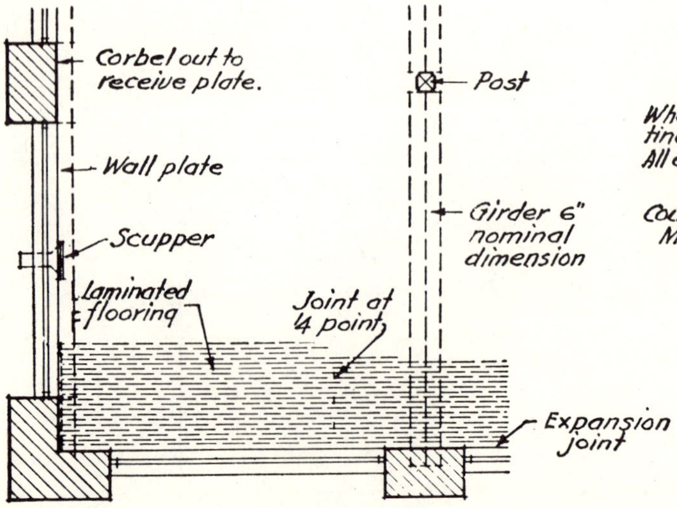
Corbel out to receive plate.
Post
Wall plate
Girder 6" nominal dimension
Scupper
Laminated flooring
Joint at 1/4 point
Expansion joint

PLAN OF CORNER BAY

NOTES

When possible run girders continuously over tops of columns.
All exposed surfaces to be dressed.

Scale 3/8" = 1'-0"
Courtesy of the National Lumber Manufacturers Association
Washington. D.C.

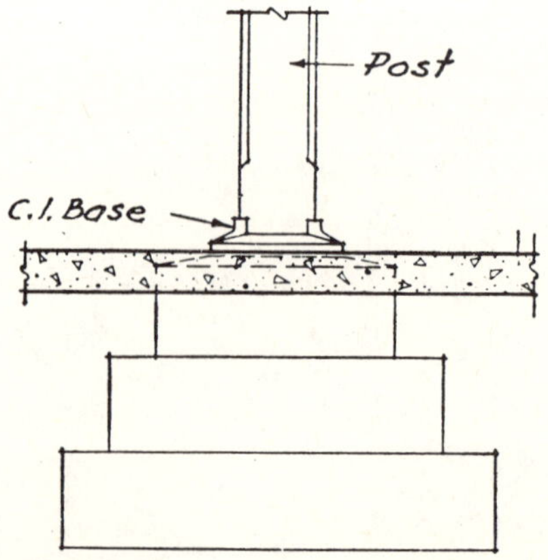
Post
C.I. Base

TYPICAL POST DETAIL

STEEL and CONCRETE CONSTRUCTION

TABLE OF CONTENTS

STRUCTURAL STEEL SHA

CONVENTIONAL RIVET SYMBOLS

SHOP RIVETS

- *Two Full Heads*
- *Countersunk and Chipped – Near Side*
- *" – Far Side*
- *" – Both Sides*
- *Countersunk, not Chipped, Max. 1/8 in. High – Near Side*
- *" – Far Side*
- *" – Both Sides*
- *Flattened to 1/4 in. High for 1/2 in. and 5/8 in. Rivets – Near Side*
- *" – Far Side*
- *" – Both Sides*
- *Flattened to 3/8 in. High for 3/4, 7/8 and 1 in. Rivets – Near Side*
- *" – Far Side*
- *" – Both Sides*

FIELD RIVETS

- *Two Full Heads*
- *Countersunk and Chipped – Near Side*
- *" – Far Side*
- *" – Both Sides*

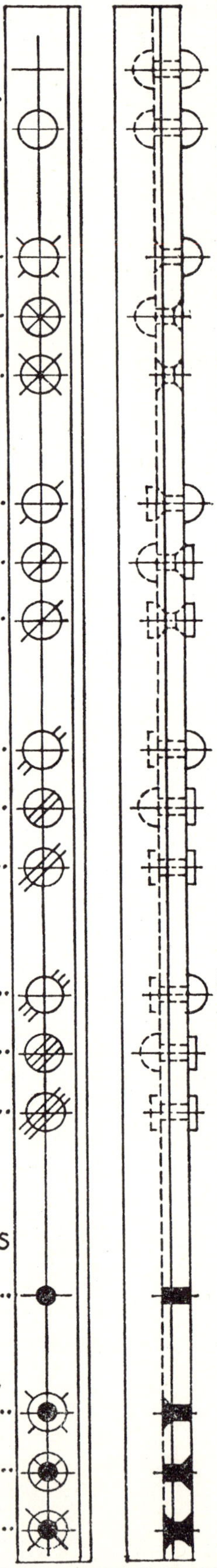

BETHLEHEM AND CARNEGIE STRUCTURA

D	WT	S	d	b	b/2+2	b/2+5
36 WF	300	1105.1	36 3/4	16 5/8	10 3/8	13 3/8
	280	1031.2	36 1/2	16 5/8		
	260	951.1	36 1/4	16 1/2	10 1/4	13 1/4
	245	892.5	36	16 1/2		
	230	835.5	35 7/8	16 1/2		
	194	663.6	36 1/2	12 1/8	8 1/8	11 1/8
	182	621.2	36 3/8	12 1/8		
	170	579.1	36 1/8	12	8	11
	160	541.0	36	12		
	150	502.9	35 7/8	12		
33 WF	240	811.1	33 1/2	15 7/8	10	13
	220	740.6	33 1/4	15 3/4	9 7/8	12 7/8
	200	669.6	33	15 3/4		
	152	486.4	33 1/2	11 5/8	7 7/8	10 7/8
	141	446.8	33 1/4	11 1/2	7 3/4	10 3/4
	130	404.8	33 1/8	11 1/2		
30 WF	210	649.9	30 3/8	15 1/8	9 5/8	12 5/8
	190	586.1	30 1/8	15	9 1/2	12 1/2
	172	528.2	29 7/8	15		
	132	379.7	30 1/4	10 1/2	7 1/4	10 1/4
	124	354.6	30 1/8	10 1/2		
	116	327.9	30	10 1/2		
	108	299.2	29 7/8	10 1/2		
27 WF	177	492.8	27 1/4	14 1/8	9 1/8	12 1/8
	160	444.5	27 1/8	14	9	12
	145	402.9	26 7/8	14		
	114	299.2	27 1/4	10 1/8	7 1/8	10 1/8
	102	266.3	27 1/8	10	7	10
	94	242.8	26 7/8	10		

D	WT	S	d	b	b/2+2	b/2+5
24 WF	160	413.5	24 3/4	14 1/8	9 1/8	12 1/8
	145	372.5	24 1/2	14	9	12
	130	330.7	24 1/4	14		
	120	299.1	24 1/4	12 1/8	8 1/8	11 1/8
	110	274.4	24 1/8	12	8	11
	100	248.9	24	12		
	94	220.9	24 1/4	9	6 1/2	9 1/2
	84	196.3	24 1/8	9		
	76	175.4	23 7/8	9		
21 WF	142	317.2	21 1/2	13 1/8	8 5/8	11 5/8
	127	284.1	21 1/4	13	8 1/2	11 1/2
	112	249.6	21	13		
	96	197.6	21 1/8	9	6 1/2	9 1/2
	82	168.0	20 7/8	9		
	73	150.7	21 1/4	8 1/4	6 1/8	9 1/8
	68	139.9	21 1/8	8 1/4		
	62	126.4	21	8 1/4		
18 WF	114	220.1	18 1/2	11 7/8	8	11
	105	202.2	18 3/8	11 3/4	7 7/8	10 7/8
	96	184.4	18 1/8	11 3/4		
	85	156.1	18 3/8	8 7/8	6 1/2	9 1/2
	77	141.7	18 1/8	8 3/4	6 3/8	9 3/8
	70	128.2	18	8 3/4		
	64	117.0	17 7/8	8 3/4		
	60	107.8	18 1/4	7 1/2	5 3/4	8 3/4
	55	98.2	18 1/8	7 1/2		
	50	89.0	18	7 1/2		
16 WF	96	166.1	16 3/8	11 1/2	7 3/4	10 3/4
	88	151.3	16 1/8	11 1/2		
	78	127.8	16 3/8	8 5/8	6 3/8	9 3/8
	71	115.9	16 1/8	8 1/2	6 1/4	9 1/4
	64	104.2	16	8 1/2		
	58	94.1	15 7/8	8 1/2		
	50	80.7	16 1/4	7 1/8	5 5/8	8 5/8
	45	72.4	16 1/8	7	5 1/2	8 1/2
	40	64.4	16	7		
	36	56.3	15 7/8	7		

D	WT	S	d	b	b/2+2	b/2+5
14 WF	426	707.4	18 3/4	16 3/4	10 3/8	13 3/8
	398	656.9	18 1/4	16 5/8		
	370	608.1	18	16 1/2	10 1/4	13 1/4
	342	599.4	17 1/2	16 3/8		
	320	492.8	16 3/4	16 3/4	10 3/8	13 3/8
	314	511.9	17 1/4	16 1/4	10 1/8	13 1/8
	287	465.5	16 3/4	16 1/8		
	264	427.4	16 1/2	16	10	13
	246	397.4	16 1/4	16		
	237	382.2	16 1/8	15 7/8		
14 WF	228	367.8	16	15 7/8	10	13
	219	352.6	15 7/8	15 7/8		
	211	339.2	15 3/4	15 3/4	9 7/8	12 7/8
	202	324.9	15 5/8	15 3/4		
	193	310.0	15 1/2	15 3/4		
	184	295.8	15 3/8	15 5/8		
	176	281.9	15 1/4	15 5/8		
	167	267.3	15 1/8	15 5/8		
	158	253.4	15	15 1/2	9 3/4	12 3/4
	150	240.2	14 7/8	15 1/2		
14 WF	142	226.7	14 3/4	15 1/2	9 3/4	12 3/4
	136	216.0	14 3/4	14 3/4	9 3/8	12 3/8
	127	202.0	14 5/8	14 3/4		
	119	189.4	14 1/2	14 5/8		
	111	176.3	14 3/8	14 5/8		
	103	163.6	14 1/4	14 5/8		
	95	150.6	14 1/8	14 1/2	9 1/4	12 1/4
	87	138.1	14	14 1/2		
	84	130.9	14 1/8	12	8	11
	78	121.1	14	12		
14 WF	74	112.3	14 1/4	10 1/8	7 1/8	10 1/8
	68	103.0	14	10	7	10
	61	92.2	13 7/8	10		
	53	77.8	14	8	6	9
	48	70.2	13 3/4	8		
	43	62.7	13 5/8	8		
	38	54.6	14 1/8	6 3/4	5 3/8	8 3/8
	34	48.5	14	6 3/4		
	30	41.8	13 7/8	6 3/4		

D	WT
12 WF	190
	161
	133
	120
	106
	99
	92
	85
	79
	72
	65
12 WF	58
	53
	50
	45
	40
	36
	31
	27
	22
	19
	16.5
	14
10 WF	112
	100
	89
	77
	72
	66
	60
	54
	49
10 WF	45
	39
	33
	29
	25
	21
	19
	17
	15
	11.5

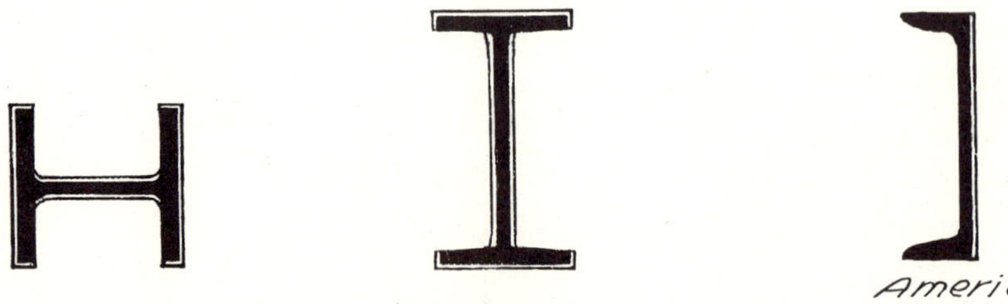

Wide flange shapes (WF)
H Column *Beam*

American Standard Channel Beam

Typical Diagrams
Showing how areas and weights of steel sections are increas

S and RIVETING SYMBOLS

ECTIONS

b	b/2+2	b/2+5
2 5/8	8 3/8	11 3/8
2 1/2		
2 3/8	8 1/4	11 1/4
2 3/8		
2 1/4		
2 1/4		
2 1/8	8 1/8	11 1/8
2 1/8		
2 1/8		
2	8	11
2		
0	7	10
0		
8 1/8	6 1/8	9 1/8
8	6	9
8		
6 5/8	5 3/8	8 3/8
6 1/2	5 1/4	8 1/4
6 1/2		
4	4	7
4		
4		
4		
—		
0 3/8	7 1/4	10 1/4
0 3/8		
0 1/4		
0 1/4	7 1/8	10 1/8
0 1/8		
0 1/8		
0 1/8		
0	7	10
0		
—		
8	6	9
8		
8		
5 3/4		
5 3/4	4 7/8	7 7/8
5 3/4		
4		
4	4	7
4		
4		

D	WT	S	d	b	b/2+2	b/2+5
8 WF	67	60.4	9	8 1/4	6 1/8	9 1/8
	58	52.0	8 3/4	8 1/4		
	48	43.2	8 1/2	8 1/8		
	40	35.5	8 1/4	8 1/8		
	35	31.1	8 1/8	8	6	9
	31	27.4	8	8		
	28	24.3	8	6 1/2	5 1/4	8 1/4
	24	20.8	7 7/8	6 1/2		
	20	17.0	8 1/8	5 1/4	4 5/8	7 5/8
	17	14.1	8	5 1/4		
	15	11.8	8 1/8	4	4	7
	13	9.9	8	4		
	10	7.8	7 7/8	4		
8C	34.3	28.9	8	8	6	9
6 WF	25	16.8	6 3/8	6	5	8
	20	13.4	6 1/4	6		
	16	10.1	6 1/4	4	4	7
	15.5	10.1	6	6	5	8
	12	7.24	6	4	4	7
	8.5	5.07	5 7/8	4		
6C	25	15.7	6	6	5	8
	20	12.9	6	6		
5 WF	18.9	9.5	5	5	4 1/2	7 1/2
	18.5	9.9	5 1/8	5		
	16	8.5	5	5		
4C	13	5.2	4	4	4	7
4B	13	5.45	4 1/8	4	4	7
4 WF	10	4.16	4	4	4	7

AMER. STD. CHANNEL SECT.

D	WT	S	d	b	SEE DETAILS
18 [	58	74.5	18	4 1/4	
	51.9	69.1	18	4 1/8	
	45.8	63.7	18	4	
	42.7	61.0	18	4	
15 [	50	53.6	15	3 3/4	
	40	46.2	15	3 1/2	
	33.9	41.7	15	3 3/8	
13 [	50	48.1	13	4 3/8	
	40	41.7	13	4 1/8	
	35	38.6	13	4 1/8	
	31	36.5	13	4	
12 [	30	26.9	12	3 1/8	
	25	23.9	12	3	
	20.7	21.4	12	3	
10 [	30	20.6	10	3	
	25	18.1	10	2 7/8	
	20	15.7	10	2 3/4	
	15.3	13.4	10	2 5/8	
9 [	20	13.5	9	2 5/8	
	15	11.3	9	2 1/2	
	13.4	10.5	9	2 3/8	
8 [	18.75	10.9	8	2 1/2	
	13.75	9.0	8	2 3/8	
	11.5	8.1	8	2 1/4	
7 [	14.75	7.7	7	2 1/4	
	12.25	6.9	7	2 1/4	
	9.8	6.0	7	2 1/8	
6 [	13.0	5.8	6	2 1/8	
	10.5	5.0	6	2	
	8.2	4.3	6	1 7/8	
5 [	9.0	3.5	5	1 7/8	
	6.7	3.0	5	1 3/4	
4 [	7.25	2.3	4	1 3/4	
	5.4	1.9	4	1 5/8	
3 [	6.0	1.4	3	1 5/8	
	5.0	1.2	3	1 1/2	
	4.1	1.1	3	1 3/8	

AMER. STD. BEAM SECT.

D	WT	S	d	b	b/2+2	b/2+5
24 I	120	250.9	24	8	6	9
	105.9	234.3	24	7 7/8		
	100	197.6	24	7 1/4	5 5/8	8 5/8
	90	185.8	24	7 1/8		
	79.9	173.9	24	7	5 1/2	8 1/2
20 I	95	160.0	20	7 1/4	5 5/8	8 5/8
	85	150.2	20	7	5 1/2	8 1/2
	75	126.3	20	6 3/8	5 1/4	8 1/4
	65.4	116.9	20	6 1/4	5 1/8	8 1/8
18 I	70	101.9	18	6 1/4	5 1/8	8 1/8
	54.7	88.4	18	6	5	8
15 I	50	64.2	15	5 5/8	4 7/8	7 7/8
	42.9	58.9	15	5 1/2	4 3/4	7 3/4
12 I	50	50.3	12	5 1/2	4 3/4	7 3/4
	40.8	44.8	12	5 1/4	4 5/8	7 5/8
	35	37.8	12	5 1/8		
	31.8	36.0	12	5	4 1/2	7 1/2
10 I	35	29.2	10	5	4 1/2	7 1/2
	25.4	24.4	10	4 5/8	4 3/8	7 3/8
8 I	23.0	16.0	8	4 1/8	4 1/8	7 1/8
	18.4	14.2	8	4	4	7
7 I	20	12.0	7	3 7/8	4	7
	15.3	10.4	7	3 5/8	3 7/8	6 7/8
6 I	17.25	8.7	6	3 5/8	3 7/8	6 7/8
	12.5	7.3	6	3 3/8	3 3/4	6 3/4
5 I	14.75	6.0	5	3 1/4	3 5/8	6 5/8
	10	4.8	5	3	3 1/2	6 1/2
4 I	9.5	3.3	4	2 3/4	3 3/8	6 3/8
	7.7	3.0	4	2 5/8		
3 I	7.5	1.9	3	2 1/2	3 1/4	6 1/4
	5.7	1.7	3	2 3/8		

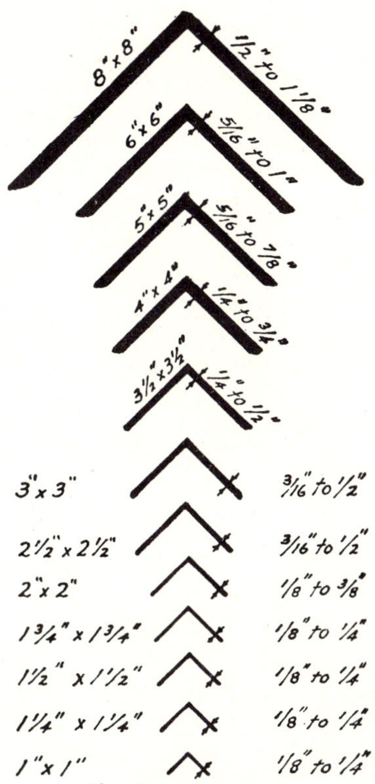

8"x8" 1/2" to 1 1/8"
6"x6" 5/16" to 1"
5"x5" 5/16" to 7/8"
4"x4" 1/4" to 3/4"
3 1/2"x3 1/2" 1/4" to 1/2"
3"x3" 3/16" to 1/2"
2 1/2"x2 1/2" 3/16" to 1/2"
2"x2" 1/8" to 3/8"
1 3/4"x1 3/4" 1/8" to 1/4"
1 1/2"x1 1/2" 1/8" to 1/4"
1 1/4"x1 1/4" 1/8" to 1/4"
1"x1" 1/8" to 1/4"

EQUAL. LEG

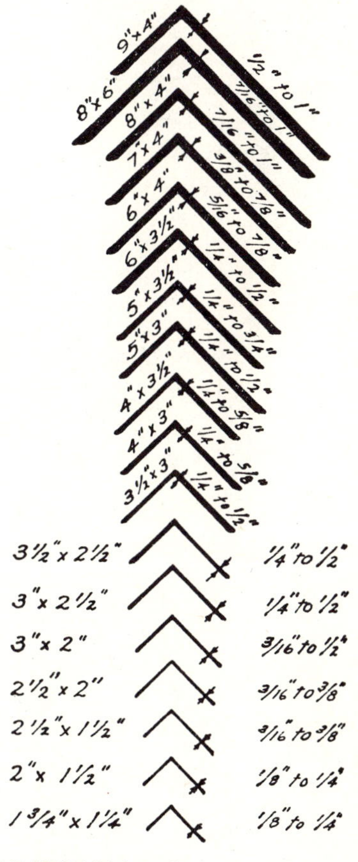

9"x4" 1/2" to 1"
8"x6" 7/16" to 1"
8"x4" 7/16" to 1"
7"x4" 3/8" to 7/8"
6"x4" 5/16" to 7/8"
6"x3 1/2" 1/4" to 1/2"
5"x3 1/2" 1/4" to 3/4"
5"x3" 1/4" to 1/2"
4"x3 1/2" 1/4" to 5/8"
4"x3" 1/4" to 5/8"
3 1/2"x3" 1/4" to 1/2"
3 1/2"x2 1/2" 1/4" to 1/2"
3"x2 1/2" 1/4" to 1/2"
3"x2" 3/16" to 1/2"
2 1/2"x2" 3/16" to 3/8"
2 1/2"x1 1/2" 3/16" to 3/8"
2"x1 1/2" 1/8" to 1/4"
1 3/4"x1 1/4" 1/8" to 1/4"

UNEQUAL LEG ANGLES

DECIMAL EQUIVALENTS OF FRACTIONS OF AN INCH

1/16	1/8	3/16	1/4	5/16	3/8	7/16	1/2	9/16	5/8	11/16	3/4	13/16	7/8	15/16	1"
.063	.125	.188	.250	.313	.375	.438	.500	.563	.625	.688	.750	.813	.875	.938	1.00

Equal
Unequal

an
rd
m

Leg Angles

the minimum.

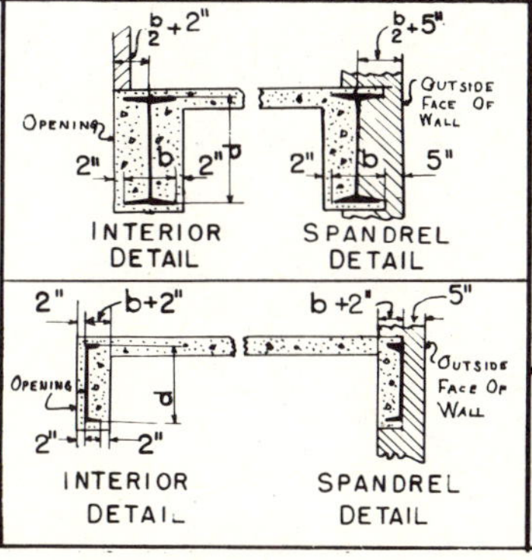

b/2+2"
b/2+5"
Outside Face Of Wall
Opening
2"
b
2"
d
2"
b
5"
INTERIOR DETAIL
SPANDREL DETAIL
2"
b+2"
b+2"
5"
Opening
d
Outside Face Of Wall
2"
2"
INTERIOR DETAIL
SPANDREL DETAIL

NOMENCLATURE

D – NOMINAL DEPTH IN INCHES
WT – WEIGHT IN LBS. PER FOOT
S – SECTION MODULUS
d – ACTUAL DEPTH IN INCHES
b – FLANGE WIDTH IN INCHES
WF – BETHLEHEM & CARNEGIE SECT.
B – BETHLEHEM SECTION
C – CARNEGIE SECTION
I – AMERICAN STANDARD SECT.

SEELYE, STEVENSON, VALUE & KNECHT
CONSULTING ENGINEERS
101 PARK AVE. NEW YORK, 17, N.Y.
DEC. '48

WELDING SYMBOLS

AMERICAN WELDING SOCIETY

SUMMARY OF STANDARD WELDING SYMBOLS

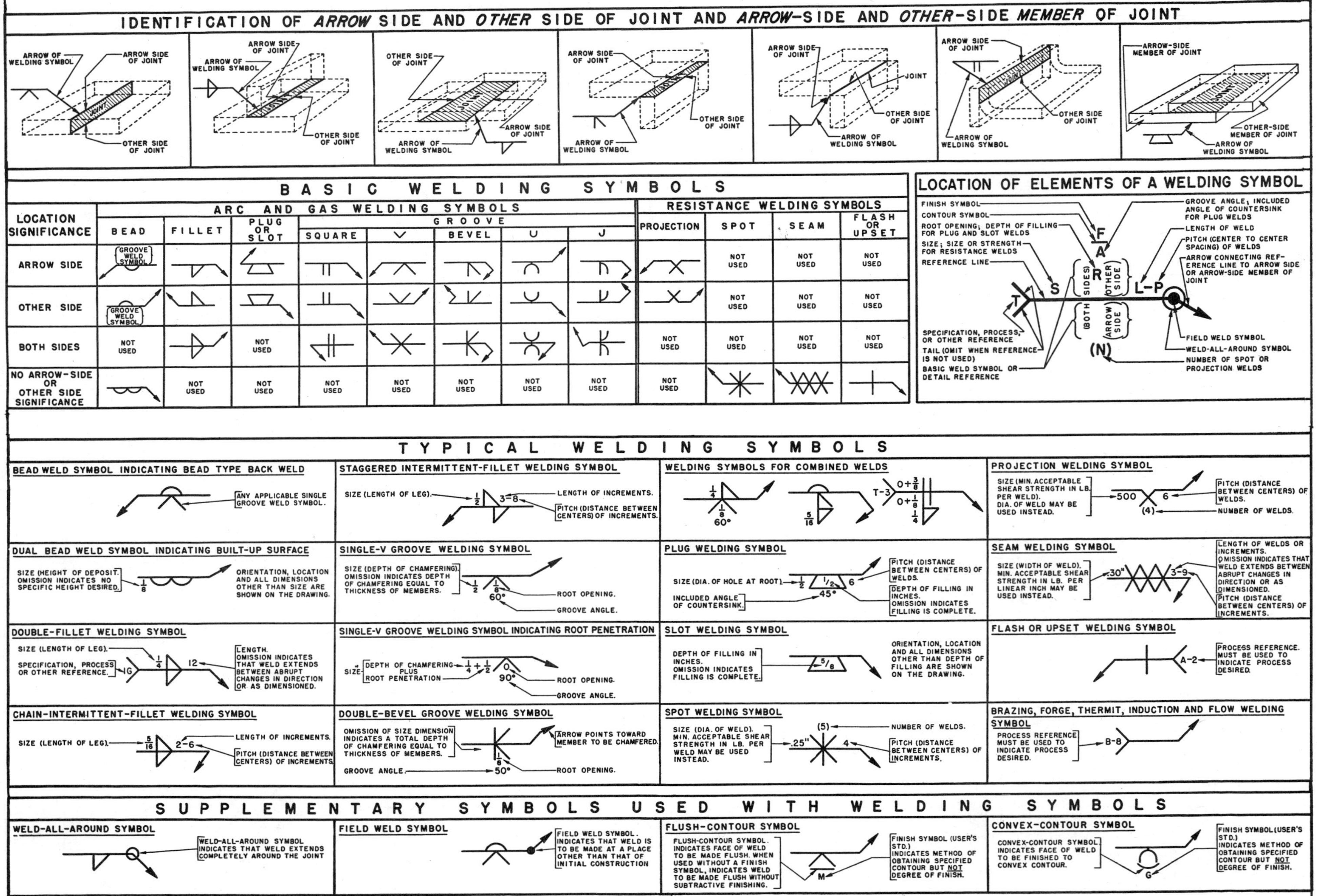
IDENTIFICATION OF ARROW SIDE AND OTHER SIDE OF JOINT AND ARROW-SIDE AND OTHER-SIDE MEMBER OF JOINT
ARROW OF WELDING SYMBOL
ARROW SIDE OF JOINT
OTHER SIDE OF JOINT
JOINT
ARROW-SIDE MEMBER OF JOINT
OTHER-SIDE MEMBER OF JOINT
BASIC WELDING SYMBOLS
LOCATION SIGNIFICANCE
ARC AND GAS WELDING SYMBOLS
BEAD
FILLET
PLUG OR SLOT
GROOVE
SQUARE
V
BEVEL
U
J
RESISTANCE WELDING SYMBOLS
PROJECTION
SPOT
SEAM
FLASH OR UPSET
ARROW SIDE
OTHER SIDE
BOTH SIDES
NO ARROW-SIDE OR OTHER SIDE SIGNIFICANCE
GROOVE WELD SYMBOL
NOT USED
LOCATION OF ELEMENTS OF A WELDING SYMBOL
FINISH SYMBOL
CONTOUR SYMBOL
ROOT OPENING; DEPTH OF FILLING FOR PLUG AND SLOT WELDS
SIZE; SIZE OR STRENGTH FOR RESISTANCE WELDS
REFERENCE LINE
SPECIFICATION, PROCESS, OR OTHER REFERENCE
TAIL (OMIT WHEN REFERENCE IS NOT USED)
BASIC WELD SYMBOL OR DETAIL REFERENCE
GROOVE ANGLE; INCLUDED ANGLE OF COUNTERSINK FOR PLUG WELDS
LENGTH OF WELD
PITCH (CENTER TO CENTER SPACING) OF WELDS
ARROW CONNECTING REFERENCE LINE TO ARROW SIDE OR ARROW-SIDE MEMBER OF JOINT
FIELD WELD SYMBOL
WELD-ALL-AROUND SYMBOL
NUMBER OF SPOT OR PROJECTION WELDS
F
A
R
S
T
L-P
(N)
(BOTH SIDES)
OTHER SIDE
ARROW SIDE
TYPICAL WELDING SYMBOLS
BEAD WELD SYMBOL INDICATING BEAD TYPE BACK WELD
ANY APPLICABLE SINGLE GROOVE WELD SYMBOL.
STAGGERED INTERMITTENT-FILLET WELDING SYMBOL
SIZE (LENGTH OF LEG).
LENGTH OF INCREMENTS.
PITCH (DISTANCE BETWEEN CENTERS) OF INCREMENTS.
1/2
3-8
WELDING SYMBOLS FOR COMBINED WELDS
1/4
1/8
60°
5/16
T-3
0+3/8
0+1/8
1/4
PROJECTION WELDING SYMBOL
SIZE (MIN. ACCEPTABLE SHEAR STRENGTH IN LB. PER WELD). DIA. OF WELD MAY BE USED INSTEAD.
500
6
(4)
PITCH (DISTANCE BETWEEN CENTERS) OF WELDS.
NUMBER OF WELDS.
DUAL BEAD WELD SYMBOL INDICATING BUILT-UP SURFACE
SIZE (HEIGHT OF DEPOSIT. OMISSION INDICATES NO SPECIFIC HEIGHT DESIRED.
1/8
ORIENTATION, LOCATION AND ALL DIMENSIONS OTHER THAN SIZE ARE SHOWN ON THE DRAWING.
SINGLE-V GROOVE WELDING SYMBOL
SIZE (DEPTH OF CHAMFERING). OMISSION INDICATES DEPTH OF CHAMFERING EQUAL TO THICKNESS OF MEMBERS.
1/2
1/8
60°
ROOT OPENING.
GROOVE ANGLE.
PLUG WELDING SYMBOL
SIZE (DIA. OF HOLE AT ROOT)
INCLUDED ANGLE OF COUNTERSINK.
1/2
1/2
6
45°
PITCH (DISTANCE BETWEEN CENTERS) OF WELDS.
DEPTH OF FILLING IN INCHES. OMISSION INDICATES FILLING IS COMPLETE.
SEAM WELDING SYMBOL
SIZE (WIDTH OF WELD). MIN. ACCEPTABLE SHEAR STRENGTH IN LB. PER LINEAR INCH MAY BE USED INSTEAD.
30"
3-9
LENGTH OF WELDS OR INCREMENTS. OMISSION INDICATES THAT WELD EXTENDS BETWEEN ABRUPT CHANGES IN DIRECTION OR AS DIMENSIONED.
PITCH (DISTANCE BETWEEN CENTERS) OF INCREMENTS.
DOUBLE-FILLET WELDING SYMBOL
SIZE (LENGTH OF LEG).
SPECIFICATION, PROCESS OR OTHER REFERENCE.
G
1/4
12
LENGTH. OMISSION INDICATES THAT WELD EXTENDS BETWEEN ABRUPT CHANGES IN DIRECTION OR AS DIMENSIONED.
SINGLE-V GROOVE WELDING SYMBOL INDICATING ROOT PENETRATION
SIZE
DEPTH OF CHAMFERING PLUS ROOT PENETRATION
1/4 + 1/2
0
90°
ROOT OPENING.
GROOVE ANGLE.
SLOT WELDING SYMBOL
DEPTH OF FILLING IN INCHES. OMISSION INDICATES FILLING IS COMPLETE.
5/8
ORIENTATION, LOCATION AND ALL DIMENSIONS OTHER THAN DEPTH OF FILLING ARE SHOWN ON THE DRAWING.
FLASH OR UPSET WELDING SYMBOL
A-2
PROCESS REFERENCE. MUST BE USED TO INDICATE PROCESS DESIRED.
CHAIN-INTERMITTENT-FILLET WELDING SYMBOL
SIZE (LENGTH OF LEG).
5/16
2-6
LENGTH OF INCREMENTS.
PITCH (DISTANCE BETWEEN CENTERS) OF INCREMENTS.
DOUBLE-BEVEL GROOVE WELDING SYMBOL
OMISSION OF SIZE DIMENSION INDICATES A TOTAL DEPTH OF CHAMFERING EQUAL TO THICKNESS OF MEMBERS.
GROOVE ANGLE.
1/8
50°
ARROW POINTS TOWARD MEMBER TO BE CHAMFERED.
ROOT OPENING.
SPOT WELDING SYMBOL
SIZE (DIA. OF WELD). MIN. ACCEPTABLE SHEAR STRENGTH IN LB. PER WELD MAY BE USED INSTEAD.
.25"
(5)
4
NUMBER OF WELDS.
PITCH (DISTANCE BETWEEN CENTERS) OF INCREMENTS.
BRAZING, FORGE, THERMIT, INDUCTION AND FLOW WELDING SYMBOL
PROCESS REFERENCE MUST BE USED TO INDICATE PROCESS DESIRED.
B-8
SUPPLEMENTARY SYMBOLS USED WITH WELDING SYMBOLS
WELD-ALL-AROUND SYMBOL
WELD-ALL-AROUND SYMBOL INDICATES THAT WELD EXTENDS COMPLETELY AROUND THE JOINT
FIELD WELD SYMBOL
FIELD WELD SYMBOL. INDICATES THAT WELD IS TO BE MADE AT A PLACE OTHER THAN THAT OF INITIAL CONSTRUCTION
FLUSH-CONTOUR SYMBOL
FLUSH-CONTOUR SYMBOL. INDICATES FACE OF WELD TO BE MADE FLUSH. WHEN USED WITHOUT A FINISH SYMBOL, INDICATES WELD TO BE MADE FLUSH WITHOUT SUBTRACTIVE FINISHING.
M
FINISH SYMBOL (USER'S STD.) INDICATES METHOD OF OBTAINING SPECIFIED CONTOUR BUT NOT DEGREE OF FINISH.
CONVEX-CONTOUR SYMBOL
CONVEX-CONTOUR SYMBOL INDICATES FACE OF WELD TO BE FINISHED TO CONVEX CONTOUR.
G
FINISH SYMBOL (USER'S STD.) INDICATES METHOD OF OBTAINING SPECIFIED CONTOUR BUT NOT DEGREE OF FINISH.

Approved as American Standard, A.S.A. Z32.2.1-1949 by American Standards Association Reaffirmed-1953.

LIGHTWEIGHT STEEL JOISTS and BEAMS

PRELIMINARY SELECTION OF LIGHTWEIGHT STEEL JOISTS AND BEAMS

The tables used on this page on depths of joists and beams are not to be used for final design but are intended to serve as an aid to the architect in speeding selection of members for preliminary design and planning

The engineering design should of course be a separate and thorough process involving a complete investigation of the pertinent conditions This page is not for that purpose.

EXAMPLE: Assume the architect has in mind a particular clear span for the building he is designing. By selecting a spacing and estimating the total load, a member can immediately be selected from the table. The architect can then proceed with preliminary design studies.

NOTE: "Total Load" = Live Load plus Dead Load. Dead load used in tables includes weight of joist or beam. For recommended Live loads, see page on "Weights of Materials". Local code will govern.

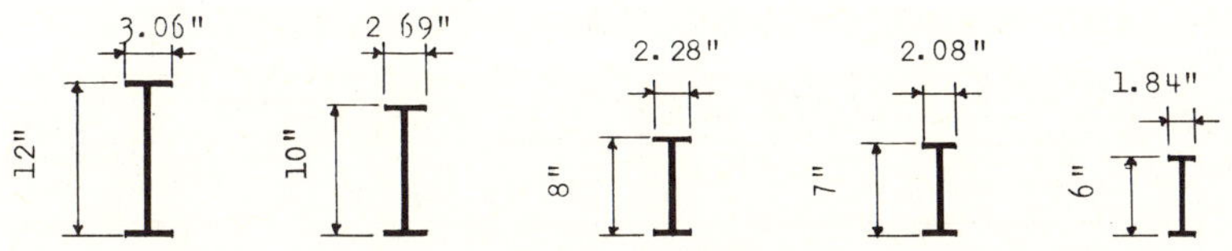
3.06"
2.69"
2.28"
2.08"
1.84"
12"
10"
8"
7"
6"

J & L JUNIOR BEAMS

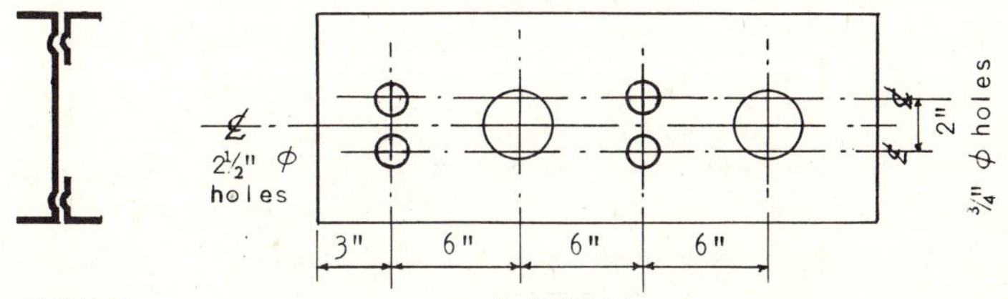
2½" ϕ holes
¾" ϕ holes
2"
3"
6"
6"
6"

SECTION ELEVATION

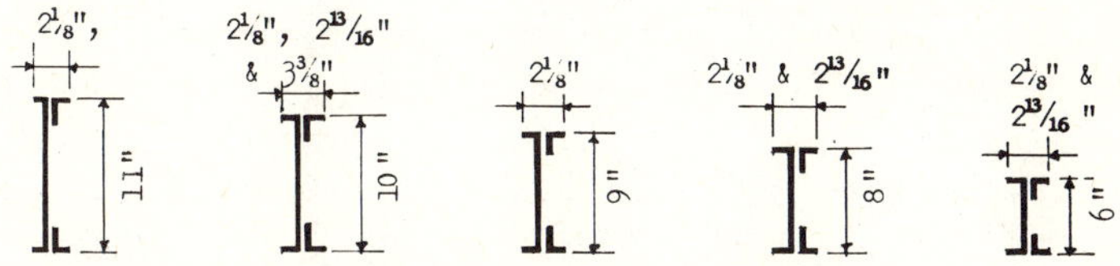
2⅛",
11"
2⅛", 2 13/16" & 3 3/8"
10"
2⅛"
9"
2⅛" & 2 13/16"
8"
2⅛" & 2 13/16"
6"

LIGHTSTEEL JOIST SIZES

DEPTHS (IN INCHES) OF J & L JUNIOR BEAMS FOR PRELIMINARY DESIGNS

TOTAL LOAD psf.	SPACING (inches)	SPAN IN FEET						
		10	12	14	16	18	20	22
80	12	6	6	6	6	7	7	8
	16	6	6	6	7	8	8	10
	20	6	6	6	7	8	10	10
	24	6	6	7	7	8	10	10
100	12	6	6	6	6	7	8	10
	16	6	6	6	7	8	10	10
	20	6	6	7	7	8	10	10
	24	6	6	7	8	10	10	12
120	12	6	6	6	7	8	8	10
	16	6	6	7	7	8	10	10
	20	6	6	7	8	10	10	12
	24	6	7	7	8	10	10	12
140	12	6	6	6	7	8	10	10
	16	6	6	7	8	8	10	10
	20	6	7	7	8	10	10	12
	24	6	7	8	10	10	12	12
160	12	6	6	6	7	8	10	10
	16	6	6	7	8	10	10	12
	20	6	7	8	10	10	12	12
	24	6	7	8	10	10	12	12
180	12	6	6	7	8	10	10	10
	16	6	7	8	8	10	10	12
	20	6	7	8	10	10	12	12
	24	7	8	10	10	12	12	-

NOTE: For wider spacing see manufacturer's literature.

DEPTHS (INCHES) OF LIGHTWEIGHT STEEL JOISTS FOR PRELIMINARY DESIGN

TOTAL LOAD psf.	SPACING (inches)	SPAN IN FEET						
		10	12	14	16	18	20	22
80	12	6	6	6	8	8	10	10
	16	6	6	8	8	10	10	10
	20	8	8	10	-	-	-	-
	24	8	8	10	-	-	-	-
100	12	6	6	8	8	10	10	10
	16	6	8	8	10	-	-	-
	20	8	8	-	-	-	-	-
	24	8	-	-	-	-	-	-
120	12	6	6	8	8	10	10	10
	16	8	8	10	10	-	-	-
	20	8	-	-	-	-	-	-
140	12	6	8	8	10	10	10	-
160	12	6	8	10	10	-	-	-
180	12	6	8	10	10	-	-	-

NOTE: Consult manufacturer's literature for weights to determine economical members.

BRIDGING FOR J & L JUNIOR BEAMS

JOIST SPAN	BRIDGING SPACING
To 14'-0"	1 row near center of span
14'-0" to 21'-0"	2 rows approx. at ⅓ points of span
21'-0" & over	3 rows approx. at ¼ points of span

BRIDGING FOR LIGHTSTEEL JOISTS

JOIST SPAN	BRIDGING SPACING
To 14'-0"	1 row at center of span
14'-0" to 21'-0"	2 rows ¼ span apart, symmetrical around center of span
21'-0" & over	3 rows, ¼ span apart

J & L DATA CHECKED BY JONES & LAUGHLIN STEEL CORPORATION

LIGHTSTEEL DATA CHECKED BY PENN METAL COMPANY

SHORT SPAN OPEN WEB BAR JOISTS

PRELIMINARY SELECTION OF SHORT SPAN BAR JOISTS

The table below on Depths of Short Span Bar Joists is not to be used for final joist design, but is intended to serve as an aid to the architect in speeding selection of bar joists for preliminary design and planning.

The engineering design should of course be a separate and thorough process, involving a complete investigation of the pertinent conditions. This page is not for that purpose.

EXAMPLE: assume the architect has in mind a particular clear span for the building he is designing. By selecting a joist spacing and estimating the total load, a joist can immediately be selected from the table. The architect can then proceed with preliminary design studies.

NOTE: "Total Load" = Live Load plus Dead Load. Dead load used in table below includes weight of joist. For recommended live loads, see page on "Weights of Materials". Local codes will govern.

Joist designation in table is that generally used on structural plans.

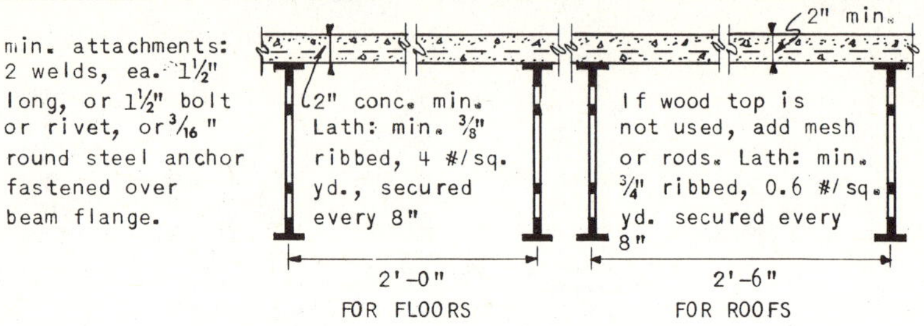
min. attachments: 2 welds, ea. 1½" long, or 1½" bolt or rivet, or 3/16" round steel anchor fastened over beam flange.
2" min.
2" conc. min. Lath: min. 3/8" ribbed, 4 #/sq. yd., secured every 8"
If wood top is not used, add mesh or rods. Lath: min. 3/4" ribbed, 0.6 #/sq. yd. secured every 8"
2'-0"
FOR FLOORS
2'-6"
FOR ROOFS

MAXIMUM JOIST SPACING

DIAGONAL BRIDGING SPACING	
JOIST SPAN	MAXIMUM SPACING
to 14'-0"	1 row, center of span (roofs only)
14'-0" to 21'-0"	2 rows approx. 1/4" span apart, symmetrical about center
21'-0" to 32'-0"	3 rows at 1/4 points of span
32'-0" to 40'-0"	4 rows at 1/5 points of span
NOTE: No span to exceed 24 times joist depth. Above bridging is in addition to safety header at center of span (floors only).	

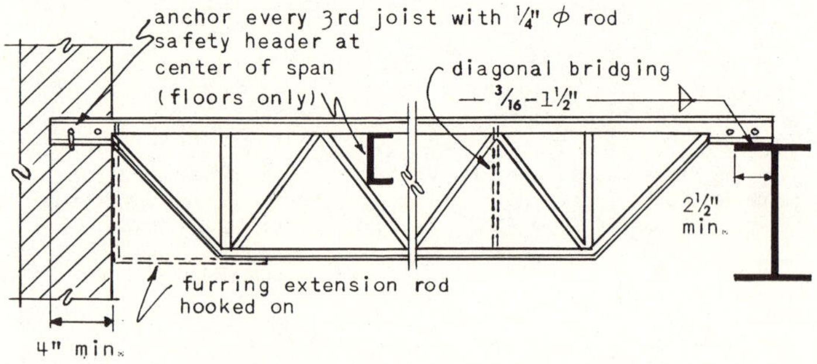
anchor every 3rd joist with 1/4" φ rod
safety header at center of span (floors only)
diagonal bridging — 3/16-1½"
2½" min.
furring extension rod hooked on
4" min.

SECTION THRU JOIST BEARING

FIRE RESISTANCE RATINGS		
HRS.	TOP SLAB	CEILING
3/4	1" T&G on 2" x 2" wood strips attached to joists.	3/4" sanded gyp. plas. on metal or wire lath.
1 to 1½	2" reinf. conc., or 2" precast reinf. gypsum tile	3/4" portland cement sand plas. or 3/4" sanded gyp. plas.
2	2¼" reinf. conc., or 2" reinf. gyp. tile with 1/4" mortar finish	3/4" sanded gyp. plas.
2½	2" reinf. conc., or 2" reinf. gyp. tile with 1/4" mortar finish	1" neat gyp. plas. or gyp.-vermiculite plas.
	2½" reinf. conc.	7/8" sanded gyp. plas.
3	2½" reinf. conc., or 2" reinf. gyp. tile with 1/2" mortar finish	1" neat gyp. plas. or 3/4" gyp.-vermiculite plas.
*	2" conc. fl. slab on metal lath or 2¾" reinf. portland cement conc. plank	1" gyp.-vermiculite plas. on metal lath
4	2½" reinf. conc. or 2" reinf. gyp. slabs with 1/2" mortar finish	1" gyp.-vermiculite plas. on metal lath.
Ratings are by Nat'l. Bur. of Standards, except for *: NBFU.		

DEPTH OF SHORT SPAN BAR JOISTS FOR PRELIMINARY ASSUMPTIONS

(To find depth of joist, drop last figure. E.g., 126 joist is 12 inches deep.)

TOTAL LOAD, psf	JOIST SPAC'G, inches	CLEAR SPAN, Feet												
		8	10	12	14	16	18	20	22	24	26	28	30	32
80	20	81	81	81	82	82	103	103	124	124	145	146	166	166
	24	81	81	82	82	102	103	123	125	125	146	146	166	167
	30	81	82	82	102	103	104	124	126	126	146	147	167	187
100	20	81	81	82	82	103	103	104	125	126	146	146	166	167
	24	81	82	82	102	103	104	125	126	126	146	147	167	187
	30	81	82	102	123	104	145	145	---	186	186	187	207	---
120	20	81	82	82	102	103	104	125	126	126	146	147	167	187
	24	81	82	82	123	123	145	145	126	186	186	187	207	---
	30	81	82	---	123	---	145	---	--	---	---	---	---	---
140	20	81	82	82	123	123	124	125	126	146	147	167	207	---
	24	81	82	102	123	---	145	---	---	186	---	---	---	---
160	20	81	82	123	---	145	---	---	186	---	---	---	---	---
180	12	81	81	82	102	103	104	124	125	145	146	147	167	167
	20	81	82	---	123	---	145	---	---	---	---	---	---	---
200	12	81	82	82	102	103	104	125	126	126	146	147	167	187

Data checked by Elwyn E. Seelye, Consulting Engineer

LONG SPAN OPEN WEB BAR JOISTS

PRELIMINARY SELECTION OF LONG SPAN BAR JOISTS

The table below on Depth of Long Span Bar Joists is not to be used for final joist design but is intended to serve as an aid to the architect in speeding selection of bar joists for preliminary design and planning.

The engineering design should of course be a separate and thorough process, involving a complete investigation of the pertinent conditions. This page is not for that purpose.

EXAMPLE: assume the architect has in mind a particular clear span for the building he is designing. By selecting a joist spacing and estimating the total load, a joist can immediately be selected from the table. The architect can then proceed with preliminary design studies.

NOTE: "Total Load" equals Live Load plus Dead Load. Dead load used in table below includes weight of joist. For recommended live loads, see page on "Weights of Materials". Local codes will govern.

Joists will span to 96'-0" of clear opening, but from approximately 70'-0" to 96'-0" are primarily for roof construction only.

Joists given within heavy boxes are for roof construction only. Shallow joist allowable because span may be 24 x depth for roof joists.

Joist designation in table is that generally used on structural plans.

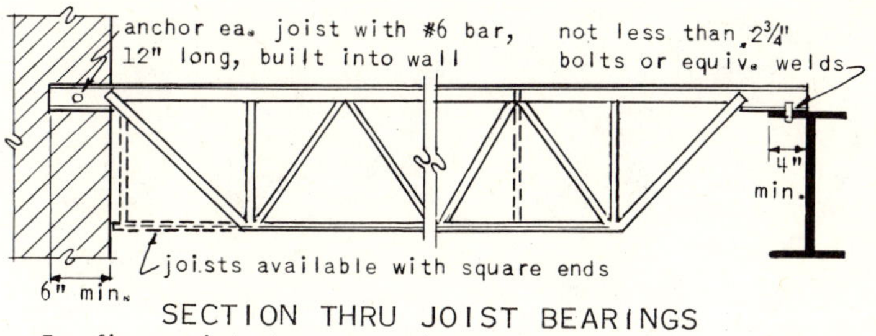
anchor ea. joist with #6 bar, 12" long, built into wall
not less than 2¾" bolts or equiv. welds
4" min.
joists available with square ends
6" min.

SECTION THRU JOIST BEARINGS

For fire-resistant construction, see page on "Short Span Open Web Bar Joists"

BRIDGING SPACING	
JOIST TYPE	MAXIMUM SPACING
Suffix 2 thru 8	10'-0" o.c.
" 9 " 16	12'-0" o.c.
" 17 " 19	16'-0" o.c.

Maximum spacing not to exceed values given above for each joist type. Joist span not to exceed 24 x depth for roofs, 20 x depth for floors. When bearing on masonry, limit clear spans to 80'-0".

DEPTH OF LONG SPAN BAR JOISTS FOR PRELIMINARY ASSUMPTIONS

(The number preceding letter is joist depth. E.g., 32L13 is 32 inches deep.)

TOTAL LOAD, psf	JOIST SPAC'G.	CLEAR SPAN, feet 25	30	35	40	45	50	55	60	65	70
100	2' o.c.	18L02	18L02	18L04	20L05	24L06	28L06	32L07	32L08	36L09	36L10
				24L04	24L04	28L06	32L07	36L08	36L08	40L09	44L10
	4' o.c.	18L05	18L07	18L10	20L11	24L12	28L13	32L13	32L14	36L15	36L16
				24L08	24L10	28L11	32L12	36L13	36L14	40L14	44L15
120	2' o.c.	18L02	18L04	18L05	20L06	24L07	28L08	32L08	32L10	36L11	36L12
				24L04	24L06	28L06	32L07	36L08	36L09	40L10	44L11
	4' o.c.	18L06	18L09	18L12	20L13	24L13	28L14	32L15	32L16	36L16	36L17
				24L10	24L12	28L13	32L13	36L14	36L15	40L16	44L16
140	2' o.c.	18L02	18L04	18L07	20L08	24L08	28L09	32L10	32L12	36L12	36L13
				24L06	24L07	28L08	32L08	36L10	36L11	40L12	44L12
	4' o.c.	18L08	18L11	20L13	24L13	28L18	32L15	32L16	36L17	40L17	40L18
				24L12				36L16			44L18
160	2' o.c.	18L04	18L06	18L08	20L09	24L10	28L10	32L11	32L13	36L13	36L14
				24L06	24L08	28L09	32L10	36L11	36L12	40L13	44L13
180	2' o.c.	18L04	18L06	18L08	20L10	24L11	28L11	32L12	32L13	36L14	36L15
				24L07	24L09	28L10	32L11	36L12	36L13	40L13	44L14
200	2' o.c.	18L05	18L07	18L10	20L11	24L12	28L12	32L13	32L14	36L15	36L16
				24L08	24L10	28L11	32L12	36L13	36L14	40L14	44L15
220	2' o.c.	18L06	18L08	18L11	20L12	24L13	28L13	32L14	32L15	36L16	36L16
				24L09	24L11	28L12	32L13	36L13	36L15	40L15	44L16
240	2' o.c.	18L06	18L09	18L12	20L13	24L13	28L13	32L15	32L16	36L16	36L17
				24L10	24L12	28L13	32L13	36L14	36L15	40L16	44L16

Data checked by Elwyn E. Seelye, Consulting Engineer

LALLY COLUMNS

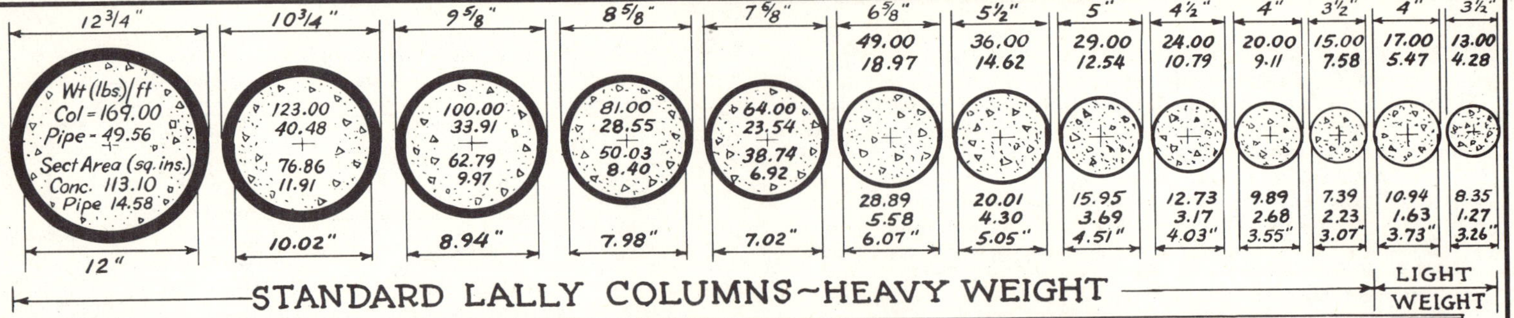
12 3/4"
Wt (lbs)/ft
Col = 169.00
Pipe - 49.56
Sect Area (sq. ins.)
Conc. 113.10
Pipe 14.58
12"
10 3/4"
123.00
40.48
76.86
11.91
10.02"
9 5/8"
100.00
33.91
62.79
9.97
8.94"
8 5/8"
81.00
28.55
50.03
8.40
7.98"
7 6/8"
64.00
23.54
38.74
6.92
7.02"
6 5/8"
49.00
18.97
28.89
5.58
6.07"
5 1/2"
36.00
14.62
20.01
4.30
5.05"
5"
29.00
12.54
15.95
3.69
4.51"
4 1/2"
24.00
10.79
12.73
3.17
4.03"
4"
20.00
9.11
9.89
2.68
3.55"
3 1/2"
15.00
7.58
7.39
2.23
3.07"
4"
17.00
5.47
10.94
1.63
3.73"
3 1/2"
13.00
4.28
8.35
1.27
3.26"
STANDARD LALLY COLUMNS~HEAVY WEIGHT
LIGHT WEIGHT

EXAMPLE of LALLY COL. DESIGN WITH ECCENTRIC LOADS

GIVEN:
9'-0" Unbraced Hgt. of Column.
Concentric load = 80 Kips
One Eccentric load = 10 Kips and one 5 Kips.

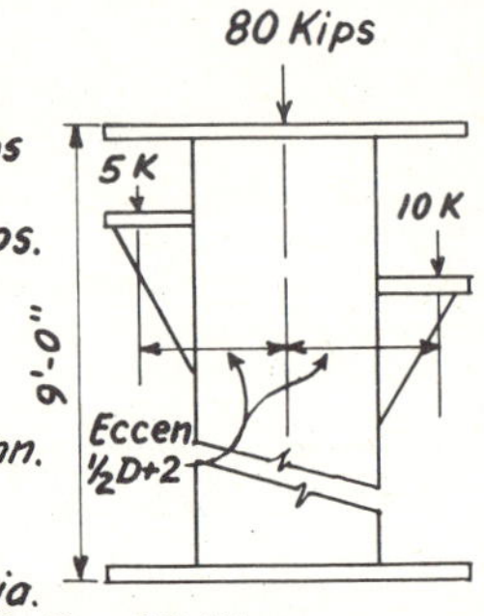
80 Kips
5 K
10 K
9'-0"
Eccen
1/2D+2

FIND:
Required Size of Column.

SOLUTION:
1. Assume a col. 6 5/8" Dia.
2. Direct Load = 80 + 10 + 5 = 95 Kips
3. Resultant eccentric load 10 − 5 = 5 Kips
4. Bending moment = $5(\frac{6\frac{5}{8}}{2}+2)$ = 26,500" lbs.
5. From safe loads table for 6 5/8" dia. col. the equivalent direct load = $\frac{26,500}{10,000} \times 7.4 = 19.5$ K.
6. Equivalent total load = 95 + 19.5 = 114.5 Kips.
7. From "Safe loads" table, a 6 5/8" dia. col. with 9'-0" unbraced height is good for 116 K. {NOTE: FOR OTHER ECCENTRIC LOAD CONDITIONS, SEE FOLLOWING SHEET.

SAFE LOADS (IN THOUSANDS OF POUNDS)

DIA. OF COL. in inches	MAX. LENGTH (feet)	Unbraced Length of Column (in feet)															*(f) ECCENTRIC LOADS
		6	7	8	9	10	11	12	13	14	15	16	17	18	19	20	
3 1/2	9.0	26.1	24.2	22.2	20.3												
4	9.0	35.6	33.4	31.2	29.0												
3 1/2	11.64	37.9	35.1	32.3	29.4	26.7	24.0										13.3
4	13.37	49.2	46.1	43.1	40.1	37.0	33.9	30.9	27.9								11.9
4 1/2	15.10	61.8	58.5	55.3	52.0	48.8	45.5	42.3	39.0	35.8	32.5						10.8
5	16.83	75.6	72.0	68.6	65.2	61.7	58.2	54.7	51.3	47.8	44.3	40.9	37.4				9.8
5 1/2	18.78	92.1	88.3	84.6	80.8	77.1	73.3	69.6	65.8	62.1	58.3	54.6	50.8	47.1	43.3		8.3
6 5/8	22.45	128.3	124.2	120.0	115.8	111.7	107.5	103.4	99.2	95.0	90.9	86.7	82.6	78.4	74.2	70.1	7.4
7 5/8	25.92	166.0	161.4	156.9	152.3	147.8	143.2	138.6	134.1	129.7	125.0	120.5	115.9	111.4	106.8	102.3	6.7
8 5/8	29.38	211.1	206.1	201.1	196.1	191.0	186.0	181.0	175.9	170.9	165.9	160.8	155.8	150.8	145.8	140.7	5.8
9 5/8	32.84	259.2	253.8	248.3	242.8	237.4	231.9	226.5	221.0	215.6	210.1	204.6	199.2	193.7	188.3	182.8	5.4
10 3/4	36.74	319.1	313.1	307.2	301.3	295.4	289.4	283.5	277.6	271.6	265.7	259.7	253.8	247.9	241.9	236.0	4.9
12 3/4	43.77	421.9	415.4	408.8	402.3	395.8	389.2	382.8	376.2	369.7	363.2	356.7	350.1	343.6	337.1	330.6	4.2

* FOR EACH 10,000 IN. LBS. UNBALANCED MOMENT ON COLUMN, ADD THE NO. OF KIPS AS SHOWN TO THE SUM OF ALL VERTICAL LOADS. SAFE LOAD FORMULA: $P=(A_c+12A_s)(1600-24\,L/d)$ WHERE P = SAFE CARRYING CAPACITY IN LBS. A_c = AREA OF CONC. IN SQ. IN., A_s = AREA OF STEEL IN SQ. IN., L = LENGTH OF COL. IN INCHES, d = DIA. OF COL IN IN.

STANDARD BASE PLATES AND CAPS

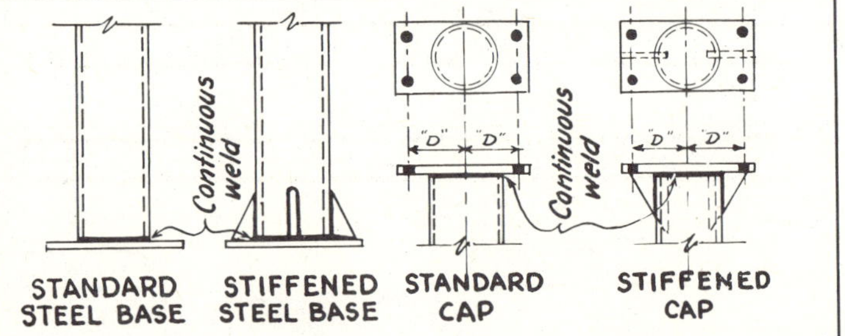
Continuous weld
"D"
"D"
Continuous weld
"D"
"D"
STANDARD STEEL BASE
STIFFENED STEEL BASE
STANDARD CAP
STIFFENED CAP

BASE PLATES *					CAPS		
COL. DIA	SIZE of BASE	SAFE LOAD IN KIPS	THICKNESS of BASE		DISTANCE "D"		THICKNESS OF CAP
			Standard	Stiffened	Standard	Stiffened	
3 1/2	8 × 8	32.0	5/8	1/2	3 1/4	4 1/4	1/2
4	9 × 9	40.5	3/4	1/2	3 1/2	4 1/2	1/2
4 1/2	10 × 10	50.0	7/8	1/2	3 3/4	4 3/4	1/2
5	12 × 12	72.0	1	1/2	4	5	5/8
5 1/2	14 × 14	98.0	1 1/4	3/4	4 1/4	5 1/4	5/8
6 5/8	16 × 16	128.0	1 1/4	3/4	4 3/4	6 1/4	3/4
7 5/8	18 × 18	162.0	1 1/2	3/4	5	6 3/4	3/4
8 5/8	20 × 20	200.0	1 3/4	3/4	5 3/4	7 1/4	3/4
9 5/8	22 × 22	242.0	1 3/4	3/4	6 1/4	7 3/4	3/4
10 3/4	24 × 24	288.0	2	7/8	7	8 1/4	3/4
12 3/4	28 × 28	392.0	2 1/4	7/8	8	9	3/4

* ASSUMED BEARING OF BASES = 500 lbs/sq. in.

NOTE: *To insure that new steel pipe of the proper thickness is furnished, always specify the weight in lbs. per. ft. of the col. on plans as given in diagrams.*

STANDARD & FIREPROOF LALLY COLUMNS

Load Bearing Shaft
Concrete Fill
Steel Shaft
Standard Lally Col.
Fireproofed Lally Col.

TYPICAL DETAILS

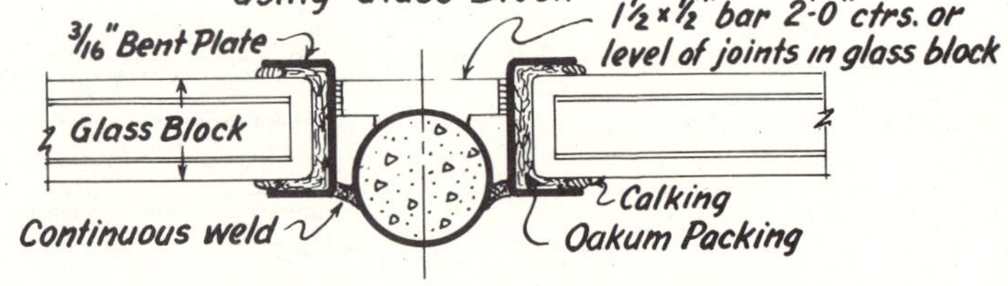
Using Glass Block
3/16" Bent Plate
1 1/2 × 1/2" bar 2'-0" ctrs. or level of joints in glass block
Glass Block
Calking
Oakum Packing
Continuous weld

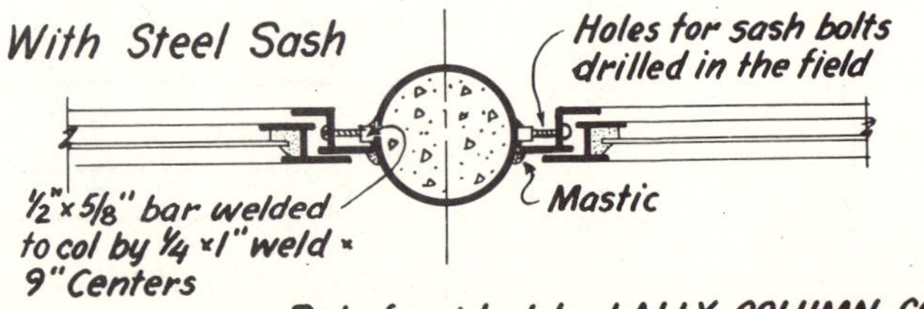
With Steel Sash
Holes for sash bolts drilled in the field
Mastic
1/2" × 5/8" bar welded to col by 1/4 × 1" weld × 9" Centers

Data furnished by LALLY COLUMN CO.

LALLY COLUMNS

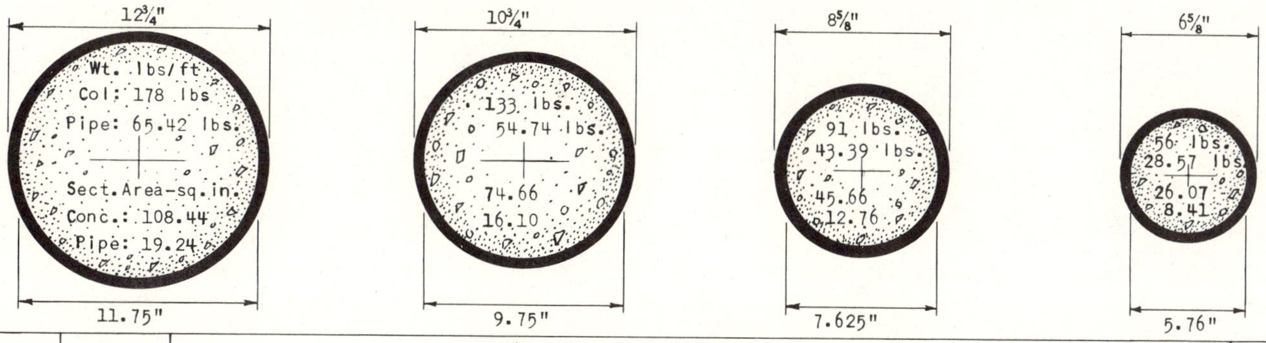

12¾"
Wt. lbs/ft
Col: 178 lbs
Pipe: 65.42 lbs.
Sect. Area–sq. in.
Conc.: 108.44
Pipe: 19.24
11.75"
10¾"
133 lbs.
54.74 lbs.
74.66
16.10
9.75"
8⅝"
91 lbs.
43.39 lbs.
45.66
12.76
7.625"
6⅝"
56 lbs.
28.57 lbs
26.07
8.41
5.76"

DIA. OF COL. in inches	MAX. LENGTH in feet	SAFE LOAD IN THOUSANDS OF POUNDS UNBRACED LENGTH OF COLUMN - IN FEET																(f) Ecc. Loads 10,000 in lbs. Bend. Mo.
		10	11	12	13	14	15	16	17	18	19	20	24	28	32	36	40	
6⅝	21.95	148	143	137	132	126	121	115	110	104	99	93						7.7
8⅝	28.78	250	244	239	232	225	219	212	206	199	192	185	157	129				6.0
10¾	36.28	356	349	342	335	328	321	314	306	298	292	285	255	225	197	169		4.8
12¾	43.35	468	460	452	444	436	428	420	412	405	397	389	360	328	296	264	232	4.1

EXTRA HEAVYWEIGHT LALLY COLUMNS

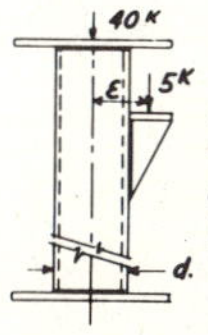

40K
5K
e
d.

Direct Load = $40^K + 5^K = 45^K$
Eccentric Load = 5^K
Bending Moment = $5(\frac{1}{2}d+2)$ *in/lbs* = M
Equiv. Direct Load = $\frac{M}{10,000} \times f = C$
Total Col. Load = $(45+C)^K$

Standard Bracket 1 Ecc. load

CASE A

Direct Load = $80^K + 10^K + 5^K = 95^K$
Resultant Ecc. Load = $10^K - 5^K = 5^K$
Bending Moment = $5(\frac{1}{2}d+2)$ *in/lbs* = M
Equiv. Direct Load = $\frac{M}{10,000} \times f = C$
Total Col. Load = $(95+C)^K$

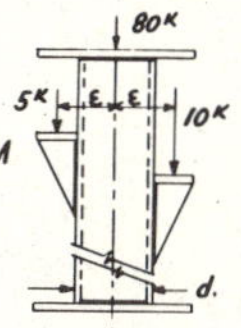

80K
5K
e
e
10K
d.

Standard Bracket 2 Ecc. loads

CASE B

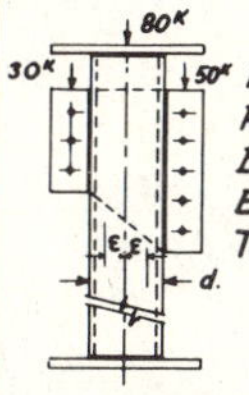

80K
30K
50K
e
e
d.

Direct Load = $80^K + 50^K + 30^K = 160^K$
Resultant Ecc. Load = $50^K - 30^K = 20^K$
Bending Mo. = $20 \times 0.3d$ *in/lbs* = M
Equiv. Direct Load = $\frac{M}{10,000} \times f = C$
Total Col. Load = $(160+C)^K$

Thru-Plate 2 Ecc. loads

CASE C

Determine moment in inch pounds with eccentricity "e" and transform into equivalent direct load by applying factor (f)

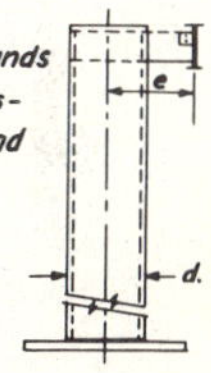

e
d.

Thru-Plate with load at rt. angles

CASE D

Methods of determining equivalent direct loads for each 10,000 in lbs bending monent using factors (f) given in safe load tables

ECCENTRIC LOAD MOVEMENT

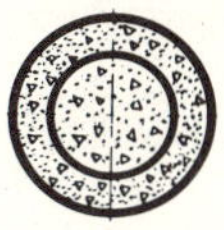

The difference in dia. of pipes min. of 4"

PIPE REINFORCEMENT

ANGLE REINFORCEMENT

Dia. of circle on which rods are located 2" less than dia. of pipe

ROD REINFORCEMENT

To increase the safe load capacity of a LALLY COLUMN, steel rod pipe or angle reinforcement may be embedded in the concrete. These methods of reinforcement are valuable where the diameter of the column must be limited, as for example, to eliminate pilaster projections in partitions or walls. The reinforcement is cut and placed to achieve full bearing on cap and base plates. Safe loads for reinforced LALLY COLUMNS are computed by the same formula as for unreinforced columns in which A_s represents the total area of the outer shell plus the reinforcement.

REINFORCED LALLY COLUMNS

Type 1
Single line of holes

Type 2
Double line of holes

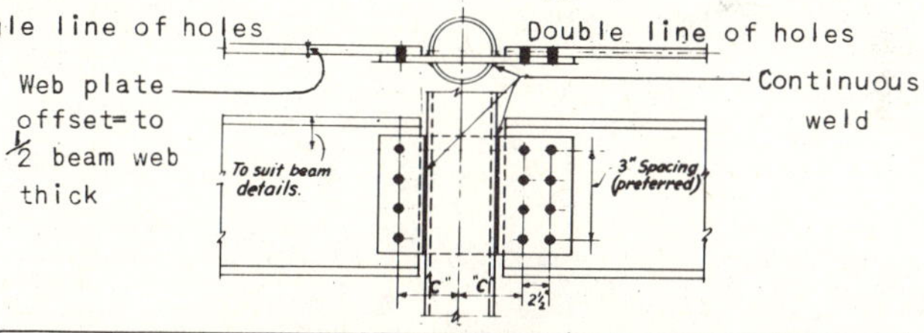

Web plate offset = to ½ beam web thick
Continuous weld
To suit beam details.
3" Spacing (preferred)
C
C
2½

DISTANCE "C" FROM THE C/L OF COL. TO THE FIRST LINE OF HOLES			
Dia. of Col.	Distance "C"	Dia. of Col.	Distance "C"
3½	3¾	7⅝	5⅞
4	4	8⅝	6⅜
4½	4¼	9⅝	6⅞
5	4½	10¾	7⅜
5½	4¾	12¾	8⅜
6⅝	5⅜		

THRU-WEB PLATE CONNECTIONS

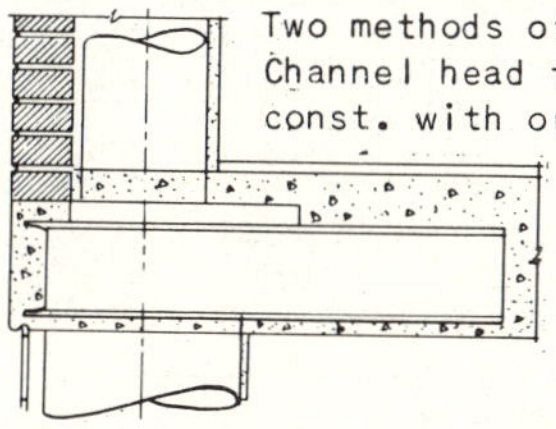

Two methods of adapting Lally Channel head to skeleton panel wall const. with or without spandel beam

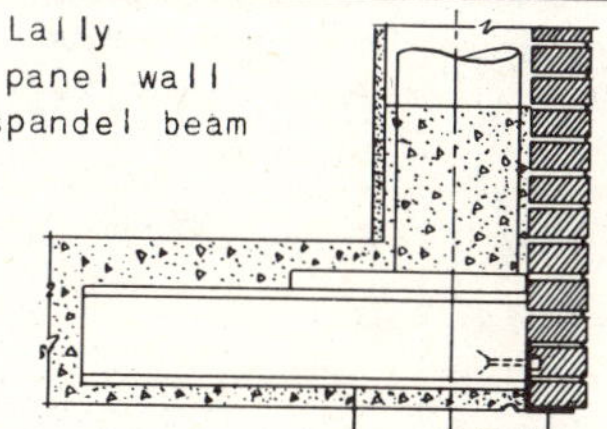

Outer arms of steel head can be omitted on exterior columns when spandel beam is designed both to support the column band load & to resist the torsion incident to negative restraint of the floor band

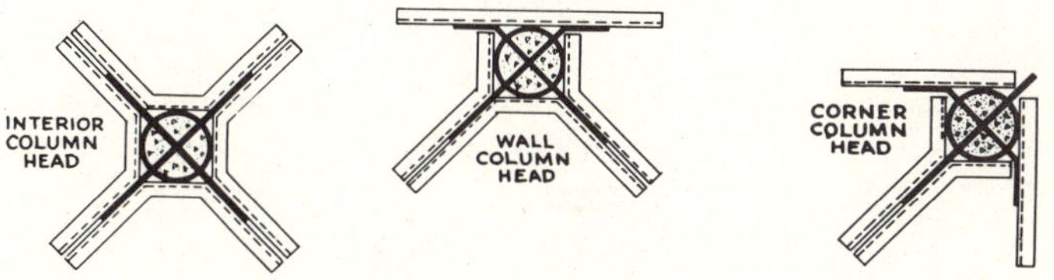

INTERIOR COLUMN HEAD
WALL COLUMN HEAD
CORNER COLUMN HEAD

TYPICAL CHANNEL HEADS

For safe loads of all connections & detail information of Lally Equidepth const. see Lally Col. Handbook

LALLY EQUIDEPTH CONSTRUCTION

MASONRY and STEEL LINTELS

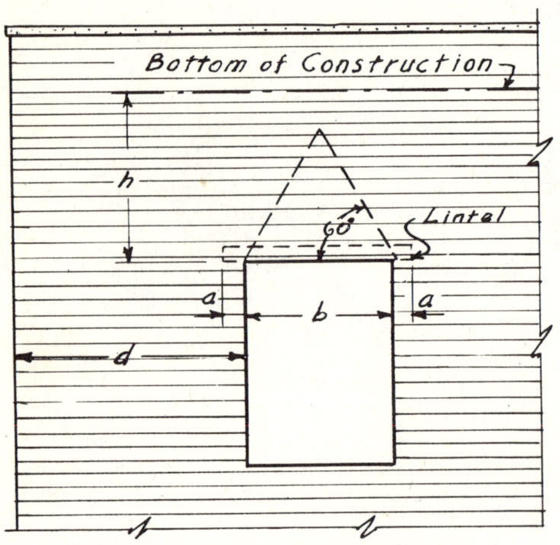
Bottom of Construction
h
Lintel
60°
a
b
a
d

SIMPLE LINTEL WITH ARCH ACTION

$M = .072Wb^3 + .108Wb^2a$

Used to determine the size of lintel required if distance "h" (to floor load) is equal to or greater than "b," and "d" at end walls is equal to or greater than "b".

NOTE:

In this type of lintel "W" is calculated as the weight of one square foot of wall × the area of the 60° triangle.

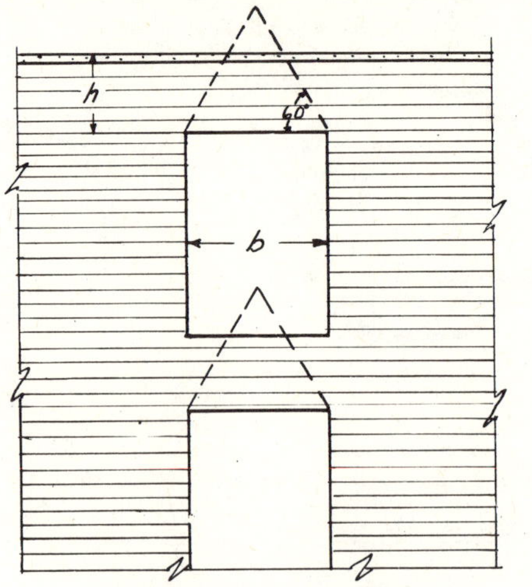
h
60°
b

SIMPLE LINTEL WITHOUT ARCH ACTION

$M = .125Whb^2 + .25Wbha$

Used to determine the size of lintel required if "h" is less than .6 "b" or if there is no arch action.

SYMBOLS USED

M = Maximum moment in ft.-lbs
W = Weight of wall in lbs/sq.ft.
b = clear span in feet
W' = floor load in lbs./ lineal ft.
h = height in feet
a = end bearing of lintel in ft.

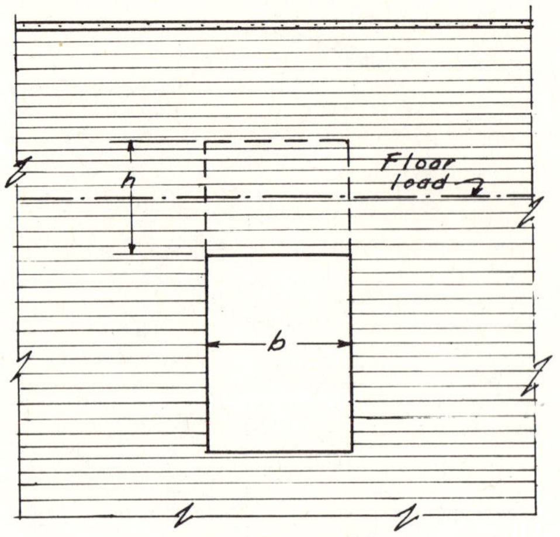
h
Floor load
b

LINTEL WITH FLOOR LOAD

$M = .125(Wh+W')b^2 + .25(Wh+W')ba$

Used to determine the size of lintel required if the bottom of floor construction is below "h" when "h" is equal to "b".

NOTE

This type of lintel must be designed to carry floor load (W') plus wall of "h" height.

TYPES of LINTEL CONDITIONS and their FORMULAE for MAX. BENDING MOMENT

These tables found on following pages can be used to determine the size lintel required for given spans.

LIST OF TABLES:

HOLLOW CLAY TILE LINTELS in TILE WALLS – № & SIZE of REINF. BARS REQ'D.

LINTEL SECTIONS	LINTEL SIZE	CLEAR SPAN	FLOOR LOAD IN LBS per SQ. FT. None	200	400	600	800	1000	WT. of TILE WALL (lbs/sq.ft.)
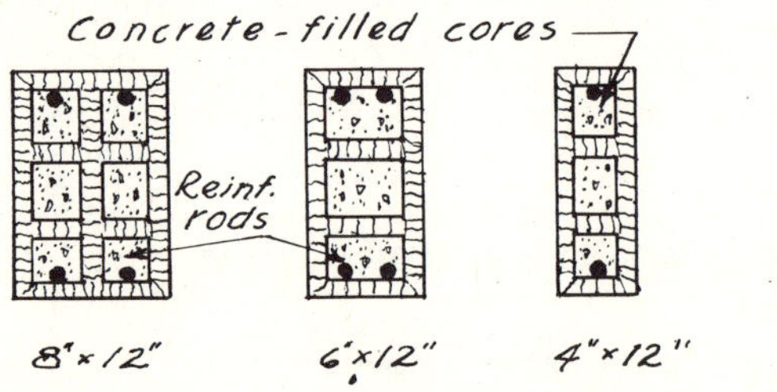 Concrete-filled cores Reinf. rods 8"×12" 6"×12" 4"×12"	8×12	4'-0"	Two #3ϕ	Two #3ϕ	Two #3ϕ	Two #3ϕ	Two #3ϕ	Two #3ϕ	46
		5'-0"							
		6'-0"			Two #4ϕ	Two #4ϕ			
	6×12	4'-0"	Two #3ϕ	Two #3ϕ	Two #3ϕ	Two #3ϕ	Two #3ϕ		41
		5'-0"							
		6'-0"							
	4×12	4'-0"	One #3ϕ	One #3ϕ	One #3ϕ	One #4ϕ			32
		5'-0"			One #4ϕ				
		6'-0"		One #4ϕ					
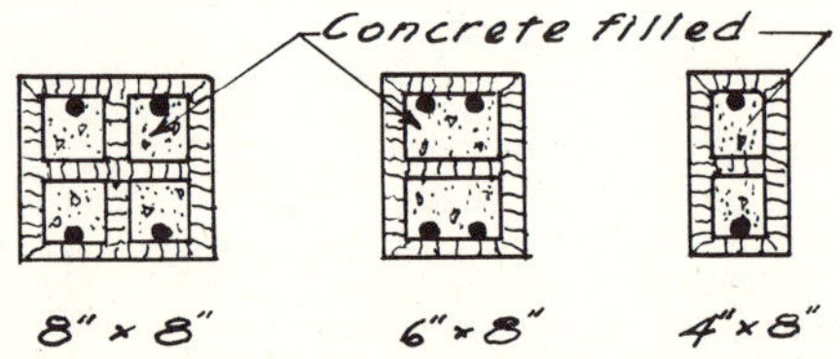 Concrete filled 8"×8" 6"×8" 4"×8" NOTE: All bars shown are top and bottom	8×8	4'-0"	Two #3ϕ	Two #3ϕ	Two #3ϕ	Two #3ϕ			46
		5'-0"			Two #4ϕ				
		6'-0"							
	6×8	4'-0"	Two #3ϕ	Two #3ϕ	Two #3ϕ	Two #3ϕ			41
		5'-0"							
		6'-0"							
	4×8	4'-0"	One #3ϕ	One #3ϕ					32
		5'-0"		One #2ϕ					
		6'-0"							

Data by Elwyn E. Seelye, Consulting Engineer

LOOSE STEEL and PRECAST CONCRETE LINTELS

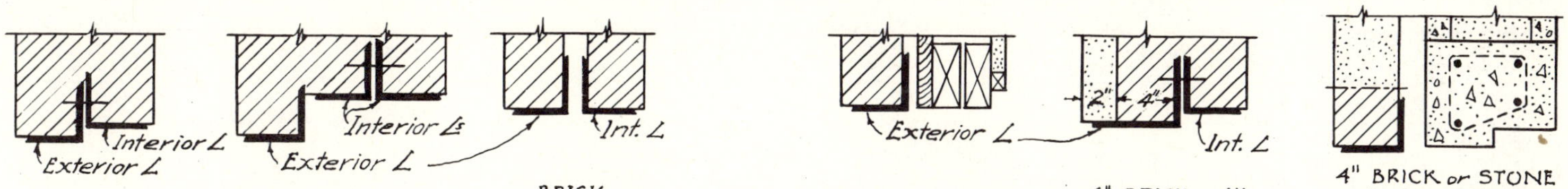
Interior ∠
Exterior ∠
Interior ∠s
Exterior ∠
Int. ∠
Exterior ∠
Int. ∠
2"
4"

8" BRICK — 12" BRICK — BRICK CAVITY WALL — BRICK VENEER — 4" BRICK with 2" STONE FACING — 4" BRICK or STONE with CONC. BLOCK or CLAY TILE.

LOOSE STEEL LINTELS for MASONRY — No. & SIZE of ANGLES REQ'D

CLEAR SPAN	EXTERIOR ANGLES for BRICK or STONE, No floor load: 4"	EXTERIOR ANGLES for BRICK or STONE, No floor load: 4"+2" stone facing	Wall Thickness	INTERIOR ANGLES — Maximum Floor Loads per Foot of Span: None	250	500	750	1000	1250	1500
4'-0" or less	∠-3½x3½x5/16	∠-3½x5x5/16	8	∠-3½x3½x5/16	∠-3½x3½x5/16	∠-3½x3½x5/16	∠-4x3½x5/16	∠-5x3½x5/16	∠-5x3½x3/8	∠-5x3½x7/16
			12	2∠s-3½x3½x5/16	2∠s 3½x3½x5/16	2∠s 3½x3½x5/16	2∠s 3½x3½x5/16	2∠s 3½x3½x5/16	2∠s 4x3½x5/16	2∠s 4x3½x5/16
5'-0"	∠-3½x3½x5/16	∠-3½x5x5/16	8	∠-3½x3½x5/16	∠-3½x3½x5/16	∠-5x3½x5/16	∠-5x3½x3/8	∠-5x3½x7/16	∠-6x3½x3/8	∠-7x4x3/8
			12	2∠s 3½x3½x5/16	2∠s 3½x3½x5/16	2∠s 3½x3½x5/16	2∠s 4x3½x5/16	2∠s 5x3½x5/16	2∠s 5x3½x5/16	2∠s 5x3½x3/8
6'-0"	∠-4x3½x5/16	∠-5x5x5/16	8	∠-4x3½x5/16	∠-5x3½x5/16	∠-5x3½x3/8	∠-6x3½x3/8	∠-7x4x3/8	∠-7x4x7/16	∠-7x4x7/16
			12	2∠s 4x3½x5/16	2∠s 4x3½x5/16	2∠s 5x3½x5/16	2-∠s 5x3½x5/16	2∠s 5x3½x3/8	2∠s 6x3½x3/8	2∠s 6x3½x3/8
7'-0"	∠-4x3½x5/16	∠-5x5x5/16	8	∠-4x3½x5/16	∠-5x3½x3/8	∠-6x4x3/8	∠-7x4x3/8	∠-8x4x7/16	∠-8x4x7/16	∠-8x4x½
			12	2∠s 4x3½x5/16	2∠s 5x3½x5/16	2∠s 5x3½x3/8	2∠s 6x3½x3/8	2∠s 6x4x3/8	2∠s 7x4x3/8	2∠s 7x4x3/8
8'-0"	∠-5x3½x5/16	∠-5x5x5/16	8	∠-5x3½x5/16	∠-6x3½x3/8	∠-7x4x3/8	∠-8x4x7/16	∠-8x4x½	∠-9x4x½	∠-9x4x9/16
			12	2∠s 5x3½x5/16	2∠s 5x3½x7/16	2∠s 6x3½x3/8	2∠s 7x4x3/8	2∠s 7x4x3/8	2∠s 7x4x7/16	2∠s 8x4x7/16
9'-0"	∠-5x3½x3/8	∠-5x5x3/8	8	∠-5x3½x3/8	∠-7x4x3/8	∠-8x4x7/16	∠-8x4x½	∠-9x4x½	∠-9x4x9/16	∠-9x4x¾
			12	2∠s 5x3½x3/8	2∠s 6x3½x3/8	2∠s 7x4x3/8	2∠s 7x4x7/16	2∠s 8x4x7/16	2∠s 8x4x7/16	2∠s 8x4x½
10'-0"	∠-6x3½x3/8	∠-5x5x½	8	∠-6x3½x3/8	∠-8x4x7/16	∠-8x4x½	∠-9x4x½	∠-9x4x5/8	∠-9x4x¾	∠-9x4x7/8
			12	2∠s 6x3½x3/8	2∠s 7x4x3/8	2∠s 8x4x7/16	2∠s 8x4x½	2∠s-8x4x½	2∠s 9x4x½	2∠s 9x4x½

6" min. bearing required for all lintels except - single angles below heavy line require 8"; below dash line, 10". Omit floor load on lintel when distance to bottom of floor construction is greater than width of opening. Interior & exterior angles in 8" walls and interior angles in 12" walls are bolted together when clear span of opening is over 6'-0". For economy, a double channel with pipe separators may be substituted for a pair of interior angles: 2-6" [ ] 8.2# for 2-7"x4"x3/8" & under; 2-7" [ ] 9.8# for 2-7"x4"x7/16; 2-8" [ ] 11.5# for 2-8"x4"x½" & under; 2-9" [ ] 13.4# for 2-9"x4"x½" & under. When masonry lighter than brick is used over interior angles floor load may be increased by the difference in weight per sq. ft. times the width of the opening. Interior angles have been designed for floor load plus brick masonry of ht. = width of opening. fs = 20,000#/□". Deflection max. 1/700 span.

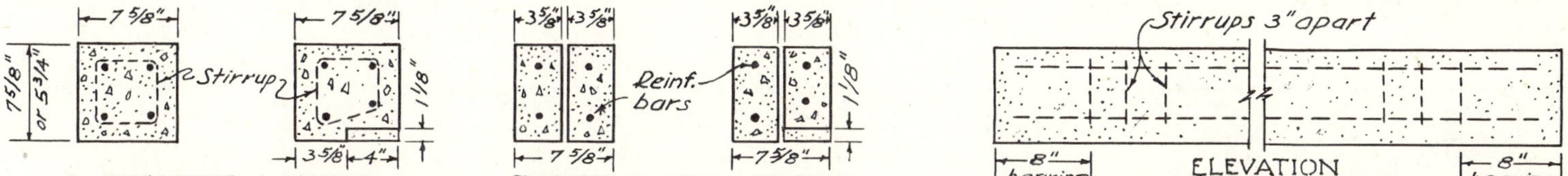
7 5/8"
7 5/8"
7 5/8" or 5 3/4"
Stirrup
1 1/8"
3 5/8"
4"
3 5/8"
3 5/8"
Reinf. bars
3 5/8"
3 5/8"
1 1/8"
7 5/8"
7 5/8"
Stirrups 3" apart
8" bearing
8" bearing

ONE PIECE LINTELS — TWO PIECE SPLIT LINTELS — ELEVATION of ONE PIECE LINTEL

PRECAST CONCRETE LINTELS — No. & SIZE of REINF. BARS REQUIRED

LINTEL SIZE	CLEAR SPAN	LINTEL IN BRICK WALL 80#/□' — Max. Floor Load in lbs per foot of clear span: None	250	500	750	1000	LINTEL IN CONCRETE BLOCK WALL 50#/□' — Max. Floor Load in lbs per ft. of clear span: None	250	500	750	1000
5¾"x7⅝"	4'-0"	Two #3 φ	Two #4 φ				Two #3 φ	Two #4 φ	Two #4 φ		
	5'-0"	Two #3 φ					Two #3 φ				
	6'-0"	Two #4 φ					Two #3 φ				
	7'-0"						Two #4 φ				
7⅝"x7⅝"	4'-0"	Two #3 φ	Two #3 φ	Two #4 φ	Two #4 φ	Two #5 φ [2]	Two #3 φ	Two #3 φ	Two #4 φ	Two #4 φ	Two #4 φ [2]
	5'-0"	Two #3 φ	Two #4 φ	Two #5 φ	Two #5 φ [5]	Two #6 φ [5]	Two #3 φ	Two #4 φ	Two #4 φ	Two #5 φ [4]	Two #6 φ [4]
	6'-0"	Two #4 φ	Two #5 φ	Two #6 φ [7]	Two #7 φ [7]	Two #8 φ [7]	Two #3 φ	Two #4 φ	Two #5 φ [7]	Two #6 φ [7]	Two #7 φ [7]
	7'-0"	Two #4 φ	Two #6 φ [7]	Two #8 φ [7]			Two #3 φ	Two #5 φ	Two #6 φ [7]	Two #7 φ [7]	
	8'-0"	Two #5 φ	Two #8 φ [7]				Two #4 φ	Two #6 φ [7]	Two #7 φ [7]		
	9'-0"	Two #6 φ					Two #4 φ	Two #8 φ [7]			
	10'-0"	Two #7 φ					Two #5 φ				

Lintels are modular sizes. fc = 3000#/□"; fs = 20,000#/□." [4] in table = no. of stirrups at each end of lintel. Lintels above heavy line require bars in bottom only, location of which must be indicated on lintel by fabricator. Lintels below heavy line require top & bottom bars the same size & stirrups as indicated. Two piece-split lintels can be used only if above heavy line & are not to carry floor loads unless bottom of floor construction is at least 12" above top of lintel. To use one piece lintel in 12" walls, increase reinf. to 3 bars or equiv. area & increase allowable floor loads by 50%.

Data by Elwyn E. Seelye, Consulting Engineer

CONCRETE "U" LINTELS, STEEL BEAMS and COLUMNS

PRECAST CONCRETE "U" LINTELS - NUMBER & SIZE of REINF. BARS REQUIRED

SECTION

6" LINTEL
5 5/8" wide
7 5/8" high

8" LINTEL
7 5/8" wide
7 5/8" high

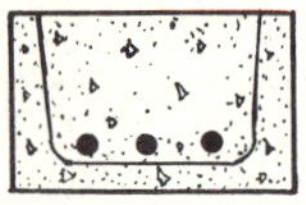

12" LINTEL
11 5/8" wide
7 5/8" high

TABLE

CLEAR SPAN	WIDTH OF WALL	NO. & SIZE OF REINF'G BARS
6'-0" & under	6"	Two #3 φ
8'-0" max.		Two #4 φ
6'-0" & under	8"	Two #3 φ
8'-0" max.		Two #4 φ
6'-0" & under	12"	Three #3 φ
8'-0" max.		Three #4 φ

NOTES

This type lintel is used to carry concrete block or lighter wall construction only. It is not recommended to carry any floor loads.

STEEL BEAMS for LIGHT CONSTRUCTION ~ MAX. UNIFORM LOADS in KIPS

TYPES of BEAMS - SIZES and WEIGHTS

SPAN	5I	*6B		6I	7I	*8B		8WF	8I	*10B			10WF	10I	*12B				12WF	12I
	10#	8.5#	12#	12.5#	15.3#	10#	13#	17#	18.4#	11.5#	15#	17#	21#	25.4#	14#	16.5#	19#	22	27#	31.8#
8'-0"	8.0	8.5	12.1	12.2	17.3	13.0	16.5	24.0	24.0	17.5	23.0	27.0	36.0	41.0	25.0	29.0	36.0	42.0	57.0	60.0
9'-0"	7.1	7.5	10.7	10.8	15.4	11.5	14.6	21.0	21.0	15.6	20.0	24.0	32.0	36.0	22.0	26.0	32.0	38.0	50.0	53.0
10'-0"	6.4	6.8	9.7	9.7	13.9	10.4	13.2	18.8	18.9	14.0	18.4	22.0	29.0	33.0	19.7	23.0	29.0	34.0	45.0	48.0
11'-0"	5.8	6.1	8.8	8.8	12.6	9.4	12.0	17.1	17.2	12.7	16.7	19.6	26.0	30.0	17.9	21.0	26.0	31.0	41.0	44.0
12'-0"		5.6	8.0	8.1	11.6	8.7	11.0	15.7	15.8	11.7	15.3	18.0	24.0	27.0	16.4	19.4	24.0	28.0	38.0	40.0
13'-0"		5.2	7.4	7.3	10.7	8.0	10.1	14.5	14.6	10.8	14.2	16.6	22.0	25.0	15.2	17.9	22.0	26.0	35.0	37.0
14'-0"					9.9	7.4	9.4	13.4	13.5	10.0	13.1	15.4	21.0	23.0	14.1	16.7	20.0	24.0	32.0	34.0
15'-0"					9.2	6.9	8.8	12.5	12.6	9.3	12.3	14.4	19.1	22.0	13.2	15.6	19.0	23.0	30.0	32.0
16'-0"						6.5	8.2	11.7	11.8	8.7	11.5	13.5	17.9	20.0	12.3	14.6	17.8	21.0	28.0	30.0
17'-0"						6.1	7.7	11.1	11.1	8.2	10.8	12.7	16.9	19.1	11.6	13.7	16.8	19.8	27.0	28.0
18'-0"										7.8	10.2	12.0	15.9	18.1	11.0	13.0	15.9	18.7	25.0	27.0
19'-0"										7.4	9.7	11.4	15.1	17.1	10.4	12.3	15.0	17.8	24.0	25.0
20'-0"										7.0	9.2	10.8	14.3	16.3	9.9	11.7	14.3	16.9	23.0	24.0

Loads below heavy lines cause deflection over 1/360 th of span. All loads are based on beams secured against lateral deflection. Unit stresses based on $M = \frac{Wl}{8}$; 20,000 lbs. per square inch.
*Bethlehem sections. Kip = 1000 lbs. (For beams not shown see A.I.S.C. handbook.)

STEEL COLUMNS for LIGHT CONSTRUCTION - MAX. CONCENTRIC LOADS in KIPS

TYPES of COLUMNS - SIZES and WEIGHTS

UNBRAC'D HEIGHT of COLUMN	I Miscellaneous				○ Standard Pipe Column				○ Extra Strong Pipe Column				● Double Extra Strong Pipe Column			
	*4M 13#	5M 18.9#	6WF 15.5#	*6WF 20#	3" 7.58#	3½" 9.11#	4" 10.79#	5" 14.62#	3" 10.25#	3½" 12.51#	4" 14.98#	5" 20.78#	3" 18.58#	3½" 22.85#	4" 27.54#	5" 38.55#
6'-0"	54	83	73	92	33	42	50	70	45	58	70	99	80	103	130	183
7'-0"	50	80	71	89	31	40	48	69	42	55	67	97	75	98	124	179
8'-0"	46	76	69	86	30	38	47	68	40	53	65	96	70	93	118	176
9'-0"	40	71	66	83	28	36	46	66	37	50	62	93	64	87	113	170
10'-0"	34	66	63	79	26	35	44	64	35	47	60	91	59	82	108	165
11'-0"	30	61	60	74	23	32	42	62	31	43	57	88	53	75	101	159
12'-0"	25	55	56	69	21	30	40	61	28	40	54	85	48	68	94	154

Loads below heavy lines are for secondary members with l/r ratio between 120 and 200. Steel pipes are assumed to have properties of A.S.T.M.- A7. For other column data, see page titled "Lally Columns".
*Carnegie sections. Kip = 1000 pounds.

Data by Elwyn E. Seelye, Consulting Engineer

CONCRETE REINFORCEMENT

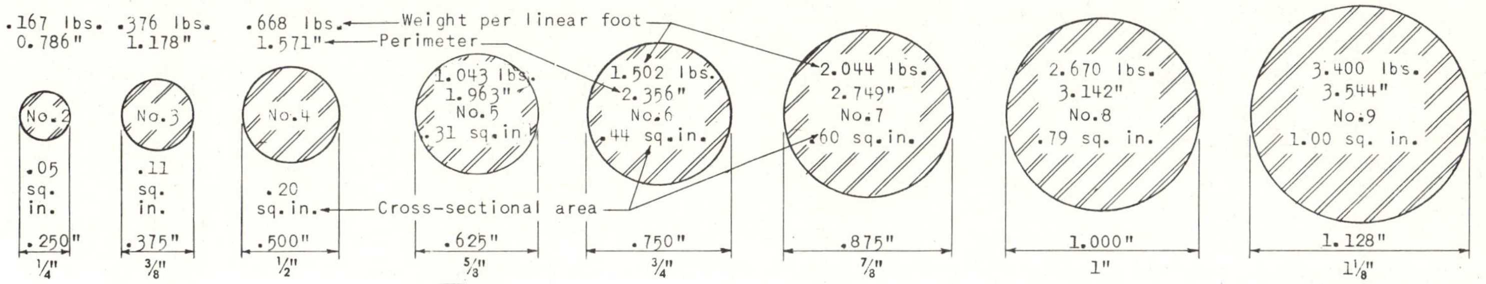
.167 lbs.
0.786"
No.2
.05 sq. in.
.250"
1/4"
.376 lbs.
1.178"
No.3
.11 sq. in.
.375"
3/8"
.668 lbs.
1.571"
No.4
.20 sq.in.
.500"
1/2"
Weight per linear foot
Perimeter
Cross-sectional area
1.043 lbs.
1.963"
No.5
.31 sq.in.
.625"
5/8"
1.502 lbs.
2.356"
No.6
.44 sq.in.
.750"
3/4"
2.044 lbs.
2.749"
No.7
.60 sq.in.
.875"
7/8"
2.670 lbs.
3.142"
No.8
.79 sq. in.
1.000"
1"
3.400 lbs.
3.544"
No.9
1.00 sq. in.
1.128"
1 1/8"

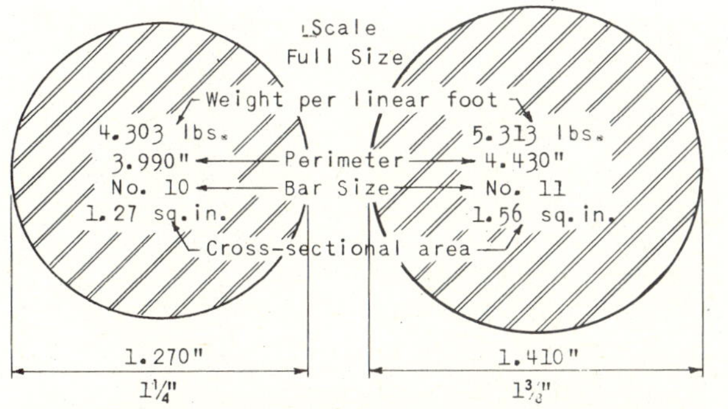
Scale Full Size
Weight per linear foot
4.303 lbs.
3.990"
Perimeter
No. 10
Bar Size
1.27 sq.in.
Cross-sectional area
5.313 lbs.
4.430"
No. 11
1.56 sq. in.
1.270"
1 1/4"
1.410"
1 3/8"

Note: Bar sizes indicated by numbers from No.2 to No.11

STANDARD CONCRETE REINFORCING BARS

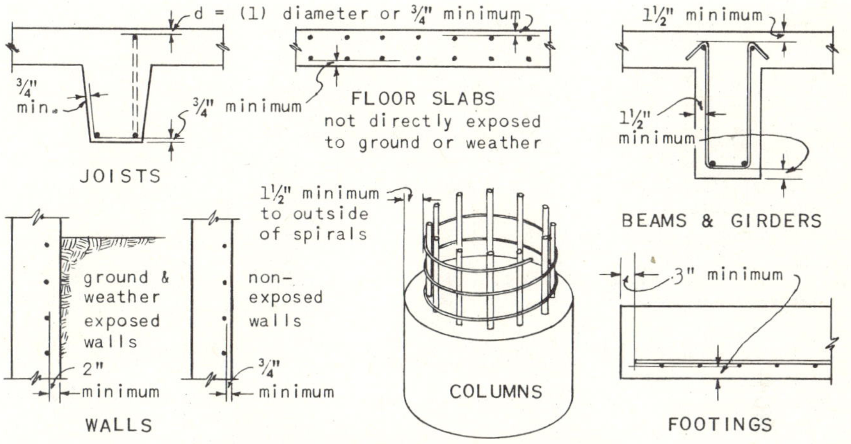
d = (1) diameter or 3/4" minimum
3/4" min.
3/4" minimum
JOISTS
FLOOR SLABS
not directly exposed
to ground or weather
1 1/2" minimum
1 1/2" minimum
BEAMS & GIRDERS
ground & weather exposed walls
2" minimum
non-exposed walls
3/4" minimum
WALLS
1 1/2" minimum to outside of spirals
COLUMNS
3" minimum
FOOTINGS

REINFORCEMENT PROTECTION

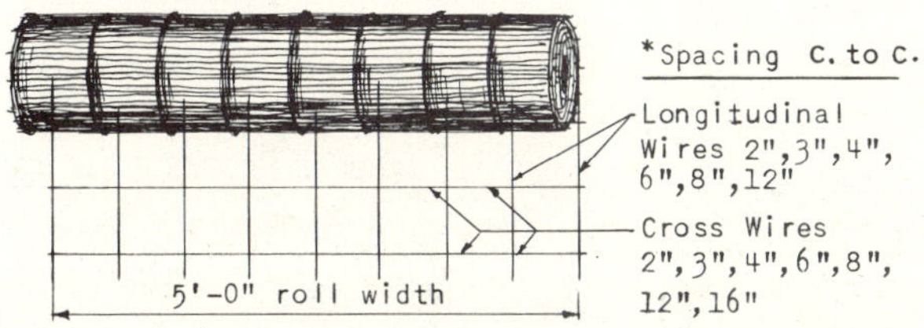
*Spacing C. to C.
Longitudinal Wires 2",3",4", 6",8",12"
Cross Wires 2",3",4",6",8", 12",16"
5'-0" roll width

ELECTRICALLY WELDED WIRE FABRIC REINFORCING

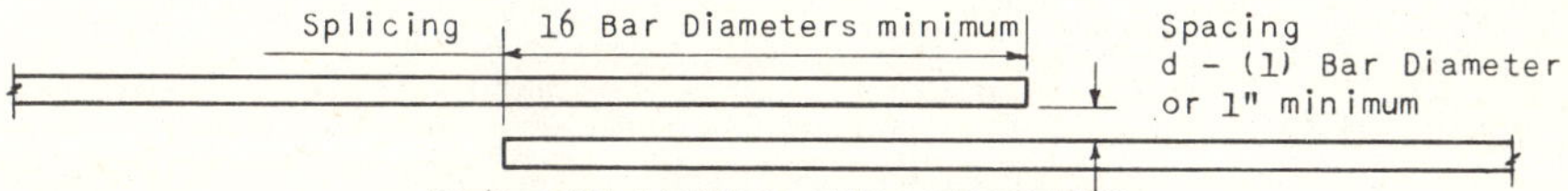
Splicing
16 Bar Diameters minimum
Spacing
d - (1) Bar Diameter
or 1" minimum

BAR SPLICING AND SPACING

STANDARD STEEL WIRE SIZES AND GAUGES				
Diameter inches	A.S.& W. Gauge	Diameter inches	Area sq. in.	Pounds per Foot
1/2		.5000	.19635	.6668
	7/0	.4900	.18857	.6404
15/32		.46875	.17257	.5861
	6/0	.4615	.16728	.5681
7/16		.4375	.15033	.5105
	5/0	.4305	.14556	.4943
13/32		.40625	.12962	.4402
	4/0	.3938	.12180	.4136
3/8		.3750	.11045	.3751
	3/0	.3625	.10321	.3505
11/32		.34375	.092806	.3152
	2/0	.3310	.086049	.2922
5/16		.3125	.076699	.2605
	0	.3065	.073782	.2506
	1	.2830	.062902	.2136
9/32		.28125	.062126	.2110
	2	.2625	.054119	.1823
1/4		.2500	.049087	.1667
	3	.2437	.046645	.1584
	4	.2253	.039867	.1354
7/32		.21875	.037583	.1276
	5	.2070	.033654	.1143
	6	.1920	.028953	.09832
3/16		.1875	.027612	.09377
	7	.1770	.024606	.08356
	8	.1620	.020612	.07000
5/32		.15625	.019175	.06512
	9	.1483	.017273	.05866
	10	.1350	.014314	.04861
1/8		.125	.012272	.04168
	11	.1205	.011404	.03873
	12	.1055	.0087147	.02969
3/32		.09375	.0069029	.02344
	13	.0915	.0065755	.02233
	14	.0800	.0050266	.01707
	15	.0720	.0040715	.01383
1/16	16	.0625	.0030680	.01042
	17	.0540	.0022902	.007778

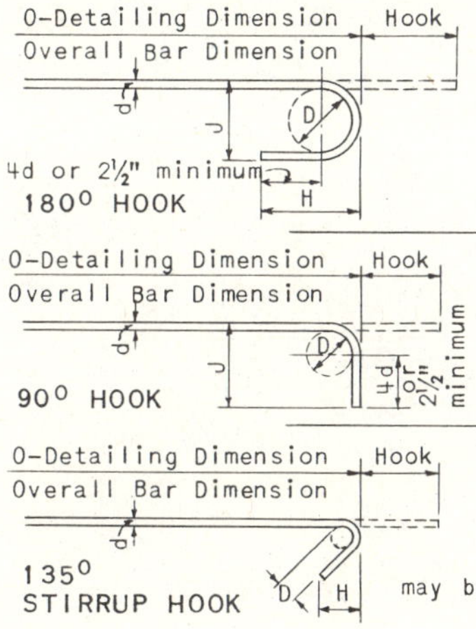
0-Detailing Dimension
Hook
Overall Bar Dimension
4d or 2 1/2" minimum
180° HOOK
0-Detailing Dimension
Hook
Overall Bar Dimension
4d or 2 1/2" minimum
90° HOOK
0-Detailing Dimension
Hook
Overall Bar Dimension
135°
STIRRUP HOOK

180° HOOK:
d = (1) Bar Diameter
D = 6d for No.2 to No. 7 Bars
D = 8d for No.8 to No. 11 Bars
J = D + 2d
H = 5d + D/2
minimum H = 2 1/2" + d + D/2

90° HOOK:
d = (1) Bar Diameter
D = 6d for No.2 to No. 7 bars
D = 8d for No.8 to No. 11 bars
J = 5d + D/2
minimum J = 2 1/2" + d + D/2

135° STIRRUP HOOK:
d = (1) Bar Diameter
D = 5d for No.2 to No. 5 Bars
H = 1" + d + D/2

When supporting bars are used, stirrup hooks may be bent to the diameter of the supporting bars

ANCHORAGE

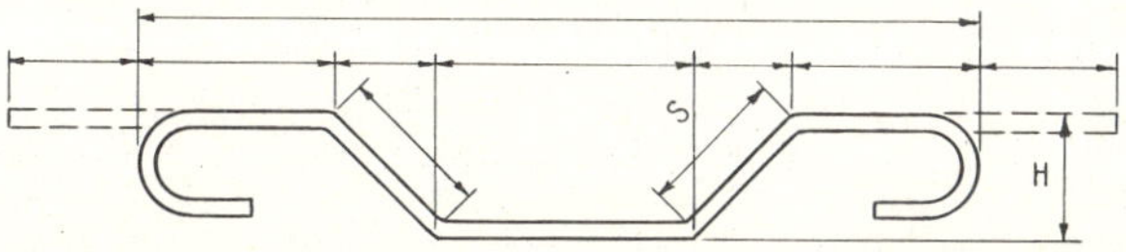

45° BAR BEND
S = 1.414H
to the nearest 1/2"

DIMENSIONING

*Welded Wire Fabric available in sheets and rolls, in 0 to 14 gauge wire.

NOTE: Bar Sizes are "Simplified Practice Recommendation R 26-52" U.S. Department of Commerce

TEMPERATURE REINFORCEMENT

in percentage of cross-sectional area of concrete

REINFORCEMENT	CONCRETE INTERIOR	CONCRETE EXTERIOR
Plain Bars	.25%	.30%
Deformed Bars	.20%	.25%
Welded Wire Mesh	.18%	.22%

DATA BY: CONCRETE REINFORCING STEEL INSTITUTE

PRECAST CONCRETE for WALLS

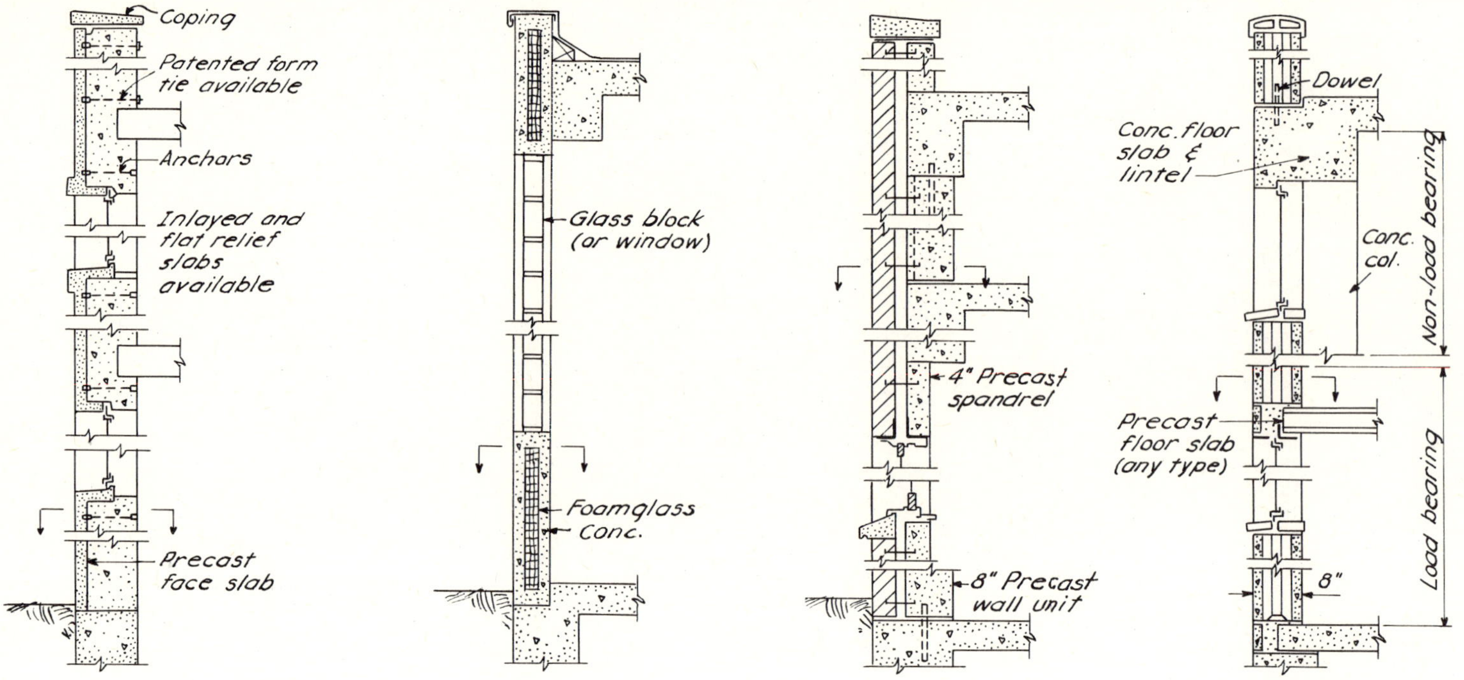
Coping
Patented form tie available
Anchors
Inlayed and flat relief slabs available
Precast face slab
Glass block (or window)
Foamglass
Conc.
4" Precast spandrel
8" Precast wall unit
Dowel
Conc. floor slab & lintel
Conc. col.
Non-load bearing
Precast floor slab (any type)
Load bearing
8"

SECTIONS

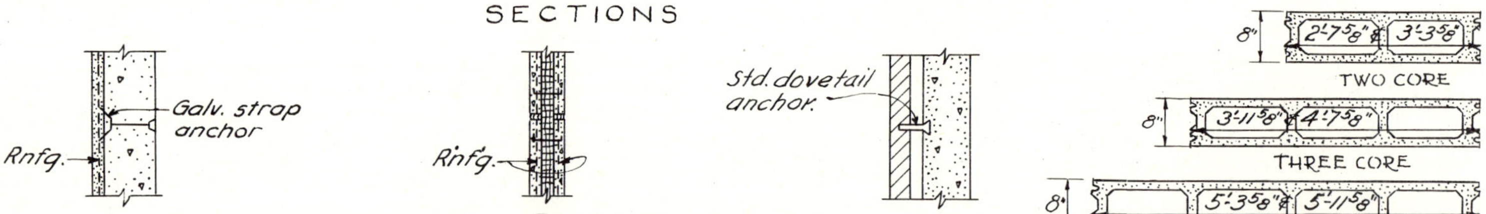
Galv. strap anchor
Rnfg.
R'nfg.
Std. dovetail anchor.
8"
2'-7 5/8" & 3'-3 5/8"
TWO CORE
3'-11 5/8" & 4'-7 5/8"
THREE CORE
5'-3 5/8" & 5'-11 5/8"
FOUR CORE

PLANS

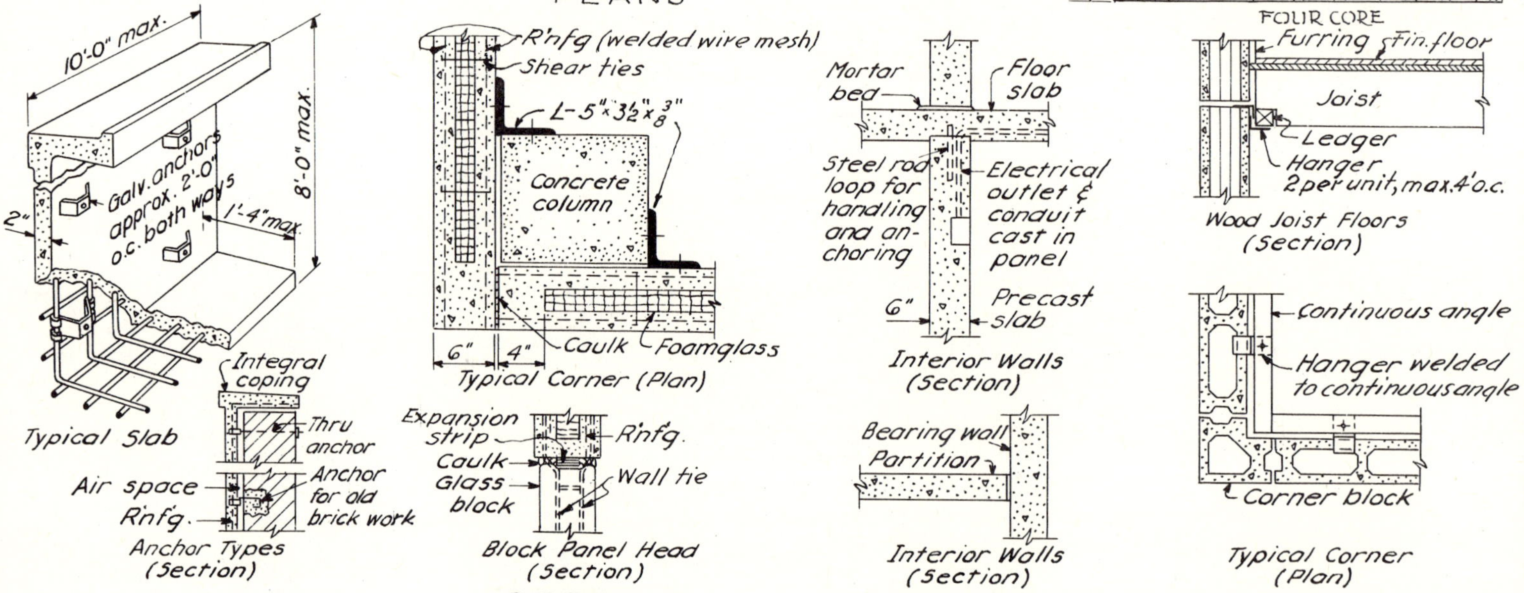
10'-0" max.
8'-0" max.
Galv. anchors approx. 2'-0" o.c. both ways
1'-4" max.
2"
Typical Slab
Integral coping
Thru anchor
Anchor for old brick work
Air space
R'nfg.
Anchor Types (Section)
R'nfg (welded wire mesh)
Shear ties
L-5"x3½"x3/8"
Concrete column
Caulk
Foamglass
6"
4"
Typical Corner (Plan)
Expansion strip
Caulk
Glass block
R'nfg.
Wall tie
Block Panel Head (Section)
Mortar bed
Floor slab
Steel rod loop for handling and anchoring
Electrical outlet & conduit cast in panel
Precast slab
6"
Interior Walls (Section)
Bearing wall
Partition
Interior Walls (Section)
Furring
Fin. floor
Joist
Ledger
Hanger 2 per unit, max. 4'o.c.
Wood Joist Floors (Section)
Continuous angle
Hanger welded to continuous angle
Corner block
Typical Corner (Plan)

DETAILS

To 100□' in area (20-60□' most econ.) @ 25#/□', 2" thick, of mixed aggregates. 7500 p.s.i. concrete. To 50□', 2¼" thick, reconstructed, polished granite. Above slab used as face form for concrete wall. Can be used with any type masonry back-up or bolted to wood or steel framing. (Made by: Mo-Sai Associates)

FACING SLAB
Factory cast.

40-60□' in area, 5" and 6" thick, u = .16. Concrete veneer to 6000 p.s.i. Cast with windows, door frames, etc., in place. Generally floor-height slabs. Made by: Pittsburgh Corning Corp.

CONCRETE-GLASS SANDWICH
Site or nearby cast.

Cast as complete wall sections with windows and door frames, wiring, conduits, etc., in place. Type of veneering optional. Can be used alone as facing.

TILT-UP SOLID-BACK SLAB
Site cast.

Height up to 10'-0"
Weight:
38#/□' Light weight conc.
50#/□' Standard conc.
"U" factor ±.33
Mortar joints 3/8" to form modular widths.
Made by:
Precast Building Sections Inc.

HOLLOW-CORE PANEL SLAB
Factory cast.

PRECAST CONCRETE JOISTS

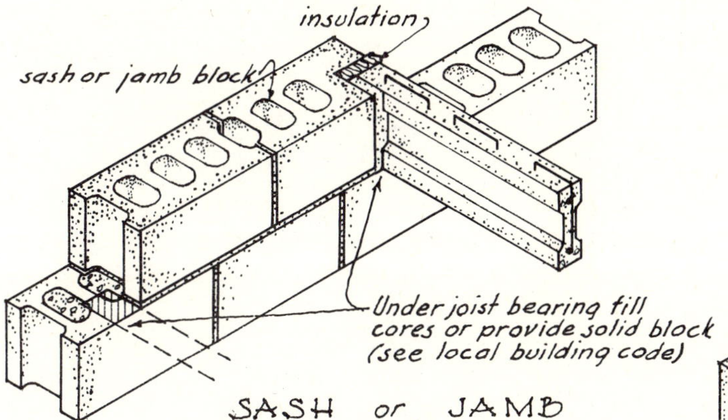
insulation
sash or jamb block
Under joist bearing fill cores or provide solid block (see local building code)

SASH or JAMB BLOCK BRIDGING

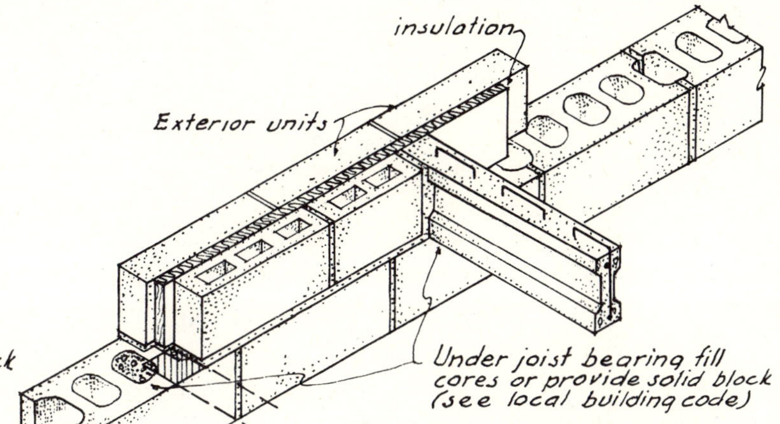
insulation
Exterior units
Under joist bearing fill cores or provide solid block (see local building code)

4"x 8"x 16" CONCRETE BRIDGING UNITS

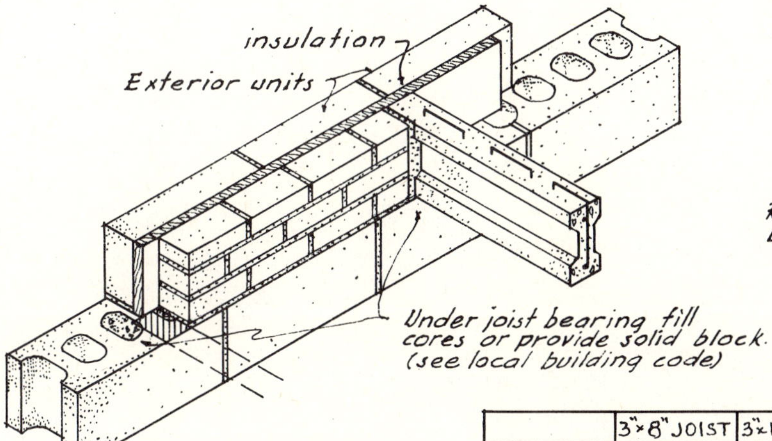
insulation
Exterior units
Under joist bearing fill cores or provide solid block. (see local building code)

BRICK BRIDGING

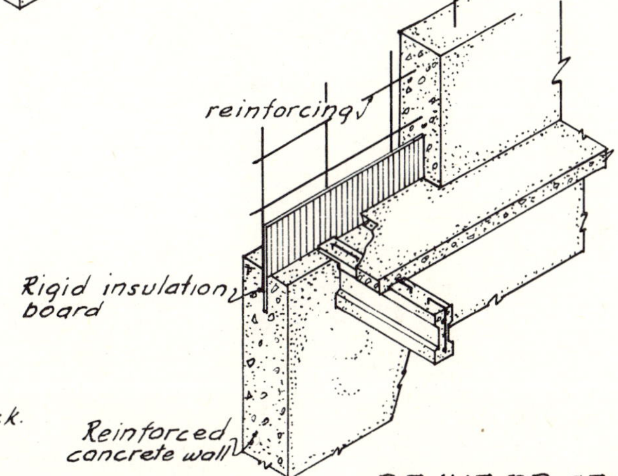
reinforcing
Rigid insulation board
Reinforced concrete wall

REINFORCED CONCRETE WALL

	3"x 8" JOIST	3"x 10" JOIST	4"x 12" JOIST
Sect'l Area	18.2 sq. in.	22.1 sq. in.	33.4 sq. in.
Max. Span	16 feet	20 feet	24 feet

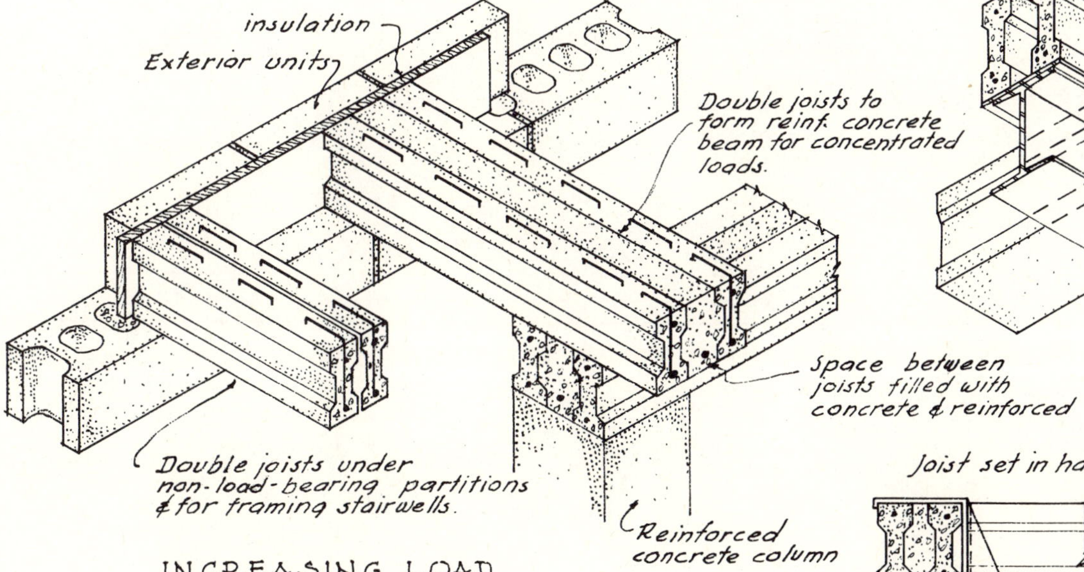
insulation
Exterior units
Double joists to form reinf. concrete beam for concentrated loads.
Space between joists filled with concrete & reinforced
Double joists under non-load-bearing partitions & for framing stairwells.
Reinforced concrete column

INCREASING LOAD CAPACITY OF JOISTS

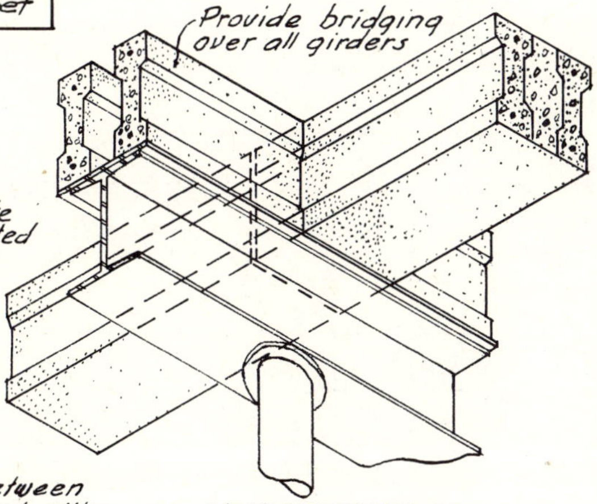
Provide bridging over all girders

STRUCTURAL GIRDERS

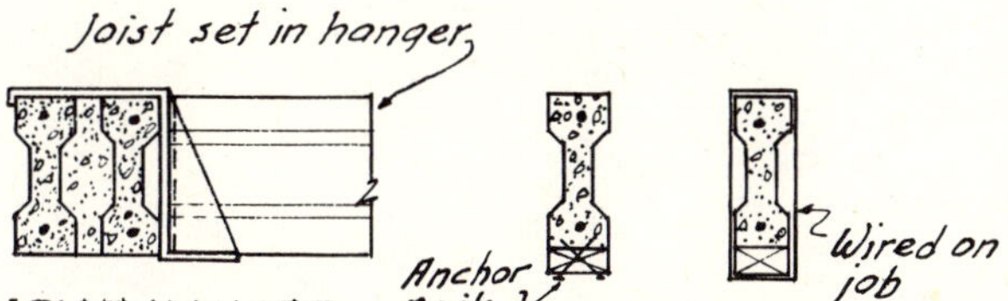
Joist set in hanger
Anchor nails
Wired on job

JOIST HANGER

NAILING STRIPS

TYPICAL BRIDGING DETAILS

Data checked by: Elwyn E. Seelye, Consulting Engineer.

CONCRETE JOIST FLOOR CONSTRUCTION

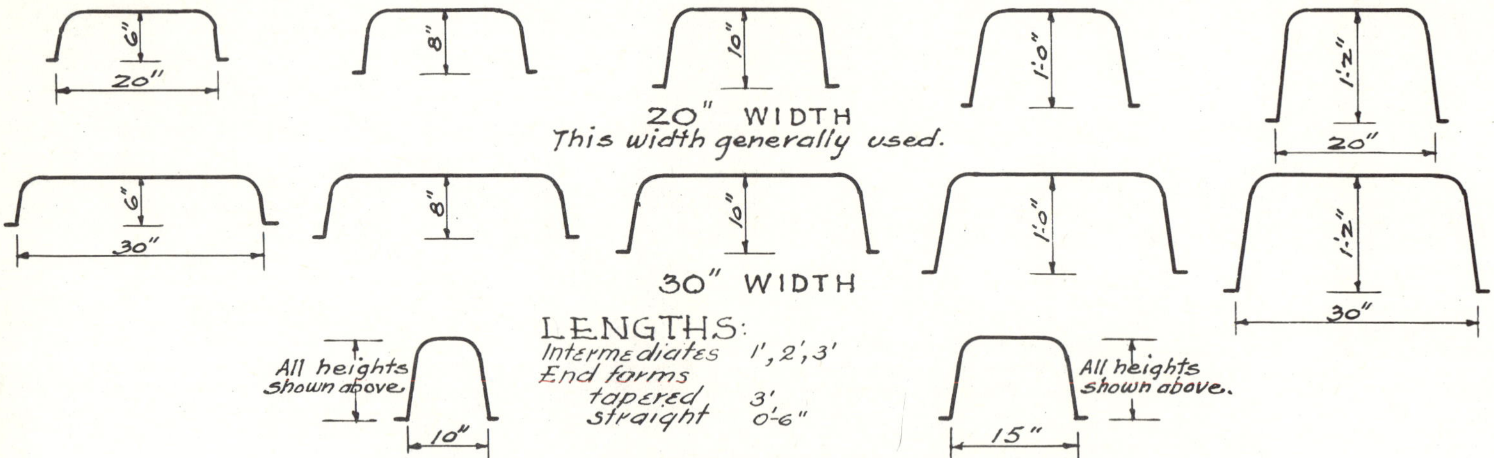
6"
20"
8"
10"
1'-0"
1'-2"
20"
20" WIDTH
This width generally used.
6"
30"
8"
10"
1'-0"
1'-2"
30"
30" WIDTH
LENGTHS:
Intermediates 1', 2', 3'
End forms
tapered 3'
straight 0'-6"
All heights shown above.
10"
All heights shown above.
15"

SPECIAL WIDTHS FOR FILLER FORMS ONLY.

STANDARD SIZES OF FLANGE TYPE FORMS

Scale: 1/2" = 1'-0"

Other sizes are made, but these are U.S. Dept. of Commerce Simplified Practice Recommendation - R 87-32
These are used for ribbed floor construction & concrete

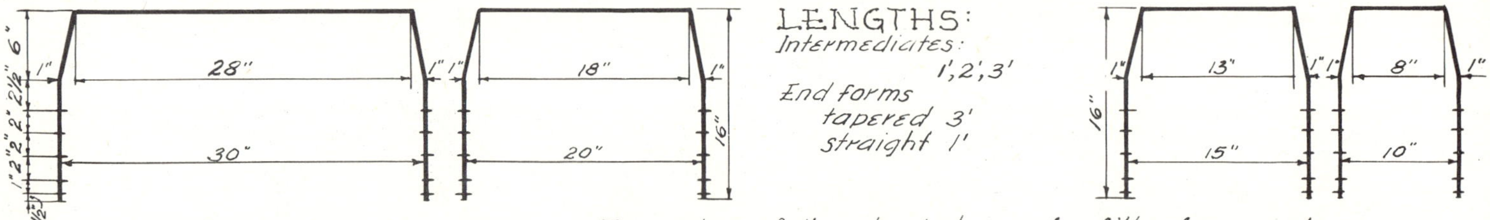
6"
2 1/2"
2"
2"
2"
1/2"
1"
28"
1"
30"
1"
18"
1"
20"
16"
LENGTHS:
Intermediates:
1', 2', 3'
End forms
tapered 3'
straight 1'
16"
1"
13"
1"
15"
1"
8"
1"
10"

STANDARD WIDTHS

Forms shown fully extended; adjust to heights dimensioned at left.

for filler forms only.

SPECIAL WIDTHS

STANDARD SIZES OF ADJUSTABLE TYPE FORMS

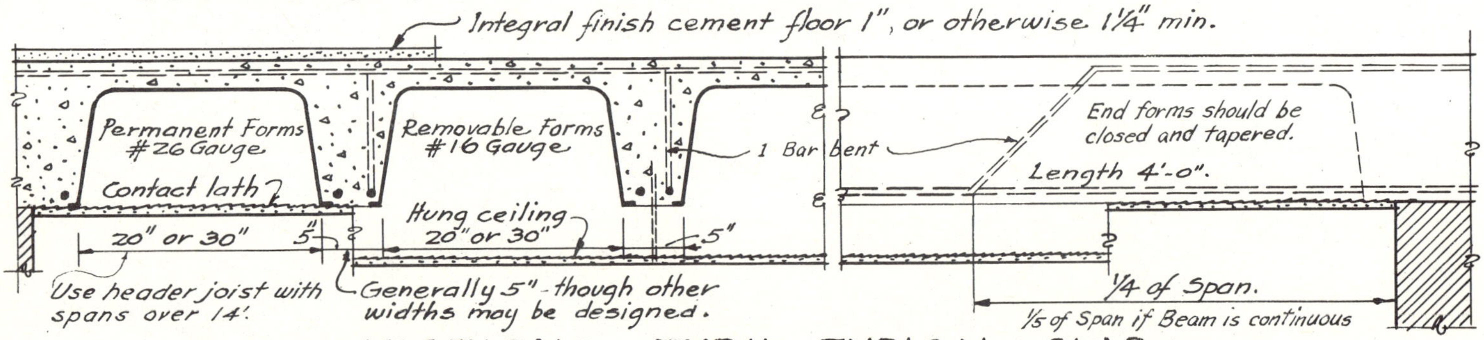
Integral finish cement floor 1", or otherwise 1 1/4" min.
Permanent Forms #26 Gauge
Contact lath
Removable Forms #16 Gauge
1 Bar Bent
End forms should be closed and tapered.
Length 4'-0".
Hung ceiling
20" or 30"
5"
20" or 30"
5"
Use header joist with spans over 14'.
Generally 5" - though other widths may be designed.
1/4 of Span.
1/5 of Span if Beam is continuous

SECTIONS THRU TYPICAL SLAB

TOP SLAB THICKNESS & FORM SIZES [no steel given] FOR PRELIMINARY ASSUMPTION												
TYPE OF BUILDING	LIVE LOAD	5" Beam used.	SPAN IN FEET.									
			10	12	14	16	18	20	22	24	26	28
RESIDENCE OR APARTMENT BLDG.	40	Slab Thk. Form Size	2" 4"×20"	2" 6"×20"	2" 6"	2" 6"	2" 8"	2" 10"	2" 12"	2 1/2" 12"	2 1/2" 12"	3" 14"
OFFICE BUILDING	50 60	Slab Form	2" 4"×20"	2" 6"×20"	2" 6"	2" 8"	2" 10"	2" 10"	2" 10"	2 1/2" 12"	2 1/2" 12"	3" 14"
SCHOOL - COLLEGE	75 80	Slab Form	2" 4"×20"	2" 6"×20"	2" 6"	2" 8"	2" 10"	2" 10"	2" 10"	2 1/2" 12"	2 1/2" 12"	3" 14"
STORES - PUBLIC SPACE	100	Slab Form	2" 6"×20"	2" 6"×20"	2" 8"	2" 8"	2" 10"	2" 10"	2" 12"	2 1/2" 12"	2 1/2" 14"	3" 14"
OTHER USES	125	Slab Form	2" 6"×20"	2" 6"×20"	2" 8"	2" 8"	2" 10"	2" 10"	2" 12"	2 1/2" 12"	2 1/2" 14"	3" 14"

REMOVABLE FORMS to be #16 Gauge smooth steel. PERMANENT FORMS to be #26 Gauge corrugated. High removable forms are often used and beam depth determined by forms. For contact lath use 3/8" rib lath 3.44 # per sq. ft. For furring rods use 3/8" pencil rods.

FLANGE & ADJUSTABLE TYPE FORMS FOR FLOOR SLABS

Data checked by Elwyn E. Seelye, Consulting Engineer.

FLOOR CONSTRUCTION

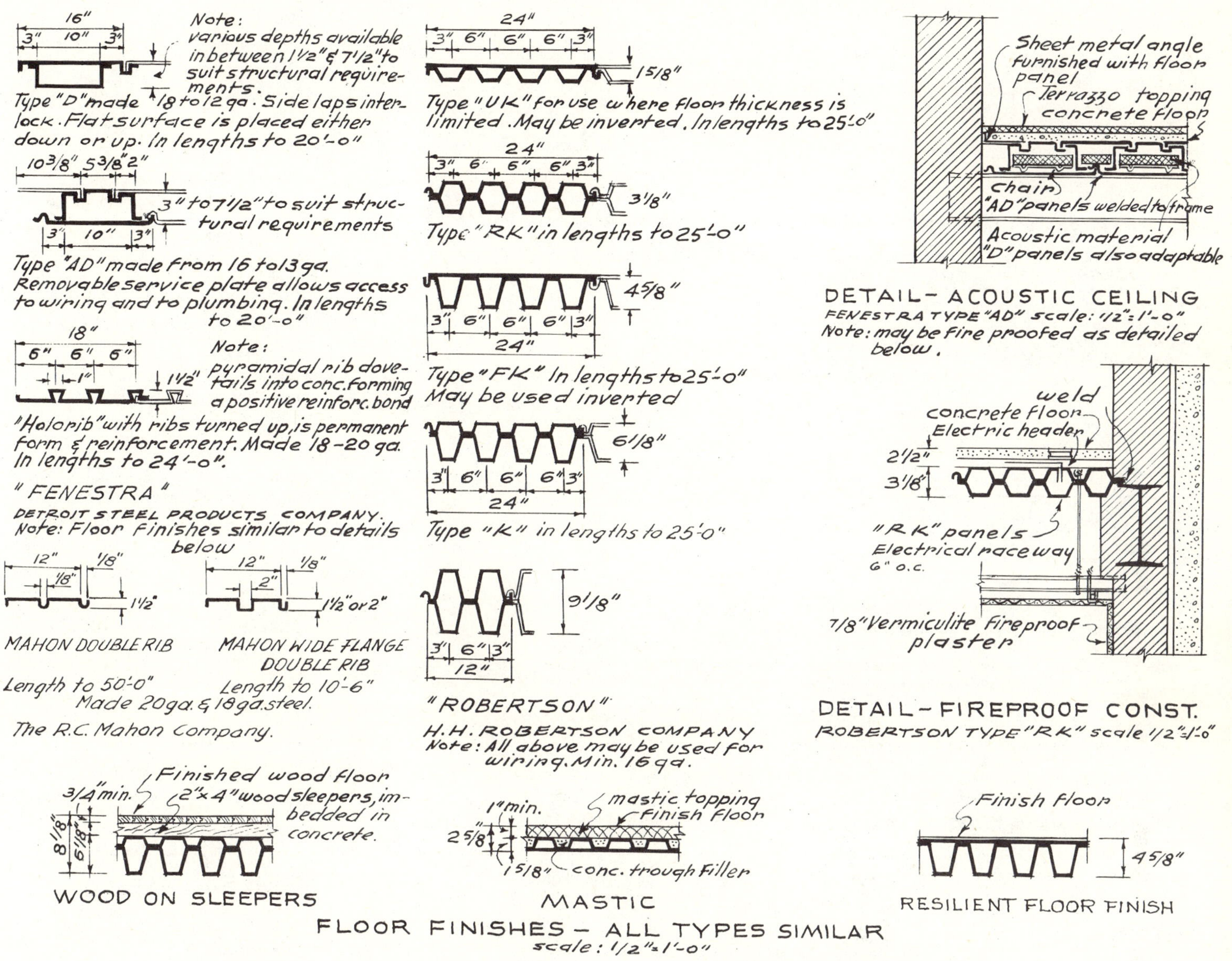
16"
3" 10" 3"
Note: various depths available in between 1 1/2" & 7 1/2" to suit structural requirements.
Type "D" made 18 to 12 ga. Side laps interlock. Flat surface is placed either down or up. In lengths to 20'-0"
10 3/8" 5 3/8" 2"
3" to 7 1/2" to suit structural requirements
3" 10" 3"
Type "AD" made from 16 to 13 ga. Removable service plate allows access to wiring and to plumbing. In lengths to 20'-0"
18"
6" 6" 6"
1"
1 1/2"
Note: pyramidal rib dovetails into conc. forming a positive reinforc. bond
"Holorib" with ribs turned up, is permanent form & reinforcement. Made 18-20 ga. In lengths to 24'-0".
"FENESTRA"
DETROIT STEEL PRODUCTS COMPANY.
Note: Floor finishes similar to details below
12" 1/8"
1/8"
1 1/2"
12" 1/8"
2"
1 1/2" or 2"
MAHON DOUBLE RIB
MAHON WIDE FLANGE DOUBLE RIB
Length to 50'-0"
Length to 10'-6"
Made 20 ga. & 18 ga. steel.
The R.C. Mahon Company.
24"
3" 6" 6" 6" 3"
1 5/8"
Type "UK" for use where floor thickness is limited. May be inverted. In lengths to 25'-0"
24"
3" 6" 6" 6" 3"
3 1/8"
Type "RK" in lengths to 25'-0"
4 5/8"
3" 6" 6" 6" 3"
24"
Type "FK" In lengths to 25'-0" May be used inverted
6 1/8"
3" 6" 6" 6" 3"
24"
Type "K" in lengths to 25'-0"
9 1/8"
3" 6" 3"
12"
"ROBERTSON"
H.H. ROBERTSON COMPANY
Note: All above may be used for wiring. Min. 16 ga.
Sheet metal angle furnished with floor panel
Terrazzo topping
concrete floor
Chain
"AD" panels welded to frame
Acoustic material
"D" panels also adaptable
DETAIL - ACOUSTIC CEILING
FENESTRA TYPE "AD" scale: 1/2" = 1'-0"
Note: may be fire proofed as detailed below.
weld
concrete floor
Electric header
2 1/2"
3 1/8"
"RK" panels
Electrical raceway 6" o.c.
7/8" Vermiculite fireproof plaster
DETAIL - FIREPROOF CONST.
ROBERTSON TYPE "RK" scale 1/2" = 1'-0"
Finished wood floor
3/4" min.
2"x4" wood sleepers, imbedded in concrete.
8 1/8"
6 1/8"
WOOD ON SLEEPERS
1" min.
mastic topping
Finish floor
2 5/8"
1 5/8"
conc. trough filler
MASTIC
Finish floor
4 5/8"
RESILIENT FLOOR FINISH
FLOOR FINISHES - ALL TYPES SIMILAR
scale: 1/2" = 1'-0"

STEEL FLOOR DECKS - TYPES & DETAILS

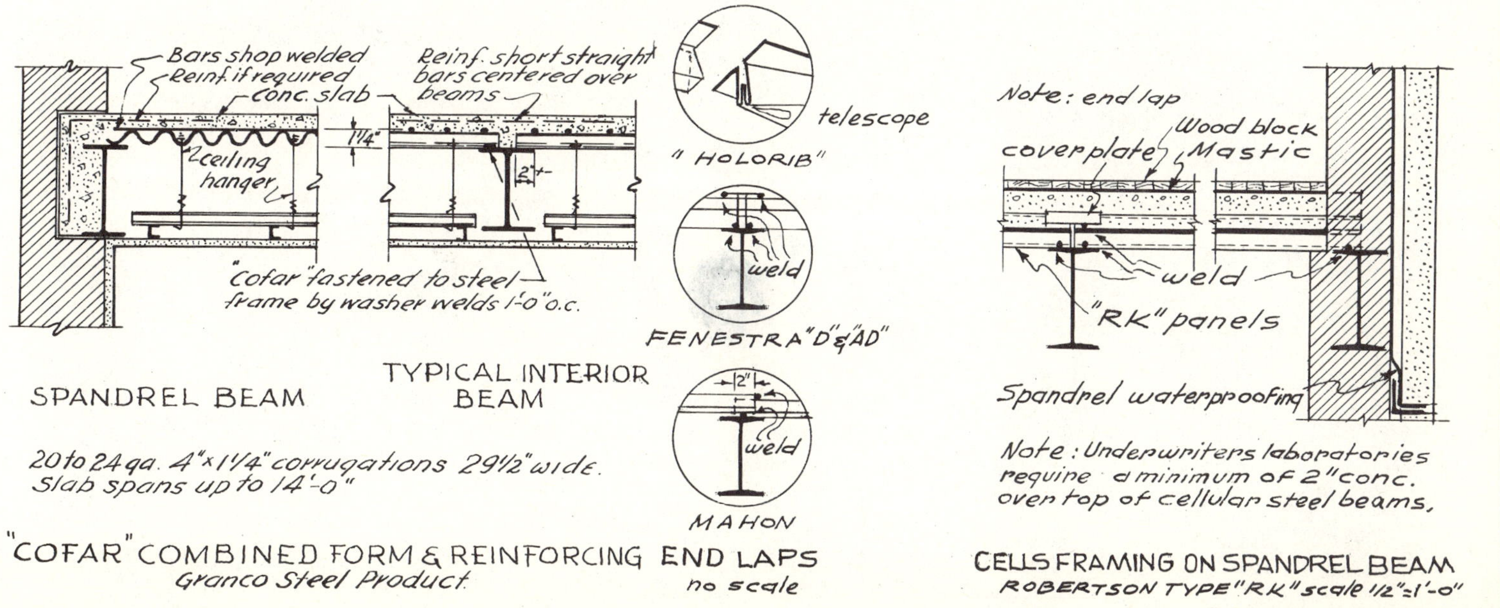
Bars shop welded
Reinf. if required
Conc. slab
ceiling hanger
Reinf. short straight bars centered over beams
1 1/4"
2"
"Cofar" fastened to steel frame by washer welds 1'-0" o.c.
SPANDREL BEAM
TYPICAL INTERIOR BEAM
20 to 24 ga. 4" x 1 1/4" corrugations 29 1/2" wide.
Slab spans up to 14'-0"
"COFAR" COMBINED FORM & REINFORCING
Granco Steel Product
telescope
"HOLORIB"
weld
FENESTRA "D" & "AD"
2"
weld
MAHON
END LAPS
no scale
Note: end lap
Wood block
cover plate
Mastic
weld
"RK" panels
Spandrel waterproofing
Note: Underwriters laboratories require a minimum of 2" conc. over top of cellular steel beams.
CELLS FRAMING ON SPANDREL BEAM
ROBERTSON TYPE "RK" scale 1/2" = 1'-0"

FLOOR CONSTRUCTION

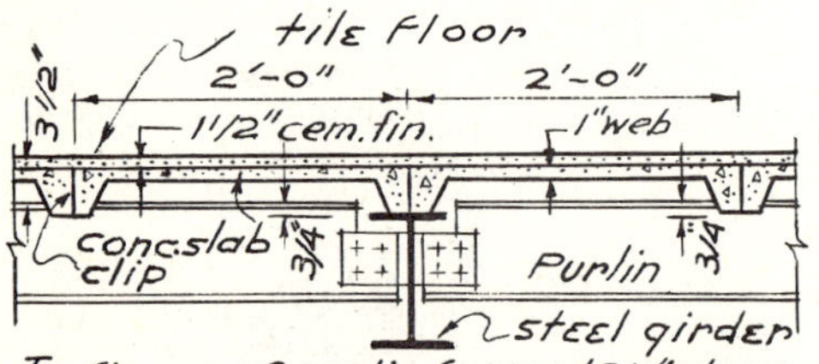
tile floor
3 1/2"
2'-0"
2'-0"
1 1/2" cem. fin.
1" web
conc. slab clip
3/4
Purlin
3/4
steel girder

Top flanges of purlin framed 3/4" above girder.

Note: Standard width of slabs is 2'-0" but special slabs are available from 9" to 2'-6" wide. Standard lengths are economical 6'-0" to 8'-0" long but are obtainable up to 10'-0" lengths. Lengths are precut to fit steel spacing. Max. recommended span for floors 6'-0"

Section — AA

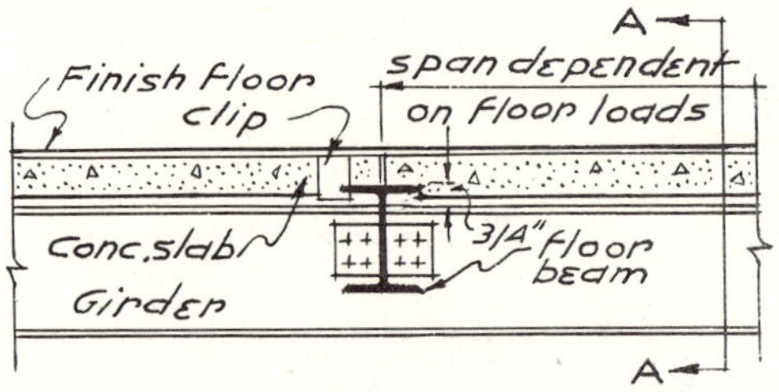
A
Finish floor
clip
span dependent on floor loads
Conc. slab
3/4" floor beam
Girder
A

Note: Slabs are laid directly on steel purlins and may be lapped over the purlin flange.

PORETE MFG. CO.

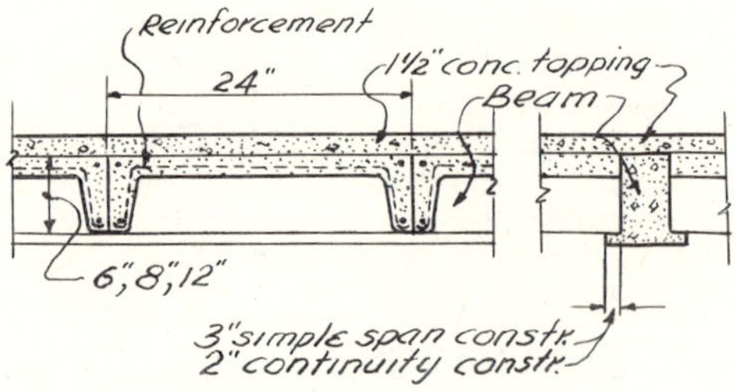
Reinforcement
24"
1 1/2" conc. topping
Beam
6", 8", 12"
3" simple span constr.
2" continuity constr.

6" channel 20'-0" max. spans
8" channel 26'-0" max. spans
12" channel 26'-0" max. spans

Note: For continuity expand reinforcement into concrete beam.

CHANNEL SLAB
The Geo. Rackle and Sons Co.

LONG SPAN CHANNEL SLABS

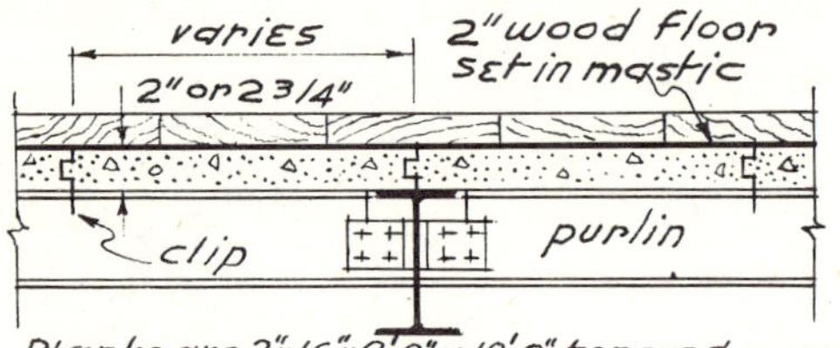
varies
2" wood floor set in mastic
2" or 2 3/4"
clip
purlin

Planks are 2"×16"×9'-0" or 10'-0" tongue & groove 4 sides: or 2"-2 3/4"×23"×length to fit beam spacing tongue & groove 2 sides: or 2"-2 3/4"×24"×length to fit beam spacing, square edge. Any floor fin. may be applied. May be nailed to wood beams. Max. spans 2"-5'-0", 2 3/4"-6'-0"

"PORETE" NAILABLE PLANK
scale 1/2"=1'-0"

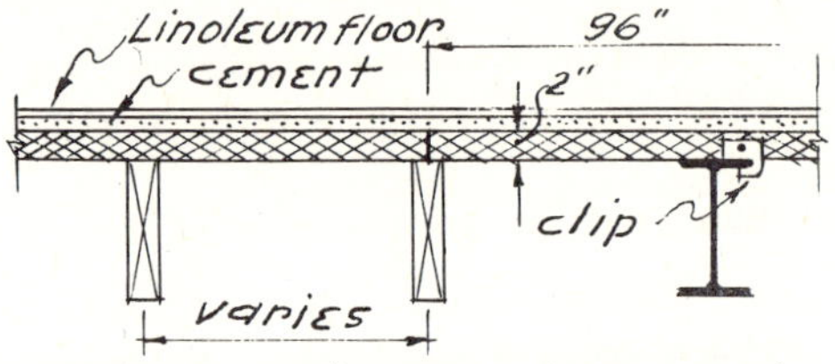
Linoleum floor
cement
96"
2"
clip
varies

Slabs are 2" or 3"×24"×96" nailed to wood joists or clipped to steel joists on 16", 20" or 24" centers. A 1/2" to 1" field cement finish is applied, and may be left exposed or covered with tile or linoleum.

INSULATING AND ACOUSTICAL
"POREX" SLABS
scale 1/2"=1'-0"

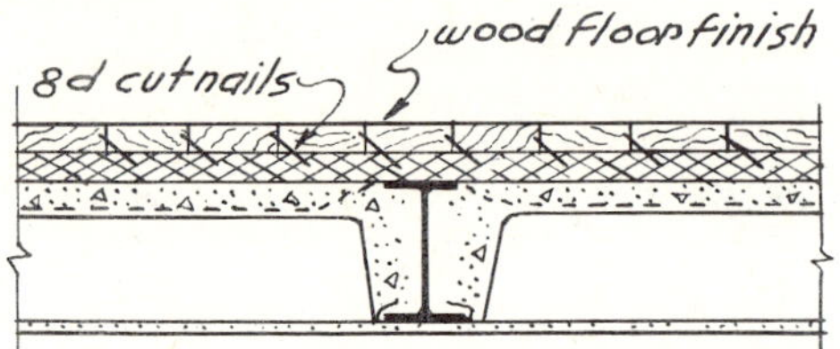
8d cut nails
wood floor finish

A 2" layer of "Porete" nail fill conc. is poured on top of the concrete slab. The wood flooring is nailed directly to this base as soon as it is set & dried.

"PORETE" NAILING CONCRETE
scale 1/2"=1'-0"

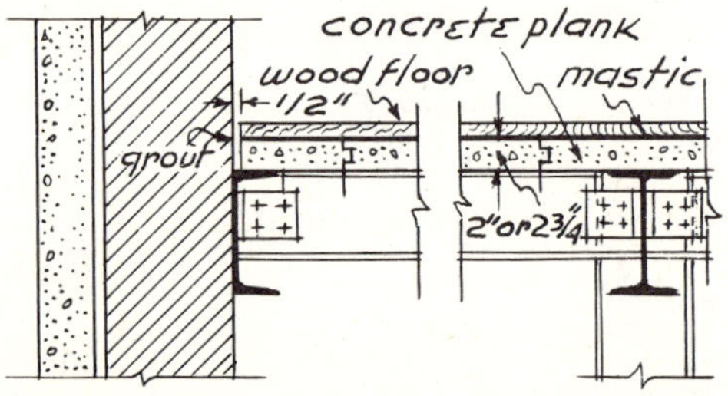
concrete plank
wood floor
mastic
1/2"
grout
2" or 2 3/4"

Planks are 2" or 2 3/4"×16"×any length to 10'-0". 2" planks will span to 4'-0", 2 3/4" planks will span to 5'-0". Sides are tongue & grooved, ends square. Plank goes from steel to steel. On bar joists 16" to 2'-0" o.c. stagger joints & use 10' length t. & g. 4 sides.

CONCRETE PLANK
scale 1/2"=1'-0"

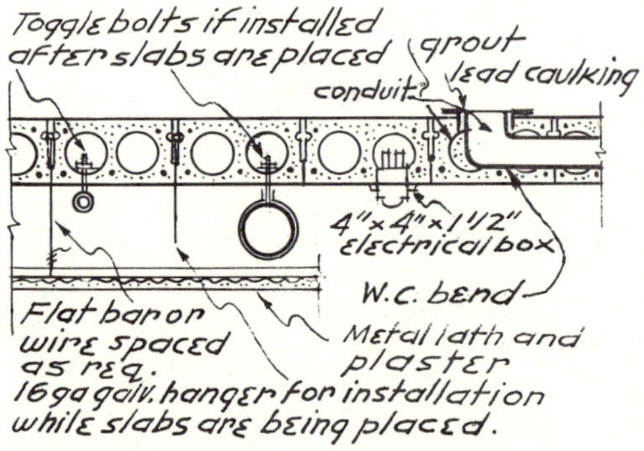
Toggle bolts if installed after slabs are placed
grout
lead caulking
conduit
4"×4"×1 1/2" electrical box
W.C. bend
Flat bar or wire spaced as req.
Metal lath and plaster
16 ga galv. hanger for installation while slabs are being placed.

HANGERS — ELECTRICAL — PLUMBING DETAILS

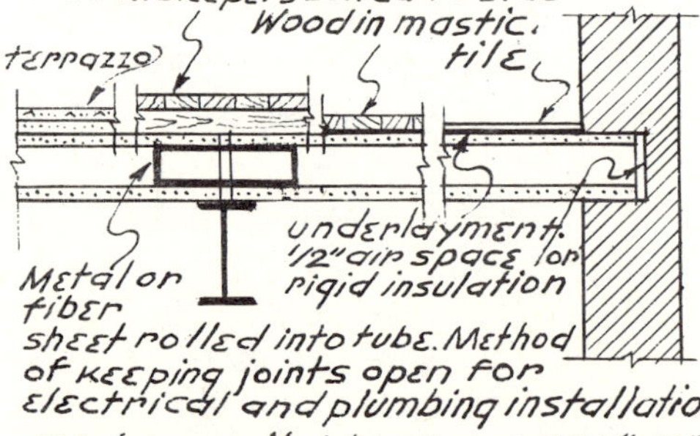
Wood on sleepers bolted to slab
Wood in mastic
terrazzo
tile
underlayment
1/2" air space or rigid insulation
Metal or fiber sheet rolled into tube. Method of keeping joints open for electrical and plumbing installation

Slabs available 6"×12", 6 5/6"×12", 6"×16" and 8"×16" to 26'-8" in 1" variations of length to 22'-6". Any floor fin. may be applied.

FLOORING AND JOINT DETAILS

FLEXICORE FLOOR SLAB
scale 1/2"=1'-0"

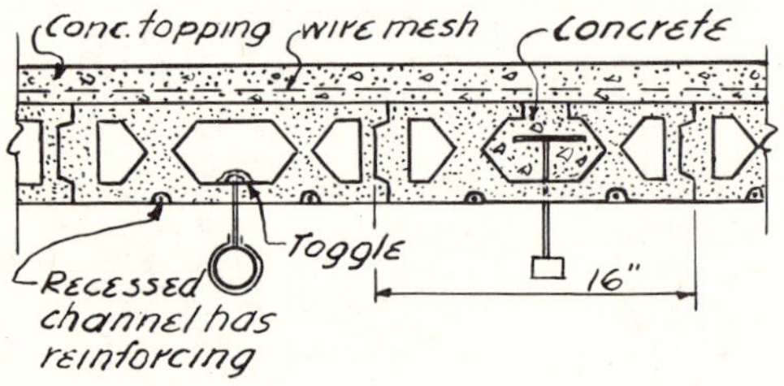
Conc. topping
wire mesh
concrete
Toggle
16"
Recessed channel has reinforcing

4"×16" spans 16'-0"
6"×16" spans 20'-0"
8"×16" spans 26'-0"

"DOX" SLAB
Multiplex Concrete Company Inc.

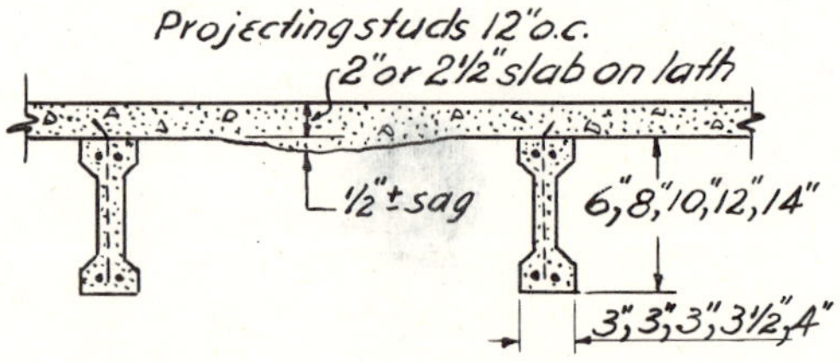
Projecting studs 12" o.c.
2" or 2 1/2" slab on lath
1/2" ± sag
6", 8", 10", 12", 14"
3", 3", 3", 3 1/2", 4"

"LITH-I-BAR" Lengths 36'-0" and over 2" to 2 1/2" concrete slab or precast on top

"LITH-I-BAR" CONC. JOISTS
The Dextone Co.

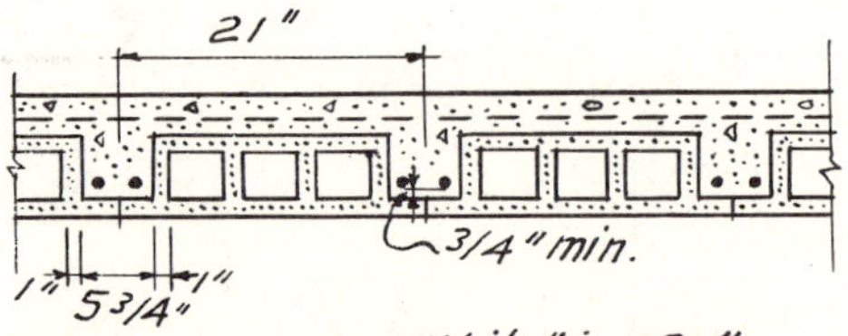
21"
3/4" min.
1"
5 3/4"
1"

"WAYLITE" soffitile is 5 5/8" or 7 5/8"×21" with 2 1/2" poured floor provides an acoustical ceiling.

"WAYLITE" SOFFITILE
scale 1/2"=1'-0"

ROOF CONSTRUCTION TYPES

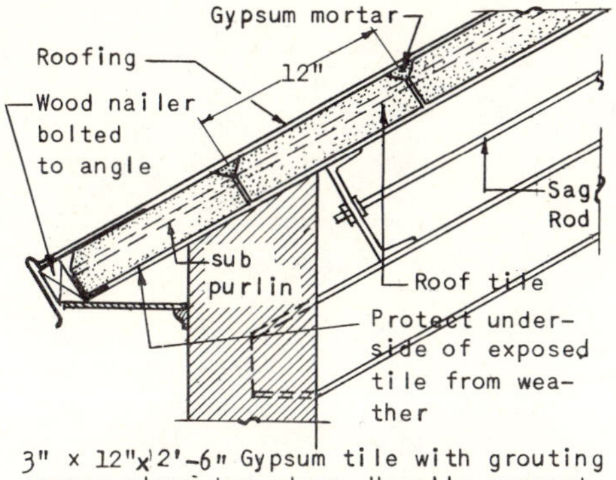
Gypsum mortar
Roofing
12"
Wood nailer bolted to angle
Sag Rod
sub purlin
Roof tile
Protect under-side of exposed tile from weather

3" x 12"x 2'-6" Gypsum tile with grouting groove along top edges. Usually supported by steel tee sub-purlins. For flat or sloped roof

3" SHORT SPAN GYPSUM ROOF TILE (Nailable)

UNITED STATES GYPSUM

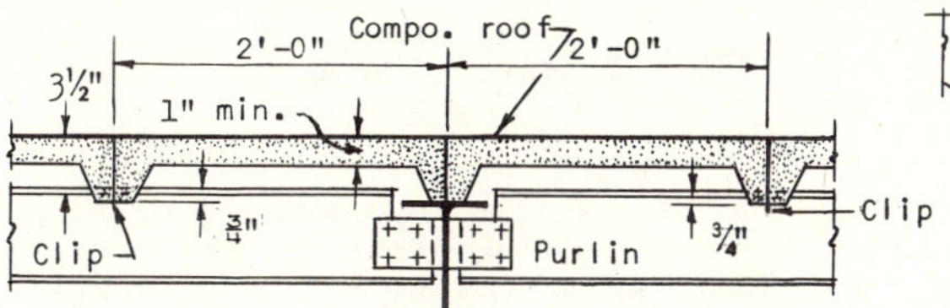
Compo. roof
$3\frac{1}{2}$"
2'-0"
2'-0"
1" min.
Clip
$\frac{3}{4}$"
Purlin
$\frac{3}{4}$"
Clip

Standard width of slabs is 2'-0" but special slabs are obtainable from 9" to 2'-6" wide. Standard lengths are economical 6'-0" to 8'-0" long but are obtainable up to 10'-0" long. Lengths are pre-cut to fit steel purlin spacing and joints are pointed.
May also be used for sloping roofs with wood nailer inserts for nailing built-up roofing.
Note : Top flanges of purlins framed $\frac{3}{4}$" above girder.

LONG SPAN CHANNEL SLAB

CONCRETE PLANK CO., INC.

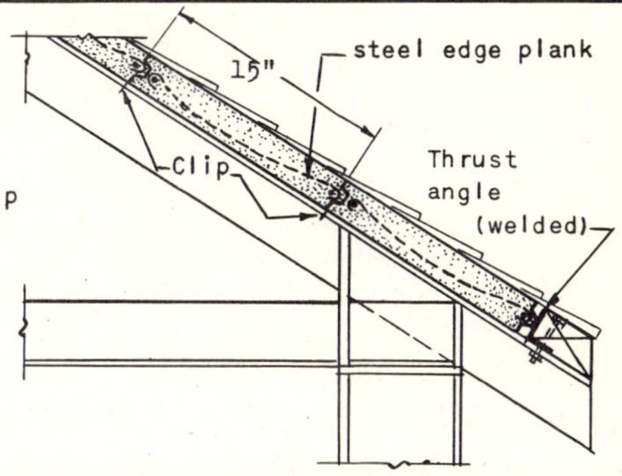
15"
steel edge plank
Clip
Thrust angle (welded)

2"x 1'-3" x 10'-0" steel edge plank spans 8'-0". Safety load 96"/sq ft. T&G four sides. Nailable for flat or sloped roof

STEEL EDGE CRETEPLANK

Note: Creteplank without steel edges 2" x 16" x 9'-0" Spans 7'-0"

MARTIN FIREPROOFING CO.

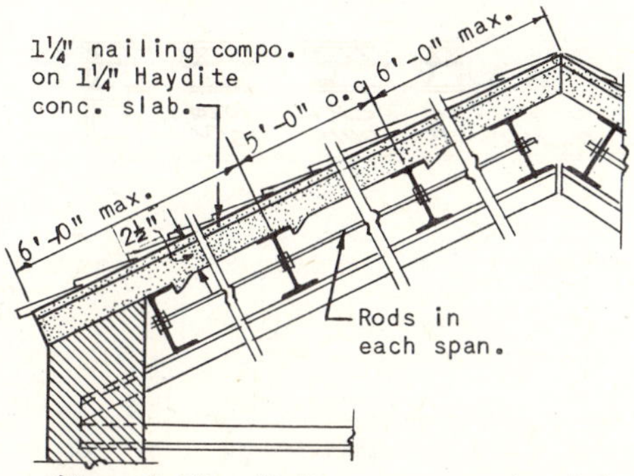
$1\frac{1}{4}$" nailing compo. on $1\frac{1}{4}$" Haydite conc. slab.
5'-0" o.c.
6'-0" max.
6'-0" max.
$2\frac{1}{2}$"
Rods in each span.

$2\frac{1}{2}$" x 2'-0" x 6'-0" max. concrete slab
Weight 18#/sq.'
When purlins frame into rafters or trusses, frame purlin tops $\frac{3}{4}$" above. Equalize slab lengths including overhang. Avoid combination of long & short lengths

NAILING CONCRETE ROOF SLAB

THE GEORGE RACKLE AND SONS CO.

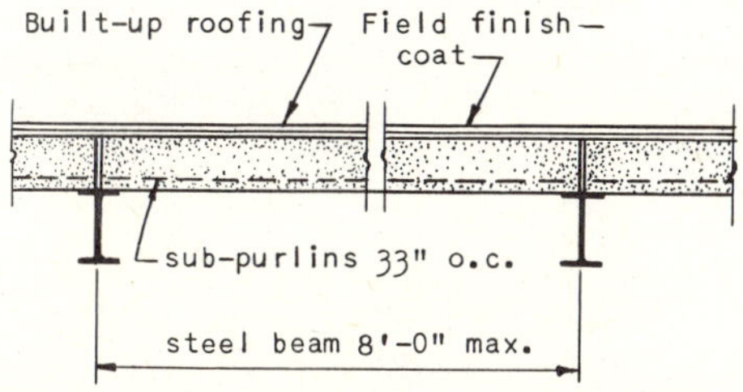
Built-up roofing
Field finish coat
sub-purlins 33" o.c.
steel beam 8'-0" max.

Slab: 2" or 3"x 2'-8"x 8'-0" weight 9#/sq.'
Slab covered by a $\frac{3}{8}$" field finish coat. Flanged channel or bulb tee sub-purlins may be used.

POREX SLAB ON STEEL SUB-PURLINS

Insulating & Acoustical

PORETE MFG. COMPANY

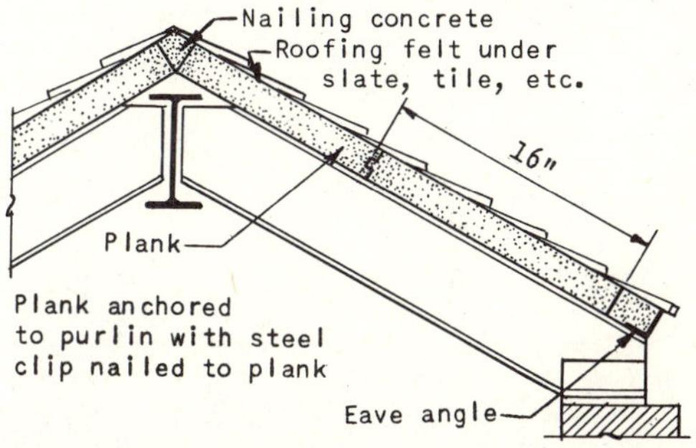
Nailing concrete
Roofing felt under slate, tile, etc.
16"
Plank
Plank anchored to purlin with steel clip nailed to plank
Eave angle

2" x 16" x any length to 10'-0" spans 7'-0"
$2\frac{3}{4}$" x 16" x any length to 8'-0"
Sides of plank are T&G, ends square.
When laid on bar joists 16" to 24" o.c. Stagger joints and use all 10'-0" plank T&G four sides.
May also be used for flat roof.

CONCRETE PLANK

CONCRETE PLANK CO.

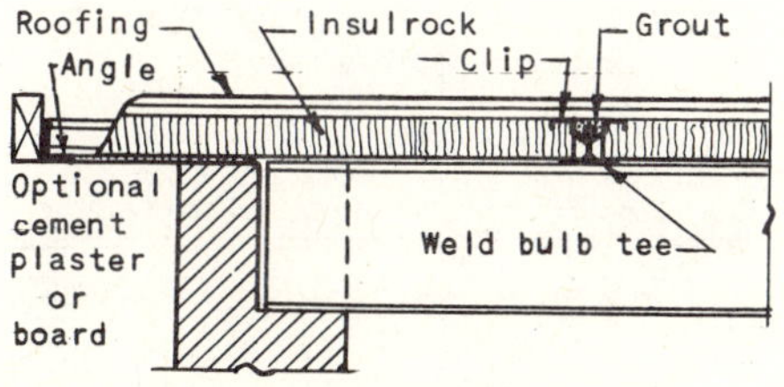
Roofing
Insulrock
Grout
Angle
Clip
Optional cement plaster or board
Weld bulb tee

2'-8"x 8'-0"x 2" or 3" thick
Spans 8'-0" (combined with bulb tee).
Insulrock, roof slabs applied to steel joist spaced 24", 32" or 48" o.c.
May also be used on sloped roofs.

INSULROCK INSULATED SLAB

INSULROCK CORPORATION

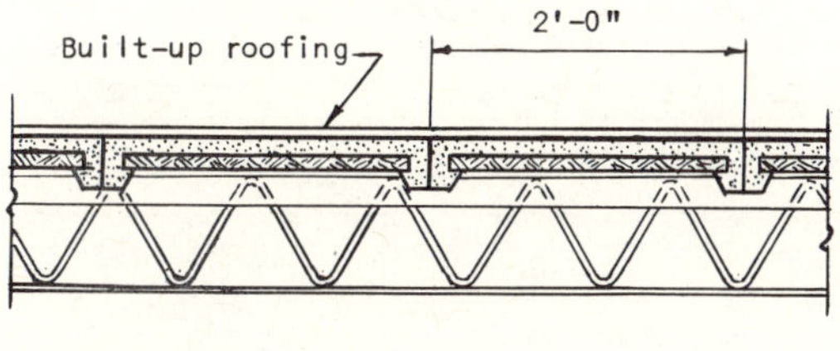
Built-up roofing
2'-0"

$3\frac{1}{2}$" x 2'-0" x length of beam
Spans 8'-0" max.
May also be used on sloped roof

INSULATING & ACOUSTICAL CHANNEL SLAB

(With Porex or Fiberglass soffit)

POREX MFG. CO.

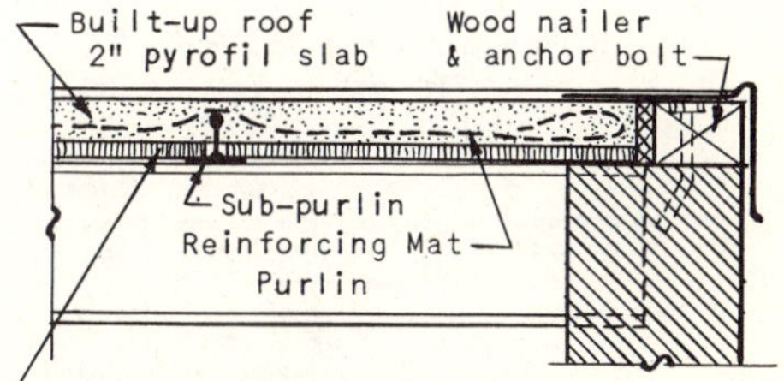
Built-up roof
2" pyrofil slab
Wood nailer & anchor bolt
Sub-purlin
Reinforcing Mat
Purlin

$\frac{1}{2}$" sheetrock or
1" USG insulation form - board or
Pyroform or
1" USG Acoustical form-board

PYROFILL ROOF DECK

UNITED STATES GYPSUM

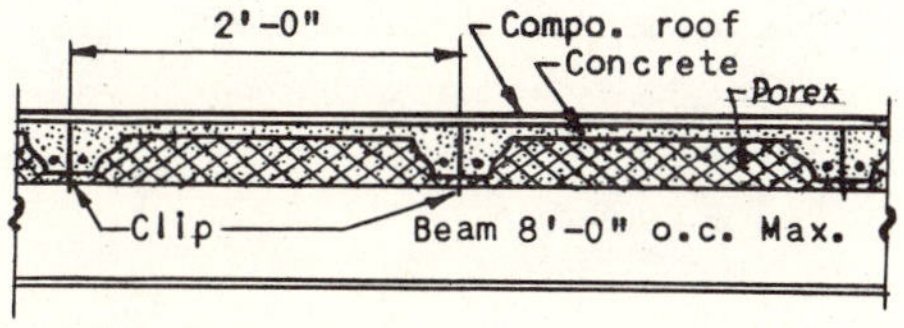
2'-0"
Compo. roof
Concrete
Porex
Clip
Beam 8'-0" o.c. Max.

$3\frac{1}{4}$" x 2'-0" x length of beam space
weight 14#/sq.'

POREX (COMPOSITE) PLANK INSULATING & ACOUSTICAL

PORETE MFG. CO.

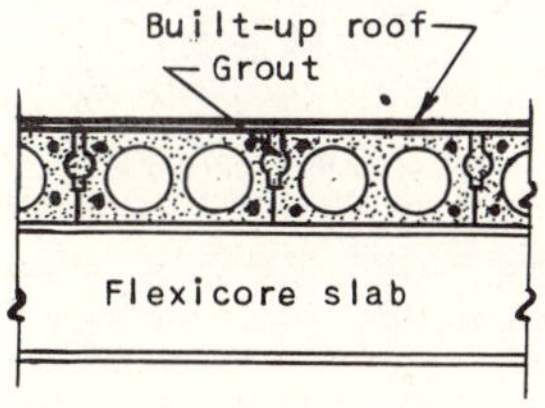
Built-up roof
Grout
Flexicore slab

Note: 6"x12" also suitable for curved saw-tooth or sloped roof

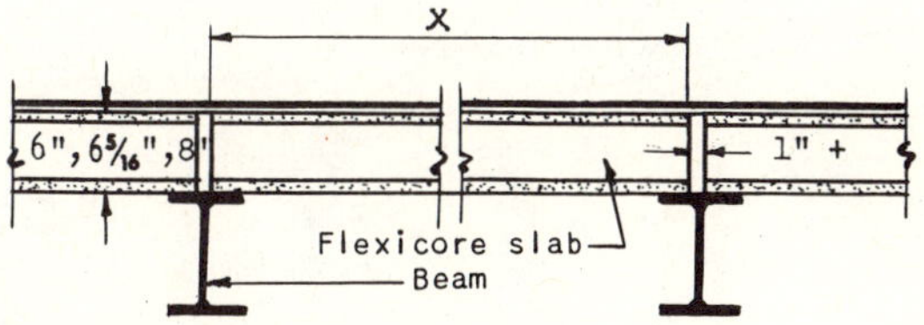
X
6", $6\frac{5}{16}$", 8"
1" +
Flexicore slab
Beam

6" x 12" x length up to 22'-6"
6" x 16" x length up to 22'-6"
$6\frac{5}{16}$" x 16" x length up to 22'-6"
8" x 16" x length up to 26'-8"
} X
All lengths are in inch variations.

"FLEXICORE" ROOF SLAB

FLEXICORE CO. INC.

ROOF CONSTRUCTION

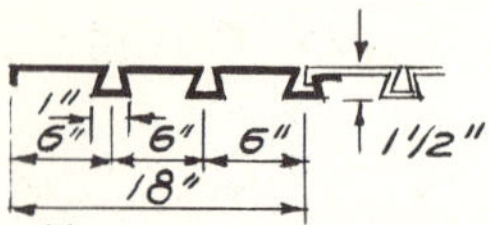
1"
6"
6"
6"
18"
1 1/2"

"Holorib" made 18-20 ga. In lengths to 24'-0" for multiple purlin spacing. Roof may be finished with slate, tile, composition or shingles above insulation.

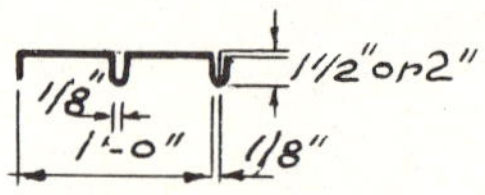
1 1/2" or 2"
1/8"
1'-0"
1/8"

Made in 20 & 18 ga. In lengths required to center endlaps directly over purlins. May span two or more purlins. May be used on flat, pitched, warped or arch roof framing. Acoustical matl. may be fitted to underside.

"MAHON"

THE R. C. MAHON COMPANY

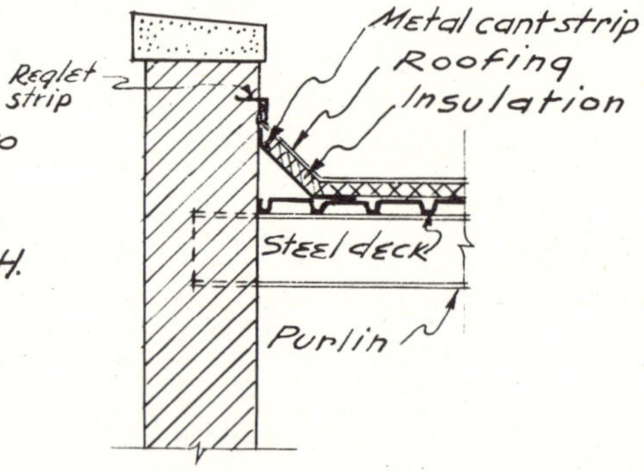
Metal cant strip
Roofing
Insulation
Reglet strip
Steel deck
Purlin

TYPICAL PARAPET WALL DETAIL
scale 1/2"=1'-0"

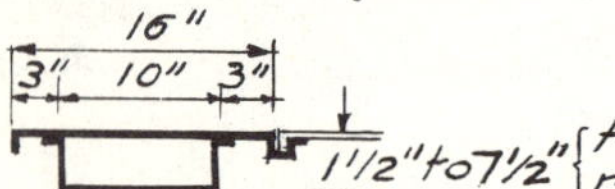
16"
3"
10"
3"
1 1/2" to 7 1/2" {to suit structural requirements

Type "D" made 18 to 12 ga. Side laps interlock. Flat surface is placed either down or up. In lengths to 20'-0"

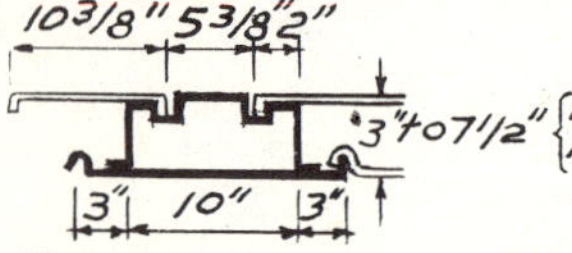
10 3/8"
5 3/8"
2"
3" to 7 1/2" {to suit structural requirements
3"
10"
3"

Type "AD" made from 16 to 13 ga. Lower plate may be perforated for acoustical treatment. For truss to truss long roof spans. To 20'-0"

"FENESTRA"

DETROIT STEEL PRODUCTS COMPANY

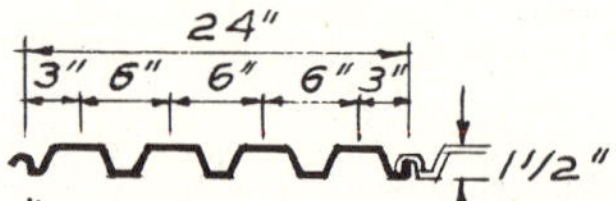
24"
3"
6"
6"
6"
3"
1 1/2"

"Q deck No 3" is economical for short spans (to 8') Maximum length in steel is 35'-0", In "Galbestos" is 12'-0"

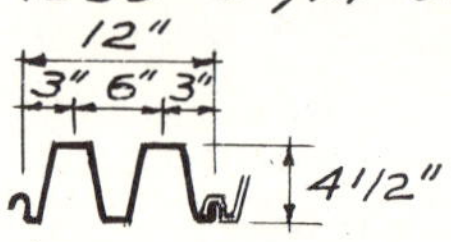
12"
3"
6"
3"
4 1/2"

"Q deck No 12" Is economical in long spans to 15'. Max. length 25' in steel

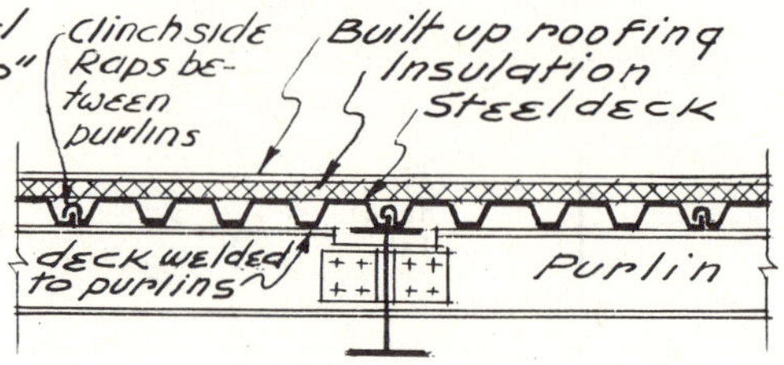
Clinch side laps between purlins
Built up roofing
Insulation
Steel deck
deck welded to purlins
Purlin

Note: Purlins should be framed to beam so that flanges are flush top.

TYPICAL DETAIL
scale: 1/2"=1'-0"

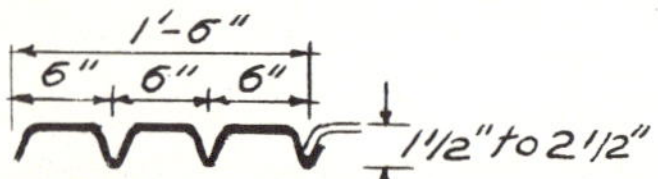
1'-6"
6"
6"
6"
1 1/2" to 2 1/2"

Fabricated in depths of 1 1/2", 1 3/4", 2" & 2 1/2" and 18, 20, 22 ga. In lengths to 22'-6" for multiple purlin spacing. Furnished in Cop-R-Loy steel or Softite galv.

"TRI-RIB"

WHEELING CORRUGATING COMPANY

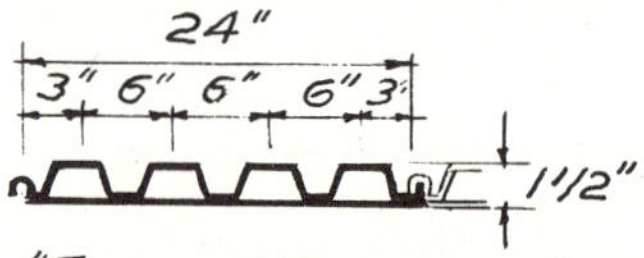
24"
3"
6"
6"
6"
3"
1 1/2"

"Type UK" For spans to 12', fluted or flat ceiling. Cells may be used for electrical raceways. Max. length 35'-0" steel only.

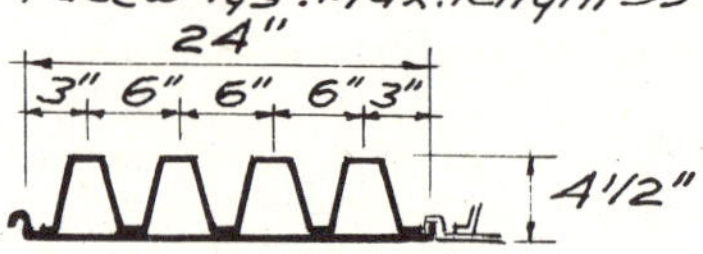
24"
3"
6"
6"
6"
3"
4 1/2"

"Type FK" For spans to 20'-0", fluted or flat ceiling. Cells may be used for electrical raceways. Max. length 35'-0" steel only.

"ROBERTSON"

H. H. ROBERTSON COMPANY.

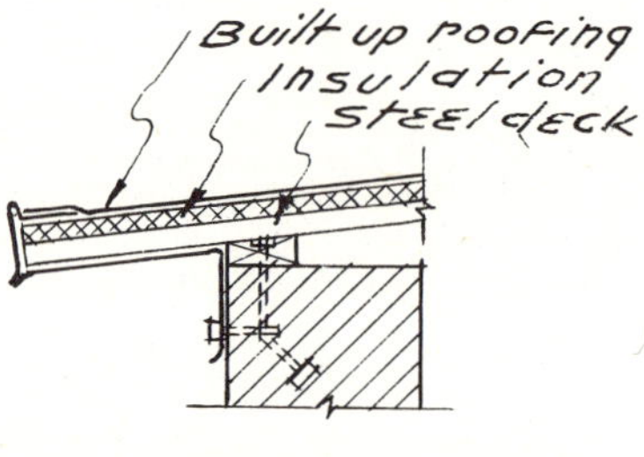
Built up roofing
Insulation
Steel deck

TYPICAL DETAIL AT EAVE
scale: 1/2"=1'-0"

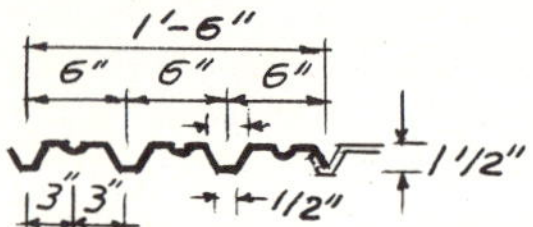
1'-6"
6"
6"
6"
1 1/2"
3"
3"
1/2"

Made 18 & 20 ga. in lengths to 24'-0" May be used on flat, pitched or warped roof framing.

U.S.G.

UNITED STATES GYPSUM CO.

STEEL ROOF DECKS - TYPES & DETAILS

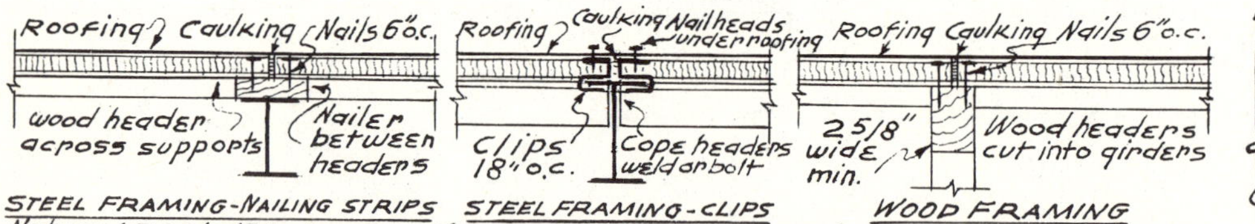
Roofing
Caulking
Nails 6" o.c.
wood header across supports
Nailer between headers
Roofing
Caulking
Nail heads under roofing
Clips 18" o.c.
Cope headers weld or bolt
Roofing
Caulking
Nails 6" o.c.
2 5/8" wide min.
Wood headers cut into girders
STEEL FRAMING-NAILING STRIPS
STEEL FRAMING-CLIPS
WOOD FRAMING

Notes: 1. Panels 1 9/16" or 2" × 4' × 8' maximum. 2. Wood or steel supports 4'-0" o.c. one way & up to 8'-0" the other way. 3. Nail heads directly on surface of cemesto or clip under roofing: nails 1" from edge of panel. 4. 1/4" space between panel edges filled with caulking.

"CEMESTO" PANELS FOR ROOF DECKS
THE CELOTEX CORPORATION scale 1/2"=1'-0"

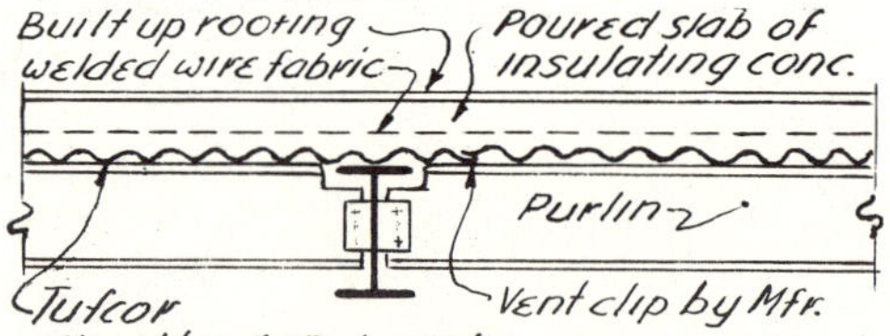
Built up roofing
welded wire fabric
Poured slab of insulating conc.
Purlin
Tufcor
Vent clip by Mfr.

Sheet lap ±3" at purlin
Deep corrugated, high tensile (80000 psi yield strength) steel 18 ga to 24 ga. 3" × 3/4" corrugations. Sheet lengths up to 14'-4" spans to 7'-0"

"TUFCOR" DECK WITH INSULATING CONCRETE FILL
Granco Steel Products Co.

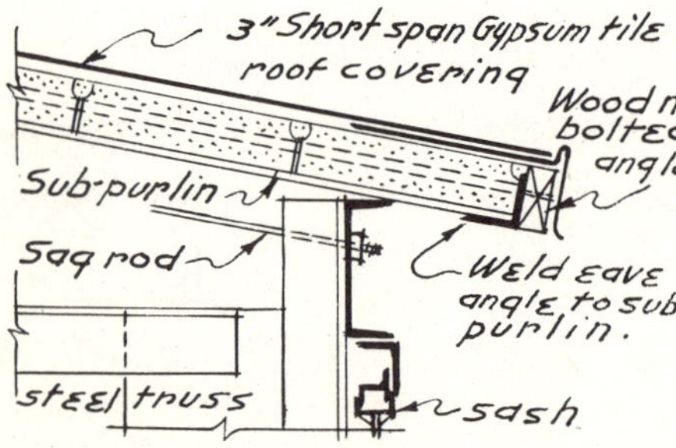
3" Short span Gypsum tile roof covering
Wood nailer bolted to angle
Sub-purlin
Sag rod
Weld eave angle to sub-purlin.
steel truss
sash

GYPSUM TILE (NAILING)
scale 3/4"=1'-0"
UNITED STATES GYPSUM CO.

Sub-purlins 2'-0 5/8" o.c. for acoustical formboard, 2'-8 5/8" for gypsum formboard and insulating formboard. Size depends on main purlin spacing

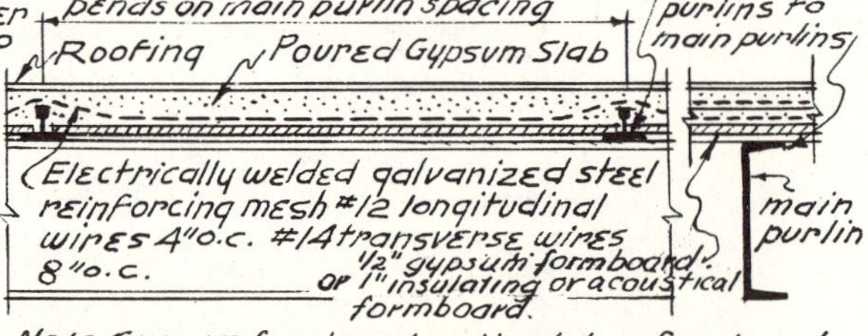
Roofing
Poured Gypsum Slab
Weld sub. purlins to main purlins
Electrically welded galvanized steel reinforcing mesh #12 longitudinal wires 4" o.c. #14 transverse wires 8" o.c.
1/2" gypsum formboard or 1" insulating or acoustical formboard.
main purlin

Note: Gypsum formboard and insulating formboard furnished in lengths to fit main purlin spacing. Maximum 10'-0". Acoustical formboard is 1" thick by 12" wide × 24" long and has T & G edges. Length spans from sub-purlin to sub-purlin.

POURED GYPSUM CONCRETE
scale 3/4"=1'-0"

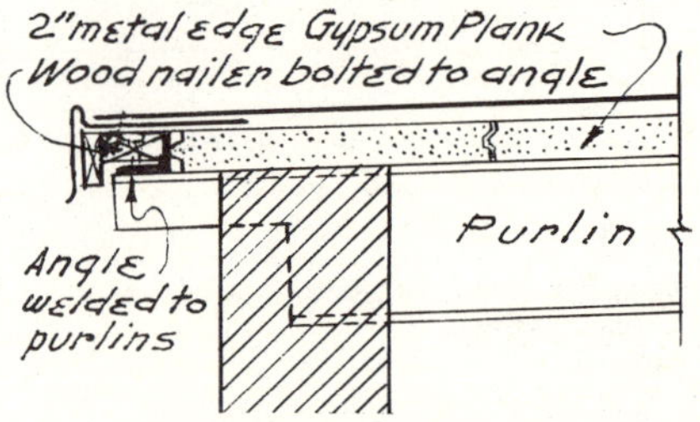
2" metal edge Gypsum Plank
Wood nailer bolted to angle
Purlin
Angle welded to purlins

GYPSUM PLANK
scale 3/4"=1'-0"
UNITED STATES GYPSUM CO.

SAFE DEPOSIT *and* BANK VAULTS

Placement of the safe deposit and bank vault (s) should be seriously studied. In all cases the vault should be placed along a side wall or the rear wall, or, if possible, in a rear corner. If the bank has a basement or if it is a split level building, place the vault area on the lower level. Bearing walls may be utilized in the construction of a vault.

Vault construction should provide fire and water, as well as burglary protection. The floors, walls and ceiling are usually of reinforced concrete, with an inner lining of steel. Vault doors, walls, floors and ceilings are always chosen to conform with insurance requirements. The maximum burglary resistance rating for a vault, including the door, is a No. 10 classification, which obtains the lowest insurance rate, with higher rates for lower classifications. All wall constructions and the vault door shown on this page conform with the No. 10 classification. The recommended fire resistance rating of 6 hours or more is obtained with walls "C" thru "J".

For further information see "Manual of Burglary Insurance," issued by the National Bureau of Casualty Underwriters, 60 John Street, New York City, and "Merchandise Vaults and Safes", issued by National Board of Fire Underwriters, 85 John Street, New York City.

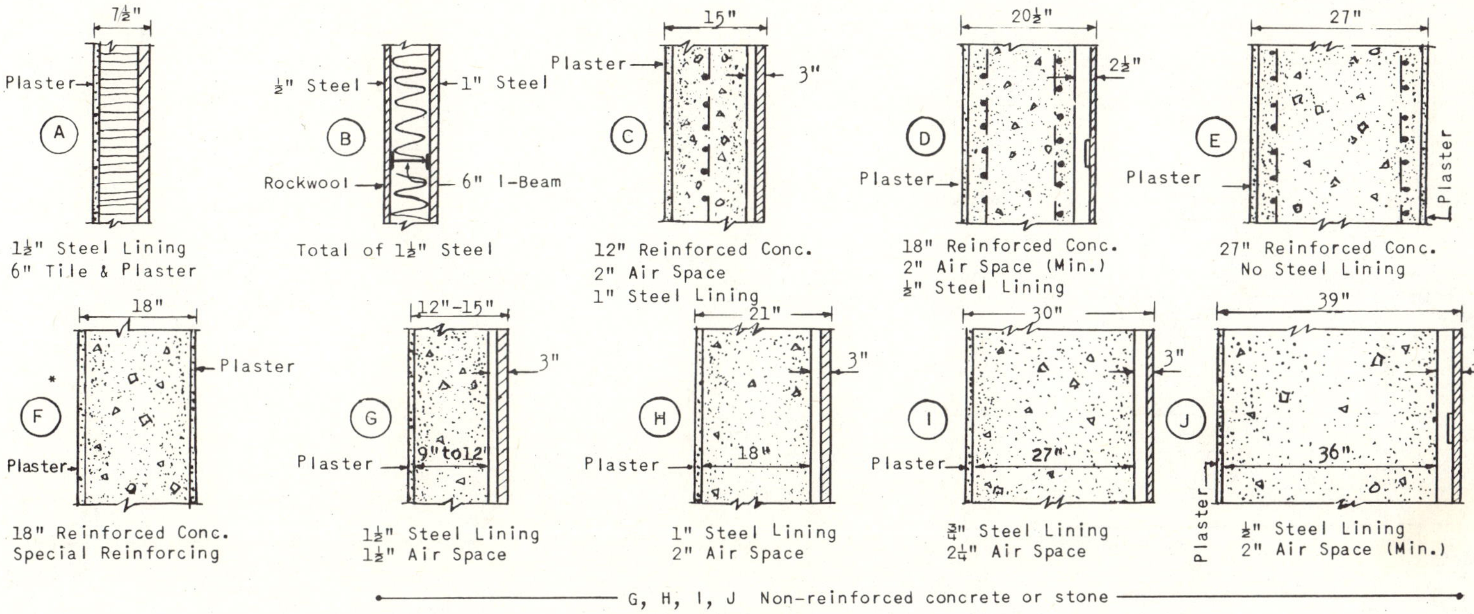
A
7½"
Plaster
1½" Steel Lining
6" Tile & Plaster
B
½" Steel
1" Steel
Rockwool
6" I-Beam
Total of 1½" Steel
C
15"
Plaster
3"
12" Reinforced Conc.
2" Air Space
1" Steel Lining
D
20½"
2½"
Plaster
18" Reinforced Conc.
2" Air Space (Min.)
½" Steel Lining
E
27"
Plaster
Plaster
27" Reinforced Conc.
No Steel Lining
F
18"
Plaster
Plaster
18" Reinforced Conc.
Special Reinforcing
G
12"-15"
3"
9" to 12"
Plaster
1½" Steel Lining
1½" Air Space
H
21"
3"
18"
Plaster
1" Steel Lining
2" Air Space
I
30"
3"
27"
Plaster
¾" Steel Lining
2¼" Air Space
J
39"
3"
36"
Plaster
½" Steel Lining
2" Air Space (Min.)
G, H, I, J Non-reinforced concrete or stone

VAULT WALLS

*No specific requirements are set forth for size or spacing or reinforcing steel when used, except for "F" above. In this case the following listed reinforcing systems should be used: Bates Truss Joint, Laclede Anchor, Havemeyer, Lock-Steel, Massillon, Rivet-Grip, Ryerson Steel-Crete, Strauss H-Beam, Truscon Kahn Bar. These should provide reinforcement of 21 lbs. per sq. ft.

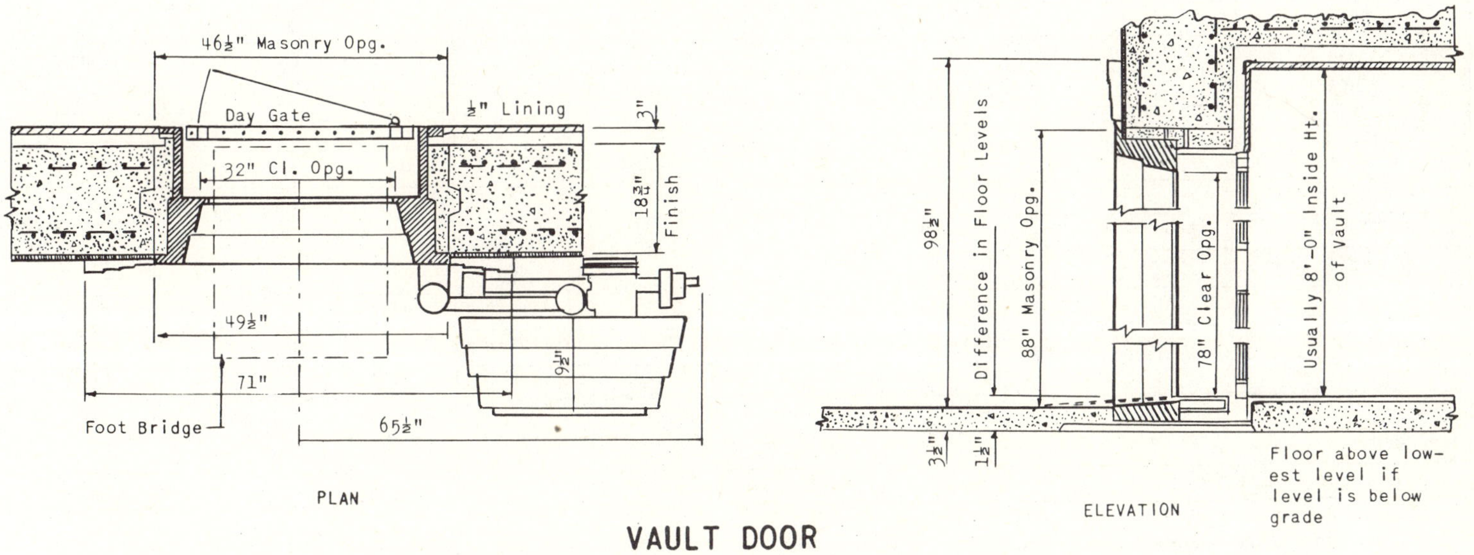
46½" Masonry Opg.
Day Gate
½" Lining
3"
32" Cl. Opg.
18¾"
Finish
49½"
9½"
71"
Foot Bridge
65½"
PLAN
98½"
Difference in Floor Levels
88" Masonry Opg.
78" Clear Opg.
Usually 8'-0" Inside Ht. of Vault
3½"
1½"
Floor above lowest level if level is below grade
ELEVATION

VAULT DOOR

The various types of wall construction and the door thickness above are for No. 10 burglary classification. Wall construction "C" thru "J" and door have fire resistance rating of 6 hrs. or more.

DATA BY MOSLER SAFE CO.

CONSTRUCTION OF VAULTS

FLOOR FRAMING SYSTEMS COMPARED

NUMBER	FLOOR SYSTEM	BASE PRICE OCT. 1954 ¢ PER SQ. FT.	ADAPTABILITY FOR TERRAZZO FINISH	SUITABILITY FOR WINTER CONSTRUCTION	INSURANCE AND SAFETY FROM FIRE	HOW FOOL-PROOF IS THIS CONSTRUCTION?	EFFECT ON COST OF SUPPORTING STRUCTURAL STEEL	ABSENCE OF SUITABLE CINDERS	NUMBER
1	REINF. CONC.-LONG SPAN	¢159.5	O.K.	handicapped	O.K.	insp'n req'd	basic	O.K.	1
2	REINF. CONC.-LOW COST HOUSING	149.7	O.K.	handicapped	O.K.	insp'n req'd	basic	O.K.	2
3	REINF. CONC.-BEAM AND SLAB	194.8	O.K.	handicapped	O.K.	insp'n req'd	basic	O.K.	3
4	OPEN WOOD JOIST (NON-FIREPROOF)	215.0*	not recomm'd	O.K.	poor	O.K.	credit	O.K.	4
5	PRECAST CONC. I-BEAM	181.1	not recomm'd	O.K.	O.K.	O.K.	basic	O.K.	5
6	OPEN WEB STEEL JOISTS(BAR JOISTS)	187.4	not recomm'd	fair	handicapped	O.K.	credit	O.K.	6
7	2" CONCRETE PLANK	197.5	not recomm'd	O.K.	handicapped	O.K.	credit	O.K.	7
8	GYPSUM PLANK	204.5	not recomm'd	O.K.	handicapped	O.K.	credit	O.K.	8
9	2¾" CONCRETE PLANK	208.1	not recomm'd	O.K.	handicapped	O.K.	credit	O.K.	9
10	REPUBLIC - ONE WAY	201.8	O.K.	handicapped	O.K.	insp'n req'd	basic	O.K.	10
11	REPUBLIC-TWO WAY SLAG BLOCK	226.3	O.K.	handicapped	O.K.	insp'n req'd	basic	O.K.	11
12	SCHUSTER - TWO WAY TILE	226.3	O.K.	handicapped	O.K.	insp'n req'd	basic	O.K.	12
13	STEEL & CINDER CONC. ARCHES	207.0	O.K.	fair	O.K.	O.K.	basic	debit	13
14	GRITCRETE	193.9	O.K.	fair	O.K.	O.K.	basic	O.K.	14
15	ROBERTSON Q-FLOOR	223.5	O.K.	O.K.	handicapped	O.K.	credit	O.K.	15
16	METAL TILE (TIN PAN)	205.2	O.K.	handicapped	O.K.	insp'n req'd	basic	O.K.	16
17	COFAR	208.8	O.K.	fair	handicapped	insp'n req'd	credit	O.K.	17
18	LONG SPAN TUBE	243.7	O.K.	handicapped	O.K.	insp'n req'd	basic	O.K.	18

NUMBER	FLOOR SYSTEM	BASE FOR ASPHALT TILE, LINOLEUM, STUCK DN. WOOD	FLAT CEILING REQUIRED	RUGGEDNESS FOR ROLLING OR CONCENTRATED LOADS	CONDUIT SPACE PROVIDED	SOUND TRANSMISSION	PLASTER BOND	PERMANENCY	NUMBER
1	REINF. CONC.-LONG SPAN	O.K.	O.K.	O.K.	O.K.	O.K.	not recomm'd	O.K.	1
2	REINF. CONC.-LOW COST HOUSING	O.K.	O.K.	O.K.	O.K.	O.K.	not recomm'd	O.K.	2
3	REINF. CONC.-BEAM AND SLAB	O.K.	debit 15¢	O.K.	O.K.	O.K.	not recomm'd	O.K.	3
4	OPEN WOOD JOIST (NON-FIREPROOF)	credit 42¢	O.K.	handicapped	O.K.	poor	O.K.	fair	4
5	PRECAST CONC. I-BEAM	O.K.	O.K.	not recomm'd	fill pref'd	O.K.	O.K.	O.K.	5
6	OPEN WEB STEEL JOISTS(BAR JOISTS)	O.K.	O.K.	not recomm'd	O.K.	fl.fill essent'l	O.K.	fair	6
7	2" CONCRETE PLANK	O.K.	O.K.	not recomm'd	O.K.	fl.fill essent'l	O.K.	fair	7
8	GYPSUM PLANK	O.K.	O.K.	not recomm'd	O.K.	fl.fill essent'l	O.K.	fair	8
9	2¾" CONCRETE PLANK	O.K.	O.K.	not recomm'd	O.K.	fl.fill essent'l	O.K.	fair	9
10	REPUBLIC - ONE WAY	O.K.	O.K.	O.K.	fill pref'd	O.K.	O.K.	O.K.	10
11	REPUBLIC - TWO WAY SLAG BLOCK	O.K.	O.K.	O.K.	fill pref'd	O.K.	O.K.	O.K.	11
12	SCHUSTER - TWO WAY TILE	O.K.	O.K.	O.K.	fill pref'd	O.K.	O.K.	O.K.	12
13	STEEL & CINDER CONC. ARCHES	O.K.	debit 15¢	**	fill pref'd	O.K.	care	O.K.	13
14	GRITCRETE	O.K.	debit 15¢	**	fill pref'd	O.K.	?	O.K.	14
15	ROBERTSON Q-FLOOR	O.K.	O.K.	not recomm'd	basic	O.K.	O.K.	fair	15
16	METAL TILE (TIN PAN)	O.K.	O.K.	handicapped	O.K.	O.K.	O.K.	O.K.	16
17	COFAR	O.K.	debit	O.K.	O.K.	O.K.	O.K.	fair	17
18	LONG SPAN TUBE	O.K.	debit	O.K.	?	O.K.	O.K.	O.K.	18

*includes finish oak floor. **stone concrete preferred.

The table above shows basic costs and how they are modified by considerations of suitability.

Costs of various floor systems given above and on the following page are built up from materials required for a particular panel 20' x 45'; 60 lbs. live load; 20,000 lbs. stress in the steel; open web steel joist stresses in accordance with specs. of the Steel Joist Institute; semi-continuous conditions for those systems where continuity is practical; no account taken for supporting beams and columns.

Prices shown are for the New York City area, based on Oct. 1954 costs, and may be varied in accordance with Engineering News Record Bldg. Cost Index curves. Example: if $3.00 is given for a system and the index later drops 10% below Oct. 1954, revise cost to $2.70. Costs given include all overhead profit, insurance, etc., except general contractor's profit.

Data checked by Elwyn E. Seelye, Consulting Engineer

FLOOR FRAMING SYSTEMS COMPARED

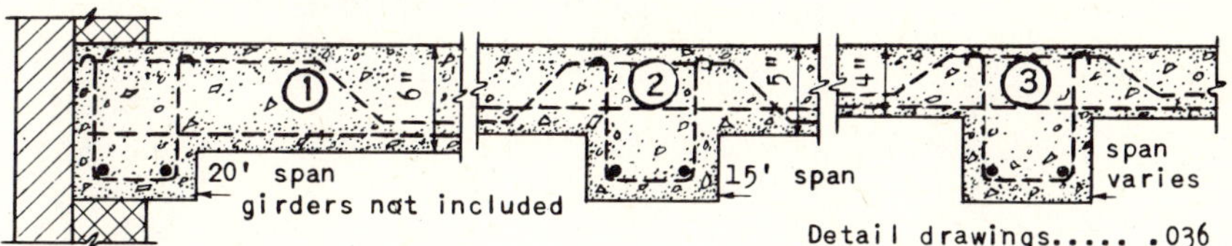
1
6"
20' span
girders not included
2
5"
15' span
4"
3
span varies

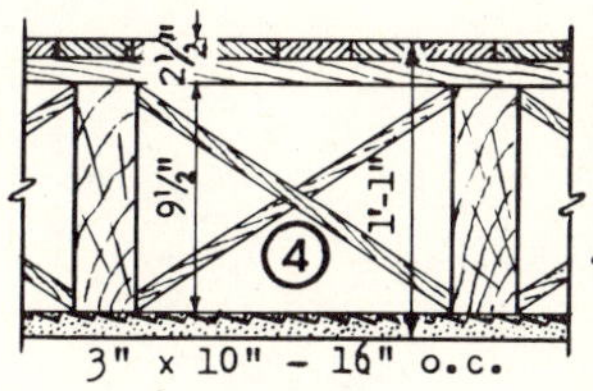
4
9½"
11-1"
3" x 10" - 16" o.c.

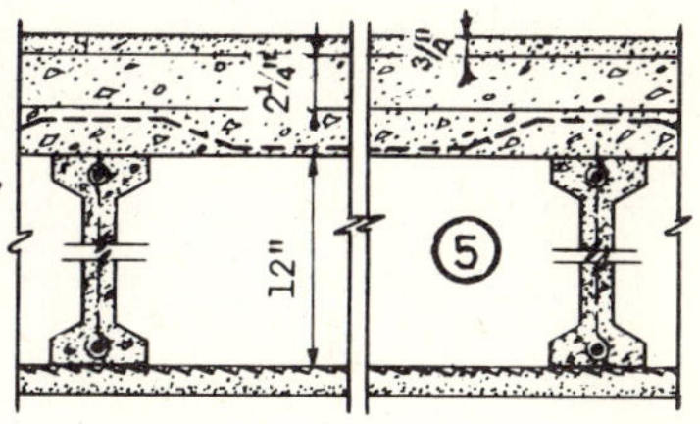
5
12"

Item	#1	#2
Conc. for slab, .5 cu.ft./sq.ft. (#2: .43 cu.ft.)	.408	.357
Reinf'g steel 2.25 psf (#2: 2 psf)	.347	.300
Forms, 1 sq.ft.	.600	.600
Steel trowel finish	.120	.120
2 coats cem.paint	.120	.120
Total	$1.595	$1.497

4 hr. fire resistance

REINFORCED CONCRETE SLAB

#1-LONG SPAN **#2-LOW COST HOUSING**

#3	
Detail drawings	.036
Stone conc., .42 cu.ft./sq.ft.	.342
3 psf	.450
Incl beams	.800
	.120
Smooth forms, trimming, 2 coats cem.paint	.200
	$1.948
If plast'd, deduct	-.200
Add for plaster	+.336
	$2.084

#3-BEAM AND SLAB

#4	
Lumber, 2 FBM/sq.ft., incl. joists, bridging	.550
Lath	.120
Plaster, 3 coats	.280
Sheath'g (sub-fl.)	.300
Oak flooring	.900
	$2.150

non-fireproof

#4-WOOD JOISTS

#5	
Conc. joist	.670
Slab, 20 cu.ft.	.200
Lath	.222
Plaster, 3 coats	.280*
$2\frac{1}{4}$" conc.fl.fill	.111
$\frac{3}{4}$" cement finish	.180
Detail drawings	.018
Steeltex	.130*
	$1.811

4 hr. fire resistance

#5-PRECAST CONC. I-BEAM

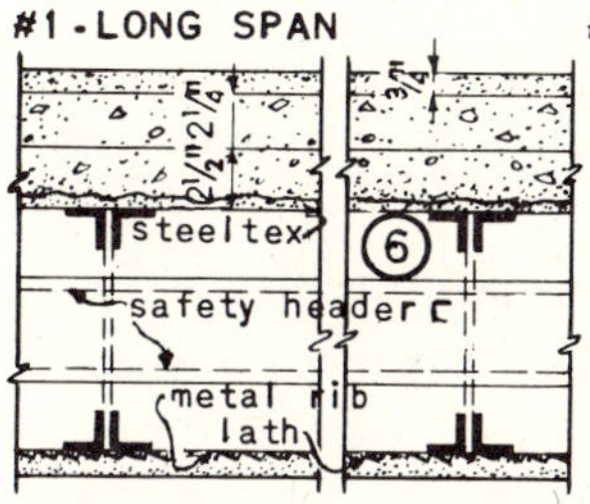
6
steeltex
safety header
metal rib lath

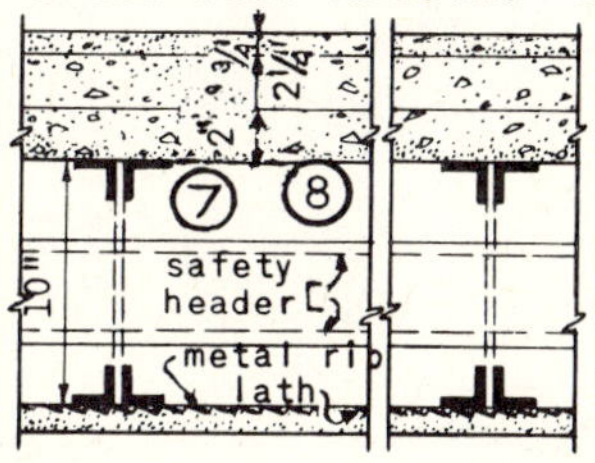
7
8
safety header
metal rib lath

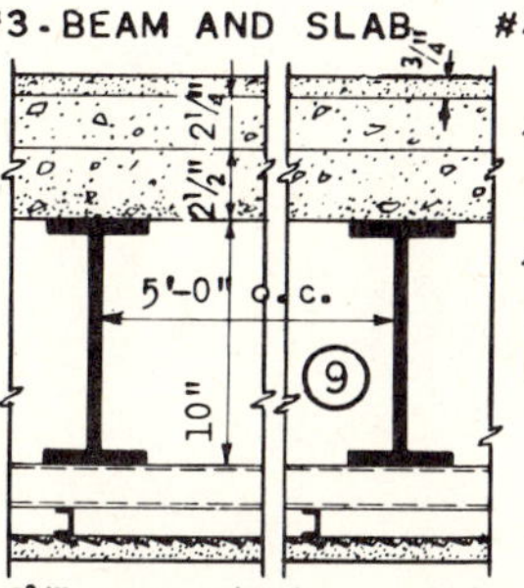
5'-0" o.c.
10"
9

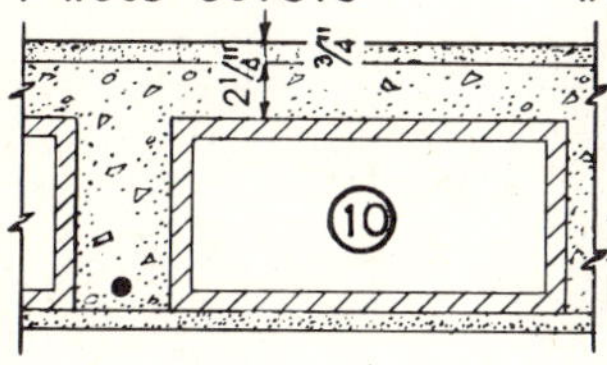
10

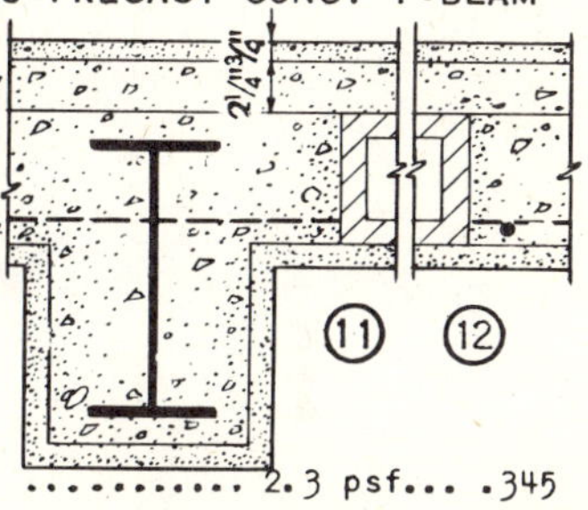
11
12

#6	
Bar joist, 4.3 psf	.624
$2\frac{1}{2}$" stone conc., .20 cu.ft./sq.ft.	.200
Lath	.222*
Plaster, 3 coats	.280*
$2\frac{1}{4}$" conc.fl.fill	.111
$\frac{3}{4}$" cement finish	.180
Channel head'r .4 psf	.060
Detail drawings	.022
Pencil rods .3 psf	.045
Steeltex	.130*
	$1.874

3-hr. fire resistance

#6-OPEN WEB STEEL (BAR JOISTS)

#7	
4 psf	.580
2" conc.plank	.520
(Lath, as #6)	.222*
(Plaster, as #6)	.280*
(Conc.fl.fill, as #6)	.111
(Cement finish, as #6)	.180
(Channel head'r, as #6)	.060
(Detail drawings, as #6)	.022
	$1.975

#9	
$2\frac{3}{4}$" conc.plank	.550
(Lath, as #6)	.222*
(Plaster, as #6)	.280*
(Conc.fl.fill, as #6)	.111
(Cement finish, as #6)	.180
Struc. steel	.560
Furring	.278
	$2.181

1 to 2 hr. fire resistance

#7-2" CONC. PLANK **#9-2$\frac{3}{4}$" CONC. PLANK**

#8-GYPSUM PLANK comparable with conc. plank. Cost in place: 35¢/sq. ft.

#10	
Reinf'g steel, 1.7 psf	.255
Conc., .24 cu.ft/sq.ft	.240
8" tile	.330
Forms, 1 sq.ft.	.600
Plaster, 3 coats	.280
$2\frac{1}{4}$" conc.fl.fill	.111
$\frac{3}{4}$" cem. finish	.180
Detail drawings	.022
	$2.018

#11	
(Reinf'g steel) 2.3 psf	.345
.21 cu.ft./sq.ft.	.210
7" tile, 1 sq.ft.	.300
(Forms, as #10)	.600
incl. beams	.280
(Conc.fl.fill, as #10)	.111
(Cem. finish, as #10)	.180
(Detail drawings, as #10)	.022
Steel for 1 side beam	.215
	$2.263

4 hr. fire resistance

#10-ONE WAY - REPUBLIC - #11-TWO WAY

#12-SCHUSTER - comparable to #11 -Two Way

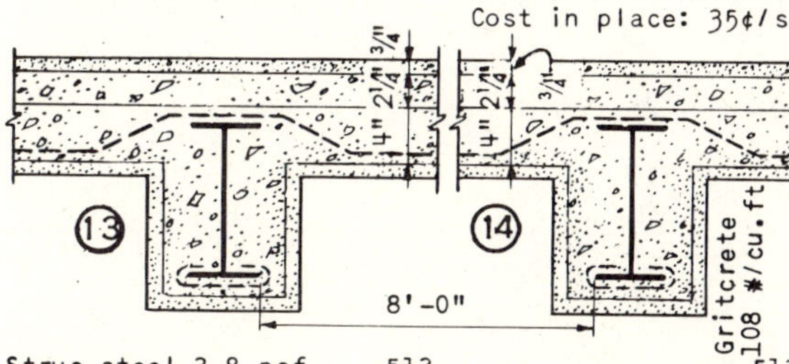
13
8'-0"
14
Gritcrete 108 #/cu.ft

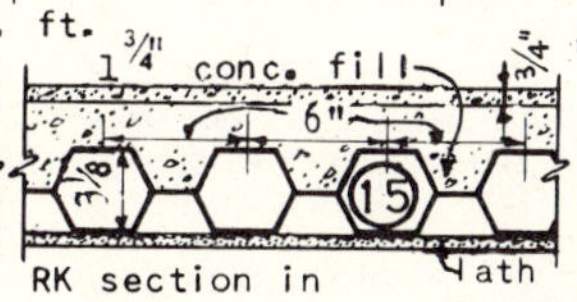
$1\frac{3}{4}$" conc. fill
6"
15
lath

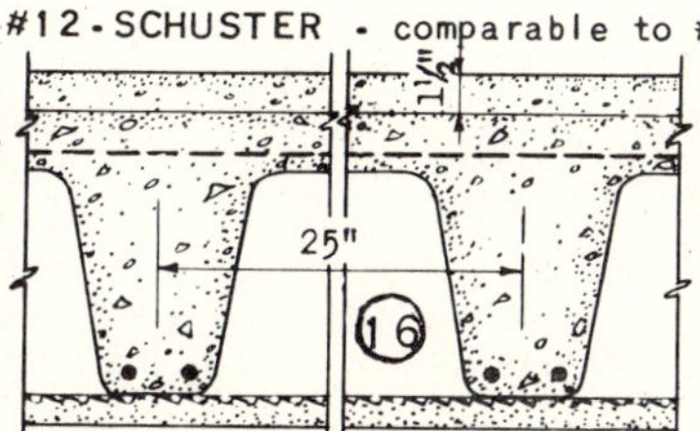
25"
16

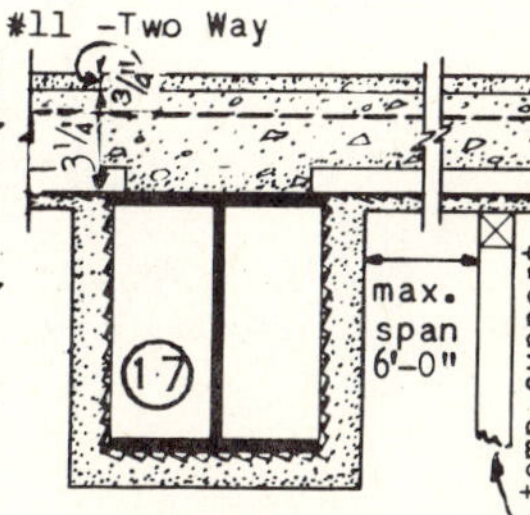
17
max. span 6'-0"
temp. support

#13	
Struc.steel 3.8 psf	.513
Mesh, 1 sq. ft.	.141
Cinder conc. .42 cu.ft./sq.ft.	.389
Forms, 1 sq.ft. hung from steel, incl. beams‡	.400
Plaster, bonds & 2 coats incl. beams	.336
$2\frac{1}{4}$" conc.fl.fill	.111
$\frac{3}{4}$" cement finish	.180
	$2.070

‡ add 10¢/sq.ft. outside New York City

#14	
(Struc.steel, as #13)	.513
(Mesh, as #13)	.141
"Gritcrete" .42 cu.ft./sq.ft.	.389
1 sq.ft., incl.bms.	.400
Smooth forms, trim'g. 2 coats cem.paint.	.200
(Conc.fl.fill)	.116
(Cement finish, as #13)	.180
	$1.939
If plast'd deduct	-.200
Add for plaster	+.336
	$2.075

4 - hr. fire resistance

#13-STEEL AND CINDER CONCRETE ARCHES **#14-GRITCRETE (AEROCRETE)**

*Substitute mineral a.t. & furring chan. for lath & plas.: add 65¢-(28+13)=24¢.

#15	
RK section in place	1.210
$1\frac{3}{4}$" conc.fl.fill	.087
$\frac{3}{4}$" cem. finish	.180
Lath	.120
Plaster, 3 coats	.336
Struc. steel, 2.4 lbs	.322
	2.235

1 to 2 hr. fire resistance

#15-ROBERTSON "Q" FLOOR

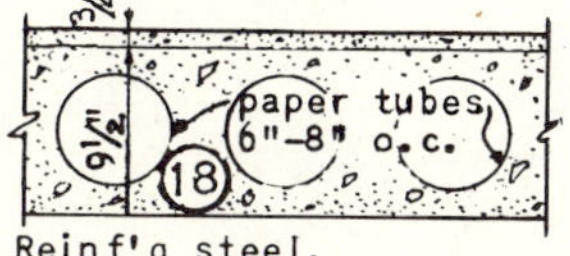
paper tubes 6"-8" o.c.
18

#18	
Reinf'g steel, 3.74 psf	.561
Conc. .5 cu.ft/sq.ft	.400
Forms	.600
Tubes 1.5 lin.ft./sq.ft.	.270
$\frac{3}{4}$" cem.finish	.180
Smooth forms, 2 coats cem.paint	.200
	$2.211

4-hr. fire resistance

#18-LONG SPAN TUBE FLR.

#16	
Reinf'g steel 2 psf	.300
Conc. .4 cu.ft./sq.ft.	.400
Lath	.222
Metal tile 20.0	
Forms 40.0	
Total	.600‡
Plaster, 3 coats	.280
Detail drawings	.035
$1\frac{1}{2}$" cem. finish	.215
	$2.052

‡ Increase 8¢ for small job. Decrease 3¢ for large, well-organized job where pans may be reused at least three times.

4 hr. fire resistance

#16-METAL TILE (TIN PAN)

combination form & reinf'g (Cofar)

#17	
Fin	.180
Slab	.322
Reinf'g .367#lbs	.055
Cofar 24 ga	.590
Struc.steel 3.6#	.485
Plaster	.336
Lath	.120
	$2.088
For sprayed insulat'n deduct lath, plas.	-.456
Add, spray insulat'n	+.350
	$1.982

3 hr. fire resistance

#17-COFAR FLOOR

Data checked by Elwyn E. Seelye, Consulting Engineer

MASONRY CONSTRUCTION

TABLE OF CONTENTS

WALL THICKNESSES : N.Y. CITY CODE

FOUNDATION WALLS

GENERAL CASE

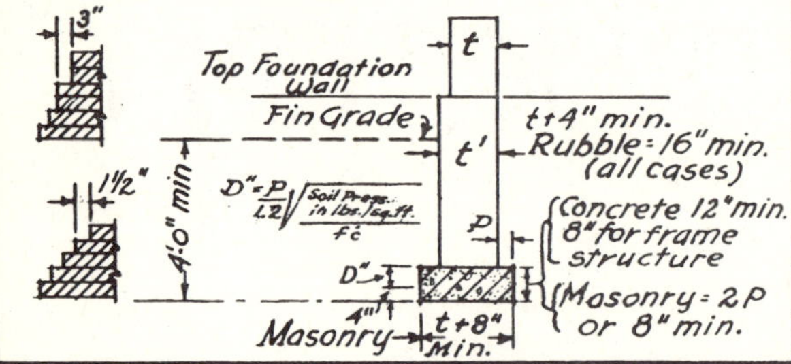
3"
1½"
Top Foundation Wall
Fin Grade
4'-0" min.
t
t'
t+4" min.
Rubble = 16" min. (all cases)
D" = P / 12 √(Soil Press. in lbs./sq.ft. / fc)
P
Concrete 12" min. 8" for frame structure
D"
Masonry = 2P or 8" min.
4"
Masonry
t+8" Min.

PRIVATE DWELLINGS

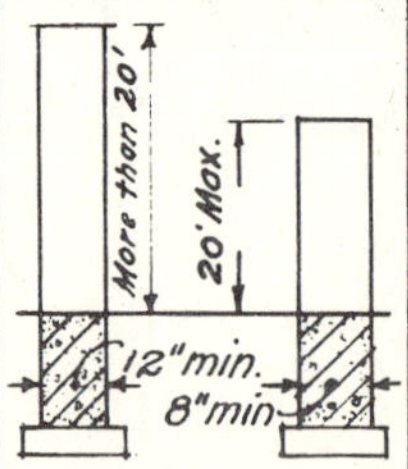
More than 20'
20' Max.
12" min.
8" min.

OTHER STRUCTURES

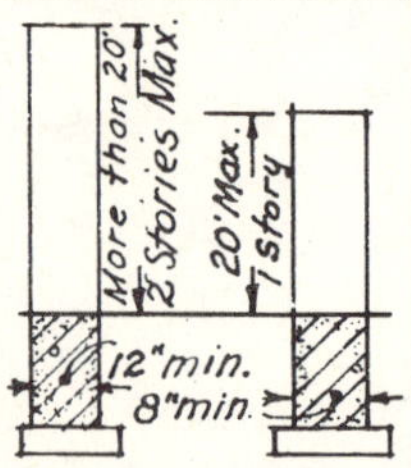
More than 20'
2 Stories Max.
20' Max.
1 Story
12" min.
8" min.

HOLLOW BLOCK (NO BASEMENT)

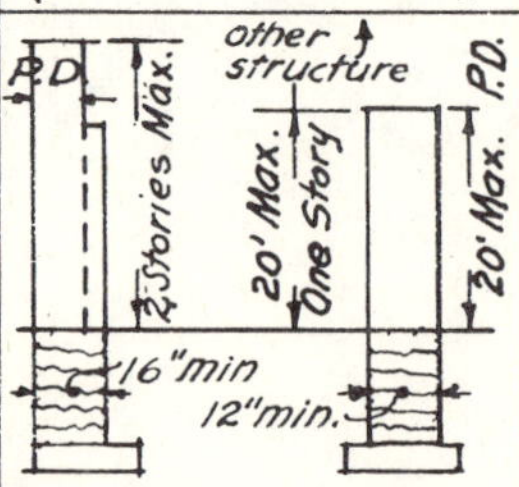
P.D.
other structure
2 Stories Max.
20' Max.
One Story
20' Max.
P.D.
16" min
12" min.

HOLLOW BLOCK SUPERSTRUCTURE

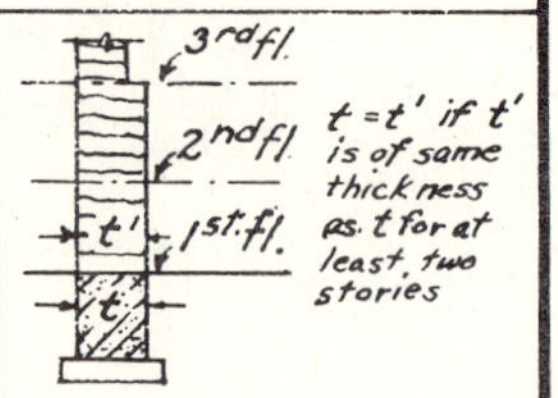
3rd fl.
2nd fl
1st fl.
t'
t
t = t' if t' is of same thickness as t for at least two stories

CURTAIN WALLS

SOLID MASONRY — HOLLOW BLOCK; or WALL

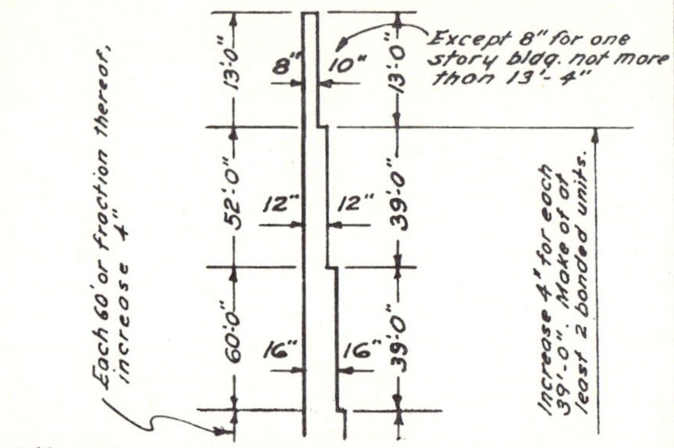
8"
10"
13'-0"
13'-0"
Except 8" for one story bldg. not more than 13'-4"
52'-0"
12"
12"
39'-0"
60'-0"
16"
16"
39'-0"
Each 60' or fraction thereof, increase 4"
Increase 4" for each 39'-0". Make of at least 2 bonded units.

When horizontal distance between supports exceeds 20'-0" increase wall thickness 4" for each additional 10' or fraction.

PANEL (SKELETON) WALLS

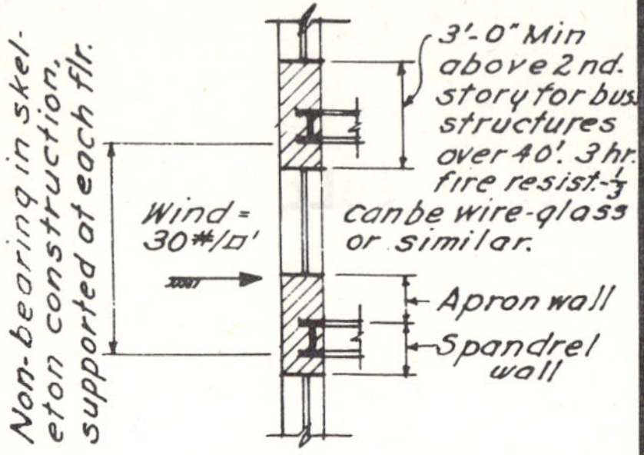
Non-bearing in skeleton construction, supported at each flr.
Wind = 30#/□'
3'-0" Min above 2nd. story for bus. structures over 40'. 3 hr. fire resist. ⅓ can be wire-glass or similar.
Apron wall
Spandrel wall

FIRE WALLS

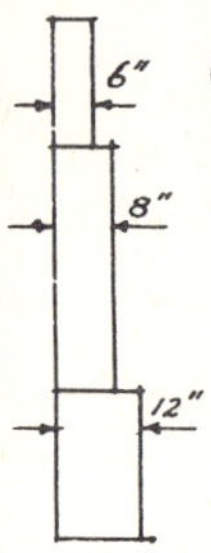
6"
8"
12"

6": (If not loaded) Reinf. Conc.; 6" solid cinder conc. blocks plaster 2 sides.

8": Solid brick; solid structural units; plain conc.; solid cinder conc. blocks; 8" hollow conc. blks (1½" thick shells) plastered 2 sides; 8" hollow clay tile (3 cells) plastered 2 sides.

12": 12" hollow clay tile blocks (2 unit, 3 cells) plastered 2 sides; 12" hollow conc. (2 cells - 1½" web.)

WALL THICKNESSES for FIRE RATINGS

MATERIAL	4 hr.	3 hr.	2 hr.	1 hr.
Reinforced Concrete	6"	5"	4"	—
Brick	8"	8"	8"	4"
Concrete Block (Hollow)	12", 8"*	8"	8"	3"*
Clay Tile (Hollow)	12", 8"*	6"‡	4"*	3"*

* Plastered both sides
‡ Plastered one side only.

PARTITIONS

Non-bearing wall, one story or less in height.

Under 12' high	–	3" thick
12' to 16' "	–	4" "
16' " 20' "	–	6" "
20' " 24' "	–	8" "

BEARING WALLS

SOLID MASONRY

GENERAL CASE

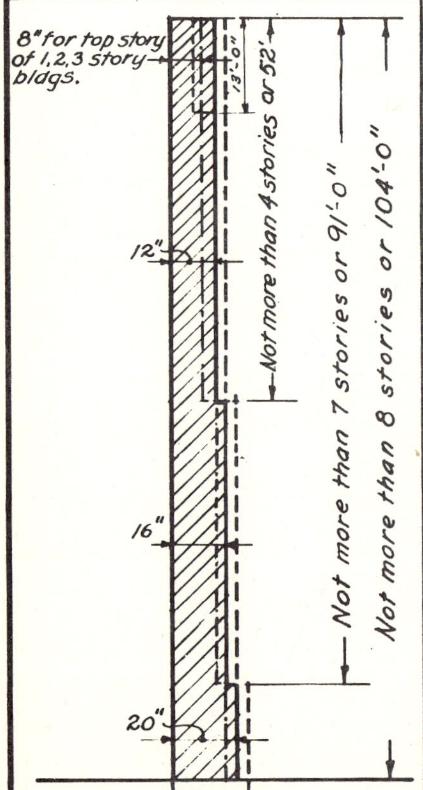
8" for top story of 1, 2, 3 story bldgs.
13'-0"
Not more than 4 stories or 52'
12"
Not more than 7 stories or 91'-0"
Not more than 8 stories or 104'-0"
16"
20"

Also see Private Dwelling 35' high or less & Mixed Occupancy

BLDGS UNDER 75'

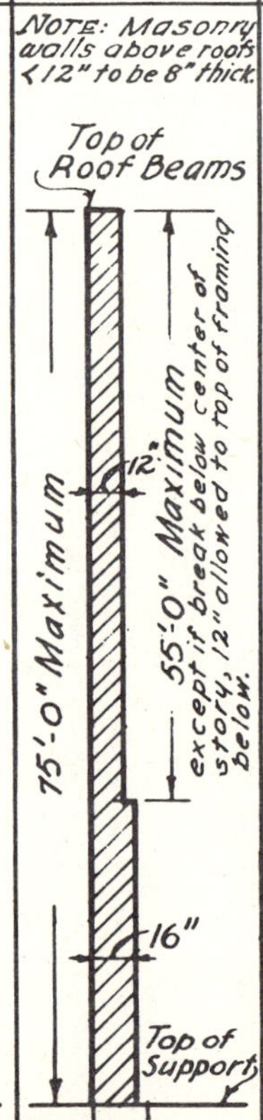
NOTE: Masonry walls above roofs <12" to be 8" thick.
Top of Roof Beams
75'-0" Maximum
12"
55'-0" Maximum except if break below center of story, 12" allowed to top of framing below.
16"
Top of Support

Bldgs under 75' high need not exceed above thickn's.

REINF. CONCRETE

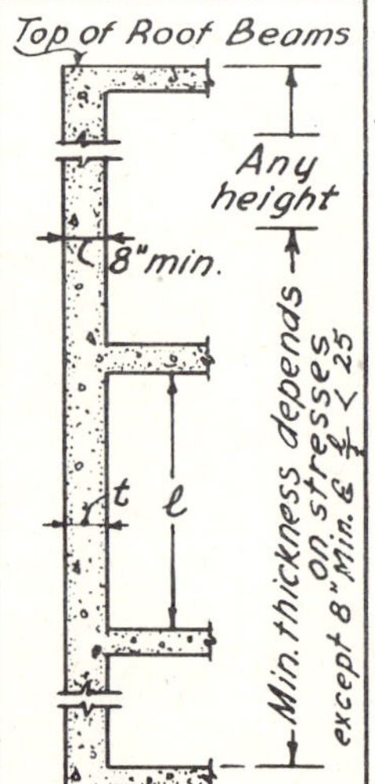
Top of Roof Beams
Any height
8" min.
t
l
Min. thickness depends on stresses except 8" Min. & l/t < 25

HOLLOW or CAVITY

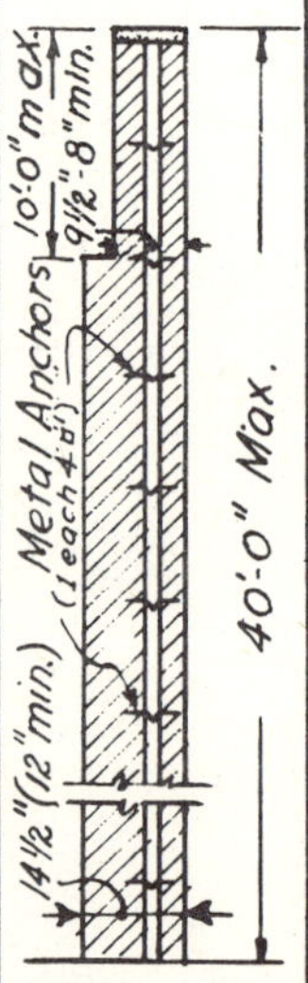
10'-0" max.
9½"-8" min.
Metal Anchors (1 each 4 sf)
40'-0" Max.
14½" (12" min.)

HOLLOW BLOCK

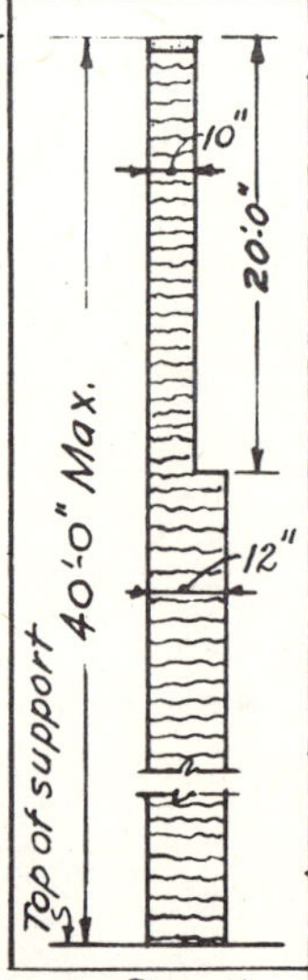
10"
20'-0"
40'-0" Max.
12"
Top of support

Also see Private Dwell. 35'-0" high or less and Mixed occupancies.

PRIVATE DWELLINGS 35'-0" high or less MIXED OCCUPANCIES 25'-0" wide or less and less than 3 stories

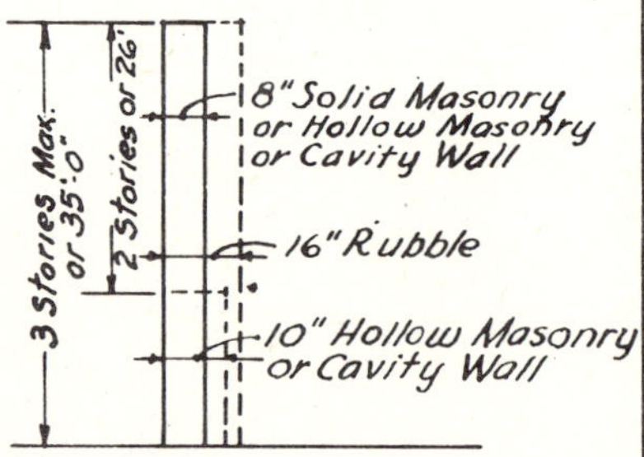
3 Stories Max. or 35'-0"
2 Stories or 26'
8" Solid Masonry or Hollow Masonry or Cavity Wall
16" Rubble
10" Hollow Masonry or Cavity Wall

INTERIOR BEARING WALLS RESIDENCE-STRUCTURES

BEARING BOTH SIDES — BEARING 1 SIDE or NON-BEARING

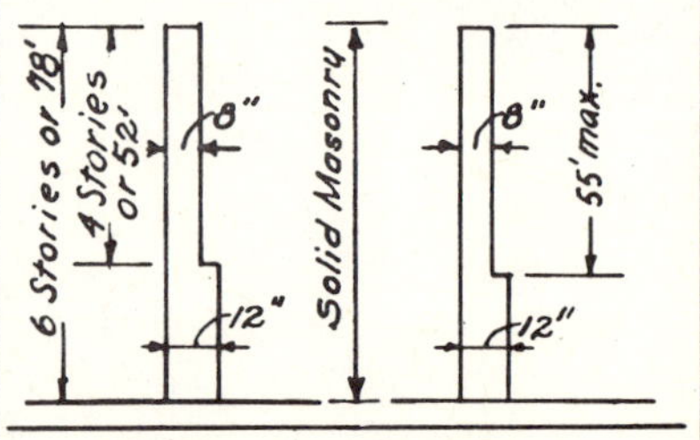
6 Stories or 78'
4 Stories or 52'
8"
12"
Solid Masonry
8"
55' max.
12"

Max. horizontal clear length of walls 30'-0". Interior bearing walls of structure same as bearing walls.

GENERAL NOTES

Walls must be increased if:

a.) Openings exceed 50%
b.) Clear horizontal span exceeds 26' for bearing walls (see code)
c.) Unsupported hgt. greater than 20 to 1.
d.) Foundations walls are more than 13' deep bet. horiz. supports
e.) Necessary to resist wind.

ISOLATED PIER

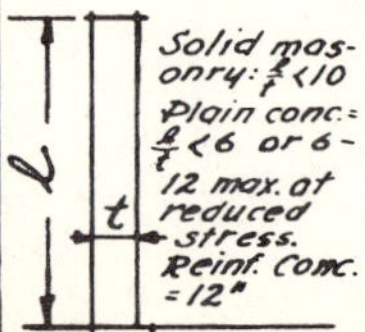
l
t
Solid masonry: l/t < 10
Plain conc.: l/t < 6 or 6-12 max. at reduced stress.
Reinf. Conc. = 12"

Data checked by: Elwyn E. Seelye, Consulting Engineer.

BRICKWORK

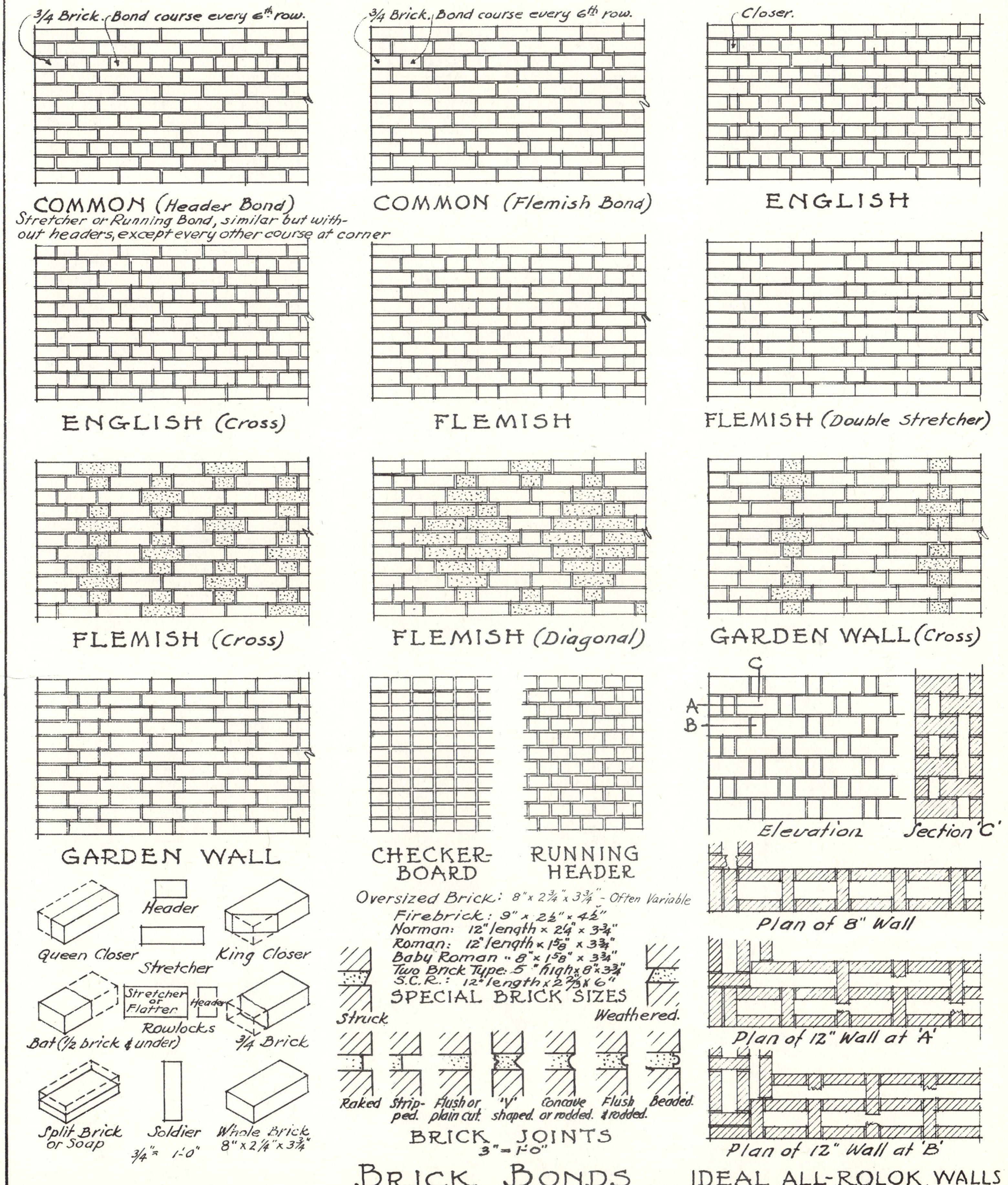
3/4 Brick. Bond course every 6th row.
COMMON (Header Bond)
Stretcher or Running Bond, similar but without headers, except every other course at corner
3/4 Brick. Bond course every 6th row.
COMMON (Flemish Bond)
Closer.
ENGLISH
ENGLISH (Cross)
FLEMISH
FLEMISH (Double Stretcher)
FLEMISH (Cross)
FLEMISH (Diagonal)
GARDEN WALL (Cross)
GARDEN WALL
CHECKER-BOARD
RUNNING HEADER
C
A
B
Elevation
Section 'C'
Header
Queen Closer
Stretcher
King Closer
Stretcher or Flatter
Header
Rowlocks
Bat (1/2 brick & under)
3/4 Brick
Split Brick or Soap
Soldier
Whole Brick 8" x 2 1/4" x 3 3/4"
3/4" = 1'-0"
Oversized Brick: 8" x 2 3/4" x 3 3/4" - Often Variable
Firebrick: 9" x 2 1/2" x 4 1/2"
Norman: 12" length x 2 1/4" x 3 3/4"
Roman: 12" length x 1 5/8" x 3 3/4"
Baby Roman " 8" x 1 5/8" x 3 3/4"
Two Brick Type: 5" high x 8" x 3 3/4"
S.C.R.: 12" length x 2 2/3" x 6"
SPECIAL BRICK SIZES
Struck
Weathered.
Raked
Stripped.
Flush or plain cut.
'V' shaped.
Concave or rodded.
Flush & rodded.
Beaded.
BRICK JOINTS
3" = 1'-0"
Plan of 8" Wall
Plan of 12" Wall at 'A'
Plan of 12" Wall at 'B'
IDEAL ALL-ROLOK WALLS

BRICK BONDS

Scale 1/2" = 1'-0"

Checked by Structural Clay Products Institute

HORIZONTAL BRICK COURSES

# OF BRICKS & JOINTS	LENGTH OF COURSE ¼" Joints	⅜" Joints	½" Joints	⅝" Joints	¾" Joints
1 brk. & 0 jt.	0'-8"	0'-8"	0'-8"	0'-8"	0'-8"
1½ brks. & 1 jt.	1'-0¼"	1'-0⅜"	1'-0½"	1'-0⅝"	1'-0¾"
2 brks. & 1 jt.	1'-4¼"	1'-4⅜"	1'-4½"	1'-4⅝"	1'-4¾"
2½ brks. & 2 jts.	1'-8½"	1'-8¾"	1'-9"	1'-9¼"	1'-9½"
3 brks. & 2 jts.	2'-0½"	2'-0¾"	2'-1"	2'-1¼"	2'-1½"
3½ brks. & 3 jts.	2'-4¾"	2'-5⅛"	2'-5½"	2'-5⅞"	2'-6¼"
4 brks. & 3 jts.	2'-8¾"	2'-9⅛"	2'-9½"	2'-9⅞"	2'-10¼"
4½ brks. & 4 jts.	3'-1"	3'-1½"	3'-2"	3'-2½"	3'-3"
5 brks. & 4 jts.	3'-5"	3'-5½"	3'-6"	3'-6½"	3'-7"
5½ brks. & 5 jts.	3'-9¼"	3'-9⅞"	3'-10½"	3'-11⅛"	3'-11¾"
6 brks. & 5 jts.	4'-1¼"	4'-1⅞"	4'-2½"	4'-3⅛"	4'-3¾"
6½ brks. & 6 jts.	4'-5½"	4'-6¼"	4'-7"	4'-7¾"	4'-8½"
7 brks. & 6 jts.	4'-9½"	4'-10¼"	4'-11"	4'-11¾"	5'-0½"
7½ brks. & 7 jts.	5'-1¾"	5'-2⅝"	5'-3½"	5'-4⅜"	5'-5¼"
8 brks. & 7 jts.	5'-5¾"	5'-6⅝"	5'-7½"	5'-8⅜"	5'-9¼"
8½ brks. & 8 jts.	5'-10"	5'-11"	6'-0"	6'-1"	6'-2"
9 brks. & 8 jts.	6'-2"	6'-3"	6'-4"	6'-5"	6'-6"
9½ brks. & 9 jts.	6'-6¼"	6'-7⅜"	6'-8½"	6'-9⅝"	6'-10¾"
10 brks. & 9 jts.	6'-10¼"	6'-11⅜"	7'-0½"	7'-1⅝"	7'-2¾"
10½ brks. & 10 jts.	7'-2½"	7'-3¾"	7'-5"	7'-6¼"	7'-7½"
11 brks. & 10 jts.	7'-6½"	7'-7¾"	7'-9"	7'-10¼"	7'-11½"
11½ brks. & 11 jts.	7'-10¾	8'-0⅛	8'-1½"	8'-2⅞"	8'-4¼"
12 brks. & 11 jts.	8'-2¾"	8'-4⅛"	8'-5½"	8'-6⅞"	8'-8¼"
12½ brks. & 12 jts.	8'-7"	8'-8½"	8'-10"	8'-11½"	9'-1"
13 brks. & 12 jts.	8'-11"	9'-0½"	9'-2"	9'-3½"	9'-5"
13½ brks. & 13 jts.	9'-3¼"	9'-4⅞"	9'-6½"	9'-8⅛"	9'-9¾"
14 brks. & 13 jts.	9'-7¼"	9'-8⅞"	9'-10½"	10'-0⅛"	10'-1¾"
14½ brks. & 14 jts.	9'-11½"	10'-1¼"	10'-3"	10'-4¾"	10'-6½"
15 brks. & 14 jts.	10'-3½"	10'-5¼"	10'-7"	10'-8¾"	10'-10½"
15½ brks. & 15 jts.	10'-7¾"	10'-9⅝"	10'-11½"	11'-1⅜"	11'-3¼"
16 brks. & 15 jts.	10'-11¾"	11'-1⅝"	11'-3½"	11'-5⅜"	11'-7¼"
16½ brks. & 16 jts.	11'-4"	11'-6"	11'-8"	11'-10"	12'-0"
17 brks. & 16 jts.	11'-8"	11'-10"	12'-0"	12'-2"	12'-4"
17½ brks. & 17 jts.	12'-0¼"	12'-2⅜"	12'-4½"	12'-6⅝"	12'-8¾"
18 brks. & 17 jts.	12'-4¼"	12'-6⅜"	12'-8½"	12'-10⅝"	13'-0¾"
18½ brks. & 18 jts.	12'-8½"	12'-10¾"	13'-1"	13'-3¼"	13'-5½"
19 brks. & 18 jts.	13'-0½"	13'-2¾"	13'-5"	13'-7¼"	13'-9½"
19½ brks. & 19 jts.	13'-4¾"	13'-7⅛"	13'-9½"	13'-11⅞"	14'-2¼"
20 brks. & 19 jts.	13'-8¾"	13'-11⅛"	14'-1½"	14'-3⅞"	14'-6¼"
20½ brks. & 20 jts.	14'-1"	14'3½"	14'-6"	14'-8½"	14'-11"
21 brks. & 20 jts.	14'-5"	14'-7½"	14'-10"	15'-0½"	15'-3"
21½ brks. & 21 jts.	14'-9¼"	14'-11⅞"	15'-2½"	15'-5⅛"	15'-7¾"
22 brks. & 21 jts.	15'-1¼"	15'-3⅞"	15'-6½"	15'-9⅛"	15'-11¾"
22½ brks. & 22 jts.	15'-5½"	15'-8¼"	15'-11"	16'-1¾"	16'-4½"
23 brks. & 22 jts.	15'-9½"	16'-0¼"	16'-3"	16'-5¾"	16'-8½"
23½ brks. & 23 jts.	16'-1¾"	16'-4⅝"	16'-7½"	16'-10⅜"	17'-1¼"
24 brks. & 23 jts.	16'-5¾"	16'-8⅝"	16'-11½"	17'-2⅜"	17'-5¼"
24½ brks. & 24 jts.	16'-10"	17'-1"	17'-4"	17'-7"	17'-10"
25 brks. & 24 jts.	17'-2"	17'-5"	17'-8"	17'-11"	18'-2"
25½ brks. & 25 jts.	17'-6¼"	17'-9⅜"	18'-0½"	18'-3⅝"	18'-6¾"
26 brks. & 25 jts.	17'-10¼"	18'-1⅜"	18'-4½"	18'-7⅝"	18'-10¾"
26½ brks. & 26 jts.	18'-2½"	18'-5¾"	18'-9"	19'-0¼"	19'-3½"
27 brks. & 26 jts.	18'-6½"	18'-9¾"	19'-1"	19'-4¼"	19'-7½"
27½ brks. & 27 jts.	18'-10¾"	19'-2⅛"	19'-5½"	19'-8⅞"	20'-0¼"
28 brks. & 27 jts.	19'-2¾"	19'-6⅛"	19'-9½"	20'-0⅞"	20 -4¼"
28½ brks. & 28 jts.	19'-7"	19'-10½"	20'-2"	20'-5½"	20'-9"
29 brks. & 28 jts.	19'-11"	20'-2½"	20'-6"	20'-9½"	21'-1"
29½ brks. & 29 jts.	20'-3¼"	20'-6⅞"	20'-10½"	21'-2⅛"	21'-5¾"
30 brks. & 29 jts.	20'-7¼"	20'-10⅞"	21'-2½"	21'-6⅛"	21'-9¾"
30½ brks. & 30 jts.	20'-11½"	21'-3¼"	21'-7"	21'-10¾"	22'-2½"
31 brks. & 30 jts.	21'-3½"	21'-7¼"	21'-11"	22'-2¾"	22'-6½"
31½ brks. & 31 jts.	21'-7¾"	21'-11⅝"	22'-3½"	22'-7⅜"	22'-11¼"
32 brks. & 31 jts.	21'-11¾"	22'-3⅝"	22'-7½"	22'-11⅜"	23'-3¼"
32½ brks. & 32 jts.	22'-4"	22'-8"	23'-0"	23'-4"	23'-8"
33 brks. & 32 jts.	22'-8"	23'-0"	23'-4"	23'-8"	24'-0"
33½ brks. & 33 jts.	23'-0¼"	23'-4⅜"	23'-8½"	24'-0⅝"	24'-4¾"
34 brks. & 33 jts.	23'-4¼"	23'-8⅜"	24'-0½"	24'-4⅝"	24'-8¾"
34½ brks. & 34 jts.	23'-8½"	24'-0¾"	24'-5"	24'-9¼"	25'-1½"
35 brks. & 34 jts.	24-0½"	24'-4¾"	24'-9"	25-1¼"	25'-5½"
35½ brks. & 35 jts.	24'-4¾"	24'-9⅛"	25'-1½"	25'-5⅞"	25'-10¼"
36 brks. & 35 jts.	24'-8¾"	25'-1⅛"	25'-5½"	25'-9⅞"	26'-2¼"
36½ brks. & 36 jts.	25'-1"	25'-5½"	25'-10"	26'-2½"	26'-7"
37 brks. & 36 jts.	25'-5"	25'-9½"	26'-2"	26'-6½"	26'-11"
37½ brks. & 37 jts.	25'-9¼"	26'-1⅞"	26'-6½"	26'-11⅛"	27'-3¾"
38 brks. & 37 jts.	26'-1¼"	26'-5⅞"	26'-10½"	27'-3⅛"	27'-7¾"
38½ brks. & 38 jts.	26'-5½"	26'-10¼"	27'-3"	27'-7¾"	28'-0½"
39 brks. & 38 jts.	26'-9½"	27'-2¼"	27'-7"	27'-11¾"	28'-4½"
39½ brks. & 39 jts.	27'-1¾"	27'-6⅝"	27'-11½"	28'-4⅜"	28'-9¼"
40 brks. & 39 jts.	27'-5¾"	27'-10⅝"	28'-3½"	28'-8⅜"	29'-1¼"
40½ brks. & 40 jts.	27'-10"	28'-3"	28'-8"	29'-1"	29'-6"
41 brks. & 40 jts.	28'-2"	28'-7"	29'-0"	29'-5"	29'-10"
41½ brks. & 41 jts.	28'-6¼"	28'-11⅜"	29'-4½"	29'-9⅝"	30'-2¾"
42 brks. & 41 jts.	28'-10¼"	29'-3⅜"	29'-8½"	30'-1⅝"	30'-6¾"
42½ brks. & 42 jts.	29'-2½"	29'-7¾"	30'-1"	30'-6¼"	30'-11½"
43 brks. & 42 jts.	29'-6½"	29'-11¾"	30'-5"	30'-10¼"	31'-3½"
43½ brks. & 43 jts.	29'-10¾"	30'-4⅛"	30'-9½"	31'-2⅞"	31'-8¼"
44 brks. & 43 jts.	30'-2¾"	30'-8⅛"	31'-1½"	31'-6⅞"	32'-0¼"
44½ brks. & 44 jts.	30'-7"	31'-0½"	31'-6"	31'-11½"	32'-5"
45 brks. & 44 jts.	30'-11"	31'-4½"	31'-10"	32'-3½"	32'-9"
45½ brks. & 45 jts.	31'-3¼"	31'-8⅞"	32'-2½"	32'-8⅛"	33'-1¾"
46 brks. & 45 jts.	31'-7¼"	32'-0⅞"	32'-6½"	33'-0⅛"	33'-5¾"
46½ brks. & 46 jts.	31'-11½"	32'-5¼"	32'-11"	33'-4¾"	33'-10½"
47 brks. & 46 jts.	32'-3½"	32'-9¼"	33'-3"	33'-8¾"	34'-2½"
47½ brks. & 47 jts.	32'-7¾"	33'-1⅝"	33'-7½"	34'-1⅜"	34'-7¼"
48 brks. & 47 jts.	32'-11¾"	33'-5⅝"	33'-11½"	34'-5⅜"	34'-11¼"
48½ brks. & 48 jts.	33'-4"	33'-10"	34'-4"	34'-10"	35'-4"
49 brks. & 48 jts.	33'-8"	34'-2"	34'-8"	35'-2"	35'-8"
49½ brks. & 49 jts.	34'-0¼"	34'-6⅜"	35'-0½"	35'-6⅝"	36'-0¾"
50 brks. & 49 jts.	34'-4¼"	34'-10⅜"	35'-4½"	35'-10⅝"	36'-4¾"
50½ brks. & 50 jts.	34'-8½"	35'-2¾"	35'-9"	36'-3¼"	36'-9½"
51 brks. & 50 jts.	35'-0½"	35'-6¾"	36'-1"	36'-7¼"	37'-1½"
51½ brks. & 51 jts.	35'-4¾"	35'-11⅛"	36'-5½"	36'-11⅞"	37'-6¼"
52 brks. & 51 jts.	35'-8¾"	36'-3⅛"	36'-9½"	37'-3⅞"	37'-10¼"
52½ brks. & 52 jts.	36'-1"	36'-7½"	37'-2"	37'-8½"	38'-3"
53 brks. & 52 jts.	36'-5"	36'-11½"	37'-6"	38'-0½"	38'-7"
53½ brks. & 53 jts.	36'-9¼"	37'-3⅞"	37'-10½"	38'-5⅛"	38'-11¾"
54 brks. & 53 jts.	37-1¼"	37'-7⅞"	38'-2½"	38'-9⅛"	39'-3¾"
54½ brks. & 54 jts.	37'-5½"	38'-0¼"	38'-7"	39'-1¾"	39'-8½"
55 brks. & 54 jts.	37'-9½"	38'-4¼"	38'-11"	39'-5¾"	40'-0½"
55½ brks. & 55 jts.	38'-1¾"	38'-8⅝"	39'-3½"	39'-10⅜"	40'-5¼"
56 brks. & 55 jts.	38'-5¾"	39'-0⅝"	39'-7½"	40'-2⅜"	40'-9¼"
56½ brks. & 56 jts.	38'-10"	39'-5"	40'-0"	40'-7"	41'-2"
57 brks. & 56 jts.	39'-2"	39'-9"	40'-4"	40'-11"	41'-6"
57½ brks. & 57 jts.	39'-6¼"	40'-1⅜"	40'-8½"	41'-3⅝"	41'-10¾"
58 brks. & 57 jts.	39'-10¼"	40'-5⅜"	41'-0½"	41'-7⅝"	42'-2¾"
58½ brks. & 58 jts.	40'-2½"	40'-9¾"	41'-5"	42'-0¼"	42'-7½"
59 brks. & 58 jts.	40'-6½"	41'-1¾"	41'-9"	42'-4¼"	42'-11½"
59½ brks. & 59 jts.	40'-10¾"	41'-6⅛"	42'-1½"	42'-8⅞"	43'-4¼"
60 brks. & 59 jts.	41'-2¾"	41'-10⅛"	42'-5½"	43'-0⅞"	43'-8¼"

EXAMPLE OF USE (WITH ¼" JOINTS)

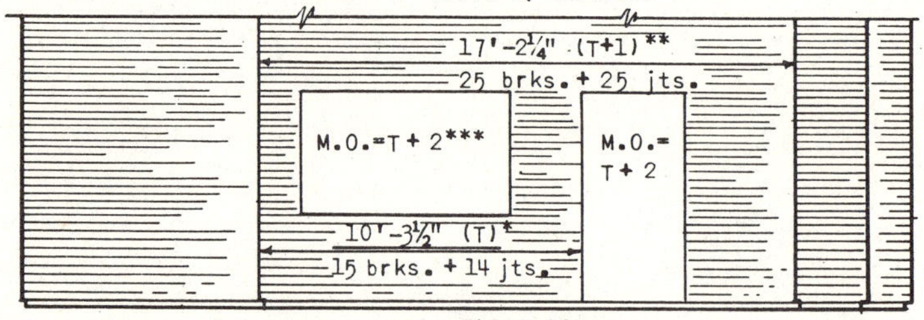

17'-2¼" (T+1) **
25 brks. + 25 jts.
M.O.=T+2***
M.O.=
T+2
10'-3½" (T)*
15 brks. + 14 jts.

ELEVATION

* T : Dimensions & no. of joints as given in above table, i.e. one joint less than the number of bricks.

** T+1: One brick joint added to figure given in table, i.e. number of bricks & joints equal.

*** T+2: Two brick joints added to figure given in table, i.e. one joint more than the number of bricks.

Table figures underlined.

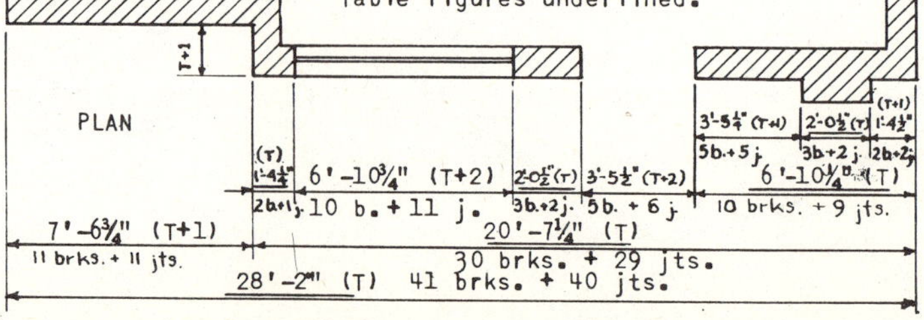

T+1
PLAN
(T)
1'-4½"
6'-10¾" (T+2)
2'-0½" (T)
3'-5½" (T+2)
2b+1j.
10 b. + 11 j.
3b.+2j.
5b. + 6 j.
3'-5¼" (T+1)
2'-0½" (T)
(T+1)
1'-4½"
5b.+5j.
3b+2j.
2b+2j.
6'-10¼" (T)
10 brks. + 9 jts.
7'-6¾" (T+1)
11 brks. + 11 jts.
20'-7¼" (T)
30 brks. + 29 jts.
28'-2" (T) 41 brks. + 40 jts.

VERTICAL BRICK COURSES

# OF BRICKS & JOINTS	HEIGHT				
	1/4" JOINTS	3/8" JOINTS	1/2" JOINTS	5/8" JOINTS	3/4" JOINTS
1 brk. & 1 jt.	2½"	2⅝"	2¾"	2⅞"	3"
2 brks. & 2 jts.	5"	5¼"	5½"	5¾"	6"
3 brks. & 3 jts.	7½"	7⅞"	8¼"	8⅝"	9"
4 brks. & 4 jts.	10"	10½"	11"	11½"	1'-0"
5 brks. & 5 jts.	1'-0½"	1'-1⅛"	1'-1¾"	1'-2⅜"	1'-3"
6 brks. & 6 jts.	1'-3"	1'-3¾"	1'-4½"	1'-5¼"	1'-6"
7 brks. & 7 jts.	1'-5½"	1'-6⅜"	1'-7¼"	1'-8⅛"	1'-9"
8 brks. & 8 jts.	1'-8"	1'-9"	1'-10"	1'-11"	2'-0"
9 brks. & 9 jts.	1'-10½"	1'-11⅝"	2'-0¾"	2'-1⅞"	2'-3"
10 brks. & 10 jts.	2'-1"	2'-2¼"	2'-3½"	2'-4¾"	2'-6"
11 brks. & 11 jts.	2'-3½"	2'-4⅞"	2'-6¼"	2'-7⅝"	2'-9"
12 brks. & 12 jts.	2'-6"	2'-7½"	2'-9"	2'-10½"	3'-0"
13 brks. & 13 jts.	2'-8½"	2'-10⅛"	2'-11¾"	3'-1⅜"	3'-3"
14 brks. & 14 jts.	2'-11"	3'-0¾"	3'-2½"	3'-4¼"	3'-6"
15 brks. & 15 jts.	3'-1½"	3'-3⅜"	3'-5¼"	3'-7⅛"	3'-9"
16 brks. & 16 jts.	3'-4"	3'-6"	3'-8"	3'-10"	4'-0"
17 brks. & 17 jts.	3'-6½"	3'-8⅝"	3'-10¾"	4'-0⅞"	4'-3"
18 brks. & 18 jts.	3'-9"	3'-11¼"	4'-1½"	4'-3¾"	4'-6"
19 brks. & 19 jts.	3'-11½"	4'-1⅞"	4'-4¼"	4'-6⅝"	4'-9"
20 brks. & 20 jts.	4'-2"	4'-4½"	4'-7"	4'-9½"	5'-0"
21 brks. & 21 jts.	4'-4½"	4'-7⅛"	4'-9¾"	5'-0⅜"	5'-3"
22 brks. & 22 jts.	4'-7"	4'-9¾"	5'-0½"	5'-3¼"	5'-6"
23 brks. & 23 jts.	4'-9½"	5'-0⅜"	5'-3¼"	5'-6⅛"	5'-9"
24 brks. & 24 jts.	5'-0"	5'-3"	5'-6"	5'-9"	6'-0"
25 brks. & 25 jts.	5'-2½"	5'-5⅝"	5'-8¾"	5'-11⅞"	6'-3"
26 brks. & 26 jts.	5'-5"	5'-8¼"	5'-11½"	6'-2¾"	6'-6"
27 brks. & 27 jts.	5'-7½"	5'-10⅞"	6'-2¼"	6'-5⅝"	6'-9"
28 brks. & 28 jts.	5'-10"	6'-1½"	6'-5"	6'-8½"	7'-0"
29 brks. & 29 jts.	6'-0½"	6'-4⅛"	6'-7¾"	6'-11⅜"	7'-3"
30 brks. & 30 jts.	6'-3"	6'-6¾"	6'-10½"	7'-2¼"	7'-6"
31 brks. & 31 jts.	6'-5½"	6'-9⅜"	7'-1¼"	7'-5⅛"	7'-9"
32 brks. & 32 jts.	6'-8"	7'-0"	7'-4"	7'-8"	8'-0"
33 brks. & 33 jts.	6'-10½"	7'-2⅝"	7'-6¾"	7'-10⅞"	8'-3"
34 brks. & 34 jts.	7'-1"	7'-5¼"	7'-9½"	8'-1¾"	8'-6"
35 brks. & 35 jts.	7'-3½"	7'-7⅞"	8'-0¼"	8'-4⅝"	8'-9"
36 brks. & 36 jts.	7'-6"	7'-10½"	8'-3"	8'-7½"	9'-0"
37 brks. & 37 jts.	7'-8½"	8'-1⅛"	8'-5¾"	8'-10⅜"	9'-3"
38 brks. & 38 jts.	7'-11"	8'-3¾"	8'-8½"	9'-1¼"	9'-6"
39 brks. & 39 jts.	8'-1½"	8'-6⅜"	8'-11¼"	9'-4⅛"	9'-9"
40 brks. & 40 jts.	8'-4"	8'-9"	9'-2"	9'-7"	10'-0"
41 brks. & 41 jts.	8'-6½"	8'-11⅝"	9'-4¾"	9'-9⅞"	10'-3"
42 brks. & 42 jts.	8'-9"	9'-2¼"	9'-7½"	10'-0¾"	10'-6"
43 brks. & 43 jts.	8'-11½"	9'-4⅞"	9'-10¼"	10'-3⅝"	10'-9"
44 brks. & 44 jts.	9'-2"	9'-7½"	10'-1"	10'-6½"	11'-0"
45 brks. & 45 jts.	9'-4½"	9'-10⅛"	10'-3¾"	10'-9⅜"	11'-3"
46 brks. & 46 jts.	9'-7"	10'-0¾"	10'-6½"	11'-0¼"	11'-6"
47 brks. & 47 jts.	9'-9½"	10'-3⅜"	10'-9¼"	11'-3⅛"	11'-9"
48 brks. & 48 jts.	10'-0"	10'-6"	11'-0"	11'-6"	12'-0"
49 brks. & 49 jts.	10'-2½"	10'-8⅝"	11'-2¾"	11'-8⅞"	12'-3"
50 brks. & 50 jts.	10'-5"	10'-11¼"	11'-5½"	11'-11¾"	12'-6"
51 brks. & 51 jts.	10'-7½"	11'-1⅞"	11'-8¼"	12'-2⅝"	12'-9"
52 brks. & 52 jts.	10'-10"	11'-4½"	11'-11"	12'-5½"	13'-0"
53 brks. & 53 jts.	11'-0½"	11'-7⅛"	12'-1¾"	12'-8⅜"	13'-3"
54 brks. & 54 jts.	11'-3"	11'-9¾"	12'-4½"	12'-11¼"	13'-6"
55 brks. & 55 jts.	11'-5½"	12'-0⅜"	12'-7¼"	13'-2⅛"	13'-9"
56 brks. & 56 jts.	11'-8"	12'-3"	12'-10"	13'-5"	14'-0"
57 brks. & 57 jts.	11'-10½"	12'-5⅝"	13'-0¾"	13'-7⅞"	14'-3"
58 brks. & 58 jts.	12'-1"	12'-8¼"	13'-3½"	13'-10¾"	14'-6"
59 brks. & 59 jts.	12'-3½"	12'-10⅞"	13'-6¼"	14'-1⅝"	14'-9"
60 brks. & 60 jts.	12'-6"	13'-1½"	13'-9"	14'-4½"	15'-0"
61 brks. & 61 jts.	12'-8½"	13'-4⅛"	13'-11¾"	14'-7⅜"	15'-3"
62 brks. & 62 jts.	12'-11"	13'-6¾"	14'-2½"	14'-10¼"	15'-6"
63 brks. & 63 jts.	13'-1½"	13'-9⅜"	14'-5¼"	15'-1⅛"	15'-9"
64 brks. & 64 jts.	13'-4"	14'-0"	14'-8"	15'-4"	16'-0"
65 brks. & 65 jts.	13'-6½"	14'-2⅝"	14'-10¾"	15'-6⅞"	16'-3"
66 brks. & 66 jts.	13'-9"	14'-5¼"	15'-1½"	15'-9¾"	16'-6"
67 brks. & 67 jts.	13'-11½"	14'-7⅞"	15'-4¼"	16'-0⅝"	16'-9"
68 brks. & 68 jts.	14'-2"	14'-10½"	15'-7"	16'-3½"	17'-0"
69 brks. & 69 jts.	14'-4½"	15'-1⅛"	15'-9¾"	16'-6⅜"	17'-3"
70 brks. & 70 jts.	14'-7"	15'-3¾"	16'-0½"	16'-9¼"	17'-6"
71 brks. & 71 jts.	14'-9½"	15'-6⅜"	16'-3¼"	17'-0⅛"	17'-9"
72 brks. & 72 jts.	15'-0"	15'-9"	16'-6"	17'-3"	18'-0"
73 brks. & 73 jts.	15'-2½"	15'-11⅝"	16'-8¾"	17'-5⅞"	18'-3"

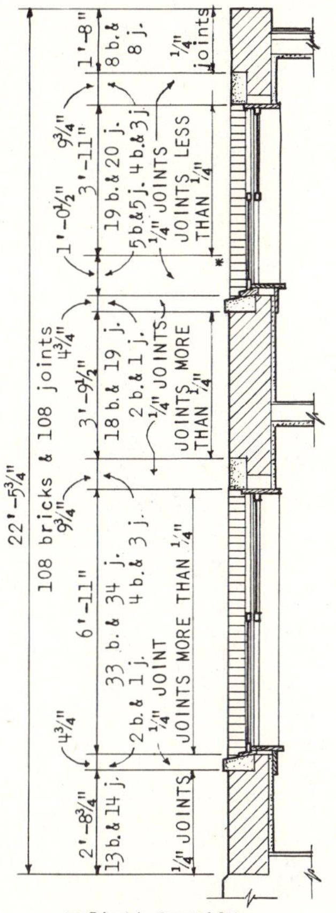
22'-5¾"
108 bricks & 108 joints
1'-8"
8 b.& 8 j.
1/4" joints
19 b.& 20 j.
JOINTS LESS THAN 1/4"
18 b.& 19 j.
JOINTS MORE THAN 1/4"
33 b.& 34 j.
JOINTS MORE THAN 1/4"
13 b.& 14 j.
1/4" JOINTS

TYPICAL SECTION
Scale: 3/16" = 1'-0"

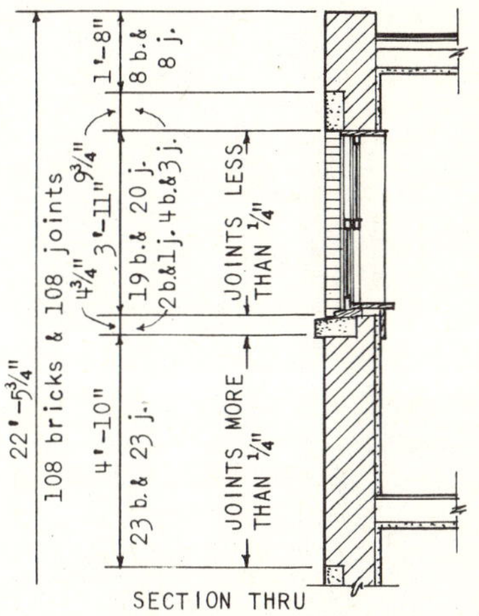
22'-5¾"
108 bricks & 108 joints
1'-8"
8 b.& 8 j.
19 b.& 20 j.
JOINTS LESS THAN 1/4"
4'-10"
23 b.& 23 j.
JOINTS MORE THAN 1/4"

SECTION THRU
NON-TYPICAL WINDOW
Scale: 3/16" = 1'0"

NOTE: Where window, door, vent, etc., dimensions and details are predetermined, sizes of brick joints must be varied somewhat at different points of the building. In order to keep brick courses on the same line around the entire building, it is necessary to key all wall sections to each other.
*In the drawing shown, notice that the course of brick below the non-typical window sill must occur on the same line on every wall of the building - even though this window may occur on only one wall.

BRICK COURSES ADJUSTED TO DIMENSIONS

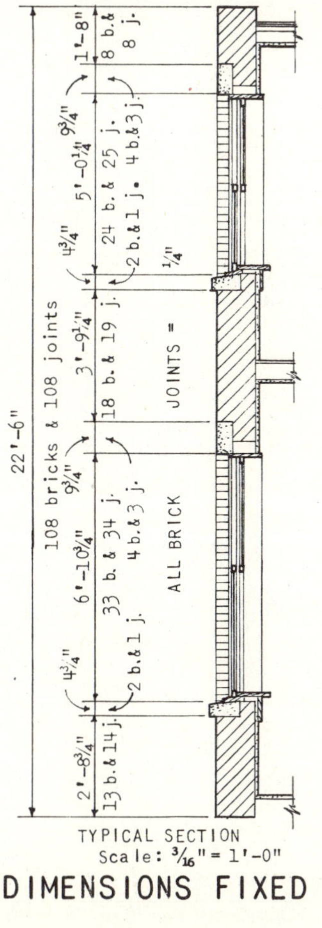
22'-6"
108 bricks & 108 joints
1'-8"
8 b.& 8 j.
24 b.& 25 j.
18 b.& 19 j.
JOINTS =
33 b.& 34 j.
ALL BRICK
13 b.& 14 j.

TYPICAL SECTION
Scale: 3/16" = 1'-0"

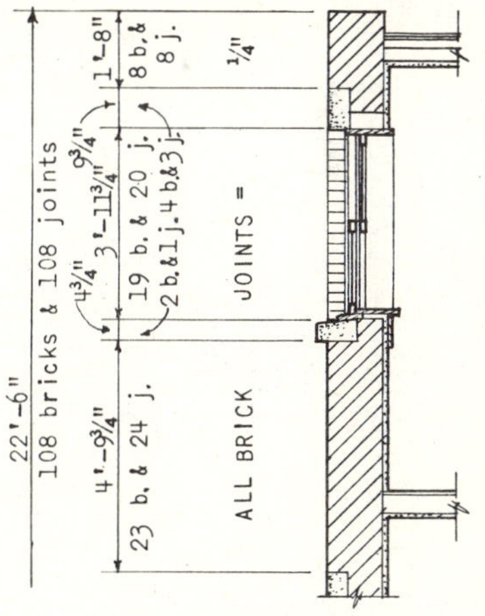
22'-6"
108 bricks & 108 joints
1'-8"
8 b.& 8 j.
19 b.& 20 j.
JOINTS =
23 b.& 24 j.
ALL BRICK

SECTION THRU
NON-TYPICAL WINDOW
Scale: 3/16" = 1'-0"

NOTE: Windows, doors, vents and other masonry opening details must be adjusted to achieve even brick coursing around entire bldg. Size of brick joint may be predetermined or may depend on the height of windows used.

Other details - doors, vents, etc.- must be adjusted with reference to the brick coursing.

DIMENSIONS FIXED BY BRICK COURSES

BRICK COURSES - MODULAR

4" × 2⅔" × 8" NOMINAL

Brick sizes:

For ¼" joint	3¾" × 2½" × 7¾"
* For ⅜" joint	3⅝" × 2⅜" × 7⅝"
** For ½" joint	3½" × 2¼" × 7½"

4" × 2⅔" × 12" NOMINAL

Brick sizes:

For ¼" joint	3¾" × 2½" × 11¾"
* For ⅜" joint	3⅝" × 2⅜" × 11⅝"
** For ½" joint	3½" × 2¼" × 11½"

S.C.R. 6" × 2⅔" × 12" NOMINAL

For ½" joint 5½" × 2⅙" × 11½"

Joint selected determines brick size.
3 courses = 2 modules (8")

Nominal heights of 2⅔" courses to ℄ of joint. Read from bottom up.

Course	Height	Course	Height
32	7'-1⅓"	65	14'-5⅓"
31	6'-10⅔"	64	14'-2⅔"
30	6'-8"	63	14'-0"
29	6'-5⅓"	62	13'-9⅓"
28	6'-2⅔"	61	13'-6⅔"
27	6'-0"	60	13'-4"
26	5'-9⅓"	59	13'-1⅓"
25	5'-6⅔"	58	12'-10⅔"
24	5'-4"	57	12'-8"
23	5'-1⅓"	56	12'-5⅓"
22	4'-10⅔"	55	12'-2⅔"
21	4'-8"	54	12'-0"
20	4'-5⅓"	53	11'-9⅓"
19	4'-2⅔"	52	11'-6⅔"
18	4'-0"	51	11'-4"
17	3'-9⅓"	50	11'-1⅓"
16	3'-6⅔"	49	10'-10⅔"
15	3'-4"	48	10'-8"
14	3'-1⅓"	47	10'-5⅓"
13	2'-10⅔"	46	10'-2⅔"
12	2'-8"	45	10'-0"
11	2'-5⅓"	44	9'-9⅓"
10	2'-2⅔"	43	9'-6⅔"
9	2'-0"	42	9'-4"
8	1'-9⅓"	41	9'-1⅓"
7	1'-6⅔"	40	8'-10⅔"
6	1'-4"	39	8'-8"
5	1'-1⅓"	38	8'-5⅓"
4	10⅔"	37	8'-2⅔"
3	8"	36	8'-0"
2	5⅓"	35	7'-9⅓"
1	2⅔"	34	7'-6⅔"
		33	7'-4"

4" × 3" × 8" NOMINAL

Brick sizes:

* For ⅜" joint	3⅝" × 2⅝" × 7⅝"
** For ½" joint	3½" × 2½" × 7½"

Joint selected determines brick size.
4 courses = 3 modules (12")

Nominal heights of 3" courses to ℄ of joint. Read from bottom up.

Course	Height	Course	Height
31	7'-9"	63	15'-9"
30	7'-6"	62	15'-6"
29	7'-3"	61	15'-3"
28	7'-0"	60	15'-0"
27	6'-9"	59	14'-9"
26	6'-6"	58	14'-6"
25	6'-3"	57	14'-3"
24	6'-0"	56	14'-0"
23	5'-9"	55	13'-9"
22	5'-6"	54	13'-6"
21	5'-3"	53	13'-3"
20	5'-0"	52	13'-0"
19	4'-9"	51	12'-9"
18	4'-6"	50	12'-6"
17	4'-3"	49	12'-3"
16	4'-0"	48	12'-0"
15	3'-9"	47	11'-9"
14	3'-6"	46	11'-6"
13	3'-3"	45	11'-3"
12	3'-0"	44	11'-0"
11	2'-9"	43	10'-9"
10	2'-6"	42	10'-6"
9	2'-3"	41	10'-3"
8	2'-0"	40	10'-0"
7	1'-9"	39	9'-9"
6	1'-6"	38	9'-6"
5	1'-3"	37	9'-3"
4	1'-0"	36	9'-0"
3	9"	35	8'-9"
2	6"	34	8'-6"
1	3"	33	8'-3"
		32	8'-0"

4" × 4" × 8" NOMINAL

Brick sizes:

For ¼" joint	3¾" × 3¾" × 7¾"
* For ⅜" joint	3⅝" × 3⅝" × 7⅝"
** For ½" joint	3½" × 3½" × 7½"

4" × 4" × 12" NOMINAL

Brick sizes:

For ¼" joint	3¾" × 3¾" × 11¾"
* For ⅜" joint	3⅝" × 3⅝" × 11⅝"
** For ½" joint	3½" × 3½" × 11½"

Joint selected determines brick size.
1 course = 1 module (4")

Nominal heights of 4" courses to ℄ of joint. Read from bottom up.

Course	Height	Course	Height
21	7'-0"	43	14'-4
20	6'-8"	42	14'-0
19	6'-4"	41	13'-8"
18	6'-0"	40	13'-4"
17	5'-8"	39	13'-0"
16	5'-4"	38	12'-8"
15	5'-0"	37	12'-4"
14	4'-8"	36	12'-0"
13	4'-4"	35	11'-8"
12	4'-0"	34	11'-4"
11	3'-8"	33	11'-0"
10	3'-4"	32	10'-8"
9	3'-0"	31	10'-4"
8	2'-8"	30	10'-0"
7	2'-4"	29	9'-8"
6	2'-0"	28	9'-4"
5	1'-8"	27	9'-0"
4	1'-4"	26	8'-8"
3	1'-0"	25	8'-4"
2	8"	24	8'-0"
1	4"	23	7'-8"
		22	7'-4"

Not all sizes made in all sections of U.S.; check with local mfrs. for sizes available. Grid lines (— - —) are 4" modules. * ⅜" joint used for facing brick; ** ½" joint for glazed & structural units and building brick.

Data checked by Structural Clay Products Institute

S.C.R. BRICK

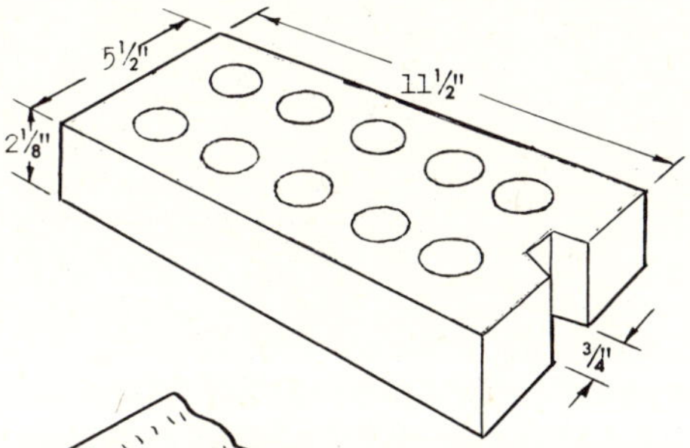
5½"
11½"
2⅛"
¾"

typical furring clip

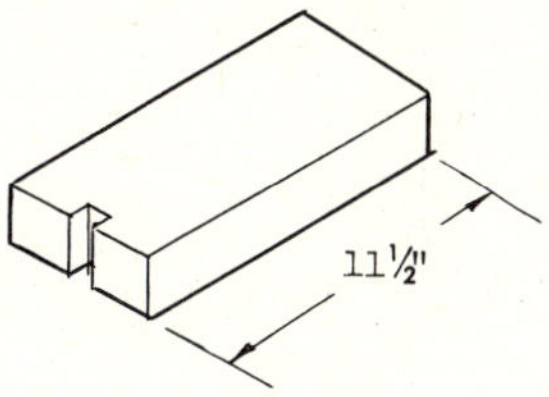
11½"

nominal 12" length & 6" width...full unit

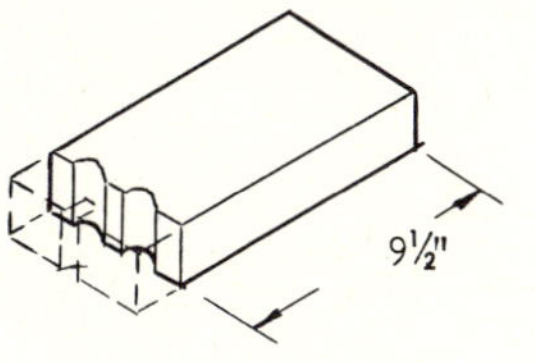
9½"

nominal 10" length

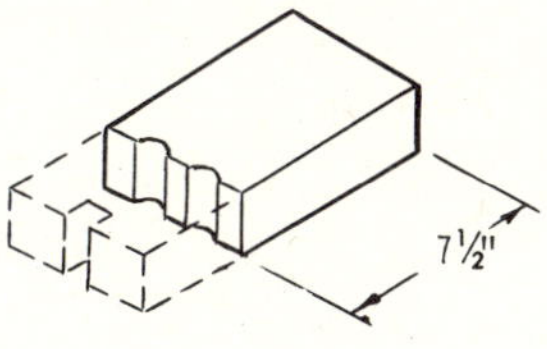
7½"

nominal 8" length

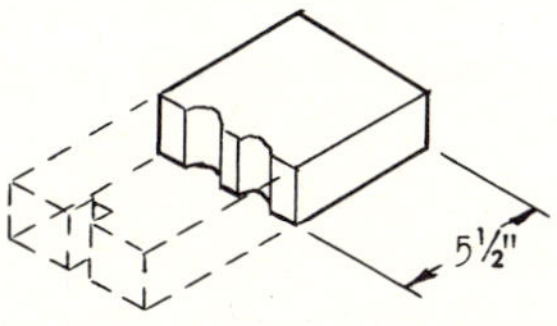
5½"

nominal 6" length

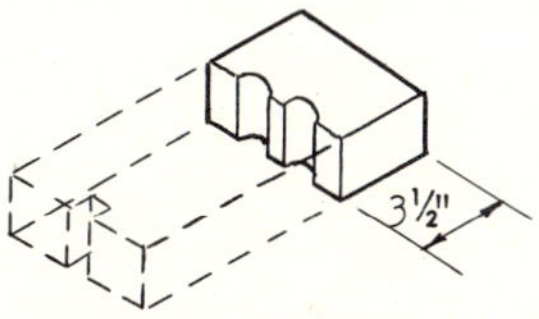
3½"

nominal 4" length

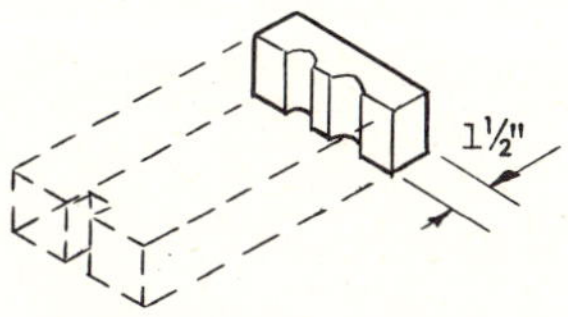
1½"

nominal 2" length closure

For vertical coursing S.C.R. modular see page on "Brick Courses—Modular," first column.

For all horizontal S.C.R. modular coursing, joints=multiples of 12" minus last joint. Ex.—If wall is 15' long you have 15 S.C.R. bricks + 14 joints = 14'-11½"

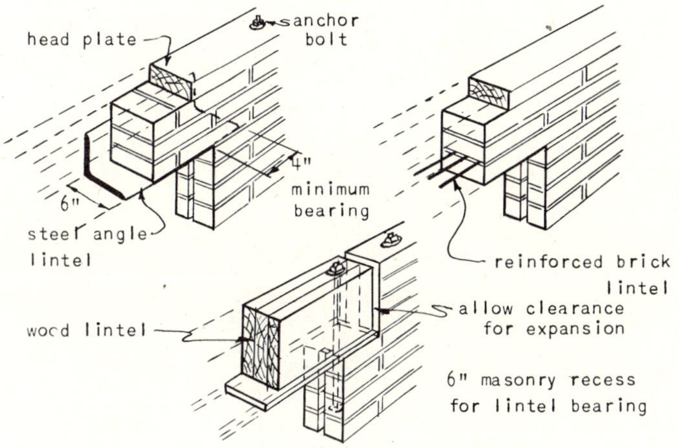
head plate
anchor bolt
4" minimum bearing
6"
steel angle lintel
reinforced brick lintel
wood lintel
allow clearance for expansion
6" masonry recess for lintel bearing

S.C.R. LINTEL CONSTRUCTION

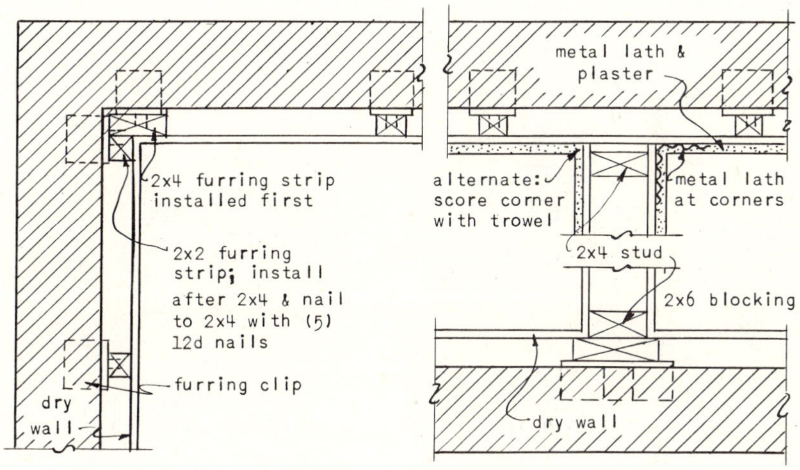
metal lath & plaster
2x4 furring strip installed first
alternate: score corner with trowel
metal lath at corners
2x2 furring strip; install after 2x4 & nail to 2x4 with (5) 12d nails
2x4 stud
2x6 blocking
furring clip
dry wall
dry wall

S.C.R. FURRING DETAILS PLANS

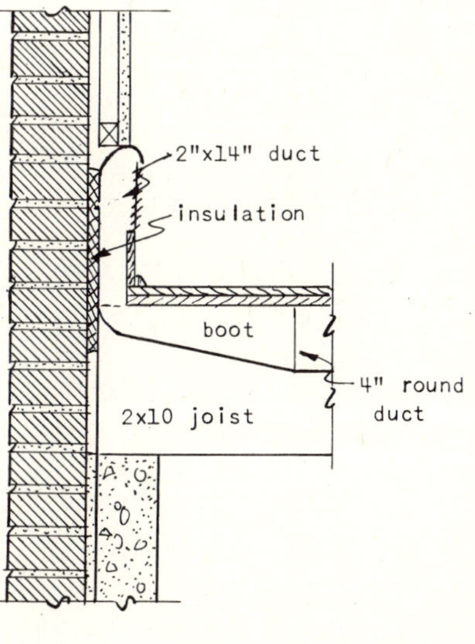
2"x14" duct
insulation
boot
4" round duct
2x10 joist

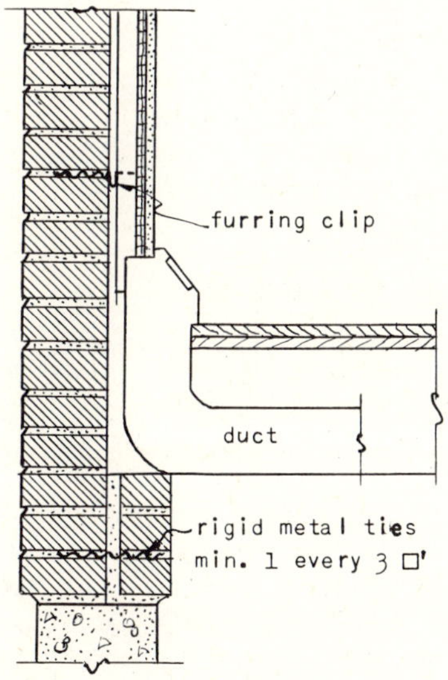
furring clip
duct
rigid metal ties min. 1 every 3 □'

Building Codes do not permit pipe or duct chases to be built into walls less than 8" in nominal thickness & require at least 4" of masonry between back of chase & outside face of wall

TYPICAL DUCT & PIPE INSTALLATION

TYPE OF INTERIOR FINISH AND INSULATION (2x2-IN. FURRING)	U FACTOR
1. 1" roll insulation, ½" insulating board lath, ½" vermiculite plaster	0.12
2. 1" roll insulation, ⅜" gypsum lath, ¾" vermiculite plaster	0.14
3. 1" roll insulation, metal lath, ¾" vermiculite plaster	0.15
4. 1" roll insulation, ⅜" gypsum board (dry wall)	0.16
5. 1" roll insulation, metal lath, ¾" gypsum plaster	0.16
6. 1" roll insulation, ⅜" gypsum lath, ½" gypsum plaster	0.16
7. ⅜" gypsum lath with aluminum foil, ½" vermiculite plaster	0.23
8. ½" insulating board lath, ½" vermiculite plaster	0.23
9. ½" insulating board lath, ½" gypsum plaster	0.25
10. ⅜" gypsum lath with aluminum foil, ½" gypsum plaster	0.25
11. ½" gypsum board (dry wall) with aluminum foil	0.26
12. Metal lath, ¾" vermiculite plaster	0.33
13. ⅜" gypsum lath, ½" vermiculite plaster	0.33
14. ⅜" gypsum lath, ½" gypsum plaster	0.37
15. Metal lath, ¾" gypsum plaster	0.40

DATA SUPPLIED BY STRUCTURAL CLAY PRODUCTS INSTITUTE

S.C.R. BRICK DETAILS

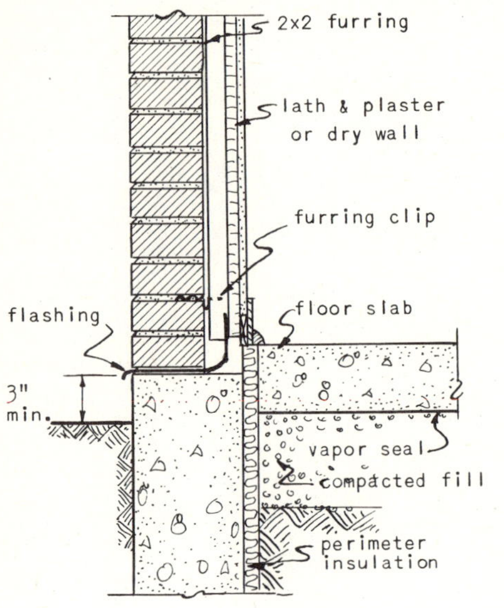
2x2 furring
lath & plaster or dry wall
furring clip
flashing
floor slab
3" min.
vapor seal
compacted fill
perimeter insulation

SLAB ON GRADE

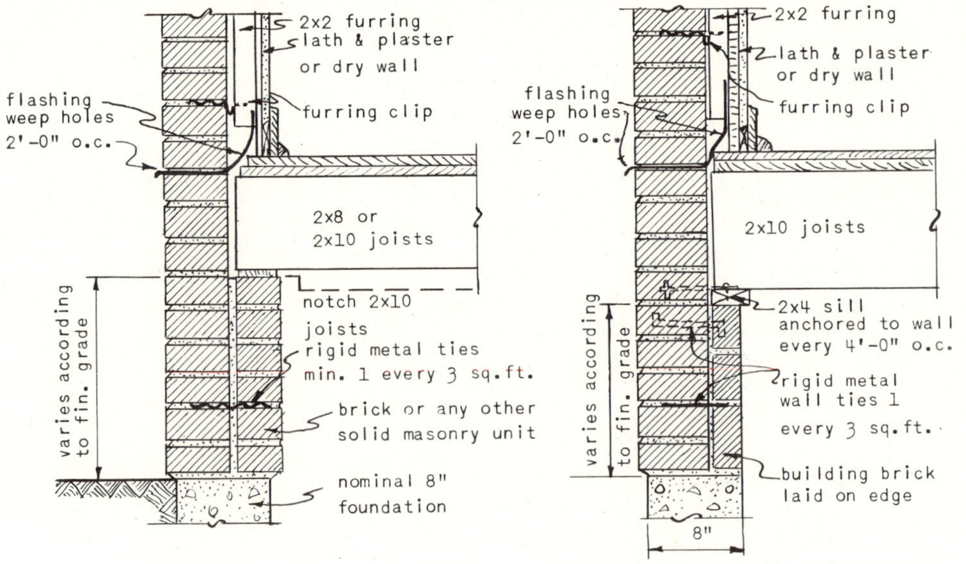
2x2 furring
lath & plaster or dry wall
flashing
weep holes 2'-0" o.c.
furring clip
2x8 or 2x10 joists
varies according to fin. grade
notch 2x10 joists
rigid metal ties min. 1 every 3 sq.ft.
brick or any other solid masonry unit
nominal 8" foundation
2x2 furring
lath & plaster or dry wall
flashing
weep holes 2'-0" o.c.
furring clip
2x10 joists
2x4 sill anchored to wall every 4'-0" o.c.
varies according to fin. grade
rigid metal wall ties 1 every 3 sq.ft.
building brick laid on edge
8"

CRAWL SPACE OR BASEMENT

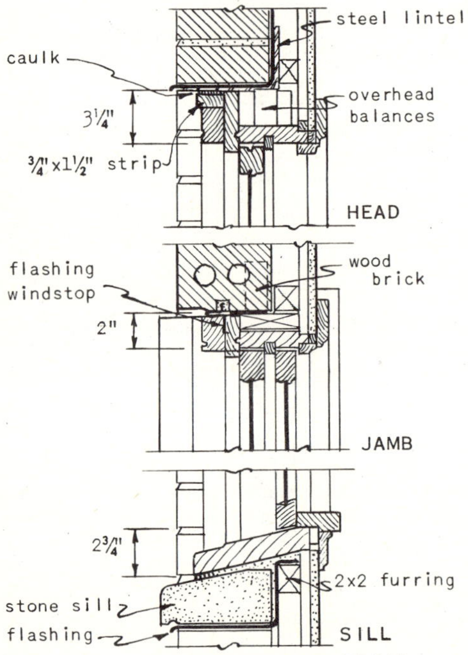
steel lintel
caulk
3¼"
overhead balances
¾"x1½" strip
HEAD
flashing windstop
wood brick
2"
JAMB
2¾"
2x2 furring
stone sill
flashing
SILL

WOOD DOUBLE HUNG

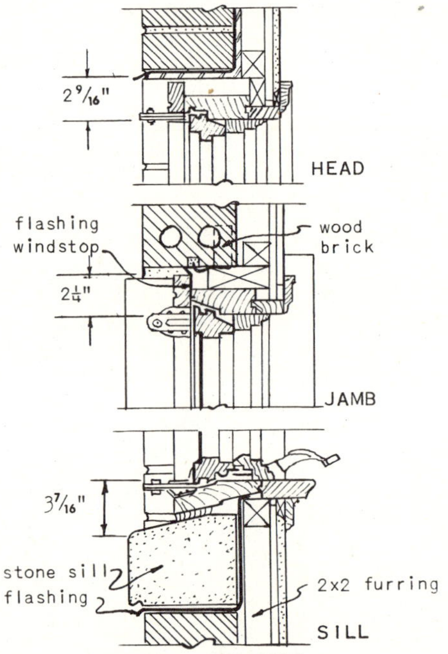
2 9/16"
HEAD
flashing windstop
wood brick
2¼"
JAMB
3 7/16"
stone sill
flashing
2x2 furring
SILL

WOOD CASEMENT

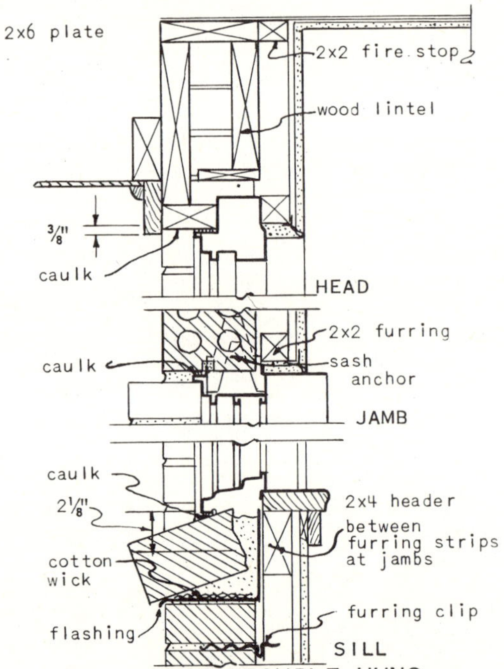
2x6 plate
2x2 fire stop
wood lintel
3/8"
caulk
HEAD
2x2 furring
caulk
sash anchor
JAMB
caulk
2⅛"
2x4 header between furring strips at jambs
cotton wick
flashing
furring clip
SILL

STEEL DOUBLE HUNG

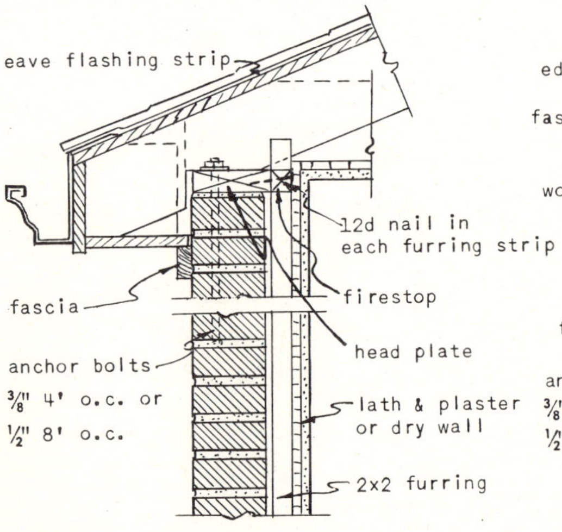
eave flashing strip
12d nail in each furring strip
fascia
firestop
anchor bolts 3/8" 4' o.c. or 1/2" 8' o.c.
head plate
lath & plaster or dry wall
2x2 furring

EAVE

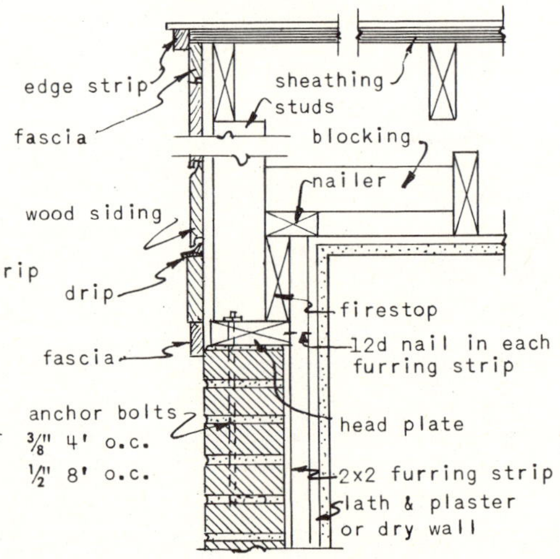
edge strip
sheathing
studs
fascia
blocking
nailer
wood siding
drip
firestop
fascia
12d nail in each furring strip
anchor bolts 3/8" 4' o.c. 1/2" 8' o.c.
head plate
2x2 furring strip
lath & plaster or dry wall

WOOD GABLE

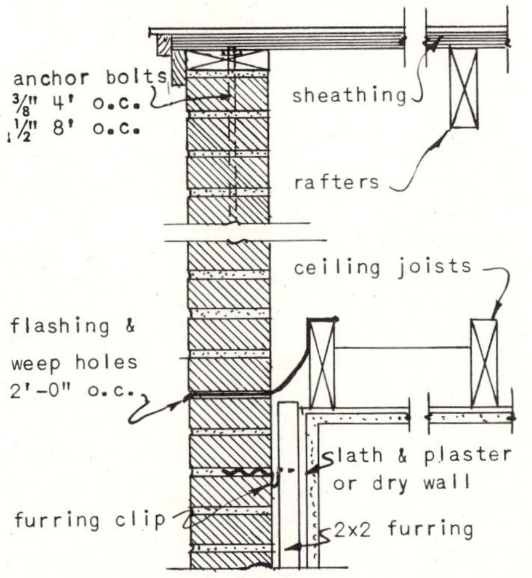
anchor bolts 3/8" 4' o.c. 1/2" 8' o.c.
sheathing
rafters
ceiling joists
flashing & weep holes 2'-0" o.c.
lath & plaster or dry wall
furring clip
2x2 furring

MASONRY GABLE

DATA SUPPLIED BY STRUCTURAL CLAY PRODUCTS INSTITUTE

BRICK WALLS

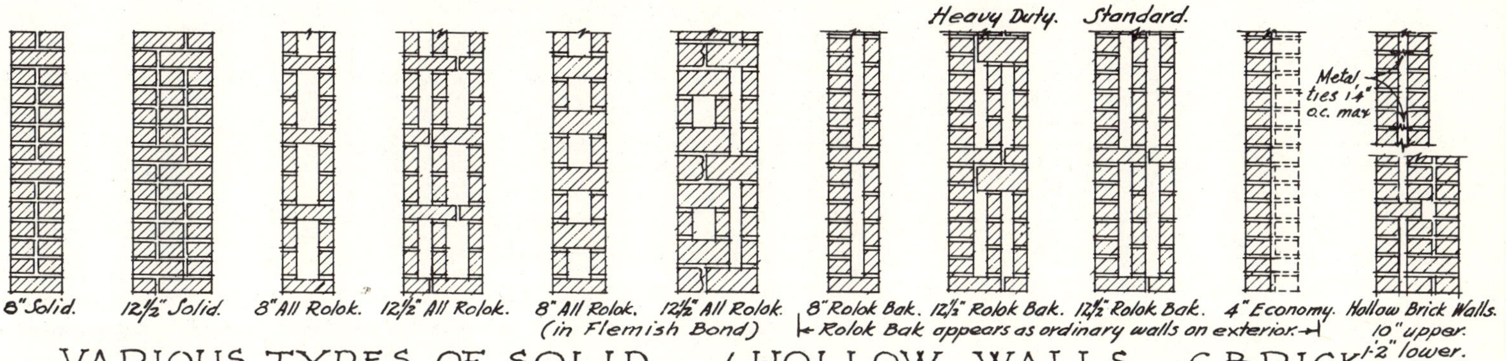
Heavy Duty.
Standard.
Metal ties 1'-4" o.c. max
8" Solid.
12½" Solid.
8" All Rolok.
12½" All Rolok.
8" All Rolok. (in Flemish Bond)
12½" All Rolok.
8" Rolok Bak.
12½" Rolok Bak.
12½" Rolok Bak.
4" Economy.
Rolok Bak appears as ordinary walls on exterior.
Hollow Brick Walls. 10" upper. 1'-2" lower.

VARIOUS TYPES OF SOLID and HOLLOW WALLS of BRICK
3/8" = 1'-0"

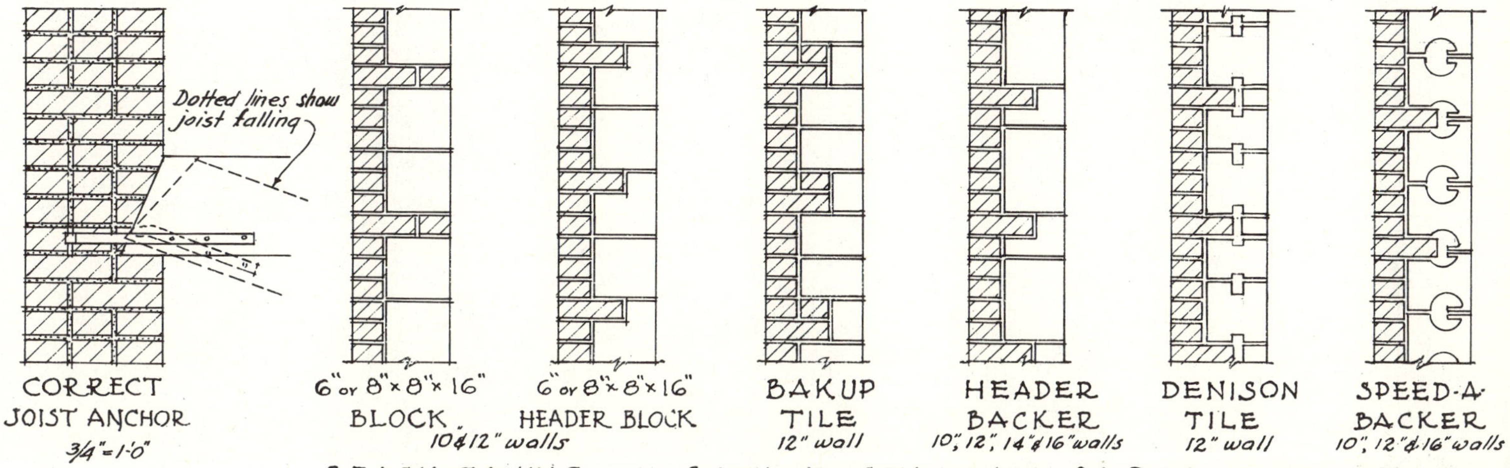
Dotted lines show joist falling
CORRECT JOIST ANCHOR
3/4" = 1'-0"
6" or 8" × 8" × 16" BLOCK
10 & 12" walls
6" or 8" × 8" × 16" HEADER BLOCK
BAKUP TILE
12" wall
HEADER BACKER
10", 12", 14" & 16" walls
DENISON TILE
12" wall
SPEED-A-BACKER
10", 12" & 16" walls

BRICK FACING with BACK-UP CONCRETE BLOCK or CLAY TILE
½" = 1'-0"

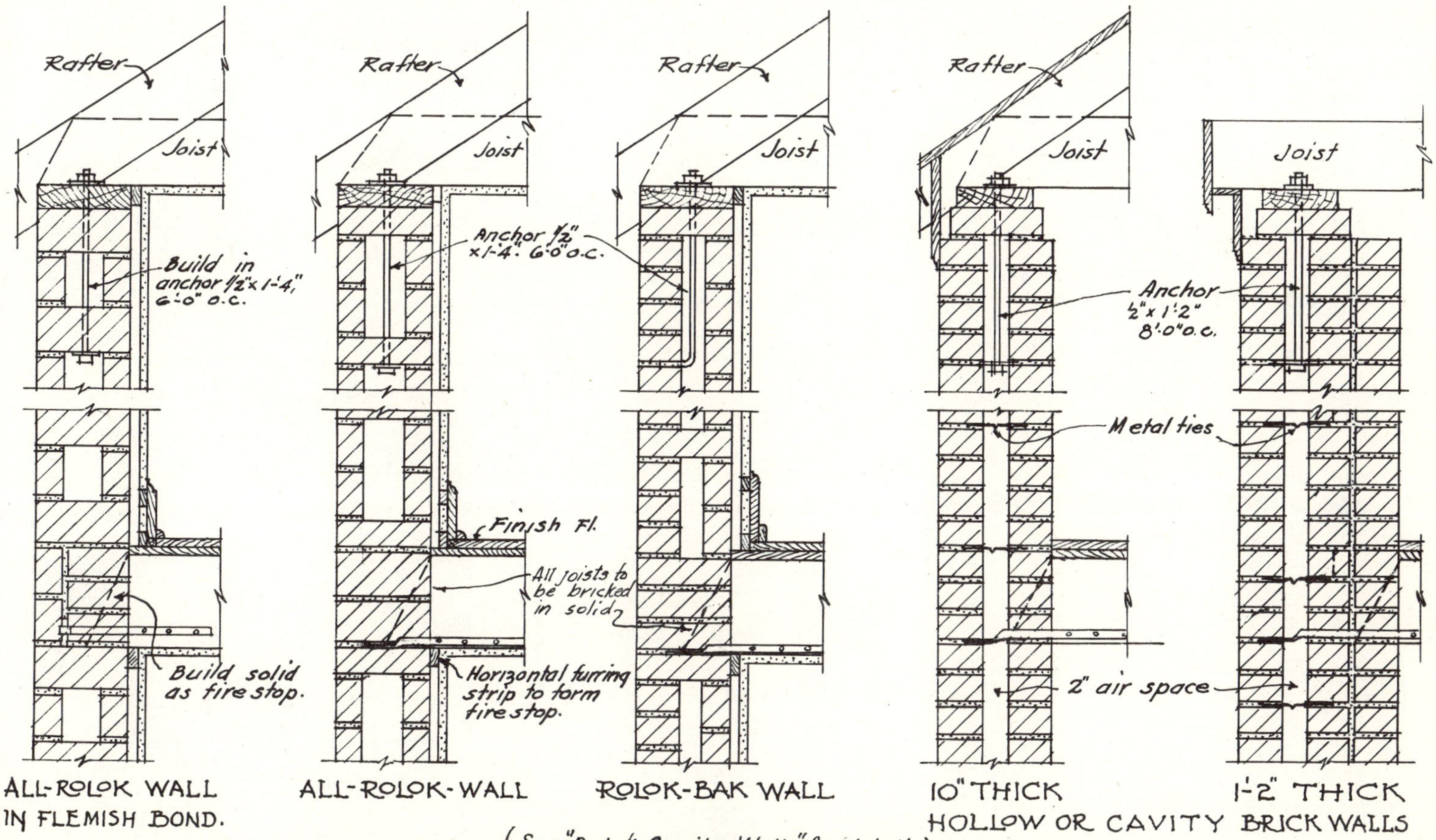
Rafter
Joist
Build in anchor ½" × 1'-4", 6'-0" o.c.
Anchor ½" × 1'-4" 6'-0" o.c.
Anchor ½" × 1'-2" 8'-0" o.c.
Metal ties
Finish Fl.
All joists to be bricked in solid
Build solid as fire stop.
Horizontal furring strip to form fire stop.
2" air space
ALL-ROLOK WALL IN FLEMISH BOND.
ALL-ROLOK-WALL
ROLOK-BAK WALL
10" THICK
1'-2" THICK
HOLLOW OR CAVITY BRICK WALLS

(See "Brick Cavity Walls" for details)
3/4" = 1'-0"

Data checked by Structural Clay Products Institute

BRICK - CAVITY & SERPENTINE WALLS

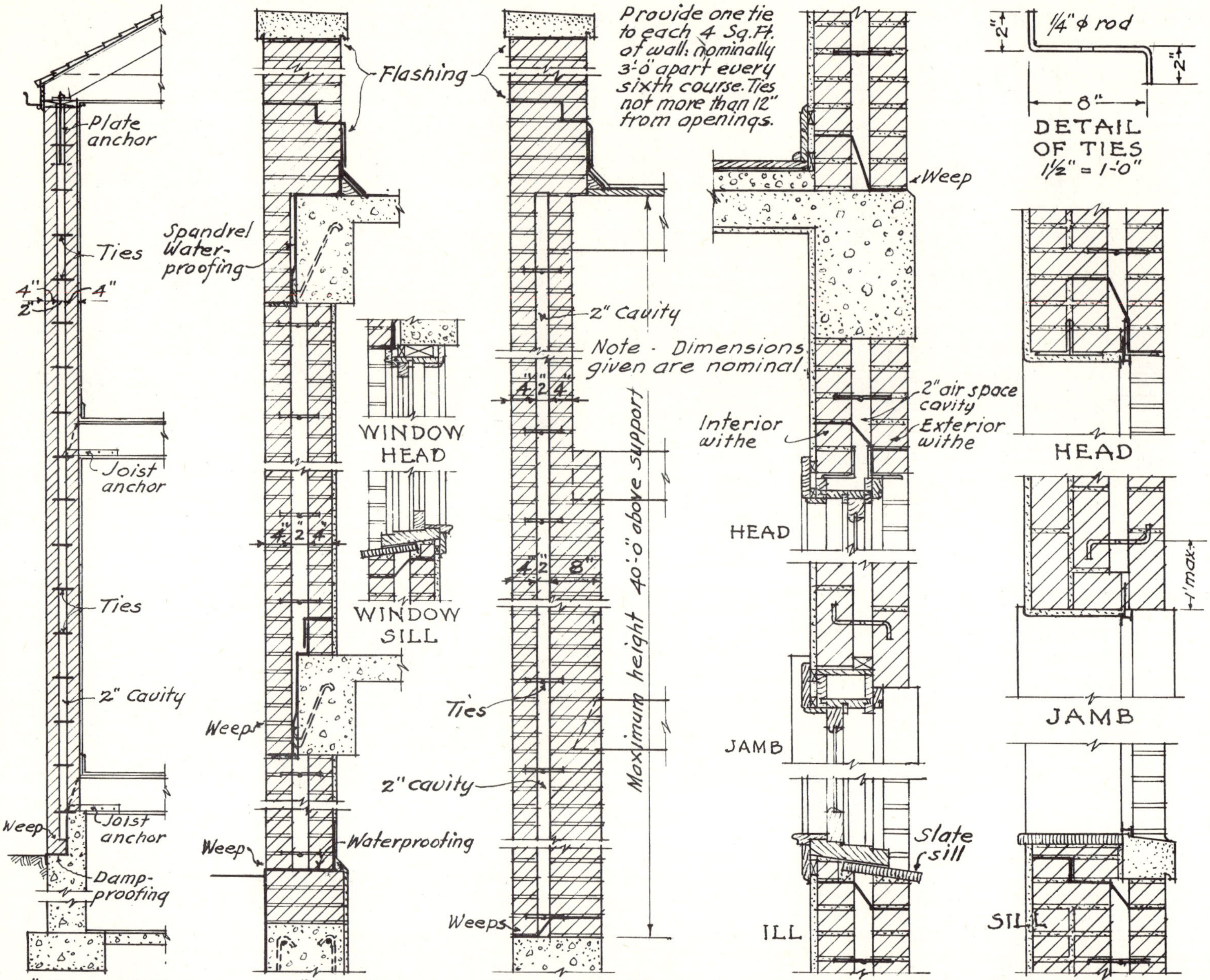
Plate anchor
Spandrel Water-proofing
Ties
4"
2"
4"
Joist anchor
Ties
2" Cavity
Weep
Joist anchor
Damp-proofing
Flashing
4" 2" 4"
Weep
2" cavity
Waterproofing
Weep
WINDOW HEAD
WINDOW SILL
Provide one tie to each 4 Sq.Ft. of wall: nominally 3'-0" apart every sixth course. Ties not more than 12" from openings.
2" Cavity
Note - Dimensions given are nominal.
4" 2" 4"
4" 2" 8"
Maximum height 40'-0" above support
Ties
Weeps
Weep
2" air space cavity
Interior withe
Exterior withe
HEAD
JAMB
Slate sill
ILL
1/4" ϕ rod
2"
2"
8"
DETAIL OF TIES
1 1/2" = 1'-0"
HEAD
1' max.
JAMB
SILL

10" LOAD BEARING 1/4" = 1'-0" | 10" PANEL | 1/2" = 1'-0" | 14" LOAD BEARING | D.H. WINDOWS | CASEMENT WINDOWS 3/4" = 1'-0"

CAVITY WALLS

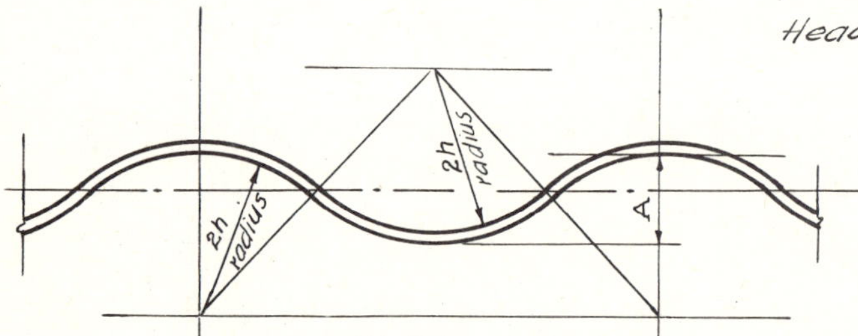
2h radius
2h radius
A

PLAN

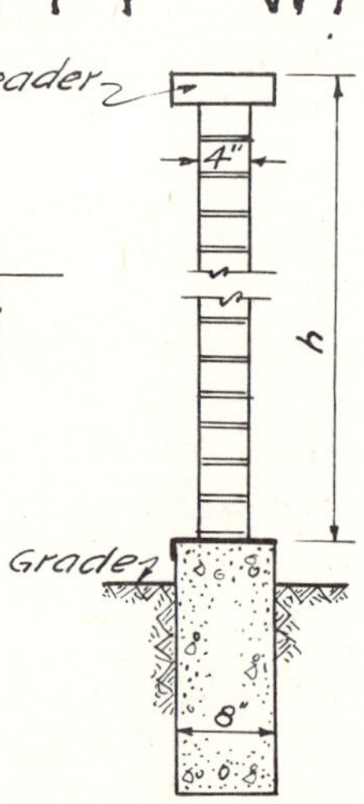
Header
4"
h
Grade
8"

SECTION

Four inch thick Serpentine walls have been built with radii up to 20'-0" in the South.
Radii under 7'-0" are advisable in the North.
Use Running Bond.

Relationships of 4" Serpentine walls		
height above foundation (h)	max. radius no more than 2h	min. distance A no less $\frac{h}{2}$
2'-0"	4'-0"	1'-0"
2'-6"	5'-0"	1'-3"
3'-0"	6'-0"	1'-6"
3'-6"	7'-0"	1'-9"
4'-0"	8'-0"	2'-0"
4'-6"	9'-0"	2'-3"
5'-0"	10'-0"	2'-6"
5'-6"	11'-0"	2'-9"
6'-0"	12'-0"	3'-0"

Note: no reinforcing used in wall.

4" BRICK SERPENTINE WALL

Data checked by Structural Clay Products Institute

MASONRY ARCHES

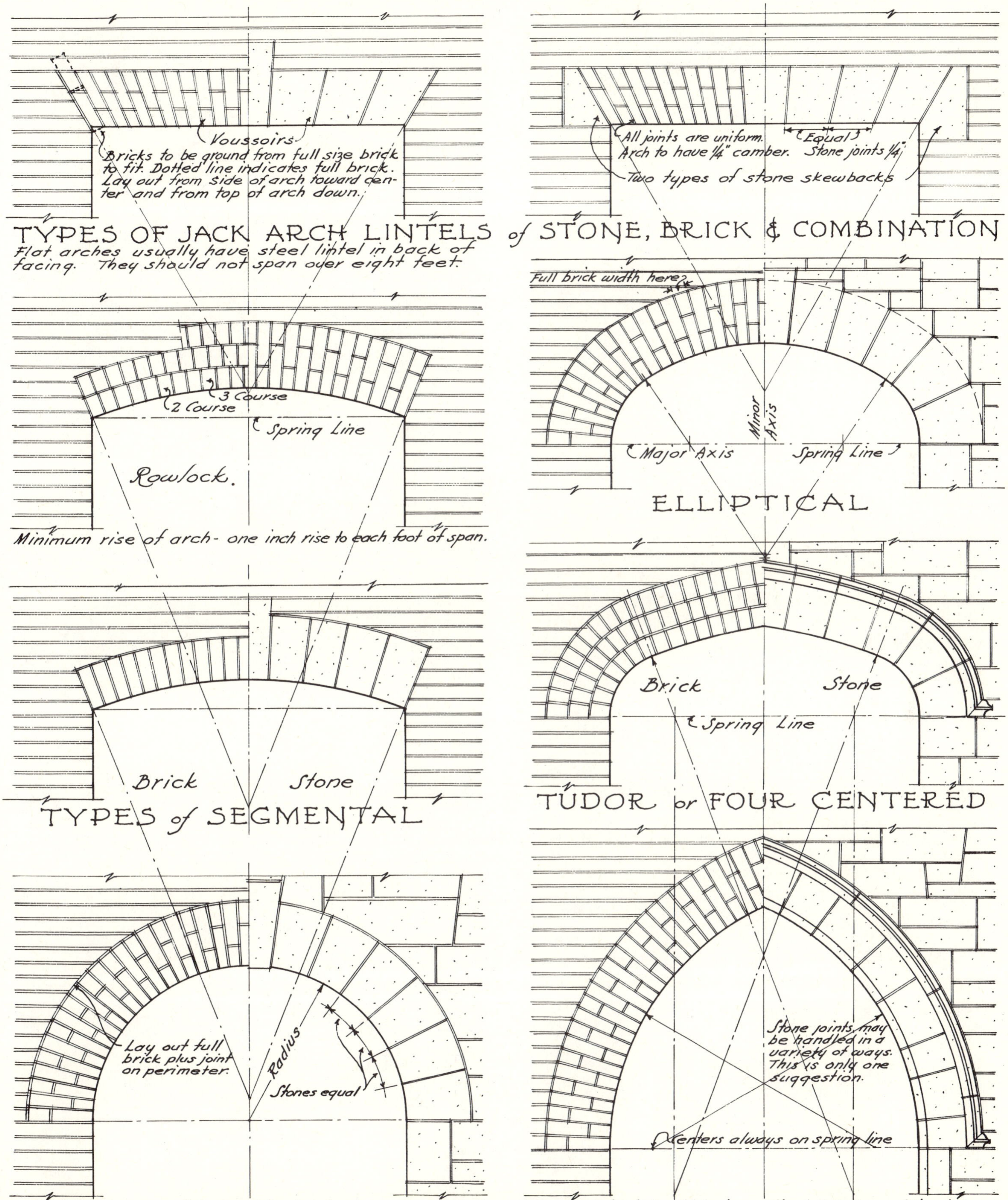
Voussoirs
Bricks to be ground from full size brick to fit. Dotted line indicates full brick. Lay out from side of arch toward center and from top of arch down.
All joints are uniform.
Arch to have 1/4" camber.
Equal
Stone joints 1/4
Two types of stone skewbacks
TYPES OF JACK ARCH LINTELS of STONE, BRICK & COMBINATION
Flat arches usually have steel lintel in back of facing. They should not span over eight feet.
Full brick width here
3 Course
2 Course
Spring Line
Rowlock.
Minimum rise of arch - one inch rise to each foot of span.
Minor Axis
Major Axis
Spring Line
ELLIPTICAL
Brick
Stone
TYPES of SEGMENTAL
Brick
Stone
Spring Line
TUDOR or FOUR CENTERED
Lay out full brick plus joint on perimeter.
Radius
Stones equal
Stone joints may be handled in a variety of ways. This is only one suggestion.
Centers always on spring line

All bricks, except in Rowlock Arch, are rubbed or shaped brick; this is called "Gauge Work".

ROMAN or SEMI-CIRCULAR — GOTHIC or POINTED

Stone joints 1/4" if with brickwork. Joints in stonework without bricks may be 1/4" or for fine work 3/16".

1/2" = 1'-0" scale

Data checked by Structural Clay Products Institute

CONCRETE BLOCKS

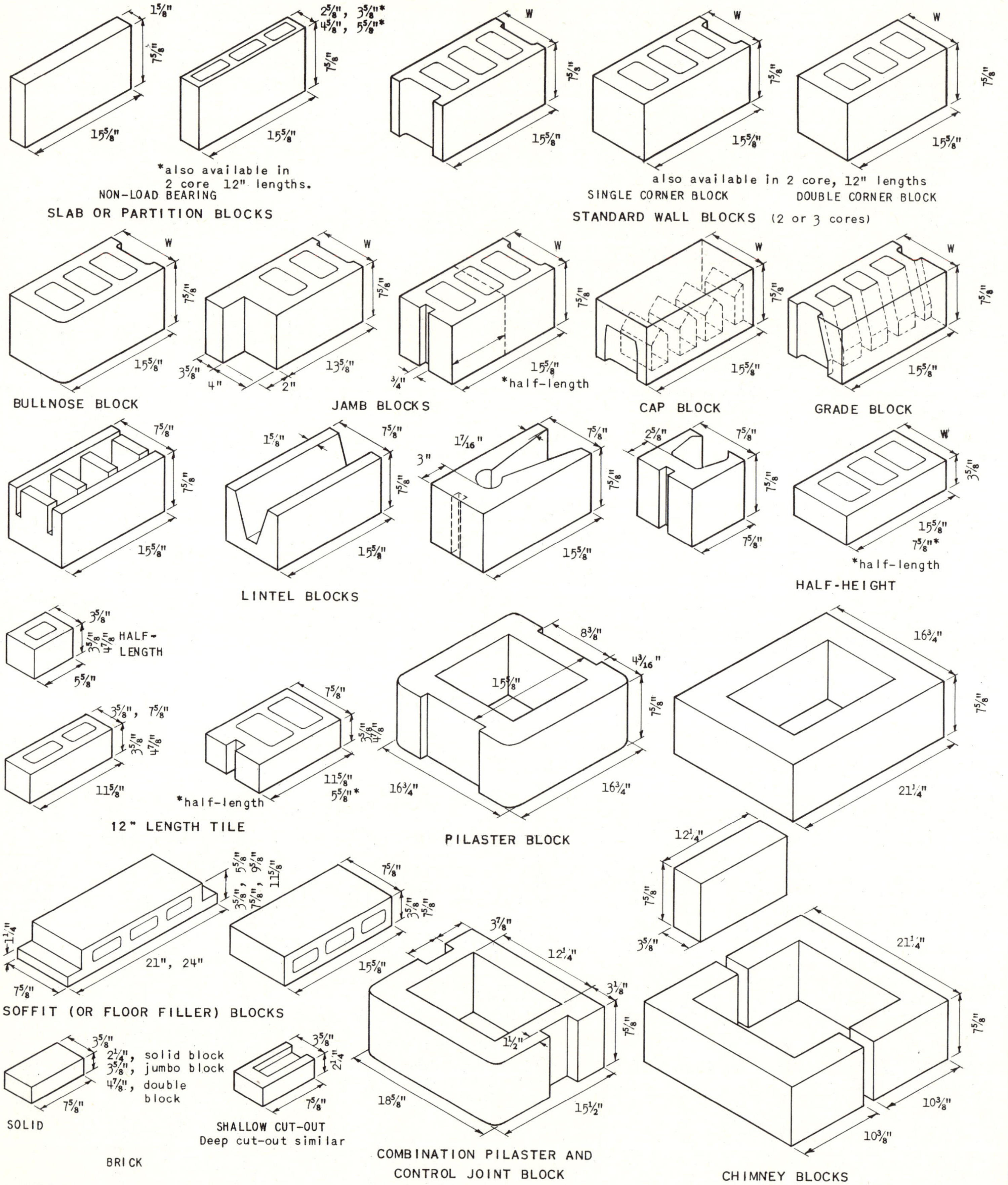
1 5/8"
7 5/8"
15 5/8"
2 5/8", 3 5/8"*
4 5/8", 5 5/8"*
7 5/8"
15 5/8"
*also available in
2 core 12" lengths.
NON-LOAD BEARING
SLAB OR PARTITION BLOCKS
W
7 5/8"
15 5/8"
also available in 2 core, 12" lengths
SINGLE CORNER BLOCK
DOUBLE CORNER BLOCK
STANDARD WALL BLOCKS (2 or 3 cores)
BULLNOSE BLOCK
3 5/8"
4"
2"
13 5/8"
3/4"
*half-length
JAMB BLOCKS
CAP BLOCK
GRADE BLOCK
1 5/8"
1 7/16"
3"
2 5/8"
LINTEL BLOCKS
3 5/8"
7 5/8"*
*half-length
HALF-HEIGHT
3 5/8"
3 5/8" 4 7/8"
HALF-LENGTH
5 5/8"
3 5/8", 7 5/8"
11 5/8"
5 5/8"*
*half-length
12" LENGTH TILE
8 3/8"
4 3/16"
16 3/4"
PILASTER BLOCK
16 3/4"
21 1/4"
12 1/4"
1 1/4"
21", 24"
3 5/8", 5 5/8", 7 5/8", 9 5/8", 11 5/8"
SOFFIT (OR FLOOR FILLER) BLOCKS
3 7/8"
3 1/8"
1 1/2"
18 5/8"
15 1/2"
10 3/8"
2 1/4", solid block
3 5/8", jumbo block
4 7/8", double block
SOLID
SHALLOW CUT-OUT
Deep cut-out similar
BRICK
COMBINATION PILASTER AND
CONTROL JOINT BLOCK
CHIMNEY BLOCKS

Data checked by Columbia Machine Works, Vancouver, Wash. "W" - indicates available widths of 7 5/8", 9 5/8", 11 5/8".
For load bearing specs., see ASTM C90-52, ASA-A79.
For non-load bearing specs., see ASTM C129-52, ASA-A80.

CONCRETE BLOCK WALLS

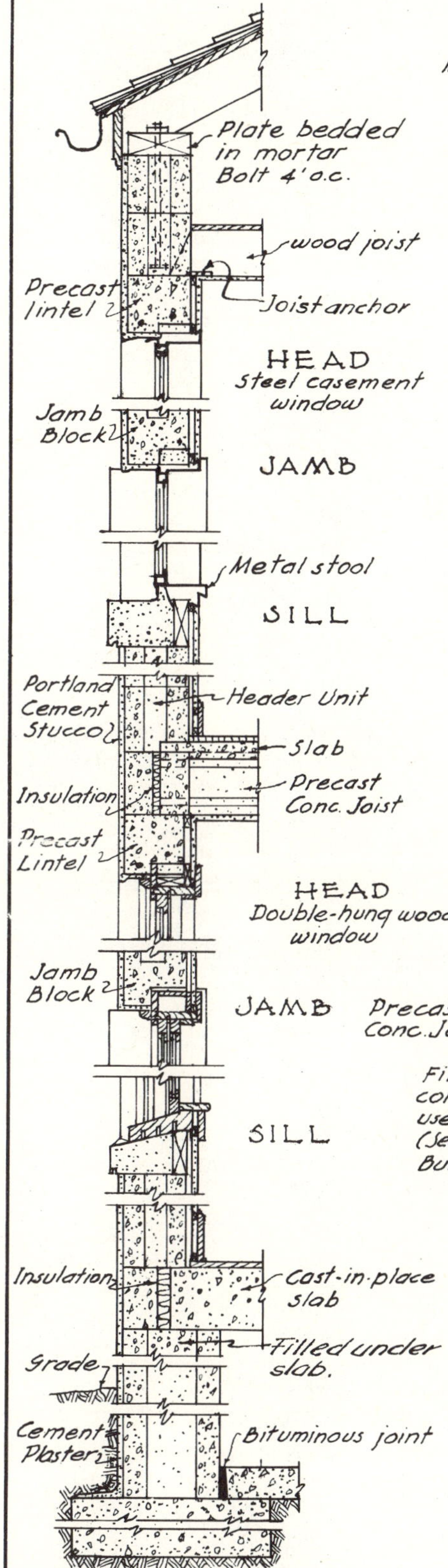
Plate bedded in mortar Bolt 4' o.c.
wood joist
Precast lintel
Joist anchor
HEAD
Steel casement window
Jamb Block
JAMB
Metal stool
SILL
Portland Cement Stucco
Header Unit
Slab
Insulation
Precast Conc. Joist
Precast Lintel
HEAD
Double-hung wood window
Jamb Block
JAMB
SILL
Insulation
Cast-in-place slab
Filled under slab.
Grade
Cement Plaster
Bituminous joint

BLOCK and STUCCO WALL SECTION
Scale 2" = 1'-0"

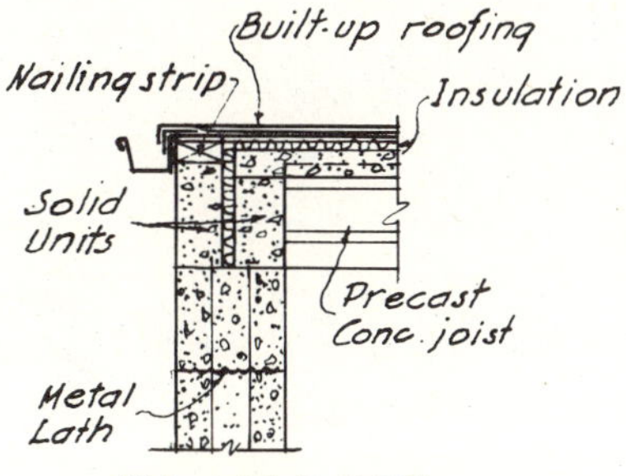
Built-up roofing
Nailing strip
Insulation
Solid Units
Precast Conc. joist
Metal Lath

FLAT ROOF

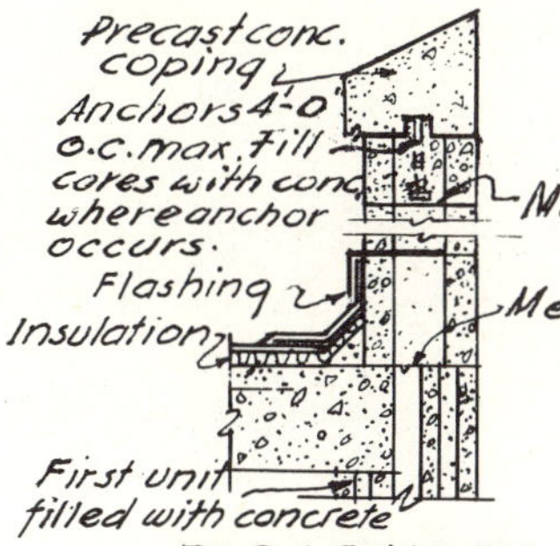
Precast conc. coping
Anchors 4'-0" o.c. max. Fill cores with conc. where anchor occurs.
Metal lath
Flashing
Metal tie
Insulation
First unit filled with concrete

PARAPET ON CAVITY WALL

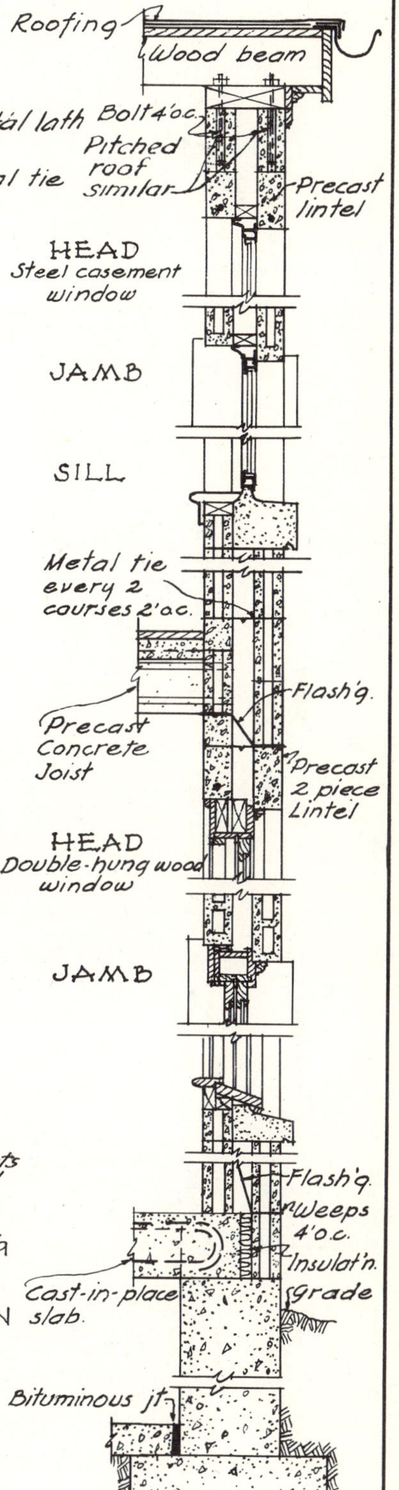
Roofing
Wood beam
Bolt 4' o.c.
Pitched roof similar
Precast lintel
HEAD
Steel casement window
JAMB
SILL
Metal tie every 2 courses 2' o.c.
Flash'g.
Precast Concrete Joist
Precast 2 piece Lintel
HEAD
Double-hung wood window
JAMB
Flash'g.
Weeps 4' o.c.
Insulat'n.
Cast-in-place slab.
Grade
Bituminous jt.

CAVITY WALL SECTION
Scale ½" = 1'-0"

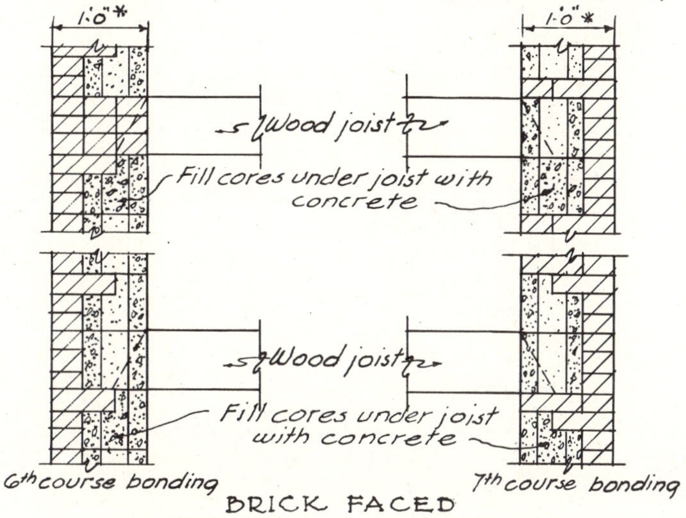
1'-0"*
1'-0"*
Wood joist
Fill cores under joist with concrete
Wood joist
Fill cores under joist with concrete
6th course bonding
7th course bonding

BRICK FACED CONCRETE MASONRY WALL
*indicates nominal dimension

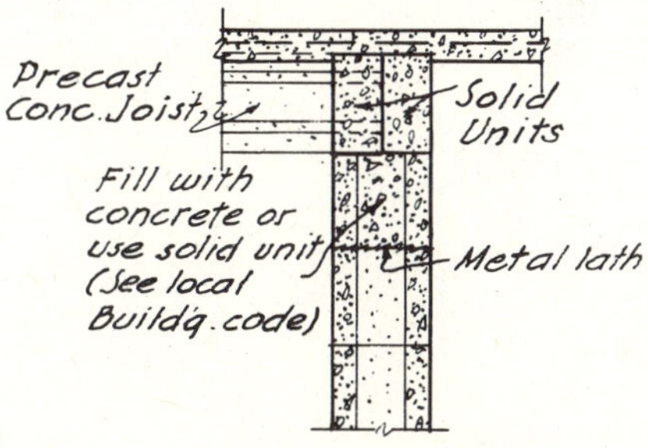
Precast Conc. Joist
Solid Units
Fill with concrete or use solid unit (See local Build'g. code)
Metal lath

8" INTERIOR BEARING WALLS
Section

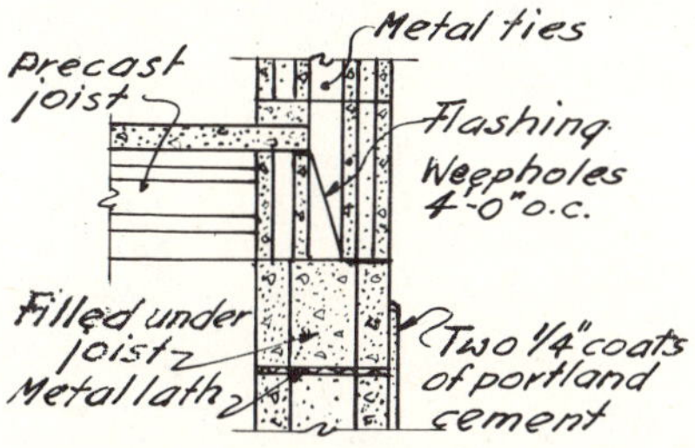
Metal ties
Precast joist
Flashing
Weepholes 4'-0" o.c.
Filled under joist
Metal lath
Two ¼" coats of portland cement

CONCRETE JOISTS BEARING ON FOUNDATION WALL

CAVITY WALL SECTION

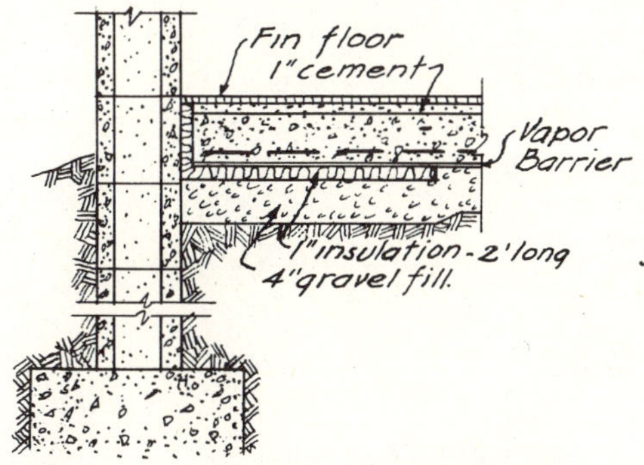
Fin floor 1" cement
Vapor Barrier
1" insulation - 2' long
4" gravel fill.

CONCRETE FLOOR on GROUND for HOUSE WITHOUT BASEMENT

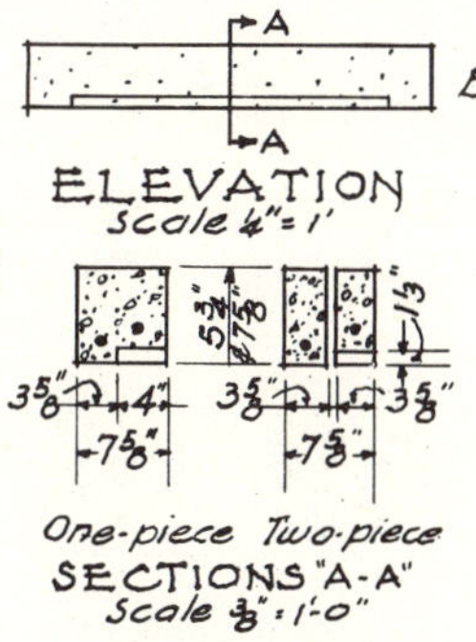
A
A
ELEVATION
Scale ¼" = 1'
One-piece Two-piece
SECTIONS "A-A"
Scale ⅜" = 1'-0"

PRECAST CONCRETE LINTEL

NOTE: Course under slab or joist to be solid or concrete filled.

NOTE: For footing drains see information on waterproofing & dampproofing of basements.

Scale ½" = 1'-0" unless otherwise noted. Mortar joints = ⅜"

CONCRETE BLOCK WALLS

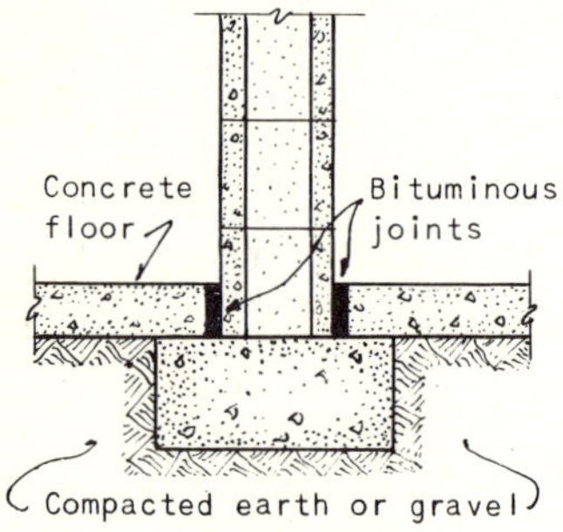
Concrete floor
Bituminous joints
Compacted earth or gravel

BEARING

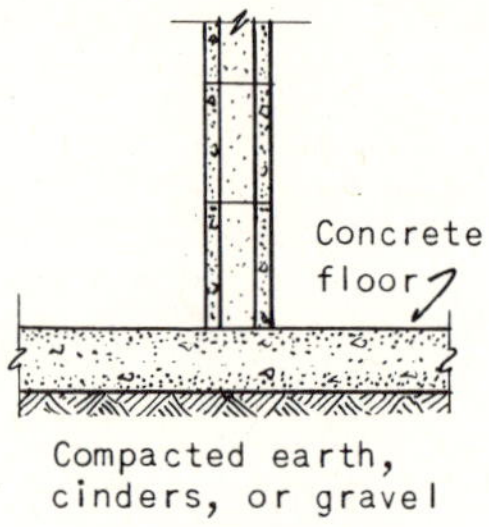
Concrete floor
Compacted earth, cinders, or gravel

NON-BEARING

INTERIOR WALLS ON GRADE

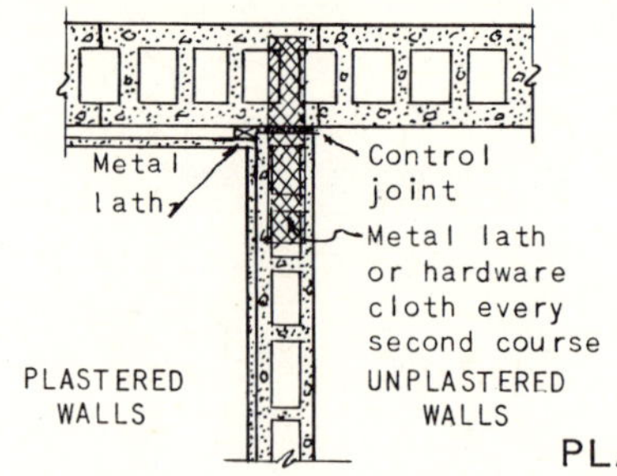
Metal lath
Control joint
Metal lath or hardware cloth every second course
PLASTERED WALLS
UNPLASTERED WALLS

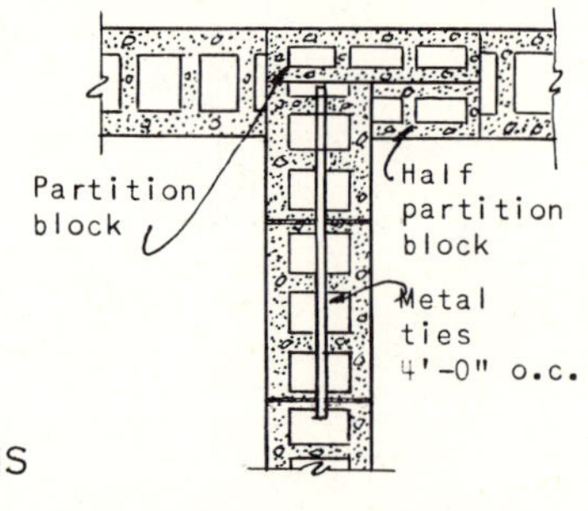
Partition block
Half partition block
Metal ties 4'-0" o.c.

PLANS

BEARING & NON-BEARING

BOTH WALLS BEARING

BONDING OF INTERSECTING WALLS

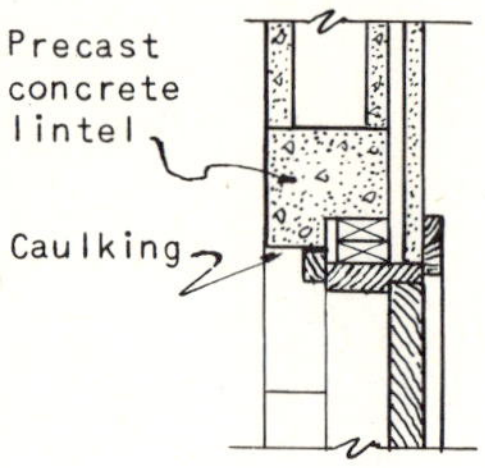
Precast concrete lintel
Caulking

HEAD

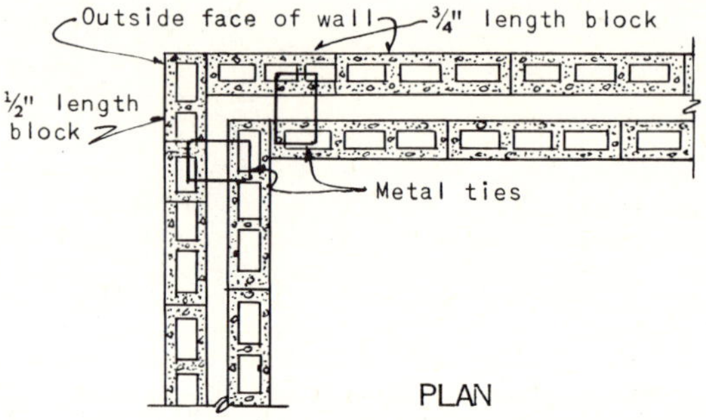
Outside face of wall
¾" length block
½" length block
Metal ties

PLAN

CORNER CONSTRUCTION, CAVITY WALL

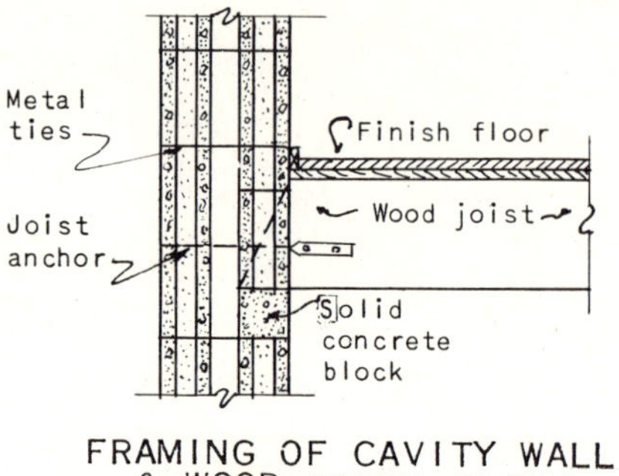
Metal ties
Finish floor
Wood joist
Joist anchor
Solid concrete block

FRAMING OF CAVITY WALL & WOOD JOIST FLOOR

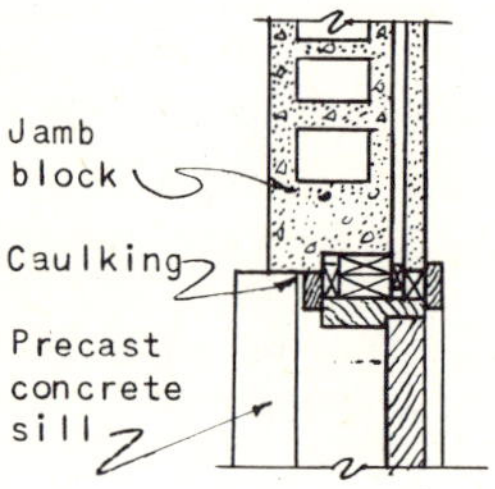
Jamb block
Caulking
Precast concrete sill

JAMB

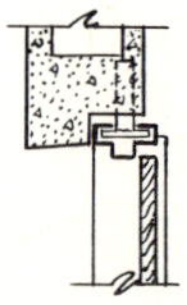

METAL FRAME JAMB

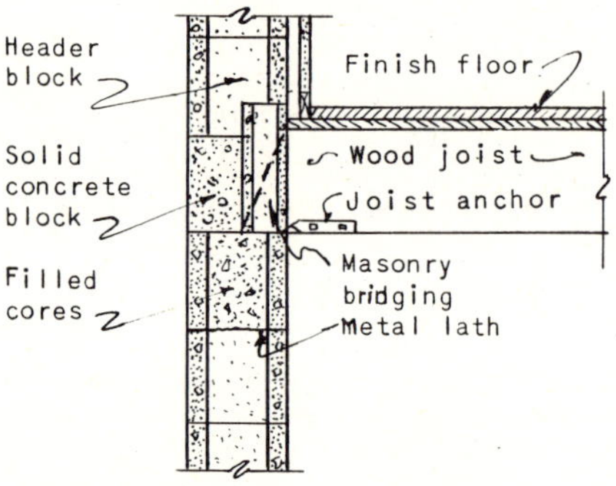
Header block
Finish floor
Solid concrete block
Wood joist
Joist anchor
Filled cores
Masonry bridging
Metal lath

FRAMING OF WALL & WOOD JOIST FLOOR

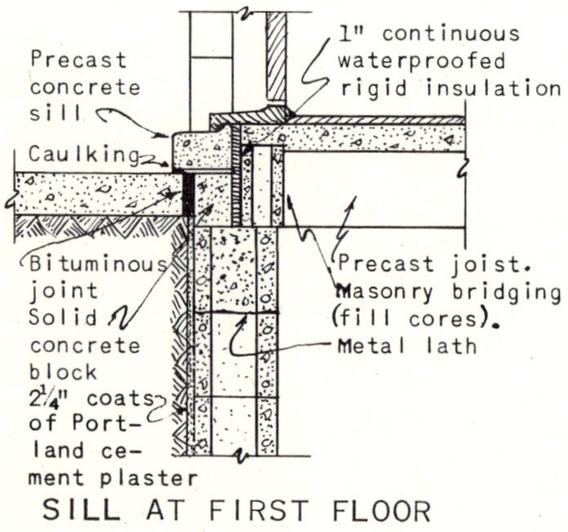
Precast concrete sill
1" continuous waterproofed rigid insulation
Caulking
Bituminous joint
Solid concrete block
2¼" coats of Portland cement plaster
Precast joist. Masonry bridging (fill cores).
Metal lath

SILL AT FIRST FLOOR

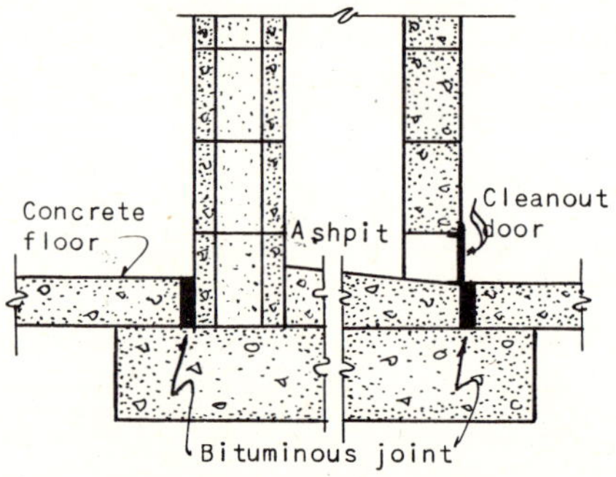
Concrete floor
Ashpit
Cleanout door
Bituminous joint

ON INTERIOR WALL

NOTE: raise ashpit above floor level for convenience in sweeping out.

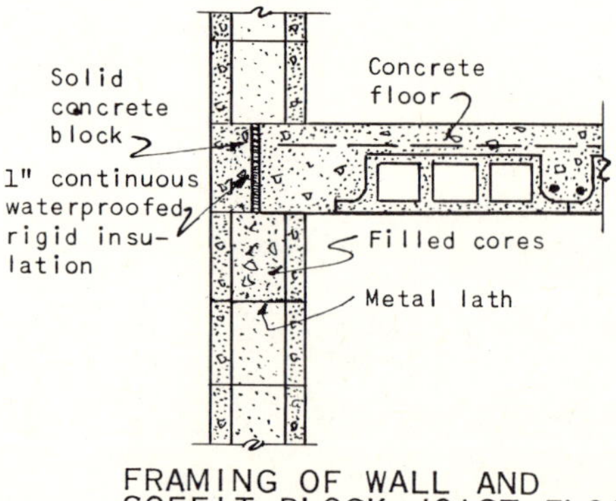
Solid concrete block
1" continuous waterproofed rigid insulation
Concrete floor
Filled cores
Metal lath

FRAMING OF WALL AND SOFFIT BLOCK JOIST FLOOR (CONCRETE BLOCK JOIST FLOOR SIMILAR)

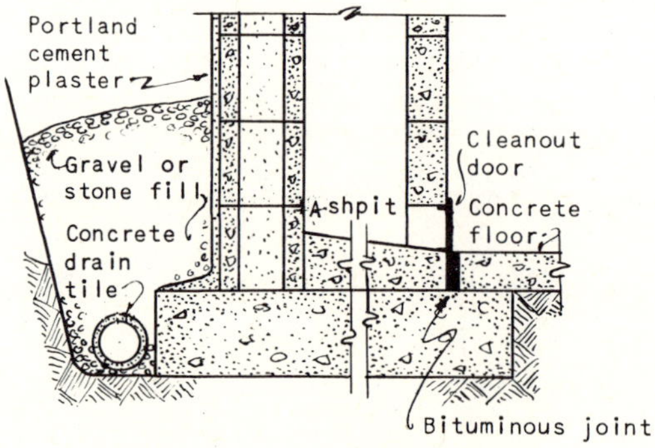
Portland cement plaster
Gravel or stone fill
Concrete drain tile
Ashpit
Cleanout door
Concrete floor
Bituminous joint

ON EXTERIOR WALL

CHIMNEY FOOTINGS

Scale all drawings: ½" = 1'-0"

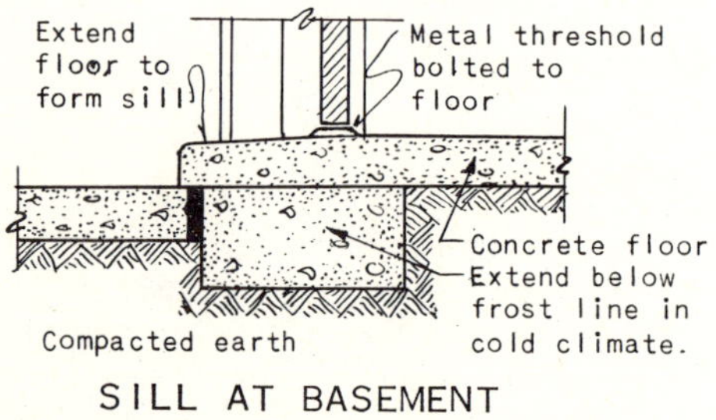
Extend floor to form sill
Metal threshold bolted to floor
Concrete floor
Extend below frost line in cold climate.
Compacted earth

SILL AT BASEMENT

SECTION AT WOOD DOOR

TYPICAL SECTIONS AT WALL AND FLOOR

CONCRETE BLOCK WALL CONTROL JOINTS

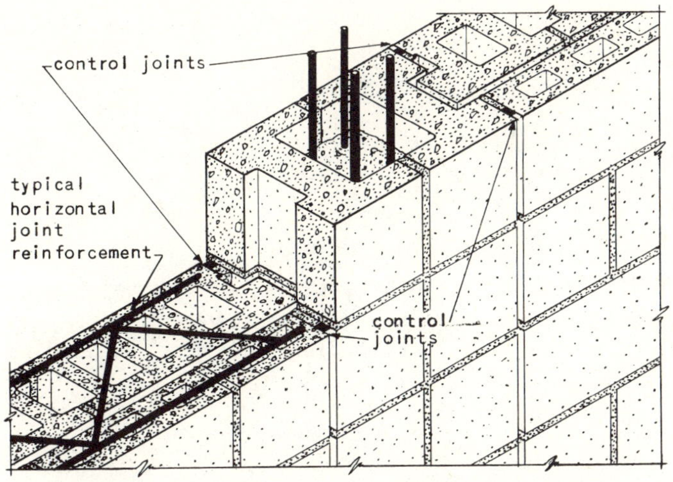
control joints
typical horizontal joint reinforcement
control joints

FLUSH WALL PILASTER AND CONTROL JOINT

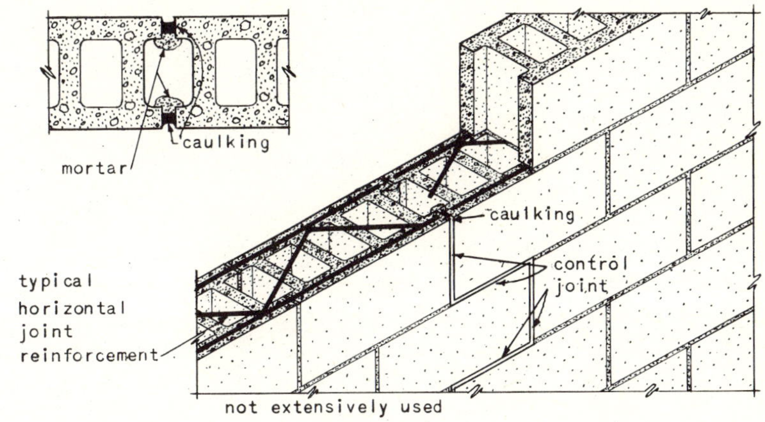
caulking
mortar
caulking
control joint
typical horizontal joint reinforcement
not extensively used

STAGGERED CONTROL JOINT

NOTE: horizontal reinforcement spacing to be 24" o.c. max. Closer spacing recommended (1) in long walls with few control joints, (2) at points of high horizontal stress concentrations.

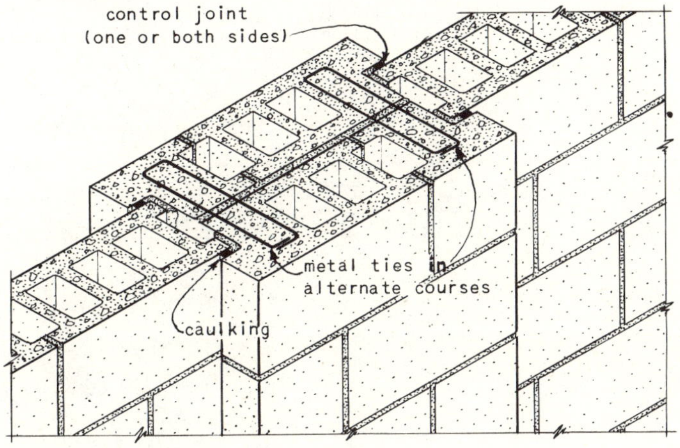
control joint
(one or both sides)
metal ties in alternate courses
caulking

CONTROL JOINT AT PIER

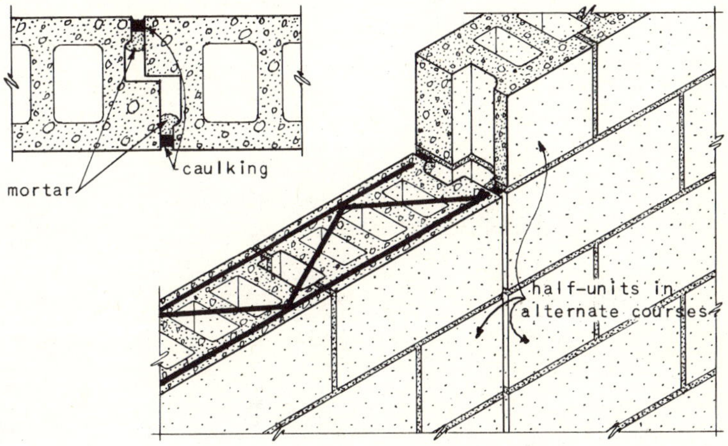
mortar
caulking
half-units in alternate courses

STRAIGHT CONTROL JOINT

CONTROL JOINTS IN FLUSH WALLS

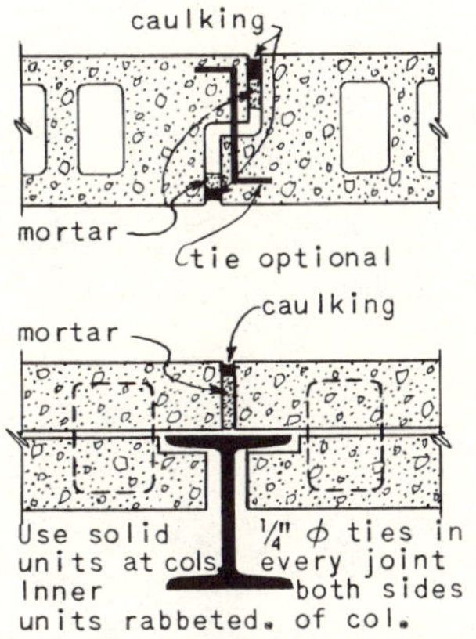
caulking
mortar
tie optional
mortar
caulking
Use solid units at cols. Inner units rabbeted.
1/4" ϕ ties in every joint both sides of col.

PLANS
ALTERNATE DETAILS OF FLUSH WALL CONTROL JOINTS

CONTROL JOINTS:
are for relieving contraction and other stresses in masonry by providing a continuous vertical separation thru the wall thickness.

1. In plain exterior walls (no openings) and interior walls in unheated buildings control joint spacing should be:

$$S = 5\sqrt{h} \text{ to } 6\sqrt{h}$$

where S = spacing and h = wall height.

2. In interior walls in heated buildings, allow slightly greater spacing.

3. In walls with openings, max. spacing should not exceed 20'.

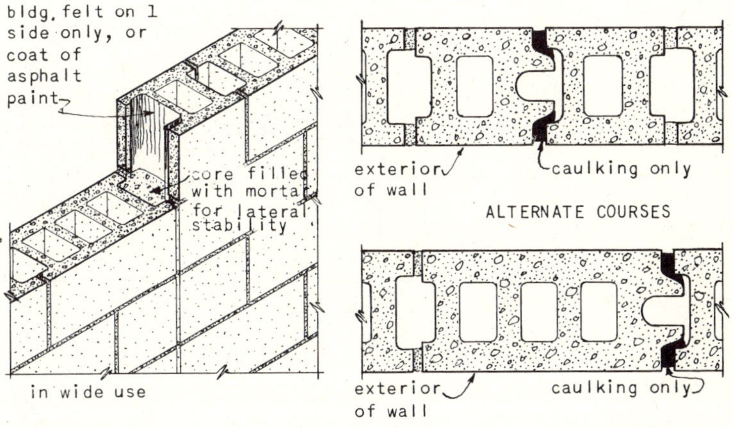
bldg. felt on 1 side only, or coat of asphalt paint
core filled with mortar for lateral stability
in wide use
exterior of wall
caulking only
ALTERNATE COURSES
exterior of wall
caulking only

SHEAR RESISTING, FLUSH WALL CONTROL JOINTS.

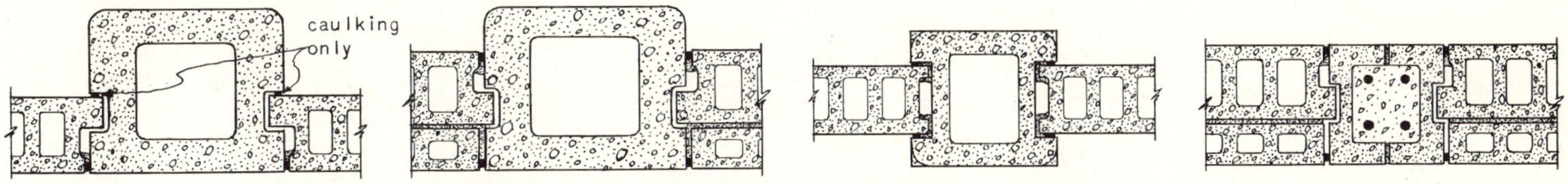
caulking only

PLANS OF CONTROL JOINTS AT WALL AND PILASTERS

Scale: 1/2" = 1'-0"

NOTE: in forming control joints, rake mortar to a depth of 3/4".

DATA CHECKED BY NATIONAL CONCRETE MASONRY ASSOCIATION

STRUCTURAL CLAY TILE for COMBINATION BRICK & TILE WALLS

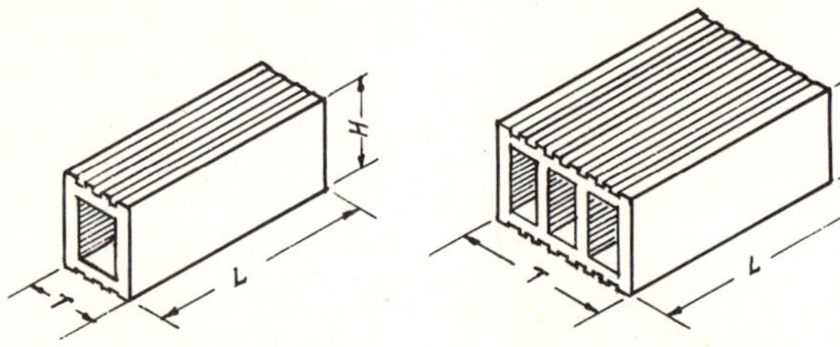

BAKUP

	T	H	L
Mod.	3½"	4⅚"	11½"
Typ.	3¾"	5"	12"

	T	H	L
Mod.	7½"	4⅚"	11½"
Typ.	8"	5"	12"

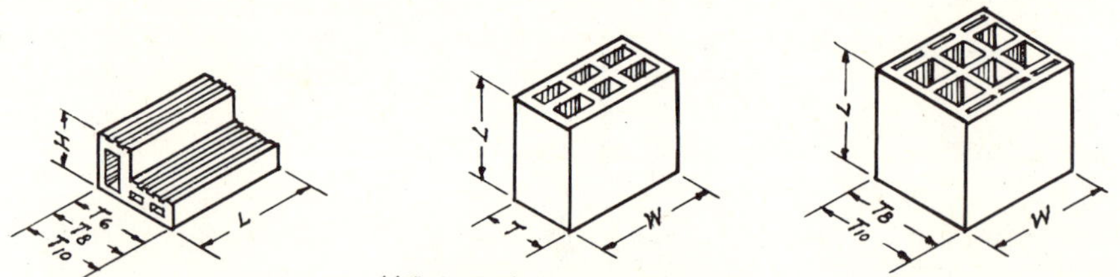

HEADER - BACKER

	T_6	T_8	T_{10}	H	L
Mod.	5½"	7½"	9½"	4⅚"	11½"
Typ.	6"	8"	10"	5"	12"

	T	W	L
Mod.	5½"	11½"	10⅙"
Typ.	6"	12"	10½"

	T_8	T_{10}	W	L.
Mod.	7½"	9½"	11½"	10⅙"
Typ.	8"	10"	12"	10½"

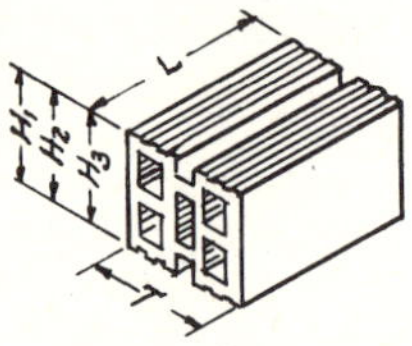

DENISON TILE

	T	H_1	H_2	H_3	L
Mod.	7½"	4⅚"	7½"	10⅙"	11½"
Typ.	8"	5"	7¾"	10½	12"

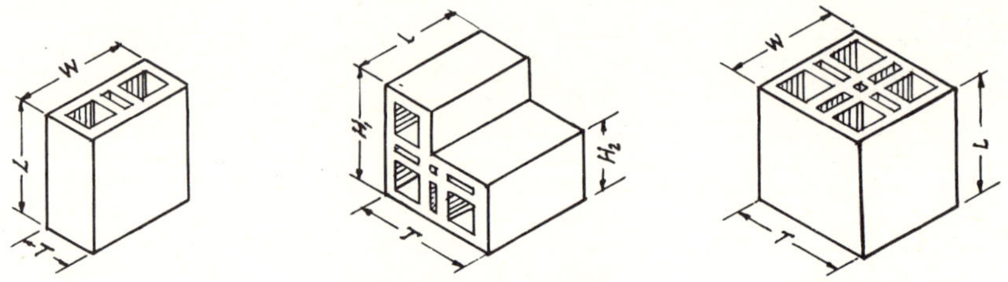

HEATH CUBES

	T	W	L
Mod.	3½"	7½"	7½"
Typ.	3¾"	7¾"	7⅞"

	T	H_1	H_2	L
Mod.	7½"	7½"	4⅚"	7½"
Typ.	7¾"	7¾"	5"	7⅞"

	T	W	L
Mod.	7½"	7½"	7½"
Typ.	7¾"	7¾"	7⅞"

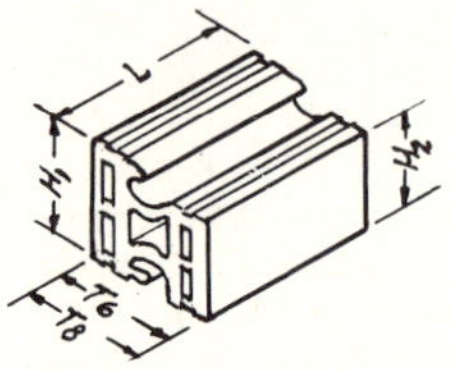

SPEED-A-BACKER

	T_6	T_8	H_1	H_2	L.
Mod.	5½"	7½"	7½"	6⅙"	11½"
Typ.	5⅞"	7¾"	7¾"	6⅜"	12"

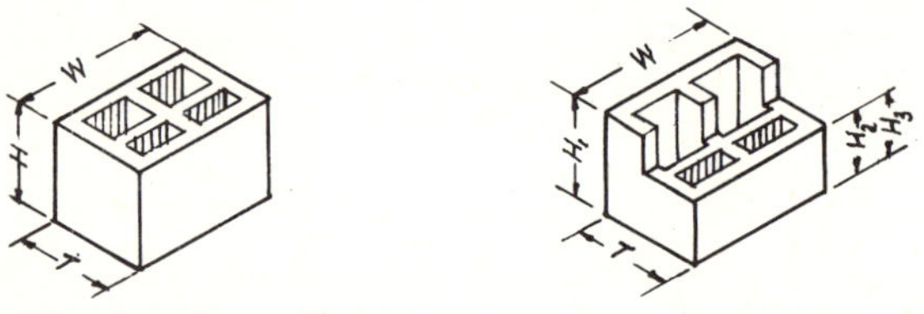

RARITILE

	T	W	H
Mod.	7½"	11½"	7½"
Typ.	7¾"	12"	7¾"

	T	W	H_1	H_2	H_3
Mod.	7½"	11½	7½"	4⅚"	6⅙"
Typ.	7¾"	12"	7¾"	5"	6⅜"

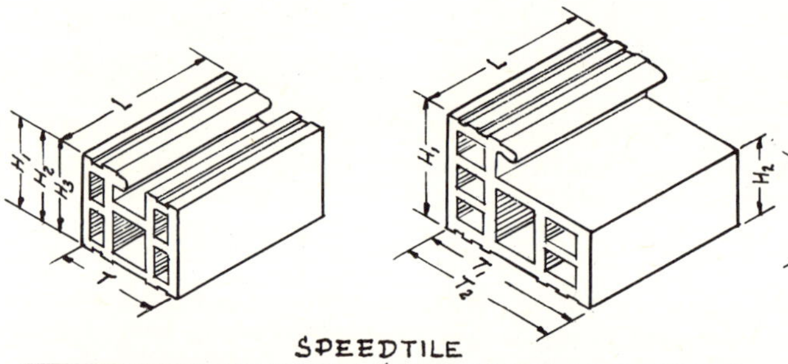

SPEEDTILE

	T	H_1	H_2	H_3	L
Mod.	7½"	4⅚"	6⅙"	7½"	11½"
Typ.	7¾"	5"	6¼"	7¾"	12"

	T_1	T_2	H_1	H_2	L
Mod.	7½"	11½"	7½"	4⅚"	11½"
Typ.	7¾"	11¾	7¾"	5"	12"

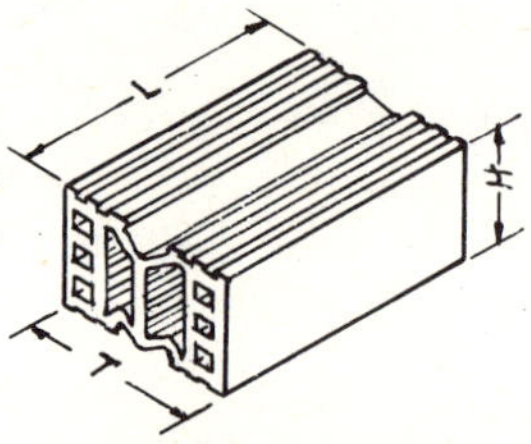

LEAK-PRUF

	T	H	L
Mod.	7½"	4⅚"	11½"
Typ.	8"	5"	12"

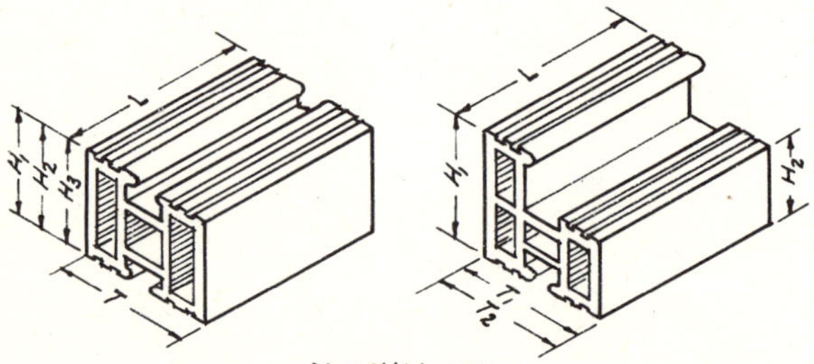

KWIKLAY

	T	H_1	H_2	H_3	L
Mod.	7½"	4⅚"	6⅙"	7½"	11½"
Typ.	7¾"	5"	6⅜"	7⅝	12"

	T_1	T_2	H_1	H_2	L
Mod.	7½"	11½"	7½"	4⅚"	11½"
Typ.	7¾"	11¾"	7⅝"	5"	12"

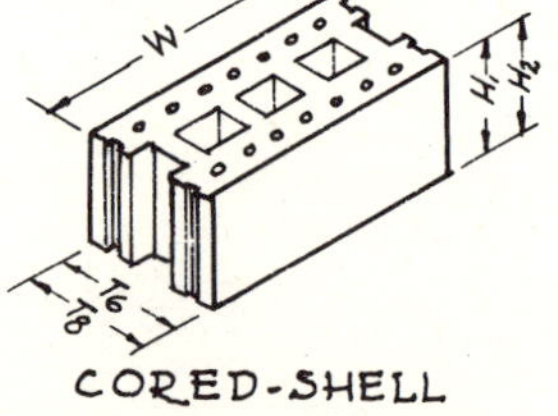

CORED-SHELL

	T_6	T_8	W	H_1	H_2
Mod.	5½"	7½"	11½"	3½"	4⅚"
Typ	5¾"	8"	12"	3¾"	5"

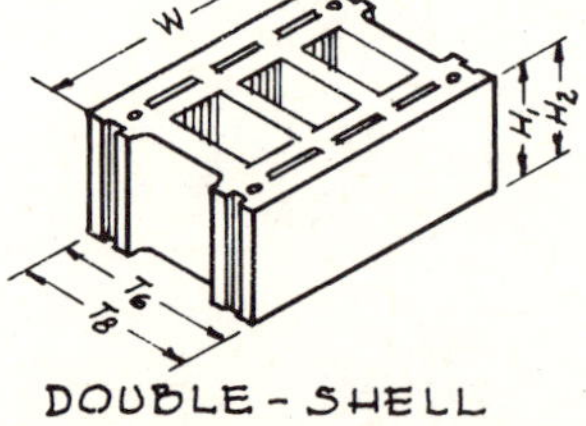

DOUBLE-SHELL

	T_6	T_8	W	H_1	H_2
Mod.	5½"	7½"	11½"	3½"	4⅚"
Typ.	5¾"	8"	12"	3¾"	5"

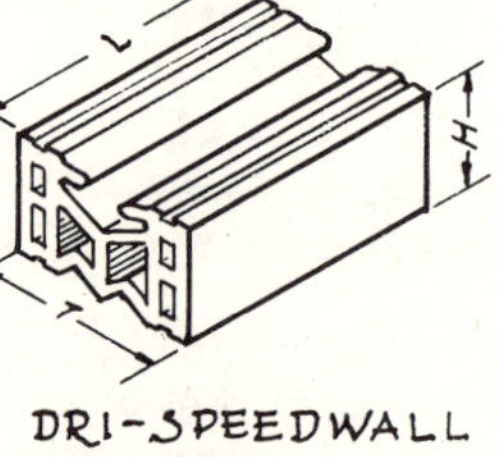

DRI-SPEEDWALL

	T	H	L
Mod.	7½"	4⅚"	11½"
Typ.	8"	5"	12"

Mod. = actual modular size of tile. Typ. = actual typical (non-modular) size of tile. Standard mortar joint for structural clay tile is ½".

Recommendations of the Structural Clay Products Institute - 1956

STRUCTURAL CLAY TILE

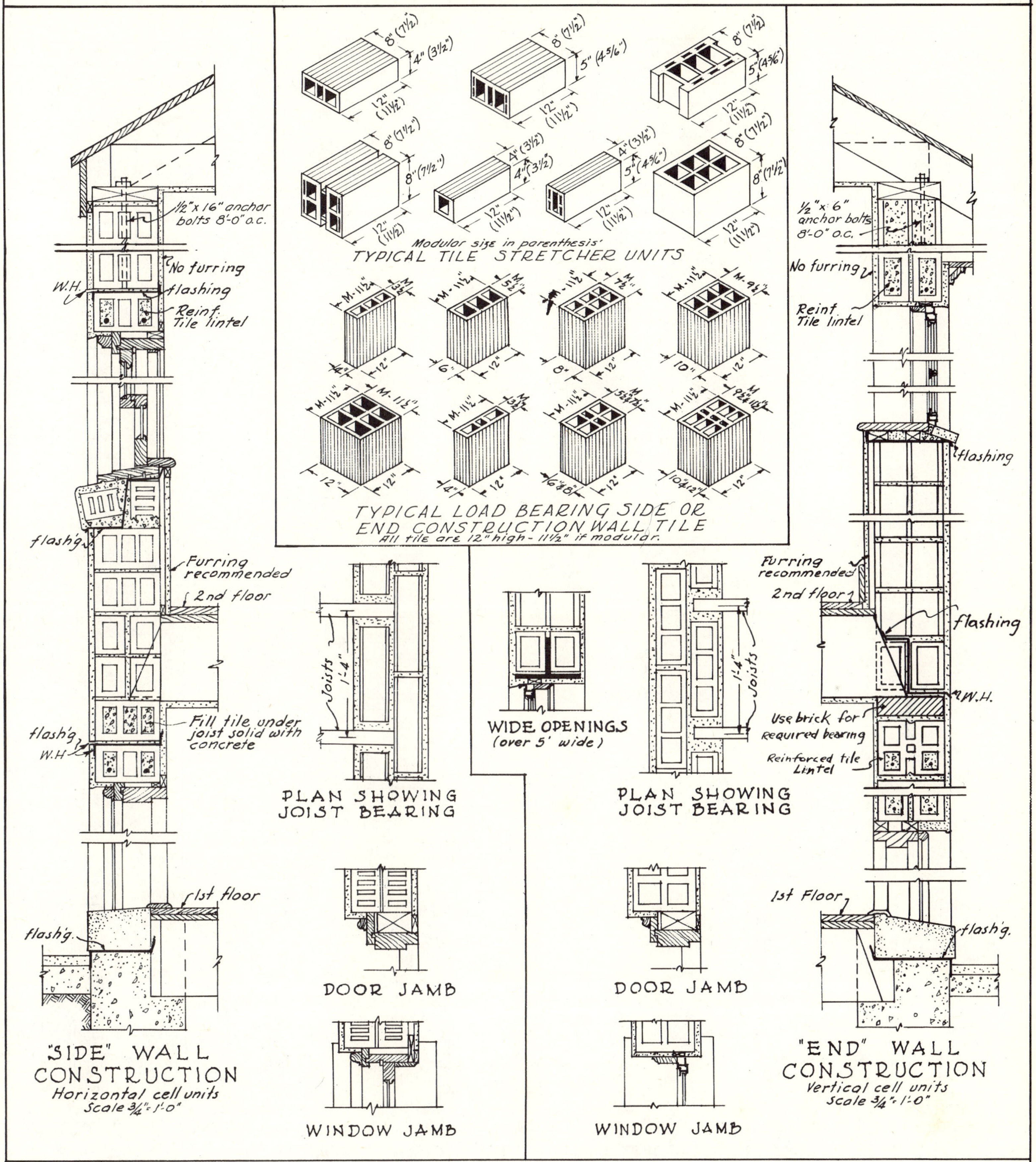
8" (7½")
4" (3½")
12" (11½")
5" (4⅚")
Modular size in parenthesis
TYPICAL TILE STRETCHER UNITS
TYPICAL LOAD BEARING SIDE OR END CONSTRUCTION WALL TILE
All tile are 12" high - 11½" if modular.
½" x 16" anchor bolts 8'-0" o.c.
No furring
W.H.
flashing
Reinf. Tile lintel
flash'g.
Furring recommended
2nd floor
Fill tile under joist solid with concrete
1st floor
"SIDE" WALL CONSTRUCTION
Horizontal cell units
Scale ¾" = 1'-0"
Joists 1'-4"
PLAN SHOWING JOIST BEARING
DOOR JAMB
WINDOW JAMB
WIDE OPENINGS (over 5' wide)
½" x 6" anchor bolts 8'-0" o.c.
Use brick for required bearing
Reinforced tile Lintel
1st Floor
"END" WALL CONSTRUCTION
Vertical cell units
Scale ¾" = 1'-0"

All tile sizes figured for use with standard ½" mortar joint

EXTERIOR WALL CONSTRUCTION with STUCCO FINISH

Recommendations of the Structural Clay Products Institute, 1956

STRUCTURAL CLAY TILE

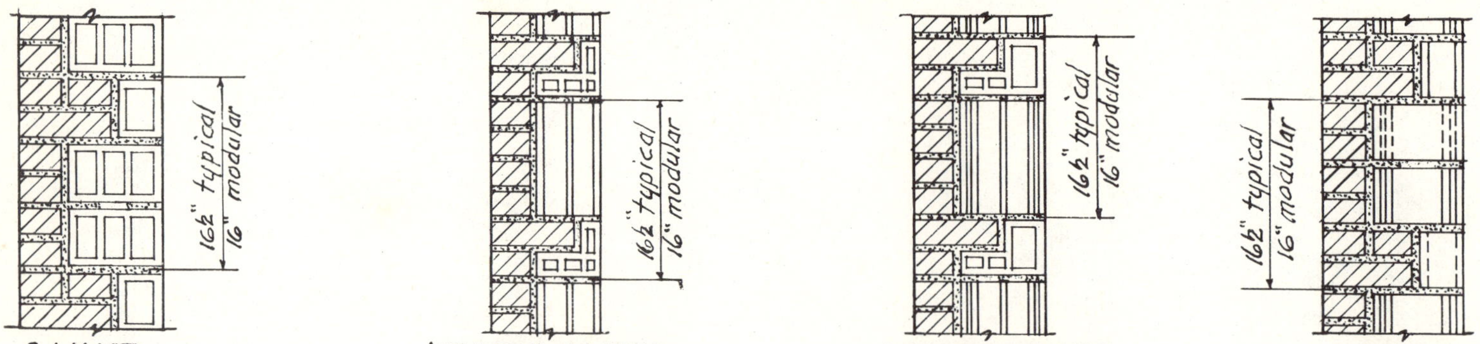
16½" typical
16" modular

BAKUP 12" wall — HEADER-BACKER 10" wall — HEADER-BACKER 12" wall — CORED or DOUBLE-SHELL 12" wall

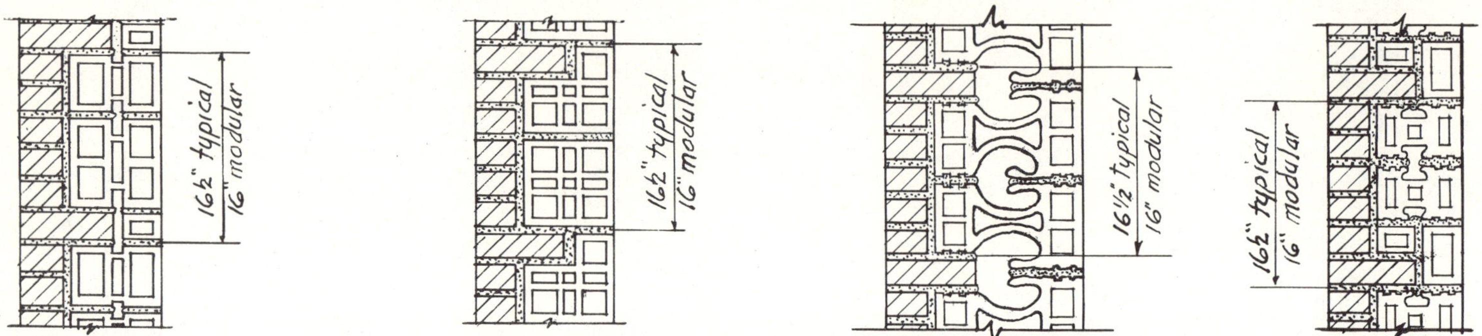
16½" typical
16" modular
16½" typical
16" modular

DENISON 12" wall — HEATH CUBE 12" wall — SPEED-A-BACKER 16" wall — KWIKLAY 8"x5⅓"x12" unit 12" wall

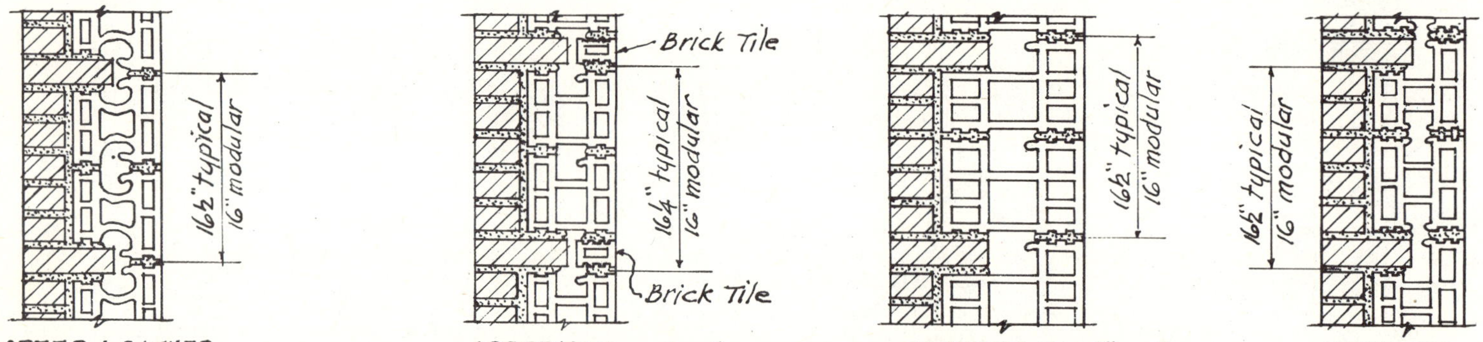
16½" typical
16" modular
Brick Tile
16¼" typical
16" modular
Brick Tile

SPEED-A-BACKER 12" wall — SPEEDTILE - 12" wall — SPEEDTILE - 16" wall — KWIKLAY 12" wall

TYPES OF BONDING *for* COMBINATION BRICK & TILE WALLS

Other combinations of units may be used for any desired header interval.

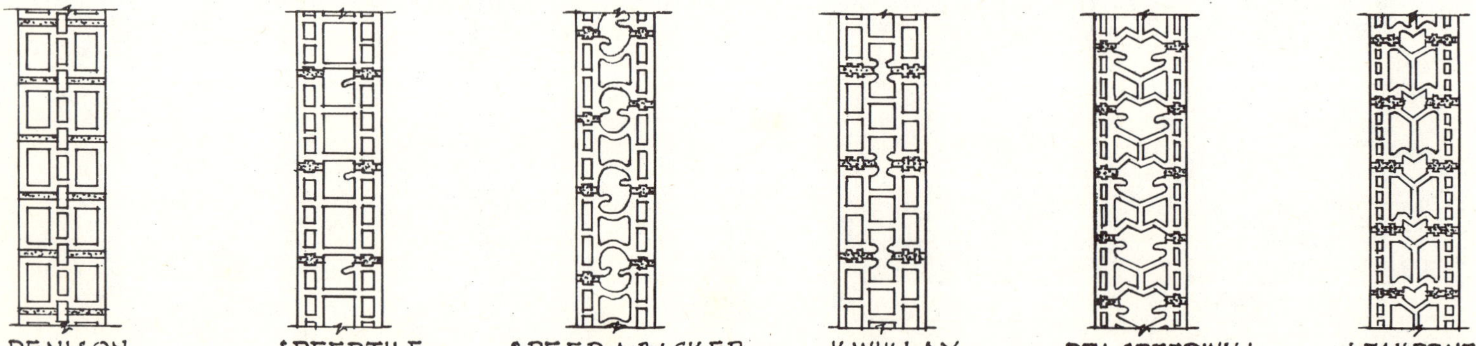

DENISON — SPEEDTILE — SPEED-A-BACKER — KWIKLAY — DRI-SPEEDWALL — LEAK-PRUF

TYPES OF NON-CONTINUOUS JOINT, SINGLE UNIT STRUCTURAL CLAY TILE WALLS

Scale ¾" = 1'-0"

Scoring not indicated on sections. Tile is made by most manufacturers to make combination walls 10", 12", 14", 16" thick. Mortar for both brick and back-up tile to be 1 part Portland Cement, 1 part lime, and 5 to 6 parts clean sharp sand. Mortar beds to be ½" thick; parging recommended back of brick or for face of tile.

Recommendations of the Structural Clay Products Institute - 1955

STRUCTURAL CLAY TILE

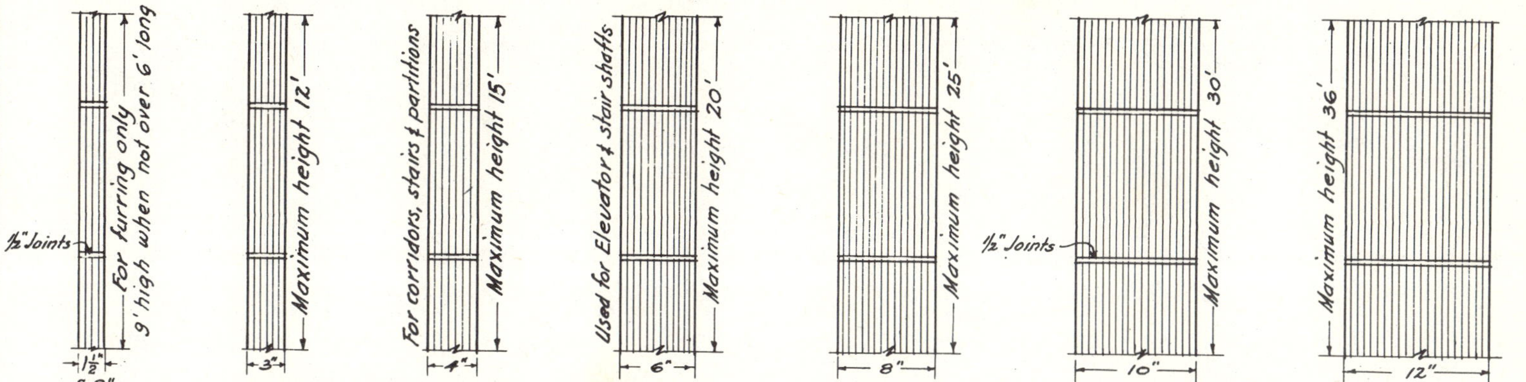
½" Joints
For furring only 9' high when not over 6' long
1½" & 2"
Maximum height 12'
3"
For corridors, stairs & partitions
Maximum height 15'
4"
Used for Elevator & stair shafts
Maximum height 20'
6"
Maximum height 25'
8"
½" Joints
Maximum height 30'
10"
Maximum height 36'
12"

SECTIONS THRO' PARTITIONS; AND HEIGHTS ALLOWABLE.

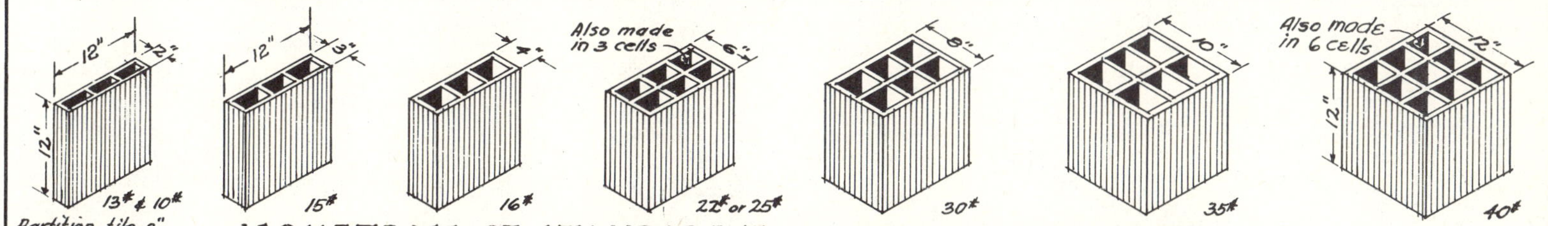
12"
2"
12"
13# & 10#
12"
3"
15#
4"
16#
Also made in 3 cells
6"
22# or 25#
8"
30#
10"
35#
Also made in 6 cells
12"
12"
40#

Partition tile 2" wide and 3" wide; also made as split furring.

ISOMETRICS OF STANDARD TILES USED IN ABOVE PARTITIONS.

STANDARD TILE PARTITIONS

Same size tiles are used for Long Span floors below.

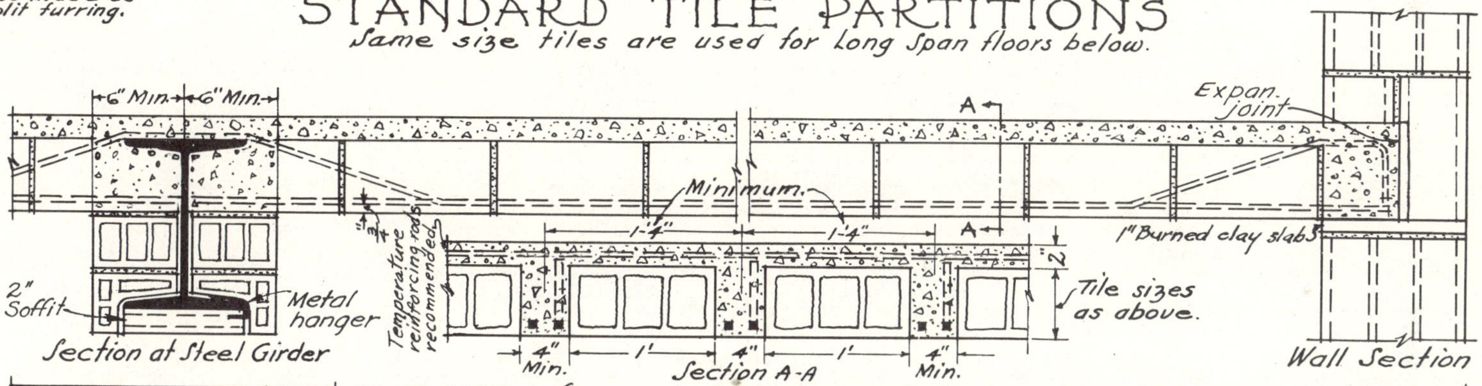
6" Min.
6" Min.
A
Expan. joint
Minimum
¾"
Temperature reinforcing rods recommended
1'-4"
1'-4"
A
1" Burned clay slabs
2
Tile sizes as above.
2" Soffit
Metal hanger
4" Min.
1'
4"
1'
4" Min.

Section at Steel Girder

Section A-A

Wall Section

ONE WAY (Long span) COMBINATION FLOOR

Economical for medium loads - spanning 16' to 28'.

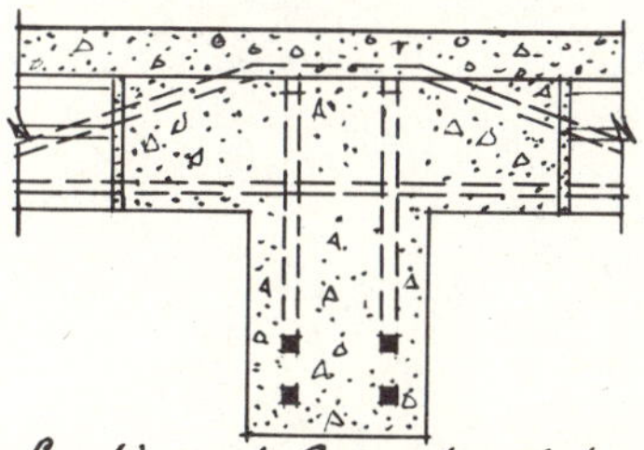

Section at Concrete girder

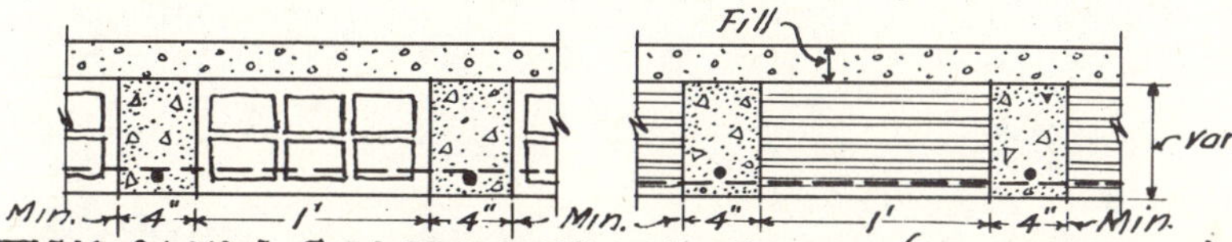
Fill
variable 3" to 12"
Min.
4"
1'
4"
Min.
4"
1'
4"
Min.

TWO WAY COMBINATION FLOOR (SCHUSTER)

Economical where bearing is had on four walls.

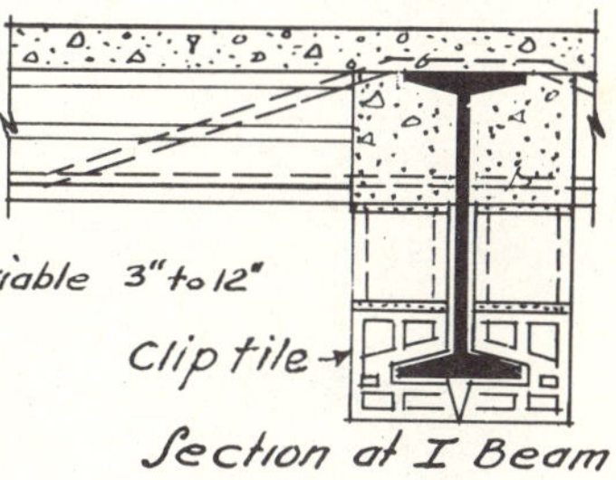
Clip tile

Section at I Beam

THICKNESS OF ONE-WAY SLABS - FOR PRELIMINARY ASSUMPTION ONLY																
Type of Building	Live Load	Span						Type of Building	Live Load	Span						
		8'	12'	16'	20'	24'	28'			8'	12'	16'	20'	24'	28'	
Residence or Apartment	40	6	6	8	10	12	14	Public Assembly	100	8	8	10	12	14	–	
Office Building	60	6	6	8	12	14	–	Heavy Duty Building	120	8	8	10	12	14	–	
School or College	75	6	6	10	10	14	–	Side Walks	250	10	10	12	14	–	–	

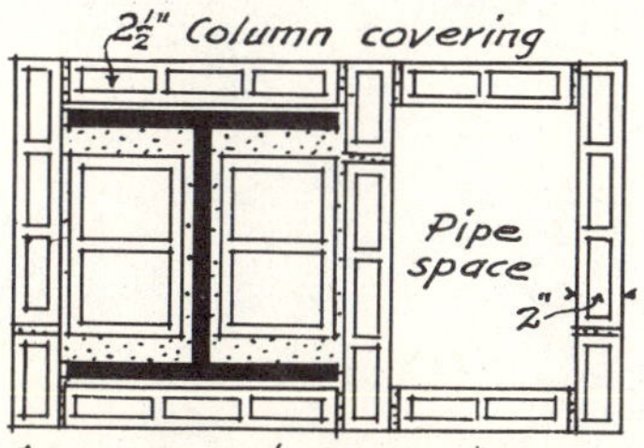
2½" Column covering
Pipe space
2"

COLUMN & PIPE CHASE

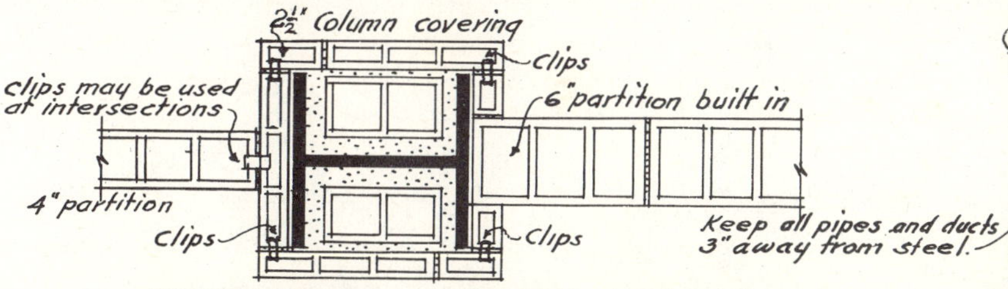
2½" Column covering
Clips
clips may be used at intersections
6" partition built in
4" partition
Clips
Clips

PARTITIONS JOINING COLUMN

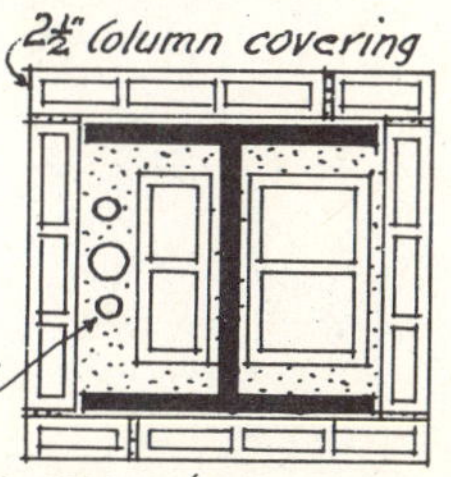
2½" Column covering
Keep all pipes and ducts 3" away from steel.

PIPES at COLUMN

In N.Y. City & East 2½"×8"×12" tile with 1" web is used, elsewhere 3"×12"×12" partition tile is also used; for exterior cols. use 4"×12"×12" tile.

Scale ¾" = 1'-0"

COLUMN FIREPROOFING

Recommendations of the Structural Clay Products Institute, 1956

STRUCTURAL CLAY FACING TILE - GLAZED & UNGLAZED

Shapes are made in Series based on face dimensions of the stretcher unit. The Standard depth or bed of full shapes in all series is generally 3¾" and that of soaps 1¾". A variety of shapes are available in all series. Series are lettered.

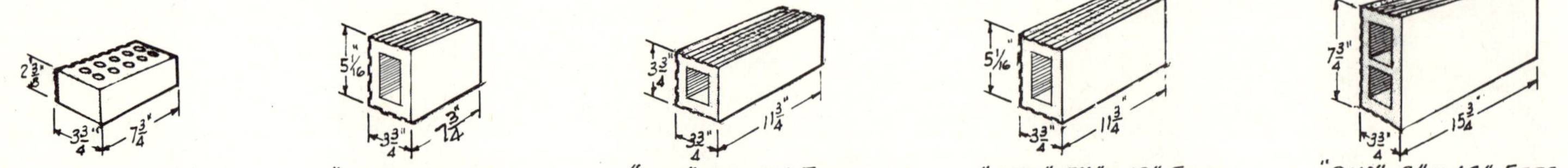

"4S" 2⅔" x 8" Face — "4DC" 5⅓" x 8" Face — "6PC" 4" x 12" Face (Not generally available) — "6TC" 5⅓" x 12" Face — "8W" 8" x 16" Face

STRETCHERS OF STANDARD SERIES

SERIES "4S" (1 BRICK EQUIV.) — SERIES "4D" (2 BRICK EQUIV.) — SERIES "6P" (2¼ BRICK EQUIV.) — SERIES "6T" (3 BRICK EQUIV.) — SERIES "8W" (6 BRICK EQUIV.)

(All sizes shown are modular.)

STANDARD - FINISHES & COLORS

CERAMIC COLOR GLAZE			UNGLAZED	CLEAR GLAZE	SALT GLAZE
FINISH	Satin		FINISH - Smooth	FINISH - Glossy	FINISH - Glossy
SINGLE COLOR FIELD SHADES	MULTI - COLOR FIELD SHADES	SINGLE COLOR TRIM SHADES	COLORS	COLORS	COLORS
White Blue Light Gray Ivory Sunlight Yellow Light Green Coral Tan Ocular Green	Gray mottle White mottle Green mottle Cream mottle	Black	Light Gray Cream Light Buff Golden Buff Gray Manganese Spot Cream Manganese Spot	Clear Glaze	Cream Tone Buff Tone

TYPES OF UNITS

SOLID MASONRY UNITS: { *Multi-cored or uncored unit whose NET cross-sectional area in every plane parallel to the Bearing surface is 75% or more of its GROSS cross-sectional area measured in the same plane.*

HOLLOW MASONRY UNITS: *A unit whose NET cross-sectional area in any plane parallel to the bearing surface is less than 75% of its gross cross-sectional area measured in the same plane.*

Type & direction of scoring and coring are optional with each manufacturer. When intended for exterior use, the absorbtion of the body should be limited in accord with Facing Tile Institute Standard Specifications.

GRADING RULES

	CERAMIC GLAZED STRUCTURAL FACING TILE	CLEAR GLAZED STRUCTURAL FACING TILE	SALT GLAZED STRUCTURAL FACING TILE	SMOOTH UNGLAZED STRUCTURAL FACING TILE
First Quality	Select Quality	Select Quality	Select Quality	Select Quality
Second Quality	"B" Quality	Standard Quality	Standard Quality	

SERIES "6T", 5⅓" x 12" *(Three brick equivalent)* SIMILAR SHAPES IN OTHER SIZES

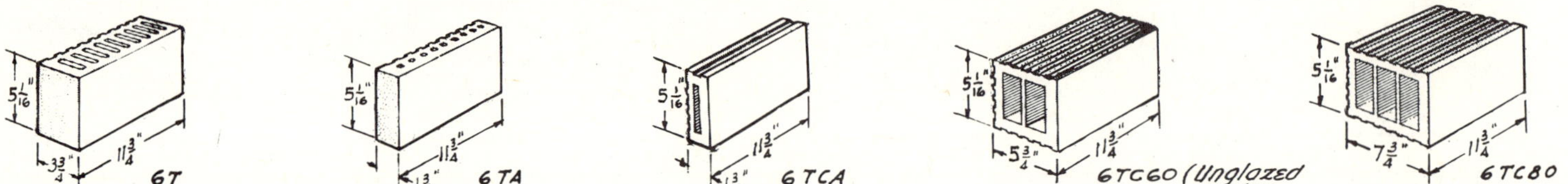

6T — Stretcher - scored or unscored backs
6TA — Soap Stretcher
6TCA — Soap Stretcher
6TC60 (Unglazed only) — 6" Stretcher
6TC80 — 8" Stretcher

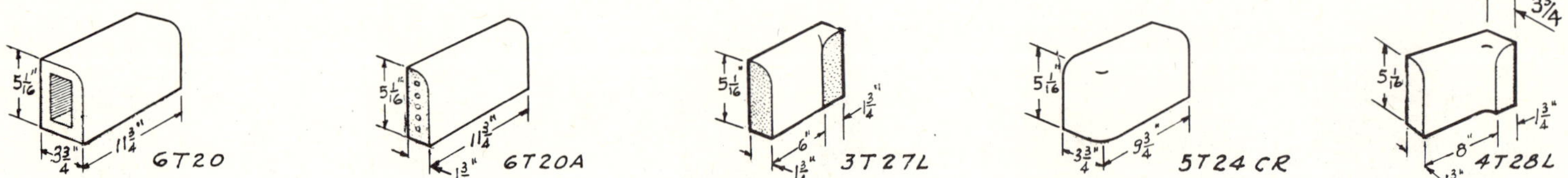

6T20 — Bullnose sill or cap 4" reveal, also square
6T20A — Soap Bullnose sill or cap, 2" reveal also square
3T27L — Bullnose sill or cap, internal square corner
5T24 CR — Bullnose sill or cap, Bullnose corner, also soap, square corner
4T28L — Bullnose sill or cap, coved internal corner

(All shapes available in opposite hand)

Data from Handbook of Facing Tile Institute - Washington, D.C.

Continued on next page

STRUCTURAL CLAY FACING TILE - GLAZED & UNGLAZED

Continued from preceding page

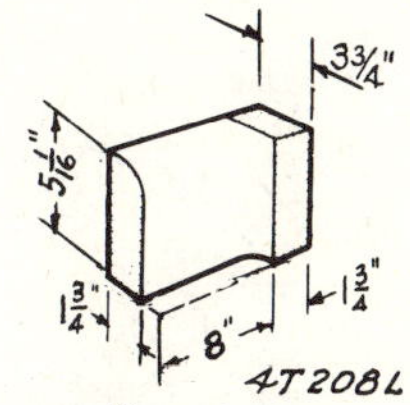

4T208L
Bullnose coved internal corner, Sill or Cap.

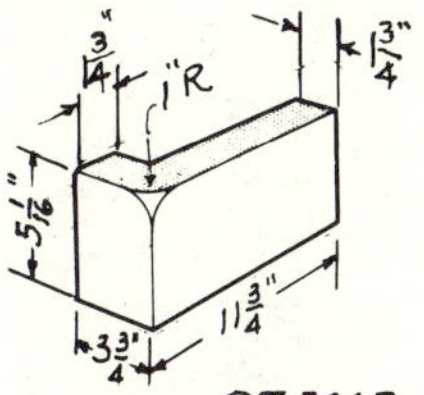

6T304R
Starter for bullnose sill or jamb. Also use with slope sills.

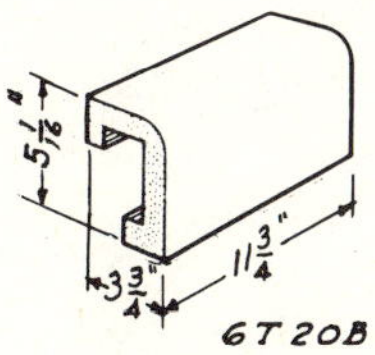

6T20B
Bullnose sill or cap, 4" reveal.

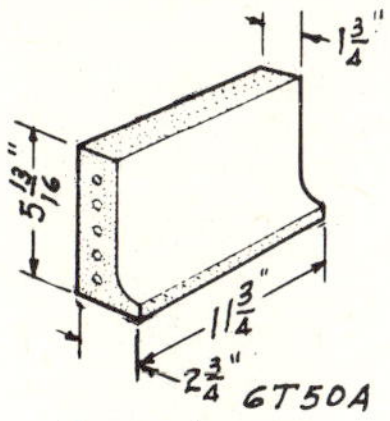

6T50A
Cove base stretcher.

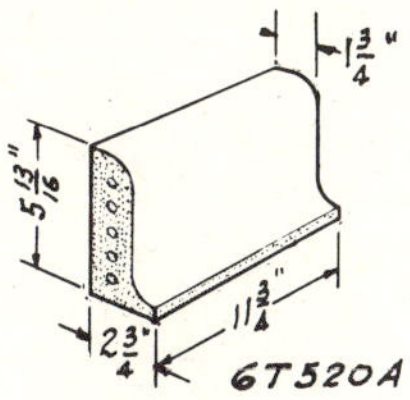

6T520A
Round top cove base stretcher.

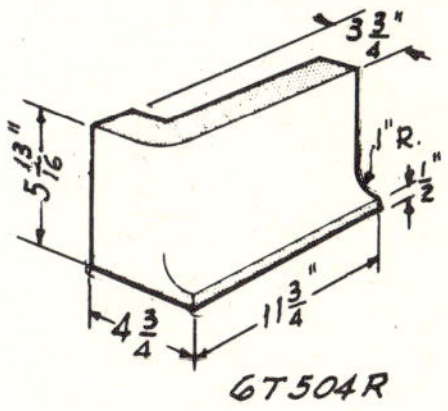

6T504R
Cove base, bullnose jamb or starter 4" return.

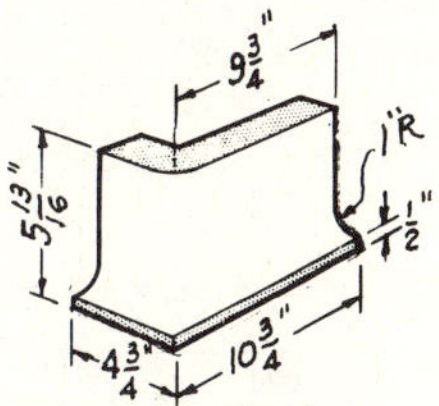

5T54R
Cove base bullnose corner, 4" return.

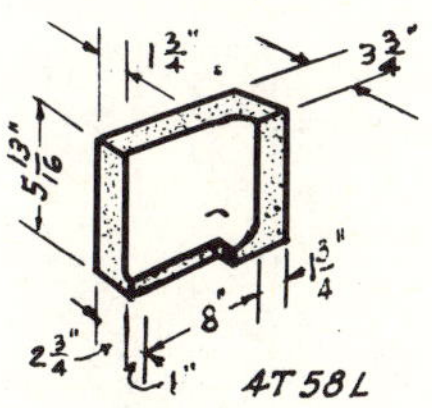

4T58L
Cove base, coved internal corner.

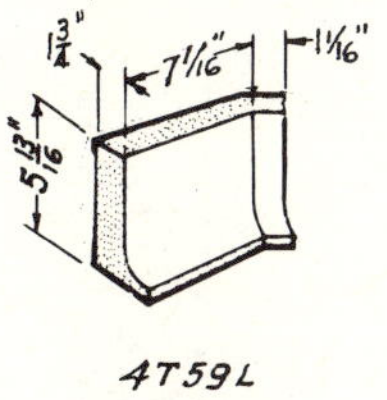

4T59L
Cove base octagonal internal corner.

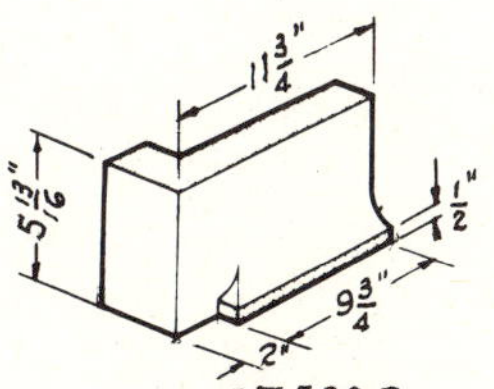

6T502R
Cove base starter, also square jamb.

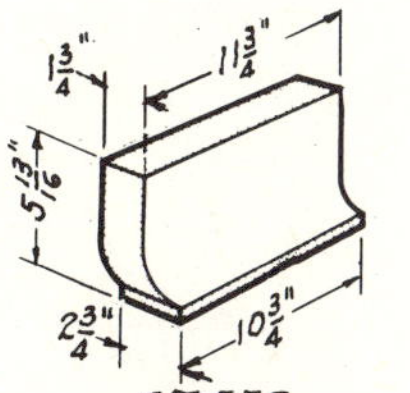

6T57R
Coped cove base internal (square corner).

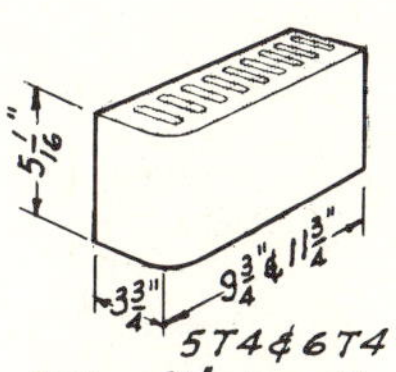

5T4 & 6T4
5T4 = 9 3/4" length
6T4 = 11 3/4" length
Bullnose corner, also jamb or starter.

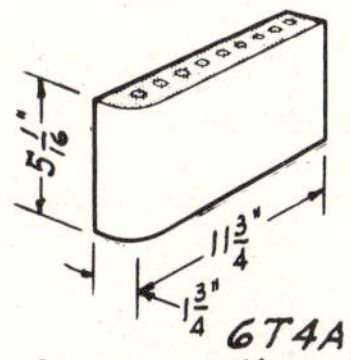

6T4A
Soap, bullnose jamb or starter 2" return.

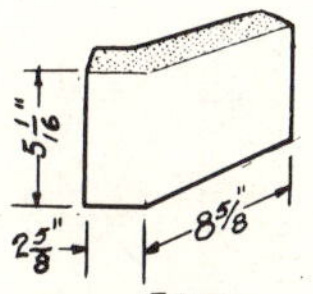

5T6
Octagonal External Corner.

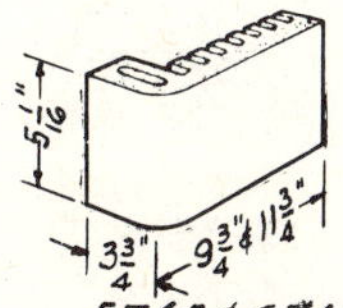

5T4B & 6T4B
5T4B = 9 3/4" length
6T4B = 11 3/4" length
Bullnose corner, also jamb or starter.

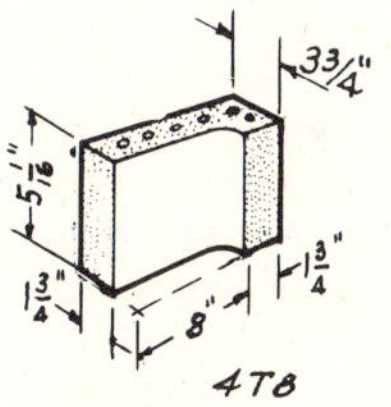

4T8
Coved internal corner.

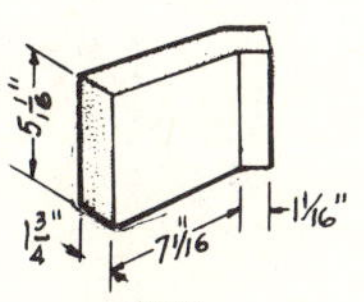

4T9
Octagonal internal corner.

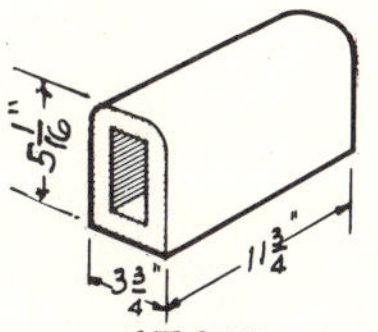

6T20D
Bullnose coping, sill, cap or lintel. 4" wall.

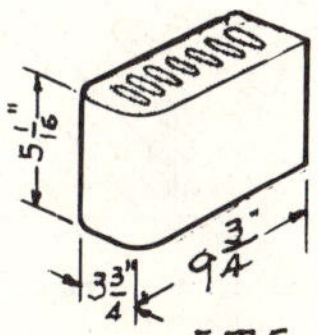

5T5
Bullnose full end, 4" wall.

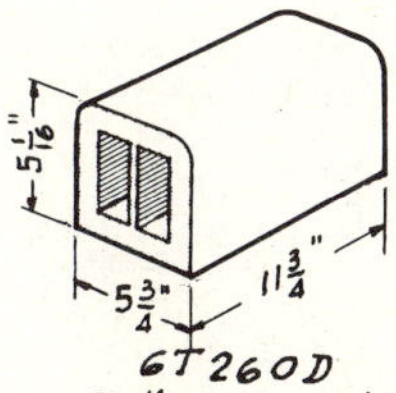

6T260D
Bullnose coping, sill, cap or lintel. 6" wall.

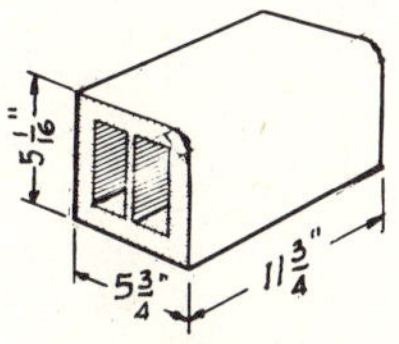

6T260
Bullnose cap or sill.

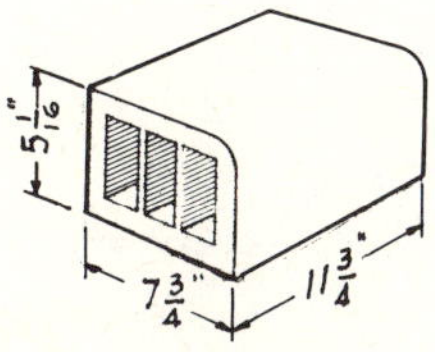

6T280
Bullnose coping, sill, cap or lintel. 8" reveal.

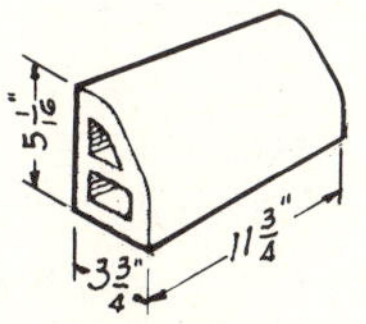

6T70
Slope sill, 4" reveal.

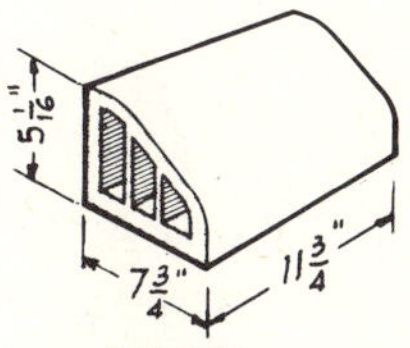

6T780
Slope sill, 8" reveal.

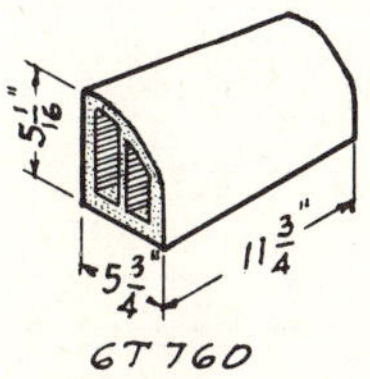

6T760
Slope sill, 6" reveal.

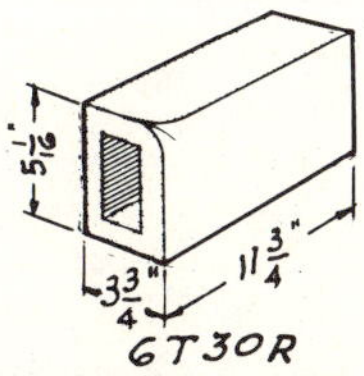

6T30R
Bullnose miter.

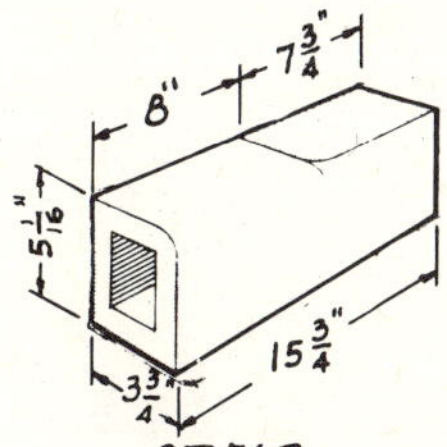

8T31R
Bullnose sill miter.

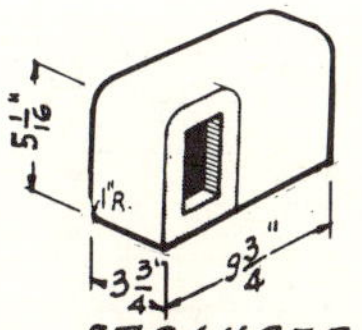

5T24X27R
Bullnose coping, sill, cap or lintel.

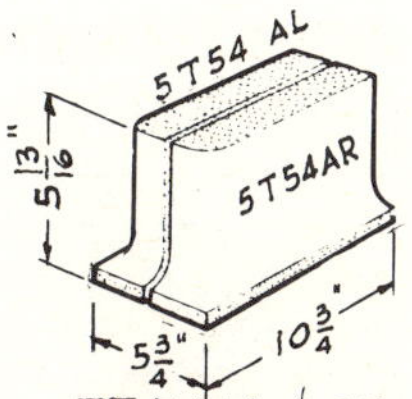
5T54 AL
5T54AR

5T54 AL & AR
Cove base bullnose end 4" wall.

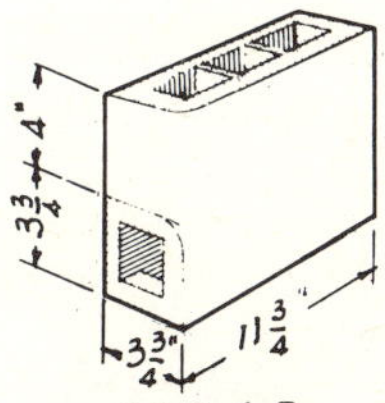

6T34R
Bullnose jamb miter used with sills and lintels.

(All sizes shown are modular)
(All shapes available in opposite hand)

SERIES "6T" - 5 1/3 x 12" (Three brick Equivalent) SIMILAR SHAPES IN OTHER SIZES

Data from Handbook of Facing Tile Institute - Washington, D.C.

STRUCTURAL CLAY FACING TILE-GLAZED & UNGLAZED

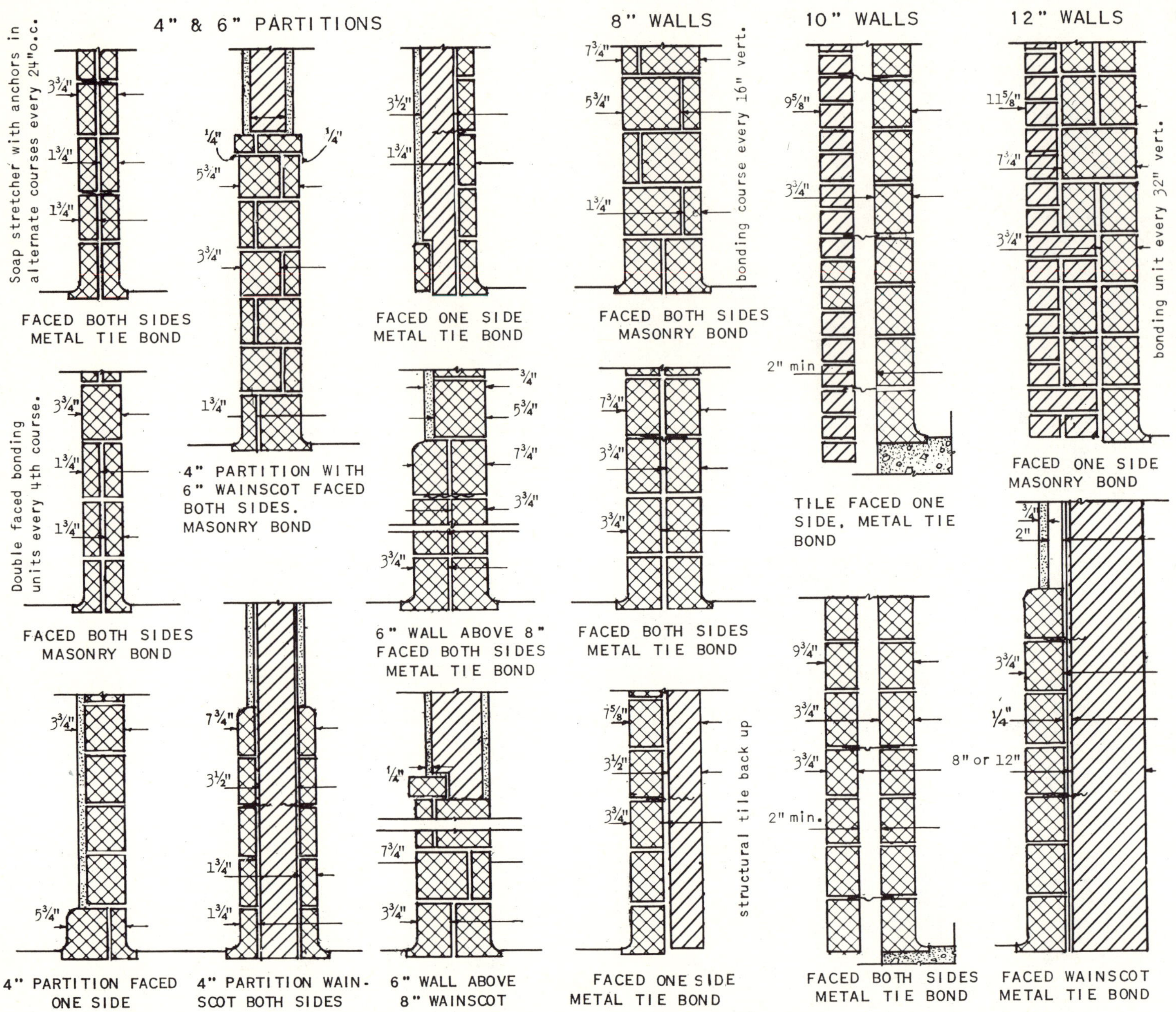
4" & 6" PARTITIONS
8" WALLS
10" WALLS
12" WALLS
Soap stretcher with anchors in alternate courses every 24" o.c.
FACED BOTH SIDES METAL TIE BOND
4" PARTITION WITH 6" WAINSCOT FACED BOTH SIDES. MASONRY BOND
FACED ONE SIDE METAL TIE BOND
FACED BOTH SIDES MASONRY BOND
bonding course every 16" vert.
TILE FACED ONE SIDE, METAL TIE BOND
FACED ONE SIDE MASONRY BOND
bonding unit every 32" vert.
Double faced bonding units every 4th course.
FACED BOTH SIDES MASONRY BOND
6" WALL ABOVE 8" FACED BOTH SIDES METAL TIE BOND
FACED BOTH SIDES METAL TIE BOND
2" min
4" PARTITION FACED ONE SIDE
4" PARTITION WAINSCOT BOTH SIDES
6" WALL ABOVE 8" WAINSCOT
FACED ONE SIDE METAL TIE BOND
structural tile back up
2" min.
FACED BOTH SIDES METAL TIE BOND
8" or 12"
FACED WAINSCOT METAL TIE BOND

Where metal anchors are indicated space them not more than 16" vertically & 24" horizontally.

TYPICAL WALL SECTIONS - UNITS 5 1/3" HIGH

COURSES	HEIGHT	COURSES	HEIGHT	COURSES	HEIGHT
1	5⅓"	14	6'- 2⅔"	27	12'- 0"
2	10⅔"	15	6'- 8"	28	12'- 5⅓"
3	1'- 4"	16	7'- 1⅓"	29	12'-10⅔"
4	1'- 9⅓"	17	7'- 6⅔"	30	13'- 4"
5	2'- 2⅔"	18	8'- 0"	31	13'- 9⅓"
6	2'- 8"	19	8'- 5⅓"	32	14'- 2⅔"
7	3'- 1⅓"	20	8'-10⅔"	33	14'- 8"
8	3'- 6⅔"	21	9'- 4"	34	15'- 1⅓"
9	4'- 0"	22	9'- 9⅓"	35	15'- 6⅔"
10	4'- 5⅓"	23	10'- 2⅔"	36	16'- 0"
11	4'-10⅔"	24	10'- 8"	37	16'- 5⅓"
12	5'- 4"	25	11'- 1⅓"	38	16'-10⅔"
13	5'- 9⅓"	26	11'- 6⅔"	39	17'- 4"

WALLS, PARTITION & FURRING OF 5 1/3" UNITS

DATA FROM HANDBOOK OF THE FACING TILE INSTITUTE-WASHINGTON, D.C.

GYPSUM PARTITIONS

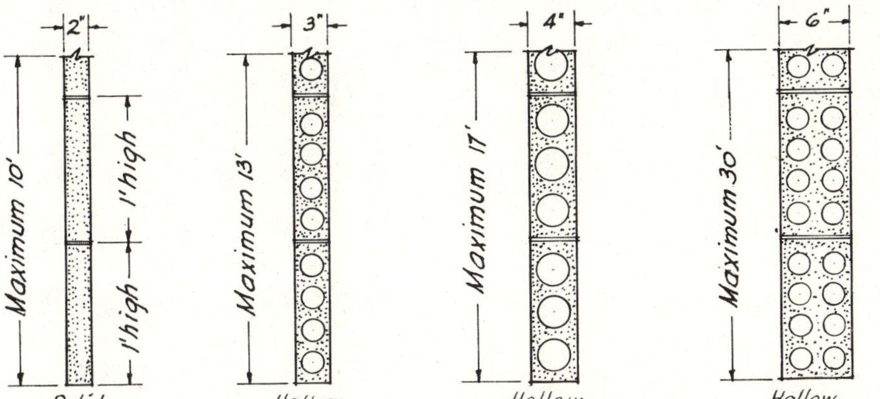

2"
3"
4"
6"
Maximum 10'
Maximum 13'
Maximum 17'
Maximum 30'
1' high
1' high

Solid
11.5 # per ☐
20.5 # per ☐

Hollow
12 # per ☐
21 # per ☐

Hollow
15.5 # per ☐
24.5 # per ☐

Hollow
22 # per ☐
31 # per ☐

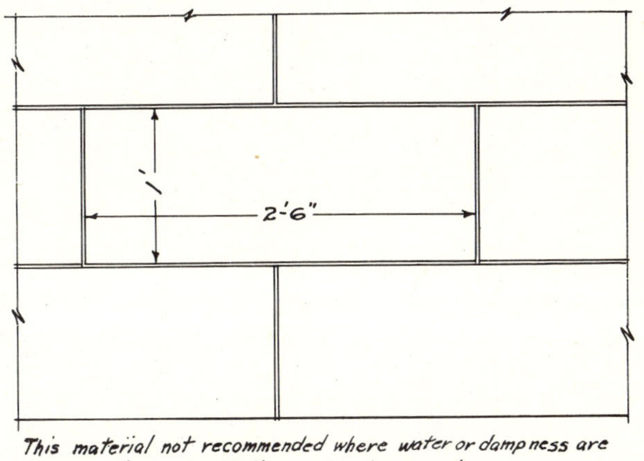

1'
2'-6"

Top row of weights are without plaster, bottom row with two sides plastered; Weight of plaster may be reduced by using Light Weight aggregate in place of sand aggregate.

This material not recommended where water or dampness are likely to exist such as baths, pools, showers, etc. Partitions are set on base courses of hollow clay tile or concrete block in basements or where cement, terrazzo or tile floors occur.

The limits of heights are the Underwriters Laboratories Recommendation.

SECTIONS THRO' PARTITIONS. ELEVATION.

GYPSUM PARTITION TILE

3/4" = 1'

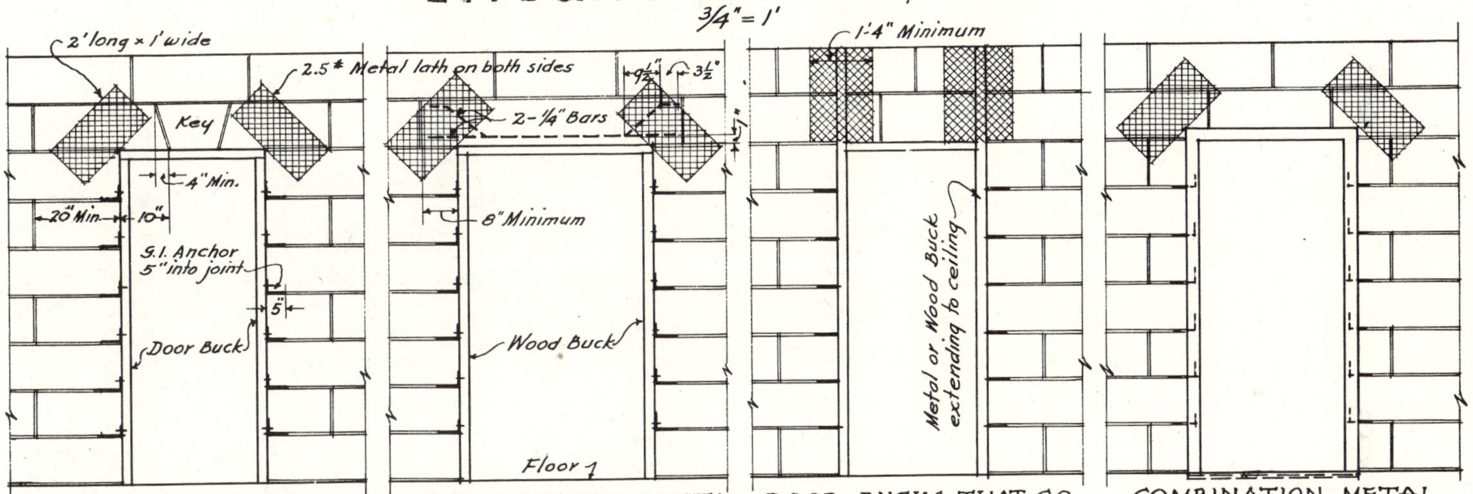

2' long × 1' wide
2.5 # Metal lath on both sides
Key
4" Min.
20" Min.
10"
G.I. Anchor
5" into joint
5"
Door Buck
2-1/4" Bars
4 1/2"
3 1/2"
7"
8" Minimum
Wood Buck
Floor
1'-4" Minimum
Metal or Wood Buck extending to ceiling

JACK ARCH LINTELS 1'-10" TO 4' WIDE.

REINFORCED GYPSUM LINTEL FOR OPENINGS 4' TO 7'.

DOOR BUCKS THAT GO TO THE CEILING.

COMBINATION METAL BUCK AND TRIM.

Lintels up to 1'-10" can be spanned with Tile with 4" Minimum bearing.

LINTELS AND BUCKS FOR PARTITIONS.

1/4" = 1'

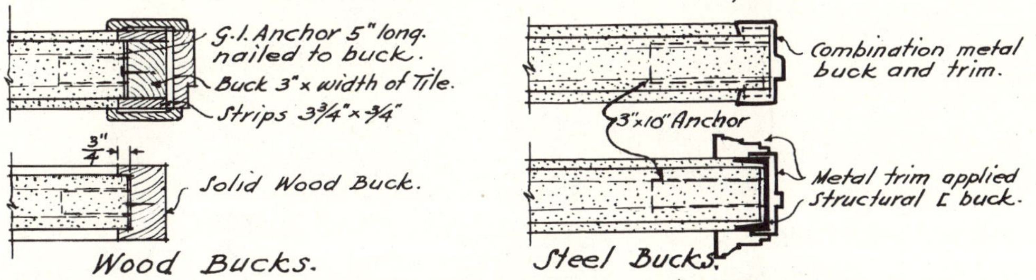

G.I. Anchor 5" long nailed to buck.
Buck 3" × width of Tile.
Strips 3 3/4" × 3/4"
3/4"
Solid Wood Buck.
Wood Bucks.
Combination metal buck and trim.
3" × 10" Anchor
Metal trim applied
Structural [buck.
Steel Bucks.

TYPES OF BUCKS Scale 3/4" = 1'-0"

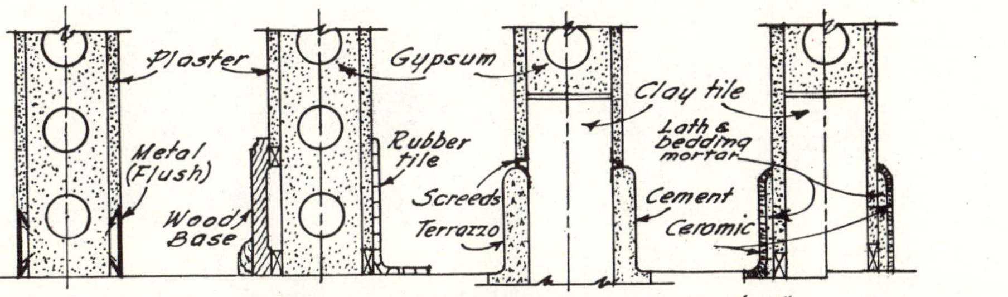

Plaster
Gypsum
Metal (Flush)
Wood Base
Rubber tile
Screeds
Terrazzo
Clay tile
Lath & bedding mortar
Cement
Ceramic

TYPES OF BASES 1 1/2" = 1'-0"

Where excessive moisture is expected, 12" struct. clay tile block 1st course.

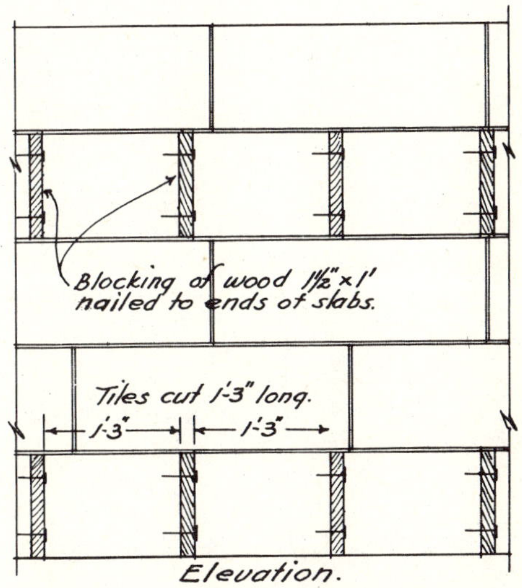

Blocking of wood 1 1/2" × 1' nailed to ends of slabs.
Tiles cut 1'-3" long.
1'-3"
1'-3"
Elevation.

METHOD OF PROVIDING NAILING FOR HEAVY FIXTURES. Such as Blackboards etc.

1/2" = 1'

STONE WORK

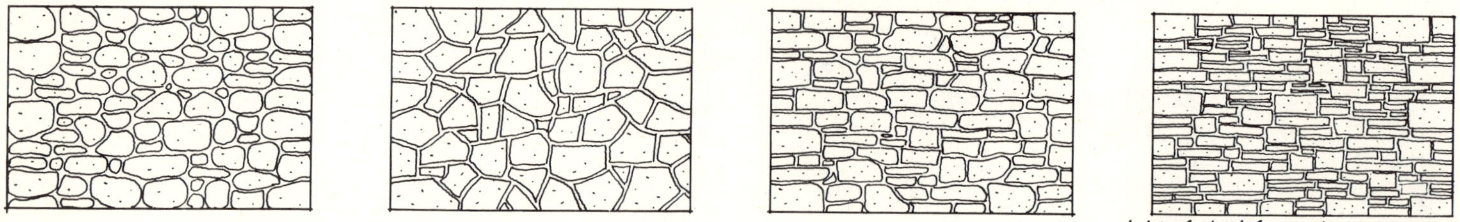

UNCOURSED FIELDSTONE ROUGH OR ORDINARY. — POLYGONAL, MOSAIC OR RANDOM. — COURSED

TYPES OF RUBBLE MASONRY

Laid of stratified stone fitted on job. It is between rubble & ashlar. Finish is quarry face, seam face or split. Called rubble ashlar in granite.

SQUARED-STONE MASONRY.

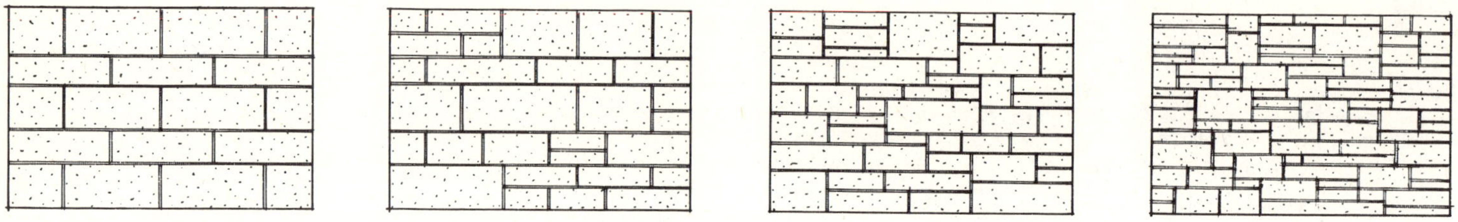

RANGE. *Coursed* — BROKEN RANGE. — RANDOM *Interrupted coursed* — RANGE. *Coursed (Long stones)*

TYPES OF ASHLAR MASONRY

This is stone that is sawed, dressed, squared or Quarry faced.

ELEVATIONS SHOWING FACE JOINTING FOR STONE.

Draft line
Chat Sawed
similar
Tooled margin

- For both hard and soft stones. **Rock or Pitch Face.**
- Smooth, but saw mark visible. All stones. **Sawed Finish (Gang).**
- More marked than sawed. Soft stones. **Shot Sawed (Rough).**
- Smooth finish with some texture. Soft stones. **Machine Finish (Planer).**
- May be coarse, medium or fine. Usually on hard stones. **Pointed Finish.**
- After pointing on hard stones. **Pean Hammered.**

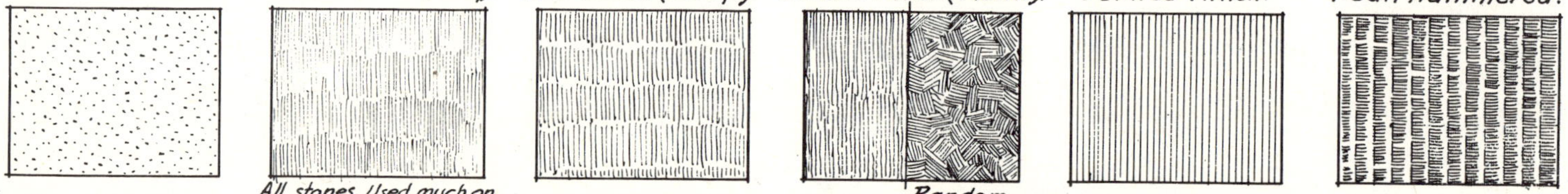

- For soft stones **Bush-hammered.**
- All stones. Used much on granite. 4 to 8 cut in 7/8". **Patent Bush-hammered**
- For soft stones. **Drove or Boasted.**
- Random For soft stones. **Hand Tooled.**
- Tool marks may be 2 to 10 per inch. **Machine Tooled.**
- For soft stones. **Tooth-chisel.**

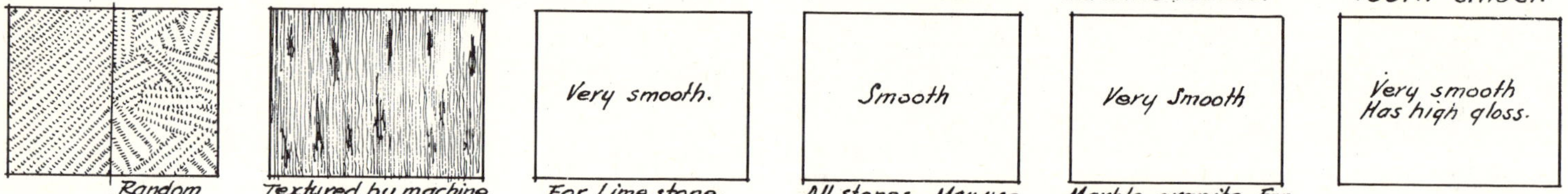
Very smooth.
Smooth
Very Smooth
Very smooth
Has high gloss.

- Random For soft stones. **Crandalled.**
- Textured by machine For Limestone **Plucker Finish.**
- For Limestone. Done by machine **Carborundum Finish.**
- All stones. May use sand or carborundum. **Rubbed (Wet).**
- Marble, granite. For interior work. Soft stones. **Honed (rubbed first).**
- Marble and Granite. **Polished (honed first).**

STONE FINISHES.

Seam face and split face (or Quarry face) not shown as they are not worked finishes.

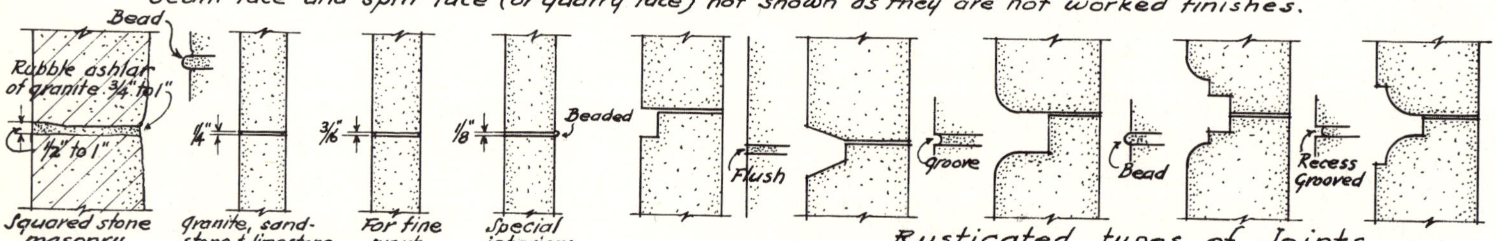
Bead
Rubble ashlar of granite 3/4" to 1"
1/2" to 1"
1/4"
3/16"
1/8"
Beaded
Flush
Groove
Bead
Recess Grooved

Squared stone masonry — Granite, sand-stone & limestone ashlar. General use. — For fine work. Limestone — Special interiors — Rusticated types of Joints.

STONE JOINTS

TYPES, FINISH AND JOINTING OF STONE MASONRY.

A perch is nominally 16'-6" long, 1'-0" high & 1'-6" thick = 24¾ cu.ft. In some localities 16½ & 22 cu.ft. are used.

STONE WORK and BACKING

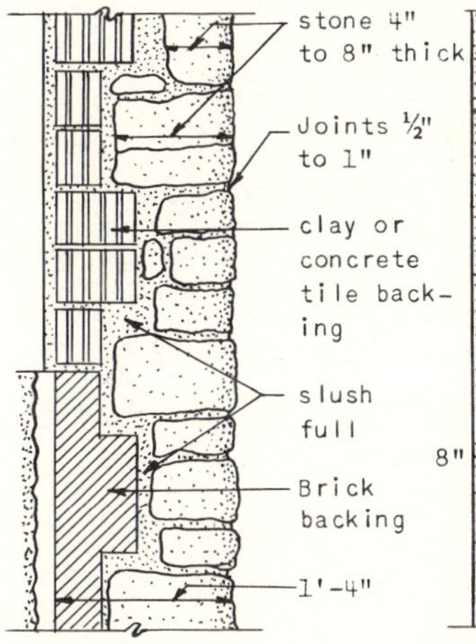
stone 4" to 8" thick
Joints ½" to 1"
clay or concrete tile backing
slush full
Brick backing
1'-4"

BONDED TO CLAY TILE, BRICK OR CONCRETE BLOCK

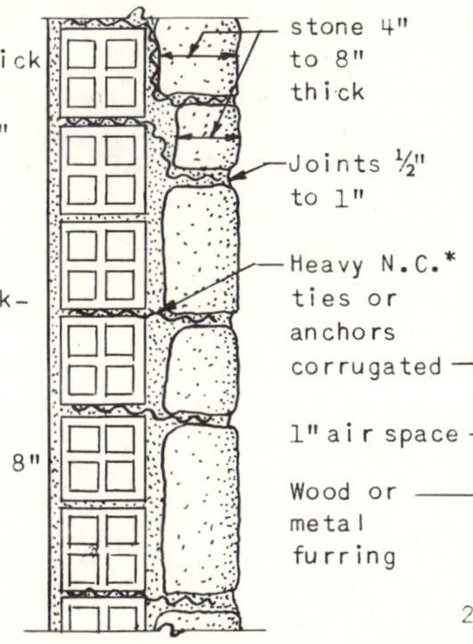
stone 4" to 8" thick
Joints ½" to 1"
Heavy N.C.* ties or anchors corrugated
1" air space
Wood or metal furring
8"

CLAY OR CONCRETE BLOCK WITH TIES

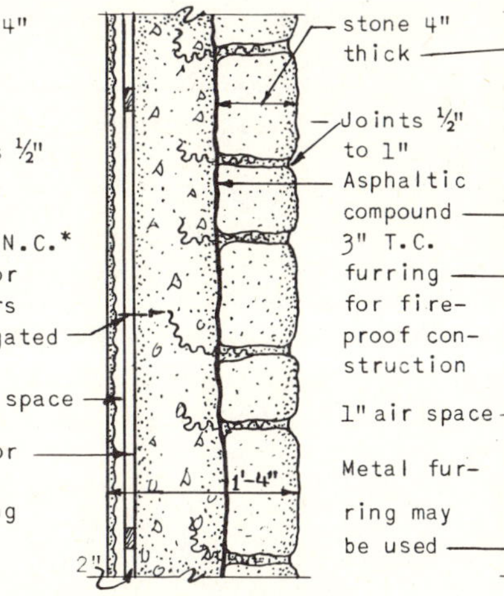
stone 4" thick
Joints ½" to 1"
Asphaltic compound
3" T.C. furring for fire-proof construction
1" air space
Metal furring may be used
1'-4"
2"

CONCRETE BACKING
Conc. in contact with stone will stain stone. Allow air space between or, as shown, face conc. with asphalt compound

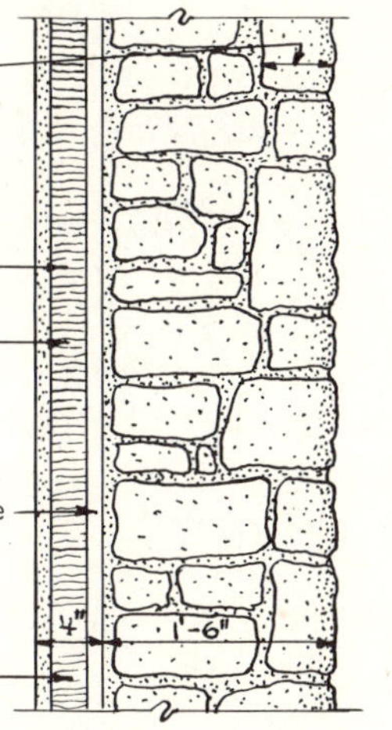
4"
1'-6"

BACKED WITH OTHER STONE

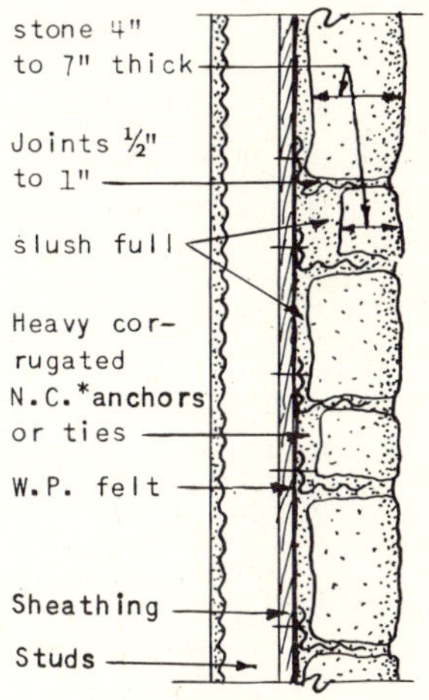
stone 4" to 7" thick
Joints ½" to 1"
slush full
Heavy corrugated N.C.*anchors or ties
W.P. felt
Sheathing
Studs

STONE VENEER ON WOOD FRAME

Ties or anchors approximately 16" o.c. both ways.

TYPICAL METHODS OF BACKING SQUARED-STONE OR GRANITE FACING

(Not recommended for buildings over two stories high)

DRESSING & FINISH FOR THIS TYPE OF STONE: Rough squared as to length & rise – Bed & joints split or pitched approximately square to face. Faces pitched out of wind. Finish: 1. Rock Face 2. Seam Face 3. Split or Quarry Face. – Joints ½" to 1" of 1 part cement (non-staining), 1 part lime & 1 part sand.

***N.C. = Non-corrosive**

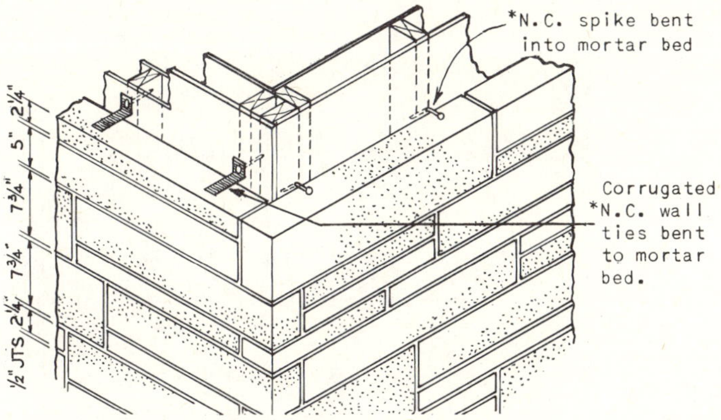
*N.C. spike bent into mortar bed
Corrugated *N.C. wall ties bent to mortar bed.
2¼"
5"
7¾"
7¾"
2¼"
½" JTS

FRAME BACKING

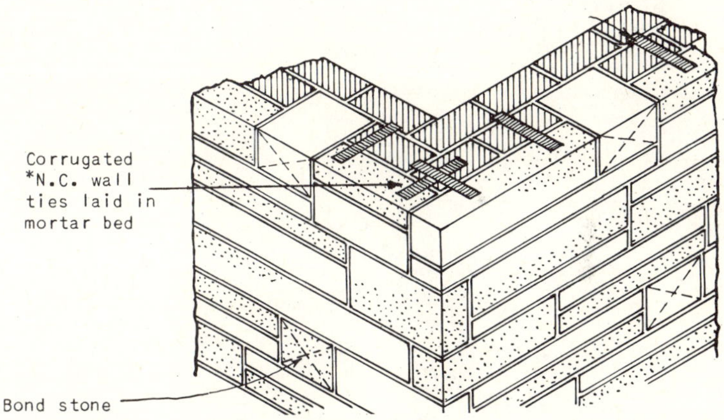
Corrugated *N.C. wall ties laid in mortar bed
Bond stone

BRICK BACKING

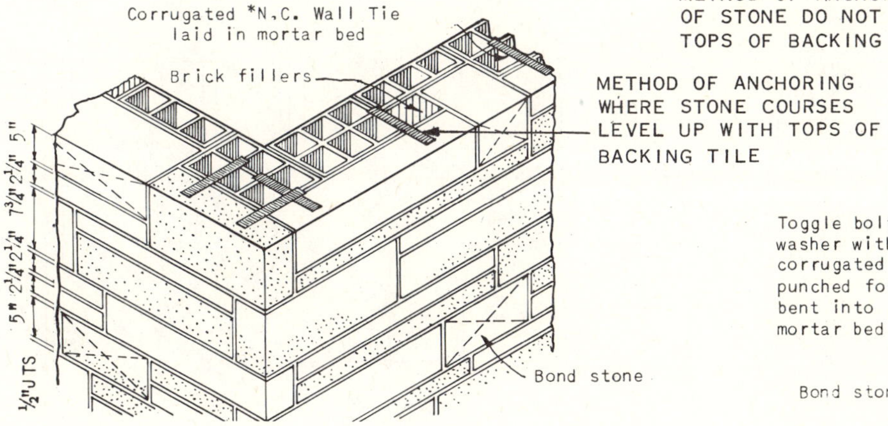
Corrugated *N.C. Wall Tie laid in mortar bed
Brick fillers
METHOD OF ANCHORING WHERE STONE COURSES LEVEL UP WITH TOPS OF BACKING TILE
5"
2¼"
7¾"
2¼"
2¼"
5"
½"JTS
Bond stone

HOLLOW TILE BACKING

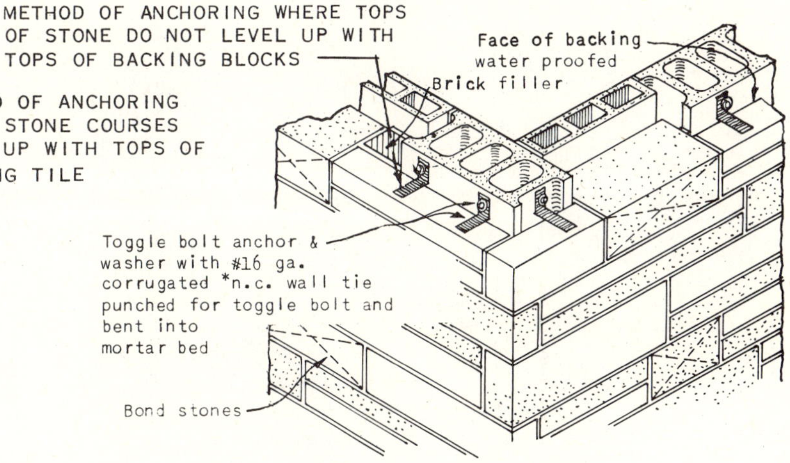
METHOD OF ANCHORING WHERE TOPS OF STONE DO NOT LEVEL UP WITH TOPS OF BACKING BLOCKS
Face of backing water proofed
Brick filler
Toggle bolt anchor & washer with #16 ga. corrugated *n.c. wall tie punched for toggle bolt and bent into mortar bed
Bond stones

CONCRETE BLOCK BACKING

*non-corrosive

BACKING FOR CUT STONE

DATA BY INDIANA LIMESTONE INSTITUTE

CUT STONE

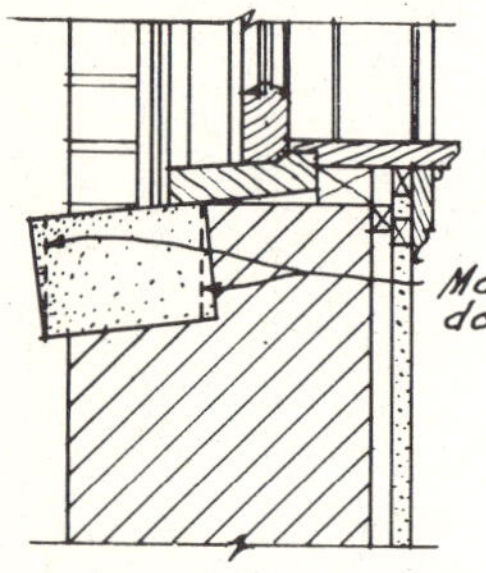
May be cut on dotted line

ECONOMICAL SILL
Made of a strip fitted to form wash

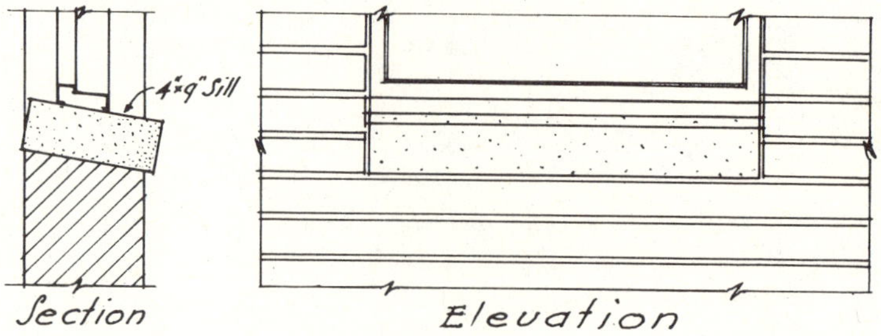
4"x9" Sill
Section
Elevation

SLIP SILL
Used for Factory and other economical construction

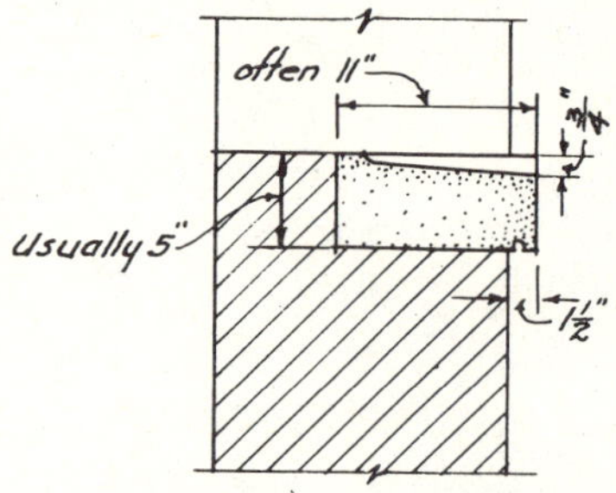
often 11"
3/4
Usually 5"
1 1/2"

LUG SILL WITH DRIP

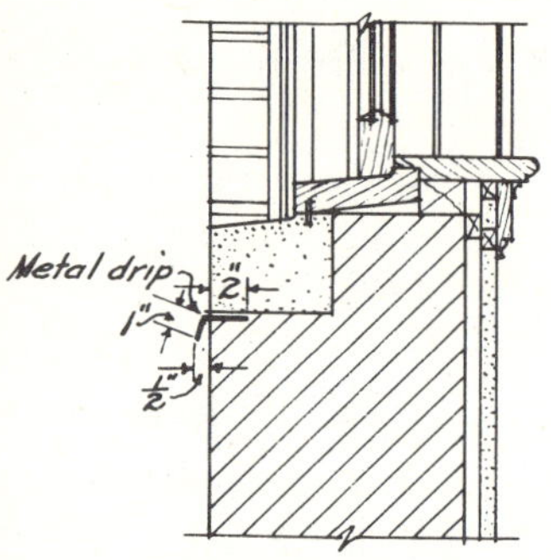
Metal drip
2"
1"
1/2"

METAL DRIP ON FLUSH SILL.

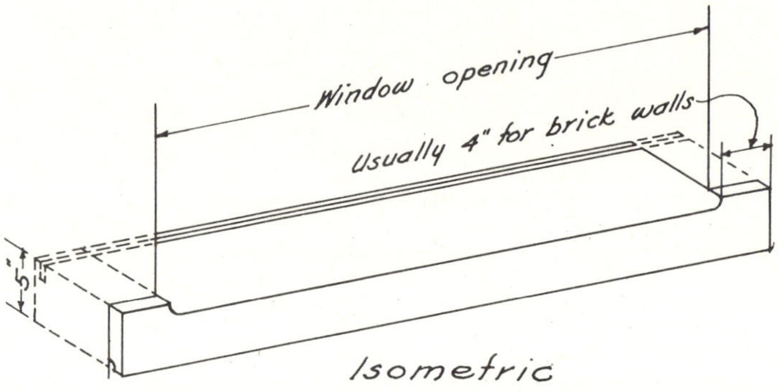
Window opening
Usually 4" for brick walls
5"
Isometric

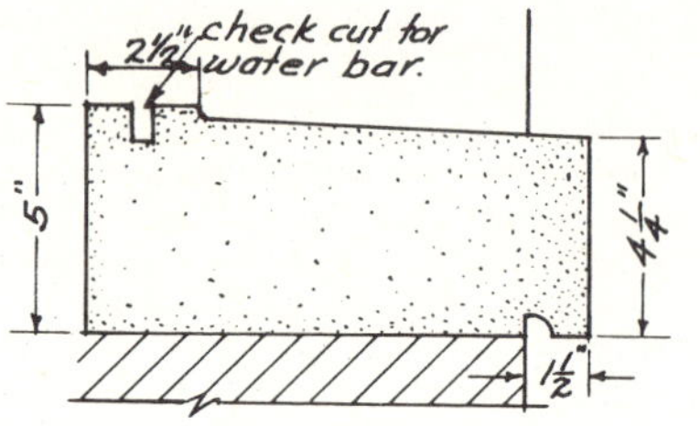
2 1/2" check cut for water bar.
5"
4 1/4"
1 1/2"

Section
Showing check for water bar.

Lug sill may be a true lug sill with throated wash like this or a plain bevelled sill 4" to 8" longer than opening.

LUG SILL
Recommended by "Stone Setting."

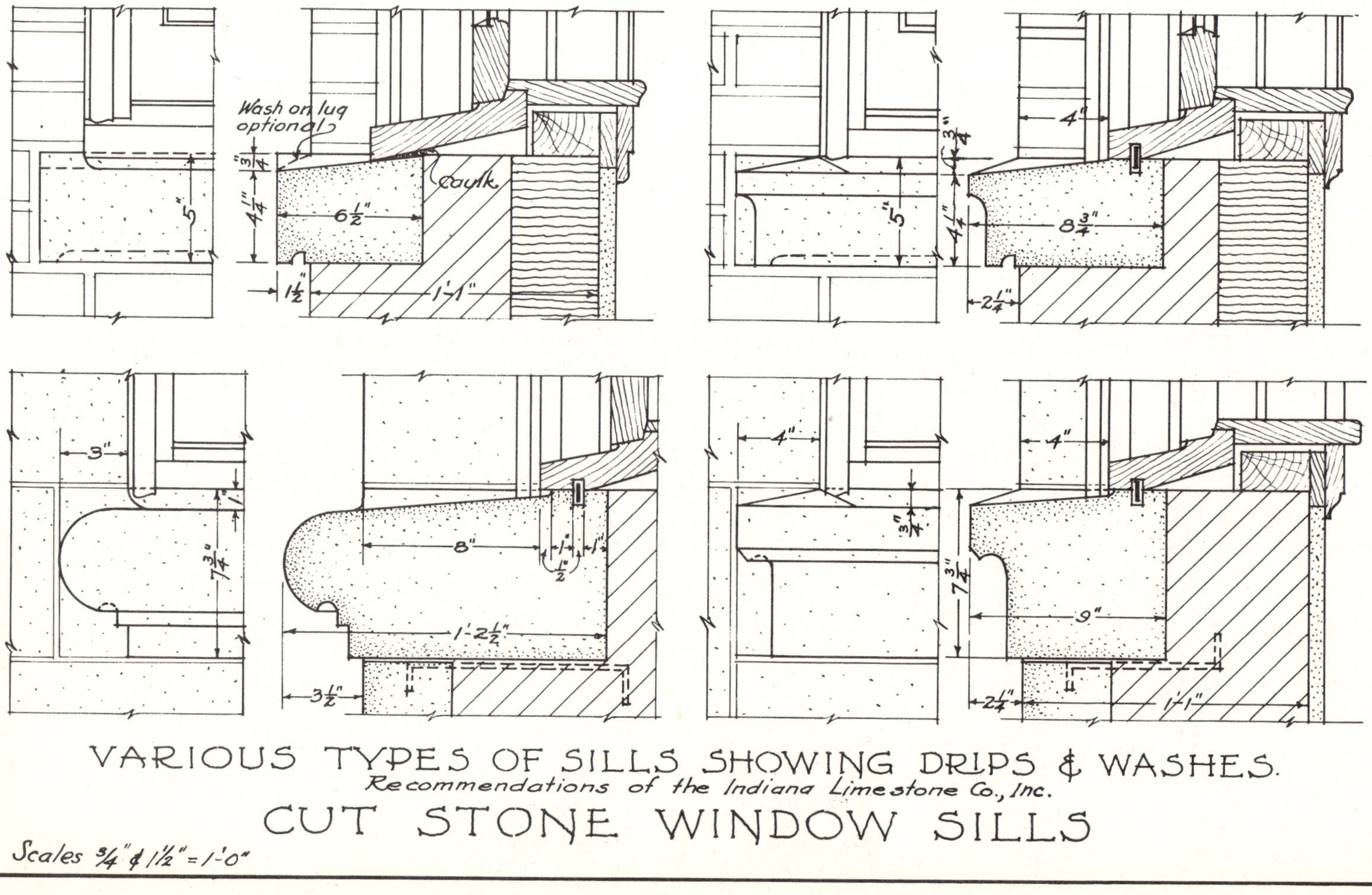
Wash on lug optional
3/4
4 1/4"
6 1/2"
Caulk
5"
1 1/2"
1'-1"
4"
3/4"
4 1/4"
8 3/4"
5"
2 1/4"
3"
1"
7 3/4"
8"
1"
1/2"
1'-2 1/2"
3 1/2"
4"
3/4"
4"
7 3/4"
9"
2 1/4"
1'-1"

VARIOUS TYPES OF SILLS SHOWING DRIPS & WASHES.
Recommendations of the Indiana Limestone Co., Inc.

CUT STONE WINDOW SILLS

Scales 3/4" & 1 1/2" = 1'-0"

CUT STONE

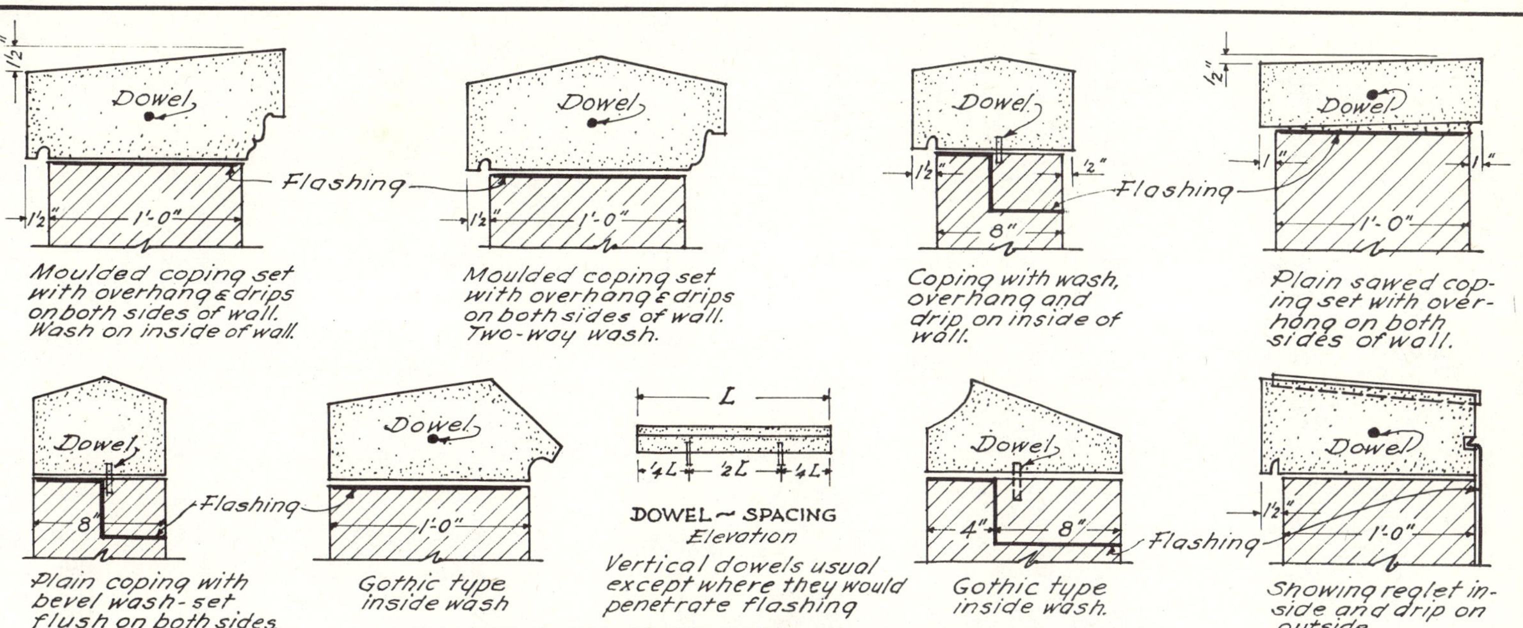
Dowel
Flashing
1½"
1'-0"
½"
8"
1"
L
¼L
½L
DOWEL ~ SPACING
Elevation
4"

Moulded coping set with overhang & drips on both sides of wall. Wash on inside of wall.

Moulded coping set with overhang & drips on both sides of wall. Two-way wash.

Coping with wash, overhang and drip on inside of wall.

Plain sawed coping set with overhang on both sides of wall.

Plain coping with bevel wash-set flush on both sides.

Gothic type inside wash

Vertical dowels usual except where they would penetrate flashing

Gothic type inside wash.

Showing reglet inside and drip on outside.

TYPES OF CUT STONE COPINGS

Scale 1" = 1'-0"

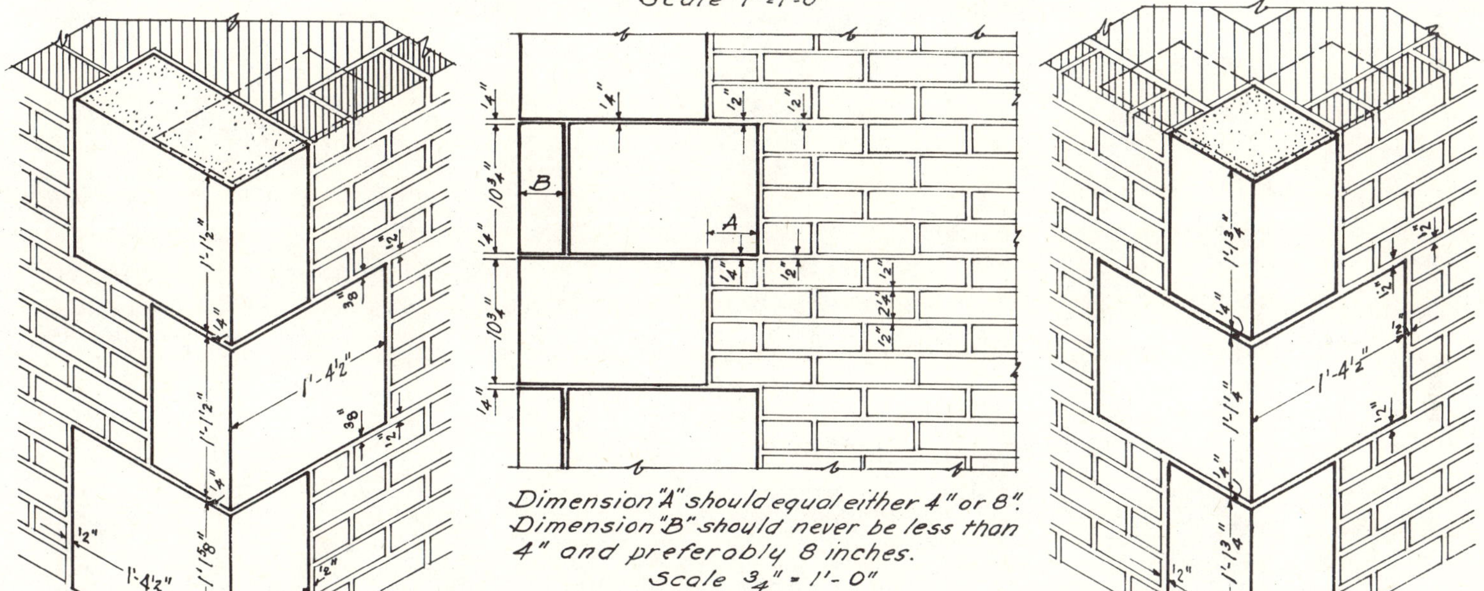
1'-1½"
1'-4½"
1'-1⅝"
⅜"
¼"
½"
8"
B
A
10¾"
2¼"
1'-1¾"
1'-1¼"

Dimension "A" should equal either 4" or 8".
Dimension "B" should never be less than 4" and preferably 8 inches.
Scale ¾" = 1'-0"

MINIMUM DIMENSIONS for BRICK WORK

ISOMETRIC

ISOMETRIC

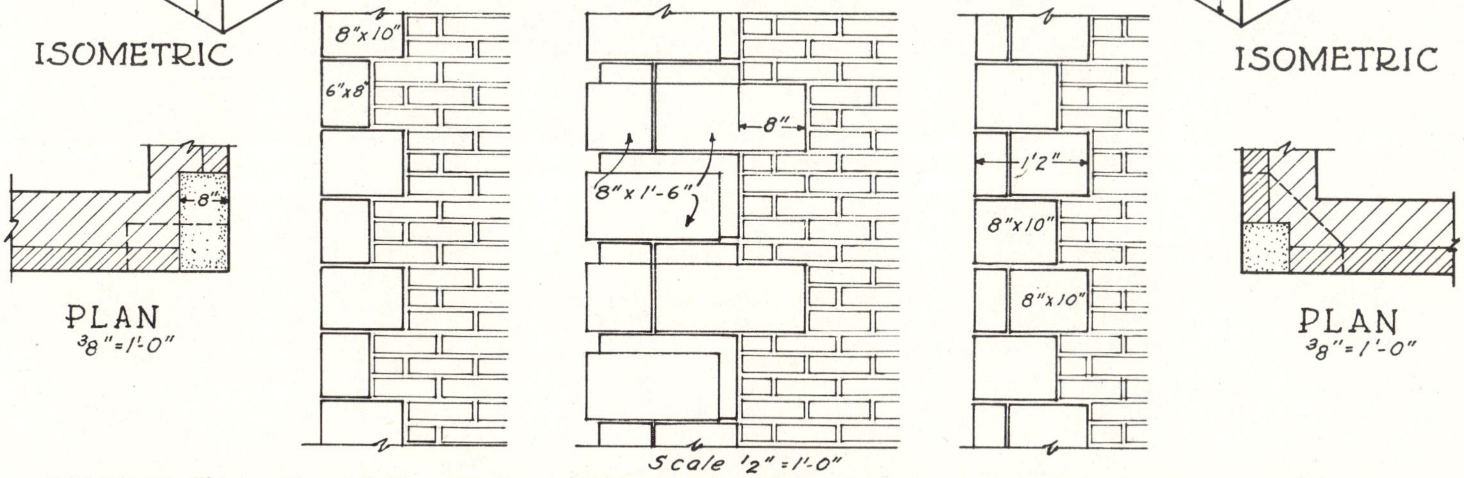
8"x10"
6"x8"
8"
8"x 1'-6"
1'2"

PLAN
⅜" = 1'-0"

PLAN
⅜" = 1'-0"

Scale ½" = 1'-0"

TYPES OF CUT STONE QUOINS FOR USE WITH BRICK

COPINGS AND QUOINS OF CUT STONE

Data checked by Indiana Limestone Co. Inc.

CUT STONE

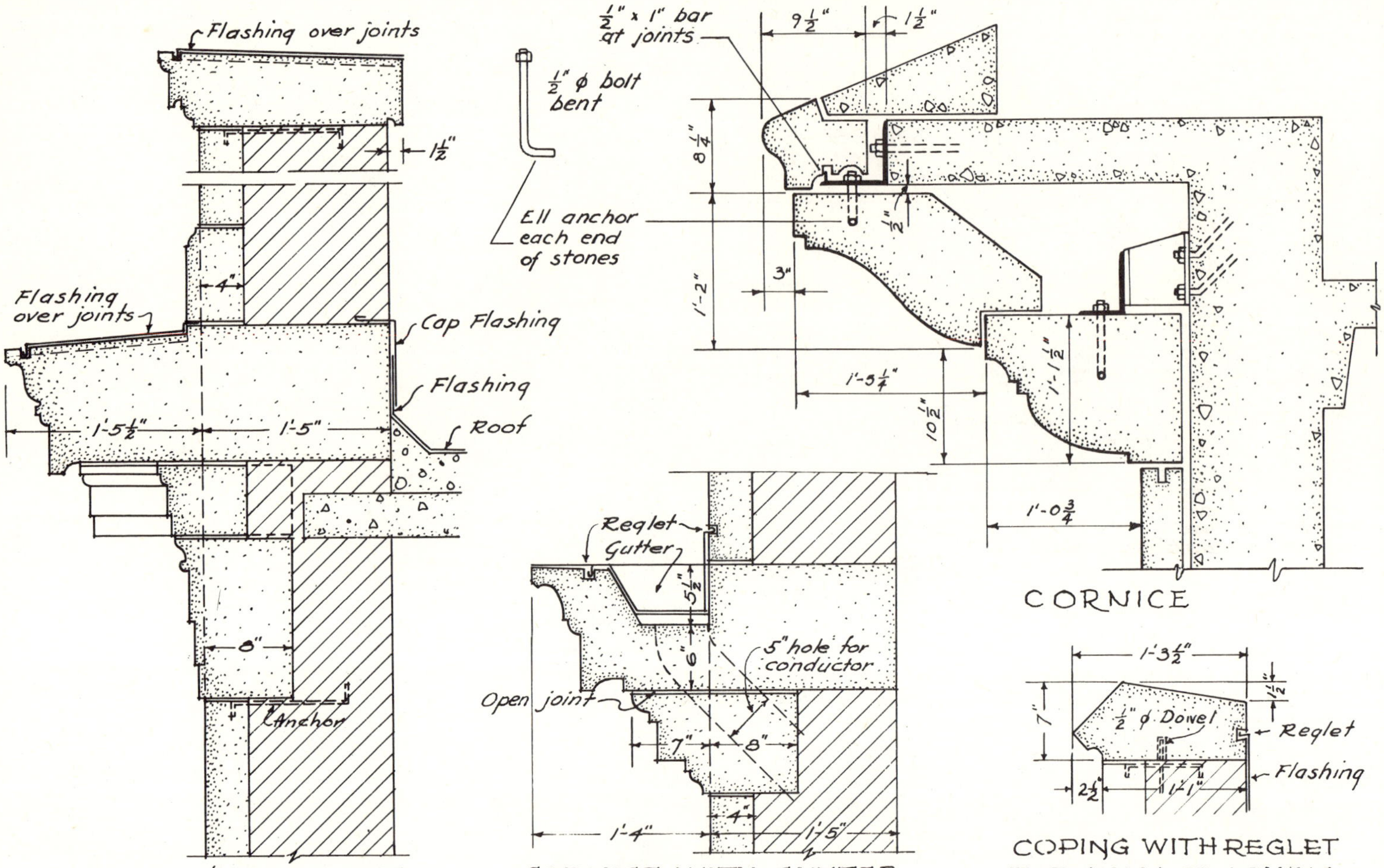
Flashing over joints
1½"
½" ϕ bolt bent
Ell anchor each end of stones
4"
Flashing over joints
Cap Flashing
Flashing
Roof
1'-5½"
1'-5"
8"
Anchor
½" x 1" bar at joints
9½"
1½"
8¼"
½"
3"
1'-2"
1'-5¼"
1'-1½"
10½"
1'-0¾"
Reglet
Gutter
5½"
6"
5" hole for conductor
Open joint
7"
8"
4"
1'-4"
1'-5"
1'-3½"
½"
7"
½" ϕ Dowel
Reglet
Flashing
2½"
1'-1"

CORNICE & PARAPET

CORNICE WITH GUTTER

COPING WITH REGLET FOR WALL FLASHING

CORNICE

SECTIONS THROUGH TYPICAL TYPES OF STONE CORNICES

3/4" = 1'-0"

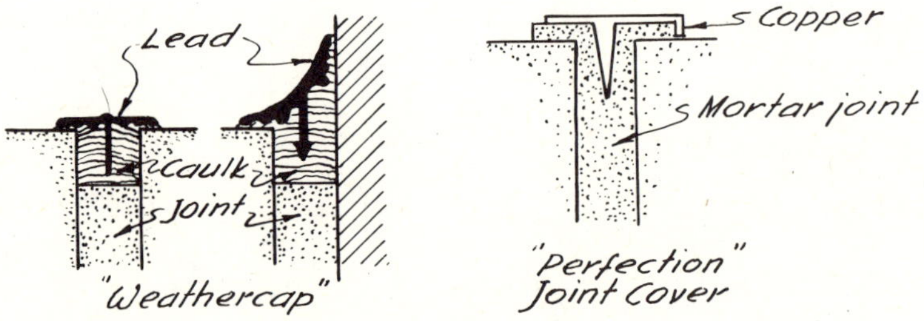
Lead
Caulk
Joint
Copper
Mortar joint

"Weathercap"

"Perfection" Joint Cover

ALTERNATE COVERING for MORTAR JOINTS

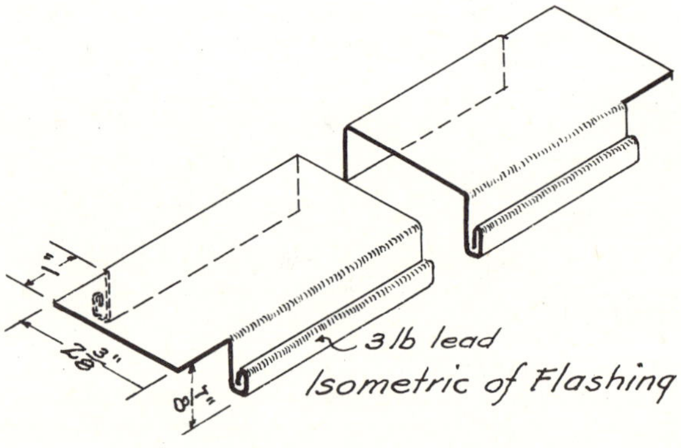
1"
2⅜"
1"
3 lb lead

Isometric of Flashing

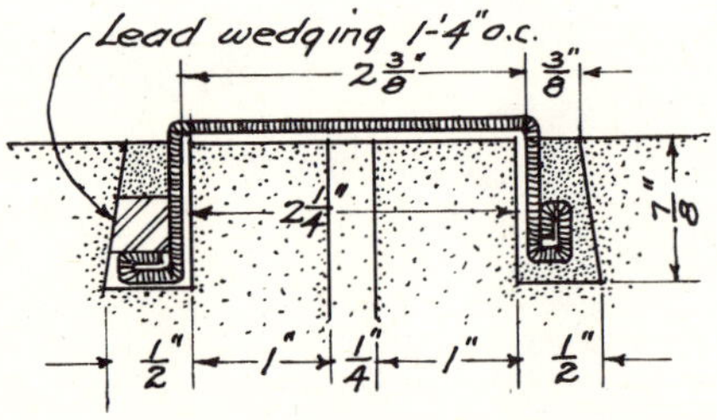
Lead wedging 1'-4" o.c.
2⅜"
⅜"
7/8"
2¼"
½"
1"
¼"
1"
½"

Fasten flashing into reglet with soft lead, wedging 1'-4" on centers and fill with elastic cement over. Do not use molten lead in reglet.

For other stone details of copings, parapets etc. see sheets preceding & following.

DETAILS OF FLASHING OVER STONE JOINTS

LIMESTONE CORNICES SHOWING FLASHING

Recommendations of the Indiana Limestone Co., Inc.

GRANITE

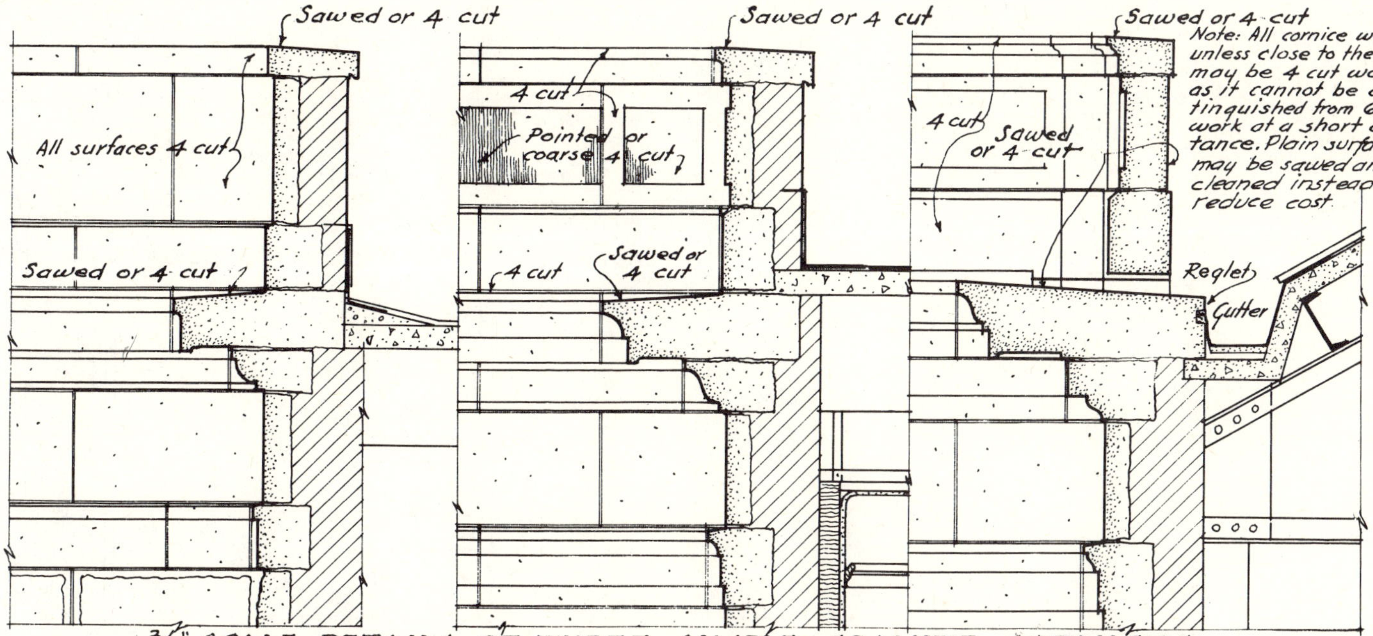
Sawed or 4 cut
Sawed or 4 cut
Sawed or 4 cut
Note: All cornice work, unless close to the eye, may be 4 cut work as it cannot be distinguished from 6 cut work at a short distance. Plain surfaces may be sawed and cleaned instead to reduce cost.
All surfaces 4 cut
4 cut
Pointed or coarse 4 cut
4 cut
Sawed or 4 cut
Sawed or 4 cut
4 cut
Sawed or 4 cut
Reglet
Gutter

3/4" SCALE DETAILS OF THREE SIMPLE GRANITE CORNICES.

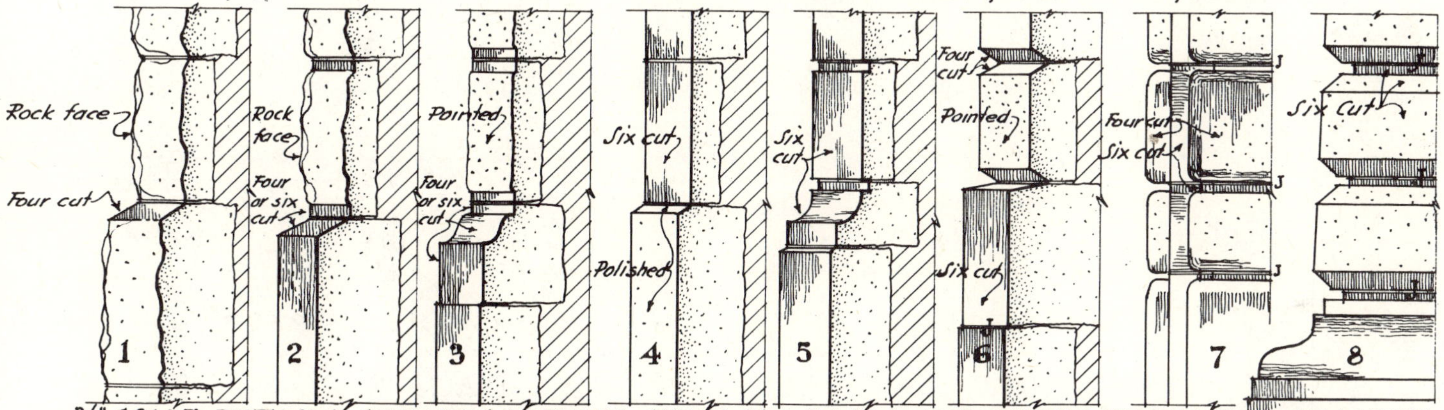
Rock face
Four cut
Rock face
Four or six cut
Pointed
Four or six cut
Six cut
Polished
Six cut
Four cut
Pointed
Six cut
Four cut
Six cut
Six Cut
1
2
3
4
5
6
7
8

3/4" SCALE DETAILS SHOWING VARIOUS SURFACES, BASES AND RUSTICATIONS FOR GRANITE

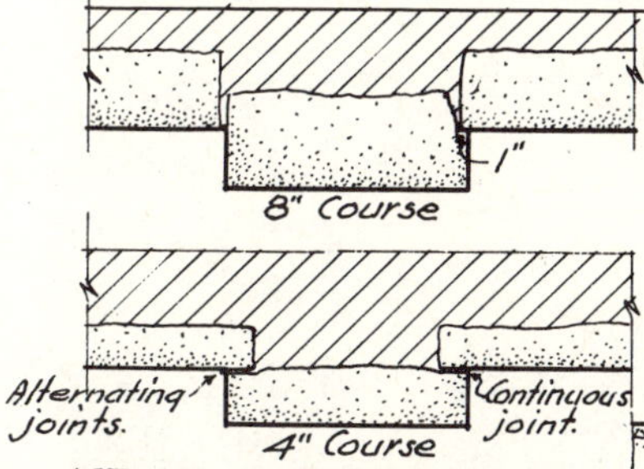
1"
8" Course
Alternating joints.
Continuous joint.
4" Course

METHODS OF BONDING PILASTERS.

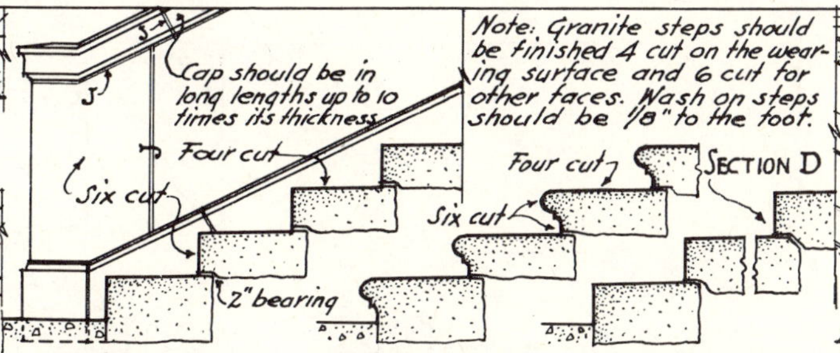
Cap should be in long lengths up to 10 times its thickness.
Four cut
Six cut
2" bearing
Note: Granite steps should be finished 4 cut on the wearing surface and 6 cut for other faces. Wash on steps should be 1/8" to the foot.
Four cut
Six cut
SECTION D

SECTION A SECTION B SECTION C

SECTIONS SHOWING BEARINGS FOR GRANITE STEPS.
Bearings shown at C & D are used to prevent sliding of stones when flight of steps is wide. C is practical & less expensive than D.

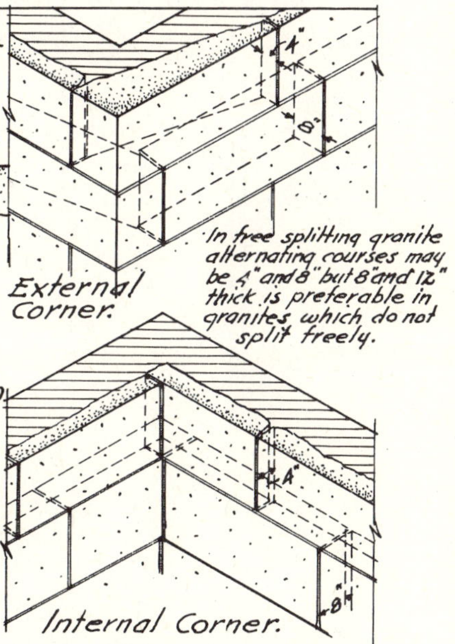
A"
B"
External Corner.
In free splitting granite alternating courses may be 4" and 8" but 8" and 12" thick is preferable in granites which do not split freely.
A"
B"
Internal Corner.

1/4" SCALE DETAILS SHOWING BONDING OF CORNERS.

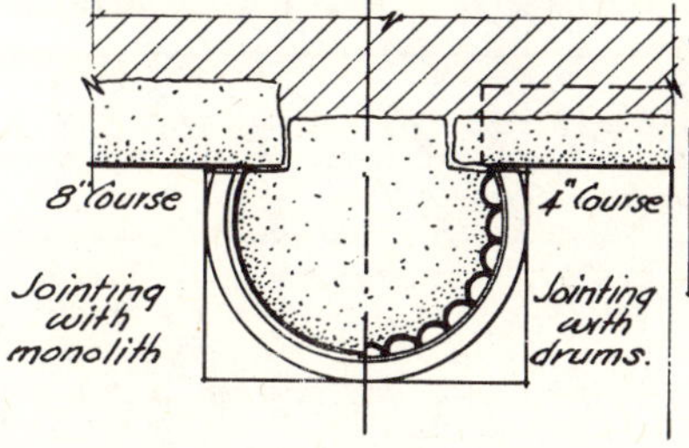
8" Course
4" Course
Jointing with monolith
Jointing with drums.

3/8" SCALE PLANS OF BONDS OF PILASTERS & COLUMNS.

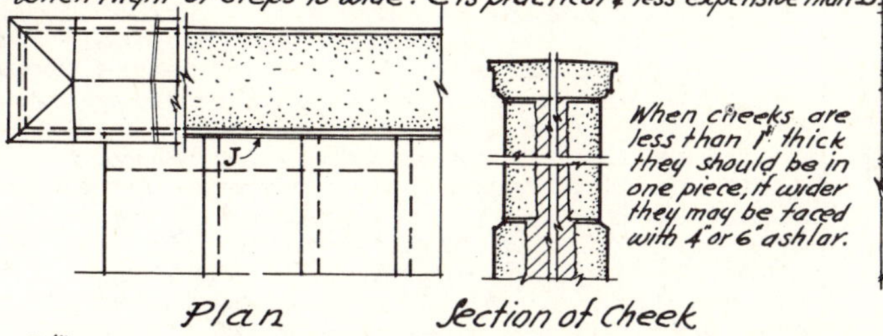
J
When cheeks are less than 1' thick they should be in one piece, if wider they may be faced with 4" or 6" ashlar.
Plan
Section of Cheek

3/8" SCALE DETAILS OF TYPICAL STAIR CONSTRUCTION.

TYPICAL GRANITE DETAILS *showing* PRACTICAL METHODS *of* CONSTRUCTION.

Recommendations of the National Building Granite Quarries Association.

ADOBE DETAILS

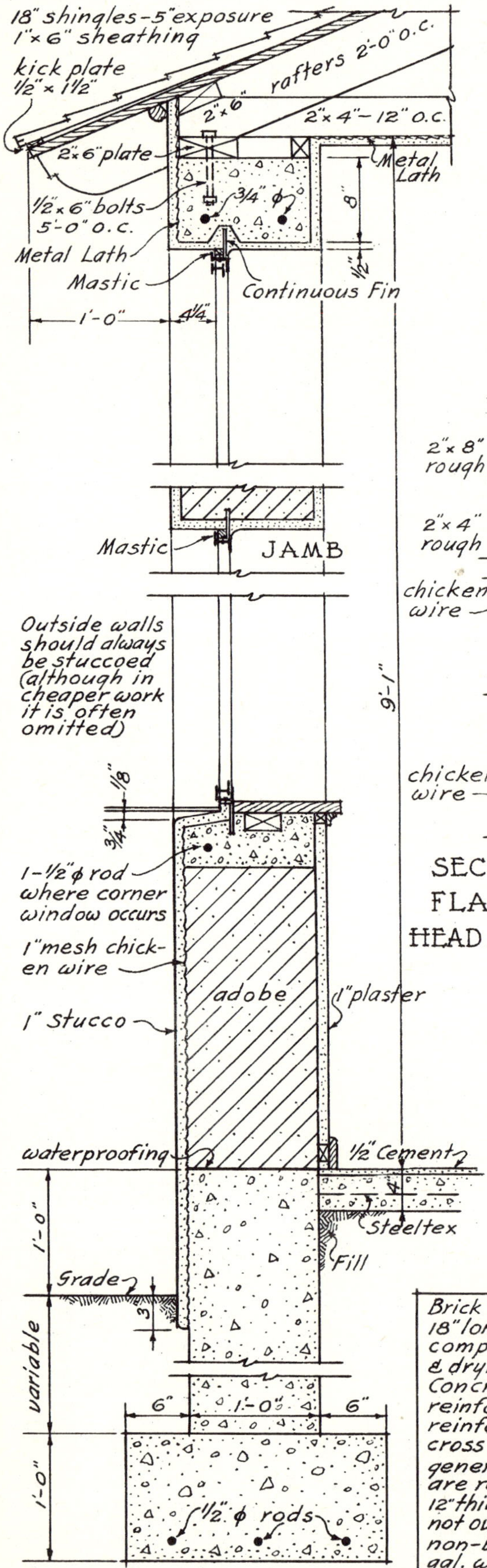

18" shingles-5" exposure
1"×6" sheathing
kick plate 1/2"×1 1/2"
rafters 2'-0" o.c.
2"×6"
2"×4"-12" o.c.
2"×6" plate
Metal Lath
3/4" ϕ
8"
1/2"×6" bolts 5'-0" o.c.
Metal Lath
Mastic
Continuous Fin
1/2"
1'-0"
4 1/4"
Mastic
JAMB
Outside walls should always be stuccoed (although in cheaper work it is often omitted)
9'-1"
1/8
3/4
1-1/2"ϕ rod where corner window occurs
1"mesh chicken wire
adobe
1"plaster
1" Stucco
waterproofing
1/2" Cement
Steeltex
Fill
Grade
3
1'-0"
variable
6"
1'-0"
6"
1'-0"
1/2" ϕ rods

WALL SECTION SHOWING PITCHED ROOF

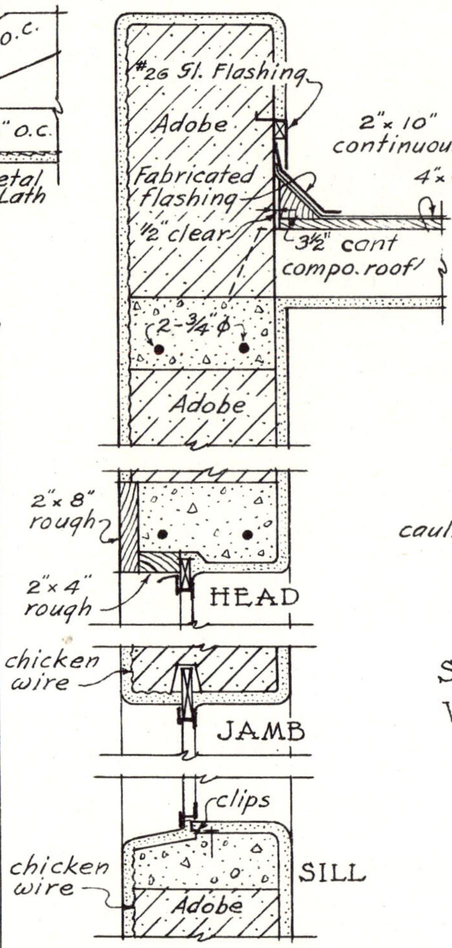

#26 Gl. Flashing
Adobe
2"×10" continuous
Fabricated flashing
1/2" clear
3 1/2" cant compo. roof
2-3/4 ϕ
Adobe
2"×8" rough
2"×4" rough
HEAD
chicken wire
JAMB
clips
chicken wire
Adobe
SILL

SECTION SHOWING FLAT ROOF, & WINDOW HEAD in SANTA FE STYLE

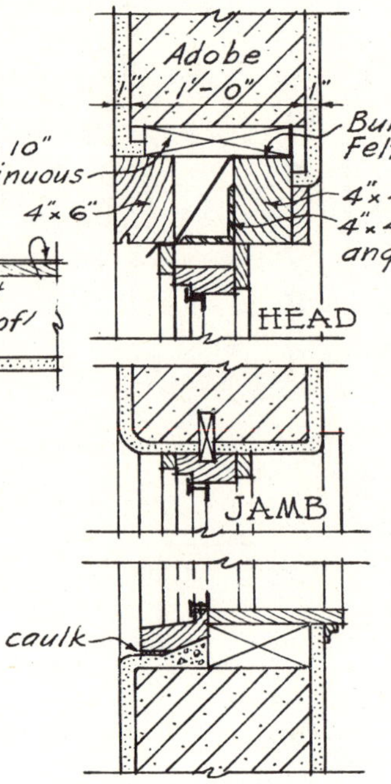

Adobe
1" 1'-0" 1"
Building Felt
4"×6"
4"×4"
4"×4"×1/4" angle
HEAD
JAMB
caulk

STEEL SASH IN WOOD FRAME (Good Work)

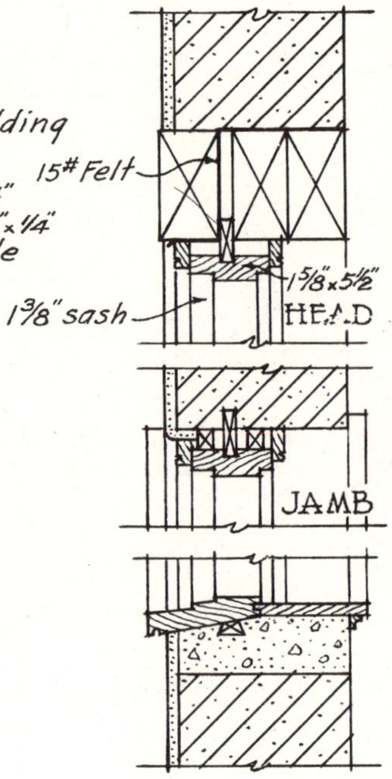

15# Felt
1 5/8"×5 1/2"
1 3/8" sash
HEAD
JAMB

WOOD SASH in CHEAP CONSTRUCTN

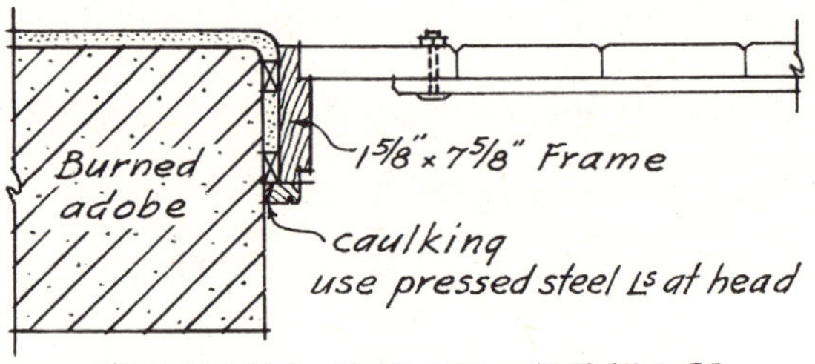

Burned adobe
1 5/8"×7 5/8" Frame
caulking
use pressed steel Ls at head

FRONT DOOR DETAIL

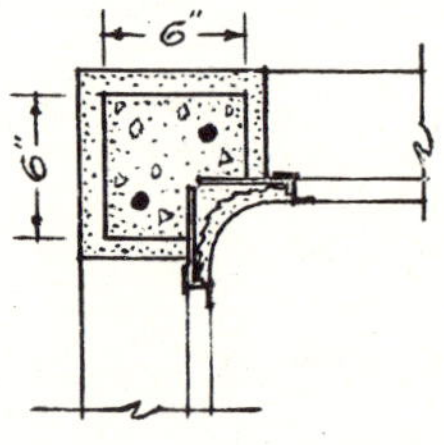

6"
6"

MULLION IN CORNER WINDOW

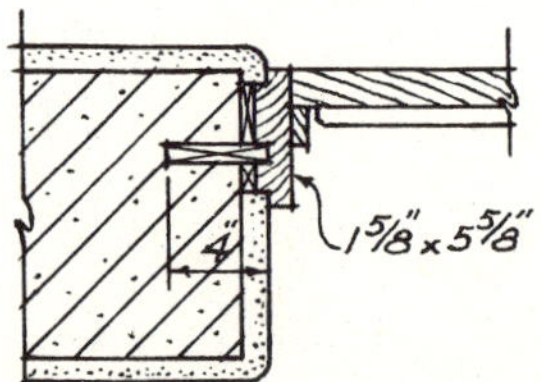

1 5/8"×5 5/8"
4"

DOOR JAMB & HEAD IN INTERIOR ADOBE WALLS, (omit fin in head)

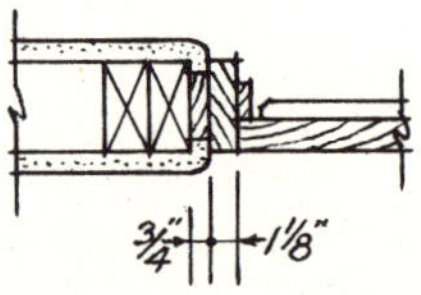

3/4"
1/8"

DOOR JAMB AND HEAD IN STUD WALL

Brick sizes = New Mexico, 3" high × 10" deep × 14" long. Arizona = 4" high × 12" deep × 18" long. Adobe bricks are either sun or kiln dried; mortar is similar in composition to the brick. In laying up, allow time for equalizing of settlement & drying of mortar, & lay in uniform stages throughout the structure. Concrete beams are not always necessary at roof plate, but a continuous reinforced collar beam is recommended at this point, not less than 6" thick, reinforced with rods whose cross sectional area is at least 1/4 of 1% of cross sectional area of the course; when used as window lintel they are generally 8" deep & reinforced same as collar beam. 4" concrete beams are recommended under window sills; but not reinforced. One story walls 12" thick in Arizona; 10" in New Mexico & not to exceed 12' in height; two story not over 22' in height = 18" thick at 1st. floor & 12" at second. Interior partitions, non-bearing 8" min., bonded & toothed into side walls or with metal mesh bond of gal. wire mesh. Stud walls anchored to adobe walls with 3" perf. gal. strap anchors, with ends hooked 10" into adobe. Min. pitch for shingled roofs 4" rise to 12" min.

This sheet prepared with the assistance of Richard A. Morse & Arthur T. Brown, Architects., Tucson, Arizona.

FIREPLACES and CHIMNEYS

TABLE OF CONTENTS

FIREPLACES

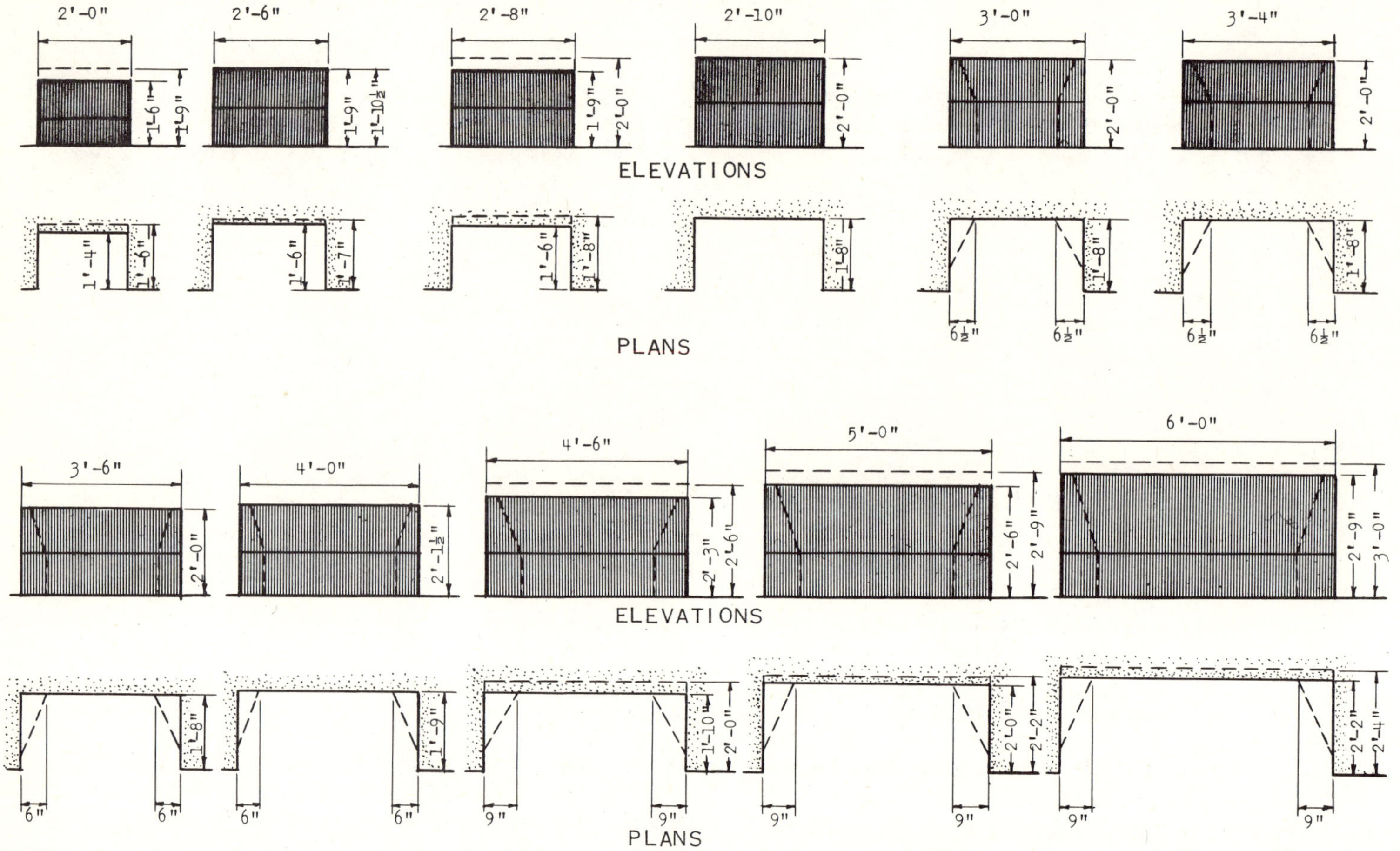

2'-0"
2'-6"
2'-8"
2'-10"
3'-0"
3'-4"
1'-6"
1'-9"
1'-9"
1'-10½"
1'-9"
2'-0"
2'-0"
2'-0"
2'-0"
ELEVATIONS
1'-4"
1'-6"
1'-6"
1'-7"
1'-6"
1'-8"
1'-8"
1'-8"
1'-8"
6½"
6½"
6½"
6½"
PLANS
3'-6"
4'-0"
4'-6"
5'-0"
6'-0"
2'-0"
2'-1½"
2'-3"
2'-6"
2'-6"
2'-9"
2'-9"
3'-0"
ELEVATIONS
1'-8"
1'-9"
1'-10"
2'-0"
2'-0"
2'-2"
2'-2"
2'-4"
6"
6"
6"
6"
9"
9"
9"
9"
9"
9"
PLANS

To select logs: allow 3" minimum clearance between log and each side of fireplace. Smaller logs thus used with splay. Splay fireplace for heating purposes. (See following page.) Larger openings than those shown may have hoods to lower openings or hobs to raise inner hearth.

Scale: ¼" =1'-0"

SIZES OF FIREPLACE OPENING

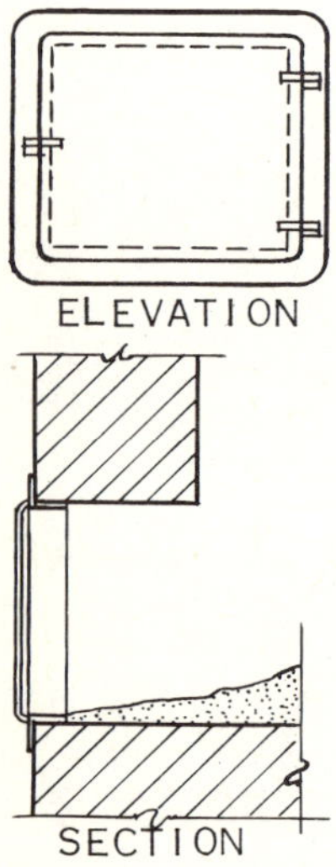

ELEVATION
SECTION

The following are clear opening sizes, as generally manufactured:

height		width
5"	x	7"
8"	x	8", 10"
8½"	x	10", 10½"
10"	x	12"
12"	x	8", 12", 16"
15"	x	12", 15"
18"	x	24"
24"	x	24", 30", 36" (Also used for stack cleanouts)

Average shovel size is 9¼" to 10½"
Oversize shovel size is 13"

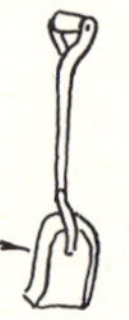

CLEANOUT OR ASHPIT DOORS

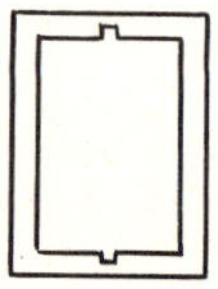

PLAN

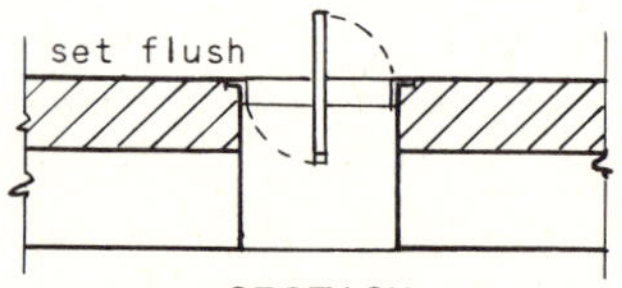

set flush
SECTION

TILTING TYPE

Usual size (hearth opening)

4" x 8"	7" x 10"	9½" x 5½"
4½"x 9"	8" x 4½"	
5" x 8"	8" x 5"	

ASH DUMPS

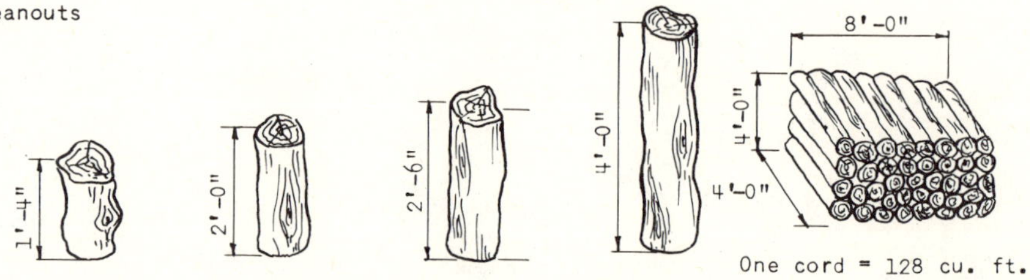

1'-4"
2'-0"
2'-6"
4'-0"
8'-0"
4'-0"
4'-0"

One cord = 128 cu. ft.

USUAL LOG SIZES

Data checked by Frederic N. Whitley, P.E., Consulting Fireplace Engineer

SPECIAL FIREPLACES

DESIGN OF SPECIAL FIREPLACES

The open floor plan makes useful multi-opening and free standing fireplaces. Design requirements for such fireplaces vary from those of conventional fireplaces. The following rules of thumb are given to aid in achieving proper function of these newer fireplaces.

Trouble factors encountered in fireplace design for the newer fireplaces are:

1. Too small a flue.
2. Damper throat too narrow.

Mr. Frederic N. Whitley, chimney expert and fireplace engineer, is recognized by architects, engineers and builders as the authority on fireplace design. He advises that proper functioning of fireplaces is dependent not only on fireplace and flue design but also on the following:

1. Height of flue and its projection above various types of roofs.
2. Neighboring and adjoining conditions, such as terrain, trees and buildings.
3. Wind directions and climate.

He also states that certain cross-draft conditions within a room may cause fireplace types marked by asterisk (*) to smoke, without regard to the design of the chimney or fireplace.

Fireplace types:

1. Fireplace open front and side.
*2. Fireplace open front and back.
3. Fireplace open three sides (one long and two short sides).
*4. Fireplace open three sides (two long and one short side).
*5. Fireplace open four sides.

Rules of thumb design data follow:

*FIREPLACE FRONT AND BACK

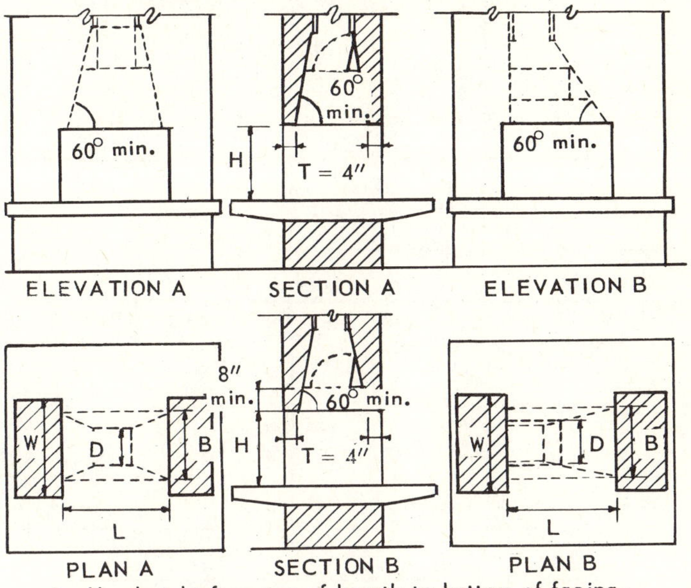
60° min.
H
T = 4″
ELEVATION A
SECTION A
ELEVATION B
8″ min.
W
D
B
L
PLAN A
SECTION B
PLAN B

1. H = height from top of hearth to bottom of facing.
2. B (depth of burning area) = 5/6 H minus 8″, but never less than 24″.
3. W (width of fireplace) = B plus T plus T.
4. D (damper at bottom of flue, Sect. A) = free area of flue.
5. D (damper closer to fire, Sect. B) = twice free area of flue. Set damper a minimum 8″ (preferably 12″) from bottom of smoke chamber. Operatable part of damper when open should extend entire length of smoke chamber, as shown.
6. Flue: free area = 1/12 of H x 2L.

FIREPLACE OPEN FRONT AND SIDE

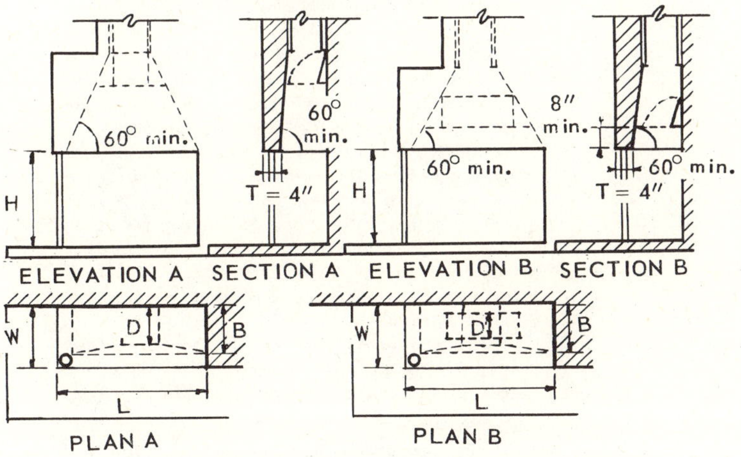
60° min.
H
T = 4″
8″ min.
ELEVATION A
SECTION A
ELEVATION B
SECTION B
W
D
B
L
PLAN A
PLAN B

1. H = height from top of hearth to bottom of facing.
2. B (depth of burning area) = 2/3 H minus 4″.
3. W (width of fireplace) = B plus T.
4. D (damper at bottom of flue, Sect. A) = free area of flue.
5. D (damper closer to fire, Sect. B) = twice the free area of the flue. Set damper a minimum 8″ (preferably 12″) from bottom of smoke chamber. Operatable part of damper when open should extend entire length of smoke chamber, as shown.
6. Flue: free area (i.e., inside dimensions of flue) = 1/12 of H x (L plus W).

FIREPLACE OPEN THREE SIDES
(one long and two short sides)

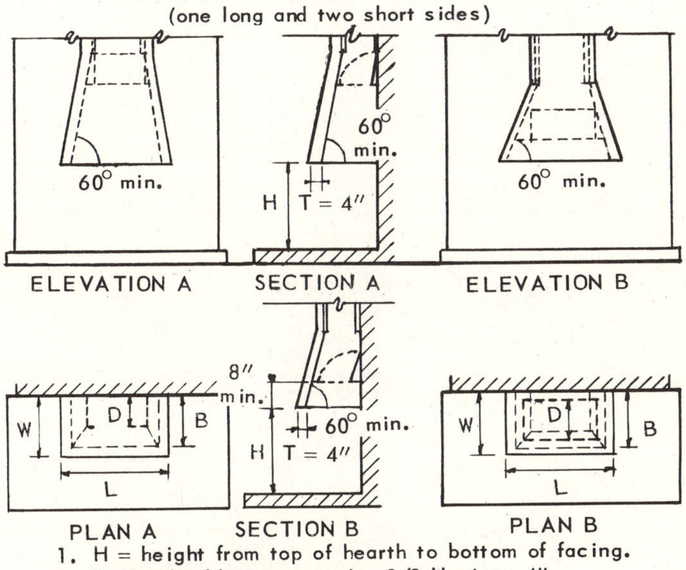
60° min.
H
T = 4″
ELEVATION A
SECTION A
ELEVATION B
8″ min.
W
D
B
L
PLAN A
SECTION B
PLAN B

1. H = height from top of hearth to bottom of facing.
2. B (depth of burning area) = 2/3 H minus 4″.
3. W (width of fireplace) = B plus T.
4. D (damper at bottom of flue, Sect. A) = free area of flue.
5. D (damper closer to fire, Sect. B) = twice free area of flue. Set damper a minimum 8″ (preferably 12″) from bottom of smoke chamber. Operatable part of damper when open should extend entire length of smoke chamber, as shown.
6. Flue: free area = 1/12 of H x (L plus 2W).

SPECIAL FIREPLACES

DESIGN OF SPECIAL FIREPLACES

*FIREPLACE OPEN THREE SIDES
(two long and one short side)

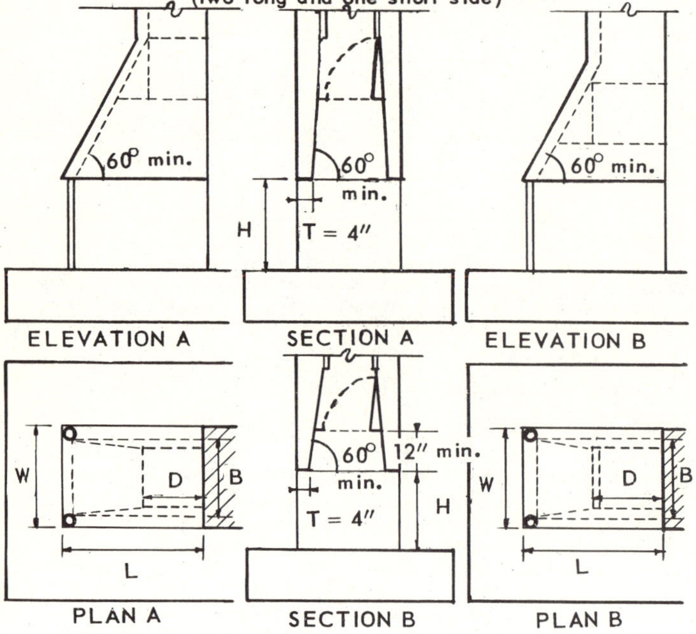
60° min.
60° min.
H
T = 4″
60° min.
ELEVATION A
SECTION A
ELEVATION B
W
D
B
L
60° 12″ min.
min.
T = 4″
H
W
D
B
L
PLAN A
SECTION B
PLAN B

1. H = height from top of hearth to bottom.
2. B*(depth) of burning area) = 5/6 H minus 8″, but never less than 24″.
3. W (width of fireplace) = B plus T plus T.
4. D (damper at bottom of flue, Sect. A) = free area of flue.
5. D (damper closer to fire, Sect. B) = twice free area of flue. Set damper a minimum of 12″ from bottom of smoke chamber. Operatable part of damper when open should extend entire length of smoke chamber, as shown.
6. Flue: free area = 1/12 of H x (2L plus W).

*FIREPLACE OPEN FOUR SIDES

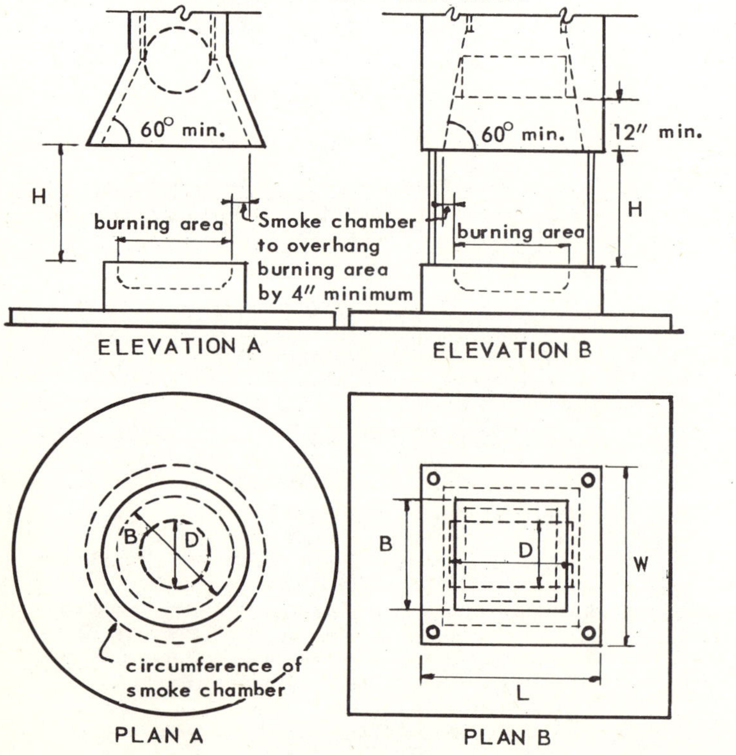
60° min.
H
burning area
Smoke chamber to overhang burning area by 4″ minimum
60° min.
12″ min.
H
burning area
ELEVATION A
ELEVATION B
B
D
circumference of smoke chamber
B
D
W
L
PLAN A
PLAN B

1. H (height from top of hearth to bottom of facing) must never exceed the longest dimension of the burning area. It is recommended that H never exceed 28″.
2. B (burning area, circular fireplace, Elev. A) = 32″ minimum diameter.
3. B (burning area, square or rectangular fireplace) = 24″ minimum dimension.
4. D (damper at bottom of flue, Elev. A) = area of flue.
5. D (damper closer to fire, Elev. B) = twice flue area. Set damper a minimum of 12″ from bottom of smoke chamber. Operatable part of damper when open should extend entire length of smoke chamber, as shown.
6. Flue, circular fireplace: free area = 1/12 of H x 3.14 x (B plus 8″).
7. Flue, square or rectangular fireplace: free area = 1/12 of H x (2L plus 2W).

In addition to proper damper and flue size, the flue height and fresh air necessary to support combustion are factors which should not be overlooked in fireplace design. The following rules of thumb make allowance for these factors.

1. In a one story flat roofed building the flue should extend 8'-0″ above the roof.
2. In a flat roofed building of two or more stories the flue should extend 6'-0″ above the roof.
3. In a one story pitched roof building the flue should extend 4'-0″ above the roof ridge.
4. In a pitched roof building of two or more stories the flue should extend 4'-0″ above the roof ridge.
5. Fresh air to support combustion and proper draft is often supplied by crack leakage around doors and windows. It can also be supplied by leaving a space between the floor and the bottoms of doors in the room where the fireplace is located. However, in air-conditioned buildings, where cracks and crevices are weatherstripped and insulated, it is more of a problem to supply the proper quantity of fresh air. The following formulas indicate the quantities of fresh air necessary for the various fireplaces. Letters shown in formulas are on the diagrams for each fireplace.

   Fireplace open front and side: cubic feet per minute of fresh air = (L plus W) x H x 60. Fireplace open front and back: c.f.m. fresh air = 2L x H x 60.

   Fireplace open three sides (one long and two short sides): c.f.m. fresh air = (L plus 2W) x H x 60.

   Fireplace open three sides (two long and one short side): c.f.m. fresh air = (2L plus W) x H x 60.

   Fireplace open four sides:
   Circular: c.f.m. fresh air = 3.14 x (B plus 8″) x H x 60.

   Square or rectangular: c.f.m. fresh air = (2L plus 2W) x H x 60.

NOTE: Consult local building codes on all details of fireplace construction and chimney heights.

SPECIAL FIREPLACES

This and the following pages show examples of special fireplaces. Variations in design may be achieved by use of different dampers.

1. Low dampers with separate lintels and more elaborate masonry work. Two dampers often required.
2. High dampers with integral lintels and a minimum of masonry work.

Relative costs will vary with each condition

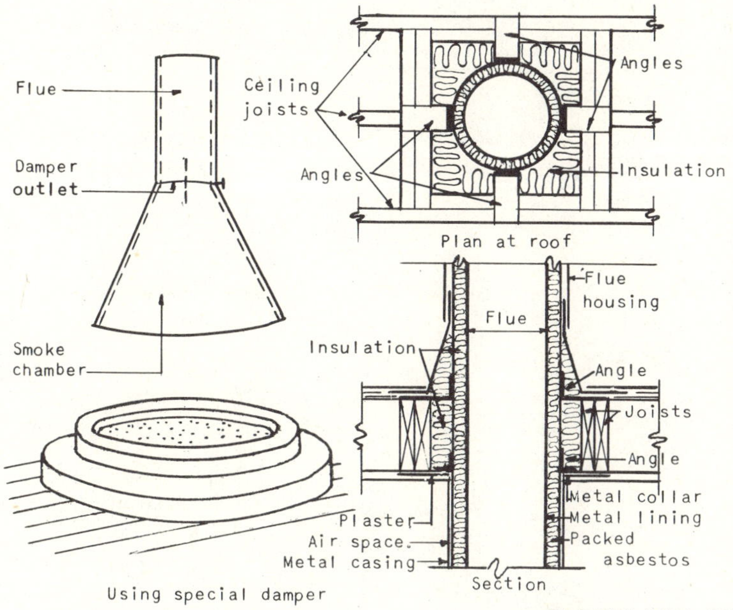
Flue
Damper outlet
Smoke chamber
Ceiling joists
Angles
Angles
Insulation
Plan at roof
Flue
Flue housing
Insulation
Angle
Joists
Angle
Metal collar
Metal lining
Packed asbestos
Plaster
Air space
Metal casing
Section

Using special damper

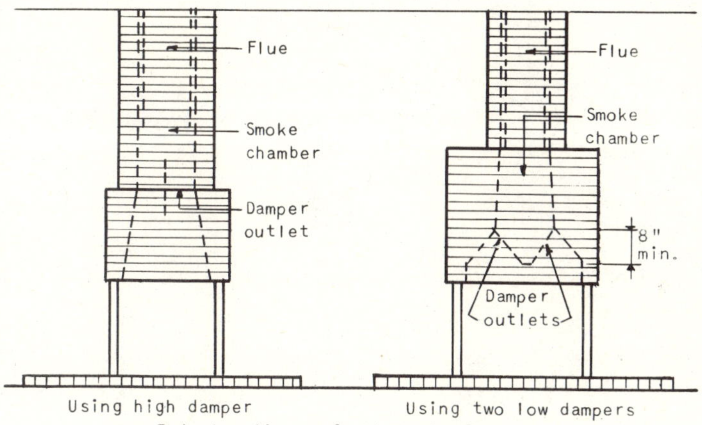
Flue
Smoke chamber
Damper outlet
Flue
Smoke chamber
8" min.
Damper outlets
Using high damper
Using two low dampers

End elevations of alternate fireplace

FIREPLACE OPEN FOUR SIDES

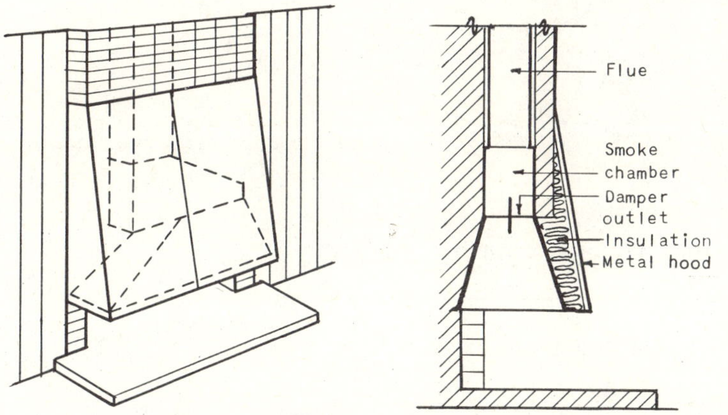
Flue
Smoke chamber
Damper outlet
Insulation
Metal hood

Using high damper

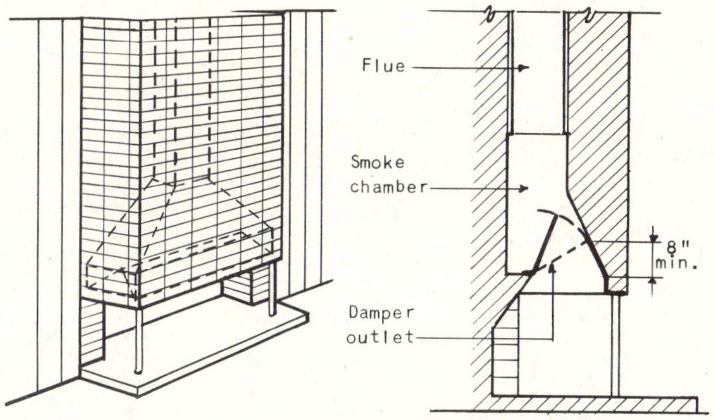
Flue
Smoke chamber
8" min.
Damper outlet

Using low damper

FIREPLACE OPEN THREE SIDES
(one long and two short sides)

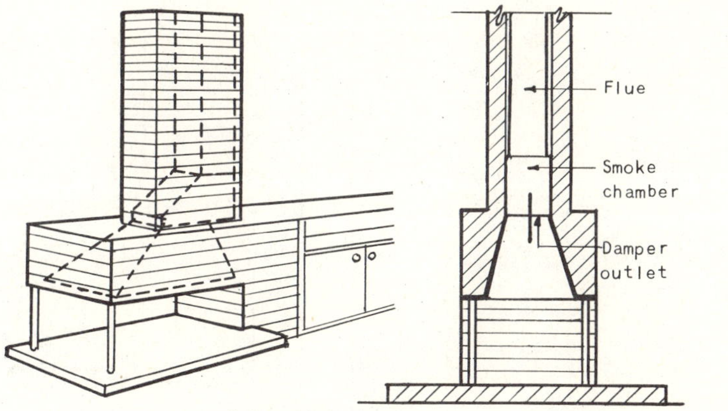
Flue
Smoke chamber
Damper outlet

Using high damper

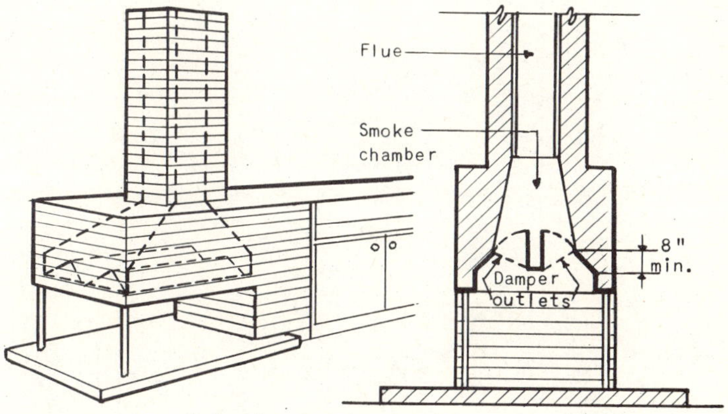
Flue
Smoke chamber
8" min.
Damper outlets

Using two low dampers

FIREPLACE OPEN THREE SIDES
(two long and one short side)

EXAMPLES OF SPECIAL FIREPLACES USING STOCK DAMPERS

SPECIAL FIREPLACES

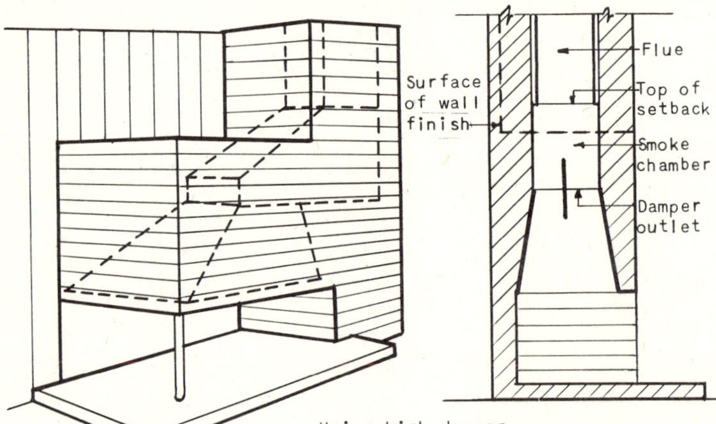
Surface
of wall
finish
Flue
Top of
setback
Smoke
chamber
Damper
outlet

Using high damper

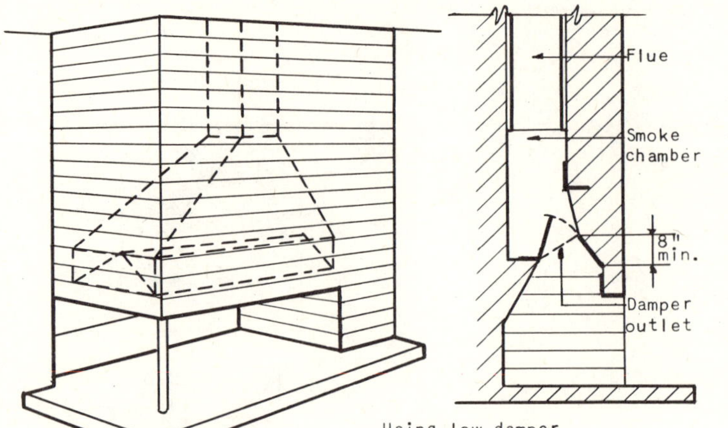
Flue
Smoke
chamber
8"
min.
Damper
outlet

Using low damper

FIREPLACE OPEN FRONT AND SIDE

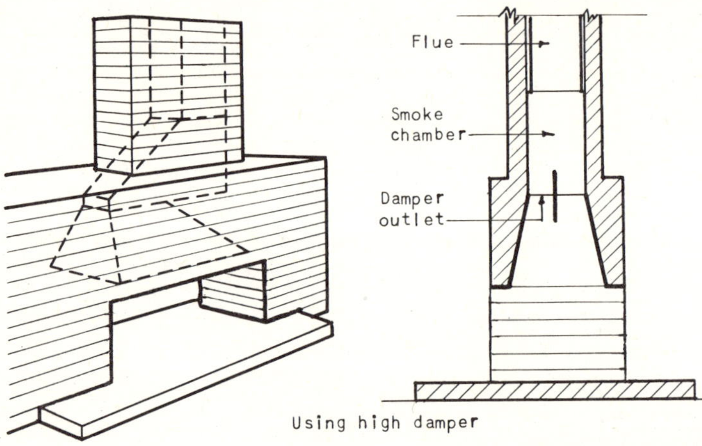
Flue
Smoke
chamber
Damper
outlet

Using high damper

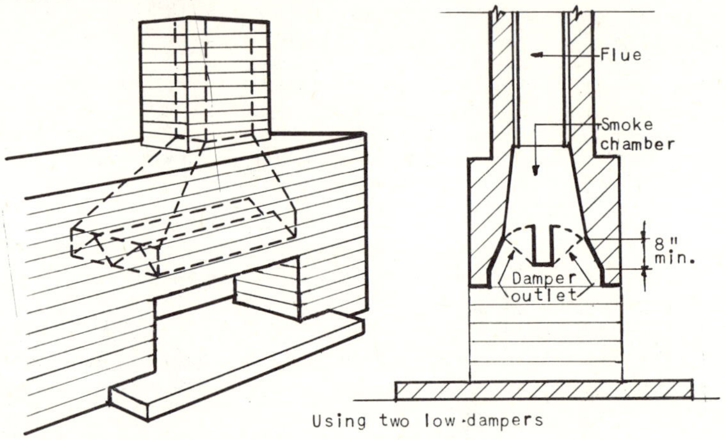
Flue
Smoke
chamber
8"
min.
Damper
outlet

Using two low-dampers

FIREPLACE OPEN FRONT AND BACK

EXAMPLES OF SPECIAL FIREPLACES USING STOCK DAMPERS

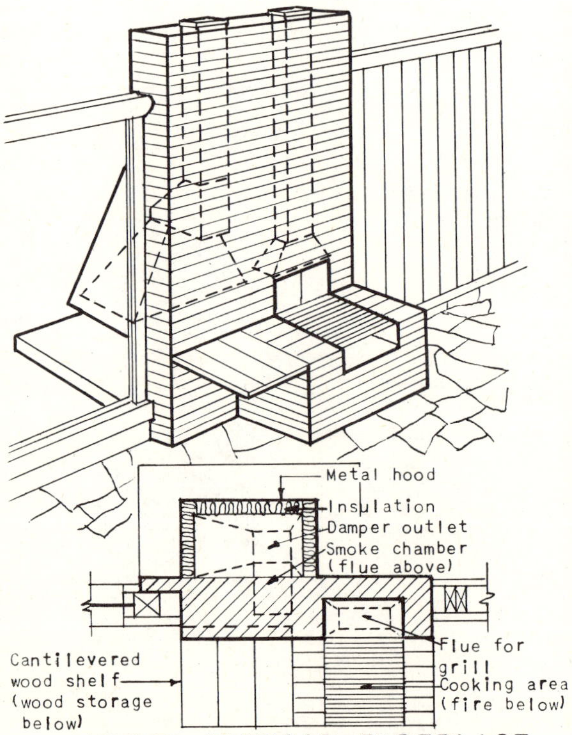
Metal hood
Insulation
Damper outlet
Smoke chamber
(flue above)
Flue for
grill
Cooking area
(fire below)
Cantilevered
wood shelf
(wood storage
below)

INDOOR-OUTDOOR FIREPLACE

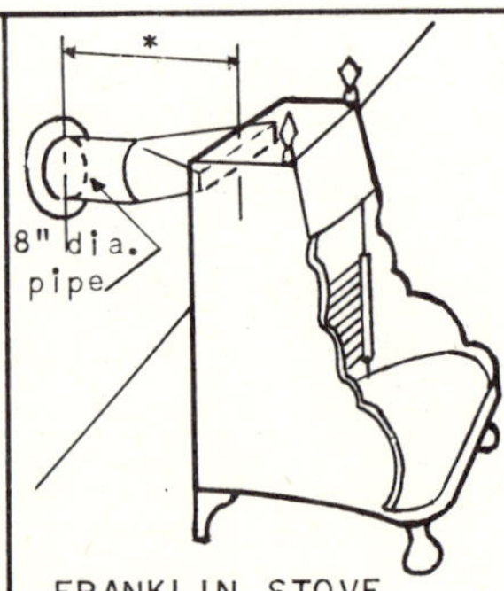
*
8" dia.
pipe

* Minimum clearances

A. Incombustible lath and plaster
   1. without shield-12"
   2. with shield-6"

B. Wood lath and plaster
   1. without shield-20"
   2. with shield-9"

FRANKLIN STOVE

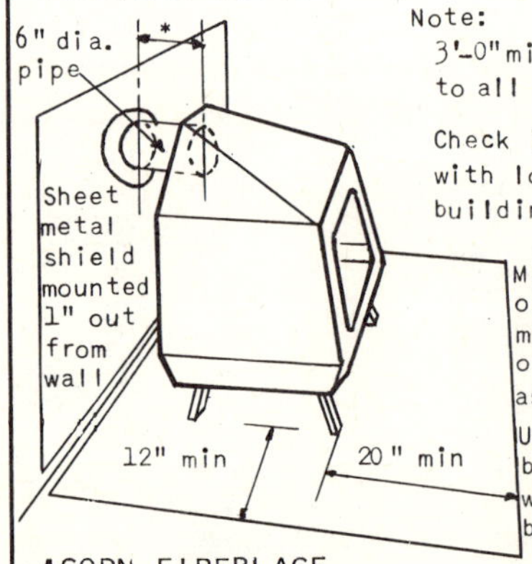
6" dia.
pipe
*
Sheet
metal
shield
mounted
1" out
from
wall
12" min
20" min

Note:
3'-0" min. clearance to all woodwork

Check installation with local building codes

Masonry hearth or 24 ga. min. metal shield over 1/4" asbestos board

Unit may also be hung from wall by brackets.

ACORN FIREPLACE

PORTABLE METAL FIREPLACES

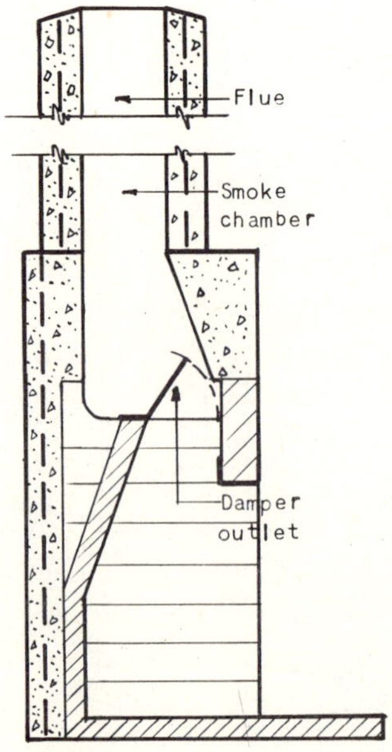
Flue
Smoke
chamber
Damper
outlet

Section

Courtesy of Don Scholz

PRECAST CONCRETE FIREPLACE

SPECIAL FIREPLACES and DAMPERS

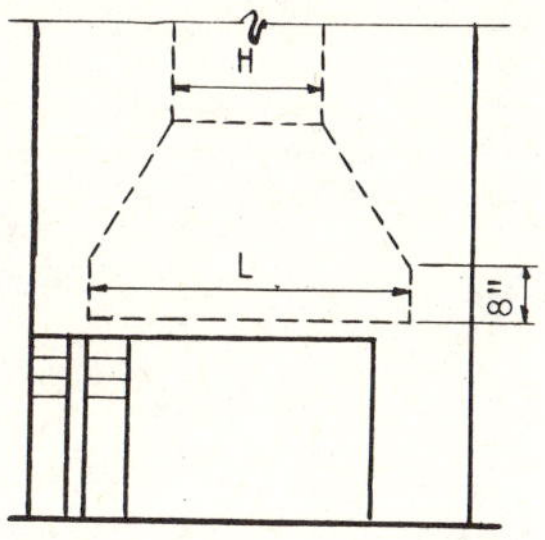
H
L
8"

ELEVATION

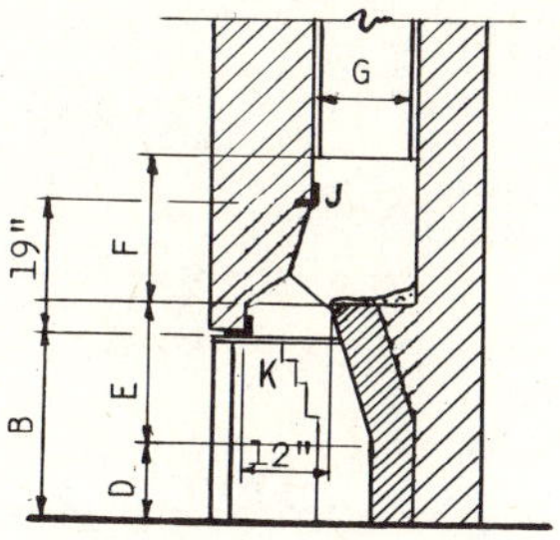
G
J
19"
F
K
12"
B
E
D

SECTION

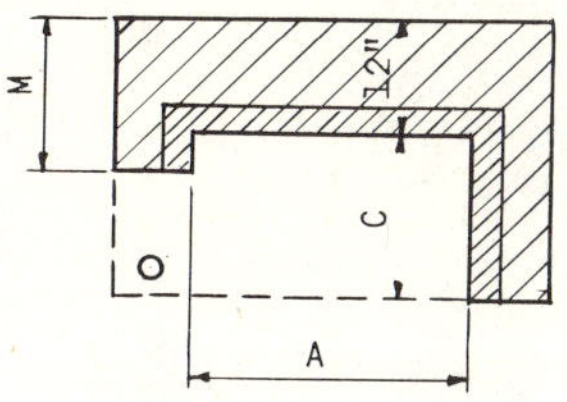
M
12"
C
A

PLAN

NOTE:
Back flange of damper must be fully supported on masonry to protect from heat. Do NOT build in solidly at ends; allow for expansion.
Facing allowed for-4", This will vary with material used.

ANGLE SIZES: "J" below
A: 3" x 3" x 3/16"
B: 3½"x 3" x ¼"

DAMPER NO.	A	B	C	D	E	F	OLD FLUE SIZE G	OLD FLUE SIZE H	NEW FLUE SIZE G	NEW FLUE SIZE H	L	M	ANGLE J (2 REQ'D.)	PLATE LINTEL K	CORNER POST HT.
528	28	26½	16	14	20	29⅓	13	13	12	12	36	16	A-36"	11 x 16	26½
532	32	26½	16	14	20	32	13	13	12	16	40	16	A-42"	11 x 16	26½
536	36	26½	16	14	20	35	13	13	12	16	44	16	A-48"	11 x 16	26½
540	40	29	16	14	20	35	13	18	16	16	48	16	B-54"	11 x 16	29
548	48	29	20	14	24	43	13	18	16	16	56	20	B-60"	11 x 16	29

FIREPLACE OPEN FRONT AND SIDE (PROJECTING CORNER)

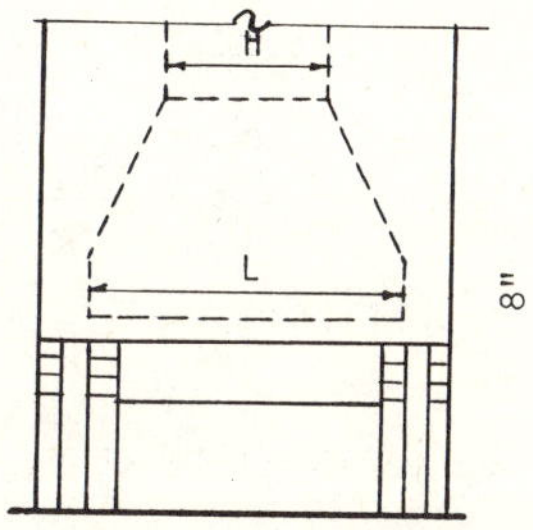
H
L
8"

ELEVATION

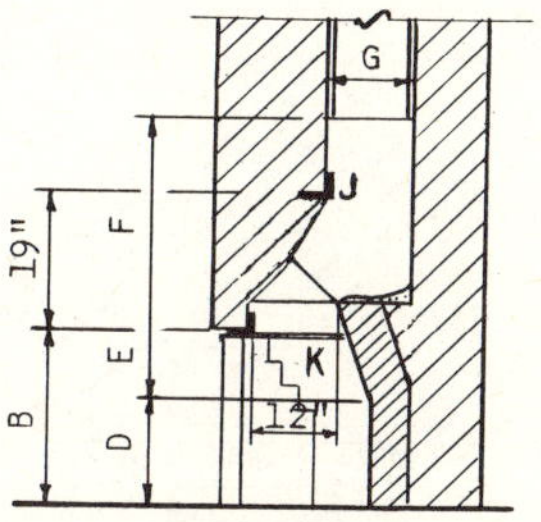
G
J
19"
F
K
12"
B
E
D

SECTION

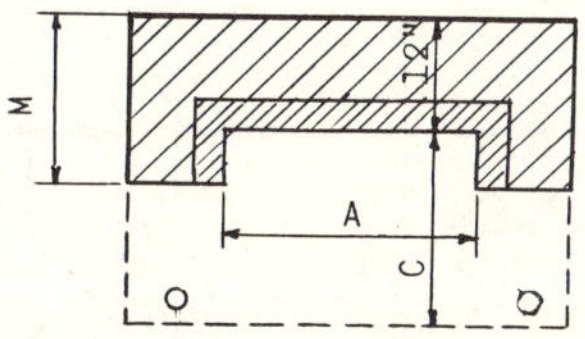
M
12"
A
C

PLAN

NOTE:
Support back flange of damper on masonry. Do not build in solidly at ends.

ANGLE SIZES: "J" below
A: 3" x 3" x 3/16"
B: 3½"x 3" x ¼"

DAMPER NO.	A	B	C	D	E	F	OLD FLUE SIZE G	OLD FLUE SIZE H	NEW FLUE SIZE G	NEW FLUE SIZE H	L	M	ANGLE J (2 REQ'D.)	PL. LINTEL K (2 REQ'D.)	CORNER POST HT. (2 REQ'D.)
528	28	26½	20	14	18	27	13	13	12	16	36	20	A-42"	11 x 16	26½
532	32	26½	20	14	18	32	13	13	16	16	40	20	A-48"	11 x 16	26½
536	36	26½	20	14	18	32	13	18	16	16	44	20	A-48"	11 x 16	26½
540	40	29	20	14	21	35	13	18	16	16	48	20	B-54"	11 x 16	29
548	48	29	20	14	21	40	13	18	16	20	56	20	B-60"	11 x 16	29

FIREPLACE OPEN THREE SIDES (2 SHORT, 1 LONG)

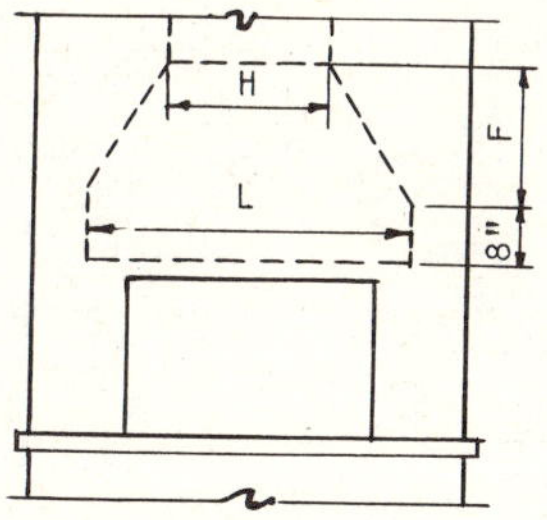
H
L
F
8"

ELEVATION

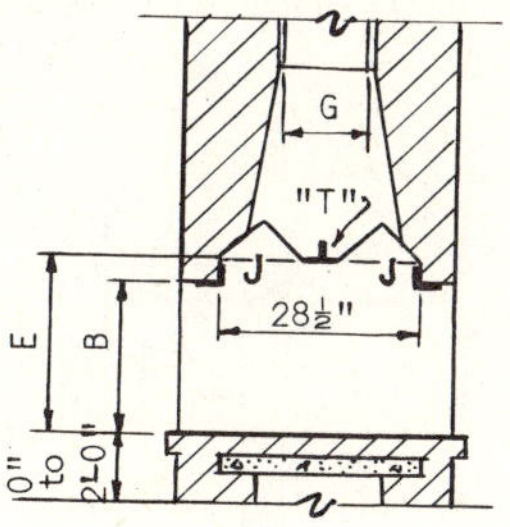
G
"T"
J
J
28½"
E
B
0" to 2-0"

SECTION

Fireplace open three sides (1 short 2 long) similar to this

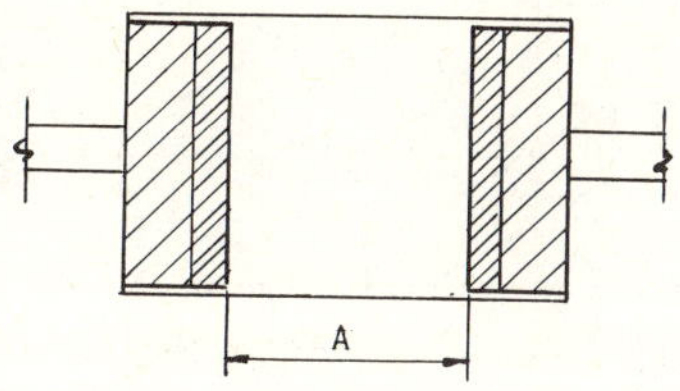
A

PLAN

NOTE:
Tee and damper not to be built in solidly at ends.

*Denotes "2 required."

ANGLE SIZES: "J" below
A: 3" x 3" x 3/16"
B: 3½"x 3" x ¼"

DAMPER NO.*	A	B	E	F	OLD FLUE SIZE G	OLD FLUE SIZE H	NEW FLUE SIZE G	NEW FLUE SIZE H	ANGLE J*	L	TEE LENGTH
528	28	24	35	19	13	13	12	16	A-36"	36	35
532	32	29	35	21	13	18	16	16	A-40"	40	39
536	36	29	35	21	13	18	16	20	A-42"	44	43
540	40	29	35	27	18	18	16	20	A-48"	48	47
548	48	32	37	32	18	18	20	20	B-54"	56	55

FIREPLACE OPEN FRONT AND BACK

SPECIAL FIREPLACES USING DONLEY DAMPERS

All dimensions given in inches. Scale: ¼" = 1'-0"

NON-MODULAR FLUE SIZES for FIREPLACES

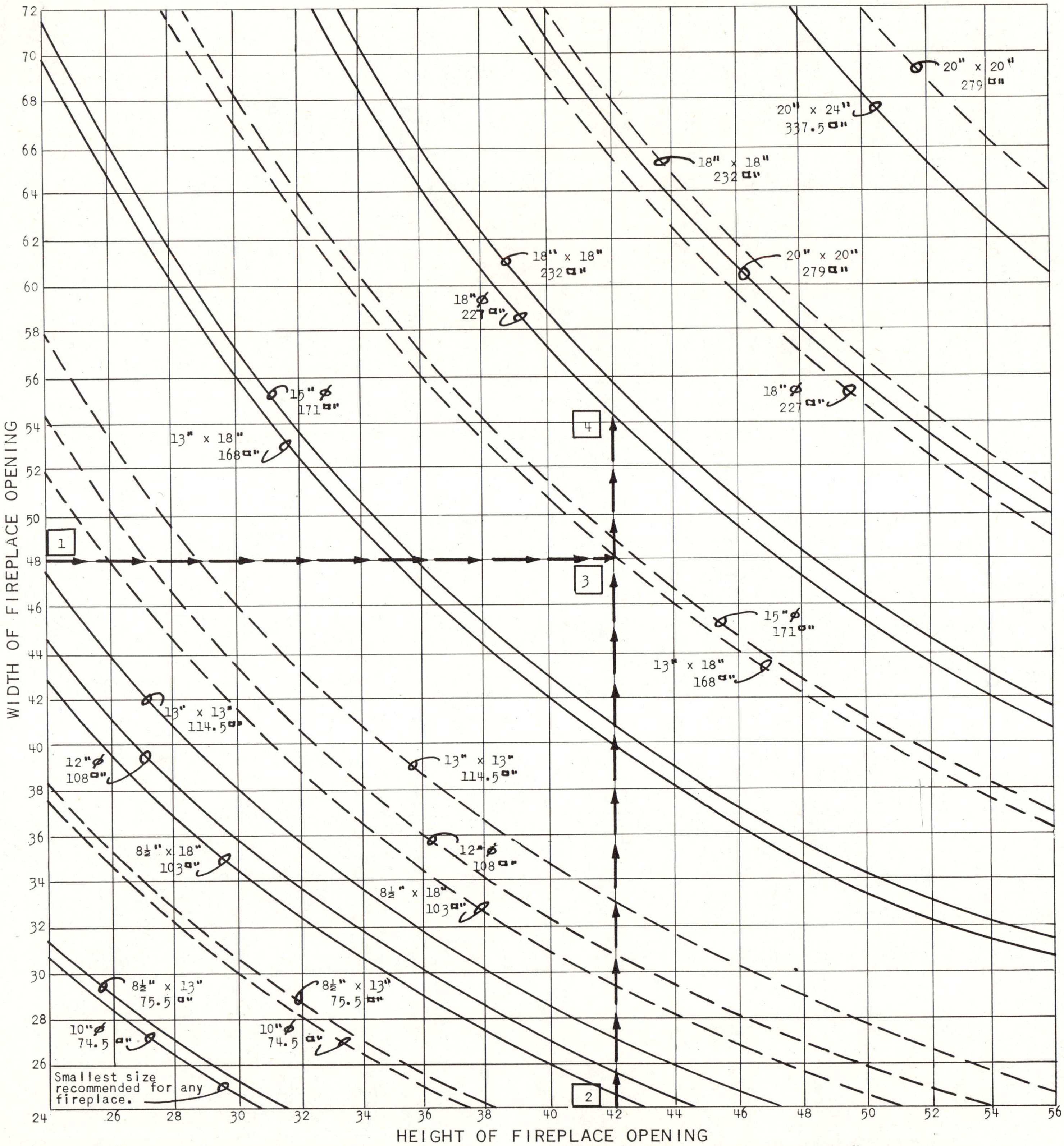

WIDTH OF FIREPLACE OPENING
HEIGHT OF FIREPLACE OPENING
20" x 20" 279 □"
20" x 24" 337.5 □"
18" x 18" 232 □"
18" x 18" 232 □"
20" x 20" 279 □"
18" Ø 227 □"
18" Ø 227 □"
15" Ø 171 □"
13" x 18" 168 □"
15" Ø 171 □"
13" x 18" 168 □"
13" x 13" 114.5 □"
12" Ø 108 □"
13" x 13" 114.5 □"
12" Ø 108 □"
8½" x 18" 103 □"
8½" x 18" 103 □"
8½" x 13" 75.5 □"
8½" x 13" 75.5 □"
10" Ø 74.5 □"
10" Ø 74.5 □"
Smallest size recommended for any fireplace.
1
2
3
4

PROBLEM: Find proper flue size, at 1/10 fireplace area, for fireplace 48" wide and 42" high.

SOLUTION:
1. Find fireplace width at left of chart.
2. Find fireplace height at bottom of chart.
3. Follow width and height lines to their intersection.
4. Proper flue size will be nearest curve (for 1/10 area) above intersection; in this case, 18" Ø. For rectangular flue, continue to next curve for 1/10 area: 18" x 18".

Charts based on minimum net inside flue areas.
For chimney less than 35' high, use 1/10 ratio for flue; if over 35', use 1/12 ratio. If flue is less than 20' high, it is advisable to use next larger flue size, unless intersection falls well below the curve.

——————— =	recommended flue size: 1/10 of fireplace area.
— — — — — =	absolute minimum flue size: 1/12 area of fireplace.

Data checked by Frederic N. Whitley, P.E., Consulting Fireplace Engineer.

FLUES - NON-MODULAR

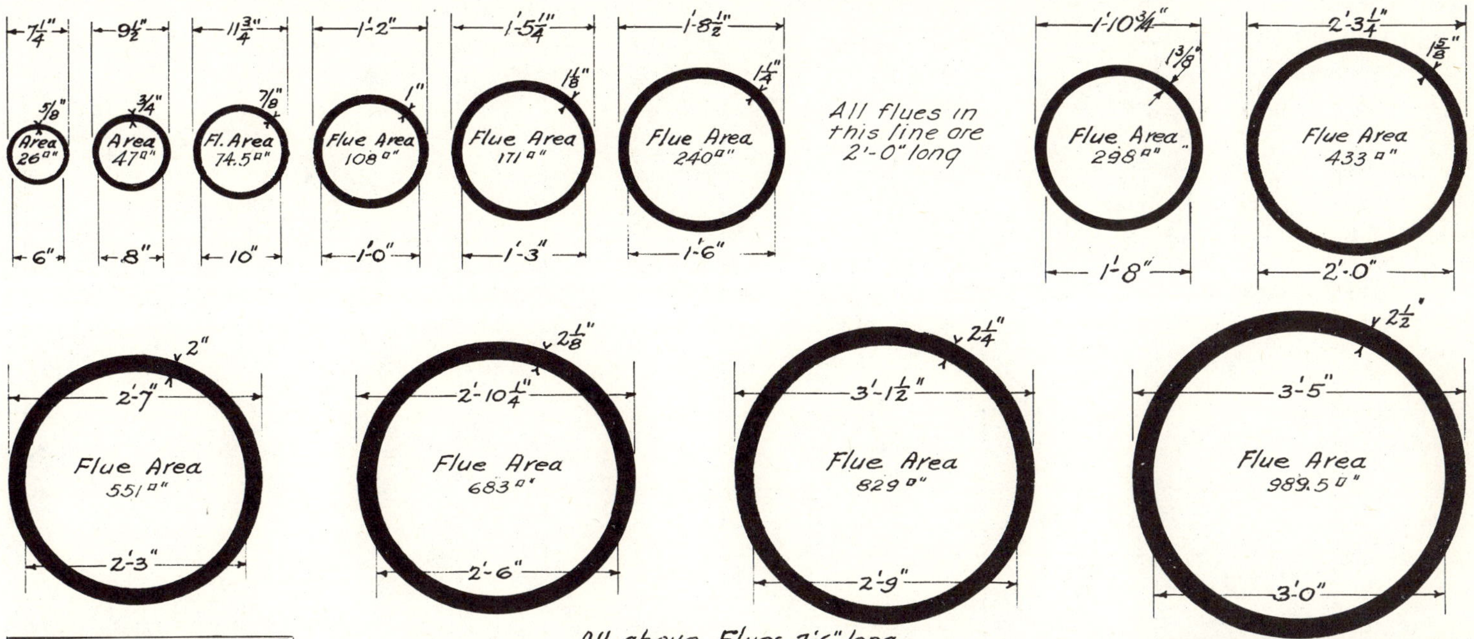
7¼"
⅝"
Area 26□"
6"
9½"
¾"
Area 47□"
8"
11¾"
⅞"
Fl. Area 74.5□"
10"
1'-2"
1"
Flue Area 108□"
1'-0"
1'-5¼"
1⅛"
Flue Area 171□"
1'-3"
1'-8½"
1¼"
Flue Area 240□"
1'-6"
All flues in this line are 2'-0" long
1'-10¾"
1⅜"
Flue Area 298□"
1'-8"
2'-3¼"
1⅝"
Flue Area 433□"
2'-0"
2"
2'-7"
Flue Area 551□"
2'-3"
2⅛"
2'-10¼"
Flue Area 683□"
2'-6"
2¼"
3'-1½"
Flue Area 829□"
2'-9"
2½"
3'-5"
Flue Area 989.5□"
3'-0"

All above Flues 2'-6" long

NOTE: All flue areas on this page are MINIMUM NET inside areas

ROUND FLUE LININGS

Nominal Flue Sizes for Round Flues is interior diameter

SPECIFY: inside diameters for round flues, outside dimensions for square or rectangular flues.

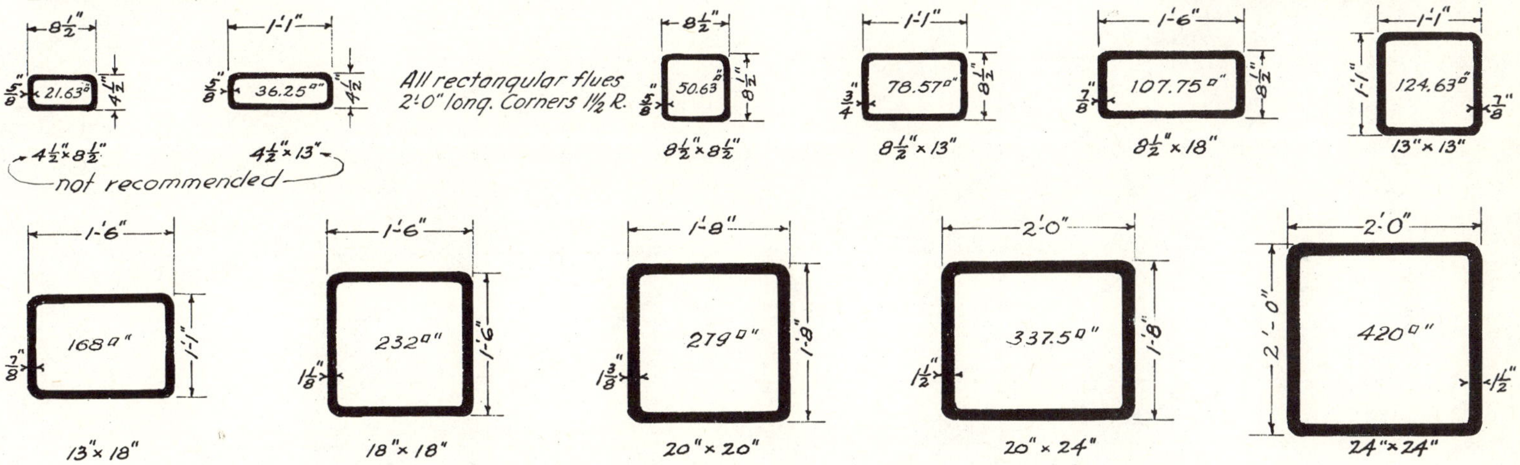
8½"
⅝"
21.63□"
4½"
4½"×8½"
1'-1"
⅝"
36.25□"
4½"
4½"×13"
not recommended
All rectangular flues 2'-0" long. Corners 1½ R.
8½"
⅝"
50.63□"
8½"
8½"×8½"
1'-1"
¾"
78.57□"
8½"
8½"×13"
1'-6"
⅞"
107.75□"
8½"
8½"×18"
1'-1"
1'-1"
124.63□"
⅞"
13"×13"
1'-6"
⅞"
168□"
1'-1"
13"×18"
1'-6"
1⅛"
232□"
1'-6"
18"×18"
1'-8"
1⅜"
279□"
1'-8"
20"×20"
2'-0"
1½"
337.5□"
1'-8"
20"×24"
2'-0"
2'-0"
420□"
1½"
24"×24"

RECTANGULAR FLUE LININGS

Nominal Flue size for Rectangular Flues is Exterior Dimension -- Interior Areas only are shown.

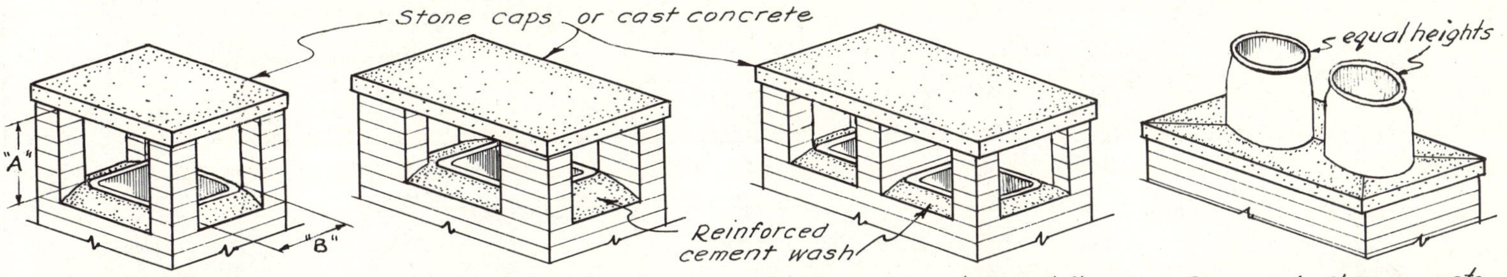
Stone caps or cast concrete
equal heights
"A"
"B"
Reinforced cement wash

Chimney hoods to prevent downdraft due to adjoining hills, buildings, trees, etc.

Water protection for seldom used flue.

Best method: Withe bet. flues

Cheapest: Chimney pots.

METHODS of PREVENTING SMOKE from ONE FLUE GOING DOWN an UNUSED FLUE

Open two sides of chimney hood must be larger than flue area.
"A" should be ¼ greater than "B" on all hooded chimneys.

CHIMNEY HOODS & POTS

Fireplace Flue Sizes:- 1/10 Area of Fireplace opening recommended. Absolute minimum size:- 1/12 area of Fireplace opening. Flues should never be less than 70□" for fireplace of 840□" opening or smaller.
Flues for Stoves and Ranges and Room Heaters:- 39 Sq. In. minimum using Rectangular flue, or 6" dia. (inside) using Round Flue.
Flues for Gas Furnaces, Boilers and Automatic Water Heaters to be same size as for Coal.
Vents for other Gas fired equipment may be smaller, but should never be less than 10 square inches.

Data checked by: Frederic N. Whitley, P.E., Consulting Fireplace Engineer.

MODULAR FLUE SIZES for FIREPLACES

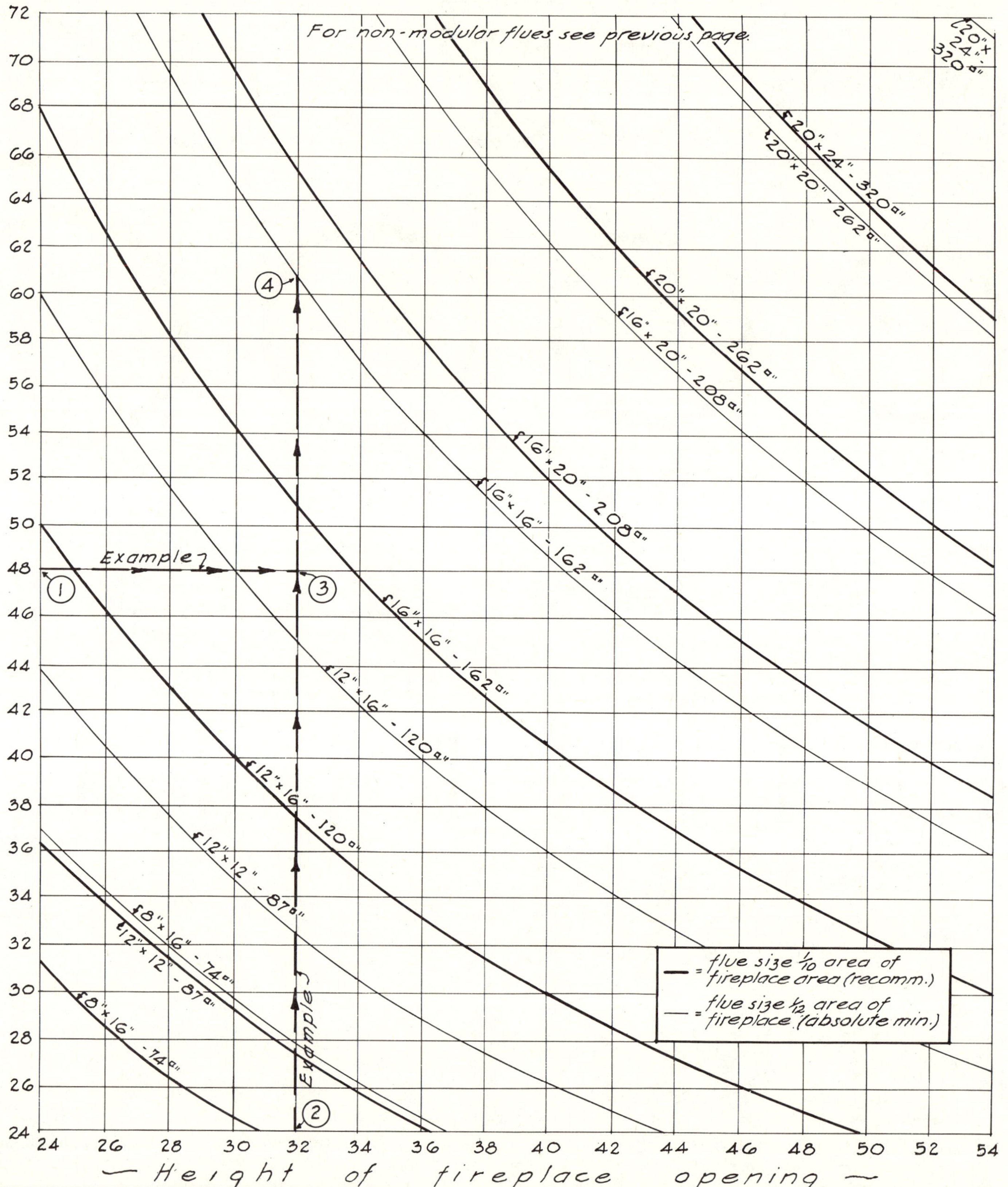
For non-modular flues see previous page.
— Width of fireplace opening —
— Height of fireplace opening —
72
70
68
66
64
62
60
58
56
54
52
50
48
46
44
42
40
38
36
34
32
30
28
26
24
24 26 28 30 32 34 36 38 40 42 44 46 48 50 52 54
Example
Example
1
2
3
4
20"×24"-320□"
20"×20"-262□"
16"×20"-208□"
16"×16"-162□"
12"×16"-120□"
12"×12"-87□"
8"×16"-74□"
= flue size 1/10 area of fireplace area (recomm.)
= flue size 1/12 area of fireplace (absolute min.)

Problem : Find proper modular flue size (@ 1/12 fireplace area) for fireplace 48" wide and 32" high.

Solution : ① Find 48" fireplace width at left of chart.
② Find 32" fireplace height at bottom of chart.
③ Follow width line across and height line up until they intersect.
④ Proper flue size will be nearest curve indicating 1/12 fireplace area above intersection (16"×16").

Modular flues only made in rectangular sizes. If round flue is desired for modular chimney, use non-modular round flue.

Chart based on net flue areas. If flue is less than 20' high it is advisable to use next larger flue size unless the intersection ③ falls well below the fireplace area curve.

Data checked by: Wm Demarest, Sec'y for Modular Coordination, American Institute of Architects.

FLUES and CHIMNEYS

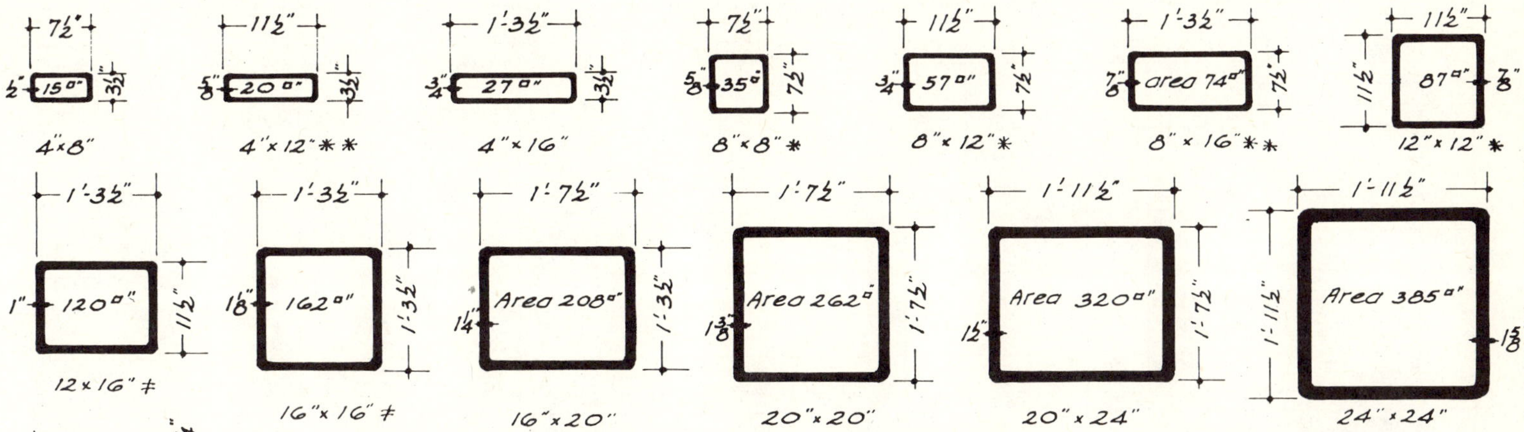
7½"
15□"
3½"
4"x8"
11½"
20□"
4"x12" **
1'-3½"
27□"
4"x16"
35□"
8"x8" *
57□"
8"x12" *
area 74□"
8"x16" **
87□"
12"x12" *
1'-3½"
120□"
12x16" #
162□"
16"x16" #
1'-7½"
Area 208□"
16"x20"
Area 262□"
20"x20"
1'-11½"
Area 320□"
20"x24"
Area 385□"
24"x24"

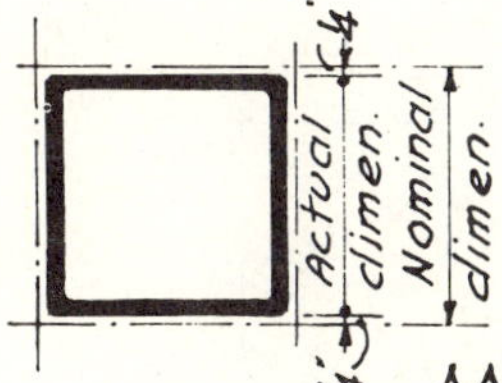
Actual dimen.
Nominal dimen.

Dimensions shown above are actual dimensions of flues. Sizes under diagrams are nominal dimensions. (See diag. at left). Areas shown are min. net inside areas. Wall thicknesses shown are min. req'd. Outside corner radius shall be no more than one-fourth the smallest distance between outside of walls. Modular rectangular flues are 2'-0" long. For proper flue size for fireplaces see page titled: "Modular Flue Sizes for Fireplaces." * Widely available. ** Available in the Southwest. # Available in Ohio and Southwest.

MODULAR RECTANGULAR FLUE LININGS

Data checked by: Wm. Demarest, Sec'y for Modular Coordination, American Institute of Architects

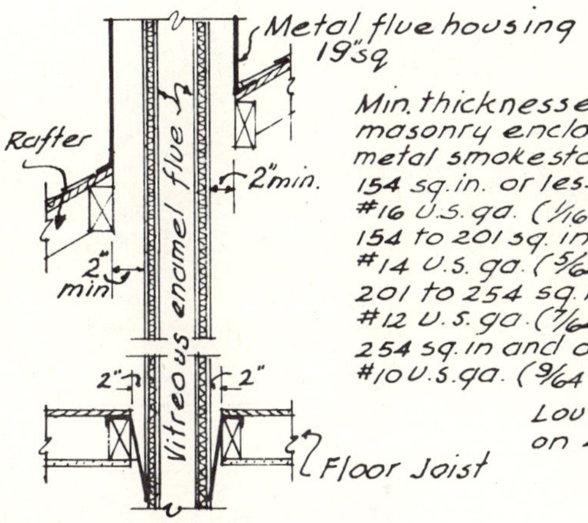
Metal flue housing 19"sq.
Rafter
2" min.
2" min
Vitreous enamel flue
2"
2"
Floor Joist

Min. thicknesses for masonry enclosed metal smokestack:
154 sq. in. or less #16 U.S. ga. (1/16");
154 to 201 sq. in #14 U.S. ga. (5/64"+);
201 to 254 sq. in. #12 U.S. ga. (7/64"-);
254 sq. in and over #10 U.S. ga. (9/64"-).

PREFABRICATED "VITROLINER" FLUE

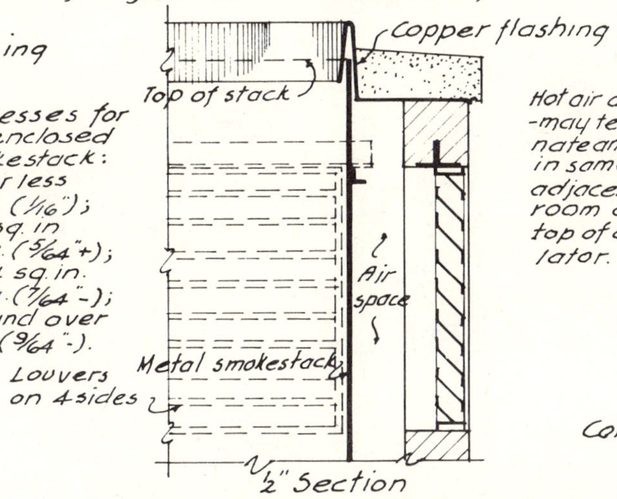
Copper flashing
Top of stack
Air space
Metal smokestack
Louvers on 4 sides
½" Section

TOP of METAL SMOKESTACK with BRICK SURROUNDS

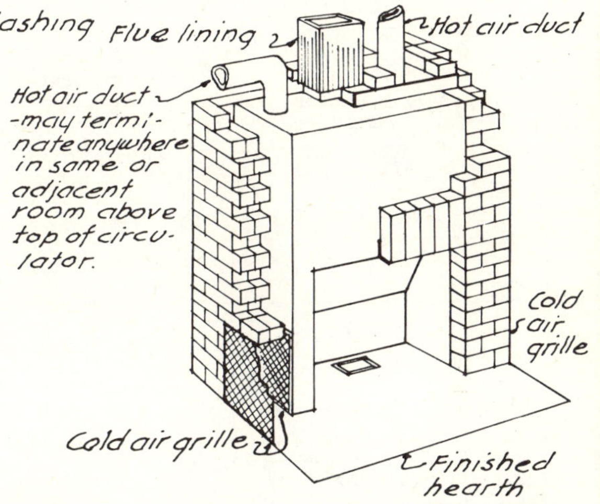
Flue lining
Hot air duct
Hot air duct -may terminate anywhere in same or adjacent room above top of circulator.
Cold air grille
Cold air grille
Finished hearth

HEAT CIRCULATOR within FIREPLACE

Drawings below apply to reinforced conc., as well as to solid masonry.

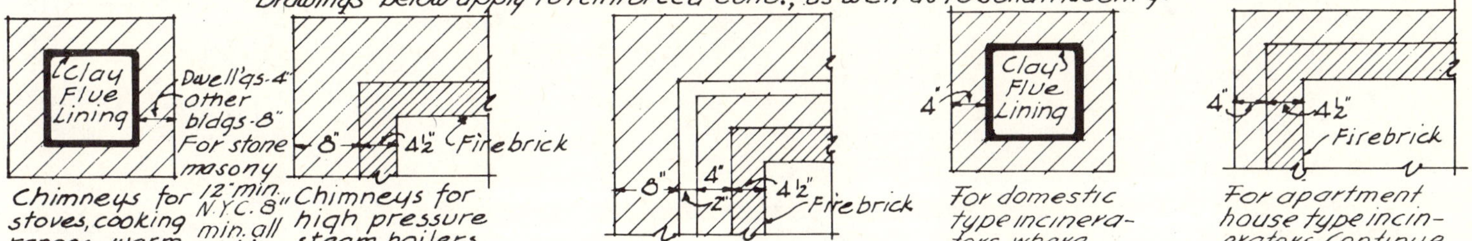
Clay Flue Lining
Dwell'gs-4" other bldgs-8" For stone masonry 12" min. N.Y.C. 8" min. all buildings incl. residences
8"
4½"
Firebrick
8"
4"
2"
4½"
Firebrick
4"
Clay Flue Lining
4"
4½"
Firebrick

Chimneys for stoves, cooking ranges, warm air, hot water & low pressure steam heating furnaces, low heat industrial appliances, portable type incinerators, fireplaces.

LOW HEAT APPLIANCES

Chimneys for high pressure steam boilers, smoke houses, and other medium heat appliances other than incinerators. Continue fire-brick up 25' min. N.Y.C. firebrick up 50' min.

MEDIUM HEAT APPLIANCES

Chimneys for cupolas, brass furnaces, porcelain baking kilns, and other high heat appliances.

HIGH HEAT APPLIANCES

For domestic type incinerators where fire box or charging compartment is not larger than 5 cubic feet

For apartment house type incinerators. Continue fire brick up 10' above roof of combustion chamber for grate area 7□' or less; 40' above for grate area exceeding 7□'

For residence bldgs., institutional bldgs., churches, schools & restaurants.

CHIMNEYS for INCINERATORS

MINIMUM CHIMNEY REQUIREMENTS

Recommendations of the National Board of Fire Underwriters

DAMPERS

DAMPER SIZES								FINSHED FIREPLACE OPENG							ROUGH BRICKWORK							
Control		Throat			Overall			Width	Height	Depth	Back	Vert. Back	Slope Back	Throat	Width	Depth	Smoke chamb	Flue Lining Sizes				
Poker	Rotary	Bot.																Rectangular		Round	Modular	
No.	No.	T	A	O	L	B	W	A	B	C	D	E	F	G	H	I	J	K	L M	Ø	K	L M
224	324	24	17 5/16	4 1/4	28 1/2	21	9 7/8	24	24	16	11	14	15	8 3/4	32	20	19	11 3/4	8 1/2 × 8 1/2	8	10	8 × 12
230	330	30	23 5/16	4 1/4	34 1/2	27	9 7/8	26 28 30	24 24 29	16 16 16	13 15 17	14 14 14	15 15 18	8 3/4 8 3/4 8 3/4	34 36 38	20 20 20	21 21 24	12 3/4 11 1/2 12 1/2	8 1/2 × 8 1/2 8 1/2 × 13 8 1/2 × 13	8 10 10	11 12 13	8 × 12 8 × 12 12 × 12
233	333	33	26 5/16	4 1/4	37 1/2	30	9 7/8	32	29	16	19	14	21	8 3/4	40	20	24	13 1/2	8 1/2 × 13	10	14	12 × 12
236	336	36	29 5/16	4 1/4	40 1/2	33	9 7/8	36	29	16	23	14	21	8 3/4	44	20	27	15 1/2	13 × 13	12	76	12 × 12
242	342	42	35 5/16	4 1/4	46 1/2	39	9 7/8	40 42	29 32	16 16	27 29	14 14	21 23	8 3/4 8 3/4	48 50	20 20	29 32	17 1/2 18 1/2	13 × 13 13 × 13	12 12	16 17	12 × 16 16 × 16
248	348	48	41 5/16	4 1/4	52 1/2	45	9 7/8	48	32	18	33	14	23	8 3/4	56	22	37	21 1/2	13 × 13	15	20	16 × 16
254	—	54	42 1/2	7	58 1/2	46	14 5/8	54	37	20	37	16	27	13	68	24	45	25	13 × 18	15	26	16 × 16
260	—	60	49 1/2	7	64 1/2	53	14 5/8	60 60	37 40	22 22	42 42	16 16	27 29	13 13	72 72	27 27	45 45	27 27	13 × 18 18 × 18	15 18	26 26	16 × 20 16 × 20
272	—	72	60 1/2	7	76 1/2	64	14 5/8	72	40	22	54	16	29	13	84	27	56	33	18 × 18	18	32	20 × 20
*284	*384	84	73 1/2	7	88 1/2	77	14 5/8	84	40	24	64	20	26	13	96	29	67	36	20 × 20	20	36	20 × 24
*296	*396	96	85 3/4	7	100 1/2	89	14 5/8	96	40	24	76	20	26	13	108	29	75	42	24 × 24	22	42	20 × 24

* Two valve plates.

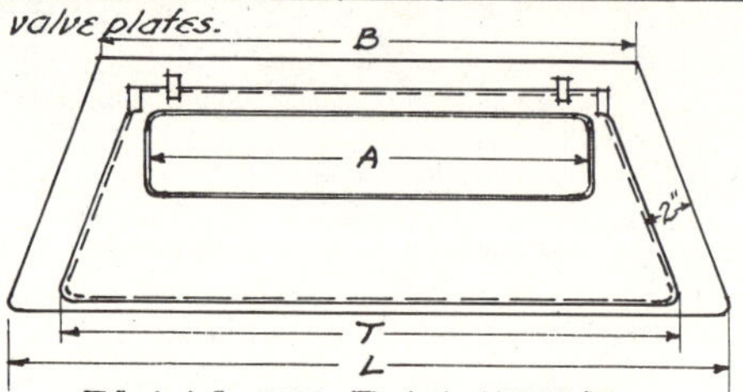
B
A
2"
T
L

PLAN OF DAMPER

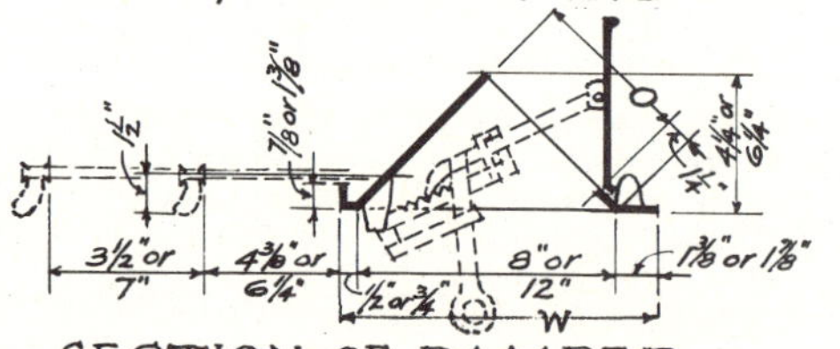
3 1/2" or 7"
4 3/4" or 6 1/4"
8" or 12"
1 1/8" or 1 7/8"
W

SECTION OF DAMPER

Where two dimensions are shown the smaller applies to Dampers 248-348 and under, the larger to 254-354 & over. Both operating devices are shown.

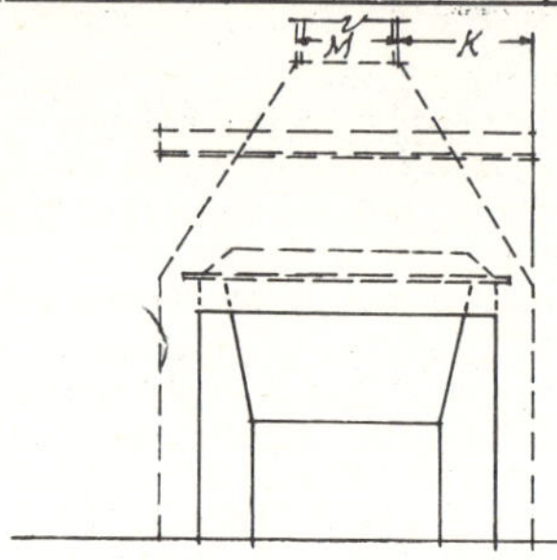
M
K

ELEVATION

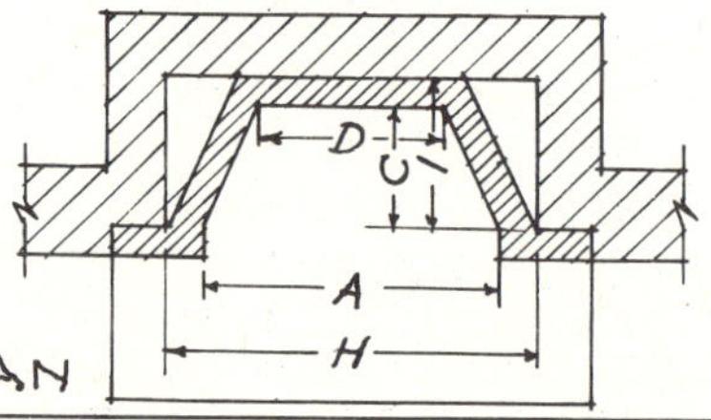
D
C
I
A
H

PLAN

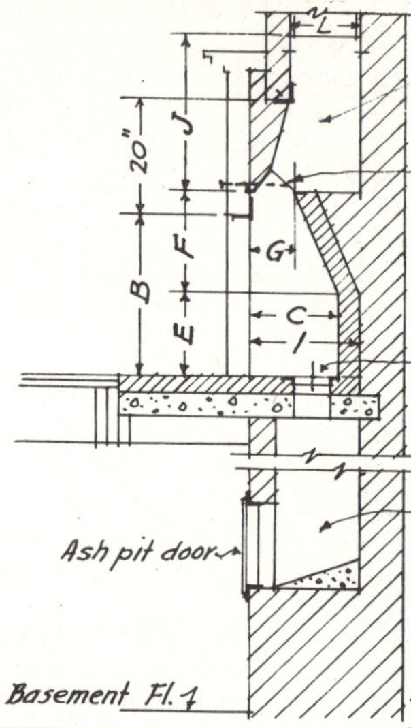
L
J
20"
Smoke Chamber
Damper
F
G
B
C
E
I
Ash dump
Ash pit
Ash pit door
Basement Fl.

SECTION

DONLEY THROAT and DAMPER

Size No.	L	WD	D	F	H	B	P	O	C	K	E	Rect. Flue Lining. outside	Round Flue Lining. Inside
24 *	26 1/2"	24"	13"	10 1/2"	4 1/2	21 1/2"	20"	17"	2"	4 1/4"	2 3/4"	8 1/2" × 8 1/2"	8"
30 *	32 1/2"	30"	"	"	"	27 1/2"	26"	23"	"	"	"	8 1/2" × 13"	10"
36 *	38 1/2"	36"	"	"	"	33 1/2"	32"	29"	"	"	"	13" × 13"	12"
42 *	44 1/2"	42"	"	"	"	39 1/2"	38"	35"	"	"	"	13" × 13"	12"
48 *	50 1/2"	48"	"	"	"	45 1/2	44"	41"	"	"	"	13" × 18"	15"

SPECIFICATIONS OF SUTTON DOME DAMPERS

Select damper in which WD = Fireplace opening. If Fireplace opening is between two WD sizes always select WD that is next larger. Example: Fireplace width = 40", use No. 42 damper.

* The letter W used after size no. is used to indicate Worm Gear Control.
The letter L used after size no. is used to indicate Long Ratchet Control.
The letter S used after size no. is used to indicate Short Ratchet Control.

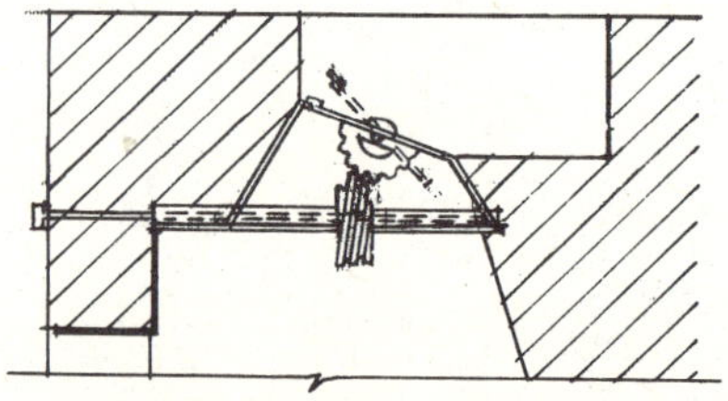

WORM GEAR CONTROL

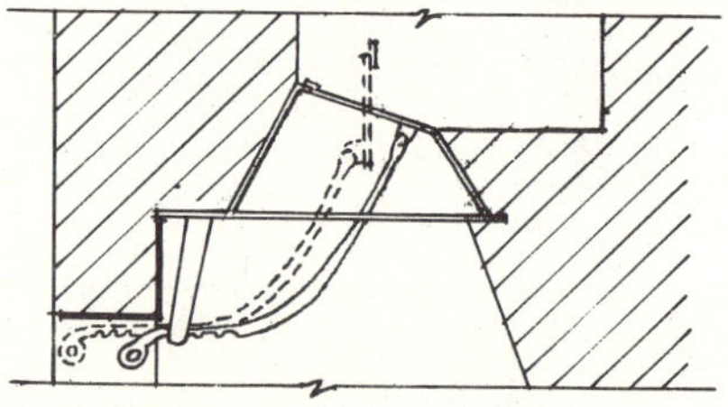

LONG RATCHET (POKER) CONTROL

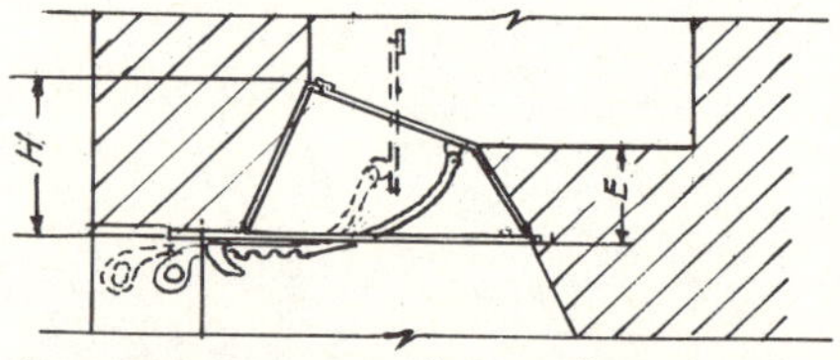
H
E

SHORT RATCHET (POKER) CONTROL

"SUTTON" DOME DAMPERS

PLAN OF DAMPER

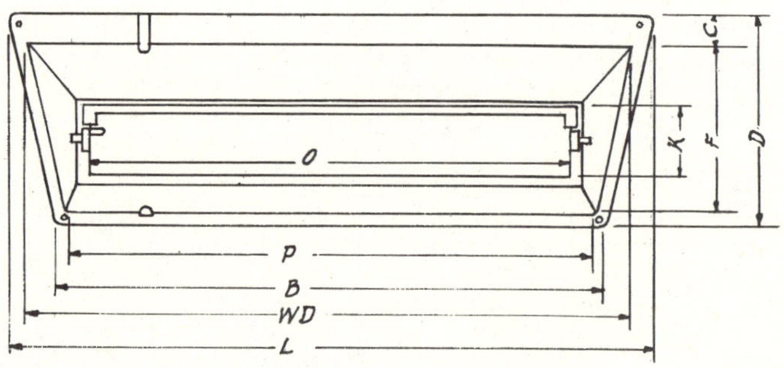
C
K
F
D
O
P
B
WD
L

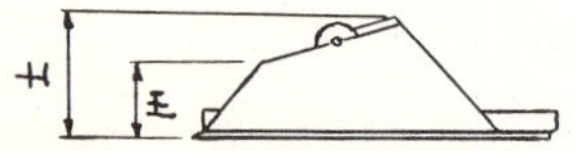
H
E

END ELEVATION

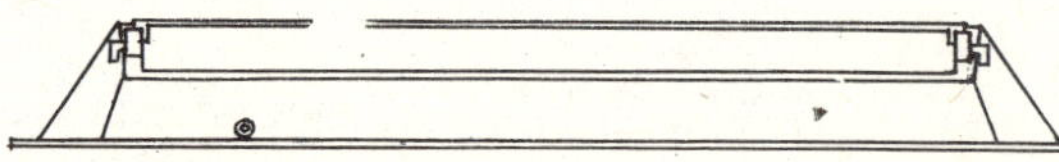

REAR ELEVATION

SUTTON THROAT and DAMPER

DAMPERS

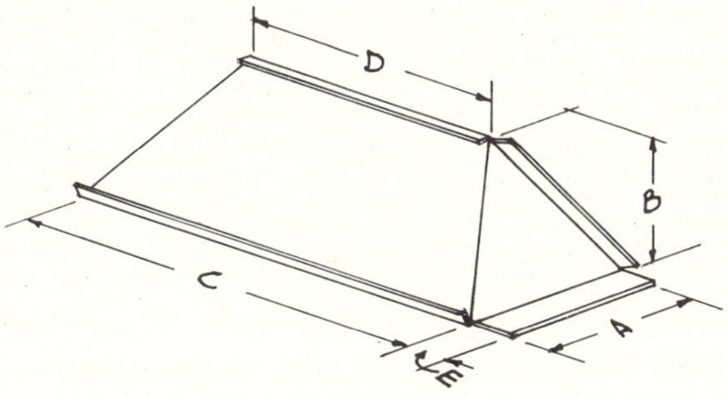
D
B
C
A
E

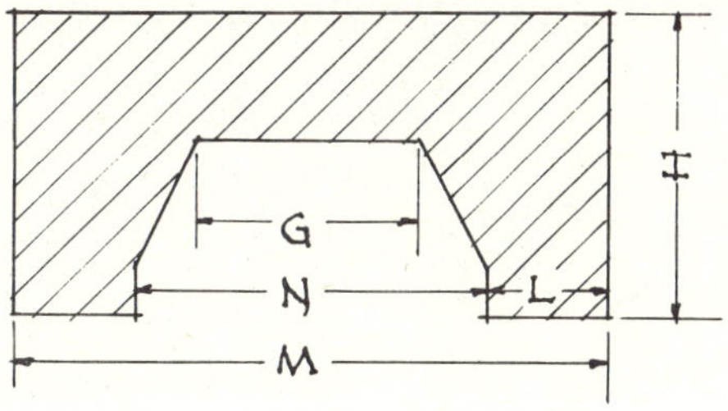
G
N
L
M
H

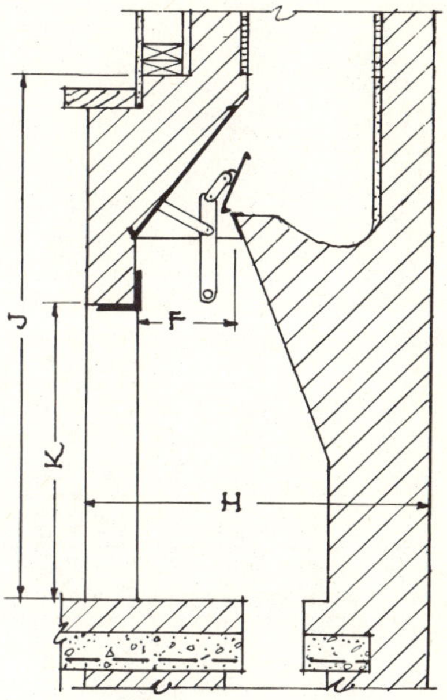
J
F
K
H

No.	A	B	C	D	E	F	G	H	J	K	L	M	N
30	10	12	29	16	2½	10¼	20 to 22	30 to 34	54	27 to 30	12½ to 16½	53 to 65	28 to 32
36	10	12	35	22	2½	10¼	26 to 28	30 to 34	54	27 to 30	12½ to 16½	58 to 70	33 to 37
42	10	12	41	28	2½	10¼	32 to 34	34 to 38	57	30 to 33	16½ to 20½	75 to 84	39 to 43
48	10	12	47	34	2½	10¼	38 to 40	38 to 42	63	33 to 39	20½ to 25	82 to 89	46 to 51
54	15	18	53	40	2½	10¼	44 to 46	42 to 48	69	39 to 45	25 to 29	95 to 104	52 to 56
60	15	18	59	46	2½	10¼	50 to 52	48 to 56	78	48 to 54	29 to 42	102 to 120	58 to 62

Dimensions given in table & diagrams are in inches.

SECTION

"SUPERIOR" FORM DAMPER

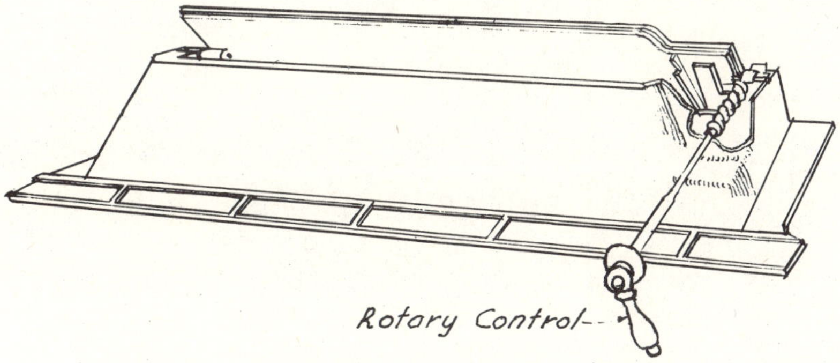
Rotary Control

MADE IN POKER, ROTARY & CHAIN CONTROL

Number	Fireplace Width	Overall Length	Overall Depth	Crated Weight
B 24	24"	28¼"	13⅝"	32#
B 30	30"	34⅜"	13⅝"	38#
B 33	33"	37¼"	13⅝"	40#
B 36	36"	40½"	13⅝"	47#
B 42	42"	46½"	13⅝"	53#
B 48	48"	52½"	13⅝"	59#
B 54	54"	59¼"	15½"	76#
B 60	60"	64½"	16⅜"	100#

SCHEDULE OF SIZES

PEERLESS THROATS and DAMPERS

Damper No.	24A26	28A30		32A34		36A38		40A42		44A46		48A50		52A54		58A60	
A, in.	28¼	32¼		36¼		40¼		44¼		48¼		52¼		56¼		62¼	
B, in.	26¾	30¾		34¾		38¾		42¾		46¾		50¾		54¾		60¾	
C, in.	24	28		32		36		40		44		48		52		58	
Finished Opening: Width, in.	26	28	30	32	34	36	38	40	42	44	46	48	50	52	54	58	60
Height, in.	28	28	30	30	30	31	31	31	31	32	32	32	34	34	34	36	36
Firebox depth, in.	16	16	16	16	16	18	18	18	18	18	18	20	20	20	20	22	22
Flue size, in.	8½ × 13	8½ × 13		13 × 13								13 × 18				18 × 18	

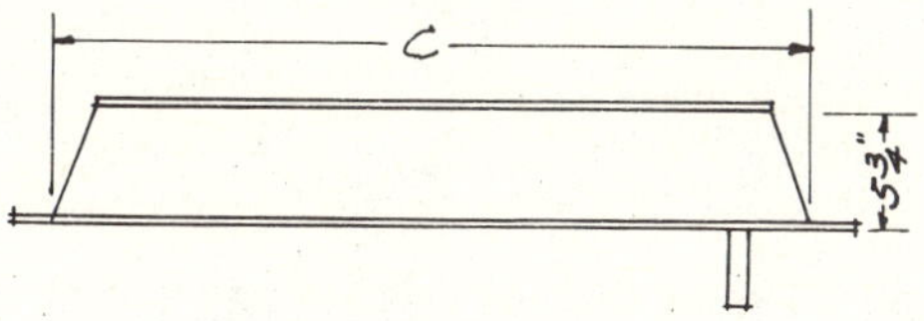
C
5¾"

ELEVATION

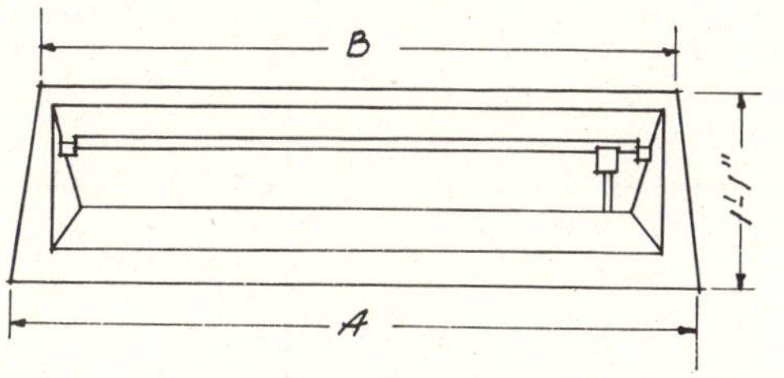
B
11"
A

PLAN

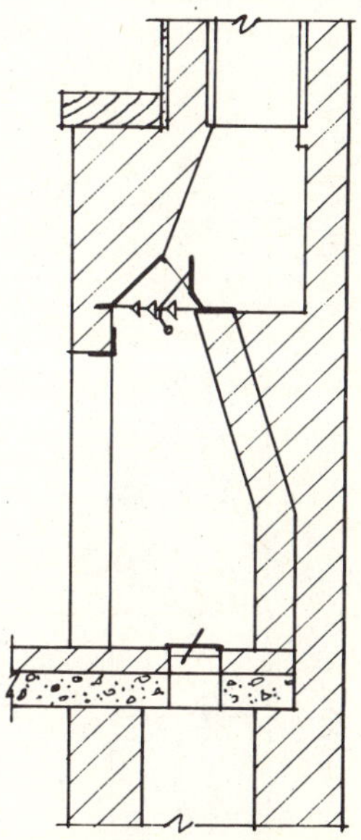

SECTION

MAJESTIC THROATS and DAMPERS

DAMPERS

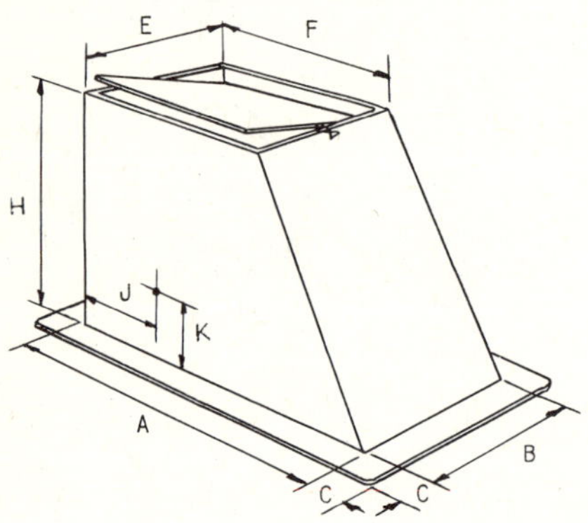
E
F
H
J
K
A
B
C
C

RATED SIZE A x B	FLUE OUTLET E x F	HEIGHT H	ROTARY J	HANDLE K
26 x 26	18 x 18	17	8	5
30 x 16	13 x 18	17	8	9
34 x 20	18 x 18	17	8	9
38 x 20	18 x 18	25	8	11
42 x 20	18 x 24	25	8	11
50 x 24	20 x 24	28	8	15

Lintel width "C" is 3" width on all sides.
Handle location can be reversed to opposite side of damper.
NOTE: Keep masonry ½" from metal.

UNIVERSAL "BENEFORM" DAMPER DIMENSIONS

HEARTH SIZES & MAXIMUM OPENING HEIGHTS

TYPE	DAMPER A x B	HEARTH SIZE Width x Depth	Max. Height of Opening Using Flue Tile Size					
			8½ x 13	13 x 13	13 x 18	18 x 18	20 x 24	24 x 24
CONVENTIONAL (ONE OPENING)	26 x 26	26 x 30	36	46	56	--	--	--
	30 x 16	30 x 20	32	42	52	--	--	--
	34 x 20	34 x 24	30	38	48	--	--	--
	38 x 20	38 x 24	28	36	46	56	--	--
	42 x 20	42 x 24	26	34	44	54	--	--
	50 x 24	50 x 28	22	30	38	56	--	--
OPEN FRONT AND SIDE (PROJECTING CORNER)	26 x 26	30 x 30	--	28	36	46	56	--
	30 x 16	34 x 20	--	30	38	48	--	--
	34 x 20	38 x 24	--	26	34	44	54	--
	38 x 20	42 x 24	--	24	34	42	48	--
	42 x 20	46 x 24	--	24	32	40	48	--
	50 x 24	54 x 28	--	20	28	36	44	--
OPEN FRONT AND BACK	26 x 26	---	--	28	36	44	--	--
	30 x 16	30 x 24	--	24	32	42	--	--
	34 x 20	34 x 28	--	22	30	38	46	--
	38 x 20	38 x 28	--	20	28	36	42	--
	42 x 20	42 x 28	--	--	26	34	40	48
	50 x 24	50 x 32	--	--	22	30	36	42
OPEN THREE SIDES (2 SHORT, 1 LONG)	26 x 26	34 x 30	--	20	26	34	37	--
	30 x 16	38 x 20	--	22	30	38	--	--
	34 x 20	42 x 24	--	20	27	35	41	--
	38 x 20	46 x 24	--	--	25	33	39	--
	42 x 20	50 x 24	--	--	24	32	38	44
	50 x 24	58 x 24	--	--	21	28	34	40
	NOTE: This table is for a fireplace which projects fully into the room. If fireplace is half recessed, use table for fireplace open front and side (projecting corner).							
OPEN THREE SIDES (2 LONG, 1 SHORT)	26 x 26	30 x 34	--	21	27	35	38	--
	30 x 16	34 x 24	--	20	26	34	--	--
	34 x 20	38 x 28	--	--	22	30	36	--
	38 x 20	42 x 28	--	--	--	29	35	--
	42 x 20	46 x 28	--	--	--	28	34	40
	50 x 24	58 x 32	--	--	--	24	30	36
OPEN ALL SIDES	26 x 26	34 x 34	--	--	20	28	32	--
	30 x 16	38 x 24	--	--	22	30	--	--
	34 x 20	42 x 28	--	--	20	28	32	--
	38 x 20	46 x 28	--	--	--	26	31	--
	42 x 20	50 x 28	--	--	--	24	30	35
	50 x 24	58 x 32	--	--	--	21	27	32
	Use 26" x 26" damper size for round or square hearths, others for rectangular.							

NOTE: Opening heights are based on a chimney height (measured from hearth level) of 20 feet. For 18' chimneys, reduce given height by 1"; for 16', 2"; for 14', 4". Hearth sizes are based on a 4" thick facing. Do not exceed 6" facing thickness.

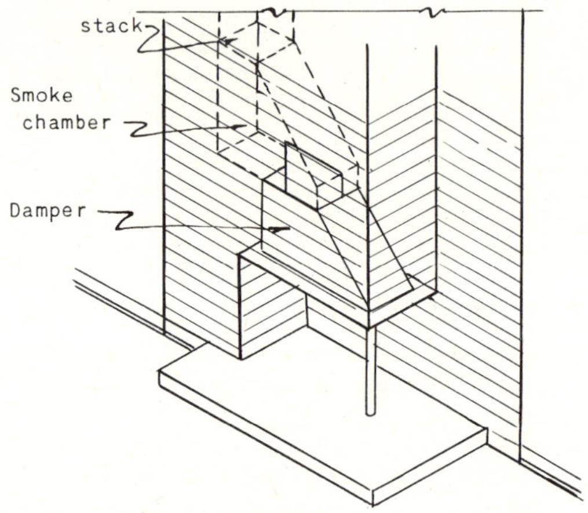
stack
Smoke chamber
Damper

UNIVERSAL DAMPER IN PLACE

SHOWING SMOKE CHAMBER ABOVE IT. LEADING TO STACK.

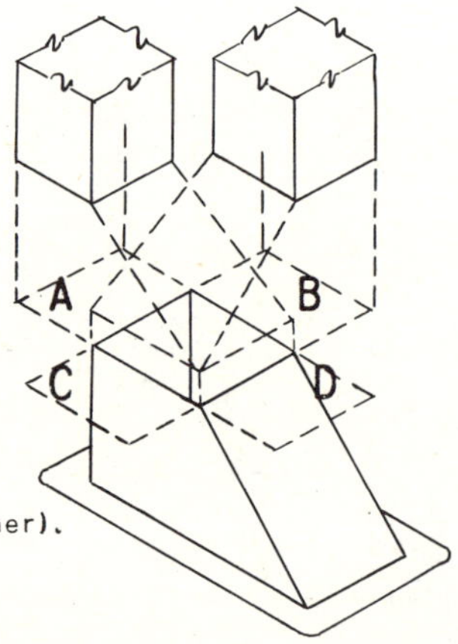
A
B
C
D

Use of smoke chamber with variable position allows flue stack to be offset without slanting or turning the flue. Four possible positions (A, B, C, D) are shown above. By reversing the damper there are four more positions available. NOTE: flue tile must never be set directly above damper outlet.

ALTERNATE FLUE LOCATIONS

All dimensions given on this page are in inches.

Data approved by Bennett-Ireland, Inc. Norwich, New York.

FIREPLACES

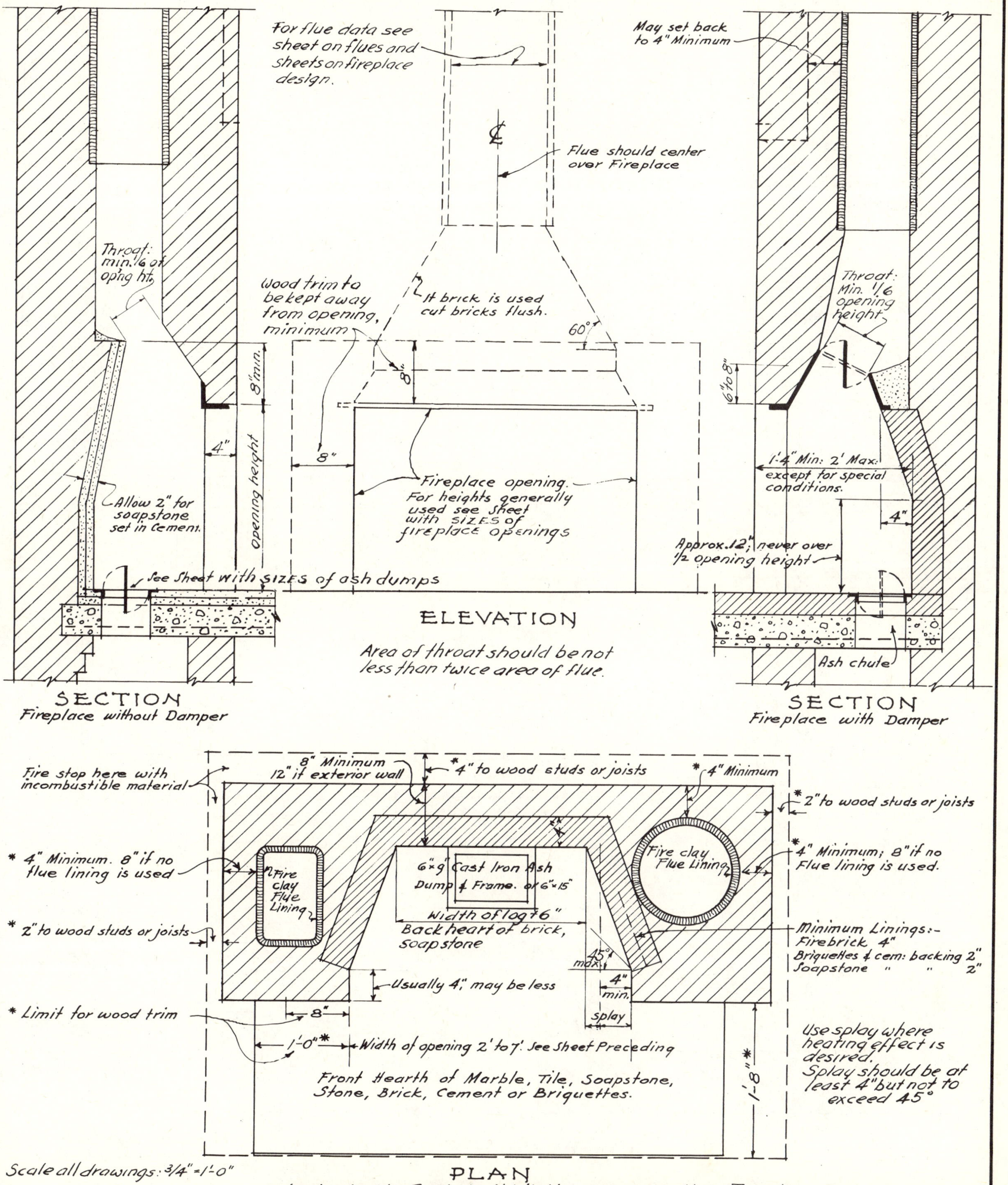
For flue data see sheet on flues and sheets on fireplace design.
Flue should center over Fireplace
May set back to 4" Minimum
Throat: min. 1/6 of opng ht.
Wood trim to be kept away from opening, minimum
If brick is used cut bricks flush.
60°
8"
8" min.
4"
opening height
Allow 2" for soapstone set in Cement.
See Sheet with SIZES of ash dumps
Fireplace opening. For heights generally used see Sheet with SIZES of fireplace openings
Throat: Min. 1/6 opening height
6" to 8"
1'-4" Min: 2' Max: except for special conditions.
Approx. 12", never over 1/2 opening height
Ash chute
ELEVATION
Area of throat should be not less than twice area of flue.
SECTION
Fireplace without Damper
SECTION
Fireplace with Damper
Fire stop here with incombustible material
8" Minimum
12" if exterior wall
* 4" to wood studs or joists
* 4" Minimum
* 2" to wood studs or joists
* 4" Minimum. 8" if no flue lining is used
Fire clay Flue Lining
6"x9" Cast Iron Ash Dump & Frame. or 6"x15"
Fire clay Flue Lining
* 4" Minimum; 8" if no Flue lining is used.
Width of log + 6"
Back heart of brick, soapstone
* 2" to wood studs or joists
Minimum Linings:-
Firebrick 4"
Briquettes & cem: backing 2"
Soapstone " " 2"
45° max.
4" min.
Usually 4", may be less
* Limit for wood trim
8"
splay
1'-0"*
Width of opening 2' to 7'. See Sheet Preceding
1'-8"*
Use splay where heating effect is desired.
Splay should be at least 4" but not to exceed 45°
Front Hearth of Marble, Tile, Soapstone, Stone, Brick, Cement or Briquettes.
Scale all drawings: 3/4" = 1'-0"
PLAN

Data checked by Frederic N. Whitley, P.E., consulting Fireplace Engineer

* National Board of Fire Underwriters recommendation

FIREPLACES

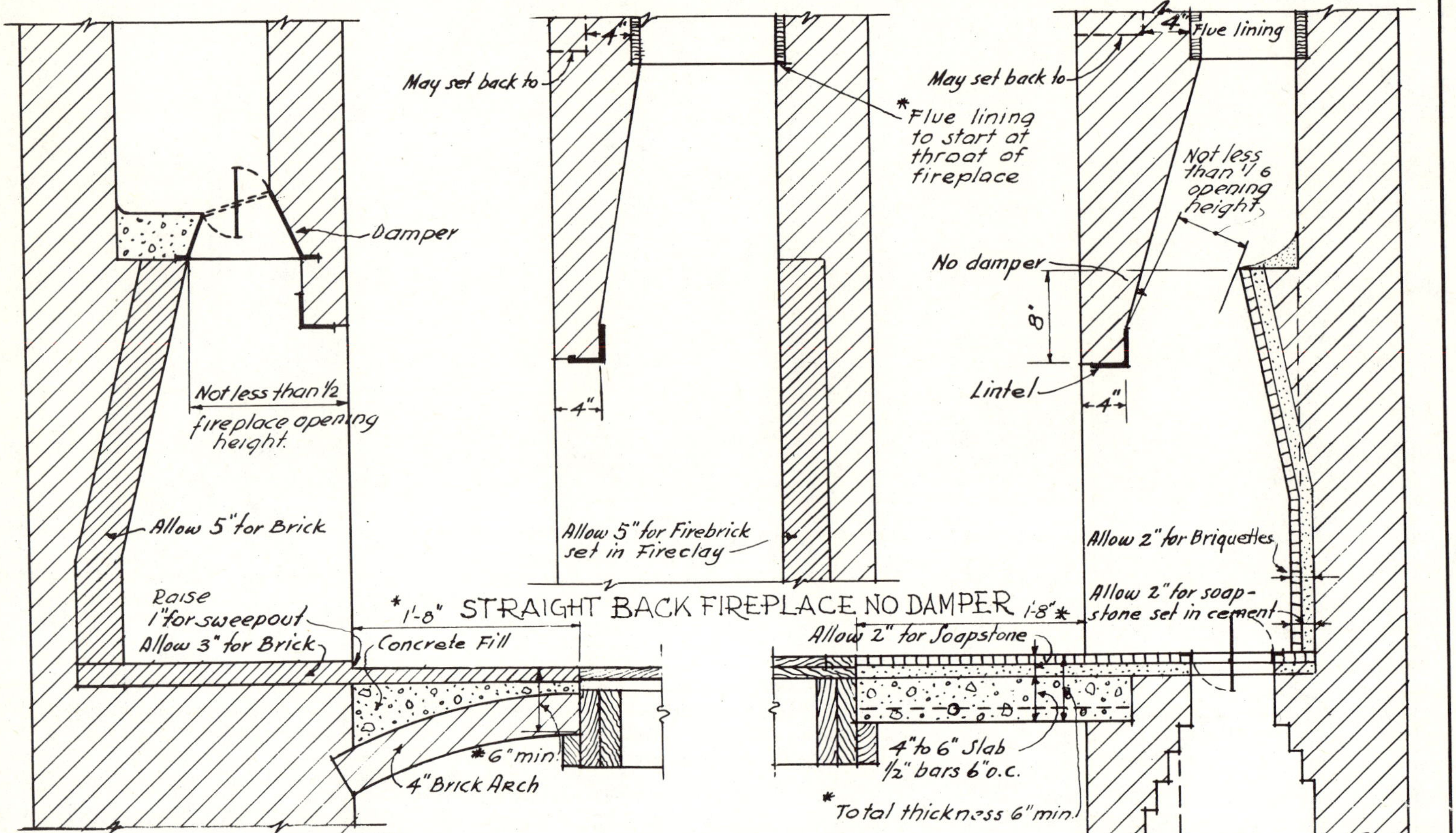
May set back to
4"
May set back to
4"
Flue lining
*Flue lining to start at throat of fireplace
Not less than 1/6 opening height
Damper
No damper
8"
Lintel
4"
4"
Not less than 1/2 fireplace opening height.
Allow 5" for Brick
Allow 5" for Firebrick set in Fireclay
Allow 2" for Briquettes
Allow 2" for soap-stone set in cement
Raise 1" for sweepout
Allow 3" for Brick
1'-8" STRAIGHT BACK FIREPLACE NO DAMPER 1'-8"
Concrete Fill
Allow 2" for Soapstone
*6" min.
4" Brick Arch
4" to 6" Slab
1/2" bars 6" o.c.
*Total thickness 6" min.

FIREPLACE *with* DAMPER
Placed high - Brick Trimmer Arch.

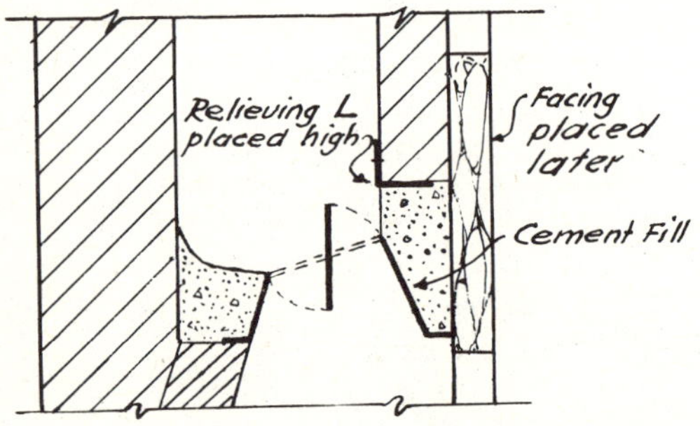
Relieving L placed high
Facing placed later
Cement Fill

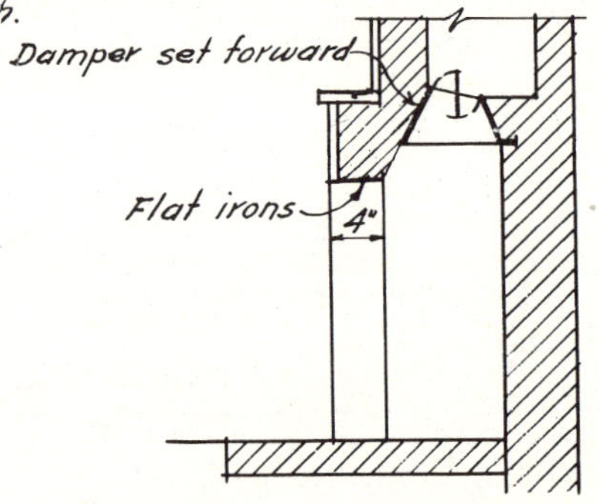
Damper set forward
Flat irons
4"

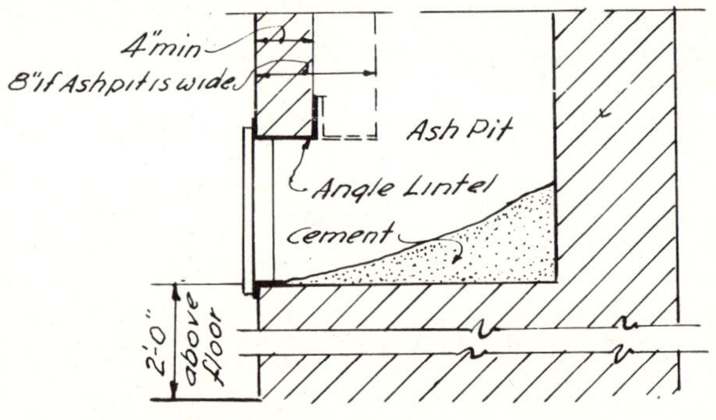
4" min
8" if Ashpit is wide
Ash Pit
Angle Lintel
Cement
2'-0" above floor

WHEN ROUGH
WORK FINISHED FIRST
Angle supports rough work - Damper and Fireplace finished later

PROJECTING MANTEL
Scale: 3/8" = 1'-0"

FIREPLACE *without* DAMPER
SLAB TRIMMER ARCH, ASH PIT

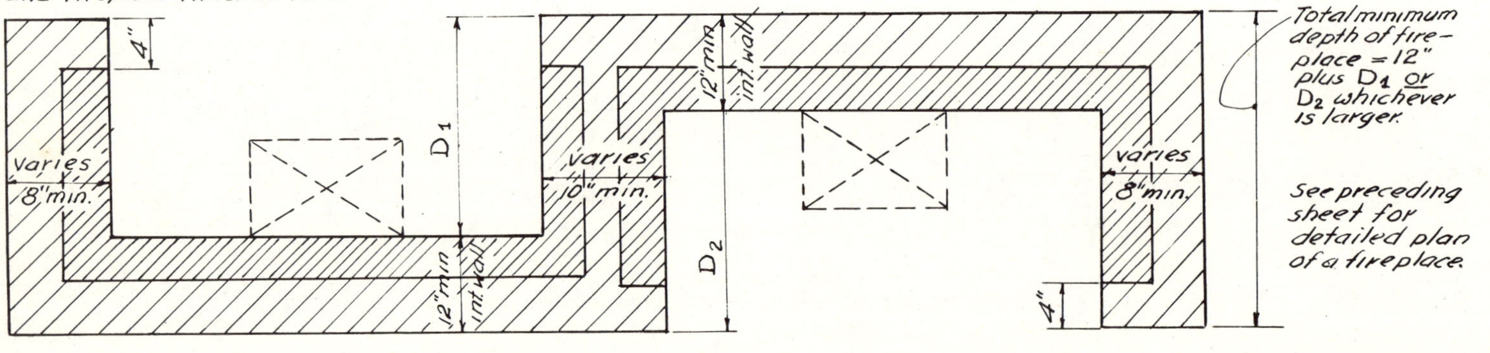
4"
D1
12" min
int. wall
varies
8" min.
varies
10" min.
varies
8" min.
D2
12" min
int. wall
4"
Total minimum depth of fire-place = 12" plus D1 or D2 whichever is larger.
See preceding sheet for detailed plan of a fireplace.

SIDE-BY-SIDE FIREPLACES

Scale all drawings unless noted: 3/4" = 1'-0"

* National Board of Fire Underwriters recommendation.
Data checked by Frederic N. Whitley, P.E., Consulting Fireplace Engineer

CHIMNEYS

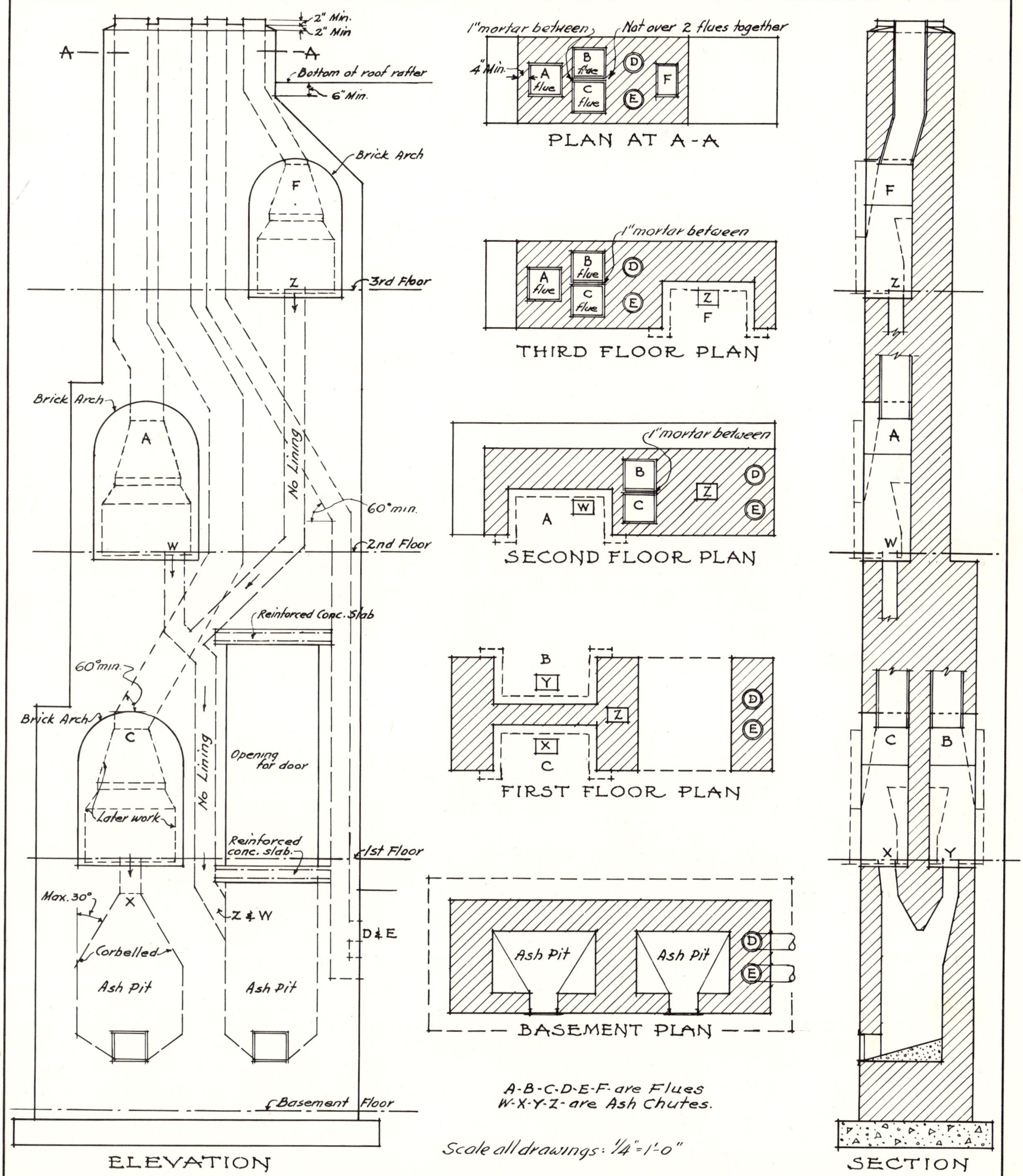
2" Min.
2" Min
A — A
Bottom of roof rafter
6" Min.
Brick Arch
F
Z
3rd Floor
Brick Arch
A
No Lining
60° min.
W
2nd Floor
Reinforced Conc. Slab
60° min.
Brick Arch
C
No Lining
Opening for door
Later work
Reinforced conc. slab.
1st Floor
Max. 30°
X
Z & W
D & E
Corbelled
Ash Pit
Ash Pit
Basement Floor
ELEVATION
1" mortar between
Not over 2 flues together
4" Min.
A flue
B flue
C flue
D
E
F
PLAN AT A-A
1" mortar between
A flue
B flue
C flue
D
E
Z
F
THIRD FLOOR PLAN
1" mortar between
B
C
Z
D
E
W
A
SECOND FLOOR PLAN
B
Y
Z
D
E
X
C
FIRST FLOOR PLAN
Ash Pit
Ash Pit
D
E
BASEMENT PLAN
A-B-C-D-E-F- are Flues
W-X-Y-Z- are Ash Chutes.
Scale all drawings: 1/4" = 1'-0"
F
Z
A
W
C
B
X
Y
SECTION

CHIMNEY CONSTRUCTION *indicating* FIREPLACES *to be* BUILT LATER

Data checked by: Frederic N. Whitley, P.E., Consulting Fireplace Engineer

CHIMNEYS

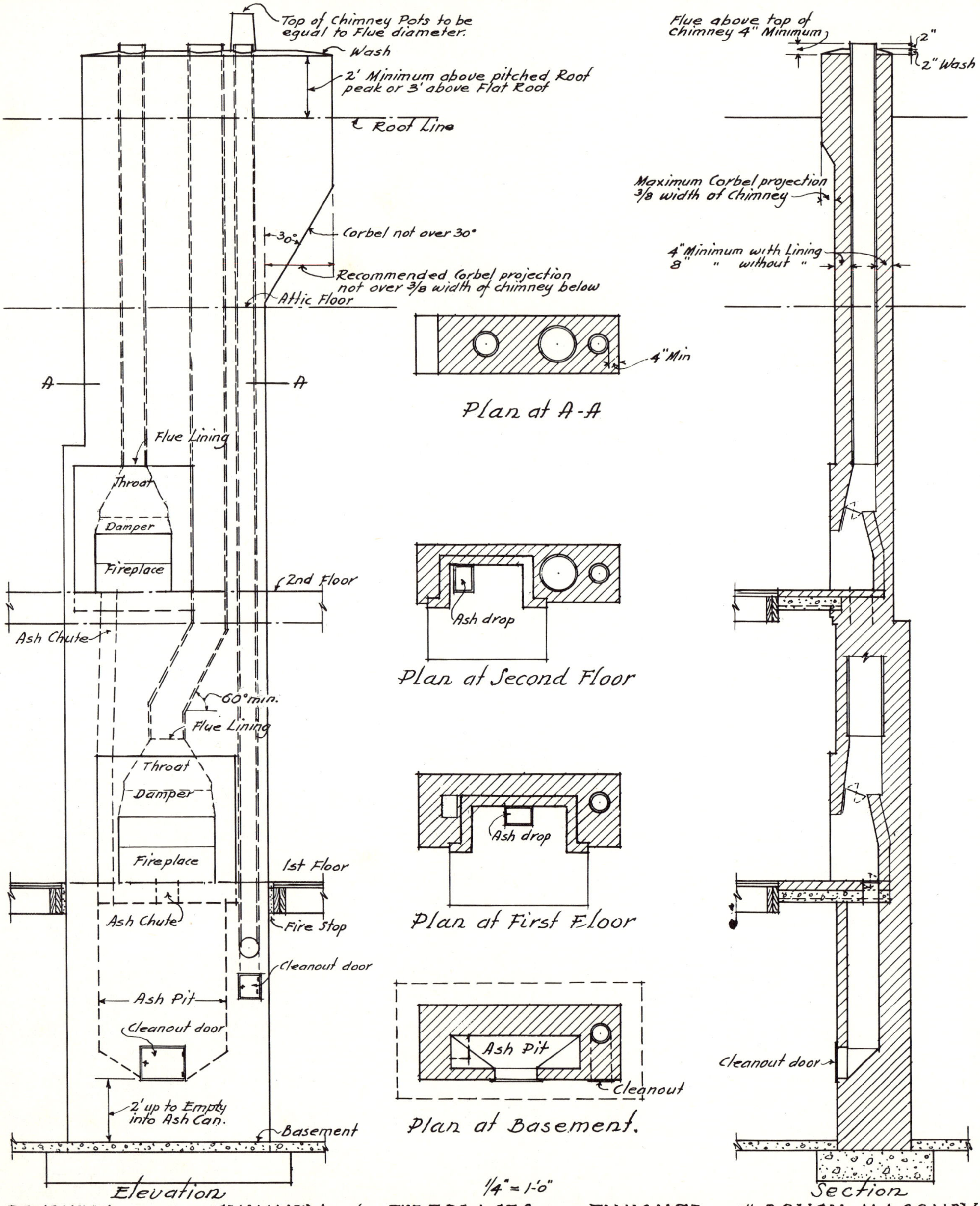

Top of Chimney Pots to be equal to Flue diameter.
Wash
2' Minimum above pitched Roof peak or 3' above Flat Roof
Roof Line
30°
Corbel not over 30°
Recommended Corbel projection not over 3/8 width of chimney below
Attic Floor
A
A
Flue Lining
Throat
Damper
Fireplace
2nd Floor
Ash Chute
60° min.
Flue Lining
Throat
Damper
Fireplace
1st Floor
Ash Chute
Fire Stop
Cleanout door
Ash Pit
Cleanout door
2' up to Empty into Ash Can.
Basement
Elevation
4" Min
Plan at A-A
Ash drop
Plan at Second Floor
Ash drop
Plan at First Floor
Ash Pit
Cleanout
Plan at Basement.
1/4" = 1'-0"
Flue above top of chimney 4" Minimum
2"
2" Wash
Maximum Corbel projection 3/8 width of Chimney
4" Minimum with Lining
8" " without "
Cleanout door
Section

DRAWING showing CHIMNEY when FIREPLACES are FINISHED with ROUGH MASONRY

See other sheet for type of Chimney that omits Fireplace during Rough Construction.

Data checked by: Frederic N. Whitley, P.E., Consulting Fireplace Engineer.

CHIMNEYS

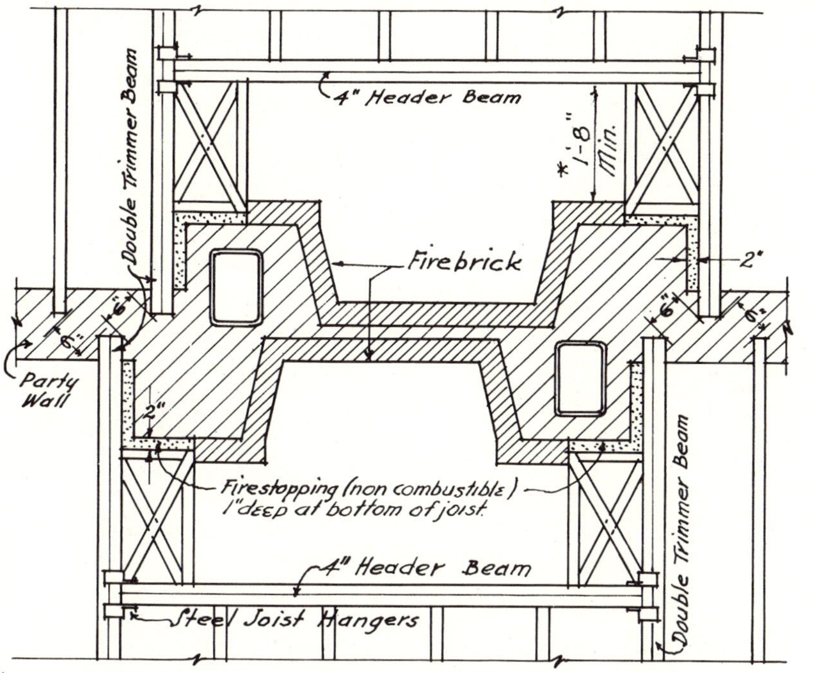
4" Header Beam
*1'-8" Min.
Double Trimmer Beam
Firebrick
2"
6"
6"
6"
6"
Party Wall
2"
Firestopping (non combustible) 1" deep at bottom of joist.
4" Header Beam
Steel Joist Hangers
Double Trimmer Beam

*FIREPLACES BACK TO BACK IN PARTY WALL SHOWING SPACING BETWEEN JOISTS
3/8"=1'-0"

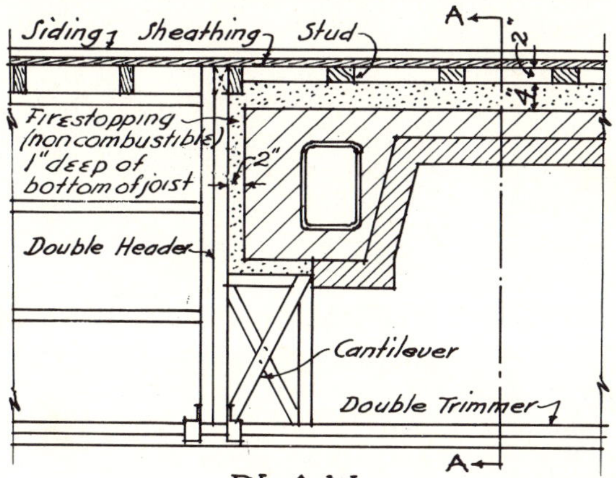
Siding
Sheathing
Stud
A
2"
4"
Firestopping (noncombustible) 1" deep of bottom of joist
2"
Double Header
Cantilever
Double Trimmer
A

PLAN

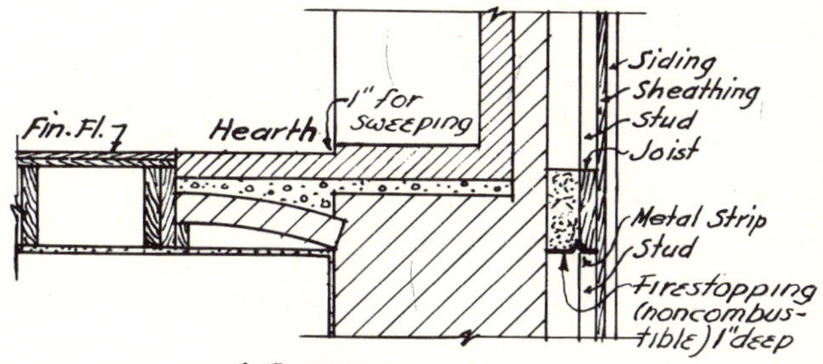
Fin. Fl.
Hearth
1" for sweeping
Siding
Sheathing
Stud
Joist
Metal Strip
Stud
Firestopping (noncombustible) 1" deep

SECTION A-A

**FIREPLACE IN EXTERIOR FRAME WALL- BRICKWORK CONCEALED
3/8"=1'-0"

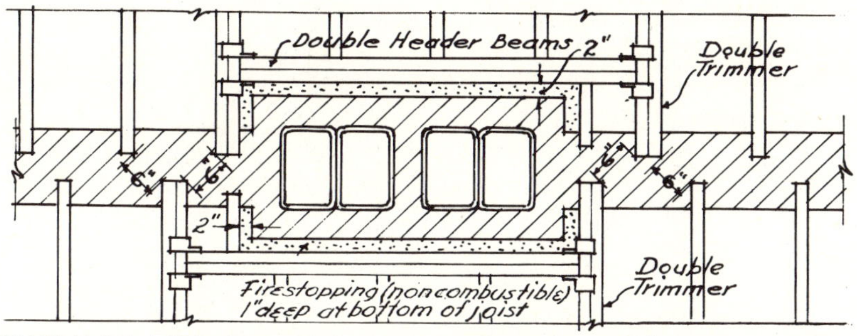
Double Header Beams
2"
Double Trimmer
6"
6"
6"
6"
2"
Firestopping (noncombustible) 1" deep at bottom of joist
Double Trimmer

*CHIMNEY IN PARTY WALL SHOWING SPACING BETWEEN JOISTS AND FIRESTOPPING
3/8"=1'-0"

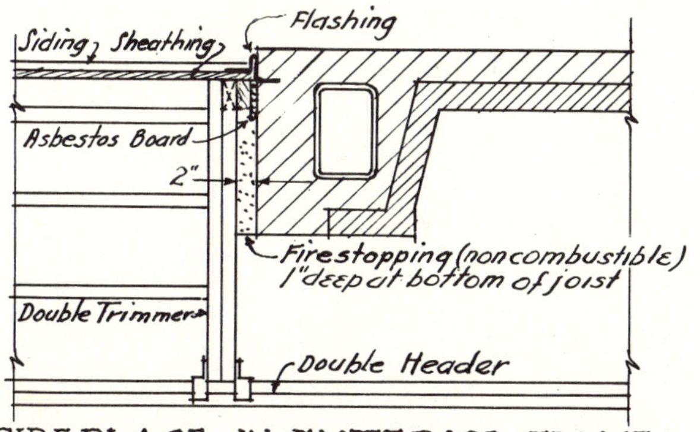
Siding
Sheathing
Flashing
Asbestos Board
2"
Firestopping (noncombustible) 1" deep at bottom of joist
Double Trimmer
Double Header

** FIREPLACE IN EXTERIOR FRAME WALL - BRICKWORK EXPOSED.
3/8"=1'-0"

NOTE: Fireplace splay is for heating purposes only.

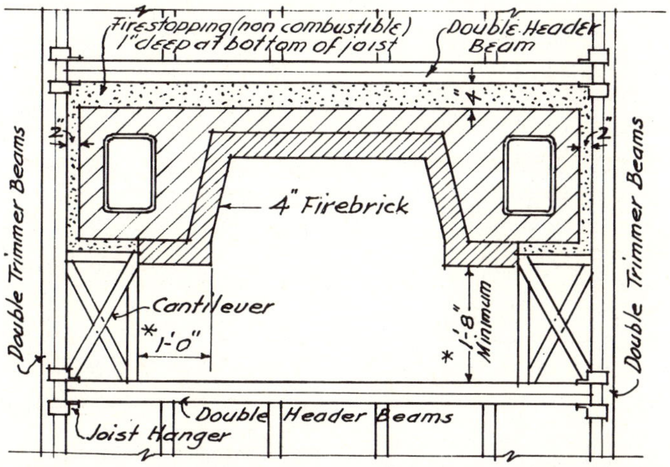
Firestopping (non combustible) 1" deep at bottom of joist
Double Header Beam
4"
2"
2"
Double Trimmer Beams
4" Firebrick
Cantilever
*1'-0"
*1'-8" Minimum
Double Trimmer Beams
Double Header Beams
Joist Hanger

*FIREPLACE FRAMING & FIRESTOPPING
3/8"=1'-0"

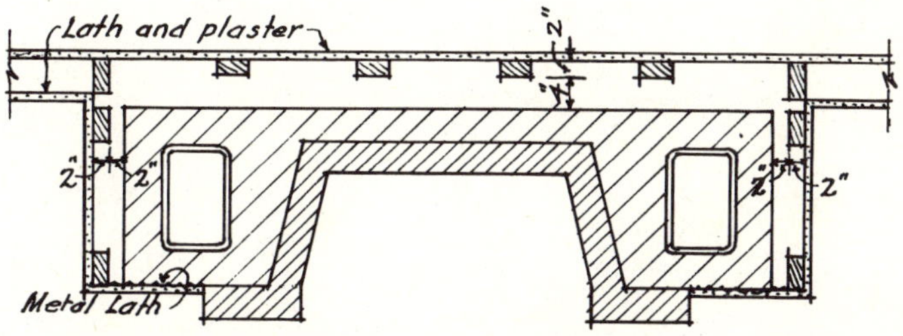
Lath and plaster
2"
2"
2"
2"
2"
Metal Lath

*FIREPLACE IN FRAME PARTITION
3/8"=1'-0"

CHIMNEYS & FIREPLACES *showing* FRAMING & FIRESTOPPING *in* WOOD CONSTN

* Recommendations of the National Board of Fire Underwriters.
** Recommendations of National Lumber Manufacturers Association.

FLUES

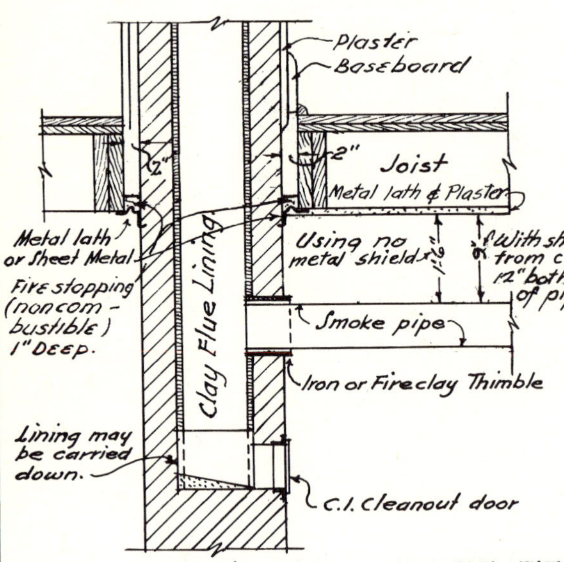
Plaster
Baseboard
2"
Joist
Metal lath & Plaster
Metal lath or Sheet Metal
Fire stopping (noncombustible) 1" Deep.
Using no metal shield
1'6"
9"
With sheet metal shield 1" from ceiling and extending 12" both sides entire length of pipe.
Clay Flue Lining
Smoke pipe
Iron or Fireclay Thimble
Lining may be carried down.
C.I. Cleanout door

SMOKE PIPE for STOVES, H.W. HEATERS & SMALL RANGES–CONNECTIONS & CLEARANCES.

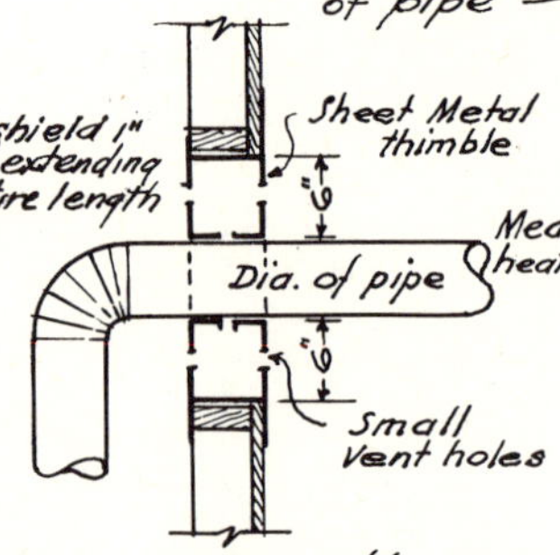
Sheet Metal thimble
6"
Medium heat appliances
Dia. of pipe
Small Vent holes

STOVE PIPE through FRAME PARTITION.

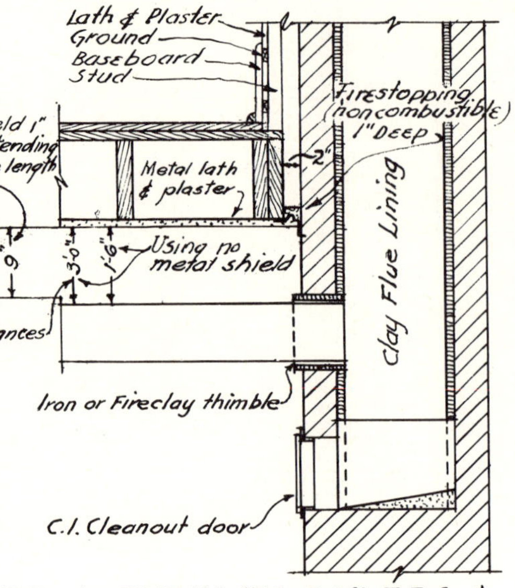
Lath & Plaster
Ground
Baseboard
Stud
Firestopping (noncombustible) 1" Deep
With sheet metal shield 1" from ceiling and extending 12" both sides entire length of pipe
Metal lath & plaster
2"
9"
3'0"
1'6"
Using no metal shield
Clay Flue Lining
Iron or Fireclay thimble
C.I. Cleanout door

SMOKE PIPE for FURNACES, BOILERS & LARGE RANGES–CONNECTIONS & CLEARANCES.

SMOKE PIPE CONNECTIONS and CLEARANCES

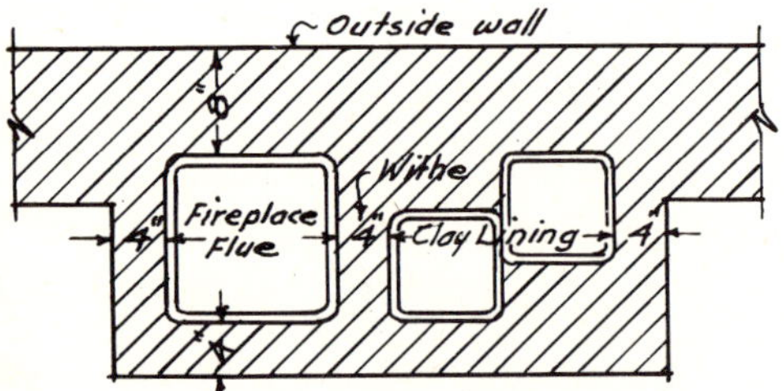
Outside wall
8"
Withe
Fireplace Flue
4"
Clay Lining
4"

FLUE ARRANGEMENT, OUTSIDE BRICK WALL

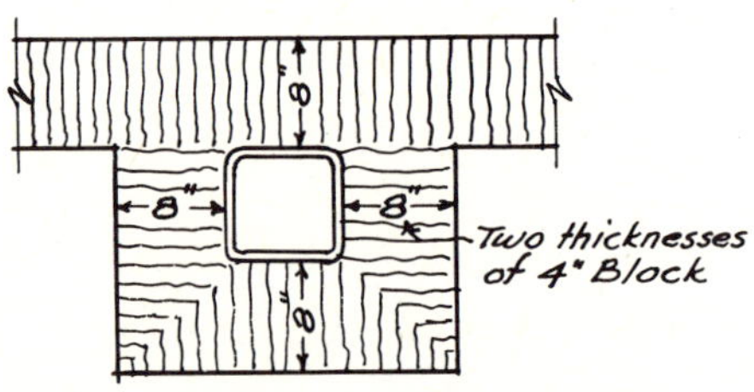
8"
8"
8"
Two thicknesses of 4" Block
8"

FLUE LINING IN OUTSIDE HOLLOW TILE WALL.
Not to be used except in connection with Hollow Tile Wall.

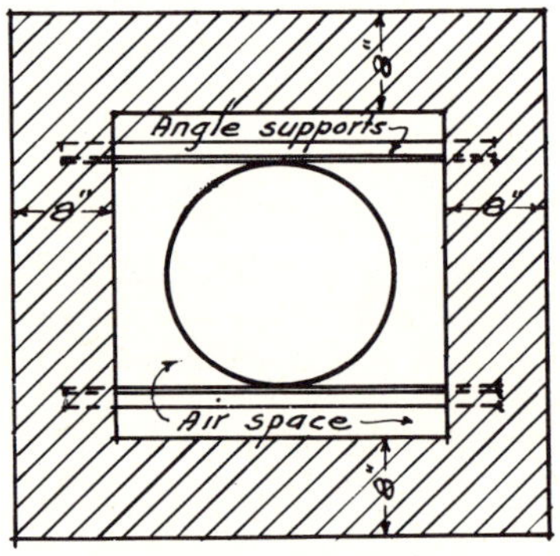
8"
Angle supports
8"
8"
Air space
8"

STEEL STACK SURROUNDED with BRICK
Used for large Boilers

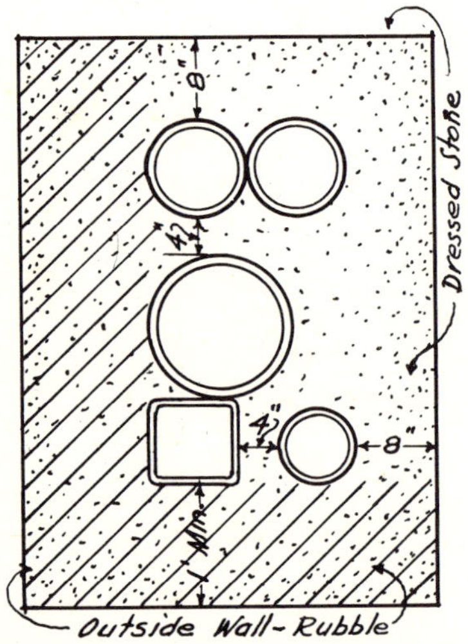
8"
Dressed Stone
4"
4"
8"
1' Min.
Outside Wall–Rubble

FLUE ARRANGEMENTS IN STONE CHIMNEY

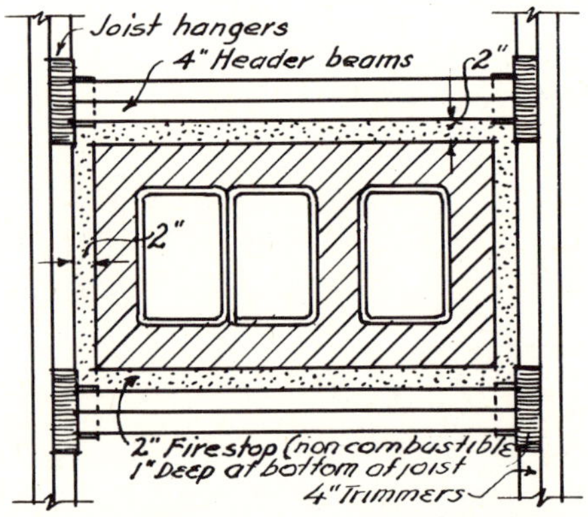
Joist hangers
4" Header beams
2"
2"
2" Firestop (non combustible) 1" Deep at bottom of joist
4" Trimmers

FRAMING (WOOD) AROUND CHIMNEY

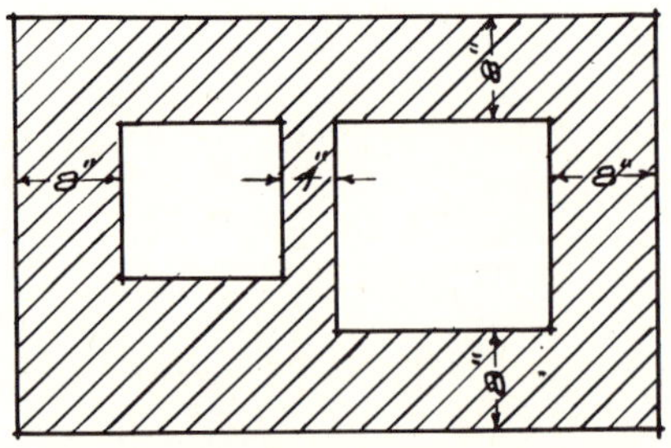
8"
8"
4"
8"
8"

REQUIRED PROTECTION AROUND UNLINED FLUES

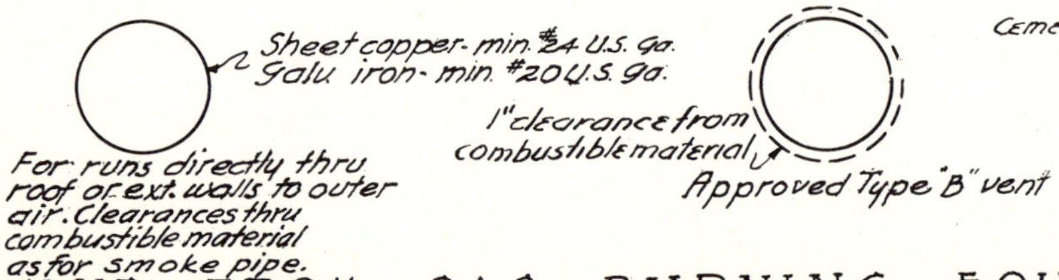
Sheet copper- min. #24 U.S. Ga.
Galv. iron- min. #20 U.S. Ga.
For runs directly thru roof or ext. walls to outer air. Clearances thru combustible material as for smoke pipe.
1" clearance from combustible material
Approved Type "B" vent

FLUE FROM GAS BURNING EQUIPMENT.
May be without masonry

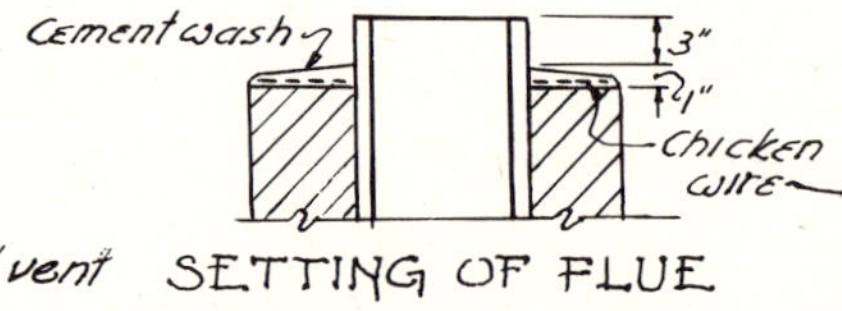
Cement wash
3"
1"
Chicken wire

SETTING OF FLUE LINING without POT

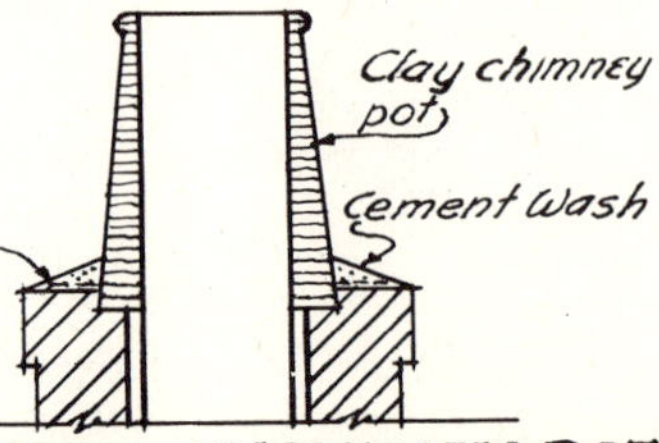
Clay chimney pot
Cement Wash

SETTING of CHIMNEY POT

Recommendations of the National Board of Fire Underwriters.

OUTDOOR FIREPLACES and BARBECUES

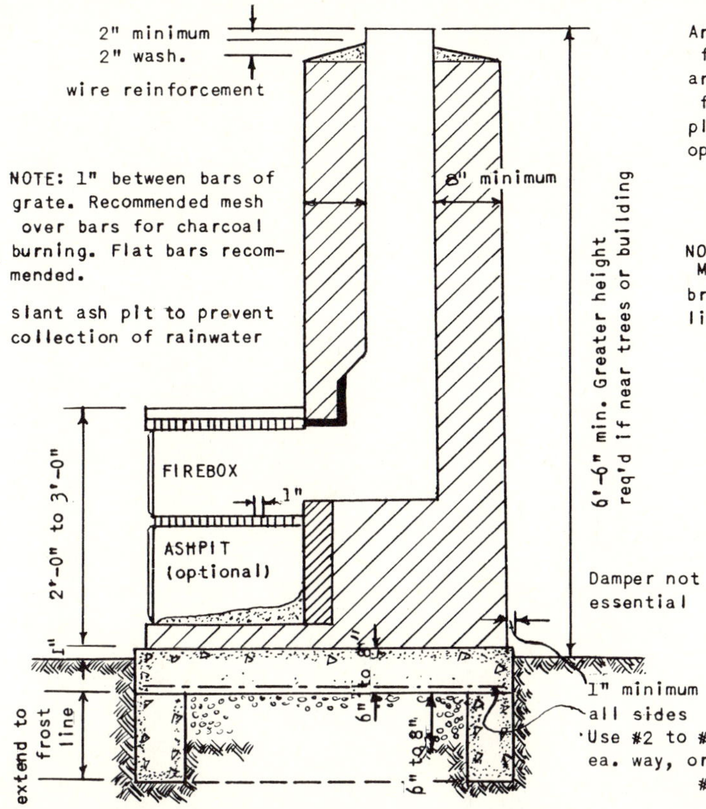
2" minimum
2" wash.
wire reinforcement
NOTE: 1" between bars of grate. Recommended mesh over bars for charcoal burning. Flat bars recommended.
slant ash pit to prevent collection of rainwater
8" minimum
6'-6" min. Greater height req'd if near trees or building
FIREBOX
1"
ASHPIT (optional)
2'-0" to 3'-0"
1"
Damper not essential
extend to frost line
6" to 8"
1" minimum all sides
Use #2 to #4 bars, 6" o.c. ea. way, or 6" mesh #10 x #10

SECTION THRU CHIMNEYED BARBECUE-FIREPLACE
Scale: ½" = 1'-0"

Area of flue:
for barbecue, ⅛ area of opening;
for outdoor fireplace, $\frac{1}{10}$ area of opening (firebox door)

NOTE:
May use either firebrick or clay flue lining.

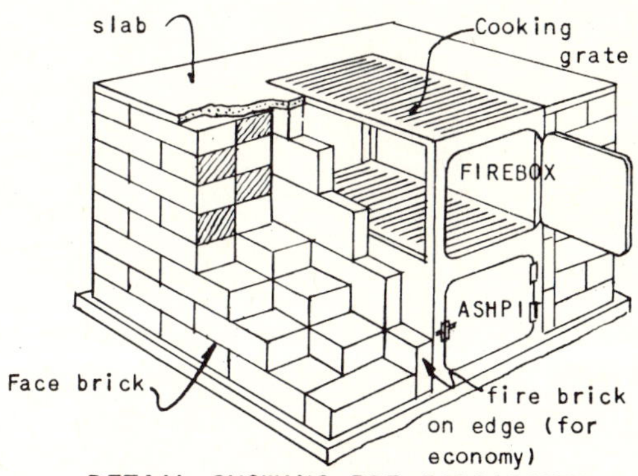
slab
Cooking grate
FIREBOX
ASHPIT
Face brick
fire brick on edge (for economy)

DETAIL SHOWING PRE-FABRICATED EQUIPMENT IN PLACE

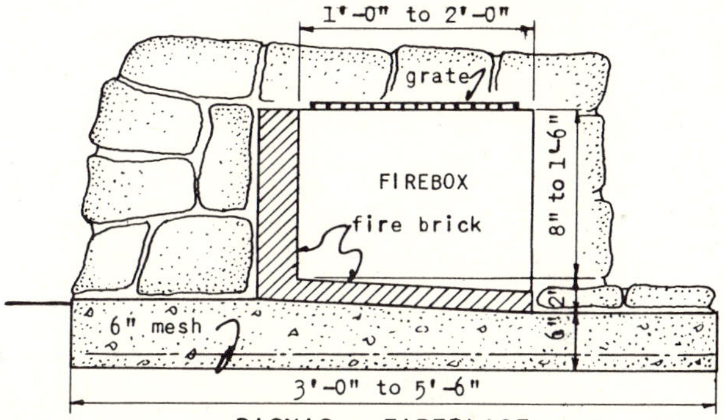
1'-0" to 2'-0"
grate
FIREBOX
fire brick
8" to 1'-6"
6" mesh
6"
3'-0" to 5'-6"

PICNIC FIREPLACE
Scale: ½" = 1'-0"

With fixed grill, x = 6" to 10" for charcoal fuel.
x = 10" to 12" for wood fuel.
With movable grill, x = 6" min; 12" max. + 2" allowance for bed of coals

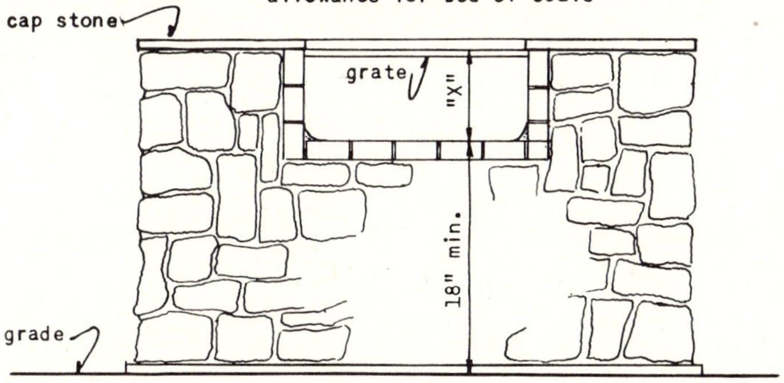
cap stone
grate
"X"
18" min.
grade

ELEVATION OF BARBECUE
Scale: ½" = 1'-0"
Chimney not required if charcoal is only fuel used.

FIREPLACE MATERIALS

MATERIAL	CHARACTERISTICS
brick, concrete block	economical, easy to handle
fine-grained sandstone	resists damaging
limestone, shale	spall or chip when exposed to heat, sudden temperature changes
granite	may spall or crack when exposed to heat
Lava rock	resists heat

PREFABRICATED METAL EQUIPMENT*

EQUIPMENT		WIDTH	HEIGHT	DEPTH	MANUFACTURER
Oven door		12½"	15½"	--	Donley
Oven		13"	10½"	18"	Majestic
Firebox doors		12"	8" 10"	-- --	
		10"	12"	--	Sutton
Ashpit doors		12"	8" 12"	--	Donley
		12"	8" 10"		Majestic
		10"	12"		Sutton
assembled units	4 grates, hinged top, firebox & door, ashpit door	16½"	13⅜"	28"	Donley
	3 grates & 1 solid top sect'n or 2 grates & 2 solid top sections, firebox & door ashpit door				
	2 grates, firebox door, ashpit door	13⅛" 15⅛" 22¼"	21⅛" 27⅞"	26" 29"	Majestic
Grates		12"	--	16" 20" 24"	Donley
		12"	--	12" 18" 24"	Majestic
		22¼"	--	20⅜"	
		4¾"	--	18" 22"	
Top grill		25½"	--	14½"	Sutton

*Consult mfr's catalogues for details.

WATERPROOFING and EXPANSION JOINTS

TABLE OF CONTENTS

WATERPROOFING & DAMPPROOFING OF RESIDENTIAL BASEMENTS

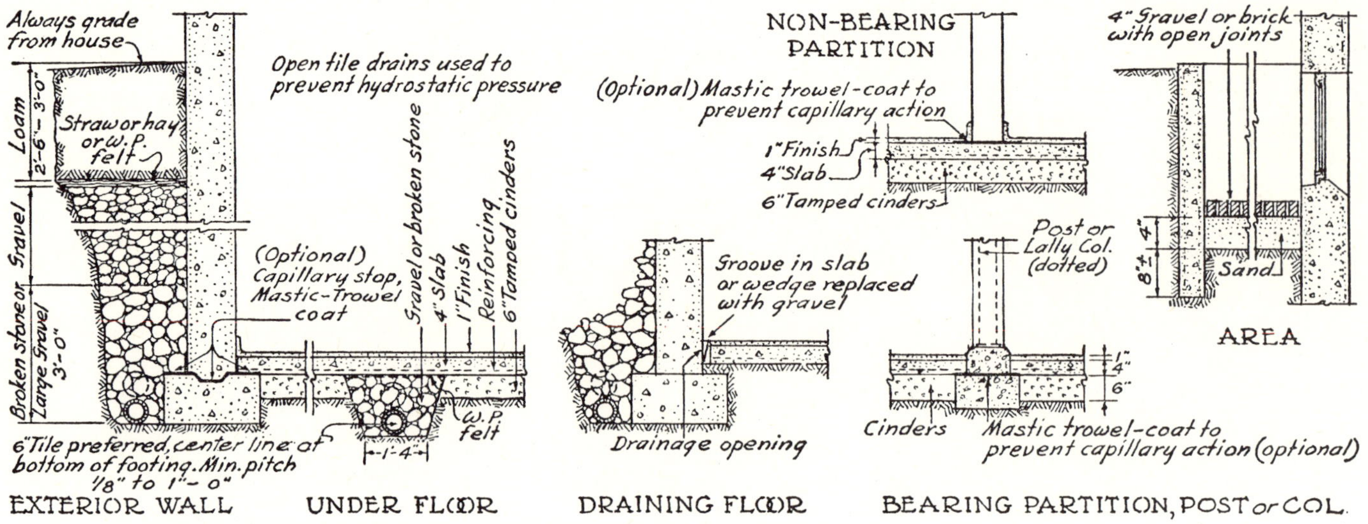
Always grade from house
Loam 2'-6" - 3'-0"
Straw or hay or W.P. felt
Broken stone or Gravel
Large Gravel 3'-0"
Open tile drains used to prevent hydrostatic pressure
(Optional) Capillary stop, Mastic-Trowel coat
Gravel or broken stone
4" Slab
1" Finish
Reinforcing
6" Tamped cinders
6" Tile preferred, center line at bottom of footing. Min. pitch 1/8" to 1'-0"
1'-4"
W.P. felt
NON-BEARING PARTITION
(Optional) Mastic trowel-coat to prevent capillary action
1" Finish
4" Slab
6" Tamped cinders
Groove in slab or wedge replaced with gravel
Drainage opening
Post or Lally Col. (dotted)
Cinders
Mastic trowel-coat to prevent capillary action (optional)
1"
4"
6"
4" Gravel or brick with open joints
4"
8"±
Sand
AREA
EXTERIOR WALL
UNDER FLOOR
DRAINING FLOOR
BEARING PARTITION, POST or COL.

RECOMMENDED DETAILS for NON-WATERPROOFED BASEMENT WALLS & FLOORS
With precautions against entry of surface water

Note: For Pits, inserts & Boiler protection see other sheet. Caulk all sleeves thru floors & walls.

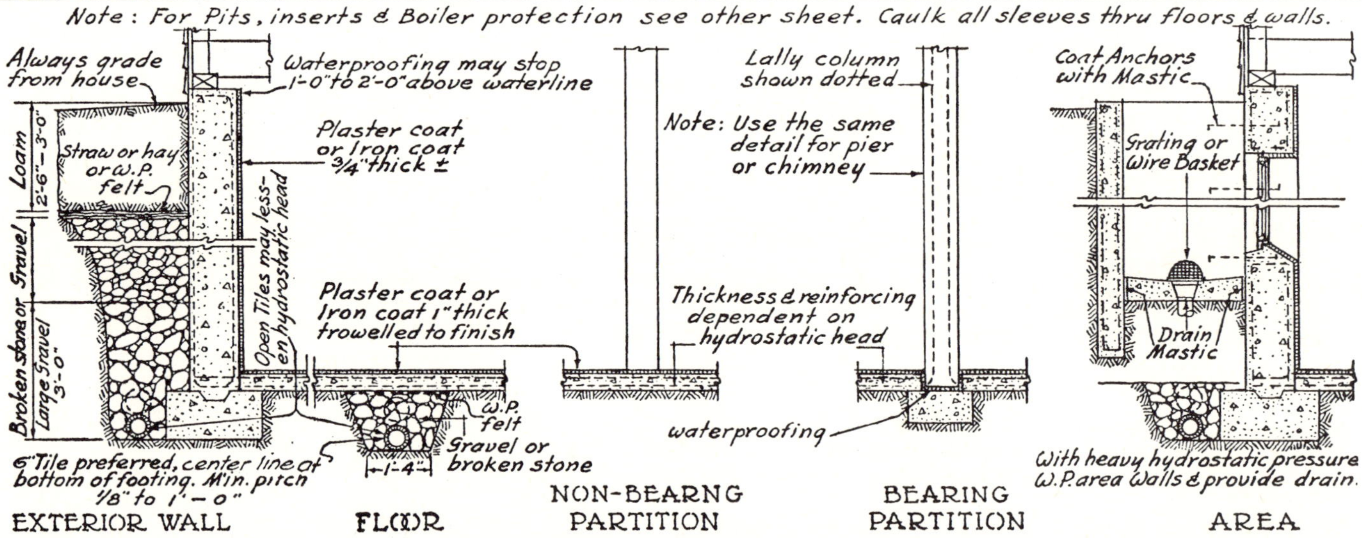
Always grade from house
Loam 2'-6" - 3'-0"
Straw or hay or W.P. felt
Broken stone or Gravel
Large Gravel 3'-0"
Waterproofing may stop 1'-0" to 2'-0" above waterline
Plaster coat or Iron coat 3/4" thick ±
Open Tiles may lessen hydrostatic head
Plaster coat or Iron coat 1" thick trowelled to finish
W.P. felt
Gravel or broken stone
1'-4"
6" Tile preferred, center line at bottom of footing. Min. pitch 1/8" to 1'-0"
Lally column shown dotted
Note: Use the same detail for pier or chimney
Thickness & reinforcing dependent on hydrostatic head
waterproofing
Coat Anchors with Mastic
Grating or Wire Basket
Drain
Mastic
With heavy hydrostatic pressure W.P. area Walls & provide drain.
EXTERIOR WALL
FLOOR
NON-BEARNG PARTITION
BEARING PARTITION
AREA

RECOMMENDED DETAILS for BASEMENT WALLS & FLOORS. INTERNALLY WATERPROOFED
Using "Plaster Coat" or Iron Coat method

Note: For Pits & other details see other sheet. Caulk all sleeves thru floors & walls.

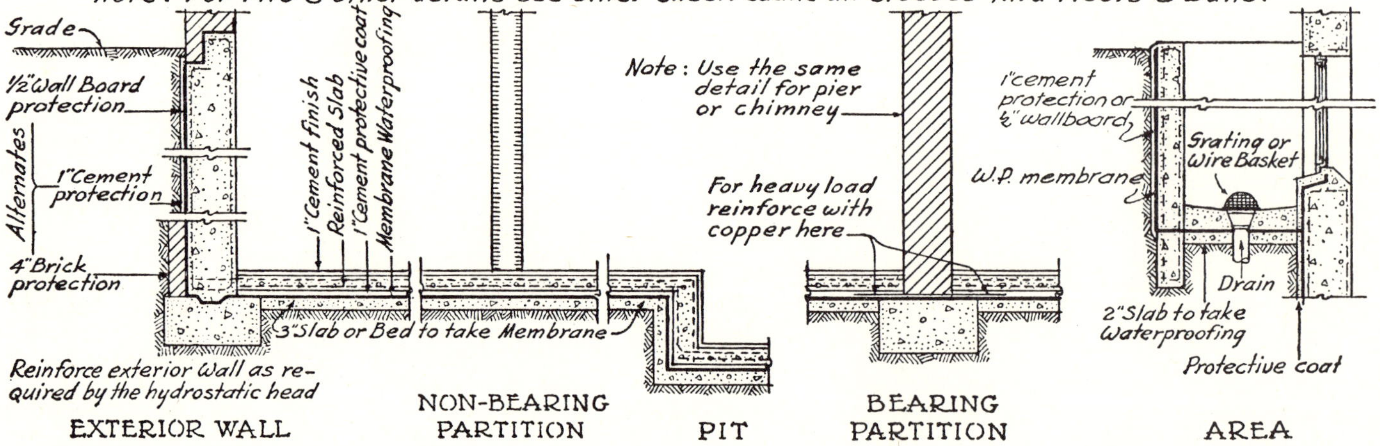
Grade
1/2" Wall Board protection
Alternates
1" Cement protection
4" Brick protection
1" Cement finish
Reinforced Slab
1" Cement protective coat
Membrane Waterproofing
3" Slab or Bed to take Membrane
Reinforce exterior Wall as required by the hydrostatic head
Note: Use the same detail for pier or chimney
For heavy load reinforce with copper here
1" cement protection or 1/2" wallboard
Grating or Wire Basket
W.P. membrane
Drain
2" Slab to take Waterproofing
Protective coat
EXTERIOR WALL
NON-BEARING PARTITION
PIT
BEARING PARTITION
AREA

RECOMMENDED DETAILS for BASEMENT WALLS & FLOORS. MEMBRANE WATERPROOFED

Scale of all drawings 1/4" = 1'-0"

WATERPROOFING

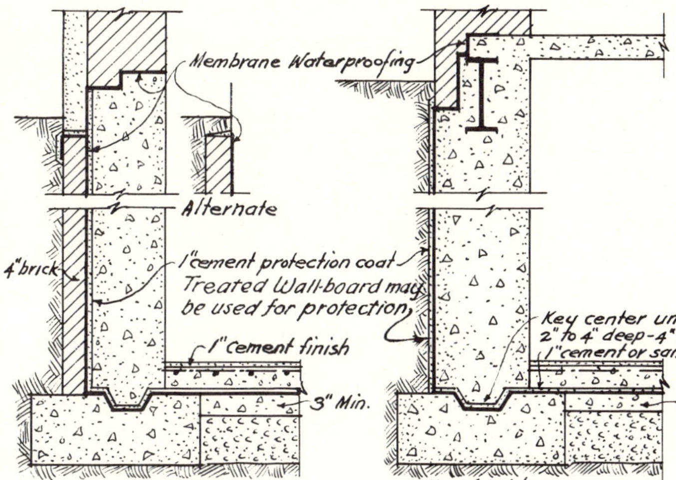

Membrane Waterproofing
Alternate
4" brick
1" cement protection coat
Treated Wall-board may be used for protection
1" Cement finish
3" Min.
Key center under wall 2" to 4" deep-4" to 6" wide.
1" cement or sand protection
3" Min.

For Heavy Pressure — For Light Pressure

EXTERIOR WALLS

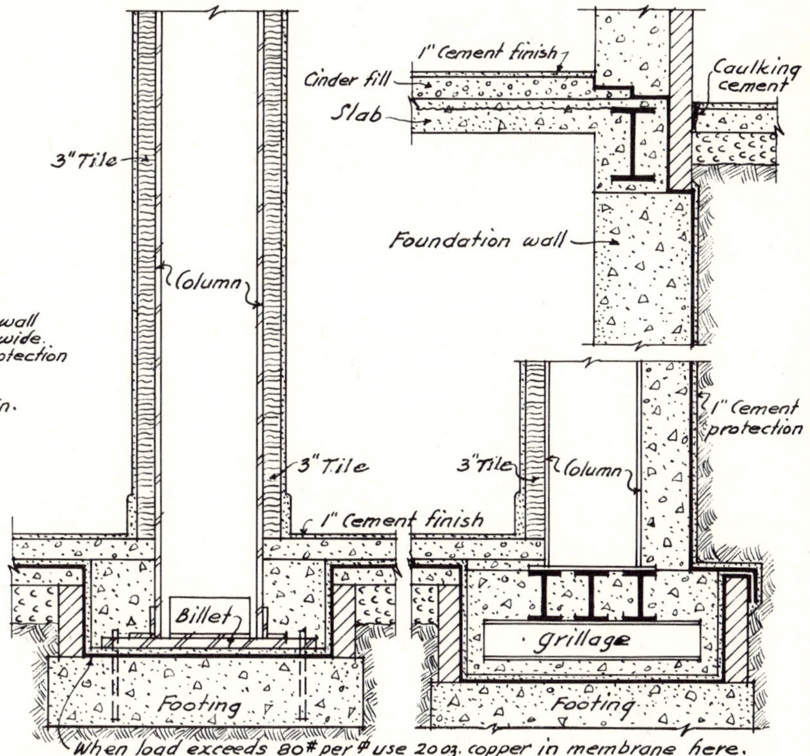

3" Tile
Column
3" Tile
1" Cement finish
Billet
Footing
1" Cement finish
Cinder fill
Slab
Caulking cement
Foundation wall
1" Cement protection
3" Tile
Column
grillage
Footing
When load exceeds 80# per □" use 20 oz. copper in membrane here.

INTERIOR COLUMN-EXTERIOR COLUMN

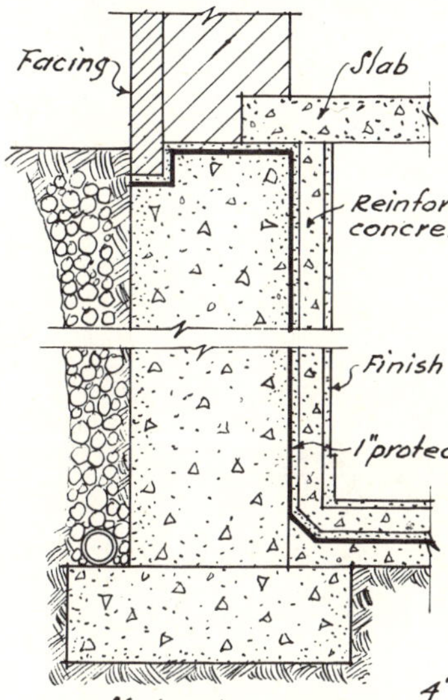

Facing
Slab
Reinforced concrete
Finish
1" protection coat

Not advisable
To be used only when not feasible to W.P. on outside.

WALL W.P. ON INSIDE

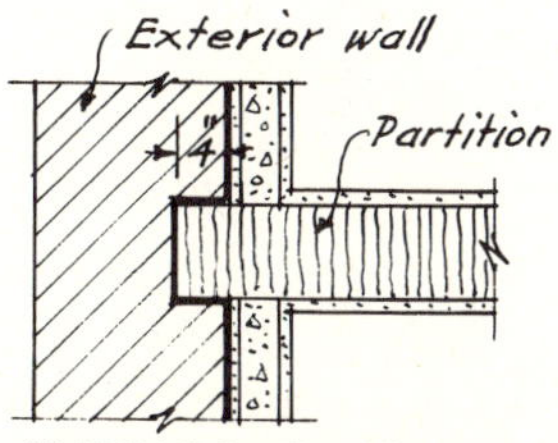

Exterior wall
4"
Partition

INTERIOR W.P. AT PARTITION

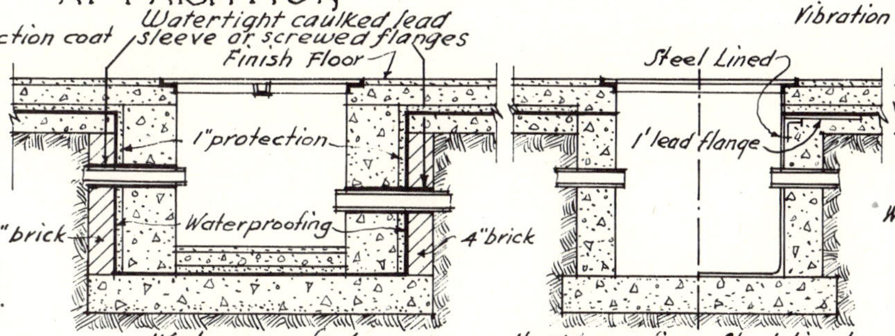

Watertight caulked lead sleeve or screwed flanges
Finish Floor
1" protection
Waterproofing
4" brick
4" brick
Steel Lined
1" lead flange

Waterproofed — No Waterproofing. Steel Lined

SUMP PITS

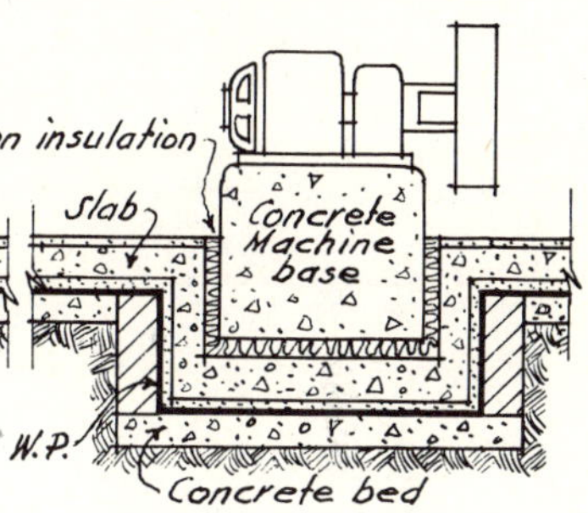

Vibration insulation
Slab
Concrete Machine base
W.P.
Concrete bed

MACHINE FOUNDATION

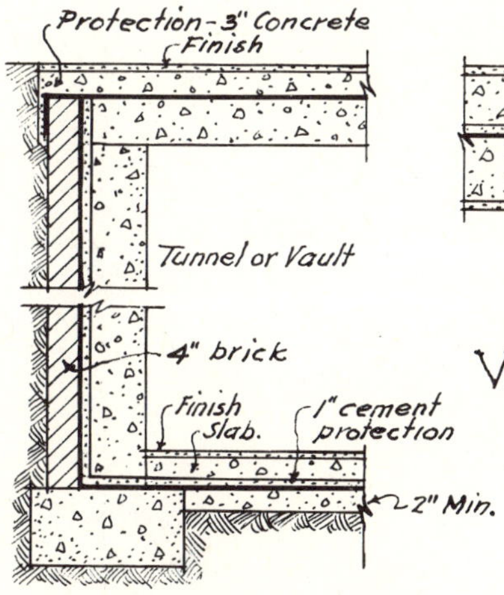

Protection-3" Concrete
Finish
Tunnel or Vault
4" brick
Finish Slab.
1" cement protection
2" Min.

SECTION thro TUNNEL

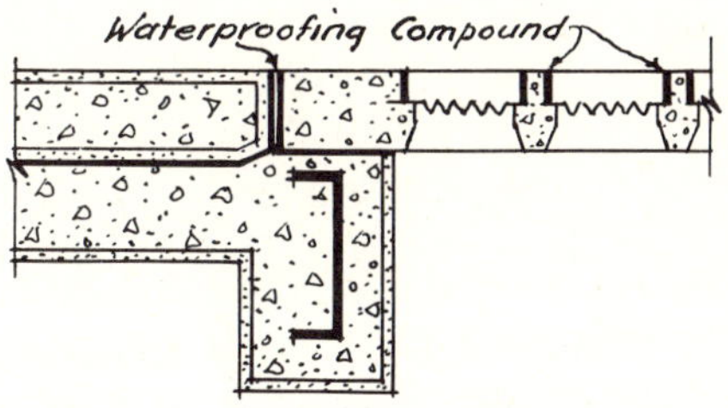

Waterproofing Compound

VAULT LIGHT

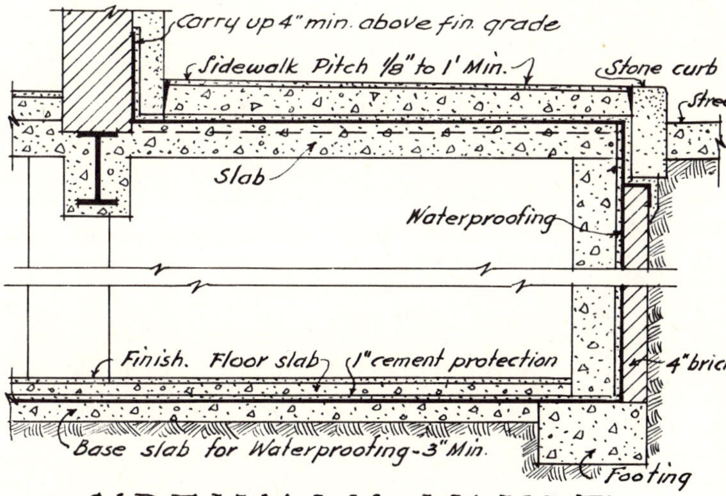

Carry up 4" min. above fin. grade
Sidewalk Pitch 1/8" to 1' Min.
Stone curb
Street
Slab
Waterproofing
Finish. Floor slab
1" cement protection
4" brick
Base slab for Waterproofing-3" Min.
Footing

SIDEWALK VAULT

Sizes, depth of Slab and reinforcing are omitted as they are always variable.
Methods as developed by the Minwax Company

MEMBRANE WATERPROOFING BELOW GRADE

Data checked by: Minwax Co. & Western Waterproofing Co., Inc. 3/8"=1'-0"

WATERPROOFING

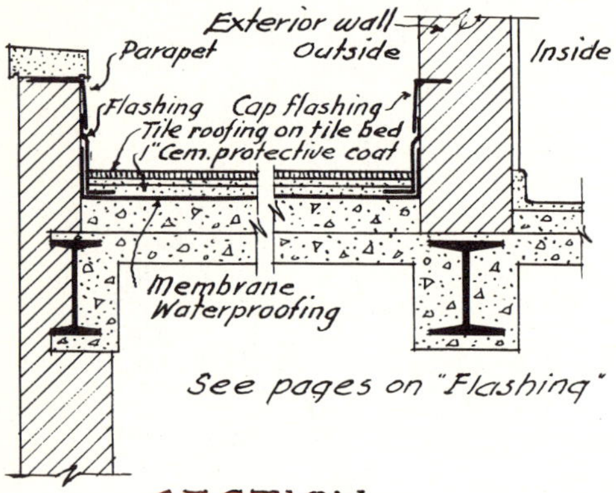
Exterior wall
Parapet
Outside
Inside
Flashing
Cap flashing
Tile roofing on tile bed
1" Cem. protective coat
Membrane Waterproofing
See pages on "Flashing"

SECTION
FLAT ROOF

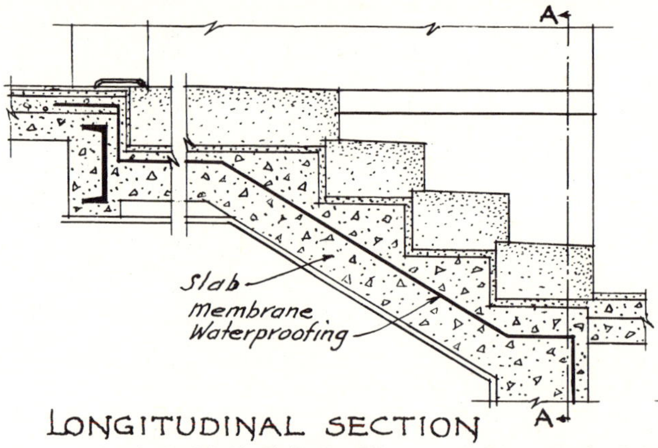
A
Slab
Membrane Waterproofing
A

LONGITUDINAL SECTION

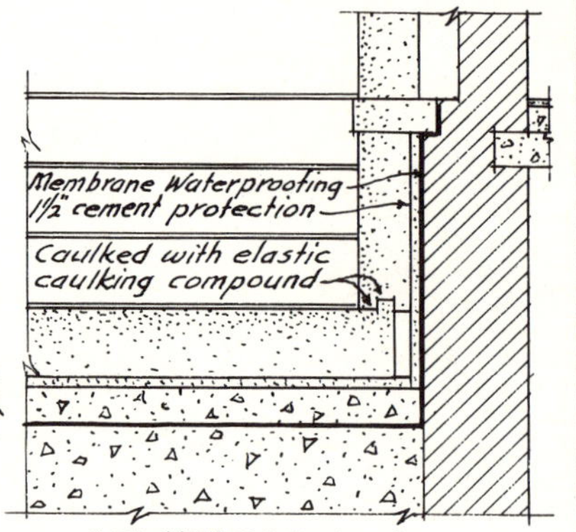
Membrane Waterproofing
1½" cement protection
Caulked with elastic caulking compound

SECTION A-A

OUTSIDE STONE STEPS

Variables, such as Dimensions & Reinforcing omitted
3/8" = 1'

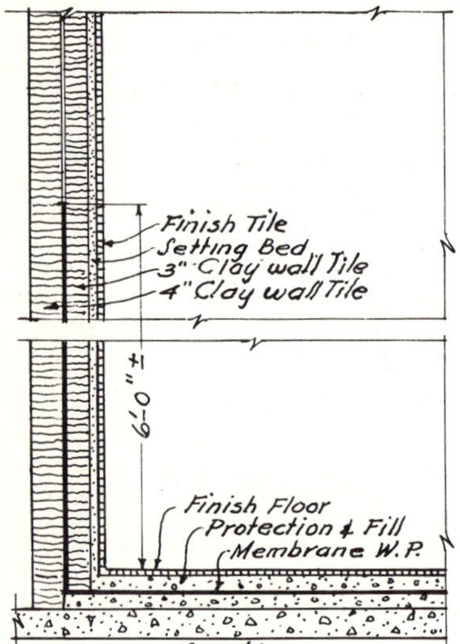
Finish Tile
Setting Bed
3" Clay wall Tile
4" Clay wall Tile
6'-0" ±
Finish Floor
Protection & Fill
Membrane W.P.

Section
GANG SHOWER

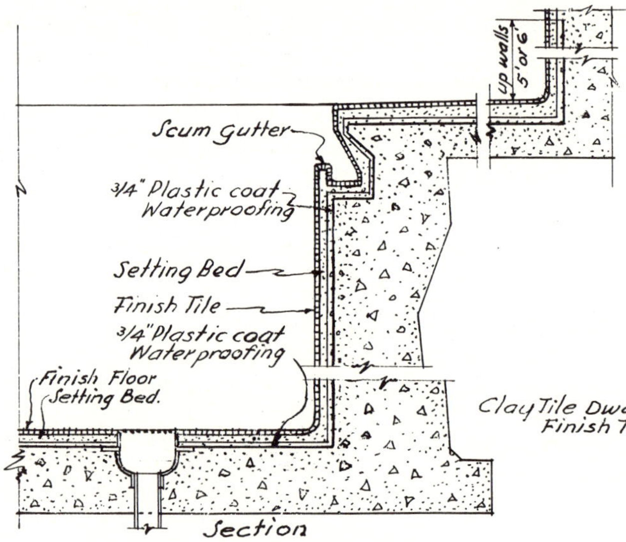
Up walls 5' or 6'
Scum Gutter
3/4" Plastic coat Waterproofing
Setting Bed
Finish Tile
3/4" Plastic coat Waterproofing
Finish Floor
Setting Bed.

Section
SWIMMING POOL

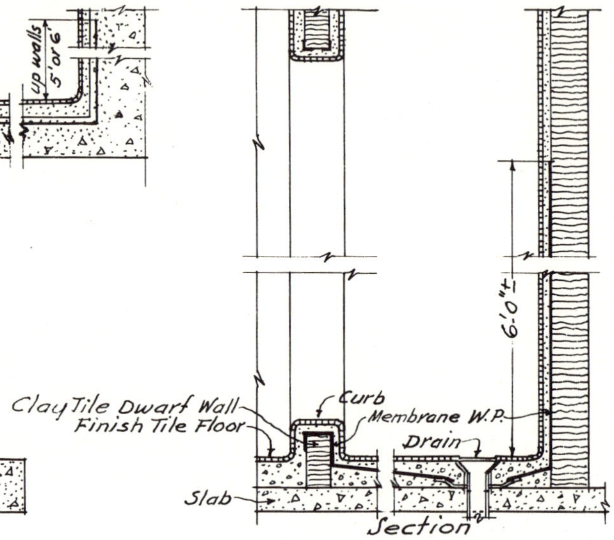
6'-0" ±
Clay Tile Dwarf Wall
Finish Tile Floor
Curb
Membrane W.P.
Drain
Slab

Section
SHOWER STALL

MEMBRANE WATERPROOFING ABOVE GRADE
3/8" = 1'

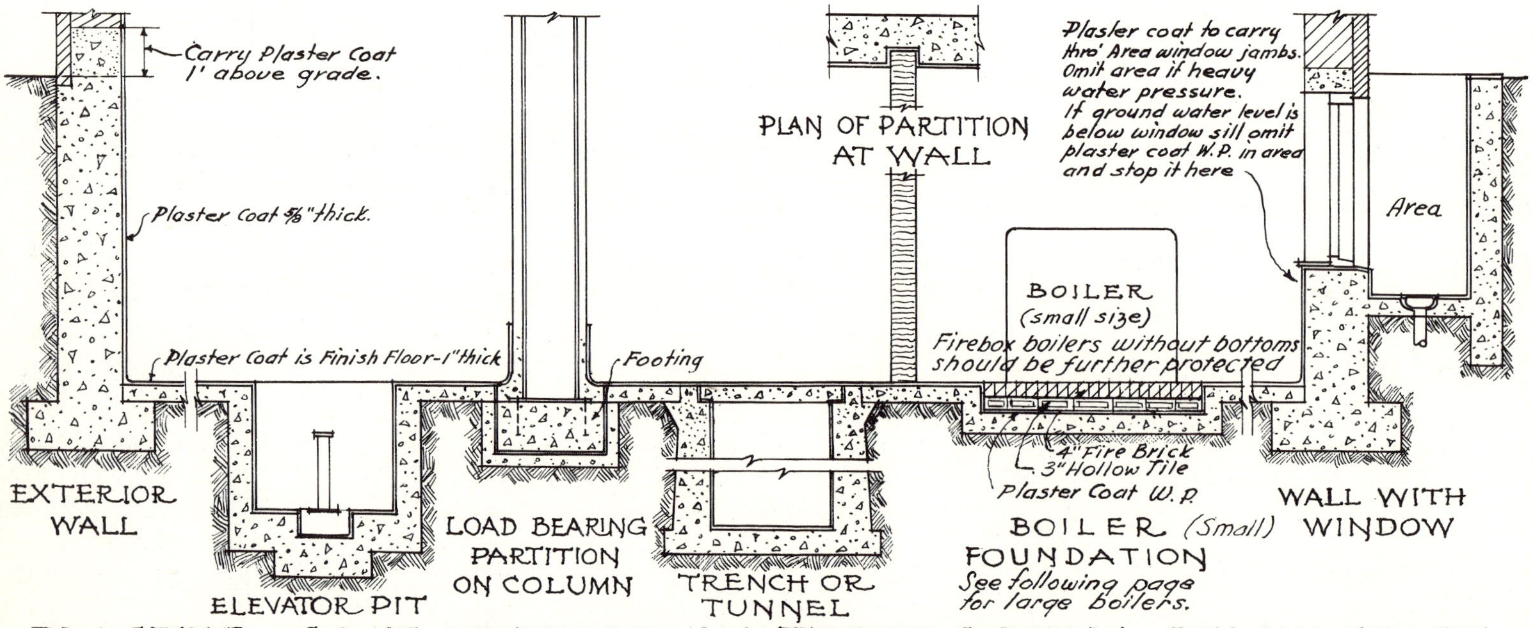
Carry Plaster Coat 1' above grade.
Plaster Coat 5/8" thick.
Plaster Coat is Finish Floor-1" thick
Footing
PLAN OF PARTITION AT WALL
Plaster coat to carry thro' Area window jambs. Omit area if heavy water pressure. If ground water level is below window sill omit plaster coat W.P. in area and stop it here
Area
BOILER (small size)
Firebox boilers without bottoms should be further protected
4" Fire Brick
3" Hollow Tile
Plaster Coat W.P.
EXTERIOR WALL
ELEVATOR PIT
LOAD BEARING PARTITION ON COLUMN
TRENCH OR TUNNEL
BOILER (Small) FOUNDATION
See following page for large boilers.
WALL WITH WINDOW

PLASTER COAT METHOD - WATERPROOFING - BELOW GRADE

All variables such as dimensions and reinforcement are omitted as they depend on actual conditions of each job.
Data Checked by: Western Waterproofing Co., Inc. 1/4" = 1'

WATERPROOFING - PLASTER COAT

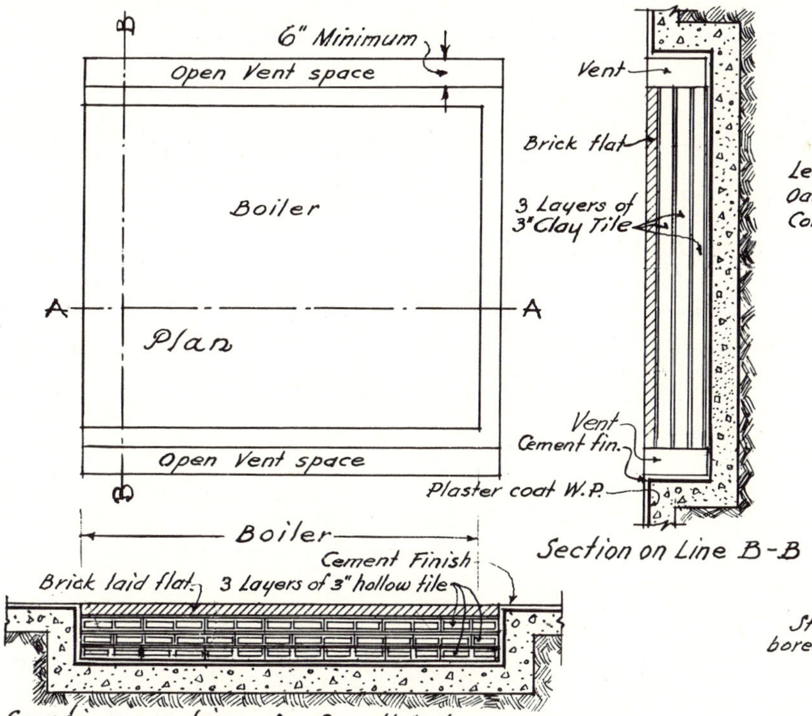
6" Minimum
Open Vent space
Boiler
Plan
A
A
B
B
Open Vent space
Vent
Brick flat
3 Layers of 3" Clay Tile
Vent
Cement fin.
Plaster coat W.P.
Section on Line B-B
Boiler
Cement Finish
Brick laid flat
3 Layers of 3" hollow tile
Section on Line A-A 1/4"=1'

INSULATION TO PROTECT W.P. UNDER BOILERS
PLASTER COAT METHOD

Similar method may be used with Membrane Waterproofing. Method developed by the Western Waterproofing Company, Inc.

If headroom permits, insulation may be built on top of boiler room floor without pit.

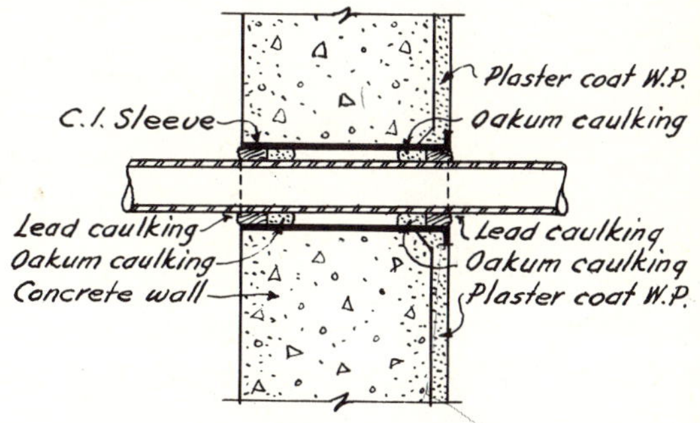
Plaster coat W.P.
C.I. Sleeve
Oakum caulking
Lead caulking
Oakum caulking
Concrete wall
Lead caulking
Oakum caulking
Plaster coat W.P.

STEAM PIPE THRO WALL
3/4"=1'

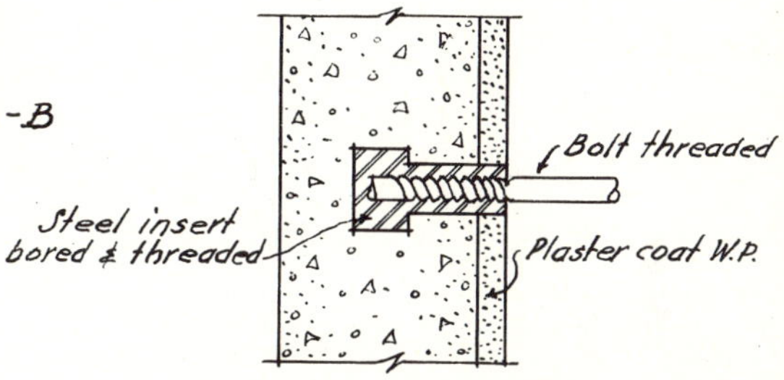
Bolt threaded
Steel insert bored & threaded
Plaster coat W.P.

BOLT ANCHORAGE.
SECTION
1½"=1'

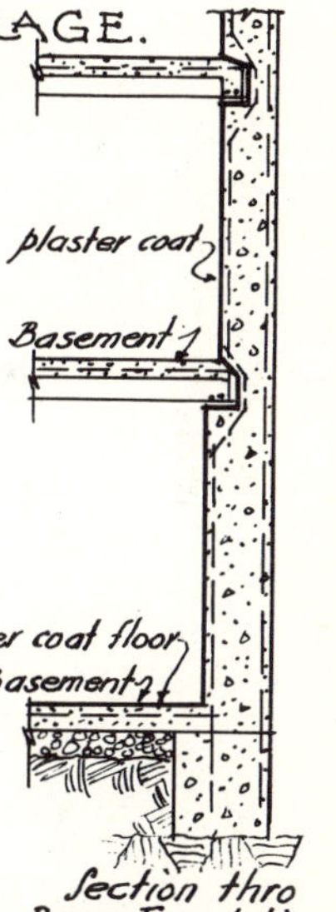
plaster coat
Basement
Plaster coat floor
Sub-Basement

Section thro Deep Foundation.

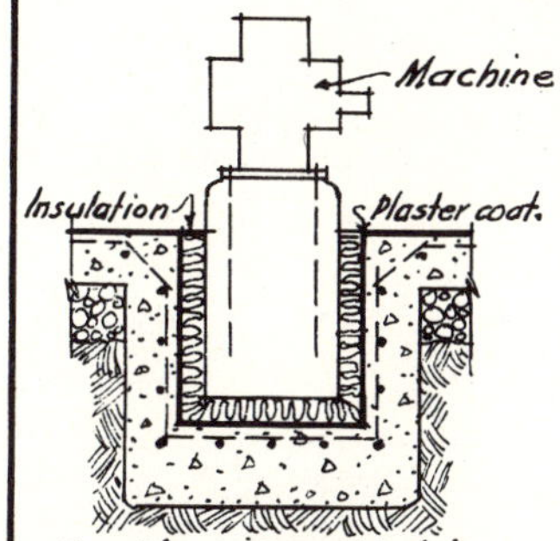
Machine
Insulation
Plaster coat.

Machine Foundation with insulation under

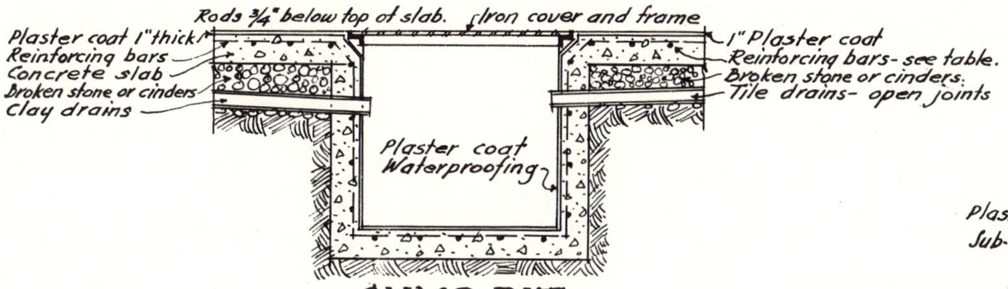
Rods 3/4" below top of slab.
Iron cover and frame
Plaster coat 1" thick
Reinforcing bars
Concrete slab
Broken stone or cinders
Clay drains
1" Plaster coat
Reinforcing bars - see table.
Broken stone or cinders.
Tile drains - open joints
Plaster coat Waterproofing

SUMP PIT

HEAD OF WATER ABOVE BOTTOM OF SLAB	SPAN	6'-0"	8'-0"	10'-0"	12'-0"	14'-0"	16'-0"	18'-0"	20'-0"	22'-0"	24'-0"	LIFTING PRESSURE IN POUNDS PER SQ. FT.
1'	Slab	4"	4"	4"	4"							62½
	Steel	3/8ϕ-12"	3/8ϕ-12"	3/8ϕ-12"	3/8ϕ-12"							
2'	Slab	4"	4"	4"	4½"	5"	5½"	6"	6"	6½"	6½"	125
	Steel	3/8ϕ-12"	3/8ϕ-7½"	3/8ϕ-5"	1/2ϕ-7½"	1/2ϕ-7"	1/2ϕ-6½"	1/2ϕ-6½"	1/2ϕ-5½"	1/2ϕ-5½"	1/2ϕ-4½"	
3'	Slab	4"	4½"	5"	5½"	6"	7"	7½"	8"	8"	8½"	187½
	Steel	3/8ϕ-7½"	3/8ϕ-5"	1/2ϕ-7"	5/8ϕ-9"	5/8ϕ-8"	5/8ϕ-8"	5/8ϕ-7"	5/8ϕ-6½"	5/8ϕ-5½"	5/8ϕ-5½"	
4'	Slab	4"	5"	6"	6½"	7½"	8"	9"	9½"	10"	10½"	250
	Steel	3/8ϕ-5"	1/2ϕ-9"	1/2ϕ-6"	1/2ϕ-5"	5/8ϕ-7"	5/8ϕ-6"	5/8ϕ-6"	3/4ϕ-8"	3/4ϕ-7"	3/4ϕ-6½"	
6'	Slab	4¾"	6"	7"	8"	9"	10"	11"	11½"	12½"	13½"	375
	Steel	1/2ϕ-7"	1/2ϕ-5"	5/8ϕ-7"	5/8ϕ-6"	5/8ϕ-5"	5/8ϕ-4½"	5/8ϕ-4"	3/4ϕ-5½"	3/4ϕ-5"	3/4ϕ-5"	
8'	Slab	5½"	7"	8"	9½"	10½"	11½"	13"	14"	15"	15½"	500
	Steel	1/2ϕ-6"	5/8ϕ-7½"	3/4ϕ-8½"	3/4ϕ-7½"	7/8ϕ-8½"	7/8ϕ-7½"	7/8ϕ-7"	7/8ϕ-6½"	7/8ϕ-6"	7/8ϕ-6"	
10'	Slab	6"	7½"	9"	10½"	12"	13"	14½"	15½	16½"	18"	625
	Steel	1/2ϕ-5"	3/4ϕ-9"	7/8ϕ-10"	7/8ϕ-8½"	7/8ϕ-7½"	7/8ϕ-6½"	7/8ϕ-6"	7/8ϕ-5½"	7/8ϕ-5"	7/8ϕ-5"	

Table based on simple span - Concrete stress 650 lbs per Sq." and steel 16000# Mix: 1-2-4. Provide distribution rods 3/8"ϕ - 12" o.c. for slabs 8" and less, and 1/2"ϕ 12" o.c. for thicker slabs running perpendicular to main reinforcing and wired thereto. Slabs are designed to resist upward pressure of heads indicated. Table redrawn by courtesy of the Western Waterproofing Company, Inc.

THICKNESS & REINFORCING *of* SLAB FOR WATERHEADS *from* 1 *to* 10 FEET - SPANS 6' *to* 24'

Data checked by: Western Waterproofing Co., Inc.

DAMPPROOFING & WATERPROOFING of COPINGS, SPANDRELS & SILLS

Caulk all joints in copings. Stop fabric flashing ½" back of face of wall.

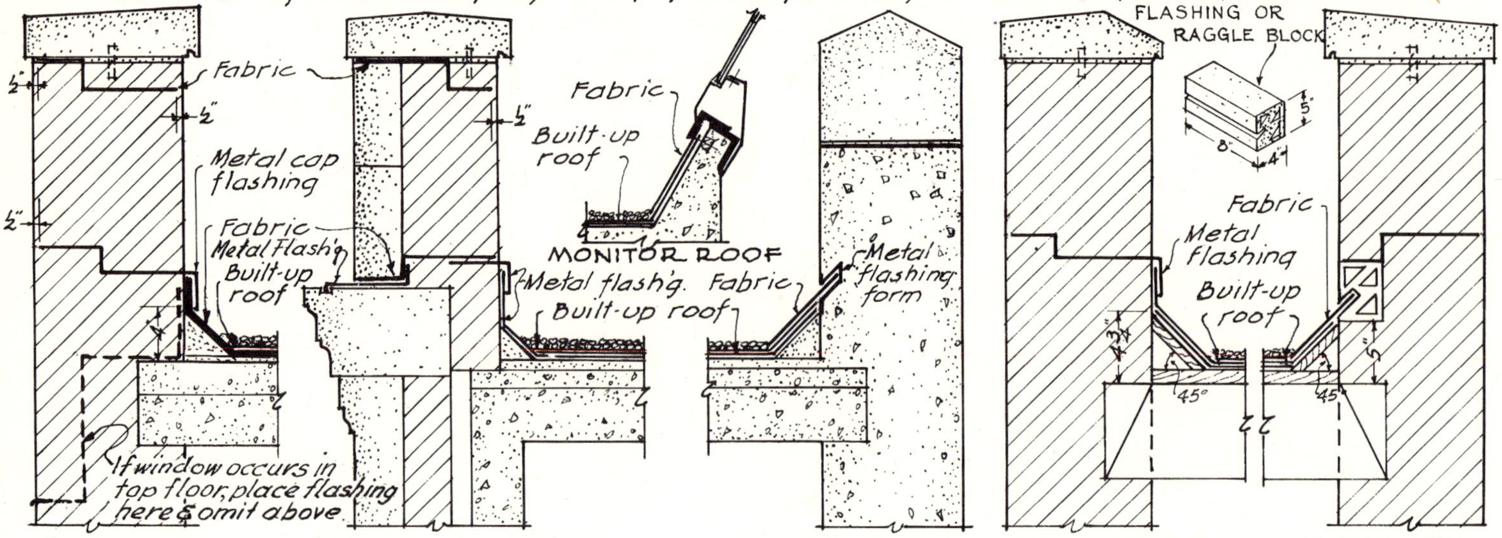

Fabric
½"
Metal cap flashing
Fabric
Metal Flash'g
Built-up roof
If window occurs in top floor, place flashing here & omit above.
Fabric
Built-up roof
MONITOR ROOF
Metal flash'g. Fabric
Built-up roof
Metal flashing form
FLASHING OR RAGGLE BLOCK
Fabric
Metal flashing
Built-up roof
45°

SEPARATE CAP & COPING FLASHING
Used for high parapet wall

CONCR. ROOF and WALL

FLASHING for LOW PARAPET

WATERPROOFING of COPINGS with FABRIC and MASTIC MATERIALS

For copper flashing see "Flashing" pages.
Scale ¾" = 1'-0"

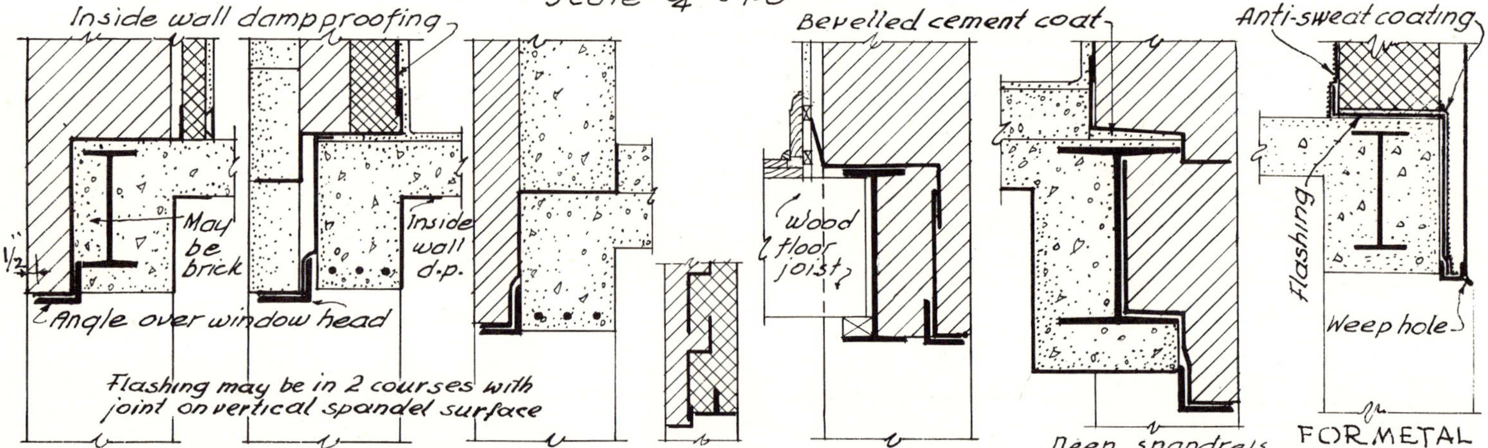

Inside wall dampproofing
May be brick
Angle over window head
Inside wall d.p.
Flashing may be in 2 courses with joint on vertical spandrel surface
Bevelled cement coat
Wood floor joist
Anti-sweat coating
Flashing
Weep hole

FOR BLOCK FURRING

FOR CONCRETE BEAM

PRE-FORMED W.P.

TURNUP with FURRING

Deep spandrels 15" or over
TWO COURSE W.P.

FOR METAL OR GLASS FACING

SPANDREL WATERPROOFING with FABRIC and MASTIC

All joints to lap minimum of 3". Flash up at all columns 6" min. (see dwg. at right), and up all chases, cutouts, etc. Bevelled cement finish on slab over flanges of spandrel beams. Trowel coat of mastic on cement and on all steel that fabric is to rest on or against. Apply impregnated felt or cloth as system calls for. Some systems call for a second coat of mastic on horizontal surfaces. Apply mastic on all jts. where fabric laps, at all pipes, ducts, etc. Apply mastic to both sides of turned-up inside ends of fabric. See manufacturers' catalogs for materials and application. Fabric as used on this page refers to all flashing materials except sheet metals. It includes felts, fabrics, bituminous compounds (alone or in combination or as coatings for metal or wire work).

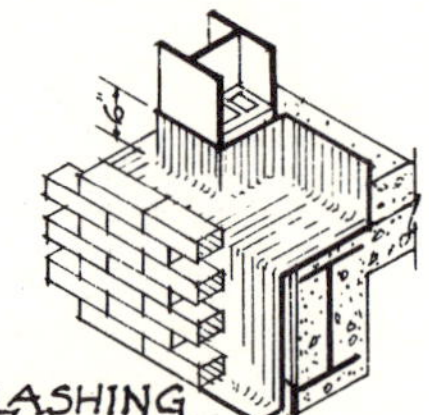

6"

FLASHING at COLUMNS

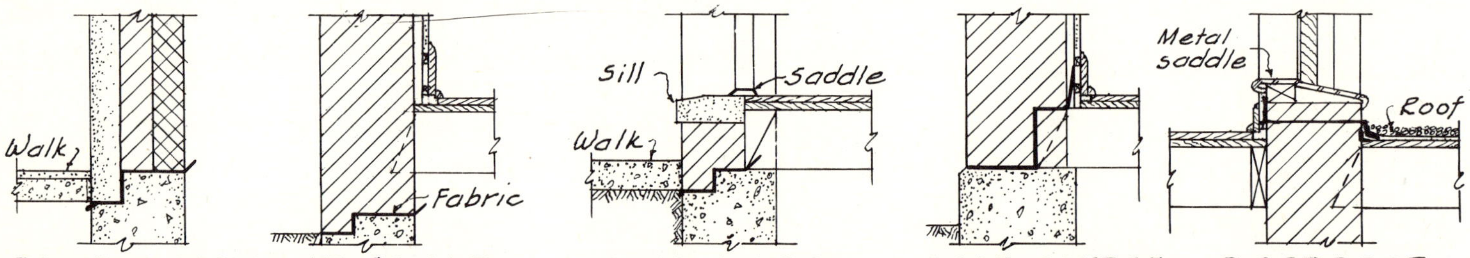

Walk
Fabric
Sill
Saddle
Walk
Metal saddle
Roof

DAMPPROOFING AT GRADE

BASE COURSE AT DOOR SILL

BASE COURSE ABOVE GRADE

ROOF DOOR SADDLE

DAMP COURSES - SILLS and AT GRADE

Data Checked by: Western Waterproofing Co., Inc.

EXPANSION JOINTS

THERMAL EXPANSION FACTORS of MATERIALS

(inches per degree)

METALS		MASONRY	
Aluminum (wrought)	.0000128	Brick	.0000031
Bronze	.0000101	Clay tile	.0000033
Copper	.0000098	Concrete	.0000065
Lead	.0000159	Granite	.0000040
Monel	.0000078	Limestone	.0000038
Steel (medium)	.0000067	Marble	.0000056
Zinc	.0000178	Plaster	.0000092

GLASS (common) .0000047

Width of expansion joint is generally assumed as 1" (one inch). Actual amount of expansion may be determined as follows:

FORMULA

Multiply span (in inches) of material x 100° (average difference in F. temperature between winter & summer) x the factor of expansion of the material. { Span" x 100° F. x Factor }

NOTES

A complete separation should be made between old & new construction by expansion joints. A complete frame of columns and beams should be on both sides of the joint but no structural connections between the two frames. Because roofs expand more than walls, expansion joints are sometimes placed in roof slabs and top floor walls under 200 ft. Expansion joints are used in cold storage plants, breweries, etc., where the temperature is at an unusual degree. Steel trusses with spans over 45 ft. should be free to move laterally at one end. A slip joint should be provided between foundation & walls that contain transecting joints. (the foundation, being underground, is but little affected by the temperature of the air).

Joints should be installed around machinery foundations to isolate vibration & permit differential settlement in floor.

FILLERS USED IN EXPANSION JOINTS

Premoulded

A. Composition (asphalt, vegetable fibre. B. Jute (rubber coated). C. Sponge rubber. D. Cork & asphalt composition. E. Cork. Standard thicknesses of premould. fillers 1/4", 3/8", 1/2", 3/4", 1".

Mastic

A. Asphalt compound
B. Rubberized asphalt comp'd. (various colors)

TABLE OF MAXIMUM ALLOWANCES

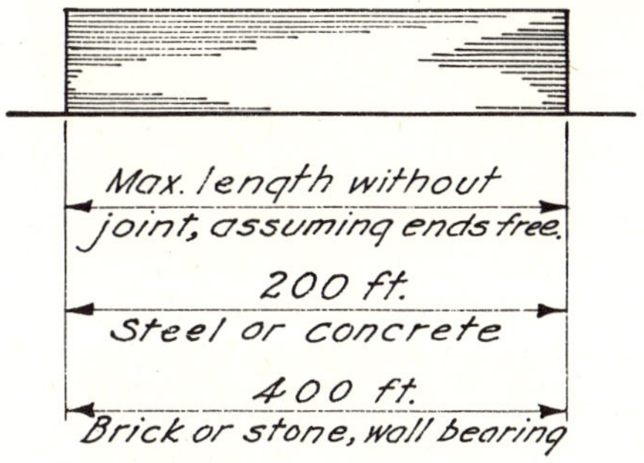

Max. length without joint, assuming ends free.
200 ft.
Steel or concrete
400 ft.
Brick or stone, wall bearing

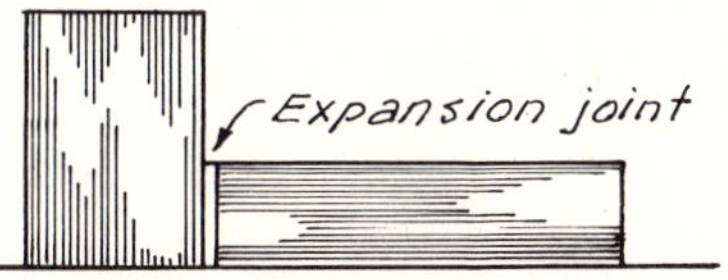

Expansion joint

A. New building adjoining existing bldg.
B. Long, low building abutting high bldg.
C. Wings adjoining main structure.

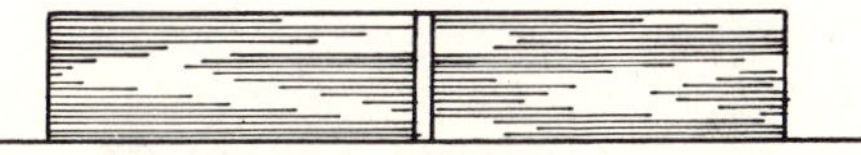

Long buildings

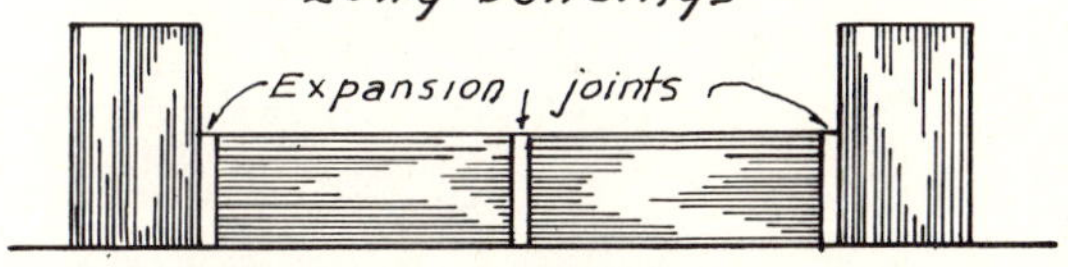

Expansion joints

Long, low building between high wings

LOCATIONS OF EXPANSION JOINTS
Diagrammatic Elevations
no scale

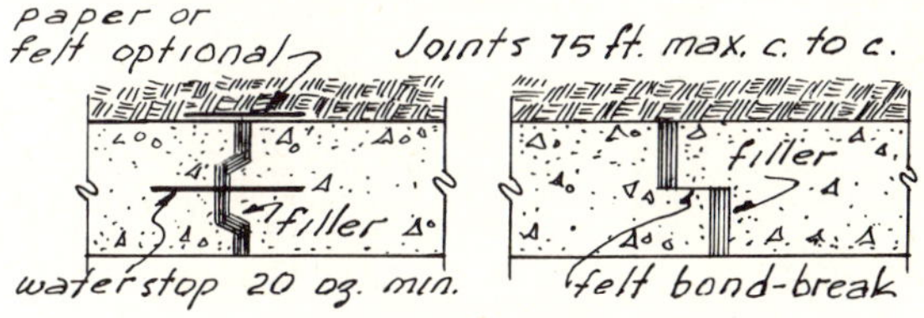

paper or felt optional
Joints 75 ft. max. c. to c.
filler
filler
waterstop 20 oz. min.
felt bond-break

JOINTS in RETAINING WALLS
1/2" = 1'-0"

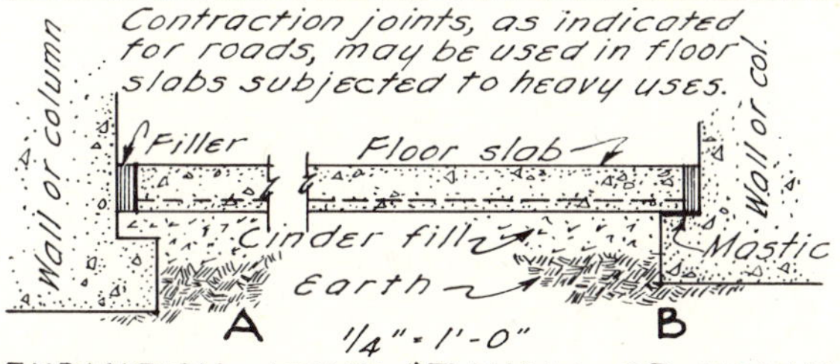

Contraction joints, as indicated for roads, may be used in floor slabs subjected to heavy uses.
Wall or column
Filler
Floor slab
Wall or col.
Cinder fill
Mastic
Earth
A
B
1/4" = 1'-0"

EXPANSION JOINT AT WALL OR COLUMN

Detail A used for heavy loads in 1 story bldgs. where pressure is greater under floor slab than under footing

Detail B used in multi-story bldgs. where pressure is greater under footing than under floor slab.

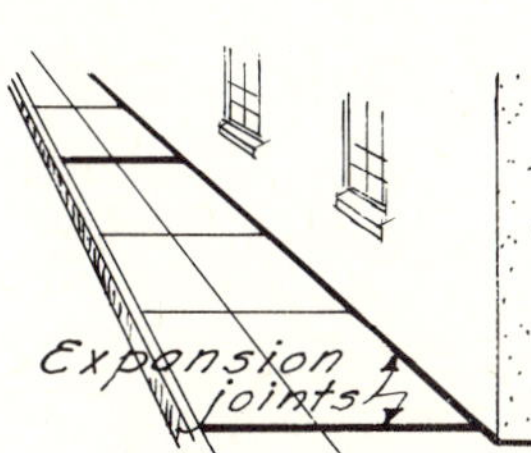

Expansion joints

JOINTS in CONCRETE WALKS
1/2" joints spaced 30' c. to c.

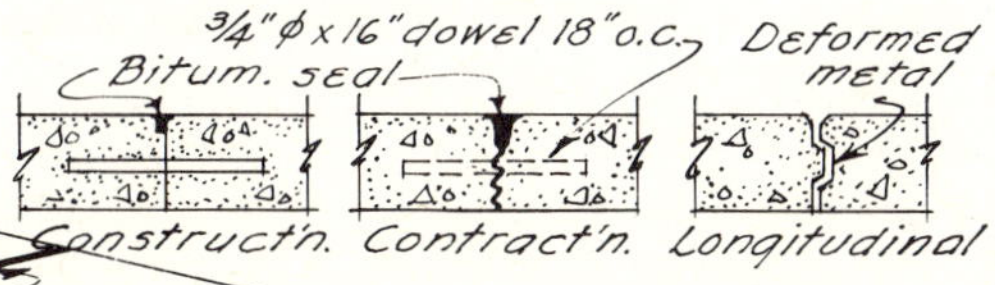

3/4" ϕ x 16" dowel 18" o.c.
Bitum. seal
Deformed metal
Constructn.
Contract'n.
Longitudinal

Stone copings are to be doweled to masonry but also set with frequent mastic joints

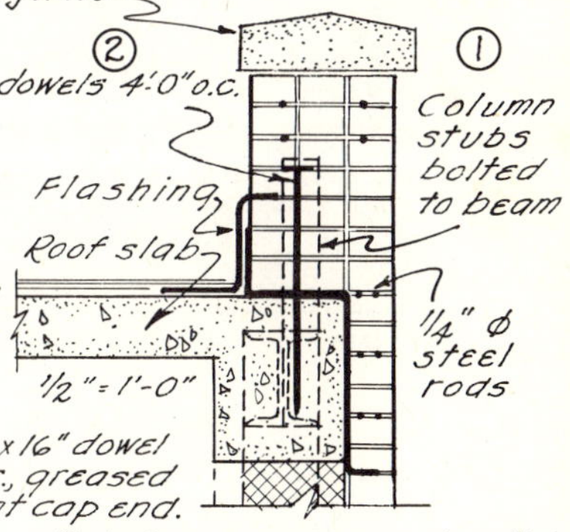

2
1
1/2" ϕ dowels 4'-0" o.c.
Column stubs bolted to beam
Flashing
Roof slab
1/4" ϕ steel rods
1/2" = 1'-0"

Reinforcing parapet walls against temp. strains by the use of horizontal steel rods & ① col. stubs in steel structures. ② dowels in concrete construct.

SPACING of JOINTS in CONCRETE ROAD SLABS

Non-reinforced slabs - contraction joints from 15'-25' depending on aggregate & climate. Expansion joints 90'-120' depending on temp. ranges. Reinf. slabs 40'-60' depending on reinf. & climate. Contraction joints seldom used.

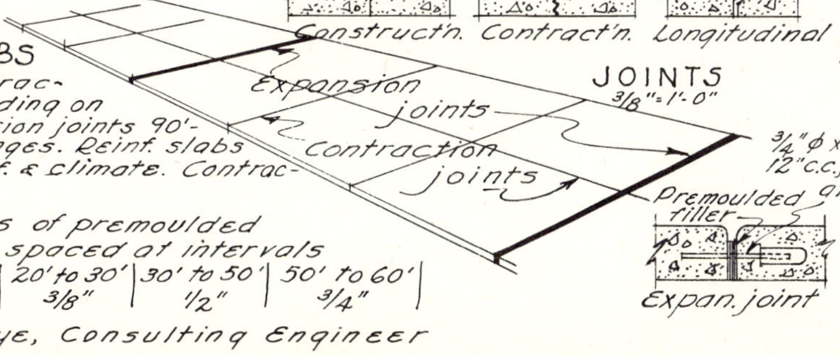

Expansion joints
Contraction joints
JOINTS
3/8" = 1'-0"
3/4" ϕ x 16" dowel 12" c.c., greased at cap end.
Premoulded filler
Expan. joint

Suggested thicknesses of premoulded filler for expansion joints spaced at intervals of:

of:	15' to 20'	20' to 30'	30' to 50'	50' to 60'
Thickness of filler:	1/4"	3/8"	1/2"	3/4"

Approved by Elwyn E. Seelye, Consulting Engineer

EXPANSION JOINTS – FLOORS

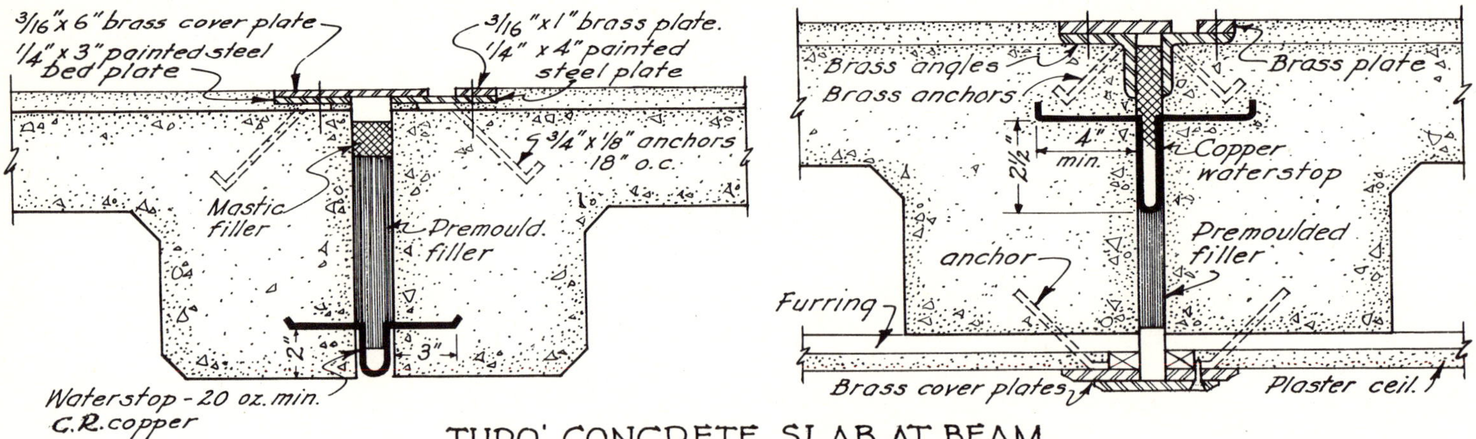
3/16"x 6" brass cover plate
1/4" x 3" painted steel bed plate
3/16" x 1" brass plate.
1/4" x 4" painted steel plate
3/4" x 1/8" anchors 18" o.c.
Mastic filler
Premould. filler
2"
3"
Waterstop - 20 oz. min. C.R. copper
Brass angles
Brass anchors
Brass plate
4" min.
2½"
Copper waterstop
Premoulded filler
anchor
Furring
Brass cover plates
Plaster ceil.

THRO' CONCRETE SLAB AT BEAM

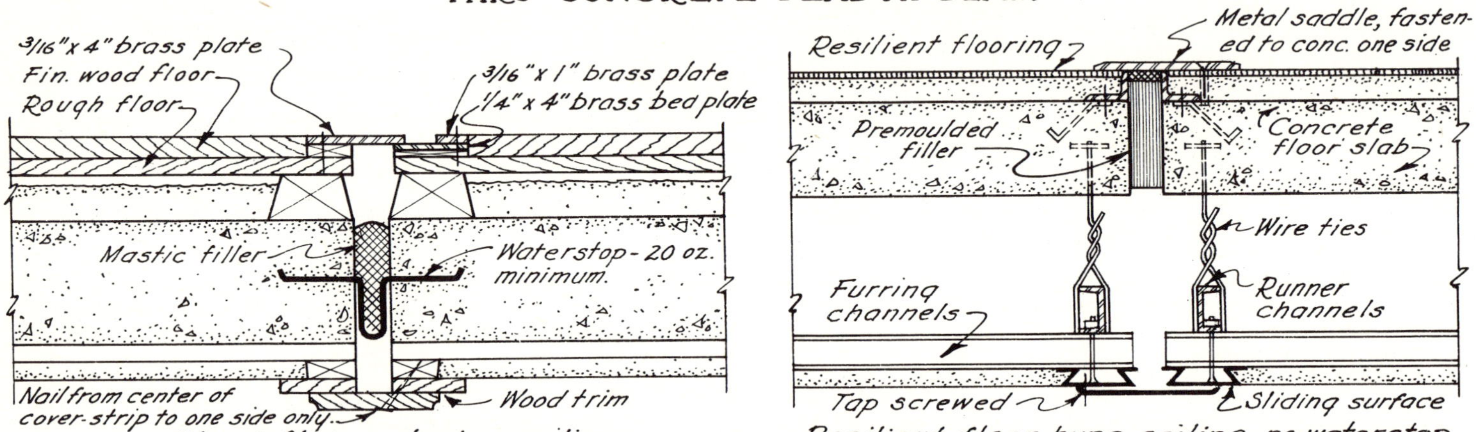
3/16" x 4" brass plate
Fin. wood floor
Rough floor
3/16" x 1" brass plate
1/4" x 4" brass bed plate
Mastic filler
Waterstop - 20 oz. minimum.
Nail from center of cover-strip to one side only.
Wood trim
Resilient flooring
Metal saddle, fastened to conc. one side
Premoulded filler
Concrete floor slab
Wire ties
Furring channels
Runner channels
Tap screwed
Sliding surface

Wood floor - plaster ceiling — *Resilient floor-hung ceiling - no waterstop*

THRO' CONCRETE SLABS

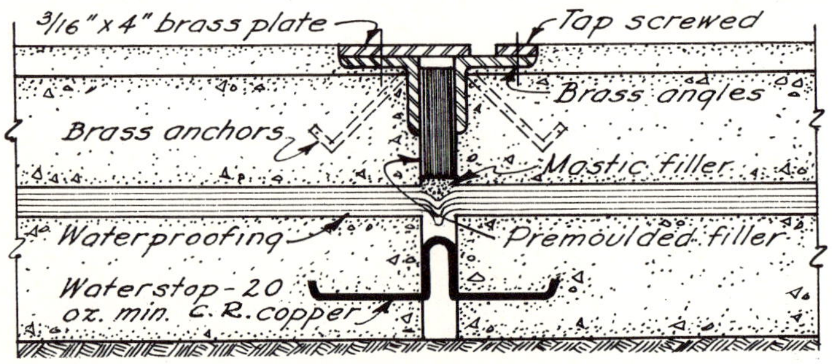
3/16" x 4" brass plate
Tap screwed
Brass angles
Brass anchors
Mastic filler
Waterproofing
Premoulded filler
Waterstop - 20 oz. min. C. R. copper

THRO' WATERPROOFED SLAB ON EARTH

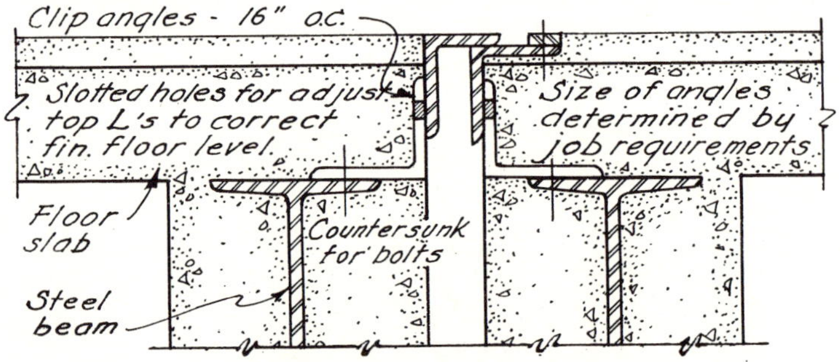
Clip angles - 16" o.c.
Slotted holes for adjust top L's to correct fin. floor level.
Size of angles determined by job requirements.
Floor slab
Countersunk for bolts
Steel beam

THRO' FLOOR SLAB ON STEEL BEAMS

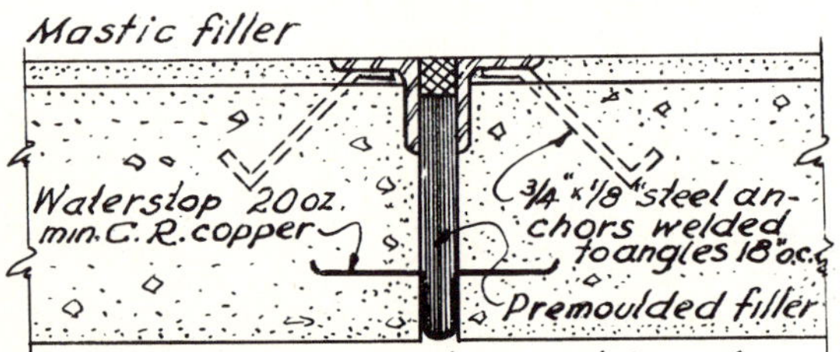
Mastic filler
Waterstop 20 oz. min. C. R. copper
3/4" x 1/8" steel anchors welded to angles 18" o.c.
Premoulded filler

Appearance not considered

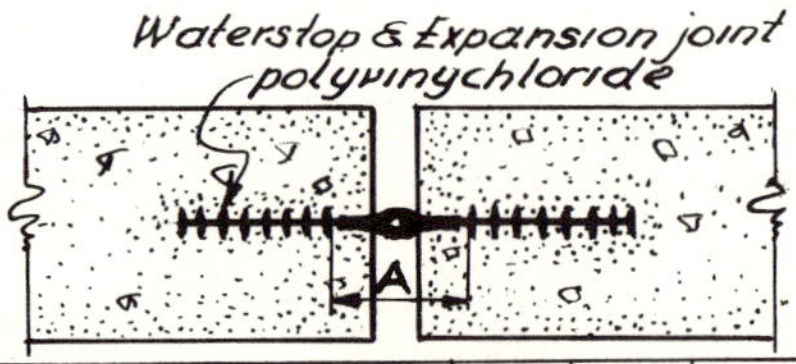
Waterstop & Expansion joint polyvinychloride
A

Sizes	2¼"	3¾"	6"	9"
Suggested max. head of water	25'	50'	100'	150'
Max. elongation of A	½"	1"	1¼"	1½"

Data supplied by: "Electrovert, New York, Montreal, Toronto."

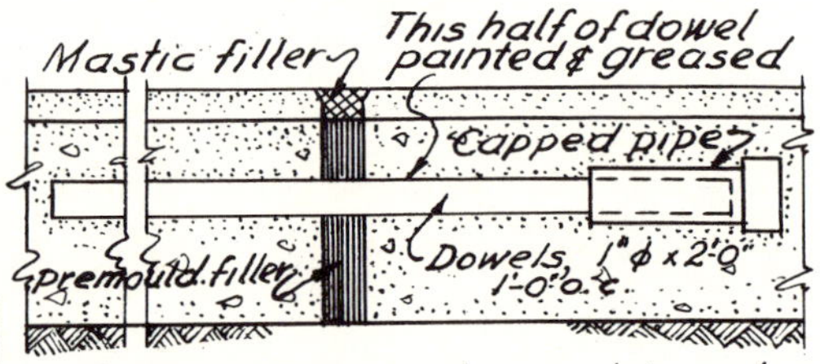
Mastic filler
This half of dowel painted & greased
Capped pipe
Premould. filler
Dowels, 1" ϕ x 2'0" 1'-0" o.c.

Appearance not considered

THRO' UTILITY FLOOR SLABS

Scale 1½" = 1'-0"

Waterstops - 20 oz. cold rolled copper, 8'-0" lengths. Ends lapped ¾" & soldered. Lead may be used to fill joints instead of mastic filler where traffic is severe. Deformed reinforcing bars should never pass through an expansion joint. Reinforcing not shown.

Data checked by the National Assoc. of Architectural Metal Mfrs., & the Copper & Brass Research Assoc.

EXPANSION JOINTS - WALLS

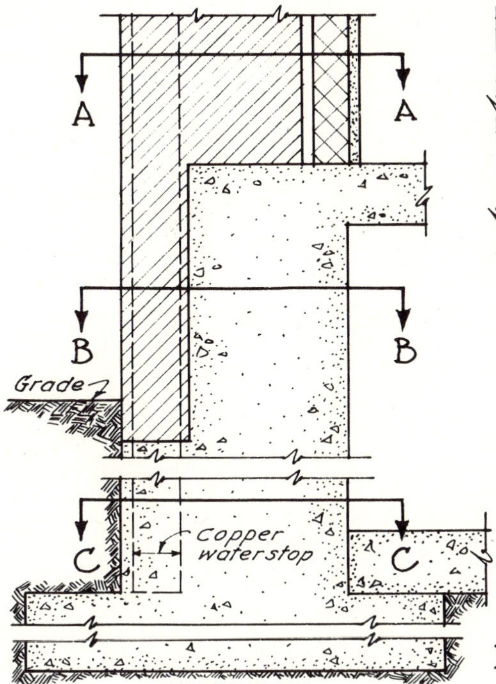
A
A
B
B
Grade
C
C
Copper waterstop

SECTION

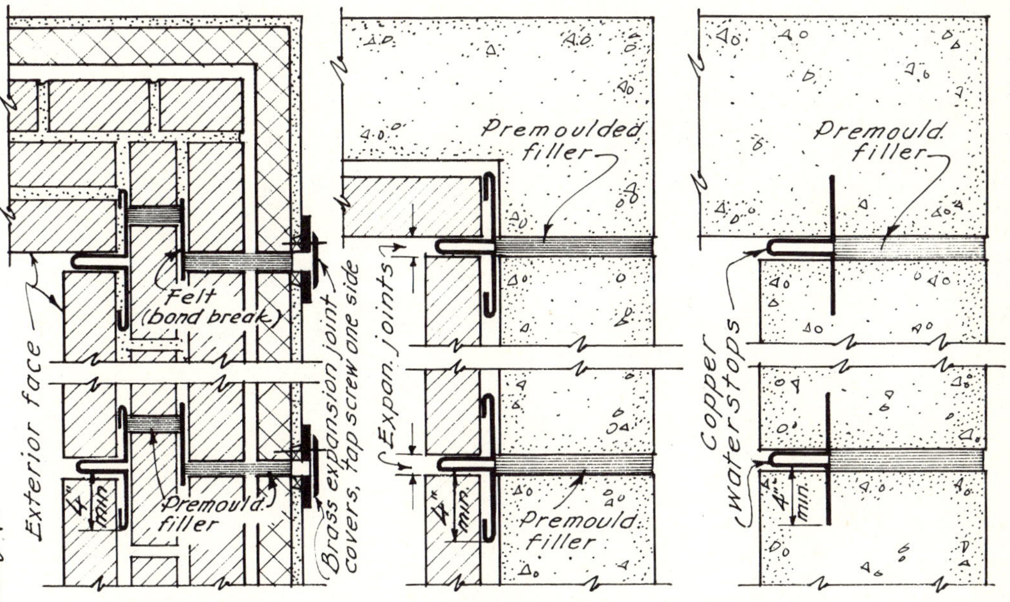
Exterior face
Felt (bond break)
Premould. filler
4" min.
Brass expansion joint covers, tap screw one side
Premoulded filler
Expan. joints
4" min.
Premould. filler
Premould. filler
Copper waterstops
4" min.

PLAN A-A PLAN B-B PLAN C-C

EXTERIOR STRAIGHT WALLS & IN-CORNERS

Scale 1" = 1'-0"

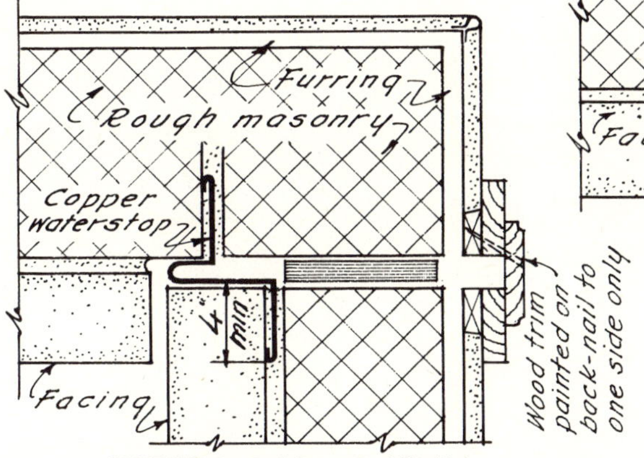
Furring
Rough masonry
Copper waterstop
4 min.
Facing
Wood trim painted on back-nail to one side only

INTERIOR WOOD TRIM

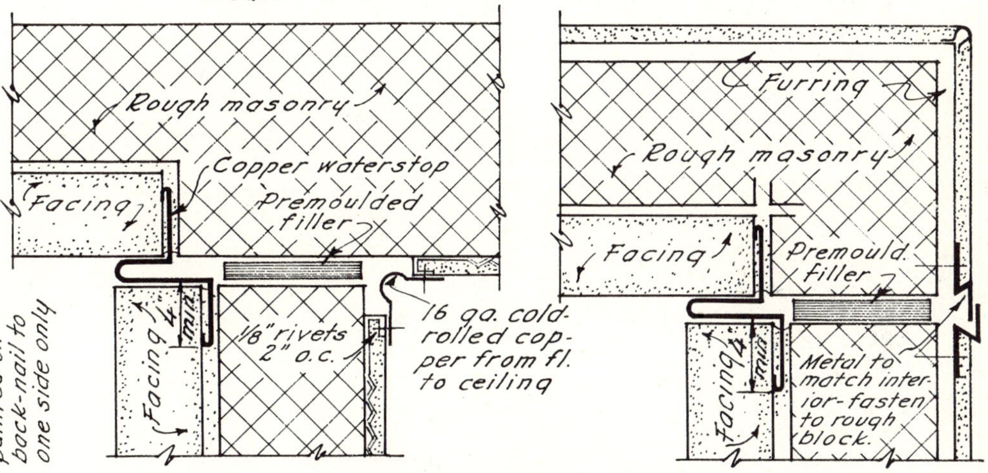
Rough masonry
Copper waterstop
Facing
Premoulded filler
Facing
4 min.
1/8" rivets 2" o.c.
16 ga. cold-rolled copper from fl. to ceiling
Furring
Rough masonry
Facing
Premould. filler
Facing
4 min.
Metal to match interior-fasten to rough block.

INTERIOR METAL TRIM

IN-CORNER OF EXTERIOR WALLS

Scale 1½" = 1'-0"

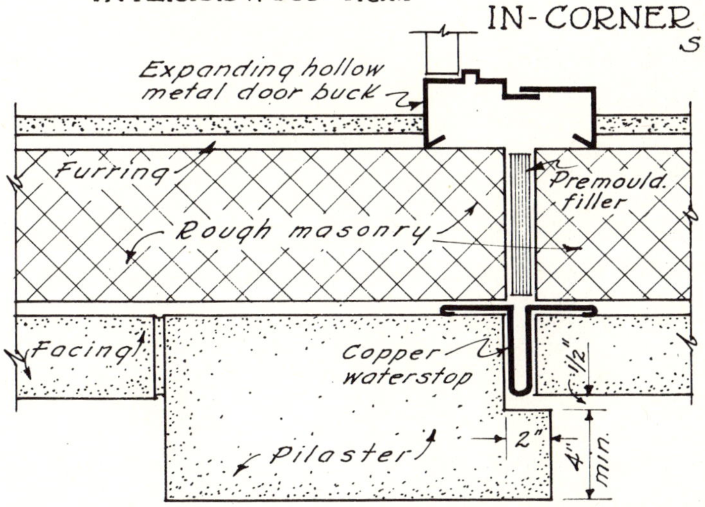
Expanding hollow metal door buck
Furring
Premould. filler
Rough masonry
Facing
Copper waterstop
1½"
2"
4" min.
Pilaster

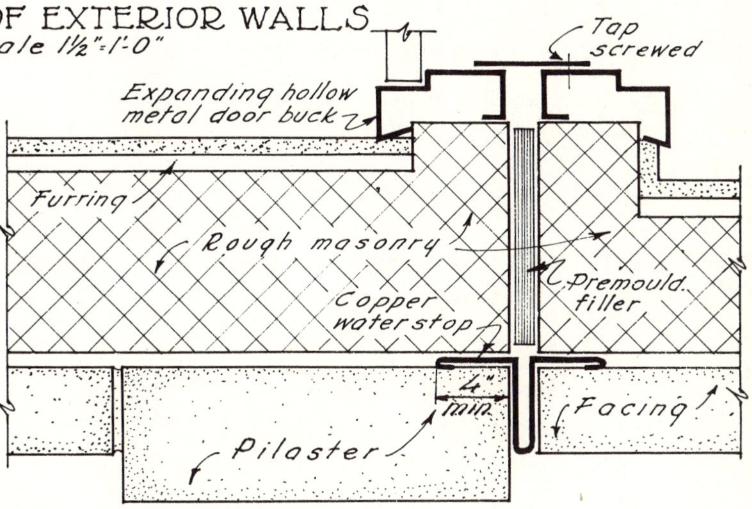
Tap screwed
Expanding hollow metal door buck
Furring
Rough masonry
Premould. filler
Copper waterstop
4" min.
Facing
Pilaster

JOINTS AT BREAK IN EXTERIOR WALLS

with hollow metal door bucks on interior. Scale 1½" = 1'-0"

Diagrams show suggested schemes for expansion joints to be adapted to specific uses. Indicated facing and rough masonry may be of any material. Waterstops are 20 oz. cold rolled copper, 8'-0" lengths, from footing to eave or top of parapet wall. Above grade, lap end joints 4", unsoldered; below grade, end jts. soldered.

Data checked by the Copper & Brass Research Assoc., & the National Assoc. of Architectural Metal Mfrs.

EXPANSION JOINTS – ROOFS & WALLS

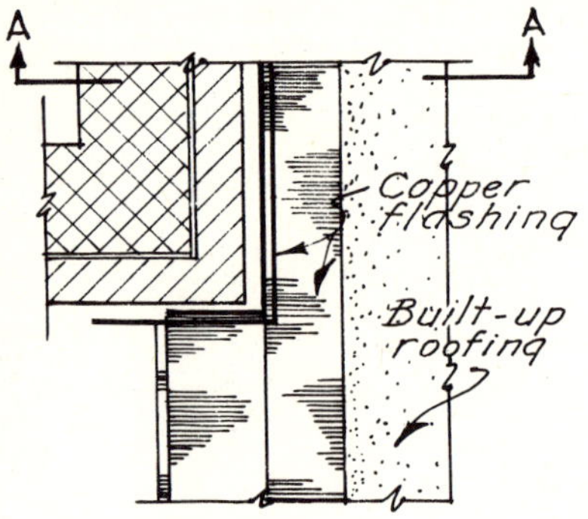

A
A
Copper flashing
Built-up roofing

PLAN
1/2" = 1'-0"

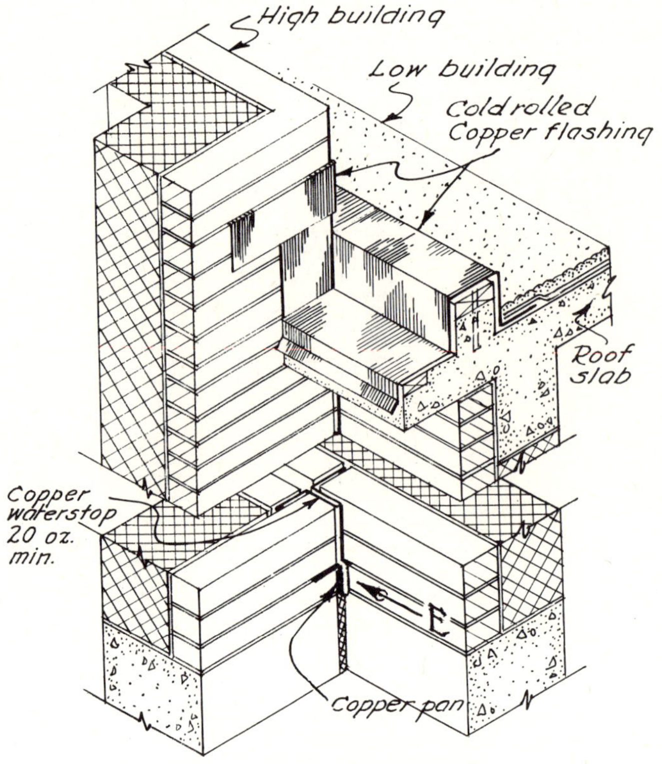

High building
Low building
Cold rolled Copper flashing
Roof slab
Copper waterstop 20 oz. min.
E
Copper pan

ISOMETRIC
1/2" = 1'-0"

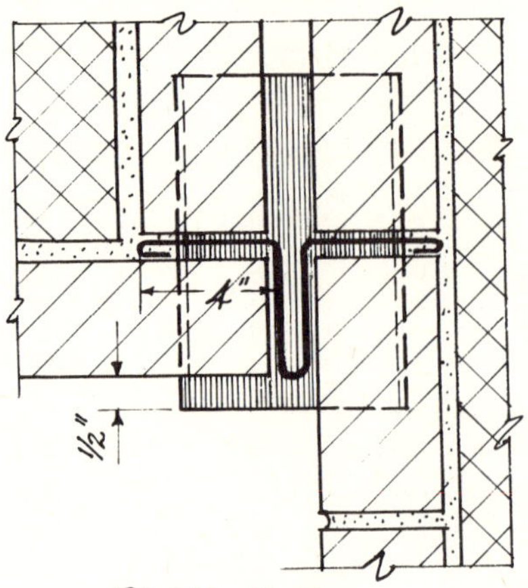

4"
1/2"

PLAN B·B

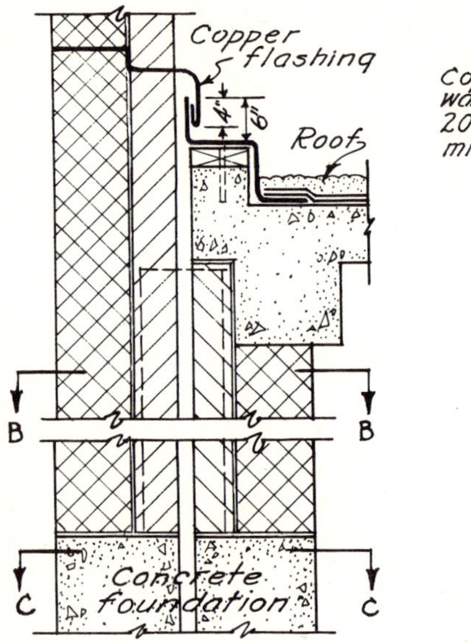

Copper flashing
4"
8"
Roof
B
B
Concrete foundation
C
C

SECTION A·A 1/2" = 1'-0"

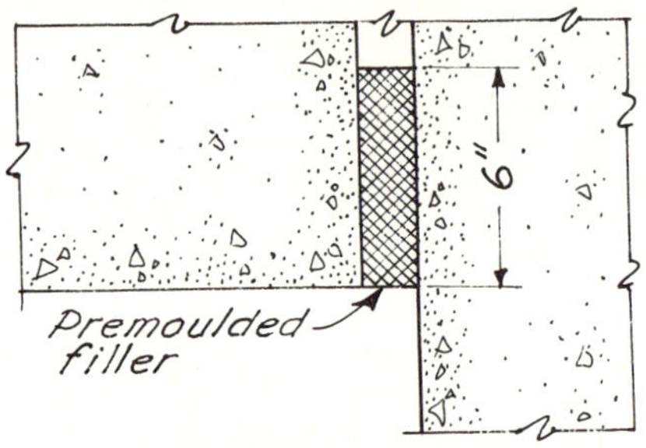

6"
Premoulded filler

PLAN C·C

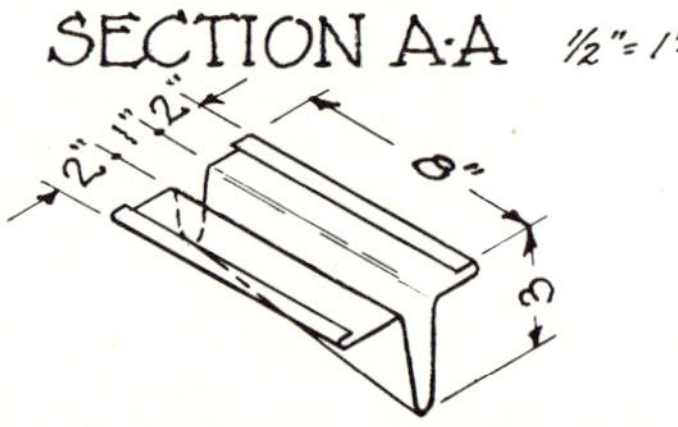

2"
1"
2"
8"
3"

Isometric of Copper Pan 1" = 1'-0"

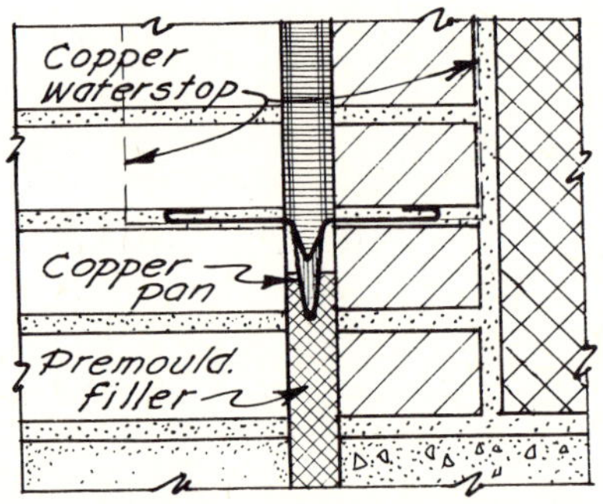

Copper waterstop
Copper pan
Premould. filler

ELEVATION E
Scale 1 1/2" = 1'-0" unless noted

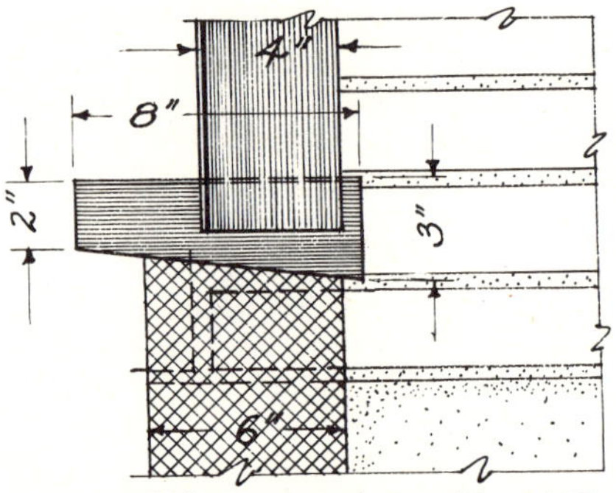

4"
8"
2"
3"
6"

DETAIL AT COPPER PAN

If basement is required to be water tight continue waterstop to footing (see "Expansion Joints - Walls")

JOINT AT INTERSECTION of HIGH & LOW BUILDINGS

All copper shown to be Cold Rolled - roofing temper

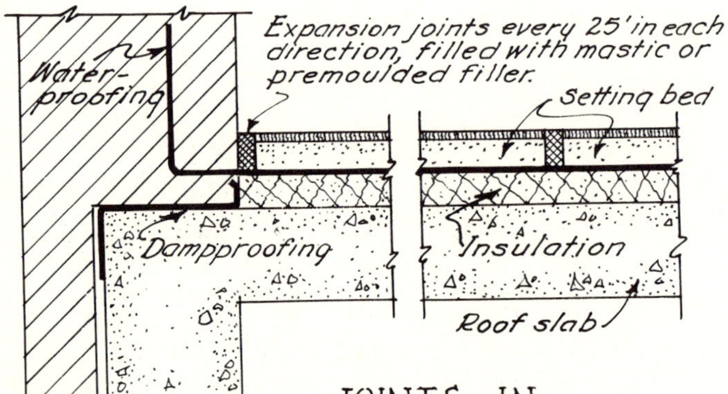

Expansion joints every 25' in each direction, filled with mastic or premoulded filler.
Water-proofing
Setting bed
Dampproofing
Insulation
Roof slab

JOINTS IN CERAMIC TILE ROOF 1" = 1'-0"

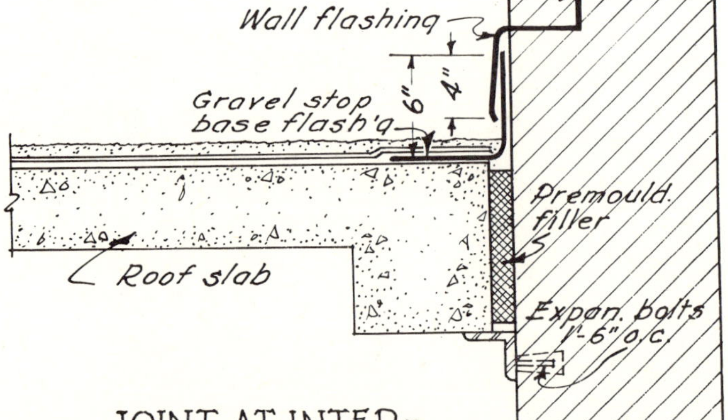

Wall flashing
Gravel stop base flash'g
6"
4"
Premould. filler
Roof slab
Expan. bolts 1'-6" o.c.

JOINT AT INTERSECTING ROOF & WALL

Data checked by the National Assoc. of Archt. Metal Mfrs., & the Copper & Brass Research Assoc.

EXPANSION JOINTS - ROOFS

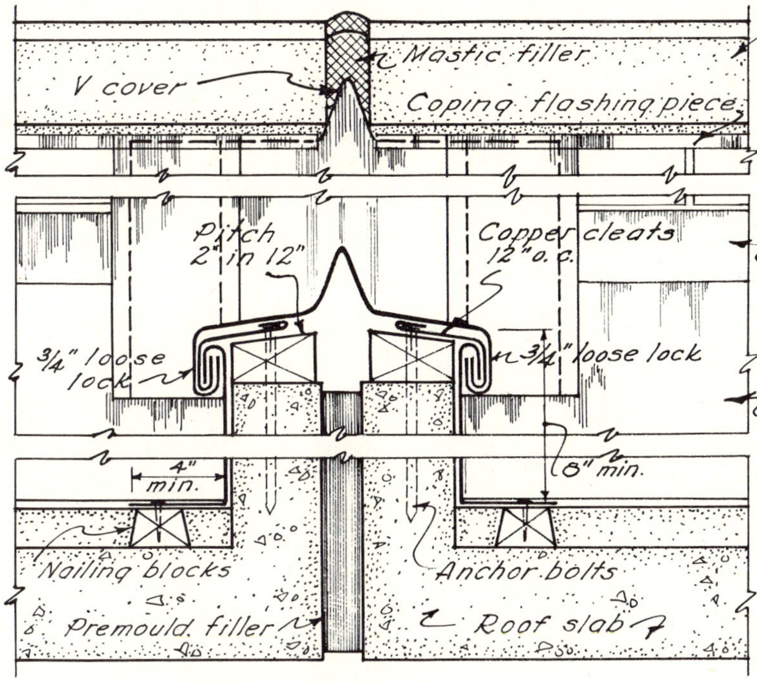

Mastic filler
V cover
Coping flashing piece
Pitch 2" in 12"
Copper cleats 12" o.c.
3/4" loose lock
3/4" loose lock
4" min.
8" min.
Nailing blocks
Anchor bolts
Premould. filler
Roof slab

*** SECTION A-A**
Thro' roof curbs

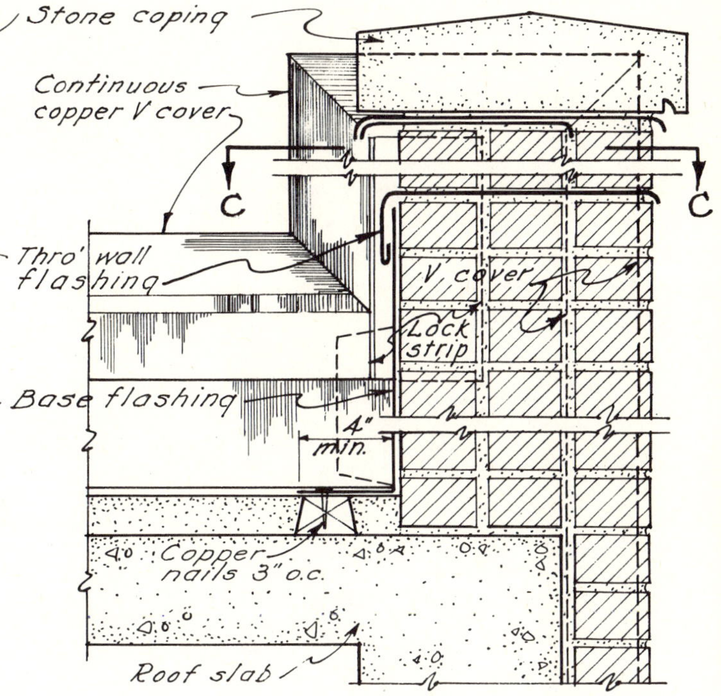

Stone coping
Continuous copper V cover
C
C
Thro' wall flashing
V cover
Lock strip
Base flashing
4" min.
Copper nails 3" o.c.
Roof slab

*** SECTION B-B**
Thro' parapet wall

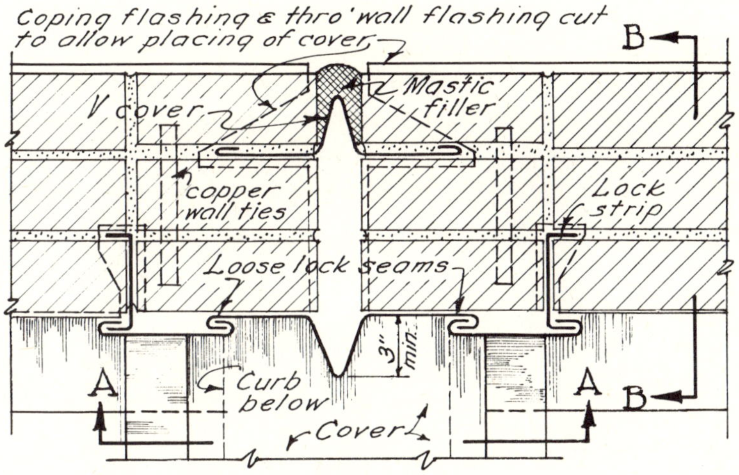

Coping flashing & thro' wall flashing cut to allow placing of cover
B
Mastic filler
V cover
copper wall ties
Lock strip
Loose lock seams
3" min.
A
Curb below
A
B
Cover

*** PLAN C-C**
Thro' parapet wall
1½" = 1'-0"

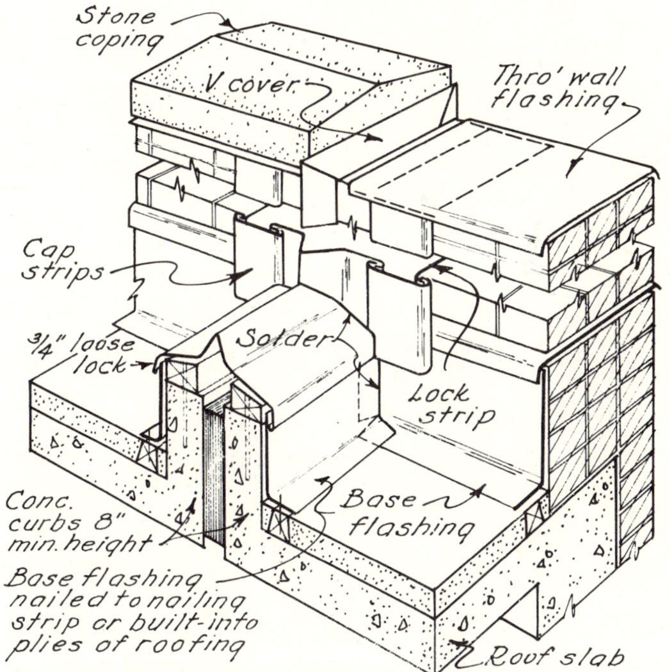

Stone coping
V cover
Thro' wall flashing
Cap strips
3/4" loose lock
Solder
Lock strip
Conc. curbs 8" min. height
Base flashing
Base flashing nailed to nailing strip or built-into plies of roofing
Roof slab

*** PERSPECTIVE**

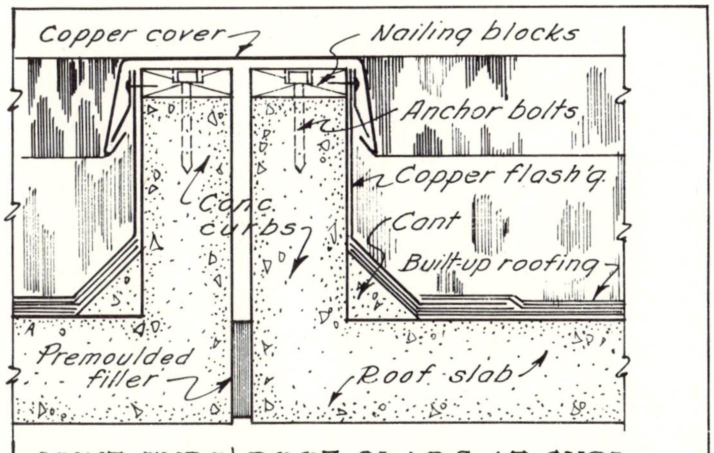

Copper cover
Nailing blocks
Anchor bolts
Copper flash'g.
Conc. curbs
Cant
Built-up roofing
Premoulded filler
Roof slab

JOINT THRO' ROOF SLABS AT CURB
Scale 1" = 1'-0"

Cover over curbs made up of 20 oz. C.R. copper, 8' lengths, 6" unsoldered lap joints. Cover for outside of wall made up of 8' lengths 2" laps built into masonry. Base flashings made in 8' lengths joined with ¾" locked & soldered seams, except every third joint (24'), to be made with a 3" loose-lock filled with elastic cement or white lead. Cover piece, cap strings & lock strips made of 20 oz. soft copper. The rest of the metal made of 20 oz. cold rolled copper.

*Data from the Copper & Brass Research Assoc.

EXTERIOR WALL FACINGS and VENEERS

TABLE OF CONTENTS

BRICK VENEER

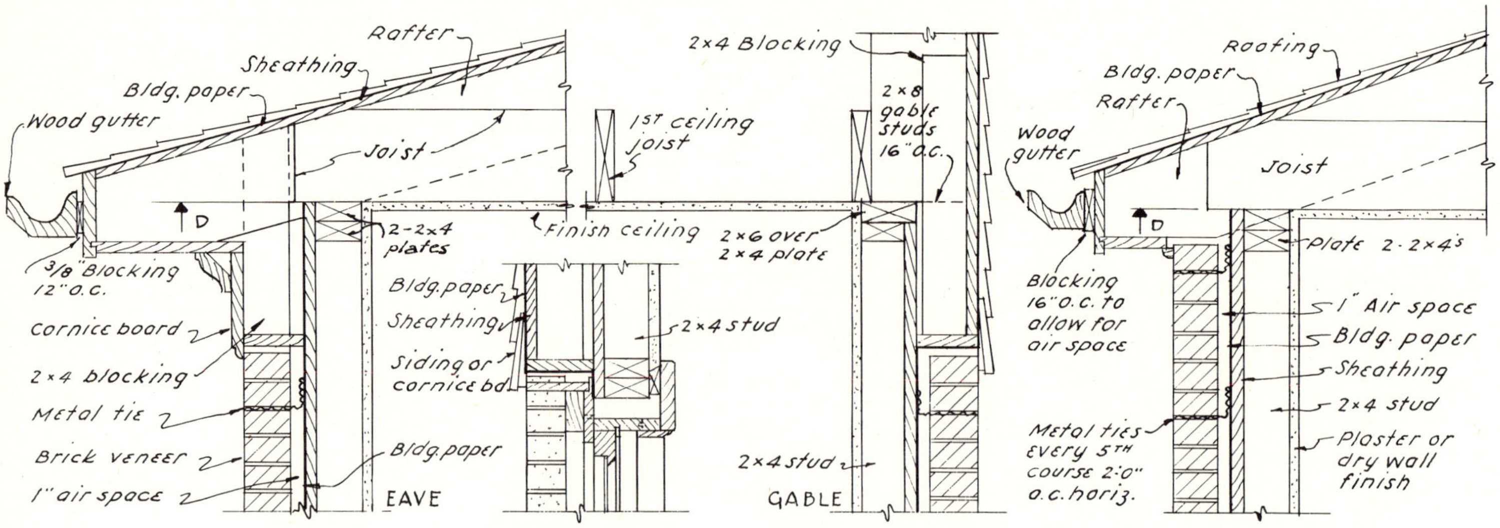
Rafter
Sheathing
Bldg. paper
Wood gutter
Joist
D
3/8" Blocking 12" o.c.
Cornice board
2×4 blocking
Metal tie
Brick veneer
1" air space
2-2×4 plates
Bldg. paper
EAVE
1st ceiling joist
Finish ceiling
Bldg. paper
Sheathing
Siding or cornice bd
2×4 stud
2×4 Blocking
2×8 gable studs 16" o.c.
2×6 over 2×4 plate
2×4 stud
GABLE
Roofing
Bldg. paper
Rafter
Wood gutter
Joist
Blocking 16" o.c. to allow for air space
Plate 2-2×4's
1" Air space
Bldg. paper
Sheathing
2×4 stud
Metal ties every 5th course 2'-0" o.c. horiz.
Plaster or dry wall finish

WINDOW HEAD (For window with brick above & below, see Window pages.)

EAVES, GABLE and WINDOW

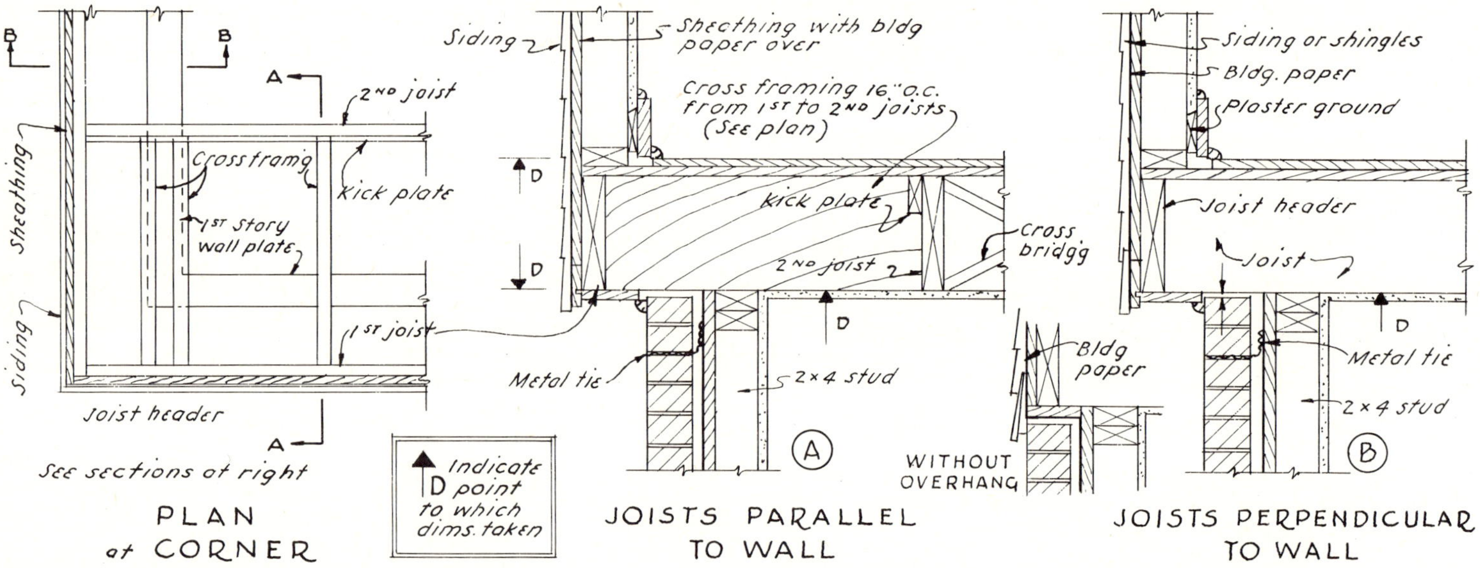
B
B
A
2nd joist
Sheathing
Cross framg
Kick plate
1st story wall plate
Siding
1st joist
Joist header
A
See sections at right
PLAN at CORNER
Indicate D point to which dims. taken
Siding
Sheathing with bldg paper over
Cross framing 16" o.c. from 1st to 2nd joists (See plan)
D
Kick plate
Cross bridg'g
D
2nd joist
D
Metal tie
2×4 stud
A
Bldg paper
WITHOUT OVERHANG
JOISTS PARALLEL TO WALL
Siding or shingles
Bldg. paper
Plaster ground
Joist header
Joist
D
Metal tie
2×4 stud
B
JOISTS PERPENDICULAR TO WALL

BRICK VENEER with WOOD SIDING on SECOND STORY

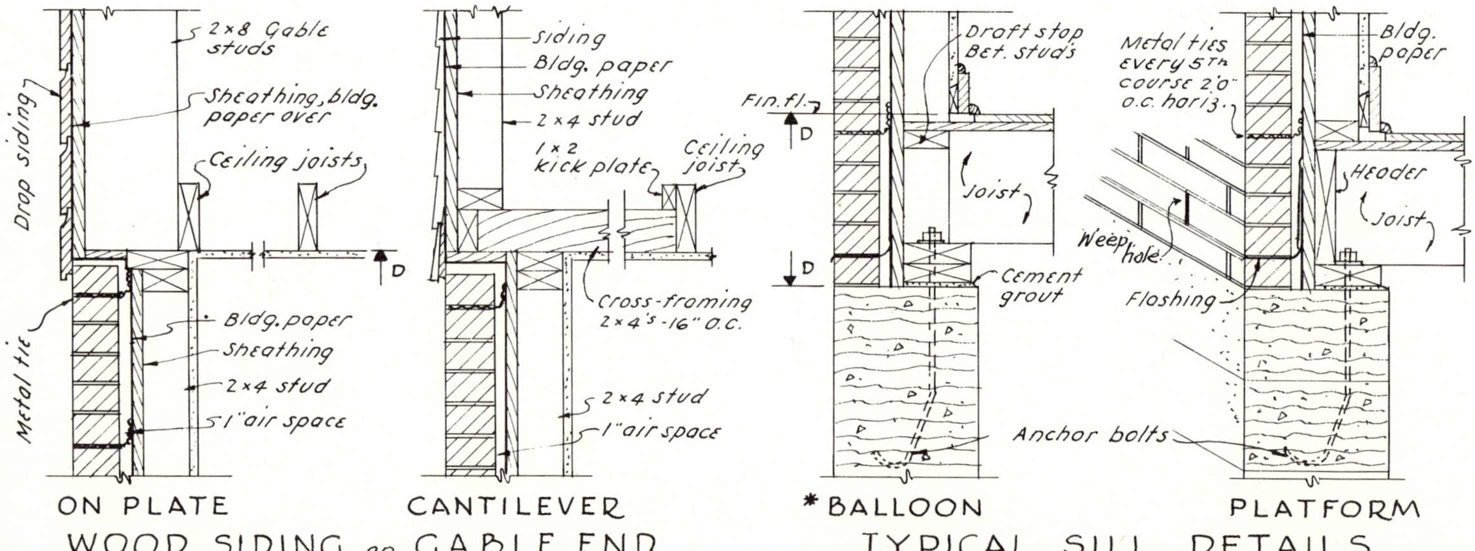
2×8 Gable studs
Drop siding
Sheathing, bldg. paper over
Ceiling joists
D
Metal tie
Bldg. paper
Sheathing
2×4 stud
1" air space
ON PLATE
Siding
Bldg. paper
Sheathing
2×4 stud
1×2 kick plate
Ceiling joist
Cross-framing 2×4's-16" o.c.
2×4 stud
1" air space
CANTILEVER
Draft stop Bet. stud's
Fin. fl.
D
Joist
D
Cement grout
Anchor bolts
*BALLOON
Metal ties every 5th course 2'-0" o.c. horiz.
Bldg. paper
Header
Joist
Weep hole
Flashing
PLATFORM

WOOD SIDING on GABLE END or SECTION at CHANGE of MATERIAL

TYPICAL SILL DETAILS

*Preferred for 2 story bldgs, due to less shrinkage.

Scale: 3/4" = 1'-0"

Adapted from data by National Lumber Manufacturers Association

ARCHITECTURAL TERRA COTTA - EXTERIOR

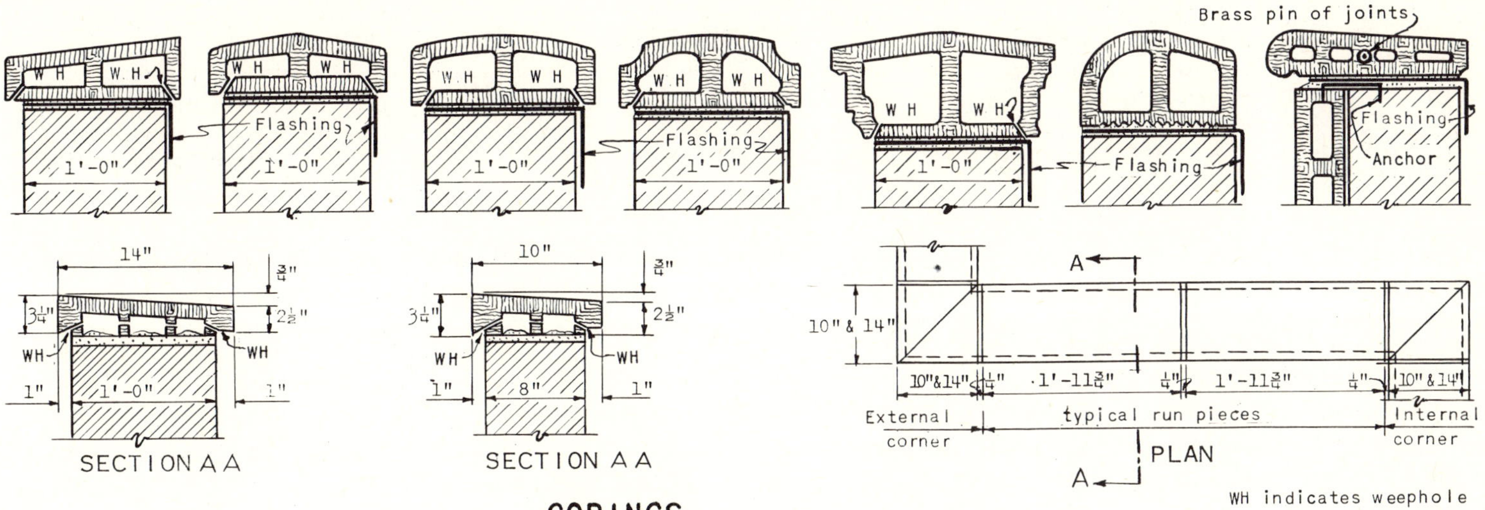
Brass pin of joints
W H
WH
Flashing
1'-0"
Anchor
14"
10"
3/4"
$3\frac{1}{4}$"
$2\frac{1}{2}$"
WH
1"
8"
SECTION A A
SECTION A A
A
10" & 14"
10"&14"
$\frac{1}{4}$"
1'-$11\frac{3}{4}$"
External corner
typical run pieces
Internal corner
PLAN
WH indicates weephole

COPINGS

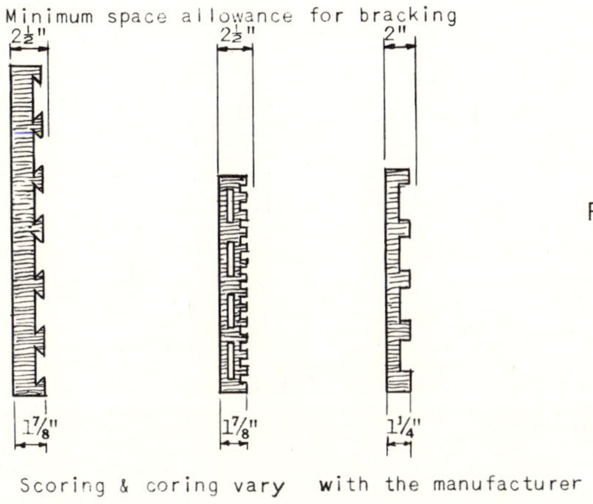
Minimum space allowance for bracking
$2\frac{1}{2}$"
$2\frac{1}{2}$"
2"
$1\frac{7}{8}$"
$1\frac{7}{8}$"
$1\frac{1}{4}$"
Scoring & coring vary with the manufacturer

SECTIONS OF FACING ASHLAR

Scale $\frac{3}{4}$" = 1'-0"

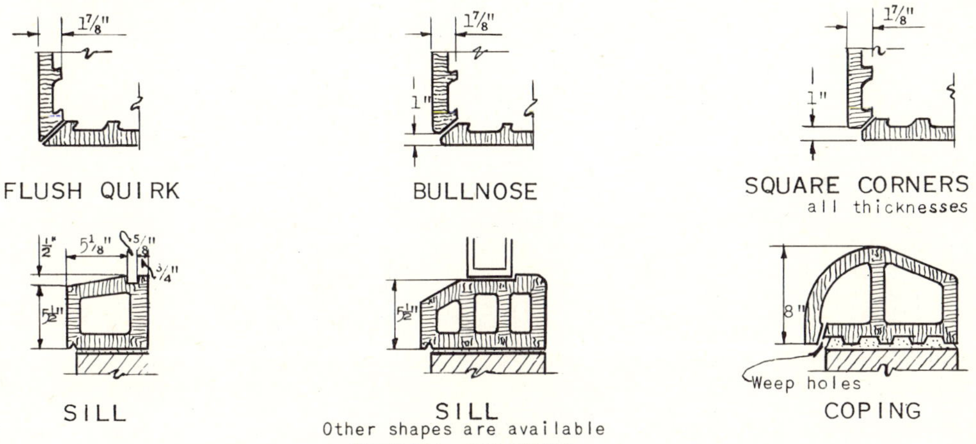
$1\frac{7}{8}$"
1"
FLUSH QUIRK
BULLNOSE
SQUARE CORNERS
all thicknesses
$\frac{1}{2}$"
$5\frac{1}{8}$"
5/8"
3/4"
$5\frac{1}{2}$"
8"
Weep holes
SILL
SILL
Other shapes are available
COPING

STOCK SHAPES
HEAVY EXTRUDED ASHLARS

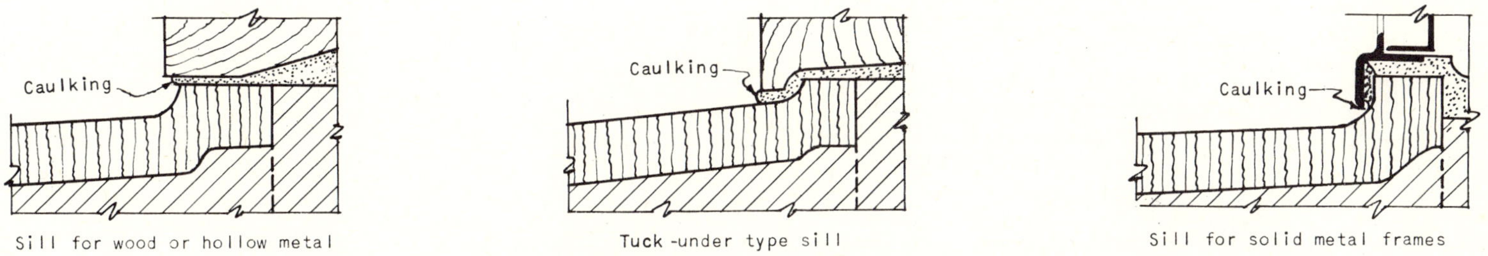
Caulking
Caulking
Caulking
Sill for wood or hollow metal
Tuck-under type sill
Sill for solid metal frames

VARIOUS TYPES OF SILLS

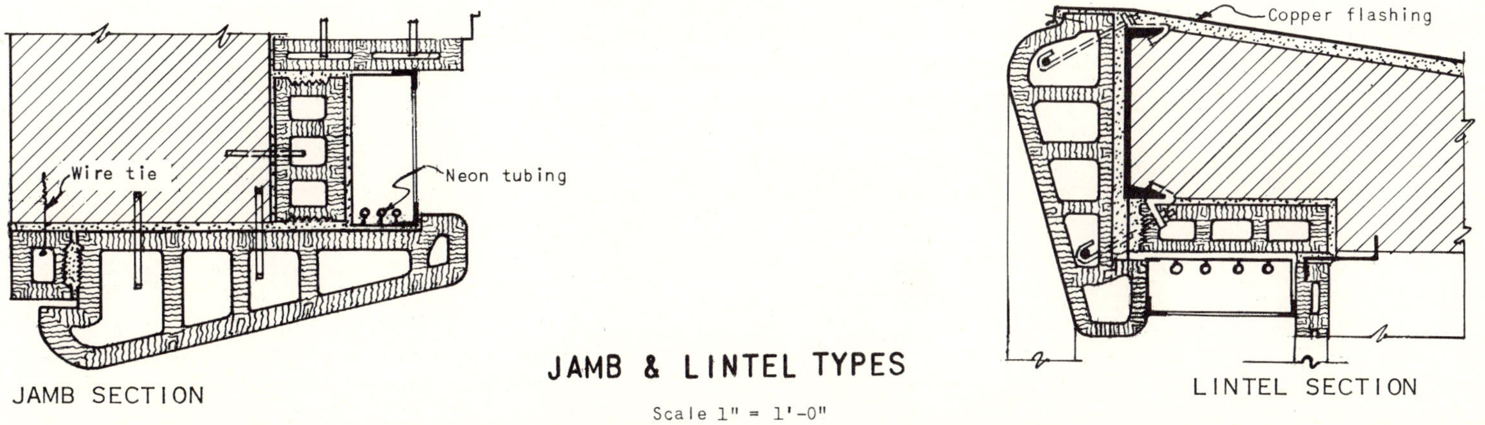
Wire tie
Neon tubing
JAMB SECTION
Copper flashing
LINTEL SECTION

JAMB & LINTEL TYPES

Scale 1" = 1'-0"

Data supplied by: Federal Seaboard Terra Cotta Corporation

ARCHITECTURAL TERRA COTTA - EXTERIOR

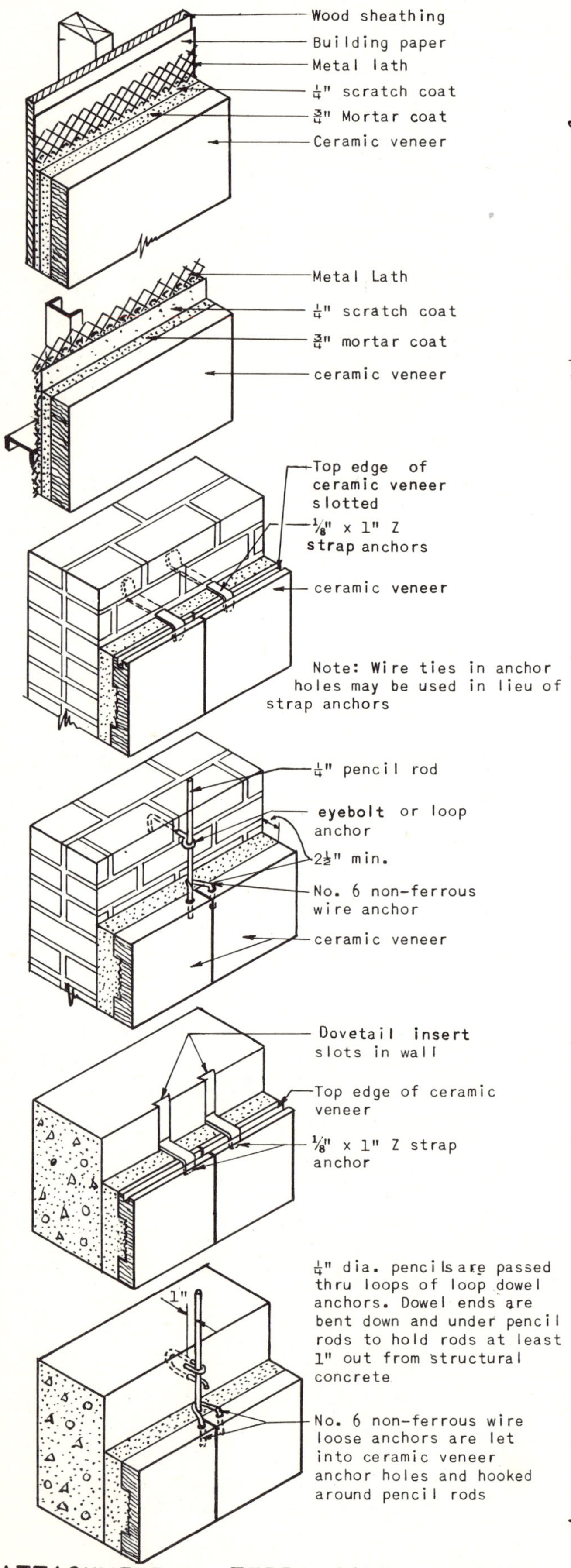
Wood sheathing
Building paper
Metal lath
1/4" scratch coat
3/4" Mortar coat
Ceramic veneer
Metal Lath
1/4" scratch coat
3/4" mortar coat
ceramic veneer
Top edge of ceramic veneer slotted
1/8" x 1" Z strap anchors
ceramic veneer
Note: Wire ties in anchor holes may be used in lieu of strap anchors
1/4" pencil rod
eyebolt or loop anchor
2 1/2" min.
No. 6 non-ferrous wire anchor
ceramic veneer
Dovetail insert slots in wall
Top edge of ceramic veneer
1/8" x 1" Z strap anchor
1"
1/4" dia. pencils are passed thru loops of loop dowel anchors. Dowel ends are bent down and under pencil rods to hold rods at least 1" out from structural concrete
No. 6 non-ferrous wire loose anchors are let into ceramic veneer anchor holes and hooked around pencil rods

ATTACHMENT OF TERRA COTTA VENEER

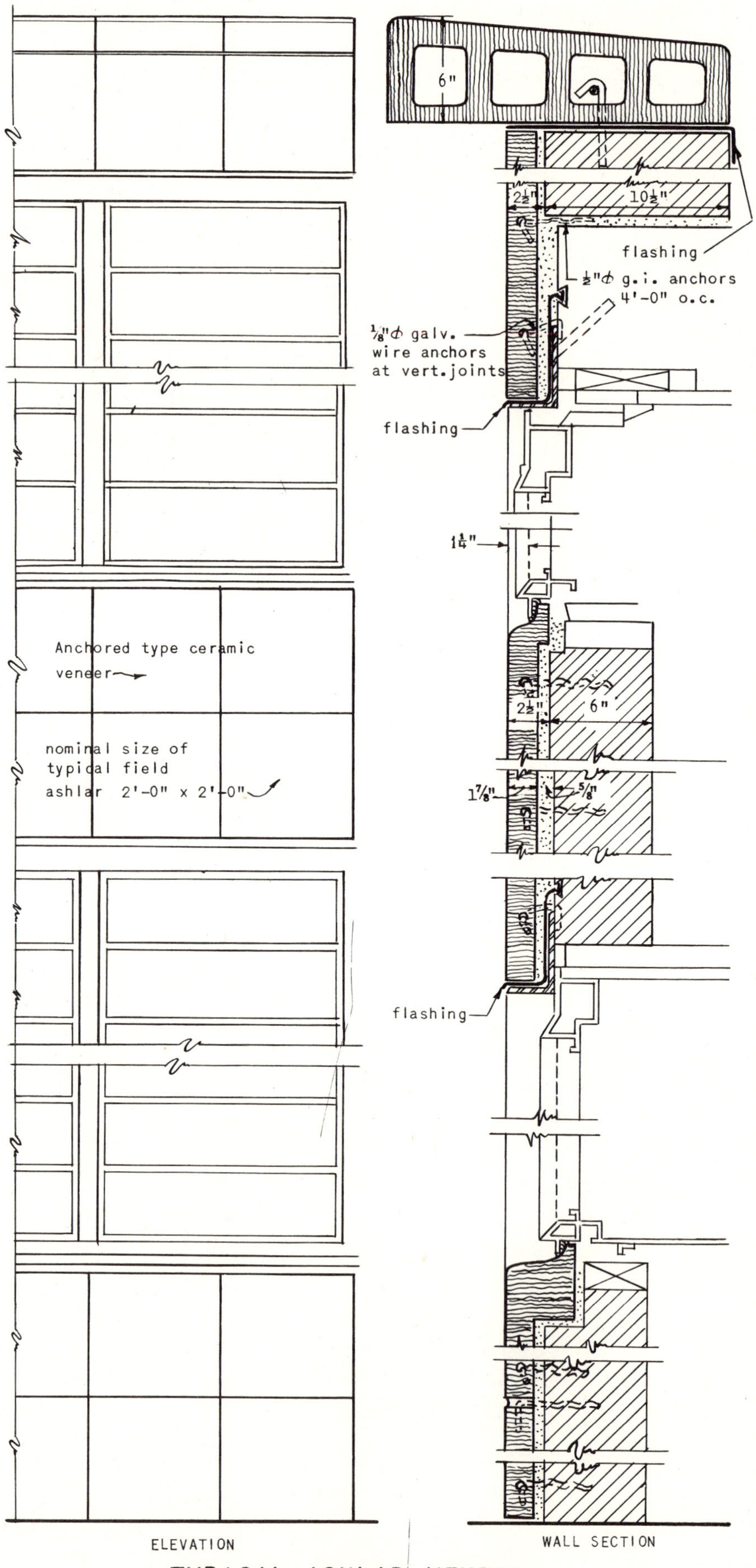
Anchored type ceramic veneer
nominal size of typical field ashlar 2'-0" x 2'-0"
ELEVATION
6"
2 1/2"
10 1/2"
flashing
1/2"Φ g.i. anchors 4'-0" o.c.
1/8"Φ galv. wire anchors at vert. joints
flashing
1 1/4"
2 1/2"
6"
1 7/8"
5/8"
flashing
WALL SECTION

TYPICAL ASHLAR VENEER

Data supplied by: Federal Seaboard Terra Cotta Corporation

ARCHITECTURAL TERRA COTTA and CERAMIC VENEER

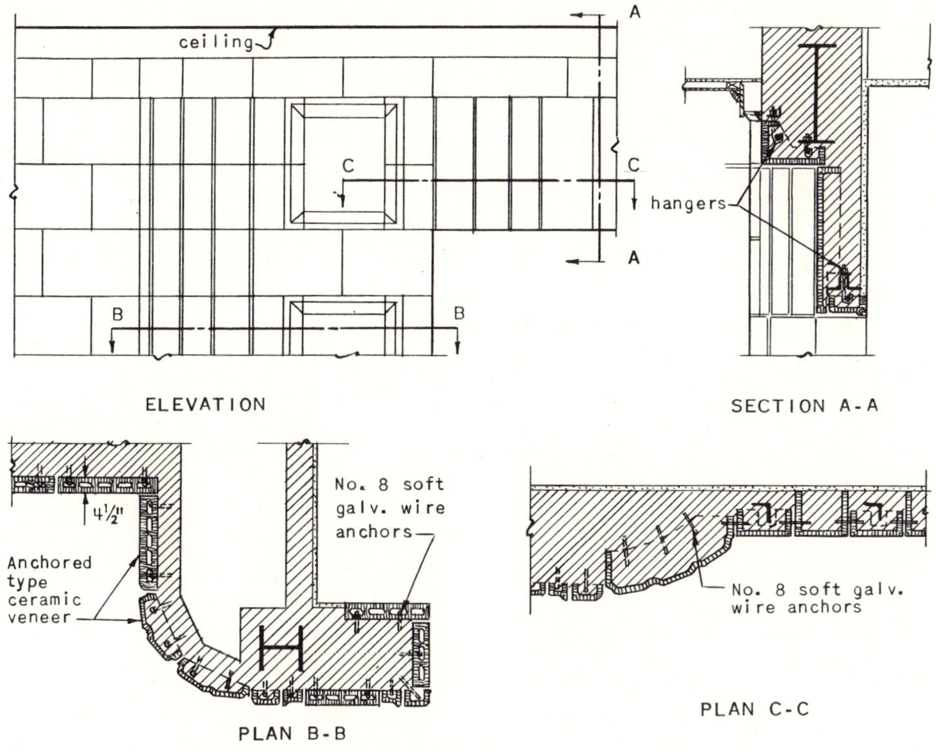
ceiling
A
C
C
A
B
B
ELEVATION
hangers
SECTION A-A
4½"
Anchored type ceramic veneer
No. 8 soft galv. wire anchors
PLAN B-B
No. 8 soft galv. wire anchors
PLAN C-C

CORNER OF PROSCENIUM ARCH

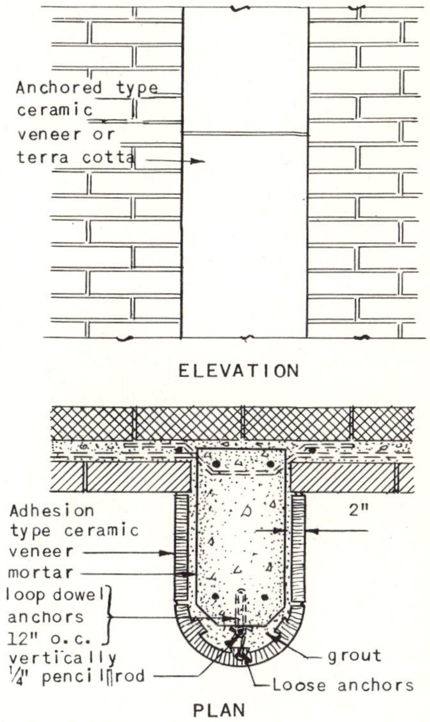
Anchored type ceramic veneer or terra cotta
ELEVATION
Adhesion type ceramic veneer
mortar
loop dowel anchors 12" o.c. vertically
¼" pencil rod
2"
grout
Loose anchors
PLAN

PILASTER

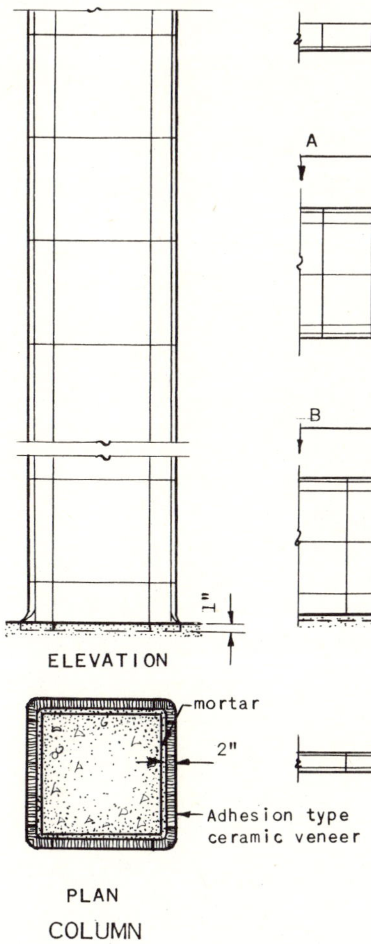
1"
ELEVATION
mortar
2"
Adhesion type ceramic veneer
PLAN
COLUMN

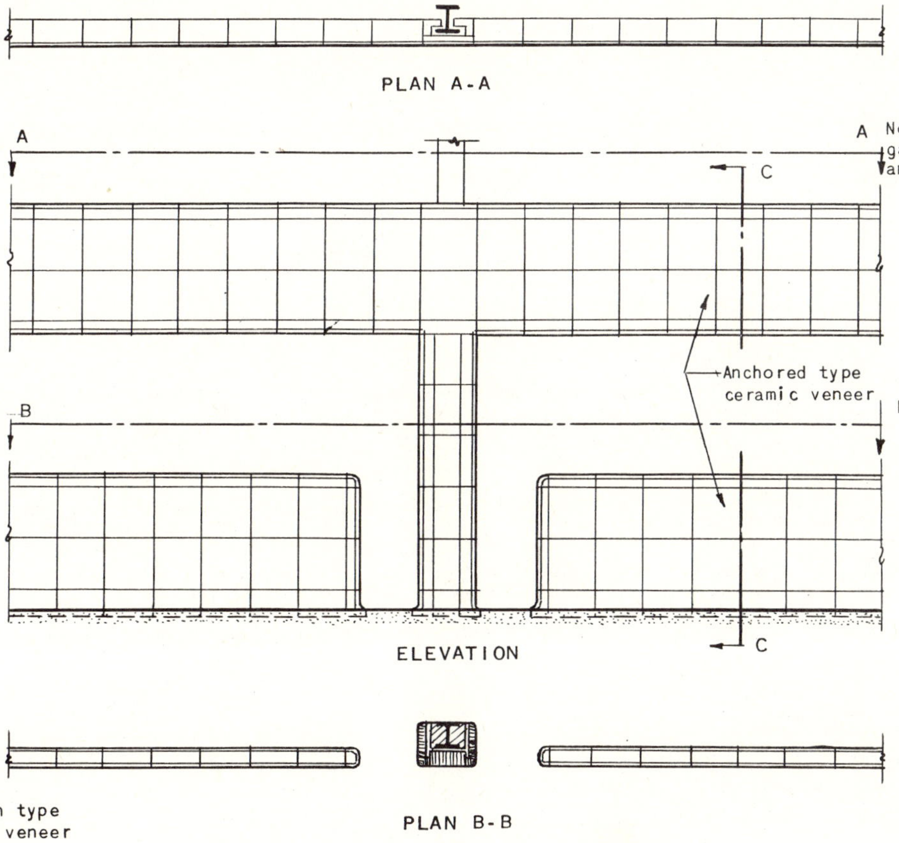
PLAN A-A
A
A
C
Anchored type ceramic veneer
B
B
ELEVATION
C
PLAN B-B

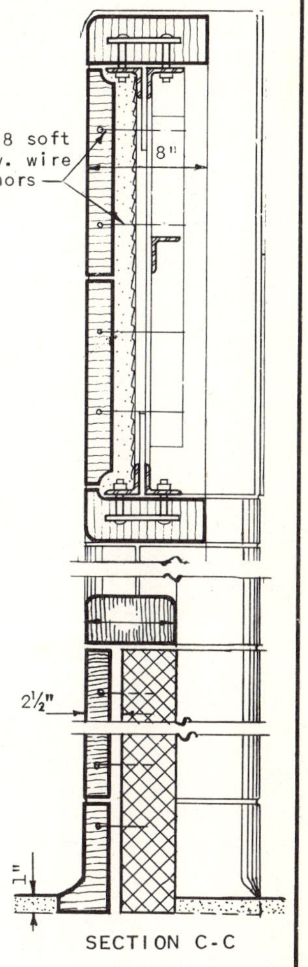
No. 8 soft galv. wire anchors
8"
2½"
1"
SECTION C-C

WALL & COLUMNS

CERAMIC VENEER, ANCHOR TYPE

NO SCALE

DATA SUPPLIED BY: FEDERAL SEABOARD TERRA COTTA CORP

ARCHITECTURAL TERRA COTTA

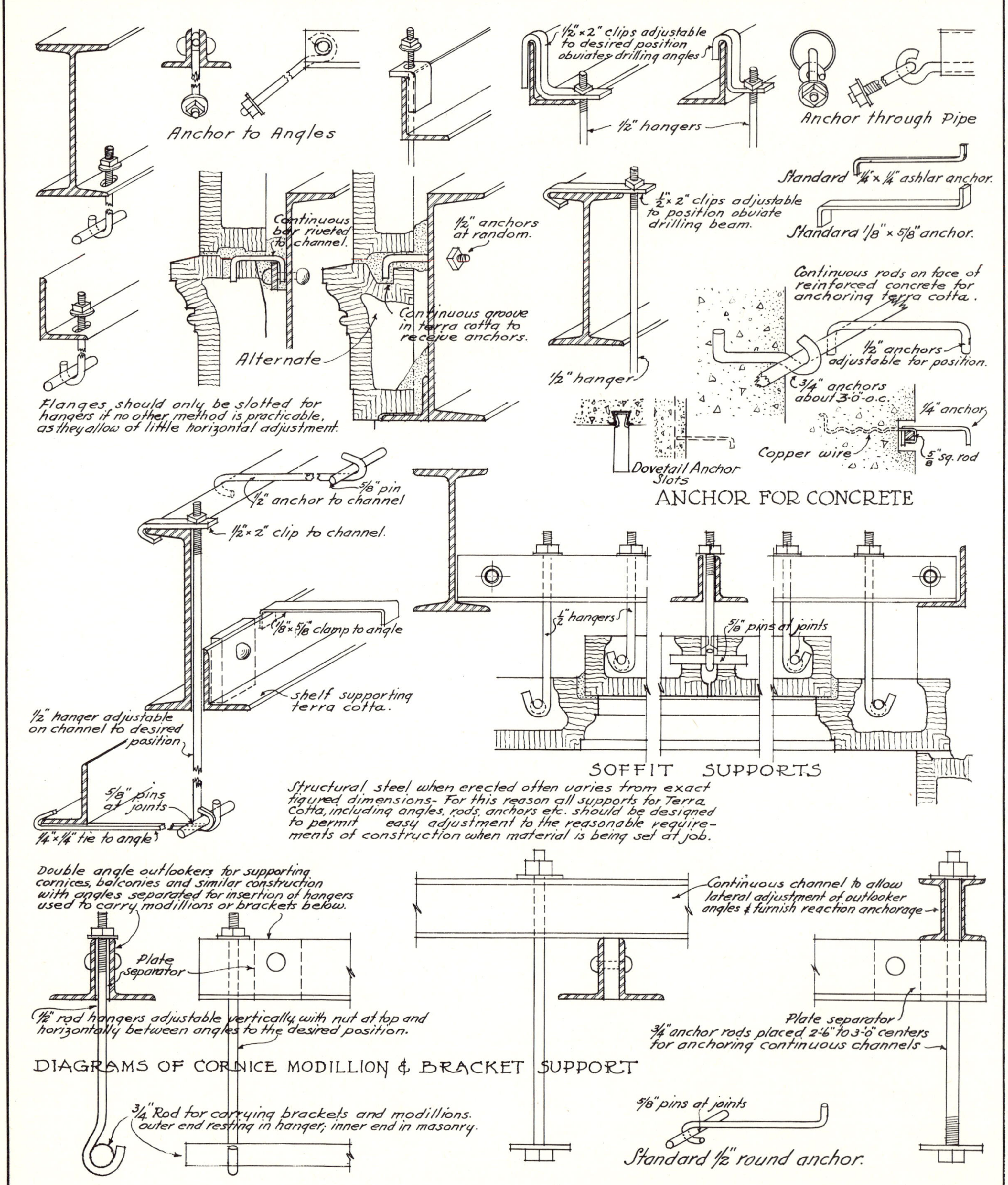
Anchor to Angles
1/2"×2" clips adjustable to desired position obuiates drilling angles
1/2" hangers
Anchor through Pipe
Standard 1/4×1/4 ashlar anchor.
Standard 1/8"×5/8" anchor.
Continuous bar riveted to channel.
1/2" anchors at random.
Continuous groove in terra cotta to receive anchors.
Alternate
1/2"×2" clips adjustable to position obuiate drilling beam.
1/2" hanger
Continuous rods on face of reinforced concrete for anchoring terra cotta.
1/2" anchors adjustable for position.
3/4" anchors about 3'-0" o.c.
1/4" anchor
Copper wire
5/8" sq. rod
Dovetail Anchor Slots
ANCHOR FOR CONCRETE
Flanges should only be slotted for hangers if no other method is practicable, as they allow of little horizontal adjustment.
5/8" pin
1/2" anchor to channel
1/2"×2" clip to channel.
1/8×5/8" clamp to angle
shelf supporting terra cotta.
1/2" hanger adjustable on channel to desired position
5/8" pins at joints
1/4"×1/4" tie to angle
1/2" hangers
5/8" pins at joints
SOFFIT SUPPORTS
Structural steel when erected often varies from exact figured dimensions- For this reason all supports for Terra Cotta, including angles, rods, anchors etc. should be designed to permit easy adjustment to the reasonable requirements of construction when material is being set at job.
Double angle outlookers for supporting cornices, balconies and similar construction with angles separated for insertion of hangers used to carry modillions or brackets below.
Plate separator
1/2" rod hangers adjustable vertically, with nut at top and horizontally between angles to the desired position.
Continuous channel to allow lateral adjustment of outlooker angles & furnish reaction anchorage
Plate separator
3/4" anchor rods placed 2'-6" to 3'-0" centers for anchoring continuous channels
DIAGRAMS OF CORNICE MODILLION & BRACKET SUPPORT
3/4" Rod for carrying brackets and modillions. outer end resting in hanger; inner end in masonry.
5/8" pins at joints
Standard 1/2" round anchor.

USE of ANCHORS, HANGERS, STRAPS, CLAMPS & CLIPS in SETTING T. C.

Data checked by: Federal Seaboard Terra Cotta Corporation

STONE FACING

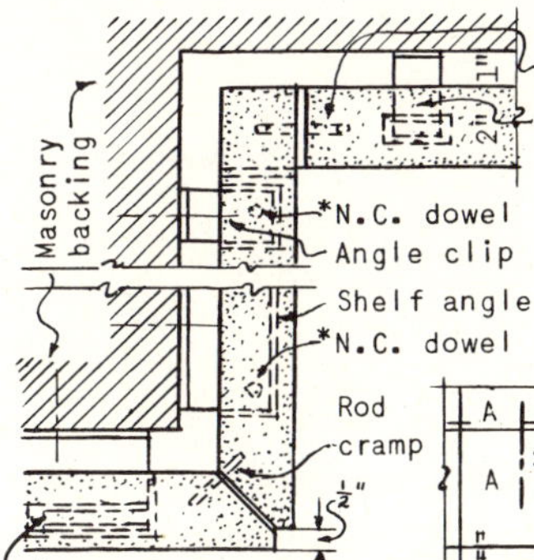
Rod cramp
φ Bars welded to clip
Masonry backing
*N.C. dowel
Angle clip
Shelf angle
*N.C. dowel
Rod cramp
½"
φ Bars welded to shelf angle

INSIDE & OUTSIDE CORNER PLAN
Scale: 1½" = 1'- 0"

*N.C. = Non-corrosive

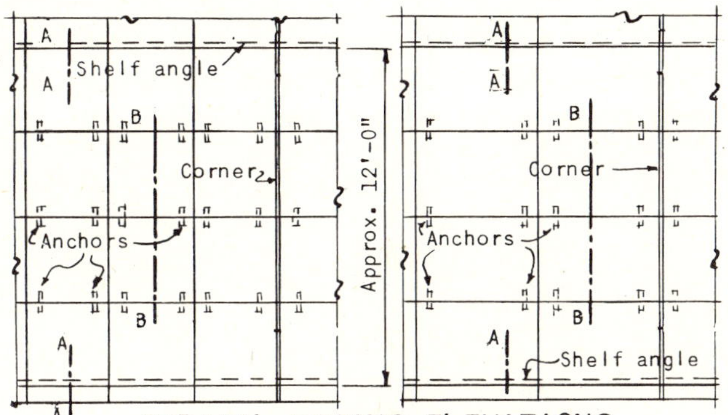
A
Shelf angle
B
Corner
Anchors
Approx. 12'-0"
A
B
Corner
Anchors
Shelf angle

TYPICAL FACING ELEVATIONS
Scale: ⅛" = 1'-0"

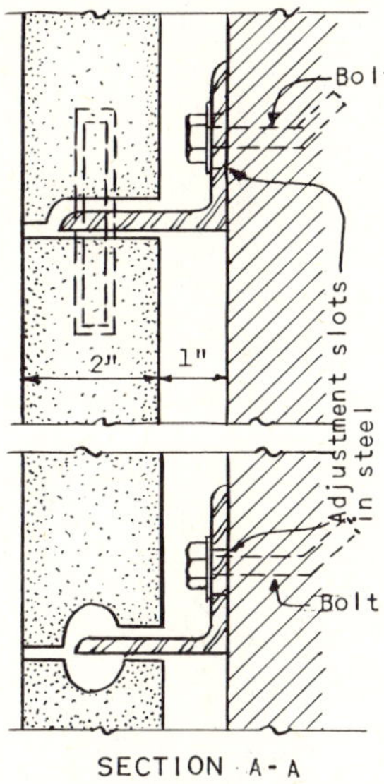
Bolt
2"
1"
Adjustment slots in steel
Bolt

SECTION A-A
SHELF ANGLE TREATMENTS

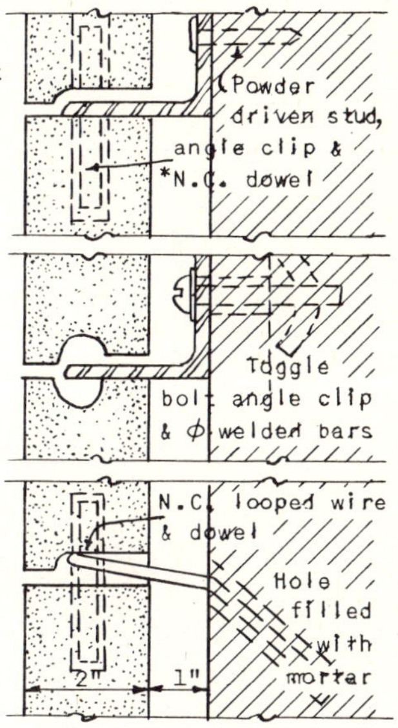
Powder driven stud, angle clip & *N.C. dowel
Toggle bolt angle clip & φ welded bars
N.C. looped wire & dowel
Hole filled with mortar
2"
1"

SECTION B-B
ANCHOR METHODS

Scale: 3" = 1'-0"

APPLICATION OF 2" LIMESTONE FACING

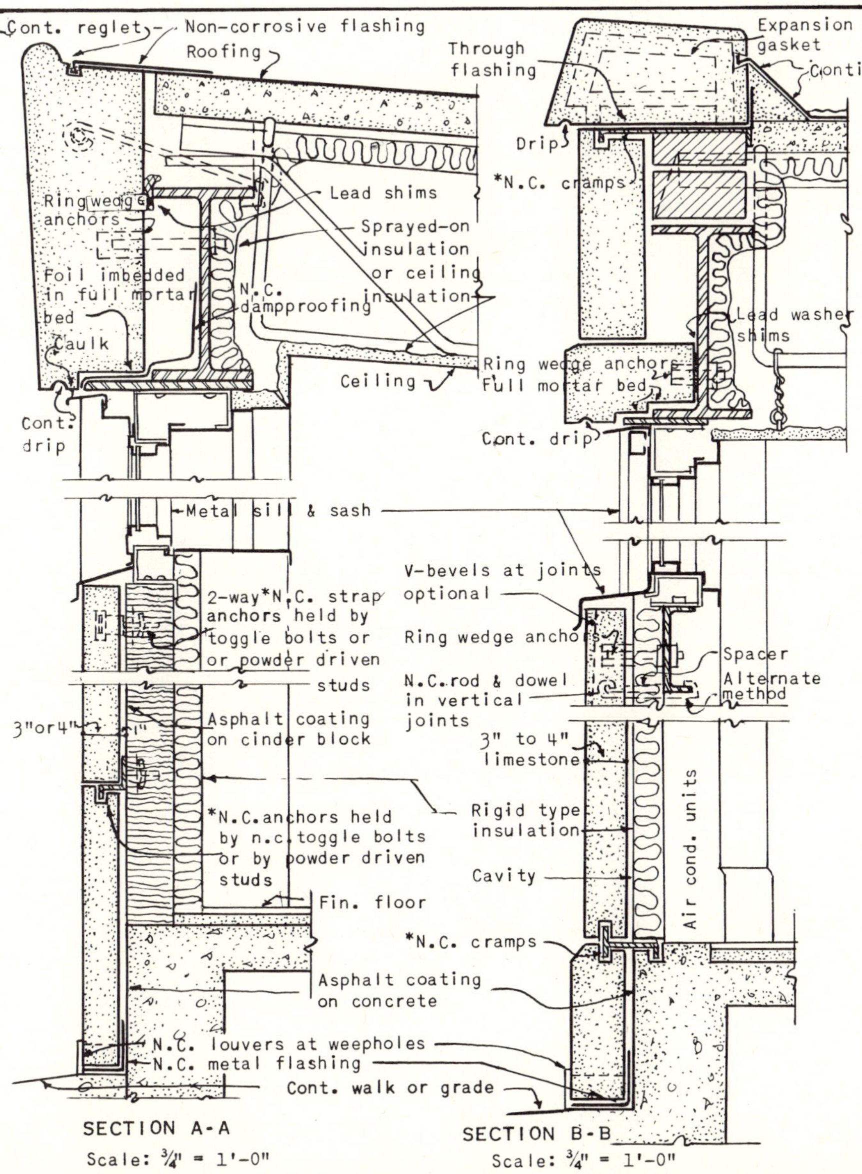
Cont. reglet
Non-corrosive flashing
Roofing
Ring wedge anchors
Lead shims
Sprayed-on insulation or ceiling insulation
Foil imbedded in full mortar bed
N.C. dampproofing
Caulk
Ceiling
Cont. drip
Metal sill & sash
2-way *N.C. strap anchors held by toggle bolts or or powder driven studs
3"or4"
1"
Asphalt coating on cinder block
*N.C. anchors held by n.c. toggle bolts or by powder driven studs
Fin. floor
Asphalt coating on concrete
N.C. louvers at weepholes
N.C. metal flashing
Cont. walk or grade
Through flashing
Expansion gasket
Continuous reglet & flashing
Drip
*N.C. cramps
Lead washer shims
Ring wedge anchors
Full mortar bed
Cont. drip
V-bevels at joints optional
Ring wedge anchor
Spacer
Alternate method
N.C. rod & dowel in vertical joints
3" to 4" limestone
Rigid type insulation
Cavity
Air cond. units
*N.C. cramps

SECTION A-A
Scale: ¾" = 1'-0"

SECTION B-B
Scale: ¾" = 1'-0"

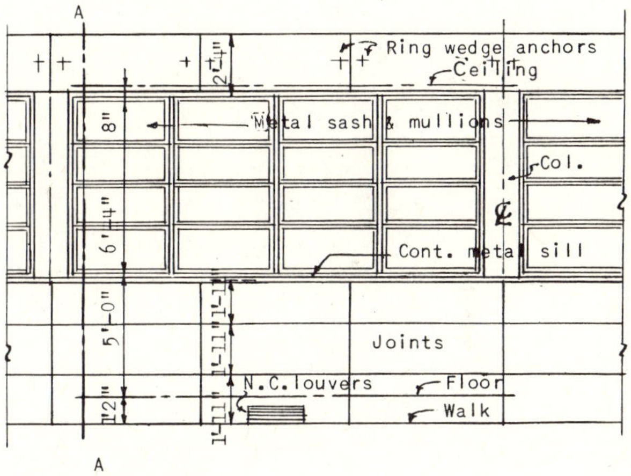
A
Ring wedge anchors
Ceiling
2'-4"
8"
Metal sash & mullions
Col.
℄
6'-4"
Cont. metal sill
5'-0"
1'-11"
1'-11"
Joints
N.C. louvers
Floor
12"
Walk
1'-11"
A

ELEVATION NO. 1
Scale: ⅛" = 1'-0"

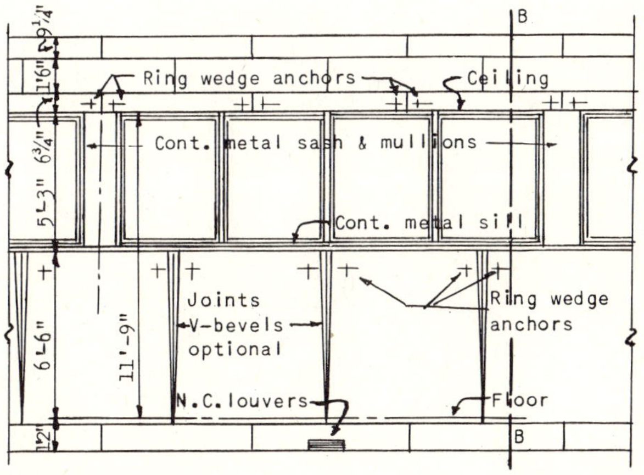
B
9¼"
1'6"
Ring wedge anchors
Ceiling
6¾"
Cont. metal sash & mullions
5'-3"
Cont. metal sill
Joints V-bevels optional
Ring wedge anchors
6'-6"
11'-9"
N.C. louvers
Floor
12"
B

ELEVATION NO. 2 (Air conditioned building)
Scale: ⅛" = 1'-0"

*Non-corrosive

ONE STORY BUILDINGS WITH STONE FACING

DATA BY INDIANA LIMESTONE INSTITUTE

EXTERIOR MARBLE, SOAPSTONE & GRANITE VENEER

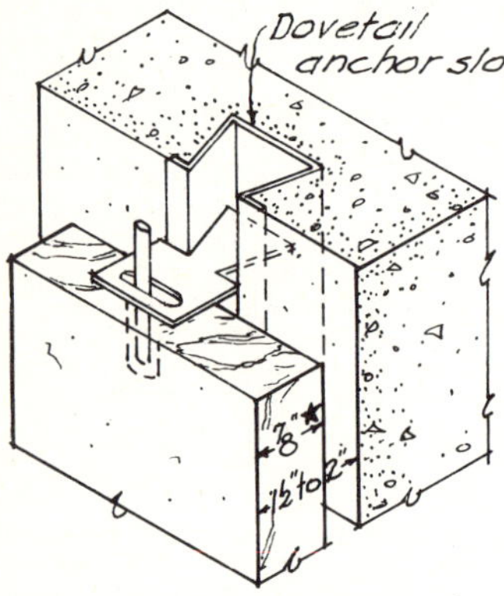
Dovetail anchor slot
7/8"★
1½" to 2"

MARBLE VENEER on CONCRETE

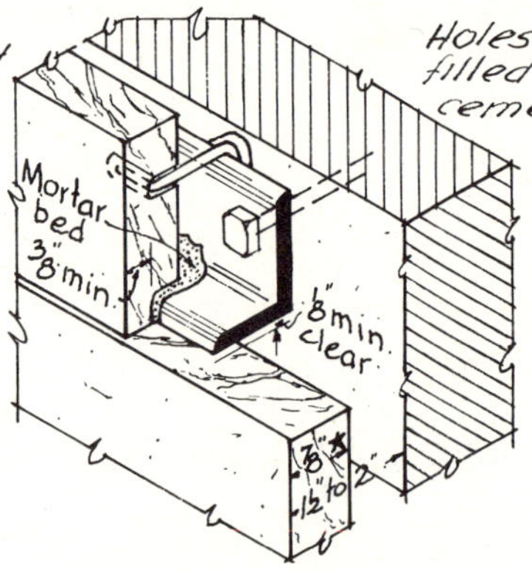
Mortar bed 3/8" min.
3/8" min. clear
7/8"★
1½" to 2"

INTERMEDIATE SUPPORTS

Where more than two stories high, marble should be supported by intermediate angle support at each upper story.

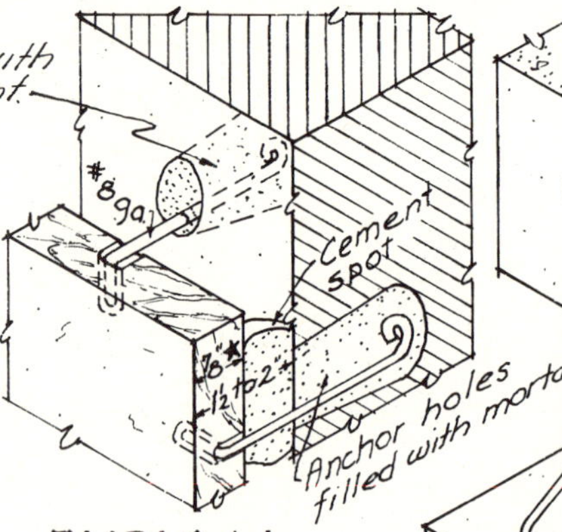
Holes filled with cement
#8 ga.
Cement spot
7/8"★
1½" to 2"
Anchor holes filled with mortar

TYPICAL ANCHORS

Recom. no. of anchors:
Slabs 2# to 4# - 3
Slabs 4# to 12# - 4
Slabs 12# to 20# - 6
Slabs over 20# - 1 per 3#

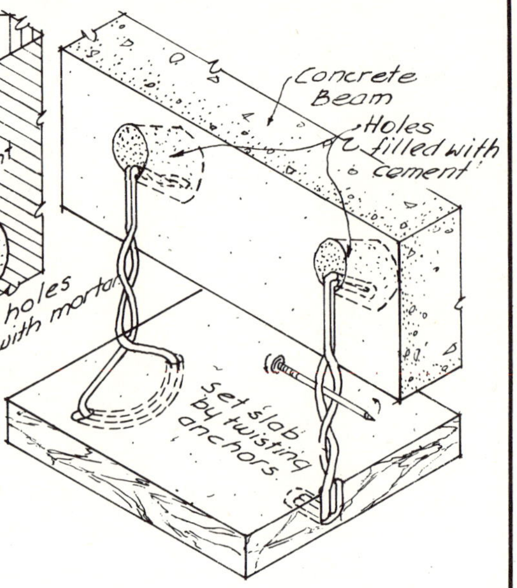
Concrete Beam
Holes filled with cement
Set slab by twisting anchors

HUNG SOFFIT of LINTEL

★ Thickness of plain ashlar areas: 2 stories high or less - 7/8" or 1¼"; more than 2 stories high - 1¼", 1½" or 2". See local bldg. code for allowable heights and anchors.

METHODS of ANCHORING EXTERIOR MARBLE VENEER

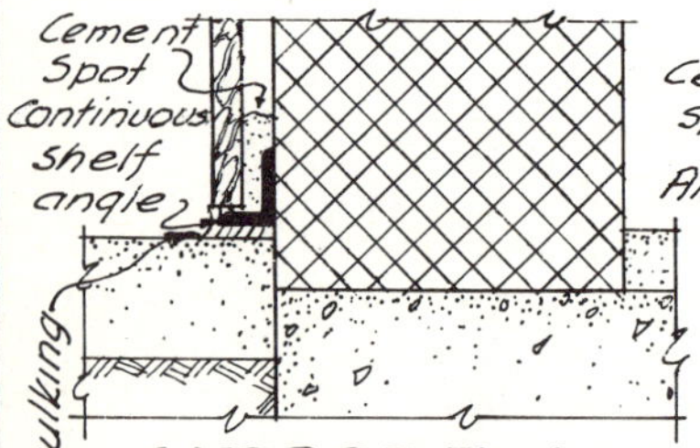
Cement Spot
Continuous shelf angle
Mastic caulking

SUPPORT at SIDEWALK

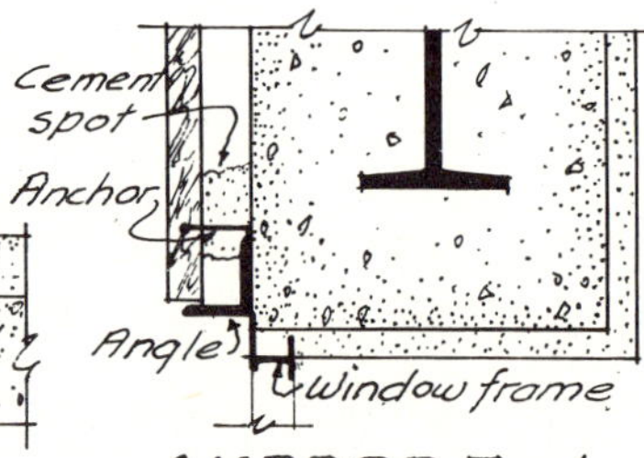
Cement spot
Anchor
Angle
Window frame

SUPPORT at SPANDREL

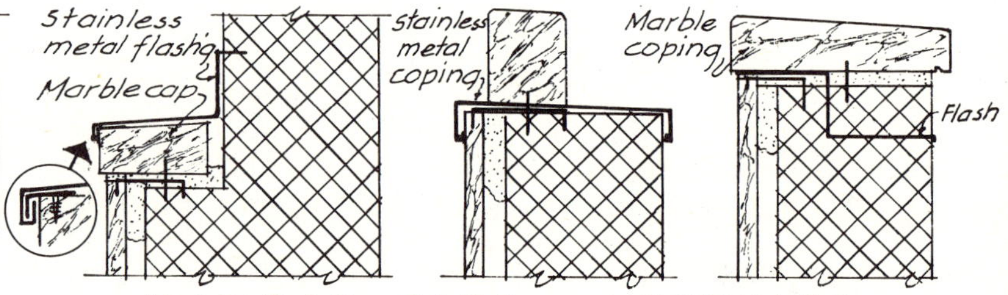
Stainless metal flashg.
Marble cap
Stainless metal coping
Marble coping
Flash

MARBLE CAPS and COPINGS

Joints for exterior marble or soapstone veneer usually ⅛" but may be less than 1/16"; use neat white Portland cement or non-staining pointing mastic with plastic or aluminum cushions spaced to support the weight. Use spots of non-staining Portland cement and accelerator or bonding cement behind slabs at or near anchors and also not spaced over 18" apart. Marble up to 2" thick may also be set with plasticized synthetic resin bonding cement without anchors. Use same number of these cement spots as number of anchors which would otherwise be required.

Scale of sections - 1½" = 1'-0"

EXTERIOR MARBLE and SOAPSTONE VENEER

Data by Marble Institute of America, Inc.

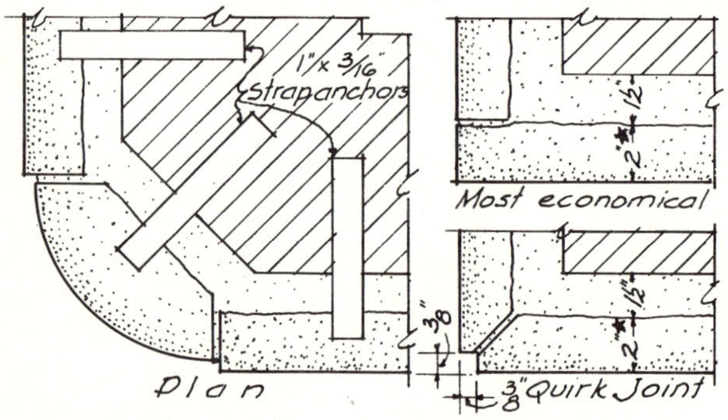
1" x 3/16" Strap anchors
Plan
1½"
2"★
Most economical
3/8"
3/8" Quirk Joint

CORNER DETAILS

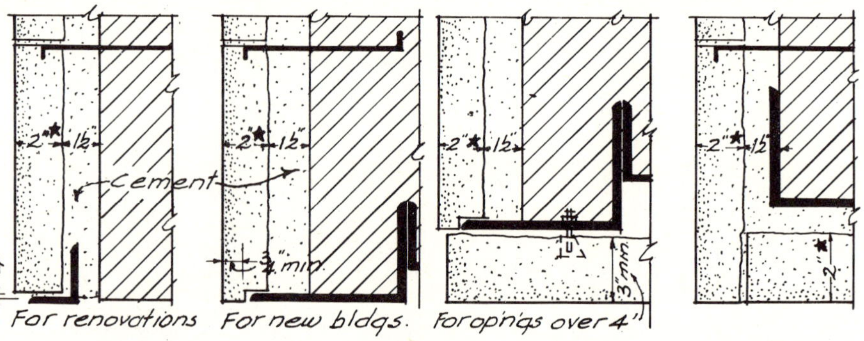
2"★
1½"
Cement
4"
¾" min.
3" min.
For renovations
For new bldgs.
For opngs over 4'

LINTEL & SOFFIT SECTIONS

¼" mortar joints usually used, but 3/16" or ⅛" may be used for close work. Anchors to be galvanized or non-corroding (for sizes see page "Anchoring of Stonework"). 2 anchors to be used in top bed of each stone. ★ Thickness of granite veneer varies 1" to 2½", but 2" is most commonly used. Granite veneer lintels should not be load bearing. Back may be parged or slushed full. See local bldg. code for allowable heights and anchors. Largest practical slab - 8' high x 12' wide. Scale of details - 1½" = 1'-0".

EXTERIOR GRANITE VENEER

Data checked by: National Building Granite Quarries Association.

CUT STONE

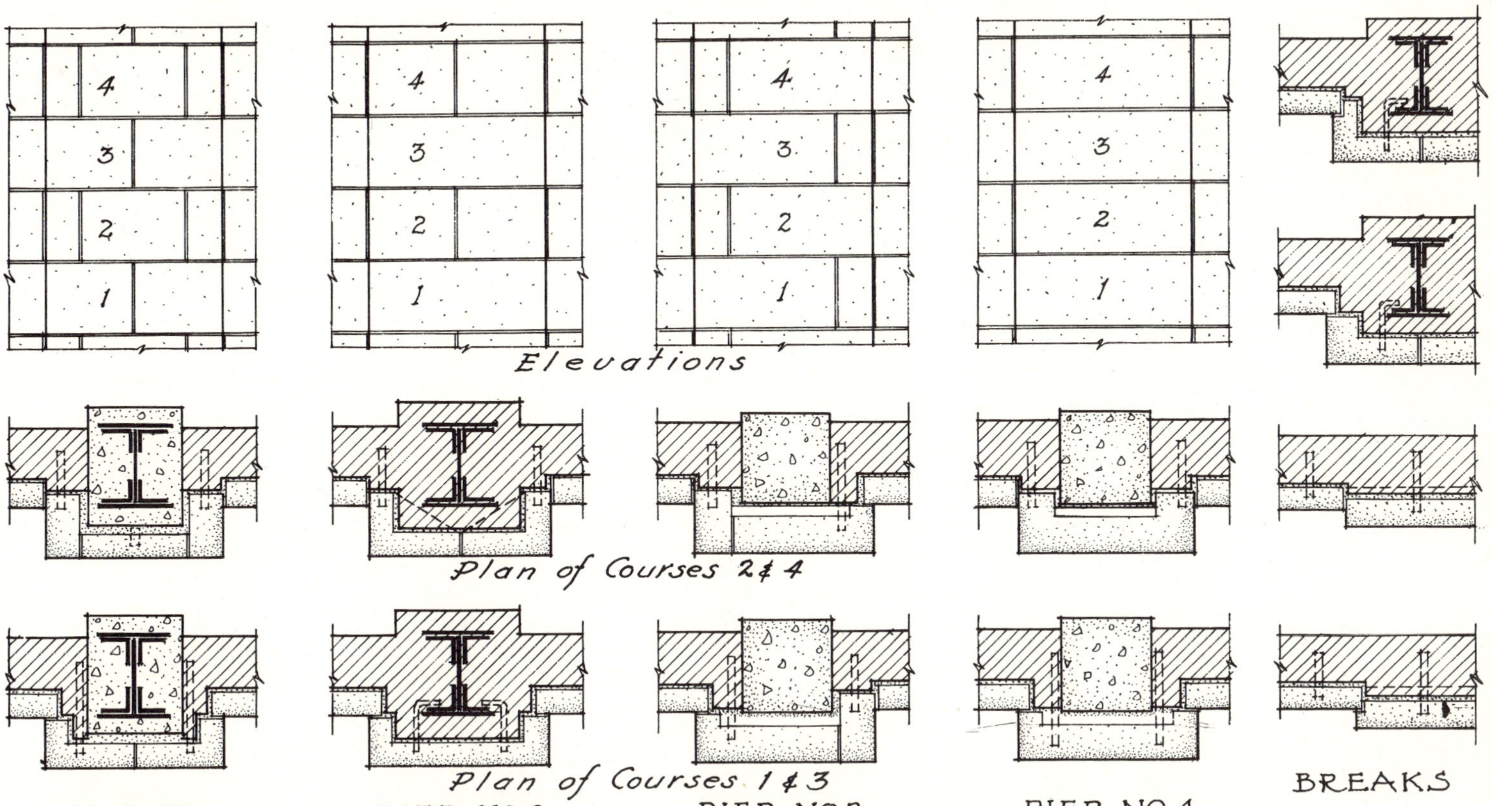
4
3
2
1
Elevations
Plan of Courses 2 & 4
Plan of Courses 1 & 3
BREAKS
PIER NO.1
PIER NO.2
PIER NO.3
PIER NO.4

METHODS of JOINTING and ANCHORING at PIERS and BREAKS

3/8" = 1'-0"

4"

TYPES OF LINTELS

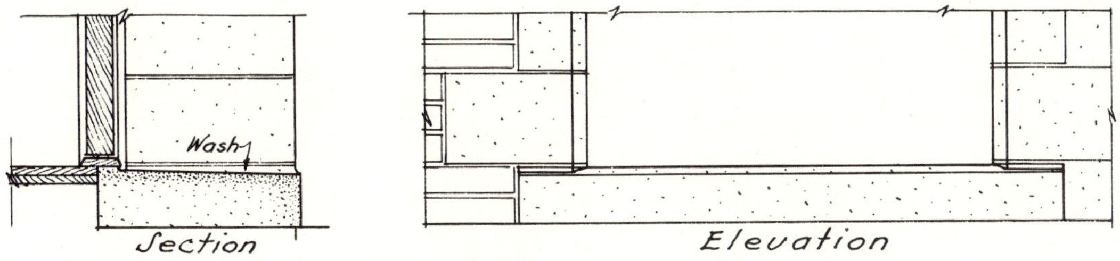
Wash
Section
Elevation

DOOR SILL

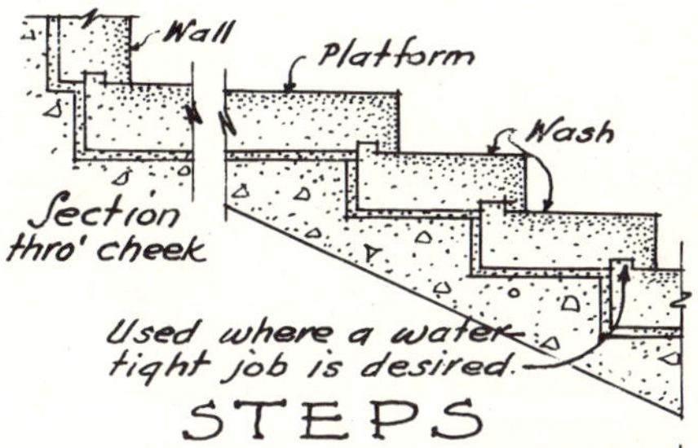
Wall
Platform
Wash
Section thro' cheek
Used where a water-tight job is desired.

STEPS

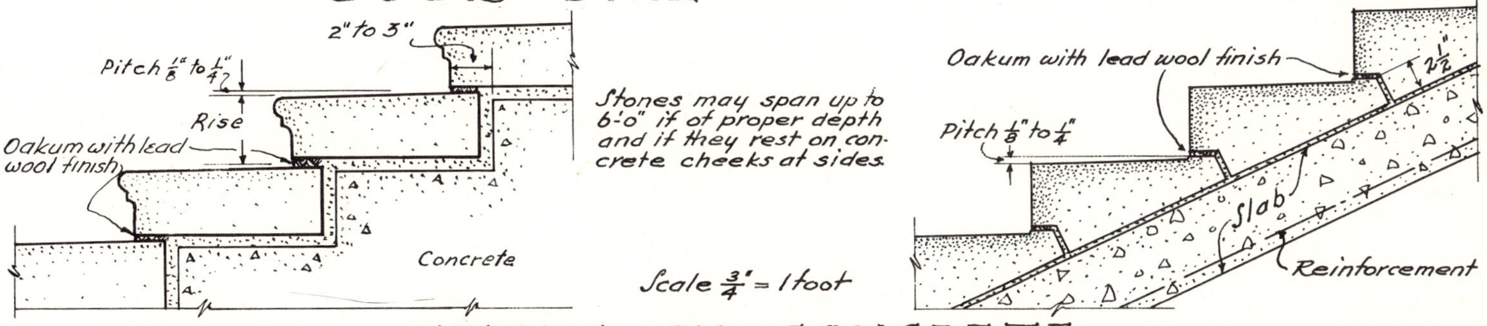
2" to 3"
Pitch 1/8" to 1/4"
Rise
Oakum with lead wool finish
Stones may span up to 6'-0" if of proper depth and if they rest on concrete cheeks at sides.
Concrete
Scale 3/4" = 1 foot
Oakum with lead wool finish
2 1/2"
Pitch 1/8" to 1/4"
Slab
Reinforcement

STEPS ON CONCRETE

JOINTING & ANCHORING CUT-STONE PIERS; LINTELS & STEPS

Data checked by the Indiana Limestone Co. Inc.

CUT STONE

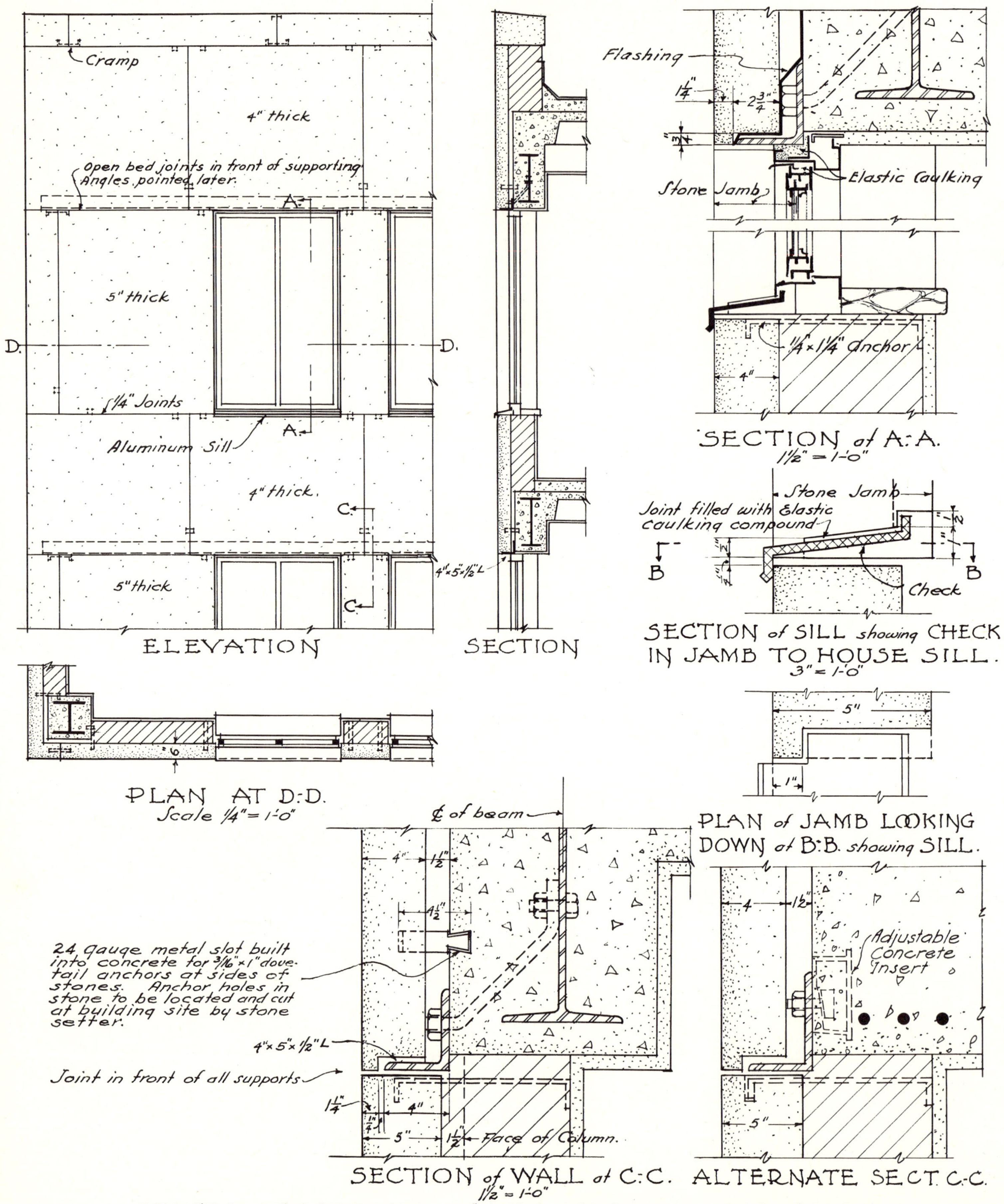
Cramp
4" thick
Open bed joints in front of supporting Angles pointed later.
A
5" thick
D.
D.
1/4" Joints
Aluminum Sill
A.
4" thick.
C.
5" thick
C.
ELEVATION
4"x5"x1/2"L
SECTION
Flashing
1 1/4"
2 3/4"
3/4"
Elastic Caulking
Stone Jamb
1 1/4"x1 1/4" Anchor
4"
SECTION of A:A.
1 1/2" = 1'-0"
Stone Jamb
Joint filled with Elastic caulking compound
B
B
Check
SECTION of SILL showing CHECK IN JAMB TO HOUSE SILL.
3" = 1'-0"
PLAN AT D:D.
Scale 1/4" = 1'-0"
5"
1"
PLAN of JAMB LOOKING DOWN at B:B. showing SILL.
℄ of beam
4"
1 1/2"
4 1/2"
24 gauge metal slot built into concrete for 3/16"x1" dove-tail anchors at sides of stones. Anchor holes in stone to be located and cut at building site by stone setter.
4"x5"x1/2"L
Joint in front of all supports
1 1/4"
4"
1"
5"
1 1/2"
Face of Column.
4
1 1/2"
Adjustable Concrete Insert
5"
SECTION of WALL at C:C.
1 1/2" = 1'-0"
ALTERNATE SECT. C-C.

HIGH COURSE CUT STONE FACING

Recommendation of the Indiana Limestone Company, Inc.

ANCHORING of STONEWORK

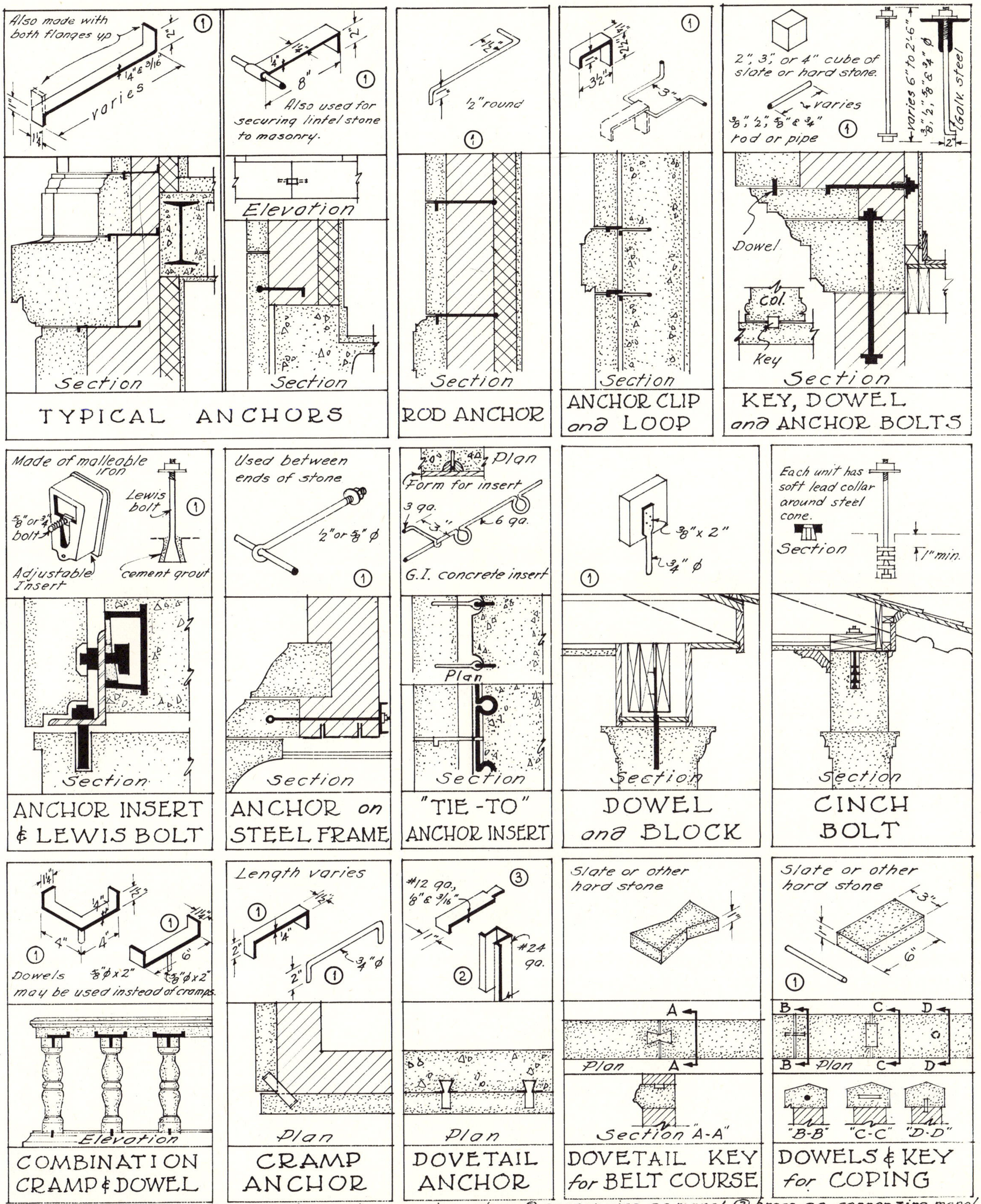
Also made with both flanges up
varies
Section
Also used for securing lintel stone to masonry.
Elevation
Section
TYPICAL ANCHORS
½" round
Section
ROD ANCHOR
Section
ANCHOR CLIP and LOOP
2", 3", or 4" cube of slate or hard stone.
varies
rod or pipe
varies 6" to 2'-6"
Galv. steel
Dowel
Col.
Key
Section
KEY, DOWEL and ANCHOR BOLTS
Made of malleable iron
Lewis bolt
Adjustable Insert
cement grout
Section
ANCHOR INSERT & LEWIS BOLT
Used between ends of stone
Section
ANCHOR on STEEL FRAME
Plan
Form for insert
3 ga.
6 ga.
G.I. concrete insert
Plan
Section
"TIE-TO" ANCHOR INSERT
Section
DOWEL and BLOCK
Each unit has soft lead collar around steel cone.
Section
1" min.
Section
CINCH BOLT
Dowels may be used instead of cramps.
Elevation
COMBINATION CRAMP & DOWEL
Length varies
Plan
CRAMP ANCHOR
#12 ga.
#24 ga.
Plan
DOVETAIL ANCHOR
Slate or other hard stone
Plan
Section "A-A"
DOVETAIL KEY for BELT COURSE
Slate or other hard stone
Plan
"B-B"
"C-C"
"D-D"
DOWELS & KEY for COPING

Materials: ① Galv. steel, copper, brass, bronze, zinc, alum., ② copper, zinc, g.s. monel, ③ brass, g.s., copper, zinc, monel.

Data checked by Indiana Limestone Co. Inc.

STRUCTURAL GLASS-GENERAL & EXTER· DETAILS

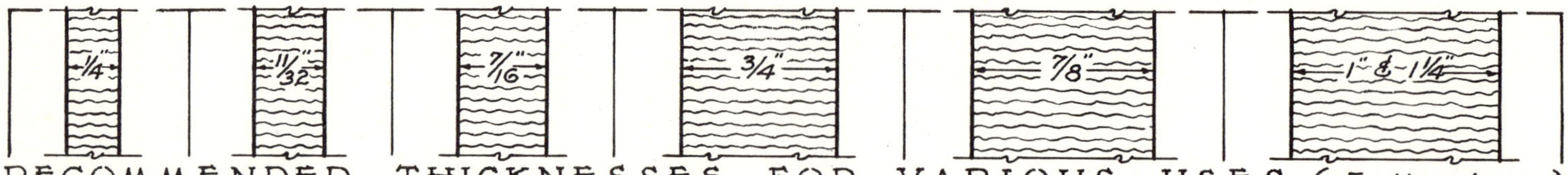
1/4"
11/32"
7/16"
3/4"
7/8"
1" & 1 1/4"

RECOMMENDED THICKNESSES FOR VARIOUS USES (Full-size)

1/4"	11/32"	7/16"	3/4"	7/8"	1" & 1 1/4"
Obscure glazing Black only	Ceilings Wall panels Wall ashlar Aprons Bath tub facing Store fronts (Small pieces)	*Wall panels *Wainscots Aprons, Caps, Strips Bases, Plinths Bulkheads *Store fronts Laminated stall partitions	Trim Window stools Caps, strips, Bases, plinths * = seldom used.	Trim Laminated partition Deal plates Solid partitions Counter tops	Seats — 1 1/4" Deal plates Toilet stiles — 1 1/4" Solid partitions Counter tops Urinal stalls — 1" Lintels — 1 1/4"

M'nfr's: "Carrara" — Pittsburgh Plate Glass Co.
"Vitrolite" — Libbey-Owens-Ford Glass Co.

RECOMMENDED SIZE LIMITATIONS

USE	MATERIAL	MAXIMUM AREA	LIMITATIONS
Exterior	Vitrolite	6 sq. ft.	3'-0" max. horiz. width — 4'-0" max. height
	Carrara	6 sq. ft. if 15'-0" or more above grade 10 sq. ft. from grade to 15'-0" above same	
Interior Slabs	Vitrolite	15 sq. ft.	3'-0" x 5'-0"
	Carrara	15 sq. ft.	
Ashlar	Vitrolite	8" x 12" & 8" x 16", and { 12" x 16", 16" x 16", 24" x 24" }	Other sizes may be secured
	Carrara	8" x 16" (standard)	" " " " "
Toilet stall		25 sq. ft.	Up to 5' x 5'
Ceilings		4 sq. ft.	

COLORS	FINISHES
Vitrolite standard colors: White, black, jade, alomptan, light gray, dark grey, red, cadet blue, cactus green, in 11/32" only. Carrara: Black-all thicknesses except 1"; White, ivory, gray-all thick. except 1/4", 1". Tranquil green all thick. except 1/4", 3/4", 1". Beige, forest green, blue, wine, orange in 11/32" only.	Standard surfaces Vitrolite: Mechanically ground and polished. Carrara: Mech. polished, suede (lower luster). VARIOUS decorative finishes secured by sand. blasting, griding wheels and enlarging.

EXTERIOR DETAILS

Scale 3" = 1'-0"

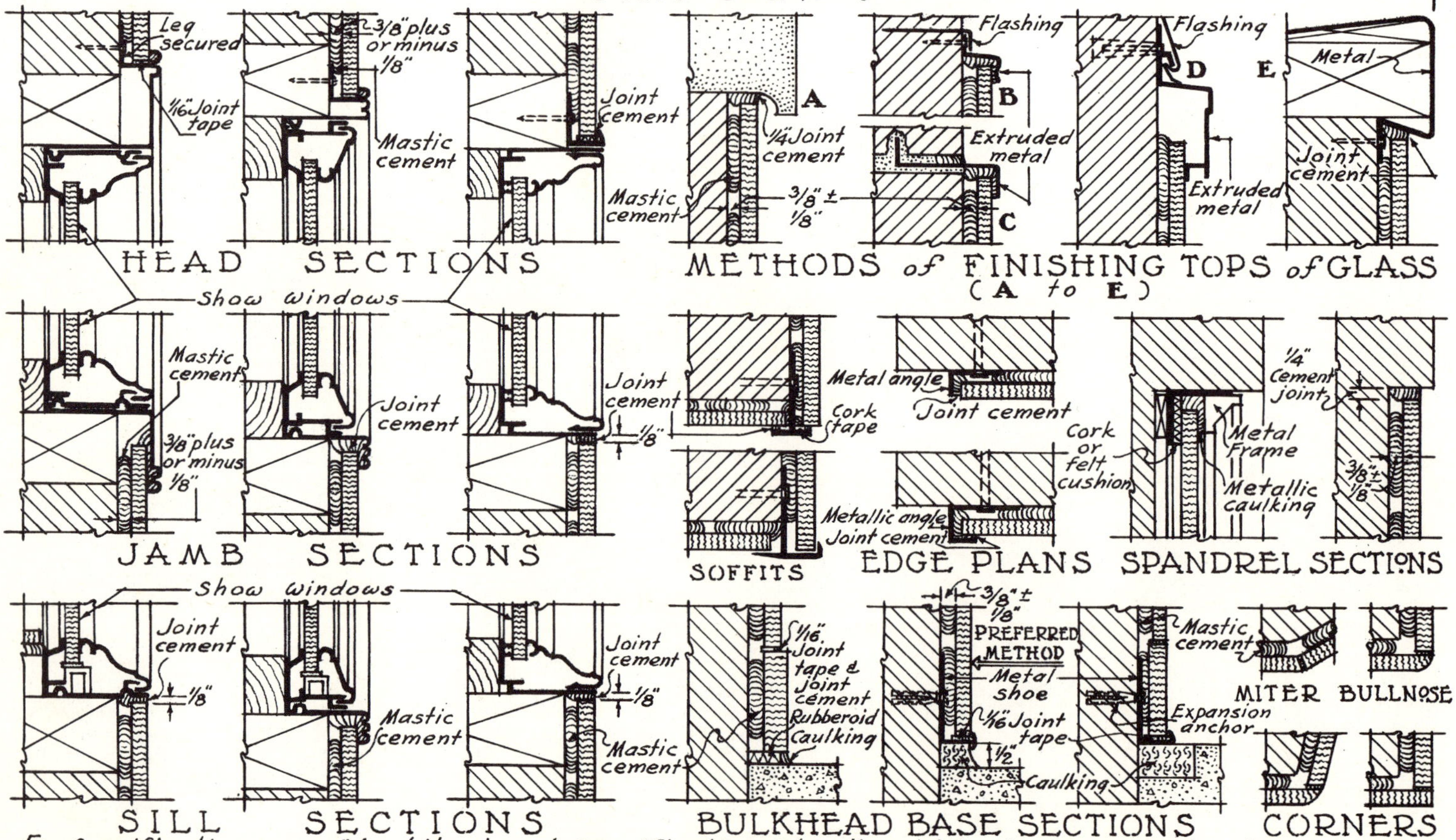
Leg secured
1/16" Joint tape
3/8" plus or minus 1/8"
Mastic cement
Joint cement
HEAD SECTIONS
Show windows
A
1/4" Joint cement
Mastic cement
3/8" ± 1/8"
Flashing
B
Extruded metal
C
D
E
Metal
Joint cement
Extruded metal
METHODS of FINISHING TOPS of GLASS (A to E)
Mastic cement
3/8" plus or minus 1/8"
Joint cement
1/8"
JAMB SECTIONS
Metal angle
Cork tape
Metallic angle
Joint cement
SOFFITS
Joint cement
Cork or felt cushion
EDGE PLANS
1/4" Cement joint
Metal Frame
Metallic caulking
3/8" ± 1/8"
SPANDREL SECTIONS
Show windows
Joint cement
1/8"
Mastic cement
SILL SECTIONS
1/16" Joint tape & Joint cement
Rubberoid Caulking
3/8" ± 1/8"
PREFERRED METHOD
Metal shoe
1/16" Joint tape
1/2"
Caulking
Mastic cement
Expansion anchor
BULKHEAD BASE SECTIONS
MITER
BULLNOSE
CORNERS

For Specifications see "Architectural Specifications" by Harold R. Sleeper; Structural Glass Division.

ASBESTOS-CEMENT ROOFING and SIDING

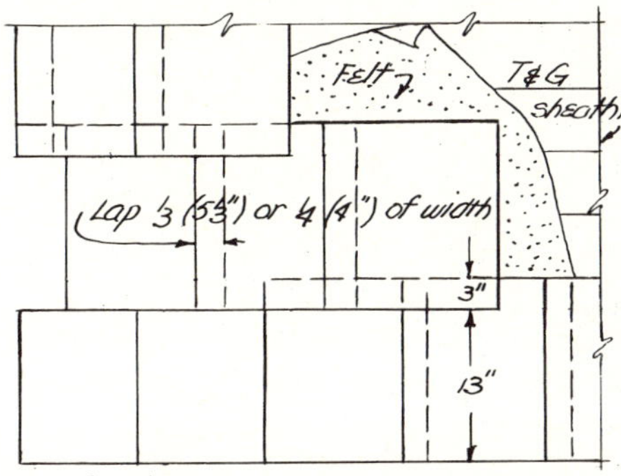
Felt
T&G sheathing
Lap 1/3 (5 1/3") or 1/4 (4") of width
3"
13"

Substantially single coverage. Requires less material than American.

RANCH, SCOTCH or DUTCH LAP METHOD

24"
16"
8"&16"
12"

8" width used for "American". Exp. 7 1/8"
16" width used for "Dutch". Exp. 13"
12" width used for "Ranch". Some mfrs. vary slightly.

INDIVIDUAL SHINGLE

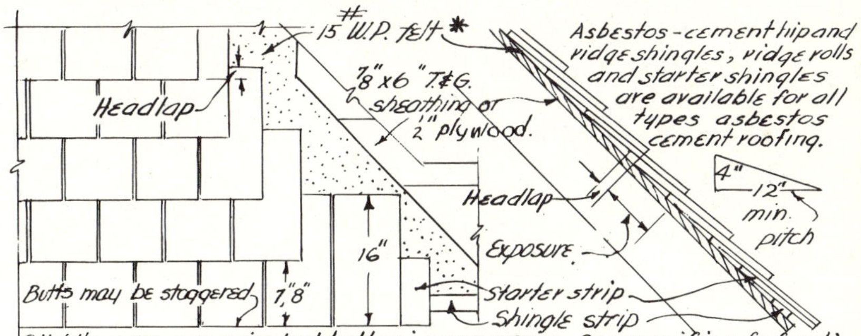
15# W.P. felt *
Headlap
7/8" x 6" T&G. sheathing or 1/2" plywood.
Asbestos-cement hip and ridge shingles, ridge rolls and starter shingles are available for all types asbestos cement roofing.
4"
12"
min. pitch
Headlap
Exposure
16"
Butts may be staggered
7 1/8"
Starter strip
Shingle strip

Slightly more expensive but better in appearance. See specific mfr. for dim.

AMERICAN METHOD (Individual shingle)

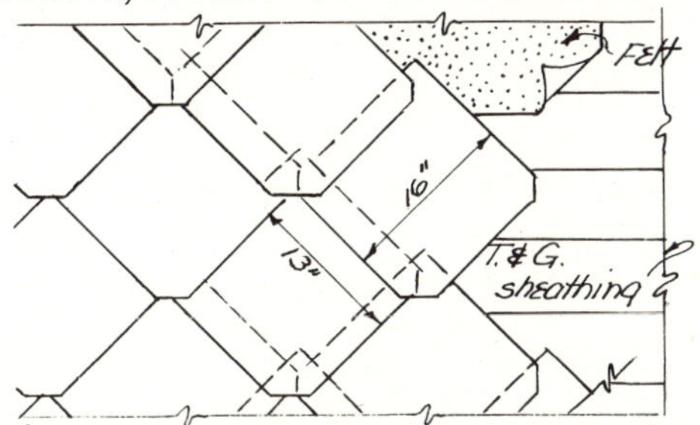
Felt
16"
13"
T&G. sheathing

Inexpensive but not as waterproof as Am.

FRENCH or HEXAGONAL METHOD

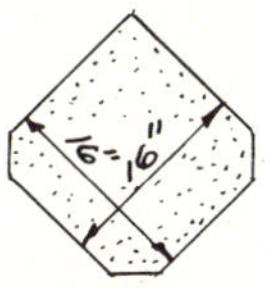
16"=16"

Exposure 13" x 13".

FRENCH or HEXAGONAL INDIVIDUAL SHINGLE

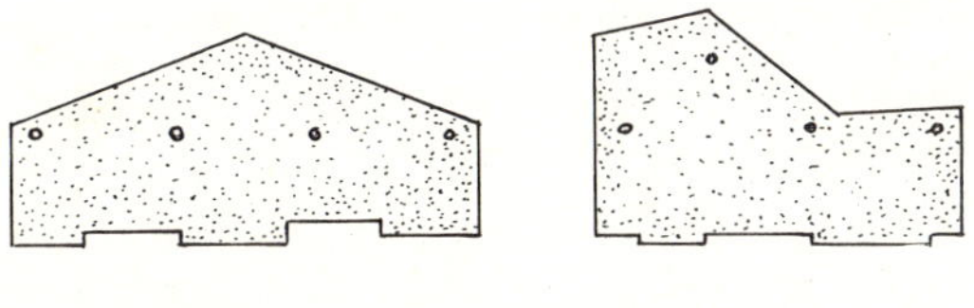

Size, design and lay up varies with mfr. Gives effect of individual layup. Min. pitch 5" in 12".

MULTIPLE UNIT (AMERICAN COLONIAL) STRIP SHINGLES

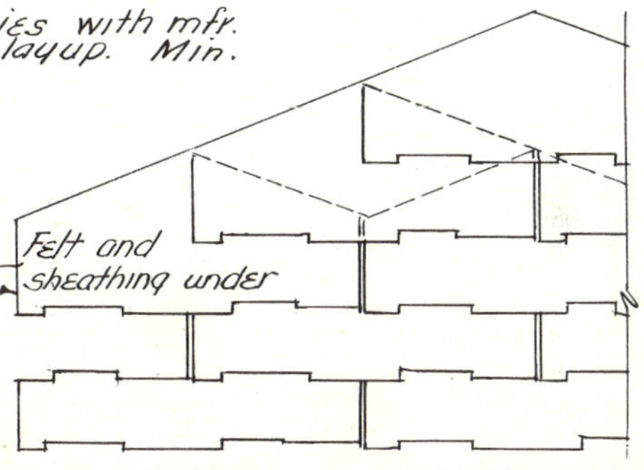
Felt and sheathing under

MULTIPLE UNIT METHOD

All shingles have uniform thickness of 5/32". Use 1 1/4" galv. or aluminum needlepoint nails. Min. slope: 5" in 12" for all shingles, over single layer under playment (30# asphalt felt *) recommended. Consult manufacturers for lesser slopes.

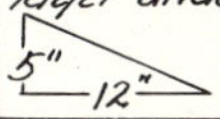
5"
12"

ASBESTOS-CEMENT ROOFING SHINGLES

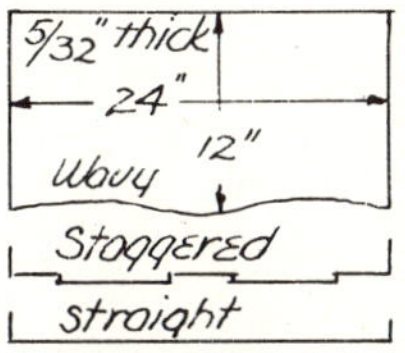
5/32" thick
24"
12"
Wavy
Staggered
straight

SIDING SHINGLES

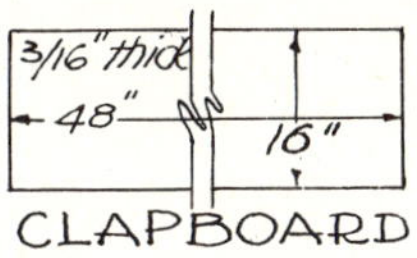
3/16" thick
48"
16"

CLAPBOARD

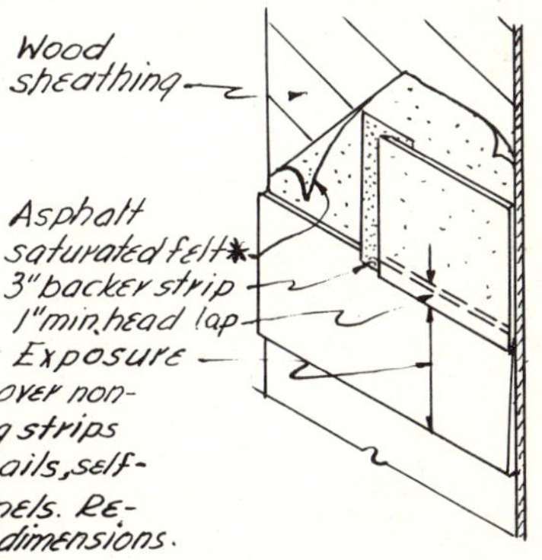
Wood sheathing
Asphalt saturated felt *
3" backer strip
1" min. head lap
Exposure

Asbestos-cement siding may be applied over non-lumber sheathing using wood undercoursing strips or insulating backer board. Use 1 1/4" galv. nails, self-clinching nails or specially designed channels. Refer to mfrs. data for proper fasteners and dimensions.

ASBESTOS-CEMENT SIDING

ASBESTOS-CEMENT SHEET SIZES*

TYPE	USES	SIZES 1/8"	3/16"	1/4"	3/8"
"F" (flexible)	Interiors & exteriors requiring high strength & density, smooth surface, low moisture absorption	32" & 48" x 48" & 96"	32" & 48" x 48" & 96"	32" & 48" x 48" & 96"	32" & 48" x 48" & 96"
"U" (utility)	Interiors & exteriors general utility & construction.		32" & 48" x 48" & 96"	32" & 48" x 48" & 96"	32" & 48" x 48" & 96"

*Both "F" & "U" 48" width are specified in Federal Specification SS-S-283a - Color; stone grey. Sheets up to 1/4" thick do not have to be drilled for nailing. Nails: galv. or alum., min. th. 1" plus sheet thickness. Nail 8"-12" o.c. on all edges, 16" o.c. on intermediate studs.

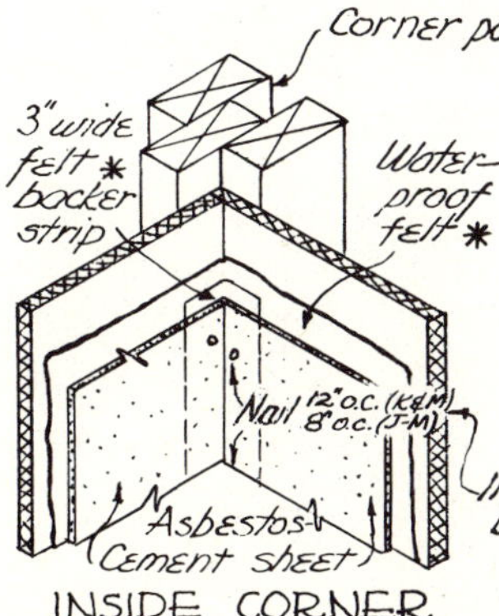
Corner post
3" wide felt * backer strip
Water-proof felt *
Nail 12" o.c. (K&M) 8" o.c. (J-M)
Insulation board
Asbestos Cement sheet

INSIDE CORNER

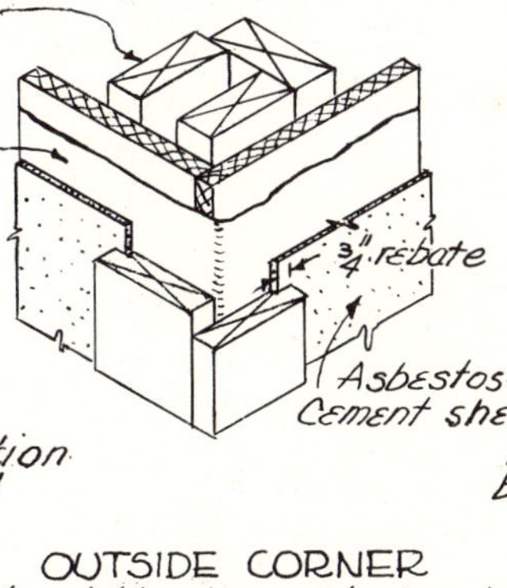
3/4" rebate
Asbestos-Cement sheet

OUTSIDE CORNER

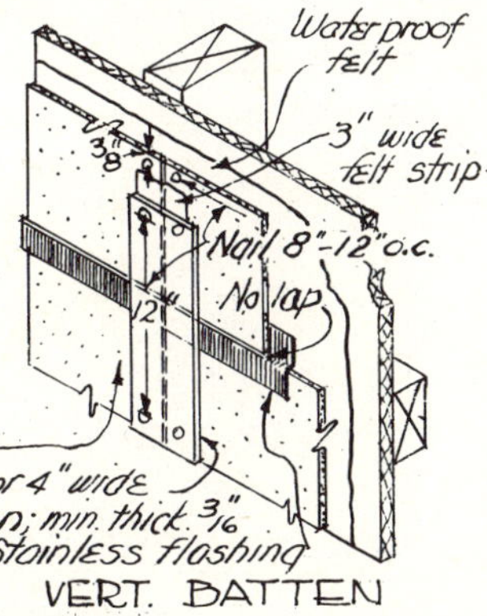
Waterproof felt
3" wide felt strip
1/2
3/8
Nail 8"-12" o.c.
No lap
12
2", 3" or 4" wide batten; min. thick. 3/16
Stainless flashing

VERT. BATTEN

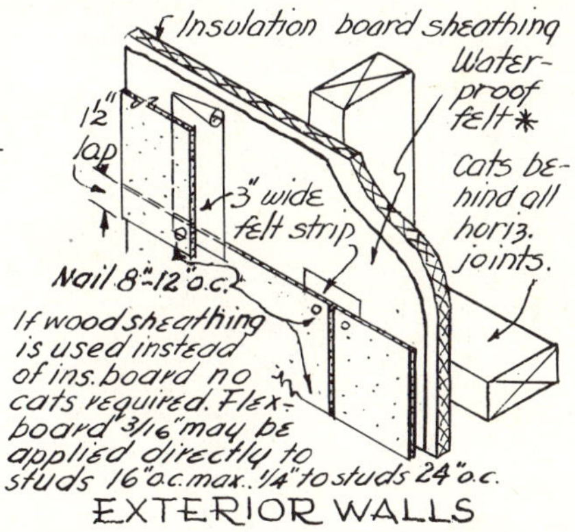
Insulation board sheathing
Water-proof felt *
1 1/2" lap
3" wide felt strip
Cats behind all horiz. joints.
Nail 8"-12" o.c.
If wood sheathing is used instead of ins. board no cats required. Flexboard 3/16" may be applied directly to studs 16" o.c. max., 1/4" to studs 24" o.c.

EXTERIOR WALLS

* Note: all underlay material should be designated as breather type.

ASBESTOS-CEMENT BOARD - EXTERIOR WALLS

Data checked by Asbestos-Cement Products Association.

CORRUGATED ASBESTOS SIDING

For standard sizes, weights, etc., and roofing details, see preceding page. For additional flashing, see "Flashing" pages.

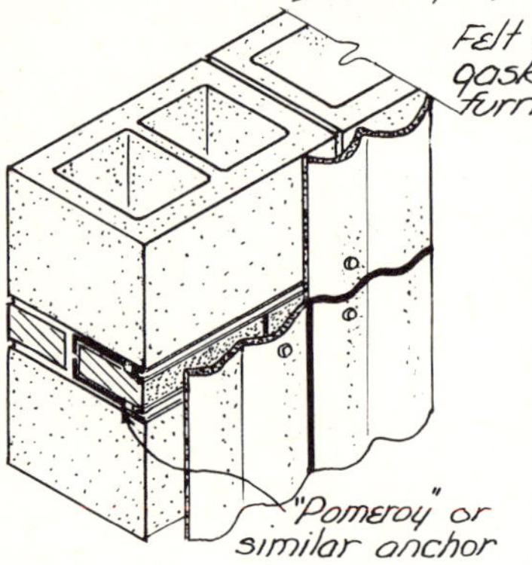
Felt or metal
gasket on
furring strip
"Pomeroy" or
similar anchor

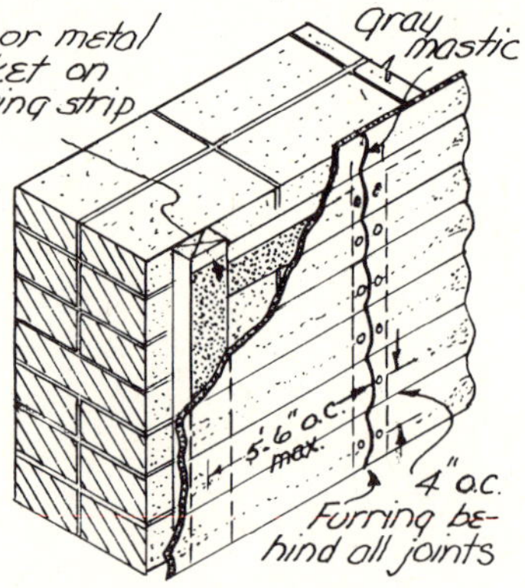
Gray
mastic
5'-6" o.c.
max.
4" o.c.
Furring be-
hind all joints

WITHOUT FURRING | WITH FURRING

CORR. ASBESTOS on MASONRY

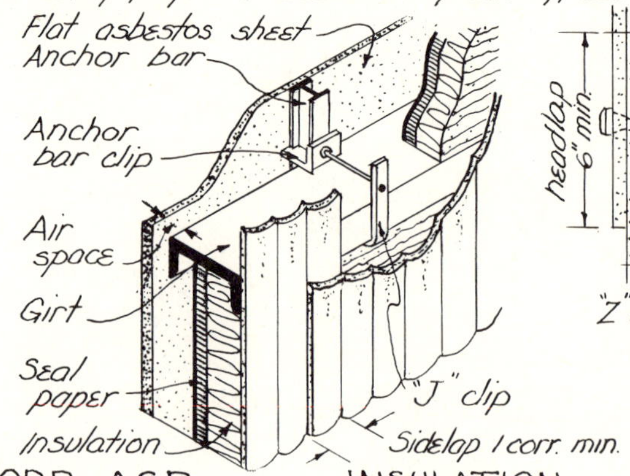
Flat asbestos sheet
Anchor bar
Anchor
bar clip
Air
space
Girt
Seal
paper
Insulation
"J" clip
Sidelap 1 corr. min.

CORR. ASB. and INSULATION on STEEL FRAME

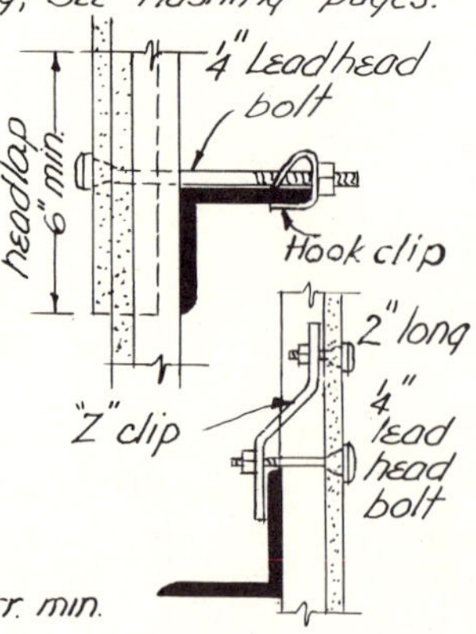
¼" Leadhead
bolt
headlap
6" min.
Hook clip
2" long
"Z" clip
¼"
lead
head
bolt

ALTERNATE SECTIONS

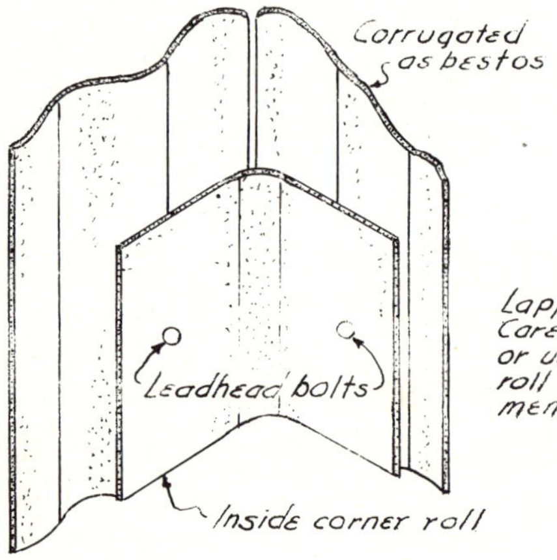
Corrugated
asbestos
Leadhead bolts
Inside corner roll

INSIDE CORNER

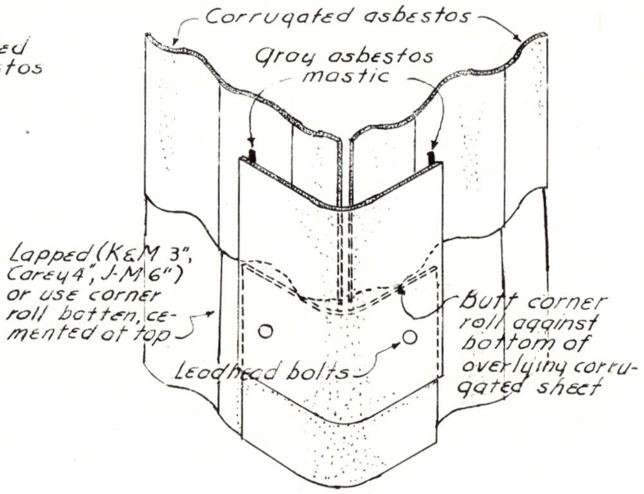
Corrugated asbestos
Gray asbestos
mastic
Lapped (K&M 3",
Carey 4", J-M 6")
or use corner
roll batten, ce-
mented at top
Leadhead bolts
Butt corner
roll against
bottom of
overlying corru-
gated sheet

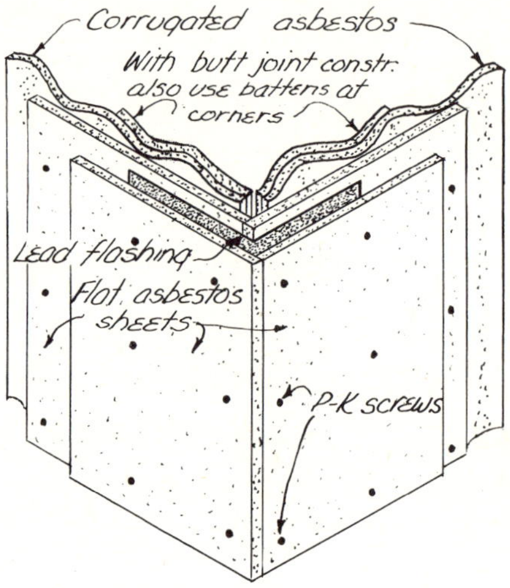
Corrugated asbestos
With butt joint constr.
also use battens at
corners
Lead flashing
Flat asbestos
sheets
P-K screws

OUTSIDE CORNER - ALTERNATES

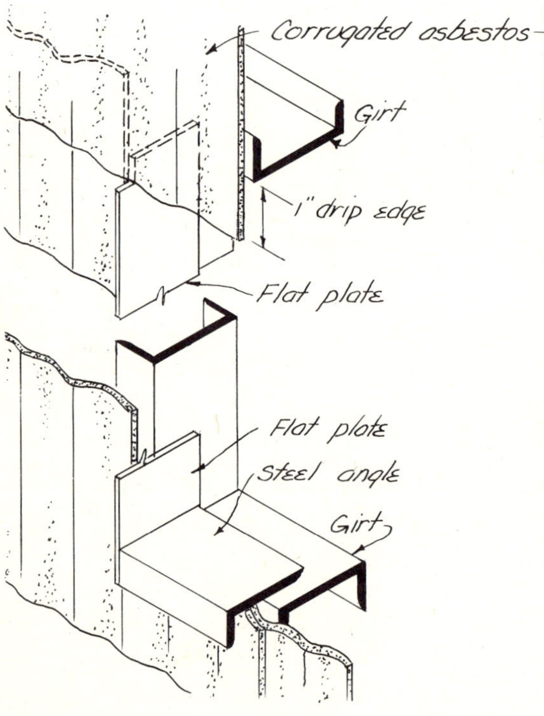
Corrugated asbestos
Girt
1" drip edge
Flat plate
Flat plate
Steel angle
Girt

WINDOW DETAIL

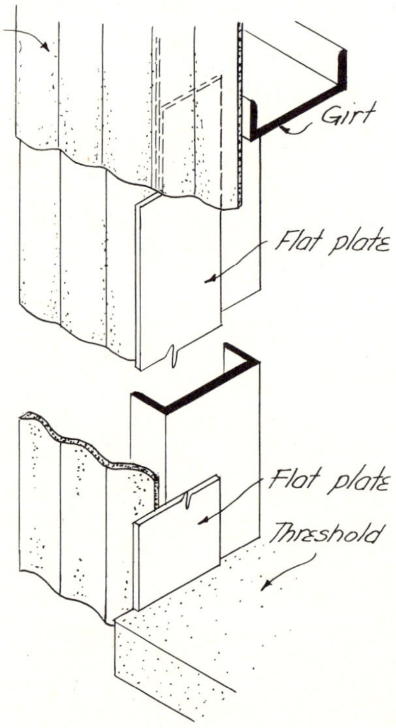
Girt
Flat plate
Flat plate
Threshold

DOOR DETAIL

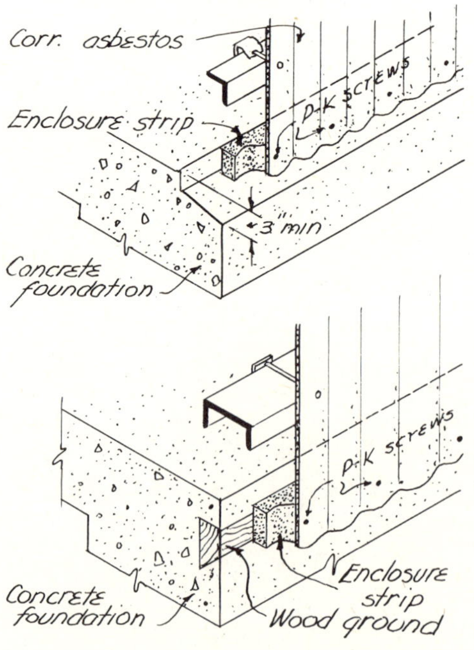
Corr. asbestos
Enclosure strip
P-K screws
3" min.
Concrete
foundation
P-K screws
Concrete
foundation
Enclosure
strip
Wood ground

ALTERNATE SILL DETAILS

Checked by Keasbey & Mattison Co., Johns-Manville, Philip Carey Mfg. Co., and National Gypsum Co.

PORCELAIN ENAMEL on STEEL

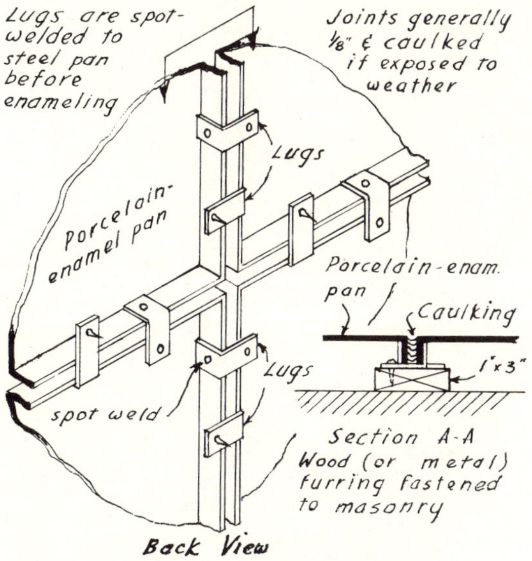

Lugs are spot-welded to steel pan before enameling
Joints generally 1/8" & caulked if exposed to weather
Lugs
Porcelain-enamel pan
Porcelain-enam. pan
Caulking
1"x3"
Lugs
spot weld
Section A-A
Wood (or metal) furring fastened to masonry

Back View

Pans can be fastened to furring on two adjacent sides. Lugs from the remaining two sides are forced under previously fastened panels.

NOTE: METHODS VARY. CONSULT MANUFACTURER

PAN & LUG METHOD OF FASTENING

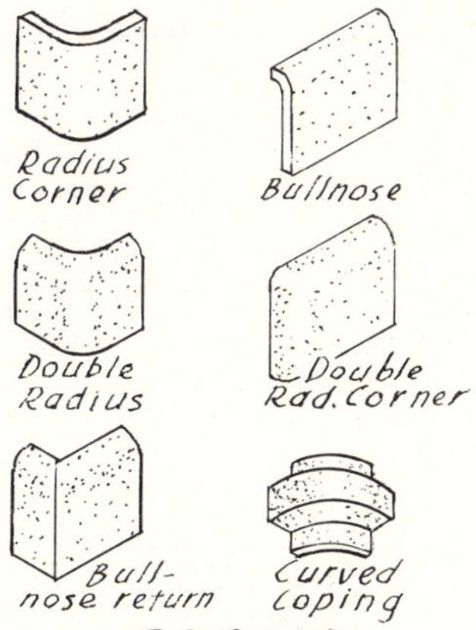

Radius Corner
Bullnose
Double Radius
Double Rad. Corner
Bull-nose return
Curved coping

FORMS

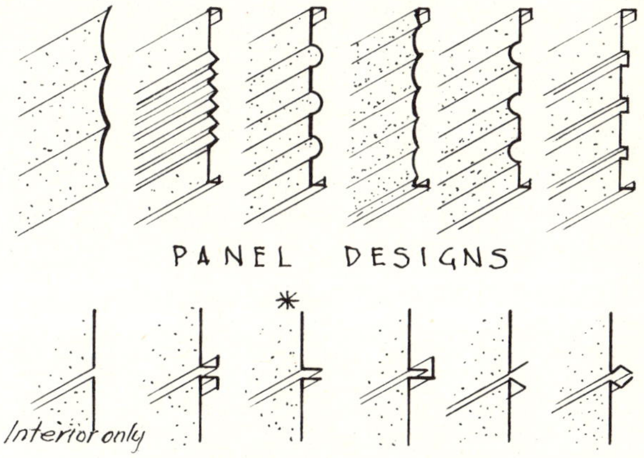

*
Interior only

PANEL DESIGNS

TYPES OF FLANGES

Any shape which can be made in sheet metal by rolling, braking, spinning or cutting & welding can be porcelain enameled. Die stamped shapes are easier to enamel than welded. The max. panel area for practical use is 10 to 12 sq. ft. Plywood or insulating board may be used to deaden metallic ring when struck, increase rigidity and reduce heat loss. Some mfrs. laminate backing to panels; or spray on a 1/8" backing. In most cases, backing is optional. Cutting or drilling holes in porcelain-enameled units is not recommended. Min. radius of edges should be no less than 3/16" radius. Gauges of metal #20 to #16, determined by design.

* type of panel shown in details

PORCELAIN-ENAMEL FASTENING & BASIC DESIGN DATA

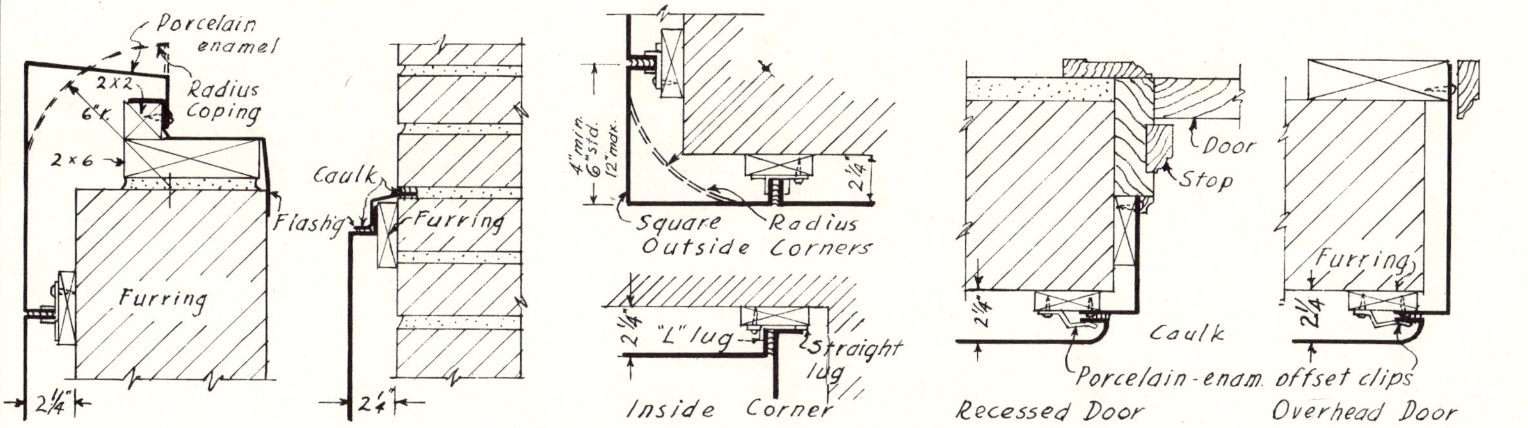

Porcelain enamel
2x2
Radius Coping
6"r.
2x6
Flashing
Furring
2¼"
Caulk
Furring
2¼"
4" min. 6" std. 12" max.
2¼
Square Outside Corners
Radius
2¼"
"L" lug
Straight lug
Inside Corner
Door
Stop
2¼"
Caulk
Porcelain-enam. offset clips
Furring
2¼
Recessed Door
Overhead Door

COPING — FLASHING — CORNERS — JAMB SECTIONS *Heads similar*

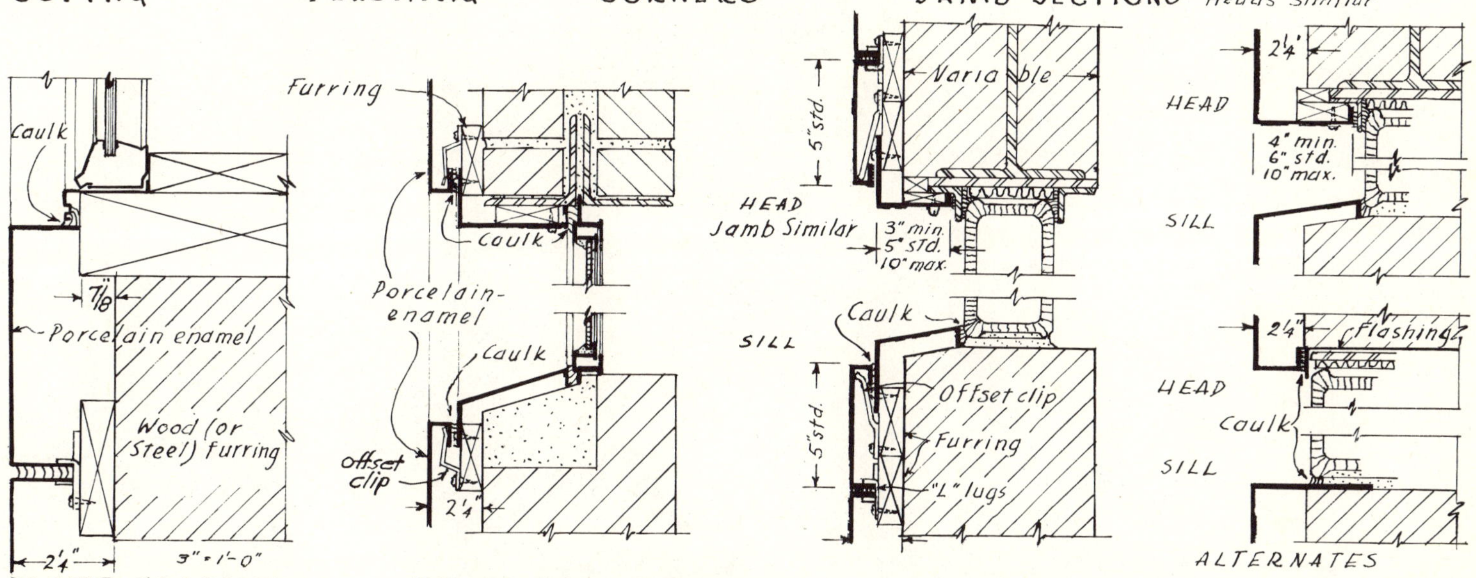

Caulk
7/8"
Porcelain enamel
Wood (or Steel) furring
2¼"
3" = 1'-0"
Furring
Caulk
Porcelain-enamel
Caulk
offset clip
2¼"
5" std.
Variable
HEAD
Jamb Similar
3" min. 5" std. 10" max.
SILL
Caulk
5" std.
Offset clip
Furring
"L" lugs
2¼"
HEAD
4" min. 6" std. 10" max.
SILL
2¼"
Flashing
HEAD
Caulk
SILL
ALTERNATES

PLATE GLASS SILL — STEEL SASH DETAIL — GLASS BLOCK DETAIL

Application details 1½" = 1'-0" unless otherwise indicated

TYPICAL APPLICATIONS

Data by the Porcelain Enamel Institute

CURTAIN WALLS

TABLE OF CONTENTS

PANEL WALL CONSTRUCTION-TYPES and DEFINITIONS

PANEL WALL

Exterior non-load bearing wall whose outer surface may or may not form exterior facing of building and whose interior surface may or may not form the interior finish. May rest on building structure or may be hung from structure.

MASONRY PANEL WALL

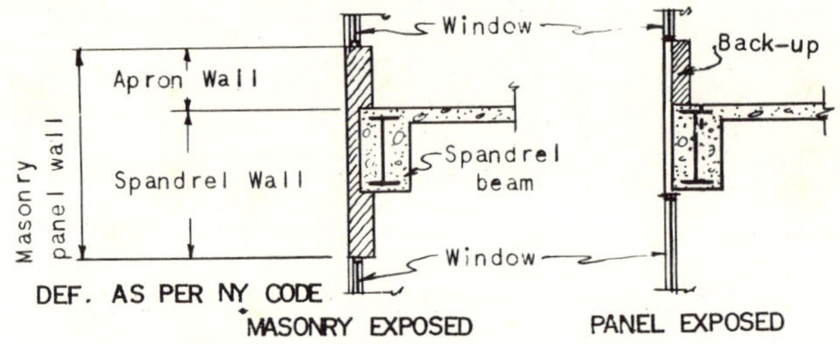
Window
Back-up
Apron Wall
Spandrel Wall
Masonry panel wall
Spandrel beam
Window
DEF. AS PER NY CODE
MASONRY EXPOSED
PANEL EXPOSED

Exterior non-load bearing wall whose outer surface may form exterior bld'g face or it may be used back of panel curtain wall to provide fire rating as required by local code. In latter case sometimes called "back-up."

PANEL CURTAIN WALL

Exterior non-load bearing wall made of panels: 1. attached directly to bld'g structure with adjustable attachments, or 2. mounted on supports (subframe), which in turn are attached to bld'g structure by adjustable attachments. Exterior surface of panels forms face of building; interior surface may or may not form interior finish.

MASONRY OR CONCRETE PANEL CURTAIN WALL

TYPES (VISUAL CHARACTERISTIC):

1. Spandrel
2. Grid
3. Sheathed

SUPPORT METHODS

1. Panels connected directly to structure.
2. Panels or wall units connected to subframe erected independent of the panels.

ASSEMBLY FOR ERECTION

1. Assembly of individual panels with or without trim.

PANEL TYPES

1. Window panel
2. Skin (Marble, stone, concrete)
3. Closed sandwich (concrete)

METAL PANEL CURTAIN WALL

TYPES (VISUAL CHARACTERISTIC):

1. Spandrel
2. Mullion
3. Grid
4. Sheathed (including industrial)

SUPPORT METHODS

1. Panels connected directly to structure.
2. Panels or wall units connected to subframe erected independent of the panels.

ASSEMBLY FOR ERECTION

1. Assembly of individual panels with or without trim.
2. Assembly of wall units: each unit composed of several panels with or without trim.

PANEL TYPES

1. Window panel
2. Skin
3. Open sandwich
4. Closed sandwich

PANEL CURTAIN WALLS-DEFINITIONS and GUIDE to SELECTION

PANEL CURTAIN WALL: Exterior non-load bearing wall made up of panels ① attached directly to bld'g structure with an adjustable attachment, or ② mounted on supports (subframe), which in turn, are attached to bld'g structure by adjustable attachments. Exterior surface of panels forms face of bld'g; interior surface may or may not form interior finish.

SUPPORTS: Structural elements independent of structural framing made of angles, plates, channels, etc., to which panels are attached. Supports may be ① integral with panel construction or ② a subframe erected independently of panel construction.

ADJUSTABLE ATTACHMENTS: Angles, plates & brackets with devices which allow for three plane adjustment to compensate for minor irregularities in the bld'g structure; used to attach supports to bld'g structure.

PANEL for PANEL CURTAIN WALL: Single element of any size or shape made of one material or assembly of materials, one side of which forms exterior bld'g face and which protects the bld'g from weather.

WINDOW TYPE PANEL: Transparent glass and frame incorporated in panel curtain wall.

SKIN TYPE PANEL: Panel made of one material.

SANDWICH TYPE PANEL: Panel made of assembly of several materials.

OPEN SANDWICH TYPE PANEL: Sandwich panel with top and bottom edges closed.

CLOSED SANDWICH TYPE PANEL: Sandwich panel in which all edges of panel are closed except for weep holes and vents.

WALL UNIT: Preassembly of several panels of any type. Units may or may not incl. trim, may be one or several stories high.

TYPES OF PANEL CURTAIN WALL (See following pages for details.)

SPANDREL TYPE	MULLION TYPE	GRID TYPE	SHEATHED TYPE	SHEATHED TYPE (INDUSTRIAL)
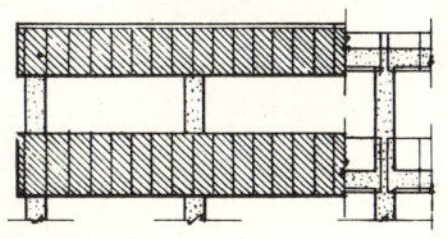	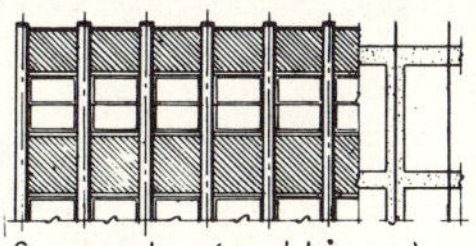	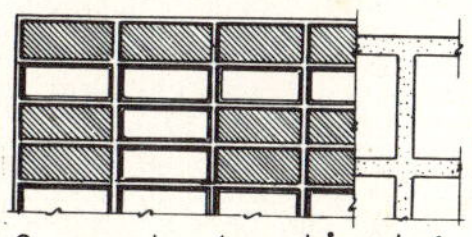	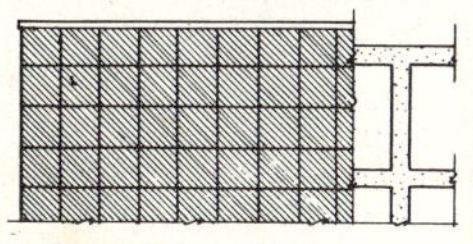	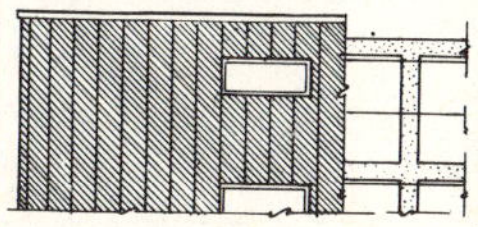
Supports not a primary element of expression.	Supports (mullions) clearly expressed.	Supports (vertical & horizontal members) clearly expressed.	Supports not expressed.	Supports not expressed.
VISUAL CHARACTERISTIC AND SIZE LIMITATIONS				
Horizontal line dominant. Joints vertical. Length of spandrel unlimited. Width of interlocking panels 4'-4" max., height 8'-0" max.	Vertical lines dominant. ℄ to ℄ of mullions, generally 4'-5". Width of panels max. 4'-4", height max. 8'-0".	Vertical & horizontal line equally dominant. Area between support members 32 sq. foot max. Width of panels 4'-4" max., height, 8'-0" max.	Non-lineal pattern. Joints vert. & hor. usually without trim, individual panel size: max. width 3'-10", max. height 8'-0"	Non-lineal pattern. Joints vertical. Panel size: width approx. 4', height 60' max.

TYPES OF PANELS / EXTERIOR PANEL MATERIAL

	Types of panels	Exterior panel material
Spandrel	Skin	Metal, Stone
Spandrel	Open Sandwich	Metal
Spandrel	Closed Sandwich	Metal, Precast conc.
Mullion	Skin	Metal, Stone, Glass
Mullion	Open Sandwich	Metal
Mullion	Closed Sandwich	Metal
Grid	Skin	Metal, Marble, Stone, Glass
Grid	Open Sandwich	Metal, Glass
Grid	Closed Sandwich	Metal
Sheathed	Skin	Stone
Sheathed	Closed Sandwich	Metal, Precast conc.
Sheathed (Industrial)	Skin	Metal
Sheathed (Industrial)	Open Sandwich	Metal

ASSEMBLY METHODS (for erection)

1. By individual panels.
2. By wall units

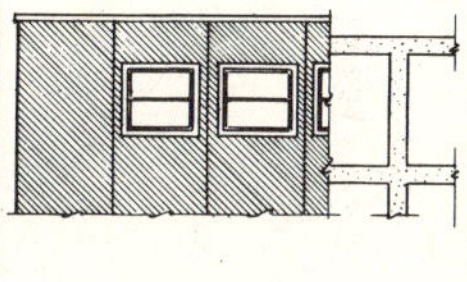

SIZE LIMITATIONS

Wall units width 6'-0" max. Heights 1 to several stories

Supports for wall units are usually modification of those used for individual panels.

WALL UNIT

SUPPORTS

There are two basic supporting methods which may be employed to achieve any of the basic types of panel curtain walls; ① support elements integral with the panel ② support elements used as a subframe erected independently of panels.

BASIC SUBFRAME (SUPPORT) SYSTEMS FOR PANEL CURTAIN WALL TYPES

The six basic types of support systems are shown diagramatically below. In order to achieve a special architectural treatment a support system may be composed of a combination of those shown.

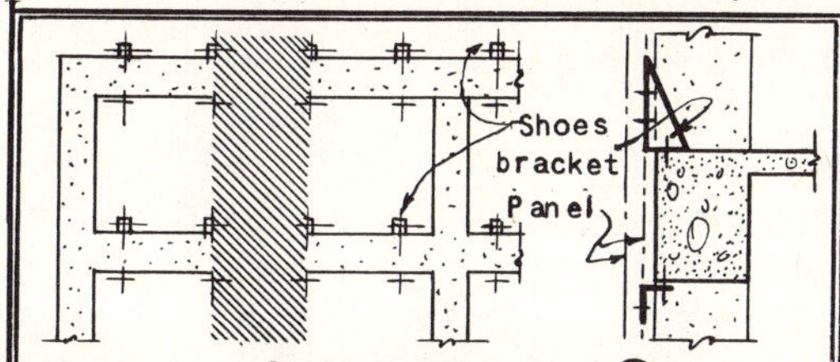
Shoes
bracket
Panel

Elevation SHEATHED WALL UNIT ① Section

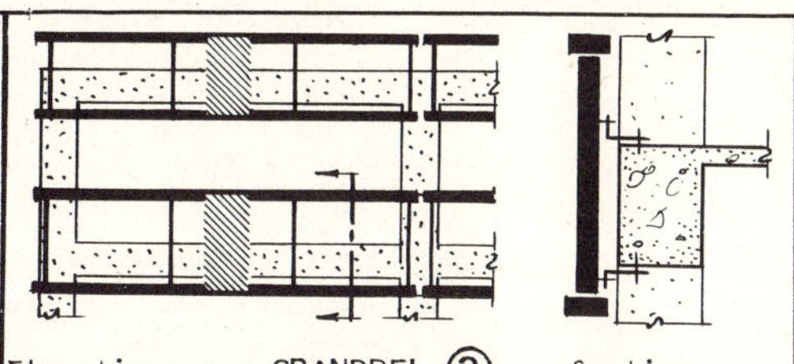

Elevation SPANDREL ② Section

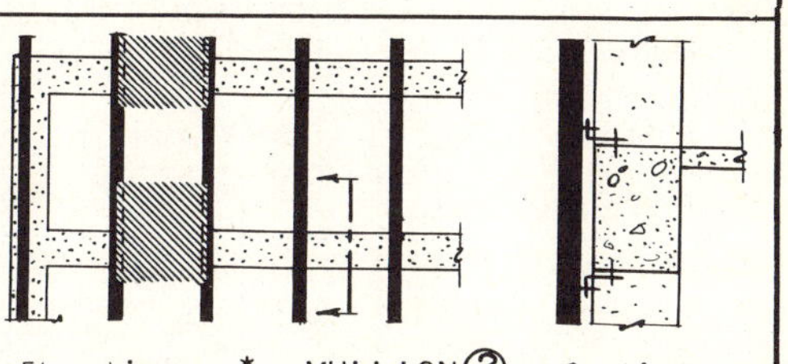

Elevation * MULLION② Section

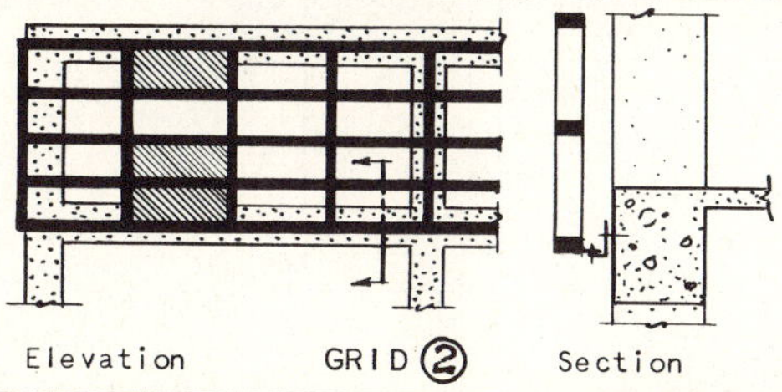

Elevation GRID ② Section

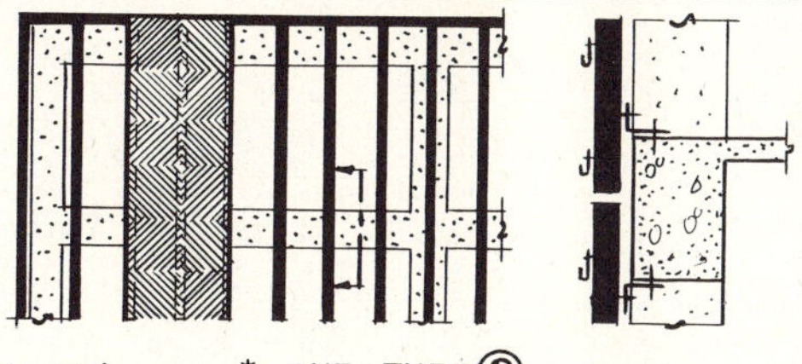

Elevation * SHEATHED② Section

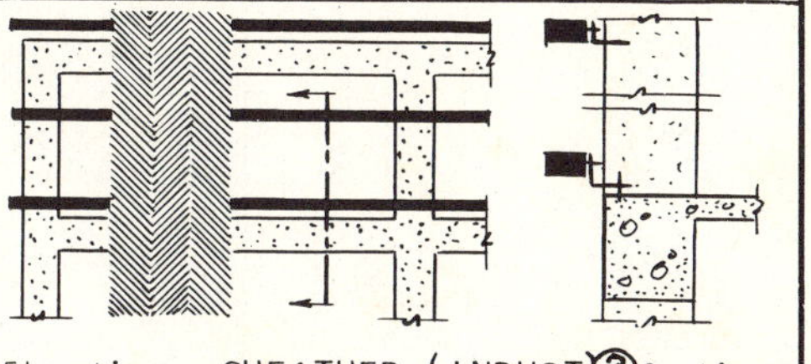

Elevation SHEATHED (INDUST.)② Section

Legend: Building structure; supports; Panel; Jointed panels; Adjustable attachment

* Note: Support system for precast concrete and stone differs (see detail pages).

METAL PANEL CURTAIN WALLS, ATTACHMENTS and DESIGN DATA

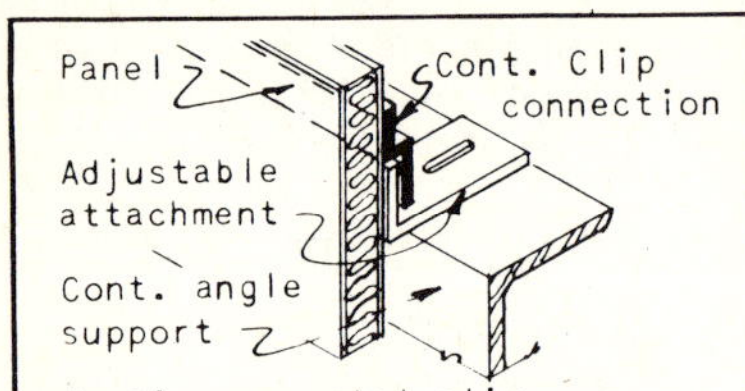
Panel
Cont. Clip connection
Adjustable attachment
Cont. angle support

Continuous metal clip welded to back of the panel.

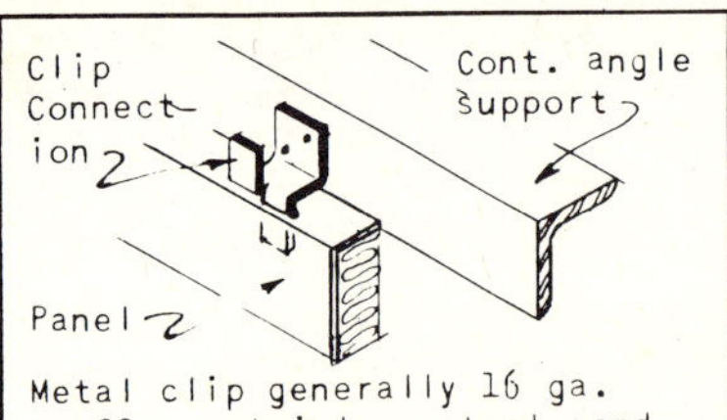
Clip Connection
Cont. angle support
Panel

Metal clip generally 16 ga. to 20 ga. stainless steel, and spaced approx. 12" O.C.

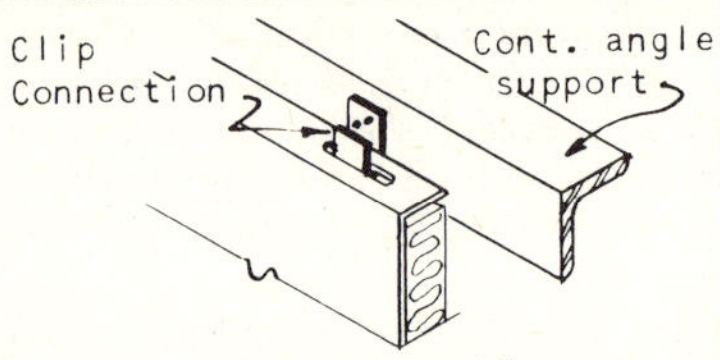
Clip Connection
Cont. angle support

Metal clip generally 16 ga. to 20 ga. stainless steel, and spaced approx. 12" o.c.

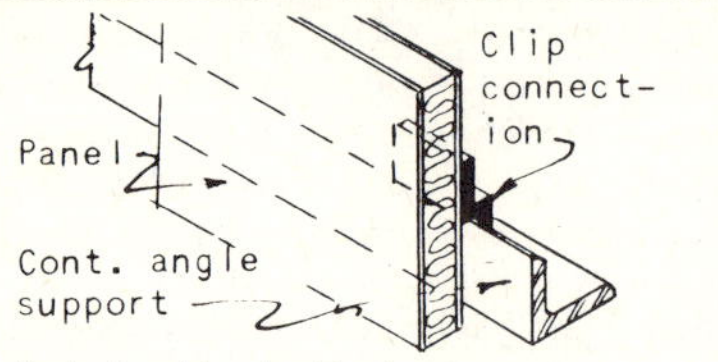
Clip connection
Panel
Cont. angle support

Metal clip bolted or welded to back of the panel.

PANEL CONNECTIONS TO SUPPORTS

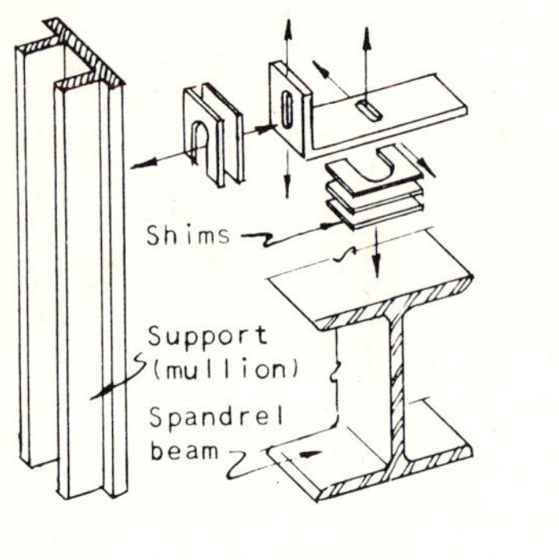
Shims
Support (mullion)
Spandrel beam

Steel angle with slots and shims for adjustment in three planes. as shown by arrows. Use a good hot dipped galv. steel clips for alum. curtain wall support system

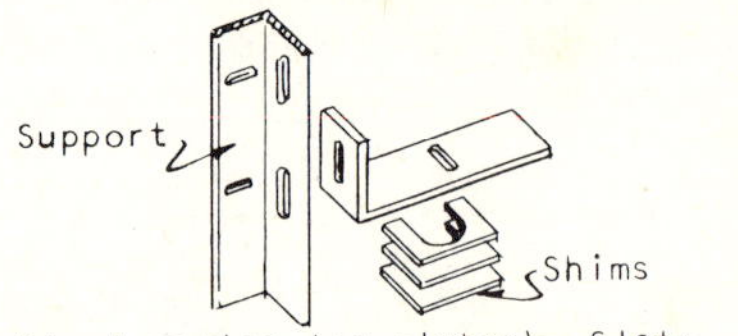
Support
Shims

Steel angles (or plates). Slots and shims for adjustment.

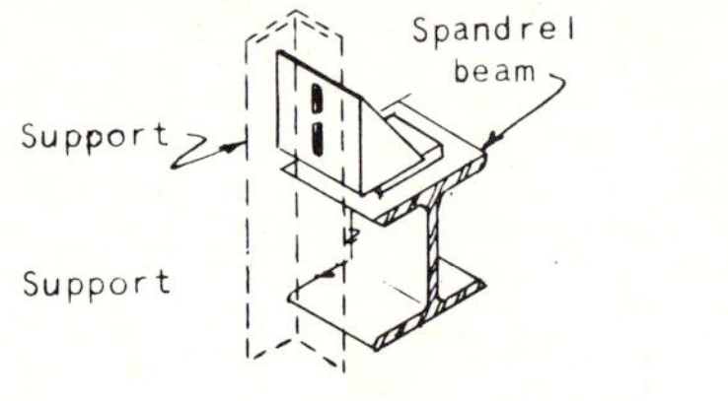
Spandrel beam
Support
Support

Metal shoes fabricated of steel plates & welded to bld'g structure. Shims & slots for adjustm't.

STEEL STRUCTURE

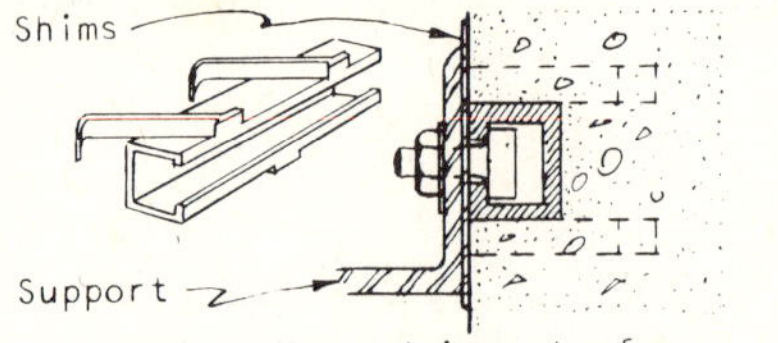
Shims
Support

Continuous slotted insert, from 12" to 60" long. Hooked anchor-legs on top & bottom.

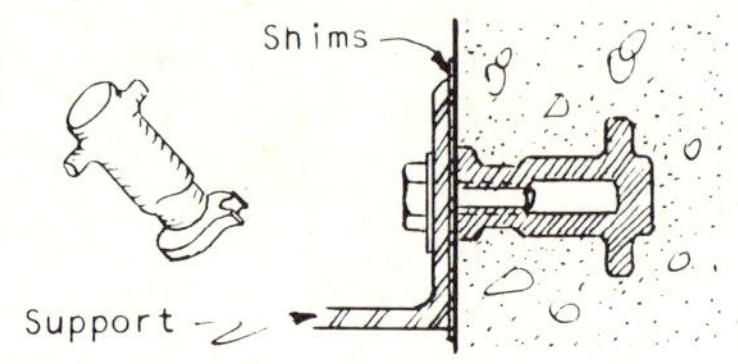
Shims
Support

Threaded insert, cast from malleable iron. Utilize full strength of the bolt. For 1/4", 3/8", 1/2", 5/8", 3/4" bolts

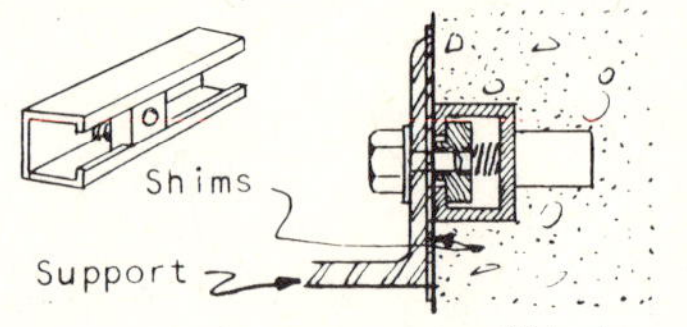
Shims
Support

Unistrut insert up to 20' long Continuous slot permits attachment any where along the length of channel; provides anchorage of 4" intervals.

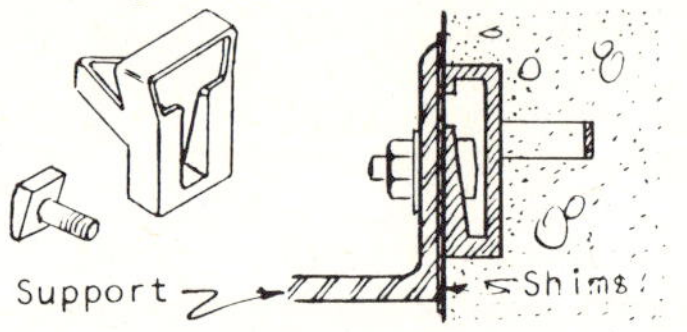
Support
Shims

Peerless wedge insert. For support with adjustment.

CONCRETE STRUCTURE

ADJUSTABLE ATTACHMENT

GENERAL DESIGN DATA FOR CURTAIN WALL PANELS

Panel types are skin, open sandwich, and closed sandwich. Thickness of sandwich panels depends on the insulation material used to obtain a specific "U" factor or fire resistance value. Skin panels may be used with rigid type insulation or back-up walls. Panel manufacturers guarantee only the panels themselves. Since joints in the curtain wall provide the least resistance to air and moisture penetration it is advisable to specify that one party be responsible for the manufacture and erection of supports, sash, panels, and trim.

Panel joints are designed for flexibility to allow for expansion and contraction due to temperature changes. Removal of panels, control of moisture, heat loss and electrolysis of materials must also be considered.

Edges of metal sandwich type panels are designed with profiles to fit component parts of specific support system to be used.

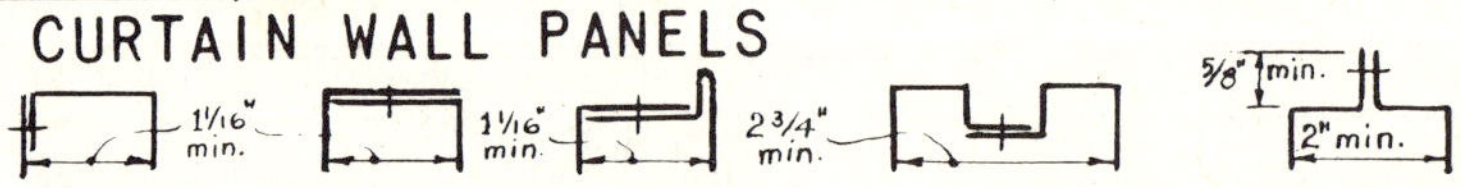
1 1/16" min.
1 1/16" min.
2 3/4" min.
5/8" min.
2" min.

STANDARD EDGE PROFILES OF PANELS MFG. BY A.P.C.O. CO.

Joints are protected with plastic gaskets, caulking compounds, or a combination of both. The erector should be consulted in the selection of protective materials.

The architect may develop new profile, skin features and joints for metal panels if a job is of sufficient size to warrant making special forming rolls or dies. If either bent or extruded forms will serve the same purpose, the bent forms are least expensive.

A wide selection of colored panels is available in porcelain, enamel, or electrochemically created finishes at little or no extra cost.

It is advisable to consult local building code for fire protection ratings before selecting curtain wall panels.

PANEL INSULATING MATERIAL

Any type of insulation may be used in closed-sandwich type (closed all sides); open-sandwich panels (closed two sides) and skin panels require rigid type insulation.

The following table indicates various types of insulation materials, their size, thickness, weight, moisture and fire resistance qualities. The cost shown is of the insulation only (cost per sq. foot one inch thick) and not total panel cost.

Insulating material	Wt.#/sq'	Thick.	Sizes	Conductivity BTU/inch	Moisture resist.	Fire resistance	Termal expansion	Cost	Remarks
Gypsum board	5.23	1/4", 3/8", 1/2"	4'x6' to 12'	1.41	Poor	Excellent		12¢	
Asbestos cement *	3.75	11/16" to 2"	4'x6', 8', 9', 10', 12'	.40	Fair (Expands)	Incombustible	Negligible	40¢	
Calcium silicate **	3.00	1/2" to 2"	4'x8', 10', 12'	.75	Poor	Excellent	Negligible	High	
Cemented excelsior	2.3	1' to 3 1/2"	32"x96"	.45	Fair (Expands)	Incombustible	Negligible	11 to 12.5¢	
Foamglass	.75	2" to 5"	12"x18"	.39	Excellent	Incombustible	Negligible	13¢	Vapor proof
Paper honeycomb ↕	.7			.39	Fair	Poor	Negligible	16¢	Batts resist
Cork board	.6	1" to 6"	12"x36" to 36"x36"	.26	Fair	Fire retardant	Negligible		fire to 450°,
Glass Fiber Board	.47	1" to 4"	24"x48"	.24	Good	Incombustible	Negligible	6.5¢	Fibers to 1000°
Aluminum honeycomb	.4				Excellent	Incombustible	High	80¢	
Paper honeycomb	.3	to 6"		.58	Fair	Poor	Negligible	12¢	
Mineral Wool	.25			.27	Fair	Excellent	Negligible	2¢	Vapor proof
Polystyrene foam	.16			.27	Excellent	Self-extenguish.	Negligible		1 to 5 mix shrinks
Pumice concrete	8.0			2.42	Poor	Excellent	Small		considerably
Perlite concrete	2.6			.77	Poor	Excellent	Small		in curing
Foam concrete	2.5			.6	Good	Excellent	Small	10¢	1 to 6 mix shrinks
Vermiculite concrete	2.25			.76	Poor	Excellent	Small		considerably
Sprayed asbestos	.9	1/2" to 2"		.26	Good	Excellent			in curing

*With fiberboard core ** Marinite, ↕ With perlite fill. NOTE: costs are approximate.

CHART DATA FROM "CURTAIN WALLS OF STAINLESS STEEL" A STUDY BY PRINCETON UNIVERSITY SCHOOL OF ARCHITECTURE. PUBLISHED BY AMERICAN IRON AND STEEL INSTITUTE.

PANEL CURTAIN WALLS - CLOSED SANDWICH and SKIN TYPE PANELS

CLOSED SANDWICH TYPE PANELS

Following are some of the available stock panels. Notes below the panels list the outer skin, the core of insulation and the inner skin, as indicated from top to bottom in the drawings. P.E. indicates porcelain enamel finish. Letters and numbers shown are those used in manufacturers' catalogs. Panels may be assembled by lamination-adhesion of skins to core, or mechanically assembled by joining outer skin and inner skin with welds, screws, rivets, dowels, etc. Flat panel faces are made by either adhesion to nonflexible board or by cementitious fill, which is generally mechanically assembled. The latter panels are guaranteed for 50 yrs.

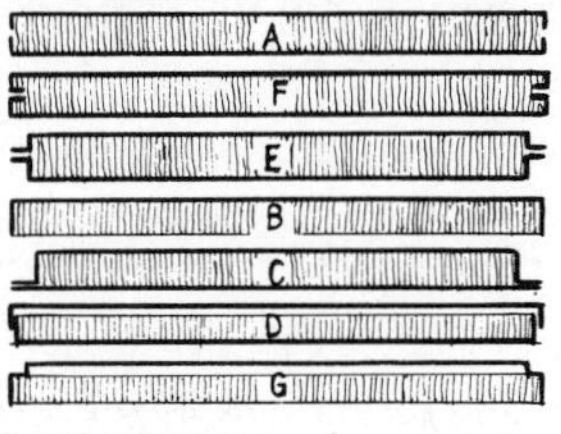

A
F
E
B
C
D
G

Laminated.
Metal with or without P.E.
Celotex, Kaylo, marinite, paper honeycomb, wood, light wt. conc. gypsum-etc.
Painted steel, alum., stainless steel or sheet metal.
Thick. A,F,E, 2" or 4" B&D $\frac{3}{4}$" to $1\frac{1}{4}$", C&G $\frac{3}{4}$" to $1\frac{1}{4}$" plus air space. "U" factor dependent on insul. value.

"A" "B" "C" "D" "E" "F" "G"

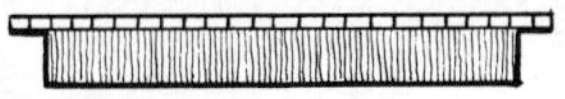

Laminated.
16 ga. P.E. iron
$\frac{1}{4}$" alum. honeycomb
22 ga. electro-galv. steel
$1\frac{1}{2}$" Fiberglas
18 ga. galv. paint. steel
Size: 5'-0"x10'-0" max.
Weight: 7 lbs./sq.ft.
"U" factor: 0.144

"C"

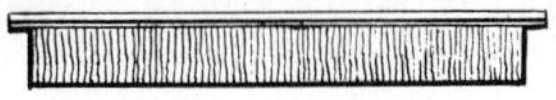

Laminated.
corrugated P.E. steel separated from back by vinyl gasket (air space)
2" foamglass
18 ga. galv. paint. steel
Size: 3'-6"x10'-1" max.
Weight 6.5 lbs./sq.ft.
"U" factor: 0.15

"E"

Laminated.
16 ga. P.E. steel
$1\frac{1}{2}$" Insulrock
16 ga. P.E. steel
Size: 10'-0" x 5'-0"
Weight 12 lbs./sq.ft.
"U" factor: 0.235

"D"

Laminated.
16 ga. P.E. Steel
Foamglass, Fiberglas celotex or light wt. conc.
Size 5'-0"x10'-0" max.
"U" factor: 0.30
No backing or with galv. steel, wall board etc.

"F"

INGRAM-RICHARDSON MFG. CO.

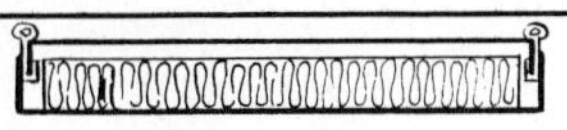

16 ga. P.E. steel
Air space
Fiberglas 6 lbs. density
P.E. galv. steel
Size: up to 12 sq. ft.
Weight: 6 lbs./sq.ft.
"U" factor: 0.236
Thickness $1\frac{1}{4}$" to 3"

"A"

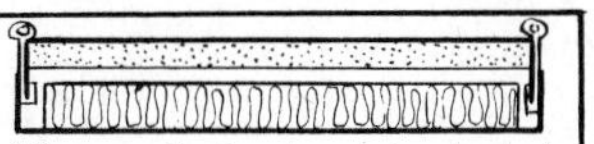

16 ga. P.E. steel & shrink proof gypsum base metal
Air space
Fiberglas 6 lbs. density
P.E. galv. steel.
Size: 20 sq. ft.
Weight: 8 lbs./sq.ft.
"U" factor: 0.227
Thickness $2\frac{1}{8}$"

"C"

DAVIDSON ENAMEL PRODUCTS, INC.

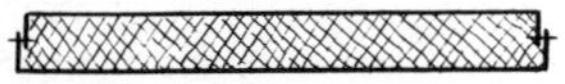

18 ga. P.E. iron.
2" Foamglas.
18 ga. galv. steel.
Size: 3'-0"x8'-0" max.
Weight 7 lbs./sq.ft.
"U" factor: 0.16.

NO. 1

16 ga. P.E. steel
$\frac{1}{4}$" air space
$1\frac{1}{2}$" Fiberglas
18 ga. galv. steel
Size 3'-0"x8'-0" max.
Weight 7 lbs./sq.ft.
"U" factor: 0.20

NO. 2

ATLAS ENAMELING COMPANY

Top
Bottom & sides

Laminated.
20 ga. P.E. iron $\frac{3}{16}$"
asbestos cement board
26 ga. zinc-coated steel
P.F.-615 Fiberglas $\frac{3}{16}$" or $\frac{1}{4}$" ASB cement board or zinc-coated steel
Size 4'-0"x10'-0" max.

thick.	Wt lbs/sq'	"U"
$1\frac{1}{2}$"	7.2 & 8.0	.24
2"	7.5 & 8.2	.14

"T-10"

VERTICAL SECTION

Laminated.
20 ga. P.E. Iron
Paper honeycomb
20 ga. P.E. iron or 20 ga. zinc-coated steel sheet
Size: 4'-0"x10'-0" max.

thick.	Wt lbs/sq'	"U"
1"	3.4 & 3.6	.33
$1\frac{1}{2}$"	3.5 & 3.7	.30

"T-30"

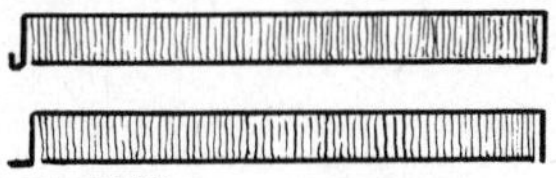

HORIZONTAL SECTION

Laminated.
20 ga. P.E. steel
1", $1\frac{1}{2}$" or 2" rigid Fiberglas 20 ga. P.E. steel
Size 4'-0"x10'-0" max.

thick.	Wt lbs/sq'	"U"
1"	5.4 & 5.0	.29
$1\frac{1}{2}$"	5.6 & 5.7	.20
2"	6.3 & 6.4	.15

"T-20"

TEXLITE INC.

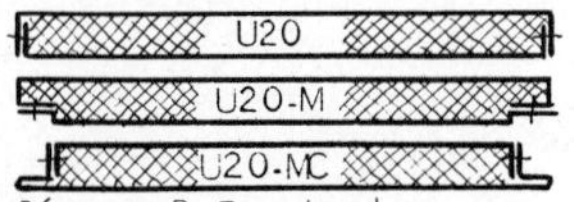

U20
U20-M
U20-MC

16 ga. P.E. steel.
Preformed fiber glass.
P.E. steel, galv. iron, alum., stainless steel.
Vinyl edge seal.
Size: 20 sq.ft. max.
Max. width 4'-0". "U" factor: 1" thick 0.20, $1\frac{1}{2}$" thick. 0.15, 2" thick 0.12

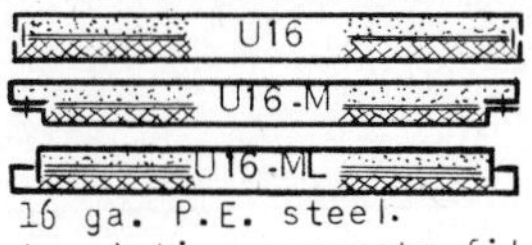

U16
U16-M
U16-ML

16 ga. P.E. steel.
Insulating concrete fill.
Foil vapor barrier,
Fiberglas.
P.E. galv. iron, alum., st. steel.
Size: 4'-0" max. width x 8'-0" max.
"U" factor: 2" thick 0.16

Available with variations to suit job requirements

THE ERIE ENAMELING COMPANY

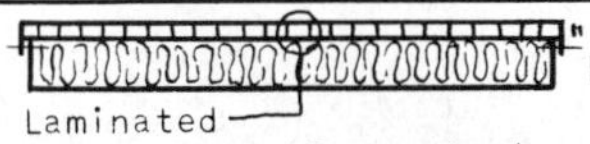

"LA 500A"

Laminated
18 or 20 ga. P.E. steel
$\frac{1}{2}$" aluminum honeycomb
24 ga. zinc-bonded steel (separator)
1" or $1\frac{1}{2}$" Fiberglas 16, 18 or 20 ga passivated zinc-bonded steel

Fiberglas thick.	Wt/sq. ft.	"U" factor
1"	6.75	.20
$1\frac{1}{2}$"	7.00	.15

"LA 501 A"

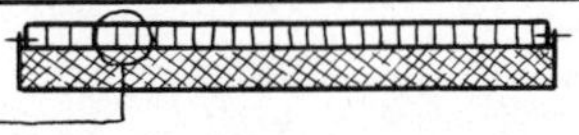

Laminated
18 or 20 ga. P.E. steel
$\frac{1}{4}$" aluminum honeycomb
24 ga. zinc-bonded steel (separator)
$1\frac{1}{2}$" or 2" Foamglass 16, 18 or 20 ga passivated zinc-bonded steel

Foam glass thick	Wt/sq. ft.	"U" factor
$1\frac{1}{2}$"	7.25	.21
2"	7.75	.16

SEAPORCEL METALS INC.

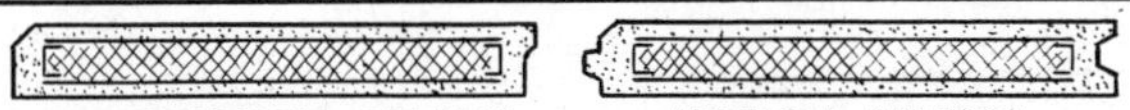

HORIZONTAL SECTION
VERTICAL SECTION

$1\frac{3}{4}$" concrete, $1\frac{1}{2}$" insulation, $1\frac{3}{4}$" concrete
Size: 8'x8'x5" thick., 8'x10'x5" thick.
"U" factor 0.14.
Outer skin may be of an aggregate (such as granite) or an applied finish (such as ceramics). Panel has cast-in metal attachment.

" PRECAST CONCRETE "

THE MARIETA CONCRETE CORP.

SKIN TYPE PANELS

May be of metal, marble, glass, or stone. Metal sections are shop assembled on stiffening members in panels generally 4'-0" wide.

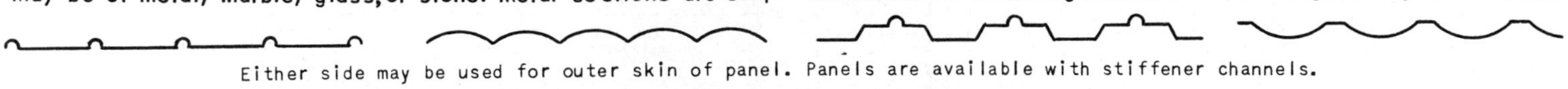

Either side may be used for outer skin of panel. Panels are available with stiffener channels.

BASIC SHAPES OF ROLLED STAINLESS STEEL

ALLEGHENY LUDLUM STEEL CORP.

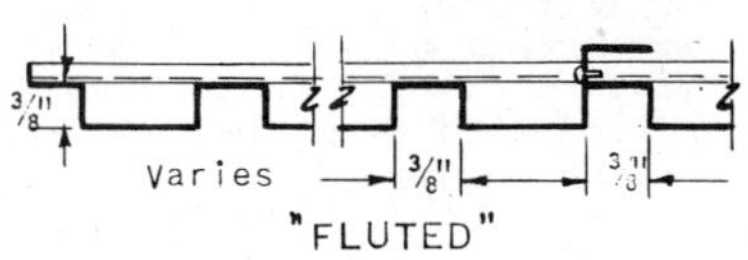

$\frac{3}{8}$"
Varies
$\frac{3}{8}$"
$\frac{3}{8}$"

"FLUTED"

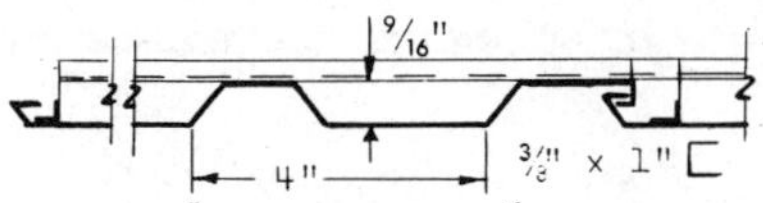

$\frac{9}{16}$"
4"
$\frac{3}{8}$" x 1"

"CORRUGATED"

Extruded or sheet aluminum; height: 30'-0" max.

ATLAS ENAMELING CO.

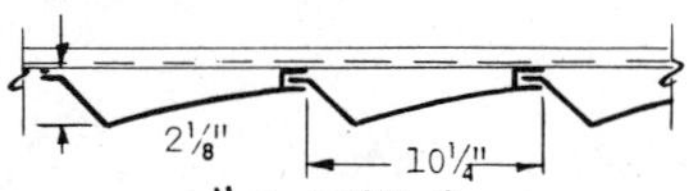

$2\frac{1}{8}$"
$10\frac{1}{4}$"

"V $10\frac{1}{4}$"

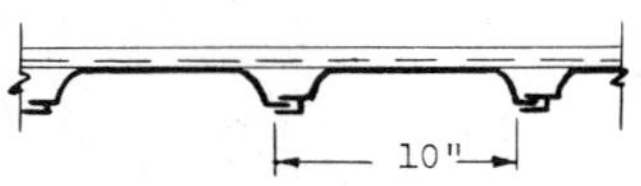

10"

Extruded or sheet aluminum; height: 30'-0" max.

ALUMINUM STRUCTURES INC.

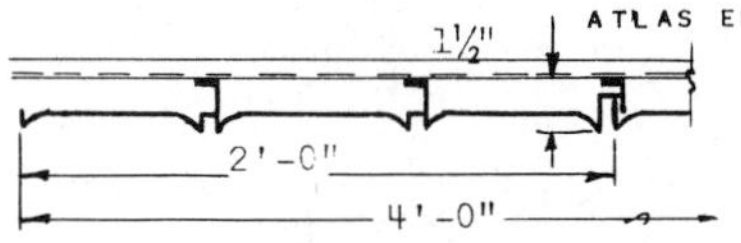

$1\frac{1}{2}$"
2'-0"
4'-0"

"3C"

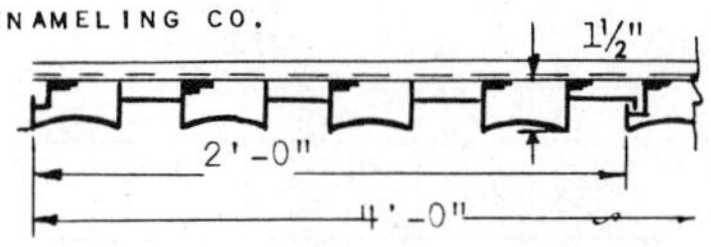

$1\frac{1}{2}$"
2'-0"
4'-0"

"4C"

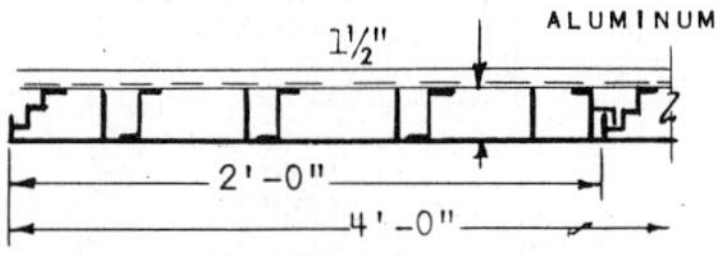

$1\frac{1}{2}$"
2'-0"
4'-0"

"4F"

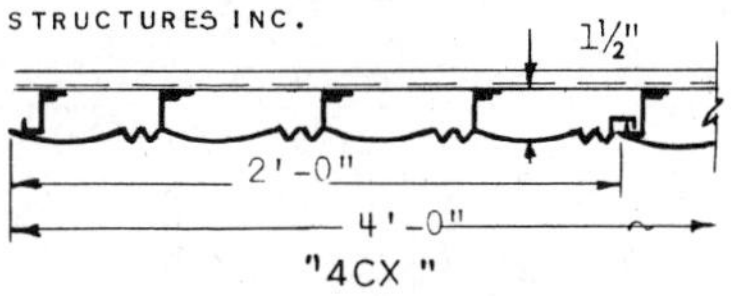

$1\frac{1}{2}$"
2'-0"
4'-0"

"4CX"

Extruded or sheet aluminum. Natural color alumilite. Electrolytically created integral colors or P.E. colors. Size 4'-0" wide stan. & up to 30' high.

ALUMINUM STRUCTURES INC.

PANEL CURTAIN WALLS - SKIN and OPEN SANDWICH TYPE PANELS

SKIN TYPE PANELS (Cont.)

MARBLE DATA BY: MARBLE INSTITUTE OF AMERICA

Max. size: 3'x4¼" thick. Material: Group A sound marble veneer. Finish: natural, sand, grit, hone and polish.
Note: In general the MIA recommends the sand finish for exterior.

GLASS DATA BY: PITTSBURGH PLATE GLASS COMPANY

SPANDRELITE: Max size: 4'x7'x9/32" thick . Material: fused-on glass ceramic colors. Finish: opaque, polished and twill.
CARRARA: Max. Size: 6'-2"x10'-10"x11/32", 3/8", ½" thick. Material: Homogeneous colored glass. Finish: polished and suede.
TWINDOW: Max. Size: 70 sq. ft. (Solex Twindow 50 sq. ft.) x 1 1/16" thick. Material: double glazed insulating glass units, combination of polished glass, rough plate, solex and Carrara. Finish: polished and rough one side.

STONE DATA BY: INDIANA LIMESTONE INSTITUTE

Max. Size: 8'-0"x4'-0"x3" thick, 6'-0"x3'-6"x2" thick, 4'-0"x3'-0"x1¼" thick. Finish: sand, sawed, smooth, planer or rubbed. Recommended finish: smooth and planer.

OPEN SANDWICH TYPE PANELS

The following metal panels are stock items. Core of insulation may be any rigid type. U-factors are for the specific insulation mentioned. Panels are not laminated unless so noted. Letters and numbers shown are those used in manufacturers catalogues to designate their panels. P.E. indicates porcelain enamel finish.

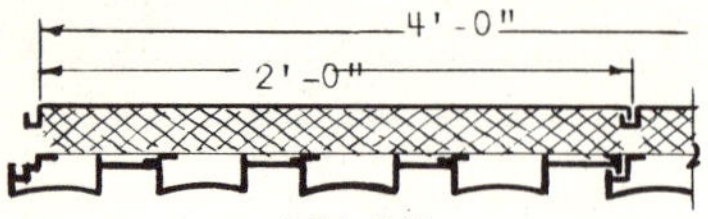
4'-0"
2'-0"

*"4-C"

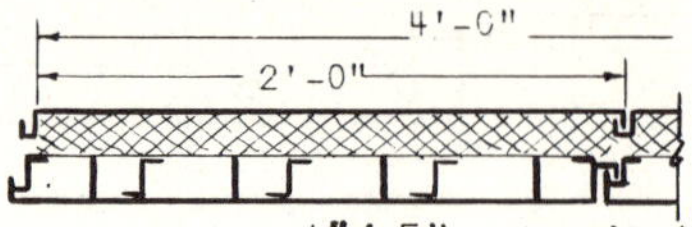
4'-0"
2'-0"

*"4-F"

longitudinal stiffening

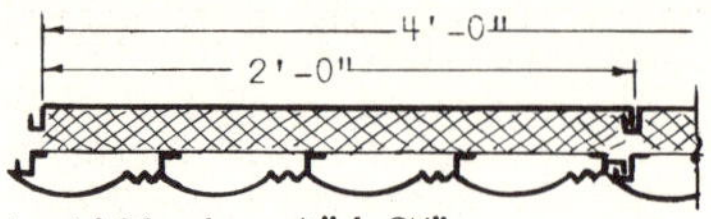
4'-0"
2'-0"

*"4-CX"

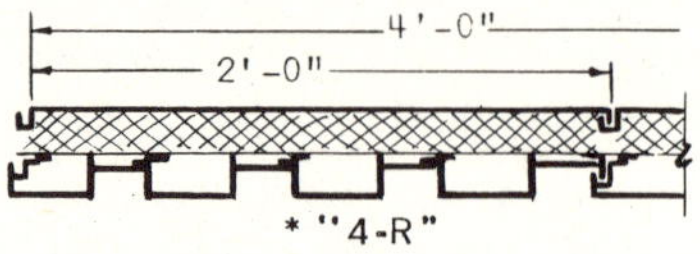
4'-0"
2'-0"

*"4-R"

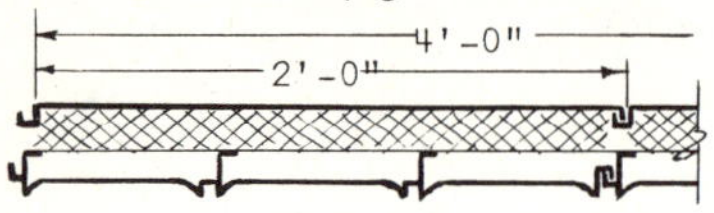
4'-0"
2'-0"

*"3-C"

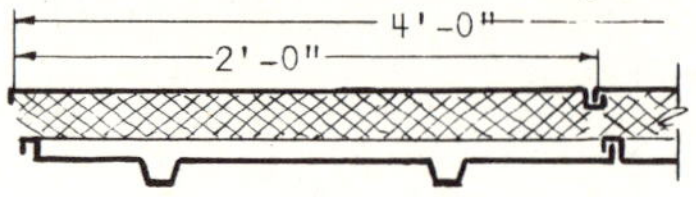
4'-0"
2'-0"

*RIBBED SHEET

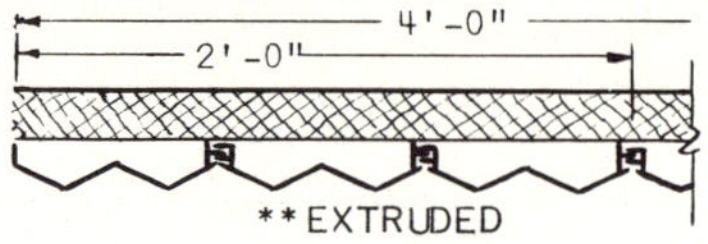
4'-0"
2'-0"

**EXTRUDED

**PRESSED FORMED

Size: 4'-0"x3¼" thick x up to 30' height. Outer skin: extruded or sheet aluminum. Finish: natural color alumilite, Electrolytically created integral color surface, porcelain enamel colors. Inner skin: Coated steel, plain or patterned aluminum, plywood, hard board, fiberboard, asbestos board, or other composition board. Core: 1½" fiber glass, U factor 0.13 for over 6' high.

*ALUMINUM STRUCTURES INC.

**OVERLY MANUFACTURING CO.

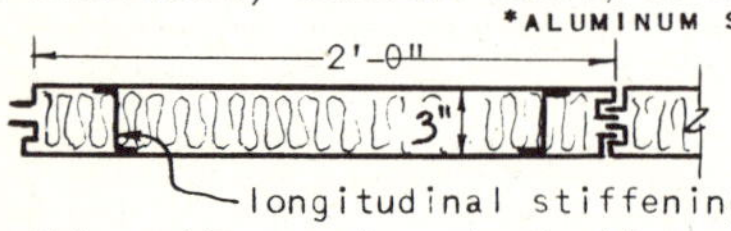
2'-0"
3"

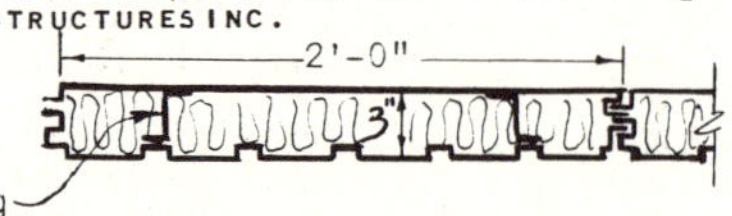
2'-0"
3"

longitudinal stiffening

Skins: 18 ga. galv. steel, 18 ga. galv. color bond, steel painted with one coat of baked on enamel, 16 B & S ga. alum., 20 ga. stainless steel. Core: 3" fiber glass of 2½" lbs. density
Size 8'-0"x3' thick. x up to 20' heights. Weight (steel) 5.6#/sq' (alum.) 3#/sq' "U" factor 0.15

FLUSH FLUTED

THE STEEL CRAFT MFG. CO.

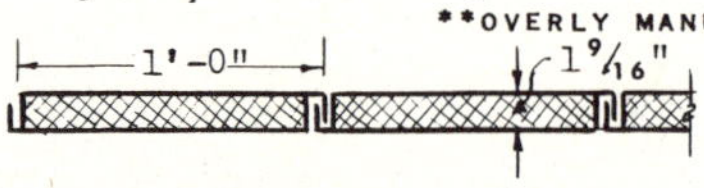
1'-0"
1 9/16"

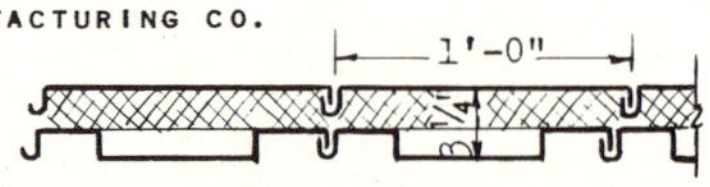
1'-0"

Outer skin: 18 ga. galv. steel, 16 B&S alum., 20 ga. stainless steel. Core: 1½" Fiberglass. Inner skin: 18 ga., 20 ga galv. steel. Size: 1'-0" x 1 9/16" x up to 30' height, 1'-0" x 3¼" x up to 60' height.

"U" factor 0.40 "U" factor 0.15

FLUSH FLUTED

THE R.C. MAHON COMPANY

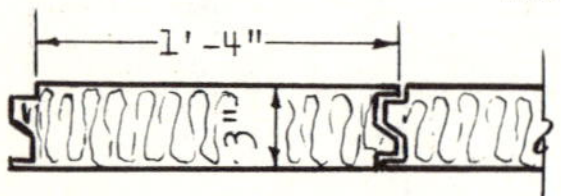
1'-4"
3"

May be used vertically or horiz. size 1'-4"x3"x length, Core: 3" Boro-silicate, glass fiber type; 2# density

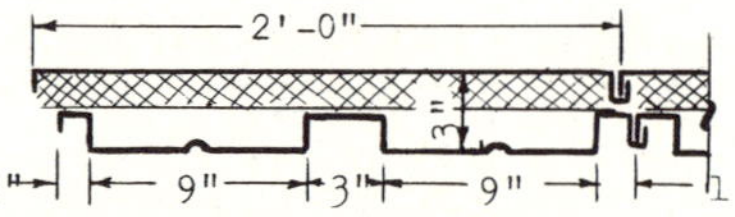
2'-0"
3"
1'2"
9"
3"
9"
1

Size 2'x0"x3" x length. Core: 1½" Boro-silicate, glass fiber type 2# density

U factor .13 to .22 depend'g on panel type & material

"C" Fenestra "F" Fenestra

	Gauge & Material		Wt. per sq. ft.	Max. allowable span between supports
	Inner skin	Outer skin		
"C"	18 P.S. 16 B&S, Al 16 B&S, Al	18 P.S. 16 B&S, Al 18 P.S.	6.50 3.00 4.50	13'-3" 9'-5" 11'-4"
"F"	18 galv.s. 16 B&S, Al 16 B&S, Al	18 galv.s. 18 galv.s. 16 B&S, Al	5.70 4.10 2.70	12'-6" 8'-6" 8'-6"
P.S. = painted steel; Al. = aluminum; S = steel				

DETROIT STEEL PRODUCTS CO.

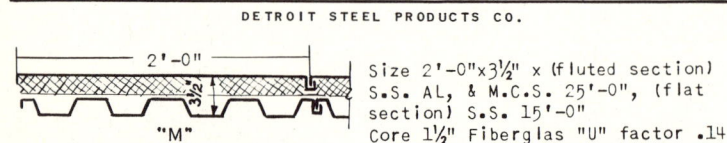

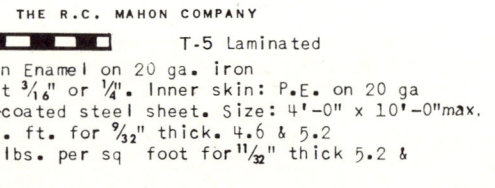

T-5 Laminated

Outer skin: Porcelain Enamel on 20 ga. iron
Core: asbestos cement 3/16" or ¼". Inner skin: P.E. on 20 ga iron or 26 ga. zinc-coated steel sheet. Size: 4'-0" x 10'-0"max.
Wt. lbs. per sq. ft. for 9/32" thick. 4.6 & 5.2
"U" factor 1.12 Wt. lbs. per sq foot for 11/32" thick 5.2 & 5.9 "U" factor.1.08.

TEXLITE INC.

Laminated. 18 ga. P.E. Steel
1", 1½", 2" paper honeycomb
18 to 24 ga. passivated zinc-bonded steel.

L.P. 300

Core thick.	Wt/sq'	"U" factor
1" 1½" 2"	3.5 3.6 3.7	.425 .34 .275

Available also with perlite

Laminated. 18 ga. P.E. Steel
¼", ½", ¾" alum. honeycomb
18 to 24 ga. passivated zinc-bonded steel.

L.A. 300

Core thick.	Wt/sq'	"U" factor
¼" ½" ¾"	4.50 4.75 5.00	

Laminated
18 ga. P.E. Steel
1/8", ¼" cement asbestos board
18 to 24 ga passivated zinc-bonded steel.

L.C. 300

Core thick.	Wt/sq'	"U" factor
1/8" ¼"	5.50 6.75	

Laminated. 18 ga. P.E. Steel
1/8" cement asbestos board
24 ga zinc-bonded steel
1" PF-615 Fiberglas
Aluminum foil
1/8" cement asbestos board, or 18 to 24 ga passivated zinc-bonded steel.
Wt/sq' 5.50 lbs. "U" factor .20

ST-600

Panels designed for installation in conjunction with standard wall frames. Can be modified to suit any frame.

SEAPORCEL METALS, INC.

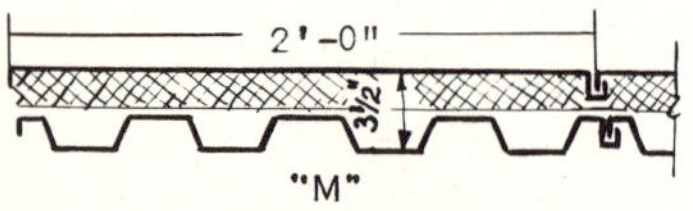
2'-0"
3½"

"M"

Size 2'-0"x3½" x (fluted section) S.S. AL, & M.C.S. 25'-0", (flat section) S.S. 15'-0"
Core 1½" Fiberglas "U" factor .14

	Gauge & Material inner skin & outerskin	Wt. per sq. ft.	Max. allowable span between supports
"M"	18 B & S, Al 14 B & S, Al 20 S.S. 18 M.S.C.	5 5 7 7	8'-0" 10'-0" 12'-0" 12'-6"
Al = Aluminum; SS = Stainless steel; M.S.C. = Mettalic Coated steel			

H.H. ROBERTSON CO.

METAL PANEL CURTAIN WALLS-SPANDREL TYPE

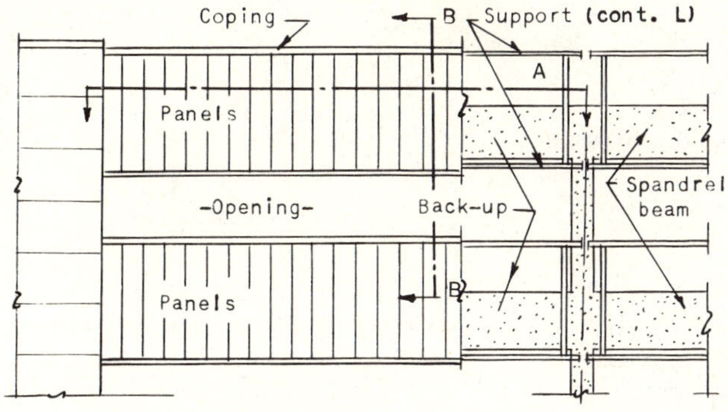
Coping
B
Support (cont. L)
A
Panels
-Opening-
Back-up
Spandrel beam
Panels
B

ELEVATION

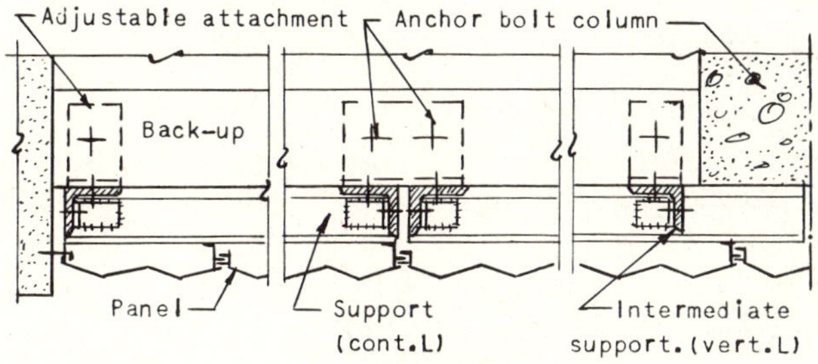
Adjustable attachment
Anchor bolt column
Back-up
Panel
Support (cont.L)
Intermediate support.(vert.L)

SECTION A-A

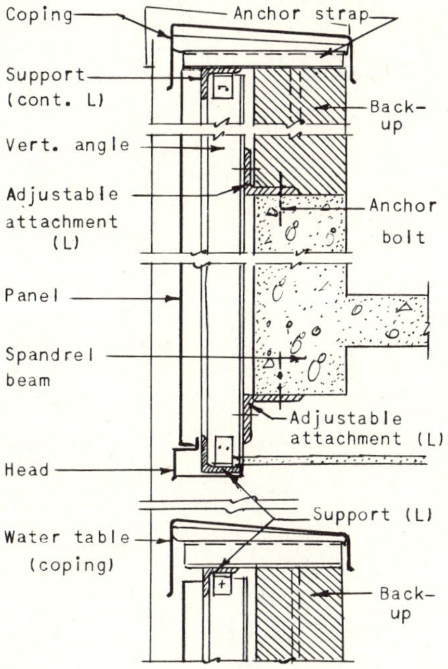
Coping
Anchor strap
Support (cont. L)
Back-up
Vert. angle
Adjustable attachment (L)
Anchor bolt
Panel
Spandrel beam
Adjustable attachment (L)
Head
Support (L)
Water table (coping)
Back-up

SECTION B-B

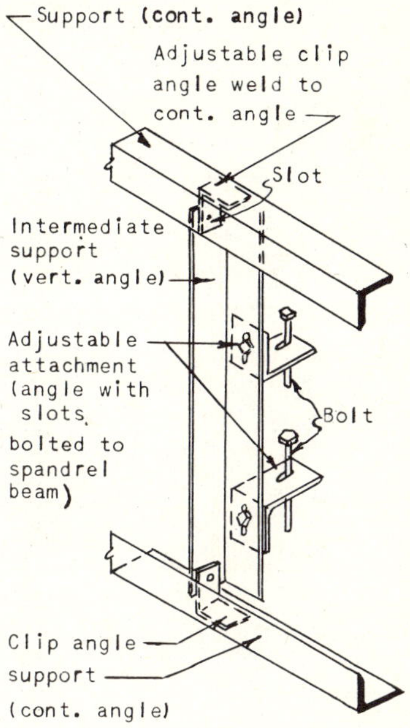
Support (cont. angle)
Adjustable clip angle weld to cont. angle
Slot
Intermediate support (vert. angle)
Adjustable attachment (angle with slots bolted to spandrel beam)
Bolt
Clip angle support (cont. angle)

SUPPORT & ADJUSTABLE ATTACHMENT

Angles (adjustable attachment) anchor to top of slab and bottom of spandrel beam. Continuous angle support attached to vertical member by means of clip angles. Panels are suspended and secured to supports by screws or by welding. Back-up wall and air space acts as insulation. Stainless steel screws should be used with aluminum sheets.

SPANDREL TYPE (Metalskin type panels)

DATA CHECKED BY: OVERLY MANUFACTURING CO.

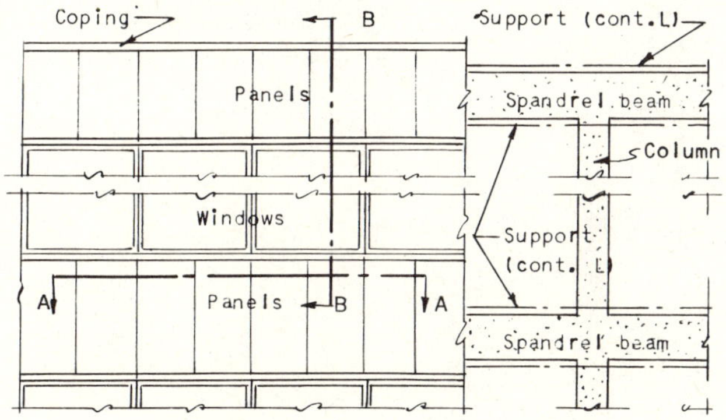
Coping
B
Support (cont.L)
Panels
Spandrel beam
Column
Windows
Support (cont. L)
A
Panels
B
A
Spandrel beam

ELEVATION

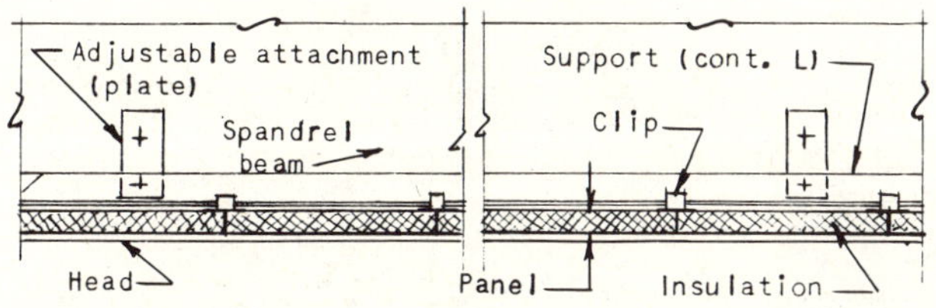
Adjustable attachment (plate)
Spandrel beam
Support (cont. L)
Clip
Head
Panel
Insulation

PLAN AT A-A

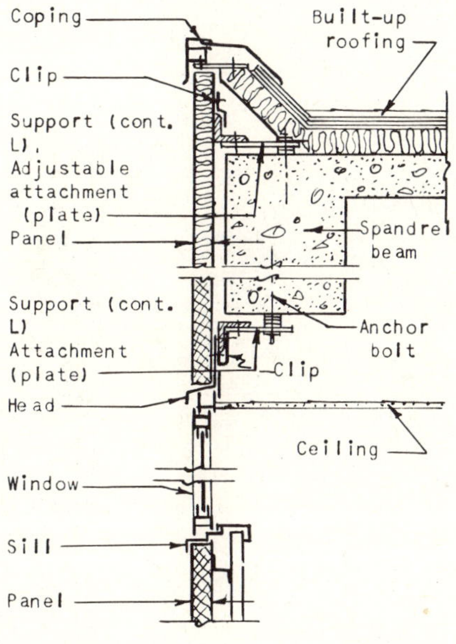
Coping
Built-up roofing
Clip
Support (cont. L),
Adjustable attachment (plate)
Panel
Spandrel beam
Support (cont. L)
Attachment (plate)
Anchor bolt
Clip
Head
Ceiling
Window
Sill
Panel

SECTION B-B

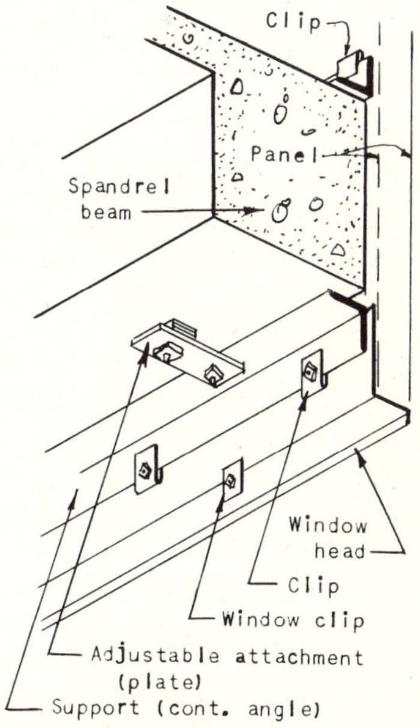
Clip
Panel
Spandrel beam
Window head
Clip
Window clip
Adjustable attachment (plate)
Support (cont. angle)

SUPPORT & ADJUSTABLE ATTACHMENT

Adjustable attachment plates anchor to top slab and bottom of spandrel beam. Continuous angle (supports) are bolted to adjustable attachment plates. Panels are suspended from support members by clips which are part of the panel itself. Head sill and windows are connected with panels by clips.

SPANDREL TYPE with WINDOWS (Metal open sandwich type panels)

DATA BY ALLEGHENY LUDLUM STEEL CORP.

METAL PANEL CURTAIN WALLS-MULLION and GRID TYPE

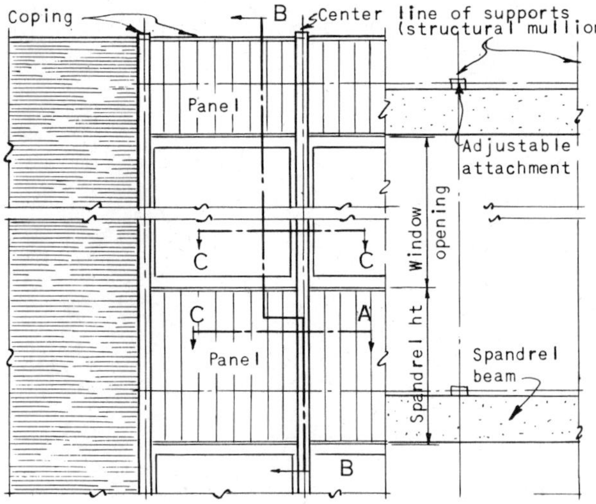
Coping
B
Center line of supports (structural mullions)
Panel
Adjustable attachment
Window opening
C
C
C
A
Spandrel ht
Panel
Spandrel beam
B

ELEVATION

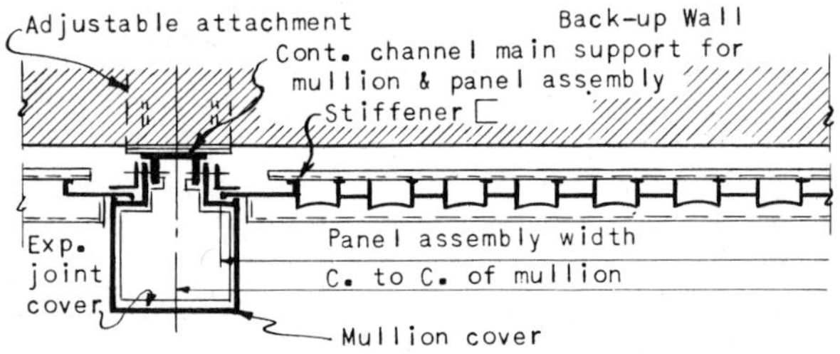
Adjustable attachment
Back-up Wall
Cont. channel main support for mullion & panel assembly
Stiffener
Exp. joint cover
Panel assembly width
C. to C. of mullion
Mullion cover

SECTION A-A

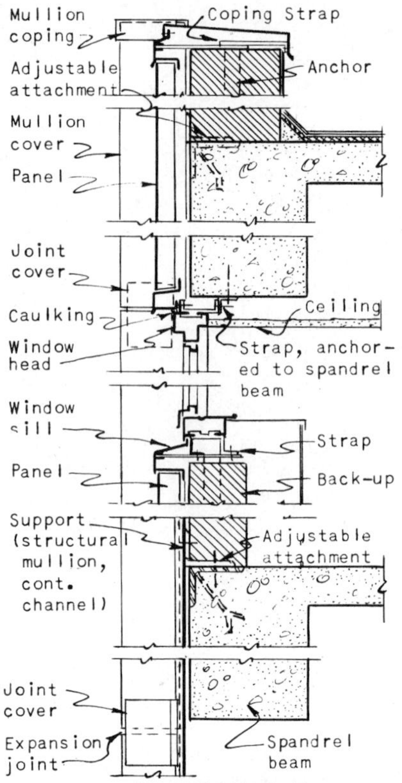
Mullion coping
Coping Strap
Adjustable attachment
Anchor
Mullion cover
Panel
Joint cover
Caulking
Ceiling
Window head
Strap, anchored to spandrel beam
Window sill
Strap
Panel
Back-up
Support (structural mullion, cont. channel)
Adjustable attachment
Joint cover
Expansion joint
Spandrel beam

SECTION B-B

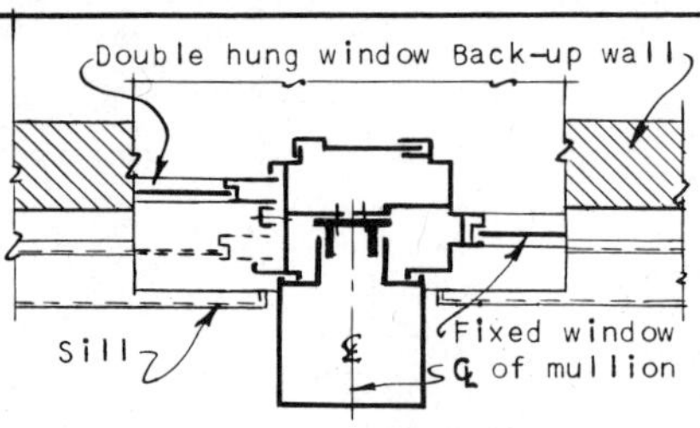
Double hung window
Back-up wall
Sill
Fixed window
℄ of mullion

SECTION C-C

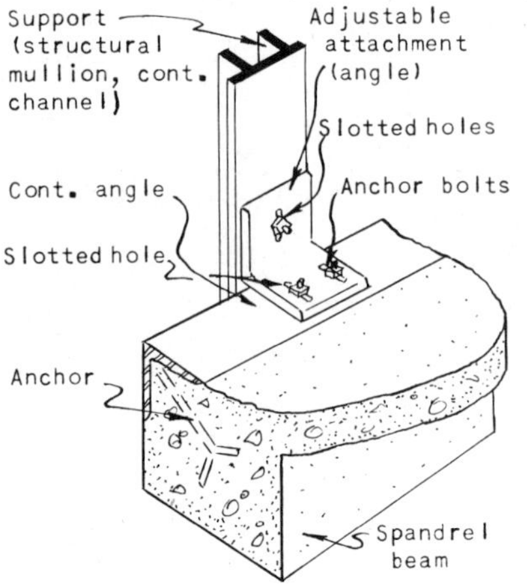
Support (structural mullion, cont. channel)
Adjustable attachment (angle)
Slotted holes
Cont. angle
Anchor bolts
Slotted hole
Anchor
Spandrel beam

SUPPORT & ADJUSTABLE ATTACHMENTS

Continuous channel, main support for mullion cover, is attached to spandrel beam by angle (adjustable attachment). Mullion cover is screwed to support. Space between mullions is filled with panels & windows. Panels are attached & suspended from mullion supports. Straps act as anchor for window and add rigidity to the panel. Straps are anchored to the bottom of the spandrel beam and back-up wall.

MULLION TYPE (Metal skin type, non-insulated panels)

DATA BY: ALUMINUM COMPANY OF AMERICA

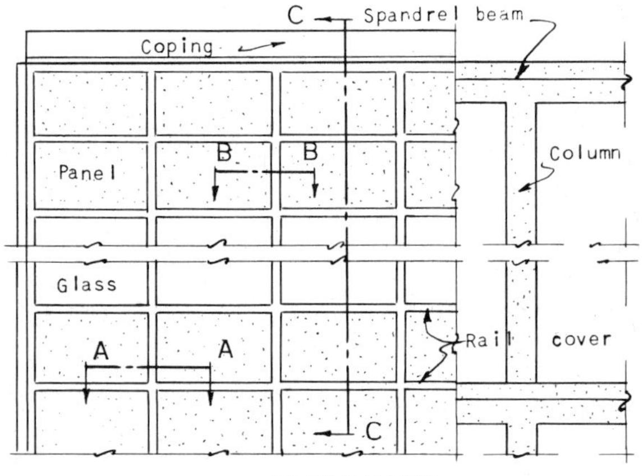
C
Spandrel beam
Coping
Column
Panel
B
B
Glass
Rail
cover
A
A
C

ELEVATION

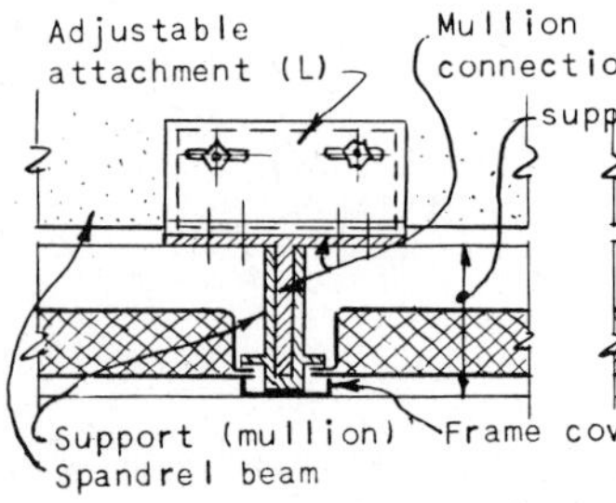
Adjustable attachment (L)
Mullion connection
support (rail)
Support (mullion)
Spandrel beam
Frame cover

PLAN AT A-A

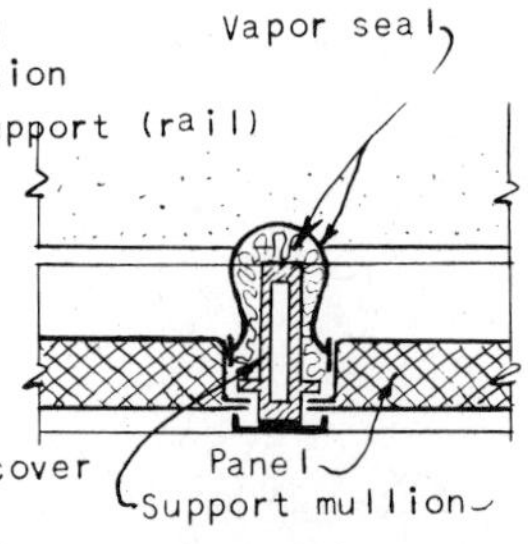
Vapor seal
Panel
Support mullion

PLAN AT B-B

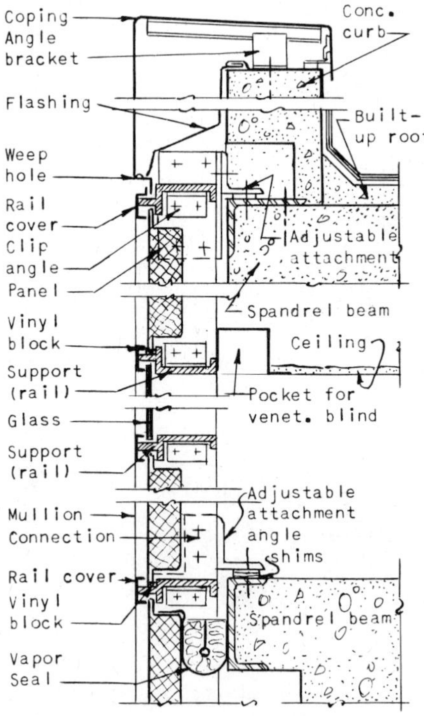
Coping
Angle bracket
Conc. curb
Flashing
Built-up roof
Weep hole
Rail cover
Clip angle
Panel
Adjustable attachment
Spandrel beam
Vinyl block
Ceiling
Support (rail)
Pocket for venet. blind
Glass
Support (rail)
Adjustable attachment angle
Mullion Connection
shims
Rail cover
Vinyl block
Spandrel beam
Vapor Seal

SECTION C-C

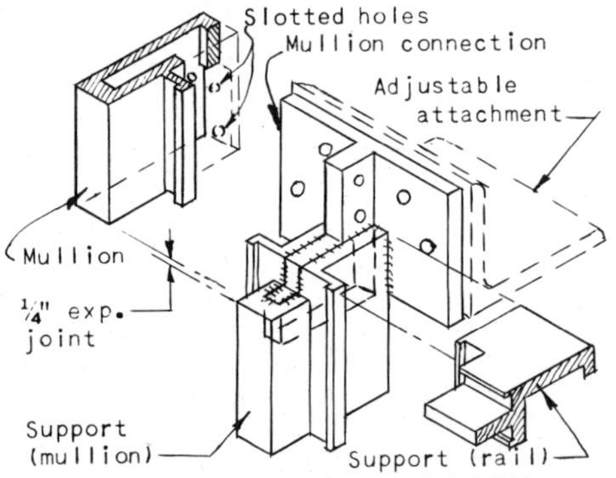
Slotted holes
Mullion connection
Adjustable attachment
Mullion
1/4" exp. joint
Support (mullion)
Support (rail)

CONNECTION OF MULLION AT EXPANSION JOINT

NOTE: Adjustable attachment (angle) bolts to mullion connection and anchors to spandrel beam.

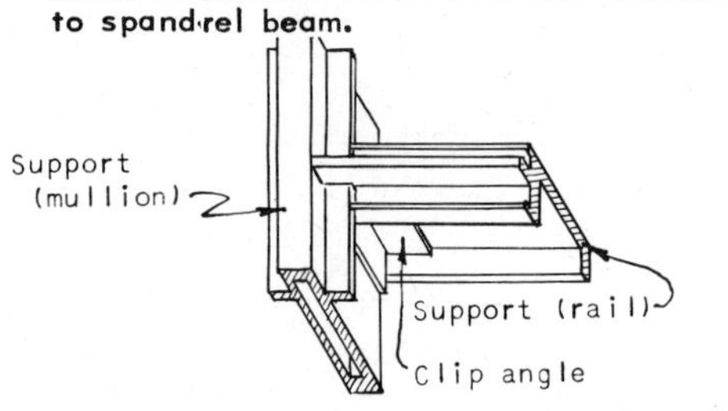
Support (mullion)
Support (rail)
Clip angle

MULLION & RAIL CONNECTION

Continuous aluminum support frame is composed of rails and mullions. Mullion is suspended and attached to spandrel beam by angle (adjustable attachment). Space between frame is filled with box panels & windows which are held in place by aluminum frame cover screwed to mullion & rail.

GRID TYPE (Metal closed sandwich type panels)

DATA BY: INGRAM-RICHARDSON MANUFACTURING CO.

METAL PANEL CURTAIN WALLS-SHEATHED TYPE

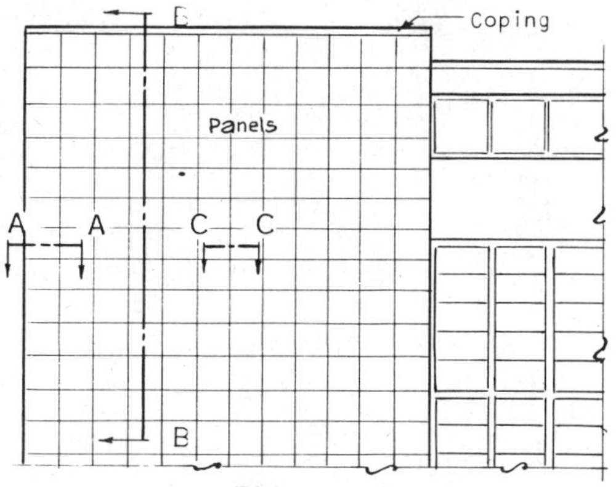
Coping
B
Panels
A
A
C
C
B

ELEVATION

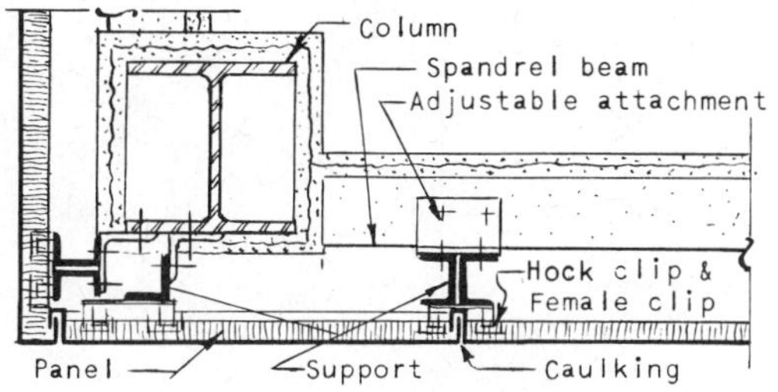
Column
Spandrel beam
Adjustable attachment
Hock clip &
Female clip
Panel
Support
Caulking

PLAN AT CORNER A-A

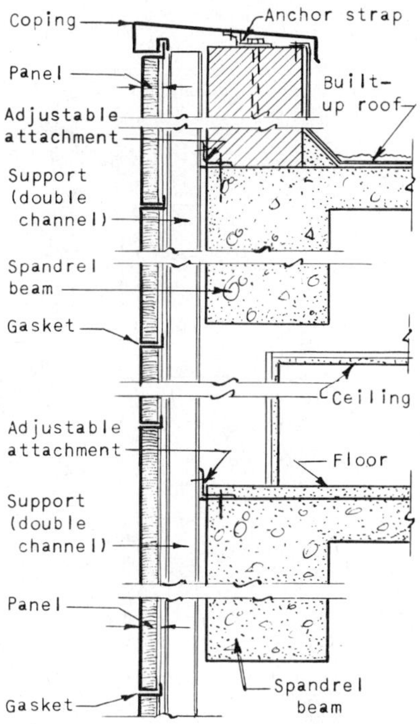
Coping
Anchor strap
Panel
Built-
up roof
Adjustable
attachment
Support
(double
channel)
Spandrel
beam
Gasket
Ceiling
Adjustable
attachment
Floor
Support
(double
channel)
Panel
Spandrel
beam
Gasket

SECTION B-B

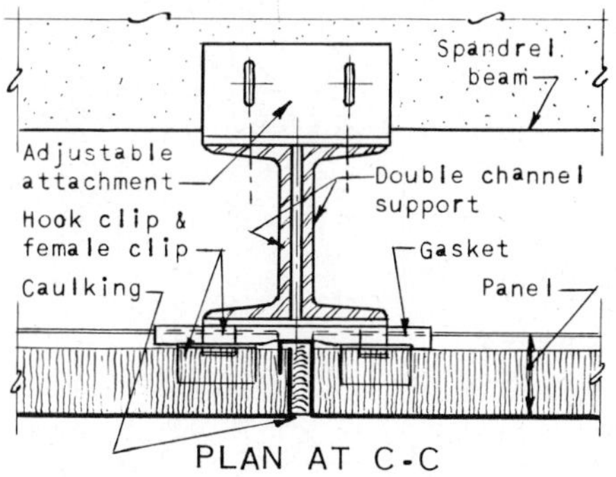
Spandrel
beam
Adjustable
attachment
Double channel
support
Hook clip &
female clip
Gasket
Caulking
Panel

PLAN AT C-C

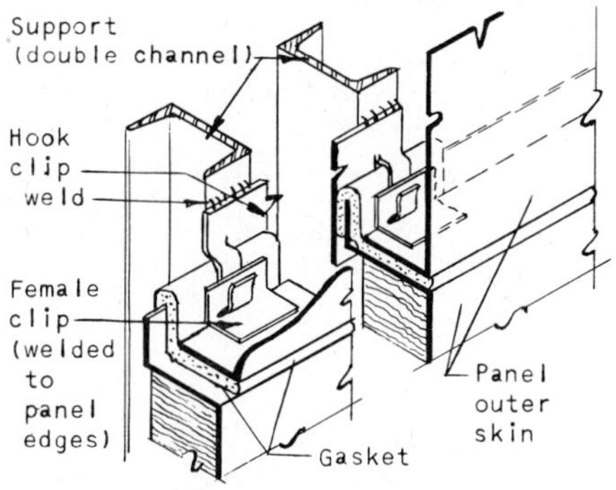
Support
(double channel)
Hook
clip
weld
Female
clip
(welded
to
panel
edges)
Panel
outer
skin
Gasket

SUPPORT, HOCK AND FEMALE CLIP

Erection of this type of curtain wall follows the following sequence. First course of panels is set in place, with vinyl gasket installed on top edge of panels. Hook clips are set on top of gasket and along support members, pressed down into gasket and welded to support members. Second course of panels is set in place so that the female clips at the bottom of the panels engage with the hook clips welded to supports. Repeat same operation for each new course of panels. The weather tightness of the horizontal joints depends on the pressure exerted when placing and welding the hook clips. Vertical joints are weather protected by interlocking shape of panel edges and caulking.

SHEATHED TYPE (Metal closed sandwich type panels)

DATA BY: TEXLITE INC.

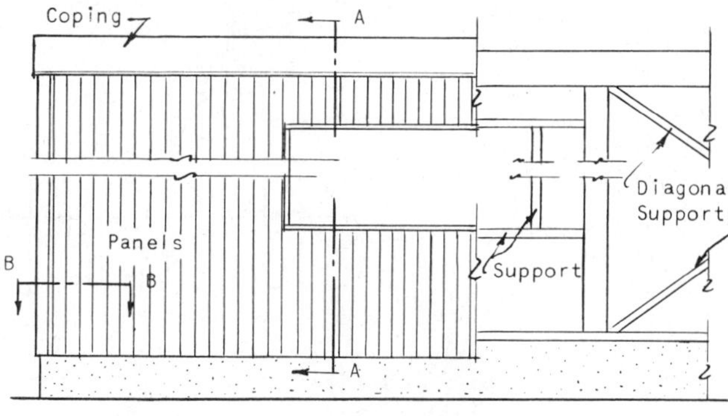
Coping
A
Diagonal
Supports
Panels
B
B
Support
A

ELEVATION

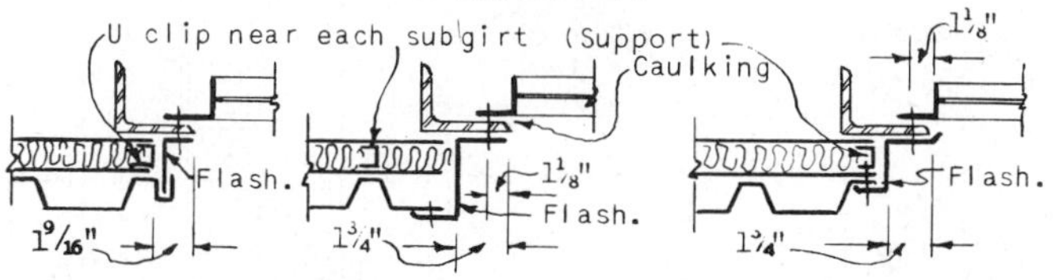
U clip near each subgirt (Support)
Caulking
$1\frac{1}{8}$"
Flash.
$1\frac{1}{8}$"
Flash.
Flash.
$1\frac{9}{16}$" dia.
$1\frac{3}{4}$"
$1\frac{3}{4}$"

FLASHING DETAILS AT WINDOW

Check the accuracy of wall grit alignment within tolerances set by AISC before placing any panels. Caulk all female lips on both faces of panels before erecting panels. Fasten panels to every girt, three fasteners per 24" panel width. Fasteners to structural steel may be: self tapping screws or welded. Stainless steel screws should be used with aluminum sheets. Flashing should be fastened with 1/4" dia. stainless steel metal screws 24" o.c. max.

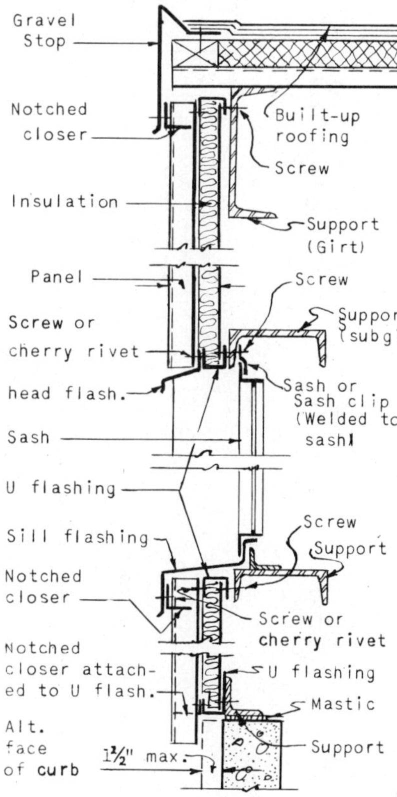
Gravel
Stop
Notched
closer
Built-up
roofing
Screw
Insulation
Support
(Girt)
Panel
Screw
Screw or
cherry rivet
Support
(subgirt)
head flash.
Sash or
Sash clip
(Welded to
sash)
Sash
U flashing
Sill flashing
Screw
Support
Notched
closer
Screw or
cherry rivet
Notched
closer attach-
ed to U flash.
U flashing
Mastic
Alt.
face
of curb
$1\frac{1}{2}$" max.
Support

SECTION A-A

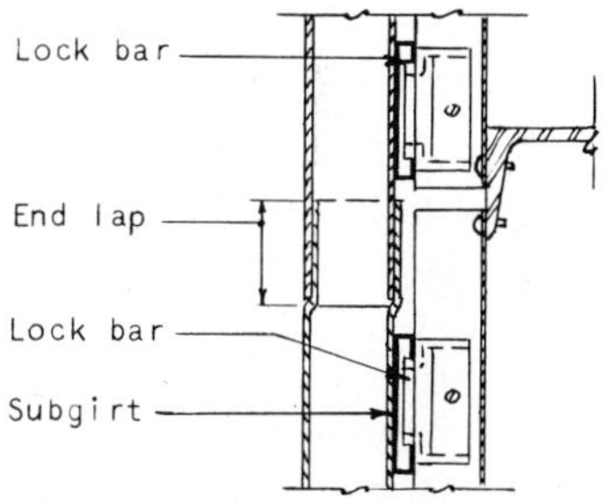
Lock bar
End lap
Lock bar
Subgirt

SECTION AT END LAP
(Horizontal panel joint)

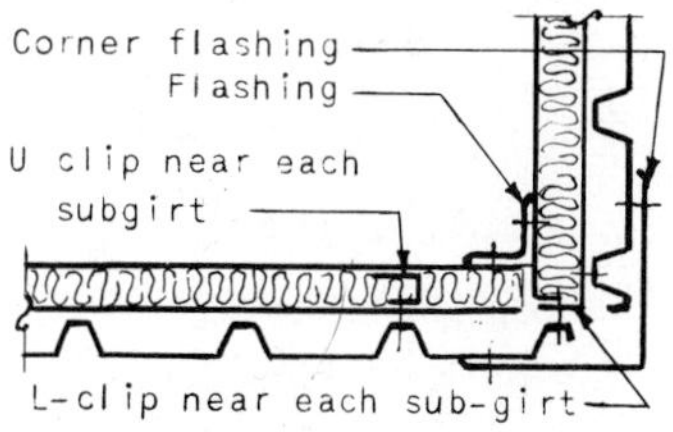
Corner flashing
Flashing
U clip near each
subgirt
L-clip near each sub-girt

PLAN AT B-B

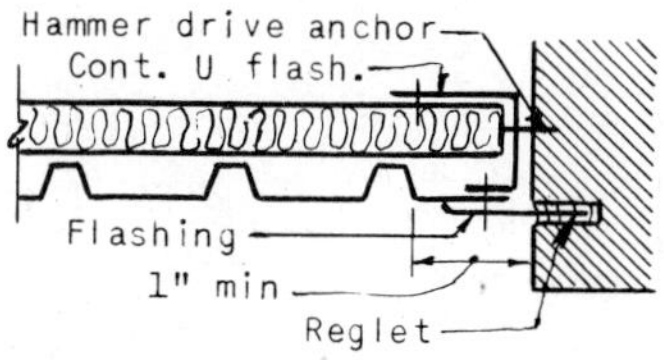
Hammer drive anchor
Cont. U flash.
Flashing
1" min
Reglet

PLAN AT INTERSECTION WITH MASONRY

SHEATHED (INDUSTRIAL) TYPE (Metal open sandwich type panels)

DATA BY: H.H. ROBERTSON CO

METAL and MASONRY PANEL CURTAIN WALLS

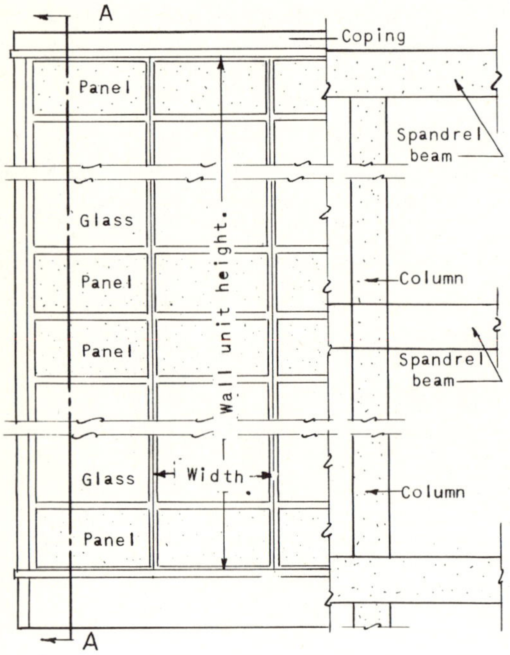
A
Coping
Panel
Spandrel beam
Glass
Wall unit height
Panel
Column
Panel
Spandrel beam
Glass
Width
Column
Panel
A

ELEVATION

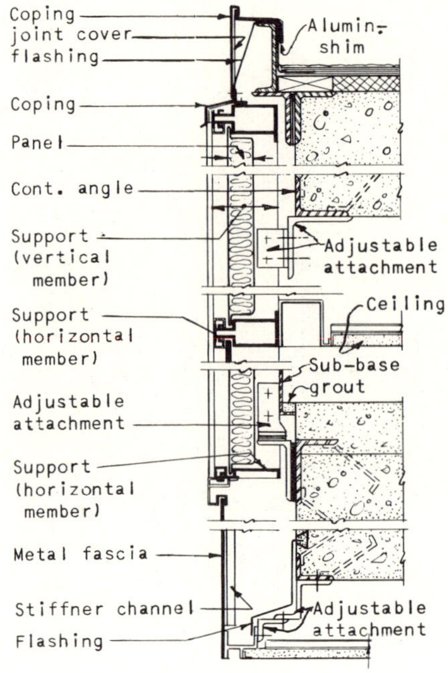
Coping joint cover flashing
Alumin. shim
Coping
Panel
Cont. angle
Support (vertical member)
Adjustable attachment
Ceiling
Support (horizontal member)
Sub-base grout
Adjustable attachment
Support (horizontal member)
Metal fascia
Stiffner channel
Adjustable attachment
Flashing

SECTION A-A

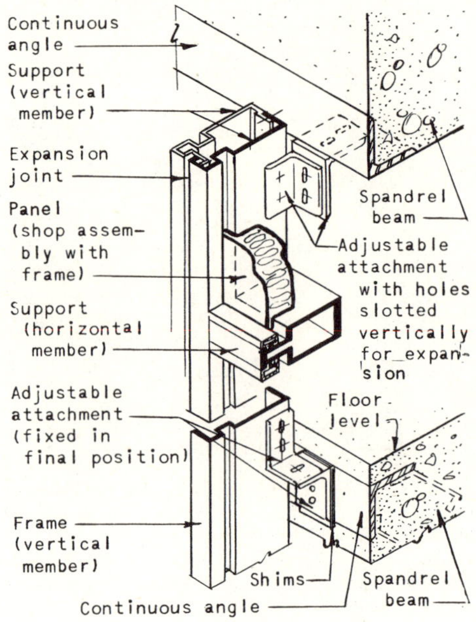
Continuous angle
Support (vertical member)
Expansion joint
Spandrel beam
Panel (shop assembly with frame)
Adjustable attachment with holes slotted vertically for expansion
Support (horizontal member)
Floor level
Adjustable attachment (fixed in final position)
Frame (vertical member)
Shims
Spandrel beam
Continuous angle

SUPPORT AND ADJUSTABLE ATTACHMENT

Wall unit shop assembled, of extruded aluminum supports, panels, and glass. Vertical support members are attached to spandrel beam by adjustable attachments made of angles. Horizontal expansion is taken up at the vertical support members. Expansion joints should be 1/16" for 4' to 5' width.

WALL UNIT ASSEMBLY (Metal wall unit two stories high)

DATA BY: KAWNEER COMPANY

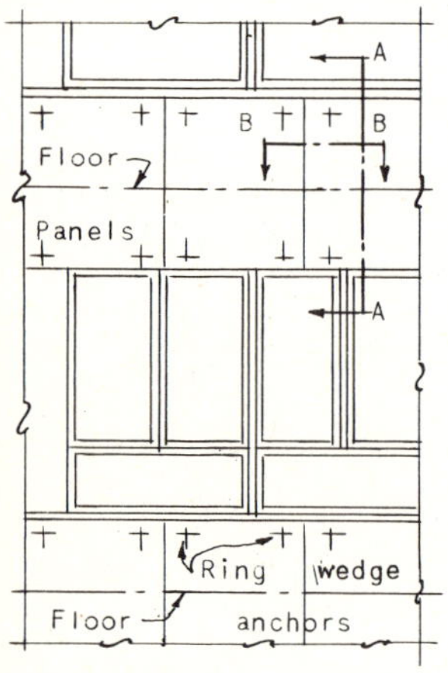
A
B
B
Floor
Panels
A
Ring wedge
Floor anchors

ELEVATION

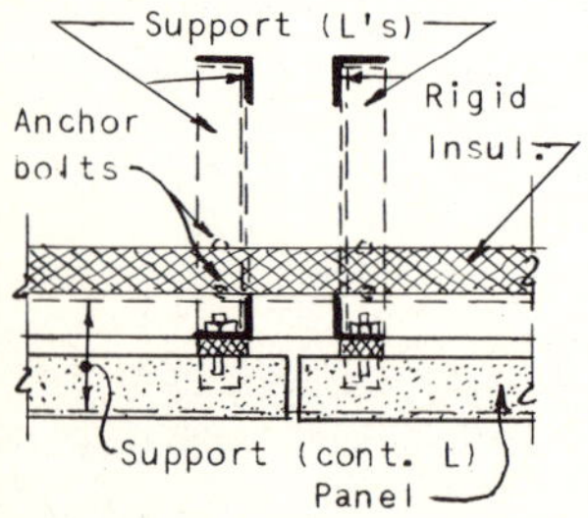
Support (L's)
Anchor bolts
Rigid Insul.
Support (cont. L)
Panel

PLAN AT B-B

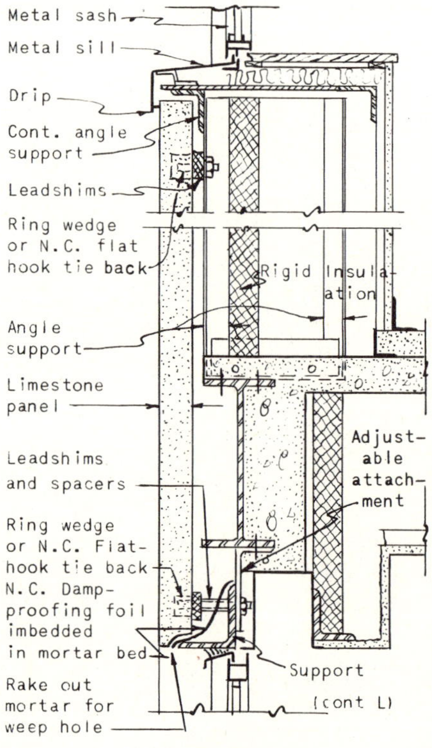
Metal sash
Metal sill
Drip
Cont. angle support
Leadshims
Ring wedge or N.C. flat hook tie back
Rigid Insulation
Angle support
Limestone panel
Leadshims and spacers
Adjustable attachment
Ring wedge or N.C. Flat-hook tie back
N.C. Damp-proofing foil imbedded in mortar bed
Support (cont L)
Rake out mortar for weep hole

SECTION A-A

SPANDREL TYPE (Stone skin type panels)

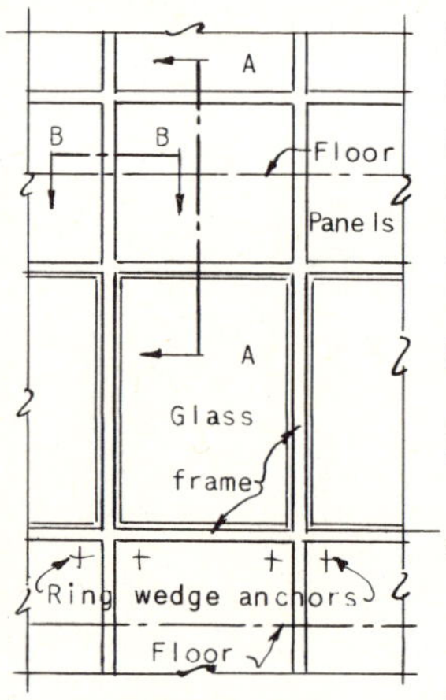
A
B
B
Floor
Panels
A
Glass
frame
Ring wedge anchors
Floor

ELEVATION

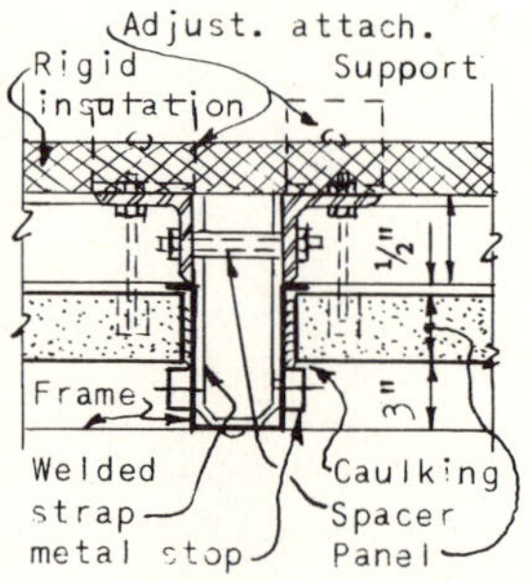
Adjust. attach.
Rigid insulation
Support
1/2"
3"
Frame
Welded strap metal stop
Caulking
Spacer
Panel

PLAN AT B-B

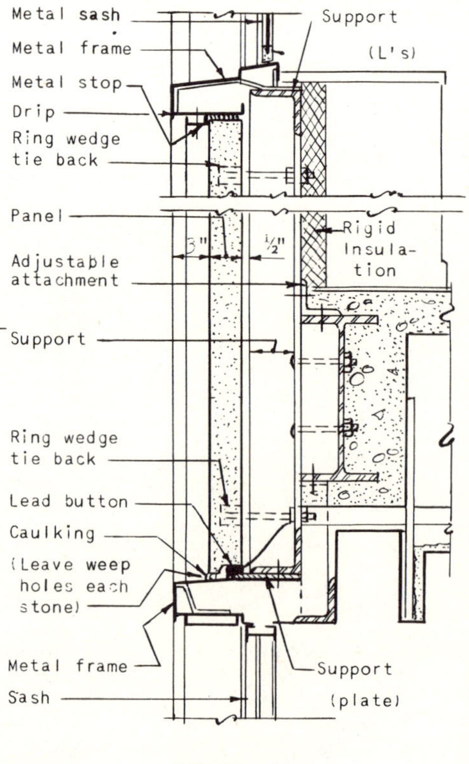
Metal sash
Support (L's)
Metal frame
Metal stop
Drip
Ring wedge tie back
Panel
3"
1/2"
Rigid Insulation
Adjustable attachment
Support
Ring wedge tie back
Lead button
Caulking
(Leave weep holes each stone)
Metal frame
Support (plate)
Sash

SECTION A-A

GRID TYPE (Stone skin type panels)

DATA BY: INDIANA LIMESTONE INSTITUTE

MASONRY and CONCRETE PANEL CURTAIN WALLS

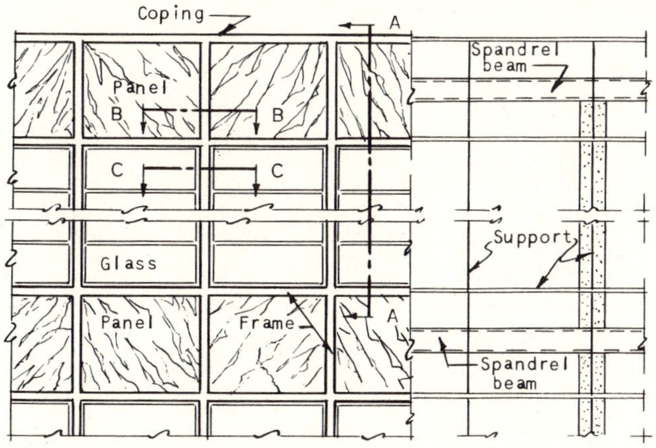
Coping
A
Spandrel beam
Panel
B
B
C
C
Glass
Support
Panel
Frame
A
Spandrel beam

ELEVATION

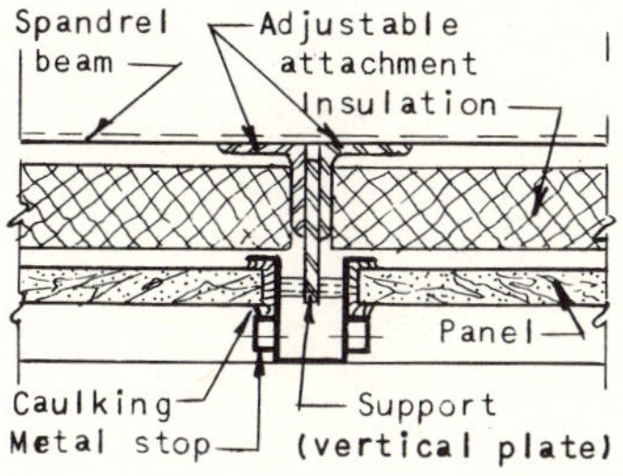
Spandrel beam
Adjustable attachment
Insulation
Panel
Caulking
Metal stop
Support (vertical plate)

PLAN AT B-B

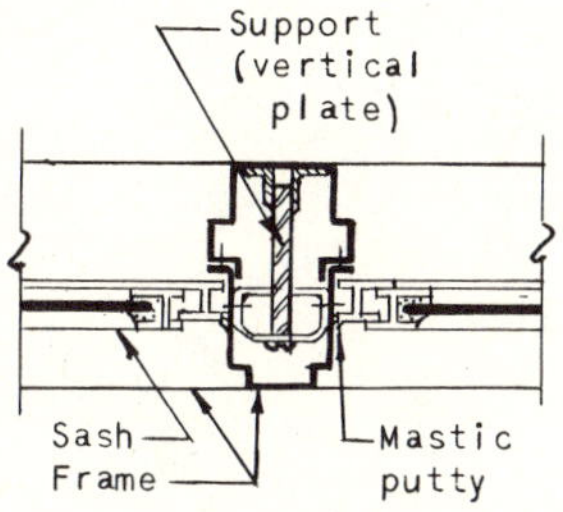
Support (vertical plate)
Sash
Frame
Mastic putty

PLAN AT C-C

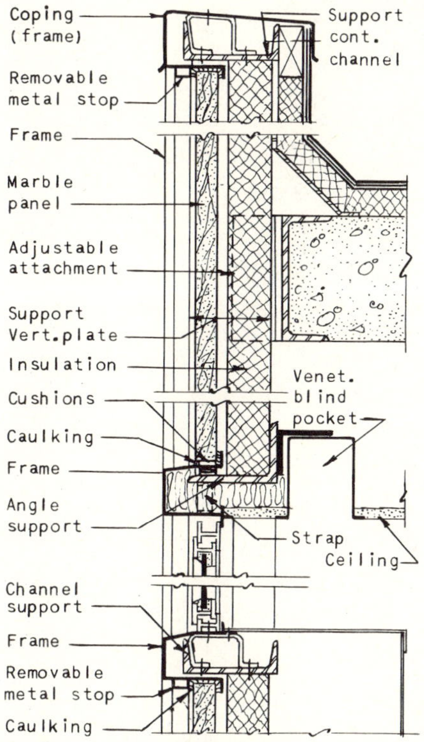
Coping (frame)
Support cont. channel
Removable metal stop
Frame
Marble panel
Adjustable attachment
Support Vert. plate
Insulation
Cushions
Venet. blind pocket
Caulking
Frame
Angle support
Strap
Ceiling
Channel support
Frame
Removable metal stop
Caulking

SECTION A-A

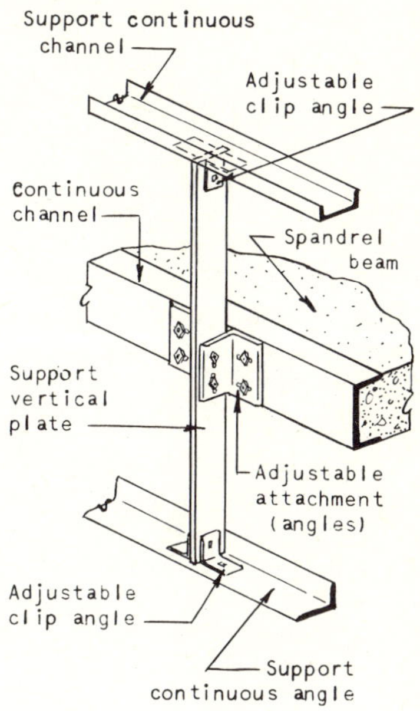
Support continuous channel
Adjustable clip angle
Continuous channel
Spandrel beam
Support vertical plate
Adjustable attachment (angles)
Adjustable clip angle
Support continuous angle

SUPPORT & ADJUSTABLE ATTACHMENT

Support made of continuous channels, cont. angles, and vertical plate, is anchored to spandrel beam by adjustable attachment (angles). Panels are set on and completely supported by non-staining and non-corrosive metal frame which is screwed to support. Edges of panels should not rest directly against metal frame. Weight bearing edges resting on plastic or alum. cushions spaced to support weight of panel. All edges, incl. adjoining surface should be fully caulked or pointed with non-staining mastic pointing compound. Metal stop to keep panel in place is screwed to metal frame. Rigid insulation backing-up panel depends on desired "U" factor.

GRID TYPE (Marble skin type panels with insulation)

DATA SUPPLIED BY: MARBLE INSTITUTE OF AMERICA

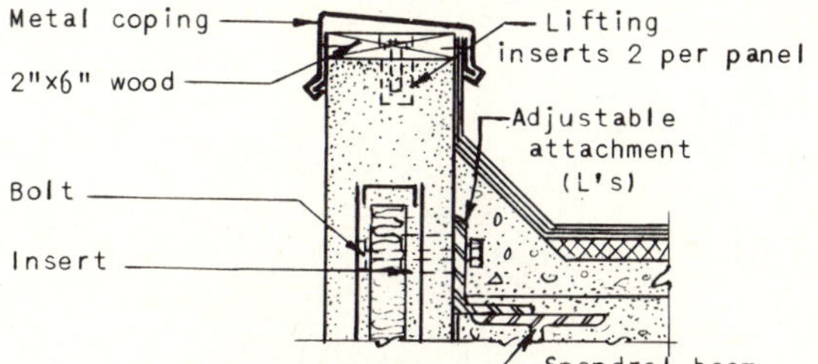
Metal coping
Lifting inserts 2 per panel
2"x6" wood
Adjustable attachment (L's)
Bolt
Insert
Spandrel beam

COPING

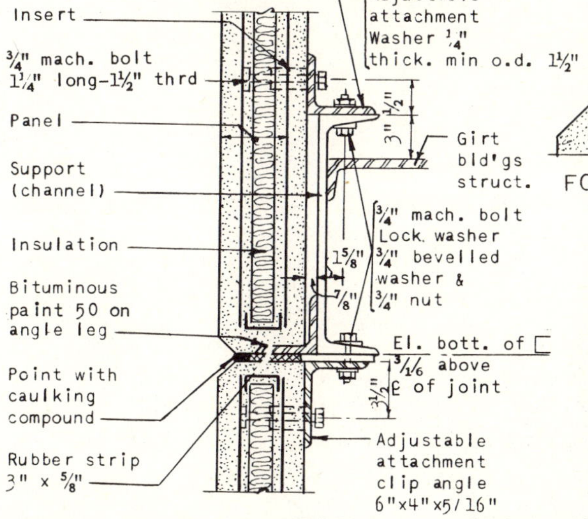
Insert
Adjustable attachment
Washer 1/4" thick. min o.d. 1½"
3/4" mach. bolt 1¼" long-1½" thrd
Panel
Girt bld'gs struct.
Support (channel)
Insulation
3/4" mach. bolt Lock washer 3/4" bevelled washer & 3/4" nut
Bituminous paint 50 on angle leg
El. bott. of [above ℄ of joint
Point with caulking compound
Rubber strip 3" x 5/8"
Adjustable attachment clip angle 6"x4"x5/16"

HORIZ. JOINT AT SUPPORT

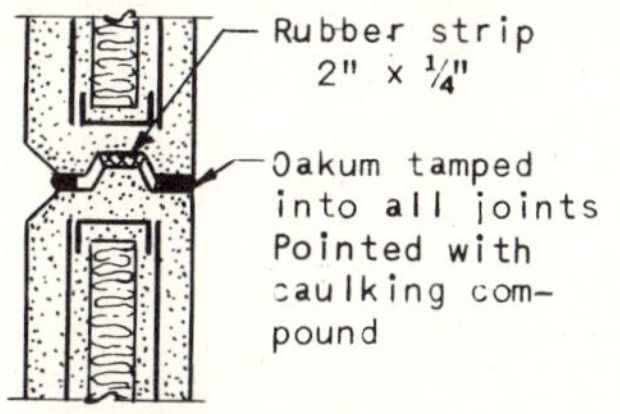
Rubber strip 2" x 1/4"
Oakum tamped into all joints Pointed with caulking compound

VERTICAL JOINT

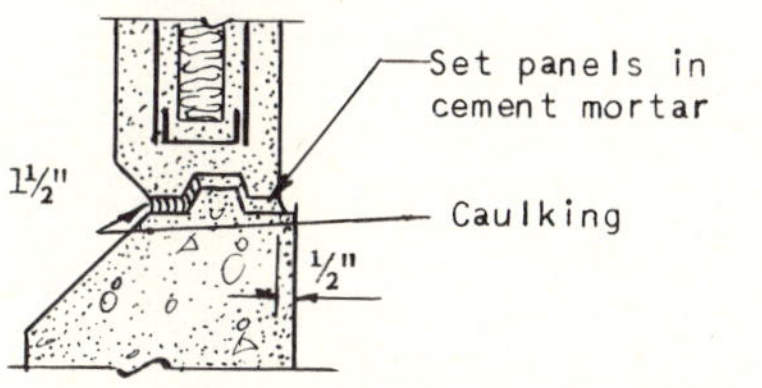
Set panels in cement mortar
Caulking
½"

FOUNDATION OR STARTER COURSE

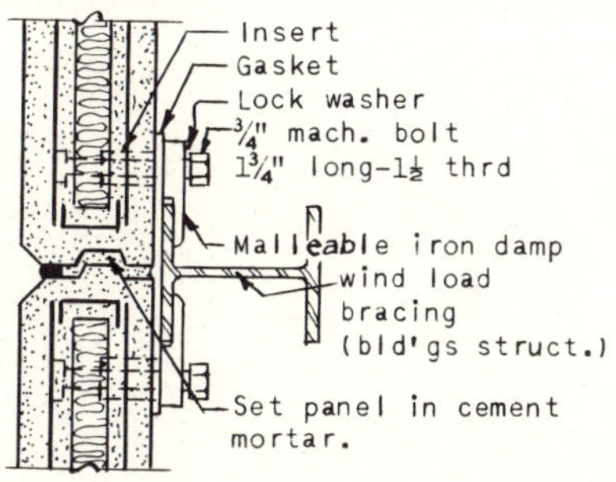
Insert
Gasket
Lock washer
3/4" mach. bolt 1¾" long-1½ thrd
Malleable iron damp wind load bracing (bld'gs struct.)
Set panel in cement mortar.

HORIZ. JOINT AT WIND LOAD BRACING

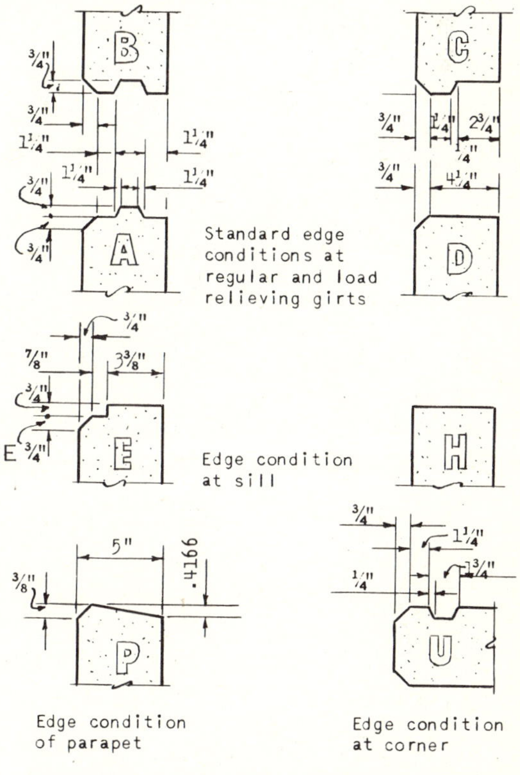
B
C
A
D
Standard edge conditions at regular and load relieving girts
E
Edge condition at sill
H
5"
.4166
P
Edge condition of parapet
U
Edge condition at corner

TYPICAL PANEL EDGE CONNECTIONS

Scale 1" = 1'-0"

SHEATHED TYPE (Precast insulated concrete, closed sandwich type panels)

DATA SUPPLIED BY: MARIETTA CONCRETE CORPS

ROOFING and SHEET METAL

TABLE OF CONTENTS

MISCELLANEOUS DATA

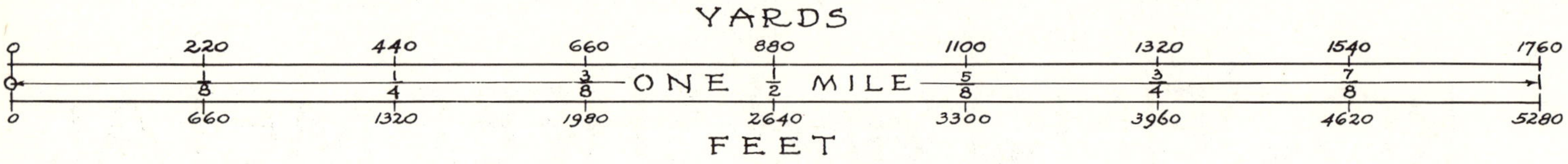
YARDS
0
220
440
660
880
1100
1320
1540
1760
ONE MILE
1/8
1/4
3/8
1/2
5/8
3/4
7/8
0
660
1320
1980
2640
3300
3960
4620
5280
FEET

GALVANIC ACTION OF METALS

The following metals are arranged in order of galvanic activity. Do not place metals far apart on this list in contact with each other.

- *Aluminum*
- *Zinc*
- *Galv. iron*
- *Tin on steel*
- *Lead, hard*
- *Stainless steel*
- *Copper*
- *Monel*

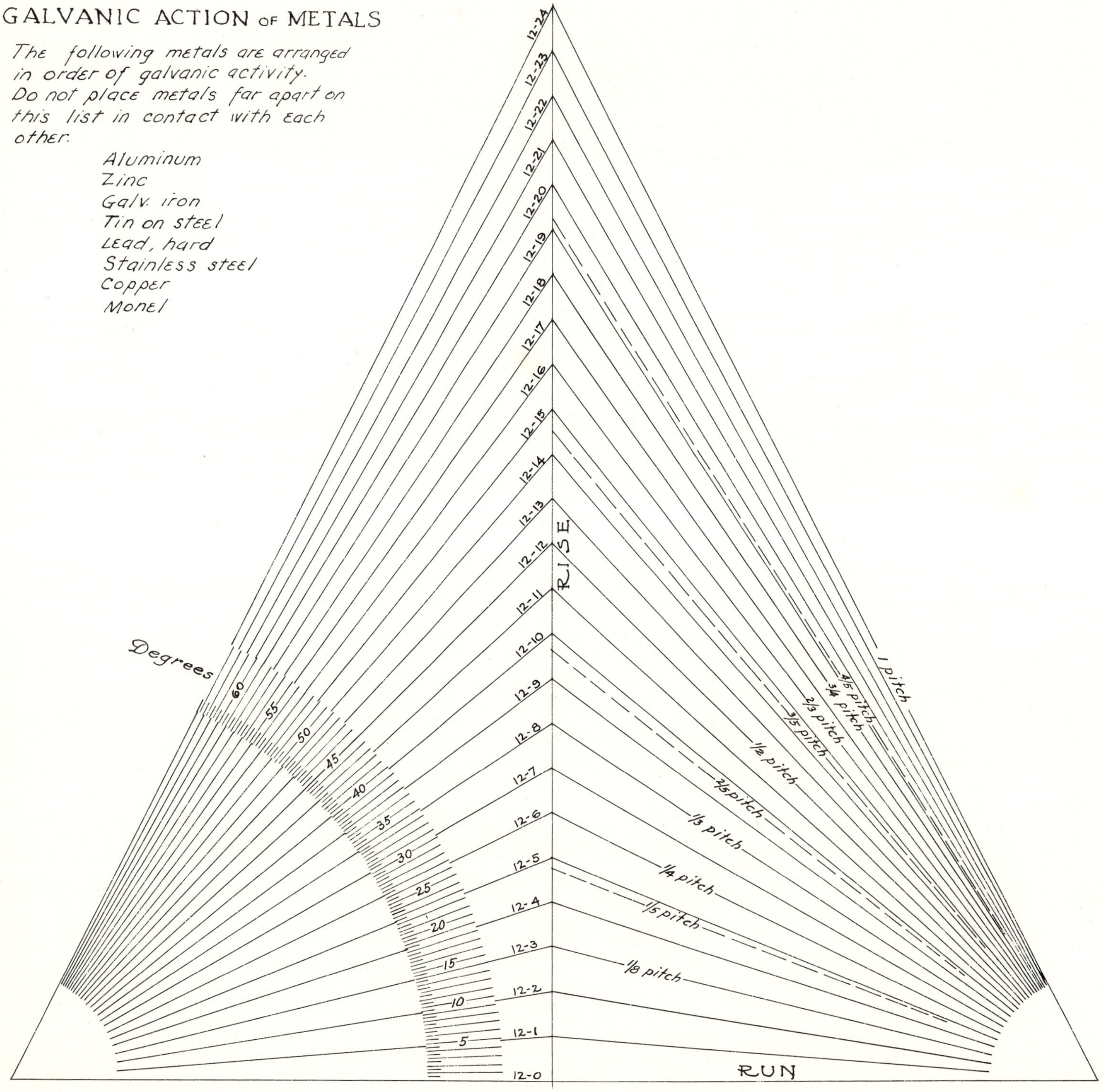
12-24
12-23
12-22
12-21
12-20
12-19
12-18
12-17
12-16
12-15
12-14
12-13
12-12
12-11
12-10
12-9
12-8
12-7
12-6
12-5
12-4
12-3
12-2
12-1
12-0
RISE
RUN
Degrees
60
55
50
45
40
35
30
25
20
15
10
5
1 pitch
4/5 pitch
3/4 pitch
2/3 pitch
3/5 pitch
1/2 pitch
2/5 pitch
1/3 pitch
1/4 pitch
1/5 pitch
1/8 pitch

ROOF SLOPES *in* RUN & RISE, PITCHES *and* DEGREES

BUILT-UP ROOFING and ROLL ROOFING

BUILT-UP FLAT ROOF WITH SLAG or GRAVEL FINISH

Max. slopes
asphalt 2" to 4" in 12"
tarred 1/2" to 4" in 12"
Scale 1" = 1'-0"

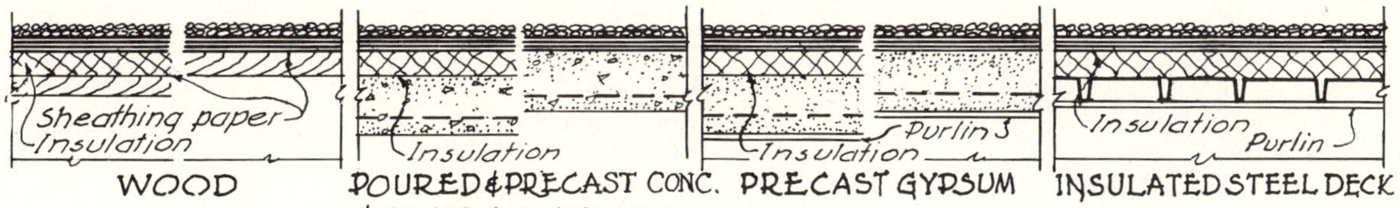

Sheathing paper
Insulation
WOOD
Insulation
POURED & PRECAST CONC. & POURED GYPSUM
Insulation
Purlins
PRECAST GYPSUM
Insulation
Purlin
INSULATED STEEL DECK

BUILT-UP STEEP ROOF WITH MINERAL SURFACE FINISH

Min. slope 3" in 12"
Max. slope 5" in 12"
Scale 1" = 1'-0"

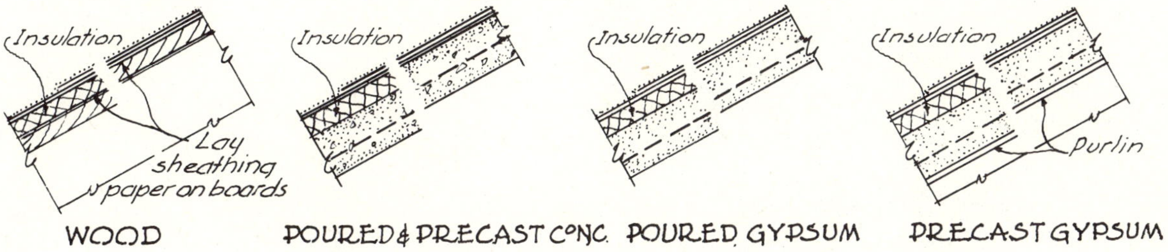

Insulation
Lay sheathing paper on boards
WOOD
Insulation
POURED & PRECAST CONC.
Insulation
POURED GYPSUM
Insulation
Purlin
PRECAST GYPSUM

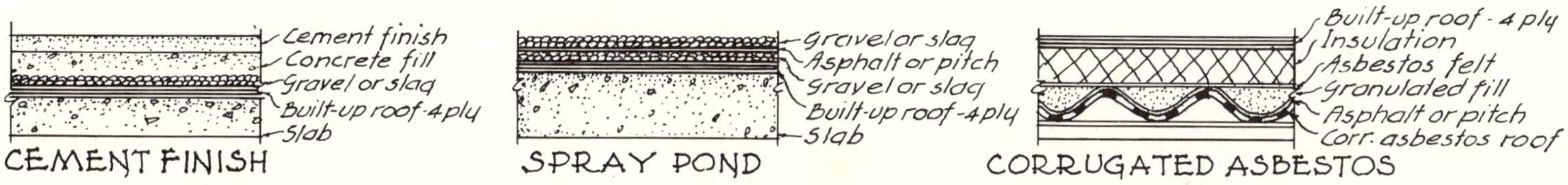

Cement finish
Concrete fill
Gravel or slag
Built-up roof - 4 ply
Slab
CEMENT FINISH
Gravel or slag
Asphalt or pitch
Gravel or slag
Built-up roof - 4 ply
Slab
SPRAY POND
Built-up roof - 4 ply
Insulation
Asbestos felt
Granulated fill
Asphalt or pitch
Corr. asbestos roof
CORRUGATED ASBESTOS

SPECIAL BUILT-UP ROOFS

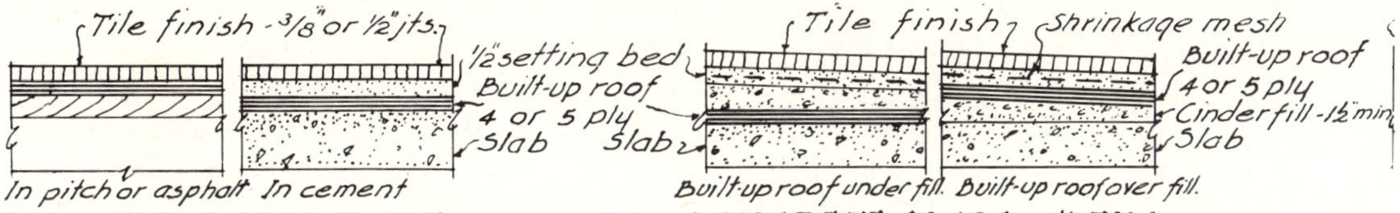

Tile finish - 3/8" or 1/2" jts.
1/2" setting bed
Built-up roof
4 or 5 ply
Slab
In pitch or asphalt
In cement
WOOD ROOF
CONC. ROOF
Tile finish
Shrinkage mesh
Built-up roof
4 or 5 ply
Cinder fill - 1 1/2" min.
Slab
Slab
Built-up roof under fill.
Built-up roof over fill.
CONCRETE SLABS with FILL

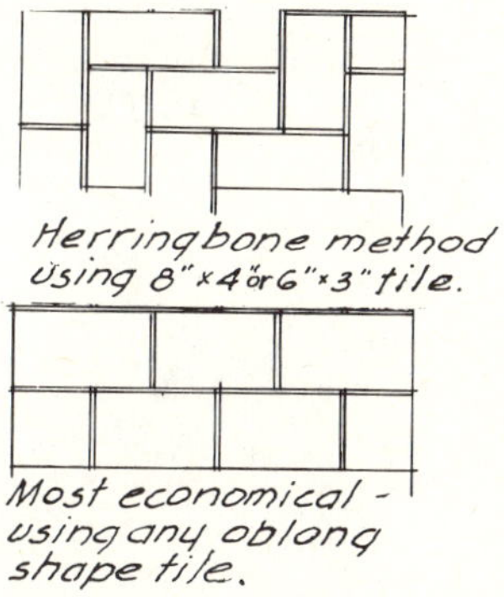

Herringbone method using 8"×4" or 6"×3" tile.
Most economical - using any oblong shape tile.

Materials:
Quarry (Promenade) tiles are usually used but other floor tile may be used. Standard sizes are: Square, 9", 8", 6", 4", 2 3/4". Oblong: 9"×6", 8"×4", 8"×3 3/4", 6"×2 3/4". Provide expansion joint every 12'-0" in both directions for tiles set in cement. Max. slope 1/4" in 12"

TILE ROOFS - FLAT

Roll roofing is best for structures where long maintenance free service is not important. Permanence may be achieved where appearance not a consideration by applying asphalt coatings at intervals of 5 to 10 years.

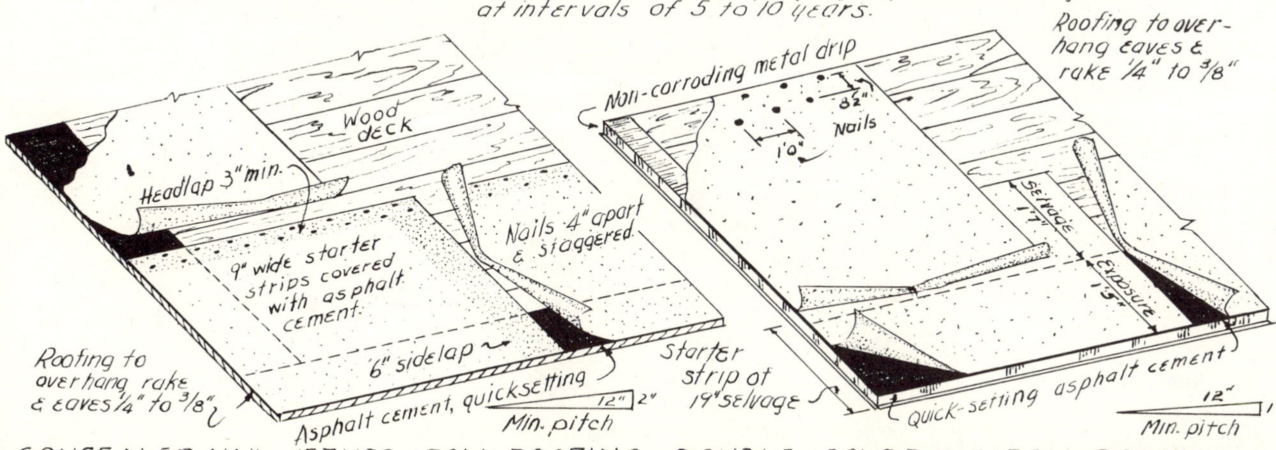

Wood deck
Headlap 3" min.
9" wide starter strips covered with asphalt cement.
Nails 4" apart & staggered.
6" sidelap
Roofing to overhang rake & eaves 1/4" to 3/8"
Asphalt cement, quicksetting
12"
2"
Min. pitch
Non-corroding metal drip
8 1/2"
Nails
1'0"
Roofing to overhang eaves & rake 1/4" to 3/8"
Selvage 17"
Exposure 1'5"
Starter strip at 19" selvage
Quick-setting asphalt cement
12"
1"
Min. pitch

CONCEALED NAIL METHOD - ROLL ROOFING

DOUBLE COVERAGE ROLL ROOFING

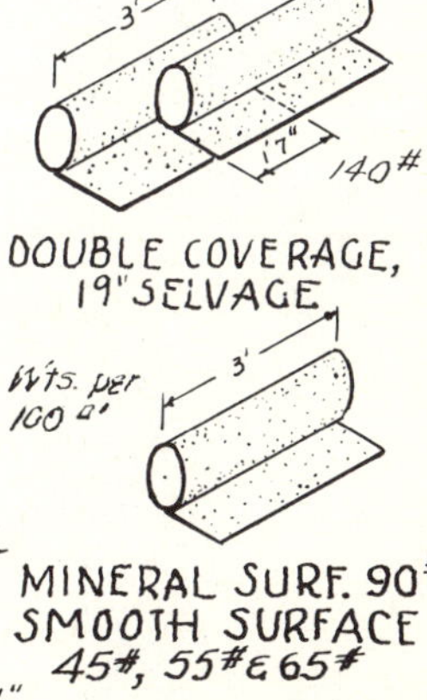

3'
17"
140#
DOUBLE COVERAGE, 19" SELVAGE
Wts. per 100 □'
3'
MINERAL SURF. 90#
SMOOTH SURFACE 45#, 55# & 65#

ASPHALT ROLL ROOFING

Data from the Asphalt Roofing Industry Bureau

ASPHALT SHINGLES

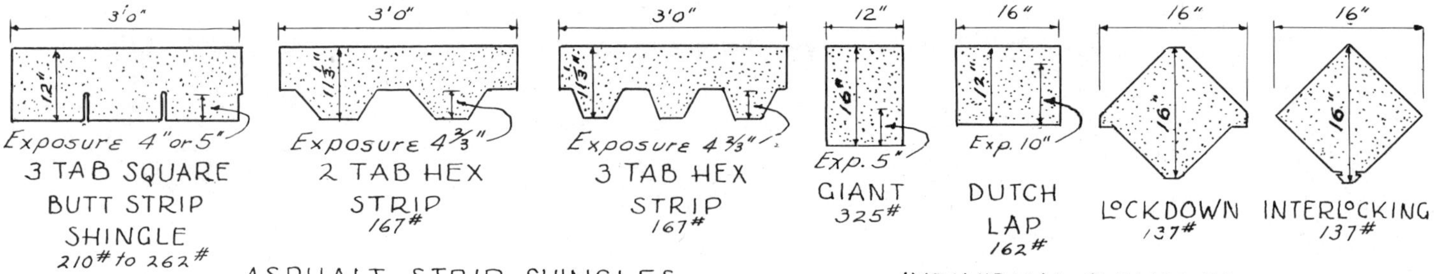

3'0"
12"
Exposure 4" or 5"
3 TAB SQUARE BUTT STRIP SHINGLE
210# to 262#
3'0"
11 3/4"
Exposure 4 2/3"
2 TAB HEX STRIP
167#
3'0"
11 3/4"
Exposure 4 2/3"
3 TAB HEX STRIP
167#
12"
16"
Exp. 5"
GIANT
325#
16"
12"
Exp. 10"
DUTCH LAP
162#
16"
16"
LOCKDOWN
137#
16"
16"
INTERLOCKING
137#

ASPHALT STRIP SHINGLES INDIVIDUAL SHINGLES

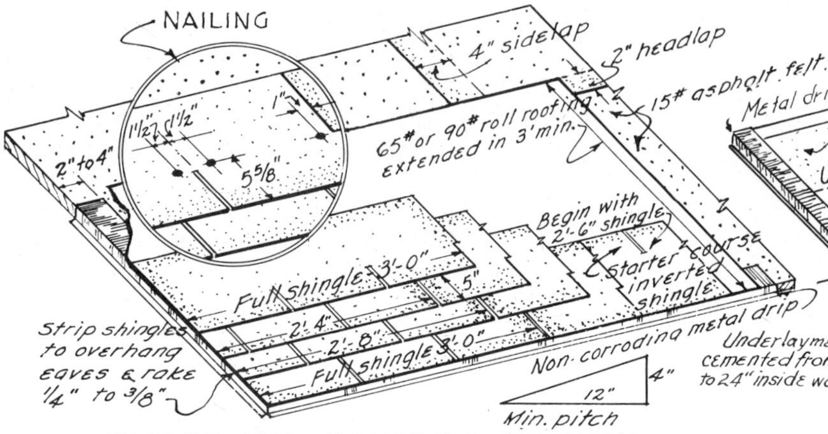

NAILING
4" sidelap
2" headlap
15# asphalt felt
1 1/2"
1 1/2"
1"
5 5/8"
65# or 90# roll roofing extended in 3' min.
2" to 4"
Begin with 2'-6" shingle
Starter course inverted shingle
Full shingle 3'-0"
5"
2'-4"
2'-8"
Full shingle 3'-0"
Strip shingles to overhang eaves & rake 1/4" to 3/8"
Non-corroding metal drip
12"
4"
Min. pitch

THREE TAB SQUARE BUTT STRIPS
4" exposure req'd for windy locations. 5" more economical.

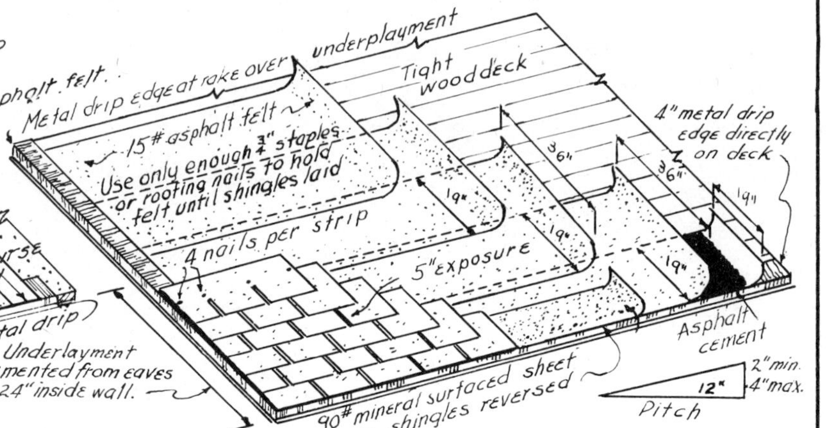

underplayment
Metal drip edge at rake over
Tight wood deck
15# asphalt felt
Use only enough 3/4" staples or roofing nails to hold felt until shingles laid
4" metal drip edge directly on deck
36"
36"
19"
19"
19"
19"
4 nails per strip
5" exposure
Asphalt cement
Underlayment cemented from eaves to 24" inside wall.
90# mineral surfaced sheet or shingles reversed
12"
2" min.
4" max.
Pitch

THREE TAB SQUARE BUTT STRIPS
LOW SLOPE ROOF

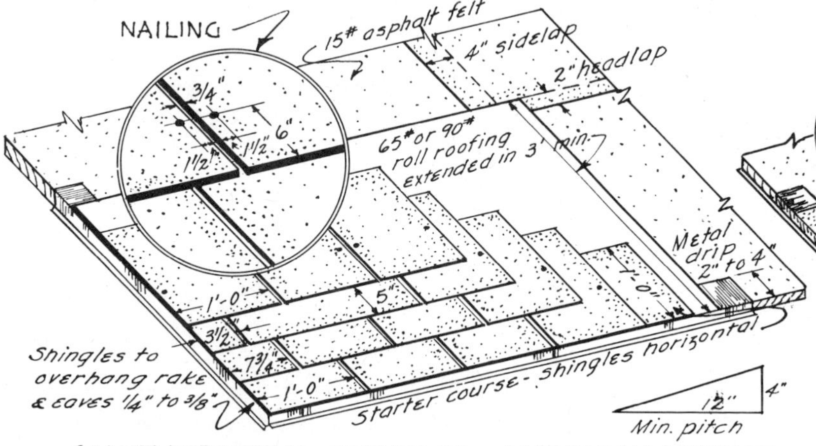

NAILING
15# asphalt felt
4" sidelap
2" headlap
3/4"
6"
1 1/2"
1 1/2"
65# or 90# roll roofing extended in 3' min.
Metal drip 2" to 4"
1'-0"
5"
1'-0"
3 1/2"
7 3/4"
1'-0"
Shingles to overhang rake & eaves 1/4" to 3/8"
Starter course - shingles horizontal
12"
4"
Min. pitch

GIANT INDIVIDUAL SHINGLES - AMERICAN METHOD

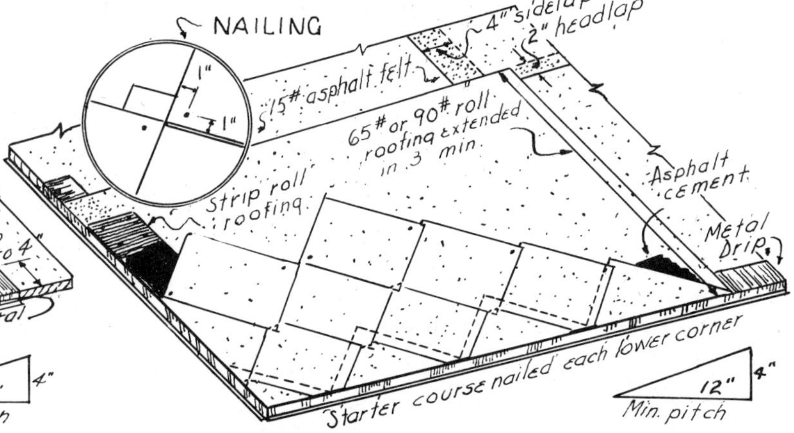

NAILING
1"
1"
4" sidelap
2" headlap
15# asphalt felt
65# or 90# roll roofing extended in 3' min.
Strip roll roofing
Asphalt cement
Metal Drip
Starter course nailed each lower corner
12"
4"
Min. pitch

INTERLOCKING SHINGLES
For windy locations

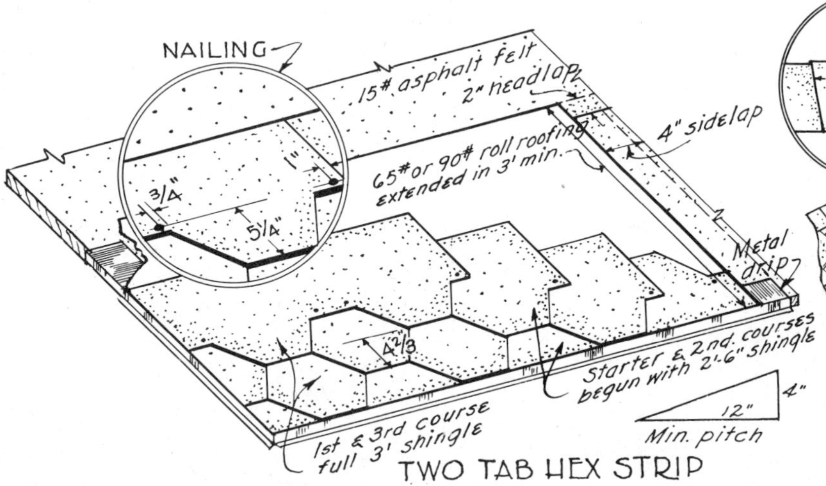

NAILING
15# asphalt felt
2" headlap
4" sidelap
1"
3/4"
5 1/4"
65# or 90# roll roofing extended in 3' min.
Metal drip
4 2/3"
Starter & 2nd. courses begun with 2'-6" shingle
1st & 3rd course full 3' shingle
12"
4"
Min. pitch

TWO TAB HEX STRIP

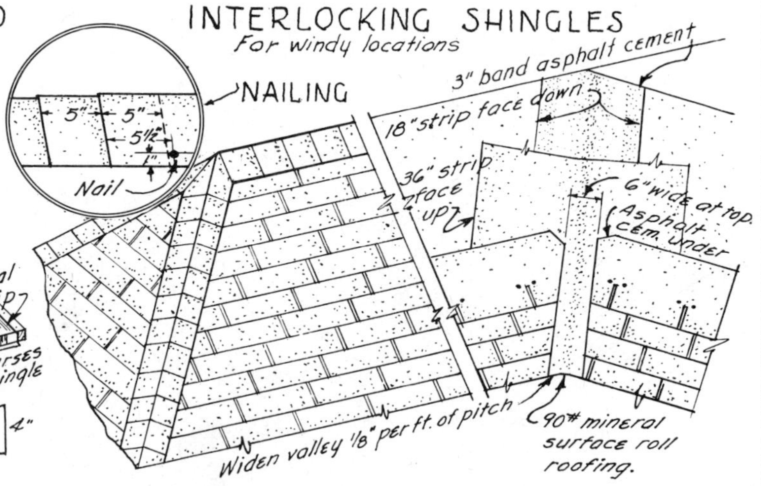

NAILING
5"
5"
5 1/2"
1"
Nail
3" band asphalt cement
18" strip face down
36" strip face up
6" wide at top
Asphalt cem. under
Widen valley 1/8" per ft. of pitch
90# mineral surface roll roofing.

HIPS & RIDGES VALLEY FLASHING

Flashing may be all metal, or all asphalt or may be asphalt base & metal cap. Non-staining metal pref'd for cap flashg.
Data on this page from the Asphalt Roofing Industry Bureau.

WOOD SHINGLES

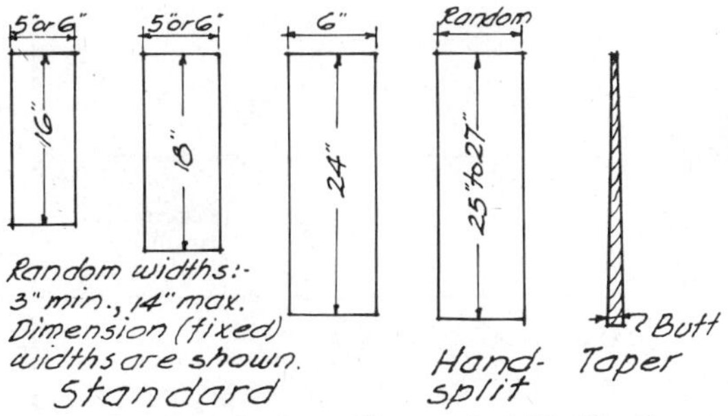
5" or 6"
5" or 6"
6"
Random
16"
18"
24"
25" to 27"
Random widths:- 3" min., 14" max. Dimension (fixed) widths are shown.
Standard
Hand-split
Taper
Butt

THICKNESSES & NAILS		
16" long	5 butts = 2"	3d
18" "	5 butts = 2¼"	3d
24" "	4 butts = 2"	4d
25" to 27"	1 butt = ½"	5d or 6d
25" to 27"	1 " = ⅝" to 1¼"	7d or 8d

EXPOSURE for ROOFING				
Shingle length	16"	18"	24"	27"
Pitch 5-12 or steeper	5"	5½"	7½"	8"
Pitch 3-12 or 4-12	3¾"	4¼"	5¾"	

EXPOSURE for SIDING				
Shingle length	16"	18"	24"	27"
Single course	7½"	8½"	11½"	12"
Double course	12"	14"	16"	16½"
Exposures shown are max.				

For double-coursing, use small-headed 5d nails. Always use hot zinc-dip nails. 3"-12" is min. pitch recommended for roofs with wood shingles.

SHINGLE SIZES, EXPOSURES, AND NAILING

Durable woods for shingles: Tidewater Red Cypress-No 1, Bests, Primes, Economy or Clipper grade. Red Cedar-Certigrade No 1, No 2 & No 3. Redwood No 1, No 2 VG or No 3 VG grade. For longer life, shingles should be painted with creosote stain. Some shingles are pre-dipped in stain. Siding shingles may be treated as above, or with house paint.

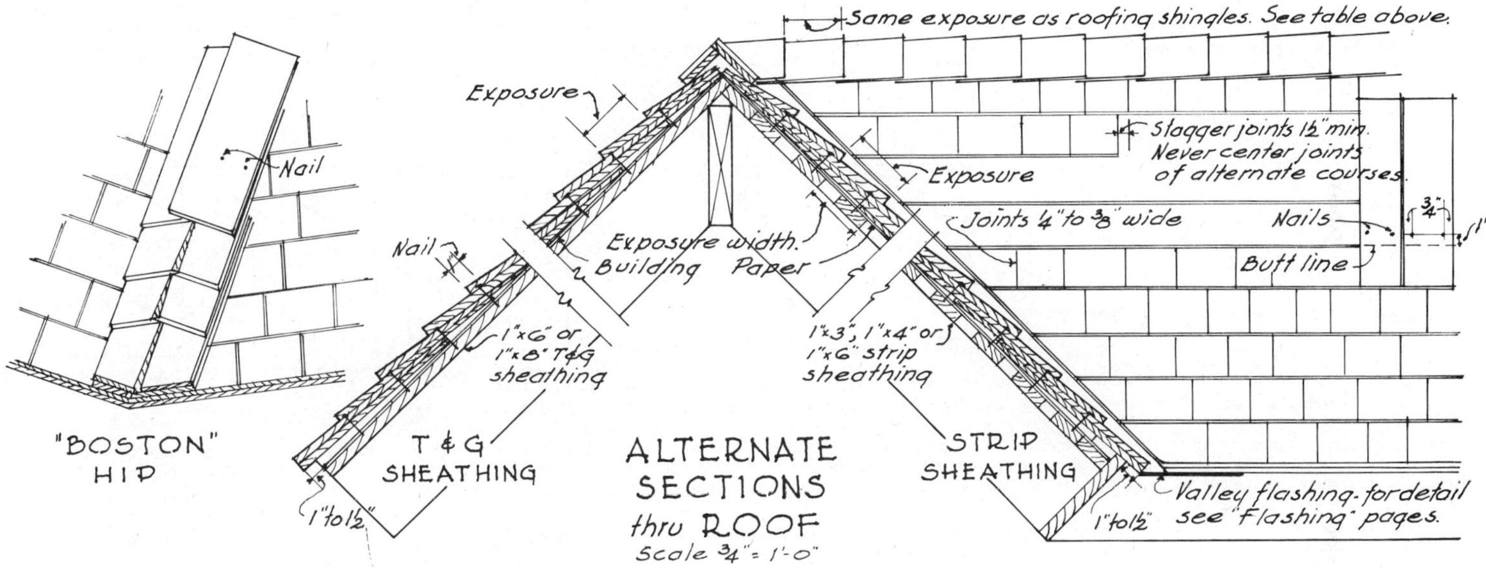
Same exposure as roofing shingles. See table above.
Nail
"BOSTON" HIP
Exposure
Stagger joints 1½" min. Never center joints of alternate courses.
Exposure
Joints ¼" to ⅜" wide
Nails
¾"
1"
Butt line
Exposure width.
Building Paper
Nail
1"x6" or 1"x8" T&G sheathing
1"x3", 1"x4" or 1"x6" strip sheathing
T & G SHEATHING
STRIP SHEATHING
1" to 1½"
1" to 1½"
Valley flashing-for detail see "Flashing" pages.

ALTERNATE SECTIONS thru ROOF
Scale ¾" = 1'-0"

WOOD SHINGLE ROOFS

For exposures see table at top of page.

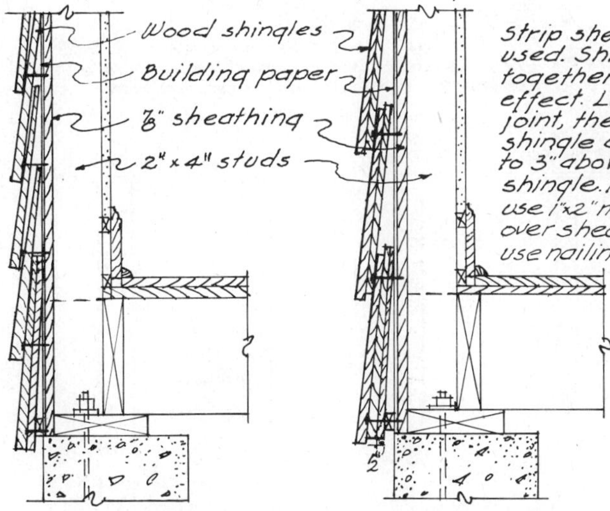
Wood shingles
Building paper
⅞" sheathing
2"x4" studs
Note: In place of undercourse shingles, asphalt impregnated backer board in 4" widths may be substituted.

SINGLE COURSING   DOUBLE COURSING

Strip sheathing may be used. Shingles laid close together give continuous effect. Laid with ⅛" to ⅜" joint, they give individual shingle effect. Nail 2" to 3" above butt of outside shingle. For fibre board sheath'g. use 1"x2" nailing strips horizontal over sheathing. For gypsum use nailing strips or "E-S" nail.

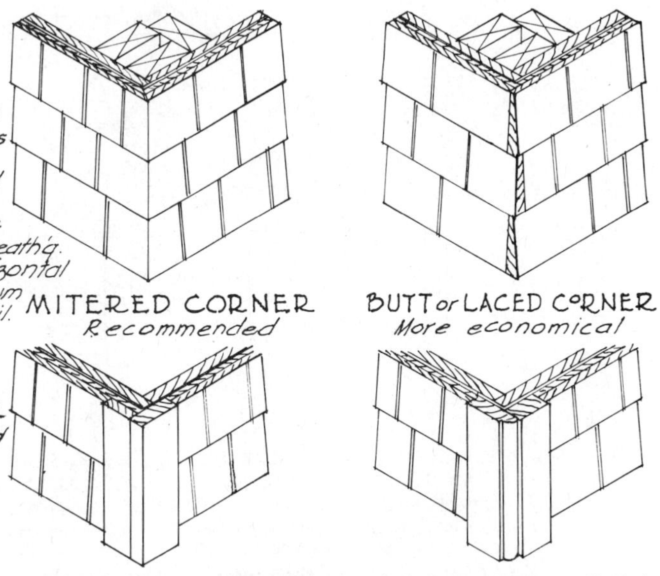

MITERED CORNER
Recommended

BUTT or LACED CORNER
More economical

ALTERNATE CORNERS with CORNER BOARDS
Use of corner boards is recommended.

WOOD SHINGLE SIDING
Scale ¾" = 1'-0"

SLATE ROOFING

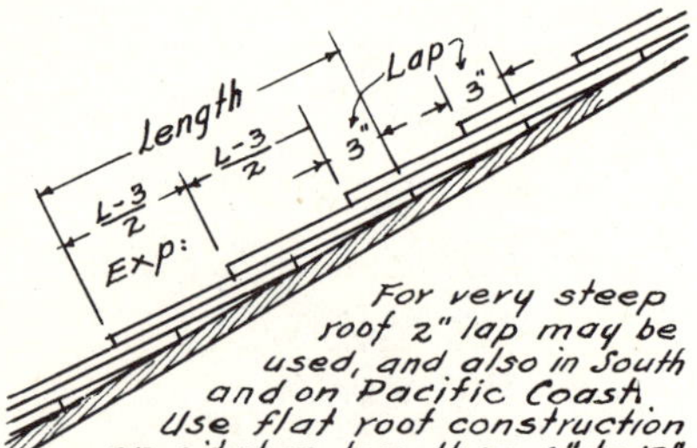
Length
Lap
L-3/2
L-3/2
Exp:
3"
3"

For very steep roof 2" lap may be used, and also in South and on Pacific Coast. Use flat roof construction on pitches less than 4" to 12". For vertical walls use a 2" lap.

LAP and EXPOSURE

Terms

"Textural" is a rough textured slate roof with uneven butts and a variation of thickness or size; generally not applied to slate over 3/8" thick.
"Graduated" Roof is a textural roof of large size slates, and more variation in thickness, size and colour.

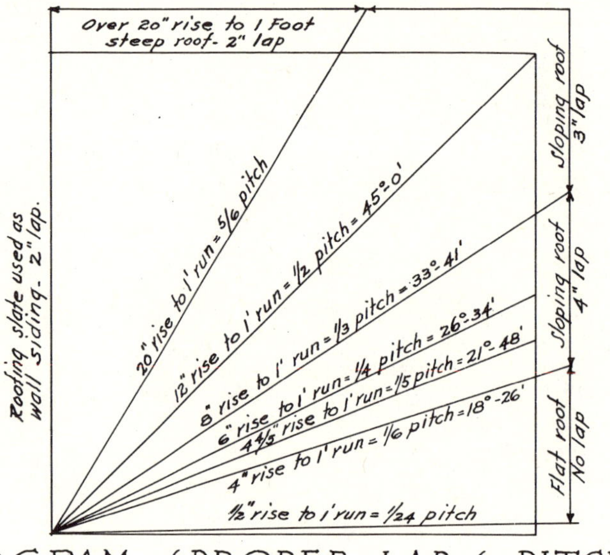
Over 20" rise to 1 Foot steep roof - 2" lap
Roofing slate used as wall siding. 2" lap.
20" rise to 1' run = 5/6 pitch
12" rise to 1' run = 1/2 pitch = 45°-0'
8" rise to 1' run = 1/3 pitch = 33°-41'
6" rise to 1' run = 1/4 pitch = 26°-34'
4 4/5" rise to 1' run = 1/5 pitch = 21°-48'
4" rise to 1' run = 1/6 pitch = 18°-26'
1/2" rise to 1' run = 1/24 pitch
Sloping roof 3" lap
Sloping roof 4" lap
Flat roof No lap

DIAGRAM of PROPER LAP for PITCHES

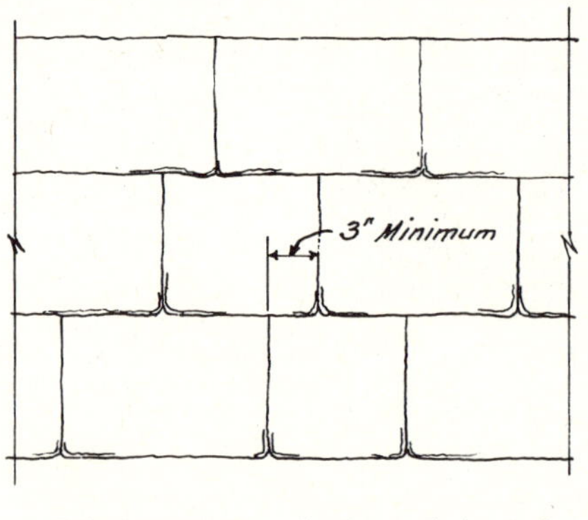
3" Minimum

PROPER JOINTING

Felt

With Commercial Standard Slate use 15# saturated Felt.
With Textural roofs use 30# Felt.
With Graduated roofs use 30# for 3/4" slates and 45# 55# or 65# prepared roll roofing for heavier.

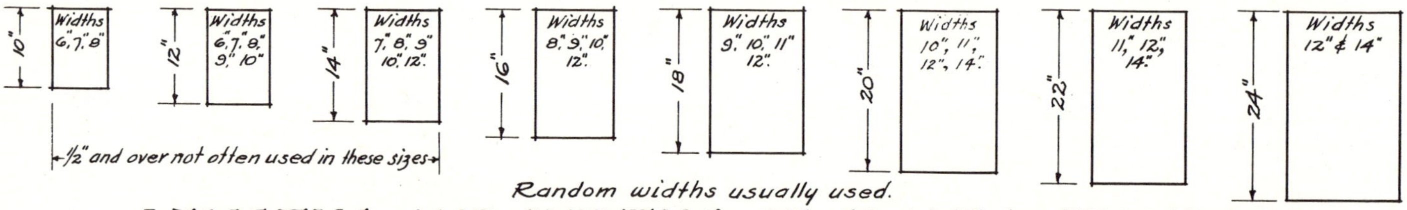
10"
Widths 6", 7", 8"
12"
Widths 6", 7", 8", 9", 10"
14"
Widths 7", 8", 9" 10", 12"
16"
Widths 8", 9", 10", 12"
18"
Widths 9", 10", 11" 12"
20"
Widths 10", 11", 12", 14"
22"
Widths 11", 12", 14"
24"
Widths 12" & 14"
1/2" and over not often used in these sizes

Random widths usually used.

LENGTHS AND WIDTHS OF SLATES-STANDARD

The above Slates are all split in these thicknesses:- 3/16", 1/4", 3/8", 1/2", 3/4", 1", 1 1/4", 1 1/2", 1 3/4" and 2".

Commercial Standard is the Quarry run of 3/16" thickness and includes tolerable variations above and below 3/16".
"Full 3/16" Slate" or "3/16" or "not less than 3/16" indicates hand picked selection with minimum variation.
On other sizes reasonable plus tolerances only are permissable; thus a 1/2" slate must be full 1/2" or slightly thicker.

A Square of Roofing Slate means a sufficient number of slates of any size to cover 100 Square Feet with 3" lap.
For Flat Roofs a Square would cover more than 100 Square Feet.

STANDARD NOMENCLATURE FOR SLATE COLOR.

Black	Gray	Purple	Green	Red
Blue Black	Blue Gray	Mottled Purple & Green	Purple Variegated.	

The above should be preceded by the word "Unfading" or "Weathering."
Other colors and combinations are termed specials.

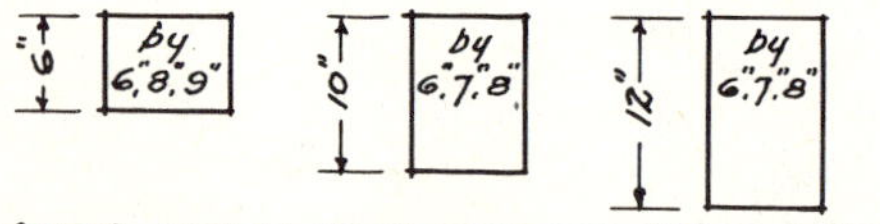
6"
by 6", 8", 9"
10"
by 6", 7", 8"
12"
by 6", 7", 8"

SIZE OF SLATE FOR FLAT ROOF

Thickness for Flat Roofs

Ordinary and light service 3/16" thick. For Promenade or Heavy Service 1/4" to 3/8".
For Special Terraces, Walks etc. 3/4" to 1 1/4" may be used & set in cement. (Editors' Note)
The above sizes & recommendations are Dept. of Commerce Simplified Practice Recommendations R-14-28.

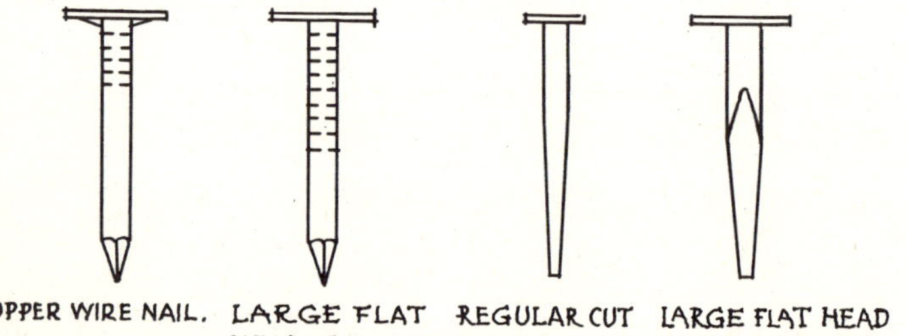

COPPER WIRE NAIL. Similar to steel wire nail; used for flashing but not for slate.

LARGE FLAT HEAD COPPER WIRE NAIL. Usual type for good work.

REGULAR CUT COPPER NAIL. Not good for slate.

LARGE FLAT HEAD CUT COPPER ROOFING NAIL. This type not good.

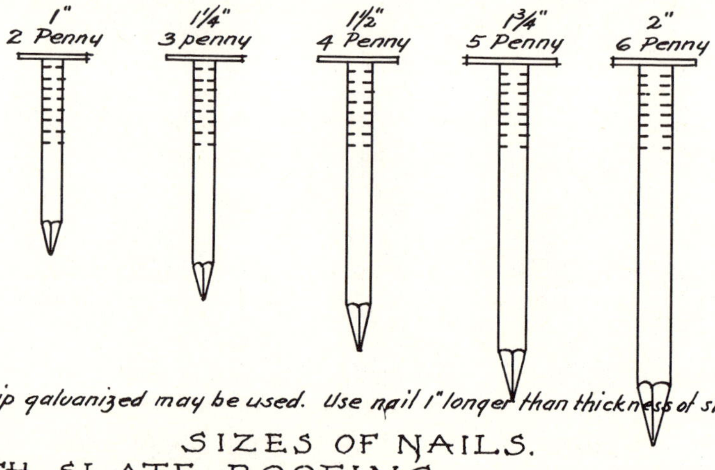
1" 2 Penny
1 1/4" 3 penny
1 1/2" 4 Penny
1 3/4" 5 Penny
2" 6 Penny

Nails should be of copper or yellow metal. In dry climates hot dip galvanized may be used. Use nail 1" longer than thickness of slate.

TYPES OF NAILS. SIZES OF NAILS.

NAILS FOR USE WITH SLATE ROOFING.

STANDARD SLATE SIZES - ROOFING NAILS - COLORS & LAP OF SLATE ROOFS.

Data checked by Vermont Structural Slate Co., Inc.

SLATE ROOFING

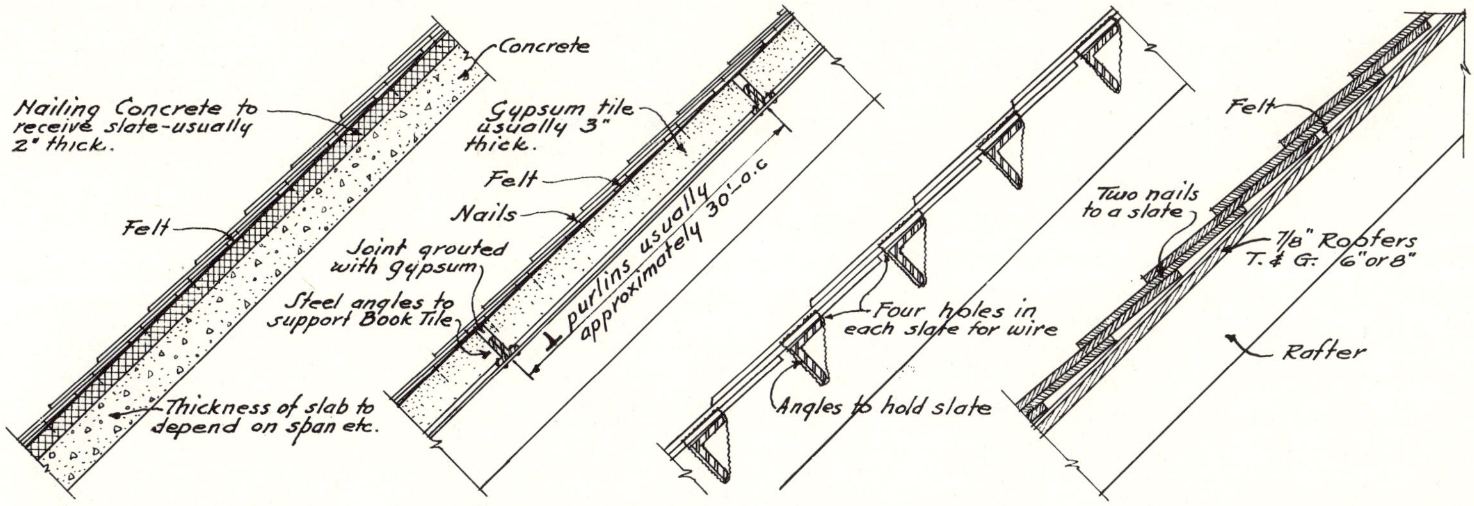
Concrete
Nailing Concrete to receive slate-usually 2" thick.
Felt
Thickness of slab to depend on span etc.
Gypsum tile usually 3" thick.
Felt
Nails
Joint grouted with gypsum
Steel angles to support Book Tile
⊥ purlins usually approximately 30'-0" o.c.
Four holes in each slate for wire
Angles to hold slate
Felt
Two nails to a slate
7/8" Roofers T. & G. 6" or 8"
Rafter

NAILING CONCRETE ON CONCRETE SLAB. | GYPSUM BOOK TILE ON STEEL ANGLES. | SLATE WIRED TO STEEL ANGLES. | WOOD RAFTER TO RECEIVE SLATE.

TYPES of ROOFS to RECEIVE SLATE.

3/4" = 1'-0"

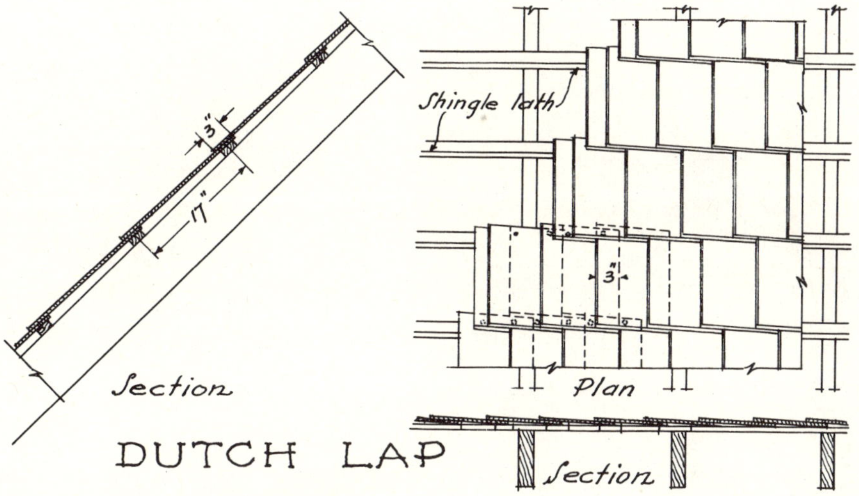
3"
17"
Section
Shingle lath
3"
Plan
Section

DUTCH LAP

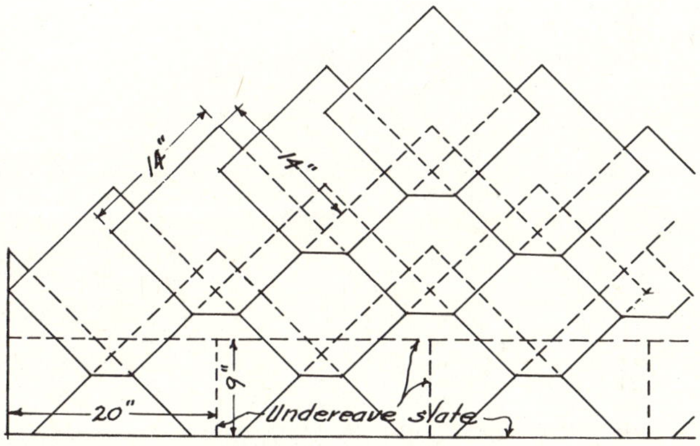
14"
14"
9"
20"
Undereave slate

Roof slate sometimes 12"×12", with undereave slate 17"×8".

FRENCH METHOD

Also known as "Hexagonal" or "Diagonal."

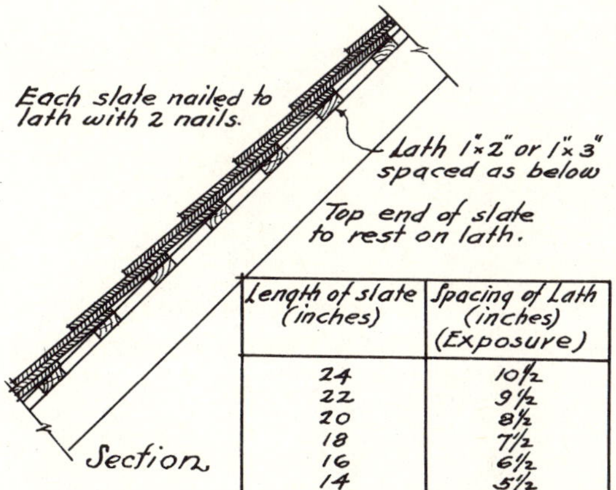
Each slate nailed to lath with 2 nails.
Lath 1"×2" or 1"×3" spaced as below
Top end of slate to rest on lath.
Section

Length of slate (inches)	Spacing of Lath (inches) (Exposure)
24	10½
22	9½
20	8½
18	7½
16	6½
14	5½
12	4½

LAYING on WOOD LATH

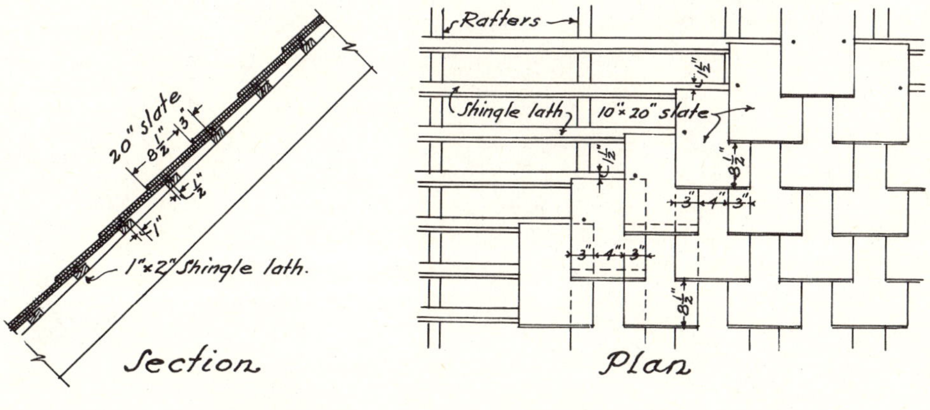
20" slate
8½"
3"
½"
1"
1"×2" Shingle lath.
Section
Rafters
Shingle lath
10"×20" slate
1½"
1½"
8½"
3" 4" 3"
3" 4" 3"
8½"
Plan

OPEN SLATING

For use where ventilation is desired.

VARIOUS METHODS OF LAYING SLATE.

1/2" = 1'-0"

See "Roof Construction" sheet

TYPES of ROOFS to RECEIVE SLATE and LAYING SLATE ROOFS.

Data checked by Vermont Structural Slate Co., Inc.

SLATE ROOFING

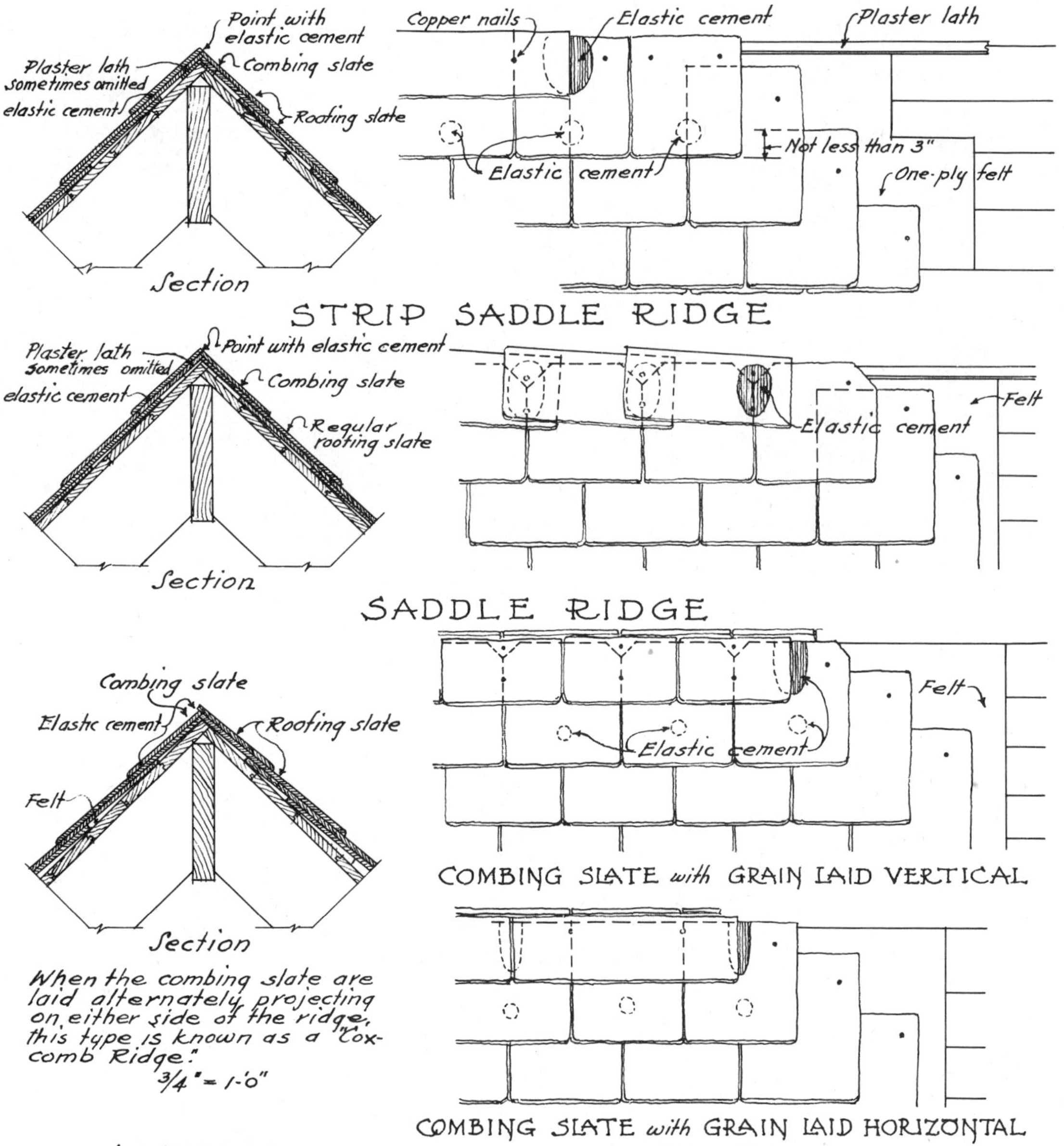
Point with elastic cement
Plaster lath sometimes omitted
Combing slate
elastic cement
Roofing slate
Copper nails
Elastic cement
Plaster lath
Not less than 3"
Elastic cement
One-ply felt
Section
STRIP SADDLE RIDGE
Plaster lath sometimes omitted
Point with elastic cement
Combing slate
elastic cement
Regular rooting slate
Felt
Elastic cement
Section
SADDLE RIDGE
Combing slate
Elastic cement
Roofing slate
Felt
Felt
Elastic cement
Section
COMBING SLATE with GRAIN LAID VERTICAL
When the combing slate are laid alternately projecting on either side of the ridge, this type is known as a "Cox-comb Ridge."
3/4" = 1'-0"
COMBING SLATE with GRAIN LAID HORIZONTAL

SECTIONS ELEVATIONS

TWO TYPES OF COMB RIDGES
SLATE ROOF RIDGES

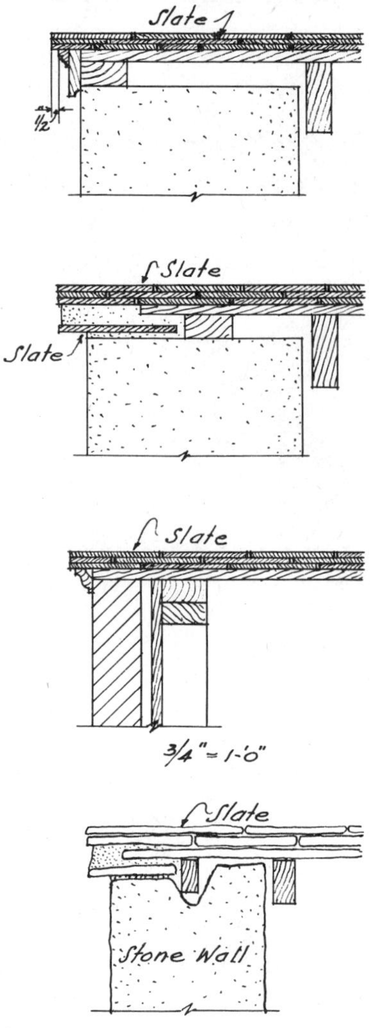
Slate
1/2
Slate
Slate
Slate
3/4" = 1'-0"
Slate
Stone Wall

SECTIONS
RAKES of GABLES

Scale - 3/4" = 1'-0"

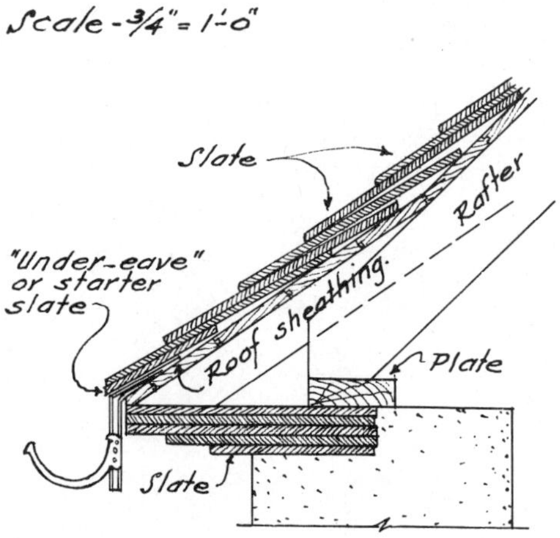
Slate
Rafter
"Under-eave" or starter slate
Roof sheathing
Plate
Slate

EAVE

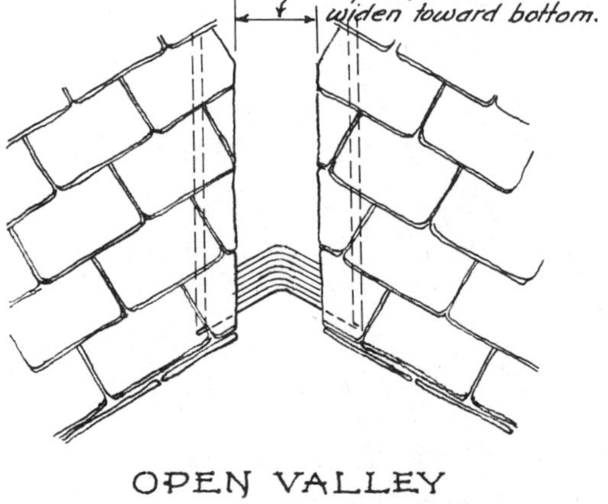
Taper 1/8" to 1'-0". widen toward bottom.

OPEN VALLEY

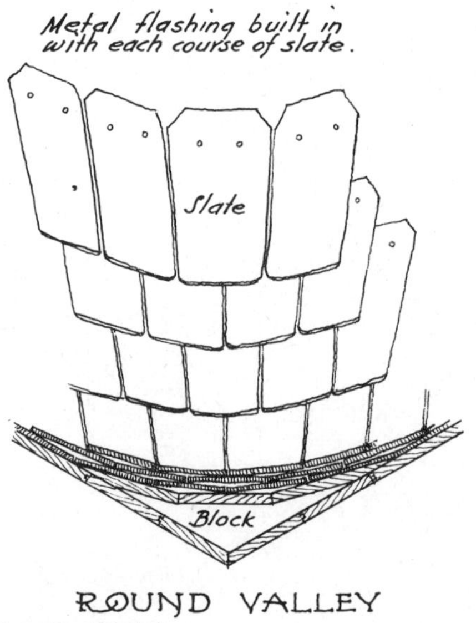
Metal flashing built in with each course of slate.
Slate
Block

ROUND VALLEY

TYPES OF VALLEYS

See "Flashing" Sheets

SLATE ROOFS showing RIDGES, VALLEYS, RAKES & EAVES

Data checked by Vermont Structural Slate Co., Inc.

SLATE ROOFING

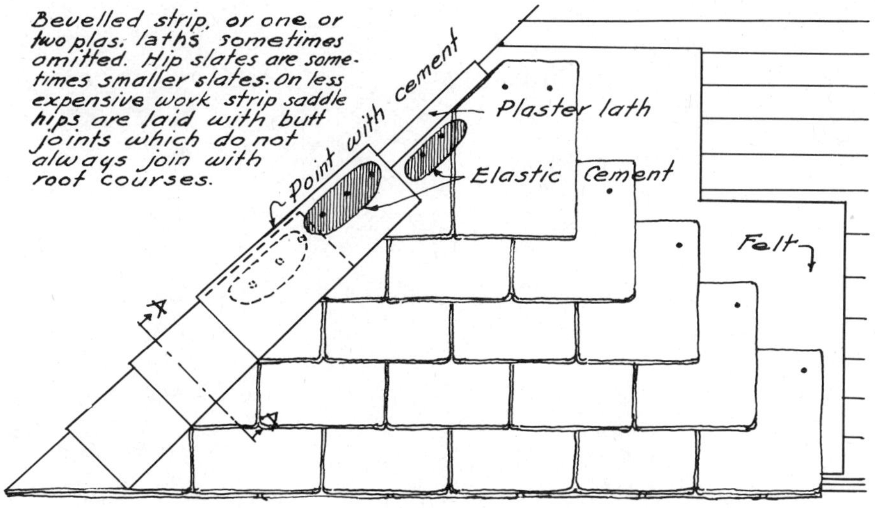
Bevelled strip, or one or two plas. laths sometimes omitted. Hip slates are sometimes smaller slates. On less expensive work strip saddle hips are laid with butt joints which do not always join with roof courses.
Point with cement
Plaster lath
Elastic Cement
Felt
A
A

THE SADDLE HIP.

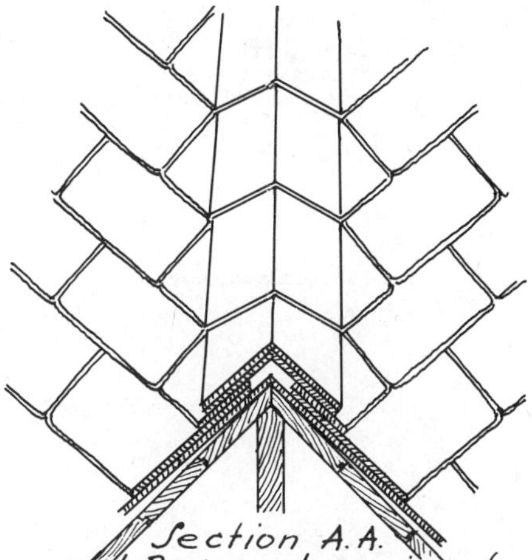

Section A.A. and Perspective view of Saddle Hip.

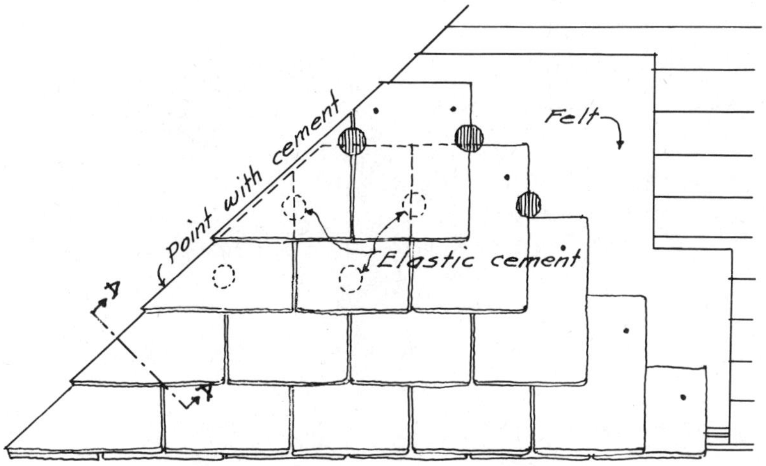
Point with cement
Felt
Elastic cement
A
A

THE MITRED HIP

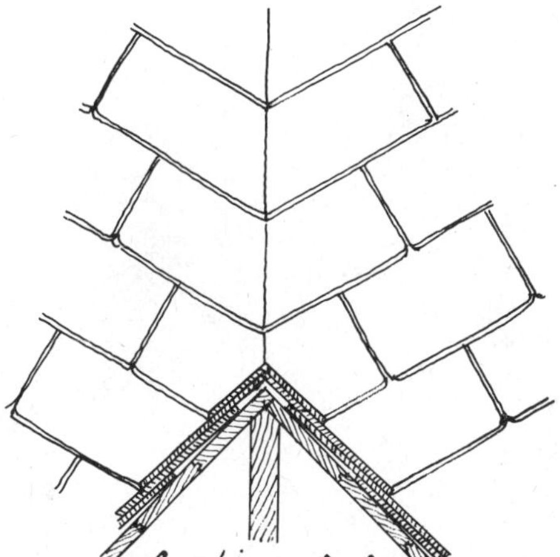

Section A-A Perspective View of Mitred Hip

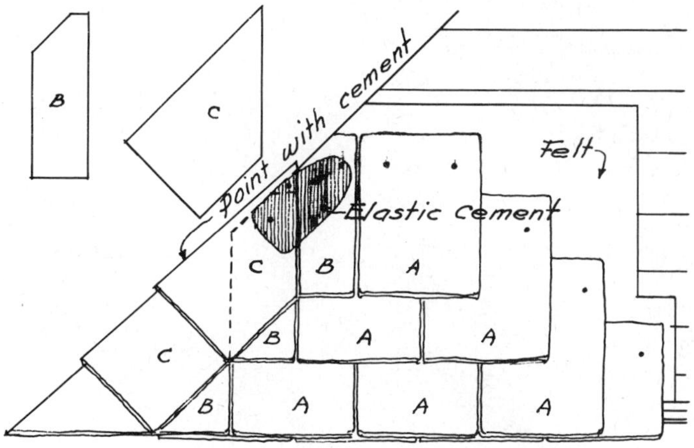
B
C
Point with cement
Elastic Cement
Felt
C
B
A
A
A
C
B
B
A
A
A

THE BOSTON HIP

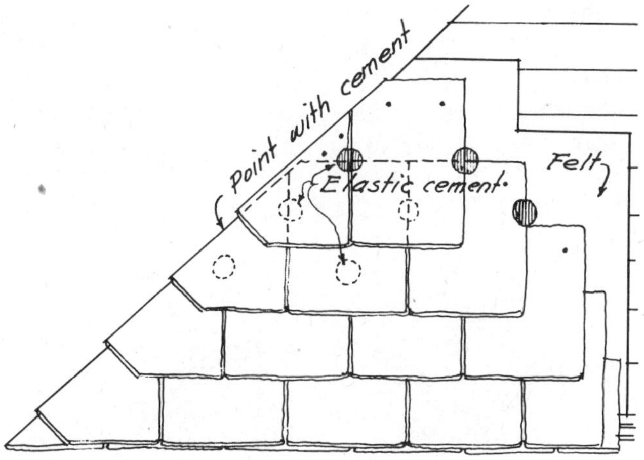
Point with cement
Elastic cement
Felt

THE FANTAIL HIP.

SLATE ROOF HIPS

Data checked by Vermont Structural Slate Co., Inc.

CLAY TILE ROOFING

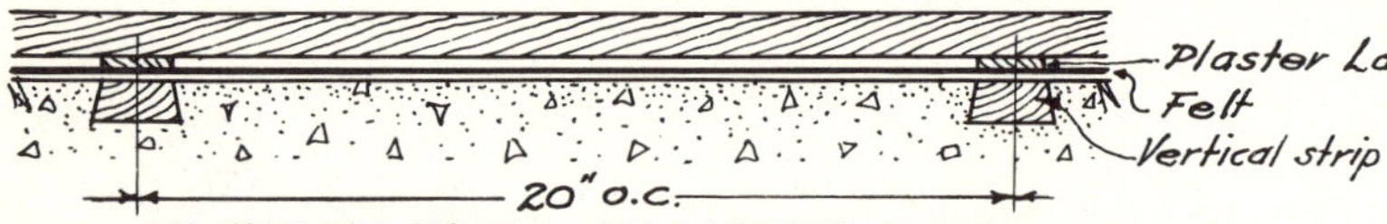
Plaster Lath
Felt
Vertical strip
20" o.c.

SECTION THRO CONCRETE ROOF.
Application of wood strips to concrete roof base.
Exact spacing of horizontal strips determined by shade of tiles.

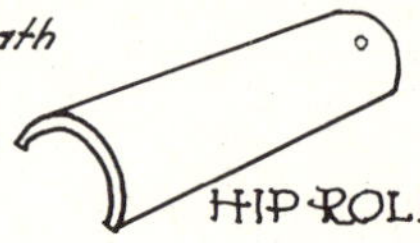

HIP ROLL

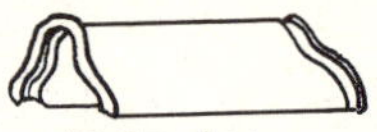

RIDGE

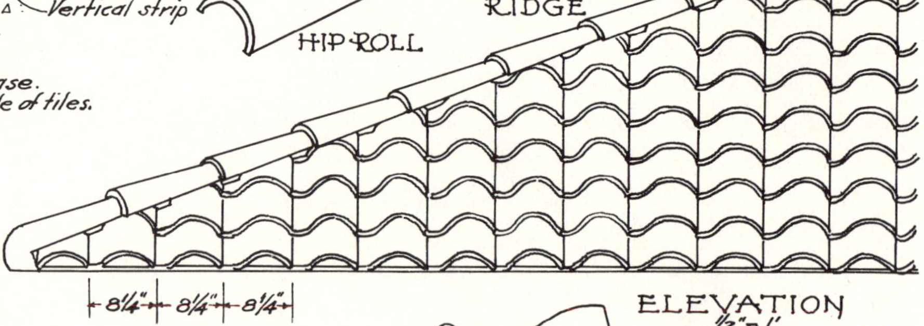
8¼" 8¼" 8¼"

ELEVATION
½" = 1'

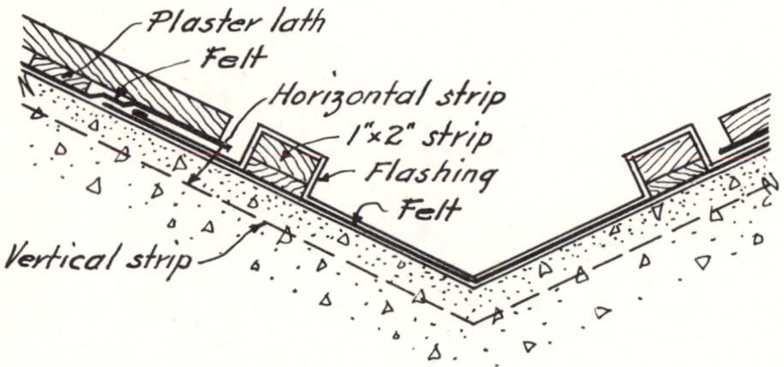
Plaster lath
Felt
Horizontal strip
1"×2" strip
Flashing
Felt
Vertical strip

SECTION THRO' VALLEY ON CONCRETE ROOF.

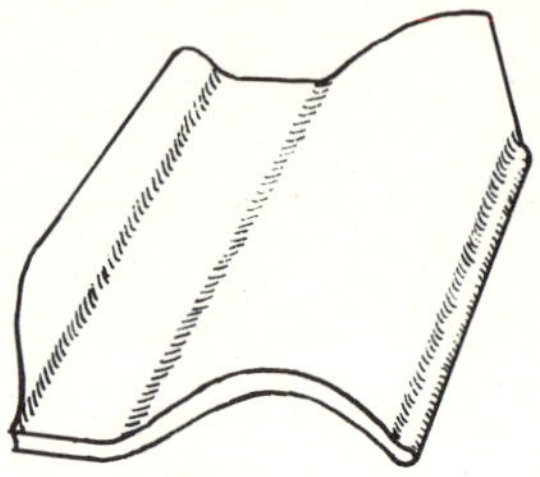

TILE

Length Average 13¼"
Width " 9¾"
Aver. length exposure 10¼"
Weight per Sq. = 900# ±

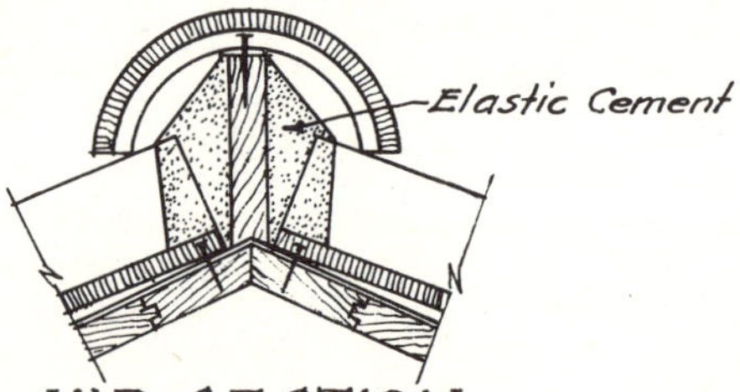
Elastic Cement

HIP SECTION
Showing Hip Roll.

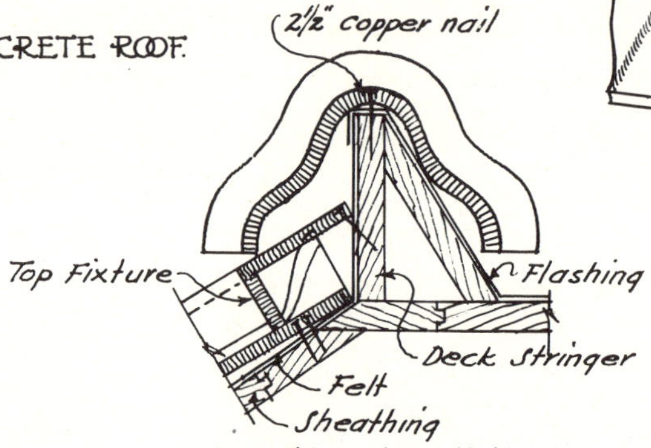
2½" copper nail
Top Fixture
Flashing
Deck Stringer
Felt
Sheathing

DECK SECTION
Showing Ridge

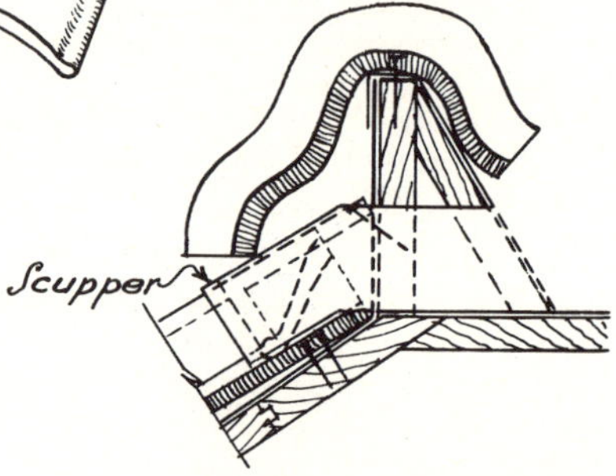
Scupper

DECK SECTION
Showing cut-off ridge and 3"×4" Scuppers draining deck.

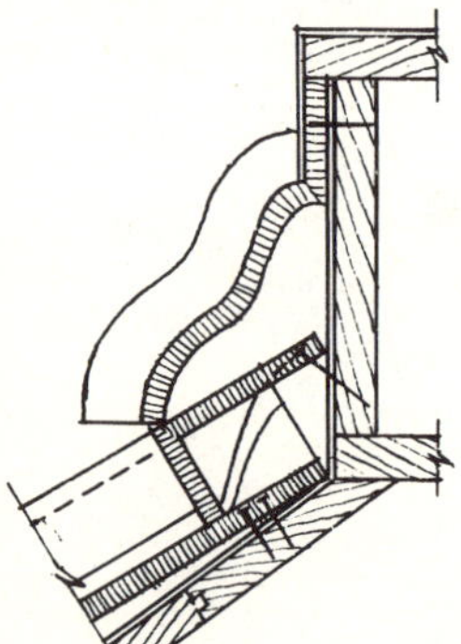

DECK SECTION SHOWING
DECK MOULD RAISED FLANGE

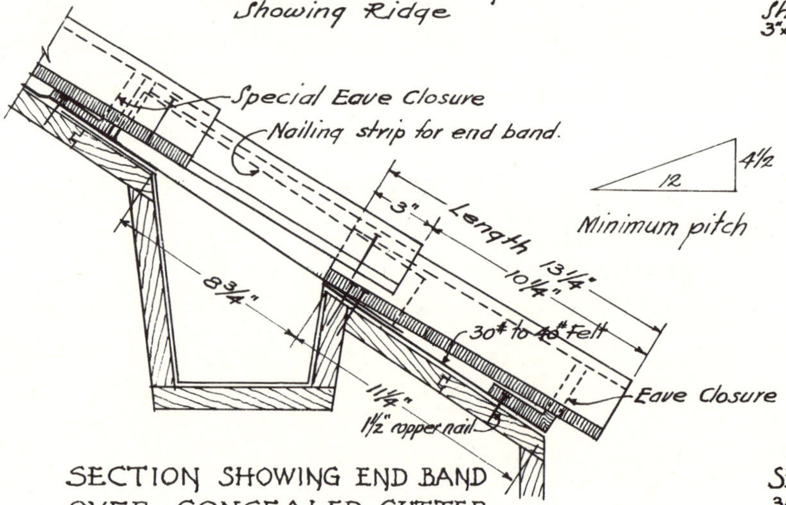
Special Eave Closure
Nailing strip for end band.
3"
Length 13¼"
10¼"
8¾"
30# to 40# Felt
1¼"
1½" copper nail
Eave Closure
12
4½
Minimum pitch

SECTION SHOWING END BAND
OVER CONCEALED GUTTER

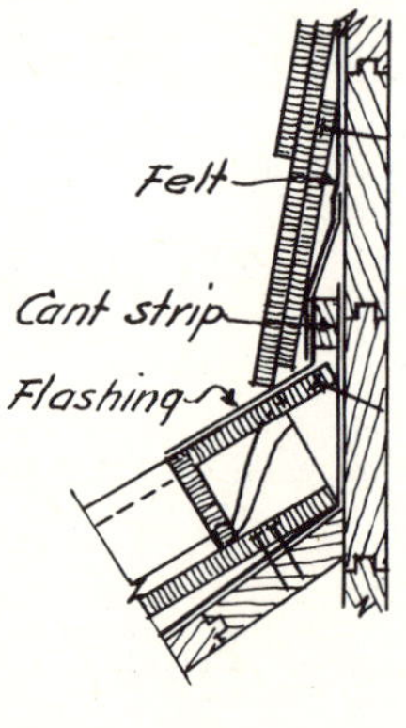
Felt
Cant strip
Flashing

SECTION OF FLASHING UNDER
⅜" FLAT SHINGLE TILE.

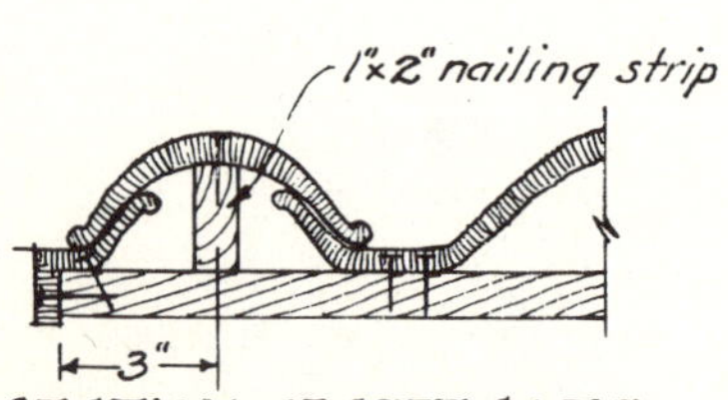
1"×2" nailing strip
3"

SECTION OF LEFT GABLE
RAKE AND END BAND.

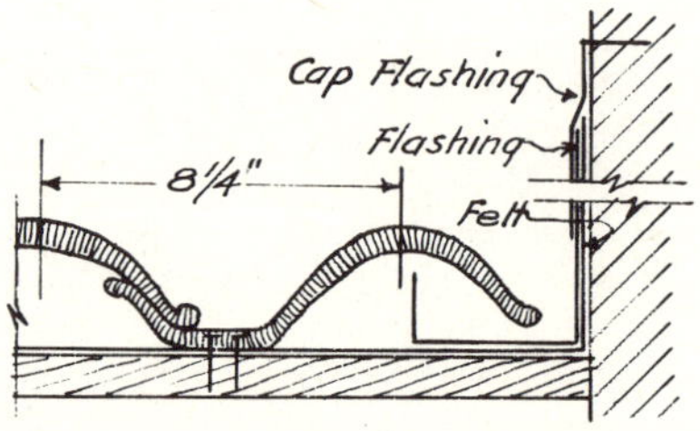
Cap Flashing
Flashing
8¼"
Felt

SECTION OF FLASHING
UNDERSIDE OF TILES.

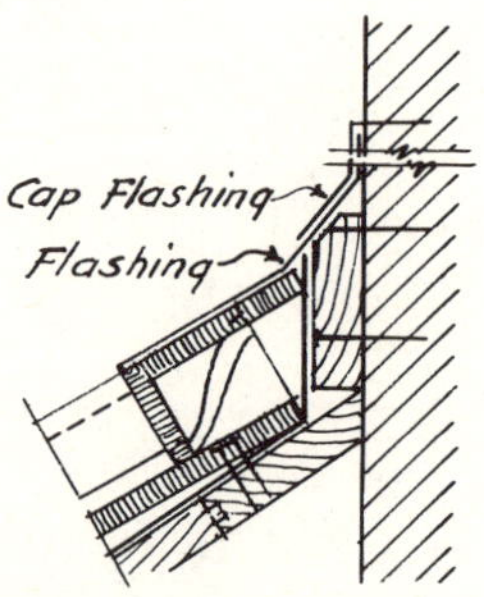
Cap Flashing
Flashing

SECTION OF FLASHING
OVER TOP OF TILES.

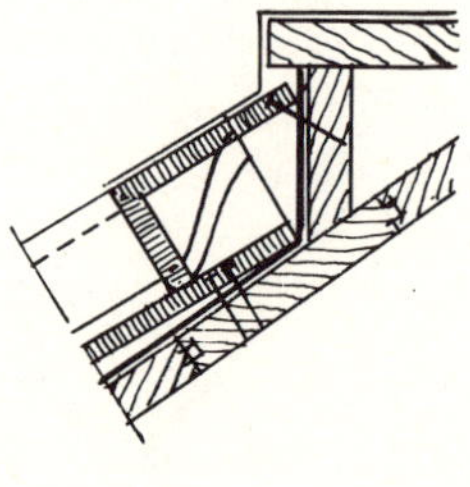

DECK SECTION OF FLASHING
OVER TOP OF TILES.

Scale 1½" = 1'0"

SPANISH TILES

Recommendations of the Ludowici-Celadon Co.

CLAY TILE ROOFING

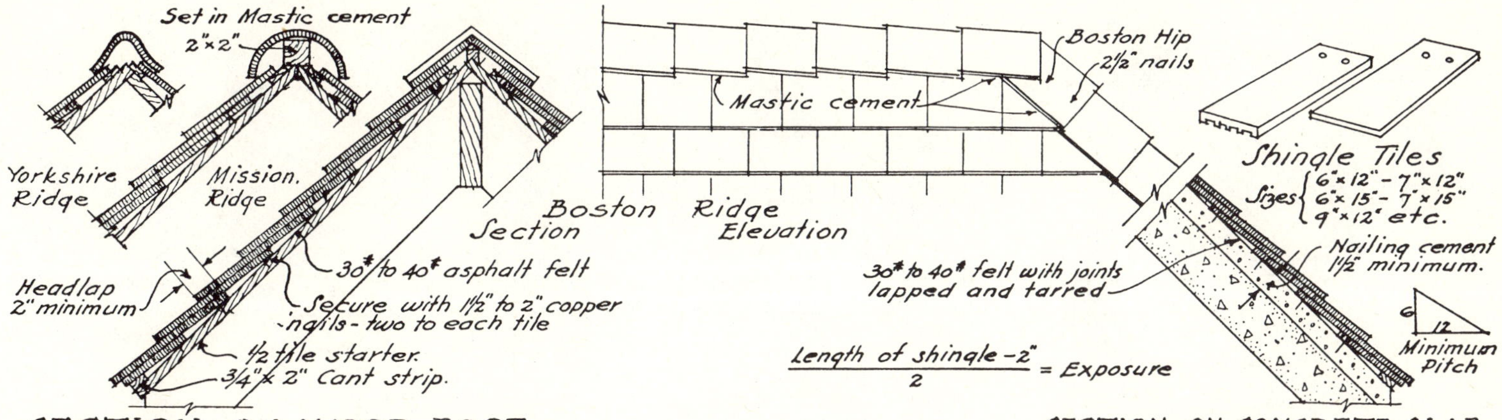
Set in Mastic cement
2"×2"
Yorkshire Ridge
Mission Ridge
Boston Ridge Section
Elevation
Headlap 2" minimum
30# to 40# asphalt felt
Secure with 1½" to 2" copper nails - two to each tile
½ tile starter.
3/4" × 2" Cant strip.
Mastic cement
Boston Hip
2½" nails
Shingle Tiles
Sizes { 6"×12" - 7"×12"
6"×15" - 7"×15"
9"×12" etc.
Nailing cement 1½" minimum.
30# to 40# felt with joints lapped and tarred
6
12
Minimum Pitch
Length of shingle - 2" / 2 = Exposure

SECTION - ON WOOD ROOF. SECTION - ON CONCRETE SLAB

SHINGLE TILES

Flashing is similar to that for slate – For use on walls see "Exterior Walls" sheet

½" = 1'-0"

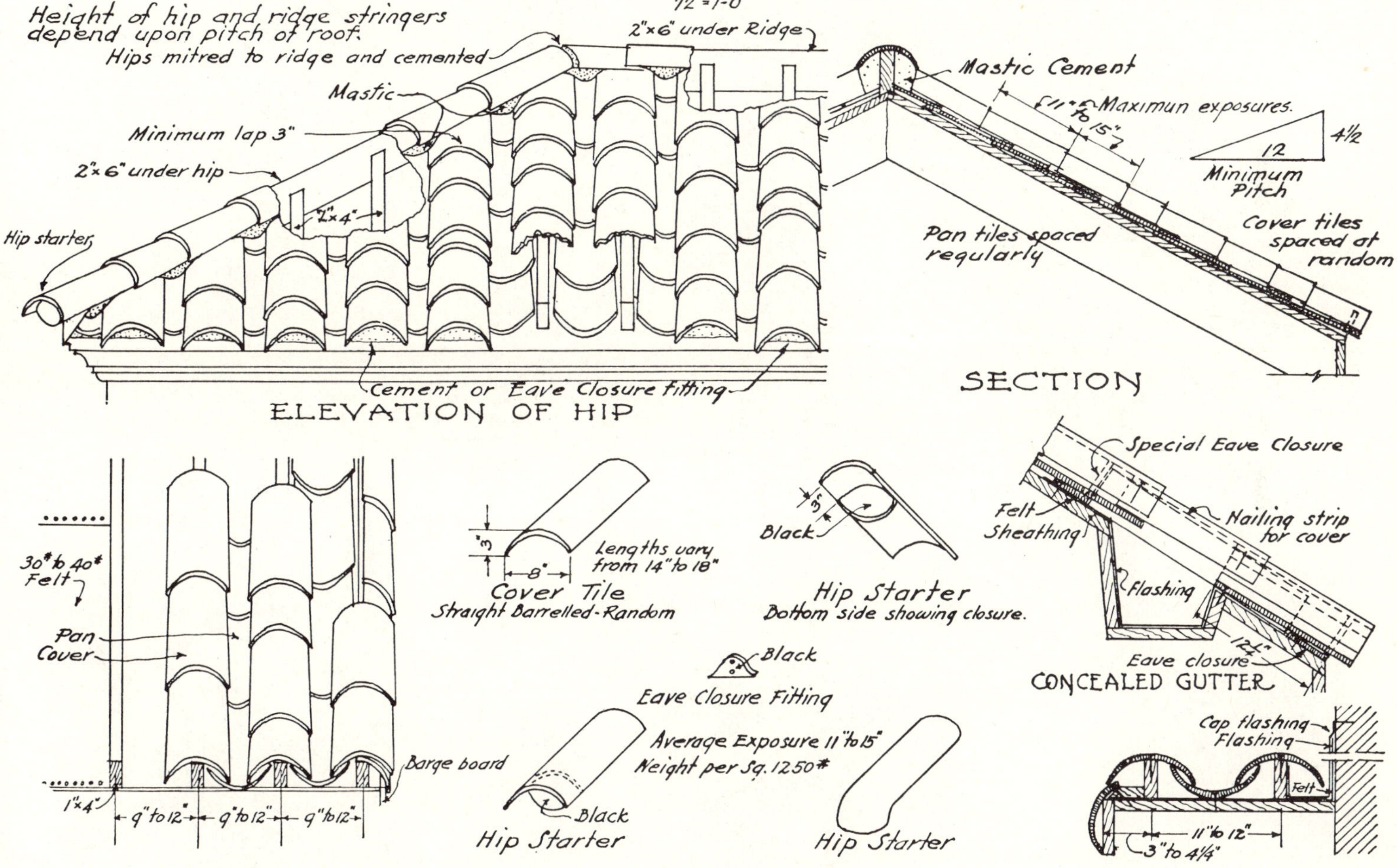
Height of hip and ridge stringers depend upon pitch of roof.
Hips mitred to ridge and cemented
2"×6" under Ridge
Mastic
Minimum lap 3"
2"×6" under hip
2"×4"
Hip starter
Cement or Eave Closure fitting
ELEVATION OF HIP
Mastic Cement
11" to 15" Maximum exposures.
4½
12
Minimum Pitch
Pan tiles spaced regularly
Cover tiles spaced at random
SECTION
30# to 40# Felt
Pan
Cover
Barge board
1"×4"
9" to 12"
9" to 12"
9" to 12"
3"
8"
Lengths vary from 14" to 18"
Cover Tile
Straight Barrelled - Random
3"
Black
Hip Starter
Bottom side showing closure.
Black
Eave Closure Fitting
Average Exposure 11" to 15"
Weight per Sq. 1250#
Black
Hip Starter
Hip Starter
Special Eave Closure
Felt
Sheathing
Nailing strip for cover
Flashing
12"
Eave closure
CONCEALED GUTTER
Cap flashing
Flashing
Felt
11" to 12"
3" to 4¼"

RAKE ½" = 1'-0" STRAIGHT BARREL MISSION TILE. SPLIT COVER GABLE RAKE ¾" = 1'-0"

Sizes vary according to Manufacturer; see Catalogues for exact sizes. – Also manufactured with tapered covers and straight pans; and tapered covers with tapered pans.

CLAY ROOFING TILES

For flashing of clay tile roof, see pages on Flashing

For other tile roofs such as promenade or quarry tile, see page "Built-up roofing"

CLAY TILE ROOFING

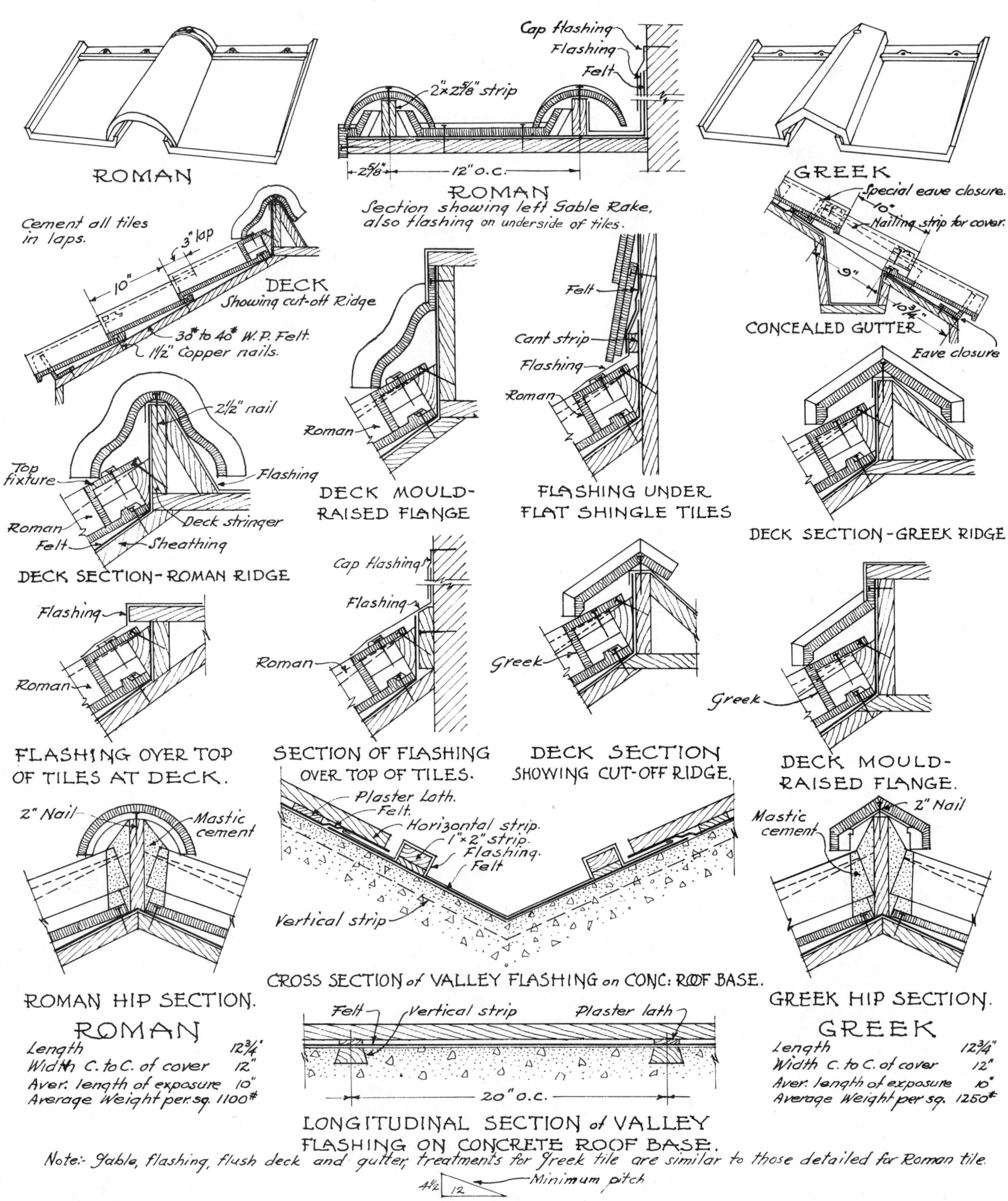
ROMAN
Cap flashing
Flashing
Felt
2"×2 5/8" strip
2 5/8"
12" o.c.
ROMAN
Section showing left Gable Rake, also flashing on underside of tiles.
GREEK
Special eave closure.
10"
Nailing strip for cover.
9"
10 3/4"
CONCEALED GUTTER
Eave closure
Cement all tiles in laps.
3" lap
10"
DECK
Showing cut-off Ridge
30# to 40# W. P. Felt.
1 1/2" Copper nails.
Roman
DECK MOULD-RAISED FLANGE
Felt
Cant strip
Flashing
Roman
FLASHING UNDER FLAT SHINGLE TILES
2 1/2" nail
Top fixture
Flashing
Roman
Deck stringer
Felt
Sheathing
DECK SECTION-ROMAN RIDGE
DECK SECTION-GREEK RIDGE
Flashing
Roman
FLASHING OVER TOP OF TILES AT DECK.
Cap flashing
Flashing
Roman
SECTION OF FLASHING OVER TOP OF TILES.
Greek
DECK SECTION SHOWING CUT-OFF RIDGE.
Greek
DECK MOULD-RAISED FLANGE.
2" Nail
Mastic cement
ROMAN HIP SECTION.
Plaster Lath.
Felt.
Horizontal strip.
1"×2" strip.
Flashing.
Felt
Vertical strip
CROSS SECTION of VALLEY FLASHING on CONC: ROOF BASE.
Mastic cement
2" Nail
GREEK HIP SECTION.
Felt
Vertical strip
Plaster lath
20" o.c.
LONGITUDINAL SECTION of VALLEY FLASHING ON CONCRETE ROOF BASE.
4 1/2
12
Minimum pitch

ROMAN

Length	12 3/4"
Width C. to C. of cover	12"
Aver. length of exposure	10"
Average Weight per sq.	1100#

GREEK

Length	12 3/4"
Width C. to C. of cover	12"
Aver. length of exposure	10"
Average Weight per sq.	1250#

Note:- Gable, flashing, flush deck and gutter, treatments for Greek tile are similar to those detailed for Roman tile.

ROMAN and GREEK TYPES of ROOFING TILES

Recommendations of the Ludowici-Celadon Co.

1 1/2" = 1'-0"

CLAY TILE ROOFING

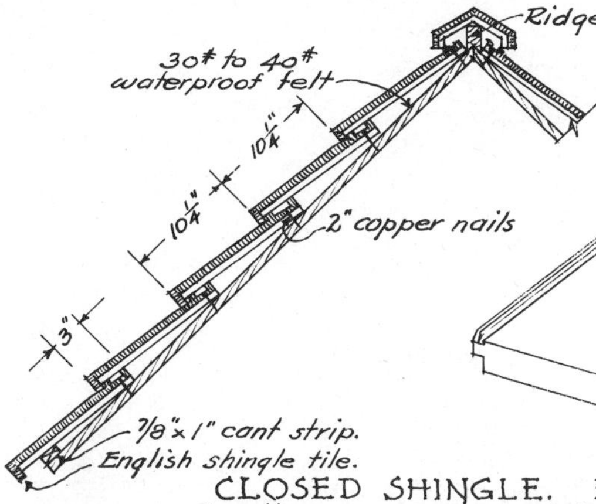
Ridge stringer
30# to 40#
waterproof felt
10¼"
10¼"
2" copper nails
3"
7/8"x1" cant strip.
English shingle tile.

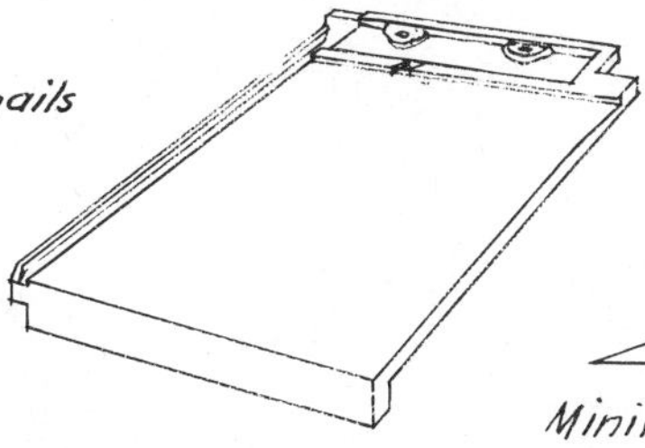

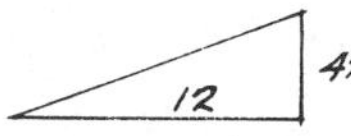
12
4½

Minimum pitch.

CLOSED SHINGLE.		ENGLISH SHINGLE.	
Length	11"	Length	13¼"
Width	8¾"	Width	8¾"
Average length - Exposure.	8"	Average length - Exposure	10⅛"
" width - "	8"	" width - "	7¾"

Average weight per Square = 900#

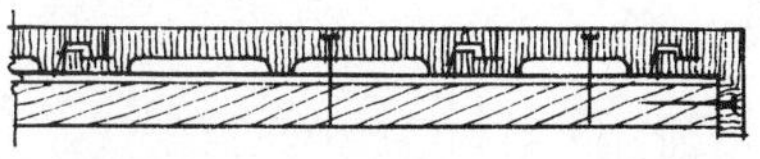

SECTION - RIGHT GABLE RAKE AND END BAND.

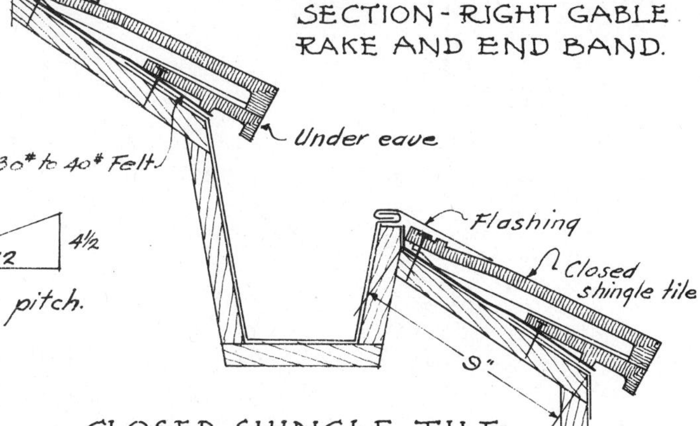
Under eave
30# to 40# Felt
Flashing
Closed
shingle tile
9"

CLOSED SHINGLE TILE
Section showing Sunken Gutter.
When English Shingle Tiles are used, undereaves are omitted and distance below gutter is 11¼".

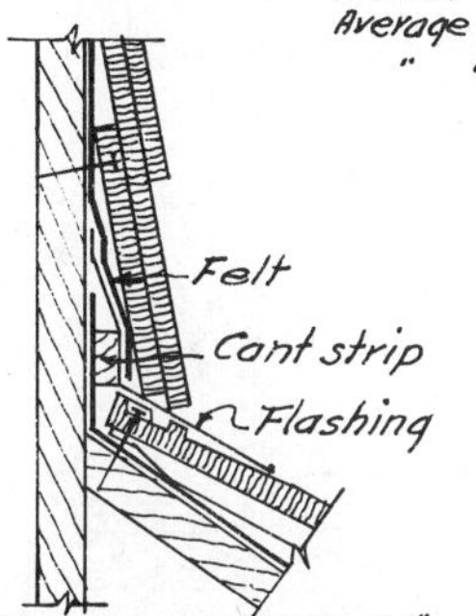
Felt
Cant strip
Flashing

FLASHING UNDER ⅜" FLAT SHINGLE TILE.

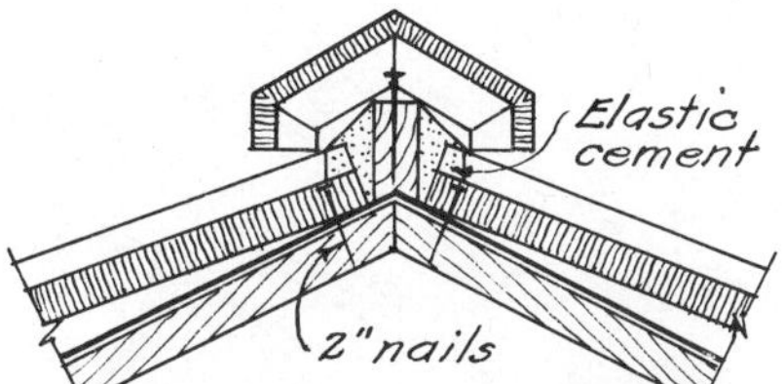
Elastic
cement
2" nails

HIP ROLL USED WITH CLOSED SHINGLE TILE.

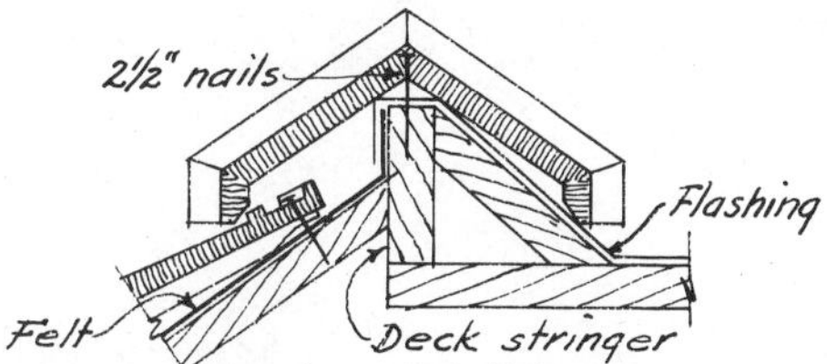
2½" nails
Flashing
Felt
Deck stringer

DECK SECTION SHOWING RIDGE.

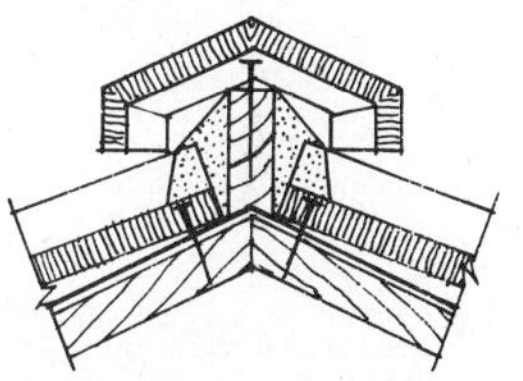

HIP ROLL USED WITH ENGLISH SHINGLE TILE.

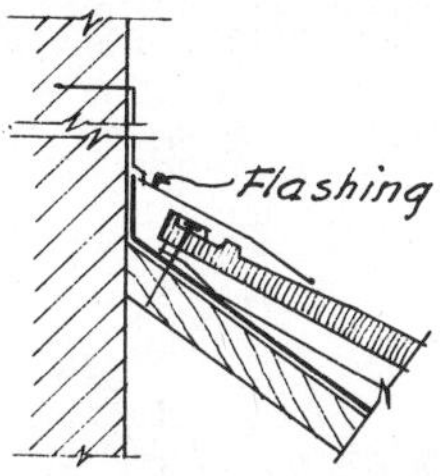
Flashing

SECTION - FLASHING OVER TOP OF TILES.

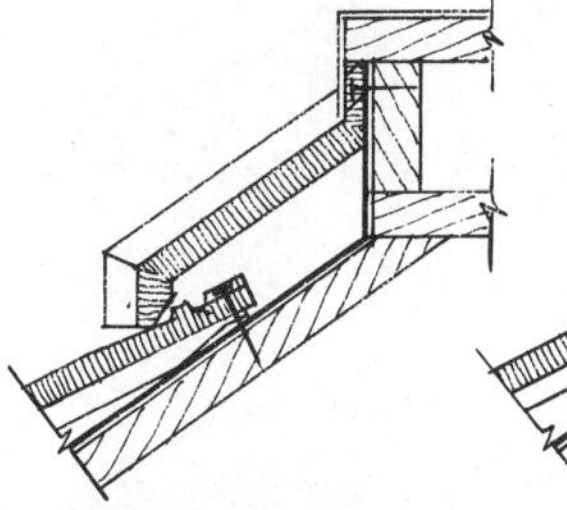

SECTION - DECK MOULD RAISED FLANGE.

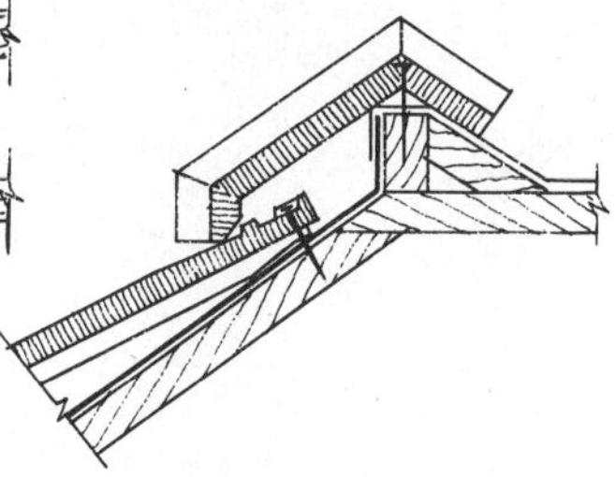

DECK SECTION CUT-OFF RIDGE.

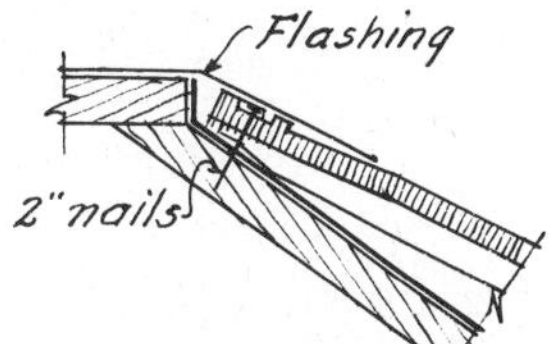
Flashing
2" nails

DECK SECTION - FLASHING OVER TOP OF TILES.

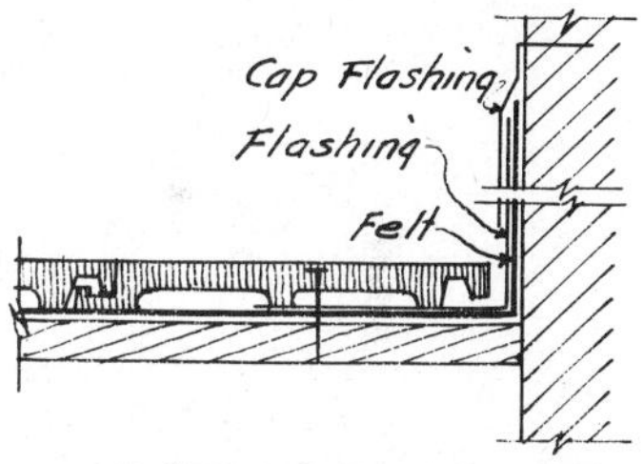
Cap Flashing
Flashing
Felt

SECTION - FLASHING UNDERSIDE OF TILES.

INTERLOCKING TILE - ENGLISH AND CLOSED.

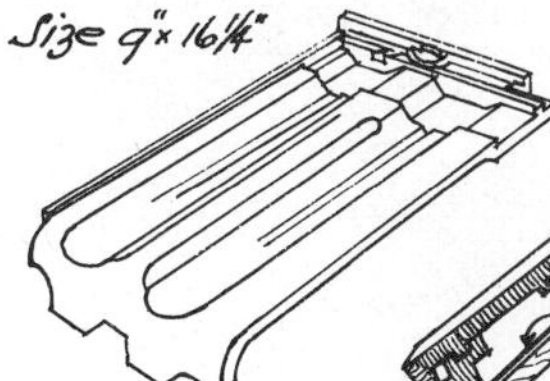
Size 9"x 16¼"

FRENCH TILE

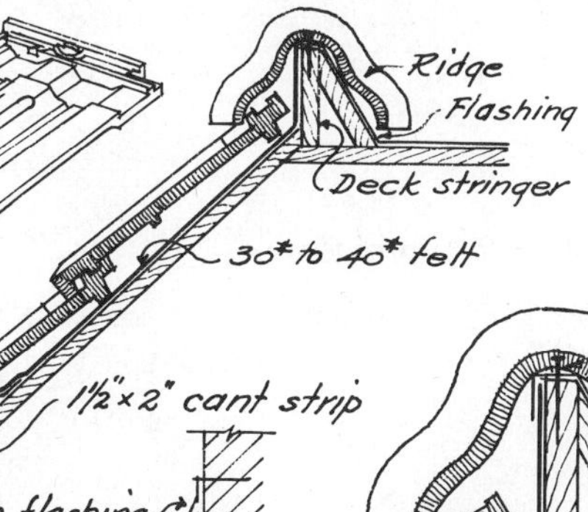
Ridge
Flashing
Deck stringer
30# to 40# felt
1½"x 2" cant strip

SECTION - RIGHT GABLE RAKE
Cement all Tile in laps.

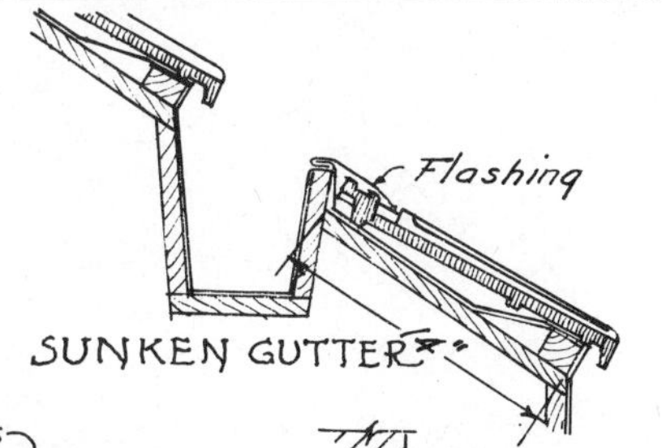
Flashing

SUNKEN GUTTER

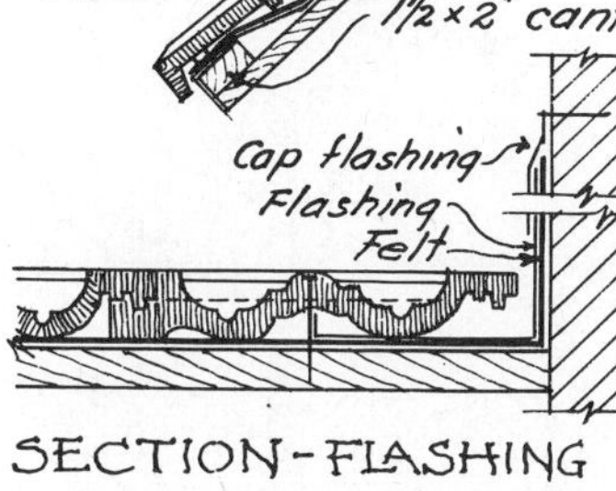
Cap flashing
Flashing
Felt

SECTION - FLASHING UNDER SIDE OF TILES.

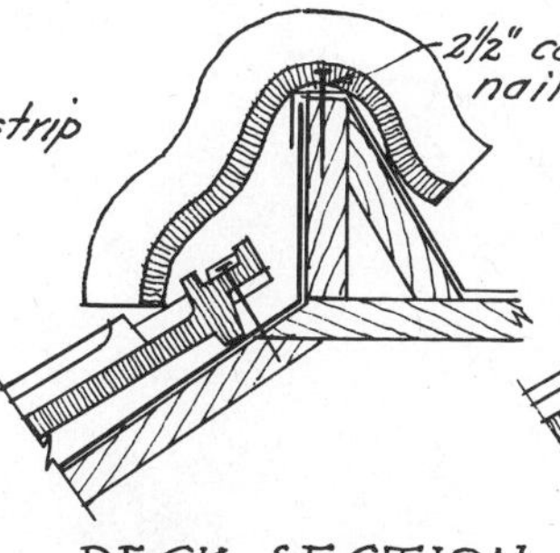
2½" copper
nails

DECK SECTION CUT-OFF RIDGE.

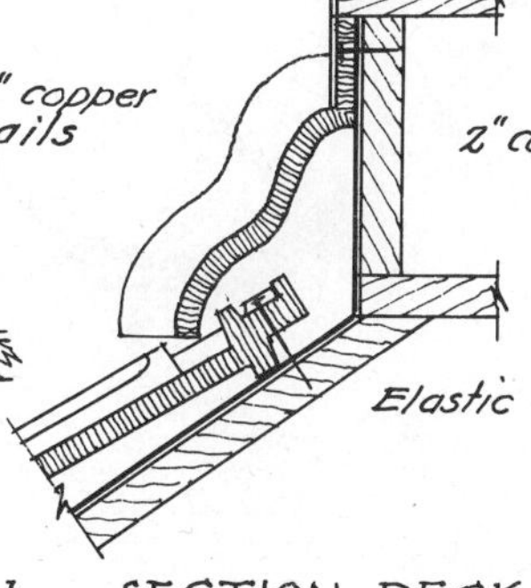

SECTION - DECK MOULD RAISED FLANGE.

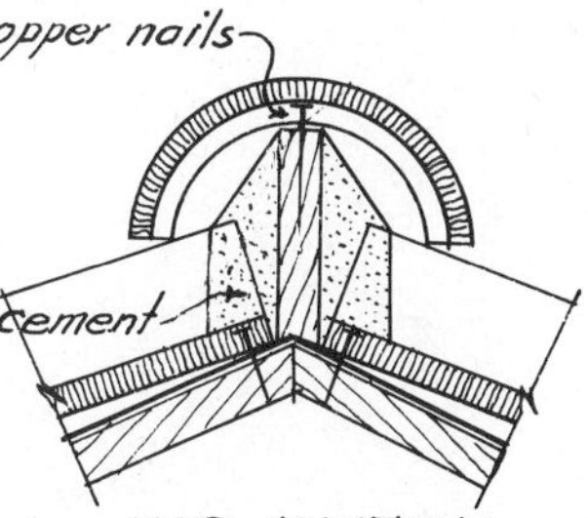
2" copper nails
Elastic cement

HIP SECTION SHOWING HIP ROLL.

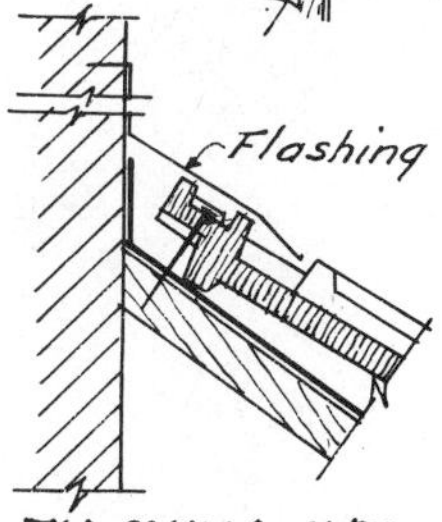
Flashing

FLASHING OVER TOP OF TILES.

FRENCH TILES

Recommendations of the Ludowici - Celadon Co.

CORRUGATED ASBESTOS ROOFING

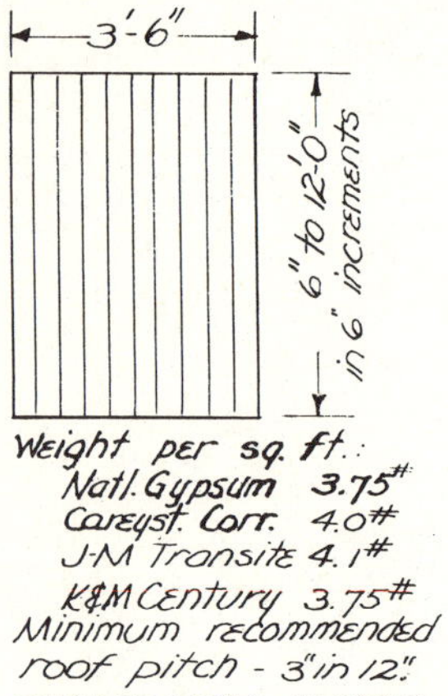

3'-6"
6" to 12'-0" in 6" increments
Weight per sq. ft.:
Nat'l. Gypsum 3.75#
Careyst. Corr. 4.0#
J-M Transite 4.1#
K&M Century 3.75#
Minimum recommended roof pitch - 3" in 12".

STANDARD SHEET

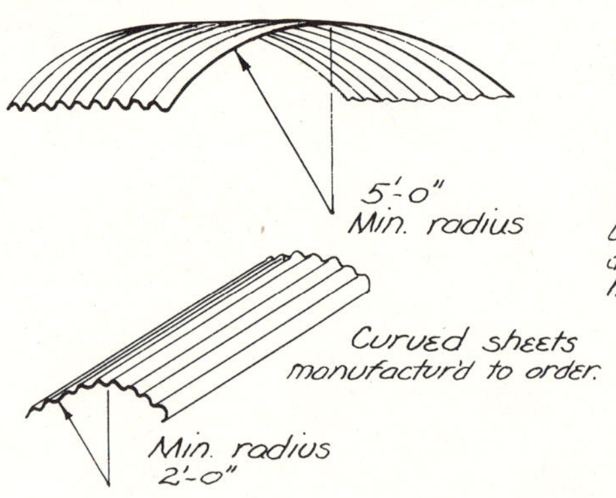

5'-0" Min. radius
Curved sheets manufactur'd to order.
Min. radius 2'-0"

CURVED CORRUGATED SHEETS

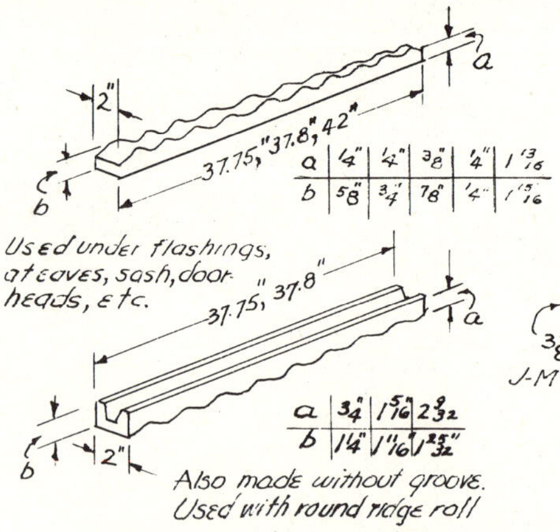

2"
37.75", 37.8", 42"
a
b
a | 1/4" | 1/4" | 3/8" | 1/4" | 1 13/16
b | 5/8" | 3/4" | 7/8" | 1/4" | 1 15/16
Used under flashings, at eaves, sash, door heads, etc.
37.75", 37.8"
a | 3/4" | 1 5/16 | 2 9/32
b | 1 1/4" | 1 1/16 | 1 25/32
2"
Also made without groove. Used with round ridge roll

ENCLOSURE (FILLER) STRIPS

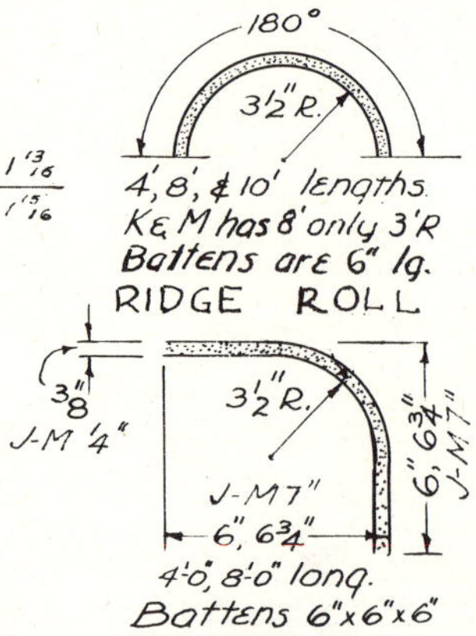

180°
3 1/2" R.
4', 8', & 10' lengths.
K&M has 8' only 3'R
Battens are 6" lg.
RIDGE ROLL
3/8"
J-M 1/4"
3 1/2" R.
J-M 7"
6", 6 3/4"
6", 6 3/4" J-M 7"
4'-0", 8'-0" long.
Battens 6"x6"x6"

CORNER ROLL

STANDARD SHAPES

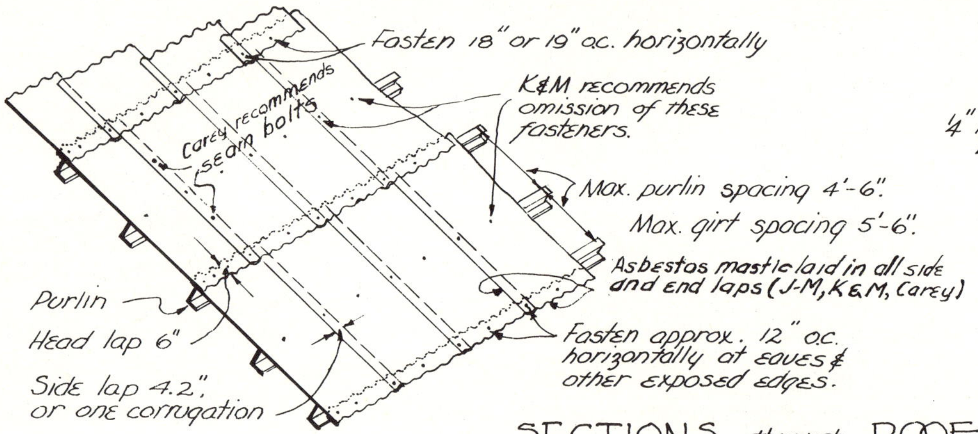

Fasten 18" or 19" o.c. horizontally
Carey recommends seam bolts
K&M recommends omission of these fasteners.
Max. purlin spacing 4'-6".
Max. girt spacing 5'-6".
Asbestos mastic laid in all side and end laps (J-M, K&M, Carey)
Purlin
Head lap 6"
Side lap 4.2", or one corrugation
Fasten approx. 12" o.c. horizontally at eaves & other exposed edges.

SECTIONS through ROOF

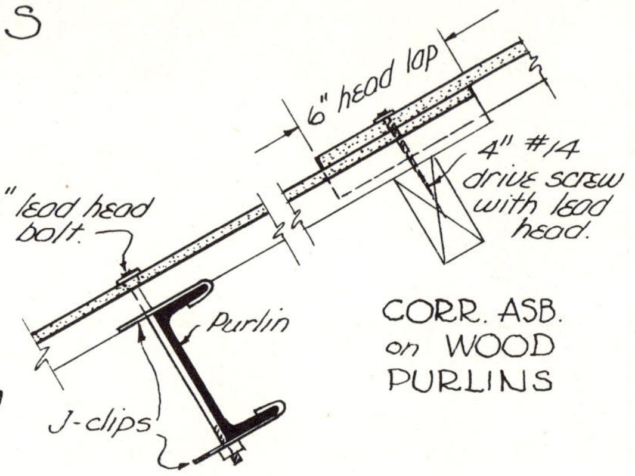

6" head lap
4" #14 drive screw with lead head.
1/4" lead head bolt.
Purlin
J-clips
CORR. ASB. on WOOD PURLINS

CORR. ASBESTOS on STEEL PURLIN
Consult mfrs. for other anchoring

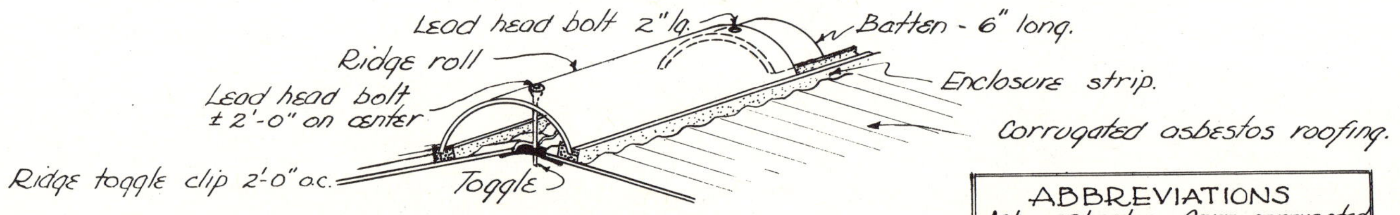

Lead head bolt 2" lg.
Batten - 6" long.
Ridge roll
Enclosure strip.
Lead head bolt ± 2'-0" on center
Corrugated asbestos roofing.
Ridge toggle clip 2'-0" o.c.
Toggle

DETAIL of RIDGE

ABBREVIATIONS
Asb. = asbestos Corr. = corrugated
K&M = Keasbey & Mattison Co.
J-M = Johns-Manville
Careyst. Corr. = Careystone Corrugated

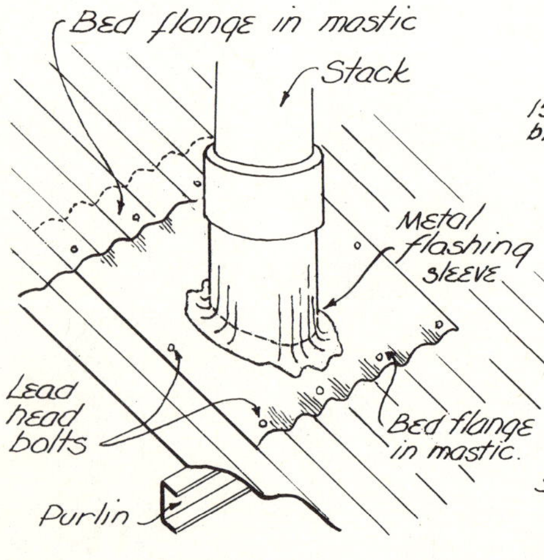

Bed flange in mastic
Stack
Metal flashing sleeve
Lead head bolts
Bed flange in mastic.
Purlin

STACK or VENT FLASHING

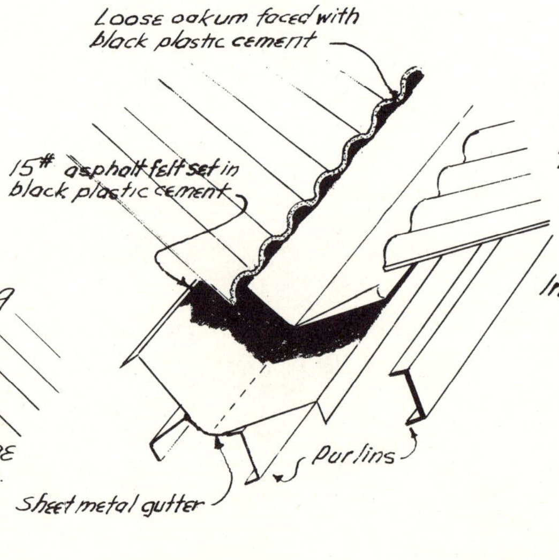

Loose oakum faced with black plastic cement
15# asphalt felt set in black plastic cement
Purlins
Sheet metal gutter

VALLEY FLASHING

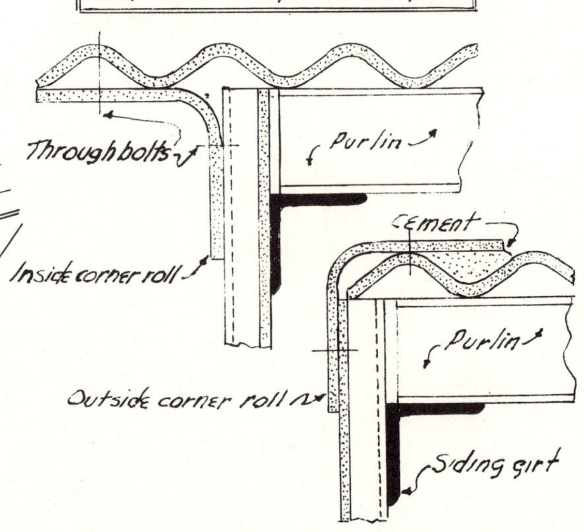

Through bolts
Purlin
Inside corner roll
Cement
Purlin
Outside corner roll
Siding girt

GABLE FLASHING

For add'l details see "Flashing." Data. ch'k'd by Keasbey & Mattison Co., Johns-Manville, Philip Carey Mfg. Co., & National Gypsum Co.

CANVAS ROOFING & PLASTIC ROOF DOMES

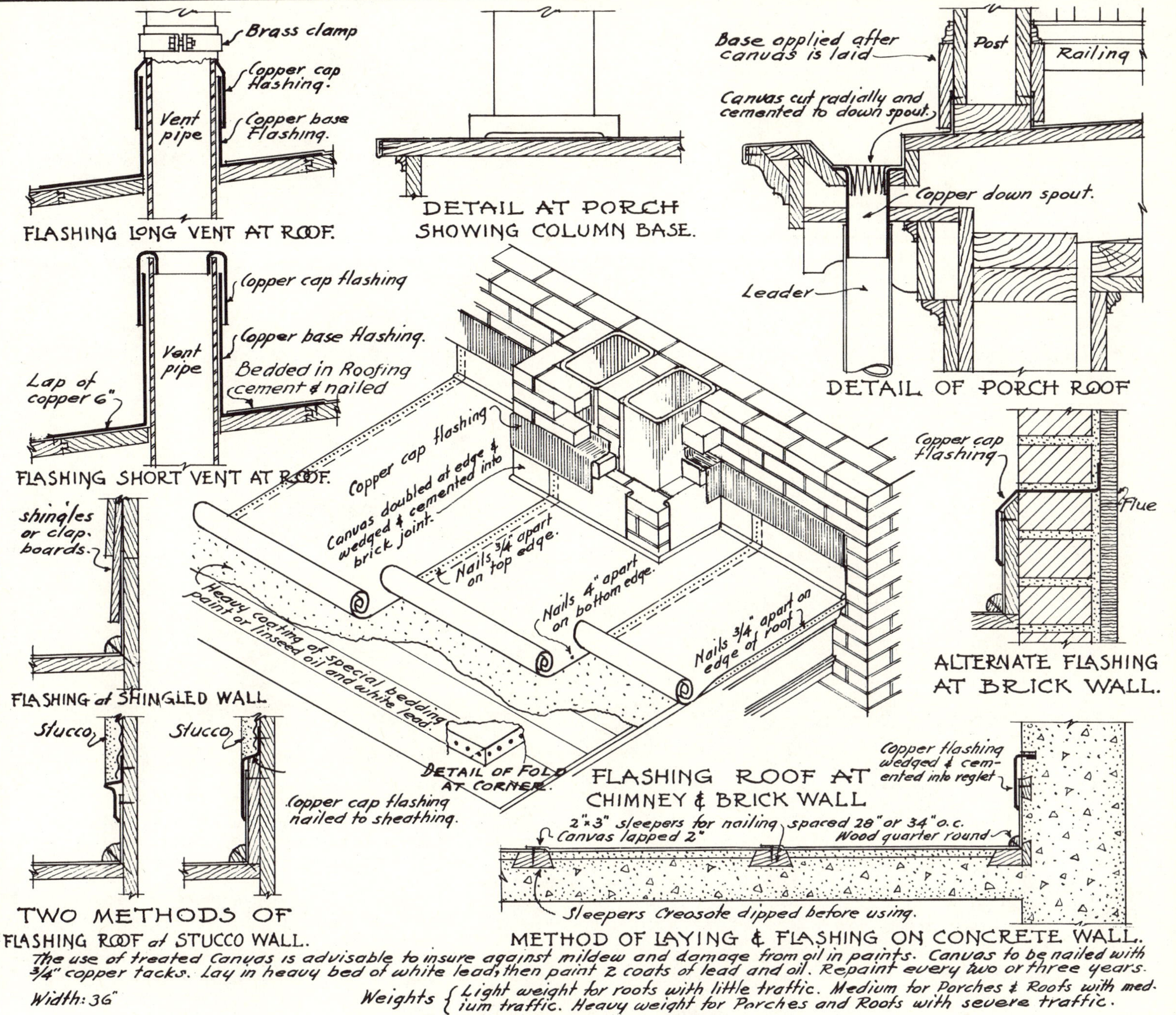
Brass clamp
Copper cap flashing.
Vent pipe
Copper base flashing.
FLASHING LONG VENT AT ROOF.
DETAIL AT PORCH SHOWING COLUMN BASE.
Base applied after canvas is laid
Post
Railing
Canvas cut radially and cemented to down spout.
Copper down spout.
Leader
DETAIL OF PORCH ROOF
Copper cap flashing
Vent pipe
Copper base flashing.
Bedded in Roofing cement & nailed
Lap of copper 6"
FLASHING SHORT VENT AT ROOF.
Copper cap flashing
Canvas doubled at edge & wedged & cemented into brick joint.
Nails 3/4" apart on top edge.
Nails 4" apart on bottom edge.
Nails 3/4" apart on edge of roof
Heavy coating of special bedding paint or linseed oil and white lead.
DETAIL OF FOLD AT CORNER.
FLASHING ROOF AT CHIMNEY & BRICK WALL
Copper cap flashing
Flue
ALTERNATE FLASHING AT BRICK WALL.
shingles or clap. boards.
FLASHING at SHINGLED WALL
Stucco
Stucco
Copper cap flashing nailed to sheathing.
TWO METHODS OF FLASHING ROOF at STUCCO WALL.
Copper flashing wedged & cemented into reglet
2"×3" sleepers for nailing, spaced 28" or 34" o.c.
Canvas lapped 2"
Wood quarter round
Sleepers Creosote dipped before using.
METHOD OF LAYING & FLASHING ON CONCRETE WALL.

The use of treated Canvas is advisable to insure against mildew and damage from oil in paints. Canvas to be nailed with 3/4" copper tacks. Lay in heavy bed of white lead, then paint 2 coats of lead and oil. Repaint every two or three years.

Width: 36"

Weights { *Light weight for roofs with little traffic. Medium for Porches & Roofs with medium traffic. Heavy weight for Porches and Roofs with severe traffic.*

CANVAS ROOFING

AP

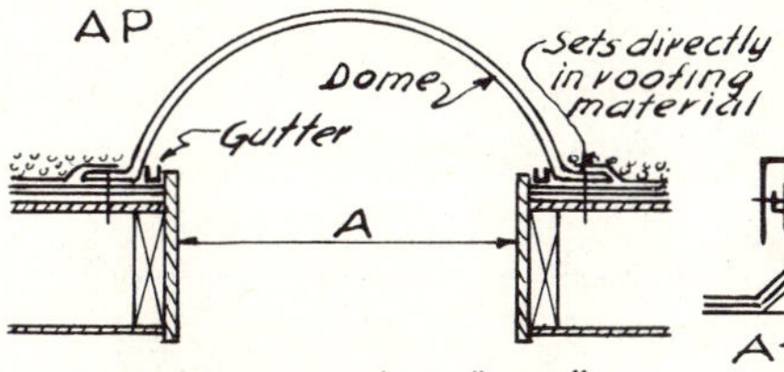
Dome
Sets directly in roofing material
Gutter
A

A- 16"×16", 24", 32", 48"
24"×24", 32", 48"
32"×32", 48"
48"×48", 72"

FOR USE DIRECTLY ON THE ROOF

W**

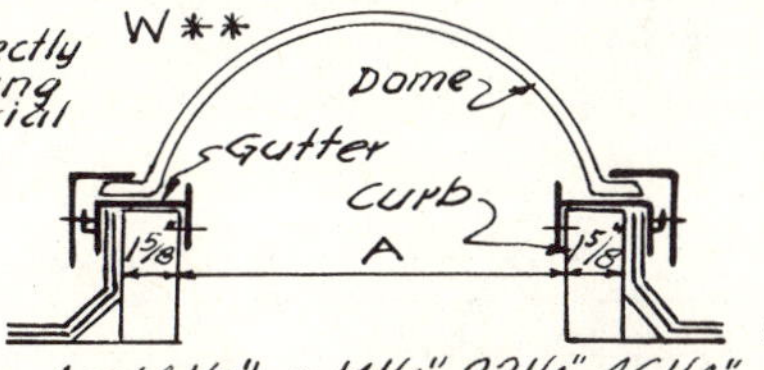
Dome
Gutter
Curb
1 5/16
A
1 5/16

A- 14 1/4" × 14 1/4", 22 1/4", 46 1/4"
19" × 19"
30 1/4" × 30 1/4", 46 1/4"
37" × 37", 75"
55" × 55"
57 1/2" × 69 1/2", 89 1/2"
93 1/4" × 113 1/4"

W**

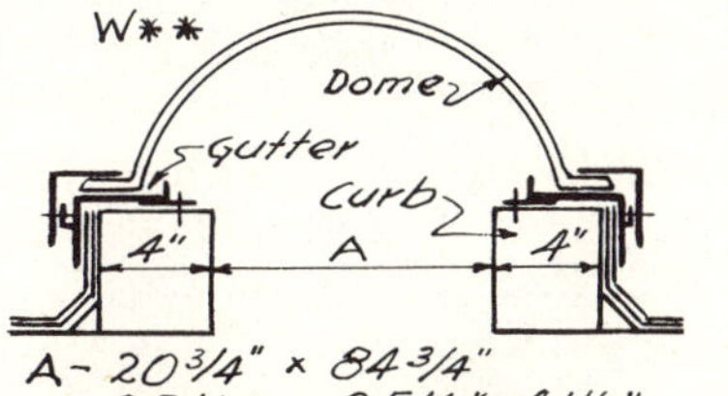
Dome
Gutter
Curb
4"
A
4"

A- 20 3/4" × 84 3/4"
25 1/2" × 25 1/2", 41 1/2"
32 1/4" × 32 1/2", 70 1/4"
50 1/4" × 50 1/4"
52 3/4" × 64 3/4", 84 3/4"
70 1/4" × 70 1/4"
88 1/2" × 108 1/2"

Other sizes available

FOR USE ON CURB CONSTRUCTION

M

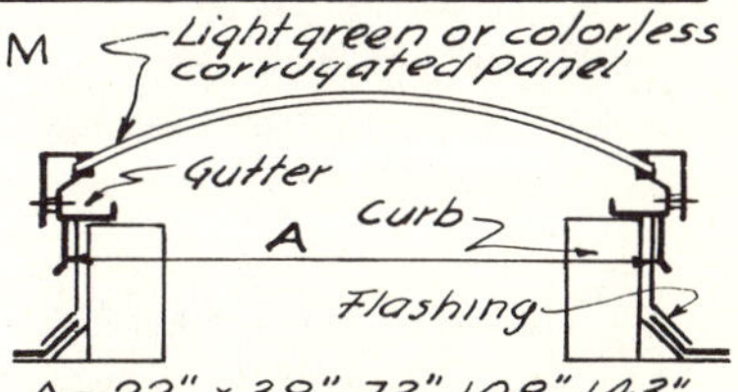
Light green or colorless corrugated panel
Gutter
Curb
A
Flashing

A- 22"×38", 73", 108", 143"
34"×38", 73", 108", 143"
38"×38"
46"×38", 73", 108", 143"
58"×38", 73", 108", 143"
70"×73", 108", 143"

Available in any custom shape and with prefabricated curb.

W & P CIRCULAR DOMES *dia. 19"*, 24", 31", 43", 54", 67", 79", 91".*

*Note: Domes are made in clear colorless or white translucent plastic. * = Mfrd. only by "P" ** = Similar domes also mfrd. by "P"*

PLASTIC ROOF DOMES

Data supplied by: AP = Architectural Plastic, Inc. W = Wasco Products, Inc. M = The Marco Co. P = Plastic Products of Texas.

ALUMINUM ROOFING and SIDING

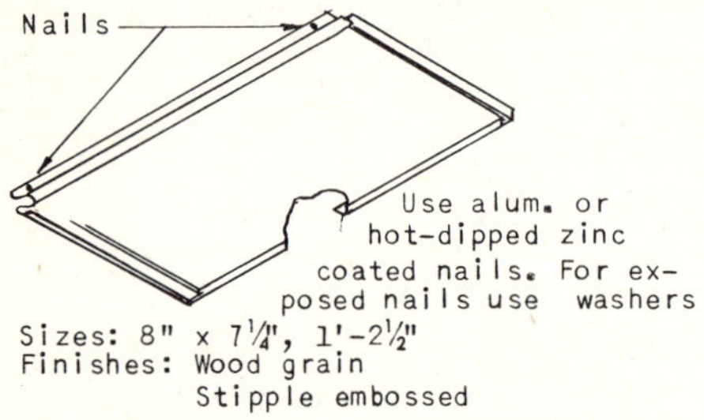
Nails
Use alum. or hot-dipped zinc coated nails. For exposed nails use washers
Sizes: 8" x 7¼", 1'-2½"
Finishes: Wood grain
Stipple embossed

INTERLOCKING SHINGLE

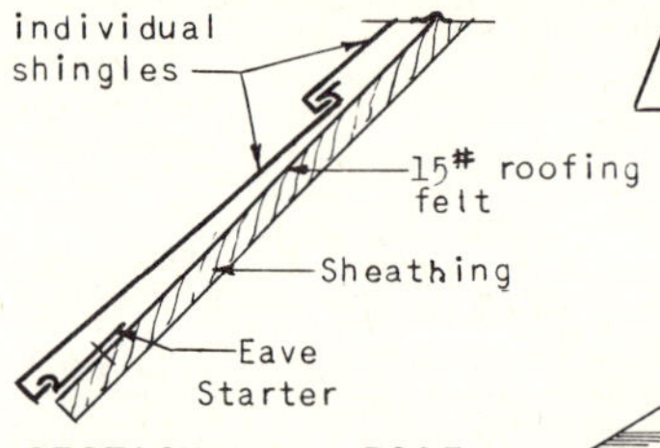
individual shingles
15# roofing felt
Sheathing
Eave Starter

SECTION THRU ROOF

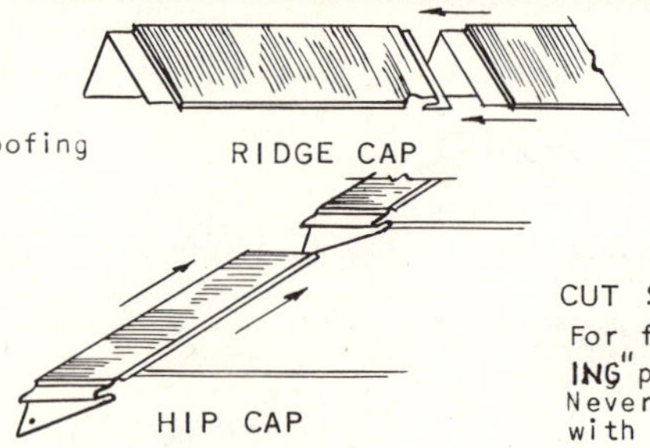
RIDGE CAP
HIP CAP

MANUFACTURED BY: REYNOLDS METALS CO.

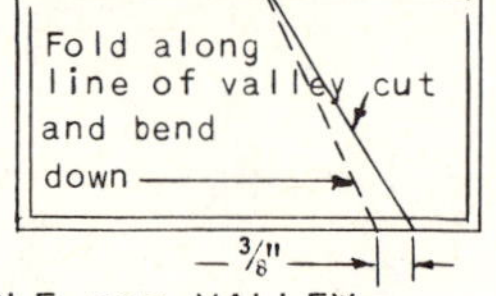
Fold along line of valley cut and bend down
3/8"

CUT SHINGLE FOR VALLEY

For flashing details see "FLASHING" pages, but use alum. only. Never use copper in contact with aluminum.

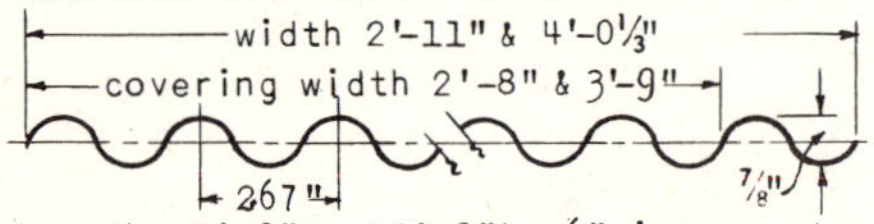
width 2'-11" & 4'-0⅓"
covering width 2'-8" & 3'-9"
2.67"
7/8"

Length: 5'-0" to 12'-0" by 6" increments
Thickness: .024" for 2'-11" width.
.032" for 4'-0⅓" width.
Finishes : Plain mill, No. E-5 pattern, stucco texture.

LOAD CARRYING CAPACITY					
Purlin spacing	Uniform load lbs/sq'		Purlin spacing	Uniform load lbs/sq'	
	.024"	.032"		.024"	.032"
3'-6"	79	106	6'-0"	27	35
4'-0"	60	80	6'-6"	23	29
4'-6"	48	63	7'-0"	20	25
5'-0"	39	50	7'-6"	17	22
5'-6"	32	41			

*‡ CORRUGATED ROOFING

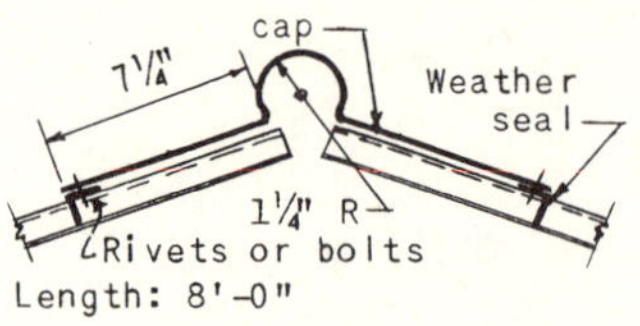
cap
7¼"
Weather seal
1¼" R
Rivets or bolts
Length: 8'-0"

RIDGE CAP

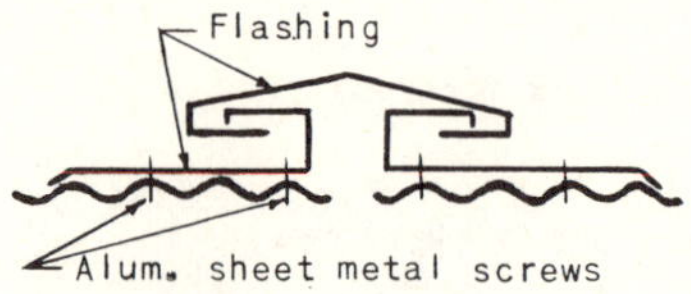
Flashing
Alum. sheet metal screws

ROOFING EXPANSION JOINT

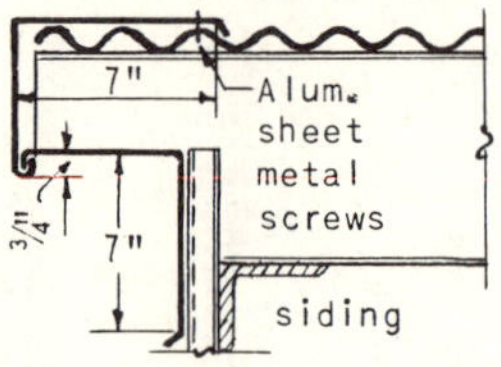
7"
Alum. sheet metal screws
3/4"
7"
siding

GABLE

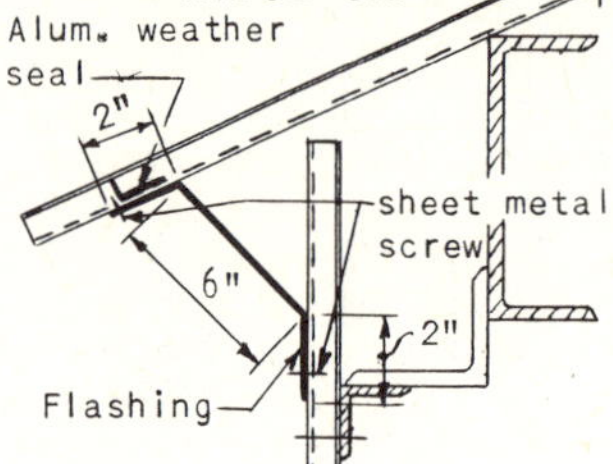
Alum. weather seal
2"
sheet metal screw
6"
2"
Flashing

EAVE

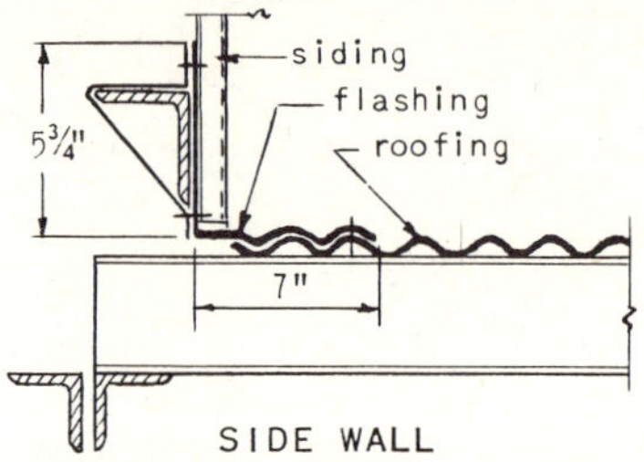
siding
flashing
roofing
5¾"
7"

SIDE WALL

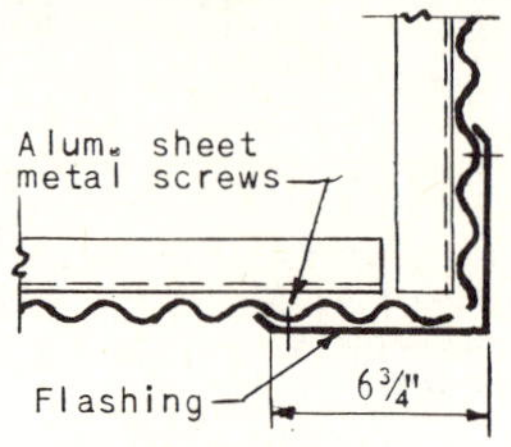
Alum. sheet metal screws
Flashing
6¾"

CORNER

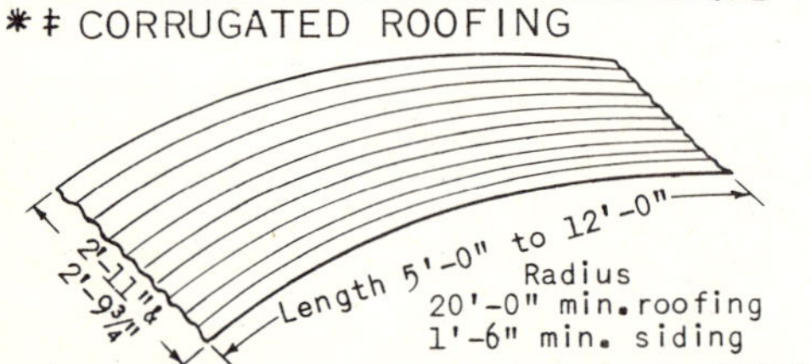
2'-11" & 2'-9¾"
Length 5'-0" to 12'-0"
Radius
20'-0" min. roofing
1'-6" min. siding

*‡ CORRUGATED ROOFING & SIDING

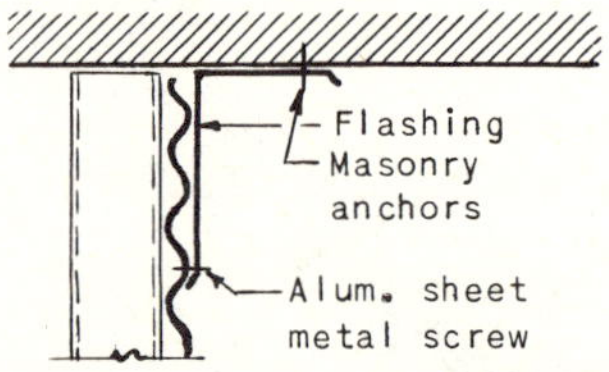
Flashing
Masonry anchors
Alum. sheet metal screw

SIDING to MASONRY

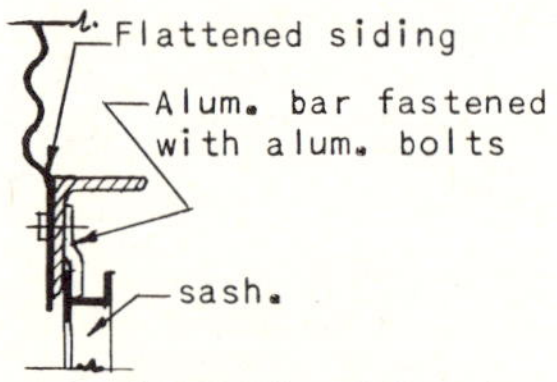
Flattened siding
Alum. bar fastened with alum. bolts
sash.

WINDOW JAMB

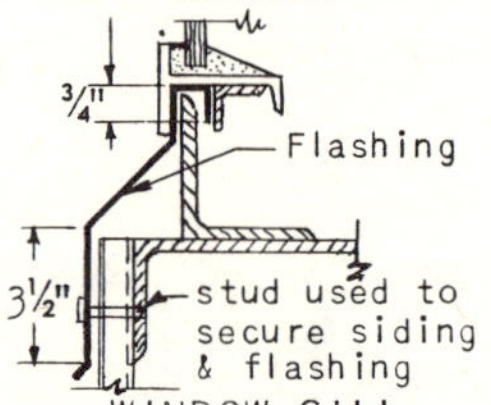
3/4"
Flashing
3½"
stud used to secure siding & flashing

WINDOW SILL

* FLASHING DETAILS Scale 1" = 1'-0"

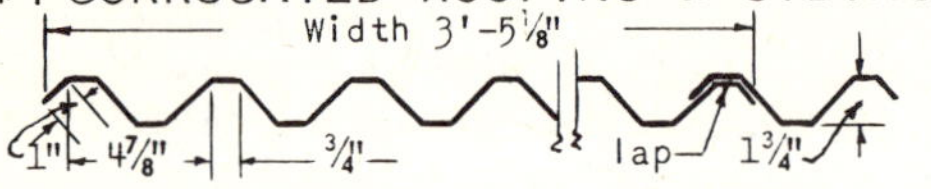
Width 3'-5⅛"
1"
4⅞"
3/4"
lap
1¾"

* V-BEAM ROOFING & SIDING

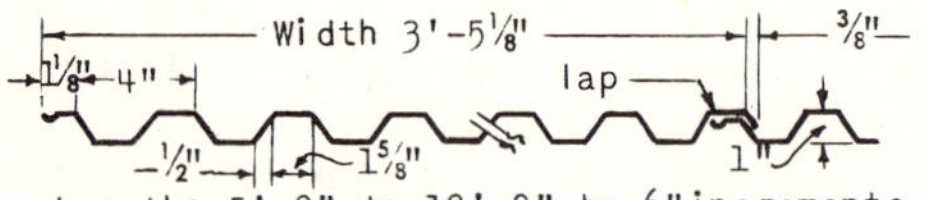
Width 3'-5⅛"
3/8"
1/8"
4"
lap
1/2"
1⅝"
1"

Length: 5'-0" to 18'-0" by 6" increments
Thickness: .032"
Finish : No. E-5 pattern, stucco texture

*‡ RIBBED INDUSTRIAL SIDING

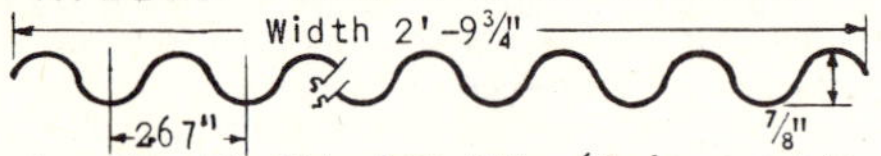
Width 2'-9¾"
2.67"
7/8"

Length: 5'-0" to 12'-0" by 6" increments
Thickness: .024" & .032"
Finish : Plain mill, No. E-5 pattern stucco texture.

*‡ CORRUGATED SIDING

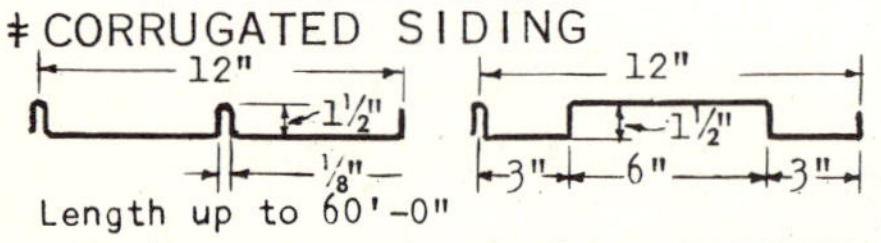
12"
1½"
1/8"
12"
1½"
3"
6"
3"

Length up to 60'-0"

** DOUBLE RIB 3-6-3 FLUTED

CORRUGATED ROOFING (Minimum roof pitch 3" in 12")
End lap should be 6" min.; side lap, 1½ corrugation. Fasten only through crown of corrugation. Space of fasteners every fourth corrugation; for extreme wind conditions, space at every third corrugation. For side lap fasteners space 12" o.c. max.

V-BEAM ROOFING (Minimum roof pitch 3" in 12")
End laps should be 6" min.; side lap, one rib. Fasten only through valley of rib Space fasteners every rib at end of supports. For side lap fasteners, space 12" o. c. max.

V-BEAM SIDING
End lap should be 4"; side lap one rib. Fasten only through valley of corrugation. Space fasteners every rib at ends of sheet and every other rib at intermediate supports. For side lap fasteners, space 12" o.c. max.

CORRUGATED SIDING
End lap should be 4" min.; side lap, one corrugation. Fastening may be through high or low corrugation. Spacing of fasteners every fourth corrugation; for extreme wind, every third corrugation. For side lap fasteners space 12" o.c. max.

DOUBLE RIB & 3-6-3 FLUTED SIDING
End lap should be 2" min. After plates are in position, weld to supporting members.

NOTE: Side lap should be laid away from prevailing wind.

DATA SUPPLIED BY: * ALUMINUM CO. OF AMERICA, ‡ REYNOLDS METALS CO., ** THE R.C. MAHON CO.

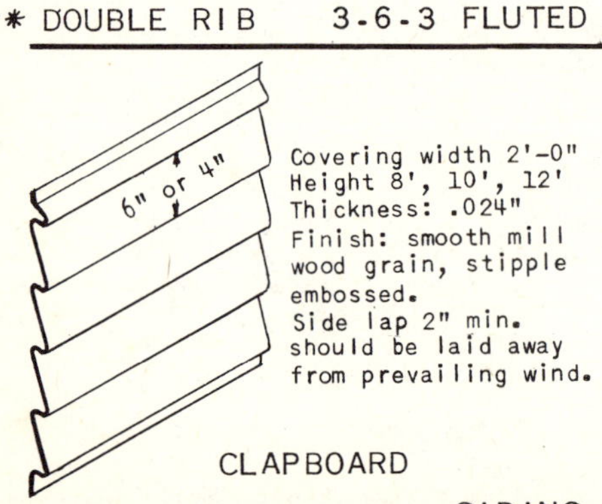
6" or 4"
Covering width 2'-0"
Height 8', 10', 12'
Thickness: .024"
Finish: smooth mill wood grain, stipple embossed.
Side lap 2" min. should be laid away from prevailing wind.

CLAPBOARD

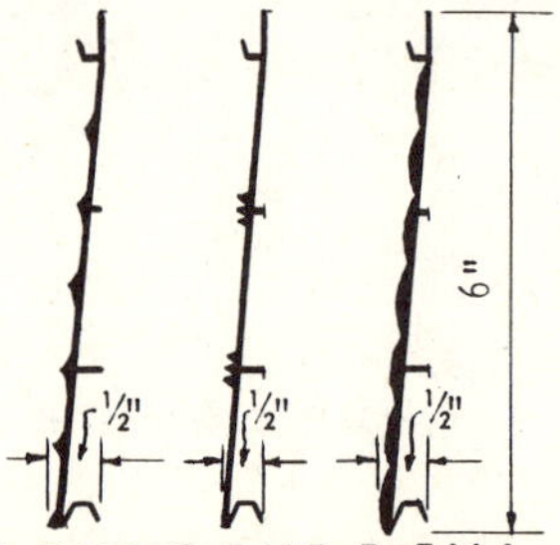
6"
1/2"
1/2"
1/2"
P-5413 P-5415 P-5414

EXTRUSIONS

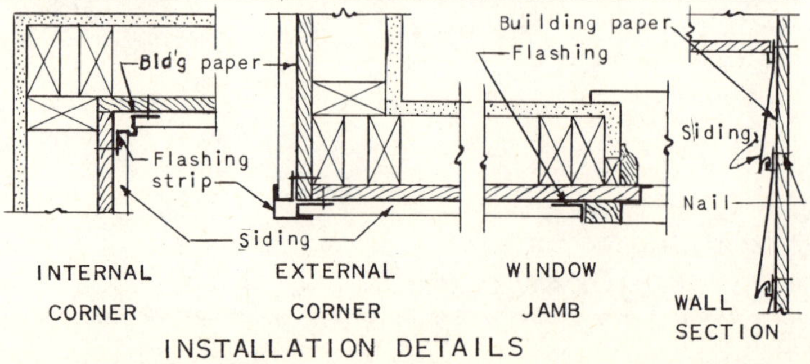
Bld'g paper
Flashing strip
Siding
Building paper
Flashing
Siding
Nail
INTERNAL CORNER
EXTERNAL CORNER
WINDOW JAMB
WALL SECTION

INSTALLATION DETAILS

SIDING

MANUFACTURED BY: REYNOLDS METAL CO.

GALVANIZED STEEL ROOFING and SIDING

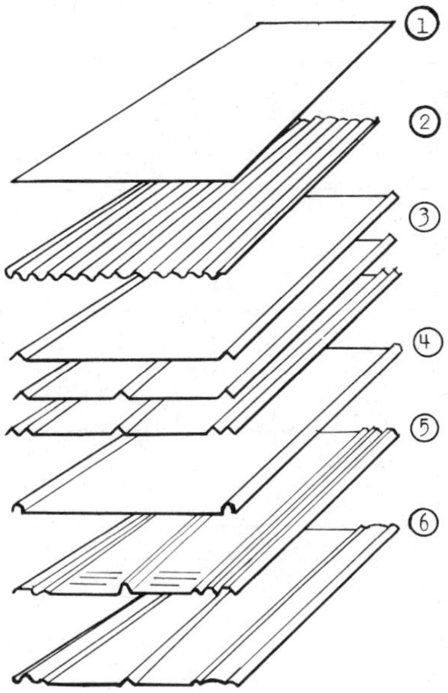
①
②
③
④
⑤
⑥

STANDARD SHEET SIZES						
USE	TYPES	MFG*	GAUGES	WIDTH	LENGTH ‡	TO WEATHER
Roofing & siding	① PLAIN SHEET					
	26½" wide sheet	R	24 & lighter	26½"	50'	24"
		B	26 to 29	26½"	50'**	24"
	② CORRUGATED SHEET					
	1¼" Corrugations	R	20 & lighter	26" or 27½"	5'-12'	24"
		B	20 to 29	25" or 26"	6'-12'	24"
	2½" Corrugations	R	16 & lighter	26" or 27½"	5'-12'	24"
		B	14 to 29	26" or 27½"	6'-12'	24"
	③ V-CRIMP SHEETS					
	2 V-crimped	R	26 to 29	25⅛"	6'-12'	24"
	3 V-crimped	R	26 to 29	25"	6'-12'	24"
	5 V-crimped	R	26 to 29	26"	6'-12'	24"
		B	26 thru 29	26"	6'-12'	24"
	④ PRESSED STANDING SEAM SHEET					
		R	24 & lighter	24"+	5'-12'	24"
	⑤ TRIPLE-DRAIN SHEET					
		R	26, 28, 29		5'-12'	24"
	⑥ STORMPROOF SHEET					
		B	26, 28, 29	26⅛"	6'-12'	24"

* R = Republic Steel Corporation * B = Bethlehem Steel Company
‡ Lengths are restricted to multiples of 1 ft.
** Made up of 4 sheets with double cross lock seams

Bethlehem & Republic

WITHOUT NAILING FLANGE WITH NAILING FLANGE
Recommended for use with V-crimp & plain sheets

Bethlehem & Republic

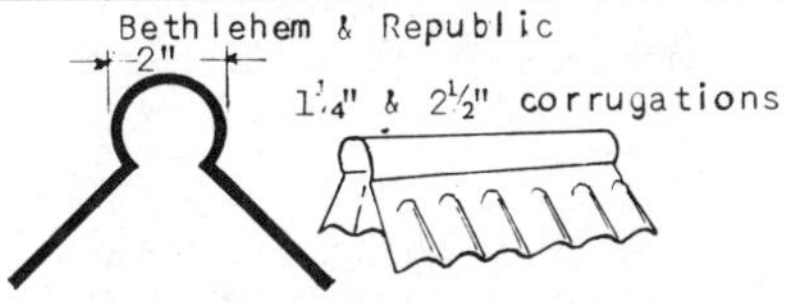
2"
1¼" & 2½" corrugations

R: 10" to 12" girths
B: 8", 10", 12" & 14" girths
CORRUGATED

Republic

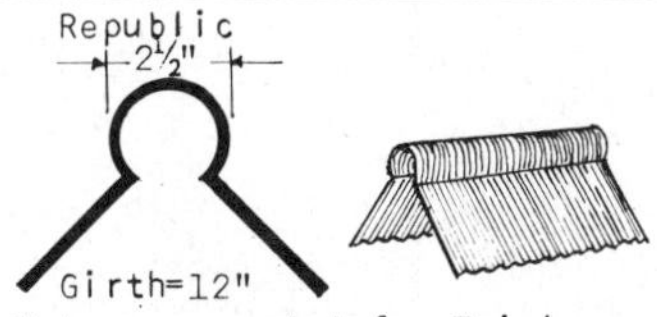
2½"
Girth=12"

Not recommended for Triple-Drain roofing sheets
CRIMPED

Bethlehem & Republic

B: 4¼"
R: 5"

Finisher on hip angles or plain ridge cap.
PLAIN OR CRIMPED

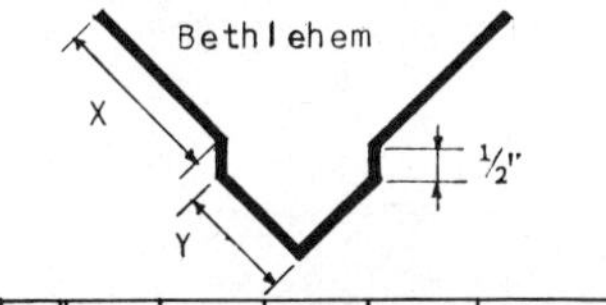
Bethlehem
X
Y
½"

X	3"	3½"	4"	4½"	5½"
Y	1½"	2"	2½"	3"	4"

Girths: 10", 12", 14", 16" & 20"
FORMED VALLEY
NOTE: Rolled valley available in 50' length, girths 8" to 30"

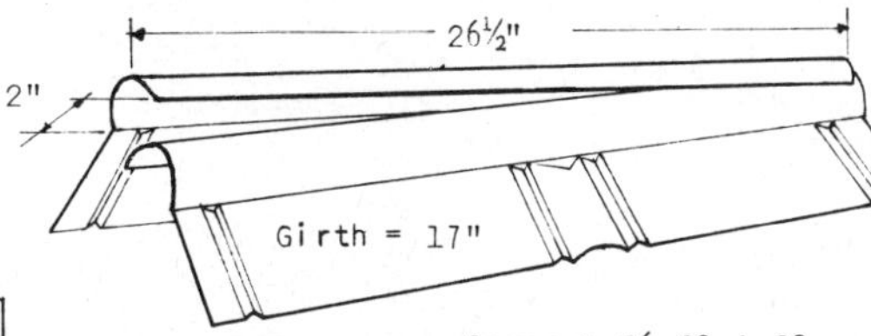
26½"
2"
Girth = 17"

Gauges: 26, 28 & 29
FOR STORMPROOF ROOFING SHEETS

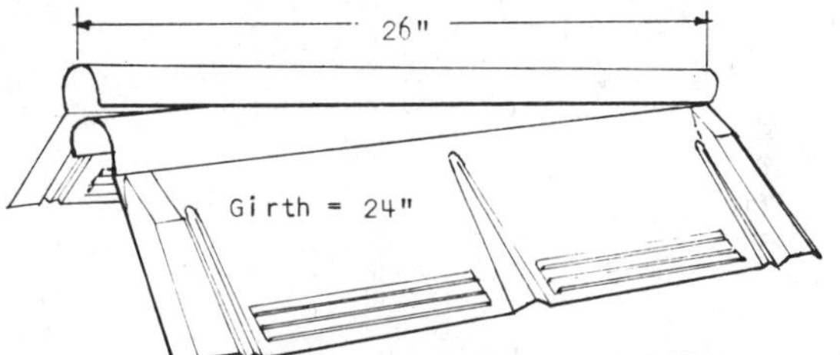
26"
Girth = 24"

FOR TRIPLE-DRAIN ROOF

2-PIECE ADJUSTABLE RIDGE ROLLS

NOTE: The girth is the width of sheet required to form the shape.

FORMED RIDGE ROLLS

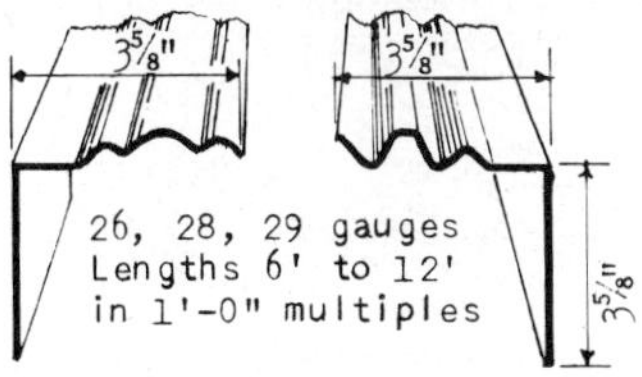
3⅝"
3⅝"
3⅝"
26, 28, 29 gauges
Lengths 6' to 12'
in 1'-0" multiples

GABLE-END FINISHER GABLE-END STARTER

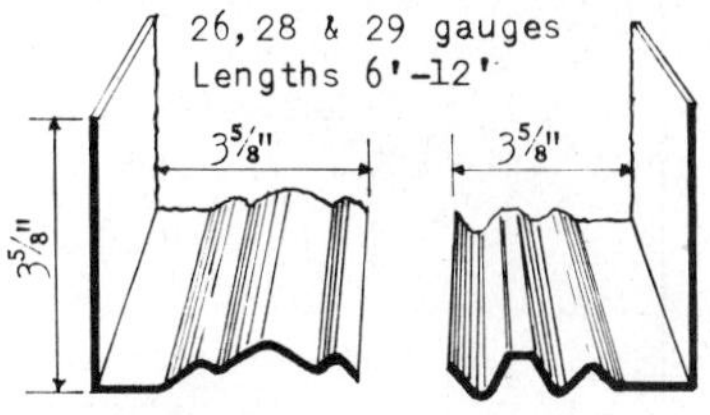
26, 28 & 29 gauges
Lengths 6'-12'
3⅝"
3⅝"
3⅝"

SIDE-WALL FINISHER SIDE-WALL STARTER

STORMPROOF

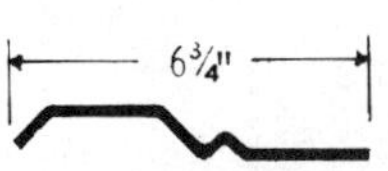
6¾"

GABLE-END FINISHER

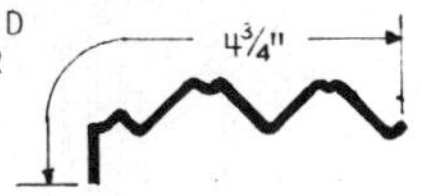
4¾"

GABLE-END STARTER

NOTE: Finisher laps over roofing sheet. Starter goes under roofing sheet.

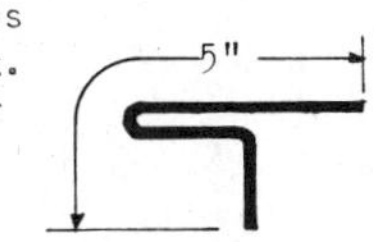
5"

OVERHANGING EAVES DRIP

TRIPLE-DRAIN

STORMPROOF & TRIPLE-DRAIN ACCESSORIES

Bethlehem & Republic

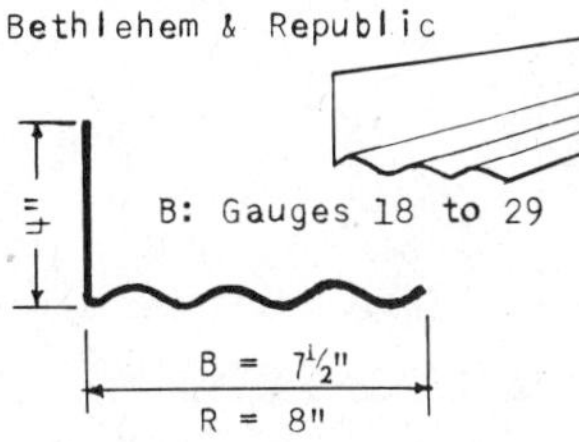
4"
B: Gauges 18 to 29
B = 7½"
R = 8"

CORRUGATED SIDE-WALL FLASHING

Bethlehem & Republic

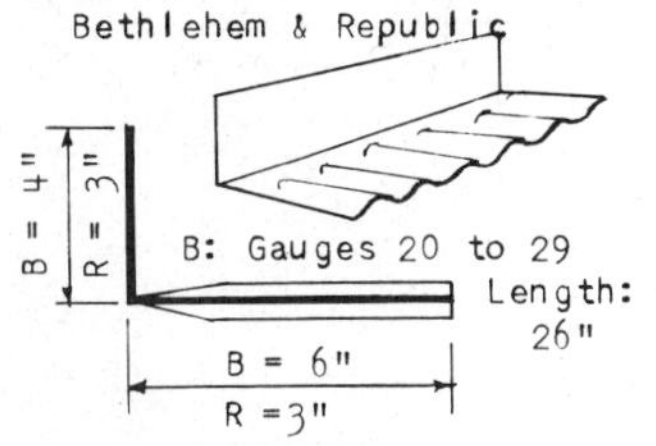
B = 4"
R = 3"
B: Gauges 20 to 29
Length: 26"
B = 6"
R = 3"

CORRUGATED END-WALL FLASHING

CORRUGATED SHEET ACCESSORIES

NOTE: Bethlehem ridge rolls, valley, and corrugated side-wall flashing available in lengths up to 10'-0".

NOTE:
For plain roll roofing details see "Zinc Roofing".
For construction details of corrugated and other types of sheet roofing see "Protected Metal Roofing & Siding".

DATA CHECKED BY REPUBLIC STEEL CORPORATION & BETHLEHEM STEEL COMPANY

PROTECTED METAL ROOFING and SIDING

TYPES

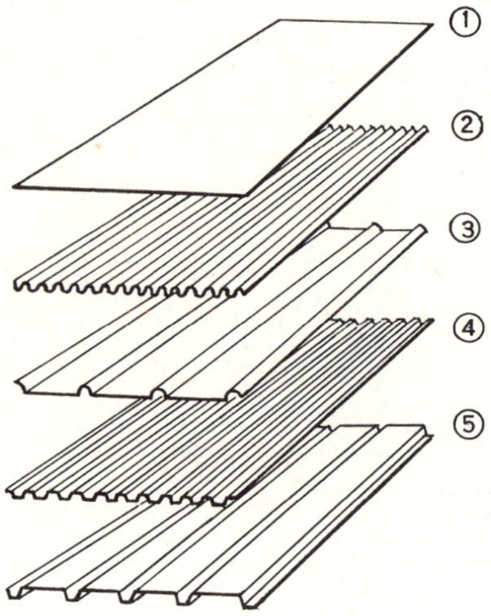

①
②
③
④
⑤

STANDARD SHEET SIZES

USE	TYPES	MFG.*	GAUGES	WIDTH	LENGTH	TO WEATHER
Roofing & siding	① PLAIN SHEET					
	36" width	ASB P R	18,20,22,24 18,20,22,24,26 22,24,26,28	36"	0-12'	
For roofing only	② CORRUGATED SHEET					
	2½" corrugations 2⅝" corrugations	ASB P R	18,20,22,24 18,20,22,24,26 18,20,22,24	33"	0-12'	29¼" 29½" 29¾"
For siding only	② CORRUGATED SHEET					
	2½" corrugations 2⅝" corrugations	ASB P R	18,20,22,24 18,20,22,24,26 18,20,22,24	34" 34" 33"	0-12'	31½" 32" 29¾"
Roofing & siding	③ MANSARD SHEET					
	6$\frac{1}{16}$" corrugations	ASB P R	18,20,22,24 20,22,24	33" 32⅜" 33"	0-12'	29¾" 30" 30"
	④ "V" BEAM SHEET					
	5.3" corrugations	ASB P R	18,20,22,24	30½" 29" 29"	0-12'	27¼" 26¾" 26¾"
Roof deck	⑤ 5 RIBS					
		P	18,20,22	24"	0-24'	24"

* ASB = American Steel Band Co. P = Plasteel R = Robertson Co.
Note: "P" lengths can be had in multiples of one foot
ASB & R can be had in any length up to 12'-0"; not restricted to multiples of one foot

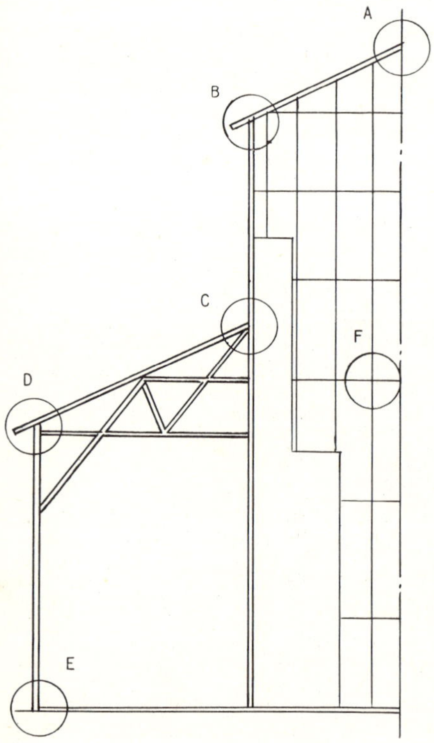

A
B
C
D
E
F

CORRUGATED SHEETS OVER STEEL FRAME

Data supplied by: American Steel Band.

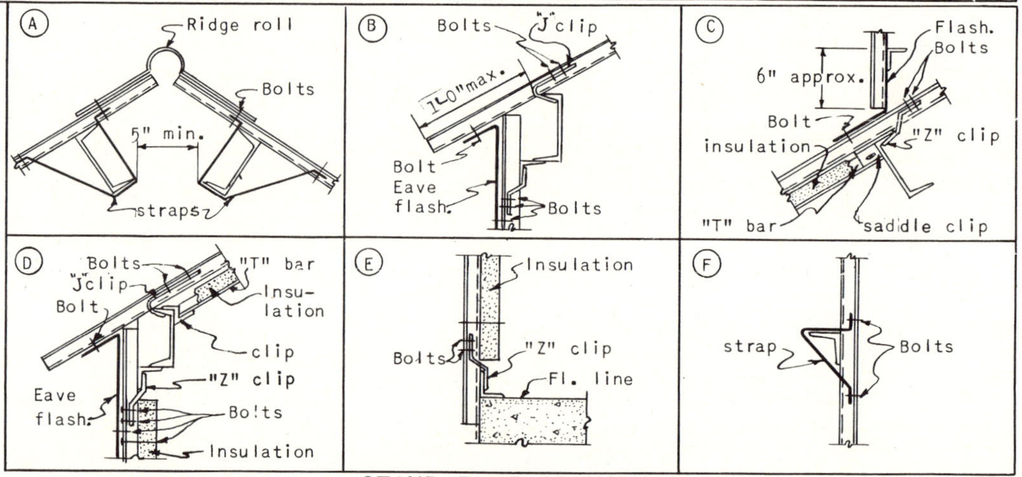

A
Ridge roll
Bolts
5" min.
straps
B
Bolts
"J" clip
1'-0" max.
Bolt
Eave flash.
Bolts
C
Flash.
Bolts
6" approx.
Bolt
insulation
"Z" clip
"T" bar
saddle clip
D
Bolts
"J" clip
Bolt
"T" bar
Insu-lation
clip
"Z" clip
Eave flash.
Bolts
Insulation
E
Insulation
Bolts
"Z" clip
Fl. line
F
strap
Bolts

STANDARD FASTENING

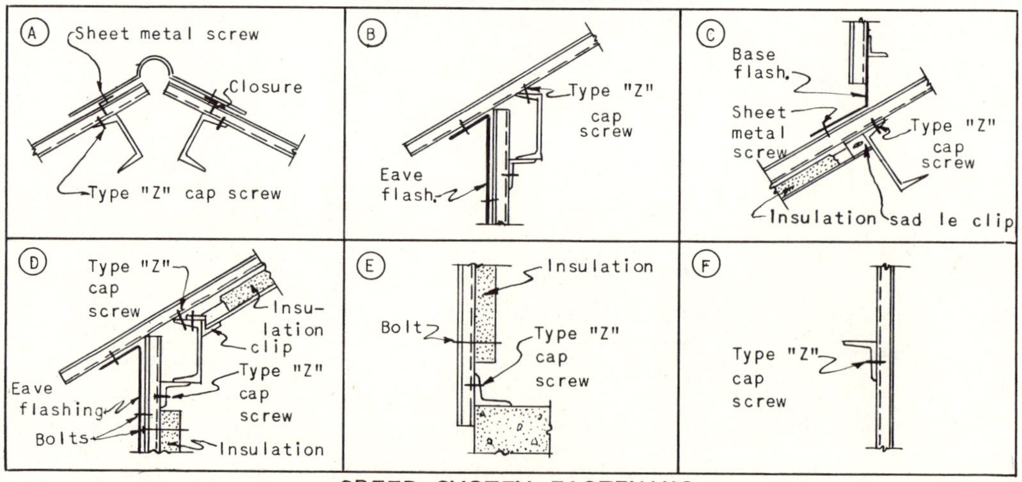

A
Sheet metal screw
Closure
Type "Z" cap screw
B
Type "Z" cap screw
Eave flash.
C
Base flash.
Sheet metal screw
Type "Z" cap screw
Insulation
sad le clip
D
Type "Z" cap screw
Insu-lation
clip
Type "Z" cap screw
Eave flashing
Bolts
Insulation
E
Insulation
Bolt
Type "Z" cap screw
F
Type "Z" cap screw

SPEED SYSTEM FASTENING

CONSTRUCTION DETAILS

Note: The principles of correct detailing of protected metal roofing are in general similar to those which apply to galvanized iron and aluminum roofing with the exception that bolts and nuts are used in place of rivets. For details of sandwich (insulation type) and V crimp roofings see pages on galvanized iron and aluminum roofings.

COPPER ROOFING

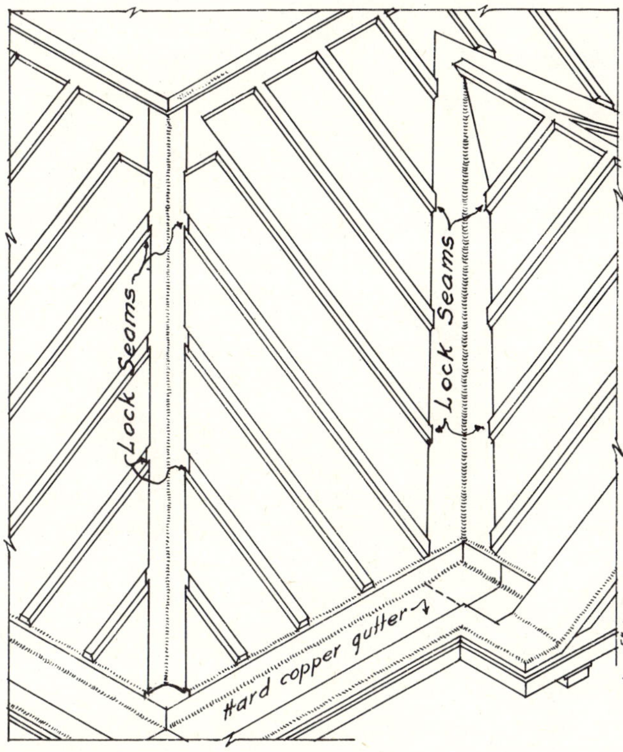
Lock Seams
Lock Seams
Hard copper gutter

SPACING OF RIBS
Spacing of ribs or battens is dependent on design. Economical spacings for stock copper sheets are 21" with 23" next. Using 2"x2" battens spacing is 3" less than width of sheet; sheets are manufactured in multiples of 2". Cross seams usually 96" apart and soldered, only when roof is less than 15° Pitch. Ribs are nailed to roof.

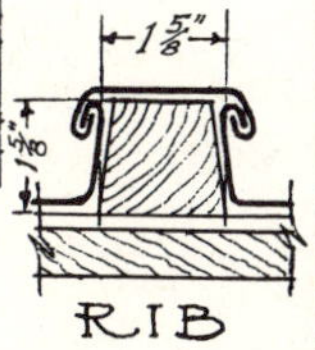
1 5/8"
1 5/8"

RIB

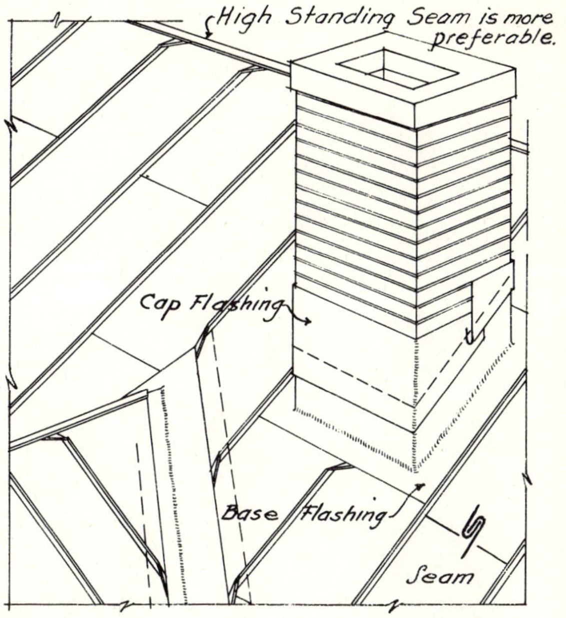
High Standing Seam is more preferable.
Cap Flashing
Base Flashing
Seam

1"

STANDING SEAM

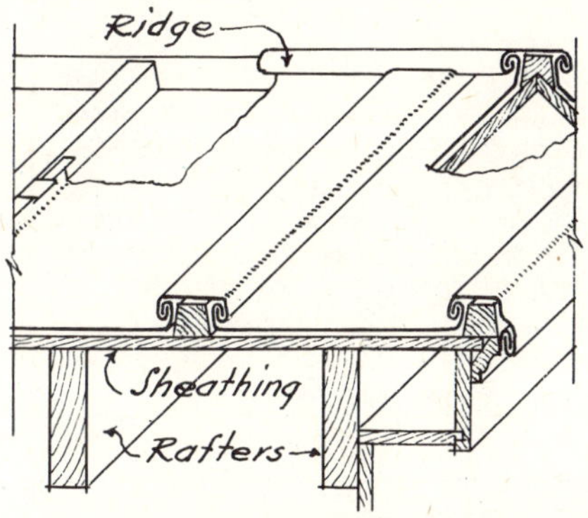
Ridge
Sheathing
Rafters

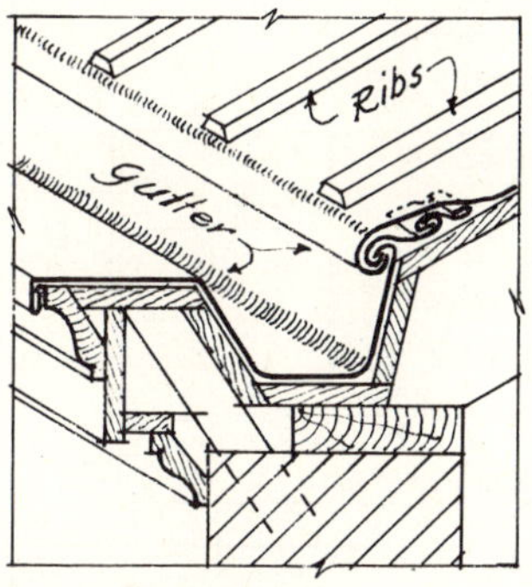
Ribs
Gutter

RIBBED SEAM ROOF
For pitches not less than 3" to 12"

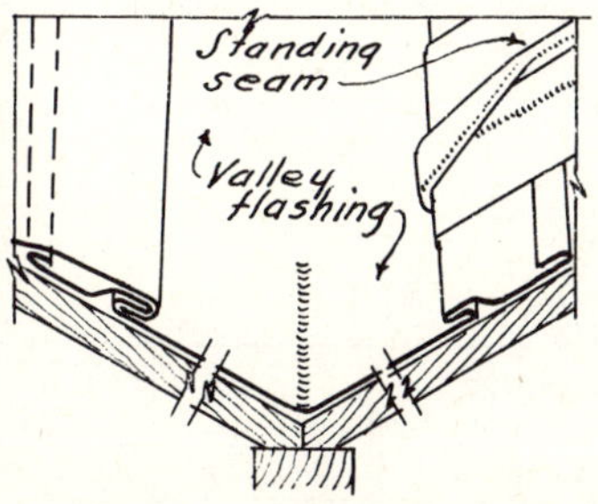
Standing seam
Valley flashing

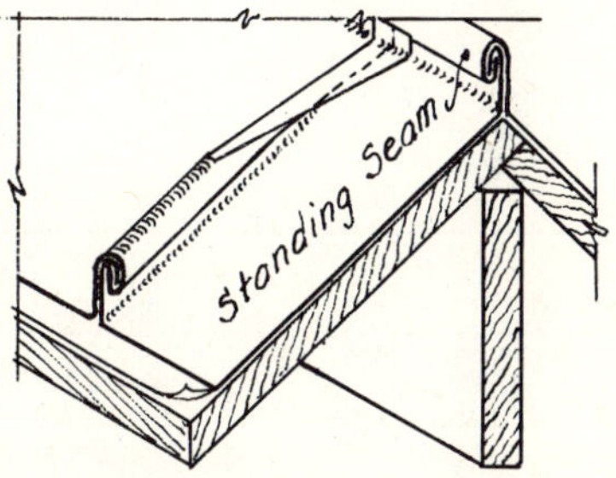
Standing Seam

SEAM AT VALLEY. SEAM AT RIDGE.
(Seam at gutter similar.)

Spacing of seams is dependent on design. Using usual 1" high seam, spacing of seams is 3 1/4" less than the width of a sheet; that is a 24" sheet would result in 20 3/4" spacing of seams. Cross seams are usually 96" apart, and soldered when roof is under 15° steep. All copper secured by cleats.

STANDING SEAM ROOF
For pitches 2 1/2" to 12" or steeper.

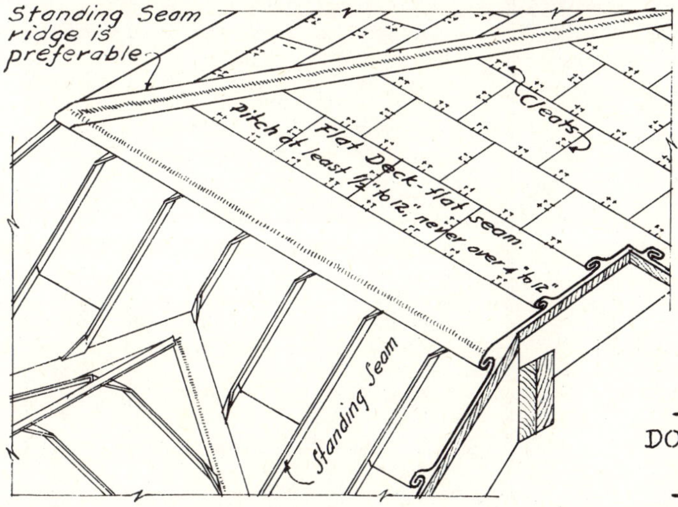
Standing Seam ridge is preferable
Cleats
Pitch at least 1/4" to 12", never over 4" to 12"
Flat Deck - flat seam.
Standing Seam

STANDING

DOUBLE LOCK

1"
Solder

SINGLE LOCK

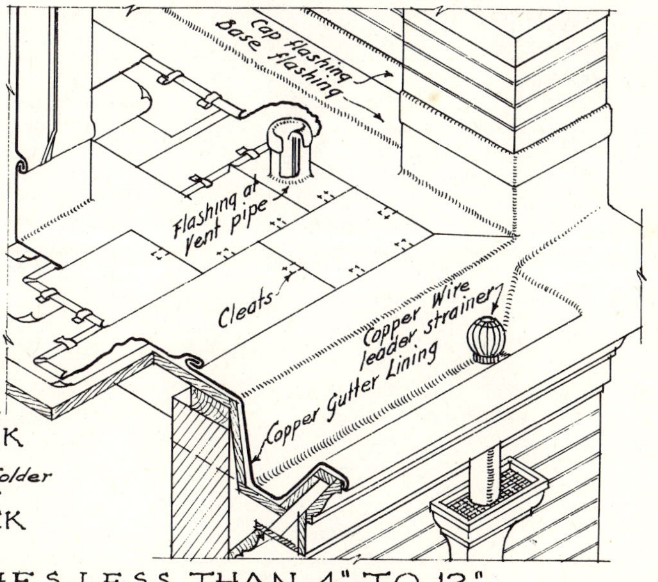
Cap flashing
Base flashing
Flashing at Vent pipe
Cleats
Copper Wire leader strainer
Copper Gutter Lining

Sheet size usually used 16" x 18" with 3/4" lock on all sides. Seams may be soldered or white leaded.

FLAT SEAM ROOFS - FOR PITCHES LESS THAN 4" TO 12".

COPPER ROOFING (16 & 20 oz. COPPER)
Methods recommended by the Copper and Brass Research Association.

MONEL ROOFING

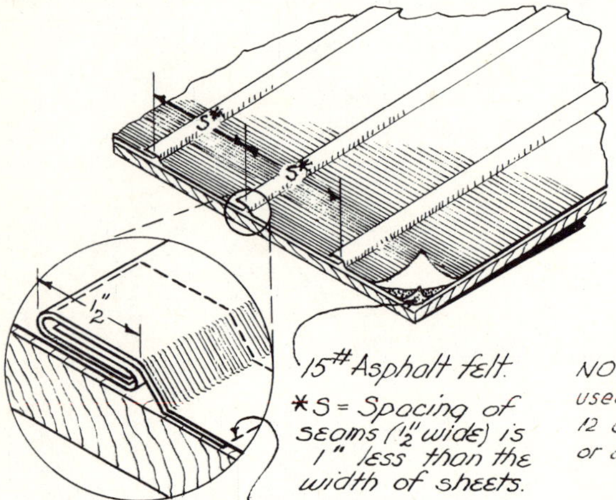
S*
S*
1/2"
15# Asphalt felt
*S = Spacing of seams (1/2" wide) is 1" less than the width of sheets.
Metal cleats 1'-0" o.c.

LOCKED FLAT SEAM

For pitches less than 3 to 12. Recommended for smaller roof areas.

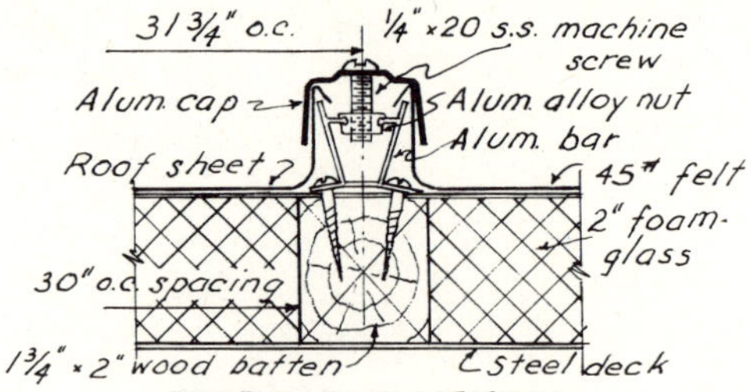
31 3/4" o.c.
1/4" × 20 s.s. machine screw
Alum. cap
Alum. alloy nut
Alum. bar
Roof sheet
45# felt
2" foam-glass
30" o.c. spacing
1 3/4" × 2" wood batten
Steel deck

TYPE B BATTEN

Used on flat or domed roofs

Scale: 3" = 1'-0"

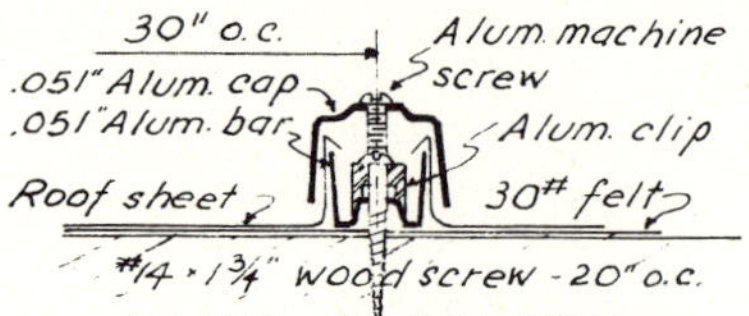
30" o.c.
Alum. machine screw
.051" Alum. cap
.051" Alum. bar
Alum. clip
Roof sheet
30# felt
#14 × 1 3/4" wood screw - 20" o.c.

TYPE A BATTEN

Scale: 3" = 1'-0"

NOTE: These battens used for pitches 3 to 12 or over and flat or domed roofs.

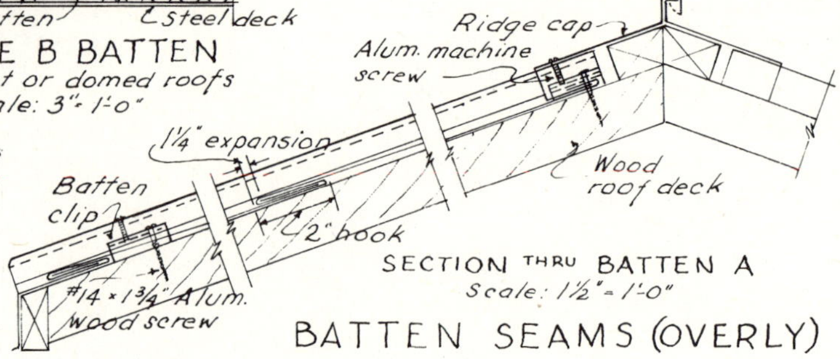
Ridge cap
Alum. machine screw
1 1/4" expansion
Wood roof deck
Batten clip
2" hook
#14 × 1 3/4" Alum. wood screw

SECTION THRU BATTEN A

Scale: 1 1/2" = 1'-0"

Data supplied by: Overly Mfg. Company

BATTEN SEAMS (OVERLY)

These aluminum battens are often used with Monel roofing but may be used with any other type of non-corrosive metal roofing.

The following maximum sheet widths are recommended to insure against buckling: For No. 26 gauge; 20" wide. For No. 25 gauge & heavier; 24" wide.

Scale 1/4" = 1'-0". Details at 1/2 full size.

TYPES of SEAMS

SHEET WEIGHTS & SIZES

U.S.S. GAUGE	MAX. WIDTH & LENGTH*	THICKNESS	WGT. #/□'	U.S.S. GAUGE	MAX. WIDTH & LENGTH*	THICKNESS	WGT. #/□'
Most commonly used gauges.				No. 21	36"×120"	.034	1.56
No. 26	36"×96"	.018"	0.827	" 20	36"×120"	.037	1.70
" 25	36"×120"	.021"	0.965	" 19	36"×120"	.043	1.98
" 24	36"×120"	.025"	1.15	" 18	36"×120"	.050	2.30
Other available gauges.				" 17	36"×120"	.056	2.57
No. 23	36"×120"	.028"	1.29	" 16	36"×120"	.062	2.85
" 22	36"×120"	.031"	1.42				

*St'd widths are 30 & 36" St'd lengths; 96" & 120" (Except .018" only 96" lengths)

Notes: Do not nail through roofing sheets. Use monel clips, cleats and nails for attachment. All bends and seams should be made with a radius at least equal to twice the thickness of the sheet. Cleats should be spaced 10"-12" o.c. The strongest joints can be obtained by lock-seaming, spot welding, or other means. Joints should allow for expansion of metal. For flashing, see pages on flashing.

RECOMMENDED GAUGES for SPECIFIC USES

USE	U.S.S. GAUGE
BATTEN SEAM ROOFING	
24" wide	#25
valleys & 20" wide	26
eaves	24
cover strips	26
CLEATS	26
COPING COVER	
edge strips on wood copings	24
edge strips on stone copings	22
standing seam	26
flat sheet coping	25
CORNICES & BELT COURSES	
edge strip on wood cornices	24
edge strip on stone cornices	22
belt courses	22
flat covering	25
COUNTER, BASE & CAP FLASHINGS	
counter flashings	26
cap flashings	26
(cont.) base, over 10" wide	#25
base, 10" and under	26
EAVES FLASHINGS	26
EXPANSION JOINTS	
exterior walls	26
roof curbs	25
"V" cover and floors	26
FLAT SEAM ROOFING	25
GRAVEL STOPS	
stops	25
edge strips	24
GUTTERS	
gutter linings	
36" girth & smaller	25
36" to 48" girth	24
48" girth & larger	22
molded gutters	25
hung gutters	26
gutter expansion joints	26
LEADERS	
downspouts	26
heads	26
straps	26
LOUVERS (STATIONARY)	
(cont.) frame covering	#26
louver slats (under 6'-0")	25
louver slats (over 6'-0")	24
vertical strips	24
SIDINGS (BULKHEADS - ELEVATOR PENTHOUSES, & STAIRCASE SHAFTS.)	
crimped, keyed, and corrugated sheets	26
flat sheets	25
SKYLIGHTS	
caps	25
condensation gutter	26
STANDING SEAM ROOFING	
24" wide	25
valleys & 20" wide	26
eaves	24
THRU WALL FLASHING	
flashings	26
VALLEY FLASHINGS	
with wood or asphalt shingles	26
with slate or tile roofing	24

Data on this sheet submitted by the International Nickel Company, Inc.

TIN ROOFING

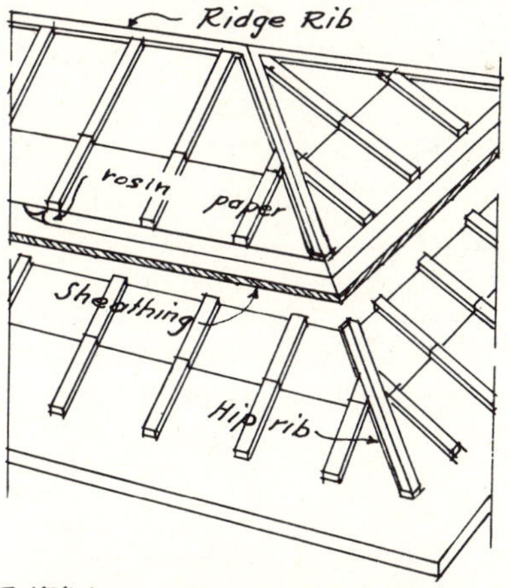
Ridge Rib
rosin paper
Sheathing
Hip rib

BATTEN or RIBBED ROOF.

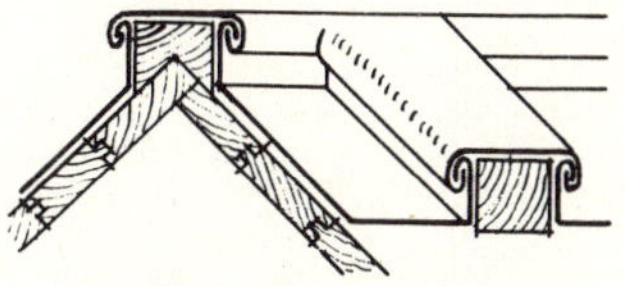

RIB SEAM FINISH AT RIDGE

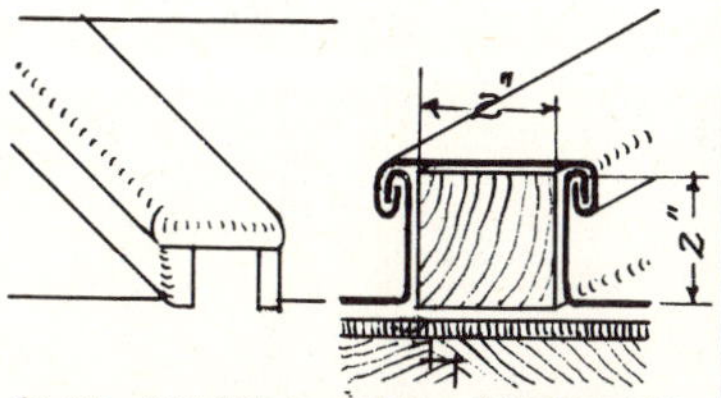
2"
2"

RIB END. RIB-SECTION.

See "Zinc" and "Copper Roofing" sheets for full details. All plates secured to ribs 1'-0" apart by cleats. Ribs nailed to sheathing. All cross seams to be flat locked and soldered. No nails to be driven thro' sheets. Ribs may be of any size desired but 2" x 2" is usual size. Sheets 20" x 28" or other standard sizes – See below

BATTEN or RIBBED SEAM ROOF.

FINISH of VALLEY OR GUTTER

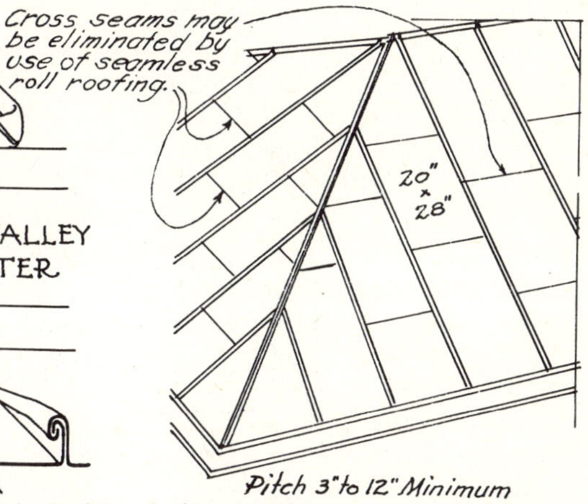
Cross seams may be eliminated by use of seamless roll roofing.
20" x 28"

Pitch 3" to 12" Minimum

STANDING SEAM ROOF.

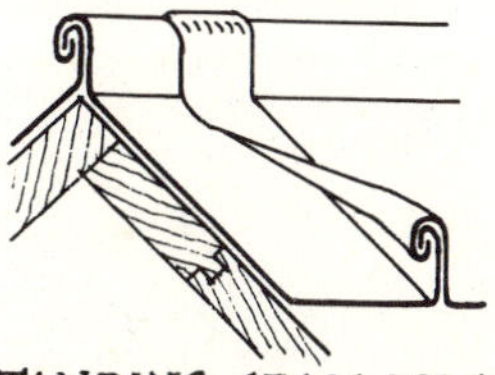

STANDING SEAM RIDGE.

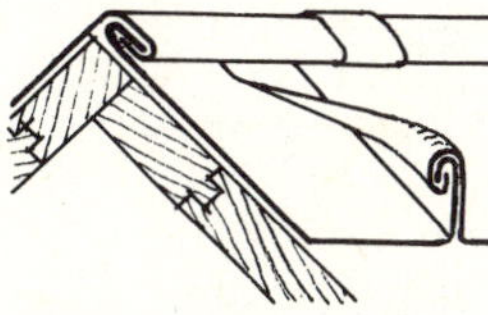

RIDGE COMB finished WITH FLAT SEAL.

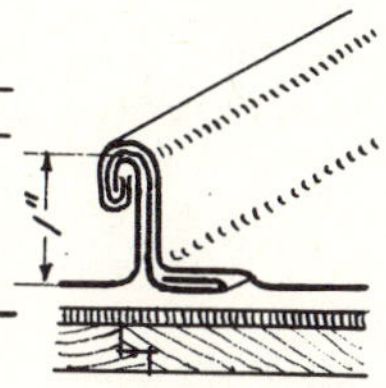
1"

STANDING SEAM DOUBLE LOCKED

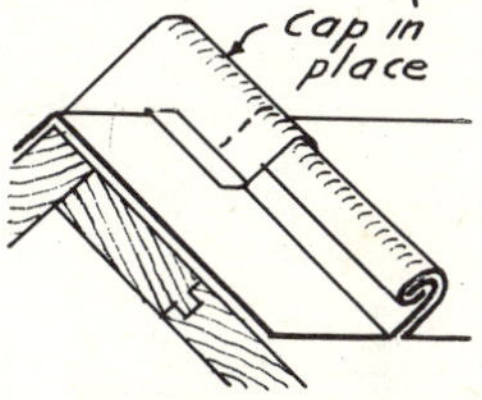
Cap in place

SEAM CAPPED RIDGE

For use on steep roofs; slope must be not less than 3" to 12". Sheet size usually used is 20" x 28", seam takes 2 3/4" from width of sheet. Cleats secure sheets to roof and are spaced 12" o.c. maximum. Cross seams to be flat locked and soldered. Use 2-7/8" nails to a cleat and space 8" apart. Nailing tin directly is not advised.

STANDING SEAM ROOF.

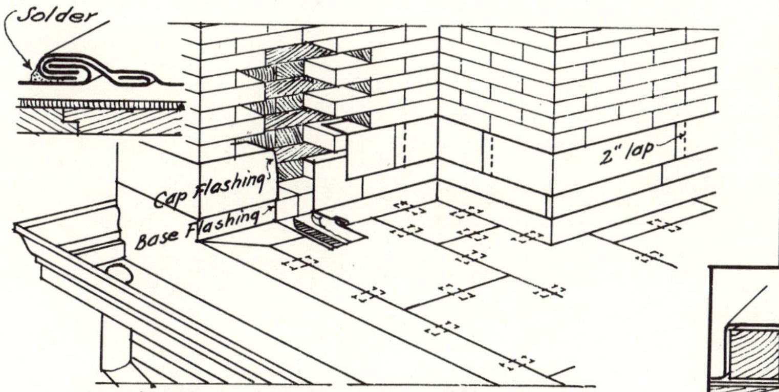
Solder
2" lap
Cap Flashing
Base Flashing

FLAT SEAM ROOF

(For Pitches less than 3" to 12")

Pitch roof not less than 1/2" to 12". Sheets are 14" x 12" and allow 1 1/2" on both dimensions for seams. Attach to roof (narrow way) with cleats - two to 14". Solder with half & half solder after malleting seams flat.

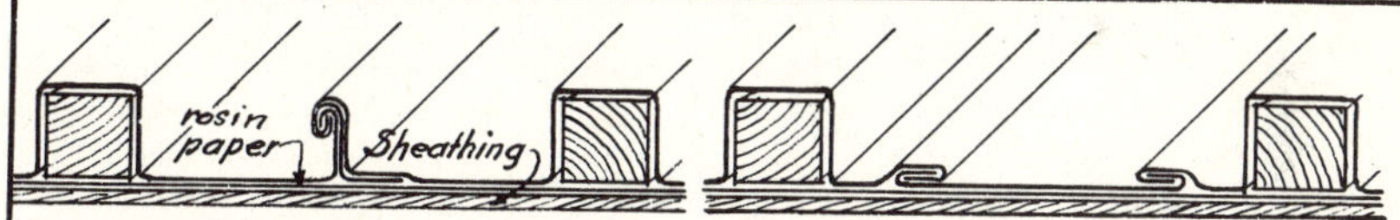
rosin paper
Sheathing

STANDING SEAM AND RIB SEAM.

FLAT SEAM AND RIB SEAM.

COMBINATION TYPES OF ROOFS.

Notes

Lay tin on rosin paper, no tar paper under rosin paper. Paint underside with iron oxide and oil. Prime top with same paint and finish with 2 coats of oil. For flashing and leaders & Gutters see sheets of those titles.

Weights and Gauges of Tin Plate (Terne Plate) - without Tin finish -

Gauge No.	Weight per □' in ounces	Weight per □' in pounds	Thickness	Stock Sizes	Recommended Use
IC (30) IX (28)	9. 11.1	.56 .69	.0122 .0155	14"x20", 20"x28", 14"x96", 20"x96", 24"x96", 28"x96", 28"x120" " " 50 ft. rolls of IC & IX gauge seamless Terne roofing available in 14", 24" & 28" widths from Follansbee Steel Corp.	For flat seams, All roofs, flashings, IC or IX for standing seams IX for gutters & valleys.
26 24	No longer available.				

Expansion of Tin .825" per 100' per 100°. Coating is:- mixture of lead & tin. Weights from 20 to 40 lbs per box (112 sheets 20" x 28"). The term "long terne" applies to the 40lb; 40# is the best to use for good work. Copper steel alloy base is proving successful in prolonging life of this metal. Roofs should be repainted every 3 or 4 years.

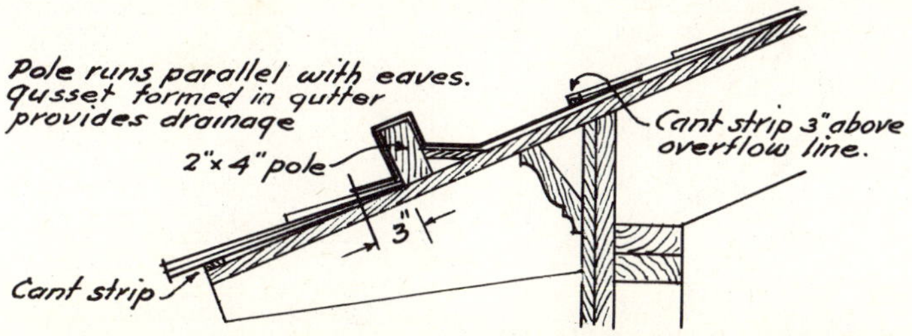
Pole runs parallel with eaves. Gusset formed in gutter provides drainage
2" x 4" pole
Cant strip 3" above overflow line.
3"
Cant strip

POLE GUTTER in SHINGLE ROOF.

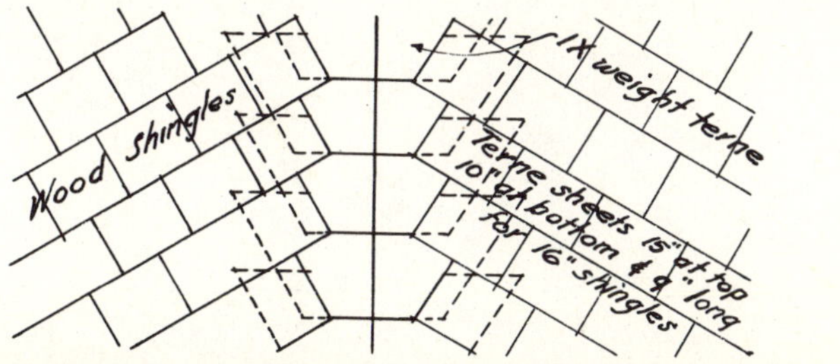
Wood Shingles
IX weight terne
Terne sheets 15" at top 10" at bottom & 9" long for 16" shingles

FLASHING CLOSE VALLEY SHINGLE ROOF.

Data checked by (Tern Plate) Follansbee Steel Corp.

LEAD ROOFING and PRECAST ROOFING

Weight per □'	Thickness in inches	Use for which it is recommended	Lengths
2½# hard	1/24	Cap & base flash'g. Batten roofing if less than 24" o.c.	For cap flashing, batten caps, gutter lining 8'-0"
3# hard	3/64	Other roofing, cornice flashing, gutter lining.	For all other purposes. 4'-0"
4# *	1/16	Special roofing conditions & shower pans.	
6# soft	3/32	Scalloped edgings. Ornaments.	Stock widths are rolled 24", 30" & 36" wide
8# soft	1/8		

* hard or soft.

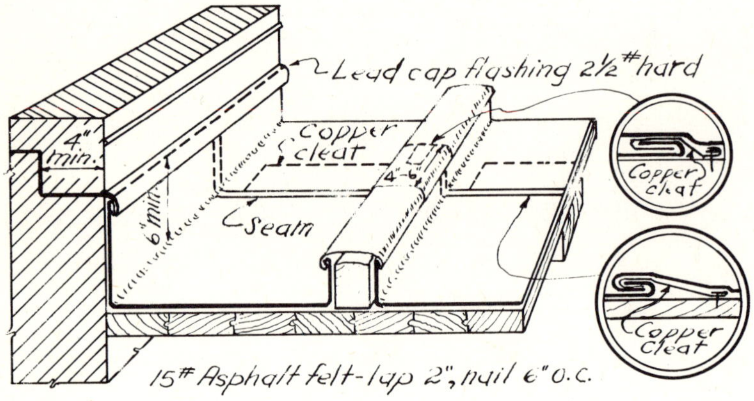
Lead cap flashing 2½# hard
4" min.
Copper cleat
4"-6"
6" min.
Seam
Copper cleat
Copper cleat
15# Asphalt felt-lap 2", nail 6" o.c.

LEAD ROOFING

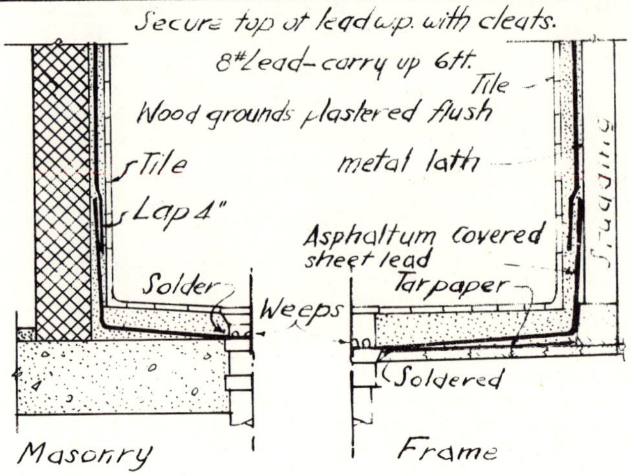
Secure top of lead up. with cleats.
8# Lead-carry up 6ft.
Tile
Wood grounds plastered flush
Tile
metal lath
Lap 4"
Asphaltum covered sheet lead
Solder
Weeps
Tarpaper
Soldered
Masonry
Frame

WATERPROOFING SHOWER STALLS

Joint for adjacent pieces or cap or base flashing.

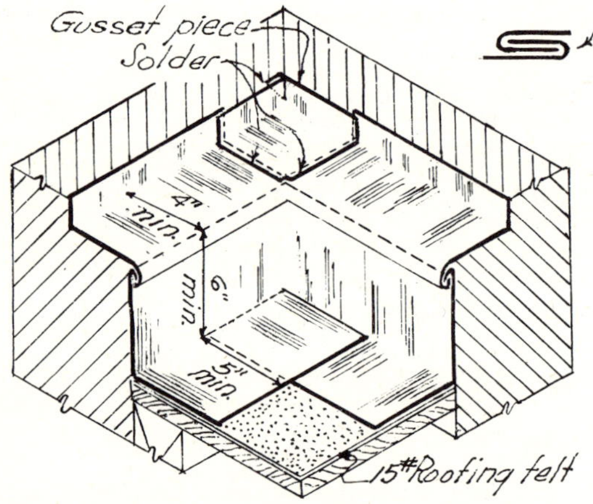
Gusset piece
Solder
4" min.
6" min.
5" min.
15# Roofing felt

Base flashing on roofs pitched less than 3 in 12 shall be loose locked together. Loose locks to turn back 1¼" & allow 1/8" clearance between fold & edge of adjoining sheets. All loose locks and laps to be set in non-hardening compound. Where flashing turns corners fold or insert gusset. Solder fold or gusset at corners only. Use 2½# hard lead for cap & base flashing.

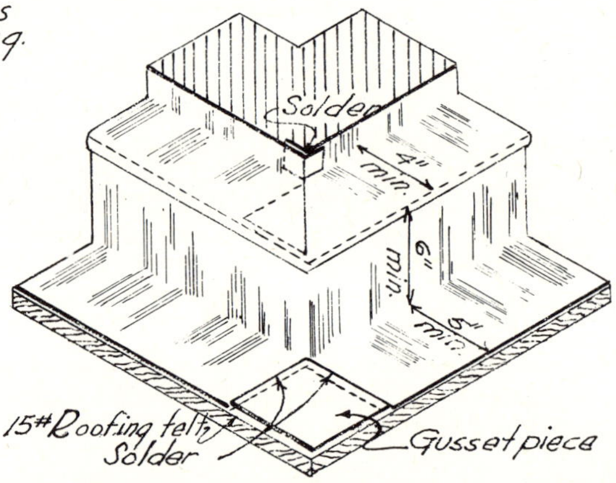
Solder
4" min.
6" min.
5" min.
15# Roofing felt
Solder
Gusset piece

FLASHING INTERIOR CORNER

FLASHING EXTERIOR CORNER

Never nail lead, but secure with lead, copper or lead-coated copper cleats which are nailed with two hard copper wire nails. Secure lead to masonry with cleats or lead cap flashing strip. All cleats to be approx. 10" o.c. On steep roofs run cleats continuously in horizontal plane and secure them 12" o.c. Do not solder loose lock seams. Lap all vertical joints 3" min. Vertical surfaces over 18" high to have seams 18" apart. Lead expands but does not contract. Max. expansion of .02/ft. 12 lbs. of lead per 100□' is usual for lead-ctd. copper. Where lead is in contact with masonry coat with asphaltum.

LEAD ROOFING, FLASHING & W.P.

Data checked by Lead Industries Association.

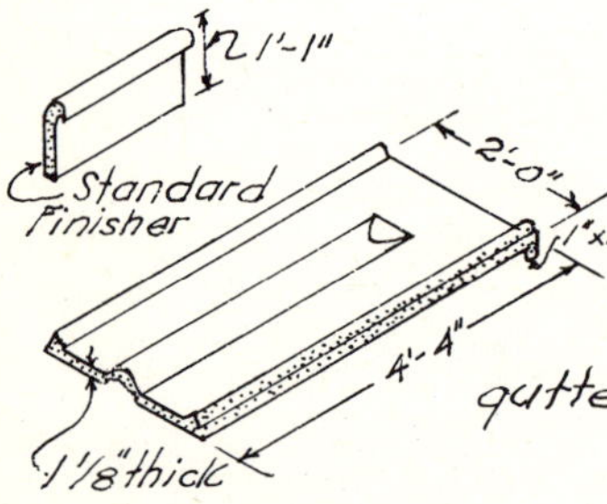
2'-1"
Standard Finisher
2'-0"
1"x1" hook
4'-4"
1 1/8" thick

STANDARD SLAB

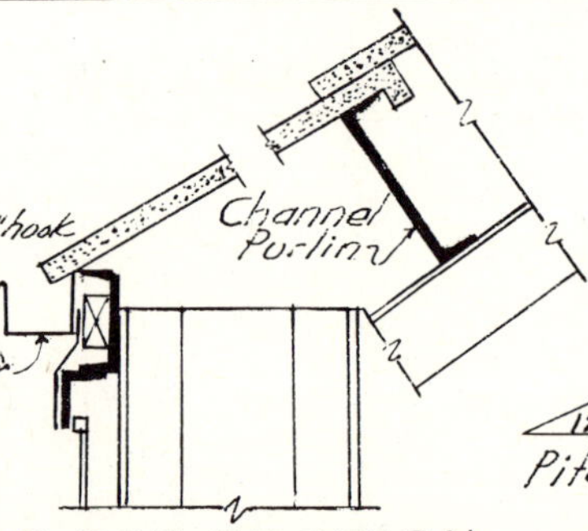
Channel Purlin
gutter

ROOF SECTION

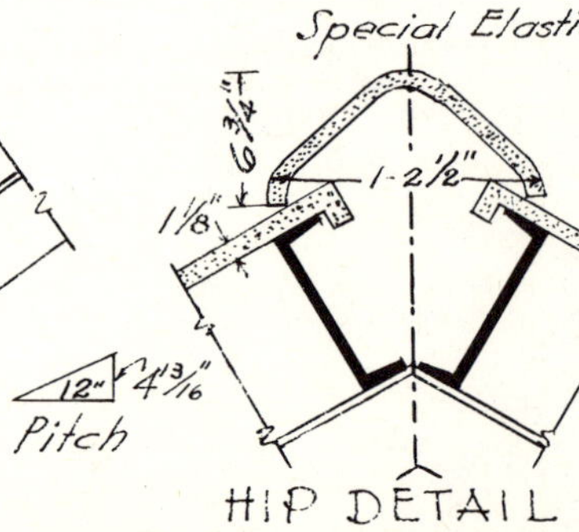
Special Elastic Cement
6¾"
1-2½"
1 1/8"
12"
4 13/16
Pitch

HIP DETAIL

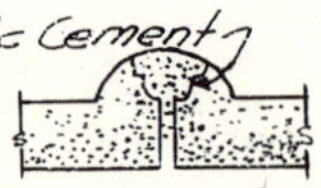

JOINT

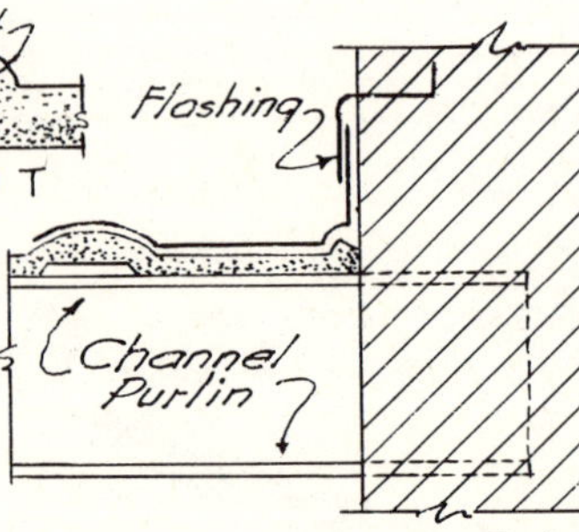
Flashing
Channel Purlin

WALL SECTION

PRECAST CONCRETE ROOFING.

These slabs do not need any additional roof surfacing

Data checked by Federal Cement Tile Co.

ZINC ROOFING

Note: Standard battens are 1-5/8" high for slope 4" to 12" or more.

For slopes less than 4" to 12" battens should be 2-5/8" high to avoid water leakage.

In the batten system metal is laid between parallel wooden batten strips which run from ridge to eave.

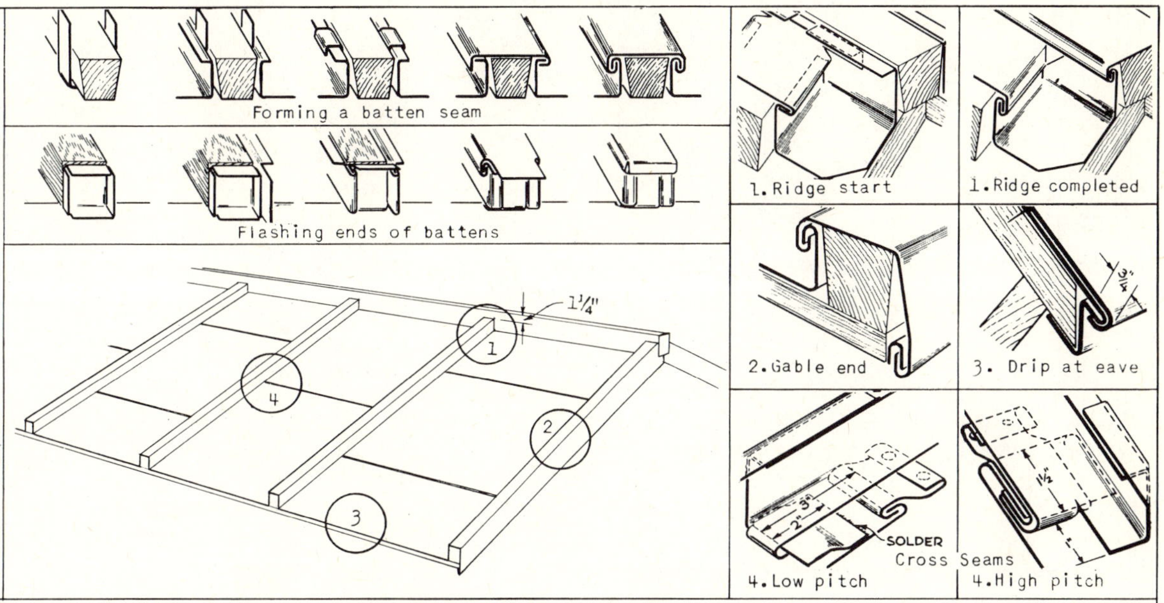
Forming a batten seam
Flashing ends of battens
1¼"
1
2
3
4
1. Ridge start
1. Ridge completed
2. Gable end
3. Drip at eave
SOLDER
Cross Seams
4. Low pitch
4. High pitch

Standard battens (1⅝"x 1⅝") spaced 2¼" o.c. less than width of sheet. When battens are not over 30" o.c. use .028" or thicker zinc.
Large battens (2⅝"x 2⅝") " 3" " " " " " " " " " " " 40" " " .032" " " ".
When battens are not over 18" o.c. use .024" or thicker zinc. Battens over 40" wide not recommended.

SPACING OF BATTENS & WEIGHTS OF ZINC

BATTEN SEAM

Note: Used on roofs with slopes of 4" to 12" or more.

Use a minimum of .024' zinc in narrow strips. Standard width 20".

Zinc may be had in either sheets or coils, the latter to be cut into lengths of not more than 8'. Seams 17½" oc. All sheets are secured by clips 1"x3" long nailed to roof 8" to 10" o.c.

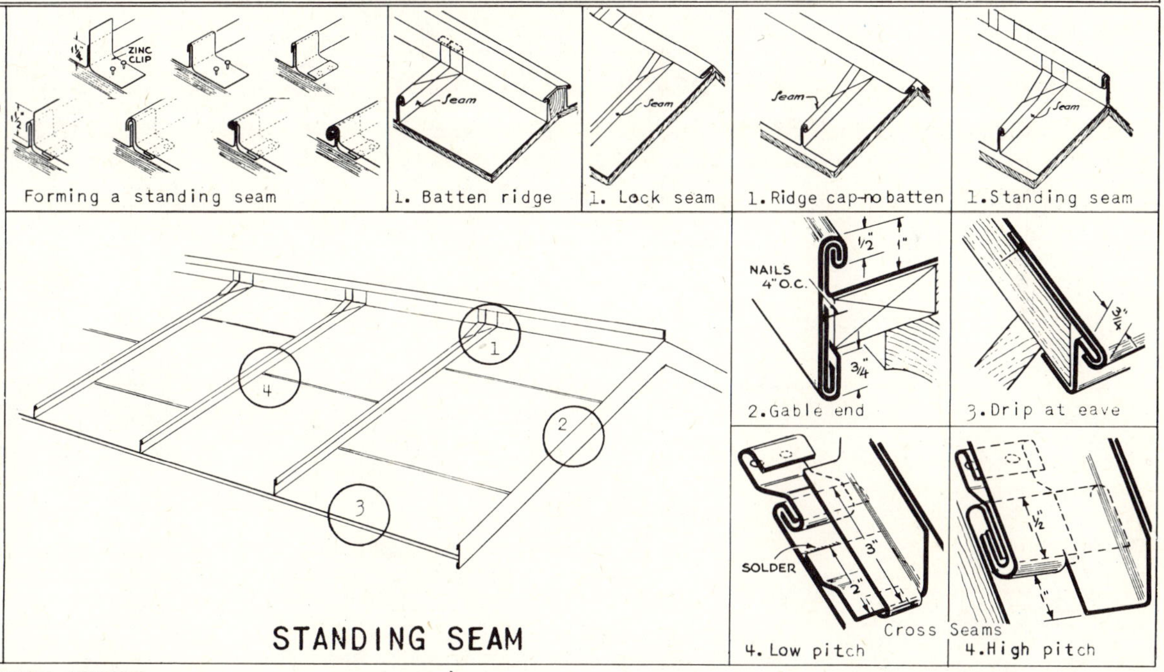
ZINC CLIP
Forming a standing seam
Seam
1. Batten ridge
1. Lock seam
1. Ridge cap-no batten
1. Standing seam
1
2
3
4
NAILS 4" O.C.
2. Gable end
3. Drip at eave
SOLDER
Cross Seams
4. Low pitch
4. High pitch

STANDING SEAM

ZINC GAUGES

Note: Specify decimal thickness to be used as too thin a metal will not give satisfactory service. .024" or thicker is recommended for roofing while .020" or thicker is used for flashing, leaders & gutters etc. Weight of zinc 20% less than weight of copper.

Ga. No.	Ounces per sq. ft.	Thickness in inches	Ga. No.	Ounces per sq. ft.	Thickness in inches
9	10.72	.018	17	29.92	.050
10	12.00	.020	18	32.96	.055
11	14.40	.024	19	36.00	.060
12	16.80	.028	20	41.92	.070
13	19.20	.032	21	48.00	.080
14	21.60	.036	22	53.92	.090
15	24.00	.040	23	60.00	.100
16	26.88	.045	24	75.20	.125

For FLASHING, LEADERS & GUTTERS see pages of those titles

Note: Zinc can be used safely in direct contact with lead, tin & aluminum. With other metals insulation is required because of electrolysis. Zinc is not affected in contact with most lumber. When used with redwood or red cedar it should be coated with asphaltum paint. Do not use zinc where acid fumes occur. Zinc expands ¼" per 10' sheet in temperature change from 0' to 120'. Always use hot-dipped gal. nails with zinc and a glossy, saturated & coated paper under it. May be painted immediately after installation if zinc metallic paint is used.

Zinc Sizes = Sheets (.018" or thicker)-up to 5' wide, 8' long-Standard 3'x8'. Strips (.018" or thicker) to 1'8" wide; flat lengths to 12'; coils, any size.

DATA SUPPLIED BY AMERICAN ZINC INSTITUTE

TERMITE CONTROL

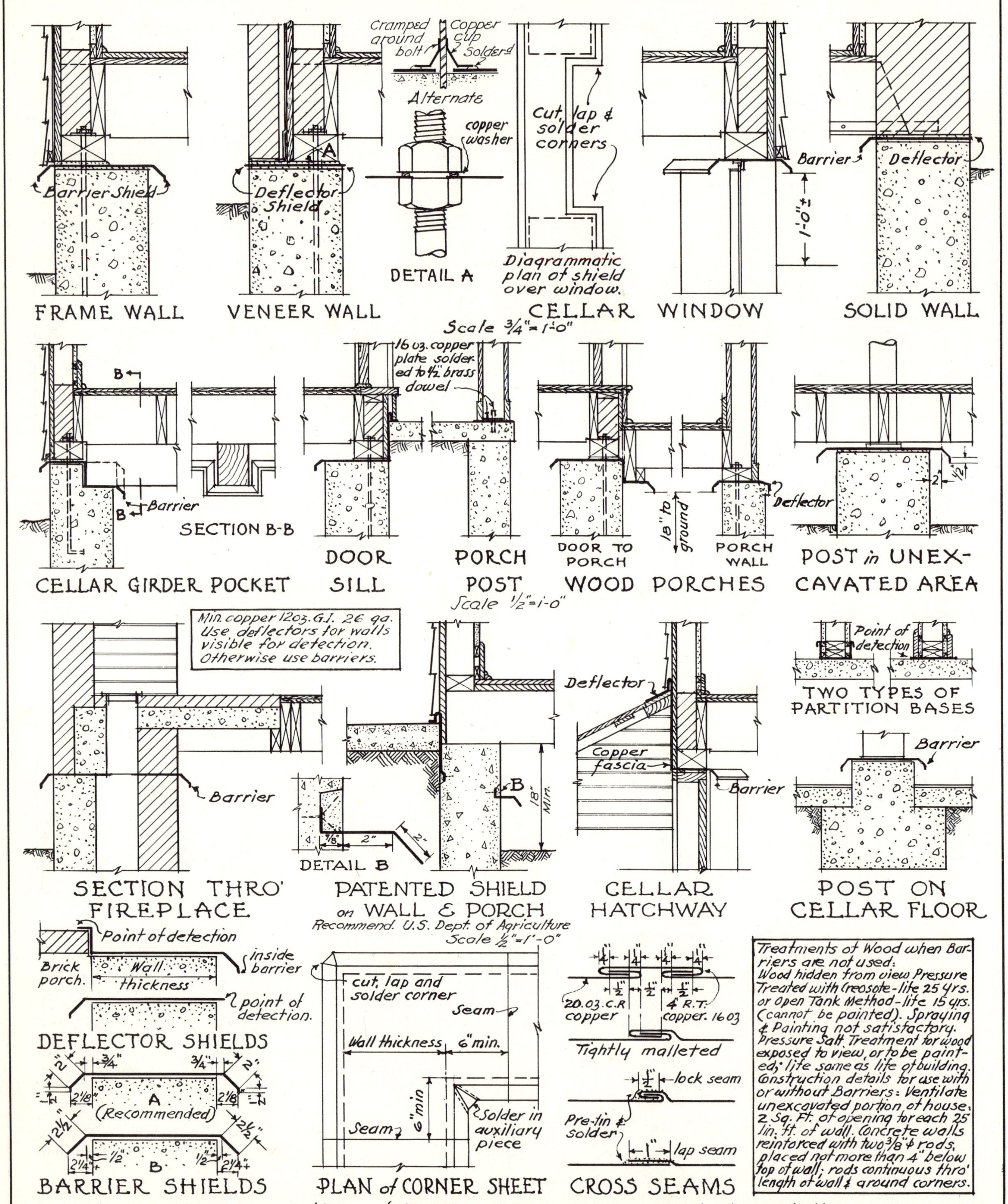
Cramped around bolt
Copper cup & Solderd
Alternate
copper washer
DETAIL A
Cut, lap & solder corners
Diagrammatic plan of shield over window.
Barrier Shield
Deflector Shield
Barrier
Deflector
1'-0"±
FRAME WALL
VENEER WALL
CELLAR WINDOW
SOLID WALL
Scale 3/4"=1'-0"
16 oz. copper plate soldered to ½" brass dowel
B
Barrier
SECTION B-B
18" to ground
Deflector
CELLAR GIRDER POCKET
DOOR SILL
PORCH POST
DOOR TO PORCH
PORCH WALL
WOOD PORCHES
POST in UNEXCAVATED AREA
Scale ½"=1'-0"
Min. copper 12oz. G.I. 26 ga. Use deflectors for walls visible for detection. Otherwise use barriers.
Point of detection
TWO TYPES OF PARTITION BASES
Barrier
Deflector
Copper fascia
Barrier
18" Min.
DETAIL B
Barrier
SECTION THRO' FIREPLACE
PATENTED SHIELD on WALL & PORCH
Recommend. U.S. Dept. of Agriculture
Scale ½"=1'-0"
CELLAR HATCHWAY
POST ON CELLAR FLOOR
Point of detection
Brick porch.
Wall thickness
inside barrier
point of detection.
DEFLECTOR SHIELDS
A (Recommended)
B
BARRIER SHIELDS
cut, lap and solder corner
Seam
Wall thickness
6" min.
6" min
Seam
Solder in auxiliary piece
PLAN of CORNER SHEET
20 oz. C.R copper
4" R.T. copper. 16 oz
Tightly malleted
lock seam
Pre-tin & solder
lap seam
CROSS SEAMS
Treatments of Wood when Barriers are not used: Wood hidden from view Pressure Treated with Creosote-life 25 yrs. or Open Tank Method-life 15 yrs. (cannot be painted). Spraying & Painting not satisfactory. Pressure Salt Treatment for wood exposed to view, or to be painted; life same as life of building. Construction details for use with or without Barriers: Ventilate unexcavated portion of house: 2 Sq. Ft. of opening for each 25 lin. ft. of wall. Concrete walls reinforced with two 3/8"ϕ rods, placed not more than 4" below top of wall; rods continuous thro' length of wall & around corners.

Recommendations of the Copper & Brass Research Association

FLASHING

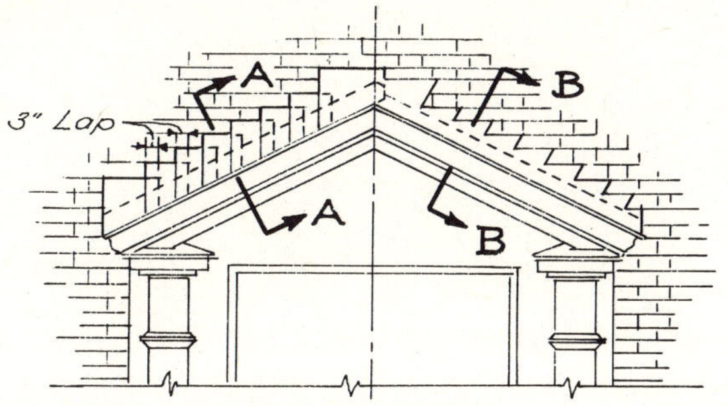
3" Lap
A
A
B
B

ELEVATION
3/8" = 1'-0"

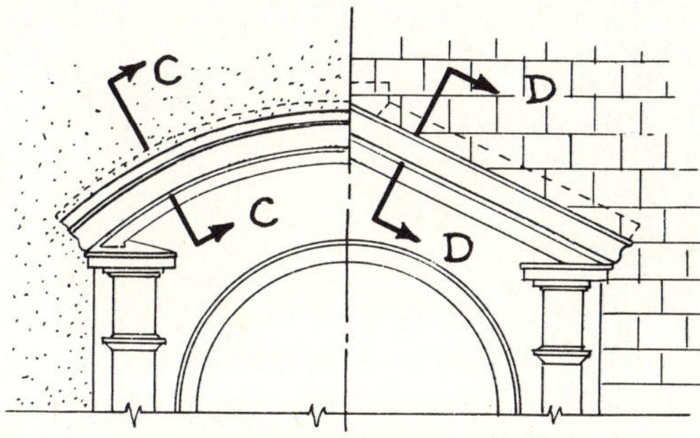
C
C
D
D

ELEVATION
3/8" = 1'-0"

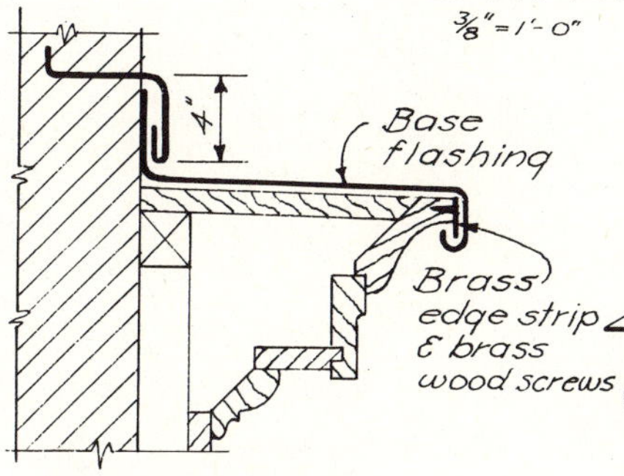
4"
Base flashing
Brass edge strip & brass wood screws

SECTION A-A

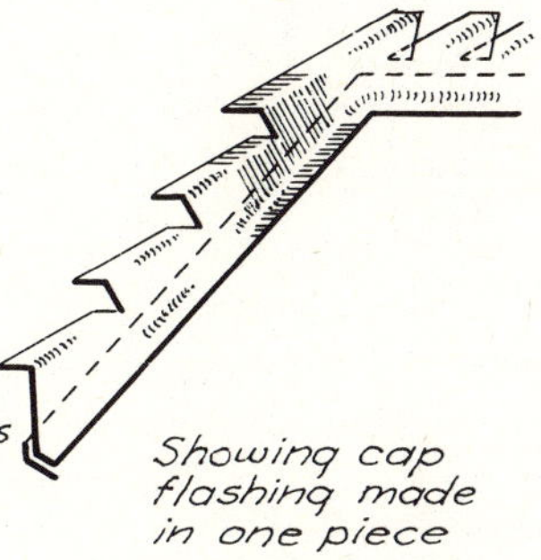
Showing cap flashing made in one piece

SECTION B-B

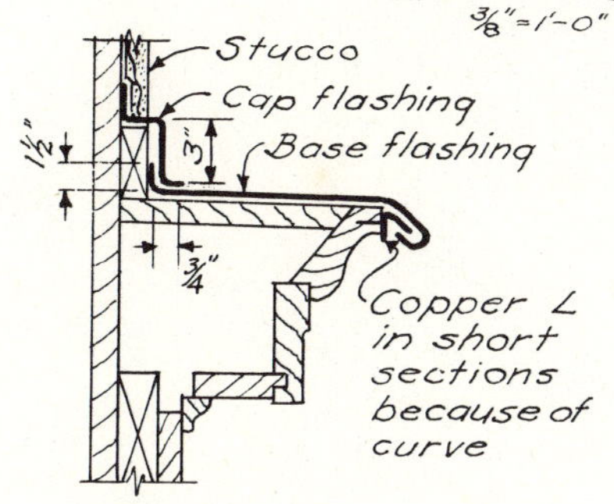
Stucco
Cap flashing
1½"
3"
Base flashing
¾"
Copper L in short sections because of curve

SECTION C-C

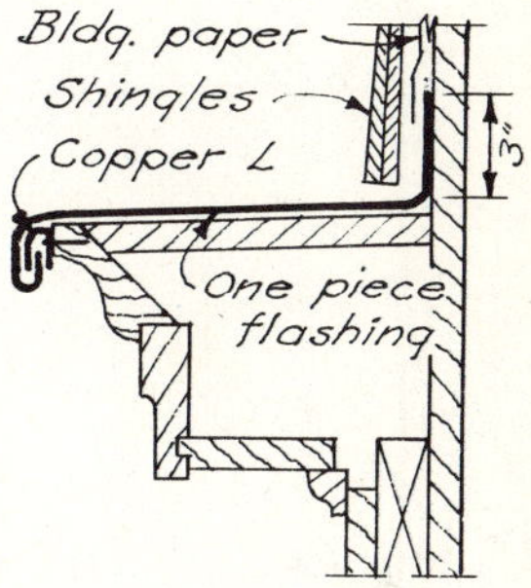
Bldg. paper
Shingles
Copper L
3"
One piece flashing

SECTION D-D

ENTRANCE FLASHING
1" = 1'-0"

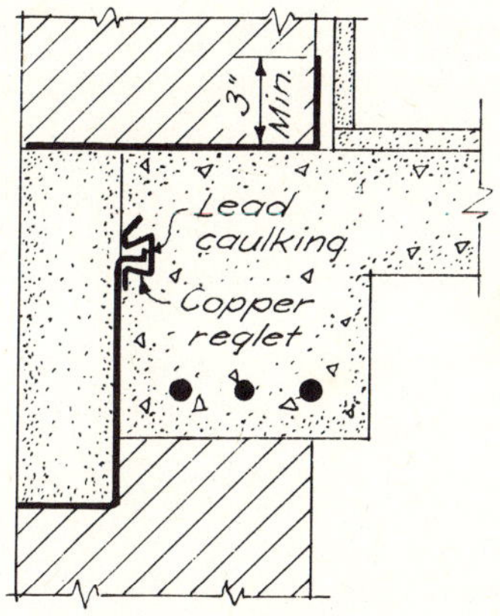
3" Min.
Lead caulking
Copper reglet

FLUSH STONE

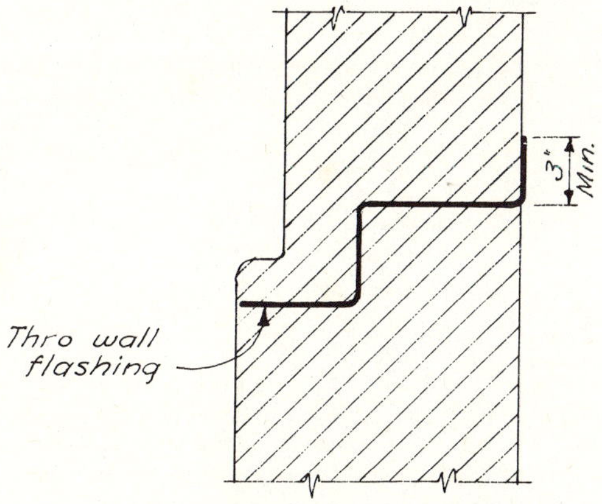
3" Min.
Thro wall flashing

MOULDED BRICK

BELT COURSES
1" = 1'-0"

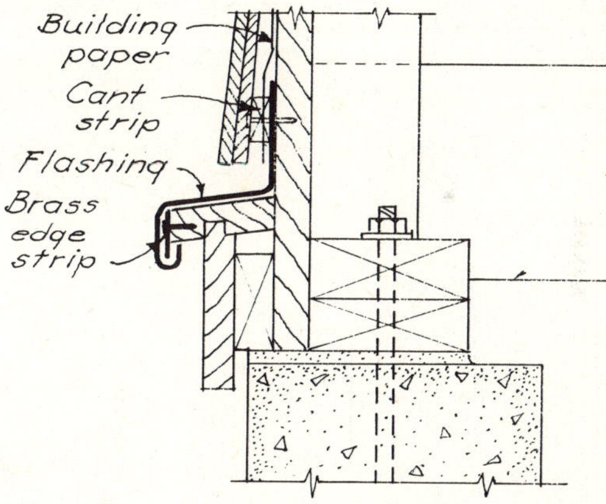
Building paper
Cant strip
Flashing
Brass edge strip

WOOD WATER TABLE
1½" = 1'-0"

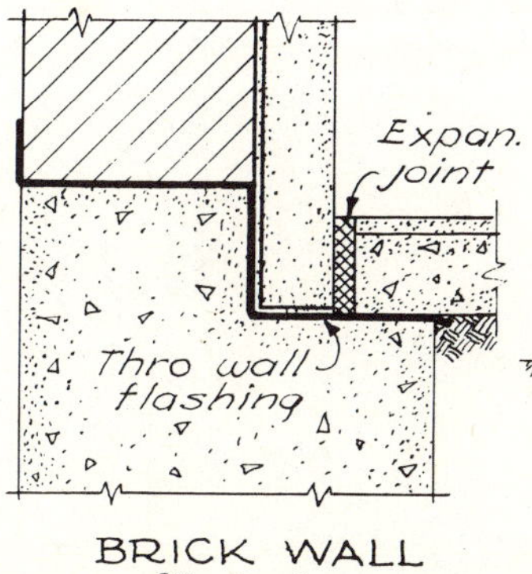
Expan. joint
Thro wall flashing

BRICK WALL
¾" = 1'-0"

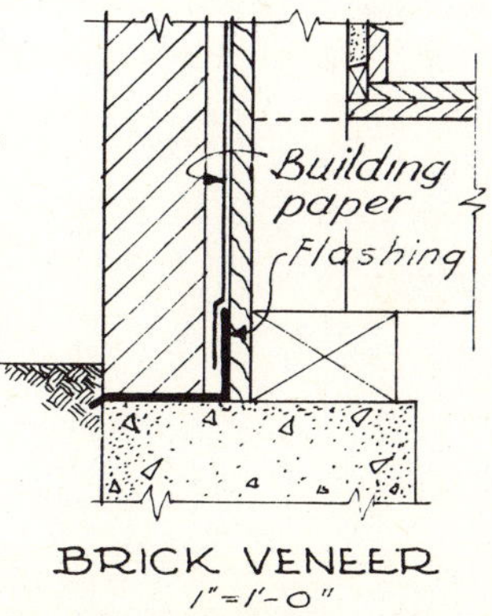
Building paper
Flashing

BRICK VENEER
1" = 1'-0"

BASE COURSES

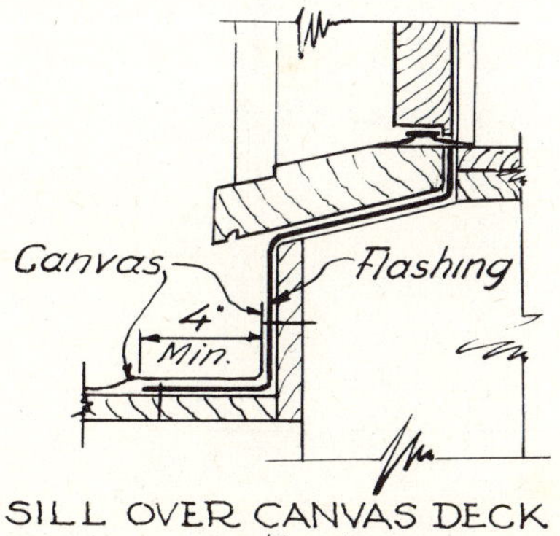
Canvas
4" Min.
Flashing

SILL OVER CANVAS DECK
1½" = 1'-0"

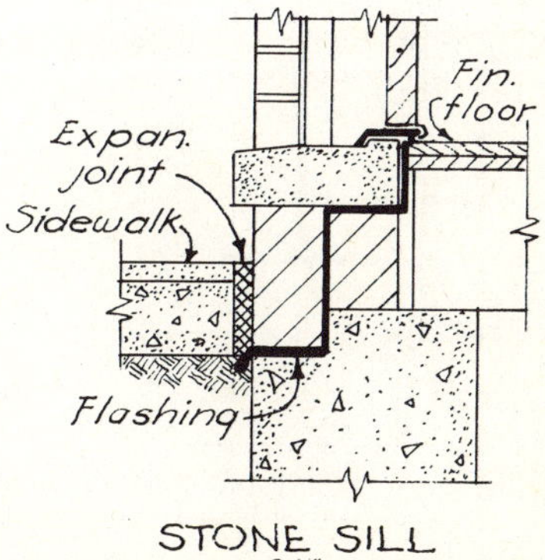
Fin. floor
Expan. joint
Sidewalk
Flashing

STONE SILL
¾" = 1'-0"

DOOR SILLS

Recommendation of Copper & Brass Research Association

FLASHING

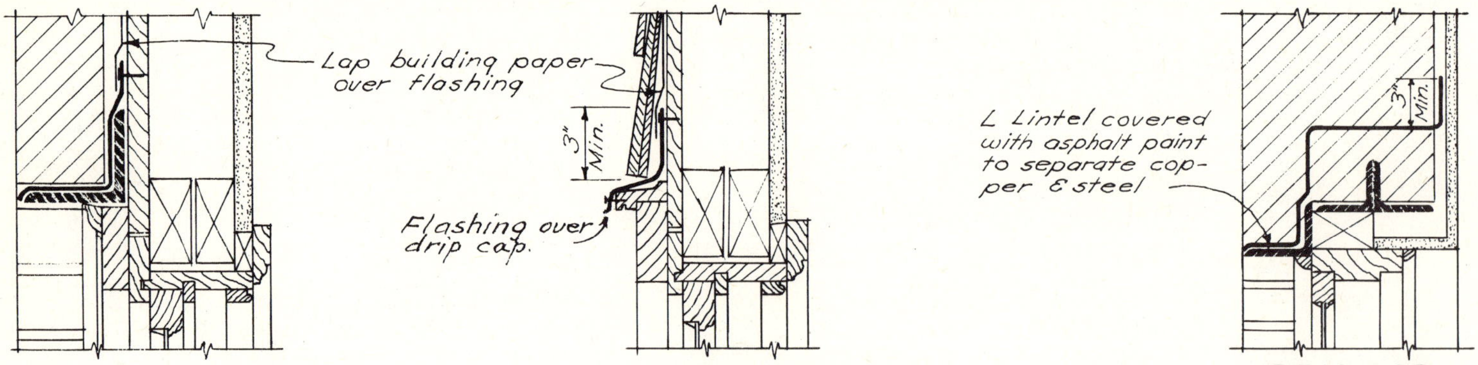
Lap building paper over flashing
3" Min.
Flashing over drip cap
∠ Lintel covered with asphalt paint to separate copper & steel
3" Min.

BRICK VENEER
1½" = 1'-0"

WOOD FRAME
1½" = 1'-0"

BRICK OR STONE LINTEL
1" = 1'-0"

WINDOW HEADS

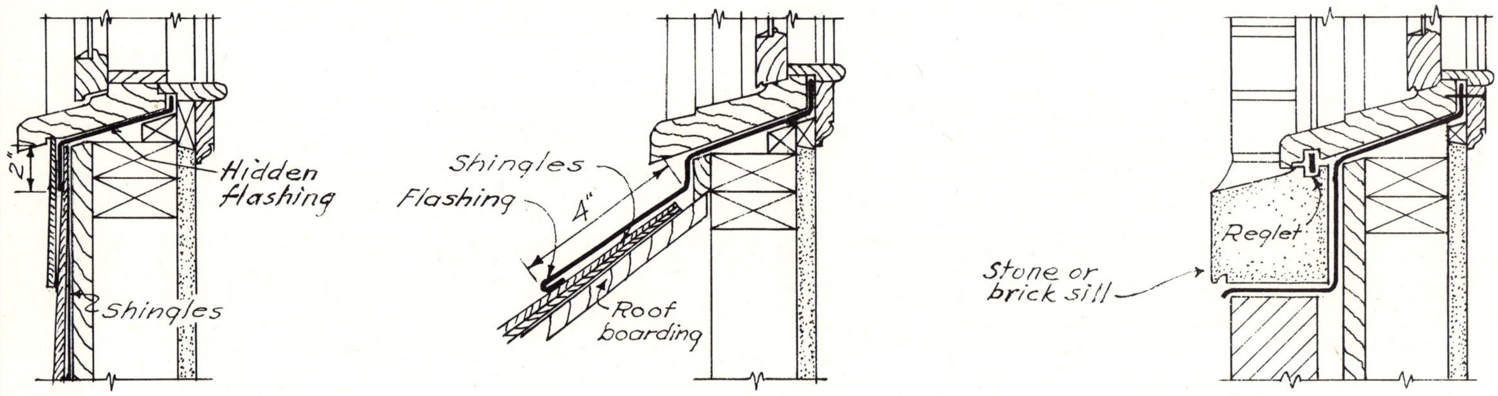
2"
Hidden flashing
Shingles
Shingles
Flashing
4"
Roof boarding
Reglet
Stone or brick sill

WOOD FRAME

DORMER

BRICK VENEER
Always use flashing under brick sills

WINDOW SILLS
1½" = 1'-0"

See - Cavity wall, building veneer, stone work pages.

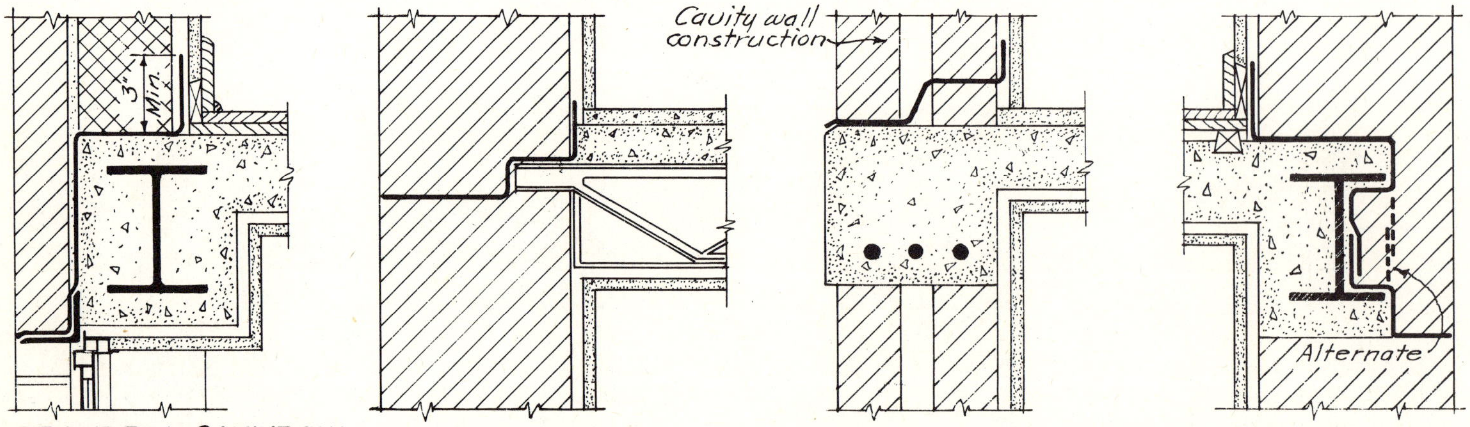
3" Min.
Cavity wall construction
Alternate

SPANDREL & WINDOW HEAD FLASHING

OPEN WEB JOIST

SPANDREL BEAM

OPEN WEB SPANDREL

SPANDRELS
1" = 1'-0"

Recommendation of Copper & Brass Research Association.

FLASHING

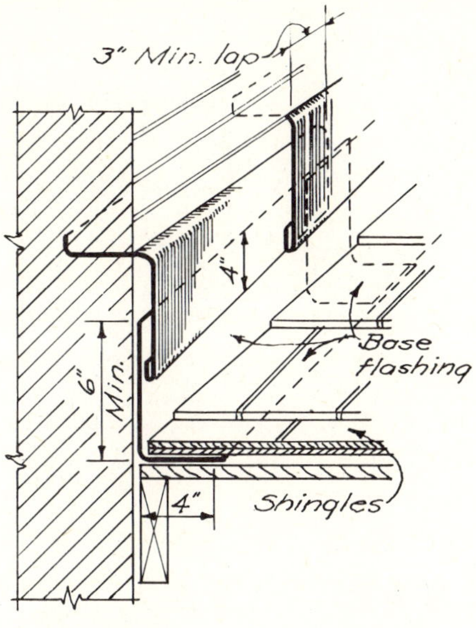
3" Min. lap
4"
6" Min.
Base flashing
4"
Shingles

STEPPED FLASHING

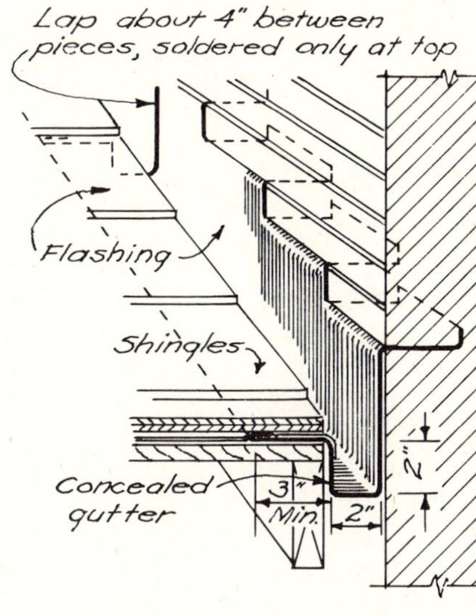
Lap about 4" between pieces, soldered only at top
Flashing
Shingles
Concealed gutter
3" Min.
2"
2"

STEPPED ONE PIECE FLASHING

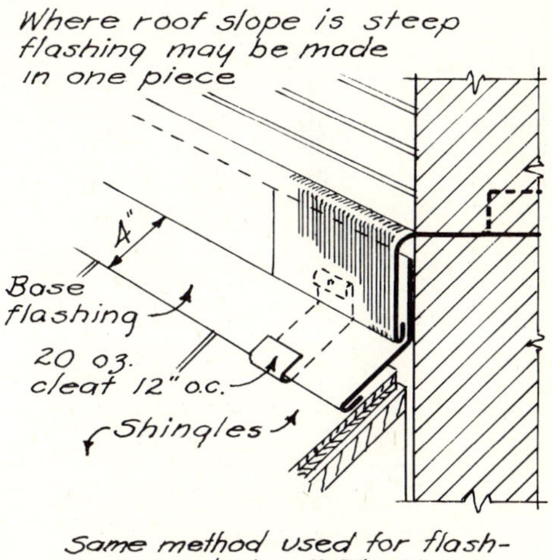
Where roof slope is steep flashing may be made in one piece
4"
Base flashing
20 oz. cleat 12" o.c.
Shingles

Same method used for flashing shingled wall. Flashing in one piece carried up under bottom row of shingles 4" min.

TOP OF ROOF FLASHING

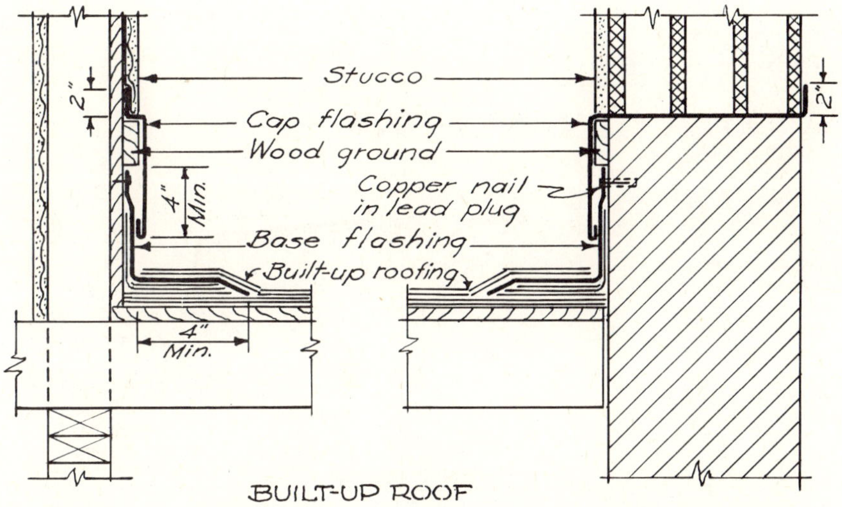
Stucco
2"
Cap flashing
Wood ground
4" Min.
Copper nail in lead plug
Base flashing
Built-up roofing
4" Min.
2"

BUILT-UP ROOF

STUCCO ON WOOD WALL STUCCO ON MASONRY WALL

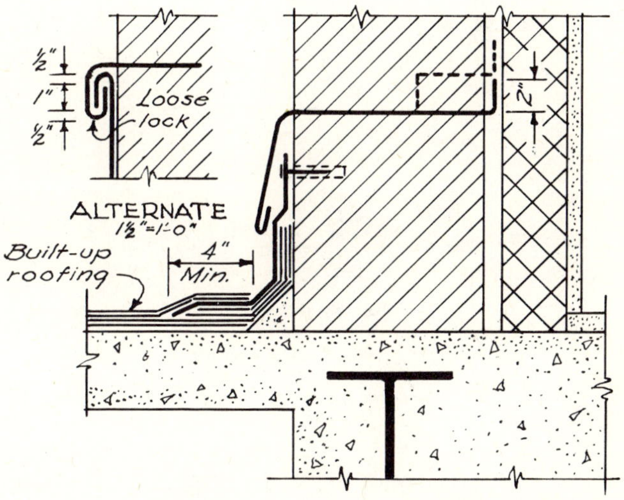
½"
1"
½"
Loose lock
ALTERNATE
1½"=1'-0"
Built-up roofing
4" Min.
2"

THRO' WALL FLASHING

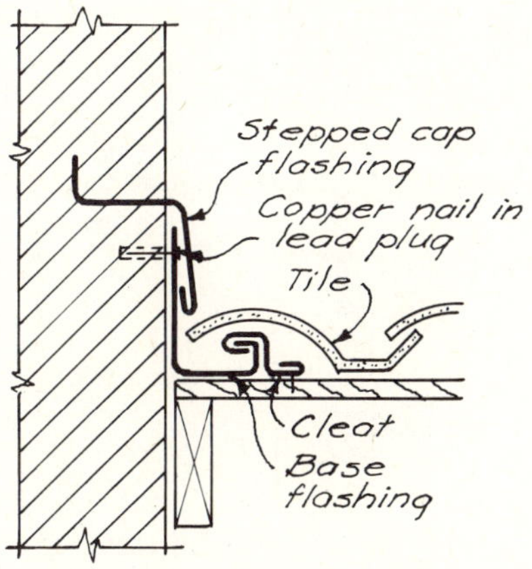
Stepped cap flashing
Copper nail in lead plug
Tile
Cleat
Base flashing

TILE ROOF

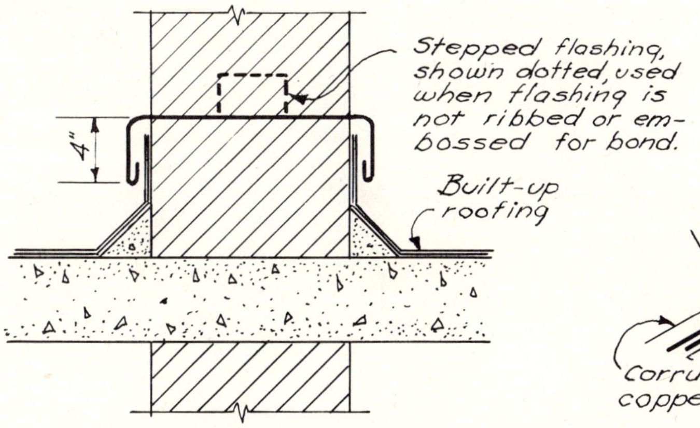
Stepped flashing, shown dotted, used when flashing is not ribbed or embossed for bond.
4"
Built-up roofing

FIREWALL FLASHING

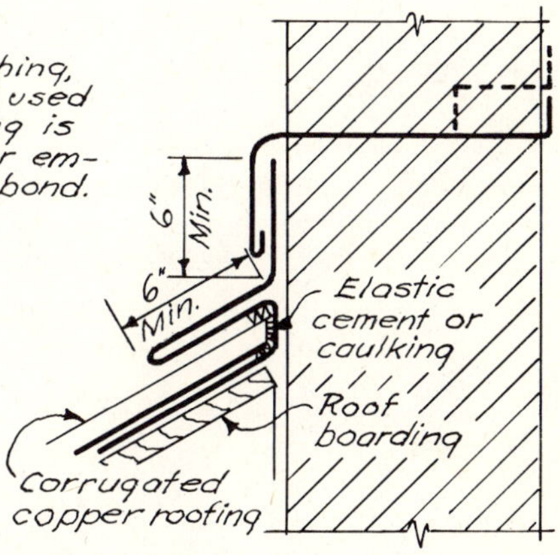
6" Min.
6" Min.
Elastic cement or caulking
Roof boarding
Corrugated copper roofing

CORRUGATED COPPER ROOF

FLASHING AT JUNCTURES OF ROOFS & WALLS

1" = 1'-0"

Recommendation of Copper & Brass Research Association

FLASHING

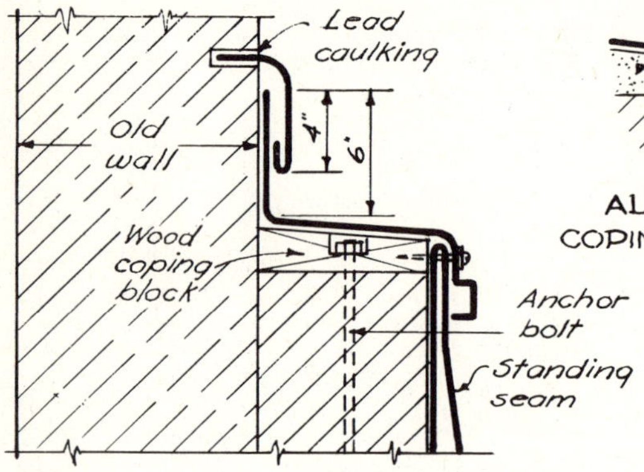
Lead
caulking
Old
wall
4"
6"
Wood
coping
block
Anchor
bolt
Standing
seam

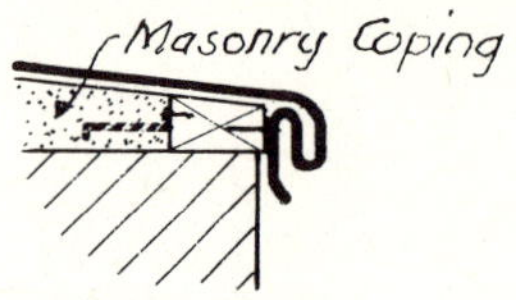
Masonry Coping

ALTERNATE
COPING & DRIP

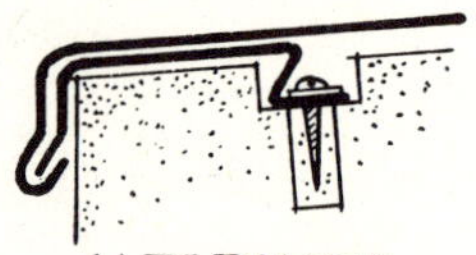

ALTERNATE
COPING & DRIP

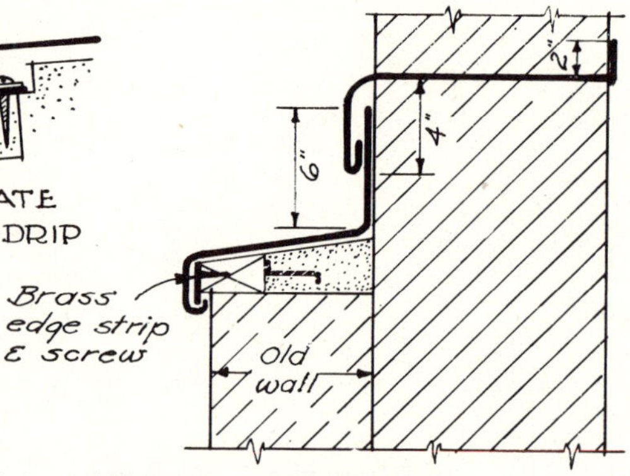
2"
6"
4"
Brass
edge strip
& screw
Old
wall

NEW WALL BELOW EXISTING WALL

NEW WALL ABOVE EXISTING WALL

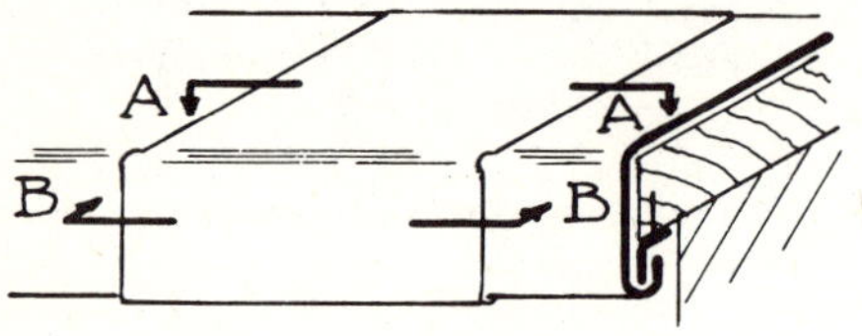
A
A
B
B

LOOSE LOCK
EXPANSION CAP
Located every 30 ft.

Copper sheet with flat locked seams soldered. If width exceeds 24", crimp or standing seam is provided for movement.

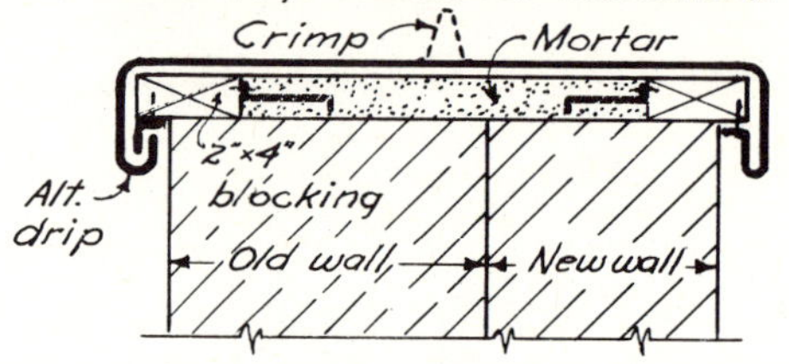
Crimp
Mortar
2"x4"
blocking
Alt.
drip
Old wall
New wall

SECTION A-A

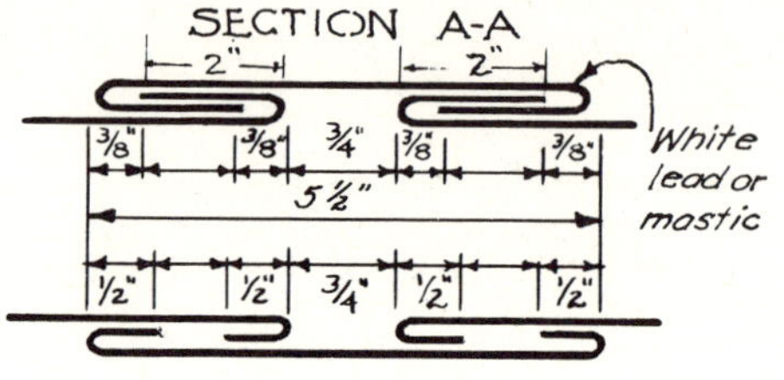
2"
2"
3/8"
3/8"
3/4"
3/8"
3/8"
5 1/2"
1/2"
1/2"
3/4"
1/2"
1/2"
White
lead or
mastic

SECTION B-B

NEW WALL LEVEL WITH EXISTING WALL

FLASHING BETWEEN OLD & NEW WALLS

1" = 1'-0"

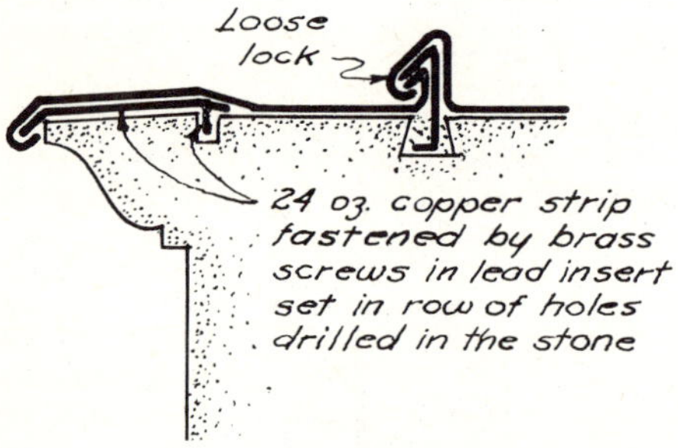
Loose
lock
24 oz. copper strip
fastened by brass
screws in lead insert
set in row of holes
drilled in the stone

STONE CORNICE
1" = 1'-0"

Large sheets are not caulked directly into reglets as movement from temperature changes will tear them. Use auxiliary strips set in reglets.

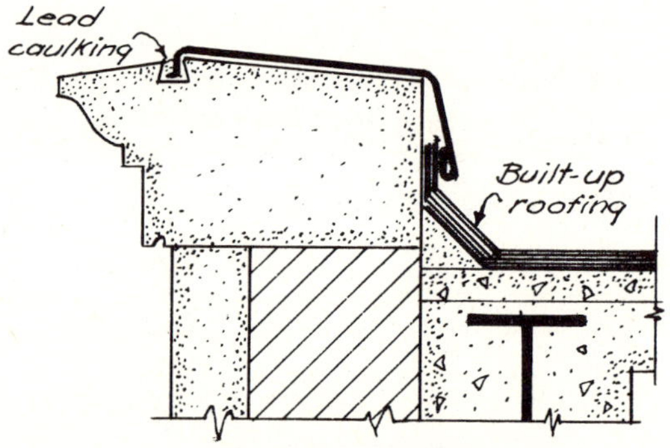
Lead
caulking
Built-up
roofing

STONE CORNICE
1" = 1'-0"

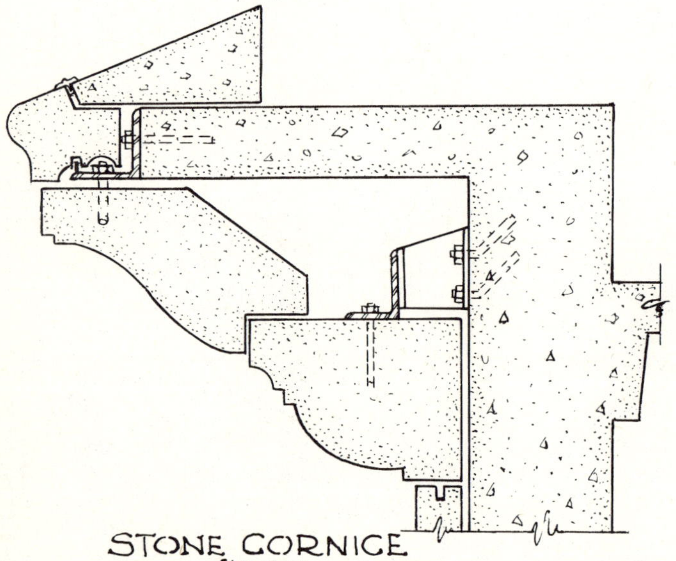

STONE CORNICE
3/4" = 1'-0"

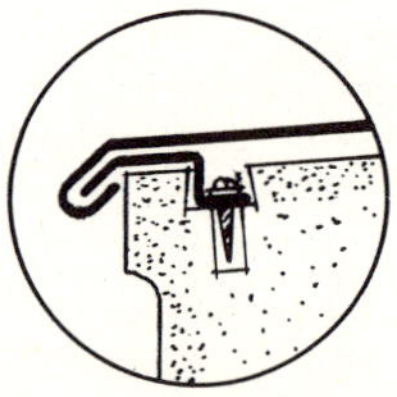

ALTERNATE
DRIP A

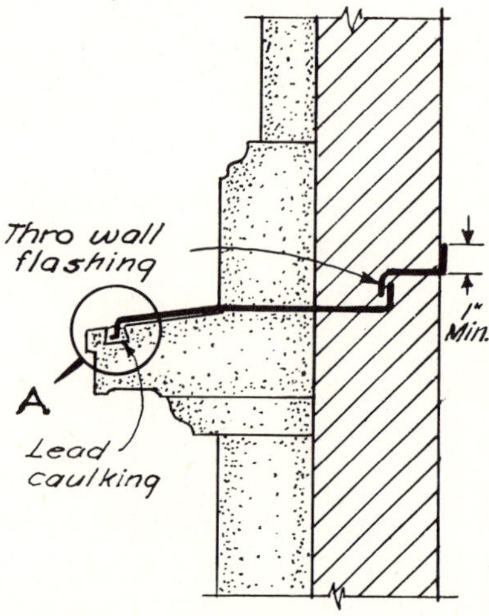
Thro wall
flashing
1"
Min.
A
Lead
caulking

STONE CORNICE
3/4" = 1'-0"

CORNICE FLASHING

Recommendation of Copper & Brass Research Association.

FLASHING

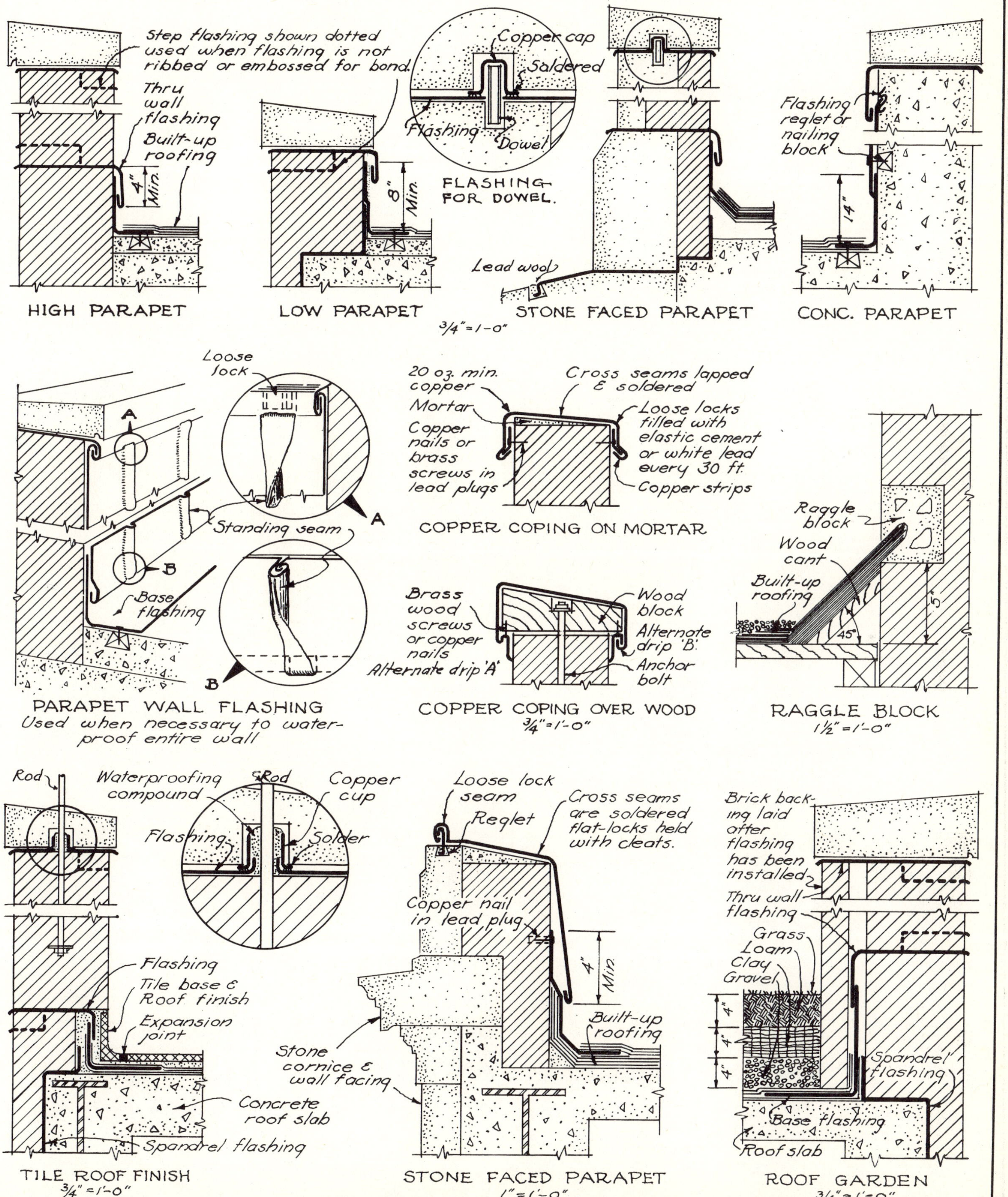
Step flashing shown dotted used when flashing is not ribbed or embossed for bond.
Thru wall flashing
Built-up roofing
4" Min.
HIGH PARAPET
8" Min.
LOW PARAPET
Copper cap
Soldered
Flashing
Dowel
FLASHING FOR DOWEL.
Lead wool
STONE FACED PARAPET
3/4" = 1-0"
Flashing reglet or nailing block
14"
CONC. PARAPET
Loose lock
A
Standing seam
B
Base flashing
PARAPET WALL FLASHING
Used when necessary to waterproof entire wall
20 oz. min. copper
Mortar
Cross seams lapped & soldered
Copper nails or brass screws in lead plugs
Loose locks filled with elastic cement or white lead every 30 ft.
Copper strips
COPPER COPING ON MORTAR
Brass wood screws or copper nails
Alternate drip 'A'
Wood block
Alternate drip 'B'.
Anchor bolt
COPPER COPING OVER WOOD
3/4" = 1'-0"
Raggle block
Wood cant
Built-up roofing
45°
5"
RAGGLE BLOCK
1 1/2" = 1'-0"
Rod
Waterproofing compound
℄ Rod
Copper cup
Flashing
Solder
Flashing
Tile base & Roof finish
Expansion joint
Concrete roof slab
Spandrel flashing
TILE ROOF FINISH
3/4" = 1'-0"
Loose lock seam
Reglet
Cross seams are soldered flat-locks held with cleats.
Copper nail in lead plug
4" Min.
Built-up roofing
Stone cornice & wall facing
STONE FACED PARAPET
1" = 1'-0"
Brick backing laid after flashing has been installed
Thru wall flashing
Grass
Loam
Clay
Gravel
4"
4"
4"
Spandrel flashing
Base flashing
Roof slab
ROOF GARDEN
3/4" = 1'-0"

Recommendation of Copper & Brass Research Association

FLASHING

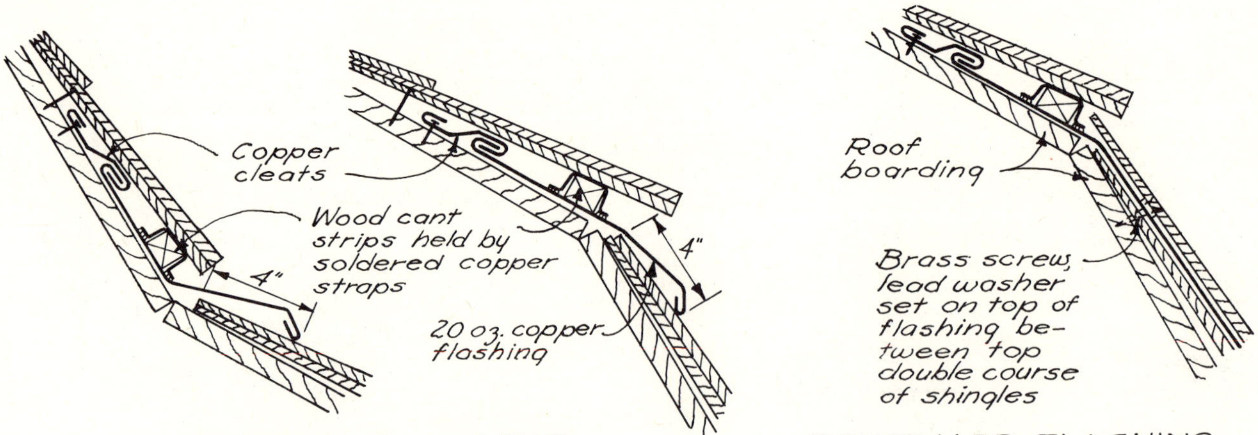
Copper cleats
Wood cant strips held by soldered copper straps
4"
4"
20 oz. copper flashing
Roof boarding
Brass screw, lead washer set on top of flashing between top double course of shingles

EXPOSED FLASHING

CONCEALED FLASHING

CHANGE IN ROOF SLOPE FLASHING

1½" = 1'-0"

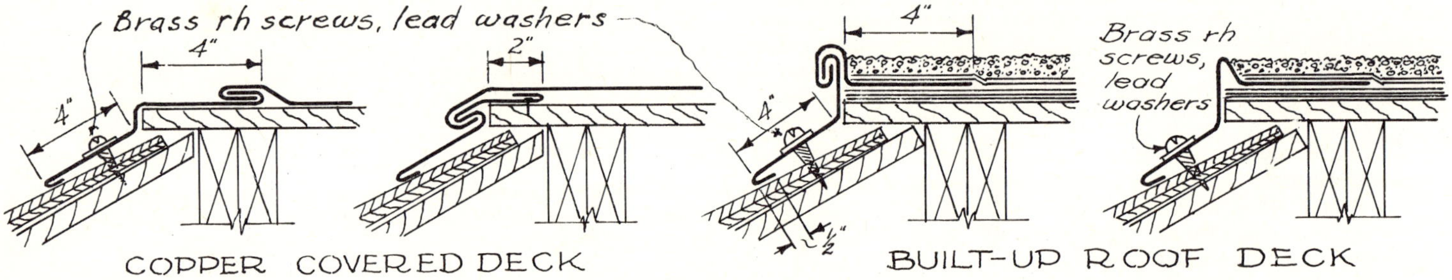
Brass rh screws, lead washers
4"
4"
2"
4"
4"
½"
Brass rh screws, lead washers

COPPER COVERED DECK

BUILT-UP ROOF DECK

SLOPED SHINGLED ROOF JOINING FLAT DECK

1½" = 1'-0"

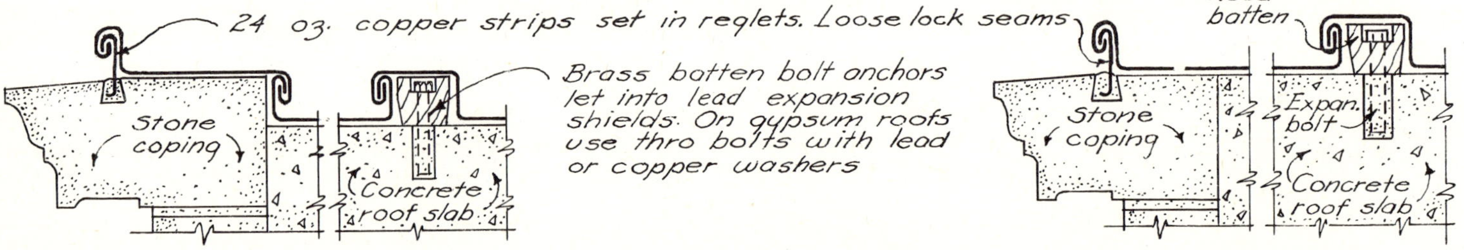
24 oz. copper strips set in reglets. Loose lock seams
Stone coping
Concrete roof slab
Brass batten bolt anchors let into lead expansion shields. On gypsum roofs use thro bolts with lead or copper washers
Wood batten
Stone coping
Expan. bolt
Concrete roof slab

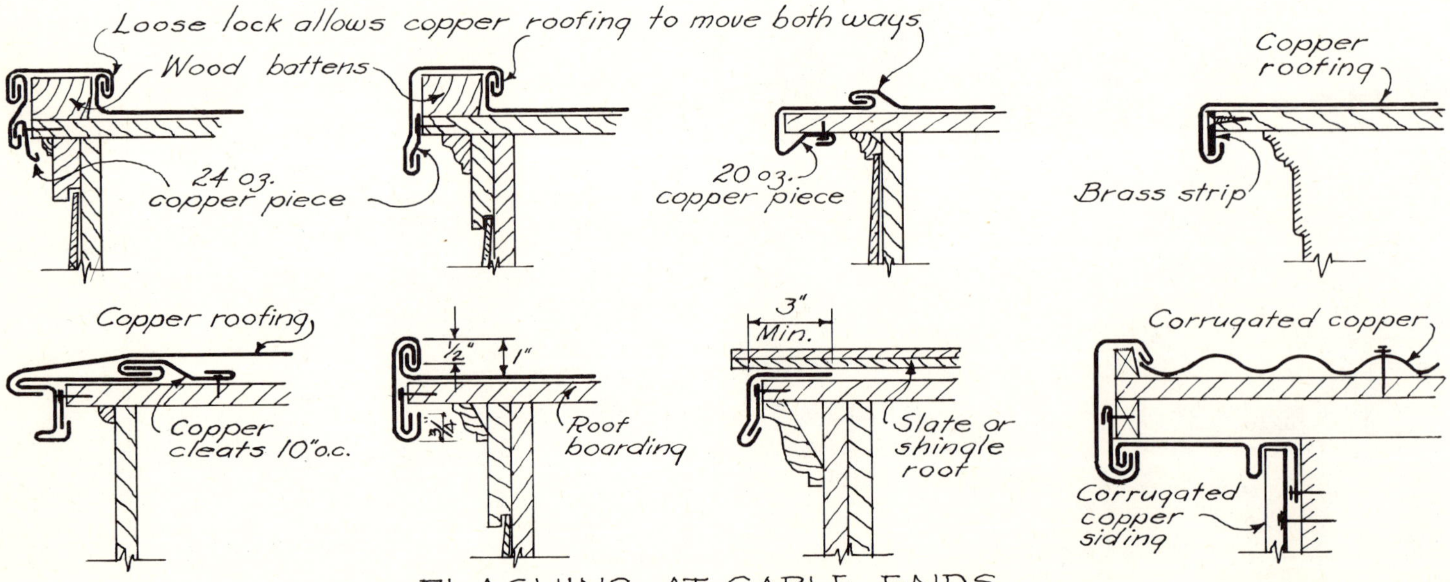
Loose lock allows copper roofing to move both ways
Wood battens
24 oz. copper piece
20 oz. copper piece
Copper roofing
Brass strip
Copper roofing
Copper cleats 10" o.c.
½"
1"
Roof boarding
3" Min.
Slate or shingle roof
Corrugated copper
Corrugated copper siding

FLASHING AT GABLE ENDS

1½" = 1'-0"

Recommendation of Copper & Brass Research Association

FLASHING

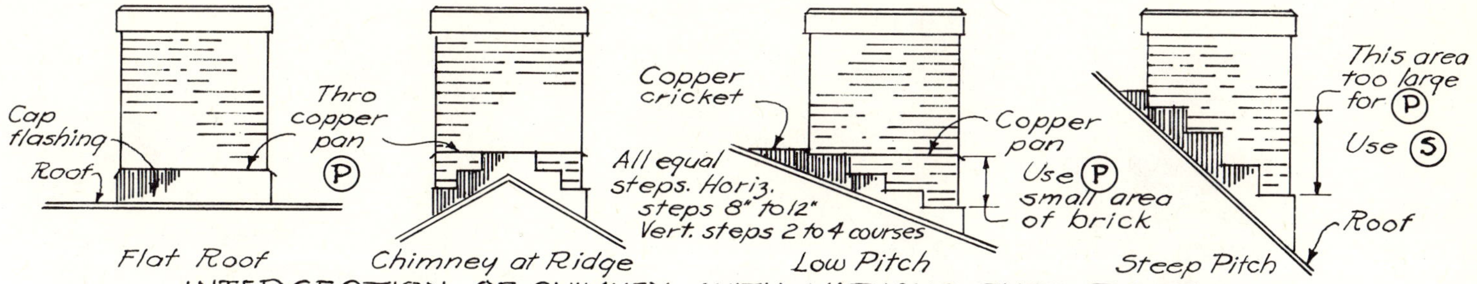

Cap flashing
Roof
Thro copper pan
P
Copper cricket
All equal steps. Horiz. steps 8" to 12" Vert. steps 2 to 4 courses
Copper pan
Use P small area of brick
This area too large for P
Use S
Roof
Flat Roof
Chimney at Ridge
Low Pitch
Steep Pitch

INTERSECTION OF CHIMNEY WITH VARIOUS TYPE ROOFS

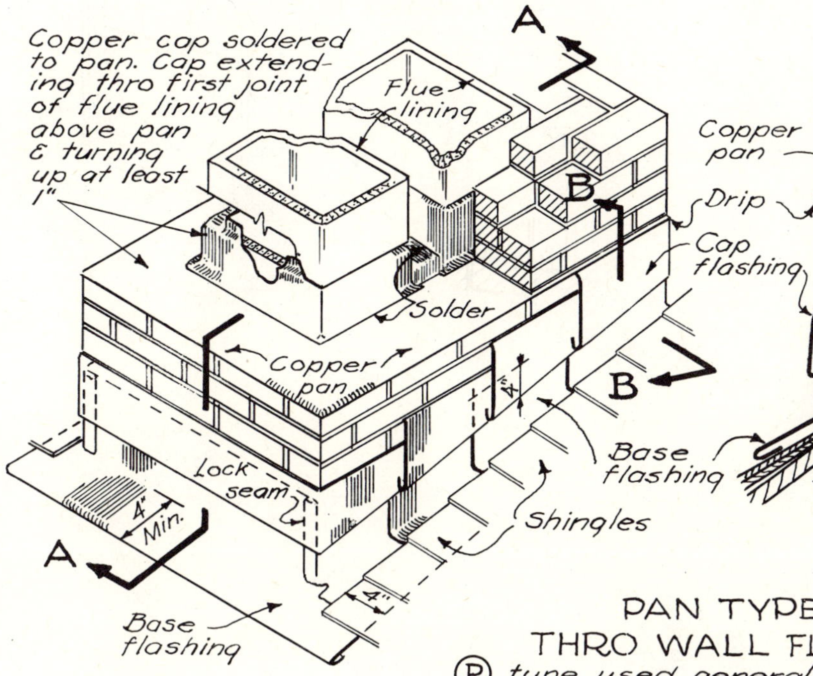

Copper cap soldered to pan. Cap extending thro first joint of flue lining above pan & turning up at least 1"
A
Flue lining
B
Solder
Copper pan
Lock seam
4" Min.
A
Base flashing
4"
B
Shingles

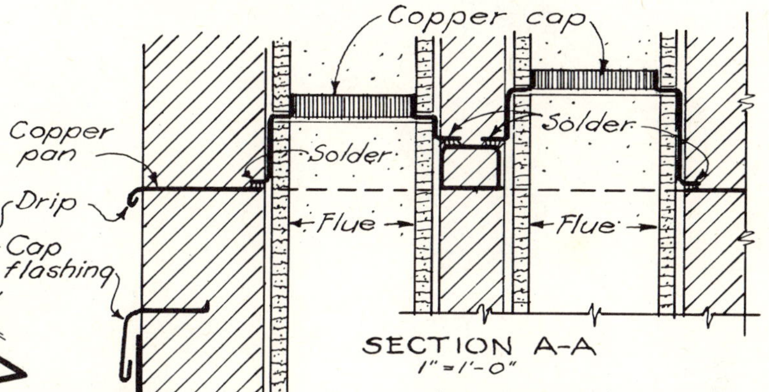

Copper cap
Copper pan
Solder
Solder
Drip
Flue
Flue
Cap flashing
Base flashing
Flue lining
SECTION A-A
1" = 1'-0"

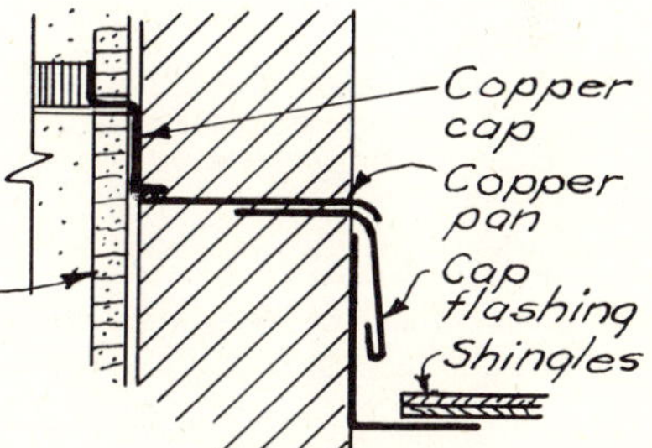

Copper cap
Copper pan
Cap flashing
Shingles
SECT. B-B
1" = 1'-0"

PAN TYPE (P)
THRO WALL FLASHING
(P) type used generally except on steep roofs or where large area of brick is exposed between copper pan & lower cap flashing

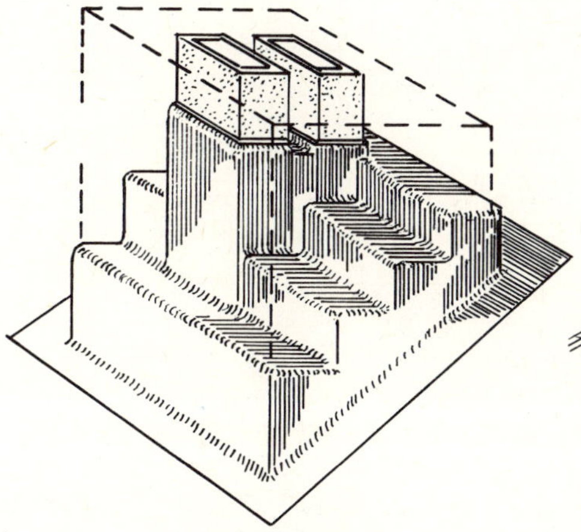

STEPPED
THRO FLASHING
TYPE (S)

This type of thro wall flashing used for steep roofs or where a large area of brick is exposed to the weather. In chimneys built of stone rubble or ashlar this type of flashing is especially recommended.

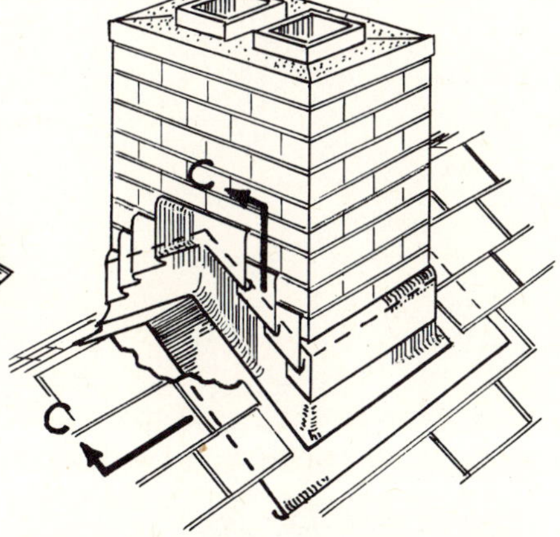

C
C

FLASHING AT RIDGE

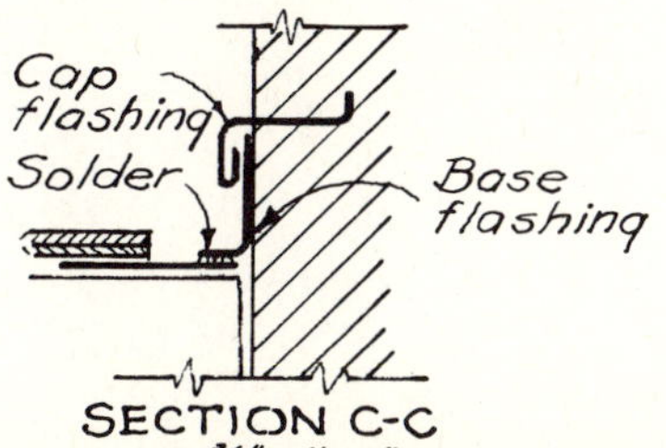

Cap flashing
Solder
Base flashing

SECTION C-C
3/4" = 1'-0"

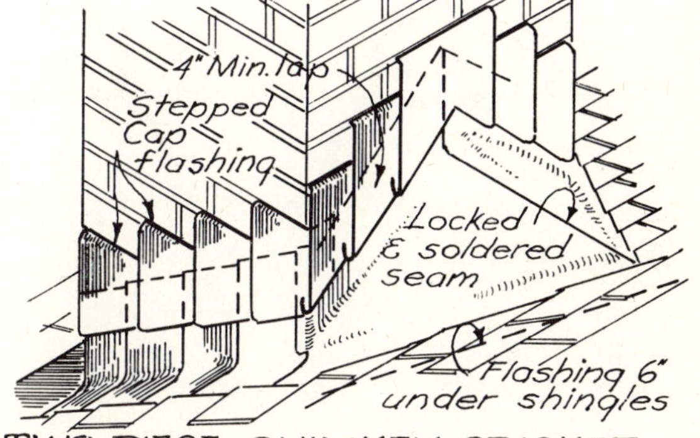

4" Min. lap
Stepped Cap flashing
Locked & soldered seam
Flashing 6" under shingles

TWO PIECE CHIMNEY CRICKET

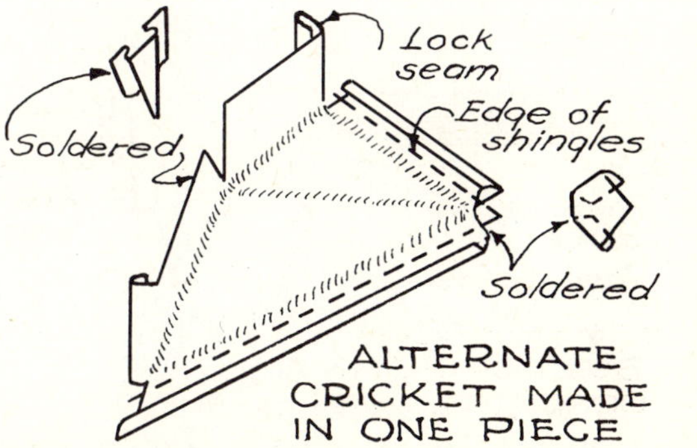

Lock seam
Edge of shingles
Soldered
Soldered

ALTERNATE CRICKET MADE IN ONE PIECE

Recommendation of Copper & Brass Research Association

FLASHING

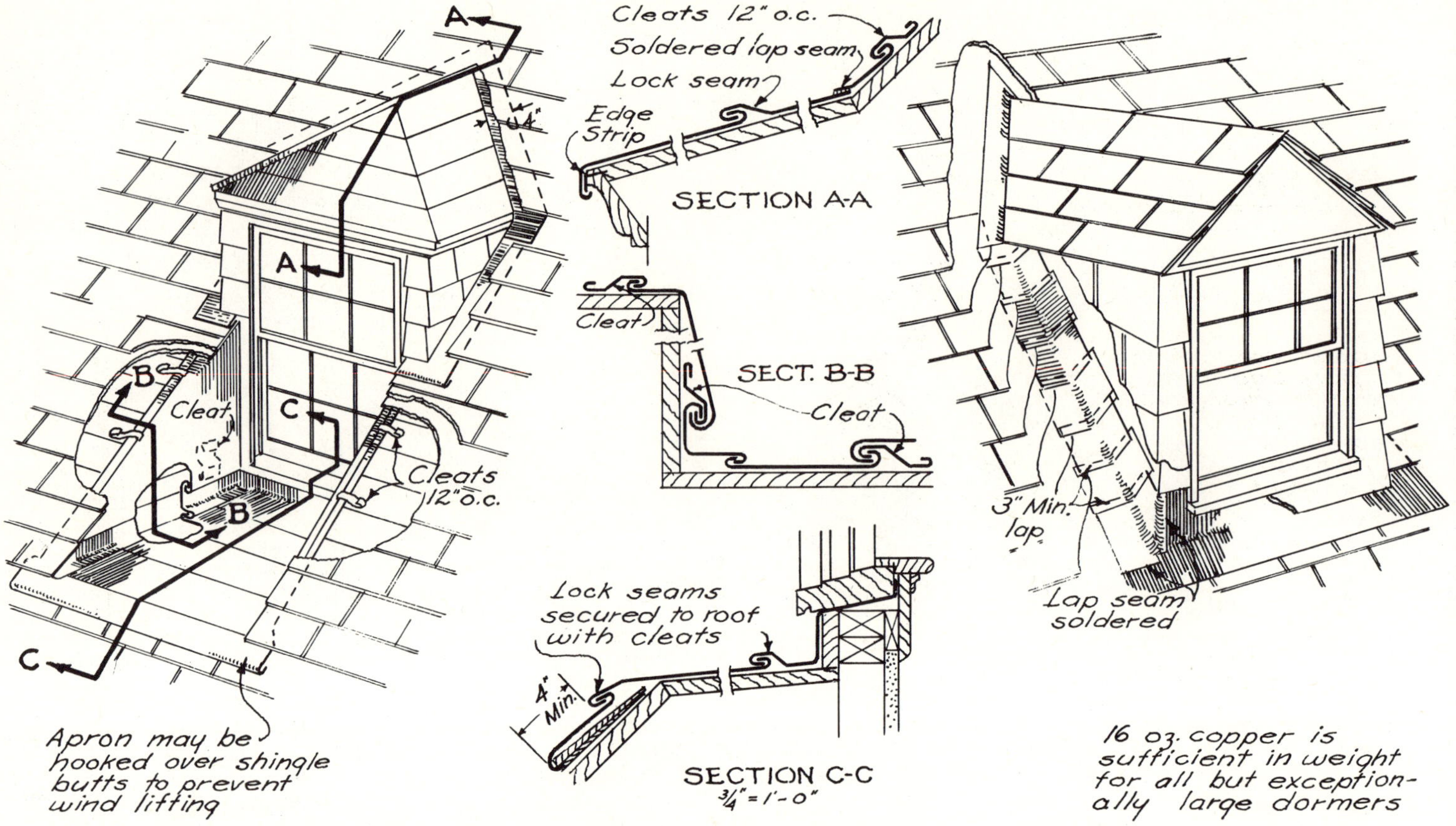
A
A
B
B
C
C
Cleat
Cleats 12" o.c.
1/4"
Apron may be hooked over shingle butts to prevent wind lifting
Cleats 12" o.c.
Soldered lap seam
Lock seam
Edge Strip
SECTION A-A
Cleat
SECT. B-B
Cleat
Lock seams secured to roof with cleats
4" Min.
SECTION C-C
3/4" = 1'-0"
3" Min. lap
Lap seam soldered
16 oz. copper is sufficient in weight for all but exceptionally large dormers

DORMER FLASHING

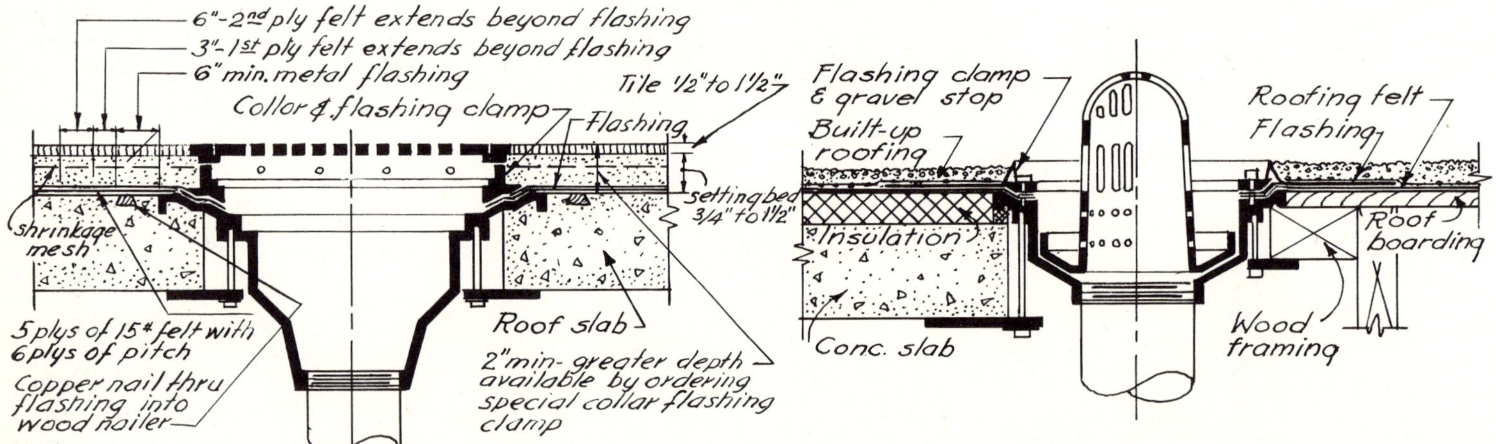
6"-2nd ply felt extends beyond flashing
3"-1st ply felt extends beyond flashing
6" min. metal flashing
Collar & flashing clamp
Flashing
Tile 1/2" to 1 1/2"
setting bed 3/4" to 1 1/2"
shrinkage mesh
5 plys of 15# felt with 6 plys of pitch
Copper nail thru flashing into wood nailer
Roof slab
2" min- greater depth available by ordering special collar flashing clamp
Flashing clamp & gravel stop
Built-up roofing
Insulation
Conc. slab
Roofing felt
Flashing
Roof boarding
Wood framing

ROOF DRAIN IN CONCRETE SLAB WITH PROMENADE TOP

ROOF DRAIN IN CONCRETE SLAB — WOOD CONST.

ROOF DRAINS

1 1/2" = 1'-0"

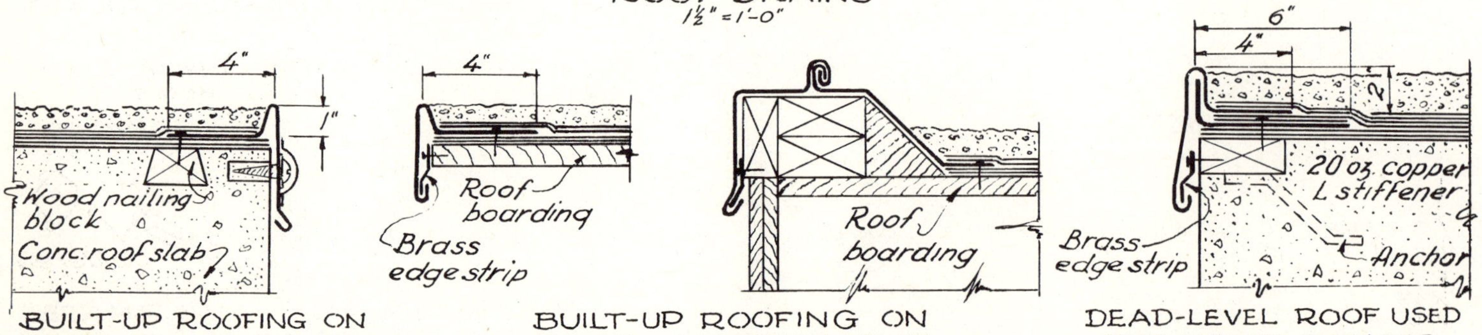
4"
1"
Wood nailing block
Conc. roof slab
4"
Roof boarding
Brass edge strip
Roof boarding
6"
4"
2"
20 oz. copper L stiffener
Brass edge strip
Anchor

BUILT-UP ROOFING ON CONCRETE ROOF SLAB

BUILT-UP ROOFING ON WOOD CONSTRUCTION

DEAD-LEVEL ROOF USED FOR WATER COOLING

GRAVEL STOPS & EAVES

1 1/2" = 1'-0"

Recommendation of Copper & Brass Research Ass'n.

FLASHING

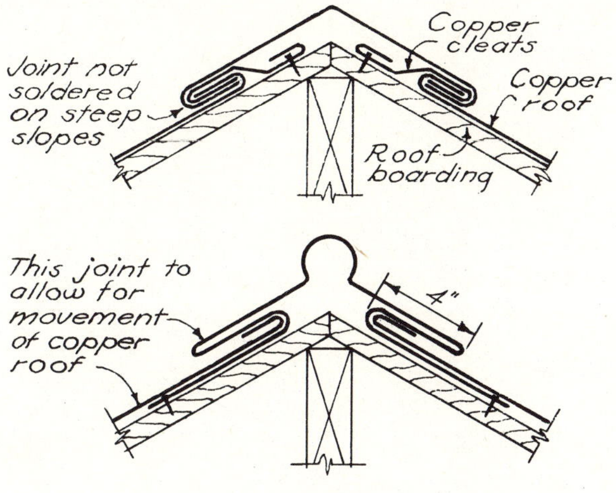
Joint not soldered on steep slopes
Copper cleats
Copper roof
Roof boarding
This joint to allow for movement of copper roof
4"

FOR COPPER ROOFS

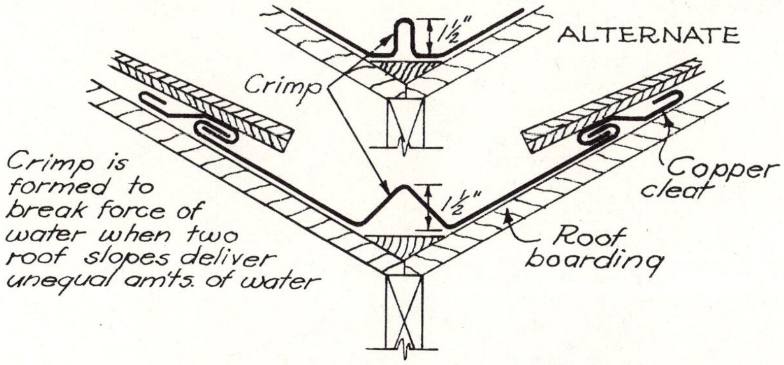
1½"
ALTERNATE
Crimp
Crimp is formed to break force of water when two roof slopes deliver unequal am'ts. of water
1½"
Copper cleat
Roof boarding

CRIMP IN VALLEY

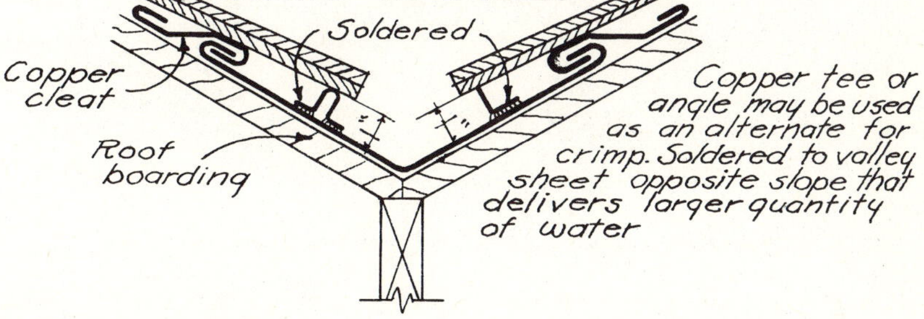
Soldered
Copper cleat
Roof boarding
Copper tee or angle may be used as an alternate for crimp. Soldered to valley sheet opposite slope that delivers larger quantity of water

TEE OR ANGLE IN VALLEY (Alternate for crimp)

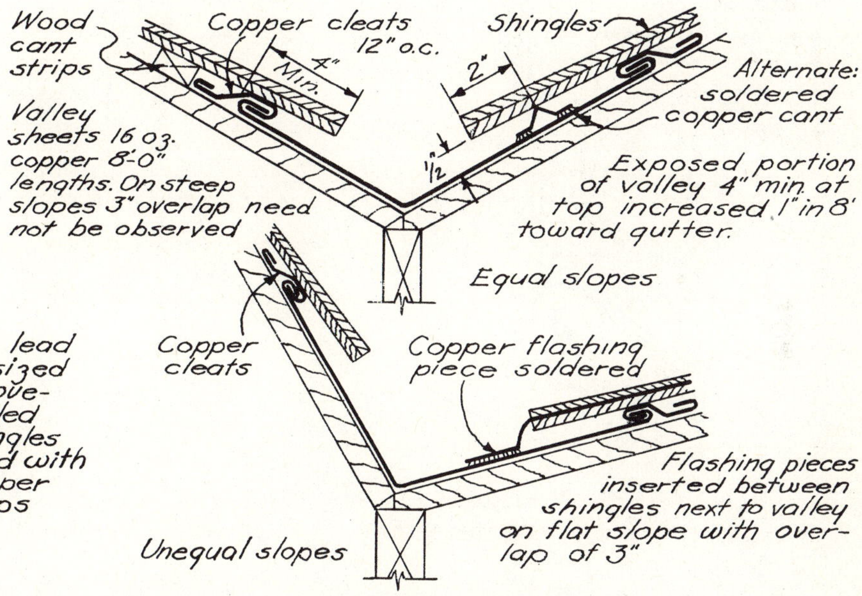
Wood cant strips
Copper cleats 12" o.c.
4" Min.
Shingles
2"
Alternate: soldered copper cant
Valley sheets 16 oz. copper 8'-0" lengths. On steep slopes 3" overlap need not be observed
1½"
Exposed portion of valley 4" min. at top increased 1" in 8' toward gutter.
Equal slopes
Copper cleats
Copper flashing piece soldered
Flashing pieces inserted between shingles next to valley on flat slope with overlap of 3"
Unequal slopes

OPEN VALLEY

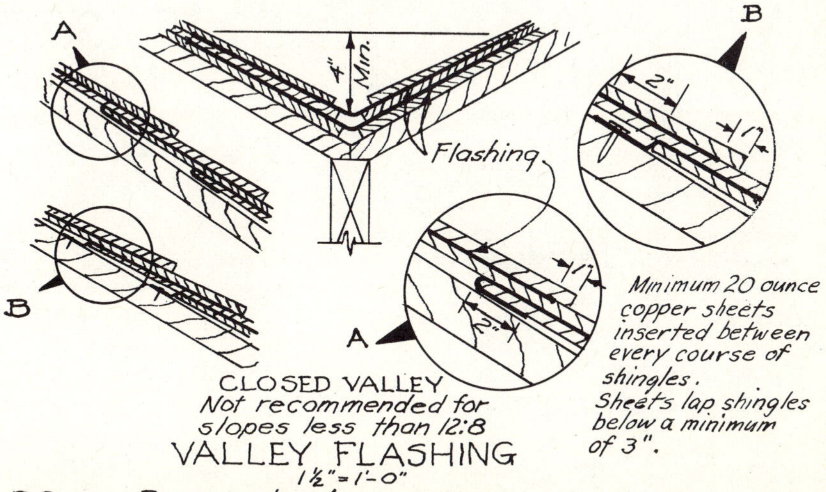
A
4" Min.
B
Flashing
2"
B
A
2"
Minimum 20 ounce copper sheets inserted between every course of shingles.
Sheets lap shingles below a minimum of 3".

CLOSED VALLEY
Not recommended for slopes less than 12:8

VALLEY FLASHING
1½"=1'-0"

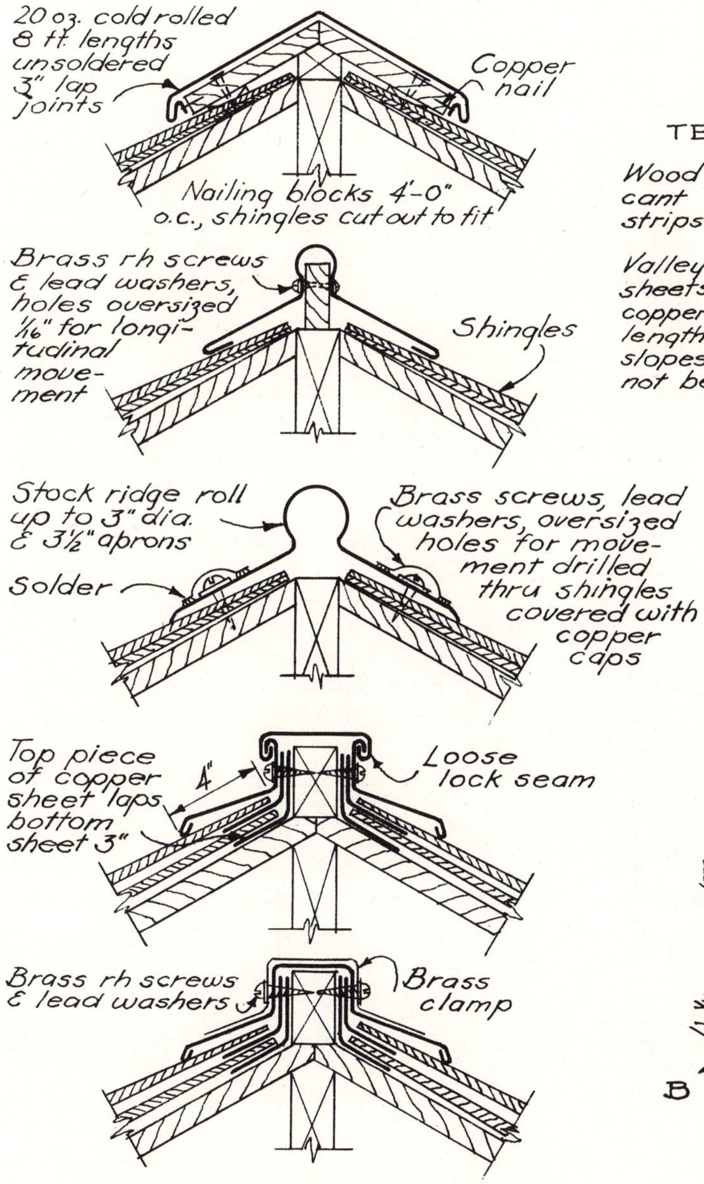
20 oz. cold rolled 8 ft. lengths unsoldered 3" lap joints
Copper nail
Nailing blocks 4'-0" o.c., shingles cut out to fit
Brass rh screws & lead washers, holes oversized 1/16" for longitudinal movement
Shingles
Stock ridge roll up to 3" dia. & 3½" aprons
Solder
Brass screws, lead washers, oversized holes for movement drilled thru shingles covered with copper caps
Top piece of copper sheet laps bottom sheet 3"
4"
Loose lock seam
Brass rh screws & lead washers
Brass clamp

FOR SHINGLE TYPE ROOFS
HIP & RIDGE FLASHING
1½"=1'-0"

Recommendation of Copper & Brass Research Association

FLASHING

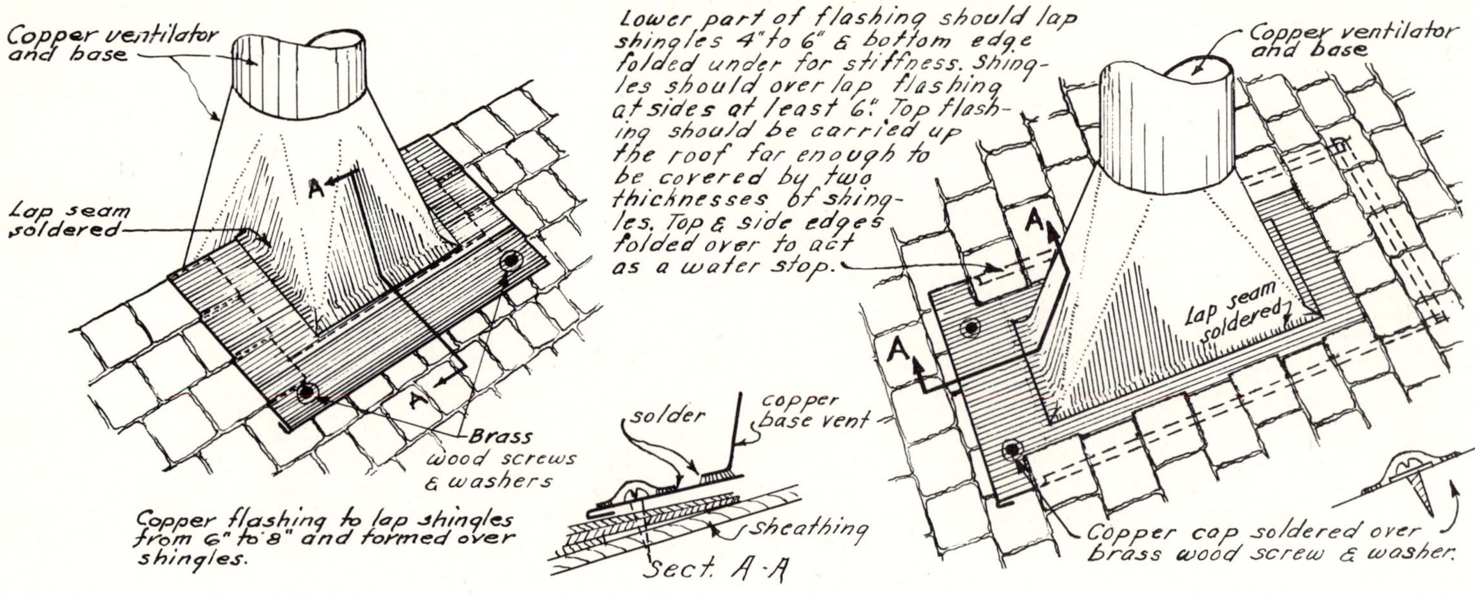
Copper ventilator and base
Lap seam soldered
Brass wood screws & washers
Copper flashing to lap shingles from 6" to 8" and formed over shingles.
Lower part of flashing should lap shingles 4" to 6" & bottom edge folded under for stiffness. Shingles should over lap flashing at sides at least 6". Top flashing should be carried up the roof far enough to be covered by two thicknesses of shingles. Top & side edges folded over to act as a water stop.
solder
copper base vent
sheathing
Sect. A-A
Copper ventilator and base
Lap seam soldered
Copper cap soldered over brass wood screw & washer.

VENTILATOR ON RIDGE OF SHINGLE ROOF. VENTILATOR ON SLOPE OF SHINGLE ROOF.

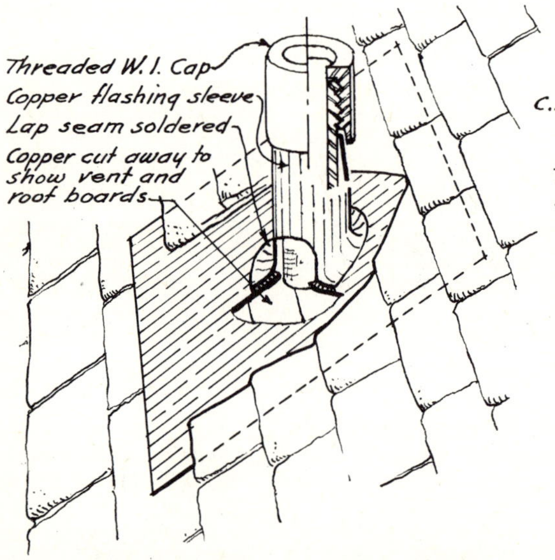
Threaded W.I. Cap
Copper flashing sleeve
Lap seam soldered
Copper cut away to show vent and roof boards

VENT PIPE THROUGH A SLOPING SHINGLE ROOF.

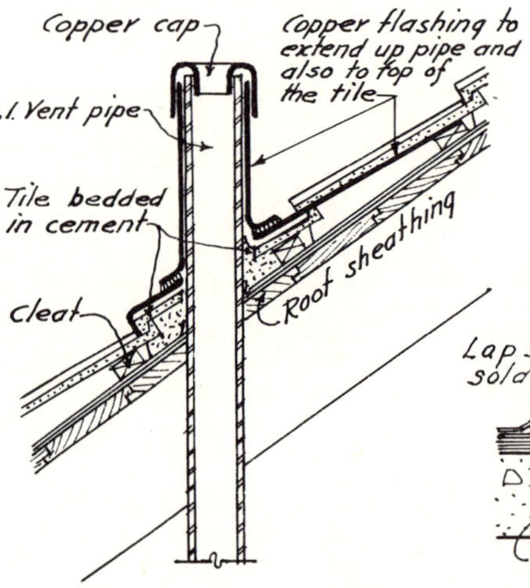
Copper cap
Copper flashing to extend up pipe and also to top of the tile
C.I. Vent pipe
Tile bedded in cement
Cleat
Roof sheathing

CAST IRON VENT THRO' CONCRETE TILE

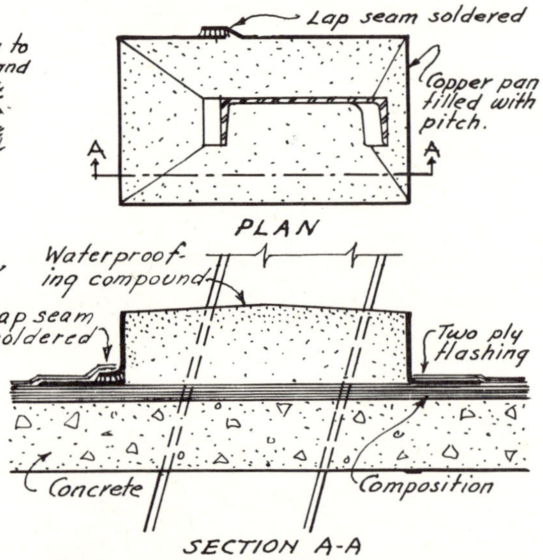
Lap seam soldered
Copper pan filled with pitch.
PLAN
Waterproofing compound
Lap seam soldered
Two ply flashing
Concrete
Composition
SECTION A-A

STEEL STRUCTURAL MEMBER THROUGH CONCRETE.

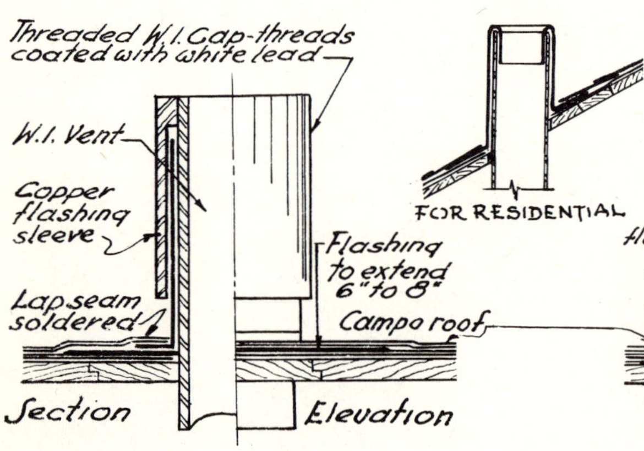
Threaded W.I. Cap-threads coated with white lead
W.I. Vent
Copper flashing sleeve
Flashing to extend 6" to 8"
Lap seam soldered
Campo roof
FOR RESIDENTIAL
Section
Elevation

FLASHING FOR IRON VENT *with* SCREW CAP

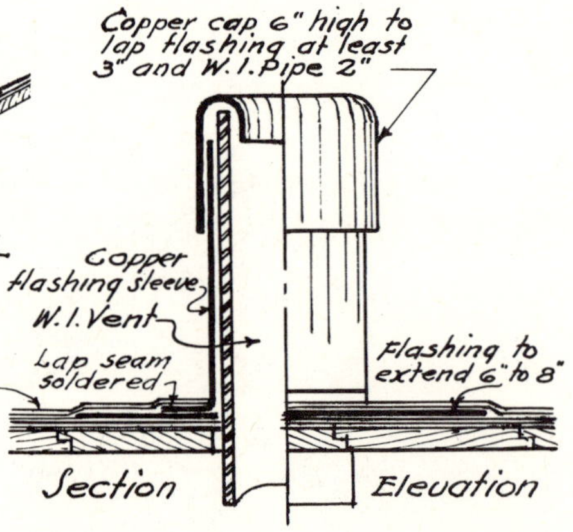
Copper cap 6" high to lap flashing at least 3" and W.I. Pipe 2"
Copper flashing sleeve
W.I. Vent
Lap seam soldered
Flashing to extend 6" to 8"
Section
Elevation

FLASHING FOR IRON VENT *with* COPPER CAP

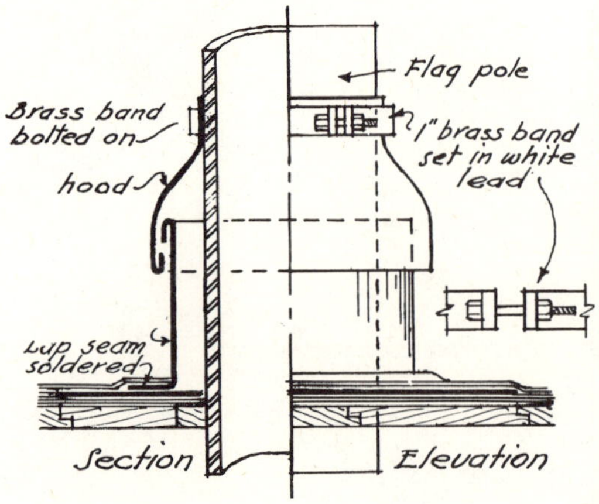
Flag pole
Brass band bolted on
1" brass band set in white lead
hood
Lap seam soldered
Section
Elevation

FLASHING *for* FLAG POLE

COPPER FLASHING *for* ROOF VENTS, VENTILATORS, FLAG POLES ETC:

Methods recommended by the Copper and Brass Research Association.

COPPER ROOFING & FLASHING

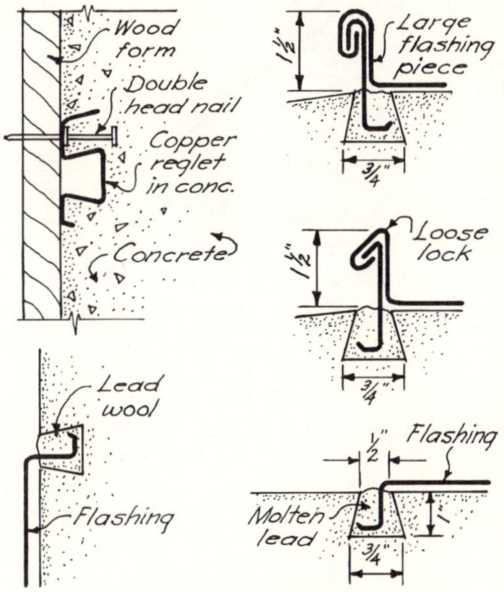

Wood form
Double head nail
Copper reglet in conc.
Concrete
1½"
Large flashing piece
¾"
Loose lock
1½"
¾"
Lead wool
Flashing
½"
Flashing
Molten lead
1"
¾"

DETAILS of REGLETS
3" = 1'-0"

Lead caulking need not be continuous nor filled to very top of reglet. Lead plugs may be driven in at 12" intervals, space intervening & reglet top filled with elastic cem.

UNSOLDERED (Loose lap)
When loose lap seams are used on slopes amt. of lap determined by pitch.

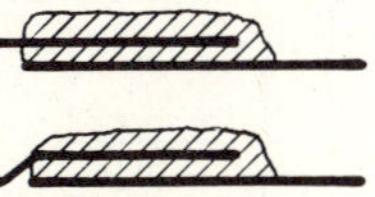

SOLDERED
Pretin edge of sheet for solder, ½" min. wider than fin. seam. 1" lap for 20 oz., 1¼" for 20 to 24.

HEAVY SHEETS RIVETED

LAP SEAMS

HOOK LOCK
Pieces hooked together & joint malleted down.

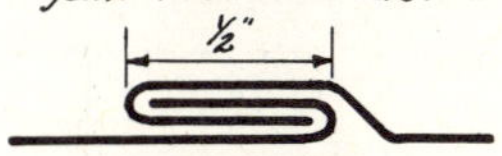

½"

FLAT LOCK
Developed from hook seam by use of grooving iron. Used where not room enough for hook lock.

DOUBLE LOCK
Virtually standing seam bent flat. Used to avoid soldering or to allow expansion & contraction

LOCK SEAMS

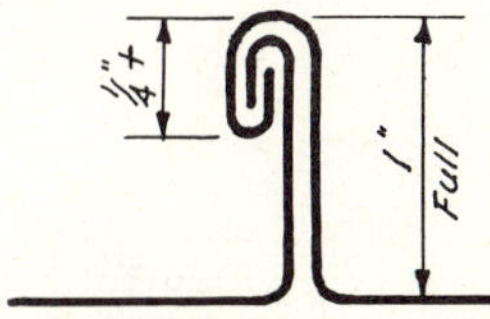

1¼"+
1" Full

STANDING SEAM
This seam allows for expansion & contraction

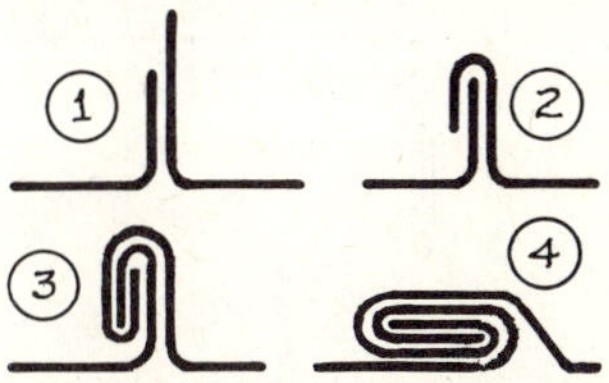

1
2
3
4

DEVELOPMENT of DOUBLE LOCK or STANDING SEAM

2"

Point driven into sheathing on new roofs. Slate butts rest against loop.

For slate roofs already laid. Hook over upper edge of slate.

For old roofs. Also soldered to copper roofs.

Spacing: Approx. 18" staggered in both directions
COPPER WIRE SNOW GUARDS (3 or 4 rows)

ADJUSTABLE BRACKET & PIPE SNOW GUARD
Spacing of brackets 6' max. Brass pipe & bronze plate fastening & brackets.
Also made with 3 pipes.

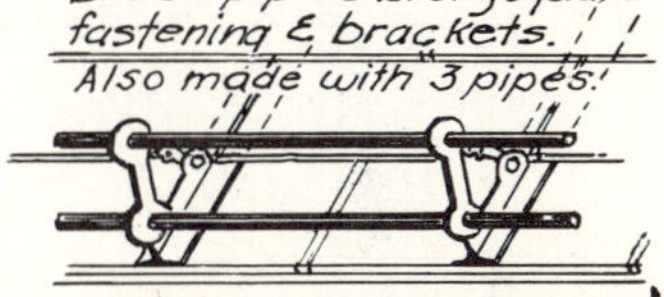

TEMPER & WEIGHT of COPPER SHEET & SHAPES FOR VARIOUS USES

NOTE: CR = cold rolled; S = Soft; * Membrane flashing

WHERE USED	TEMPER & WEIGHT Oz. per ft.²	WHERE USED	TEMPER & WEIGHT Oz. per ft.²	WHERE USED	TEMPER & WEIGHT Oz. per ft.²	WHERE USED	TEMPER & WEIGHT Oz. per ft.²
Cant Strips	16 CR	-Jambs	3* or 6 S	Gutters, Built-in - Apron	16 CR	-Batten Covers	16 CR
Chimneys	16 CR	-Sills	16 CR	-Lining	Varies	-Lock Strips	16 CR
Dormer Roofs	16 or 20 CR	Gable Ends	20 CR	-Lock Strip	Varies	-Valleys	16 CR
Dowels, Rods, Struts	16 or 20 CR	Hips	20 CR	-Half Round, Hanging	16 CR	-Standing Seam - Pan	16 or 20 CR
Edge Strips	16 to 32 CR	Hips, Saddle	16 CR	-Molded (or Box)	16 CR	-Roll	16 or 20 CR
Flashings:		Masonry Veneer	10 S	-Pole	16 CR	-Small Hse.	10 CR
Base, Low	16 CR	Ridges	16 CR	Leaders	16 CR	-Valleys	16 CR
Base, High	20 CR	Thro-Wall - Concealed	6 or 10 S	Leader Heads	16 or 20 CR	-Flat Seam - Cleats	20 CR
Belt Courses, Stone	20 CR	-Exposed, Wide	16 S	Leader Straps	16 CR	-Sheets	20 CR
Cap (Counter)	16 CR	-Exposed, Narrow	10 S	Louvres - Frame Covering	16 S	-Corrugated - Sheets	20 CR
Cavity Wall	10 S	Valleys, Closed - Slate or Tile	20 CR	-Slats	20 CR	Scuppers	20 CR
Copings	20 CR	-Wood	16 CR	Outlets - Gutter	16 to 24 CR	Siding - Standing Seam	20 CR
Cornices, Stone	20 CR	Valleys, Open - Slate or Tile	24 CR	-Roof	16 to 32 CR	-Flat Seam	20 CR
Cornices, Wood	16 CR	-Wood	16 CR	Roofing - Batten Seam - 20" pans	16 CR	-Corrugated	16 CR
Door & Window - Heads	3* or 6 S	Gravel Stops	16 or 20 CR	-24" pans	20 CR	Vents & Ventilators	16 or 20 CR

STANDARD SIZES of SHEET COPPER, SOFT & COLD-ROLL

WEIGHT Oz. per ft.²	WIDTH Inches			LENGTH Inches
32	24	30	36	96
24	24	30	36	96
20	24	30	36	96
1.8	24	30	36	96
1.6	24	30	36	96
1.4	24	30	36	96

STANDARD SIZES of STRIP COPPER

WEIGHT Oz. per ft.²	SIZE Inches	WEIGHT Oz. per ft.²	SIZE Inches
32	20 × 96	16	15 × 96
24	20 × 96	16	14 × 96
20	20 × 96	16	12 × 96
18	20 × 96	16	10 × 96
16	20 × 120	14	20 × 96
16	20 × 96	10	16 × 72

NOTE: The above weights & sizes are generally preferred but additional weights & sizes are available. Strip is also generally available in rolls of 16 oz. copper in widths varying from 6" to 20" & from about 50' to 100' in length, depending on width, weighing between 80 & 100 lbs.
Details of Copper Roofing & Flashing applicable to Zinc Roofing & Flashing. For information on Zinc Roofing see page of that title.

Recommendation of Copper & Brass Research Association.

GRAVEL STOPS and WATER TABLES

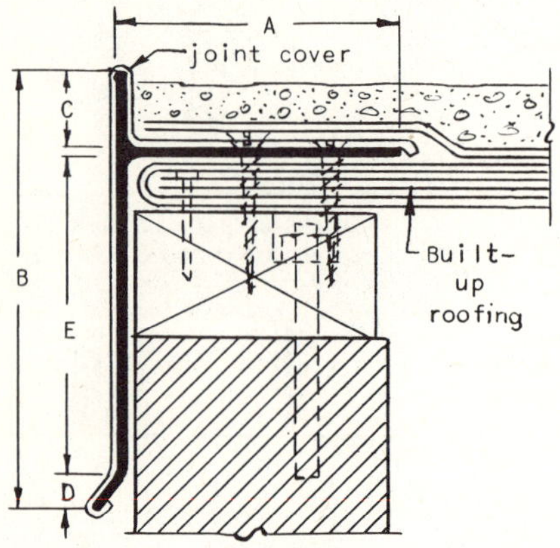
A
joint cover
C
B
E
D
Built-
up
roofing

TYPE E

SECTION	A	B	C	D	E
42058	4"	5"	1"	7/16"	3/32"
42054	4"	3 1/2"	5/8"	9/32"	3/32"
42063	4"	7 3/4"	5/8"	1/4"	1/8"
39259	4"	6 1/2"	3/4"	3/8"	3/32"
66588	4"	6"	1 1/2"	3/8"	3/32"

Note: Type E available in sections shown above.

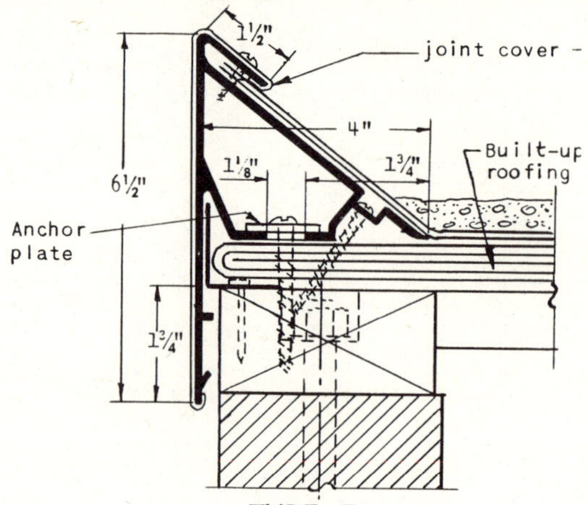
1 1/2"
joint cover
4"
6 1/2"
1 1/8"
1 3/4"
Built-up
roofing
Anchor
plate
1 3/4"

TYPE F

DATA SUPPLIED BY ALUMINUM COMPANY OF AMERICA

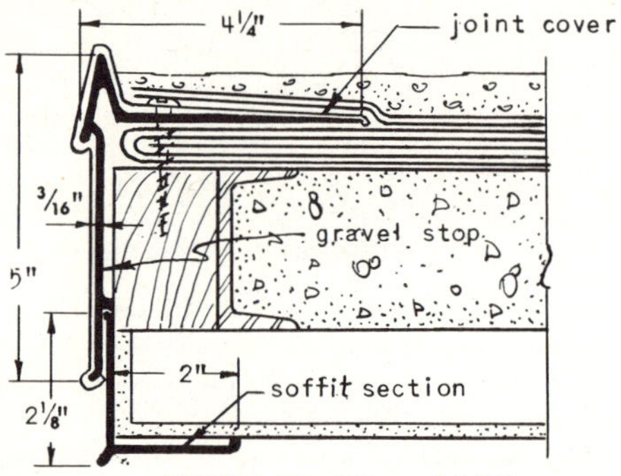
4 1/4"
joint cover
3/16"
gravel stop
5"
2"
soffit section
2 1/8"

SECTION NO. 3133

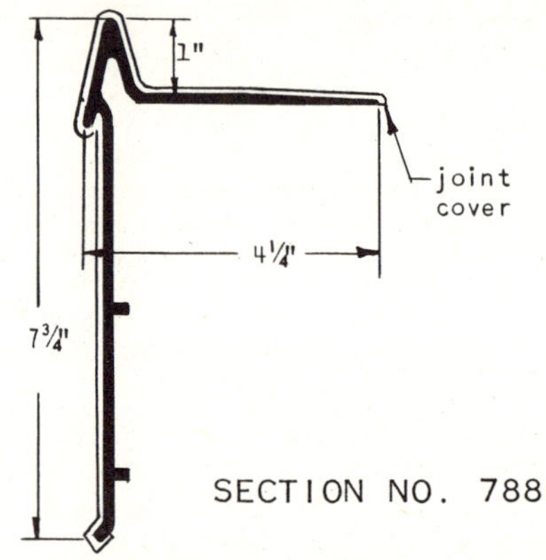
1"
joint
cover
4 1/4"
7 3/4"

SECTION NO. 7886

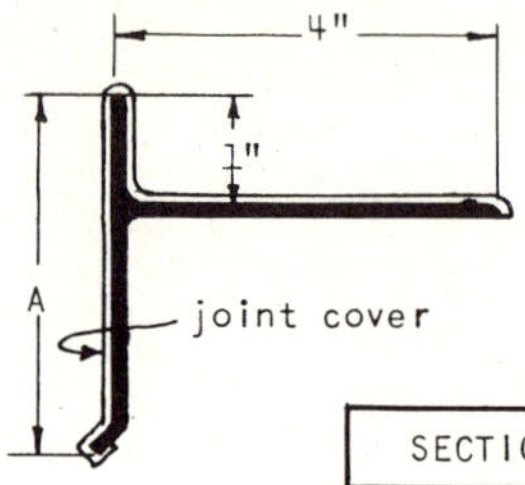
4"
1"
A
joint cover

SECTION	A
4632	3 1/2"
9852	5"
8972	6 1/2"
13011	7 3/4"

All gravel stops available in 10'-0" length

DATA SUPPLIED BY REYNOLDS METALS COMPANY

ALUMINUM GRAVEL STOPS

scale 3" = 1'-0"

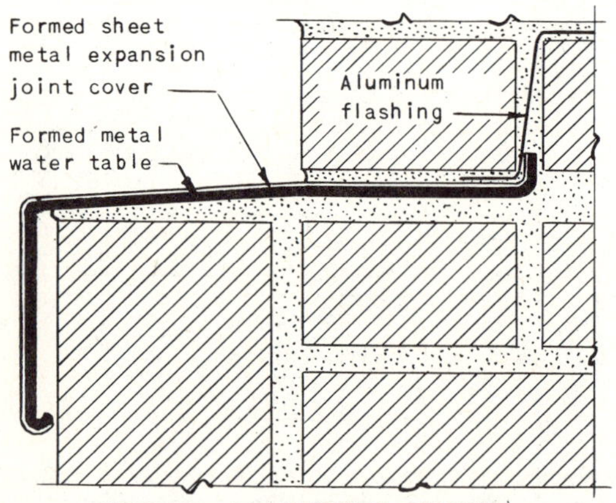
Formed sheet
metal expansion
joint cover
Aluminum
flashing
Formed metal
water table

FORMED ALUMINUM SHEET

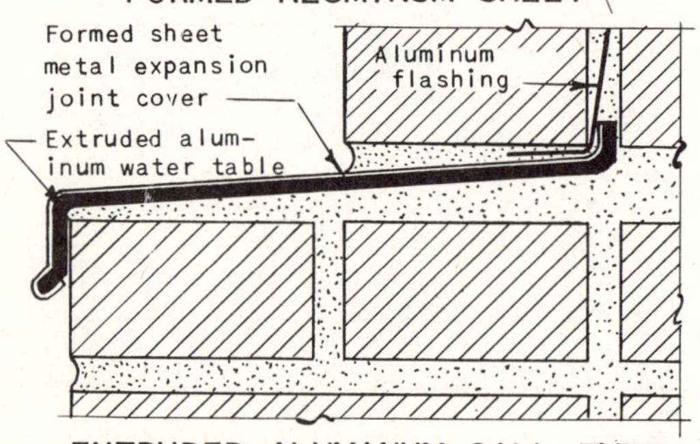
Formed sheet
metal expansion
joint cover
Aluminum
flashing
Extruded alum-
inum water table

EXTRUDED ALUMINUM SILL TYPE

See page on Metal Sills

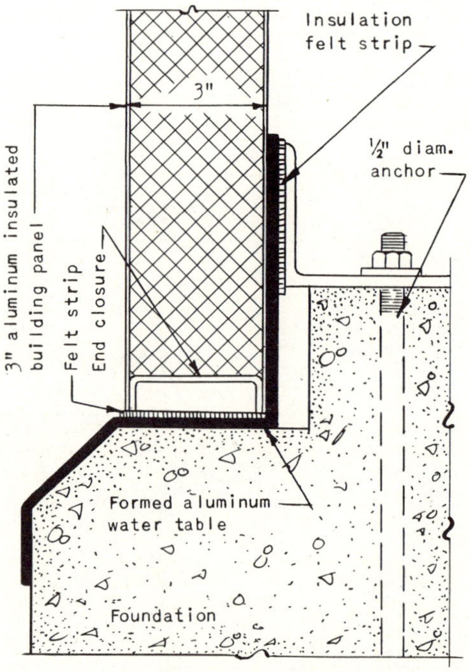
Insulation
felt strip
3"
1/2" diam.
anchor
3" aluminum insulated
building panel
Felt strip
End closure
Formed aluminum
water table
Foundation

FORMED ALUMINUM
DETROIT STEEL PRODUCTS
CO. "C" PANEL WALL

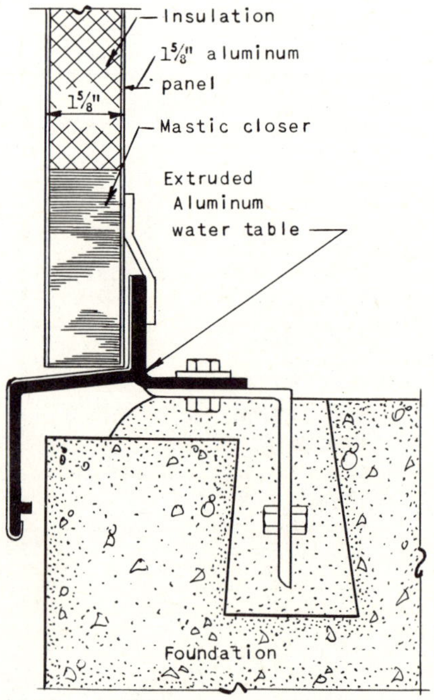
Insulation
1 5/8" aluminum
panel
1 5/8"
Mastic closer
Extruded
Aluminum
water table
Foundation

EXTRUDED ALUMINUM
PANEL WALL

H. H. Robertson Co.

EXTRUDED & FORMED METAL WATER TABLES

scale: 3" = 1'-0"

ALUMINUM COPINGS

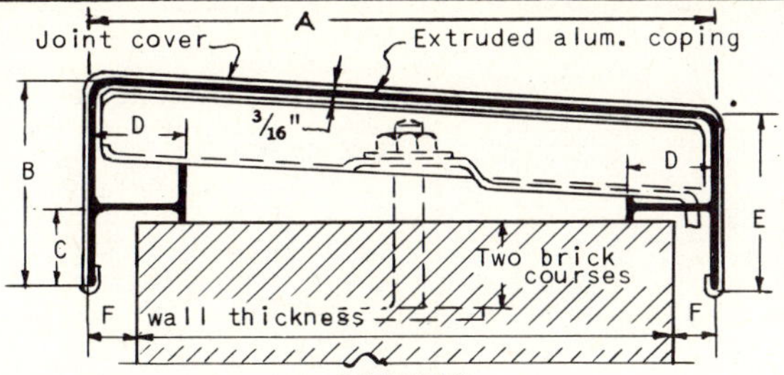
A
Joint cover
Extruded alum. coping
3/16"
D
D
B
C
E
Two brick courses
F
wall thickness
F

SECTION

TYPE	A	B	C	D	E	F
G-8	9½"	3⅛"	1¼"	1½"	2⅝"	¾"
G-12	14"	3⅞"	1¼"	1¾"	3$\frac{3}{16}$"	¾"

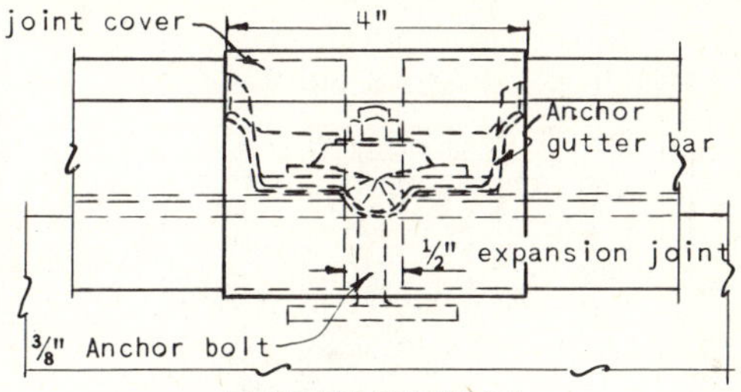
joint cover
4"
Anchor gutter bar
½" expansion joint
⅜" Anchor bolt

REAR ELEVATION

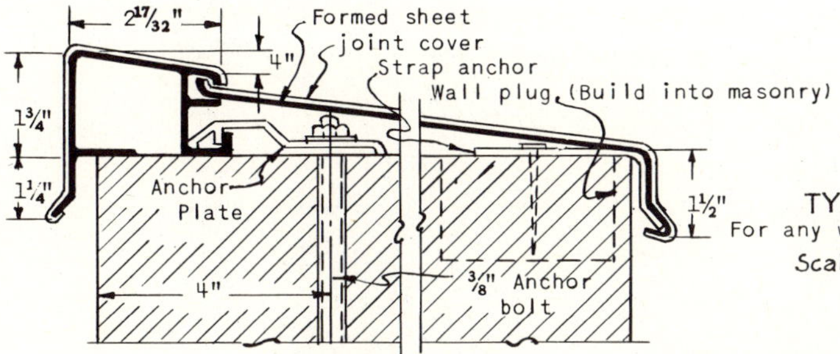
2$\frac{17}{32}$"
Formed sheet
joint cover
Strap anchor
Wall plug (Build into masonry)
4"
1¾"
1¼"
Anchor Plate
1½"
4"
⅜" Anchor bolt

SECTION

TYPE A-46
For any wall thickness
Scale 3" = 1'-0"

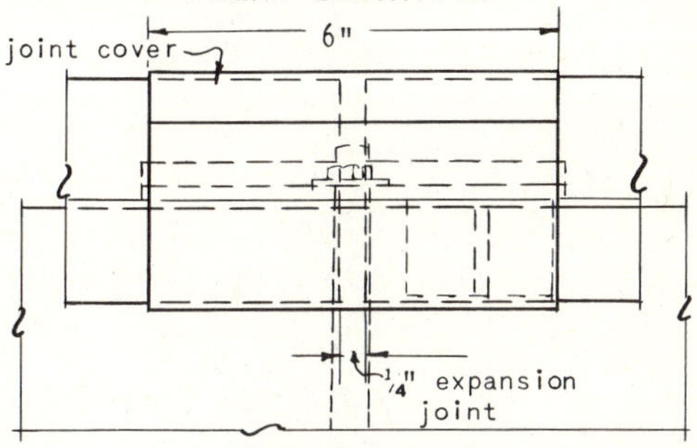
joint cover
6"
¼" expansion joint

REAR ELEVATION

MANUFACTURED BY: ALUMINUM CO. OF AMERICA

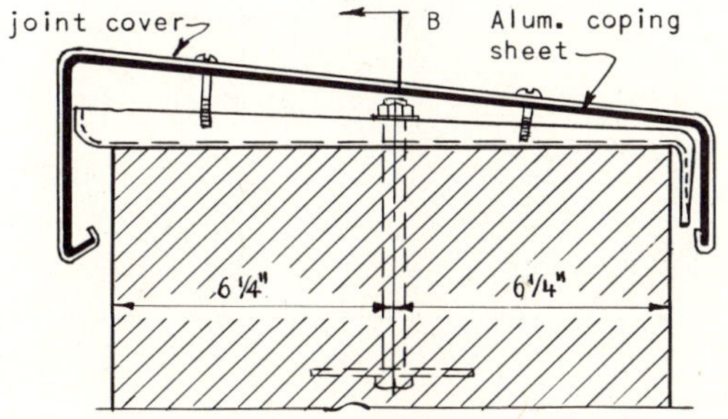
joint cover
B
Alum. coping sheet
6¼"
6¼"

SECTION

Similar prefabricated copings may be formed of any corrosion-resistant metal. Standard shapes are formed for walls 8½ & 12½" width. Various fascia profiles may be integrated in the standard const.

Recommended gauge of coping
Aluminum............................ 14 B & S ga.
Stainless steel.................. 24 U.S. ga.
Copper...................... 24 ounce cold rolled
Monel...24 ga.

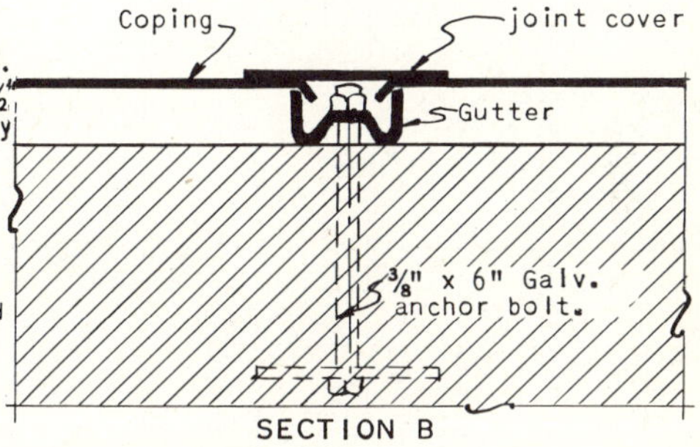
Coping
joint cover
Gutter
⅜" x 6" Galv. anchor bolt.

SECTION B

OVERLY MFG. CO. GOODWIN

Scale 2" = 1'-0"

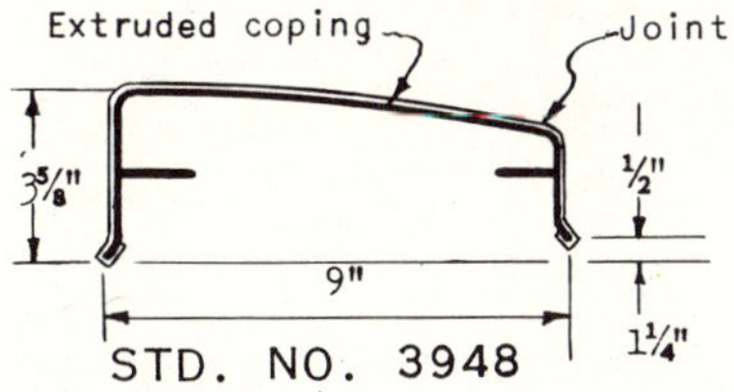
Extruded coping
Joint cover
3⅝"
½"
9"
1¼"

STD. NO. 3948

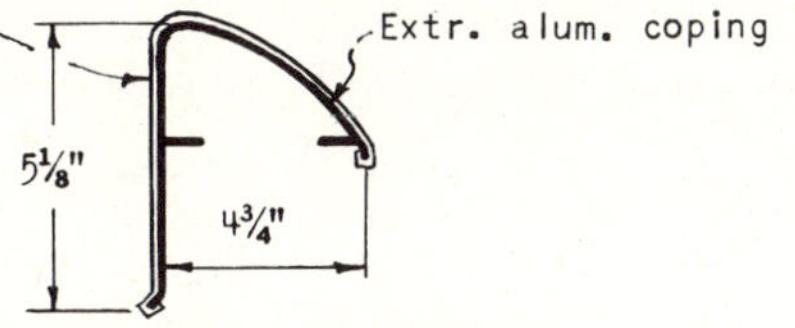
Extr. alum. coping
5⅛"
4¾"

STD. NO. P-3909

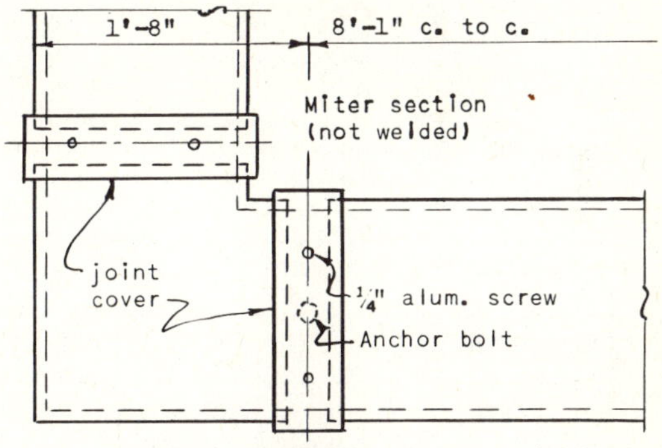
1'-8"
8'-1" c. to c.
Miter section (not welded)
joint cover
¼" alum. screw
Anchor bolt

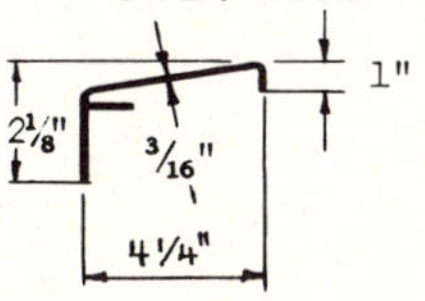
1"
2⅛"
3/16"
4¼"

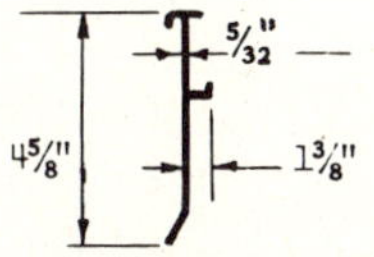
5/32
4⅝"
1⅜"

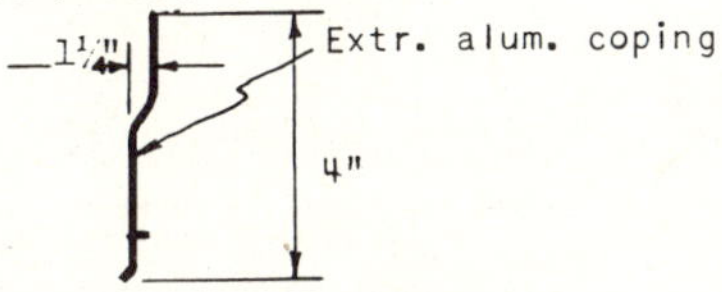
1¼"
Extr. alum. coping
4"

STD. NO. P-3131 STD.NO. 3947 STD. NO. 3223

Installation same as shown at top of this page

MANUFACTURED BY: REYNOLDS METALS COMPANY.

NOTE: Coping available in 10'-0" length.

Scale: 1½" = 1'-0"

PLAN

OVERLY MFG. CO. GOODWIN.

Similar corners are available for above shown copings.

Scale: 2" = 1'-0"

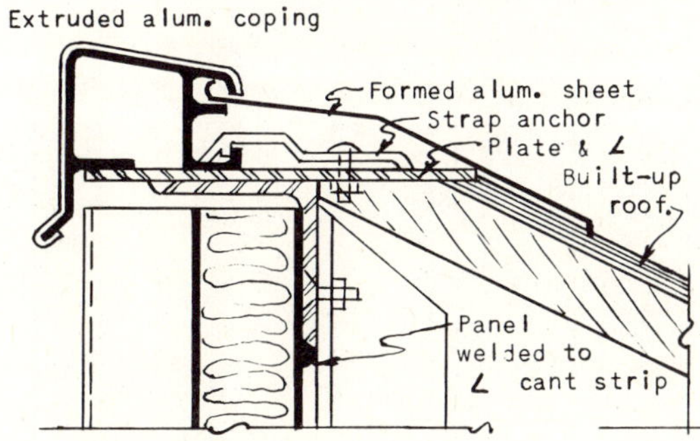
Extruded alum. coping
Formed alum. sheet
Strap anchor
Plate & ∠
Built-up roof.
Panel welded to ∠ cant strip

FLAT ROOF
CANT STRIP WITH DECK

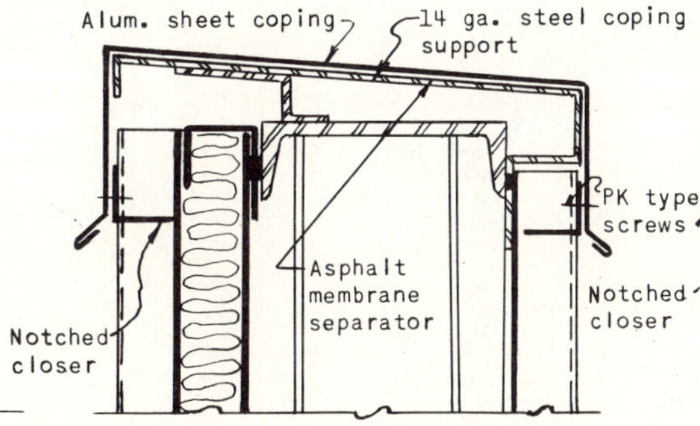
Alum. sheet coping
14 ga. steel coping support
PK type screws
Asphalt membrane separator
Notched closer
Notched closer

PARAPET WALL (FRAMED TYPE)

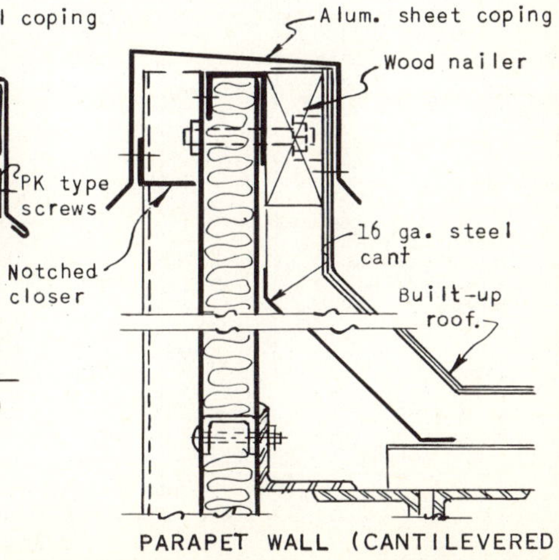
Alum. sheet coping
Wood nailer
16 ga. steel cant
Built-up roof.

PARAPET WALL (CANTILEVERED)

Q PANEL TYPE
H.H. ROBERTSON COMPANY

LEADER & GUTTER - SIZE REQUIREMENTS

WIDTHS of RECTANGULAR GUTTERS *(For level gutters. If slope exceeds 2% gutter is narrowed & deepened)*

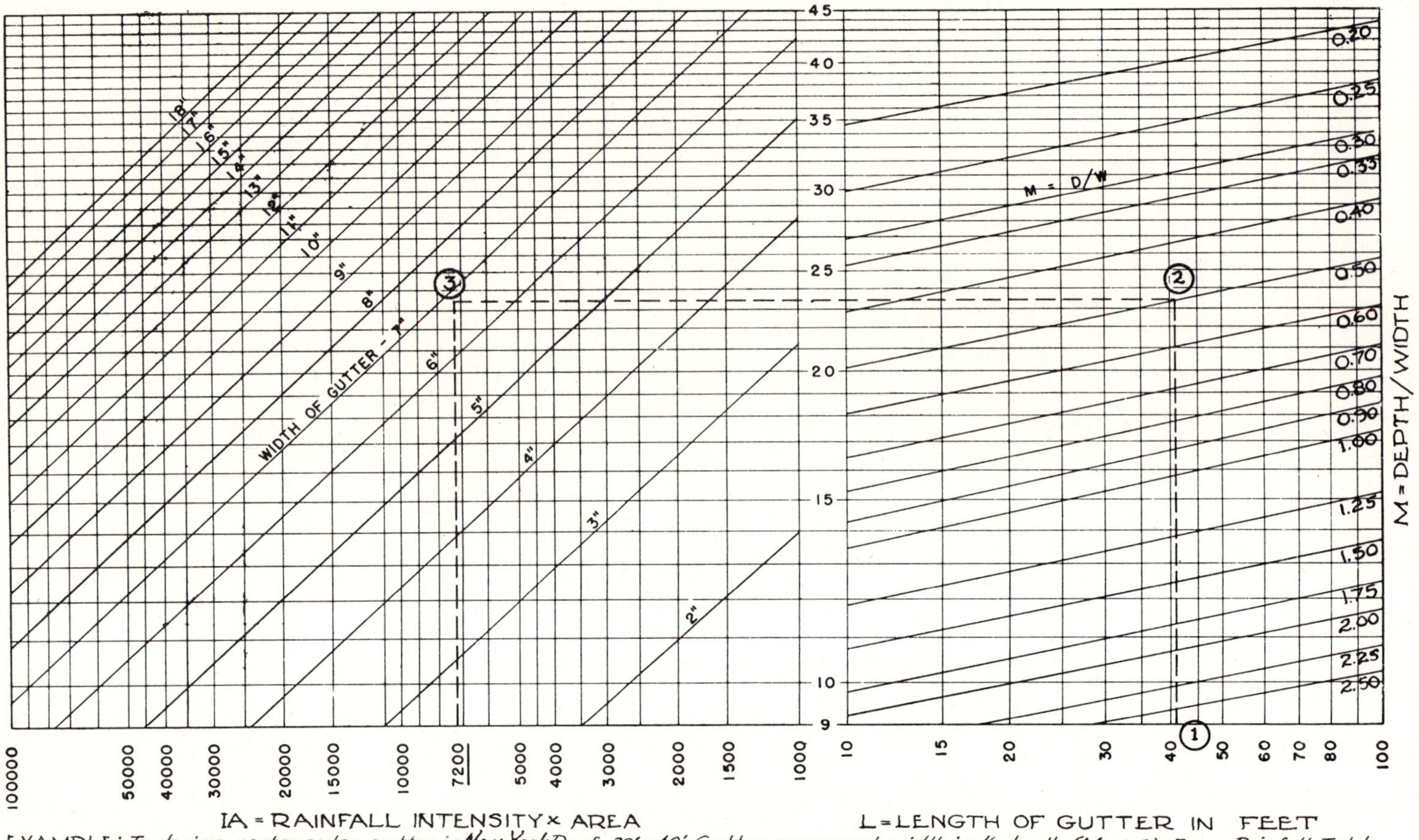
45
40
35
30
25
20
15
10
9
18"
17"
16"
15"
14"
13"
12"
11"
10"
9"
8"
WIDTH OF GUTTER - 7"
6"
5"
4"
3"
2"
③
②
①
M = D/W
0.20
0.25
0.30
0.33
0.40
0.50
0.60
0.70
0.80
0.90
1.00
1.25
1.50
1.75
2.00
2.25
2.50
M = DEPTH/WIDTH
100000
50000
40000
30000
20000
15000
10000
7200
5000
4000
3000
2000
1500
1000
10
15
20
30
40
50
60
70
80
100
IA = RAINFALL INTENSITY × AREA
L = LENGTH OF GUTTER IN FEET

EXAMPLE: *To design rectangular gutter in* ***New York*** *Roof 20'×40'. Gutter assumed width is ½ depth (M = 0.5). From Rainfall Table Intensity I = 9"/hr. Area drained A = 800 sq. ft. IA = 7200. Start at ① on Rect. Gutter Graph using L = 40' for Gutter length & follow vertically to intersection ② with oblique line M = 0.5. Follow hor. to intersection ③ with vert. line IA = 7200. Point of intersection occurs between gutter widths of 6" & 7". Required width is 7" & depth is 3½".*

EXAMPLE: *To design semi-circular gutter in Buffalo. Roof Area = 800 sq.ft. From Rainfall table Intensity = 10"/hr. Using Semi-Circ. Gutter graph find intersection of 800 sq.ft. & 10"/hr. to be 8" which is required gutter width.*

EXAMPLE: *To design leader in Knoxville. Roof Area drained per leader = 3000 sq.ft. From Rainfall Table 1 sq. in. of leader serves 200 sq.ft. of roof area. Therefore 15 sq.in. is required. From Leader Dimensions Table select either 5" round, octagonal or square or 4"×5" rectangular.* (NOTE: *Gutter design is for large Buildings.*)

RAINFALL DATA & DRAINAGE FACTORS

CITIES	MAXIMUM RECORD STORMS		CITIES	MAXIMUM RECORD STORMS	
NOTE: *Roof drainage data based on assumption that for intensity of 8"/Hr. 1 sq.in. of leader drains 150 sq.ft.*	*Intensity in In./Hr. lasting for 5 minutes*	*Sq.ft. of roof drained per sq. in. of leader area.*		*Intensity in In./Hr. lasting for 5 minutes*	*Sq. ft. of roof drained per sq. in. of leader area.*
Albany, N.Y.	7	175	New Orleans, La.	9	150
Atlanta, Ga.	9	130	New York, N.Y.	9	130
Boston, Mass.	7	175	Norfolk, Va.	8	150
Buffalo, N.Y.	10	120	Philadelphia, Pa.	8	150
Chicago, Ill.	7	175	Pittsburg, Pa.	9	175
Detroit, Mich.	10	175	St. Louis, Mo.	7	110
Duluth, Minn.	7	175	St. Paul, Minn.	7	150
Kansas City, Mo.	10	120	San Francisco, Cal.	4	400
Knoxsville, Tenn.	7	200	Savannah, Ga.	9	150
Louisville, Ky.	9	150	Seattle, Wash.	3	600
Memphis, Tenn.	9	120	Washington, D.C.	10	150
Montgomery, Ala.	8	175	*Checked by U.S. Weather Bureau*		

DIMENSIONS of LEADERS

TYPE	AREA sq. in.	NOM. SIZE
Plain Round	7.07	3"
	12.57	4"
	19.63	5"
	28.27	6"
Corrugated Round	5.94	3"
	11.04	4"
	17.72	5"
	25.97	6"
Polygon Octagonal	6.36	3"
	11.30	4"
	17.65	5"
	25.40	6"
Square Corrugated	3.80	2"
	7.73	3"
	11.70	4"
	18.75	5"
Plain Rectangular	3.94	1¾"×2¼"
	6.00	2"×3"
	8.00	2"×4"
	12.00	3"×4"
	20.00	4"×5"
	24.00	4"×6"

WIDTHS of SEMI-CIRC. GUTTERS

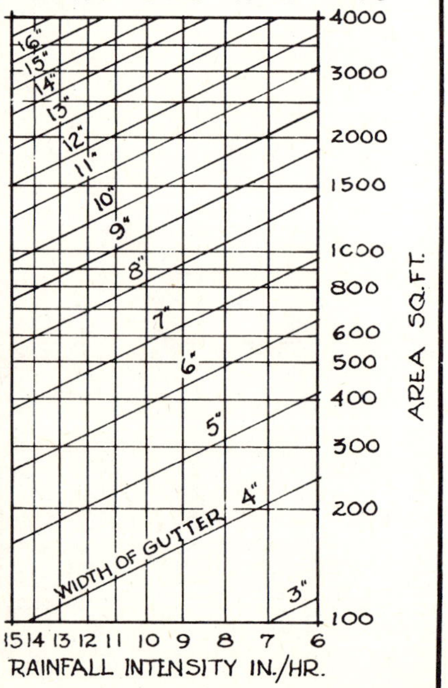
16"
15"
14"
13"
12"
11"
10"
9"
8"
7"
6"
5"
WIDTH OF GUTTER 4"
3"
4000
3000
2000
1500
1000
800
600
500
400
300
200
100
AREA SQ.FT.
15 14 13 12 11 10 9 8 7 6
RAINFALL INTENSITY IN./HR.

Recommendation of Copper & Brass Research Assn.

GUTTERS & LEADERS

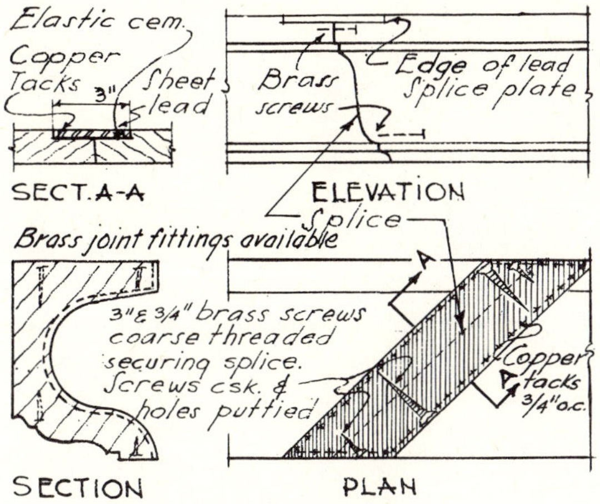
Elastic cem.
Copper Tacks
3"
Sheet lead
SECT. A-A
Brass screws
Edge of lead Splice plate
ELEVATION
Splice
Brass joint fittings available
3" & 3/4" brass screws coarse threaded securing splice. Screws csk. & holes puttied
Copper tacks 3/4" o.c.
A
SECTION
PLAN

SPLICED JOINT
1½" = 1'-0"

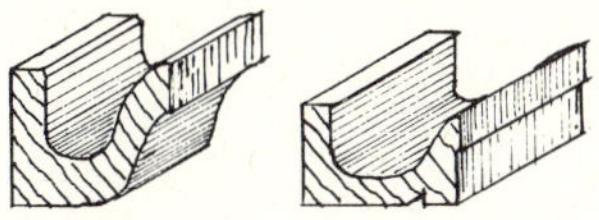

REDWOOD GUTTERS

Sizes	Sizes
3" x 4"	3" x 4"
4" x 4"	4" x 4"
4" x 6"	

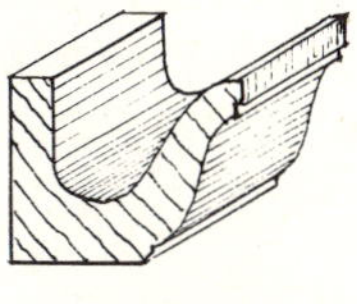

FIR GUTTER
Sizes
3"x5", 4"x5", 4"x6",
5"x7".
Length up to 40'

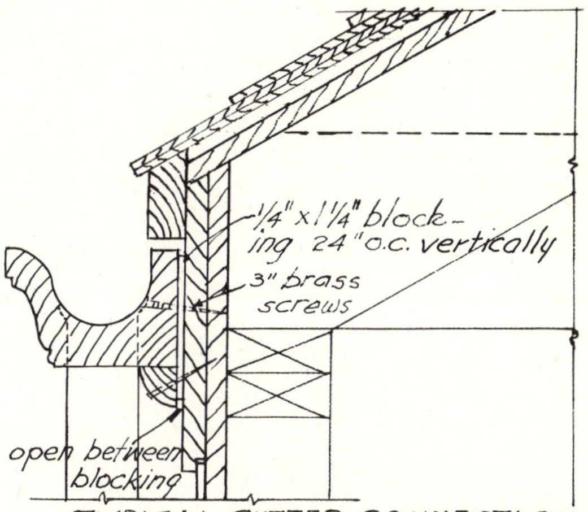
1/4" x 1 1/4" blocking 24" o.c. vertically
3" brass screws
open between blocking

TYPICAL GUTTER CONNECTION
1½" = 1'-0"

WOOD GUTTERS & LEADERS

Data checked by: Long Fir Gutter Co. Cadiz, Ohio.

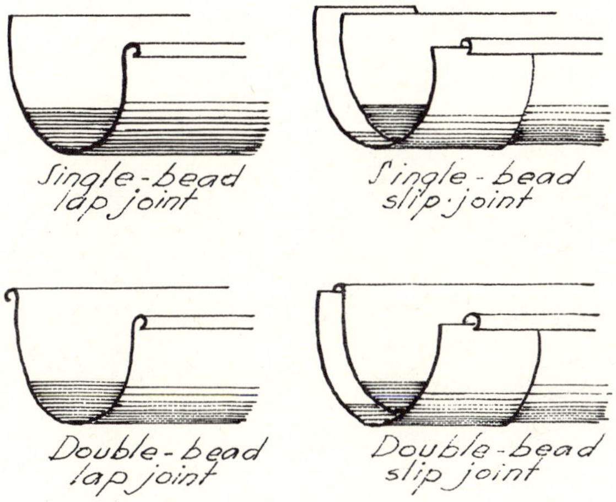
Single-bead lap joint
Single-bead slip joint
Double-bead lap joint
Double-bead slip joint

HALF ROUND GUTTERS

Copper: All above types in 4" to 10" diam.
Stainless Steel: Single bead in 4" to 10" diam.
Aluminum: Single bead lap joint in 5" diam.
Galv. Iron: All above types in 3½" to 8" diam.
Lengths 10'. Double bead is stiffer than single bead and permits wider hanger spacing, but is more difficult to line inside bead against roof. With considerable slope lengths may be lapped 3" and left unsoldered.

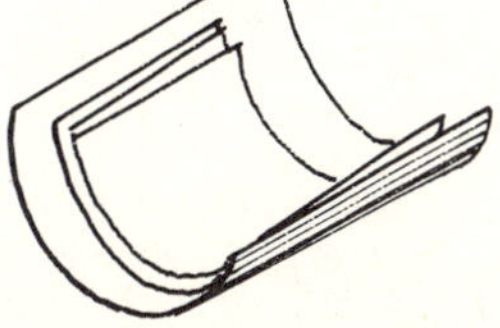

SLIP JOINT CONNECTION
Set 30' apart to provide for expansion & contraction in long runs of lap gutters.
Joints between are lapped & soldered. Slip joint not soldered.

GUTTER DESIGN for SMALL RESIDENTIAL WORK

Avoid gutters under 4" wide.
Min. slope 1/16" per ft. required.
Min. depth equal to ½ & max. depth not over ¾ of width.
If leader spacing is less than 20' use a gutter same size as leader. If leader spacing is over 20' add 1" to leader dia. for every add'l 30' on peak roofs, 1" for every add'l 40' on flat.

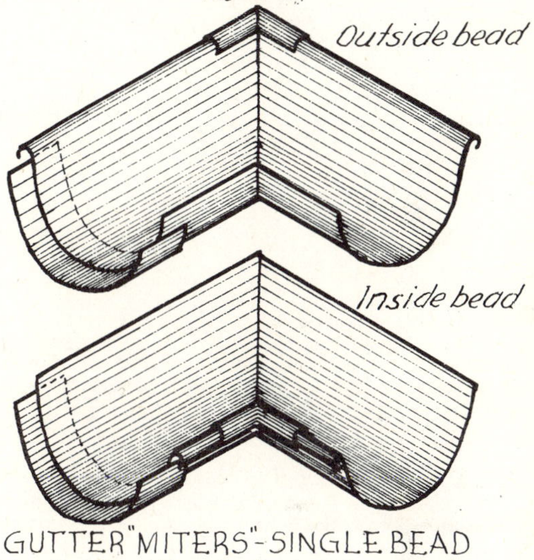
Outside bead
Inside bead

GUTTER "MITERS" - SINGLE BEAD
Available without slip joint connection & in double bead or box gutter type

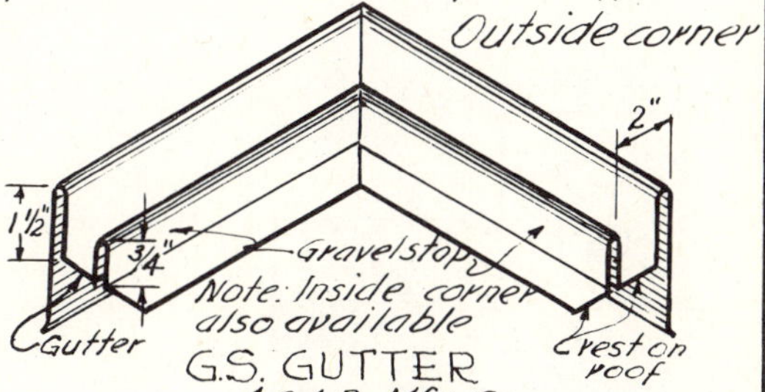
Outside corner
2"
1½"
3/4"
Gravelstop
Note: Inside corner also available
Gutter
Crest on roof

G.S. GUTTER
A.G.A.R. Mfr. Co.

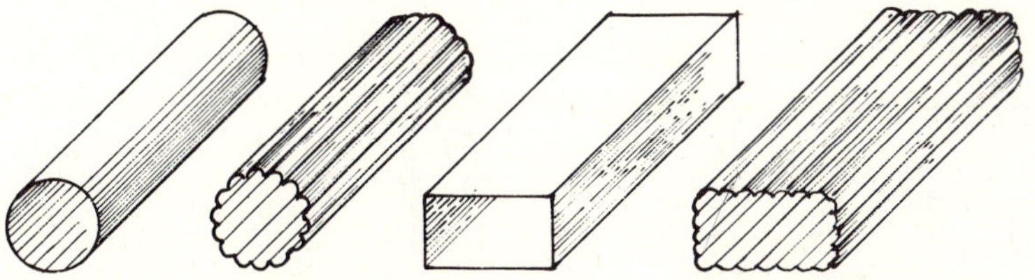
Plain round
Corrugated round
Plain rectangular
Corrugated rectangular

METAL LEADERS (downspouts)

Copper: See Leader Dimension Table on other page.
Galvanized Iron: Same sizes as Copper.
Stainless Steel: 2" to 6" round & 2" to 5" rect. plain & corrug.
Aluminum 3" round & 2⅜" x 3¼" rect. plain & corrug.
Lengths 10'. General rule: 1 sq. in. of leader to 100 sq. ft. of roof area drained. Corrugated resists bursting from freezing best.

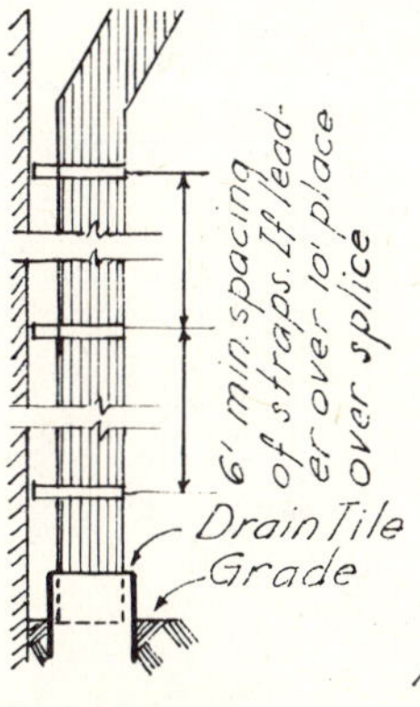
6' min. spacing of straps. If leader over 10' place over splice
Drain Tile
Grade

LEADER WITH TILE SHOE

TABLE OF GALVANIC ACTIVITY

WEIGHTS of SHEET METAL

Metal	for leader	for Gutter
Aluminum	23ga	25ga.
Zinc	11-13ga	12-13ga
Galv. Iron	24-26ga	24-26ga
Tin on Steel	1x	1x
Lead, hard	4-8lbs.	4-8lbs.
Stain. Steel	28ga.	28ga
Copper	16oz.	16oz.
Monel	26ga.	25-26ga.

Above metals are arranged in order of galvanic activity. Metals far apart in this table should not be in contact with each other.

STOCK METAL GUTTERS

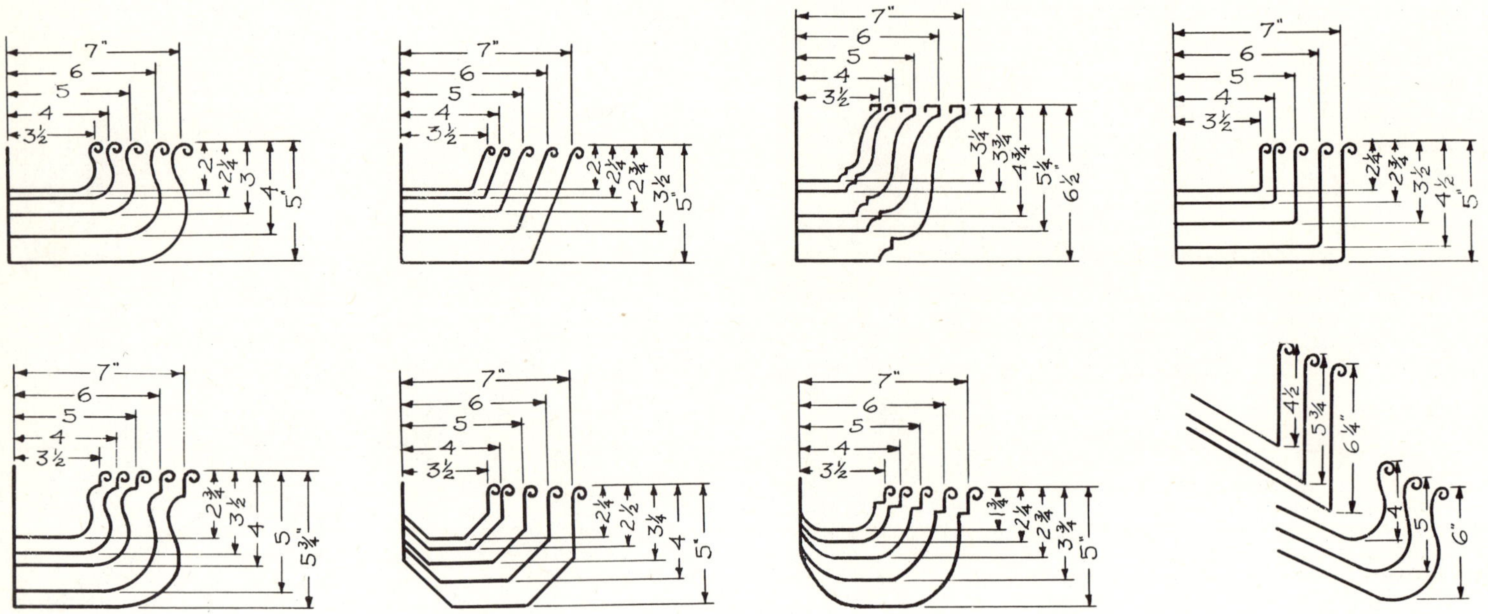

ZINC COATED SHEET ~ "ARMCO ZINCGRIP"
Armco Steel Corporation

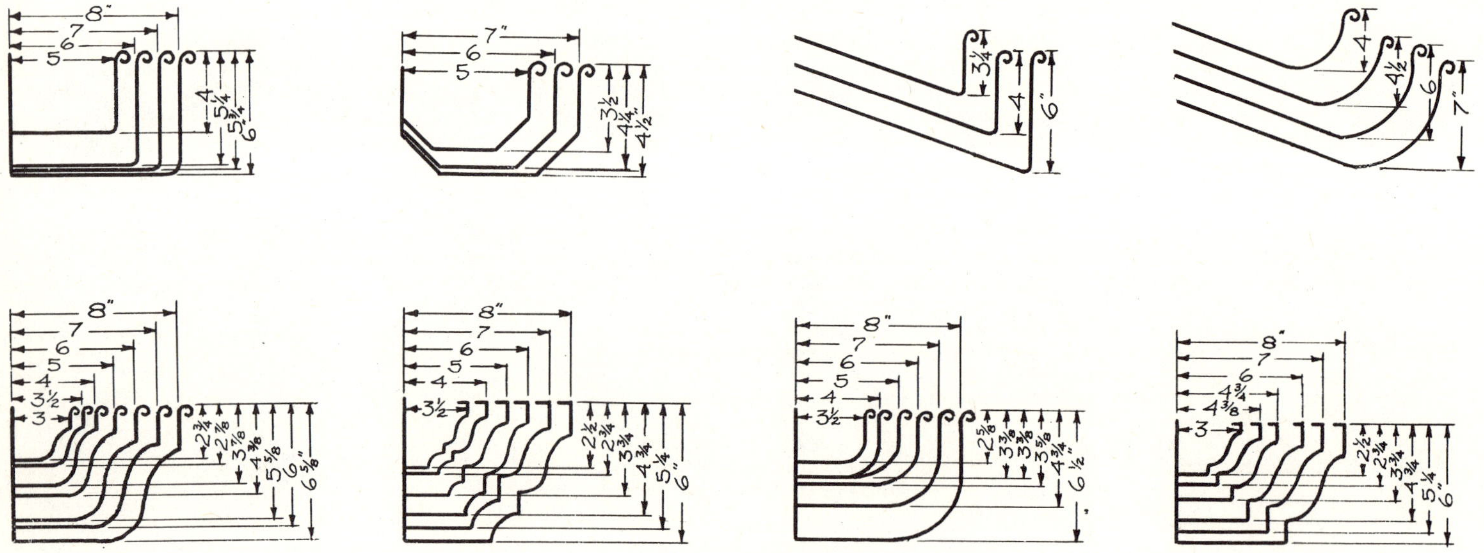

STAINLESS STEEL
Sharon Steel Company

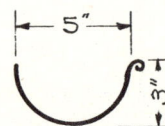

ALUMINUM
Reynolds Metals Co.

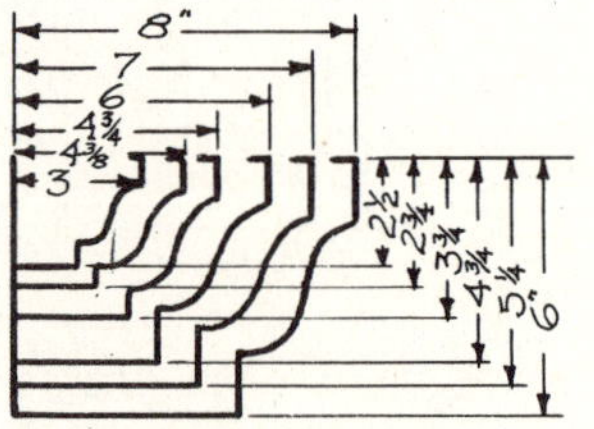

STYLE "K" *(stock)*

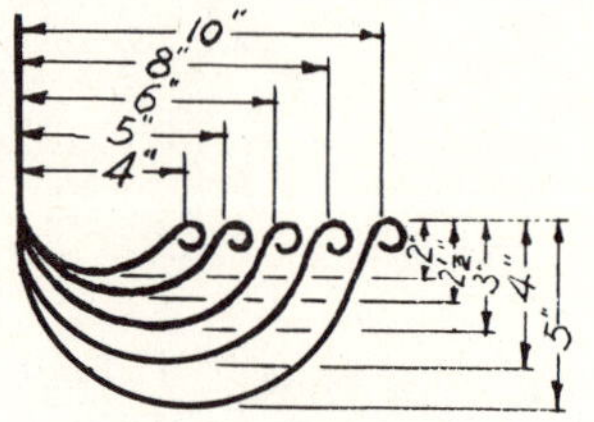

HALF ROUND COPPER

Chase Copper & Brass Co. Inc.

NOTE: *All sizes shown in inches. See following page for weights*

GUTTER & LEADER ACCESSORIES

All sheetmetal items shown on this sheet are available from sheetmetal distributors

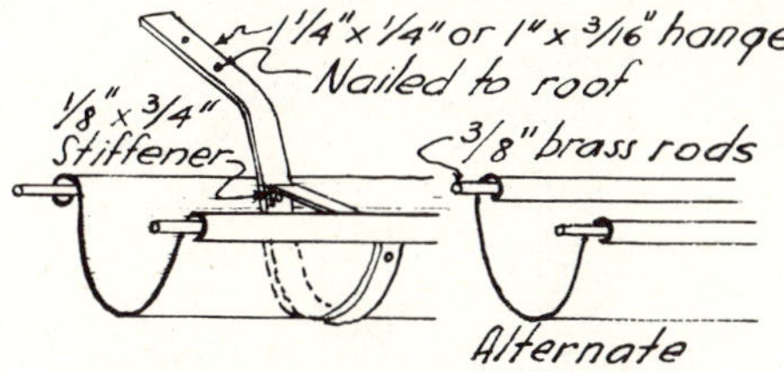
1¼"x¼" or 1"x 3/16" hanger
Nailed to roof
1/8"x¾" Stiffener
3/8" brass rods
Alternate

FIXED STRAP HANGER OF BRASS - SPECIAL
(For the best class of residence) Space hangers 3'-0" o.c. for 1"x 3/16" hanger and 3'-6" o.c. for 1¼"x¼" hanger.

Gutter screens available.

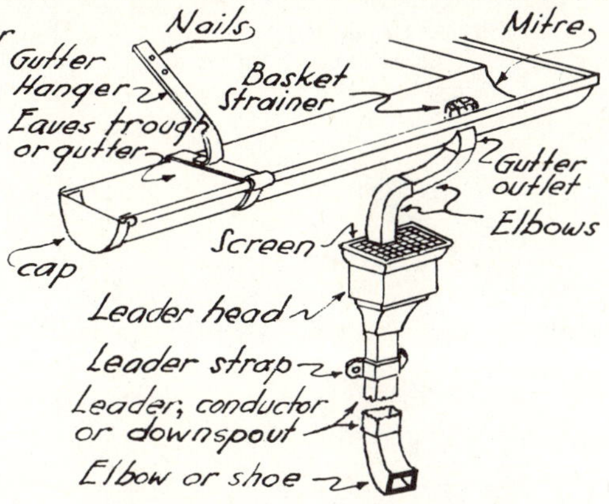
Nails
Mitre
Gutter Hanger
Basket Strainer
Eaves trough or gutter
Gutter outlet
Elbows
Screen
cap
Leader head
Leader strap
Leader; conductor or downspout
Elbow or shoe

PARTS of a GUTTER

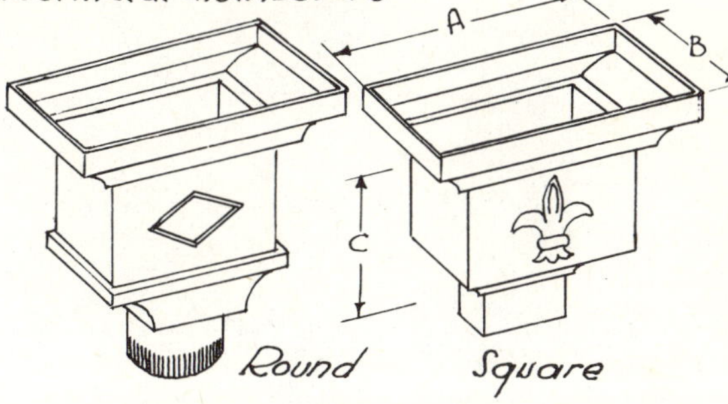
A
B
C
Round
Square

STOCK LEADER HEADS					
SIZE	OUTLET		A	B	C
	Square	Round			
Small	2"x3"	3"	9"	5½"	7½"
	3"x4"	4"	10"	6"	7½"
Large	2"x3"	3"	10"	6"	9"
	3"x4"	4"	11"	6½"	9"

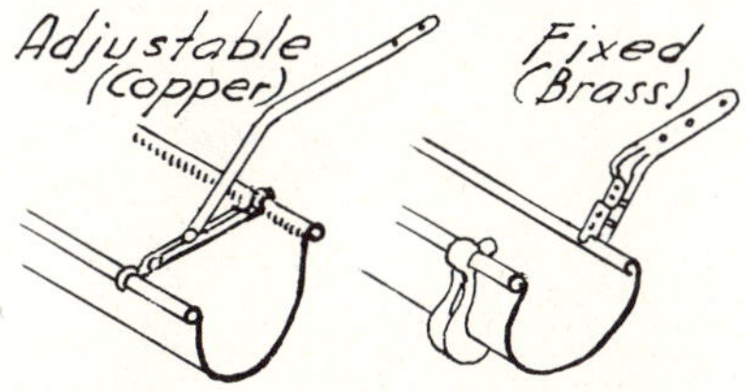
Adjustable (Copper)
Fixed (Brass)

STOCK STRAP HANGERS COPPER & BRASS
Spaced not over 2'-6" o.c. Blocking between bldg. & gutter essential to provide for overflow.

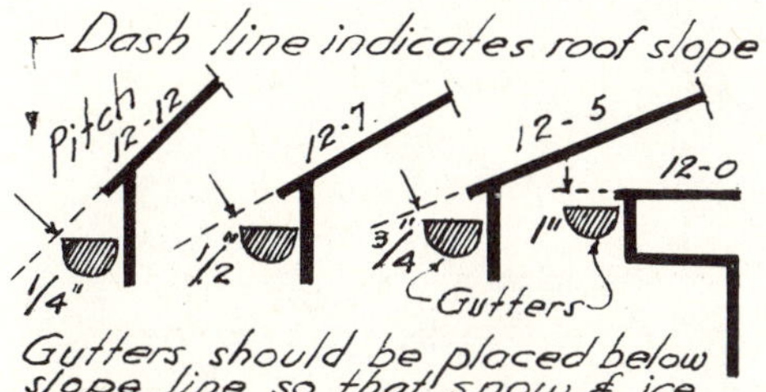
Dash line indicates roof slope
Pitch 12-12
12-7
12-5
12-0
¼"
½"
¾"
1"
Gutters

Gutters should be placed below slope line so that snow & ice can slide clear. Steeper pitch requires less clearance.
PLACING of GUTTERS

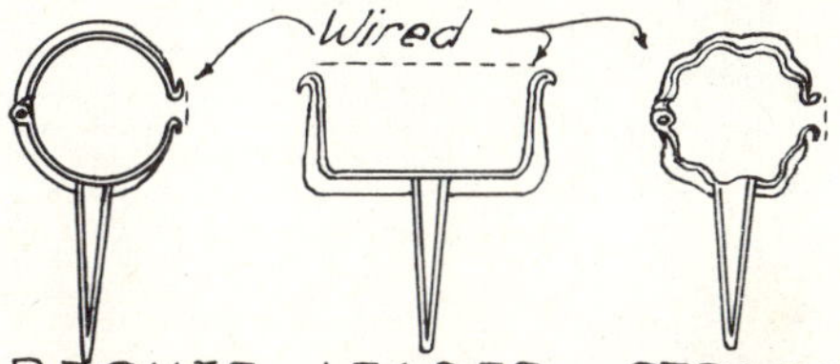
Wired

BRONZE LEADER STRAPS
Set 6'-0" apart min.

COPPER ELBOWS and SHOES

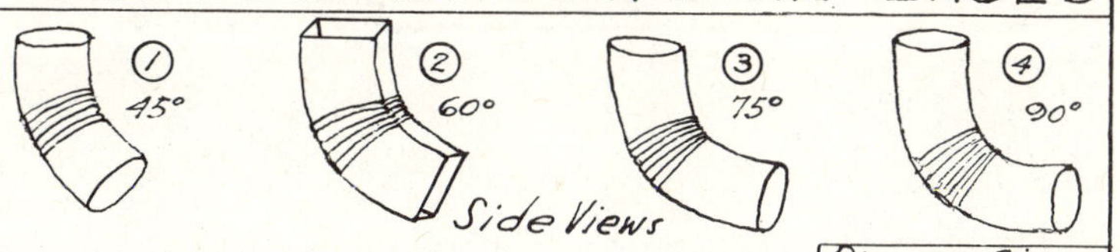
1 45°
2 60°
3 75°
4 90°
Side Views

			Dia. or size			
Elbows	Round	Plain & corrugated #1,2,3,4	2"	3"	5"	6"
	Square	" " "	2"	3"	5"	
Shoes	Round	" " #3	2"	3"	5"	6"
	Square	Corrugated only #3	2"	3"	5"	

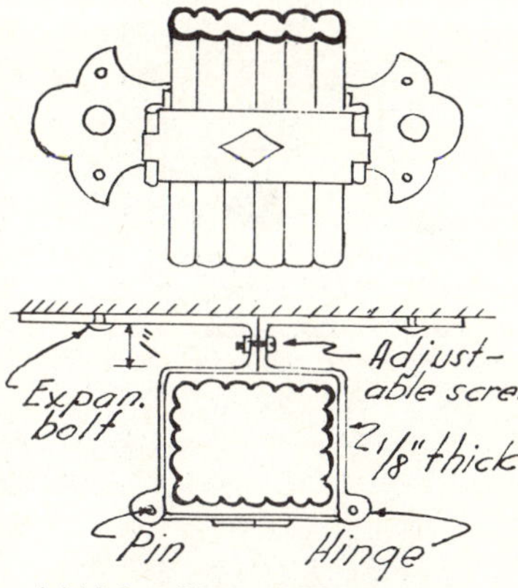
Adjustable screw
Expan. bolt
1/8" thick
Pin
Hinge

HINGED LEADER STRAP - BRONZE.
Loose pin in left side permits removal of leader without taking strap off wall. Also made for round leaders.

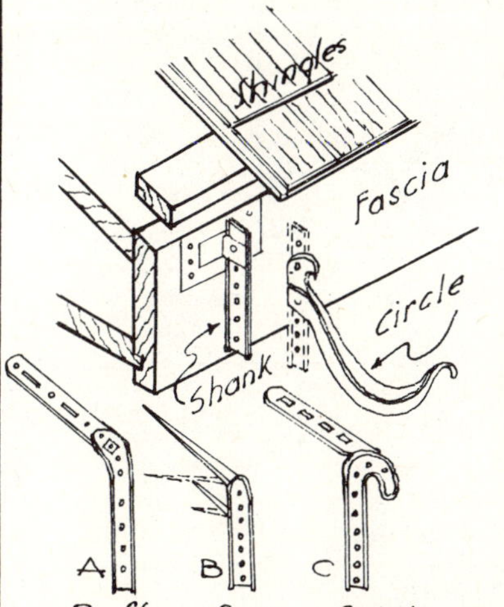
Shingles
Fascia
Circle
Shank
A
B
C

Rafter Spike Subshingle
BRONZE HANGERS
A Nailed to side of rafter
B Spiked into rafter or fascia
C Adjustable, nailed under shingles. Others available.

CAST IRON DOWNSPOUT SHOES

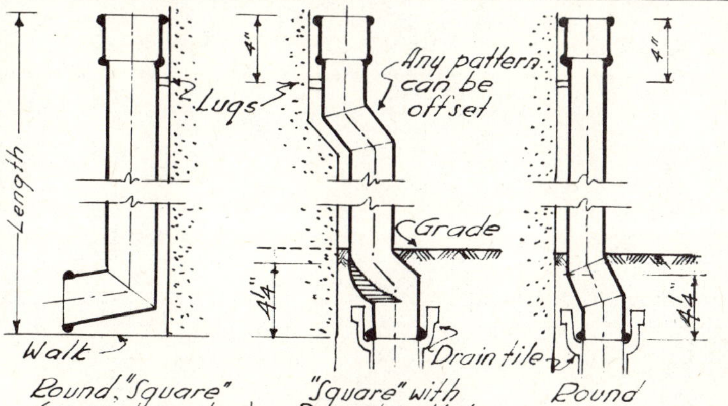
Length
4"
Lugs
Any pattern can be offset
Grade
4¼"
Walk
Drain tile
Round, "Square" (or rectangular)
"Square" with Round Outlet
Round

Available lengths from 12" to 72" in increments of 6 inches; Plain, fluted or panel designs.

SQUARE & RECTANGULAR								ROUND			
Spout size	2"x2"	2"x3"	3"x3"	3"x4"	4"x4"	4"x5"	4"x6"	Spout dia.	3"	4"	5"
Outlet dia.	3"	3"	4"	4"	4"	4"	5"	Outlet dia.	3"	4"	5"

Contractor's Foundry, Inc.

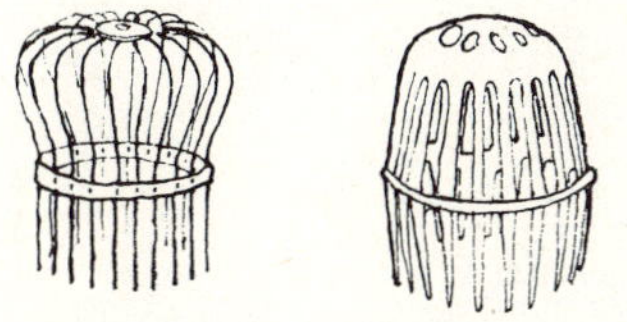

Copper Wire Cast Bronze
BASKET STRAINERS
Copper wire type also made in square form to fit standard gutter outlets. Cast Bronze made 3, 4, 5, 6, 7, 8, in. round. 2"x3", 3"x4" sq.

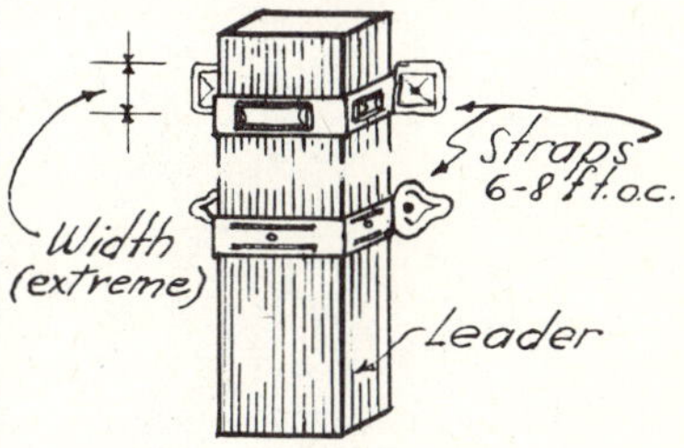
Straps 6-8 ft. o.c.
Width (extreme)
Leader

COPPER LEADER STRAPS
Variety of ornamentation available. Lengths 13" to 20". Widths 1½"-4 3/8"

Data by Copper & Brass Research Association

BUILT-IN GUTTERS

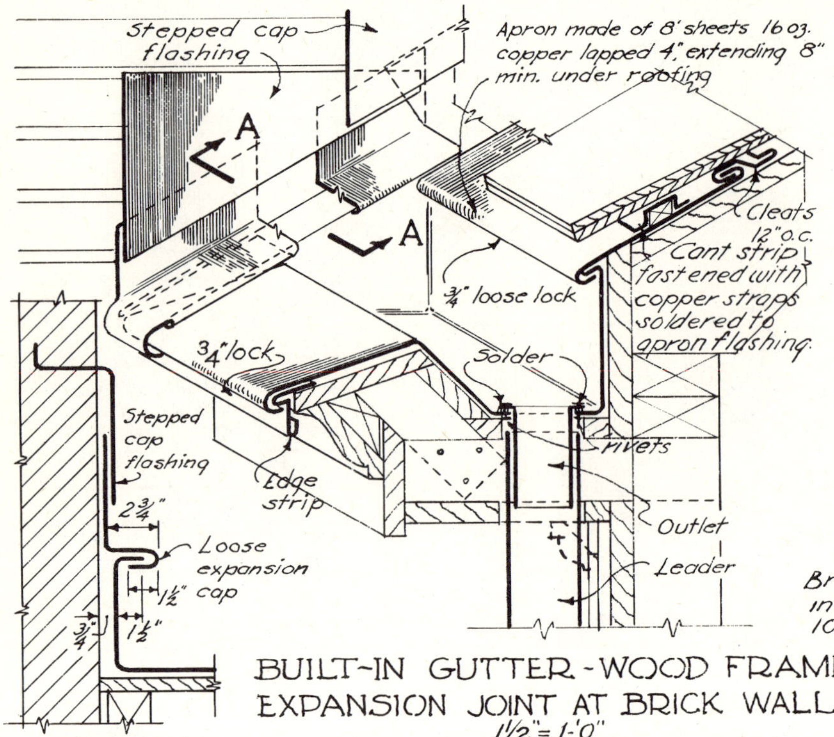
Stepped cap flashing
Apron made of 8' sheets 16 oz. copper lapped 4" extending 8" min. under roofing
A
A
Cleats 12" o.c.
Cant strip fastened with copper straps soldered to apron flashing.
3/4" loose lock
3/4" lock
Solder
Stepped cap flashing
Edge strip
Rivets
Outlet
Leader
2 3/4"
Loose expansion cap
1/2"
1 1/2"
3/4"

BUILT-IN GUTTER-WOOD FRAME.
EXPANSION JOINT AT BRICK WALL
1½" = 1'-0"

SECTION A-A
1" = 1'-0"

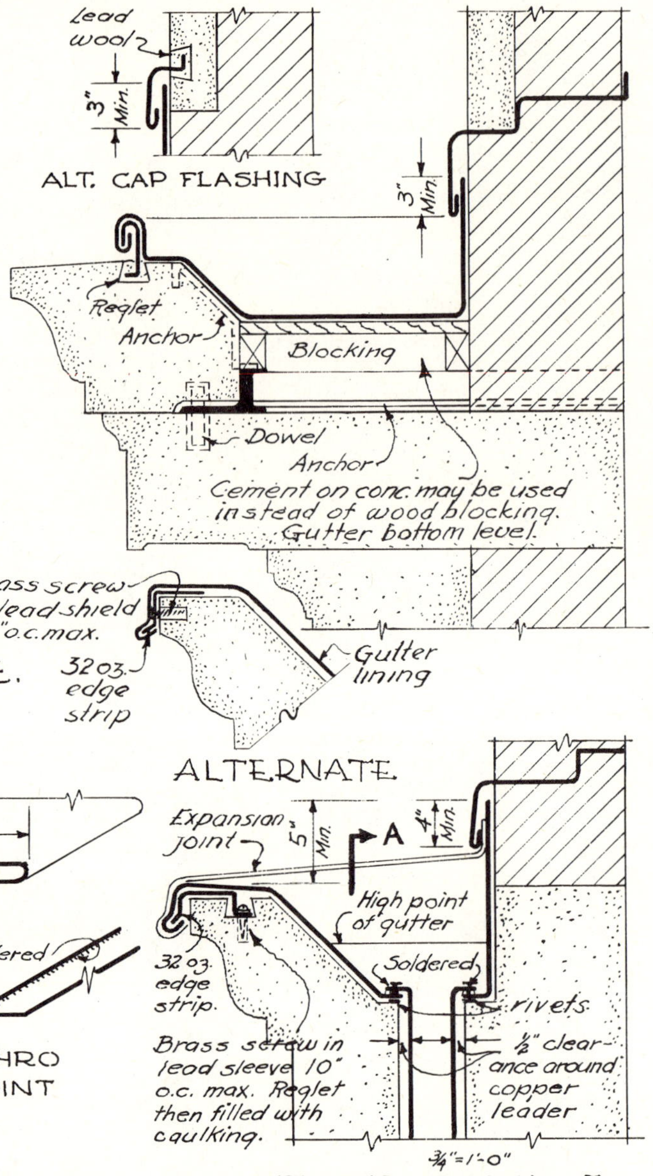
Lead wool
3" Min.
ALT. CAP FLASHING
3" Min.
Reglet
Anchor
Blocking
Dowel
Anchor
Cement on conc. may be used instead of wood blocking. Gutter bottom level.
Brass screw in lead shield 10" o.c. max.
32 oz. edge strip
Gutter lining
ALTERNATE
Expansion joint
5" Min.
4" Min.
A
High point of gutter
32 oz. edge strip.
Soldered
rivets
Brass screw in lead sleeve 10" o.c. max. Reglet then filled with caulking.
1/2" clearance around copper leader
3/4" = 1'-0"

IN STONE CORNICE.

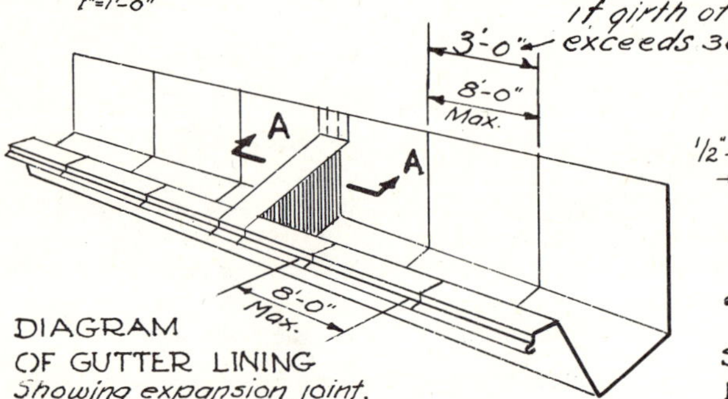
3'-0" if girth of gutter exceeds 36"
8'-0" Max.
A
A
8'-0" Max.

DIAGRAM
OF GUTTER LINING
Showing expansion joint.
Gutter lining fixed at downspout moving to ℄ from expansion joint

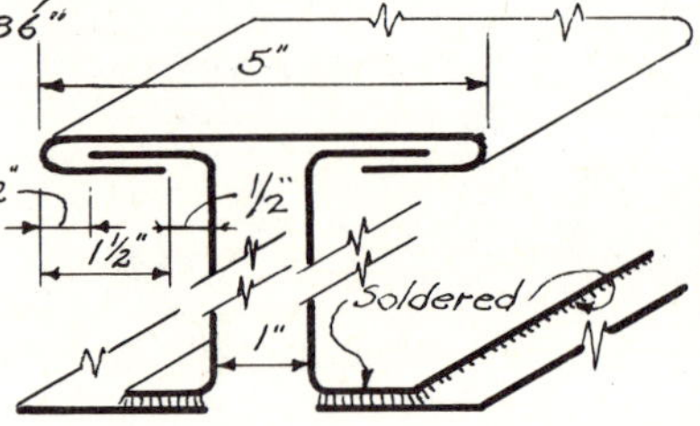
5"
1/2"
1/2"
1 1/2"
Soldered
1"

SECTION A-A THRO
EXPANSION JOINT
3" = 1'-0"

*DETERMINATION OF GAUGE *and* EXPANSION JOINT LOCATION *for* COPPER GUTTER LININGS

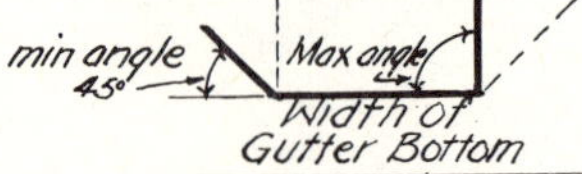
min angle 45°
Max angle
Width of Gutter Bottom

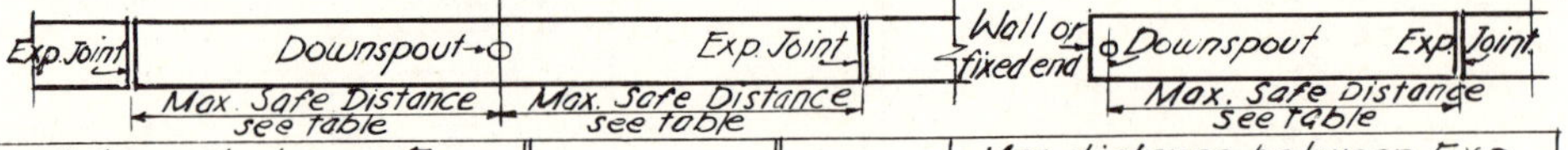
Exp. Joint
Downspout
Exp. Joint
Max. Safe Distance see table
Max. Safe Distance see table
Wall or fixed end
Downspout
Exp. Joint
Max. Safe Distance see table

Weight of Cold Rolled Copper in Ounces	Width of Gutter Bottom	Max. distance between Exp. Joint & Downspout, in ft. Angle of Gutter Sides				
		90° 45°	90° 60°	90° 90°	60° 60°	45° 45°
16	6	18'-6"	19'-6"	21'-6"	17'-6"	15'-0"
	8	16'-0"	17'-6"	19'-0"	15'-0"	13'-0"
	10	14'-0"	15'-0"	16'-6"	13'-0"	11'-0"
24	8	26'-0"	28'-0"	31'-0"	25'-0"	22'-0"
	10	23'-0"	25'-0"	27'-0"	22'-0"	19'-6"
	12	21'-0"	22'-6"	24'-6"	20'-0"	17'-6"

Weight of Cold Rolled Copper in Ounces	Width of Gutter Bottom	Max. distance between Exp. Joint & Downspout, in ft. Angle of Gutter Sides				
		90° 45°	90° 60°	90° 90°	60° 60°	45° 45°
20	6	24'-0"	26'-0"	29'-0"	23'-0"	20'-0"
	8	20'-6"	22'-0"	24'-6"	19'-6"	17'-0"
	10	18'-0"	19'-6"	21'-6"	17'-0"	15'-0"
32	10	40'-6"	43'-6"	47'-6"	39'-0"	34'-6"
	12	37'-6"	39'-6"	43'-0"	35'-6"	31'-6"
	14	34'-6"	36'-6"	40'-0"	32'-6"	29'-0"

Gutter linings must be unrestrained, except at downspouts. Built-in gutters are lined with cold rolled Copper. Sheets of 16 & 20 oz. are joined by ¾" wide locked & soldered seams. Sheets of 24 & 32 oz. are joined by 1½" wide lapped, riveted & soldered seams. Rivets are copper 3/16" dia. with burrs under peened heads. Rivets spaced 3" o.c., two rows staggered.

BUILT-IN GUTTERS

Recommendation of Copper & Brass Research Association
** Data recommendation of Revere Copper & Brass Incorporated*

CORRUGATED WIRE GLASS

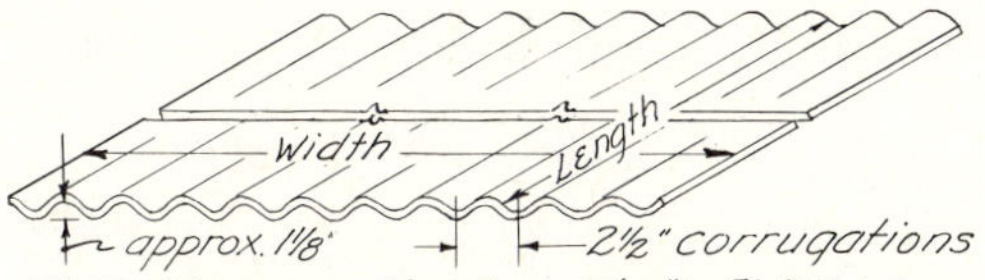
Width
Length
approx. 1 1/8"
2 1/2" corrugations

H.H.R. Max. size: 2'-3 1/2" W. × 12'-0" L. × 7/16" thick.
Standard lengths: 4'-6" to 5'-8" by 2" increment
Max. clear spans: Skylight 5'-0", Side wall, Sash and Monitors 8'-0"
P.W.G. Max. size: 2'-3 3/4" W. × 10'-6" L. × 7/16" thick
Max. clear spans: Side walls and monitors 8'-0"
H.H.R. & P.W.G. available in white flint & blue tinted glass also in frosted finish to reduce glare. Weight: 6 1/4#/sq.'

STANDARD SHEETS

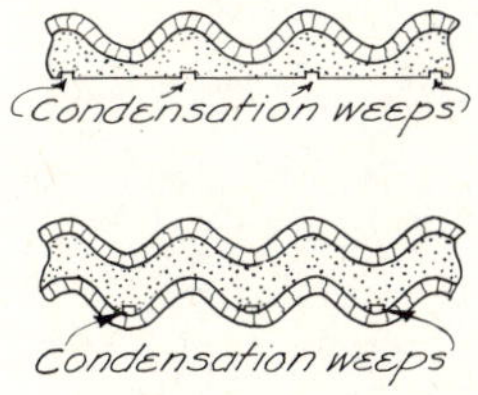
Condensation weeps
Condensation weeps

SEALING STRIPS

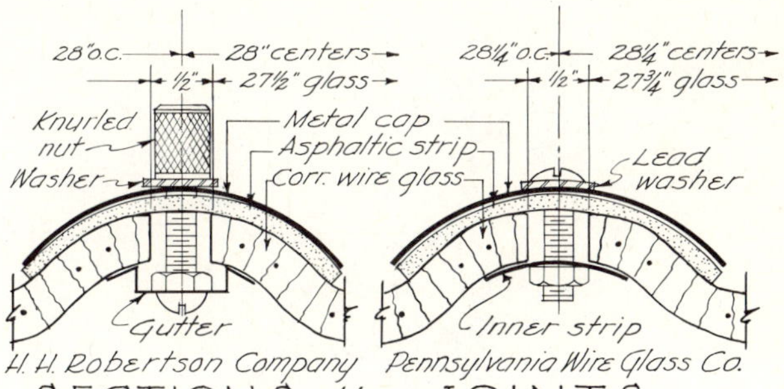
28" o.c.
28" centers
1/2"
27 1/2" glass
Knurled nut
Washer
Metal cap
Asphaltic strip
Corr. wire glass
Gutter
H. H. Robertson Company
28 1/4" o.c.
28 1/4" centers
1/2"
27 3/4" glass
Lead washer
Inner strip
Pennsylvania Wire Glass Co.

SECTIONS thru JOINTS

NOTE: Corrugated wire glass is also used in stationary & top-hinged monitors and, stationary & pivoted side-wall windows.

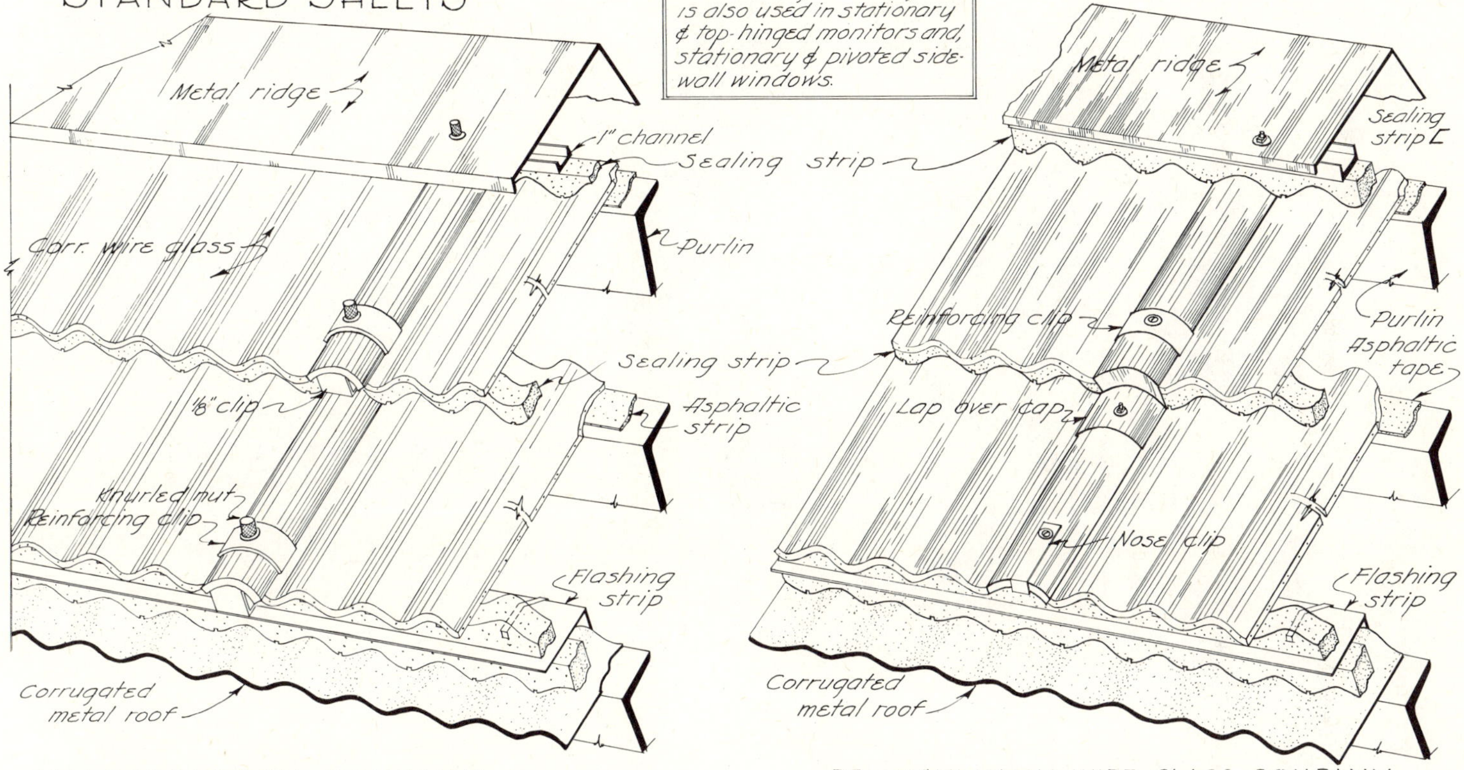
Metal ridge
1" channel
Sealing strip
Corr. wire glass
Purlin
Sealing strip
1/8" clip
Asphaltic strip
Knurled nut
Reinforcing clip
Flashing strip
Corrugated metal roof
Metal ridge
Sealing strip
Sealing strip [
Reinforcing clip
Purlin
Asphaltic tape
Lap over cap
Nose clip
Flashing strip
Corrugated metal roof

H. H. ROBERTSON COMPANY — PENNSYLVANIA WIRE GLASS COMPANY

TYPICAL CORRUGATED WIRE GLASS ROOF CONSTRUCTION

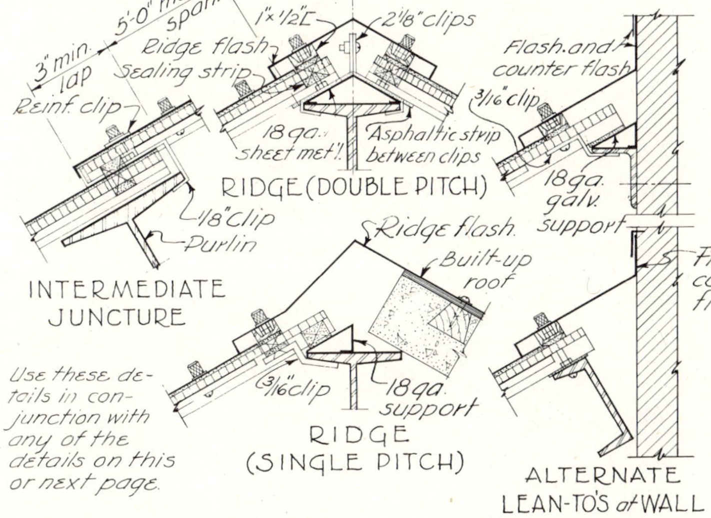
5'-0" max. span.
3" min. lap
Ridge flash
Sealing strip
Reinf. clip
1/8" Clip
Purlin
INTERMEDIATE JUNCTURE
1" × 1/2" [
2 1/8" clips
18 ga. sheet met'l.
Asphaltic strip between clips
RIDGE (DOUBLE PITCH)
Flash. and counter flash
3/16" clip
18 ga. galv. support
Ridge flash.
Built-up roof
3/16" clip
18 ga. support
RIDGE (SINGLE PITCH)
Flash. & counter flashing
ALTERNATE LEAN-TO'S at WALL
Use these details in conjunction with any of the details on this or next page.

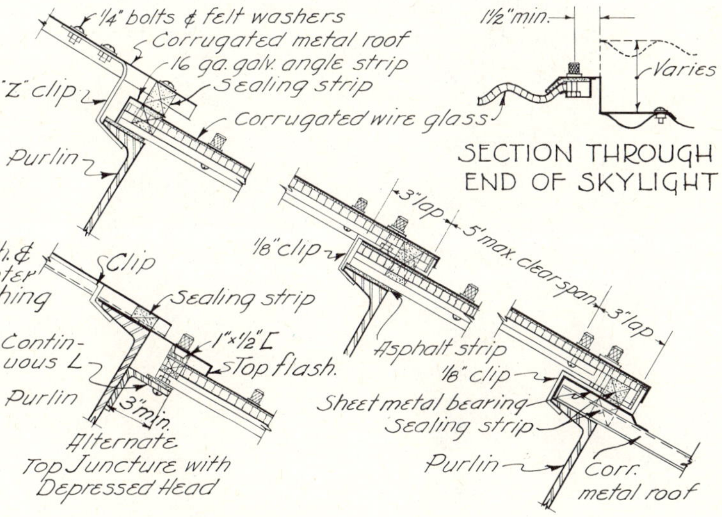
1/4" bolts & felt washers
Corrugated metal roof
16 ga. galv. angle strip
Sealing strip
"Z" clip
Corrugated wire glass
Purlin
1 1/2" min.
Varies
SECTION THROUGH END OF SKYLIGHT
3" lap
5' max. clear span
3" lap
1/8" clip
Clip
Sealing strip
Continuous L
1" × 1/2" [
Top flash.
Purlin
3" min.
Alternate Top Juncture with Depressed Head
Asphalt strip
1/8" clip
Sheet metal bearing
Sealing strip
Purlin
Corr. metal roof

CORRUGATED WIRE GLASS SKYLIGHT DETAILS FOR ANY KIND OF ROOF

CORRUGATED WIRE GLASS SKYLIGHT in CORRUGATED METAL ROOF

construction details from H. H. Robertson Company   Scale 1 1/2" = 1'-0"

CORRUGATED WIRE GLASS

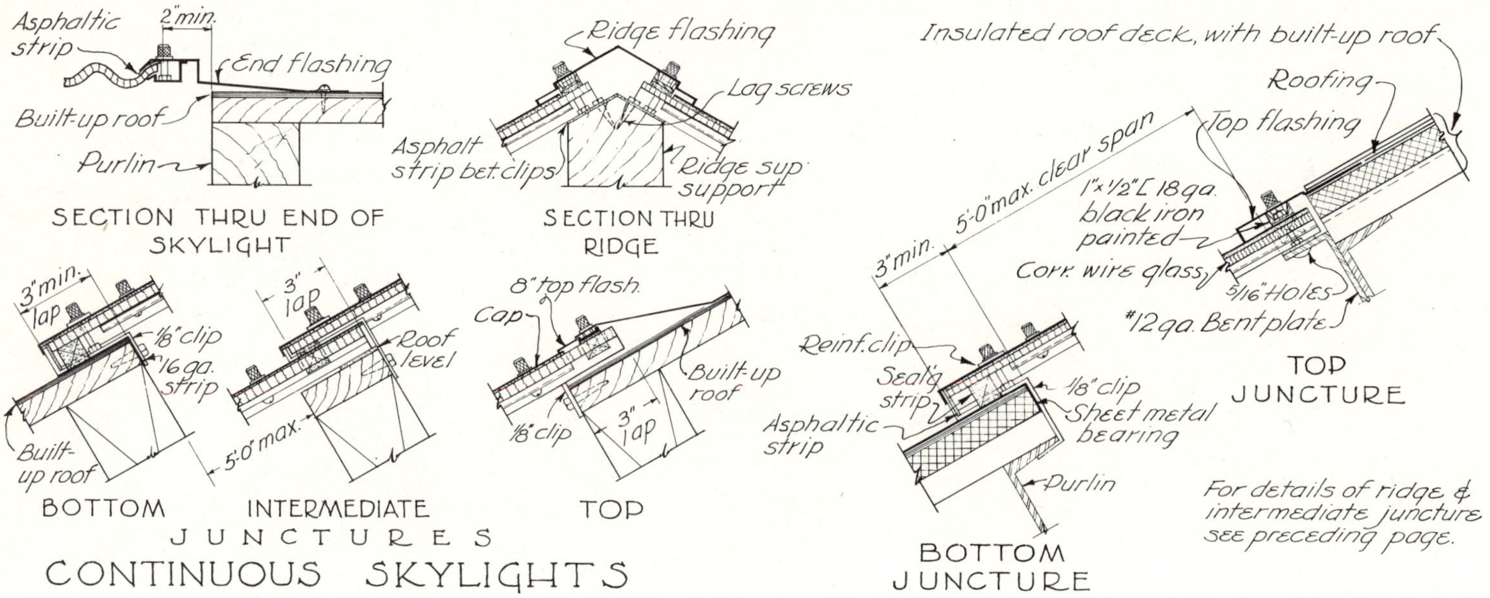

Asphaltic strip
2" min.
End flashing
Built-up roof
Purlin
SECTION THRU END OF SKYLIGHT
Ridge flashing
Lag screws
Asphalt strip bet. clips
Ridge sup. support
SECTION THRU RIDGE
3" min. lap
1/8" clip
16 ga. strip
Built-up roof
3" lap
Roof level
5'-0" max.
8" top flash.
Cap
Built-up roof
1/8" clip
3" lap
BOTTOM
INTERMEDIATE
TOP
JUNCTURES
Insulated roof deck, with built-up roof
Roofing
Top flashing
5'-0" max. clear span
3" min.
1"×1/2" [18 ga. black iron painted
Corr. wire glass
5/16" HOLES
#12 ga. Bent plate
TOP JUNCTURE
Reinf. clip
Seal'g strip
1/8" clip
Sheet metal bearing
Asphaltic strip
Purlin
BOTTOM JUNCTURE
For details of ridge & intermediate juncture see preceding page.

CONTINUOUS SKYLIGHTS

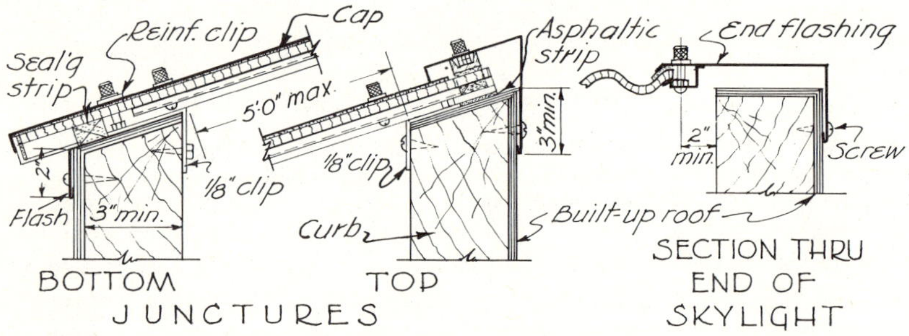

Cap
Reinf. clip
Seal'g strip
5'-0" max.
2"
Flash
3" min.
1/8" clip
BOTTOM
Asphaltic strip
1/8" clip
3" min.
Curb
Built-up roof
TOP
JUNCTURES
End flashing
2" min.
Screw
SECTION THRU END OF SKYLIGHT

HATCH TYPE SKYLIGHTS

SKYLIGHTS on WOOD BUILT-UP ROOFS

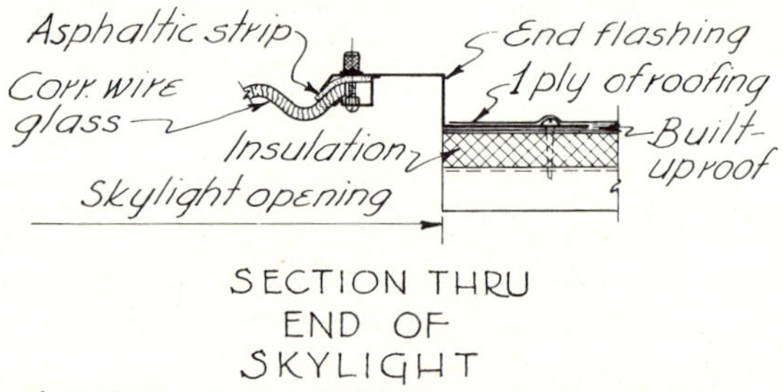

Asphaltic strip
End flashing
Corr. wire glass
1 ply of roofing
Insulation
Built-up roof
Skylight opening
SECTION THRU END OF SKYLIGHT

SKYLIGHTS on STEEL DECK ROOF

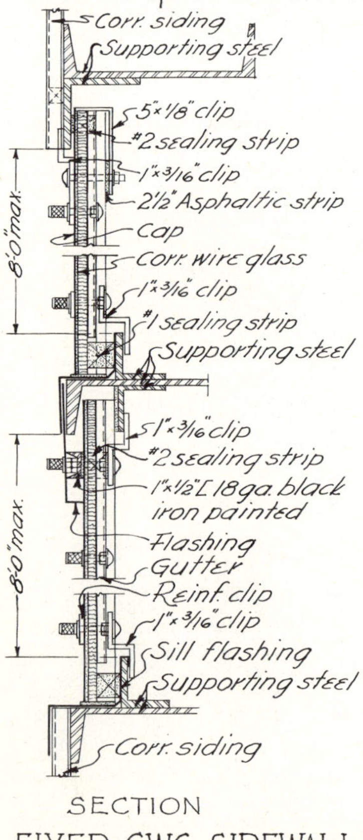

Corr. siding
Supporting steel
5"×1/8" clip
#2 sealing strip
1"×3/16" clip
2 1/2" Asphaltic strip
Cap
Corr. wire glass
1"×3/16" clip
#1 sealing strip
Supporting steel
8'-0" max.
1"×3/16" clip
#2 sealing strip
1"×1/2" [18 ga. black iron painted
Flashing
Gutter
Reinf. clip
1"×3/16" clip
Sill flashing
Supporting steel
8'-0" max.
Corr. siding
SECTION

FIXED C.W.G. SIDEWALL

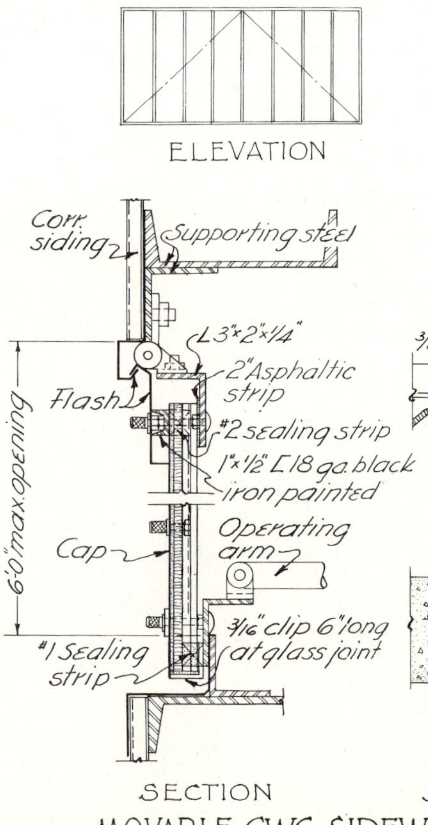

ELEVATION
Corr. siding
Supporting steel
L 3"×2"×1/4"
2" Asphaltic strip
Flash
#2 sealing strip
1"×1/2" [18 ga. black iron painted
Cap
Operating arm
6'-0" max. opening
3/16" clip 6" long at glass joint
#1 Sealing strip
SECTION

MOVABLE C.W.G. SIDEWALL

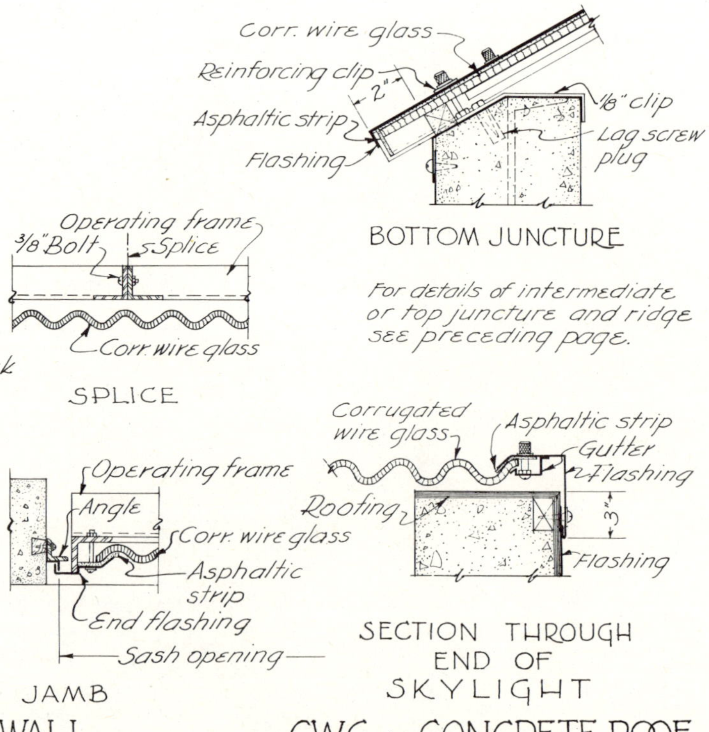

Corr. wire glass
Reinforcing clip
2"
Asphaltic strip
Flashing
1/8" clip
Lag screw plug
BOTTOM JUNCTURE
For details of intermediate or top juncture and ridge see preceding page.
Operating frame
3/8" Bolt
Splice
Corr. wire glass
SPLICE
Operating frame
Angle
Corr. wire glass
Asphaltic strip
End flashing
Sash opening
JAMB
Corrugated wire glass
Asphaltic strip
Gutter
Flashing
Roofing
3"
Flashing
SECTION THROUGH END OF SKYLIGHT

C.W.G. in CONCRETE ROOF

construction details from H. H. Robertson Company   Scale: 1½" = 1'-0"

SKYLIGHTS

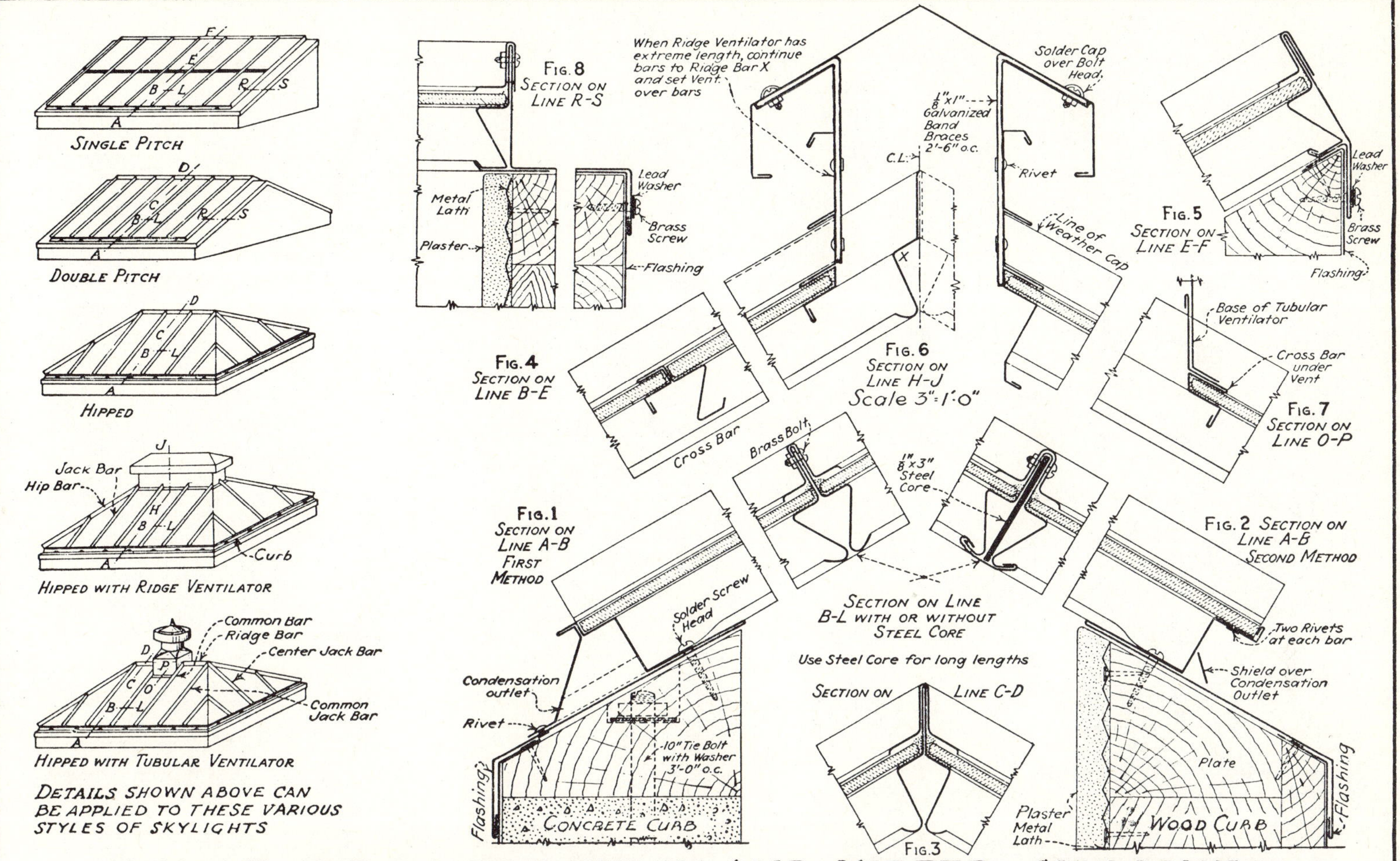

Single Pitch
Double Pitch
Hipped
Jack Bar
Hip Bar
Curb
Hipped with Ridge Ventilator
Common Bar
Ridge Bar
Center Jack Bar
Common Jack Bar
Hipped with Tubular Ventilator
Details shown above can be applied to these various styles of skylights
Fig. 8 Section on Line R-S
Metal Lath
Plaster
Lead Washer
Brass Screw
Flashing
When Ridge Ventilator has extreme length, continue bars to Ridge Bar X and set Vent. over bars
1/8"x1" Galvanized Band Braces 2'-6" o.c.
C.L.
Rivet
Solder Cap over Bolt Head
Line of Weather Cap
Fig. 6 Section on Line H-J
Scale 3"=1'-0"
Fig. 5 Section on Line E-F
Lead Washer
Brass Screw
Flashing
Fig. 4 Section on Line B-E
Cross Bar
Base of Tubular Ventilator
Cross Bar under Vent
Fig. 7 Section on Line O-P
Fig. 1 Section on Line A-B First Method
Brass Bolt
1/8"x3" Steel Core
Solder Screw Head
Condensation outlet
Rivet
10" Tie Bolt with Washer 3'-0" o.c.
Flashing
Concrete Curb
Section on Line B-L with or without Steel Core
Use Steel Core for long lengths
Section on Line C-D
Fig. 3
Fig. 2 Section on Line A-B Second Method
Two Rivets at each bar
Shield over Condensation Outlet
Plate
Plaster
Metal Lath
Wood Curb
Flashing

SINGLE AND DOUBLE PITCH AND HIPPED SKYLIGHTS

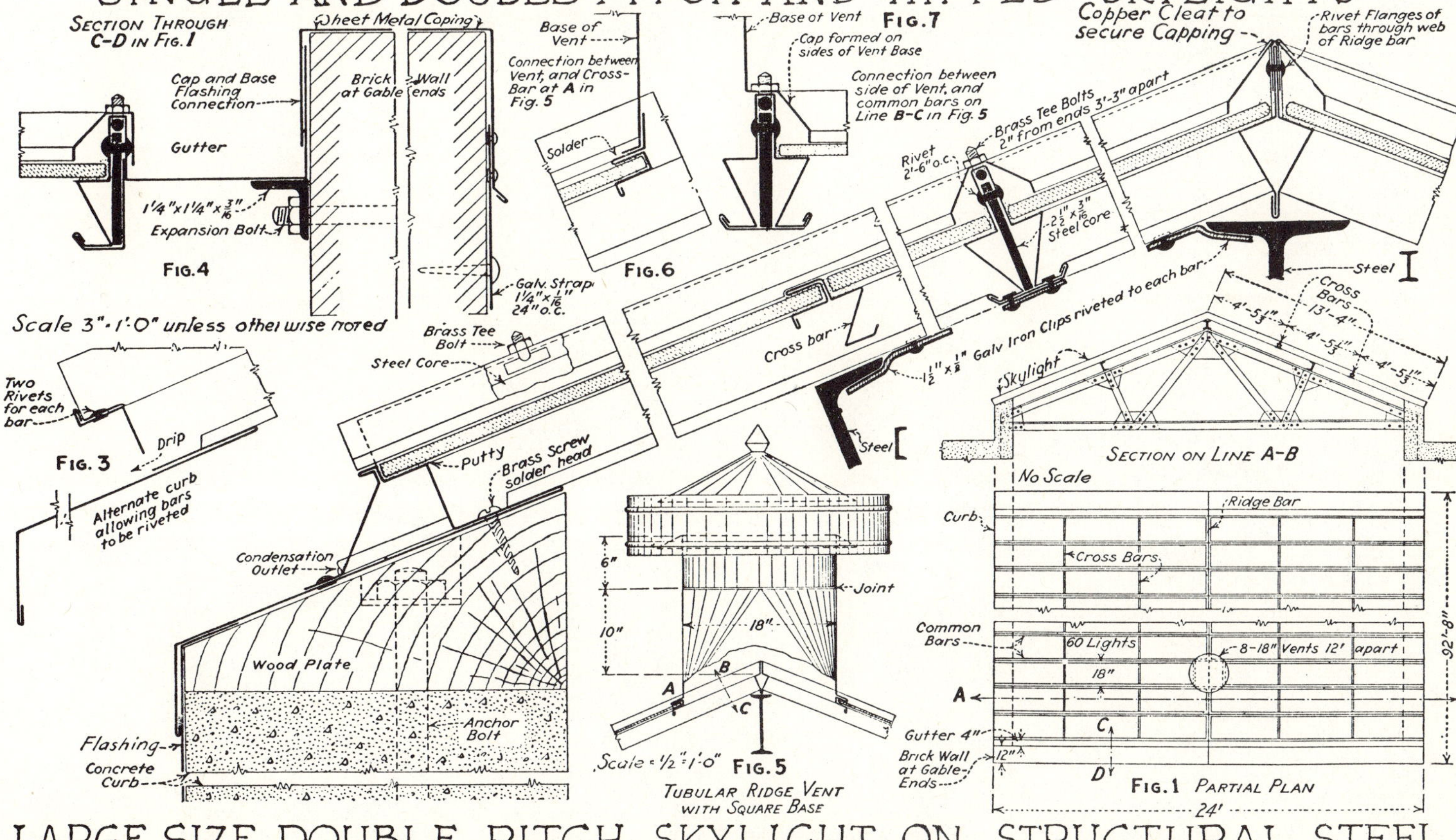

Section Through C-D in Fig. 1
Sheet Metal Coping
Cap and Base Flashing Connection
Brick Wall at Gable ends
Gutter
1¼"x1¼"x3/16"
Expansion Bolt
Fig. 4
Galv. Strap 1¼"x1/16" 24" o.c.
Scale 3"=1'-0" unless otherwise noted
Base of Vent
Connection between Vent, and Cross-Bar at A in Fig. 5
Solder
Fig. 6
Base of Vent
Fig. 7
Cap formed on sides of Vent Base
Connection between side of Vent, and common bars on Line B-C in Fig. 5
Copper Cleat to secure Capping
Rivet Flanges of bars through web of Ridge bar
Brass Tee Bolts 2" from ends 3'-3" apart
Rivet 2'-6" o.c.
2½"x3/16" Steel Core
Steel I
1½"x⅛" Galv Iron Clips riveted to each bar
Cross bar
Steel [
Brass Tee Bolt
Steel Core
Two Rivets for each bar
Drip
Fig. 3
Alternate curb allowing bars to be riveted
Putty
Brass Screw solder head
Condensation Outlet
Wood Plate
Anchor Bolt
Flashing
Concrete Curb
6"
10"
18"
Joint
Scale=½"=1'-0"
Fig. 5
Tubular Ridge Vent with Square Base
Cross Bars 13'-4"
4'-5⅓"
Skylight
Section on Line A-B
No Scale
Curb
Ridge Bar
Cross Bars
Common Bars
60 Lights
18"
8-18" Vents 12' apart
Gutter 4"
Brick Wall at Gable-Ends
12"
92'-8"
24'
Fig. 1 Partial Plan

LARGE SIZE DOUBLE PITCH SKYLIGHT ON STRUCTURAL STEEL

Data checked by: Sheet Metal Contractors' Nat'l. Assn., Inc.

SKYLIGHTS

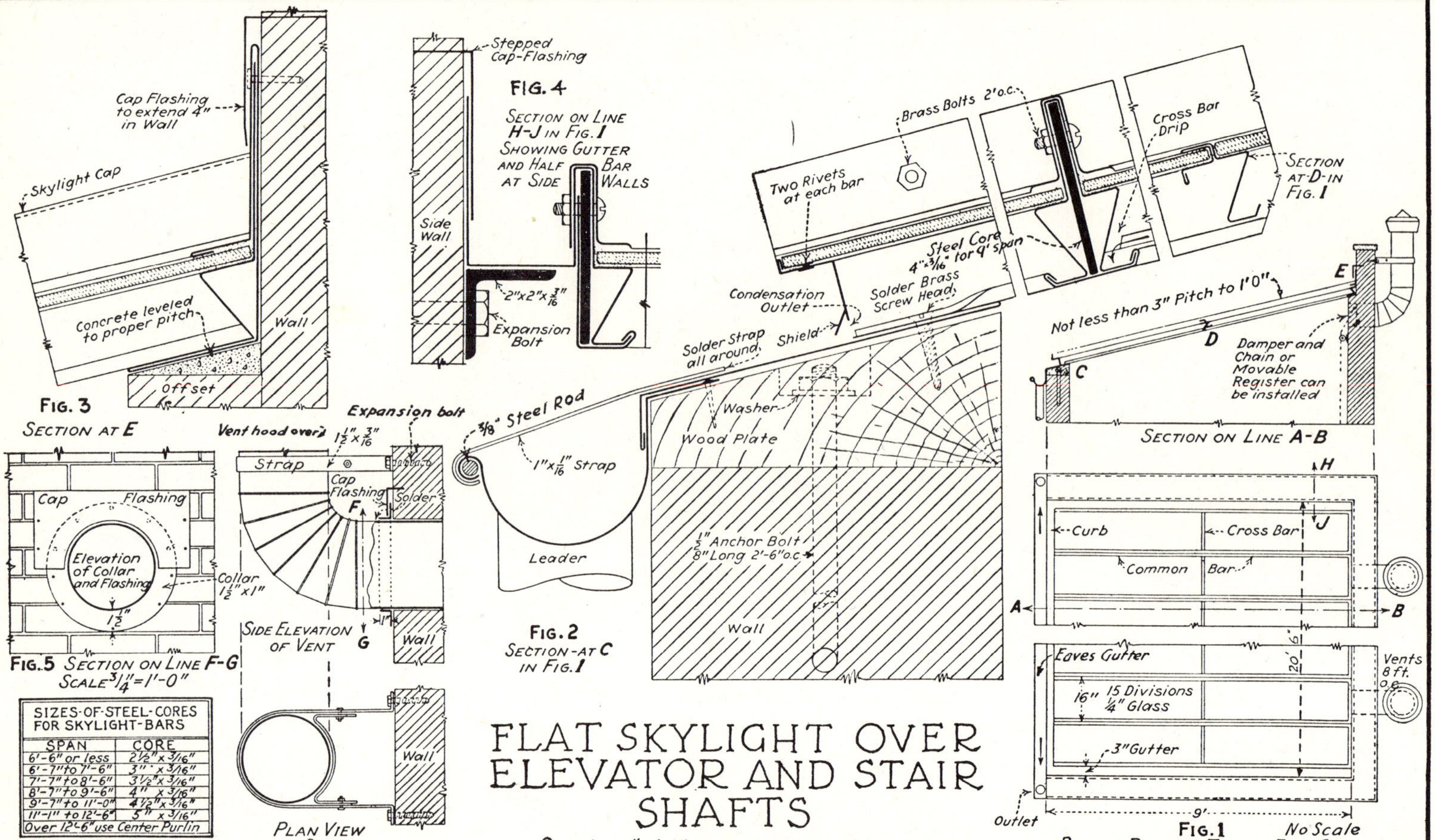

Cap Flashing to extend 4" in Wall
Skylight Cap
Concrete leveled to proper pitch
Wall
Offset
FIG. 3
SECTION AT E
Stepped Cap-Flashing
FIG. 4
SECTION ON LINE H-J IN FIG. I SHOWING GUTTER AND HALF BAR AT SIDE WALLS
Side Wall
2"x2"x3/16"
Expansion Bolt
Brass Bolts 2' o.c.
Two Rivets at each bar
Cross Bar Drip
SECTION AT D IN FIG. I
Steel Core 4"x3/16" for 9' span
Condensation Outlet
Solder Brass Screw Head
Solder Strap all around
Shield
Not less than 3" Pitch to 1'0"
Damper and Chain or Movable Register can be installed
SECTION ON LINE A-B
Expansion bolt
Vent hood over
1 1/2" x 3/16"
Strap
3/8" Steel Rod
1"x1/16" Strap
Washer
Wood Plate
Cap Flashing
Solder
Leader
1/2" Anchor Bolt 8" Long 2'-6" o.c.
Wall
FIG. 2
SECTION AT C IN FIG. I
Cap
Flashing
Elevation of Collar and Flashing
Collar 1 1/2" x 1"
1 1/2"
FIG. 5 SECTION ON LINE F-G
SCALE 3/4"=1'-0"
SIDE ELEVATION OF VENT
PLAN VIEW OF STRAP
Curb
Cross Bar
Common
Bar
Eaves Gutter
16"
15 Divisions 1/4" Glass
3" Gutter
20'-6"
Vents 8 ft. o.c.
Outlet
9'
FIG. 1
No Scale
PARTIAL PLAN OF TYPICAL FLAT SKYLIGHT MINUS STEEL FRAMING

SIZES OF STEEL CORES FOR SKYLIGHT BARS	
SPAN	CORE
6'-6" or less	2 1/2" x 3/16"
6'-7" to 7'-6"	3" x 3/16"
7'-7" to 8'-6"	3 1/2" x 3/16"
8'-7" to 9'-6"	4" x 3/16"
9'-7" to 11'-0"	4 1/2" x 3/16"
11'-1" to 12'-6"	5" x 3/16"
Over 12'-6" use Center Purlin	

Spacing of Bars not to exceed 1'-6" o.c.

FLAT SKYLIGHT OVER ELEVATOR AND STAIR SHAFTS

Scale 3" = 1'0" unless otherwise noted

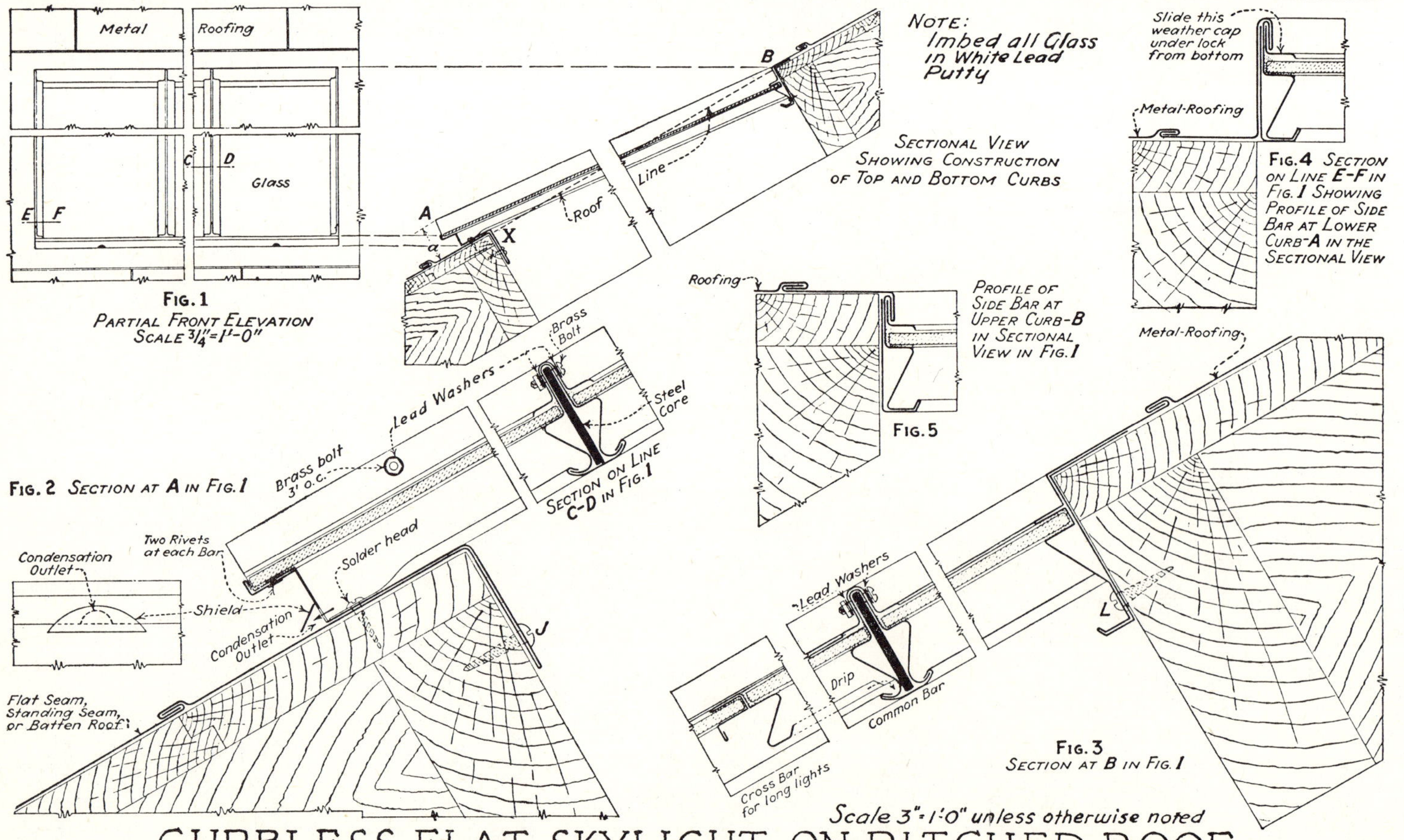

Metal
Roofing
Glass
FIG. 1
PARTIAL FRONT ELEVATION
SCALE 3/4"=1'-0"
NOTE: Imbed all Glass in White Lead Putty
Roof
Line
SECTIONAL VIEW SHOWING CONSTRUCTION OF TOP AND BOTTOM CURBS
Slide this weather cap under lock from bottom
Metal-Roofing
FIG. 4 SECTION ON LINE E-F IN FIG. I SHOWING PROFILE OF SIDE BAR AT LOWER CURB-A IN THE SECTIONAL VIEW
Roofing
PROFILE OF SIDE BAR AT UPPER CURB-B IN SECTIONAL VIEW IN FIG. I
FIG. 5
Lead Washers
Brass Bolt
Steel Core
SECTION ON LINE C-D IN FIG. I
Brass bolt 3' o.c.
FIG. 2 SECTION AT A IN FIG. I
Two Rivets at each Bar
Solder head
Condensation Outlet
Shield
Flat Seam, Standing Seam, or Batten Roof
Drip
Common Bar
Cross Bar for long lights
FIG. 3
SECTION AT B IN FIG. I

Scale 3" = 1'0" unless otherwise noted

CURBLESS FLAT SKYLIGHT ON PITCHED ROOF

Data checked by: Sheet Metal Contractors' Nat'l. Assn., Inc.

ROOF COVERINGS

The following pages show the various types of roof finishes available. For comparative purposes, many factors important in choosing a roof finish are listed. These factors include a description of material, the minimum and maximum slopes, method of application, guaranty available, and the cost of various finishes. The costs per square foot are based on normal quantity of the type of roofing used in the Eastern Area. Prices may vary 30% due to competition, size of job, and location. Costs are costs to owner, including installation, over-head and profit.

BUILT-UP ROOFING

TYPE	DESCRIPTION	SLOPE MAX.	SLOPE MIN.	WGT.	SIZE	COSTS (Sq. ft.)	M'F'RS. BOND	UNDER-LAY	FASTENER	APPLICATION	LAP	COLOR & TEXTURE	U.L.R.
ASPHALT SATURATED FELT WITH a) SLAG b) GRAVEL c) MARBLE CHIPS	Wood or Nailable Deck 5-Ply	2"to 4" in 12"	0 to 1/8" in 12"	525#/sq. 625#/sq.	36" wide rolls	a) .22 b) .22 c) .24	20 yr.	Rosin Sheathing	Galvanized nails & Asphalt	5-Layers #15 A.S.F. & Gravel or slag imbedded in hot asphalt	19" & 24½"	Rough Various colors	Class A
	4-Ply	do.	do.	480#/sq. 580#/sq.	do.	a-b). 19 c) .21	15 yr.	do.	do.	Similar to above but use 4-Layers #15 A.S.F.	19"	do.	do.
	Non-combustible or insulated Deck 4-Ply	do.	do.	550#/sq. 650#/sq.	do.	a-b). 23 c) .25	20 yr.	Asphalt coat	do.	do.	27½"	do.	do.
	3-Ply	do.	do.	505#/sq. 605#/sq.	do.	a-b). 20 c) .22	15 yr.	do.	do.	Similar to above but use 3-Layers #15 A.S.F.	24-2/3"	do.	do.
PITCH SATURATED FELT WITH a) SLAG b) GRAVEL c) MARBLE CHIPS	Wood or Nailable Deck 5-Ply	½" to 2" in 12"	0"in 12"	530#/sq. 630#/sq.	do.	a-b). 22 c) .24	20 yr.	Rosin Sheathing	Galv. nails & Pitch	5-Layer #15 P.S.F. & Gravel or slag imbedded in hot pitch	19" & 24½"	do.	do.
	4-Ply	do.	do.	490#/sq. 590#/sq.	do.	a-b). 19 c) .21	15 yr.	do.	do.	Similar to above but use 4-Layers of #15 P.S.F	19"	do.	do.
	Non-combustible or insulated Deck 4-Ply	do.	do.	560#/sq. 660#/sq.	do.	a-b). 23 c) .25	20 yr.	Pitch coat	do.	do.	27½"	do.	do.
	3-Ply	do.	do.	520#/sq. 620#/sq.	do.	a-b). 20 c) .22	15 yr.	do.	do.	Similar to above but use 3-Layers of #15 P.S.F.	24-2/3"	do.	do.
	Wood or Nailable Deck 3-Ply	2"in 12"	0"in 12"	490#/sq. 590#/sq.	do.	a-b). 18½ c). 20½	10 yr.	Rosin Sheathing	do.	1-#30 P.S.F. & 2-#15 P.S.F. & Gravel or slag	19"	do.	do.
SMOOTH SURFACE ASPHALT	Wood or Nailable Deck 3 or 4-Ply	6"in 12"	½"in 12"	160#/sq.	do.	.16	10 yr.	do.	Galv. nails & Asphalt	1-#30 A.S.F. & 2-#15 A.S.F. (or 4#15 A.S.F.) & Asphalt coat	19"	Smooth: Black	Class C
	On Concrete Deck 3-Ply	3"in 12"	do.	194#/sq.	do.	.17	10 yr.	Asphalt Primer	do.	3-#15 A.S.F. & asphalt coating	24-2/3"	do.	do.
MINERAL SURFACE	Wood or Nailable Decks 4-Ply	9"in 12"	3"in 12"	235#/sq.	do.	.24	15 yr.	None	Galv. nails & Asphalt	2-#15 A.S.F. & 2-19" Mineral Surfaced Roofing	19"	Rough: Various Colors	do.
	4-Ply	do.	do.	200#/sq.	do.	.24	10 yr.	do.	do.	Similar but less asphalt	do.		do.
	Concrete Deck 4-Ply	do.	do.	270#/sq.	do.	.25	15 yr.	Asphalt Primer	do.	2-#15 A.S.F. & 2-19" Mineral Surfaced Roofing	do.	do.	do.
	3-Ply	do.	do.	225#/sq.	do.	.23	10 yr.	do.	do.	Similar but 1-#15 A.S.F.	do.	do.	do.
ALUMINUM FOIL	Aluminum and chips over built-up roof	3"in 12"	-	265#/sq. 365#/sq.	.002" Thick Foil	.30	20 yr. Material Guar.	1-30# & 2-15# Felts	Aluminum nails & cement	Aluminum applied over Asphalt roof & imbedded with marble chips.	3" End lap 3" Side lap	do.	Class A
ASPHALT ROLL ROOFING	Mica Surface one side	-	2"to3" in 12"	65#/sq.	36" wide 36' long	.10	Contractor would normally furnish two year guaranty for these types	None	Galvanized or Aluminum nails & Asphalt Cement	Nail to wood sheathing cement all laps	19"	do.	Class C
	Gun Metal both sides	-	do.	55#/sq.	do.	.10		do.		do.	2"	Gray Smooth	do.
	Mica Surface both sides	-	do.	45#/sq.	do.	.10		do.	do.	do.	19"	Rough Various colors	None
	Mineral Surfaced	-	do.	90 to 95#/sq.	do.	.12		do.	do.	do.	2"to 4" Head 4"to 6" side.		Class C
	Pattern Edge Roll	-	4"in 12"	105#/sq.	32"& 36"W. 42'& 48' L.	.15		do.	do.	do.	2" Side lap 14" or 16" Exposure	do.	do.
	19" Selvedge Double coverage	-	1"in 12"	140#/sq.	36" wide 36' long	.18		do.	do.	do.	19" Head lap 17" Exposure	do.	do.
	Smooth Roll	-	2"in 12"	65#/sq. 55#/sq. 45#/sq.	32"& 36"W. 36'-0" L.	.10 .10 .10		None	do.	do.	2" Head lap 4" Side lap	Black: Smooth	do. do. None

ABBREVIATIONS: A.S.F.-ASPHALT SATURATED FELT; EXP.-EXPOSURE; GA.-GAUGE; GUAR.-GUARANTY; L-LENGTH; M'F'R'S-MANUFACTURERS; P.S.F.-PITCH SATURATED FELT; SQ.FT.-SQUARE FOOT; U.L.R.-UNDERWRITERS LABORATORY RATING; W.-WIDTH; #/SQ.-POUNDS PER SQUARE; A.S.As.F.-ASPHALT SATURATED ASBESTOS FELT; P.S.As.F.-PITCH SATURATED ASBESTOS FELT.

PREPARED IN CONSULTATION WITH TURNER CONSTRUCTION COMPANY

ROOF COVERINGS

BUILT-UP ROOFING (cont.)

TYPE	DESCRIPTION	SLOPE MAX.	SLOPE MIN.	WGT.	SIZE	COSTS SQ.FT.	M'F'R'S BOND	UNDER-LAY	FASTENER	APPLICATION	LAP	COLOR & TEXTURE	U.L.R.
PROMENADE ROOF	For use under Promenade Tile	1"in 12"	0"in 12"	275#/sq.	36" wide rolls	.20	None	Pitch Coat	Pitch	4 - 15# P.S.F. 1 - 15# P.S.F.	19" 2"	Black Smooth	—
ASBESTOS FELT	Asphalt Saturated Asbestos Felt. Over Insulation	6"in 12"	½"in 12"	145 to 190#/sq.	32"& 36" Wide Rolls	.22 .19 .18	20 yr. 15 yr. 10 yr.	— — —	Nails & Asphalt	4 - 15 lb. A.S.A$_S$.F 3 - 15 lb. A.S.A$_S$.F 2 - 15 lb. A.S.A$_S$.F,1#15 A.S.F.	24½" 22" 17"	do.	Class A with Covering
	Pitch Saturated Asbestos Felt. Over Insulation	½"in 12"	0"in 12"	do.	do.	.21 .18	20 yr. 15 yr.	— —	Nails & Pitch	4 - 15 lb. P.S.A$_S$.F 3 - 15 lb. P.S.A$_S$.F	24½" 22"	do.	do.
	Asbestos felt may also be applied over a wood deck or over a non-combustible deck.												
PREPARED ASBESTOS FELT	A.S. A$_S$. F. Smooth Surface		2"in 12"	85#/sq	32" W. 40'6" L.	15	Normal. 2 yr. con-tractor Guar.	—	Galvanized Nails & Asphalt Cement	Applied directly over T. & G. wood sheathing cement Horizontal Laps	2" Head lap Butt Sides	Various colors Smooth	Class C
	Granule Surfaced		3"in 12"									Rough	
	White Top		3"in 12"									White, Smooth	

ROOFING SHINGLES

TYPE	DESCRIPTION	SLOPE MAX.	SLOPE MIN.	WGT.	SIZE	BUTT. THICK.	COST SQ.FT.	GUAR-ANTY	UNDER-LAY	FASTENER	APPLICATION	LAP OR EXPOSURE	COLOR & TEXTURE	U.L.R.
ASBESTOS	American Individual		4"to 5" in 12"	285 to 300#/sq 600#/sq	8"to 9½" W. 16" to 18½" L.	5/32" or 1/4"	Varies widely	10 to 15 Years	Saturated Felt or Water-proof Paper.	Galv. Iron, Copper or Aluminum Nails	Laid on matched roofer's covered with waterproof paper or slater's felt.	2" Head lap 5" to 7" Exposure	Smooth: Various Colors	Class B
	American Duplex (2 shingles)		do.	285 to 300#/sq	16"to 17½"W. 16"to 18½"L.	5/32"	do			do.		do.	do.	do.
	Dutch or Scotch		5" in 12"	260#/sq	16"to 24" W. 12"to 16" L.	do.	do			do.	do.	3" Head lap 4" Side lap	do.	do.
	French or Hexagonal		do.	245 to 265#/sq	16" x 16"	do.	do		do.	do.	do.	3" Head lap 3" Side lap	do.	do.
	American Strip (3 Shingles)		do.	300#/sq	16"to 32"W. L. varies	do.	do		do.	do.	do.	2" Head lap	do.	do.
	3-Tab Hexagonal Strip (3 Shingles)		do.	245 to 265#/sq	36" W. 11 1/3" L	do.	do		do.	do.	do.	4 2/3" Exp.	do.	do.
ASPHALT	Asbestos-Plastic Coating - 3 Tabs		4"in 12"	325#/sq	36" W. 12" L.	3/8"	do	10 Yrs.	do.	do.	do.	2" Head lap 5" Exposure	do.	Class A
	Strip Shingle 3 tab		3"in 12"	300#/sq	36" wide 15" long	.2"	do.	10 yrs.	15# felt	galv. iron or alu. nails	laid on 6"-9" T & G wood decking	5" exposure 5" lead lap	course mineral many colors	Class C
	Individual Dutch lap		4"in 12"	160#/sq	12"L.x16" W.	.16" to .2"	do	do	Asphalt Felt or Roll Roofing	Copper, Zinc Galv. Iron or Aluminum Nails	Laid on matched roofers covered with Asphalt Felt or Roll Roofing	2" Head lap 3" Side lap	Rough Various Colors	do.
	Individual American		do.	320#/sq	16"L.x12" W.	do.	do	do.				6" Head lap 5" Exposure		do.
	Strip Shingles 3-Tabs		do.	210 to 275#/sq	36" Wide 12" Long	do	do	do	do.	do.	do.	2" Head lap 5" Exposure	do.	do.
	Hexagonal Strip 2 or 3 Tabs		do.	167#/sq	36" Wide 11 1/3" L	do	do	do	do	do.	do.	2" Head lap 4 2/3" Exp	do.	do.
	Inter-locking Standard		do.	170#/sq	19"x19 3/8"	do	do	do	do	do.	do.	2 to 3½"Head 4¼" Side lap	do.	do.
	Inter-locking Double Coverage		do.	230#/sq	19¾"x23 3/8" 18½"x20"	do	do	do	do	do.	do.	4½" Head lap 6 7/8"Side lap	do.	do.
	Lockdown		do.	135 to 162#/sq	16" x 16"	do.	do	None	do.	Copper Staple	do.	2½" Side & Head lap	do.	do.
ALUMINUM	4-Way Interlocking		4"to 5" in. 12"	40#/sq	8" x 7¼" 8" x 14½"	3/8"	60 60	None	#15 or #30 Felt	Aluminum Nails	Over solid deck sheathing.	Interlocking	Smooth & Embossed. Many Colors	—
SLATE	Sloping Roofs Standard	20"in. 12"	4"in 12"	750#/sq 900#/sq	10"to 26" Long	3/16" 1/4" &	.93 .98	20 yrs.	15#Felt 30#Felt	Copper or Galv. Iron nails & Slater's Cement.	Applied to tight sheathing or nailing compound.	4" Lap up to 8" in 12" slope 3" lap over 8" in 12"	Smooth or Rustic. Many Colors	—
	Sloping Roofs Textural			1400#/sq	6" to 14" wide	3/8"	1.05		30#Felt					
	Sloping Roofs Graduated			1800#/sq 2700#/sq		1/2" & 3/4"	1.06 1.07		45 or 65# Roll Roof					

PREPARED IN CONSULTATION WITH TURNER CONSTRUCTION COMPANY

ROOF COVERINGS

ROOFING SHINGLES & TILES (cont.)

TYPE	DESCRIPTION	SLOPE MAX.	SLOPE MIN.	WGT.	SIZE	BUTT. THICK.	COST SQ. FT.	GUARANTY	UNDERLAY	FASTENER	APPLICATION	LAP OR EXPOSURE	COLOR & TEXTURE	U.L.R.
SLATE	Flat Promenade Roofs or Heavy Use Special Walks Terraces, etc.		½" in 12"	3600#/sq	9" x 10" to 9" x 18" 1" Thick	—	2.00	Depends on Location	Built-up Roofing	Cement	Laid in 1" Cement Bed	—	Various colors & Textures	—
WOOD	Red Cedar Redwood Cypress White Cedar Southern Pine	Vert-ical	3" to 6" in 12"	200#/sq	16", 18", 24" & 27" Long 2½" to 16" Long	3/8" to 1/2" (5/8" to 1" special)	Varies widely do.	15 yrs. extended if dipped	Roofer's Felt	Galvanized or Copper Nails.	Laid on felt over spaced or solid sheathing. Shingles spaced not less than 1/4" apart or more than 3/8".	Exposures 4½" for 16"L. 5½" for 18"L. 7½" for 24"L. 8" for 27"L.	do.	—
	Handsplit & pre-stained handsplit	do.	do.	200 to 250#/sq	25"-27" L. W. varies	1/2" to 1 1/4"	do.	do.	do.	do.		8" to 10" Exposure	Rough Many Colors	—
CLAY TILE	French Corrugated		4½" to 5" in 12"	1000 to 1600#/sq	9" x 16"	3/8"	do.	20 yrs.	30# or 40# Felt	Copper Nails	Tile Laid over Asphalt Felt	3" Head lap 1½" Side lap	Blues, Grays Greens, Reds Fire Flashed & natural colors. Smooth or Lightly Scored	Class A
	Spanish-rounded		4½" in 12"	850#/sq	9¼" W. 13¾" L.	1/2"	do.	do.	do.	do.	do.	3" Head lap		do.
	Barrel-Mission curved		do.	1350#/sq	14" to 18" L. 6" to 8" W.	1/2"	do.	do.	do.	do.	Wood strip under each cover tile for Nailing	do.		do.
	Shingle-Flat		6" in 12"	1500 to 1750#/sq	12" to 15" L. 6" to 7" W.	3/8", 1/2, 9/16, 5/8, 1"	do.	20 yrs.	30# or 40# Felt	Copper Nails	Tile laid over Asphalt Felt	2" Head lap over third course above	Blues, Grays Greens, Reds Smoothed or Scored	Class A
	Interlocking Flat English		4" in 12"	800#/sq	13¼" Long 8" Wide	3/4" & 7/8"	do.	do.	do.	do.	do.	3" Head lap		do.
	Interlocking Closed		4½" in 12"	900#/sq	11" long 8¾" Wide	do.	do.	do.	do.	do.	do.	do.	do.	do.
	Roman		4½" in 12"	1400#/sq	12¾" L.	1"	do.	do.	do.	do.	do.	2¾" Head lap	do.	do.
	Greek		do.	1450#/sq	do.	—	do.	do.	do.	do.	do.	do.	do.	do.
	Promenade or Quarry Tile	2" in 12"	1/4" in 12"	900#/sq	2¾" to 9" square; 6x2¾" or 9" 8x3¾" or 4"	1/2" to 1 3/8"	do.	do.	Built-up Roof	Cement Mortar	Set in bed of cement Mortar	None	Red. Smooth or Non-skid	do.
CEMENT TILE	Bermuda		2½" in 12"	1050#/sq	15¾" x 8¾"	2"	.35	None	30# Felt	Cement Mortar	Over underlay apply roll roofing. 90# Set Tile in Mortar bed.	13½" x 9" Exp.	Many Pastel Colors. Rough	—
	Flat Shingle		do.	900#/sq	15" x 8¼"	1"	.32	do.	do.	do.		13½" x 8½" Exp.		—
	Spanish		do.	900#/sq	15" x 8¾"	—	.32	do.	do.	do.		13" x 8½" Exp.		—
CONCRETE PANEL	Pre-Cast Panel		4 3/16" in 12"	1600#/sq	4'-4" L. 2'-0" W.	1 1/8" T.	.75	5 yrs.	None	Elastic Compound Concrete Hook	Tile laid with shoulder hooked over purlin. Joints filled with mastic.	3½" min. 7" max. Head lap	Red, Smooth	—
PORCELAIN ENAMEL	Steel Base with enamel fused to it.		3" in 12"	225#/sq	Approx. 10¾" x 12½"	—	1.70	Indefinite depends on location.	30# Felt	Galvanized or Copper head Nails	Laid on Tongue & groove roofing. Felt to overlap each previous course.	2½" horizontal lap 10" x 10" Exposure.	Many Colors & Textures	—

* pre-dipping costs 1½¢ extra per sq. ft.

PREPARED IN CONSULTATION WITH TURNER CONSTRUCTION COMPANY.

ROOF COVERINGS

The following pages show the various types of roof finishes available for use in small construction. For comparative purposes, many factors important in choosing a roof finish are listed. These factors include a description of the material, the minimum and maximum slopes, method of application, guaranty available, and the cost of various finishes. The costs per square foot are based on normal quantity of the type of roofing used in the Eastern Area. Prices may vary 30% due to competition, size of job, and location. Prices include installation.

CORRUGATED & CRIMPED ROOFING

TYPE	DESCRIPTION	SLOPE MAX.	SLOPE MIN.	WGT.	SIZE	THICK	COST SQ.FT	GUARANTY	UNDER-LAY	FASTENER	APPLICATION	LAP OR EXPOSURE	COLOR & TEXTURE	U.L.R.
IRON & STEEL; OR GALVANIZED IRON	1¼" Corrugations Iron & Steel		3" in 12"	75# to 200#	25"& 26" W. 6'-0" to 12'-0" L.	26 to 18 ga.	26 ga. .33 18 ga. .54	10 yr.	55# Felt over wood	Nails or Clips	Nail to wood Clip to Steel	1½ to 2 Corr. sidelap. 6" Endlap	Bright - lustre & Smooth	-
	1¼" Corr. Galvanized		do.	90# to 215#		do.		do.		do.	do.			-
	2½" Corr. Iron & Steel		do.	75# to 200#	26"& 27½"W. 6'-0" to 12'-0" L.	do.	do.	do.	do.	do.	do.	do.	do.	-
	2½" Corr. Galvanized		do.	90# to 215#		do.	do.	do.	do.	do.	do.	do.	do.	-
STEEL WITH COMPOSITE COVERING	Covering 1¼ Corr. of b only	Cement side-laps for slopes below 3"in 12"		101 to 205#/sq.	23", 33" & 34" W. 6'to 12' L.	24 gauge	.75	a) 1 yr. b) 1–10 yr. c) 1–10 yr. depends on locat-ion	-	Lead Headed Nails or bolts	Nail to wood Clip to Steel	do.	Mica	-
	a) primer, adhesive, asbestos, sealer. 2½ Corr. a.	do		185 to 300#/sq.	33" Wide up to 12'L.	24 ga. 18 ga.	.71 .81		-	Stainless Steel bolts or screws	Screw to wood Bolt to Steel	1½ sidelap 6" endlap	Black Aluminum	-
	b) primer, asphalt-plastic, mica. b.		2" in 12"	101 to 251#/sq.	26",27½",33" & 34" W. 6'to 12'L.	24 ga. 18 ga.	.75 .87		-	Lead headed nails or bolts	Nail to wood Bolt to Steel	1 to 2 Corr. sidelap 6" endlap	Mica	-
	2.67Corr. c-only		2" in 12"	129 to 255#/sq.	33" W. up to 12'L.	24 ga. 18 ga.	.75 .87		-	Stainless Steel & Nickel-Copper Screws	Screwed into Steel members	1½ sidelap 6" to 12" end.	Black, Maroon Aluminum	-
	c) Zinc, Felt, Sealer. V-Beam a.		2" in 12"	142 to 350#/sq.	Up to 12'L. 29½" W.	24 ga. 18 ga.	.75 .88	up to 10 yrs. depends on locat-ion	-	Lead, Stainless Steel or Nickel-Copper Bolts or Screws	Screwed or nailed to wood; screwed or bolted to steel	6" endlap 1½ to 2 corrugation sidelap	Mica. Black Maroon Aluminum	-
	b.		2"in12"		29" W.	24 ga. 18 ga.	.79 .96							
	c.		1½"in12"		29" W.	24 ga. 18 ga.	.80 .93							
	5-V crimp b-only	Cement side-laps for slopes below 4"in 12"		101 to 251#/sq.	26" Wide 6'-0" to 12'-0" L	26 ga.	.70	1-10 years	-	Lead headed nails or bolts	Nail to wood Bolt to steel	24" exposure	Mica	-
	Mansard a.		4" in 12"	129 to 225#/sq.	33" Wide up to 12'L.	24 ga. 20 ga.	.71 .76	do	-	Stainless Steel or Nickel-Copper Screws & Bolts	Screw to wood Screw or bolt to Steel	1 to 1½ corr. sidelap 6" to 12" endlap	Black Maroon Aluminum	-
	c.		4" in 12"			24 ga. 20 ga.	.75 .81							
COPPER	2½"Corrugation		4" in 12	100 to 165#/sq.	27½" Wide	20 ounce	1.40	10 yr.		Copper or copper alloy nails or screws	Insulate from other metals	1½ to 2 Corr. sidelap 6" endlap	Copper Smooth	-
	Copper clad corrugated sheet		do.	do.	do.	26 ga. 18 ga.	.93 1.14	do.	-		do.		do.	-
	Copper bearing steel	1¼" & 2½"Corrugations					Same as galvanized iron							
	Copper molybdenum iron 1¼ corr.		3" in 12"	84 to 286#/sq.	24" Wide 5'to 12'L.	28 ga. 20 ga.	.30 .50	1-10 yrs.	-	Copper or Copper Alloy nails or screws	Can be used on open decks	1½ to 2 Corr. sidelap 6" endlap	Copper, smooth	-
	2½ corr.		do.	do.	do.	28 ga. 16 ga.	.30 .55	do.	-		do.		do.	-
ALUMINUM	Corrugations 1¼" & 2½"		3" in 12"	56#/sq.	5'to 12'L. 26" W.	.024"T. .019"T.	.60	10 yrs.	do.	Aluminum nails Screws or Clips	Nail to wood Screw or rivet weld to steel	1½,2,2½ Corr.side 6"or 8"end.	Smooth	-
	2.67"				35"or48"W.	.032"T.							Smooth or embossed	
	Curved Corrugated	-	-	do.	do.	do.	.70	15 yrs.	do.		Min. radius of curvature 30"	do.	do.	-
	5-V crimp		3" in 12"	30#/sq. 41#/sq.	5'-to 12' L. 26" wide	26 ga 24 ga	.40 .43	do	do.	do.	Over solid or near solid sheathing	2 crimp side 6"or 8" end.	Smooth or embossed	-
CORRUGATED ASBESTOS CEMENT	4.2 corrugation		3"or4" in 12"	375 to 410#/sq.	6"to 12'-0" long 42" Wide	1½" overall thick	.80	10 yrs.	none	Lead headed Bolt or screw	Screw to Wood Bolt to Steel	1 corrugated sidelap 6" endlap	Smooth Gray	-
	Curved 2'-0" min. 5'-0" min.	radius radius	W. L.	do.	6'to 12'-0" L.,42"W.	do.	1.15 to 2.75	do.	do.	do.	do.	do.	do.	-

PREPARED IN CONSULTATION WITH TURNER CONSTRUCTION COMPANY

ROOF COVERINGS

CORRUGATED ROOFING (Con't)

TYPE	DESCRIPTION	SLOPE MAX.	SLOPE MIN.	WGT.	SIZE	THICK	COST SQ.FT.	GUAR-ANTY	UNDER-LAY	FASTENER	APPLICATION	LAP OR EXPOSURE	COLOR & TEXTURE	U.L.R
GLASS	2½" Corrugations		3"or 4" in 12"	630#/sq.	0 to 12'-0"L. 42" Wide	3/8"	2.75	depends on location	None	Sheet Metal Cap & Bolts	Clipped to Purlins	3" endlap	White & Amber	-
PLASTIC	1¼",2½",2.67" & 4.2"Corrugation 5-V crimp		3"or 4" in 12"	50 to 70#/sq.	2' to 12'-0"L. 26" to 42" Wide	.065" to .097"	1.47	None	do.	Nails, Bolts or clips	Fastened to Structural Members	1"or 1½" Corrugation sidelap	Smooth or Rough Many Colors	-
PORCELAIN ENAMEL	2½ Corrugations		2" in 12"	139 to 248#/sq.	27½" W. up to 12'L.	24 ga. 18 ga.	.88 1.00	depends on site 10 yrs +	-	Screws	Screw to wood or steel	1½"corr. sidelap	Many Colors Smooth	-

STANDING SEAM, FLAT SEAM & BATTEN SEAM ROOFING

TYPE	DESCRIPTION	SLOPE MAX.	SLOPE MIN.	WGT.	SIZE	THICK	COST SQ.FT.	GUAR-ANTY	UNDER-LAY	FASTENER	APPLICATION	LAP OR EXPOSURE	COLOR & TEXTURE	U.L.R
ALUMINUM	Batten Seam		1½"in 12"	60 to 92#/sq.	31½"x120" sheet	.032"	1.16	15 yrs.	30 lb. Felt	Aluminum nails or screws & cleats	Sheet placed in Batten & cap is screwed over.	-	Smooth Mill Finish	-
COPPER	Standing Seam Pan or Roll Method		2½"in 12"	80 or 125#/sq.	16"x72"	10 oz.	1.36	do.	15 lb. Felt & Rosin Paper	Copper or Bronze Nails & Cleats	Sheets locked together to form Standing Seams	-	Smooth: Weathers Green	-
					20"x48" 20"x96"	16 oz.	1.70							
					24"x96"	20 oz.	1.97							
	Batten Seam Pan Method		3" in 12"	253#/sq.	20"or 24" W. 8'-0" L.	16 oz.	1.27	None	do.	do.	Place pans between battens and cap over	-	do.	-
			1½"in 12"	do.	do.	20 oz.	1.48	15 yrs.	do.	do.		-	do.	-
	Flat Seam	4" in 12"	¼" in 12"	150#/sq.	16"x18" best size	20 oz.	2.21	do.	15 lb. Felt	do.	Seams, Locked & soldered	-	do.	-
COPPER MOLYB-DENUM IRON ALLOY	Standing Seam Roll Method		2" in 12"	81 to 130#/sq.	26½" W. 50'-0"L.	24 ga.& Lighter	.87	1-10 yrs.			Used only over a tight deck	24" Exp.	Smooth	-
	Pressed Standing Seam		-	79 to 183#/sq.	25" W. 5' to 12'L.	do.	.80	do.			do.	do.	do.	-
COPPER BEARING STEEL	Standing Seam Roll Method		2" in 12"	81 to 130#/sq.	26½" W. 50'-0"L.	24 ga.& Lighter	.87	do.			do.	do.	do.	-
	Pressed Standing Seam		-	79 to 183#/sq.	25" W. 5' to 12'L.	do.	.80	do.			do.	do.	do.	-
LEAD +6 TO 7.5% ANTIMONY	Batten and Standing seams Regular or Special batten Seams not over 24" o.c.		Varies	Approx. 300#/sq.	Average 2'-0"x4'-0" maximum; Special 4'-0"x6'-0" maximum	2½# = 1/24" 3# = 3/64" 4# = 1/16"	R / S 1.50 / 1.70 1.63 / 1.83 1.90 / 2.10	15 to 20 yrs.	15 lb. Felt	Cleats lead coated steel or hard copper alloy nails	Sheets joined by means of Locked Seams Laid on smooth roof surface.	1" turnover on lap seams	Weathers to gray. Many Textures	-
NICKEL COPPER ALLOY	Batten Seam		3"in12" 1½"in12"	26 ga.= 86#/sq. 25 ga.= 101#/sq.	20" Wide or 24" Wide	26 ga.= .018" 25 ga.= .021"	1.77	None 15 yrs.	30 lb. Felt	Nickel-Copper Cleats & Nails	do.	-	Slate gray or combination of gray-green & brown	-
	Standing Seam		3"in12"				1.75	None	15 lb. Felt	do.	do.	-		-
	Flat Seam	3" in 12"		do.	do.	26 ga. 25 ga.	1.95 1.96	None	15 lb. Felt	do.	do.	-	do.	-
STAINLESS STEEL			1½" in 12"	227#/sq.		28 ga.	2.06	20 yrs. or better		Stainless Steel Nails & Screws	Lap Seamed & Soldered	-	Bright or Satin Finish	-
TIN (TERNE PLATE) 80% LEAD 20% TIN	Batten Seam		2" in 12"	1C = 62#/sq. 1X = 76#/sq.	14",20",24" &28" Wide X20",24" 28",96" & 120" or 50'-0" Long	1C ga.= .0122 T. 1X ga.= .0155 T.	# / IC / IX 8 / .83 / .87	1 yr.	Rosin sized paper	Terne cleats & roofing nails	Use Double Lock Unsoldered Seam	11" to 19" Exp.	May be painted any Color	-
	Standing Seam		do.				20 / .92 / .95 40 / .99 / 1.01	1 yr.	do.	do.	do.	11" to 25" Exp.		-
	Flat Seam	2" in 12"	½" in 12"	do.	do.	do.	8 / 1.01 / 1.04 20 / 1.10 / 1.12 40 / 1.17 / 1.21	10-15 yrs.	do.	do.	Single Lock Seam Soldered	12½" to 26½" Exp.	do.	-

ABBREVIATIONS - A.S.F. - Asphalt Saturated Felt; Exp.-Exposure; Ga.-gauge; Guar.-Guaranty; L-Length; M'f'rs-Manufacturers; P.S.F.-Pitch Saturated Felt; Sq.ft.-Square foot; U.L.R.-Underwriters Laboratory Rating; W-Width; #/sq.-pounds per square; A.S.As.F-Asphalt Saturated Asbestos Felt & P.S.As.F.-Pitch Saturated Asbestos Felt; R-Regular; S-Special.

PREPARED IN CONSULTATION WITH TURNER CONSTRUCTION COMPANY

ROOF COVERINGS

STANDING SEAM, FLAT SEAM & BATTEN SEAM ROOFING (Con't)

TYPE	DESCRIPTION	SLOPE MAX.	SLOPE MIN.	WGT.	SIZE	THICK	COST SQ.FT.	GUARANTY	UNDERLAY	FASTENER	APPLICATION	LAP OR EXPOSURE	COLOR & TEXTURE	U.L.R
GALVANIZED IRON & STEEL	Standing Seam		2" in 12"	88 to 130#/sq.	26½" Wide 50'-0" Long	28 ga. 24 ga.	.78 .84	1-10 yrs.	None	Galvanized Nails & Cleats	Use Double lock Seam	24" Exp.	Smooth: Metallic	-
	Pressed Standing Seam		6" in 12"	79 to 183#/sq.	26½" Wide 5' to 12' L.	28 to 22 ga.	-	do.	do.	do.	-	do.	do.	-
	Double or Triple Drain Sheets		6" in 12"	92 to 106#/sq.	26½" Wide 6'-0" to 12'-0" L.	29 ga. to 26 ga.	-	do.	do.	Lead Seal Nails	Sheets nailed to Wood Deck	24" Exp. 6" endlap	do.	-
ZINC	Batten Seam		3" in 12"	75 to 150#/sq.	20", 30", 36" & 40" W.	15 ga. to 11 ga.	10 ga.= 1.13 11 ga.= 1.21 15 ga.= 1.59	15-20 yrs.	Glassy Saturated & coated paper	Galvanized Nails & Cleats	Laid on a Smooth un-Obstructed Surface covered with sheathing paper	-	Weathers to gray	-
	Standing Seam		2" in 12"	100 to 200#/sq.	20" Wide 7'-0" or 8'-0" L.	#10 Zinc								
	Flat Seam Max. Area 200 Sq. Ft.				14" x 20" maximum	#10 Zinc	1.33	do.	do.	do.	do.	-	do.	-

FIBERBOARD ROOFING

TYPE	DESCRIPTION	SLOPE MAX.	SLOPE MIN.	WGT.	SIZE	THICK	COST SQ.FT.	GUARANTY	UNDERLAY	FASTENER	APPLICATION	LAP OR EXPOSURE	COLOR & TEXTURE	U.L.R
FIBERBOARD TILE	Cane Fiberboard impregnated with bituminous	1" in 12"	½" in 12"	201#/sq.	24½" x 49" 23¾" x 21½" 23¾" x 49"	1/2" 3/16" 3/16"	1.00	None	3-Ply built-up roof	Asphalt Plastic Compound	Apply Tile on 15# Felt over Built-up roof	Rabbeted Edges	Black Green Red	Class A
FIBERBOARD CORE WITH COVERING (ALL BOARD FACTORY FABRICATED)	90# asphalt applied over fiberboard at factory		2½" to 3" in 12"	360#/sq.	15-3/16" Wide 8'-0" Long	1½"T.	-	-	None	Aluminum Nails	Sheets nailed & sealed with mastic	13" Exposure	Rough	None
	Copper Sleeve over fiberboard Core		do.	do.	do.	do.	-	-	None	Copper Nails	do.	do.	Smooth: Weathers Green	do.
	Aluminum Sleeve over fiberboard		do.	do.	do.	do.	-	-	None	Aluminum Nails	do.	do.	Smooth: Aluminum	do.
	Aluminum Foil Plus Felt & marble chips over fiber-board core		do.	do.	do.	do.	-	-	None	do.	do.	do.	Rough: Various Colors	do.

CANVAS

TYPE	DESCRIPTION	SLOPE MAX.	SLOPE MIN.	WGT.	SIZE	THICK	COST SQ.FT.	GUARANTY	UNDERLAY	FASTENER	APPLICATION	LAP OR EXPOSURE	COLOR & TEXTURE	U.L.R
LIGHT WGT MEDIUM " HEAVY "	Cotton Duck or specially treated cotton fabric	Flat		15 oz. 18 oz. 21 oz.	30" or 36" Wide	-	.30 .34 .38	5 yrs.	Heavy coat of Linseed Oil	Galvanized or Copper Tacks	Applied to wood deck cover with 1 coat of lead & Oil paint & 1 coat of deck paint	1½" or 2" lap	Paint any Color	-

CEMENT FINISH

TYPE	DESCRIPTION	SLOPE MAX.	SLOPE MIN.	WGT.	SIZE	THICK	COST SQ.FT.	GUARANTY	UNDERLAY	FASTENER	APPLICATION	LAP OR EXPOSURE	COLOR & TEXTURE	U.L.R
CEMENT FINISH	Laid over built-up roof	Flat		Varies	Varies	1" Finish Coat	*.35	-	4-Ply Built-up roof	Poured Concrete	Cement Finish over concrete fill	-	-	-

*does not include fill

PLASTIC ROOFING

TYPE	DESCRIPTION	SLOPE MAX.	SLOPE MIN.	WGT.	SIZE	THICK	COST SQ.FT.	GUARANTY	UNDERLAY	FASTENER	APPLICATION	LAP OR EXPOSURE	COLOR & TEXTURE	U.L.R
VINYL	Vinyl Spray	any pitch		13#/sq.	6-8 Plys	.02" to .04"	.45	12 to 15 yrs.	None	None	Spray on dry & clean surface	-	Many colors & Textures	-
NEOPRENE	Neoprene latex & dehydrating powder	pitch only for drainage		150#/sq. 200#/sq.	Varies	3/16" to 3/8"	1.00	10 yrs.	Felt	None	Mopped on a firm deck	-	Many Colors	-

PREPARED IN CONSULTATION WITH TURNER CONSTRUCTION COMPANY

STAIRS

TABLE OF CONTENTS

STAIR TREAD-RISER PROPORTION FORMULAE

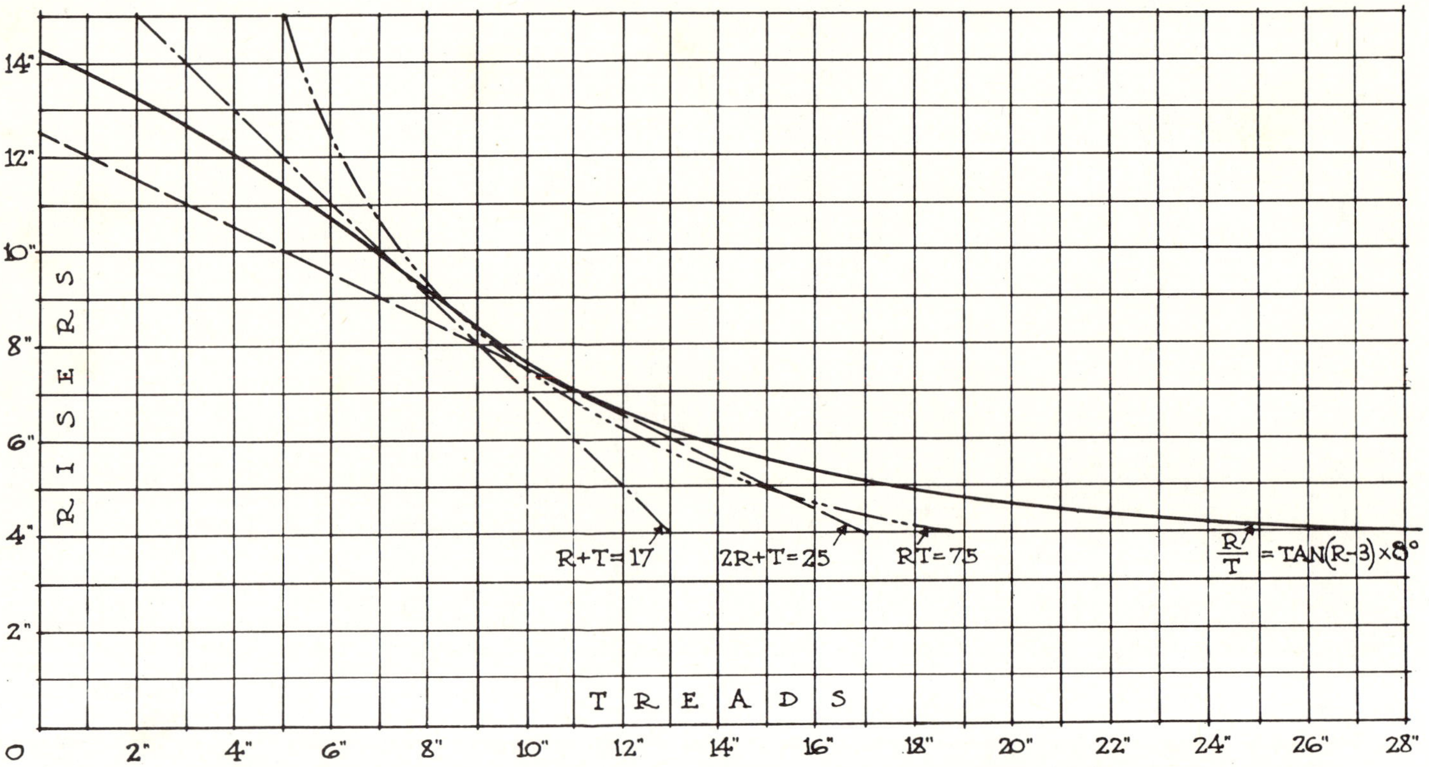
RISERS
TREADS
14"
12"
10"
8"
6"
4"
2"
0
2"
4"
6"
8"
10"
12"
14"
16"
18"
20"
22"
24"
26"
28"
R+T=17
2R+T=25
RT=75
R/T = TAN(R-3)×8°

COMPARISON OF VARIOUS STAIR TREAD-RISER PROPORTION FORMULAE

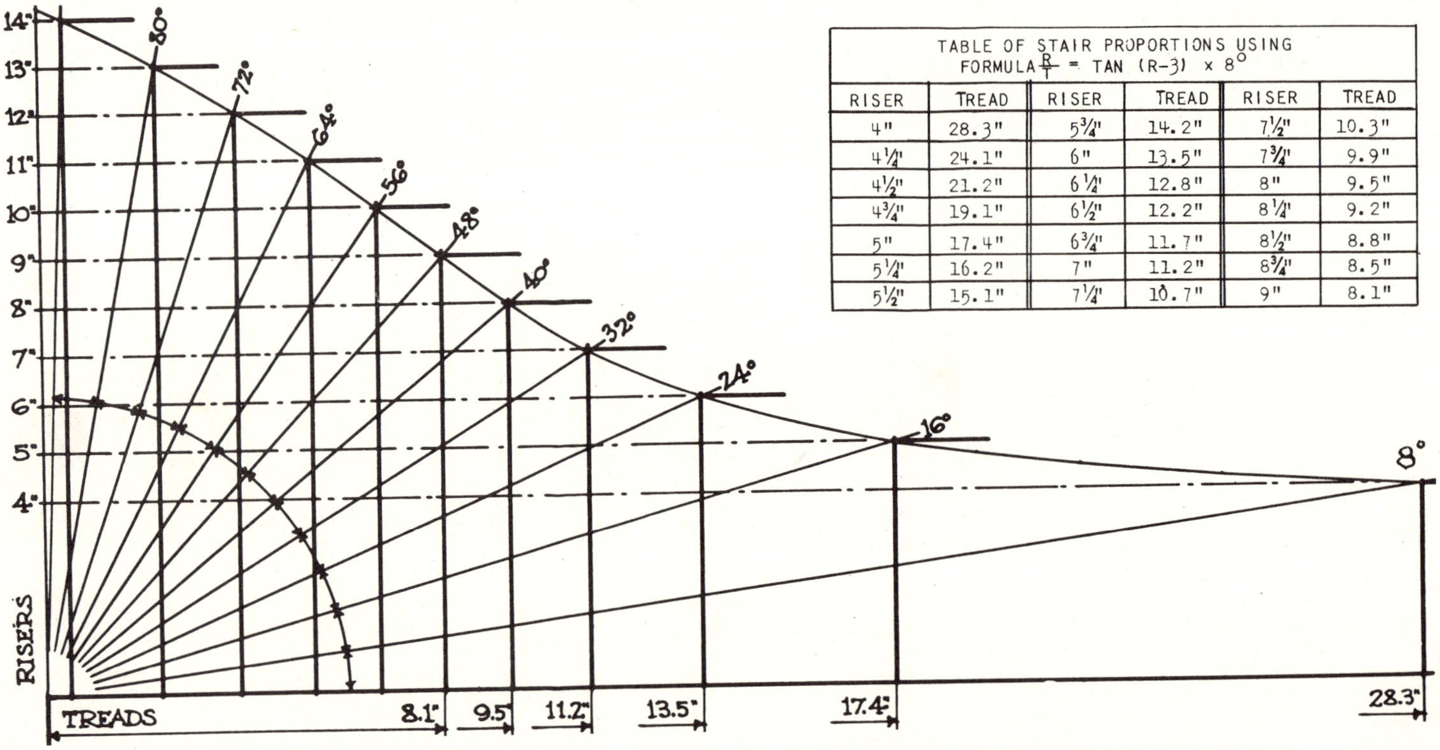
RISERS
TREADS
14"
13"
12"
11"
10"
9"
8"
7"
6"
5"
4"
80°
72°
64°
56°
48°
40°
32°
24°
16°
8°
8.1"
9.5"
11.2"
13.5"
17.4"
28.3"

TABLE OF STAIR PROPORTIONS USING FORMULA $\frac{R}{T}$ = TAN (R-3) x 8°

RISER	TREAD	RISER	TREAD	RISER	TREAD
4"	28.3"	5¾"	14.2"	7½"	10.3"
4¼"	24.1"	6"	13.5"	7¾"	9.9"
4½"	21.2"	6¼"	12.8"	8"	9.5"
4¾"	19.1"	6½"	12.2"	8¼"	9.2"
5"	17.4"	6¾"	11.7"	8½"	8.8"
5¼"	16.2"	7"	11.2"	8¾"	8.5"
5½"	15.1"	7¼"	10.7"	9"	8.1"

EXAMPLE: Assuming riser height of 8", find size of tread necessary for proper stair proportion.

Formula $\frac{R}{T}$=TAN. (R-3) x 8°

$$\frac{8}{T} = \frac{\text{TAN.}(8-3)\times 8^\circ}{1} = \frac{\text{TAN. } 5\times 8^\circ}{1} = \frac{\text{TAN. } 40^\circ}{1}$$

(in logarithm tables, tan. 40° = .83910)

$$\frac{8}{T} = \frac{.83910}{1}$$

.83910T = 8

$$T = \frac{8}{.83910} = 9.5340"$$

Tread = 9½"

STAIR PROPORTIONS USING FORMULA $\frac{R}{T}$ = TAN (R-3)8° OR T=R×COT(R-3)8°

FORMULA BY JAMIESON PARKER. A.I.A.

STAIR DATA

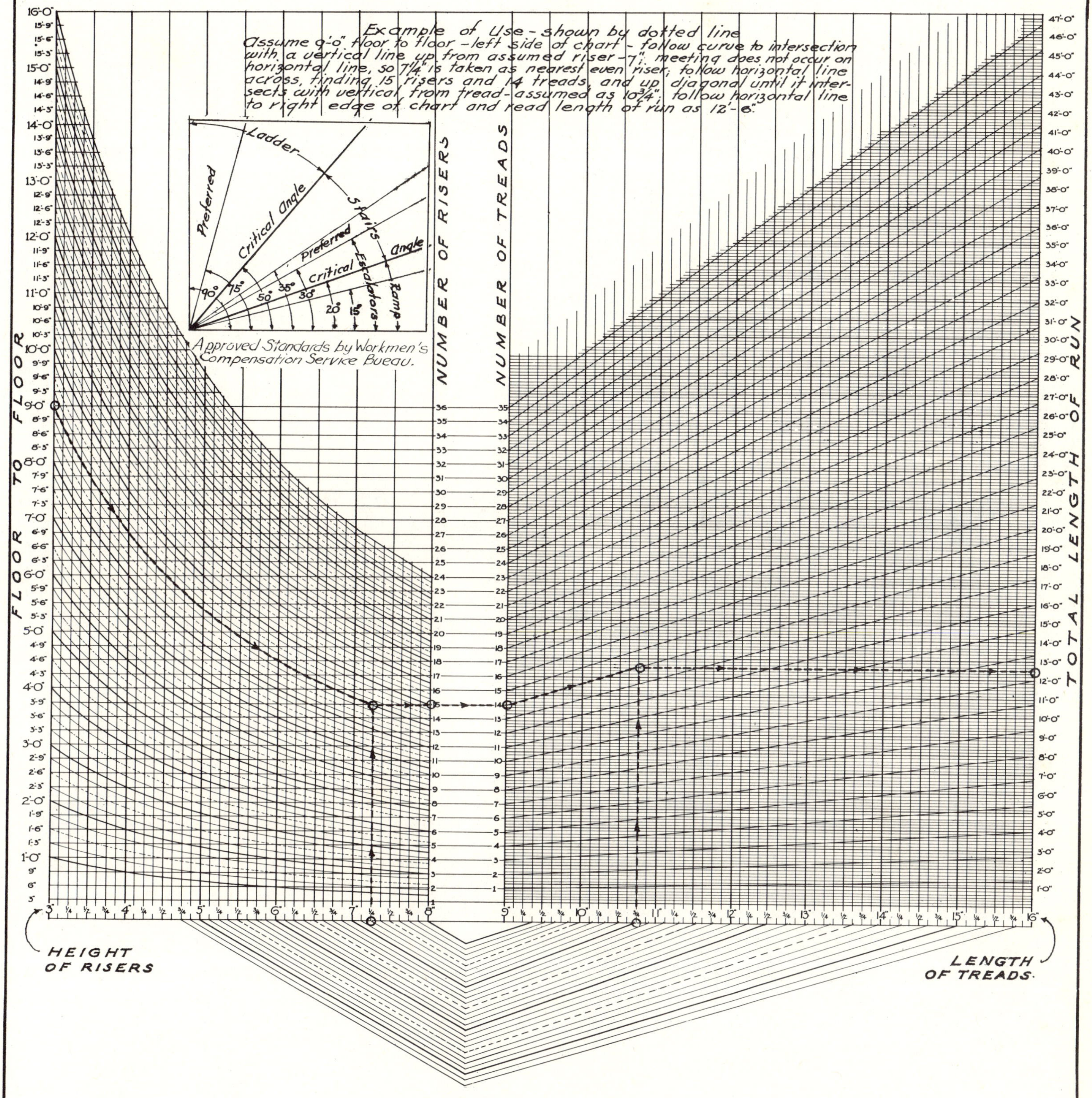
Example of Use - shown by dotted line
Assume 9'-0" floor to floor - left side of chart - follow curve to intersection with a vertical line up from assumed riser - 7"; meeting does not occur on horizontal line, so 7¼" is taken as nearest even riser; follow horizontal line across, finding 15 risers and 14 treads, and up diagonal until it intersects with vertical from tread - assumed as 10¾"; follow horizontal line to right edge of chart and read length of run as 12'-6".
Ladder
Preferred
Critical Angle
Stairs
Preferred
Critical
Angle
Escalators
Ramp
90°
75°
50°
35°
30°
20°
15°
Approved Standards by Workmen's Compensation Service Bueau.
FLOOR TO FLOOR
NUMBER OF RISERS
NUMBER OF TREADS
TOTAL LENGTH OF RUN
HEIGHT OF RISERS
LENGTH OF TREADS

Lines connecting treads & risers are based on product of tread & riser = 75 (about); these lines may be disregarded & any other rule substituted. They do not apply to exterior stairs.

Another rule commonly used is: run & riser = 17½; Run equals tread less nosing.

Recommendations: minimum width of tread with nosing = 11", except stairs with open risers. Maximum width of tread with nosing = 15". Maximum height of riser = 7¾", min. 6"

Conceived by Frederick L. Ackerman, Architect.

WOOD STAIRS

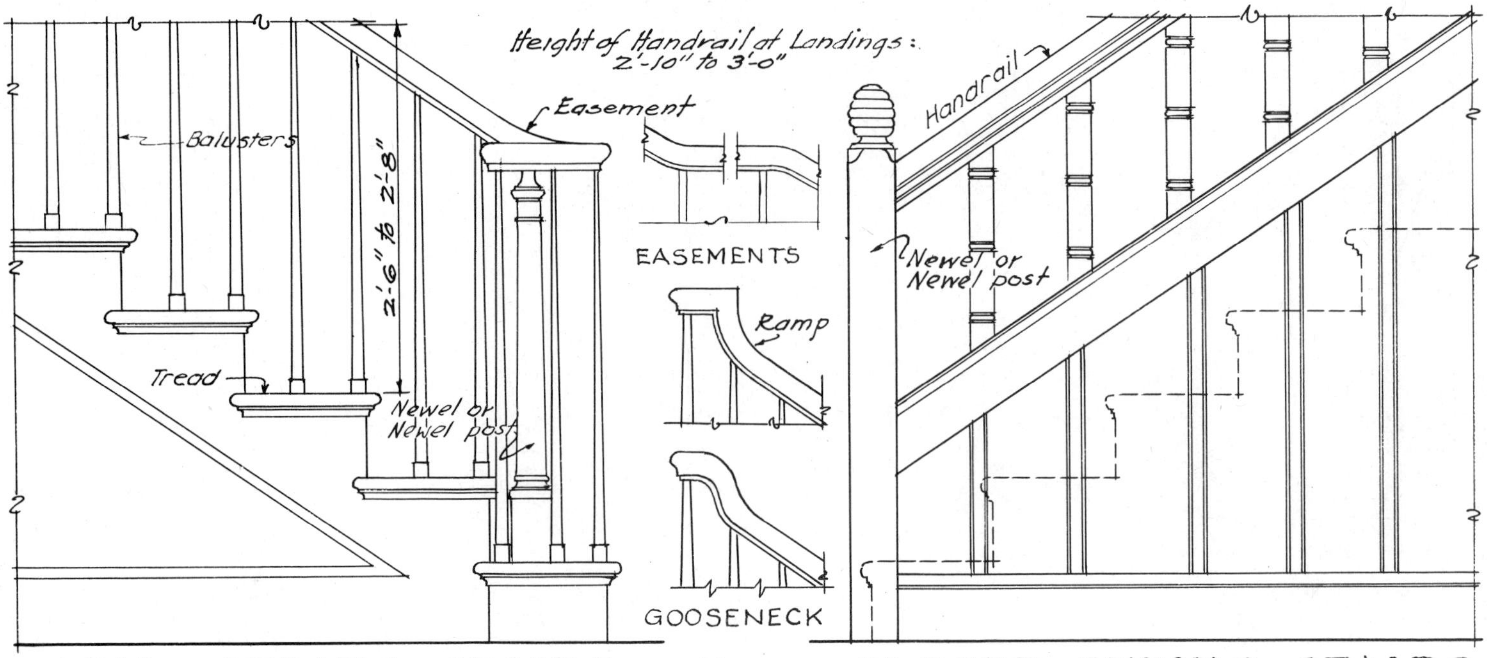
Height of Handrail at Landings: 2'-10" to 3'-0"
Easement
Balusters
2'-6" to 2'-8"
Tread
Newel or Newel post
EASEMENTS
Ramp
GOOSENECK
Handrail
Newel or Newel post

OPEN STRING STAIRS 3/4" = 1'-0" CLOSED STRING STAIRS

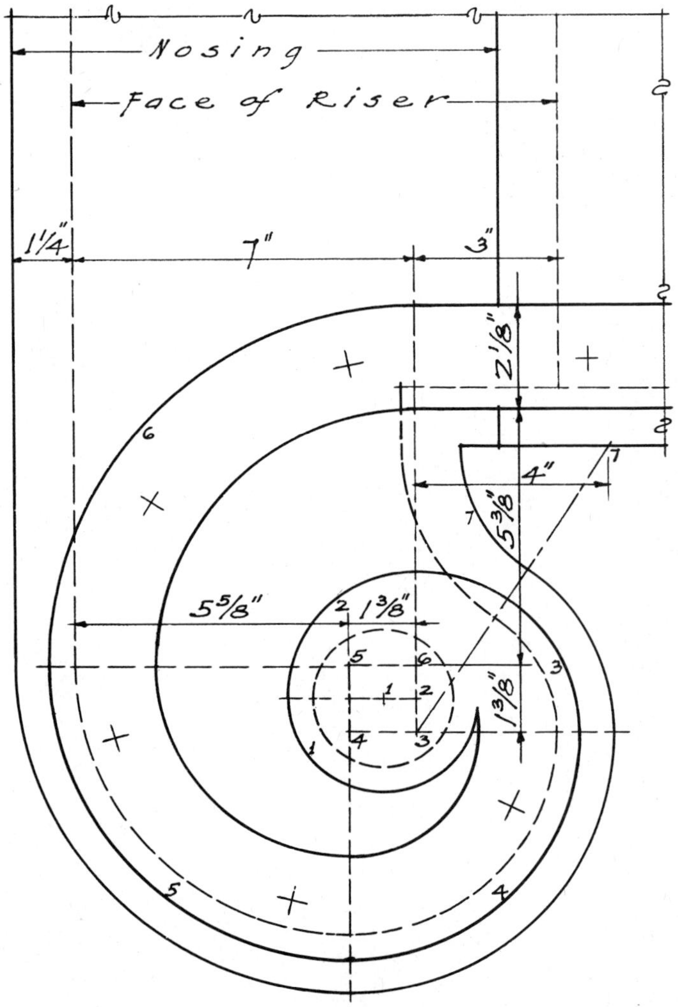
Nosing
Face of Riser
1 1/4"
7"
3"
2 1/8"
4"
5 3/8"
5 5/8"
1 3/8"
1 3/8"

DETAIL of a SIMPLE VOLUTE
3" = 1'-0"

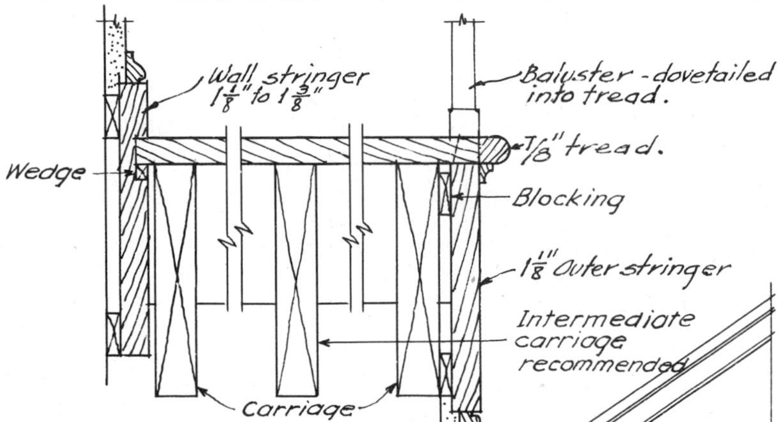
Wall stringer 1 1/8" to 1 3/8"
Baluster - dovetailed into tread.
Wedge
7/8" tread.
Blocking
1 1/8" Outer stringer
Intermediate carriage recommended
Carriage

SECTION thru WALL and OUTER STRINGS
1 1/2" = 1'-0"

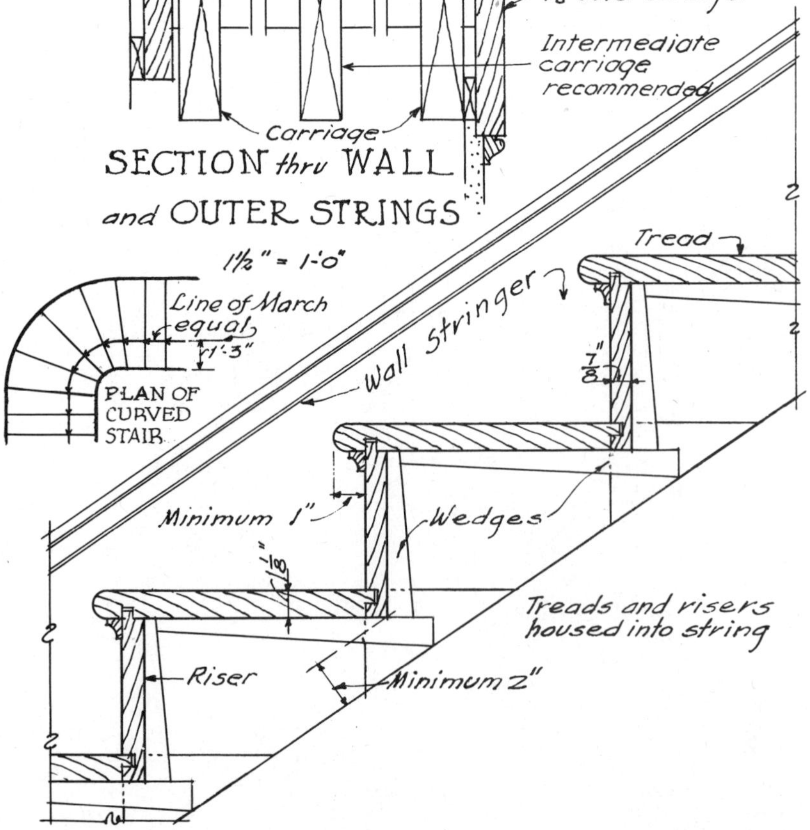
Line of March equal
1'-3"
PLAN OF CURVED STAIR
Tread
Wall Stringer
7/8"
Minimum 1"
Wedges
1/16"
Treads and risers housed into string
Riser
Minimum 2"

SECTION thru TREADS and RISERS
1 1/2" = 1'-0"

DISAPPEARING STAIRS

THE BESSLER DISAPPEARING STAIRWAY Cº AKRON, OHIO.

Model	A Floor to Floor	B Fin. Open. Width	C Fin. Open. Length	D Operat. Space	E Floor Run
35 & 50	7' - 7"	2' - 0"	5' - 6"	4' - 1"	5' - 4"
	8' - 1"	2' - 0"	5' - 6"	4' - 8"	5' - 8"
	8' - 7"	2' - 0"	5' - 6"	5' - 3"	6' - 0"
	9' - 1"	2' - 0"	5' - 6"	5' - 10"	6' - 4"
	9' - 7"	2' - 0"	6' - 0"	5' - 10"	6' - 8"
	10' - 1"	2' - 0"	6' - 0"	6' - 6"	6' - 11"
	10' - 7"	2' - 0"	6' - 0"	7' - 1"	7' - 4"
45 & 60	7' - 7"	2' - 6"	5' - 6"	4' - 1"	5' - 4"
	8' - 1"	2' - 6"	5' - 6"	4' - 8"	5' - 8"
	8' - 7"	2' - 6"	5' - 6"	5' - 3"	6' - 0"
	9' - 1"	2' - 6"	5' - 6"	5' - 10"	6' - 4"
	9' - 7"	2' - 6"	6' - 0"	5' - 10"	6' - 8"
	10' - 1"	2' - 6"	6' - 0"	6' - 6"	6' - 11"
	10' - 7"	2' - 6"	6' - 0"	7' - 1"	7' - 4"
75	7' - 7"	2' - 6"	5' - 10"	4' - 1"	5' - 4"
	8' - 1"	2' - 6"	5' - 10"	4' - 8"	5' - 8"
	8' - 7"	2' - 6"	5' - 10"	5' - 3"	6' - 0"
	9' - 1"	2' - 6"	5' - 10"	5' - 10"	6' - 4"
	9' - 7"	2' - 6"	6' - 0"	5' - 10"	6' - 8"
	10' - 1"	2' - 6"	6' - 0"	6' - 6"	6' - 11"
	10' - 7"	2' - 6"	6' - 0"	7' - 1"	7' - 4"
89	7' - 7"	2' - 6"	5' - 10"	4' - 4"	6' - 5"
	8' - 1"	2' - 6"	5' - 10"	4' - 11"	6' - 10"

Model	A Floor to Floor	B Fin. Open. Width	C Fin. Open. Length	D Operat. Space	E Floor Run
89	8' - 7"	2' - 6"	5' - 10"	5' - 7"	7' - 3"
	9' - 1"	2' - 6"	6' - 0"	6' - 2"	7' - 7"
	9' - 7"	2' - 6"	6' - 4"	6' - 4"	8' - 0"
	10' - 1"	2' - 6"	6' - 8"	6' - 8"	8' - 4"
	10' - 7"	2' - 6"	6' - 11"	7' - 1"	8' - 9"
97	7' - 7"	2' - 6"	5' - 10"	4' - 4"	6' - 5"
	8' - 1"	2' - 6	5' - 10"	4' - 11"	6' - 10"
	8' - 7"	2' - 6"	5' - 10"	5' - 7"	7' - 3"
	9' - 1"	2' - 6"	6' - 0"	6' - 2"	7' - 7"
	9' - 7"	2' - 6"	6' - 4"	6' - 4"	8' - 0"
	10' - 1"	2' - 6"	6' - 8"	6' - 8"	8' - 4"
	10' - 7"	2' - 6"	6' - 11"	7' - 1"	8' - 9"
	11' - 1"	2' - 6"	7' - 3"	7' - 6"	9' - 2"
	11' - 7"	2' - 6"	7' - 6"	7' - 9"	9' - 6"
	12' - 1"	2' - 6"	7' - 9"	8' - 1"	9' - 10"
	12' - 7"	2' - 6"	8' - 1"	8' - 5"	10' - 3"
	13' - 1"	2' - 6"	8' - 4"	8' - 9"	10' - 8"
	13' - 7"	2' - 6"	8' - 8"	9' - 1"	11' - 0"
	14' - 1"	2' - 6"	9' - 0"	9' - 5"	11' - 5"
	14' - 7"	2' - 6"	9' - 3"	9' - 8"	11' - 9"
	15' - 1"	2' - 6"	9' - 6"	10' - 3"	12' - 3"
	15' - 7"	2' - 6"	9' - 9"	10' - 9"	12' - 10"
	16' - 1"	2' - 6"	10' - 1"	11' - 1"	13' - 1"

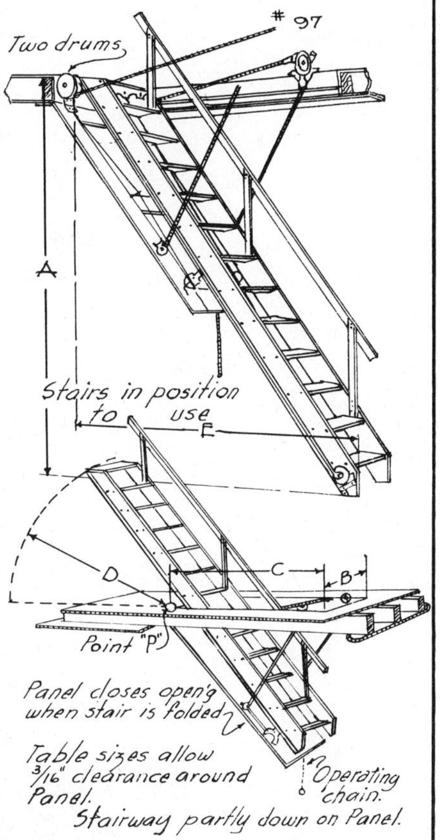

97
Two drums
A
Stairs in position to use
E
D
C
B
Point "P"
Panel closes open'g when stair is folded
Table sizes allow 3/16" clearance around Panel.
Operating chain.
Stairway partly down on Panel.

Model 97 similar with 2 drums at top.

CRAIG COMPANY.
Columbus, Georgia.

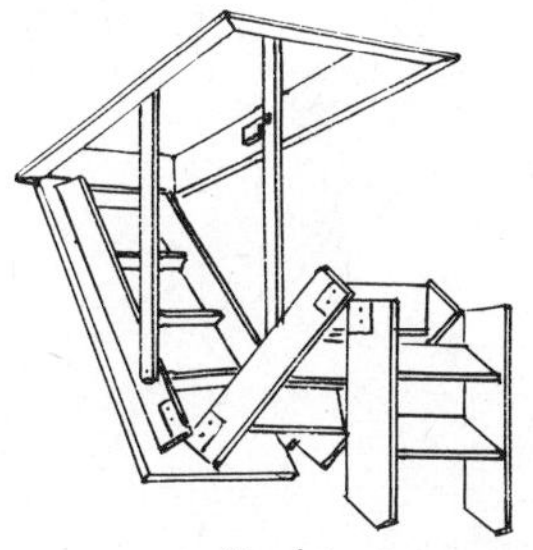

Fold-A-Away

Model	Ceiling Ht.	Floor Run	Fin. Opng.
Fold-A-Away	Up to 9'	5'-7"	24"x52"
Slide-A-Fold	Up to 9'2"	5'-7"	24"x52"
36" min. clearance above attic floor			

Slide-A-Fold.

FARLEY & LOETSCHER MFG. Cº
Dubuque, Iowa.

Ceiling Height C	Run D	Run B
8' - 1"	5'-1"	5'-7"
8' - 7"	5'-4"	6'-0"
9' - 1"	5'-8"	6'-4"
9' - 7"	4'-10"	6'-4"
Finished Opening 2'-4" x 5'-0"		
3'-0" minimum clearance above attic floor.		

Shipped assembled.

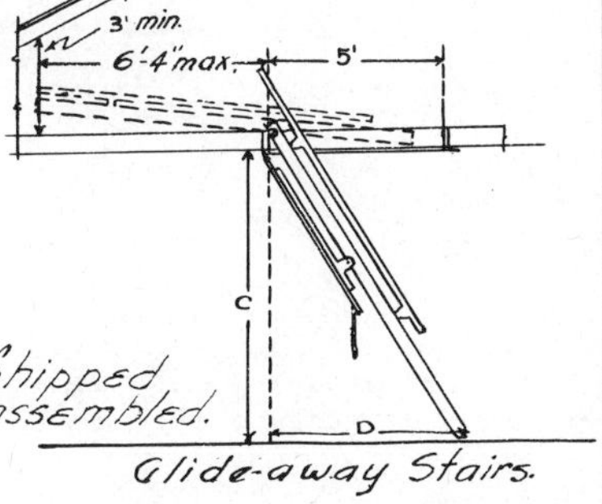

3' min.
6'-4" max.
5'
C
D

Glide-away Stairs.

THE MARSCHKE COMPANY.
St. Paul, 8, Minnesota.

Sizes and Opening Dimensions.

No.	Model	Clg. height maximum	Rough Opening Width	Rough Opening Length	Finished Opening Width	Finished Opening Length
24	Telefold	10' - 3"	2' - 2"	4' - 6"	2' - 0"	4' - 4"
36	Junior	9' - 1½"	2' - 2"	4' - 6"	2' - 0"	4' - 4"
48	Standard	10' - 1½"	2' - 6"	5' - 2"	2' - 4"	5' - 0"
66	Standard	11' - 7"	2' - 6"	6' - 0"	2' - 4"	5' - 10"

These stairs fold within the size of the ceiling opening when closed & require no rafter clearance. Jambs are furnished. #24 slides on itself then folds; two sections. Other models are counterbalanced by springs and fold in three sections.

STAIRS - GENERAL PURPOSE

(PAN TYPE)

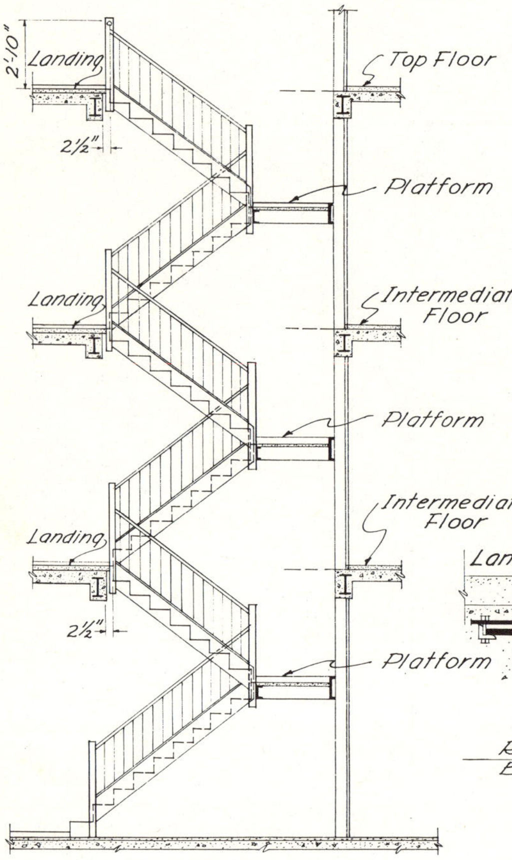
2'-10"
Landing
Top Floor
2½"
Platform
Landing
Intermediate Floor
Platform
Intermediate Floor
Landing
2½"
Platform

SECTION A-A
1/8" = 1'-0"

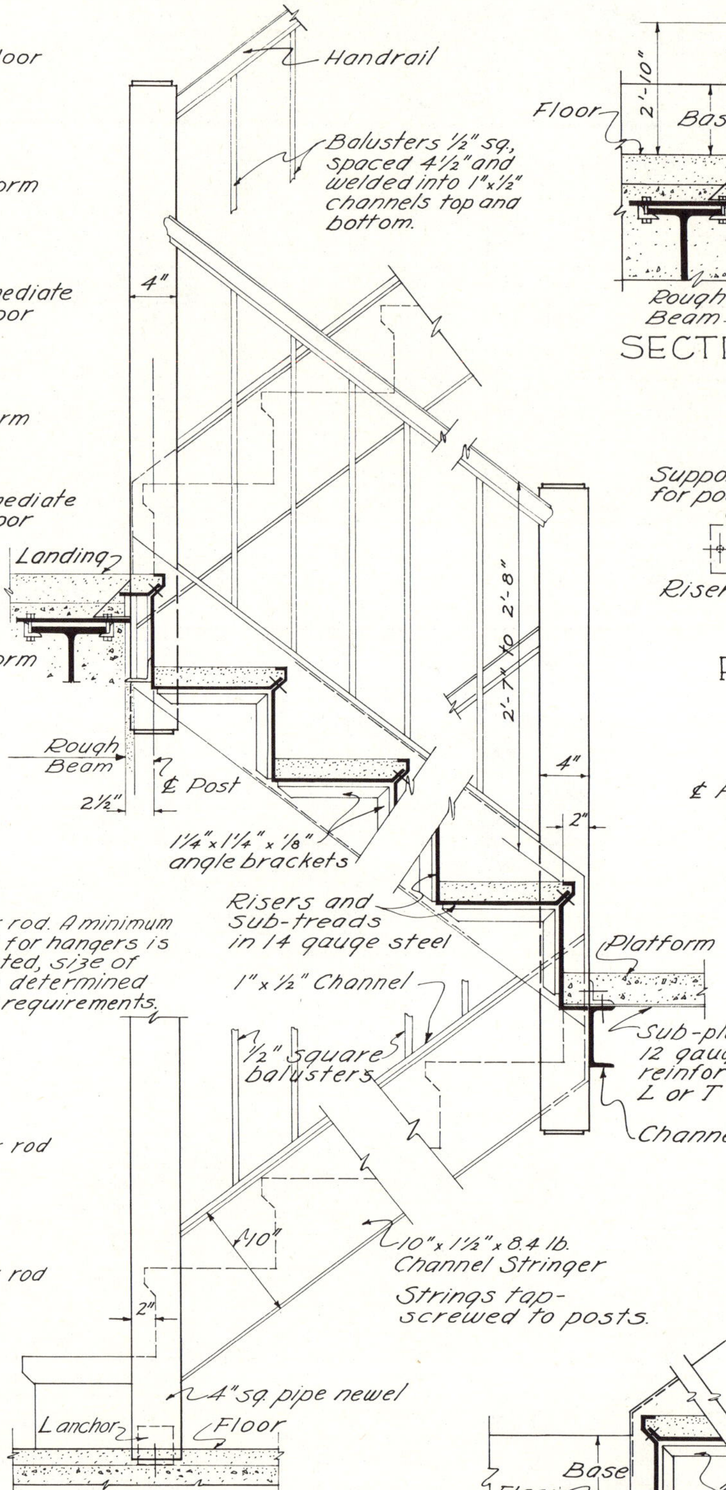
Handrail
Balusters ½" sq. spaced 4½" and welded into 1"x½" channels top and bottom.
4"
Landing
Rough Beam
2½"
℄ Post
1¼"x1¼"x⅛" angle brackets
2'-8"
2'-7" to
4"
2"
Risers and Sub-treads in 14 gauge steel
Platform
1"x½" Channel
½" square balusters
Sub-platforms 12 gauge steel reinforced with L or T stiffeners
Channel
10"
10"x1½"x8.4 lb. Channel Stringer
Strings tap-screwed to posts.
2"
4" sq. pipe newel
L anchor
Floor

SECTION 1-1
3/4" = 1'-0"

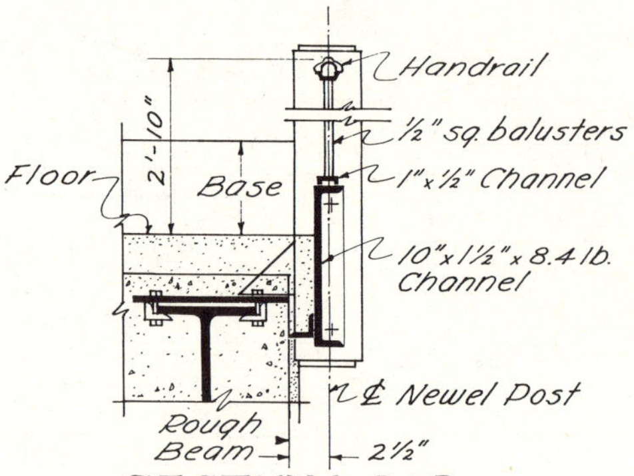
Handrail
½" sq. balusters
1"x½" Channel
2'-10"
Floor
Base
10"x1½"x8.4 lb. Channel
℄ Newel Post
Rough Beam
2½"

SECTION 3-3

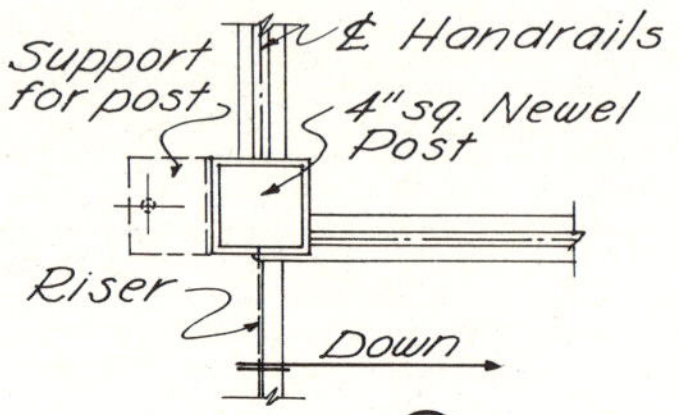
℄ Handrails
Support for post
4" sq. Newel Post
Riser
Down

PLAN 5

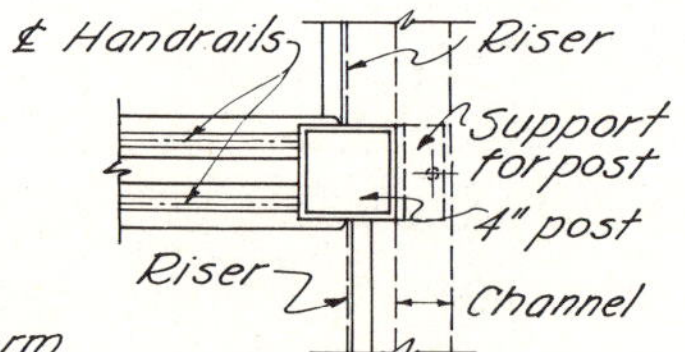
℄ Handrails
Riser
Support for post
4" post
Riser
Channel

PLAN 4

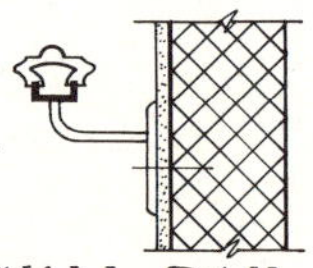

WALL RAIL

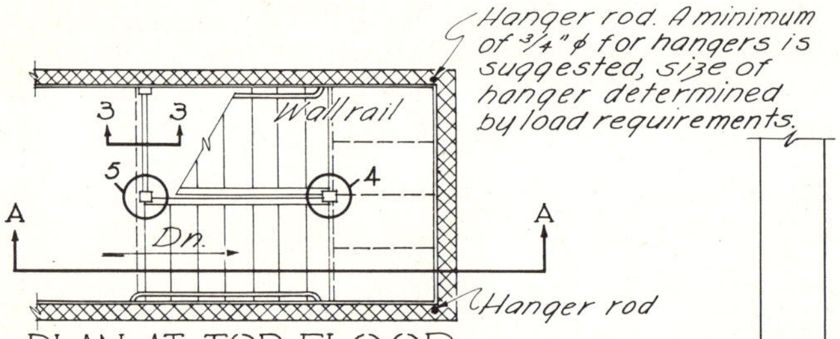
Hanger rod. A minimum of ¾" ϕ for hangers is suggested, size of hanger determined by load requirements.
3
3
Wall rail
5
4
A
A
Dn.
Hanger rod

PLAN AT TOP FLOOR

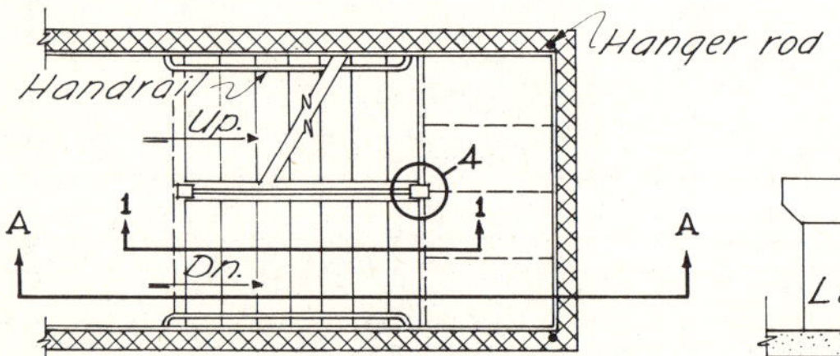
Hanger rod
Handrail
Up.
4
1
1
A
A
Dn.

PLAN AT INTERMEDIATE FLOORS

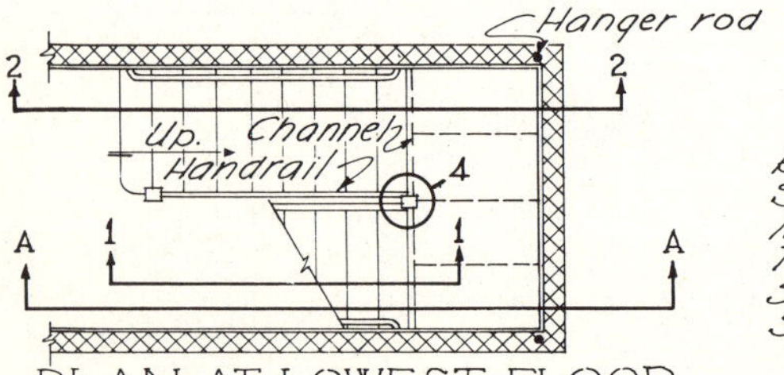
Hanger rod
2
2
Up.
Channel
Handrail
4
A
1
1
A

PLAN AT LOWEST FLOOR
1/8" = 1'-0"

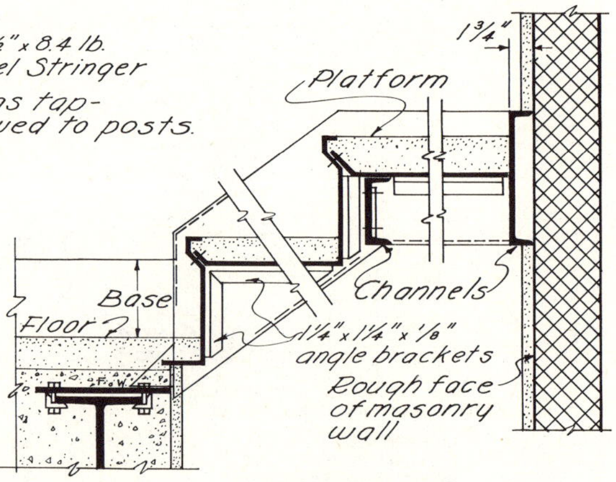
1¾"
Platform
Base
Floor
Channels
1¼"x1¼"x⅛" angle brackets
Rough face of masonry wall

SECTION 2-2
3/4" = 1'-0"

ALTERNATES:

Riser brackets may be omitted.
Struts may be used in place of hangers.
Newels and railings may be of other design.
Tread brackets may be other size angles or bars.
Strings may be channels, flat plates or formed plates.
Sub-treads, Risers and sub-platforms may be heavier gauge.

Data reviewed by National Assoc. of Architectural Metal Mfrs.

STAIRS - OPEN WELL

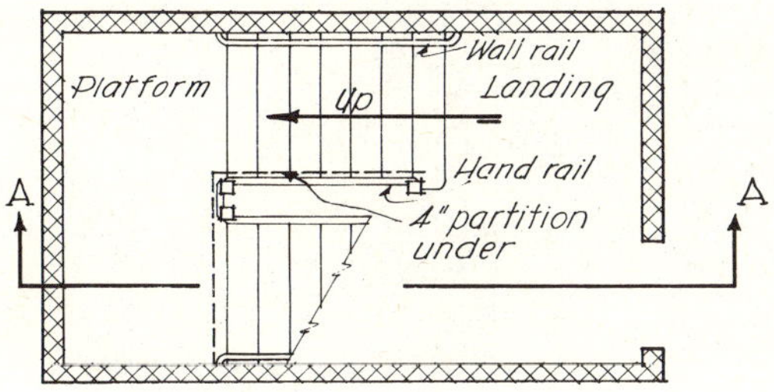

Platform
Wall rail
Landing
Up
Hand rail
4" partition under
A
A

BOTTOM FLOOR PLAN

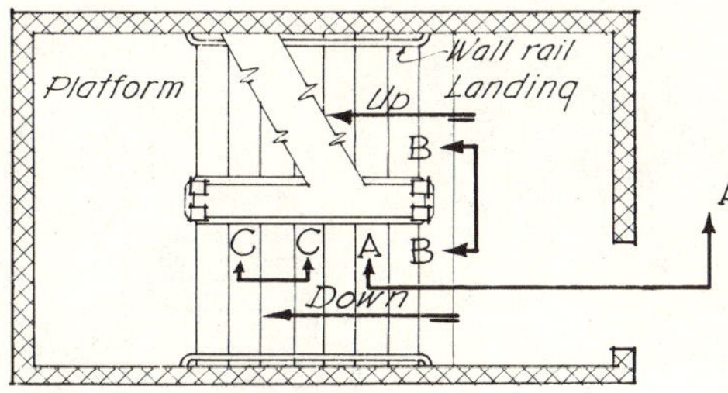

Platform
Wall rail
Landing
Up
B
B
C
C
A
Down

INTERMEDIATE FLOOR PLAN
Scale 1/8" = 1'-0"

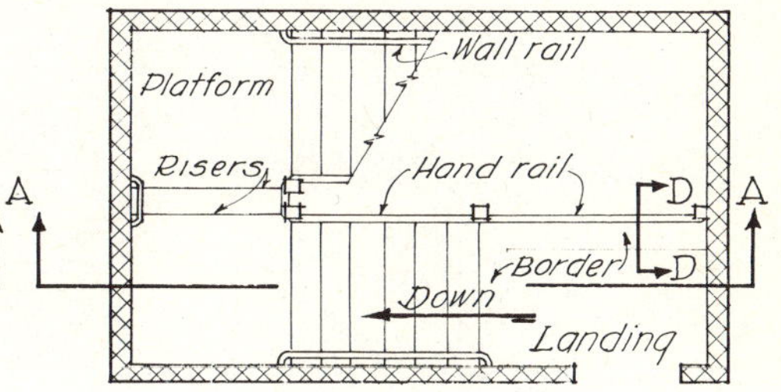

Platform
Wall rail
Risers
Hand rail
A
A
D
D
Border
Down
Landing

TOP FLOOR PLAN

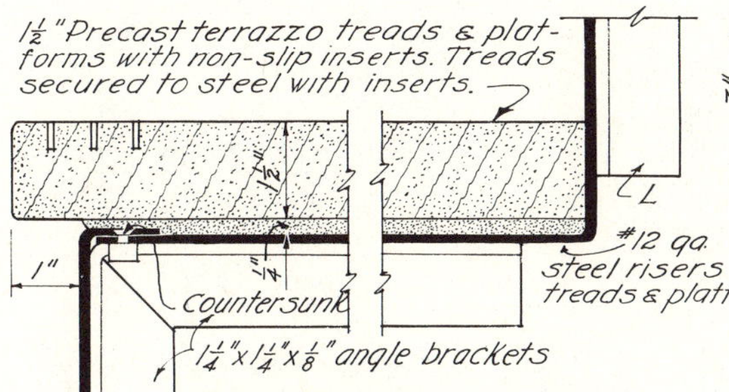

1½" Precast terrazzo treads & platforms with non-slip inserts. Treads secured to steel with inserts.
1½"
¼"
1"
L
#12 ga. steel risers treads & platf.
Countersunk
1¼"x1¼"x⅛" angle brackets

SECTION C-C
Scale 3" = 1'-0"

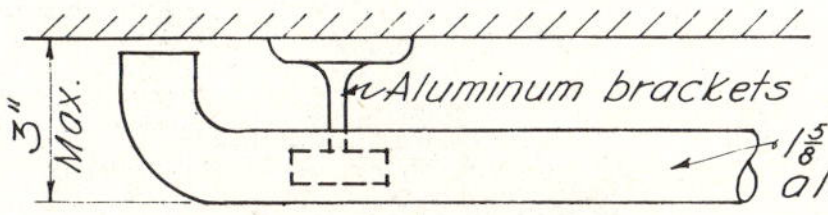

3" Max.
Aluminum brackets
1⅝" o.d. alum.

RETURN OF HAND RAIL TO WALL
Scale 1½" = 1'-0"

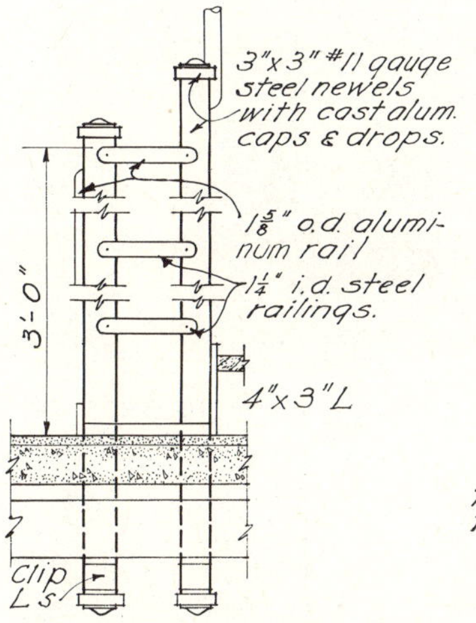

3"x3" #11 gauge steel newels with cast alum. caps & drops.
1⅝" o.d. aluminum rail
1¼" i.d. steel railings.
3'-0"
4"x3" L
Clip L's

SECT B-B THRO' LANDING
Scale ½" = 1'-0"

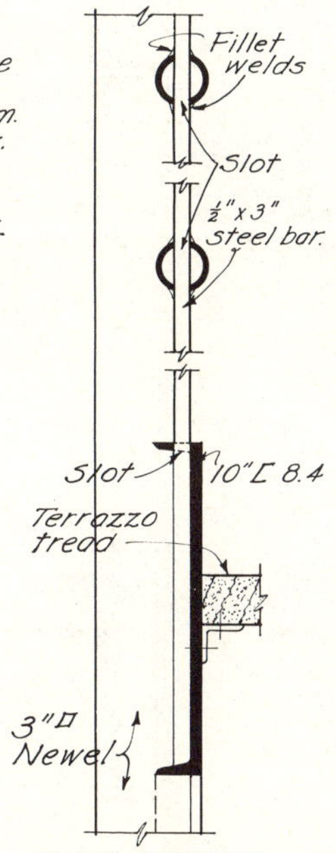

Fillet welds
Slot
½"x3" steel bar.
Slot
10" [8.4
Terrazzo tread
3" □ Newel

RAIL DETAIL
Scale 1½" = 1'-0"

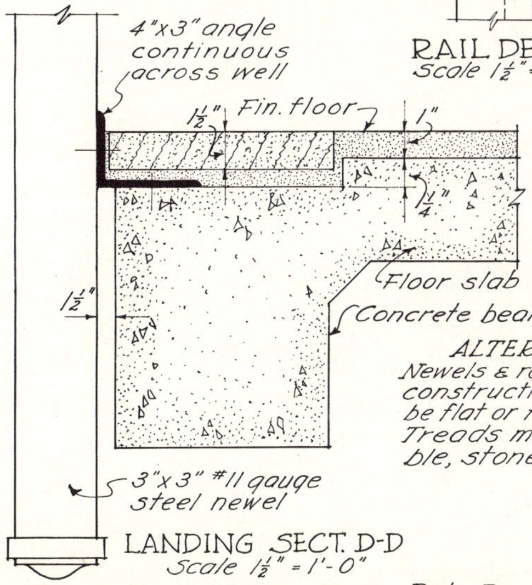

4"x3" angle continuous across well
1½"
Fin. floor
1"
¼"
Floor slab
Concrete beam
1½"
3"x3" #11 gauge steel newel

LANDING SECT. D-D
Scale 1½" = 1'-0"

ALTERNATES:
Newels & railings of other construction. Strings may be flat or formed plates. Treads may be of marble, stone or slate.

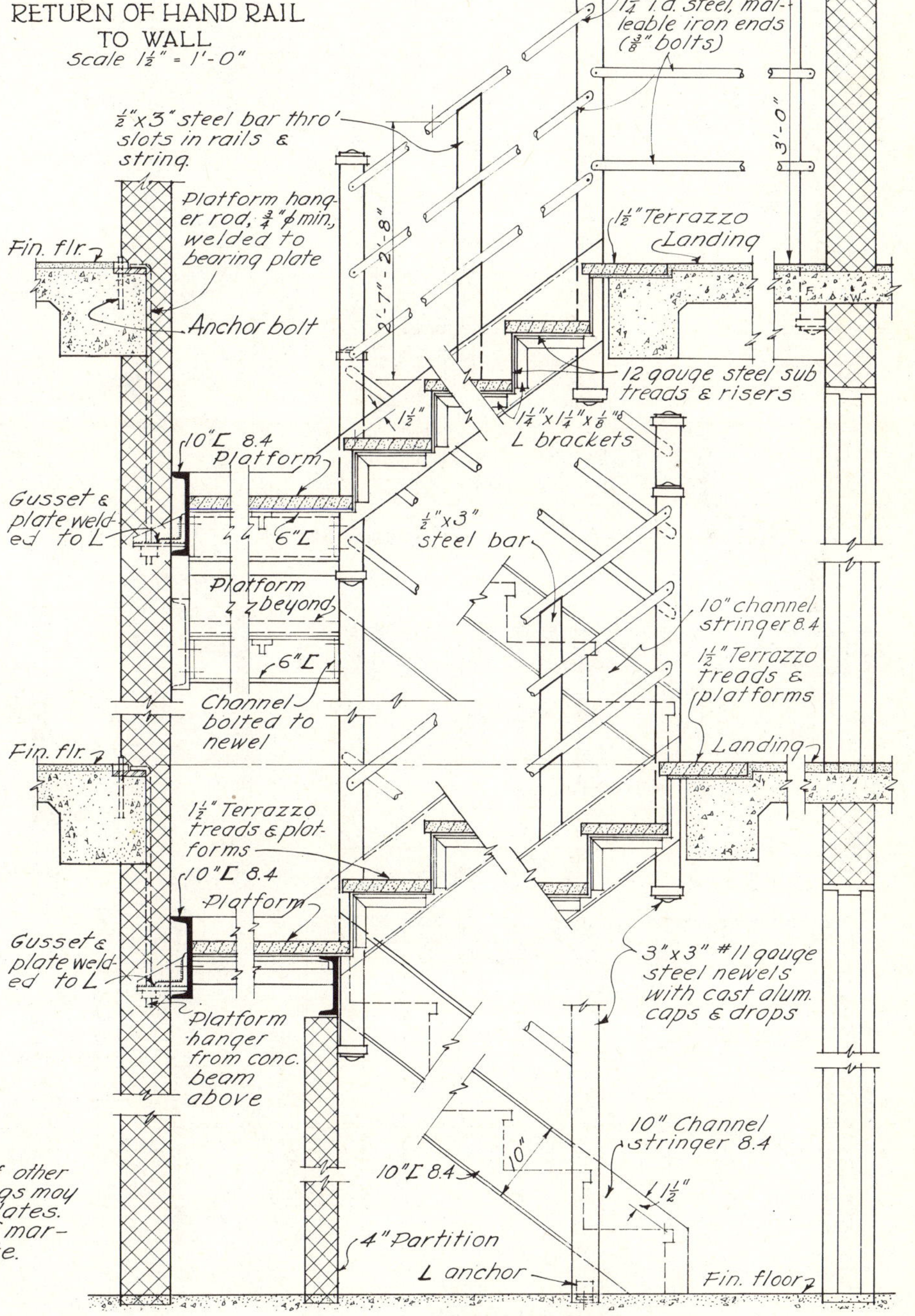

1⅝" o.d. alum. top rails, cast alum. ends. Wall rail similar.
1¼" i.d. steel, malleable iron ends (⅜" bolts)
3'-0"
½"x3" steel bar thro' slots in rails & string.
Platform hanger rod, ¾"φ min, welded to bearing plate
Fin. flr.
Anchor bolt
2'-7"-2'-8"
1½" Terrazzo Landing
12 gauge steel sub treads & risers
1½"
1¼"x1¼"x⅛" L brackets
10" [8.4
Platform
Gusset & plate welded to L
6" [
½"x3" steel bar
Platform beyond
6" [
Channel bolted to newel
10" channel stringer 8.4
1½" Terrazzo treads & platforms
Landing
Fin. flr.
1½" Terrazzo treads & platforms
10" [8.4
Platform
Gusset & plate welded to L
Platform hanger from conc. beam above
3"x3" #11 gauge steel newels with cast alum. caps & drops
10" Channel stringer 8.4
10"
10" [8.4
1½"
4" Partition
L anchor
Fin. floor

SECTION A-A
Scale ½" = 1'-0

Data Reviewed by the National Assoc. of Architectural Metal Mfrs.

STEEL STAIRS

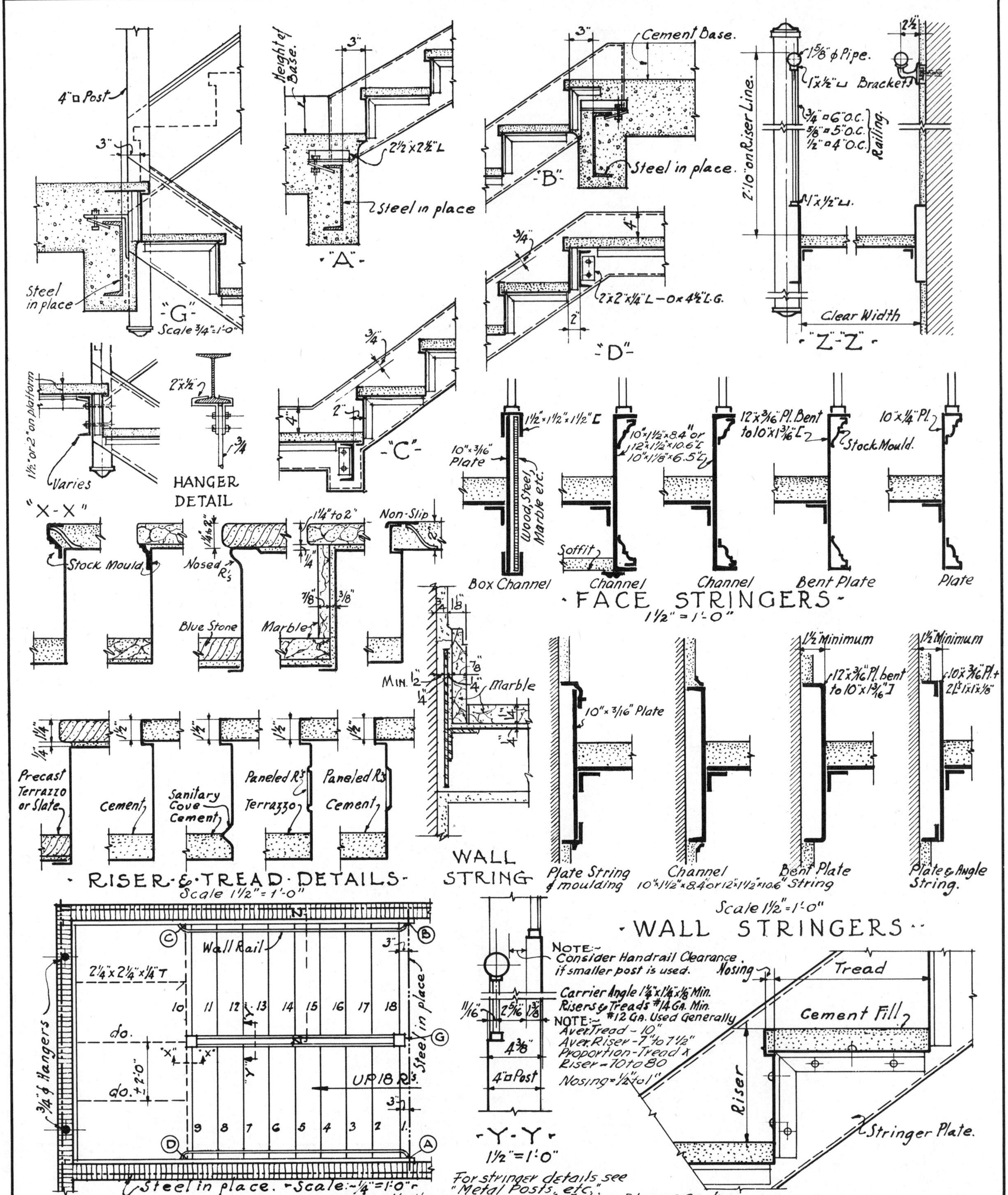
4" □ Post
3"
Steel in place
"G"
Scale 3/4"=1'-0"
Height of Base.
3"
2½"x2½" L
Steel in place
"A"
3"
Cement Base.
Steel in place.
"B"
3/4"
4"
2"x2"x1/4" L – 0 x 4½" L.G.
2"
"D"
2½"
1⅝" φ Pipe.
1"x½" ⊔ Bracket
3/4" □ 6" O.C.
5/8" □ 5" O.C.
1/2" □ 4" O.C.
Railing.
2'-10" on Riser Line.
1"x½" ⊔
Clear Width
"Z-Z"
3/4"
4"
2"
"C"
1½" or 2" on platform
Varies
"X-X"
2"x½"
3/4
HANGER DETAIL
1½"x1½"x1½" L
10"x3/16" Plate
Wood, Steel, Marble etc.
10"x1½"x8.4" or 12"x1½"x10.6" [10"x1⅛"x6.5" [
12"x3/16" Pl. Bent to 10"x1⅜" [
Stock Mould.
10"x1/4" Pl.
Soffit
Box Channel
Channel
Channel
Bent Plate
Plate
· FACE STRINGERS ·
1½" = 1'-0"
Stock Mould
Nosed R's
1¼" to 2"
Non-Slip
Blue Stone
Marble
7/8"
3/8"
Precast Terrazzo or Slate
Cement
Sanitary Cove Cement
Paneled R's Terrazzo
Paneled R's Cement
· RISER · & · TREAD · DETAILS ·
Scale 1½" = 1'-0"
MIN. ½"
Marble
WALL STRING
10" x 3/16" Plate
1½" Minimum
12"x3/16" Pl. bent to 10"x1⅜" [
1½" Minimum
10"x3/16" Pl. + 2 L's 1"x1"x1/8"
Plate String & moulding
Channel 10"x1½"x8.4" or 12"x1½"x10.6"
Bent Plate String
Plate & Angle String.
Scale 1½" = 1'-0"
· WALL STRINGERS ·
N
C
B
Wall Rail
3"
2¼"x2¼"x1/4" T
10 11 12 13 14 15 16 17 18
do.
do.
±2'-0"
"X"
"Y"
UP 18 R's.
Steel in place
G
3/4" φ Hangers
3"
9 8 7 6 5 4 3 2 1
D
A
Steel in place. – Scale – 1/4" = 1'-0"
NOTE:– Consider Handrail Clearance if smaller post is used.
Carrier Angle 1¼"x1¼"x1/8" Min.
Risers & Treads #14 GA. Min. #12 GA. Used Generally
NOTE:–
Aver. Tread – 10"
Aver. Riser – 7" to 7½"
Proportion – Tread x Riser = 70 to 80
Nosing = ½" to 1"
11/16"
2 5/16"
1⅜"
4⅜"
4" □ Post
· Y · Y ·
1½" = 1'-0"
Nosing
Tread
Cement Fill
Riser
Stringer Plate.
For stringer details see "Metal Posts, etc."

Prepared with the assistance of Julius Blum & Co., Inc.
Data checked by · National Association of Architectural Metal Mfrs. & Julius Blum & Co., Inc.

STAIRS-INDUSTRIAL, POWER HOUSE, ETC.

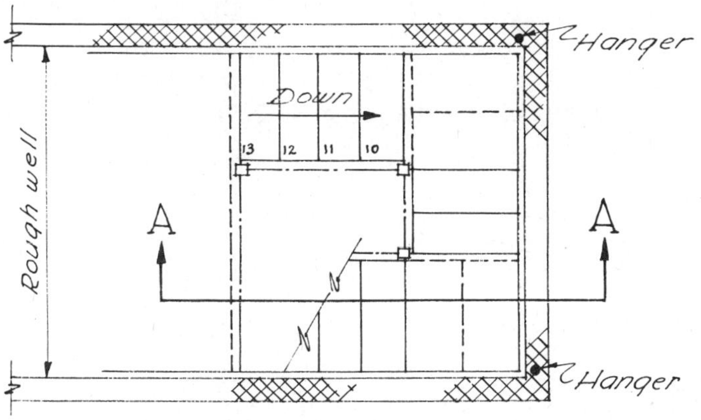
Hanger
Down
13
12
11
10
A
A
Rough well
Hanger

TOP FLOOR PLAN

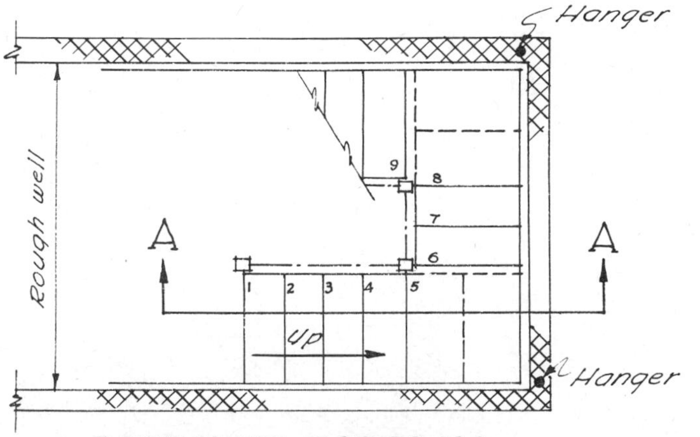
Hanger
Rough well
9
8
7
6
A
A
1
2
3
4
5
Up
Hanger

BOTTOM FLOOR PLAN
Scale: 1/4" = 1'-0"

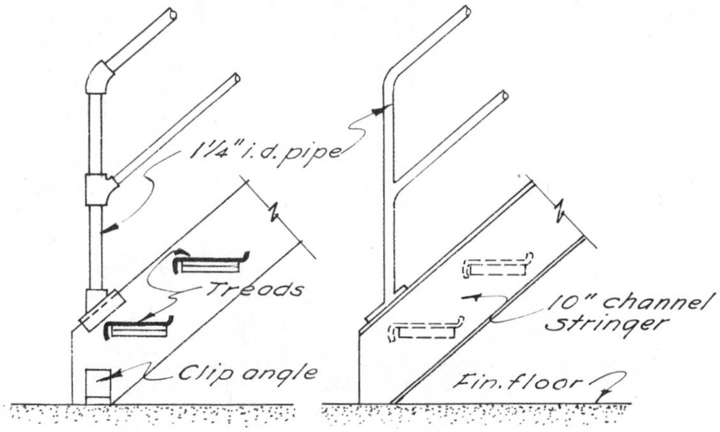
1 1/4" i.d. pipe
Treads
Clip angle
10" channel stringer
Fin. floor

WITH FITTINGS WELDED

ALTERNATE NEWEL POSTS
Scale: 1/2" = 1'-0"

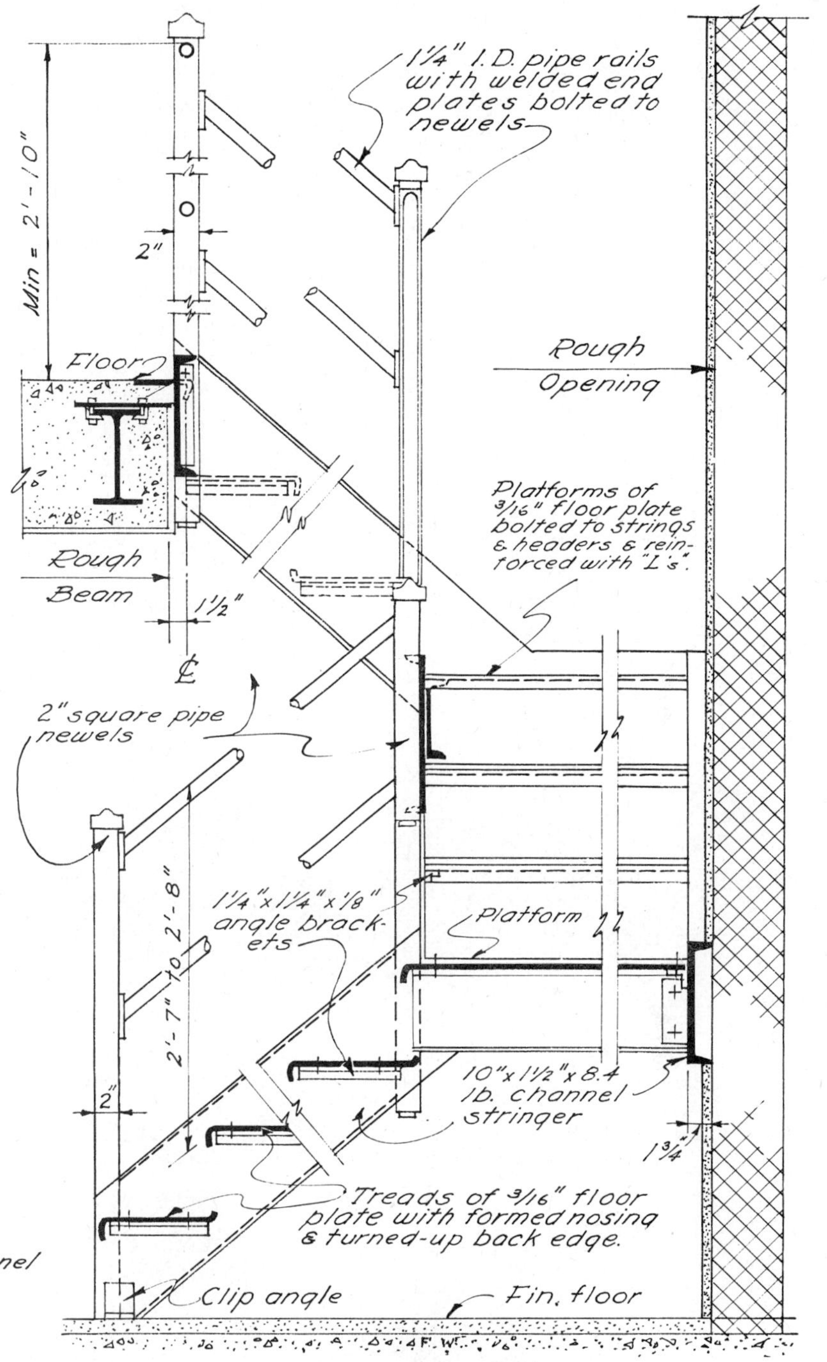
1 1/4" I.D. pipe rails with welded end plates bolted to newels
Min = 2'-10"
2"
Floor
Rough Beam
1 1/2"
℄
Rough Opening
Platforms of 3/16" floor plate bolted to strings & headers & reinforced with "L's".
2" square pipe newels
2'-7" to 2'-8"
1 1/4" x 1 1/4" x 1/8" angle brackets
Platform
10" x 1 1/2" x 8.4 lb. channel stringer
1 3/4"
2"
Treads of 3/16" floor plate with formed nosing & turned-up back edge.
Clip angle
Fin. floor

SECTION A-A
3/4" = 1'-0"

ALTERNATES:

Strings may be channels, flat plates or formed plates.
Floorplate thickness may be varied to suit stair width & load.
Tread brackets may be other size "L's" or bars.
Struts may be used in place of hangers.
Strings, Newels & Railings may be welded as a unit, where conditions permit.
Wall rails, where required, may be of pipe with wall brackets or with ends returned to plates bolted to wall.

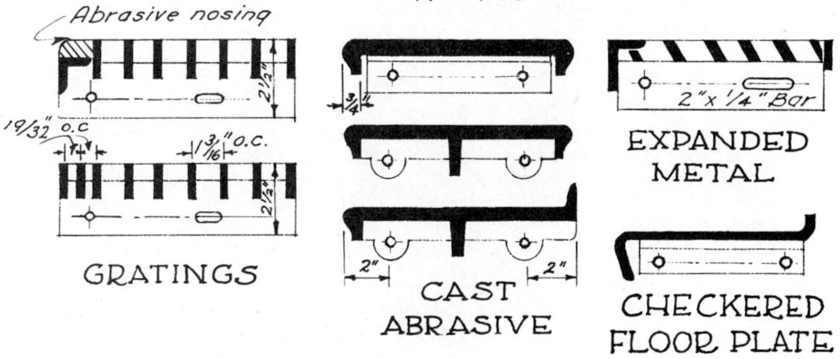
Abrasive nosing
2 1/2"
19/32" o.c.
1/4"
1 3/16" o.c.
2 1/4"
GRATINGS
3/4"
2"
2"
CAST ABRASIVE
2" x 1/4" Bar
EXPANDED METAL
CHECKERED FLOOR PLATE

ALTERNATE TYPE TREADS
Scale: 1 1/2" = 1'-0"

Data supplied by National Assoc. of Architectural Metal Mfrs.

SAFETY TREADS and NOSINGS

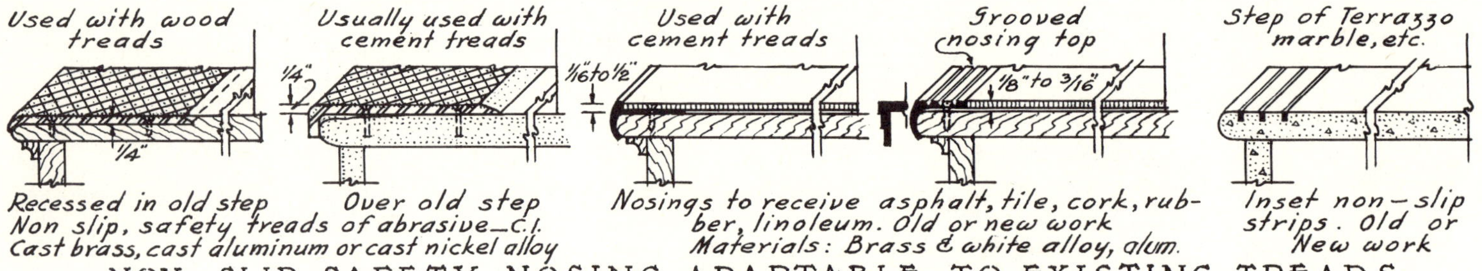
Used with wood treads
Usually used with cement treads
Used with cement treads
Grooved nosing top
Step of Terrazzo marble, etc.
1/4"
1/4"
1/16 to 1/2"
1/8" to 3/16"
Recessed in old step
Over old step
Non slip, safety treads of abrasive—C.I.
Cast brass, cast aluminum or cast nickel alloy
Nosings to receive asphalt, tile, cork, rubber, linoleum. Old or new work
Materials: Brass & white alloy, alum.
Inset non-slip strips. Old or New work

NON-SLIP, SAFETY NOSING ADAPTABLE TO EXISTING TREADS

Scale 1½" = 1'-0"

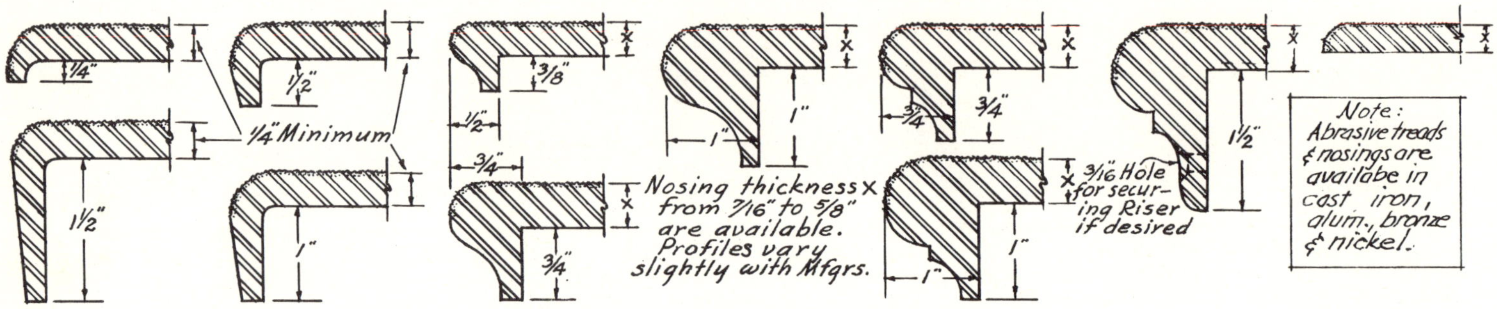
1/4"
1/2"
1/4" Minimum
1 1/2"
1"
3/8"
1/2"
3/4"
3/4"
x
1"
1"
3/4"
3/4"
1 1/2"
Nosing thickness x from 7/16" to 5/8" are available. Profiles vary slightly with Mfgrs.
3/16" Hole for securing Riser if desired
1"
1"
Note: Abrasive treads & nosings are availabe in cast iron, alum., bronze & nickel.

STOCK TYPE LIPS   STOCK TYPE CAST ABRASIVE NOSING

Scale: Half Full Size

width	5"	6"	7"	8"	9"	10"
Hole spacing A	2"	3"	3½"	4"	5"	6"

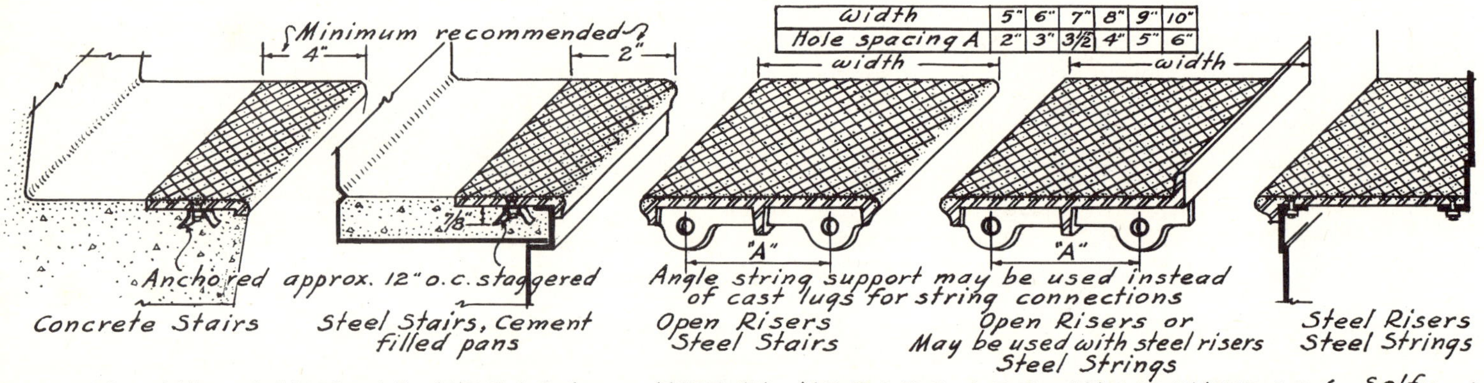
Minimum recommended
4"
2"
width
width
7/8"
"A"
"A"
Anchored approx. 12" o.c. staggered
Angle string support may be used instead of cast lugs for string connections
Concrete Stairs
Steel Stairs, Cement filled pans
Open Risers Steel Stairs
Open Risers or May be used with steel risers Steel Strings
Steel Risers Steel Strings

NON-STRUCTURAL TREADS   THESE TREADS ARE STRUCTURAL (Self-Supporting)

Scale 1½" = 1'-0"

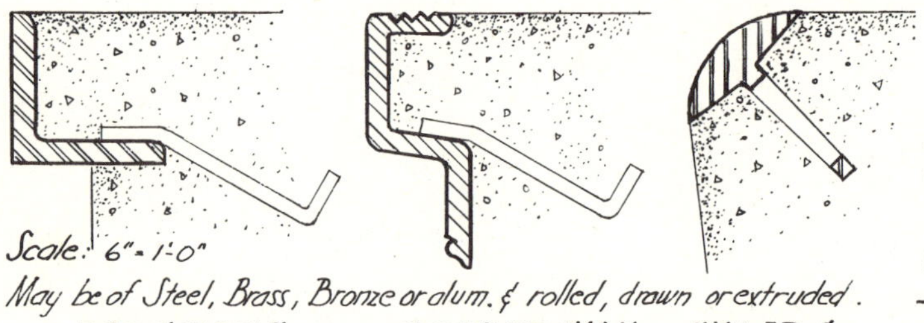
Scale: 6" = 1'-0"

May be of Steel, Brass, Bronze or alum. & rolled, drawn or extruded.

NOSINGS for CONCRETE STAIRS

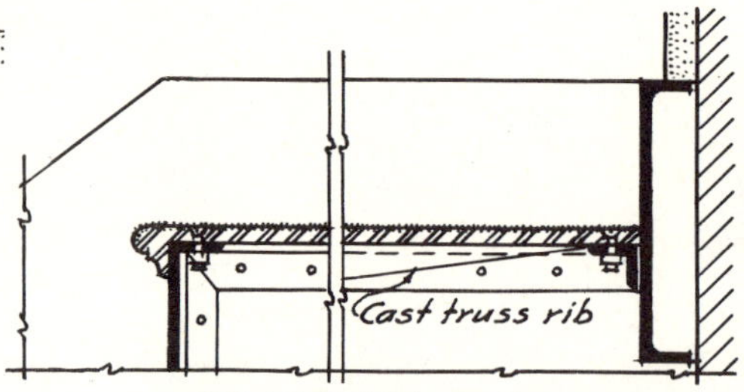
Cast truss rib

SECTION A-A

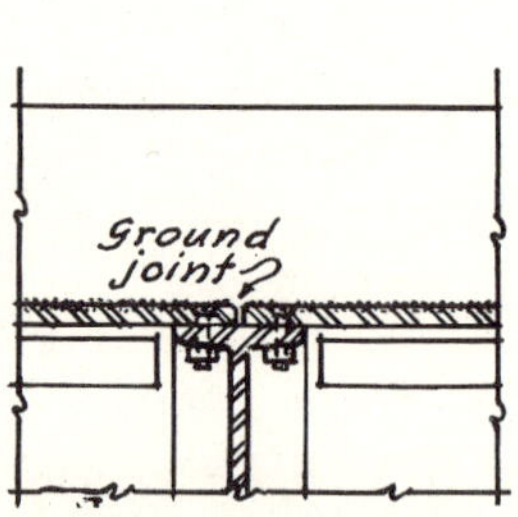
Ground joint

SECTION B-B

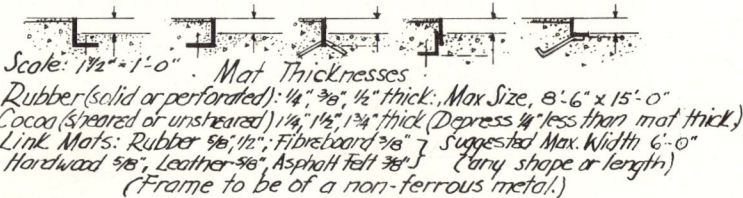

Scale: 1½" = 1'-0"   Mat Thicknesses

Rubber (solid or perforated): ¼", ⅜", ½" thick.; Max Size, 8'-6" x 15'-0"
Cocoa (sheared or unsheared) 1¼", 1½", 1¾" thick (Depress ¼" less than mat thick.)
Link Mats: Rubber 5/16", ½"; Fibreboard ⅜"; Hardwood 5/16", Leather 5/16", Asphalt felt ⅜" } Suggested Max. Width 6'-0" (any shape or length)
(Frame to be of a non-ferrous metal.)

Plate sizes are limited to 44" x 80" or 44" x 90"
Plate thicknesses increase with size from ½" to ¾"
Material: Cast abrasive iron.

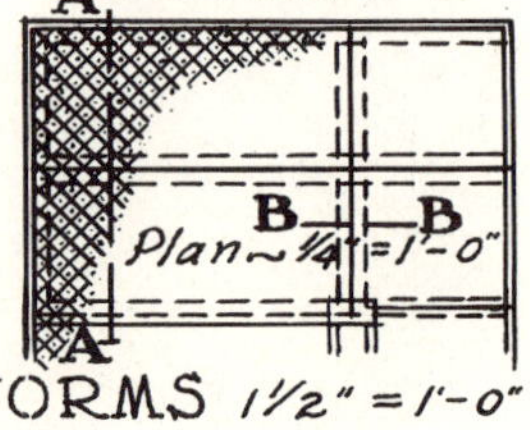
A
B
B
A
Plan ¼" = 1'-0"

SAFETY TREAD PLATFORMS 1½" = 1'-0"

Scale: 1½" = 1'-0"

MAT SINKAGE

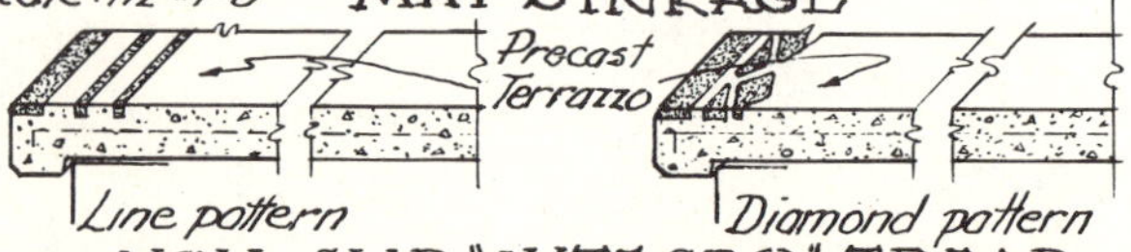
Precast Terrazzo
Line pattern
Diamond pattern

NON-SLIP "INTEGRO" TREAD

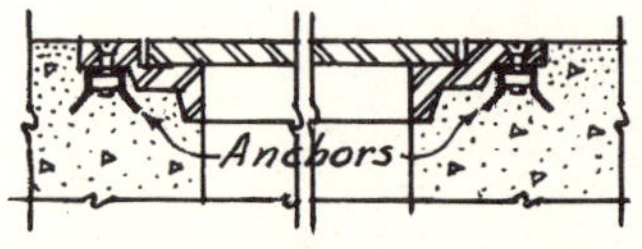
Anchors

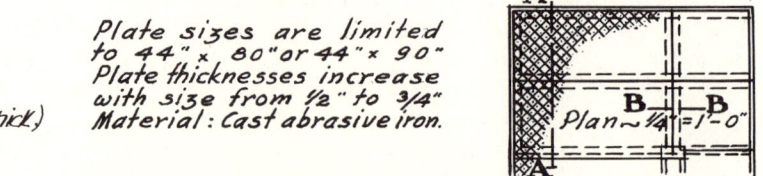

Made in abrasive cast iron. Cover thickness from ½" for 24" span to ¾" for 44" span.

Scale 1½" = 1'-0"

TRENCH COVER & FRAME CAST ABRASIVE

Data reviewed by: National Association of Architectural Metal Mfrs.

METAL FLOOR PLATES & TREADS

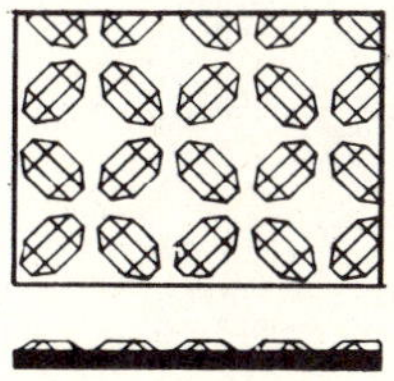
Fig. 1

Fig. 2

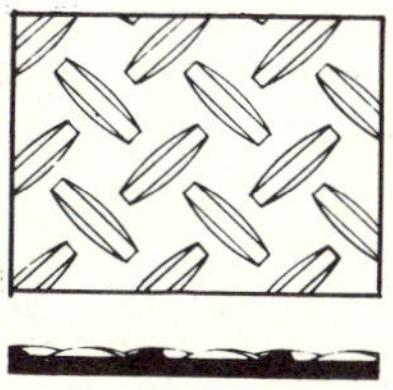
Fig. 3

Fig. 4

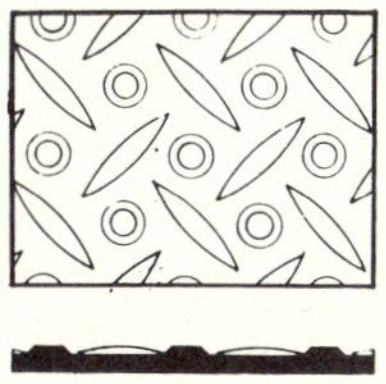
Fig. 5

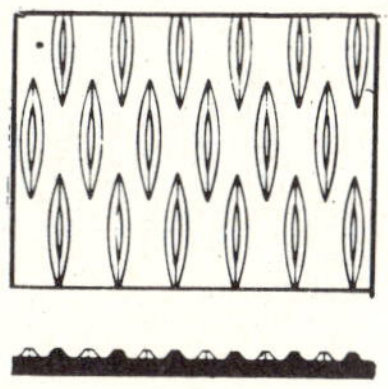
Fig. 6

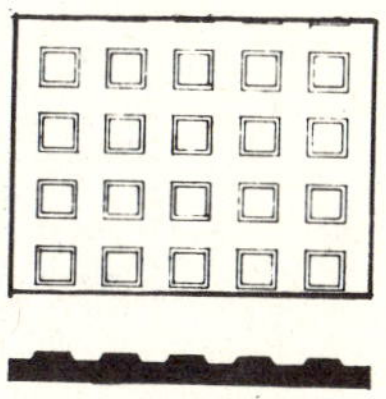
Fig. 7

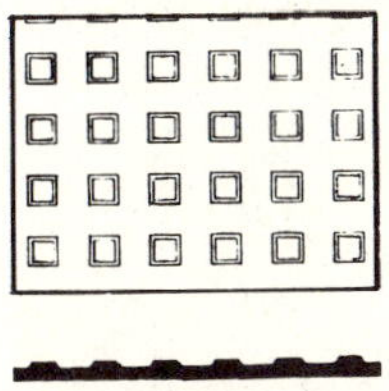
Fig. 8

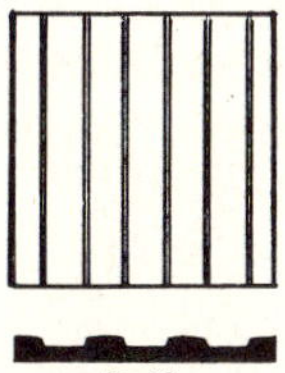
Fig. 10

Fig. 11

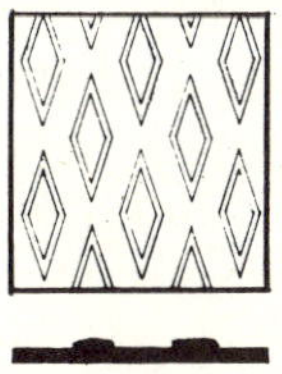
Fig. 12

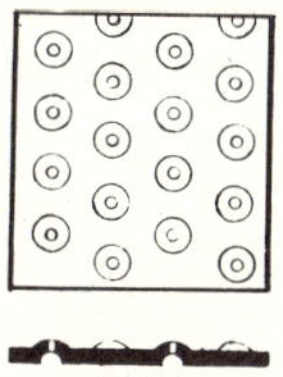
Fig. 13

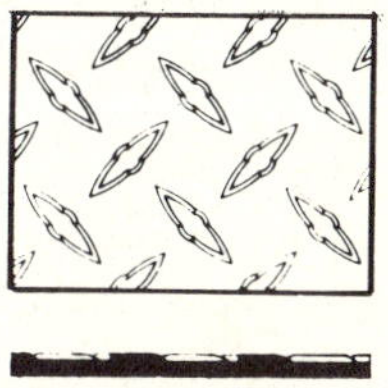
Fig. 9

FLOOR PLATE PATTERNS 1/2"=1'-0"

Structural supports or stiffeners are usually employed to carry the entire load, the plate thickness thus being kept to a minimum. Where plates are to be used for spanning openings with only end supports, plate thicknesses should be determined from the table of allowable loads and deflections below.

THICKNESS of FLOOR PLATES, and METALS in which they are ROLLED

THICKNESS	FIGURE NUMBERS												
	1	2	3	4	5	6	7	8	9	10	11	12	13
18 ga.						●							
16 ga.			●			●		●					●
14 ga.			●			●		●					●
13 ga.			●			●		●					
12 ga.			●			●		●					●
10 ga.													●
1/8"	●		●			●	●	●	●	●	●	●	
3/16"	●	●	●	●	●	●	●		●	●	●	●	
1/4"	●	●	●	●	●	●	●		●	●	●	●	
5/16"	●	●	●	●	●	●	●			●	●	●	
3/8"	●	●	●	●	●	●	●		●	●	●	●	
7/16"	●	●					●			●		●	
1/2"	●	●		●	●		●		●	●		●	
5/8"	●	●		●	●		●			●		●	
3/4"	●	●		●	●					●			
7/8"				●	●								
1"				●	●								
METAL													
Steel	●	●	●	●	●	●	●	●		●	●	●	●
Aluminum									●				

Check stock lists for currently available floor plates as all thicknesses and metals are not always available. Patterns #4, 6, and 11 may be obtained in aluminum, brass, copper, monel metal, nickel, lead, zinc, or magnesium, when required quantities are sufficient to warrant mill rollings.

Thickness of plate is taken through body excluding raised portion.

ALLOWABLE UNIFORM LOADS in POUNDS PER SQUARE FOOT & DEFLECTIONS in INCHES (weight of plate included; fibre stress 16,000 lbs. per square inch)

PLATE THICKNESS (inches)	SPANS													
	1'-0"	1'-6"	2'-0"	2'-6"	3'-0"	3'-6"	4'-0"	4'-6"	5'-0"	5'-6"	6'-0"	6'-6"	7'-0"	7'-6"
1/8	332	148	83	53	37									
	.132	.298	.530	.830	1.190									
3/16	750	334	188	120	83	61	47							
	.088	.198	.353	.551	.794	1.082	1.410							
1/4	1 332	591	333	213	148	109	83	66	53	44				
	.066	.149	.265	.414	.596	.812	1.060	1.340	1.660	2.000				
5/16	2 086	927	522	333	232	170	130	103	83	66	58	49		
	.053	.119	.212	.331	.477	.650	.848	1.07	1.325	1.603	1.907	2.236		
3/8	3 008	1 337	752	482	334	246	188	149	120	100	84	70	61	53
	.044	.098	.176	.274	.396	.540	.705	.891	1.101	1.333	1.585	1.859	2.157	2.476
7/16	4 080	1 813	1 020	652	453	333	255	201	163	134	114	96	83	72
	.038	.085	.151	.236	.341	.465	.607	.767	.948	1.147	1.365	1.601	1.857	2.132
1/2	5 336	2 371	1 334	854	593	436	333	263	213	176	148	126	109	95
	.033	.074	.132	.206	.298	.406	.530	.670	.828	1.000	1.192	1.398	1.622	1.862
9/16	6 744	3 000	1 686	1 079	749	551	422	333	270	223	187	159	137	120
	.030	.066	.117	.183	.265	.361	.472	.596	.737	.892	1.060	1.244	1.444	1.657
5/8	8 336	3 705	2 084	1 334	926	681	521	412	333	275	232	197	170	148
	.027	.059	.106	.165	.238	.325	.424	.536	.662	.802	.954	1.120	1.300	1.490
11/16	10 008	4 483	2 572	1 614	1 121	823	631	498	404	333	280	238	206	179
	.024	.054	.096	.149	.216	.294	.384	.486	.600	.726	.864	1.014	1.176	1.350
3/4	12 000	5 333	3 000	1 920	1 334	980	750	593	480	396	333	284	245	213
	.022	.049	.088	.137	.198	.270	.352	.446	.551	.666	.793	.930	1.080	1.238
13/16	14 080	6 257	3 520	2 253	1 565	1 149	880	695	563	465	391	333	287	250
	.020	.046	.081	.127	183	.250	.326	.412	.509	.616	.733	.860	1.000	1.145
7/8	16 312	7 249	4 078	2 610	1 813	1 331	1 020	805	652	538	453	385	333	290
	.019	.042	.075	.117	.170	.231	.302	.382	.472	.571	.679	.797	.925	1.061
15/16	18 768	8 340	4 692	3 003	2 086	1 532	1 173	927	751	619	521	443	382	333
	.018	.039	.070	.110	.159	.217	.283	.357	.442	.535	.636	.746	.865	.993
1	21 328	9 478	5 332	3 412	2 370	1 741	1 333	1 053	853	704	592	504	435	379
	.017	.037	.066	.103	.149	.203	.265	.335	.414	.501	.596	.699	.811	.931

Deflections for loads less than shown in table are in direct proportion of the smaller load to load given in table. To find the safe concentrated load for any span, multiply the load shown in table by the span and divide by two. For example: Find the safe concentrated load for 3/8" plate on 3'-0" span: $\frac{334 \times 3}{2} = 501$ lbs.

Data from "Architectural Metal Handbook", by permission of the National Assoc. of Architectural Metal Mfrs.

SPIRAL STAIRS and NEWELS

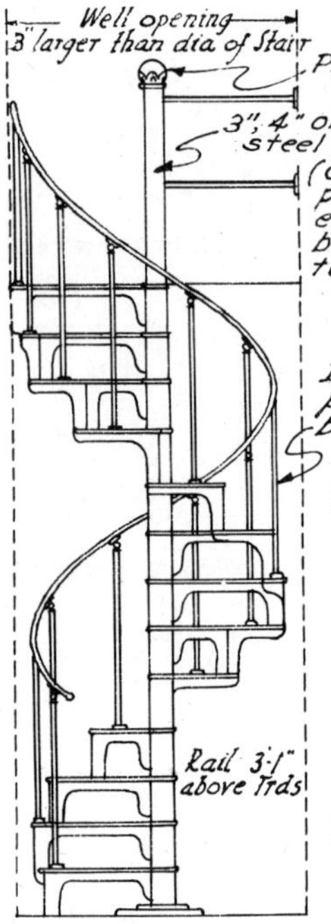
Well opening
3" larger than dia. of Stair
Pipe cap
3", 4" or larger i.d. steel ctr. pipe. (Center pipe may extend & be secured to ceiling.
1" i.d. steel pipe or steel bar balusters
Rail 3'-1" above Trds

LEFT HAND STAIR ELEV.

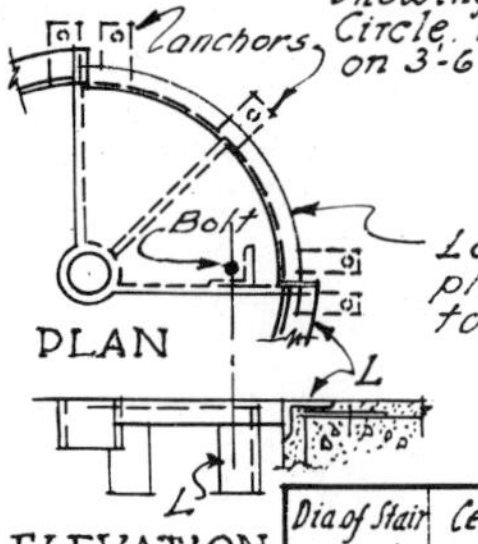
Anchors
Bolt
Landing platform atchd. to well construction
L

PLAN

ELEVATION

LEFT HAND STAIR

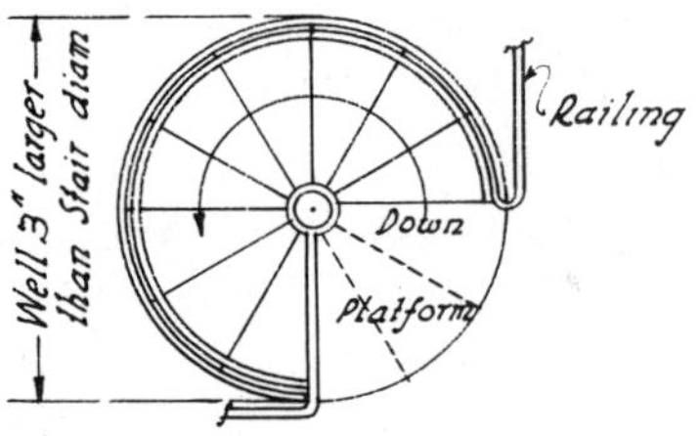
Well 3" larger than Stair diam
Railing
Down
Platform

ROUND WELL
Showing 12 Treads to the Circle. Do not use 12 Trds. on 3'-6" dia or Sq. Stair.

RIGHT HAND STAIR

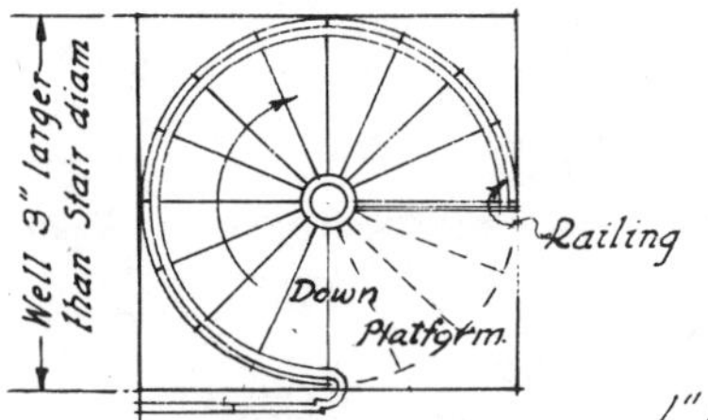
Well 3" larger than Stair diam
Railing
Down
Platform

SQUARE WELL
Showing 16 Treads to the Circle.

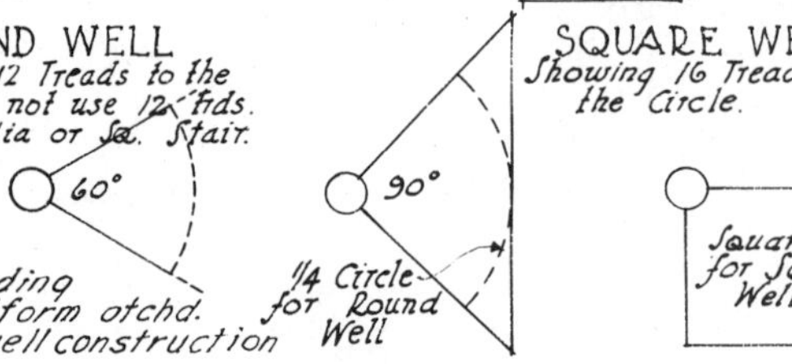
60°
90°
1/4 Circle for Round Well
Square for Sq. Well

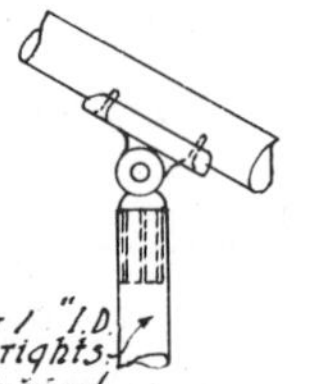
3/4" or 1" I.D. Pipe Uprights per. thread

Scale 1½"-1'-0"

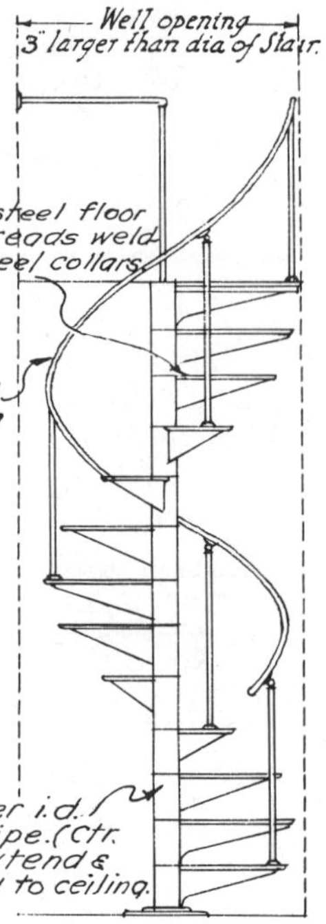
Well opening
3" larger than dia. of Stair.
Formed steel floor plate treads welded to steel collars.
1" i.d. steel pipe railing
3", 4" or larger i.d. steel ctr. pipe. (Ctr. pipe may extend & be secured to ceiling.

RIGHT HAND STAIR ELEV.

TYPES OF PLATFORMS
Other angle platforms also made.

Dia of Stair in inches	Center pipe ins.	Platform size in inches: Square	1/4 Circle	60° or 30°	Floor opening size in inches	
48"	3"	25½" x 25½"	25½" rad.	25½" alt.	51" × 51"	51" dia.
54"	4"	28½" x 28½"	28½" rad.	28½" alt.	57" × 57"	57" dia.
60"	4"	31½" x 31½"	31½" rad.	31½" alt.	63" × 63"	63" dia.
66"	4"	34½" x 34½"	34½" rad.	34½" alt.	69" × 69"	69" dia.
72"	4"	37½" x 37½"	37½" rad.	37½" alt.	75" × 75"	75" dia.
* 84"	5"	43½" x 43½"	43½" rad.	43½" alt.	87" × 87"	87" dia.
* 96"	6"	49½" x 49½"	49½" rad.	49½" alt.	99" × 99"	99" dia.

SIZES OF STAIRS, WELLS & PLATFORMS
Standard sizes are usually as above but some Mfrs. may vary.
*Sizes starred are not made by all Mfrs. 6'-6" size is sometimes made

Riser Design.

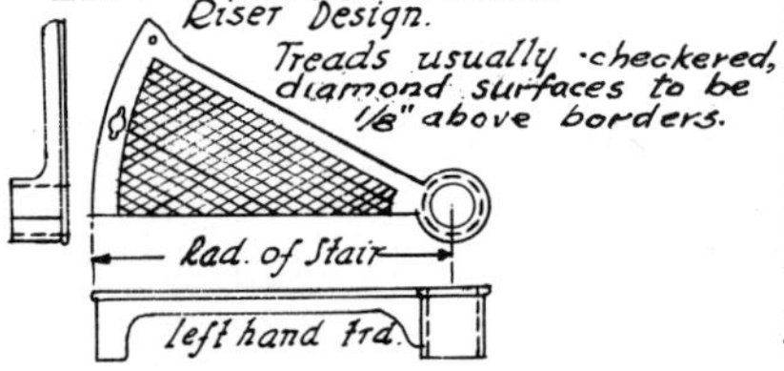
Treads usually checkered, diamond surfaces to be 1/8" above borders.
Rad. of Stair
left hand trd.

Cantilever Design.

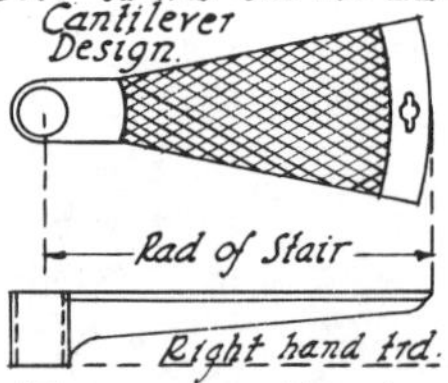
Rad. of Stair
Right hand trd.

Treads on this type stair must be firmly secured. Treads are held in position by means of set screws in the hub.

Spiral stairs are usually constructed with 12 or 16 treads to the circle. Steel or non-ferrous face strings may be used for ornamental appearance.

If using 12 Treads to Circle minimum. Riser 8½" & 90° Platform maximum
If using 16 Treads to Circle minimum. Riser 7" & Platform may be over 90°.
Minimum diameter 4'-0".

RISERS

SPIRAL STAIRS OF CAST IRON & STEEL

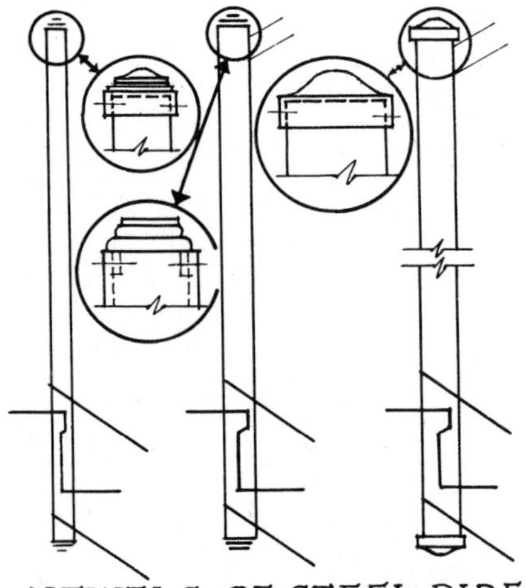

NEWELS OF STEEL PIPE & TUBING WITH CAST or PRESSED CAPS & DROPS

Sq. tubing is produced in the non-ferrous metals in several sizes & gauges. Finish can match the finish of railings, handrails & other non-ferrous metals.

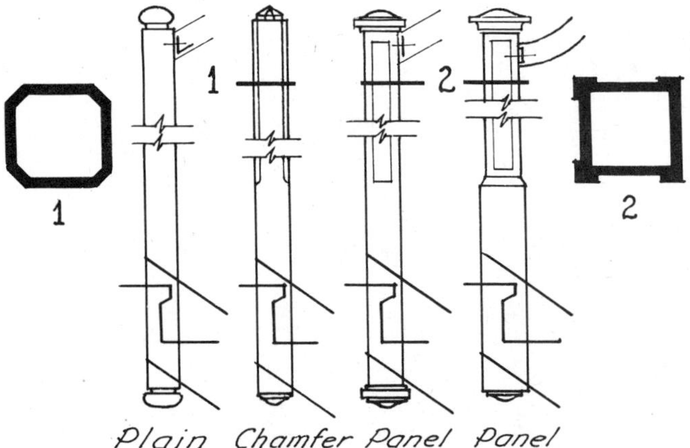
1
1
2
2

Plain — Chamfer corners — Panel — Panel with base

CAST NEWELS

Newel posts of cast metal may be manufactured in any shape, length & design required, with matching caps and drops.

SQUARE PIPE & TUBE

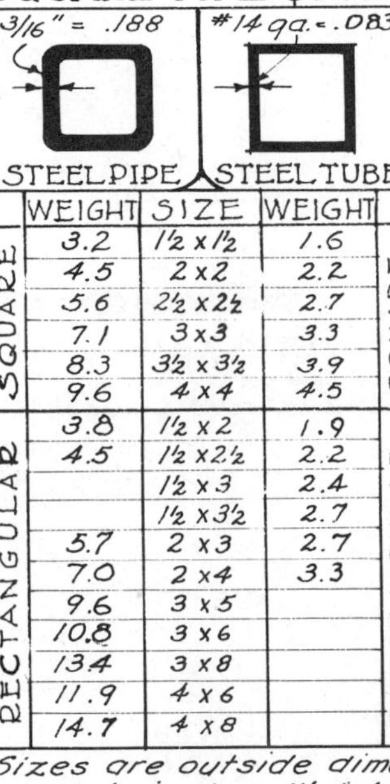
3/16" = .188
#14 ga. = .083
STEEL PIPE
STEEL TUBE

	STEEL PIPE WEIGHT	SIZE	STEEL TUBE WEIGHT
SQUARE	3.2	1½ x 1½	1.6
SQUARE	4.5	2 x 2	2.2
SQUARE	5.6	2½ x 2½	2.7
SQUARE	7.1	3 x 3	3.3
SQUARE	8.3	3½ x 3½	3.9
SQUARE	9.6	4 x 4	4.5
RECTANGULAR	3.8	1½ x 2	1.9
RECTANGULAR	4.5	1½ x 2½	2.2
RECTANGULAR		1½ x 3	2.4
RECTANGULAR		1½ x 3½	2.7
RECTANGULAR	5.7	2 x 3	2.7
RECTANGULAR	7.0	2 x 4	3.3
RECTANGULAR	9.6	3 x 5	
RECTANGULAR	10.8	3 x 6	
RECTANGULAR	13.4	3 x 8	
RECTANGULAR	11.9	4 x 6	
RECTANGULAR	14.7	4 x 8	

Sizes are outside dimensions in inches. Weights are approx. in lbs. per ft.

½" = 1'-0"

STEEL & CAST NEWELS

Data reviewed by National Assoc. of Architectural Metal Mfrs.

EXTERIOR STEPS

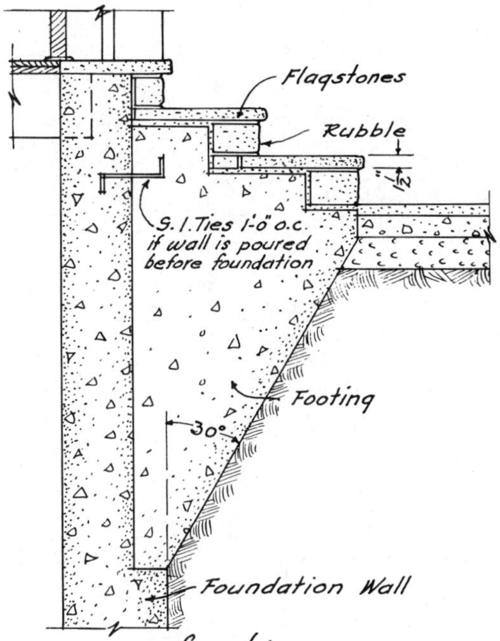

Flagstones
Rubble
1/2
S. I. Ties 1'-0" o.c. if wall is poured before foundation
Footing
30°
Foundation Wall

Section

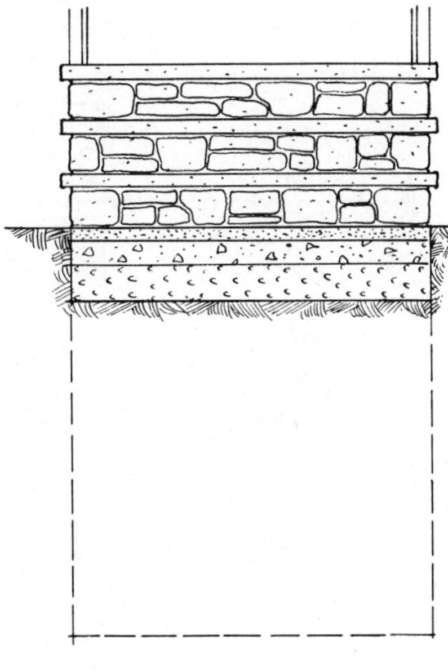

Elevation

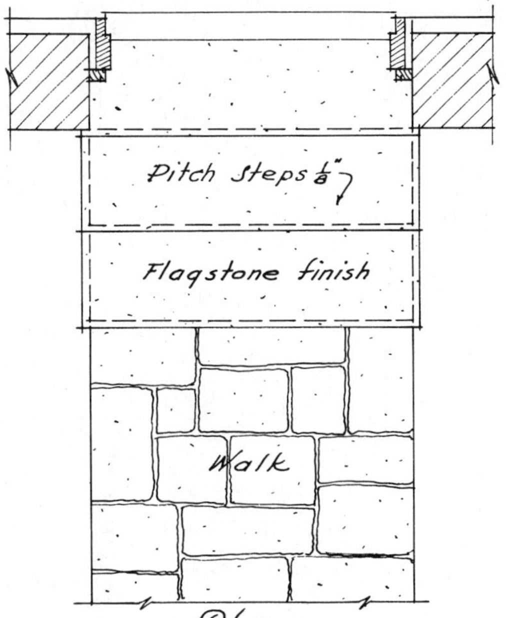

Pitch Steps 1/8"
Flagstone finish
Walk

Plan

SLOPE-BACK FOUNDATION for ENTRANCE STEPS

This type of footing will stay in place, but becomes uneconomical when there are more than three or four steps.
1/2"=1'-0"

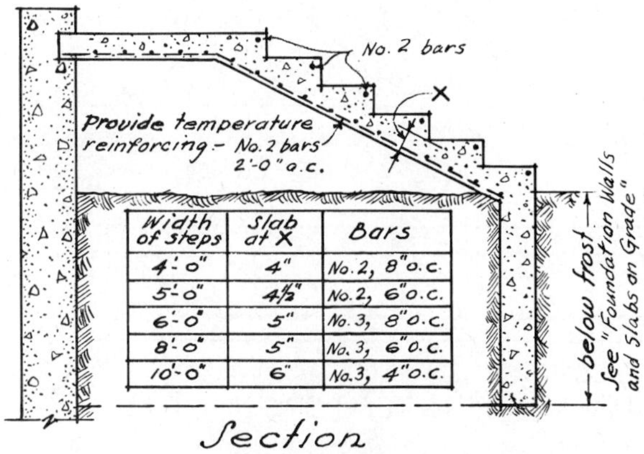

No. 2 bars
X
Provide temperature reinforcing – No. 2 bars 2'-0" o.c.
below frost
See "Foundation Walls and Slabs on Grade"

Width of steps	Slab at X	Bars
4'-0"	4"	No. 2, 8" o.c.
5'-0"	4½"	No. 2, 6" o.c.
6'-0"	5"	No. 3, 8" o.c.
8'-0"	5"	No. 3, 6" o.c.
10'-0"	6"	No. 3, 4" o.c.

Section

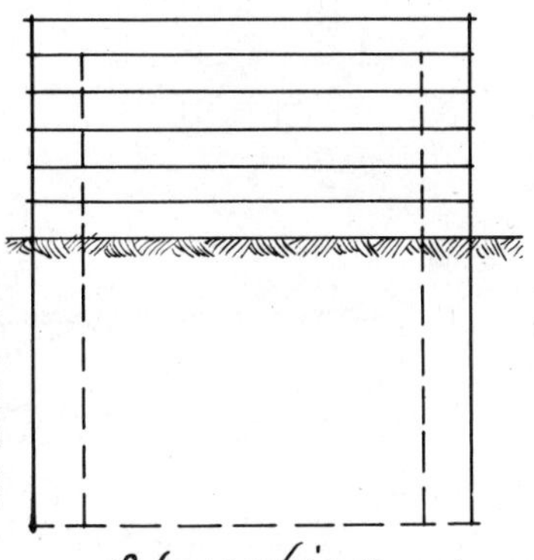

Elevation

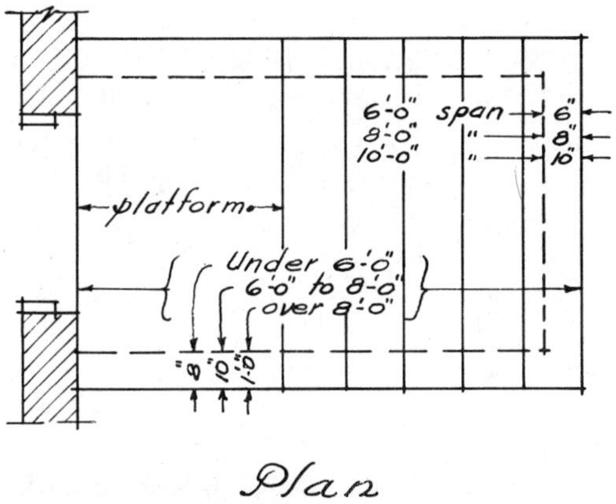

6'-0" span 6"
8'-0" " 8"
10'-0" " 10"
platform
Under 6'-0"
6'-0" to 8'-0"
over 8'-0"
8" 10" 1'-0"

Plan

SELF SUPPORTING SLAB FOR STEPS AND PLATFORM

DIAGRAMS of CONCRETE STEPS for RESIDENTIAL WORK

Finish is not indicated but slabs will take slate, flag or other finish.
1/4"=1'-0"

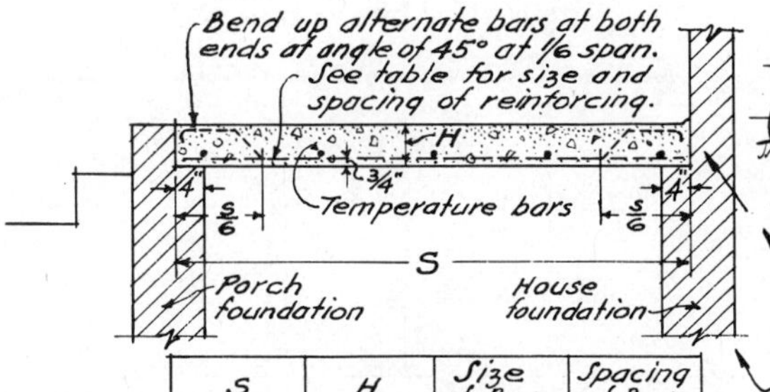

Bend up alternate bars at both ends at angle of 45° at 1/6 span. See table for size and spacing of reinforcing.
H
4"
3/4"
S/6
Temperature bars
S/6
4"
S
Porch foundation
House foundation

S	H	Size of Bars	Spacing of Bars
4'-0"	4½"	No. 2	8"
5'-0"	4½"	No. 2	6"
6'-0"	4½"	No. 3	9"
8'-0"	5"	No. 3	6"
10'-0"	5"	No. 3	4"

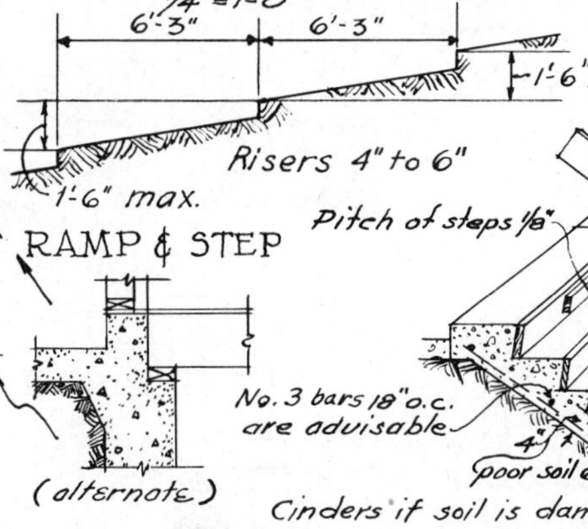

6'-3"
6'-3"
1'-6" max.
Risers 4" to 6"
1'-6" max.
RAMP & STEP
(alternate)

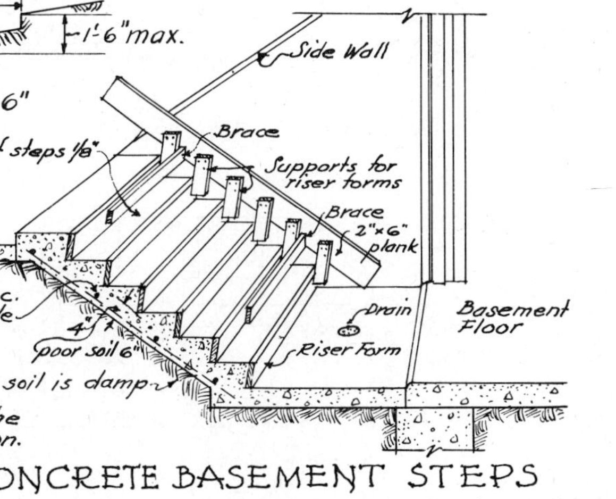

Side Wall
Brace
Pitch of steps 1/8"
Supports for riser forms
Brace
2"×6" plank
No. 3 bars 18" o.c. are advisable
4" poor soil 6"
Drain
Basement Floor
Riser Form
Cinders if soil is damp

Recommendations of the Portland Cement Association.

REINFORCED CONCRETE PORCH FLOOR

CONCRETE BASEMENT STEPS

STEPS ETC; CONCRETE, FLAGSTONE and BLUESTONE

Calculations checked by Elwyn E. Seelye. Consulting Engineer.

SCISSOR STAIRS

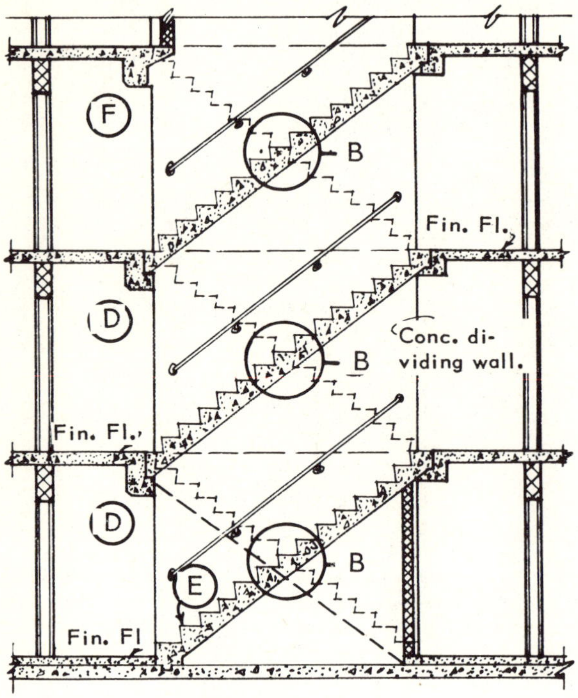
F
D
D
E
B
B
B
Fin. Fl.
Conc. dividing wall.
Fin. Fl.
Fin. Fl

SECTION A-A
Scale 1/8" = 1'-0"

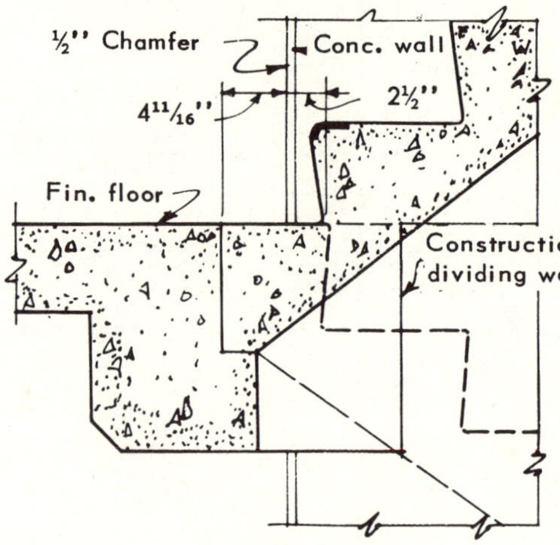
1/2" Chamfer
Conc. wall
$4^{11}/_{16}$"
2 1/2"
Fin. floor
Construction joint of dividing wall

DETAIL D

All interior steps to have non-slip nosings 3" wide and 3" short of treads at each end.

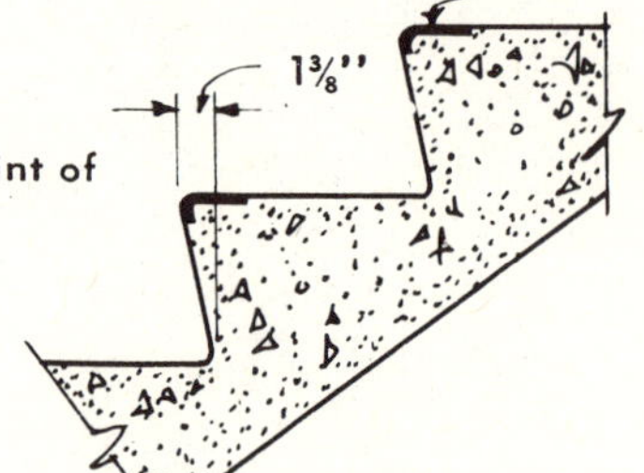
1 3/8"

DETAIL E

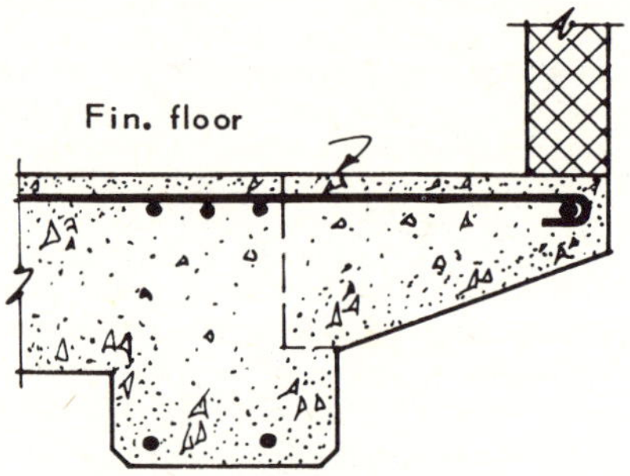
Fin. floor

DETAIL F

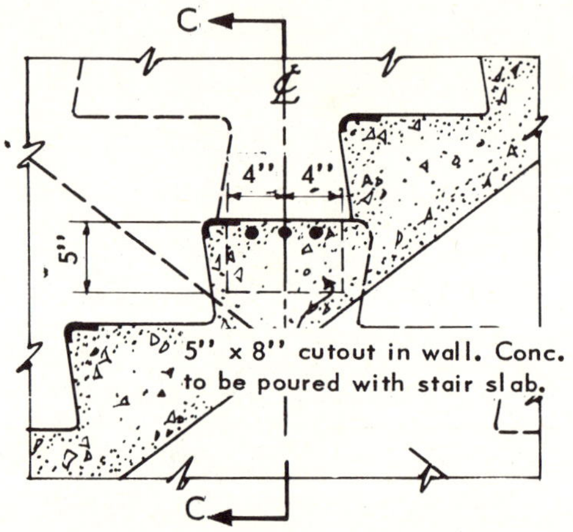
C
C
4"
4"
5"
5" x 8" cutout in wall. Conc. to be poured with stair slab.

DETAIL B

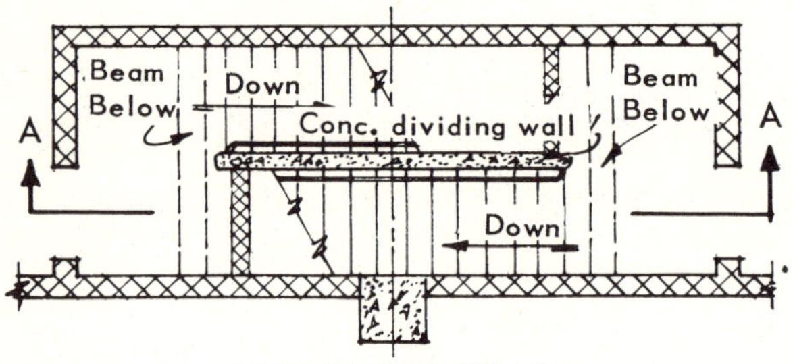
Beam Below
Down
Conc. dividing wall
Beam Below
A
A
Down

TOP FLOOR PLAN

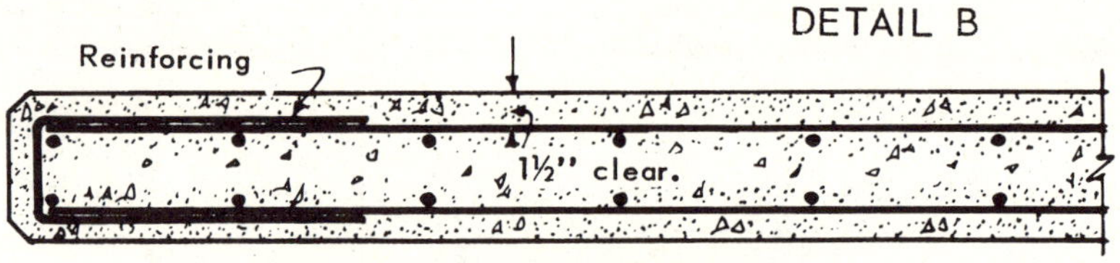
Reinforcing
1 1/2" clear.

PLAN OF CONCRETE WALL–
USED AS COLUMN–SHOWING REINFORCING

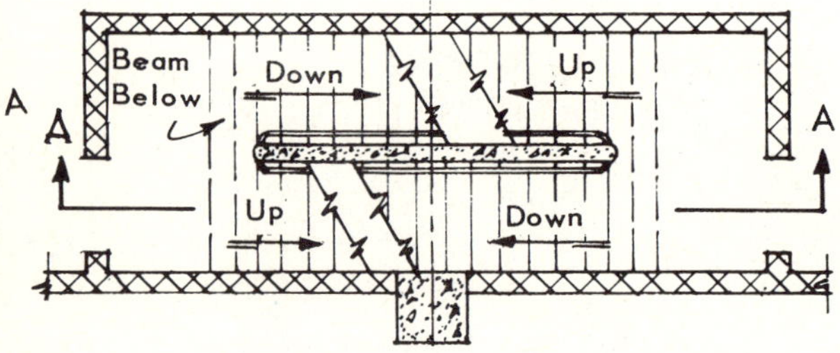
A
A
Beam Below
Down
Up
A
Up
Down

INTERMEDIATE FLOOR PLAN

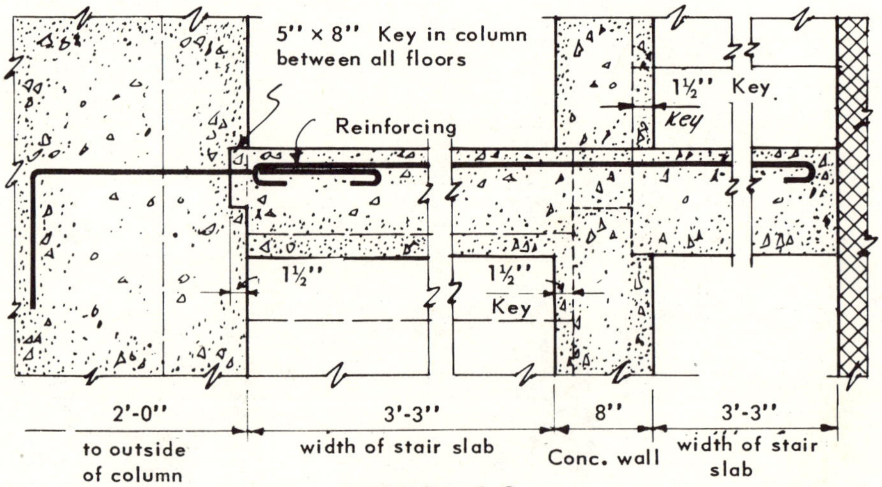
5" x 8" Key in column between all floors
Reinforcing
1 1/2" Key
Key
1 1/2"
1 1/2"
Key
2'-0"
to outside of column
3'-3"
width of stair slab
8"
Conc. wall
3'-3"
width of stair slab

SECTION C-C
Scale 3/4" = 1'-0"

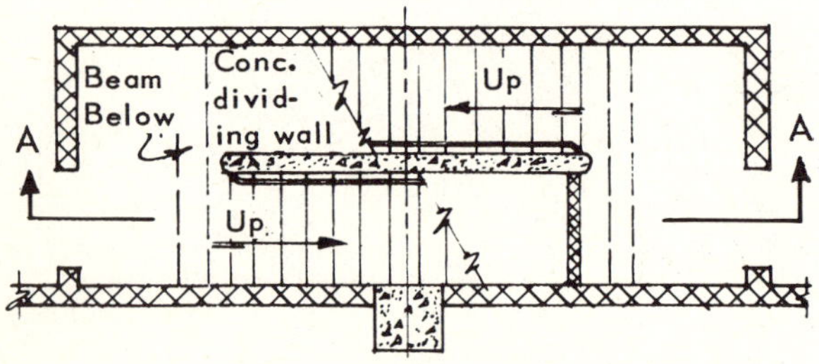
Beam Below
Conc. dividing wall
Up
A
A
Up

BOTTOM FLOOR PLAN
Scale 1/8" = 1'-0"

Scheme shown is diagrammatic only.
Design subject to specific job requirements.

METAL POSTS, BALUSTERS, RAILINGS,–ATTACHMENT, ETC.

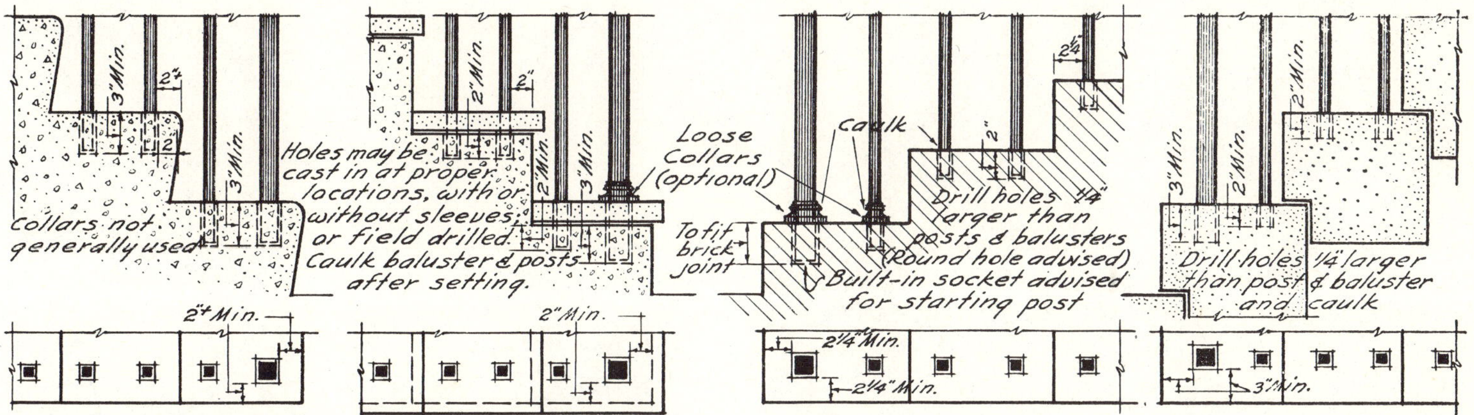
3" Min.
2"
Holes may be cast in at proper locations, with or without sleeves, or field drilled. Caulk baluster & posts after setting.
Collars not generally used
2" Min.
Loose Collars (optional)
Caulk
To fit brick joint
Drill holes 1/4" larger than posts & balusters (Round hole advised)
Built-in socket advised for starting post
2 1/4"
Drill holes 1/4 larger than post & baluster and caulk
2" Min.
2 1/4" Min.
3" Min.

CEMENT TREADS & RISERS, INTEGRAL | CEMENT RISERS, FLAG, SLATE, MARBLE TRDS.
CONCRETE STAIRS or STEPS

BRICK TREADS AND RISERS
BRICK STEPS

STONE TREADS AND RISERS
STONE STEPS

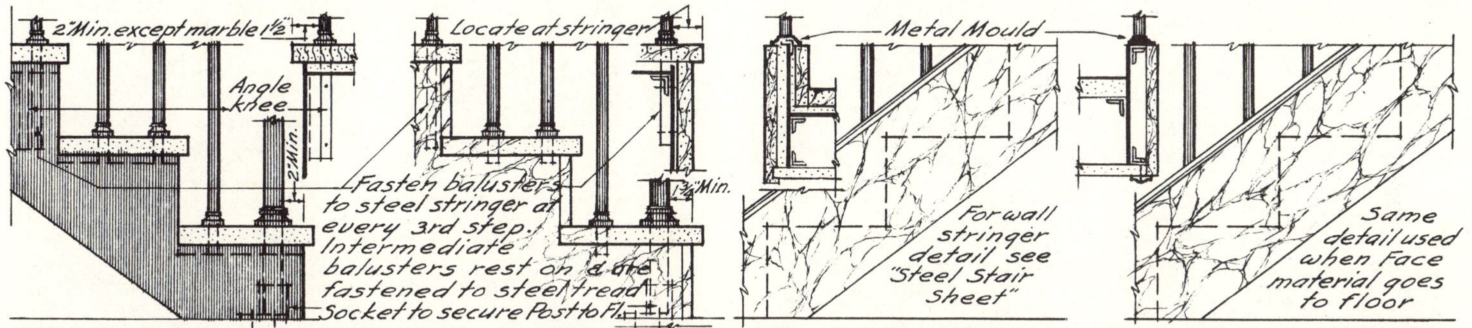
2" Min. except marble 1 1/2"
Angle knee
2" Min.
Locate at stringer
Fasten balusters to steel stringer at every 3rd step. Intermediate balusters rest on & are fastened to steel tread
Socket to secure Post to Fl.
1 3/4" Min.
Metal Mould
For wall stringer detail see "Steel Stair Sheet"
Same detail used when Face material goes to floor

MARBLE, SLATE, FLAG & PRE-CAST TERRAZZO TRDS., STEEL RS. & STRINGERS
STEEL STAIRS

MARBLE ETC. TRDS. RS. & STRINGERS | BOX or CLOSED STRINGER MARBLE FACED IN & OUT
STEEL SUB-STAIRS
Refer to "Steel Stairs"

BOX or CLOSED STRINGER FASCIA OF WOOD, MARBLE, ETC.
STEEL SUB-STAIRS

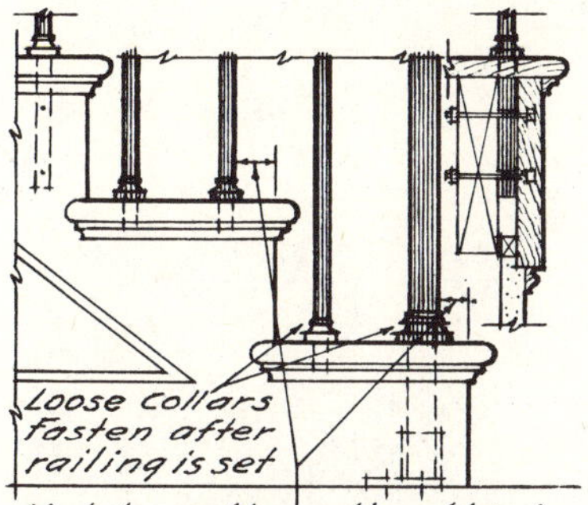
Loose collars fasten after railing is set

Not less than the thickness of the riser.
Fasten balusters to stringers every third tread.
WOOD STAIRS

NOTES

Caulking may be done with either molten lead or molten sulphur. Sulphur is the least expensive and on account of its color should be covered with collars. Do not caulk marble or wood. Collars are optional and for ornamental use with most materials but required for wood. Not required for marble and stones easily cut. Holes are drawn square, but for hard materials such as flags, blue stone, slate, brick and concrete round holes are advisable as they are easier to drill without breakage.

1/8" to 1/4" — Use round holes for materials which are hard to drill. — 1/8"

Marble 1/16" — Use square holes for materials Easy to drill such as limestone, marble, wood, etc. — 1/8" to 1/4" other than marble

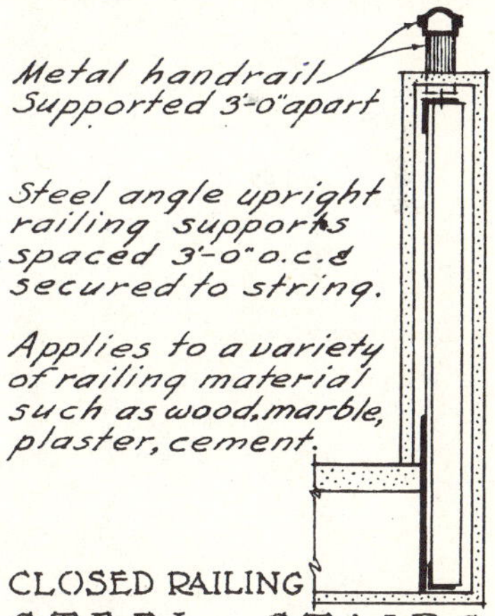
Metal handrail Supported 3'-0" apart
Steel angle upright railing supports spaced 3'-0" o.c. & secured to string.
Applies to a variety of railing material such as wood, marble, plaster, cement.

CLOSED RAILING
STEEL STAIRS

METHODS of SECURING POSTS & BALUSTERS
Scale 3/4" = 1'-0"

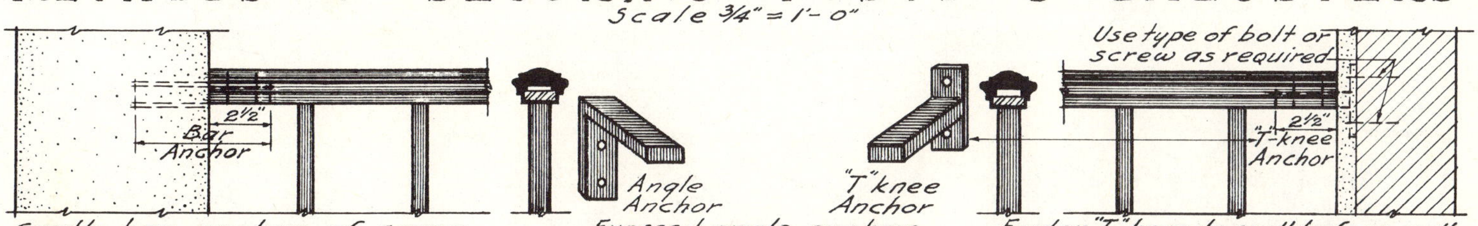
2 1/2"
Bar Anchor
Angle Anchor
"T" knee Anchor
Use type of bolt or screw as required
2 1/2"
"T" knee Anchor

Caulk bar anchor of same size as lower member of rail to wall with lead. Hole 1/4" larger than bar. Fasten bar to under side of rail.

Exposed angle anchors often used but not recommended except for very cheap work.
Scale 1 1/2" = 1'-0"

Fasten "T" knee to wall before wall finish is applied. Projecting end of knee fastens to underside of top member of rail and is same size as lower rail member.

UNFINISHED BRICK, STONE or CONCRETE | FINISH of PLASTER, STUCCO, MARBLE, ETC.
METHODS of SECURING RAILING TO WALLS

Prepared with the assistance of Julius Blum & Co., Inc.
Data reviewed by: National Association of Architectural Metal Manufacturers & Julius Blum & Co., Inc.

ALUMINUM PIPE HAND RAILINGS

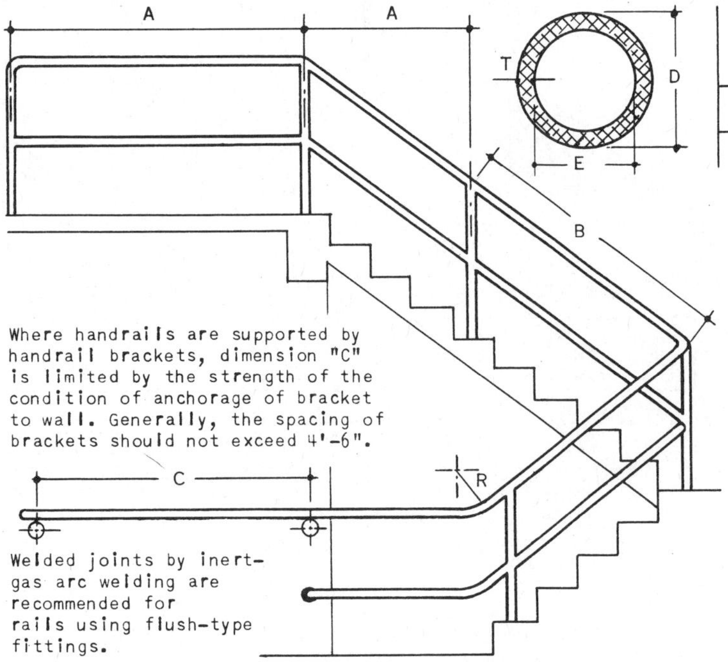

A
A
B
C
R
T
D
E

NOMINAL PIPE SIZE	"D" (INCHES)	"E" (INCHES)	"T" (INCHES)
$1\frac{1}{4}$"	1.660	1.380	0.140
$1\frac{1}{2}$"	1.990	1.610	0.145

"A" - RECOMMENDED POST SPACING:
$1\frac{1}{4}$" pipe - 5'-8"
$1\frac{1}{2}$" pipe - 7'-0"

"B" - MAXIMUM POST SPACING:
$1\frac{1}{4}$" pipe - 7'-10"
$1\frac{1}{2}$" pipe - 9'-11"

"R" - MINIMUM RADII FOR BENDS:
$1\frac{1}{4}$" pipe - $6\frac{3}{4}$"
$1\frac{1}{2}$" pipe - $7\frac{3}{4}$"

Where handrails are supported by handrail brackets, dimension "C" is limited by the strength of the condition of anchorage of bracket to wall. Generally, the spacing of brackets should not exceed 4'-6".

Welded joints by inert-gas arc welding are recommended for rails using flush-type fittings.

Pipe and fittings are stock items in $1\frac{1}{4}$" and $1\frac{1}{2}$" pipe, fittings in 35°, 40° and 90° angles. Sizes other than standard can be supplied.

UTILITY PIPE RAILINGS

DATA SUPPLIED BY THE ALUMINUM COMPANY OF AMERICA

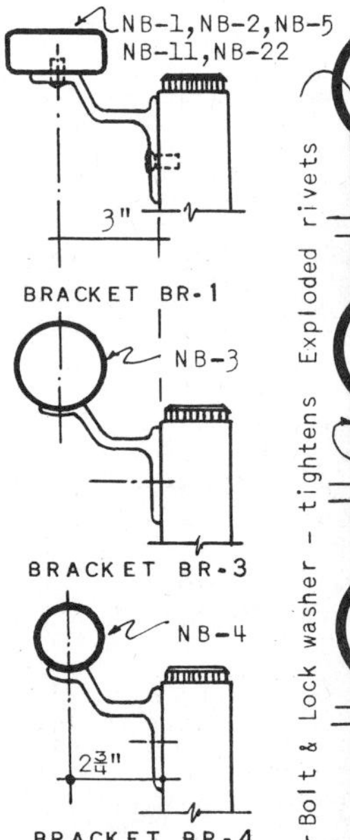

NB-1, NB-2, NB-5
NB-11, NB-22
3"
BRACKET BR-1
NB-3
BRACKET BR-3
NB-4
$2\frac{3}{4}$"
BRACKET BR-4

VERTICAL SECTIONS
Attachment of hand rails for POST 25
scale: $1\frac{1}{2}$"=1'-0"

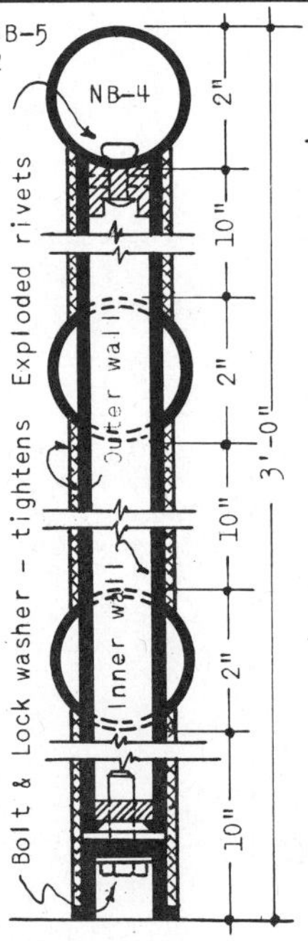

NB-4
Bolt & Lock washer - tightens Exploded rivets
Outer wall
Inner wall
2"
10"
2"
10"
2"
10"
3'-0"

VERTICAL SECTION
POST 20
scale: 3"=1'-0"

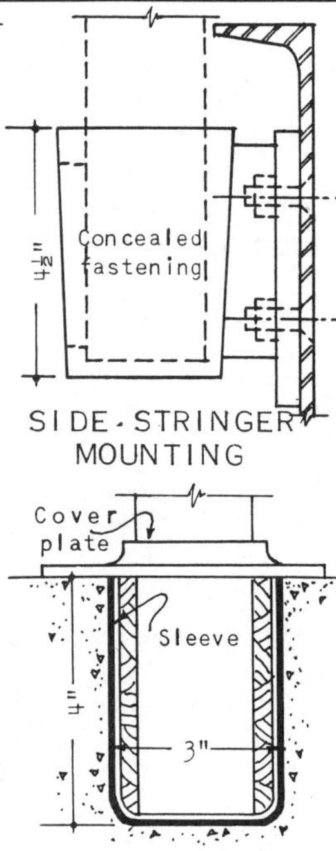

$4\frac{1}{2}$"
Concealed fastening
SIDE-STRINGER MOUNTING
Cover plate
Sleeve
4"
3"

ANCHORAGE IN CONCRETE

NOTE: All extrusions Min. ⅛" wall thickness

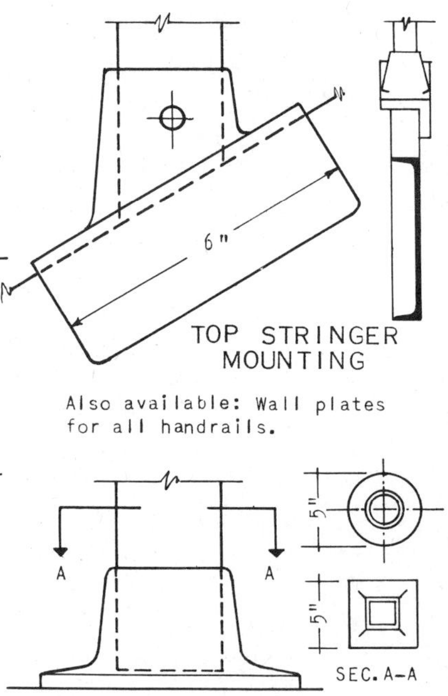

6"
TOP STRINGER MOUNTING
A
A
5"
5"
SEC. A-A

Also available: Wall plates for all handrails.

FLOOR FLANGE
(Fastens with wood screws, expansion bolts, or to suit conditions.)

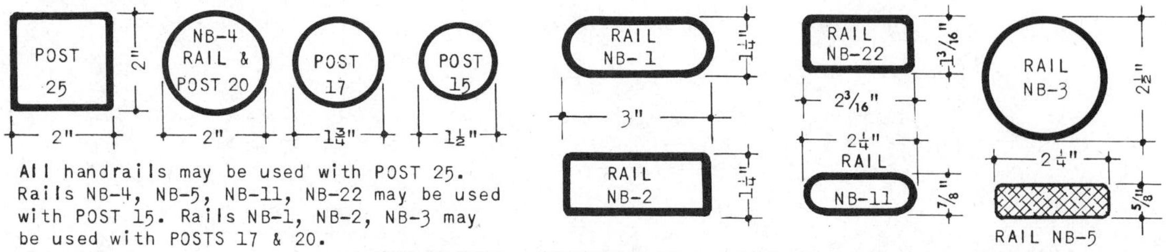

POST 25
2"
2"
NB-4 RAIL & POST 20
2"
POST 17
$1\frac{3}{4}$"
POST 15
$1\frac{1}{2}$"
RAIL NB-1
$1\frac{1}{4}$"
3"
RAIL NB-2
$1\frac{1}{4}$"
RAIL NB-22
$1\frac{3}{16}$"
$2\frac{3}{16}$"
$2\frac{1}{4}$"
RAIL NB-11
⅞"
RAIL NB-3
$2\frac{1}{2}$"
$2\frac{1}{4}$"
$\frac{5}{16}$"
RAIL NB-5

All handrails may be used with POST 25. Rails NB-4, NB-5, NB-11, NB-22 may be used with POST 15. Rails NB-1, NB-2, NB-3 may be used with POSTS 17 & 20.

LOW COST EXTRUDED ALUMINUM RAILINGS

DATA SUPPLIED BY "ECONO-RAIL" - NEWMAN BROTHERS, INC., CINCINNATI 3, OHIO

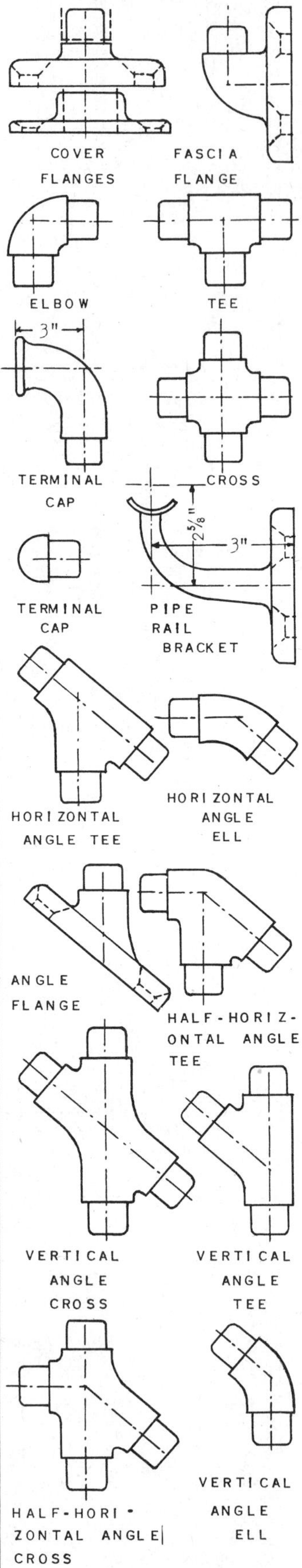

COVER FLANGES
FASCIA FLANGE
ELBOW
TEE
3"
TERMINAL CAP
CROSS
$2\frac{5}{8}$"
3"
TERMINAL CAP
PIPE RAIL BRACKET
HORIZONTAL ANGLE TEE
HORIZONTAL ANGLE ELL
ANGLE FLANGE
HALF-HORIZONTAL ANGLE TEE
VERTICAL ANGLE CROSS
VERTICAL ANGLE TEE
HALF-HORIZONTAL ANGLE CROSS
VERTICAL ANGLE ELL

STANDARD FLUSH FITTINGS
ALUMINUM CO OF AMERICA

EXTRUDED ALUMINUM HANDRAILS

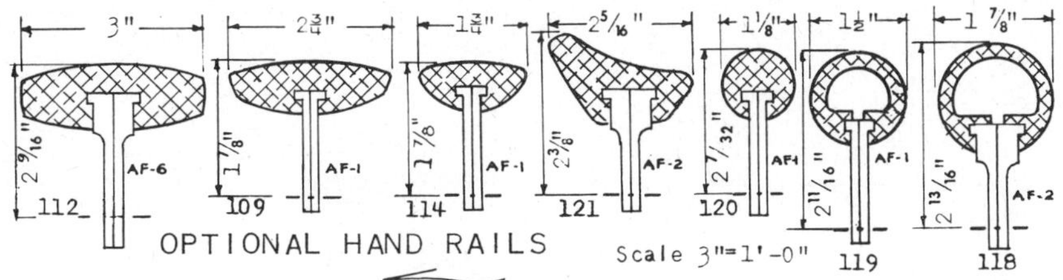
3"
2¾"
1¾"
2 5/16"
1⅛"
1½"
1 7/8"
2 9/16"
AF-6
112
1 7/8"
AF-1
109
1 7/8"
AF-1
114
2 3/8"
AF-2
121
2 7/32"
120
AF-1
2 11/16"
AF-1
119
2 13/16"
AF-2
118

OPTIONAL HAND RAILS Scale 3"=1'-0"

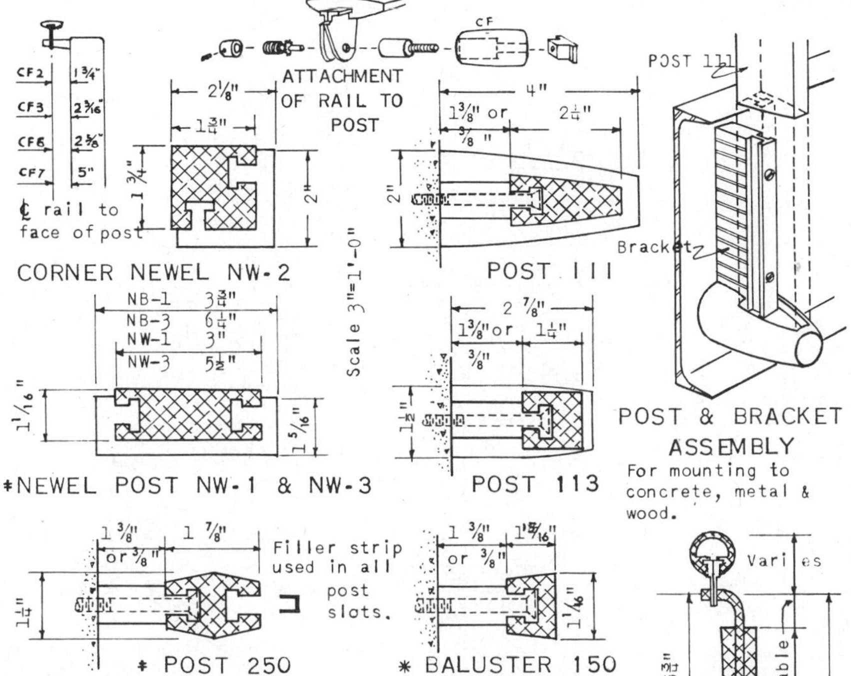
CF2 1¾"
CF3 2 3/16"
CF6 2⅜"
CF7 5"
℄ rail to face of post
2⅛"
1¾"
1¾"
2"
ATTACHMENT OF RAIL TO POST
CF
4"
1⅜" or 2¼"
⅜"
2"
Scale 3"=1'-0"
NB-1 3¾"
NB-3 6¼"
NW-1 3"
NW-3 5½"
1 1/16"
1 5/16"
2 7/8"
1⅜"or 1¼"
⅜"
1½"
1 3/8" 1 7/8"
or ⅜"
Filler strip used in all post slots.
1¼"
1 3/8" 1 15/16"
or ⅜"
1 1/16"
POST 111
Bracket
POST & BRACKET ASSEMBLY
For mounting to concrete, metal & wood.

CORNER NEWEL NW-2 POST 111

*NEWEL POST NW-1 & NW-3 POST 113

* POST 250 * BALUSTER 150

* May be used as center post with 1'-0" Max. spacing handrails on each side.

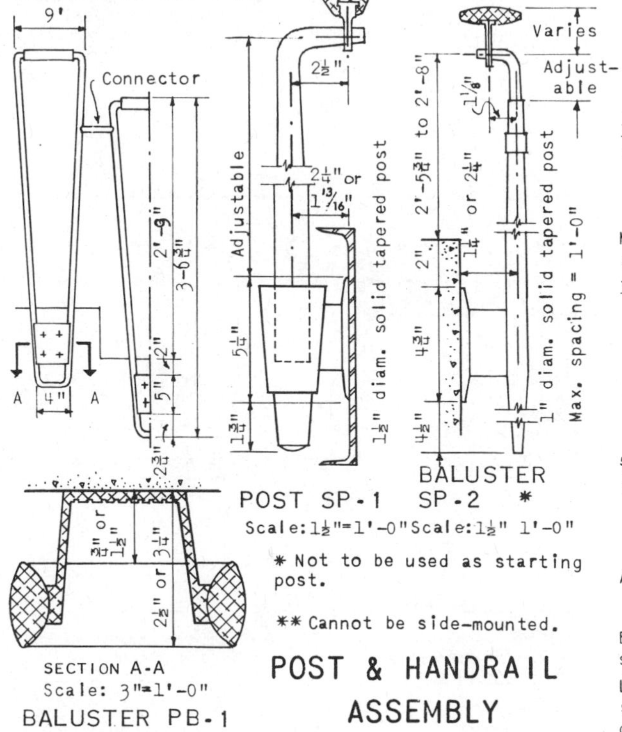
9'
Connector
A 4" A
2'-9"
3'-6¾"
2"
5"
2¾"
¾" or 1⅛"
3¼"
2½" or 3¼"
2½"
Adjustable
2¼" or 1 13/16"
5¼"
1¾"
1½" diam. solid tapered post
Varies
Adjustable
1⅛"
2'-5¾" to 2'-8"
2" or 2¼"
1¼"
4¾"
4½"
1" diam. solid tapered post
Max. spacing = 1'-0"

SECTION A-A Scale: 3"=1'-0"

BALUSTER PB-1

POST SP-1 Scale: 1½"=1'-0"

BALUSTER SP-2 ** Scale: 1½" 1'-0"

* Not to be used as starting post.

** Cannot be side-mounted.

POST & HANDRAIL ASSEMBLY

NOTE: Maximum post spacing is 4'-0" unless otherwise noted. Posts may have any amount or combination of handrails; balusters have top rails only. Not shown but available: other posts and balusters, flanges for mounting posts in concrete, wall plates, AF-3 fasteners for non-slotted rails & custom rails.

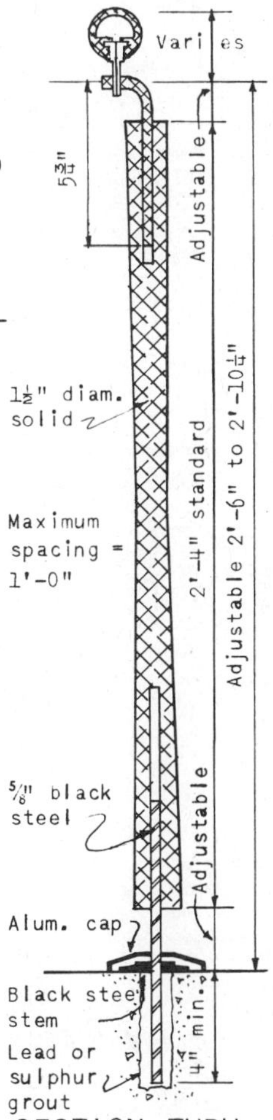
Varies
5¾"
Adjustable
1½" diam. solid
Maximum spacing = 1'-0"
2'-4" standard
Adjustable 2'-6" to 2'-10¼"
⅝" black steel
Adjustable
Alum. cap
Black steel stem
Lead or sulphur grout
4" min.

SECTION THRU BALUSTER SP-5 TYPE B * **

Scale: 1½"=1'-0"

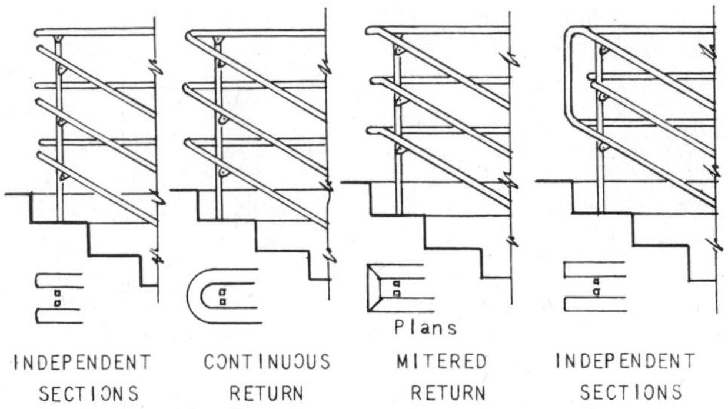
Plans
INDEPENDENT SECTIONS
CONTINUOUS RETURN
MITERED RETURN
INDEPENDENT SECTIONS

RETURNS WITHOUT NEWELS

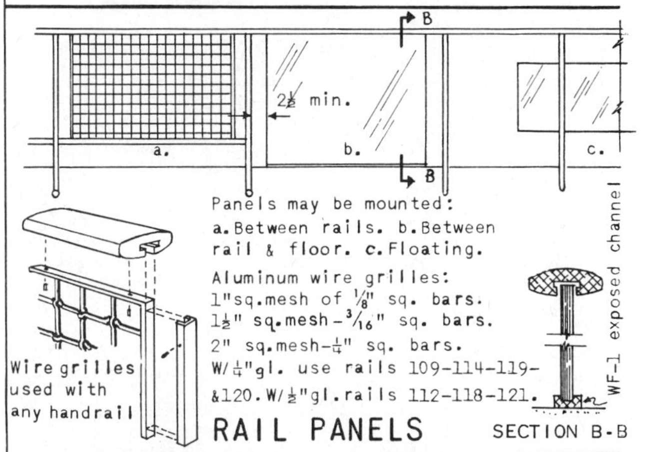
B
2½ min.
a.
b.
c.
B
Wire grilles used with any handrail
WF-1 exposed channel

Panels may be mounted: a. Between rails. b. Between rail & floor. c. Floating.

Aluminum wire grilles: 1" sq. mesh of ⅛" sq. bars. 1½" sq. mesh-3/16" sq. bars. 2" sq. mesh-¼" sq. bars. W/¼" gl. use rails 109-114-119-&120. W/½" gl. rails 112-118-121.

RAIL PANELS

SECTION B-B

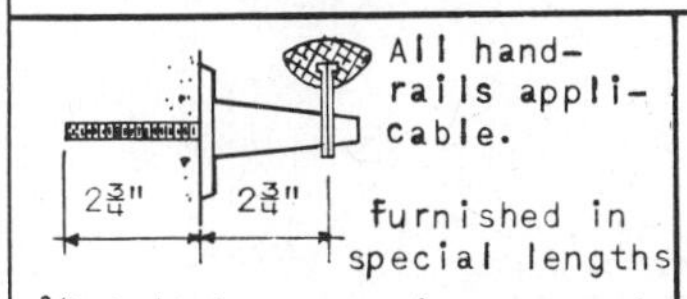
2¾"
2¾"

All handrails applicable.

furnished in special lengths

⅜" bolt for expansion or toggle

Lag screw for wood fastening.

WALL BRACKET WB-2

a.
3⅝"

a. 1⅞" for rail 118, 1⅜" for rail 119, 1" for rail 120. for rails 109, 112, 114 & 121, 3⅝" long

RAIL TERMINALS

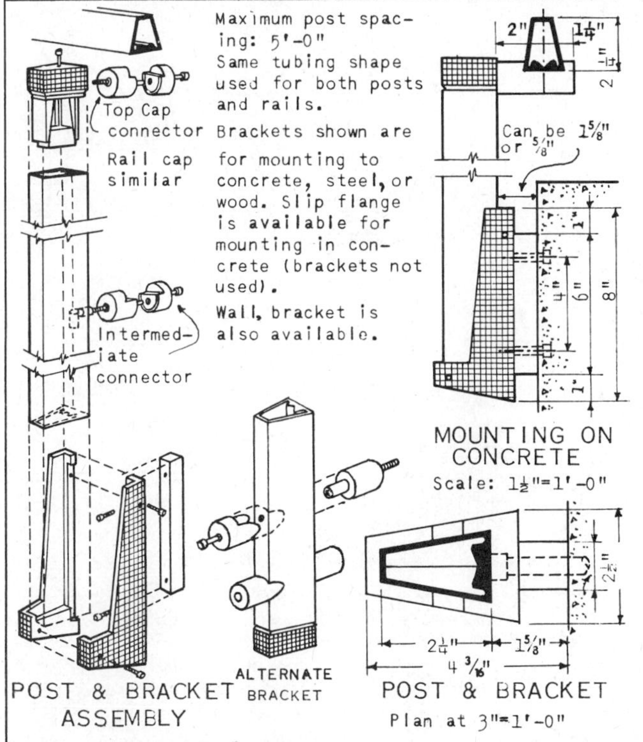
Top Cap connector
Rail cap similar
Intermediate connector
2"
1¼"
1¼"
2
Can be 1⅝" or ⅝"
1"
4"
6"
8"
1"
2¼"
2¼"
1⅝"
4 3/16"
ALTERNATE BRACKET

Maximum post spacing: 5'-0"
Same tubing shape used for both posts and rails.
Brackets shown are for mounting to concrete, steel, or wood. Slip flange is available for mounting in concrete (brackets not used).
Wall bracket is also available.

MOUNTING ON CONCRETE Scale: 1½"=1'-0"

POST & BRACKET ASSEMBLY

POST & BRACKET Plan at 3"=1'-0"

LOW COST EXTRUDED ALUM. HANDRAIL

DATA SUPPLIED BY BLUMCRAFT OF PITTSBURGH (CHECK MANUFACTURER'S CATALOGUES FOR COMPLETE DETAILS)

STEEL & IRON PIPE RAILINGS

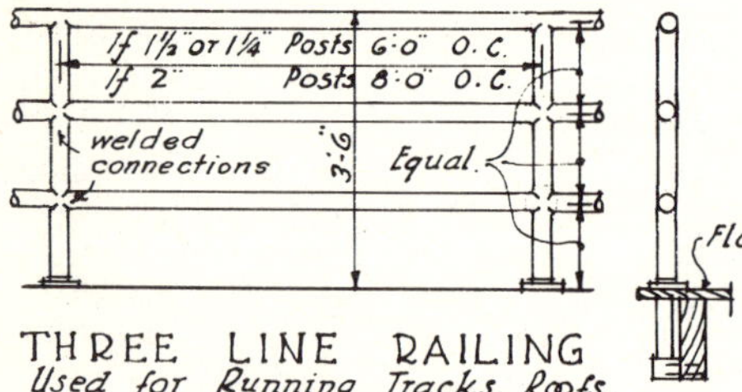
If 1½" or 1¼" Posts 6'-0" O.C.
If 2" Posts 8'-0" O.C.
welded connections
3'-6"
Equal
Floor

THREE LINE RAILING
Used for Running Tracks, Roofs, Board Walk edges.

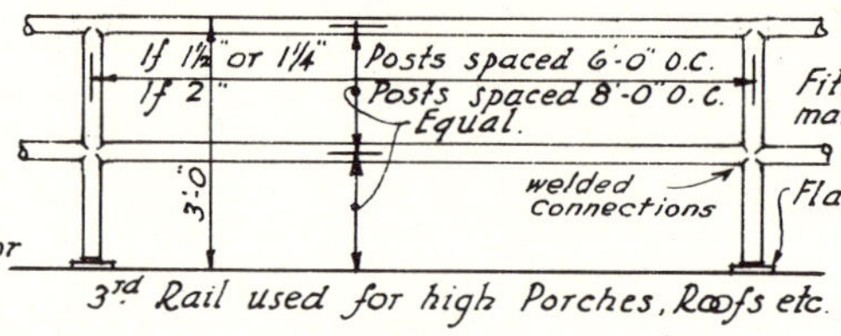
If 1½" or 1¼" Posts spaced 6'-0" O.C.
If 2" Posts spaced 8'-0" O.C.
Equal.
3'-0"
welded connections
Flanges C.I.
3rd Rail used for high Porches, Roofs etc.

TWO LINE RAILING
Type used for Areas, Pits, Roofs etc.

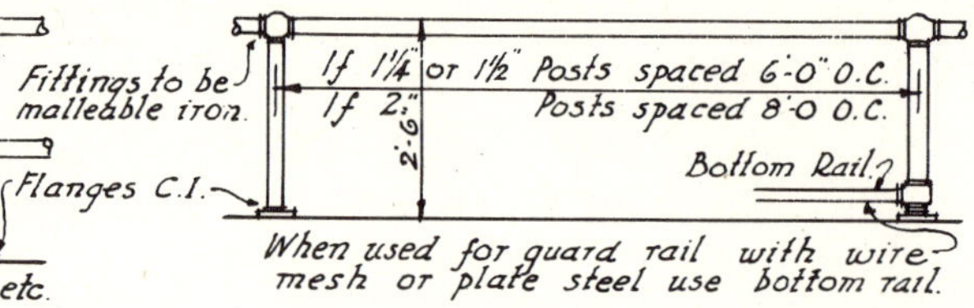
Fittings to be malleable iron.
If 1¼" or 1½" Posts spaced 6'-0" O.C.
If 2" Posts spaced 8'-0" O.C.
2'-6"
Bottom Rail
When used for guard rail with wire-mesh or plate steel use bottom rail.

SINGLE LINE RAILING
Type used for shallow Area, Yards Terraces etc.

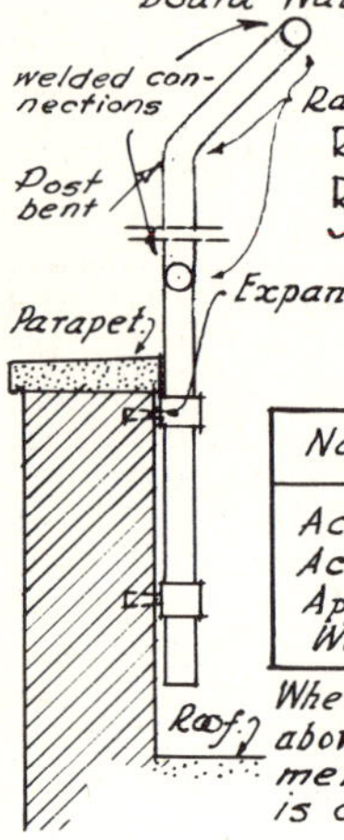
welded connections
Rail
Post bent
Expansion Bolts
Parapet
Roof

RAILING FOR ROOF COPING. Scale 3/8" = 1'-0"

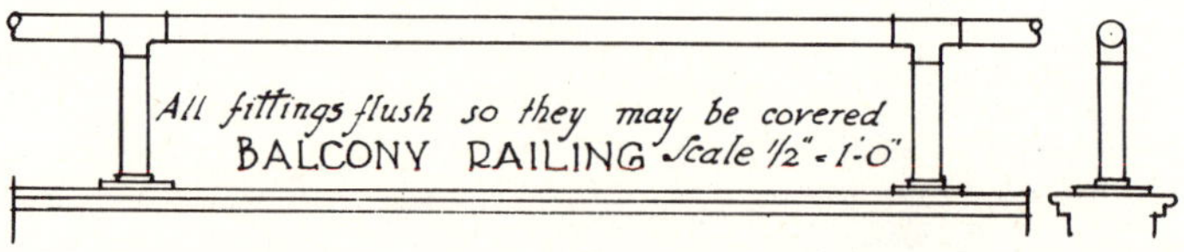
All fittings flush so they may be covered

BALCONY RAILING Scale 1/2" = 1'-0"

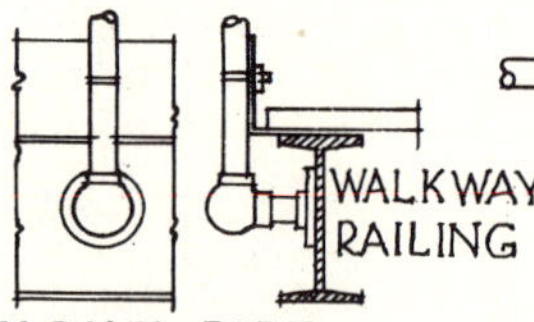

WALKWAY RAILING

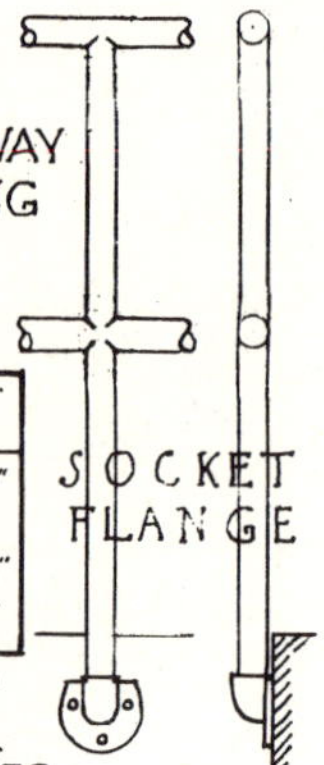

SOCKET FLANGE

GENERAL INFORMATION REGARDING STANDARD WEIGHT PIPE.
Finish is black or galvanized iron

Nominal size wrought steel pipe-ins	1/2"	3/4"	1"	1 1/4"	1 1/2"	2"	2 1/2"	3"	3 1/2"	4"	5"
Actual inside diameter - inches	.62	.82	1.05	1.38	1.61	2.07	2.47	3.07	3.55	4.03	5.05"
Actual outside diameter - inches	.84	1.05	1.32	1.66	1.90	2.38	2.88	3.50	4.00	4.50	5.56
Approximate outside - inches	7/8	1 1/16	1 5/16"	1 11/16	1 15/16	2 3/8	2 7/8	3 1/2"	4"	4 1/2	5 1/2"
Weight per foot pounds	.85	1.13	1.68	2.28	2.72	3.65	5.79	7.58	9.11	10.79	14.62

Where extra strength is necessary extra strong wrought steel may be specified. Outside diam. is same as above, inside diam. smaller. Pipe of genuine wrought iron, copper steel, stainless steel, or non-ferrous metal, also produced in the above sizes, is made & specified in "iron pipe sizes." Round pipe size is always designated by nominal I.D. Ball type fittings used only where special conditions warrant them.

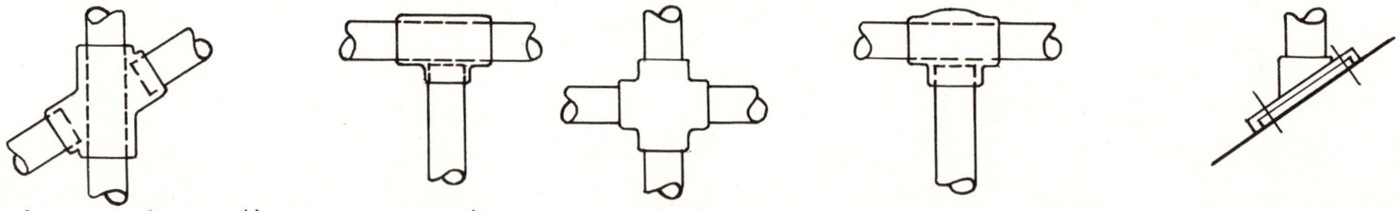

Ball pattern or plain pattern cross for ramp construction. Used with tees, elbows and side outlet fittings.

Plain pattern tee

Cross for horizontal construction

Ball pattern tee with horizontal pipe extending thro' fitting

Beveled base flange with raised lugs for adjustment to variation in pitch.

Special fittings usually available in slopes of 30°, 35°, 40° & 45°. A variation of plus or minus 2½ degrees in slope of railing permissible.

FITTINGS
1/2" = 1'-0"

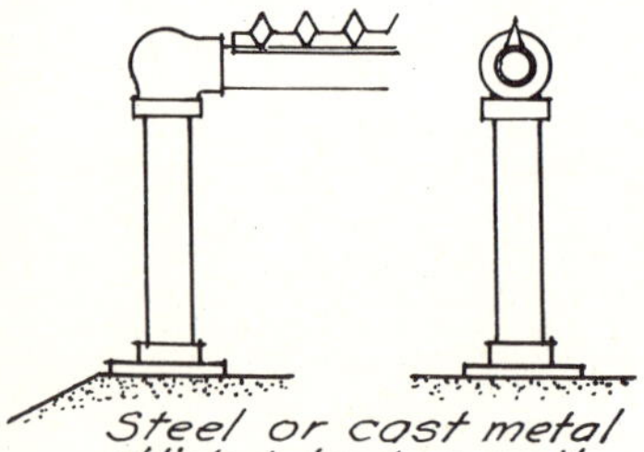

Steel or cast metal attchd. to top rail

LOAFER RAIL
1/2" = 1'-0"

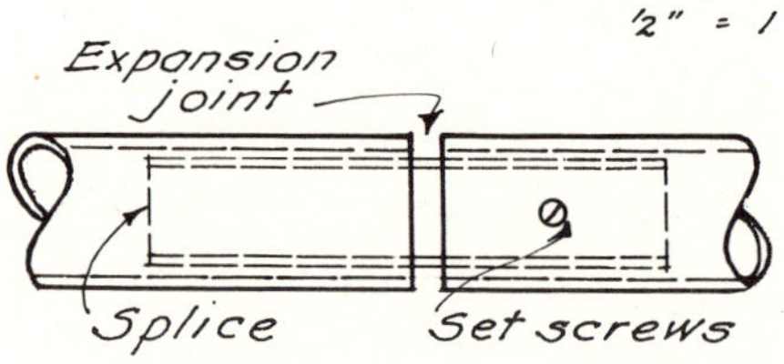
Expansion joint
Splice
Set screws

EXPANSION JOINT in LONG RAILINGS
1½" = 1'-0"

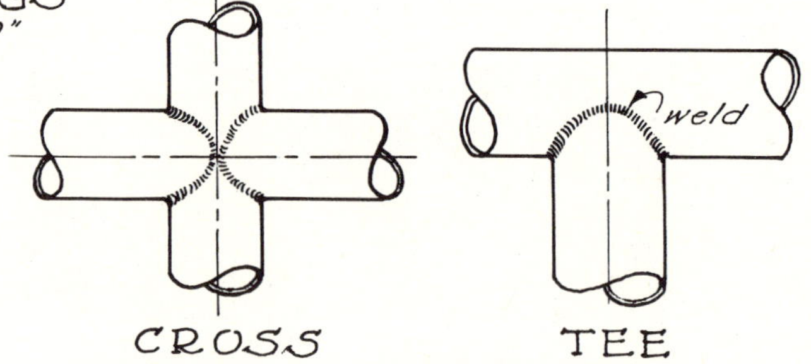
weld

CROSS TEE

WELDED CONNECTIONS
1½" = 1'-0"

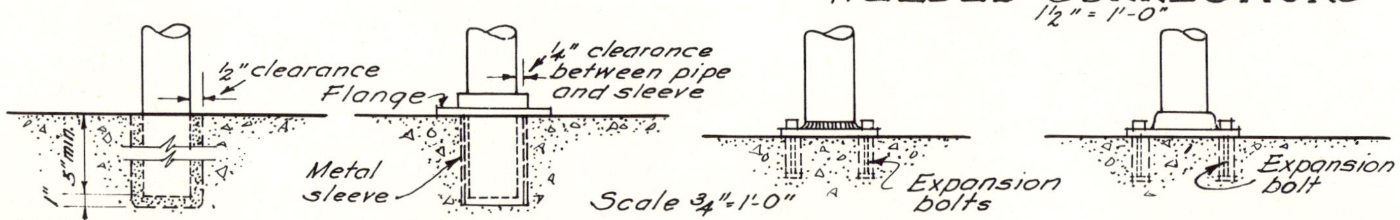
½" clearance
5" min.
1"
Flange
¼" clearance between pipe and sleeve
Metal sleeve
Expansion bolts
Expansion bolt

Scale 3/4" = 1'-0"

Post set in masonry without sleeve. Anchored with concrete or sulphur

Post set in pipe or sheet metal sleeve. Flange may be loose or fastened to post

Post welded to plate base and anchored by expansion bolts.

Post threaded into screw flange and anchored by expansion bolts.

Molten lead or lead wool may be used for anchoring, where tendency to flow is not a factor involving strength.

POST ANCHORAGE
3/4" = 1'-0"

Data reviewed by the National Assoc. of Architectural Metal Mfrs.

STEEL LADDERS and METAL TUBE RAILINGS

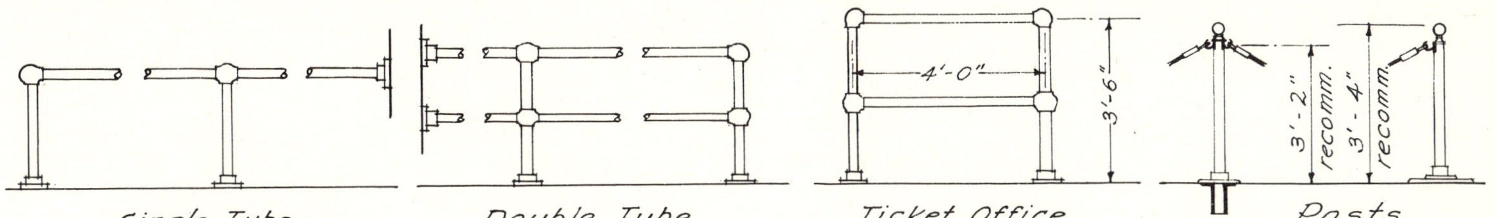
4'-0"
3'-6"
3'-2" recomm.
3'-4" recomm.

Single Tube Railing — Double Tube Railing — Ticket Office Railing

Ball Type Slip Fittings
Scale ¼" = 1'-0"

Posts
Removable — Movable

Single posts with ball caps & hooks for rope railing. Removable post is constructed with metal socket set in floor, with plug provided for socket. Movable post is free-standing on floor with large flat base of sufficient weight to hold post rigid.

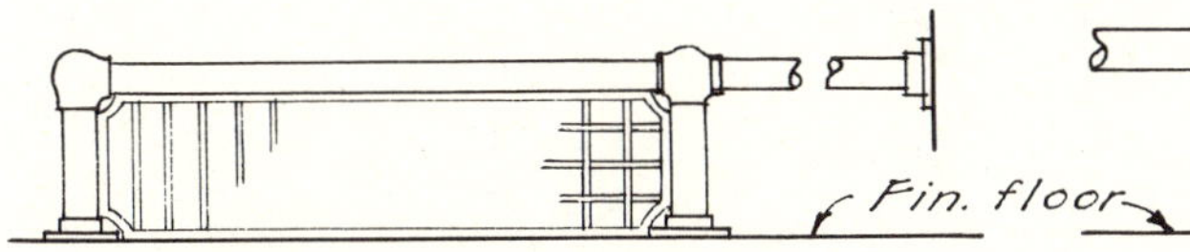
Fin. floor

Low Level Railing with or without grille

Foot Rail with stationary posts

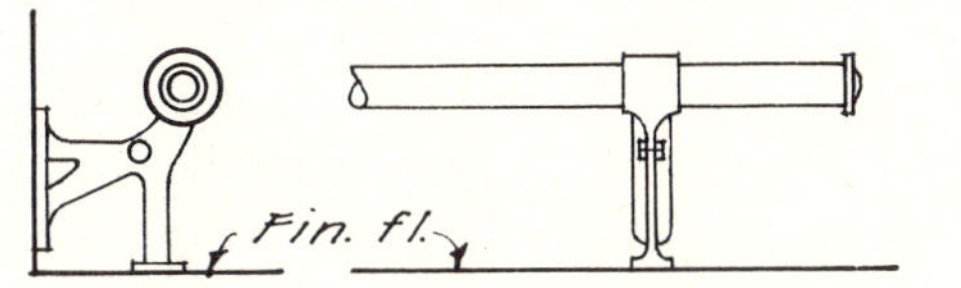
Fin. fl.

Foot Rail with Pivoted Bracket

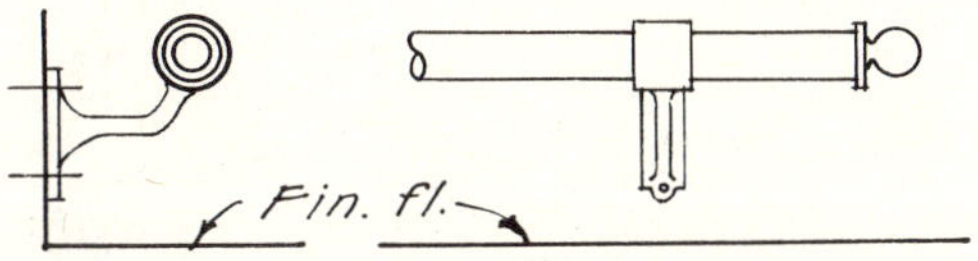
Fin. fl.

Foot Rail with Stationary Bracket
Scale ½" = 1'-0"

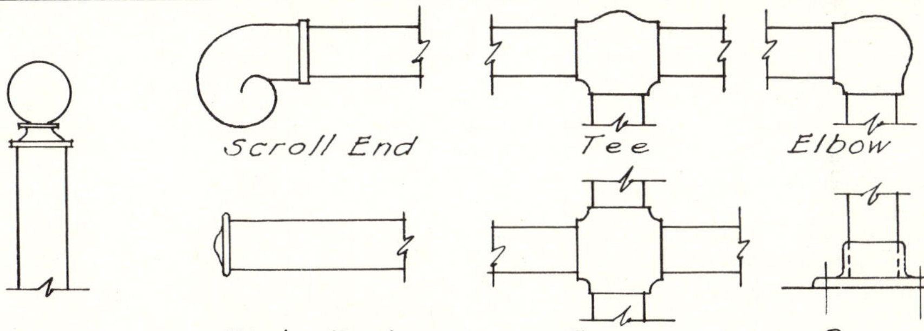

Cap — Scroll End — Tee — Elbow — Plain End — Cross — Base

Connections of tube railings usually cast ball type fittings, with tube set in fittings & welded, brazed or pinned. Fittings for tube railings available in brass, bronze, aluminum, and chromium plated metals. Railings of stainless steel tubes may be constructed with welded joints or with chromium plated fittings.

SLIP FITTINGS
1½" = 1'-0"

Railings of round tubes made in steel, stainless steel, brass, bronze, aluminum & other non-ferrous metals. Tubes always measured by o.d. Tube railings usually specified in 1", 1½", 1¾", 2", 2½", or 3" dia. & in wall thicknesses of 18, 16 or 14 ga. 18 ga. usually satisfactory in all metals except aluminum which is usually 16 ga. Base flanges & brackets are available for all usual types of railing construction. Where posts require reinforcing under heavy use, steel pipe or tube may be inserted.

TUBE RAILINGS

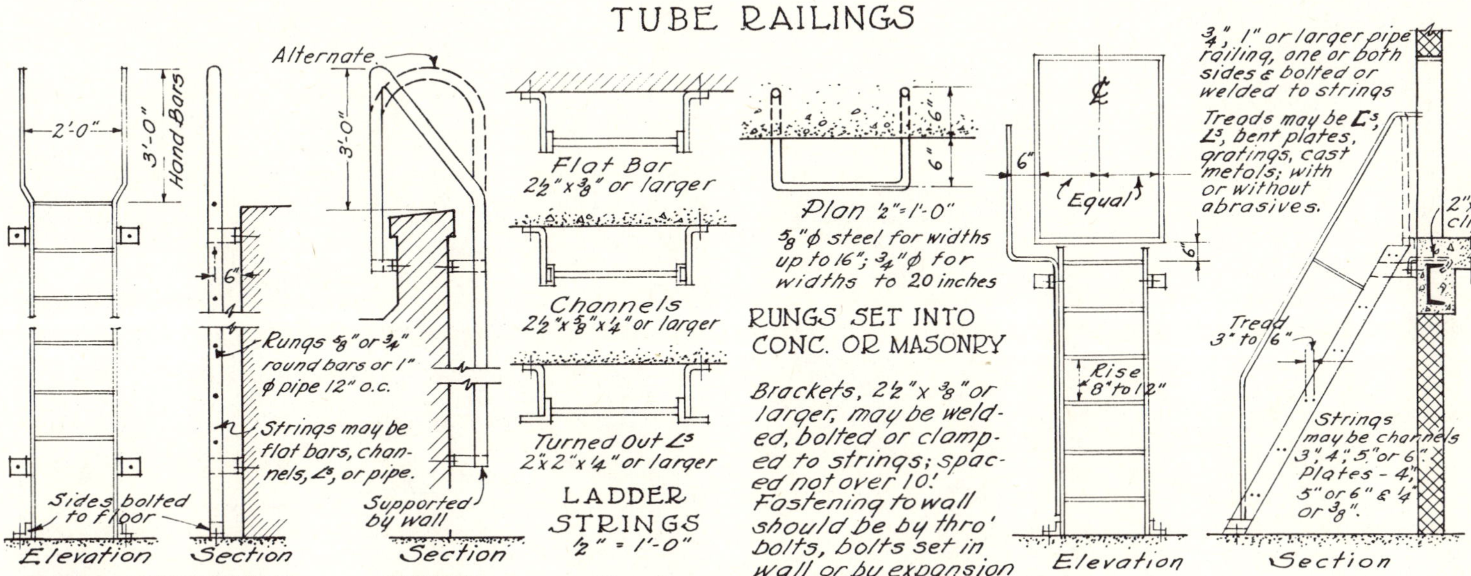
2'-0"
3'-0" Hand Bars
6"
Rungs ⅝" or ¾" round bars or 1" ϕ pipe 12" o.c.
Strings may be flat bars, channels, ∠s, or pipe.
Sides bolted to floor
Elevation
Section
Alternate
3'-0"
Supported by wall
Section
Flat Bar 2½" x ⅜" or larger
Channels 2½" x ⅝" x ¼" or larger
Turned Out ∠s 2½" x 2" x ¼" or larger
Plan ½" = 1'-0"
6"
6"
⅝" ϕ steel for widths up to 16"; ¾" ϕ for widths to 20 inches
℄
6"
Equal
6"
Rise 8" to 12"
Elevation
¾", 1" or larger pipe railing, one or both sides & bolted or welded to strings
Treads may be [s, ∠s, bent plates, gratings, cast metals; with or without abrasives.
2" x ¼" clip
Tread 3" to 6"
Strings may be channels 3", 4", 5" or 6". Plates - 4", 5" or 6" & ¼" or ⅜".
Section

SIDES EXTENDING ABOVE LANDING

SIDES OVER PARAPET

Scale ¼" = 1'-0"

LADDER STRINGS
½" = 1'-0"

RUNGS SET INTO CONC. OR MASONRY

Brackets, 2½" x ⅜" or larger, may be welded, bolted or clamped to strings; spaced not over 10'. Fastening to wall should be by thro' bolts, bolts set in wall or by expansion bolts. Rungs, ⅝" ϕ or ¾" ϕ bars usually set into holes in strings & welded together.

60° LADDER
¼" = 1'-0"

VERTICAL & SHIP LADDERS

Data reviewed by the National Association of Architectural Metal Mfrs.

FIRE ESCAPES

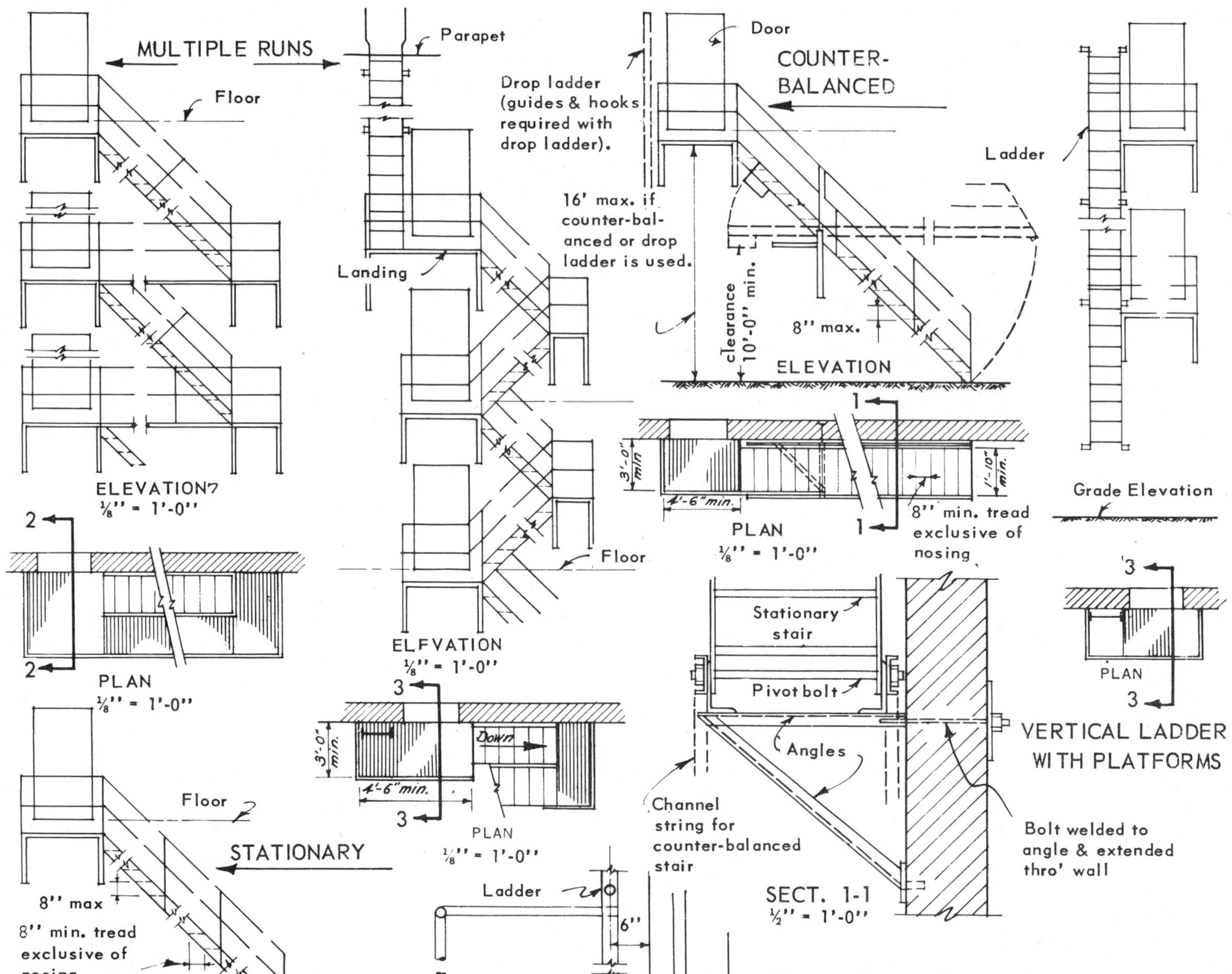

MULTIPLE RUNS
Floor
ELEVATION
1/8" = 1'-0"
PLAN
1/8" = 1'-0"
Parapet
Landing
Floor
ELEVATION
1/8" = 1'-0"
3'-0" min.
Down
4'-6" min.
PLAN
1/8" = 1'-0"
Door
COUNTER-BALANCED
Drop ladder (guides & hooks required with drop ladder).
16' max. if counter-balanced or drop ladder is used.
clearance 10'-0" min.
8" max.
ELEVATION
3'-0" min
4'-6" min.
1'-10" min.
PLAN
1/8" = 1'-0"
8" min. tread exclusive of nosing
Ladder
Grade Elevation
PLAN
VERTICAL LADDER WITH PLATFORMS
Stationary stair
Pivot bolt
Angles
Channel string for counter-balanced stair
Bolt welded to angle & extended thro' wall
SECT. 1-1
1/2" = 1'-0"
Floor
STATIONARY
8" max
8" min. tread exclusive of nosing
ELEVATION
1/8" = 1'-0"
Ladder
6"

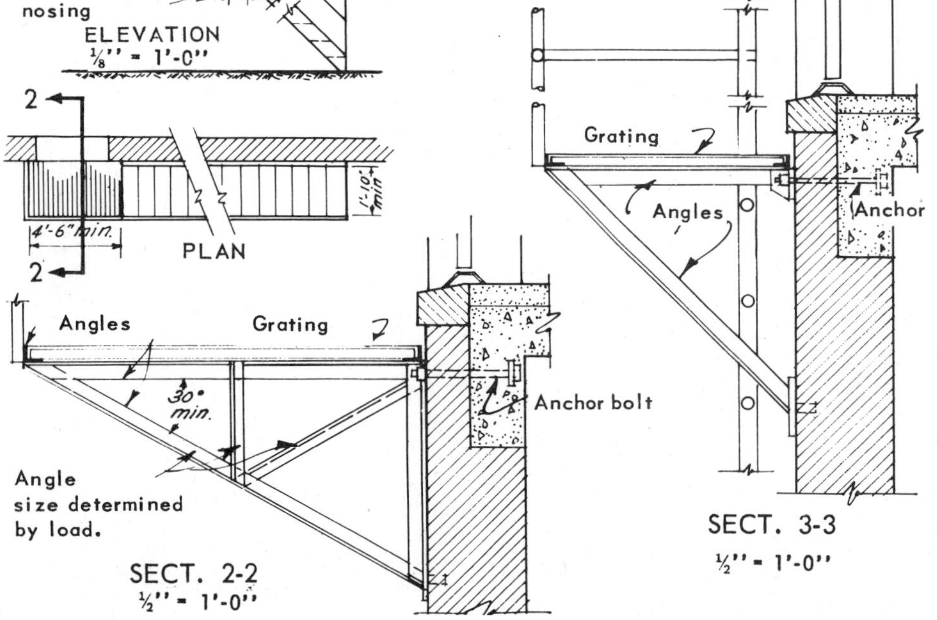

1'-10" min
4'-6" min.
PLAN
Grating
Angles
Anchor
Angles
Grating
30° min.
Anchor bolt
Angle size determined by load.
SECT. 2-2
1/2" = 1'-0"
SECT. 3-3
1/2" = 1'-0"

Fire escapes are of 4 general types:

1. Vertical ladders with platforms at exit doors & windows. This type used only for industrial bldgs. of low height.
2. Stairways supported on brackets attached to bldg. walls with platforms at exits. This type may be used for bldgs. of any height where permitted by building codes. Lower section may be counter-balanced, or drop ladder.
3. Free – standing stairways independently supported on steel columns, with platforms & walkways at exits. This type may be used for bldgs. where the construction cannot be attached to walls or piers.
4. Chute-fire escapes, used chiefly for bldgs. where persons are under institutional care.

On all fire escapes design reference must be made to state or local laws & ordinances.

Frames for platforms may be angles as shown, or channels bolted to brackets; grating may be bolted to frames or set in frame recess loose. Alternate bracket may be round or square steel usually 1" or 1¼".

Data reviewed by the National Assoc. of Architectural Metal Mfrs.

MISCELLANEOUS METALS

TABLE OF CONTENTS

METAL GUARDS

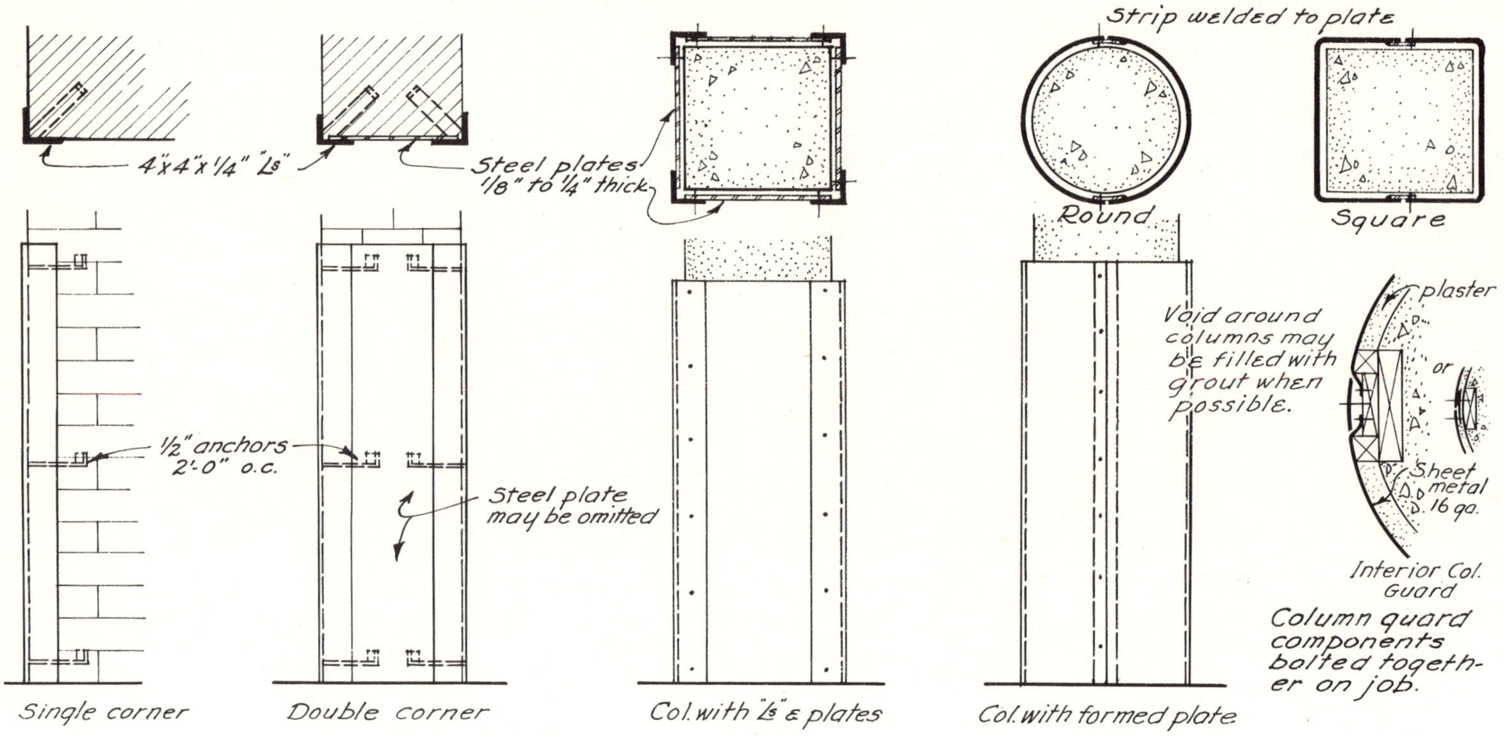
Strip welded to plate
4"x4"x1/4" "Ls"
Steel plates 1/8" to 1/4" thick
Round
Square
1/2" anchors 2'-0" o.c.
Steel plate may be omitted
Void around columns may be filled with grout when possible.
plaster
or
Sheet metal 16 ga.
Interior Col. Guard
Column guard components bolted together on job.
Single corner
Double corner
Col. with "Ls" & plates
Col. with formed plate

CORNER AND COLUMN GUARDS - 1/2" = 1'-0"

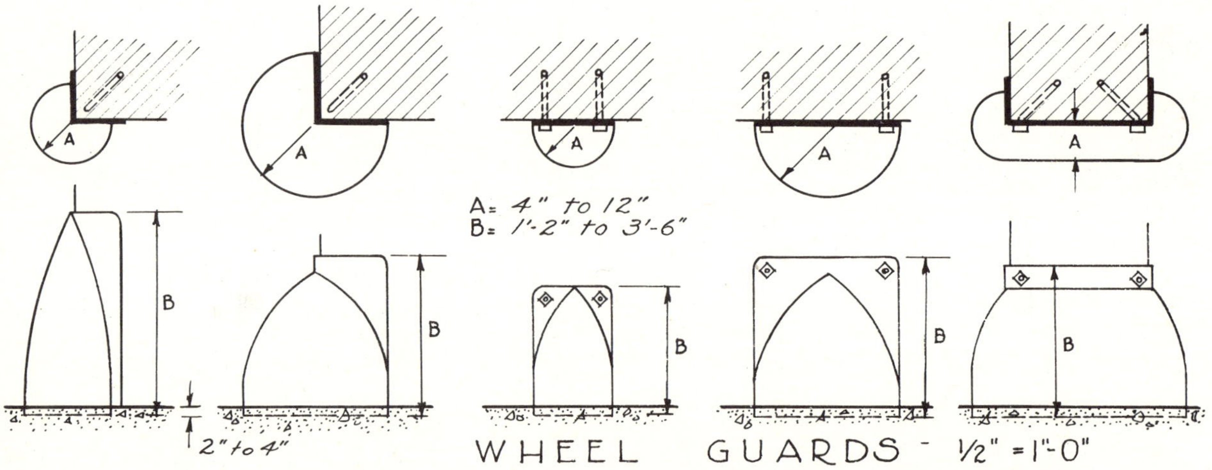
A
B
A= 4" to 12"
B= 1'-2" to 3'-6"
2" to 4"

WHEEL GUARDS - 1/2" = 1'-0"

Used for protection of door jambs, walls and corners. May be combined with corner and column guards above.
Usually made of cast iron, 1/2" minimum thickness. For heavy traffic thicker metal is required.
Other patterns are available. Sizes given are made by most manufacturers, though given pattern may vary.

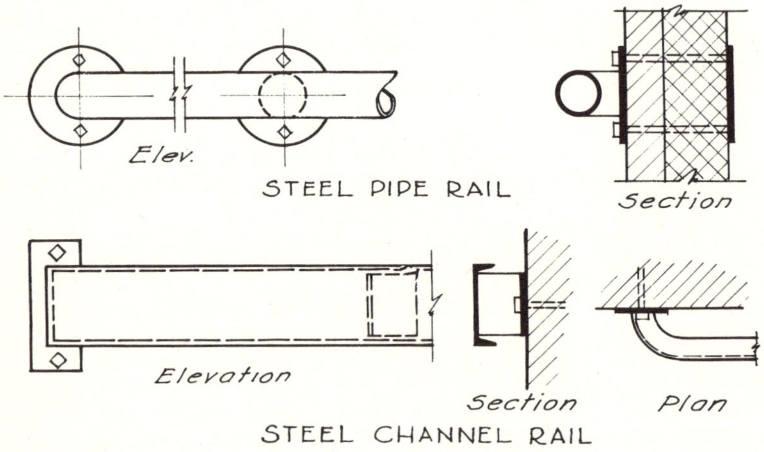
Elev.
STEEL PIPE RAIL
Section
Elevation
Section
Plan
STEEL CHANNEL RAIL

RAIL TYPE GUARDS 1/2" = 1'-0"

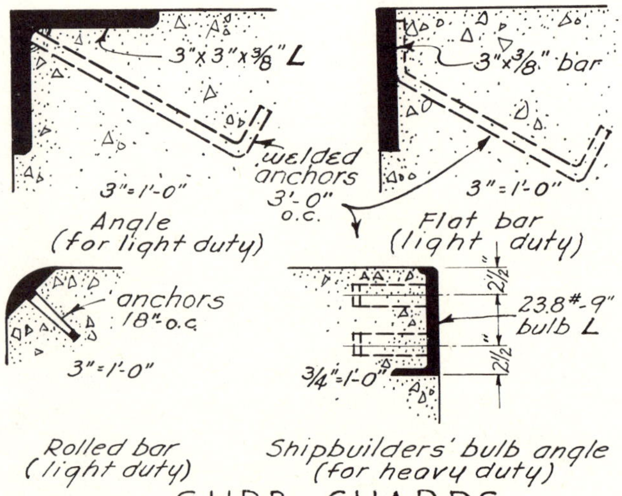
3"x3"x3/8" L
welded anchors 3'-0" o.c.
3" = 1'-0"
Angle (for light duty)
3"x3/8" bar
3" = 1'-0"
Flat bar (light duty)
anchors 18" o.c.
3" = 1'-0"
Rolled bar (light duty)
2 1/2"
23.8#-9" bulb L
2 1/2"
3/4" = 1'-0"
Shipbuilders' bulb angle (for heavy duty)

CURB GUARDS

From "Architectural Metal Handbook," by permission of the National Assoc. of Architectural Metal Mfrs.

GRATINGS

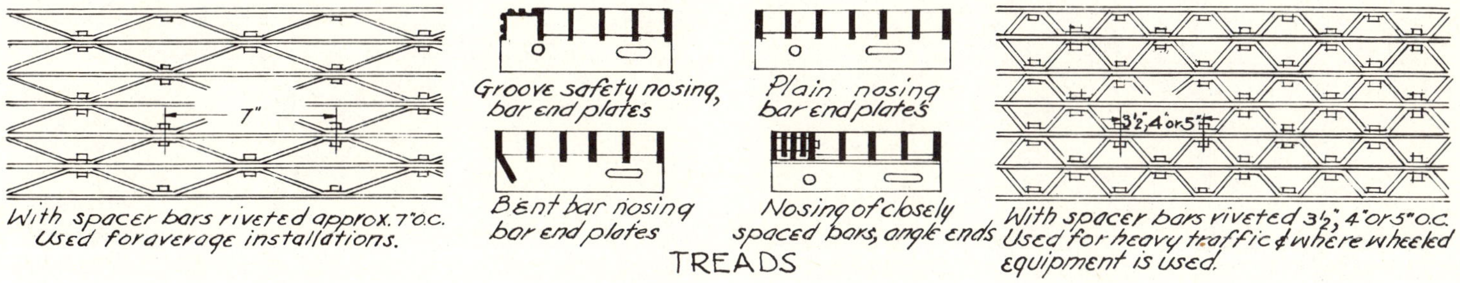
7"
With spacer bars riveted approx. 7" o.c.
Used for average installations.
Groove safety nosing, bar end plates
Plain nosing bar end plates
Bent bar nosing bar end plates
Nosing of closely spaced bars, angle ends
3½", 4" or 5"
With spacer bars riveted 3½", 4" or 5" o.c.
Used for heavy traffic & where wheeled equipment is used.
TREADS

Constructed of flat bearing bars & continuous bent spacer or reticuline bars riveted to the bearing bars. Usually with open ends or may have ends banded with flat bars of similar size as bearing bars, welded across ends. Normal bar spacing ⅞", 1", 1⅛", 1³⁄₁₆" or 1¼". For usual bar sizes, see "Table of Safe Loads for Gratings."

RETICULATED

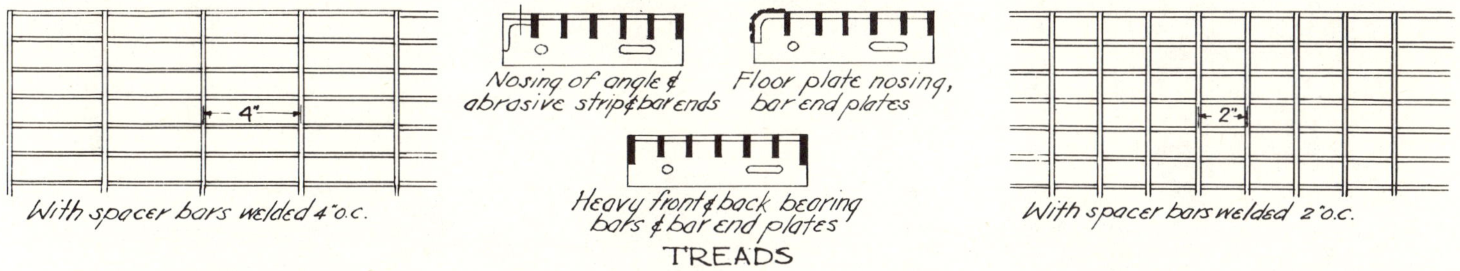
4"
With spacer bars welded 4" o.c.
Nosing of angle & abrasive strip & bar ends
Floor plate nosing, bar end plates
Heavy front & back bearing bars & bar end plates
2"
With spacer bars welded 2" o.c.
TREADS

Constructed of flat bearing bars with spacer bars at right angles. Spacer bars may be square, rectangular or other shape. Spacer bars connected to bearing bars by pressing into prepared slots, or by welding. Usually with open ends, or may have ends banded with flat bars of similar size as bearing bars welded. Nominal bar spacing ⅞", 1", 1⅛", 1³⁄₁₆". For usual bar sizes, see "Table of Safe Load for Gratings."

RECTANGULAR

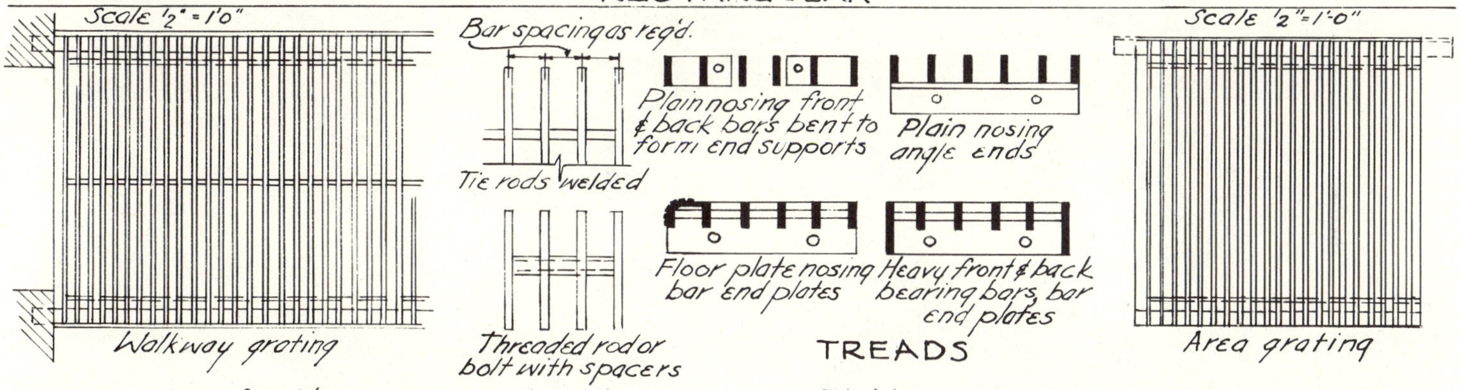
Scale ½" = 1'-0"
Walkway grating
Bar spacing as req'd.
Tie rods welded
Threaded rod or bolt with spacers
Plain nosing front & back bars bent to form end supports
Plain nosing angle ends
Floor plate nosing bar end plates
Heavy front & back bearing bars, bar end plates
TREADS
Scale ½" = 1'-0"
Area grating

Constructed of flat bars connected by rods & spacers or with rods welded. May be constructed with or without frames. When frames are required they may be flat bars, angles, or channels.

Flat bars usually 1" or 1¼" × ³⁄₁₆" or ¼" spaced 1" to 1½" o.c. Tie rods usually ⁵⁄₁₆" or ⅜" round, 15" to 18" o.c. May be constructed of larger size bars & tie rods where long spans or extra loads are involved. This type is often used for screening heavy material.

BAR & SPACER TYPE

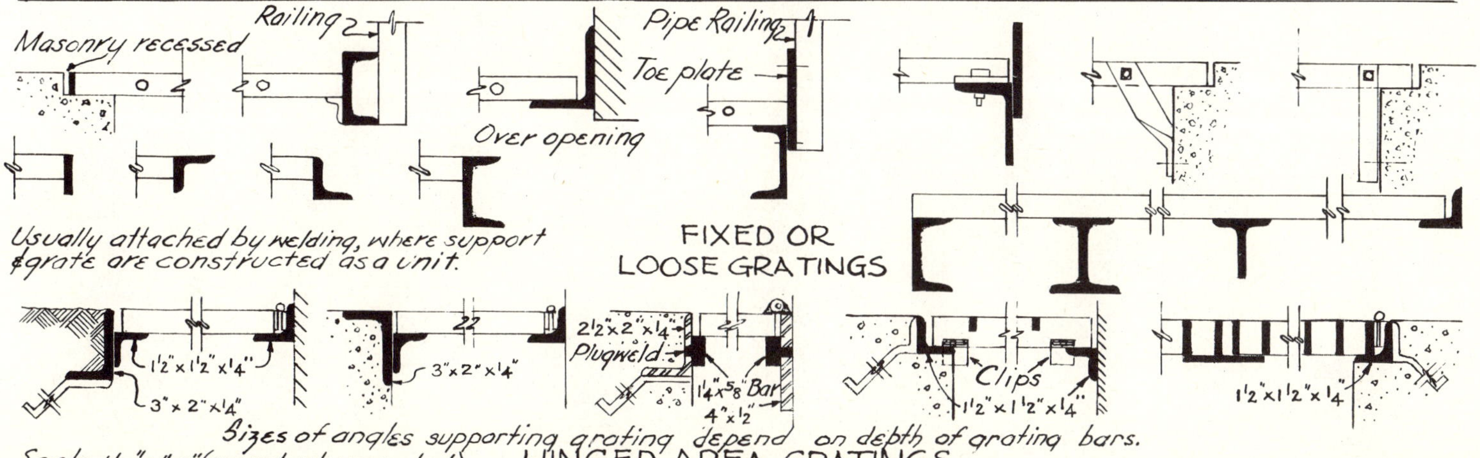
Masonry recessed
Railing
Over opening
Pipe Railing
Toe plate
Usually attached by welding, where support & grate are constructed as a unit.
FIXED OR LOOSE GRATINGS
1½" x 1½" x ¼"
3" x 2" x ¼"
3" x 2" x ¼"
2½" x 2" x ¼"
Plug weld
1¼" x ⅝" Bar
4" x ½"
Clips
1½" x 1½" x ¼"
1½" x 1½" x ¼"
Sizes of angles supporting grating depend on depth of grating bars.

Scale 1½" = 1'-0" (except where noted)

HINGED AREA GRATINGS

from "Architectural Metal Handbook," by permission of the National Association of Architectural Metal Mfrs.

LOAD DATA *for* GRATINGS (EXCEPT EXPANDED METAL)

TABLE OF SAFE LOADS

C—SAFE CONCENTRATED LOAD IN POUNDS PER FOOT OF WIDTH
U—SAFE UNIFORM LOAD IN POUNDS PER SQUARE FOOT   D DEFLECTION IN INCHES

SIZE OF BEARING BARS		SPAN IN FEET AND INCHES												
		2'-0"	2'-6"	3'-0"	3'-6"	4'-0"	4'-6"	5'-0"	5'-6"	6'-0"	6'-6"	7'-0"	8'-0"	9'-0"
3/4" × 1/8"	U	330	222	143										
	D	.085	.134	.192										
	C	330	265	215										
	D	.068	.108	.154										
3/4" × 3/16"	U	500	320	217										
	D	.085	.134	.192										
	C	500	400	325										
	D	.068	.108	.154										
1" × 1/8"	U	600	384	267	188	150								
	D	.064	.099	.143	.195	.256								
	C	600	480	400	330	300								
	D	.051	.080	.115	.156	.205								
1" × 3/16"	U	900	580	400	286	225								
	D	.064	.099	.143	.195	.256								
	C	900	725	600	500	450								
	D	.051	.080	.115	.156	.205								
1 1/4 × 1/8"	U	950	600	420	303	232	184	146	120					
	D	.051	.081	.115	.157	.205	.259	.321	.389					
	C	950	750	630	530	465	415	365	330					
	D	.041	.064	.092	.125	.163	.207	.256	.310					
1 1/4" × 3/16"	U	1425	900	633	457	350	278	220	182					
	D	.051	.081	.115	.157	.205	.259	.321	.389					
	C	1425	1125	950	800	700	625	550	500					
	D	.041	.064	.092	.125	.163	.207	.256	.310					
1 1/2" × 1/8"	U	1365	880	610	445	340	266	220	182	150	128	110		
	D	.043	.067	.094	.131	.166	.216	.267	.324	.385	.440	.522		
	C	1365	1100	915	785	680	600	550	500	450	415	385		
	D	.034	.053	.077	.104	.137	.173	.214	.259	.308	.361	.418		
1 1/2" × 3/16"	U	2050	1320	917	672	512	400	330	273	225	192	164		
	D	.043	.067	.094	.131	.166	.216	.267	.324	.385	.440	.522		
	C	2050	1650	1375	1175	1025	900	825	750	675	625	575		
	D	.034	.053	.077	.104	.137	.173	.214	.259	.308	.361	.418		
1 3/4" × 3/16"	U	2800	1780	1230	915	700	544	440	364	308	262	228	175	133
	D	.038	.057	.082	.112	.147	.185	.229	.276	.330	.387	.450	.580	.737
	C	2800	2225	1860	1600	1400	1225	1100	1000	925	850	800	700	600
	D	.029	.046	.066	.090	.117	.148	.183	.221	.264	.308	.358	.468	.593
2" × 3/16"	U	3650	2340	1618	1200	912	723	580	482	400	346	293	225	178
	D	.032	.050	.072	.099	.128	.163	.201	.243	.289	.341	.397	.516	.651
	C	3650	2925	2425	2100	1825	1625	1450	1325	1200	1125	1025	900	800
	D	.026	.040	.057	.078	.102	.129	.160	.193	.230	.269	.314	.409	.518
2 1/4" × 3/16"	U	4650	2960	2065	1515	1150	912	740	608	516	438	379	288	228
	D	.027	.044	.064	.087	.113	.148	.177	.214	.255	.305	.349	.455	.574
	C	4650	3700	3100	2650	2300	2050	1850	1675	1550	1425	1325	1150	1025
	D	.023	.035	.051	.070	.091	.115	.142	.172	.204	.240	.279	.364	.460

Spans to right of heavy line not recommended.

Maximum bending stress 16 Kips per square inch.

TABLE OF LOAD FACTORS

CLEAR OPENING		LOAD FACTOR	USES
RECTANGULAR	RETICULATED		
5/8"	3/4"	1.40	*Gratings of close spacing for protection of small shoe heels and where small trucking wheels are used.*
3/4"	7/8"	1.25	
7/8"	1"	1.00	
1"	1 1/8"	1.00	*Average spacing, for use in many industrial and commercial locations.*
1 1/8"	1 5/16"	.90	
1 1/4"	1 9/16"	.75	*Wide spacing, used in boiler and engine rooms, and many other industrial purposes.*
1 1/2"	1 11/16"	.66	
2"	2 3/16"	.50	

The Table of Load Factors may be used as an approximate guide for calculating allowable loads on gratings of various types - by applying the load factor given opposite the clear opening of the grating, to the values given in the Table of Safe Loads.
The Table of Safe Loads gives allowable loads for gratings having clear openings between bearing bars of 1", the load factor of these gratings therefore being 1.00.
The slightly larger load value of reticulated gratings over rectangular gratings for the same clear openings is due to the added load value of the reticulated bars. Other type gratings (spool-spaced, welded rods) will support equiv. loads by using heavier bearing bars.

Data from "Architectural Metal Handbook," by permission of the National Assoc. of Architectural Metal Mfrs.

EXPANDED METAL GRATINGS, TRENCH COVERS & STEEL AREA WALLS

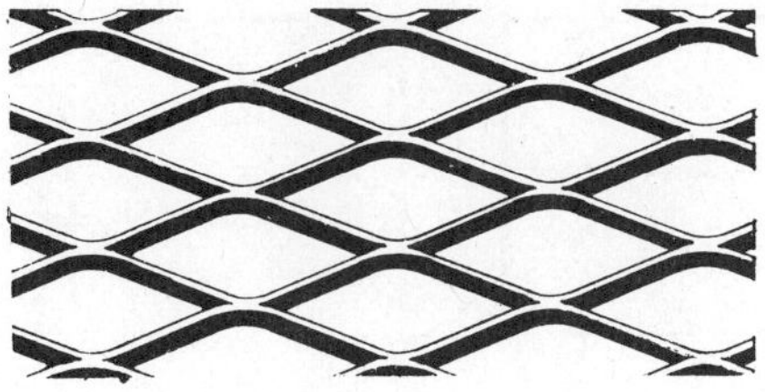

FLATTENED

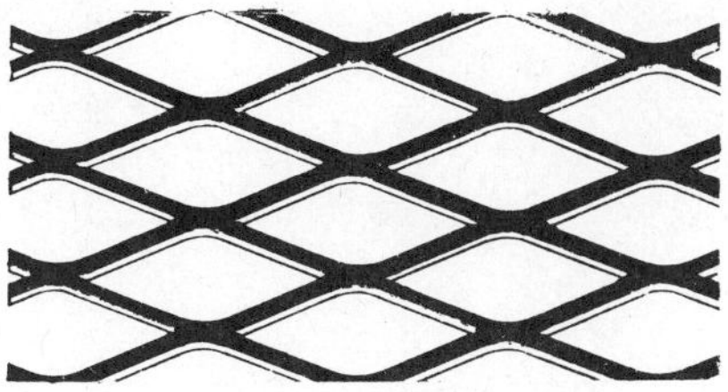

STANDARD

Flattened type used where small trucking wheels may be used.

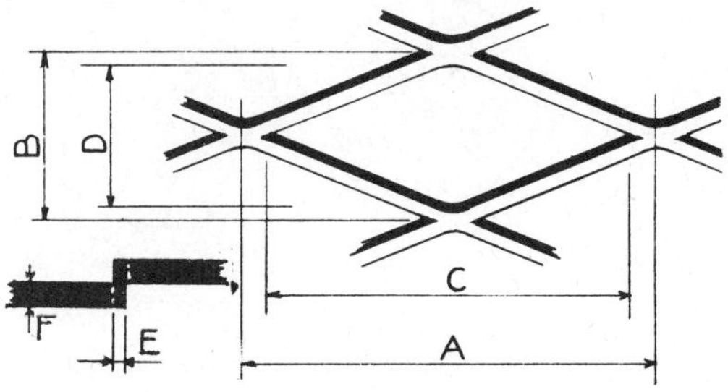
B
D
C
F
E
A

TABLE of DEFLECTIONS for 4 lb. 5.0"x1.39" GRATING								
SPAN	2'-0"		2'-6"		3'-0"		3'-6"	
LOADS	A	B	A	B	A	B	A	B
50#	.027	.032	.056	.078	.092	.167	.149	.325
100	.053	.065	.107	.156	.188	.336	.301	.650
150	.077	.095	.156	.233	.284	.501	.453	.975
200	.112	.127	.208	.311	.374	.668		

NOTE: *Welded fastenings produce less deflection than bolting.*

A - *Deflection in inches for concentrated load in pounds, applied at center of span 12" wide.*

B - *Deflection in inches for uniform load in pounds per square ft. of span.*

Ends are fastened rigidly to supports about 6" on centers.

MESH SIZES						
WEIGHT lbs/sq. ft.	DIMENSIONS in INCHES					
	MESH		OPENING		STRAND	
	A	B	C	D	E	F
3.00	5.33	1.33	3.44	.937	.187	.264
3.12	6.00	2.00	4.87	1.63	.250	.312
4.00	5.00	1.39	3.25	1.00	.224	.300
4.00	5.33	1.33	3.44	.937	.213	.300
4.27	4.00	1.41	2.87	1.00	.250	.300
6.25	5.33	1.41	3.37	.812	.312	.350

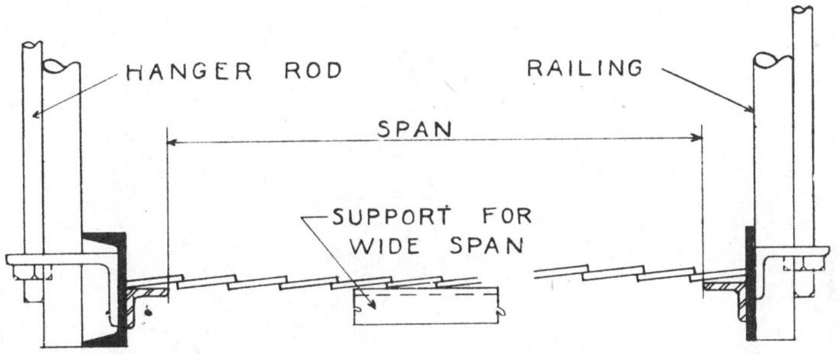
HANGER ROD
RAILING
SPAN
SUPPORT FOR
WIDE SPAN

Grating walkway with channel or flat bar frame, pipe railing and hanger rod supports. Angle, tee, or bar support may be bolted or welded between side frames for wide spans. Size of supports determined by spans and loads.

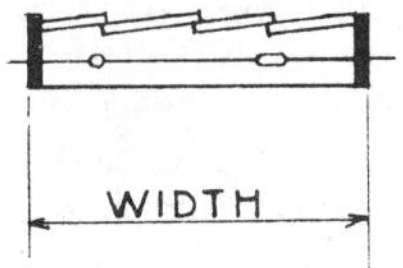
WIDTH

Tread welded to bar frame. Frame may be other constrn.

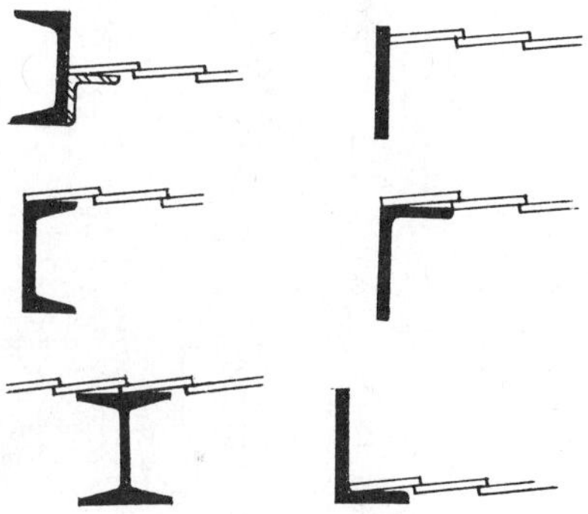

Methods of Fastening

Expanded metal gratings may be welded to bar, angle, or channel for frames and bolted into units or to structural supports. They may also be welded direct to the structural framing when conditions require. Fastenings should be approx. 6" on center

*EXPANDED METAL GRATINGS

Scale 1½" = 1'-0"

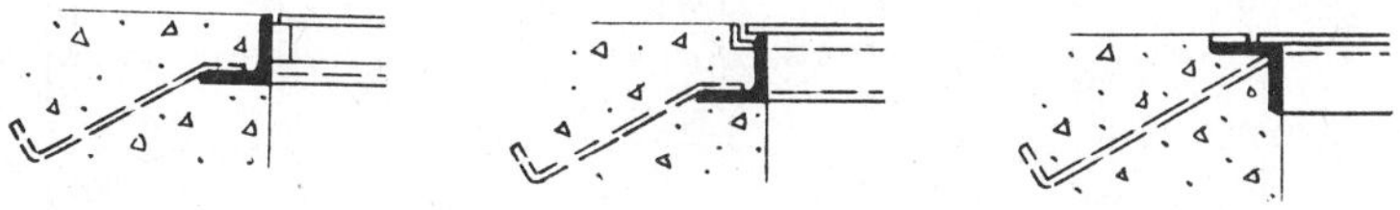

Angle details for Steel Plate type covers.
1½" = 1'-0"

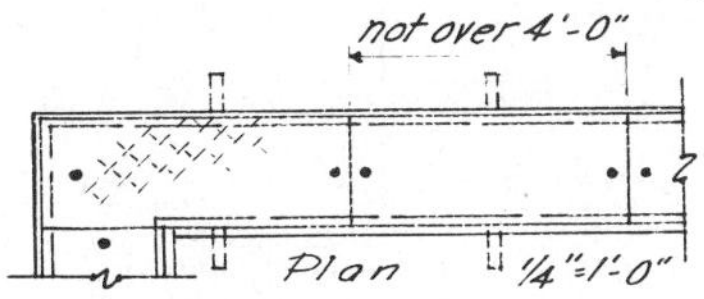
not over 4'-0"
Plan
¼" = 1'-0"

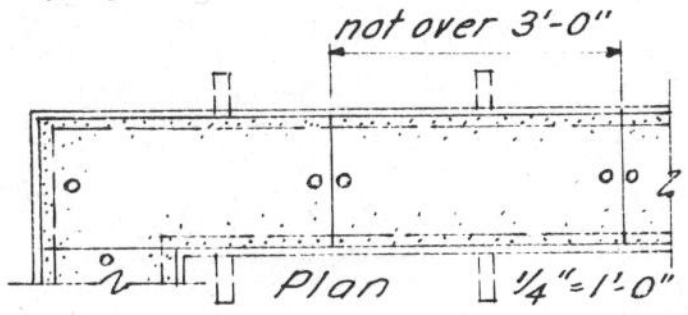
not over 3'-0"
Plan
¼" = 1'-0"

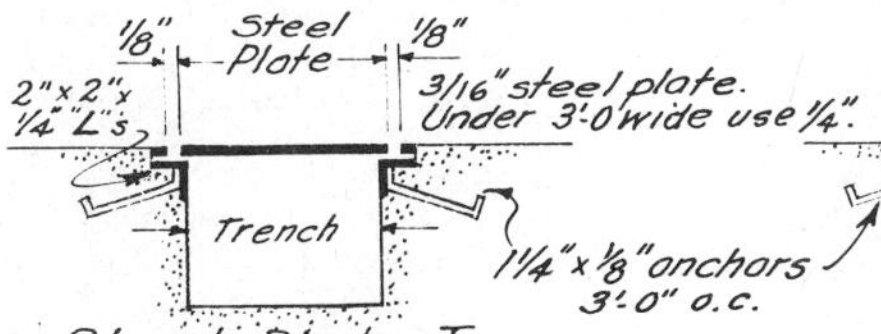
1/8"
Steel Plate
1/8"
2"x2"x¼" L's
3/16" steel plate. Under 3'-0" wide use ¼".
Trench
1¼"x⅛" anchors 3'-0" o.c.

Steel Plate Type
½" = 1'-0"

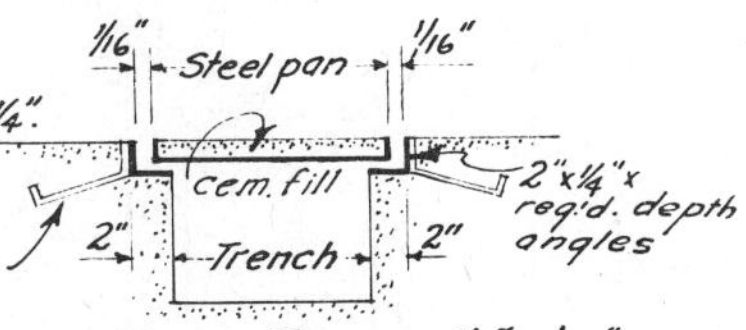
1/16"
Steel pan
1/16"
cem. fill
2"x¼"x req'd. depth angles
2"
Trench
2"

Pan Type ½" = 1'-0"

TRENCH COVERS

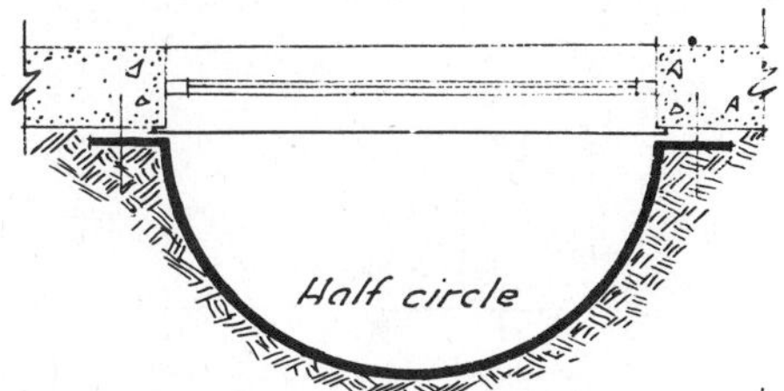
Half circle

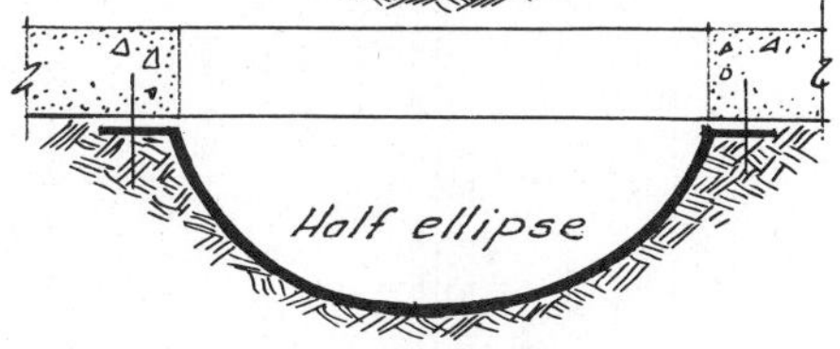
Half ellipse

Plans

Made of 16 ga. galvanized iron: corrugated or ribbed. Dia. - 2'-7" to 5'-11". Heights: 12" to 3'-0".

STEEL AREA WALLS

*From "Architectural Metal Handbook", by permission of the National Assoc. of Architectural Metal Mfrs.

LAUNDRY, WASTE and MAIL CHUTES

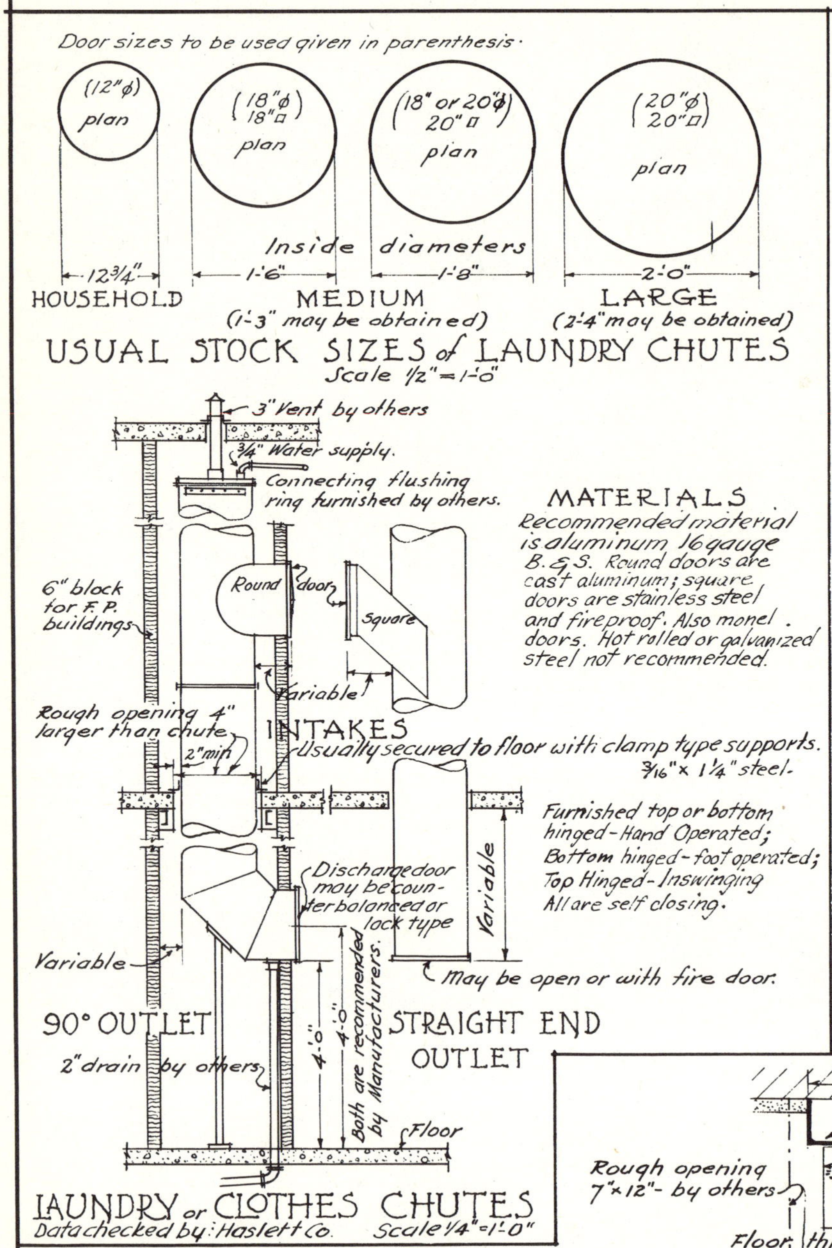
Door sizes to be used given in parenthesis.
(12"ø) plan
(18"ø 18"□) plan
(18" or 20"ø 20"□) plan
(20"ø 20"□) plan
Inside diameters
12¾"
1'-6"
1'-8"
2'-0"
HOUSEHOLD
MEDIUM
(1'-3" may be obtained)
LARGE
(2'-4" may be obtained)
USUAL STOCK SIZES of LAUNDRY CHUTES
Scale ½"=1'-0"
3" Vent by others
¾" Water supply.
Connecting flushing ring furnished by others.
6" block for F.P. buildings
Round door
Square
Variable
Rough opening 4" larger than chute
2" min
INTAKES
Usually secured to floor with clamp type supports. 3/16" x 1¼" steel.
MATERIALS
Recommended material is aluminum 16 gauge B.&S. Round doors are cast aluminum; square doors are stainless steel and fireproof. Also monel doors. Hot rolled or galvanized steel not recommended.
Furnished top or bottom hinged - Hand Operated; Bottom hinged - foot operated; Top Hinged - Inswinging. All are self closing.
Discharge door may be counterbalanced or lock type
Variable
Variable
May be open or with fire door.
4'-0"
4'-0"
Both are recommended by Manufacturers.
90° OUTLET
STRAIGHT END OUTLET
2" drain by others
Floor

LAUNDRY or CLOTHES CHUTES
Data checked by: Haslett Co. Scale ¼"=1'-0"

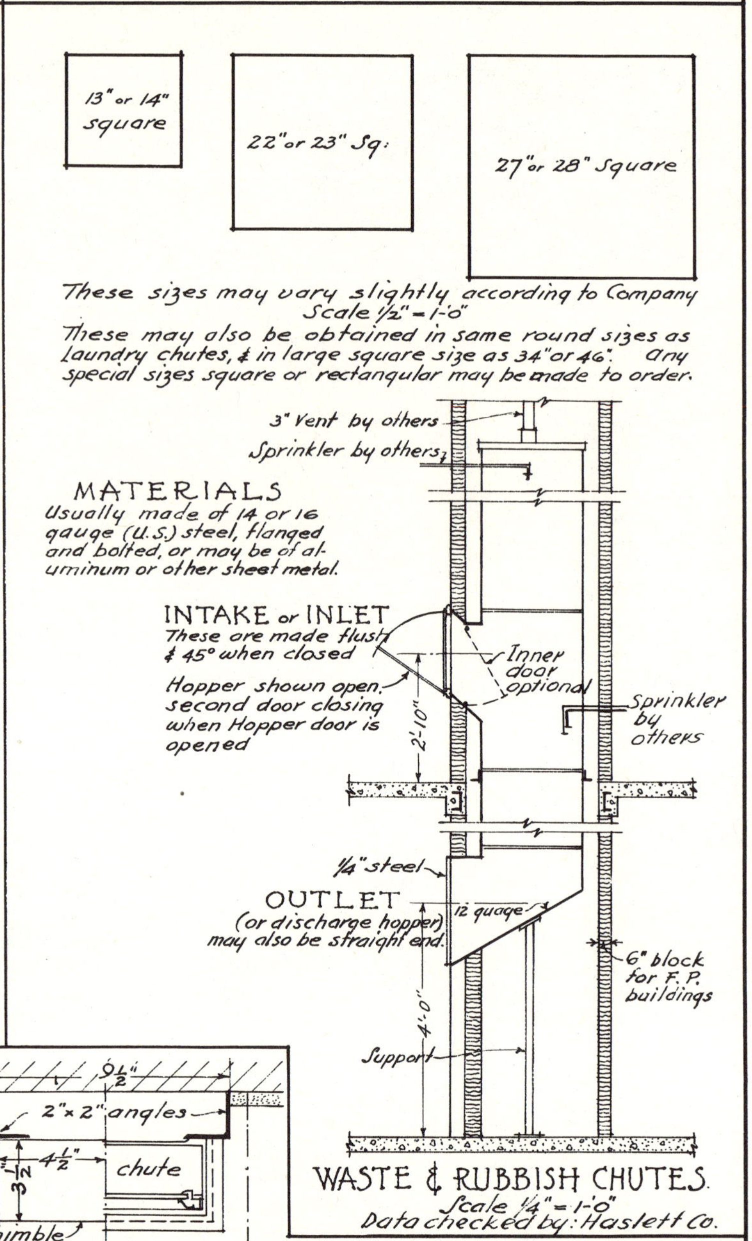
13" or 14" square
22" or 23" Sq.
27" or 28" Square
These sizes may vary slightly according to Company
Scale ½"=1'-0"
These may also be obtained in same round sizes as laundry chutes, & in large square size as 34" or 46". Any special sizes square or rectangular may be made to order.
3" Vent by others
Sprinkler by others
MATERIALS
Usually made of 14 or 16 gauge (U.S.) steel, flanged and bolted, or may be of aluminum or other sheet metal.
INTAKE or INLET
These are made flush & 45° when closed
Hopper shown open, second door closing when Hopper door is opened
Inner door optional
2'-10"
Sprinkler by others
¼" steel
OUTLET
(or discharge hopper) may also be straight end.
12 gauge
6" block for F.P. buildings
4'-0"
Support

WASTE & RUBBISH CHUTES.
Scale ¼"=1'-0"
Data checked by: Haslett Co.

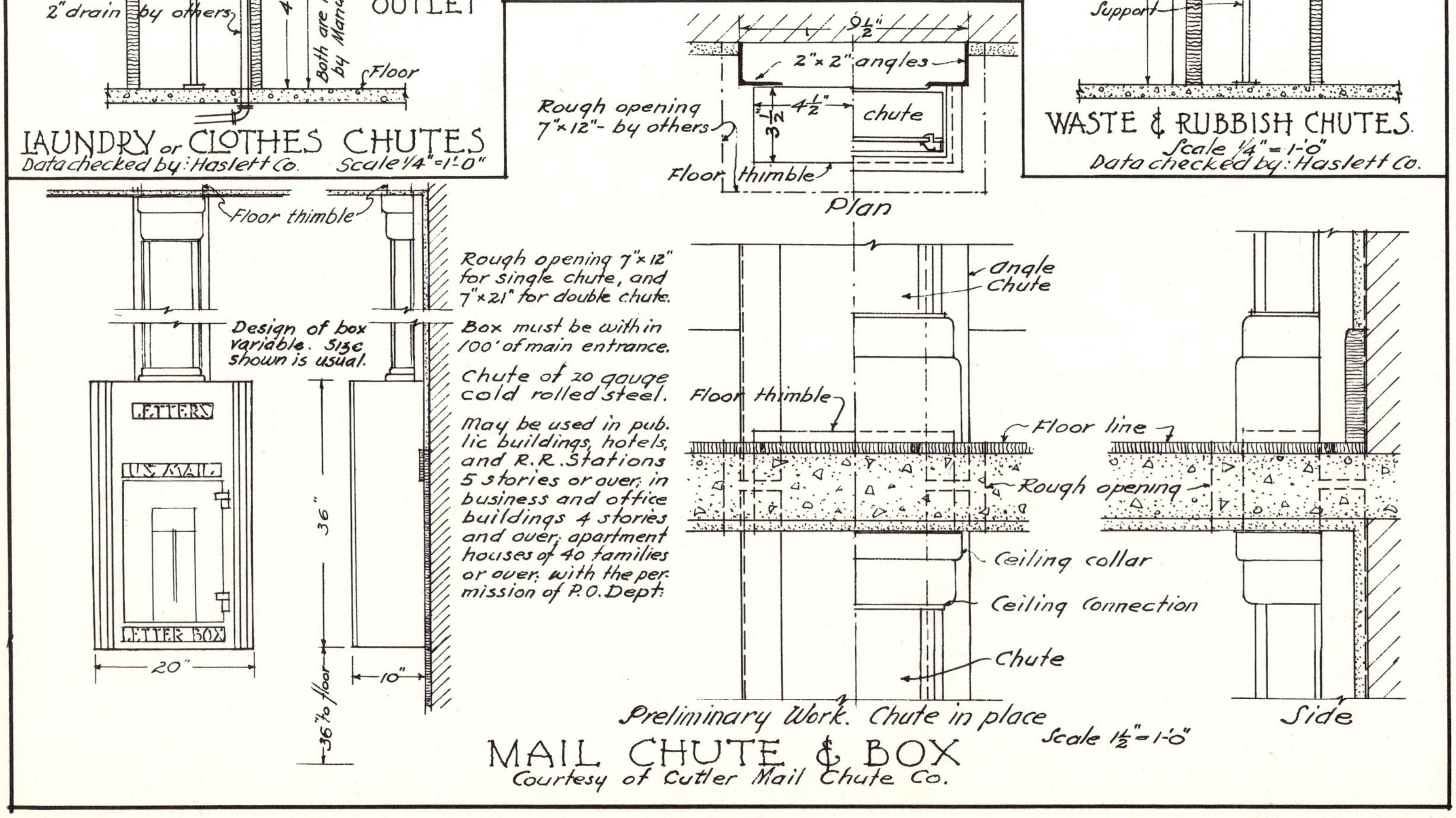
9½"
2"x2" angles
4½"
3½"
chute
Rough opening 7"x12" - by others
Floor thimble
Plan
Floor thimble
Design of box variable. Size shown is usual.
LETTERS
U.S. MAIL
LETTER BOX
20"
36"
36" to floor
10"
Rough opening 7"x12" for single chute, and 7"x21" for double chute.
Box must be within 100' of main entrance.
Chute of 20 gauge cold rolled steel.
May be used in public buildings, hotels, and R.R. Stations 5 stories or over; in business and office buildings 4 stories and over; apartment houses of 40 families or over; with the permission of P.O. Dept.
Angle Chute
Floor thimble
Floor line
Rough opening
Ceiling collar
Ceiling Connection
Chute
Preliminary Work. Chute in place
Side
Scale 1½"=1'-0"

MAIL CHUTE & BOX
Courtesy of Cutler Mail Chute Co.

ACCESS DOORS and COAL CHUTES

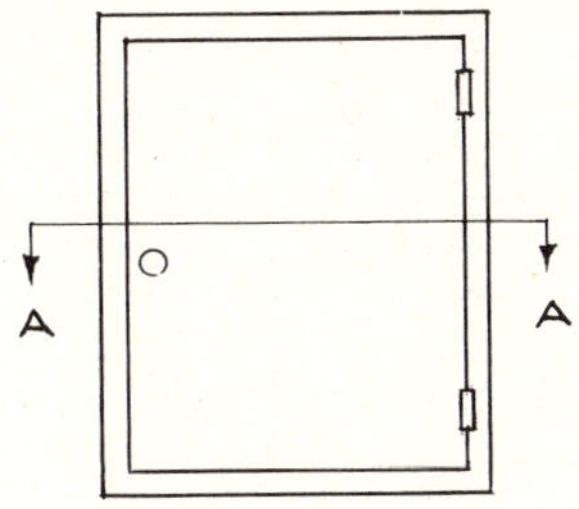
A
A

SWING TYPE

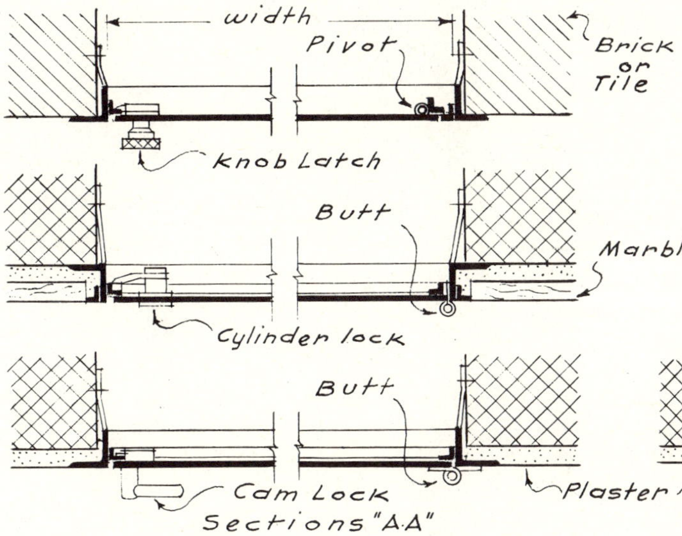
width
Pivot
Brick or Tile
knob Latch
Butt
Marble
Cylinder lock
Butt
Cam Lock
Plaster

Sections "A-A"

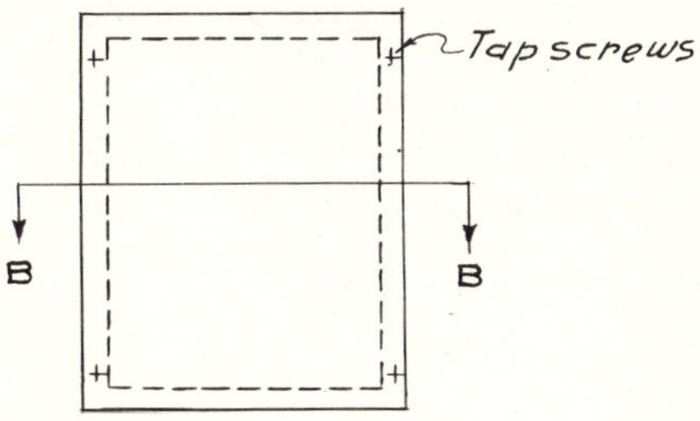
Tap screws
B
B

REMOVABLE TYPE

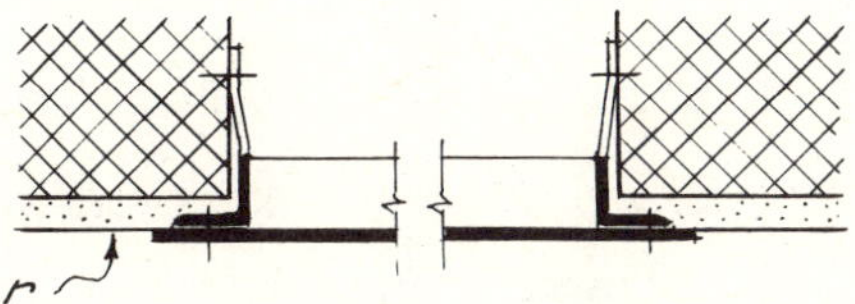

Section "B-B"

Frames usually set into bldg. construction & door constructed to fit later. Doors may be hinged, set in with clips or fastened with screws. Hinges may be butt, pivot or surface. Assorted stock sizes from 8" x 8" to 24" x 36"

A C C E S S D O O R S

sections 1 1/2" = 1'-0"

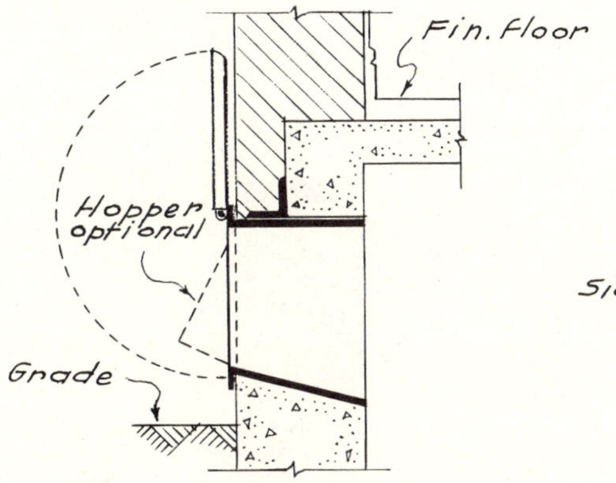
Fin. Floor
Hopper optional
Grade

FOUNDATION COAL CHUTE-SECTION

Used where the coal room ceiling is high enough above grade to allow space for the chute.

TYPE OF DOOR	NOMINAL DOOR SIZE	
	width	height
Solid steel or	24"	18"
glazed 3 lights	33"	24"

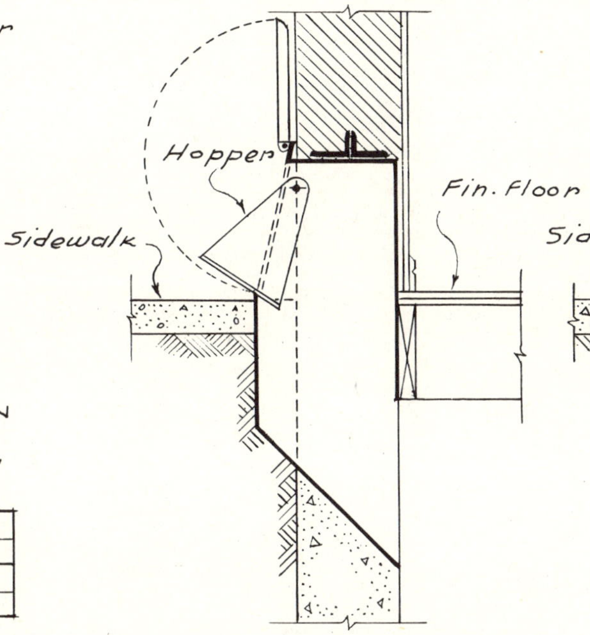
Hopper
Sidewalk
Fin. Floor

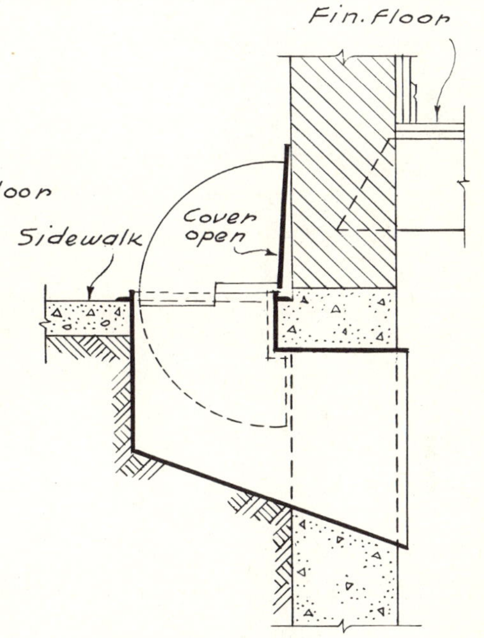
Fin. Floor
Sidewalk
Cover open

FOUNDATION COAL CHUTE-SECTION

Used where the first floor is on or near grade level. Body of the chute extending down into the foundation.

TYPE OF DOOR	NOMINAL DOOR SIZE	
	width	height
Solid steel	25"	18"
	33"	22"

GRADE LINE COAL CHUTE SECTION

Used where the first floor is on or near grade level.

TYPE OF DOOR	NOMINAL DOOR SIZE	
	width	length
cast malleable iron	26"	19"
	32"	21"
	24"	16"
steel floor plate	19"	19"
	21"	26"
	27"	32"

Scale : 1/2" = 1'-0"

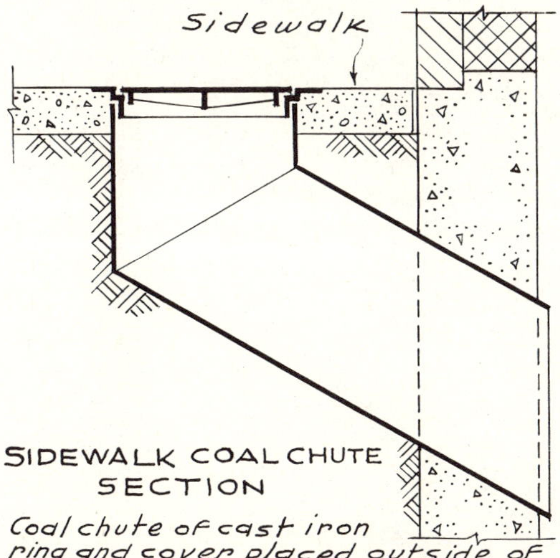
Sidewalk

SIDEWALK COAL CHUTE SECTION

Coal chute of cast iron ring and cover placed outside of building and connected to coal storage by steel hopper of 12 or 14 gauge.

Notes:

Coal chutes are usually constructed of steel or malleable iron, and are set into the building walls during construction.
The sizes given are nominal.
For exact dimensions and construction consult manufacturers.

C O A L C H U T E S

Data from "Architectural Metal Handbook" National Association of Architectural Metal Manufacturers

WOVEN WIRE GRILLES & VENTS

GAUGE of WIRE & MESH SIZE.

Wasburn & Moen Gauge

WIRE SHOWN FULL SIZE WITH DECIMAL & FRACTIONAL EQUIVALENT

Decimal	Fraction	Number	Size of Wire	Mesh	Decimal	Fraction	Number	Size of Wire	Mesh
.2437	1/4"	3		—	.1620	5/32" +	8		2"
.2253	7/32"	4		—	.1483	5/32" −	9		1¾"
.2070	13/64"	5		—	.1350	9/64"	10		1½"
.1920	3/16"	6		2½"	.1205	1/8"	11		1¼"
.1770	11/64"	7		2¼"	.1055	7/64"	12		1"
					.0915	3/32"	13		
					.0800	5/64"	14		¾"
					.0625	1/16"	16		3/8 or 1/2

RECOMMENDED USES FOR VARIOUS MESHES AND FRAMES

WIRE & MESH	FRAME	USES	NOTES
3/8" Mesh # 16 Wire 1/2" Mesh # 15 Wire Square or Diamond Mesh	1/4" Round 1/2" or 5/8" Channel 1/2" × 1/8" Flat	Radiator screens & grilles	Can be supplied in copper, brass or bronze also
3/4" Mesh # 14 Wire Square or Diamond Mesh	5/16" Round or 3/4" Channel	Air intake screens, Bird screens, Church windows	Should be galvanized after fabrication or made of bronze
1" Mesh # 12 Wire Square or Diamond Mesh	3/8" Round or 1" Channel	Basement window guards, Shelving Skylight screens, Pipe railing screens.	Diamond Mesh for strength. Round frame for exterior.
1¼" Mesh # 11 Wire Square or Diamond Mesh	3/8" Round or 1" Channel	Same as 1" Mesh # 12 wire Radiator guards	
1¼" Mesh # 8 Wire Diamond Mesh	1¼" Channel	Heavy duty partitions, as for tool cribs, elevator shafts stock rms.	Ideal for factory use where trucking is done.
1½" Mesh # 10 Wire Diamond Mesh 2" Mesh # 8 Wire	1" Channels	Stockrooms, Toolrooms, Switchboards, Transformers, Eleva. shafts, Fire escapes, Cashier cages, Office partitions, Corridors, Runways, Stair enclosures, Locker rooms, Storerooms, Gym. window guards, lockers, Elevator car tops & safety gates, Radiator guards, Porch grilles Shelves Etc.	1½" Diamond Mesh # 10 gauge wire in 1" channel frames is standard construction & is especially recommended for economy, strength & appearance.
1¾" Mesh # 9 Wire Diamond Mesh	3/8" Round 1" Channel.	Door & Window guards	Usual specification for insurance protection
2¼" Mesh # 7 Wire 2½" Mesh # 6 Wire Diamond Mesh	7/16" Round frames 1½" Channel	Wire roof signs Fences, Porch screens	Should be galvanized after fabrication

Woven wire available in stainless steel, aluminum, brass, bronze, copper, monel etc. Wire flat, square or round, pressed, crimp.

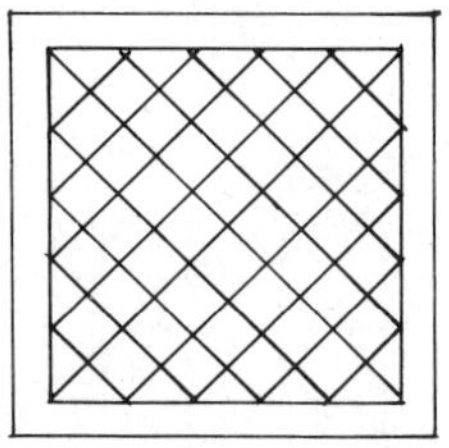

DIAMOND MESH VENT

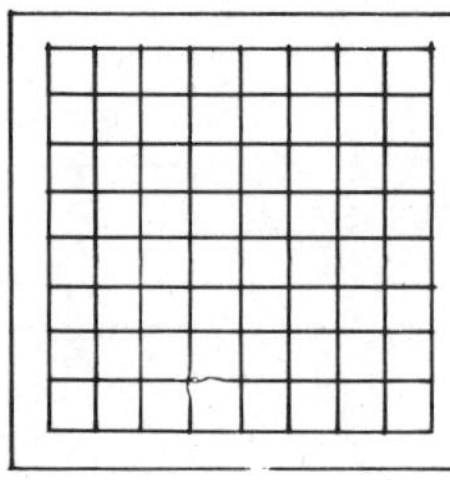

SQUARE MESH GRILLES

Mesh	3/4"	1"	1¼"	1½"
Wire	14	12	11	10

Frame - Angles 1" to 2"
" Channels 3/4 to 1½"

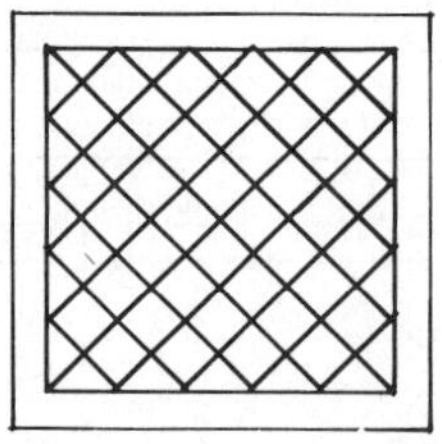

FLATWIRE DIAMOND RADIATOR GRILLES

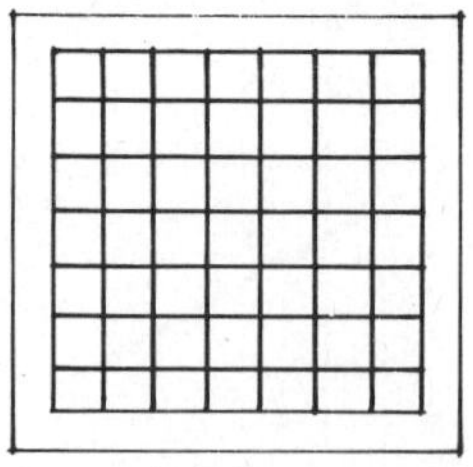

FLATWIRE SQUARE & BANK CAGES

Mesh	3/4"	1"	1¼"	1½"	2"
Flatwire	3/16"	3/16"-1/4	1/4"-5/16	5/16"-3/8	3/8"

Frame - Angles 1" to 2" - Channels 3/4 to 1½"

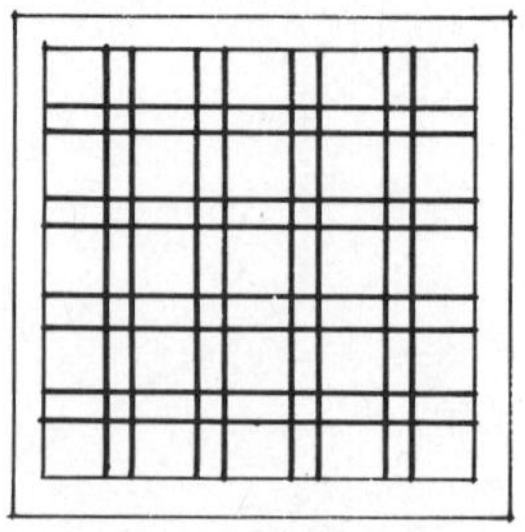

DOUBLE STRAND FLATWIRE SQUARE

Many designs available

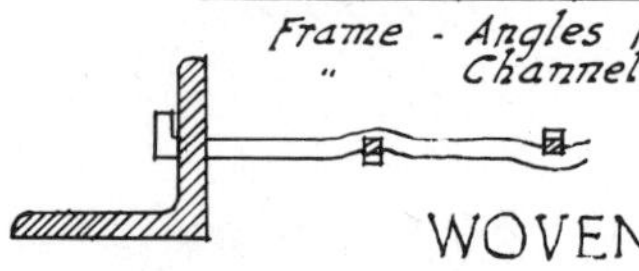

Angle Frame

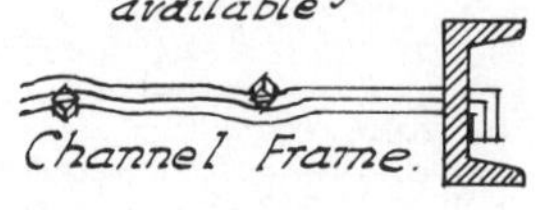

Channel Frame.

WOVEN WIRE FOR VENTS RADIATOR GRILLES & BANK SCREENS.

Data checked by: National Association of Architectural Metal Manufacturers

CHAIN LINK FENCES

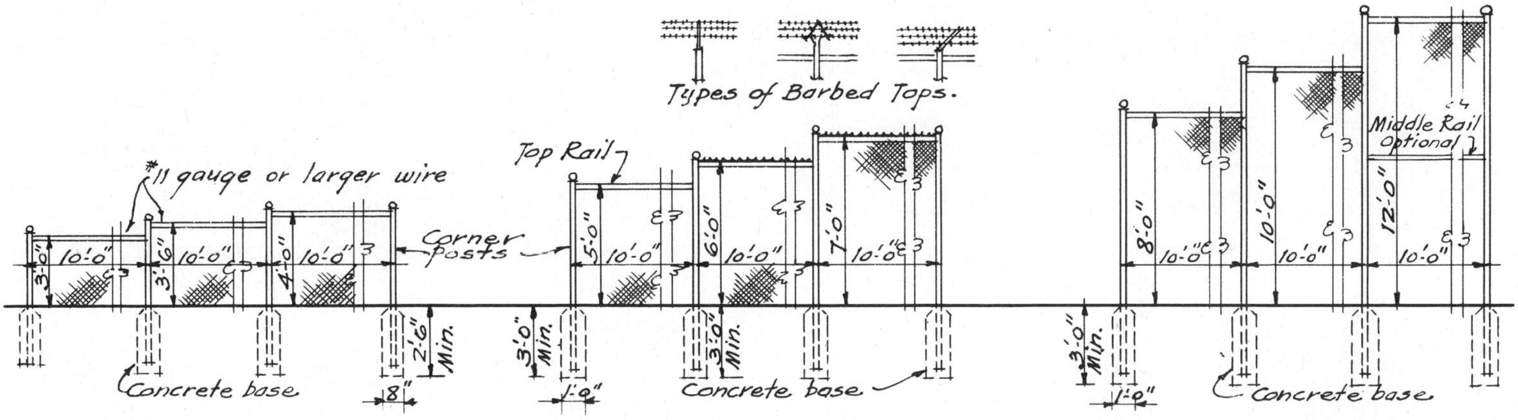
Types of Barbed Tops.
#11 gauge or larger wire
Top Rail
Corner posts
3'-0"
3'-6"
4'-0"
10'-0"
5'-0"
6'-0"
7'-0"
8'-0"
12'-0"
Middle Rail Optional
2'-6" Min.
3'-0" Min.
8"
1'-0"
Concrete base

FOR SMALL HOUSES, LAWNS, ETC.

FOR LARGE ESTATES, INDUSTRIAL, SCHOOLS, INSTITUTIONS.
Barbed Tops are often used on these.
Scale 1/8" = 1'-0".

FOR TENNIS COURTS & SPECIAL HIGH PROTECTION.

MATERIALS:

Wires- Gauge- Usually #11 or #9 W.&M. for specially rugged fence use #6. for tennis courts usually #11.
Mesh - Usually 2". For tennis courts usually 1 5/8" or 1 3/4" of chain link steel hot dip galvanized after weaving. Top and bottom selvage may be barbed or knuckled.

Corner & End Posts: For Lawn fences usually 2" O.D.
For Estate fences 2" for low and 2 1/2" for medium and 3" O.D. for heavy or high
For Tennis Courts 3"-O.D.

Line or Intermediate Posts: For Lawn 1 5/8" or 2" O.D. round.
For Estate, etc. 2", 2 1/4", 2 1/2" H or I sections.
For Tennis Courts 2 1/2" round O.D. or 2 1/4" H or I sections.

Gate Posts - The same or next size larger than the corner posts. Footings for gate posts 3'-6" deep.
Top Rails - 1 5/8" O.D. except some lawn fence may be 1 3/8" O.D.
Middle Rails - on 12'-0" fence same as top rail.
Gates - single or double any width desired.
Post Spacing - Line posts 10'-0" o.c. 8'-0" o.c. may be used on heavy construction.

The above sizes are not standard but merely represent the average sizes used.
Data checked by, National Assoc. of Architectural Metal Mfrs.

O.D. = Outside Diameter

CHAIN LINK FENCES

A.S.A SHEDULE 40 PIPE SIZES	SWING GATE OPENINGS GATE OPENINGS SINGLE GATE	GATE OPENINGS DOUBLE GATE
2 1/2"	To 6'-0"	up to 12'-0"
3 1/2"	over 6' to 13'	over 12' to 26'
6"	over 13' to 18'	over 26' to 36'
8"	over 18' to 32'	over 36' to 64'

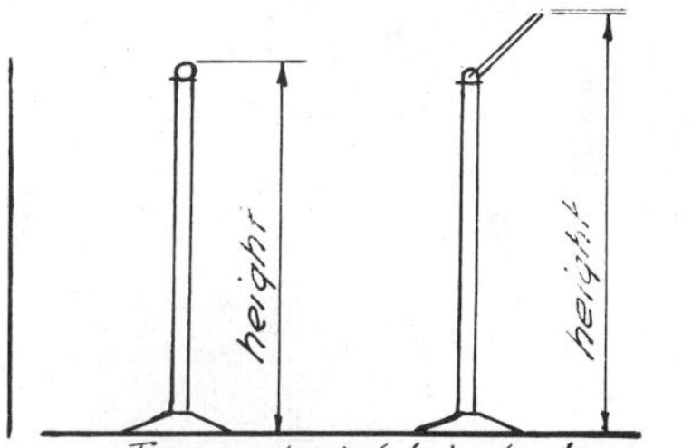
height
height

Fence height is to top of post or to top strand of barbed wire.

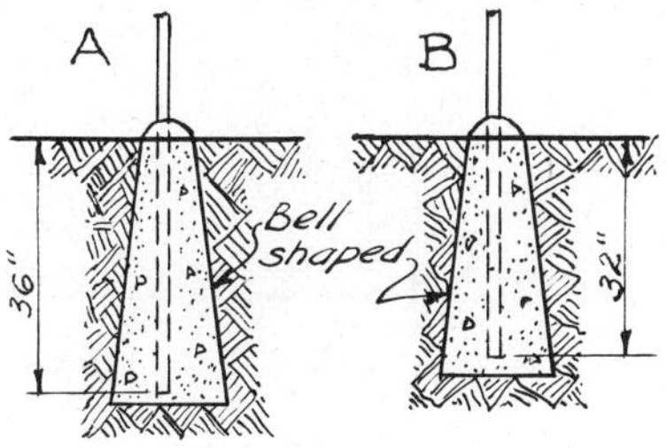
A
B
Bell shaped
36"
32"

A Terminal corner & gate post holes. 12" min. dia. at top by 40" deep. Posts set a full 36" into hole.

B Line post holes. 8" min. dia. at top by 36" deep. Posts set a full 32" into hole.

Galvanized chain link fences also made by Alcoa.

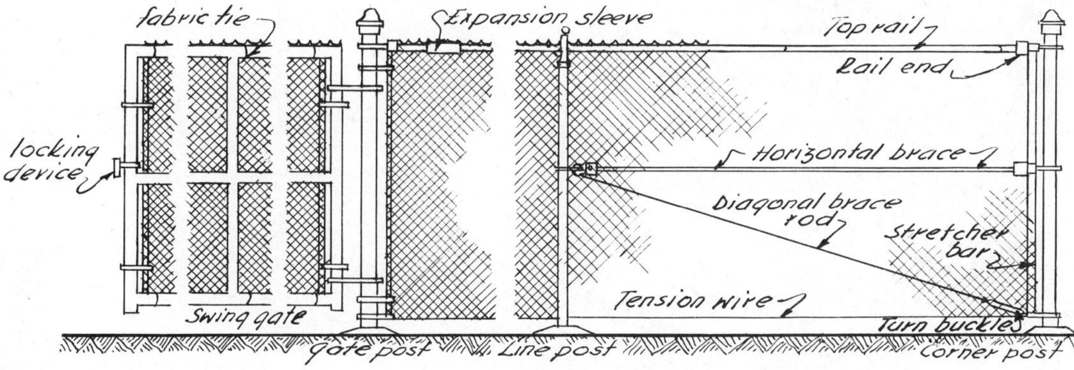
fabric tie
Expansion sleeve
Top rail
Rail end
locking device
Horizontal brace
Diagonal brace rod
Stretcher bar
Tension wire
Turn buckle
Swing gate
Gate post
Line post
Corner post

Note: For fences 5'-0" and taller a horizontal or diagonal brace, or both, is used for greater stability.
Post spacing should be equidistant and should not exceed 10'-0" o.c.

ALUMINUM CHAIN LINK FENCES

Data supplied by Aluminum Company of America.

WIREWORK

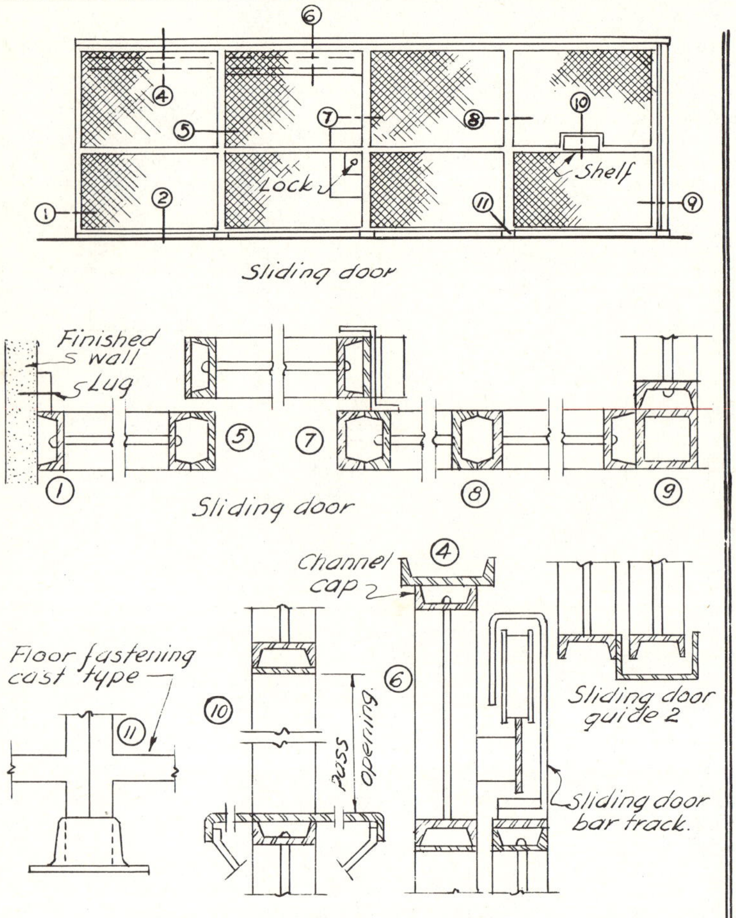
6
4
5
7
8
10
Shelf
Lock
1
2
11
9
Sliding door
Finished wall
Lug
5
7
1
Sliding door
8
9
Channel cap
4
Floor fastening cast type
11
10
Pass opening
6
Sliding door guide 2
Sliding door bar track.

WIRE MESH SLIDING DOOR PARTITION

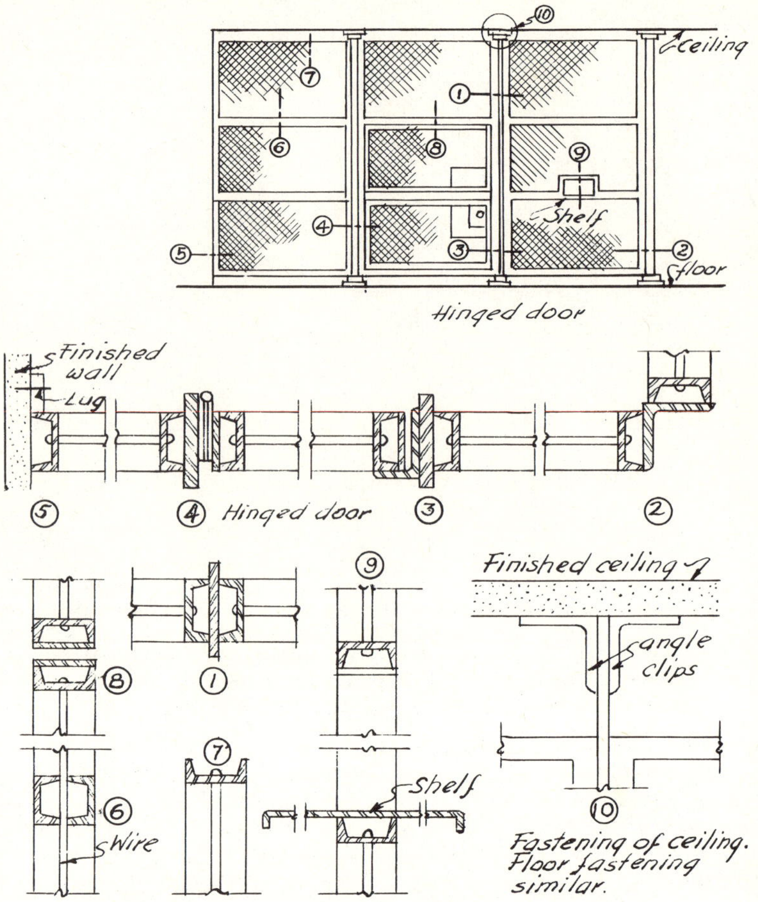
10
Ceiling
7
1
6
8
9
Shelf
5
4
3
2
Floor
Hinged door
Finished wall
Lug
5
4 Hinged door
3
2
9
Finished ceiling
angle clips
8
1
7
6
Wire
Shelf
10
Fastening of ceiling. Floor fastening similar.

FLOOR TO CEILING HINGED DOOR PARTITION

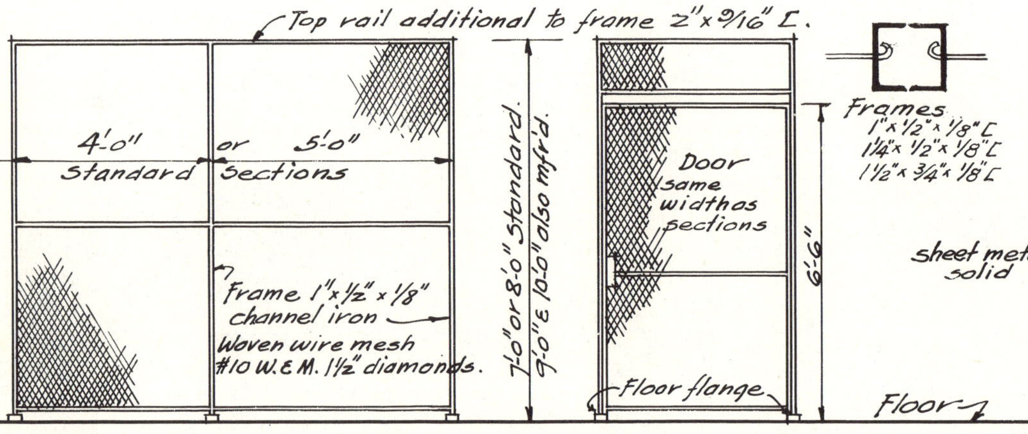
Top rail additional to frame 2" x 9/16" ⊏.
4'-0" Standard
or 5'-0" Sections
Frame 1" x 1/2" x 1/8" channel iron
Woven wire mesh #10 W. & M. 1 1/2" diamonds.
7'-0" or 8'-0" standard. 9'-0" & 10'-0" also mfr'd.
Door same width as sections
6'-6"
Floor flange
Frames 1" x 1/2" x 1/8" ⊏ 1 1/4" x 1/2" x 1/8" ⊏ 1 1/2" x 3/4" x 1/8" ⊏
Floor

STANDARD SECTIONS

Standards of the National Association of Architectural Metal Mfrs.

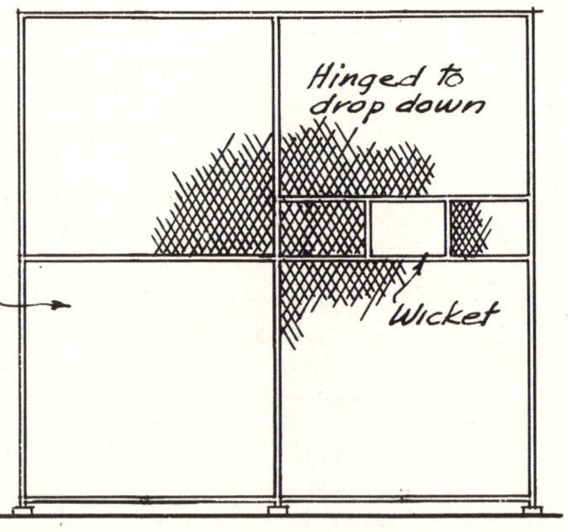
Hinged to drop down
sheet metal solid
Wicket

SPECIAL SECTIONS.

WIRE PARTITIONS.

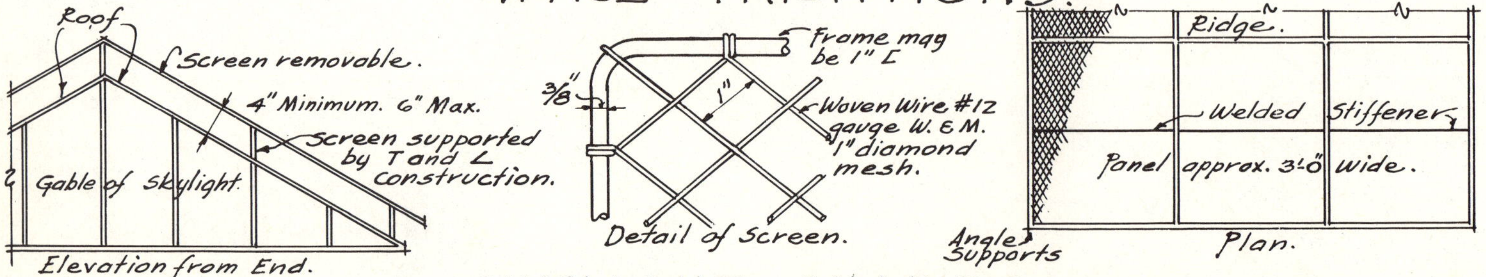
Roof
Screen removable.
4" Minimum. 6" Max.
Screen supported by T and L construction.
Gable of skylight.
Elevation from End.
Frame may be 1" ⊏
3/8"
1"
Woven Wire #12 gauge W. & M. 1" diamond mesh.
Detail of Screen.
Ridge.
Welded Stiffener
Panel approx. 3'-0" wide.
Angle Supports
Plan.

SKYLIGHT GUARDS

Data reviewed by National Association of Architectural Metal Mfrs.

WOVEN WIRE WINDOW GUARDS

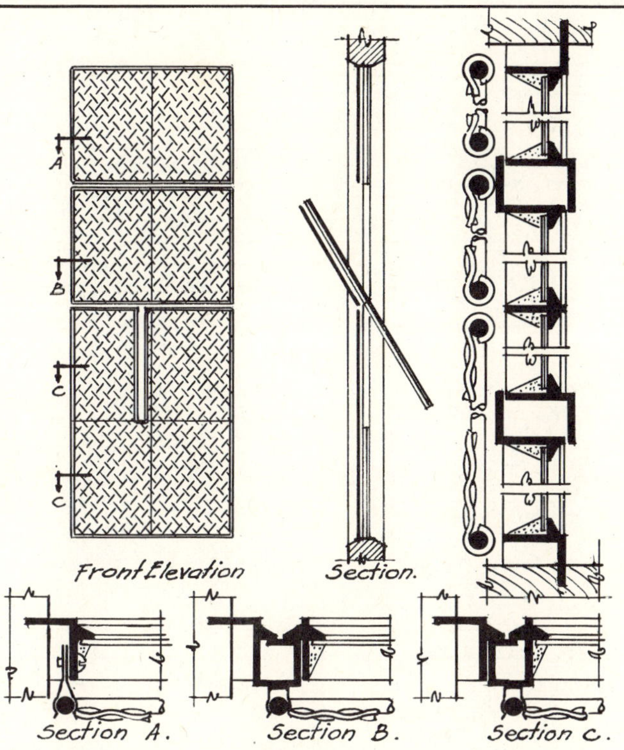
A
B
C
C
Front Elevation
Section.
Section A.
Section B.
Section C.

DETAILS OF REMOVABLE WIRE MESH WINDOW GUARDS

Applied to steel sash windows with pivoted ventilators by means of spring clips.

For sizes see footnote.

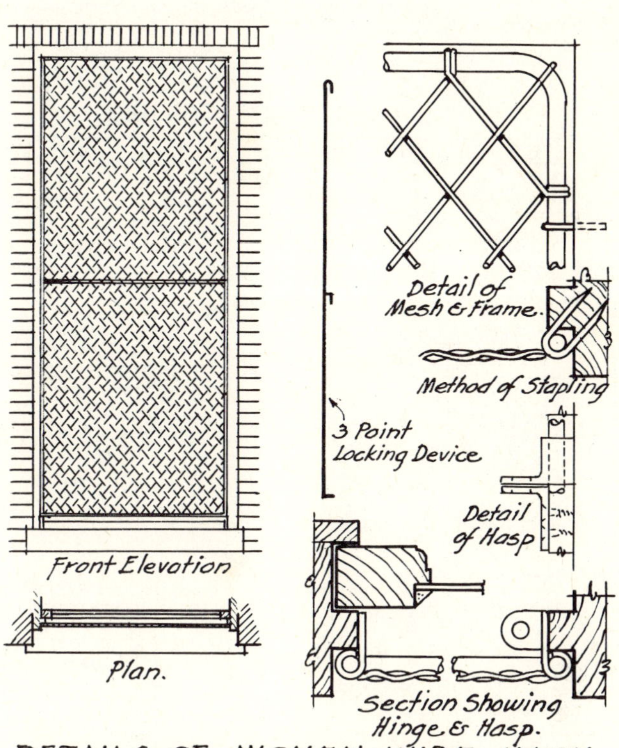
Front Elevation
Plan.
Detail of Mesh & Frame.
Method of Stapling
3 Point Locking Device
Detail of Hasp
Section Showing Hinge & Hasp.

DETAILS OF WOVEN WIRE MESH WINDOW GUARDS

Especially recommended for exterior use on windows.

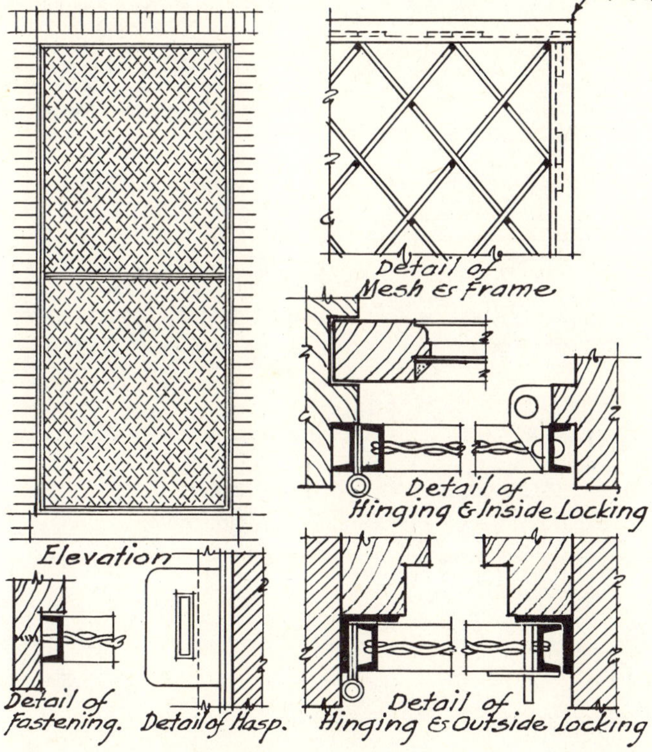
Elevation
Detail of Mesh & Frame
Detail of Hinging & Inside Locking
Detail of Fastening.
Detail of Hasp.
Detail of Hinging & Outside Locking

DOUBLE HUNG WINDOW WITH GUARD IN CHANNEL FRAME

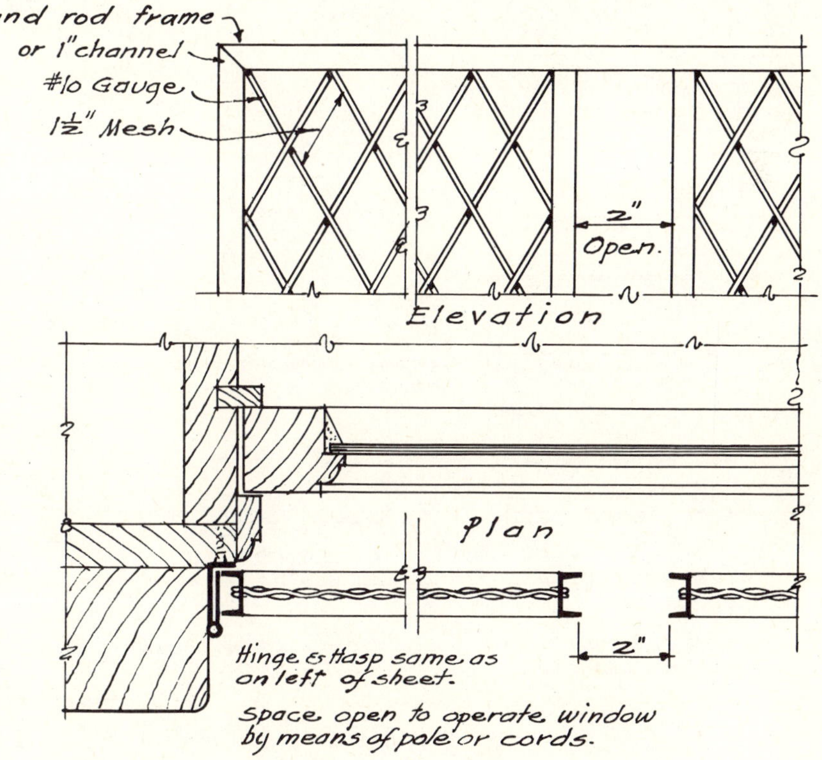
Round rod frame or 1" channel
#10 Gauge
1½" Mesh
2"
Open.
Elevation
Plan
2"
Hinge & Hasp same as on left of sheet.
Space open to operate window by means of pole or cords.

DOUBLE HUNG WINDOW WITH GUARD IN CHANNEL FRAME - TYPE FOR GYMNASIUM

CHANNEL FRAMES

Space:	Wire & Mesh:	Frame:
Basement Window guards.	1" Mesh - #12 Wire.	3/8" round or 1" channel
Other guards (except gymns). . . .	1¾" " - #9 "	3/8" " or 1" "

Data reviewed by National Association of Architectural Metal Mfrs.

GRILLES

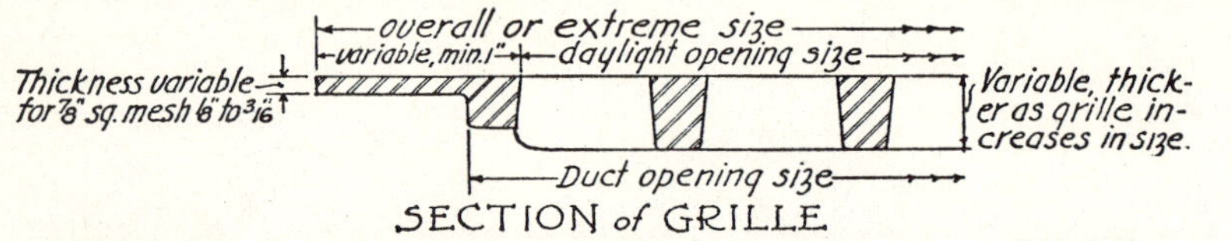
overall or extreme size
variable, min. 1"
daylight opening size
Thickness variable for 7/8" sq. mesh 1/8" to 3/16"
Variable, thicker as grille increases in size.
Duct opening size

SECTION of GRILLE

MATERIALS	STANDARD SQ. MESH OR LATTICE			
	Sq. holes	Bars	Free area	Margin
Iron, Brass, Bronze, Monel, Aluminum	1/2"	1/4"	44%	Margin is variable from 1" to 2"+
	3/4"	1/4" ±	56%	
	7/8"	1/4" ±	61%	

All details are 1/2 Full Size. "Finish" as herein used refers to finishing material adjacent to grille frame.

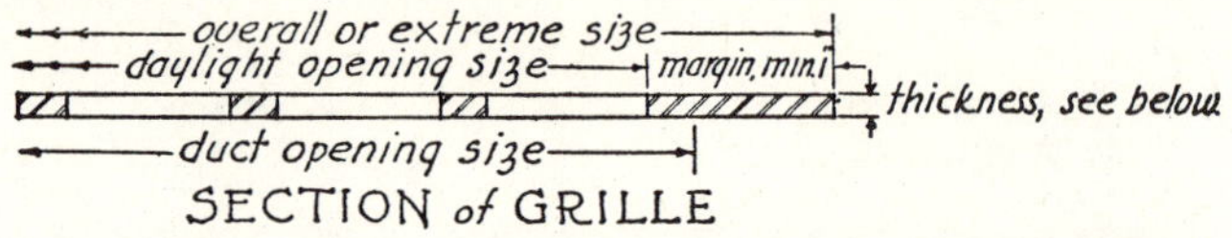
overall or extreme size
daylight opening size
margin, min. 1"
thickness, see below
duct opening size

SECTION of GRILLE

MATERIALS	STANDARD SQ. MESH			DIAGONAL MESH		
	Sq. holes	Bars	Free area	Sq. holes	Bars	Free area
B&S Gauge:- Brass, bronze, aluminum, nickel silver. U.S.S. Gauge:- Steel, monel, and stainless steel. Gauges #16 to #3, #12 most common; large grilles #10, small grilles #12 or #14	1/2"	3/16"-1/4"	48%-45%	1/2"	1/4"	43%
	5/8"	1/4"-3/8"	51%	3/4"	1/4"	56%
	3/4"	1/4"	57%	1"	1/4"	62%
	7/8"	1/4"	60%			
	1"	1/4"	65%			

CAST GRILLES

STAMPED GRILLES

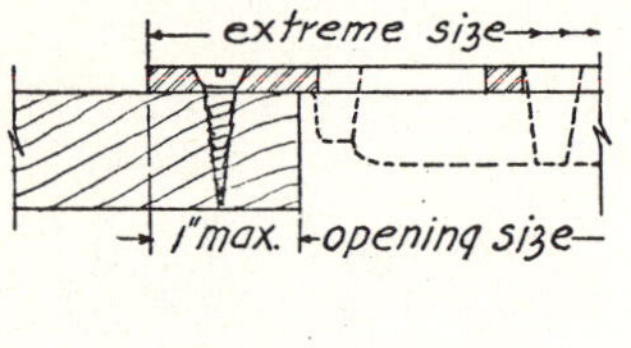
extreme size
1" max.
opening size

Over Wood Frame.

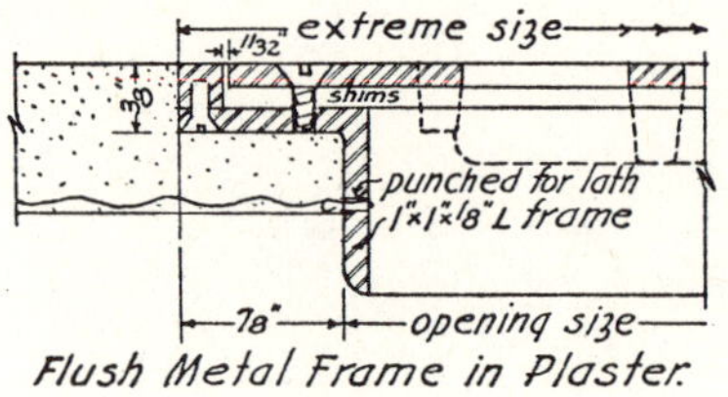
1/32
extreme size
shims
punched for lath
1"×1"×1/8" L frame
7/8"
opening size

Flush Metal Frame in Plaster.

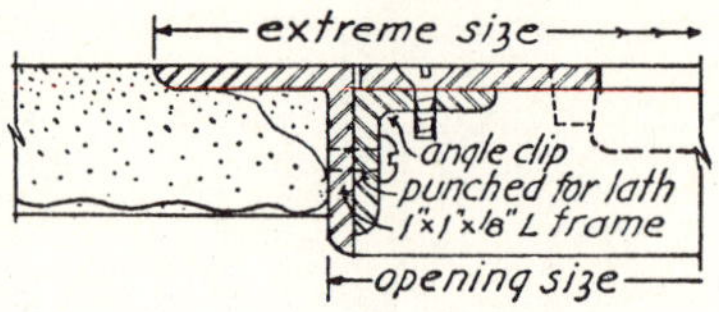
extreme size
angle clip
punched for lath
1"×1"×1/8" L frame
opening size

In Plaster with Angle Frame.

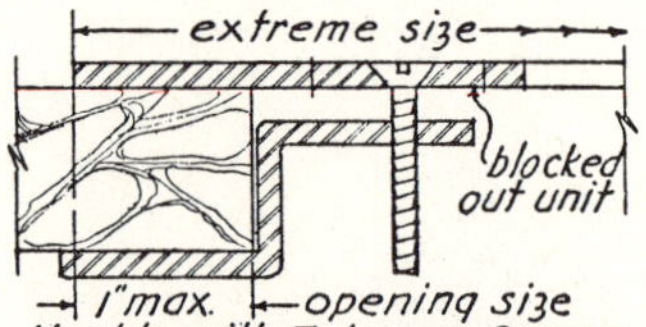
extreme size
blocked out unit
1" max.
opening size

Marble with Z Lugs & Screws through Blocked Out Unit.

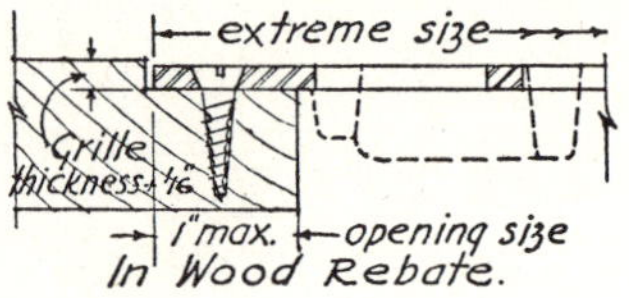
extreme size
Grille thickness +1/16
1" max.
opening size

In Wood Rebate.

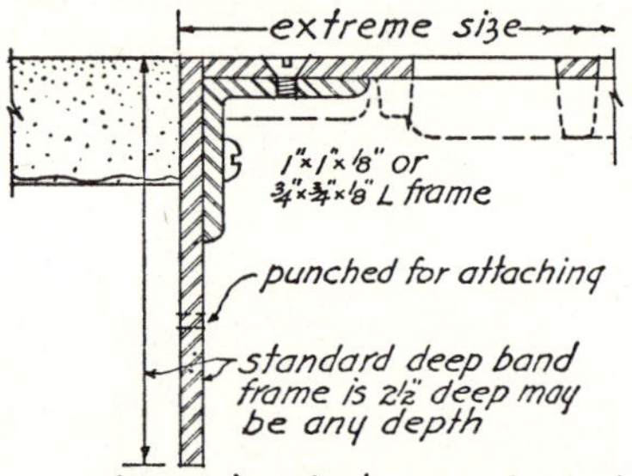
extreme size
1"×1"×1/8" or 3/4"×3/4"×1/8" L frame
punched for attaching
standard deep band frame is 2 1/2" deep may be any depth

Shown in Plaster, may be used with any finish when narrow exposed steel frame is desired.

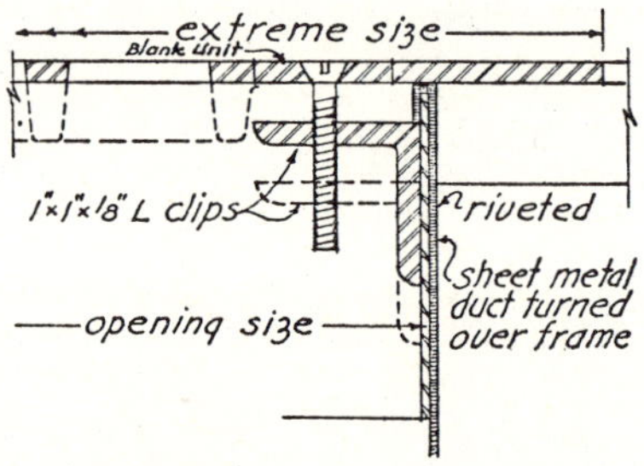
extreme size
Blank unit
1"×1"×1/8" L clips
riveted
sheet metal duct turned over frame
opening size

Attached to Steel Band Frame, may also be used with other finishes.

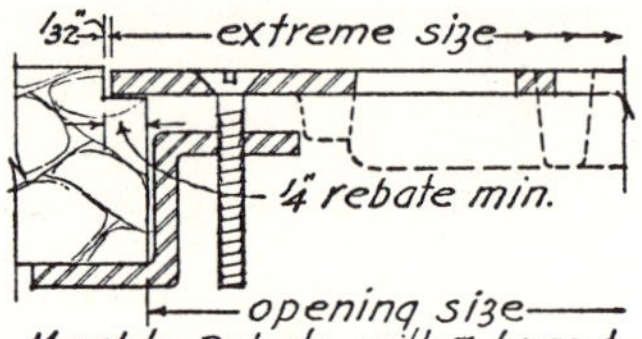
1/32
extreme size
1/4" rebate min.
opening size

Marble Rebate with Z Lugs & screws through rim.

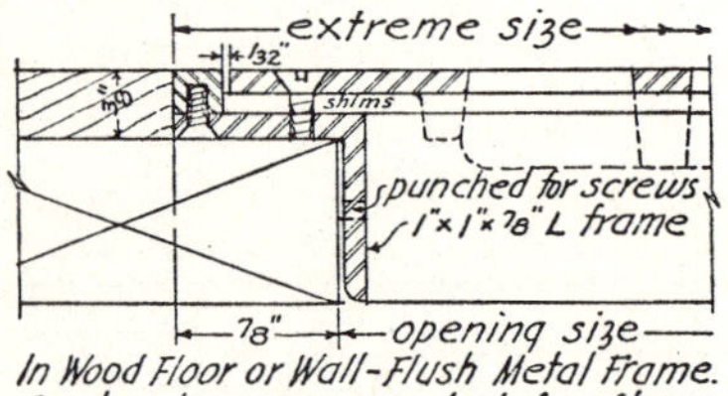
extreme size
1/32
shims
punched for screws
1"×1"×7/8" L frame
7/8"
opening size

In Wood Floor or Wall-Flush Metal Frame. Cast only recommended for floor.

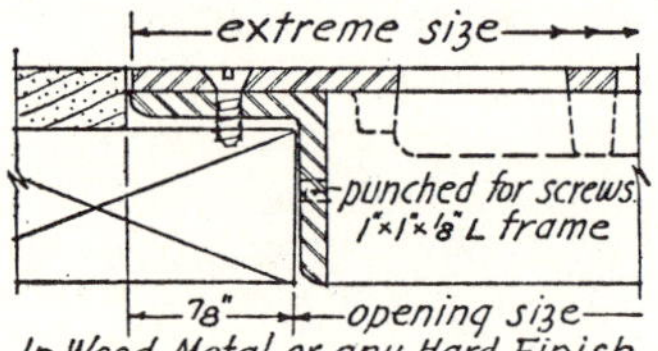
extreme size
punched for screws
1"×1"×1/8" L frame
7/8"
opening size

In Wood, Metal or any Hard Finish. Angle frame on back.

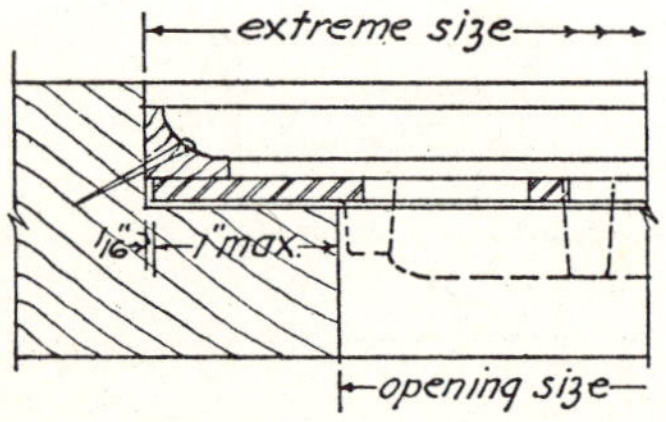
extreme size
1/16"
1" max.
opening size

In Wood Rebate with Mould.

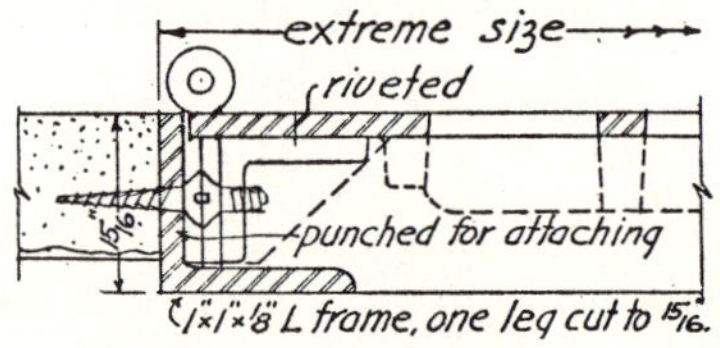
extreme size
riveted
15/16"
punched for attaching
1"×1"×1/8" L frame, one leg cut to 15/16.

For any Finish where Narrow Frame is desired. With Reverse Angle Frame on back. Hinged with Exposed Butt.

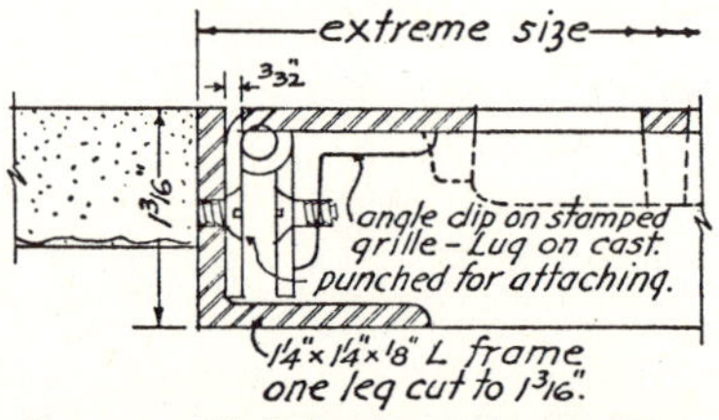
3/32
extreme size
1 3/16"
angle clip on stamped grille - Lug on cast.
punched for attaching.
1 1/4"×1 1/4"×1/8" L frame
one leg cut to 1 3/16".

For any Finish where Narrow Frame is desired. Reversed Angle Frame. Hinged with Recessed Butt.

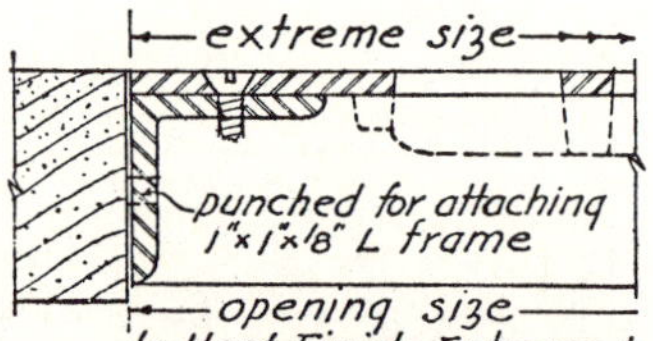
extreme size
punched for attaching
1"×1"×1/8" L frame
opening size

In Hard Finish. Extreme & Opening Sizes are the same. Reversed Angle Frame on Back.

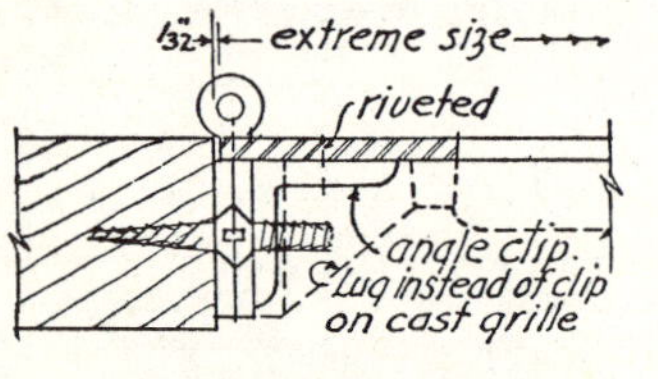
1/32
extreme size
riveted
angle clip.
Lug instead of clip on cast grille

With Angle Clip Hinged with Exposed Butt.

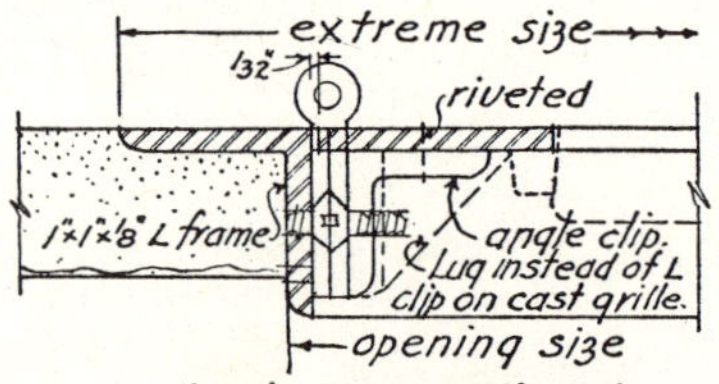
extreme size
1/32
riveted
1"×1"×1/8" L frame
angle clip.
Lug instead of L clip on cast grille.
opening size

Angle Frame Hinged with Exposed Butt.

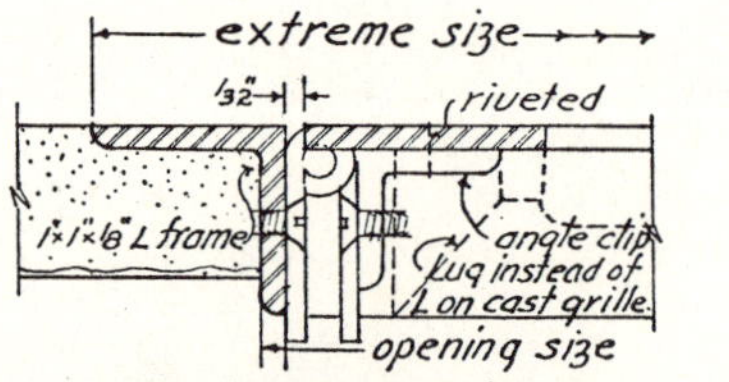
extreme size
1/32
riveted
1"×1"×1/8" L frame
angle clip
Lug instead of L on cast grille.
opening size

Angle Frame Hinged with Recessed Butt.

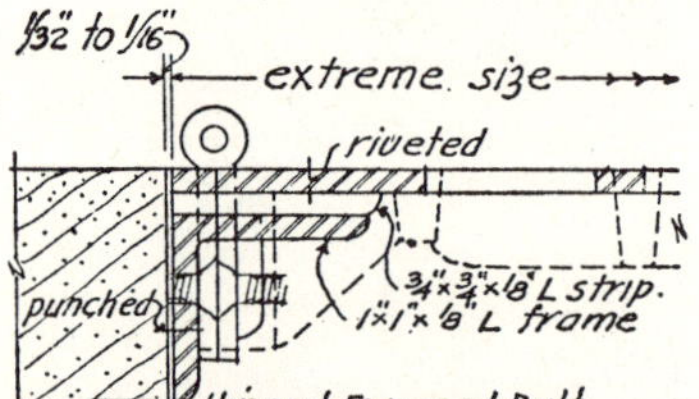
1/32" to 1/16"
extreme size
riveted
punched
3/4"×3/4"×1/8" L strip.
1"×1"×1/8" L frame

Hinged Exposed Butt
Extreme & Opening Size are the same. Reverse Angle Frame on Back.

IN WOOD FRAME — IN PLASTER FINISH — IN MARBLE & HARD TYPE FINISH

STAMPED or CAST GRILLES (cast are shown dotted)

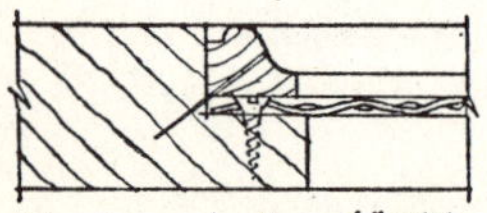

For Panels Max. 1-2' Wide.

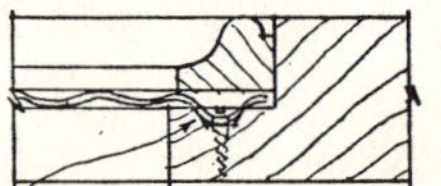

Groove to Tighten Mesh.

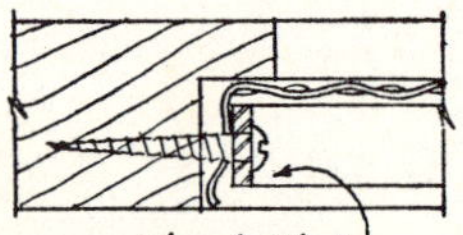

Steel Strip

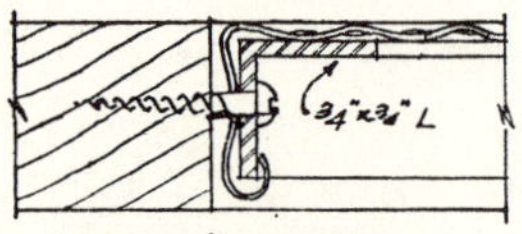
3/4"×3/4" L

Angle Frame

SECURED IN WOOD

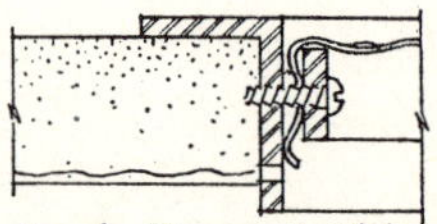

Angle Frame & Strip.

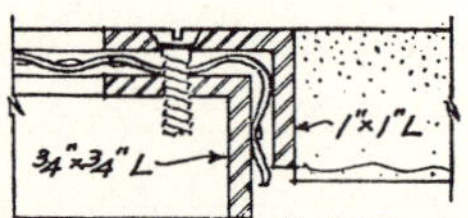
1"×1" L
3/4"×3/4" L

2 Angles and Screws

IN PLASTER

WOVEN WIRE MESH

Data reviewed by National Assoc. of Architectural Metal Mfrs.

MISCELLANEOUS STEEL SHAPES

HOT ROLLED STEEL

WIDTH (Inches)	STRIPS, BANDS B.W. Gauge 16	14	12	10	FLATS Thickness in inches 1/8	3/16	1/4	5/16	3/8	7/16	1/2	9/16	5/8	11/16	3/4	13/16	7/8	1	1 1/8	1 1/4	1 3/8	1 1/2	1 5/8	1 3/4	1 7/8	2
3/8	●	●	●	●	●	●	●																			
1/2	●	●	●	●	●	●	●	●	●																	
5/8	●	●	●	●	●	●	●	●	●		●															
3/4	●	●	●	●	●	●	●	●	●	●	●		●													
7/8	●	●	●	●	●	●	●	●	●	●	●		●		●											
1	●	●	●	●	●	●	●	●	●	●	●		●		●		●									
1 1/8	●	●	●	●	●	●	●	●	●		●		●		●		●									
1 1/4	●	●	●	●	●	●	●	●	●	●	●		●		●		●	●								
1 3/8			●	●	●	●	●	●	●	●	●		●		●		●									
1 1/2	●	●	●	●	●	●	●	●	●	●	●		●		●		●	●		●						
1 3/4	●	●	●	●	●	●	●	●	●	●	●		●		●		●	●		●		●				
2	●	●	●	●	●	●	●	●	●	●	●		●		●		●	●	●	●		●		●		
2 1/4	●	●	●	●	●	●	●	●	●	●	●		●		●		●	●		●		●				●
2 1/2	●	●	●	●	●	●	●	●	●	●	●		●		●		●	●	●	●		●		●		●
2 3/4	●	●	●	●	●	●	●	●	●	●	●		●		●		●	●		●		●		●		
3	●	●	●	●	●	●	●	●	●	●	●		●		●		●	●	●	●		●		●		●
3 1/4				●	●	●	●	●	●	●	●		●		●		●	●		●						
3 1/2	●	●	●	●	●	●	●	●	●	●	●		●		●		●	●		●		●		●		●
4	●	●	●	●	●	●	●	●	●	●	●		●		●		●	●	●	●		●		●		●
4 1/2				●	●	●	●	●	●	●	●		●		●		●	●		●		●		●		●
5				●	●	●	●	●	●	●	●		●		●		●	●	●	●		●		●		●
5 1/2				●	●	●	●	●	●	●	●		●		●		●	●		●		●		●		
6				●	●	●	●	●	●	●	●		●		●		●	●	●	●		●		●		●
ROUNDS						●	●	●	●	●	●	●	●	●	●	●	●	●	●	●	●	●	●	●	●	●
HALF-ROUNDS									●		●		●		●		●	●	●	●		●		●		●
HEXAGONS											●	●	●	●	●	●	●	●	●	●	●	●	●	●	●	●
SQUARES							●	●	●	●	●	●	●	●	●	●	●	●	●	●	●	●	●	●	●	●
PLATES							●	●	●	●	●		●		●		●	●		●		●		●		●

ANGLES*

Nom. Size	Thickness (inches)			
Square Root - Equal Leg				
3/8 x 3/8 x	3/32			
1/2 x 1/2 x	3/32	1/8		
5/8 x 5/8 x	3/32	1/8		
3/4 x 3/4 x	3/32	1/8		
7/8 x 7/8 x	3/32			
1 x 1 x	3/32	1/8		
1 1/4 x 1 1/4 x	1/8	3/16		
1 1/2 x 1 1/2 x	1/8	3/16	1/4	
1 3/4 x 1 3/4 x	3/16			
2 x 2 x	5/32	3/16	1/4	
Bar Size - Unequal Leg				
1 x 5/8 x	1/8			
1 x 3/4 x	1/8			
1 3/8 x 7/8 x	1/8	3/16		
1 1/2 x 1 1/4 x	3/16			
1 3/4 x 1 1/4 x	1/8	3/16		
2 x 1 1/4 x	3/16	1/4		
2 x 1 1/2 x	1/8	3/16	1/4	
2 1/2 x 1 1/2 x	3/16	1/4	5/16	
2 1/2 x 2 x	3/16	1/4	5/16	3/8
Square Root - Unequal Leg				
3/4 x 3/8 x	3/32	1/8		
1 x 5/8 x	1/8			
1 1/4 x 3/4 x	3/32	1/8		
1 3/8 x 7/8 x	3/32			
1 1/2 x 3/4 x	1/8			
1 1/2 x 1 x	1/8			
2 x 1 x	1/8			

a
b
a
b
c

Square Root Tee — *Bar Size or Structural Tee* — *Square Root Unequal Leg Angle* — *Bar Size or Str'l. Unequal Leg Angle* — *Square Root Equal Leg Angle* — *Bar Size or Str'l. Zee* — *Square Root Zee*

TEES - Nominal sizes & their thicknesses

Bar Size				*Structural*			*Square Root*	
3/4 x 3/4 x	1/8			3 x 2 1/2 x	5/16		1/2 x 1/2 x	3/32
7/8 x 7/8 x	1/8			3 x 3 x	5/16	3/8	5/8 x 5/8 x	3/32
1 x 1 x	1/8	3/16		4 x 2 1/2 x	3/8		3/4 x 3/4 x	3/32
1 1/4 x 1 1/4 x	1/8	3/16	1/4	4 x 3 x	3/8		3/4 x 1 x	1/8
1 1/2 x 1 1/2 x	3/16	1/4		4 x 4 x	1/2		3/4 x 1 3/16 x	5/32
1 3/4 x 1 3/4 x	3/16	1/4		5 x 3 1/8 x	1/2		3/4 x 1 3/8 x	1/8
2 x 1 1/2 x	1/4							
2 x 2 x	1/4	5/16						
2 1/4 x 2 1/4 x	1/4							
2 1/2 x 2 1/2 x	1/4	5/16						

ZEES - Nominal sizes & their thicknesses

Bar Size (a b c)		*Structural* (a b c)				*Square Root* (a b c)		SHEETS
1 1/4 x 1 3/4 x 1 3/4 x	3/16	2 11/16 x 3 x 2 11/16 x	1/4	3/8	1/2	1/2 x 1 x 5/8 x	1/8	*Revised U.S.S. Ga. Thickness*
1 1/4 x 1 3/4 x 2 1/8 x	7/32	3 1/16 x 4 x 3 1/16 x	1/4			1/2 x 1 x 9/16 x	5/32	3/16"
1 3/4 x 1 3/4 x 1 3/4 x	3/16	3 1/8 x 4 1/16 x 3 1/8 x	5/16	1/2		1/2 x 1 1/16 x 7/8 x	1/8	8
		3 3/16 x 4 1/8 x 3 3/16 x	3/8			1/2 x 1 3/16 x 5/8 x	5/32	10
		3 1/4 x 5 x 3 1/4 x	5/16	1/2		1/2 x 1 3/8 x 5/8 x	5/32	12
		3 5/16 x 5 1/16 x 3 5/16 x	3/8			5/8 x 1 3/16 x 3/4 x	1/8	14
		3 1/2 x 6 x 3 1/2 x	3/8			5/8 x 1 3/8 x 3/4 x	3/16	16
		3 5/8 x 6 1/8 x 3 5/8 x	1/2			3/4 x 1 3/8 x 1 3/16 x	1/8	18
								20

*See "Structural Shapes & Riveting Symbols" page for angle data. Bar Size denotes tees, zees, angles, & channels whose largest dimen. under 3".

Data from "Architectural Metal Handbook," permission of the National Assoc. of Architectural Metal Mfrs.

STEEL CHANNELS, PIPE and TUBING

STEEL PIPE

ROUND

Nom. i.d. Size (inches)	Outside Diameter (inches)	Inside Diameter (i.d.) inches: Standard	Extra Strong	Double Ex. Strong
1/8	.405	.269	.215	
1/4	.540	.364	.302	
3/8	.675	.493	.423	
1/2	.840	.622	.546	.252
3/4	1.050	.824	.742	.434
1	1.315	1.049	.957	.599
1 1/4	1.660	1.380	1.278	.896
1 1/2	1.900	1.610	1.500	1.100
2	2.375	2.067	1.939	1.503
2 1/2	2.875	2.469	2.323	1.771
3	3.500	3.068	2.900	2.300
3 1/2	4.000	3.548	3.364	2.728
4	4.500	4.026	3.826	3.152
5	5.563	5.047	4.813	4.063
6	6.625	6.065	5.761	4.897
8	8.625	7.981	7.625	6.875
10	10.750	10.020	9.750	
12	12.750	12.000	11.750	

SQUARE

Outside Dimension (inches)	Wall Thickn's (inches)
1 x 1	1/8
1 x 1	3/16
1 1/4 x 1 1/4	135
1 1/4 x 1 1/4	3/16
1 1/2 x 1 1/2	9/64
1 1/2 x 1 1/2	3/16
1 1/2 x 1 1/2	1/4
2 x 2	145
2 x 2	3/16
2 x 2	1/4
2 1/2 x 2 1/2	3/16
3 x 3	1/8
3 x 3	3/16
3 x 3	1/4
3 1/2 x 3 1/2	3/16
4 x 4	3/16
4 x 4	1/4
5 x 5	3/16
6 x 6	3/16
7 x 7	3/16
8 x 8	3/16

RECTANGULAR

Outside Dimension (inches)	Wall Thickn's (inches)
2 x 1 1/2	9/64
2 x 1 1/2	3/16
2 1/2 x 1 1/2	3/16
3 x 2	3/16
4 x 2	3/16
4 x 3	3/16
5 x 3	3/16
5 x 4	3/16
6 x 3	3/16
6 x 4	3/16
7 x 3	3/16
7 x 4	3/16
8 x 3	3/16
8 x 4	3/16
9 x 3	3/16
9 x 4	3/16
10 x 4	3/16

STEEL TUBING

SQUARE

Nom. Size (inches)	Wall Thickness (B.W gauge)						
3/8 x 3/8	20	18					
1/2 x 1/2	20	18	16				
5/8 x 5/8	20	18	16				
3/4 x 3/4	20	18	16	13	11		
7/8 x 7/8	20	18	16	13			
1 x 1	20	18	16	14	12	3/16"	
1 1/8 x 1 1/8	18	16					
1 1/4 x 1 1/4	18	17	16	14	11	10	3/16"
1 3/8 x 1 3/8	18	17	16				
1 1/2 x 1 1/2	18	16	14	11	10		
1 3/4 x 1 3/4	18	16	14	11	3/16"		
2 x 2	16	14	13	11	3/16"	1/4"	
2 1/4 x 2 1/4	1/4"						
2 1/2 x 2 1/2	16	14	11	1/4"			
3 x 3	16	14	11	3/16"			
3 1/2 x 3 1/2	14	3/16"					
4 x 4	14	11	10	3/16"			

RECTANGULAR

Nom. Size (inches)	Wall Thick's (B.W. ga.)	
3/8 x 3/4	16	
3/8 x 1	16	
3/8 x 2	14	
3/4 x 1 1/2	14	
1 x 1 1/2	14	
1 x 2	14	
1 x 2 1/2	14	
1 x 3	14	
1 x 3 1/2	14	
1 1/4 x 1 3/4	14	
1 1/4 x 2	14	
1 1/4 x 2 1/2	16	14
1 1/4 x 3	14	
1 1/4 x 3 1/2	14	
1 1/2 x 2	14	
1 1/2 x 2 1/2	14	
1 1/2 x 3	14	
1 1/2 x 3 1/2	14	
2 x 3	14	
2 x 4	14	

HEXAGONAL

Size (inches)	Wall Thickness (B.W. ga.)		
1/2	18		
5/8	20	18	16
3/4	20	18	16
7/8	20	16	
1	16		
1 1/16	20		

TWISTED SQUARE

Size (inches)	Wall Thick (B.W. ga.)
1/2 x 1/2	20
5/8 x 5/8	20
3/4 x 3/4	20
7/8 x 7/8	20
1 x 1	20
1 1/4 x 1 1/4	20
1 1/2 x 1 1/2	18
2 x 2	18

ROUND

Size

Nominal Outside Diameters of 3/32" to 12" in intervals of 1/32" for the small sizes; 1/16", 1/8", 1/4" for the medium sizes and 1/2" for the larger sizes. Wall Thicknesses are varied and numerable.

STEEL CHANNELS

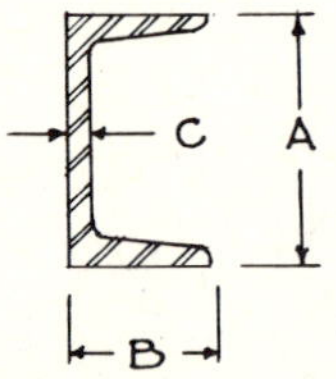

C
A
B

BAR SIZE

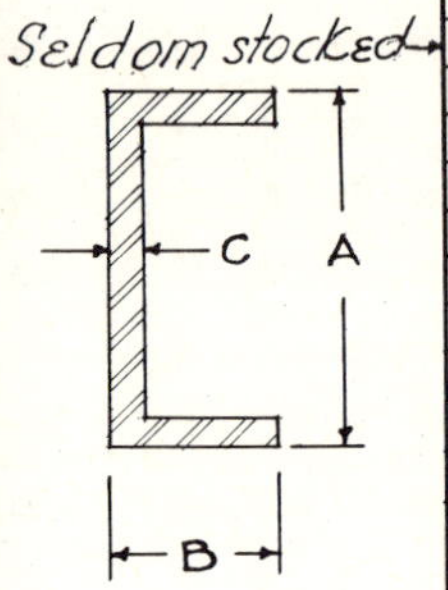

Seldom stocked
C
A
B

SQUARE ROOT

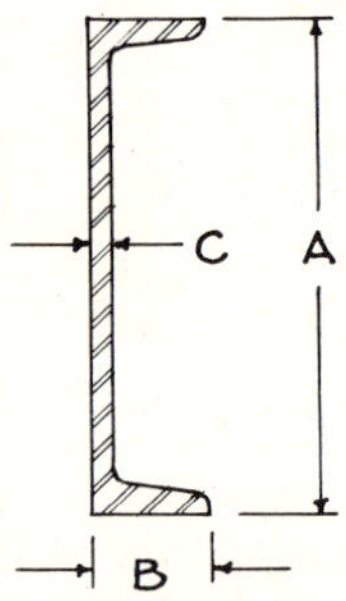

C
A
B

STAIR STRING

BAR SIZE

A	B	C	Wt./ft. (lbs)
1/2	1/4	1/8	.28
3/4	5/16	1/8	.50
3/4	3/8	#15	.40
3/4	3/8	1/8	.52
7/8	3/8	1/8	.58
7/8	7/16	1/8	.69
1	3/8	1/8	.68
1	1/2	1/8	.79
1 1/8	9/16	3/16	1.16
1 1/4	1/2	1/8	.93
1 1/2	1/2	1/8	1.04
1 1/2	1/2	1/4	1.53
1 1/2	9/16	3/16	1.36
1 1/2	3/4	1/8	1.17
1 1/2	1 1/2	3/16	2.65
1 3/4	1/2	3/16	1.55
2	1/2	1/8	1.34
2	9/16	3/16	1.76
2	5/8	1/4	2.10
2	1	1/8	1.59
2	1	3/16	2.32
2 1/2	5/8	3/16	2.27

SQUARE ROOT

A	B	C	Wt./ft. (lbs)
1/2	1/2	3/32	.33
5/8	5/8	3/32	.47
5/8	15/16	3/32	.58
3/4	3/4	3/32	.56
7/8	7/8	3/32	.65
1	1	1/8	1.00
1 3/16	1	5/32	1.50
1 1/4	1 1/4	1/8	1.35
1 5/16	2	1/8	2.25
1 1/2	3/4	1/8	1.17
1 1/2	1 1/2	1/8	1.75
1 3/4	11/16	1/8	1.12
2	1	1/8	1.45
2	2	5/32	2.64
2 3/8	2 1/4	3/16	4.23

STAIR STRING

A	B	C	Wt./ft. (lbs)
10	1 1/8	.150	6.5
10	1 1/2	.170	8.4
12	1 1/2	.190	10.6

Round steel pipe is specified by "Nominal Inside Diameter" (followed by the terms – "Standard," "Extra-Strong," or "Double-Extra Strong." Non-ferrous round pipe is specified by I.P.S. (iron pipe size). Large Round Steel O.D. Pipe 14" & over in diameter is specified by outside diameter (o.d.), wall thicknesses varying from 1/4" to 1." Also measured by outside dimension are rectangular & square pipe, & all shapes of tubing.

For channel sizes other than those listed, see page "Structural Steel & Riveting Symbols."

Standard · Extra Strong · Double Extra Strong · Square · Rectangular

STEEL PIPE

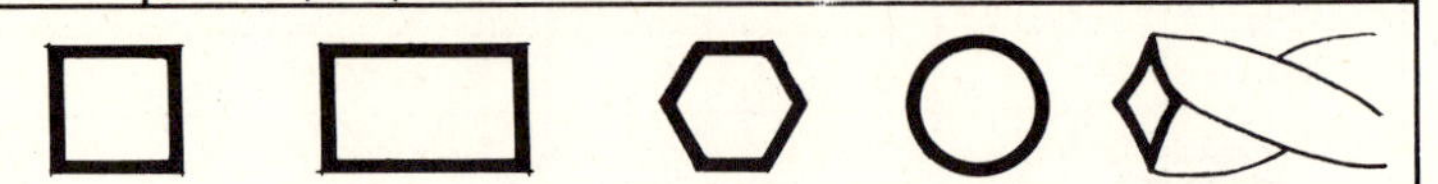

Square · Rectangular · Hexagonal · Round · Twisted Square

STEEL TUBING

Data from "Architectural Metal Handbook" by permission of the National Assoc. of Architectural Metal Manufactrs.

TURNSTILES

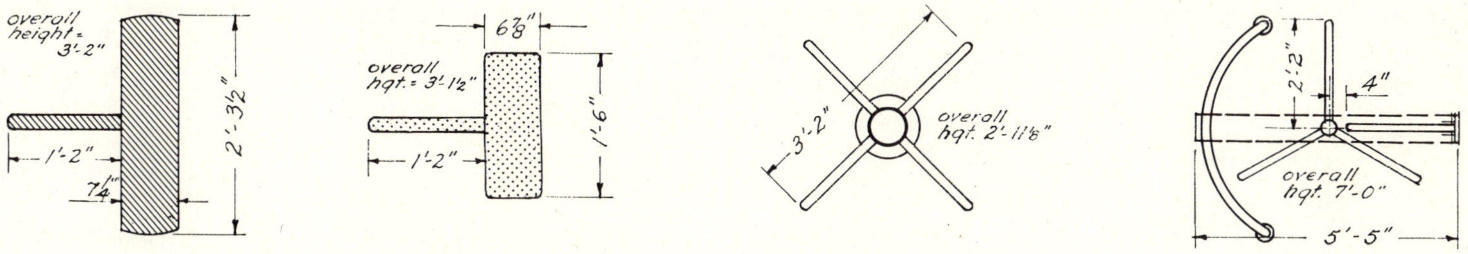
overall height = 3'-2"
2'-3½"
1'-2"
7¼"
6⅞"
overall hgt. = 3'-1½"
1'-6"
1'-2"
3'-2"
overall hgt. 2'-11⅛"
2'-2"
4"
overall hgt. 7'-0"
5'-5"

SLOT & ATTENDED DROP ARM — TRAFFIC CONTROL SPACE-SAVING TYPES ½" = 1'-0"

RIGID ARM TRAFFIC CONTROL ⅜" = 1'-0"

BAFFLE EXIT GATE ¼" = 1'-0"

BASIC TYPES of TURNSTILES

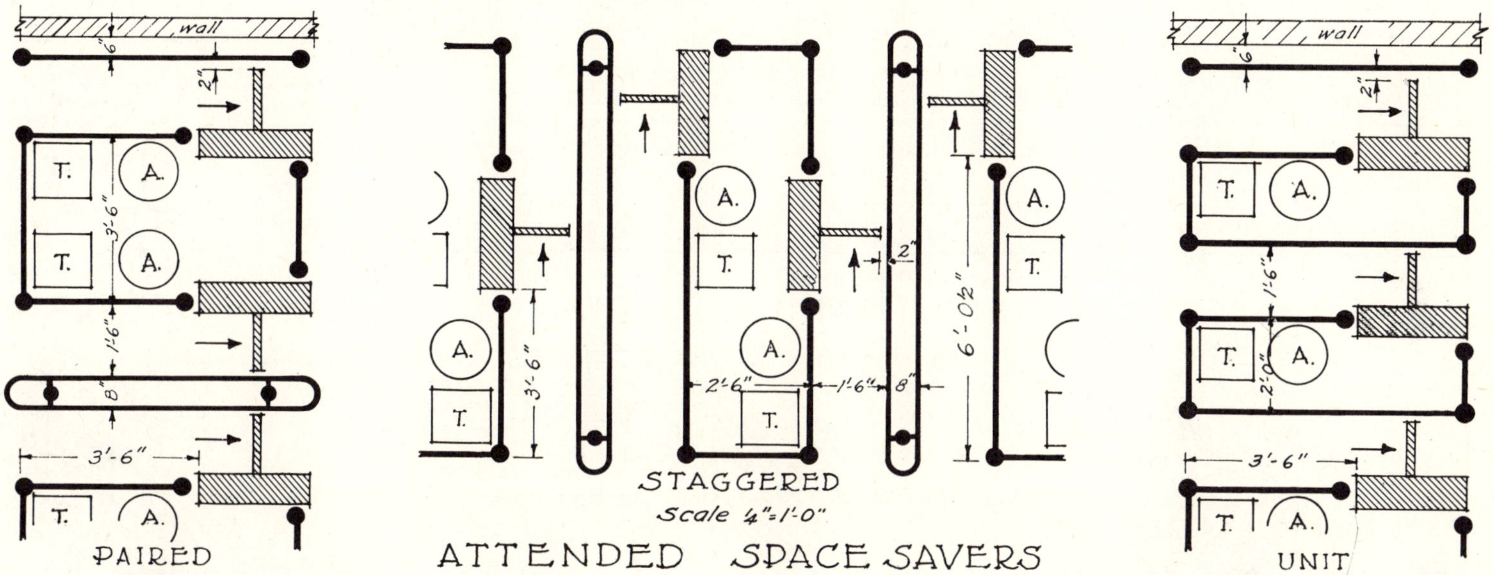
wall
6"
2"
T.
A.
3'-6"
1'-6"
8"
3'-6"
2'-6"
1'-6"
6'-0½"
2'-0"
STAGGERED
Scale ¼" = 1'-0"

PAIRED — ATTENDED SPACE SAVERS — UNIT

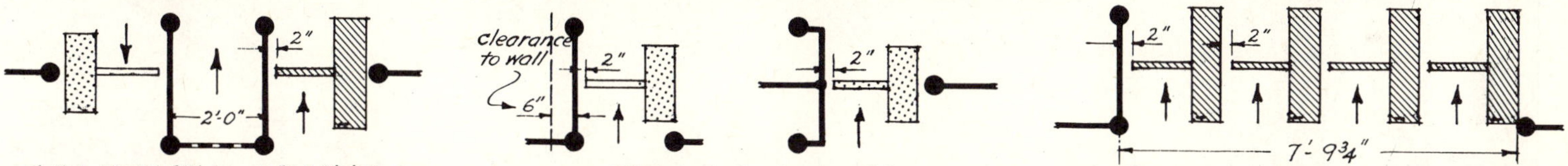
2"
2'-0"
clearance to wall
6"
7'-9¾"

COMBINED UNITS ¼" = 1'-0" — TRAFFIC CONTROL ¼" = 1'-0" — SLOT TYPE - GROUPED ¼" = 1'-0"

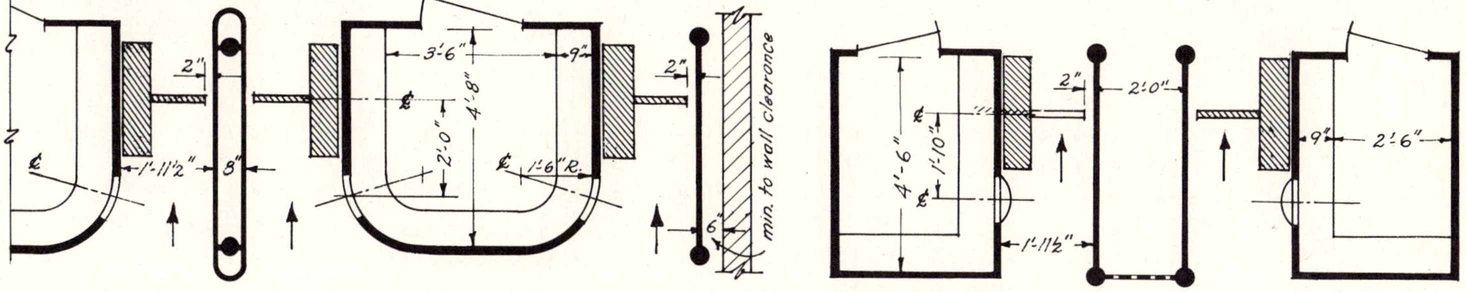
2"
3'-6"
9"
4'-8"
2'-0"
1'-11½"
8"
1'-6"R.
6"
min. to wall clearance
4'-6"
1'-10"
2'-0"
2'-6"

CASHIER ATTENDED - BOOTHS ¼" = 1'-0"

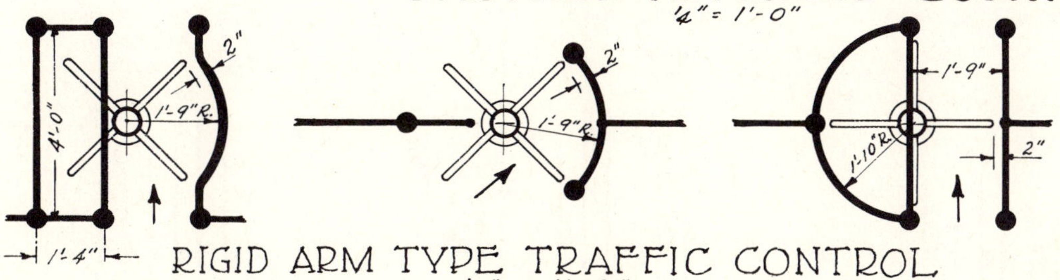
4'-0"
2"
1'-9"R.
1'-4"
1'-9"
1'-10"R.

RIGID ARM TYPE TRAFFIC CONTROL ¼" = 1'-0"

SYMBOLS

●—● 1½" standard pipe rail	Ⓐ Attendant
- - - Pass gate	T. Ticket box

NOTES

From floor to top of arms = 2'-10", except Baffle type. Floor to top of rails 36" min., 39" max. for Rigid Arm type; others 34". Clearances: arm ends to rail = 2"; rail to walls = 6 inches.

TYPICAL INSTALLATIONS

Data by Perey Turnstile Company

FLAGS & POLES

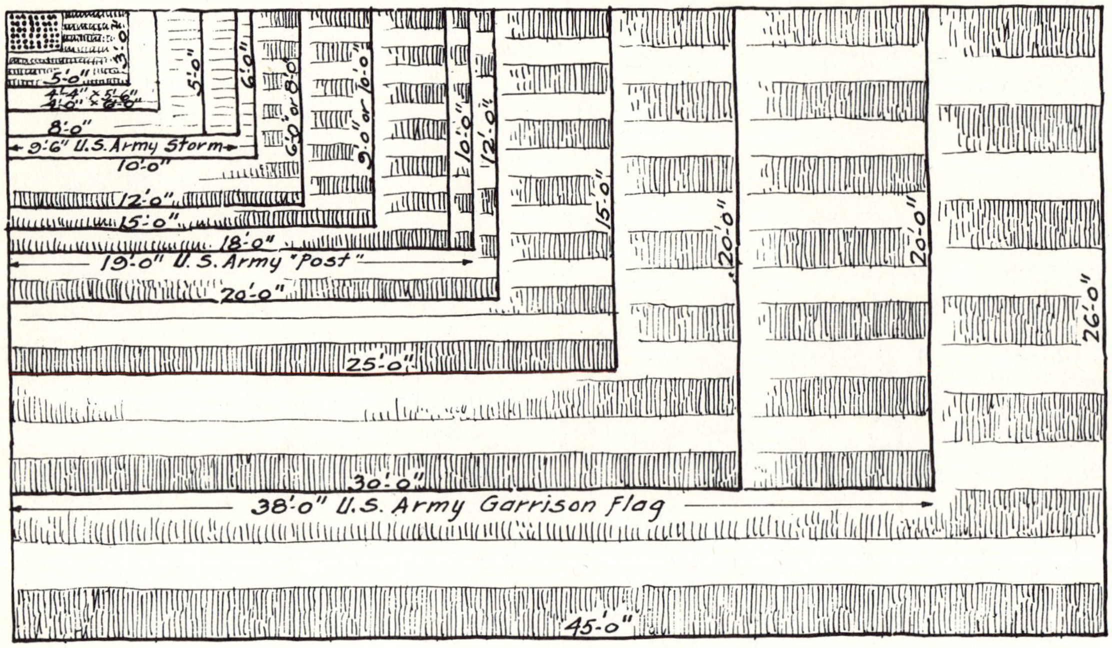
5'-0"
4'-4" × 5'-6"
4'-0" × 6'-8"
5'-0"
6'-0"
6'-0" or 8'-0"
8'-0"
9'-6" U.S. Army Storm
10'-0"
9'-0" or 10'-0"
10'-0"
12'-0"
12'-0"
15'-0"
18'-0"
19'-0" U.S. Army "Post"
20'-0"
15'-0"
20'-0"
20'-0"
25'-0"
26'-0"
30'-0"
38'-0" U.S. Army Garrison Flag
45'-0"

1/8" = 1'-0"

U.S. FLAG SIZES USUALLY MANUFACTURED & USED.

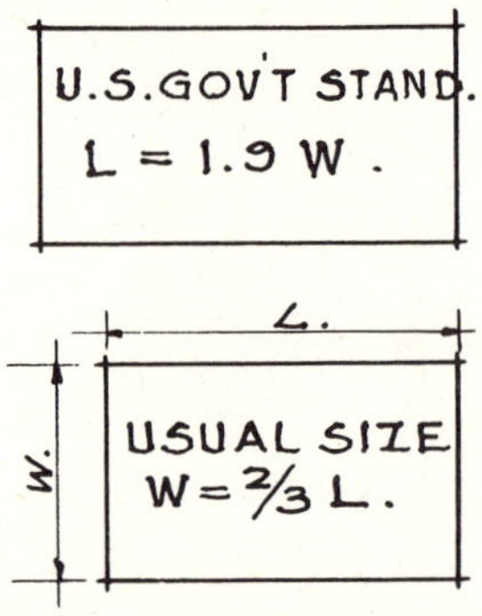
U.S. GOV'T STAND.
L = 1.9 W.
L.
W.
USUAL SIZE
W = 2/3 L.

PROPORTIONS OF U.S. FLAG.

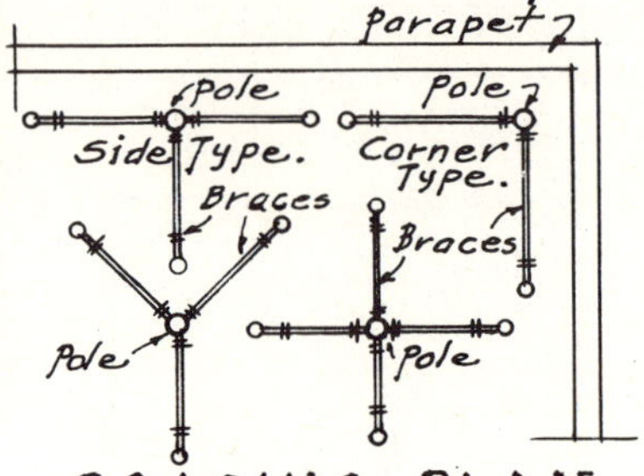
Parapet
Pole
Pole
Side Type.
Corner Type.
Braces
Braces
Pole
Pole

BRACING PLAN

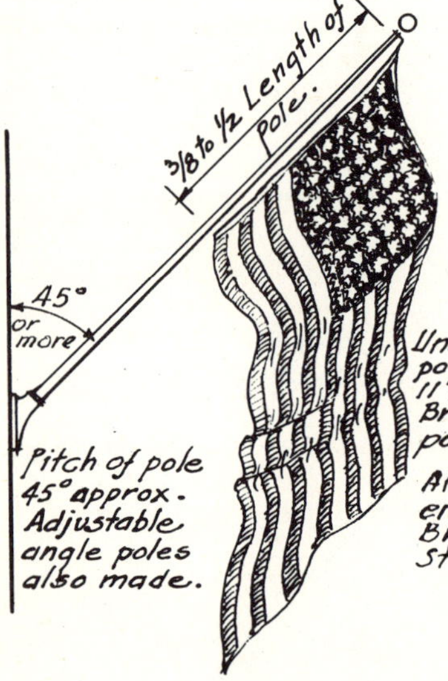
3/8 to 1/2 Length of Pole.
45° or more
Pitch of pole 45° approx. Adjustable angle poles also made.
Unbraced outrigger poles 7', 8', 9', 10', 11', 12 Ft. long. Braced outrigger poles 14' to 30' long.
Also available in entatis tapered Bronze, Aluminum, Stainless steel etc.

OUTRIGGER POLES FOR FLAGS ON BUILDING FRONTS.

For stormy weather smaller flags than those listed must be used

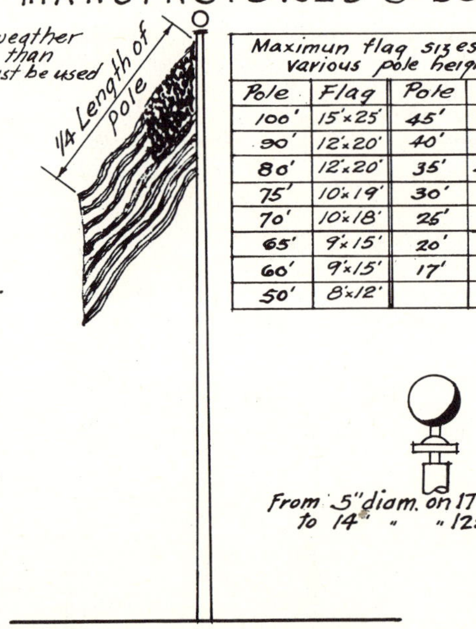
1/4 Length of pole
From 5" diam. on 17' Pole, to 14" " " 125' ".

Maximun flag sizes for various pole heights.

Pole	Flag	Pole	Flag
100'	15'×25'	45'	6'×12'
90'	12'×20'	40'	6'×10'
80'	12'×20'	35'	5'×9'-6"
75'	10'×19'	30'	5'×8'
70'	10'×18'	25'	4'×6'
65'	9'×15'	20'	3'×5'
60'	9'×15'	17'	3'×5'
50'	8'×12'		

POLE ON GROUND.

1/3 Length of Pole.

Relation of Hgt. of Pole to Bldg:
20 Ft. Pole on Bldg 1-2 Stories.
25 " " " " 3 to 5 "
33'-35' " " " 6 " 10 "
40'-50' " " " 11 " 15 "
60-75 " " " over 15 "
This rule serves for preliminary assumptions.

FOR FLAGS ON ROOFS.

For stormy weather - smaller flags than the above are generally used.

SIZE OF FLAG IN RELATION TO POLE HEIGHT

Tilting Poles for Roof are also available.

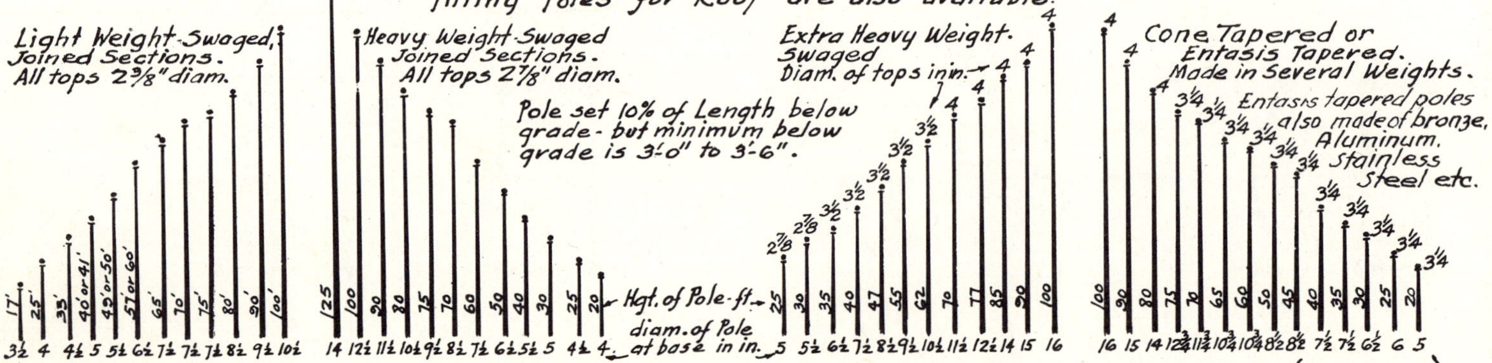
Light Weight Swaged, Joined Sections. All tops 2 3/8" diam.
Heavy Weight Swaged Joined Sections. All tops 2 7/8" diam.
Pole set 10% of Length below grade - but minimum below grade is 3'-0" to 3'-6".
Extra Heavy Weight. Swaged Diam. of tops in in.
Cone Tapered or Entasis Tapered. Made in Several Weights.
Entasis tapered poles also made of bronze, Aluminum, Stainless Steel etc.
Hgt. of Pole-ft.
diam. of Pole at base in in.
17' 25' 35' 40' or 41' 45' or 50' 57' or 60' 65' 70' 75' 80' 90' 100'
3½ 4 4½ 5 5½ 6½ 7½ 7½ 8½ 9½ 10½
125 100 90 80 75 70 60 50 40 30 25 20
14 12½ 11½ 10½ 9½ 8½ 7½ 6½ 5½ 5 4½ 4
25 30 35 40 47 55 62 70 77 85 90 100
5 5½ 6½ 7½ 8½ 9½ 10½ 11½ 12½ 14 15 16
100 90 80 75 70 65 60 50 45 40 35 30 25 20
16 15 14 12½ 11½ 10½ 10½ 8½ 8½ 7½ 7½ 6½ 6 5

POLE SIZES & TYPES AS GENERALLY MANUFACTURED (STEEL)

TOWER CLOCKS and BELLS

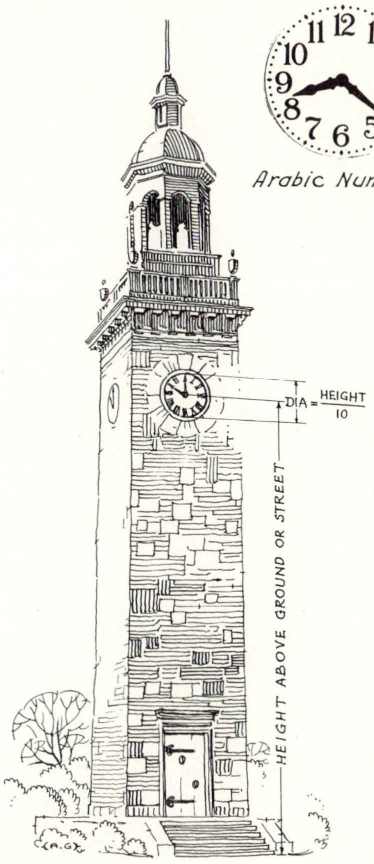
DIA = HEIGHT/10
HEIGHT ABOVE GROUND OR STREET

SIZE of CLOCK RELATIVE TO HEIGHT ABOVE GRADE

Arabic Numbers
Roman Numbers
Skeleton Dial
No Numbers

DIAL TYPES

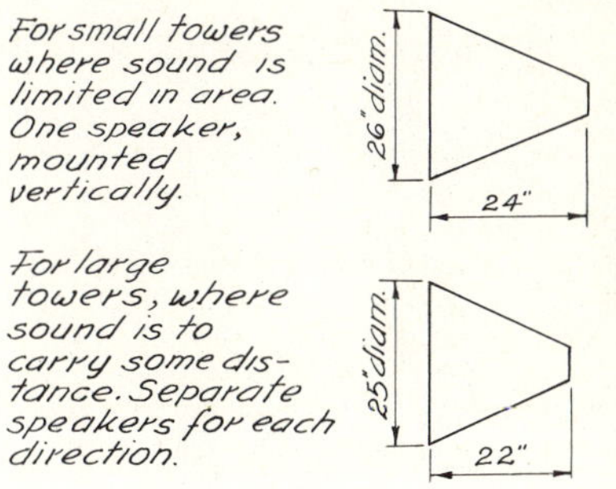
For small towers where sound is limited in area. One speaker, mounted vertically.
26" diam.
24"
For large towers, where sound is to carry some distance. Separate speakers for each direction.
25" diam.
22"

SPEAKERS

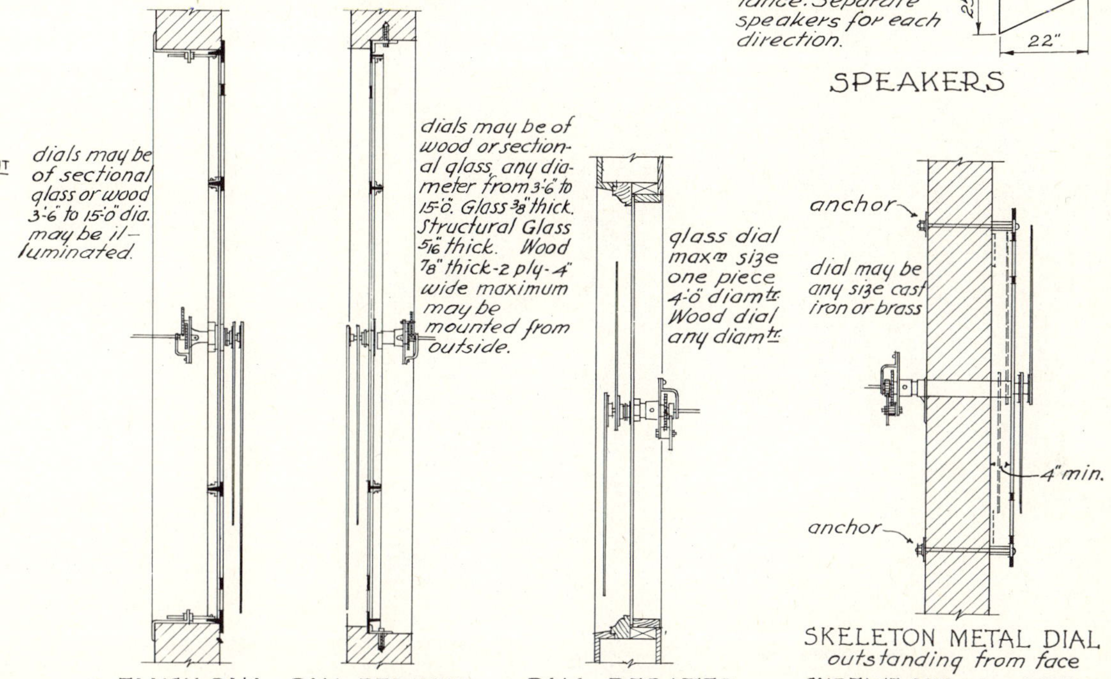
dials may be of sectional glass or wood 3'-6" to 15'-0" dia. may be illuminated.
dials may be of wood or sectional glass, any diameter from 3'-6" to 15'-0". Glass 3/8" thick. Structural Glass 5/16" thick. Wood 7/8" thick-2 ply-4" wide maximum may be mounted from outside.
glass dial maxm size one piece 4'-0" diamtr. Wood dial any diamtr.
anchor
dial may be any size cast iron or brass
4" min.
anchor

FLUSH DIAL *in masonry* — DIAL REBATED *in masonry* — DIAL REBATED *in frame* — SKELETON METAL DIAL *outstanding from face* SURFACE DIAL *shown DOTTED numerals on wall*

SECTIONS thro' DIALS

Standard dials made up to 15'-0" dia. and specials up to 50'-0" Standard dials made in multiples of 6"

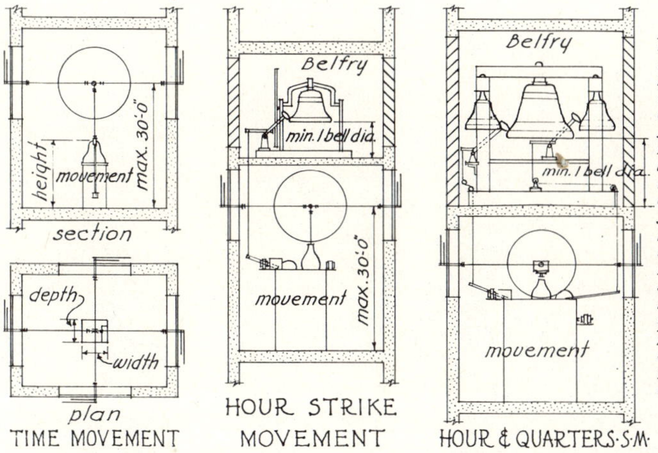
height
movement
max. 30'-0"
section
depth
width
plan
Belfry
min. 1 bell dia.
movement
max. 30'-0"
Belfry
min. 1 bell dia.
movement

TIME MOVEMENT — HOUR STRIKE MOVEMENT — HOUR & QUARTERS·S·M·

Types of clocks= 1. Time movement. 2. Time & strike movement. 3. Time-strike-&-quarter-strike movemt. Belfry= Place over movement if practical. Make openings max. size. Head of opening near ceiling & sill near floor. See Mfrs. Cat. for exact movement sizes, which vary according to number of dials, size of dials, and type of clock. Movements= Many horizontal locations possible, directly behind dial is preferable. Electric movement indicated & now largely used.

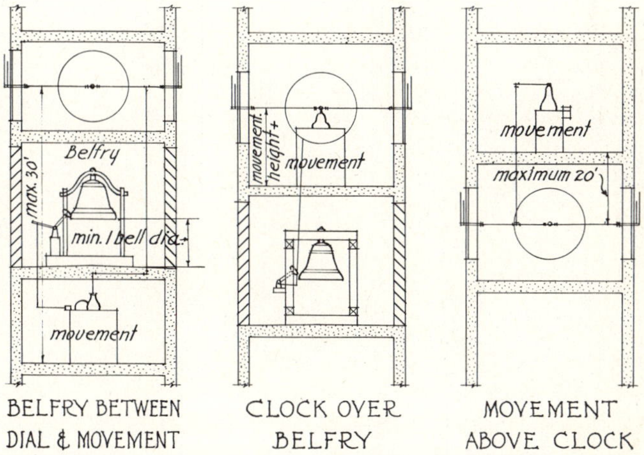
max. 30'
Belfry
min. 1 bell dia.
movement
movement height +
movement
maximum 20'

BELFRY BETWEEN DIAL & MOVEMENT — CLOCK OVER BELFRY — MOVEMENT ABOVE CLOCK

DIAGRAMMATIC ARRANGEMENTS and RECOMMENDATIONS - CLOCK TOWER ELEMENTS

CHURCH BELL DATA

Medium Tone	Weight lbs	Size		Mounting	
		Diameter	Height	Outside Frame	Dia. Wheel
D	400 lbs	2'-3"	1'-10"	3'-5" × 3'-8"	4'-4"
C sharp	450 lbs	2'-4"	2'-0"	3'-5" × 3'-8"	4'-4"
C	500 lbs	2'-5"	2'-0"	3'-5" × 3'-8"	4'-4"
B	600 lbs	2'-7"	2'-1"	3'-8" × 3'-11"	4'-9"
B	700 lbs	2'-9"	2'-3"	3'-11" × 4'-2"	4'-9"
B flat	800 lbs	2'-10"	2'-4"	3'-11" × 4'-2"	5'-6"
A	900 lbs	3'-0"	2'-5"	4'-2" × 4'-6"	5'-9"
A	1000 lbs	3'-1"	2'-7"	4'-2" × 4'-6"	5'-9"
A flat	1200 lbs	3'-3"	2'-9"	4'-8" × 4'-9"	6'-3"
G	1500 lbs	3'-6"	3'-0"	4'-10" × 4'-10"	6'-6"

CHURCH BELL DATA

Medium Tone	Weight lbs	Size		Mounting	
		Diameter	Height	Outside Frame	Dia. Wheel
F sharp	1800 lbs	3'-9"	3'-1"	5'-5" × 5'-7"	7'-0"
F	2000 lbs	3'-10"	3'-3"	5'-5" × 5'-7"	7'-0"
E	2500 lbs	4'-2"	3'-5"	5'-9" × 6'-0"	7'-0"
E flat	3000 lbs	4'-5"	3'-7"	6'-4" × 6'-8"	7'-8"
D	3500 lbs	4'-8"	3'-9"	6'-4" × 6'-8"	7'-8"
C sharp	4000 lbs	4'-10"	3'-11"	7'-4" × 7'-2"	8'-6"
C	4500 lbs	5'-1"	4'-1"	7'-4" × 7'-2"	8'-6"
C	5000 lbs	5'-3"	4'-2"	7'-4" × 7'-2"	8'-6"
B	6000 lbs	5'-7"	4'-5"	7'-4" × 7'-2"	8'-6"
B flat	7000 lbs	5'-9"	4'-8"	8'-11" × 9'-2"	9'-6"

Data checked by: Electric Time Co., Inc.; Howard Clock Products Inc.; Stromberg time Corp.

DOORS, BUCKS, WINDOWS and EQUIPMENT

TABLE OF CONTENTS

STOCK WOOD DOORS

STANDARD SIZES
INTERIOR DOORS
Ponderosa Pine:
1'-6" x {6'-6", 6'-8"}
2'-0", 2'-4", 2'-6", 2'-8" x {6'-0", 6'-6", 6'-8", 7'-0"}
3'-0" x {6'-8", 7'-0"}

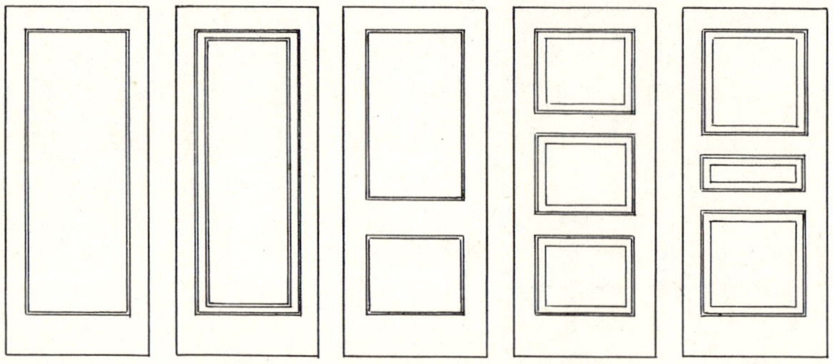

ONE PANEL
INSERT FRAME
TWO PANEL
3 EQUAL PANEL
3 UNEQUAL PANEL

PINE (CS120-53)	#100		#101		#102		#103		#104	
FIR (CS73-51)		F20		F2		F82		F3		F33
Stiles & top rail	$4\frac{3}{4}$"	$4\frac{9}{16}$"	$4\frac{1}{4}$"	$4\frac{9}{16}$"	$4\frac{3}{4}$"	$4\frac{9}{16}$"	$4\frac{3}{4}$"	$4\frac{9}{16}$"	$4\frac{3}{4}$"	$4\frac{9}{16}$"
Lock rail					8"	$7\frac{3}{8}$"			$7\frac{7}{8}$"	
Intermed. rails							$4\frac{5}{8}$"	$2\frac{1}{4}$"	$4\frac{11}{16}$"	$4\frac{1}{2}$"
Muntins (vert.)										
Bottom rail	$9\frac{5}{8}$"	$9\frac{3}{8}$"	$9\frac{1}{4}$-$9\frac{1}{2}$"	$9\frac{3}{8}$"	$9\frac{5}{8}$"	$9\frac{3}{8}$"	$9\frac{5}{8}$"	$9\frac{3}{8}$"	8"	$9\frac{3}{8}$"

STANDARD SIZES
INTERIOR DOORS
Douglas Fir:
2'-0", 2'-4", 2'-6", 2'-8", 3'-0" x {6'-0", 6'-6", 6'-8", 7'-0"}

4 PANEL
5 CROSS PANEL
6 PANEL COLONIAL
8 EQUAL PANEL
15 EQUAL PANEL

PINE (CS120-53)	#106		#107		#108		#109		#113	
FIR (CS73-51)		F44		F5		F66		F88		
Stiles & Top Rail	$4\frac{3}{4}$"	$4\frac{9}{16}$"	$4\frac{3}{4}$"	$4\frac{9}{16}$"	$4\frac{3}{4}$"	$4\frac{9}{16}$"	$4\frac{3}{4}$"	$4\frac{9}{16}$"	$4\frac{3}{4}$"	
Lock Rail	8"	$7\frac{3}{8}$"			8"	$7\frac{3}{8}$"				
Intermed. Rails			$4\frac{5}{8}$"	$4\frac{1}{2}$"	$3\frac{7}{8}$"	$4\frac{1}{2}$"	$3\frac{1}{4}$"	$3\frac{3}{8}$"	$2\frac{1}{8}$"	
Muntins (vert.)	$4\frac{5}{8}$"	$4\frac{1}{2}$"			$3\frac{7}{8}$"	$4\frac{1}{2}$"	$4\frac{5}{8}$"	$3\frac{3}{8}$"	$2\frac{1}{8}$"	
Bottom Rail	$9\frac{5}{8}$"	$9\frac{3}{8}$"	$9\frac{5}{8}$"	$9\frac{3}{8}$"	$9\frac{5}{8}$"	$9\frac{3}{8}$"	$9\frac{5}{8}$"	$9\frac{3}{8}$"	$9\frac{5}{8}$"	

STANDARD THICKNESS PINE INTERIOR DOORS: All $1\frac{3}{8}$" & $1\frac{3}{4}$" except doors 2'-4" wide and less, which are $1\frac{3}{8}$". Fir Doors: all $1\frac{3}{8}$" & $1\frac{3}{4}$".

INTERIOR DOORS

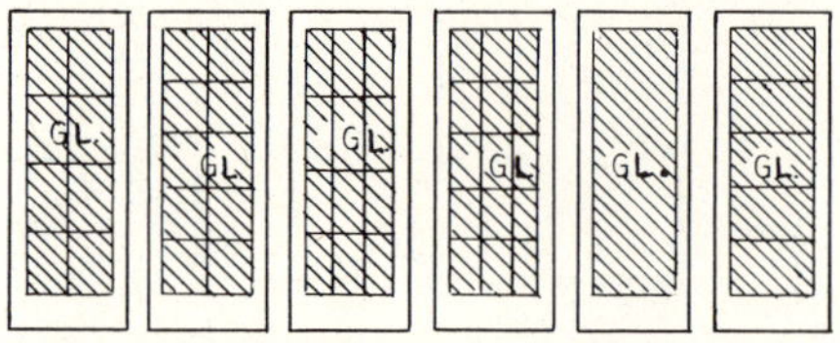

GL.

INTERIOR FRENCH OR CASEMENT DOORS, RIM AND HORIZONTAL-LIGHT DOORS

Door Sizes: 2'-4", 2'-6" x {6'-6", 6'-8", 7'-0"}; 2'-8", 3'-0" x {6'-8", 7'-0"}

Door thickness: $1\frac{3}{8}$" & $1\frac{3}{4}$"
Stiles & top rail: $4\frac{3}{4}$"
Bottom rail: $9\frac{5}{8}$"

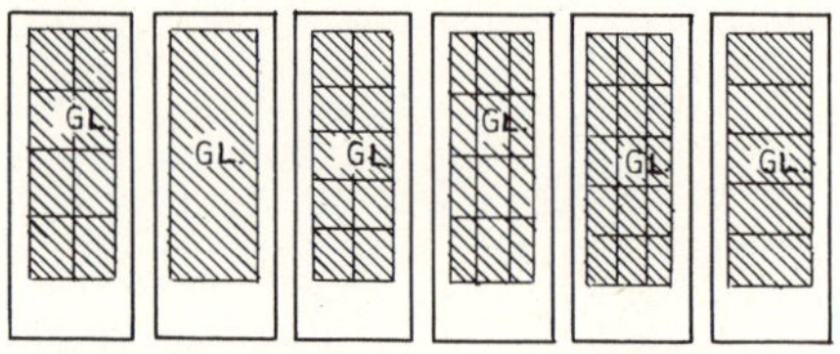

GL.

EXTERIOR FRENCH OR CASEMENT DOORS, HORIZONTAL-LIGHT DOOR

(Rim door similar but also in 7'-6" & 8'-0" heights)

Door Sizes: 2'-8", 3'-0", 3'-4" x {6'-8", 7'-0"}

Door thickness: $1\frac{3}{8}$" & $1\frac{3}{4}$" except $1\frac{3}{4}$" only for doors over 3'-0"
Stiles: $5\frac{1}{2}$" ($6\frac{1}{2}$" for doors over 3'-0")
Top rail: $6\frac{1}{2}$"
Bottom rail: 1'-$6\frac{1}{2}$"

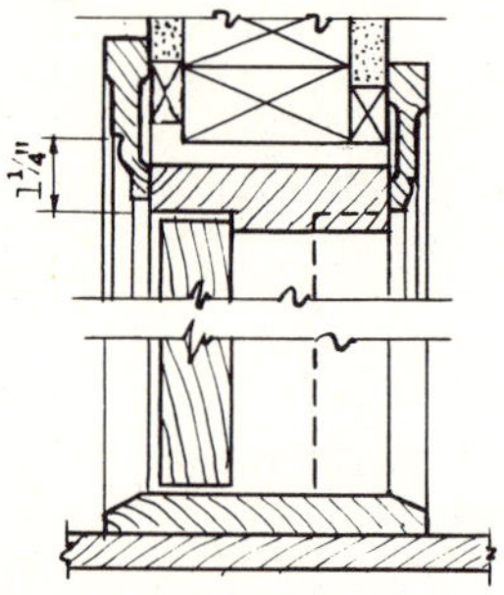

$1\frac{1}{4}$"
HEAD
(Jamb similar)
SILL

TYPICAL INTERIOR DOOR FRAME

GL.

Stock standard types in pine. $1\frac{3}{4}$" thickness. Hts 6'-8" & 7'-0". Widths 2'-8", 3'-0", 3'-4"

ENTRANCE DOORS

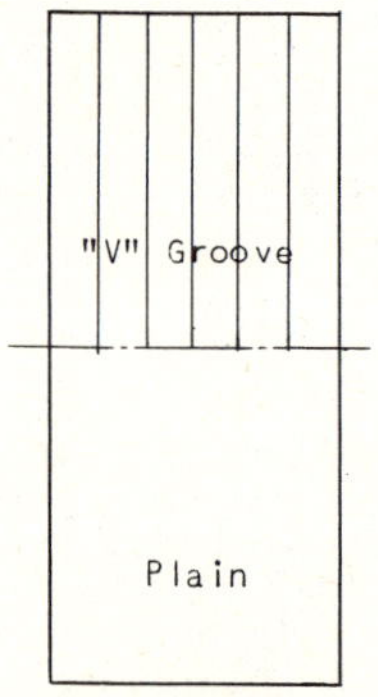

"V" Groove
Plain

FLUSH DOORS

$1\frac{3}{4}$" thick in all exterior and interior sizes.

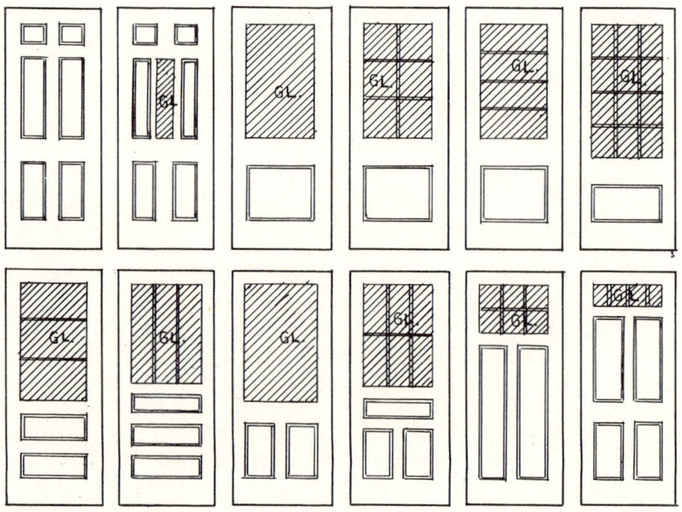

GL.

Typical standard types in pine & fir. Various other types stocked.

EXTERIOR DOORS

Data obtained from U.S. Commerce Department Standards 73-51 and 120-53.

STOCK WOOD DOORS and FRAMES

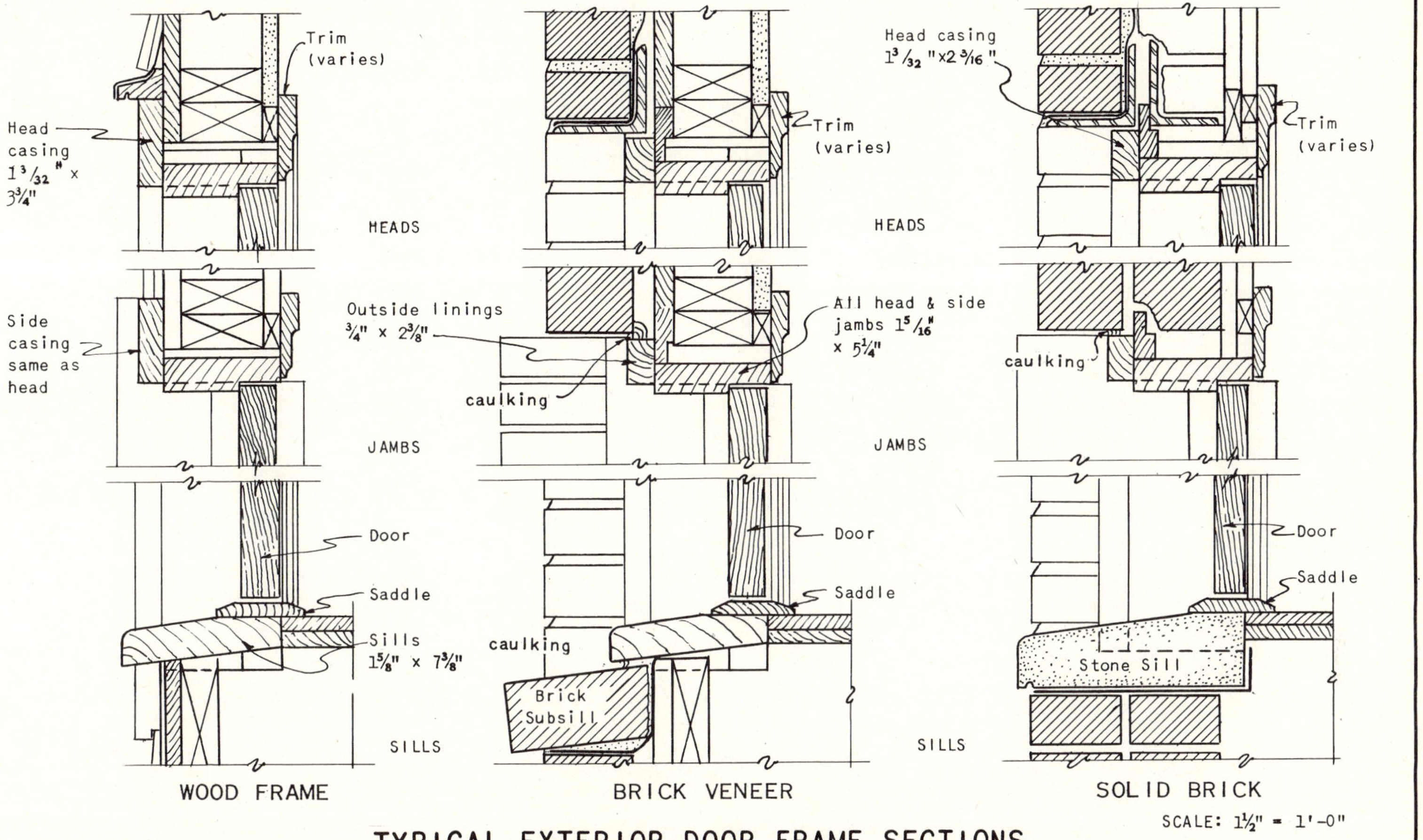
Trim (varies)
Head casing 1 3/32" x 3 3/4"
HEADS
Side casing same as head
JAMBS
Door
Saddle
Sills 1 5/8" x 7 3/8"
SILLS
WOOD FRAME
Outside linings 3/4" x 2 3/8"
caulking
Trim (varies)
All head & side jambs 1 5/16" x 5 1/4"
Door
Saddle
caulking
Brick Subsill
BRICK VENEER
Head casing 1 3/32" x 2 3/16"
Trim (varies)
HEADS
caulking
JAMBS
Door
Saddle
Stone Sill
SILLS
SOLID BRICK
SCALE: 1½" = 1'-0"

TYPICAL EXTERIOR DOOR FRAME SECTIONS

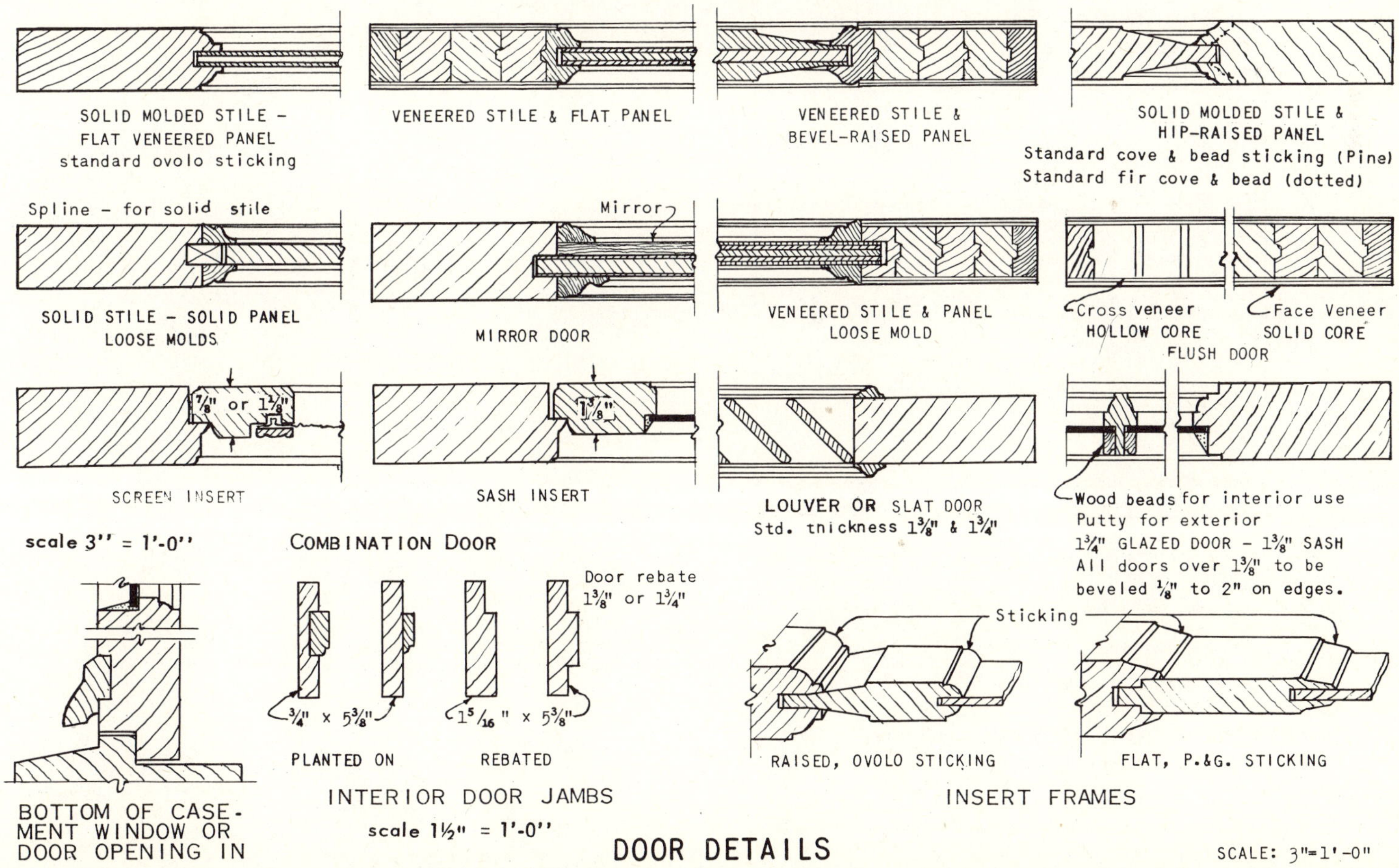
SOLID MOLDED STILE - FLAT VENEERED PANEL standard ovolo sticking
VENEERED STILE & FLAT PANEL
VENEERED STILE & BEVEL-RAISED PANEL
SOLID MOLDED STILE & HIP-RAISED PANEL
Standard cove & bead sticking (Pine)
Standard fir cove & bead (dotted)
Spline - for solid stile
SOLID STILE - SOLID PANEL LOOSE MOLDS
Mirror
MIRROR DOOR
VENEERED STILE & PANEL LOOSE MOLD
Cross veneer
HOLLOW CORE
Face Veneer
SOLID CORE
FLUSH DOOR
7/8" or 1 1/8"
SCREEN INSERT
1 3/8"
SASH INSERT
LOUVER OR SLAT DOOR
Std. thickness 1 3/8" & 1 3/4"
Wood beads for interior use
Putty for exterior
1 3/4" GLAZED DOOR - 1 3/8" SASH
All doors over 1 3/8" to be beveled 1/8" to 2" on edges.
scale 3" = 1'-0"
COMBINATION DOOR
Door rebate 1 3/8" or 1 3/4"
3/4" x 5 3/8"
1 5/16" x 5 3/8"
PLANTED ON
REBATED
INTERIOR DOOR JAMBS
scale 1½" = 1'-0"
BOTTOM OF CASEMENT WINDOW OR DOOR OPENING IN
Sticking
RAISED, OVOLO STICKING
FLAT, P.&G. STICKING
INSERT FRAMES

DOOR DETAILS

SCALE: 3"=1'-0"

HOLLOW METAL, KALAMEIN and TIN CLAD DOORS

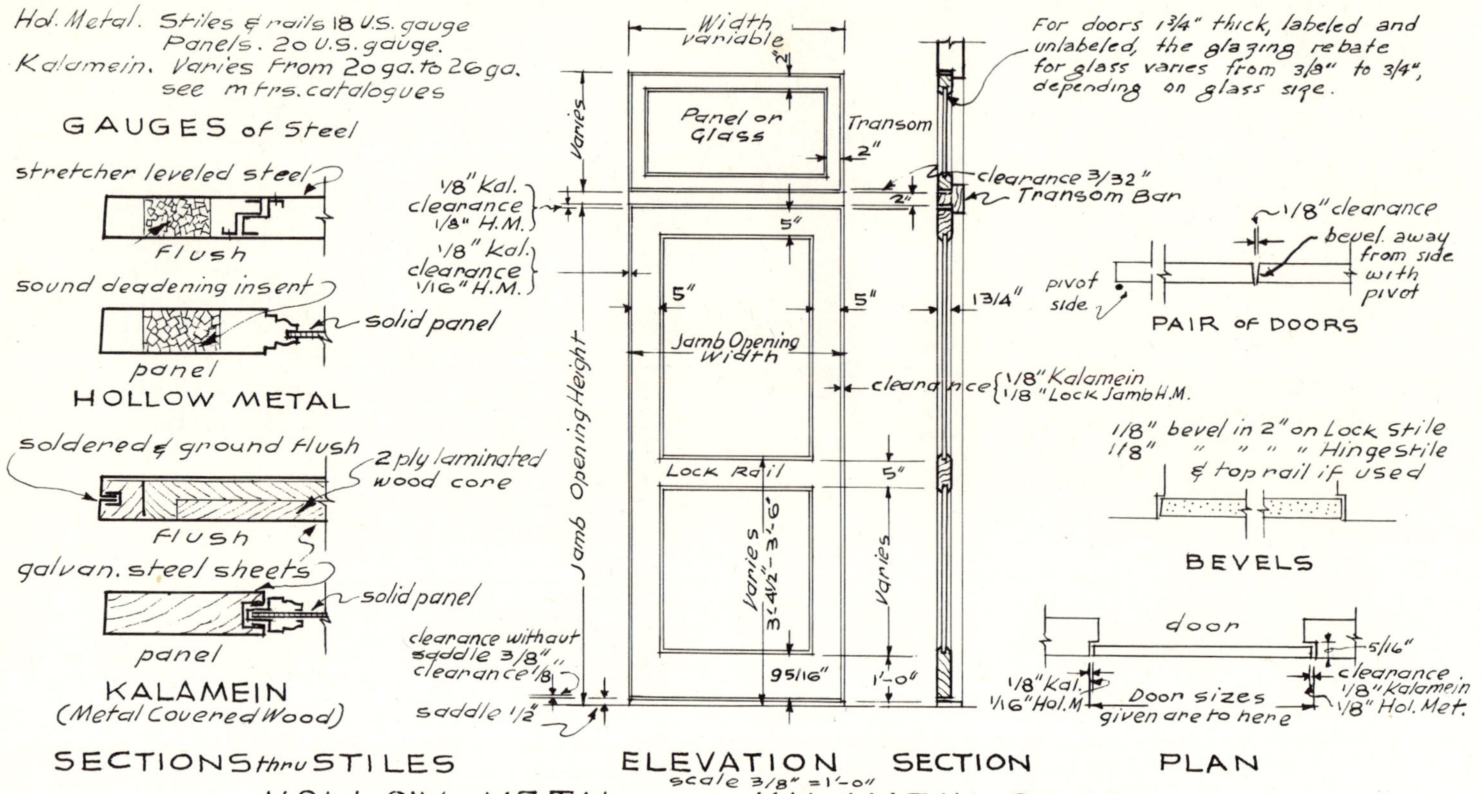

Hol. Metal. Stiles & rails 18 U.S. gauge
Panels. 20 U.S. gauge.
Kalamein. Varies from 20 ga. to 26 ga.
see mfrs. catalogues
GAUGES of Steel
stretcher leveled steel
Flush
sound deadening insert
solid panel
panel
HOLLOW METAL
soldered & ground flush
2 ply laminated wood core
Flush
galvan. steel sheets
solid panel
panel
KALAMEIN
(Metal Covered Wood)
Width variable
2"
Varies
Panel or Glass
Transom
2"
1/8" Kal. clearance 1/8" H.M.
1/8" Kal. clearance 1/16" H.M.
5"
5"
5"
Jamb Opening Width
Jamb Opening Height
Lock Rail
5"
Varies 3'-4½"-3'-6"
Varies
clearance without saddle 3/8"
clearance 1/8
saddle 1/2"
9 5/16"
1'-0"
clearance 3/32"
Transom Bar
1 3/4"
clearance {1/8" Kalamein, 1/8" Lock Jamb H.M.
For doors 1 3/4" thick, labeled and unlabeled, the glazing rebate for glass varies from 3/8" to 3/4", depending on glass size.
1/8" clearance
bevel away from side with pivot
pivot side
PAIR OF DOORS
1/8" bevel in 2" on Lock Stile
1/8" " " " Hinge Stile & top rail if used
BEVELS
door
5/16"
1/8" Kal.
1/16" Hol. M.
Door sizes given are to here
clearance 1/8" Kalamein 1/8" Hol. Met.
SECTIONS thru STILES
ELEVATION
scale 3/8" = 1'-0"
SECTION
PLAN

HOLLOW METAL and KALAMEIN DOORS

Data checked by Nat'l Kalamein Co., Inc.

Hollow metal doors available in classes A, B, C, D, E; Kalamein doors available in classes B, C, D, E.

NATIONAL BOARD OF FIRE UNDERWRITERS CLASSIFICATION OF FIRE DOORS

CLASS	APPLICATIONS
A	In walls between separate buildings or sections of buildings, and in firewalls. No glass, or panels. Door on both sides of wall. 3 hr. rating.
B	In enclosures of vertical communications thru bldgs: stairway enclosures, fire towers, shafts, fire partitions, refuse vaults, incinerator rooms, incinerator chutes, in walls and partitions within stage enclosures, or separating garages from other occupancies. Max. of 100 sq. in. in wire glass. 12" max. vert. or horiz. dimension. 1½ hr. rating.
C	In corridor or room partitions. Max. of 1296 sq in. in each light. 1/4" thick wire glass. 3/4 hr. rating.
D	In exterior walls subject to severe fire exposure. No glass or panels. 1½ hr. rating.
E	In exterior walls subject to moderate fire exposure. Max. of 720 sq. in. in each light. 1/4" thick wire glass. 3/4 hr. rating.

Consult underwriters' literature for frame types, etc. Both door and frame must be of required label to meet fire underwriters' regulations.

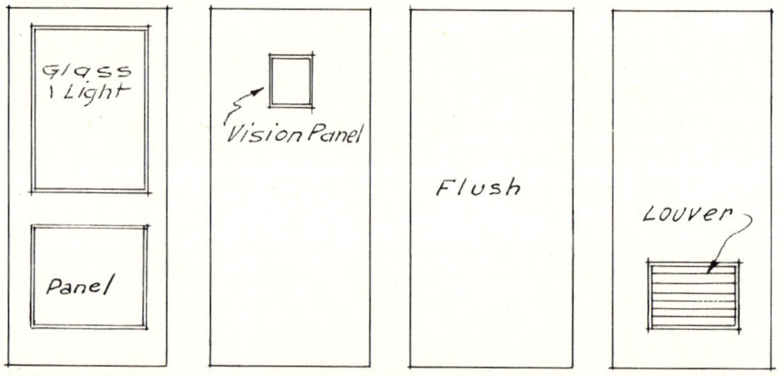

Glass 1 Light
Panel
Vision Panel
Flush
Louver

TYPICAL HOLLOW METAL & KALAMEIN DOORS

Many combinations available. Sizes vary with type.

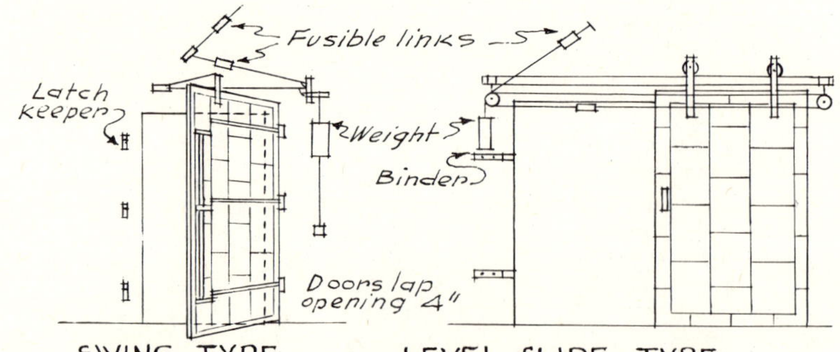

Fusible links
Latch keeper
Weight
Binder
Doors lap opening 4"
SWING TYPE
LEVEL SLIDE TYPE

Also available: vertical and inclined slide types. 3 ply door has class A label; 2 ply, classes B, C, D, E.

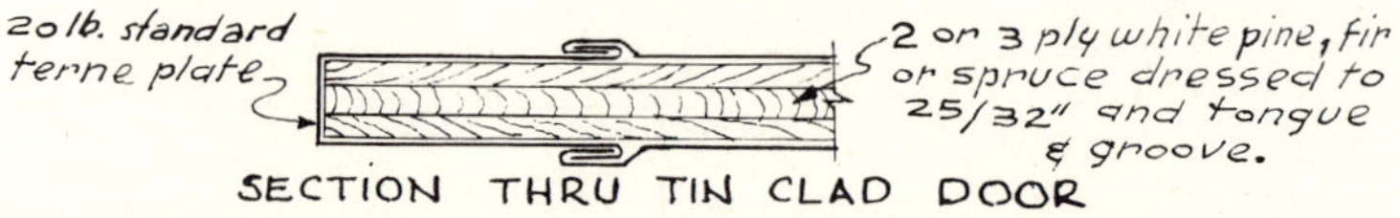

20 lb. standard terne plate
2 or 3 ply white pine, fir or spruce dressed to 25/32" and tongue & groove.

SECTION THRU TIN CLAD DOOR

TIN CLAD AUTOMATIC FIRE DOORS

HOLLOW METAL DOORS

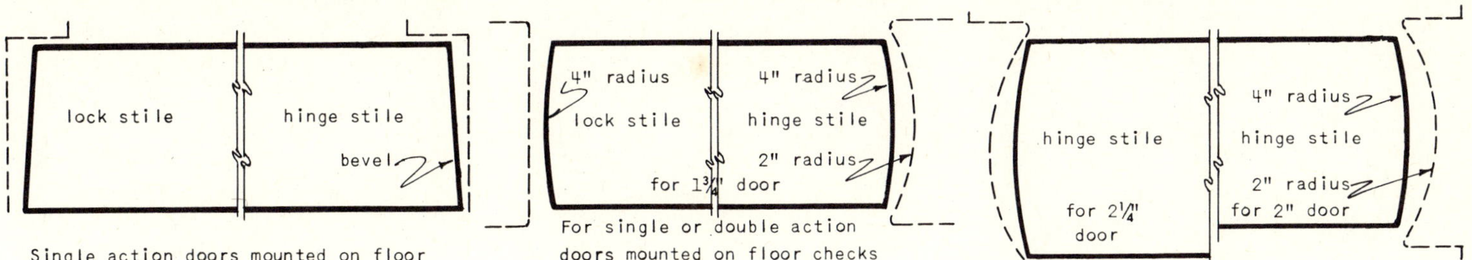
lock stile
hinge stile
bevel
4" radius
lock stile
4" radius
hinge stile
2" radius
for 1¾" door
hinge stile
4" radius
hinge stile
2" radius
for 2¼" door
for 2" door

Single action doors mounted on floor checks or pivots with offset arms.

For single or double action doors mounted on floor checks or pivots with center hung arms.

For single or double action doors mounted on floor checks or pivots with center hung arms.

SINGLE SWINGING DOORS

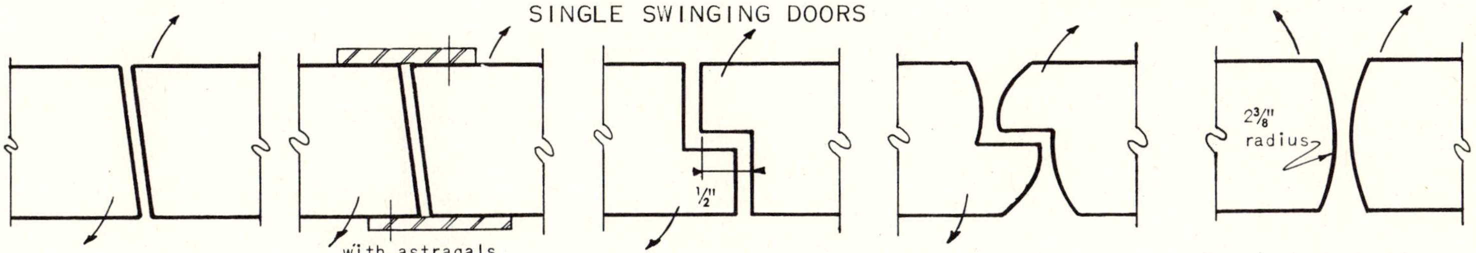
with astragals
½"
2⅜" radius

Used for "In and Out" doors mounted on single action floor checks or pivots with center hung arms, or doors hung on butts.

For single or double action doors mounted on floor checks or pivots with center hung arms.

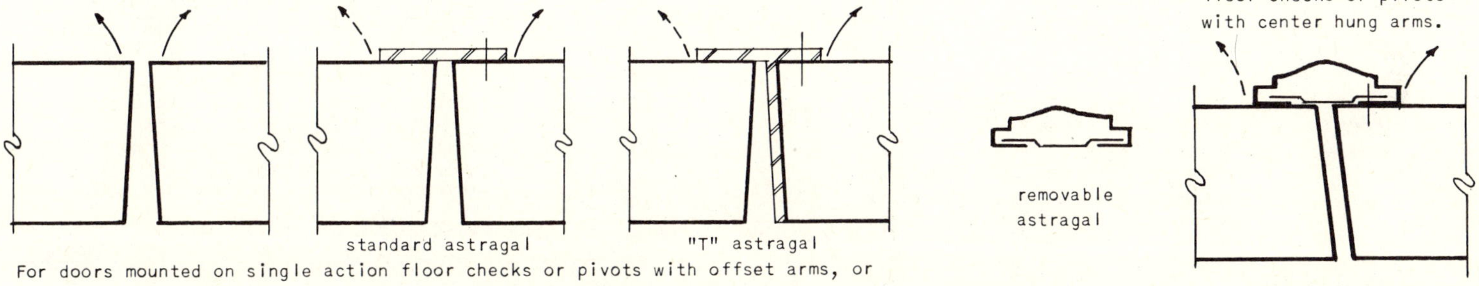
standard astragal
"T" astragal
removable astragal
astragal mounted on outside

For doors mounted on single action floor checks or pivots with offset arms, or doors hung on butts. Without astragal, both doors active.

bevel standard always ⅛" in 2"

For doors mounted on single action floor checks or pivots with offset arms, or doors hung on butts. Both doors active.

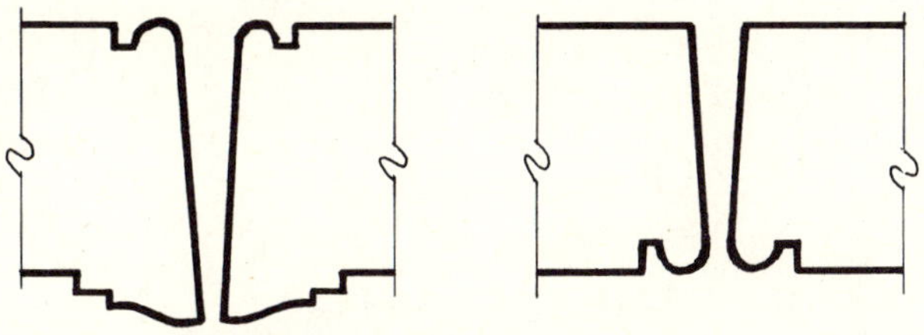

active leaf
inactive leaf

DOOR SWINGS

DOUBLE SWINGING DOORS

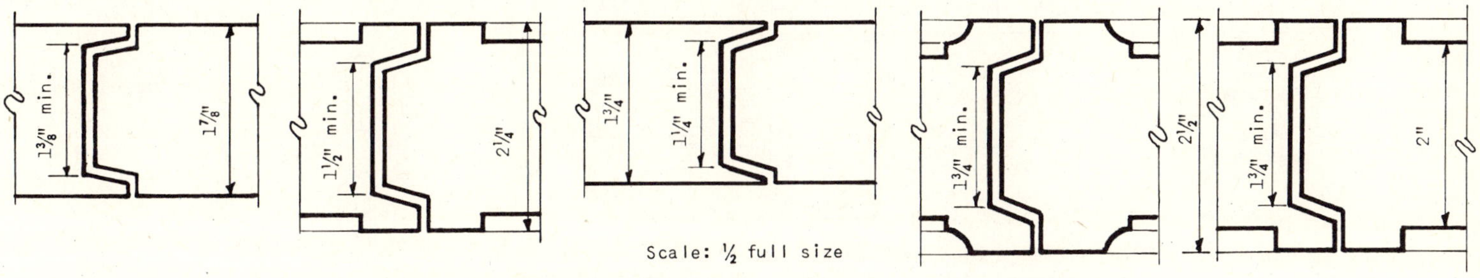
1⅜" min.
1⅞"
1½" min.
2¼"
1¾"
1¼" min.
1¾" min.
2½"
1¾" min.
2"

Scale: ½ full size

SLIDING DOORS, MEETING STILES, DOUBLE DOORS

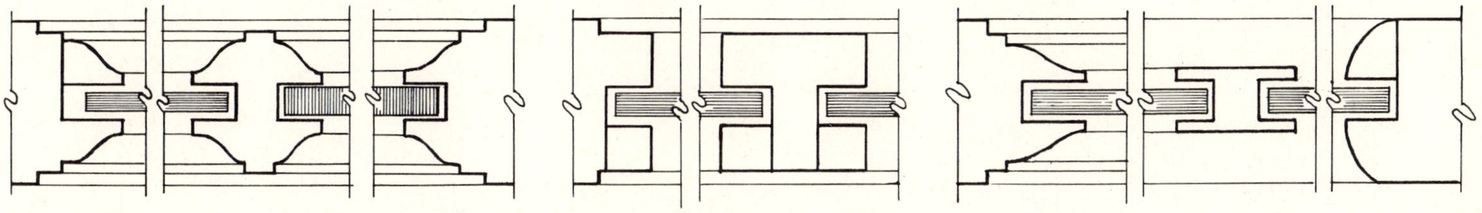

RAILS, STILES & MUNTINS, PANELED AND GLAZED

NOTE: Right hand leaf is usually active leaf, left hand leaf, inactive.

Data checked by American Society of Architectural Hardware Consultants.

Standard H.M. door thickness: 1¾"

GLASS DOORS - ENTRANCE

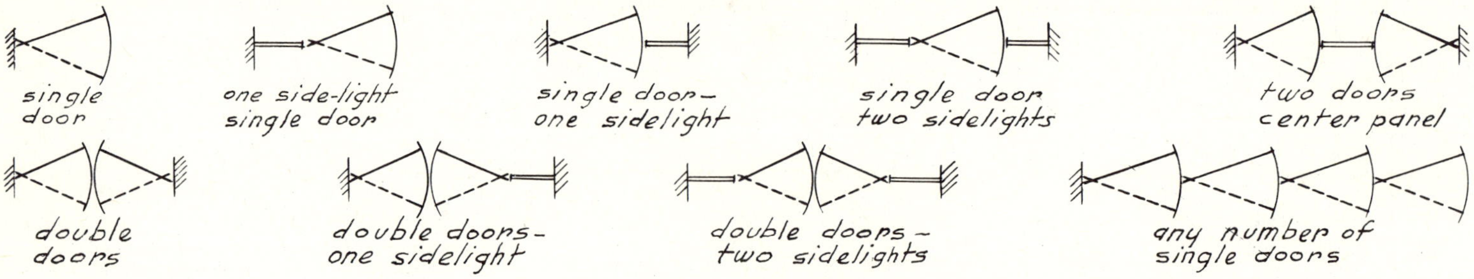
single door
one side-light single door
single door - one sidelight
single door two sidelights
two doors center panel
double doors
double doors - one sidelight
double doors - two sidelights
any number of single doors

SEVERAL POSSIBLE DOUBLE-ACTING DOOR ARRANGEMENTS

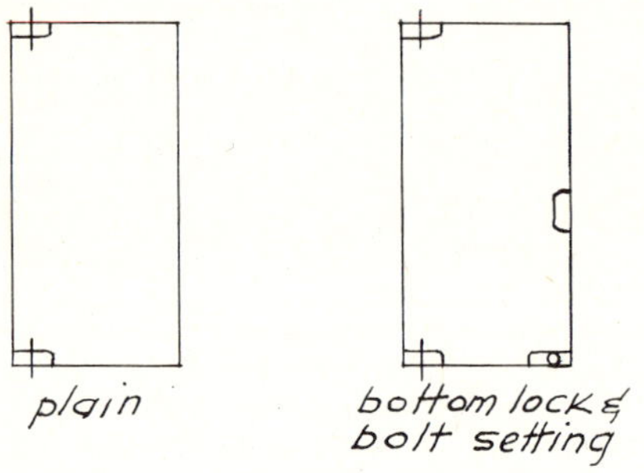
plain
bottom lock & bolt setting

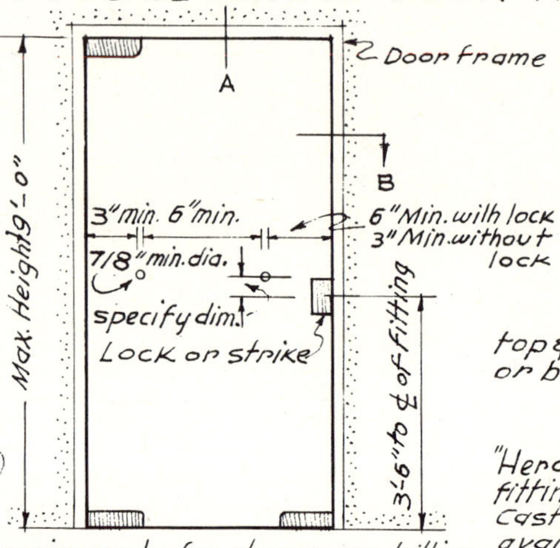
Door frame
A
B
Max. Height 9'-0"
3" min. 6" min.
6" Min. with lock
3" Min. without lock
7/8" min. dia.
specify dim.
Lock or strike
3'-6" to ℄ of fitting

Requirements for clearances; drilling

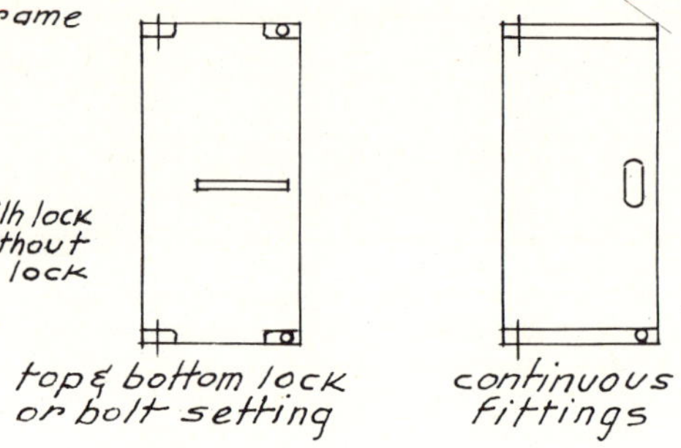
top & bottom lock or bolt setting
continuous fittings

SIZES

Both "Herculite" (Pittsburgh Plate Glass Co.) & "Tuf-flex" (Libbey-Owens-Ford Glass Co.) are available in thickness of 1/2" & 3/4", widths up to 48", lengths up to 108".

FINISHES

"Herculite" Doors are available with fittings of Alumilited Aluminum & Cast Bronze. "Tuf-flex" fittings are available in Chrome Plating in addition to the above mentioned finishes.

Data checked by Libbey-Owens-Ford Glass Co. (Tuf-flex) & Pittsburgh Plate Glass Co. (Herculite)

TEMPERED GLASS DOORS (Frameless)

Note: Fabrication of doors must be done before tempering.

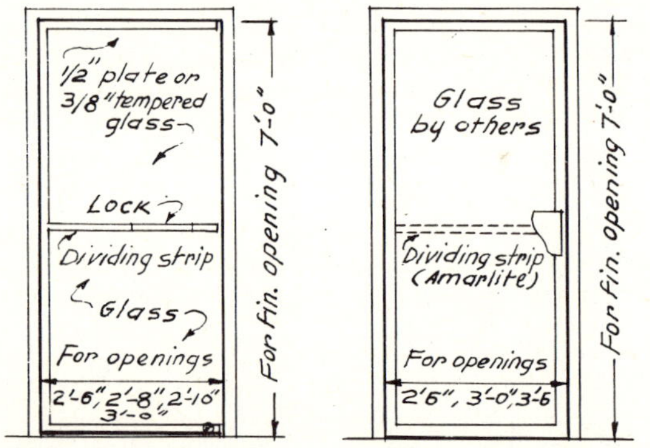
1/2" plate or 3/8" tempered glass
Lock
Dividing strip
Glass
For openings
2'-6", 2'-8", 2'-10" 3'-0"
For fin. opening 7'-0"
Glass by others
Dividing strip (Amarlite)
For openings
2'6", 3'-0", 3'-6"
For fin. opening 7'-0"

Double door widths 5'-0", 5'-4", 5'-8", 6'-0" Bronze, stainless steel. In aluminum widths to 42" single, 84" double ("Temprex")

Double door widths 5'-0", 6'-0" & 7'-0" In Extruded aluminum. stock doors

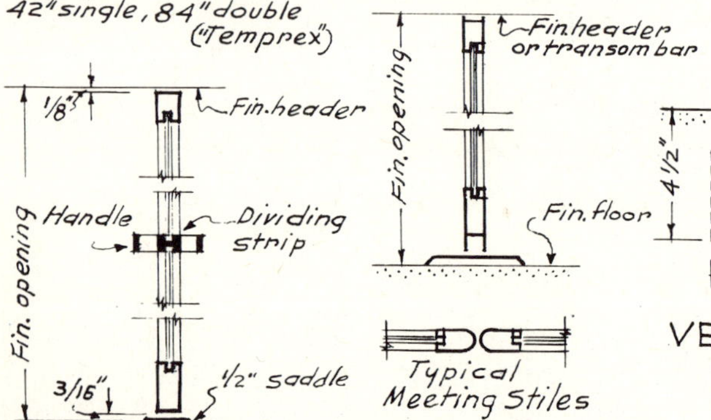
1/8"
Fin. header
Handle
Dividing strip
Fin. opening
3/16"
1/2" saddle
Fin. header or transom bar
Fin. opening
Fin. floor
Typical Meeting Stiles

SINGLE STILE "Fulite"

NARROW STILES "Kawneer"; "Visulite"; "Amarlite".

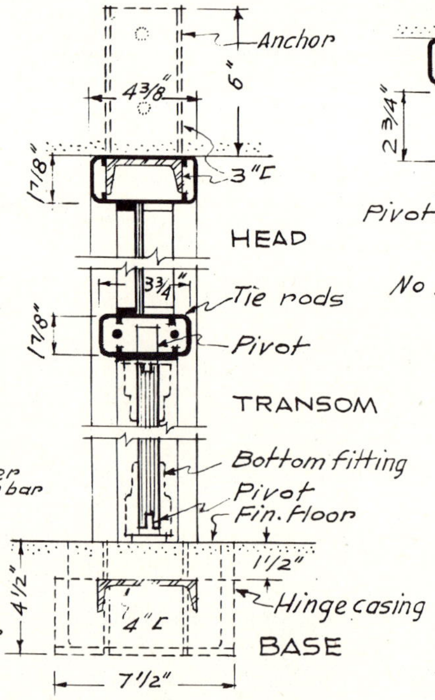
Anchor
4 3/8"
6"
1 7/8"
3" [
HEAD
3 3/4"
Tie rods
1 7/8"
Pivot
TRANSOM
Bottom fitting
Pivot
Fin. Floor
1 1/2"
4 1/2"
4" [
Hinge casing
BASE
7 1/2"

VERTICAL SECTION (A)

Scale: 1 1/2" = 1'-0"

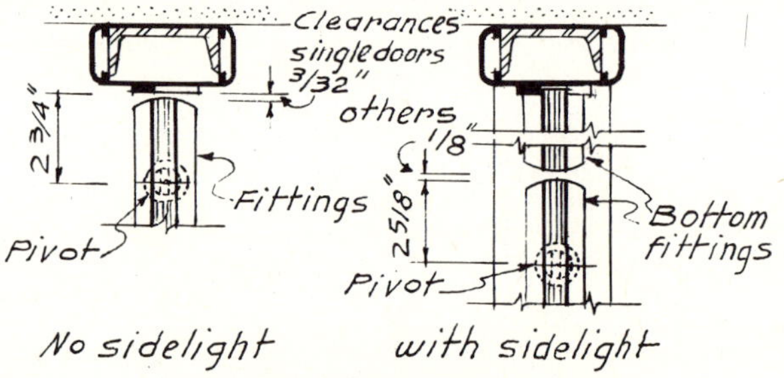
Clearances single doors 3/32" others 1/8"
2 3/4"
Fittings
Pivot
2 5/8"
Bottom fittings
Pivot
No sidelight
with sidelight

JAMB SECTIONS (B)

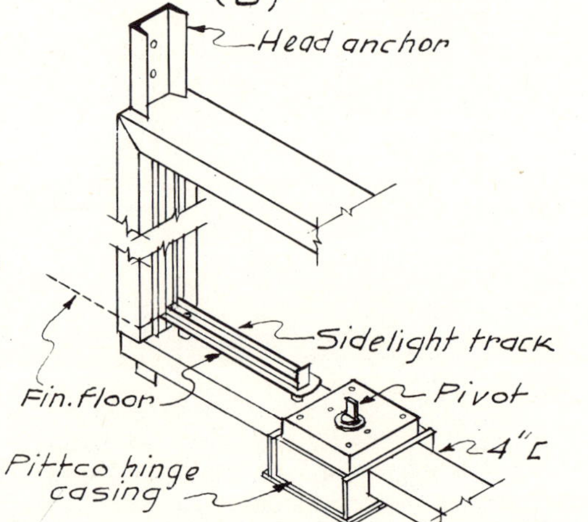
Head anchor
Sidelight track
Pivot
4" [
Fin. Floor
Pittco hinge casing

PERSPECTIVE of FRAME for SIDELIGHT

GLASS DOORS (Tempered or Plain Plate Glass) WITH FRAMES

HERCULITE DOOR FRAMES for Tempered Glass Doors

Data checked by Amer. Art Metals Co. (Amarlite), Martin Katz Corp. (Visulite), Schacht Asso. Inc. (Fulite)

LIGHT WEIGHT STEEL INTERIOR DOORS and FRAMES

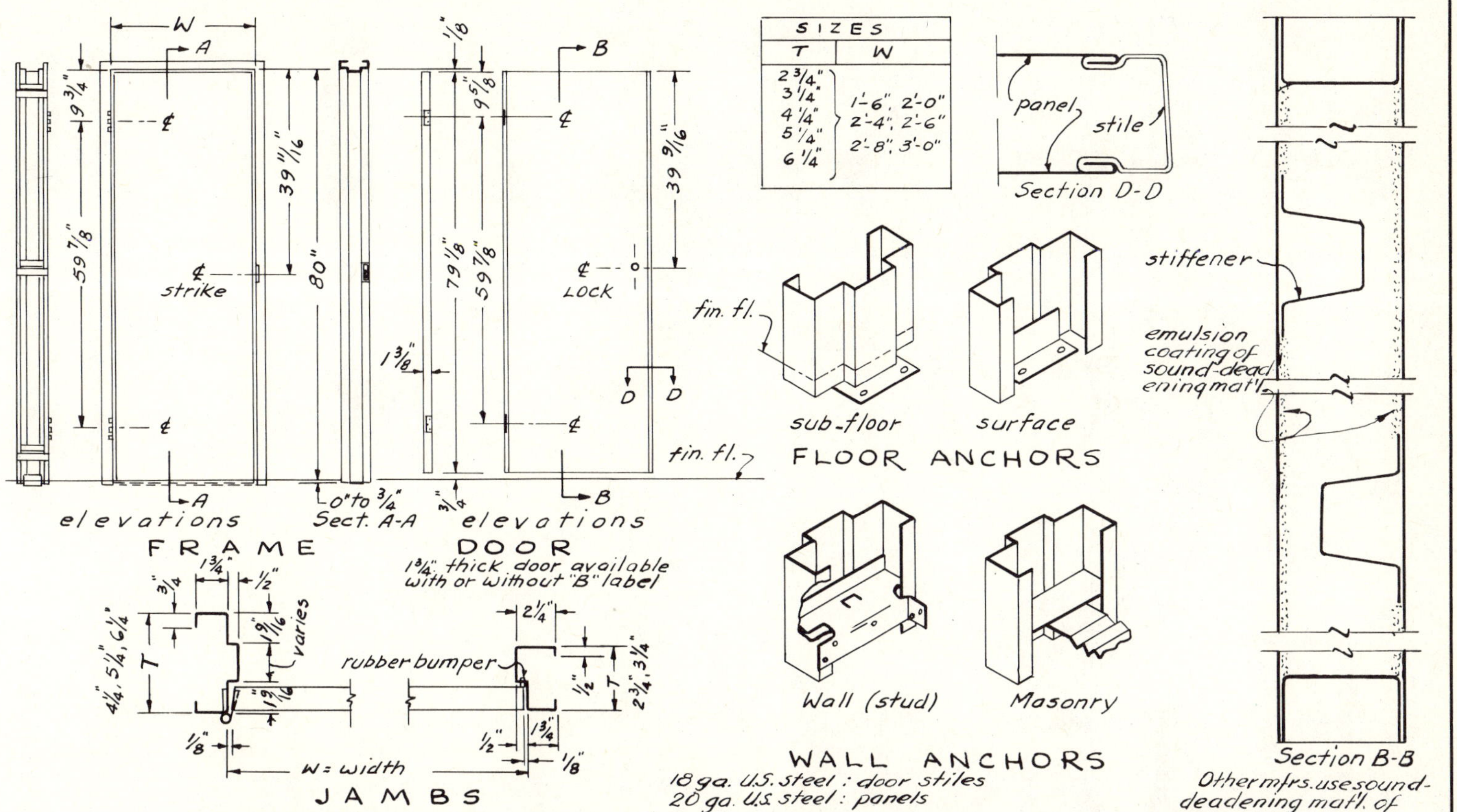

W
A
9 3/4
59 7/8
39 11/16
80"
¢
¢ strike
0" to 3/4"
elevations
Sect. A-A
FRAME
1/8
B
9 5/8
39 9/16
79 1/8
59 7/8
1 3/8"
¢ LOCK
D D
fin. fl.
3/4
elevations
DOOR
1 3/4" thick door available with or without "B" label
3/4
1 3/4"
1/2"
9/16
varies
T
4 1/4, 5 1/4, 6 1/4
1/8"
W = width
rubber bumper
2 1/4"
1/2"
2 3/4, 3 1/4
1 3/4
1/8"
JAMBS
panel
stile
Section D-D
fin. fl.
sub-floor
surface
FLOOR ANCHORS
Wall (stud)
Masonry
WALL ANCHORS
18 ga. U.S. steel : door stiles
20 ga. U.S. steel : panels
stiffener
emulsion coating of sound-deadening mat'l.
Section B-B
Other mfrs. use sound-deadening mat'l. of asbestos, rock wool, fiber glass, etc.

SIZES	
T	W
2 3/4" 3 1/4" 4 1/4" 5 1/4" 6 1/4"	1'-6", 2'-0" 2'-4", 2'-6" 2'-8", 3'-0"

INTERIOR DOOR and FRAME UNITS

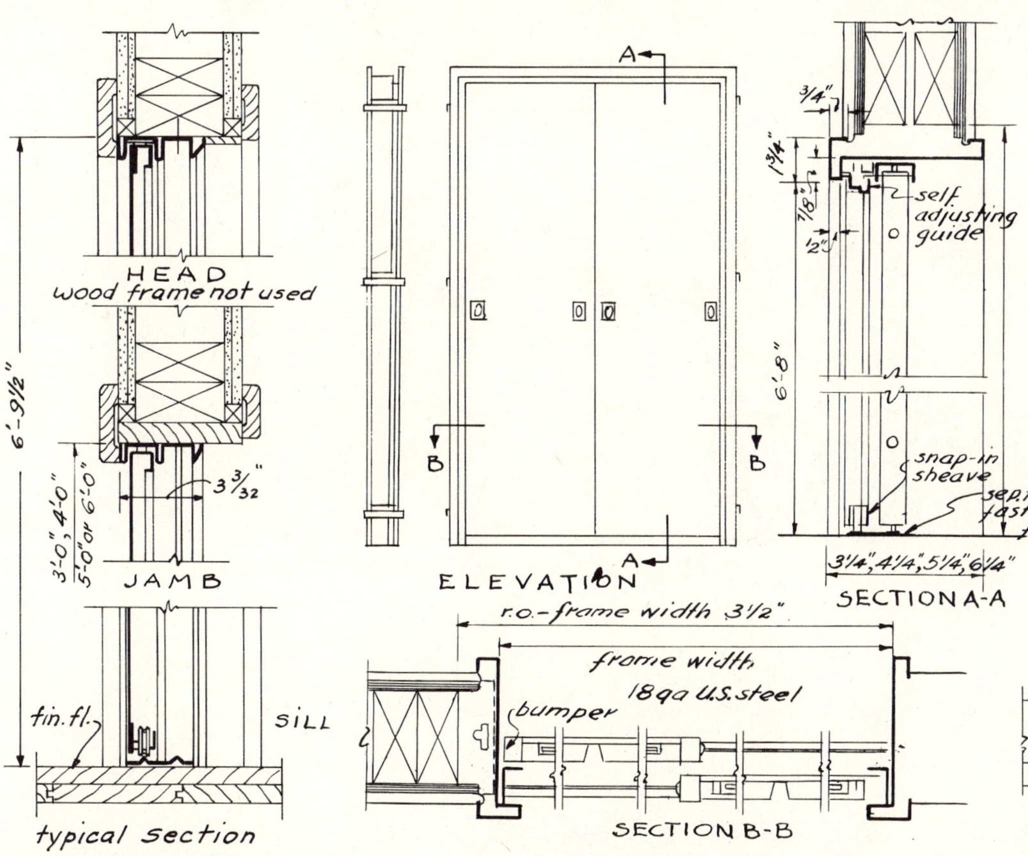

HEAD
wood frame not used
6'-9 1/2"
3 3/32"
3'-0", 4'-0"
5'-0" or 6'-0"
JAMB
fin. fl.
SILL
typical section
A
B
B
A
ELEVATION
3/4"
1 3/4"
1/8"
1/2"
self adjusting guide
6'-8"
snap-in sheave
set track fastens to floor
3 1/4", 4 1/4", 5 1/4", 6 1/4"
SECTION A-A
r.o.-frame width 3 1/2"
frame width
18 ga U.S. steel
bumper
SECTION B-B

KNOCKED DOWN UNIT
24 ga. U.S. steel.

DOORS & FRAME UNITS

SLIDING CLOSET DOORS 1 1/2" = 1'-0"

Data by American Welding & Manufacturing Co.

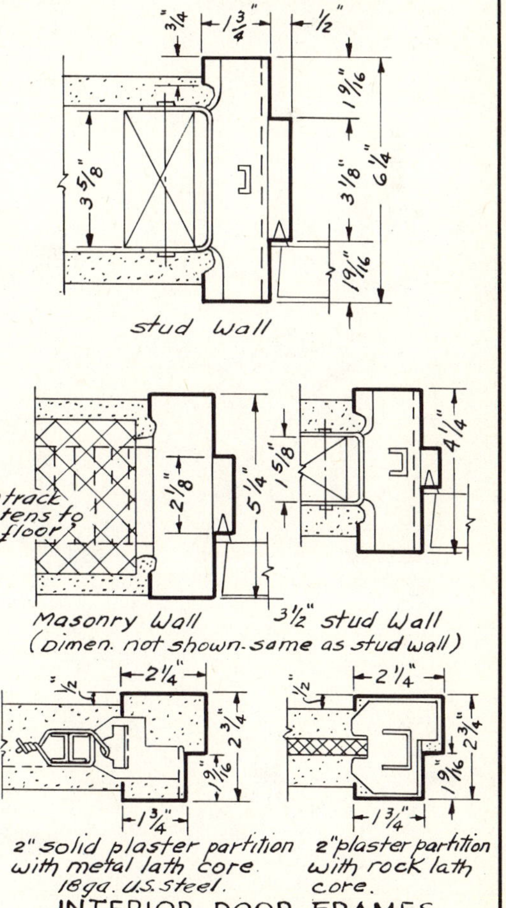

3/4
1 3/4"
1/2"
1 9/16
3 5/8
3 1/8"
6 1/4"
1 9/16
stud wall
2 1/8"
5 1/4"
1 5/8
4 1/4"
Masonry Wall
3 1/2" stud Wall
(Dimen. not shown-same as stud wall)
2 1/4"
1/2
2 3/4"
1 9/16"
1 3/4"
2" solid plaster partition with metal lath core
18 ga. U.S. steel.
2" plaster partition with rock lath core.

INTERIOR DOOR FRAMES IN TYPICAL WALL SECTIONS

REVOLVING DOORS

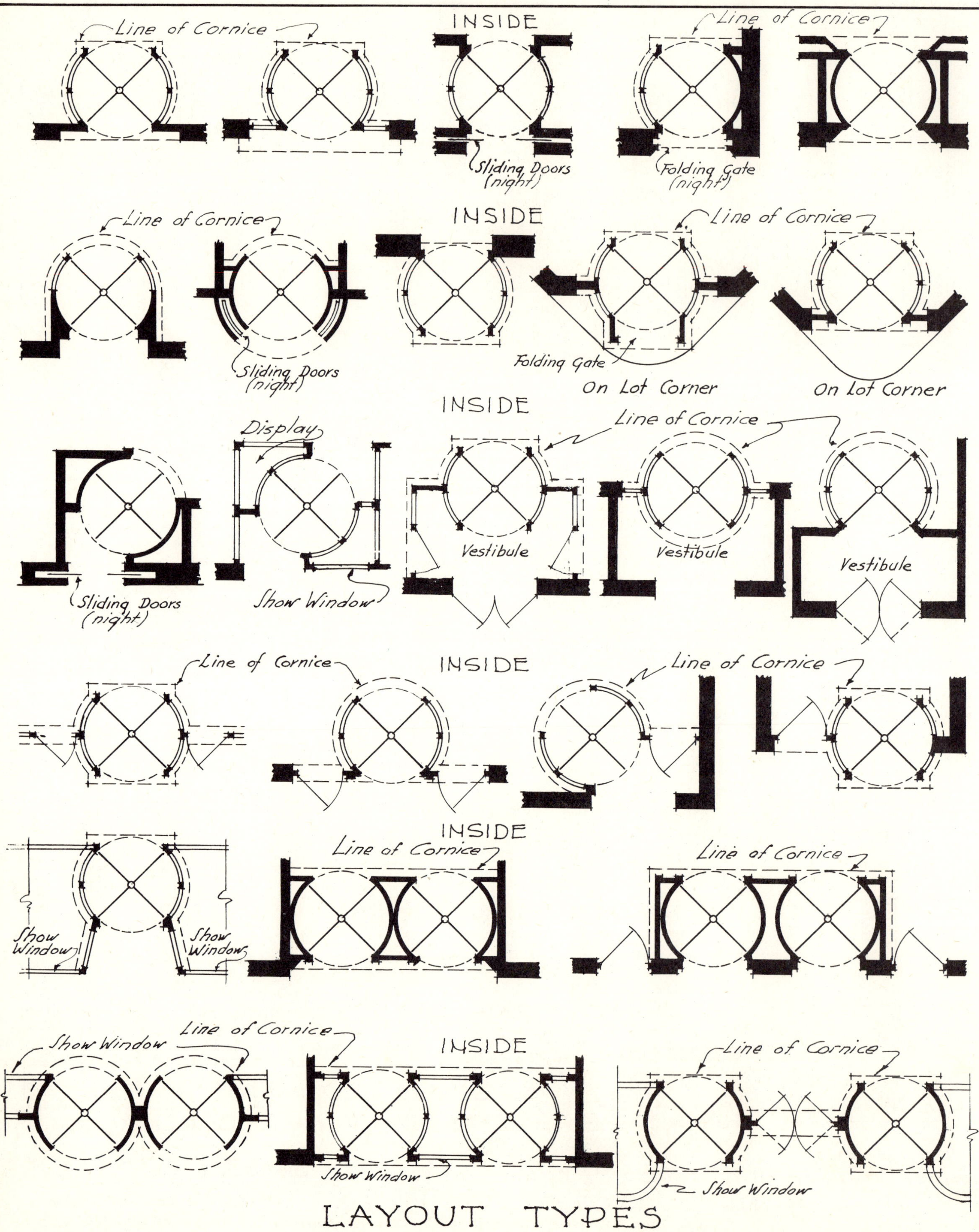

Line of Cornice
INSIDE
Line of Cornice
Sliding Doors (night)
Folding Gate (night)
Line of Cornice
INSIDE
Line of Cornice
Sliding Doors (night)
Folding Gate
On Lot Corner
On Lot Corner
INSIDE
Display
Line of Cornice
Vestibule
Vestibule
Vestibule
Sliding Doors (night)
Show Window
Line of Cornice
INSIDE
Line of Cornice
INSIDE
Line of Cornice
Line of Cornice
Show Window
Show Window
Show Window
Line of Cornice
INSIDE
Line of Cornice
Show Window
Show Window

LAYOUT TYPES

REVOLVING DOORS

KEY TO DIMENSIONS

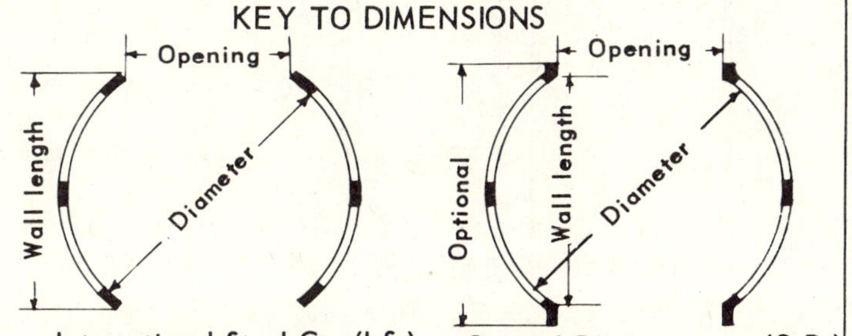
Opening
Wall length
Diameter
Opening
Optional
Wall length
Diameter

International Steel Co. (I.S.) General Bronze Corp. (G.B.)

SIZES OF STANDARD DOORS (plan)

Diameter	Opening		Wall length	
	I.S.	G.B.	I.S.	G.B.
5'-6"	3'-8¾"	3'-8¾"	4'-3¼"	4'-0½"
5'-8"		3'-10⅛"		4'-2"
5'-10"	3'-11½"	3'-11½"	4'-6⅛"	4'-3⅜"
6'-0"	4'-1"	4'-0⅞"	4'-7 7/16"	4'-4⅞"
6'-2"	4'-2½"	4'-2⅜"	4'-8 13/16"	4'-6¼"
6'-4"	4'-4"	4'-3¾"	4'-10⅛"	4'-7⅝"
*6'-6"	4'-5¼"	4'-5⅛"	4'-11 11/16"	4'-9⅛"
6'-8"	4'-6¾"	4'-6⅝"	5'-1"	4'-10½"
6'-10"	4'-8"	4'-8"	5'-2⅝"	4'-11⅞"
7'-0"	4'-9½"	4'-9½"	5'-3 15/16"	5'-1¼"
7'-2"	4'-11"	4'-10⅞"	5'-5¼"	5'-2¾"
7'-4"	5'-0⅜"	5'-0¼"	5'-6 11/16"	5'-4⅛"
7'-6"	5'-1¾"	5'-1⅝"	5'-8 3/16"	5'-5⅝"
7'-8"		5'-3"		5'-7"
7'-10"		5'-4½"		5'-8⅜"
8'-0"		5'-5⅞"		5'-9¾"

* International Steel mfr. this size for stock in stainless steel, bronze, aluminum & mild steel. (6'-10" high.)

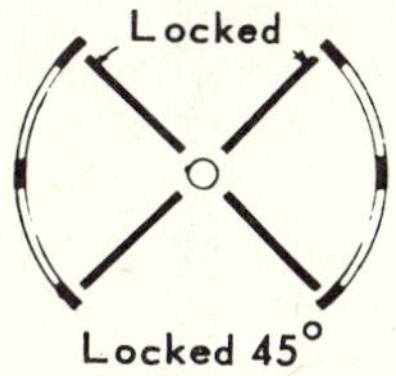
Locked

Locked 45°

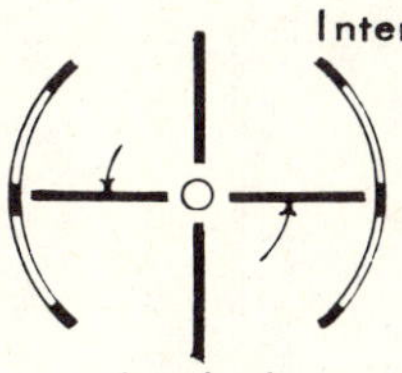
Interior

Locked

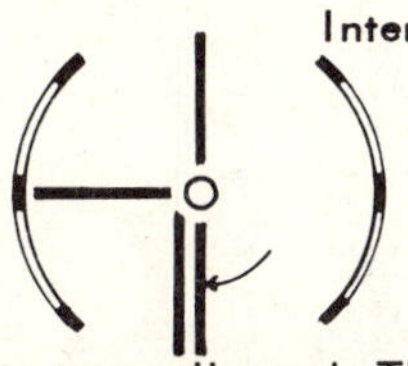
Interior

One wing collapsed. This may be used for night swing door, or for passage of large, bulky objects.

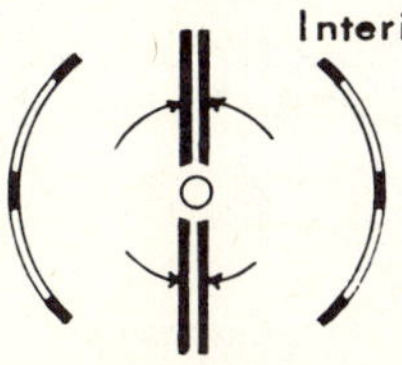
Interior

Central open wings folded in pairs.

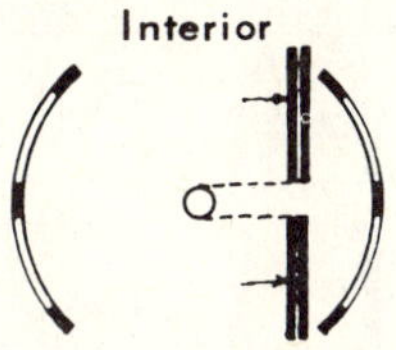
Interior

Full open-side, with the wings folded in pairs.

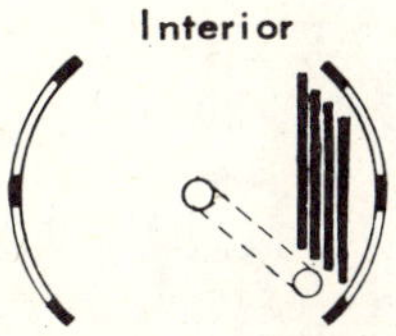
Interior

Full open-side, with the wings book-folded. This type seldom used.

Interior

Panic-collapsed, wings book folded in center

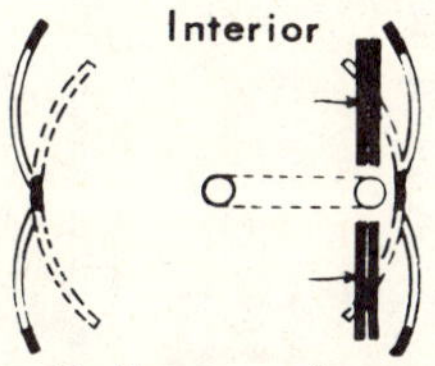
Interior

Full open-wing aside

Solid lines show flexed wall to provide for wider passage

PLANS of WINGS POSITION

Scale: 1/8" = 1'-0"

Note: Three wing door types are available

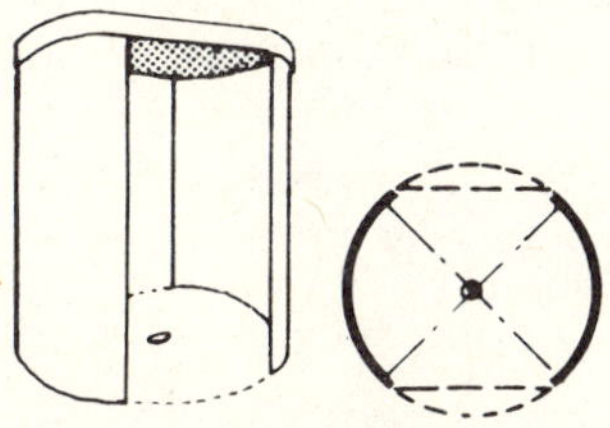

Solid wall exposed with heavy cornice. Concealed mechanism.

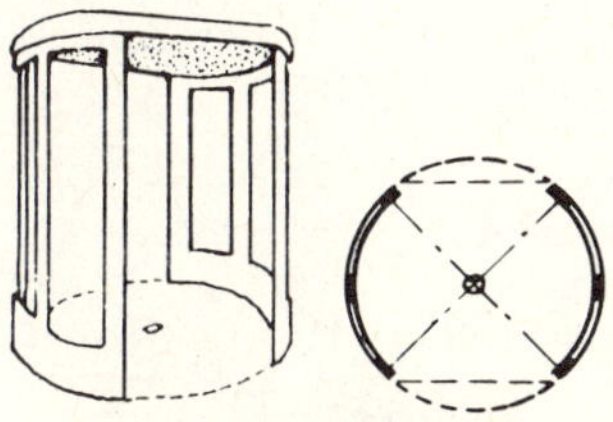

Glazed wall with heavy cornice. Concealed mechanism.

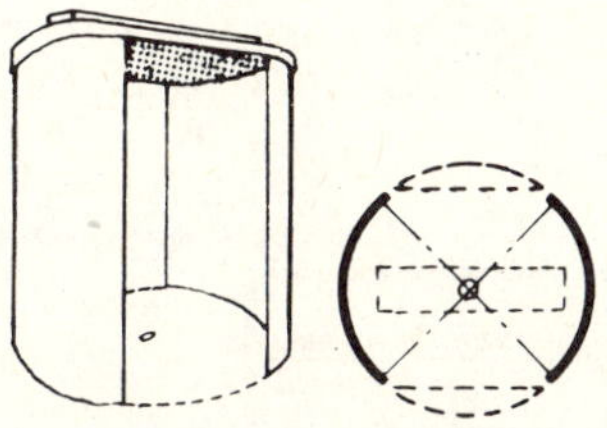

*Solid wall exposed with light cornice. Mechanism boxed.

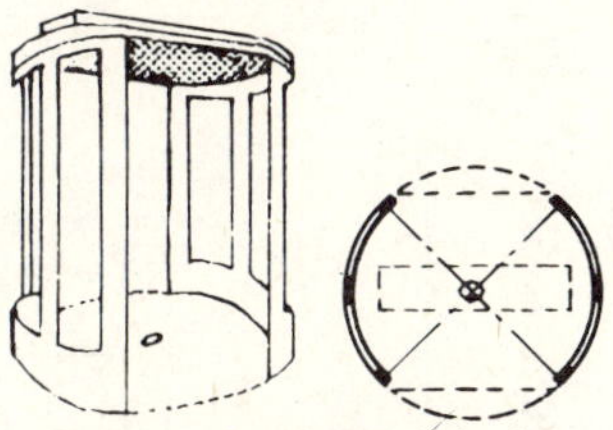

Glazed wall with light cornice. Mechanism boxed.

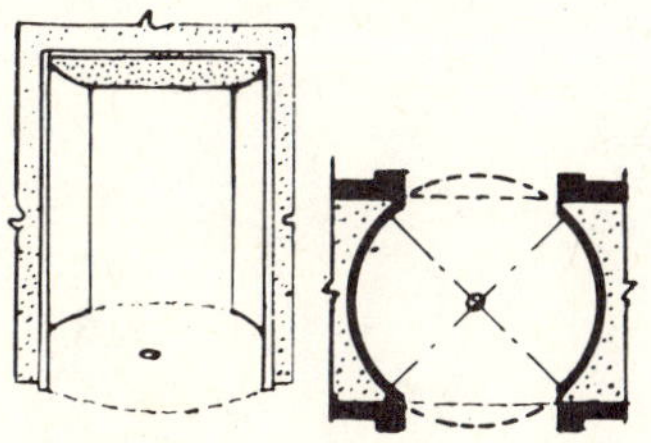

Walls built-in

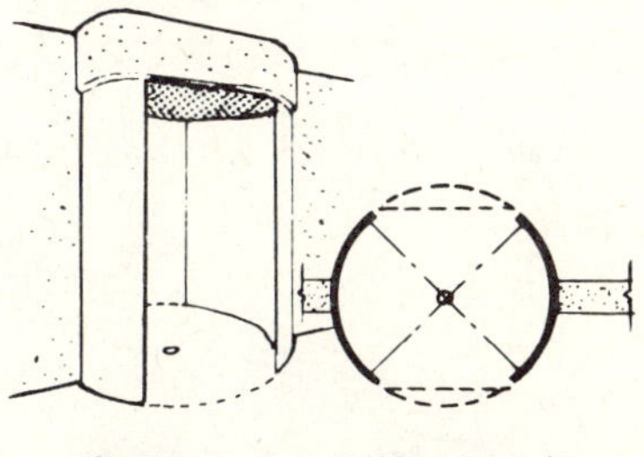

Walls exposed. Head built in. Walls can either be glazed or solid.

ENCLOSURE DESIGN TYPES

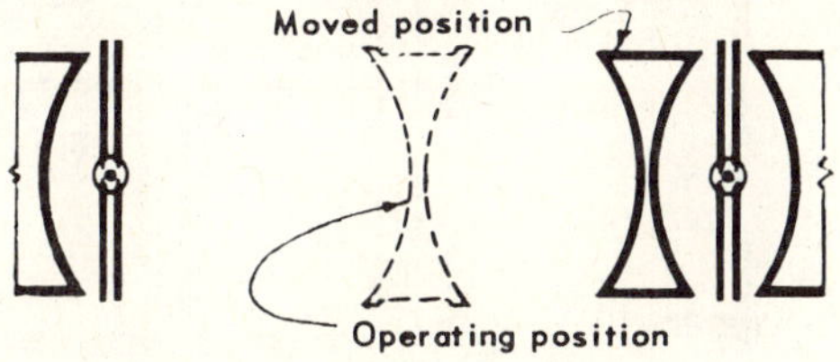
Moved position
Operating position

A two door entrance transforms into a large opening for automobiles, display, etc.

MOVABLE ENCLOSURE WALLS

* A 2" cornice can be obtained by placing mechanism in floor; with this arrangement wings cannot be moved to side.

REVOLVING DOORS

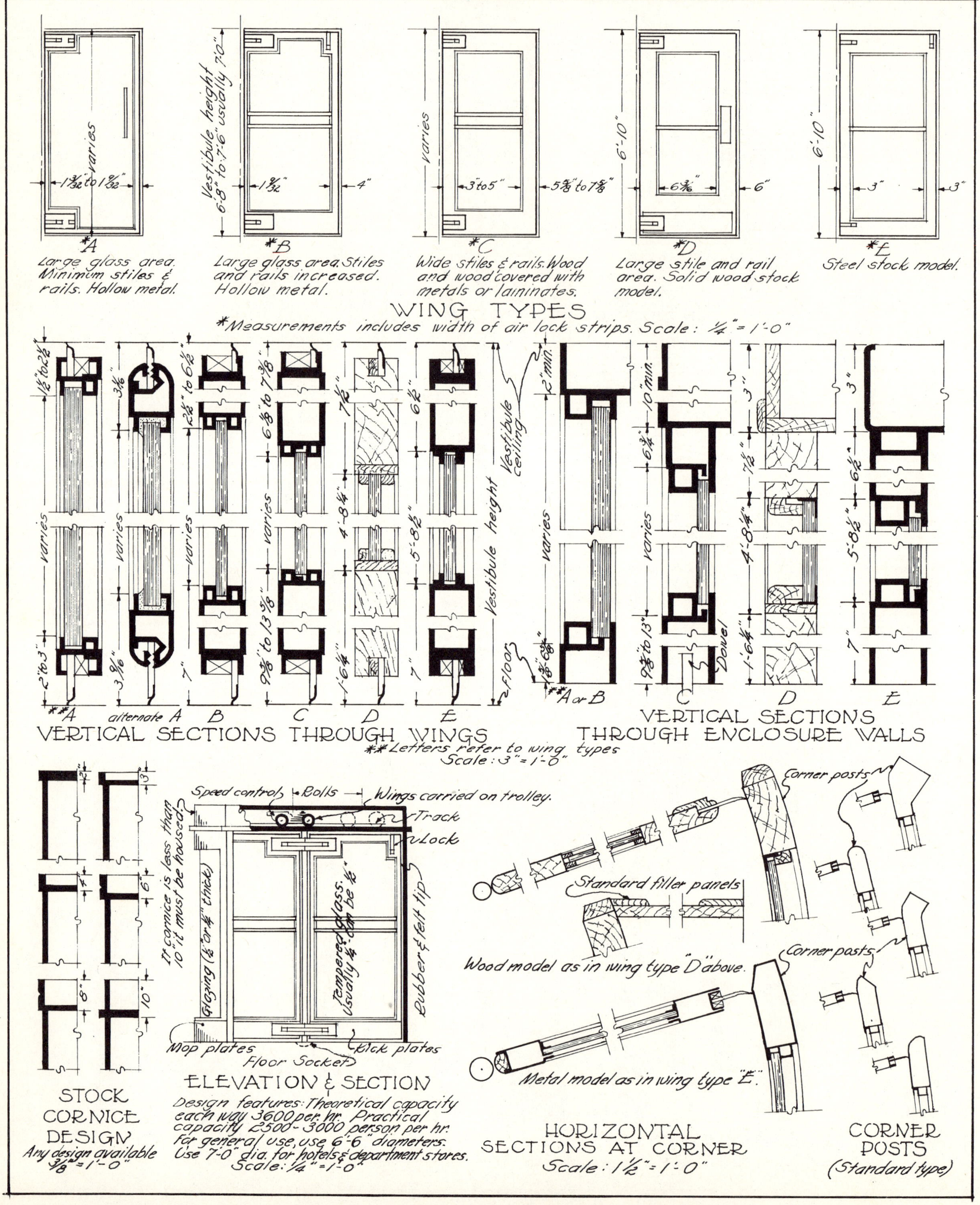
varies
1 3/32" to 1 9/32"
*A
Large glass area. Minimum stiles & rails. Hollow metal.
Vestibule height 6'-8" to 7'-6" usually 7'-0"
1 9/32"
4"
*B
Large glass area. Stiles and rails increased. Hollow metal.
varies
3" to 5"
5 5/8" to 7 5/8"
*C
Wide stiles & rails. Wood and wood covered with metals or laminates.
6'-10"
6 3/16"
6"
*D
Large stile and rail area. Solid wood stock model.
6'-10"
3"
3"
*E
Steel stock model.
WING TYPES
*Measurements includes width of air lock strips. Scale: 1/4" = 1'-0"
1 1/2" to 2 1/2"
varies
2" to 3"
3 1/16"
varies
3 5/16"
2 1/2" to 6 1/2"
varies
7"
6 5/8" to 7 3/8"
varies
9 5/8" to 13 5/8"
7 1/2"
4'-8 1/4"
1'-6 1/4"
6 1/2"
5'-8 1/2"
7"
Vestibule ceiling
Vestibule height
Floor
**A
alternate A
B
C
D
E
VERTICAL SECTIONS THROUGH WINGS
**Letters refer to wing types
Scale: 3" = 1'-0"
2" min.
varies
3 5/8"
6 5/8"
10" min.
6 3/4"
varies
9 5/8" to 13"
Dowel
3"
7 1/2"
4'-8 1/4"
1'-6 1/4"
3"
6 1/2"
5'-8 1/2"
7"
**A or B
C
D
E
VERTICAL SECTIONS THROUGH ENCLOSURE WALLS
3"
3"
4"
6"
8"
10"
STOCK CORNICE DESIGN
Any design available
3/8" = 1'-0"
Speed control
Rolls
Wings carried on trolley.
Track
Lock
If cornice is less than 10" it must be housed.
Glazing (1/8" or 1/4" thick)
Tempered glass. Usually 1/4". Can be 1/2"
Rubber & felt tip
Mop plates
Kick plates
Floor Socket
ELEVATION & SECTION
Design features: Theoretical capacity each way 3600 per. hr. Practical capacity 2500-3000 person per hr. For general use, use 6'-6" diameters. Use 7'-0" dia. for hotels & department stores.
Scale: 1/4" = 1'-0"
Corner posts
Standard filler panels
Wood model as in wing type "D" above.
Corner posts
Metal model as in wing type "E".
HORIZONTAL SECTIONS AT CORNER
Scale: 1 1/2" = 1'-0"
CORNER POSTS
(Standard type)

STORAGE ROOMS and STORAGE VAULTS, FIRE-RESISTING

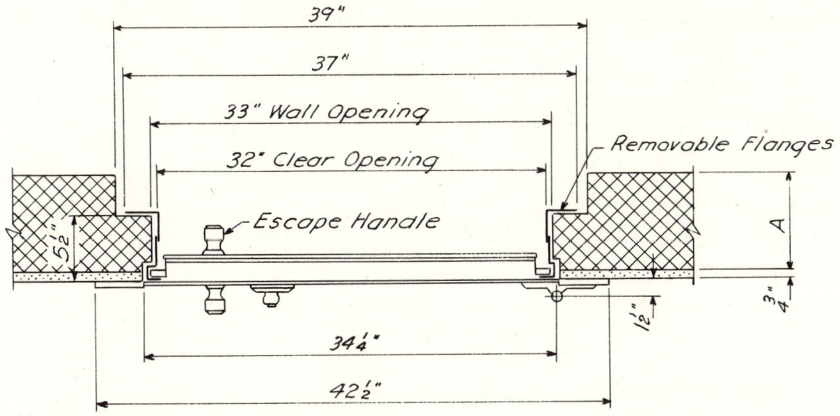
39"
37"
33" Wall Opening
32" Clear Opening
Removable Flanges
Escape Handle
A
$5\frac{1}{2}$"
$\frac{3}{4}$"
$1\frac{1}{2}$"
$34\frac{1}{4}$"
$42\frac{1}{2}$"

Note:
Dimensions are for both ½ hr. & 1 hr. doors. Masonry and plaster completed before setting door. No grouting. Use for records, wine storage, silver (house) storage. Floor and ceiling thicknesses same as for walls.

MINIMUM WALL THICKNESSES RECOMMENDED BY THE NATIONAL FIRE PROTECTION ASSOCIATION:

A { Reinforced Concrete .... 6"; Brick .... 8"; Hollow Concrete Masonry .... 8" } Exclusive of finish

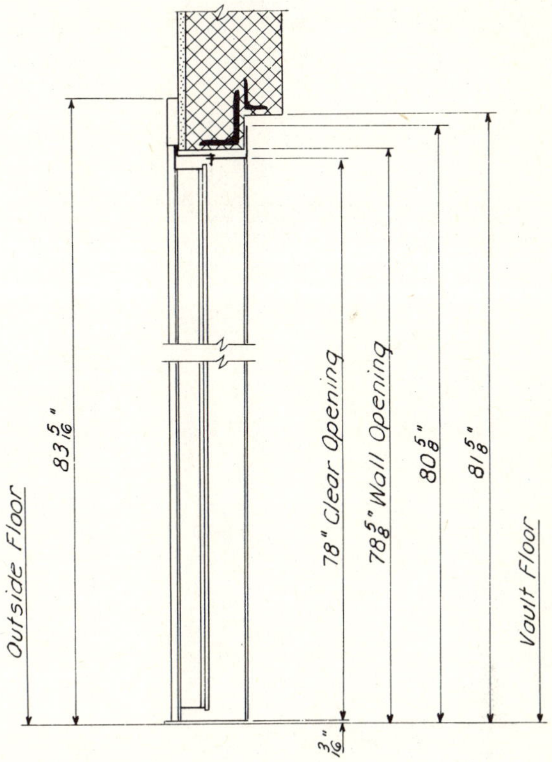
Outside Floor
$83\frac{5}{16}$"
78" Clear Opening
$78\frac{5}{8}$" Wall Opening
$80\frac{5}{8}$"
$81\frac{5}{8}$"
Vault Floor
$\frac{3}{16}$"

ONE-HALF HOUR & ONE HOUR FILE STORAGE ROOMS

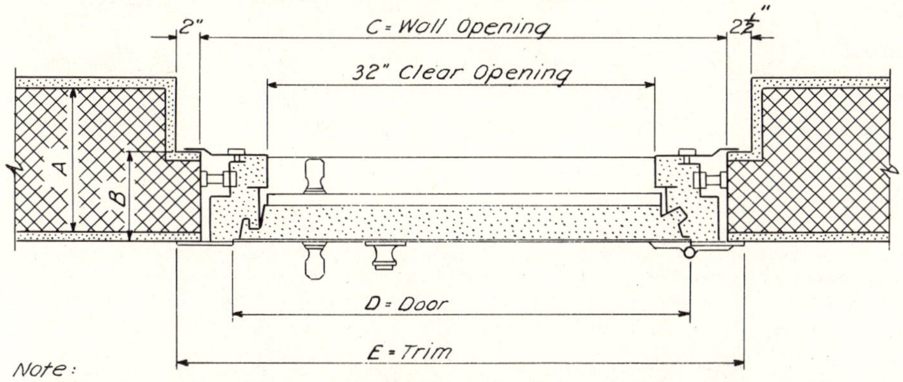
2"
C = Wall Opening
$2\frac{1}{2}$"
32" Clear Opening
A
B
D = Door
E = Trim

Note:
Masonry and plaster completed before setting door. No grouting. Floor and ceiling thicknesses same as for walls.

	A*	B	C	D	E	F	G	H	USE
2 HR.	6" Reinf. Conc. 8" Brick 8" Hol. Conc. Mas.	$7\frac{1}{2}$"	$43\frac{1}{2}$"	$37\frac{11}{16}$"	$46\frac{11}{16}$"	$85\frac{11}{16}$"	$84\frac{1}{8}$"	$9\frac{3}{8}$"	Books, papers
4 HR.	8" Reinf. Conc. 12" Brick	$9\frac{1}{2}$"	$43\frac{1}{2}$"	$37\frac{11}{16}$"	$46\frac{11}{16}$"	$85\frac{11}{16}$"	$84\frac{1}{8}$"	$9\frac{3}{8}$"	Fur storage, valuable papers
6 HR.	10" Reinf. Conc. 12" Brick	$11\frac{1}{2}$"	$45\frac{1}{2}$"	$38\frac{7}{16}$"	$49\frac{15}{16}$"	$87\frac{7}{16}$"	$85\frac{1}{4}$"	$12\frac{7}{16}$"	Books, silver (house) storage, valuable papers

* Minimum thicknesses recommended by THE NATIONAL FIRE PROTECTION ASSOCIATION.

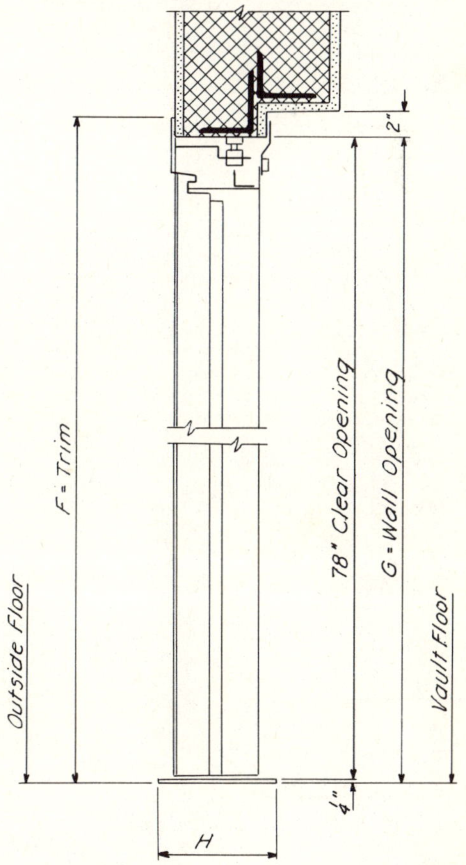
2"
F = Trim
78" Clear Opening
G = Wall Opening
Outside Floor
Vault Floor
$\frac{1}{4}$"
H

TWO HOUR, FOUR HOUR & SIX HOUR VAULTS

Scale: $\frac{3}{4}$" = 1'-0"

Courtesy of The Mosler Safe Co.

SIDEWALK DOORS and HATCHWAYS

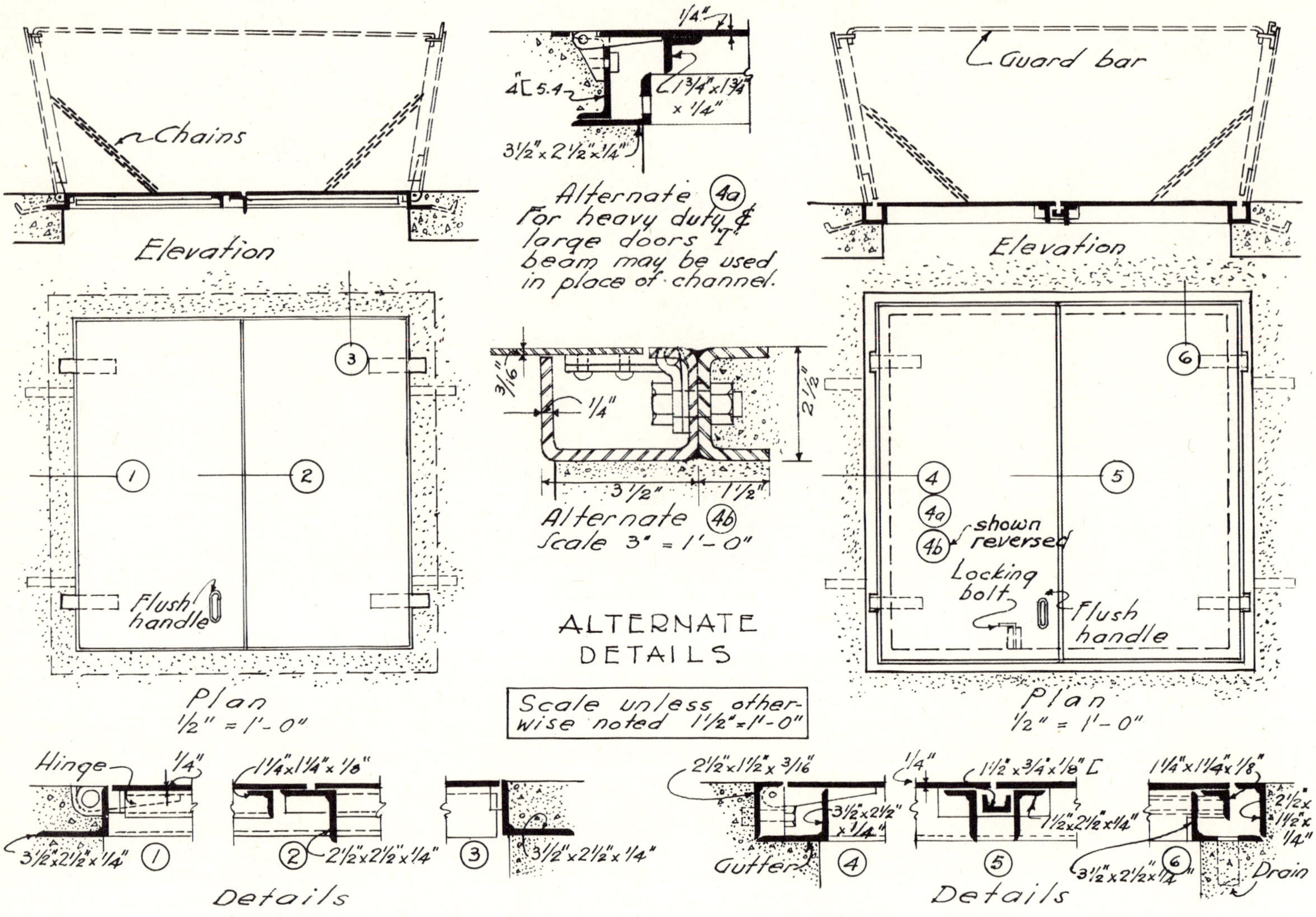
Chains
Elevation
1/4"
4[5.4
1 3/4" x 1 3/4" x 1/4"
3 1/2" x 2 1/2" x 1/4"
Alternate 4a
For heavy duty & large doors "I" beam may be used in place of channel.
Guard bar
Elevation
3
1
2
Flush handle
Plan
1/2" = 1'-0"
3/16"
1/4"
2 1/2"
3 1/2"
1 1/2"
Alternate 4b
Scale 3" = 1'-0"
ALTERNATE DETAILS
Scale unless otherwise noted 1 1/2" = 1'-0"
6
4
5
4a
4b
shown reversed
Locking bolt
Flush handle
Plan
1/2" = 1'-0"
Hinge
1/4"
1 1/4" x 1 1/4" x 1/8"
3 1/2" x 2 1/2" x 1/4"
1
2
2 1/2" x 2 1/2" x 1/4"
3
3 1/2" x 2 1/2" x 1/4"
Details
STANDARD FRAME
2 1/2" x 1 1/2" x 3/16"
1/4"
1 1/2" x 3/4" x 1/8" [
1 1/4" x 1 1/4" x 1/8"
3 1/2" x 2 1/2" x 1/4"
1 1/2" x 2 1/2" x 1/4"
2 1/2" x 1 1/2" x 1/4"
Gutter
4
5
6
3 1/2" x 2 1/2" x 1/4"
Drain
Details
WITH GUTTER and DRAIN

*SIDEWALK DOORS

Doors are usually of steel reinforced with angles, tees, or bars; & may also be of aluminum floor plate for weight reduction, & of abrasive or safety type metal. Frames are usually of structural shapes with anchors into masonry or floor construction. They may be of cast iron, steel or non-ferrous metals. Hinges can be set flush or on the surface & may be of cast iron, or steel, fitted with brass or bronze pins, or made entirely of non-ferrous metals. Lifting handles usually set flush are essential where doors are to be operated from above. Locking is usually by a heavy barrel bolt on the underside. Other methods may be used. Guard bars & chains are required to hold doors in open position & to protect the opening. The number of leaves on sidewalk doors may be 1, 2, 3, 4 or more & for large openings, there may be removable supports set in the frame. Door leaves of floor plate for ordinary construction may be 3/16" or 1/4" thickness with stiffeners to support the load. Plates of greater thickness may be used. For deflections & allowable loads, see page, "Metal Floor Plates & Treads." Automatic opening & closing may be arranged for sidewalk elevators, hoists or lifts.

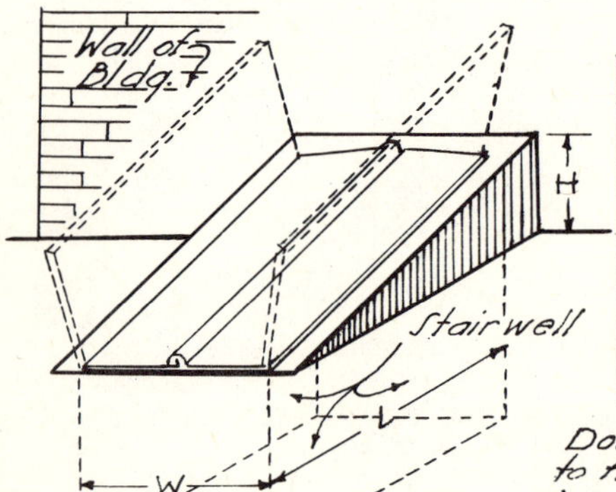
Wall of Bldg.
H
Stairwell
L
W

OPENINGS			
Door Size	A	4'-6"	L
		3'-4"	W
		2'-0½"	H
	B	5'-0"	L
		3'-8"	W
		1'-10"	H
	C	5'-8"	L
		4'-0"	W
		1'-7½"	H

Doors are made to fit above openings. Others to order.

CELLAR DOORS
The Bilco Company

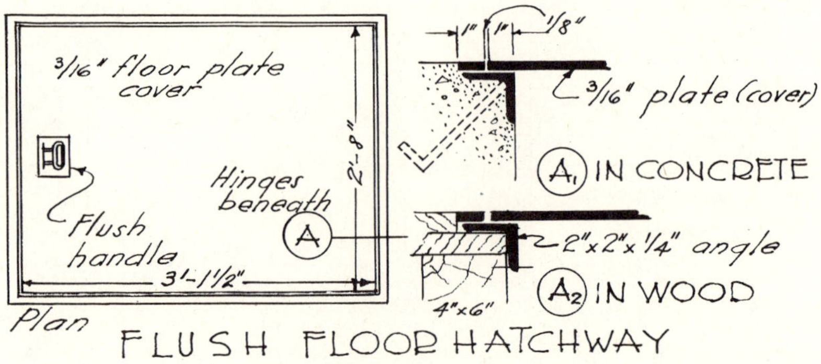
3/16" floor plate cover
Flush handle
Hinges beneath
A
2'-8"
3'-1 1/2"
Plan
1"
1"
1/8"
3/16" plate (cover)
A1 IN CONCRETE
2" x 2" x 1/4" angle
4" x 6"
A2 IN WOOD

FLUSH FLOOR HATCHWAY

*Data from "Architectural Metals Handbook" by permission of the National Assoc. of Architectural Metal Mfrs.

METAL DOOR BUCKS-GENERAL

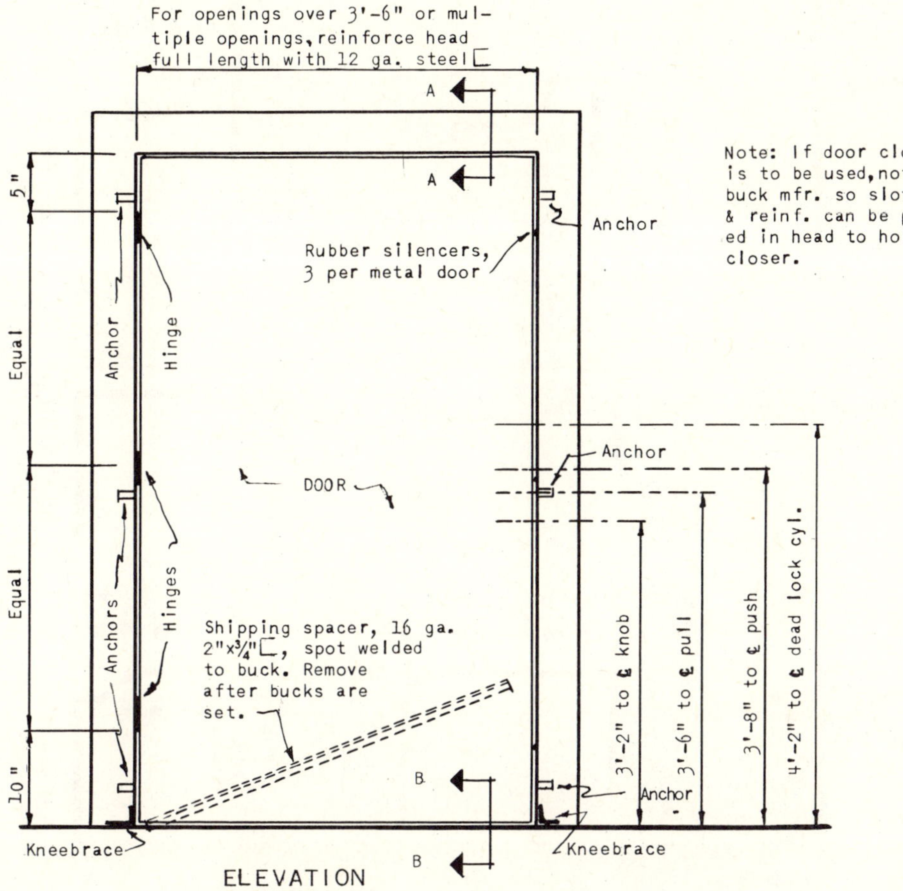
For openings over 3'-6" or multiple openings, reinforce head full length with 12 ga. steel ⊏
A
A
5"
Equal
Equal
10"
Anchor
Hinge
Anchor
Rubber silencers, 3 per metal door
DOOR
Anchor
Anchors
Hinges
Shipping spacer, 16 ga. 2"x¾"⊏, spot welded to buck. Remove after bucks are set.
3'-2" to ℄ knob
3'-6" to ℄ pull
3'-8" to ℄ push
4'-2" to ℄ dead lock cyl.
Anchor
B
B
Kneebrace
Kneebrace

ELEVATION
Scale ½"=1'-0"

BUCK ON FINISHED FLOOR

Note: If door closer is to be used, notify buck mfr. so slots & reinf. can be placed in head to hold closer.

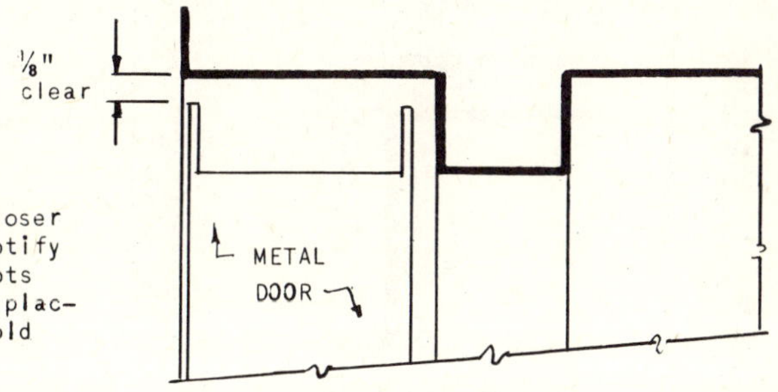
⅛" clear
METAL DOOR

SECTION A-A

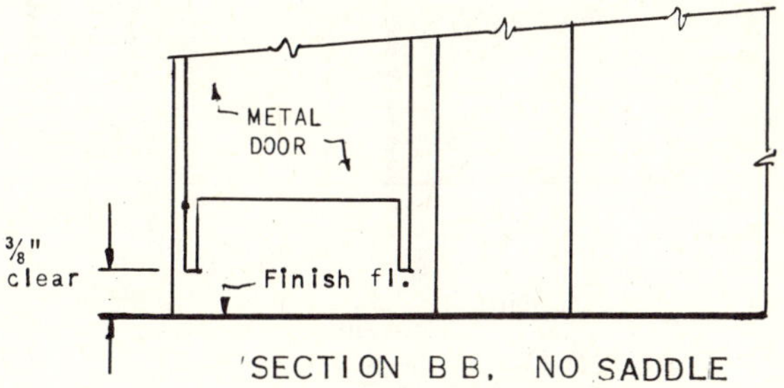
METAL DOOR
⅜" clear
Finish fl.

SECTION B B, NO SADDLE

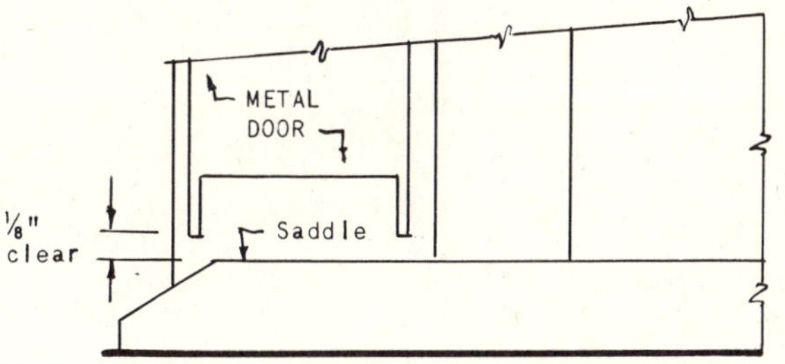
METAL DOOR
⅛" clear
Saddle

SECTION B-B, WITH SADDLE

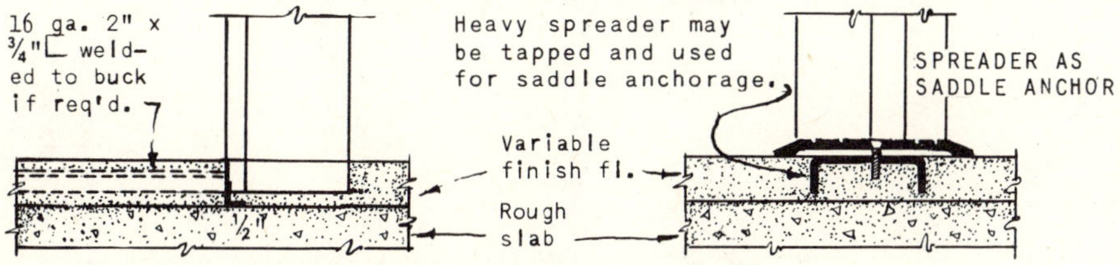
16 ga. 2" x ¾"⊏ welded to buck if req'd.
½"
Heavy spreader may be tapped and used for saddle anchorage.
SPREADER AS SADDLE ANCHOR
Variable finish fl.
Rough slab

Scale: 1"=1'-0"

BUCK ON ROUGH SLAB

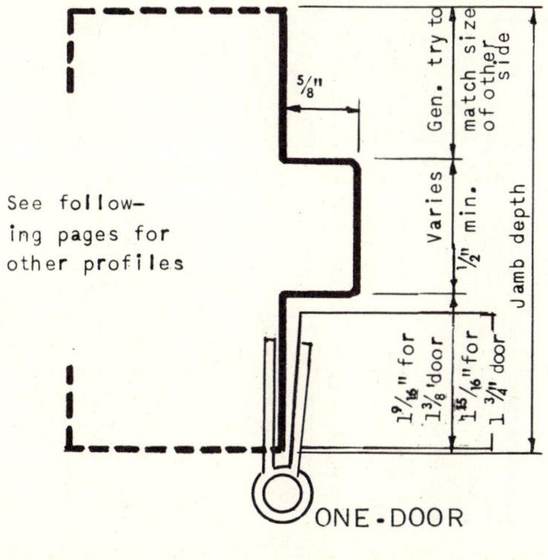
⅝"
Gen. try to match size of other side
Varies
½" min.
Jamb depth
1⁹⁄₁₆" for 1⅜" door
1¹⁵⁄₁₆" for 1¾" door
See following pages for other profiles

ONE-DOOR

Note: Always check clearance with hardware to be used.

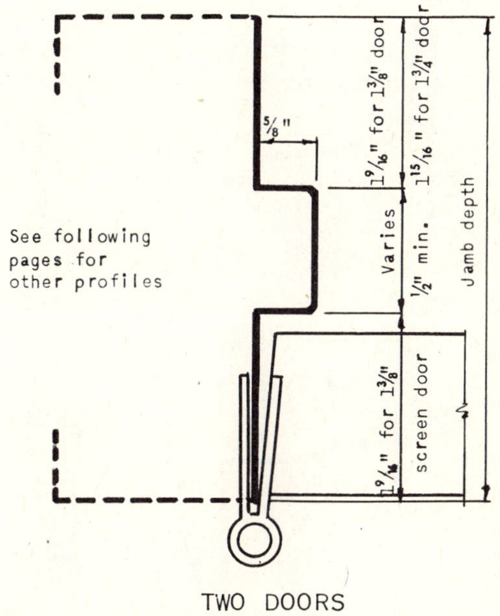
⅝"
1⁹⁄₁₆" for 1⅜" door
1¹⁵⁄₁₆" for 1¾" door
Varies
½" min.
Jamb depth
1⁹⁄₁₆" for 1⅜" screen door
See following pages for other profiles

TWO DOORS

TYPICAL BUCK DETAILS

Scale: half size

STANDARD METAL BUCK TRIM PROFILES

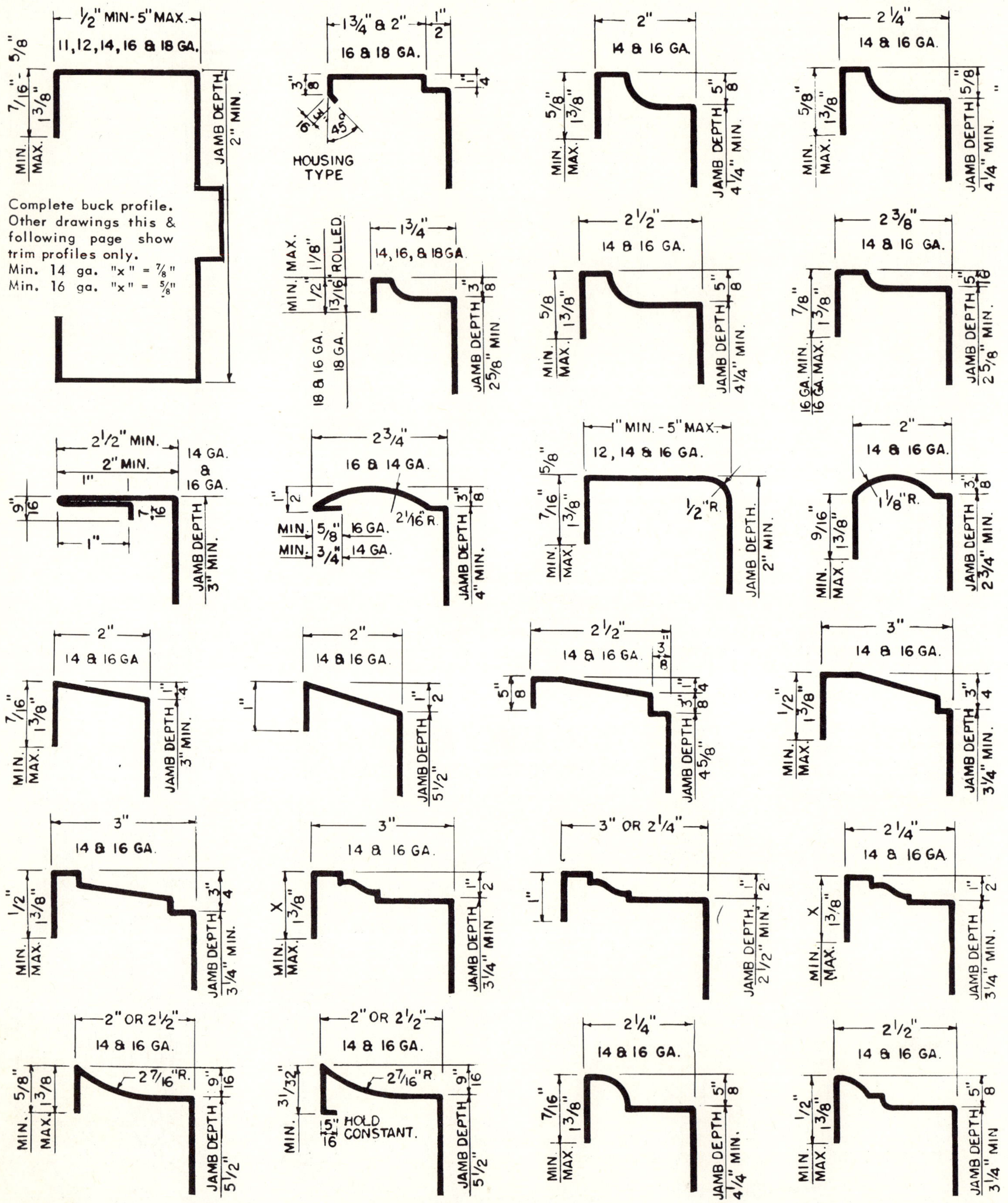
1/2" MIN-5" MAX.
11, 12, 14, 16 & 18 GA.
JAMB DEPTH 2" MIN.
MIN. MAX.
Complete buck profile. Other drawings this & following page show trim profiles only.
Min. 14 ga. "x" = 7/8"
Min. 16 ga. "x" = 5/8"
1 3/4" & 2"
16 & 18 GA.
HOUSING TYPE
45°
2"
14 & 16 GA.
JAMB DEPTH 4 1/4" MIN.
2 1/4"
14 & 16 GA.
JAMB DEPTH 4 1/4" MIN.
1 3/4"
14, 16, & 18 GA.
1 1/8" ROLLED
18 & 16 GA.
18 GA.
JAMB DEPTH 2 5/8" MIN.
2 1/2"
14 & 16 GA.
JAMB DEPTH 4 1/4" MIN.
2 3/8"
14 & 16 GA.
16 GA. MIN.
16 GA. MAX.
JAMB DEPTH 2 5/8" MIN.
2 1/2" MIN.
2" MIN.
1"
14 GA. & 16 GA.
JAMB DEPTH 3" MIN.
2 3/4"
16 & 14 GA.
2 1/16" R.
MIN. 5/8" 16 GA.
MIN. 3/4" 14 GA.
JAMB DEPTH 4" MIN.
1" MIN. - 5" MAX.
12, 14 & 16 GA.
1/2" R.
JAMB DEPTH 2" MIN.
2"
14 & 16 GA.
1 1/8" R.
JAMB DEPTH 2 3/4" MIN.
2"
14 & 16 GA.
JAMB DEPTH 3" MIN.
2"
14 & 16 GA.
JAMB DEPTH 5 1/2"
2 1/2"
14 & 16 GA.
JAMB DEPTH 4 5/8"
3"
14 & 16 GA.
JAMB DEPTH 3 1/4" MIN.
3"
14 & 16 GA.
JAMB DEPTH 3 1/4" MIN.
3"
14 & 16 GA.
JAMB DEPTH 3 1/4" MIN
3" OR 2 1/4"
JAMB DEPTH 2 1/2" MIN.
2 1/4"
14 & 16 GA.
JAMB DEPTH 3 1/4" MIN.
2" OR 2 1/2"
14 & 16 GA.
2 7/16" R.
JAMB DEPTH 5 1/2"
2" OR 2 1/2"
14 & 16 GA.
2 7/16" R
5/16" HOLD CONSTANT.
JAMB DEPTH 5 1/2"
2 1/4"
14 & 16 GA.
JAMB DEPTH 4 1/4" MIN.
2 1/2"
14 & 16 GA.
JAMB DEPTH 3 1/4" MIN

NOTE: The above profiles and dimensions are those of one manufacturer only and are shown to indicate the scope of jamb trim available Other manufacturers' profiles and sizes may vary slightly from these.

DATA BY AETNA STEEL PRODUCTS CORP

SPECIAL METAL BUCK TRIM PROFILES

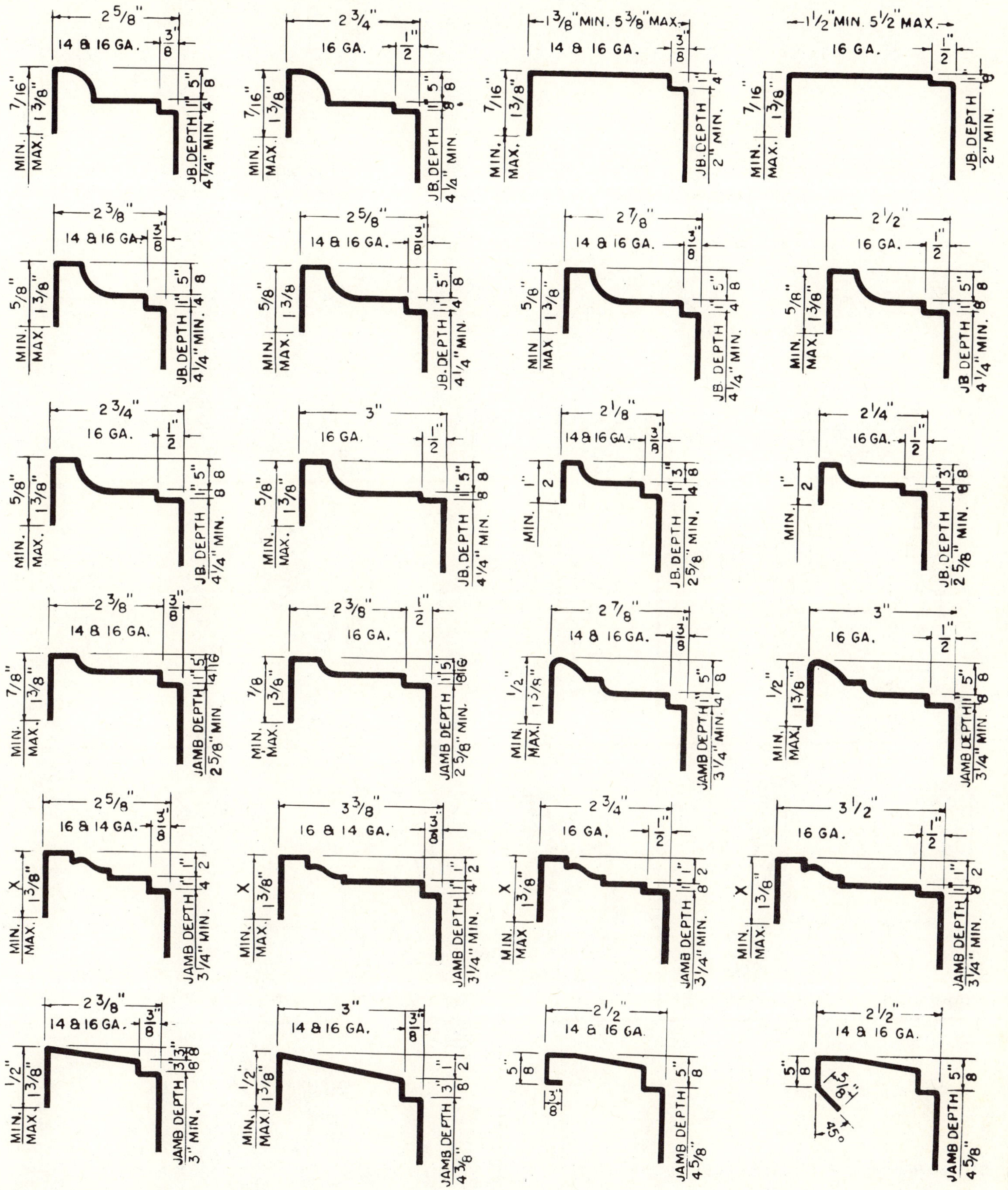

NOTE: The above profiles and dimensions are those of one manufacturer only and are shown to indicate the scope of jamb trim available. Other manufacturers' profiles and sizes may vary slightly from these. Min. 14 ga. "x" = 7/8"; min. 16 ga. "x" = 5/8".

DATA BY AETNA STEEL PRODUCTS CORP.

DOOR BUCK ANCHORAGES and SPECIAL ACCESSORIES

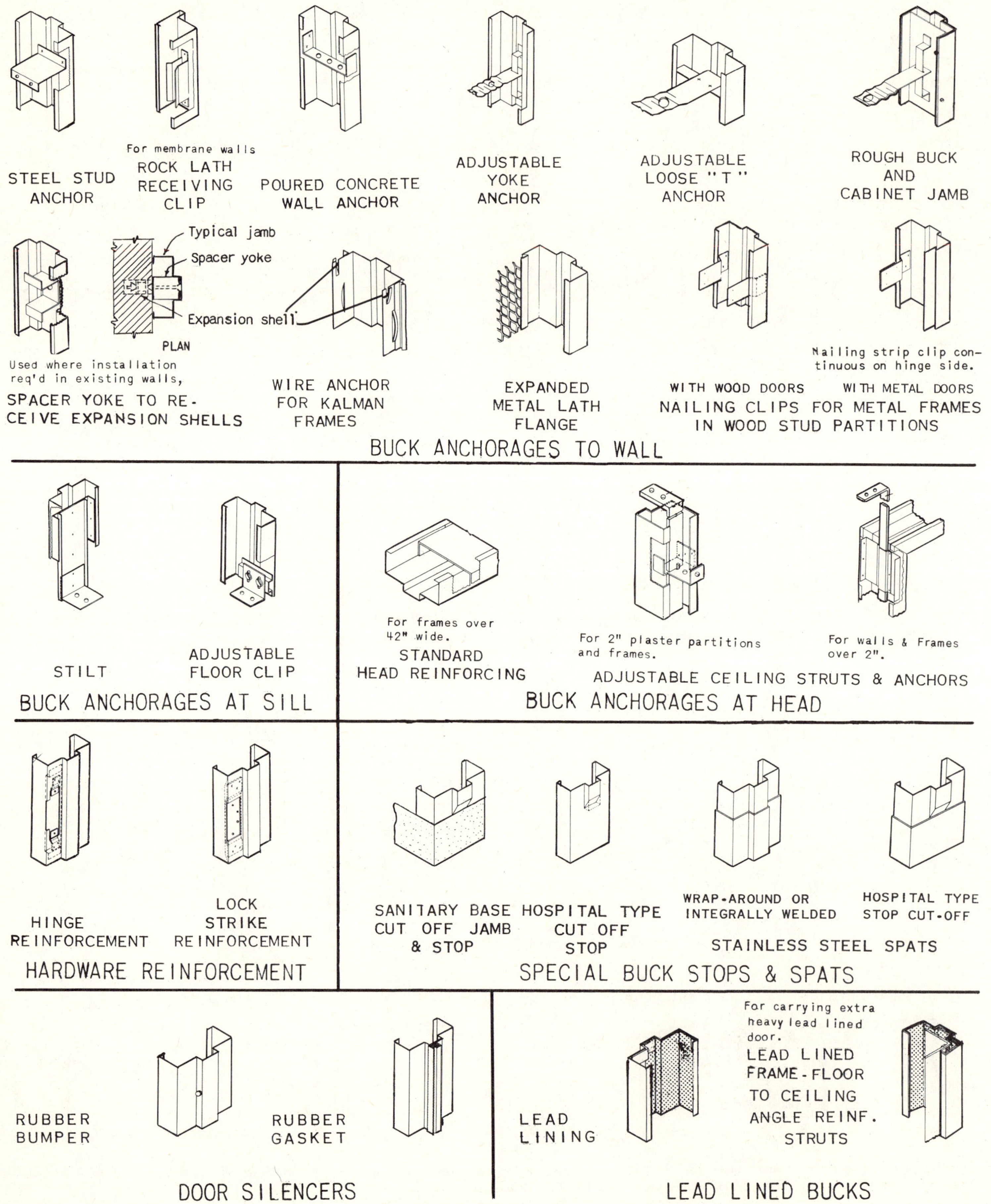
STEEL STUD ANCHOR
For membrane walls
ROCK LATH RECEIVING CLIP
POURED CONCRETE WALL ANCHOR
ADJUSTABLE YOKE ANCHOR
ADJUSTABLE LOOSE "T" ANCHOR
ROUGH BUCK AND CABINET JAMB
Typical jamb
Spacer yoke
Expansion shell
PLAN
Used where installation req'd in existing walls,
SPACER YOKE TO RECEIVE EXPANSION SHELLS
WIRE ANCHOR FOR KALMAN FRAMES
EXPANDED METAL LATH FLANGE
Nailing strip clip continuous on hinge side.
WITH WOOD DOORS
WITH METAL DOORS
NAILING CLIPS FOR METAL FRAMES IN WOOD STUD PARTITIONS
BUCK ANCHORAGES TO WALL
STILT
ADJUSTABLE FLOOR CLIP
BUCK ANCHORAGES AT SILL
For frames over 42" wide.
STANDARD HEAD REINFORCING
For 2" plaster partitions and frames.
For walls & Frames over 2".
ADJUSTABLE CEILING STRUTS & ANCHORS
BUCK ANCHORAGES AT HEAD
HINGE REINFORCEMENT
LOCK STRIKE REINFORCEMENT
HARDWARE REINFORCEMENT
SANITARY BASE CUT OFF JAMB & STOP
HOSPITAL TYPE CUT OFF STOP
WRAP-AROUND OR INTEGRALLY WELDED
HOSPITAL TYPE STOP CUT-OFF
STAINLESS STEEL SPATS
SPECIAL BUCK STOPS & SPATS
RUBBER BUMPER
RUBBER GASKET
DOOR SILENCERS
LEAD LINING
For carrying extra heavy lead lined door.
LEAD LINED FRAME-FLOOR TO CEILING ANGLE REINF. STRUTS
LEAD LINED BUCKS

DATA BY OVERLY MANUFACTURING CO.

HOUSING and RESIDENTIAL METAL BUCKS; WOOD DOOR FRAMES and JAMBS

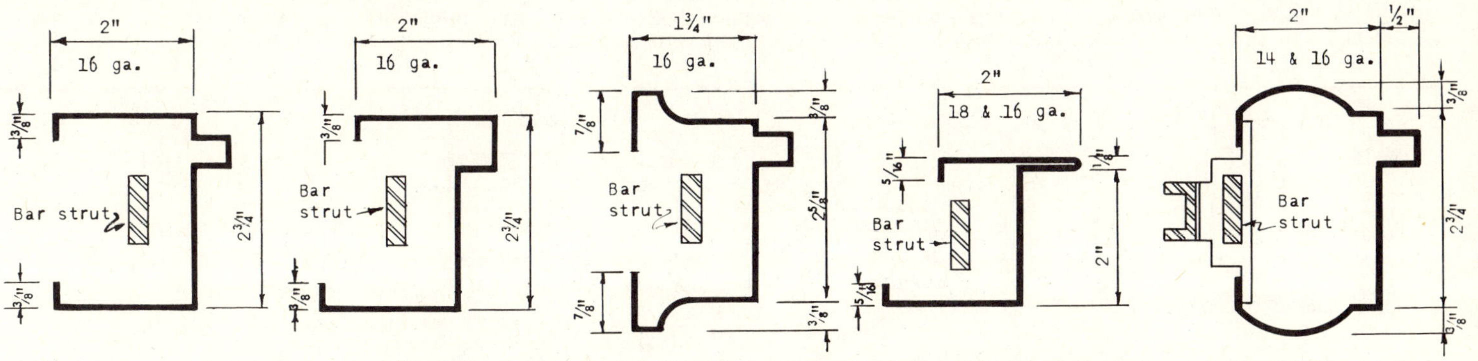
2"
16 ga.
Bar strut
2¾"
1¾"
18 & 16 ga.
14 & 16 ga.
½"
⅜"
⅞"
5/16"
2"

STANDARD HOUSING METAL BUCK & TRIM

DATA BY AETNA STEEL PRODUCTS CORP. Scale: ⅜" = 1'-0"

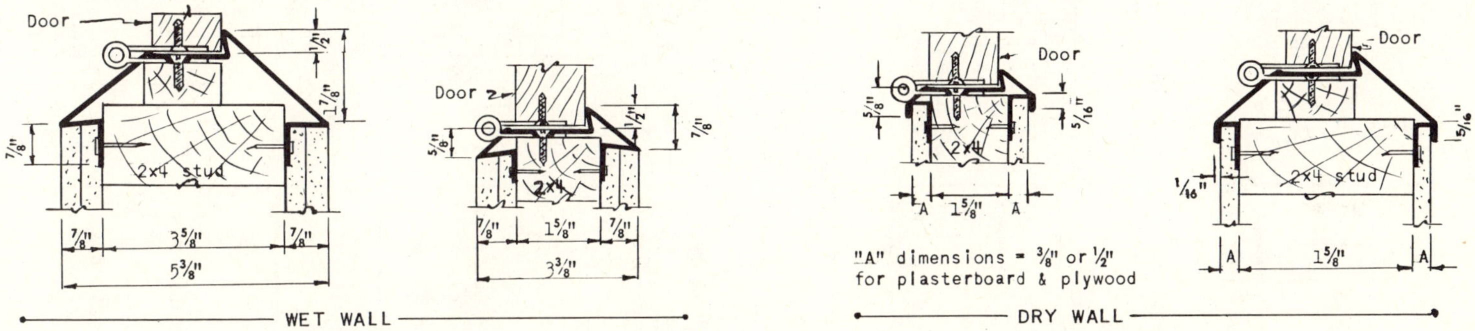
Door
2x4 stud
2x4
⅞"
3⅝"
5⅜"
1⅝"
3⅜"
1½"
1⅞"
5/16"
1/16"
A
"A" dimensions = ⅜" or ½"
for plasterboard & plywood
WET WALL
DRY WALL

LIGHT DUTY METAL BUCK FOR RESIDENTIAL CONSTRUCTION

DATA BY TRIMCO METAL PRODUCTS Scale 3" = 1'-0"

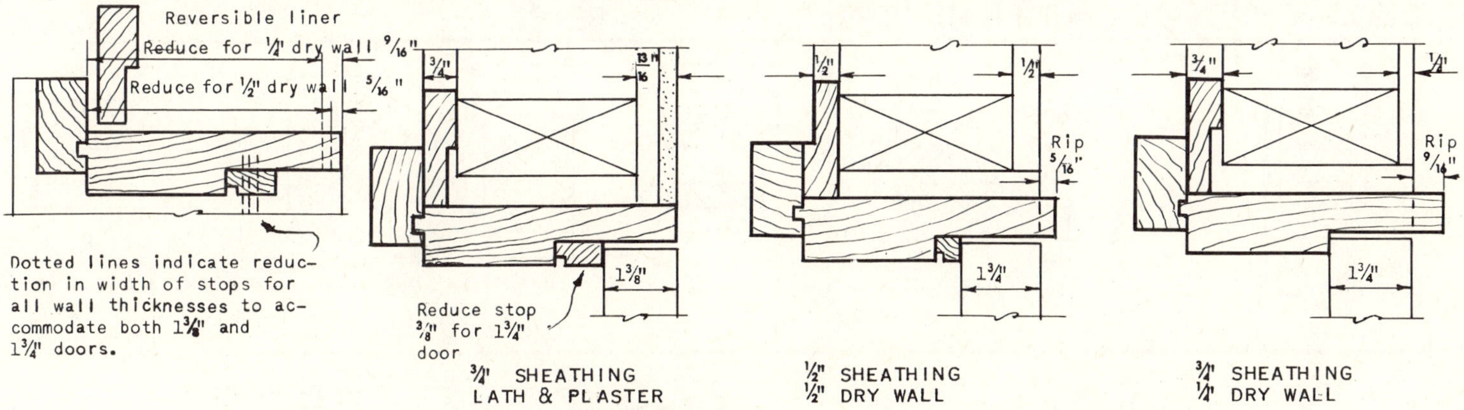
Reversible liner
Reduce for ¼" dry wall 9/16"
Reduce for ½" dry wall 5/16"
Dotted lines indicate reduction in width of stops for all wall thicknesses to accommodate both 1⅜" and 1¾" doors.
Reduce stop ⅜" for 1¾" door
1⅜"
1¾"
Rip 5/16"
Rip 9/16"
¾" SHEATHING
LATH & PLASTER
½" SHEATHING
½" DRY WALL
¾" SHEATHING
½" DRY WALL

STOCK ALL-PURPOSE EXTERIOR WOOD DOOR FRAME

DATA BY NATIONAL DOOR MANUFACTURERS ASSOCIATION Scale 3" = 1'-0"

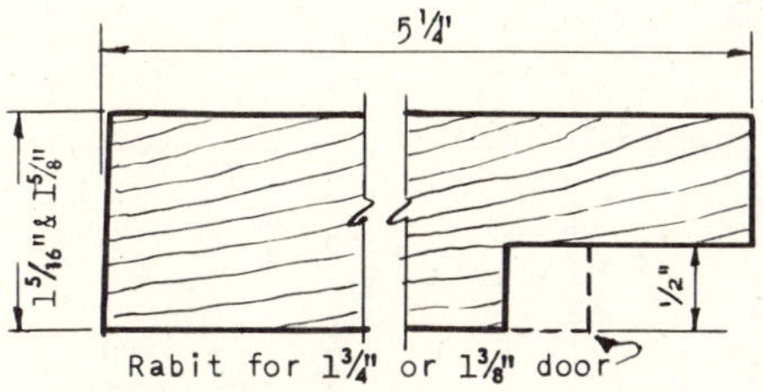
5¼"
1 5/16" & 1⅝"
½"
Rabit for 1¾" or 1⅜" door

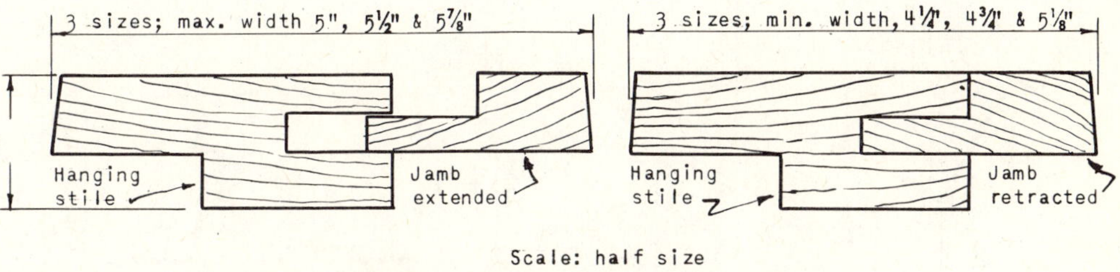
3 sizes; max. width 5", 5½" & 5⅞"
3 sizes; min. width, 4¼", 4¾" & 5⅛"
1¼"
Hanging stile
Jamb extended
Jamb retracted
Scale: half size

STOCK WOOD DOOR JAMB

DATA BY NAT'L DOOR MFRS. ASSOC.

ADJUSTABLE WOOD DOOR JAMB

DATA BY CURTIS WOODWORK

METAL DOOR BUCKS *related to* PARTITIONS *and* WALL CONDITIONS

GENERAL: Before dimensioning bucks it is necessary to study them in relation to actual thicknesses of wall materials and finishes where they will be located. The following drawings illustrate typical solutions to a number of common wall conditions.

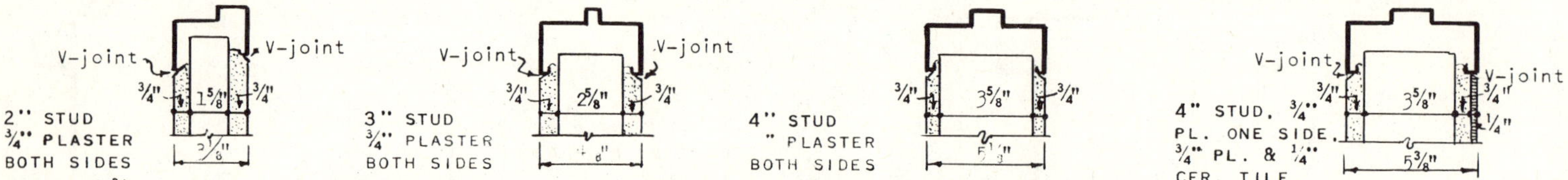
V-joint
V-joint
3/4"
1 5/8"
3/4"
2" STUD
3/4" PLASTER
BOTH SIDES
3/4"
2 5/8"
3/4"
3" STUD
3/4" PLASTER
BOTH SIDES
3/4"
3 5/8"
3/4"
4" STUD
" PLASTER
BOTH SIDES
3/4"
3 5/8"
1/4"
5 3/8"
4" STUD, 3/4" PL. ONE SIDE, 3/4" PL. & 1/4" CER. TILE OTHER SIDE

Note: If 3/8" gypsum lath & plaster is used in place of metal lath & plaster, dimension is 7/8" instead of 3/4" as shown. Change overall dimension as required.

FRAME CONSTRUCTION

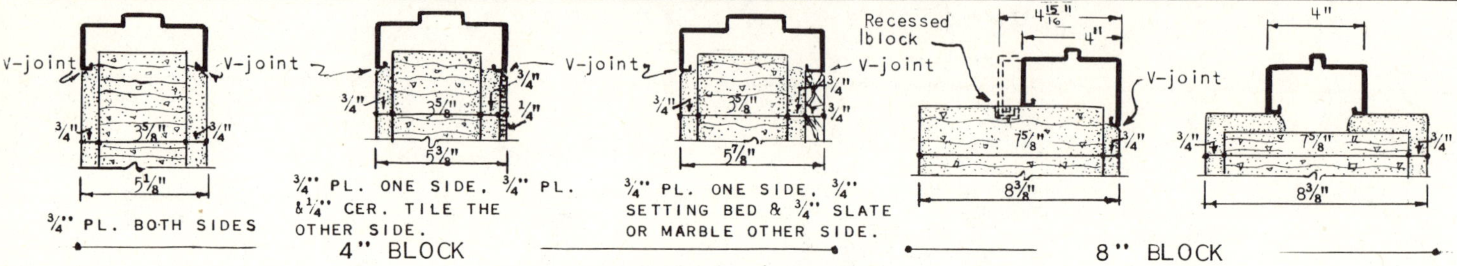
V-joint
V-joint
3/4"
3 5/8"
3/4"
5 1/8"
3/4" PL. BOTH SIDES
3/4"
3 5/8"
3/4"
1/4"
5 3/8"
3/4" PL. ONE SIDE, 3/4" PL. & 1/4" CER. TILE THE OTHER SIDE.
3 5/8"
5 7/8"
3/4" PL. ONE SIDE, 3/4" SETTING BED & 3/4" SLATE OR MARBLE OTHER SIDE.
4" BLOCK
Recessed block
4 15/16"
4"
7 5/8"
8 3/8"
4"
7 5/8"
8 3/8"
8" BLOCK

CONCRETE BLOCK

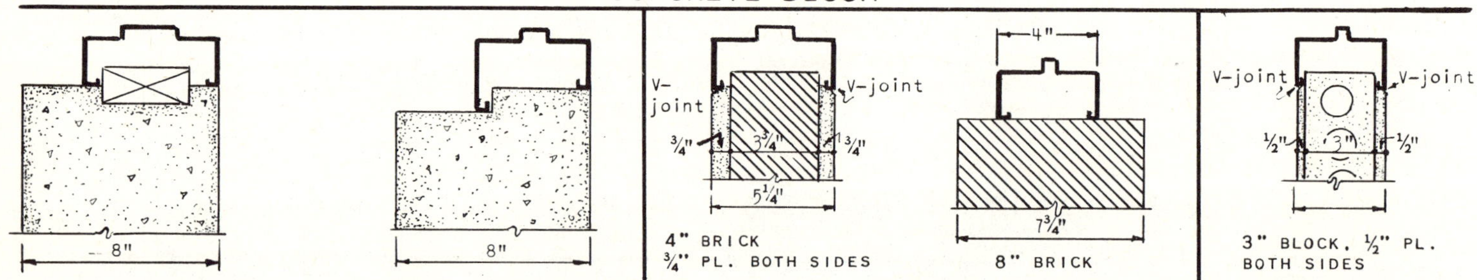
8"
8"
V-joint
V-joint
3/4"
3 3/4"
3/4"
5 1/4"
4" BRICK
3/4" PL. BOTH SIDES
4"
7 3/4"
8" BRICK
V-joint
V-joint
1/2"
3"
1/2"
3" BLOCK, 1/2" PL. BOTH SIDES

8" CONC.-EXTERIOR BUCKS WITH WIND STOPS

BRICK

GYPSUM BLOCK

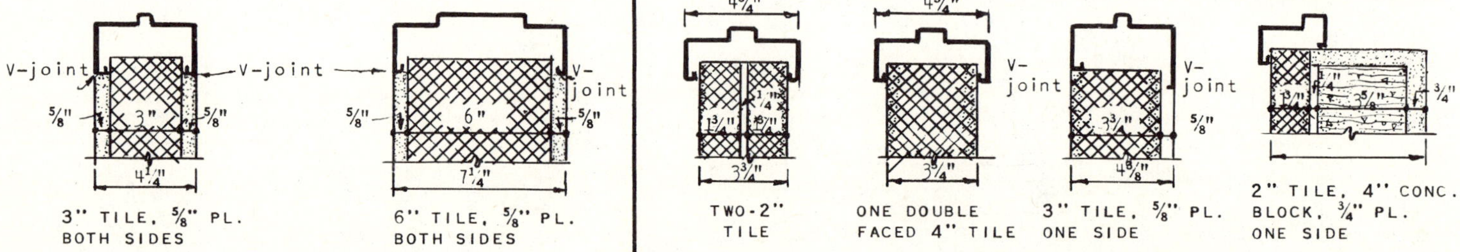
V-joint
V-joint
5/8"
3"
5/8"
4 1/4"
3" TILE, 5/8" PL. BOTH SIDES
V-joint
5/8"
6"
5/8"
7 1/4"
6" TILE, 5/8" PL. BOTH SIDES
4 3/4"
3 3/4"
TWO-2" TILE
4 3/4"
3 3/4"
ONE DOUBLE FACED 4" TILE
V-joint
3 3/4"
4 3/8"
3" TILE, 5/8" PL. ONE SIDE
V-joint
5/8"
3 5/8"
3/4"
2" TILE, 4" CONC. BLOCK, 3/4" PL. ONE SIDE

CLAY TILE

GLAZED FACING TILE

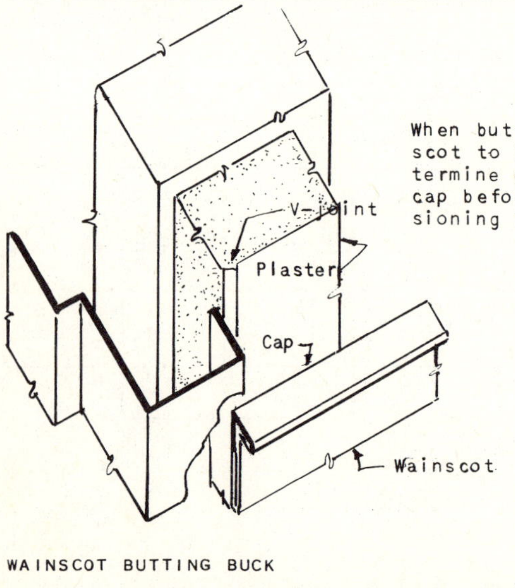
V-joint
Plaster
Cap
Wainscot

When butting wainscot to buck determine depth of cap before dimensioning buck.

WAINSCOT BUTTING BUCK

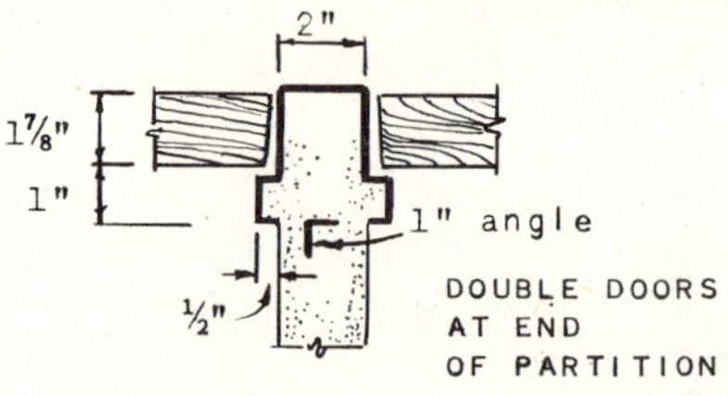
2"
1 7/8"
1"
1" angle
1/2"

DOUBLE DOORS AT END OF PARTITION

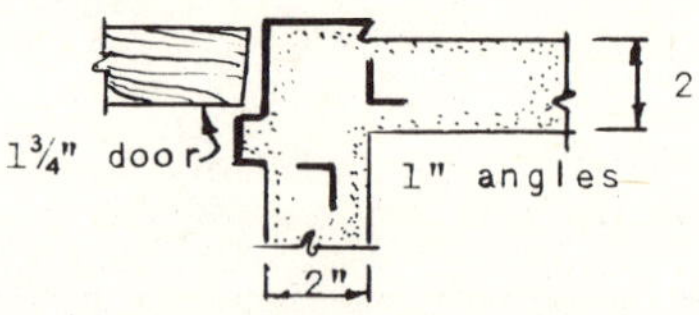
2"
1 3/4" door
1" angles
2"

DOOR AT PARTITION CORNER

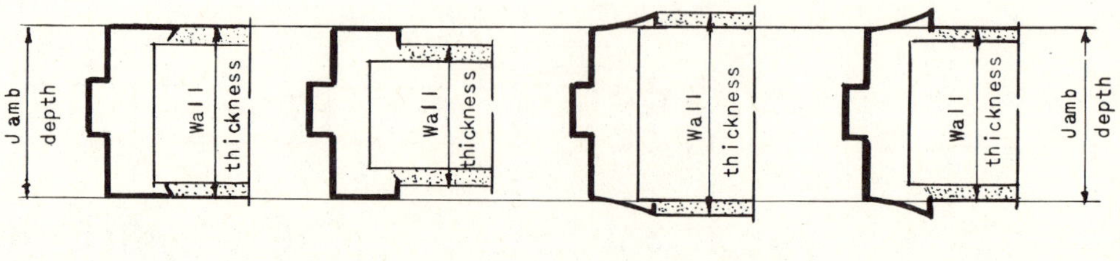
Jamb depth
Wall thickness
Wall thickness
Wall thickness
Wall thickness
Jamb depth

JAMB DEPTH AS AFFECTED BY JAMB PROFILE AND TRIM USE

SPECIAL CONDITIONS

WOOD and KALAMEIN OVERHEAD DOORS

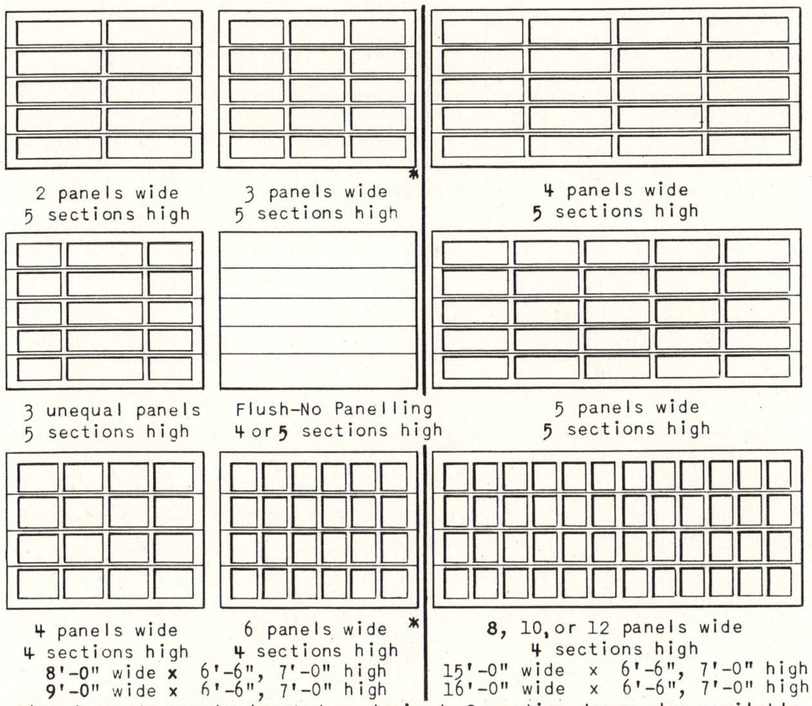

2 panels wide
5 sections high
3 panels wide
5 sections high
4 panels wide
5 sections high
3 unequal panels
5 sections high
Flush-No Panelling
4 or 5 sections high
5 panels wide
5 sections high
4 panels wide
4 sections high
8'-0" wide x 6'-6", 7'-0" high
9'-0" wide x 6'-6", 7'-0" high
6 panels wide *
4 sections high
8, 10, or 12 panels wide
4 sections high
15'-0" wide x 6'-6", 7'-0" high
16'-0" wide x 6'-6", 7'-0" high

Glazed panels may be located as desired. 3 section doors also available.
NOTE: Other stock designs and sizes available varying with manufacturers.
*Also available 8'-0" wide x 7'-6", 8'-0" high.

STANDARD STOCK DOOR DESIGNS AND SIZES
Scale: 1/8" = 1'-0"

HEIGHT	SECTIONS
—— to 6'-6"	2 - 3
6'-6" to 8'-6"	3 - 5
8'-6" to 10'-6"	4 - 6
10'-6" to 12'-6"	5 - 7
12'-6" to 14'-6"	6 - 8
14'-6" to 16'-6"	7 - 9
16'-6" to 18'-6"	8 - 10
18'-6" to 20'-6"	10 - 11
Over 20'-6"	✢

WIDTH	PANELS
—— to 10'-6"	1 - 8
10'-6" to 12'-6"	1 - 12
12'-6" to 14'-0"	3 - 12
14'-0" to 16'-0"	3 - 16
16'-0" to 18'-0"	4 - 16
18'-0" to 20'-0"	4 - 16
20'-0" to 24'-0"	6 - 18
24'-0" to 28'-0"	6 - 18
28'-0" to 30'-0"	8 - 16

✢ Intermediate sections of all doors may not exceed 2'-0" in height; the number of sections required for any height door follows this rule.

SECTION AND PANEL SCHEDULE FOR ALL WOOD DOORS

NOTE: Special Doors, maximum size 38'-0" wide x 18'-0" high. Weight of a standard wood door is approximately 3½ pounds per square foot (includes hardware). Glass is double strength. Doors with wicket or pass doors, ventilating screens, or louvers are also available.

SPECIAL DOOR DESIGNS AND SIZES

WOOD OVERHEAD DOORS

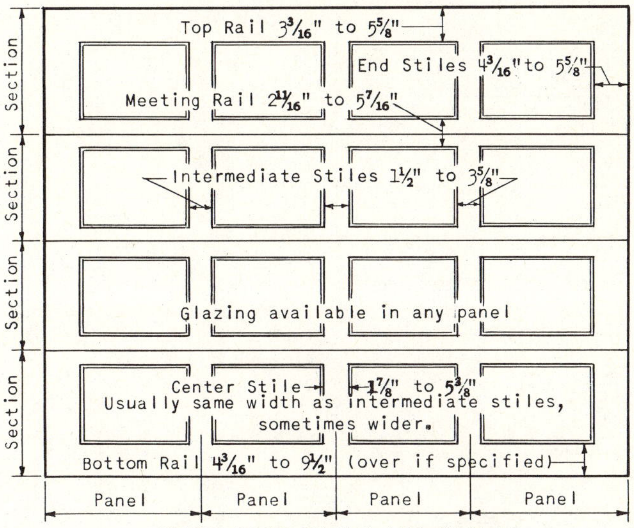

Top Rail 3 3/16" to 5 5/8"
End Stiles 4 3/16" to 5 5/8"
Meeting Rail 2 11/16" to 5 7/16"
Intermediate Stiles 1½" to 3 5/8"
Glazing available in any panel
Center Stile 1 7/8" to 5 3/8"
Usually same width as intermediate stiles, sometimes wider.
Bottom Rail 4 3/16" to 9½" (over if specified)
Section
Section
Section
Section
Panel
Panel
Panel
Panel

STOCK DOOR RAILS AND STILES
Scale: 3/8" = 1'-0"

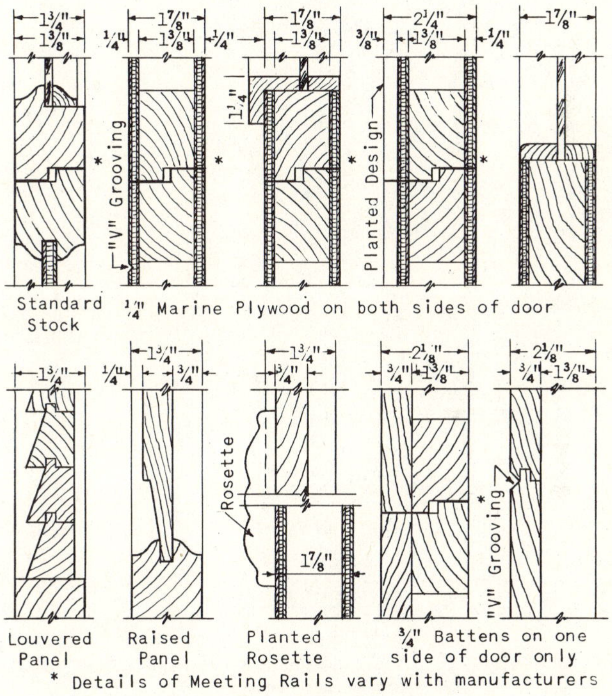

1 3/4"
1 3/8"
1 7/8"
1/4"
1 3/8"
1/4"
1 7/8"
1 3/8"
2 1/4"
3/8"
1 3/8"
1/4"
1 7/8"
1 1/4"
"V" Grooving
Planted Design
Standard Stock
1/4" Marine Plywood on both sides of door
1 3/4"
1/4"
1 1/4"
3/4"
1 3/4"
1/4"
2 1/8"
3/4"
1 3/8"
2 1/8"
3/4"
1 3/8"
Rosette
1 7/8"
"V" Grooving
Louvered Panel
Raised Panel
Planted Rosette
3/4" Battens on one side of door only

* Details of Meeting Rails vary with manufacturers

TYPICAL WOOD DOOR CONSTRUCTION DETAILS
Scale: 3/16" = 1'-0"

KALAMEIN DOORS (METAL COVERED WOOD)

Kalamein doors have no label or fire rating but are fire retardant. Maximum Size: 24'-0" wide x 18'-0" high weighing approximately 6½ pounds per square foot (including hardware), and are all made to order.

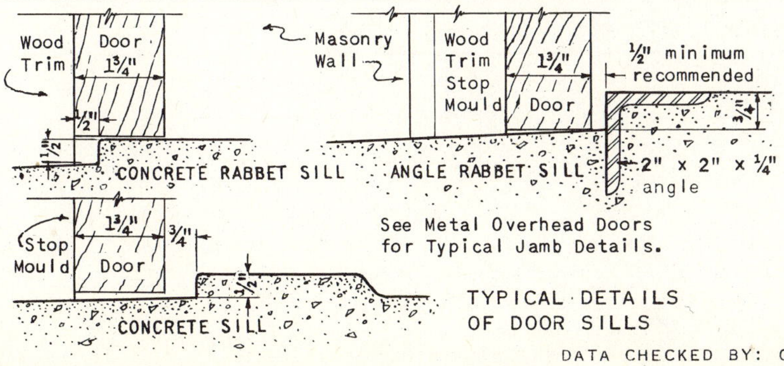

Wood Trim
Door
1 3/4"
1/2"
1/2"
CONCRETE RABBET SILL
Masonry Wall
Wood Trim Stop Mould
1 3/4"
Door
1/2" minimum recommended
ANGLE RABBET SILL
2" x 2" x 1/4" angle
Stop Mould
1 3/4"
3/4"
Door
1/2"
CONCRETE SILL
See Metal Overhead Doors for Typical Jamb Details.

TYPICAL DETAILS OF DOOR SILLS

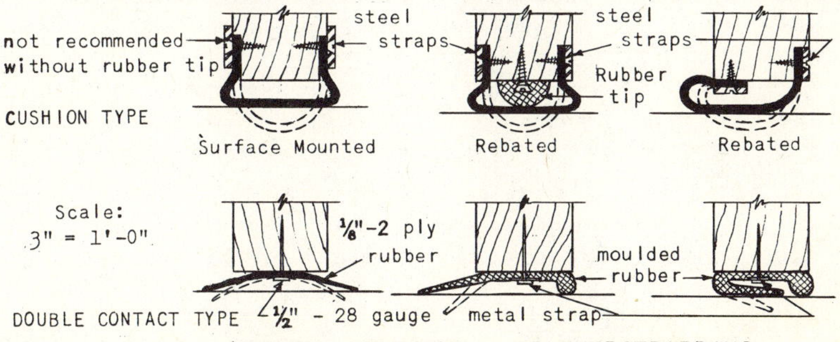

not recommended without rubber tip
CUSHION TYPE
steel straps
Surface Mounted
steel straps
Rubber tip
Rebated
Rebated
Scale: 3" = 1'-0"
1/8"-2 ply rubber
moulded rubber
DOUBLE CONTACT TYPE
1/2" - 28 gauge metal strap

RUBBER ASTRAGALS - WEATHERSTRIPPING

DATA CHECKED BY: OVERHEAD DOOR CORPORATION

METAL OVERHEAD DOORS

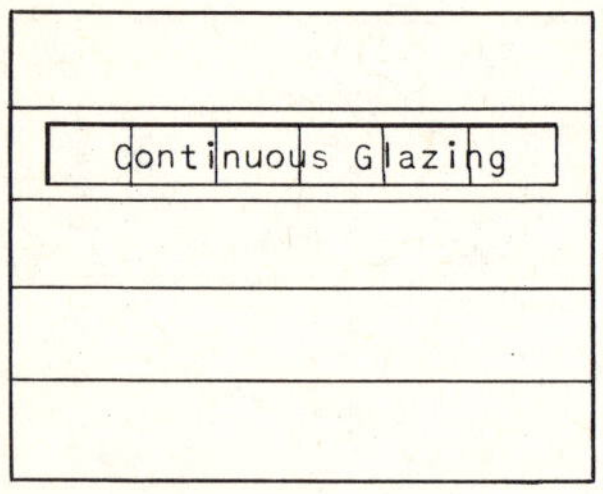
Continuous Glazing

Maximum Size of Galvanized Steel Doors is:
50'-0" wide x 21'-0" high (hangar doors)

Steel Doors are available in flush panels only of 16 gauge bonderized, or galvanized steel with 1.75 ounces zinc coating per square foot.

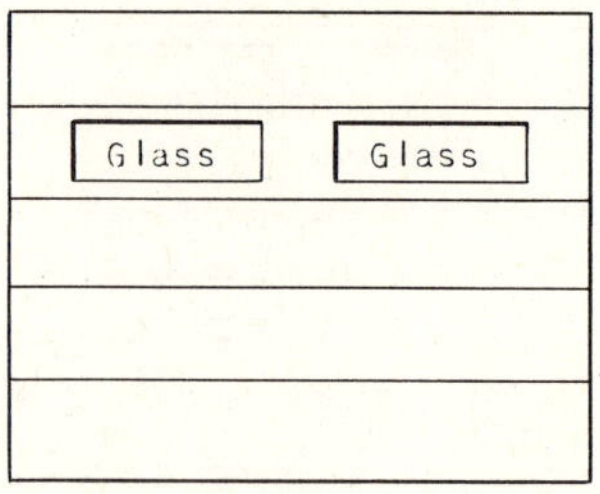
Glass
Glass

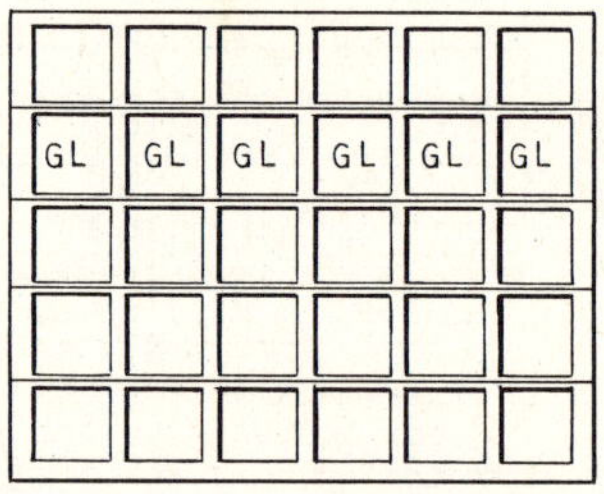
GL
GL
GL
GL
GL
GL

Aluminum Doors are similar to Wood Doors

Maximum Size:
38'-0" wide x 18'-0" high

Scale:
$\frac{3}{16}$" = 1'0"

GALVANIZED STEEL DOORS

CONTINUOUS INTERLOCKING HINGE CONSTRUCTION* TUBULAR STILE CONSTRUCTION†

Weight of bonderized or galvanized steel doors is approximately 6½ pounds per square foot (including hardware). Glazing is generally 10" high for all steel doors, width is variable. Glazing may be located as desired.

ALUMINUM DOORS

EXTRUDED TUBULAR ALUMINUM CONSTRUCTION†

Weight, panelling, sections, sizes, and glazing are similar to, or the same as, wood overhead doors. Not available in flush panelling.

NOTE: All metal doors are made to order, and are available with wicket (pass) doors, or screened, louvered, or perforated sections.

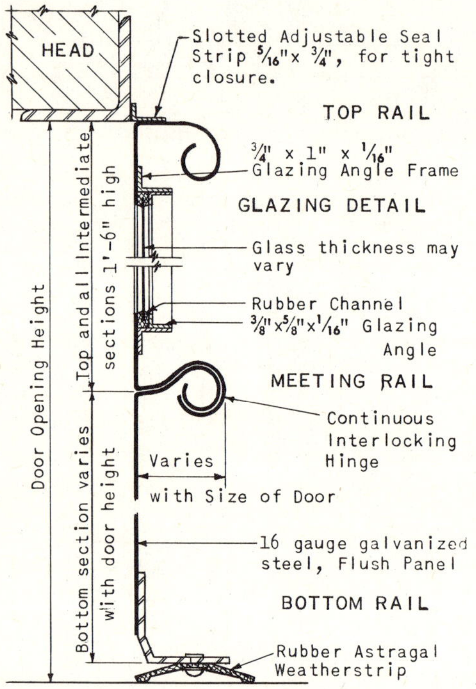
HEAD
Slotted Adjustable Seal Strip 5/16"x 3/4", for tight closure.
TOP RAIL
3/4" x 1" x 1/16" Glazing Angle Frame
GLAZING DETAIL
Glass thickness may vary
Rubber Channel
3/8"x5/8"x1/16" Glazing Angle
MEETING RAIL
Continuous Interlocking Hinge
Varies with Size of Door
16 gauge galvanized steel, Flush Panel
BOTTOM RAIL
Rubber Astragal Weatherstrip
Door Opening Height
Top and all Intermediate sections 1'-6" high
Bottom section varies with door height

CONTINUOUS INTERLOCKING HINGE*

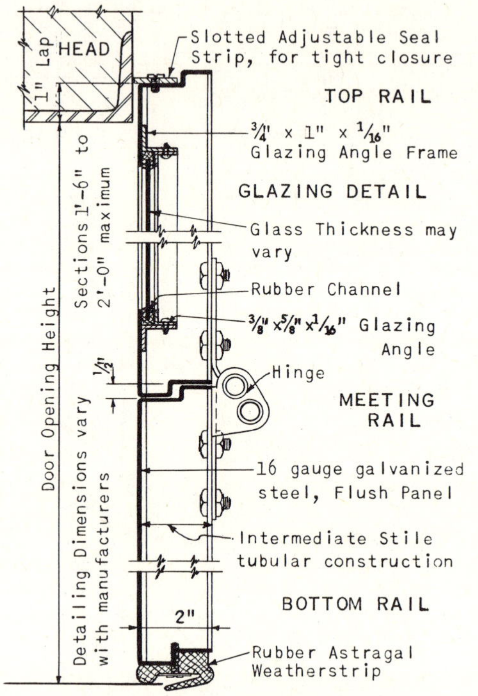
HEAD
1" Lap
Slotted Adjustable Seal Strip, for tight closure
TOP RAIL
3/4" x 1" x 1/16" Glazing Angle Frame
GLAZING DETAIL
Glass Thickness may vary
Rubber Channel
3/8"x5/8"x1/16" Glazing Angle
1/2"
Hinge
MEETING RAIL
16 gauge galvanized steel, Flush Panel
Intermediate Stile tubular construction
BOTTOM RAIL
2"
Rubber Astragal Weatherstrip
Door Opening Height
Sections 1'-6" to 2'-0" maximum
Detailing Dimensions vary with manufacturers

TUBULAR STILE CONSTRUCTION†

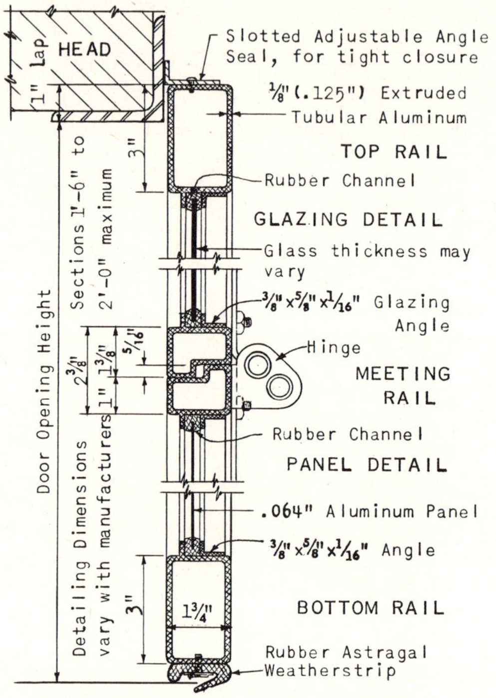
HEAD
1" Lap
Slotted Adjustable Angle Seal, for tight closure
1/8"(.125") Extruded Tubular Aluminum
TOP RAIL
3"
Rubber Channel
GLAZING DETAIL
Glass thickness may vary
3/8"x5/8"x1/16" Glazing Angle
Hinge
MEETING RAIL
2 3/8"
1"
1 3/8"
5/16"
Rubber Channel
PANEL DETAIL
.064" Aluminum Panel
3/8"x5/8"x1/16" Angle
BOTTOM RAIL
3"
1 3/4"
Rubber Astragal Weatherstrip
Door Opening Height
Sections 1'-6" to 2'-0" maximum
Detailing Dimensions vary with manufacturers

EXTRUDED TUBULAR ALUMINUM†

TYPICAL DOOR SECTIONS

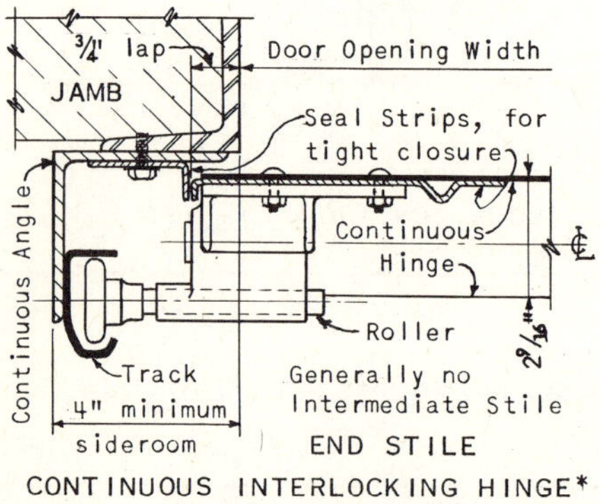
3/4" lap
Door Opening Width
JAMB
Seal Strips, for tight closure
Continuous Hinge
Continuous Angle
Roller
Track
4" minimum sideroom
2 9/16"
Generally no Intermediate Stile
END STILE

CONTINUOUS INTERLOCKING HINGE*

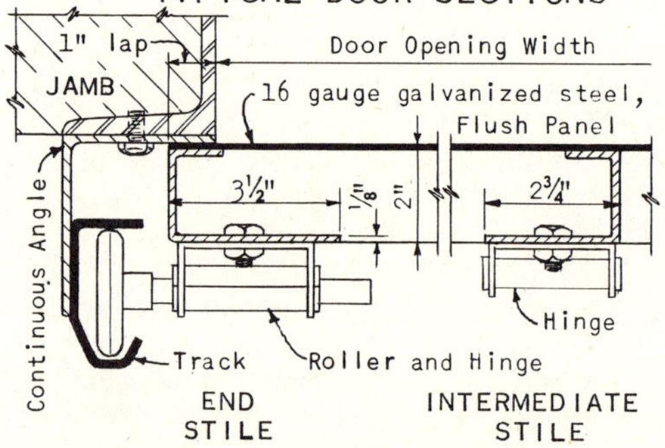
1" lap
Door Opening Width
JAMB
16 gauge galvanized steel, Flush Panel
3 1/2"
1/8"
2"
2 3/4"
Continuous Angle
Track
Roller and Hinge
Hinge
END STILE
INTERMEDIATE STILE

TUBULAR STILE CONSTRUCTION†

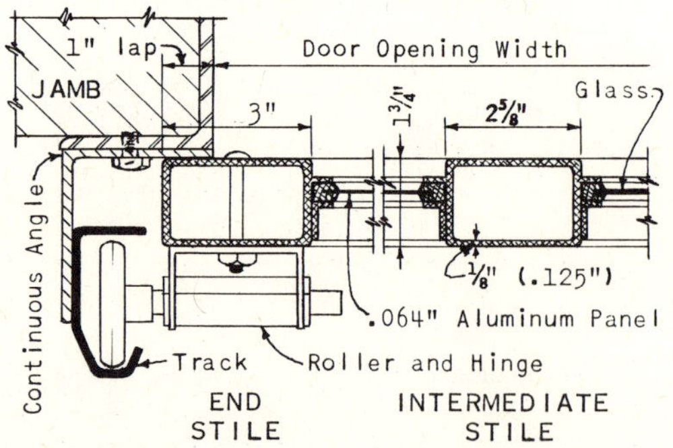
1" lap
Door Opening Width
JAMB
Glass
3"
1 3/4"
2 5/8"
Continuous Angle
1/8" (.125")
.064" Aluminum Panel
Track
Roller and Hinge
END STILE
INTERMEDIATE STILE

EXTRUDED TUBULAR ALUMINUM†

METAL OVERHEAD DOOR DETAILS - TYPICAL JAMB AND DOOR SECTIONS

Scale: $\frac{3}{16}$" = 1'-0"

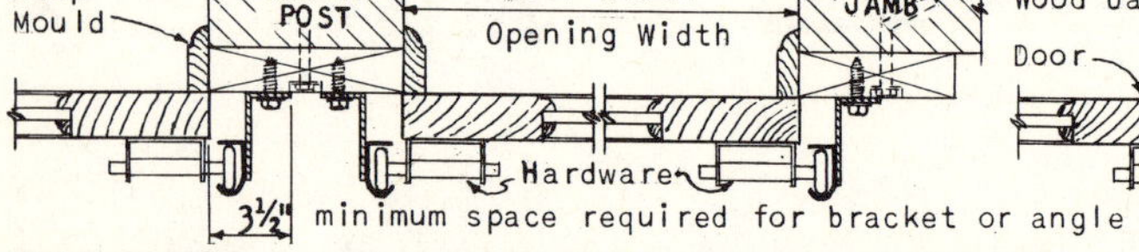
Stop Mould
CENTER POST
Door Width
Opening Width
JAMB
Hardware
3 1/2" minimum space required for bracket or angle

WOOD CASING — FOR WOOD OR METAL DOORS

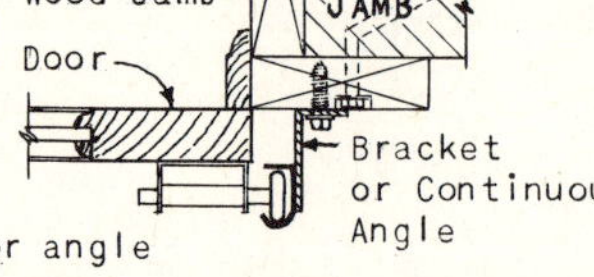
Wood Jamb
JAMB
Door
Bracket or Continuous Angle

WOOD JAMB — FOR WOOD OR METAL DOORS

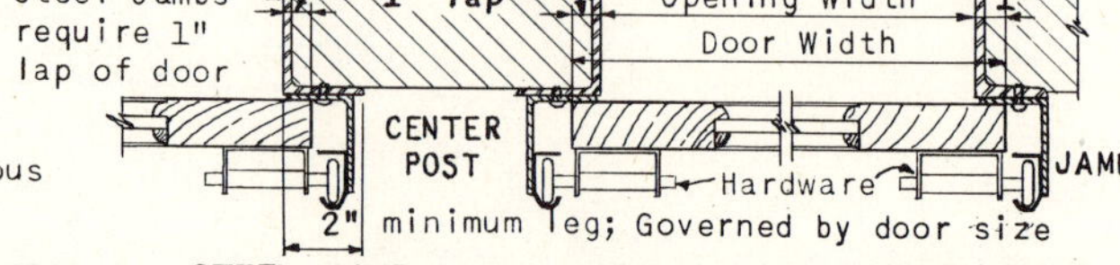
Steel Jambs require 1" lap of door
1" lap
Opening Width
Door Width
1"
CENTER POST
Hardware
JAMB
2" minimum leg; Governed by door size

STEEL JAMB — FOR METAL AND LARGE WOOD DOORS

Minimum Center Post dimensions are generally governed by Structural and Building Code requirements. N.Y.C. Municipal Code: Maximum Height of solid masonry piers set in portland cement mortar - 10 times least dimension of pier.

Scale: 1" = 1'-0"

TYPICAL JAMB AND CENTER POST DETAILS

NOTE: Metal doors and large or heavy wood doors require 1" lap of door at casings or jambs.

DATA CHECKED BY: * KINNEAR MANUFACTURING CO., INC. †OVERHEAD DOOR CO., INC.

OVERHEAD DOORS-TRACK LOCATIONS and CLEARANCES

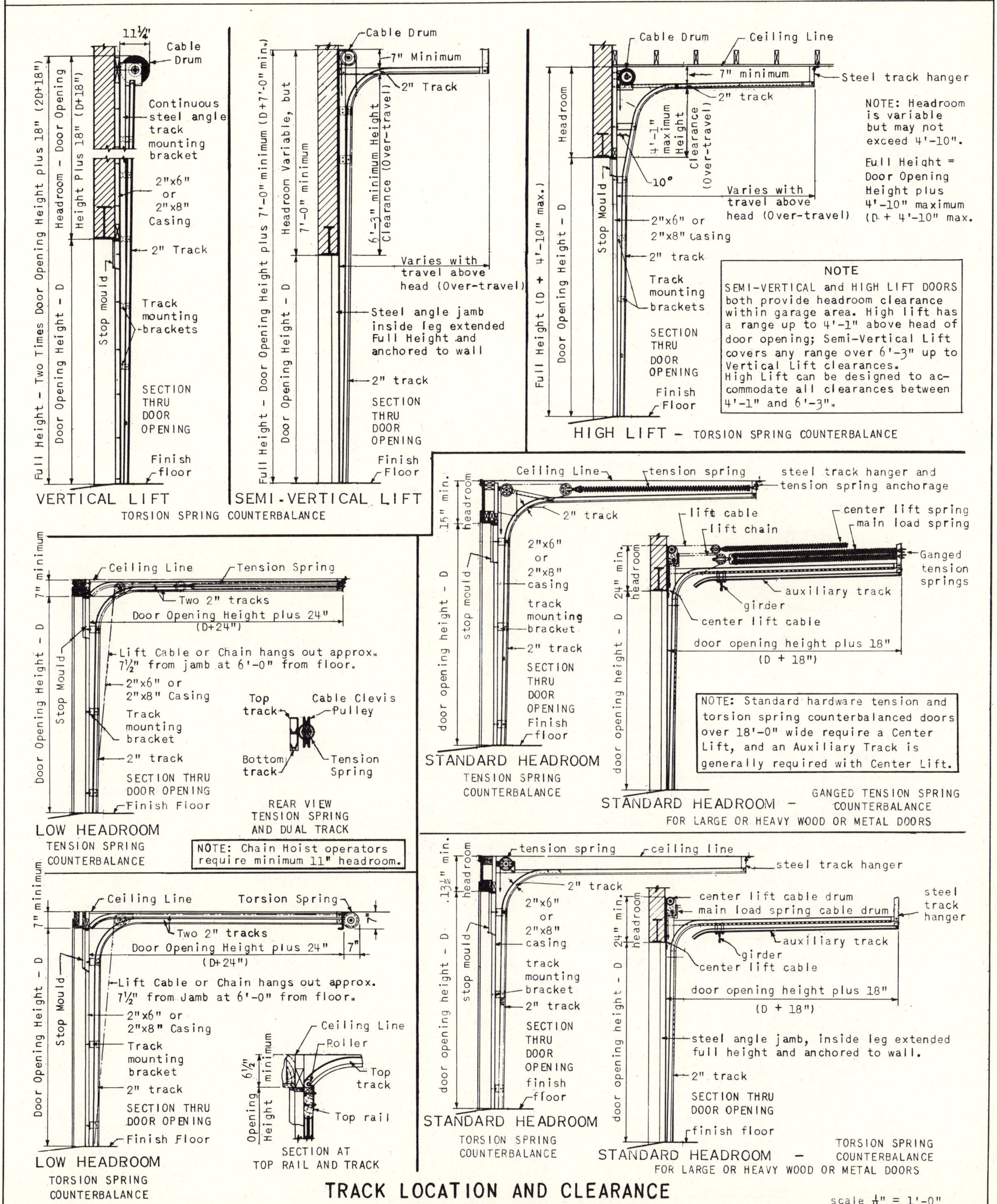
11¼"
Cable Drum
Continuous steel angle track mounting bracket
2"x6" or 2"x8" Casing
2" Track
Track mounting brackets
Stop mould
Full Height - Two Times Door Opening Height plus 18" (2D+18")
Headroom - Door Opening Height Plus 18" (D+18")
Door Opening Height - D
SECTION THRU DOOR OPENING
Finish floor
VERTICAL LIFT
Cable Drum
7" Minimum
2" Track
Full Height - Door Opening Height plus 7'-0" minimum (D+7'-0" min.)
Headroom Variable, but 7'-0" minimum
6'-3" minimum Height Clearance (Over-travel)
Varies with travel above head (Over-travel)
Steel angle jamb inside leg extended Full Height and anchored to wall
2" track
SECTION THRU DOOR OPENING
Finish Floor
SEMI-VERTICAL LIFT
TORSION SPRING COUNTERBALANCE
Cable Drum
Ceiling Line
7" minimum
Steel track hanger
2" track
NOTE: Headroom is variable but may not exceed 4'-10".
Full Height = Door Opening Height plus 4'-10" maximum (D + 4'-10" max.
Headroom
4'-1" maximum Height
Clearance (Over-travel)
10°
Varies with travel above head (Over-travel)
2"x6" or 2"x8" casing
2" track
Track mounting brackets
Stop Mould
Full Height (D + 4'-10" max.)
Door Opening Height - D
SECTION THRU DOOR OPENING
Finish Floor
NOTE
SEMI-VERTICAL and HIGH LIFT DOORS both provide headroom clearance within garage area. High lift has a range up to 4'-1" above head of door opening; Semi-Vertical Lift covers any range over 6'-3" up to Vertical Lift clearances. High Lift can be designed to accommodate all clearances between 4'-1" and 6'-3".
HIGH LIFT - TORSION SPRING COUNTERBALANCE
7" minimum
Ceiling Line
Tension Spring
Two 2" tracks
Door Opening Height plus 24" (D+24")
Lift Cable or Chain hangs out approx. 7½" from jamb at 6'-0" from floor.
2"x6" or 2"x8" Casing
Track mounting bracket
2" track
Stop Mould
Door Opening Height - D
SECTION THRU DOOR OPENING
Finish Floor
Top track
Cable Clevis Pulley
Bottom track
Tension Spring
REAR VIEW TENSION SPRING AND DUAL TRACK
LOW HEADROOM
TENSION SPRING COUNTERBALANCE
NOTE: Chain Hoist operators require minimum 11" headroom.
Ceiling Line
tension spring
steel track hanger and tension spring anchorage
15" min. headroom
2" track
2"x6" or 2"x8" casing
track mounting bracket
2" track
stop mould
door opening height - D
SECTION THRU DOOR OPENING
Finish floor
STANDARD HEADROOM
TENSION SPRING COUNTERBALANCE
lift cable
lift chain
center lift spring
main load spring
Ganged tension springs
24" min. headroom
auxiliary track
girder
center lift cable
door opening height plus 18" (D + 18")
door opening height - D
NOTE: Standard hardware tension and torsion spring counterbalanced doors over 18'-0" wide require a Center Lift, and an Auxiliary Track is generally required with Center Lift.
STANDARD HEADROOM - GANGED TENSION SPRING COUNTERBALANCE
FOR LARGE OR HEAVY WOOD OR METAL DOORS
7" minimum
Ceiling Line
Torsion Spring
7"
Two 2" tracks
Door Opening Height plus 24" (D+24")
7"
Lift Cable or Chain hangs out approx. 7½" from Jamb at 6'-0" from floor.
2"x6" or 2"x8" Casing
Track mounting bracket
2" track
Stop Mould
Door Opening Height - D
SECTION THRU DOOR OPENING
Finish Floor
Ceiling Line
Roller
6½" minimum
Top track
Opening Height
Top rail
SECTION AT TOP RAIL AND TRACK
LOW HEADROOM
TORSION SPRING COUNTERBALANCE
13½" min. headroom
tension spring
ceiling line
steel track hanger
2" track
2"x6" or 2"x8" casing
track mounting bracket
2" track
stop mould
door opening height - D
SECTION THRU DOOR OPENING
finish floor
STANDARD HEADROOM
TORSION SPRING COUNTERBALANCE
center lift cable drum
main load spring cable drum
steel track hanger
24" min. headroom
auxiliary track
girder
center lift cable
door opening height plus 18" (D + 18")
steel angle jamb, inside leg extended full height and anchored to wall.
2" track
door opening height - D
SECTION THRU DOOR OPENING
finish floor
STANDARD HEADROOM - TORSION SPRING COUNTERBALANCE
FOR LARGE OR HEAVY WOOD OR METAL DOORS

TRACK LOCATION AND CLEARANCE

DATA CHECKED BY: OVERHEAD DOOR CORPORATION

scale ¼" = 1'-0"

OVERHEAD DOORS-ANCHORAGE and CLEARANCES

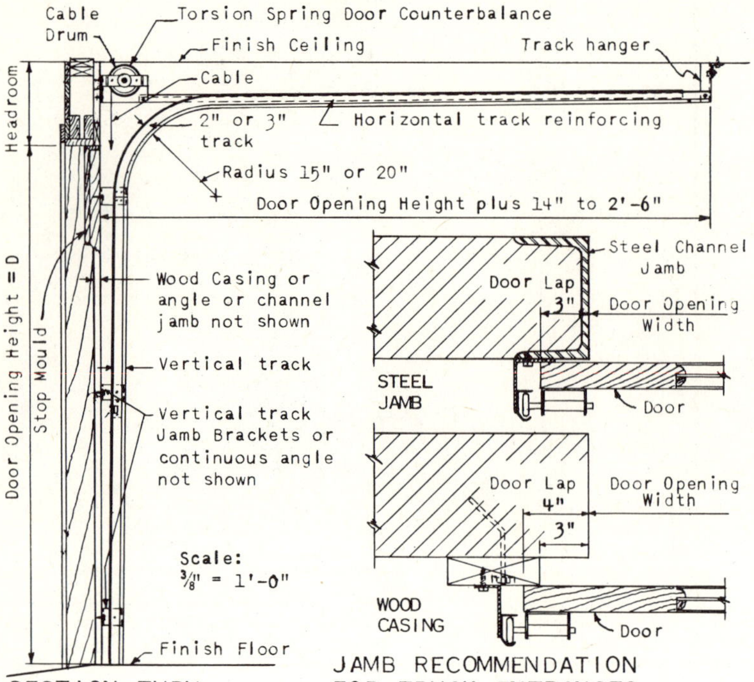
Cable Drum
Torsion Spring Door Counterbalance
Finish Ceiling
Track hanger
Cable
Headroom
2" or 3" track
Horizontal track reinforcing
Radius 15" or 20"
Door Opening Height plus 14" to 2'-6"
Door Opening Height = D
Stop Mould
Wood Casing or angle or channel jamb not shown
Vertical track
Vertical track Jamb Brackets or continuous angle not shown
Scale: 3/8" = 1'-0"
Finish Floor
Steel Channel Jamb
Door Lap 3"
Door Opening Width
STEEL JAMB
Door
Door Lap 4"
3"
Door Opening Width
WOOD CASING
Door

SECTION THRU DOOR OPENING

JAMB RECOMMENDATION FOR TRUCK ENTRANCES
Scale: 1½" = 1'-0"

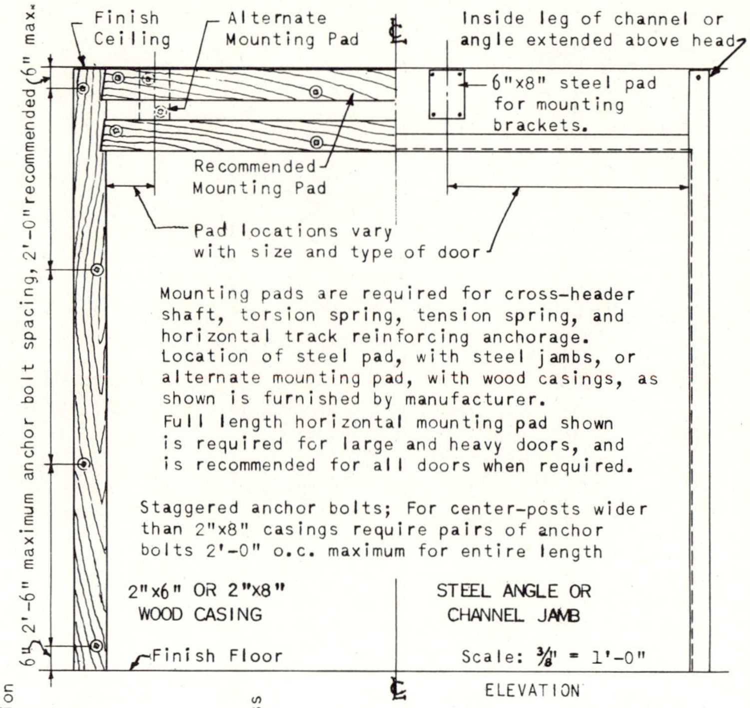
6" 2'-6" maximum anchor bolt spacing, 2'-0" recommended 6" max.
Finish Ceiling
Alternate Mounting Pad
Inside leg of channel or angle extended above head
6"x8" steel pad for mounting brackets.
Recommended Mounting Pad
Pad locations vary with size and type of door
Mounting pads are required for cross-header shaft, torsion spring, tension spring, and horizontal track reinforcing anchorage. Location of steel pad, with steel jambs, or alternate mounting pad, with wood casings, as shown is furnished by manufacturer.
Full length horizontal mounting pad shown is required for large and heavy doors, and is recommended for all doors when required.
Staggered anchor bolts; For center-posts wider than 2"x8" casings require pairs of anchor bolts 2'-0" o.c. maximum for entire length
2"x6" OR 2"x8" WOOD CASING
STEEL ANGLE OR CHANNEL JAMB
Finish Floor
Scale: 3/8" = 1'-0"

ELEVATION

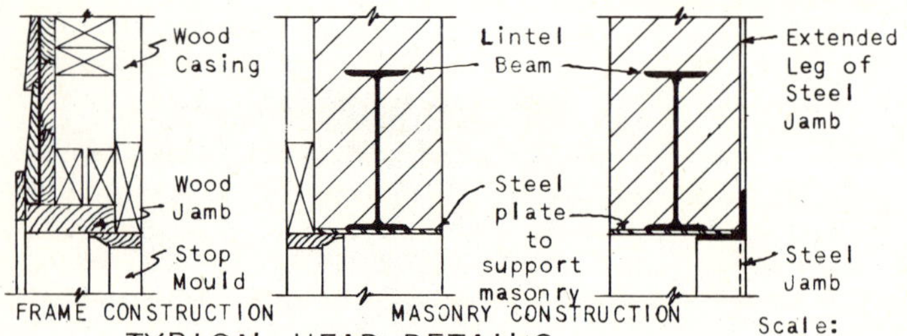
Wood Casing
Wood Jamb
Stop Mould
Lintel Beam
Steel plate to support masonry
Extended Leg of Steel Jamb
Steel Jamb
FRAME CONSTRUCTION
MASONRY CONSTRUCTION
Scale: 3/4" = 1'-0"

TYPICAL HEAD DETAILS

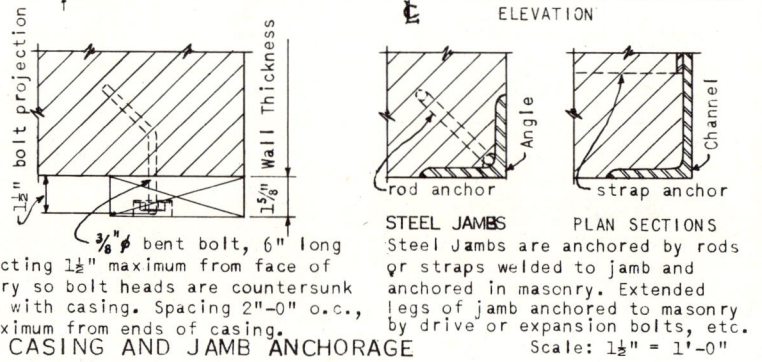

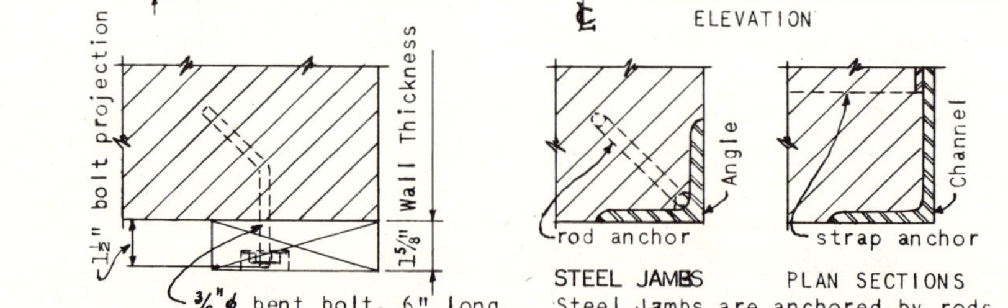
1½" bolt projection
Wall Thickness
1 5/8"
3/8"φ bent bolt, 6" long projecting 1½" maximum from face of masonry so bolt heads are countersunk flush with casing. Spacing 2"-0" o.c., 6" maximum from ends of casing.
Angle
rod anchor
Channel
strap anchor
STEEL JAMBS
PLAN SECTIONS
Steel Jambs are anchored by rods or straps welded to jamb and anchored in masonry. Extended legs of jamb anchored to masonry by drive or expansion bolts, etc.
Scale: 1½" = 1'-0"

CASING AND JAMB ANCHORAGE

WOOD OVERHEAD DOOR CLEARANCE

NOTE: AREA OF DOORS GOVERNS CLEARANCES — CHOICE OF EITHER MAXIMUM WIDTH OR MAXIMUM HEIGHT

		MANUAL OPERATION						CHAIN HOIST OPERATOR REQUIRED*																				
AREA	in sq. ft.	72 □'			120 □'			120 □'			160 □'			180 □'			180 □'			240 □'			360 □'			500 □		
WIDTH	in ft.-in.	9'-0"			16'-0"			16'-0"			18'-0"			18'-0"			22'-0"			24'-0"			30'-0"			40'-0"		
HEIGHT	in ft.-in.	8'-0"			8'-0"			12'-0"			12'-0"			14'-0"			18'-0"			18'-0"			25'-0"			25'-0"		
DOOR TYPE	COUNTER-BALANCE †	HEAD ROOM	SIDE ROOM	CENTER POST	HEAD ROOM	SIDE ROOM	CENTER POST	HEAD ROOM	SIDE ROOM	CENTER POST	HEAD ROOM	SIDE ROOM	CENTER POST	HEAD ROOM	SIDE ROOM	CENTER POST	HEAD ROOM	SIDE ROOM	CENTER POST	HEAD ROOM	SIDE ROOM	CENTER POST	HEAD ROOM	SIDE ROOM	CENTER POST	HEAD ROOM	SIDE ROOM	CENTER POST
VERTICAL LIFT	TORSION SPRINGS	D+18"	5"	10"	D+18"	5"	10"	D+18"	7"	14"	D+18"	7"	14"	D+22"	7"	14"	D+24"	7"	14"	D+24"	7"	14"	D+24"	8½"	17"	D+36"	10"	20"
SEMI-VERTICAL OR HIGH LIFT	TORSION SPRINGS	Varies	7½"	15"	Varies	5"	10"	Varies	7"	14"	Varies	7"	14"	Varies	7"	14"	Varies	7"	14"	Varies	7"	14"	Varies	8½"	17"	Varies	10"	20"
STANDARD HEADROOM	TENSION OR TORSION SPRINGS	15"	3¼"	7"	15"	3¼"	7"	15"	5"	10"	16"	6"	12"	18"	6"	12"	22"	6½"	13"	22"	6½"	13"	24"	8½"	17"	30"	10"	20"
LOW HEADROOM ‡	TENSION OR TORSION SPRINGS	7"	3¼"	7"	11½"	3¼"	7"	11½"	6"	12"	12"	6½"	13"	12"	6½"	13"	14"	7½"	15"	14"	7½"	15"						

Example:
With Door Area 160 □' or less and maximum width = 18'-0" maximum height will be:
160 sq. ft. ÷ 18'-0" width = 8.88 feet maximum height
or
maximum height = 12'-0" maximum width will be:
160 sq. ft. ÷ 12'-0" height = 13.33 feet maximum width

NOTE: Clearances given are for Wood Doors only. All metal and Kalamein doors are made to order and require special consideration.

*CHAIN HOIST INSTALLATIONS: See Chain Hoist Minimum Sideroom Clearances for additional space required for chain hoist mounting.

†VERTICAL AND SEMI-VERTICAL LIFT DOORS also available with weight counter balance, chain hoist and motor operator as required

‡LOW HEADROOM CLEARANCES given raise door and hardware completely above head of door opening. Low Headroom Doors can be installed with no headroom, but door and hardware will project 7" below ceiling or head of door opening.

DATA CHECKED BY: OVERHEAD DOOR CORPORATION

OVERHEAD DOOR OPERATORS-CHAIN HOIST and MOTOR

OVERHEAD DOOR OPERATORS

TYPES OF OPERATORS: Manual, Chain Hoist, Electric Operator

Residential doors are generally manually operated. A motor operator is recommended for two-car doors, and is necessary where electronic (radio) control is desired.

Commercial and Industrial doors are generally Chain Hoist operated. Chain Hoist is recommended for Wood Doors exceeding 160 square feet, 16'–0" wide or 13'–0" high, and for Metal Doors exceeding 120 square feet, 15'–0" wide or 12'–0" high. An Electric Motor-Chain Hoist Operator is recommended for all Metal Doors, heavy, wide, or high doors, and where the door is operated frequently.

CHAIN HOIST OPERATORS

NOTE: All chain hoist operators require additional sideroom clearance. Operator may be mounted on left, or right side as shown; on the left greater sideroom is required. Dimensions shown are from door jamb to projection of operator.

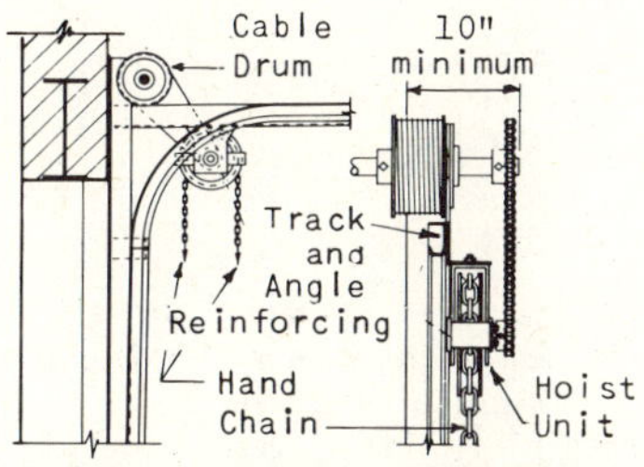
Cable
Drum
10"
minimum
Track
and
Angle
Reinforcing
Hand
Chain
Hoist
Unit

MOUNTED ON AND BELOW HORIZONTAL TRACK REINFORCING ANGLE

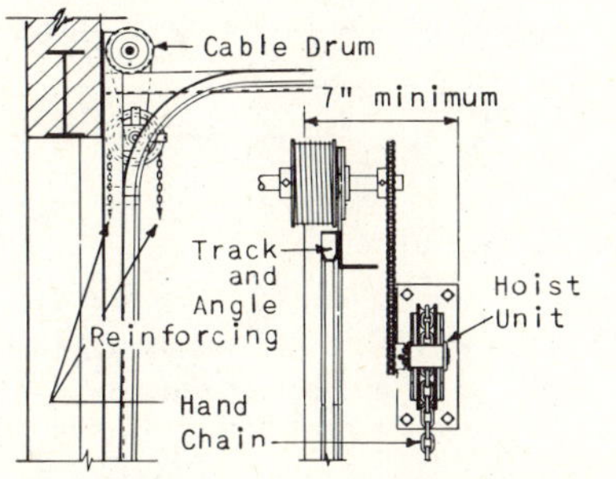
Cable Drum
7" minimum
Track
and
Angle
Reinforcing
Hoist
Unit
Hand
Chain

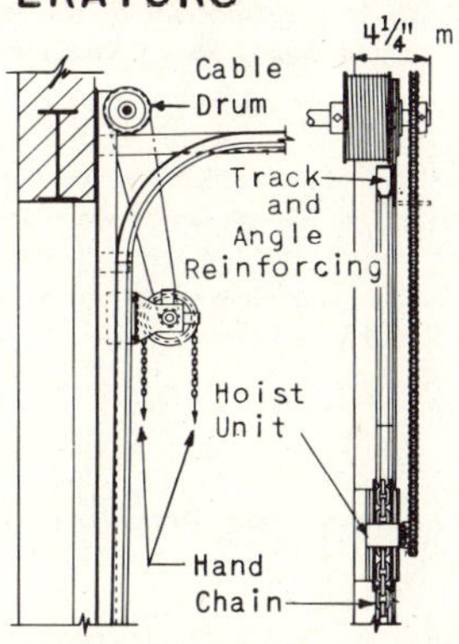
4¼" minimum
Cable
Drum
Track
and
Angle
Reinforcing
Hoist
Unit
Hand
Chain

WALL MOUNTED TO SIDE AND BELOW HORIZONTAL TRACK AND CABLE DRUM

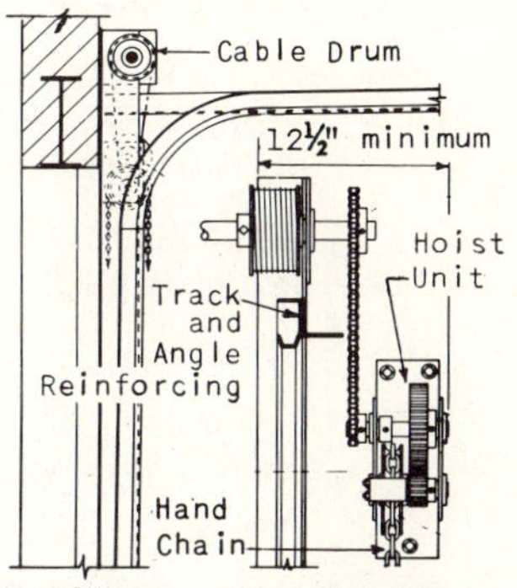
Cable Drum
12½" minimum
Hoist
Unit
Track
and
Angle
Reinforcing
Hand
Chain

JAMB MOUNTED BELOW HORIZONTAL TRACK AND CABLE DRUM
For large or heavy doors

CHAIN HOIST - MINIMUM SIDEROOM CLEARANCES

ELECTRIC MOTOR OPERATORS

TYPES OF MOTOR OPERATORS:

1. Drawbar Operator: chain drive with drawbar, carriage and track
2. Cross-Header Shaft Operator: coupled drive, operator coupled to cross-header shaft (disengageable emergency chain hoist operator optional)

TYPES OF MOTOR OPERATOR CONTROLS:

1. Push Button Switch (two buttons for open and close or three buttons for open, close, and stop).
2. Key Switch (two positions for open and close).
3. Chain Pull Switch (weatherproof).
4. Safety Switch (bar at bottom of door; door stops if obstructed).
5. Electronic (radio) Control (button in car dashboard)

NOTE: Emergency chain hoist operator is not available for drawbar motor operators. Only drawbar operators are available with electronic control. Electronic control is rarely used on heavier (industrial or commercial) door installations. Cross-header shaft operators are never used on smaller or residential doors. Only cross-header shaft operators are applicable to weight counterbalanced doors. Either type operator is operable with either tension or torsion spring counterbalance.

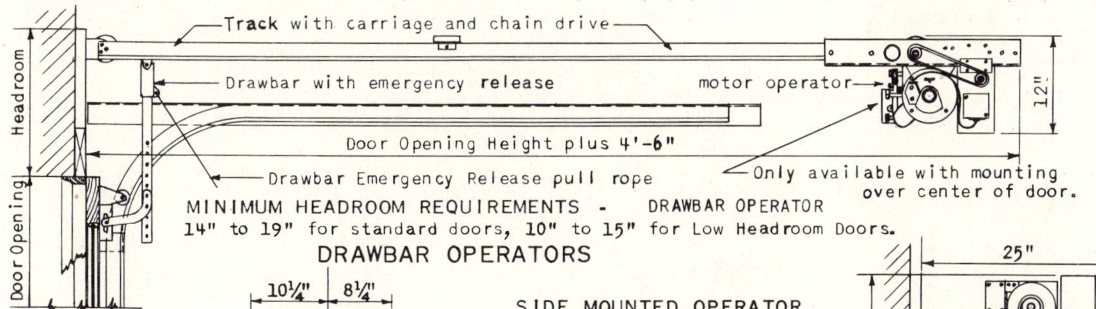
Track with carriage and chain drive
Headroom
Drawbar with emergency release
motor operator
12"
Door Opening Height plus 4'-6"
Drawbar Emergency Release pull rope
Only available with mounting
over center of door.
Door Opening

MINIMUM HEADROOM REQUIREMENTS - DRAWBAR OPERATOR
14" to 19" for standard doors, 10" to 15" for Low Headroom Doors.

DRAWBAR OPERATORS

MINIMUM HEADROOM REQUIREMENTS CROSS-HEADER SHAFT OPERATOR	
CENTER MOUNTED	
without girder	29½"
with girder	32½"
SIDE MOUNTED	
without girder	17½"
with girder	20½"
Low Headroom	10" to 12"

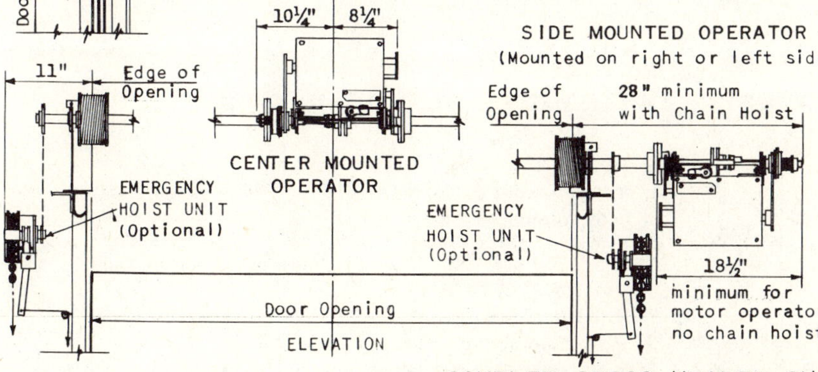
11"
Edge of
Opening
10¼"
8¼"
CENTER MOUNTED
OPERATOR
EMERGENCY
HOIST UNIT
(Optional)
SIDE MOUNTED OPERATOR
(Mounted on right or left side)
Edge of
Opening
28" minimum
with Chain Hoist
EMERGENCY
HOIST UNIT
(Optional)
18½"
minimum for
motor operator
no chain hoist
Door Opening
ELEVATION

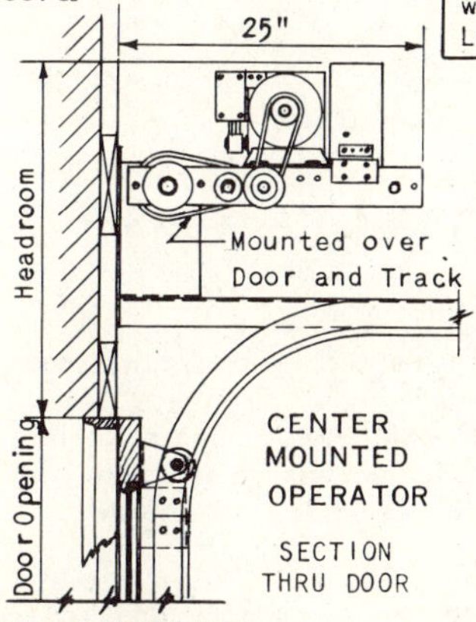
25"
Headroom
Mounted over
Door and Track
Door Opening
CENTER
MOUNTED
OPERATOR
SECTION
THRU DOOR

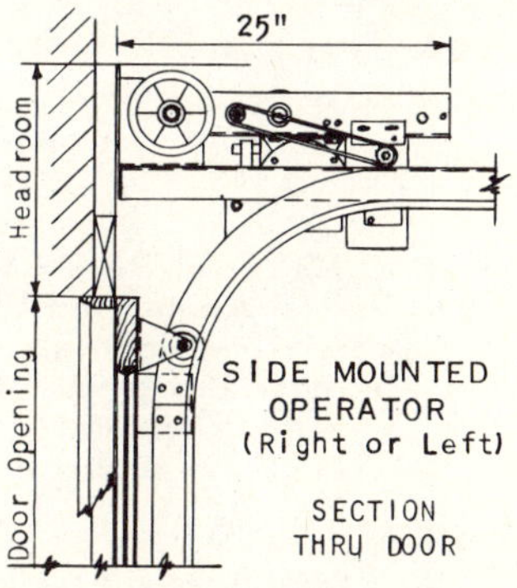
25"
Headroom
Door Opening
SIDE MOUNTED
OPERATOR
(Right or Left)
SECTION
THRU DOOR

Scale: ½" = 1'-0"

COUPLED CROSS-HEADER SHAFT OPERATOR

MOTOR OPERATORS - MINIMUM CLEARANCES

NOTE: Headroom clearance varies as noted in Table Above.

DATA CHECKED BY: OVERHEAD DOOR CORPORATION

FOLDING PARTITIONS

Folding partitions may be used to solve a variety of partitioning problems in gymnasiums, classrooms and commercial buildings. In gymnasiums, a large regulation playing court with spectator seating may be quickly and effectively divided into two or more gymnasiums for regular student use.

Folding partitions shown are all of the top-hung type which do not require bottom grooves or a track in the gymnasium floor. Other types of folding and rolling partitions are available with floor guides.

Folding partitions on this and the following page may be obtained with manual, mechanical, or automatic electric operation.

The diagram at the right shows possible variations in the installation of folding partitions.

Consult manufacturers for exact dimensions and installation details.

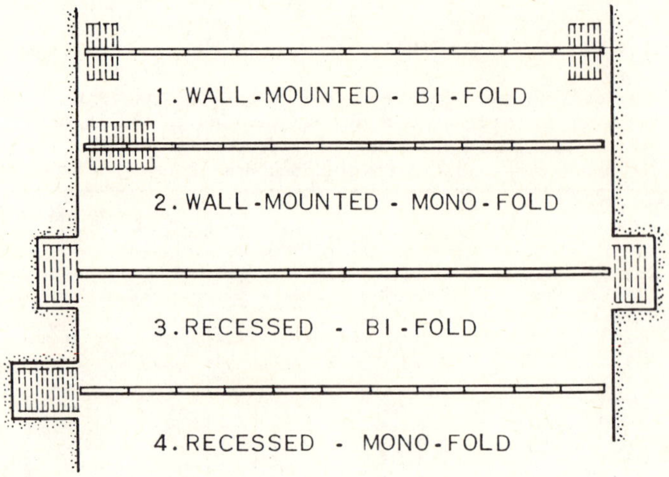
1. WALL-MOUNTED - BI-FOLD
2. WALL-MOUNTED - MONO-FOLD
3. RECESSED - BI-FOLD
4. RECESSED - MONO-FOLD

NOTE: For mono-fold partitions, the opening must contain an odd number of equal-width panels. Each part of a bi-fold partition must contain an odd number of equal width panels.

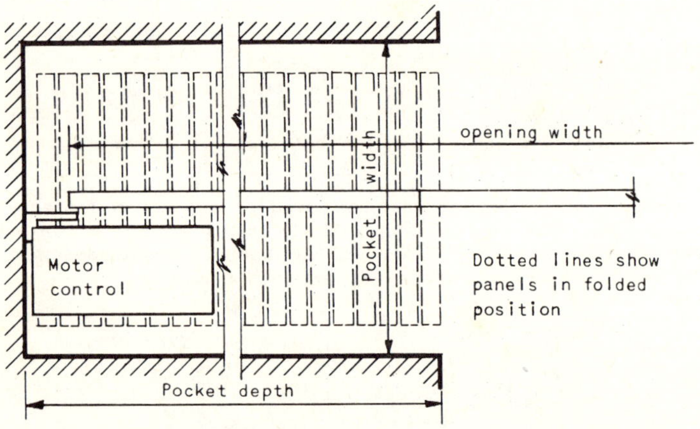
opening width
Pocket width
Motor control
Dotted lines show panels in folded position
Pocket depth

PLAN-POCKET RECESS WITHOUT DOORS

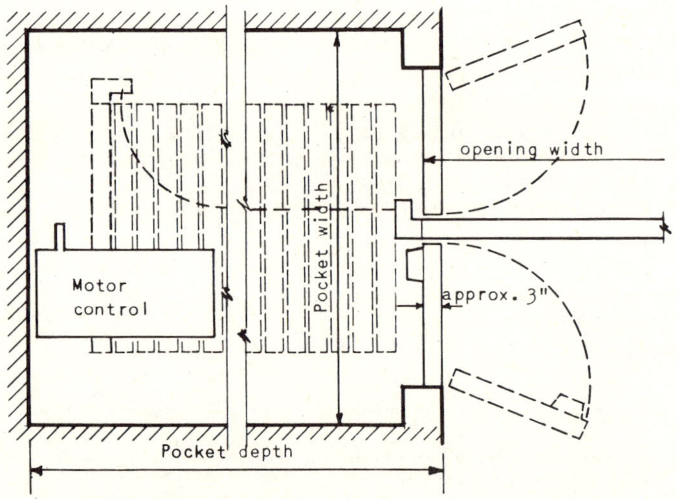
opening width
Pocket width
Motor control
approx. 3"
Pocket depth

PLAN-POCKET RECESS WITH DOORS

TO DETERMINE NUMBER OF PANELS AND DIMENSIONS OF RECESS

FOR NUMBER OF PANELS:

1. Divide opening width by 4'-0" to determine the approximate number of doors.
2. Increase this number to meet requirements for the type of operation (Mono-fold: Odd number of doors in total width. Bi-fold: Odd number of doors in 1/2 total width).

FOR DOOR WIDTH:

Divide total opening width by number of doors. (Maximum width = 4'-1½". Minimum width = 3'-0"). Door width should be as near 4'-0" as possible and not less than 3'-0" as narrow doors are not stable.

FOR POCKET WIDTH:

1. Without recess doors – Door Width + 1'-0"
2. With manual recess doors – Door Width + 1'-6"
3. With automatic recess doors – Door Width + 2'-0"

FOR POCKET DEPTH:

1. Without recess doors – 3¾" x no. of doors + 1'-0"
2. With manual recess doors – 3¾" x no. of doors + 1'-6"
3. With automatic recess doors – 3¾" x no. of doors + 1'-0"

Manufacturers recommend manually operated doors as they close the pocket whether partition is extended or folded.

FOLDING PARTITIONS

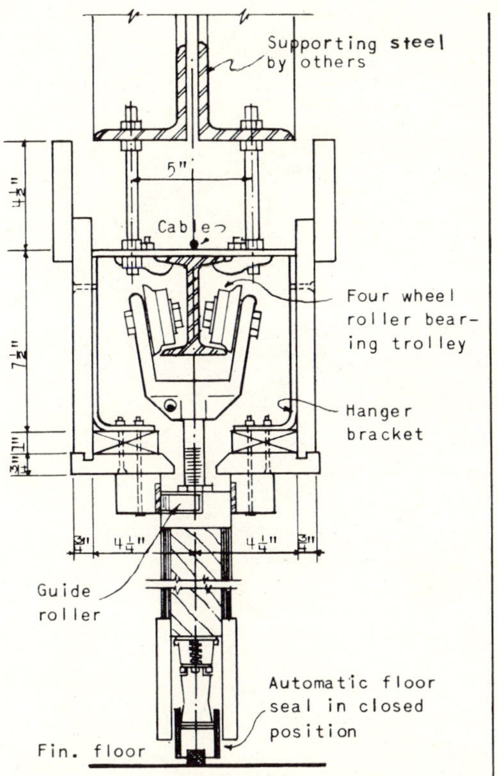

Supporting steel by others
5"
Cable
Four wheel roller bearing trolley
Hanger bracket
4½"
7½"
Guide roller
Automatic floor seal in closed position
Fin. floor

HORN DIVISION
BRUNSWICK-BALKE-COLLENDER CO.

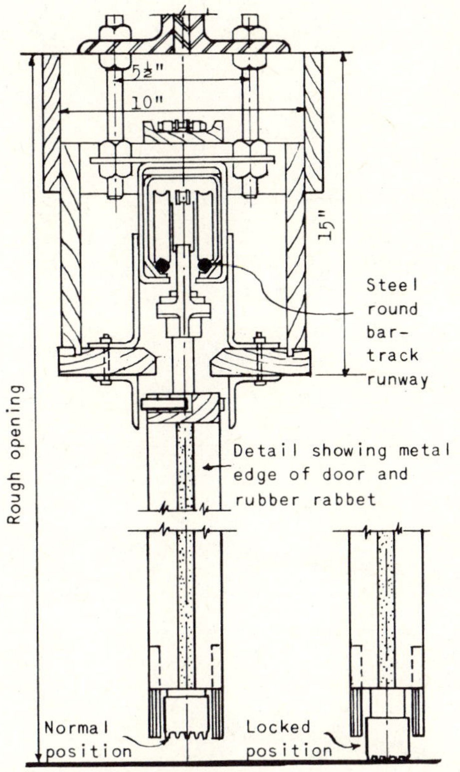

5½"
10"
15"
Steel round bar-track runway
Rough opening
Detail showing metal edge of door and rubber rabbet
Normal position
Locked position

RICHARDS-WILCOX
MANUFACTURING CO.

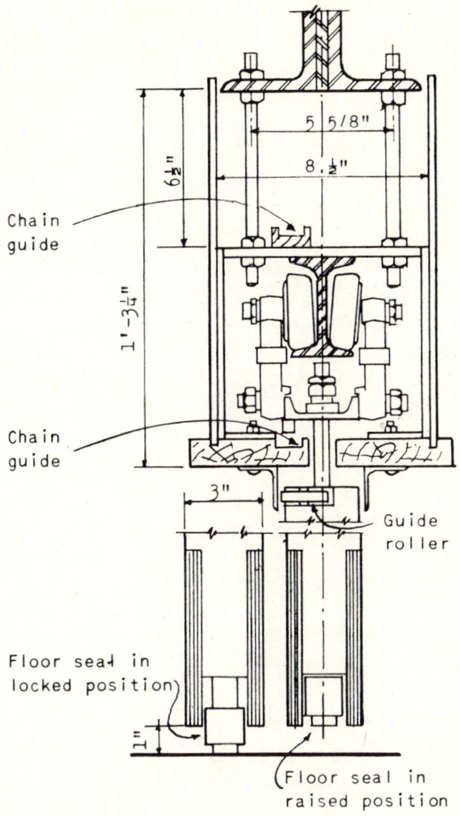

5 5/8"
8 ½"
6½"
1'-3¼"
Chain guide
Chain guide
3"
Guide roller
Floor seal in locked position
1"
Floor seal in raised position

WAYNE IRON WORKS

VERTICAL SECTIONS THROUGH DOOR AND HANGER ASSEMBLY

Bi-fold partitions require two jambs of type "A"

Mono-fold partitions require one jamb of type "A" and one jamb of type "B"

Scale of all drawings: 1½" = 1'-0"

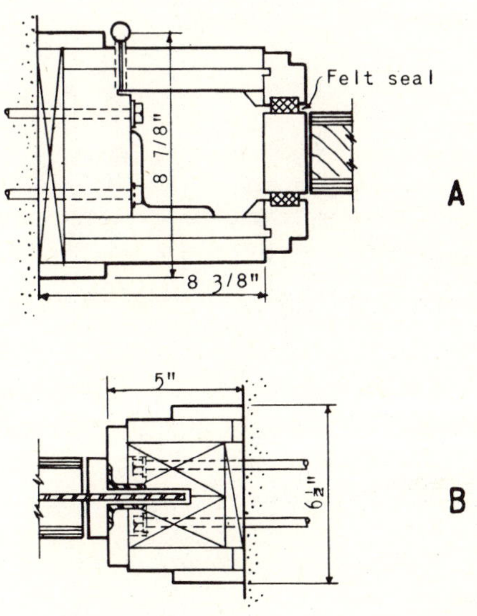

Felt seal
8 7/8"
8 3/8"
A
5"
6½"
B

HORN DIVISION
BRUNSWICK-BALKE-COLLENDER CO.

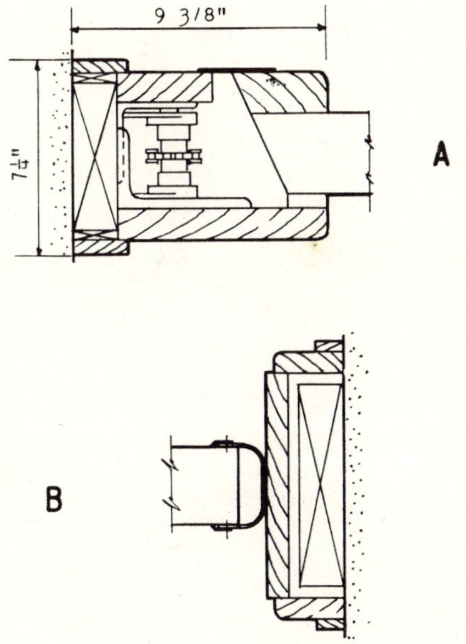

9 3/8"
7¼"
A
B

RICHARDS-WILCOX
MANUFACTURING CO.

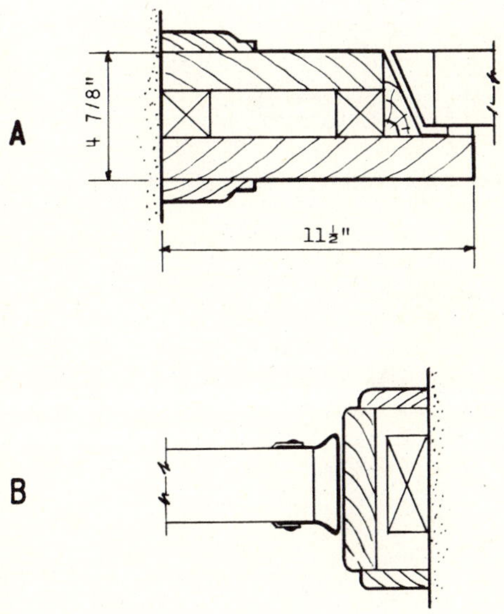

4 7/8"
A
11½"
B

WAYNE IRON WORKS

JAMB DETAILS

EXTERIOR SADDLES and WEATHERSTRIPPING

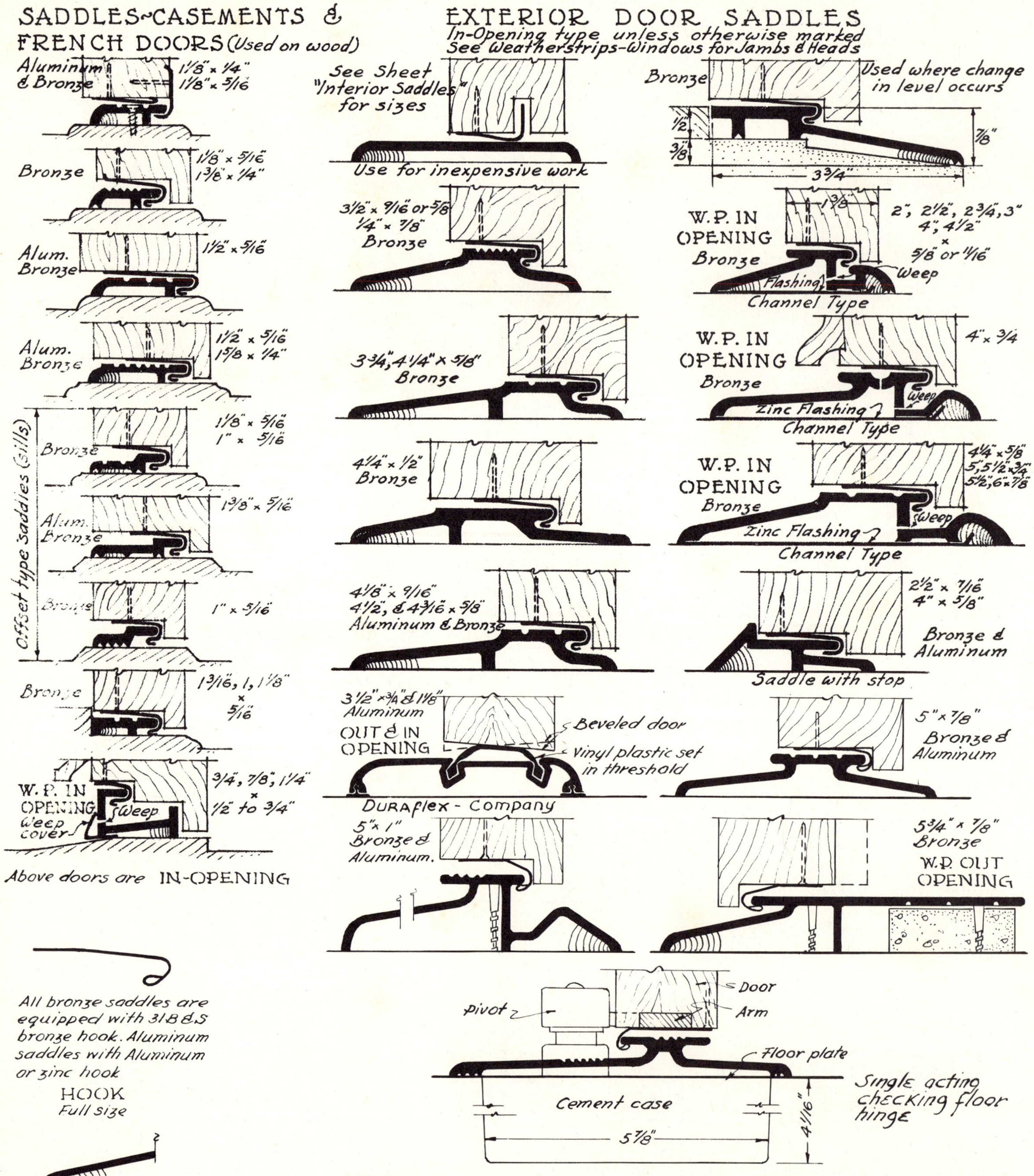

SADDLES~CASEMENTS & FRENCH DOORS (Used on wood)
Aluminum & Bronze
1 1/8" × 1/4"
1 1/8" × 5/16"
Bronze
1 1/8" × 5/16"
1 3/8" × 1/4"
Alum. Bronze
1 1/2" × 5/16"
Alum. Bronze
1 1/2" × 5/16"
1 5/8 × 1/4"
Offset type saddles (sills)
Bronze
1 1/8" × 5/16"
1" × 5/16"
Alum. Bronze
1 3/8" × 5/16"
Bronze
1" × 5/16"
Bronze
1 3/16, 1, 1 1/8" × 5/16
W.P. IN OPENING
Weep
Weep cover
3/4", 7/8", 1 1/4" × 1/2" to 3/4"
Above doors are IN-OPENING
EXTERIOR DOOR SADDLES
In-Opening type unless otherwise marked
See Weatherstrips-Windows for Jambs & Heads
See Sheet "Interior Saddles" for sizes
Use for inexpensive work
Bronze
Used where change in level occurs
1/2
3/8
7/8"
3 3/4"
3 1/2" × 9/16" or 5/8
1/4" × 7/8"
Bronze
W.P. IN OPENING
Bronze
1 3/8
2", 2 1/2", 2 3/4", 3"
4", 4 1/2"
×
5/8 or 11/16"
Flashing
Weep
Channel Type
3 3/4", 4 1/4" × 5/8"
Bronze
W.P. IN OPENING
Bronze
4" × 3/4
Zinc Flashing
Weep
Channel Type
4 1/4" × 1/2"
Bronze
W.P. IN OPENING
Bronze
4 1/4" × 5/8"
5", 5 1/2" × 3/4"
5 1/2", 6" × 7/8"
Weep
Zinc Flashing
Channel Type
4 1/8" × 9/16"
4 1/2", & 4 3/16" × 5/8"
Aluminum & Bronze
2 1/2" × 7/16"
4" × 5/8"
Bronze & Aluminum
Saddle with stop
3 1/2" × 3/4" & 1 1/8"
Aluminum
OUT & IN OPENING
Beveled door
Vinyl plastic set in threshold
Duraflex - Company
5" × 7/8"
Bronze & Aluminum
5" × 1"
Bronze & Aluminum.
5 3/4" × 7/8"
Bronze
W.P. OUT OPENING
All bronze saddles are equipped with 31 B & S bronze hook. Aluminum saddles with Aluminum or zinc hook
HOOK
Full size
INDICATION for CAULKING
Pivot
Door
Arm
Floor plate
Cement case
5 7/8"
4 1/16"
Single acting checking floor hinge

NOTES: Saddles vary in details from the above as they are not standardized. Typical types are shown "W.P." types are advised for in-opening doors if uncovered. Saddles also termed thresholds & sills.

SOUND, NOISE, LIGHT, DIRT & DRAFT PROOF WEATHERSTRIPS

Scale 6" = 1'-0"

Data checked by Zero Weather Stripping Co. Inc.

INTERIOR METAL SADDLES (THRESHOLDS)

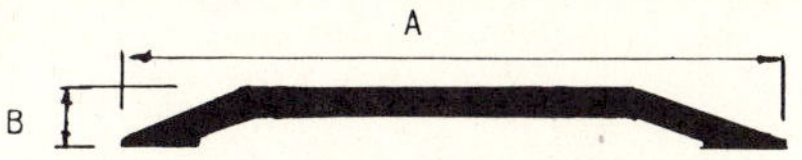
A
B

BRASS		ALUMINUM				BRONZE	
A	B	A	B	A	B	A	B
3"	1/4"	4 5/64	5/32	4, 4 5/64 5&6"	1/2"	2 1/2, 3"	1/4"
2 1/4"	3/16"	2 1/4"	3/16"			4, 5 & 6"	1/2"
4, 5 & 6"	1/2"	2 1/2, 3	1/4"				
		2 1/4"	3/8"	4"	7/16"		

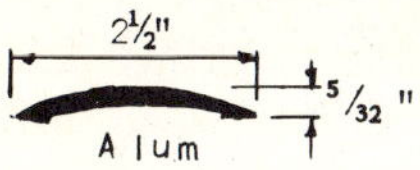
2 1/2"
5/32"
Alum

PLAIN TYPES

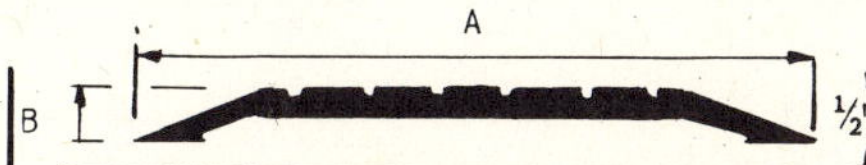
A
B

BRASS		ALUM.		BRONZE		STEEL	
A	B	A	B	A	B	A	B
3, 3 1/2, 4, 5 &6"	1/2"	3, 4, 5, 6, 6 1/4 7, 7 1/2"	1/2"	3"	5/16"	3&4"	1/2"
				3"	3/8"	5 1/2"	9/16"
				4, 4 1/2, 5, 6 &7"	1/2"	5 1/2" &7"	5/8"
		3, 4 5&6"	5/8"	6&7"	5/8"		

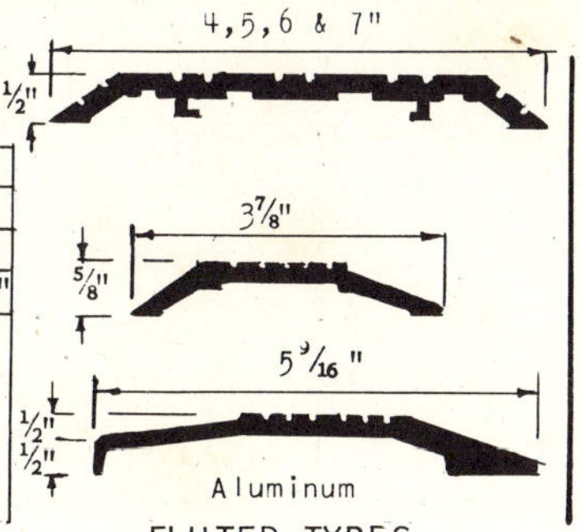
4, 5, 6 & 7"
1/2"
3 7/8"
5/8"
5 9/16"
1/2"
1/2"
Aluminum

FLUTED TYPES

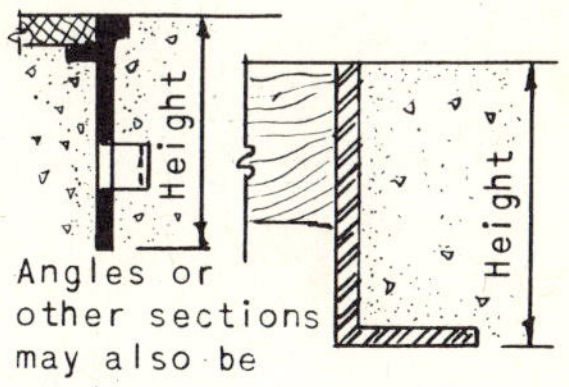
Height
Height

Angles or other sections may also be used

Used for division of flrs. of different materials

JOINT STRIPS (PARTING BARS)

Note: Threshold profiles vary somewhat from mfr. to mfr. Slots for fluted type are 1/8"± radius and are spaced approx. 1/2" c. to c. Std. length is 18' to 20' or saddles may be ordered cut to size. Anchors to wood floors are screws: to terrazzo or cement floors, screws in fiber plugs or expansive metal anchors; to concrete, screws tapped to clips set in concrete.

INTERIOR METAL SADDLES & JOINT STRIPS

DATA CHECKED BY NATIONAL ASSOCIATION OF ARCHITECTURAL METAL MANUFACTURERS

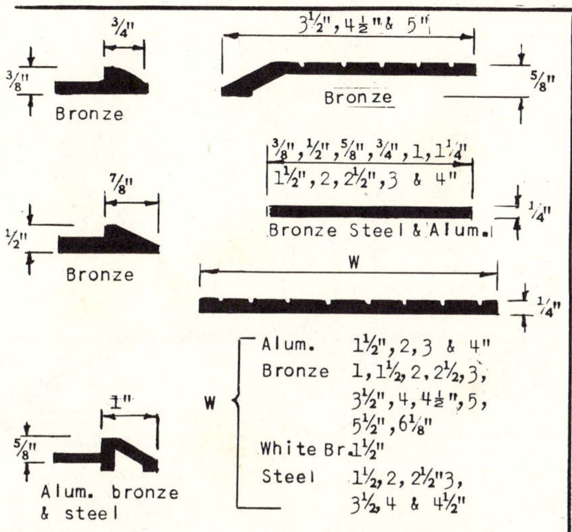
3/4"
3/8"
Bronze
3 1/2", 4 1/2" & 5"
5/8"
Bronze
7/8"
1/2"
Bronze
3/8", 1/2", 5/8", 3/4", 1, 1 1/4"
1 1/2", 2, 2 1/2", 3 & 4"
1/4"
Bronze Steel & Alum.
W
1/4"
1"
5/8"
Alum. bronze & steel
W
Alum. 1 1/2", 2, 3 & 4"
Bronze 1, 1 1/2, 2, 2 1/2, 3, 3 1/2", 4, 4 1/2", 5, 5 1/2", 6 1/8"
White Br. 1 1/2"
Steel 1 1/2, 2, 2 1/2"3, 3 1/2, 4 & 4 1/2"

ASSEMBLED SADDLE COMPONENTS

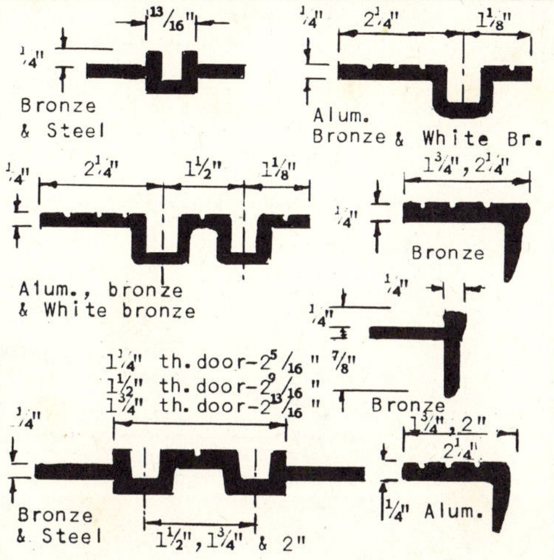
13/16"
1/4"
Bronze & Steel
1/4"
2 1/4"
1 1/8"
Alum. Bronze & White Br.
1/4"
2 1/4"
1 1/2"
1 1/8"
Alum., bronze & White bronze
1 3/4", 2 1/4"
1/4"
Bronze
1/4"
1/4"
1 1/4" th. door-2 5/16" 7/8"
1 1/2" th. door-2 9/16"
1 3/4" th. door-2 13/16"
Bronze
1/4"
Bronze & Steel
1 1/2", 1 3/4" & 2"
1 3/4", 2"
2 1/4"
1/4" Alum.

SLIDING DOOR SADDLE COMPONENTS

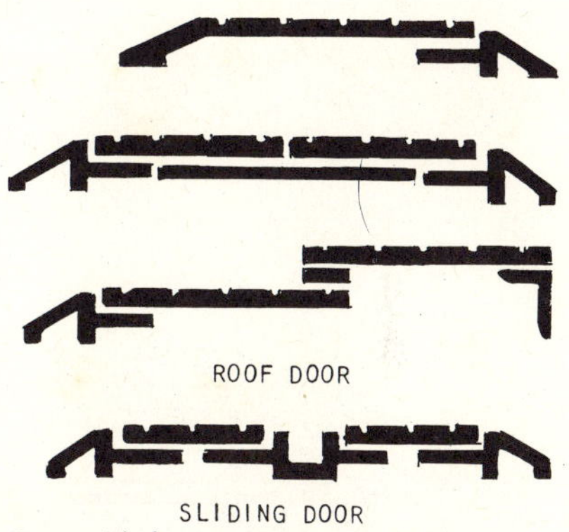
ROOF DOOR
SLIDING DOOR

By combining components saddles may be made to any width. Joints will not show as flute pattern is identical.

TYPICAL ASSEMBLED SADDLES

DATA BY JULIUS BLUM & CO., INC.

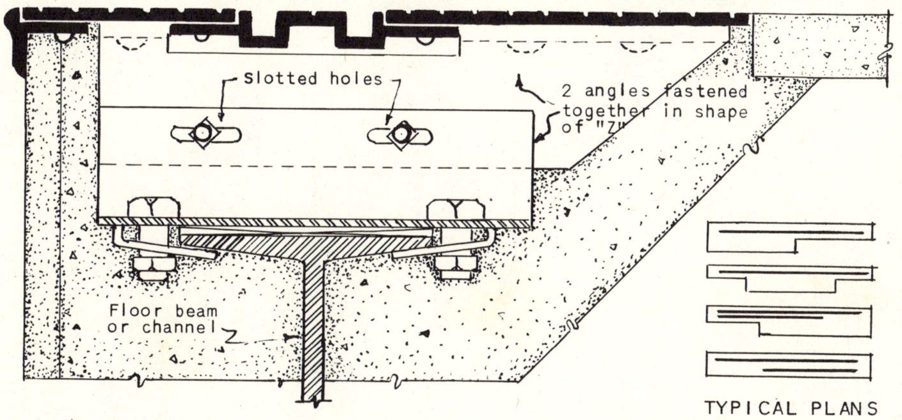
Slotted holes
2 angles fastened together in shape of "Z"
Floor beam or channel

TYPICAL PLANS

Scale 3"=1'-0"

TYPICAL ELEVATOR SADDLE CONSTRUCTION

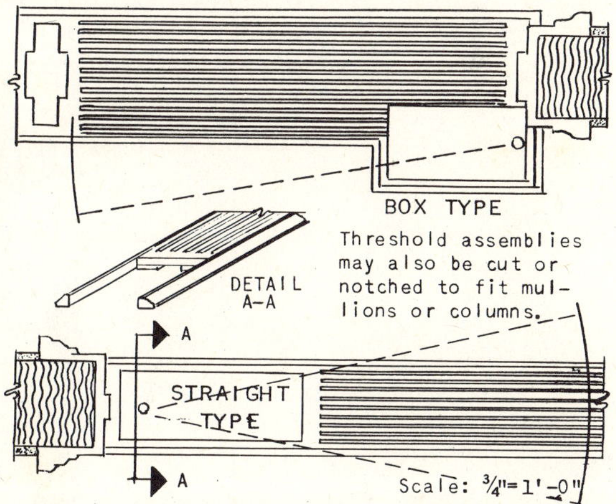
BOX TYPE
DETAIL A-A
A
STRAIGHT TYPE
A

Threshold assemblies may also be cut or notched to fit mullions or columns.

Scale: 3/4"=1'-0"

TYPICAL CUTOUTS FOR FLOOR HINGES

DATA BY JULIUS BLUM & CO., INC.

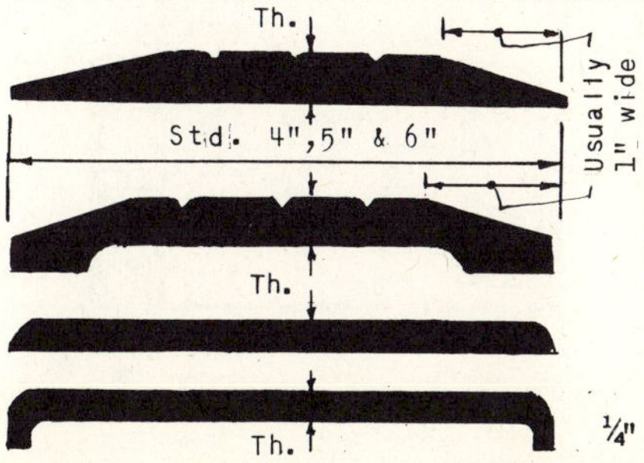
Th.
Usually 1" wide
Std. 4", 5" & 6"
Th.
Th.
1/4"

RECOMMENDED PRACTICE

TH.	IRON	BRONZE	ALUMINUM	NICKEL
1/4"		to 6" wide	to 10" wide	to 6" wide
5/16"	to 6" wide	to 10" wide	to 18" wide	to 10" wide
3/8"	to 12" wide	to 18" wide	to 24" wide	to 14" wide
7/16"	to 24" wide	to 24" wide	to 36" wide	to 18" wide
1/2"	to 30" wide	to 30" wide	to 42" wide	to 24" wide
5/8"	to 42" wide	to 42" wide	to 42" wide	to 30" wide
3/4"	to 42" wide	to 42" wide	to 42" wide	to 30" wide

Length, to 9'-6". When width exceeds 32", length should not exceed 7'-6".

1"

Min. th. 1/2" for iron, 3/8" for bronze, aluminum & nickel.

1"

Saddles with floor hinge cut-outs, as shown above also available

CAST METAL SADDLES WITH OR WITHOUT ABRASIVE CONTENT

DATA BY AMERICAN ABRASIVE METALS COMPANY

WEATHERSTRIPS for DOORS

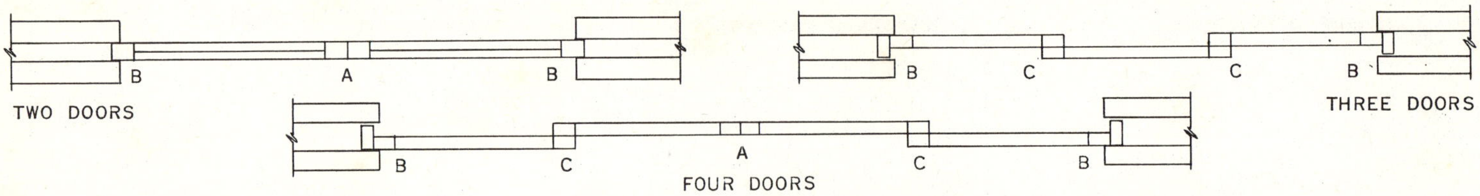
B
A
B
TWO DOORS
B
C
C
B
THREE DOORS
B
C
A
C
B
FOUR DOORS

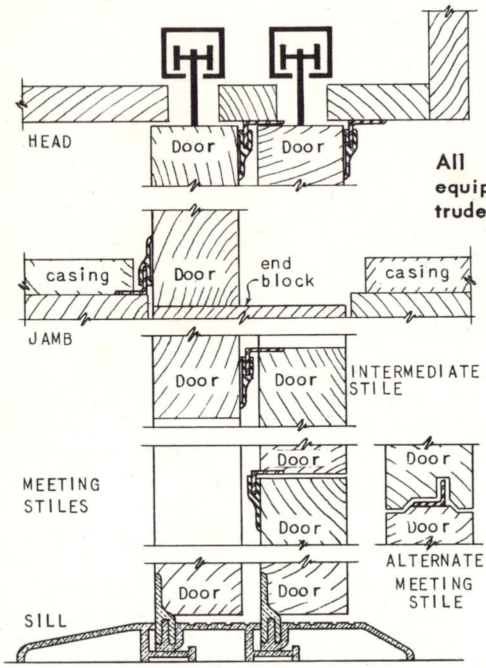
HEAD
Door
Door
casing
Door
end block
casing
JAMB
Door
Door
INTERMEDIATE STILE
MEETING STILES
Door
Door
Door
Door
ALTERNATE MEETING STILE
SILL
Door
Door

All sliding door equipment is extruded bronze.

SECTION Scale: 3"=1'-0"

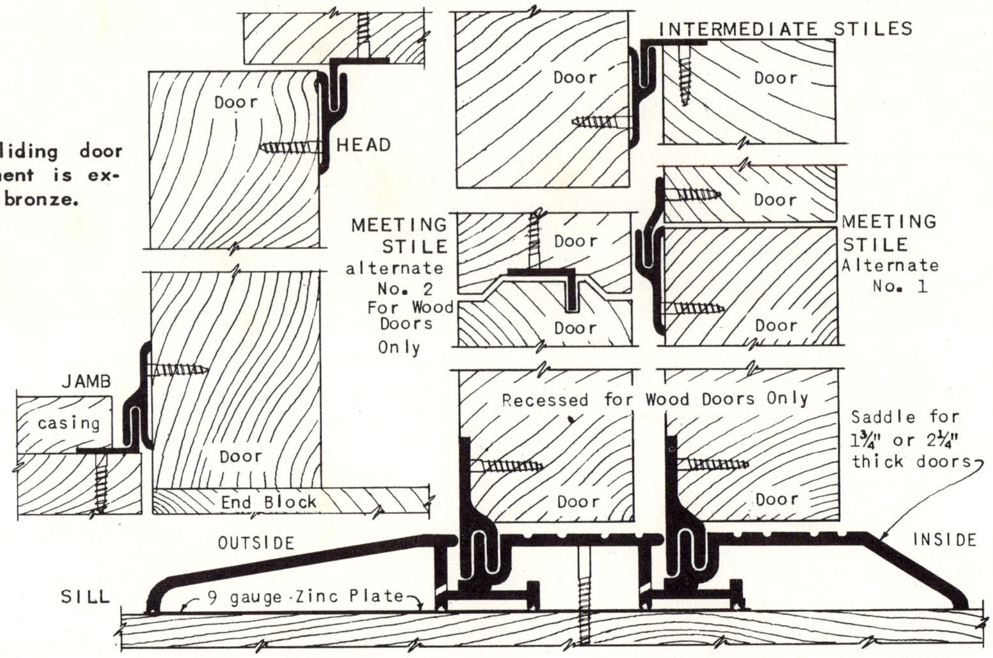
Door
HEAD
INTERMEDIATE STILES
Door
Door
Door
MEETING STILE alternate No. 2 For Wood Doors Only
Door
Door
Door
MEETING STILE Alternate No. 1
Door
JAMB
casing
Door
End Block
Recessed for Wood Doors Only
Door
Door
Saddle for 1¾" or 2¼" thick doors
OUTSIDE
INSIDE
SILL
9 gauge Zinc Plate

DETAILS Scale: Half Full Size

SLIDING DOORS

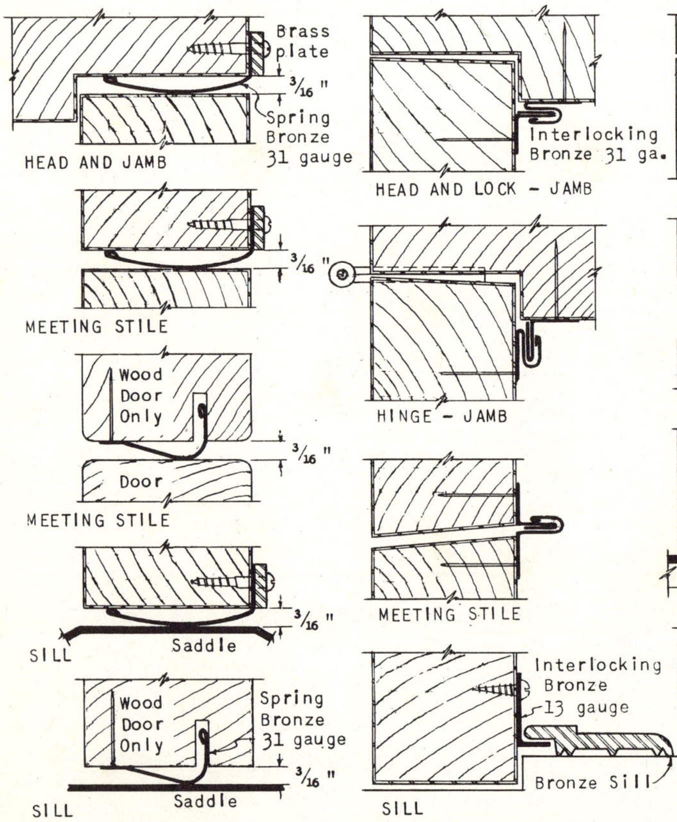
Brass plate
3/16"
Spring Bronze 31 gauge
HEAD AND JAMB
Interlocking Bronze 31 ga.
HEAD AND LOCK - JAMB
3/16"
MEETING STILE
HINGE - JAMB
Wood Door Only
3/16"
Door
MEETING STILE
MEETING STILE
3/16"
SILL
Saddle
Wood Door Only
Spring Bronze 31 gauge
3/16"
SILL
Saddle
Interlocking Bronze 13 gauge
Bronze Sill
SILL

WEATHER STRIPPING FOR DIRT AND DRAFT PROOFING DOORS

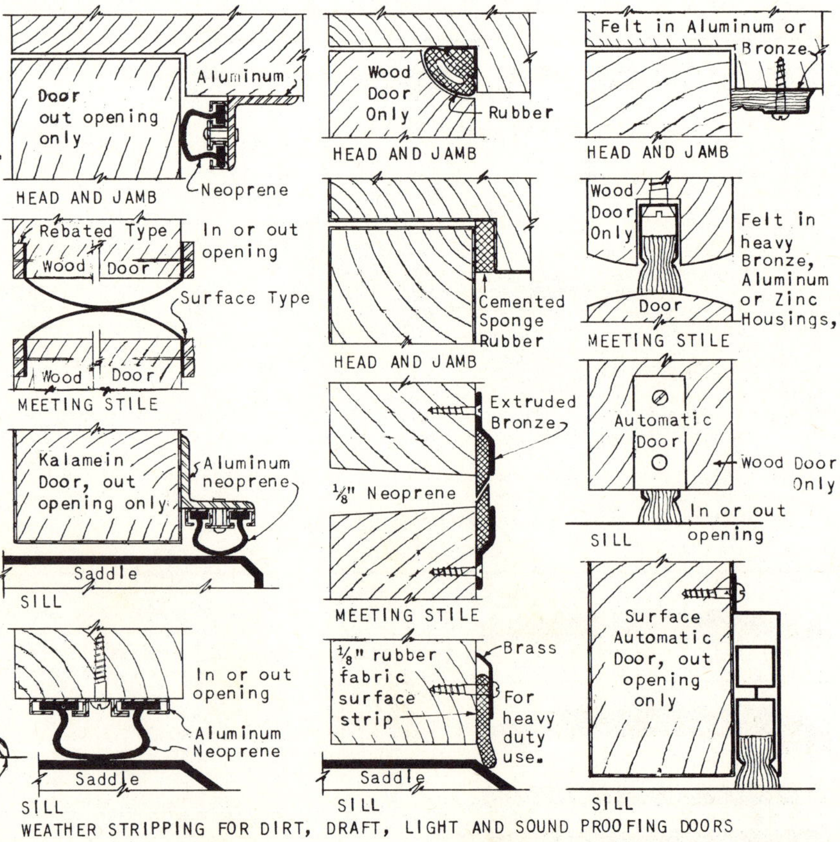
Aluminum
Door out opening only
HEAD AND JAMB
Neoprene
Wood Door Only
Rubber
HEAD AND JAMB
Felt in Aluminum or Bronze
HEAD AND JAMB
Rebated Type
Wood
Door
In or out opening
Surface Type
Wood
Door
MEETING STILE
Cemented Sponge Rubber
HEAD AND JAMB
Wood Door Only
Felt in heavy Bronze, Aluminum or Zinc Housings,
Door
MEETING STILE
Kalamein Door, out opening only
Aluminum neoprene
Saddle
SILL
Extruded Bronze
1/8" Neoprene
MEETING STILE
Automatic Door
Wood Door Only
In or out opening
SILL
In or out opening
Aluminum Neoprene
Saddle
SILL
1/8" rubber fabric surface strip
Brass
For heavy duty use.
Saddle
SILL
Surface Automatic Door, out opening only
SILL

WEATHER STRIPPING FOR DIRT, DRAFT, LIGHT AND SOUND PROOFING DOORS

WEATHER STRIPPING

Scale: Half Full Size

Applicable to all door types except where noted!

DATA CHECKED BY ZERO WEATHER STRIPPING CO. INC.

WEATHERSTRIPS ~ WINDOWS

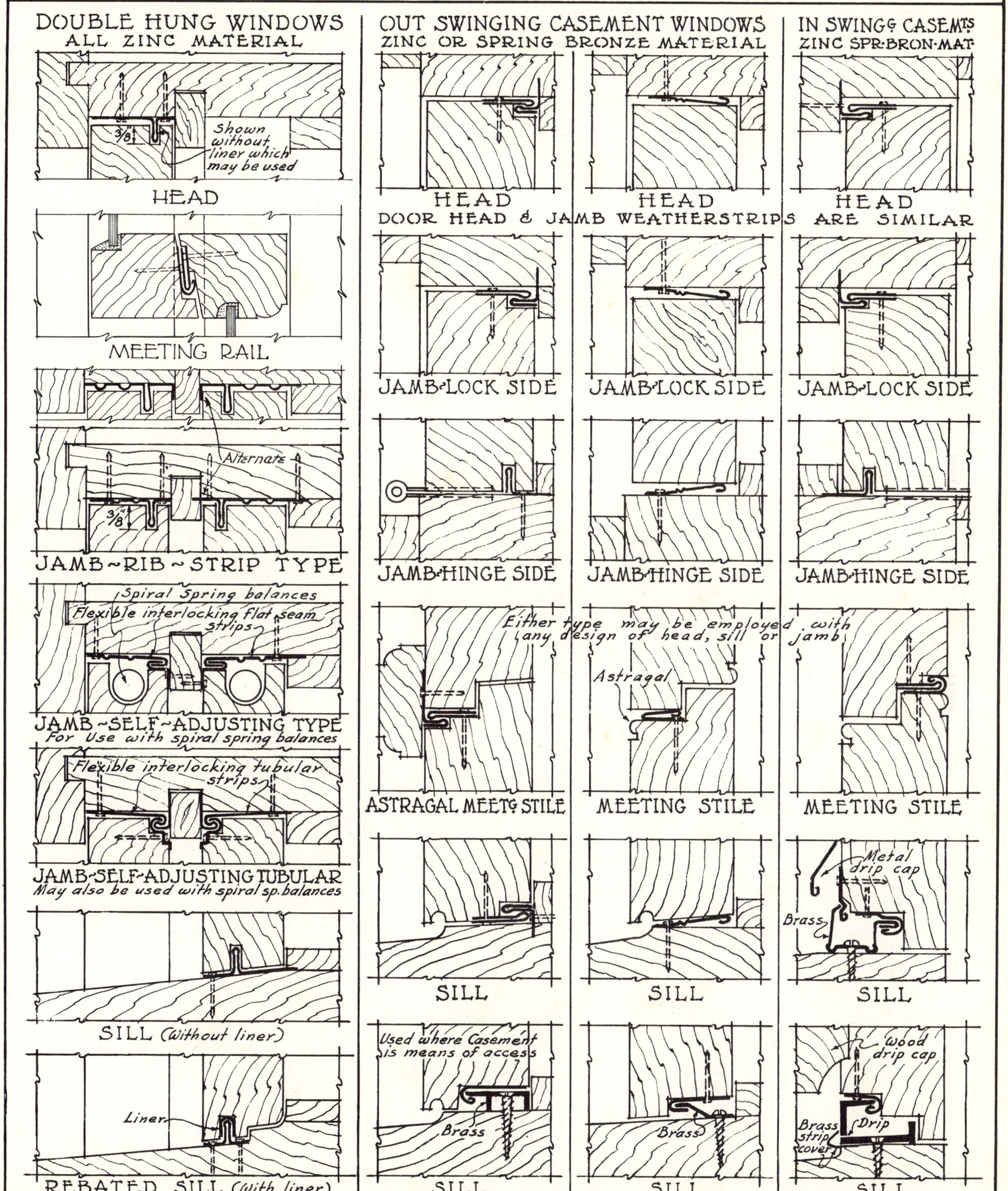
DOUBLE HUNG WINDOWS
ALL ZINC MATERIAL
3/8"
Shown without liner which may be used
HEAD
MEETING RAIL
Alternate
3/8"
JAMB ~ RIB ~ STRIP TYPE
Spiral Spring balances
Flexible interlocking flat seam strips
JAMB ~ SELF ~ ADJUSTING TYPE
For Use with spiral spring balances
Flexible interlocking tubular strips
JAMB~SELF~ADJUSTING TUBULAR
May also be used with spiral sp. balances
SILL (Without liner)
Liner
REBATED SILL (With liner)
OUT SWINGING CASEMENT WINDOWS
ZINC OR SPRING BRONZE MATERIAL
HEAD
HEAD
DOOR HEAD & JAMB WEATHERSTRIPS ARE SIMILAR
JAMB~LOCK SIDE
JAMB~LOCK SIDE
JAMB~HINGE SIDE
JAMB~HINGE SIDE
Either type may be employed with any design of head, sill or jamb
Astragal
ASTRAGAL MEET'G STILE
MEETING STILE
SILL
SILL
Used where Casement is means of access
Brass
SILL
Brass
SILL
IN SWING'G CASEM'TS
ZINC SPR·BRON·MAT·
HEAD
JAMB~LOCK SIDE
JAMB~HINGE SIDE
MEETING STILE
Metal drip cap
Brass
SILL
Wood drip cap
Brass strip cover
Drip
SILL

Note: Manufacturers standard types vary in details from the typical types shown above. For Detailed Specifications see Architectural Specifications by Harold R. Sleeper. Data checked by: Zero Weather Stripping Co.

Scale: 6" = 1'-0"

WOOD, CERAMIC and MASONRY SADDLES

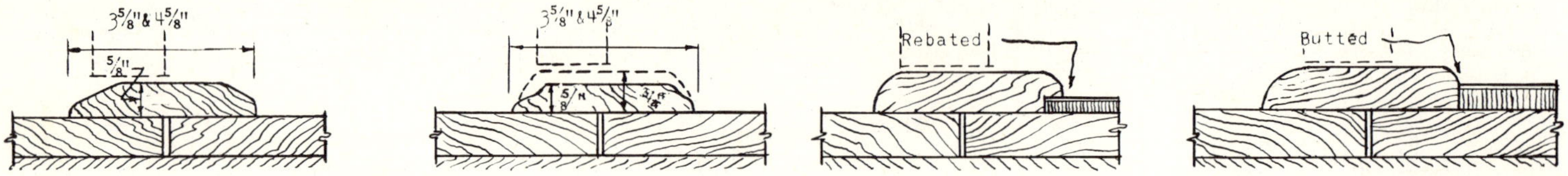
3⅝" & 4⅝"
⅝"
3⅝" & 4⅝"
⅝"
¾"
Rebated
Butted

STOCK TYPES — FLOORS AT DIFFERENT LEVELS

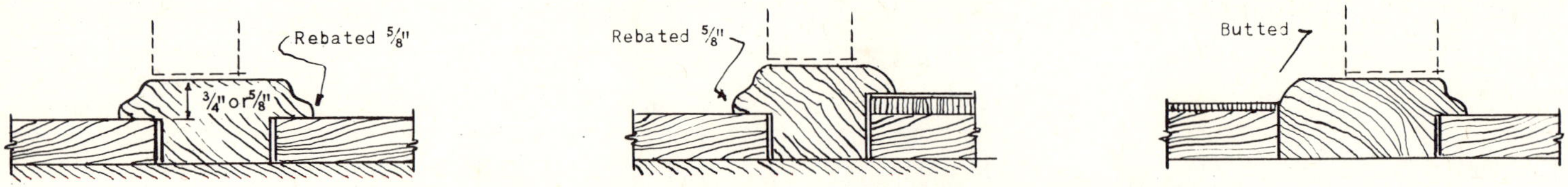
Rebated ⅝"
¾" or ⅝"
Rebated ⅝"
Butted

THICK REBATED TYPES FOR BETTER WORK

WOOD SADDLES ON WOOD FLOORING

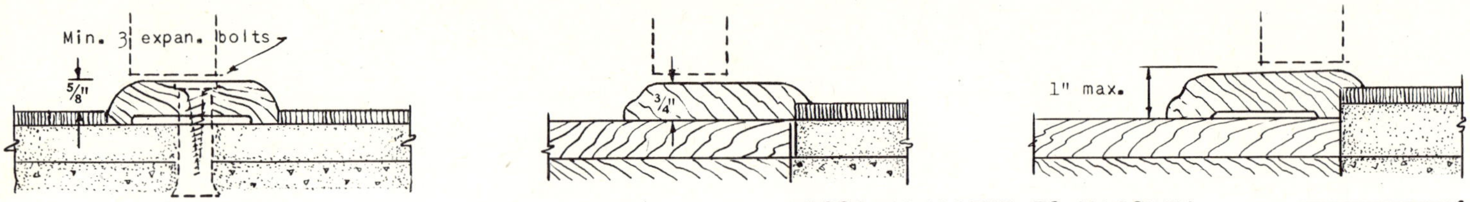
Min. 3 expan. bolts
⅝"
¾"
1" max.

WOOD ON CEMENT — WOOD ADJACENT TO MASONRY

WOOD SADDLES ON MASONRY

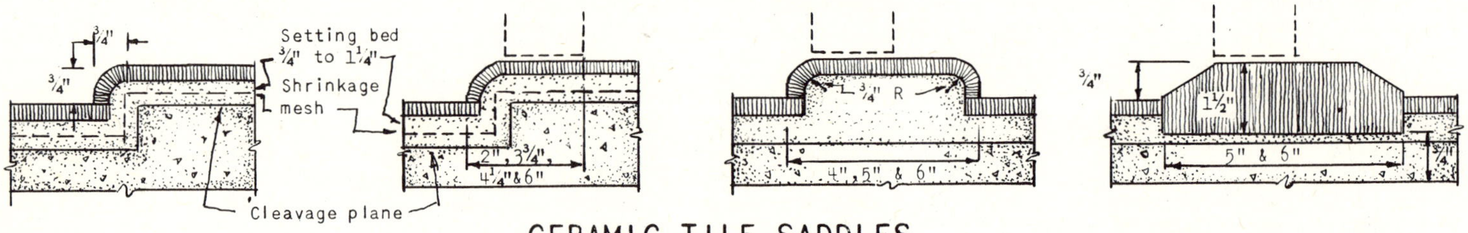
¾"
¾"
Setting bed
¾" to 1¼"
Shrinkage
mesh
Cleavage plane
2", 3¾"
4¼" & 6"
¾" R
4", 5" & 6"
¾"
1½"
5" & 6"
¾"

CERAMIC TILE SADDLES

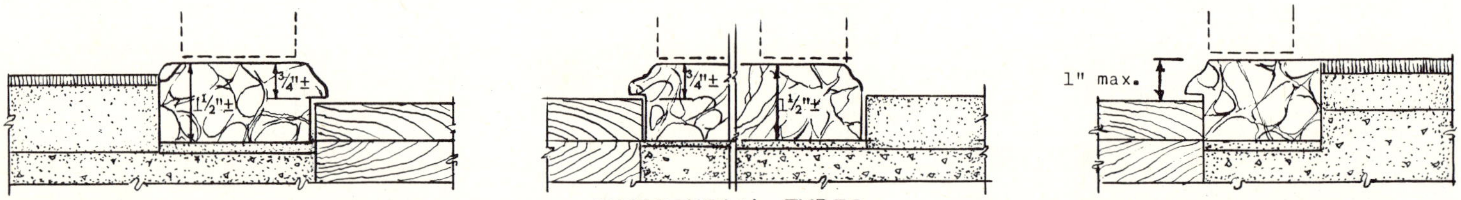
¾"±
1½"±
¾"±
1½"±
1" max.

RESIDENTIAL TYPES

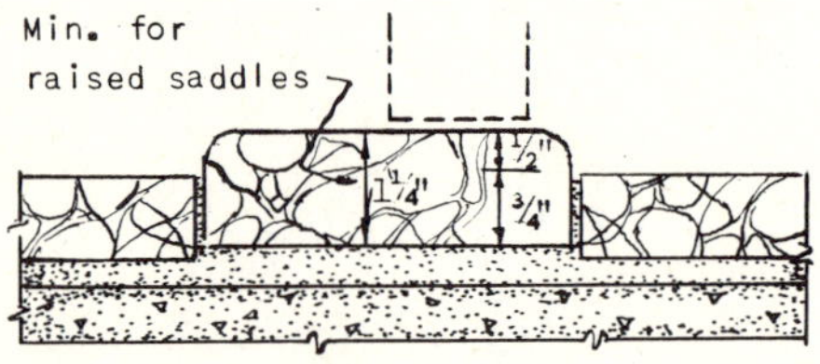
Min. for
raised saddles
½"
1¼"
¾"

Marble, slate and bluestone available in stock thicknesses of ⅞", 1¼", 1½" & 2"

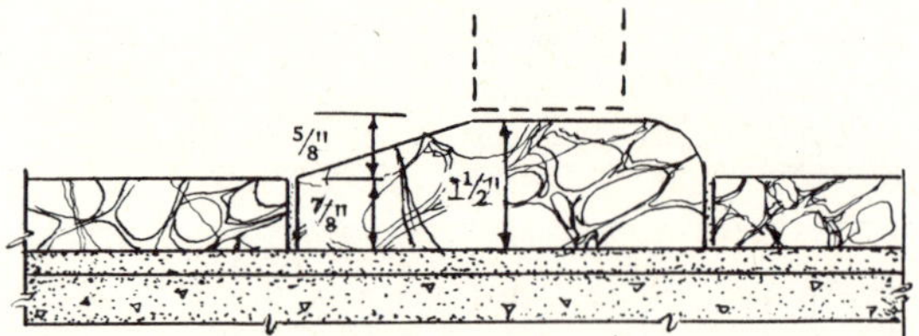
⅝"
⅞"
1½"

COMMERCIAL TYPES

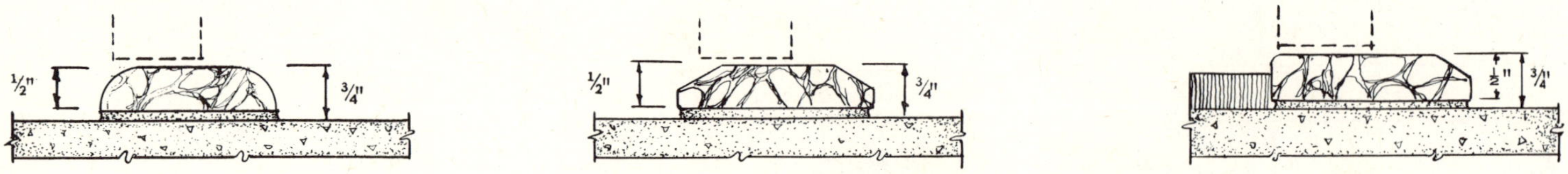
½"
¾"
½"
¾"
½"
¾"

SHALLOW OVERFLOOR TYPES

MARBLE, SLATE, BLUESTONE & PRECAST TERRAZZO SADDLES

Scale 3" = 1"-0"

GENERAL: Width of saddles variable, usually not less than width of jamb. Saddles should be cut around door stop and trim. Secure to wood with screws; wood and metal saddles to masonry with screws and expansion bolts or similar attachments; tile and masonry saddles with cement mortar. Hard flooring (not asphalt tile) may butt against or under saddle. Rebates recommended for soft floors.

MULTI-USE WOOD FRAME MEMBER

The following details illustrate how one single wood mill-member may be used to form all parts of the frames for windows, doors. panels and glass, including their heads, jambs, sills, mullions and posts.

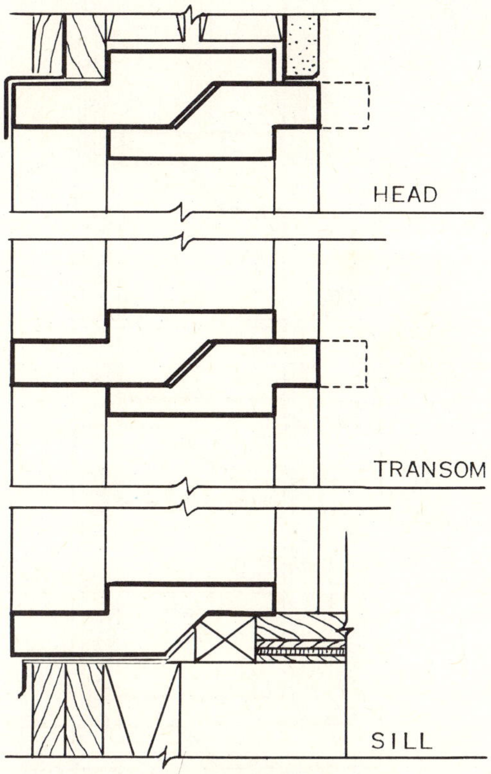
HEAD
TRANSOM
SILL

HORIZONTAL MEMBERS

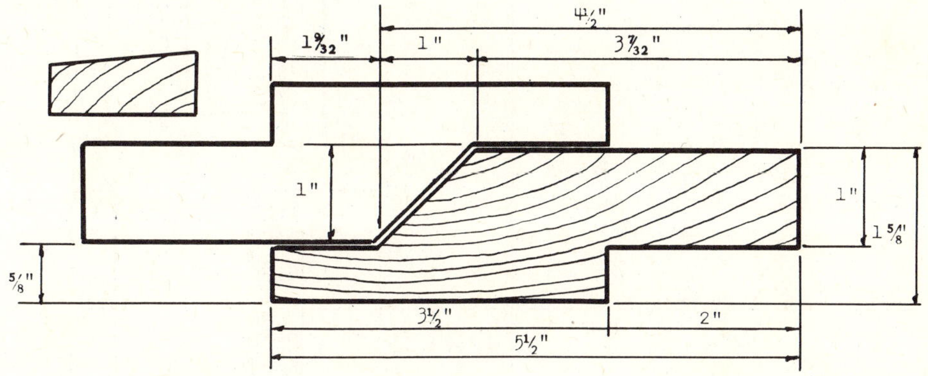
4½"
1 9/32"
1"
3 7/32"
1"
1"
1 5/8"
5/8"
3½"
2"
5½"

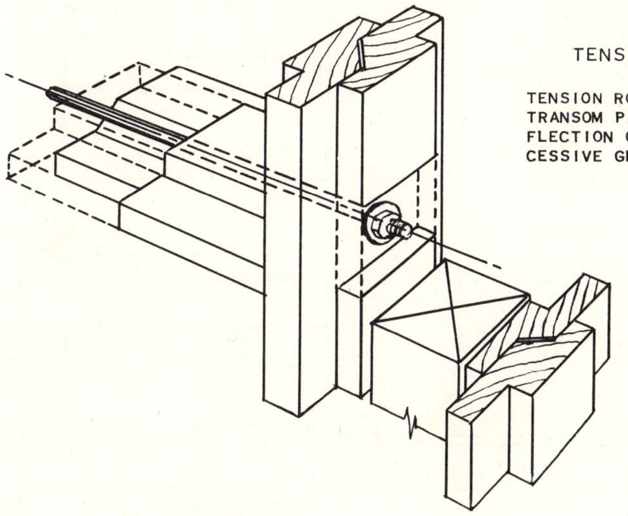

TENSION ROD DETAIL

TENSION RODS MAY BE PLACED THRU TRANSOM PIECES TO DECREASE DEFLECTION OF TRANSOM UNDER EXCESSIVE GLASS OR PANEL LOADS.

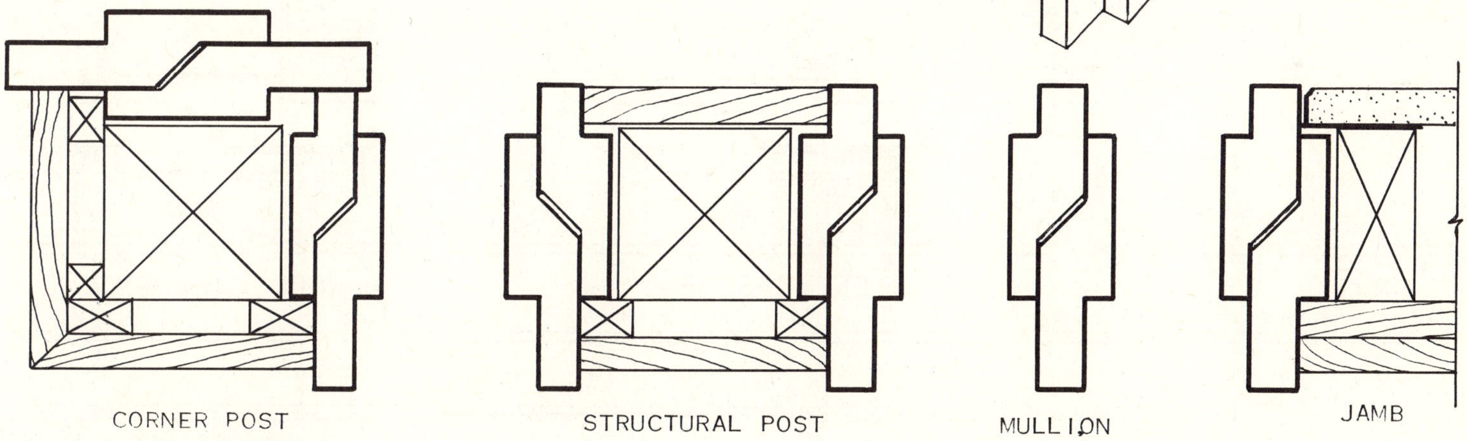
CORNER POST
STRUCTURAL POST
MULLION
JAMB

VERTICAL MEMBERS

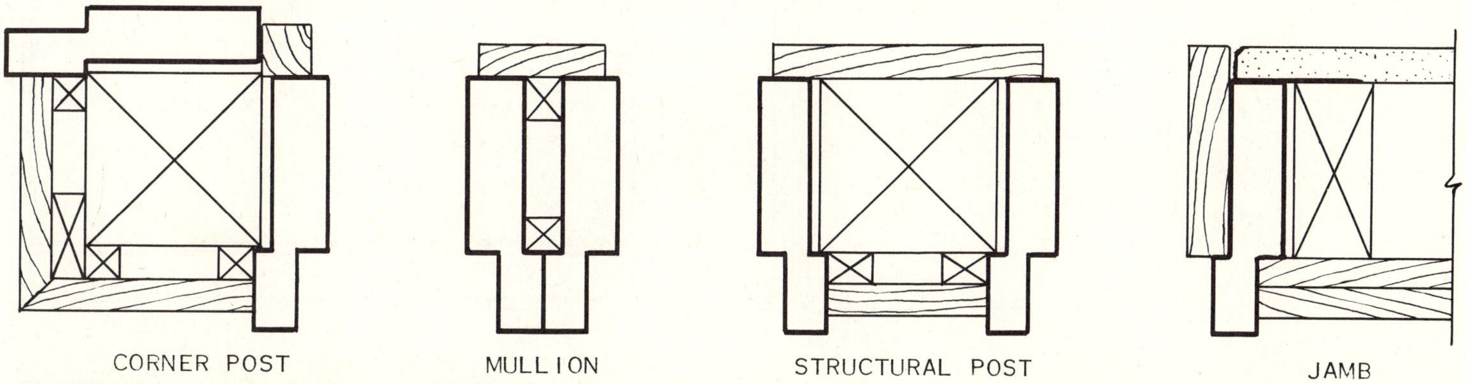
CORNER POST
MULLION
STRUCTURAL POST
JAMB

ALTERNATE VERTICAL MEMBERS

MULTI-USE WOOD FRAME MEMBER

FLASHING IS OPTIONAL.
INTERIOR NOSE MAY BE CUT TO FINISH FLUSH WITH WALL.
WHEN HANGING DOOR, CUTS MUST BE MADE TO FIT DOOR FLUSH WITH WALL.
(SEE DOOR DETAIL 16-19)

ADDITIONAL BLOCKING IS NECESSARY FOR DOUBLE GLAZING.
FIXED PANEL & FIXED GLASS DETAILS ARE SIMILAR.
SCREENS OR INTERIOR STORM SASH OPTIONAL WHEN USING OUT-SWINGING CASEMENTS.
PUTTY MAY BE USED IN PLACE OF STOPS ON SMALL FIXED GLASS.

FLASHING AND METAL DOOR SADDLE OPTIONAL.
(SEE 4, 8, 12, 15, 19.)

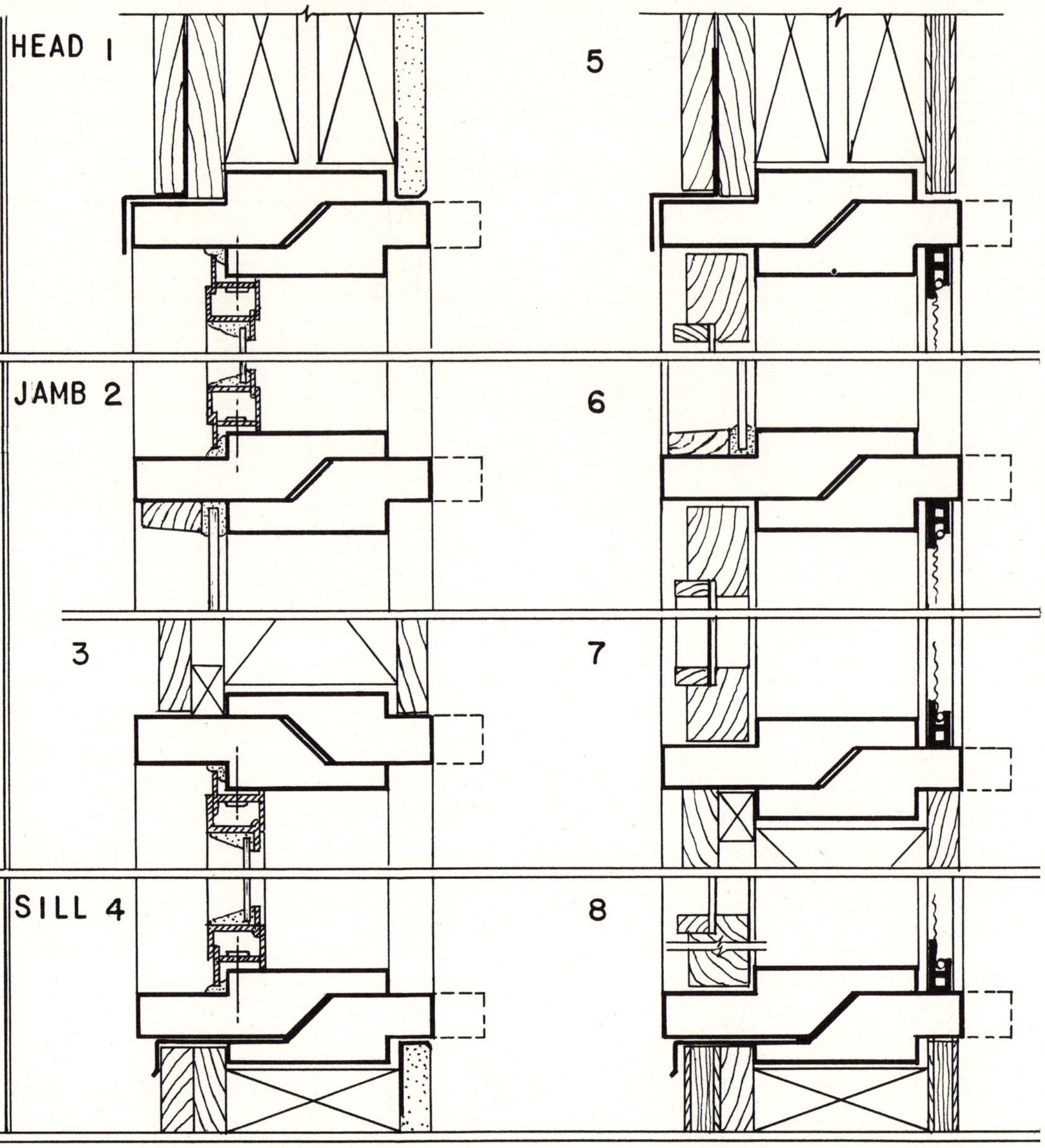
HEAD 1
5
JAMB 2
6
3
7
SILL 4
8

STEEL CASEMENT

WOOD CASEMENT

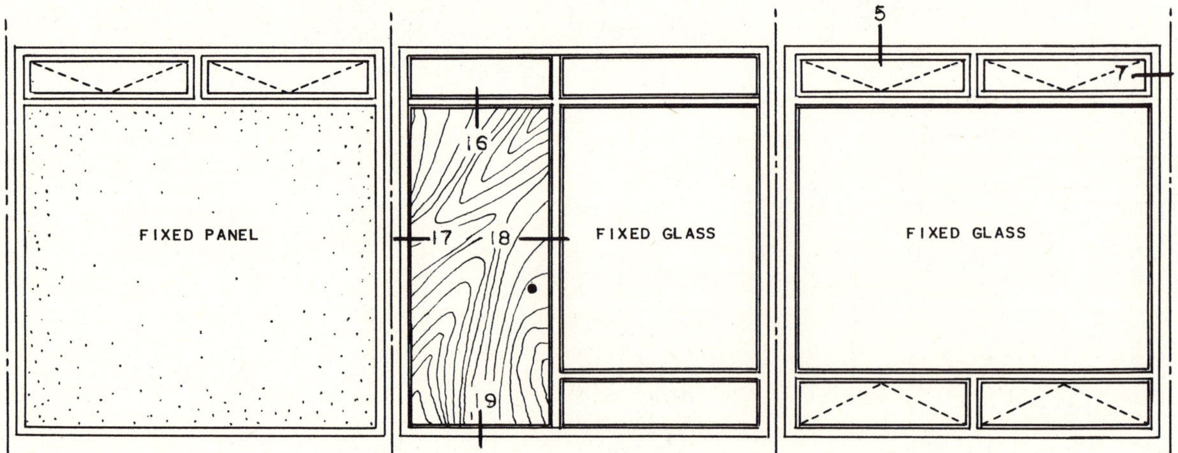
5
7
16
FIXED PANEL
17
18
FIXED GLASS
FIXED GLASS
19

ELEVATIONS (ELEVATIONS BASED ON POSTS 8'-0" O.C.)

MULTI-USE WOOD FRAME MEMBER

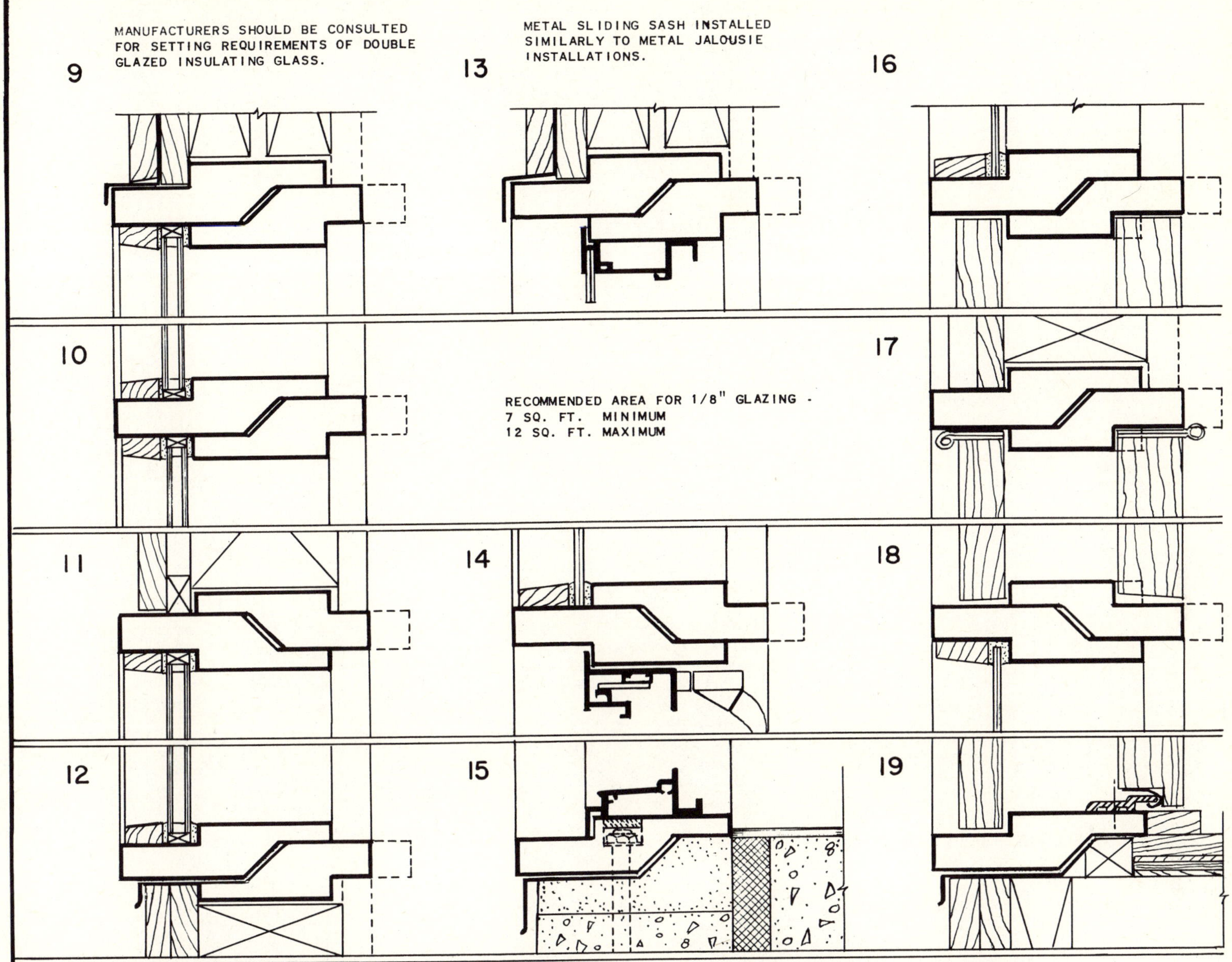
MANUFACTURERS SHOULD BE CONSULTED FOR SETTING REQUIREMENTS OF DOUBLE GLAZED INSULATING GLASS.
METAL SLIDING SASH INSTALLED SIMILARLY TO METAL JALOUSIE INSTALLATIONS.
RECOMMENDED AREA FOR 1/8" GLAZING -
7 SQ. FT. MINIMUM
12 SQ. FT. MAXIMUM
9
10
11
12
13
14
15
16
17
18
19

DOUBLE GLAZING | JALOUSIE & SLIDING SASH | DOOR

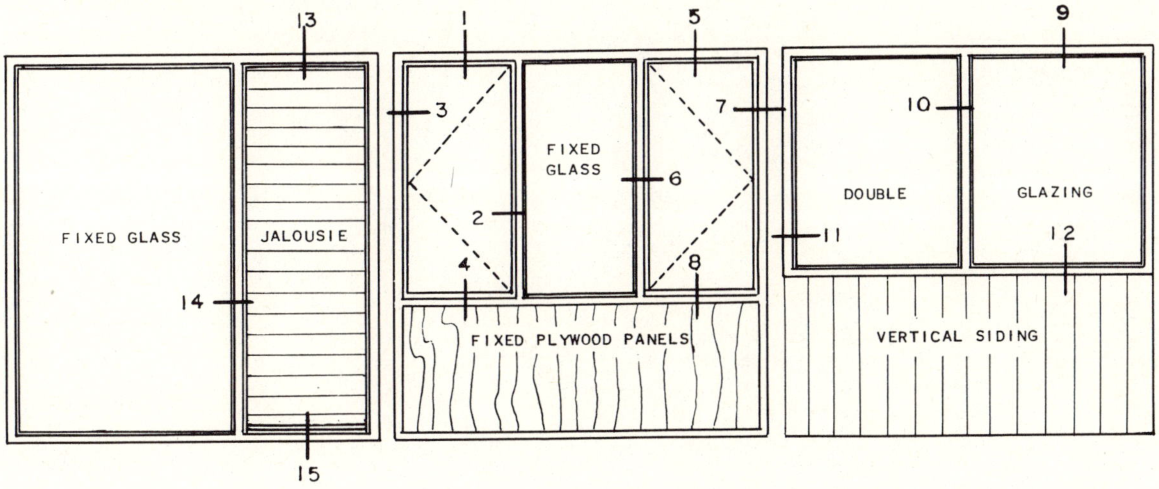
FIXED GLASS
JALOUSIE
FIXED GLASS
FIXED PLYWOOD PANELS
DOUBLE
GLAZING
VERTICAL SIDING
1
2
3
4
5
6
7
8
9
10
11
12
13
14
15

WOOD CASEMENT WINDOWS

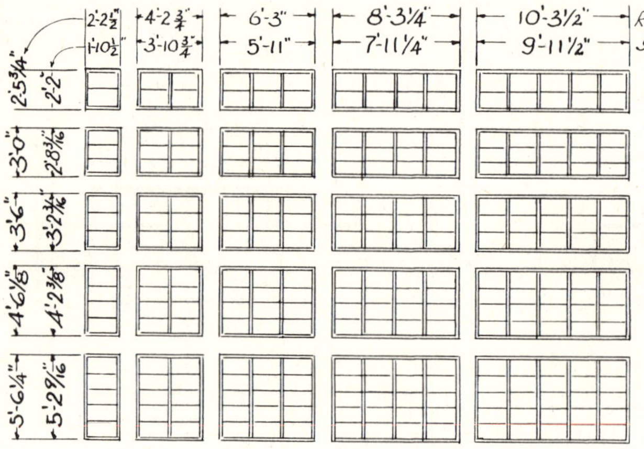
2'-2½" 4'-2¾" 6'-3" 8'-3¼" 10'-3½" Rgh. stud opg.
1'-10½" 3'-10¾" 5'-11" 7'-11¼" 9'-11½" Sash opg.
2'-5¾" 2'-2"
3'-0" 2'-8³⁄₁₆"
3'-6" 3'-2³⁄₁₆"
4'-6⅛" 4'-2⅜"
5'-6¼" 5'-2⁹⁄₁₆"

SERIES "W"

CASEMENT SASH UNITS

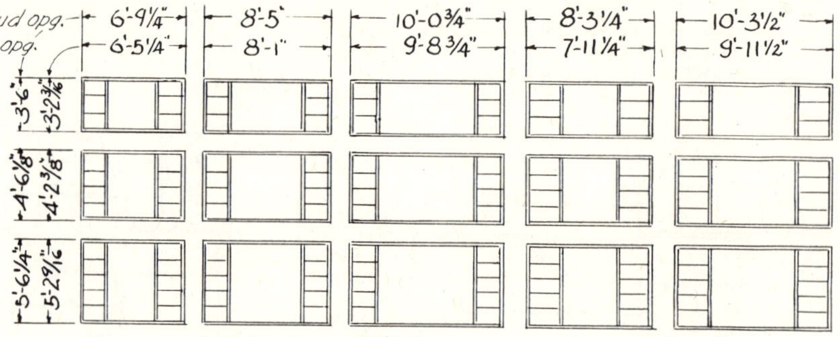
6'-9¼" 8'-5" 10'-0¾" 8'-3¼" 10'-3½"
6'-5¼" 8'-1" 9'-8¾" 7'-11¼" 9'-11½"
3'-6" 3'-2³⁄₁₆"
4'-6⅛" 4'-2⅜"
5'-6¼" 5'-2⁹⁄₁₆"

SERIES "N"* SERIES "W"

*Series "N" not stocked on west coast

CASEMENT PICTURE WINDOW UNITS

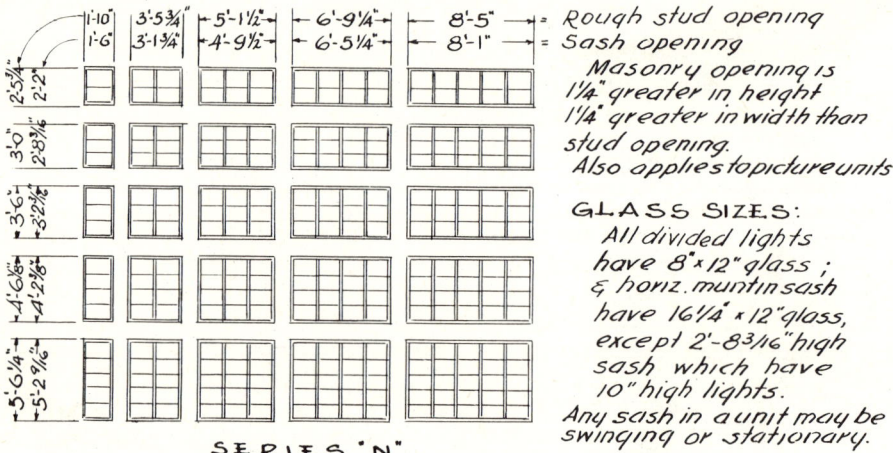

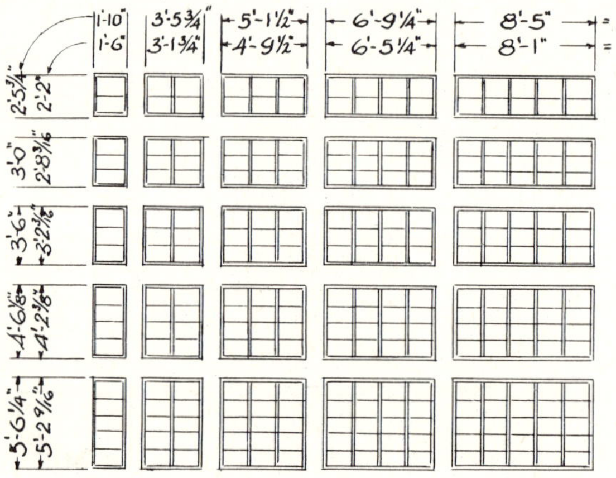
1'-10" 3'-5¾" 5'-1½" 6'-9¼" 8'-5" = Rough stud opening
1'-6" 3'-1¾" 4'-9½" 6'-5¼" 8'-1" = Sash opening
2'-5¾" 2'-2"
3'-0" 2'-8³⁄₁₆"
3'-6" 3'-2³⁄₁₆"
4'-6⅛" 4'-2⅜"
5'-6¼" 5'-2⁹⁄₁₆"

Masonry opening is 1¼" greater in height 1¼" greater in width than stud opening. Also applies to picture units

GLASS SIZES:
All divided lights have 8" x 12" glass; & horiz. muntin sash have 16¼" x 12" glass, except 2'-8³⁄₁₆" high sash which have 10" high lights.
Any sash in a unit may be swinging or stationary.

SERIES "N"

CASEMENT SASH UNITS

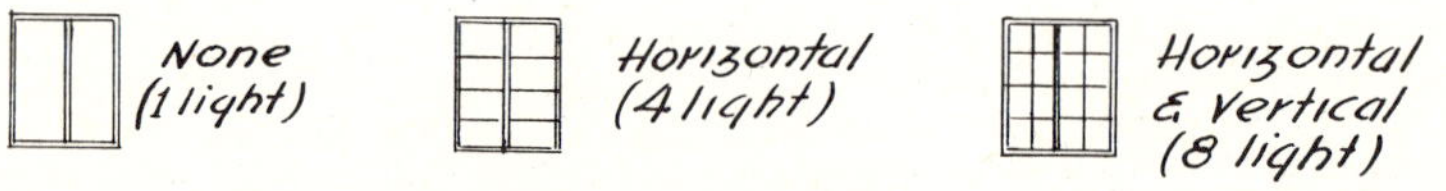
None
(1 light)
Horizontal
(4 light)
Horizontal
& Vertical
(8 light)

MUNTIN TYPES
(4'-2⅜" height as example)

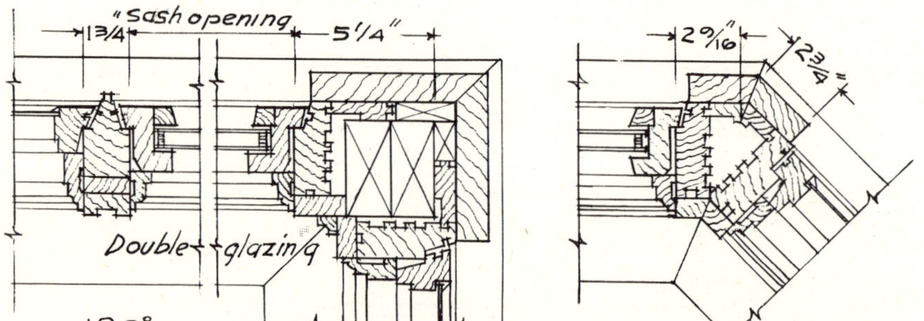
1¾
"Sash opening
5¼"
Double glazing
2⁹⁄₁₆"
2¾"

180° MULLION CORNER 45° BY MULLION

Angle iron or steel pipe column may be used in place of 2×4's. Sash may be swinging or stationary. (Made from standard units).

Made from standard units. Exterior & interior casings are not furnished by mfr.

MULLION and CORNER PLANS

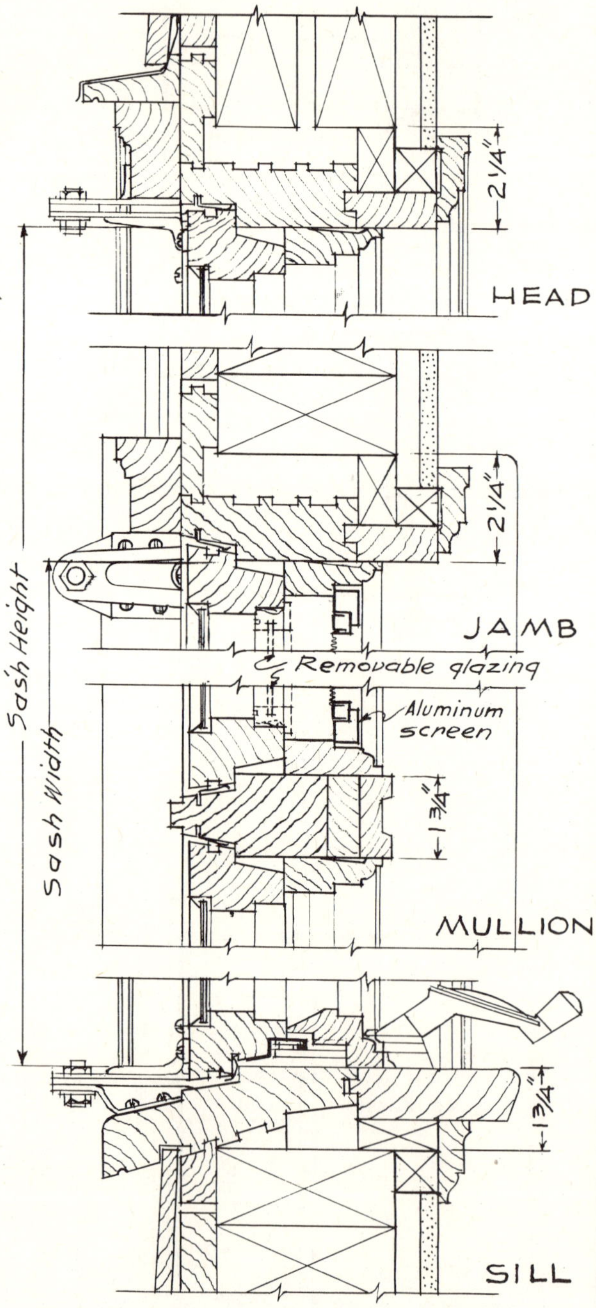
2¼"
HEAD
2¼"
JAMB
Removable glazing
Aluminum screen
1¾"
Sash Height
Sash Width
MULLION
1¾"
SILL

TYPICAL SECTION 3" = 1'-0"

STOCK WOOD CASEMENT UNITS

Data by Andersen Corporation, Bayport, Minnesota.

WOOD CASEMENT WINDOW UNITS

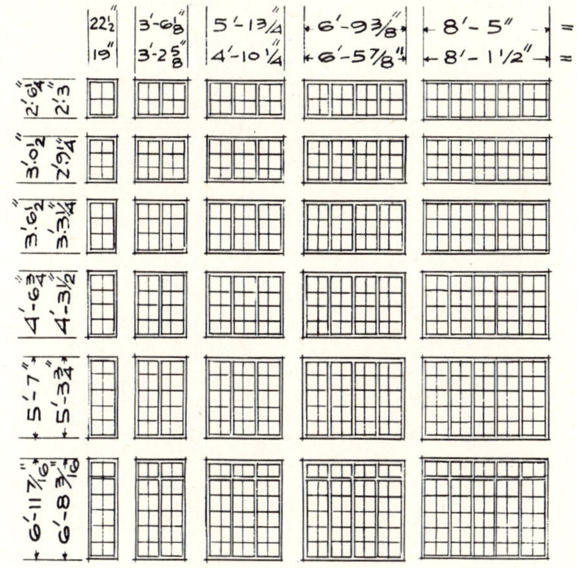
22½" | 3'-6⅛" | 5'-1¾" | 6'-9⅜" | 8'-5" = Rough stud opening
19" | 3'-2⅝" | 4'-10¼" | 6'-5⅞" | 8'-1½" = Sash opening
2'-6¼" 2'-3
3'-0½" 2'-9¼"
3'-6½" 3'-3¼"
4'-6¾" 4'-3½"
5'-7" 5'-3¾"
6'-11⁷⁄₁₆" 6'-8³⁄₁₆"

Masonry opening is 3½" greater in width and 2⅞" greater in height than stud opening

SASH SIZES

Glass sizes: 8"x12" standard except 2'-9¼" high sash in which case lights are 8"x10"

Units are packed in cartons unassembled with all parts machined and prefitted including operating hardware, pre-fit screens (optional) and insulating glass (optional). All sash are factory assembled including glazing.

Range of sizes stocked in specific areas may vary.

Transom type casement installation is not a stock item but can be obtained on special order.

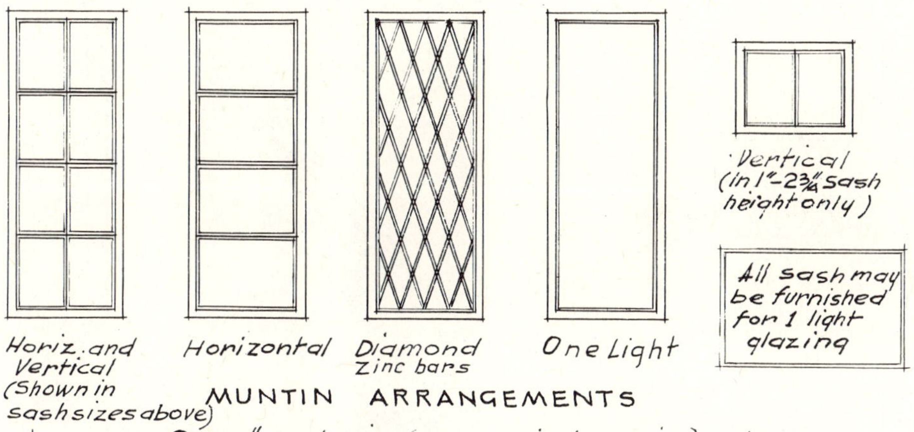
Horiz. and Vertical (Shown in sash sizes above)
Horizontal
Diamond Zinc bars
One Light
Vertical (in 1'-2¾" sash height only)
All sash may be furnished for 1 light glazing

MUNTIN ARRANGEMENTS

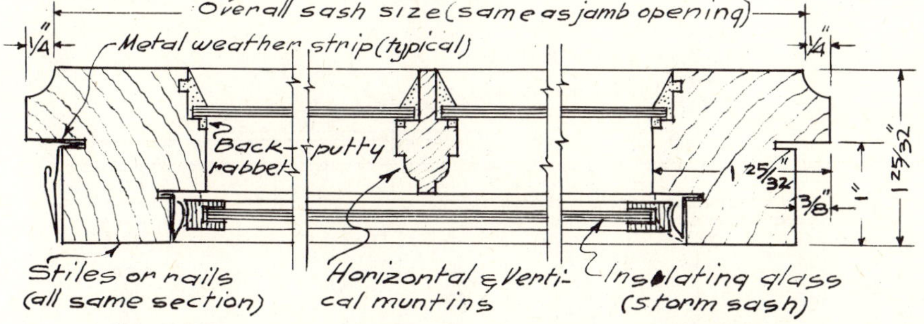
Overall sash size (same as jamb opening)
¼"
Metal weather strip (typical)
¼"
Back-putty rabbet
1 25/32"
1"
⅜"
1 25/32"
Stiles or rails (all same section)
Horizontal & Vertical muntins
Insulating glass (storm sash)

SECTION OF CASEMENT SASH MEMBERS

Insulating glass set in metal came. Dotted line indicates glass bead if insulating glass is not required. Scale: One-half full size.

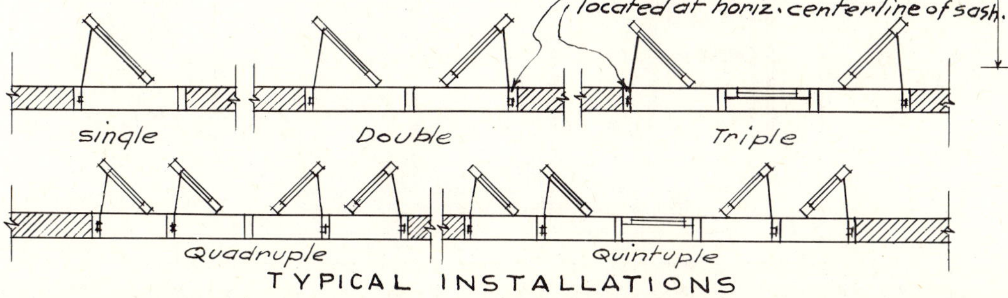
Casement operating hardware located at horiz. centerline of sash.
Single
Double
Triple
Quadruple
Quintuple

TYPICAL INSTALLATIONS

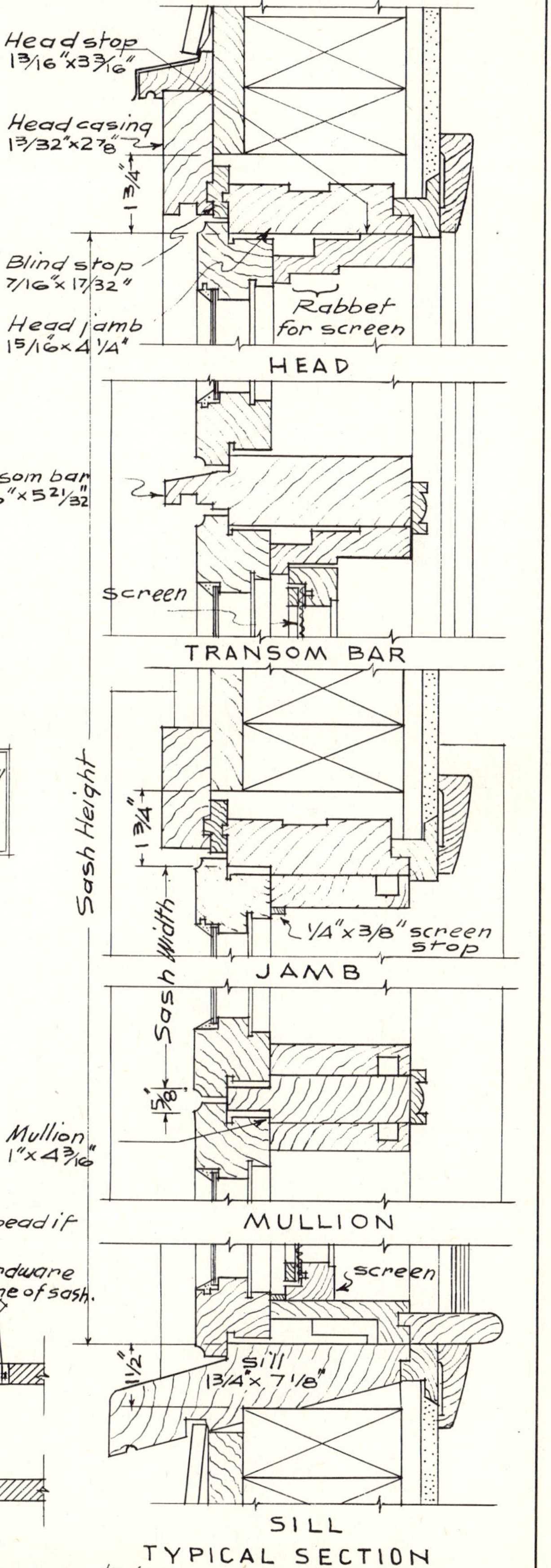
Head stop 1³⁄₁₆"x3³⁄₁₆"
Head casing 1³⁄₃₂"x2⅞"
1¾
Blind stop ⁷⁄₁₆"x1⁷⁄₃₂"
Rabbet for screen
Head jamb 1⁵⁄₁₆"x4¼"
HEAD
Transom bar 1¹¹⁄₁₆"x5²¹⁄₃₂"
Screen
TRANSOM BAR
Sash Height
1¾
Sash Width
¼"x⅜" screen stop
JAMB
⅝
Mullion 1"x4³⁄₁₆"
MULLION
Screen
1½
Sill 1¾"x7⅛"
SILL

TYPICAL SECTION

3" = 1'-0"

Data by Curtis Companies Incorporated

DORMER WINDOWS - CASEMENT

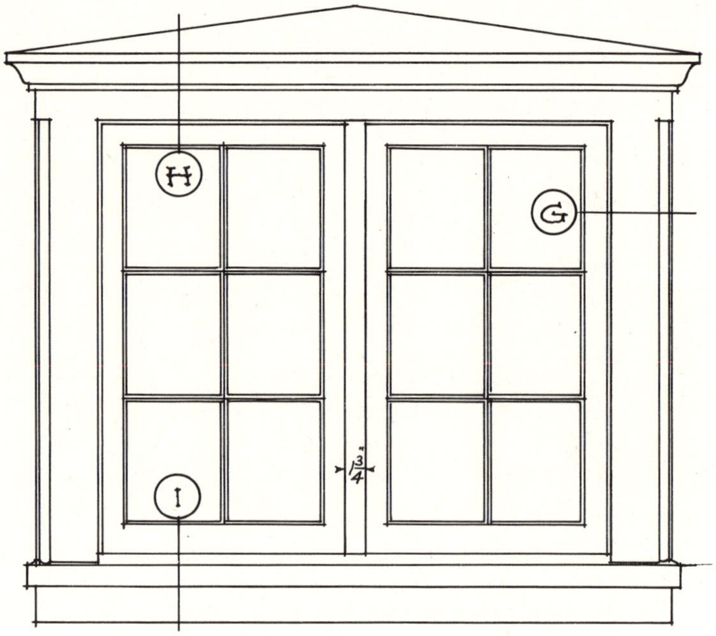
H
G
I
1¾"

WOOD CASEMENTS

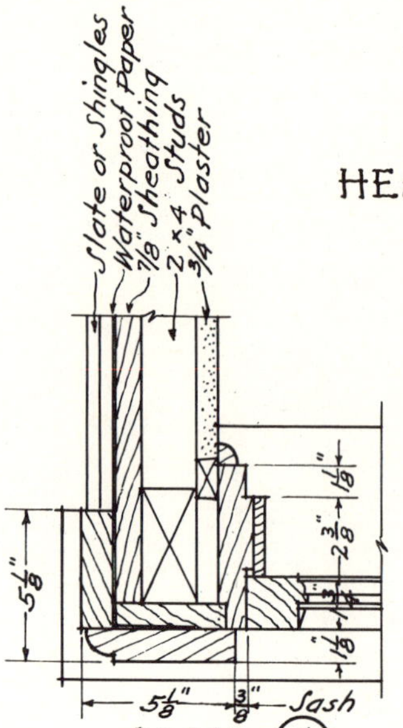
Slate or Shingles
Waterproof Paper
⅞" Sheathing
2 × 4 Studs
¾" Plaster
5⅛"
⅞"
2⅜"
1¾"
1⅛"
5⅛"
⅜"
Sash

JAMB (G)

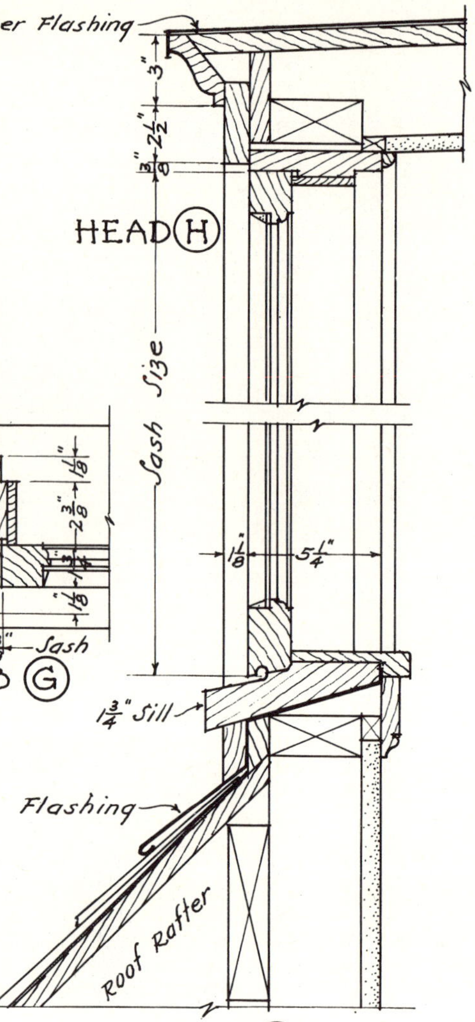
Copper Flashing
3"
2½"
⅜"
HEAD (H)
Sash Size
1⅛"
5¼"
1¾" Sill
Flashing
Roof Rafter

SILL (I)

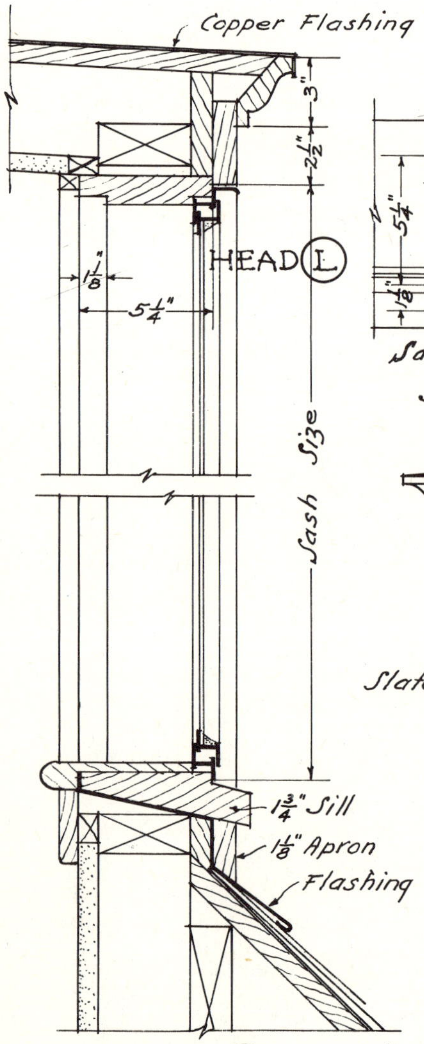
Copper Flashing
3"
2½"
HEAD (L)
1⅛"
5¼"
Sash Size
1¾" Sill
1⅛" Apron
Flashing

SILL (M)

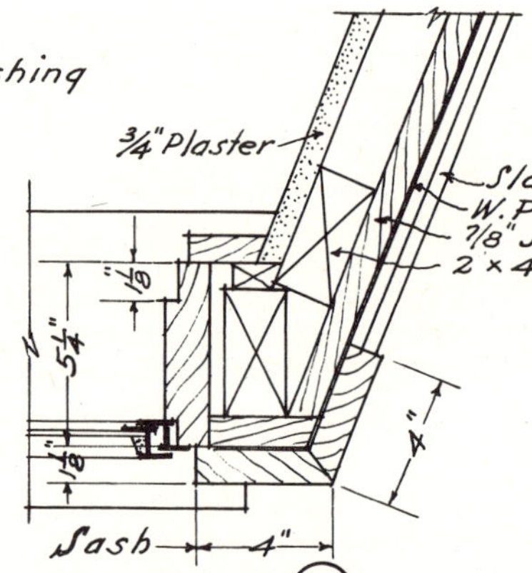
¾" Plaster
Slate or Shingles
W.P. Paper
⅞" Sheathing
2 × 4" Studs
⅞"
5¼"
1⅛"
4"
Sash
4"

JAMB (K)

¾" = 1'-0". Details 1½" = 1'-0"

L
Slate or Shingle
K
M

STEEL CASEMENTS *in* SPLAYED DORMER

WOOD DOUBLE HUNG WINDOWS, NON-STOCK

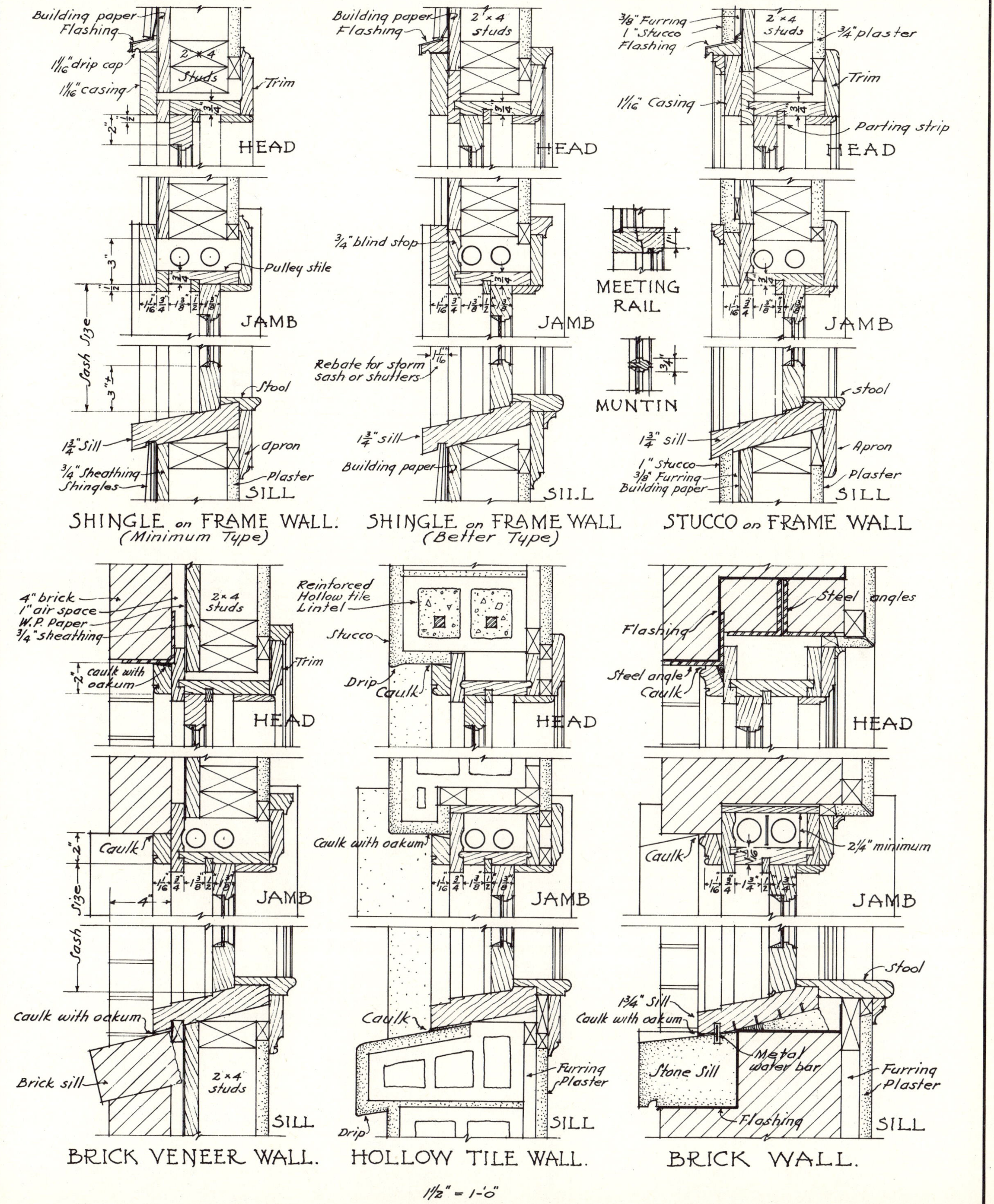
Building paper
Flashing
1 1/16" drip cap
1 1/16" casing
2 x 4 Studs
Trim
HEAD
Pulley stile
JAMB
Sash Size
Stool
1 3/4" Sill
Apron
3/4" Sheathing
Shingles
Plaster
SILL
SHINGLE on FRAME WALL.
(Minimum Type)
2" x 4 studs
3/4" blind stop
Rebate for storm sash or shutters
1 3/4" sill
Building paper
SHINGLE on FRAME WALL
(Better Type)
MEETING RAIL
MUNTIN
3/8" Furring
1" Stucco
Flashing
3/4" plaster
1 1/16" Casing
Parting strip
stool
1" Stucco
3/8" Furring
Building paper
STUCCO on FRAME WALL
4" brick
1" air space
W.P. Paper
3/4" sheathing
caulk with oakum
Caulk
Caulk with oakum
Brick sill
2 x 4 studs
BRICK VENEER WALL.
Reinforced Hollow tile Lintel
Stucco
Drip
Caulk with oakum
Furring
Plaster
HOLLOW TILE WALL.
Steel angles
Flashing
Steel angle
Caulk
2 1/4" minimum
Stool
1 3/4" Sill
Caulk with oakum
Metal water bar
Stone Sill
Flashing
BRICK WALL.
1 1/2" = 1'-0"

DORMER WINDOWS - DOUBLE HUNG

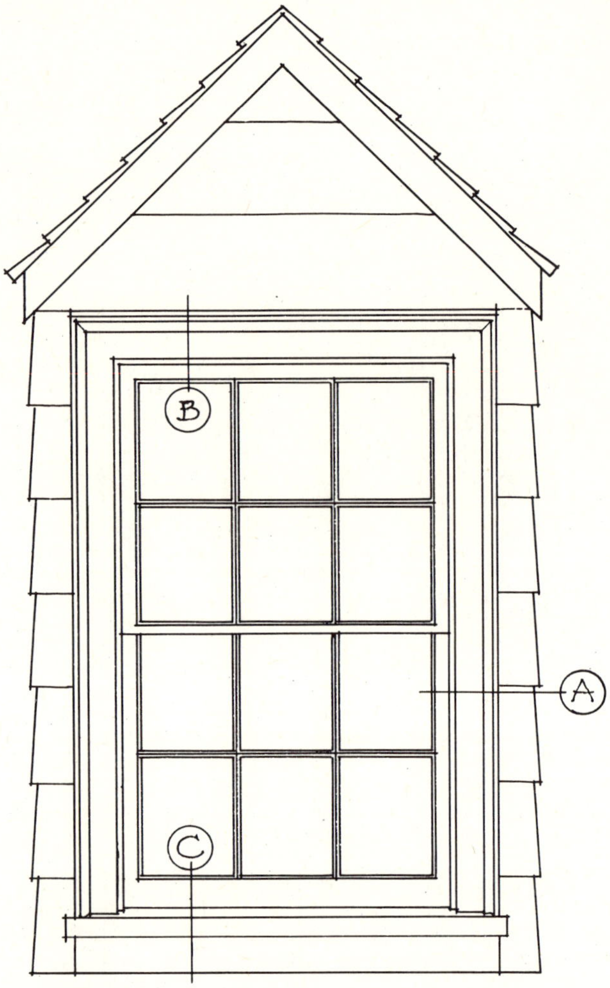
B
A
C

SHINGLED DORMER
3/4" = 1'-0"

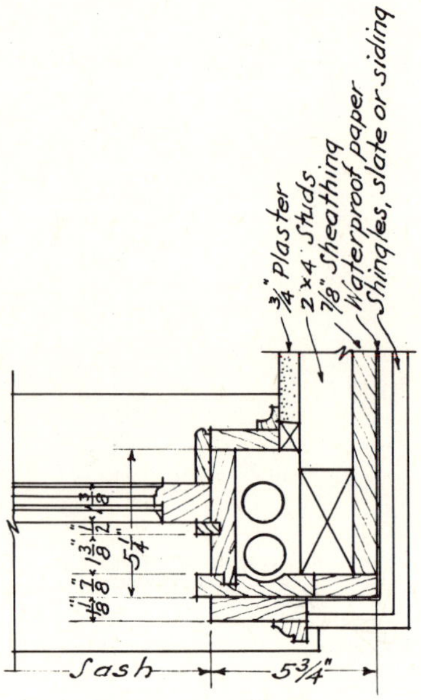
3/4" Plaster
2 x 4 Studs
7/8" Sheathing
Waterproof paper
Shingles, slate or siding
Sash
5 3/4"

JAMB (A)

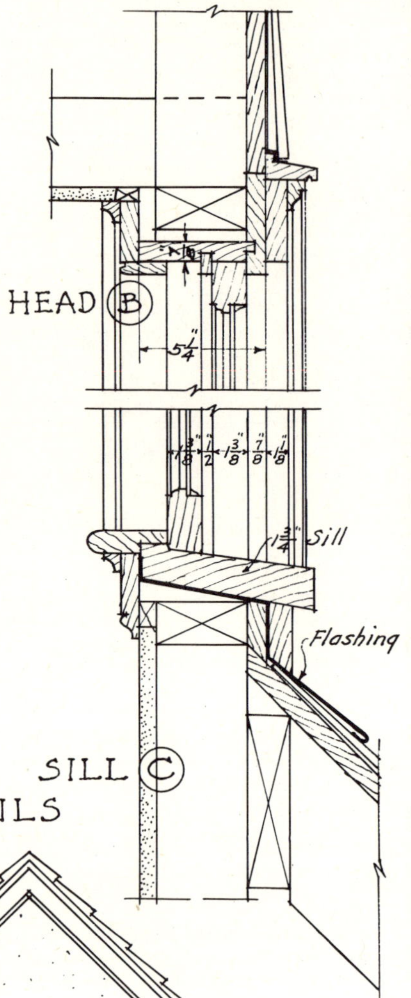
5 1/4"
1 3/4" Sill
Flashing

HEAD (B)

SILL (C)

1½" SCALE DETAILS

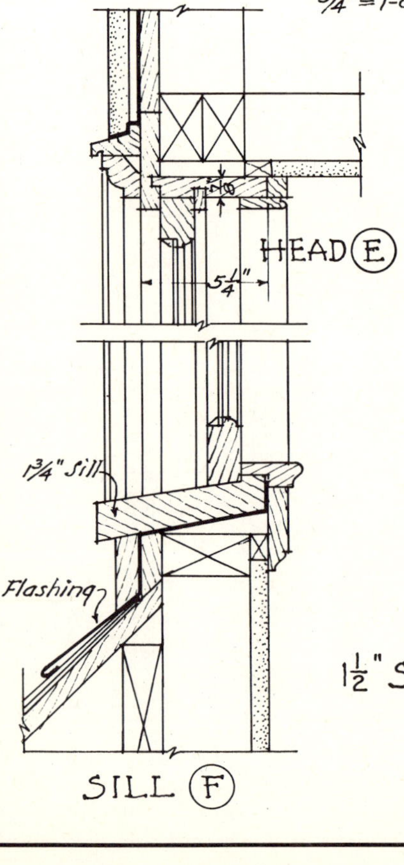
5 1/4"
1 3/4" Sill
Flashing

HEAD (E)

SILL (F)

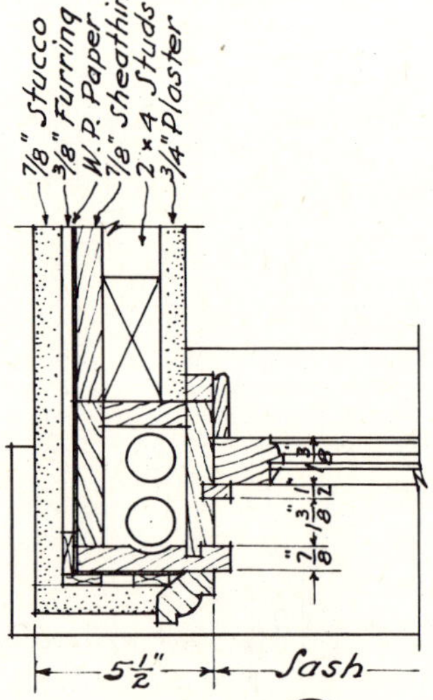
7/8" Stucco
3/8" Furring
W. P. Paper
7/8" Sheathing
2 x 4 Studs
3/4" Plaster
5 1/2"
Sash

JAMB (D)

1½" SCALE DETAILS

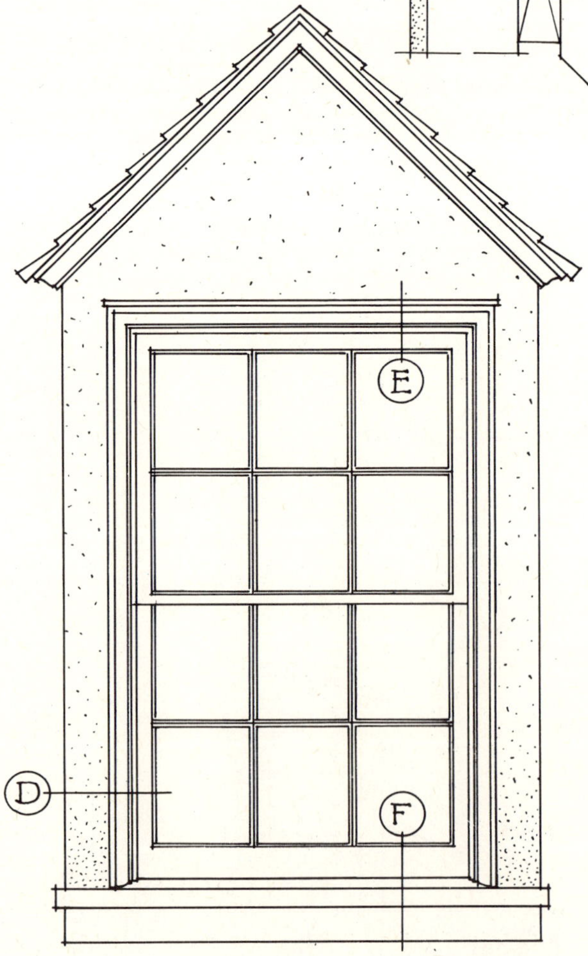
E
D
F

STUCCOED DORMER
3/4" = 1'-0"

MODULAR WOOD DOUBLE HUNG WINDOWS

STANDARD WINDOW TYPES →

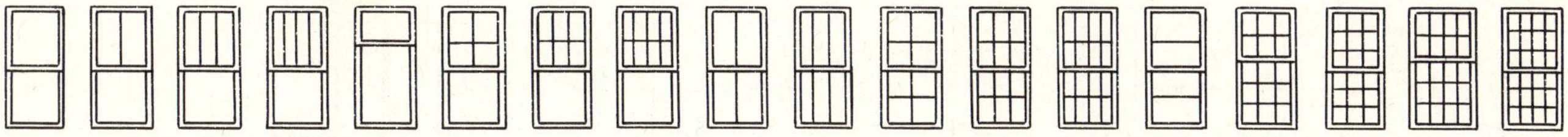
A
B
C
D
E
F
G
H
I
J
K
L
M
N
O
P
Q
R

FACE MEASURE of	A–E	F–H	I	J	K	L	M	N	O–P	Q–R
Stiles	A–H: $1\frac{29}{32}$"		I–L: $1\frac{21}{32}$"				M–N: $1\frac{29}{32}$"		$1\frac{21}{32}$"	$1\frac{29}{32}$"
Top Rail	$1\frac{29}{32}$"	$1\frac{21}{32}$"	I–J: $1\frac{29}{32}$"		K–M: $1\frac{21}{32}$"			$1\frac{29}{32}$"	O–R: $1\frac{29}{32}$"	
Bottom Rail	A–J: 3"				K–M: $2\frac{3}{4}$"			3"	O–R: 3"	
Vertical Bar	B–D: $\frac{3}{16}$"	$\frac{3}{16}$"	$\frac{7}{16}$"	$\frac{3}{16}$"	$\frac{7}{16}$"	L–M: $\frac{3}{16}$"		–	O–R: $\frac{3}{16}$"	
Muntin (Horiz.)		$\frac{3}{16}$"			K–M: $\frac{3}{16}$"			$\frac{7}{16}$"	O–R: $\frac{3}{16}$"	
Check Rail	A–R: All check or plain rails $1\frac{3}{32}$"									

MODULAR DOUBLE HUNG WINDOWS - SIZES of STANDARD TYPES

HEIGHT of OPENING*	WIDTH of OPENING* 1'-4"	1'-8"	2'-0"	2'-4"	2'-8"	3'-0"	3'-4"	3'-8"	4'-0"	4'-4"
2'-6"	ABFN	ABFN	ACGN	ACGJN						
2'-10"	ABFN	ABFN	ACGN	ACGN	ACGJN	ADHJN	ADHN			
3'-2"	ABFN	ABFN	ACGILN	ACGI˙LN	ACGIN	ADHIJN	ADHIN			
3'-6"	ABFN	ABFN	ACGI LN	ACGI˙LN	ACGIN	ADHIJN	ADHIN	ADHN	ADHN	
3'-10"	ABFN	ABF KN	˙ACG˙IKLN	˙ACG˙I˙LN	ACG˙ILN	ADHIJLMN	ADHIN	ADHN	ADHN	
4'-2"	ABFN	ABFKN	ACGILN	ACGILN	ACGIN	ADHIN	ADHIN	ADHN	ADHN	
4'-6"	ABFN	ABF KN	˙ACGI KLN	˙ACG˙IK˙LN	ACG˙I LN	ADHI LMN	ADHI LMN	ADEHLMN	ADEHN	ADEHMN
4'-10"	ABFN	ABFKN	˙ACGI KLN	˙ACG˙ILNO	ACG˙I LN	ADHILNQ	ADEHIMN	ADEHIMN	ADEHN	ADEHN
5'-2"	ABFN	ABFN	ACGI KLN	˙ACG˙I K˙LN	ACG˙I LN	ADHI LMN	ADEHI˙LMN	ADEHIMN	ADEHN	ADEHMN
5'-6"	ABFN	ABFN	ACGIKLN	ACG˙INOP	ACGI LNO	ADHI LNOQR	ADHINOQ	ADEHIMNQ	ADEHN	ADEHNQ
5'-10"	ABFN	ABFN	ACGKN	ACGI KN	ACGI KLN	ADHI LN	ADHI˙LMN	ADEHIMN	ADEHN	ADHMN
6'-2"		ABFN	ACGN	ACGIN	ACGINO	ADHIN	ADHINQ	ADHN	ADHN	ADEHN
6'-6"		ABFN	ACG KN	ACGI KNOP	ACGI KLNOP	ADHI LNOPQR	ADHI˙LNOPQR	ADHMNQR	ADHN	ADHMNQR

*Windows are made $\frac{1}{8}$" narrower and $\frac{1}{16}$" shorter than given opening size. Sizes are for $1\frac{3}{8}$" check rail windows. Types preceded by ˙ are also available as standard in $1\frac{1}{8}$" plain rail windows. Face measures of members are the same except: A, I - top rail $2\frac{7}{16}$", bottom rail $2\frac{7}{16}$"; L - top rail $2\frac{3}{16}$", bottom rail $2\frac{3}{16}$". Other plain rail, non-modular sizes available.

Scale of details: 3" = 1'-0"

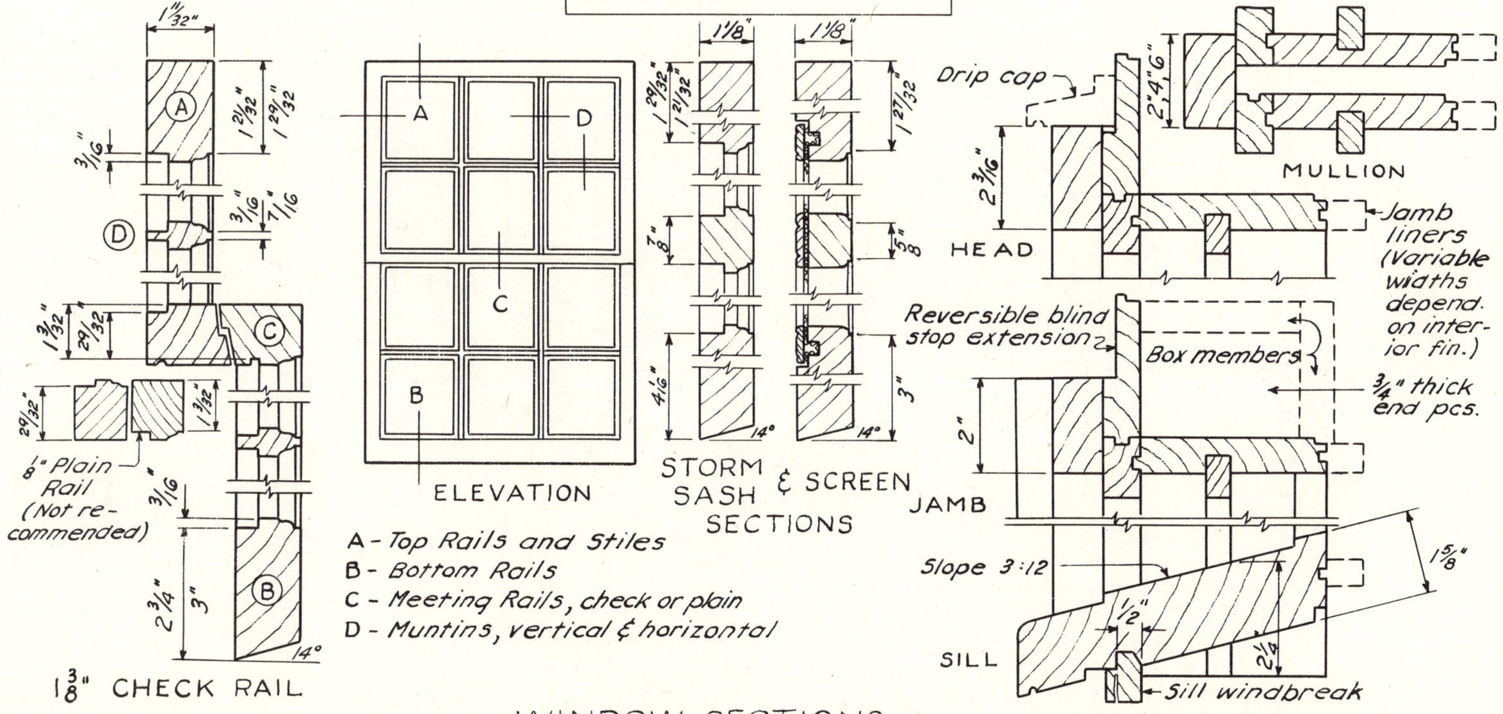
$1\frac{11}{32}$"
A
$1\frac{21}{32}$"
$1\frac{29}{32}$
$\frac{3}{16}$
D
$\frac{3}{16}$"
$\frac{7}{16}$
$1\frac{3}{32}$"
$\frac{29}{32}$
C
$\frac{29}{32}$"
$1\frac{3}{32}$
$1\frac{1}{8}$" Plain Rail (Not recommended)
$\frac{3}{16}$
B
$2\frac{3}{4}$
3"
14°
$1\frac{3}{8}$" CHECK RAIL
A
D
C
B
ELEVATION
A - Top Rails and Stiles
B - Bottom Rails
C - Meeting Rails, check or plain
D - Muntins, vertical & horizontal
$1\frac{1}{8}$"
$1\frac{1}{8}$"
$1\frac{29}{32}$"
$1\frac{21}{32}$"
$1\frac{27}{32}$
$\frac{7}{8}$"
$\frac{5}{8}$"
$4\frac{1}{16}$"
3"
14°
14°
STORM SASH & SCREEN SECTIONS
Drip cap
$2\frac{3}{16}$"
HEAD
2"-4"-6"
MULLION
Jamb liners (Variable widths depend. on interior fin.)
Reversible blind stop extension
Box members
$\frac{3}{4}$" thick end pcs.
2"
JAMB
Slope 3:12
$1\frac{5}{8}$"
$\frac{1}{2}$"
$2\frac{1}{4}$
SILL
Sill windbreak
BASIC WOOD FRAME

WINDOW SECTIONS

Data by National Woodwork Manufacturers Association, Inc.

MODULAR WOOD DOUBLE HUNG WINDOWS

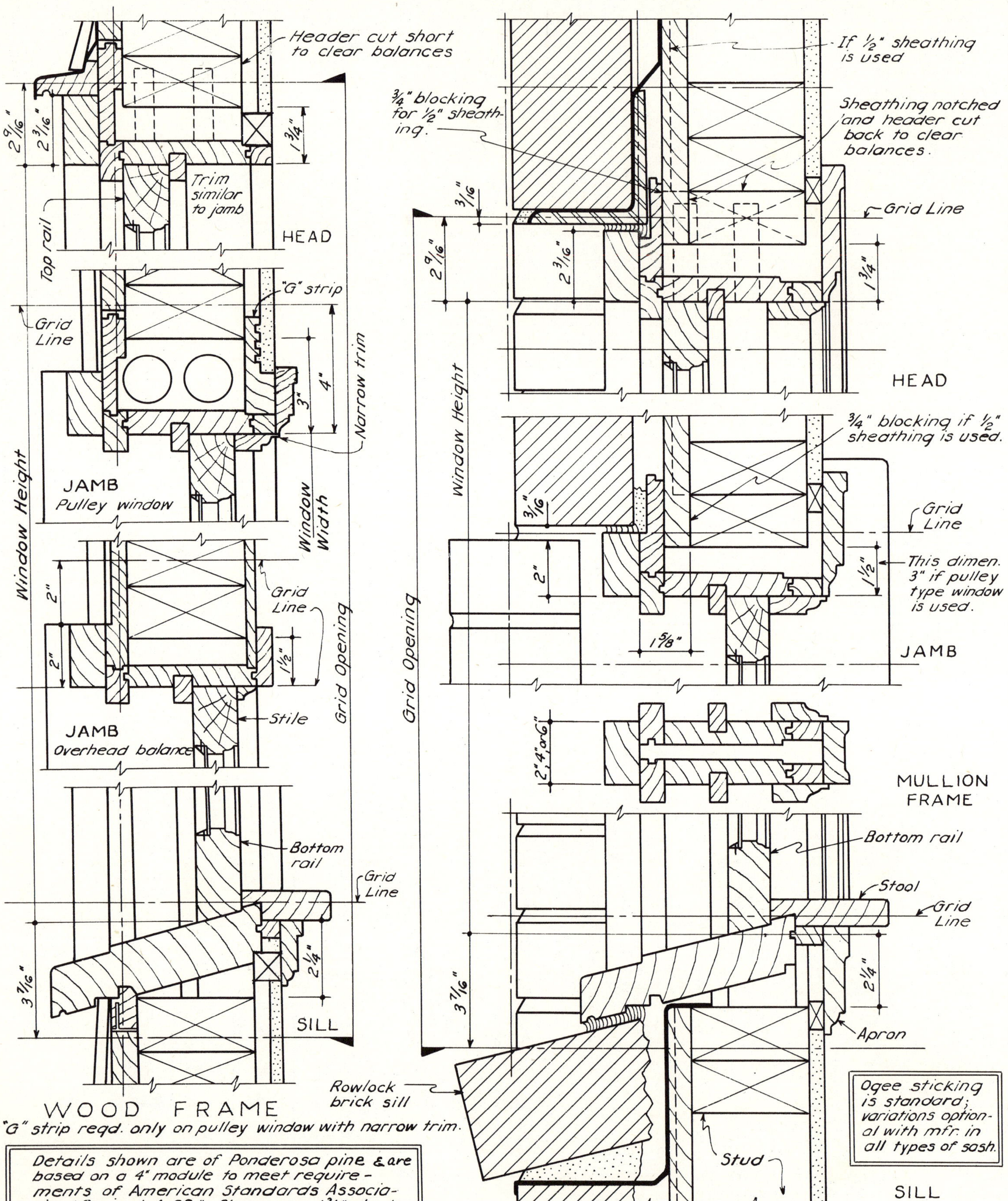
Header cut short to clear balances
Top rail
Trim similar to jamb
HEAD
"G" strip
Grid Line
Narrow trim
JAMB
Pulley window
Window Height
Window Width
Grid Opening
Grid Line
Stile
JAMB
Overhead balance
Bottom rail
Grid Line
SILL
WOOD FRAME
"G" strip reqd. only on pulley window with narrow trim.
3/4" blocking for 1/2" sheathing.
If 1/2" sheathing is used
Sheathing notched and header cut back to clear balances.
Grid Line
HEAD
3/4" blocking if 1/2" sheathing is used.
Grid Line
This dimen. 3" if pulley type window is used.
JAMB
MULLION FRAME
Bottom rail
Stool
Grid Line
Apron
Rowlock brick sill
Stud
Ogee sticking is standard; variations optional with mfr. in all types of sash.
SILL
BRICK VENEER

Details shown are of Ponderosa pine & are based on a 4" module to meet requirements of American Standards Association "Project A 62". Shown are 1 3/8" check rail windows (nominal), fin. thickness is 1 11/32".

Modular coordination in masonry wall only.

Data by National Woodwork Manufacturers Association, Inc.

Scale: 3" = 1'-0"

MODULAR WOOD DOUBLE HUNG WINDOWS

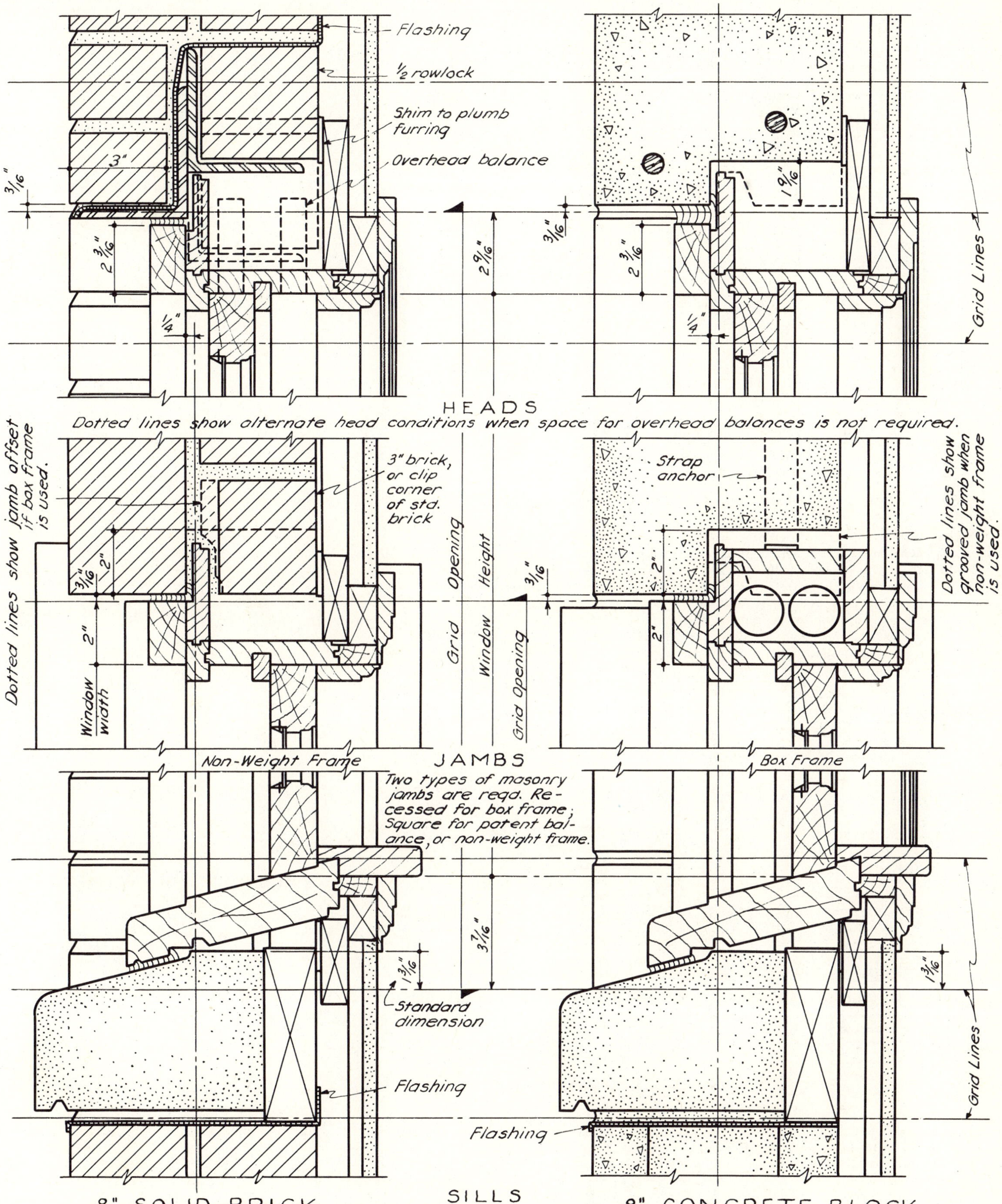
Flashing
1/2 rowlock
Shim to plumb furring
Overhead balance
3"
3/16
2 3/16"
2 9/16"
1/4"
1 9/16
Grid Lines
HEADS
Dotted lines show alternate head conditions when space for overhead balances is not required.
Dotted lines show jamb offset if box frame is used.
3" brick, or clip corner of std. brick
Strap anchor
Dotted lines show grooved jamb when non-weight frame is used.
2"
Grid Opening
Window Height
Window Opening
Grid Opening
Window width
JAMBS
Non-Weight Frame
Box Frame
Two types of masonry jambs are reqd. Recessed for box frame; Square for patent balance, or non-weight frame.
3 7/16"
1 3/16"
Standard dimension
Flashing
SILLS
8" SOLID BRICK
8" CONCRETE BLOCK

Scale 3" = 1'-0"

Data by National Woodwork Manufacturers Association, Inc.

ALUMINUM CASEMENT WINDOWS

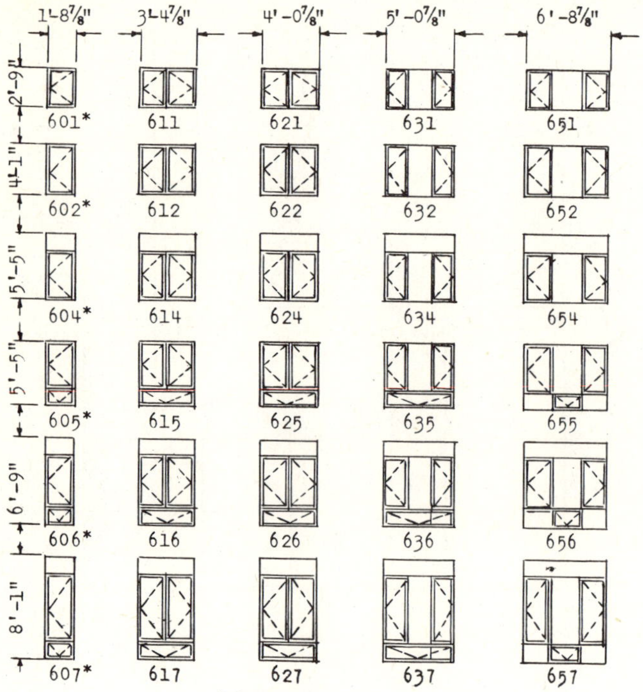
1'-8⅞"
3'-4⅞"
4'-0⅞"
5'-0⅞"
6'-8⅞"
2'-9"
4'-1"
5'-5"
5'-5"
6'-9"
8'-1"
601* 611 621 631 651
602* 612 622 632 652
604* 614 624 634 654
605* 615 625 635 655
606* 616 626 636 656
607* 617 627 637 657

COMMERCIAL

*Windows with a single ventilator may be hinged either left or right.

Sizes shown are actual window dimensions. Horizontal and/or vertical muntins may be added in commercial casement windows provided they are based on 20" or 24" bar centers for width and 16" bar centers for height. Fixed types furnished for all sizes shown. In commercial combination fixed light may be provided at sill in place of sill vent. All windows viewed from outside.

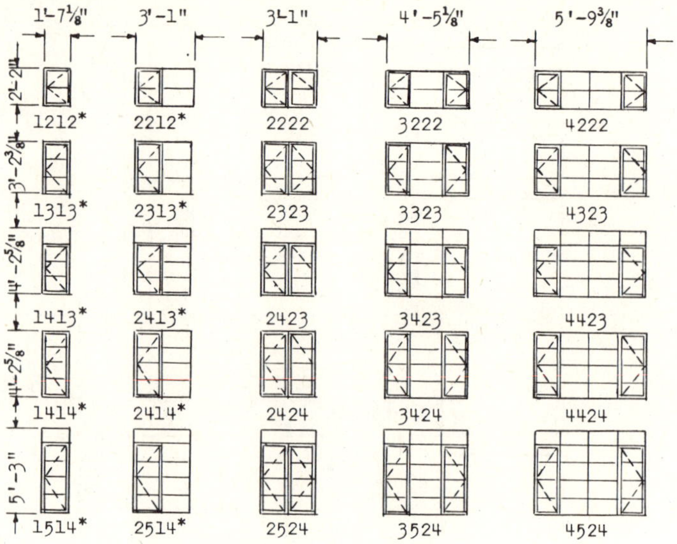
1'-7⅛"
3'-1"
3'-1"
4'-5⅛"
5'-9⅜"
2'-2½"
3'-2⅜"
4'-2⅝"
4'-2⅝"
5'-3"
1212* 2212* 2222 3222 4222
1313* 2313* 2323 3323 4323
1413* 2413* 2423 3423 4423
1414* 2414* 2424 3424 4424
1514* 2514* 2524 3524 4524

RESIDENTIAL STANDARD

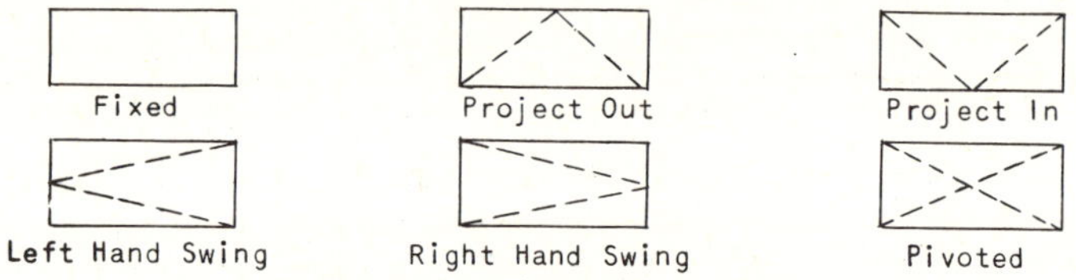
Fixed
Project Out
Project In
Left Hand Swing
Right Hand Swing
Pivoted

SYMBOLS & CONVENTIONS

(as used on architectural drawings)

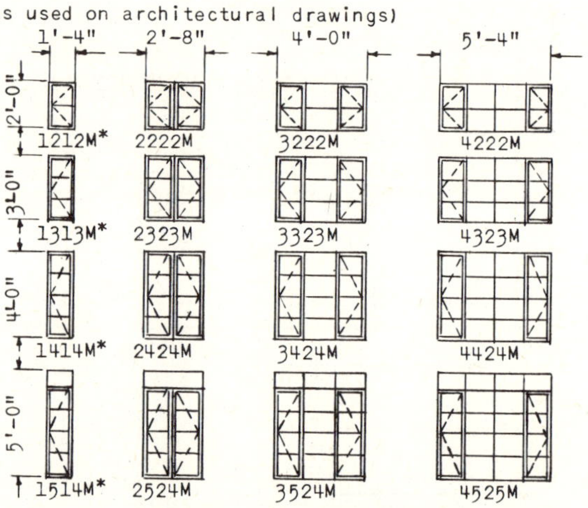
1'-4"
2'-8"
4'-0"
5'-4"
2'-0"
3'-0"
4'-0"
5'-0"
1212M* 2222M 3222M 4222M
1313M* 2323M 3323M 4323M
1414M* 2424M 3424M 4424M
1514M* 2524M 3524M 4525M

RESIDENTIAL MODULAR

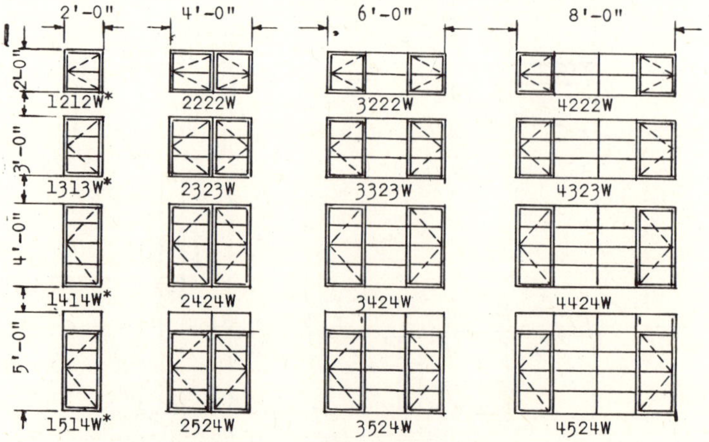
2'-0"
4'-0"
6'-0"
8'-0"
2'-0"
3'-0"
4'-0"
5'-0"
1212W* 2222W 3222W 4222W
1313W* 2323W 3323W 4323W
1414W* 2424W 3424W 4424W
1514W* 2524W 3524W 4524W

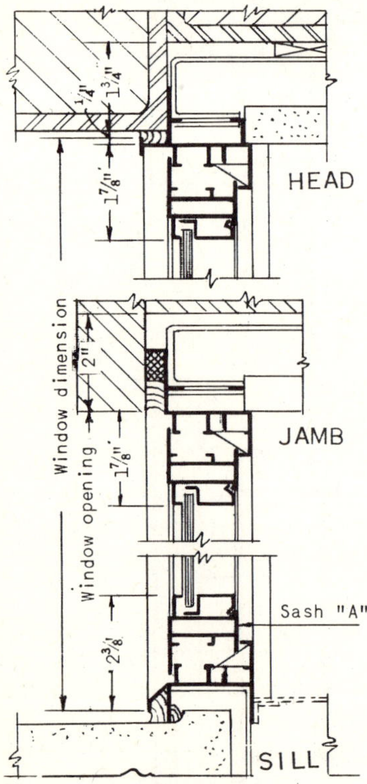
1¼"
1¾"
1⅞"
HEAD
Window dimension
2"
JAMB
1⅞"
Window opening
Sash "A"*
2⅜"
SILL

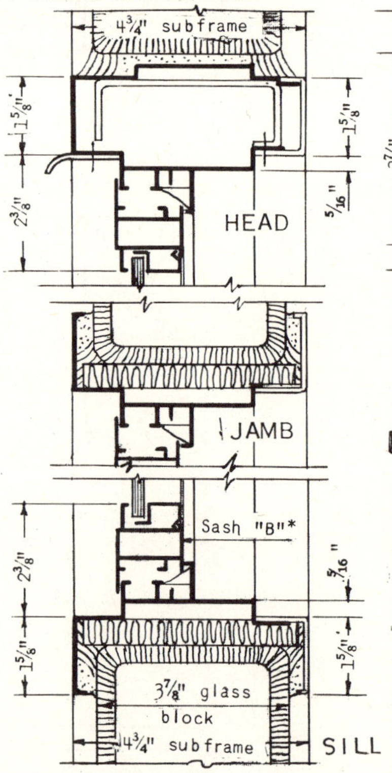
4¾" subframe
1⅝"
1⅝"
2⅜"
5/16"
HEAD
JAMB
Sash "B"*
2⅜"
5/16"
1⅝"
1⅝"
3⅞" glass block
4¾" subframe
SILL

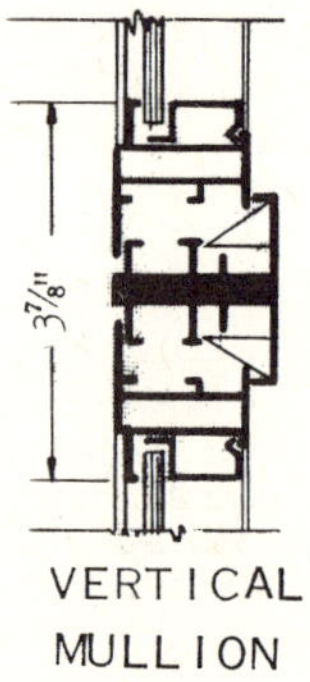
3⅞"
VERTICAL MULLION

*Sash "A" for aluminum up to 2'-0" x 5'-0". Sash "B" for larger sizes in aluminum and bronze.

IN BRICK

WITH GLASS BLOCK

RESIDENTIAL WESTERN MODULAR

Sizes shown are standard sizes of the Aluminum Window Manufacturers Association. Details are of commercial weight windows made by General Bronze Corp.(Permalite Division).

ALUMINUM PROJECTED WINDOWS

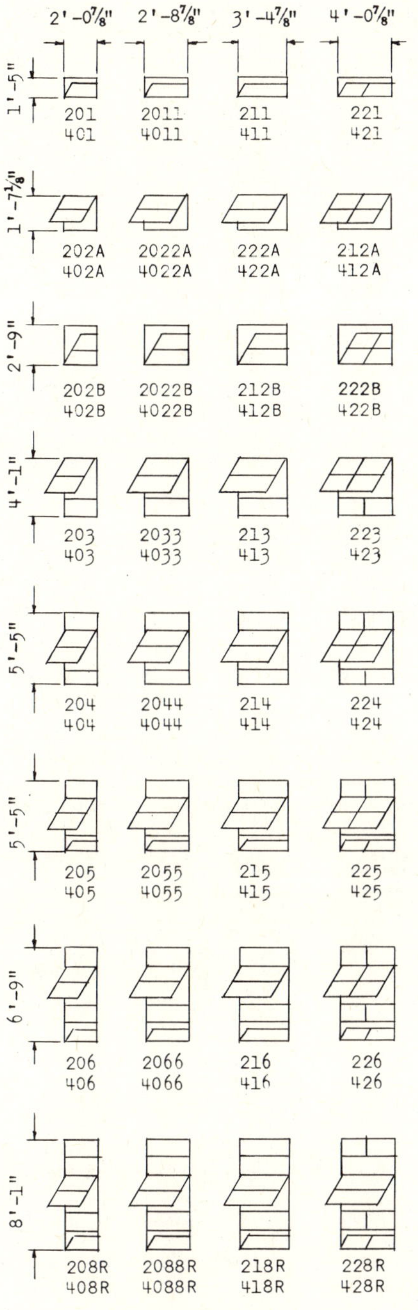
2'-0 7/8"
2'-8 7/8"
3'-4 7/8"
4'-0 7/8"
1'-5"
201 401
2011 4011
211 411
221 421
1'-7 1/8"
202A 402A
2022A 4022A
222A 422A
212A 412A
2'-9"
202B 402B
2022B 4022B
212B 412B
222B 422B
4'-1"
203 403
2033 4033
213 413
223 423
5'-5"
204 404
2044 4044
214 414
224 424
5'-5"
205 405
2055 4055
215 415
225 425
6'-9"
206 406
2066 4066
216 416
226 426
8'-1"
208R 408R
2088R 4088R
218R 418R
228R 428R

COMMERCIAL & MONUMENTAL

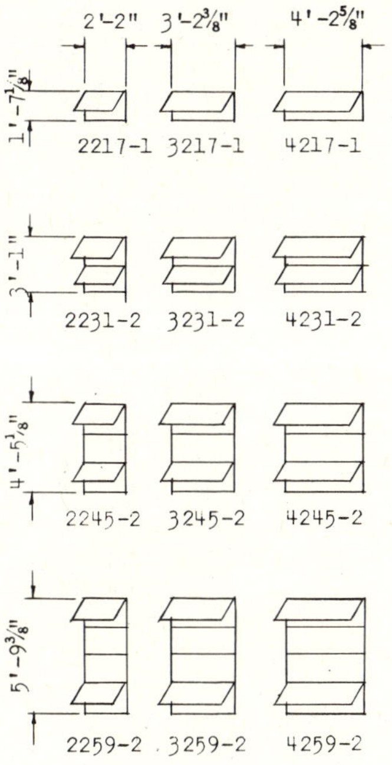
2'-2"
3'-2 3/8"
4'-2 5/8"
1'-7 1/8"
2217-1
3217-1
4217-1
3'-1"
2231-2
3231-2
4231-2
4'-5 1/8"
2245-2
3245-2
4245-2
5'-9 3/8"
2259-2
3259-2
4259-2

RESIDENTIAL

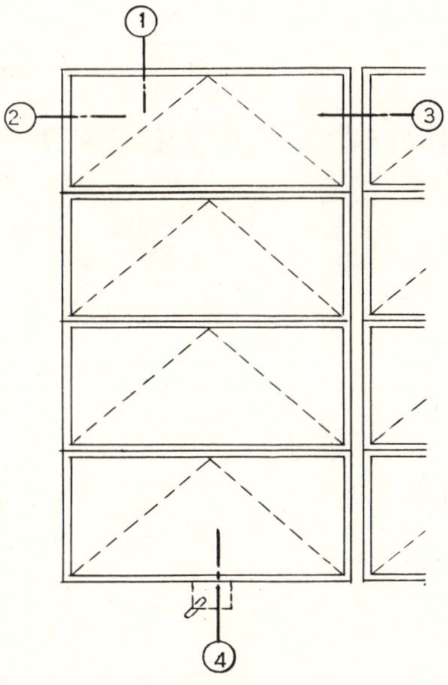
1
2
3
4

ELEVATION

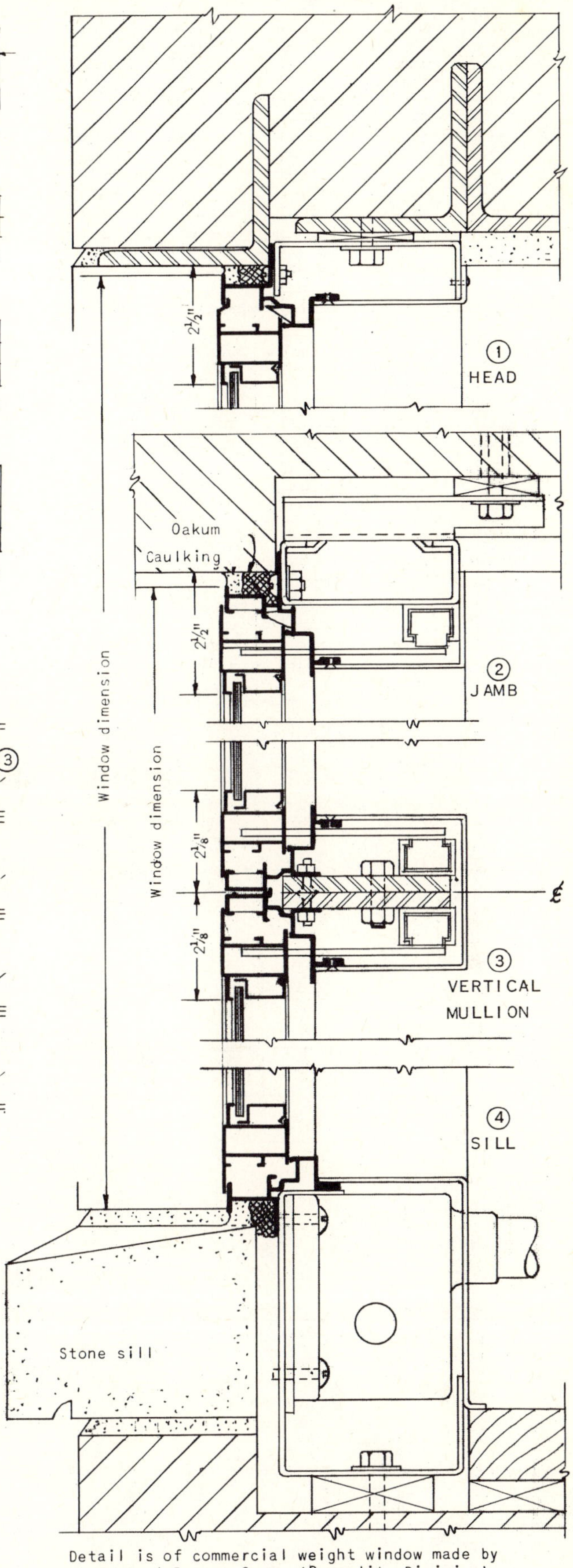
1 HEAD
2 1/2"
Oakum
Caulking
2 JAMB
Window dimension
Window dimension
2 1/8"
2 1/8"
℄
3 VERTICAL MULLION
4 SILL
Stone sill

Detail is of commercial weight window made by General Bronze Corp. (Permalite Division)

Sizes shown are standard sizes of the Aluminum Window Manufacturers Association. All dimensions shown are window dimensions. Not all manufacturers make a full range of sizes and some deviate slightly from the above standards. Fixed types furnished for all sizes shown.

In the commercial projected the 200 series indicates architectural projected; the 400 series, intermediate projected which are heavier and sturdier in construction. All vents shown to project out may be made to project in, provided all vents in the same unit project in. Vertical muntins may be added to 200 and 400 commercial series if desired provided they are based on 20" or 24" bar centers.

ALUMINUM PROJECTED WINDOWS-STANDARD SIZES

PROJECTED WINDOW WITH CONCEALED MECHANICAL OPERATION

ALUMINUM AWNING, BASEMENT and SLIDING WINDOWS

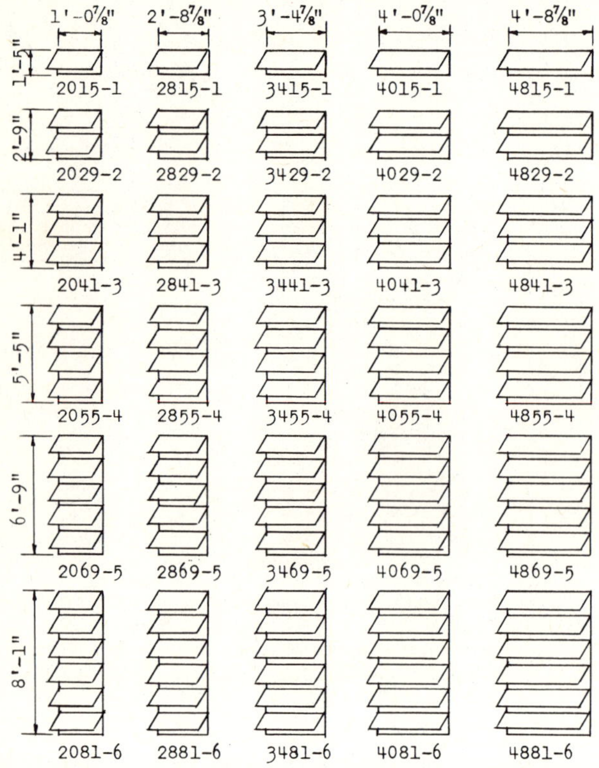
1'-0⅞" 2'-8⅞" 3'-4⅞" 4'-0⅞" 4'-8⅞"
1'-5" 2015-1 2815-1 3415-1 4015-1 4815-1
2'-9" 2029-2 2829-2 3429-2 4029-2 4829-2
4'-1" 2041-3 2841-3 3441-3 4041-3 4841-3
5'-5" 2055-4 2855-4 3455-4 4055-4 4855-4
6'-9" 2069-5 2869-5 3469-5 4069-5 4869-5
8'-1" 2081-6 2881-6 3481-6 4081-6 4881-6

COMMERCIAL AWNING

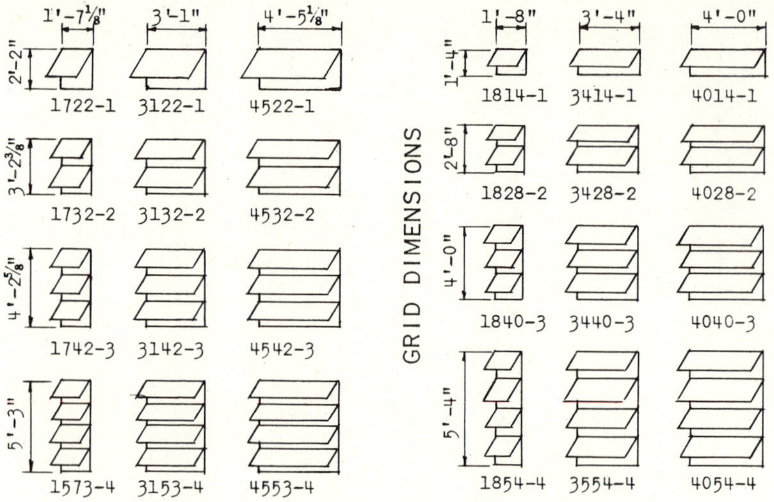
1'-7⅛" 3'-1" 4'-5⅛"
2'-2" 1722-1 3122-1 4522-1
3'-2⅜" 1732-2 3132-2 4532-2
4'-2⅝" 1742-3 3142-3 4542-3
5'-3" 1573-4 3153-4 4553-4
STANDARD
1'-8" 3'-4" 4'-0"
GRID DIMENSIONS
1'-4" 1814-1 3414-1 4014-1
2'-8" 1828-2 3428-2 4028-2
4'-0" 1840-3 3440-3 4040-3
5'-4" 1854-4 3554-4 4054-4
MODULAR

RESIDENTIAL AWNING

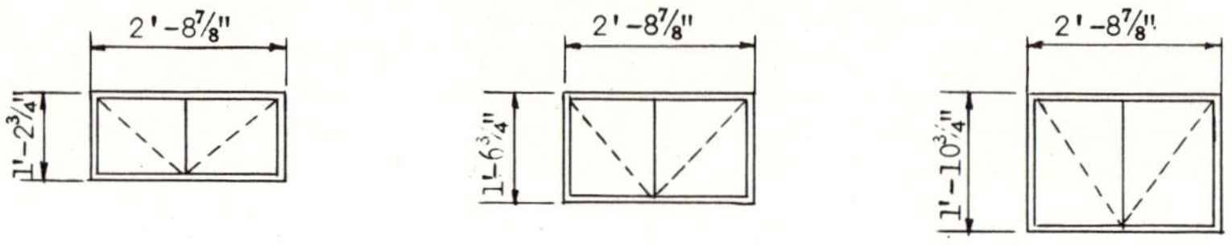
2'-8⅞" 1'-2¾"
2'-8⅞" 1'-6¾"
2'-8⅞" 1'-10¾"

BASEMENT

Sizes shown are standard sizes of the Aluminum Window Manufacturers Association. All dimensions, except as otherwise indicated, are masonry opening dimensions.

ALUMINUM AWNING & BASEMENT WINDOWS

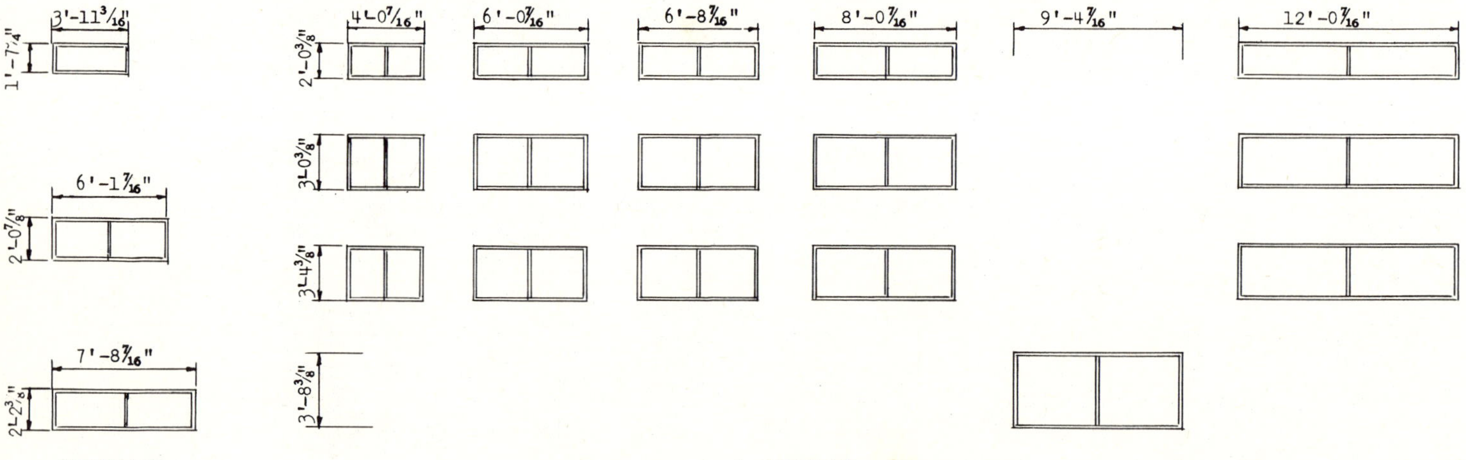
3'-11³⁄₁₆" 1'-7¼"
6'-1⁷⁄₁₆" 2'-0⅞"
7'-8⁷⁄₁₆" 2'-2⅜"
4'-0⁷⁄₁₆" 6'-0⁷⁄₁₆" 6'-8⁷⁄₁₆" 8'-0⁷⁄₁₆" 9'-4⁷⁄₁₆" 12'-0⁷⁄₁₆"
2'-0⅜" 3'-0⅜" 3'-4⅜" 3'-8⅜"
STANDARD
MODULAR

ALUMINUM SLIDING WINDOWS

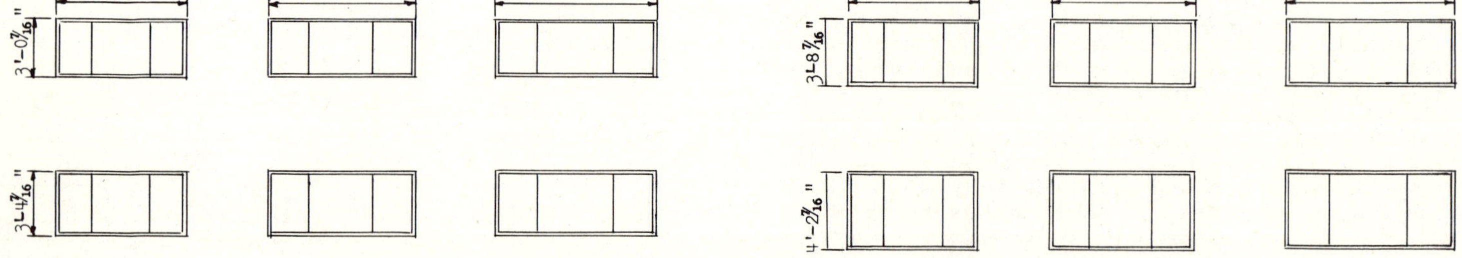
7'-0⅜" 8'-0⅜" 9'-0⅜" 7'-0⅜" 8'-0⅜" 9'-0⅜"
3'-0⁷⁄₁₆" 3'-4⁷⁄₁₆" 3'-8⁷⁄₁₆" 4'-2⁷⁄₁₆"

ALUMINUM SLIDING WINDOWS WITH FIXED CENTER SASH

Sizes shown for aluminum sliding windows and sliding windows with fixed sash are those of General Bronze Corp. (Alwintite Division). Standards have not been established for these types and consequently sizes will vary somewhat from manufacturer to manufacturer. All sizes shown indicate masonry openings.

ALUMINUM DOUBLE HUNG WINDOWS

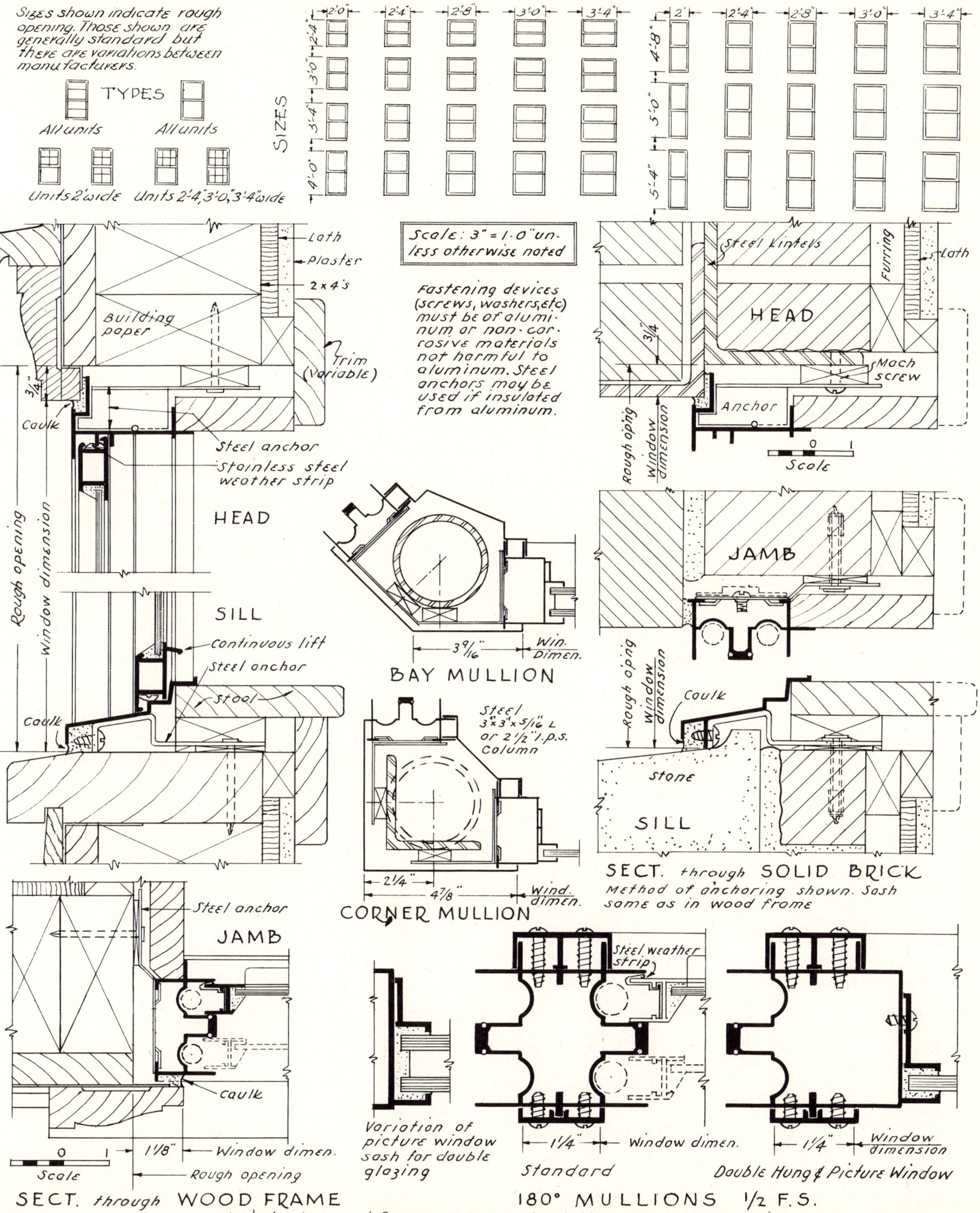
Sizes shown indicate rough opening. Those shown are generally standard but there are variations between manufacturers.
TYPES
All units
All units
Units 2' wide
Units 2'-4", 3'-0", 3'-4" wide
SIZES
2'-0"
2'-4"
2'-8"
3'-0"
3'-4"
2'-4"
3'-0"
3'-4"
4'-0"
2'
2'-4"
2'-8"
3'-0"
3'-4"
4'-8"
5'-0"
5'-4"
Scale: 3" = 1'-0" unless otherwise noted
Lath
Plaster
2 x 4's
Building paper
Trim (Variable)
3/4"
Caulk
Steel anchor
Stainless steel weather strip
Rough opening
Window dimension
HEAD
SILL
Continuous lift
Steel anchor
Stool
Caulk
Fastening devices (screws, washers, etc.) must be of aluminum or non-corrosive materials not harmful to aluminum. Steel anchors may be used if insulated from aluminum.
3 9/16"
Win. Dimen.
BAY MULLION
Steel 3" x 3" x 5/16" L or 2 1/2" I.p.s. column
2 1/4"
4 7/8"
Wind. dimen.
CORNER MULLION
Steel Lintels
Furring
Lath
HEAD
3/4
Mach screw
Anchor
Rough op'ng
Window dimension
0
1
Scale
JAMB
Rough op'ng
Window dimension
Caulk
Stone
SILL
SECT. through SOLID BRICK
Method of anchoring shown. Sash same as in wood frame
Steel anchor
JAMB
Caulk
0
1
Scale
1 1/8"
Window dimen.
Rough opening
SECT. through WOOD FRAME
Steel weather strip
Variation of picture window sash for double glazing
1 1/4"
Window dimen.
Standard
1 1/4"
Window dimension
Double Hung & Picture Window
180° MULLIONS 1/2 F.S.

Data by General Bronze Corporation (ALWINTITE DIVISION)

STEEL RESIDENTIAL DOUBLE HUNG WINDOWS

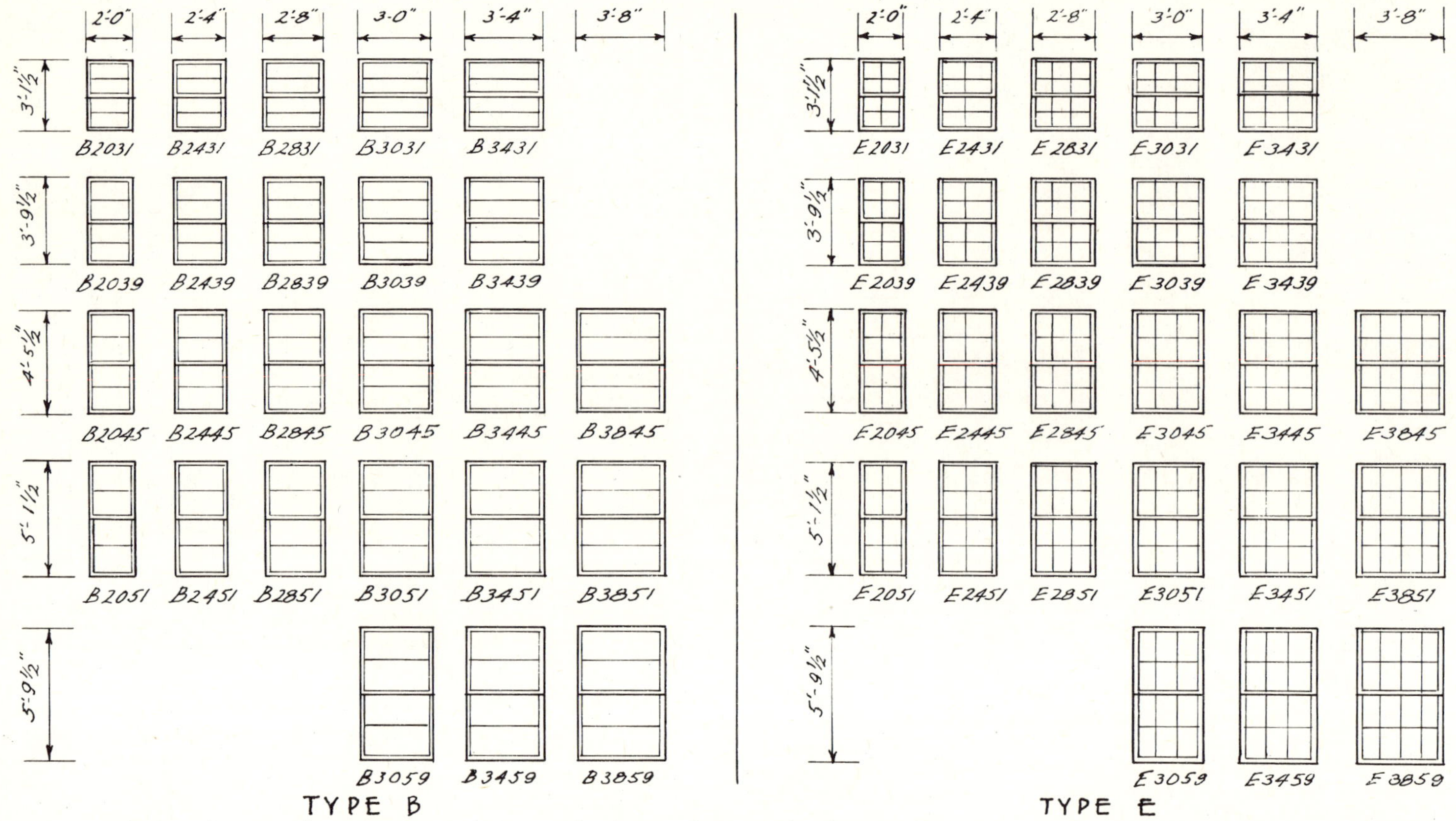
2'-0"
2'-4"
2'-8"
3'-0"
3'-4"
3'-8"
3'-1½"
B2031 B2431 B2831 B3031 B3431
3'-9½"
B2039 B2439 B2839 B3039 B3439
4'-5½"
B2045 B2445 B2845 B3045 B3445 B3845
5'-1½"
B2051 B2451 B2851 B3051 B3451 B3851
5'-9½"
B3059 B3459 B3859
TYPE B
E2031 E2431 E2831 E3031 E3431
E2039 E2439 E2839 E3039 E3439
E2045 E2445 E2845 E3045 E3445 E3845
E2051 E2451 E2851 E3051 E3451 E3851
E3059 E3459 E3859
TYPE E

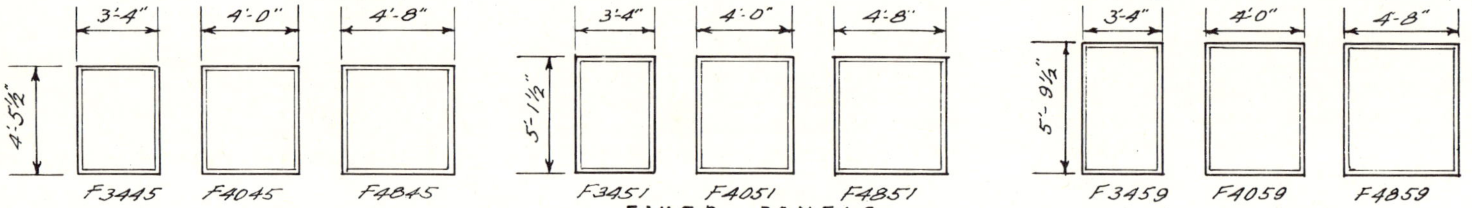
3'-4"
4'-0"
4'-8"
4'-5½"
F3445 F4045 F4845
5'-1½"
F3451 F4051 F4851
5'-9½"
F3459 F4059 F4859

FIXED PANELS

Dimensions shown are window dimensions. Stud opening dimensions equal window dimensions plus 1½" in width, and 2¼" in height. Both type B & E windows can be obtained with either top or bottom vents. However, this is not standard. Vertical or horizontal muntins may be omitted or rearranged on special orders. Types & sizes from Steel Window Institute. Scale: ⅛"=1'-0"

Note: Heavier models, both spring-balanced & counter-balanced are offered on special orders by the manufacturers for commercial type buildings. Not standard as to size or section.

STANDARD TYPES and SIZES

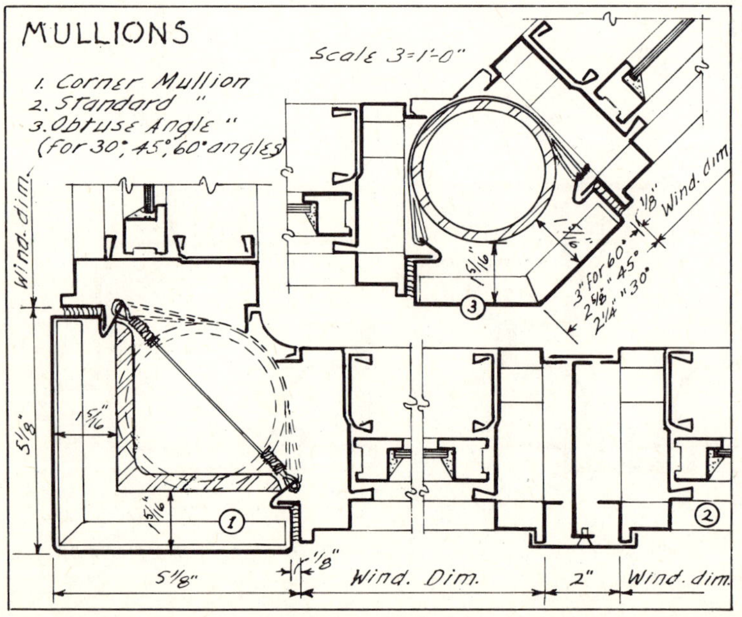
MULLIONS
1. Corner Mullion
2. Standard "
3. Obtuse Angle "
(For 30°, 45°, 60° angles)
Scale 3"=1'-0"
Wind. dim.
5⅛"
1⁵⁄₁₆"
⅛"
Wind. Dim.
2"
Wind. dim.
3" for 60°
2⅝" " 45°
2¼" " 30°

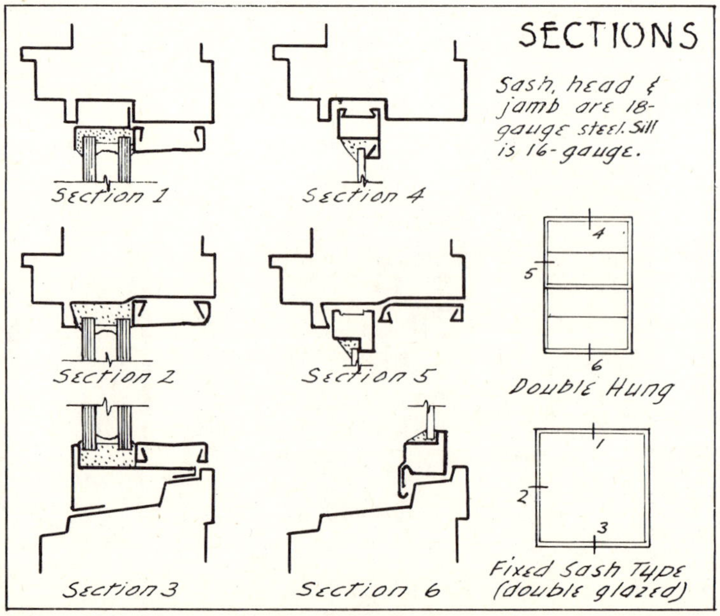
SECTIONS
Sash, head & jamb are 18-gauge steel. Sill is 16-gauge.
Section 1
Section 4
Section 2
Section 5
Section 3
Section 6
Double Hung
Fixed Sash Type (double glazed)

STEEL WINDOWS-RANCH and WESTERN CASEMENT

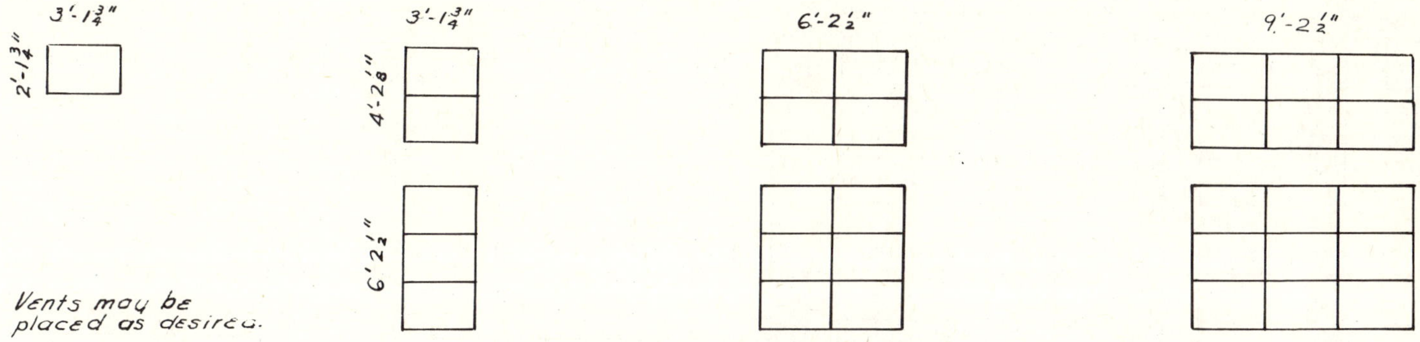
3'-1¾"
2'-1¾"
3'-1¾"
4'-2⅛"
6'-2½"
6'-2½"
9'-2½"

Vents may be placed as desired.

RANCH WINDOWS

BULLSEYE
2'-2" Dia.

Types and sizes shown are recommended only for the states of Arizona, California, Idaho, Nevada, Oregon, Utah, Washington.

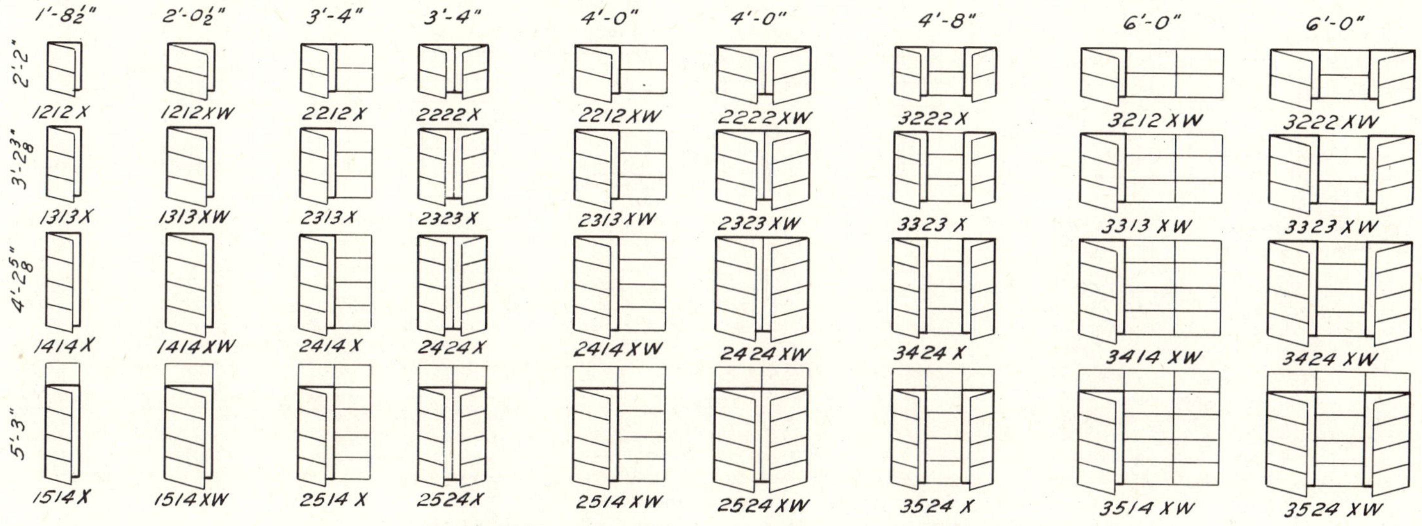
1'-8½"
2'-0½"
3'-4"
3'-4"
4'-0"
4'-0"
4'-8"
6'-0"
6'-0"
2'-2"
1212X
1212XW
2212X
2222X
2212XW
2222XW
3222X
3212XW
3222XW
3'-2⅜"
1313X
1313XW
2313X
2323X
2313XW
2323XW
3323X
3313XW
3323XW
4'-2⅝"
1414X
1414XW
2414X
2424X
2414XW
2424XW
3424X
3414XW
3424XW
5'-3"
1514X
1514XW
2514X
2524X
2514XW
2524XW
3524X
3514XW
3524XW

WAREHOUSE STOCK UNITS

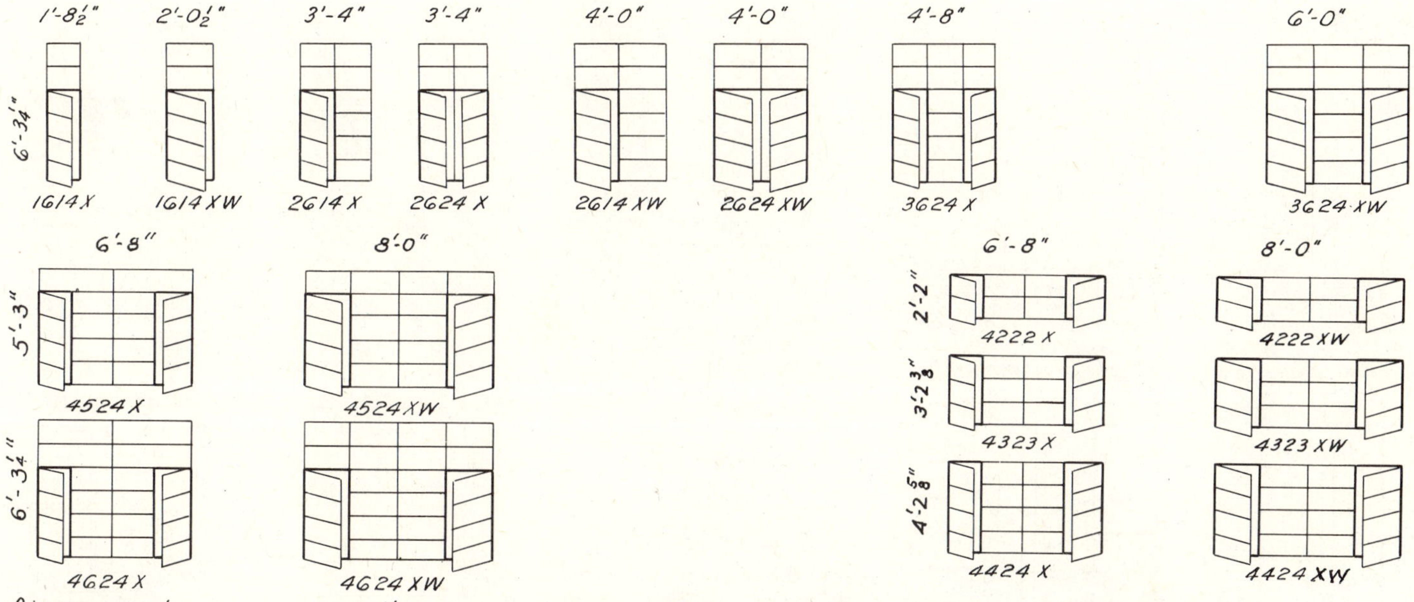
1'-8½"
2'-0½"
3'-4"
3'-4"
4'-0"
4'-0"
4'-8"
6'-0"
6'-3¼"
1614X
1614XW
2614X
2624X
2614XW
2624XW
3624X
3624XW
6'-8"
8'-0"
5'-3"
4524X
4524XW
6'-3¼"
4624X
4624XW
6'-8"
8'-0"
2'-2"
4222X
4222XW
3'-2⅜"
4323X
4323XW
4'-2⅝"
4424X
4424XW

Dimensions shown are overall out-to-out measurements. Single ventilators may swing from right or left jamb. Fixed types furnished for all sizes shown. Data by Steel Window Institute.

STANDARDS-NON-WAREHOUSE UNITS
RESIDENTIAL CASEMENT (WESTERN)

RESIDENTIAL STEEL CASEMENT WINDOWS and DOORS

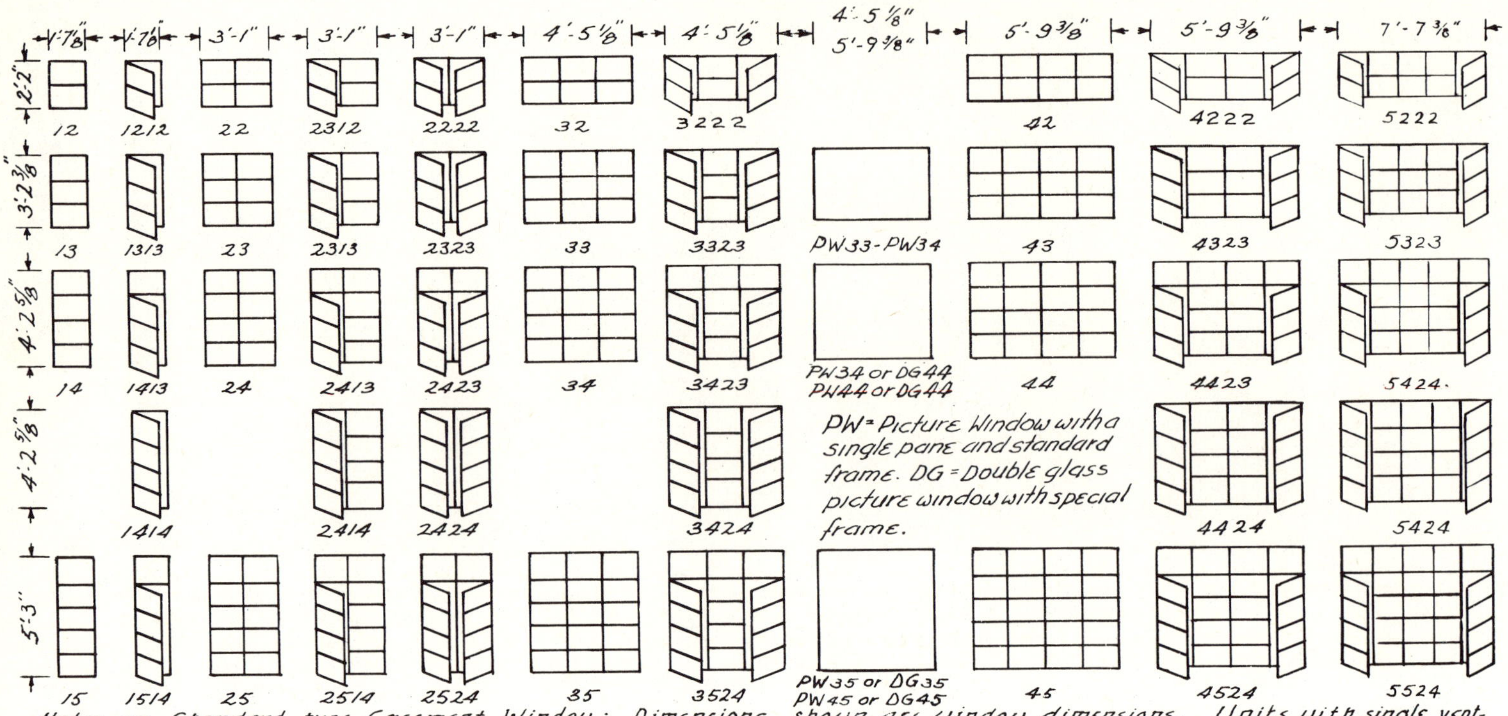
1'-7 5/8"
1'-7 5/8"
3'-1"
3'-1"
3'-1"
4'-5 1/8"
4'-5 1/8"
4'-5 1/8"
5'-9 3/8"
5'-9 3/8"
5'-9 3/8"
7'-7 3/8"
2'-2"
3'-2 3/8"
4'-2 5/8"
4'-2 5/8"
5'-3"
12
1212
22
2312
2222
32
3222
42
4222
5222
13
1313
23
2313
2323
33
3323
PW33-PW34
43
4323
5323
14
1413
24
2413
2423
34
3423
PW34 or DG44
PW44 or DG44
44
4423
5424.
1414
2414
2424
3424
PW = Picture Window with a single pane and standard frame. DG = Double glass picture window with special frame.
4424
5424
15
1514
25
2514
2524
35
3524
PW35 or DG35
PW45 or DG45
45
4524
5524

Notes on Standard type Casement Window: Dimensions shown are window dimensions. Units with single ventilators may swing from either right or left jamb. These are standard sizes of the Steel Window Institute.

Notes on Special Items (not standard): For size of masonry opening or for wood rebate dimensions, in usual construction, add 1/4" to the above sizes. This may not hold for special wood or metal surrounds. See mfrs. catalogs for such dimensions. If several units are assembled with vertical mullions add 1/8" or 1/4" (this dimension varies with mfrs.) for each mullion. If units are assembled over each other, add 1/8" for each horizontal mullion. See fol. p. for types and sizes available for the Pacific Coast, Southwest and Rocky Mountain areas. Tee or pipe type vertical mullions and Tee horizontal mullions join combinations of units. Screens and/or storm sash, wood fins, steel fins wood and/or metal surrounds are available. In ventilators, any or all muntins may be omitted. Vertical muntins may be added. Inside metal trim and casings available. Operator types: Rotary, lever, or under-screen. Apartment Casements are standard Residence Casements equipped with Simplex locking handles and friction hinges on orders of 300 or more units. Sizes of glass vary fractionally with mfrs.

Data by Steel Window Institute

RESIDENTIAL CASEMENT WINDOWS

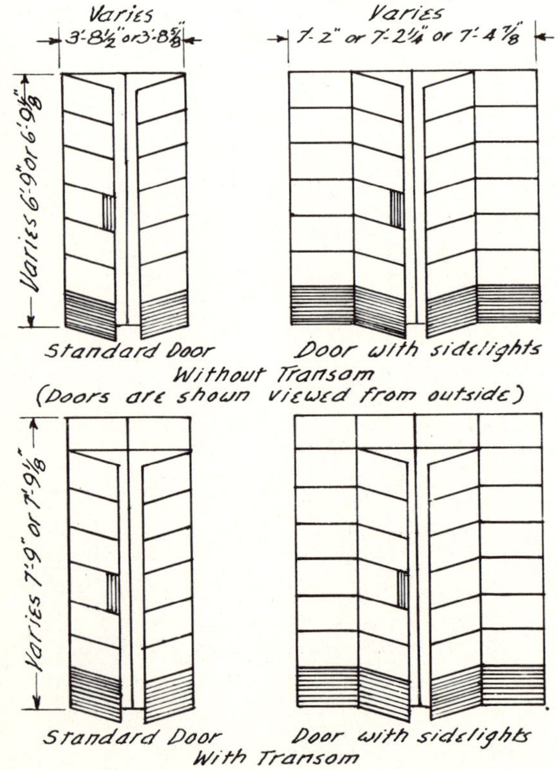
Varies
3'-8 1/2" or 3'-8 5/8"
Varies
7'-2" or 7'-2 1/4" or 7'-4 7/8"
Varies 6'-9" or 6'-9 5/8"
Standard Door
Door with sidelights
Without Transom
(Doors are shown viewed from outside)
Varies 7'-9" or 7'-9 5/8"
Standard Door
Door with sidelights
With Transom

CASEMENT DOORS

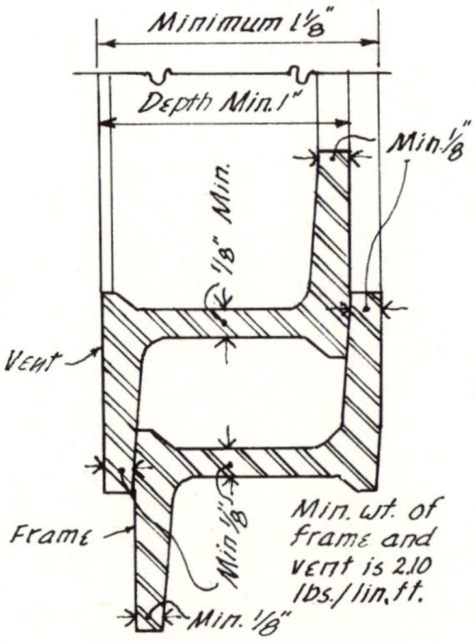
Minimum 1 1/8"
Depth Min. 1"
Min. 1/8"
1/8" Min.
Vent
Frame
Min. 1/8"
Min. 1/8"
Min. wt. of frame and vent is 2.10 lbs./lin. ft.

RESIDENCE CASEMENT

Frame and ventilator members are Z-shaped sections. These members are of steel and should not be less than 1" deep, and 1/8" in thickness. Muntins should not be less than 7/8" deep.

Scale: Full Size

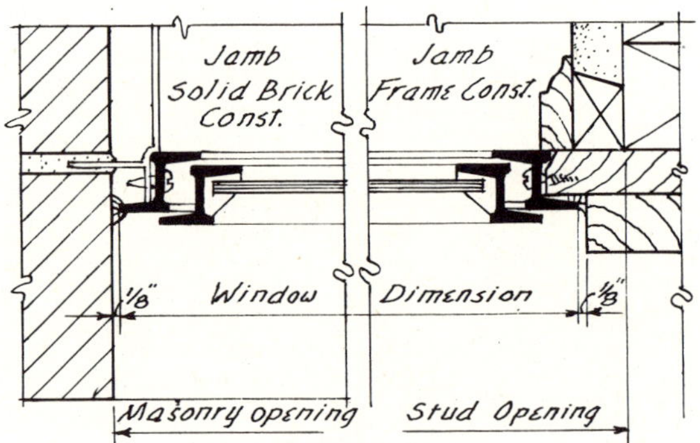
Jamb
Solid Brick Const.
Jamb
Frame Const.
1/8"
Window
Dimension
1/8"
Masonry opening
Stud Opening

PLAN

Scale: 3" = 1'-0"

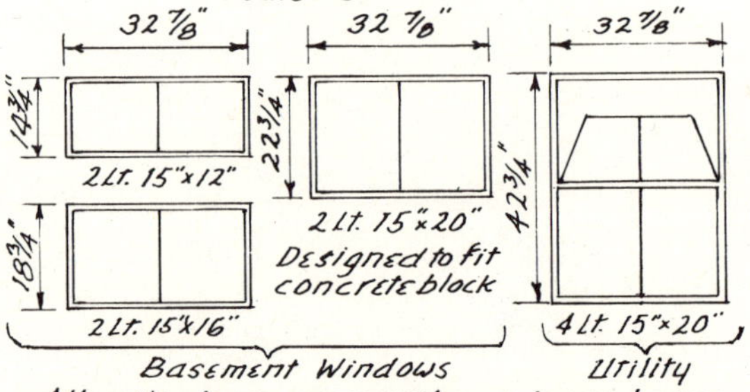
32 7/8"
32 7/8"
32 7/8"
12 3/4"
2 Lt. 15" x 12"
22 3/4"
2 Lt. 15" x 20"
Designed to fit concrete block
42 3/4"
18 3/4"
2 Lt. 15" x 16"
4 Lt. 15" x 20"
Basement Windows
Utility

All units shown are warehouse types & sizes. Bottom hinged to open in. Measurements shown are opening dimensions.

BASEMENT & UTILITY WINDOWS

(for basements, garages, areaways, etc.)

Sizes by Steel Window Institute

RESIDENTIAL STEEL CASEMENT WINDOWS, SHINGLES on FRAME

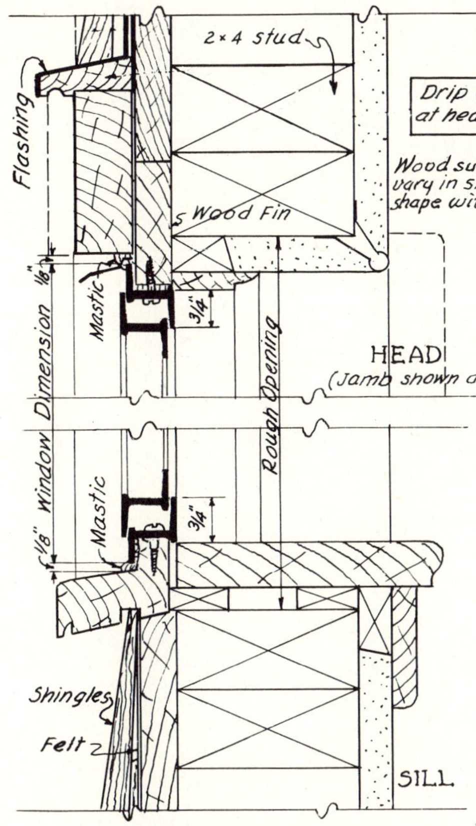
2×4 stud
Flashing
Wood Fin
1/8"
Mastic
3/4"
Window Dimension
Rough Opening
HEAD
(Jamb shown dotted)
1/8"
Mastic
3/4"
Shingles
Felt
SILL

WOOD FIN
(with plaster reveal)

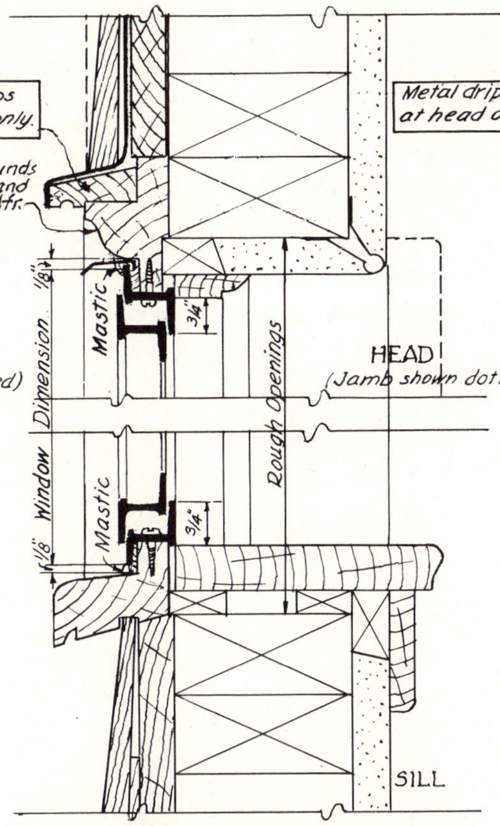
Drip caps at head only.
Wood surrounds vary in size and shape with Mfr.
1/8"
Mastic
3/4"
Window Dimension
Rough Openings
HEAD
(Jamb shown dotted)
1/8"
Mastic
3/4"
SILL

WOOD SURROUND
(with plaster reveal)

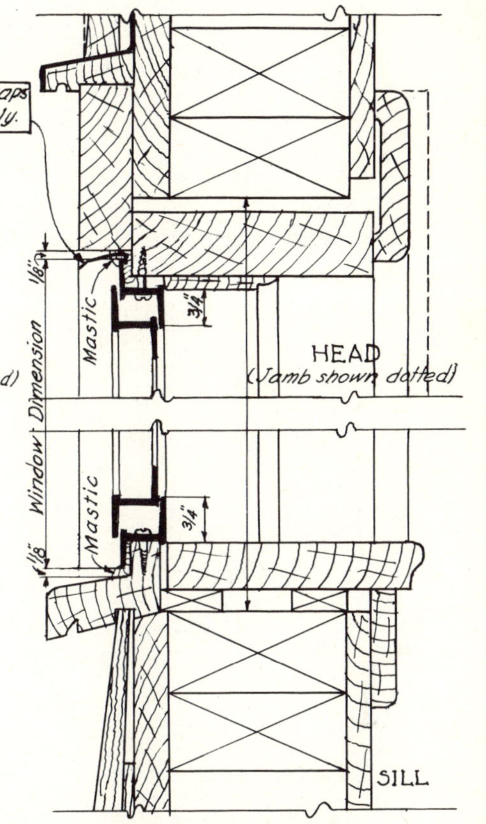
Metal drip caps at head only.
1/8"
Mastic
3/4"
Window Dimension
HEAD
(Jamb shown dotted)
1/8"
Mastic
3/4"
SILL

WOOD CASINGS
(with wood veneer interior)

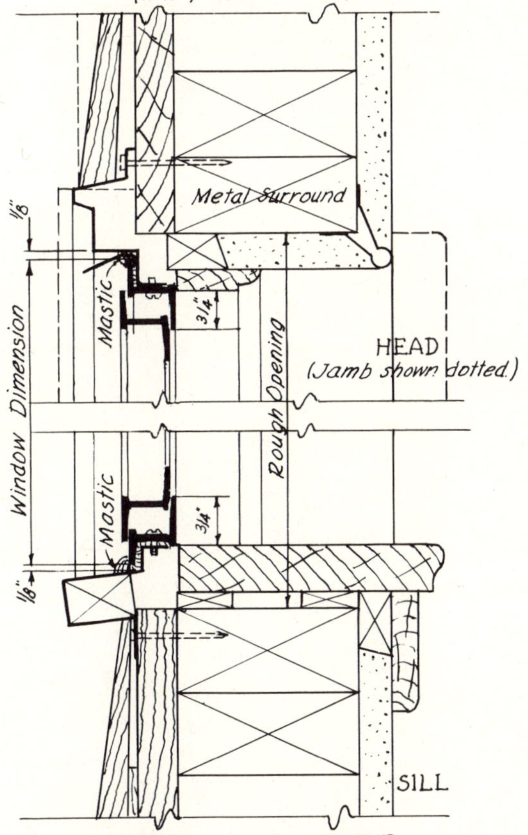
Metal Surround
1/8"
Mastic
3/4"
Window Dimension
Rough Opening
HEAD
(Jamb shown dotted)
Mastic
3/4"
1/8"
SILL

METAL SURROUND
(with plaster reveal)

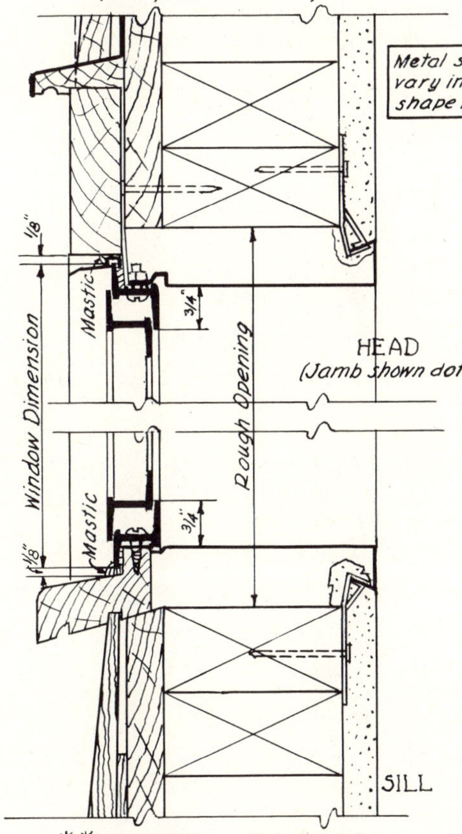
1/8"
Mastic
3/4"
Window Dimension
Rough Opening
HEAD
(Jamb shown dotted)
1/8"
Mastic
3/4"
SILL

**METAL CASING
Scale : 3"=1'0"

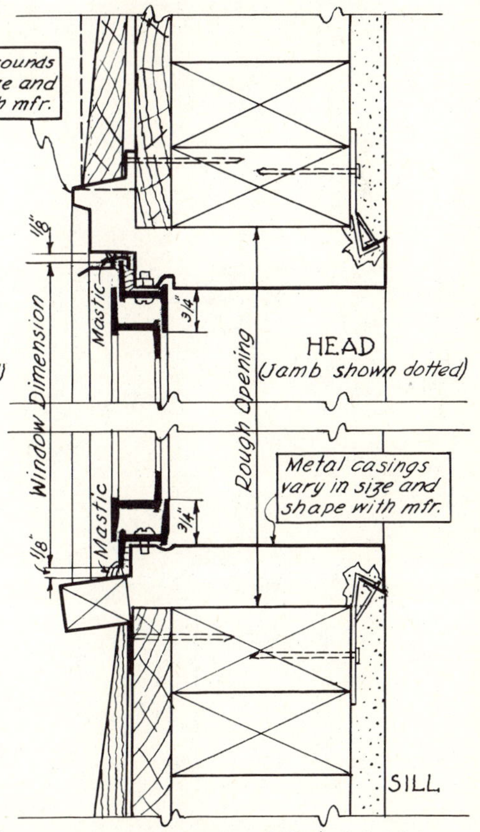
Metal surrounds vary in size and shape with mfr.
1/8"
Mastic
3/4"
Window Dimension
Rough Opening
HEAD
(Jamb shown dotted)
Metal casings vary in size and shape with mfr.
1/8"
Mastic
3/4"
SILL

*METAL SURROUND & CASING

Wood surrounds & wood fins supplied by window manufacturers only when specified. Flashing, building paper, structural lintels, blocking, woodstops, stools, aprons, inside trim, etc., are not generally supplied by window mfr. *Metal surrounds may also be used with wood casings. ** Metal casings may also be used with wood surrounds.

Details checked by Hope's Windows, Inc.

RESIDENTIAL STEEL CASEMENT WINDOWS, BRICK VENEER

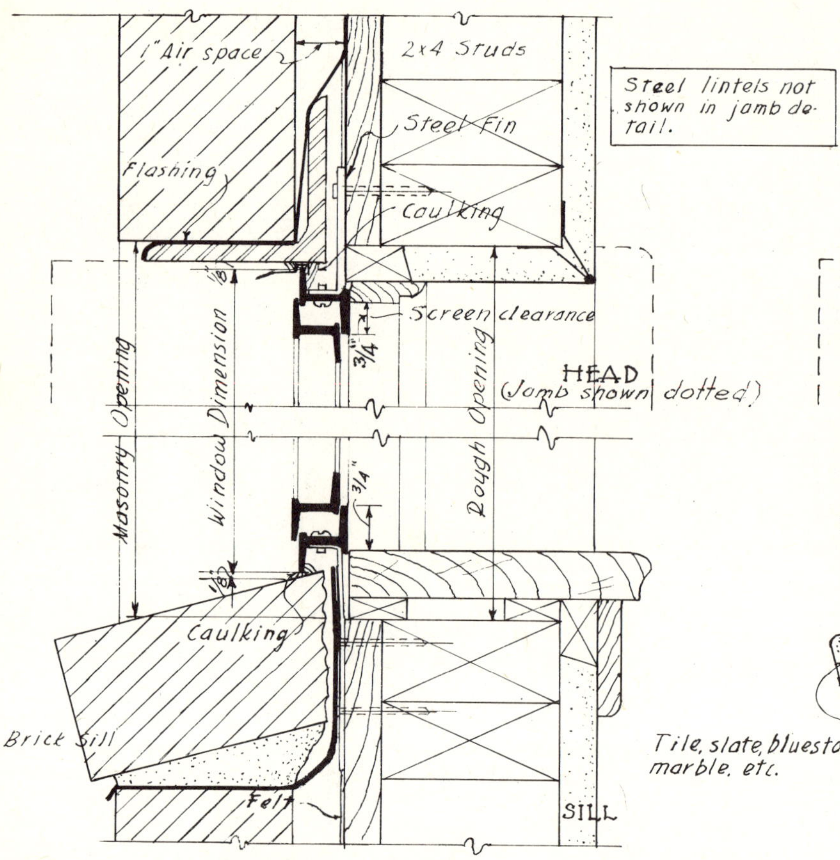

1" Air space
2x4 Studs
Steel Fin
Flashing
Caulking
Screen clearance
1/8
3/4
Masonry Opening
Window Dimension
Rough Opening
HEAD
(Jamb shown dotted)
3/4
1/8
Caulking
Brick Sill
Felt
SILL
Steel lintels not shown in jamb detail.
Tile, slate, bluestone, marble, etc.

METAL FIN
(With plaster reveal)

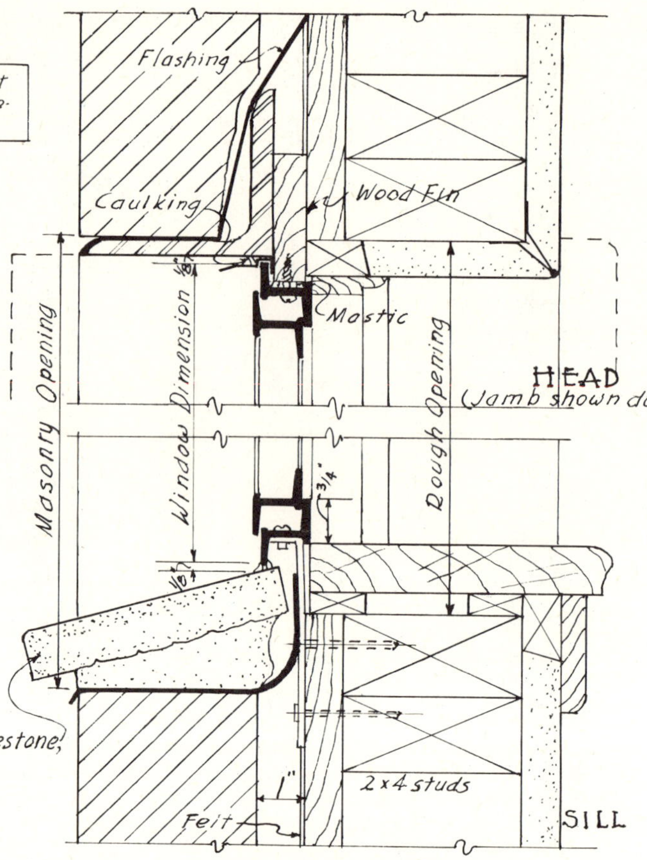

Flashing
Caulking
Wood Fin
Mastic
1/8
Masonry Opening
Window Dimension
Rough Opening
HEAD
(Jamb shown dotted)
3/4
1/8
1"
2x4 studs
Felt
SILL

WOOD FIN
(with plaster reveal)

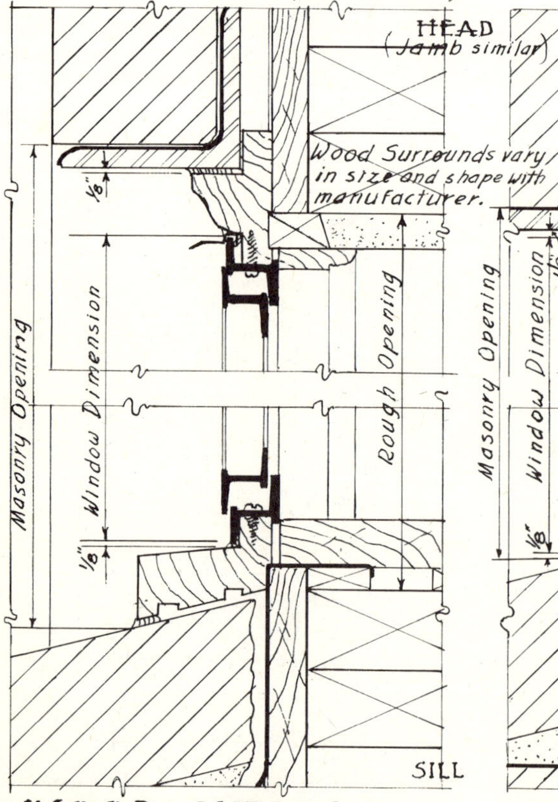

HEAD
(Jamb similar)
Wood Surrounds vary in size and shape with manufacturer.
1/8
Masonry Opening
Window Dimension
Rough Opening
1/8
SILL

WOOD SURROUNDS
(with plaster reveals)

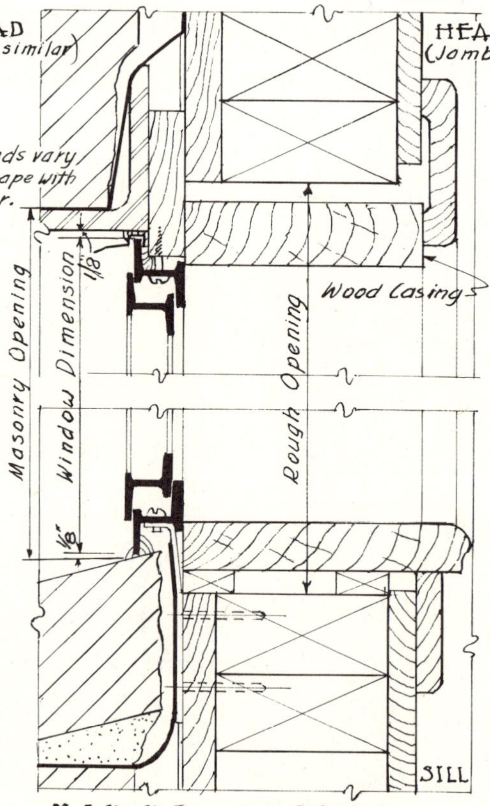

HEAD
(Jamb Similar)
Wood Casings
Masonry Opening
Window Dimension
1/8
Rough Opening
1/8
SILL

WOOD CASING
Scale 3" = 1'-0"

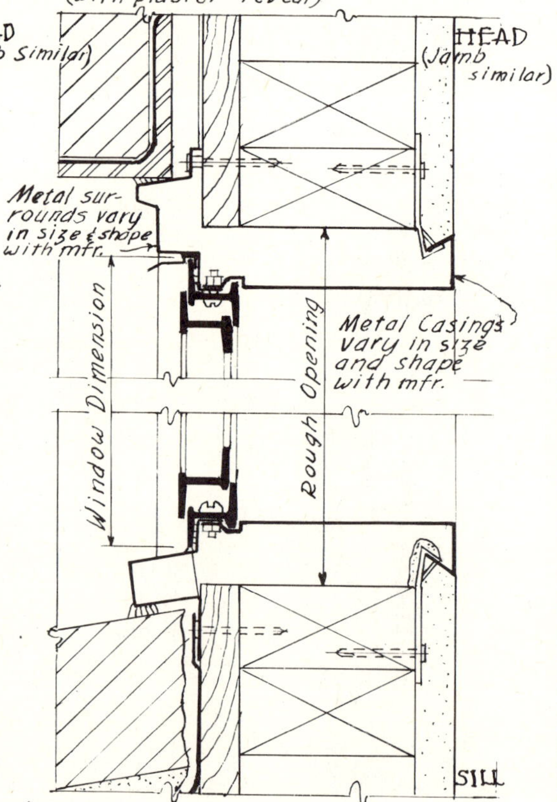

HEAD
(Jamb similar)
Metal surrounds vary in size & shape with mfr.
Window Dimension
Rough Opening
Metal Casings vary in size and shape with mfr.
SILL

*METAL SURROUND & CASING

*Metal casings may also be used with wood surrounds or with wood or metal fins. Metal surrounds may also be used with plaster or wood casings. For note on supplies furnished by Window Manufacturers see page on "Residential Steel Casement Windows, Shingles on Frame."

Details checked by Hope's Windows, Inc.

RESIDENTIAL STEEL CASEMENT WINDOWS, STUCCO on BLOCK and FRAME

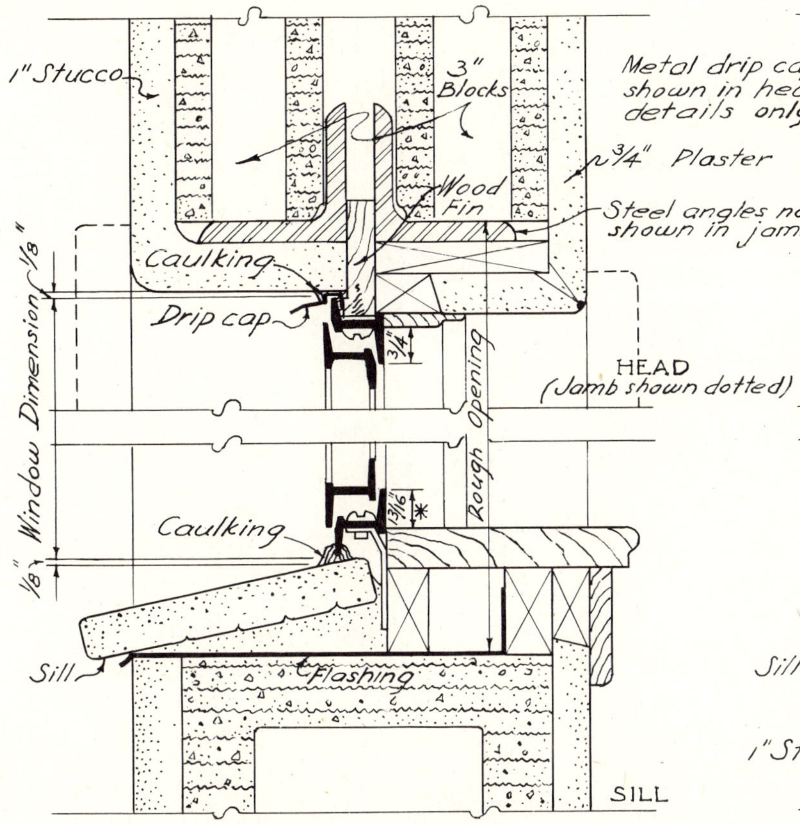
1" Stucco
3" Blocks
Metal drip caps shown in head details only.
3/4" Plaster
Wood Fin
Steel angles not shown in jamb
Caulking
1/8"
Drip cap
3/4
HEAD
(Jamb shown dotted)
Window Dimension
Rough Opening
Caulking
13/16
*
1/8"
Sill
Flashing
SILL

STEEL LINTEL
(Stucco reveal)

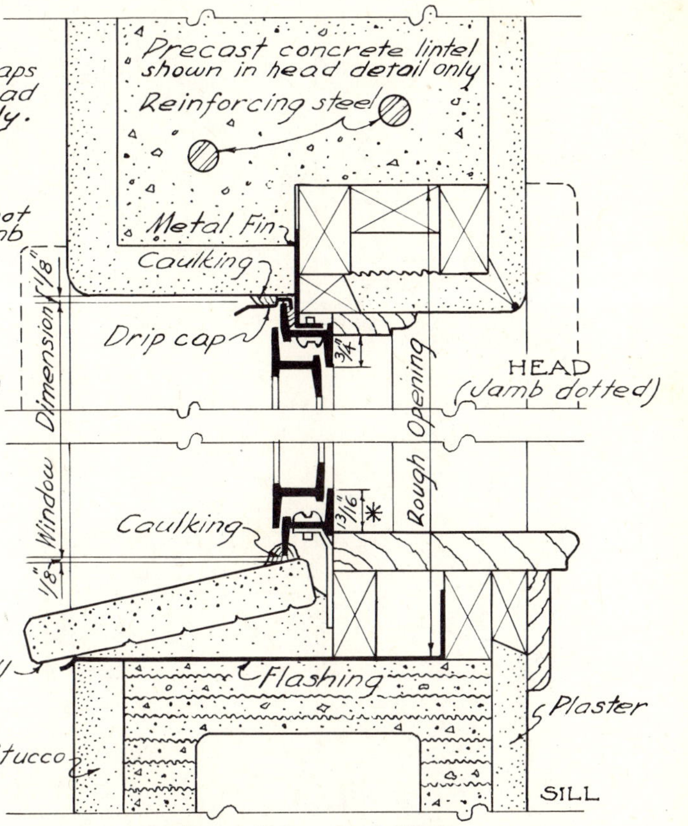
Precast concrete lintel shown in head detail only
Reinforcing steel
Metal Fin
Caulking
1/8"
Drip cap
3/4
HEAD
(Jamb dotted)
Window Dimension
Rough Opening
Caulking
13/16
*
1/8"
Sill
Flashing
Plaster
1" Stucco
SILL

PRECAST LINTEL
(Stucco reveal)

STUCCO ON BLOCK

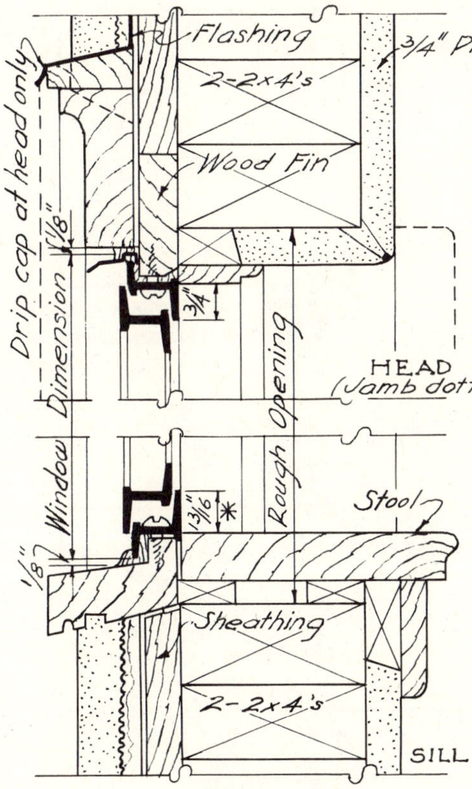
Flashing
3/4" Plaster
Drip cap at head only
2-2x4's
Wood Fin
1/8"
3/4
HEAD
(Jamb dotted)
Window Dimension
Rough Opening
3/16
*
Stool
1/8"
Sheathing
2-2x4's
SILL

WOOD FIN
(With outside trim)

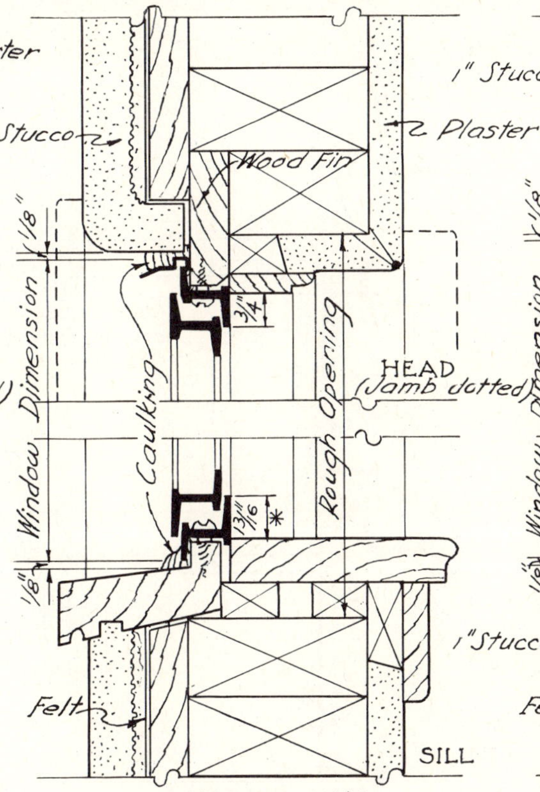
1" Stucco
Plaster
Wood Fin
1/8"
3/4
HEAD
(Jamb dotted)
Window Dimension
Caulking
Rough Opening
3/16
*
1/8"
Felt
SILL

WOOD FIN
(With stucco return)

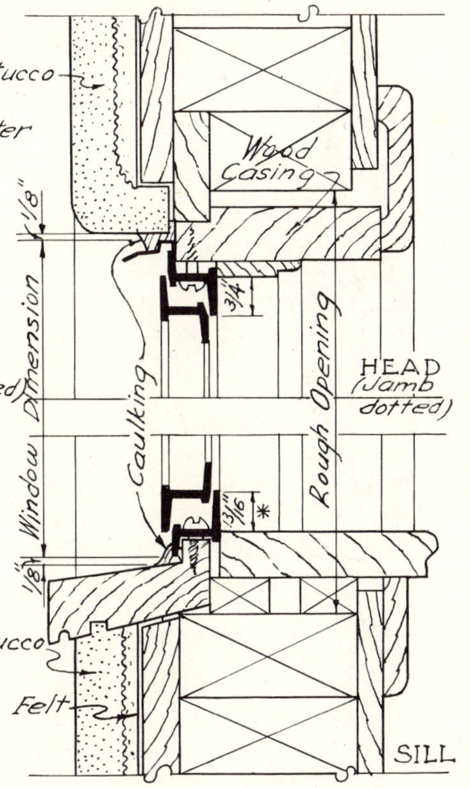
1" Stucco
Wood Casing
1/8"
3/4
HEAD
(Jamb dotted)
Window Dimension
Caulking
Rough Opening
3/16
*
1/8"
1" Stucco
Felt
SILL

WOOD CASING

STUCCO ON FRAME

* *Varies with manufacturer.*

For note on supplies furnished by window manufacturers, see page on "Residential Steel Casement Windows, Shingles on Frame." Above details checked by Hope's Windows, Inc. Scale : 3" = 1'-0"

RESIDENTIAL STEEL CASEMENT WINDOWS, SOLID BRICK WALLS

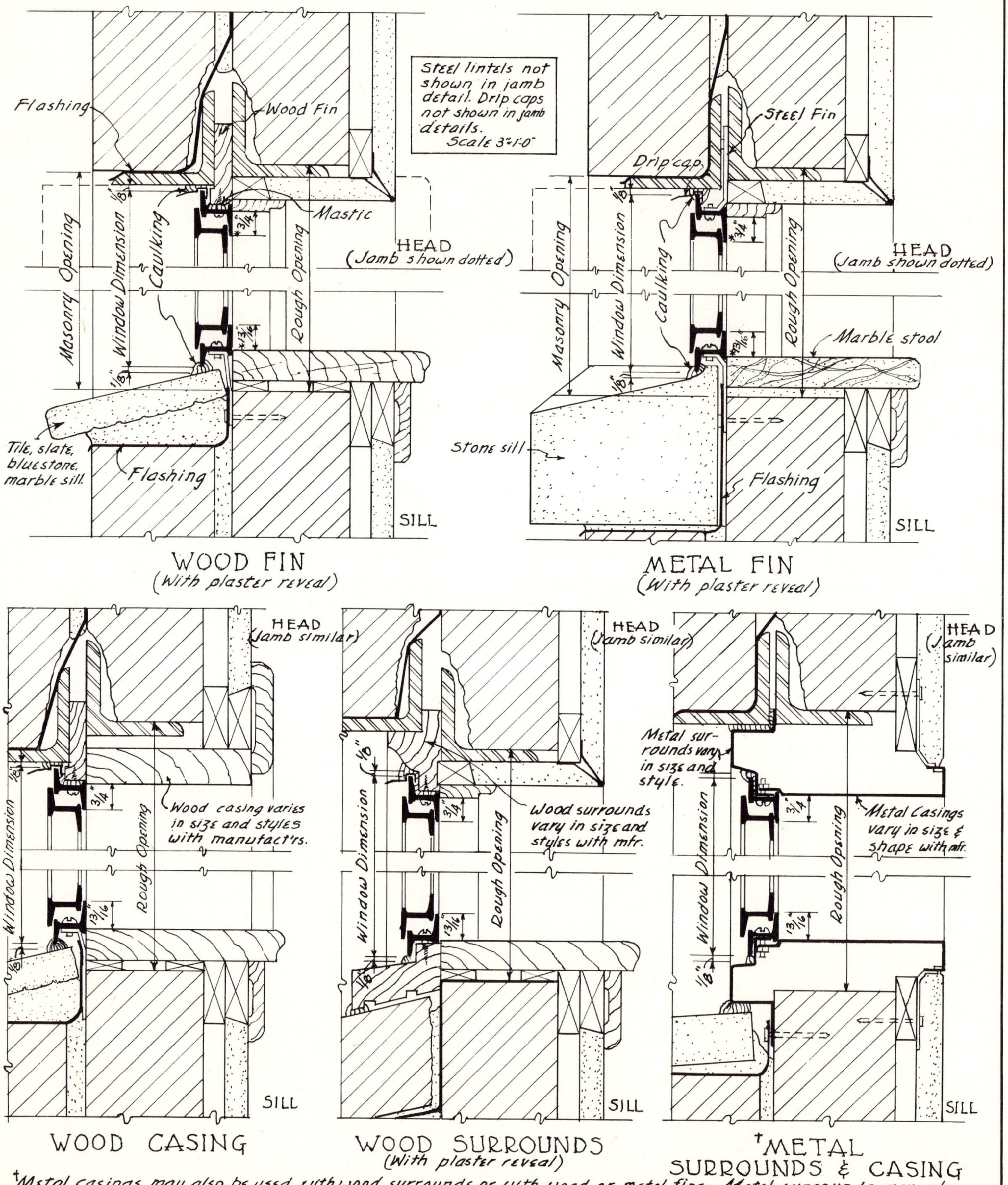
Steel lintels not shown in jamb detail. Drip caps not shown in jamb details.
Scale 3"=1'-0"
Flashing
Wood Fin
Mastic
Caulking
Masonry Opening
Window Dimension
Rough Opening
HEAD
(Jamb shown dotted)
Tile, slate, bluestone, marble sill.
Flashing
SILL
WOOD FIN
(With plaster reveal)
Steel Fin
Drip cap
Marble stool
Stone sill
Flashing
SILL
METAL FIN
(With plaster reveal)
HEAD
(Jamb similar)
Wood casing varies in size and styles with manufact'rs.
Window Dimension
Rough Opening
SILL
WOOD CASING
HEAD
(Jamb similar)
Wood surrounds vary in size and styles with mfr.
SILL
WOOD SURROUNDS
(With plaster reveal)
HEAD
(Jamb similar)
Metal surrounds vary in size and style.
Metal Casings vary in size & shape with mfr.
SILL
†METAL SURROUNDS & CASING

†Metal casings may also be used with wood surrounds or with wood or metal fins. Metal surrounds may also be used with plaster or wood casings. For note on supplies furnished by window manufacturers see page on "Residential Steel Casement Windows, Shingles on Frame" *Clearance varies with manufacturer.
Details checked by Hope's Windows, Inc.

RESIDENTIAL STEEL CASEMENT WINDOWS, MASONRY WALLS

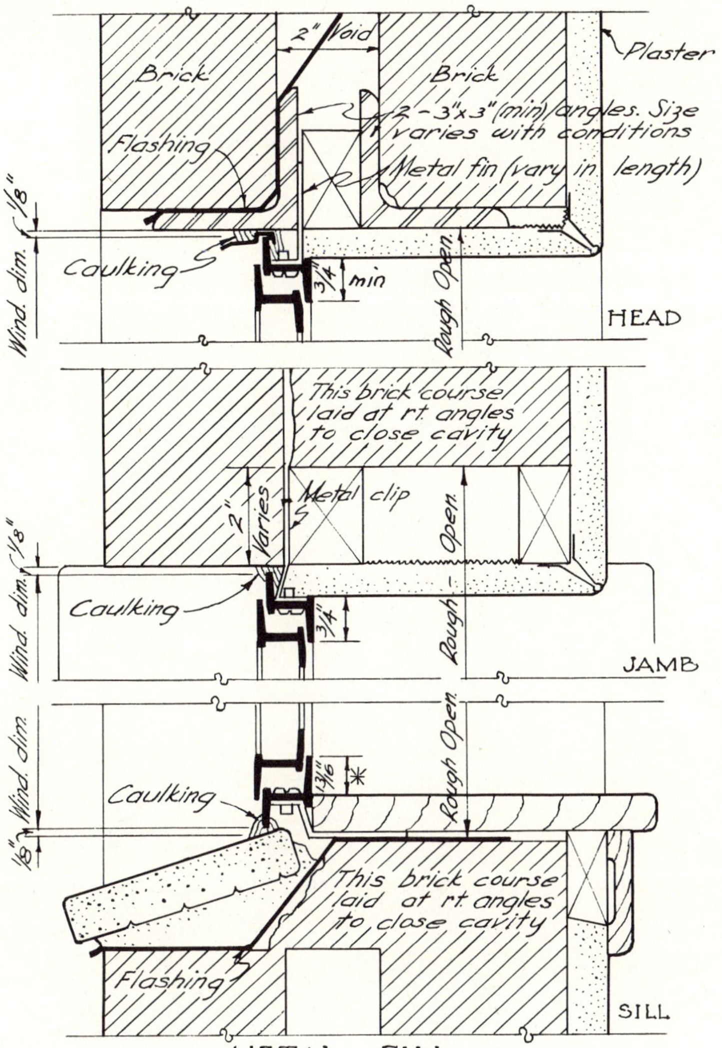
2" Void
Plaster
Brick
Brick
2-3"x3" (min) angles. Size varies with conditions
Flashing
Metal fin (vary in length)
1/8
Wind. dim.
Caulking
3/4 min
Rough Open
HEAD
This brick course laid at rt. angles to close cavity
Metal clip
2"
Varies
Caulking
3/4
Rough Open
JAMB
Wind. dim.
Caulking
13/16
*
Rough Open
1/8
This brick course laid at rt. angles to close cavity
Flashing
SILL

METAL FIN
(With 2-3"x3" steel angles as lintels)

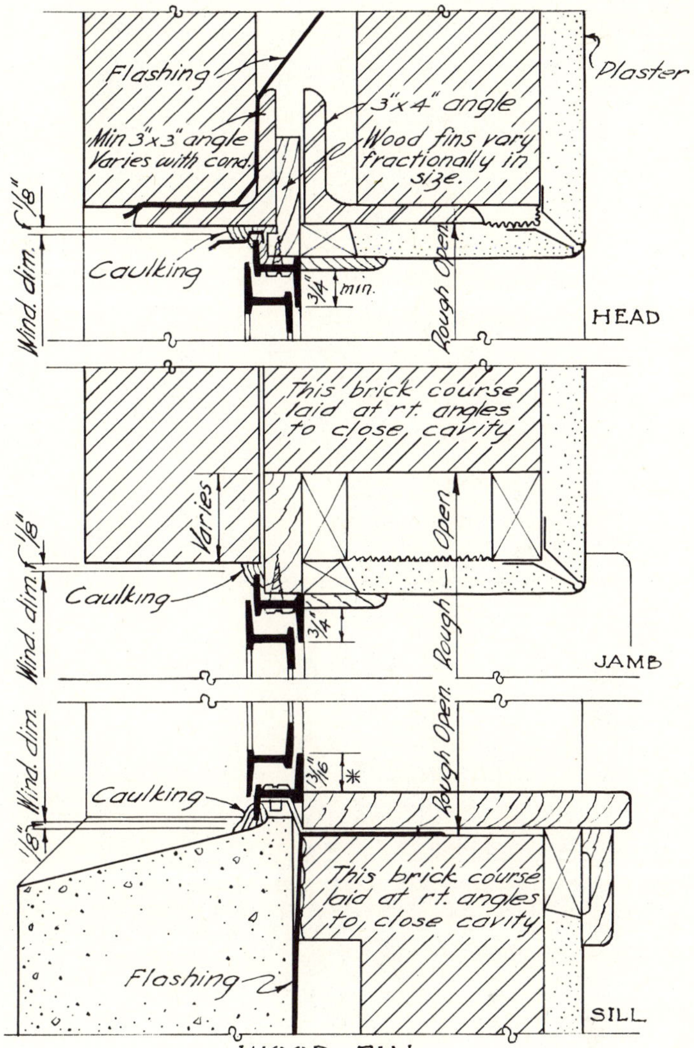
Plaster
Flashing
3"x4" angle
Min 3"x3" angle Varies with cond.
Wood fins vary fractionally in size.
1/8
Wind. dim.
Caulking
3/4 min.
Rough Open
HEAD
This brick course laid at rt. angles to close cavity
Varies
Caulking
3/4
Rough Open
JAMB
Wind. dim.
Caulking
13/16
*
Rough Open
1/8
This brick course laid at rt. angles to close cavity
Flashing
SILL

WOOD FIN
(With 1-3"x4" & 1-3"x3" steel angles as lintels)

BRICK CAVITY WALLS

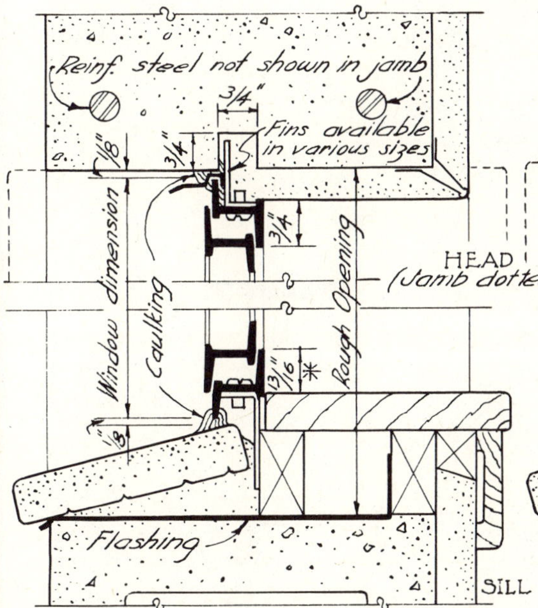
Reinf. steel not shown in jamb
3/4"
Fins available in various sizes
1/8
3/4
3/4
HEAD
(Jamb dotted)
Window dimension
Caulking
Rough Opening
13/16
*
1/8
Flashing
SILL

(Metal fin with precast lintel)

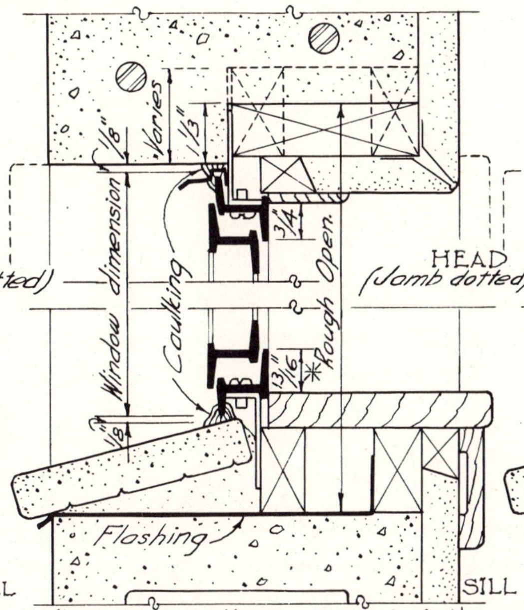
1/8
Varies
1/3
3/4
HEAD
(Jamb dotted)
Window dimension
Caulking
Rough Open.
13/16
*
1/8
Flashing
SILL

(Metal fin with precast lintel)

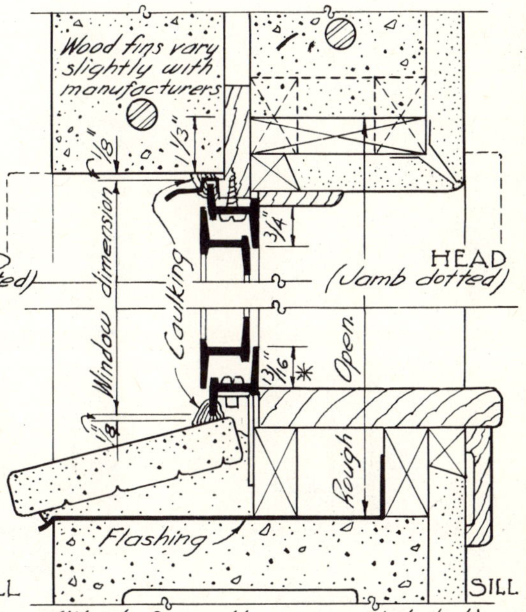
Wood fins vary slightly with manufacturers
1/8
1/3
3/4
HEAD
(Jamb dotted)
Window dimension
Caulking
Open.
Rough
13/16
*
1/8
Flashing
SILL

(Wood fin with precast lintel)

CONCRETE BLOCK or TILE WALLS

These details shown without furring; in some climates, however, furring is recommended. For note on supplies furnished by window manufacturers, see page on "Residential Steel Casement Windows, Shingles on Frame"
* Varies with manufacturer. Above details checked by Hope's Windows, Inc. Scale: 3" = 1'-0"

RESIDENTIAL STEEL CASEMENT, BAY WINDOWS

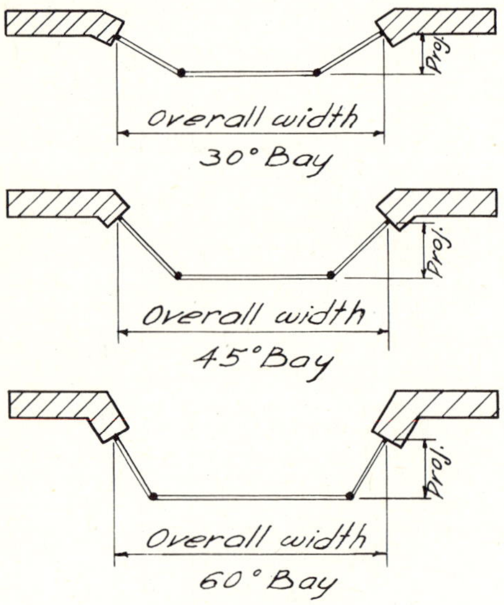
Proj.
Overall width
30° Bay
Proj.
Overall width
45° Bay
Proj.
Overall width
60° Bay

SPLAYED

ANGLE of BAY	Lights in Return	OVERALL WIDTH — Lights in Front Section *2	3	4	PROJECTION
30°	1	6'-1 1/8"	7'-5 1/4"	8'-9 1/2"	10"
	2	8'-8 1/8"	10'-0 1/4"	11'-4 1/2"	1'-6 7/8"
45°	1	5'-7 1/4"	6'-11 3/8"	8'-3 5/8"	1'-2 1/4"
	2	7'-8 1/2"	9'-0 5/8"	10'-4 7/8"	2'-2 7/8"
60°	1	4'-11 1/4"	6'-3 3/8"	7'-7 5/8"	1'-5 1/2"
	2	6'-5 1/8"	7'-9 1/4"	9'-1 1/2"	2'-9"

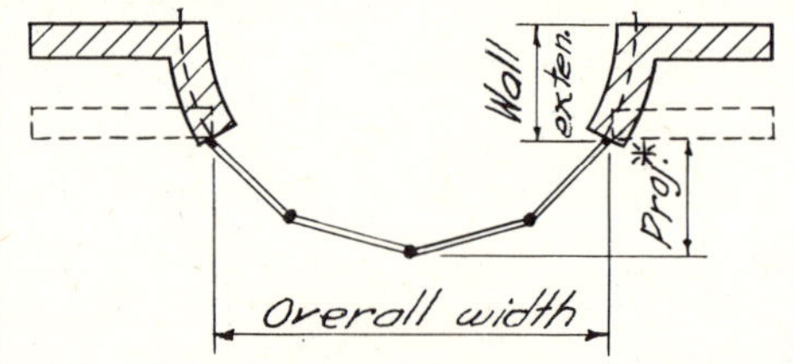
Wall exten.
Proj.*
Overall width

ROUND

* Shown below are formulae for obtaining the overall width, projection, and unit width in round bays.

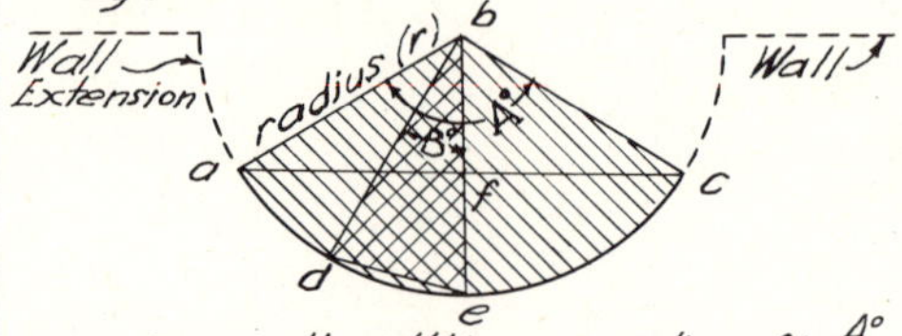
Wall Extension
Wall
radius (r)
b
B°
A°
a
c
f
d
e

ac (Overall width) = 2x radius x Sin $\frac{A°}{2}$
de (Unit width) = 2 x Sin B°/2
ef (Projection) = radius − bf (wall exten.)

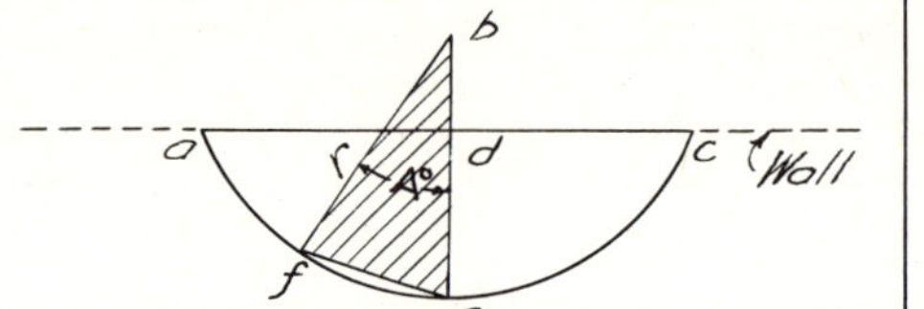
b
a
d
c
Wall
r
A°
f
e

Radius of arc (be) = [(dc)² + (de)²] ÷ (2 x de)
Overall width (ac) = wall opening (dc)
Unit width (fe) = 2 x r x Sin A°/2
Projection (de) = chord rise (de)

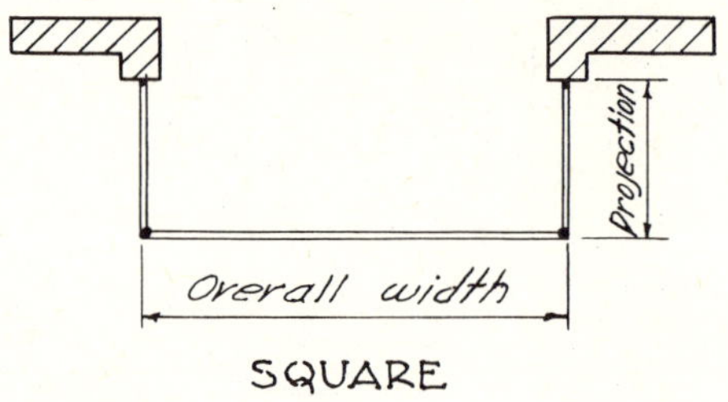
Projection
Overall width

SQUARE

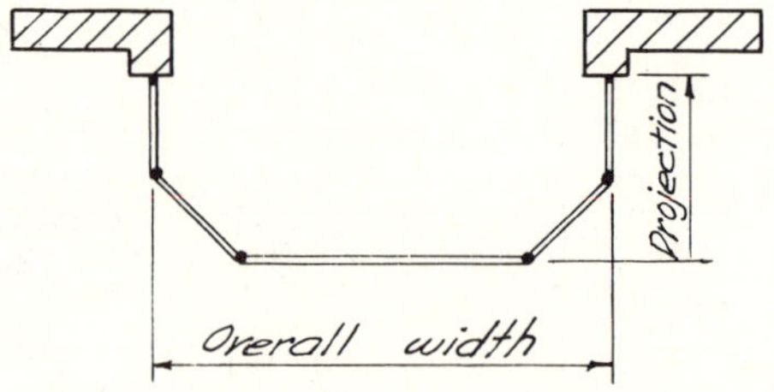
Projection
Overall width

SQUARE-SPLAYED

ANGLE of BAY	Lights in return	OVERALL WIDTH — Lights in Front Section *2	3	4	PROJECTION
SQUARE	1	3'-4"	4'-8 1/8"	6'-0 3/8"	1'-8 3/4"
	2	3'-4"	4'-8 1/8"	6'-0 3/8"	3'-2 5/8"
SQUARE SPLAYED	1	5'-8 1/4"	7'-0 3/8"	8'-4 5/8"	2'-10 7/8"
	2	7'-9 1/2"	9'-1 5/8"	10'-5 7/8"	5'-5 3/8"

* Dimensions based on single vent in returns & double (2) vented units in front.

Residence casements may be combined to form bay windows as suggested above. Such combinations require the use of bearing or non-bearing mullions. T-bar mullions cannot be used. Standard non-bearing mullions are generally supplied by the window manufacturer. These mullions are not designed to support any building construction. Structural angle shown below is only bearing mullion shown.

STANDARD BAY COMBINATIONS

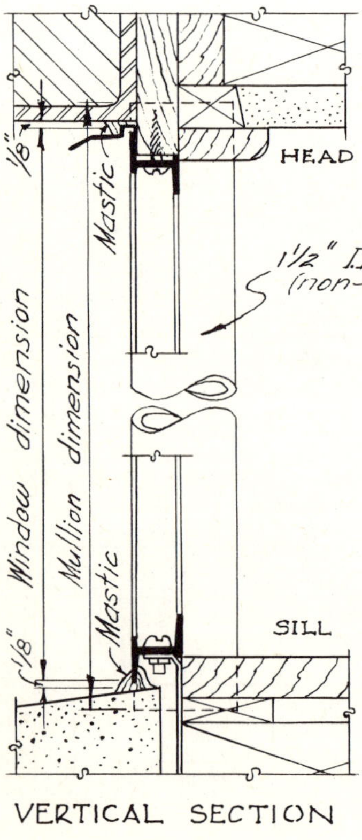
1/8"
HEAD
Mastic
1 1/2" I.D. Steel pipe (non-bearing)
Window dimension
Mullion dimension
Mastic
1/8
SILL

VERTICAL SECTION

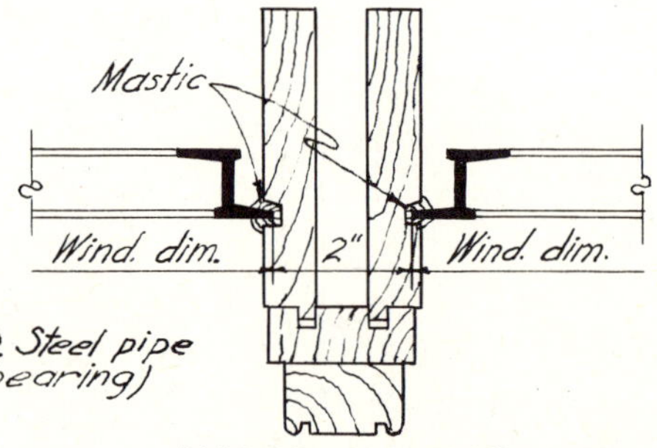
Mastic
Wind. dim.
2"
Wind. dim.

WOOD CASING

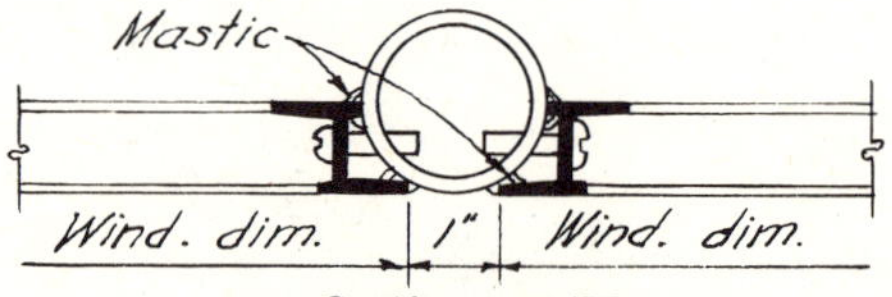
Mastic
Wind. dim.
1"
Wind. dim.

STRAIGHT
(Steel pipe mullion)

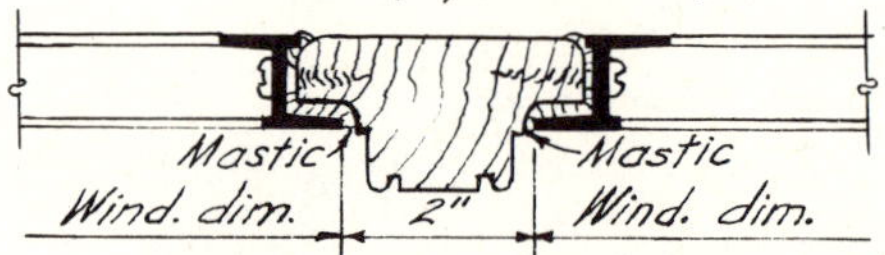
Mastic
Mastic
Wind. dim.
2"
Wind. dim.

WOOD SURROUND

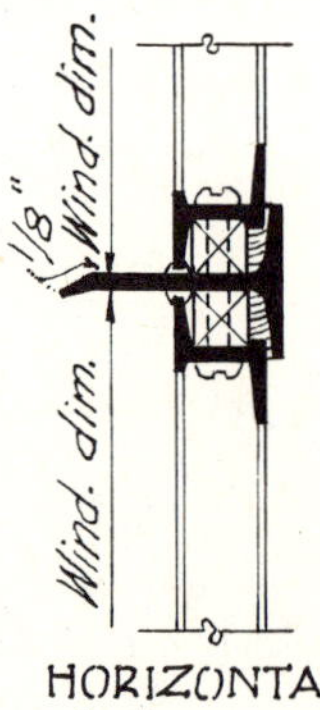
Wind. dim.
1/8"
Wind. dim.

HORIZONTAL "T"-BAR

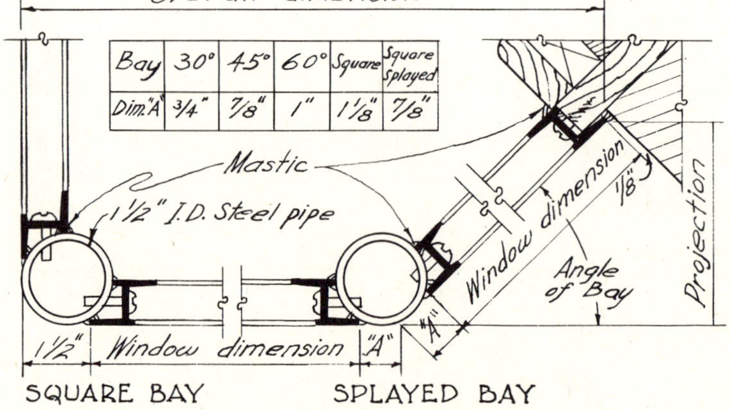
Overall dimension
Mastic
1 1/2" I.D. Steel pipe
Window dimension
1/8"
Angle of Bay
Projection
1 1/2"
Window dimension
"A"
"A"

Bay	30°	45°	60°	Square	Square Splayed
Dim. "A"	3/4"	7/8"	1"	1 1/8"	7/8"

SQUARE BAY — SPLAYED BAY

Wind. dim.
Wind. dim.
1/8"

VERTICAL "T"-BAR

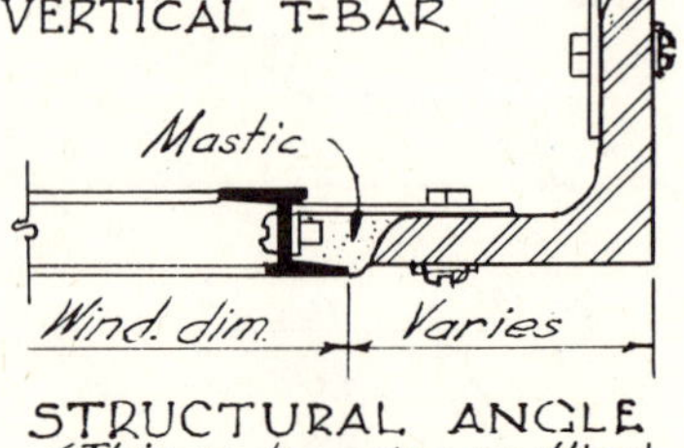
Mastic
Mastic
Wind. dim.
Varies

STRUCTURAL ANGLE
(This is bearing mullion)

MULLION DETAILS

Scale: 3" = 1'-0"

Checked by Hope's Windows, Inc.

INTERMEDIATE STEEL CASEMENT WINDOWS

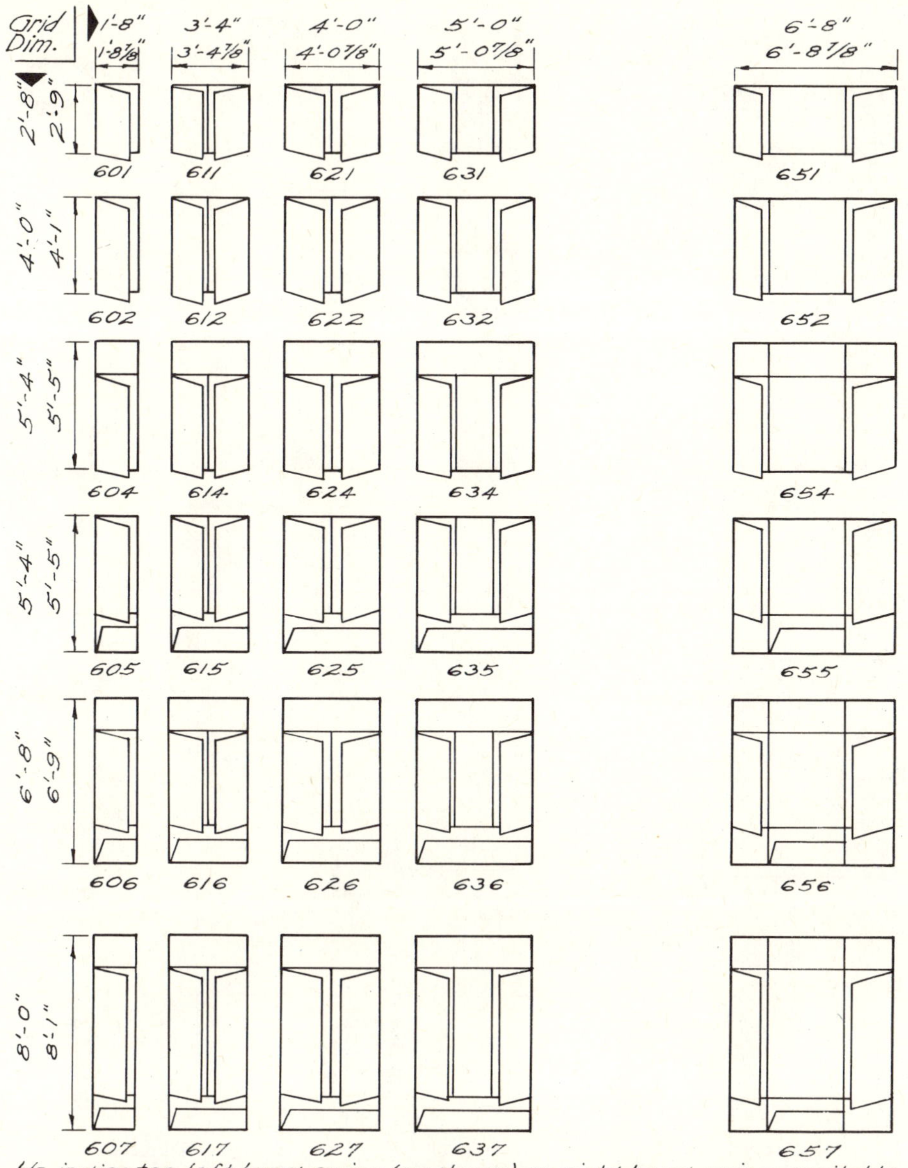
Grid Dim.
1'-8" 1'-8⅞"
3'-4" 3'-4⅞"
4'-0" 4'-0⅞"
5'-0" 5'-0⅞"
6'-8" 6'-8⅞"
2'-8" 2'-9"
601 611 621 631 651
4'-0" 4'-1"
602 612 622 632 652
5'-4" 5'-5"
604 614 624 634 654
5'-4" 5'-5"
605 615 625 635 655
6'-8" 6'-9"
606 616 626 636 656
8'-0" 8'-1"
607 617 627 637 657

L/R indicates left hand swing (as shown) or right hand swing available. Horizontal and/or vertical muntins may be added provided they are based on 20" or 24" bar centers for width, and 16" bar centers for height. Fixed or stationary units may be supplied for all types. Sill ventilators may be omitted & replaced with fixed sill lights. Measurements shown are window opening dimensions. Units are viewed from outside. These are standard sizes of the Steel Window Institute. Operator types: Rotary or handle.

INTERMEDIATE COMBINATION WINDOWS

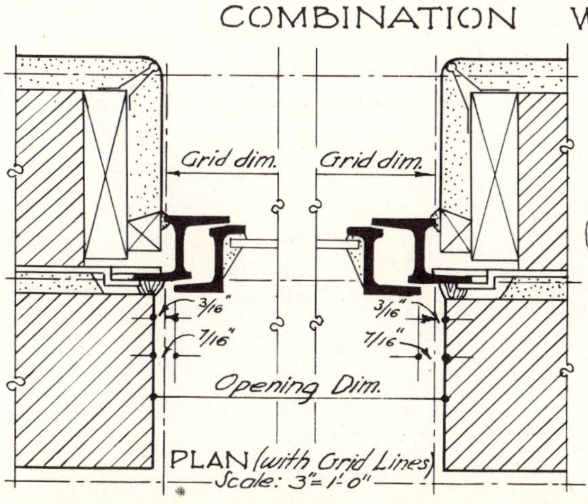
Grid dim.
Grid dim.
3/16"
7/16"
3/16"
7/16"
Opening Dim.

PLAN (with Grid Lines)
Scale: 3" = 1'-0"

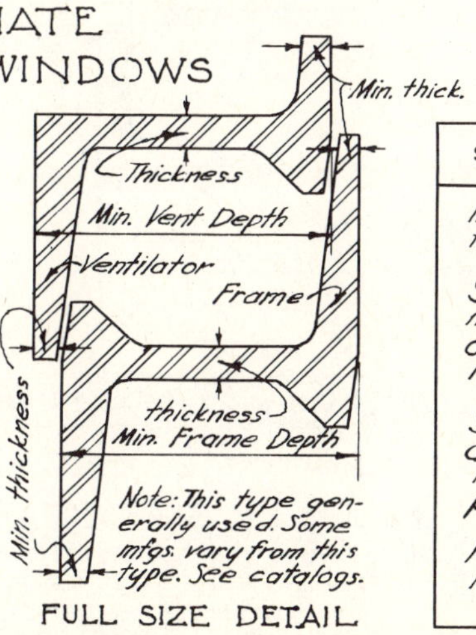
Min. thick.
Thickness
Min. Vent Depth
Ventilator
Frame
thickness
Min. Frame Depth
Min. Thickness
Note: This type generally used. Some mfgs. vary from this type. See catalogs.

FULL SIZE DETAIL

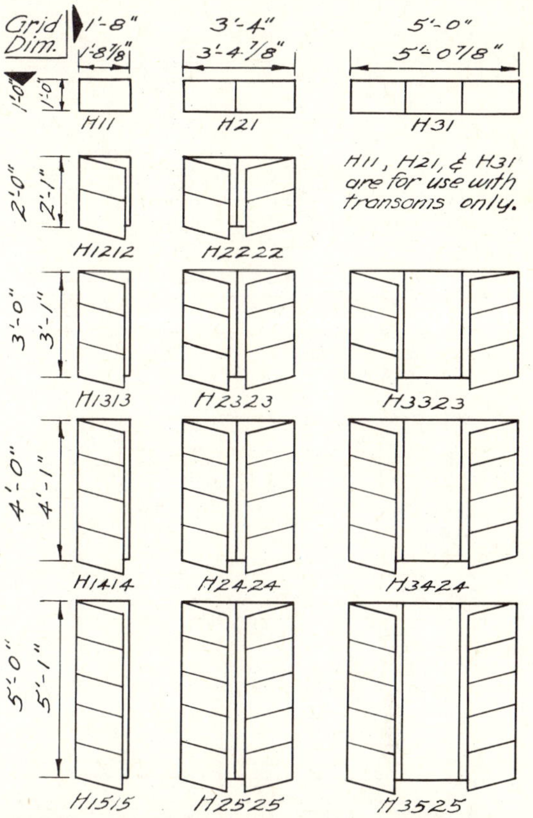
Grid Dim.
1'-8" 1'-8⅞"
3'-4" 3'-4⅞"
5'-0" 5'-0⅞"
1'-0" 1'-0"
H11 H21 H31
H11, H21, & H31 are for use with transoms only.
2'-0" 2'-1"
H1212 H2222
3'-0" 3'-1"
H1313 H2323 H3323
4'-0" 4'-1"
H1414 H2424 H3424
5'-0" 5'-1"
H1515 H2525 H3525

Note: Single ventilator units are furnished hinged at either left or right hand jamb. Glass sizes vary fractionally with different mfrs. Measurements shown are window opening dimensions. These are standard sizes of the Steel Window Institute. Units viewed from outside. Operator types: Rotary or handle. Notes on specials (not standard): Fixed units available for all vents. Muntins may be omitted.

INTERMEDIATE CASEMENTS

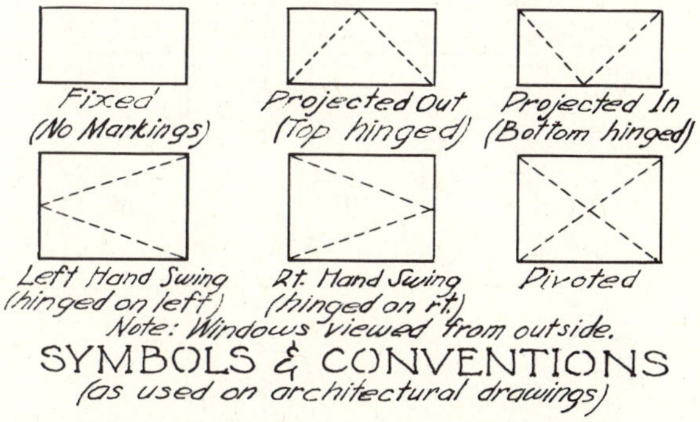
Fixed (No Markings)
Projected Out (Top hinged)
Projected In (Bottom hinged)
Left Hand Swing (hinged on left)
Rt. Hand Swing (hinged on rt.)
Pivoted

Note: Windows viewed from outside.

SYMBOLS & CONVENTIONS
(as used on architectural drawings)

SIZE AND WEIGHTS of CASEMENTS

Intermediate casement is classified as intermediate and intermediate heavy.

Size of intermediate ventilator and casement frame sections is up to 1¼". Weight of casement (vent and frame) is not less than 3#/lin. ft.

Size of intermediate heavy ventilator and casement sections is not less than 1 5/16". The minimum weight is 3½# per lin. ft.

Min. thickness equals ⅛" and weathering tolerances vary from 1/64" to 1/32".

STEEL ARCHITECTURAL and INTERMEDIATE PROJECTED WINDOWS

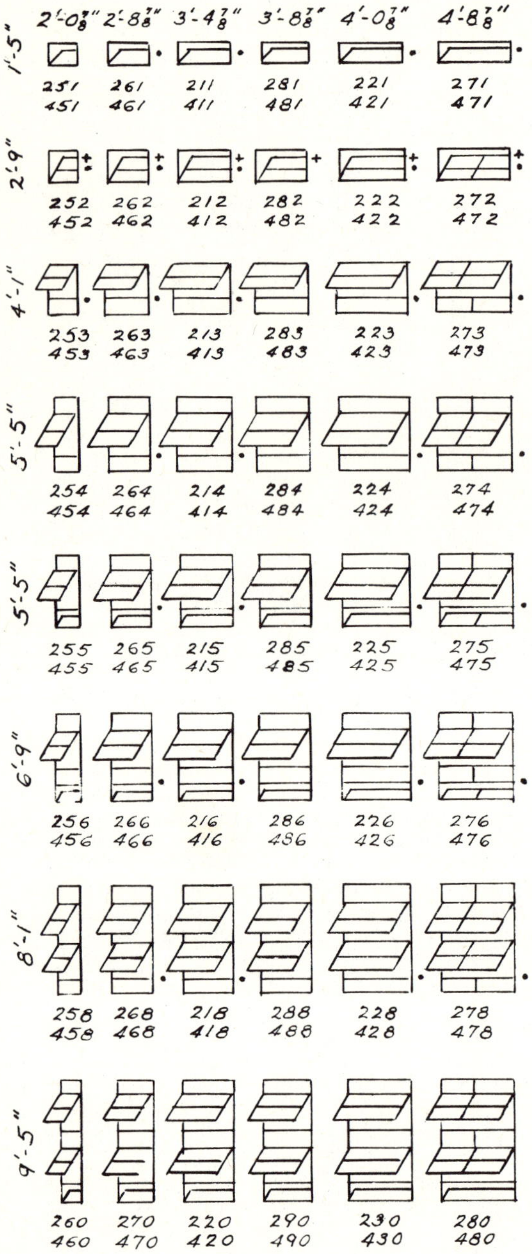
2'-0 7/8" 2'-8 7/8" 3'-4 7/8" 3'-8 7/8" 4'-0 7/8" 4'-8 7/8"
1'-5"
251 261 211 281 221 271
451 461 411 481 421 471
2'-9"
252 262 212 282 222 272
452 462 412 482 422 472
4'-1"
253 263 213 283 223 273
453 463 413 483 423 473
5'-5"
254 264 214 284 224 274
454 464 414 484 424 474
5'-5"
255 265 215 285 225 275
455 465 415 485 425 475
6'-9"
256 266 216 286 226 276
456 466 416 486 426 476
8'-1"
258 268 218 288 228 278
458 468 418 488 428 478
9'-5"
260 270 220 290 230 280
460 470 420 490 430 480

+ Also "A" series (top hinged), proj. out.
• Indicates warehouse types with swing of vents only as indicated. All windows viewed from outside.

200 series indicate Architectural Proj. 400 series indicate Intermediate Proj. Vertical muntins may be added, if desired, provided they are based on 20" or 24" bar centers. Fixed or stationary units may be supplied for all types shown. All vents shown to project out may be made to project in, provided all vents in the same unit project in. Dimensions shown are window opening dimensions. These are standard sizes of the Steel Window Institute.

STANDARD WINDOW SIZES

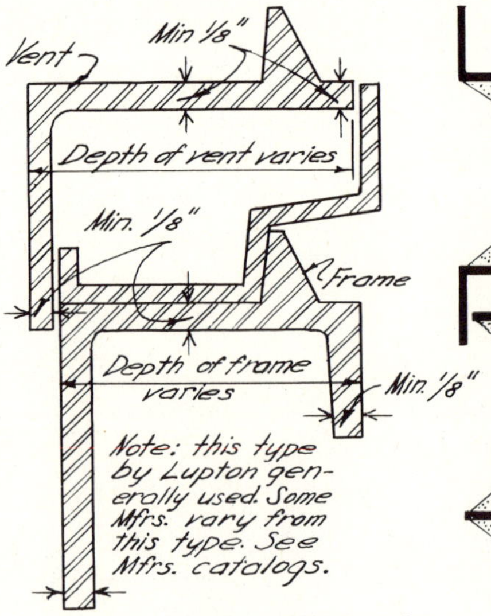
Vent
Min 1/8"
Depth of vent varies
Min. 1/8"
Frame
Depth of frame varies
Min. 1/8"
Note: this type by Lupton generally used. Some Mfrs. vary from this type. See Mfrs. catalogs.

FULL SIZE SECTION

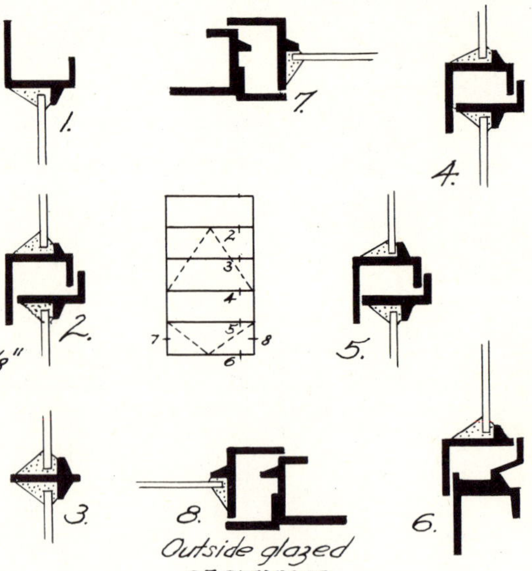
1.
2.
3.
4.
5.
6.
7.
8.
2'
3'
4'
5'
6'
7
8

Outside glazed SECTIONS

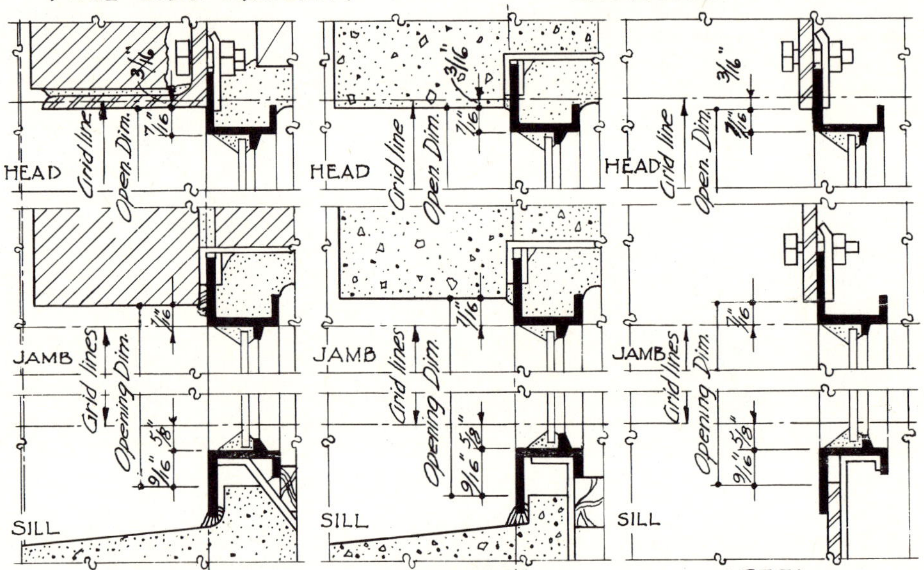
HEAD
JAMB
SILL
Grid line
Open. Dim.
3/16"
7/16"
Grid lines
Opening Dim.
5/8"
9/16"

BRICK CONCRETE STEEL
3" = 1'-0"
WALL SECTIONS

ARCHITECTURAL PROJ. WINDOW DETAILS

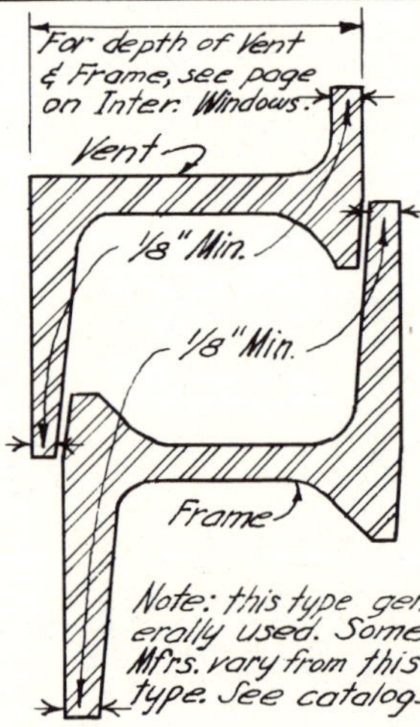
For depth of Vent & Frame, see page on Inter. Windows.
Vent
1/8" Min.
1/8" Min.
Frame
Note: this type generally used. Some Mfrs. vary from this type. See catalogs.

FULL SIZE SECTION

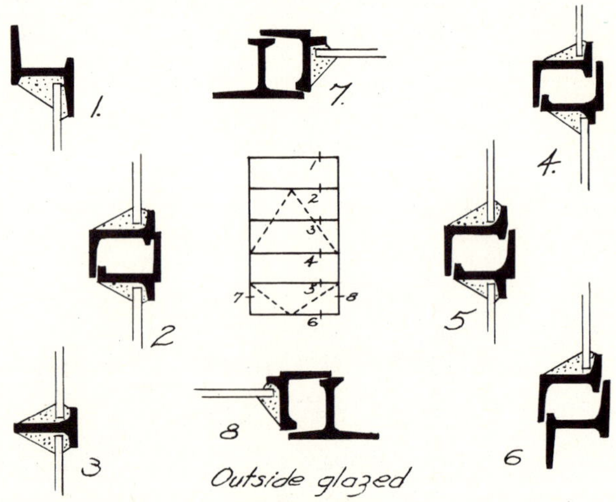
1.
2
3
4.
5
6
7.
8
1
2
3
4
5
6
7
8

Outside glazed SECTIONS

Note: For other sections, see page on "Intermediate Steel Casement Windows". See also page on "Modular Coordination."

INTERMEDIATE PROJ. WINDOW DETAILS

Checked by Hope's Windows, Inc.

STEEL COMMERCIAL PROJECTED WINDOWS

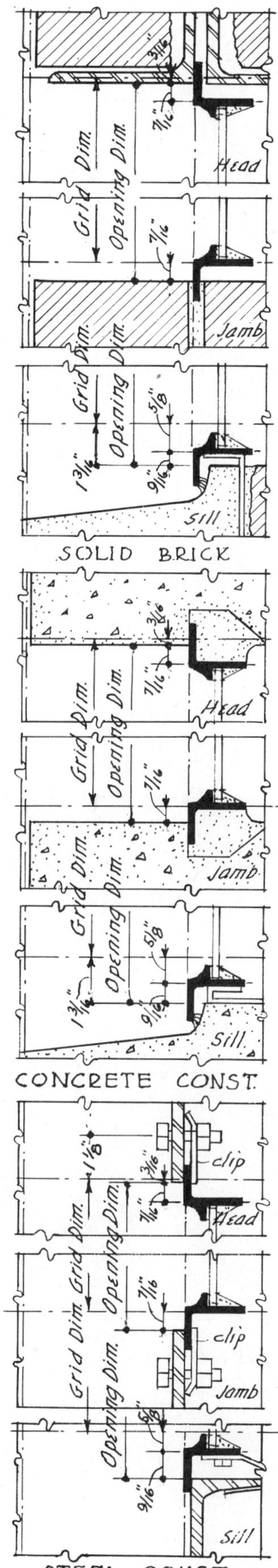
Grid Dim.
Opening Dim.
Head
Jamb
Sill
3/16
7/16
5/8
9/16
1 3/16"
clip
1 1/8

SOLID BRICK

CONCRETE CONST.

STEEL CONST.
SECTIONS
(Showing Grid) 3" = 1'-0"

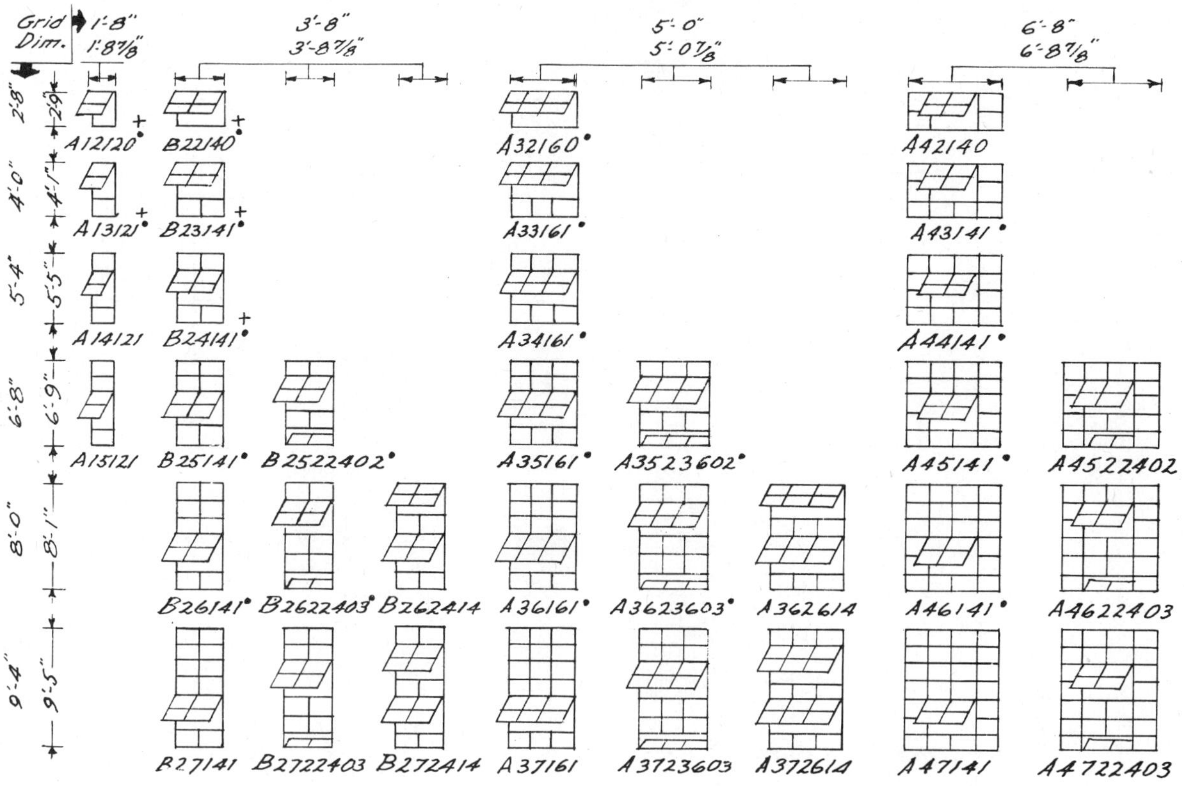
Grid Dim.
1'-8"
1'-8 7/8"
3'-8"
3'-8 7/8"
5'-0"
5'-0 7/8"
6'-8"
6'-8 7/8"
2'-8"
2'-9"
4'-0"
4'-1"
5'-4"
5'-5"
6'-8"
6'-9"
8'-0"
8'-1"
9'-4"
9'-5"
A12120 +
B22140• +
A32160•
A42140
A13121• +
B23141• +
A33161•
A43141•
A14121
B24141• +
A34161•
A44141•
A15121
B25141•
B2522402•
A35161•
A3523602•
A45141•
A4522402
B26141•
B2622403•
B262414
A36161•
A3623603•
A362614
A46141•
A4622403
B27141
B2722403
B272414
A37161
A3723603
A372614
A47141
A4722403

"A" indicates 2" x 16" bar centers; "B", 2.2" x 16" bar centers. + indicates lights made to project in and are warehouse types. Units marked "•" with vents as shown, are warehouse types and sizes.

All vents shown to project out may be made to project in provided all vents in same unit project in, but are not warehouse types.

Measurements shown are window opening dimensions with the exception of Grid Dimensions. For further information on coordinating steel windows with Grid see pages on Modular Coordination.

Operators: Latch, plus pole for vents out of reach.

All windows viewed from outside.

Above sizes are standards of the Steel Window Institute.

STANDARD WINDOW SIZES

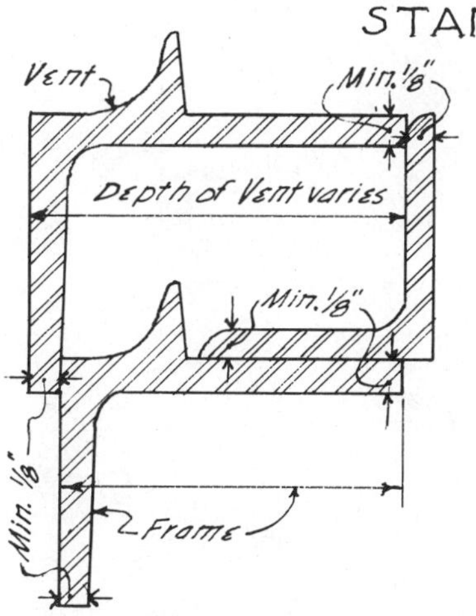
Vent
Min. 1/8"
Depth of Vent varies
Min. 1/8"
Min. 1/8"
Frame

FULL SCALE
SECTION

Note: this type generally used. Types vary in size and design with mfr. See mfrs.' catalogs.

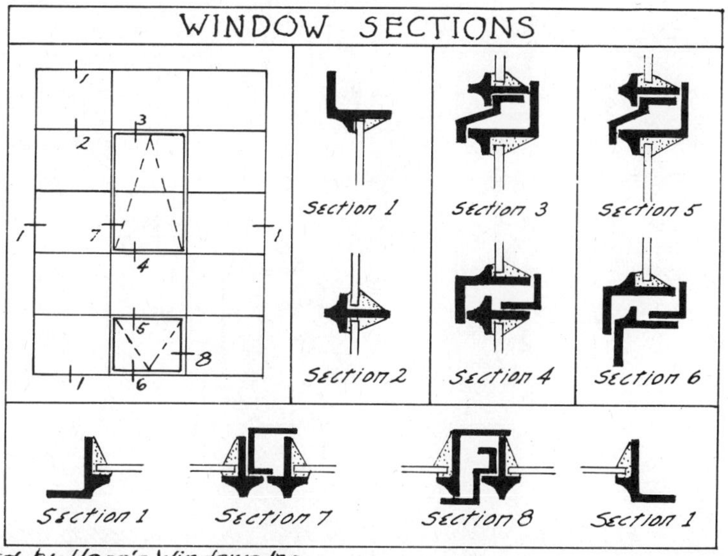
WINDOW SECTIONS
1
2
3
4
5
6
7
8
Section 1
Section 2
Section 3
Section 4
Section 5
Section 6
Section 1
Section 7
Section 8
Section 1

Details checked by Hope's Windows, Inc.

STEEL PIVOTED WINDOWS

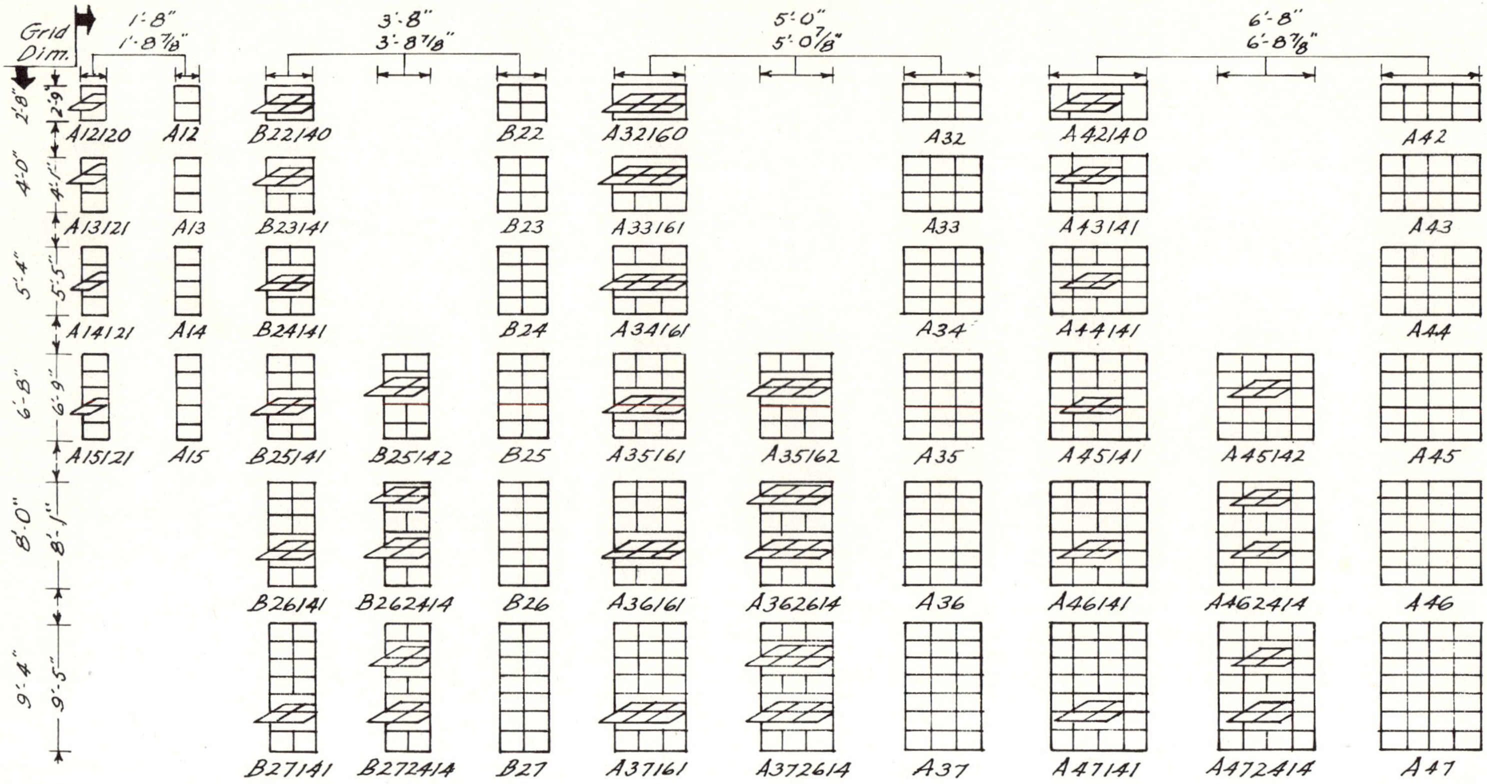
Grid Dim.
1'-8"
1'-8 7/8"
3'-8"
3'-8 7/8"
5'-0"
5'-0 7/8"
6'-8"
6'-8 7/8"
2'-8"
2'-9"
4'-0"
4'-1"
5'-4"
5'-5"
6'-8"
6'-9"
8'-0"
8'-1"
9'-4"
9'-5"
A12120 A12 B22140 B22 A32160 A32 A42140 A42
A13121 A13 B23141 B23 A33161 A33 A43141 A43
A14121 A14 B24141 B24 A34161 A34 A44141 A44
A15121 A15 B25141 B25142 B25 A35161 A35162 A35 A45141 A45142 A45
B26141 B262414 B26 A36161 A362614 A36 A46141 A462414 A46
B27141 B272414 B27 A37161 A372614 A37 A47141 A472414 A47

Notes on standard pivoted windows: "A" indicates 20"x16" bar centers; "B", 22"x16" bar centers.

All measurements with the exception of the Grid Dimensions are window opening dimensions. For information on coordinating steel windows with the grid see pages on Modular Coordination.

Ventilators are horizontally pivoted approximately 2" above center. Operators: stay bars for vents within reach, latch and chain for vents out of reach. Glass sizes vary fractionally with mfrs.

All windows viewed from outside.

Above sizes are standards of the Steel Window Institute.

PIVOTED WINDOWS

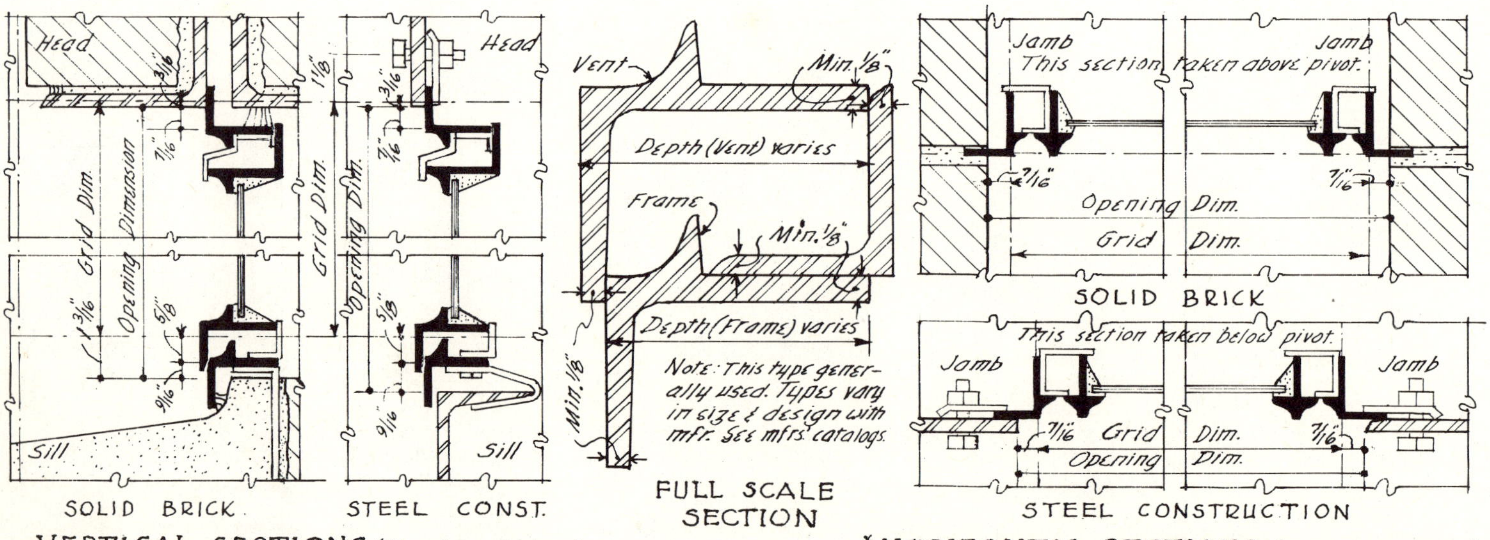
Head
3/16"
1 1/8"
7/16
Grid Dim.
Opening Dimension
1 3/16
5/8
9/16
Sill
Grid Dim.
Opening Dim.
Head
3/16
7/16
5/8
9/16
Sill
SOLID BRICK
STEEL CONST.
Vent
Min. 1/8"
Depth (Vent) varies
Frame
Min. 1/8
Depth (Frame) varies
Min. 1/8
Note: This type generally used. Types vary in size & design with mfr. See mfrs. catalogs.
FULL SCALE SECTION
Jamb
This section taken above pivot.
Jamb
7/16
7/16
Opening Dim.
Grid Dim.
SOLID BRICK
This section taken below pivot.
Jamb
Jamb
7/16
Grid Dim.
7/16
Opening Dim.
STEEL CONSTRUCTION

VERTICAL SECTIONS (Showing grid lines)
Scale: 3"=1'-0"

*HORIZONTAL SECTIONS (Showing grid lines)
Scale: 3" = 1'-0"

*When designing multiple unit openings, the total opening width may be determined by using Grid Dimensions of windows times the number of such units plus 4" for standard mullions plus 7/8" (clearance at jamb). See pages on Modular Coordination

Details checked by Hopes Windows, Inc.

STEEL PSYCHIATRIC, SECURITY and CONTINUOUS WINDOWS - DOORS

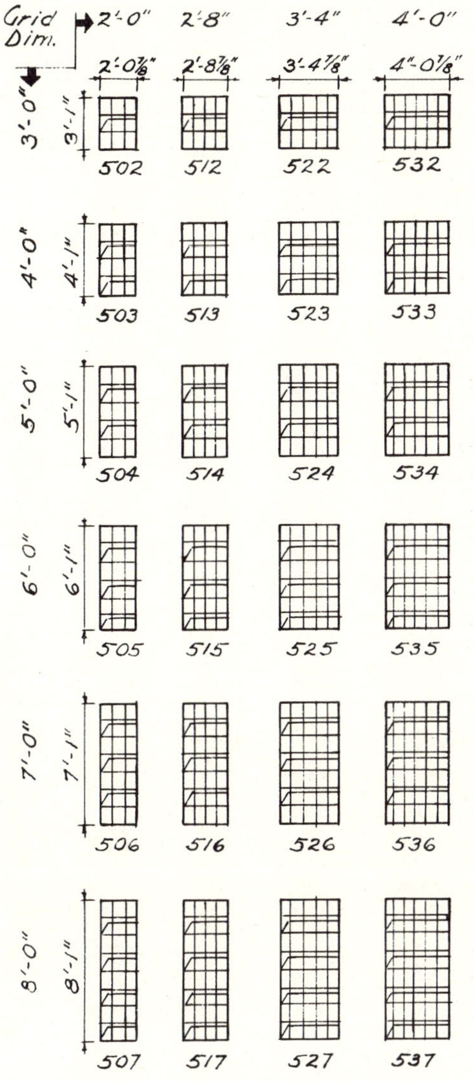

Grid Dim.
2'-0"
2'-8"
3'-4"
4'-0"
2'-0⅞"
2'-8⅞"
3'-4⅞"
4'-0⅞"
3'-0"
3'-1"
502
512
522
532
4'-0"
4'-1"
503
513
523
533
5'-0"
5'-1"
504
514
524
534
6'-0"
6'-1"
505
515
525
535
7'-0"
7'-1"
506
516
526
536
8'-0"
8'-1"
507
517
527
537

Restraining arms limit opening of ventilators to 5". Dimensions shown are opening dimensions with the exception of the Grid dimensions.

PSYCHIATRIC PROJ.

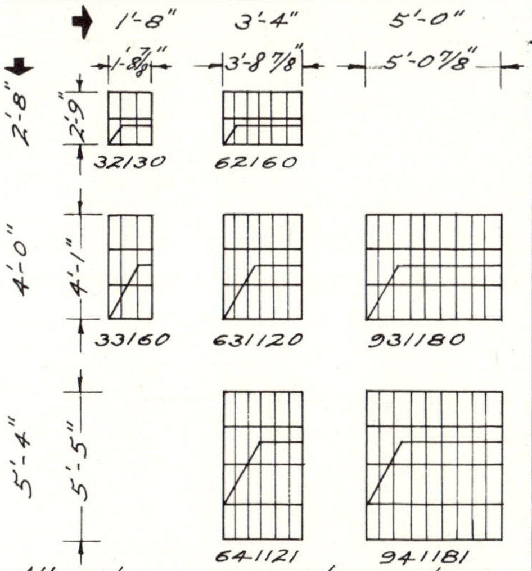

1'-8"
3'-4"
5'-0"
1'-8⅞"
3'-8 7/8"
5'-0⅞"
2'-8"
2'-9"
32130
62160
4'-0"
4'-1"
33160
631120
931180
5'-4"
5'-5"
641121
941181

All units are warehouse types. Measurements shown are opening dim. with the exception of the Grid dim. Vents open behind fixed unit muntins.

SECURITY

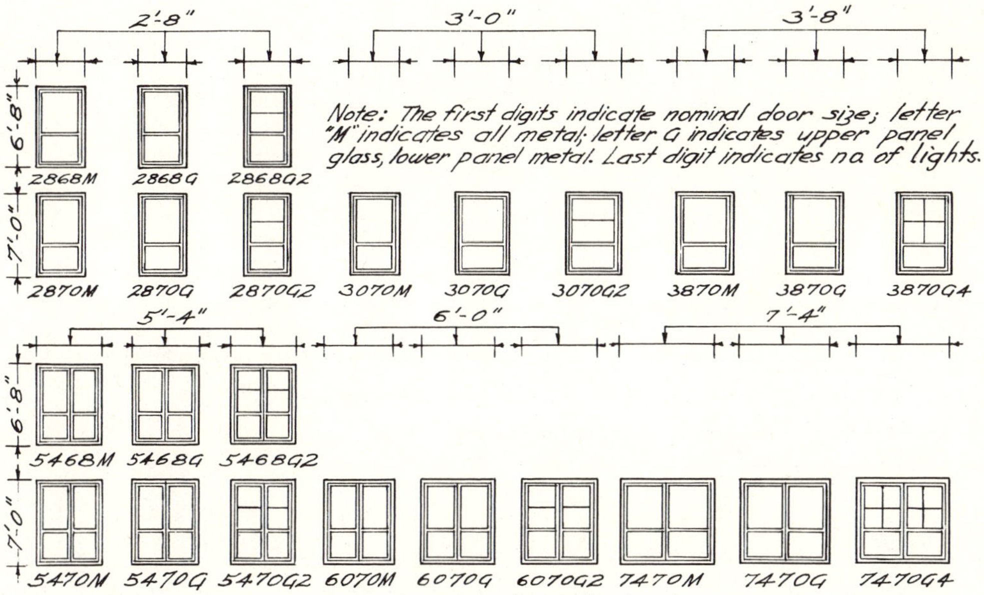

2'-8"
3'-0"
3'-8"
6'-8"
2868M
2868G
2868G2
7'-0"
2870M
2870G
2870G2
3070M
3070G
3070G2
3870M
3870G
3870G4
5'-4"
6'-0"
7'-4"
5468M
5468G
5468G2
5470M
5470G
5470G2
6070M
6070G
6070G2
7470M
7470G
7470G4

Note: The first digits indicate nominal door size; letter "M" indicates all metal; letter G indicates upper panel glass, lower panel metal. Last digit indicates no. of lights.

Note: Swing doors 6'-8" & 7'-0" high furnished standard with pressed metal frames machined for doors and hardware. They may also be installed in structural frames if desired, but such frames are furnished and machined by others. Hardware for the above doors: Mortise type Lock & Strikes (latch-bit key or cylinder-master-keyed), chain bolt (double door only), Foot bolt (double door only), push & pull plates, butts (1½ pair per leaf), door checks and door stops.

SWING DOORS

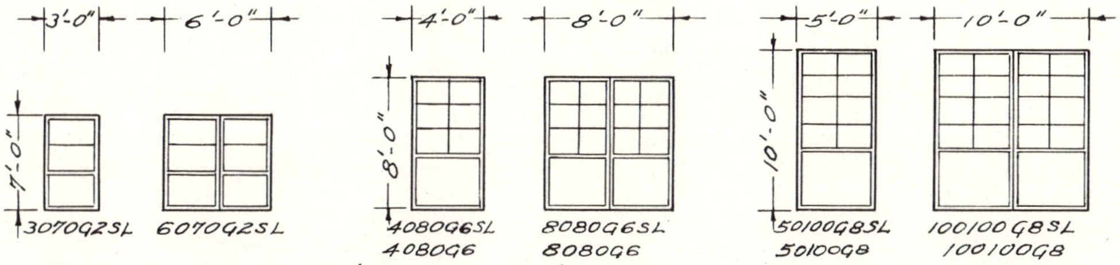

3'-0"
6'-0"
4'-0"
8'-0"
5'-0"
10'-0"
7'-0"
8'-0"
10'-0"
3070G2SL
6070G2SL
4080G6SL
4080G6
8080G6SL
8080G6
50100G8SL
50100G8
100100G8SL
100100G8

Slide doors (SL): Furnished for structural frames only. Frames furnished and machined by others. Hardware: Hasp & staple (for padlock), binder-end-stop, center stop-guides, track & hangers, trolley & clevis, and door pulls.
Large swing doors: Furnished for structural frames only. Frames furnished and machined by others. Hardware: Tee latch (for padlock), chain bolt (for double door only), foot bolt (double door only), and butts (2 pair per leaf).
Note: All doors viewed from outside. Hasp and staple inside only.

SWING and SLIDE DOORS

CONTINUOUS WINDOWS - OPERATORS

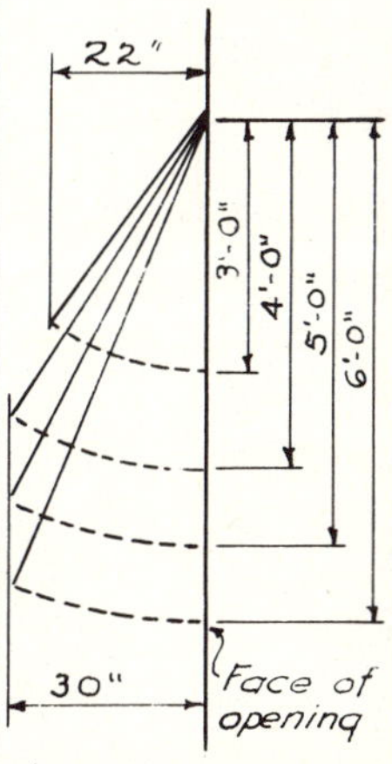

22"
3'-0"
4'-0"
5'-0"
6'-0"
30"
Face of opening

Vertical muntins on normal 2 foot centers. Standard length units at even foot op'ngs.

PIVOTED WINDOW OPERATORS

TYPE	LEVER (1" PIPE)				RACK & PINION (1" PIPE)				
CONTROL	MANUAL				MANUAL				ELEC.
	DUST*		OIL+		DUST*		OIL+		OIL INCL.
	CHAIN	ROD	CHAIN	ROD	CHAIN	ROD	CHAIN	ROD	
SASH OP. 16"	100'	80'	150'	120'	160'	140'	200'	180'	240'

PROJECTED WINDOW OPERATORS

TYPE	RACK & PINION				
CONTROL	MANUAL				ELEC.
	DUST*		OIL+		
	CHAIN	ROD	CHAIN	ROD	
	100'	90'	140'	120'	200'

TOP HUNG WINDOW OPERATORS

TYPE			RACK & PINION	TENSION	
CONTROL			MANUAL OR ELEC.	MANUAL	ELECTRIC
LIMITS	SASH	HEIGHT	1" PIPE	1" PIPE	1" PIPE
	VERT.	3'-4'-5'-6'	150'	200'	300'
	30° SLOPE	3'-0"	120'	160'	240'
		4'-0"	100'	140'	210'
		5'-0"	80'	120'	180'
		6'-0"	60'	100'	150'

*Dust-protected cast gearing: +Oil-enclosed cut gearing

These are standard sizes of the Steel Window Institute.

METAL WINDOW SILLS

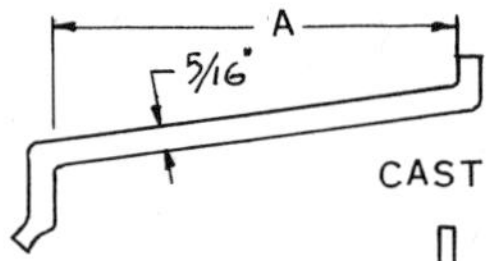
A
5/16"

A	4"	4¼"	5"

CAST IRON SILL

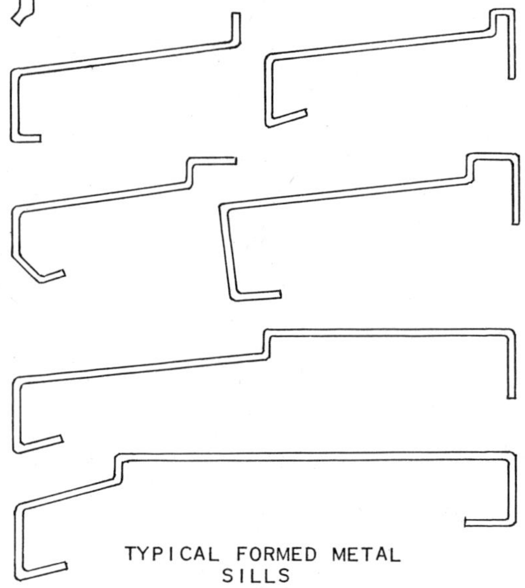

TYPICAL FORMED METAL SILLS

Data supplied by National Association of Architectural Metal Mfrs.

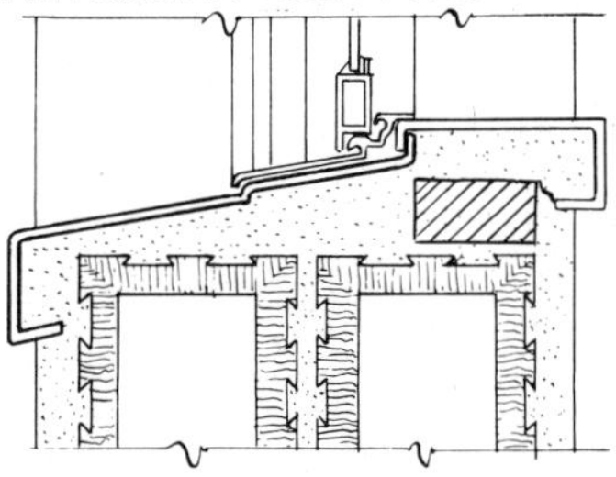

MASONRY WALL WITH METAL WINDOW FORMED SILL & STOOL

Scale: 1½" = 1'-0"

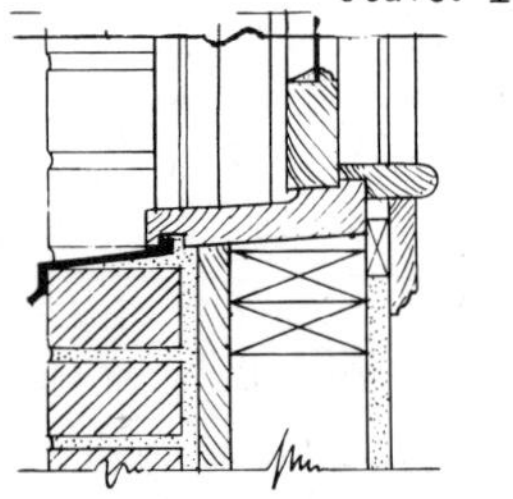

BRICK VENEER WITH WOOD WINDOW

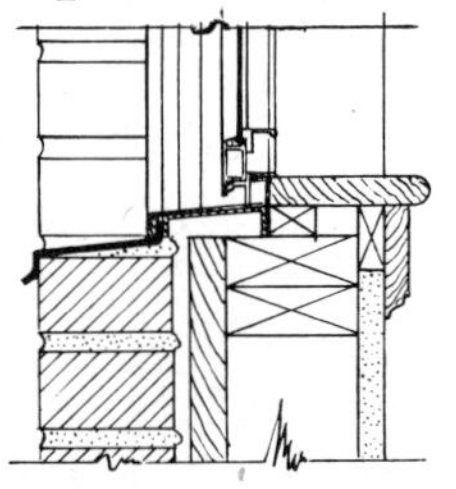

BRICK VENEER WITH ALUM. DOUBLE HUNG WINDOW

Scale: 1" = 1'-0"

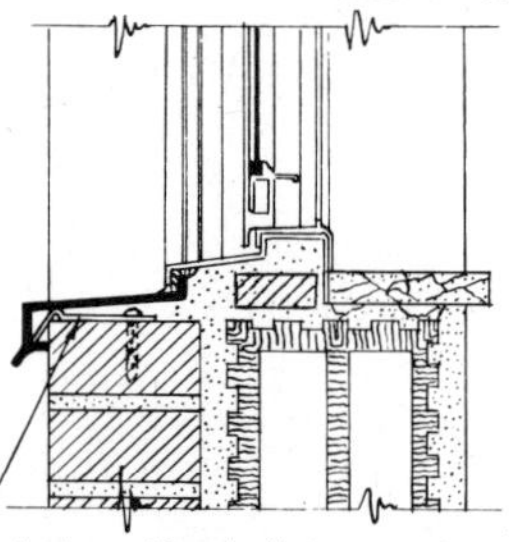

Anchor clip shall be attached with 2" cadmium plated masonry nails

MASONRY WALL WITH CONTINUOUS LINE OF DOUBLE HUNG WINDOWS

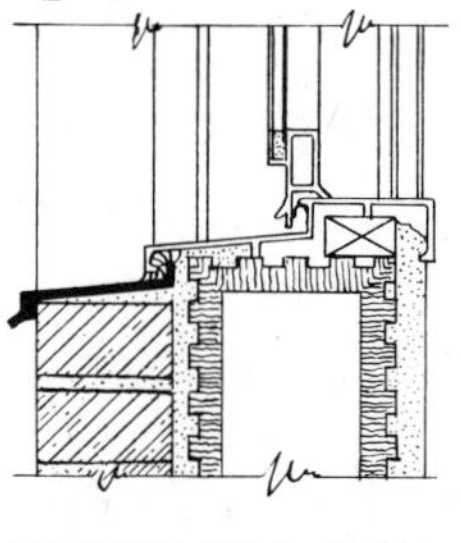

MASONRY WALL WITH ALUM. DOUBLE HUNG WINDOW

Scale: 1" = 1'-0"

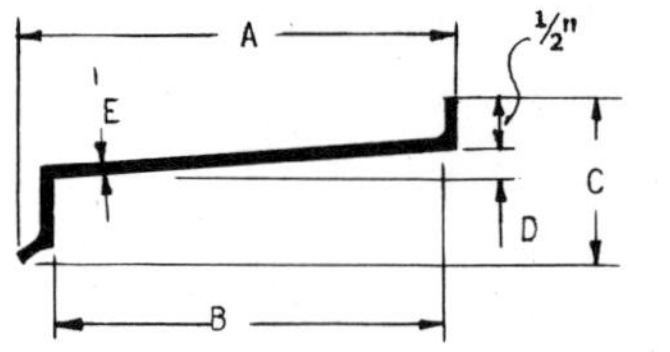
A
½"
E
C
D
B

For Lug Sills

Extend into brick joints at window jambs and allow ¼" space for expansion at ends.

For Continuous Sills

At joints allow ¼" to ⅜" for expansion and flash joints.

A	B	C	D	E	Std.No.	Mfr.	
3- 7/16"	3"	1- 9/16"	3/16"	3/32"	37734	A	
3-29/32"		1- 1/2"			P-3684	R	*
3-15/16"	3-1/2"	1-19/32"	7/32"	3/32"	37735	A	
4-13/32"		1-17/32"			P-3683	R	*
4- 7/16"	4"	1- 5/8"	1/4"	3/32"	37736	A	
4- 7/8"		1- 9/16"			3686	R	
4-15/16"	4-1/2"	1-21/32"	9/32"	3/32"	37737	A	
5- 3/8"		1- 9/16"			3687	R	
5- 7/16"	5"	1-11/16"	5/16"	3/32"	37738	A	
5- 7/8"		1- 5/8"			3685	R	
5-15/16"	5-1/2"	1-23/32"	11/32"	3/32"	37739	A	
6-15/32"		1-21/32"			P-3689	R	*
6- 1/2"	6"	1- 3/4"	3/16"	1/8"	37740	A	*
7"	6-1/2"	1-25/32"	3/16"	1/8"	37741	A	*
7- 1/2"	7"	1-13/16"	3/16"	1/8"	37742	A	*
8- 1/16"	7-1/2"	1-29/32"	1/4"	5/32"	37743	A	*
9- 1/16"	8-1/2"	1-31/32"	1/4"	5/32"	37745	A	*

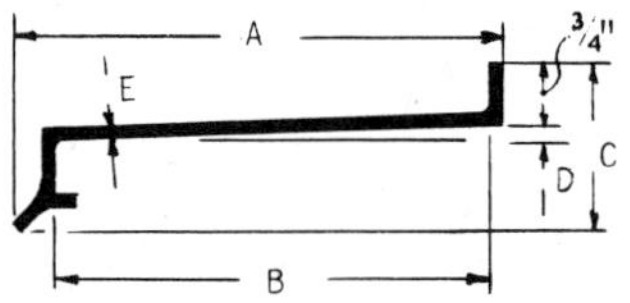
A
¾"
E
C
D
B

Used for continuous line of windows. Provide ¼" to ⅜" expansion space at jamb or butt joints of continuous sills.

A	B	C	D	E	Std.No.	Mfr.
3-1/2"	2-3/4"	1-13/16"	3/16"	1/8"	54684	A
4"	3-1/4"	1-27/32"	7/32"	1/8"	54685	A
4-1/2"	3-3/4"	1- 7/8"	1/4"	1/8"	54686 9558	A R
5"	4-1/4"	1-29/32"	9/32"	1/8"	54687 13008	A R
5-1/2"	4-3/4"	1-15/16"	5/16"	1/8"	54688 13009	A R
6"	5-1/4"	1-31/32"	11/32"	1/8"	54689	A
6-9/16"	5-3/4"	2"	3/8"	5/32"	54690	A
7-9/16"	6-3/4"	2-1/16"	7/16"	5/32"	54691	A
8-1/8"	7-1/4"	2-5/32"	15/32"	3/16"	54692	A
9-1/8"	8-1/4"	2-7/32"	17/32"	3/16"	54693	A

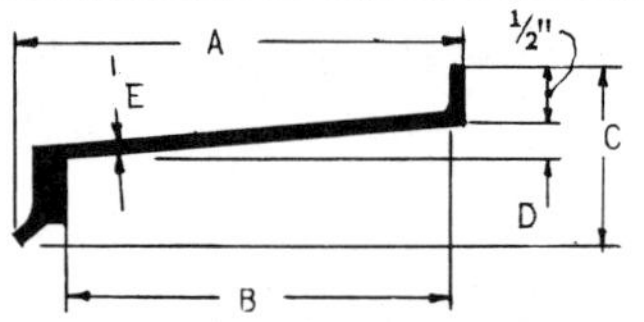
A
½"
E
C
D
B

For Slip Sills

Used with heavy section d-h window. Allow ¼" to ⅜" clearance at ends. Coulk water-tight against jamb.

A	B	C	D	E	Std.No.	Mfr.	
3- 5/8"	2-15/16	1- 9/16"	3/16"	3/16"	2013	A	*
4- 3/8"	3-11/16	1-11/16"	5/16"	3/16"	2883	A	*
4-11/16"	4"	1- 9/16"	3/16"	3/16"	1538	A	*
5- 1/8"	4- 7/16	1-11/16"	5/16"	3/16"	2826	A	*
5- 3/4"	5- 1/16	1- 9/16"	3/16"	3/16"	2231	A	*
5- 7/8"	5- 3/16	1- 9/16"	3/16"	3/16"	5454	A	*
6- 3/4"	6- 1/16	1-11/16"	5/16"	3/16"	6881	A	*
7- 3/16"	6- 1/2"	1-11/16"	5/16"	3/16"	6882	A	*
9- 3/8"	8-15/16	1- 9/16"	3/16"	3/16"	8030	A	*
10- 3/8"	9-11/16	1- 9/16"	3/16"	3/16"	8029	A	*

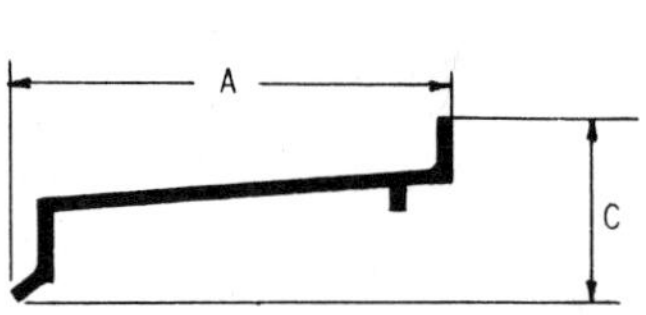
A
C

A	B	C	D	E	Std. No	Mfr.	
3-1/2"		1- 9/16"			P-3692	R	*
4"		1-19/32"			P-3691	R	*
4-1/2"		1- 5/8"			P-3690	R	*
5"		1-21/32"			P-3126	R	*
5-1/2"		1-11/16"			P-3127	R	*
6"		1-23/32"			P-3128	R	*
9-1/16"		1-29/32"			P-3230	R	*

R

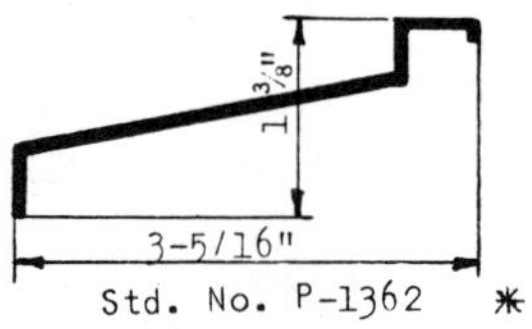
1-3/8"
3-5/16"

Std. No. P-1362 *

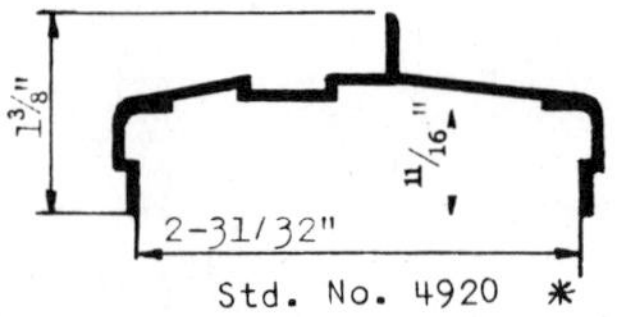
1-3/8"
11/16"
2-31/32"

Std. No. 4920 *

Not to scale

Sills may be made to fit posts or mullions, and may be mitered at corners. Sills over eight feet in length should have central anchorage to keep them in proper position.

* Non-warehouse items

Data supplied by: A = Aluminum Company of America R = Reynolds Metals Company

STORE FRONTS

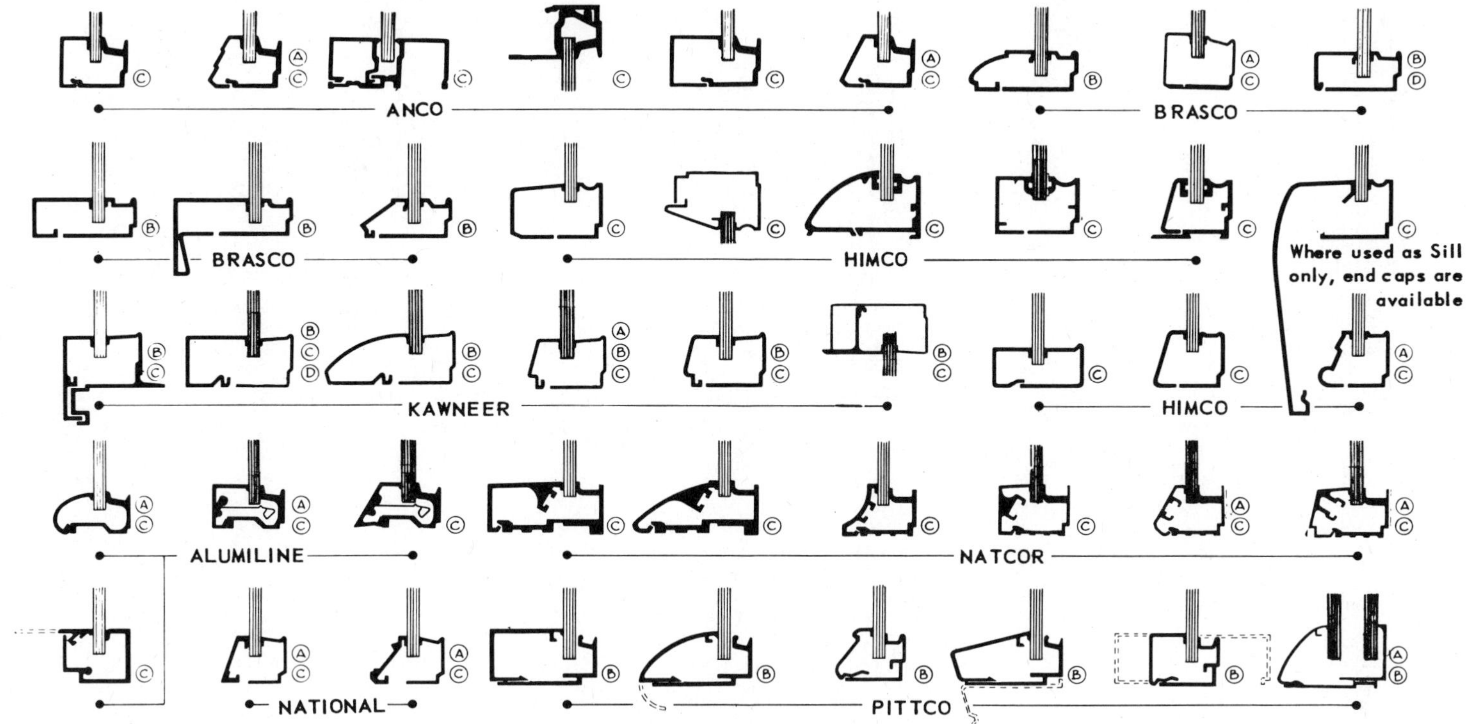
ANCO
BRASCO
BRASCO
HIMCO
Where used as Sill only, end caps are available
KAWNEER
HIMCO
ALUMILINE
NATCOR
NATIONAL
PITTCO

SELECTION OF MOULDINGS
Taken from leading manufacturers

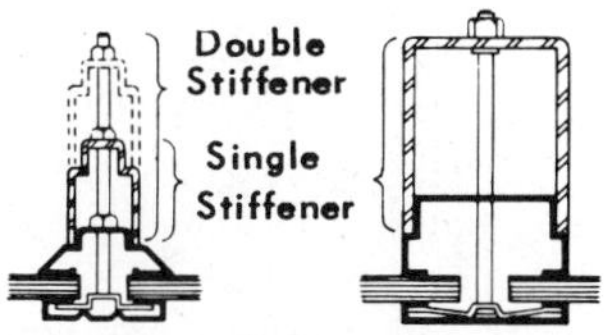
Double Stiffener
Single Stiffener

TYPICAL DIVISION BARS FOR LARGE GLASS SIZES

Where glass size is not too great. Butted Joints with Crane clips, thru bolted, may be used. Space clips approx. 3'-0" O.C.

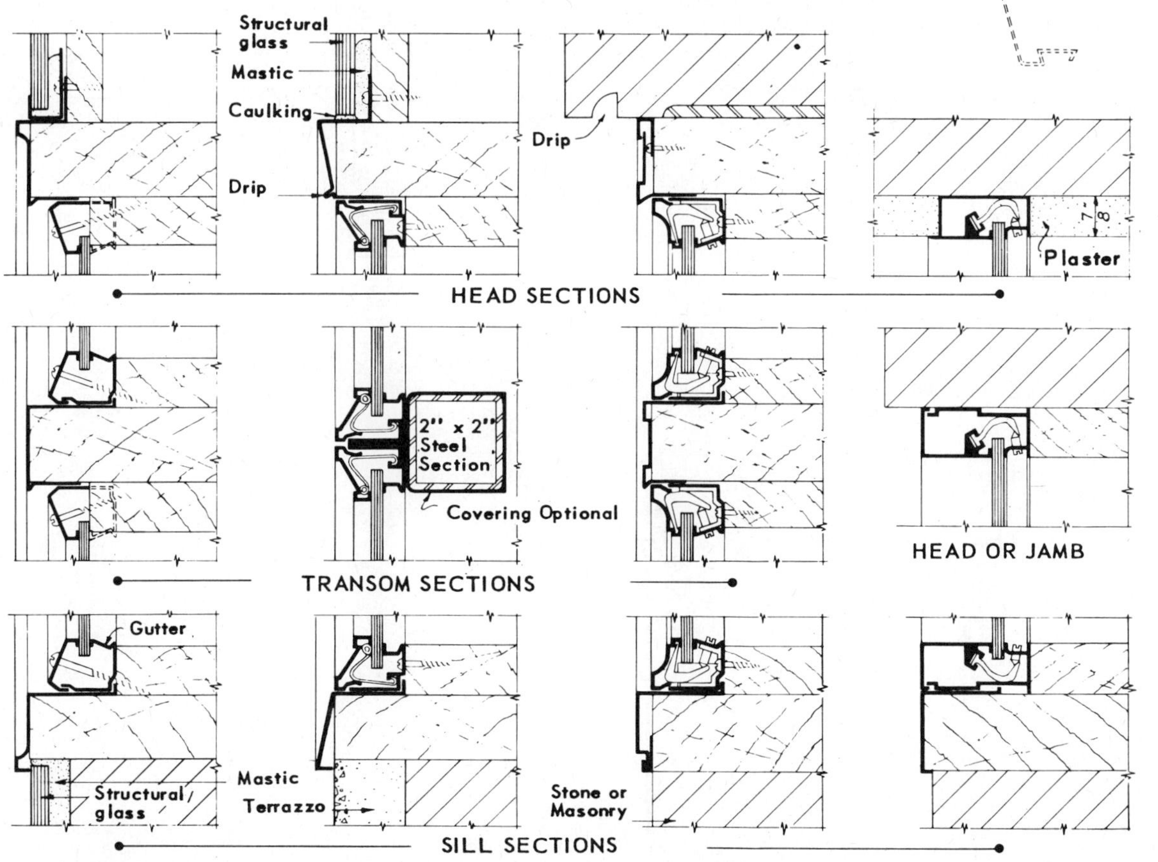
Structural glass
Mastic
Caulking
Drip
Drip
7/8
Plaster
HEAD SECTIONS
2" x 2" Steel Section
Covering Optional
TRANSOM SECTIONS
HEAD OR JAMB
Gutter
Structural glass
Mastic
Terrazzo
Stone or Masonry
SILL SECTIONS

OUTSIDE SET TYPE A
Economical Glass may be replaced from outside.

SNAP-ON TYPE B (spring clip)
No exposed screw heads. setting from outside

INSIDE SET TYPE C
Self-adjusting to glass thick. Glass not removable from outside.

FLUSH TYPE D
Eliminates projecting mouldings. Adaptable to other jambs or sills.

Scale 3" = 1'-0"

SETTING DETAILS

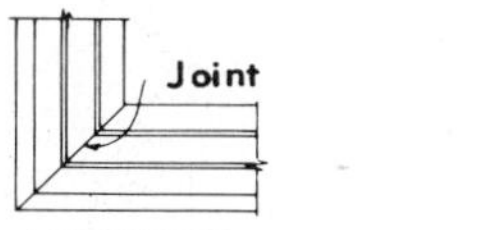
Joint

MITERED

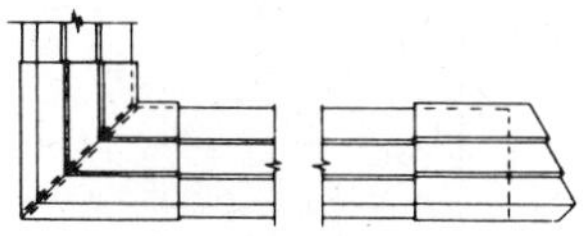

CAPPED

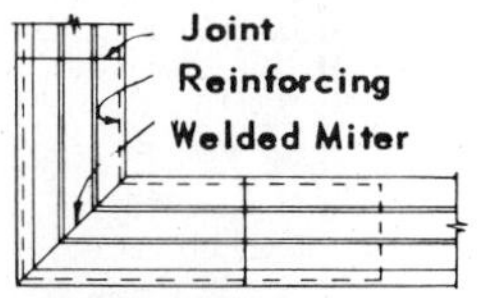
Joint
Reinforcing
Welded Miter

WELDED MITER

For Curved Glass, mouldings may be bent to radius: 12" min. for Rolled sections. 18" min. for Extruded sections.

CORNER DETAILS

Data prepared by DANIEL SCHWARTZMAN, Architect

COMBINATION SCREEN and STORM SASH

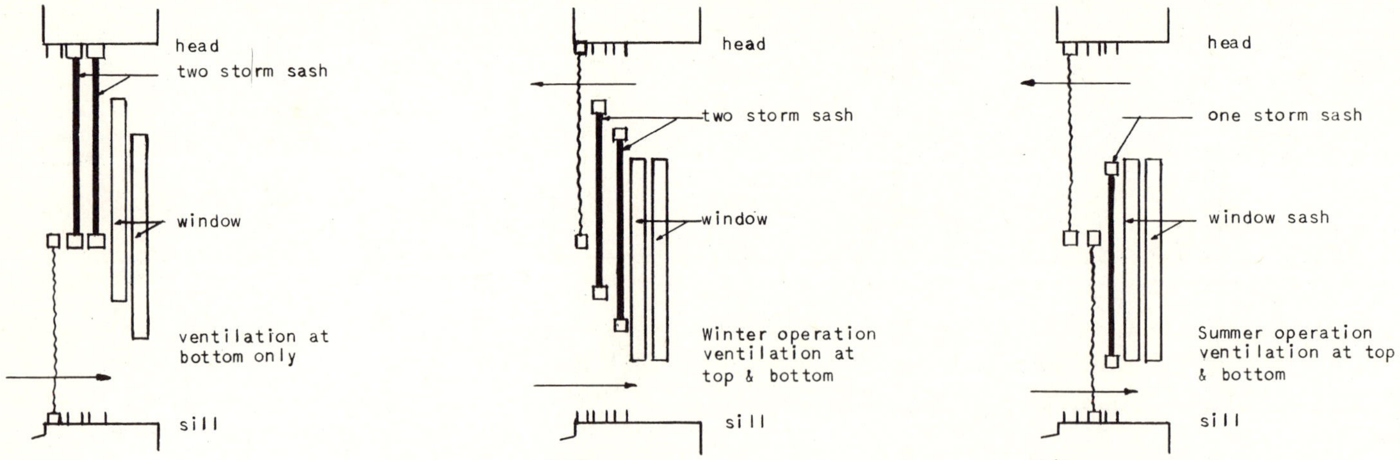
head
two storm sash
window
ventilation at
bottom only
sill
head
two storm sash
window
Winter operation
ventilation at
top & bottom
sill
head
one storm sash
window sash
Summer operation
ventilation at top
& bottom
sill

1-½ screen
2-storm sash
3 CHANNEL

1-½ screen
2-storm sash
3 CHANNEL

2-½ screens
1-storm sash
3 CHANNEL

Exterior operable ½ screen - operable storm sash.
NOTE: For proper ventilation in summer & winter two screens & storm sash sections should be used. In the winter, one screen section must be stored. In the summer one storm sash must be stored.

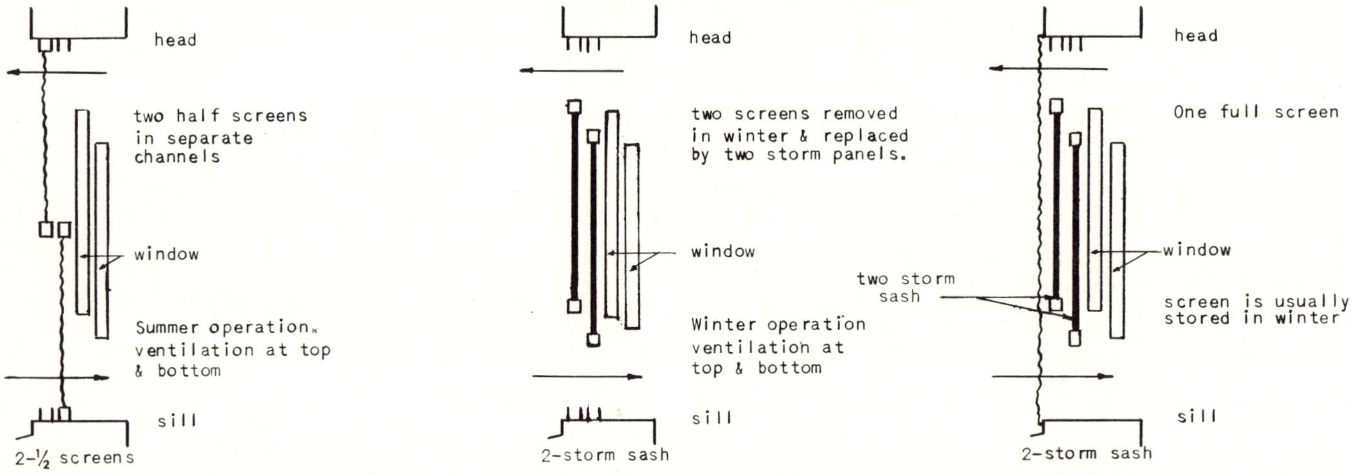
head
two half screens
in separate
channels
window
Summer operation.
ventilation at top
& bottom
sill
head
two screens removed
in winter & replaced
by two storm panels.
window
Winter operation
ventilation at
top & bottom
sill
head
One full screen
two storm
sash
window
screen is usually
stored in winter
sill

2-½ screens
2-CHANNEL

2-storm sash
2-CHANNEL

INTERCHANGEABLE STORM SASH & SCREEN PANELS.
Note: For proper ventilation screens must be stored in winter & storm sash in summer.

2-storm sash
1-fixed screen
2-CHANNEL
FIXED SCREEN & OPERABLE STORM SASH
Note: Unless sash & storm sash are of the removable type, sash may be hard to clean.

COMBINATION SCREEN & STORM SASH FOR D.H. WINDOWS

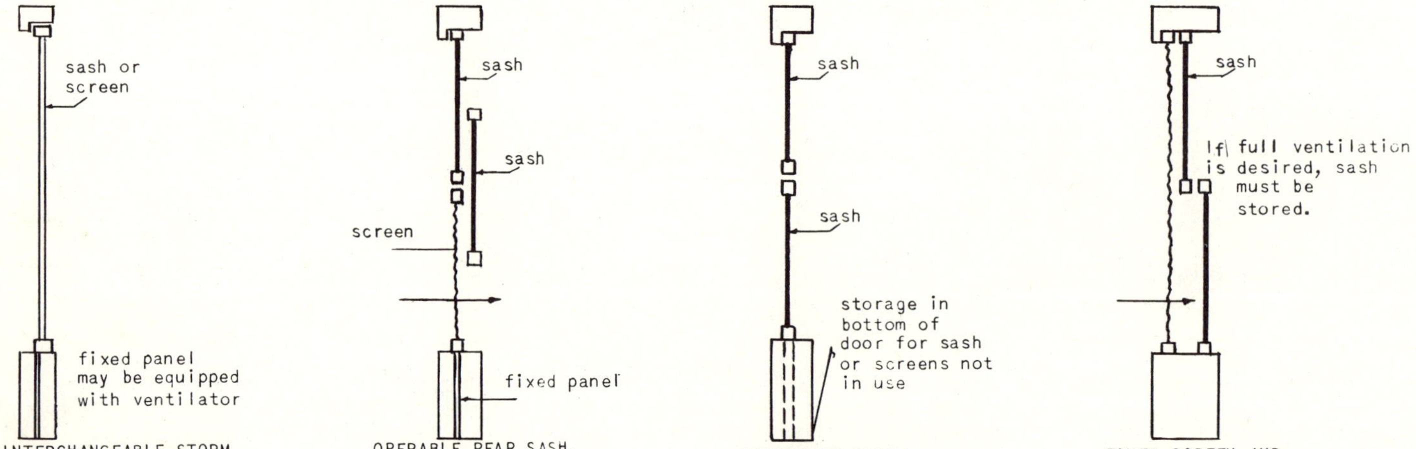
sash or
screen
fixed panel
may be equipped
with ventilator
sash
sash
screen
fixed panel
sash
sash
storage in
bottom of
door for sash
or screens not
in use
sash
If full ventilation
is desired, sash
must be
stored.

INTERCHANGEABLE STORM SASH AND SCREEN.
Note: Must store either screen or storm sash in other location.

OPERABLE REAR SASH, FIXED FRONT SASH & SCREEN
Center ventilation only.

REMOVABLE STORM SASH & SCREENS.
Note: In stormy weather sash may replace screens.

FIXED SCREEN AND OPERABLE SASH
Note: Good for screen porches

COMBINATION SCREEN & STORM DOORS

SCREENS FOR WOOD WINDOWS

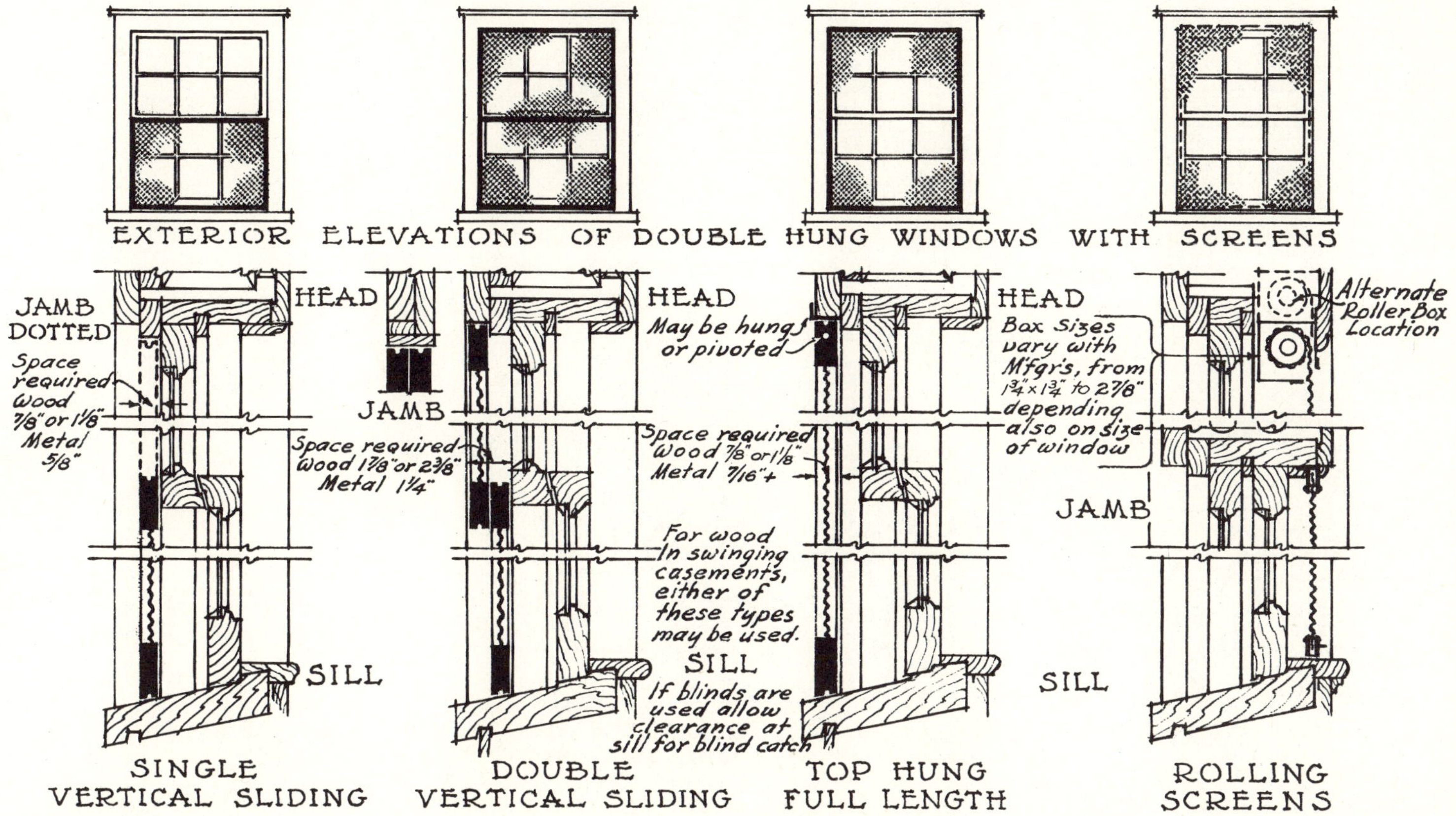
EXTERIOR ELEVATIONS OF DOUBLE HUNG WINDOWS WITH SCREENS
JAMB DOTTED
HEAD
Space required Wood 7/8" or 1 1/8" Metal 5/8"
JAMB
Space required Wood 1 7/8" or 2 3/8" Metal 1 1/4"
May be hung or pivoted
Space required Wood 7/8" or 1 1/8" Metal 7/16"+
For wood In swinging casements, either of these types may be used.
If blinds are used allow clearance at sill for blind catch
Box sizes vary with M'fgr's, from 1 3/4" x 1 3/4" to 2 7/8" depending also on size of window
Alternate Roller Box Location
SILL
SINGLE VERTICAL SLIDING
DOUBLE VERTICAL SLIDING
TOP HUNG FULL LENGTH
ROLLING SCREENS

METHODS OF SCREENING DOUBLE HUNG WINDOWS

Scale 1½" = 1'-0"

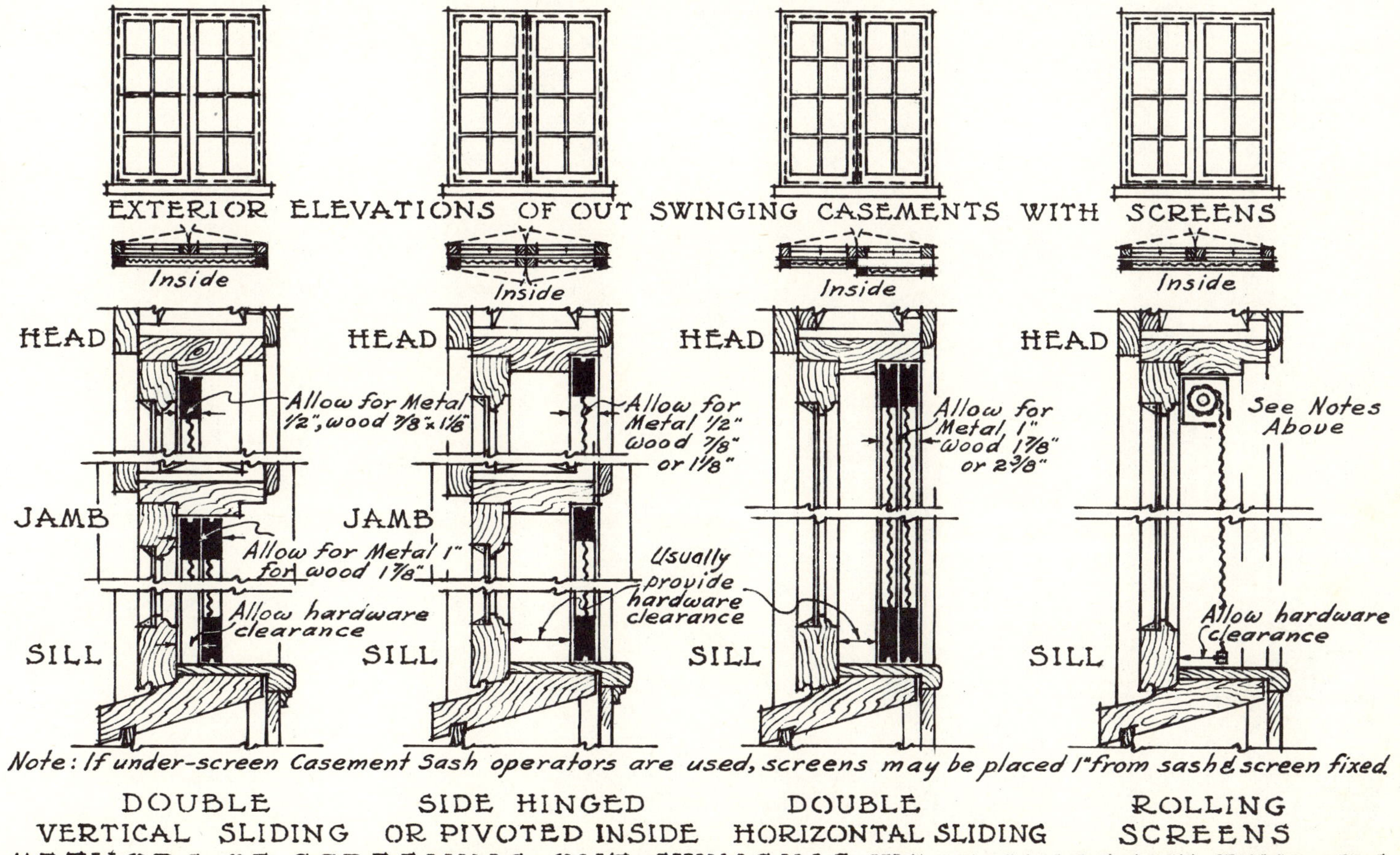
EXTERIOR ELEVATIONS OF OUT SWINGING CASEMENTS WITH SCREENS
Inside
HEAD
JAMB
SILL
Allow for Metal 1/2", wood 7/8" x 1 1/8"
Allow for Metal 1" for wood 1 7/8"
Allow hardware clearance
Allow for Metal 1/2" Wood 7/8" or 1 1/8"
Usually provide hardware clearance
Allow for Metal 1" Wood 1 7/8" or 2 3/8"
See Notes Above
Note: If under-screen Casement Sash operators are used, screens may be placed 1" from sash & screen fixed.
DOUBLE VERTICAL SLIDING
SIDE HINGED OR PIVOTED INSIDE
DOUBLE HORIZONTAL SLIDING
ROLLING SCREENS

METHODS OF SCREENING OUT SWINGING WOOD CASEMENT WINDOWS

For Detailed Specifications see "Architectural Specifications" by Harold R. Sleeper.

SCREENS for METAL WINDOWS & PORCHES

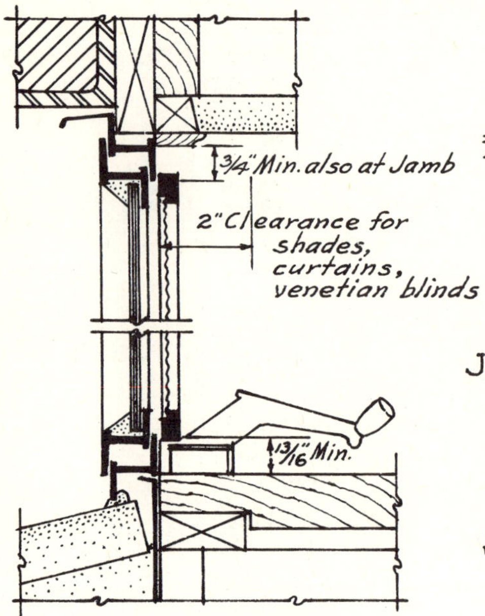
3/4" Min. also at Jamb
2" Clearance for shades, curtains, venetian blinds
13/16" Min.

FIXED SCREEN
With underscreen operator Handle is either thru hole in screen or on frame side
CASEMENT

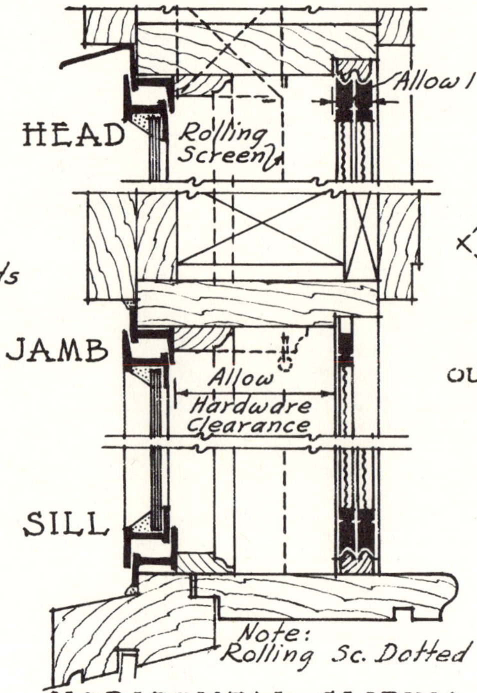
HEAD
Rolling Screen
Allow 1"
JAMB
Allow Hardware Clearance
SILL
Note: Rolling Sc. Dotted

HORIZONTAL SLIDING CASEMENT WOOD FRAME
Pivoted type screen also used

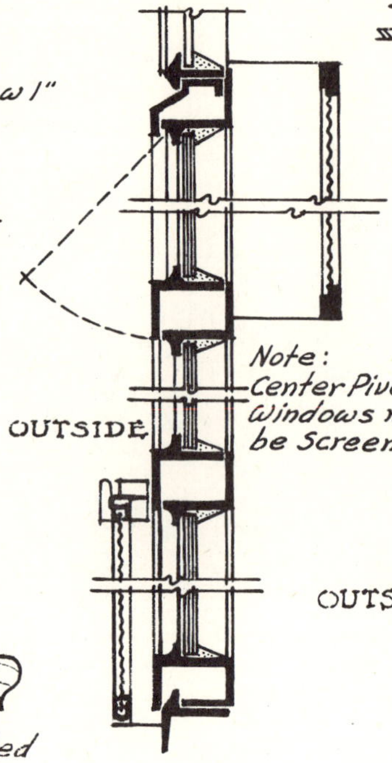
OUTSIDE
Note: Center Pivoted Windows may be Screened

PROJECTED TYPE WINDOW

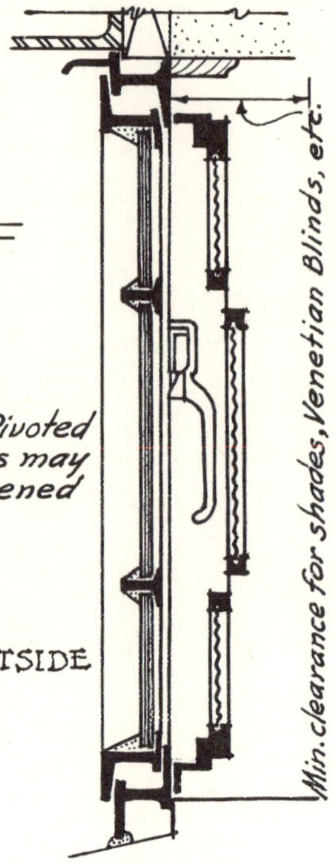
OUTSIDE
Min. clearance for shades, Venetian Blinds, etc.

SLIDING WICKET FOR CASEMENT

SCREENS for METAL CASEMENTS & METAL WINDOWS

Scale 3" = 1'-0"

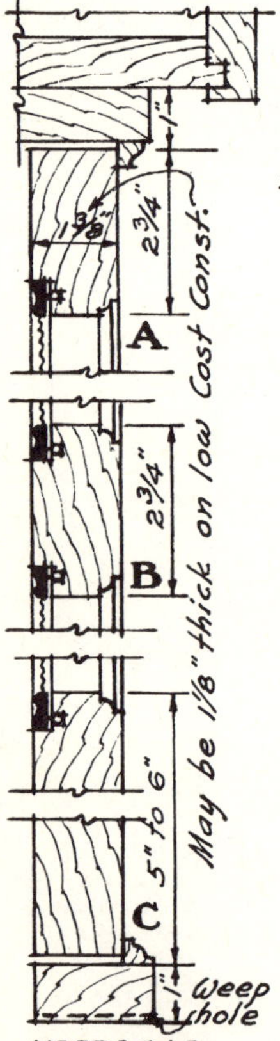
1"
1 3/8"
2 3/4"
A
2 3/4"
B
5" to 6"
C
May be 1/8" thick on low Cost Const.
Weep hole

TYPICAL SECTION SMALL PORCHES
Scale 3" = 1'-0"

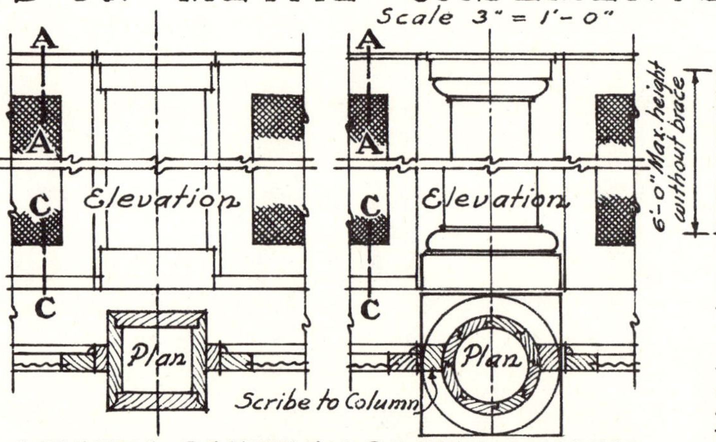
A
A
C
Elevation
C
Plan
A
A
C
Elevation
C
Plan
Scribe to Column
6'-0" Max. height without brace

SCREENS BETWEEN POSTS & COLUMNS
Scale 3/4" = 1'-0"

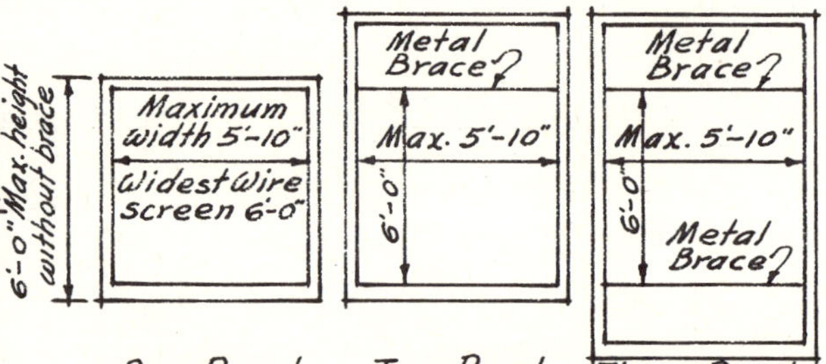
Maximum width 5'-10"
Widest Wire Screen 6'-0"
Metal Brace
Max. 5'-10"
6'-0"
Metal Brace
Max. 5'-10"
6'-0"
Metal Brace

One Panel *Two Panels* *Three Panels*
WIRE WIDTH HUNG VERTICALLY

Screen Wire: 18 x 14 Mesh or finer Wire cloth of aluminum, bronze or steel.

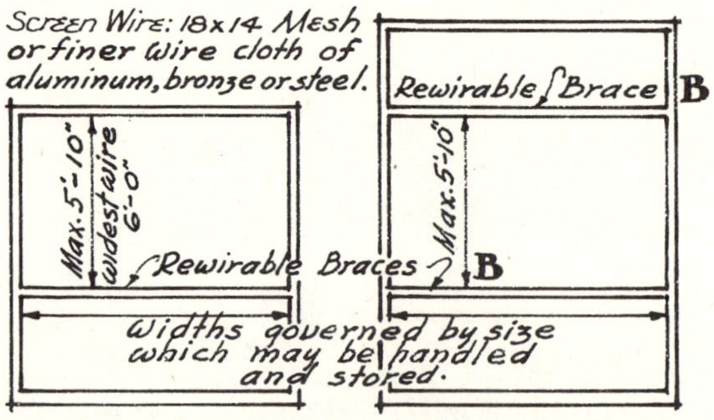
Rewirable Brace
B
Max. 5'-10"
Widest wire 6'-0"
Max. 5'-10"
Rewirable Braces
B
Widths governed by size which may be handled and stored.

WIRE WIDTH HUNG HORIZONTALLY
Rail locations governed by design. Locate rails so as not to obstruct view.
ARRANGEMENTS of PANELS for PORCHES

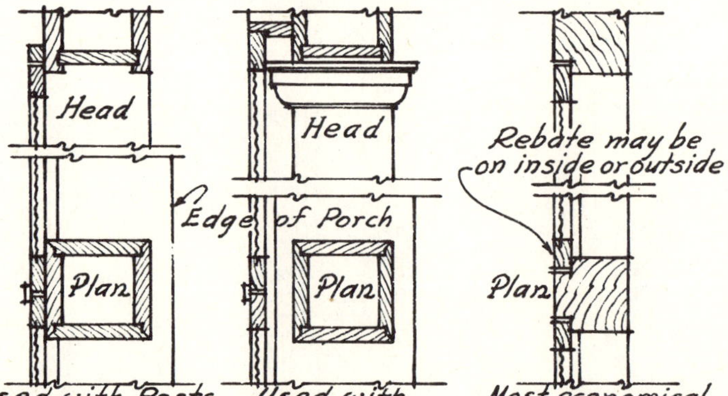
Head
Edge of Porch
Plan
Head
Plan
Rebate may be on inside or outside
Plan

Used with Posts without Caps — SCREEN ON POST
Used with Post Caps — SCREEN INSIDE
Most economical type Rebated Posts — SCREEN IN REBATE
Scale 3/4" = 1'-0"

METAL PORCH SC. FRAMES
Made of Tubular or Hollow Steel, galvanized steel, stainless steel, bronze, aluminum.
Sizes usually: 7/16" x 1 1/2", 1/2" x 1 1/2", 7/16" x 2", 1/2" x 2" or 5/8" x 2".

WOOD SCREENS for PORCHES

Note: For detailed Specifications see "Architectural Specifications" by Harold R. Sleeper

VENETIAN BLINDS

TYPE of SLAT	SIZE		PULLEY OPERATED	OSCILLATING LIFT
2" ALUMINUM	BLIND	max. width	16'	20'
		max. length	20'	16'
		max. area	120□'	245□'
		headbox size	2" h. x 2 3/8" w.	5 5/8" x 4 7/8"
	POCKET	width "W"	4 1/4"	7 1/4"
		height "H"	2 1/2" + 3/4" per linear foot of blind height	7 3/4" + 3/4" per linear foot of blind height
2" STEEL	BLIND	max. width	16'	20'
		max. length	20'	16'
		max area	80□'	140□'
		headbox size	2" h. x 2 3/8" w.	5 7/8" x 4 7/8"
	POCKET	width "W"	4 1/4"	7 1/4"
		height "H"	2 1/2" + 3/4" per linear foot of blind height	7 3/4" + 3/4" per linear foot of blind height
1 3/4" or 2" WOOD	BLIND	max. width	12'	16'
		max. length	20'	16'
		max. area	80□'	140□'
		headbox size	2" h. x 2 3/8" w	5 5/8" x 4 7/8"
	POCKET	width "W"	4 1/4"	7 1/4"
		height "H"	2 1/2" + 1 3/4" per linear foot of blind height	7 3/4" + 1 3/4" per linear foot of blind height

HORIZONTAL VENETIAN BLINDS

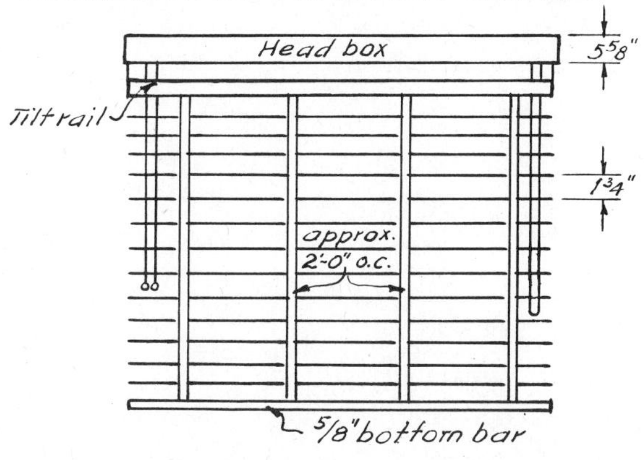
Head box
5 5/8"
Tilt rail
1 3/4"
approx. 2'-0" o.c.
5/8" bottom bar

VERTICAL BLINDS

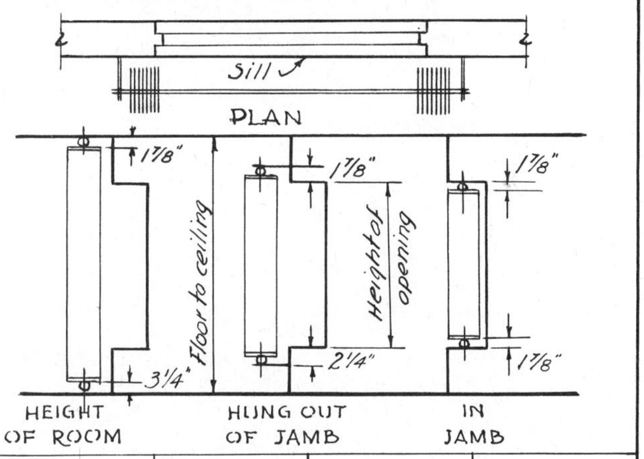
Sill
PLAN
1 7/8"
Floor to ceiling
3 1/4"
1 7/8"
Height of opening
2 1/4"
1 7/8"
1 7/8"
HEIGHT OF ROOM
HUNG OUT OF JAMB
IN JAMB

	THRU VU	SUN VERTICAL	SIMON VENTILIGHTER
Single span width limit	12'-6"	9'-0"	10'-0"
Height	up to 25'-0"	up to 25'-0"	10'-0"
Depth of vane	7"	3"	5 to 7"

Data supplied by Thru-vu Vertical Blind Corp., Sun Vertikal Blind Co. & Simon Ventilighter Co.

Aluminum and steel slat (2" only) are in general use; wood slat (2") occasional use, 1 3/4" and 2 3/8" rare use. All pulley operated blinds 69 7/8" wide and under are single pull; larger blinds use compound pull. On pulley operated blinds some manufacturers use head rail (2" to 2 1/2" wide; 3/4" to 1 1/16" thick) and tilt bar.

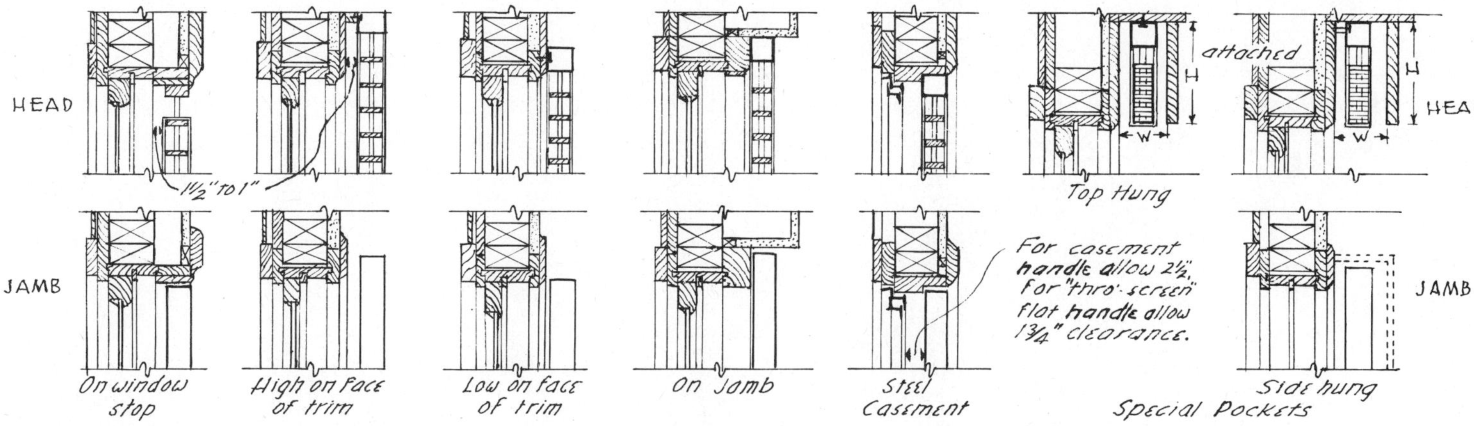
HEAD
JAMB
1 1/2" to 1"
attached
H
W
Top Hung
For casement handle allow 2 1/2". For "thro' screen" flat handle allow 1 3/4" clearance.
HEAD
JAMB
On window stop
High on face of trim
Low on face of trim
On Jamb
Steel Casement
Side hung
Special Pockets

These are the average manufacturers' recommendations and are variable. Data checked by Lester S. Simon.

GLASS, GLAZING and GLASS BLOCK

TABLE OF CONTENTS

GLASS

SINGLE GLAZING

TYPE GLASS	MFR.+	THICKNESS	WEIGHT	MAX. STOCK SIZES	QUALITY
Window-picture	LOF, PPG	1/16"	14 oz ±	36"×50" or 60U*	AA, A, B
Single strength	" "	3/32"	19 oz ±	40"×50" or 90U*	AA, A, B
Double strength	" "	1/8"	26 oz ±	60"×80" or 120U*	AA, A, B Greenhouse
Heavy sheet	" "	3/16"	40 oz ±	76"×120" or 50□'	AA, A, B
" "	AWG	"	"	86"×120"	" " "
" "	LOF, PPG	7/32"	45 oz ±	76"×120" or 60□'	" " "
" "	AWG	"	"	86"×120"	" " "
" "	"	1/4"	51 oz	86"×120"	" " "
	"	5/16"	64 oz	86"×120"	" " "
Polished Plate	LOF PPG LOF PPG.	1/8" " 1/4" "	1.64# " 3.27# "	72"×74" 76"×128" 120"×170" 130"×218"	Silvering, mirror glazing, & glazing
Heavy Plate	PPG PPG LOF PPG LOF LOF PPG LOF LOF PPG LOF PPG LOF	5/16" 3/8" " 1/2" " 5/8" 3/4" " 7/8" 1" " 1 1/4" "	4.06# 4.90# ± " 6.55# ± " 8.20# ± 9.67# 9.81# 11.44# 13.12# ± " 16.45# 16.25#	130"×218" 76"×190" 90"×130" 76"×190" 90"×130" 72"×120" 74"×160" 72"×120" 42"×96" 74"×148" 42"×96" 74"×148" 42"×96"	Selected and commercial
Plate Glass Mirrors	LOF, PPG	Any	Approx. Same as plate gl.	Reg. 80"×144" copper-back & struc 74"×140"	Silvering, mirror glazing & glazing
One-Way Mirrors	LOF	1/8" 1/4"		30"×40" 30"×60"	

TYPE GLASS	MFR.+	THICKNESS	WEIGHT	MAX. STOCK SIZES	QUALITY
Colored Plate	LOF	7/32" to 1/4"	Variable	Max. lngth 120"	Glazing
Heat Absorbant *Patterned	BRG* MGC* PPG LOF BRG* MGC*	1/8" " 1/4" " " "	1.75# ± 2.3# 3.28# ± " 3.# ± 3.4#	48"×132" 34"×132" 130"×218" Max lngth 120" 48"×136" 34"×144"	
X-Ray Lead Plate	PPG	5.35-7.35 mm	5.5#	40"×72"	
Safety Sheet-thin " SS+SS SS+DS DS+DS Safety Plate " " Heavy	PPG LOF LOF, PPG " " " " LOF PPG LOF	1/8" 5/32" 7/32" 15/64" 1/4" 1/4" 1/4" 11/32"–1"	1.62# 1.62 & 1.92 2.89# 3.08# 3.34# 3.16# " 4.52-13.16	32"×42" 7□' 15□' 15□' 15□' 48"×84" 60"×90" 30"×72"	Laminated
Bullet Resisting	LOF PPG	3/4" to 3" " " "	9.71-39.63 " "	30"×90" 60"×90"	Laminated
Patterned or light diffusing-most patterns (ribbed hammered, etc) in sizes shown.	BRG MGC SSG BRG MGC SSG	1/8" " " 7/32" " "	1.75# 2# " 2.75# 2.8# "	54"×132" 48"×132" 60"×140" 60"×136" 60×136" 60"×140"	Sizes shown are for plain
Polished Wire glass	BRG MGC SSG BRG, SSG BRG	1/4" " " 3/8" 1/2"	3.5# ± 3.4# " 5.# 6.5#	60"×144" 60"×132" 56"×144" 48"×120" 48"×100"	Finish - For special finish sizes see mfrs catalog
Patterned Wire Glass	MGC SSG BRG BRG SSG BRG	1/4" " " 3/8" 7/16" 1/2"	3.4# ± " " 5.# 5.66# 6.5#	60"×144" 56"×134" 60×144" 48"×120" 48"×120" 48"×100"	

+LOF-Libbey-Owens-Ford; PPG-Pittsburgh Plate Glass Co.; AWG-American Window Glass Co.; BRG-Blue Ridge Glass Corp. (Libbey-Owens-Ford as agent); MGC-Mississippi Glass Co.; SSG-Southwestern Sheet Glass Co. *United inch = Length + width.

WINDOW AND PLATE GLASS WIND RESISTANCE CHART
SQUARE FEET OF AREA

Glass Thickness	1/16"	3/32"	1/8"	3/16"	1/4"	5/16"	3/8"	1/2"	5/8"-1"	1 1/4"
30 mile wind	35	64	72	162	198	198				
40 mile wind	17.5	32	36	81	144	198	240			
55 mile wind	11.6	21	24	54	96	150	216			
65 mile wind	9	16	18	41	72	112	162	240		
80 mile wind	6	11	12	27	48	75	108	192		
100 mile wind	4	6	7	16	29	45	65	115		
120 mile wind	3	5	5	11	20	32	46	82	80	74

1/16", 3/32" & 1/8" glass, because of flexibility, should not be used beyond 20□'

MULTIPLE GLAZING

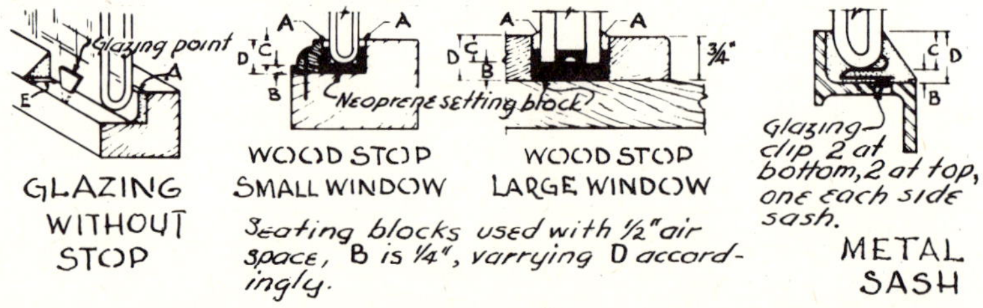

Glazing point
A
E
A
C
D
B
Neoprene setting block
3/4"
Glazing clip 2 at bottom, 2 at top, one each side sash.
GLAZING WITHOUT STOP
WOOD STOP SMALL WINDOW
WOOD STOP LARGE WINDOW
METAL SASH

Seating blocks used with 1/2" air space, B is 1/4", varrying D accordingly.

THERMOPANE △

	MAXIMUM HEIGHT		MAXIMUM LENGTH		MAXIMUM AREA IN SQUARE INCHES	AVG. NET WT. #/□'
	1/4" AIR SPACE	1/2" AIR SPACE	1/4" AIR SPACE	1/2" AIR SPACE		
DOUBLE						
1/8" All	40"	24"	76"	76"	1700	3 1/4"
3/16" Sheet	50"	50"	76"	76"	3200	5"
1/4" Polished Plate	48"	98"	132"	132"	4800 < 9600 ≤	6 1/2"
1/4" Heat Absorbent	48"	98"	132"	132"	4800 < 9600 ≤	6 1/2"
1/4" B.R.	42"	42"	100"	100"	4800	6 1/4"
7/32" B.R. Patterned	48"	48"	100"	100"	4800	6 1/4"
1/4" Tuf-Flex	40"	40"	48"	48"		6 1/2"
TRIPLE						
1/8" ALL	24"		76"		1700	5"
3/16" Sheet	42"	42"	76"	76"		7 1/2"
1/4" Polished Plate	48"	48"	100"	100"	3200 < 4800 ≤	10 1/2"
1/4" Heat Absorbent	48"	48"	100"	100"	3200 < 4800 ≤	10 1/2"

EXPLANATION OF DETAILS

SYMBOL AND EXPLANATION	D.S.A. 1/8" P.I. 1/8" FIG	3/16" SHEET GLASS		1/4" PLATE 7/32" OR 1/4" FIGURED		
GLASS SIZES	UNDER *80 U"	UNDER *80 U"	*80 U" TO 120 U"	UNDER *80 U"	OVER *80 U"	OVER *120 U"
A-Glaz. Comp. bed-width	1/8"	1/8"	1/8"	1/8"	1/8"	1/8"
B-Glaz. Clear. (all edges)	1/8"	1/4"	1/4"	1/4"	1/4"	1/4"
C-Metalized edge-depth	3/8"	3/8"	3/8"	3/8"	1/2"	1/2"
D-Total Rabbet-Depth B+C	1/2", 9/16	9/16"	5/8"	9/16"	13/16"	7/8"
E-Glazing compound.	1/2"+	5/8"+	5/8"	7/8"+	7/8"+	7/8"+

TWINDOW

**POLISHED PLATE ONLY		AIR SPACE	MAX. AREA	AVG. NET WEIGHT
Double	1/8"	1/4" and 1/2"	10□'	3 1/2 lbs
	1/4"	1/4" and 1/2"	70□'	7 1/2 lbs
**Triple	1/8"	1/4"	10□'	5 1/4 lbs
	1/4"	1/4" and 1/2"	35□'	10 1/2 lbs

* United inch - length + width. ** Other glass to order.
< 1/4" air space ≤ 1/2" air space. △ Wood stops only.

See pages on structural & corrugated glass; also pages on curtain wall panels for glass used as an exterior wall surfacing material.

MIRROR INSTALLATION

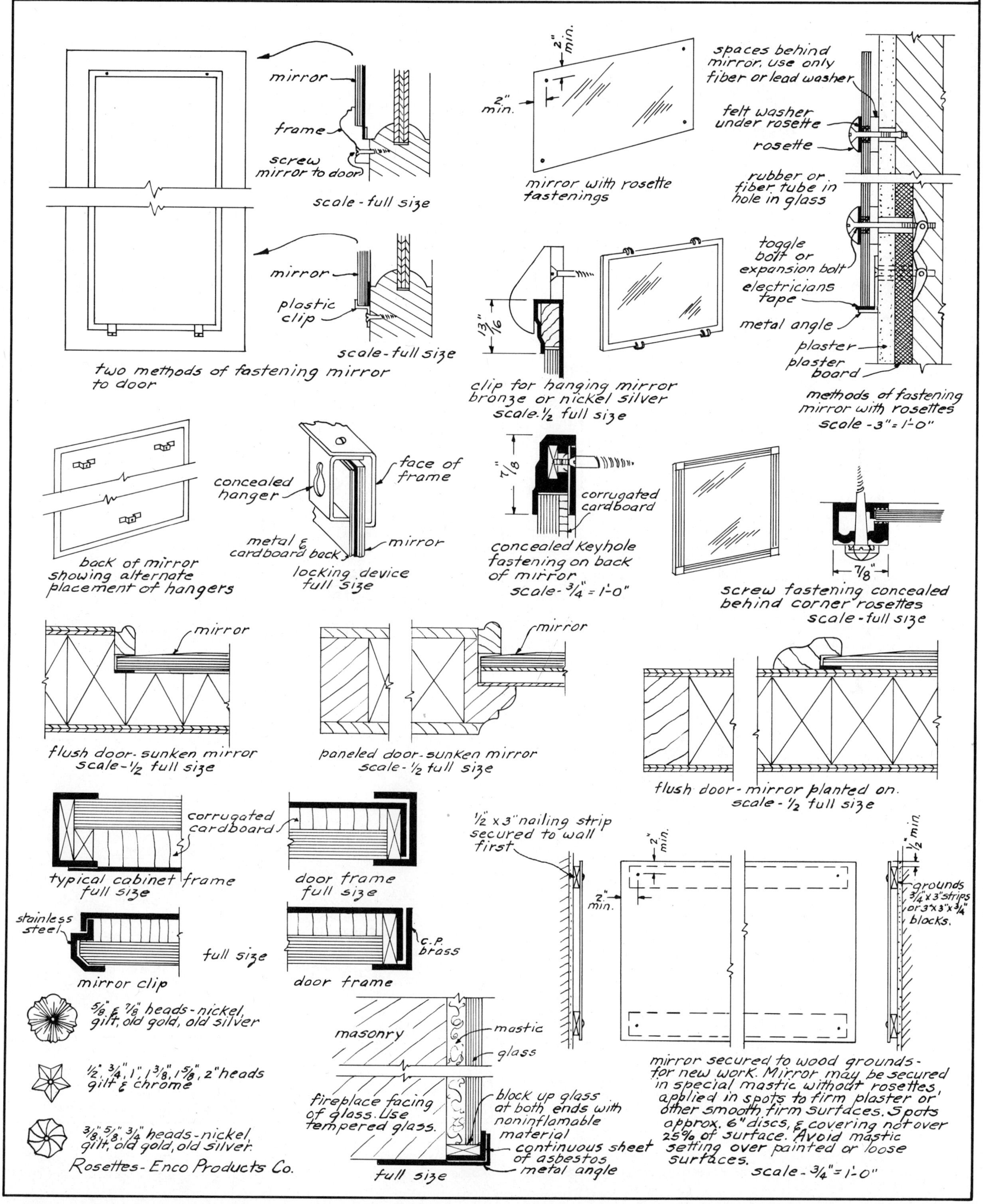
mirror
frame
screw mirror to door
scale - full size
mirror
plastic clip
scale - full size
two methods of fastening mirror to door
2" min.
2" min.
mirror with rosette fastenings
spaces behind mirror, use only fiber or lead washer
felt washer under rosette
rosette
rubber or fiber tube in hole in glass
toggle bolt or expansion bolt
electricians tape
metal angle
plaster
plaster board
methods of fastening mirror with rosettes
scale - 3" = 1'-0"
13"/16
clip for hanging mirror bronze or nickel silver
scale ½ full size
back of mirror showing alternate placement of hangers
concealed hanger
face of frame
metal & cardboard back
mirror
locking device full size
7/8
corrugated cardboard
concealed keyhole fastening on back of mirror
scale - ¾" = 1'-0"
7/8"
screw fastening concealed behind corner rosettes
scale - full size
mirror
flush door - sunken mirror
scale - ½ full size
mirror
paneled door - sunken mirror
scale - ½ full size
flush door - mirror planted on.
scale - ½ full size
corrugated cardboard
typical cabinet frame full size
door frame full size
stainless steel
full size
mirror clip
C.P. brass
door frame
⅝" & ⅞" heads - nickel, gilt, old gold, old silver
½", ¾", 1", 1⅜", 1⅝", 2" heads gilt & chrome
⅜", ⅝", ¾" heads - nickel, gilt, old gold, old silver.
Rosettes - Enco Products Co.
masonry
mastic
glass
fireplace facing of glass. Use tempered glass.
block up glass at both ends with noninflamable material
continuous sheet of asbestos
metal angle
full size
½" x 3" nailing strip secured to wall first
2" min.
2" min.
½" min.
grounds ¾" x 3" strips or 3" x 3" x ¾" blocks.
mirror secured to wood grounds - for new work. Mirror may be secured in special mastic without rosettes, applied in spots to firm plaster or other smooth firm surfaces. Spots approx. 6" discs, & covering not over 25% of surface. Avoid mastic setting over painted or loose surfaces.
scale - ¾" = 1'-0"

GLASS BLOCKS

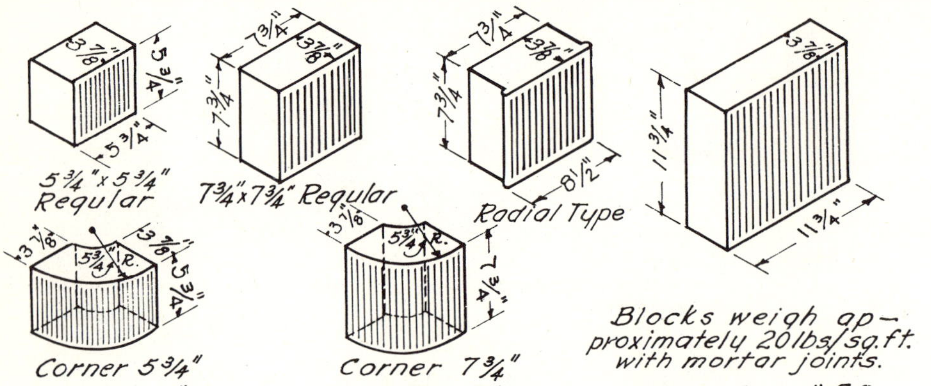
3 7/8"
5 3/4"
5 3/4"
5 3/4" x 5 3/4" Regular
7 3/4"
3 7/8"
7 3/4"
7 3/4" x 7 3/4" Regular
7 3/4"
3 7/8"
7 3/4"
8 1/2"
Radial Type
3 7/8"
11 3/4"
11 3/4"
3 7/8"
5 3/4" R.
3 7/8"
5 3/4"
3 7/8"
5 3/4" R.
7 3/4"
Blocks weigh approximately 20 lbs/sq. ft. with mortar joints.

Corner 5 3/4" — NOMINAL 6" SQ. | Corner 7 3/4" — NOMINAL 8" SQ. | NOMINAL 12" SQ

BLOCK SIZES MADE BY O-I & PC*

Scale 3/4" = 1'-0"

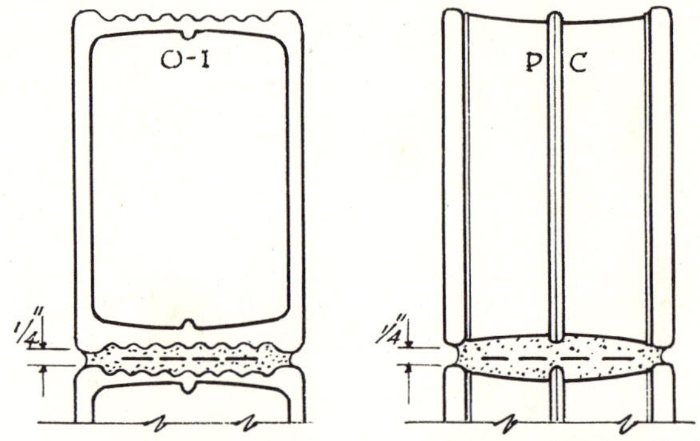
O-I
P C
1/4"
1/4"

OWENS-* ILLINOIS | PITTSBURGH CORNING

BLOCK & JOINTS

Scale 3" = 1'-0"

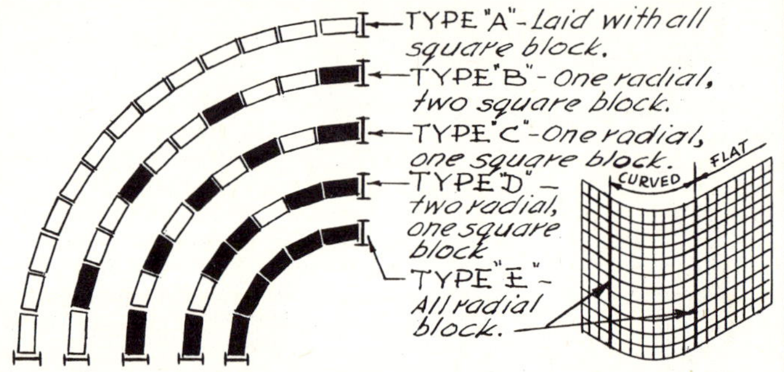
TYPE "A" - Laid with all square block.
TYPE "B" - One radial, two square block.
TYPE "C" - One radial, one square block.
TYPE "D" - two radial, one square block
TYPE "E" - All radial block.
CURVED
FLAT

CURVED PANEL LAYING RADII

OUTSIDE RADIUS	NO OF UNITS*	JOINT THICKNESS IN SIDE	JOINT THICKNESS OUT SIDE	TYPE
7 3/4" STANDARD RADIAL ‡				
2'-5" Min.	5-R	1/8"	5/8"	E
2'-10"	6-R	3/16"	3/8"	E
3'-3"	7-R	3/8"	7/16"	E
3'-8"	8-R	3/16"	1/8"	E
4'-1"	6-R+3-S	1/8"	5/16"	D
4'-4"	9-R	5/8"	9/16"	E
4'-8"	10-R	7/16"	1/4"	E
5'-0"	8-R+3-S	1/4"	1/4"	D
5'-4"	6-R+6S	1/8"	1/4"	C
5'-9"	7-R+6S	1/8"	3/16"	C
5'-9"	13-S	1/8"	5/8"	A
6'-0"	7-R+6-S	1/2"	9/16"	C
6'-4"	7-R+7-S	3/8"	3/8"	C
6'-4"	14-S	3/8"	3/4	A
6'-8"	7-R+8-S	1/4"	1/4"	C
6'-8"	15-S	1/4"	5/8"	A
7'-0"	6-R+10-S	1/8"	1/4"	B
7'-0"	16-S	1/8"	1/2"	A
7'-5"	6-R+11-S	1/8"	1/4"	B
7'-5"	17-S	1/8"	7/16"	A
7'-8"	6-R+11-S	7/16"	1/2"	B
7'-8"	17-S	7/16"	3/4"	A
7 3/4" STD. & RADIAL (CONTINUED)				
8'-0"	6-R+12-S	5/16"	7/16"	B
8'-0"	18-S	5/16"	5/8"	A
8'-4"	7-R+12-S	1/4"	1/4"	B
8'-4"	19-S	1/4"	1/2"	A
5 3/4" STANDARD ‡				
4'-3" Min.	13-S	1/8"	5/8"	A
4'-8"	14-S	1/8"	1/2"	A
5'-0"	15-S	1/8"	1/2"	A
5'-4"	16-S	1/8"	1/2"	A
5'-8"	17-S	3/16"	1/2"	A
6'-0"	18-S	3/16"	1/2"	A
6'-4"	19-S	3/16"	1/2"	A
6'-8"	20-S	1/4"	1/2"	A
7'-0"	21-S	1/4"	1/2"	A
7'-4"	22-S	1/4"	1/2"	A
No Max.				
11 3/4" STANDARD ‡				
8'-6" Min. No Max.	13-S	1/8"	5/8"	A

Max. outside joint 5/8"; min inside joint 1/8"

* S = Standard; R = Radial ‡ nominal sizes 1/4" greater
Use all square blocks for larger radii

WALL ANCHORS*

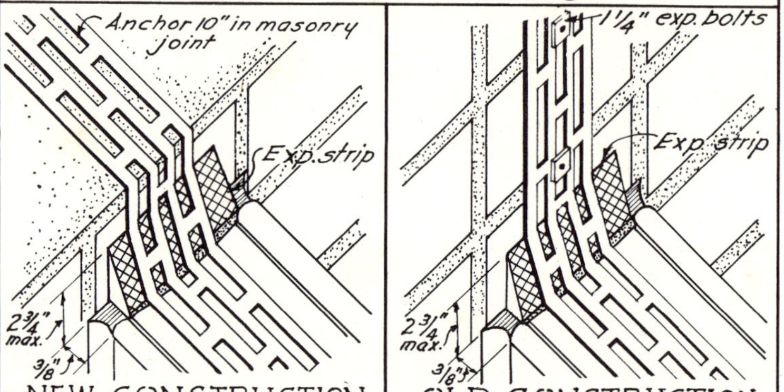
Anchor 10" in masonry joint
Exp. strip
2 3/4" max.
3/8"
1 1/4" exp. bolts
Exp. strip
2 3/4" max.
3/8"

NEW CONSTRUCTION | OLD CONSTRUCTION

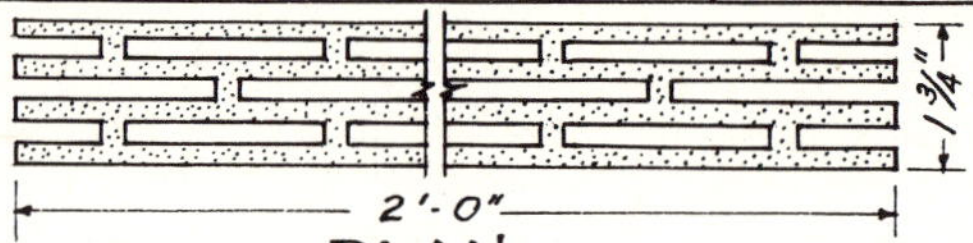
1 3/4"
2'-0"

PLAN

* Use of wall anchors limited to panels of 100# max. area without chose.

Wall anchors are 1 3/4" wide, 2'-0" long, # 20 gauge perforated steel strips, galv. Use to secure block to masonry & frame - see details. They are placed in joints with wall ties, crimped within the expansion joint and built into masonry joints 10 inches.

WALL TIES

2" c. to c.
8"
8"

PLAN

#9 ga. wires 12 to 14 ga. galv. wires welded together

Wall ties continuous in horizontal mortar joints. Lap ends of ties 6". Run to ends of panels, but not across expansion joints.

Space wall ties every 24" regardless of the size of glass blocks used.

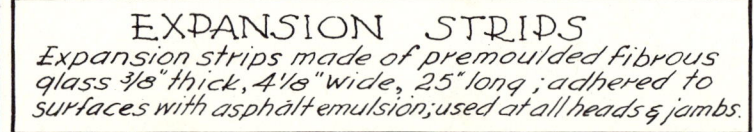

EXPANSION STRIPS

Expansion strips made of premoulded fibrous glass 3/8" thick, 4 1/8" wide, 25" long; adhered to surfaces with asphalt emulsion; used at all heads & jambs.

* Abbreviations used: PC for Pittsburgh Corning Corp., O-I for Owens-Illinois glass block mfrd. by Kimble Glass Co., a subsidiay of Owens-Illinois Glass Co. For specifications see: "Architectural Specifications" by: Harold R. Sleeper.

GLASS BLOCKS

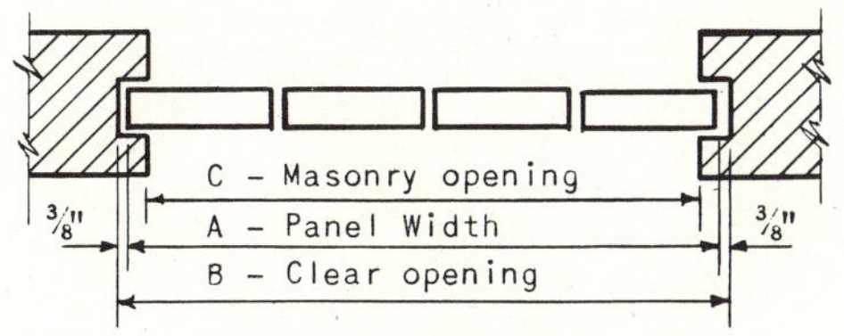
C - Masonry opening
3/8"
A - Panel Width
3/8"
B - Clear opening

CHASE CONSTRUCTION

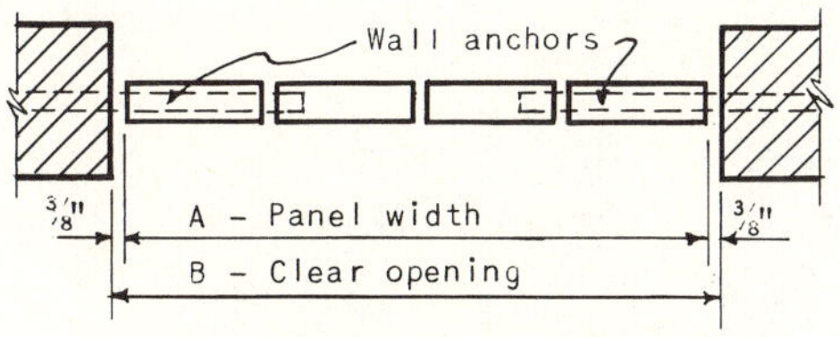
Wall anchors
3/8"
A - Panel width
3/8"
B - Clear opening

WALL ANCHOR CONSTRUCTION

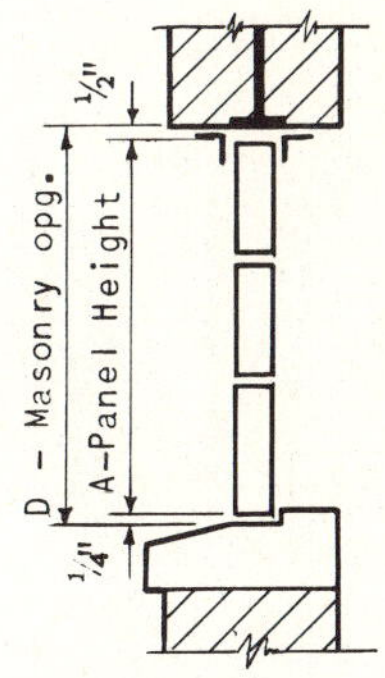
1/2"
D - Masonry opg.
A-Panel Height
1/4"

CHASE OR
WALL ANCHOR
CONSTRUCTION

Chase construction — LIMITATIONS

Maximum Panel Length .... 25 ft.
Maximum Panel Height .... 20 ft.
Maximum Panel Area .... 144 sq. ft.

Wall anchor construction — LIMITATIONS

Maximum Panel Length .... 10 ft.
Maximum Panel Height .... 10 ft.
Maximum Panel Area .... 100 ft.

NOTE: Masonry opening "D" allows for ½" Lintel Deflection.

TABLE OF DIMENSIONS

NO. OF UNITS	5¾" SQUARE BLOCKS				7¾" SQUARE BLOCKS				11¾" SQUARE BLOCKS			
	A	B	C	D	A	B	C	D	A	B	C	D
1	5¾"	6½"	2⅜"	7"	7¾"	8½"	4⅜"	9"	11¾"	1'-0½"	8⅜"	1'-1"
2	11¾"	1'-0½"	8⅜"	1'-1"	1'-3¾"	1'-4½"	1'-0⅜"	1'-5"	1'-11¾"	2'-0½"	1'-8⅜"	2'-1"
3	1'-5¾"	1'-6½"	1'-2⅜"	1'-7"	1'-11¾"	2'-0½"	1'-8⅜"	2'-1"	2'-11¾"	3'-0½"	2'-8⅜"	3'-1"
4	1'-11¾"	2'-0½"	1'-8⅜"	2'-1"	2'-7¾"	2'-8½"	2'-4⅜"	2'-9"	3'-11¾"	4'-0½"	3'-8⅜"	4'-1"
5	2'-5¾"	2'-6½"	2'-2⅜"	2'-7"	3'-3¾"	3'-4½"	3'-0⅜"	3'-5"	4'-11¾"	5'-0½"	4'-8⅜"	5'-1"
6	2'-11¾"	3'-0½"	2'-8⅜"	3'-1"	3'-11¾"	4'-0½"	3'-8⅜"	4'-1"	5'-11¾"	6'-0½"	5'-8⅜"	6'-1"
7	3'-5¾"	3'-6½"	3'-2⅜"	3'-7"	4'-7¾"	4'-8½"	4'-4⅜"	4'-9"	6'-11¾"	7'-0½"	6'-8⅜"	7'-1"
8	3'-11¾"	4'-0½"	3'-8⅜"	4'-1"	5'-3¾"	5'-4½"	5'-0⅜"	5'-5"	7'-11¾"	8'-0½"	7'-8⅜"	8'-1"
9	4'-5¾"	4'-6½"	4'-2⅜"	4'-7"	5'-11¾"	6'-0½"	5'-8⅜"	6'-1"	8'-11¾"	9'-0½"	8'-8⅜"	9'-1"
10	4'-11¾"	5'-0½"	4'-8⅜"	5'-1"	6'-7¾"	6'-8½"	6'-4⅜"	6'-9"	9'-11¾"	10'-0½"	9'-8⅜"	10'-1"
11	5'-5¾"	5'-6½"	5'-2⅜"	5'-7"	7'-3¾"	7'-4½"	7'-0⅜"	7'-5"	10'-11¾"	11'-0½"	10'-8⅜"	11'-1"
12	5'-11¾"	6'-0½"	5'-8⅜"	6'-1"	7'-11¾"	8'-0½"	7'-8⅜"	8'-1"	11'-11¾"	12'-0½"	11'-8⅜"	12'-1"
13	6'-5¾"	6'-6½"	6'-2⅜"	6'-7"	8'-7¾"	8'-8½"	8'-4⅜"	8'-9"	12'-11¾"	13'-0½"	12'-8⅜"	13'-1"
14	6'-11¾"	7'-0½"	6'-8⅜"	7'-1"	9'-3¾"	9'-4½"	9'-0⅜"	9'-5"	13'-11¾"	14'-0½"	13'-8⅜"	14'-1"
15	7'-5¾"	7'-6½"	7'-2⅜"	7'-7"	9'-11¾"	10'-0½"	9'-8⅜"	10'-1"	14'-11¾"	15'-0½"	14'-8⅜"	15'-1"
16	7'-11¾"	8'-0½"	7'-8⅜"	8'-1"	10'-7¾"	10'-8½"	10'-4⅜"	10'-9"	15'-11¾"	16'-0½"	15'-8⅜"	16'-1"
17	8'-5¾"	8'-6½"	8'-2⅜"	8'-7"	11'-3¾"	11'-4½"	11'-0⅜"	11'-5"	16'-11¾"	17'-0½"	16'-8⅜"	17'-1"
18	8'-11¾"	9'-0½"	8'-8⅜"	9'-1"	11'-11¾"	12'-0½"	11'-8⅜"	12'-1"	17'-11¾"	18'-0½"	17'-8⅜"	18'-1"
19	9'-5¾"	9'-6½"	9'-2⅜"	9'-7"	12'-7¾"	12'-8½"	12'-4⅜"	12'-9"	18'-11¾"	19'-0½"	18'-8⅜"	19'-1"
20	9'-11¾"	10'-0½"	9'-8⅜"	10'-1"	13'-3¾"	13'-4½"	13'-0⅜"	13'-5"	19'-11¾"	20'-0½	19'-8⅜"	20'-1"
21	10'-5¾"	10'-6½"	10'-2⅜"	10'-7"	13'-11¾"	14'-0½"	13'-8⅜"	14'-1"	20'-11¾"	21'-0½"	20'-8⅜"	21'-1"
22	10'-11¾"	11'-0½"	10'-8⅜"	11'-1"	14'-7¾"	14'-8½"	14'-4⅜"	14'-9"	21'-11¾"	22'-0½"	21'-8⅜"	22'-1"
23	11'-5¾"	11'-6½"	11'-2⅜"	11'-7"	15'-3¾"	15'-4½"	15'-0⅜"	15'-5"	22'-11¾"	23'-0½"	22'-8⅜"	23'-1"
24	11'-11¾"	12'-0½"	11'-8⅜"	12'-1"	15'-11¾"	16'-0½"	15'-8⅜"	16'-1"	23'-11¾"	24'-0½"	23'-8⅜"	24'-1"
25	12'-5¾"	12'-6½"	12'-2⅜"	12'-7"	16'-7¾"	16'-8½"	16'-4⅜"	16'-9"	24'-11¾"	25'-0½"	24'-8⅜"	25'-1"
26	12'-11¾"	13'-0½"	12'-8⅜"	13'-1"	17'-3¾"	17'-4½"	17'-0⅜"	17'-5"				
27	13'-5¾"	13'-6½"	13'-2⅜"	13'-7"	17'-11¾"	18'-0½"	17'-8⅜"	18'-1"				
28	13'-11¾"	14'-0½"	13'-8⅜"	14'-1"	18'-7¾"	18'-8½"	18'-4⅜"	18'-9"				
29	14'-5¾"	14'-6½"	14'-2⅜"	14'-7"	19'-3¾"	19'-4½"	19'-0⅜"	19'-5"				
30	14'-11¾"	15'-0½"	14'-8⅜"	15'-1"	19'-11¾"	20'-0½"	19'-8⅜"	20'-1"				
31	15'-5¾"	15'-6½"	15'-2⅜"	15'-7"	20'-7¾"	20'-8½"	20'-4⅜"	20'-9"				
32	15'-11¾"	16'-0½"	15'-8⅜"	16'-1"	21'-3¾"	21'-4½"	21'-0⅜"	21'-5"				
33	16'-5¾"	16'-6½"	16'-2⅜"	16'-7"	21'-11¾"	22'-0½"	21'-8⅜"	22'-1"				
34	16'-11¾"	17'-0½"	16'-8⅜"	17'-1"	22'-7¾"	22'-8½"	22'-4⅜"	22'-9"				
35	17'-5¾"	17'-6½"	17'-2⅜"	17'-7"	23'-3¾"	23'-4½"	23'-0⅜"	23'-5"				
36	17'-11¾"	18'-0½"	17'-8⅜"	18'-1"	23'-11¾"	24'-0½"	23'-8⅜"	24'-1"				
37	18'-5¾"	18'-6½"	18'-2⅜"	18'-7"	24'-7¾"	24'-8½"	24'-4⅜"	24'-9"				
38	18'-11¾"	19'-0½"	18'-8⅜"	19'-1"	25'-3¾"	25'-4½"	25'-0⅜"	25'-5"				
39	19'-5¾"	19'-6½"	19'-2⅜"	19'-7"								
40	19'-11¾"	20'-0½"	19'-8⅜"	20'-1"								
41	20'-5¾"	20'-6½"	20'-2⅜"	20'-7"								
42	20'-11¾"	21'-0½"	20'-8⅜"	21'-1"								
43	21'-5¾"	21'-6½"	21'-2⅜"	21'-7"								
44	21'-11¾"	22'-0½"	21'-8⅜"	22'-1"								
45	22'-5¾"	22'-6½"	22'-2⅜"	22'-7"								
46	22'-11¾"	23'-0½"	22'-8⅜"	23'-1"								
47	23'-5¾"	23'-6½"	23'-2⅜"	23'-7"								
48	23'-11¾"	24'-0½"	23'-8⅜"	24'-1"								
49	24'-5¾"	24'-6½"	24'-2⅜"	24'-7"								
50	24'-11¾"	25'-0½"	24'-8⅜"	25'-1"								

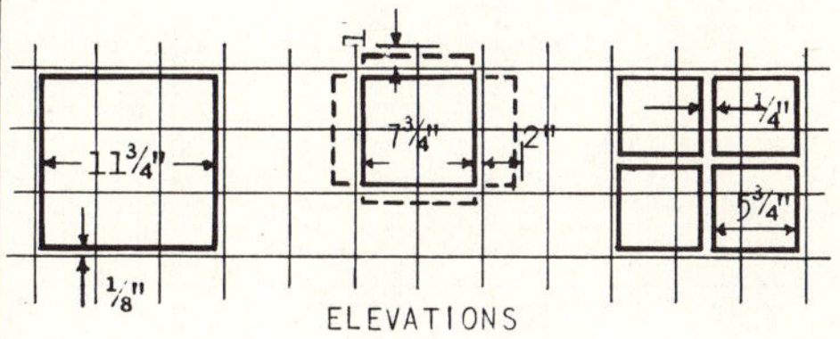
11¾"
1/8"
7¾"
2"
1/4"
5¾"

ELEVATIONS

Glass block is a modular product. Vertically, the panels may be 1" above or below the grid lines depending upon head and sill details used. Horizontally, panels may be on the grid lines or centered between, depending upon jamb details.
The above tables are based on modular coordination using ⅜" mortar joints in face brick.

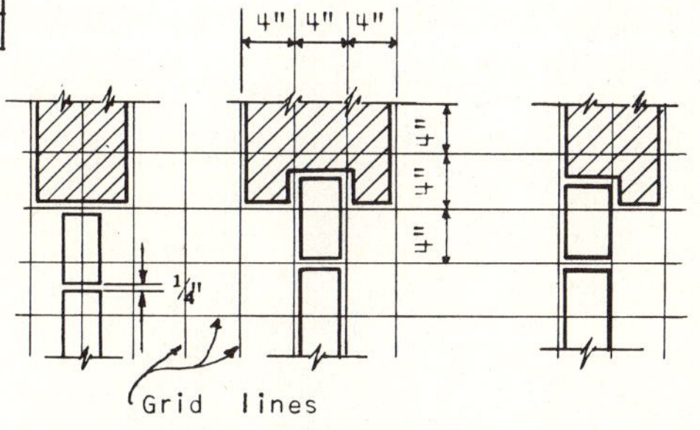
4"
4"
4"
4"
4"
1/4"
Grid lines

SECTIONS

DATA ON THIS PAGE SUPPLIED BY PITTSBURGH-CORNING CORPORATION AND OWENS-ILLINOIS GLASS CO.

GLASS BLOCKS - EXTERIOR USE

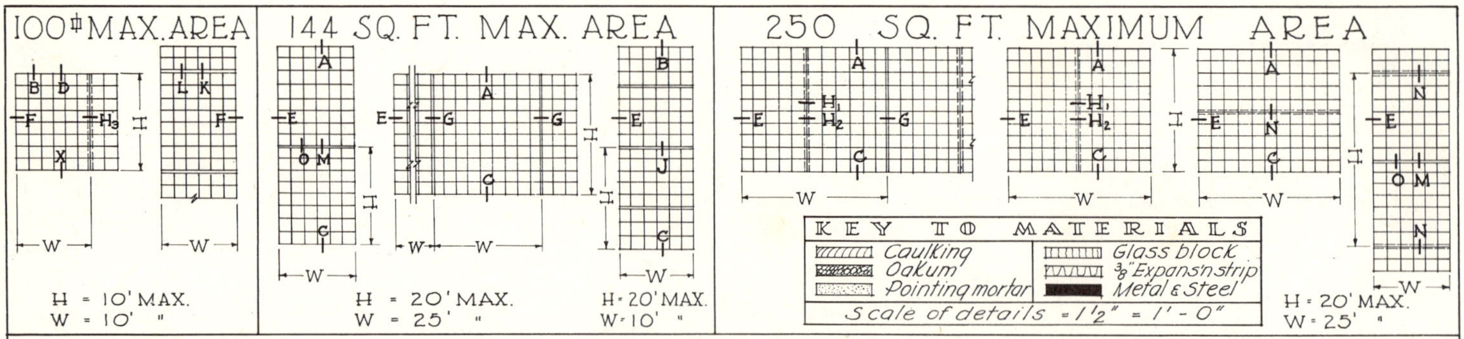

100# MAX. AREA
H = 10' MAX.
W = 10' "
144 SQ. FT. MAX. AREA
H = 20' MAX.
W = 25' "
H = 20' MAX.
W = 10' "
250 SQ. FT. MAXIMUM AREA
H = 20' MAX.
W = 25' "
KEY TO MATERIALS
Caulking
Oakum
Pointing mortar
Glass block
3/8" Expans'n strip
Metal & Steel
Scale of details = 1 1/2" = 1'-0"

Details of sections lettered above are shown below and on next page. All details shown are modular. Dimensions: Arrow indicates dimension is to grid line. Dot indicates dimension is not on grid line.

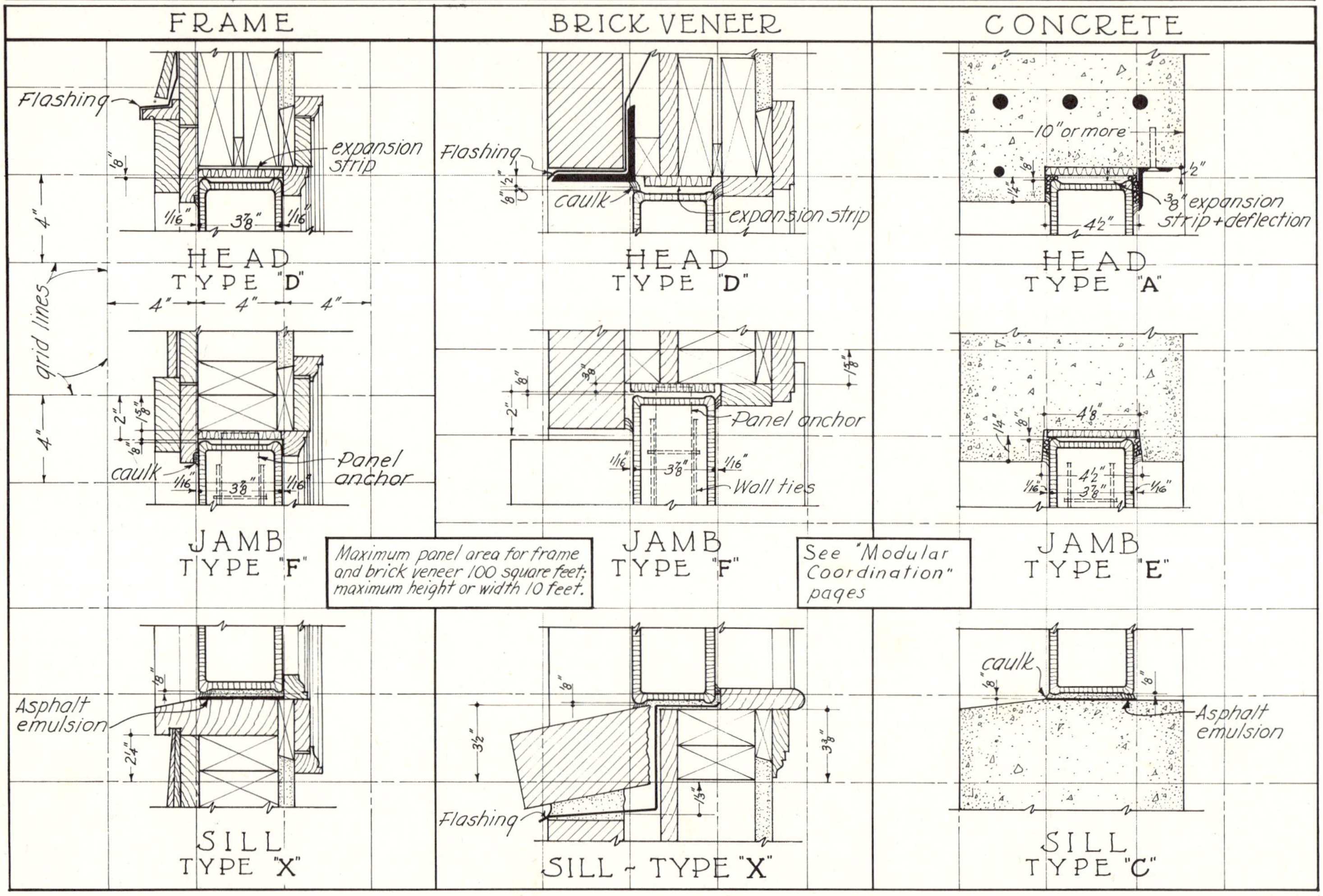

FRAME
BRICK VENEER
CONCRETE
Flashing
expansion strip
1/16" 3 7/8" 1/16"
HEAD
TYPE "D"
grid lines
4" 4" 4"
caulk
expansion strip
10" or more
3/8" expansion strip + deflection
4 1/2"
HEAD
TYPE "A"
Panel anchor
caulk
JAMB
TYPE "F"
Wall ties
JAMB
TYPE "E"
Maximum panel area for frame and brick veneer 100 square feet; maximum height or width 10 feet.
See "Modular Coordination" pages
Asphalt emulsion
SILL
TYPE "X"
Flashing
SILL - TYPE "X"
caulk
Asphalt emulsion
SILL
TYPE "C"

VERTICAL INTERMEDIATE DETAILS

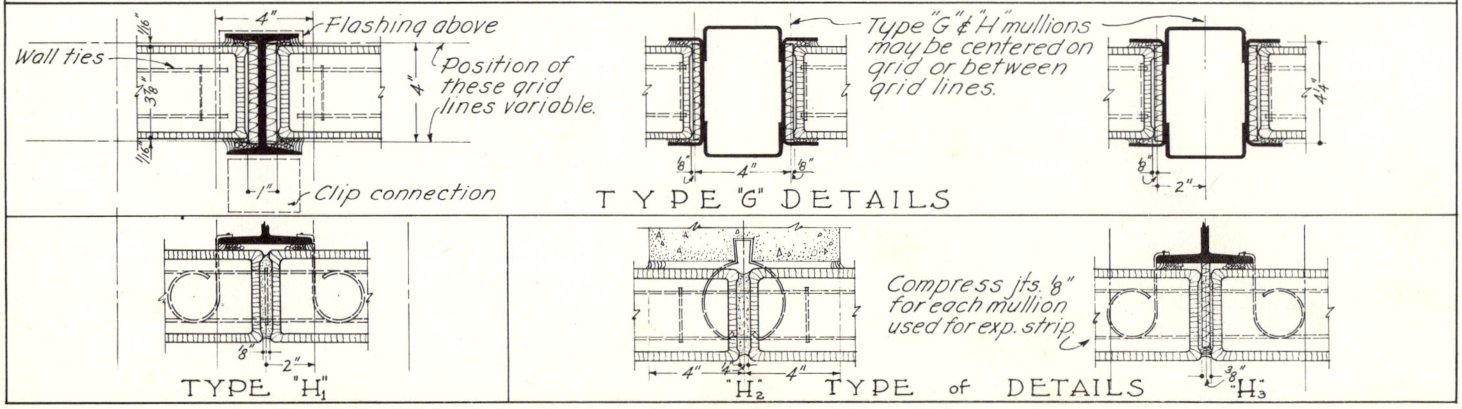

Wall ties
Flashing above
Position of these grid lines variable.
Clip connection
Type "G" & "H" mullions may be centered on grid or between grid lines.
TYPE "G" DETAILS
TYPE "H1"
Compress jts. 1/8" for each mullion used for exp. strip.
"H2"
TYPE of DETAILS
"H3"

Data checked by Pittsburgh-Corning Corporation & Owens-Illinois Glass Company

GLASS BLOCKS - EXTERIOR USE

DETAILS for BRICK CONSTRUCTION

For key to section types — see previous page.

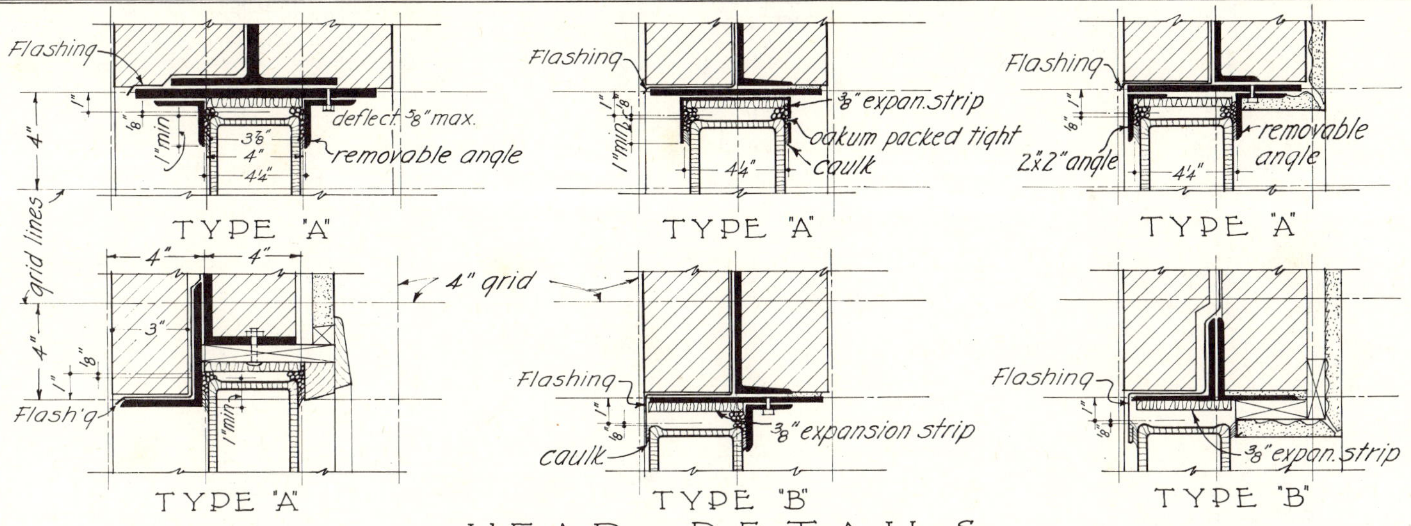

Flashing
deflect 5/8" max.
removable angle
3⅞"
4"
4¼"
1"
⅛"
1" min
4"
grid lines
TYPE "A"
Flashing
⅜" expan. strip
oakum packed tight
caulk
1" min
4¼"
TYPE "A"
Flashing
removable angle
2"x2" angle
4¼"
TYPE "A"
4"
4"
3"
Flash'g
1" min
TYPE "A"
4" grid
Flashing
caulk
⅜" expansion strip
TYPE "B"
Flashing
⅜" expan. strip
TYPE "B"

HEAD DETAILS

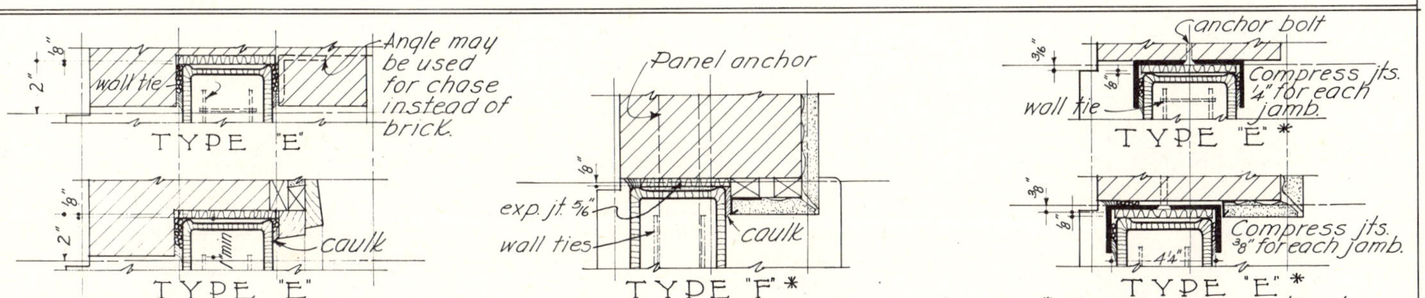

wall tie
2"
⅛"
Angle may be used for chase instead of brick.
TYPE "E"
2"
1" min
caulk
TYPE "E"
Panel anchor
exp. jt. 5/16"
wall ties
caulk
TYPE "F" *
anchor bolt
3/16"
wall tie
Compress jts. ¼" for each jamb.
TYPE "E" *
⅜"
Compress jts. ⅜" for each jamb.
4¼"
TYPE "E" *

JAMB DETAILS

* Position of vertical grid lines variable

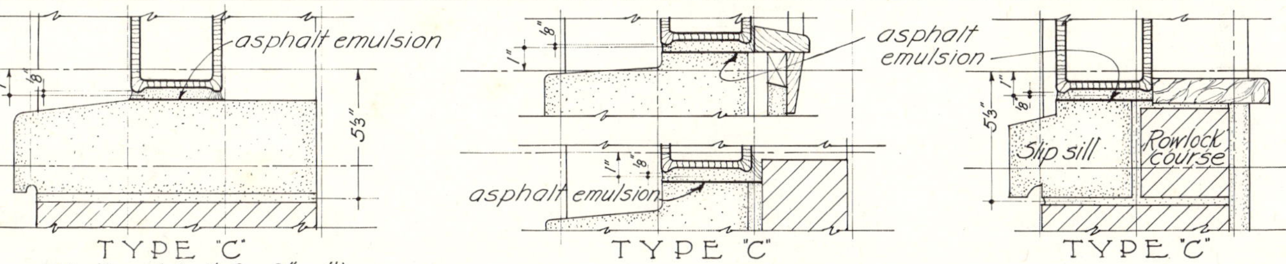

asphalt emulsion
5¾"
TYPE "C"
(Similar detail for 8" wall.)
asphalt emulsion
asphalt emulsion
TYPE "C"
Slip sill
Rowlock course
5¾"
TYPE "C"

SILL DETAILS

(Sills designed to architects details.)

Position of vertical grid lines at head, sill & vertical intermediate details varies with position of grid lines at jambs. Horizontal joints of panel usually centered on grid line or 1" below or above.

HORIZONTAL INTERMEDIATE DETAILS

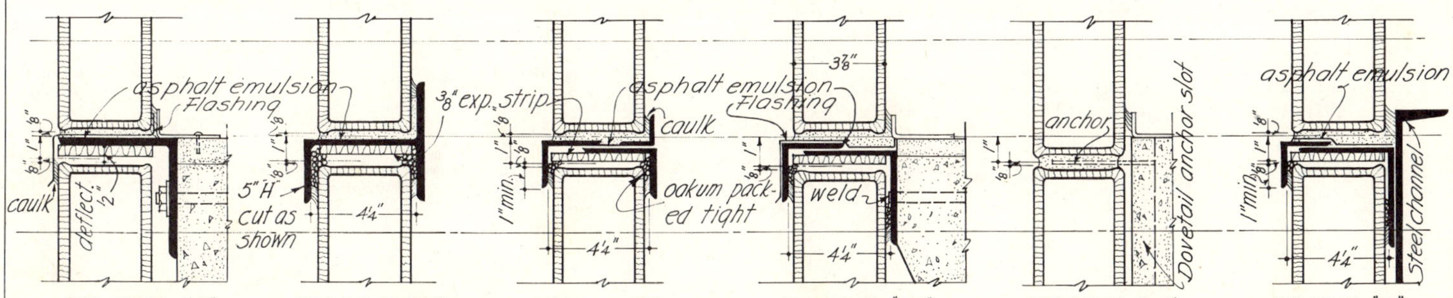

asphalt emulsion
Flashing
caulk
deflect ½"
5" H cut as shown
TYPE "J"
⅜" exp. strip
4¼"
TYPE "K"
caulk
1" min.
4¼"
TYPE "L"
asphalt emulsion
Flashing
oakum packed tight
3⅞"
weld
4¼"
TYPE "M"
anchor
Dovetail anchor slot
TYPE "N"
asphalt emulsion
1" min
4¼"
Steel channel
TYPE "O"

See "Modular Coordination" pages. Position of horizontal & vertical grid lines variable.
Scale 1½" = 1'-0"

Data checked by Pittsburgh-Corning Corporation & Owens-Illinois Glass Company

GLASS BLOCKS *with* METAL WINDOWS

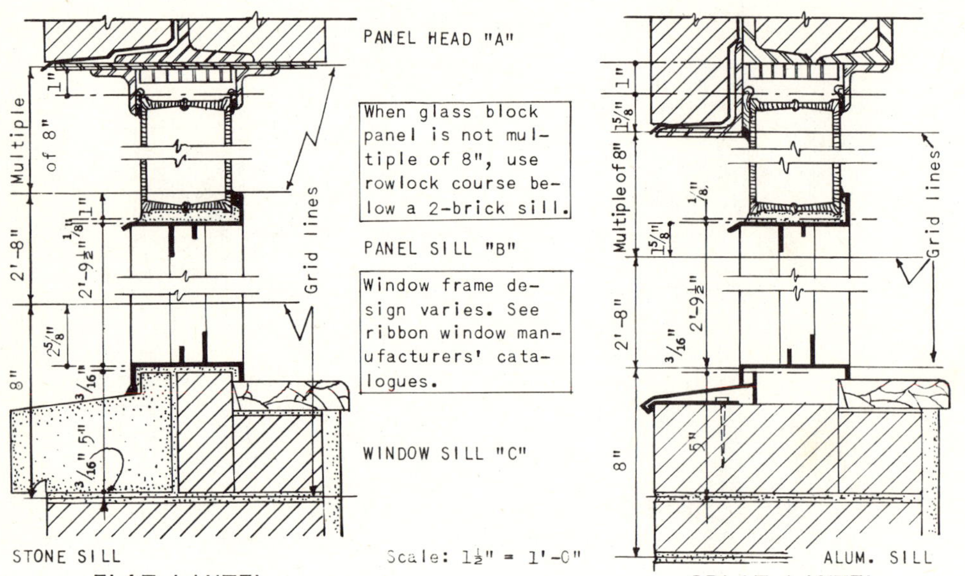
PANEL HEAD "A"
When glass block panel is not multiple of 8", use rowlock course below a 2-brick sill.
PANEL SILL "B"
Window frame design varies. See ribbon window manufacturers' catalogues.
WINDOW SILL "C"
Multiple of 8"
2'-8"
2'-9½"
8"
Grid lines
STONE SILL
Scale: 1½" = 1'-0"
ALUM. SILL
FLAT LINTEL
SPLIT LINTEL

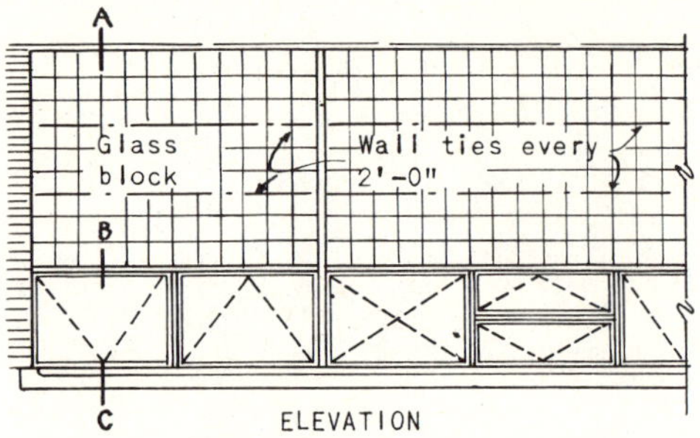
A
Glass block
Wall ties every 2'-0"
B
C
ELEVATION

The Glass Block & Ribbon Window Standards Committee has established standards for details & sizes of openings. At left are shown standard opening heights; below, standard opening widths.
Maximum opening length: 18'-0"
Maximum area: 144 sq. ft. (includes glass block panel plus ½ ribbon window area).
Maximum ventilator size: 4'-0" x 2'-9" high.
Higher windows shall have 2 or more ventilators.

MODULAR HEIGHTS

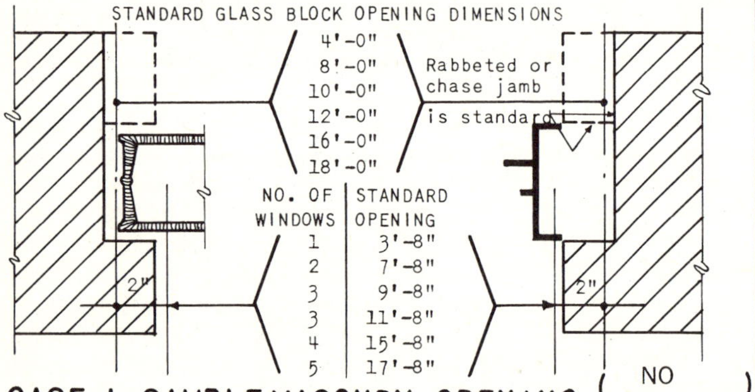
STANDARD GLASS BLOCK OPENING DIMENSIONS
4'-0"
8'-0"
10'-0"
12'-0"
16'-0"
18'-0"
Rabbeted or chase jamb is standard
NO. OF WINDOWS | STANDARD OPENING
1 | 3'-8"
2 | 7'-8"
3 | 9'-8"
3 | 11'-8"
4 | 15'-8"
5 | 17'-8"
2"

CASE 1-SIMPLE MASONRY OPENING (NO MULLIONS)

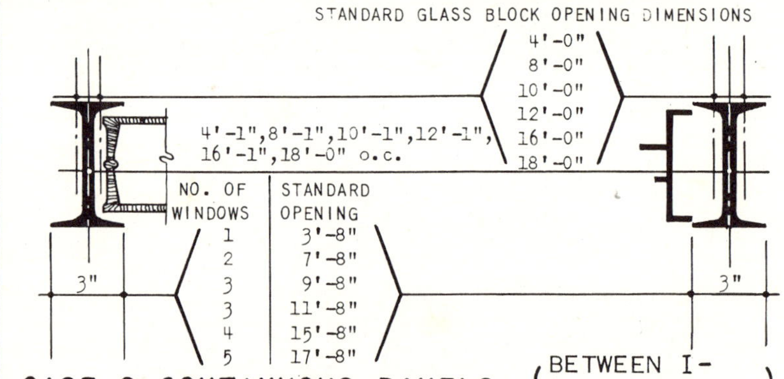
STANDARD GLASS BLOCK OPENING DIMENSIONS
4'-0"
8'-0"
10'-0"
12'-0"
16'-0"
18'-0"
4'-1",8'-1",10'-1",12'-1", 16'-1",18'-0" o.c.
NO. OF WINDOWS | STANDARD OPENING
1 | 3'-8"
2 | 7'-8"
3 | 9'-8"
3 | 11'-8"
4 | 15'-8"
5 | 17'-8"
3"

CASE 2-CONTINUOUS PANELS (BETWEEN I-BEAM MULLIONS)

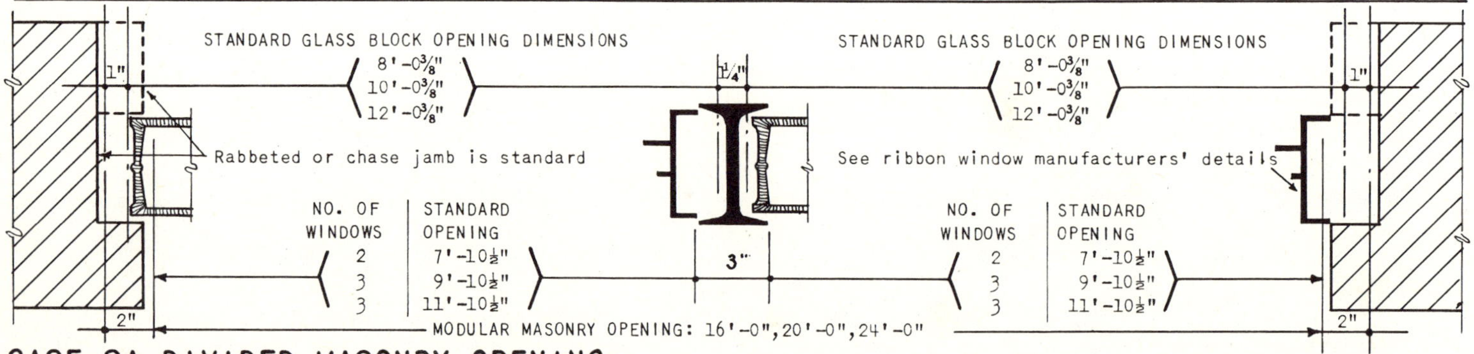
STANDARD GLASS BLOCK OPENING DIMENSIONS
8'-0⅜"
10'-0⅜"
12'-0⅜"
1"
1¼"
Rabbeted or chase jamb is standard
See ribbon window manufacturers' details
NO. OF WINDOWS | STANDARD OPENING
2 | 7'-10½"
3 | 9'-10½"
3 | 11'-10½"
3"
2"
MODULAR MASONRY OPENING: 16'-0",20'-0",24'-0"

CASE 3A-DIVIDED MASONRY OPENING (WITH ONE MULLION THROUGH GLASS BLOCK PANEL)

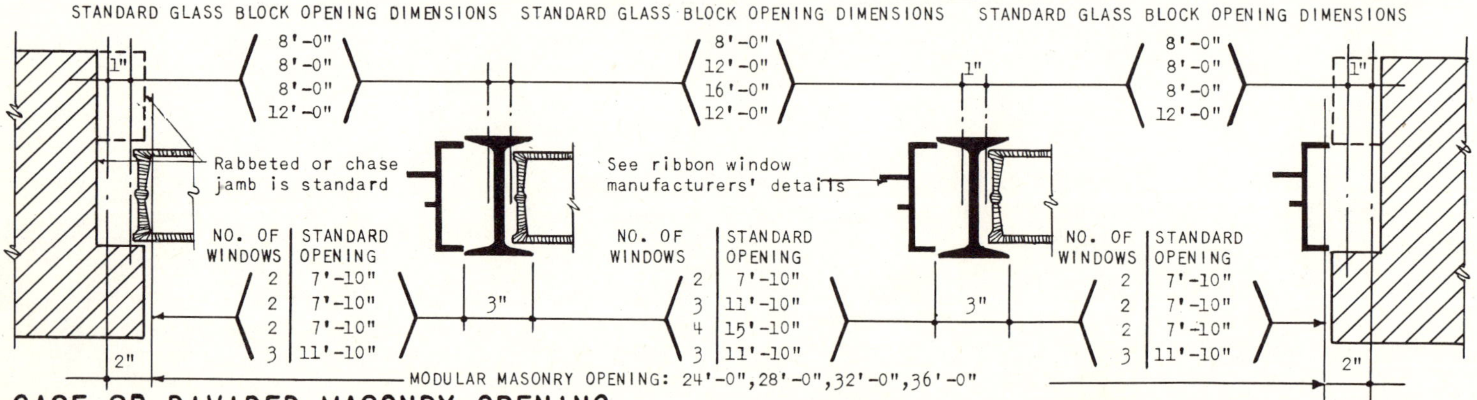
STANDARD GLASS BLOCK OPENING DIMENSIONS
8'-0"
8'-0"
8'-0"
12'-0"
STANDARD GLASS BLOCK OPENING DIMENSIONS
8'-0"
12'-0"
16'-0"
12'-0"
1"
Rabbeted or chase jamb is standard
See ribbon window manufacturers' details
NO. OF WINDOWS | STANDARD OPENING
2 | 7'-10"
2 | 7'-10"
2 | 7'-10"
3 | 11'-10"
NO. OF WINDOWS | STANDARD OPENING
2 | 7'-10"
3 | 11'-10"
4 | 15'-10"
3 | 11'-10"
3"
2"
MODULAR MASONRY OPENING: 24'-0",28'-0",32'-0",36'-0"

CASE 3B-DIVIDED MASONRY OPENING (WITH TWO MULLIONS THROUGH GLASS BLOCK PANELS)

DATA BY PITTSBURGH-CORNING CORPORATION & OWENS-ILLINOIS GLASS COMPANY

GLASS BLOCKS

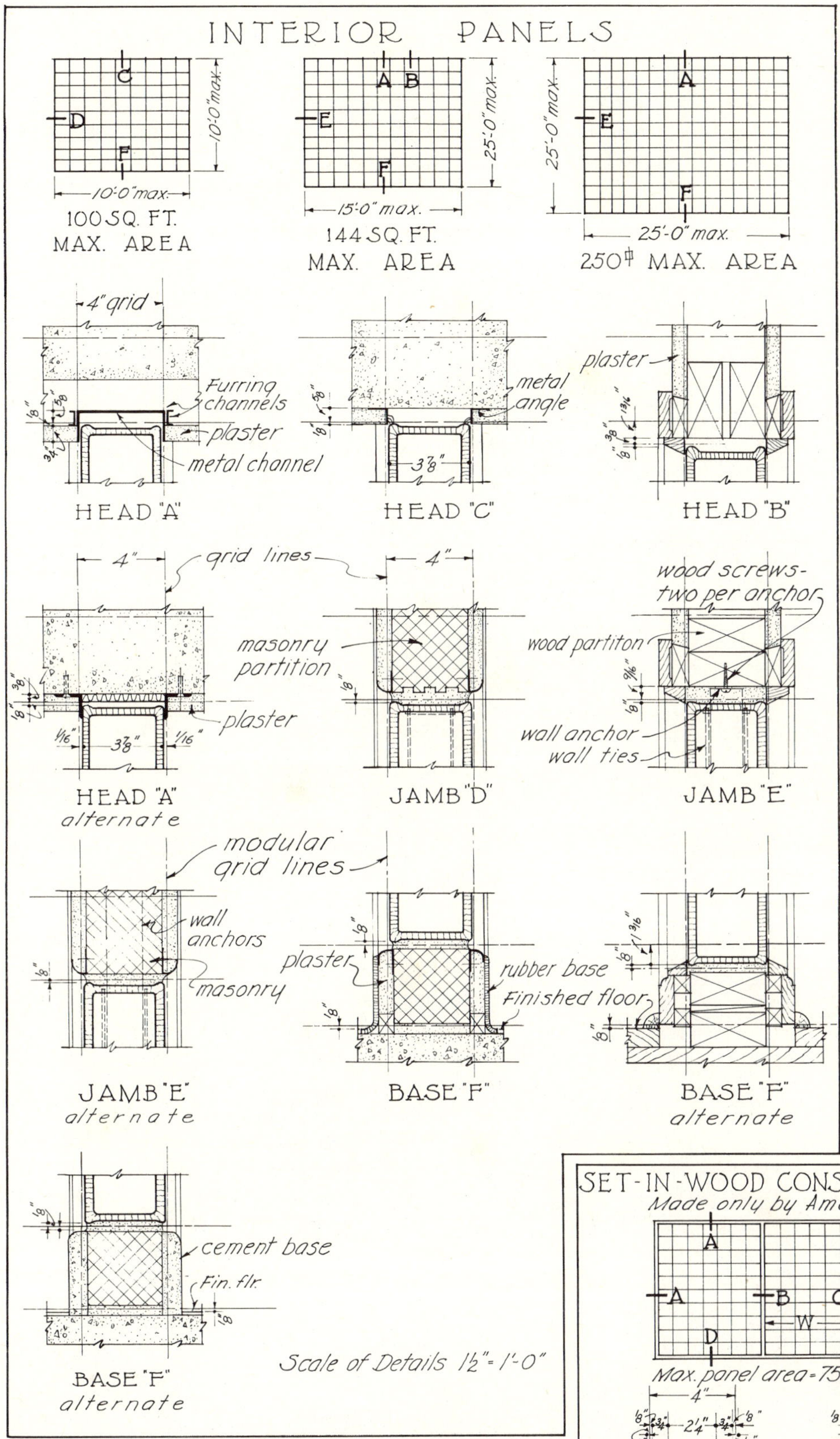
INTERIOR PANELS
C
D
F
10'-0" max.
10'-0" max.
100 SQ. FT.
MAX. AREA
A B
E
F
25'-0" max.
15'-0" max.
144 SQ. FT.
MAX. AREA
A
E
F
25'-0" max.
25'-0" max.
250# MAX. AREA
4" grid
Furring channels
plaster
metal channel
HEAD "A"
metal angle
3 7/8"
HEAD "C"
plaster
HEAD "B"
4"
grid lines
4"
masonry partition
plaster
3 7/8"
1/16"
1/16"
HEAD "A"
alternate
JAMB "D"
wood screws-
two per anchor
wood partiton
wall anchor
wall ties
JAMB "E"
modular
grid lines
wall anchors
masonry
JAMB "E"
alternate
plaster
rubber base
Finished floor
BASE "F"
BASE "F"
alternate
cement base
Fin. flr.
BASE "F"
alternate
Scale of Details 1½" = 1'-0"

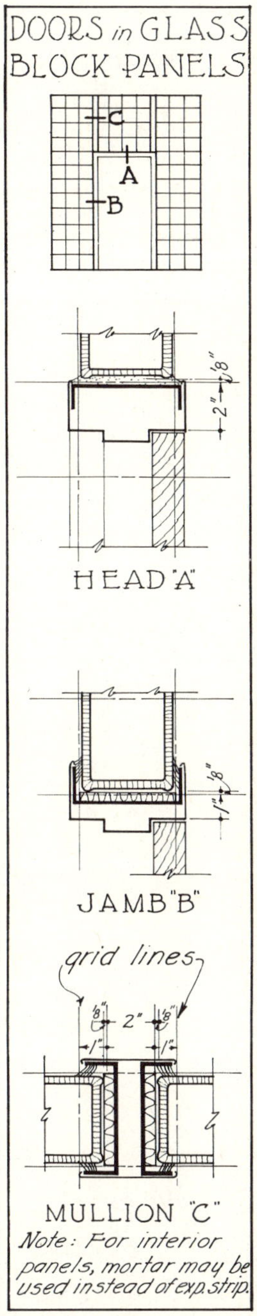
DOORS in GLASS
BLOCK PANELS
C
A
B
HEAD "A"
JAMB "B"
grid lines
2"
MULLION "C"
Note: For interior
panels, mortar may be
used instead of exp. strip.

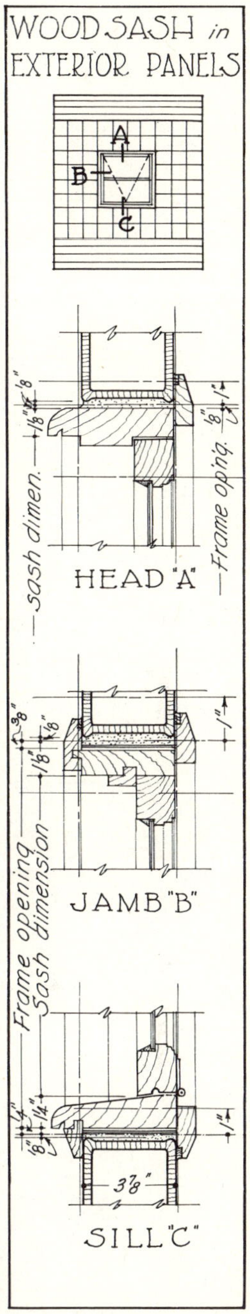
WOOD SASH in
EXTERIOR PANELS
A
B
C
sash dimen.
Frame opng.
HEAD "A"
JAMB "B"
Frame opening
Sash dimension
3 7/8"
SILL "C"

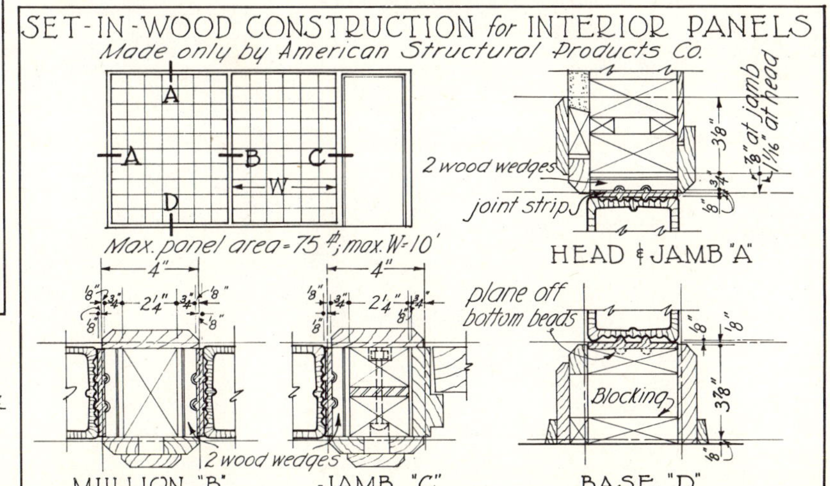
SET-IN-WOOD CONSTRUCTION for INTERIOR PANELS
Made only by American Structural Products Co.
A
A
B
C
W
D
Max. panel area = 75#; max. W = 10'
2 wood wedges
joint strip
1/8" at jamb
1/16" at head
3 7/8"
HEAD & JAMB "A"
4"
2 1/4"
4"
2 1/4"
plane off
bottom beads
Blocking
3 7/8"
2 wood wedges
MULLION "B"
JAMB "C"
BASE "D"

Construction supporting panels over 144 sq. ft. in area must be of a type which will provide for a minimum of movement and settlement.
Before glass blocks are installed in wood partitions, all wood adjacent to mortar shall be properly primed.

Data on this page by Pittsburgh-Corning Corp. & Owens-Illinois Glass Company

SEE "Modular Coordination" pages

DAYLIGHTING NOMOGRAPH

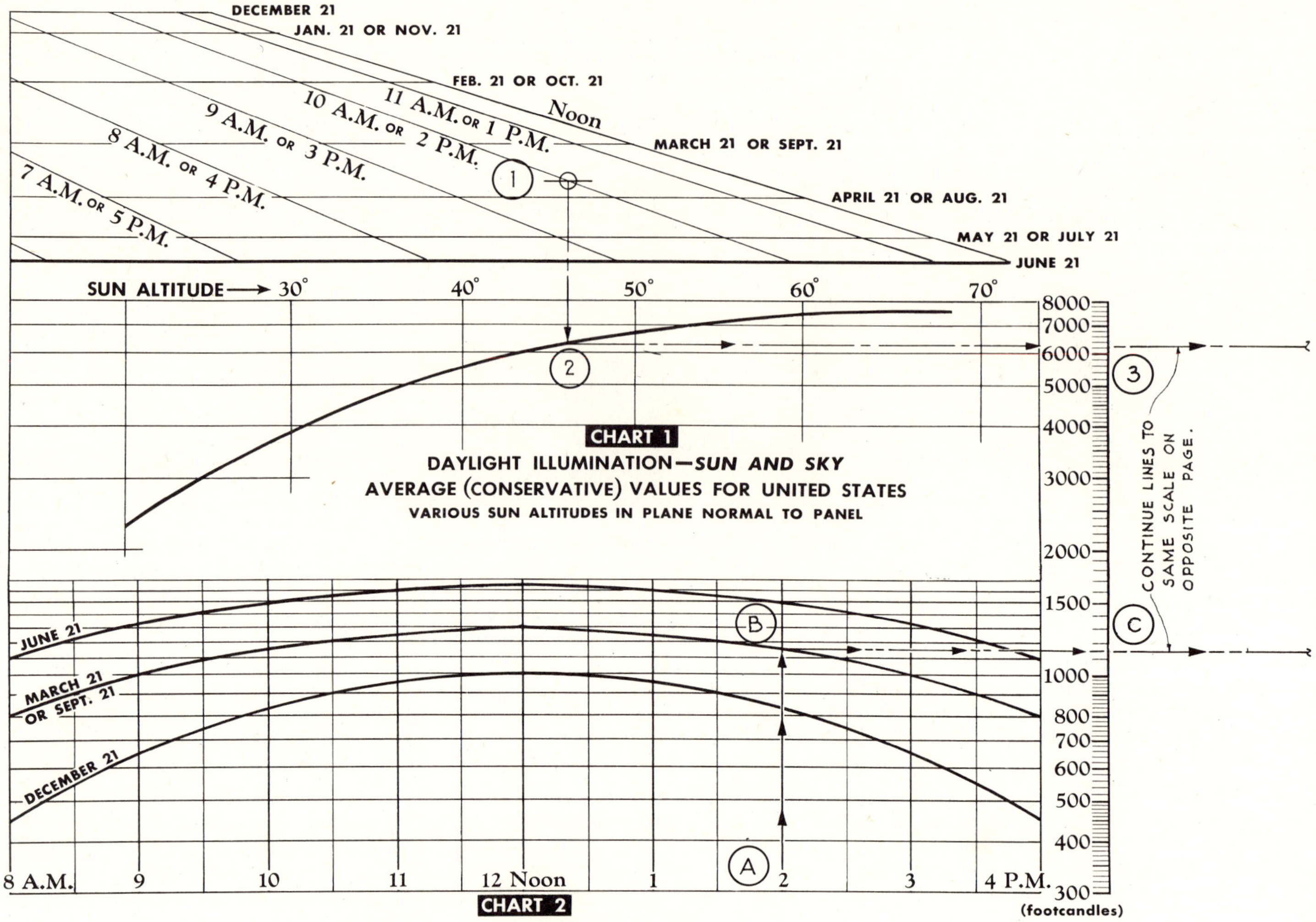
DECEMBER 21
JAN. 21 OR NOV. 21
FEB. 21 OR OCT. 21
MARCH 21 OR SEPT. 21
APRIL 21 OR AUG. 21
MAY 21 OR JULY 21
JUNE 21
Noon
11 A.M. OR 1 P.M.
10 A.M. OR 2 P.M.
9 A.M. OR 3 P.M.
8 A.M. OR 4 P.M.
7 A.M. OR 5 P.M.
SUN ALTITUDE
30°
40°
50°
60°
70°
8000
7000
6000
5000
4000
3000
2000
1500
1000
800
700
600
500
400
300
(footcandles)
CONTINUE LINES TO SAME SCALE ON OPPOSITE PAGE.
JUNE 21
MARCH 21 OR SEPT. 21
DECEMBER 21
8 A.M.
9
10
11
12 Noon
1
2
3
4 P.M.

CHART 1

DAYLIGHT ILLUMINATION—*SUN AND SKY*

AVERAGE (CONSERVATIVE) VALUES FOR UNITED STATES

VARIOUS SUN ALTITUDES IN PLANE NORMAL TO PANEL

CHART 2

DAYLIGHT ILLUMINATION—*SKY ONLY*

AVERAGE (CONSERVATIVE) VALUES FOR UNITED STATES

"CHART 1" VALUES ARE BASED ON THE SUN BEING IN A PLANE NORMAL TO THE PANEL. FOR OTHER CONDITIONS, MULTIPLY NOMOGRAPH VALUES BY THE FOLLOWING FACTORS DEPENDING ON AMOUNT OF DEPARTURE FROM NORMAL: 0° TO 15° - 1; 16° TO 30° - 4/5; 31° TO 45° - 2/3; 46° TO 60° - 1/2; 61° TO 75° - 1/3; 76° TO 90° - USE VALUE BASED ON "CHART 2" INSTEAD OF "CHART 1".

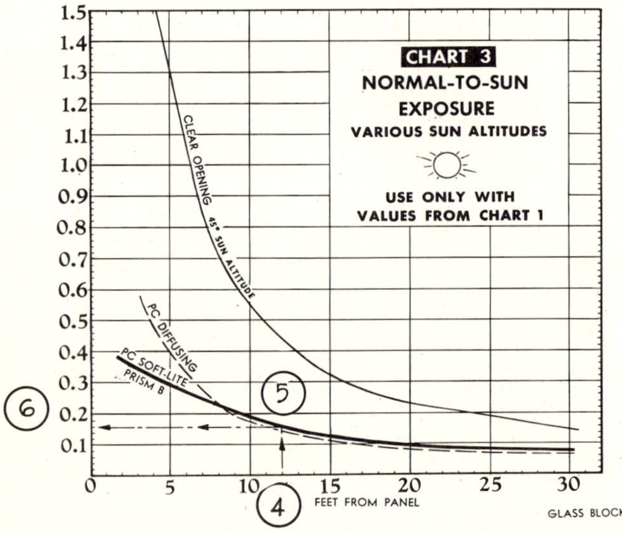
CHART 3
NORMAL-TO-SUN EXPOSURE
VARIOUS SUN ALTITUDES
USE ONLY WITH VALUES FROM CHART 1
CLEAR OPENING 45° SUN ALTITUDE
PC DIFFUSING
PC SOFT-LITE PRISM B
FEET FROM PANEL

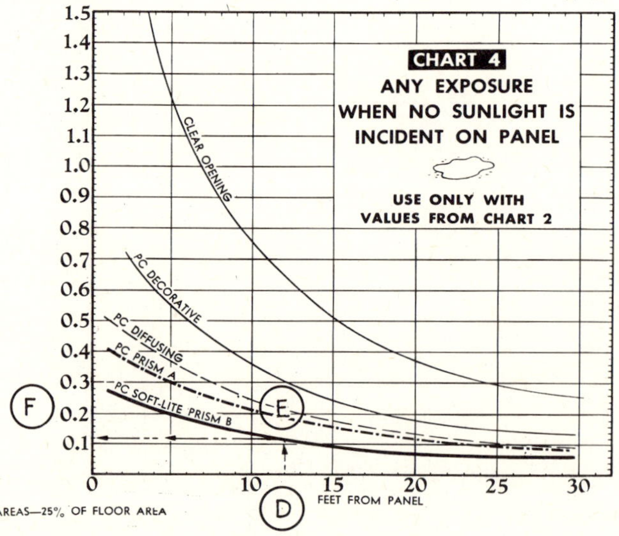
CHART 4
ANY EXPOSURE WHEN NO SUNLIGHT IS INCIDENT ON PANEL
USE ONLY WITH VALUES FROM CHART 2
CLEAR OPENING
PC DECORATIVE
PC DIFFUSING
PC PRISM A
PC SOFT-LITE PRISM B
FEET FROM PANEL

GLASS BLOCK PANEL AREAS—25% OF FLOOR AREA

FOR P.C. GLASS BLOCKS

FOR ESTIMATING DAYLIGHT ILLUMINATION ON WORKING PLANES (30″ ABOVE FLOOR) PROVIDED BY PANELS OF PITTSBURGH-CORNING GLASS BLOCKS

FOR TWO EXAMPLES SHOWN, FOLLOW CONSECUTIVELY EITHER STEPS (1),(2),(3), ETC. OR STEPS (A),(B),(C), ETC.

THE NOMOGRAPH IS BASED ON A RATIO OF PANEL AREA TO FLOOR AREA OF 25%. VALUES READ FROM IT CAN BE PROPORTIONED FOR OTHER PANEL TO FLOOR RATIOS AS FOLLOWS:

$$\text{CORRECT VALUE} = \text{NOMOGRAPH READING} \times 4 \times \frac{\text{PANEL AREA}}{\text{FLOOR AREA}}$$

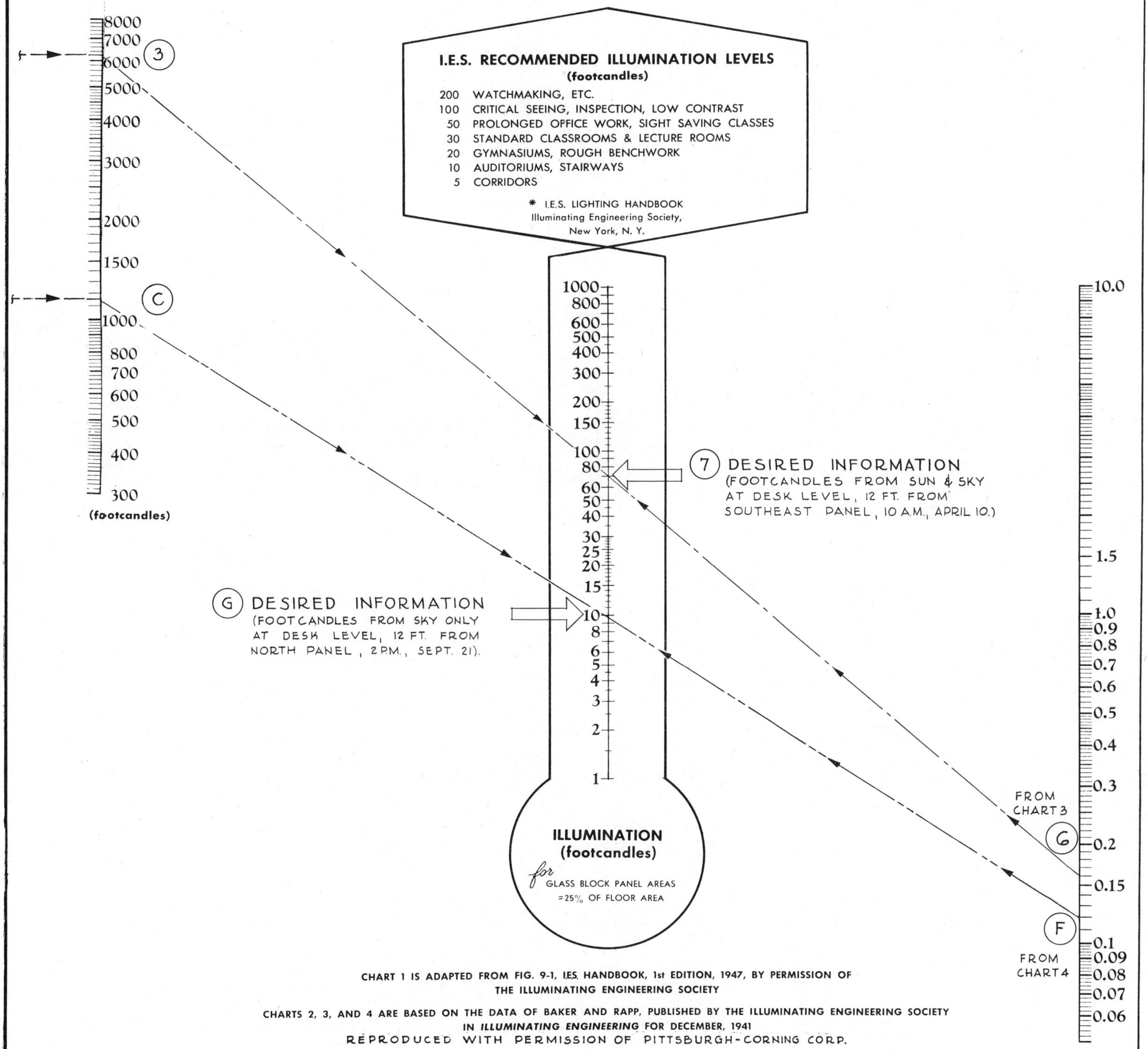

I.E.S. RECOMMENDED ILLUMINATION LEVELS
(footcandles)
200 WATCHMAKING, ETC.
100 CRITICAL SEEING, INSPECTION, LOW CONTRAST
50 PROLONGED OFFICE WORK, SIGHT SAVING CLASSES
30 STANDARD CLASSROOMS & LECTURE ROOMS
20 GYMNASIUMS, ROUGH BENCHWORK
10 AUDITORIUMS, STAIRWAYS
5 CORRIDORS
* I.E.S. LIGHTING HANDBOOK
Illuminating Engineering Society,
New York, N. Y.
8000
7000
6000
5000
4000
3000
2000
1500
1000
800
700
600
500
400
300
(footcandles)
3
C
1000
800
600
500
400
300
200
150
100
80
60
50
40
30
25
20
15
10
8
6
5
4
3
2
1
7 DESIRED INFORMATION
(FOOTCANDLES FROM SUN & SKY AT DESK LEVEL, 12 FT. FROM SOUTHEAST PANEL, 10 A.M., APRIL 10.)
G DESIRED INFORMATION
(FOOTCANDLES FROM SKY ONLY AT DESK LEVEL, 12 FT. FROM NORTH PANEL, 2 P.M., SEPT. 21).
ILLUMINATION
(footcandles)
for GLASS BLOCK PANEL AREAS
=25% OF FLOOR AREA
10.0
1.5
1.0
0.9
0.8
0.7
0.6
0.5
0.4
0.3
0.2
0.15
0.1
0.09
0.08
0.07
0.06
FROM CHART 3
6
F
FROM CHART 4

CHART 1 IS ADAPTED FROM FIG. 9-1, IES HANDBOOK, 1st EDITION, 1947, BY PERMISSION OF THE ILLUMINATING ENGINEERING SOCIETY

CHARTS 2, 3, AND 4 ARE BASED ON THE DATA OF BAKER AND RAPP, PUBLISHED BY THE ILLUMINATING ENGINEERING SOCIETY IN *ILLUMINATING ENGINEERING* FOR DECEMBER, 1941

REPRODUCED WITH PERMISSION OF PITTSBURGH-CORNING CORP.

DAYLIGHT ILLUMINATION—O-I GLASS BLOCK

TABLE I : Brightness Constant in Foot-lamberts

	8″ SIZE	12″ SIZE
Glass Block No. 63	260	280
Glass Block No. 65	350	390
Glass Block No. 65-F	330	360
Glass Block No. 80	250	290
Glass Block No. 80-F	260	275
Toplite	440	

To obtain the brightness in foot-lamberts *of O-I functional glass block for any time of year and exposure, multiply the brightness constant in Table I by the appropriate exterior illumination factor, Table II.*

The important ratio of source brightness to task illumination—for the three types of rooms in Table III is determined by dividing brightness, Table I, by illumination, Table III.

TABLE II : Exterior Illumination Factor

		12 NOON			3 P.M. WEST 9 A.M. EAST			CLEAR SKY NORTH—NO SUN	OVERCAST SKY
32° No. LAT.		12/21	2/21 10/21	4/21 8/21	12/21	2/21 10/21	4/21 8/21		
42° No. LAT.		2/21 10/21	3/21 9/21	6/21	2/21 10/21	3/21 9/21	6/21		
No. 363	S	9.6	9.0	3.8	3.3	3.8	3.0	1.4	.90
	EW	1.4	1.4	1.4	3.8	5.3	9.1	1.4	.90
No. 463	S	10	9.4	4.1	3.5	3.9	3.1	1.5	1.00
	EW	1.5	1.5	1.5	4.0	5.6	9.5	1.5	1.00
No. 365	S	7.4	7.1	4.0	3.0	3.0	2.6	1.4	.84
	EW	1.4	1.4	1.4	3.4	4.8	7.2	1.4	.84
No. 465	S	7.4	7.1	4.0	3.1	3.1	2.7	1.4	.85
	EW	1.4	1.4	1.4	3.7	4.8	7.2	1.4	.85
No. 365-F	S	5.0	4.8	2.7	2.1	2.2	1.7	.94	.58
	EW	.94	.94	.94	2.5	3.2	4.8	.94	.58
No. 465-F	S	5.3	5.0	2.8	2.1	2.2	1.9	.96	.60
	EW	.96	.96	.96	2.5	3.3	5.1	.96	.60
No. 380	S	6.1	6.1	4.4	3.2	3.1	2.7	1.5	.88
	EW	1.5	1.5	1.5	3.5	4.5	6.2	1.5	.88
No. 480	S	6.8	6.8	4.6	3.3	3.3	2.7	1.6	.96
	EW	1.6	1.6	1.6	3.8	4.9	6.9	1.6	.96
No. 380-F	S	4.5	4.5	3.0	2.3	2.0	1.8	1.0	.64
	EW	1.0	1.0	1.0	2.4	3.1	4.5	1.0	.64
No. 480-F	S	4.5	4.5	3.0	2.3	2.2	1.8	1.0	.64
	EW	1.0	1.0	1.0	2.4	3.1	4.5	1.0	.64
Toplite All Exp.		3.0	3.2	3.3	.75	1.1	2.4	—	1.0

Table III shows the illumination in standard-shape classrooms from three different sources of daylight. Continuous *unilateral* fenestration is six feet of O-I glass block above a shaded vision strip. *Toplite fenestration* is three 4′ x 4′ O-I panels. *Clerestory fenestration* is a continuous O-I glass block panel four feet high, with a nine-foot sill.

To obtain illumination from each of these sources of daylight, multiply factor in Table III (for the desired position in the room) by exterior illumination factor in Table II (for the appropriate location, time of day and year and exposure).

Note: *Figures for illumination from glass block panel do not include vision strip component. The contribution from such a shaded strip is 37 fc. at 3′ station; 6 fc. at 15′ and 3 fc. at 27′. Values are approximate for all exterior conditions cited.*

In the case of bilateral jobs, add the illumination from the unilateral fenestration to the illumination from Toplite or clerestory.

For other fenestration sizes than those shown, illumination can be approximated by a direct ratio, as follows: For variations in glass area (with floor area constant)—divide glass area used by that of room shown, and multiply this factor by illumination from Table III.

Example: *What is the approximate maximum brightness ratio and illumination in a room thirty feet square and with a main fenestration of five feet No. 463 block on south exposure, and four feet No. 480 block in clerestory on the north, for March 21, 42° north latitude, 9 A.M. (No vision strip)?*

Select the three illumination factors shown for the unilateral room in Table III. Multiply these factors by the exterior illumination factor which corresponds to No. 463 block on March 21, 9 A.M. and 42° north latitude. Do the same for the clerestory panel using non-sun exposure, clear sky. Add together figures for corresponding task position.

Illumination Factors X Exterior Illumination Factor

A = 54 × 3.9 = 210
B = 30 × 3.9 = 117
C = 21 × 3.9 = 82
(These figures are for a 6′ panel; for a 5′ panel multiply by 5/6. Then, A = 175; B = 97; C = 68.)
G = 14 × 1.6 = 22
H = 20 × 1.6 = 32
I = 36 × 1.6 = 58
Total A + G = 197 = Total Illumination at A
Total B + H = 129 = Total Illumination at B
Total C + I = 126 = Total Illumination at C

For usual observer position, the brightness of No. 463 block is 3.9 x 280 or 1100 foot-lamberts. For the No. 480, it is 1.6 x 290 or 465 foot-lamberts. Thus the maximum ratio of brightness to minimum illumination is 1100 ÷ 126 = 8.7.

TABLE III : Interior Illumination Distribution Factors

UNILATERAL

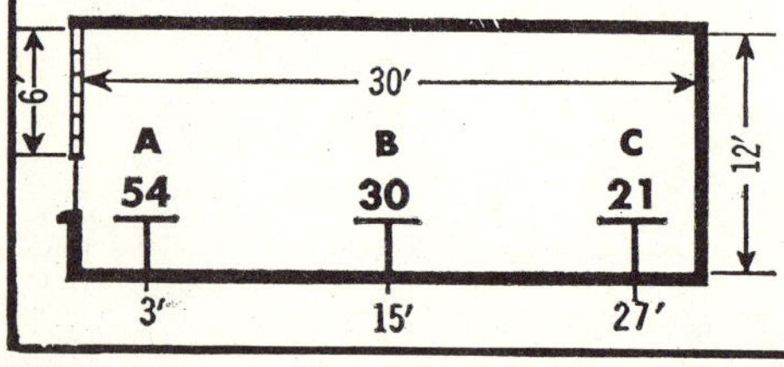
6′
30′
A
54
B
30
C
21
12′
3′
15′
27′

TOPLITE ONLY

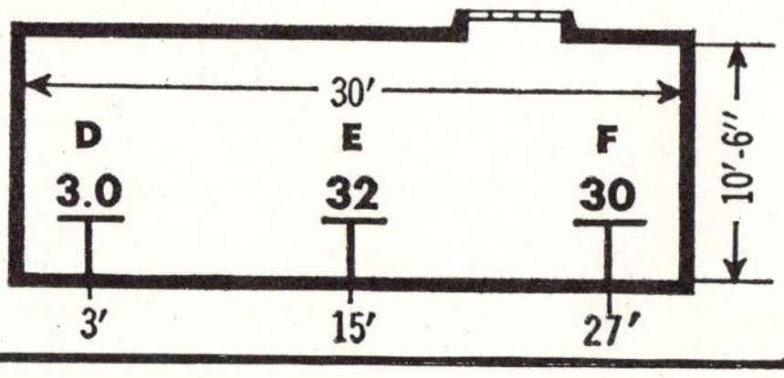
30′
D
3.0
E
32
F
30
10′-6″
3′
15′
27′

CLERESTORY ONLY

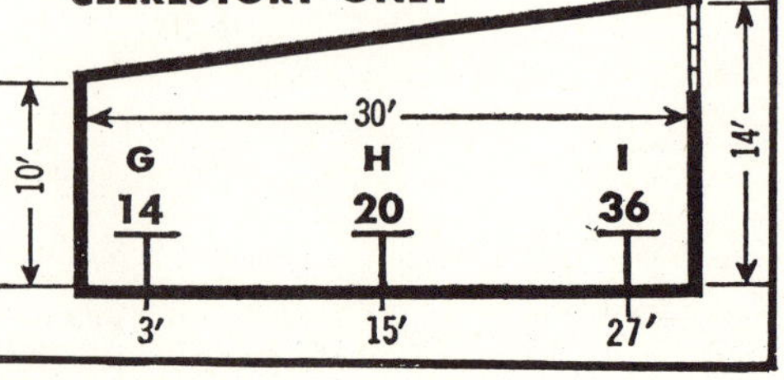
10′
30′
G
14
H
20
I
36
14′
3′
15′
27′

NOTE: This method of illumination prediction is reasonably accurate for regions where daylight intensities are at maximum. For other regions, slightly lower valves are to be expected.

DATA THIS PAGE BY KIMBLE GLASS CO., A SUBSIDIARY OF OWENS-ILLINOIS GLASS CO

CORRUGATED GLASS

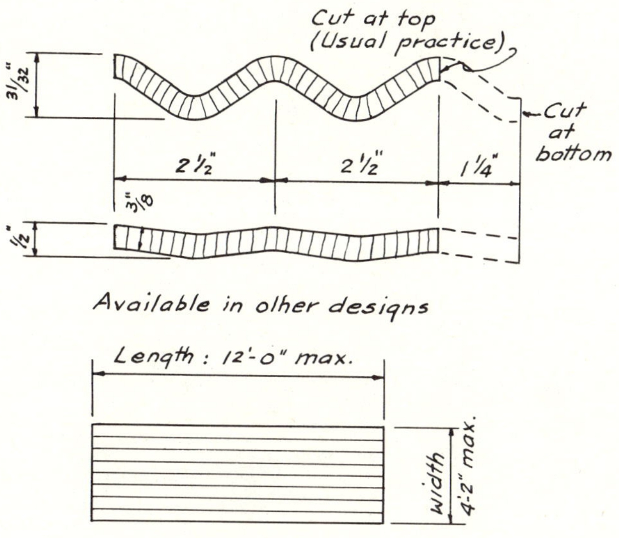

Cut at top
(Usual practice)
Cut at bottom
3 1/32"
2 1/2"
2 1/2"
1 1/4"
3/8"
1/2"
Available in other designs
Length : 12'-0" max.
width 4'-2" max.

DIMENSIONS
Scale: 4" = 1'-0"

INCL. ANGLE	INCR. IN WIDTH	INCL. ANGLE	INCR IN WIDTH
60°	5/8"	130°	5/16"
70°	5/8"	140°	1/4"
80°	9/16"	150°	3/16"
90°	9/16"	160°	1/8"
100°	1/2"	170°	1/16"
110°	7/16"	180°	0"
120°	3/8"		

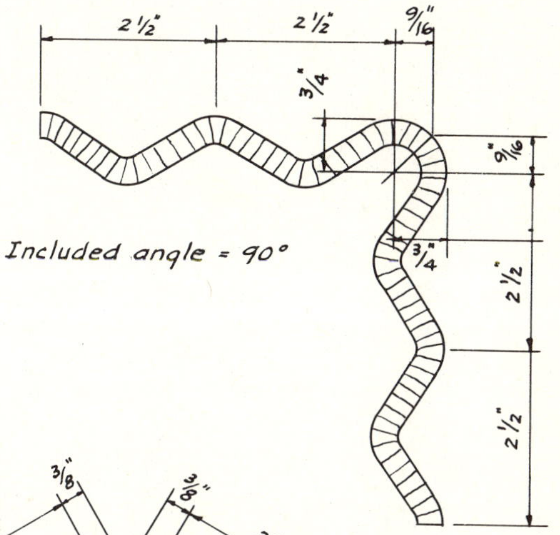

2 1/2"
2 1/2"
9/16"
3/4"
9/16"
Included angle = 90°
3/4"
2 1/2
2 1/2

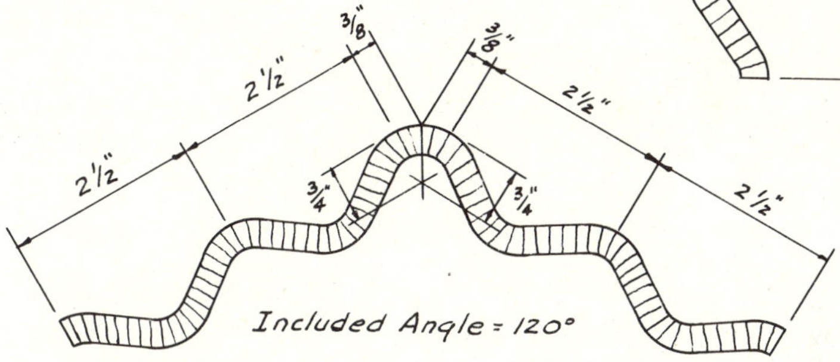

3/8"
3/8"
2 1/2"
2 1/2"
2 1/2"
2 1/2"
3/4"
3/4"
Included Angle = 120°

LAYOUT AT CORNERS
Scale : 4" = 1'-0"

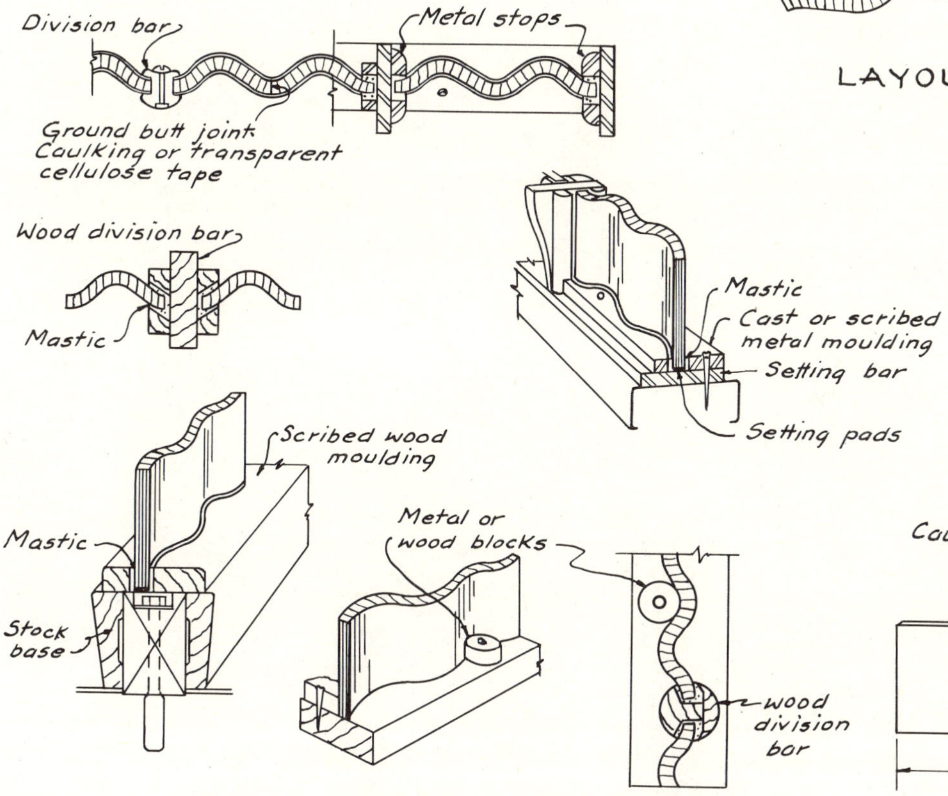

Division bar
Metal stops
Ground butt joint
Caulking or transparent cellulose tape
Wood division bar
Mastic
Mastic
Cast or scribed metal moulding
Setting bar
Setting pads
Scribed wood moulding
Mastic
Stock base
Metal or wood blocks
wood division bar

INSTALLATION DETAILS
Not to scale

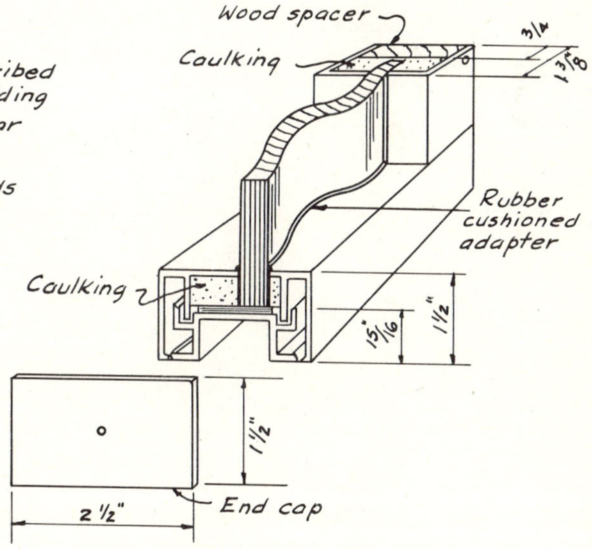

Wood spacer
Caulking
3/4
1 3/8
Rubber cushioned adapter
Caulking
15/16"
1 1/2"
1 1/2"
2 1/2"
End cap

SNAP-ON MOULDING
O. E. Stelzer

GENERAL: Do not glaze directly on hard metal, masonry or other unyielding base; where such base is necessary use wood setting blocks or other cushioning material; do not wedge glass tightly into opening.
FOR INTERIOR GLASS: Glass can be set with division bars of metal, wood or plastic, specially designed or made of stock shapes; where edges are not ground division bars should provide min. coverage of 1/2" from end of each light, and head and sill mouldings should have min. depth of 1"; mouldings of wood or metal made to fit contour of glass or straight, with contour filled by scribed wood fillers, gypsum casting plaster, putty or glazing compound; prime wood mouldings before setting. FOR EXTERIOR GLASS: Use filler, e.g. show case cement, in all butt and miter joints to insure waterproofing; use weatherproof tape between division bars and glass, inside & outside; bed glass in glazing or caulking at head, sill & jambs. Do not use plaster filler.

HARDWARE

TABLE OF CONTENTS

NAIL USES

USE (All wood sizes are nominal)	SIZE PENNY	SIZE INCHES	TYPE, MATERIAL & FINISH NOTES ETC.†
CARPENTRY-WOOD-ROUGH			
1" Thick stock	8d	2½"	Common nails
2" Thick stock	16d to 20d	3½" or 4"	Common nails
3" Thick stock	40d to 60d	5" or 6"	Common nails or spikes
Concrete Forms	variable		Common or double headed nails
Framing generally—Sizes to fit conditions	10d, 16d, 20d, 60d	3", 3½", 4", 6"	Common nails or spikes for large members
Toe nailing studs, joists, etc.	10d	3"	Common nails
Spiking usual plates & sills	16d	3½"	Common nails
Toe nailing rafters & plates	10d	3"	Common nails
Sheathing: roof & wall; Rough flooring	8d	2½"	Common nails, may be zinc coated
CARPENTRY-WOOD-FINISHING			
Moldings—Size as required		7/8", 1", 1⅛", 1¼"	Molding nails (brads)
Carpet strips, shoes	8d	2½"	Finishing or casing nails
Door & window stops & members ¼" to ½" thick	4d	1½"	Finishing or casing nails
Ceiling, trim, casing, picture mold, base balusters and members ½" to ¾" thick	6d	2"	Finishing or casing nails
Ceiling, trim, casing, base, jambs, trim and members ¾" to 1" thick	8d	2½"	Finishing or casing nails
Door & window trim, boards and other members 1" to 1¼" thick	10d	3"	Finishing or casing nails
Drop siding, 1" thick	*7d or □9d	*2¼" or □2¾"	*Siding nails — □Casing nails
Bevel siding, ½" thick	*6d or □8d	*2" or □2½"	□Finishing — *Siding
FLOORING WOOD	See wood flooring sheet for sizes & types recommended		Cut steel, wire, finishing, wire casing, flooring brads, parquet, flooring nails
LATHING			
Wood lath	3d	1¼"	Blued lath nail
Gypsum lath	3d	1¼"	Blued common
Fiber lath			
Metal lath, interior		1"	Blued lath nails, staples or offset head nails
Metal lath, exterior	*3d	*1¼"	Self furring nails (double heads). Staples or cement coated
SHEATHING or SIDING			
Asbestos 3/8" thick		1¼"	Galvanized roofing nail, 7/16" dia. head. See "Sheathing on Wood Framing" for spacing etc.
Fiber board ½" & 25/32"		1½" to 2"	Galvanized roofing nail, 7/16" dia. head. See "Sheathing on Wood Framing" for spacing etc.
Gypsum board ½"		1¾"	Galvanized roofing nail, 7/16" dia. head. See "Sheathing on Wood Framing" for spacing etc.
Plywood 5/16" & 3/8" thick	6d	2"	Common
Plywood ½" & 5/8" "	8d	2½"	Common
ROOFING & SHEET METAL			
Aluminum roofing		1¾" to 2½"	Aluminum nail, neoprene washer optional
Asbestos, corrugated or sheets	Depends on thickness		Leak proof roofing nails
Asbestos shingles		1" to 2"	See "Asbestos Cement Roofing & Siding."
Asphalt shingles			Large head roofing, galv.
Copper cleats & flashing to wood			Copper wire or cut slating nails
" " " " to prevent joints			Barbed copper nails
Clay tile	4d to 6d	1½" to 2"	See clay tile Roofing Sheets. Use copper
Prepared felt roofing		1" to 1¼"	Roofing nails or large head roofing nails; barbed preferred—Heads may be reinforced. Zinc
Shingles, wood	3d to 4d; 4d to 8d for heavy butts	usual	See "Wood Shingles, Roofg & Sidg." for sizes. Zinc coated, copper wire shingle, copper clad shingle, cut iron or cut steel
Slate	Use nails 1" larger than thickness of slate		Copper wire slating nail (large head). In dry climates zinc coated or copper clad nails may be used
Tin, Zinc roofing			Zinc coated nails—Roofing or slating
Monel roofing			Monel nail.
Nailing to sheet metal			Self tapping screws, helical drive-screws
NAILING TO CONCRETE & CEMENT MORTAR			Concrete or cement nails (hardened) or helical drive nails or drive bolts

†NOTE: For further data on nail uses see pages on specific material involved.

NAILS

COMMON NAILS
Flat Head. Diamond Point

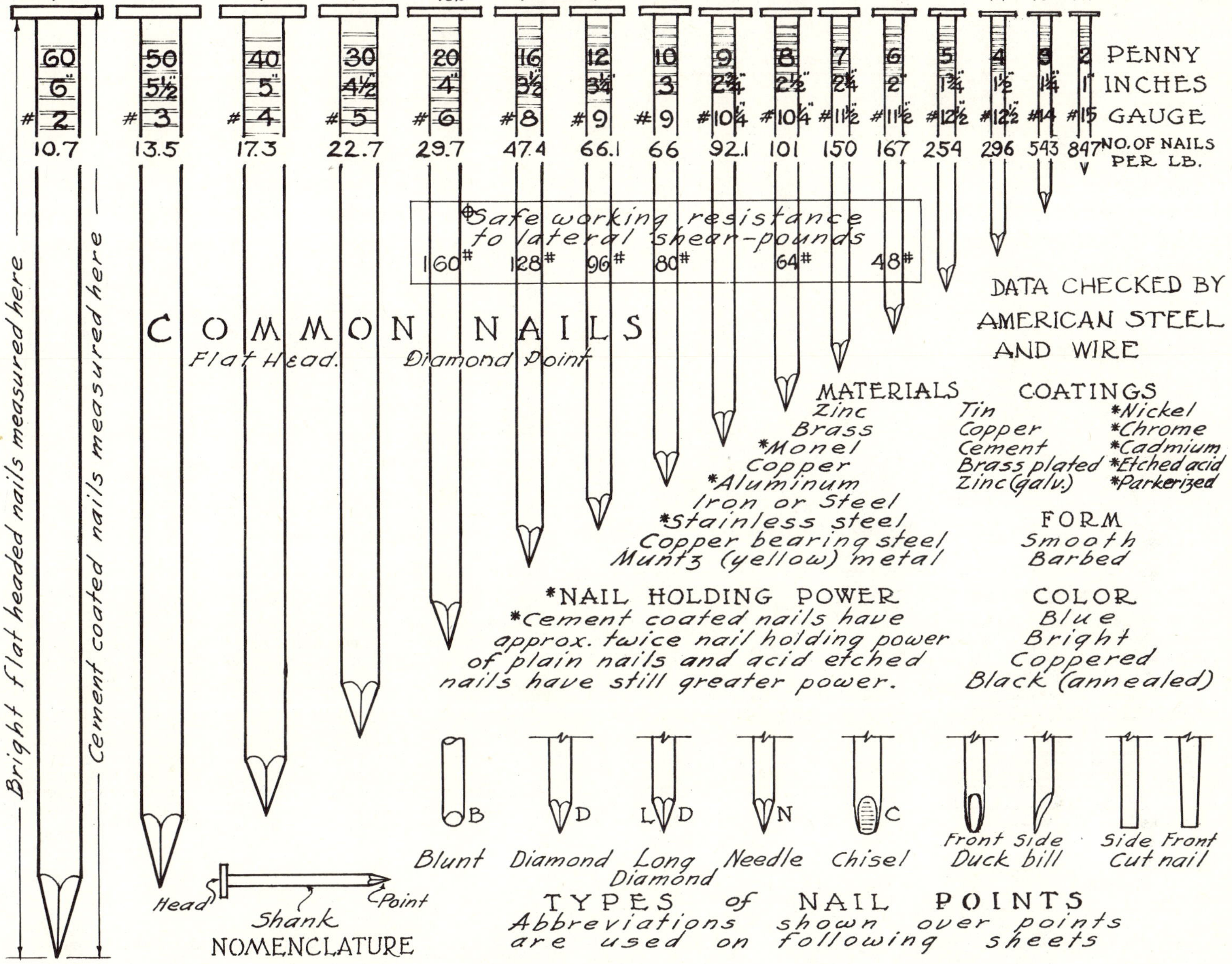

Bright flat headed nails measured here
Cement coated nails measured here

DIA. of HEAD	17/32"	1/2"	15/32"	7/16"	13/32"	11/32"	5/16"	5/16"	9/32"	9/32"	17/64"	17/64"	1/4"	1/4"	13/64"	11/64"
PENNY	60	50	40	30	20	16	12	10	9	8	7	6	5	4	3	2
INCHES	6"	5½"	5"	4½"	4"	3½"	3¼"	3	2¾"	2½"	2¼"	2"	1¾"	1½"	1¼"	1"
GAUGE	#2	#3	#4	#5	#6	#8	#9	#9	#10¼	#10¼	#11½	#11½	#12½	#12½	#14	#15
NO. OF NAILS PER LB.	10.7	13.5	17.3	22.7	29.7	47.4	66.1	66	92.1	101	150	167	254	296	543	847
⊕ Safe working resistance to lateral shear-pounds					160#	128#	96#	80#		64#		48#				

DATA CHECKED BY AMERICAN STEEL AND WIRE

MATERIALS
Zinc
Brass
*Monel
Copper
*Aluminum
Iron or Steel
*Stainless steel
Copper bearing steel
Muntz (yellow) metal

COATINGS
Tin
Copper
Cement
Brass plated
Zinc (galv.)
*Nickel
*Chrome
*Cadmium
*Etched acid
*Parkerized

FORM
Smooth
Barbed

COLOR
Blue
Bright
Coppered
Black (annealed)

***NAIL HOLDING POWER**
*Cement coated nails have approx. twice nail holding power of plain nails and acid etched nails have still greater power.

Head
Shank
Point

NOMENCLATURE

B
D
LD
N
C
Blunt
Diamond
Long Diamond
Needle
Chisel
Front Side Duck bill
Side Front Cut nail

TYPES of NAIL POINTS
Abbreviations shown over points are used on following sheets

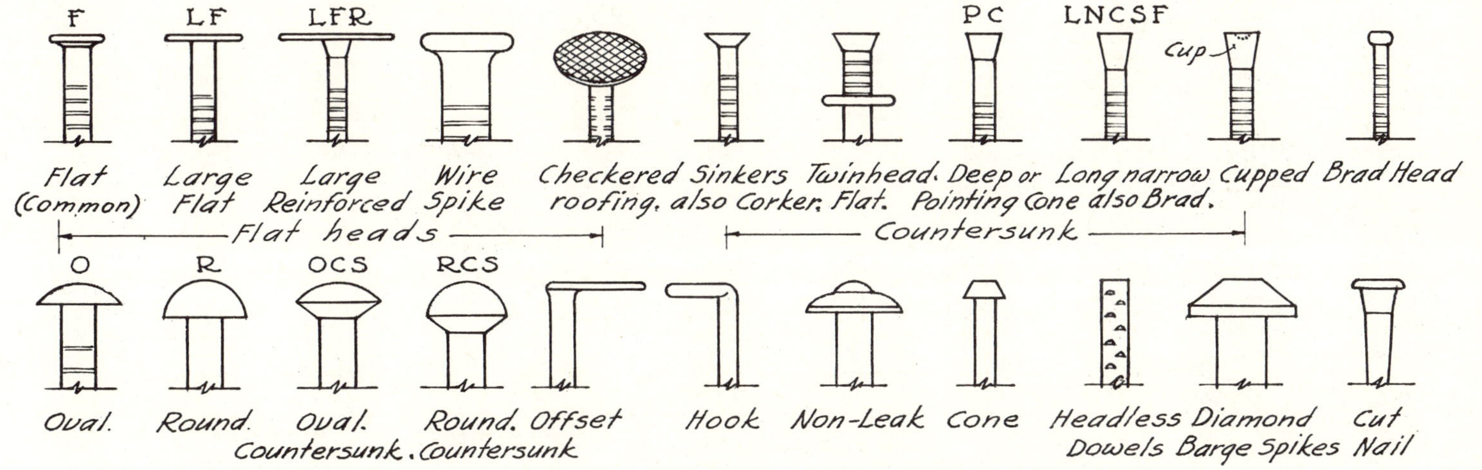

F
LF
LFR
PC
LNCSF
Cup
Flat (Common)
Large Flat
Large Reinforced
Wire Spike
Checkered roofing.
Sinkers also Corker.
Twinhead.
Deep or Flat.
Long narrow Pointing Cone
Cupped also Brad.
Brad Head
Flat heads
Countersunk
O
R
OCS
RCS
Oval.
Round.
Oval. Countersunk.
Round. Countersunk
Offset
Hook
Non-Leak
Cone
Headless Dowels
Diamond Barge Spikes
Cut Nail

TYPES of NAIL HEADS
Abbreviations shown over heads are used on following sheets.
Gauge shown is Steel Wire (Washburn & Moen)
⊕ For Nail withdrawal resistance and nail lateral resistance see Wood "Handbook" U.S. Dept. of Agriculture, prepared by Forest Products Laboratory.

NAILS

Sizes and types are taken from U.S. Federal Specification IV FF-N-101 (Part 5) unless marked *
For abbreviation for heads and points see other "Nails" sheet

NAIL TYPE	Shown 4d (1½") unless noted otherwise	SIZES	SPECIFICATION
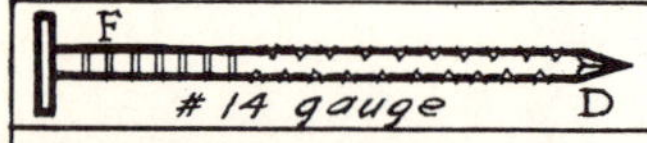 F #14 gauge D	Barbed nails	1/4" to 1½"	Cement coated, brass, steel
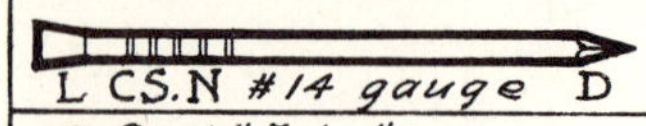 L CS.N #14 gauge D	Casing nails	2d to 40d 6d to 10d *Alum.	Bright & cement coated *Cupped heads available
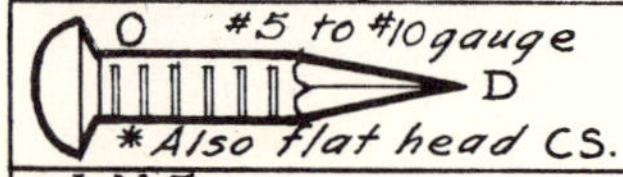 O #5 to #10 gauge D *Also flat head CS.	Cement nails also called concrete nails & hardened nails	1/2" to 3"	Smooth, bright *Oil quenched
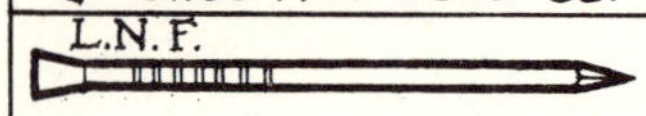 L.N.F.	Common brad Cup head available — #15 to #2 ga.	2d to 60d	Bright " — may be secured with cupped head " Cement coated {usually made in heavy gauges
 F	Cut common	2d to 60d	Steel or Iron *Plain & zinc coated
Slightly smaller gauge than bright common	Copper-clad common nails	2d to 60d	Also used for shingle nails
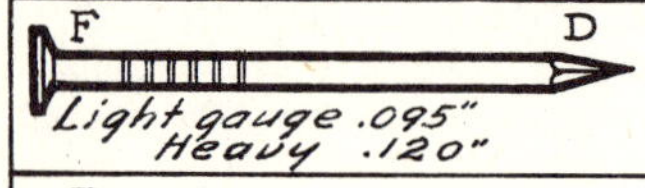 F D Light gauge .095" Heavy .120"	Common brass wire nails — Light gauge / Heavy "	*1½, 1" to 3½" 3/4 to 6"	Brass, Alum.
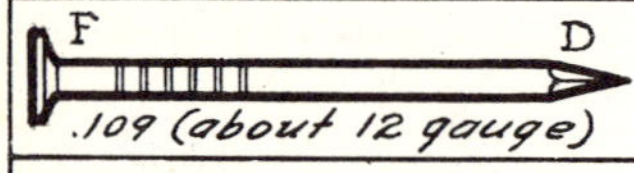 F D .109 (about 12 gauge)	Common copper wire nails; Alum.	*5/8" to 6"	Also used for shingle nails
	Standard cut nails (non-ferrous)	5/8" to 6"	Copper, muntz metal, or zinc
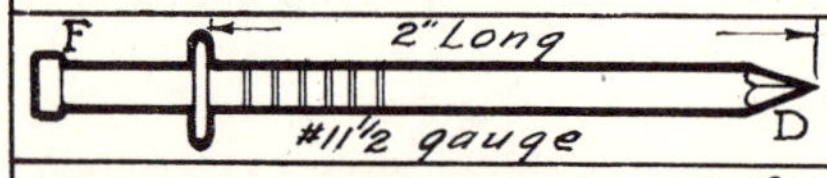 F 2" Long #11½ gauge D	Double headed	*1¾, 2", 2¼, 2½", *2¾ 3", 3½", *4", *4½"	Bright & cement coated made in several designs
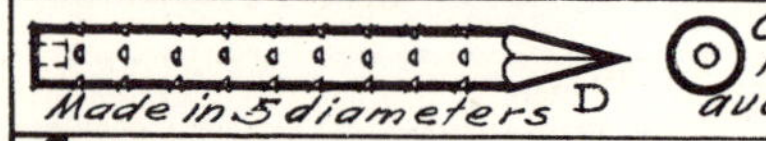 Made in 5 diameters D	Cupped head available — Dowel Pins	5/8" to 2"	Barbed — *may have cupped head
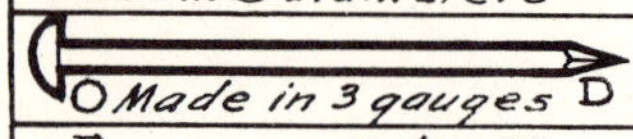 O Made in 3 gauges D	Escutcheon Pins	1/4" to 2"	Bright steel, brass plated, brass *also nickel-silver & copper & alum.
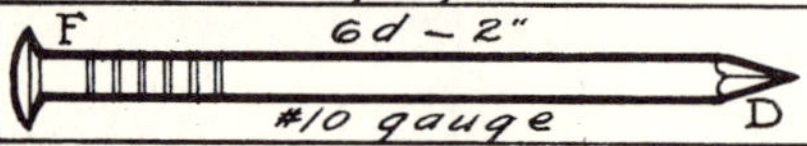 F 6d – 2" #10 gauge D	Fence nails	5d to 20d	Smooth; bright & cement coated (Gauge are heavier than common)
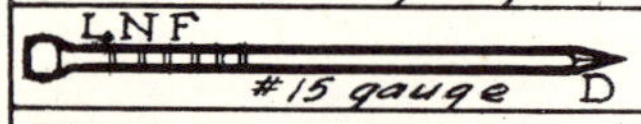 L.N.F #15 gauge D	Finishing nail, wire	2d to 20d	Smooth; *Cupped heads available (Smaller gauge than usual common brads)
	Finishing nails Cut iron & steel — Standard — 3d to 20d Fine — 6d to 10d		
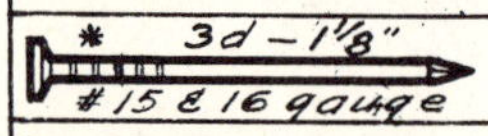 * 3d – 1⅛" #15 & 16 gauge	*Fine nails	*2d & 2d Ex. Fine *3d & 3d Ex. Fine	*Bright — Smaller gauge & heads than common nails
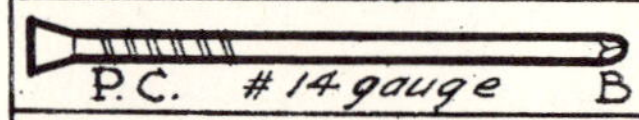 P.C. #14 gauge B	Flooring nails (Also with D point)	*3d to *20d 6d to 20d	*Bright & cement coated (different gauge) *Cupped heads available
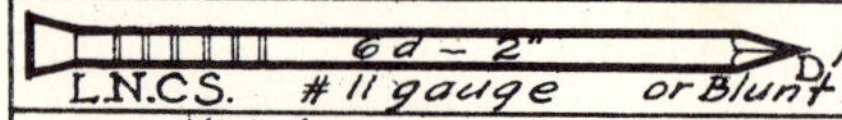 6d – 2" L.N.C.S. #11 gauge or Blunt D D	Flooring brad	6d to 20d	Smooth; bright & cement coated Cupped heads available
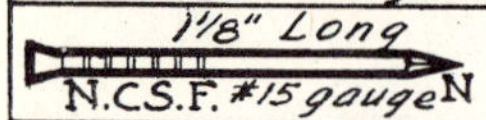 1⅛" Long N.C.S.F. #15 gauge N	Parquet flooring nail or brad	1", 1⅛", 1¼"	Smooth or barbed
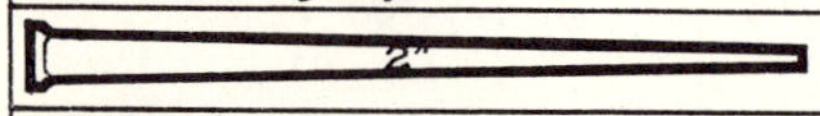 2"	Flooring nails Cut iron or steel	4d to 20d	Iron or steel
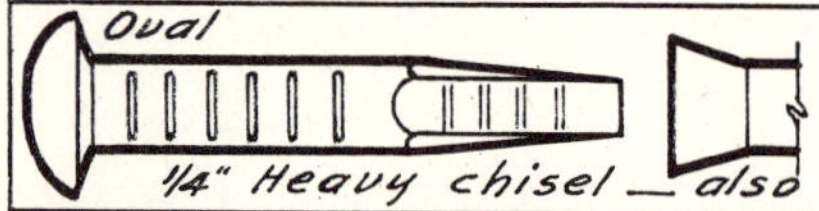 Oval 1/4" Heavy chisel — also CS. head	Hinge nails — Heavy—1/4 to 3/8 dia. Light—3/16 to 1/4 dia.	1½" to 4" Long	Smooth; bright or annealed
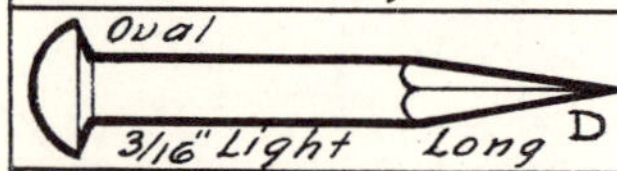 Oval 3/16" Light Long D	Hinge nails — Heavy—1/4" dia. Light—3/16" dia.	1½" to 3" also to *4"	Smooth; bright or annealed
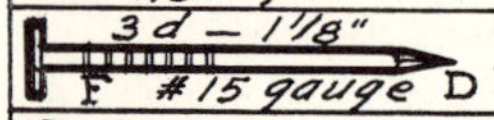 3d – 1⅛" F #15 gauge D	Lath nails (wood)	2d, 2d Light, 3d 3d Light, 3d heavy, 4d	Bright, (not recommended) blued or cement coated
 Hook 1⅛" #12 gauge	Lath nails (Metal lath) Staples #14, 15 gauge	1⅛" Staples 1" to 1½"	Bright, blued, zinc coated, annealed
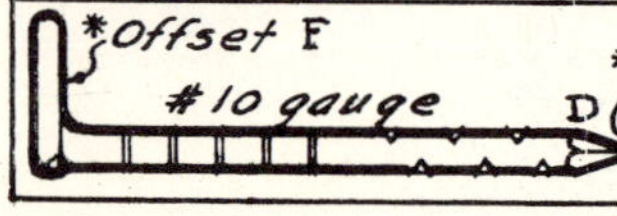 *Offset F #10 gauge D	*Lath offset head nails (For self furring metal lath)	*1¼ to *1¾	Bright, zinc coated

NAILS

Sizes and types are taken from U.S. Federal Specification IV FF-N-101 (Part 5) unless marked *
For abbreviation for heads and points see other "Nails" sheet

NAIL TYPE Shown 4d (1½") unless noted otherwise		SIZES	SPECIFICATION
 needle N.C.S.F. #14 gauge	Molding nails (brads)	7/8" to 1¼"	Smooth; bright or cement coated
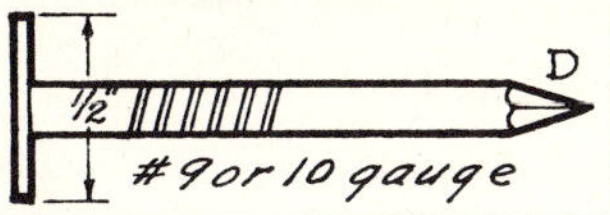 ½ D #9 or 10 gauge	Plaster-board nails Used also for wall board Rock Lath (5/16" head) →	1" to 1¾" 1⅛" to 1½" →	Smooth; bright or cement coated Blued *Aluminum
 F # 10 gauge D	Roofing nails (standard)	¾" to 2"	Bright, cement coated, zinc coated Barbed
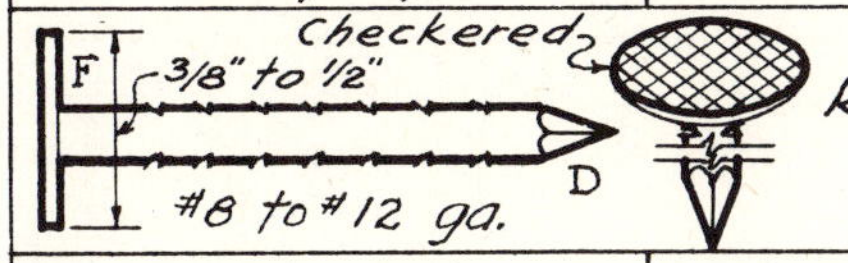 F Checkered 3/8" to ½" #8 to #12 ga. D	Roofing nails Large head	¾" to 1¾" also *2" ¾" to 2½" →	Barbed; bright or zinc coated Checkered available Aluminum (etched), neoprene washer opt'n'l.
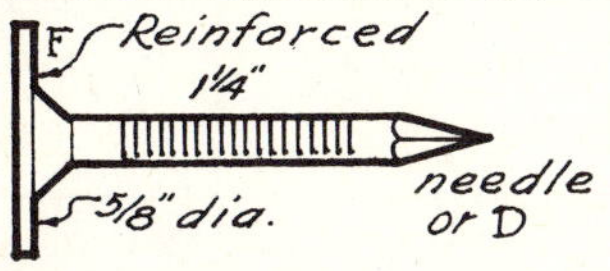 F Reinforced 1¼" 5/8" dia. needle or D	Roofing nails for prepared roofing	¾" to 1¼" #11 to #12 ga. *also #10 gauge	Bright or zinc coated
	Sheathing nails Cut copper or muntz M.	¾" to 3"	Copper or muntz metal
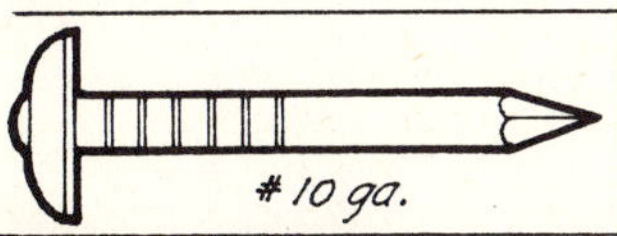 #10 ga.	*Non-leaking roofing nails	*1¾" to 2"	*Zinc coated—also with lead heads
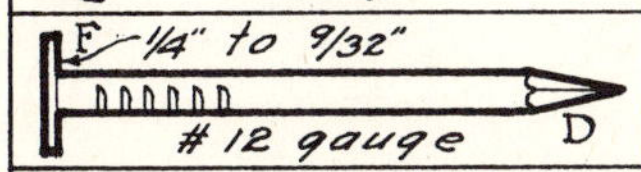 F ¼" to 9/32" # 12 gauge D	Shingle nails Large headed also available 5/16 dia.	3d to 6d 2d to 6d →	Smooth; bright or zinc coated, cement coated, light & heavy *Aluminum
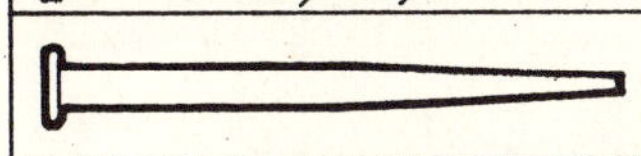	*Shingle nails Cut iron or steel	2d to 6d	Plain or zinc coated
Shingle nails, copper wire are the same as common copper wire nails Shingle nails, copper clad, are the same as copper clad common wire nails			
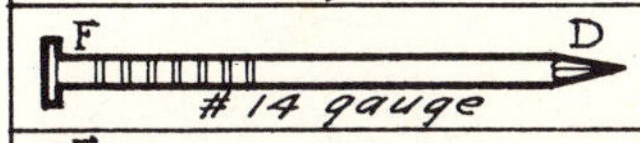 F D # 14 gauge	Siding nails	2d to 40d 6d to 10d →	Smooth; bright or cement coated Smaller diameter than common nails * Aluminum
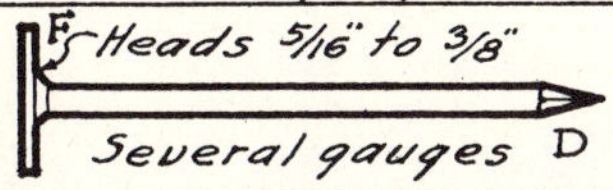 F Heads 5/16" to 3/8" Several gauges D	Slating nails—3/8" head 1" to 2" Slating nails—small heads 1" to 2" Slating nails—copper wire 7/8" to 1½"		Zinc coated Bright; cement coated and copper clad, copper
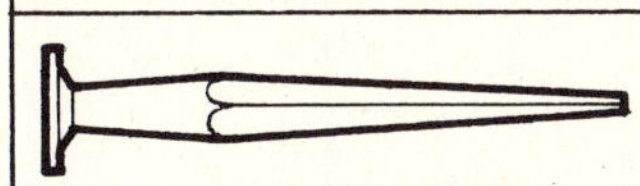	Cut slating nails non-ferrous	1¼" to 2"	Copper or muntz metal or zinc

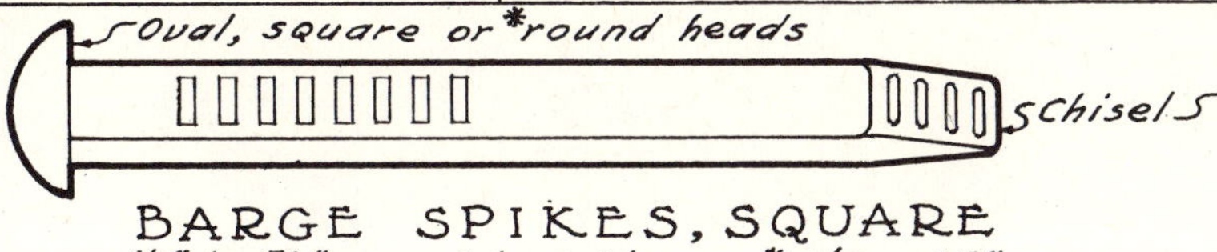

Oval, square or *round heads
Chisel

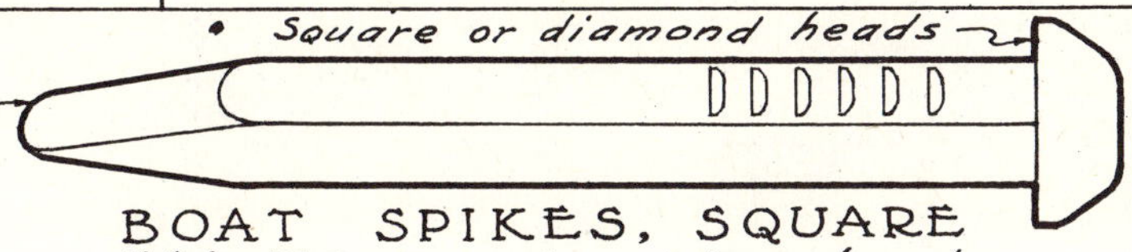

• Square or diamond heads

BARGE SPIKES, SQUARE
¼" to 5/8" sq. 3" to 12" long, *also 16"

BOAT SPIKES, SQUARE
¼" to 5/8" sq. 3" to 12" long, heads from 7/32" to 1⅛" dia.

These spikes are usually used for hard wood, made plain and zinc coated

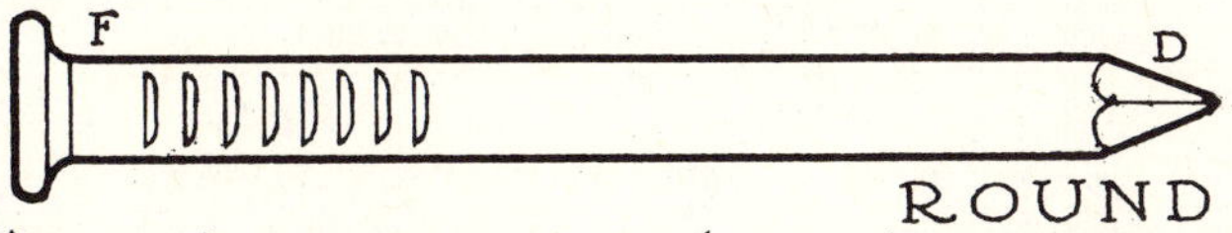

F
D

10d to 60d & 7" to 12"

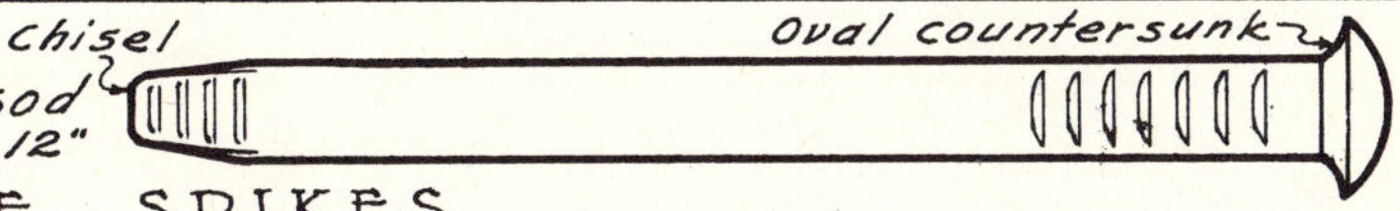

Chisel
Oval countersunk

ROUND WIRE SPIKES
*May be secured up to 16" long. Smooth; bright or zinc coated. Gauges vary from #6 to 3/8"

Gutter Spikes — 5½" to 10½", ¼" dia. oval head; chisel point; or flat head diamond point. Bright or zinc coated

Common cut iron or steel spikes — 20d to 100d (4" to 8") Plain or zinc coated

 Fetter Ring

Spirally grooved (helical) 

SCREWS, BOLTS and NUTS

GRAPHIC SIZES · B.W. Gauge & INCHES of screws & bolts. N.C. (Nat'l. Coarse) threads used in arch'l work.

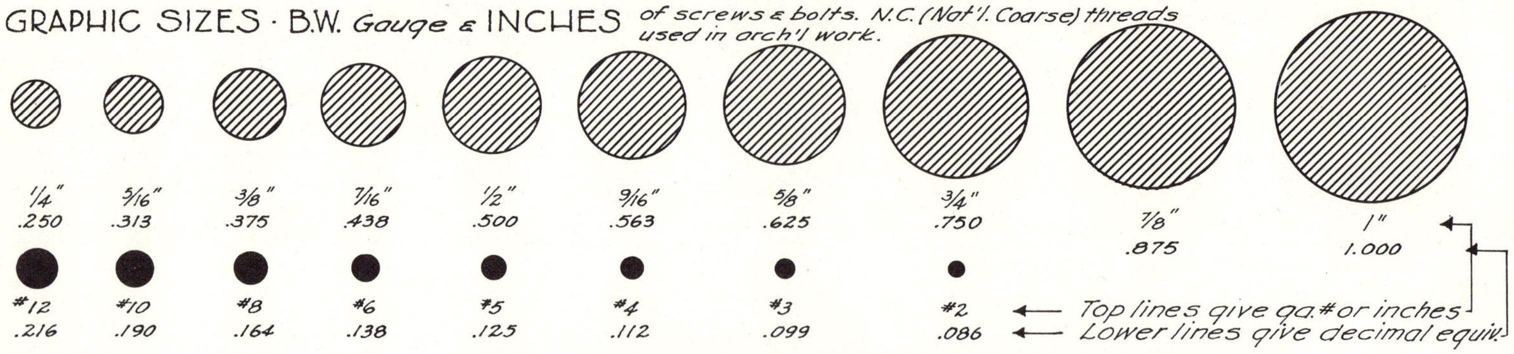

1/4" .250
5/16" .313
3/8" .375
7/16" .438
1/2" .500
9/16" .563
5/8" .625
3/4" .750
7/8" .875
1" 1.000
#12 .216
#10 .190
#8 .164
#6 .138
#5 .125
#4 .112
#3 .099
#2 .086
← Top lines give ga.# or inches
← Lower lines give decimal equiv.

SCREW & BOLT LENGTHS

SIZE		1/4"	5/16"	3/8"	7/16"	1/2"	9/16"	5/8"	3/4"	7/8"	1"
CAP SCREWS	Button-head / Flat-head	1/2"-2 1/4"	1/2"-2 3/4"	5/8"-3"	3/4"-3"	3/4"-4"	1"-4"	1"-4"	1"-4"		
CAP SCREWS	Hexagon-head	1/2"-3 1/2"	1/2"-3 1/2"	1/2"-4"	3/4"-4"	3/4"-4 1/2"	1"-4 1/2"	1"-5"	1 1/4"-5"	2"-6"	2"-6"
CAP SCREWS	Fillister-head	3/4"-3"	3/4"-3 3/4"	3/4"-3 1/2"	3/4"-3 3/4"	3/4"-4"	1"-4"	1 1/4"-4 1/2"	1 1/2"-4 1/2"	1 3/4"-5"	2"-5"
Length Intervals: 1/8" up to 1"; 1/4" from 1 1/4" to 4"; 1/2" from 4 1/2" to 6".											
BOLTS	Machine bolt	1/2"-8"	1/2"-8"	3/4"-12"	3/4"-12"	3/4"-24"	1"-30"	1"-30"	1"-30"	1 1/2"-30"	1 1/2"-30"
BOLTS	Carriage bolt	3/4"-8"	3/4"-8"	3/4"-12"	1"-12"	1"-20"	1"-20"	1"-20"	1"-20"		
Length Intervals: 1/4" up to 6"; 1/2" from 6 1/2" to 12"; by 1" over 12". Longer available.											

STOVE BOLT SIZES						1/8"		5/32"	3/16"		1/4"	5/16"	3/8"	1/2"
MACHINE SCREW SIZES		2	3	4 (40 N.C.)	4 (36 N.C.)	5	6	8	10	12	1/4"	5/16"	3/8"	1/2"
MACHINE SCREW & STOVE BOLT	Round head / Flat head	1/8"-7/8"	1/8"-7/8"	1/8"-1 1/2"	1/8"-1 1/2"	1/8"-2"	1/8"-2"	3/16"-3"	3/16"-6"	1/4"-3"	5/16"-6"	3/8"-6"	1/2"-5"	1"-4"
MACHINE SCREW & STOVE BOLT	Fillister head / Oval head	1/8"-7/8"	1/8"-7/8"	1/8"-1 1/2"	1/8"-1 1/2"	1/8"-2"	1/8"-2"	3/16"-3"	3/16"-3"	1/4"-3"	5/16"-3"	3/8"-3"	1/2"-3"	
MACHINE SCREW & STOVE BOLT	Oven head				1/8"-3/4"	3/8"-2"	1/8"-1"	3/16"-2"	1/4"-6"		3/8"-6"	3/4"-6"	3/4"-5"	
Length Intervals: 1/16" up to 1/2"; 1/8" from 5/8" to 1 1/4"; 1/4" from 1 1/2" to 3"; 1/2" from 3 1/2" to 6".														

American Standard sizes by the Amer. Inst. of Bolt, Nut and Rivet Mfrs. Many of listed items also stocked in alum., brass, copper, stainless steel, monel & bronze. Stove bolts have wider tolerances than mach. screws.

Slotted · HEADS · Phillips

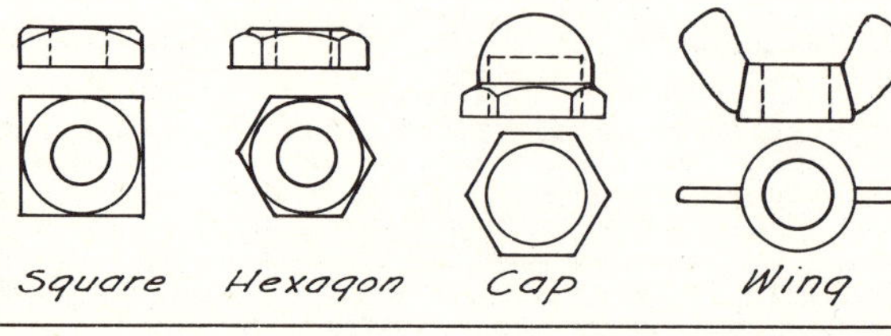

Square
Hexagon
Cap
Wing

NUT SIZES

Square & hexagon head nuts are available for all screws & bolts listed; Cap nuts for all except nos. 2, 3, 4 (40 N.C. only), 5, & 9/16". Wing nuts for all except # 2, 3, 4 (40 N.C.), 5, 9/16, 5/8, 3/4, 7/8, & 1"

Data adapted from "Architectural Metal Handbook," by permission of the National Assoc. of Architectural Metal Mfrs.

SCREWS, BOLTS, ETC.

WOOD SCREWS

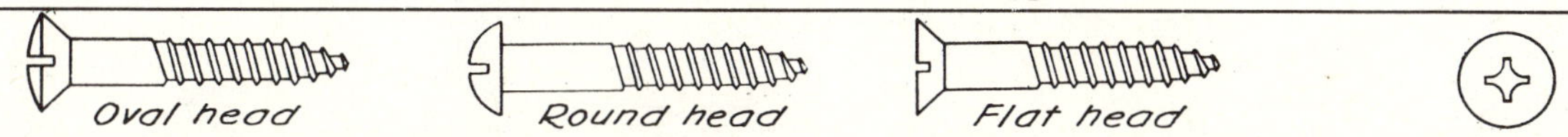

Oval head   Round head   Flat head   Phillips   Slotted

SIZE	0	1	2	3	4	5	6	7	8	9	10	11	12	14	16	18	20	24
Decimal Equivalent	.060	.073	.086	.099	.112	.125	.138	.151	.164	.177	.190	.203	.216	.242	.268	.294	.320	.372
Length	1/4"-3/8	1/4"-1/2	1/4"-3/4	1/4"-1"	1/4"-1 1/2	3/8"-1 1/2	3/8"-2 1/2	3/8"-2 1/2	3/8"-3"	1/2"-3"	1/2"-3 1/2	5/8"-3 1/2	5/8"-4"	3/4"-5"	1"-5"	1 1/4"-5"	1 1/2"-5"	3"-5"

Length Intervals: by 1/8" up to 1"; 1/4" from 1 1/4" to 3"; 1/2" from 3 1/2" to 5".

LAG BOLTS

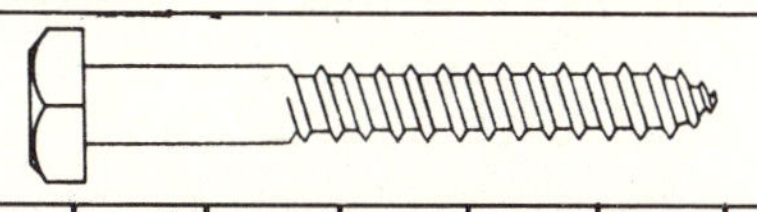

SIZE	1/4"	5/16"	3/8"	7/16"	1/2"	5/8"	3/4"	7/8"	1"
Dec. Equiv.	.250	.313	.375	.438	.500	.625	.750	.875	1.000
Length	1"-6"	1"-10"	1"-12"	1"-12"	1"-12"	1 1/2-16"	1 1/2-16"	2"-16"	2"-16"

Length Intervals: by 1/2" up to 8"; by inches over 8".

SHEET METAL & THREADING SCREWS

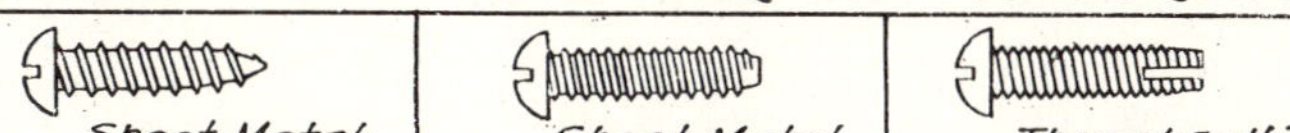

Sheet Metal-Gimlet Point	Sheet Metal-Blunt Point	Thread Cutting-Cutting Slot
Hardened, self-tapping. Used in #28 to #18 ga. sheet metal. Made in #4 to #14 sizes & usual heads.	Hardened, self-tapping. Used in #28 to #6 sheet metal; alum., plastic, slate, etc. Usual head types.	Hardened. Used in metals up to 1/4" thick. Sizes: #4 to 5/16"; in usual head types. (Flat, oval, round, etc.)

SET SCREWS

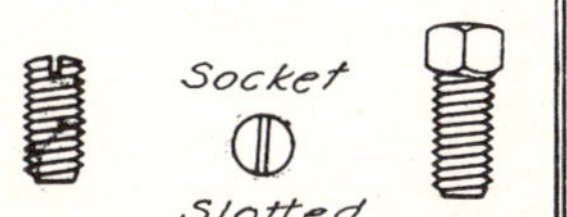

Socket   Slotted   Headless   Square Head

Headless type with socket or slotted top made in sizes #4 to 1/2"; in 1/2" to 5" lengths. Square head sizes 1/4" to 1"; 1/2" to 5" lengths.

WASHERS

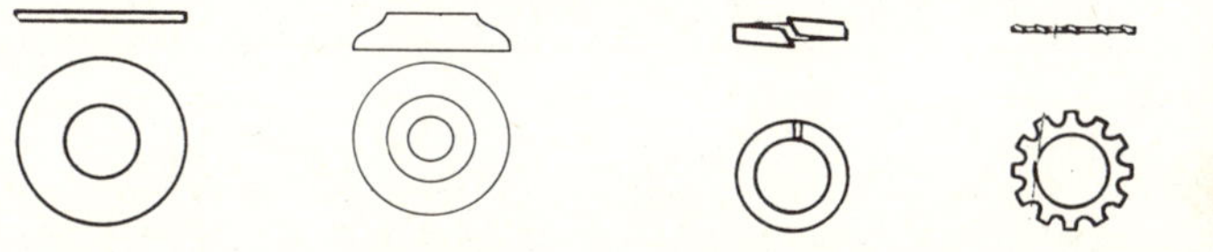

Cut	O.G. Cast	Spring Lock	External Tooth Lock
Of steel and non-ferrous metals.	Made of cast metal.	Of steel, monel metal, bronze & stainless steel.	Of steel, monel metal, phos. bronze, beryllium copper & s.s.

All types for bolts and screws of all sizes.

RIVETS

round   truss   flat   counter sunk   pan

Standard Rivets available with solid, tubular & split shanks, of steel, brass, copper, aluminum, monel metal & stainless steel; in diameters of 1/8" up to 7/16" & lengths of 3/16" up to 4 inches.

TOGGLE BOLTS

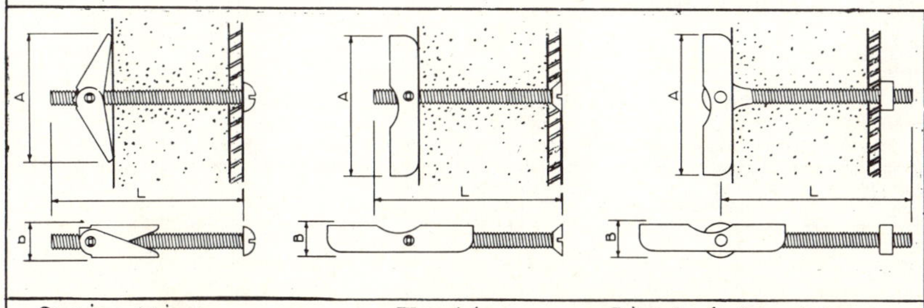

Spring wing   Tumble   Riveted tumble

SIZE		1/8"	5/32"	3/16"	1/4"	5/16"	3/8"	1/2"
Decimal Equiv.		.138	.164	.190	.250	.313	.375	.500
Spring Wing	A	1.438	1.875	1.875	2.063	2.750	2.875	4.625
	B	.375	.500	.500	.688	.875	1.000	1.250
	L	2"-4"	2 1/2"-4"	2"-6"	2 1/2-6"	3"-6"	3"-6"	4"-6"
Tumble	A	1.250	2.000	2.000	2.250	2.750	2.750	
	B	.375	.500	.500	.688	.875	.875	
	L	2"-4"	2 1/2"-4"	3"-6"	3"-6"	3"-6"	3"-6"	
Riveted Tumble	A		2.000	2.000	2.250	2.750	2.750	3.375
	B		.375	.375	.500	.625	.688	.875
	L		2 1/2-4"	3"-6"	3"-6"	3"-6"	3"-6"	3"-6"

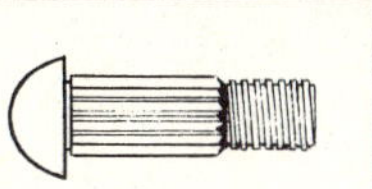

DARDELET "SELF LOCKING" Rivet Bolts

Dia. 3/8" length 1 1/8" to 2 1/4"   Dia. 3/4" length 1 1/2" to 4 1/8"
Dia. 1/2" length 1 1/4" to 2 3/4"   Dia. 7/8" length 1 11/16" to 5 1/4"
Dia. 5/8" length 1 3/8" to 3 5/8"   Dia. 1" length 2 3/16" to 5 3/8"

Length Intervals: by 1/2" up to 4" and by inches over 4".

TURNBUCKLES

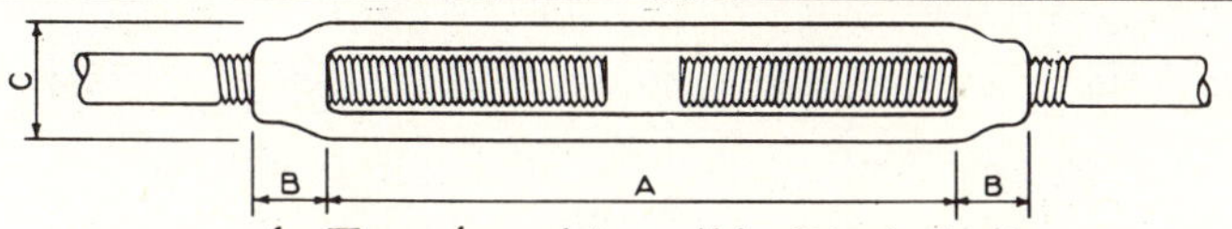
C
B
A
B

A Turnbuckle with Stub Ends

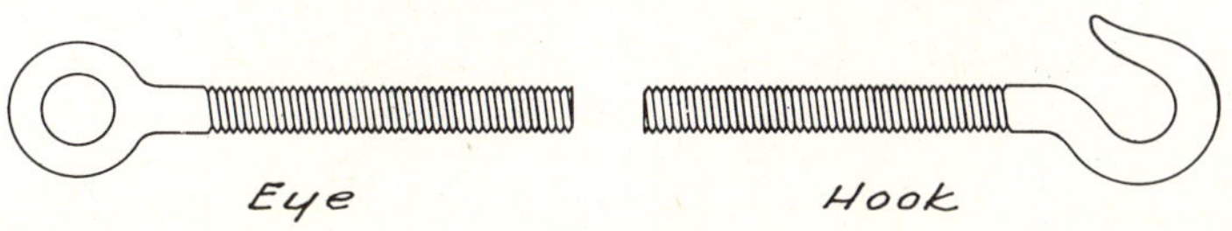

Eye   Hook

SIZE	1/4"	5/16"	3/8"	1/2"	5/8"	3/4"	7/8"	1"
Decimal Equiv.	.250	.313	.375	.500	.625	.750	.875	1.000
A	4"	4 1/2"	6"	6"	6"	6"	6"	6"
				9"	9"	9"		
				12"	12"	12"	12"	12"
B	7/16"	1/2"	9/16"	3/4"	29/32"	1 1/16"	1 7/32"	1 3/8"
C	3/4"	7/8"	31/32"	1 7/32"	1 1/2"	1 23/32"	1 7/8"	2 1/32"

Diameters over 1" available, not always stocked.

Data adapted from "Architectural Metal Handbook," by permission of the National Assoc. of Architectural Metal Mfr.

SHIELDS and ANCHORS

MACHINE-BOLT ANCHORS and SHIELDS

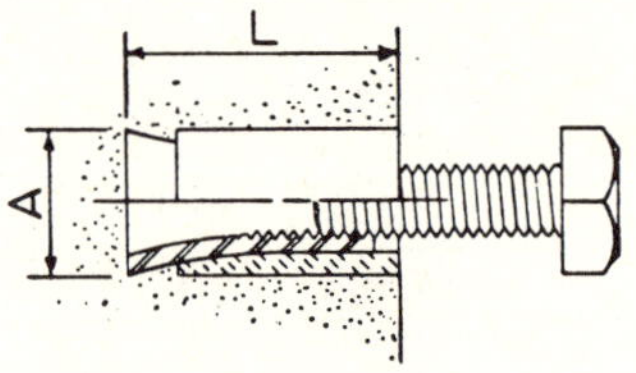
L
A

(1) Machine-Bolt Anchor Single Expanding Unit

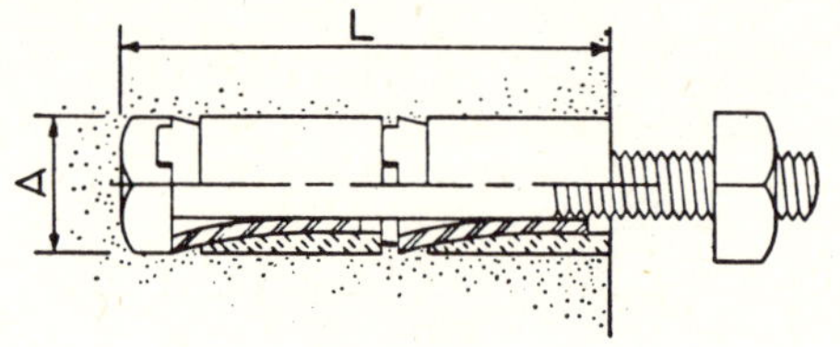
L
A

(2) Stud Anchor Multiple Expanding Units

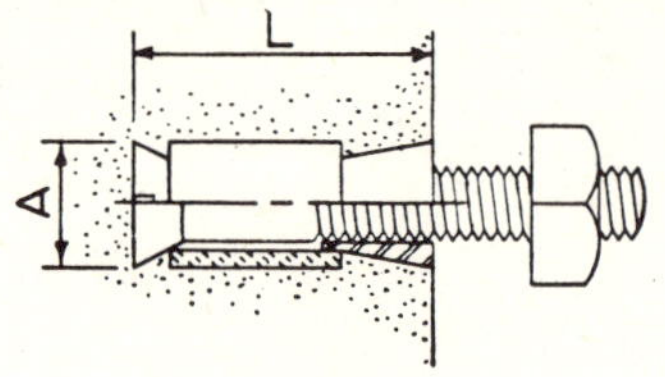
L
A

(3) Stud Anchor Single Expanding Unit

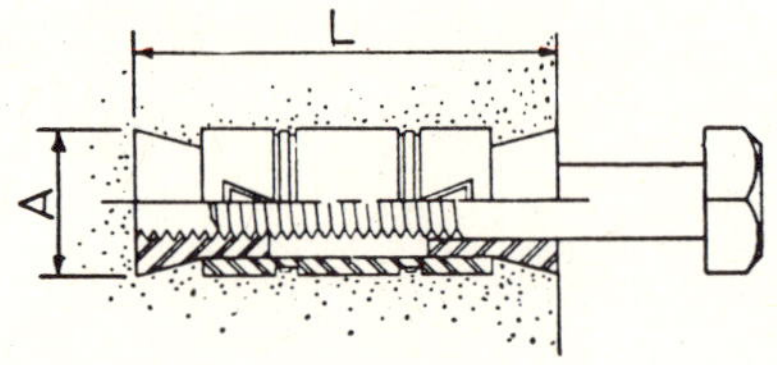
L
A

(4) Machine-Bolt Expansion Shield Double Acting

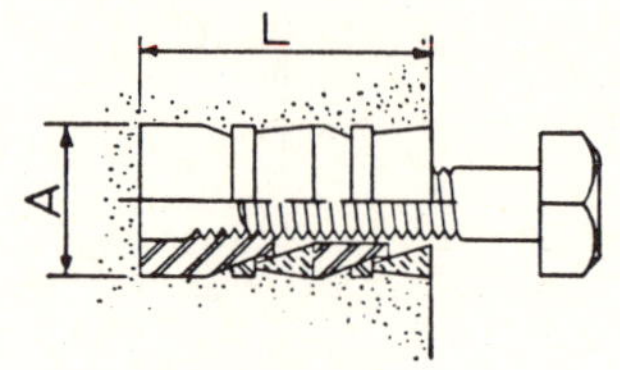
L
A

(5) Machine-Bolt Anchor Ring Wedge Multiple Expanding Unit

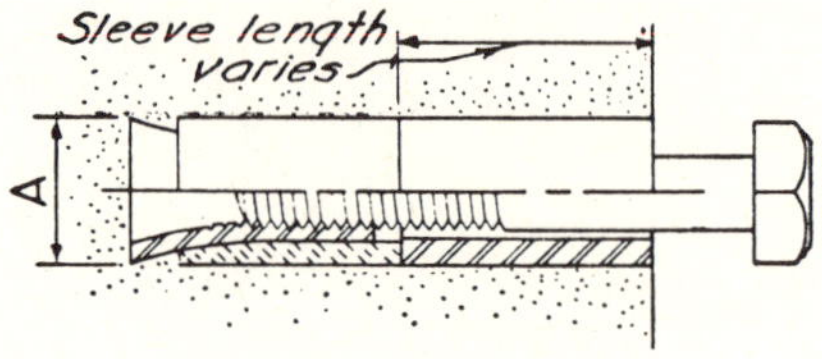
Sleeve length varies
A

(6) Machine-Bolt Anchor Single Expanding Unit with sleeve for deep setting

		6	8	10	12	1/4	5/16	3/8	7/16	1/2	5/8	3/4	7/8	1
Bolt Sizes		6	8	10	12	1/4	5/16	3/8	7/16	1/2	5/8	3/4	7/8	1
Threads per Inch		32	32	24	24	20	18	16	14	13	11	10	9	8
Decimal Equivalents		.138	164	190	216	.250	3125	375	.4375	5000	6250	.7500	8750	1.0000
Fig. 1	A	1/4	5/16	3/8	1/2	1/2	5/8	3/4	7/8	7/8	1 1/8	1 1/4	1 1/2	1 3/4
	L	3/8	1/2	5/8	7/8	7/8	1	1 1/4	1 1/2	1 1/2	2	2 1/4	2 3/4	3 1/2
Fig. 2	A							3/4	1	1	1 1/4	1 1/2	1 3/4	1 3/4
	L 1 Unit							1 5/8	1 3/4	1 3/4	2 1/2	2 3/4	4	4
	L 2 Units							2 7/8	3	3	4 1/2	4 3/4	7	7
	L 3 Units							4 1/8	4 1/4	4 1/4	6 1/2	6 7/8	10	10
Fig. 3	A					3/8	1/2	9/16		3/4	1	1 1/8		1 5/8
	L					3/4	1	1 1/8		1 1/2	1 3/4	2 1/4		3
Fig. 4	A					1/2	5/8	3/4	7/8	7/8	1	1 1/4	1 1/2	1 3/4
	L					1 5/8	1 7/8	2 1/8	2 3/8	2 3/8	2 7/8	4	4 1/2	4 7/8
Fig. 5	A			1/2		5/8	5/8	13/16		1	1 1/8	1 3/8	1 1/2	1 5/8
	L 2 Units			7/8		1 1/16	1 1/16	1 1/2		1 3/4	1 7/8	2 1/2	2 3/4	3 1/4
	L 3 Units			1 1/8		1 5/8	1 5/8	2 1/4		2 5/8	2 7/8	3 3/4	4	4 7/8

Expansion shields and anchors shown are representative of many types, some of which may be used either in single or multiple units. Many are threaded for use with the head of the bolt outside, some with head inside. Some types require setting tools to install.

LAG BOLT and WOOD SCREW SHIELDS

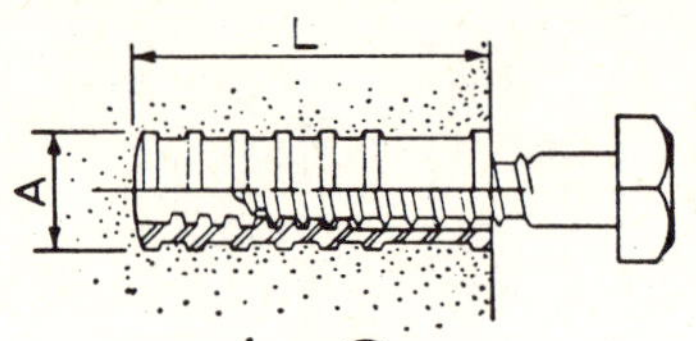
L
A

(7) Lag-Bolt Expansion Shield

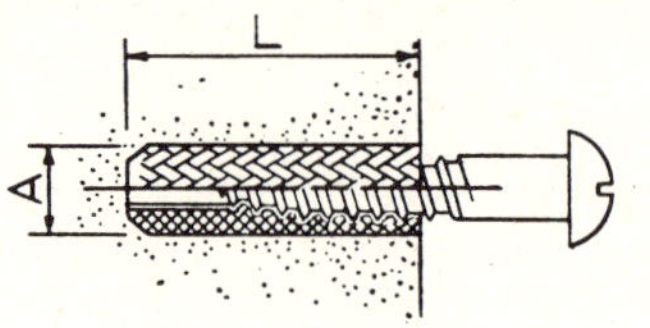
L
A

(8) Fiber-Plug for Lag Bolt or Wood Screw

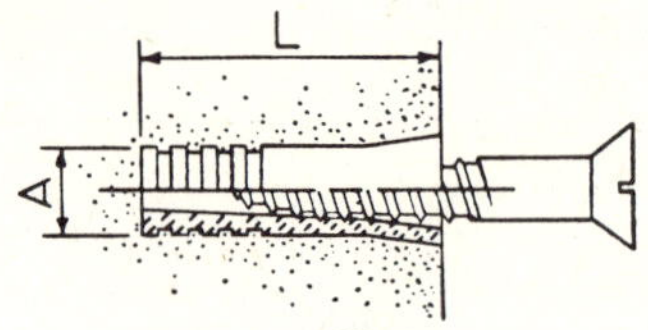
L
A

(9) Lead Shield for Lag Bolt or Wood Screw

Lag Screw Sizes										1/4			5/16	3/8	7/16	1/2	5/8	3/4
Wood Screw Sizes		5	6	7	8	9	10	11	12	14	16	18	20	24				
Decimal Equivalents		.125	.138	.151	.164	.177	.190	.203	.216	.242	.268	.294	.320	.372	.4375	.5000	.6250	.7500
Fig. 7	A									1/2			1/2	5/8		3/4	7/8	1
	L Short									1"			1 1/4"	1 3/4"		2"	2"	2"
	L Long									1 1/2"			1 3/4"	2 1/2"		3"	3 1/2"	3 1/2"
Fig. 8	A	5/32	5/32	11/64	11/64	3/16	3/16	1/4	1/4	9/32	5/16	5/16	3/8	7/16	1/2	5/8	3/4	
	L	5/8" to 1"	5/8" to 1"	5/8" to 1 1/2"	5/8" to 1 1/2"	3/4" to 1 1/2"	3/4" to 1 1/2"	3/4" to 1 1/2"	3/4" to 1 1/2"	1" to 2"	1" to 2"	1" to 2"	1" to 2"	1 1/2" to 3"	1 1/2" to 3"	2" to 3"	2 1/2" to 3 1/2"	
Fig. 9	A	1/4	1/4	1/4	1/4	5/16	5/16	5/16	3/8	3/8	7/16	7/16	9/16	9/16	11/16	3/4	7/8	
	L	1/2" to 1 1/2"	1/2" to 1 1/2"	1/2" to 1 1/2"	1/2" to 1 1/2"	1/2" to 1 1/2"	1/2" to 1 1/2"	1/2" to 1 1/2"	3/4" to 1 1/2"	3/4" to 1 1/2"	1" to 1 1/2"	1" to 1 1/2"	1" to 2"	1" to 2"	2"	2"	2" to 3 1/2"	

Data adapted from "Architectural Metals Handbook" by permission of the National Assoc. of Architectural Metal Manufacturers.

HARDWARE

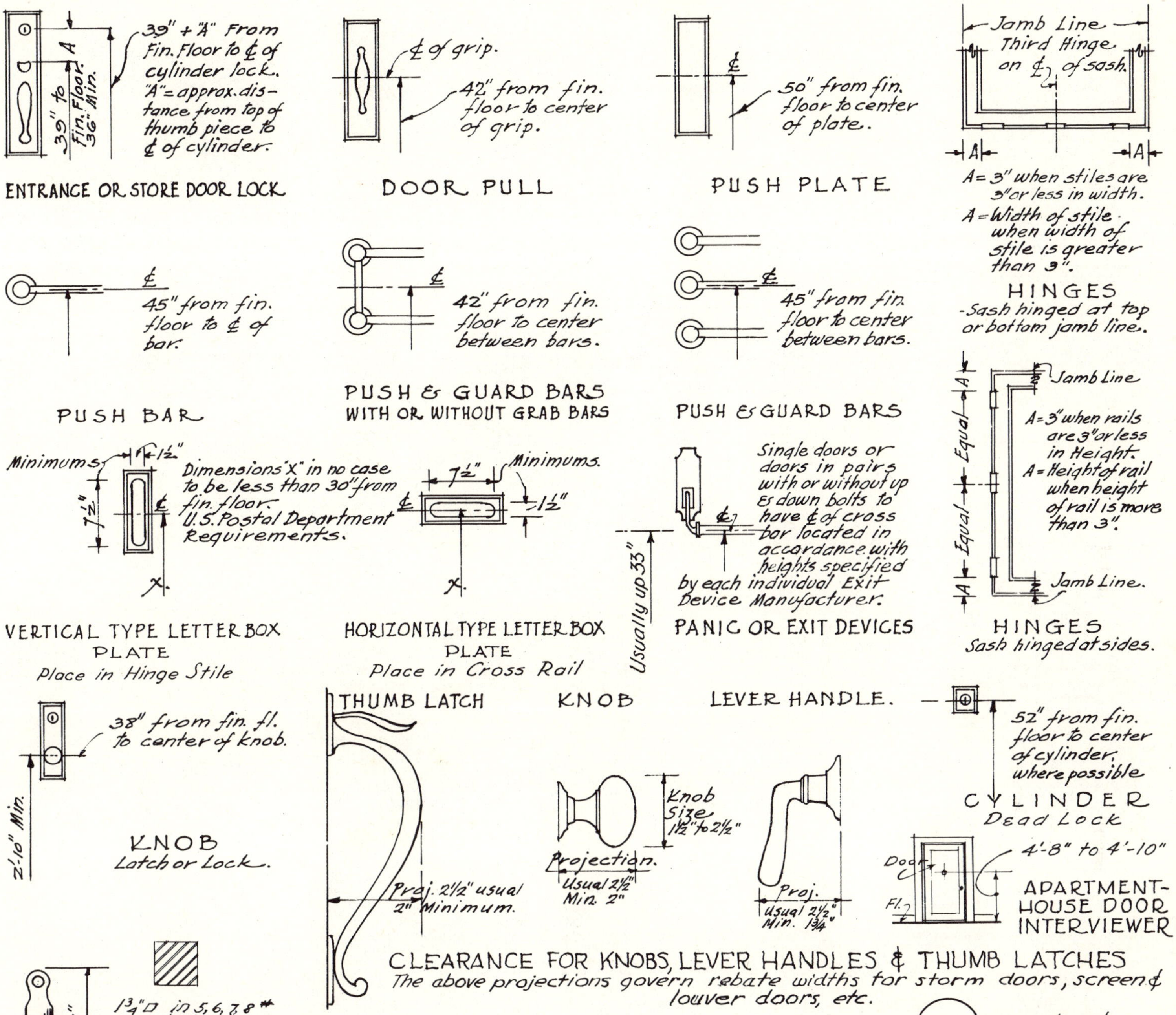

39" + "A" From Fin. Floor to ℄ of cylinder lock. "A" = approx. distance from top of thumb piece to ℄ of cylinder.
39" to Fin. Floor 36" Min.
A
ENTRANCE OR STORE DOOR LOCK
℄ of grip.
42" from fin. floor to center of grip.
DOOR PULL
℄
50" from fin. floor to center of plate.
PUSH PLATE
Jamb Line
Third Hinge on ℄ of sash.
A
A = 3" when stiles are 3" or less in width.
A = Width of stile when width of stile is greater than 3".
HINGES
-Sash hinged at top or bottom jamb line.
℄
45" from fin. floor to ℄ of bar.
PUSH BAR
℄
42" from fin. floor to center between bars.
PUSH & GUARD BARS
WITH OR WITHOUT GRAB BARS
℄
45" from fin. floor to center between bars.
PUSH & GUARD BARS
Jamb Line
A = 3" when rails are 3" or less in Height.
A = Height of rail when height of rail is more than 3".
Equal
Equal
Jamb Line.
HINGES
Sash hinged at sides.
Minimums
1½"
7½"
Dimensions "X" in no case to be less than 30" from fin. floor. U.S. Postal Department Requirements.
X
VERTICAL TYPE LETTER BOX PLATE
Place in Hinge Stile
7½"
Minimums.
1½"
℄
X
HORIZONTAL TYPE LETTER BOX PLATE
Place in Cross Rail
Usually up 33"
Single doors or doors in pairs with or without up & down bolts to have ℄ of cross bar located in accordance with heights specified by each individual Exit Device Manufacturer.
PANIC OR EXIT DEVICES
38" from fin. fl. to center of knob.
2'-10" Min.
KNOB
Latch or Lock.
THUMB LATCH
Proj. 2½" usual 2" Minimum.
KNOB
Knob Size 1½" to 2½"
Projection.
Usual 2½" Min. 2"
LEVER HANDLE.
Proj.
Usual 2½" Min. 1¾"
52" from fin. floor to center of cylinder, where possible
CYLINDER
Dead Lock
Door
Fl.
4'-8" to 4'-10"
APARTMENT-HOUSE DOOR INTERVIEWER

CLEARANCE FOR KNOBS, LEVER HANDLES & THUMB LATCHES

The above projections govern rebate widths for storm doors, screen & louver doors, etc.

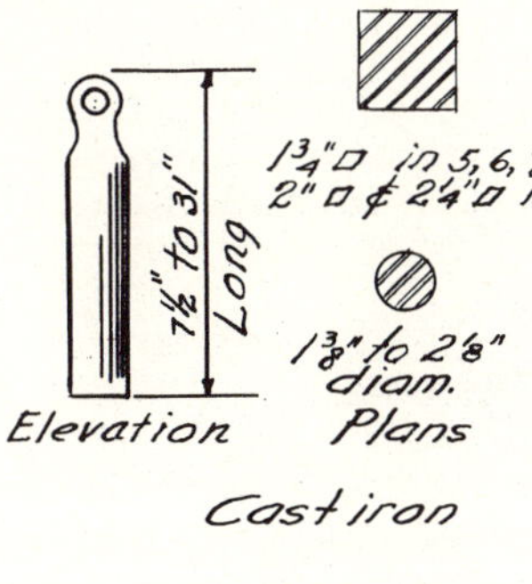

1¾"□ in 5, 6, 7, 8 lbs.
2"□ & 2¼"□ in 7, 8, 9, 10 lbs.
1⅜" to 2⅛" diam.
7½" to 31" Long
Elevation
Plans
Cast iron

SASH WEIGHTS

Pocket for sash weights generally 2¼" for residential work, 2½" for larger size weights.

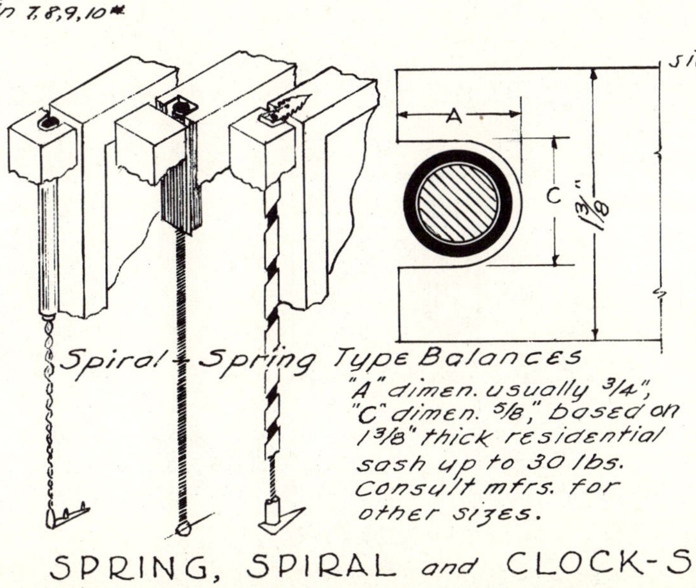

A
C
1⅜"
Spiral-Spring Type Balances
"A" dimen. usually ¾", "C" dimen. ⅝", based on 1⅜" thick residential sash up to 30 lbs. Consult mfrs. for other sizes.

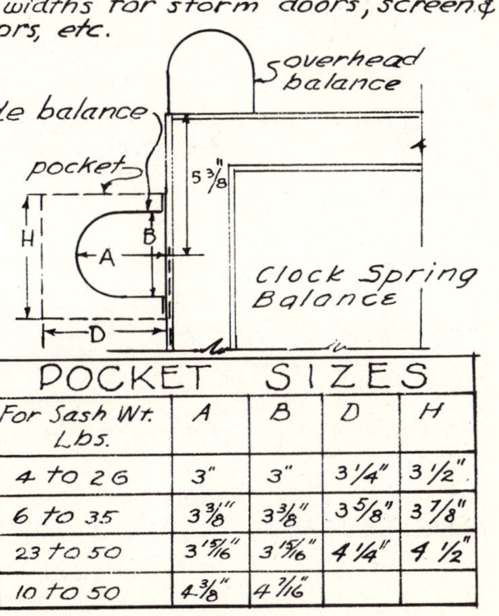

overhead balance
side balance
pocket
5⅜"
H
A
B
D
Clock Spring Balance

POCKET SIZES				
For Sash Wt. Lbs.	A	B	D	H
4 to 26	3"	3"	3¼"	3½"
6 to 35	3⅜"	3⅜"	3⅝"	3⅞"
23 to 50	3$^{15}/_{16}$"	3$^{15}/_{16}$"	4¼"	4½"
10 to 50	4⅜"	4$^{7}/_{16}$"		

Data checked by: American Society of Architectural Hardware Consultants.

SPRING, SPIRAL and CLOCK-SPRING BALANCES

DOOR HARDWARE REQUIREMENTS

RULE FOR HAND OF DOORS

Stand on side of door from which security is desired, i.e. the outside.

If butts are on left side of you with the door swinging away, it is a left hand door regular.

If butts are on left side of you with the door swinging toward you, it is a left hand door reverse.

If butts are on right side of you with the door swinging away, it is a right hand door regular.

If butts are on right side of you with the door swinging toward you, it is a right hand door reverse.

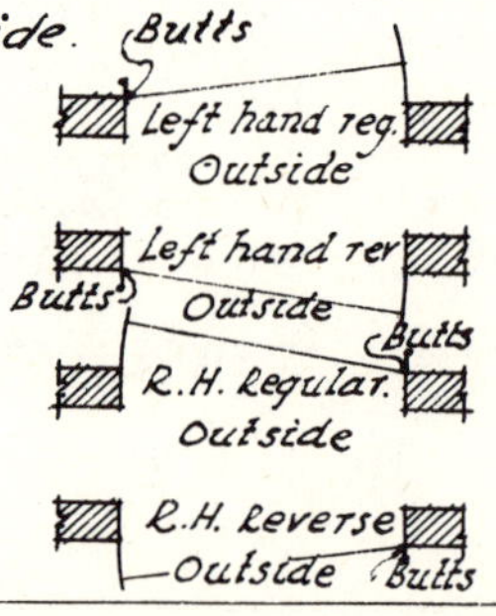

Butts
Left hand reg.
Outside
Left hand rev.
Butts
Outside
Butts
R.H. Regular.
Outside
R.H. Reverse
Outside
Butts

No Bevel 1 3/8" Door
7/64"
1 3/4" Door 7/64" Bevel
2"
1/8"
9/64"
2 1/4" Door 9/64" Bevel

BASIS OF STANDARD BEVEL 1/8" IN 2".
Full Size detail

DOOR BEVELS

These are not required on 1 3/8" or thinner doors

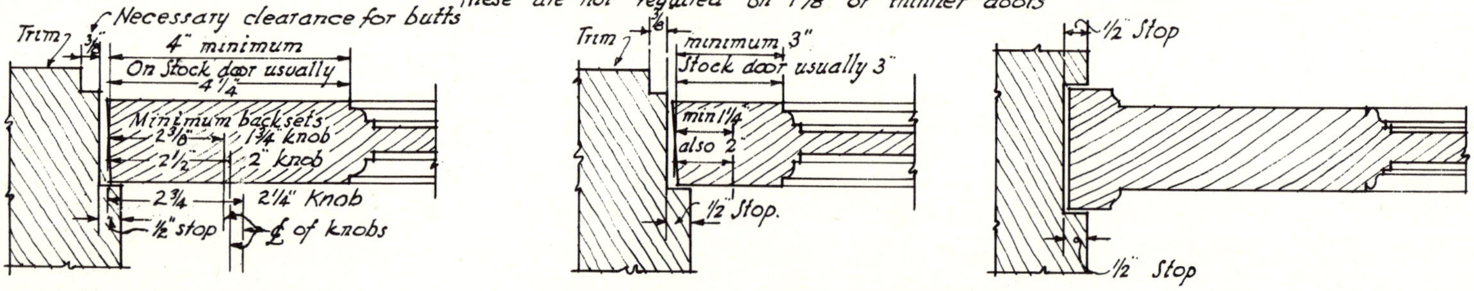

Necessary clearance for butts
Trim
3/8"
4" minimum
On Stock door usually 4 1/4"
Minimum backsets
2 3/8" 1 3/4" knob
2 1/2" 2" knob
2 3/4" 2 1/4" Knob
1/2" stop
℄ of knobs
Trim
3/8"
minimum 3"
Stock door usually 3"
min 1 1/4"
also 2"
1/2" Stop.
1/2" Stop
1/2" Stop

DOOR WITH KNOB
Using bit key or cylinder lock

DOOR WITH LEVER HANDLE
Using bit key or cylinder lock

SLIDING DOOR

These doors shown with bevel. Same dimensions hold for thinner doors

SINGLE DOORS

3" = 1'-0"

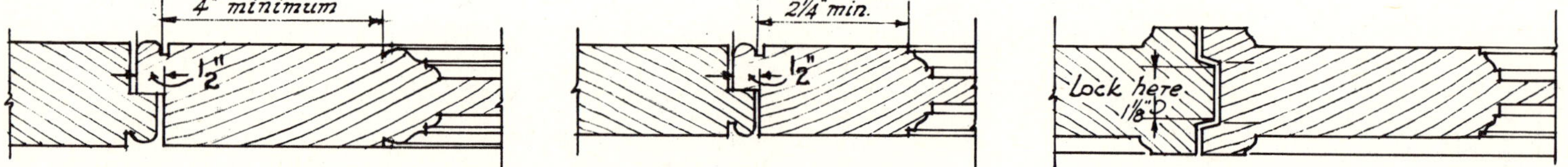

Usually 4 1/4" on Stock doors
4" minimum
1/2"
Usually 3" on Stock doors
2 1/4" min.
1/2"
Lock here
1 1/8"

Minimum for use of knobs. Minimum for lever handle

RABBETED MEETING STILE
Cylinder or bit key lock

SLIDING DOOR WITH ASTRAGAL

DOUBLE DOORS

4" minimum
Backset
2 1/2 or 2 3/4
Usual 2 1/2"
Min. 2"
Door
Screen Door
For Stock door These are usually
3"
2 1/4" min
1 1/2"
1 1/4" Backset min

SCREEN DOOR CLEARANCE

FOR KNOB.
BEVELLED FOR CYLINDER LOCK

FOR LEVER HANDLES

DOUBLE DOORS WITH FLAT ASTRAGALS

DOOR HARDWARE

Data checked by American Society of Architectural Hardware Consultants

WINDOW HARDWARE REQUIREMENTS

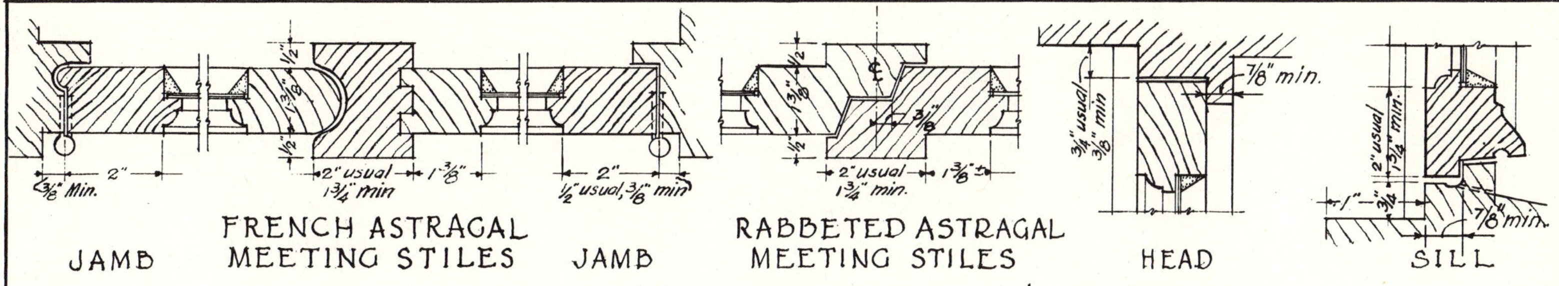
2"
3/8" Min.
2" usual
1 3/4" min
1 3/8"
1/2" usual, 3/8" min
2" usual
1 3/4" min.
1 3/8"
3/8"
7/8" min.
3/4" usual
3/8" min
2" usual
1 3/4" min.
1"
7/8" min.
JAMB
FRENCH ASTRAGAL
MEETING STILES
JAMB
RABBETED ASTRAGAL
MEETING STILES
HEAD
SILL

FOR USE WITH CREMONE BOLT & ADJUSTER

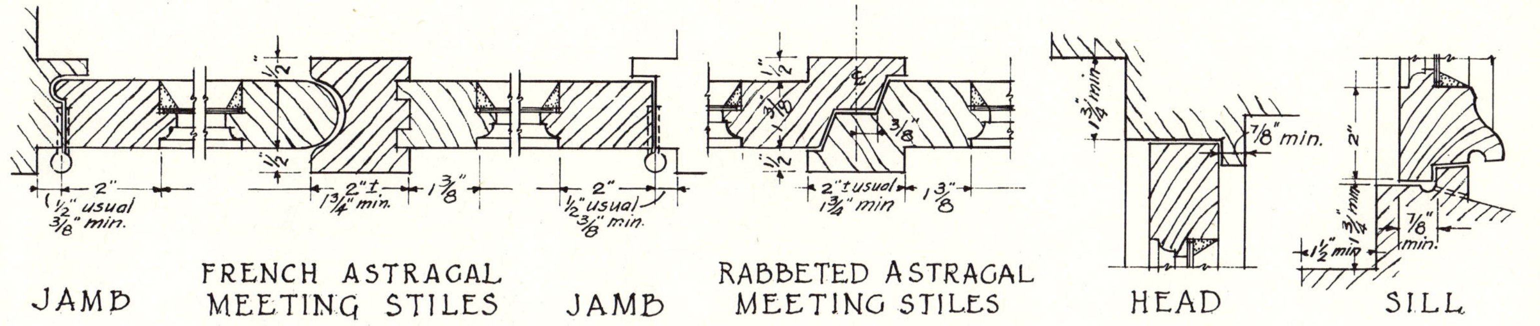
2"
1/2" usual
3/8" min.
2" ±
1 3/4" min.
1 3/8"
1/2" usual
3/8" min.
2" ± usual
1 3/4" min
1 3/8"
3/8"
1 3/4" min
7/8" min.
2"
1 3/4" min
1 1/2" min
7/8" min.
JAMB
FRENCH ASTRAGAL
MEETING STILES
JAMB
RABBETED ASTRAGAL
MEETING STILES
HEAD
SILL

FOR USE WITH ESPAGNOLETTE BOLT AND ADJUSTERS

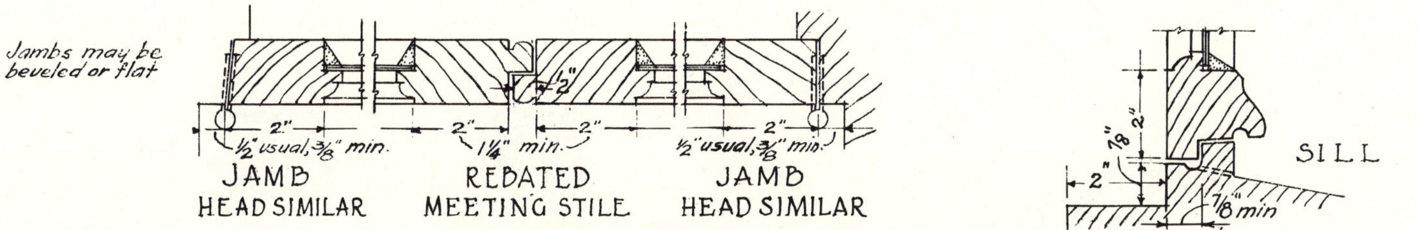
Jambs may be
beveled or flat
1/2"
2"
1/2" usual, 3/8" min.
2"
1 1/4" min.
2"
2"
1/2" usual, 3/8" min.
JAMB
HEAD SIMILAR
REBATED
MEETING STILE
JAMB
HEAD SIMILAR
2"
7/8"
2"
7/8" min
SILL

FOR USE WITH RIM or MORTISE CASEMENT FASTENER or CREMONE BOLT & ADJUSTER

Use Cremone Bolt with sash over 4'-0" high

CASEMENTS OPENING IN

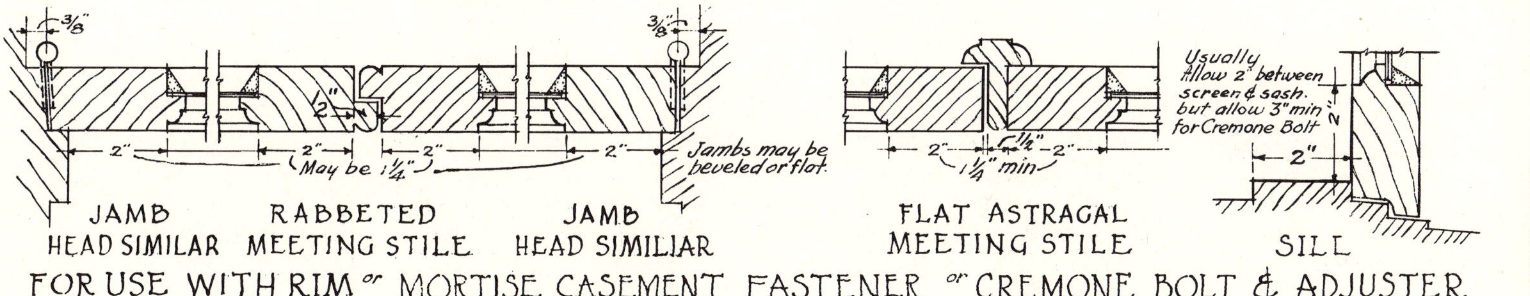
3/8"
3/8"
2"
2"
2"
May be 1 1/4"
2"
2"
Jambs may be
beveled or flat.
2"
1 1/4"
2"
1 1/4" min
Usually
Allow 2" between
screen & sash.
but allow 3" min
for Cremone Bolt
2"
2"
JAMB
HEAD SIMILAR
RABBETED
MEETING STILE
JAMB
HEAD SIMILIAR
FLAT ASTRAGAL
MEETING STILE
SILL

FOR USE WITH RIM or MORTISE CASEMENT FASTENER or CREMONE BOLT & ADJUSTER

Use Cremone Bolt with sash over 4'-0" high

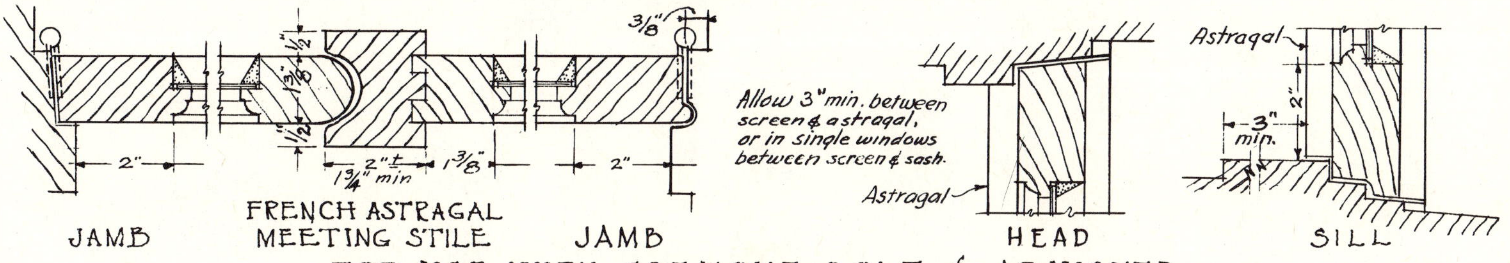
3/8"
1/2"
1 3/8"
1/2"
2"
2" ±
1 3/4" min
1 3/8"
2"
Allow 3" min. between
screen & astragal,
or in single windows
between screen & sash.
Astragal
Astragal
2"
3"
min.
JAMB
FRENCH ASTRAGAL
MEETING STILE
JAMB
HEAD
SILL

FOR USE WITH CREMONE BOLT & ADJUSTER

CASEMENTS OPENING OUT

Requirements for Single Casements the same, with the omission of meeting stile. Flat or beveled jambs, with or without tonque on hinge side, may be used.

Data checked by American Society of Architectural Hardware Consultants

3" = 1'-0"

WOOD CASEMENT HARDWARE

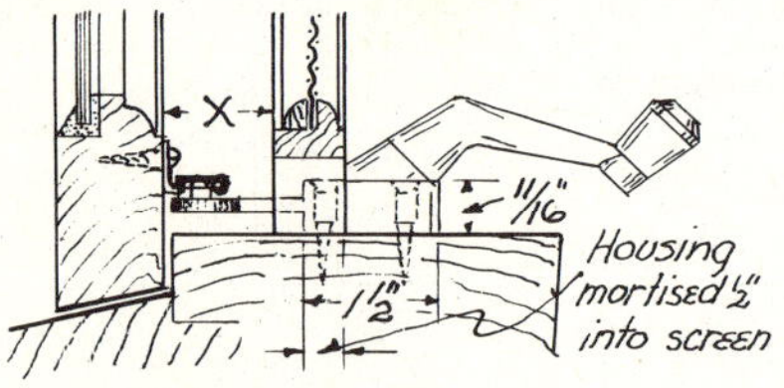
X
11/16"
1 1/2"
Housing mortised 1/2" into screen

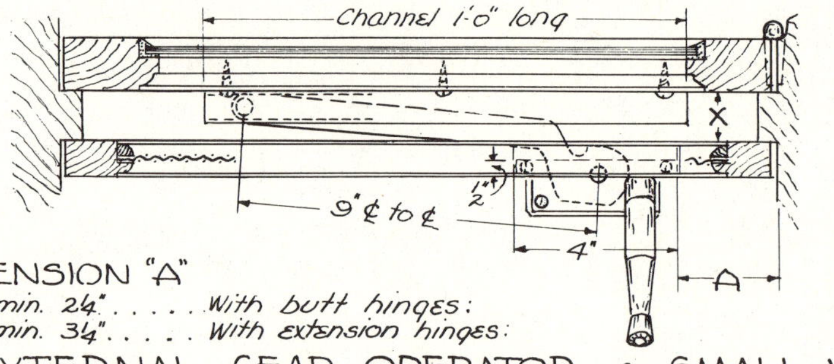
Channel 1'-0" long
X
1/2"
9" ¢ to ¢
4"
A

Standard operators are furnished with 9" arms for use with butt hinges to fit sash 14" to 20" wide; with extension hinges to fit sash 16" to 20" wide. Channel must be 15" long if extension hinges are used. Use of these operators on sash over 1'-8" wide or 3'-2" high is not recommended. Special operators are furnished with shorter arms for use with butt hinges to fit sash from 11" wide; with extension hinges to fit sash from 14" wide.

DIMENSION "X" DIMENSION "A"
min. 1"; max. 4" . . . . min. 2 1/4" . . . . . With butt hinges:
min. 1"; max. 1 1/2" . . . . min. 3 1/4" . . . . . With extension hinges:

ANGULAR DRIVE - EXTERNAL GEAR OPERATOR *for* SMALL WOOD CASEMENTS

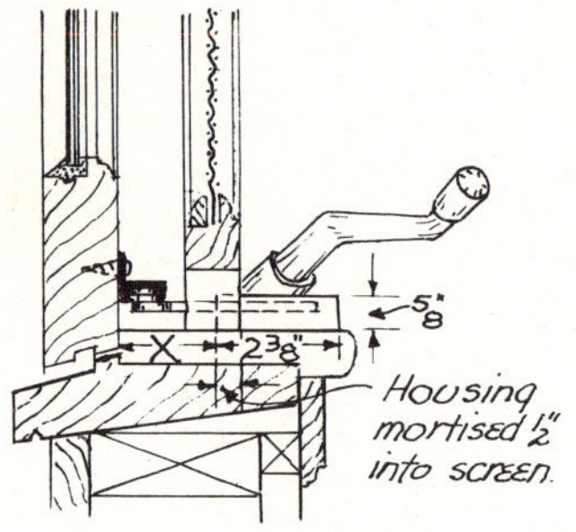
5/8"
X
2 3/8"
Housing mortised 1/2" into screen.

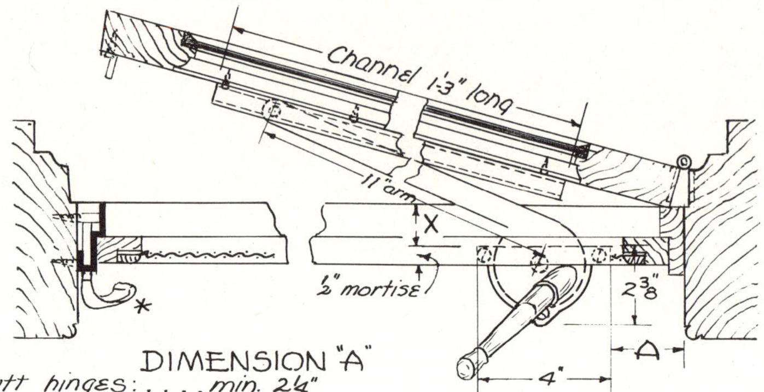
Channel 1'-3" long
11" arm
X
*
1/2" mortise
2 3/8"
A
4"

Standard operators are furnished with 11" arms for use with butt hinges to fit sash 16" to 30" wide; with extension hinges to fit sash 19" to 30" wide. Use of these operators on casements over 2'-6" wide or 6'-0" high is not recommended. Special operators can be furnished with shorter arms for use with butt hinges to fit sash from 11" wide; with extension hinges to fit sash from 17" wide. Operators may be equipped with a removable crank handle, or with a pole hook for remote operation by winding brace pole to fit special conditions.

DIMENSION "X" DIMENSION "A"
min. 1 1/8" max. 4 1/2" . . . With butt hinges: . . . . . min. 2 1/4"
min. 1 1/8" max. 3" . . . With extension hinges: . . min. 4"

ANGULAR DRIVE - INTERNAL GEAR OPERATOR *for* LARGE WOOD CASEMENTS

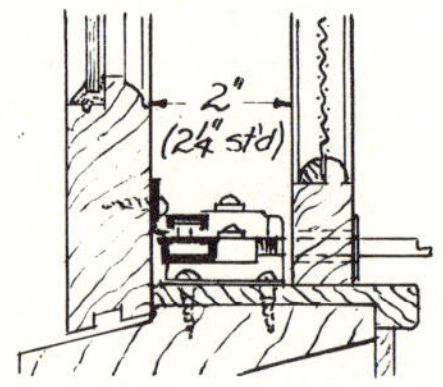
2"
(2 1/4" std)

ABOVE - STOOL INSTALLATION

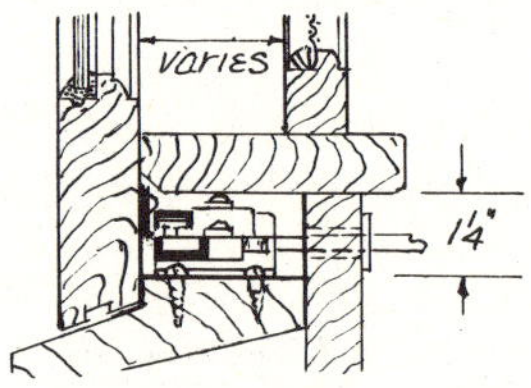
Varies
1 1/4"

UNDER - STOOL INSTALLATION

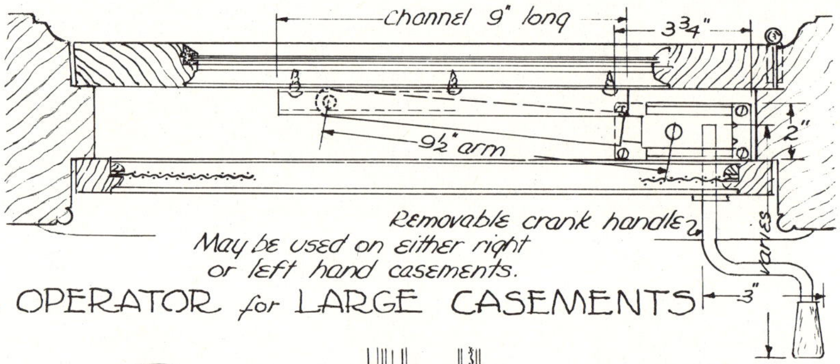
Channel 9" long
3 3/4"
2"
9 1/2" arm
Removable crank handle
Varies
3"

May be used on either right or left hand casements.

HORIZONTAL DRIVE - EXTERNAL GEAR OPERATOR *for* LARGE CASEMENTS

Length 7 1/2", 8", 8 1/2", 9", 10", 12", 13", 15", 18". Should be 2/3 of casement width. Design varies with mf'r.

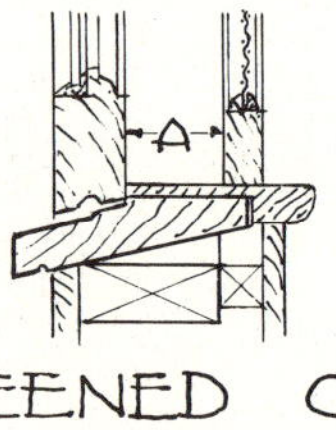
A

DIMENSION "A"
With butt hinges:
min. 1 1/4"; max. 3 1/2"
With extension hinges:
min. 1 1/2"; max. 3 1/2"
SILL

SLIDE ADJUSTER *for* NON-SCREENED CASEMENTS

All rabbets on meeting rails should be eliminated as a standard practice. Where unavoidable, a one-half inch square rabbet, not bevelled, should be used.

The term "French Window" should be applied to glazed, narrow-stile openings, hinged at the side, which do not extend to the floor. The face width of stiles for such openings should be not less than two inches.

The term "French Door" should be applied to glazed, narrow-stile openings which extend to the floor. The face width of the stiles for such openings should be not less than three inches.

DETAILS AFFECTING HARDWARE

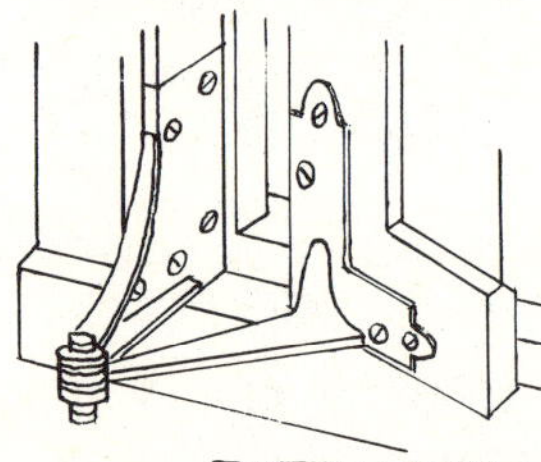

EXTENSION

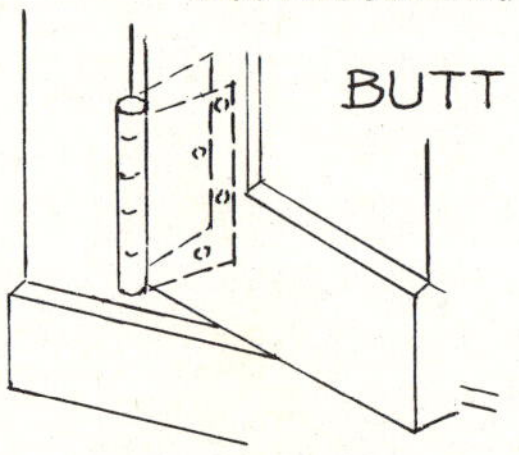

BUTT

HINGES.

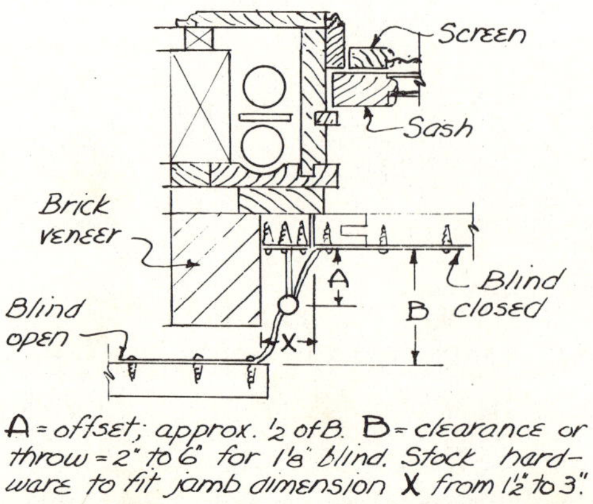
Screen
Sash
Brick veneer
A
B
Blind closed
Blind open
X

A = offset; approx. 1/2 of B. B = clearance or throw = 2" to 6" for 1 1/8" blind. Stock hardware to fit jamb dimension X from 1 1/2" to 3".

BLIND REQUIREMENTS

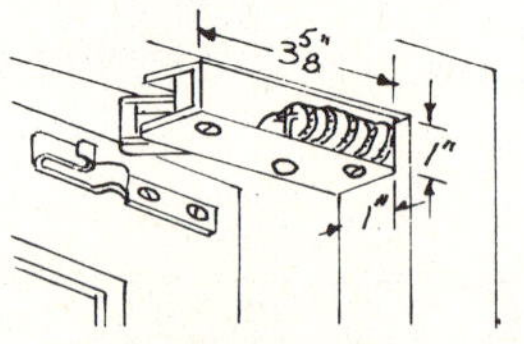
3 5/8"
1"
1"

CLOSER

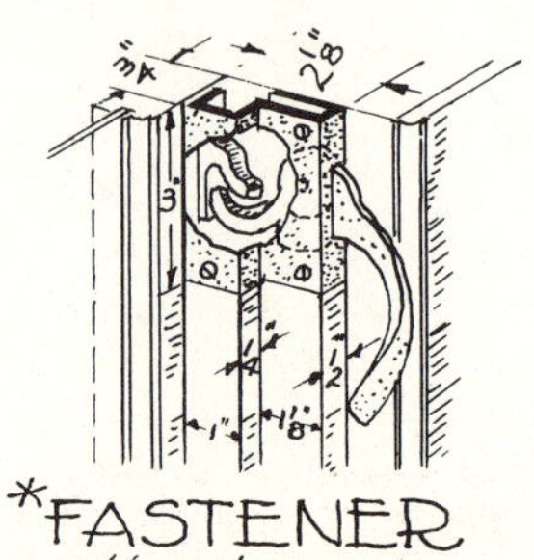

*FASTENER

Data checked by: American Society of Architectural Hardware Consultants.

HARDWARE

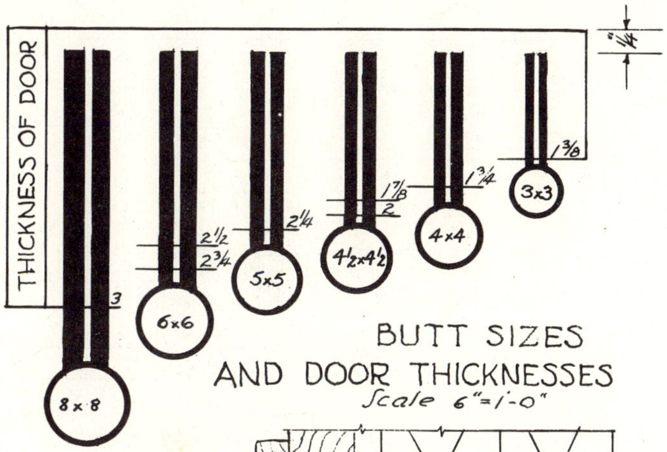
THICKNESS OF DOOR
3/4
1 3/8
3x3
1 3/4
1 7/8
2
4x4
2 1/4
4 1/2 x 4 1/2
2 1/2
2 3/4
5x5
6x6
3
8x8

BUTT SIZES AND DOOR THICKNESSES
Scale 6" = 1'-0"

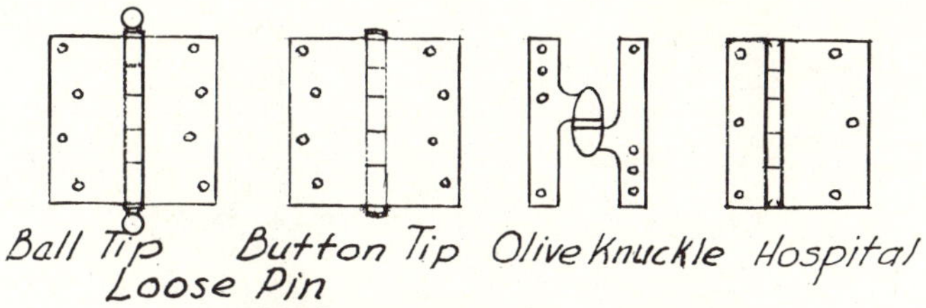
Ball Tip
Button Tip
Olive Knuckle
Hospital
Loose Pin

TYPES OF BUTT HINGES

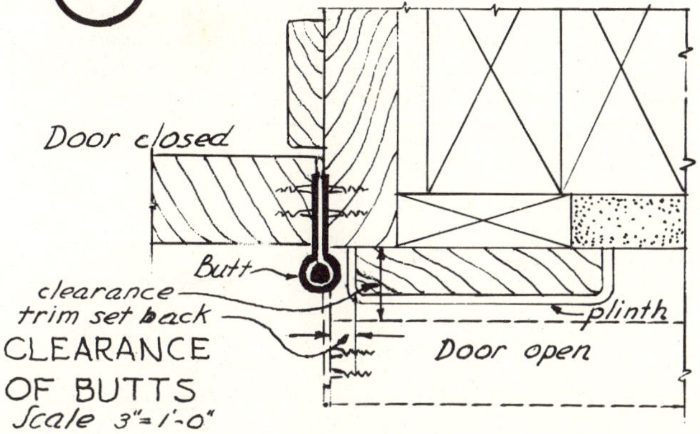
Door closed
Butt
clearance
trim set back
plinth
Door open

CLEARANCE OF BUTTS
Scale 3" = 1'-0"

CLEARANCE OF BUTTS AND SET BACK OF TRIM

STANDARD BUTT HINGE

Door Thick.	Butt Size	Max. Clear.	Set Back
1 3/8	3x3	3/4	3/8
	3 1/2 x 3 1/2	1 1/4	3/8
	4x4	1 3/4	3/8
1 3/4	4x4	1	3/8
	4 1/2 x 4 1/2	1 1/2	1/2
	5x5	2	1/2
	6x6	3	1/2
1 7/8	4 1/2 x 4 1/2	1 1/4	1/2
	5x5	1 3/4	1/2
	6x6	2 3/4	5/8

EXTRA HEAVY BUTT HINGE

Door Thick.	Butt Size	Max. Clear.	Set Back
1 3/4	4x4	1	3/8
	4 1/2 x 4 1/2	1 1/2	1/2
	5x5	2	1/2
	6x6	3	5/8
1 7/8	4 1/2 x 4 1/2	1 1/4	1/2
	5x5	1 3/4	1/2
	6x6	2 3/4	5/8
2	4 1/2 x 4 1/2	1	1/2
	5x5	1 1/2	1/2
	6x6	2 1/2	5/8

Door Thick.	Butt Size	Max. Clear.	Set Back
2 1/4	5x5	1	1/2
	6x6	2	5/8
	6x8	4	5/8
2 1/2	5x5	3/4	1/2
	6x6	1 3/4	5/8
	6x8	3 3/4	5/8
2 3/4	6x6	1 1/4	5/8
	6x8	3 1/4	5/8
3	6x6	3/4	5/8
	6x8	2 3/4	5/8
	8x6	3/4	5/8
	8x8	2 3/4	5/8

Extra heavy butts recommended for metal doors & much used doors
All dimensions given in inches

SIZES OF BUTT HINGES

THICKNESS (in inches)	WIDTH OF DOORS OR HEIGHT OF TRANSOMS	SIZE OF BUTT HINGE (in inches)
3/4 to 1 1/8 cabinet doors	To 24	2 1/2 x 2 1/2
7/8 and 1 1/8 screen or combination doors	To 36	3 x 3
1 1/8 doors	To 36	3 1/2 x 3 1/2
1 1/4 and 1 3/8 doors	To 32 over 32 to 37	3 1/2 x 3 1/2 4 x 4
1 3/4 and 1 7/8 doors	To 32 over 32 to 37 over 37 to 43 over 43 to 50	4 1/2 x 4 1/2 5 x 5 5x5 extra heavy 6x6 extra heavy
2, 2 1/4 and 2 1/2 doors	To 37 over 37 to 43 over 43 to 50	5 x 5 5x5 extra heavy 6x6 extra heavy
1 1/4 and 1 3/8 transoms	To 20 over 20 to 36	2 1/2 x 2 1/2 3 x 3
1 1/2, 1 3/4, and 1 7/8 transoms	To 20 over 20 to 36	3 x 3 3 1/2 x 3 1/2

Width of butt hinges as necessary to clear trim. Doors to 60" high inclusive require 2 butt hinges; over 60" to 90" high inclusive, 3 butt hinges; over 90" to 120" high inclusive, 4 butt hinges.

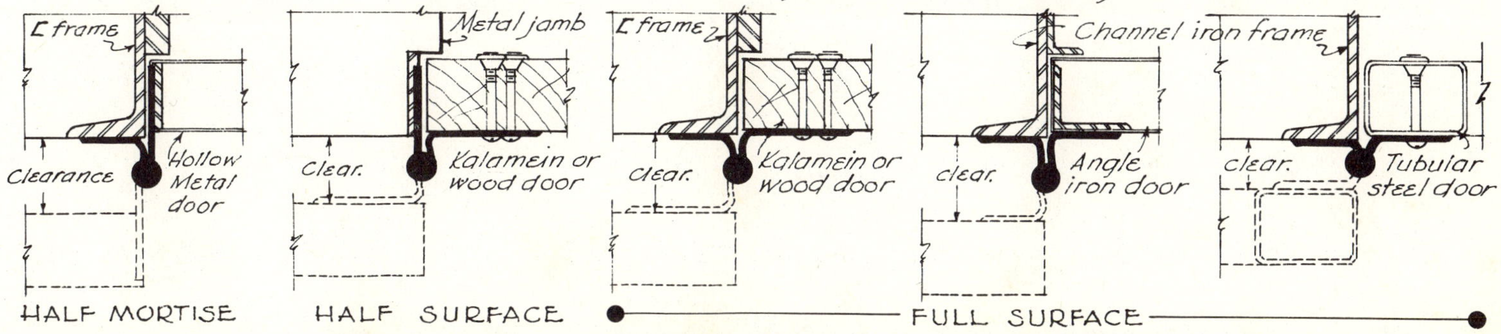
[frame
Clearance
Hollow Metal door
HALF MORTISE
Metal jamb
Clear.
Kalamein or wood door
HALF SURFACE
[frame
clear.
Kalamein or wood door
Channel iron frame
clear.
Angle iron door
clear.
Tubular steel door
FULL SURFACE

TYPICAL APPLICATION of BUTT HINGES

Full Mortise shown in wood jamb near top of page. For clearance of butts & trim set-back, see table.
Data checked by: American Society of Architectural Hardware Consultants.

SPRING HINGES, DOOR CHECKS (CLOSERS), STOPS and HOLDERS

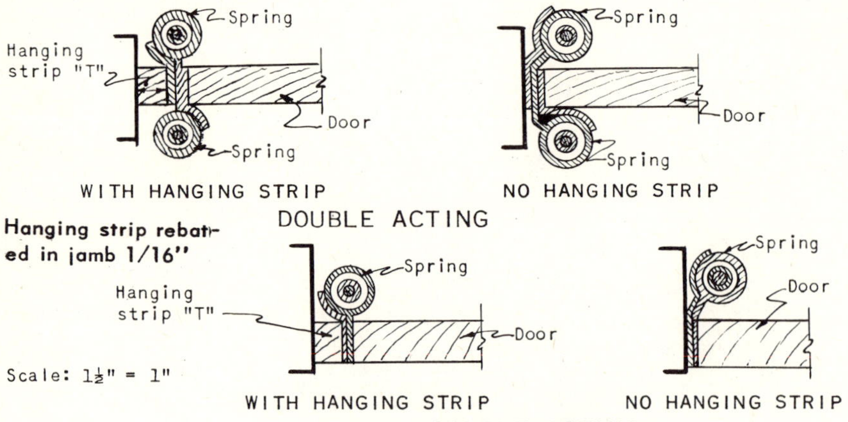
Spring
Hanging strip "T"
Door
Spring
WITH HANGING STRIP
Spring
Door
Spring
NO HANGING STRIP
DOUBLE ACTING
Hanging strip rebated in jamb 1/16"
Spring
Hanging strip "T"
Door
Scale: 1½" = 1"
WITH HANGING STRIP
Spring
Door
NO HANGING STRIP
SINGLE ACTING

SPRING BUTT HINGES

SPRING BUTT HINGE SIZES				
Hinge Sizes	Door Thickness Min.–Max.*	Max. Door Width	Max. Door Weight	Depth Hanging Strip (T)
3"	¾"–1"	2'- 2"	30#	½"
4"	⅞"–1¼"	2'- 4"	42#	⅝"
5"	1" –1½"	2'- 6"	56#	⅝"
6"	1⅛"–1¾"	2'- 8"	72#	¾"
7"	1¼"–2"	2'- 9"	90#	⅞"
8"	1½"–2¼"	2'-10"	110#	1"
10"	1¾"–2½"	3'- 0"	150#	1⅛"
12"	2¼"–3"	3'- 2"	190#	1¼"

*Max. sizes shown are for wood doors; deduct 1/8" for metal doors. Use min. thickness only for light wood doors. Check mfrs. for exact data.

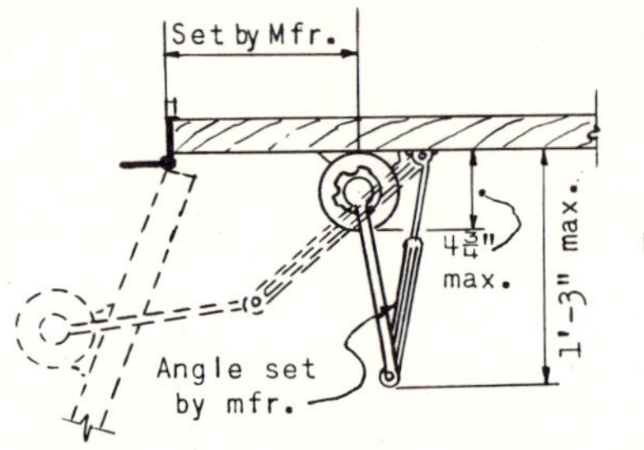
Set by Mfr.
4½" max.
1'-3" max.
Angle set by mfr.

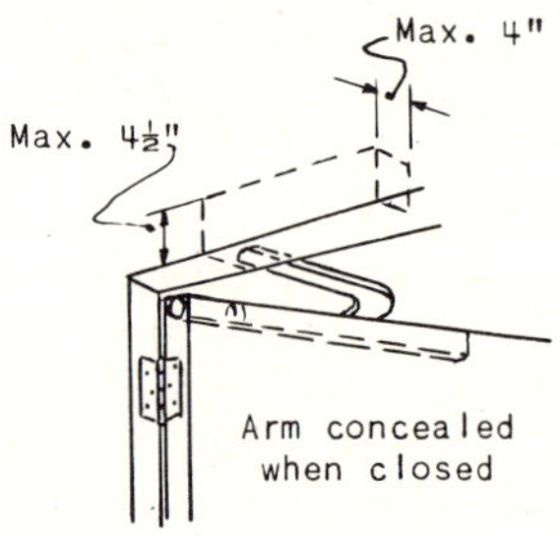
Max. 4"
Max. 4½"
Arm concealed when closed

Cylinder may be mounted on door, or either side of door head. Corner mount permits full 180° opening but reduces effective power of check for closing. For exact dimensions check with mfr., and when ordering specify max. op. angle

OVERHEAD EXPOSED

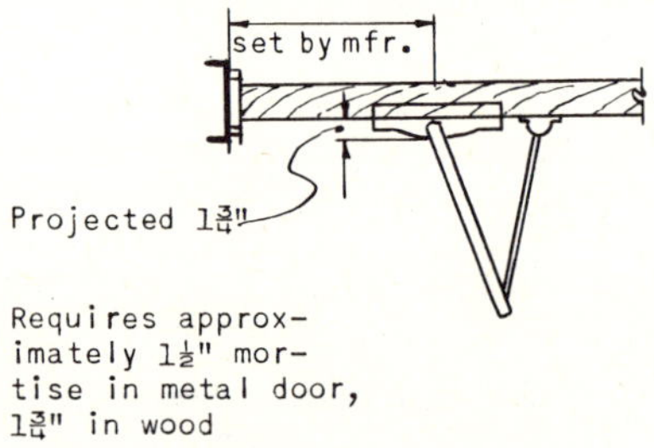
set by mfr.
Projected 1¾"
Requires approximately 1½" mortise in metal door, 1¾" in wood

OVERHEAD SEMI-CONCEALED

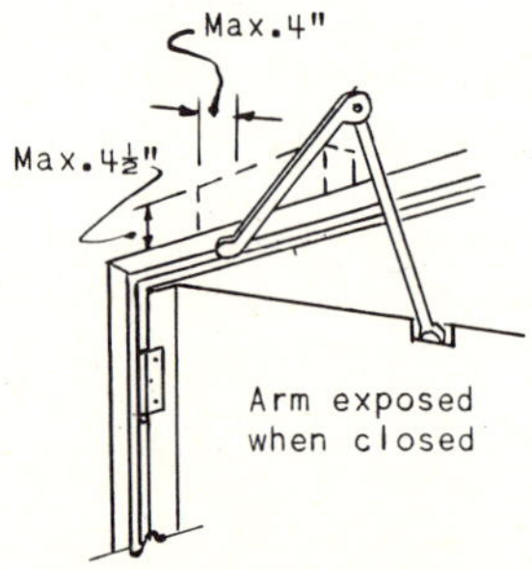
Max.4"
Max.4½"
Arm exposed when closed

OVERHEAD CONCEALED

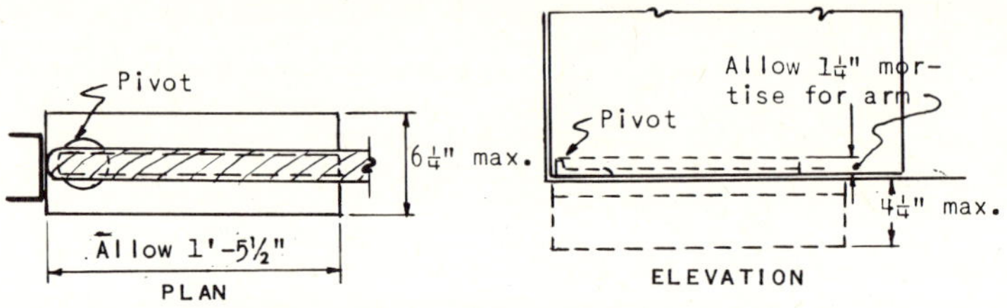
Pivot
6¼" max.
Allow 1'-5½"
PLAN
Allow 1¼" mortise for arm
Pivot
4¼" max.
ELEVATION

DOUBLE ACTING ON CENTER PIVOT

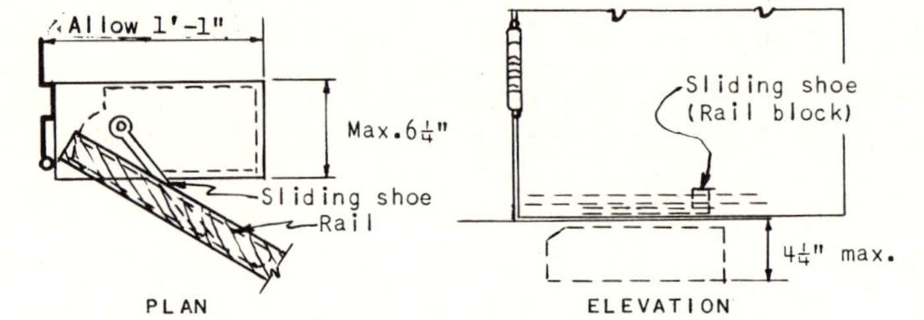
Allow 1'-1"
Max.6¼"
Sliding shoe
Rail
PLAN
Sliding shoe (Rail block)
4¼" max.
ELEVATION

SINGLE ACTING ON BUTT HINGES

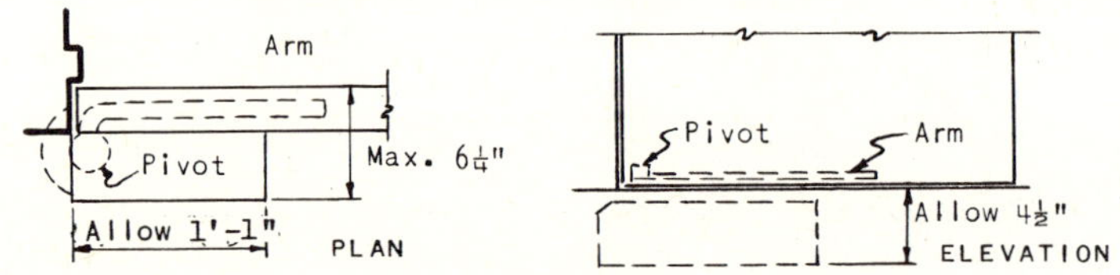
Arm
Pivot
Max. 6¼"
Allow 1'-1"
PLAN
Pivot
Arm
Allow 4½"
ELEVATION

SINGLE ACTING ON OFFSET PIVOTS

FLOOR CLOSERS

Scale: ½" = 1"

DOOR CHECKS (CLOSERS)

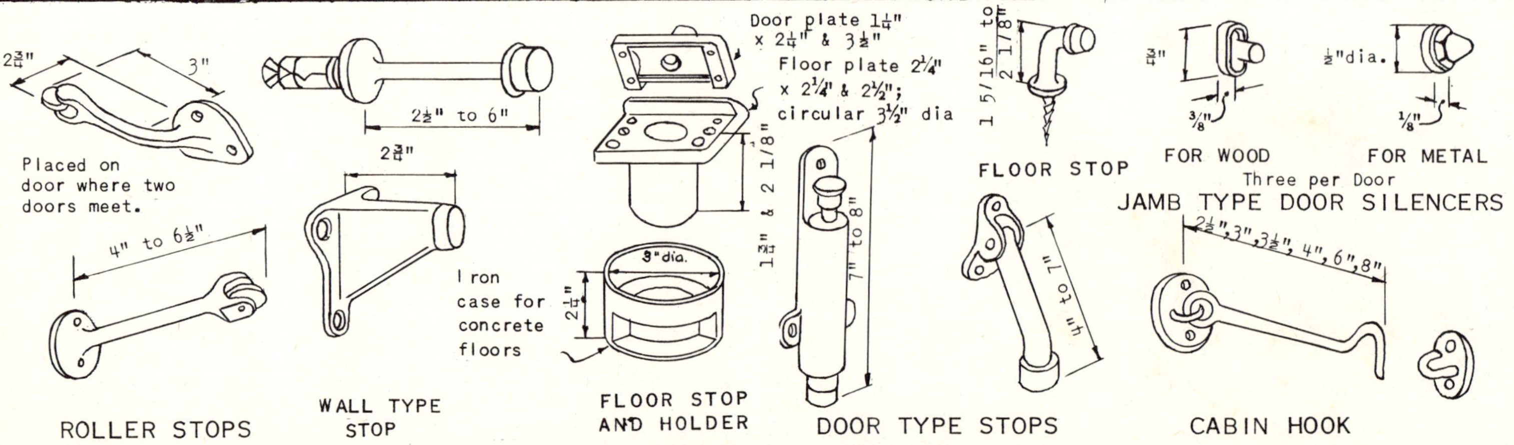
2¾"
3"
Placed on door where two doors meet.
4" to 6½"
ROLLER STOPS
2½" to 6"
2¾"
WALL TYPE STOP
Door plate 1¼" x 2¼" & 3½"
Floor plate 2¼" x 2¼" & 2½"; circular 3½" dia
1¾" & 2 1/8"
3" dia.
2¼"
Iron case for concrete floors
FLOOR STOP AND HOLDER
7" to 8"
4" to 7"
DOOR TYPE STOPS
1 5/16" to 2 1/8"
FLOOR STOP
¾"
3/8"
FOR WOOD
½"dia.
1/8"
FOR METAL
Three per Door
JAMB TYPE DOOR SILENCERS
2½",3",3½",4",6",8"
CABIN HOOK

DOOR STOPS AND HOLDERS

DATA BY THE AMERICAN SOCIETY OF ARCHITECTURAL HARDWARE CONSULTANTS

HARDWARE FINISHES

FINISHES FOR BUILDERS' HARDWARE COMMERCIAL STANDARD CS22-40
U.S. DEPT. OF COMMERCE STANDARD FINISHES FOR NORMAL USE

SYMBOL	GENERAL DESCRIPTION	METAL APPLIED TO	SAMPLES SELECTED AS STANDARD	RESTRICTIONS OR CHARACTERISTICS
USP	PRIMED FOR PAINTING	. . . .	. . . .	
US1B	BRIGHT JAPANNED	. . . .	. . . .	
US1D	DEAD BLACK	. . . .	. . . .	
US2C	CADMIUM PLATED	. . . .	. . . .	
US2G	ZINC, ELECTROPLATED	. . . .	. . . .	
US2H	ZINC, HOT DIPPED	. . . .	. . . .	
US3	BRIGHT BRASS	IRON, STEEL, WROUGHT AND CAST BRASS	YALE AZ10	
US3A	BRIGHT BRASS, NO LACQUER	WROUGHT AND CAST BRASS	. . . . . .	LIMITED TO WROUGHT AND CAST BRASS*
US4	DULL BRASS	IRON, STEEL, WROUGHT AND CAST BRASS	CORBIN EA	
US5	DULL BRASS, OXIDIZED AND RELIEVED	. . . . DO	RUSSWIN 9C	LIMITED TO ORNAMENTAL DESIGNS. PLAIN HARDWARE TO MATCH TO BE FINISH US4
US9	BRIGHT BRONZE	IRON, STEEL, WROUGHT AND CAST BRONZE	YALE BZ10	
US9A	BRIGHT BRONZE, NO LACQUER	WROUGHT AND CAST BRONZE	. . . . . .	LIMITED TO WROUGHT AND CAST BRONZE*
US10	DULL BRONZE	IRON, STEEL, WROUGHT AND CAST BRONZE	CORBIN DB	
US10A	DULL BRONZE, OXIDIZED	WROUGHT AND CAST BRONZE	READING 271	LIMITED TO PLAIN SURFACES
US10B	DULL BRONZE, OXIDIZED AND OIL RUBBED	WROUGHT AND CAST BRONZE	. . . . . .	LIMITED ON WROUGHT BRONZE TO BUTTS*
US11	DULL BRONZE, OXIDIZED AND RELIEVED	IRON, STEEL, WROUGHT AND CAST BRONZE	SARGENT 06P	LIMITED TO ORNAMENTAL DESIGNS, PLAIN HARDWARE TO MATCH TO BE FINISH US10
US11A	DULL BRONZE, OXIDIZED AND RELIEVED, OIL RUBBED	WROUGHT AND CAST BRONZE	. . . . . .	LIMITED TO WROUGHT AND CAST BRONZE*
US14	NICKEL PLATED	IRON, STEEL, WROUGHT AND CAST BRASS OR BRONZE	RUSSWIN 4	POLISHED SURFACES
US15	NICKEL PLATED, DULL	. . . . DO	LOCKWOOD 90	LIMITED TO PLAIN SURFACES
US15A	NICKEL PLATED, DULL, OXIDIZED AND RELIEVED	. . . . DO	CORBIN KE	LIMITED TO ORNAMENTAL DESIGNS
US17A	NICKEL PLATED, IMITATION HALF POLISHED IRON SANDED, OXIDIZED AND RELIEVED	IRON, STEEL, WROUGHT AND CAST BRASS OR BRONZE	STANLEY Y2	
US18	BOWER BARFF	IRON AND STEEL	YALE FX80	ABRASION RESISTANT
US18A	SANDED, RUST-RESISTING BLACK	IRON AND STEEL	YALE PX80	CORROSION RESISTANT
US19	SANDED DULL BLACK	IRON, STEEL, WROUGHT AND CAST BRASS OR BRONZE	YALE BX80, BRONZE YALE FX90 STEEL	ON IRON & STEEL, SAME AS US18A (YALE PX80).
US20	STATUARY BRONZE	WROUGHT AND CAST BRONZE (SEE RESTRICTIONS)	PENN BBZ4	LIMITED ON IRON AND STEEL TO BUTTS
US25	WHITE BRONZE METAL	WROUGHT AND CAST WHITE BRONZE	SARGENT EM	LIMITED TO WHITE BRONZE COMPOSITIONS AND TO WROUGHT WHITE BRONZE IN PUSH PLATES, KICK PLATES AND BUTTS
US25D	WHITE BRONZE METAL, DULL	WROUGHT AND CAST WHITE BRONZE	YALE NY40	DO
US26	CHROMIUM PLATED	. . . .	. . . .	POLISHED SURFACES
US26D	CHROMIUM PLATED DULL	. . . .	CORBIN DCR	DO

* WHEN FINISHES US3A, 9A, 10B, AND 11A ARE FURNISHED ON IRON OR STEEL, THEY WILL BE COATED WITH LACQUER.

As symbols for hardware finishes vary among manufacturers, it is advisable to use the above symbols. It is the intention of manufacturers to bring their standard finishes into close conformity with this standard. However it is impractical to attain an exact match. Oxidized finishes, especially statuary bronze US20, are most likely to vary in shade. Samples of standard finishes may be obtained from the National Bureau of Standards.

FURRING, LATHING and PLASTERING

TABLE OF CONTENTS

WALL FURRING and METHODS of FASTENING

"MASONRY UNIT" FURRING

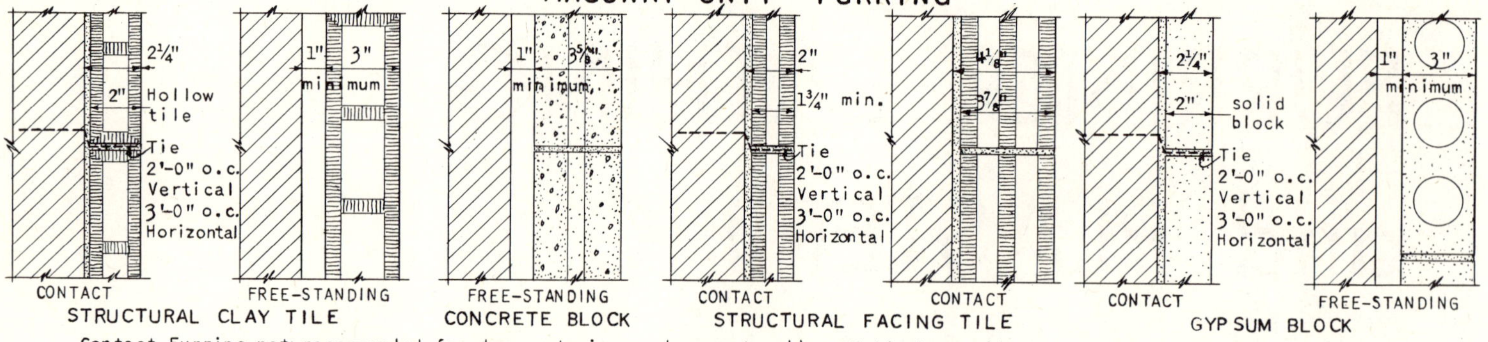
2¼"
2"
Hollow tile
Tie 2'-0" o.c. Vertical 3'-0" o.c. Horizontal
1"
3"
minimum
3⅝"
2"
1¾" min.
4⅛"
3⅞"
2¼"
2"
solid block
1"
3"
CONTACT
FREE-STANDING
STRUCTURAL CLAY TILE
FREE-STANDING
CONCRETE BLOCK
CONTACT
CONTACT
STRUCTURAL FACING TILE
CONTACT
FREE-STANDING
GYPSUM BLOCK

Contact Furring not recommended for damp exterior or basement walls; 2" block or tile not used for Free-Standing Furring.

Scale 1½" = 1'-0"

METHODS OF FASTENING FURRING TO CONCRETE OR MASONRY

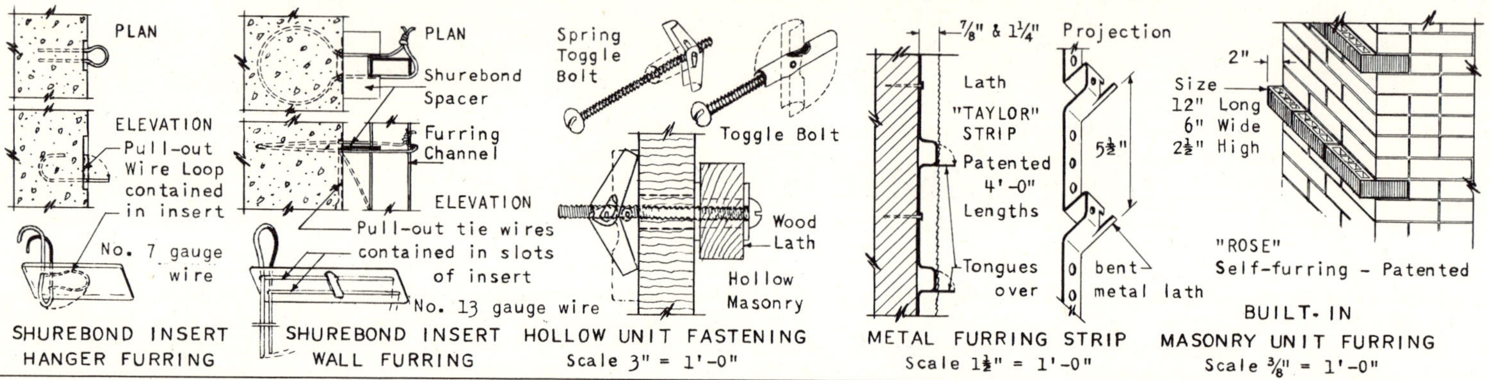
PLAN
ELEVATION
Pull-out Wire Loop contained in insert
No. 7 gauge wire
SHUREBOND INSERT HANGER FURRING
PLAN
Shurebond Spacer
Furring Channel
ELEVATION
Pull-out tie wires contained in slots of insert
No. 13 gauge wire
SHUREBOND INSERT WALL FURRING
Spring Toggle Bolt
Toggle Bolt
Wood Lath
Hollow Masonry
HOLLOW UNIT FASTENING
Scale 3" = 1'-0"
⅞" & 1¼" Projection
Lath
"TAYLOR" STRIP
Patented 4'-0" Lengths
Tongues over
5½"
bent metal lath
METAL FURRING STRIP
Scale 1½" = 1'-0"
2"
Size 12" Long 6" Wide 2½" High
"ROSE" Self-furring - Patented
BUILT-IN MASONRY UNIT FURRING
Scale ⅜" = 1'-0"

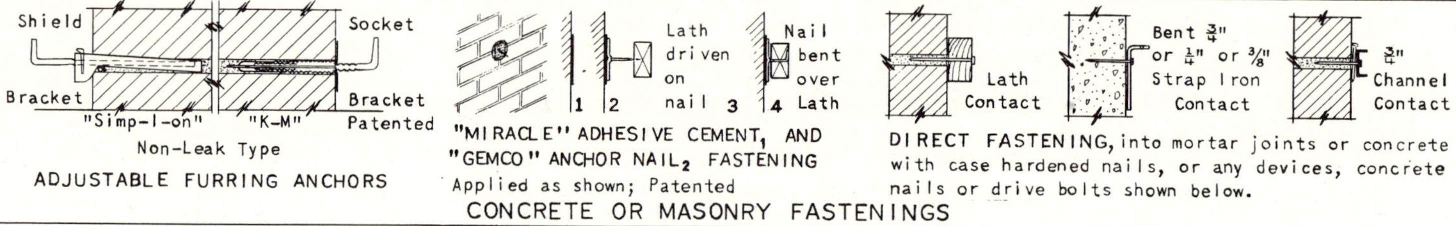
Shield
Socket
Bracket
Bracket
"Simp-l-on"
"K-M"
Patented
Non-Leak Type
ADJUSTABLE FURRING ANCHORS
Lath driven on nail
Nail bent over Lath
1
2
3
4
"MIRACLE" ADHESIVE CEMENT₁ AND "GEMCO" ANCHOR NAIL₂ FASTENING
Applied as shown; Patented
Lath Contact
Bent ¾" or ¼" or ⅜" Strap Iron Contact
¾" Channel Contact
DIRECT FASTENING, into mortar joints or concrete with case hardened nails, or any devices, concrete nails or drive bolts shown below.

CONCRETE OR MASONRY FASTENINGS

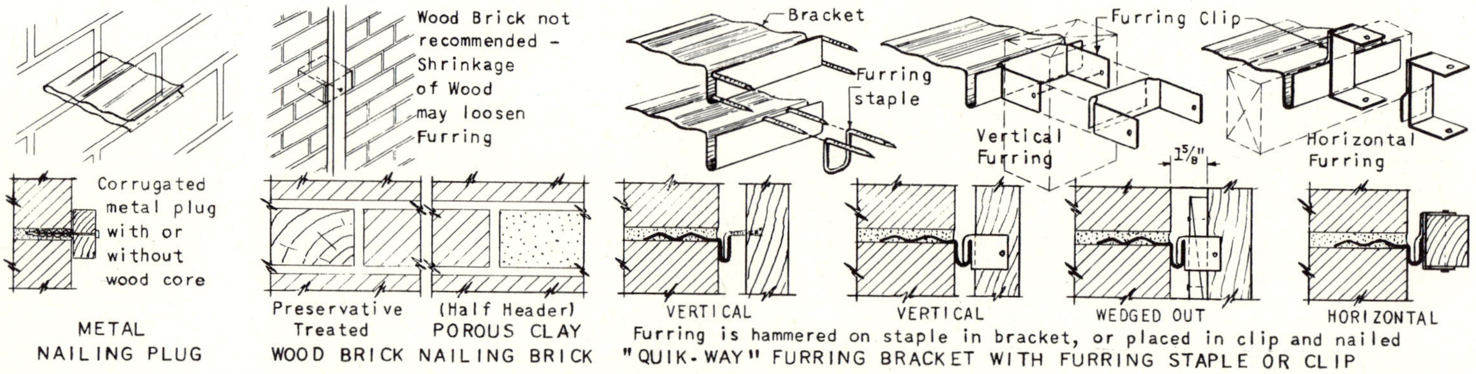
Wood Brick not recommended - Shrinkage of Wood may loosen Furring
Bracket
Furring staple
Furring Clip
Vertical Furring
Horizontal Furring
Corrugated metal plug with or without wood core
METAL NAILING PLUG
Preservative Treated WOOD BRICK
(Half Header) POROUS CLAY NAILING BRICK
1⅝"
VERTICAL
VERTICAL
WEDGED OUT
HORIZONTAL
Furring is hammered on staple in bracket, or placed in clip and nailed
"QUIK-WAY" FURRING BRACKET WITH FURRING STAPLE OR CLIP

MASONRY FASTENINGS

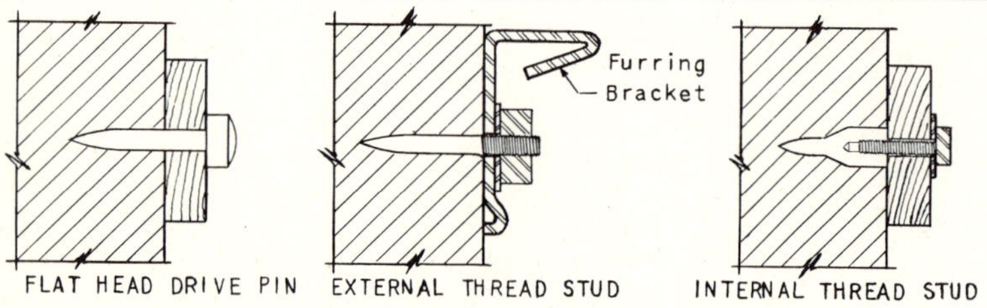
Furring Bracket
FLAT HEAD DRIVE PIN
EXTERNAL THREAD STUD
INTERNAL THREAD STUD

TYPICAL RAMMED OR DRIVEN PIN ANCHORS FOR FASTENING TO CONCRETE OR MASONRY

Scale ⅜" = 1"

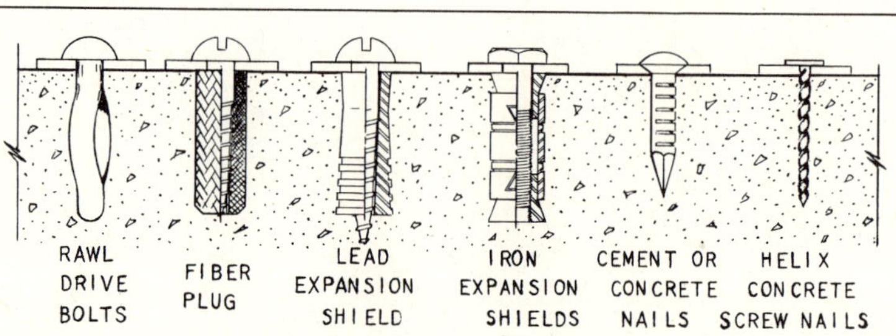
RAWL DRIVE BOLTS
FIBER PLUG
LEAD EXPANSION SHIELD
IRON EXPANSION SHIELDS
CEMENT OR CONCRETE NAILS
HELIX CONCRETE SCREW NAILS

OTHER DEVICES FOR FASTENING TO CONCRETE OR MASONRY

Scale ½" Full Size

WOOD and METAL WALL FURRING

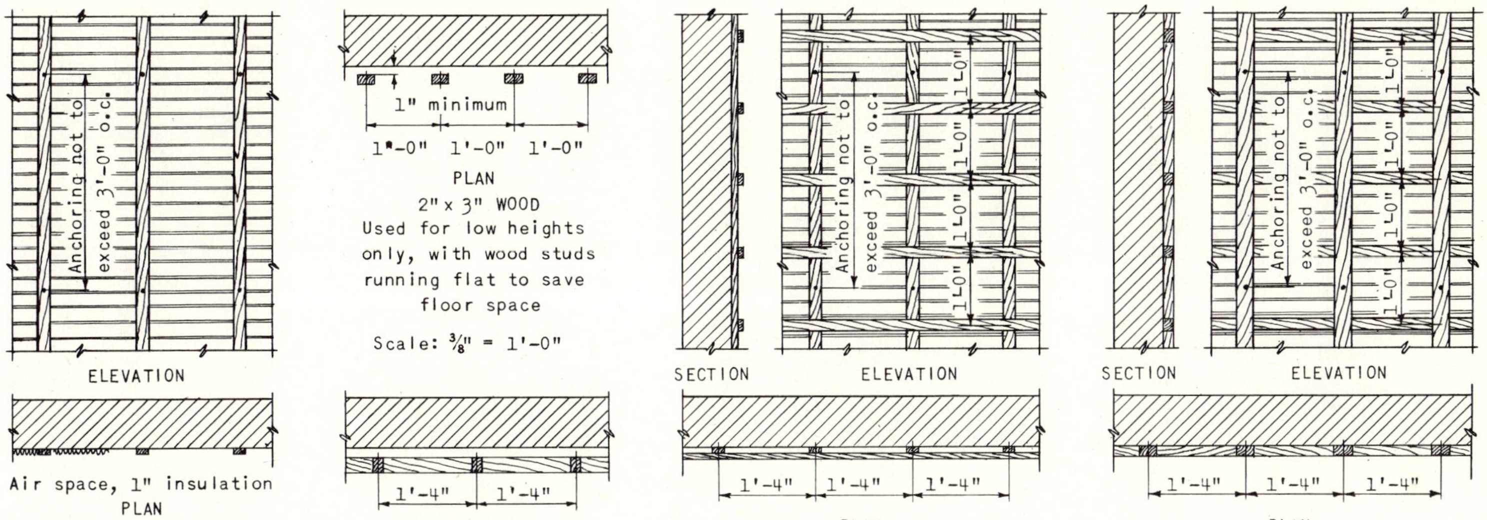
Anchoring not to exceed 3'-0" o.c.
ELEVATION
1" minimum
1'-0" 1'-0" 1'-0"
PLAN
2" x 3" WOOD
Used for low heights only, with wood studs running flat to save floor space
Scale: 3/8" = 1'-0"
SECTION
ELEVATION
Anchoring not to exceed 3'-0" o.c.
1'-0"
SECTION
ELEVATION
1'-4" 1'-4"
1'-4" 1'-4" 1'-4"

Air space, 1" insulation
PLAN
1" x 2" CONTACT WOOD
2" x 3", 2" x 4" also used
Spacing, 12"-16" o.c; depends on type and weight of lath

PLAN
2" x 3" OR 2" x 4" WOOD
FREE-STANDING
Use one row bridging

WOOD FURRING FOR HORIZONTAL PANELING
WITH BOARDS, PLANKS, METAL OR GYPSUM LATH OR WALL BOARDS

PLAN
1" x 2" CONTACT FURRING, minimum size
1" x 2" CROSS FURRING, Minimum size
Recommended for basements

PLAN
2" x 3" CONTACT FURRING
2" x 2" HEADERS OR CATS
Heavier sizes may be used

WOOD FURRING FOR VERTICAL PANELING
WITH BOARDS, PLANKS, METAL OR GYPSUM LATH OR WALL BOARDS

WOOD STUD FURRING

Scale: 3/8" = 1'-0"

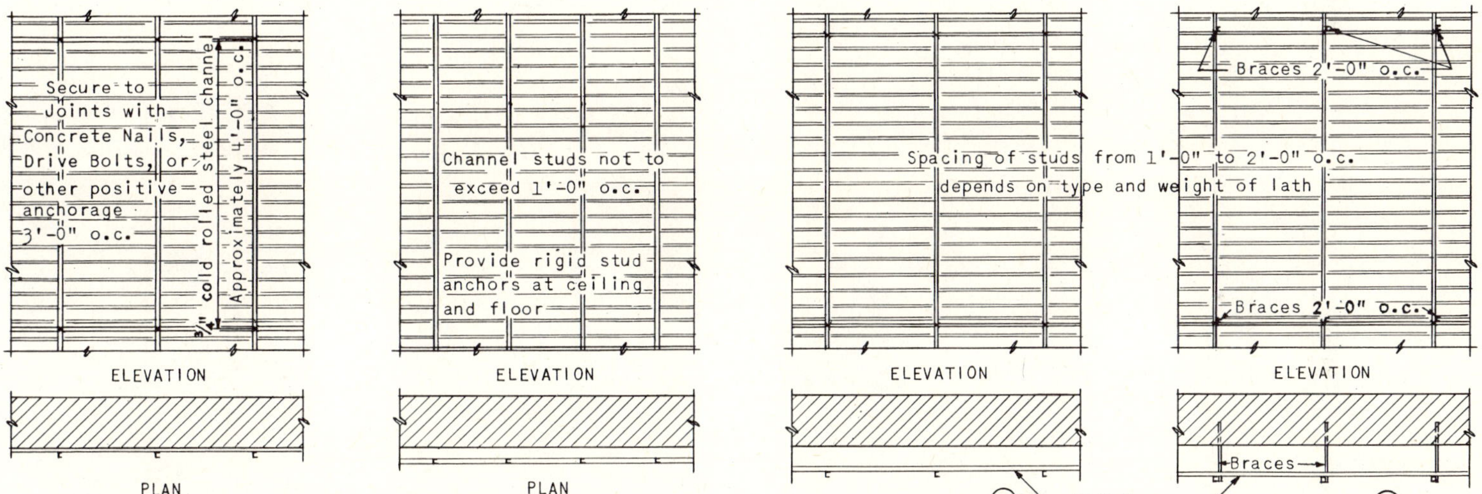
Secure to Joints with Concrete Nails, Drive Bolts, or other positive anchorage 3'-0" o.c.
3/4" cold rolled steel channel
Approximately 4'-0" o.c.
ELEVATION
Channel studs not to exceed 1'-0" o.c.
Provide rigid stud anchors at ceiling and floor
ELEVATION
Spacing of studs from 1'-0" to 2'-0" o.c. depends on type and weight of lath
ELEVATION
Braces 2'-0" o.c.
Braces 2'-0" o.c.
ELEVATION
Braces
Stiffeners

PLAN
Spacing, 12"-24" o.c., depends on type and weight of lath
CONTACT-METAL

PLAN
For low ceilings and minimum cost work
FREE-STANDING, UNBRACED

PLAN ①
FREE-STANDING, UNBRACED WITH STIFFENERS

PLAN ②
METAL BRACED AND CHANNEL STIFFENERS

STEEL CHANNEL FURRING

Scale: 3/8" = 1'-0"

FREE-STANDING FURRING

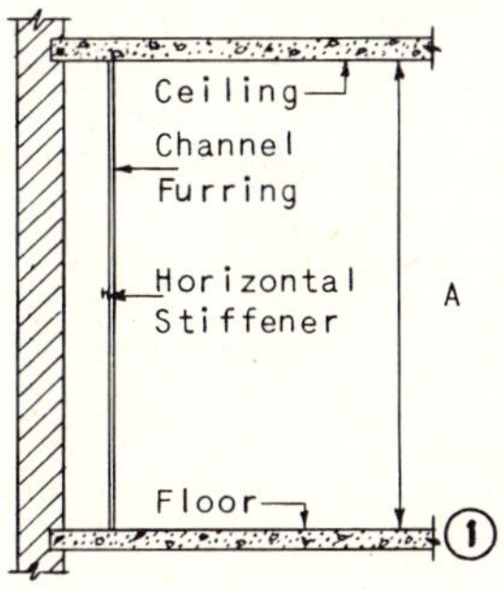
Ceiling
Channel Furring
Horizontal Stiffener
A
Floor
①

RECOMMENDED MAXIMUM HEIGHT "A" UNSUPPORTED FREE-STANDING ①		
METAL STUDS BASED ON SPACINGS	12" o.c.	16" o.c.
3/4" Channel	9'-4"	8'-0"
1 1/2" Channel	12'-0"	10'-0"
2 1/2" Prefabricated	14'-6"	12'-0"
3 1/4" Prefabricated	20'-0"	17'-0"

BRACED FURRING

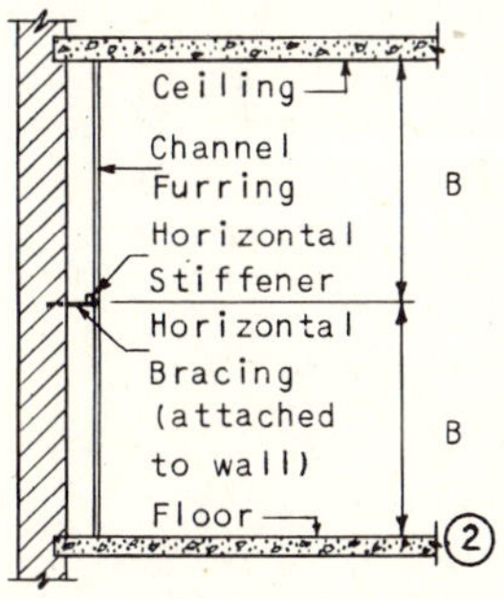
Ceiling
Channel Furring
Horizontal Stiffener
Horizontal Bracing (attached to wall)
B
B
Floor
②

RECOMMENDED MAXIMUM HEIGHT "B" BETWEEN HORIZONTAL BRACING ②		
METAL STUDS BASED ON SPACINGS	12" o.c.	16" o.c.
3/4" Channel	7'-0"	6'-0"
1 1/2" Channel	9'-4"	8'-0"
2 1/2" Prefabricated	12'-0"	10'-0"
3 1/4" Prefabricated	16'-0"	14'-0"

Horizontal stiffeners are recommended for all free-standing partitions, spaced the same as shown in Height "B" for bracing. When furring is more than 16" o.c., use one-half Height "B" spacings, with a minimum of 3'-6" o.c.
When overall height of furring exceeds Height "A", use horizontal bracing as indicated by height "B".

ALLOWABLE HEIGHTS FOR VERTICAL STEEL STUD FURRING

DATA CHECKED BY: METAL LATH MANUFACTURERS ASSOCIATION

METAL FURRING, LATHING and PLASTERING-DETAILS

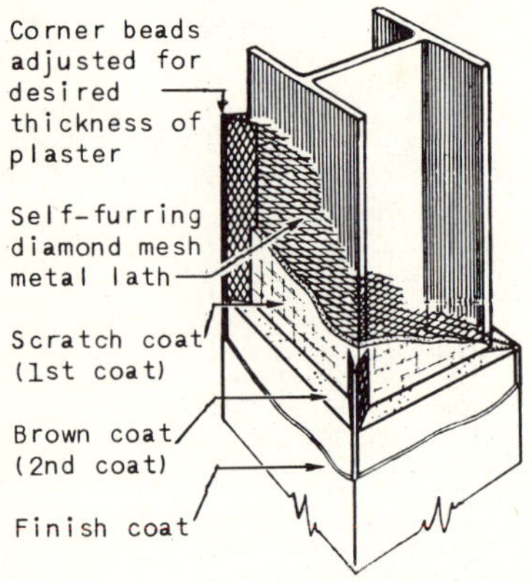
Corner beads adjusted for desired thickness of plaster
Self-furring diamond mesh metal lath
Scratch coat (1st coat)
Brown coat (2nd coat)
Finish coat

SELF-FURRING LATH

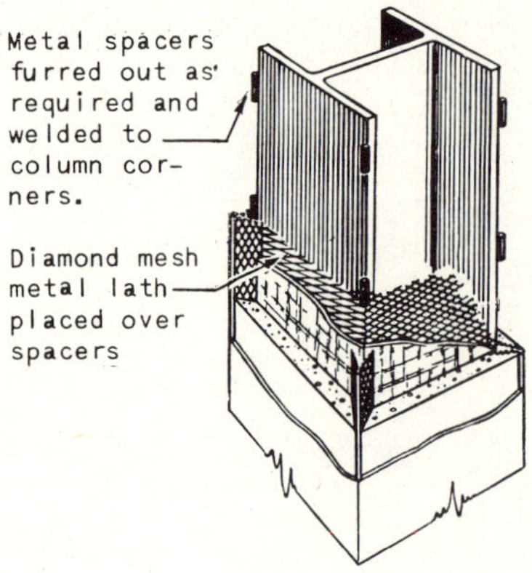
Metal spacers furred out as required and welded to column corners.
Diamond mesh metal lath placed over spacers

WELDED SPACERS

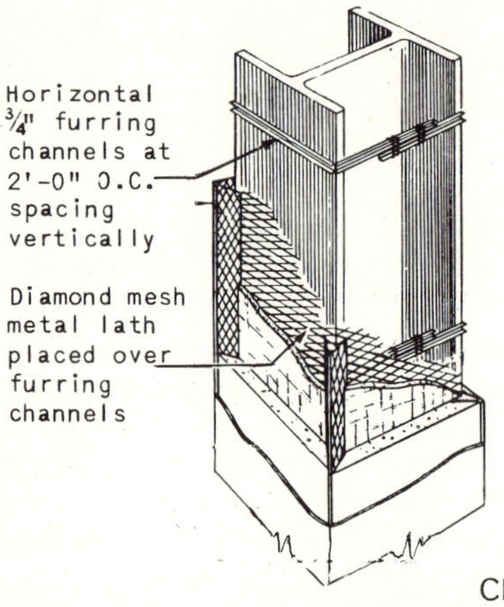
Horizontal ¾" furring channels at 2'-0" O.C. spacing vertically
Diamond mesh metal lath placed over furring channels

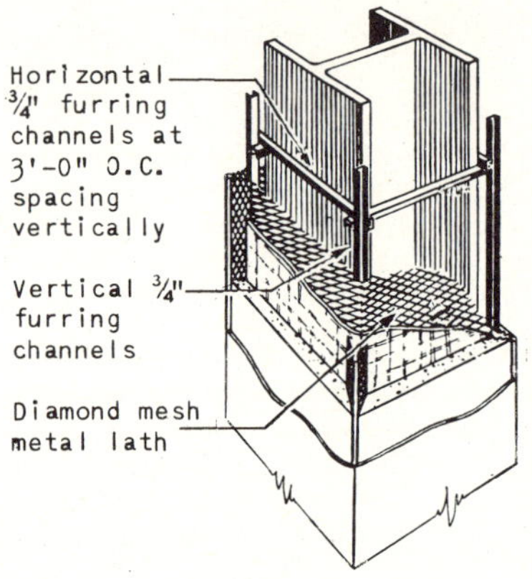
Horizontal ¾" furring channels at 3'-0" O.C. spacing vertically
Vertical ¾" furring channels
Diamond mesh metal lath

CHANNEL FURRING

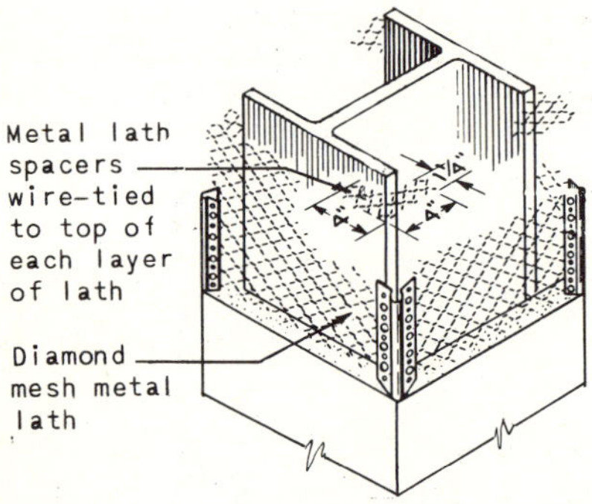
Metal lath spacers wire-tied to top of each layer of lath
Diamond mesh metal lath

METAL LATH SPACERS

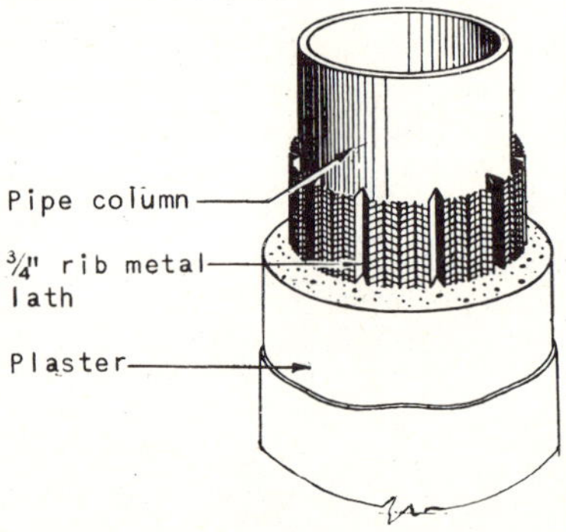
Pipe column
¾" rib metal lath
Plaster

RIB LATH ON PIPE COLUMN

COLUMN FURRING AND LATHING

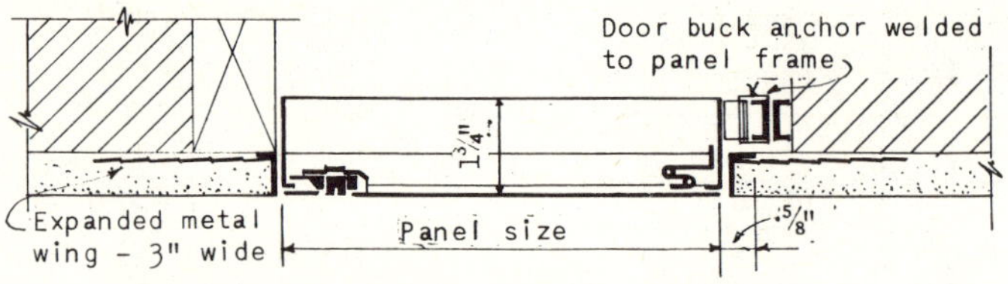
Door buck anchor welded to panel frame
1¾"
Expanded metal wing - 3" wide
Panel size
5/8"

STEEL ACCESS DOOR DETAIL

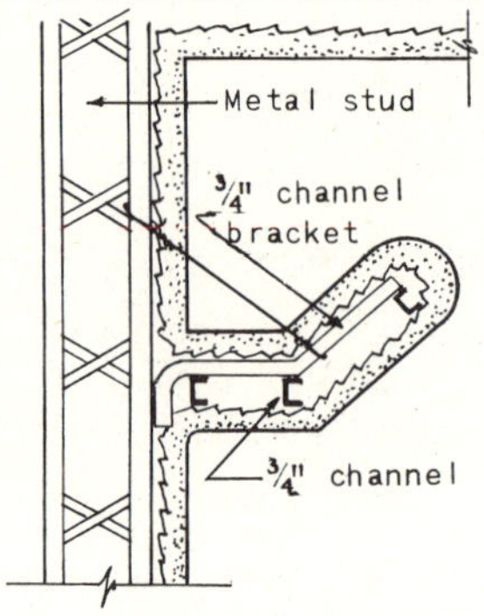
Metal stud
¾" channel bracket
¾" channel

WALL-HUNG LIGHT-TROUGH

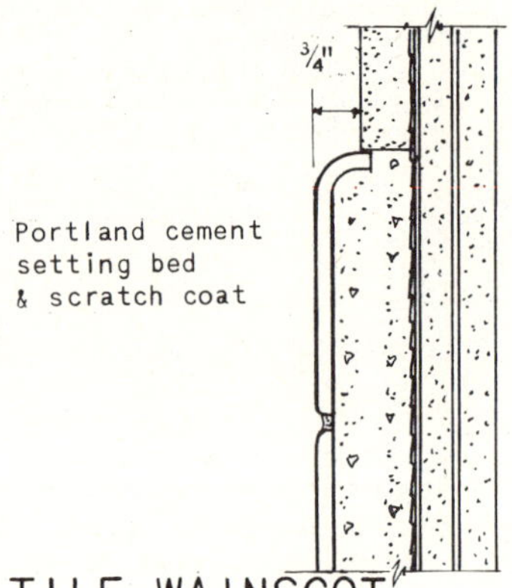
¾"
Portland cement setting bed & scratch coat

TILE WAINSCOT
FOR PLASTER PARTITIONS

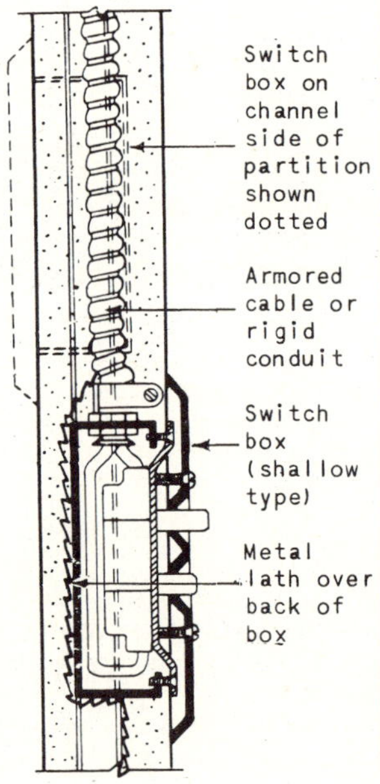
Switch box on channel side of partition shown dotted
Armored cable or rigid conduit
Switch box (shallow type)
Metal lath over back of box

WALL OUTLET IN SOLID PARTITION

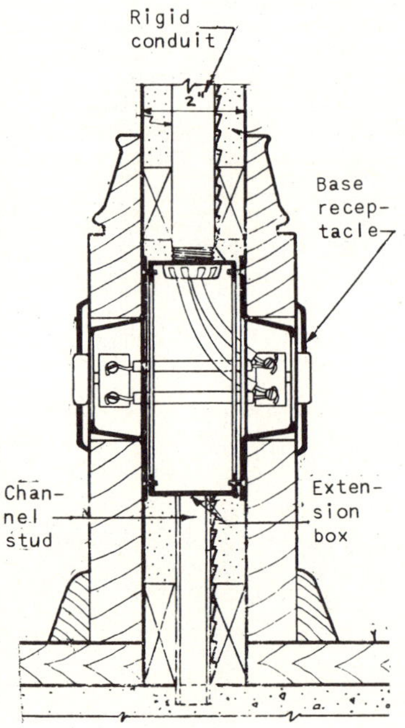
Rigid conduit
2"
Base receptacle
Channel stud
Extension box

WALL BASE DETAIL

Kifs are nailed to concrete forms to form plaster key in finished concrete.

Recommended spacing: 6" O.C. (both ways) for ceilings. 8" O.C. (both ways) for walls.

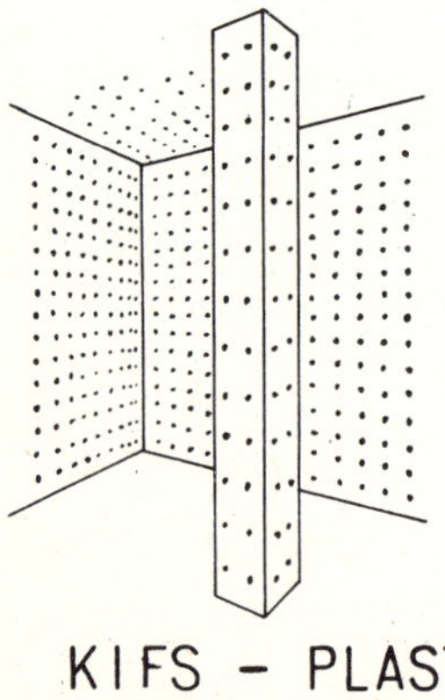

SPACING	NO. PER SQ. FT.
4" O.C. 2 ways	9
6" O.C. 2 ways	4
8" O.C. 2 ways	2¼
10" O.C. 2 ways	1½

KIFS - PLASTER KEYS FOR PLASTER ON REINFORCED CONCRETE CONSTRUCTION

SECTION THRU CEILING

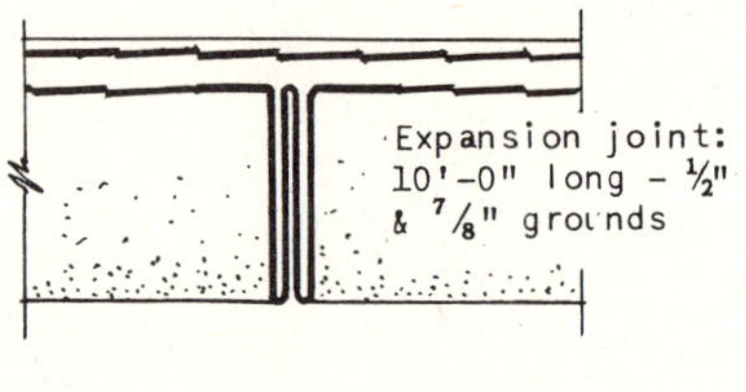
Expansion joint: 10'-0" long - ½" & 7/8" grounds

PLASTER EXPANSION JOINT

DATA CHECKED BY METAL LATH MANUFACTURERS ASSOCIATION

METAL LATH and ACCESSORIES

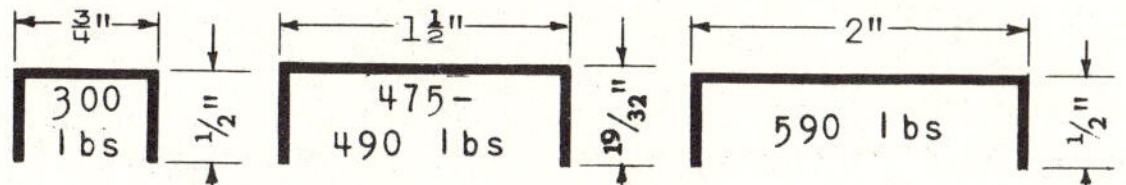

3/4"
300 lbs
1/2"
1 1/2"
475-490 lbs
19/32"
2"
590 lbs
1/2"

FURRING CHANNELS
Cold rolled steel, 16 ga. stock lengths 16 & 20 feet
Scale: 1/2 Full Size

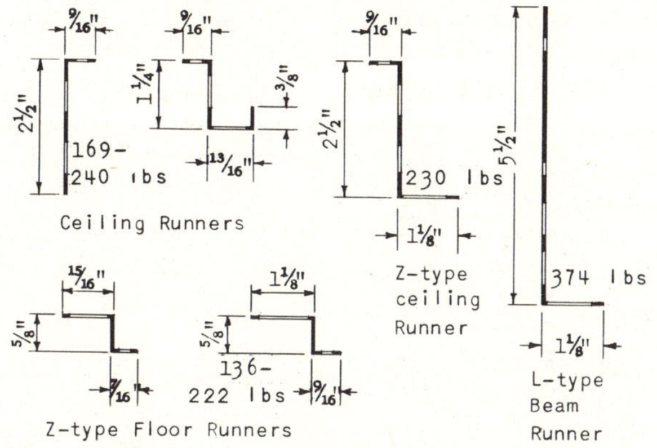

9/16"
2 1/2"
169-240 lbs
1 1/4"
3/8"
13/16"
Ceiling Runners
2 1/2"
230 lbs
1 1/8"
Z-type ceiling Runner
5 1/2"
374 lbs
1 1/8"
L-type Beam Runner
15/16"
5/8"
7/16"
1 1/8"
136-222 lbs
9/16"
Z-type Floor Runners

Note: Weights are per 1,000 linear feet.

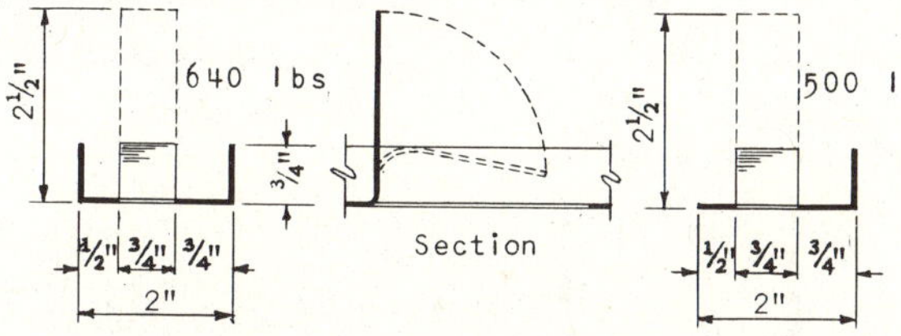

2 1/2"
640 lbs
3/4"
1/2" 3/4" 3/4"
2"
Section
2 1/2"
500 lbs
1/2" 3/4" 3/4"
2"
For Channel Studs
For Prefabricated Studs
Channel Track Floor Runners

FLOOR AND CEILING RUNNERS AND TRACKS
Galvanized steel, 18-28 ga. stock lengths 10 feet.
Scale: 1/4 Full Size

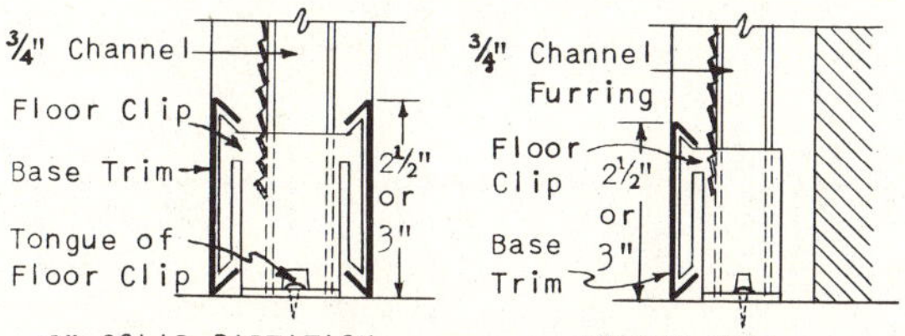

3/4" Channel
Floor Clip
Base Trim
Tongue of Floor Clip
2 1/2" or 3"
3/4" Channel Furring
Floor Clip
2 1/2" or 3"
Base Trim
2" SOLID PARTITION
FURRED WALL

FLOOR CLIPS

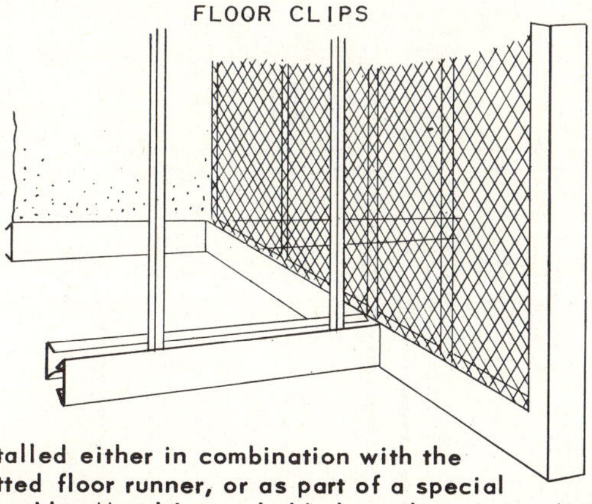

Installed either in combination with the slotted floor runner, or as part of a special assembly. Metal bases hold channel studs in alignment and also provide accurate grounds for plaster. Bases should be filled with plaster grout to give additional anchorage and to seal base for sanitation, sound insulation, and fire resistance. Made in 18-20 gauge steel, 10' lengths.

FLUSH METAL BASES

TYPES OF METAL LATH

FLAT EXPANDED LATHS

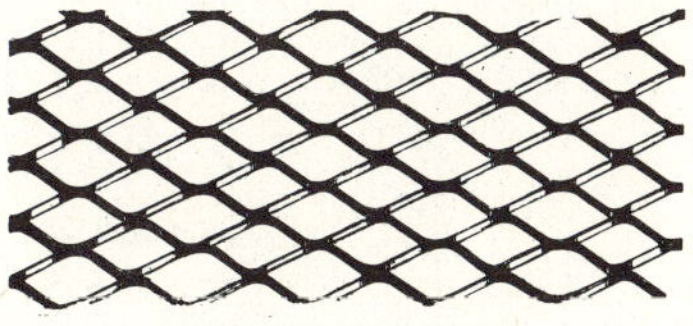

DIAMOND MESH

Used for all types of plastering, available painted or galvanized, weights 2.5 or 3.4 lbs. per sq. yd. sheet sizes 24" x 96" or 27" x 96".

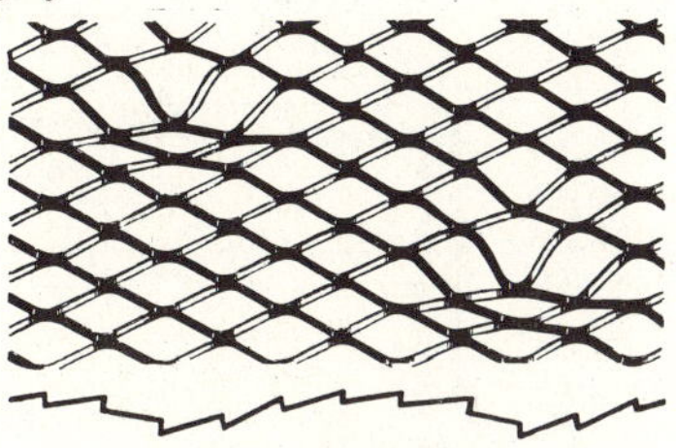

SELF FURRING

Used over old plaster or wallboard, and against interior masonry, diamond mesh lath with even indentations or "dimples", available in weights and sizes of diamond mesh lath.

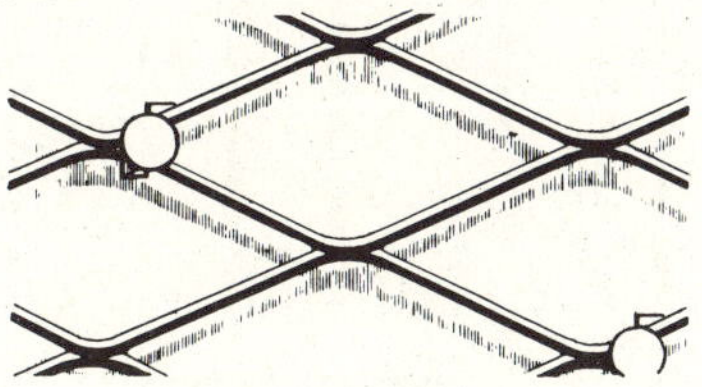

STUCCO MESH

Used as exterior stucco expanded metal reinforcing, similar to diamond mesh lath with larger openings, available weights 1.8 or 3.6 lbs. per sq. yd. sheet sizes vary.

SHEET LATH

SHEET LATHS

Used as plaster base, centering for concrete slabs, and as backing for ceramic clay tile, lath stamped into desired patterns with or without ribs from copper alloy sheet steel, painted. Available weights 4.5 lbs. per sq. yd. or over as required.

EXPANDED RIB LATHS

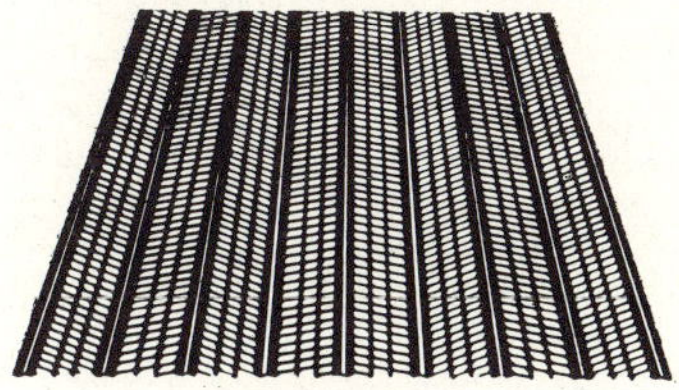

FLAT RIB

Used for all types of plastering, more rigid than diamond mesh lath, ribs not over 1/8" deep, copper alloy steel, painted, available weights 2.75 or 3.4 lbs. per sq. yd. sheet sizes 24" x 96" or 27" x 96".

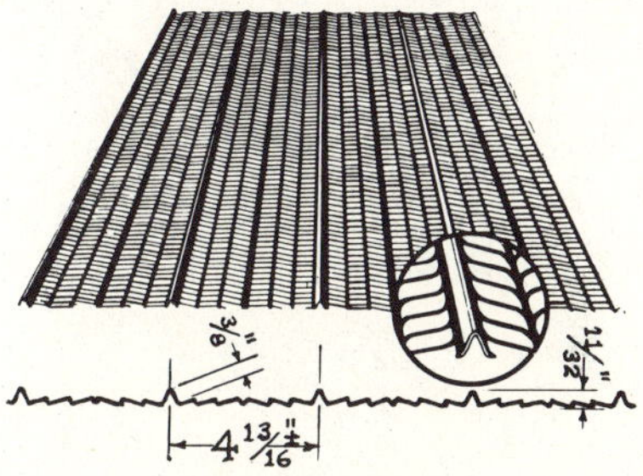

3/8"
11/32"
4 13/16"

3/8" RIB

Used as self furring lath and where greater rigidity is desired for wider spans, copper alloy steel, painted, available weights, 3.4 or 4.0 lbs. per sq. yd. sheet sizes 24" x 96" or 27" x 96".

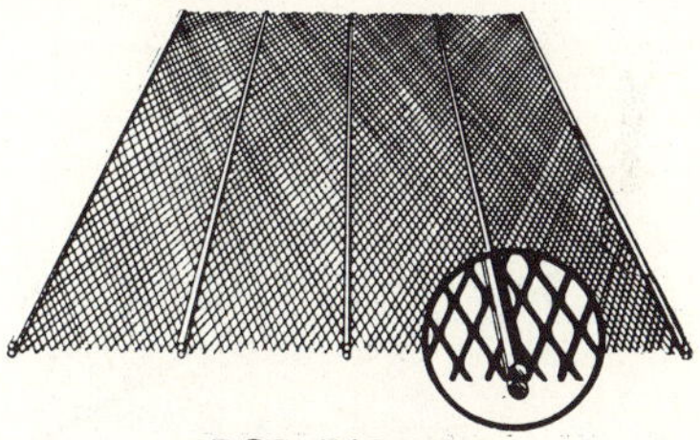

ROD RIBBED

Used as 3/8" rib lath and available in same material, weights, and sizes.

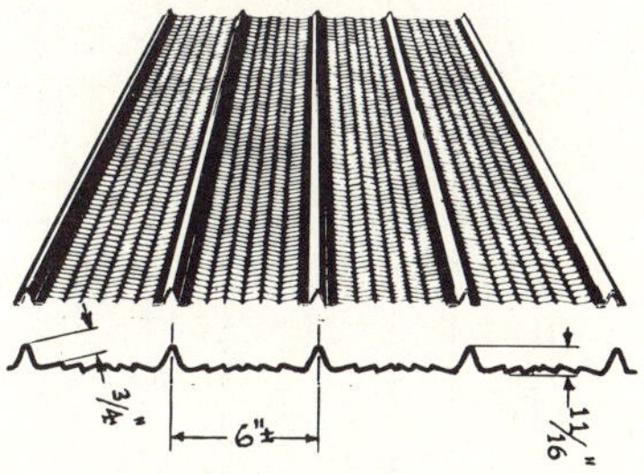

3/4"
6"
1 1/16"

3/4" RIB

Used primarily as a combination form and reinforcing (centering) for concrete floors and roofs, holds wet concrete without sagging and requires no stretching; expanded copper alloy steel, painted, available weights .60 or .75 lbs. per sq. ft., lengths vary 8, 10, and 12 feet.

DATA CHECKED BY: METAL LATH MANUFACTURERS ASSOCIATION

METAL TRIM

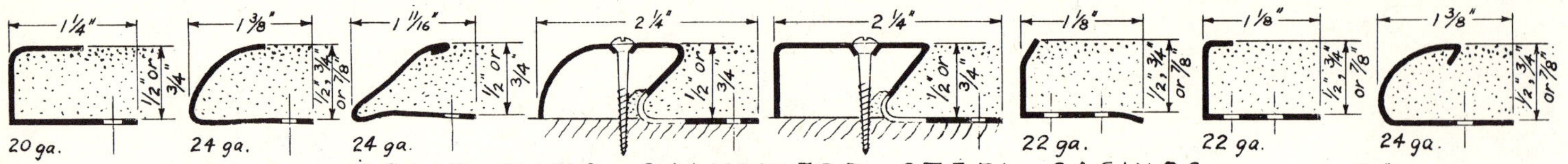
1¼"
½" or ¾
20 ga.
1⅜"
24 ga.
1 11/16"
½" or ¾
24 ga.
2¼"
½" or ¾
2¼"
½" or ¾
1⅛"
½" ¾ or ⅞
22 ga.
1⅛"
½" ¾ or ⅞
22 ga.
1⅜"
½" ¾ or ⅞
24 ga.

SOLID WING GALVANIZED STEEL CASINGS

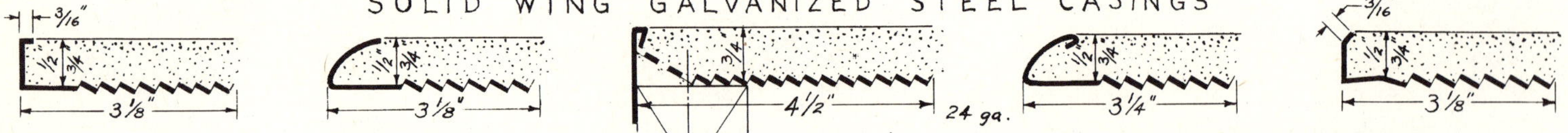
3/16"
½
¾
3⅛"
3⅛"
4½"
24 ga.
3¼"
3/16"
3⅛"

EXPANDED WING GALVANIZED STEEL CASINGS

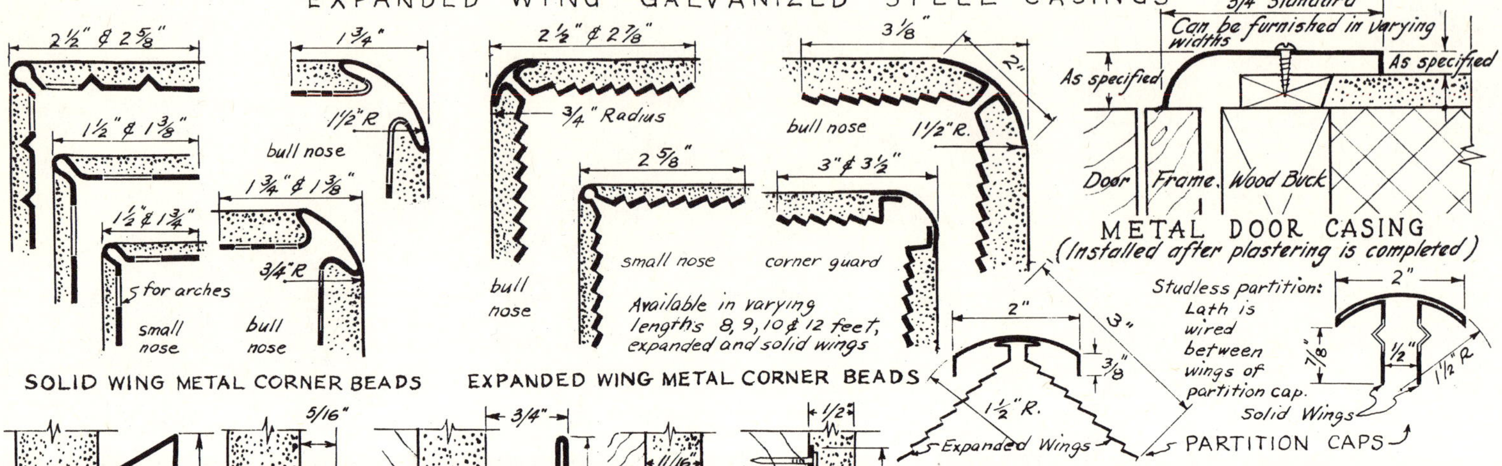
2½" & 2⅝"
1½" & 1⅜"
1½" & 1¾"
for arches
small nose
1¾"
1½"R
bull nose
1¾" & 1⅜"
¾"R
bull nose
2½" & 2⅞"
¾" Radius
bull nose
2⅝"
small nose
3⅛"
2"
bull nose
1½"R.
3" & 3½"
corner guard
Available in varying lengths 8, 9, 10 & 12 feet, expanded and solid wings
3/4" standard
Can be furnished in varying widths
As specified
As specified
Door
Frame
Wood Buck
2"
3"
⅜"
1½"R.
Expanded Wings
Studless partition: Lath is wired between wings of partition cap.
2"
⅞"
½"
1½"R
Solid Wings

SOLID WING METAL CORNER BEADS

EXPANDED WING METAL CORNER BEADS

METAL DOOR CASING
(Installed after plastering is completed)

PARTITION CAPS

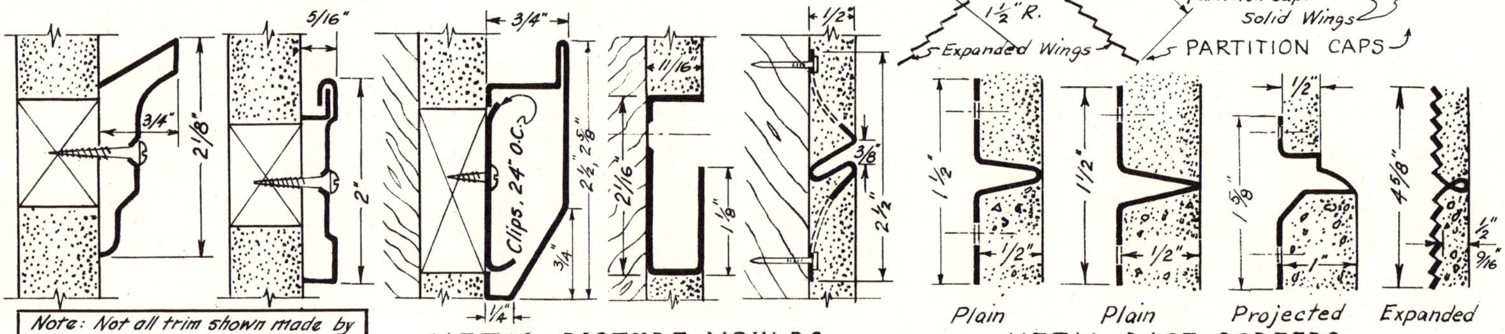
¾"
2⅛"
5/16"
2"
¾"
Clips. 24" O.C.
2½, 2⅝"
¾
¼"
11/16
2⅛"
1⅛"
½"
⅜"
2½"
1½"
½"
1½"
½"
½"
1⅝"
1"
4⅝"
½"
9/16
Plain
Plain
Projected
Expanded

Note: Not all trim shown made by all manufacturers.

METAL PICTURE MOULDS

METAL BASE SCREEDS

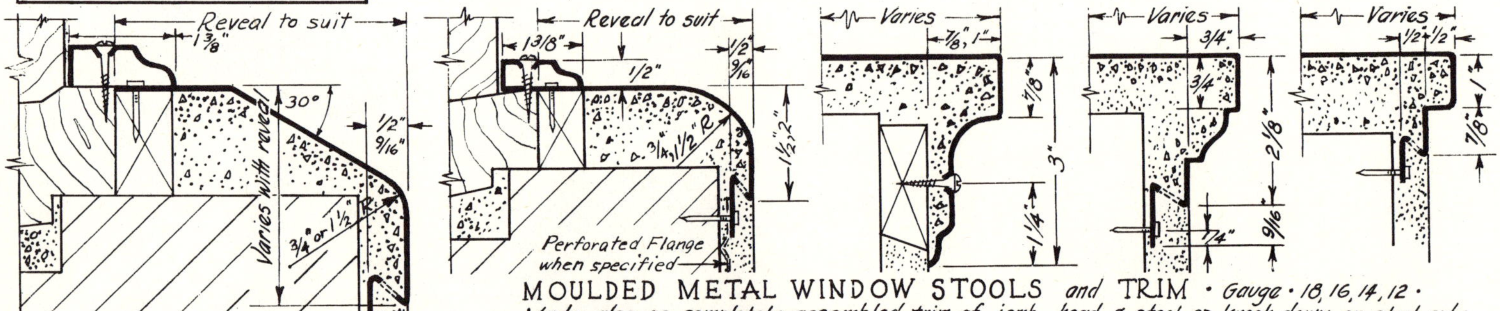
Reveal to suit
1⅜"
30°
½"
9/16"
Varies with reveal
¾" or 1½" R
Reveal to suit
1⅜"
½"
½"
9/16
¾"
1½" R
1¼", 2"
Perforated Flange when specified
Varies
⅞", 1"
⅞
3"
1¼
Varies
¾"
¾
2⅛
9/16
¼"
Varies
½" ½"
1
⅞"

MOULDED METAL WINDOW STOOLS *and* TRIM • *Gauge* • *18, 16, 14, 12* •
Made also as completely assembled trim of jamb, head & stool, or knock down or stool only

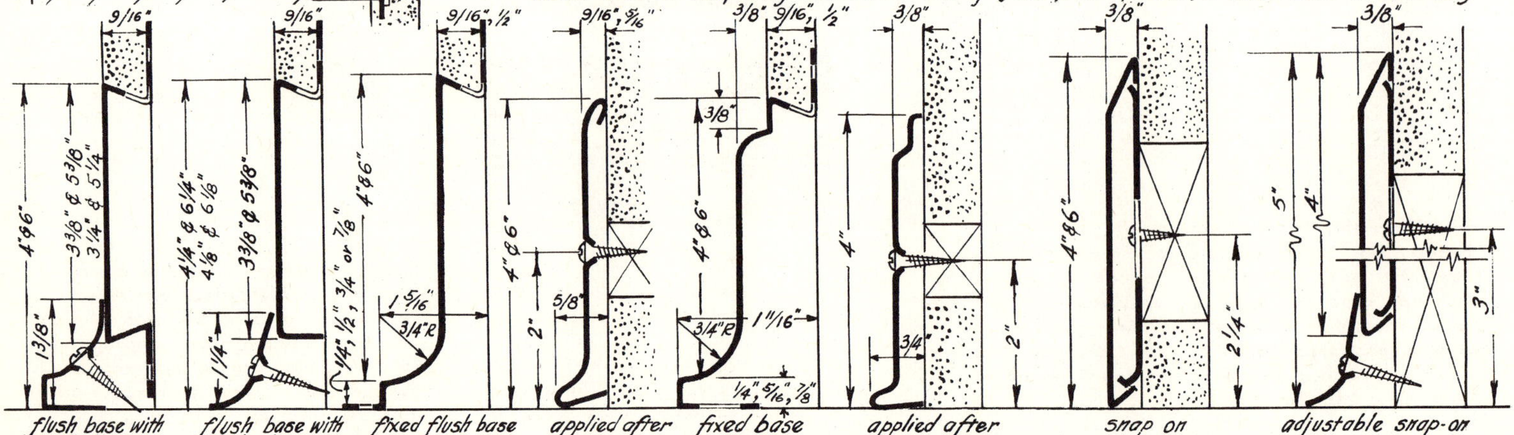
9/16"
4" & 6"
3⅜" & 5⅜"
3¼" & 5¼"
1⅜"
9/16"
4¼" & 6¼"
4⅛" & 6⅛"
3⅜" & 5⅜"
1¼"
9/16", ½"
4" & 6"
¼", ½", ¾" or ⅞"
1 5/16"
¾"R
9/16", 5/16"
4" & 6"
⅝"
2"
⅜" 9/16", ½"
⅜"
4" & 6"
¾"R
1 11/16"
¼", 5/16", ⅞
⅜"
4"
¾"
2"
⅜"
4" & 6"
2¼"
⅜"
5"
4"
3"

flush base with applied cove | *flush base with applied cove* | *fixed flush base* | *applied after* | *fixed base* | *applied after* | *snap on* | *adjustable snap-on*

10'-0" lengths • METAL BASES FOR PLASTER PARTITIONS • *18, 20 Gauge*

Data checked by: Inland Steel Products Co. & Knapp Brothers Manufacturing Co.

ERECTION and SPACING of SUPPORTS for METAL LATH PARTITIONS

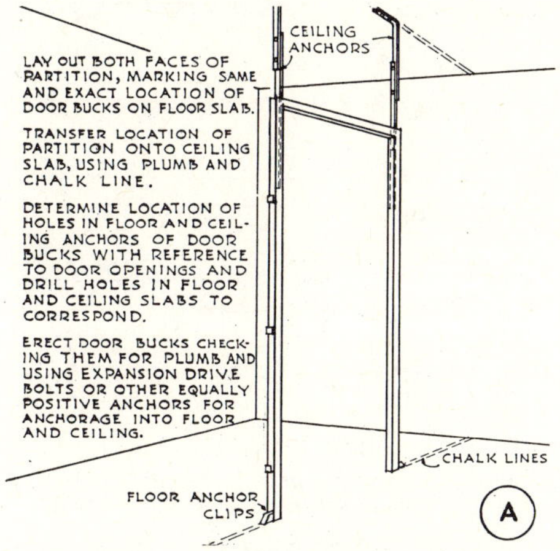
CEILING ANCHORS
LAY OUT BOTH FACES OF PARTITION, MARKING SAME AND EXACT LOCATION OF DOOR BUCKS ON FLOOR SLAB.
TRANSFER LOCATION OF PARTITION ONTO CEILING SLAB, USING PLUMB AND CHALK LINE.
DETERMINE LOCATION OF HOLES IN FLOOR AND CEILING ANCHORS OF DOOR BUCKS WITH REFERENCE TO DOOR OPENINGS AND DRILL HOLES IN FLOOR AND CEILING SLABS TO CORRESPOND.
ERECT DOOR BUCKS CHECKING THEM FOR PLUMB AND USING EXPANSION DRIVE BOLTS OR OTHER EQUALLY POSITIVE ANCHORS FOR ANCHORAGE INTO FLOOR AND CEILING.
CHALK LINES
FLOOR ANCHOR CLIPS
A

LOCATION LAYOUT, ERECTION, PLUMBING, AND ANCHORAGE OF BUCKS

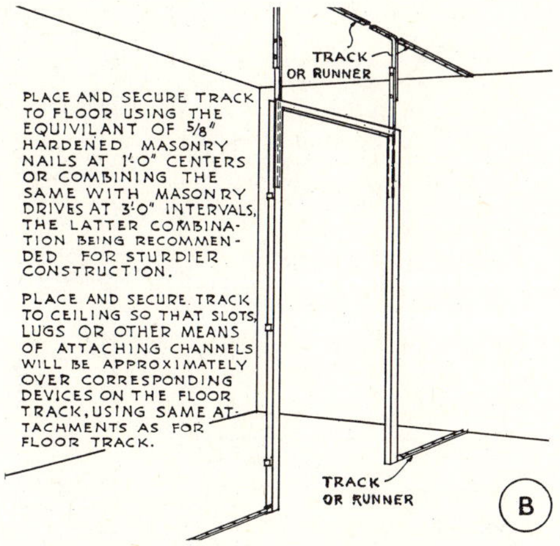
TRACK OR RUNNER
PLACE AND SECURE TRACK TO FLOOR USING THE EQUIVILANT OF 5/8" HARDENED MASONRY NAILS AT 1'-0" CENTERS OR COMBINING THE SAME WITH MASONRY DRIVES AT 3'-0" INTERVALS, THE LATTER COMBINATION BEING RECOMMENDED FOR STURDIER CONSTRUCTION.
PLACE AND SECURE TRACK TO CEILING SO THAT SLOTS, LUGS OR OTHER MEANS OF ATTACHING CHANNELS WILL BE APPROXIMATELY OVER CORRESPONDING DEVICES ON THE FLOOR TRACK, USING SAME ATTACHMENTS AS FOR FLOOR TRACK.
TRACK OR RUNNER
B

PLACING AND SECURING OF FLOOR AND CEILING TRACKS OR RUNNERS

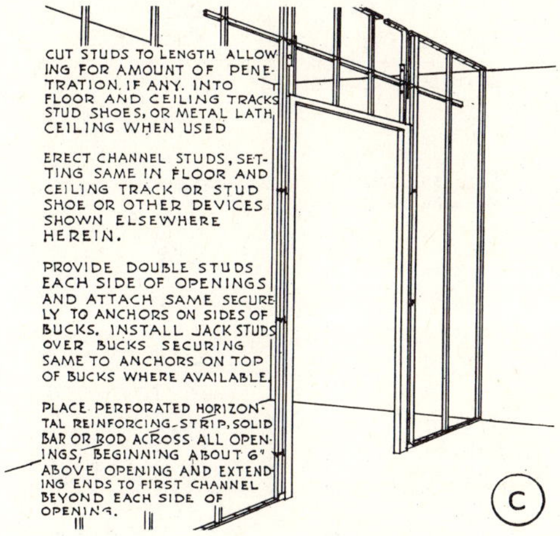
CUT STUDS TO LENGTH ALLOWING FOR AMOUNT OF PENETRATION. IF ANY. INTO FLOOR AND CEILING TRACKS STUD SHOES, OR METAL LATH CEILING WHEN USED
ERECT CHANNEL STUDS, SETTING SAME IN FLOOR AND CEILING TRACK OR STUD SHOE OR OTHER DEVICES SHOWN ELSEWHERE HEREIN.
PROVIDE DOUBLE STUDS EACH SIDE OF OPENINGS AND ATTACH SAME SECURELY TO ANCHORS ON SIDES OF BUCKS. INSTALL JACK STUDS OVER BUCKS SECURING SAME TO ANCHORS ON TOP OF BUCKS WHERE AVAILABLE.
PLACE PERFORATED HORIZONTAL REINFORCING-STRIP, SOLID BAR OR ROD ACROSS ALL OPENINGS, BEGINNING ABOUT 6" ABOVE OPENING AND EXTENDING ENDS TO FIRST CHANNEL BEYOND EACH SIDE OF OPENING.
C

ERECTION OF STUDS AND INSTALLATION OF REINFORCEMENT OVER DOOR OR WINDOW OPENINGS

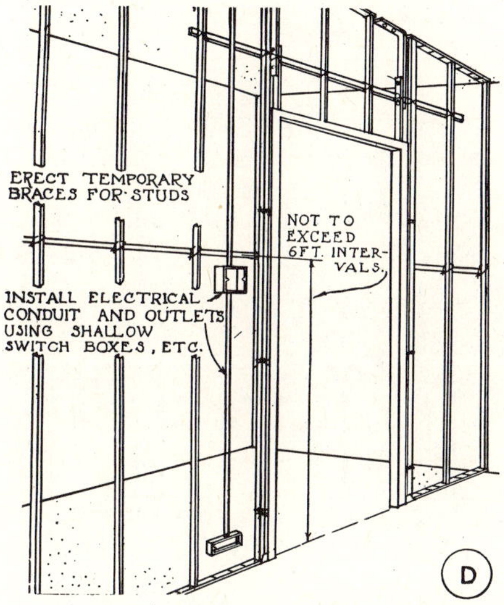
ERECT TEMPORARY BRACES FOR STUDS
NOT TO EXCEED 6FT. INTERVALS.
INSTALL ELECTRICAL CONDUIT AND OUTLETS USING SHALLOW SWITCH BOXES, ETC.
D

TEMPORARY BRACING OF STUDS, INSTALLATION OF ELECTRICAL CONDUITS, OUTLETS, ETC.

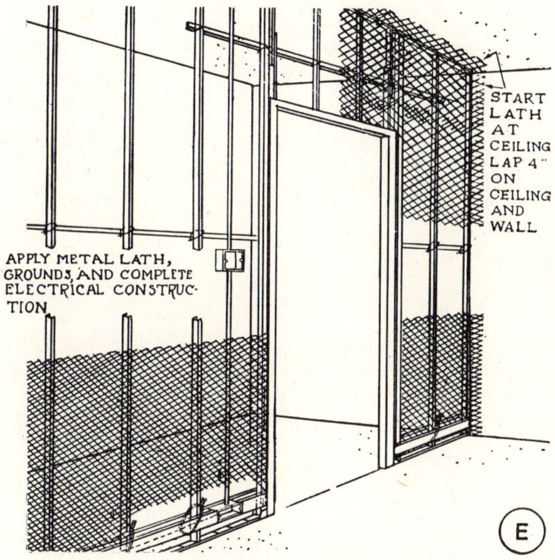
START LATH AT CEILING LAP 4" ON CEILING AND WALL
APPLY METAL LATH, GROUNDS, AND COMPLETE ELECTRICAL CONSTRUCTION
E

APPLICATION OF METAL LATH, LAPPING AT CEILINGS AND ABUTTING WALLS; APPLICATION OF GROUNDS

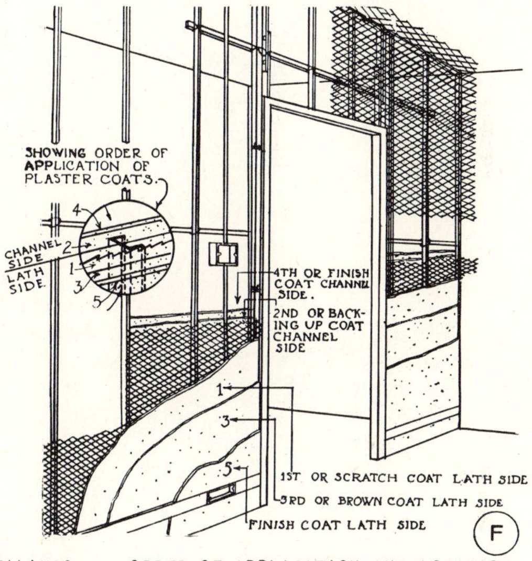
SHOWING ORDER OF APPLICATION OF PLASTER COATS.
CHANNEL SIDE
LATH SIDE
4TH OR FINISH COAT CHANNEL SIDE.
2ND OR BACKING UP COAT CHANNEL SIDE
1ST OR SCRATCH COAT LATH SIDE
3RD OR BROWN COAT LATH SIDE
FINISH COAT LATH SIDE
F

ORDER OF APPLICATION AND LOCATION OF VARIOUS PLASTER COATS

SEQUENCE OF STEPS IN THE ERECTION OF A METAL LATH AND PLASTER PARTITION

MAXIMUM SPACING OF SUPPORTS FOR METAL LATH - (INCHES)

TYPE OF LATH	MINIMUM WEIGHT OF LATH LB. PER SQ. YD.	WALLS AND PARTITION			CEILINGS	
		Wood Studs	Solid Partitions	Steel Studs Wall Furring etc.	Wood or Concrete	Steel Channel or Joists
Diamond Mesh (flat expanded)	2.5	16	16	12	0	0
	3.4	16	16	16	16	13½
Flat Rib	2.75	16	16	16	16	12
	3.4	19	24 (3)	19	19	19
3/8" Rib and Rod-Ribbed (1) (2)	3.4	24	(4)	24	24	24
	4.0	24	(4)	24	24	24
Sheet Lath (2)	4.5	24	(4)	24	24	24

(1) 3.4 lb., 3/8" Rib Lath is permissible under Concrete Joists at 27" center to center.

(2) These spacings are based on a narrow bearing surface for the lath. When supports with a relatively wide bearing surface are used, these spacings may be increased accordingly, and still assure satisfactory work.

(3) This spacing permissible for Solid Partitions not exceeding 16 feet in height. For greater heights, permanent horizontal stiffener channels or rods must be provided on channel side of partitions, every 6 feet vertically, or else spacing shall be reduced 25%.

(4) See Studless Metal Lath and Plaster Solid Partitions.

DATA CHECKED BY: METAL LATH MANUFACTURERS ASSOCIATION

WOOD STUD and 2" SOLID CHANNEL STUD PARTITIONS

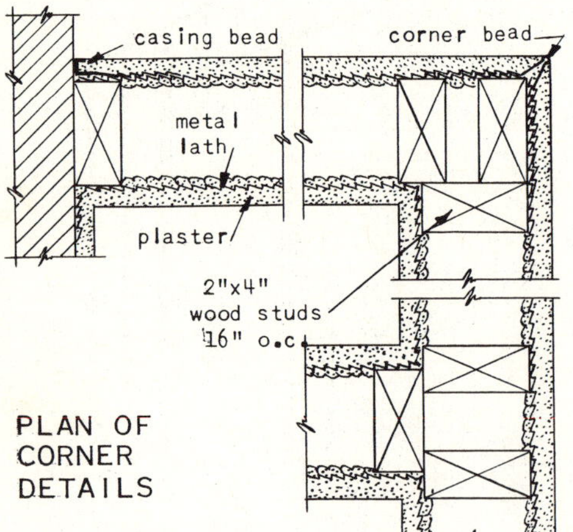
casing bead
corner bead
metal lath
plaster
2"x4" wood studs 16" o.c.

PLAN OF CORNER DETAILS

Scale: 1½" = 1'-0"

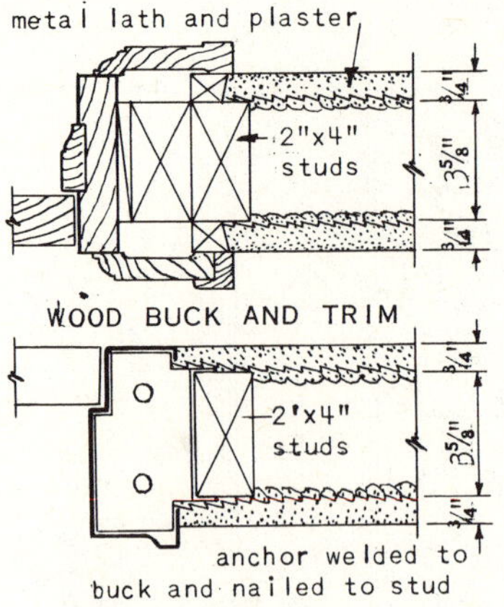
metal lath and plaster
2"x4" studs
3/4
3⅝"
3/4
WOOD BUCK AND TRIM
2"x4" studs
anchor welded to buck and nailed to stud
METAL DOOR BUCK

DOOR BUCK DETAILS

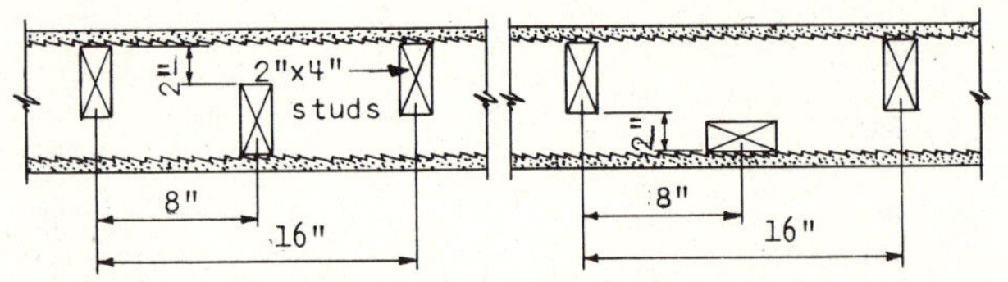
2"x4" studs
2"
8"
16"

PLAN OF DOUBLE PARTITIONS

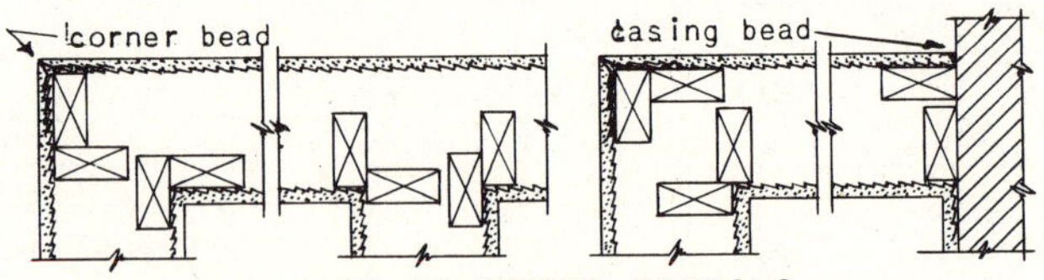
corner bead
casing bead

PLAN OF CORNER DETAILS

NOTE: For other double or sound insulating partitions, see "Sound Insulating - Hollow Metal Lath and Plaster Partitions."

WOOD STUD DOUBLE PARTITIONS

WOOD STUD PARTITIONS

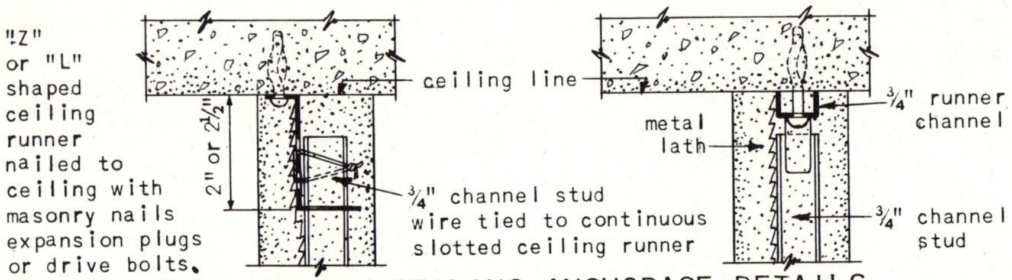
"Z" or "L" shaped ceiling runner nailed to ceiling with masonry nails expansion plugs or drive bolts.
2" or 2½"
ceiling line
¾" channel stud wire tied to continuous slotted ceiling runner
metal lath
¾" runner channel
¾" channel stud

PARTITION - CEILING ANCHORAGE DETAILS

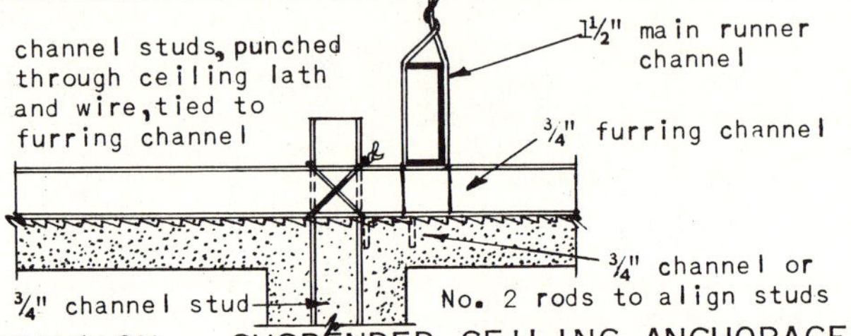
channel studs, punched through ceiling lath and wire, tied to furring channel
1½" main runner channel
¾" furring channel
¾" channel or No. 2 rods to align studs
¾" channel stud

PARTITION - SUSPENDED CEILING ANCHORAGE

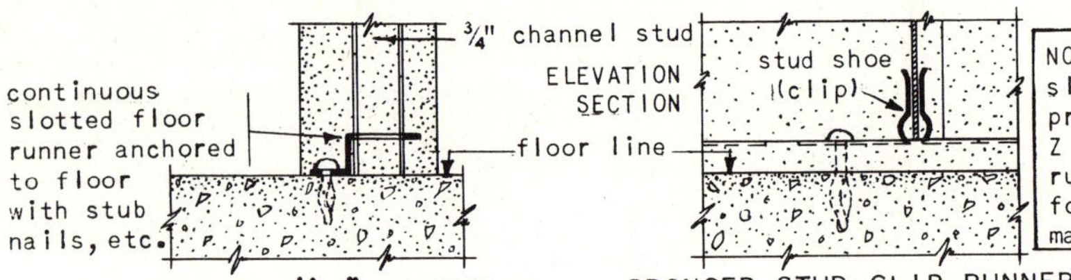
¾" channel stud
continuous slotted floor runner anchored to floor with stub nails, etc.
ELEVATION SECTION
stud shoe (clip)
floor line
SLOTTED "Z" RUNNER
PRONGED STUD CLIP RUNNER

NOTE: Numerous other slotted, notched, or pronged channel and L or Z type ceiling and floor runners are manufactured for stud anchorage. See manufacturer's catalogs.

PARTITION - BASE ANCHORAGE DETAILS

Scale: 3" = 1'-0"

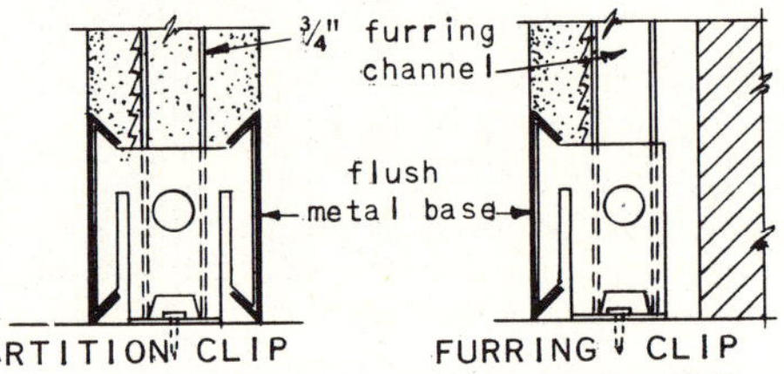
¾" furring channel
flush metal base
PARTITION CLIP
FURRING CLIP

BASE CLIP STUD ANCHORAGE

MAXIMUM ALLOWABLE HEIGHTS AND LENGTHS OF SOLID PARTITIONS FOR VARYING STUD SIZES AND PARTITION THICKNESS

MAXIMUM HEIGHT	PARTITION THICKNESS	CHANNEL SIZES AND WEIGHTS *
8 ft. 6 in.	1½"	¾" 300 lbs.
12 ft.	2"	¾" 300 lbs.
14 ft.	2¼"	¾" 300 lbs.
16 ft.	2½"	¾" 300 lbs.
18 ft.	2¾"	1½" 475 lbs.
20 ft.	3"	1½" 475 lbs.
24 ft.	3¼"	1½" 475 lbs.

* Weights per 1,000 linear feet

NOTE: Horizontal stiffeners recommended every 4'-0" o.c. vertically.
LENGTH LIMITATIONS: Partitions under 12'-0" high have no length limitations; over 12'-0" high, allowable length.
2 times height up to 16'-0" high
1½ times height up to 24'-0" high
1 times height over 24'-0" high.
Partitions exceeding allowable lengths are proportionately thicker, generally increased a minimum of 20%.

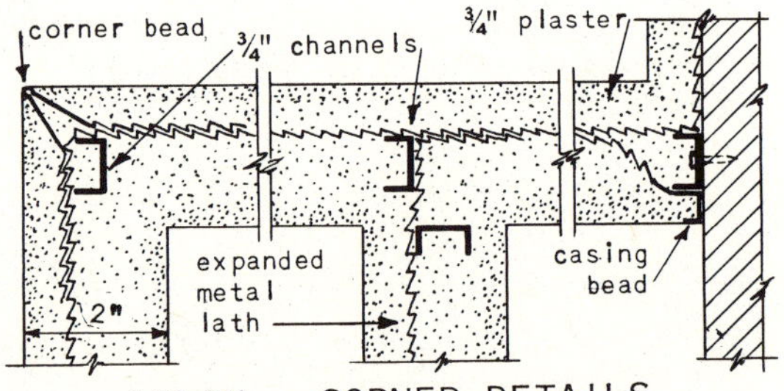
corner bead
¾" channels
¾" plaster
expanded metal lath
casing bead
2"

PLAN - CORNER DETAILS

NOTE: For required stud spacing see "Metal lath Partitions - Erection and Spacing of Supports."

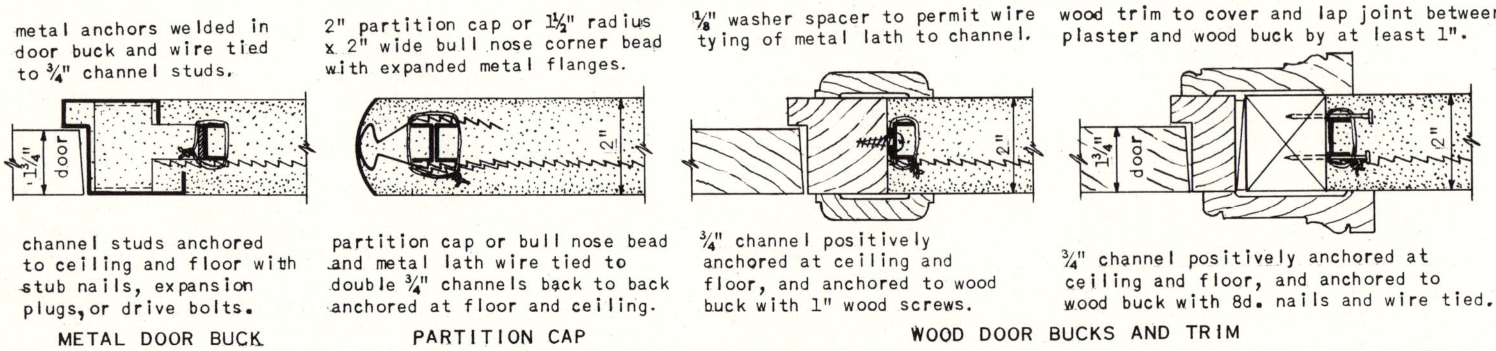
metal anchors welded in door buck and wire tied to ¾" channel studs.
2" partition cap or 1½" radius x 2" wide bull nose corner bead with expanded metal flanges.
⅛" washer spacer to permit wire tying of metal lath to channel.
wood trim to cover and lap joint between plaster and wood buck by at least 1".
1¾"
door
2"
channel studs anchored to ceiling and floor with stub nails, expansion plugs, or drive bolts.
partition cap or bull nose bead and metal lath wire tied to double ¾" channels back to back anchored at floor and ceiling.
¾" channel positively anchored at ceiling and floor, and anchored to wood buck with 1" wood screws.
¾" channel positively anchored at ceiling and floor, and anchored to wood buck with 8d. nails and wire tied.

METAL DOOR BUCK — PARTITION CAP — WOOD DOOR BUCKS AND TRIM

DOOR BUCK DETAILS

Scale: 3" = 1'-0"

2" SOLID - CHANNEL STUD PARTITIONS

DATA CHECKED BY METAL LATH MANUFACTURERS ASSOCIATION

METAL LATH and PLASTER PARTITIONS

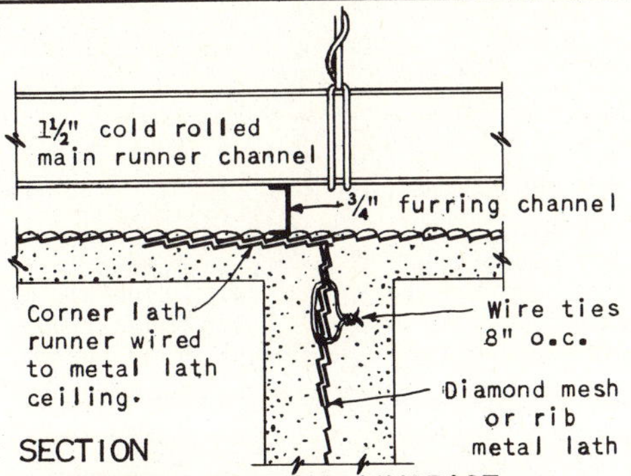
1½" cold rolled main runner channel
¾" furring channel
Corner lath runner wired to metal lath ceiling.
Wire ties 8" o.c.
Diamond mesh or rib metal lath

SECTION
SUSPENDED CEILING ACHORAGE

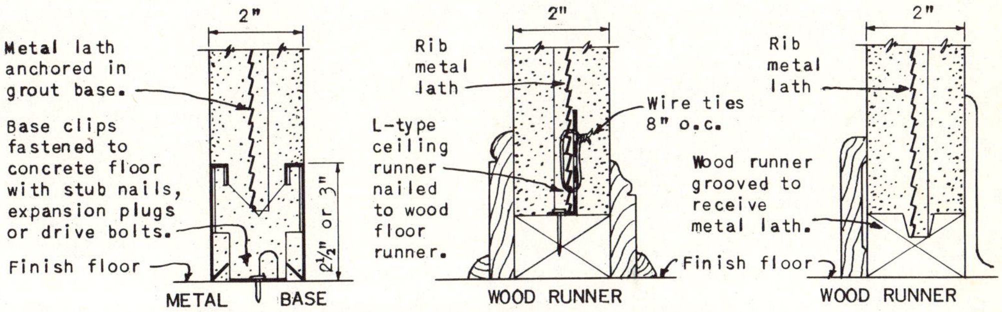
2"
Metal lath anchored in grout base.
Base clips fastened to concrete floor with stub nails, expansion plugs or drive bolts.
Finish floor
2½" or 3"
METAL BASE
2"
Rib metal lath
Wire ties 8" o.c.
L-type ceiling runner nailed to wood floor runner.
WOOD RUNNER
2"
Rib metal lath
Wood runner grooved to receive metal lath.
Finish floor
WOOD RUNNER

SECTIONS OF BASES AND ANCHORAGE DETAILS

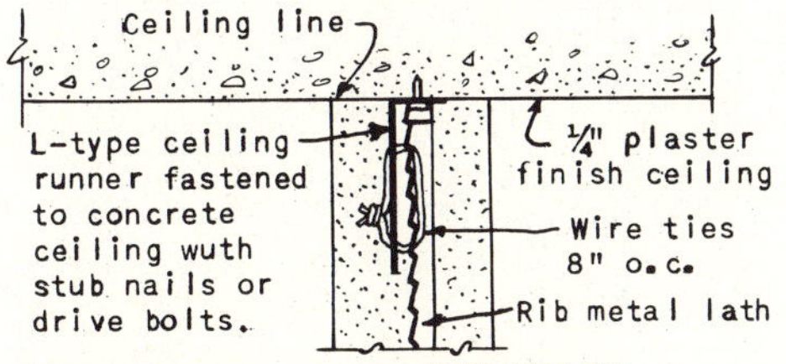
Ceiling line
L-type ceiling runner fastened to concrete ceiling wuth stub nails or drive bolts.
¼" plaster finish ceiling
Wire ties 8" o.c.
Rib metal lath

CONCRETE CEILING ANCHORAGE

NOTE: CORNER DETAILS similar to "2" Solid Stud Partitions"; Cornerite for inside corners, corner beads for outside corners, casing beads for plaster stops and grounds

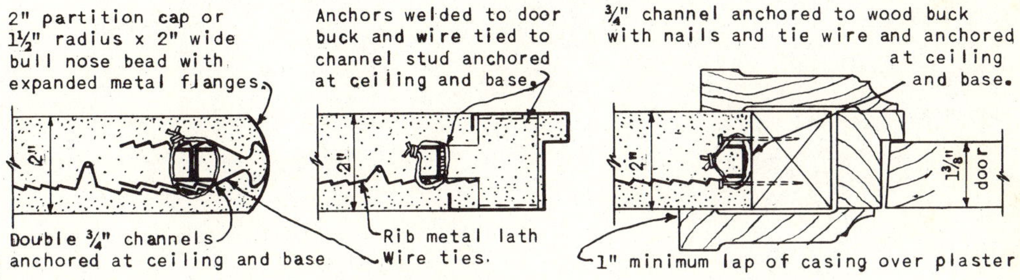
2" partition cap or 1½" radius x 2" wide bull nose bead with expanded metal flanges.
2"
Double ¾" channels anchored at ceiling and base
PARTITION CAP
Anchors welded to door buck and wire tied to channel stud anchored at ceiling and base.
2"
Rib metal lath
Wire ties.
METAL BUCK
¾" channel anchored to wood buck with nails and tie wire and anchored at ceiling and base.
2"
1⅜" door
1" minimum lap of casing over plaster
WOOD BUCK

SECTIONS OF DOOR BUCK DETAILS
Scale: 3" = 1'-0"

2" SOLID STUDLESS PARTITIONS

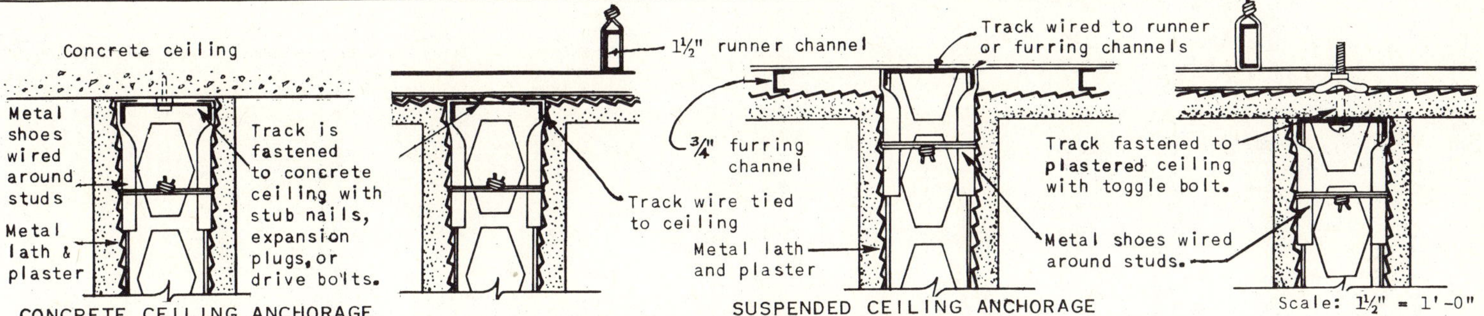
Concrete ceiling
Metal shoes wired around studs
Metal lath & plaster
Track is fastened to concrete ceiling with stub nails, expansion plugs, or drive bolts.
CONCRETE CEILING ANCHORAGE
1½" runner channel
¾" furring channel
Track wire tied to ceiling
Track wired to runner or furring channels
Metal lath and plaster
Track fastened to plastered ceiling with toggle bolt.
Metal shoes wired around studs.
SUSPENDED CEILING ANCHORAGE
Scale: 1½" = 1'-0"

SECTIONS OF CEILING ANCHORAGE DETAILS

MAXIMUM HEIGHTS OF HOLLOW (NON-BEARING) PARTITIONS*				
TYPE OF PARTITION (STUD)	PARTITION THICKNESS	STUD SPACING - C. TO C.		
		24"	19"	16"
Single row 2½" Prefabricated Studs	4"	9 ft.	14 ft.	15 ft.
Single row 3¼" Prefabricated Studs	4¾"	13 ft.	18 ft.	21 ft.
Single row 4" Prefabricated Studs	5½"	16 ft.	20 ft.	22 ft.
Single row 6" Prefabricated Studs	7½"	20 ft.	24 ft.	26 ft.
Double row ¾" Channels (Braced)	3"			14 ft
	4"			16 ft.
	5"			20 ft.

*Maximum Heights for lengths not exceeding 1½ times height.
Bearing Partitions require light weight steel studs; see Mfrs. Cat.
Thicknesses of partitions increase ½" when using rib metal lath.

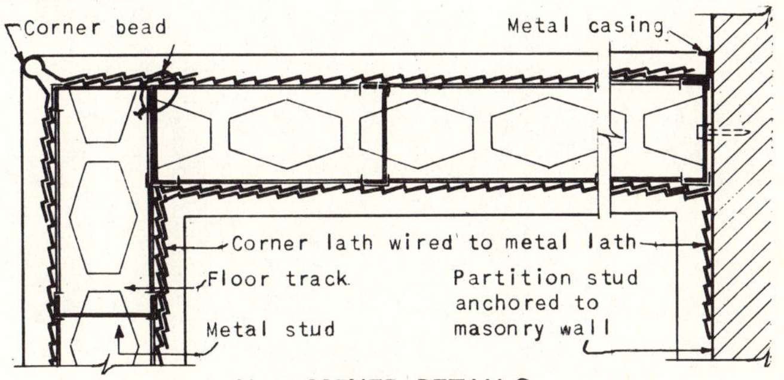
Corner bead
Metal casing
Corner lath wired to metal lath
Floor track
Metal stud
Partition stud anchored to masonry wall

PLAN - CORNER DETAILS

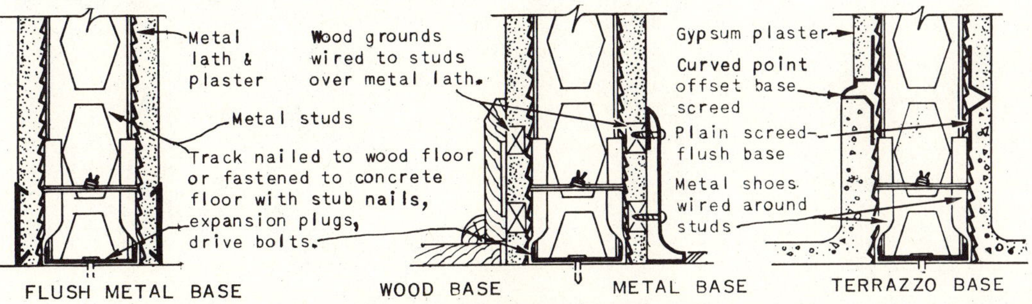
Metal lath & plaster
Metal studs
Track nailed to wood floor or fastened to concrete floor with stub nails, expansion plugs, drive bolts.
FLUSH METAL BASE
Wood grounds wired to studs over metal lath.
WOOD BASE
METAL BASE
Gypsum plaster
Curved point offset base screed
Plain screed-flush base
Metal shoes wired around studs
TERRAZZO BASE

SECTIONS OF BASES AND ANCHORAGE DETAILS

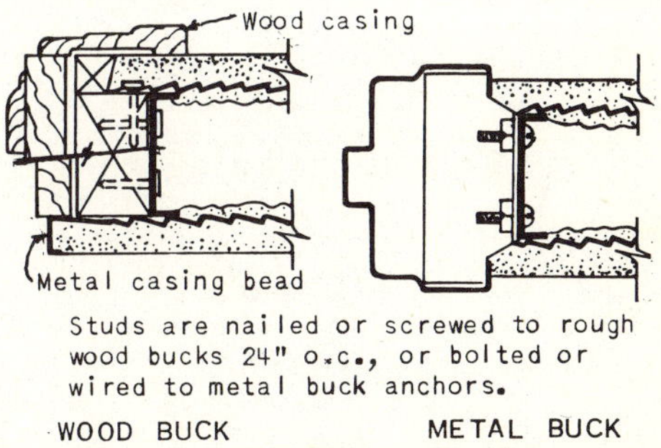
Wood casing
Metal casing bead
Studs are nailed or screwed to rough wood bucks 24" o.c., or bolted or wired to metal buck anchors.
WOOD BUCK
METAL BUCK

SECTIONS OF DOOR BUCK DETAILS

CHANNEL STUD AND PREFABRICATED METAL STUD - HOLLOW PARTITIONS

DATA CHECKED BY: METAL LATH MANUFACTURERS ASSOCIATION

METAL LATH and PLASTER PARTITIONS

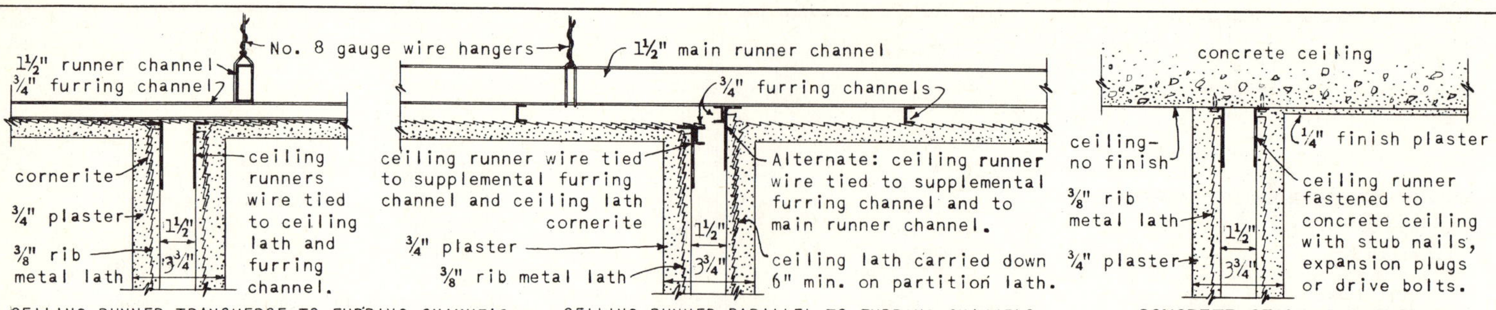
1½" runner channel
¾" furring channel
No. 8 gauge wire hangers
1½" main runner channel
¾" furring channels
cornerite
¾" plaster
⅜" rib metal lath
ceiling runners wire tied to ceiling lath and furring channel.
1½"
3¾"
ceiling runner wire tied to supplemental furring channel and ceiling lath
cornerite
¾" plaster
⅜" rib metal lath
Alternate: ceiling runner wire tied to supplemental furring channel and to main runner channel.
ceiling lath carried down 6" min. on partition lath.
concrete ceiling
ceiling-no finish
⅜" rib metal lath
¾" plaster
¼" finish plaster
ceiling runner fastened to concrete ceiling with stub nails, expansion plugs or drive bolts.

CEILING RUNNER TRANSVERSE TO FURRING CHANNELS — SUSPENDED CEILING ANCHORAGE

CEILING RUNNER PARALLEL TO FURRING CHANNELS

CONCRETE CEILING ANCHORAGE

SECTIONS - CEILING ANCHORAGE DETAILS

Scale: 1½"=1'-0"

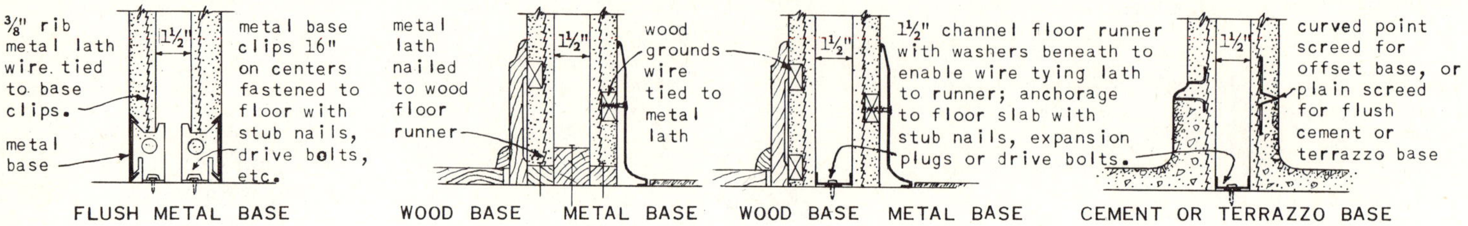
⅜" rib metal lath wire tied to base clips.
metal base
1½"
metal base clips 16" on centers fastened to floor with stub nails, drive bolts, etc.
metal lath nailed to wood floor runner
wood grounds
wire tied to metal lath
1½" channel floor runner with washers beneath to enable wire tying lath to runner; anchorage to floor slab with stub nails, expansion plugs or drive bolts.
curved point screed for offset base, or plain screed for flush cement or terrazzo base

FLUSH METAL BASE — WOOD BASE — METAL BASE — WOOD BASE — METAL BASE — CEMENT OR TERRAZZO BASE

SECTIONS - FLOOR ANCHORAGE DETAILS

Scale: 1½"=1'-0"

CORNER DETAILS are similar to 2" solid channel stud partitions; cornerite used for inside corners, corner beads for outside corners, and casing beads for termination of plaster around openings and where plaster partition butts other materials and finishes.

NOTE: Maximum height of partitions 8'-6"; Cross ties not recommended for sound insulation; Stiffeners, ¾" channels 4'-0" o.c. vertically.

HOLLOW STUDLESS PARTITION DETAILS

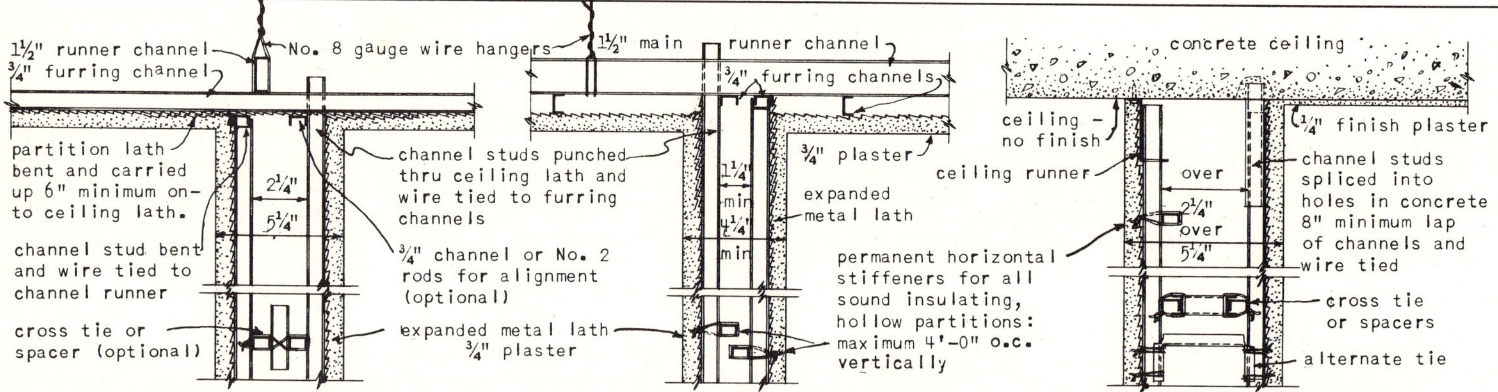
1½" runner channel
¾" furring channel
No. 8 gauge wire hangers
partition lath bent and carried up 6" minimum on-to ceiling lath.
channel stud bent and wire tied to channel runner
cross tie or spacer (optional)
2¼"
5¼"
channel studs punched thru ceiling lath and wire tied to furring channels
¾" channel or No. 2 rods for alignment (optional)
expanded metal lath
¾" plaster
1½" main runner channel
¾" furring channels
¾" plaster
1¼" min
4¼" min
expanded metal lath
permanent horizontal stiffeners for all sound insulating hollow partitions: maximum 4'-0" o.c. vertically
concrete ceiling
ceiling - no finish
ceiling runner
over 2¼"
over 5¼"
¼" finish plaster
channel studs spliced into holes in concrete 8" minimum lap of channels and wire tied
cross tie or spacers
alternate tie

PARTITION TRANSVERSE TO FURRING CHANNELS — SUSPENDED CEILING ANCHORAGE

PARTITION PARALLEL TO FURRING CHANNELS

CONCRETE CEILING ANCHORAGE

SECTIONS - CEILING ANCHORAGE DETAILS

Scale: 1½"=1'-0"

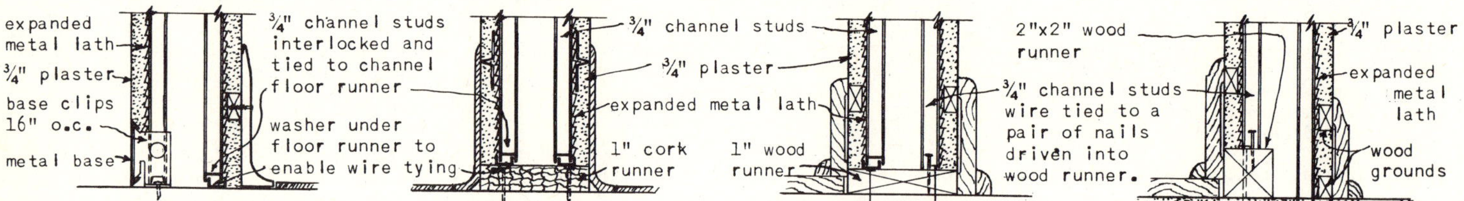
expanded metal lath
¾" plaster
base clips 16" o.c.
metal base
¾" channel studs interlocked and tied to channel floor runner
washer under floor runner to enable wire tying
¾" channel studs
¾" plaster
expanded metal lath
1" cork runner
1" wood runner
2"x2" wood runner
¾" channel studs wire tied to a pair of nails driven into wood runner.
¾" plaster
expanded metal lath
wood grounds
concrete
floor

FLUSH METAL BASE — METAL BASE — ASPHALT BASE — WOOD BASES

SECTIONS - FLOOR ANCHORAGE DETAILS

Scale: 1½"=1'-0"

NOTE: For Maximum Allowable Heights of hollow partitions see "Wood and Metal Wall Furring"; For type of lath required see "Erection and Spacing of Supports for Metal Lath Partitions"; CORNER DETAILS see "Metal Lath & Plaster Partitions"

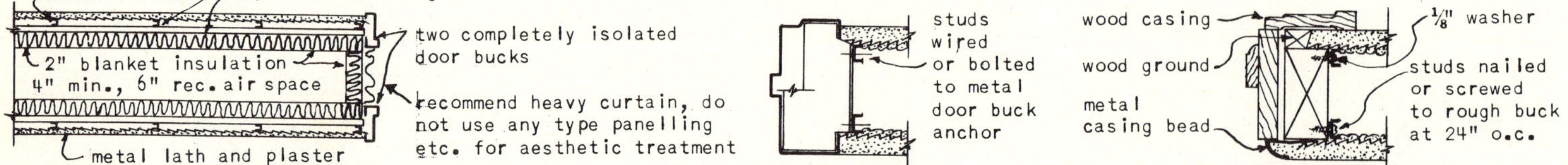
channel studs
channel stiffening
2" blanket insulation
4" min., 6" rec. air space
metal lath and plaster
two completely isolated door bucks
recommend heavy curtain, do not use any type panelling etc. for aesthetic treatment
studs wired or bolted to metal door buck anchor
wood casing
wood ground
metal casing bead
⅛" washer
studs nailed or screwed to rough buck at 24" o.c.

DOUBLE DOOR BUCK DETAIL FOR SOUND STUDIOS — METAL DOOR BUCK — WOOD BUCK

NOTE: Door Buck Anchorage details are applicable to channel stud and studless sound insulating hollow partitions.

Scale: 1½"=1'-0"

NOTE: Sound studios are completely isolated from building structure and completely insulated.

SECTIONS - DOOR BUCK ANCHORAGE

HOLLOW CHANNEL STUD PARTITION DETAILS

DATA CHECKED BY METAL LATH MANUFACTURERS ASSOCIATION

METAL LATH PARTITIONS and STUD ANCHORAGE

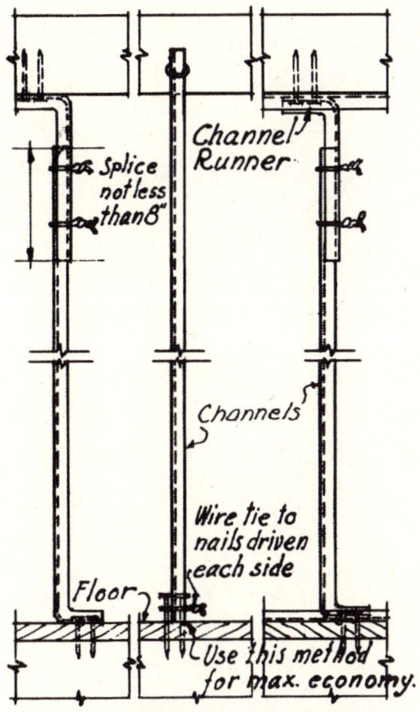

Splice not less than 8"
Channel Runner
Channels
Wire tie to nails driven each side
Floor
Use this method for max. economy.

· FOR WOOD JOIST · FLOORS

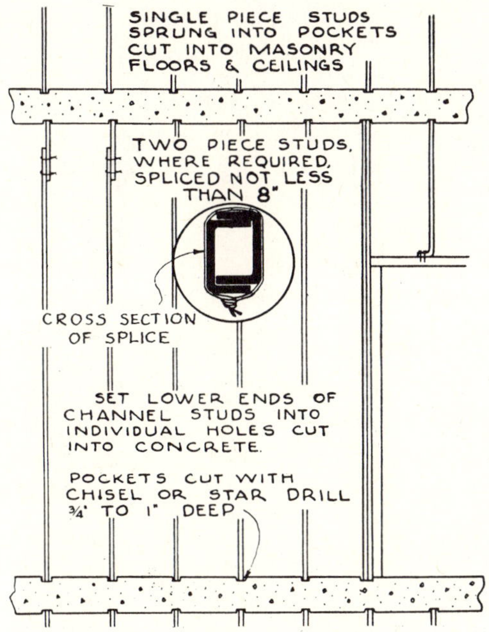

SINGLE PIECE STUDS SPRUNG INTO POCKETS CUT INTO MASONRY FLOORS & CEILINGS
TWO PIECE STUDS, WHERE REQUIRED, SPLICED NOT LESS THAN 8"
CROSS SECTION OF SPLICE
SET LOWER ENDS OF CHANNEL STUDS INTO INDIVIDUAL HOLES CUT INTO CONCRETE.
POCKETS CUT WITH CHISEL OR STAR DRILL 3/4" TO 1" DEEP

METAL STUDS SPRUNG into POCKETS CUT in MASONRY 1/4"=1'-0"

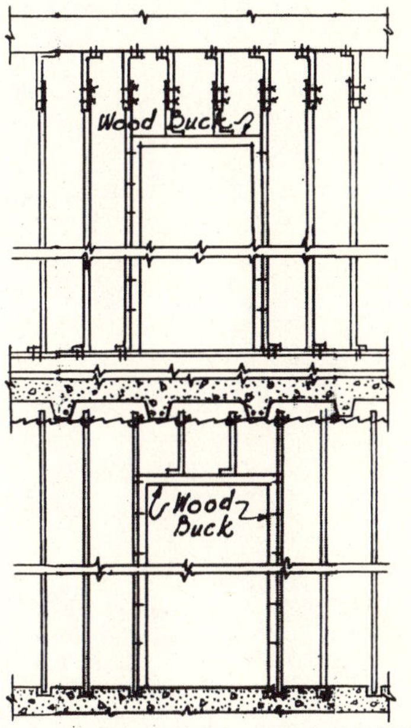

Wood Buck
Wood Buck

DOOR FRAMING - MASONRY CONSTRUCTION 3/16"=1'-0"

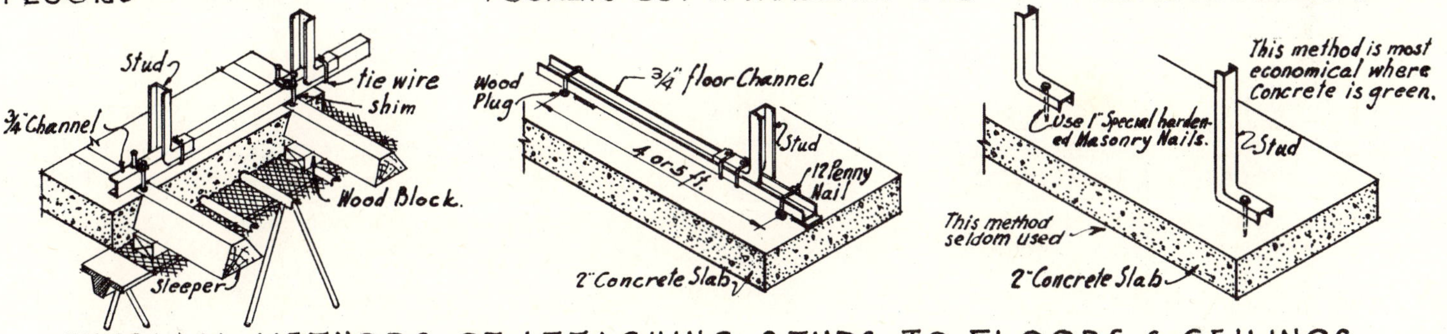

Stud
tie wire
shim
3/4" Channel
Wood Block.
Sleeper
Wood Plug
3/4" floor Channel
4 or 5 ft.
Stud
12 Penny Nail
2" Concrete Slab
This method is most economical where Concrete is green.
Use 1" Special hardened Masonry Nails.
Stud
This method seldom used
2" Concrete Slab

·TYPICAL·METHODS·OF·ATTACHING·STUDS·TO·FLOORS·&·CEILINGS·

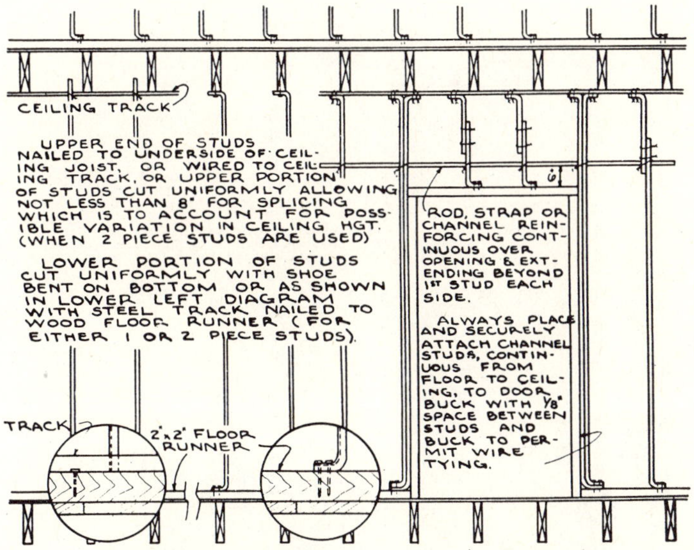

CEILING TRACK
UPPER END OF STUDS NAILED TO UNDERSIDE OF CEILING JOIST, OR WIRED TO CEILING TRACK, OR UPPER PORTION OF STUDS CUT UNIFORMLY ALLOWING NOT LESS THAN 8" FOR SPLICING WHICH IS TO ACCOUNT FOR POSSIBLE VARIATION IN CEILING HGT. (WHEN 2 PIECE STUDS ARE USED)
LOWER PORTION OF STUDS CUT UNIFORMLY WITH SHOE BENT ON BOTTOM OR AS SHOWN IN LOWER LEFT DIAGRAM WITH STEEL TRACK NAILED TO WOOD FLOOR RUNNER (FOR EITHER 1 OR 2 PIECE STUDS).
ROD, STRAP OR CHANNEL REINFORCING CONTINUOUS OVER OPENING & EXTENDING BEYOND 1ST STUD EACH SIDE.
ALWAYS PLACE AND SECURELY ATTACH CHANNEL STUDS, CONTINUOUS FROM FLOOR TO CEILING, TO DOOR BUCK WITH 1/8" SPACE BETWEEN STUDS AND BUCK TO PERMIT WIRE TYING.
TRACK
2"x2" FLOOR RUNNER

METAL STUDS ATTACHED to WOOD JOISTS or CEILING TRACK in WOOD FRAME CONSTRUCTION

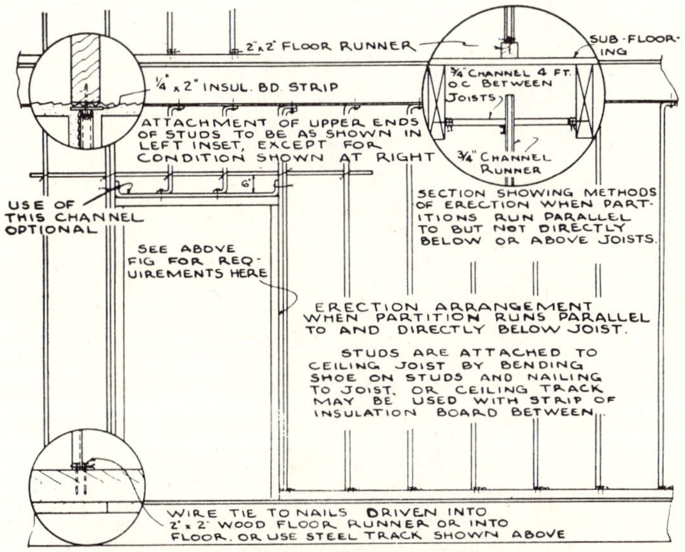

2"x2" FLOOR RUNNER
SUB-FLOORING
1/4"x2" INSUL. BD. STRIP
3/4" CHANNEL 4 FT. O.C. BETWEEN JOISTS
ATTACHMENT OF UPPER ENDS OF STUDS TO BE AS SHOWN IN LEFT INSET, EXCEPT FOR CONDITION SHOWN AT RIGHT
3/4" CHANNEL RUNNER
USE OF THIS CHANNEL OPTIONAL
SECTION SHOWING METHODS OF ERECTION WHEN PARTITIONS RUN PARALLEL TO BUT NOT DIRECTLY BELOW OR ABOVE JOISTS.
SEE ABOVE FIG FOR REQUIREMENTS HERE
ERECTION ARRANGEMENT WHEN PARTITION RUNS PARALLEL TO AND DIRECTLY BELOW JOIST.
STUDS ARE ATTACHED TO CEILING JOIST BY BENDING SHOE ON STUDS AND NAILING TO JOIST, OR CEILING TRACK MAY BE USED WITH STRIP OF INSULATION BOARD BETWEEN.
WIRE TIE TO NAILS DRIVEN INTO 2"x2" WOOD FLOOR RUNNER OR INTO FLOOR, OR USE STEEL TRACK SHOWN ABOVE

PARTITIONS RUNNING PARALLEL TO and UNDER WOOD JOISTS in WOOD FRAME CONSTRUCTION

Note: The various details of anchorage on this and the following page show methods of floor and ceiling anchorage for the studs which should not be limited to these examples alone. The methods may be used interchangeably to fit whatever conditions may be encountered. Various patented floor runners and ceiling tracks are made by the manufacturers of metal lath & metal lath accessories.

METAL STUD ANCHORAGE

Data by Metal Lath Manufacturers Association

METAL STUD ANCHORAGE

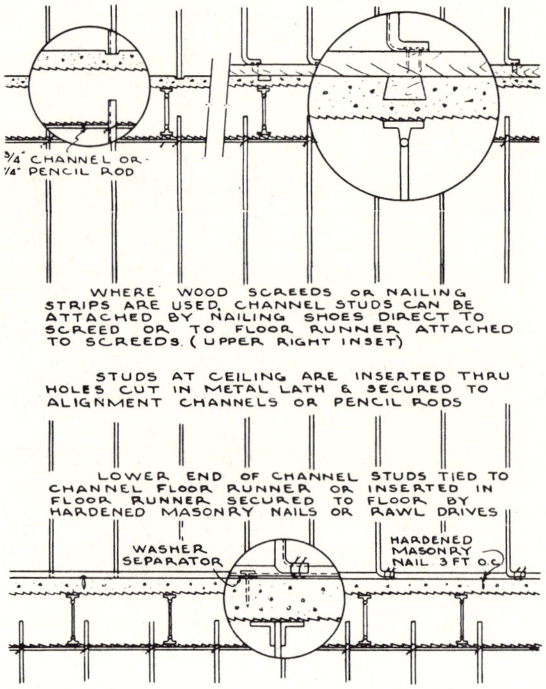
3/4" CHANNEL OR 1/4" PENCIL ROD
WHERE WOOD SCREEDS OR NAILING STRIPS ARE USED, CHANNEL STUDS CAN BE ATTACHED BY NAILING SHOES DIRECT TO SCREED OR TO FLOOR RUNNER ATTACHED TO SCREEDS. (UPPER RIGHT INSET)
STUDS AT CEILING ARE INSERTED THRU HOLES CUT IN METAL LATH & SECURED TO ALIGNMENT CHANNELS OR PENCIL RODS
LOWER END OF CHANNEL STUDS TIED TO CHANNEL FLOOR RUNNER OR INSERTED IN FLOOR RUNNER SECURED TO FLOOR BY HARDENED MASONRY NAILS OR RAWL DRIVES
WASHER SEPARATOR
HARDENED MASONRY NAIL 3 FT O.C.

METAL LATH CEILINGS
ATTACHED *to* STEEL JOISTS
~ CONTACT *or* FURRED ~

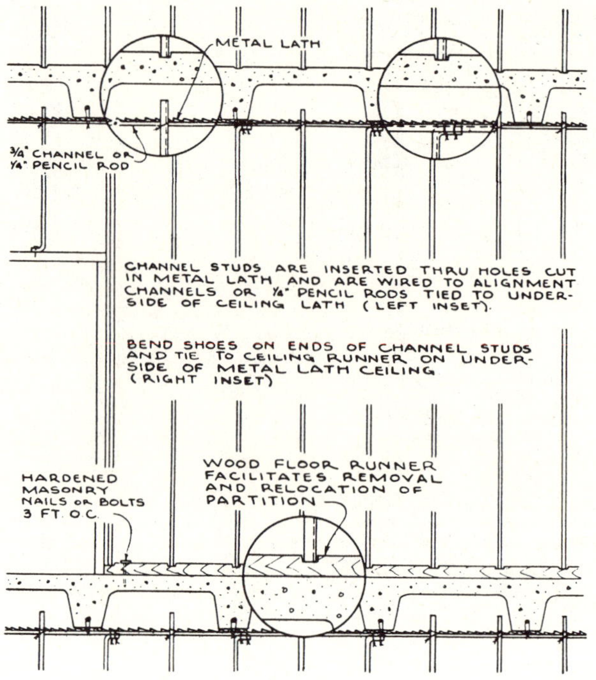
METAL LATH
3/4" CHANNEL OR 1/4" PENCIL ROD
CHANNEL STUDS ARE INSERTED THRU HOLES CUT IN METAL LATH AND ARE WIRED TO ALIGNMENT CHANNELS OR 1/4" PENCIL RODS TIED TO UNDERSIDE OF CEILING LATH (LEFT INSET)
BEND SHOES ON ENDS OF CHANNEL STUDS AND TIE TO CEILING RUNNER ON UNDERSIDE OF METAL LATH CEILING (RIGHT INSET)
HARDENED MASONRY NAILS OR BOLTS 3 FT. O.C.
WOOD FLOOR RUNNER FACILITATES REMOVAL AND RELOCATION OF PARTITION

METAL LATH CEILINGS
ATTACHED *to* CONCRETE JOISTS
~ CONTACT *or* FURRED ~

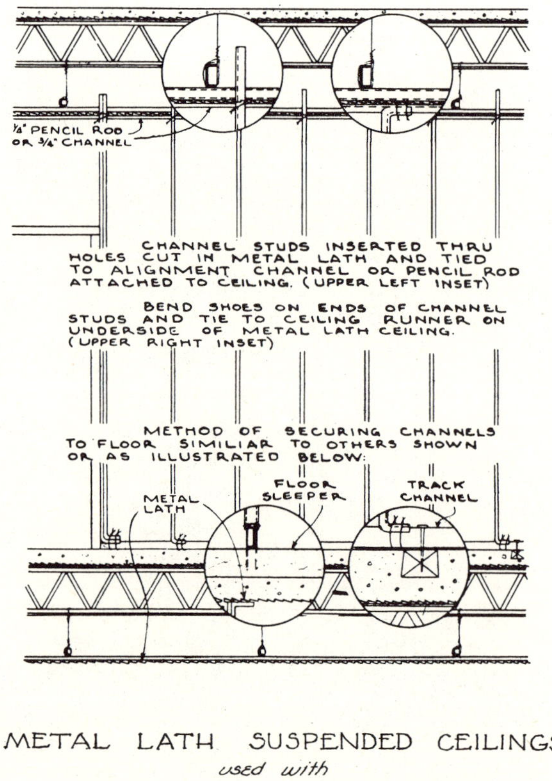
1/4" PENCIL ROD OR 3/4" CHANNEL
CHANNEL STUDS INSERTED THRU HOLES CUT IN METAL LATH AND TIED TO ALIGNMENT CHANNEL OR PENCIL ROD ATTACHED TO CEILING. (UPPER LEFT INSET)
BEND SHOES ON ENDS OF CHANNEL STUDS AND TIE TO CEILING RUNNER ON UNDERSIDE OF METAL LATH CEILING. (UPPER RIGHT INSET)
METHOD OF SECURING CHANNELS TO FLOOR SIMILIAR TO OTHERS SHOWN OR AS ILLUSTRATED BELOW:
METAL LATH
FLOOR SLEEPER
TRACK CHANNEL

METAL LATH SUSPENDED CEILINGS
used with
STEEL JOIST CONSTRUCTION

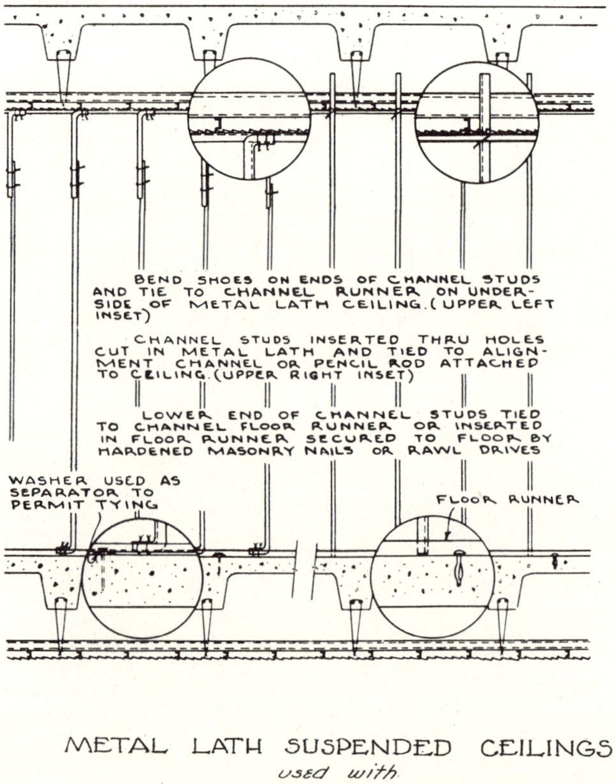
BEND SHOES ON ENDS OF CHANNEL STUDS AND TIE TO CHANNEL RUNNER ON UNDERSIDE OF METAL LATH CEILING. (UPPER LEFT INSET)
CHANNEL STUDS INSERTED THRU HOLES CUT IN METAL LATH AND TIED TO ALIGNMENT CHANNEL OR PENCIL ROD ATTACHED TO CEILING. (UPPER RIGHT INSET)
LOWER END OF CHANNEL STUDS TIED TO CHANNEL FLOOR RUNNER OR INSERTED IN FLOOR RUNNER SECURED TO FLOOR BY HARDENED MASONRY NAILS OR RAWL DRIVES
WASHER USED AS SEPARATOR TO PERMIT TYING
FLOOR RUNNER

METAL LATH SUSPENDED CEILINGS
used with
CONCRETE JOIST CONSTRUCTION

Data by Metal Lath Manufacturers Association

METAL LATH & PLASTER - CONTACT, FURRED & SUSPENDED - CEILINGS

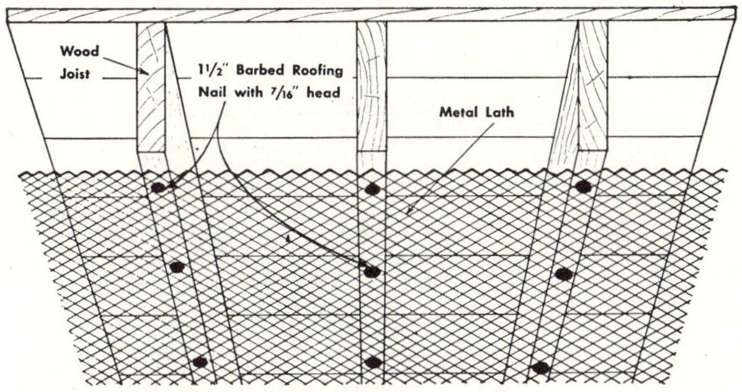
Wood Joist
1½" Barbed Roofing Nail with 7/16" head
Metal Lath

CONTACT CEILING - LATH NAILED TO WOOD JOISTS

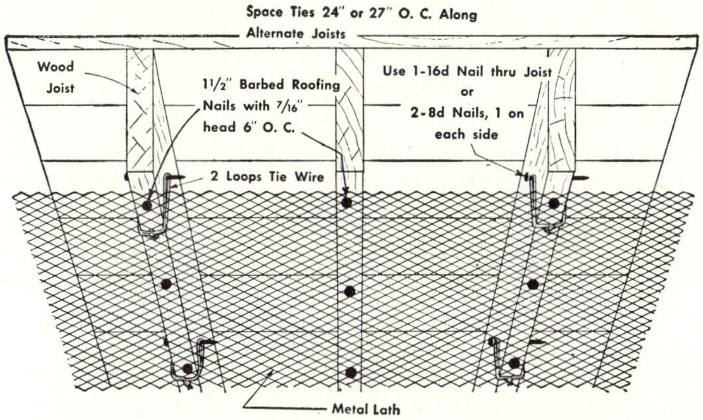
Space Ties 24" or 27" O. C. Along Alternate Joists
Wood Joist
1½" Barbed Roofing Nails with 7/16" head 6" O. C.
Use 1-16d Nail thru Joist or 2-8d Nails, 1 on each side
2 Loops Tie Wire
Metal Lath

CONTACT CEILING - LATH TIED AND NAILED TO JOISTS

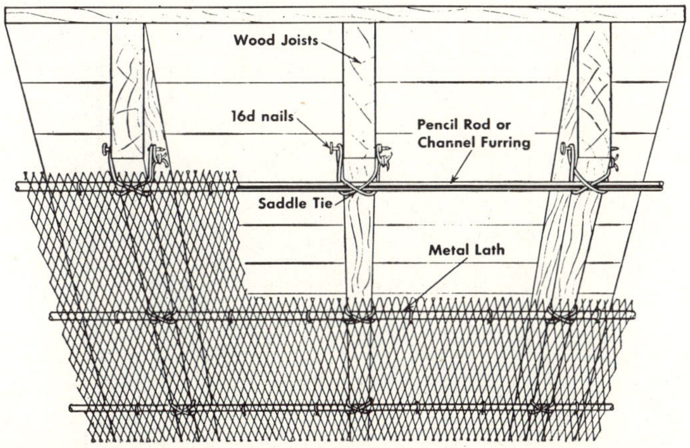
Wood Joists
16d nails
Pencil Rod or Channel Furring
Saddle Tie
Metal Lath

FURRED CEILING ON WOOD JOISTS

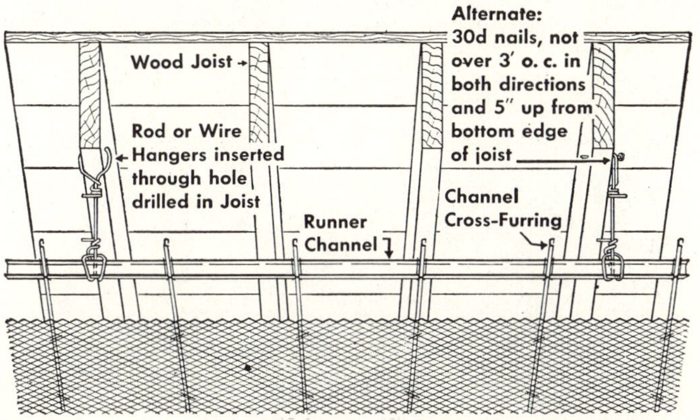
Wood Joist
Alternate: 30d nails, not over 3' o. c. in both directions and 5" up from bottom edge of joist
Rod or Wire Hangers inserted through hole drilled in Joist
Runner Channel
Channel Cross-Furring

SUSPENDED CEILING BELOW WOOD JOISTS

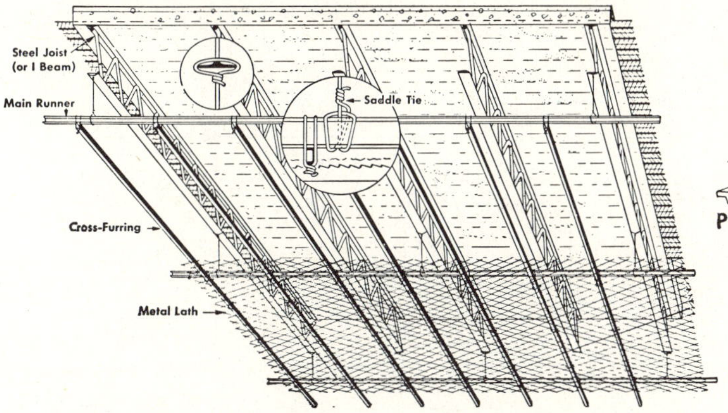
Steel Joist (or I Beam)
Main Runner
Saddle Tie
Cross-Furring
Metal Lath

SUSPENDED CEILING BELOW STEEL CONSTRUCTION

Clip or Wire Tie
Plaster
Rib Metal Lath
Open Truss Joists

CONTACT CEILING - LATH TIED TO STEEL JOISTS

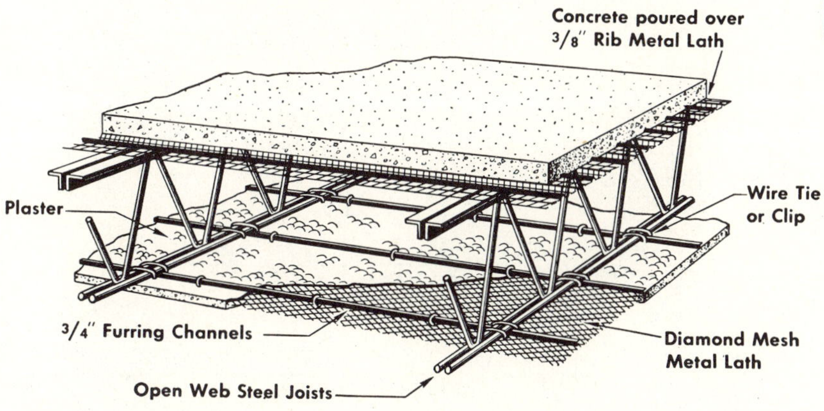
Concrete poured over 3/8" Rib Metal Lath
Plaster
Wire Tie or Clip
3/4" Furring Channels
Diamond Mesh Metal Lath
Open Web Steel Joists

FURRED CEILING ON STEEL JOISTS

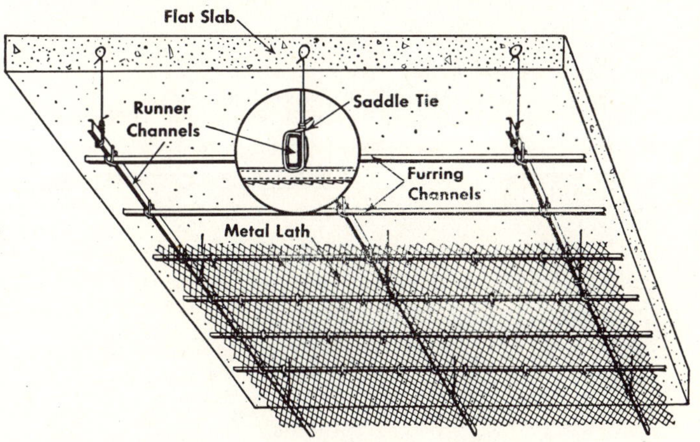
Flat Slab
Runner Channels
Saddle Tie
Furring Channels
Metal Lath

SUSPENDED CEILING BELOW CONCRETE FLAT SLAB

For applicable construction requirements see General Notes on other page

DATA CHECKED BY: METAL LATH MANUFACTURERS ASSOCIATION

METAL LATH and PLASTER CONTACT, FURRED and SUSPENDED CEILINGS

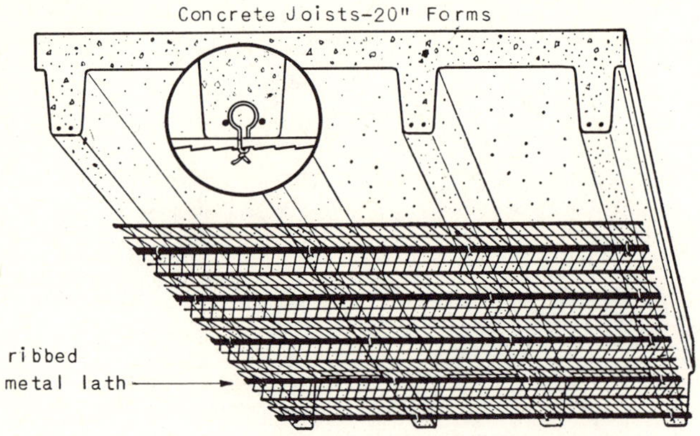
Concrete Joists-20" Forms
ribbed metal lath

CONTACT CEILING - LATH ON CONCRETE JOISTS

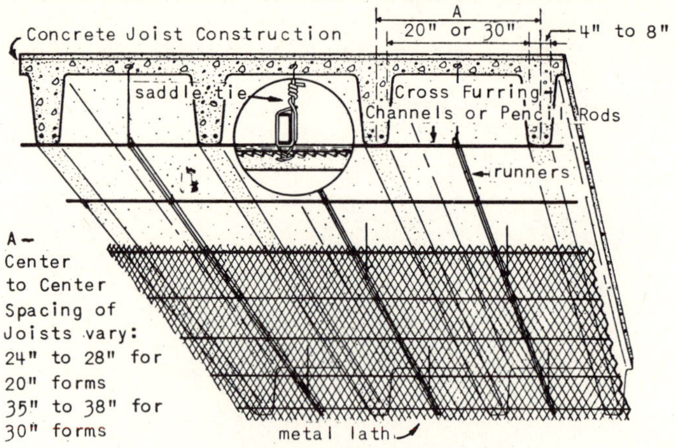
Concrete Joist Construction
A
20" or 30"
4" to 8"
saddle tie
Cross Furring Channels or Pencil Rods
runners
A- Center to Center Spacing of Joists vary: 24" to 28" for 20" forms 35" to 38" for 30" forms
metal lath

FURRED CEILING ON CONCRETE JOISTS

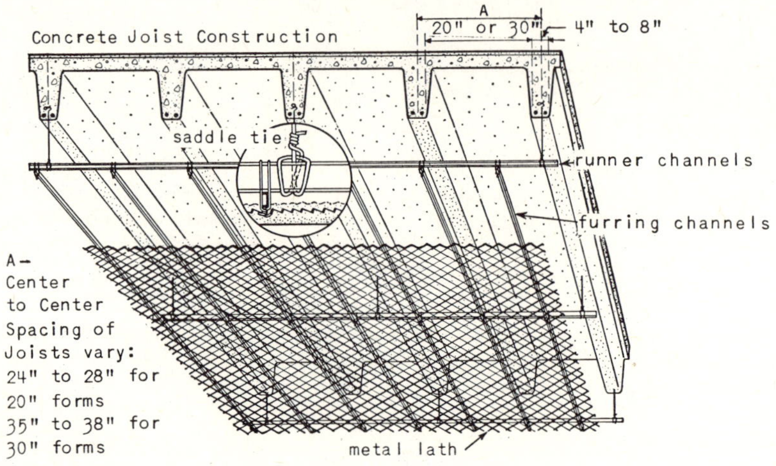
Concrete Joist Construction
A
20" or 30"
4" to 8"
saddle tie
runner channels
furring channels
A- Center to Center Spacing of Joists vary: 24" to 28" for 20" forms 35" to 38" for 30" forms
metal lath

SUSPENDED CEILING BELOW CONCRETE JOISTS

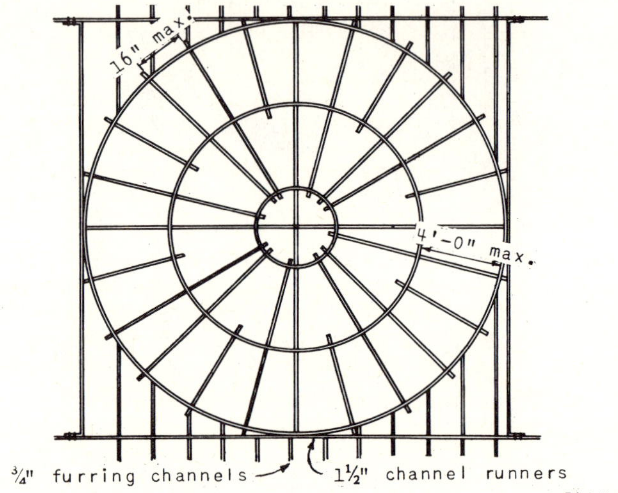
16" max.
4'-0" max.
3/4" furring channels
1½" channel runners

PLAN

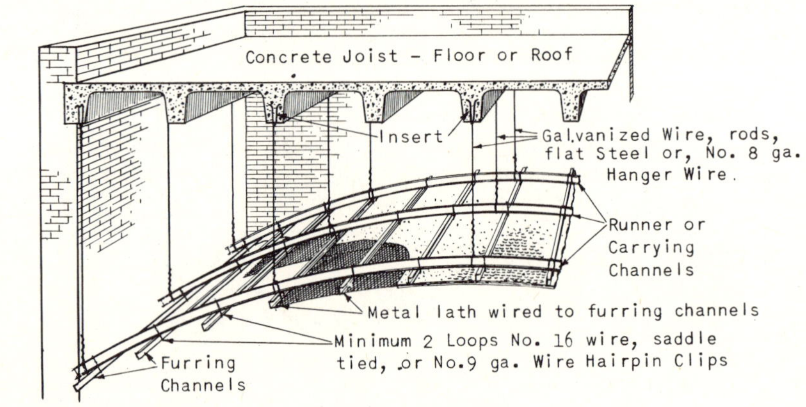
Concrete Joist - Floor or Roof
Insert
Galvanized Wire, rods, flat Steel or, No. 8 ga. Hanger Wire.
Runner or Carrying Channels
Metal lath wired to furring channels
Minimum 2 Loops No. 16 wire, saddle tied, or No.9 ga. Wire Hairpin Clips
Furring Channels

SUSPENDED - ARCHED CEILING

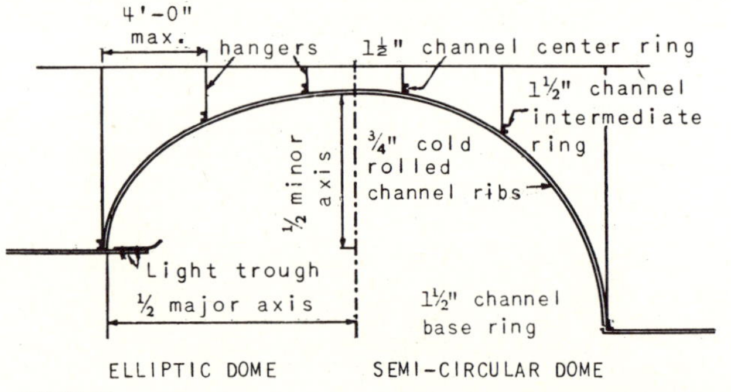
4'-0" max.
hangers
1½" channel center ring
1½" channel intermediate ring
3/4" cold rolled channel ribs
½ minor axis
Light trough
½ major axis
1½" channel base ring
ELLIPTIC DOME
SEMI-CIRCULAR DOME

SECTION

SUSPENDED - DOME CEILING

Note: For Concrete Insert Fastenings see page on Wall Furring and Methods of Fastening

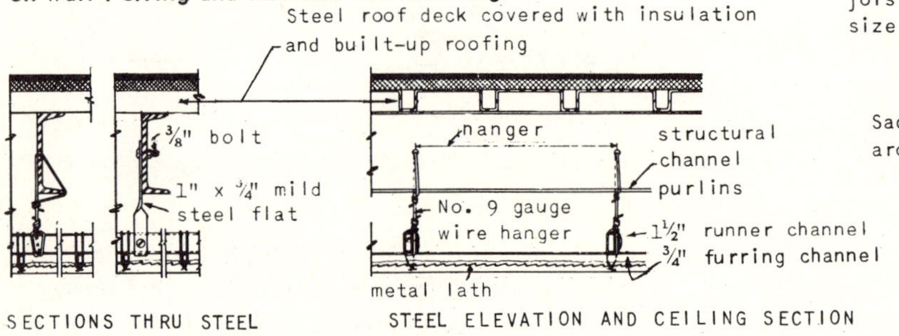
Steel roof deck covered with insulation and built-up roofing
3/8" bolt
1" x 3/4" mild steel flat
hanger
structural channel purlins
No. 9 gauge wire hanger
1½" runner channel
3/4" furring channel
metal lath
SECTIONS THRU STEEL
STEEL ELEVATION AND CEILING SECTION

STEEL DETAILS

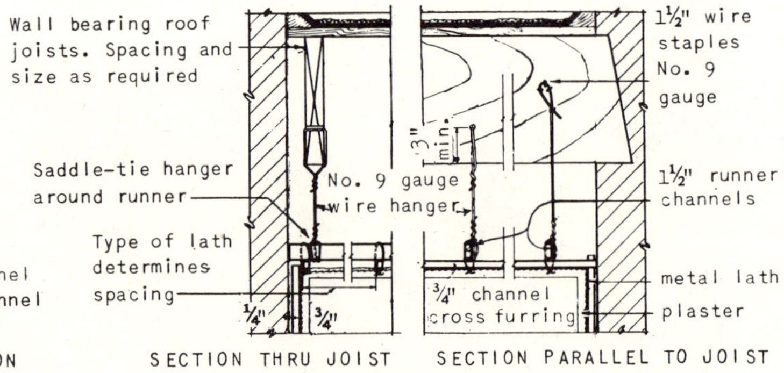
Wall bearing roof joists. Spacing and size as required
Saddle-tie hanger around runner
Type of lath determines spacing
No. 9 gauge wire hanger
3" min.
1½" wire staples No. 9 gauge
1½" runner channels
metal lath
plaster
3/4" channel cross furring
1/4"
3/4"
SECTION THRU JOIST
SECTION PARALLEL TO JOIST

WOOD DETAILS

For applicable construction requirements see General Notes on other page

DATA CHECKED BY: METAL LATH MANUFACTURERS ASSOCIATION

METAL LATH & PLASTER CONTACT, FURRED & SUSPENDED CEILINGS

GENERAL NOTES APPLICABLE TO METAL LATH AND PLASTER CEILINGS

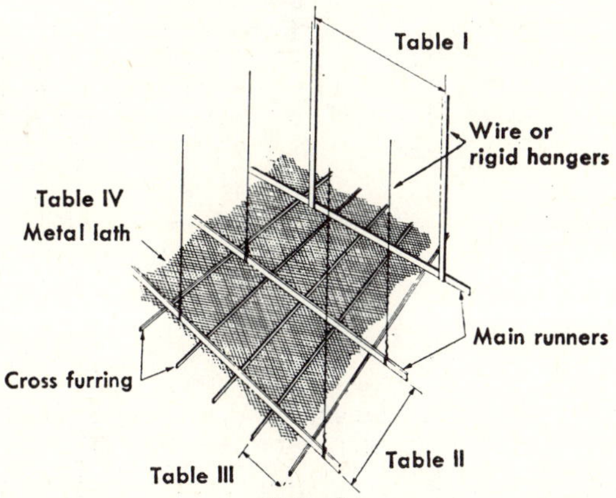
Table I
Wire or rigid hangers
Table IV
Metal lath
Main runners
Cross furring
Table III
Table II

Table I
SIZE AND SPACING OF HANGERS FOR SUSPENDED CEILINGS

Maximum Ceiling Area Supported Per Hanger	Maximum Center to Center Spacing of Hangers Along Runners	Minimum Size of Gage Galvanized Wire	Alternate Types and Sizes of Hangers for Areas Up to 16 Sq. Ft.
Up to 12.5 sq. ft.	4 ft.	No. 9	No. 8 gage galvanized wire; or 3/16″ or 1/4″ round mild steel rods; or 1 x 3/16″ flat mild steel bars

Table II
SIZE AND SPACING OF MAIN RUNNERS FOR SUSPENDED CEILINGS

Center to Center Spacing of Hangers Along Runners	Size of Cold Rolled Channel	Main Runners (Wgt. per 1,000 ft.)	Maximum Center to Center Spacing of Runners
Up to 2 ft.	3/4″	300 lbs.	3 ft.
Up to 3 ft. (1)	3/4″	300 lbs.	27 in.
Up to 3 ft.	1 1/2″	475 lbs.	4 ft.
Up to 3 ft. 6 in.	1 1/2″	475 lbs.	3 ft. 6 in.
Up to 4 ft.	1 1/2″	475 lbs.	3 ft.

Note.
Where hangers are spaced not to exceed 24″ on centers along each runner or carrying channel, cross furring channels may be omitted and lath attached crosswise and directly to runner channels; provided, however, that spacing center to center of such runner channels shall not exceed the limits specified in Table IV.

(1) This spacing for concrete joist construction only.

Table III
SIZE AND SPACING OF CROSS FURRING FOR FURRED–SUSPENDED CEILINGS

Center to Center Spacing of Supports	Cross Furring: Size, Type and Weight	Maximum Spacing
Up to 2 ft.	1/4″ Pencil Rods	12″
	3/8″ Pencil Rods	19″
Up to 2 ft. 6 in.	3/8″ Pencil Rods	12″
Up to 3 ft.	3/4″ Cold rolled channels @ 300 lbs. per 1,000 feet	24″
Up to 3 ft. 6 in.		19″
Up to 4 ft.		16″

Table IV
TYPES AND WEIGHTS OF METAL LATH, AND SPACING OF SUPPORTS

Type of Lath	Minimum Weight of Lath (Lbs. per Sq. Yd.)	Max. Allowable Spacing of Horizontal Supports (In.): Metal
Diamond Mesh (Flat Expanded)	2.5 3.4	0 13 1/3
Flat Rib	2.75 3.4	12 19
3/8″ Rib and Rod-Ribbed	3.4 4.0	24 24
Sheet Lath	4.5	24

All metal lath is applied with the long dimension of the lath across supports.

Carry metal lath down 6″ onto walls and partitions, except rib and sheet lath which is butted into corners and corner lath applied over and wired 6″ intervals along edges.

Nails or staples fastening lath directly to wood joists must provide at least 1 1/4″ penetration into underside of joists, spaced not over 6″ o.c. Supplemental tying is used in wood joist structures subject to greater-than-ordinary vibration as in: classrooms, gymnasiums, auditoriums, and other places of public assembly, and in buildings subject to earthquakes etc.; and for a higher safety factor and increased fire retardance, furring is recommended. Nails for supplemental tying must provide at least 1 1/2″ penetration at a minimum of 2″ above bottom edges of alternate joists, spaced 24″ or 27″ on centers with wire ties twisted not less than three times around projecting nail on either side of joist.

Hangers fastening lath directly to underside of concrete or concrete joists may be hairpin, hook, or loop hangers, or other inserts or equal attachments positively anchored in concrete or fastened to reinforcing; No. 14 ga. for tie wires, and No. 10 ga. when struck over to support lath.

Additional supports, hangers, or fastening between joists of larger spans are No. 10 ga. wire centered between joists or located as required, and spaced not to exceed 36″ o.c. for supporting furring channels and suspended ceilings not over 6″ below joists.

Fasten lath to wood, steel, concrete joists, furring channels, or pencil rod supports with one loop No. 16 ga. tie wire, or two loops No. 18 ga. wire, twisted beneath lath, spaced not over 6″ o.c. for fastening to furring or steel joists, not over 5″ o.c. for concrete joists, and applicable tying of side laps of lath.

Lap metal lath 1″ at ends or nest. Lap diamond mesh lath not less than 1/2″ at sides. Lap rib and sheet lath at sides by nesting outside ribs or selvage. End laps of sheets should generally occur only over supports; if between tie adequately with No. 18 ga. tie wire. Tie all laps at not over 6″ intervals.

Fasten furring or main runners to underside of wood, steel, or concrete joists with two loops No. 16 ga. tie wires, or saddle tie or wrap hangers around furring.

Run cross furring transversely to joists and runners using 3/4″ cold rolled steel channels or 1/4″ round steel pencil rods (No. 2 rods) spaced not over 12″ o.c., or 3/8″ pencil rods (No. 3 rods) spaced not over 19″ o.c. Saddle tie cross furring to runner (main) channels with two loops No. 16 ga. wire at crossings, or with equivalent clips or attachments.

Lap splicing of furring members (rods or channels) not less than 8″ (channel flanges interlocked) and tie at ends with double loops No. 16 ga. tie wire.

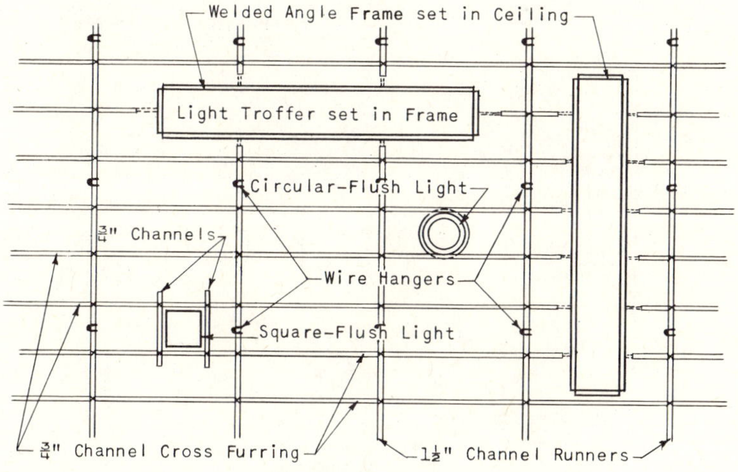
Welded Angle Frame set in Ceiling
Light Troffer set in Frame
Circular-Flush Light
3/4" Channels
Wire Hangers
Square-Flush Light
3/4" Channel Cross Furring
1 1/2" Channel Runners

PLAN - SUSPENDED CEILING LIGHTING
Scale: 1/4" = 1'-0"

DATA CHECKED BY: METAL LATH MANUFACTURERS ASSOCIATION

SUSPENDED CEILING and SOFFIT FURRING DETAILS-AIR DIFFUSERS & LIGHTING

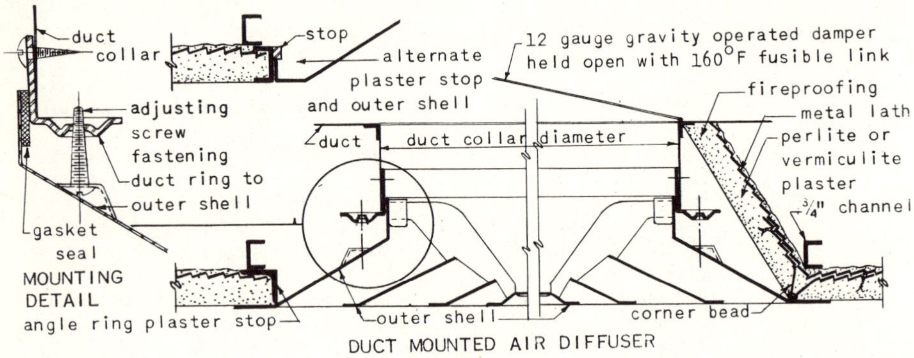
duct
collar
adjusting
screw
fastening
duct ring to
outer shell
gasket
seal
MOUNTING
DETAIL
angle ring plaster stop
stop
alternate
plaster stop
and outer shell
duct
duct collar diameter
12 gauge gravity operated damper
held open with 160°F fusible link
fireproofing
metal lath
perlite or
vermiculite
plaster
3/4" channel
outer shell
corner bead

DUCT MOUNTED AIR DIFFUSER

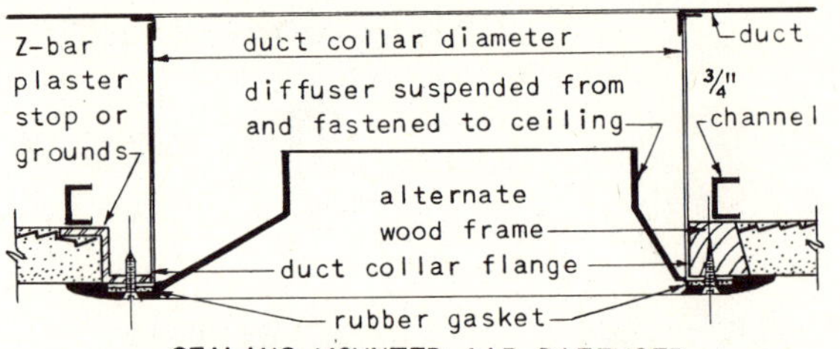
Z-bar
plaster
stop or
grounds
duct collar diameter
duct
3/4"
channel
diffuser suspended from
and fastened to ceiling
alternate
wood frame
duct collar flange
rubber gasket

CEILING MOUNTED AIR DIFFUSER

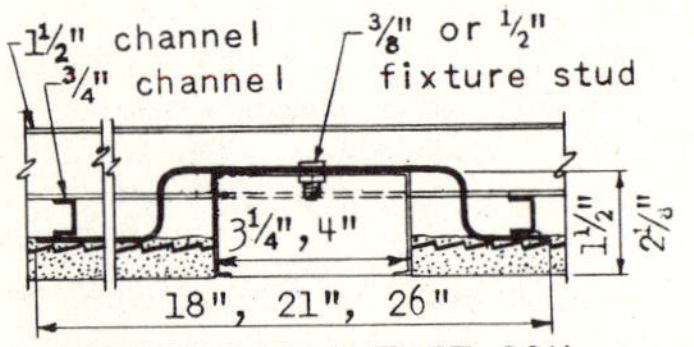
1½" channel
3/4" channel
3/8" or ½"
fixture stud
3¼",4"
1½"
2⅛"
18", 21", 26"

OFFSET-BAR OUTLET BOX HANGER

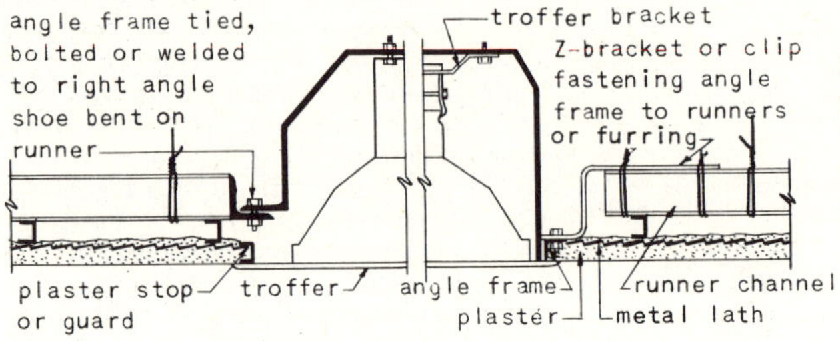
angle frame tied,
bolted or welded
to right angle
shoe bent on
runner
troffer bracket
Z-bracket or clip
fastening angle
frame to runners
or furring
plaster stop
or guard
troffer
angle frame
plaster
runner channel
metal lath

FLUSH LIGHT TROFFERS

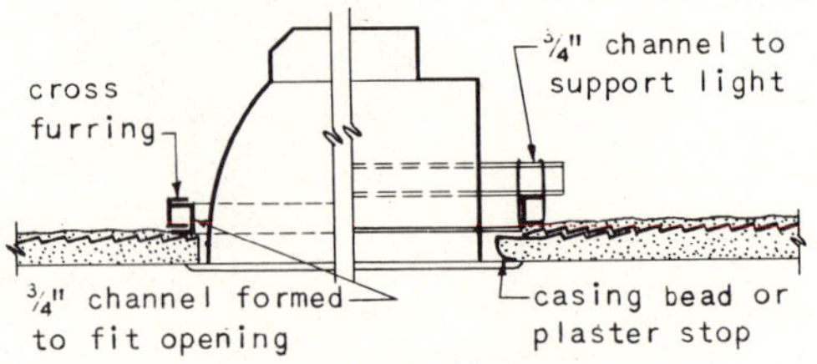
cross
furring
3/4" channel to
support light
3/4" channel formed
to fit opening
casing bead or
plaster stop

TYPICAL FLUSH LIGHTS

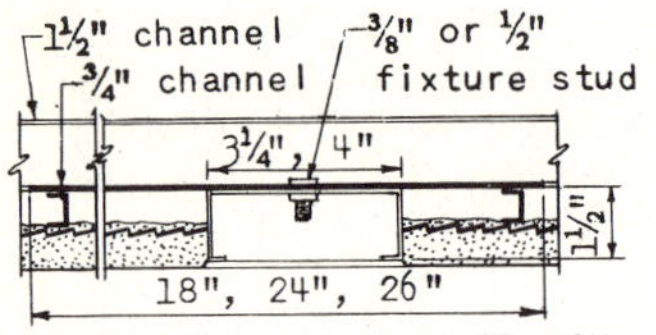
1½" channel
3/4" channel
3/8" or ½"
fixture stud
3¼",4"
1½"
18", 24", 26"

STRAIGHT-BAR OUTLET BOX HANGER

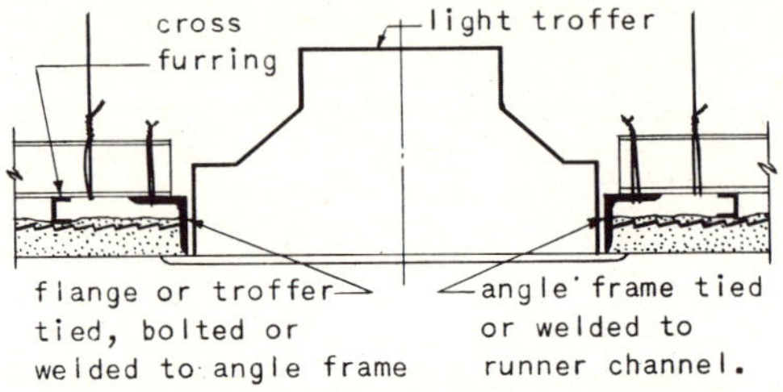
cross
furring
light troffer
flange or troffer
tied, bolted or
welded to angle frame
angle frame tied
or welded to
runner channel.

TROFFER TYPE FLUSH LIGHT

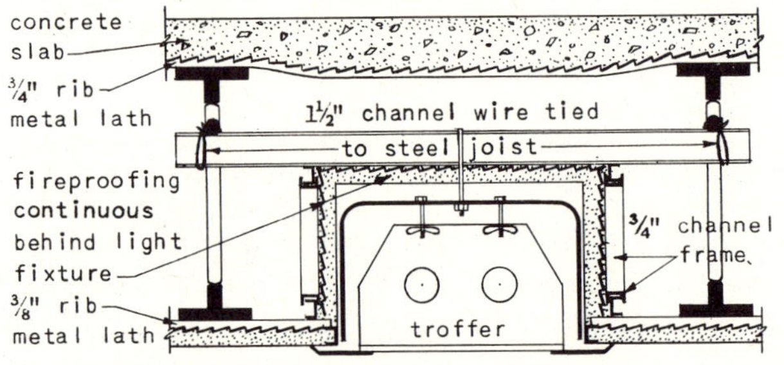
concrete
slab
3/4" rib
metal lath
1½" channel wire tied
to steel joist
fireproofing
continuous
behind light
fixture
3/8" rib
metal lath
troffer
3/4" channel
frame

TROFFER LIGHT-CEILING FIREPFOOFING UNDER STEEL JOIST FLOOR CONSTRUCTION

NOTE: Methods of attachment and types of lighting and ventilating fixtures are not limited to the details shown.
These fixtures may also be suspended from structural members or construction above with the hangers piercing the finished ceiling.

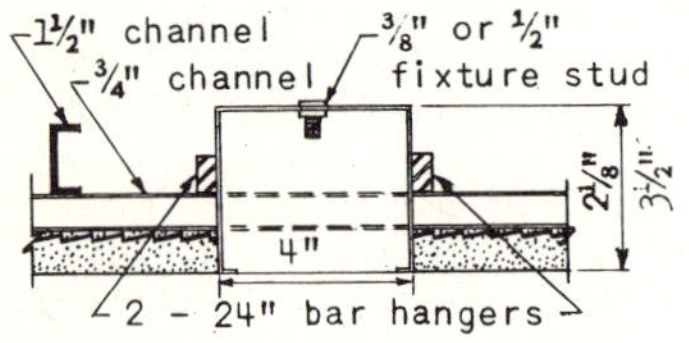
1½" channel
3/4" channel
3/8" or ½"
fixture stud
2⅛"
3½"
4"
2 - 24" bar hangers

DOUBLE-BAR OUTLET BOX HANGER

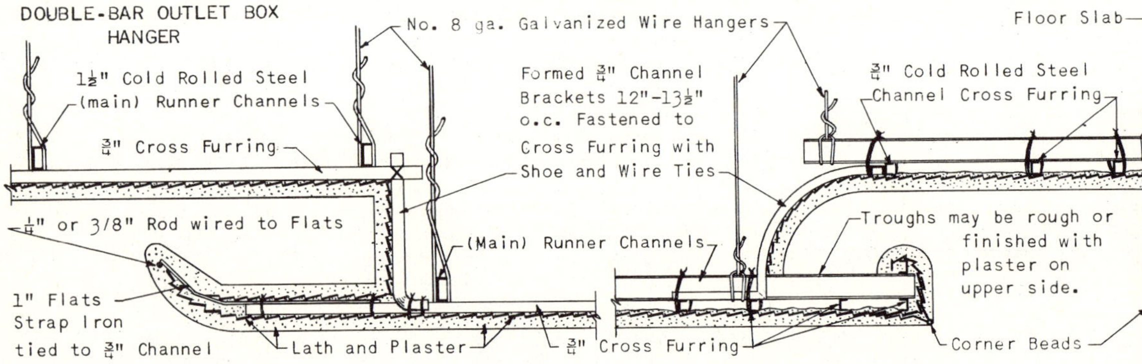
No. 8 ga. Galvanized Wire Hangers
1½" Cold Rolled Steel
(main) Runner Channels
¾" Cross Furring
Formed ¾" Channel
Brackets 12"-13½"
o.c. Fastened to
Cross Furring with
Shoe and Wire Ties
¾" Cold Rolled Steel
Channel Cross Furring
¼" or 3/8" Rod wired to Flats
(Main) Runner Channels
Troughs may be rough or
finished with
plaster on
upper side.
1" Flats
Strap Iron
tied to ¾" Channel
Lath and Plaster
¾" Cross Furring
Corner Beads

SUSPENDED CEILING LIGHT TROUGHS FOR INDIRECT LIGHTING

Scale: 1" = 1'-0"

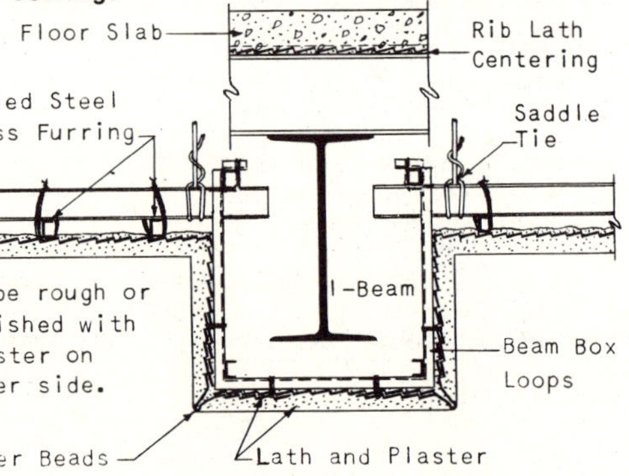
Floor Slab
Rib Lath
Centering
Saddle
Tie
I-Beam
Beam Box
Loops
Lath and Plaster

SUSPENDED CEILING BEAM

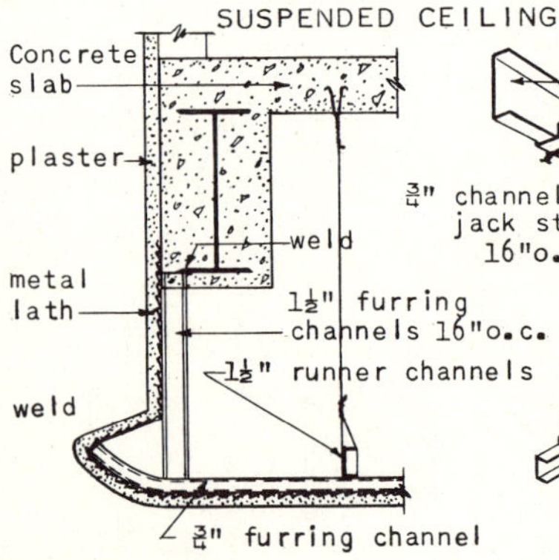
Concrete
slab
plaster
weld
metal
lath
1½" furring
channels 16"o.c.
1½" runner channels
weld
¾" furring channel

RECESSED CEILING VERTICAL FURRING DETAIL

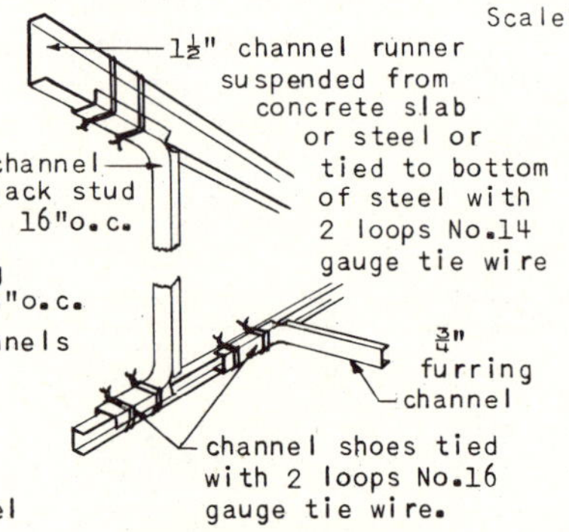
1½" channel runner
suspended from
concrete slab
or steel or
tied to bottom
of steel with
2 loops No.14
gauge tie wire
¾" channel
jack stud
16"o.c.
¾"
furring
channel
channel shoes tied
with 2 loops No.16
gauge tie wire.

SUSPENDED RECESSED CEILING FURRING DETAIL

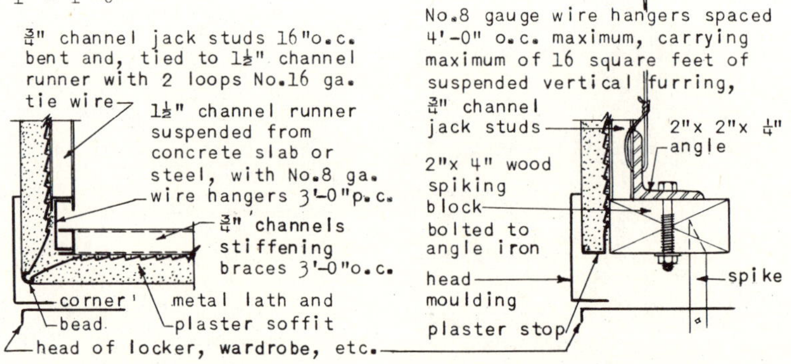
¾" channel jack studs 16"o.c.
bent and, tied to 1½" channel
runner with 2 loops No.16 ga.
tie wire
1½" channel runner
suspended from
concrete slab or
steel, with No.8 ga.
wire hangers 3'-0"o.c.
¾" channels
stiffening
braces 3'-0"o.c.
corner
bead
metal lath and
plaster soffit
head of locker, wardrobe, etc.
No.8 gauge wire hangers spaced
4'-0" o.c. maximum, carrying
maximum of 16 square feet of
suspended vertical furring,
¾" channel
jack studs
2"x 2"x ¼"
angle
2"x 4" wood
spiking
block
bolted to
angle iron
head
moulding
plaster stop
spike

SUSPENDED RECESSED CEILING FURRING ABOVE WARDROBES, CLOSETS, ETC.

RECESSED CEILING AND SOFFIT FURRING DETAILS

DATA CHECKED BY: METAL LATH MANUFACTURERS ASSOCIATION

GYPSUM LATH on WOOD STUDS and METAL FURRING

GYPSUM LATH LIMITATIONS

3/8" gypsum lath may not be used on supports over 16" o.c.
1/2" gypsum lath may not be used on supports over 24" o.c.
1/2" gypsum lath on supports over 16" o.c. requires 1/2" min. thickness (3 coats) of plaster.
Gypsum lath can be used with gypsum plasters only; bond between gypsum lath and lime or portland cement plaster is inadequate.

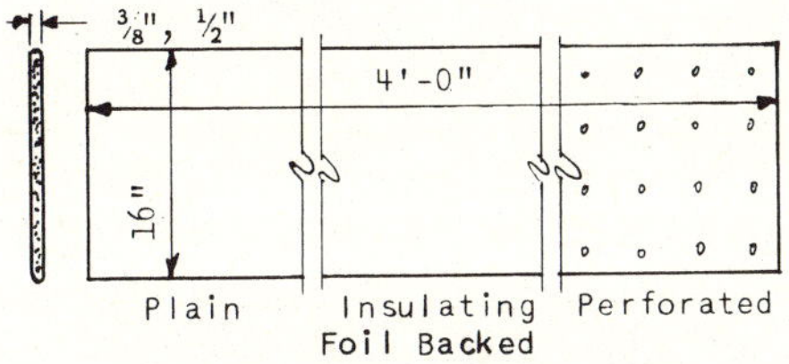

3/8", 1/2"
4'-0"
16"
Plain
Insulating Foil Backed
Perforated

Long length lath 24" wide, 12'-0" long with longitudinal v-edges, 1/2" thick, plain or insulating.

GYPSUM LATH TYPES AND SIZES

Scale: 1/2" = 1'-0"

NOTE: Gypsum lath differs from gypsum wallboard. Wallboard is used without plaster, joints being taped and spackled. Gypsum lath requires plaster finish.

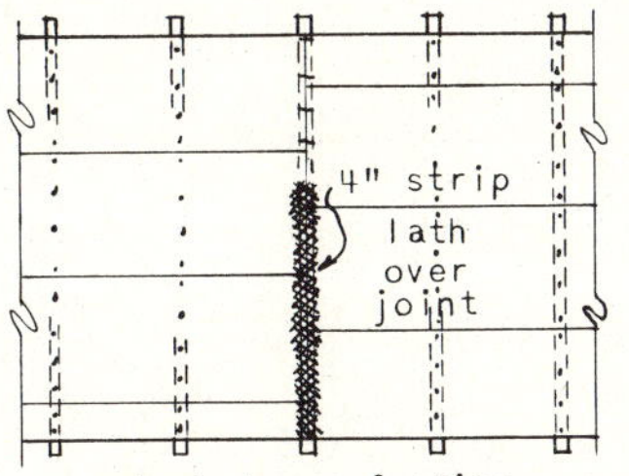

4" strip lath over joint
wood studs or furring

STAGGERED HORIZONTAL JOINTS

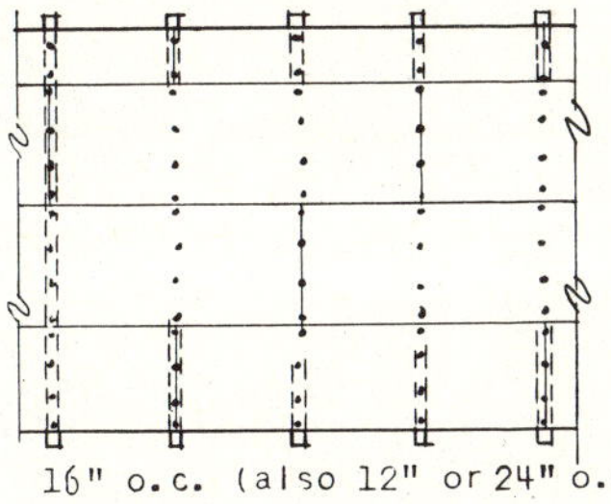

16" o.c. (also 12" or 24" o.c.)

STAGGERED VERTICAL JOINTS
SHORT EDGE OF LATH FORMING JOINTS OVER STUDS

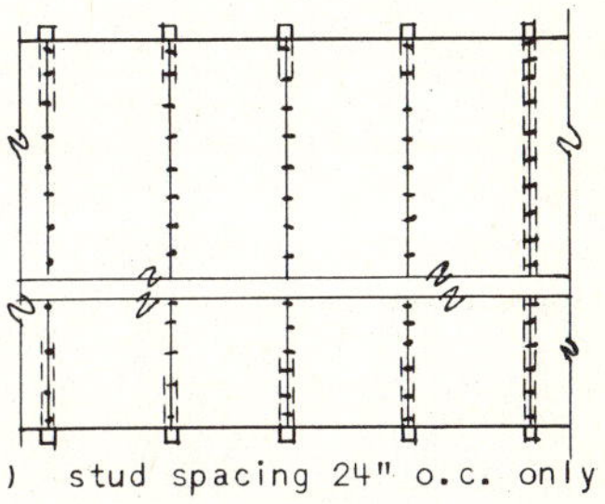

stud spacing 24" o.c. only

LONG EDGE LATH VERTICALLY
LONG EDGE OF LATH FORMING JOINTS OVER STUDS

NOTE: data given also applies to lath on ceilings below wood joists. Nails: 1 1/8" (1 1/4" for 1/2" lath), 13 ga., blued 19/16" flathead (3/8" for 1/2" lath), smooth diamond point nails, spaced 3/8" from edge of lath at approx. 5" intervals, using 4 nails per width of lath; (for 1/2" lath on studs over 16" o.c., nail spacing is 4" intervals, 5 nails per width of lath).

GYPSUM LATH NAILED TO WOOD STUDS FURRING OR CEILING JOISTS.

scale: 1/4" = 1'-0"

NOTE: strip lath reinf'g rec. over all ceiling joints

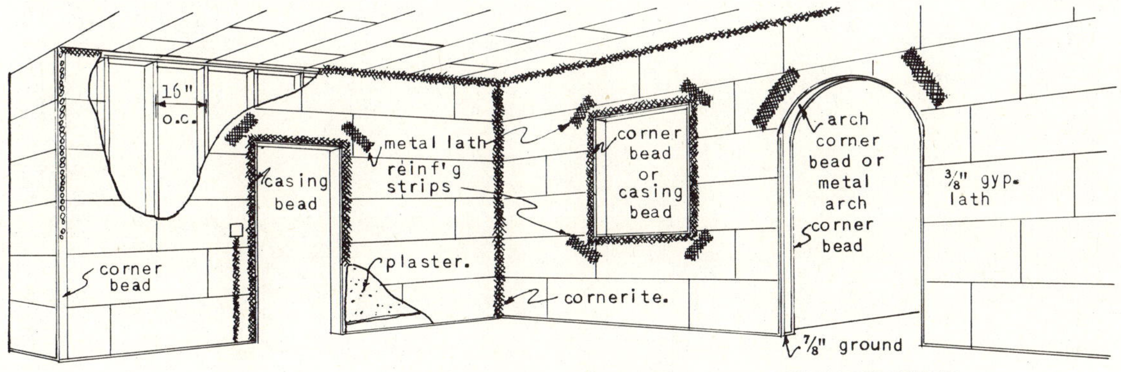

16" o.c.
metal lath reinf'g strips
casing bead
corner bead or casing bead
arch corner bead or metal arch corner bead
3/8" gyp. lath
corner bead
plaster.
cornerite.
7/8" ground

Metal lath reinforcing is required to prevent plaster cracks at corners and around openings. Expanded or perforated flange corner beads and casing beads may be used for plaster returns, corners and plaster stops.

Expanded flange arched corner bead or perforated metal arches are available for curved openings. Arched corner beads can be shaped to arch desired.

METAL LATH REINFORCING REQUIREMENTS

NOTE: applicable to all gypsum lathing

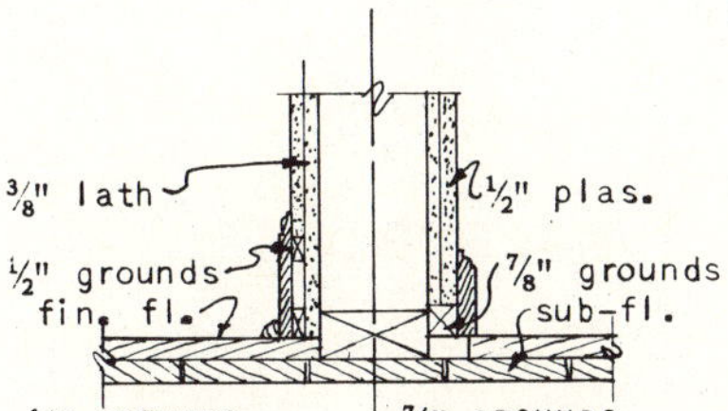

3/8" lath
1/2" plas.
1/2" grounds
fin. fl.
7/8" grounds
sub-fl.

1/2" GROUNDS OVER GYPSUM

7/8" GROUNDS OVER WOOD STUDS

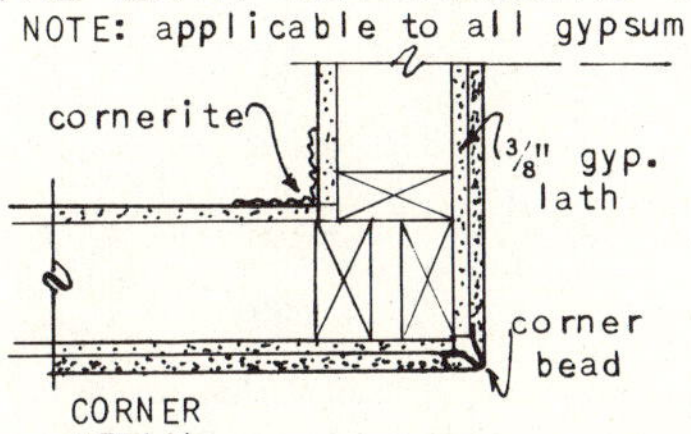

cornerite
3/8" gyp. lath
corner bead

CORNER DETAIL

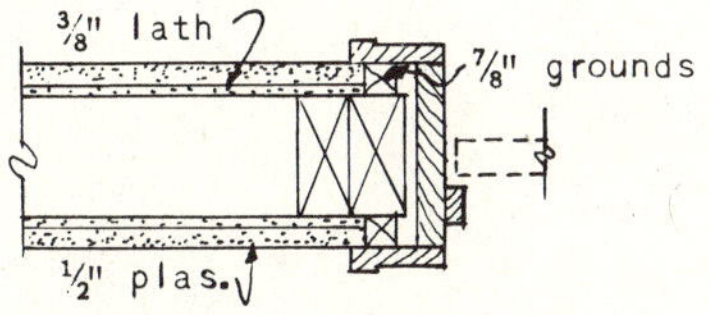

3/8" lath
7/8" grounds
1/2" plas.

WOOD DOOR BUCK DETAIL

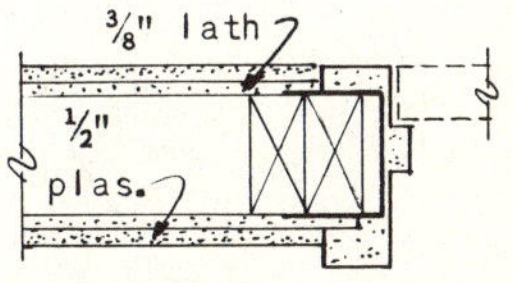

3/8" lath
1/2" plas.

METAL DOOR BUCK DETAIL

PARTITION DETAILS

scale: 1" = 1'-0"

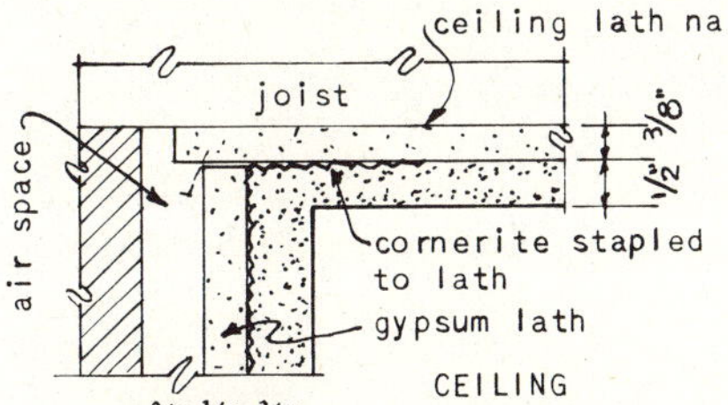

ceiling lath nailed to joist
joist
air space
1/2 3/8"
cornerite stapled to lath
gypsum lath

CEILING DETAIL

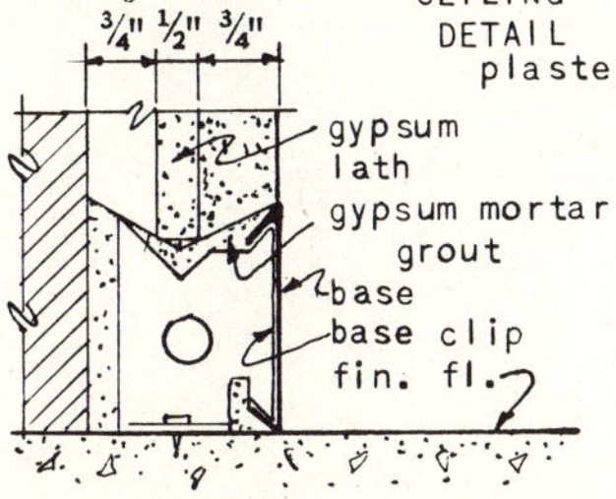

plaster
3/4" 1/2" 3/4"
gypsum lath
gypsum mortar grout
base
base clip
fin. fl.

BASE DETAIL

scale: 3" = 1'-0"

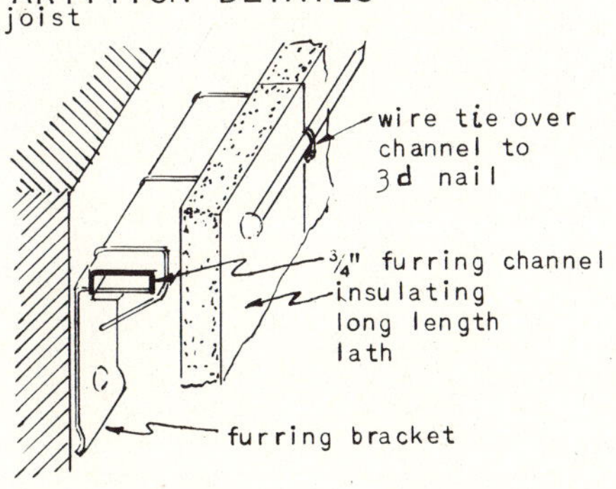

wire tie over channel to 3d nail
3/4" furring channel
insulating long length lath
furring bracket

WALL SECTION

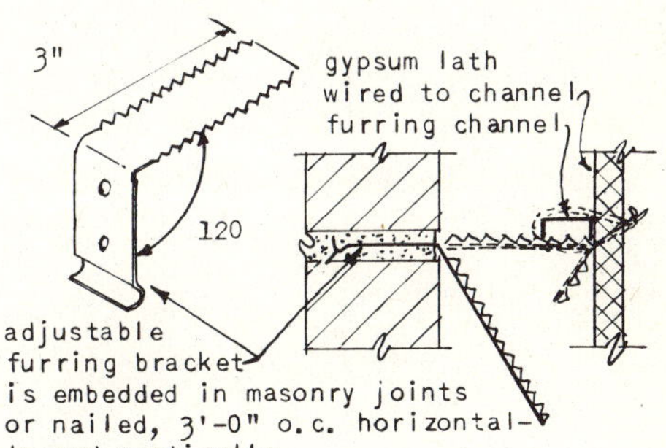

3"
gypsum lath wired to channel
furring channel
120

adjustable furring bracket is embedded in masonry joints or nailed, 3'-0" o.c. horizontally and vertically.

ADJUSTABLE WALL FURRING BRACKET

NOTE: for heavy fixture attachments install 2x4 cats between studs for solid anchoring surface.

EXTERIOR WALL FURRING

GYPSUM LATHING and PLASTERING

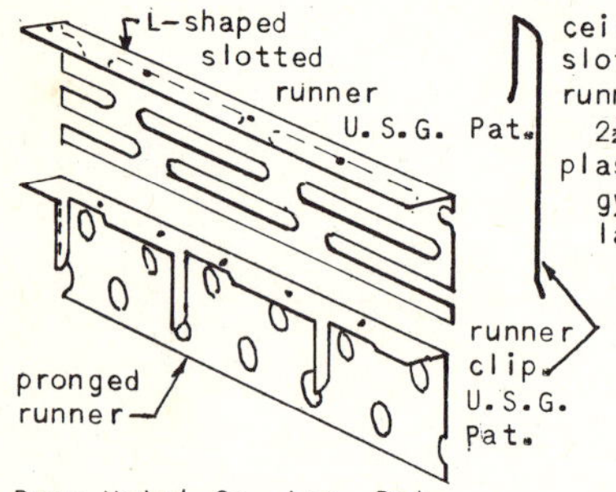
L-shaped
slotted
runner
U.S.G. Pat.
runner
clip
U.S.G.
Pat.
pronged
runner

Penn Metal Co. Inc. Pat.

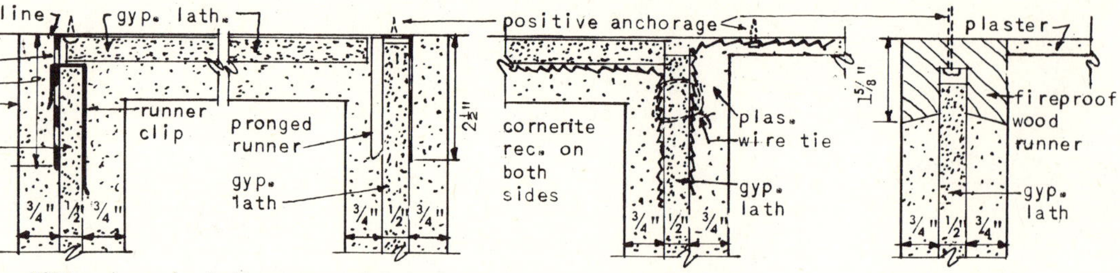
ceiling line
slotted
runner
2½"
plas.
gyp.
lath
gyp. lath
runner
clip
pronged
runner
gyp.
lath
2½"
¾" ½" ¾"
¾" ½" ¾"
positive anchorage
cornerite
rec. on
both
sides
plas.
wire tie
gyp.
lath
¾" ½" ¾"
plaster
1⅝"
fireproof
wood
runner
gyp.
lath
¾" ½" ¾"

NOTE: shown is lath on wood joists or plaster on ceiling slab.

CEILING ANCHORAGE DETAILS scale: 3" = 1" - 0"

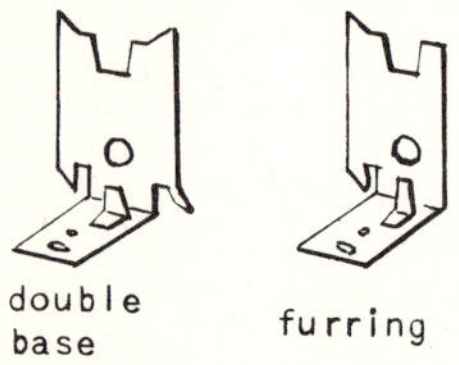
double
base
furring

BASE CLIPS

Base clips vary with manufacturers and are generally applicable only to specific metal bases and trim. Clips are designed for metal lath stud or studless partitions and studless ½" gypsum lath partitions.

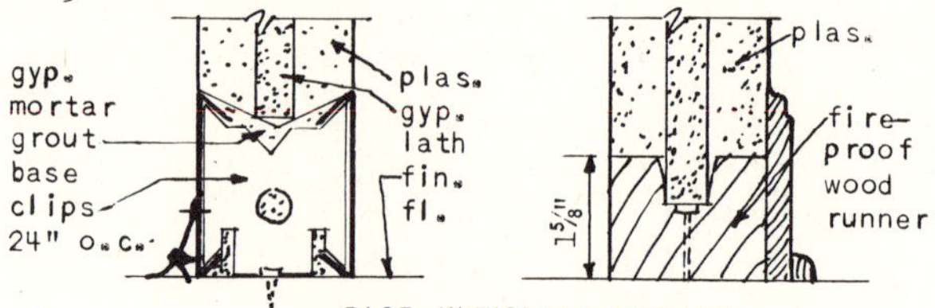
gyp.
mortar
grout
base
clips
24" o.c.
plas.
gyp.
lath
fin.
fl.
plas.
fire-
proof
wood
runner
1⅝"

BASE ANCHORAGE DETAILS

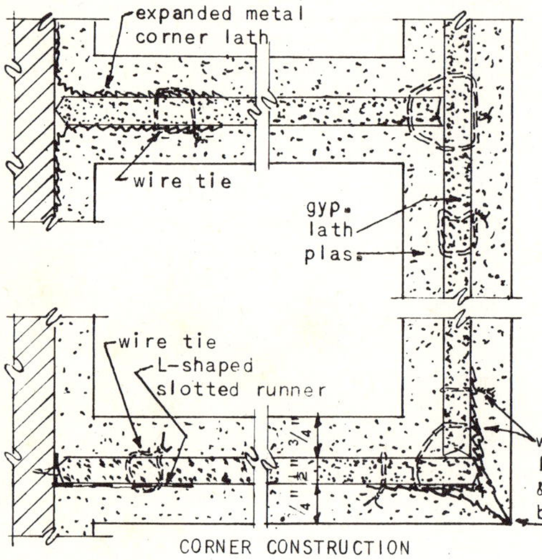
expanded metal
corner lath
wire tie
gyp.
lath
plas.
wire tie
L-shaped
slotted runner
wire tied
lath joint
& corner
bead

CORNER CONSTRUCTION

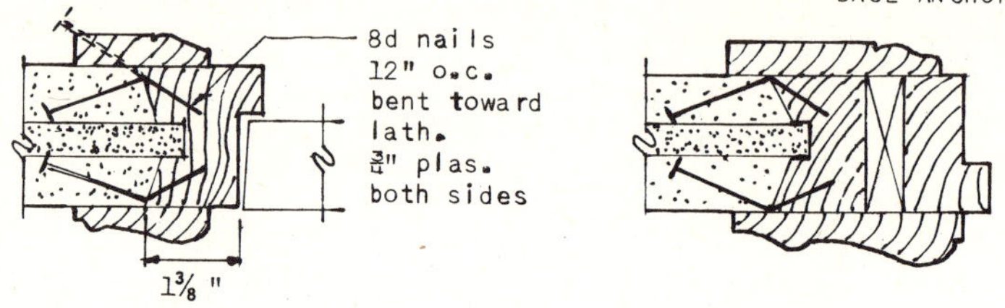
8d nails
12" o.c.
bent toward
lath.
¾" plas.
both sides
1⅜"

integral wood door buck-
may be flush, without trim, casing.

rough wood
door buck.

WOOD DOOR BUCKS

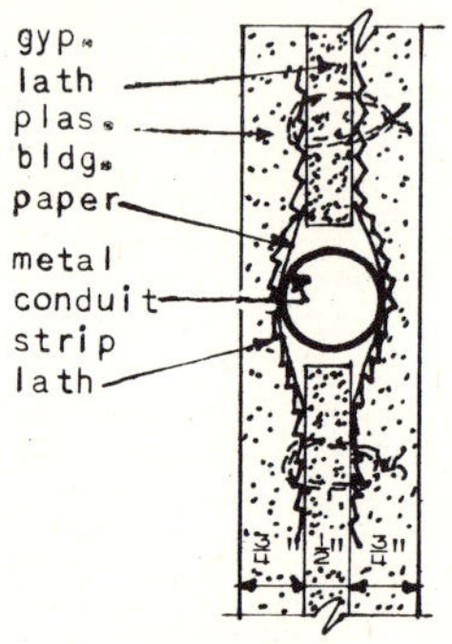
gyp.
lath
plas.
bldg.
paper
metal
conduit
strip
lath

CONDUIT OR
PIPES IN
PARTITION

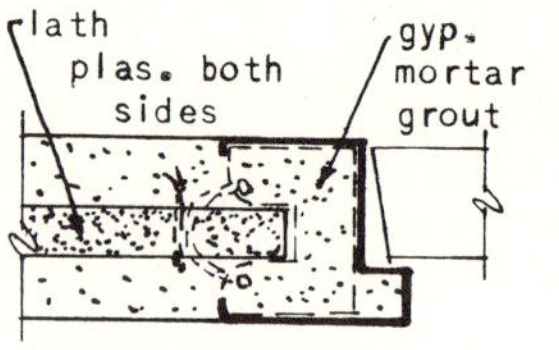
lath
plas. both
sides
gyp.
mortar
grout

METAL DOOR BUCK

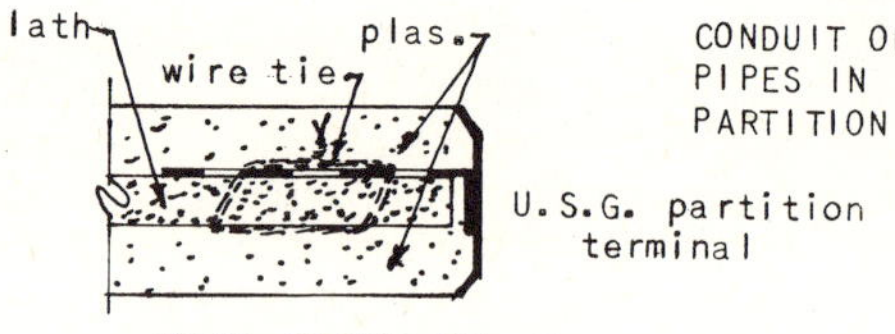
lath
wire tie
plas.
U.S.G. partition
terminal

METAL PARTITION END

scale: 3" = 1'-0"

2" SOLID GYPSUM LATH PARTITIONS

Data checked by United States Gypsum Co.

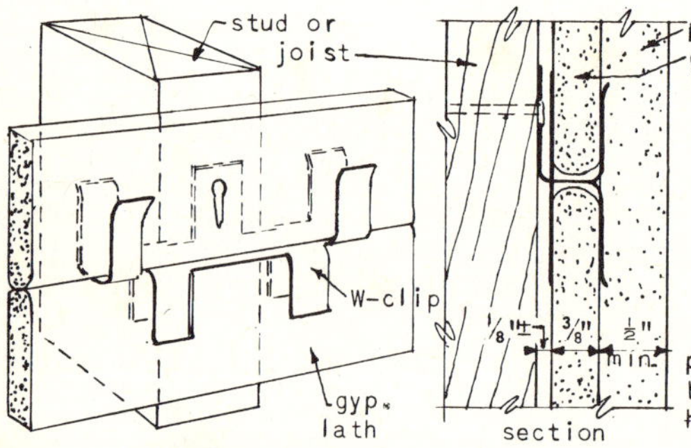
stud or
joist
W-clip
gyp.
lath
plas.
gyp.
lath
⅛" ⅜" ½"
min.
section

CEILING & WALL FIELD CLIP

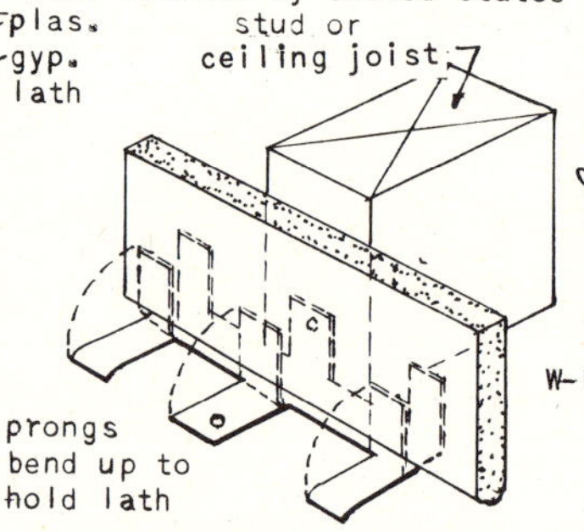
stud or
ceiling joist
prongs
bend up to
hold lath

STARTER-FINISHER CLIP

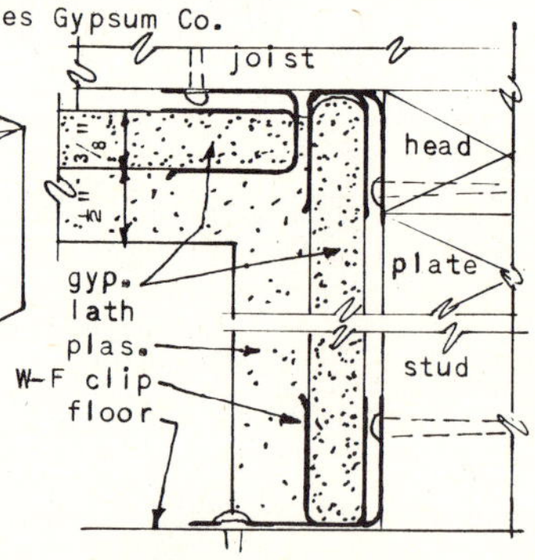
joist
head
plate
stud
gyp.
lath
plas.
W-F clip
floor

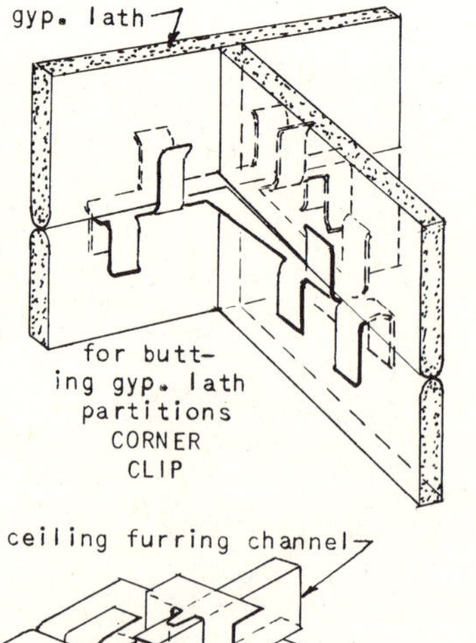
gyp. lath
for butt-
ing gyp. lath
partitions

CORNER
CLIP

SPRING CLIP LATHING SYSTEM

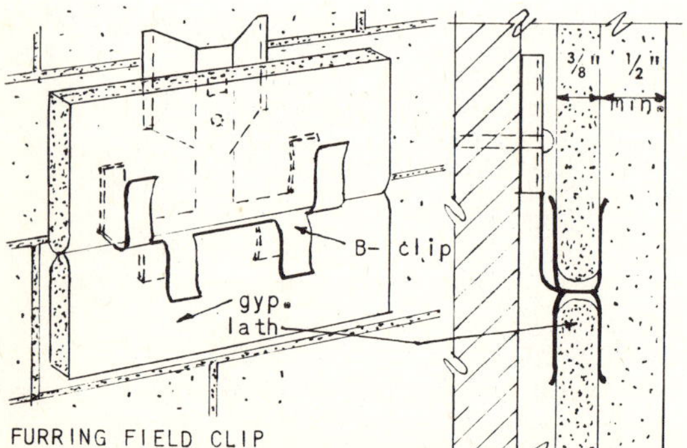
B- clip
gyp.
lath
⅜" ½"
min

FURRING FIELD CLIP

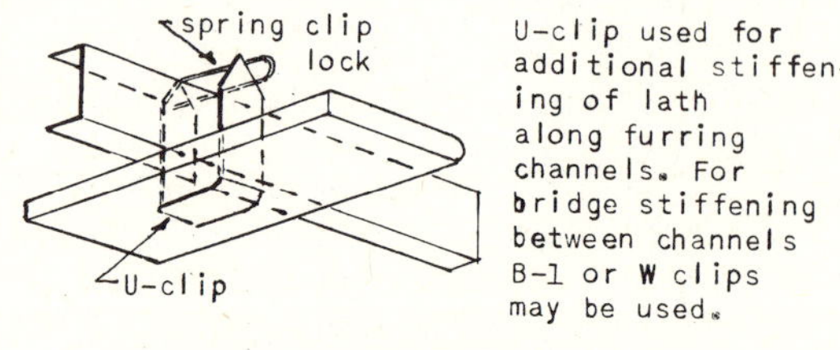
spring clip
lock
U-clip

U-clip used for additional stiffening of lath along furring channels. For bridge stiffening between channels B-1 or W clips may be used.

FURRED OR SUSPENDED CEILING
CENTER BOARD CLIP

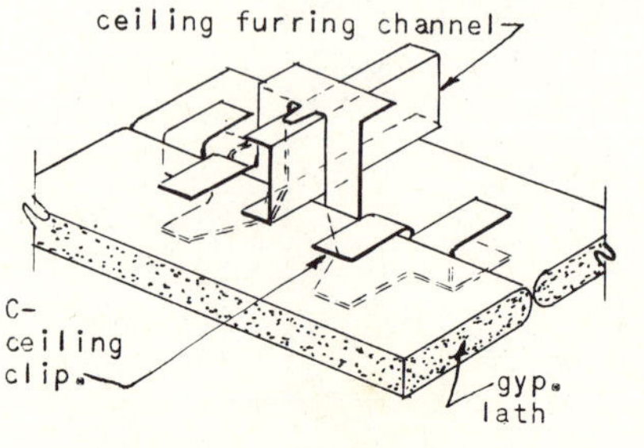
ceiling furring channel
C-
ceiling
clip.
gyp.
lath

FURRED OR SUSPENDED CEILING
- - CHANNEL FIELD CLIP

SPRING FURRING CLIPS

scale: ½ full size

Data checked by Burson Clip System, Inc.

GYPSUM LATH-RESILIENT CLIP SYSTEMS

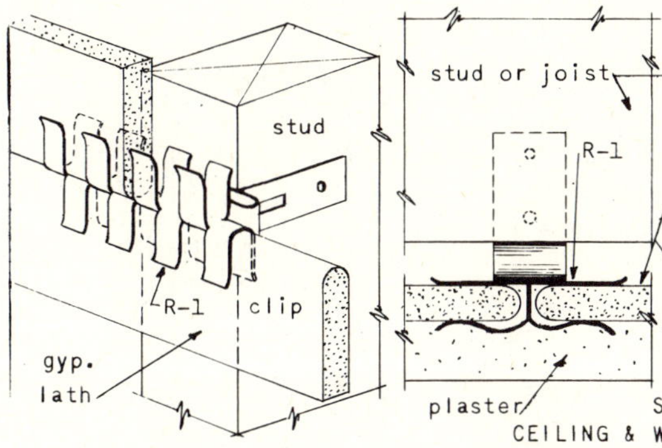
stud
R-1 clip
gyp.
lath
stud or joist
R-1
clip
gyp.
lath
3/8"
1/2"
plaster
Section
plaster

CEILING & WALL FIELD CLIP

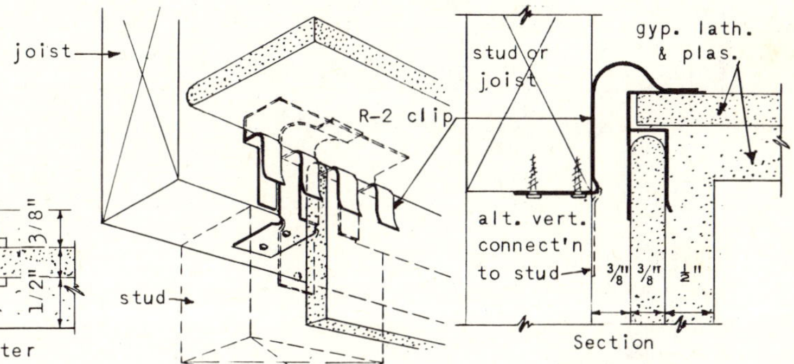
joist
R-2 clip
stud
stud or
joist
gyp. lath.
& plas.
alt. vert.
connect'n
to stud
3/8" 3/8" 1/2"
Section

CORNER CLIP

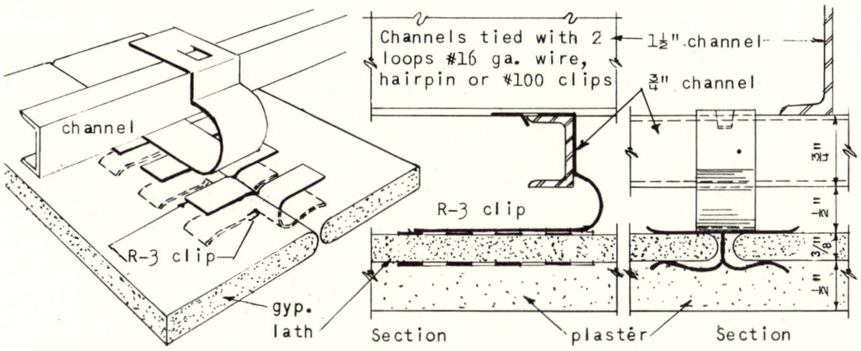
channel
R-3 clip
gyp.
lath
Channels tied with 2
loops #16 ga. wire,
hairpin or #100 clips
1½" channel
¾" channel
R-3 clip
Section
plaster
Section

CEILING CHANNEL FIELD CLIP

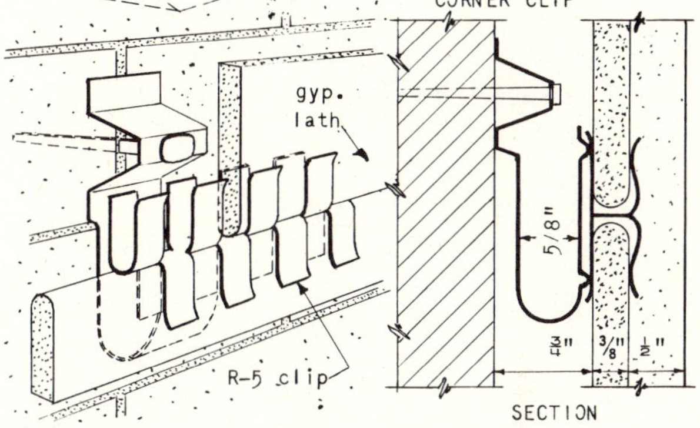
gyp.
lath
R-5 clip
5/8"
¾" 3/8" ½"
SECTION

FURRING FIELD CLIP

R-5 clip spaced 16" o.c. horizontally and vertically, attached with 10d cut steel nails, drive or toggle bolt, or other positive anchorage shown on wall furring page. See "Metal Lath Partitions and Ceilings" for hairpin and other clips.

RESILIENT SPRING CLIPS

scale: ½ full size.

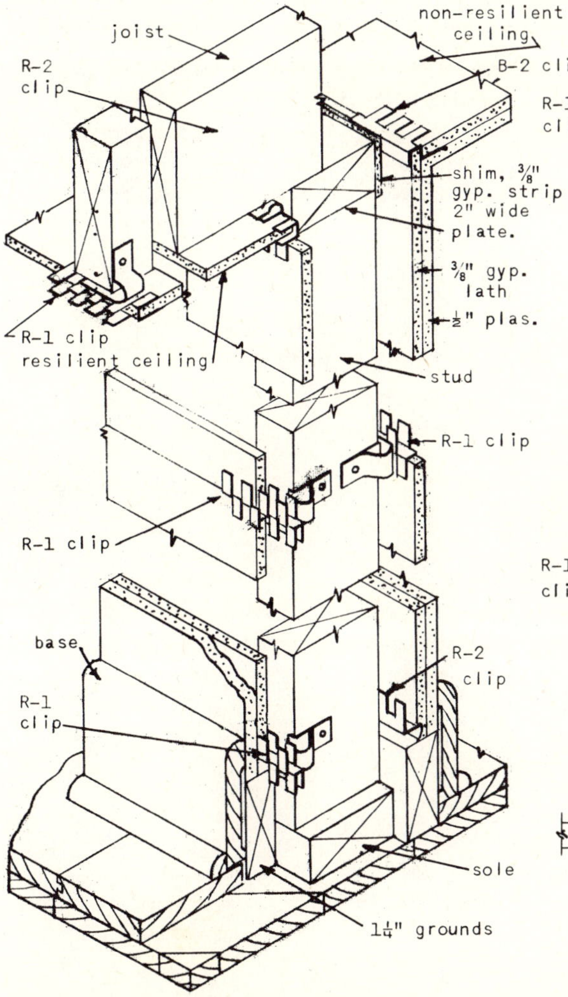
joist
R-2
clip
non-resilient
ceiling
B-2 clip
R-1
clip
shim, 3/8"
gyp. strip
2" wide
plate.
3/8" gyp.
lath
½" plas.
R-1 clip
resilient ceiling
stud
R-1 clip
R-1 clip
base
R-1
clip
R-2
clip
sole
1¼" grounds

RESILIENT LATHING SYSTEM

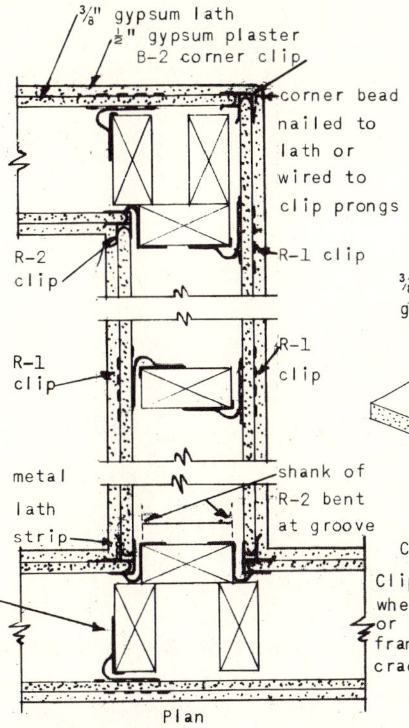
3/8" gypsum lath
½" gypsum plaster
B-2 corner clip
corner bead
nailed to
lath or
wired to
clip prongs
R-2
clip
R-1 clip
R-1
clip
R-1
clip
metal
lath
strip
shank of
R-2 bent
at groove
R-1
clip
Plan

CORNER CONSTRUCTION OF RESILIENT LATHING SYSTEM

scale: 1½" = 1'-0"

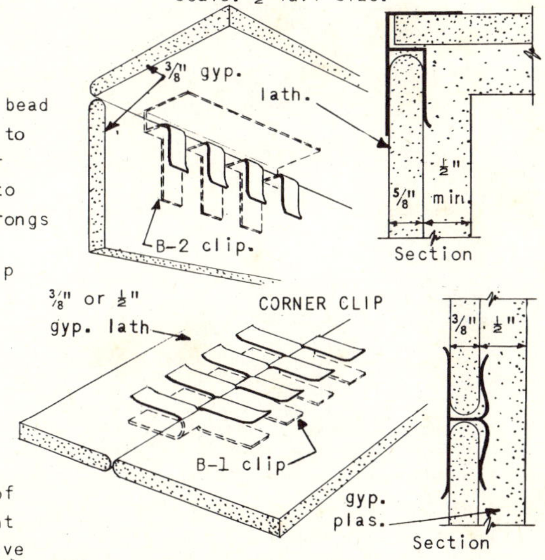
3/8" gyp.
lath.
B-2 clip.
½"
5/8" min.
Section
CORNER CLIP
3/8" or ½"
gyp. lath
B-1 clip
gyp.
plas.
3/8" ½"
Section

CEILING & WALL FIELD CLIP

Clips provide rigid alignment of gypsum lath where ends are not over studs, ceiling joists or structural members. Joints occur between framing members to resist edge and joint cracking.

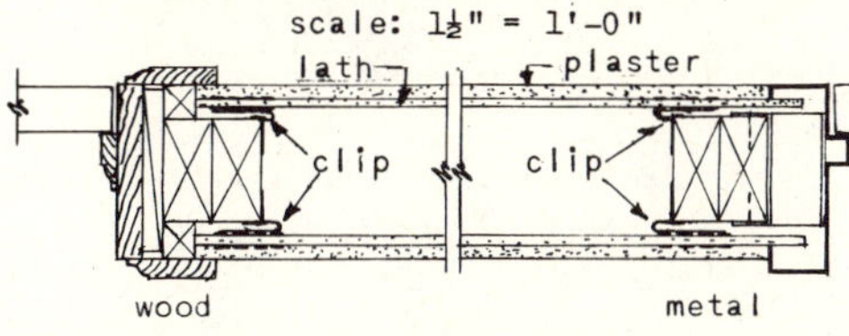
lath
plaster
clip
clip
wood
metal

DOOR BUCK DETAIL

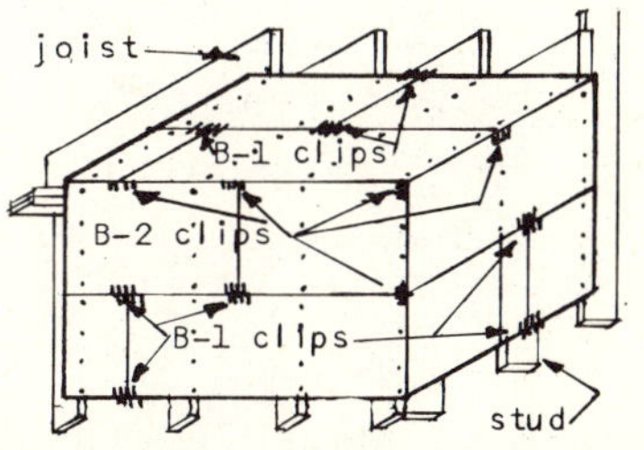
joist
B-1 clips
B-2 clips
B-1 clips
stud

BRIDGE JOINT LATHING SYSTEM ON WOOD FRAME CONSTRUCTION – SPRING BRIDGE CLIPS

Data checked by: United States Gypsum Co.

GYPSUM LATH on METAL STUD PARTITIONS

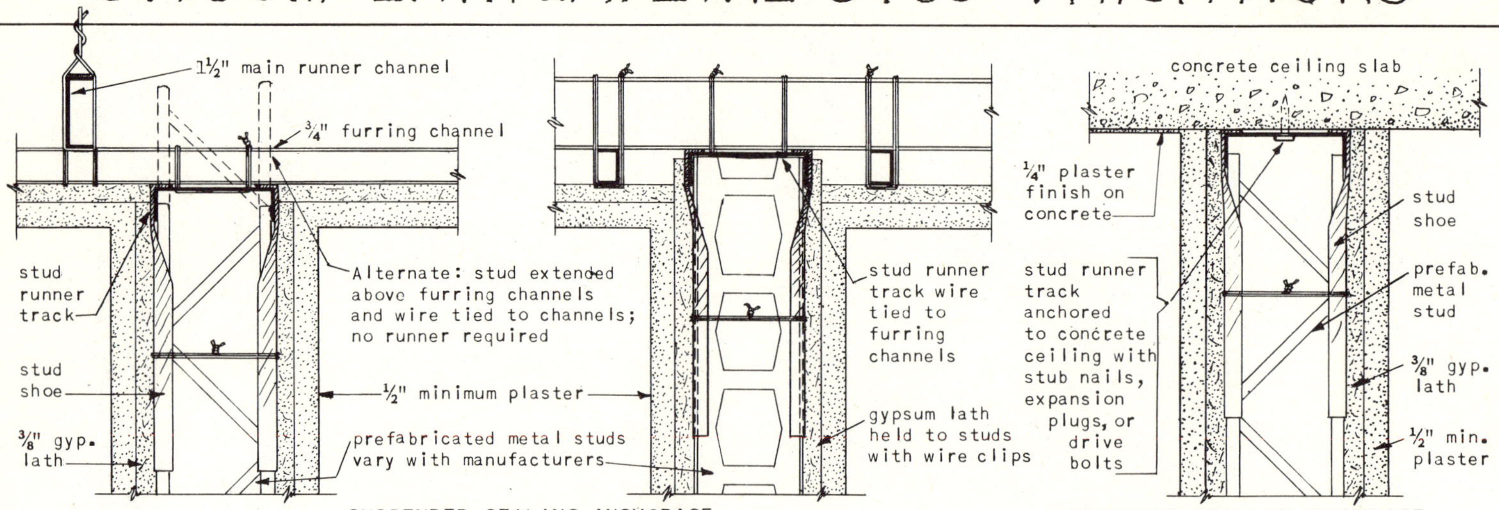
1½" main runner channel
¾" furring channel
stud runner track
Alternate: stud extended above furring channels and wire tied to channels; no runner required
stud shoe
½" minimum plaster
⅜" gyp. lath
prefabricated metal studs vary with manufacturers
stud runner track wire tied to furring channels
gypsum lath held to studs with wire clips
concrete ceiling slab
¼" plaster finish on concrete
stud runner track anchored to concrete ceiling with stub nails, expansion plugs, or drive bolts
stud shoe
prefab. metal stud
⅜" gyp. lath
½" min. plaster

SUSPENDED CEILING ANCHORAGE

CONCRETE CEILING ANCHORAGE

PARTITION - CEILING ANCHORAGE DETAILS

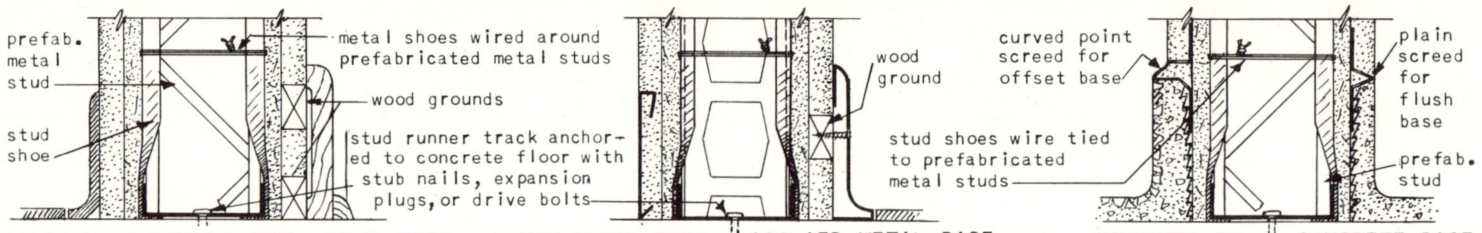
prefab. metal stud
metal shoes wired around prefabricated metal studs
wood grounds
stud shoe
stud runner track anchored to concrete floor with stub nails, expansion plugs, or drive bolts
wood ground
curved point screed for offset base
stud shoes wire tied to prefabricated metal studs
plain screed for flush base
prefab. stud

ASPHALT OR RUBBER BASE WOOD BASE FLUSH METAL BASE APPLIED METAL BASE TERRAZZO OR CONCRETE BASE

SECTIONS OF BASES AND ANCHORAGE DETAILS

Scale: 3"=1'-0"

PREFABRICATED STUD PARTITIONS		
STUD WIDTH	PARTITION THICKNESS	MAXIMUM HEIGHTS STUD SPACING 16" O.C.
2½"	4½"	14 feet
3¼"	5¼"	16 feet
4"	6"	18 feet
6"	8"	20 feet

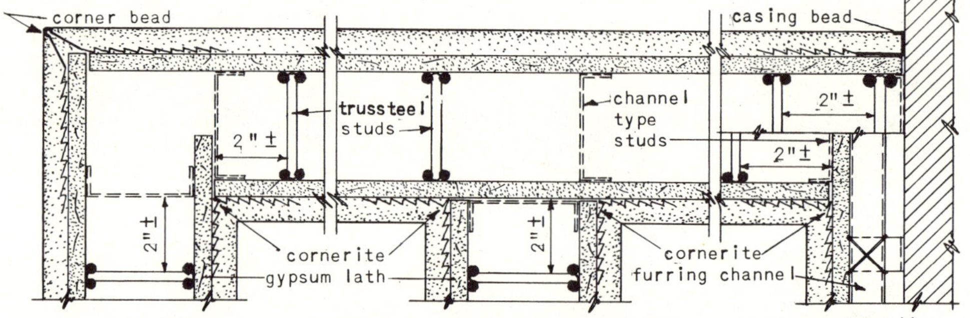
corner bead
casing bead
trussteel studs
channel type studs
2" ±
2" ±
2" ±
2" ±
2" ±
cornerite
gypsum lath
cornerite
furring channel
masonry wall

Scale: 3"=1'-0"

PLAN OF CORNER DETAILS

NOTE: Prefabricated channel type studs, shown dotted, located differently than trussteel studs shown solid.

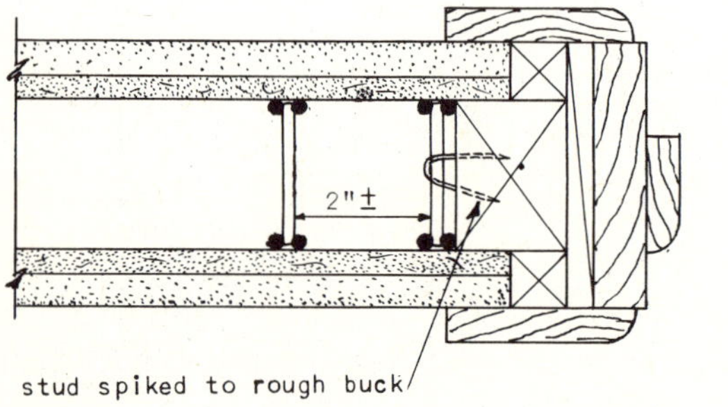
2" ±
stud spiked to rough buck

WOOD DOOR BUCK AND TRIM

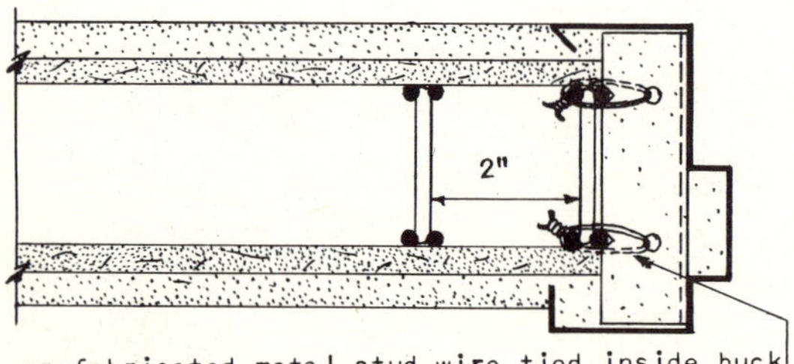
2"

prefabricated metal stud wire tied inside buck to metal strap anchors welded to buck; door buck grouted solid

METAL DOOR BUCK

DOOR BUCK DETAILS

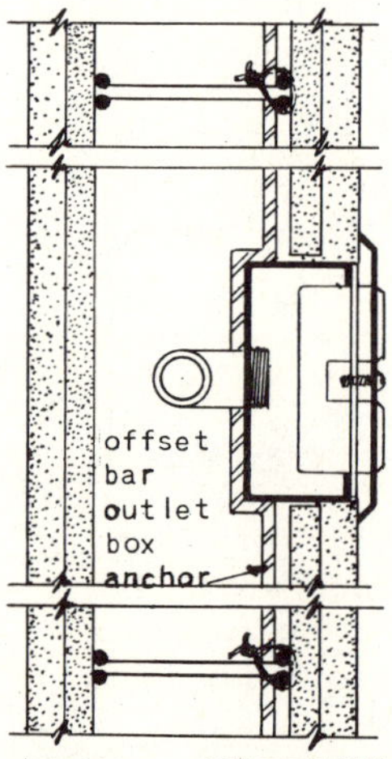
offset bar outlet box anchor

PLAN - SECTION THRU ELECTRICAL OUTLET BOX

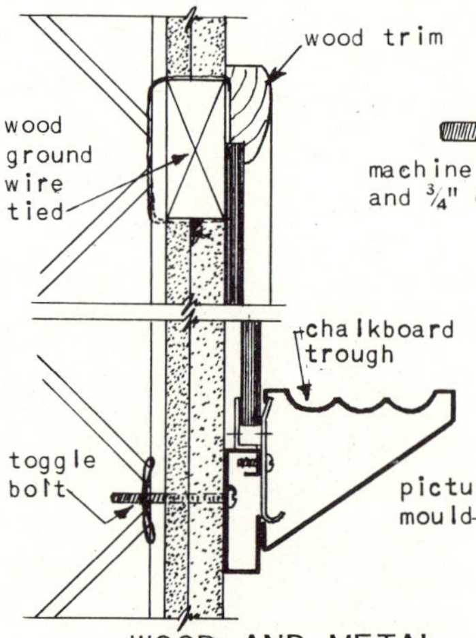
wood trim
wood ground wire tied
chalkboard trough
toggle bolt
picture mould

WOOD AND METAL TRIM ANCHORAGE

Scale: 3"=1'-0"

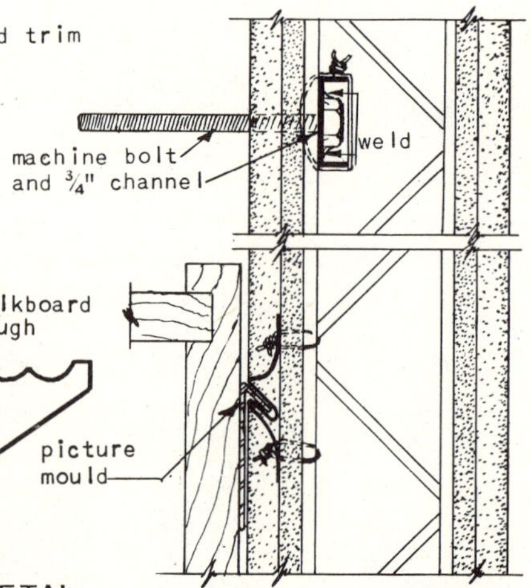
weld
machine bolt and ¾" channel

SHELF CABINET AND FIXTURE ANCHORAGE

PREFABRICATED METAL STUD - GYPSUM LATH PARTITIONS

DATA CHECKED BY UNITED STATES GYPSUM COMPANY

INTERIOR FINISHES

TABLE OF CONTENTS

CERAMIC MOSAIC, PAVERS and QUARRY TILE-TRIMMERS

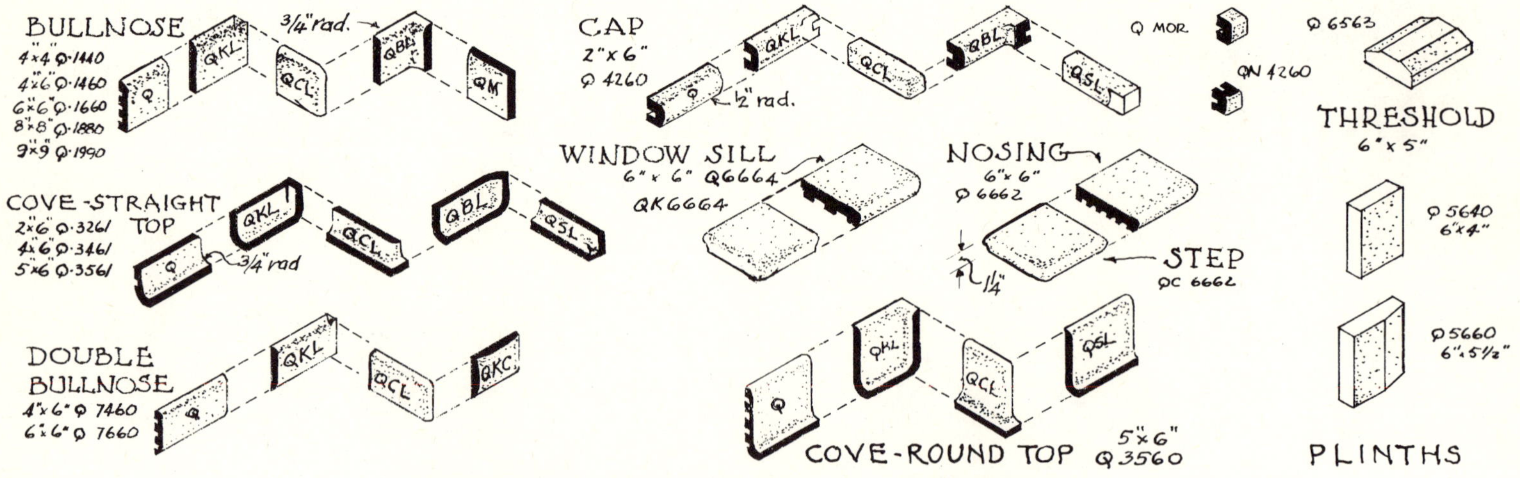
BULLNOSE
4"x4" Q·1440
4"x6" Q·1460
6"x6" Q·1660
8"x8" Q·1880
9"x9" Q·1990
3/4" rad.
CAP
2"x6"
Q 4260
1/2" rad.
Q MOR.
Q 6563
QN 4260
THRESHOLD
6"x5"
COVE-STRAIGHT TOP
2"x6" Q·3261
4"x6" Q·3461
5"x6" Q·3561
3/4" rad
WINDOW SILL
6"x6" Q6664
QK6664
NOSING
6"x6"
Q 6662
STEP
QC 6662
1/4"
Q 5640
6"x4"
DOUBLE BULLNOSE
4"x6" Q 7460
6"x6" Q 7660
Q 5660
6"x5 1/2"
COVE-ROUND TOP
5"x6"
Q 3560
PLINTHS

QUARRY TILE TRIM SHAPES

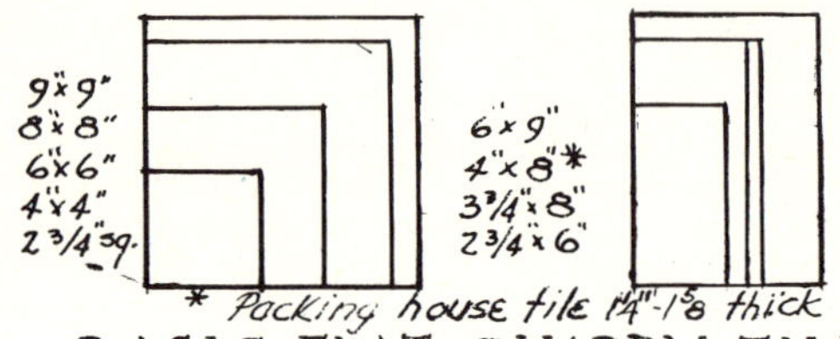
9"x9"
8"x8"
6"x6"
4"x4"
2 3/4" sq.
6"x9"
4"x8"*
3 3/4"x8"
2 3/4"x6"
* Packing house tile 1 1/4"-1 3/8" thick

BASIC FLAT QUARRY TILE

PAVER trimmers are available to meet all needs but have not yet been standardized. For information on available trim shapes, consult the manufacturer.

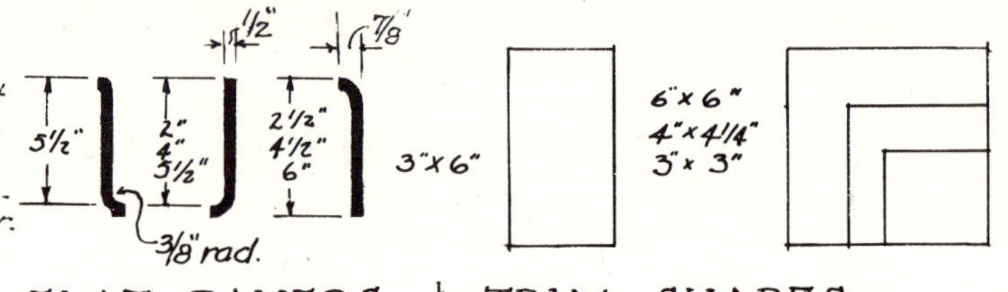
1/2"
7/8"
5 1/2"
2"
4"
5 1/2"
2 1/2"
4 1/2"
6"
3"x6"
3/8" rad.
6"x6"
4"x4 1/4"
3"x3"

BASIC FLAT PAVERS & TRIM SHAPES

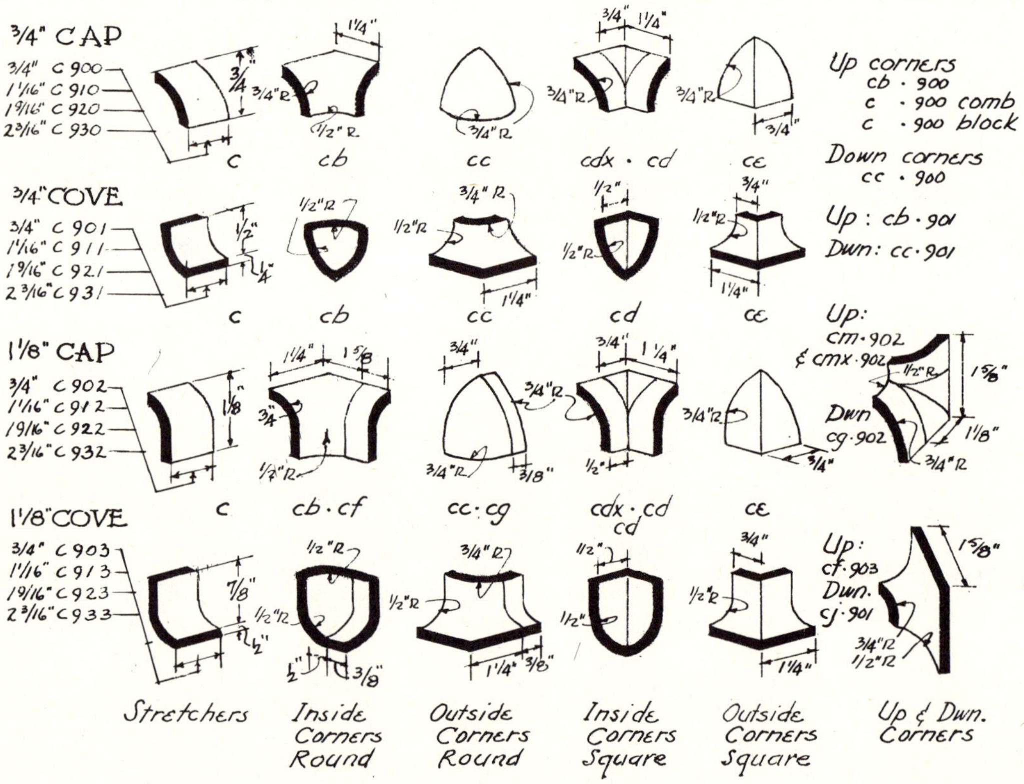
3/4" CAP
3/4" C 900
1 1/16" C 910
1 9/16" C 920
2 3/16" C 930
c cb cc cdx · cd ce
Up corners
cb · 900
c · 900 comb
c · 900 block
Down corners
cc · 900
3/4" COVE
3/4" C 901
1 1/16" C 911
1 9/16" C 921
2 3/16" C 931
c cb cc cd ce
Up : cb · 901
Dwn: cc · 901
1 1/8" CAP
3/4" C 902
1 1/16" C 912
1 9/16" C 922
2 3/16" C 932
c cb · cf cc · cg cdx · cd ce
Up:
cm · 902
& cmx · 902
Dwn
cg · 902
1 1/8" COVE
3/4" C 903
1 1/16" C 913
1 9/16" C 923
2 3/16" C 933
Up:
cf · 903
Dwn.
cj · 901
Stretchers
Inside Corners Round
Outside Corners Round
Inside Corners Square
Outside Corners Square
Up & Dwn. Corners

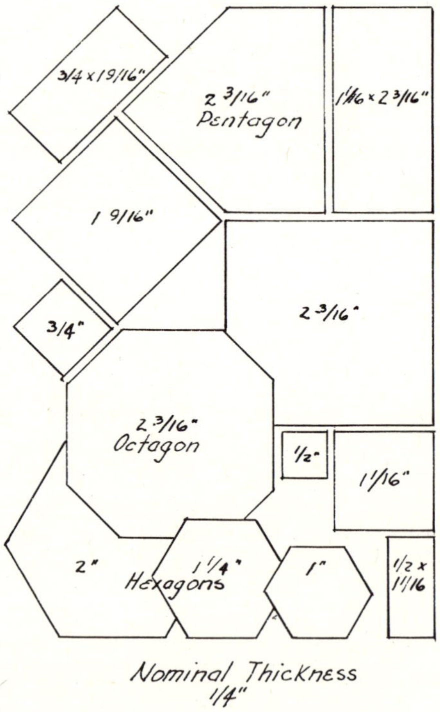
3/4 x 1 9/16"
2 3/16" Pentagon
1 1/16 x 2 3/16"
1 9/16"
3/4"
2 3/16"
2 3/16" Octagon
1/2"
1 1/16"
2"
1 1/4" Hexagons
1"
1/2 x 1 1/16
Nominal Thickness 1/4"

CERAMIC MOSAIC TRIM SHAPES
Nominal thickness 1/4"

CERAMIC MOSAIC SIZES
(Unglazed or glazed)

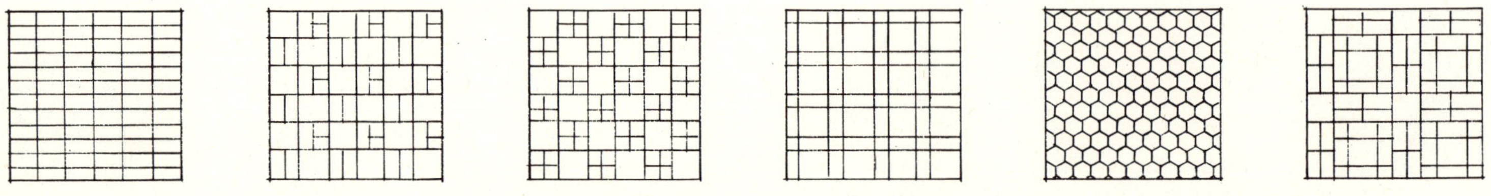

CERAMIC MOSAIC · STANDARDIZED SHEET UNITS, WHICH ARE APPROXIMATELY 1'×2'
Numerous other patterns are available

GLAZED INTERIOR TILE and TRIMMERS

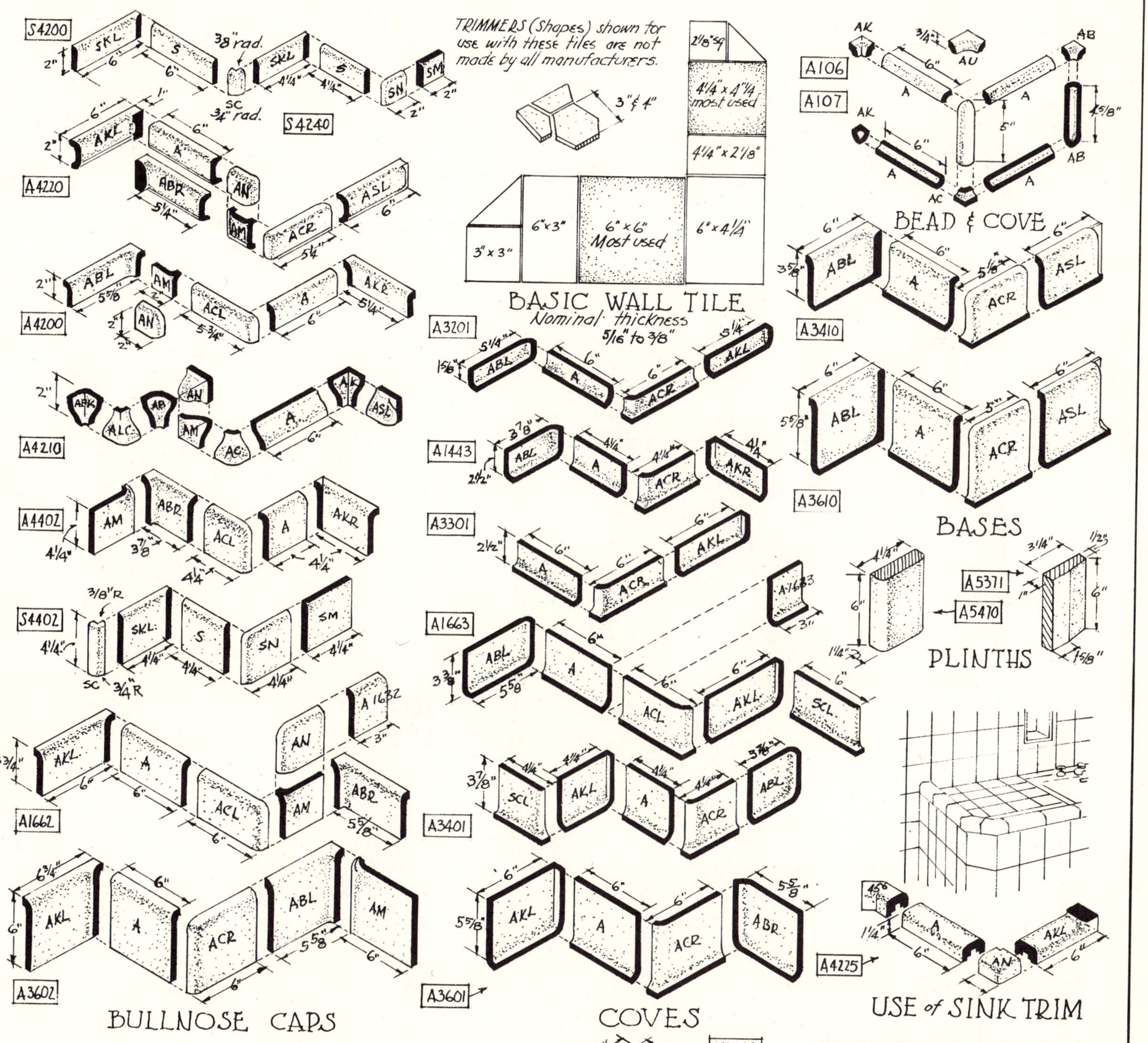
S4200
S4240
A4220
A4200
A4210
A4402
S4402
A1662
A3602
BULLNOSE CAPS
TRIMMERS (Shapes) shown for use with these tiles are not made by all manufacturers.
6" x 6" Most used
6" x 3"
3" x 3"
6" x 4 1/4"
4 1/4" x 4 1/4" most used
4 1/4" x 2 1/8"
BASIC WALL TILE
Nominal thickness 5/16" to 3/8"
A3201
A1443
A3301
A1663
A3401
A3601
COVES
A106
A107
BEAD & COVE
A3410
A3610
BASES
A5371
A5410
PLINTHS
A4225
USE of SINK TRIM

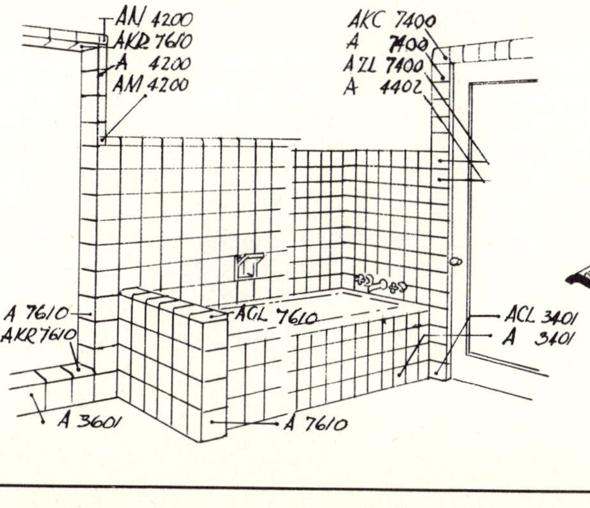
AN 4200
AKR 7610
A 4200
AM 4200
AKC 7400
A 7400
AZL 7400
A 4402
A 7610
AKR 7610
ACL 7610
ACL 3401
A 3401
A 3601
A 7610

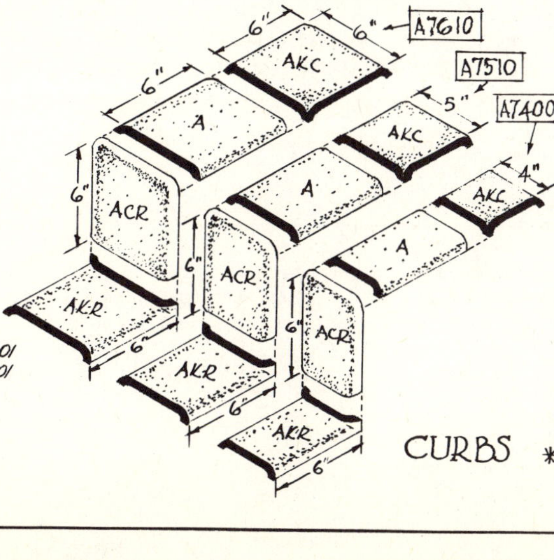
A7610
A7510
A7400
AKC
A
ACR
AKR
CURBS

PREFIX LETTERS for IDENTIFICATION

A · Standard as adopted by U.S. Simplified Practice - R. 61-44
B · 3/8" Radius, Concave
C · 3/4" Convex
K · Square Concave
L* "Left hand," also "Convex angle corner" (bottom round- top square)
M · Up angle
N · Down angle
R* Right angle
S · "Surface type" - use for adhesive installation; also, "Stop".
Z · "3 Way junction angle", Stnrd. radii: Convex 3/4", Concave 3/8".

Reversible units are listed as "ACL, "ACR"
Lone prefix "A", "S" refers to stretcher.
All companies do not manufact. all trim.
* If angle is on right side of unit, it is termed a "Left angle" & conversely.

GLAZED TILE - TYPES and SIZES

GLAZE TILE														
TYPE OF TILE	DESCRIPTION OF TILE – OUTER FINISH OR SKIN – GLAZED (IMPERVIOUS FINISH): BRIGHT	SEMI-MATTE	MATTE	CRYS-TALLINE	BODY OF TILE: IMPERVIOUS	VITREOUS	SEMI-VITREOUS	NON-VITREOUS	EDGE: CUSHION	SQUARE	SPACING: REGULAR	SELF-SPACING	BASIC SHAPE & NOMINAL SIZE – SIZE	THICK-NESS
GLAZED INTERIOR TILE	Is available in any of the four types of glazes.				Not Available	Not Available	Available	Body of tile is generally Non-Vitreous	All four glazes are available in either cushion or square edges		All four glazes are available in either regular or self-spacing edge surface		Hexigon 3 Hexigon 4 Half of Hexigons 3 and 4 6 x 9 6 x 12	Minor thickness 1/4" to 11/32" depending upon Mfg. Average 5/16" 6 x 9 & 6 x 12 tiles 1/2"
EXTRA DUTY – Subject to wear	Not Available	Not Available	Only if Certified by Mfg.	Can be Certified									2 1/8 x 2 1/8 Triangular half 2 1/8 x 2 1/8 2 1/8 x 2 1/4 4 1/4 x 4 1/4 Triangular half 4 1/4 x 4 1/4 4 1/4 x 6 3 x 3 Triangular half 3 x 3 3 x 6 6 x 6 Triangular half 6 x 6	
EXTRA DUTY – Subject to Freezing	Available	Available	Available	Available	Available	Available if Certified	Not Available	Not Available						
CERAMIC MOSAIC	Is available in any of the four types of glazes				Available	Available	Not Available	Not Available			Available	Not Available	1 9/16 x 1 9/16 Triangular half 1 9/16 1 9/16 x 47/64 47/64 x 47/64 Triangular half 47/64 47/64 x 25/64 25/64 x 25/64 2 x 2 Triangular half of 2 2 x 1 1 x 1 Triangular half of 1 1 x 1/2 1/2 x 1/2 1 15/16 x 1 15/16 Triangular half 1 15/16 1 15/16 x 31/32 31/32 x 31/32 Triangular half 31/32 31/32 x 31/64 31/64 x 31/64 2 3/16 x 2 3/16 Triangular half 2 3/16 2 3/16 x 1 3/32 1 3/32 x 1 3/32 Triangular half 1 3/32 1 3/32 x 35/64 35/64 x 35/64 Hexagonal 1 Hexagonal 1 1/4 Hexagonal 2 Halfs of Hexagons 1, 1 1/4, 2 3/4 x 3/4	1/4"
FAIENCE (HANDMADE)	Will make as desired special sizes, shapes, patterns colors etc. Consult manufacturer for further information													
FAIENCE MOSAIC (HANDMADE)														
SPECIAL PURPOSES	A tile made to correspond to any specific design qualifications desired, such as size, thickness, shape, color, or decoration, keys or lugs on back, edges, unique resistance to absorption, alkali, acid, thermal shock, physical impact or high co-efficient of friction or electrical properties.													

GLAZED TILE and its USAGE

GLAZED TILE			
RECOMMENDED JOINT SIZES	TRIMMERS	USAGE: GENERAL APPLICATION	USAGE: TYPICAL INSTALLATION
When Joint Width is not Determined by the Self-Spacing Lugs. Specify Your desired thickness From 1/16" to 1/4"		**GLAZED TILE** Have an impervious surface which will not absorb stains or change color. Used where an impervious non-staining, non-fading surface is desired. A good commercial water-proofing grout should be used for the tile joints, According to the manufacturers directions to eliminate staining of the body thru the joints.	Suitable for all uses except surfaces subject to abrasion, freezing, or excessive changes in temperature impact. Typical surfaces occur in: bathrooms, showers, operating rooms, corridors, lunch rooms, locker rooms, washrooms, closets, and powder rooms.
Generally Paper Mounted 1/16" Average Not Mounted Specify Your desired thickness 1/16" to 1/8"	See pages on Tile and Trimmers	BRIGHT TILES: Suitable for walls and ceilings, never used on floors. SEMI-MATTE: Suitable for walls, & ceilings; never used on floors. MATTE: Suitable for walls, ceiling & sometimes countertops and residential floors which are subject to a very minimum of wear. CRYSTALLINE: Suitable for walls and ceilings and residential floors and counter tops. Subject to light wear but never on a commercial floor. **BODY OF TILE:** Water absorption resistance to freezing and thawing. IMPERVIOUS: Can be used anywhere. VITREOUS: With a glazed tile, warrantee whould be obtained against freezing & thawing. SEMI-VITREOUS: Should always ask for warrantee by the manufacturers against freezing and thawing. NON-VITREOUS: Cannot be used where subject to freezing & thawing.	Can be used on any surface where glazed tile is suitable and ordinarily for exterior surfaces and should be recommended as being suitable for this purpose by the manufacturer. Bulkheads, store fronts, exterior decoration, subway entrances, light traffic floors, vestibules, fountains, drainboards.
Specify Your Desired Thickness From 1/16" 1/2"			Specified to meet specific requirements in any location.

UNGLAZED TILE - TYPES and SIZES

<table>
<tr><th colspan="12">UNGLAZED TILE</th></tr>
<tr><th rowspan="2">TYPE OF TILE</th><th colspan="9">DESCRIPTION OF TILE</th><th colspan="2">BASIC SHAPE & NOMINAL SIZE</th></tr>
<tr><th colspan="3">OUTER FINISH OR SKIN</th><th colspan="4">BODY OF TILE</th><th colspan="2">EDGE</th><th>SIZE</th><th>THICKNESS</th></tr>
<tr><th></th><th colspan="2">NON-SLIP</th><th>SMOOTH SURFACE</th><th rowspan="2">IMPERVIOUS</th><th rowspan="2">VITREOUS</th><th rowspan="2">SEMI-VITREOUS</th><th rowspan="2">NON-VITREOUS</th><th rowspan="2">CUSHION</th><th rowspan="2">SQUARE</th><th colspan="2" rowspan="3">Same as glazed ceramic mosaic</th></tr>
<tr><th></th><th>ADMIXTURE</th><th>GROOVED</th><th></th></tr>
<tr><td>CERAMIC MOSAIC</td><td>Available</td><td>Not Available</td><td>Available</td><td>Available</td><td>Available</td><td>Not Available</td><td>Not Available</td><td colspan="2">Available in either cushion or square edges</td></tr>
<tr><td>FAIENCE</td><td colspan="9" rowspan="2">Will make as desired, special sizes, shapes patterns, colors, etc. Consult Manufacturer for further information</td><td colspan="2" rowspan="2"></td></tr>
<tr><td>FAIENCE MOSAIC</td></tr>
<tr><td>PAVER</td><td rowspan="2">Available</td><td rowspan="3">Available</td><td rowspan="2">Available</td><td rowspan="4">Available</td><td rowspan="4">Available</td><td>Not Available</td><td rowspan="4">Not Available</td><td rowspan="3">Not Available</td><td rowspan="4">Available</td><td>3" x 3"
4" x 4"
4 1/4" x 4 1/4"
6" x 6"
6" x 3"</td><td>3/8" to 5/8"</td></tr>
<tr><td>QUARRY</td><td>Available</td><td>2 3/4" x 2 3/4"
4" x 4"
6" x 6"
8" x 8"
9" x 9"
6" x 2 3/4"
6" x 9"
8" x 3 3/4"
8" x 4"</td><td>Keys on bottom 1/16" to 1/4" major thickness 1/2" to 3/4"
1 1/4" to 1 5/8"</td></tr>
<tr><td>SHIP OR GALLEY</td><td rowspan="2">Not Available</td><td>Not Available</td><td rowspan="2">Not Available</td><td>6" x 6"</td><td>5/8" to 3/4"</td></tr>
<tr><td>CONDUCTIVE TILE</td><td>Not Available</td><td>Available</td><td>Available</td><td>1 9/16" x 1 9/16"
1 1/16" x 1 1/16"</td><td>1/4"</td></tr>
</table>

TERMS USED BY THE TRADE ~ ALL TILE

NATURAL CLAY TILE: A type of ceramic mosaic or paver made by either dust-pressed method or plastic method, from clays that produce a dense strong body having a distinctive, slightly textured appearance, with a high resistance to wear.
PORCELAIN TILE: A type of ceramic mosaic tile or paver tile usually formed by dust-pressed method from mixtures of refined ceramic materials to form, after firing, a vitreous or impervious tile that is dense, fine grained, smooth and characterized by clear, permanent color or granular blends thereof.
FLINT: Extremely dense and durable dust-pressed paver tile of porcelain type made from refined clays and having an impervious body.
CERAMICS: Glazed ceramic mosaic tile are often referred to loosely as "ceramics" although the word properly embodies all types of fired clay products.
STRIPS: Glazed pieces that are narrow in width compared to length. Used as decorative accents principally with glazed interior tile.

METHODS OF MANUFACTURE ~ ALL TILE

DUST PRESSED METHOD: Tile shaped or formed by pressure in metal dies from powdered or granular clay, shales and/or other ceramic materials.
PLASTIC PROCESS: Tile prepared from a clay preparation that contains enough moisture to make it plastic and usually formed by extruding from dies.
HAND MADE TILE: Tile made by hand from plastic materials having a variation in face and edges that occur from the handicraft method.

GRADES OF TILE: should conform to Simplified practice recommendation R 61-44.
STANDARD GRADE: Best grade obtainable.
SECONDS: Result of slight imperfections in manufacture that in no way affect wearing or sanitary qualities.

DESCRIPTION OF TILE
JOINT SPACING: Varies from 1/32" to 1/4"
REGULAR EDGE SURFACE: Spacing of joints established by architect generally 1/16" to 1/4"

UNGLAZED TILE and its USAGE

UNGLAZED TILE			
RECOMMENDED JOINT SIZE	TRIMMERS	USAGE	
		GENERAL APPLICATION	TYPICAL INSTALLATION
up to $4\frac{1}{4}$ x $4\frac{1}{4}$ tile $\frac{1}{8}$ to $\frac{1}{4}$ 6 x 6 tile & over $\frac{3}{16}$ to $\frac{3}{4}$ $\frac{3}{8}$" to $\frac{3}{4}$"	See pages on Tile and Trimmers	BODY STAINING QUALITIES apply only to unglazed tile as glazed tile has an impervious surface IMPERVIOUS: Resists staining VITREOUS: normally resistant to staining SEMI-VITREOUS: may or may not resist staining. A manufacturers warrantee should be obtained. NON-VITREOUS: cannot be used if tile is subject to staining. BODY OF TILE: water absorption resistance to freezing and thawing. IMPERVIOUS: can be used anywhere VITREOUS: can be used anywhere SEMI-VITREOUS: should always ask for warrantee by mfg. against freezing and thawing. NON-VITREOUS: cannot be used where subject to freezing & thawing.	Generally suitable for any use. Especially adapted to floors or other heavy duty purposes - both indoor and outdoor. Working surfaces, drainboards, toilet rooms, bathrooms, kitchens, corridors, operating rooms, delivery rooms, stables, entrances, showers, recreation rooms, stairs & landings, porches, dairies, packing houses, power and industrial plants, stove backs, swimming pools, snack bars, grease rooms.
$\frac{3}{8}$" to $\frac{3}{4}$"			Used on Ship Decks & Galley Floors
paper mounted $\frac{1}{16}$" average			

TILE DEFINITIONS

DESCRIPTION OF TILE (cont.)

EDGE: Tiles may have either square or cushion edges. The cushion edge has a slight curvature at the face edge.

square edge   cushion edge

SELF SPACING EDGE SURFACE: Lugs or protuberances on side of tile usually $\frac{1}{64}$", when butted together these lugs automatically space the tile $\frac{1}{32}$" apart.

GLAZE: Any impervious material produced by fire used to cover the body of a tile to prevent absorption of liquids and gases and to resist abrasion and impact or to give a more pleasing appearance.

BRIGHT GLAZE: A highly reflective surface which will reflect a clear image.

SEMI MATTE GLAZE: A surface with some sheen which does not reflect a clear image.

MATTE GLAZE: A surface without sheen which will not reflect an image.

GLAZE (cont.)

CRYSTALLINE GLAZE: A surface having a textural effect which may vary from a bright to a matte finish on the same piece of tile.

NON-SLIP TILE

Reduces hazard of slipping according to requirements of B.M.S. 100 entitled "Relative Slipperiness of Floor and Deck Surfaces".

NON-SLIP BY ADMIXTURE: Incorporates certain admixtures such as abrasive granules in the body or in the surface of the tile.

NON-SLIP BY GROOVES: Use of surface grooves or protuberances to decrease hazard of slipping.

BODY OF TILE

IMPERVIOUS: Body of tile having a moisture absorption of approximately 0.5 percent or less by weight.

VITREOUS: Body of tile having a moisture absorption between 0.5 to 3 percent by weight.

SEMI-VITREOUS: Body of tile having a moisture absorption between 3 to 7 percent by weight.

NON-VITREOUS: Body of tile having a moisture absorption of more than 7 percent by weight.

TILE and its USAGE, SETTING of WALL and CERAMIC MOSAIC TILE

TILE DEFINITIONS - CONT.

UNGLAZED TILE
A hard, dense tile of homogeneous composition deriving color and texture from the materials of which it is made. Colors are limited by composition, firing and degree of vitrification. Made by dust-pressed or plastic process. This group comprises the following.
CERAMIC MOSAIC TILE: Maximum of 6 square inches in face area, approximately ¼" thick, having fully vitrified or fairly dense body and produced by either the dust-pressed or plastic extrusion process. They are usually mounted on Kraft paper 2 ft. by 1 ft. to facilitate installation.
FAIENCE TILE: Made from plastic clay which presents characteristic variations in face, edge, and/or glazes that result in a hand crafted, decorative effect.
FAIENCE MOSAIC TILE: Same as faience in body and glaze, but less than 6 sq. in. in face area.

PAVER TILE: Similar to ceramic mosaic tile in composition and physical characteristics, having a face area of 6 sq. in. or more. Made by dust-pressed or plastic method. Porcelain or natural clay. Abrasive or non-abrasive.
QUARRY TILE: Unglazed tile usually 6 sq. in. or more in surface area made from natural clays or shales by a plastic extrusion process.
SPECIAL PURPOSE TILE: A tile made to correspond to any specific design qualifications desired, such as size, thickness, shape, color or decoration, keys or lugs on back, unique resistance to absorption, alkali, acid, thermal shock, physical impact, high coefficient of friction or electrical properties.
CONDUCTIVE TILE: Made by the dust-pressed or the plastic method from special body compositions or methods that result in specific properties of electrical conductivity while retaining other normal physical properties of tile.

GLAZED TILE
Floor and wall tile having an impervious white or colored, clear or opaque finish made of ceramic materials fused on the exposed surfaces. This group comprises the following;
GLAZED INTERIOR TILE: A glazed tile with a body that is usually non-vitreous. Used where the tile is not subject to excessive abrasion, impact, or to freezing and thawing.
GLAZED EXTRA DUTY TILE: Especially designed to minimize the appearance of wear when used for light duty floors and other surfaces subject to not more than light abrasion or impact. Suitable for use in locations in any climate. Such tiles should be warranteed by manufacturer.

GLAZED FAIENCE TILE: Faience tile with glaze.
GLAZED FAIENCE MOSAIC TILE: Faience mosaic tile with glaze.
GLAZED SPECIAL PURPOSE TILE: Special purpose tile with glaze.
GLAZED CERAMIC MOSAIC TILE: Ceramic mosaic tile with glaze.

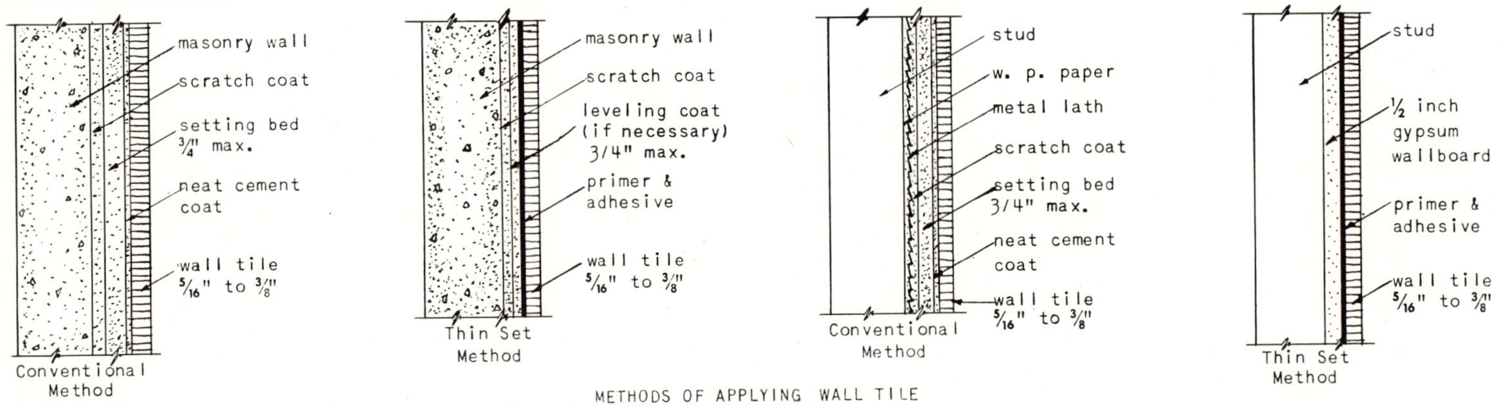
masonry wall
scratch coat
setting bed ¾" max.
neat cement coat
wall tile 5/16" to 3/8"
Conventional Method
masonry wall
scratch coat
leveling coat (if necessary) 3/4" max.
primer & adhesive
wall tile 5/16" to 3/8"
Thin Set Method
stud
w. p. paper
metal lath
scratch coat
setting bed 3/4" max.
neat cement coat
wall tile 5/16" to 3/8"
Conventional Method
stud
½ inch gypsum wallboard
primer & adhesive
wall tile 5/16" to 3/8"
Thin Set Method

METHODS OF APPLYING WALL TILE

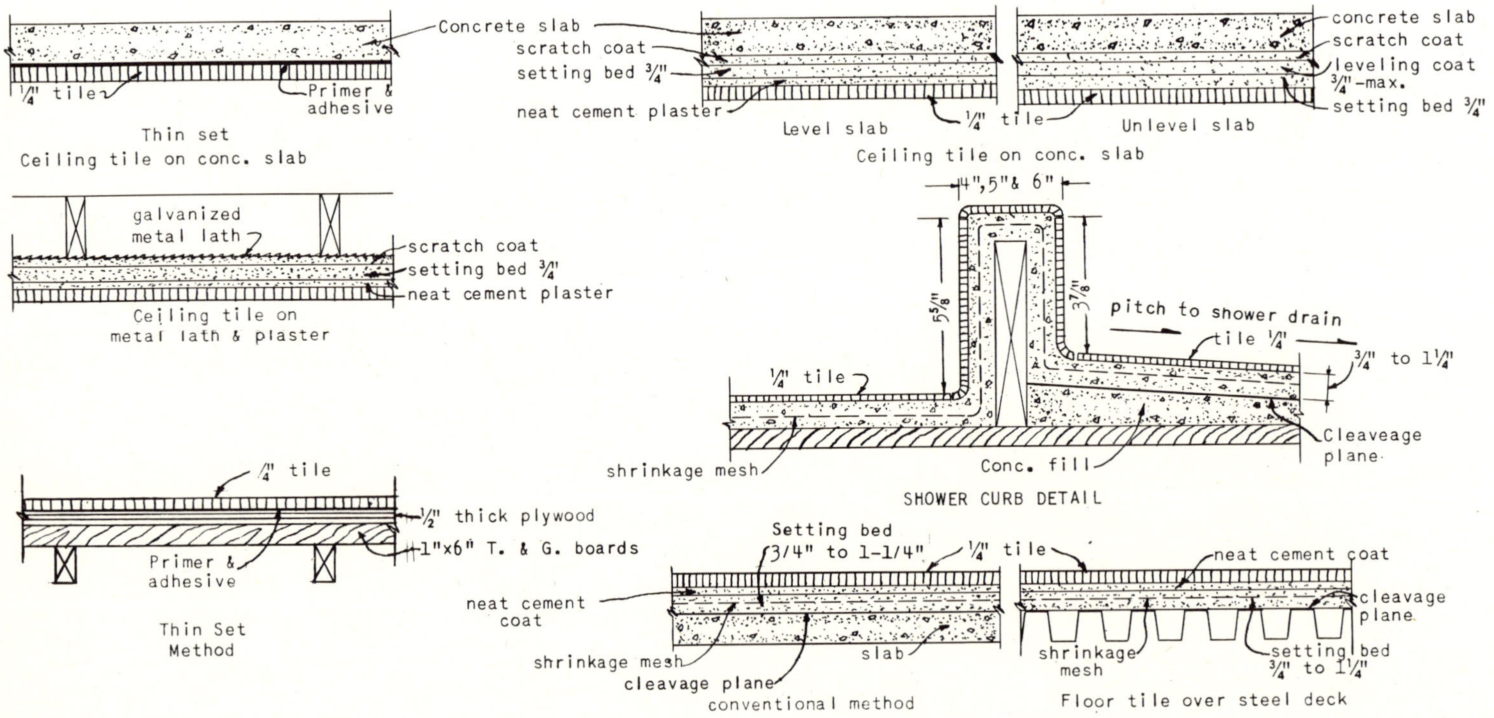
Concrete slab
¼" tile
Primer & adhesive
Thin set
Ceiling tile on conc. slab
scratch coat
setting bed ¾"
neat cement plaster
Level slab
¼" tile
Unlevel slab
concrete slab
scratch coat
leveling coat ¾"-max.
setting bed ¾"
Ceiling tile on conc. slab
galvanized metal lath
scratch coat
setting bed ¾"
neat cement plaster
Ceiling tile on metal lath & plaster
4",5"& 6"
5⅝"
3⅞"
pitch to shower drain
tile ¼"
¾" to 1¼"
¼" tile
Cleaveage plane
shrinkage mesh
Conc. fill
SHOWER CURB DETAIL
¼" tile
½" thick plywood
1"x6" T. & G. boards
Primer & adhesive
Thin Set Method
Setting bed 3/4" to 1-1/4"
¼" tile
neat cement coat
neat cement coat
cleavage plane
shrinkage mesh
slab
cleavage plane
conventional method
shrinkage mesh
setting bed ¾" to 1¼"
Floor tile over steel deck

METHODS OF APPLYING CERAMIC MOSAICS TILE TO FLOORS & CEILING

MARBLE FLOORS, WALLS & WAINSCOTS

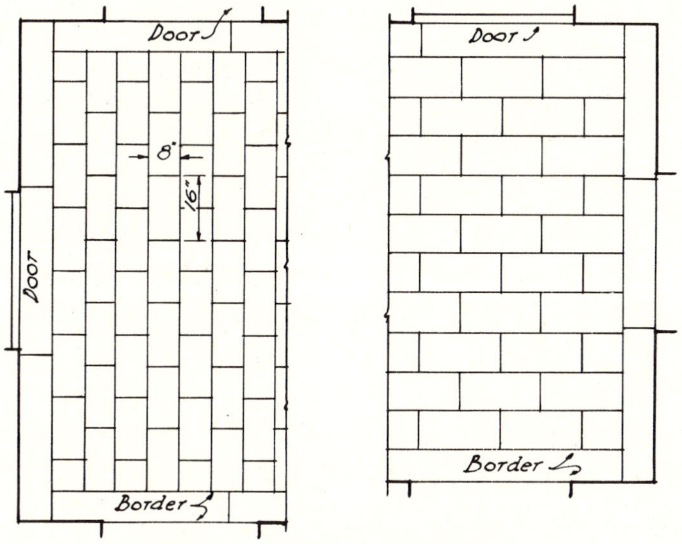
Door
Door
8"
16"
Border
Door
Border
Border

FOR CORRIDORS
Standard Sizes 8"×16", 12"×12" & 10"×20"

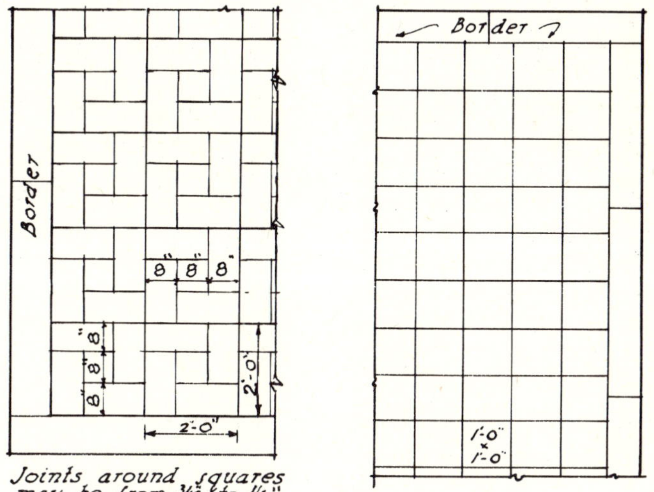
Border
8" 8" 8"
8" 8" 8"
2'-0"
2'-0"
Border
1'-0" × 1'-0"

Joints around squares may be from 3/16 to 1/4" & colored

FOR HALLS & LOBBIES

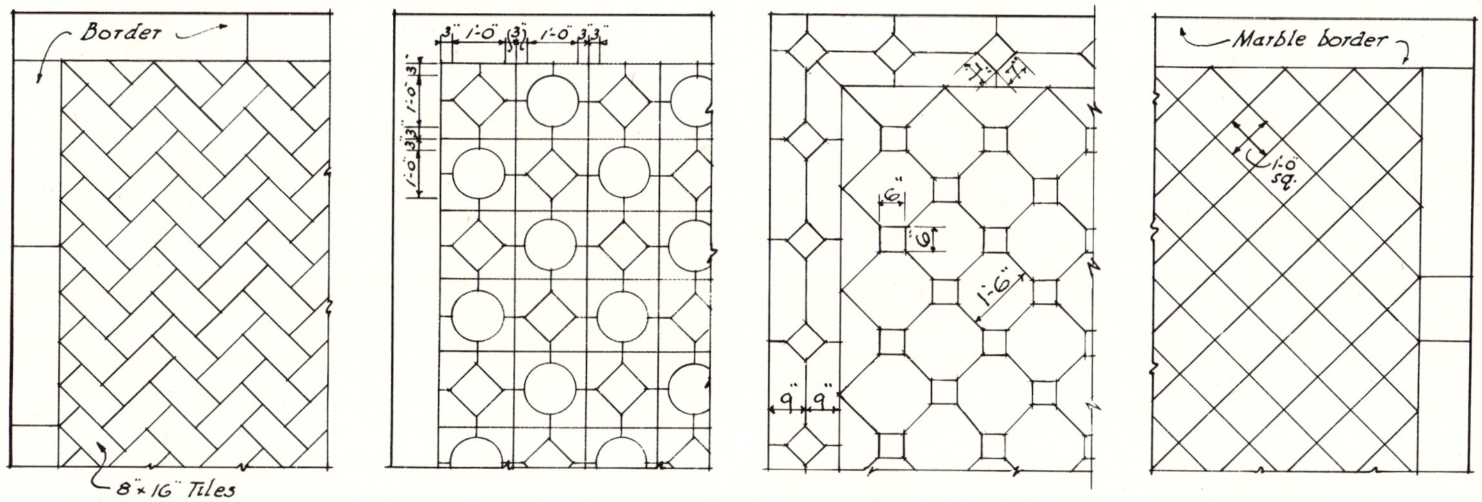
Border
3" 1'-0" 3" 1'-0" 3" 3"
1'-0" 3"
1'-0" 3" 3"
6"
6"
1'-6"
9" 9"
Marble border
1'-0" sq.
8"×16" Tiles

MARBLE TILE FLOORS (USING STANDARD SIZES)

Floor tile is a by-product and hence limited in size to not over 2 sq. ft of area per piece. Thickness is random between 3/8" and 1 1/2". If large tiles or ones of uniform thickness are used they are termed floor slabs. Floor joints 1/16". Mortar for bed of 1 part cement 3 parts sand.
Scale 1/4" = 1'-0"

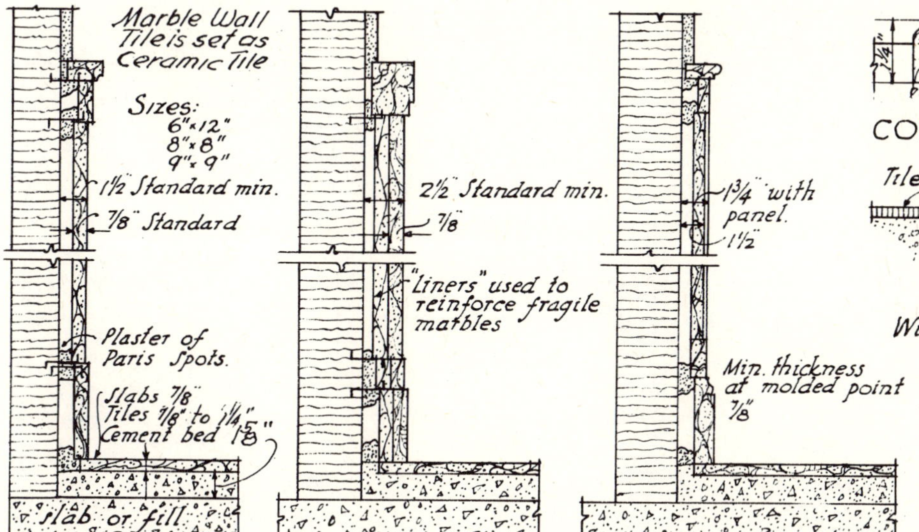
Marble Wall Tile is set as Ceramic Tile
Sizes:
6"×12"
8"×8"
9"×9"
1 1/2" Standard min.
7/8" Standard
Plaster of Paris Spots.
Slabs 7/8"
Tiles 7/8" to 1 1/4"
Cement bed 1 5/8"
slab or fill
2 1/2" Standard min.
7/8"
"Liners" used to reinforce fragile marbles
1 3/4" with panel.
1 1/2"
Min. thickness at molded point 7/8"

Plain — With Liner — With Panelling

SECTION OF WALLS OR WAINSCOTS
Scale 1" = 1'-0"

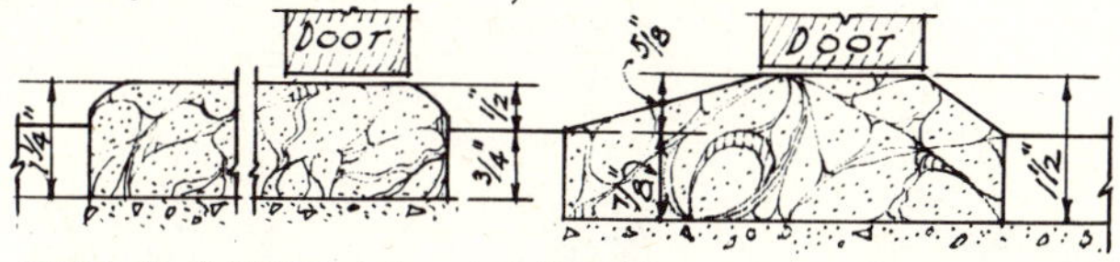
Door
Door
5/8

COMMERCIAL TYPES OF SADDLES

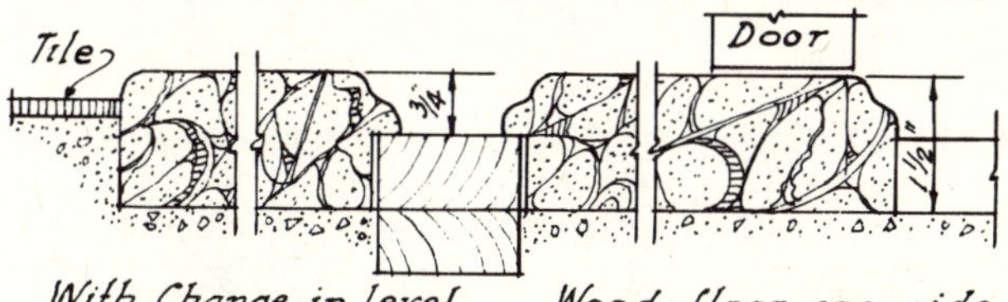
Tile
Door
3/4"
1 1/2"

With Change in level — Wood floor one side

SADDLES FOR RESIDENCES
3" = 1'-0"

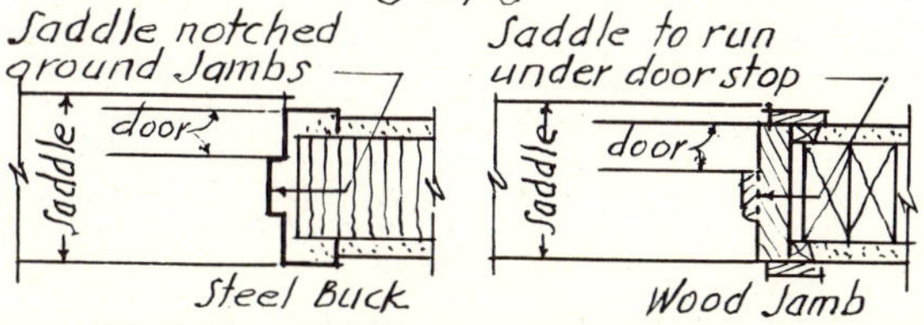
Saddle notched around Jambs
Saddle to run under door stop
door
Saddle
door
Saddle

Steel Buck — Wood Jamb

PLAN of SADDLES and JAMBS

STRUCTURAL GLASS-INTERIOR

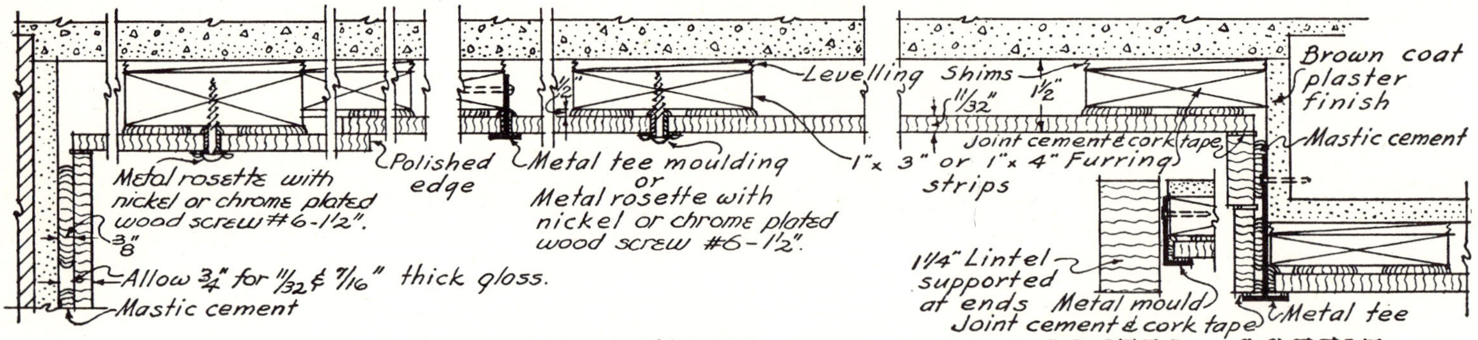
Levelling Shims
Brown coat plaster finish
1/2"
11/32"
1/2"
Joint cement & cork tape
Mastic cement
Metal rosette with nickel or chrome plated wood screw #6-1 1/2".
Polished edge
Metal tee moulding or Metal rosette with nickel or chrome plated wood screw #6-1 1/2".
1" x 3" or 1" x 4" Furring strips
3/8"
Allow 3/4" for 11/32 & 7/16" thick glass.
Mastic cement
1 1/4" Lintel supported at ends
Metal mould
Joint cement & cork tape
Metal tee

CEILING CONSTRUCTION　　LINTEL SOFFIT

Scale 3" = 1'-0"

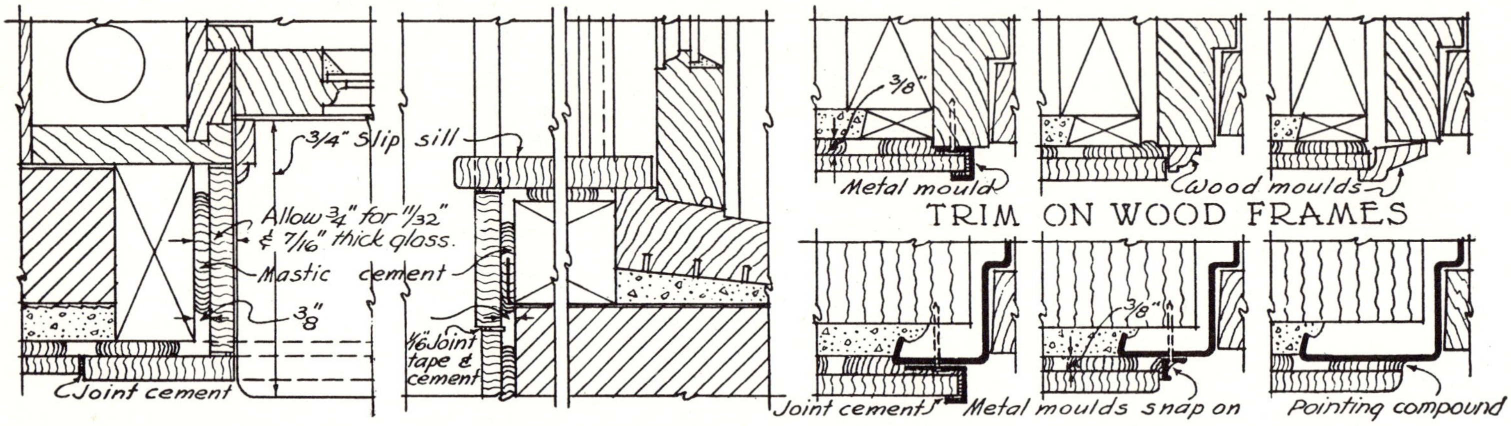
3/4" Slip sill
Allow 3/4" for 11/32" & 7/16" thick glass.
Mastic cement
3/8"
1/16" Joint tape & cement
Joint cement
3/8"
Metal mould
Wood moulds
TRIM ON WOOD FRAMES
3/8"
Joint cement
Metal moulds snap on
Pointing compound

PLAN OF WINDOW　SECTION OF WINDOW　TRIM OF METAL BUCKS

Scale 3" = 1'-0"

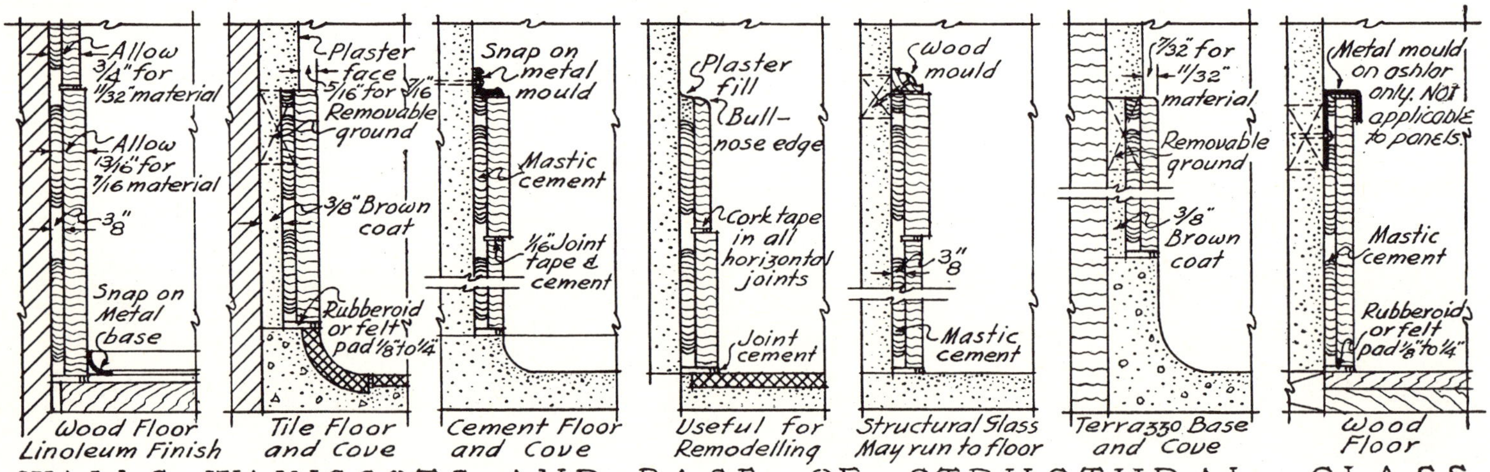
Allow 3/4" for 11/32" material
Allow 13/16" for 7/16 material
3/8"
Snap on Metal base
Wood Floor Linoleum Finish
Plaster face
5/16" for 7/16
Removable ground
3/8" Brown coat
Rubberoid or felt pad 1/8" to 1/4"
Tile Floor and Cove
Snap on metal mould
Mastic cement
1/16" Joint tape & cement
Cement Floor and Cove
Plaster fill
Bull-nose edge
Cork tape in all horizontal joints
Joint cement
Useful for Remodelling
Wood mould
3/8"
Mastic cement
Structural Glass May run to floor
7/32" for 11/32" material
Removable ground
3/8" Brown coat
Terrazzo Base and Cove
Metal mould on ashlar only. Not applicable to panels.
Mastic cement
Rubberoid or felt pad 1/8" to 1/4"
Wood Floor

WALLS WAINSCOTS AND BASE OF STRUCTURAL GLASS

Scale 3" = 1'-0"

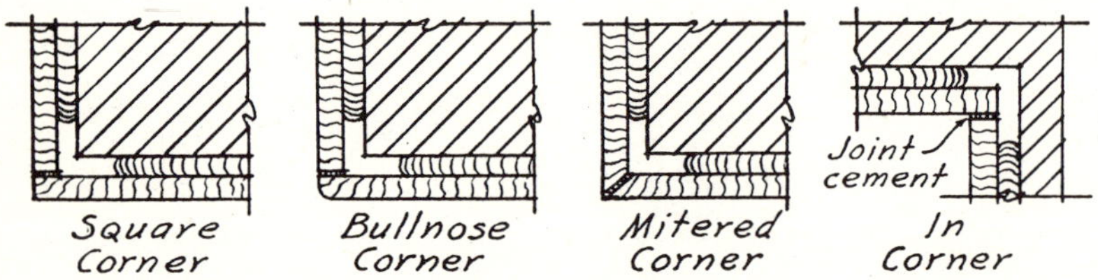
Joint cement
Square Corner
Bullnose Corner
Mitered Corner
In Corner

MATERIAL INDICATIONS AND NOTES

Structural Glass	Mastic Cement
Plaster	Ceramic Tile
Steel	Lath

For recommended thickness, sizes and colors
See previous sheet. Mastic cement applied in spots

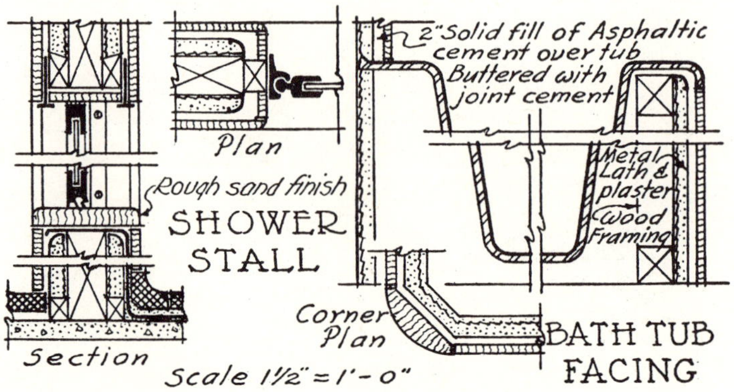
Plan
Rough sand finish
SHOWER STALL
Section
2" Solid fill of Asphaltic cement over tub
Buttered with joint cement
Metal Lath & plaster
Wood Framing
Corner Plan
BATH TUB FACING

Scale 1 1/2" = 1'-0"

For Specifications see "Architectural Specifications" by Harold R. Sleeper; Structural Glass Division.

WOOD JOINTS

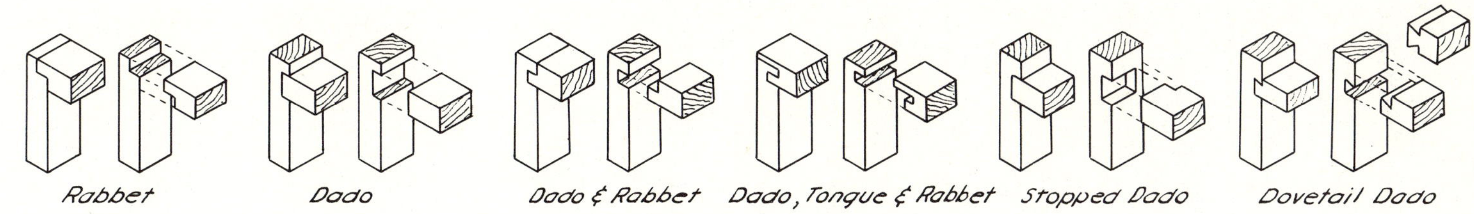
Rabbet
Dado
Dado & Rabbet
Dado, Tongue & Rabbet
Stopped Dado
Dovetail Dado

RABBET & DADO

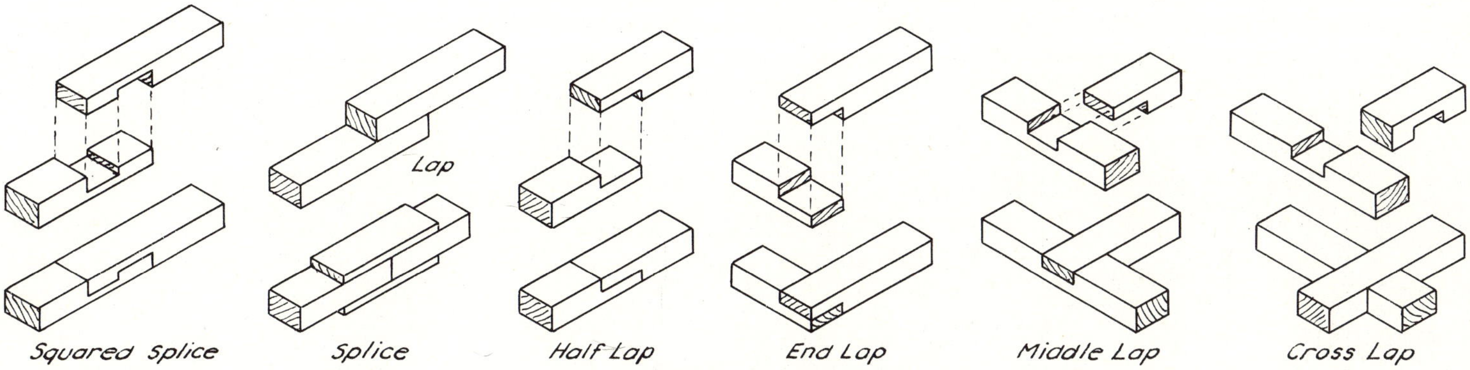
Lap
Squared Splice
Splice
Half Lap
End Lap
Middle Lap
Cross Lap

SPLICE & LAP

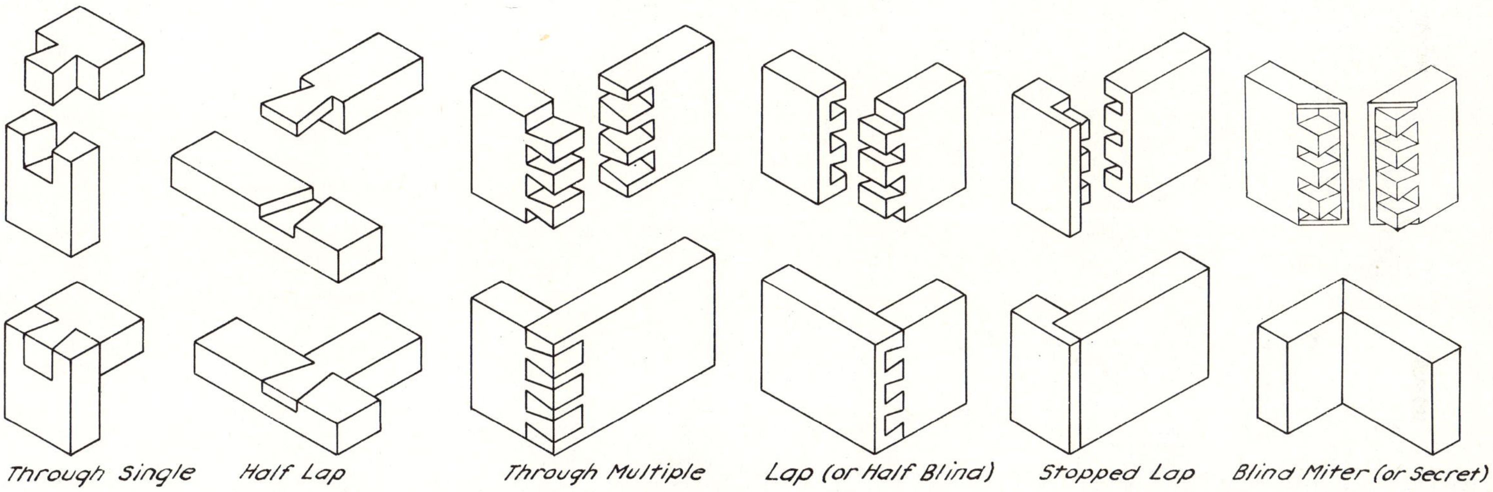
Through Single
Half Lap
Through Multiple
Lap (or Half Blind)
Stopped Lap
Blind Miter (or Secret)

DOVETAIL

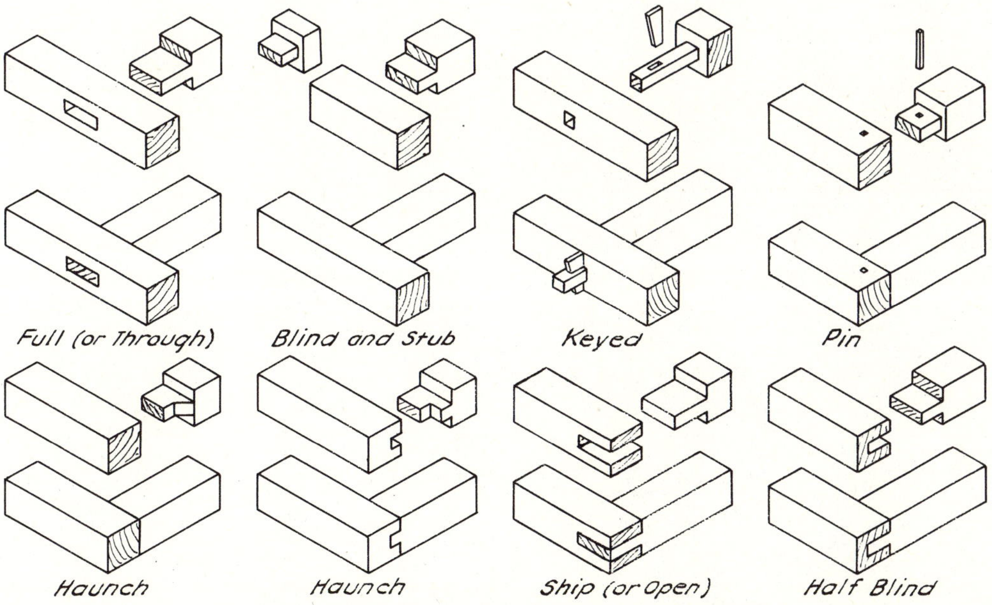
Full (or Through)
Blind and Stub
Keyed
Pin
Haunch
Haunch
Ship (or Open)
Half Blind

MORTISE & TENON

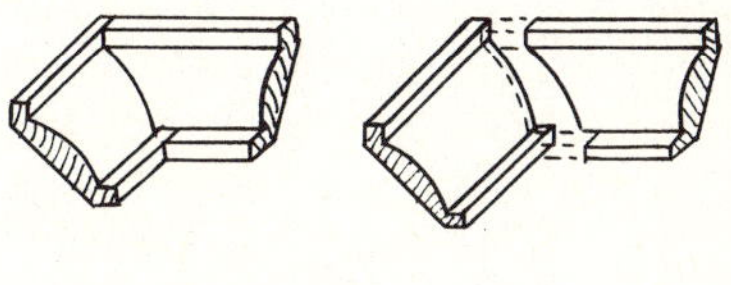

COPED

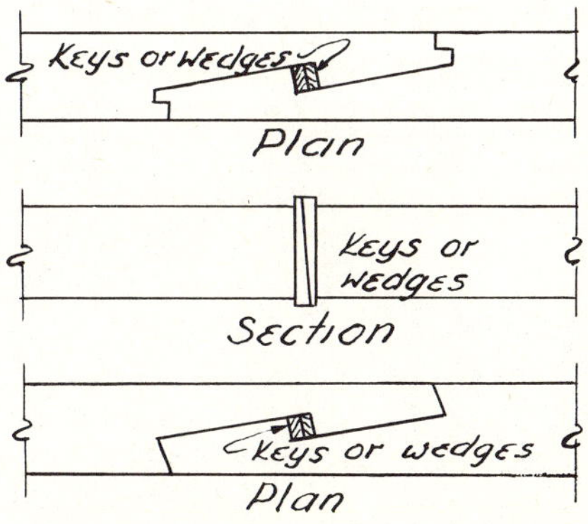
Keys or Wedges
Plan
Keys or Wedges
Section
Keys or wedges
Plan

GIRDER SPLICING

Checked by E. Nordholm of Kapp & Nordholm Company, Inc.
Mt. Vernon, N.Y.

JOINTS in WOODWORK – PANELING

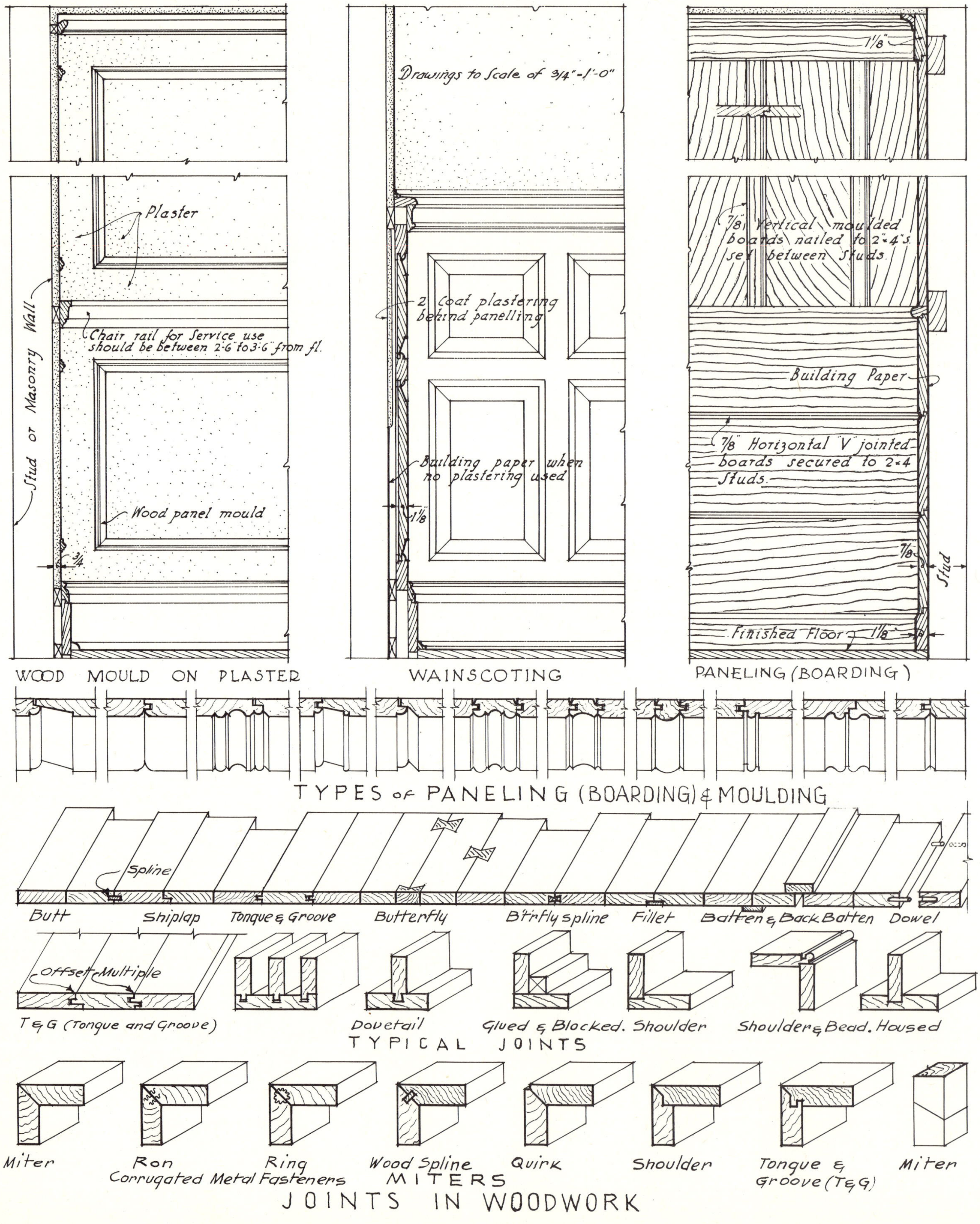

Drawings to Scale of 3/4" = 1'-0"
Plaster
Stud or Masonry Wall
Chair rail for Service use should be between 2'6" to 3'6" from fl.
Wood panel mould
3/4
2 Coat plastering behind panelling
Building paper when no plastering used
1 1/8
1 1/8"
7/8" Vertical moulded boards nailed to 2"x4"s set between Studs.
Building Paper
7/8" Horizontal "V" jointed boards secured to 2x4 Studs.
7/8"
Stud
Finished Floor
1 1/8"
WOOD MOULD ON PLASTER
WAINSCOTING
PANELING (BOARDING)
TYPES of PANELING (BOARDING) & MOULDING
Spline
Butt
Shiplap
Tongue & Groove
Butterfly
B'trfly spline
Fillet
Batten & Back Batten
Dowel
Offset
Multiple
T&G (Tongue and Groove)
Dovetail
Glued & Blocked.
Shoulder
Shoulder & Bead.
Housed
TYPICAL JOINTS
Miter
Ron
Ring
Corrugated Metal Fasteners
Wood Spline
Quirk
Shoulder
Tongue & Groove (T&G)
Miter
MITERS
JOINTS IN WOODWORK

WOOD BOOK SHELVES

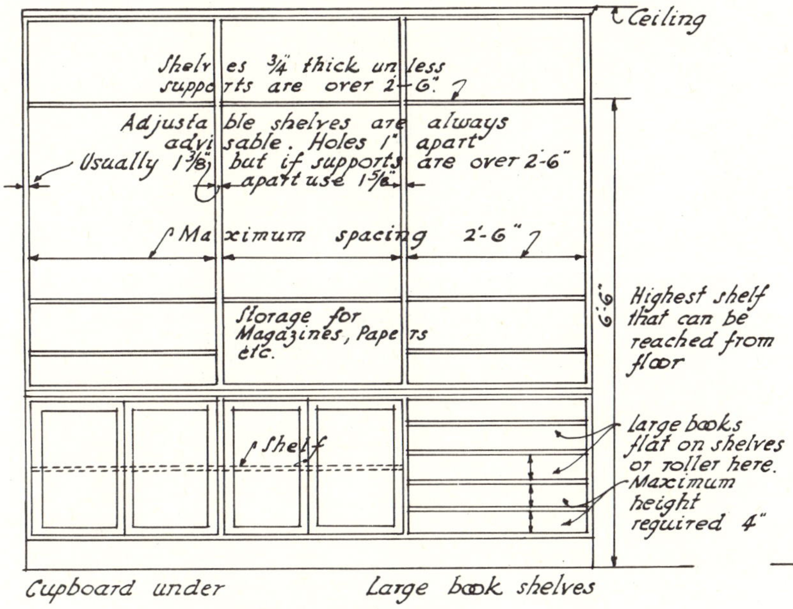
Ceiling
Shelves 3/4 thick unless supports are over 2'-6"
Adjustable shelves are always advisable. Holes 1" apart
Usually 1 3/8 but if supports are over 2'-6" apart use 1 5/8
Maximum spacing 2'-6"
6'-6"
Highest shelf that can be reached from floor
Storage for Magazines, Papers etc.
Shelf
large books flat on shelves or roller here.
Maximum height required 4"
Cupboard under
Large book shelves

ELEVATION
3/8" = 1'-0"

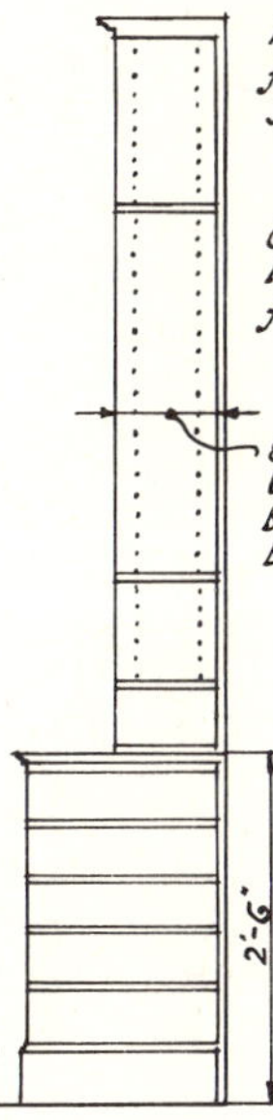
8" or 9" unless special book are to be housed
2'-6"

SECTION
3/8" = 1'-0"

All books over 1'-8" long should be housed flat. Such books usually placed on lower shelves which need not be over 4" apart

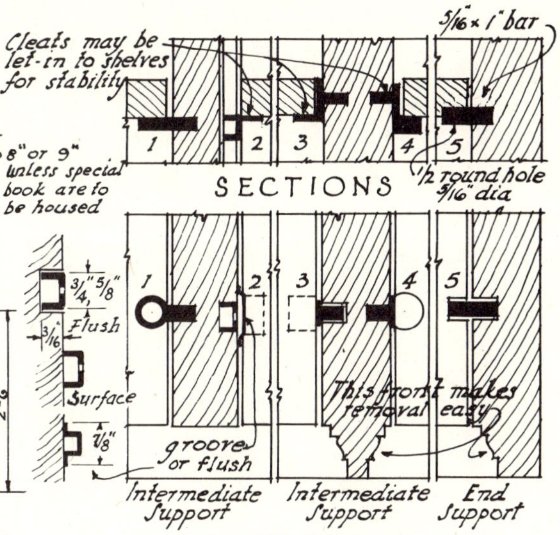
Cleats may be let-in to shelves for stability
5/16 × 1" bar
1 2 3 4 5
1/2 round hole 5/16" dia
SECTIONS
3/4", 5/8"
3/16
Flush
Surface
1/8"
groove or flush
This front makes removal easy
Intermediate Support
Intermediate Support
End Support

PLANS
SHELF PINS.
ADJUSTABLE

Pin diameters are 1/4", 5/16" or 3/8". Length of pin to go into hole 3/8" to 3/4". Pin # 2 has continuous metal strip over groove. Nos. 3 & 4 are used extensively. No. 5 is a simple bar that serves well & economically. Pin holes usually 1" on center. If shelves are rebated, on types 1, 2, 3 & 4 they cannot slide off.

Scale 3" = 1'-0".

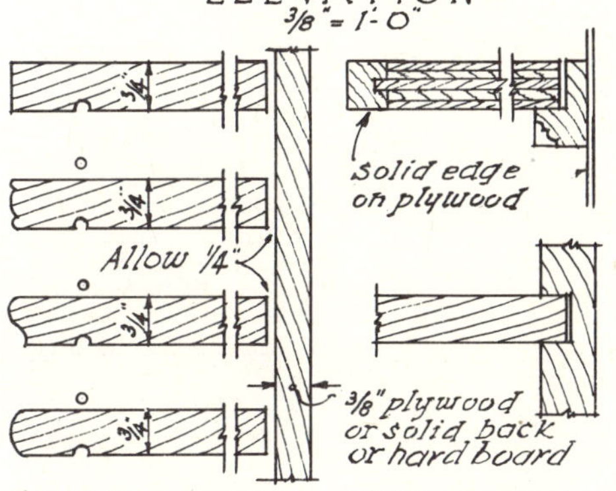
3/4
3/4
Allow 1/4"
3/4
3/4
solid edge on plywood
3/8" plywood or solid back or hard board

SHELF EDGES
Usual types

FIXED SHELVES
3" = 1'-0"

In setting up shelves place small books at top and increase to large at bottom. Allow 10" in height per shelf on center. If plywood used, wood thickness may be decreased slightly.

FOR REQUIREMENTS OF BOOKS AND FOR METAL SHELVES, SEE SHEET ON "LIBRARY EQUIPMENT"

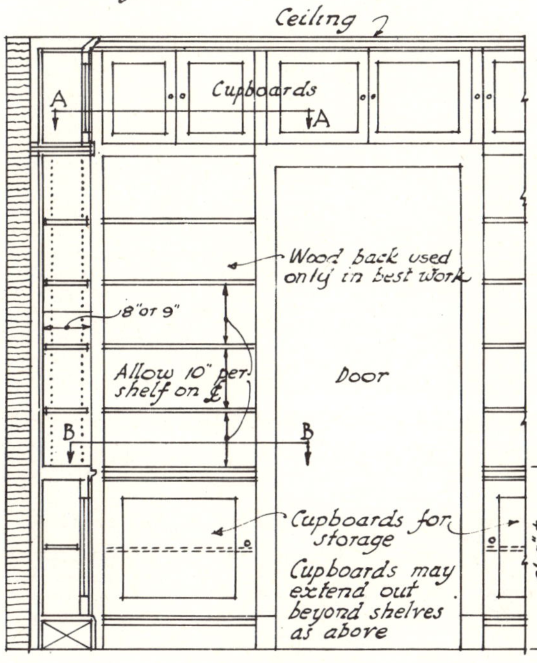
Ceiling
Cupboards
A
A
Wood back used only in best work
8" or 9"
Allow 10" per shelf on ℄
Door
B
B
Cupboards for storage
Cupboards may extend out beyond shelves as above
2'-6"±

ELEVATION
Scale 3/8"=1'-0

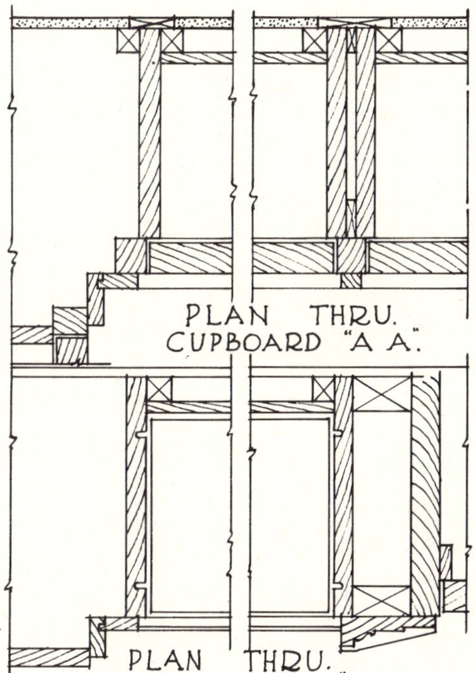
PLAN THRU.
CUPBOARD "A A".

PLAN THRU.
SHELVES "B B".

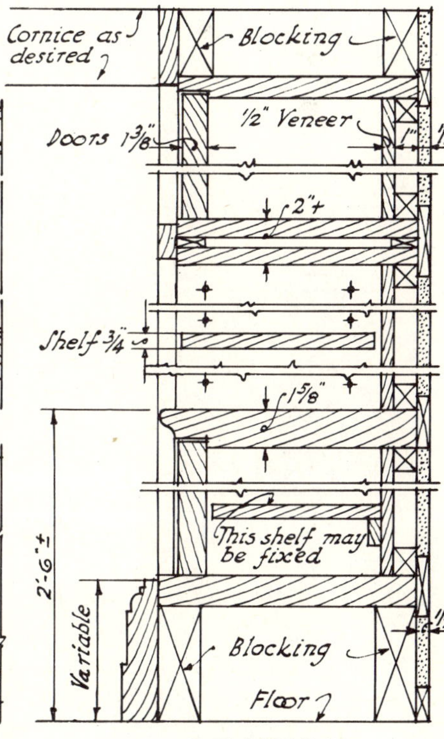
Cornice as desired
Blocking
1/2" Veneer
Doors 1 3/8
1"
1/2"
2"+
Shelf 3/4
1 5/8"
This shelf may be fixed
2'-6"±
Variable
1/2"
Blocking
Floor

SECTION
Scale 1 1/2"=1'-0".

BOOK SHELVING WITH CUPBOARDS TOP & BOTTOM

BOOK CASES

WOOD MOULDINGS - 8000 SERIES

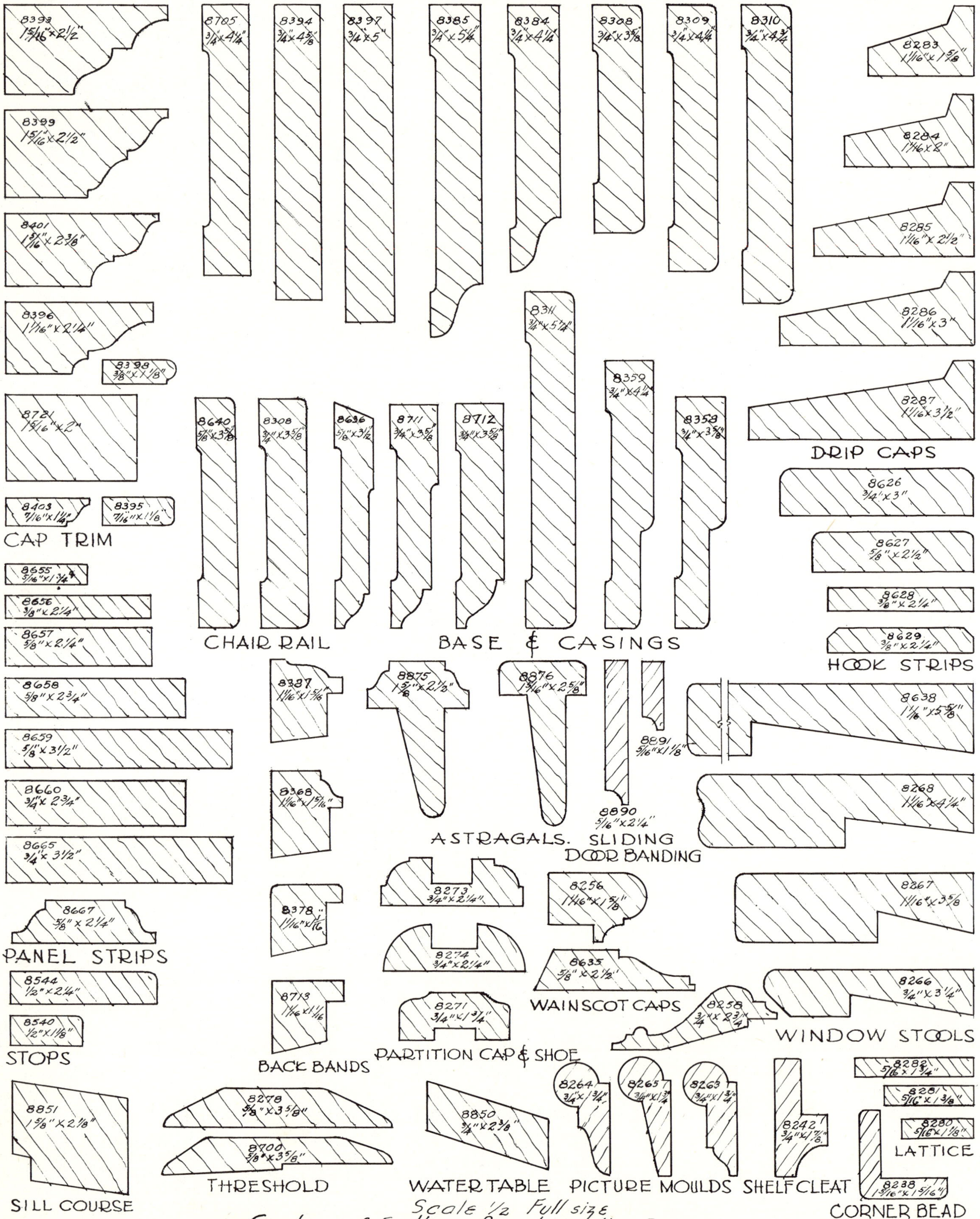
8393 1 5/16" x 2 1/2"
8399 1 5/16" x 2 1/2"
8401 1 5/16" x 2 3/8"
8396 1 1/16" x 2 1/4"
8398 3/8" x 1 1/8"
8721 1 5/16" x 2"
8403 7/16" x 1 1/4"
8395 7/16" x 1 1/8"
CAP TRIM
8655 5/16" x 1 3/4"
8656 3/8" x 2 1/4"
8657 5/8" x 2 1/4"
8658 5/8" x 2 3/4"
8659 5/8" x 3 1/2"
8660 3/4" x 2 3/4"
8665 3/4" x 3 1/2"
8667 5/8" x 2 1/4"
PANEL STRIPS
8544 1/2" x 2 1/4"
8540 1/2" x 1 1/8"
STOPS
8851 1 5/8" x 2 1/8"
SILL COURSE
8705 3/4" x 4 1/4"
8394 3/4" x 4 5/8"
8397 3/4" x 5"
8385 3/4" x 5 1/4"
8384 3/4" x 4 1/4"
8308 3/4" x 3 5/8"
8309 3/4" x 4 1/4"
8310 3/4" x 4 3/4"
8311 3/4" x 5 1/4"
8359 3/4" x 4 1/4"
8640 5/8" x 3 5/8"
8308 3/4" x 3 5/8"
8636 5/8" x 3 1/2"
8711 3/4" x 3 5/8"
8712 3/4" x 3 5/8"
8358 3/4" x 3 5/8"
CHAIR RAIL
BASE & CASINGS
8283 1 1/16" x 1 5/8"
8284 1 1/16" x 2"
8285 1 1/16" x 2 1/2"
8286 1 1/16" x 3"
8287 1 1/16" x 3 1/2"
DRIP CAPS
8626 3/4" x 3"
8627 5/8" x 2 1/2"
8628 3/8" x 2 1/4"
8629 3/8" x 2 1/4"
HOOK STRIPS
8327 1 1/16" x 1 5/16"
8875 1 5/8" x 2 1/2"
8876 1 5/16" x 2 5/8"
8891 5/16" x 1 1/8"
8890 5/16" x 2 1/4"
ASTRAGALS.
SLIDING DOOR BANDING
8368 1 1/16" x 1 5/16"
8378 1 1/16" x 1 1/16"
8713 1 1/16" x 1 1/16"
BACK BANDS
8273 3/4" x 2 1/4"
8274 3/4" x 2 1/4"
8271 3/4" x 1 3/4"
PARTITION CAP & SHOE
8256 1 1/16" x 1 5/8"
8635 5/8" x 2 1/2"
WAINSCOT CAPS
8638 1 1/16" x 5 5/8"
8268 1 1/16" x 4 1/4"
8267 1 1/16" x 3 5/8"
8266 3/4" x 3 1/4"
WINDOW STOOLS
8258 3/4" x 2 3/4"
8278 5/8" x 3 5/8"
8700 3/8" x 3 5/8"
THRESHOLD
8850 3/4" x 2 3/8"
WATER TABLE
8264 3/4" x 3/4"
8265 3/4" x 1 3/4"
8263 3/4" x 1 3/4"
PICTURE MOULDS
8242 3/4" x 1 7/8"
SHELF CLEAT
8282 5/16" x 1 3/4"
8281 5/16" x 1 3/8"
8280 5/16" x 1 1/8"
LATTICE
8238 1 5/16" x 1 5/16"
CORNER BEAD

Scale 1/2 Full size
Courtesy of Southern Pine Inspection Bureau.

WOOD MOULDINGS - 8000 SERIES

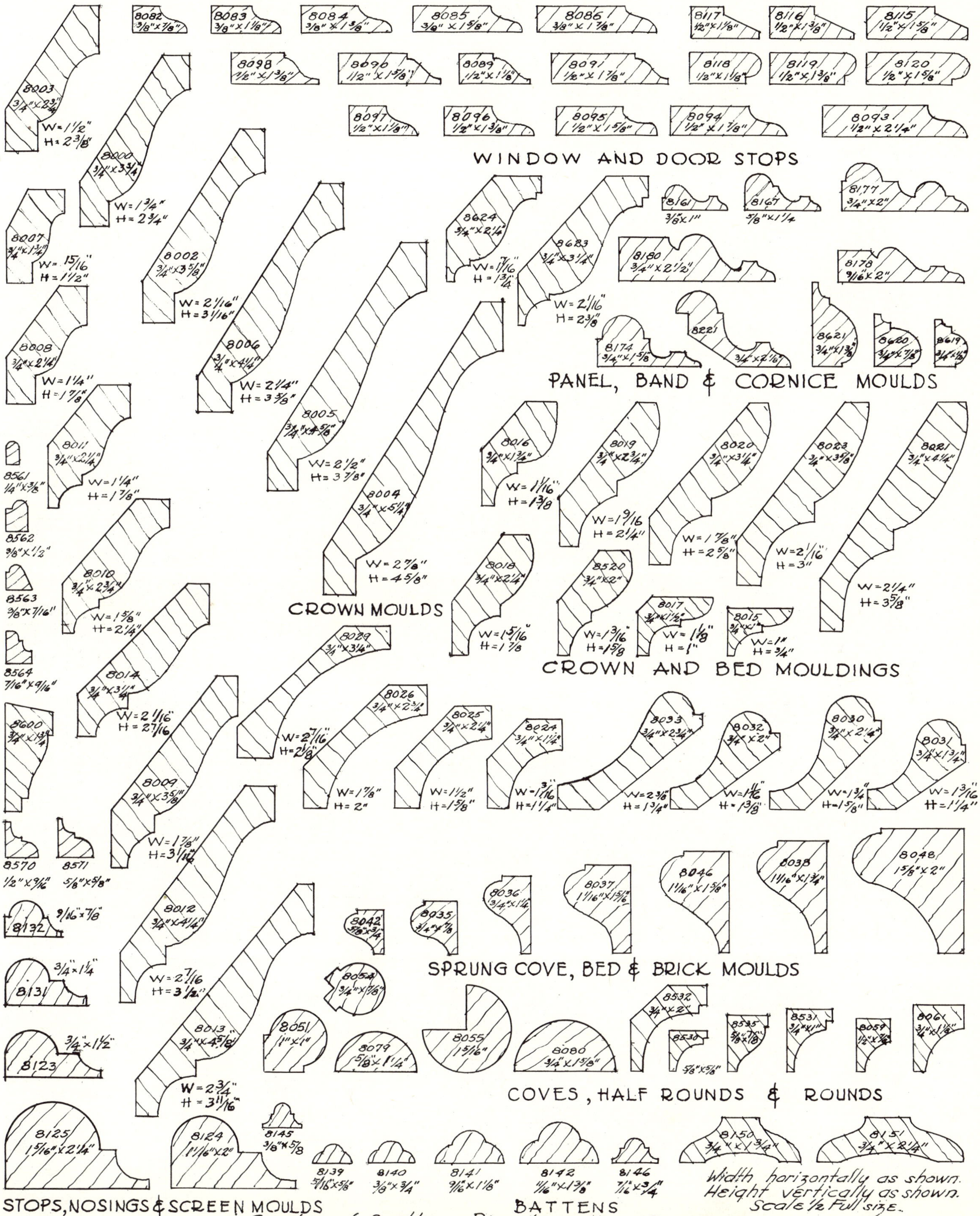
WINDOW AND DOOR STOPS
8082 3/8"×7/8"
8083 3/8"×1 1/8"
8084 3/8"×1 3/8"
8085 3/8"×1 5/8"
8086 3/8"×1 7/8"
8117 1/2"×1 1/8"
8116 1/2"×1 3/8"
8115 1/2"×1 5/8"
8098 1/2"×1 3/8"
8090 1/2"×1 5/8"
8089 1/2"×1 1/8"
8091 1/2"×1 7/8"
8118 1/2"×1 1/8"
8119 1/2"×1 3/8"
8120 1/2"×1 5/8"
8097 1/2"×1 1/8"
8096 1/2"×1 3/8"
8095 1/2"×1 5/8"
8094 1/2"×1 7/8"
8093 1/2"×2 1/4"
PANEL, BAND & CORNICE MOULDS
8161 3/8"×1"
8167 5/8"×1 1/4
8177 3/4"×2"
8624 3/4"×2 1/4" W=1 1/16 H=1 3/4
8683 3/4"×3 1/4" W=2 1/16" H=2 3/8"
8180 3/4"×2 1/2"
8178 9/16"×2"
8174 3/4"×1 5/8
8221 3/4"×2 1/16
8621 3/4"×1 3/8
8620 3/4"×7/8
8619 3/4"×1/2
CROWN MOULDS
8003 3/4"×2 3/4" W=1 1/2" H=2 3/8"
8000 3/4"×3 1/4" W=1 3/4" H=2 3/4"
8007 3/4"×1 3/4" W=15/16" H=1 1/2"
8002 3/4"×3 5/8" W=2 1/16" H=3 1/16"
8008 3/4"×2 1/4" W=1 1/4" H=1 7/8"
8006 3/4"×4 1/4" W=2 1/4" H=3 3/8"
8005 3/4"×4 5/8" W=2 1/2" H=3 7/8"
8004 3/4"×5 1/4" W=2 7/8" H=4 5/8"
8011 3/4"×2 1/4" W=1 1/4" H=1 7/8"
8010 3/4"×2 3/4" W=1 5/8" H=2 1/4"
8014 3/4"×3 1/4" W=2 1/16" H=2 7/16
8009 3/4"×3 5/8" W=1 7/8" H=3 1/16"
8012 3/4"×4 1/4" W=2 7/16 H=3 1/2"
8013 3/4"×4 5/8" W=2 3/4" H=3 11/16"
CROWN AND BED MOULDINGS
8016 3/4"×1 3/4" W=1 1/16 H=1 3/8
8019 3/4"×2 3/4" W=1 9/16 H=2 1/4"
8020 3/4"×3 1/4" W=1 7/8" H=2 5/8"
8023 3/4"×3 5/8 W=2 1/16 H=3"
8021 3/4"×4 1/4" W=2 1/4" H=3 5/8"
8018 3/4"×2 1/4 W=1 5/16" H=1 7/8
8520 3/4"×2" W=1 3/16 H=1 5/8
8017 3/4"×1 1/2" W=1 1/8" H=1"
8015 3/4"×1" W=1" H=3/4"
8029 3/4"×3 1/4" W=2 7/16" H=2 1/8"
8026 3/4"×2 3/4" W=1 7/8" H=2"
8025 3/4"×2 1/4 W=1 1/2" H=1 5/8"
8024 3/4"×1 3/4" W=1 3/16 H=1 1/4"
8033 3/4"×2 3/4" W=2 3/8 H=1 3/4"
8032 3/4"×2" W=1 1/16 H=1 3/8
8030 3/4"×2 1/4" W=1 3/4" H=1 5/8"
8031 3/4"×1 3/4" W=1 3/16 H=1 1/4"
SPRUNG COVE, BED & BRICK MOULDS
8042 5/8"×3/4
8035 3/4"×7/8
8036 3/4"×1 1/4
8037 1 1/16"×1 5/8"
8046 1 1/16"×1 3/8"
8038 1 1/16"×1 3/4
8048 1 5/8"×2"
COVES, HALF ROUNDS & ROUNDS
8054 3/4"×7/8
8051 1"×1"
8079 5/8"×1 1/4"
8055 1 5/16"
8080 3/4"×1 5/8"
8532 3/4"×2"
8530 5/8"×5/8"
8535 5/8"×7/8
8531 3/4"×1"
8059 1/2"×1/2
8061 3/4"×1 1/8"
STOPS, NOSINGS & SCREEN MOULDS
8561 1/4"×3/8"
8562 3/8"×1/2"
8563 3/8"×7/16"
8564 7/16"×9/16"
8600 3/4"×1 3/4"
8570 1/2"×9/16"
8571 5/8"×5/8"
8132 9/16"×7/8"
8131 3/4"×1 1/4"
8123 3/4"×1 1/2"
8125 1 5/16"×2 1/4"
8124 1 1/16"×2"
8145 3/8"×5/8
BATTENS
8139 5/16"×5/8"
8140 3/8"×3/4"
8141 9/16"×1 1/8"
8142 11/16"×1 3/8"
8146 7/16"×3/4
8150 3/4"×1 3/4"
8151 3/4"×2 1/4"
Width horizontally as shown.
Height vertically as shown.
Scale 1/2 Full size.

Courtesy of Southern Pine Inspection Bureau.

DOUGLAS FIR & SOFTWOOD PLYWOODS – SIZES

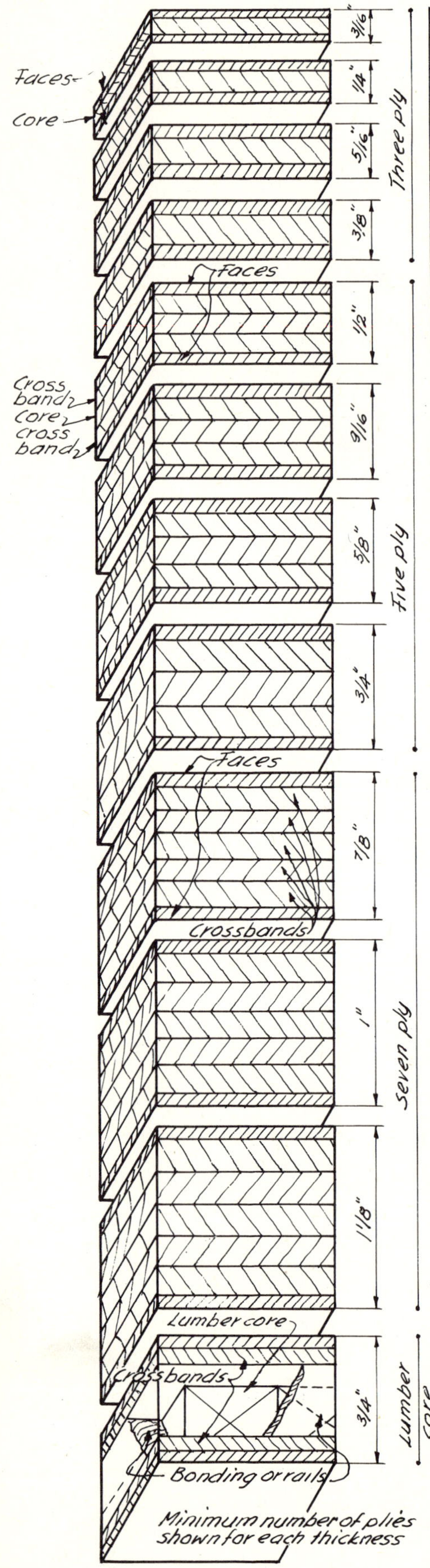

Faces
Core
Cross band
Core
Cross band
Faces
Faces
Crossbands
Lumber core
Crossbands
Bonding or rails
3/16
1/4
5/16
3/8
1/2
9/16
5/8
3/4
7/8
1"
1 1/8
3/4
Three ply
Five ply
Seven ply
Lumber core

Minimum number of plies shown for each thickness

F.S. THICKNESSES & PLYWOOD CONST.

STANDARD DOUGLAS FIR PLYWOOD SIZES

	GRADE	WIDTH × LENGTH × THICKNESS	USES
INTERIOR TYPES	A-A (Int.) A-B (Sound/Solid-int.)	30", 36", 42", 48" × 60", 72", 84", 96", 108", 120", 144" × 3/16", 1/4", 3/8", 1/2", 5/8", 3/4"	Built-ins, displays, partitions, fixtures, gen. inside
	A-D (Int.) (Plypanel)		Walls, ceilings, built-ins, cabinets, in "dry-wall" construction.
	B-D (Int.) C-(repaired) D-(Plybase) (Int.)		Base for carpeting, linoleum, & backing for wall materials.
	C-D (Sheathing-Int.) (Plyscord)	48" × 96", 108", 120", 144" × 5/16", 3/8", 1/2", 5/8"	Wall & roof sheathing, subfloors and other construction purposes.
	B-B (Conc. Form Panel-Int.) (Plyform)	48" × 96" × 1/4", 1/2", 9/16", 5/8", 3/4"	For limited re-uses in conc. form work, moisture resistant bond.
EXTERIOR TYPES	A-A (Ext.) A-B (Ext.)	30", 36", 42", 48" × 60", 72", 84", 96", 108", 120", 144" × 3/16, 1/4", 3/8", 1/2", 5/8", 3/4", 7/8, 1", 1 1/8"	All uses where permanently exposed to weather, water, etc.
	A-C (Sound 1 Side-Ext.) (Plyshield)		Siding of homes, bldgs, etc.
	B-C (Exterior Utility C-(Repaired) C-(Underlayment, Ext.)		General exterior utility use, especially painted surfaces.
	C-C (Sheathing-Ext.)	48" × 96", 108", 120", 144" × 5/16", 3/8", 1/2", 5/8"	Exterior surfacing where appearance is not important (farm bldgs, etc.)
	B-B (Conc. Form Panel-Ext.)	48" × 96" × 5/8", 3/4"	Conc. Forms requiring max. re-use, waterproof bond.

Grade stamped on edge of all panels except Plypanel, Plybase, Plyscord & Plyform, in which case grade is stamped on the back of panel. Plyshield grade is stamped on both the edge and the back.

Based on U.S. Dept. of Commerce Commercial Standard CS-45-55.

STANDARD STOCK SOFTWOOD PLYWOOD SIZES

	GRADES	WIDTH	LENGTH	1/4"	5/16"	3/8"	1/2"	5/8"	3/4"	7/8"	1"
INTERIOR	A1-A1 Int. A-A Int.	36"	72"	•					•		
			96"	•		•	•		•		
		48"	72", 84", 96" & 120"	•		•	•	•	•		
			108"	•		•			•		
			144"	•					•		
	A-B Int.	36"	96"	•		•	•	•	•		
		48"	72", 84", 96" & 120"	•		•	•	•	•		
			108" & 144"	•					•		
	A1-D Int. A-D Int.	30"	60", 72" & 120"						•		
			84" & 96"	•					•		
		36"	60"						•		
			72", 84" & 96"	•		•	•	•	•		
			120"	•					•		
		48"	60", 72", 84", 96", 108", 120", 144"	•		•	•	•	•		
	B-B Conc. form	48"	96"					•	•		
	B-D Int.	48"	84" & 96"	•		•	•	•	•		
	C-D Underlay.	48"	96"	•		•	•	•	•		
	C-D Sheathing	48"	96"		•	•	•	•	•		
			120"		•			•			
EXTERIOR	A1-A1 Ext. A-A Ext.	48"	60", 84", 108", 120" & 144"	•		•	•	•	•		
			96"	•		•	•	•	•	•	•
	A-B Ext.	48"	84"	•		•		•			
			96" & 120"	•		•	•	•	•		
			144"	•		•	•		•		
	A1-C Ext.	36"	96"	•		•	•	•	•		
	A-C Ext.	48"	72", 84" 108", 120" & 144"	•		•	•	•	•		
			96"	•		•	•	•	•		•
	B-B (Conc. form)	48"	96"					•	•		
	C-C Underlay	48"	96"	•		•	•	•	•		
	C-C Sheathing	48"	96"		•	•	•	•	•		

Based on U.S. Dept. of Commerce Commercial Standard CS 122-49 Revised

STANDARD PONDEROSA PINE & SUGAR PINE PLYWOOD SIZES

Grades		WIDTHS × LENGTHS × THICKNESS	Based on U.S. Dept. of Commerce Commercial Standard CS 157-49
Good 2 sides Good 1 Side Sound 2 Sides Sound 1 Side	Solid 2 Sides Solid 1 Side Sound 1 side Solid 1 Side	12" to 48" in 2" increments × 60", 72", 84", 96" × 1/4", 3/8", 1/2", 5/8", 3/4", 1"	
Sheathing		same as above × 5/16", 3/8", 1/2", 5/8"	

Interior only

In above tables all sheathing grades are unsanded - all others sanded 2 sides.

Data checked by: Douglas Fir Plywood Association

PLYWOOD DETAILS

STOCK SIZES OF PLYWOOD										
MFRS.	DIMENSIONS									FACING WOODS
	3-PLY			5-PLY			LUMBER CORE			
	WIDTHS	LENGTHS	TH'S	WIDTHS	LENGTHS	TH'S	WIDTHS	LENGTHS	TH'S	
U.S. Plywood (Weldwood)	24", 30" 36" & 48"	48", 60", 72" 84" & 96"	1/8" & 1/4"	24", 30" 36" & 48"	60", 72" 84" & 96"	3/8" & 1/2"	24", 30" 36" & 48"	60", 72", 84" & 96"	3/4"	Douglas fir, pine, gum, birch, korina, prima vera, maple, elm, walnut, oak, avodire, birch, cherry, etc.
Roddis Plywood (Roddiscraft)	24", 30" 36" & 48"	36", 48", 72" 84" & 96"	1/8", 3/16" & 1/4"	24", 30" 36" & 48"	36", 48", 72" 84" & 96"	3/8" & 1/2"	24", 30" 36" & 48"	36", 48", 72" 84" & 96"	3/4"	Birch, maple, oak, walnut, mahogany, prima vera, avodire, blond limba, chen chen, white ash, elm.
F. Eggers Plywood & Veneer	24", 36" & 48"	48", 60", 72", 84", 96", 120" & 144"	1/8", 3/16" & 1/4"	24", 36" & 48"	48", 60", 72", 84", 96", 120" & 144"	3/8" & 1/4"	24", 36" & 48"	48", 60", 72", 84", 96" 120" & 144"	3/4" to 2 1/4"	Birch, maple, ash, oak, elm, walnut, mahogany, prima vera, avodire, limba, cherry, gum, redwood and foreign woods.
M & M Wood Working Co.	48"	96"	1/4" & 1/8"	48"	96"	3/8" & 3/4"				California redwood.

Plywood is made of both soft and hard woods. Douglas Fir, pine and cedar are classified as soft; birch, maple, oak, ash, walnut, gum, mahogany, avodire, korina, blonde limba, chen chen and prima vera, as hardwoods. Exterior plywood is differentiated from interior in that a water proof glue (instead of water resistant) is used as a bonding agent.

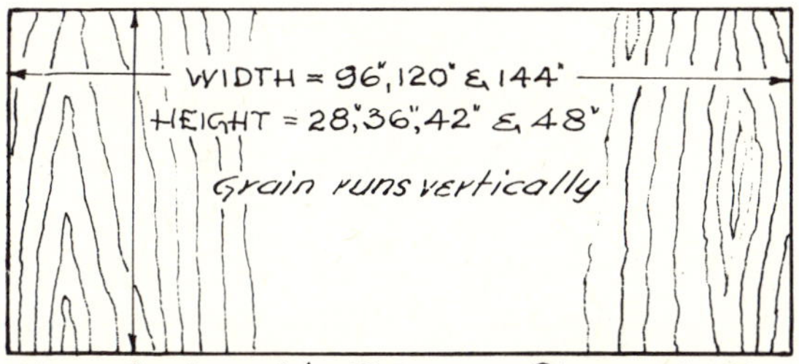
WIDTH = 96", 120" & 144"
HEIGHT = 28", 36", 42" & 48"
Grain runs vertically

Made in various hardwood faces usually good only one side.

Thickness: 3/4" lumber core construction in all sizes. 3/4" veneer core in 96" and 120" widths

Manufactured by F. Eggers, Plywood & Veneer Co. U.S. Plywood Corp. & Roddis Plywood Corp.

PLYWOOD FOR CONTERFRONTS

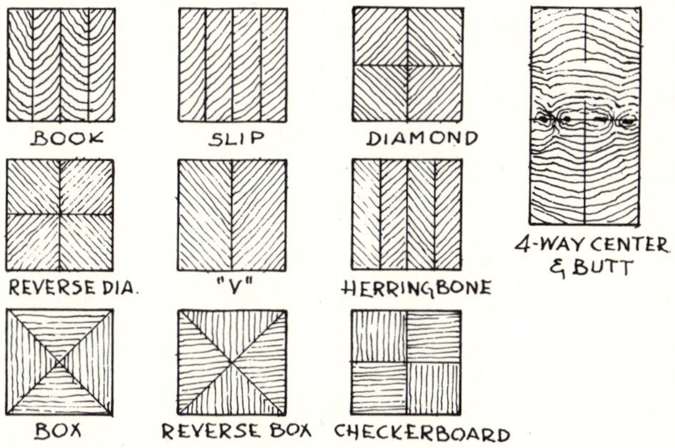
BOOK
SLIP
DIAMOND
4-WAY CENTER & BUTT
REVERSE DIA.
"V"
HERRINGBONE
BOX
REVERSE BOX
CHECKERBOARD

VENEER MATCHING

WELDEX striated Plywood

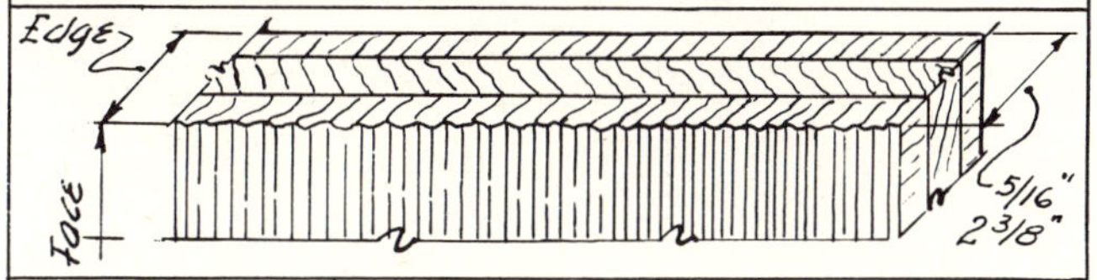
Edge
Face
5/16"
2 3/8"

WOOD	TYPE	SIZES
Fir	Interior Exterior	4'-0" x 6, 7, 8, 9 & 10 Ft. 4'-0" x 15 7/8", * 8, 9, 10 Ft.
Gum	Interior (Select or unselected)	12", 16", 24" squares & 4'-0" x 8'-0"
Mahogany (Philippine)	Interior	4'-0" x 8'-0"

* Siding - All manufactured sound one side, 3 ply plywood 5/16" thick except exterior type fir which is made 3/8" thick. Gum best for painting. Mahogany most effective when finished in natural color. Nailing same as regular Plywood.

NOVOPLY — Three ply laminate mfrd from resin treated wood particles.

WOOD	TYPE	SIZES
California Redwoods	Interior	3/8" & 3/4" thick 4'-0" x 8'-0" *
Pine & Fir mixed	Interior	3/8" thick - 4'-0" x 8'-0" *
	Interior	3/4" thick Sizes from 2'-6" x 4'-0" to 4'-0" x 8'-0" *
	Reveneering	11/16" thick

* 3/8" is intended principally for wall paneling and wainscoting and for small cabinet and sliding cabinet doors. The 3/4" panel is used for built-ins, partitions, cabinet and sliding doors and as a core stock under wood veneers and plastic laminates.

Plank weld (Reg. Pat. Pend.) Weldtex and Novoply are products of United States Plywood Corporation.

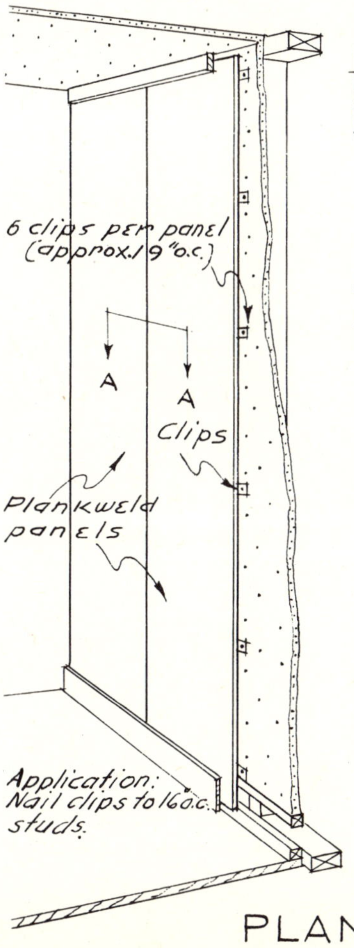
6 clips per panel (approx. 19" o.c.)
A
A
Clips
Plankweld panels
Application: Nail clips to 16" o.c. studs.

PLANKWELD

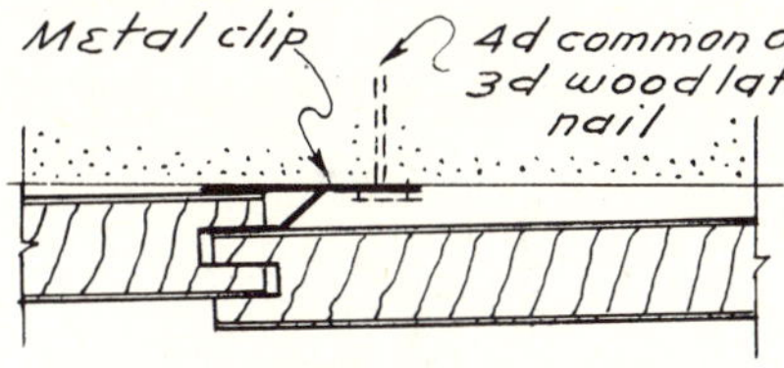
Metal clip
4d common or 3d wood lath nail

F.S. SECTION "AA"

16 1/4" wide
6', 7', & 8' long

Made of 1/4" prefin. hardwood plywood stocked in - Plain sliced oak, birch, Phil. mahogany, Korina, walnut.

TYPICAL PANEL

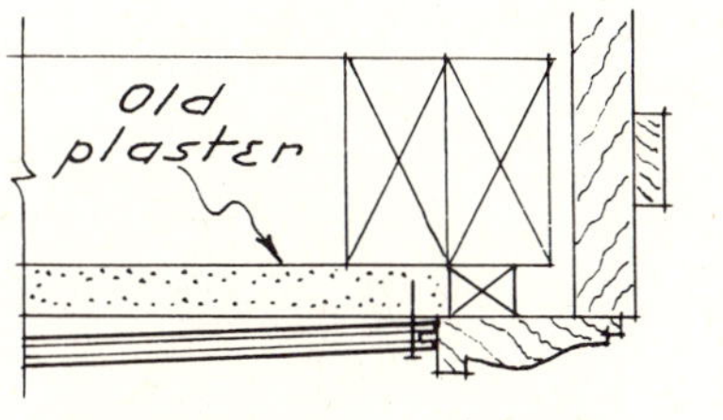
Old plaster

TYPICAL JAMB

Butted to existing casings

PLYWOOD DETAILS

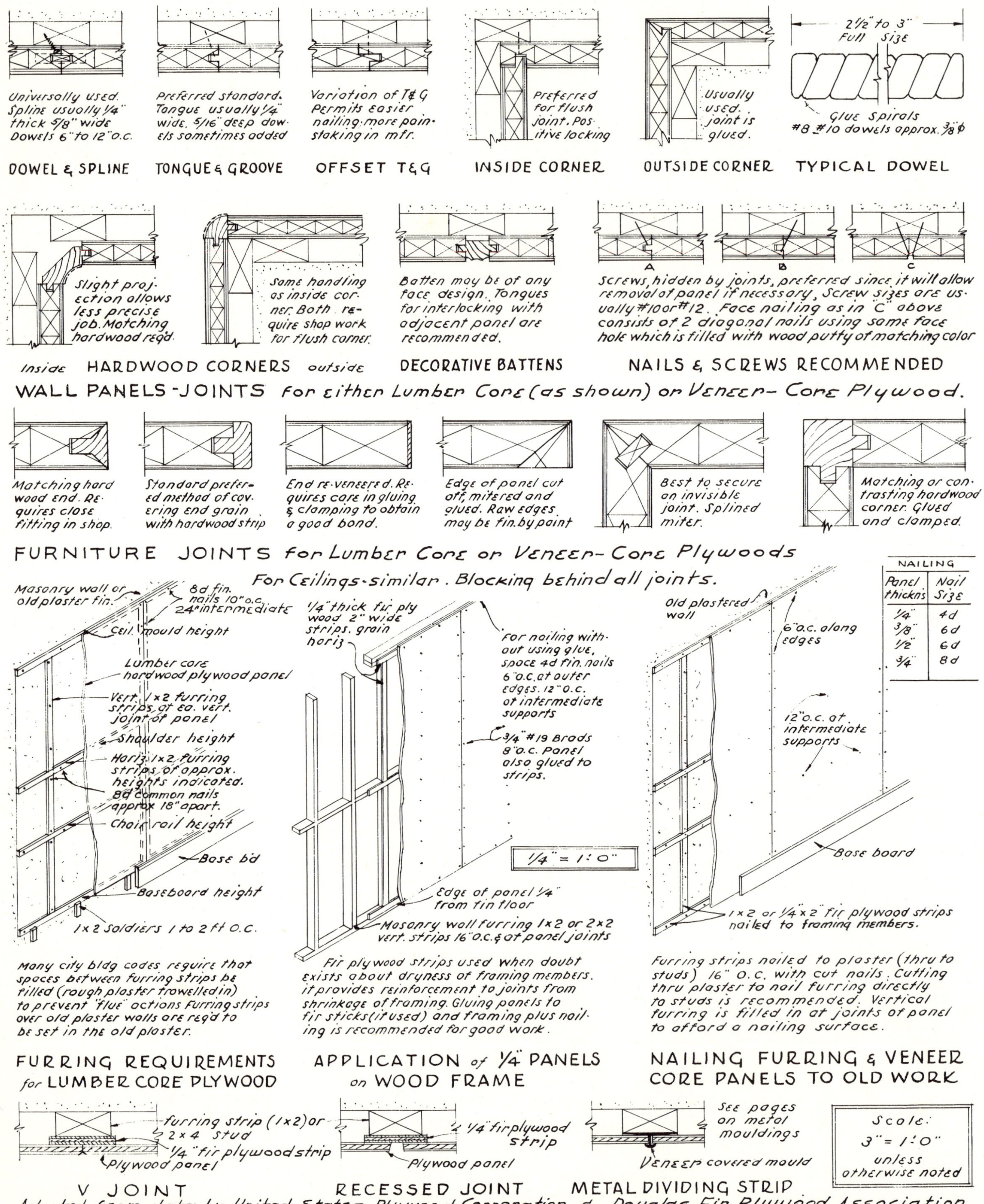
Universally used. Spline usually 1/4" thick 5/8" wide Dowels 6" to 12" o.c.
Preferred standard. Tongue usually 1/4" wide. 5/16" deep dowels sometimes added
Variation of T&G Permits easier nailing. more painstaking in mfr.
Preferred for flush joint. Positive locking
Usually used. joint is glued.
2 1/2" to 3" Full size
Glue spirals #8 - #10 dowels approx. 3/8"ϕ
DOWEL & SPLINE
TONGUE & GROOVE
OFFSET T&G
INSIDE CORNER
OUTSIDE CORNER
TYPICAL DOWEL
Slight projection allows less precise job. Matching hardwood req'd.
Same handling as inside corner. Both require shop work for flush corner.
Batten may be of any face design. Tongues for interlocking with adjacent panel are recommended.
A
B
C
Screws, hidden by joints, preferred since it will allow removal of panel if necessary. Screw sizes are usually #10 or #12. Face nailing as in "C" above consists of 2 diagonal nails using same face hole which is filled with wood putty of matching color
inside HARDWOOD CORNERS outside
DECORATIVE BATTENS
NAILS & SCREWS RECOMMENDED
WALL PANELS-JOINTS for either Lumber Core (as shown) or Veneer-Core Plywood.
Matching hard wood end. Requires close fitting in shop.
Standard preferred method of covering end grain with hardwood strip
End re-veneered. Requires care in gluing & clamping to obtain a good bond.
Edge of panel cut off, mitered and glued. Raw edges may be fin. by paint
Best to secure an invisible joint. Splined miter.
Matching or contrasting hardwood corner. Glued and clamped.
FURNITURE JOINTS for Lumber Core or Veneer-Core Plywoods
For Ceilings-similar. Blocking behind all joints.
NAILING
Panel thickn's | Nail size
1/4" | 4d
3/8" | 6d
1/2" | 6d
3/4" | 8d
Masonry wall or old plaster fin.
8d fin. nails 10" o.c. 24" intermediate
Ceil. mould height
Lumber core hardwood plywood panel
Vert. 1x2 furring strips at ea. vert. joint of panel
Shoulder height
Horiz. 1x2 furring strips of approx. heights indicated. 8d common nails approx 18" apart.
Chair rail height
Base b'd
Baseboard height
1x2 soldiers 1 to 2 ft o.c.
1/4" thick fir ply wood 2" wide strips, grain horiz.
For nailing without using glue, space 4d fin. nails 6" o.c. at outer edges. 12" o.c. at intermediate supports
3/4" #19 Brads 8" o.c. Panel also glued to strips.
1/4" = 1'-0"
Edge of panel 1/4" from fin floor
Masonry wall furring 1x2 or 2x2 vert. strips 16" o.c. & at panel joints
Old plastered wall
6" o.c. along edges
12" o.c. at intermediate supports
Base board
1x2 or 1/4"x2" fir plywood strips nailed to framing members.
Many city bldg codes require that spaces between furring strips be filled (rough plaster trowelled in) to prevent "flue" actions. Furring strips over old plaster walls are req'd to be set in the old plaster.
Fir plywood strips used when doubt exists about dryness of framing members. it provides reinforcement to joints from shrinkage of framing. Gluing panels to fir sticks (if used) and framing plus nailing is recommended for good work.
Furring strips nailed to plaster (thru to studs) 16" o.c. with cut nails. Cutting thru plaster to nail furring directly to studs is recommended. Vertical furring is filled in at joints of panel to afford a nailing surface.
FURRING REQUIREMENTS for LUMBER CORE PLYWOOD
APPLICATION of 1/4" PANELS on WOOD FRAME
NAILING FURRING & VENEER CORE PANELS TO OLD WORK
furring strip (1x2) or 2x4 stud
1/4" fir plywood strip
Plywood panel
1/4" fir plywood strip
Plywood panel
See pages on metal mouldings
Veneer covered mould
Scale: 3" = 1'-0" unless otherwise noted
V JOINT
RECESSED JOINT
METAL DIVIDING STRIP

Adapted from data by United States Plywood Corporation & Douglas Fir Plywood Association.

PLYWOOD DETAILS

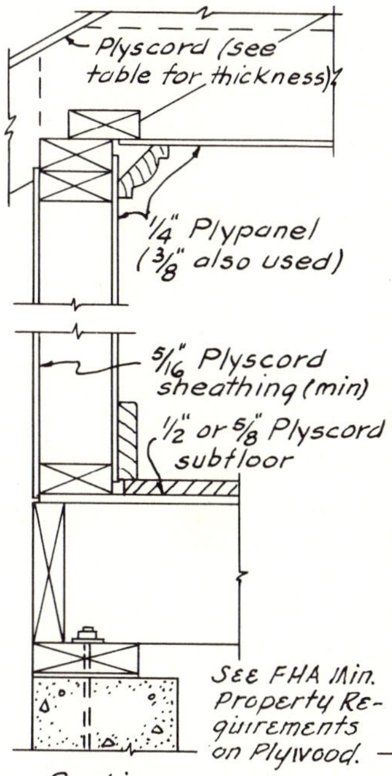
Plyscord (see table for thickness)
1/4" Plypanel (3/8" also used)
5/16" Plyscord sheathing (min)
1/2" or 5/8" Plyscord subfloor
See FHA Min. Property Requirements on Plywood.

Section

PLYWOOD ROOF SHEATHING Recommended thickness for panels lengthwise across rafters continuous over 2 or more spans. Rafters o.c.			
THICKNESS	20#/□' LOAD*	30#/□' LOAD*	40#/□' LOAD*
5/16" Plyscord +	20"	20"	20"
3/8" Plyscord +	24"	24"	24"
1/2" Plyscord +	32"	32"	30"
5/8" Plyscord +	42"	42"	39"
3/4" Plyscord + Plybase or Plypanel +	48"	47"	42"

*Deflection limited to 1/240 of span. For deflection, of 1/360 deduct 1/8 of span. + Plyscord sheathing should not be exposed to weather

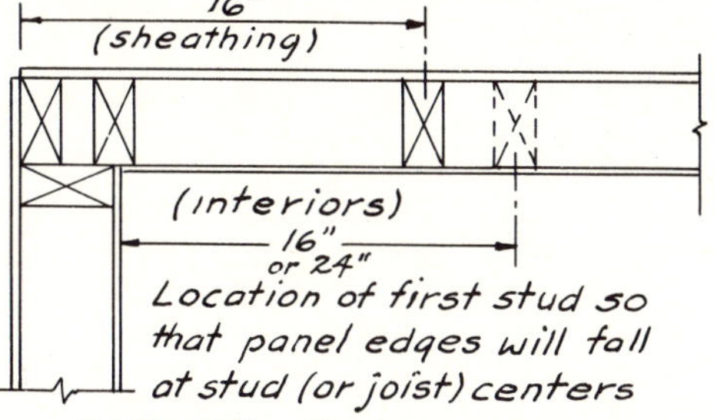
16" (sheathing)
(interiors)
16" or 24"
Location of first stud so that panel edges will fall at stud (or joist) centers

CORNER PLAN

PLYWOOD CONSTRUCTION in FRAME WALLS

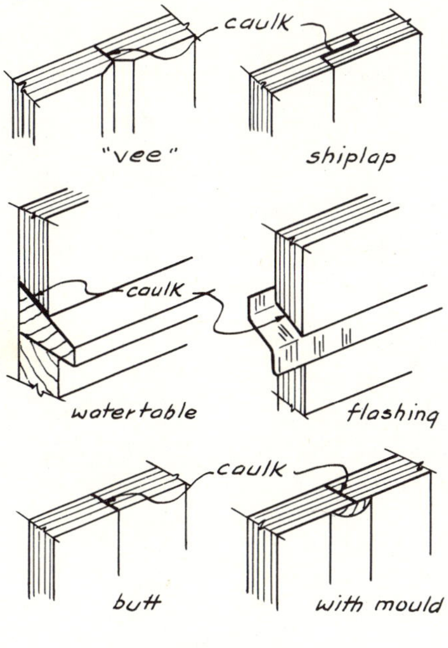
caulk
"vee"
shiplap
caulk
watertable
flashing
caulk
butt
with mould

EXTERIOR

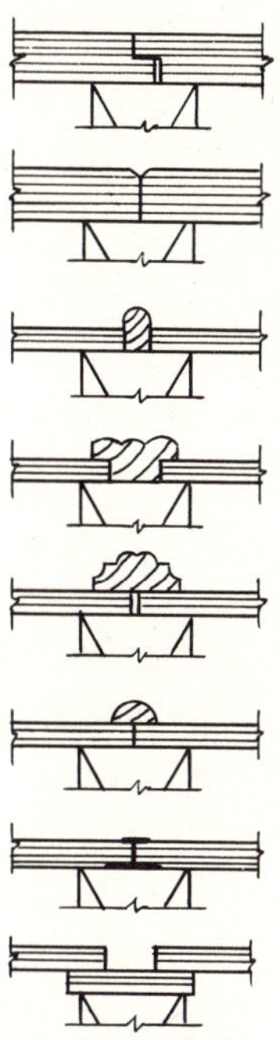

INTERIOR

JOINT SUGGESTIONS

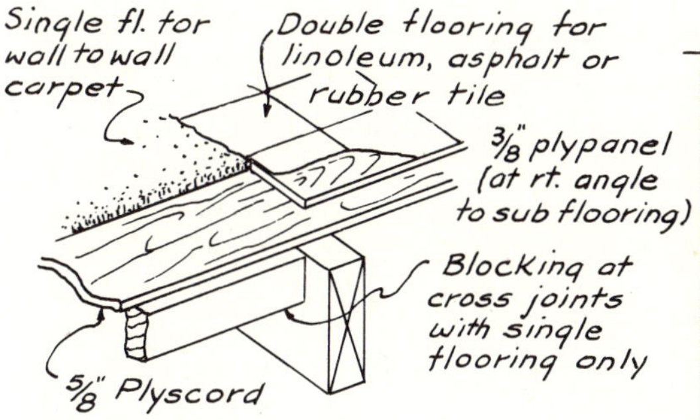
Single fl. for wall to wall carpet
Double flooring for linoleum, asphalt or rubber tile
3/8" plypanel (at rt. angle to sub flooring)
Blocking at cross joints with single flooring only
5/8" Plyscord

For economy 1/2" thickness is acceptable wherever 5/8" is shown; 1/4" for 3/8" as underlayment

PLYWOOD SUBFLOORING

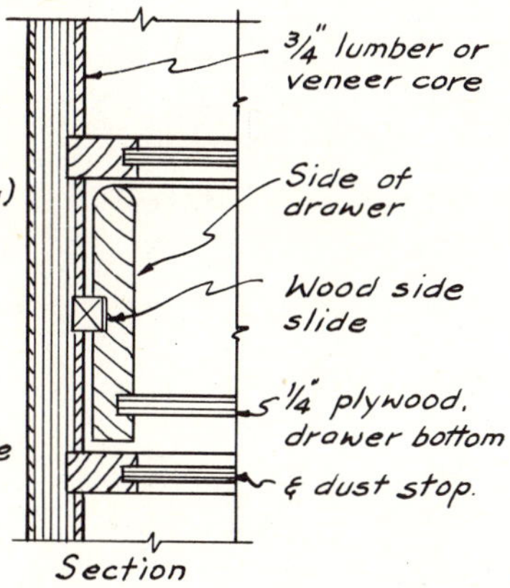
3/4" lumber or veneer core
Side of drawer
Wood side slide
1/4" plywood, drawer bottom & dust stop.

Section

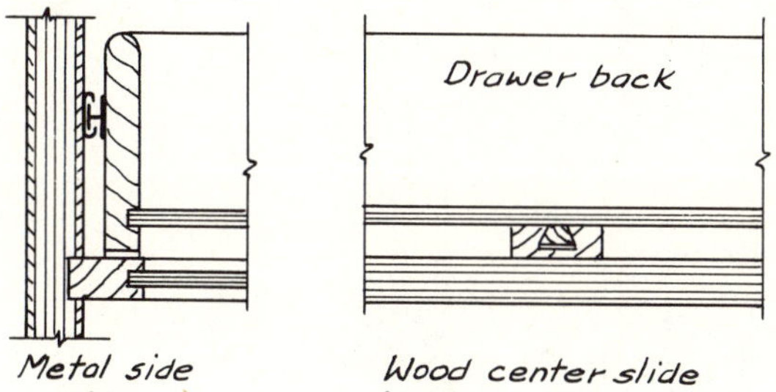
Drawer back

Metal side slide

Wood center slide (Metal available)

Many types of good metal slides, with ball bearings available

Alternates

CABINET DRAWERS - 3" = 1'-0"

APPROX. MIN. BENDING RADII Douglas Fir Plywood		
Panel Thickness	Across Grain	Parallel to Grain
1/8"	6 1/2"	10"
1/4"	15"	24"
3/8"	36"	54"
1/2"	6'-0"	8'-0"
5/8"	8'-0"	10'-0"
3/4"	10'-0"	12'-0"

Shorter radii may be obtained by steaming or wetting at the risk of rupture and possible checking & grain-raising. Installation of curved panels first is recommended.

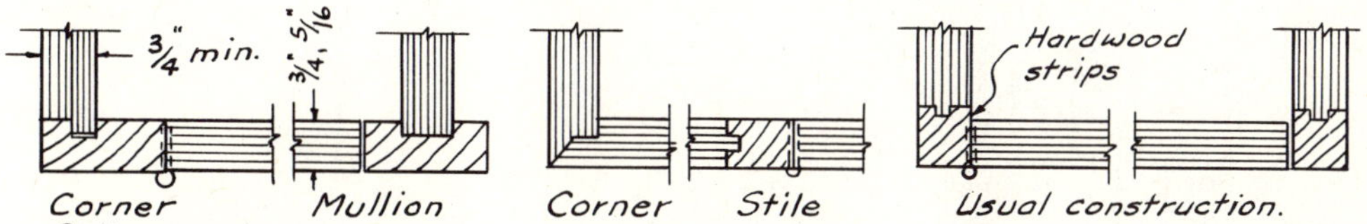
3/4" min.
3/4, 5/16
Hardwood strips

Corner Mullion
Solid member forms wardrobe door frame

Corner Stile
Good where natural fin. is continuous.

Usual construction.
Strips may be omitted (edge exposed)

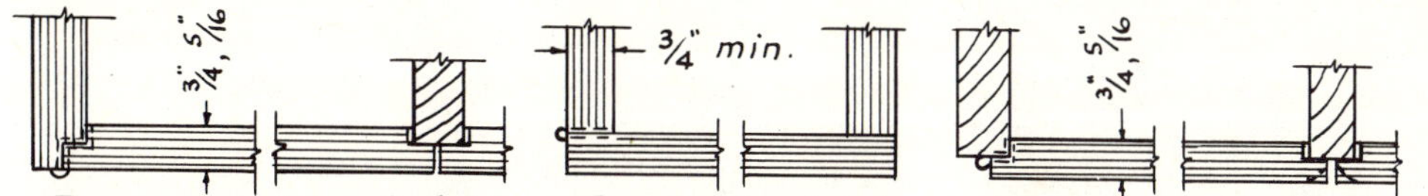
3/4, 5/16"
3/4" min.
3/4, 5/16"

Recessed door. Outside corner edge exposed.

Good only at outside corners

Raised panel effect
Edges may be rounded

FLUSH DOORS

3/4"
1/4" plywood
Usual
Back nailed
1/4" plywood
Applied mould

PANEL DOORS

WARDROBE & CABINET DOORS Scale 3" = 1'-0"

Data from Douglas Fir Plywood Association

ASBESTOS CEMENT & GYPSUM WALLBOARDS for INTERIORS

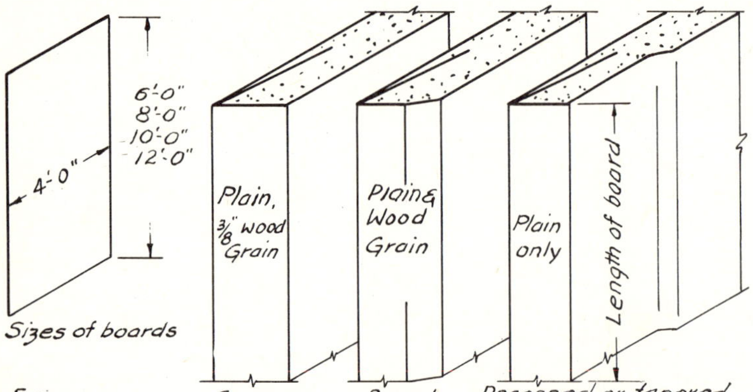
6'-0"
8'-0"
10'-0"
12'-0"
4'-0"
Sizes of boards
Plain, 3/8" wood Grain
Plain & Wood Grain
Plain only
Length of board
Edge:
Thicknesses:
Square
1/4", 3/8", 1/2"
Bevel
3/8"
Recessed or tapered
3/8", 1/2", 5/8"

BENDING RADII		
Thickness	Lengthwise	Width
1/4"	5'-0"	15'-0"
3/8"	7'-6"	25'-0"
1/2"	20'-0"	—

Shorter radii may be obtained by moistening face & back so that water will soak well into core of board

Not all sizes or edges in thicknesses shown are made by all mfrs.

1/4" over old work, vert. joints, 6d, 13 ga., 1 7/8" nails.

3/8" std. use, vert. & horizontally, 4d, 14 ga. 1 3/8" nails, except for wood grain use 4d, 16 ga. 1 1/2" brad. fin. nails.

1/2" greater rigidity, better fire protection (double thickness, staggered joints, for usual fire protection) vert. & horizontally applied 5d, 13 1/2 ga. 1 5/8" nails. Nails, unless otherwise noted, are flat head, 6"-8" o.c. on walls, 5"-7" o.c. on ceilings.

Notes: Horizontal application of recess edge boards recommended.

On ceilings place boards at right angles to joists.

Joint treatment:
1. Joint adhesive
2. Joint reinforcing.
3. Joint adhesive sanded smooth
4. Joint adhesive, thin coat.

Nails: flat heads; 3/8" board, 4d, 1 3/8", 14 ga.; 1/2" board, 5d, 1 5/8", 13 1/2 ga.; 5/8" board, 6d, 1 7/8", 13 ga.

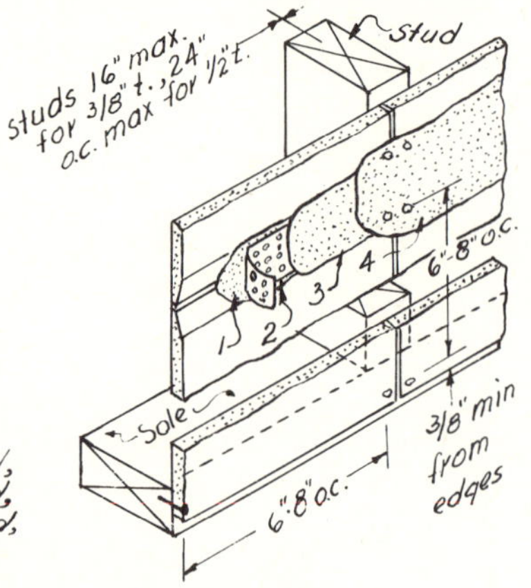
Stud
Studs 16" max. for 3/8" t., 24" o.c. max for 1/2" t.
6"-8" o.c.
Sole
1
2
3
4
3/8" min from edges
6"-8" o.c.

RECESSED EDGE JOINT

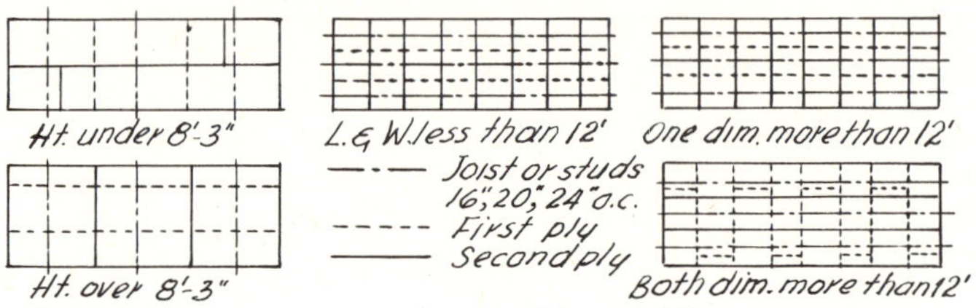
Ht. under 8'-3"
Ht. over 8'-3"
L. & W. less than 12'
One dim. more than 12'
Joist or studs 16", 20", 24" o.c.
First ply
Second ply
Both dim. more than 12'
SIDE WALLS
CEILINGS

3/8" board is used for 2-ply const.; recessed or sq. edged for 1 ply, recessed edge for 2nd ply. Facing or 2nd ply is bonded to 1st by cement approved by wall board mfr. Nail holes and joints in facing ply are finished as above.

SIZES, EDGES, USE and NAILING

LAYOUT PATTERNS-2 PLYS GYPSUM BOARD

GYPSUM WALL BOARDS

Data checked by The Gypsum Association.

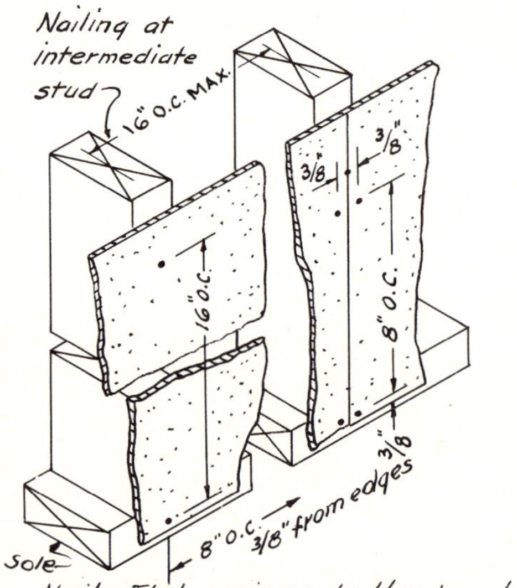
Nailing at intermediate stud
16" O.C. MAX.
3/8
3/8
16" O.C.
8" O.C.
3/8
8" O.C.
3/8" from edges
Sole

Nails: Flat, casing or button head. Drive screw nails to penetrate into solid wood. Drilling for nails and fasteners is unnecessary on type "U" or "F" boards on any thickness up to and including 1/4"

NAILS and SPACING

BENDING RADII

Minimum

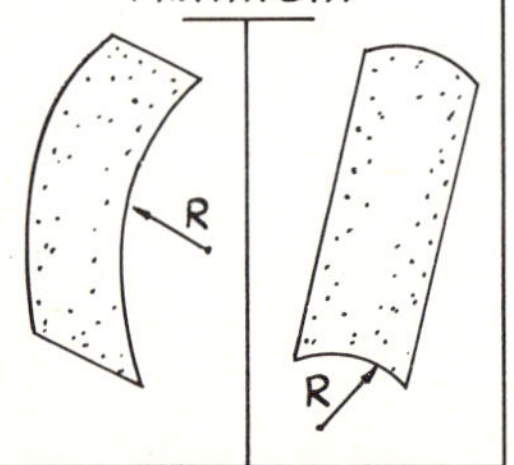
R
R

Length	Thickn.	Width
30" 36"	1/8" 3/16	36" 54"

Unscored boards only

SIZES

Boards - 4'x4', 4'x8' - 1/8" & 3/16" thick usual for interior finishes. 1/8" x 4'x4' tile-like scored boards also available

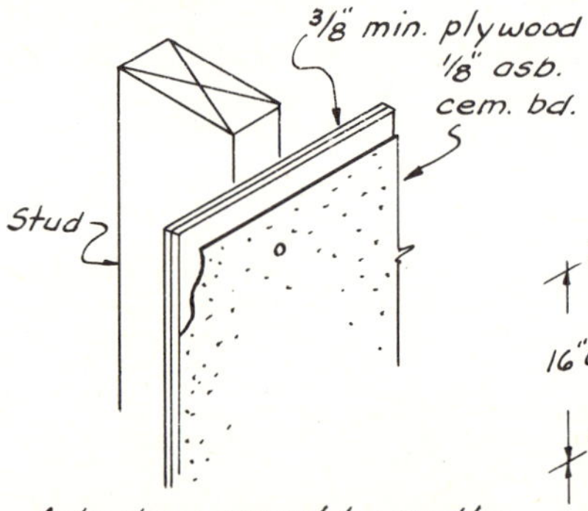
3/8" min. plywood
1/8" asb. cem. bd.
Stud

Asbestos cement board has a Underwriters' Laboratory fire resistance rating of zero combustibility, zero flame spread and zero toxic smoke production. Backing with gypsum board increases its fire resistance and is recommended. 1/8" board should have a 3/8" min gyp. backing. 3/8" asb. cem. board may be used without backing if cats are placed behind all joints.

ON WOOD STUDS OVER BACKING

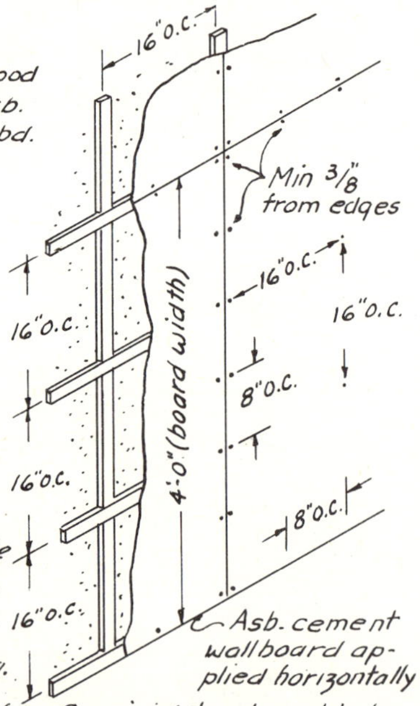
16" o.c.
Min 3/8 from edges
16" o.c.
16" o.c.
16" o.c.
8" o.c.
16" o.c.
4'-0" (board width)
8" o.c.
16" o.c.
Asb. cement wallboard applied horizontally

See joint treatment below

ON FURRING over MASONRY or PLASTER

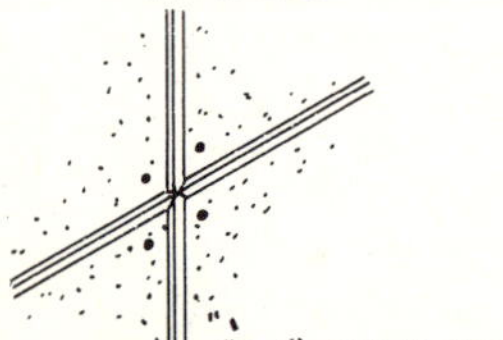

"V" JOINT

Edges of board beveled with rasp.

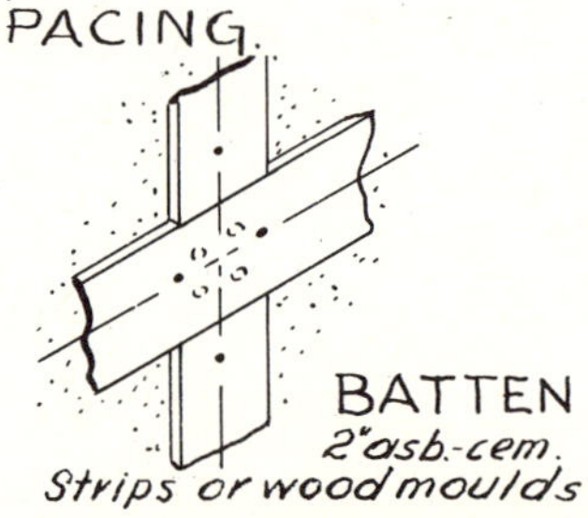

BATTEN

2" asb.-cem. Strips or wood moulds

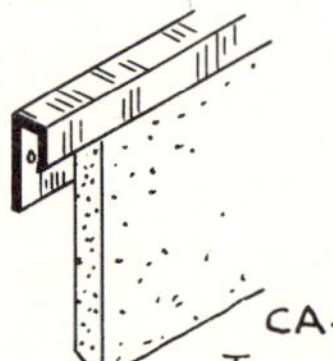

CAP

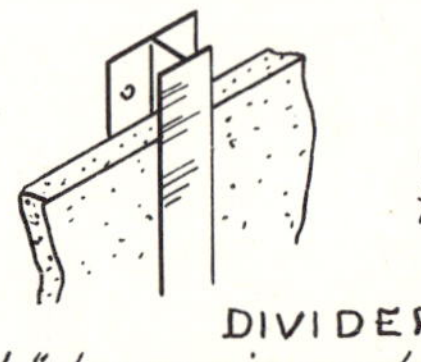

DIVIDER

To prevent "drumming add face nailing or adhesive to these board attachments

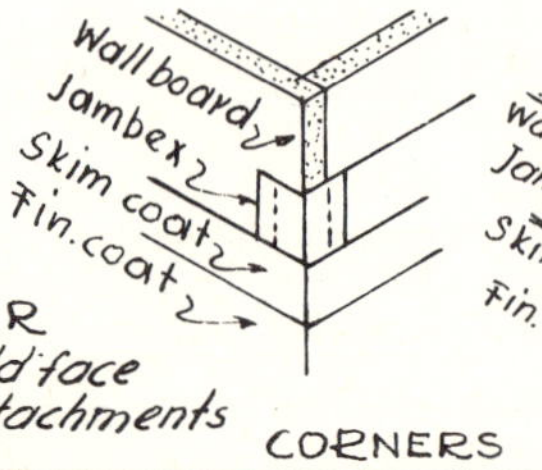
Wall board 2
Jambe x 2
Skim coat 2
Fin. coat 2

CORNERS

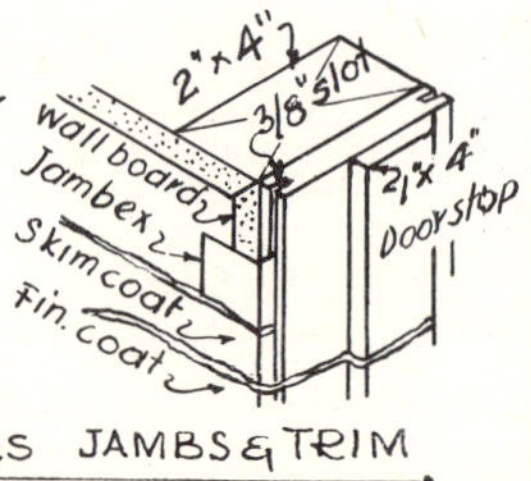
2"x4"
3/8" slot
Wall board 2
Jambe x 2
Skim coat 2
Fin. coat 2
2"x4"
Doorstop

JAMBS & TRIM

MOULDINGS

ASBESTOS CEMENT WALL BOARDS

Data checked by Asbestos Cement Products Assoc.

FIBER (vegetable) WALLBOARDS for INTERIORS

DESIGNATION		SIZES	THICKNESSES
Wallboard, Building Board, Structural Fiberboard, Insulating Board, Insulation Board or Structural Insulation Board.	Panel	Generally available in widths of 4'-0" & Lengths from 4'-0" to 12'-0" in increments of 1'-0" (No 11'-0" Lengths made). Several Boards are manufactured in sizes 8'-0" x 14'-0" & 16'-0" (Homosote & Upson). A 4'-0" x 14'-0" & 16'-0" is made (Upson). Largest Board made is 8'-0" x 18'-0" (Upson).	3/8", 15/32" (Homosote) 1/2" & 3/4"
	Plank	Generally available in widths of 8", 10", 12", 16" & in Lengths of 8'-0", 10'-0", 12'-0". A few planks are made in 6'-0" Lengths.	1/2" & 3/4"

See also "Insulating materials"

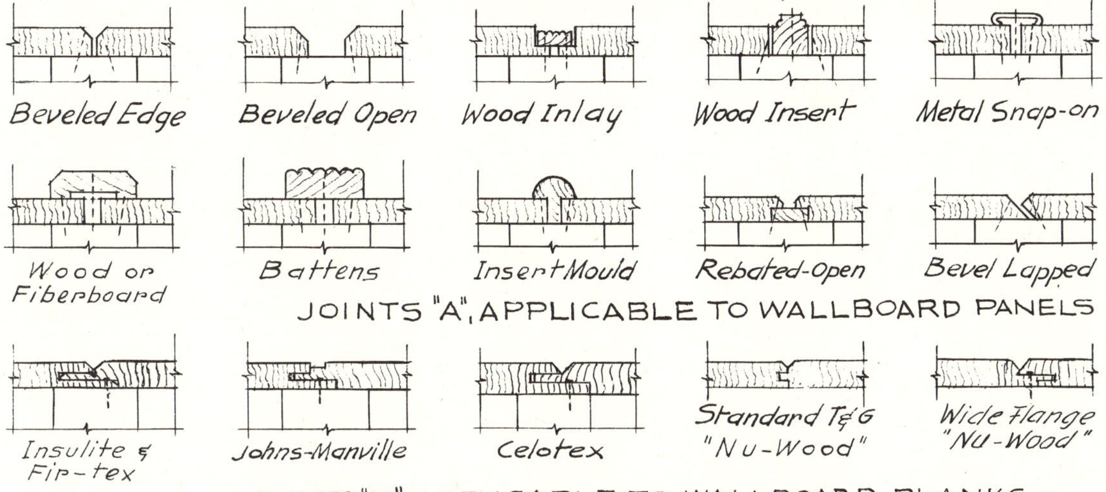

Beveled Edge
Beveled Open
Wood Inlay
Wood Insert
Metal Snap-on
Wood or Fiberboard
Battens
Insert Mould
Rebated-Open
Bevel Lapped
Insulite & Fir-tex
Johns-Manville
Celotex
Standard T&G "Nu-Wood"
Wide Flange "Nu-Wood"

JOINTS "A", APPLICABLE TO WALLBOARD PANELS

JOINTS "B", APPLICABLE TO WALLBOARD PLANKS

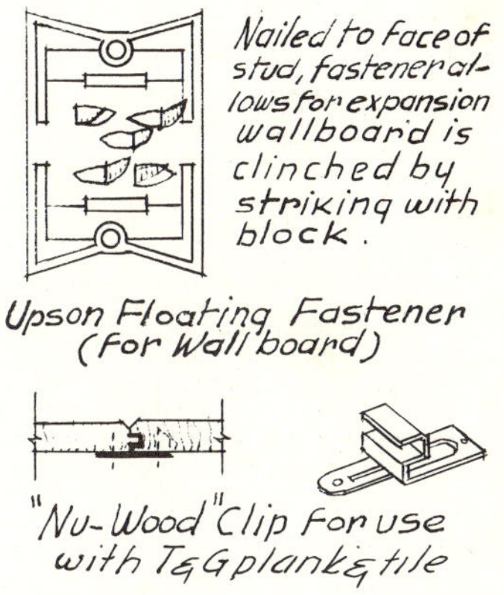

Nailed to face of stud, fastener allows for expansion wallboard is clinched by striking with block.
Upson Floating Fastener (For Wall board)
"Nu-Wood" Clip for use with T&G plank & tile

CONCEALED FASTENERS

Application of Planks & Panels to ceiling is similar to wall applications

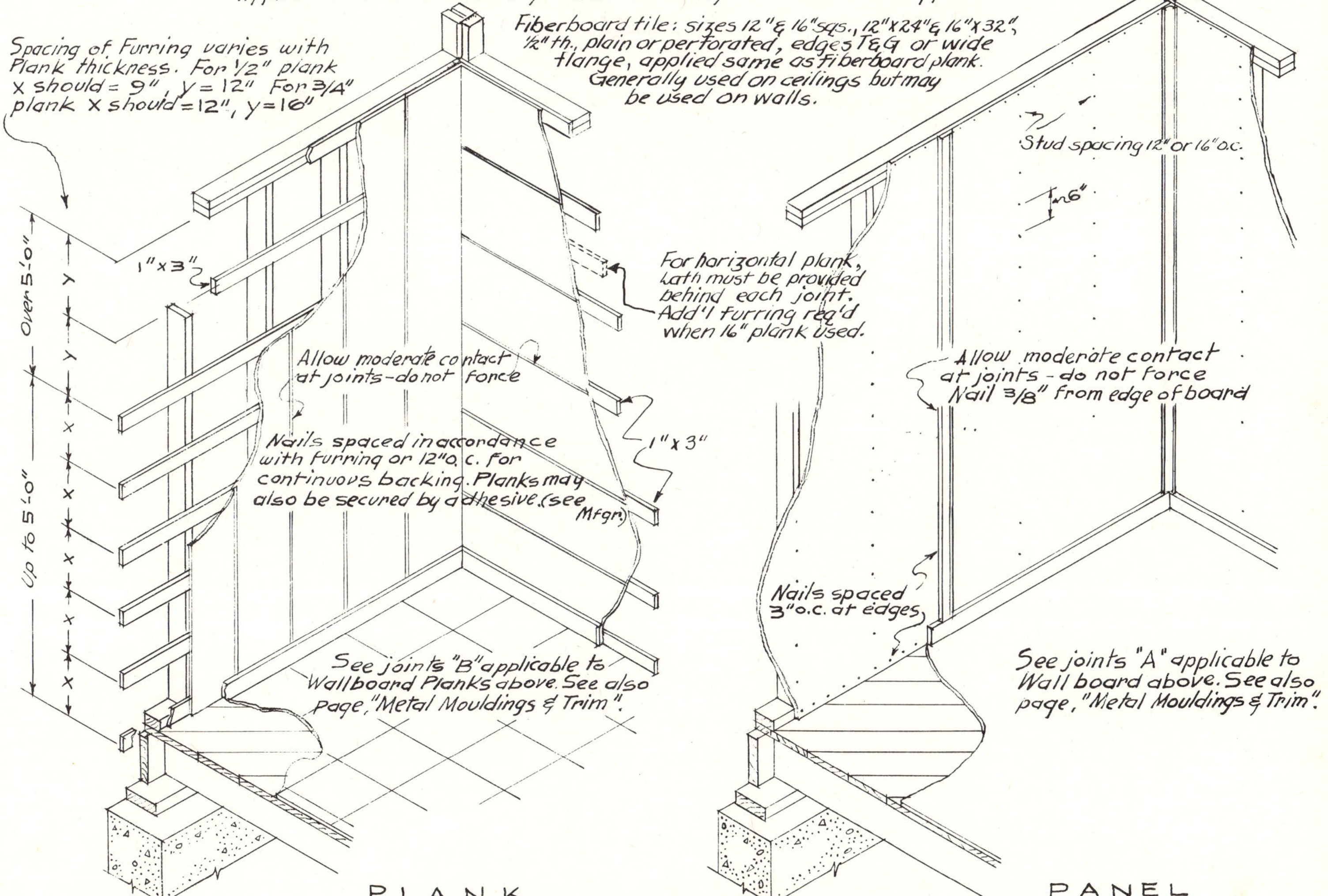

Fiberboard tile: sizes 12" & 16" sqs., 12" x 24" & 16" x 32", ½" th., plain or perforated, edges T&G or wide flange, applied same as Fiberboard plank. Generally used on ceilings but may be used on walls.
Spacing of Furring varies with Plank thickness. For ½" plank X should = 9", Y = 12" For 3/4" plank X should = 12", Y = 16"
1" x 3"
Over 5'-0"
Up to 5'-0"
Y
X
For horizontal plank, Lath must be provided behind each joint. Add'l furring req'd when 16" plank used.
Allow moderate contact at joints - do not force
Nails spaced in accordance with furring or 12" o.c. for continuous backing. Planks may also be secured by adhesive. (see Mfgr.)
1" x 3"
See joints "B" applicable to Wallboard Planks above. See also page, "Metal Mouldings & Trim".
Stud spacing 12" or 16" o.c.
6"
Allow moderate contact at joints - do not force
Nail 3/8" from edge of board
Nails spaced 3" o.c. at edges
See joints "A" applicable to Wall board above. See also page, "Metal Mouldings & Trim".
PLANK
PANEL

For Nail sizes & types, see Mfgr's. specs.

METHODS OF APPLYING INTERIOR FIBERBOARD

HARDBOARD-SIZES, DETAILS and NAILING

PRODUCT	USE OR DESCRIPTION	SURFACE	STANDARD SIZES			
			1/8"	3/16"	1/4"	5/16"
STANDARD UNTREATED	The product most commonly used for normal interior and protected exterior applications (interior finish, cabinets, displays, etc.)	Smooth 1-side	4' x 2' to 16'	4' x 3' to 16'	4' x 4', 6', 8', 12' & 16'	4' x 6', 8', 12' & 16'
		Smooth 2-sides	4' x 8' & 16'	4' x 8' & 16'	-	-
TEMPERED OR TREATED	Used wherever strength and wear are factors, Also for exterior use (Wainscots, work surfaces, siding, signs, etc.)	Smooth 1-side	4' x 2' to 16'	4' x 3' to 16'	4' x 4', 6', 8', 12' & 16'	4' x 6', 8' 12' & 16'
		Smooth 2-sides	4' x 8' & 16' 5' x 8' & 16'	4' x 8' & 16' 5' x 8' & 16'	4' - 8' & 16' 5' - 8' & 16'	-
UTILITY GRADE	A lower density hardboard suitable where service conditions are not severe (Interior finish, porch ceilings, eaves, etc.)	Smooth 1-side	-	4' x 8', 12' & 16'	4' x 8', 12' & 16'	-
		Smooth 2-sides	-	-	4' x 3', 4', 6', 8' 9', 10' & 12'	-
UNDER-LAYMENT	Underlay for asphalt tile, linoleum, etc.	Smooth 1-side	-	-	4' x 3' & 4'	-
LAP SIDING	A treated hardboard with smooth or striated surface	Smooth 1-side	-	-	12", 16" & 24" x 8', 12' & 16'	12", 16" & 24" x 8', 12' & 16'
CONCRETE FORM	Specially treated for concrete form use	Smooth 1-side	-	4' x 8' & 12'	4' x 8' & 12'	-
PERFORATED	A hardboard with holes 1" o.c. each way	S-1-S & S-2-S	2' x 3', 4', 6' & 8' 4' x 3', 4', 6' & 8'	-	2' x 3', 4', 6' & 8' 4' x 3', 4', 6' & 8'	-
STRIATED PATTERN	A treated hardboard with a combed surface	-	-	-	4' x 8', 12' & 16' 4' x 12", 16" & 24"	-
LEATHER PATTERN	A treated hardboard embossed to simulate leather	-	4' x 8' & 16'	-	-	-
TILE PATTERN	A treated hardboard scored to form 4" squares.	-	4' x 8' & 16'	-	-	-

Mfrs. & Suppliers: Masonite, uperwood, Forest Fiber Products, Oregon Lumber, U.S. Gypsum, Chapman Mfg., Flintkote, Celotex, Nat. Gypsum, Johns-Manville, Insulite, Armstrong Cork, U.S. Plywood, Dant & Russell

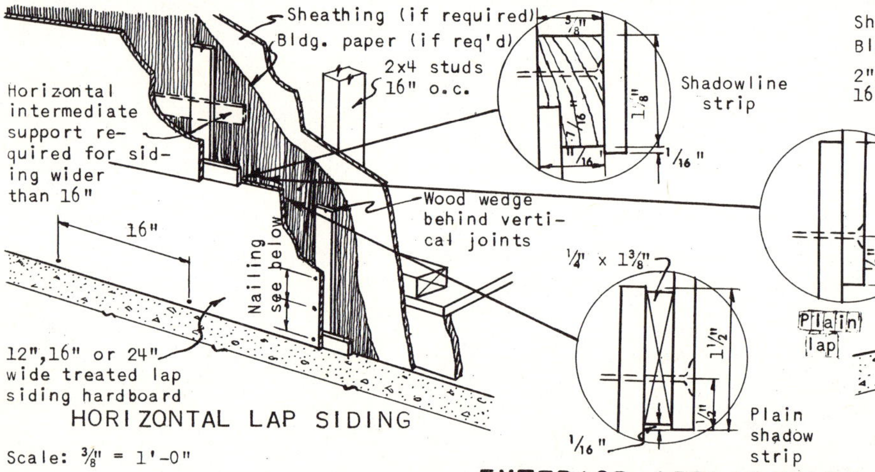

Sheathing (if required)
Bldg. paper (if req'd)
2x4 studs 16" o.c.
Horizontal intermediate support required for siding wider than 16"
16"
Nailing see below
Wood wedge behind vertical joints
12", 16" or 24" wide treated lap siding hardboard
Shadowline strip
1/16"
1/4" x 1 3/8"
Plain shadow strip

HORIZONTAL LAP SIDING

Scale: 3/8" = 1'-0"

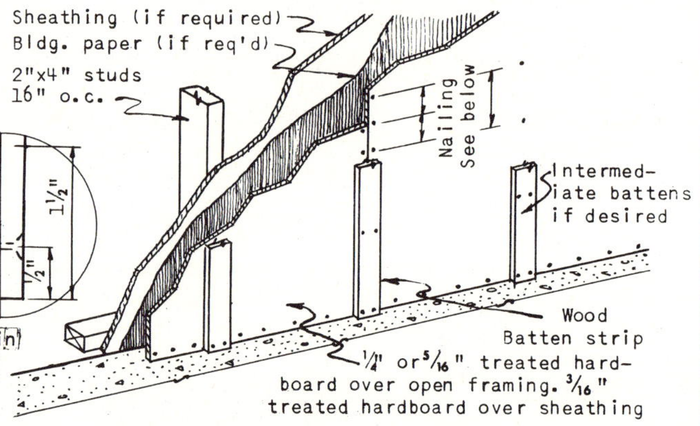

Sheathing (if required)
Bldg. paper (if req'd)
2"x4" studs 16" o.c.
Nailing See below
Intermediate battens if desired
Plain lap
Wood Batten strip
1/4" or 5/16" treated hardboard over open framing. 3/16" treated hardboard over sheathing

VERTICAL PANEL SIDING

EXTERIOR APPLICATION

	SIZES & TYPES OF HARDBOARD	WHERE USED	SIZE NAIL	TYPE*	SPACING AROUND EDGE	SPACING IN PANEL
INTERIOR	3/16" Std. & tempered	Walls & Ceilings	1¼"	C&F	4"	6"
	1/4" & 5/16" Std. & tempered		1½"	C, F	4"	6"
	.215 Underplayment	Floor	1¼"	RG, DS BB&CS	6"	6"
	3/16" & 1/4" Finished Floor	Floor	1¼"	CC	3"	6"
EXTERIOR	3/16", 1/4" & 5/16" oversheathing	vertical panel siding	2¼"	S&GB	3"	12"
	3/16", 1/4" & 5/16" no sheathing		2"	S&GB	3"	6"
	1/4" & 5/16" plain lap	Horizontal Lap siding	2½"	S&GB	3"	16"
	1/4" & 5/16" with shadow strip		3"	S&GB	3"	16"

HARDBOARD NAILING REQUIREMENTS

*C=casing nail; F=Finishing; RG=Ring grooved; DS=drive screw; BB=barbed box; CS=coated sinker; CC=coated casing; S=galvan. siding; GB=gal. box.

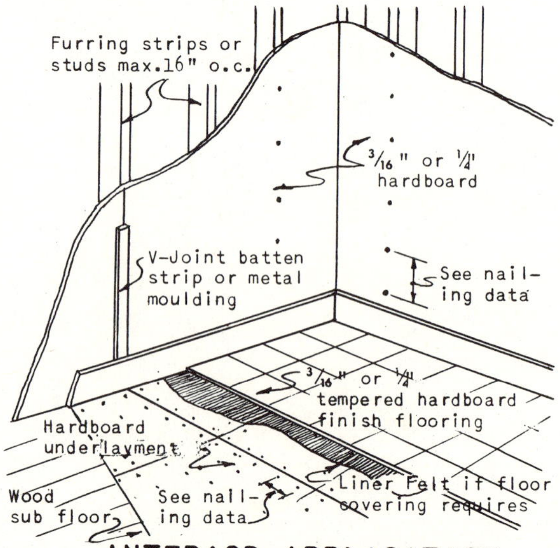

Furring strips or studs max. 16" o.c.
3/16" or 1/4" hardboard
V-Joint batten strip or metal moulding
See nailing data
3/16" or 1/4" tempered hardboard finish flooring
Hardboard underlayment
Wood sub floor
See nailing data
Liner Felt if floor covering requires

INTERIOR APPLICATION

DATA BY THE HARDBOARD ASSOCIATION

ENAMELED HARDBOARD PANELS-MISCELLANEOUS WALL TILES

PREFINISHED PLASTIC ENAMELED HARDBOARD WALL PANELS

TYPES AND SIZES			NOTES & MANUFACTURERS
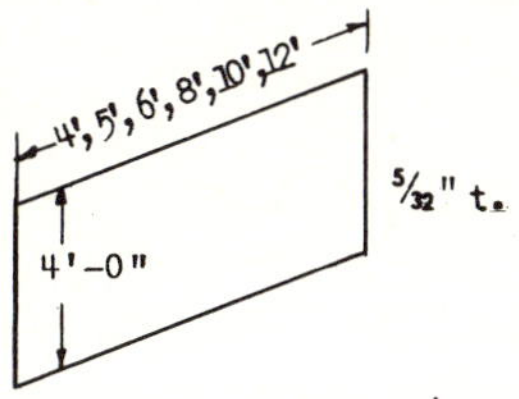4',5',6',8',10',12' 4'-0" 5/32" t.	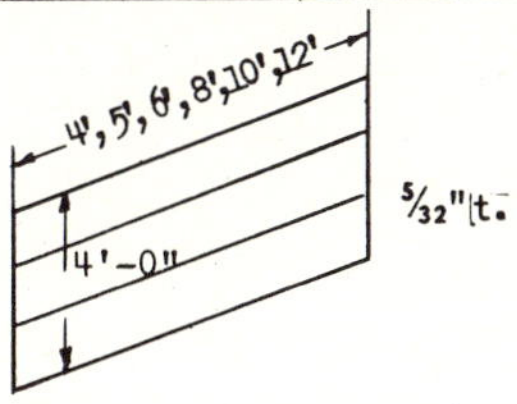4',5',6',8',10',12' 4'-0" 5/32" t.	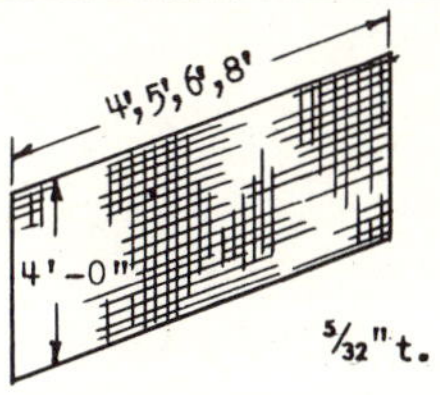4',5',6',8' 4'-0" 5/32" t.	Sizes are typical, all 4'-0" wide, 5/32" thick. Number of length-sizes available vary among manufacturers. Application by adhesives to smooth level backing such as brown coat plaster, plywood, gypboard etc. Joints may be covered with moulds. Plastic enamel is baked on tempered hard board, available with highly polished or satin finish varying with manufacturers.
PLAIN Solid colors. marble & wood patterns.	HORIZ. SCORED Solid colors. Spacing & no. of lines vary with manufacturers.	TILE PATTERN Solid colors. 4" square scoring is usual.	Brands: Barclay, Tylac, Marlite, Monowall.

Data checked by Hardboard Association

WALL TILE: METAL, ENAMELED METAL, PLASTIC, CORK & LEATHER

MANUFACTURERS	TYPES													SIZES	NOTES
	SYNTHETIC RESIN ENAMELED STEEL*	SYNTHETIC RESIN ENAM. ALUMINUM*	PORCELAIN ENAMEL ON STEEL	PORCELAIN ENAMEL ON ALUMINUM	POLISHED SATIN STAINLESS STEEL	POLISHED GRAINED STAINLESS STEEL	POLISHED COPPER	POLYSTRENE PLASTIC	VINYL-PLASTIC	PLASTIC ASBESTOS	RUBBER	CORK	LEATHER	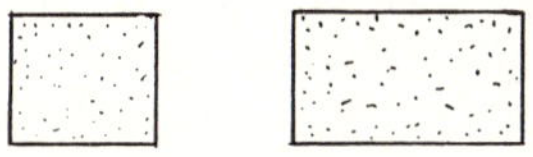 Square Rectangular TYPICAL FIELD TILE SHAPES	
Armstrong Cork												●		6"x6" & 12"; 9"x9" 12"x12"; 24"x24" & 48"	1/8", 3/16", & 5/16" th.
Bettinger Corp.			●	●										3"x4½"; 4½"x4½"; 4⅛"x8¼"; & 8¼"x8¼"	
Congoleum Nairn									●					9" x 9"	.063" th.
												●		6"x6" & 12"; 9" x 9"; 12" x 12" & 24"	1/8" & 3/16" th.
C.F. Church Mfg.								●						4¼"x4¼" & 8½"; 8½"x8½"	
Dodge Cork Co.												●		6"x6" & 12"; 9"x9"; 12"x12" & 24"; 36"x24" & 36"	1/8". 3/16", 1/4", 5/16" & 1/2" th.
Entec Products												●		2"x12";3"x4" & 8";4"x6"&12"	Cork bricks 7/8" th.
Flintkote Co.									●	●				6"x12";9"x9";12"x12"	3/32" th.
Goodyear										●				6"x6";9"x9";12"x12"	3/32", 1/8" & 3/16" th.
Hachmeister									●					4¼"x2⅛" & 4¼"	
Kentile, Inc.									●	●				9" x 9"	1/16" th.
												●		6"x6"& 12";9"x9";12"x12"&24"	3/16", 5/16" & 1/2" th.
Kiefer Tanneries													●	4½" x 4½" & 9"	1/16" impregnated pigskin
Mastic Tile Corp.								●				●		4¼"x4¼"; 8½"x8½"	1/8" & 3/16" th.
Moultile, Inc.												●		9" x 9"	1/8" & 3/16" th.
Metal Tile Products		●		●	●									5"x5" & 10"; 10"x10" & 20"	
Pittsburg Tile Co.								●						4¼"x4¼"; 8½"x8½"; 2⅛"x4¼"	Tiles interlock
Porcelain Enamel Products			●											4½"x4½"; 8¼"x8¼" 8¼" x 4⅛"	Ceramic on steel. Trade names - Veos & Starfire
Vikon Tile	●	●	●	●	●	●	●	●						4¼"x4¼" & 8½"; 6"x6"; 8½" x 8½"	Pastel, mottled & hammered textures made in aluminum
Vinyl Plastics, Inc.									●					9"x9"; 12"x12"	1/8" th.

Other Tile Shapes: Most manufacturers except cork & leather, make cap, base & outside corner tile corresponding to field sizes. Inside corners, feature strips & other shapes are available from many. *Steel is bonderized (coated with Parkers Zinc Phosphate) to prevent corrosion Aluminum may be bonderized or anodized (etched & coated with aluminum phosphate).

LAMINATED PLASTIC VENEERS

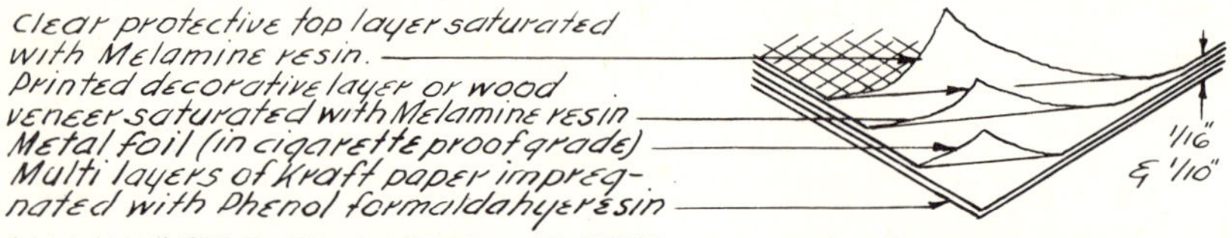
Clear protective top layer saturated with Melamine resin.
Printed decorative layer or wood veneer saturated with Melamine resin
Metal foil (in cigarette proof grade)
Multi layers of kraft paper impregnated with Phenol formaldahye resin
1/16" & 1/10"

LAMINATED PLASTIC SHEETS-GLOSS OR SATIN FINISH

Plywood with heavily grained or rotary cut top ply should not be used as figure will show thru. Gum, birch, poplar, mahogany & vertical grain fir make the best gluing surface. Contact adhesive is used for field bonding of plastic laminate to plywood or hardboard; thermosetting adhesives under pressure for shop application. Prepared veneered plywood is mfrd. under trade name Micarta, Formica & Farlite; prepared hardboard under Micartaboard, Formica beautyboard, St. Regis Panelyte, GE Texolyte & Farolex. Stock sizes are the same as for sheets.

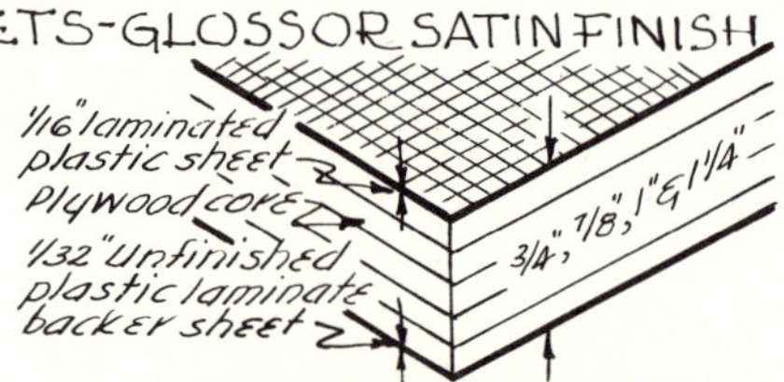
1/16" laminated plastic sheet
Plywood core
1/32" unfinished plastic laminate backer sheet
3/4", 7/8", 1" & 1 1/4"

LAMINATED PLASTIC VENEERED PLYWOOD

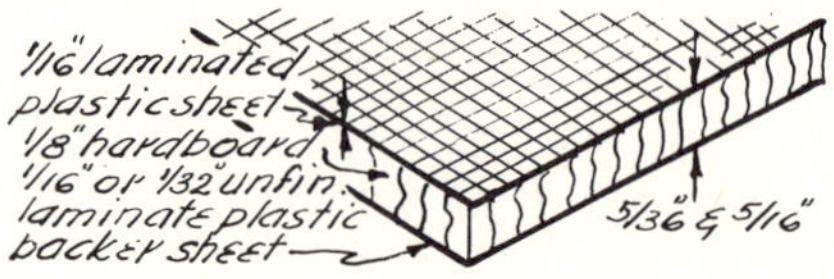
1/16" laminated plastic sheet
1/8" hardboard
1/16" or 1/32" unfin. laminate plastic backer sheet
5/36" & 5/16"

LAMINATED PLASTIC VENEERED HARDBOARD

STOCK SIZES-PLASTIC LAMINATES		
THICKNESS	PRODUCT	SIZES
1/16" standard	Consoweld	30", 36", 42" & 48" × 96", 120", & 144".
	Farlite	24", 30" & 36" × 60", 72", & 84"
	Formica	24", 30" & 36" × 60", 72", 84", 96" & 120"; 48" & 96" × 120"
	Lamin-Art.	24" × 60", 72", 96" & 120"; 30", 36" & 48" × 48", 60", 72", 96" & 120".
	Micarta	30" & 36" × 60"; 24", 30" & 48" × 72"
	Panelyte	24" × 96" & 120"; 30" × 60", 72", 96" & 120", 36" & 48" × 60", 96" & 120".
	Textolite-GE	24" × 60", 96", & 120"; 30" × 60", 72", 84", 96", 108" & 120"; 36" × 60", 72" & 96"; 48" × 96"
1/10" Rigid *	Consoweld	30", 36", 42" & 48" × 96", 120" & 144".
	Panelyte	30" & 48" × 96" & 120".
1/20" Post Forming**	Farlite	30" & 36" × 60", 72" & 84"
	Formica	24", 30", 36" × 60", 72", 84", 96", 120"; 48" × 96", 120"
	Lamin-Art	30" & 36" × 96" & 120".
	Micarta	24", 30", 36", & 48" × 96"; 30" × 84"
	Panelyte	30" & 36" × 96", & 120."
	Textolite-GE	30" & 36" × 96" & 120"; 30" × 84" & 60"

* Extra thick. Grain or stud joints will not show thru. May be applied directly on plaster, dry wall, cement block or studding with mastic type adhesive.

** For concave and convex curves, min. rad. 3/4". Generally requires shop fabrication; shaping by controled heat.

Note: Most mfrs. supply .020 and / or .045 thick unfinished backer sheets. These are applied to the unexposed side of laminated plastic veneered plywood or hardboard as illustrated and are used to prevent warpage.

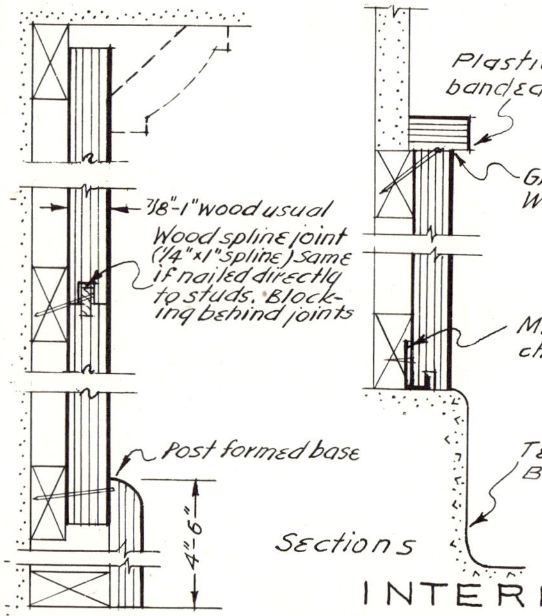
7/8"-1" wood usual
Wood spline joint (1/4"×1" spline) same if nailed directly to studs. Blocking behind joints
Post formed base
4"-6"
Plastic banded edge.
Glued Wainscot
Metal channel
Terrazzo Base

Sections

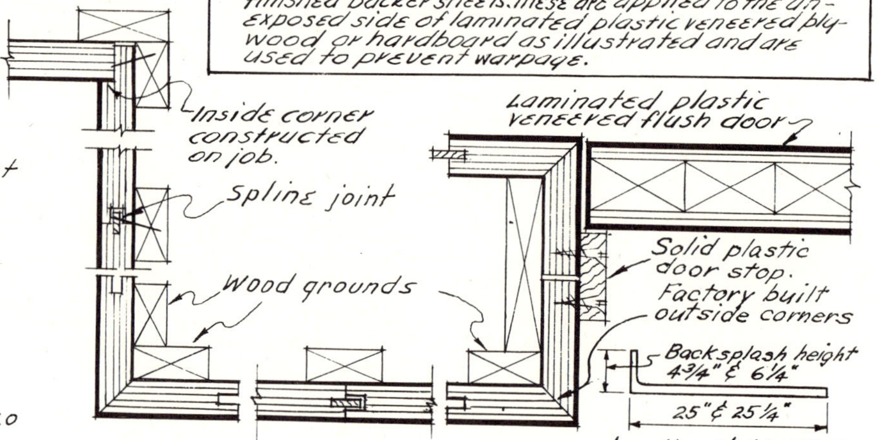
Inside corner constructed on job.
Spline joint
Wood grounds
Laminated plastic veneered flush door
Solid plastic door stop.
Factory built outside corners
Backsplash height 4 3/4" & 6 1/4"
25" & 25 1/4"

Composite Plan of a Wall Section.
scale: 3" = 1'-0"

Lengths-5', 6' & 8'. Tradenames: Consoweia Curvatop, GE Monotop, & Micarta Unitop.

INTERIOR WALL FINISH DETAILS

PREFORMED COUNTER TOPS

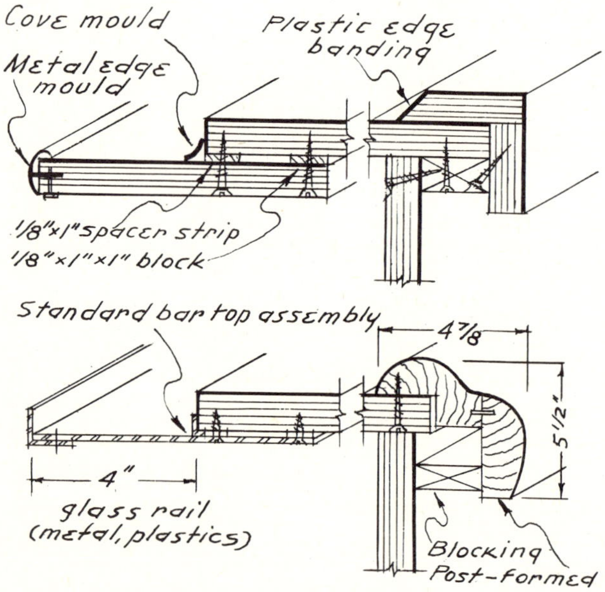
Cove mould
Metal edge mould
Plastic edge banding
1/8"×1" spacer strip
1/8"×1"×1" block
Standard bar top assembly
4 7/8
5 1/2"
4"
glass rail (metal, plastics)
Blocking
Post-formed

BAR TOPS

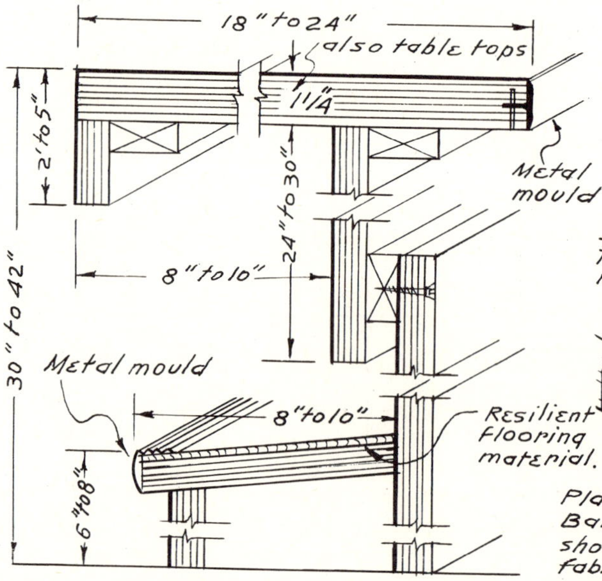
18" to 24"
also table tops
1 1/4"
2' to 5"
24" to 30"
Metal mould
8" to 10"
30" to 42"
Metal mould
8" to 10"
Resilient flooring material.
6" to 8"

LUNCH COUNTERS

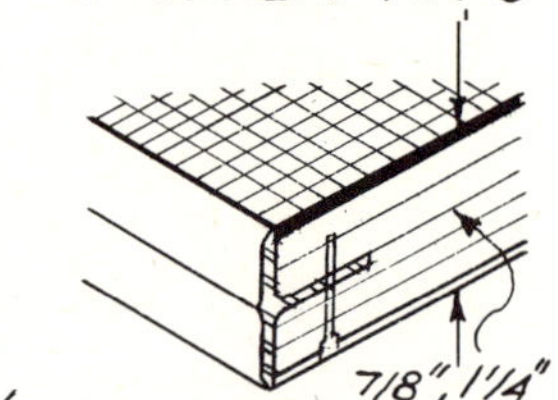
7/8", 1 1/4"

"T" metal edge
See pages on Metal Trim for various types made.

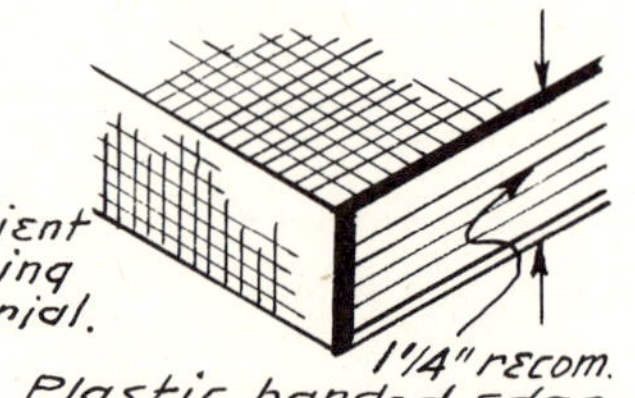
1 1/4" recom.

Plastic banded edge. Banding of edge bands should be done by fabricator.

EDGE TREATMENT

FLEXIBLE WALL COVERINGS

PAPER AND FABRIC

PAPER	WIDTH	WIDTH trimmed	LENGTH single rolls	HOW SOLD
American	20"	18"	8 yds.	(2 single) or 1 double roll
	22"	20"	7 yds.	(2 single) or 1 double roll
	24"	22"	6 yds.	triple rolls
	30"	28"	5 yds.	triple rolls
	36"	34"	4¾ yds	triple rolls
English & Canadian	22"	20½"	7 to 7¾ yds.	1½ rolls or 1 double roll
French	19½" 22", 29½	19" 20", 28"	7 yds.	single rolls
Scenic		variable		in sections
Varlar, Stainproof	25½"	24"	16⅔ yds.	by square ft.
Imperial, Scrubable	22"	20½"	7 yds.	single rolls
Marvalon, coated		46"	24 yds.	6 rolls per carton
Timbertone	36" 30"		4 & 8 yds 10 yds	double rolls
FABRIC				
Japanese Grass cloth, Shiki Silk	36"	35"	3¾ yds	double roll
Dexolium	37"	36"	30 yds	by the yard
Burlap, Canvas Fab-rik-o-na	30" 30" 36" 38"		50 yds	by the yard
Canvas printed Stylon	30"	27"	5 yds	single roll
Wall-Tex, Scrubable	24"	24"	6 yds.	single roll
Fabron, Detron	27"	26"	33¼"	double roll
Sanitas / " -pretrimmed	50½"	48" 24"	3 yds 6 yds	single rolls

SIZE OF ROOM	*NUMBER OF SINGLE ROLLS REQUIRED FOR A ROOM					YARDS OF BORDER	SINGLE ROLLS OF CEILING
	8 FT. ceiling	9 FT. ceiling	10 FT. ceiling	11 FT. ceiling	12 FT. ceiling		
8' × 10'	9	10	11	12	13	13	3
10' × 10'	10	11	13	14	15	15	4
10' × 12'	11	12	14	15	16	16	4
10' × 14'	12	14	15	16	18	17	5
12' × 12'	12	14	15	16	18	17	5
12' × 14'	13	15	16	18	19	18	6
12' × 16'	14	16	17	19	21	20	6
12' × 18'	15	17	19	20	22	21	7
12' × 20'	16	18	20	22	24	23	8
14' × 14'	14	16	17	19	21	20	6
14' × 16'	15	17	19	20	22	21	7
14' × 18'	16	18	20	22	24	23	8
14' × 20'	17	19	21	23	25	24	9
14' × 22'	18	20	22	24	27	25	10
16' × 16'	16	18	20	22	24	23	8
16' × 18'	17	19	21	23	25	25	10
16' × 20'	18	20	22	24	27	26	10
16' × 22'	19	21	23	26	28	28	11
16' × 24'	20	22	25	27	30	29	12
18' × 18'	18	20	22	24	27	26	11
18' × 20'	19	21	23	26	28	28	12

To find the number of single rolls by formula (for average house ceiling height.)

① Calculate area of wall space to be covered including window & door area.

② As all single rolls of wall paper and most wall fabric cover (36□') or 30□' allowing for trimming, the number of rolls required equals the area divided by 30.

* ③ For every door and window of average size deduct ⅔ roll.

Example: Area of wall space of a room 12' × 14' × 10' high = 520 sq. ft. and 520 sq. ft. ÷ 30 = 17⅓

Room has two windows and two doors, therefore deduct 4 × ⅔ = 2⅔

Answer: is therefore the nearest even roll above 14⅔ or 15 rolls

A double roll = two single rolls in one stick; A triple roll = 3 single rolls in one stick.

All wall paper and most wall fabric is priced by the single roll.

Felt, linoleum, rubber, plastic, and wood wall coverings, generally come in large rolls or sheets selling by the square or linear foot or by the square yard.

OTHER MATERIALS

MATERIAL	NAME	WIDTH	LENGTH single roll	HOW SOLD
FELT	Congowall-Enameled	36" & 54"	80' to 140'	by linear ft.
	Armstrong Quaker	54"	75' to 150'	by linear ft.
LINOLEUM	Armstrong Linowall	36" & 72"	45'	by sq. yd.
	Linkrusta	19½"	7½ yds	by single roll
RUBBER	Goodyear	36"	20 to 25 yds	by sq. yd.
	Wallflex. - R.C.A.	36"	20 to 25 yds	by sq. yd.
WOOD	Flexwood	18" & 24"	8', 10' & 12'	by sq. ft.
	Superflex	4'	4', 6' & 8'	by sq. ft.
	Kaligrain & Randomwood	15'	8' & 10'	by sq. ft.

MATERIAL	NAME	WIDTH	LENGTH single roll	HOW SOLD
PLASTIC	Carpenter's Vicrtex	54"	30 yds	by lin. yd.
	Dexolium	54"	30 & 50 yds	by the roll
	Dublin	54"	30'	by single roll
	Du Pont Fabrilite	54"	30 yds	by lin. yd.
	Federan Fedwall	54"	90'	by sq. ft.
	Goodyear	45"	30-38 yds	by sq. yd.
	Joanna	48" & 54"	24 yds	by sq. yd.
	Kalistron & Kalitex	54"	100'	by sq. ft.
	Lifewall	50"	29' to 36'	by sq. ft.
	Permon	48"	90'	by sq. ft.
	Velveray	24"	18'	by the roll
	Wall-Tex Guard	54"	16 yds.	by lin. yd.

METAL MOULDINGS and TRIM

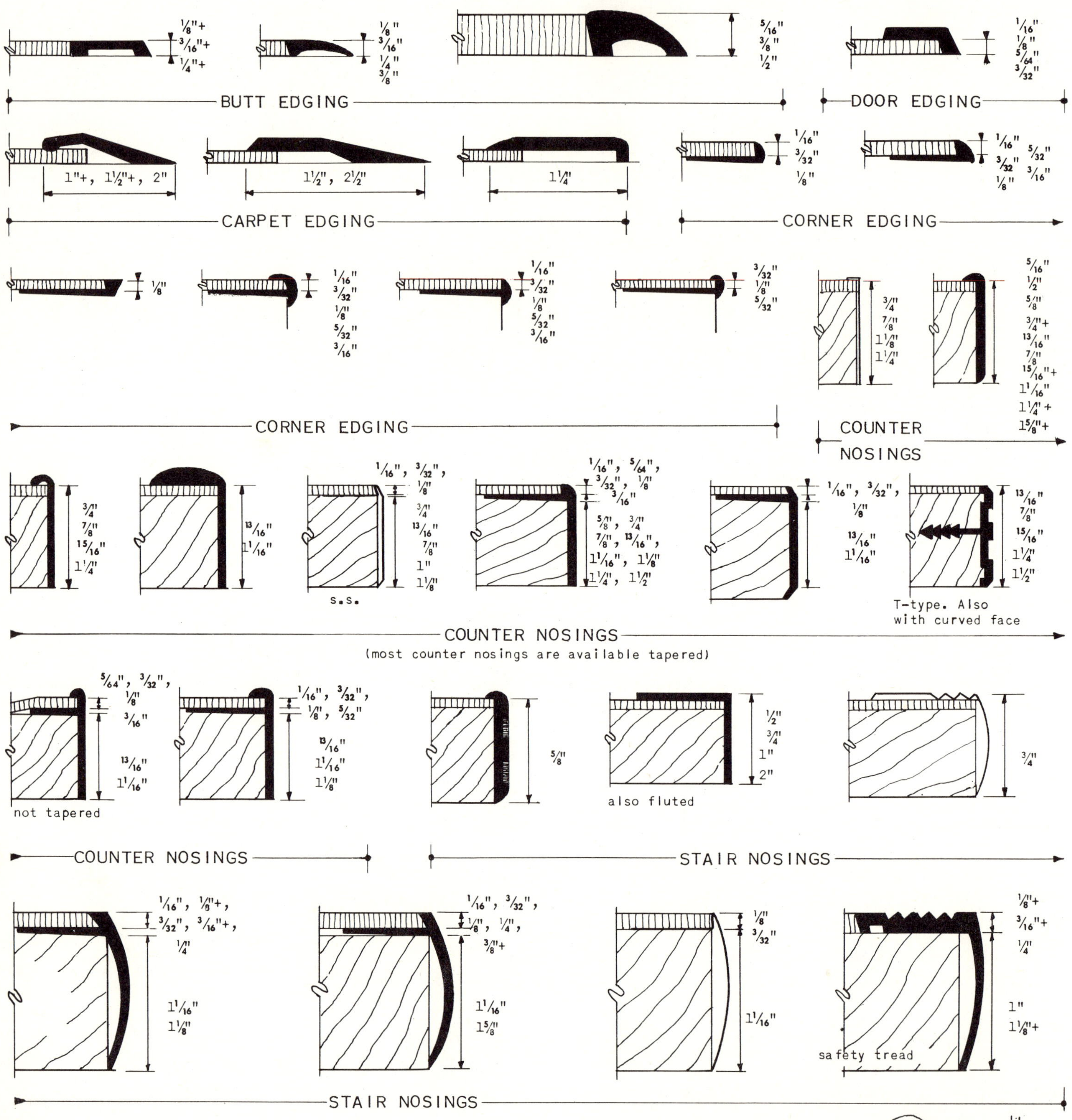
1/8"+ 3/16"+ 1/4"+
1/8" 3/16" 1/4" 3/8"
5/16" 3/8" 1/2"
1/16" 1/8" 5/64" 3/32"
BUTT EDGING
DOOR EDGING
1"+, 1½"+, 2"
1½", 2½"
1¼"
1/16" 3/32" 1/8"
1/16" 3/32" 1/8" 5/32" 3/16"
CARPET EDGING
CORNER EDGING
1/8"
1/16" 3/32" 1/8" 5/32" 3/16"
1/16" 3/32" 1/8" 5/32" 3/16"
3/32" 1/8" 5/32"
3/4" 7/8" 1⅛" 1¼"
5/16" 1/2" 5/8" 3/4"+ 13/16" 7/8" 15/16"+ 1 1/16" 1¼"+ 1⅝"+
CORNER EDGING
COUNTER NOSINGS
3/4" 7/8" 15/16" 1¼"
13/16" 1 1/16"
1/16", 3/32", 1/8"
3/4" 13/16" 7/8" 1" 1⅛"
s.s.
1/16", 5/64", 3/32", 1/8" 3/16"
5/8", 3/4" 7/8", 13/16", 1 1/16", 1⅛" 1¼", 1½"
1/16", 3/32", 1/8"
13/16" 1 1/16"
13/16" 7/8" 15/16" 1¼" 1½"
T-type. Also with curved face
COUNTER NOSINGS
(most counter nosings are available tapered)
5/64", 3/32", 1/8"
3/16"
13/16" 1 1/16"
not tapered
1/16", 3/32", 1/8", 5/32"
13/16" 1 1/16" 1⅛"
5/8"
1/2" 3/4" 1" 2"
also fluted
3/4"
COUNTER NOSINGS
STAIR NOSINGS
1/16", 1/8"+, 3/32", 3/16"+, 1/4"
1 1/16" 1⅛"
1/16", 3/32", 1/8", 1/4", 3/8"+
1 1/16" 1⅝"
1/8" 3/32"
1 1/16"
1/8"+ 3/16"+ 1/4"
1" 1⅛"+
safety tread
STAIR NOSINGS

NOTE:

All types are aluminum only unless noted thus: += brass, s.s.= stainless steel.

Mouldings shown made by:
Chromedge, Ford, Wooster, Nychrome

Not all types and sizes are made by all companies.

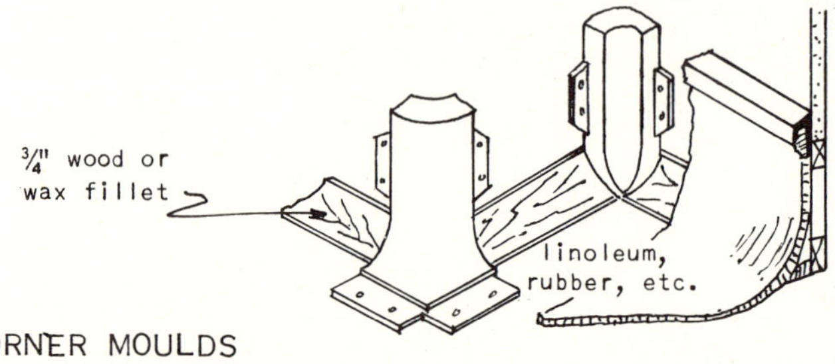
3/4" wood or wax fillet
linoleum, rubber, etc.

CORNER MOULDS
FOR "FLASHING" - TYPE COVE BASE

METAL MOULDINGS and TRIM

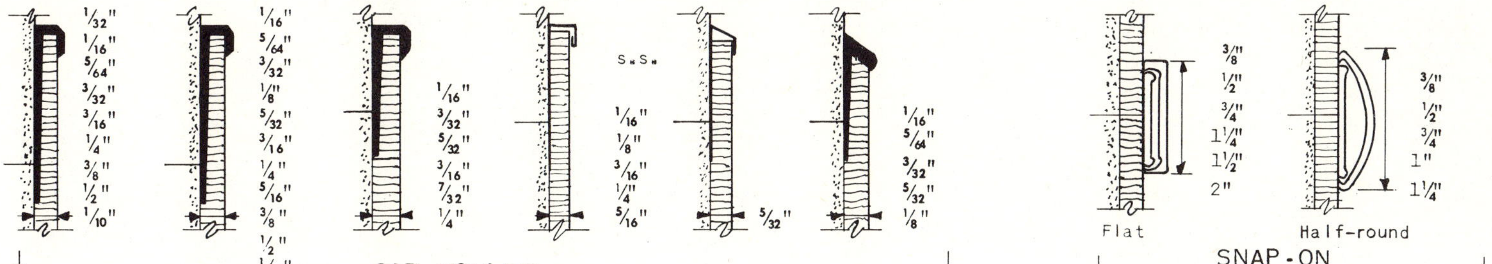
1/32" 1/16" 5/64" 3/32" 3/16" 1/4" 3/8" 1/2" 1/10"
1/16" 5/64" 3/32" 1/8" 5/32" 3/16" 1/4" 5/16" 3/8" 1/2" 1/10"
1/16" 3/32" 5/32" 3/16" 7/32" 1/4"
S.S.
1/16" 1/8" 3/16" 1/4" 5/16"
5/32"
1/16" 5/64" 3/32" 5/32" 1/8"
3/8" 1/2" 3/4" 1 1/4" 1 1/2" 2"
Flat
3/8" 1/2" 3/4" 1" 1 1/4"
Half-round

CAP MOULDS — SNAP-ON MOULDINGS

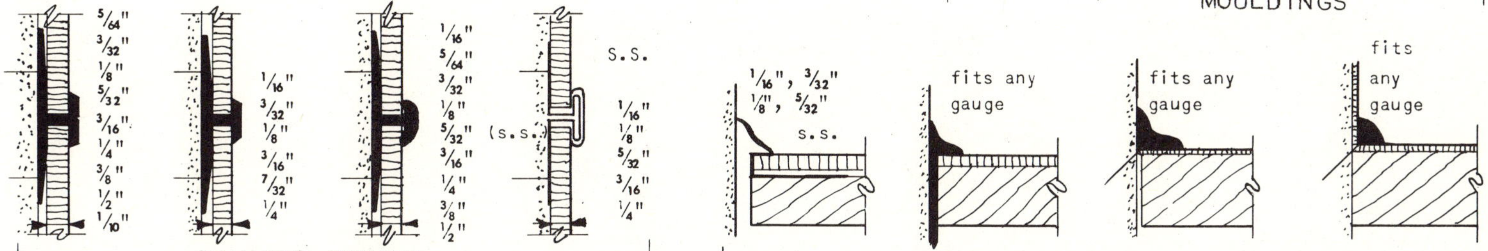
5/64" 3/32" 1/8" 5/32" 3/16" 1/4" 3/8" 1/2" 1/10"
1/16" 3/32" 1/8" 3/16" 7/32" 1/4"
1/16" 5/64" 3/32" 1/8" 5/32" 3/16" 1/4" 3/8" 1/2"
S.S.
(s.s.)
1/16" 1/8" 5/32" 3/16" 1/4"
1/16", 3/32" 1/8", 5/32"
s.s.
fits any gauge
fits any gauge
fits any gauge

DIVIDER STRIPS — COVES FOR WALL OR BACK SPLASH

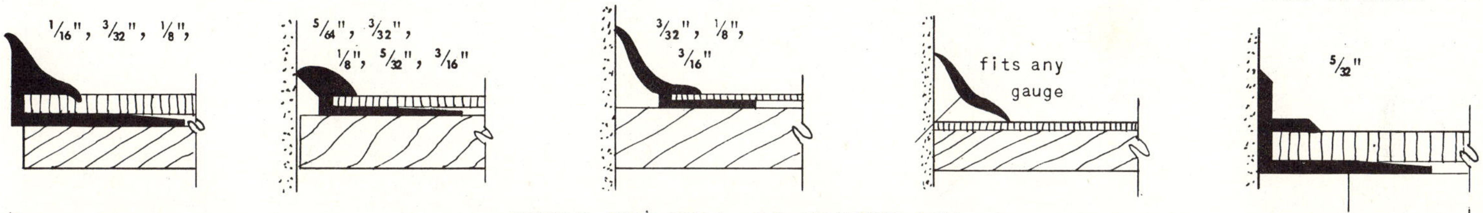
1/16", 3/32", 1/8",
5/64", 3/32", 1/8", 5/32", 3/16"
3/32", 1/8", 3/16"
fits any gauge
5/32"

COVES FOR WALL OR BACKSPLASH

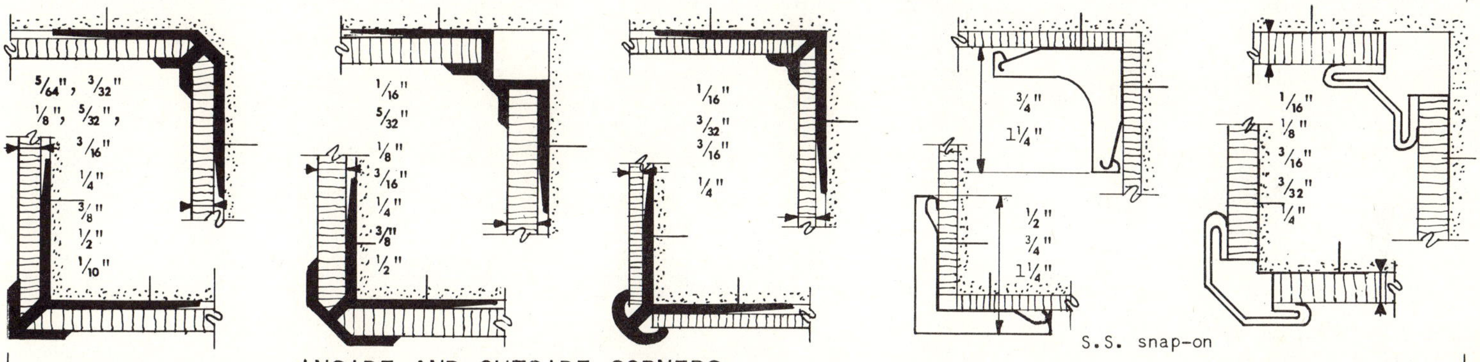
5/64", 3/32" 1/8", 5/32", 3/16" 1/4" 3/8" 1/2" 1/10"
1/16" 5/32" 1/8" 3/16" 1/4" 3/8" 1/2"
1/16" 3/32" 3/16" 1/4"
3/4" 1 1/4"
1/2" 3/4" 1 1/4"
S.S. snap-on
1/16" 1/8" 3/16" 3/32" 1/4"

INSIDE AND OUTSIDE CORNERS

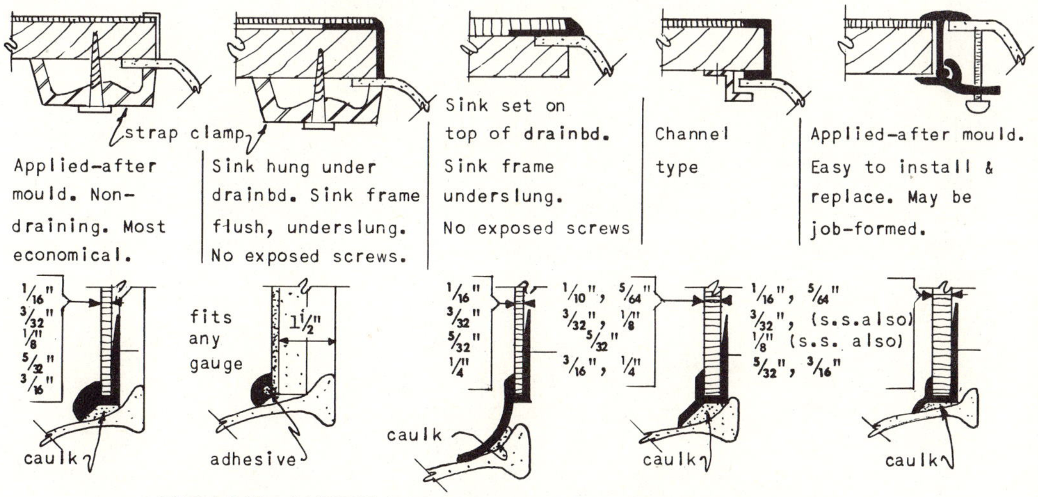
strap clamp
Applied-after mould. Non-draining. Most economical.
Sink hung under drainbd. Sink frame flush, underslung. No exposed screws.
Sink set on top of drainbd. Sink frame underslung. No exposed screws
Channel type
Applied-after mould. Easy to install & replace. May be job-formed.
1/16" 3/32" 1/8" 5/32" 3/16"
caulk
fits any gauge
1 1/2"
adhesive
1/16" 3/32" 5/32" 1/4"
1/10", 5/64" 3/32", 1/8" 5/32" 3/16", 1/4"
caulk
1/16", 5/64" 3/32", (s.s.also) 1/8" (s.s. also) 5/32", 3/16"
caulk
caulk

TYPICAL INSTALLATIONS - SINK AND TUB TRIM

NOTE: All mouldings of aluminum, unless otherwise noted (s.s.= stainless steel).
Mouldings shown made by: Chromedge, Ford, Nychrome, Wooster.
Not all types and sizes made by all manufacturers.

THICKNESS OF MATERIAL USED WITH METAL MOULDS

For walls:
Asbestos-cement bd: 1/8", 3/16"
Fiberboards (wall bd, bldg. bd, insulation bd, tile bd): 3/8", 15/32", 1/2".
Gypsum bd (plain & veneered): 1/4", 3/8", 1/2"
Hardbd: 1/8", 3/16", 1/4", 5/16"
Linoleum: 1/16"
Plastic tile: 1/16", 3/32", 1/8", 3/16"
Plastic laminates: 1/16", 1/10"
Plastic on hardbd: 5/32"
Plywood: 1/8", 3/16", 1/4", 3/8", 1/2"
Plastic on plywood: 3/4", 7/8", 1", 1 1/4"
Rubber wall covering: ± 1/16"
Wood covered metal: 1/28" plus thickness of metal

For floors:
Asphalt tile: 3/16", 1/8"
Cork tile: 1/8", 3/16", 5/16"
Linoleum: 1/16", 3/32", 1/8"
Plastic tile, vinyl: 1/16", 3/32", 3/16", 1/8"
Plastic asbestos tile: 1/16", 3/32", 1/8"
Rubber tile: 1/8", 3/16", 1/4"
Wood: 3/8" (or thinner), 13/16"

WOOD FLOORING

OAK STRIP FLOORING

FLOORING SIZES

Type	Thickness nom'l	Thickness act'l	Widths (face)			Nailing
(hollow back)	25/32"	25/32"	1½"	2"	2¼"	Blind
(grooves)	* ½"	15/32"	1½"	2"		Blind
(grooves)	* 3/8"	11/32"	1½"	2"		Blind
(flat back)	* 5/16"	10/32"	1½"	2"		Surface

*These should always be used over sub-flooring. Narrow widths cost more laid.

NAILING / QUANTITIES

Sizes (nominal)	O.C.	Nail Size	Increase fl. areas by	Counted as
25/32"×2¼"	10"	8d cut steel	33⅓ %	1"× 3"
25/32"× 2"	10"	8d " "	37½ %	1"× 2¾"
25/32"× 1½"	12"	8d " "	50 %	1"× 2¼"
½"× 2"	10"	6d wire fin.	25 %	1"× 2½"
½"× 1½"	10"	6d " "	33½ %	1"× 2"
3/8"× 2"	8"	4d wire casing	25%	1"× 2½"
3/8"× 1½"	8"	4d " "	33⅓ %	1"× 2"
5/16"× 2"	5"	1" barbed wire	—	1"× 2"
5/16"× 1½"	7(2)	Floor brad #15	—	1"× 1½"

For irregularities add 5% more for waste.

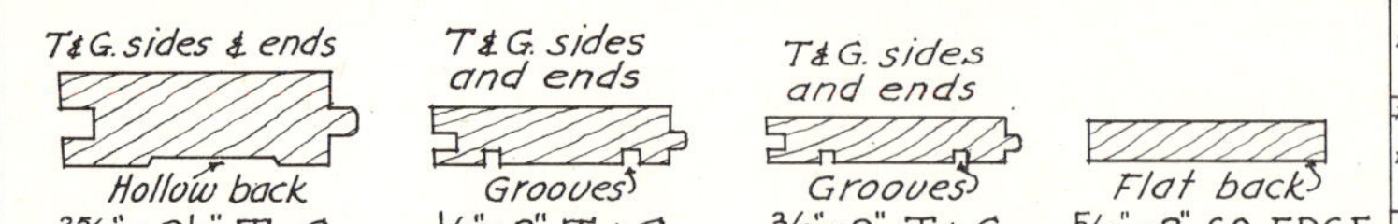

T&G. sides & ends
Hollow back
25/32"×2¼" T&G.
T&G. sides and ends
Grooves
½"×2" T&G.
T&G. sides and ends
Grooves
3/8"×2" T&G.
Flat back
5/16"×2" SQ. EDGE.

STANDARD GRADES

Grade	Allowed Defects	Bundle Lengths	Uses
Clear Quartered or Plain Sawed.	Face practically free from defects except 3/8" bright sap.	2'-0" & up. Max. of 25% under 4'-0". Aver. 4'-6"	Fine domestic work, clubs, hotels, also churches, schools.
Sap Clear Quartered.	Face practically free from defects except unlimited bright sap.	ditto.	Fine domestic work, clubs, hotels, etc.
Select Quartered or Plain Sawed.	Sap, pin worm holes, streaks, slight working imperfections, small tight knots - 1 to every 3'-0".	2'-0" and up average 4'-0"	Medium domestic work, schools, offices, stores & institutions.
#1 Common Plain Sawed.	Shall be of such nature as will make and lay a sound floor without cutting.	2'-0" and up average 3'-0"	cheap apartments, schools, stores, high class lofts & factories.
#2 Common Plain Sawed.	May contain defects of all types. Will lay a serviceable floor.	1'-3" and up average 2'-6"	Cheap apartments, lofts and factories.

Grades; do not consider the question of color.

Recommendations & Grading Rules of the National Oak Flooring Manufacturers Association, 814 Sterick Building, Memphis 3, Tennessee.

NORTHERN HARD MAPLE, BEECH, and BIRCH FLOORING (STRIP & BLOCK)

FLOORING SIZES-STRIP

Type	Thickness cut from	Thickness act	Widths (face)					
Standard			1½"	2"	2¼"	3¼"	*2½"	*3¼"
Special	1¼"	35/32"	1½"	2"	2¼"	3¼"	*2½"	*3¼"
Special	1½"				2¼"	3¼"		
Special	2"	53/32"			2¼"	3¼"		
Special	1"		1½"	2"	2¼"			
Special	1"		1½"	2"	2¼"			
Special	1"	3/8"	1½"	2"	2¼"			

*Square edged (jointed) only; other sizes T & G sides and ends.

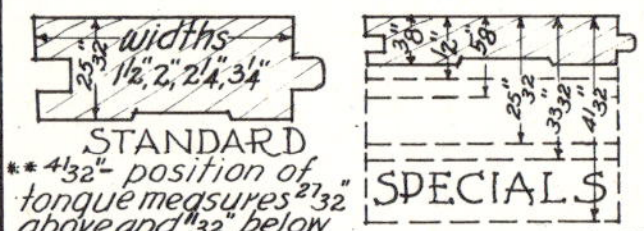

widths 1½", 2", 2¼", 3¼"
25/32"
STANDARD
3/8"
½"
5/8"
25/32"
33/32"
41/32"
SPECIALS

** 41/32" - position of tongue measures 27/32" above and 1/32" below tongue.

NAILING

Sizes actual	O.C.	Nail Size
33/32"	12" to 16"	2¼" No. 5 spiral fl. screw nail
25/32"	12" to 16"	2¼" No. 5 spiral fl. screw nail.
3/8"	9"	1½" No. 1 spiral floor screw nail

STANDARD MEASURE^MT

½" & thicker, all widths, are measured ¾" waste for matching. 3/8", all widths, is measured ½" waste for matching. Jointed flooring all widths and thicknesses; measured ¾" waste.

QUANTITIES

Width	½"-5/8"-25/32" incr. fl. area by	3/8" incr. fl. area by
1½"	50%	33⅓%
2"	37½%	25%
2¼"	33½%	22½%
3¼"	24%	
2½"	*20%	
3¼"	24%	

For thicker flooring determine number of feet for 25/32" as above and add as follows:
33/32" " — 25%
41/32" " — 50%
53/32" " — 100%
For wastage add 5% to above

STANDARD GRADES

Grade	Uses
1st Grade: Length 2' & more; not over 25% under 4 ft.	Highest standard made; fine houses, apartm^ts, churches, public bldgs, clubs, dance fls, gyms, hotels, offices, skating rinks, schools.
2nd. Grade: Length 2' & more; not over 40% under 4 ft.	Slight imperfections permitted; same use as above, but where imperfections are not objectionable, or when colored finish desired.
3rd. Grade: Length 1'4" & more; not over 60% under 4 ft.	Serviceable for factories, warehouses, workshops, farms, industrial buildings, stores, low cost housing & homes.
Special Grades	White Clear Northern Hard Maple, selected for color uniformity. Brown Clear Northern Hard Maple, selected for color uniformity. Red Clear Northern Beech, Red Clear Northern Birch, especially selected for color.

Marked color variations not a defect except in special grades

Northern Hard Maple is botanically "Acer Saccharum."

Recommendations & Grading Rules of the Maple Flooring Manufacturers Association, 35 East Wacker Drive, Chicago, Ill. Trade Mark "MFMA"

FLOORING BLOCKS (T. & G. on wood or concrete)

For Patterns, Squares, or Herringbone

Single Piece Blocks: For laying in herring bone and square patterns are side and end T&G., ½ each right and left hand matching. 25/32" & 33/32" th. in 1½", 2" & 2¼" face widths. Face lengths, as desired, from 6¾" to 13½".

FABRICATED BLOCKS or SQUARES on wood or concrete

MATERIAL	1½" STRIPS	2" STRIPS	2¼" STRIPS
Maple, Beech & Birch 25/32" & 33/32" thick	7½"×7½" & 9"×9" squares	8"×8" & 10"×10" squares	6¾"×6¾" & 9"×9" squares

Note: maple also made into single slats end-to-end pattern with face widths of 1½", 2", 2¼" & 3¼", in thicknesses 25/32", 33/32", 41/32" and 53/32". Face lengths are 8" to 16" but principally 12".

SOFTWOOD STRIP FLOORING

SIZES

FINISHED THICKNESS	FACE WIDTHS				
5/16"	1½"	2⅜"	3¼"	4¼"	5 3/16"
7/16"	"	"	"	"	"
9/16"	"	"	"	"	"
25/32"	"	"	"	"	"
1 1/16"	"	"	"	"	"
1 5/16"	"	"	"	"	"

FINISHED THICKNESS	SHIPLAP	T&G	SPLINE
25/32"	3/8" lap: 3⅛", 5⅛", 7⅛", 9⅛", 11⅛", 13⅛", 15⅛"; 2" lap: 3", 5", 7", 9", 11", 13", & 15"	¼" tongue: 3¼", 5 3/16", 7", 9" & 11"	
1 1/16"		¼" tongue: 3¼", 5 3/16", 7", 9" & 11"	
1 5/16"		¼" tongue: 3¼", 5 3/16", 7", 9" & 11"	
1⅝"	½" lap: 3", 5", 7", 9" & 11"	3/8" tongue: 3⅜", 5⅜", 7", 9" & 11"	3½", 5½", 7½", 9½" & 11½"
2⅝"	"	"	"
3⅝"	"	"	"
4⅝"	"	"	"

QUANTITIES FOR ESTIMATING

Size: Add to floor area as follows:

25/32" × 2⅜"	27%
" × 3¼"	23%
" × 5 3/16"	15%
1 1/16" × 2⅜"	58%
" × 3¼"	54%
" × 5 3/16"	43%
1 5/16" × 2⅜"	90%
" × 3¼"	85%
" × 5 3/16"	72%

Also add 3% to 5% to above for waste.

WOOD SPECIES AND GRADES AVAILABLE

SPECIES	FLAT GRAIN	EDGE GRAIN	MIXED GRAIN
Cedar, Western Red (Coast Region); Cedar, Western Red (Inland Region)	B & Btr; C; Sel. Merch; Nos. 1, 2, 3 Boards*; 1 & 2 Clear (B & Btr.); C Select; D Select; Nos. 1, 2, 3 Boards*		
Cypress, Tidewater Red; Douglas Fir (Coast Region)	A; C Sel; D; C & Btr; D; Sel. Merch.; Nos. 1, 2, 3 Boards*	Clear all heart B & Btr; C; D; V.G.	D; E
Douglas Fir (Inland Region)	B & Btr; C Sel; D Select; Nos. 1, 2, 3 Boards*		
Hemlock & Tamarack (Eastern); Hemlock (West coast)	D & Btr.; Nos. 1, 2 & 3; C & Btr, D; Select Merch.; Nos. 1, 2, 3 Boards*	Clear all heart, B & Btr; C; D; V.G.	D; E
Larch-Douglas Fir; Lodgepole Pine	B & Btr; C & D Select; Nos. 1, 2 & 3; B & Btr.; C Sel.; D Sel.; Nos. 1, 2 & 3		
Spruce, Engelman	B & Btr.; C Sel; D Sel; Nos. 1, 2, 3		
Spruce, Sitka	B & Btr. C, D.; Select Merch.; Nos. 1, 2, 3 Boards	Clear; all heart: B & Btr C	D; E
Pine, Idaho White	Supreme (B & Btr); Choice (C Sel); Quality (D Sel); Colonial (No. 1); Stering (No. 2); Standard No. 3)		
Pine, Northern White; Norway, Jack; Spruce, Eastern; Balsam Fir	B & Btr; C; D; Nos. 1, 2, & 3		
Pine, Ponderosa	1 & 2 clear (B & Btr); C Sel; D Sel; Nos 1, 2 & 3		
Pine, Southern	A; B; C; D; Nos. 2 & 3	A; B; C; D; No. 2	
Pine, Sugar	1 & 2 Clear; C Sel; D Sel; Nos. 1, 2 & 3.		

Note: See Regional Lumber Assns. for Grade-Quality-Use data. *These numerical designations may be changed to grade names with subsequent issues of Grading Rules.

Data by the National Lumber Manufacturers Assoc., 1319 18th Street, N.W., Washington, D.C.

OTHER MATERIALS

Oak, Teak, Walnut, Mahogany planks (laminated or veneer) and Pine and Oak solid planks.
Sizes not standard but usually available:-
33/32" thick, 4" to 8" wide, 4" to 12" in plain Oak and Teak.
25/32" thick, 4" to 8" wide, 4" to 12" in plain Oak and Teak.
Planks, screwed as well as nailed, plugged or butterflied.
These materials available for parquetry, in blocks (see Maple sizes).

Fin. ¼" min.
chestnut core

PLANK

DETAILS

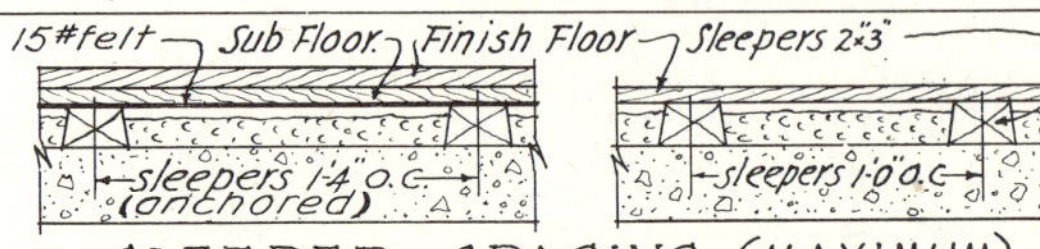

15# felt
Sub Floor
Finish Floor
Sleepers 2"×3"
sleepers 1'-4" o.c. (anchored)
sleepers 1'-0" o.c.

SLEEPER SPACING (MAXIMUM)

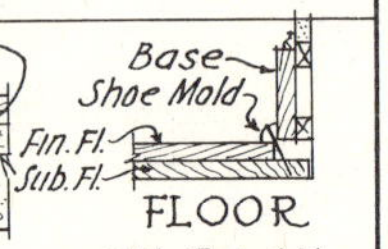

Base
Shoe Mold
Fin. Fl.
Sub. Fl.

FLOOR AT BASE.

FLOORING ON CONCRETE OVER EARTH

FLOOR FINISHES DEMANDING DRY CONDITIONS   FLOOR FINISHES TOLERATING DAMPNESS

Scale 3/4" = 1'-0"

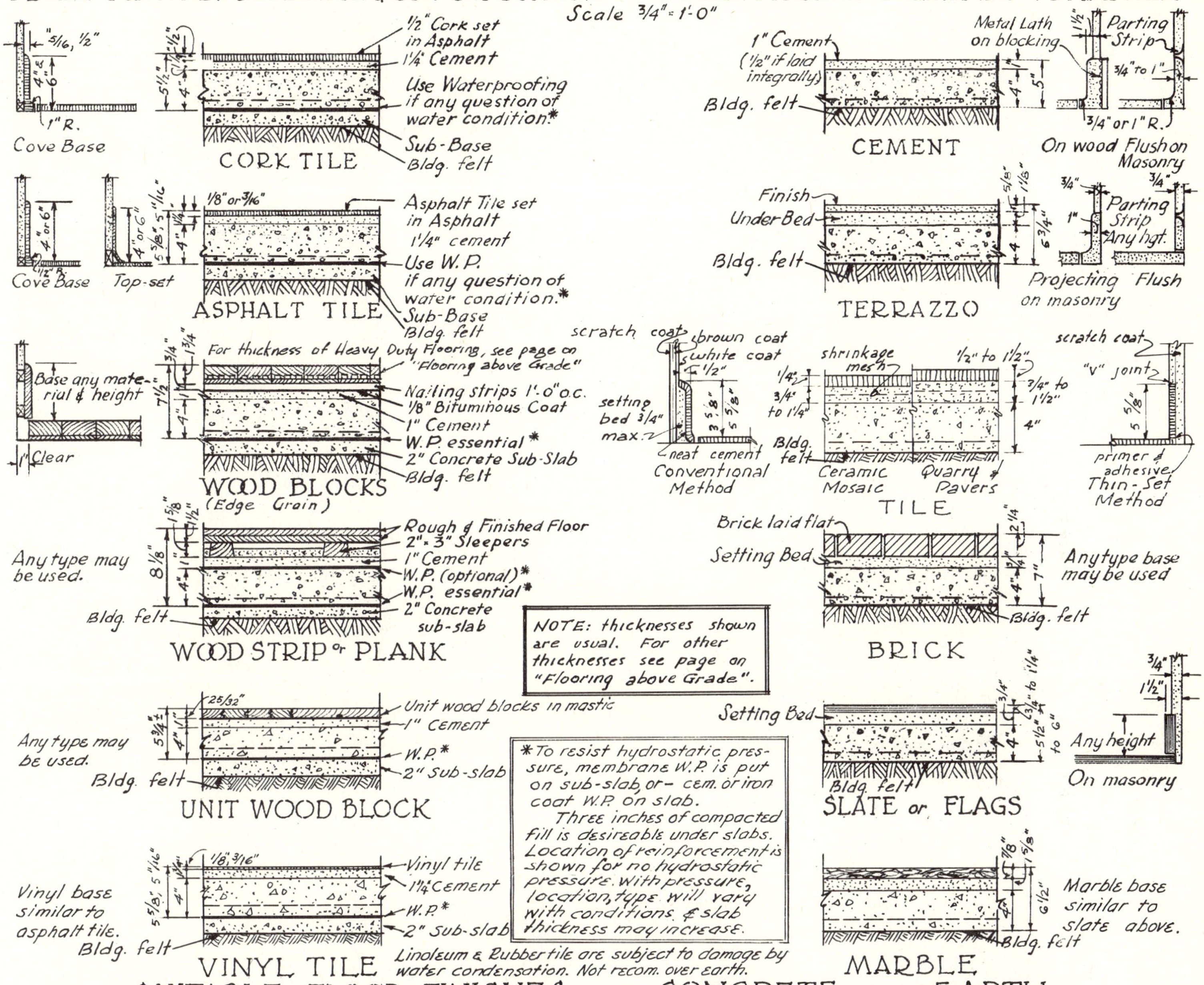
5/16, 1/2"
4" & 6"
1" R.
Cove Base
1/2" Cork set in Asphalt
1 1/4" Cement
Use Waterproofing if any question of water condition.*
Sub-Base
Bldg. felt
CORK TILE
1" Cement (1/2" if laid integrally)
Bldg. felt
CEMENT
Metal Lath on blocking
Parting Strip
3/4" to 1"
3/4" or 1" R.
On wood Flush on Masonry
1/8" or 3/16"
Asphalt Tile set in Asphalt
1 1/4" cement
Use W.P. if any question of water condition.*
Sub-Base
Bldg. felt
4" or 6"
Cove Base
Top-set
ASPHALT TILE
Finish
Under Bed
Bldg. felt
TERRAZZO
Parting Strip
Any hgt.
Projecting
Flush on masonry
Base any material & height
1" Clear
For thickness of Heavy Duty Flooring, see page on "Flooring above Grade"
Nailing strips 1'-0" o.c.
1/8" Bituminous Coat
1" Cement
W.P. essential*
2" Concrete Sub-Slab
Bldg. felt
WOOD BLOCKS (Edge Grain)
scratch coat
brown coat
white coat
setting bed 3/4" max.
neat cement
Conventional Method
shrinkage mesh
1/2" to 1 1/2"
3/4" to 1 1/2"
3/4 to 1 1/4"
Bldg. felt
Ceramic Mosaic
Quarry & Pavers
TILE
scratch coat
"V" joint
primer & adhesive
Thin-Set Method
Any type may be used.
Rough & Finished Floor
2" x 3" Sleepers
1" Cement
W.P. (optional)*
W.P. essential*
2" Concrete sub-slab
Bldg. felt
WOOD STRIP or PLANK
Brick laid flat
Setting Bed
Any type base may be used
Bldg. felt
BRICK
NOTE: thicknesses shown are usual. For other thicknesses see page on "Flooring above Grade".
Any type may be used.
Unit wood blocks in mastic
1" Cement
W.P.*
2" Sub-slab
Bldg. felt
UNIT WOOD BLOCK
*To resist hydrostatic pressure, membrane W.P. is put on sub-slab, or— cem. or iron coat W.P. on slab.
Three inches of compacted fill is desireable under slabs. Location of reinforcement is shown for no hydrostatic pressure. With pressure, location, type will vary with conditions & slab thickness may increase.
Setting Bed
Bldg. felt
SLATE or FLAGS
Any height
On masonry
Vinyl base similar to asphalt tile.
Vinyl tile
1 1/4" Cement
W.P.*
2" Sub-slab
Bldg. felt
VINYL TILE
Linoleum & Rubber tile are subject to damage by water condensation. Not recom. over earth.
Marble base similar to slate above.
Bldg. felt
MARBLE

SUITABLE FLOOR FINISHES for CONCRETE over EARTH

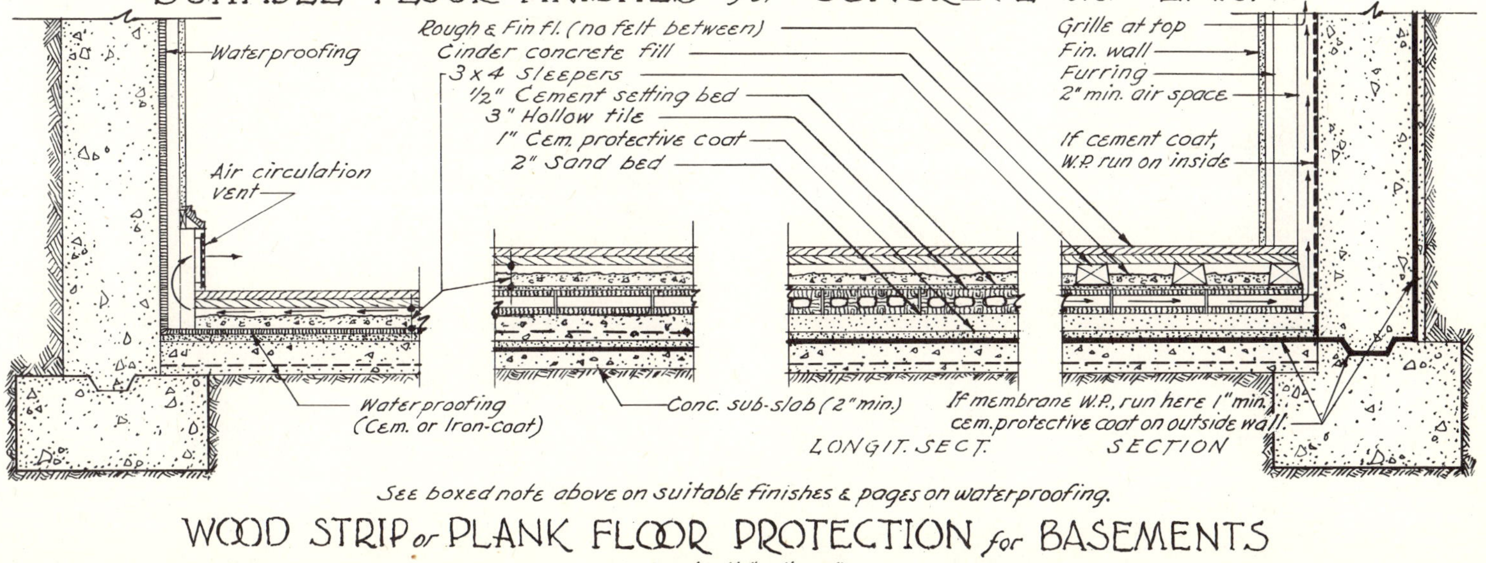
Waterproofing
Air circulation vent
Rough & Fin fl. (no felt between)
Cinder concrete fill
3 x 4 Sleepers
1/2" Cement setting bed
3" Hollow tile
1" Cem. protective coat
2" Sand bed
Grille at top
Fin. wall
Furring
2" min. air space
If cement coat, W.P. run on inside
Waterproofing (Cem. or Iron-coat)
Conc. sub-slab (2" min.)
If membrane W.P., run here 1" min. cem. protective coat on outside wall.
LONGIT. SECT.
SECTION

See boxed note above on suitable finishes & pages on waterproofing.

WOOD STRIP or PLANK FLOOR PROTECTION for BASEMENTS

Scale 1/2" = 1'-0"

FLOORING ABOVE GRADE

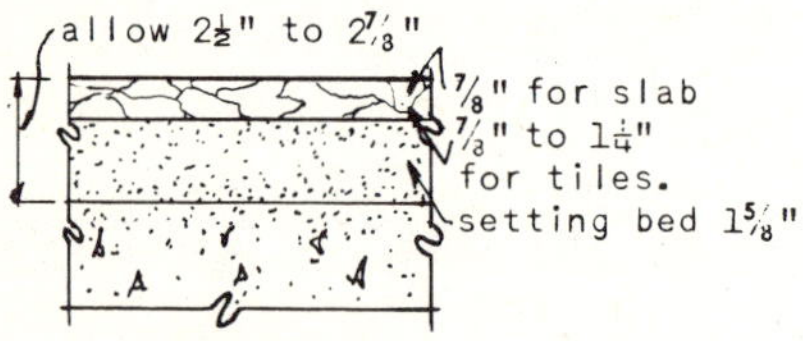
allow 2½" to 2⅞"
⅞" for slab
⅞" to 1¼"
for tiles.
setting bed 1⅝"

MARBLE

Setting depth 2⅞" + for layer of tarpaper or sand between setting bed & rough slab. For cleavage plane, place shrinkage mesh in setting bed.

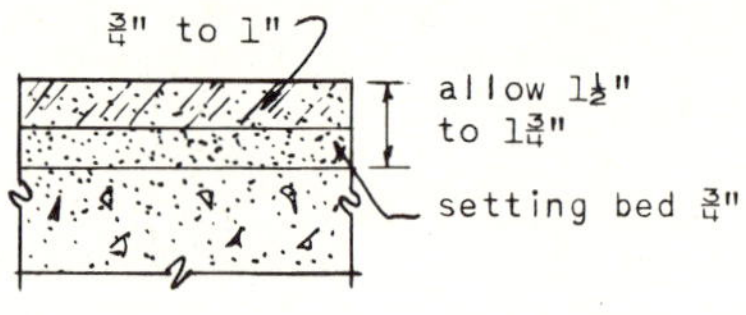
¾" to 1"
allow 1½"
to 1¾"
setting bed ¾"

SLATE

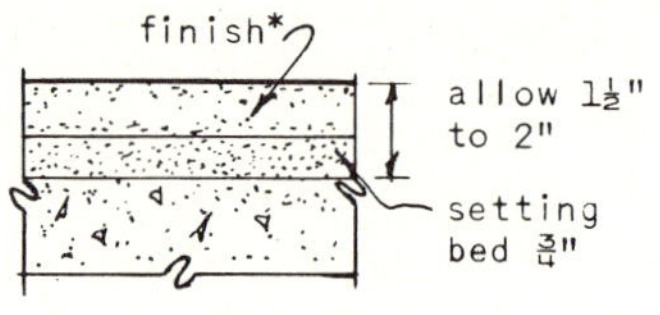
finish*
allow 1½"
to 2"
setting
bed ¾"

FLAGGING

* Quartzite ¾" to 1¼"
Sandstone 1"

Thickness of finished flooring materials on this page is based on products most generally manufactured.

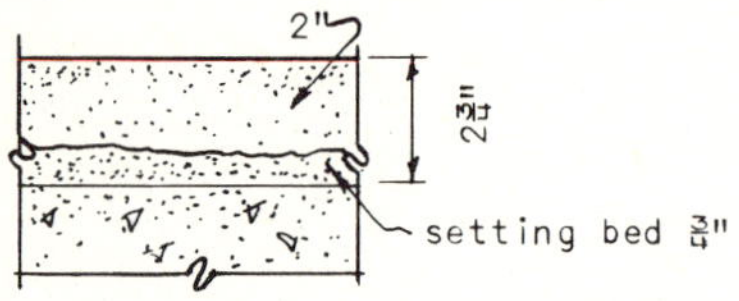
2"
2¾"
setting bed ¾"

CUTSTONE

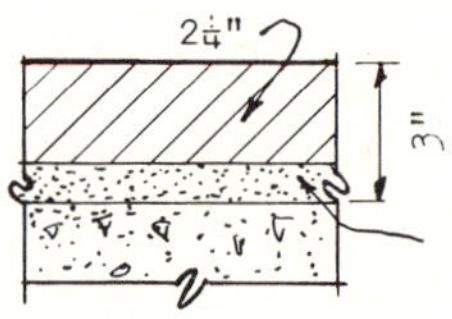
2¼"
3"

BRICKS FLAT

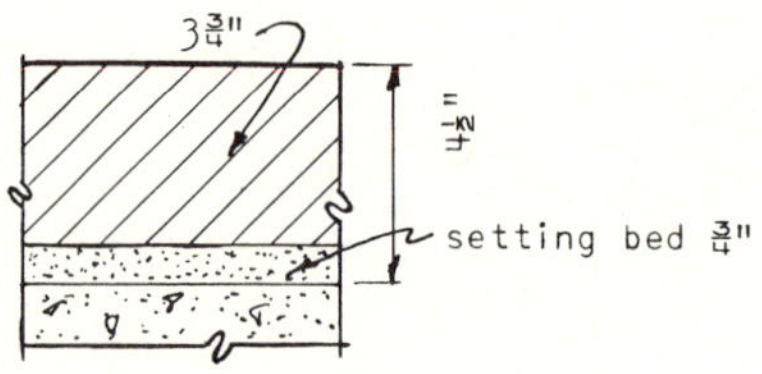
3¾"
4½"
setting bed ¾"

BRICKS ON EDGE

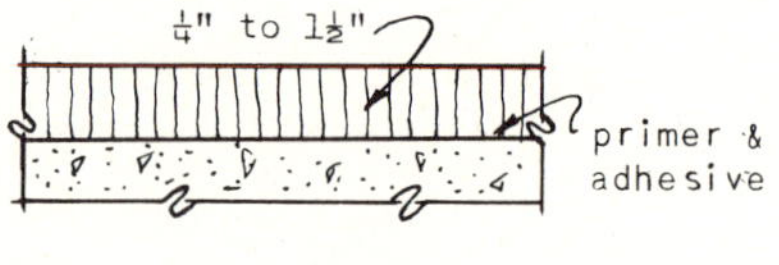
¼" to 1½"
primer &
adhesive

thin-set method

CERAMIC TILE

STONE, BRICK, AND TILE FLOORS

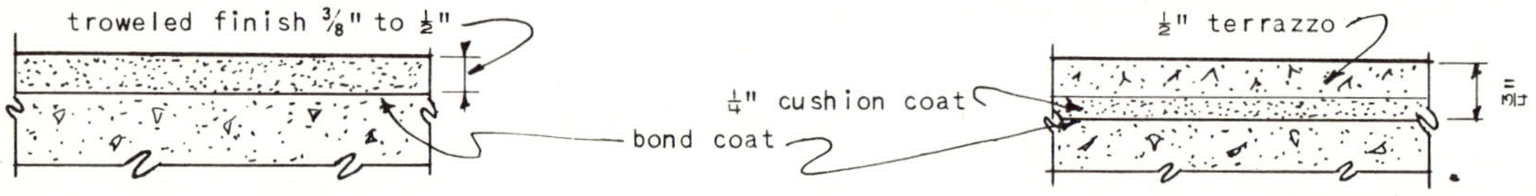
troweled finish ⅜" to ½"
bond coat
¼" cushion coat
½" terrazzo
¾"

thin-set method

ON CONCRETE

TERRAZZO ON CONCRETE

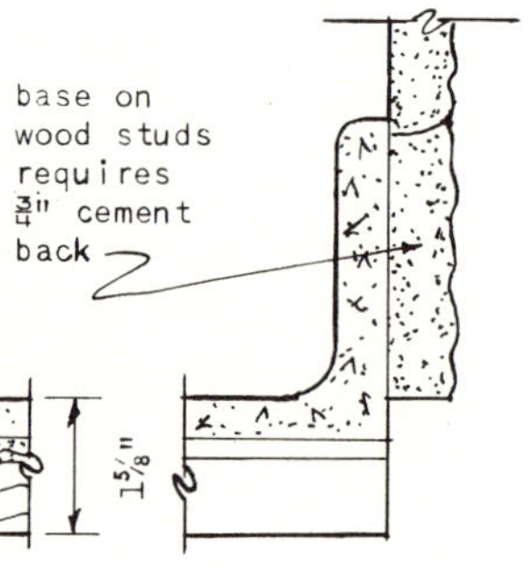
base on
wood studs
requires
¾" cement
back

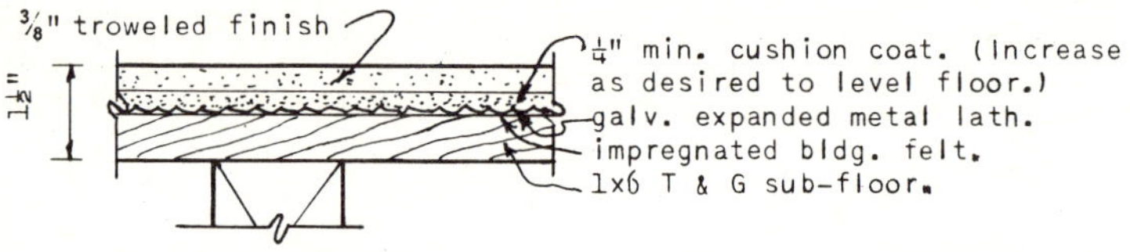
⅜" troweled finish
1½"
¼" min. cushion coat. (Increase
as desired to level floor.)
galv. expanded metal lath.
impregnated bldg. felt.
1x6 T & G sub-floor.

ON WOOD

Scale: 3" = 1'-0"

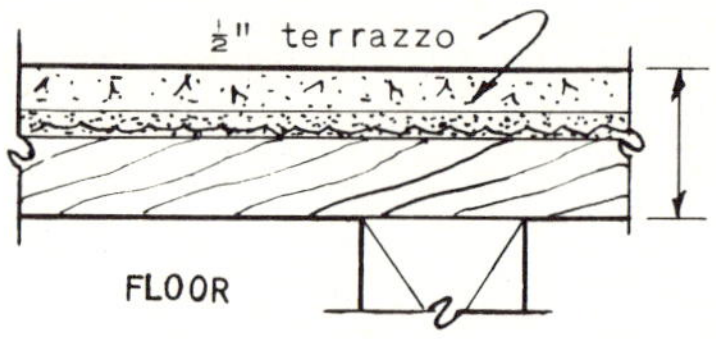
½" terrazzo
1⅝"

FLOOR

BASE

TERRAZZO ON WOOD

OXYCHLORIDE FLOORS (magnesite)

Base may be formed ½" thick as desired.

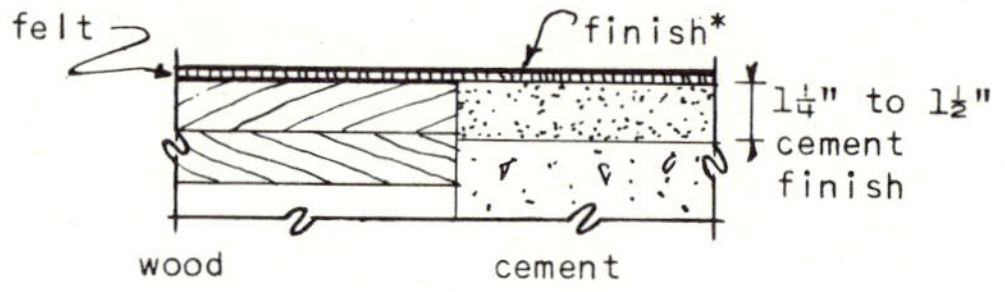
felt
finish*
1¼" to 1½"
cement
finish
wood
cement

RUBBER TILE
* ⅛", 3/16"

VINYL PLASTIC TILE
* 1/16", 3/32", ⅛", 3/16"

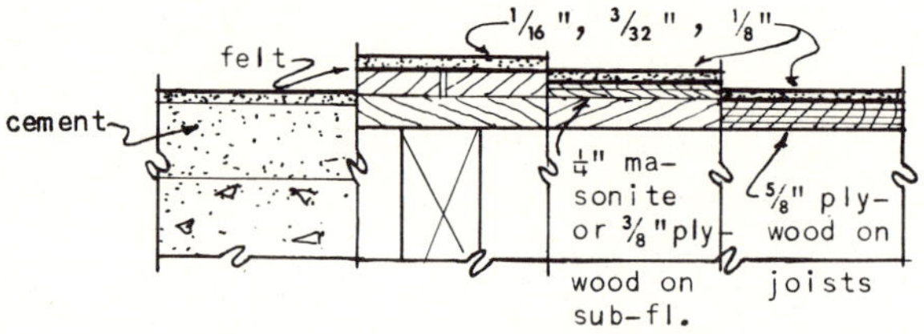
1/16", 3/32", ⅛"
felt
cement
¼" ma-
sonite
or ⅜"ply
wood on
sub-fl.
⅝" ply-
wood on
joists

LINOLEUM

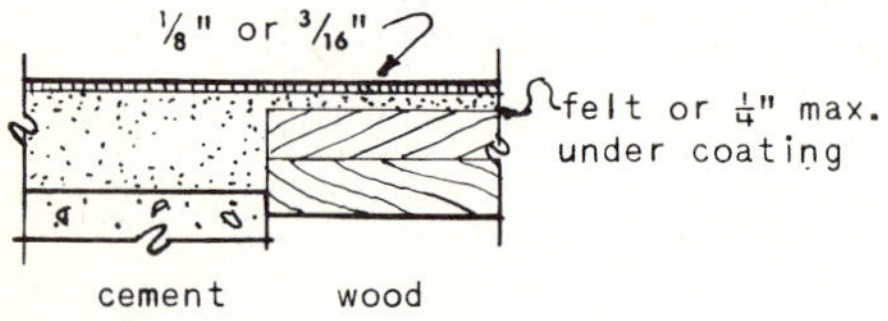
⅛" or 3/16"
felt or ¼" max.
under coating
cement
wood

ASPHALT TILE

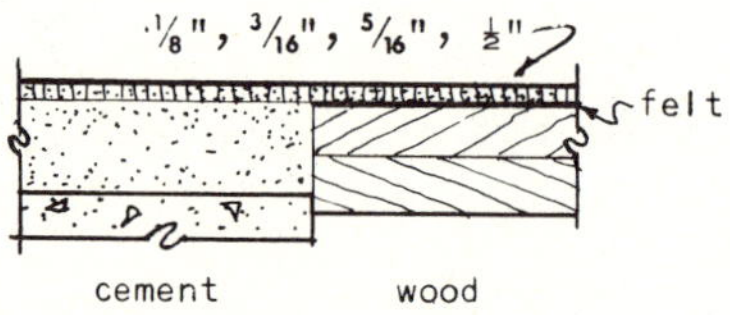
⅛", 3/16", 5/16", ½"
felt
cement
wood

CORK TILE

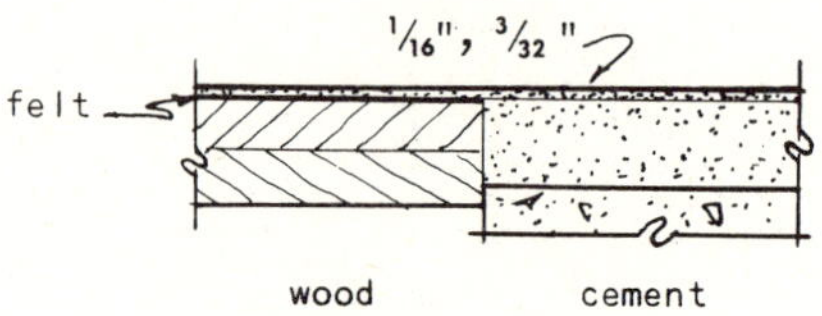
1/16", 3/32"
felt
wood
cement

LINOLEUM TILE

RESILIENT FLOORING

Scale: 1½" = 1'-0"

FLOORING ABOVE GRADE

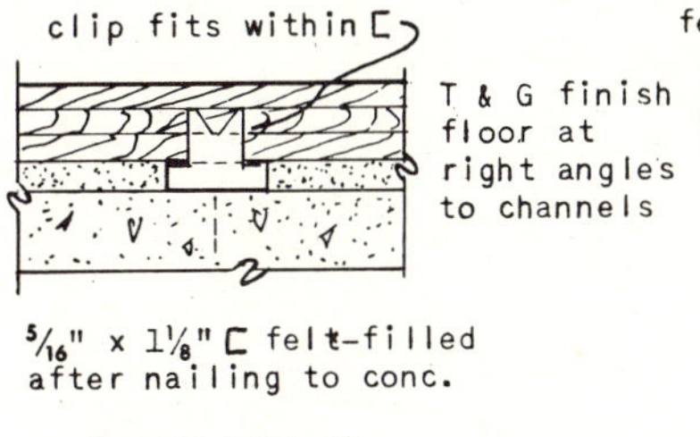
clip fits within ⊏
T & G finish floor at right angles to channels
5/16" x 1 1/8" ⊏ felt-filled after nailing to conc.

scale: 3" = 1'-0"

OVER CHANNELS

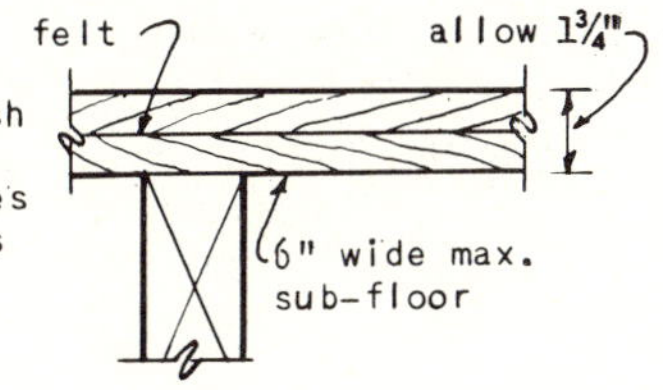
felt
allow 1 3/4"
6" wide max. sub-floor

OVER WOOD SUBFLOORS

THICKNESSES:
flat grains:
25/32", 33/32", 41/32", 53/32"
edge grain:
33/32", 1 1/4", 1 1/2", 1 3/4", 2"

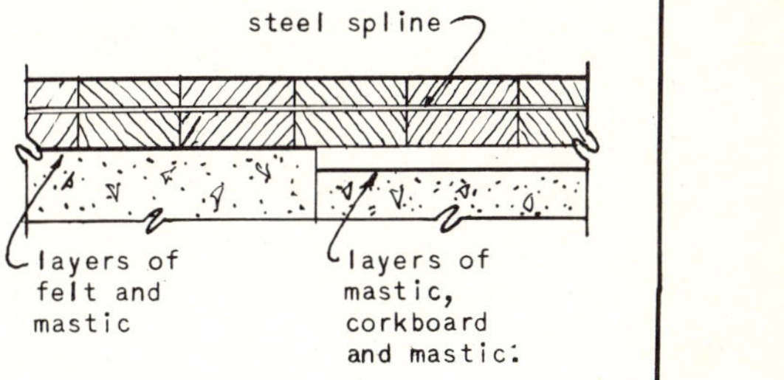
steel spline
layers of felt and mastic
layers of mastic, corkboard and mastic.

HEAVY DUTY FLOORING

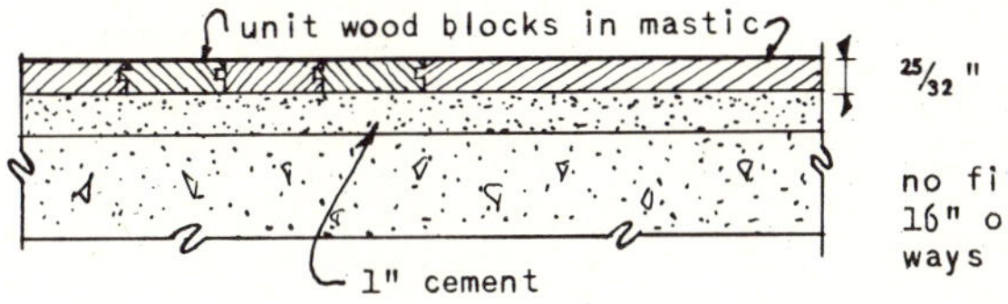
unit wood blocks in mastic
25/32"
1" cement

UNIT WOOD BLOCK

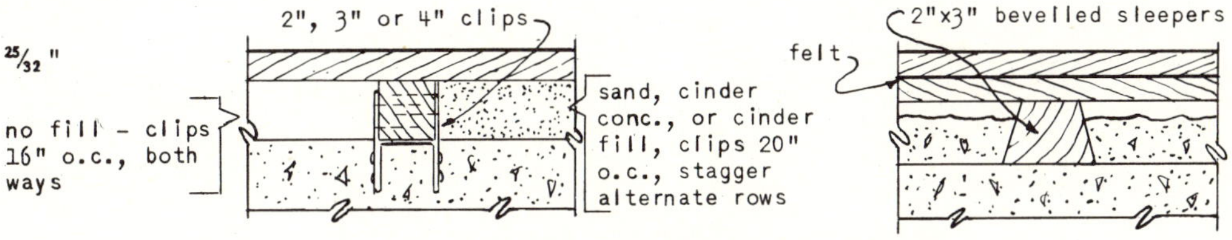
no fill - clips 16" o.c., both ways
2", 3" or 4" clips
sand, cinder conc., or cinder fill, clips 20" o.c., stagger alternate rows
felt
2"x3" bevelled sleepers

OVER SLEEPERS ON SLABS

sleepers 16" o c.
fin. wood floors usually 25/32" thick. Also made in 5/16", 3/8", 1/2" & 5/8" thicknesses.

WOOD FLOORS

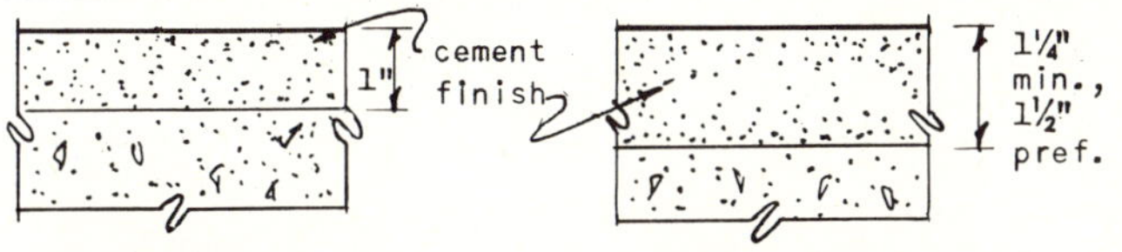
1"
cement finish
1 1/4" min., 1 1/2" pref.

INTEGRAL ON SLAB, OR SEPARATE FINISH ON CONC. FILL.

SEPARATE FINISH DIRECTLY ON SLAB, NO FILL.

scale: 3" = 1'-0"

FLOORS

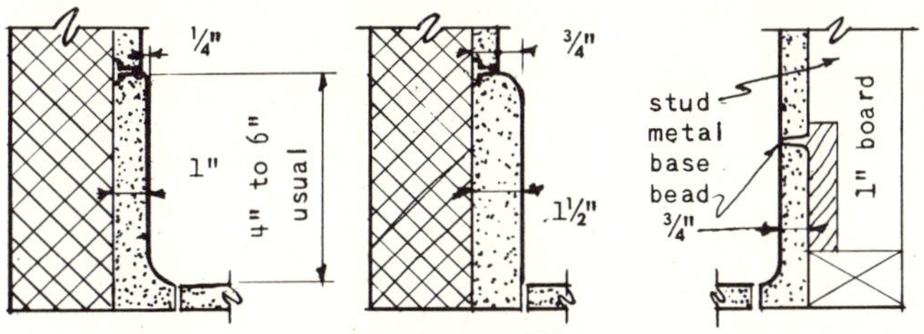
1/4"
1"
4" to 6" usual
3/4"
1 1/2"
stud
metal base bead
3/4"
1" board

PROJECTING 1/4" | PROJECTING 3/4" | FLUSH

BASES

CEMENT FLOORS AND BASES

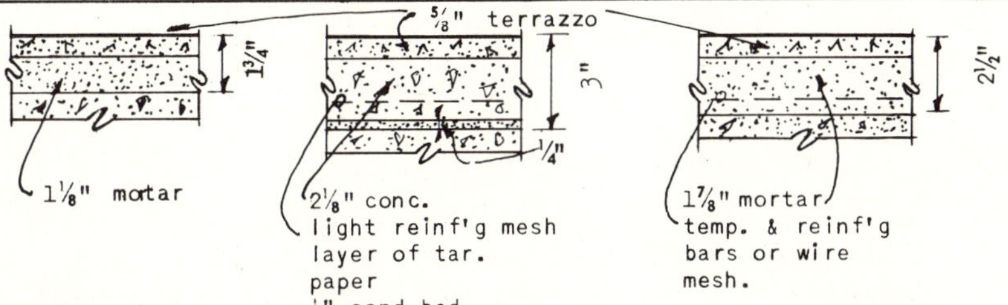
5/8" terrazzo
1 3/4"
3"
1/4"
2 1/2"
1 1/8" mortar
2 1/8" conc.
light reinf'g mesh
layer of tar. paper
1/4" sand bed.
1 7/8" mortar
temp. & reinf'g bars or wire mesh.

BONDED TO CONCRETE | SAND CUSHION OVER CONC. | DIRECTLY OVER JOISTS

FLOORS

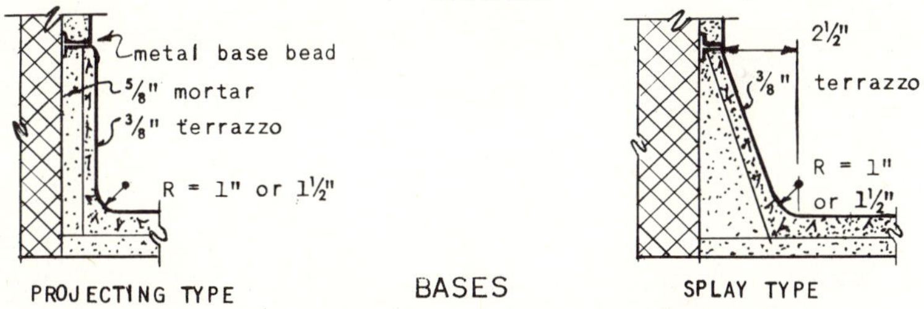
metal base bead
5/8" mortar
3/8" terrazzo
R = 1" or 1 1/2"
2 1/2"
3/8" terrazzo
R = 1" or 1 1/2"

PROJECTING TYPE | BASES | SPLAY TYPE

NOTE: separated floor to be used where vibration, shrinkage, or settlement is expected.

TERRAZZO

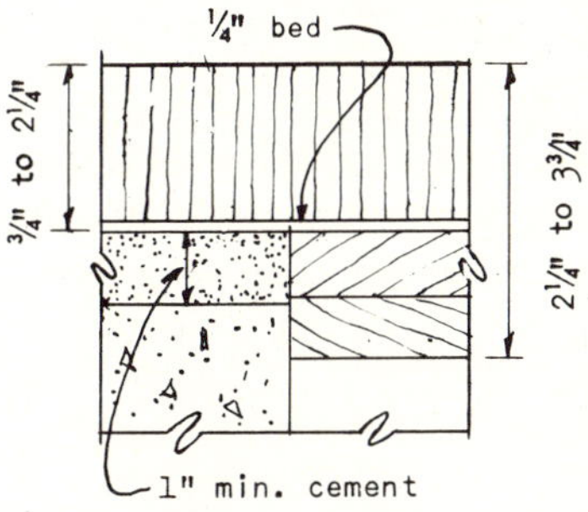
1/4" bed
3/4" to 2 1/4"
2 1/4" to 3 3/4"
1" min. cement
cement
wood

scale: 3" = 1'-0"

ASPHALT COMPOSITION

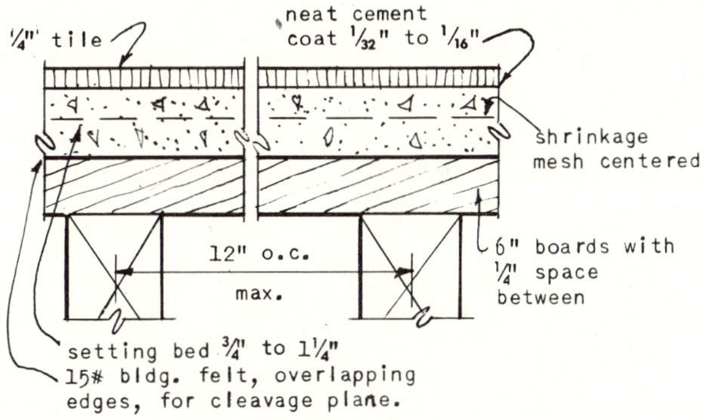
1/4" tile
neat cement coat 1/32" to 1/16"
shrinkage mesh centered
6" boards with 1/4" space between
12" o.c.
max.
setting bed 3/4" to 1 1/4"
15# bldg. felt, overlapping edges, for cleavage plane.

scale: 3" = 1'-0"

CERAMIC MOSAIC TILE ON WOOD JOISTS

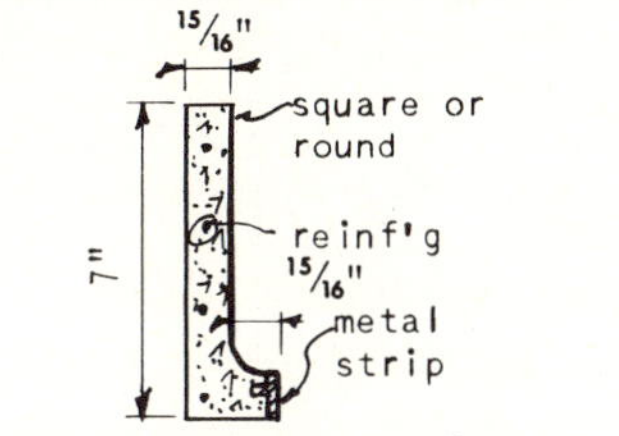
15/16"
square or round
reinf'g
15/16"
metal strip
7"

SINGLE FACE BASE. Also available: double face base for partitions.

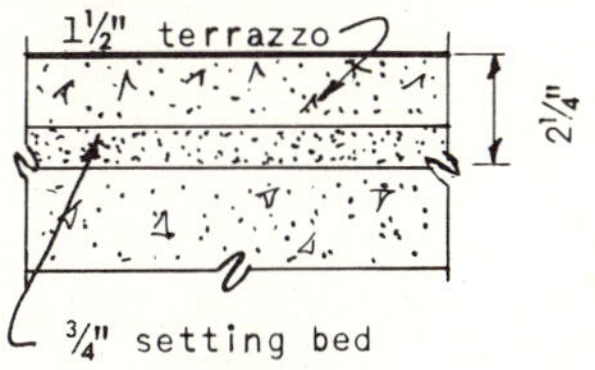
1 1/2" terrazzo
2 1/4"
3/4" setting bed

FLOOR

PRECAST TERRAZZO

scale: 1 1/2" = 1'-0" except as noted.

ACOUSTICAL CORRECTION

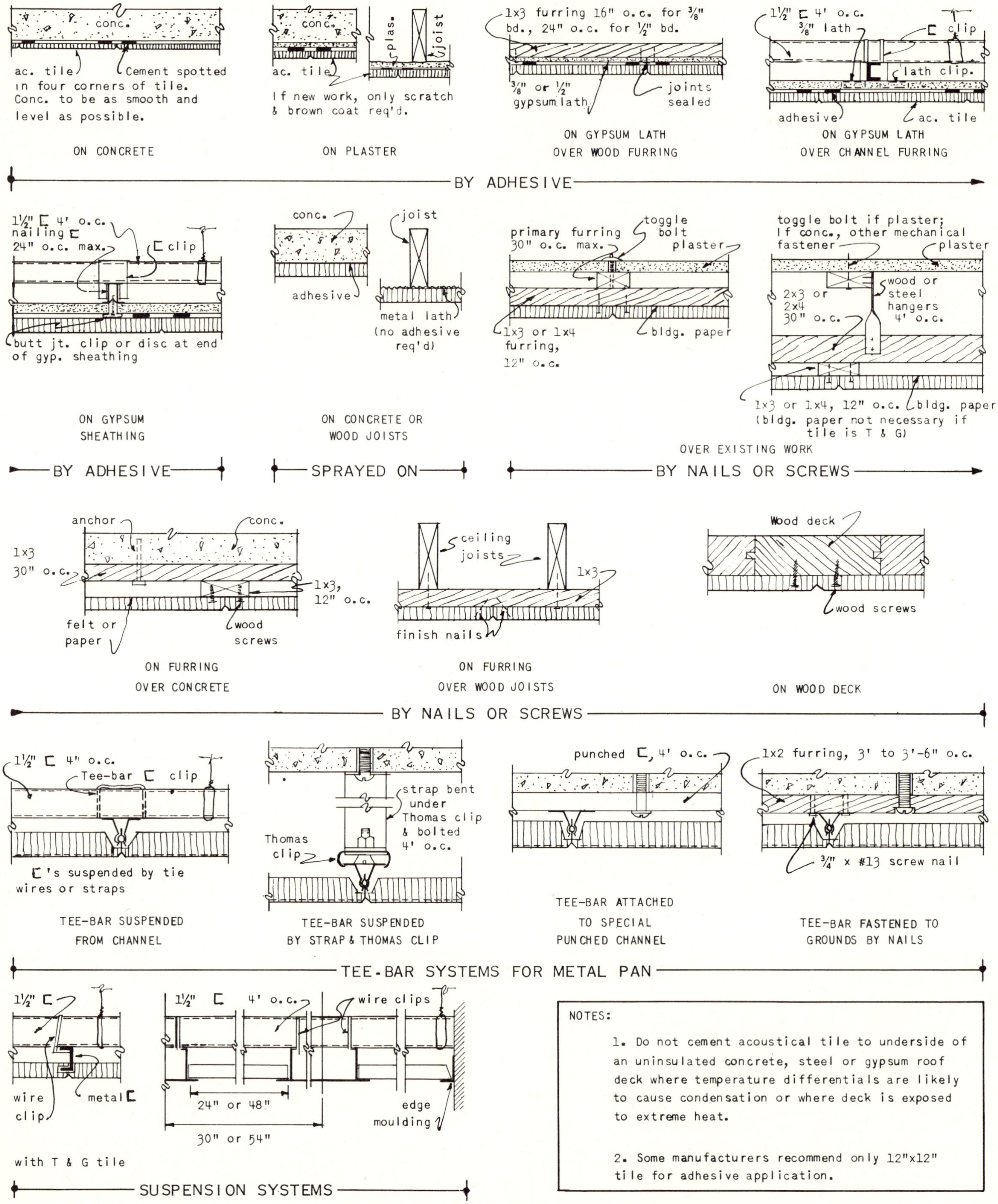
conc.
ac. tile
Cement spotted in four corners of tile. Conc. to be as smooth and level as possible.
ON CONCRETE
conc.
plas.
joist
ac. tile
If new work, only scratch & brown coat req'd.
ON PLASTER
1x3 furring 16" o.c. for 3/8" bd., 24" o.c. for 1/2" bd.
3/8" or 1/2" gypsum lath
joints sealed
ON GYPSUM LATH OVER WOOD FURRING
1½" [4' o.c.
3/8" lath
[clip
lath clip.
adhesive
ac. tile
ON GYPSUM LATH OVER CHANNEL FURRING
BY ADHESIVE
1½" [4' o.c.
nailing [24" o.c. max.
[clip
butt jt. clip or disc at end of gyp. sheathing
ON GYPSUM SHEATHING
conc.
adhesive
joist
metal lath (no adhesive req'd)
ON CONCRETE OR WOOD JOISTS
primary furring 30" o.c. max.
toggle bolt
plaster
1x3 or 1x4 furring, 12" o.c.
bldg. paper
toggle bolt if plaster; If conc., other mechanical fastener
plaster
2x3 or 2x4 30" o.c.
wood or steel hangers 4' o.c.
1x3 or 1x4, 12" o.c.
bldg. paper (bldg. paper not necessary if tile is T & G)
OVER EXISTING WORK
BY ADHESIVE
SPRAYED ON
BY NAILS OR SCREWS
anchor
conc.
1x3 30" o.c.
1x3, 12" o.c.
felt or paper
wood screws
ON FURRING OVER CONCRETE
ceiling joists
1x3
finish nails
ON FURRING OVER WOOD JOISTS
Wood deck
wood screws
ON WOOD DECK
BY NAILS OR SCREWS
1½" [4" o.c.
Tee-bar [clip
['s suspended by tie wires or straps
TEE-BAR SUSPENDED FROM CHANNEL
strap bent under Thomas clip & bolted 4' o.c.
Thomas clip
TEE-BAR SUSPENDED BY STRAP & THOMAS CLIP
punched [, 4' o.c.
TEE-BAR ATTACHED TO SPECIAL PUNCHED CHANNEL
1x2 furring, 3' to 3'-6" o.c.
3/4" x #13 screw nail
TEE-BAR FASTENED TO GROUNDS BY NAILS
TEE-BAR SYSTEMS FOR METAL PAN
1½" [
wire clip
metal [
with T & G tile
1½" [4' o.c.
wire clips
24" or 48"
30" or 54"
edge moulding
SUSPENSION SYSTEMS

NOTES:

1. Do not cement acoustical tile to underside of an uninsulated concrete, steel or gypsum roof deck where temperature differentials are likely to cause condensation or where deck is exposed to extreme heat.

2. Some manufacturers recommend only 12"x12" tile for adhesive application.

ACOUSTICAL INSTALLATION METHODS

ACOUSTICAL SUSPENDED CEILINGS

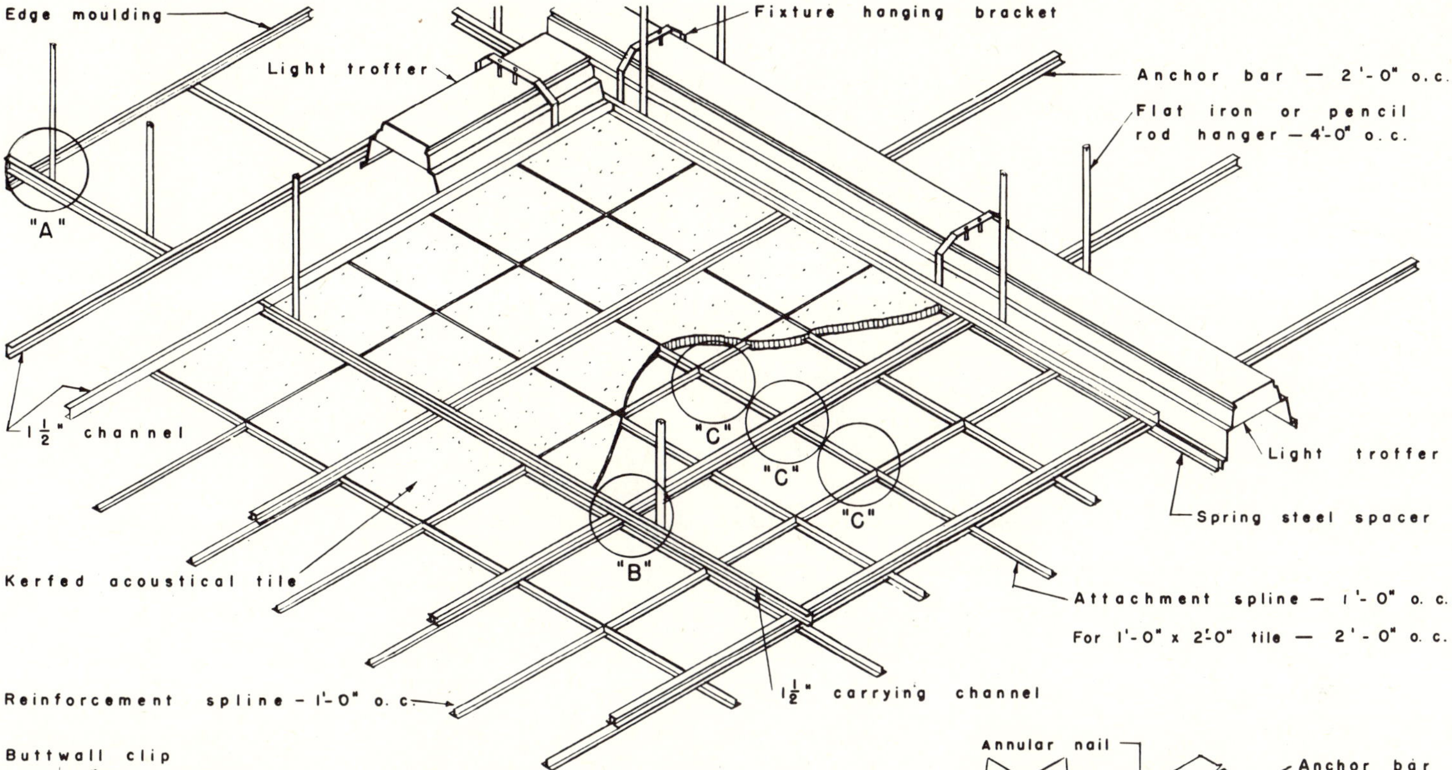
Edge moulding
Fixture hanging bracket
Light troffer
Anchor bar — 2'-0" o.c.
Flat iron or pencil rod hanger — 4'-0" o.c.
"A"
$1\frac{1}{2}$" channel
"C"
"C"
"C"
Light troffer
Spring steel spacer
"B"
Kerfed acoustical tile
Attachment spline — 1'-0" o.c.
For 1'-0" x 2'-0" tile — 2'-0" o.c.
Reinforcement spline - 1'-0" o.c.
$1\frac{1}{2}$" carrying channel

MECHANICAL INSTALLATION OF ACOUSTICAL TILE

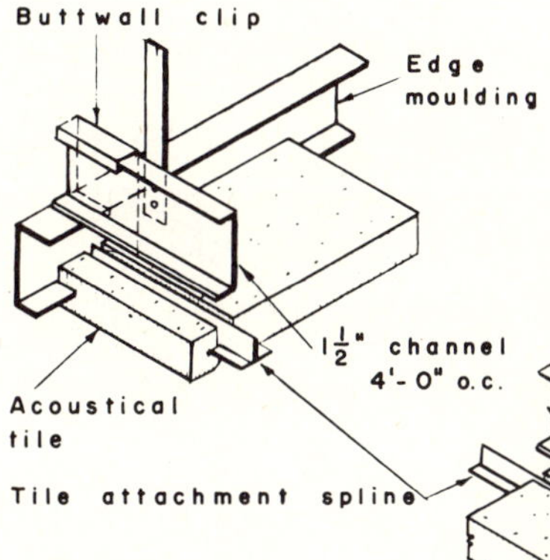
Buttwall clip
Edge moulding
$1\frac{1}{2}$" channel 4'-0" o.c.
Acoustical tile
Tile attachment spline

DETAIL "A"

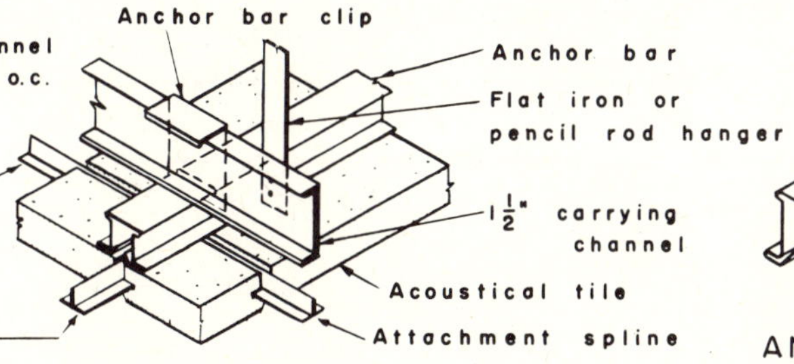
Anchor bar clip
Anchor bar
Flat iron or pencil rod hanger
$1\frac{1}{2}$" carrying channel
Acoustical tile
Tile reinforcement spline
Attachment spline

DETAIL "B"

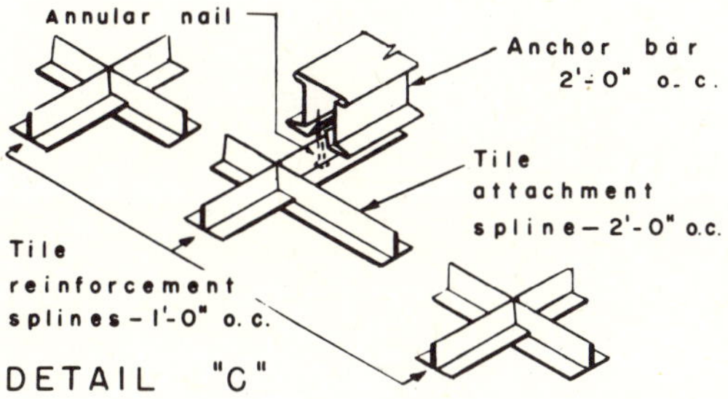
Annular nail
Anchor bar 2'-0" o.c.
Tile attachment spline - 2'-0" o.c.
Tile reinforcement splines - 1'-0" o.c.

DETAIL "C"

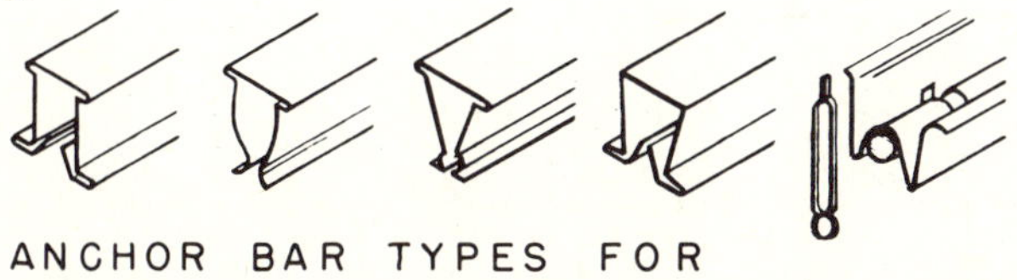

ANCHOR BAR TYPES FOR KERFED ACOUSTICAL TILE & METAL PANS

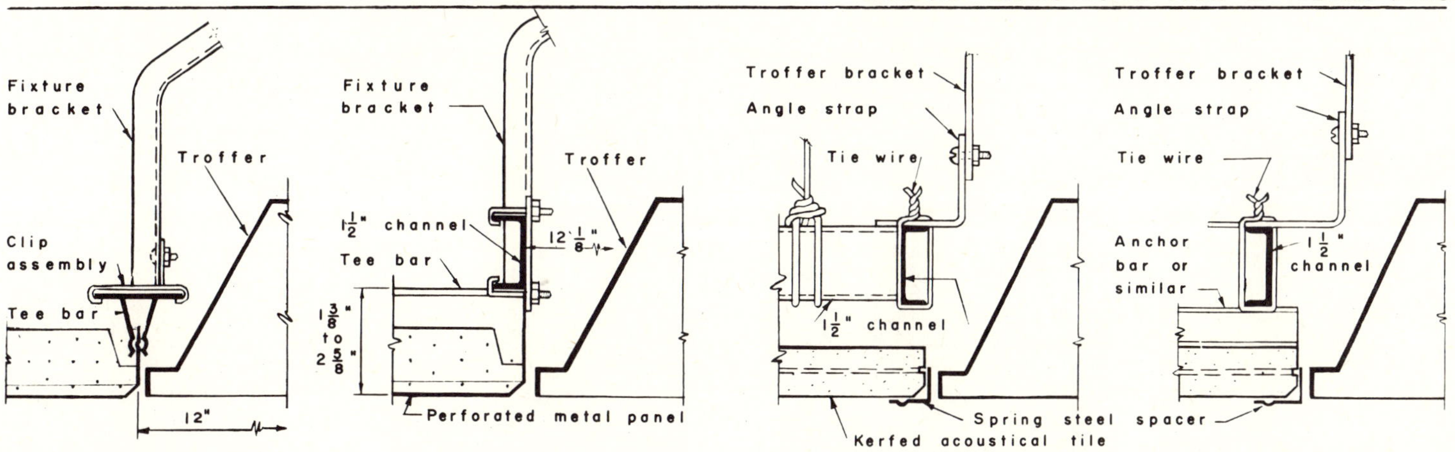
Fixture bracket
Troffer
Clip assembly
Tee bar
12"
Fixture bracket
Troffer
$1\frac{1}{2}$" channel
$12\frac{1}{8}$"
Tee bar
$1\frac{3}{8}$" to $2\frac{5}{8}$"
Perforated metal panel
Troffer bracket
Angle strap
Tie wire
$1\frac{1}{2}$" channel
Spring steel spacer
Kerfed acoustical tile
Troffer bracket
Angle strap
Tie wire
Anchor bar or similar
$1\frac{1}{2}$" channel

TROFFER SUPPORTED BY TEE BAR — WHERE TROFFER CROSSES TEE BAR

TROFFER WITH METAL PANELS

CHANNEL PERPENDICULAR TO LIGHT TROFFER — CHANNEL PARALLEL TO LIGHT TROFFER

TROFFER WITH KERFED TILE

DETAILS — INSTALLATION OF TROFFER IN SUSPENDED PANEL CEILINGS

ACOUSTICAL METAL SUSPENDED CEILINGS

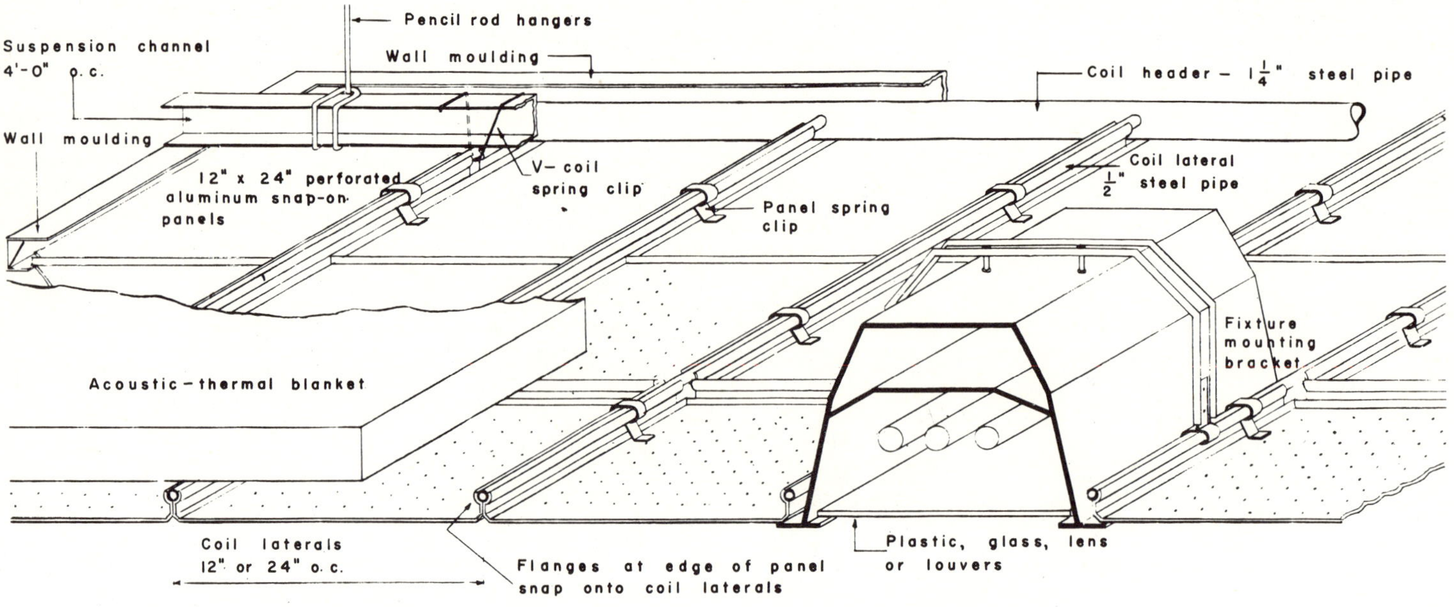
Pencil rod hangers
Suspension channel 4'-0" o.c.
Wall moulding
Coil header – 1 1/4" steel pipe
Wall moulding
12" x 24" perforated aluminum snap-on panels
V– coil spring clip
Coil lateral 1/2" steel pipe
Panel spring clip
Fixture mounting bracket
Acoustic – thermal blanket
Coil laterals 12" or 24" o.c.
Flanges at edge of panel snap onto coil laterals
Plastic, glass, lens or louvers

CEILING SYSTEM WITH RADIANT COOLING, RADIANT HEATING & ACOUSTIC CONTROL

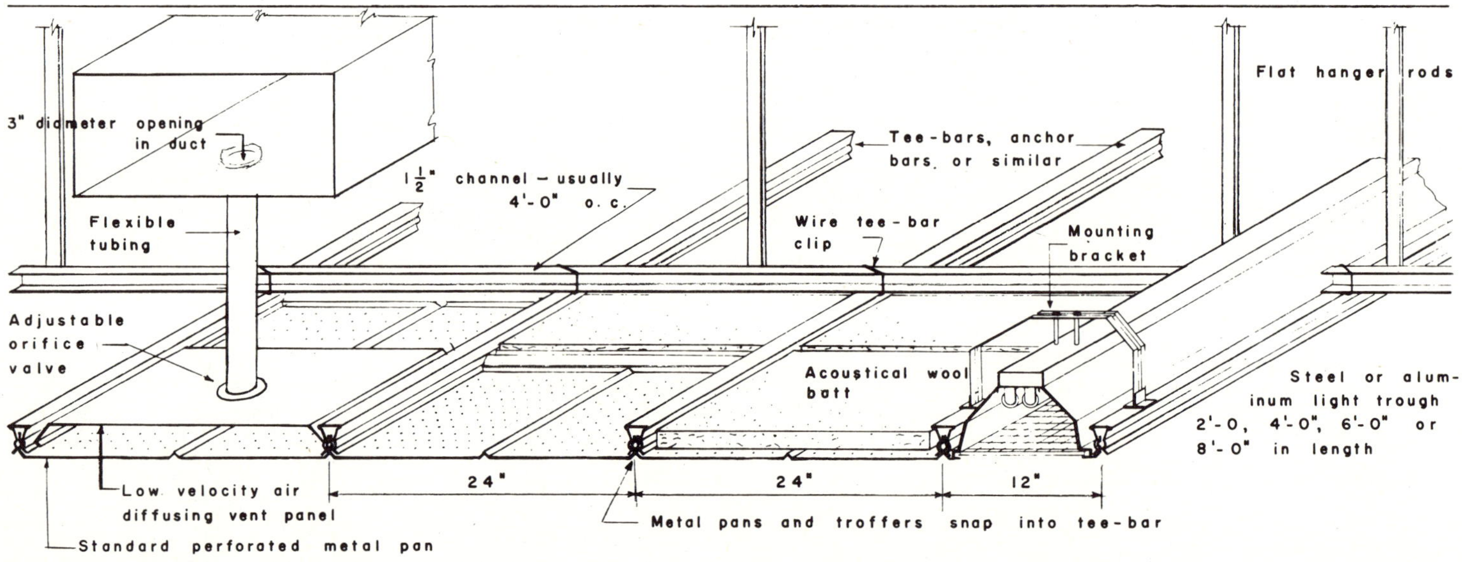
Flat hanger rods
3" diameter opening in duct
Tee-bars, anchor bars or similar
1 1/2" channel – usually 4'-0" o.c.
Flexible tubing
Wire tee-bar clip
Mounting bracket
Adjustable orifice valve
Acoustical wool batt
Steel or aluminum light trough 2'-0, 4'-0", 6'-0" or 8'-0" in length
24"
24"
12"
Low velocity air diffusing vent panel
Metal pans and troffers snap into tee-bar
Standard perforated metal pan

ACOUSTICAL METAL CEILING WITH AIR-DIFFUSING PANEL AND TROFFERS

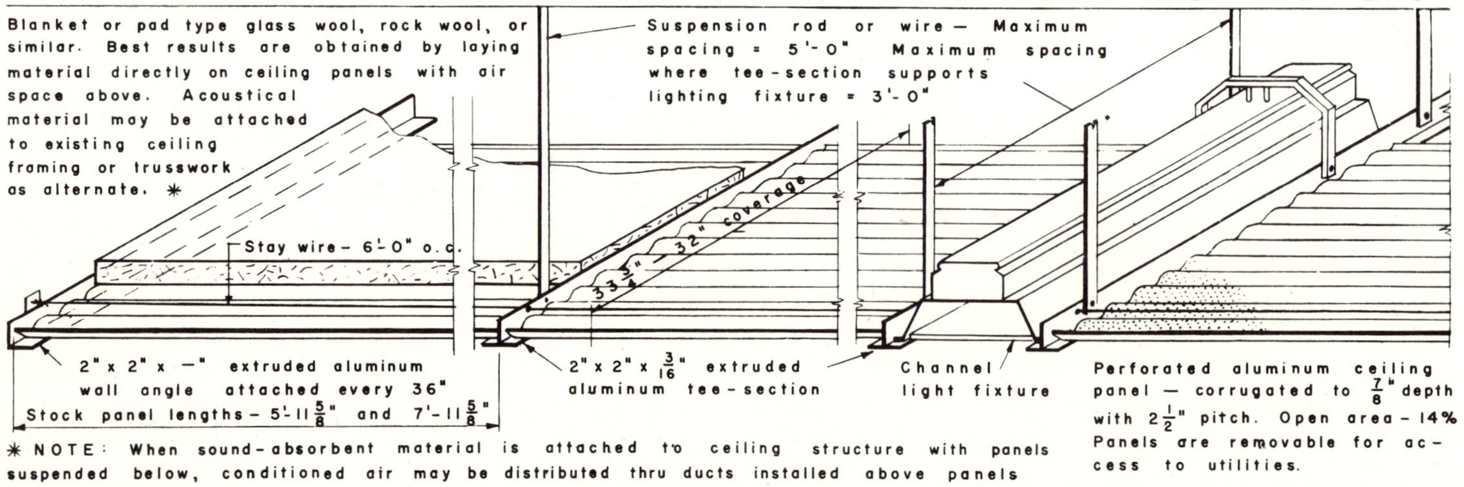
Blanket or pad type glass wool, rock wool, or similar. Best results are obtained by laying material directly on ceiling panels with air space above. Acoustical material may be attached to existing ceiling framing or trusswork as alternate. *
Suspension rod or wire – Maximum spacing = 5'-0" Maximum spacing where tee-section supports lighting fixture = 3'-0"
Stay wire – 6'-0" o.c.
33 3/4" – 32" coverage
2" x 2" x –" extruded aluminum wall angle attached every 36"
Stock panel lengths – 5'-11 5/8" and 7'-11 5/8"
2" x 2" x 3/16" extruded aluminum tee-section
Channel light fixture
Perforated aluminum ceiling panel – corrugated to 7/8" depth with 2 1/2" pitch. Open area – 14% Panels are removable for access to utilities.

* NOTE: When sound-absorbent material is attached to ceiling structure with panels suspended below, conditioned air may be distributed thru ducts installed above panels

PERFORATED METAL ACOUSTICAL CEILING SYSTEM

LOUVERED SUSPENDED CEILINGS

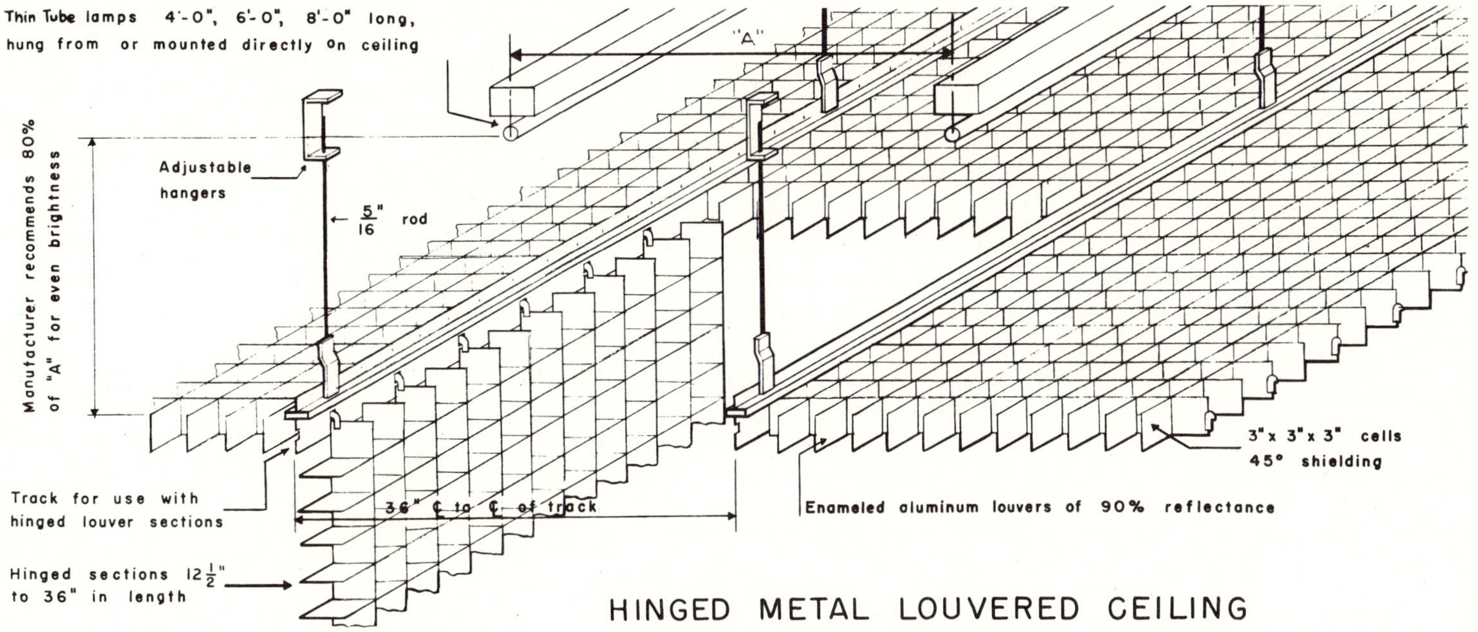
Thin Tube lamps 4'-0", 6'-0", 8'-0" long, hung from or mounted directly on ceiling
"A"
Manufacturer recommends 80% of "A" for even brightness
Adjustable hangers
5/16" rod
Track for use with hinged louver sections
36" ℄ to ℄ of track
Hinged sections 12 1/2" to 36" in length
3"x 3"x 3" cells 45° shielding
Enameled aluminum louvers of 90% reflectance

HINGED METAL LOUVERED CEILING

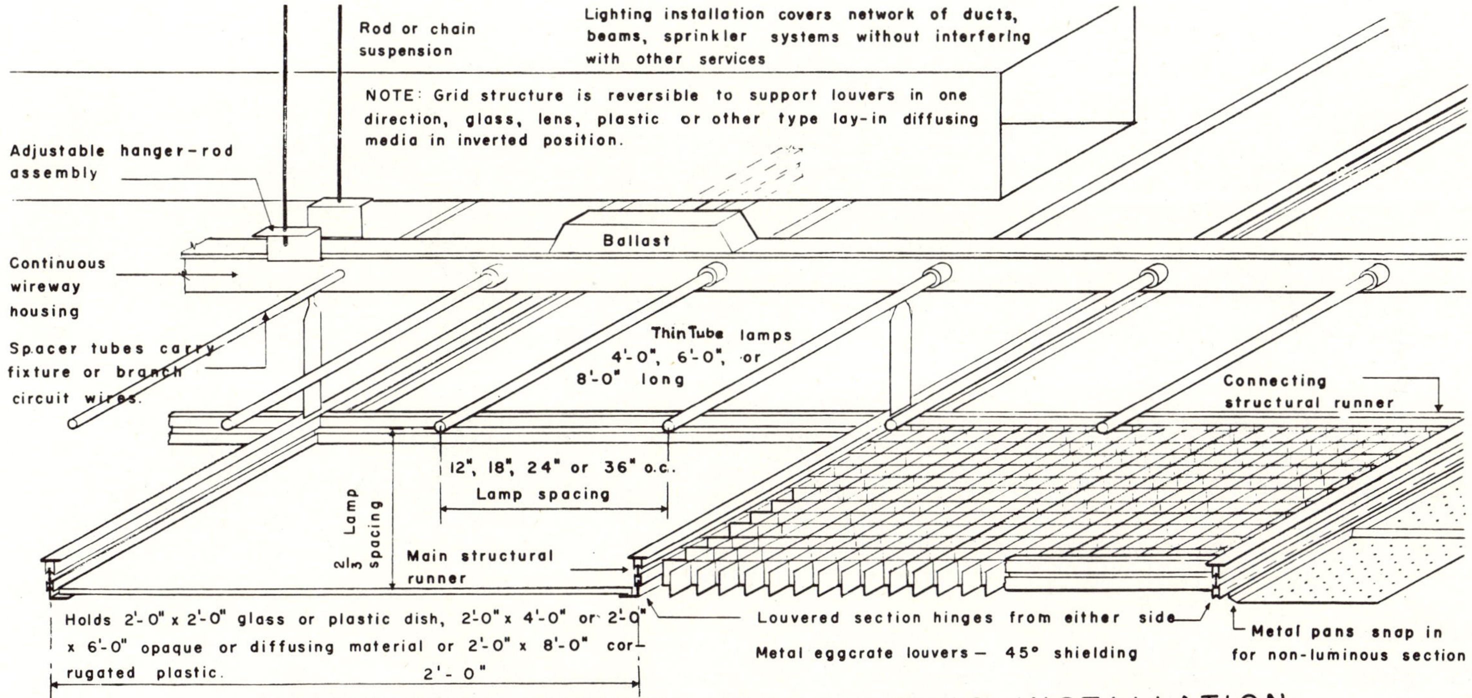
Rod or chain suspension
Lighting installation covers network of ducts, beams, sprinkler systems without interfering with other services
NOTE: Grid structure is reversible to support louvers in one direction, glass, lens, plastic or other type lay-in diffusing media in inverted position.
Adjustable hanger-rod assembly
Ballast
Continuous wireway housing
Spacer tubes carry fixture or branch circuit wires.
Thin Tube lamps 4'-0", 6'-0", or 8'-0" long
Connecting structural runner
12", 18", 24" or 36" o.c.
Lamp spacing
2/3 Lamp spacing
Main structural runner
Holds 2'-0" x 2'-0" glass or plastic dish, 2'-0" x 4'-0" or 2'-0" x 6'-0" opaque or diffusing material or 2'-0" x 8'-0" corrugated plastic.
2'-0"
Louvered section hinges from either side
Metal eggcrate louvers – 45° shielding
Metal pans snap in for non-luminous section

SUSPENSION SYSTEM FOR LIGHTING INSTALLATION WITH GRID STRUCTURE TO HOLD LIGHT-DIFFUSING PANELS

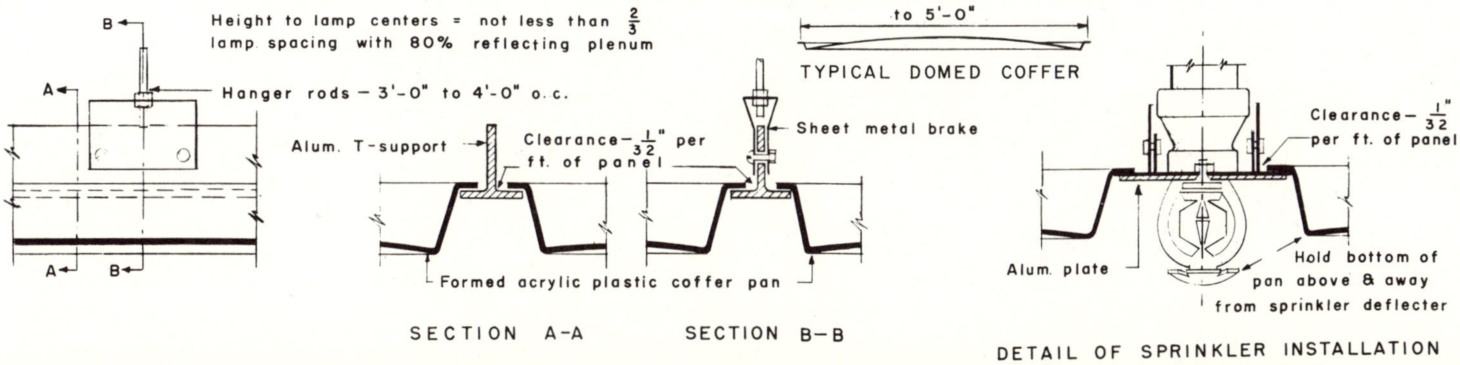
Height to lamp centers = not less than 2/3 lamp spacing with 80% reflecting plenum
B
A
Hanger rods – 3'-0" to 4'-0" o.c.
A
B
to 5'-0"
TYPICAL DOMED COFFER
Alum. T-support
Clearance – 1/32" per ft. of panel
Sheet metal brake
Formed acrylic plastic coffer pan
SECTION A–A
SECTION B–B
Clearance – 1/32" per ft. of panel
Alum. plate
Hold bottom of pan above & away from sprinkler deflecter
DETAIL OF SPRINKLER INSTALLATION

STANDARD SUPPORT DETAILS FOR FORMED PLASTIC CEILINGS

CORRUGATED PLASTIC SUSPENDED CEILINGS

NOTE: This type of plastic diffusing material may be used under sprinkler systems, as it loses corrugations at 140°, softens & falls out

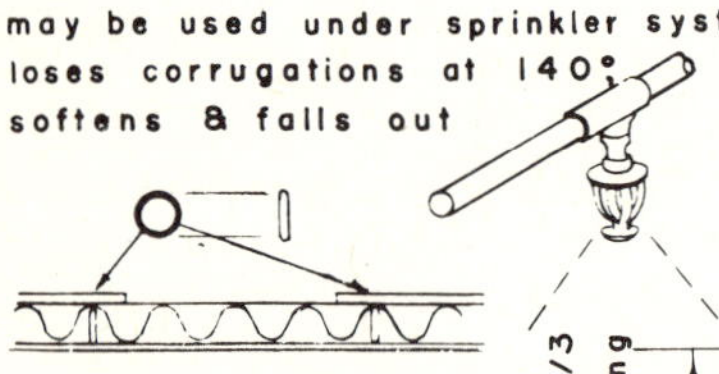

Retaining rings hold corrugated plastic firmly in place at openings and at the beginning and end of each plastic run.

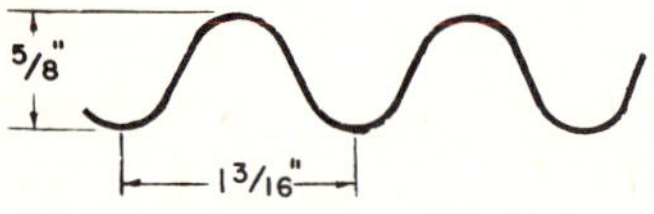

5/8"
1 3/16"

CORRUGATIONS AT HALF SIZE
Thickness = .007"

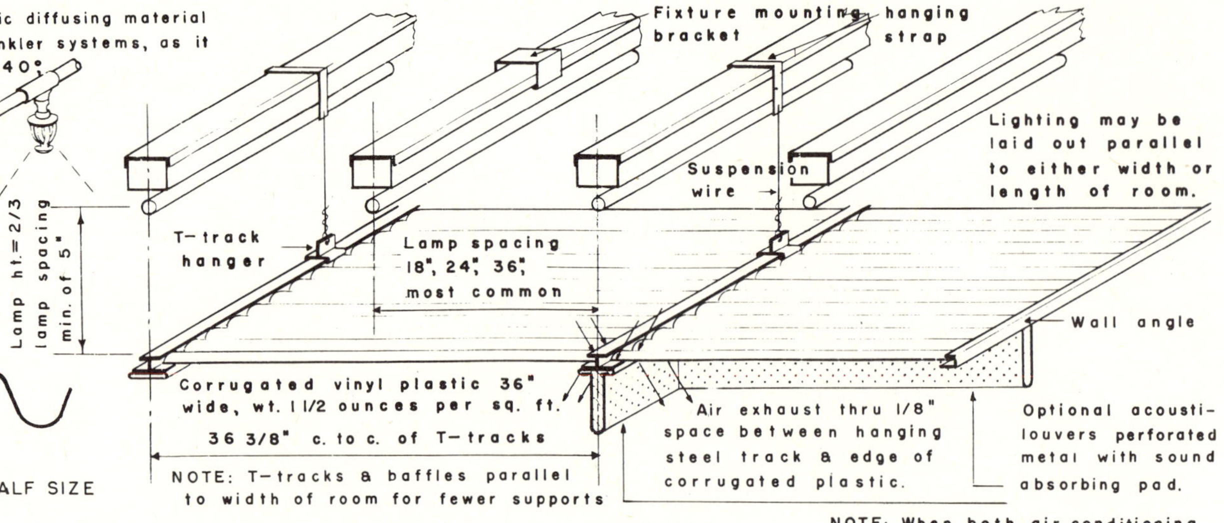

Fixture mounting bracket
hanging strap
Lighting may be laid out parallel to either width or length of room.
Suspension wire
Lamp ht. = 2/3 lamp spacing min. of 5"
T-track hanger
Lamp spacing 18", 24", 36", most common
Wall angle
Corrugated vinyl plastic 36" wide, wt. 1 1/2 ounces per sq. ft.
36 3/8" c. to c. of T-tracks
NOTE: T-tracks & baffles parallel to width of room for fewer supports
Air exhaust thru 1/8" space between hanging steel track & edge of corrugated plastic.
Optional acousti-louvers perforated metal with sound absorbing pad.

A LUMINOUS CEILING OF SELF EXTINGUISHING CORRUGATED PLASTIC WITH ACOUSTIC CORRECTION

THE PLENUM CAN BE USED FOR BOTH HEATING AND COOLING; DISTRIBUTION OF AIR CAN BE EFFECTED WITHOUT THE USE OF GRILLES OR DIFFUSERS.

NOTE: When both air conditioning and heating are supplied thru plenum, best results are obtained by use of sufficient returns placed properly high for cooling, low for heating.

Height to lamp centers = not less than 2/3 lamp spacing with 80% reflecting plenum

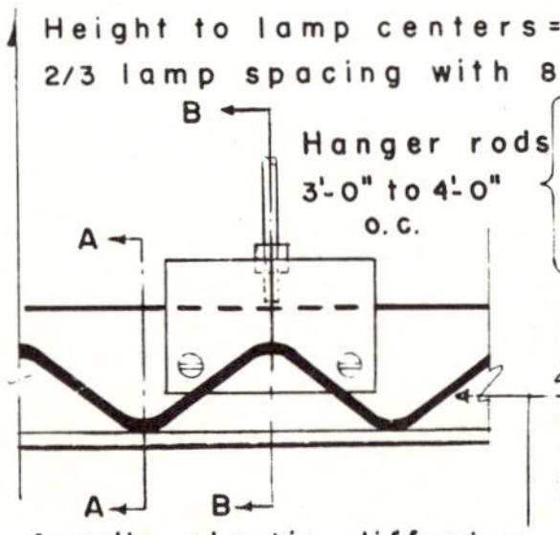

B
A
Hanger rods 3'-0" to 4'-0" o.c.
A
B

Where supports are installed in one direction only, hangers should be braced above plastic to prevent side play

Acrylic plastic diffusing panel to 1/4" thickness

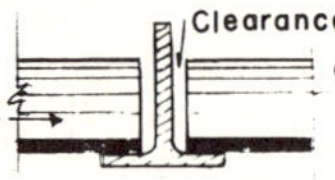

Clearance — 1/32" per ft. of panel

SECTION A-A

sheet metal brake

SECTION B-B

Alum. extrusion (supports are also available of metal or plastic extrusion)

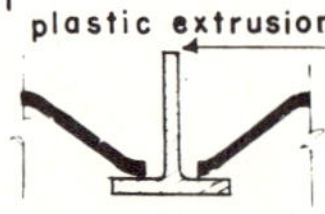

TYPICAL CROSS SUPPORT

SCALE: 3" = 1'-0"

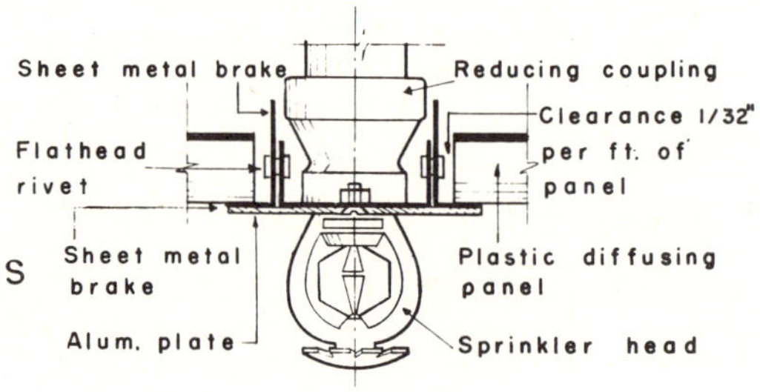

Sheet metal brake
Reducing coupling
Clearance 1/32" per ft. of panel
Flathead rivet
Sheet metal brake
Plastic diffusing panel
Alum. plate
Sprinkler head

DETAIL OF SPRINKLER INSTALLATION

Corrugated 1" frequency, $\frac{3}{8}$" amplitude	Maximum span 2'-6"	Supported 2 sides only — across corrugations
Corrugated $2\frac{1}{2}$" freq., 1" amp.	Maximum span 4'-0"	
Flat $\frac{1}{4}$" thickness	Maximum span 2'-0"	Supported 4 sides
Formed coffer pans	Maximum span 5'-0"	Supported 4 sides

OTHER STANDARD SUPPORT DETAILS FOR PLASTIC CEILINGS

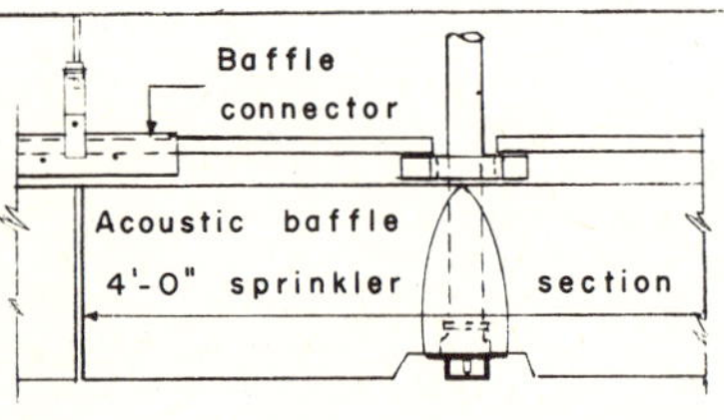

Baffle connector
Acoustic baffle
4'-0" sprinkler section

SPRINLER INSTALLATION IN BAFFLE

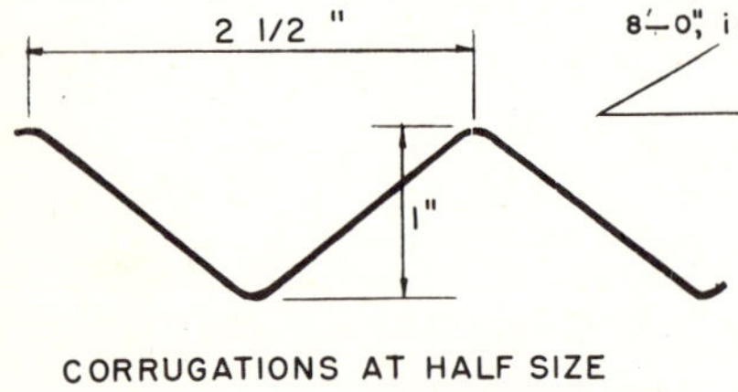

2 1/2"
1"

CORRUGATIONS AT HALF SIZE
Thickness = .06" or greater

Air passage — 3.2 sq. in. per sq. ft. of ceiling

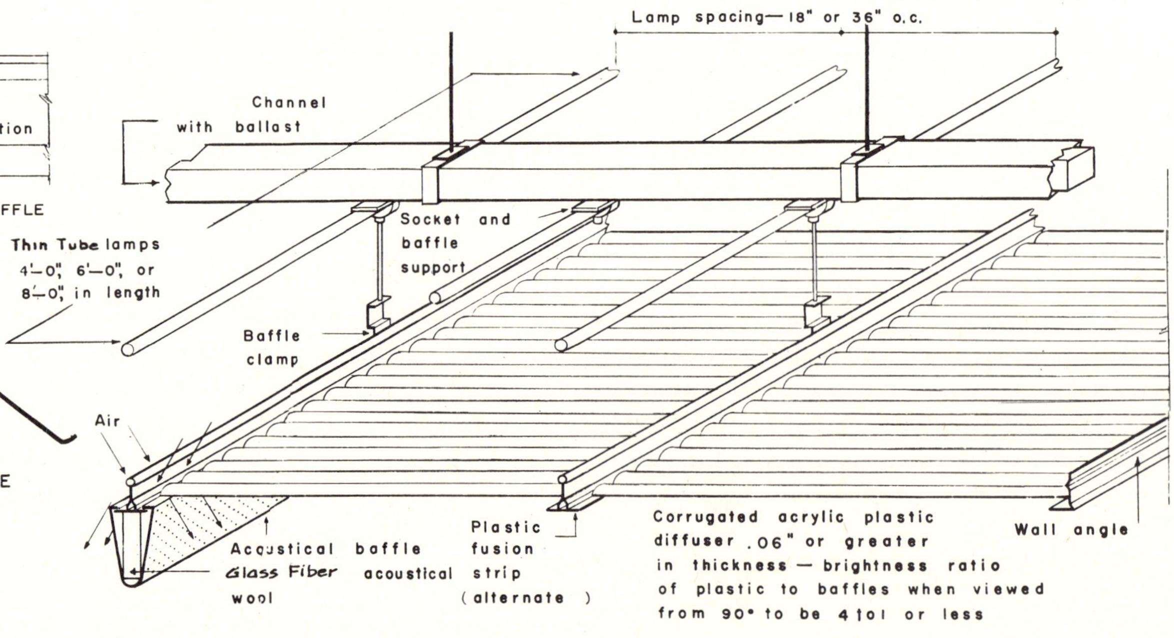

Lamp spacing — 18" or 36" o.c.
Channel with ballast
Socket and baffle support
Thin Tube lamps 4'-0", 6'-0", or 8'-0", in length
Baffle clamp
Air
Acoustical baffle
Glass Fiber acoustical wool
Plastic fusion strip (alternate)
Corrugated acrylic plastic diffuser .06" or greater in thickness — brightness ratio of plastic to baffles when viewed from 90° to be 4 to 1 or less
Wall angle

LUMINOUS CEILING SYSTEM OF CORRUGATED PLASTIC

FURNITURE, ACCESSORIES, EQUIPMENT and STORAGE

TABLE OF CONTENTS

SLIDE and MOVIE PROJECTION

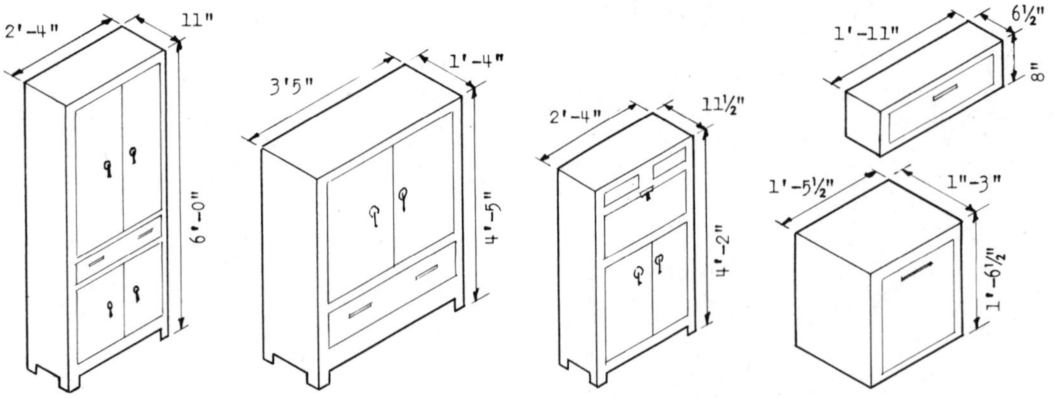
2'-4"
11"
6'-0"
3'5"
1'-4"
4'-5"
2'-4"
11½"
4'-2"
1'-11"
6½"
8"
1'-5½"
1"-3"
1'-6½"

STORAGE CABINETS

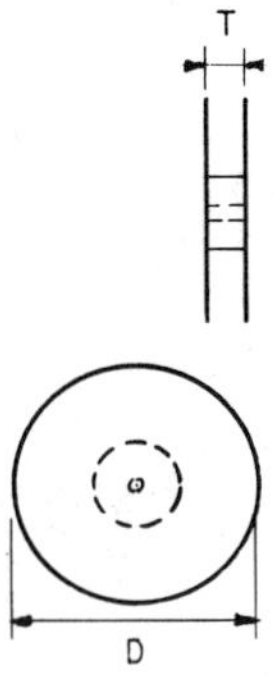
T
D

REEL SIZES		
REEL FOOT	D in.	T in.
200*	5	7/16
400	7	3/4
800	9 7/8	3/4
1600	14	3/4
2000	15	3/4

*for 8mm only. Others for 16mm only.

PROJECTOR REELS

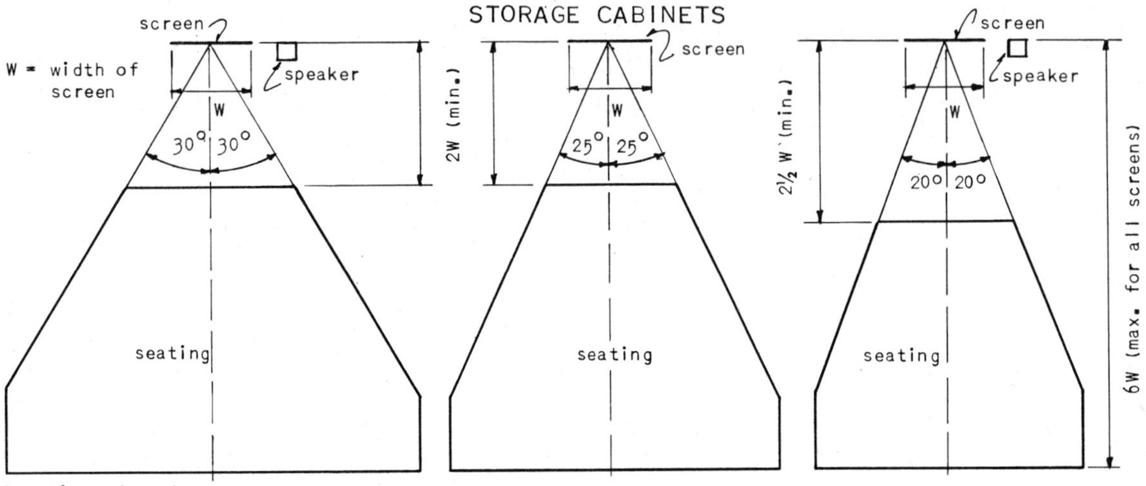
screen
W = width of screen
speaker
W
30° 30°
2W (min.)
seating
screen
W
25° 25°
seating
screen
speaker
2½ W (min.)
W
20° 20°
seating
6W (max. for all screens)

Location of projector depends on type of projector, focal length of lens used, and character of material being projected.

MATTE SCREEN — ALUMINIZED METALLIC SCREEN — BEADED SCREEN

(Smaller angle is better for color stereo projection)

RECOMMENDED SEATING LAYOUTS

SEATING CAPACITY		
SCREEN WIDTH (aisle included)	SEATING AREA Sq. ft.	CAPACITY AT 6 SQ. FT. PER PERSON
40"	135	23
50"	238	40
60"	340	50
70"	482	80
7'	654	110
8'	848	141
9'	1078	180
10'	1338	220
11'	1650	276
12'	2000	334

AVERAGE SLIDE PROJECTOR DISTANCE (ft.) ACCORDING TO SCREEN WIDTH

WIDTH OF SCREEN FOR 3 SLIDE TYPES*

PROJECTOR LENS FOCAL LENGTH	40" (3'-4")			50" (4'-2")			60" (5'-0")			70" (5'-10")			84" (6'-0")			96" (8'-0")			108" (9'-0")			120" (10'-0")			144" (12'-0")		
	stereo	2x2	2¼ x 2¼	stereo	2x2	2¼ x 2¼	stereo	2x2	2¼ x 2¼	stereo	2x2	2¼ x 2¼	stereo.	2x2	2¼ x 2¼	stereo	2x2	2¼ x 2¼	stereo	2x2	2¼ x 2¼	stereo	2x2	2¼ x 2¼	stereo	2x2	2¼ x 2¼
3"	7	11	-	9	14	-	11	17	-	13	19	-	16	23	-	18	27	-	20	30	-	22	33	-	27	40	-
4"	10	15	-	12	19	-	15	22	-	17	26	-	21	31	-	24	36	-	27	40	-	30	44	-	36	53	-
5"	12	19	8	16	23	10	19	28	12	22	32	14	26	39	16	30	44	19	34	50	21	37	56	23	45	68	28
6"	15	22	9	19	28	12	22	33	14	26	39	16	31	47	19	36	53	22	40	60	25	45	67	28	54	80	33
7"	17	26	11	22	32	14	26	39	16	30	45	19	37	55	23	42	62	26	47	70	29	52	78	33	63	94	39
8"	20	29	-	25	37	-	30	45	-	35	52	-	42	62	-	48	71	-	54	80	-	60	89	-	72	107	-
9"	-	-	14	-	-	17	-	-	21	-	-	24	-	-	29	-	-	33	-	-	38	-	-	42	-	-	50

* 2"x2" slides are 35 mm film, mounted; 2¼"x2¼" slides are 120 or 620 film, unmounted.

MOVIE PROJECTOR DISTANCE (ft.)

lens focal lgth.		WIDTH OF SCREEN								
16mm.	8mm.	40"	50"	60"	70"	84"	8'	9'	10'	12'
1½"	¾"	13	17	21	24	30	34	38	42	50
2"	1"	18	23	27	32	39	44	50	55	66
2½"	-	22	27	33	38	46	53	59	66	79
3"	-	26	33	40	46	55	63	71	79	95
3½"	1½"	30	37	45	54	62	72	80	90	107

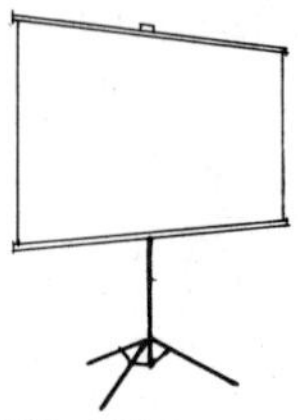

TRIPOD TYPE
fl. to tripod ht. usually 3' to 4'. (adjustable).

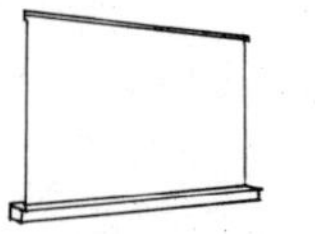

TABLE OR WALL-HUNG TYPE

(Similar type is ceiling-or-wall-hung).

SCREENS

SCREEN SIZES:

Tripod type: 30"x40" to 72"x96"

Table-or-wall-hung: 18"x24" to 36"x36"

Ceiling-or-wall-hung: 30"x40" to 72"x96"; 6'x8' to 15'x20' (electrically operated: 6'x8' to 12'x12'; 11'x14' to 18'x18').

Date checked by Bell & Howell Co. Eastman Kodak Co., Radiant Mfg. Co.

RADIOS, PHONOGRAPHS, JUKE BOXES

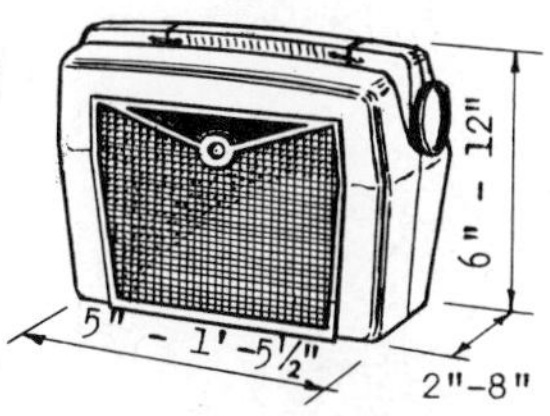
6" – 12"
5" – 1'-5½"
2"-8"

PORTABLE

5"-10"
10" – 13"
6½"-7"

RADIO-CLOCK

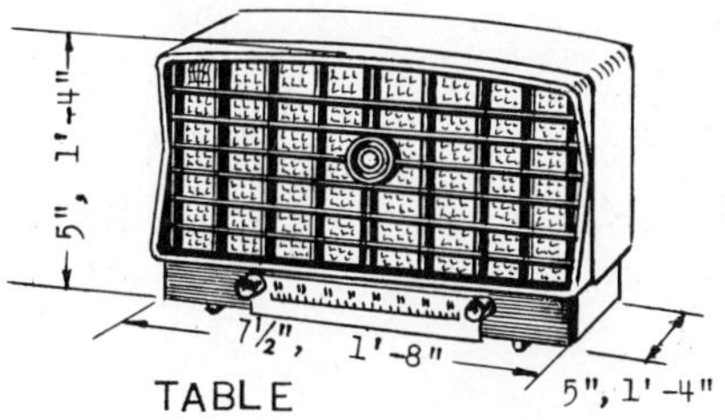
5", 1'-4"
7½", 1'-8"
5", 1'-4"

TABLE

RADIOS

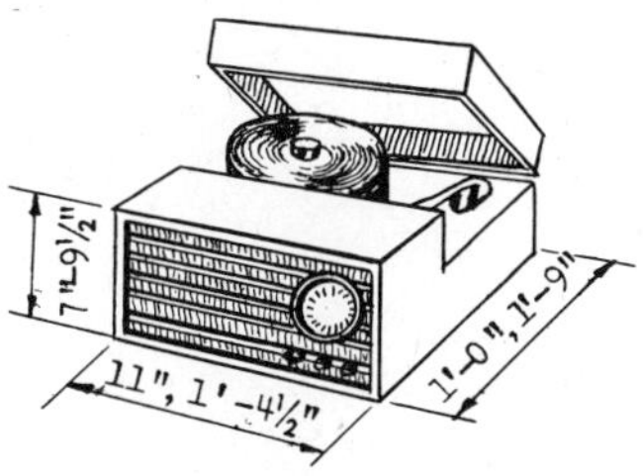
7"-9½"
11", 1'-4½"
1'-0", 1'-9"

TABLE

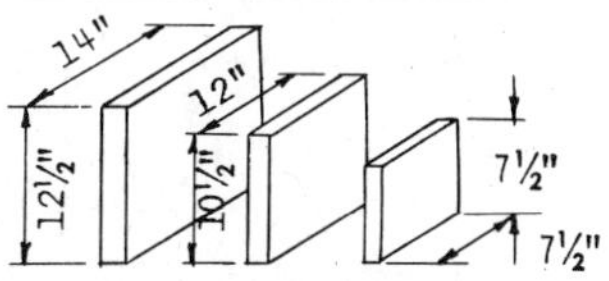
14"
12½"
12"
10½"
7½"
7½"
12" 10" 7"
33 & 78 RPM 45 RPM

RECORD ALBUMS

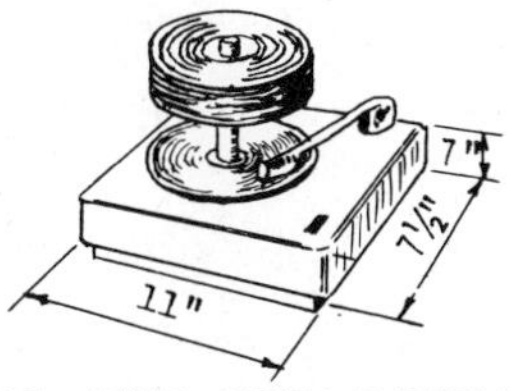
7"
7½"
11"

45 RPM ATTACHMENT

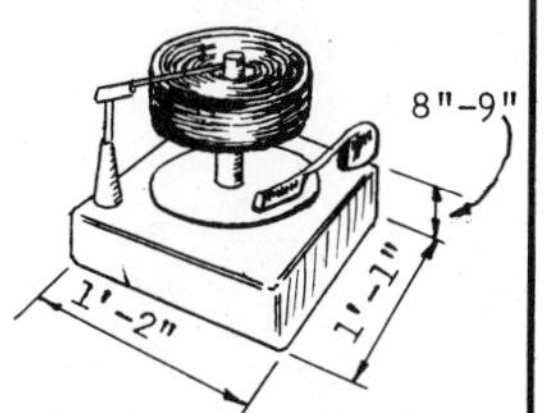
8"-9"
1'-2"
1'-1"

3-SPEED ATTACHMENT

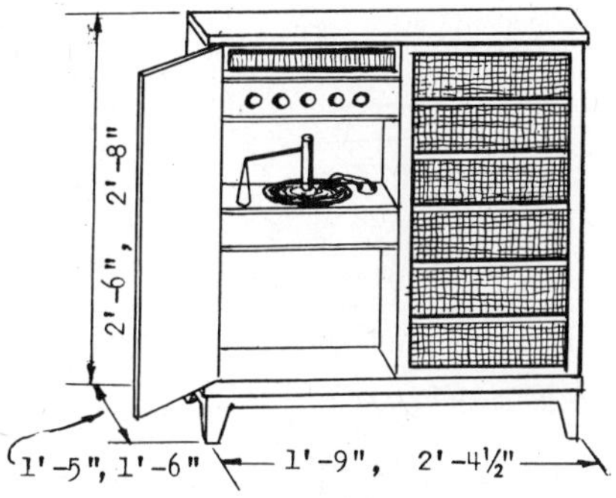
2'-6", 2'-8"
1'-5", 1'-6"
1'-9", 2'-4½"

CONSOLETTE

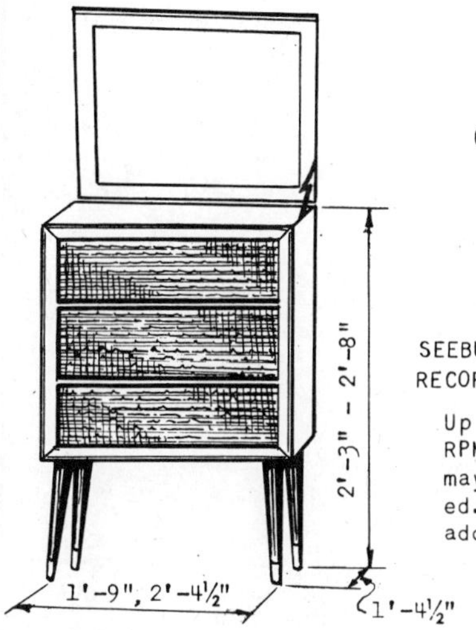
2'-3" – 2'-8"
1'-9", 2'-4½"
1'-4½"

CONSOLETTE

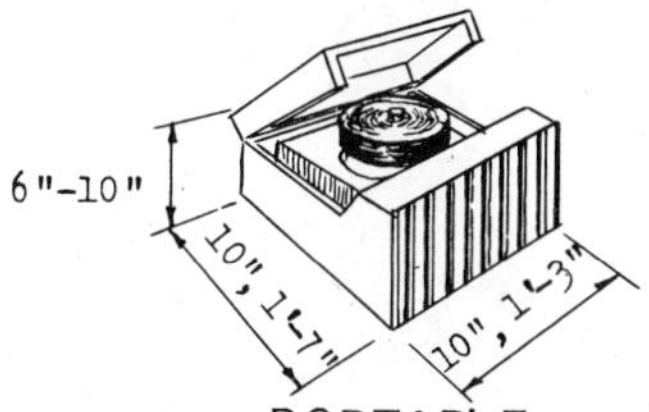
6"-10"
10", 1'-7"
10", 1'-3"

PORTABLE

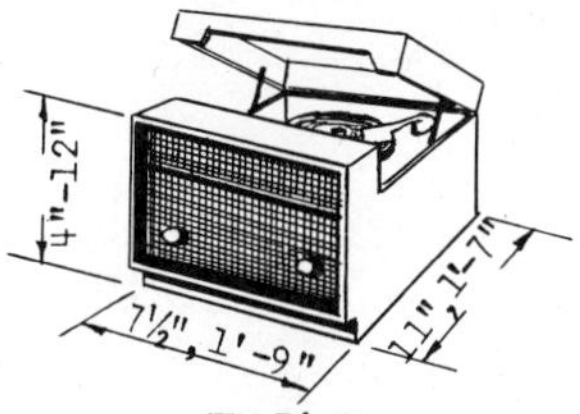
4"-12"
7½", 1'-9"
11", 1'-7"

TABLE

SEEBURG VERTICAL RECORD PLAYER

Up to 100-45 RPM's. Unit may be recessed. Requires add'l speaker

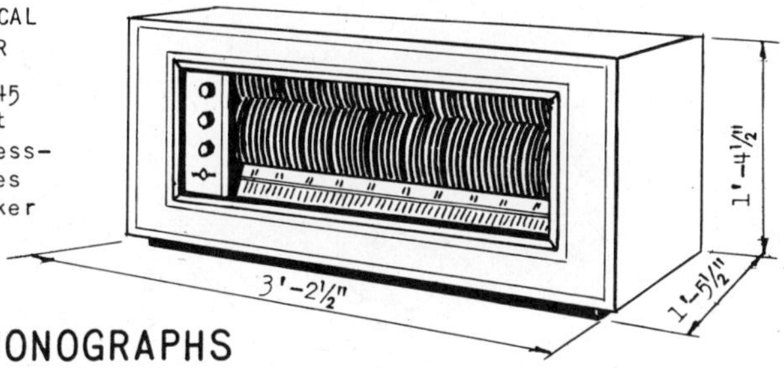
1'-4½"
3'-2½"
1'-5½"

PHONOGRAPHS

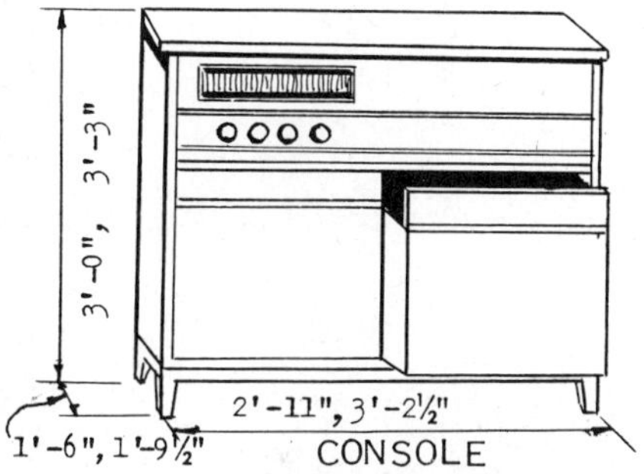
3'-0", 3'-3"
2'-11", 3'-2½"
1'-6", 1'-9½"

CONSOLE

COMBINATION RADIO-PHONOGRAPHS

Note: Dimensions shown are nominal. Sizes vary from mfr. to mfr. and from model to model by the same mfr.

JUKE BOX & ACCESSORY SIZES

MFR.	NO. OF SELECTIONS	RECORD TYPE *	SIZES H	SIZES W	SIZES D	APPROX. WT.
WURLITZER	48	45 or 78 RPM	53½"	29⅜"	26⅞"	315#
	104	45 RPM	55½"	31⅞"	27½"	308#
	104	45 & 78 Mixed	56¾"	38¼"	27⅞"	448#
	104†	45 RPM	33½"	33⅝"	26"	231#
SEEBURG	100	45 RPM	59"	35"	26"	315#
	100†	45 RPM	27½"	36"	23"	208#

*45 RPM records are 7" dia.; 78 RPM, 10" dia.
†Concealed type.

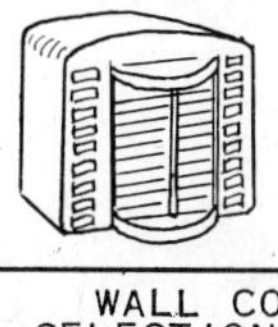

May also be counter or table mounted

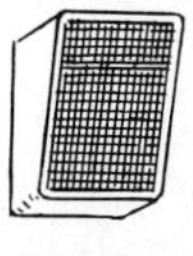

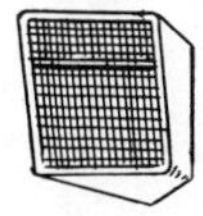

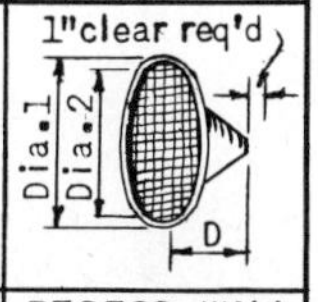
1"clear req'd
Dia.1
Dia.2
D

	WALL COIN & SELECTION BOXES				WALL SPEAKERS			CORNER SPEAKERS			RECESS. WALL & CEIL. SPEAK.		
	NO. OF SELECTIONS	SIZE H.	SIZE W.	SIZE D.	SIZE H.	SIZE W.	SIZE D.	SIZE H.	SIZE W.	SIZE D.	SIZE Dia.1	SIZE Dia.2	SIZE D.
W	48 & 104	12½"	11¾"	7⅜"	8" 12" 18"	24" 24" 24"	14" 14" 14"	13" 21¾"	19" 16"	10" 10½"			
S	100	12¾"	12¼"	5⅞"	18⅞"	22⅞"	10½"	18⅞"	22⅞"	10½"	14½"	12"	5¾"

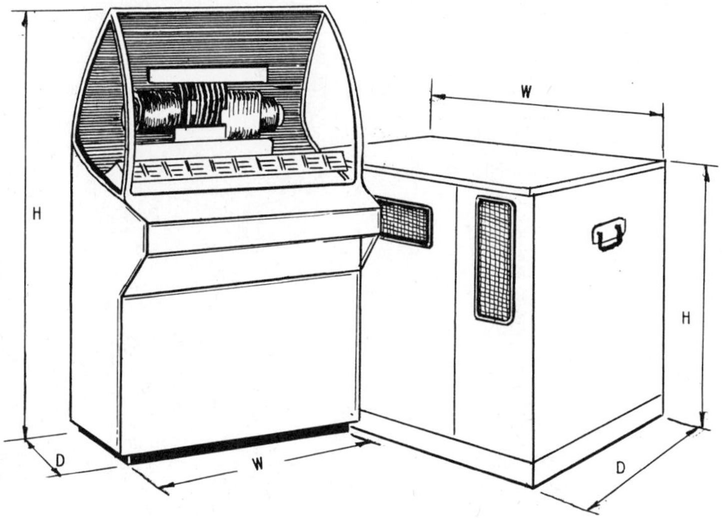
H
W
D
W
H
D

FLOOR TYPE CONCEALED TYPE

Floor type has a coin box & selection mechanism incorporated; additional wall coin & selection boxes may be added. Concealed type requires wall coin & selection boxes for operation.

JUKE BOXES

FURNITURE

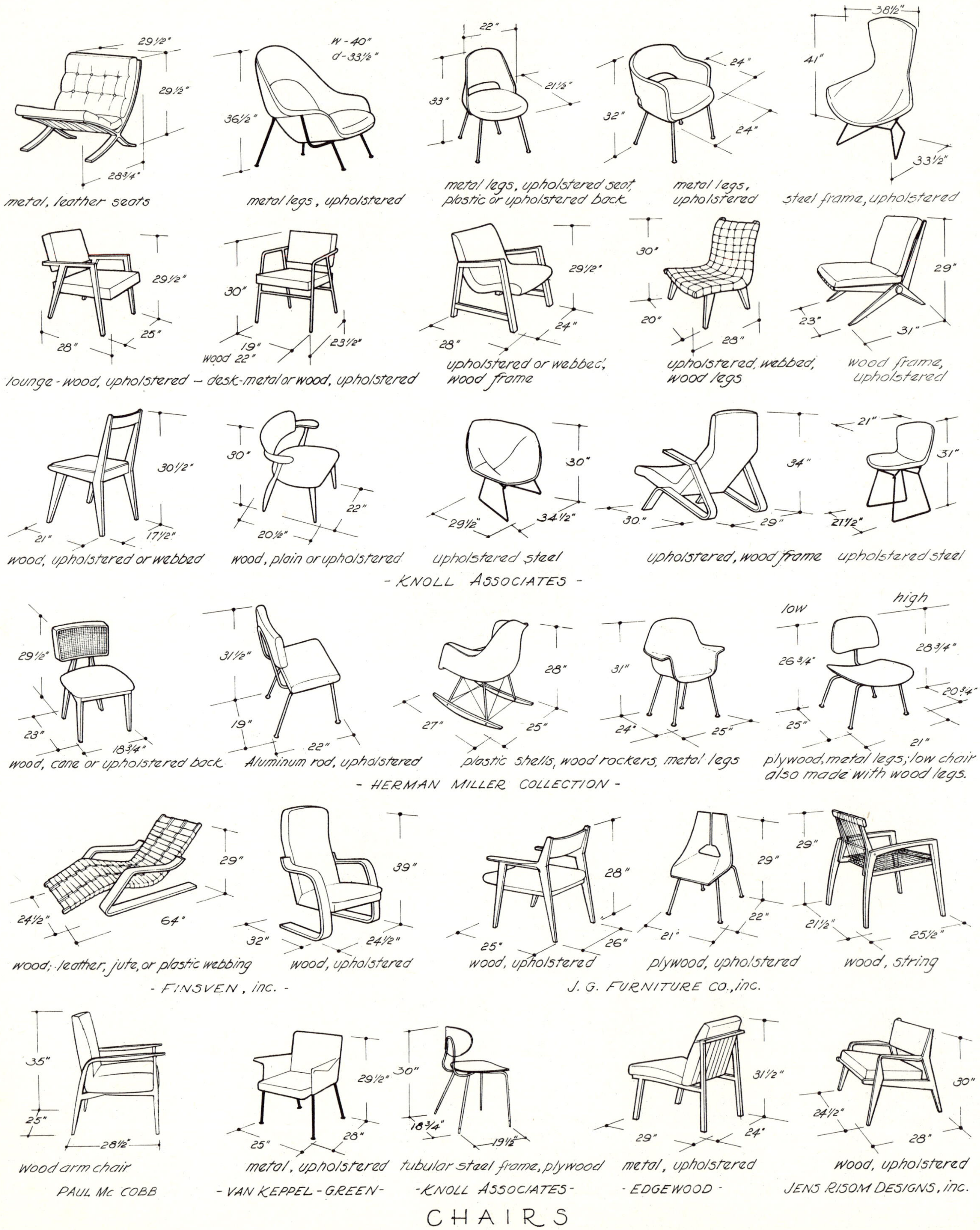
29 1/2"
29 1/2"
28 3/4"
metal, leather seats
w - 40"
d - 33 1/2"
36 1/2"
metal legs, upholstered
22"
21 1/2"
33"
metal legs, upholstered seat, plastic or upholstered back
24"
32"
24"
metal legs, upholstered
38 1/2"
41"
33 1/2"
steel frame, upholstered
29 1/2"
28"
25"
30"
19"
wood 22"
23 1/2"
lounge - wood, upholstered — desk-metal or wood, upholstered
29 1/2"
28"
24"
upholstered or webbed, wood frame
30"
20"
28"
upholstered, webbed, wood legs
29"
23"
31"
wood frame, upholstered
30 1/2"
21"
17 1/2"
wood, upholstered or webbed
30"
22"
20 1/2"
wood, plain or upholstered
30"
29 1/2"
34 1/2"
upholstered steel
34"
30"
29"
upholstered, wood frame
21"
31"
21 1/2"
upholstered steel
- KNOLL ASSOCIATES -
29 1/2"
23"
18 3/4"
wood, cane or upholstered back
31 1/2"
19"
22"
Aluminum rod, upholstered
28"
27"
25"
31"
24"
25"
plastic shells, wood rockers, metal legs
low
high
26 3/4"
28 3/4"
20 3/4"
25"
21"
plywood, metal legs; low chair also made with wood legs.
- HERMAN MILLER COLLECTION -
29"
24 1/2"
64"
wood; leather, jute, or plastic webbing
39"
32"
24 1/2"
wood, upholstered
- FINSVEN, inc. -
28"
25"
26"
wood, upholstered
29"
21"
22"
plywood, upholstered
29"
21 1/2"
25 1/2"
wood, string
J. G. FURNITURE CO., inc.
35"
25"
28 1/2"
wood arm chair
PAUL Mc COBB
29 1/2"
25"
28"
metal, upholstered
- VAN KEPPEL - GREEN -
30"
18 3/4"
19 1/2"
tubular steel frame, plywood
- KNOLL ASSOCIATES -
31 1/2"
29"
24"
metal, upholstered
- EDGEWOOD -
30"
24 1/2"
28"
wood, upholstered
JENS RISOM DESIGNS, inc.

CHAIRS

FURNITURE

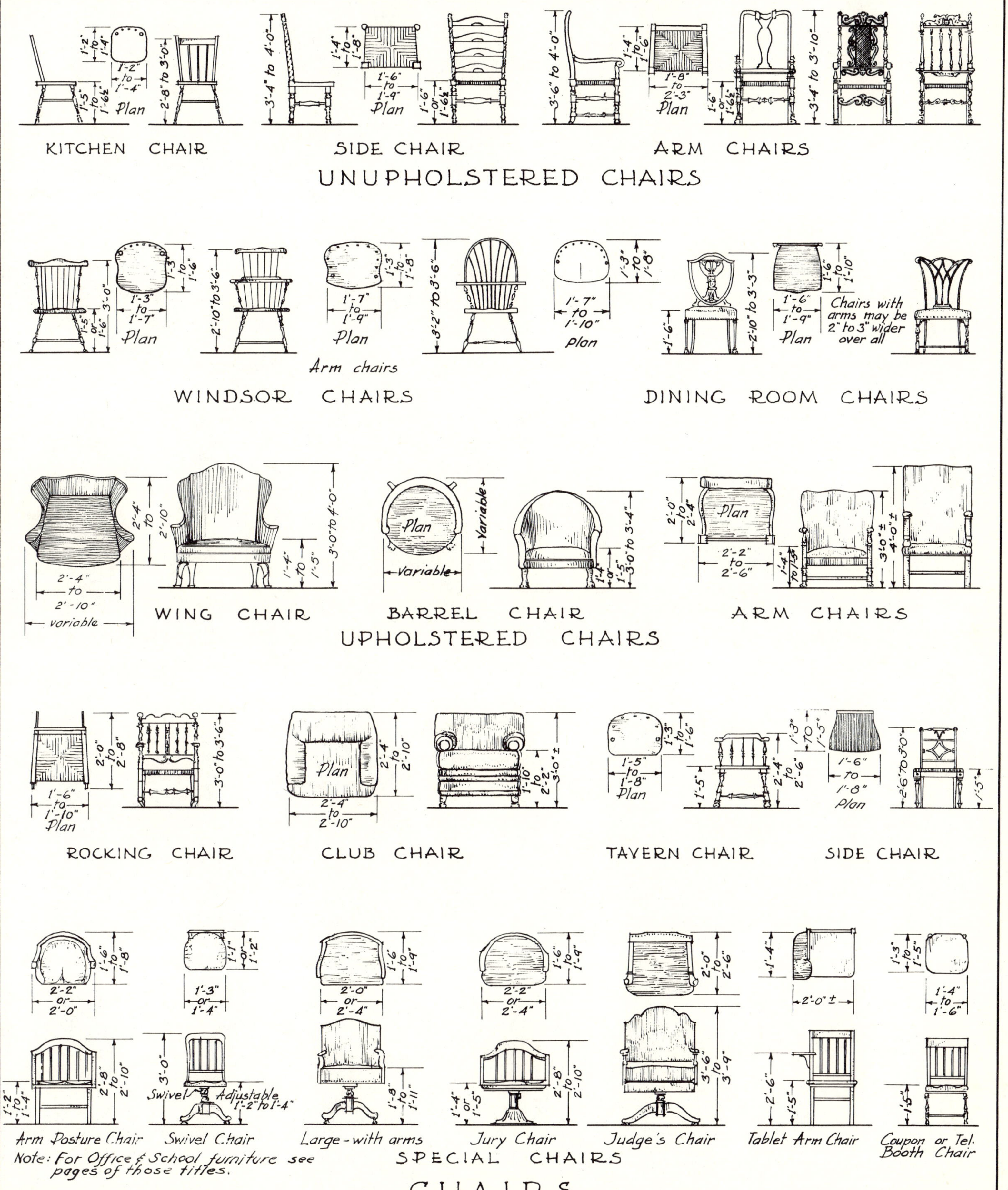
KITCHEN CHAIR
SIDE CHAIR
ARM CHAIRS
UNUPHOLSTERED CHAIRS
Plan
Arm chairs
WINDSOR CHAIRS
Chairs with arms may be 2" to 3" wider over all
DINING ROOM CHAIRS
WING CHAIR
BARREL CHAIR
ARM CHAIRS
UPHOLSTERED CHAIRS
ROCKING CHAIR
CLUB CHAIR
TAVERN CHAIR
SIDE CHAIR
Arm Posture Chair
Swivel Chair
Large-with arms
Jury Chair
Judge's Chair
Tablet Arm Chair
Coupon or Tel. Booth Chair
Note: For Office & School furniture see pages of those titles.
SPECIAL CHAIRS

CHAIRS

1/4"=1'-0"

FURNITURE

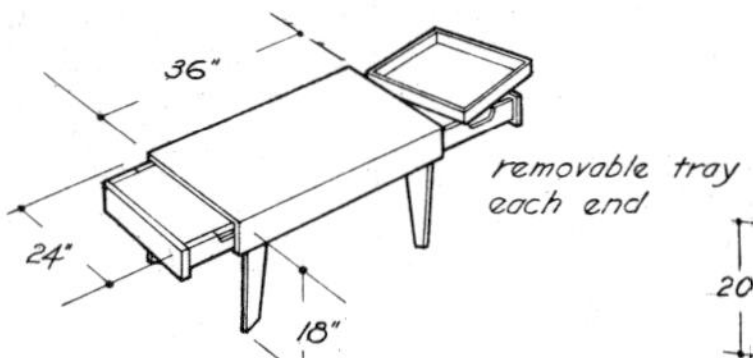
36"
24"
18"
removable tray each end

extends 18" each end - extended length 72". Underside of removable trays forms extension top.

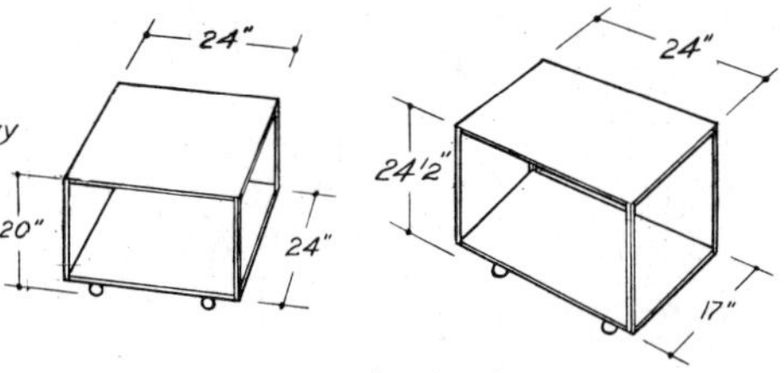
24"
20"
24"
24"
24½"
17"

mobile tables - plastic top & shelf metal frames

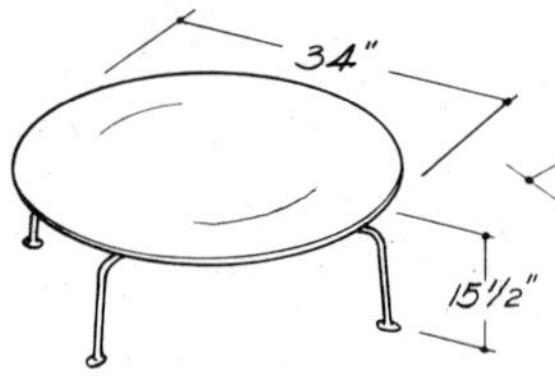
34"
15½"

wood top, metal legs

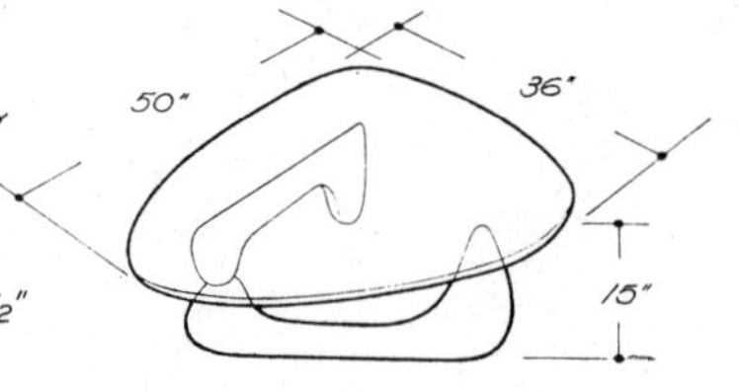
50"
36"
15"

removable glass top, pivoted wood base

- HERMAN MILLER COLLECTION -

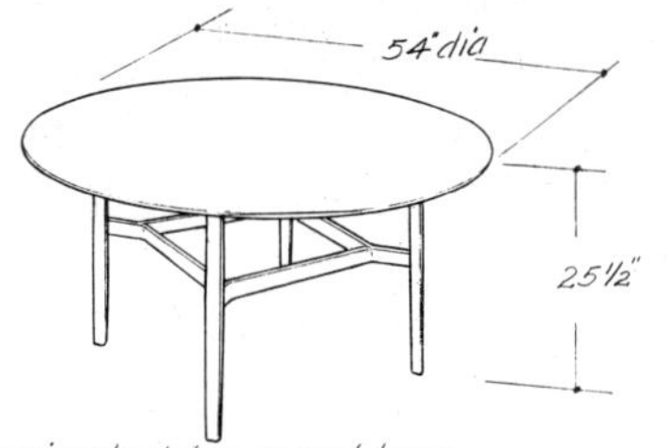
54" dia
25½"

laminated top, wood legs.

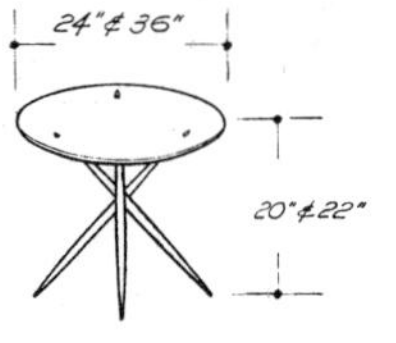
24" & 36"
20" & 22"

demountable

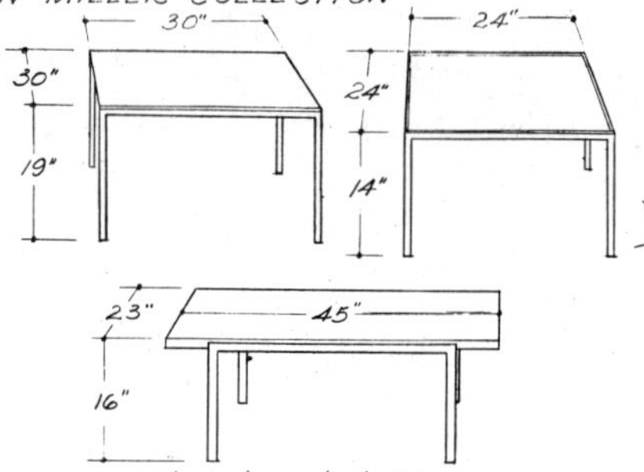
30"
30"
19"
24"
24"
14"
23"
45"
16"

structural tables

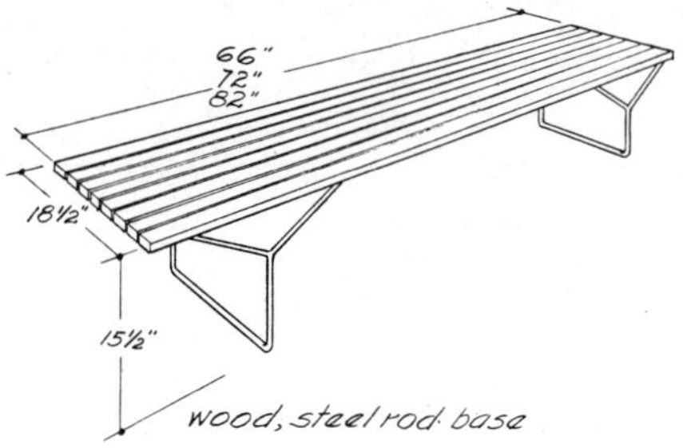
66"
72"
82"
18½"
15½"

wood, steel rod base

- KNOLL ASSOCIATES -

see below
14"
18½"

table, platform-bench, available in the following lengths... 48", 56 3/16", 68", 72" 92" & 102"

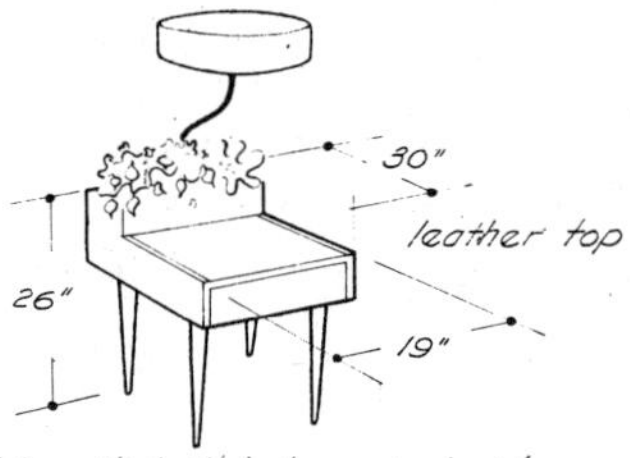
30"
leather top
26"
19"

table, with built-in lamp & plant box

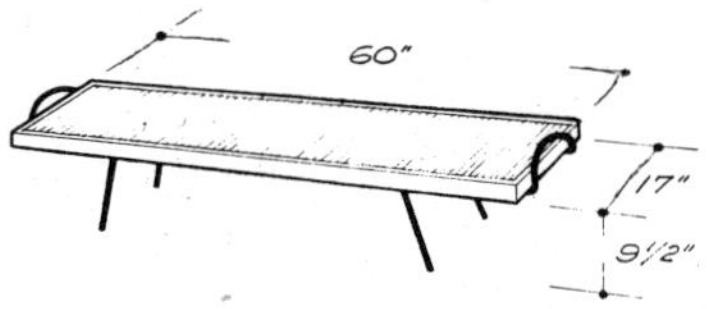
60"
17"
9½"

wood, metal legs

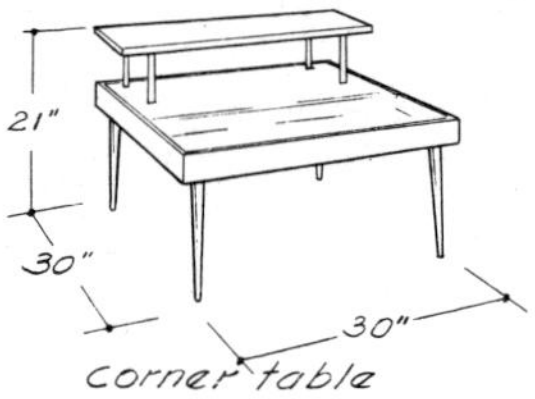
21"
30"
30"

corner table

- HERMAN MILLER COLLECTION -

- LA VERNE -

PAUL McCOBB

COFFEE & OCCASIONAL TABLES

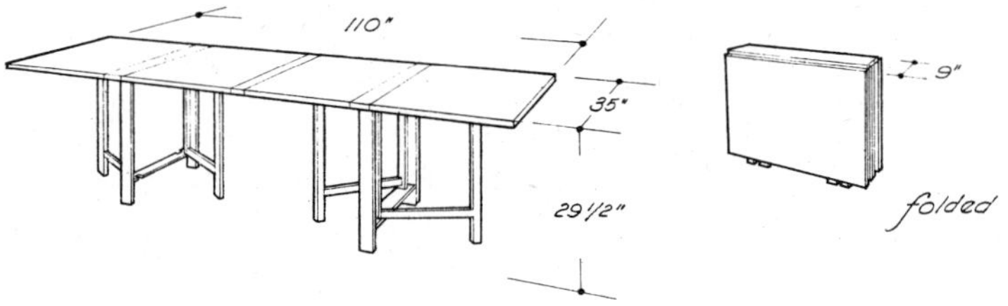
110"
35"
29½"
9"
folded

Wood, extends to seat 12, folds to a width of 9"

- BONNIERS -

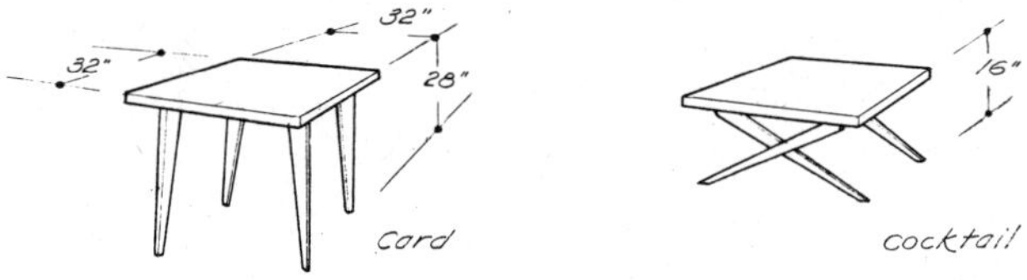
32"
32"
28"
card
16"
cocktail

legs slide, fold to form card or cocktail table.

- STERLING FURNITURE, INC. -

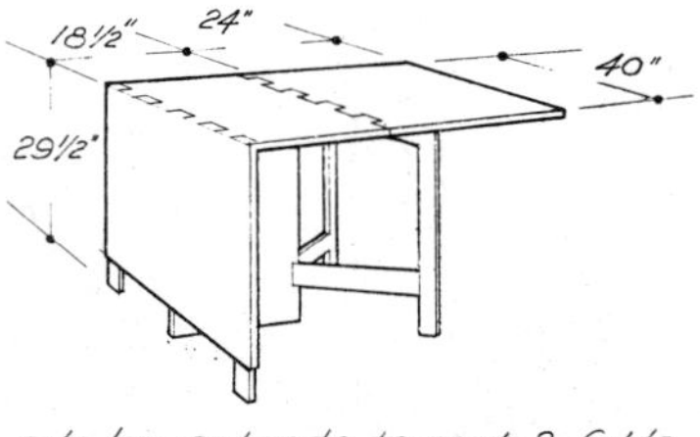
18½"
24"
40"
29½"

gate leg, extends to seat 8, folds, to line up with other Miller cases

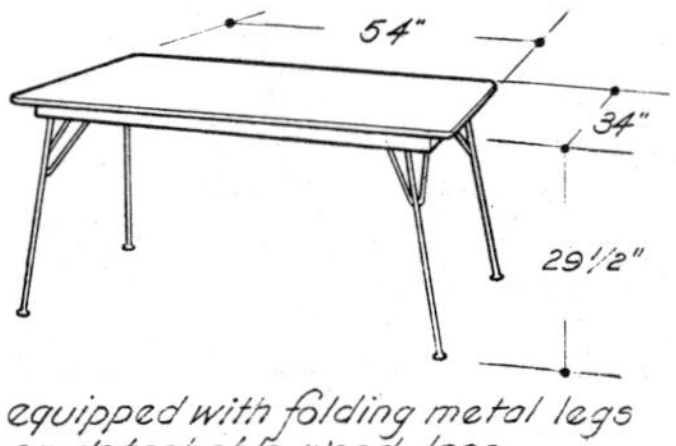
54"
34"
29½"

equipped with folding metal legs or detachable wood legs

- HERMAN MILLER COLLECTION -

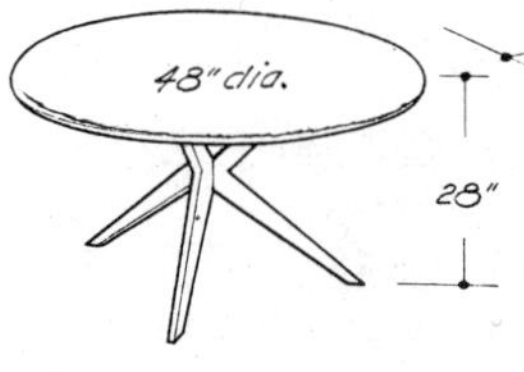
48" dia.
28"

- KNOLL ASSOCIATES -

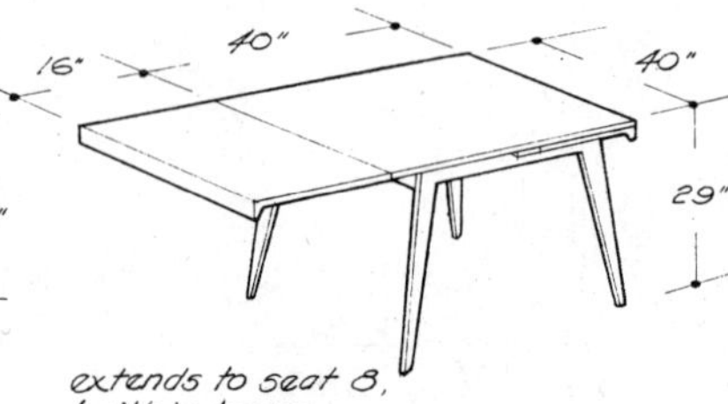
16"
40"
40"
29"

extends to seat 8, built-in leaves

- JENS RISOM -

DINING TABLES

FURNITURE

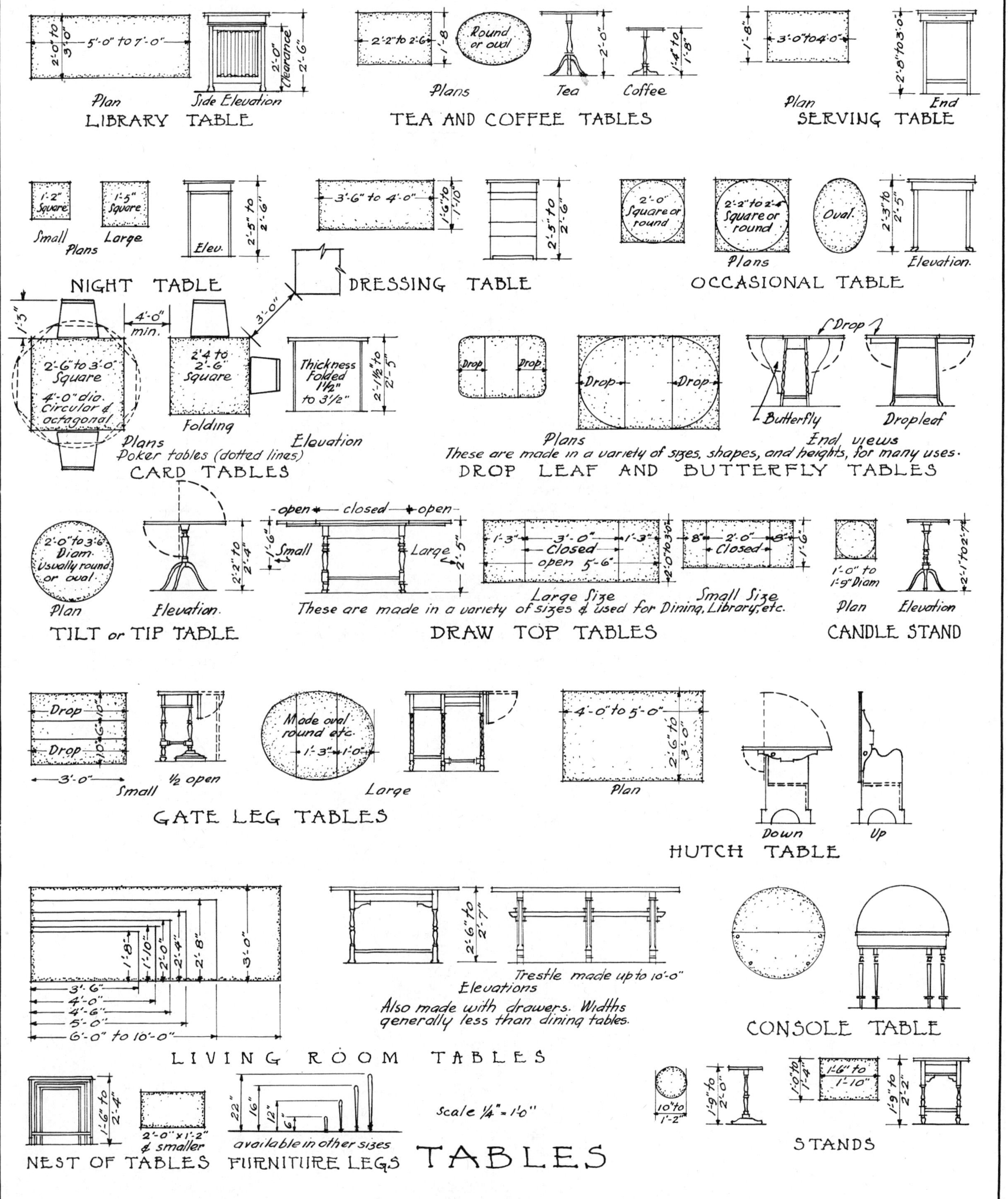
LIBRARY TABLE
Plan
Side Elevation
5'-0" to 7'-0"
2'-0" to 3'-0"
2'-0" clearance
2'-6"
TEA AND COFFEE TABLES
Plans
Tea
Coffee
2'-2" to 2'-6"
1'-8"
Round or oval
2'-0"
1'-4" to 1'-8"
SERVING TABLE
Plan
End
3'-0" to 4'-0"
1'-8"
2'-8" to 3'-0"
NIGHT TABLE
1'-2" Square
1'-5" Square
Small
Large
Plans
Elev.
2'-5" to 2'-6"
DRESSING TABLE
3'-6" to 4'-0"
1'-6" to 1'-10"
2'-5" to 2'-6"
OCCASIONAL TABLE
2'-0" Square or round
2'-2" to 2'-4" Square or round
Oval
Plans
Elevation
2'-3" to 2'-5"
CARD TABLES
1'-5"
4'-0" min.
3'-0"
2'-6" to 3'-0" Square
4'-0" dia. Circular & octagonal
2'-4" to 2'-6" square
Folding
Thickness Folded 1½" to 3½"
2'-1½" to 2'-5"
Plans
Poker tables (dotted lines)
Elevation
DROP LEAF AND BUTTERFLY TABLES
Drop
Plans
Butterfly
Dropleaf
End views
These are made in a variety of sizes, shapes, and heights, for many uses.
TILT or TIP TABLE
2'-0" to 3'-6" Diam. Usually round or oval.
Plan
Elevation.
2'-2" to 2'-4"
DRAW TOP TABLES
-open- -closed- -open-
1'-6"
Small
Large
2'-5"
1'-3"
3'-0"
Closed
open 5'-6"
2'-0" to 3'-0"
8"
2'-0"
Closed
Large Size
Small Size
These are made in a variety of sizes & used for Dining, Library, etc.
CANDLE STAND
1'-0" to 1'-9" Diam
Plan
Elevation
2'-1" to 2'-7"
GATE LEG TABLES
Drop
10"-6"-10"
3'-0"
Small
½ open
Made oval round etc.
1'-3"
1'-0"
Large
HUTCH TABLE
4'-0" to 5'-0"
2'-6" to 3'-0"
Plan
Down
Up
LIVING ROOM TABLES
1'-8"
1'-10"
2'-0"
2'-4"
2'-8"
3'-0"
3'-6"
4'-0"
4'-6"
5'-0"
6'-0" to 10'-0"
2'-6" to 2'-7"
Trestle made up to 10'-0"
Elevations
Also made with drawers. Widths generally less than dining tables.
CONSOLE TABLE
NEST OF TABLES
1'-6" to 2'-4"
2'-0" x 1'-2" & smaller
22"
16"
12"
6"
available in other sizes
FURNITURE LEGS
scale ¼" = 1'-0"
TABLES
10" to 1'-2"
1'-9" to 2'-0"
1'-0" to 1'-4"
1'-6" to 1'-10"
1'-9" to 2'-2"
STANDS

FURNITURE

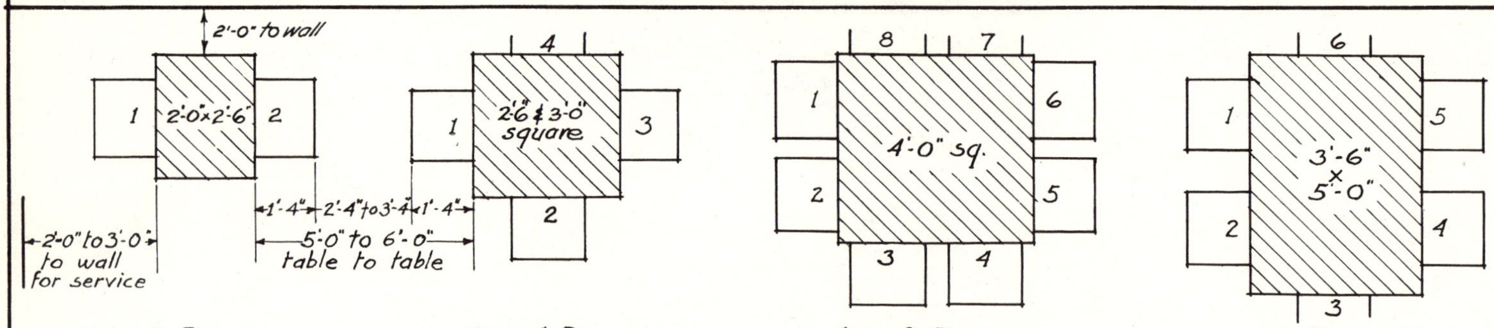
2'-0" to wall
1
2'-0"×2'-6"
2
2'-0" to 3'-0" to wall for service
1'-4"
2'-4" to 3'-4"
1'-4"
5'-0" to 6'-0" table to table
4
1
2'-6" & 3'-0" square
3
2
8
7
1
6
4'-0" sq.
2
5
3
4
6
1
5
3'-6" × 5'-0"
2
4
3

2 Persons | 3 or 4 Persons | 6 to 8 Persons | 6 Persons

SQUARE TABLES

For diagonal spacing see "Restaurant" sheets.

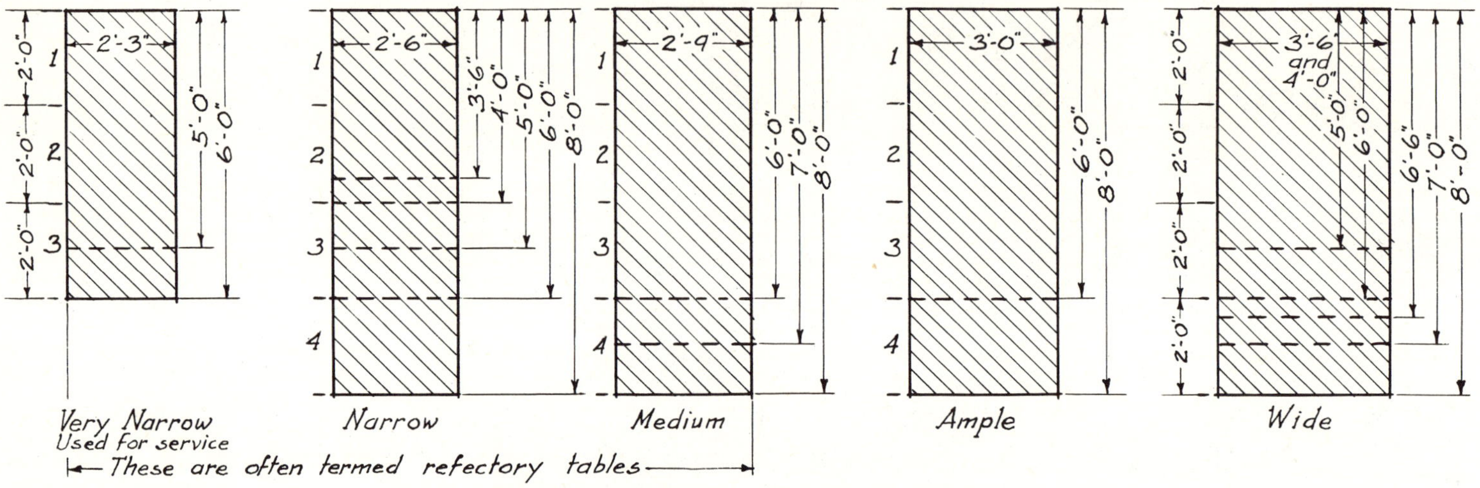
2'-3"
2'-0"
2'-0"
2'-0"
5'-0"
6'-0"
1
2
3
2'-6"
3'-6"
4'-0"
5'-0"
6'-0"
8'-0"
4
2'-9"
6'-0"
7'-0"
8'-0"
3'-0"
6'-0"
8'-0"
3'-6" and 4'-0"
5'-0"
6'-0"
6'-6"
7'-0"
8'-0"
Very Narrow
Used for service
Narrow
Medium
Ample
Wide
These are often termed refectory tables

RECTANGULAR TABLES

Allowance for chairs & aisles as above.

FOR COMFORTABLE SEATING ALLOW 2'-0" FOR EACH PERSON – MINIMUM IS 1'-10" PER P.

Tables accommodate same number if seats are placed at ends except on wide table where two extra are cared for.

Table sizes are not standard but are sizes that are generally manufactured – many other sizes are available.

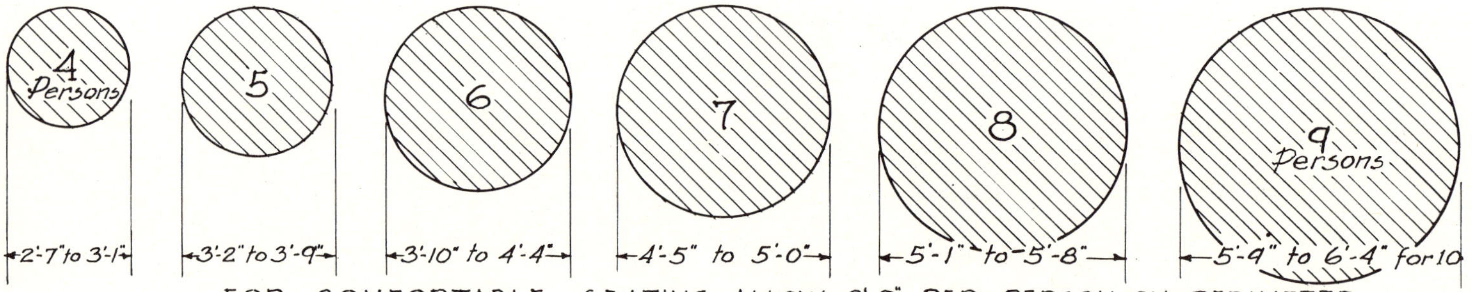
4 Persons
5
6
7
8
9 Persons
2'-7" to 3'-1"
3'-2" to 3'-9"
3'-10" to 4'-4"
4'-5" to 5'-0"
5'-1" to 5'-8"
5'-9" to 6'-4" for 10

FOR COMFORTABLE SEATING ALLOW 2'-0" PER PERSON ON PERIMETER

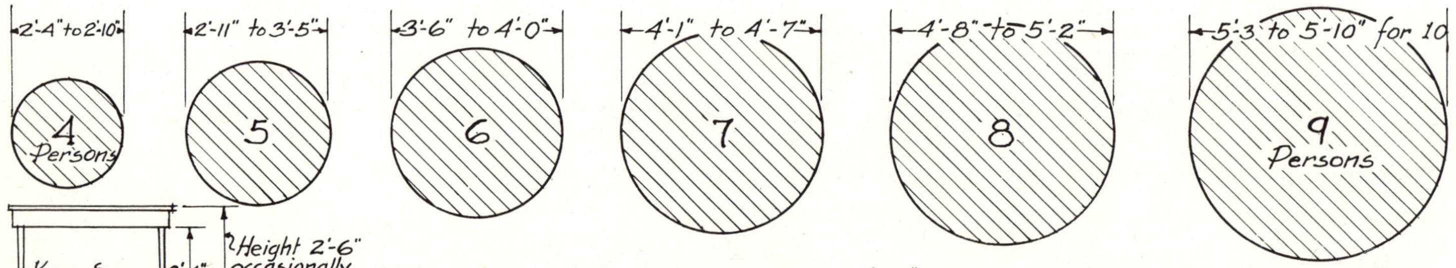
2'-4" to 2'-10"
2'-11" to 3'-5"
3'-6" to 4'-0"
4'-1" to 4'-7"
4'-8" to 5'-2"
5'-3" to 5'-10" for 10
4 Persons
5
6
7
8
9 Persons

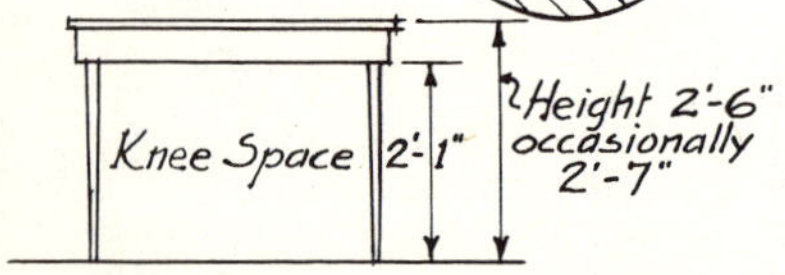
Knee Space
2'-1"
Height 2'-6" occasionally 2'-7"

SNUG SEATING; ALLOWING 1'-10" PER PERSON ON PERIMETER

ROUND TABLES

Table section

Allowance for chairs and aisles same as indicated for square tables.

In preliminary planning allow 10 sq. ft. to 16 sq. ft. per person – 12 sq. ft. is good average.

1/4" = 1'-0"

TABLES

FURNITURE

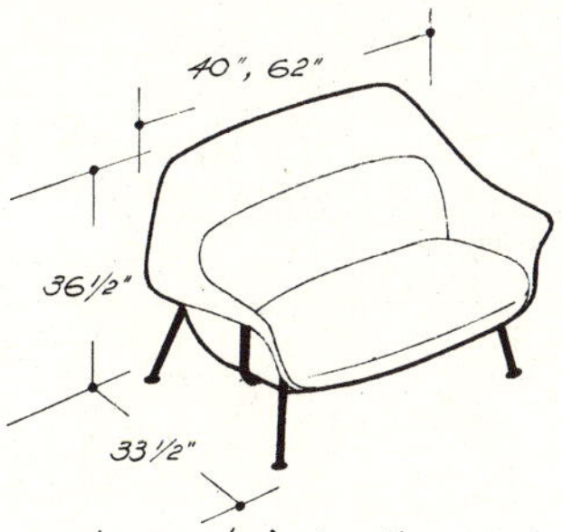
40", 62"
36½"
33½"
made as chair & settee - upholstered, metal legs.

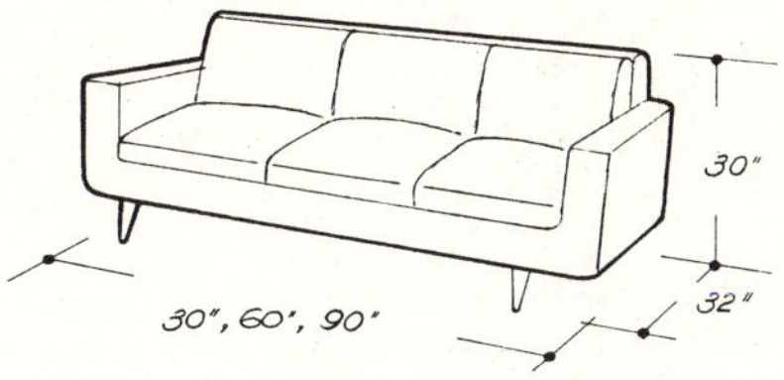
30"
30", 60", 90"
32"
made as chair, settee & sofa, upholstered

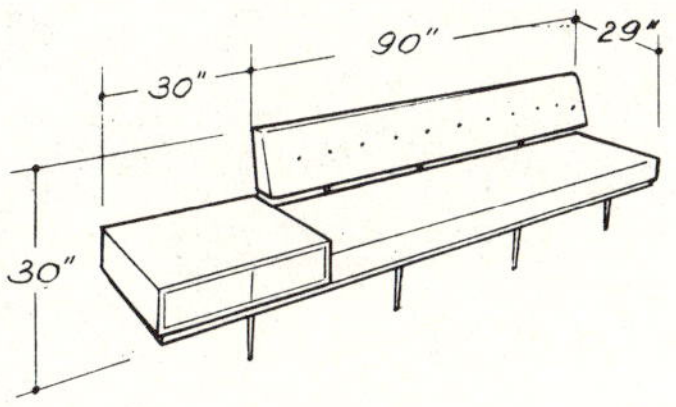
90"
29"
30"
30"
steel frame, upholstered

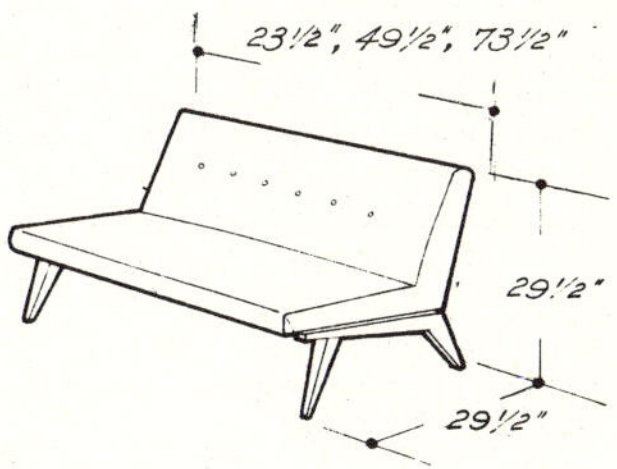
23½", 49½", 73½"
29½"
29½"
made as chair, settee & sofa, upholstered

- KNOLL ASSOCIATES -

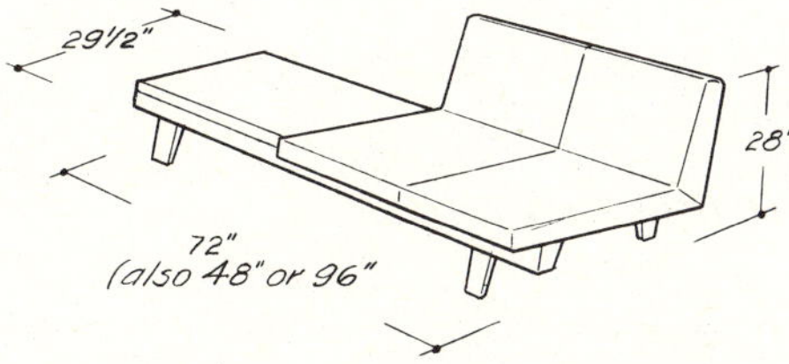
29½"
28"
72"
(also 48" or 96"
modular table tops, upholstered and loose cushion units in any desired arrangement on metal base 4', 6', or 8' long

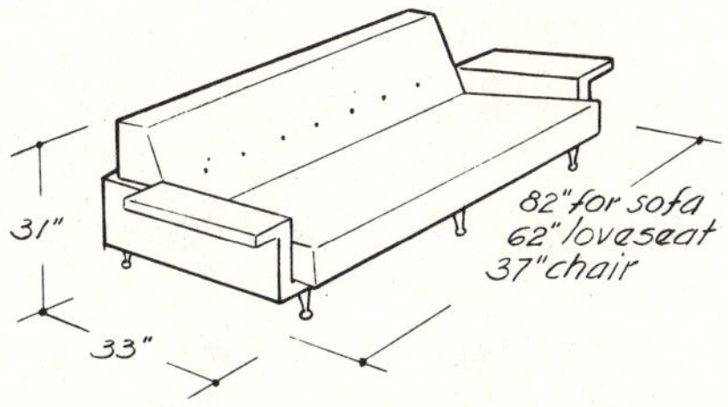
31"
33"
82" for sofa
62" loveseat
37" chair
Upholstered chair, loveseat, & sofa, aluminum legs.

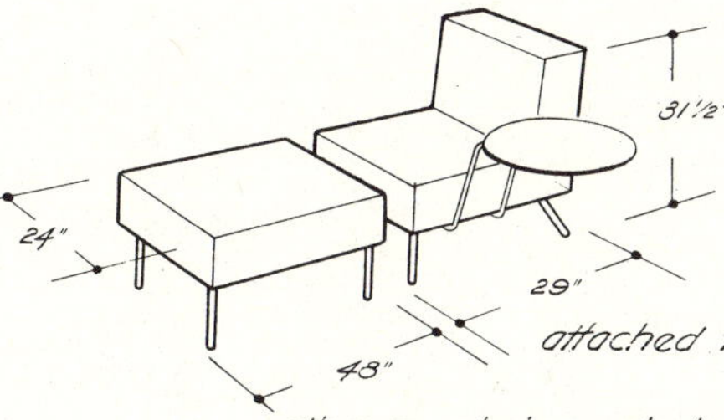
31½"
24"
29"
48"
attached tray
ottoman, chair - upholstered, metal legs

- HERMAN MILLER COLLECTION -

UPHOLSTERED CHAIRS, SETTEES & SOFAS

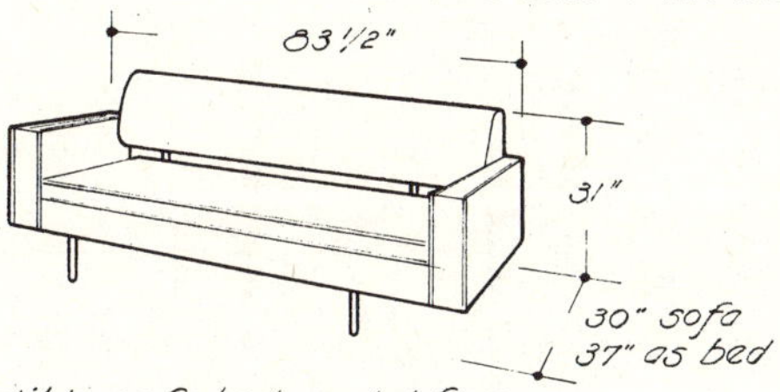
83½"
31"
30" sofa
37" as bed
convertible sofa bed, metal frame

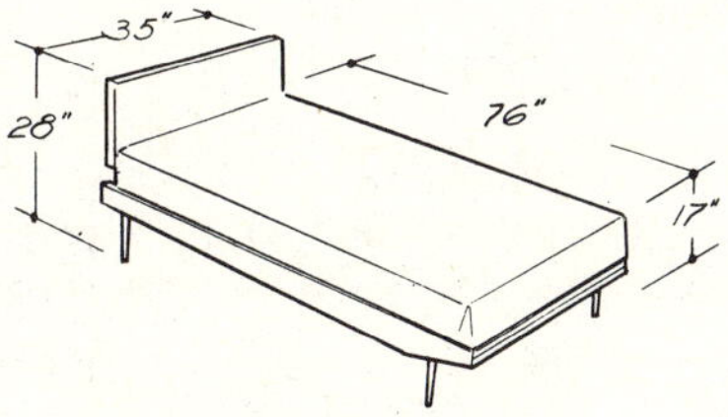
35"
28"
76"
17"
bed, steel frame

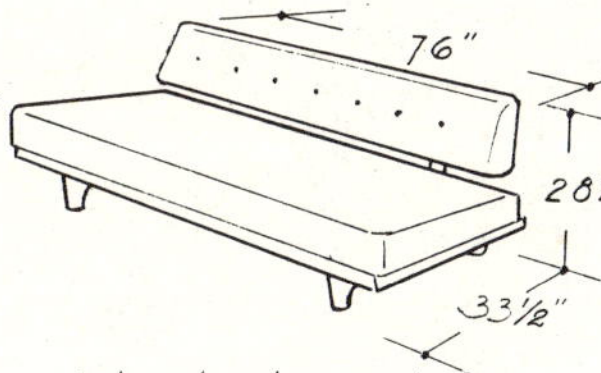
76"
28½"
33½"
day bed, wood frame

- KNOLL ASSOCIATES -

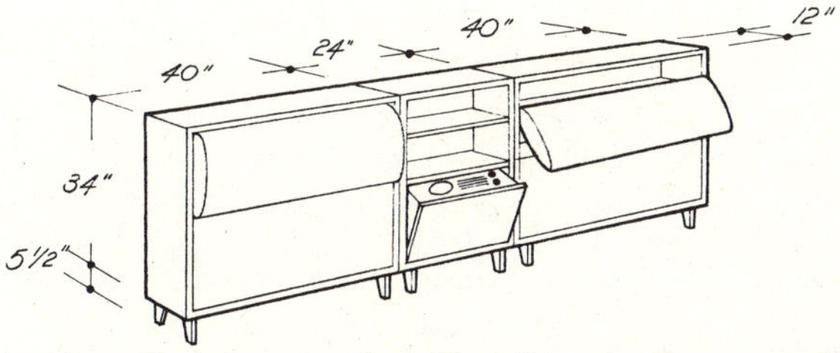
40"
24"
40"
12"
34"
5½"
series of storage units with tilting head rest, radio

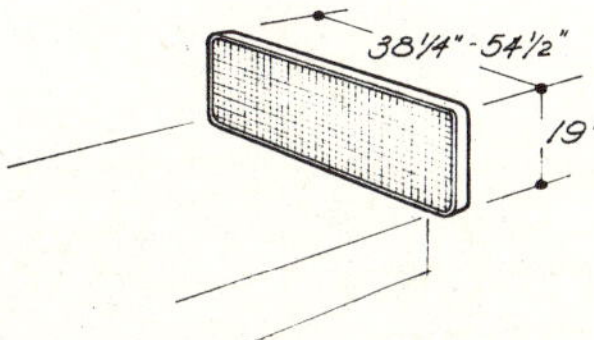
38¼" - 54½"
19"
wall - hung headboard

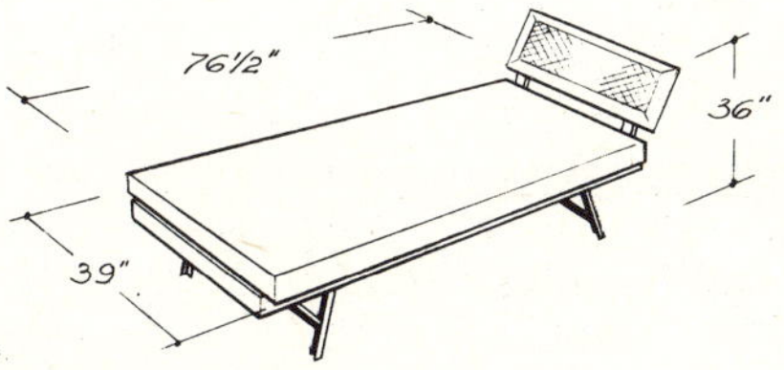
76½"
36"
39"
bed, wood frame, cane head board. metal legs.

- HERMAN MILLER COLLECTION -

BEDS & HEADBOARDS

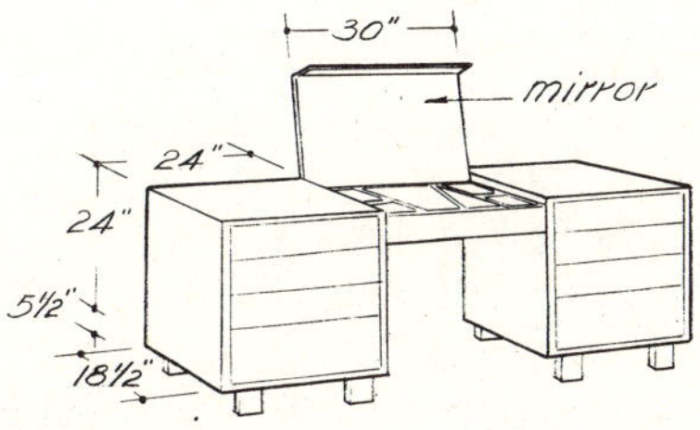
30"
mirror
24"
24"
5½"
18½"
vanity may be suspended between any two 24" cabinets on 5½" legs.

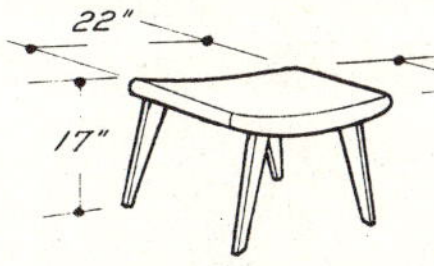
22"
15½"
17"
upholstered

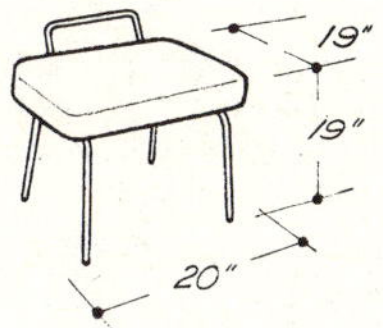
19"
19"
20"

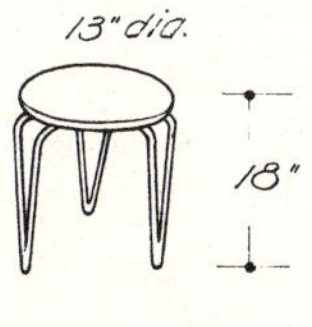
13" dia.
18"
wood

- KNOLL ASSOCIATES

stools

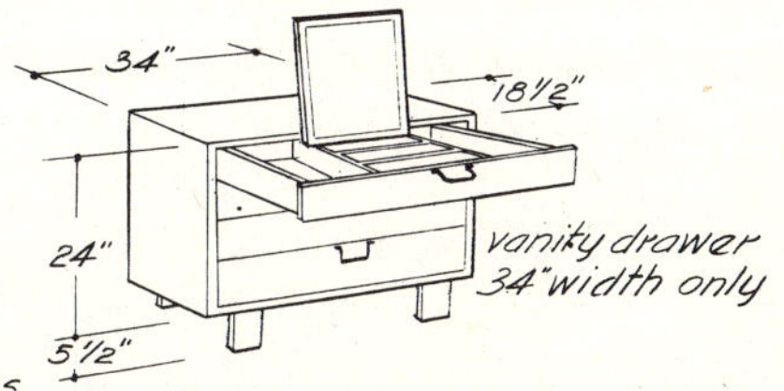
34"
18½"
24"
5½"
vanity drawer 34" width only

cabinet available also in 24" width, various drawer & door combinations - on legs or bench.

- HERMAN MILLER COLLECTION -

STOOLS & VANITIES

FURNITURE

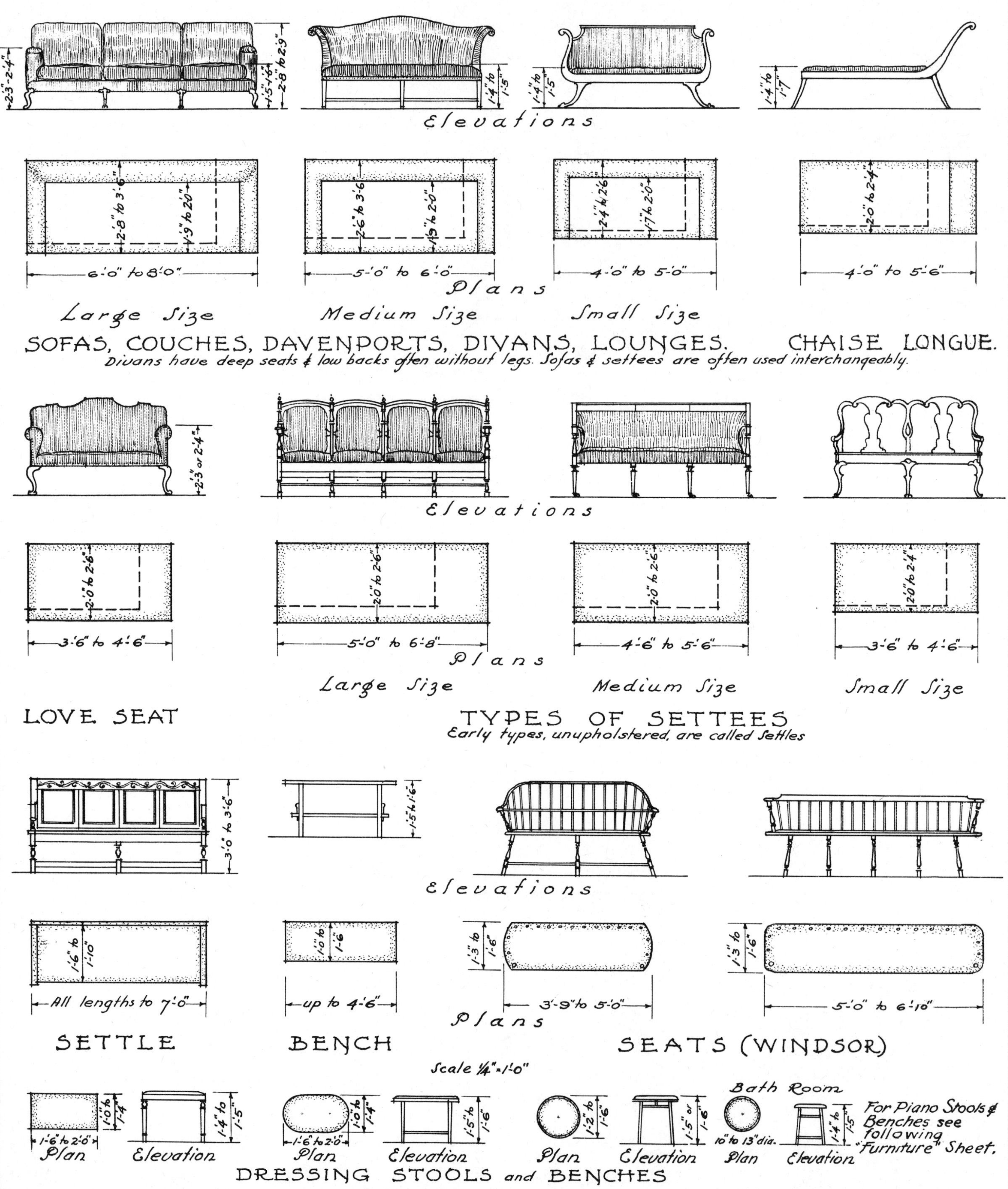
2'-3"-2'-4"
1'-5"-1'-6"
2'-8" to 2'-9"
1'-4" to 1'-5"
1'-4" to 1'-5"
1'-4" to 1'-7"
Elevations
2'-8" to 3'-6"
1'-9" to 2'-0"
6'-0" to 8'-0"
2'-6" to 3'-6"
1'-9" to 2'-0"
5'-0" to 6'-0"
2'-4" to 2'-6"
1'-7" to 2'-0"
4'-0" to 5'-0"
2'-0" to 2'-4"
4'-0" to 5'-6"
Plans
Large Size
Medium Size
Small Size
SOFAS, COUCHES, DAVENPORTS, DIVANS, LOUNGES.
CHAISE LONGUE.
Divans have deep seats & low backs often without legs. Sofas & settees are often used interchangeably.
2'-3" or 2'-4"
Elevations
2'-0" to 2'-6"
3'-6" to 4'-6"
2'-0" to 2'-6"
5'-0" to 6'-8"
2'-0" to 2'-6"
4'-6" to 5'-6"
2'-0" to 2'-4"
3'-6" to 4'-6"
Plans
Large Size
Medium Size
Small Size
LOVE SEAT
TYPES OF SETTEES
Early types, unupholstered, are called Settles
3'-0" to 3'-6"
1'-5" to 1'-6"
Elevations
1'-6" to 1'-10"
All lengths to 7'-0"
1'-0" to 1'-6"
up to 4'-6"
1'-3" to 1'-6"
3'-9" to 5'-0"
1'-3" to 1'-6"
5'-0" to 6'-10"
Plans
SETTLE
BENCH
SEATS (WINDSOR)
Scale 1/4" = 1'-0"
1'-0" to 1'-4"
1'-6" to 2'-0"
Plan
1'-4" to 1'-5"
Elevation
1'-0" to 1'-4"
1'-6" to 2'-0"
Plan
1'-5" to 1'-6"
Elevation
1'-2" to 1'-6"
Plan
1'-5" or 1'-6"
Elevation
Bath Room
10" to 13" dia.
Plan
1'-4" to 1'-5"
Elevation
For Piano Stools & Benches see following "Furniture" Sheet.
DRESSING STOOLS and BENCHES

SEATS - SOFAS - CHAISE LONGUE - SETTLES - BENCHES - COUCHES - DIVANS - LOUNGES

FURNITURE

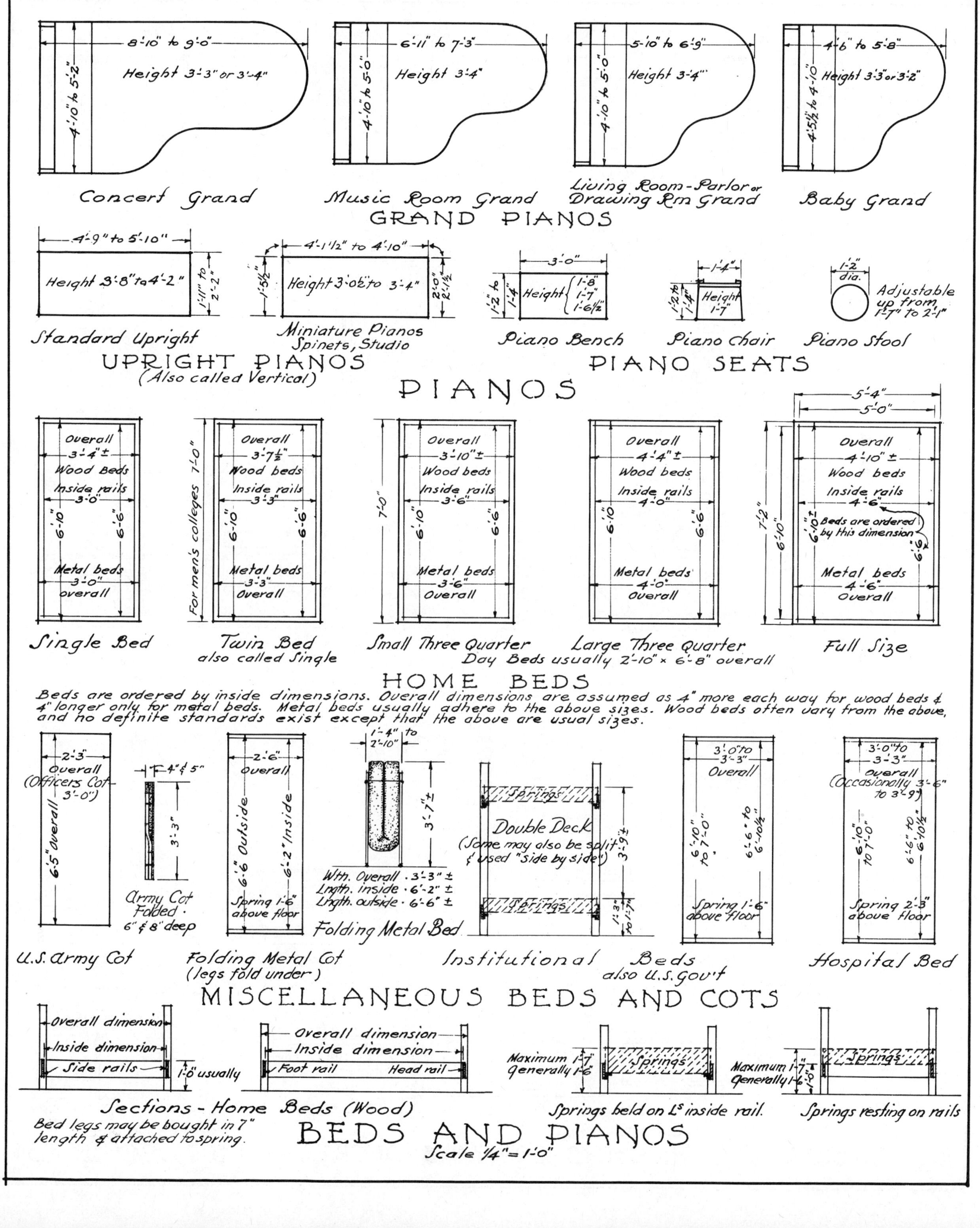
8'-10" to 9'-0"
4'-10" to 5'-2"
Height 3'-3" or 3'-4"
Concert Grand
6'-11" to 7'-3"
4'-10" to 5'-0"
Height 3'-4"
Music Room Grand
5'-10" to 6'-9"
4'-10" to 5'-0"
Height 3'-4"
Living Room-Parlor or Drawing Rm Grand
4'-6" to 5'-8"
4'-5½" to 4'-10"
Height 3'-3" or 3'-2"
Baby Grand
GRAND PIANOS
4'-9" to 5'-10"
Height 3'-8" to 4'-2"
1'-11" to 2'-2"
Standard Upright
4'-1½" to 4'-10"
1'-5½"
Height 3'-0½" to 3'-4"
2'-0" to 2'-1½"
Miniature Pianos Spinets, Studio
UPRIGHT PIANOS
(Also called Vertical)
3'-0"
1'-2" to 1'-4"
Height 1'-8" 1'-7" 1'-6½"
Piano Bench
1'-4"
1'-2" to 1'-4"
Height 1'-7"
Piano Chair
1'-2" dia.
Adjustable up from 1'-7" to 2'-1"
Piano Stool
PIANO SEATS
PIANOS
Overall 3'-4" ±
Wood Beds
Inside rails 3'-0"
6'-10"
6'-6"
Metal beds 3'-0" overall
Single Bed
For men's colleges 7'-0"
Overall 3'-7½"
Wood beds
Inside rails 3'-3"
6'-10"
6'-6"
Metal beds 3'-3" Overall
Twin Bed
also called Single
7'-0"
Overall 3'-10" ±
Wood beds
Inside rails 3'-6"
6'-10"
6'-6"
Metal beds 3'-6" Overall
Small Three Quarter
Overall 4'-4" ±
Wood beds
Inside rails 4'-0"
6'-10"
6'-6"
Metal beds 4'-0" Overall
Large Three Quarter
Day Beds usually 2'-10" × 6'-8" overall
5'-4"
5'-0"
7'-2"
6'-10"
Overall 4'-10" ±
Wood beds
Inside rails 4'-6"
6'-10"
Beds are ordered by this dimension
6'-6"
Metal beds 4'-6" Overall
Full Size
HOME BEDS
Beds are ordered by inside dimensions. Overall dimensions are assumed as 4" more each way for wood beds & 4" longer only for metal beds. Metal beds usually adhere to the above sizes. Wood beds often vary from the above, and no definite standards exist except that the above are usual sizes.
2'-3" Overall (Officers Cot 3'-0")
6'-5" Overall
U.S. Army Cot
4" & 5"
3'-3"
Army Cot Folded · 6" & 8" deep
2'-6" Overall
6'-6" Outside
6'-2" Inside
Spring 1'-6" above floor
Folding Metal Cot
(legs fold under)
1'-4" to 2'-10"
3'-7" ±
Wth. Overall · 3'-3" ±
Lngth. inside · 6'-2" ±
Lngth. outside · 6'-6" ±
Folding Metal Bed
Springs
Double Deck
(Some may also be split & used "side by side")
3'-9" ±
Springs
1'-3" to 1'-7"
Institutional Beds
also U.S. Gov't
3'-0" to 3'-3" Overall
6'-10" to 7'-0"
6'-6" to 6'-10½"
Spring 1'-6" above floor
3'-0" to 3'-3" overall (Occasionally 3'-6" to 3'-9")
6'-10" to 7'-0"
6'-6" to 6'-10½"
Spring 2'-3" above floor
Hospital Bed
MISCELLANEOUS BEDS AND COTS
Overall dimension
Inside dimension
Side rails
1'-6" usually
Overall dimension
Inside dimension
Foot rail
Head rail
Sections - Home Beds (Wood)
Bed legs may be bought in 7" length & attached to spring.
Maximum 1'-7"
Generally 1'-6"
Springs
Springs held on L^s inside rail.
Maximum 1'-7"
Generally 1'-6"
Springs
Springs resting on rails
BEDS AND PIANOS
Scale 1/4" = 1'-0"

FURNITURE

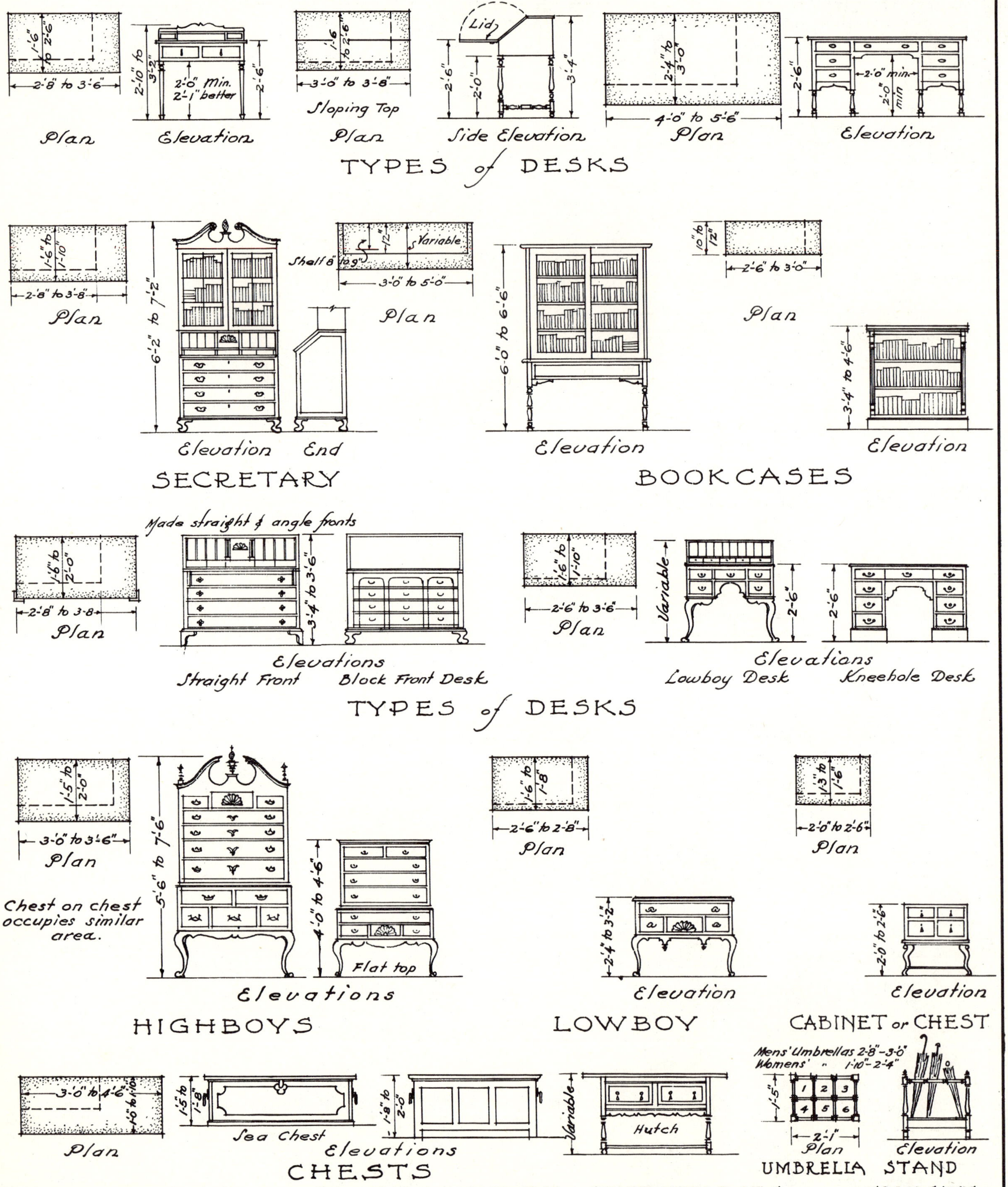
1'-6" to 2'-6"
2'-8" to 3'-6"
Plan
2'-10" to 3'-2"
2'-0" Min.
2'-1" better
2'-6"
Elevation
1'-6" to 2'-6"
3'-0" to 3'-8"
Sloping Top
Plan
Lid
2'-6"
2'-0"
3'-4"
Side Elevation
2'-4" to 3'-0"
4'-0" to 5'-6"
Plan
2'-6"
2'-0" min.
2'-0" min
Elevation
TYPES of DESKS
1'-6" to 1'-10"
2'-8" to 3'-8"
Plan
6'-2" to 7'-2"
Elevation
End
SECRETARY
12"
Variable
Shelf 8" to 9"
3'-0" to 5'-0"
Plan
6'-0" to 6'-6"
Elevation
10" to 12"
2'-6" to 3'-0"
Plan
3'-4" to 4'-6"
Elevation
BOOKCASES
Made straight & angle fronts
1'-6" to 2'-0"
2'-8" to 3'-8"
Plan
3'-4" to 3'-6"
Elevations
Straight Front
Block Front Desk
1'-6" to 1'-10"
2'-6" to 3'-6"
Plan
Variable
2'-6"
2'-6"
Elevations
Lowboy Desk
Kneehole Desk
TYPES of DESKS
1'-5" to 2'-0"
3'-0" to 3'-6"
Plan
Chest on chest occupies similar area.
5'-6" to 7'-6"
4'-0" to 4'-6"
Flat top
Elevations
HIGHBOYS
1'-6" to 1'-8"
2'-6" to 2'-8"
Plan
2'-4" to 3'-2"
Elevation
LOWBOY
1'-3" to 1'-6"
2'-0" to 2'-6"
Plan
2'-0" to 2'-6"
Elevation
CABINET or CHEST
3'-0" to 4'-6"
1'-0" to 1'-10"
Plan
1'-5" to 1'-8"
Sea Chest
1'-8" to 2'-0"
Variable
Hutch
Elevations
CHESTS
Mens' Umbrellas 2'-8"-3'-0"
Womens' " 1'-10"-2'-4"
1'-5"
1 2 3
4 5 6
2'-1"
Plan
Elevation
UMBRELLA STAND

DESKS - BOOKCASES - HIGHBOYS - LOWBOYS - SECRETARIES and CHESTS

1/4" = 1'-0"

FURNITURE

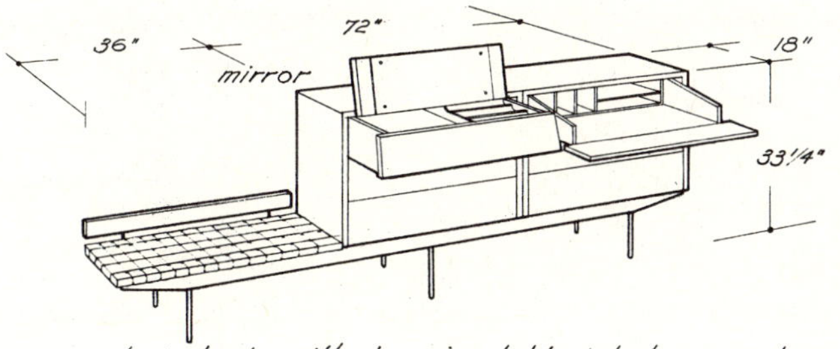
36"
72"
mirror
18"
33 1/4"

luggage rack & chests with dressing table & desk compartments

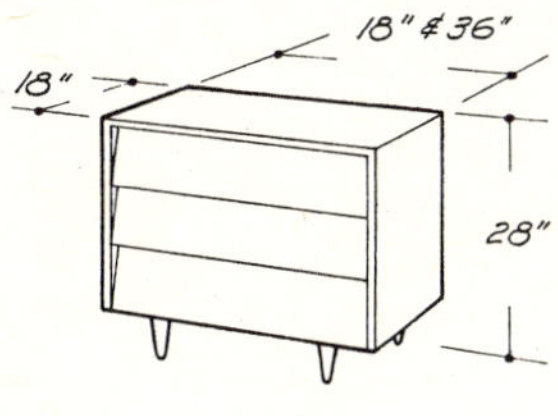
18" & 36"
18"
28"

chest

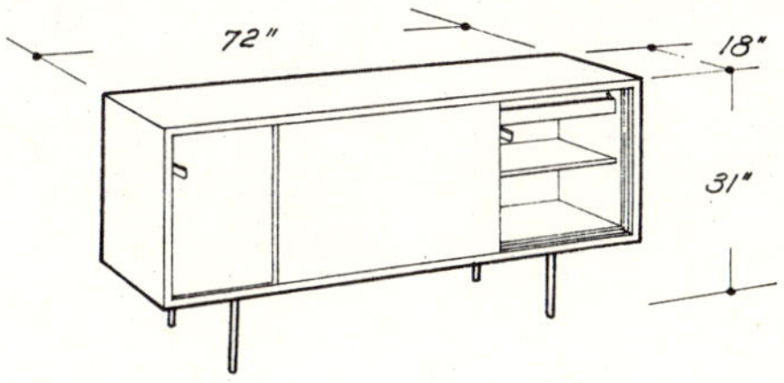
72"
18"
31"

sideboard

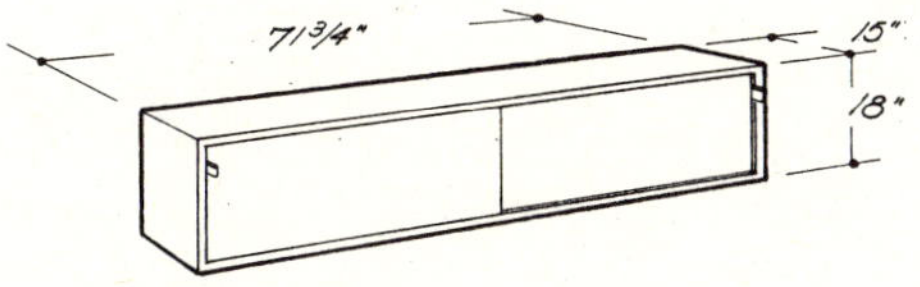
71 3/4"
15"
18"

wall-hung cabinet - sliding doors

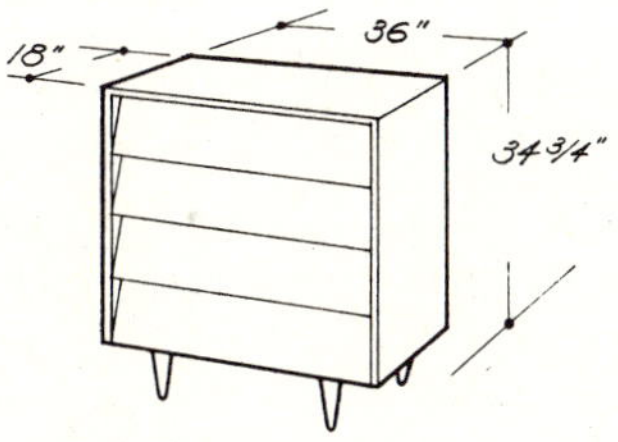
36"
18"
34 3/4"

chest

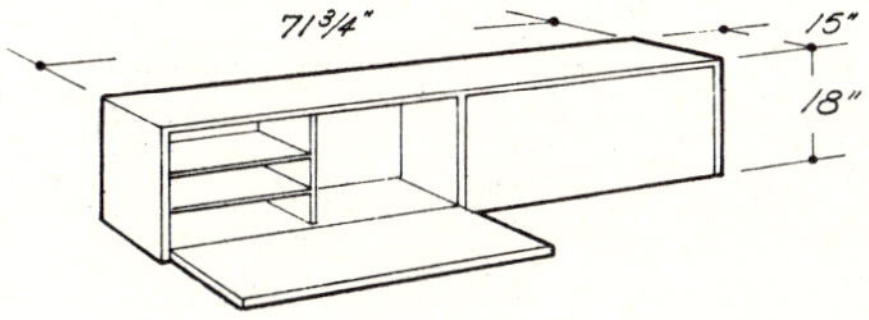
71 3/4"
15"
18"

wall-hung cabinet - folding doors

- KNOLL ASSOCIATES -

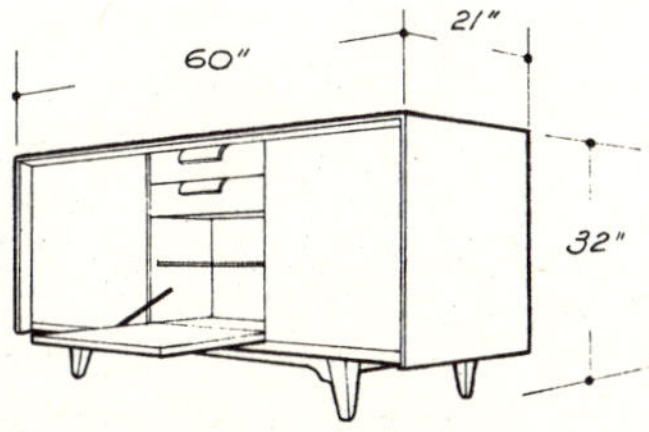
60"
21"
32"

sideboard: 2 felt lined drawers, bottle cabinet, 3 adjustable shelves each side.

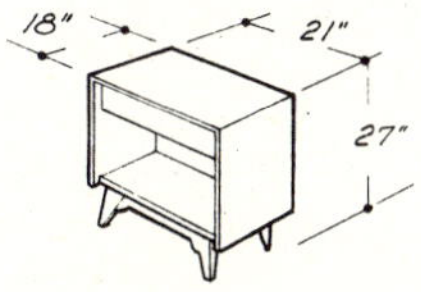
18"
21"
27"

cabinet, with drawer

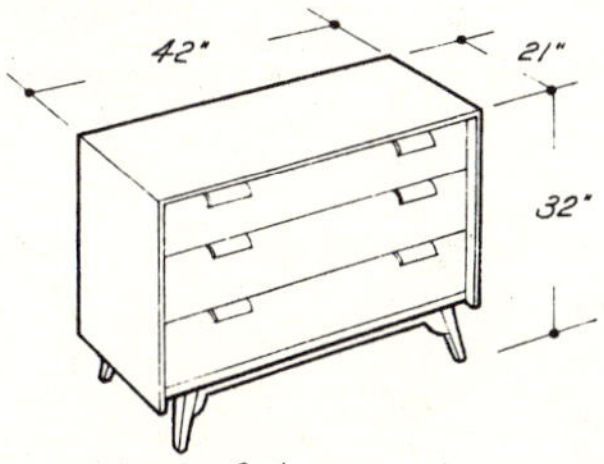
42"
21"
32"

chest of drawers

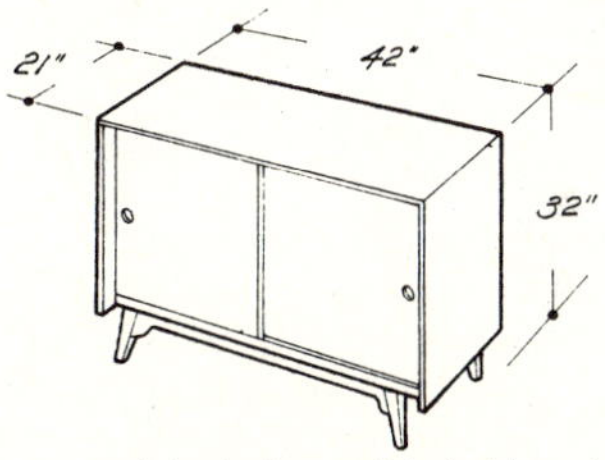
21"
42"
32"

cabinet, two adjustable shelves, sliding doors

JENS RISOM -

17 1/4"
33 9/16"
29 1/2"

chest-metal frame. Colored lacquer, plastic top.

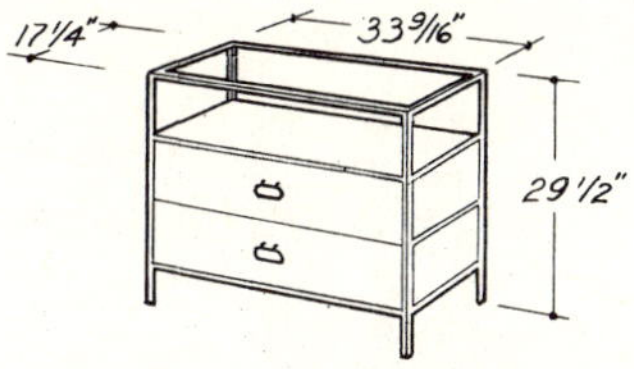
17 1/4"
33 9/16"
29 1/2"

chest with glass top. Metal frame, colored lacquer.

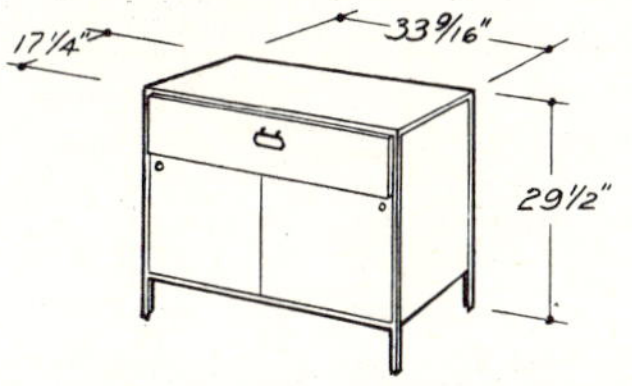
17 1/4"
33 9/16"
29 1/2"

chest with sliding doors-metal frame, colored lacquer, plastic top.

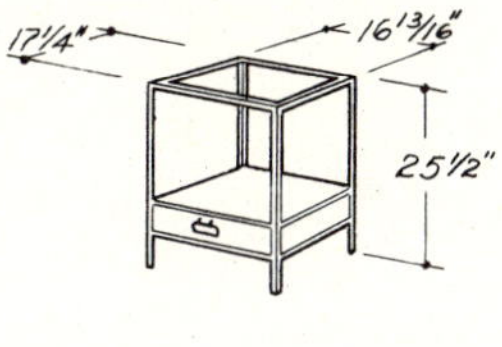
17 1/4"
16 13/16"
25 1/2"

end table or night stand, glass top. Metal frame.

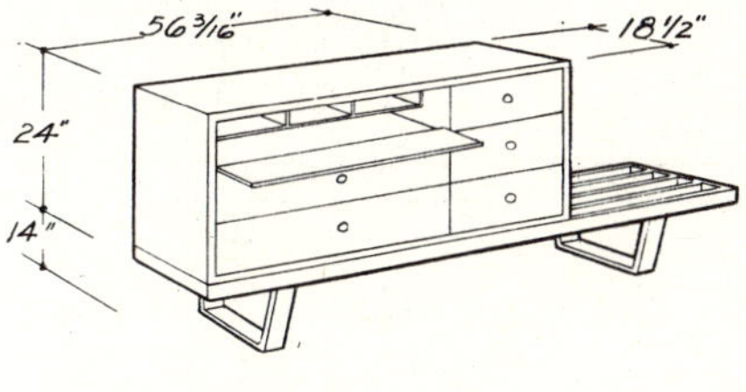
56 3/16"
18 1/2"
24"
14"

desk-chest unit available on bench to form luggage rack or on legs.

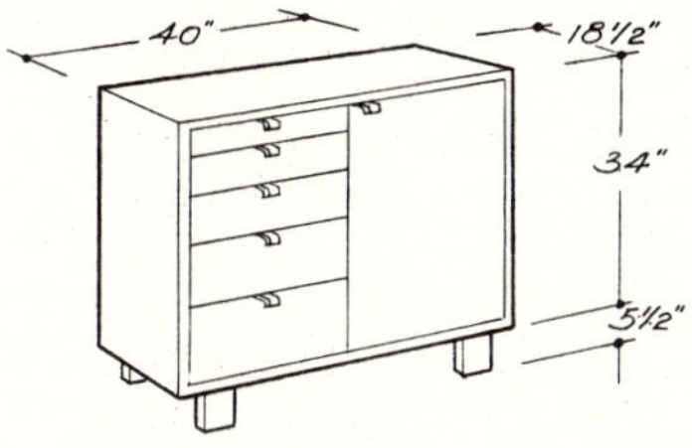
40"
18 1/2"
34"
5 1/2"

cabinet mounted on legs or bench-various drawer & door arrangements.

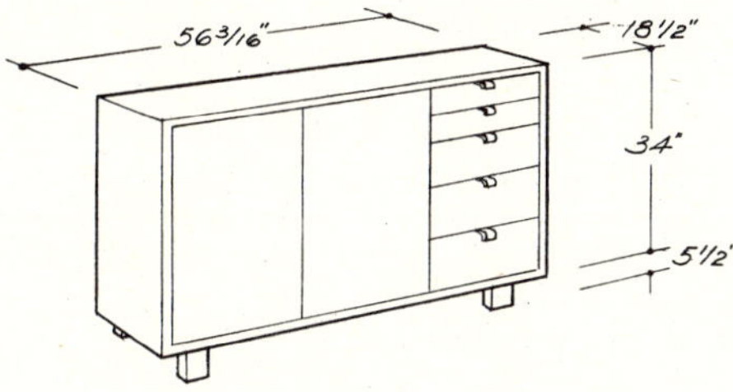
56 3/16"
18 1/2"
34"
5 1/2"

chest-cabinet-also with 5 large drawers and one small door. On legs or bench.

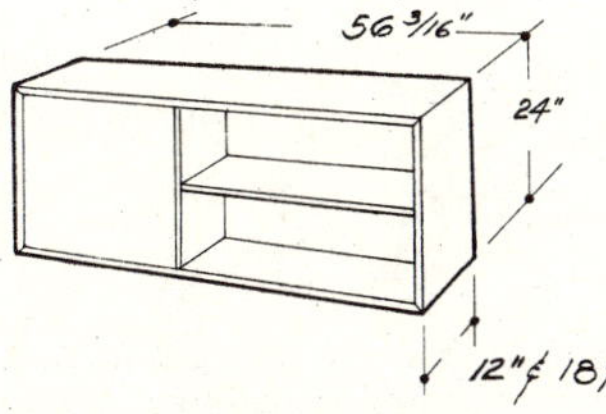
56 3/16"
24"
12" & 18 1/2"

cabinet available in two widths & several shelf & door arrangements. May be wall-hung or mounted on legs or bench.

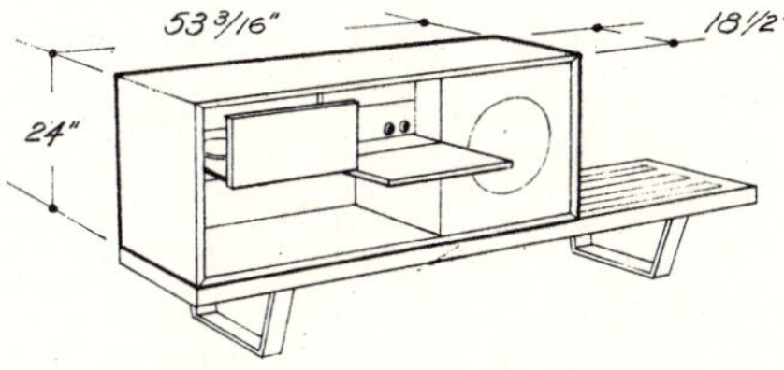
53 3/16"
18 1/2"
24"

radio-record player console-with record storage. Other types also available.

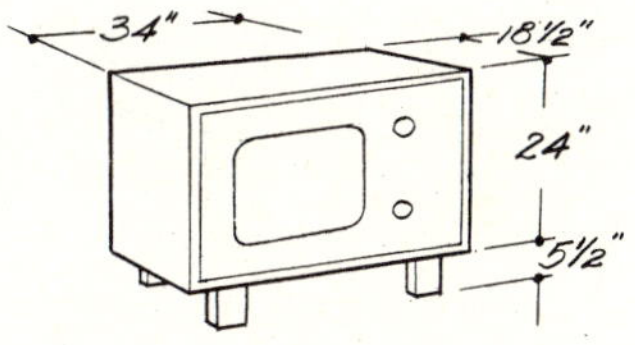
34"
18 1/2"
24"
5 1/2"

television cabinet. Also for use on bench to match radio phonograph at left.

- HERMAN MILLER COLLECTION -

CHESTS, CABINETS & CASES

FURNITURE

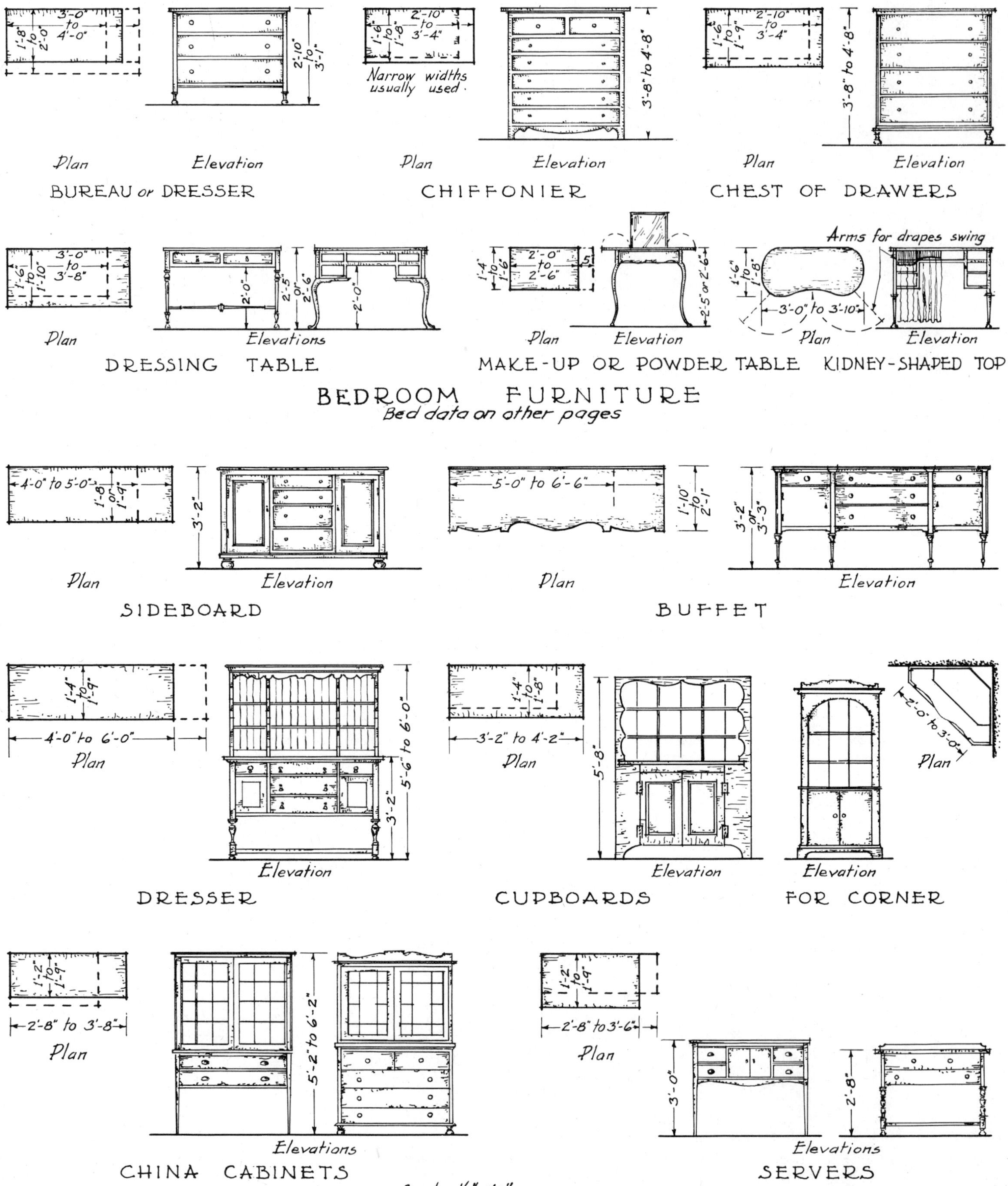
3'-0" to 4'-0"
1'-8" to 2'-0"
2'-10" to 3'-1"
Plan
Elevation
BUREAU or DRESSER
2'-10" to 3'-4"
1'-6" to 1'-8"
Narrow widths usually used.
3'-8" to 4'-8"
Plan
Elevation
CHIFFONIER
2'-10" to 3'-4"
1'-6" to 1'-9"
3'-8" to 4'-8"
Plan
Elevation
CHEST OF DRAWERS
3'-0" to 3'-8"
1'-6" to 1'-10"
2'-0"
2'-5" or 2'-6"
2'-0"
Plan
Elevations
DRESSING TABLE
2'-0" to 2'-6"
1'-4" to 1'-6"
2'-5" or 2'-6"
Plan
Elevation
MAKE-UP OR POWDER TABLE
Arms for drapes swing
1'-6" to 1'-8"
3'-0" to 3'-10"
Plan
Elevation
KIDNEY-SHAPED TOP
BEDROOM FURNITURE
Bed data on other pages
4'-0" to 5'-0"
1'-8" or 1'-9"
3'-2"
Plan
Elevation
SIDEBOARD
5'-0" to 6'-6"
1'-10" to 2'-1"
3'-2" or 3'-3"
Plan
Elevation
BUFFET
1'-4" to 1'-9"
4'-0" to 6'-0"
Plan
5'-6" to 6'-0"
3'-2"
Elevation
DRESSER
1'-4" to 1'-8"
3'-2" to 4'-2"
Plan
5'-8"
Elevation
CUPBOARDS
2'-0" to 3'-0"
Plan
Elevation
FOR CORNER
1'-2" to 1'-9"
2'-8" to 3'-8"
Plan
5'-2" to 6'-2"
Elevations
CHINA CABINETS
1'-2" to 1'-9"
2'-8" to 3'-6"
Plan
3'-0"
2'-8"
Elevations
SERVERS

Scale 1/4" = 1'-0"

DINING ROOM AND BEDROOM FURNITURE

STANDARD SIZES, HOUSEHOLD LINEN, RUGS and CARPETS

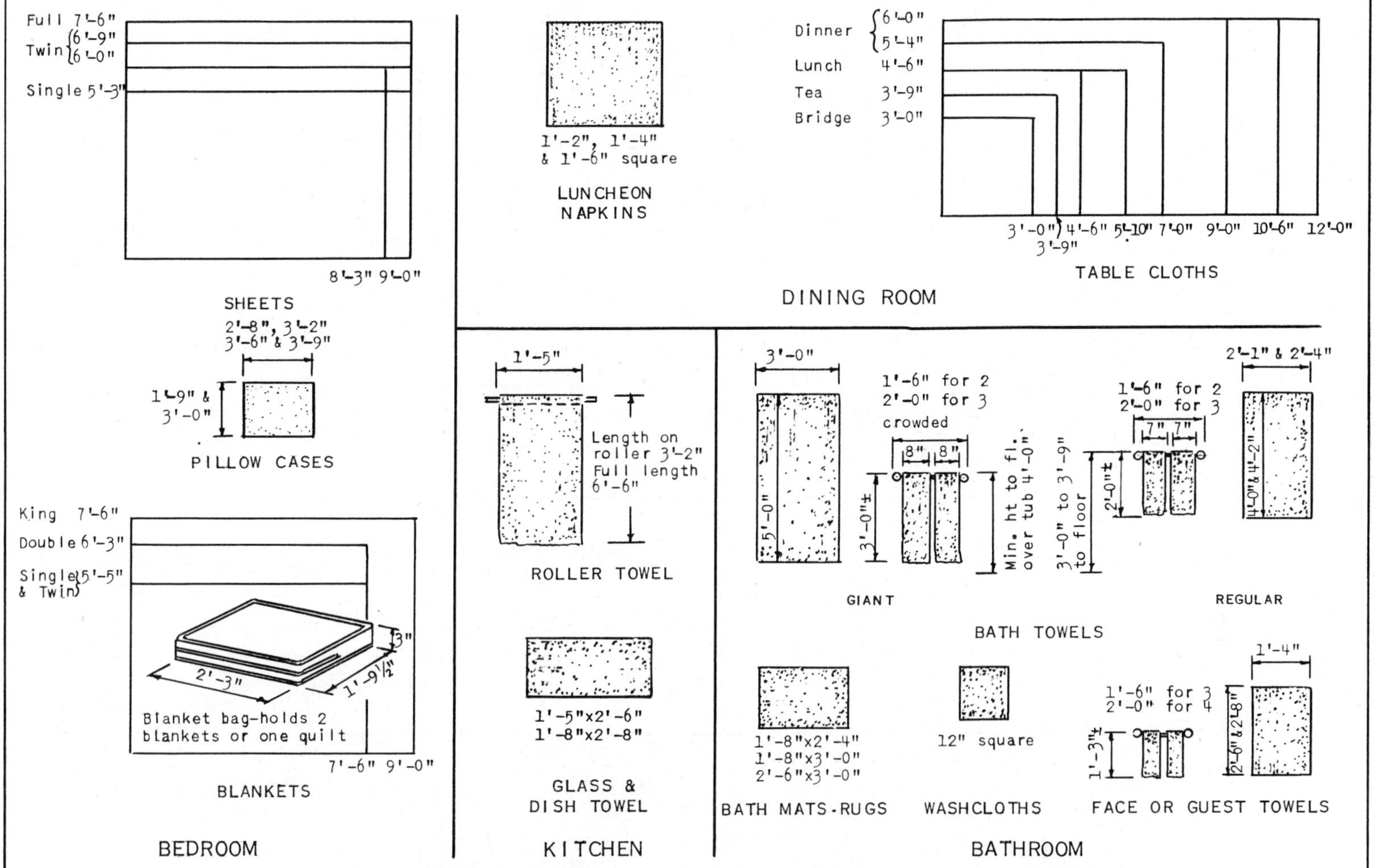
Full 7'-6"
Twin 6'-9" 6'-0"
Single 5'-3"
8'-3" 9'-0"
SHEETS
2'-8", 3'-2"
3'-6" & 3'-9"
1'-9" & 3'-0"
PILLOW CASES
King 7'-6"
Double 6'-3"
Single 5'-5" & Twin
3"
2'-3"
1'-9½"
Blanket bag-holds 2 blankets or one quilt
7'-6" 9'-0"
BLANKETS
BEDROOM
1'-2", 1'-4" & 1'-6" square
LUNCHEON NAPKINS
Dinner 6'-0" 5'-4"
Lunch 4'-6"
Tea 3'-9"
Bridge 3'-0"
3'-0" 4'-6" 5'-10" 7'-0" 9'-0" 10'-6" 12'-0"
3'-9"
TABLE CLOTHS
DINING ROOM
1'-5"
Length on roller 3'-2"
Full length 6'-6"
ROLLER TOWEL
1'-5"x2'-6"
1'-8"x2'-8"
GLASS & DISH TOWEL
KITCHEN
3'-0"
5'-0"
1'-6" for 2
2'-0" for 3
crowded
8" 8"
3'-0"±
Min. ht to fl. over tub 4'-0"
GIANT
3'-0" to 3'-9" to floor
2'-0"±
1'-6" for 2
2'-0" for 3
7" 7"
2'-1" & 2'-4"
4'-0" & 4'-2"
REGULAR
BATH TOWELS
1'-8"x2'-4"
1'-8"x3'-0"
2'-6"x3'-0"
BATH MATS-RUGS
12" square
WASHCLOTHS
1'-4"
1'-6" for 3
2'-0" for 4
1'-3"±
2'-6" & 2'-8"
FACE OR GUEST TOWELS
BATHROOM

LINEN FOR BEDROOM, DINING ROOM, KITCHEN & BATH

CARPETS: Broadloom carpeting is made in standard widths of 2'-3", 9'-0" and 15'-0" by all manufacturers. Some also have standard widths of 3'-0" & 18'-0". All widths obtainable in any length. Hall and stair carpets are 27" wide.
SCATTER RUGS: Sizes 1'-6" x 2'-6" to 4'-0" x 6'-0", in any material, are considered as such.

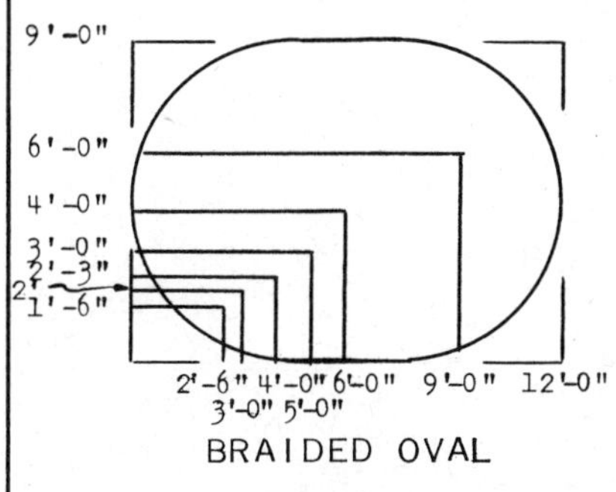
9'-0"
6'-0"
4'-0"
3'-0"
2'-3"
2'
1'-6"
2'-6" 4'-0" 6'-0" 9'-0" 12'-0"
3'-0" 5'-0"
BRAIDED OVAL

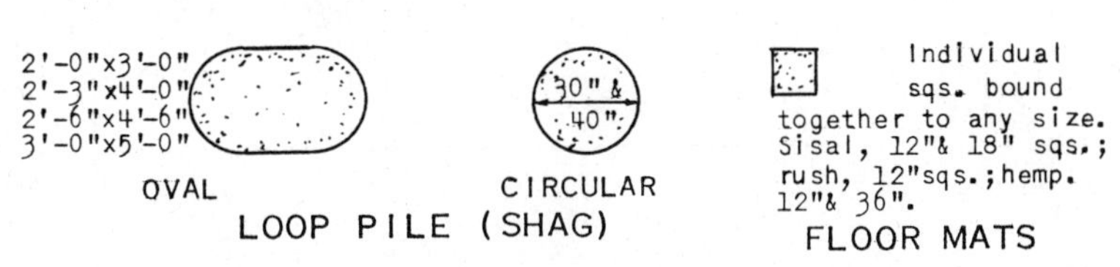
2'-0"x3'-0"
2'-3"x4'-0"
2'-6"x4'-6"
3'-0"x5'-0"
OVAL
30" & 40"
CIRCULAR
LOOP PILE (SHAG)
Individual sqs. bound together to any size. Sisal, 12" & 18" sqs.; rush, 12" sqs.; hemp. 12" & 36".
FLOOR MATS

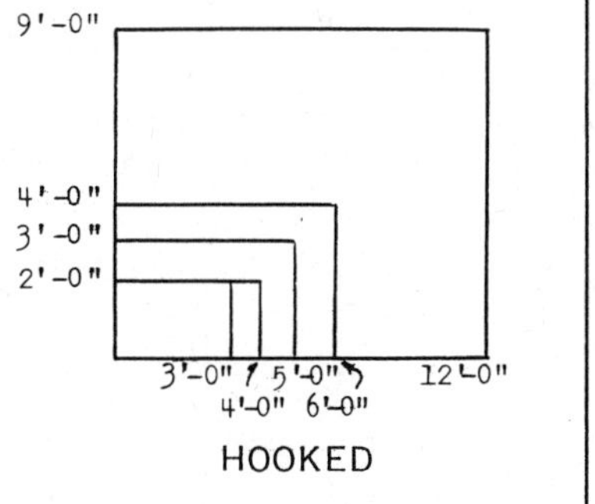
9'-0"
4'-0"
3'-0"
2'-0"
3'-0" 5'-0" 12'-0"
4'-0" 6'-0"
HOOKED

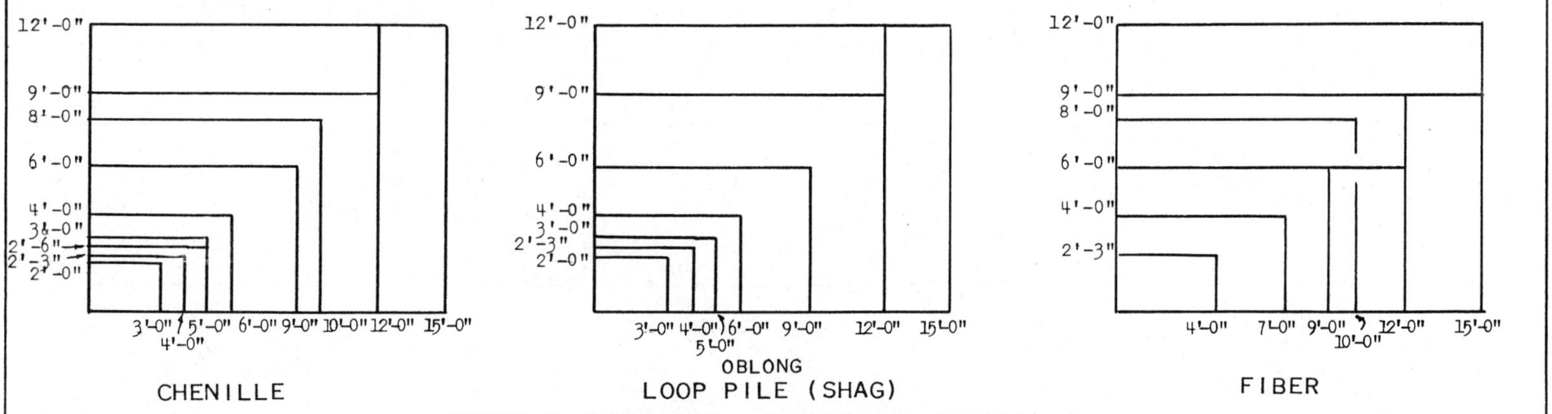
12'-0"
9'-0"
8'-0"
6'-0"
4'-0"
3'-0"
2'-6"
2'-3"
2'-0"
3'-0" 5'-0" 6'-0" 9'-0" 10'-0" 12'-0" 15'-0"
4'-0"
CHENILLE
12'-0"
9'-0"
6'-0"
4'-0"
3'-0"
2'-3"
2'-0"
3'-0" 4'-0" 6'-0" 9'-0" 12'-0" 15'-0"
5'-0"
OBLONG
LOOP PILE (SHAG)
12'-0"
9'-0"
8'-0"
6'-0"
4'-0"
2'-3"
4'-0" 7'-0" 9'-0" 12'-0" 15'-0"
10'-0"
FIBER

RUGS & CARPETS: STANDARD SIZES

FOLDED FLATWORK-LINEN

DIMENSIONS FOLDED FLATWORK BED, BATH, TABLE & KITCHEN LINEN			
ITEMS	SIZES	FOLDS	FOLDED & STACKED DIMENSIONS
SHEETS	6'-9"x12'-0"	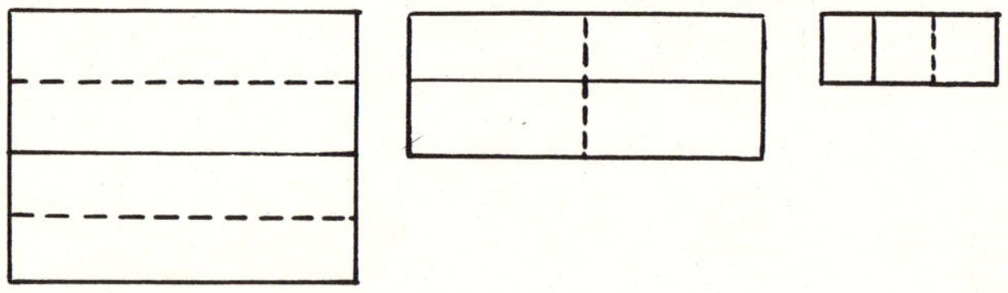	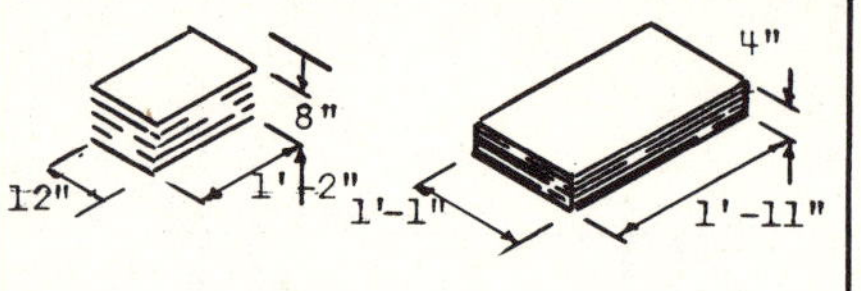4" 8" 12" 1'-2" 1'-1" 1'-11" 6 HIGH
SHEETS	6'-0"x12'-0"	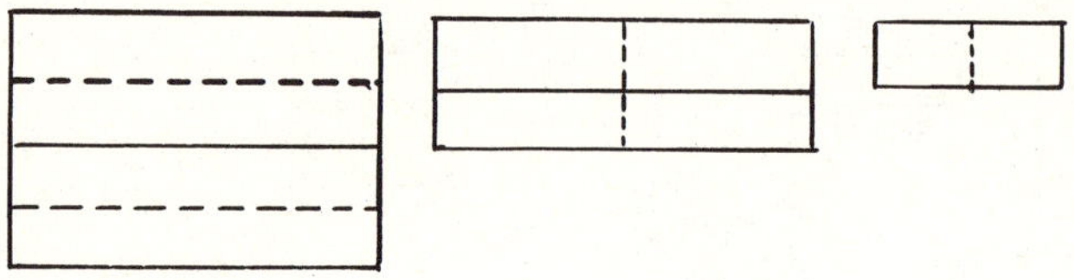	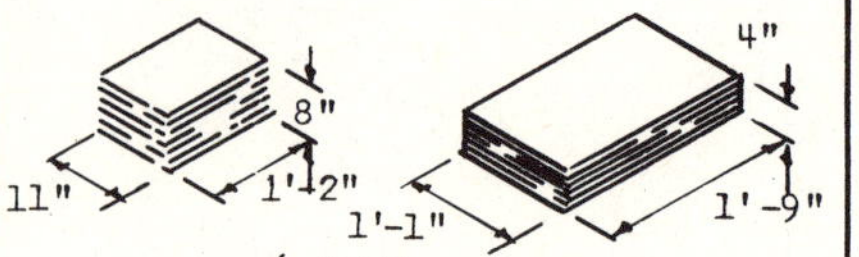4" 8" 11" 1'-2" 1'-1" 1'-9" 6 HIGH
PILLOW CASES	1'-9"x2'-8"	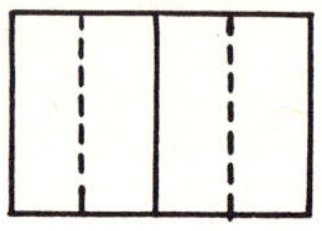	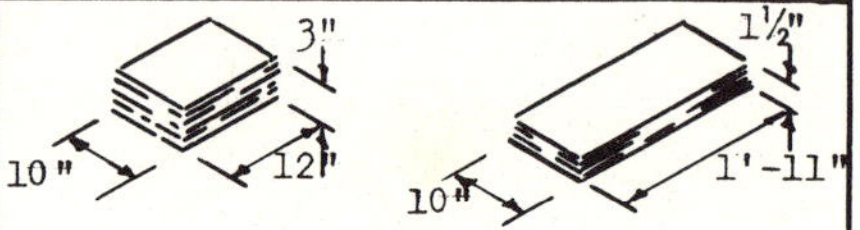3" 1½" 10" 12" 10" 1'-11" 6 HIGH
FACE TOWELS	1'-6"x2'-8"	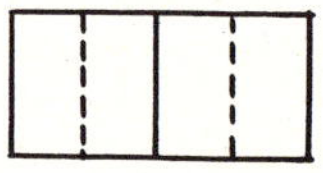	12 HIGH 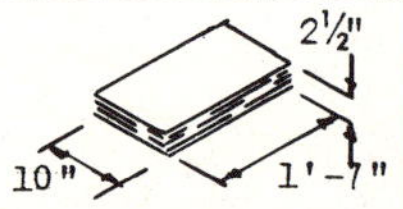2½" 10" 1'-7"
HAND TOWELS	1'-3"x1'-6"	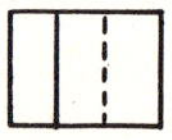	12 HIGH 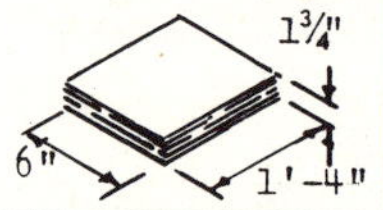1¾" 6" 1'-4"
BATH TOWELS	2'-0"x3'-8"		6 HIGH 8½" 13" 13"
WASH CLOTHS	12"x12"		12 HIGH 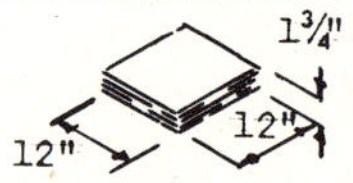1¾" 12" 12"
BATH MATS	1'-8"x2'-4"	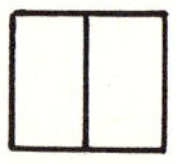	6 HIGH 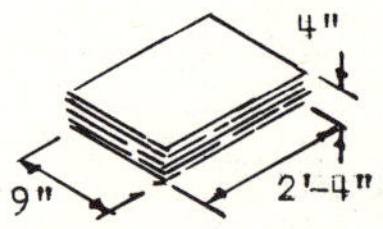4" 9" 2'-4"
BATH RUGS	1'-8"x3'-0" 2'-6"x3'-0"	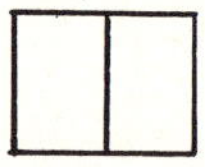	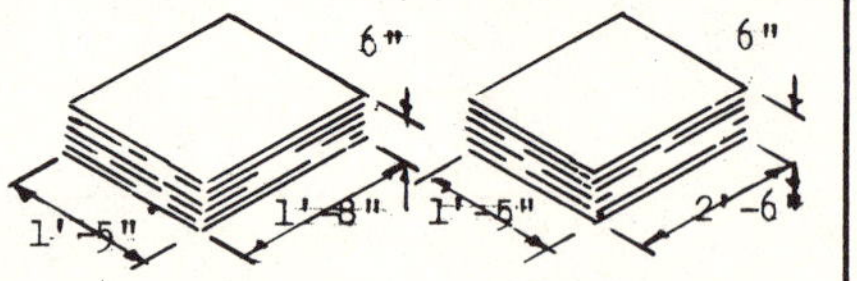6" 6" 1'-5" 1'-8" 1'-5" 2'-6" 1'-8" x 3'-0" 2'-6" x 3'-0" 6 HIGH
NAPKINS	16"x16" 18"x18"		2½" 3½" 16" x 16" 18" x 18" 12 HIGH
DISH TOWELS	1'-7"x2'-4"	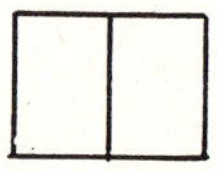	Stacked flat in bundles of 25 & folded in half 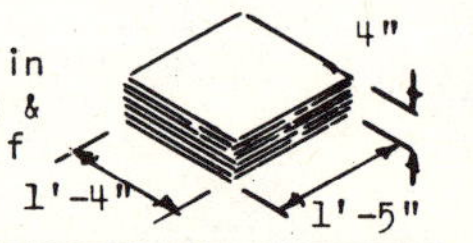4" 1'-4" 1'-5"

DATA BY THE AMERICAN LAUNDRY MACHINERY CO.

APPAREL

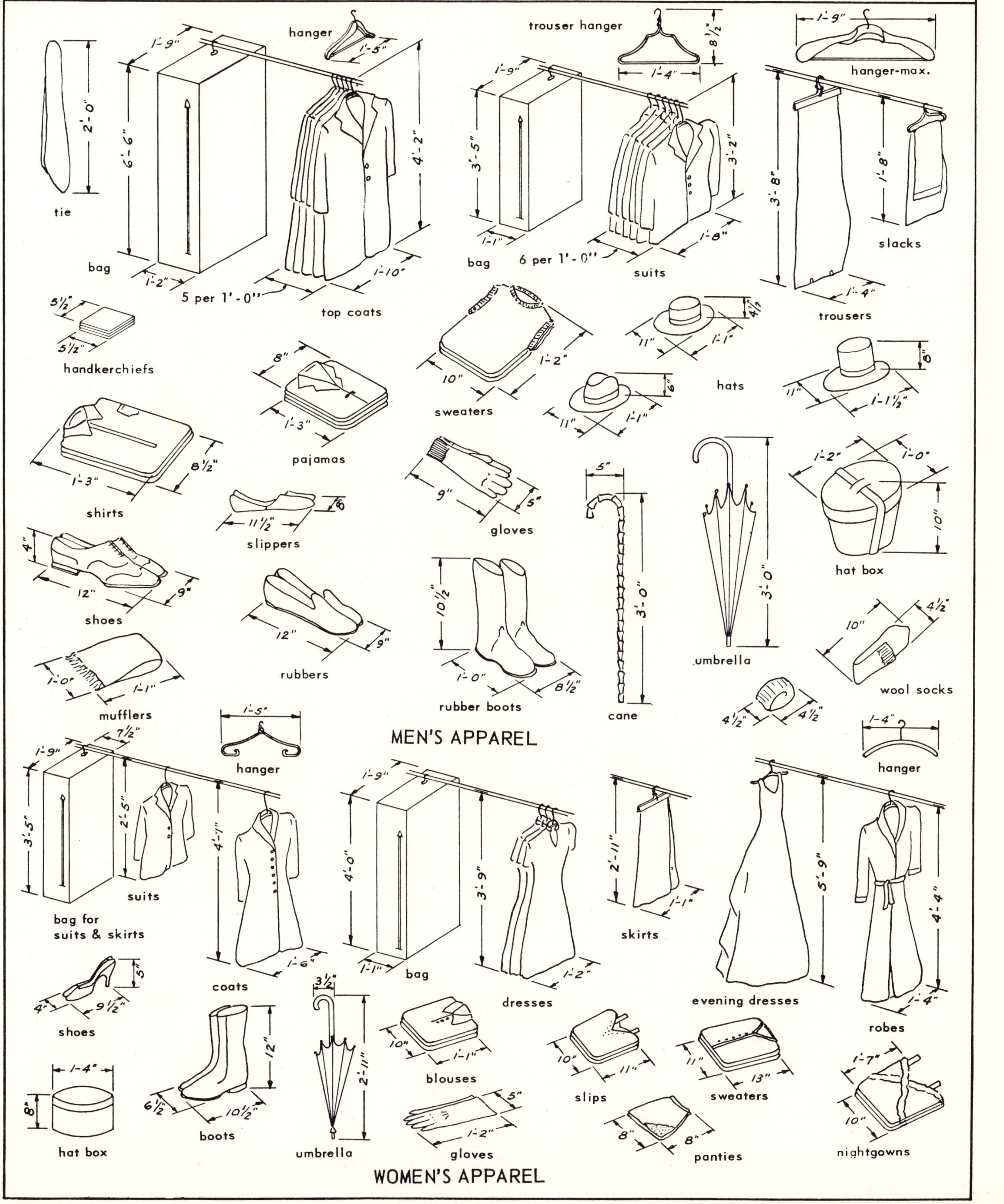
tie
2'-0"
bag
1'-9"
6'-6"
1'-2"
5 per 1'-0"
hanger
1'-5"
4'-2"
1'-10"
top coats
trouser hanger
8½"
1'-4"
1'-9"
3'-5"
1'-1"
bag
6 per 1'-0"
3'-2"
1'-8"
suits
hanger-max.
3'-8"
1'-8"
slacks
1'-4"
trousers
5½"
5½"
handkerchiefs
8"
1'-3"
pajamas
10"
1'-2"
sweaters
11"
1'-1"
4½"
11"
1'-1"
6"
hats
11"
1'-1½"
8"
1'-3"
8½"
shirts
11½"
6"
slippers
9"
5"
gloves
5"
3'-0"
cane
3'-0"
umbrella
1'-2"
1'-0"
10"
hat box
4"
12"
9"
shoes
12"
9"
rubbers
10½"
1'-0"
8½"
rubber boots
10"
4½"
wool socks
4½"
4½"
1'-0"
1'-1"
mufflers
1'-5"
hanger
MEN'S APPAREL
1'-4"
hanger
1'-9"
7½"
3'-5"
2'-5"
suits
bag for
suits & skirts
4'-7"
1'-6"
coats
1'-9"
4'-0"
1'-1"
bag
3'-9"
1'-2"
dresses
2'-11"
1'-1"
skirts
5'-9"
evening dresses
4'-4"
1'-4"
robes
5"
4"
9½"
shoes
1'-4"
8"
hat box
12"
6½"
10½"
boots
3½"
2'-11"
umbrella
10"
1'-1"
blouses
5"
1'-2"
gloves
10"
11"
slips
11"
13"
sweaters
8"
8"
panties
1'-7"
10"
nightgowns
WOMEN'S APPAREL

HOUSEHOLD and SPORTS EQUIPMENT

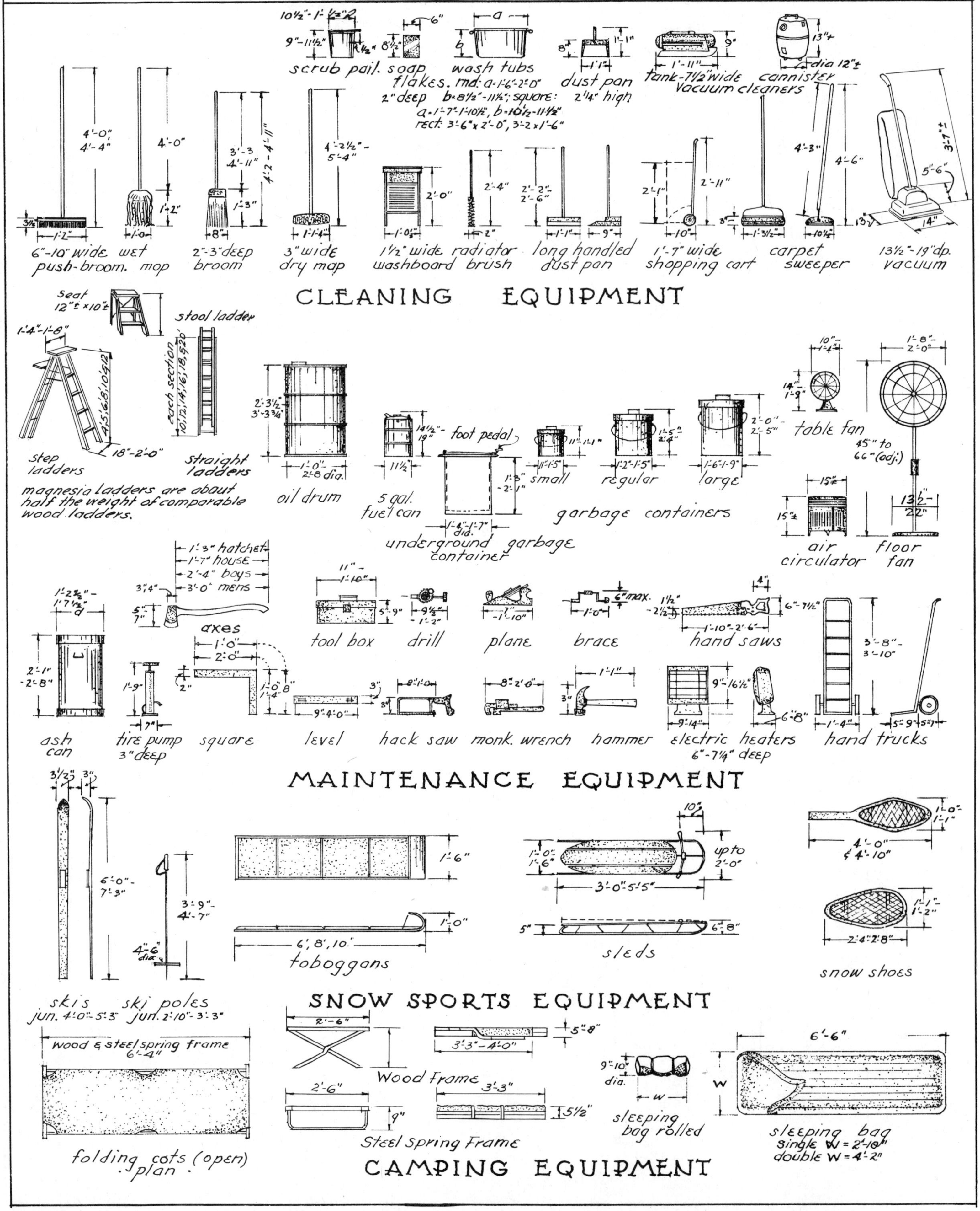
scrub pail
soap flakes
wash tubs
rnd: a=1'-6"-2'-0" 2" deep b=8½"-11½"; square: a=1'-7"-1'-10½", b=10½-11½"
rect: 3'-6"x2'-0", 3'-2x1'-6"
dust pan
2¼" high
tank-7½" wide
cannister
vacuum cleaners
6"-10" wide push-broom.
wet mop
2"-3" deep broom
3" wide dry mop
1½" wide washboard
radiator brush
long handled dust pan
1'-7" wide shopping cart
carpet sweeper
13½"-19" dp. vacuum
CLEANING EQUIPMENT
seat 12"± x 10"±
stool ladder
step ladders
each section 10,12,14,16,18,&20'
straight ladders
magnesia ladders are about half the weight of comparable wood ladders.
oil drum
foot pedal
5 gal. fuel can
underground garbage container
small
regular
large
garbage containers
table fan
45" to 66" (adj.)
air circulator
floor fan
1'-3" hatchet
1'-7" house
2'-4" boys
3'-0" mens
axes
tool box
drill
plane
brace
hand saws
ash can
tire pump 3" deep
square
level
hack saw
monk. wrench
hammer
electric heaters 6"-7¼" deep
hand trucks
MAINTENANCE EQUIPMENT
up to 2'-0"
toboggans
sleds
snow shoes
skis jun. 4'-0"-5'-3"
ski poles jun. 2'-10"-3'-3"
SNOW SPORTS EQUIPMENT
wood & steel spring frame 6'-4"
folding cots (open) plan
Wood frame
Steel Spring Frame
sleeping bag rolled
sleeping bag single W = 2'-10" double W = 4'-2"
CAMPING EQUIPMENT

LUGGAGE

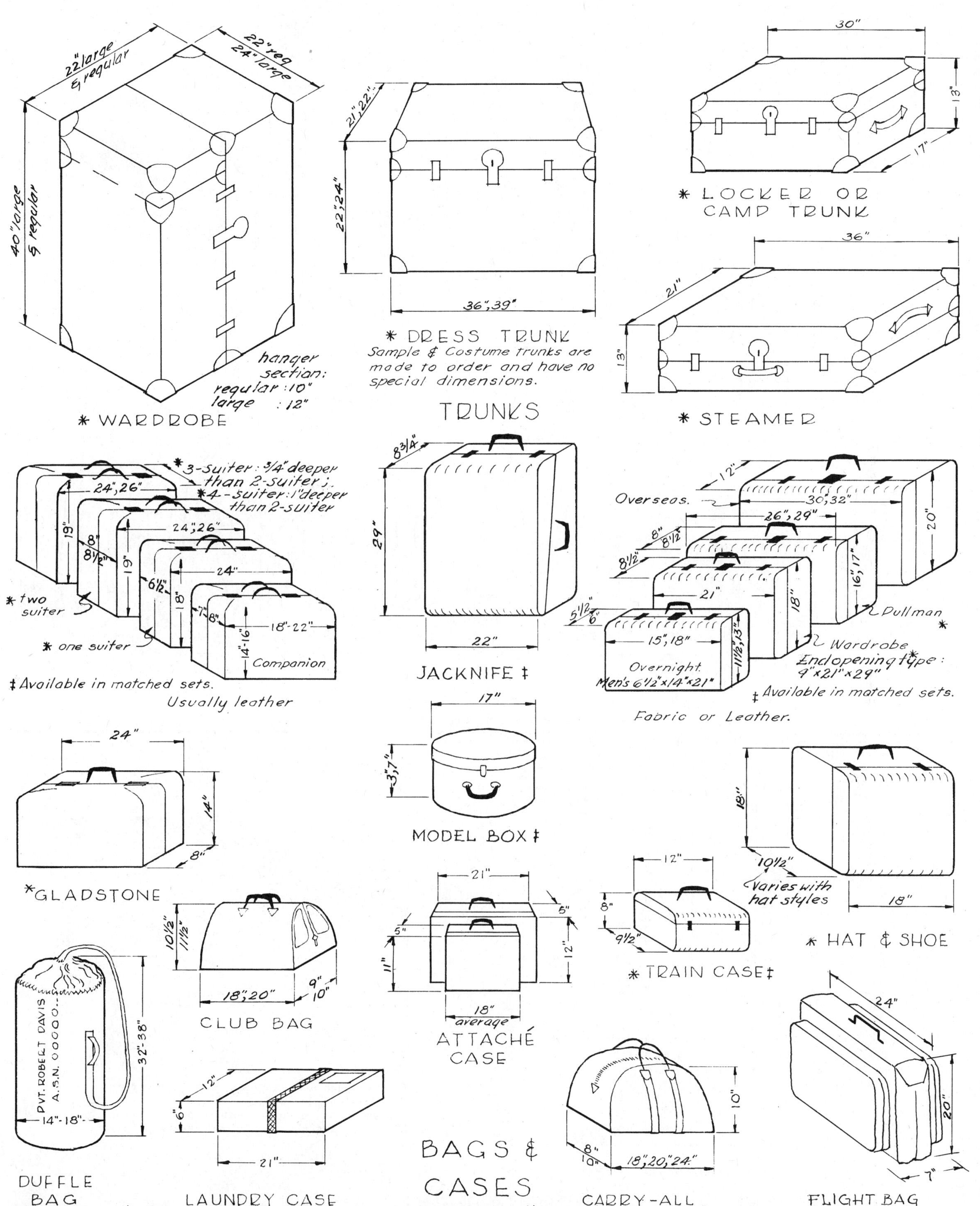
22" large & regular
22" reg.
24" large
40" large & regular
hanger section:
regular : 10"
large : 12"
* WARDROBE
21", 22"
22", 24"
36", 39"
* DRESS TRUNK
Sample & Costume trunks are made to order and have no special dimensions.
TRUNKS
30"
13"
17"
* LOCKER OR CAMP TRUNK
36"
21"
13"
* STEAMER
* 3-suiter: 3/4" deeper than 2-suiter;
* 4-suiter: 1" deeper than 2-suiter
24", 26"
19"
8"
8 1/2"
24", 26"
19"
6 1/2"
18"
24"
7"
8"
18"-22"
14"-16"
Companion
* two suiter
* one suiter
‡ Available in matched sets.
Usually leather
8 3/4"
29"
22"
JACKNIFE ‡
12"
Overseas.
30", 32"
20"
8"
8 1/2"
26", 29"
8 1/2"
16", 17"
21"
18"
5 1/2"
6"
15", 18"
11 1/2", 13"
Overnight.
Men's 6 1/2"×14"×21"
Pullman *
Wardrobe
Endopening type*: 9"×21"×29"
‡ Available in matched sets.
Fabric or Leather.
24"
14"
8"
*GLADSTONE
17"
3", 7"
MODEL BOX ‡
18"
10 1/2"
Varies with hat styles
18"
* HAT & SHOE
10 1/2"
11 1/2"
18", 20"
9"
10"
CLUB BAG
21"
5"
5"
11"
12"
18" average
ATTACHÉ CASE
12"
8"
9 1/2"
* TRAIN CASE ‡
PVT. ROBERT DAVIS
A.S.N. 00000
32"-38"
14"-18"
DUFFLE BAG
12"
6"
21"
LAUNDRY CASE
BAGS & CASES
10"
8"
10"
18", 20", 24"
CARRY-ALL
24"
20"
7"
FLIGHT BAG

* from U.S. Dept. of Commerce Simplified Practice Recommendation R215-46. Dimensions are minimum.
‡ Available in matched sets.

MUSICAL INSTRUMENTS and ELECTRONIC ORGANS

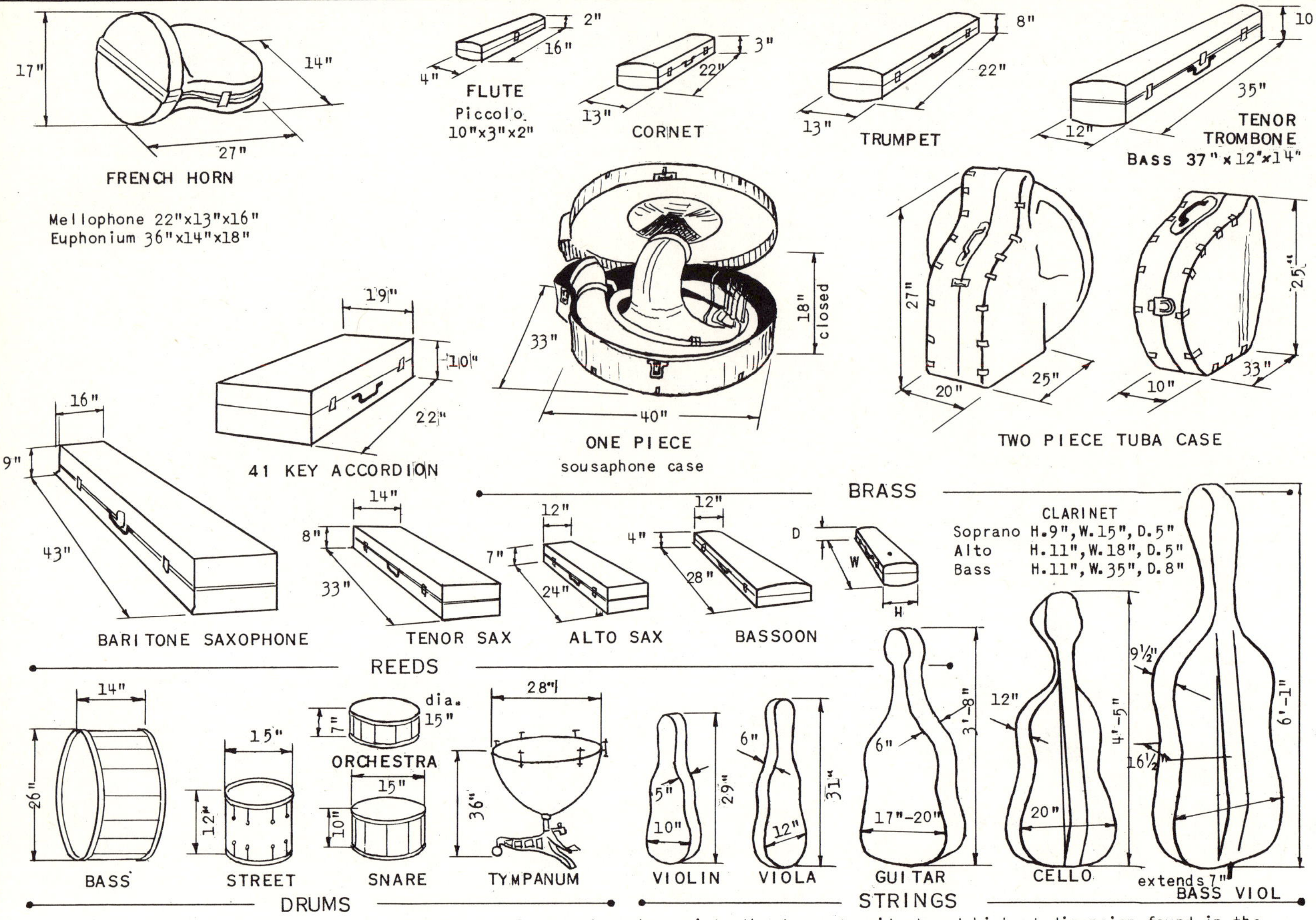
17"
14"
27"
FRENCH HORN
Mellophone 22"x13"x16"
Euphonium 36"x14"x18"
2"
16"
4"
FLUTE
Piccolo
10"x3"x2"
3"
22"
13"
CORNET
8"
22"
13"
TRUMPET
10"
35"
12"
TENOR
TROMBONE
BASS 37"x12"x14"
19"
10"
22"
41 KEY ACCORDION
18" closed
33"
40"
ONE PIECE
sousaphone case
27"
20"
25"
25"
10"
33"
TWO PIECE TUBA CASE
16"
9"
43"
BARITONE SAXOPHONE
14"
8"
33"
TENOR SAX
12"
7"
24"
ALTO SAX
12"
4"
28"
BASSOON
D
W
H
BRASS
CLARINET
Soprano H.9",W.15",D.5"
Alto H.11",W.18",D.5"
Bass H.11",W.35",D.8"
REEDS
14"
26"
BASS
15"
12"
STREET
7"
dia. 15"
ORCHESTRA
15"
10"
SNARE
28"
36"
TYMPANUM
DRUMS
5"
10"
29"
VIOLIN
6"
12"
31"
VIOLA
6"
17"-20"
3'-8"
GUITAR
12"
20"
4'-5"
CELLO
9½"
16½"
6'-1"
extends 7"
BASS VIOL
STRINGS

Dimensions shown are maximum of several models. If several styles exist, the longest, widest and highest dimension found in the group are given.

MUSICAL INSTRUMENT CASE SIZES

DATA BY C.G. CONN LTD.

MFR.	ORGANS: MODEL AND/OR TYPE	SIZES** H.	W.	D1	D2	APP. WT.	TONE BOXES*: MODEL	SIZES** H.	W.	D	APP. WT.
BALDWIN	40 Spinet†	38"	46"	26"		250#	Q	60"	38"	22"	187#
	45 Console†	42"	52"	30"	42"	414	N&NR	40"	31"	18"	116
	5 Console	44"	53"	29"	43"	430	J	39"	27"	18"	123
	10 Console	48"	65"	36"	55"	689					
HAMMOND	Spinet†	35"	46"	26"		243#	ER20	39"	31"	18"	144#
	Chord†	35"	43"	21"		156	F40	40"	33"	29"	228
	Home	39"	49"	29"	50"	450	H40	48"	34"	17"	162
	Church	39"	49"	29"	47"	450	JR20	40"	30"	16"	120
WURLITZER	44 Spinette†	37"	46"	26"		275#	400	47"	21"	20"	125#
	4600 Contemp.	41"	52"	28"	41"	575	626	40"	37"	25"	250
	4602 Tradition	41"	52"	28"	46"	600	800	47"	35"	20"	250
	4800 Concert	47"	61"	32	45"	750					
CONN	500 Minuett	35"	47"	21"		175#	110	38"	33"	19"	112#
	700 Artist	42"	51"	27"	38"	270	119	38"	32"	18"	95
	810 Classic	47"	55"	29"	46"	380	159	49"	37"	21"	132
							210	47"	34"	18"	152
							219	45"	32"	17"	120
							259	22" 45"	45" 48"	16" 24"	262

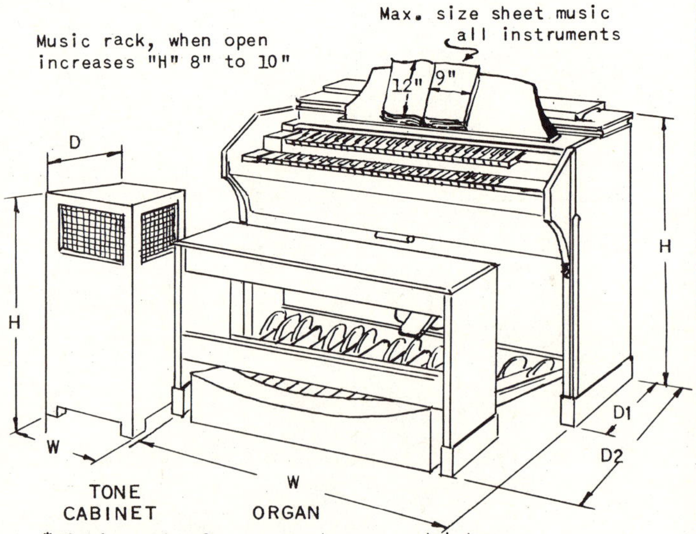
Max. size sheet music all instruments
Music rack, when open increases "H" 8" to 10"
12"
9"
D
H
H
W
W
D1
D2
TONE CABINET
ORGAN

*Within each mfr. any number or model tone box can be used with any organ.
**Dimensions are to nearest inch above fraction.
†These organs have their own speakers built in.

NOTE: Organ and tone box models listed are in current production. For best accustical results consult mfr. on organ and tone box placement. 3/4" conduit is required for cable from organ to tone cabinet if wiring is to be concealed.

ELECTRONIC ORGANS

STORAGE UNITS and CLOSET FRONTS

DEPTH	WIDTH	HEIGHT	MANUFACTURE	MATERIALS & FINISHES
2'-0"	2' 3' 4' 5'	7'-7½"	The Mengel Co.	Units are obtainable with plywood or composition board, fronts in varying grades and textures, ranging from paint grade to finished hardwood panels.
2'-3"	3' 4' 5'	7'-6"	Standard model manufactured locally.	
10" 1'-6" 1'-9" 2'-2"	3' 4' 5' 6'	7'-7½"	"Nova" Homosote Co.	These units are the same material for the front and accessories but the inner walls and backs are made of composition hard board.

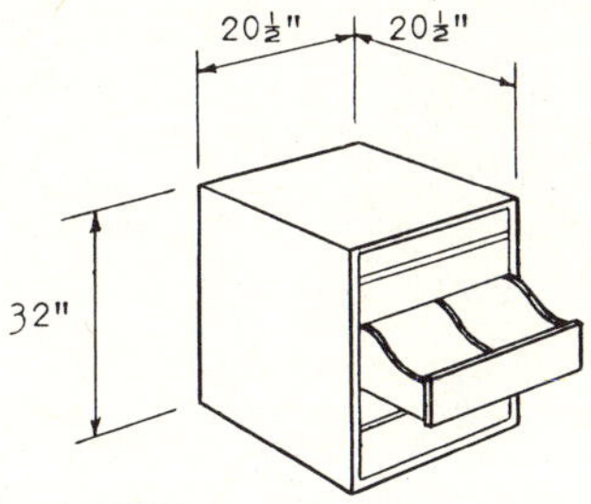

20½"
20½"
32"

TRAY CHEST

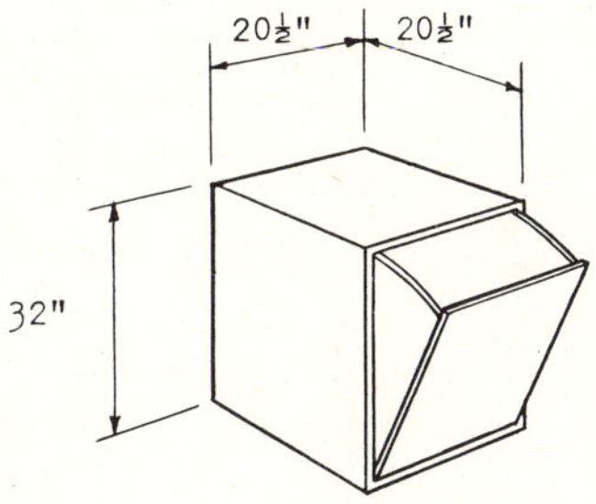

20½"
20½"
32"

HAMPER

WARDROBE CABINET
Available with or without shelves, vertical partitions or door front. For use as nonbearing walls with any combination of accessories shown.

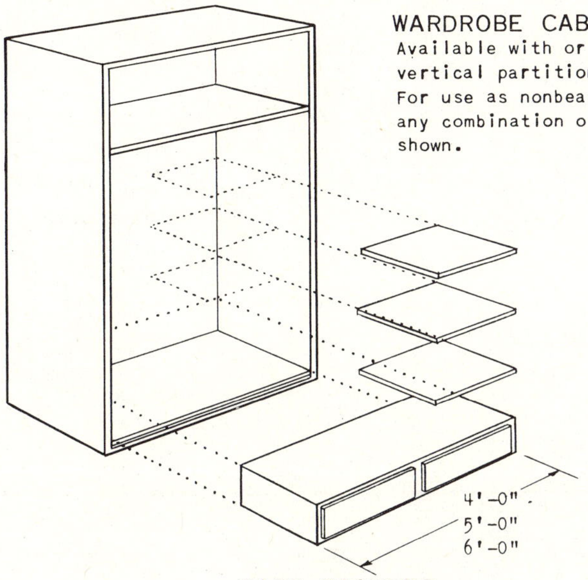

4'-0"
5'-0"
6'-0"

BASE DRAWERS

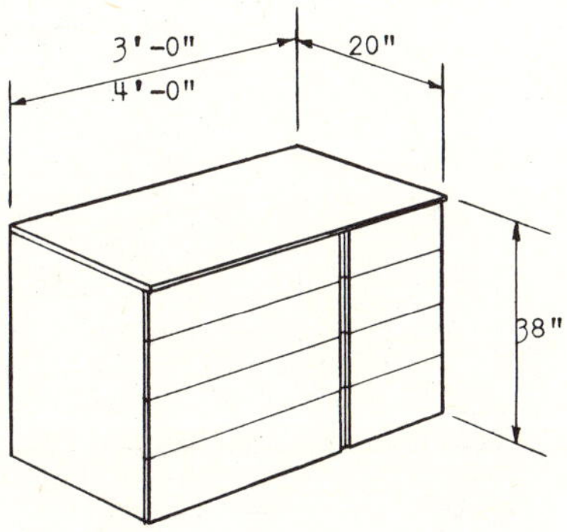

3'-0"
4'-0"
20"
38"

DRESSER

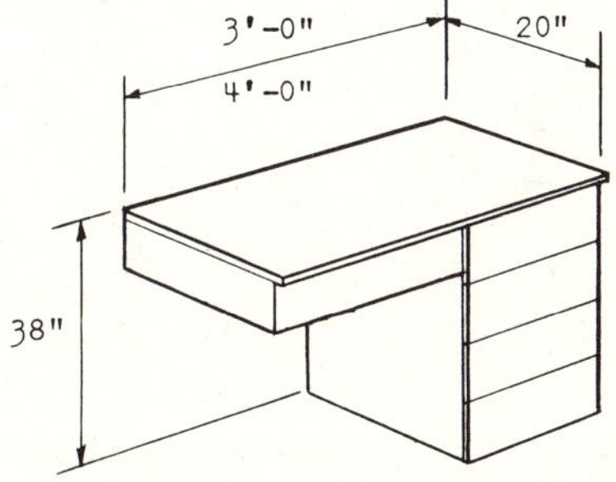

3'-0"
4'-0"
20"
38"

VANITY - DESK

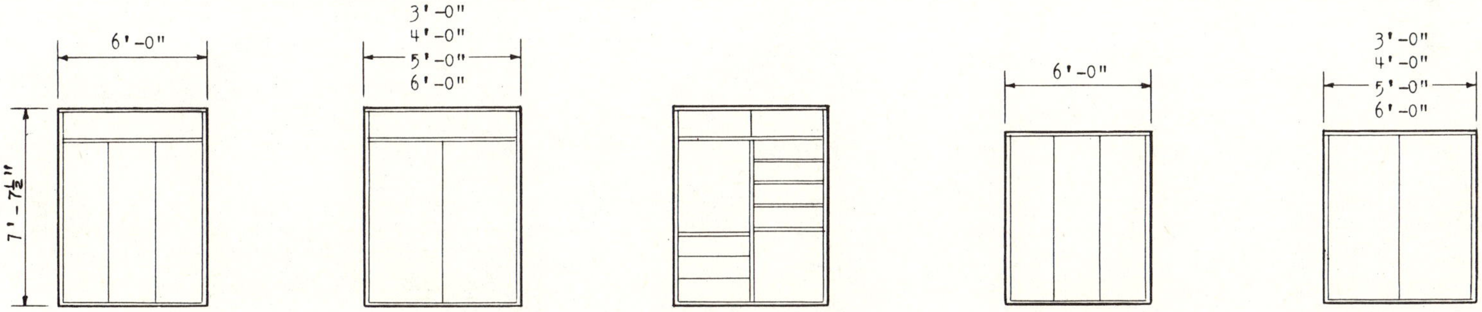

6'-0"
7'-7½"
3'-0"
4'-0"
5'-0"
6'-0"
6'-0"
3'-0"
4'-0"
5'-0"
6'-0"

3 DOOR SHELF OVER — 2 DOOR SHELF OVER — SHELVES & DRAWERS INTERCHANGEABLE — 3 DOOR — 2 DOOR

CLOSET FRONTS - May be used with standard stud-wall construction. Available in 3, 4, 6, foot widths with or without upper shelves.

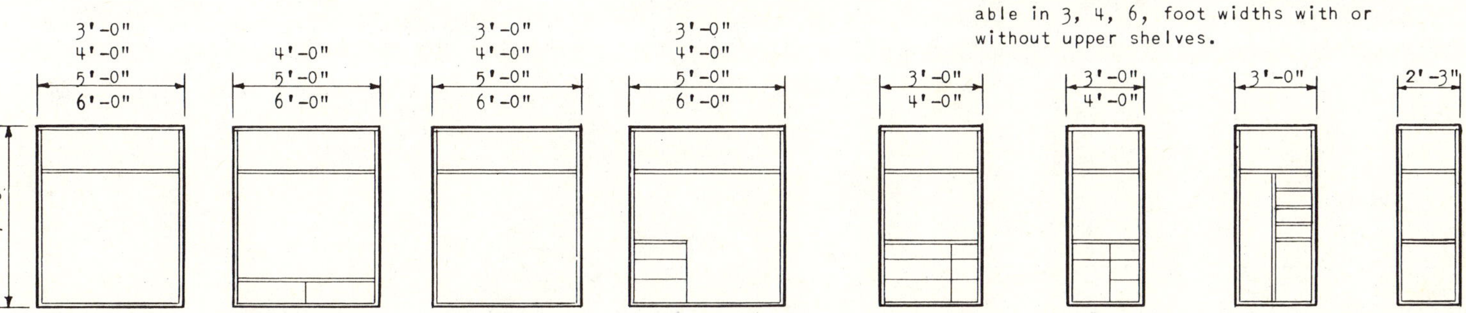

3'-0"
4'-0"
5'-0"
6'-0"
4'-0"
5'-0"
6'-0"
3'-0"
4'-0"
5'-0"
6'-0"
3'-0"
4'-0"
5'-0"
6'-0"
3'-0"
4'-0"
3'-0"
4'-0"
3'-0"
2'-3"
7'-6"

WARDROBE — WARDROBE LOWER DRAWERS — STORAGE CABINET — WARDROBE TRAY CHEST — DRESSER — VANITY-DESK (Without door fronts) — LINEN & STORAGE CLOSETS

STORAGE UNIT & CLOSET FRONTS

CLOTHES and BED CLOSETS

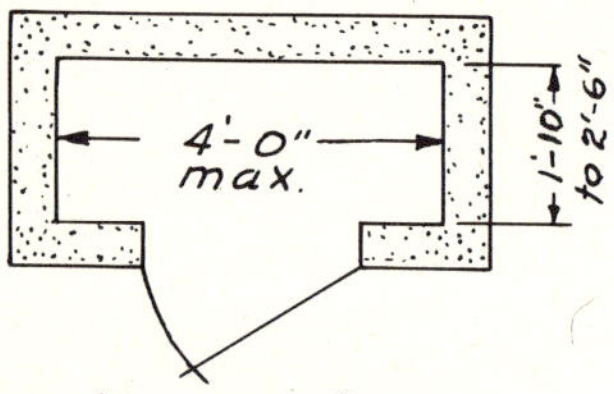
4'-0" max.
1'-10" to 2'-6"

swing door for closet less than 4'-0" with no space for sliding doors

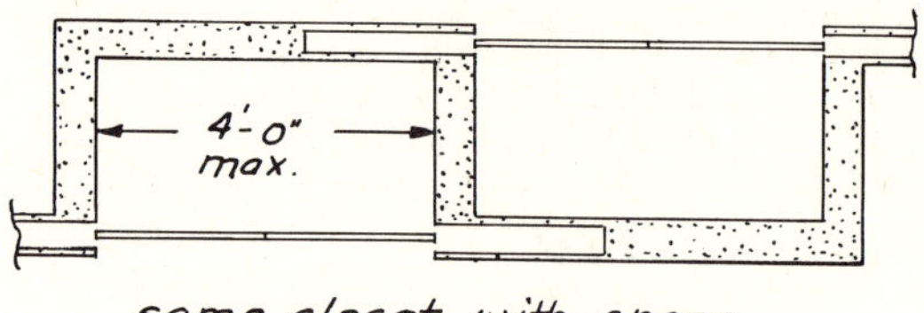
4'-0" max.

same closet with space for sliding doors.

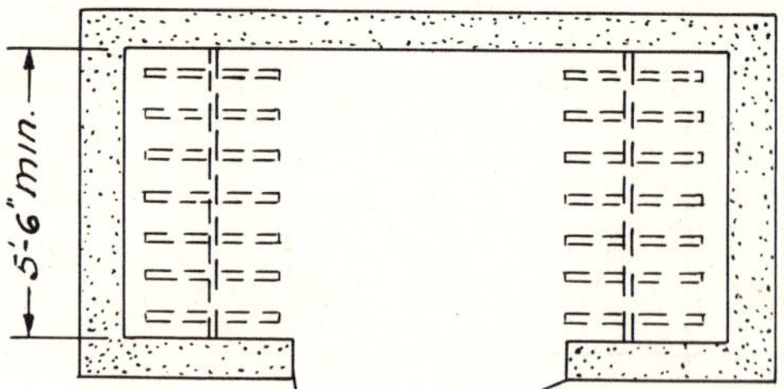
5'-6" min.

swing door for walk-in closet

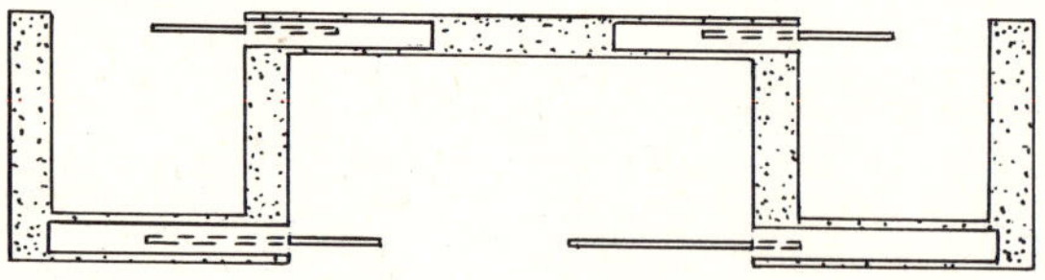

sliding doors with pockets doors up to 3'-0" wide

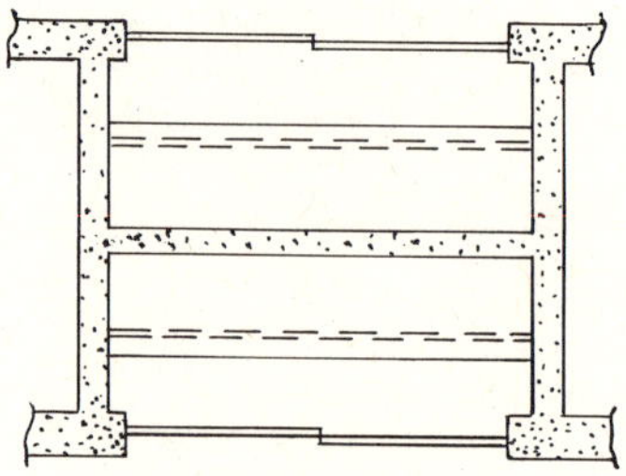

shallow closets back to back

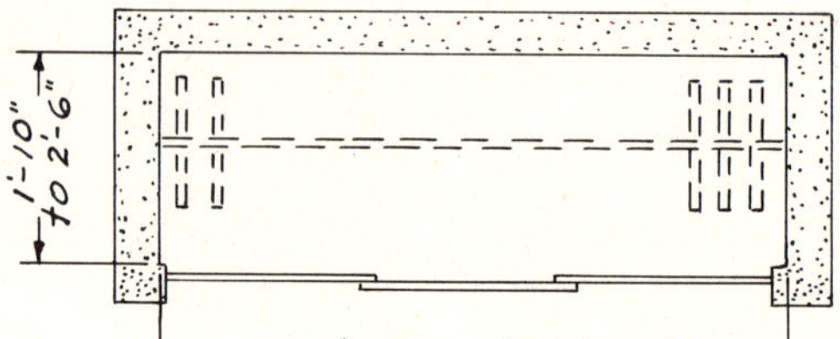
1'-10" to 2'-6"

2 doors - 4'-0" to 6'-0"
3 doors - 6'-0" to 9'-0
shallow closet with sliding doors

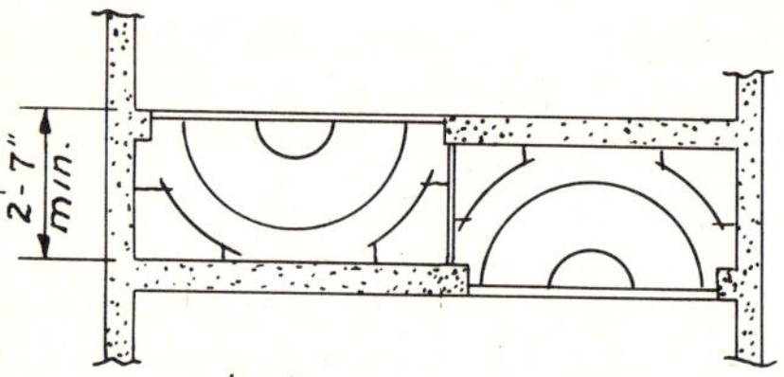
2'-7" min.

between rooms complete separation

REVOLVADOR

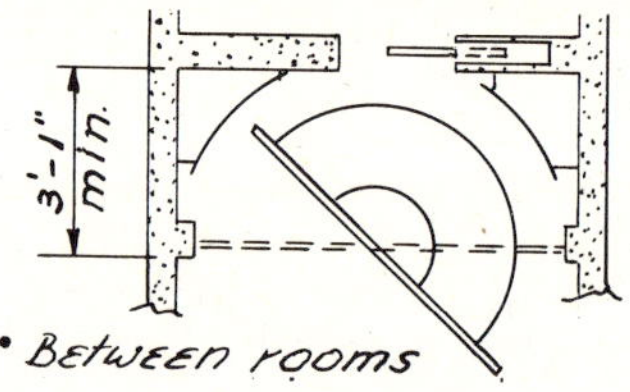
3'-1" min.

Between rooms

CLOTHES CLOSETS

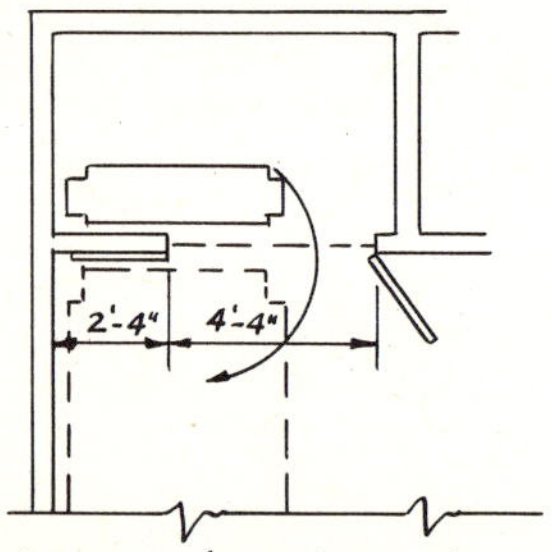
2'-4"
4'-4"

doors-width, two 2'-2" height-6'-8" or 7'-0"- bed pocket 2'-4" bed clearance 7'-6" wall to foot end of bed when lowered in room.

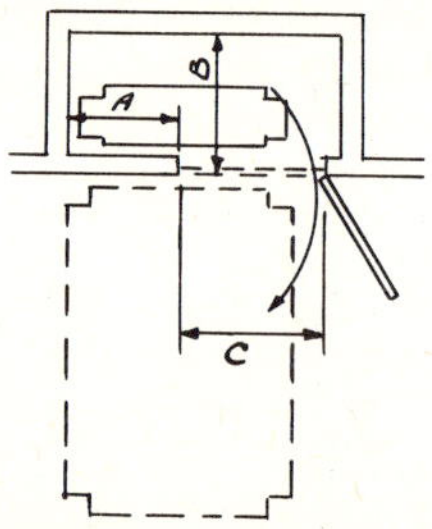
A
B
C

width of bed	A	B	C
4'-6"	2'-4"	3'-0"	3'-0"
4'-0"	2'-1"	2'-10"	2'-10"
3'-3"	1'-9"	2'-8"	2'-8"

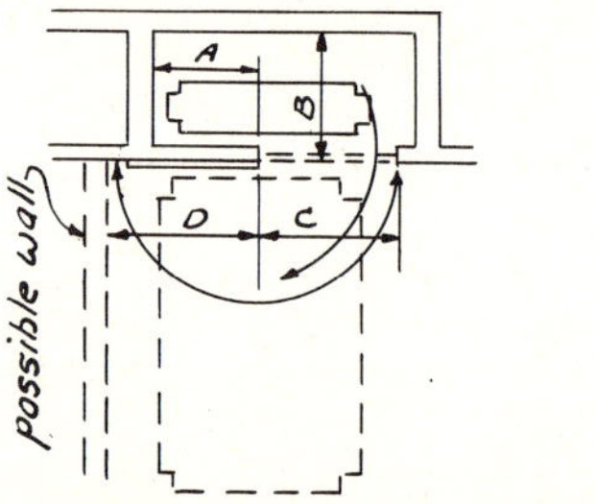
A
B
D
C
possible wall

width of bed	A	B	C	D
4'-6"	2'-4"	3'-1"	3'-0"	3'-2
4'-0"	2'-1"	2'-11"	2'-10"	3'-0"
3'-3"	1'-9"	2'-9"	2'-8"	2'-10"

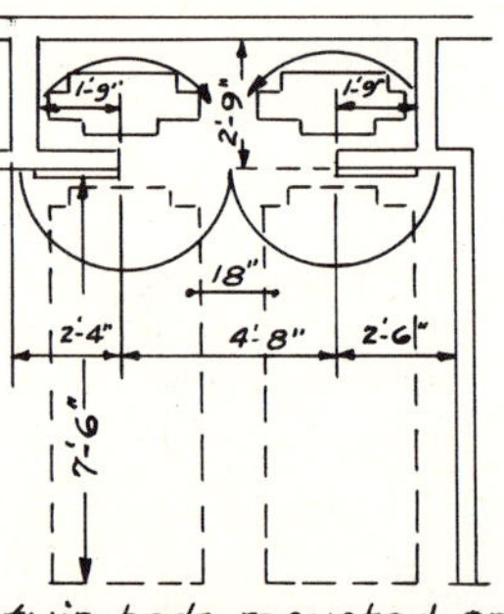
1'-9"
2'-9"
1'-9"
18"
2'-4"
4'-8"
2'-6"
7'-6"

twin beds mounted on opposite jambs and emerging through two doors.

PIVOT TYPES

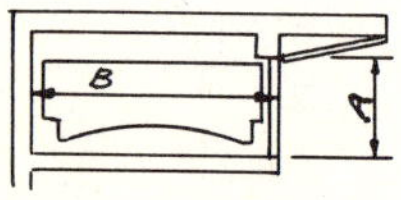
B
A

Bed	A	B
4'-6"	2'-2"	5'-0"
3'-3"	2'-2"	3'-9"

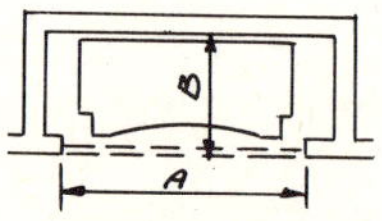
B
A

Bed	A	B
4'-6"	5'	2'-2"
3'-3"	4'	2'-2"

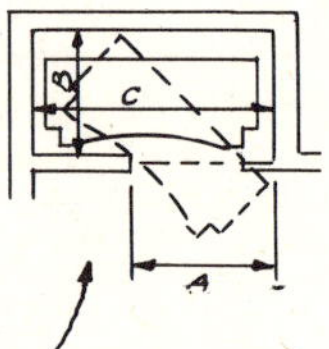
B
C
A

3'-0" door				2'-10" door			2'-8" door		
Bed	A	B	C	A	B	C	A	B	C
4'-6"	3'-0"	32"	61"	34"	34"	61"	32"	36"	61"
3'-3"	3'-0"	28"	47"	34"	29"	47"	32"	31"	47"

ROLLER TYPES

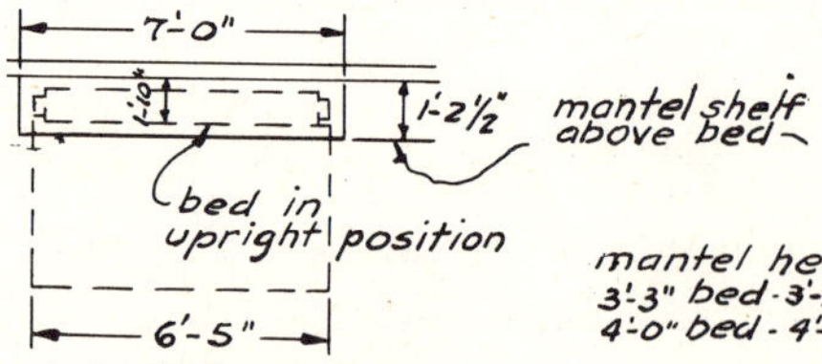
7'-0"
1'-10"
1'-2½"
montel shelf above bed
bed in upright position
6'-5"

mantel height for 3'-3" bed-3'-5" for 4'-0" bed - 4'-6"

SIDE BED

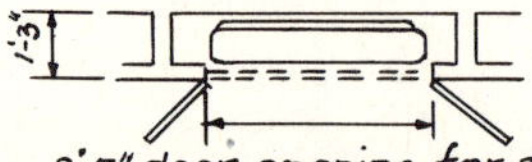
1'-3"

3'-7" door opening for 3'-3" bed-4'-10" door opening for 4'-6" bed.

ECONOMY RECESS

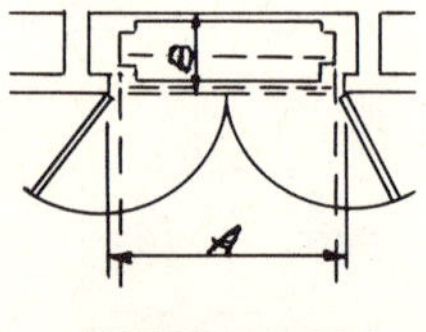
B
A

TYPE "A" Projects forward 9" when open

Bed	A	B
4'-6"	5'-0"	19"
4'-0"	4'-6"	19"
3'-3"	3'-9"	19"

TYPE "B" Does not project forward

Bed	A	B
4'-6"	4'-10"	17¼"
3'-3"	8'-7"	17¼"

RECESS TYPES

BED CLOSETS

Data by the Murphy Door Bed Co.

TRAYS & SHELVES, SHOE & HAT RACKS

1'-0"
1'-0"
1'-3" to 1'-5"
1'-2"
5/8
3/4
Usually 6'-8", also 6'-10" and 7'-0"
Drawer Guides
2"
TRAY HEIGHTS
Flat silver, 2" and 3"
Linen, doilies, luncheon sets, lace, 2"
Face towels, pillow cases, 8"-10"
Sheets, bath towels, table cloths, 1'-0"
Collars, socks, handkerchiefs, 3"
Sweaters and shirts 6" to 8"
Underwear, etc 4" to 6"
4'-0" ± usual. May be 4'-6" for men.
Drawer Guides
Lift hand holes

"A" SECTION ½ "A" ELEV. ½ "B" ELEV. "B" SECTION

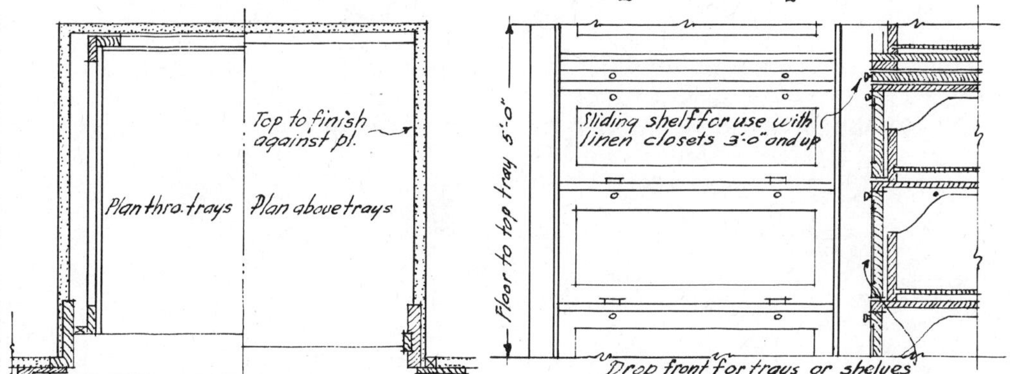
Top to finish against pl.
Plan thro. trays
Plan above trays
Floor to top tray 5'-0"
Sliding shelf for use with linen closets 3'-0" and up
Drop front for trays or shelves where doors are omitted.

"B" Plan similar

"A" PLAN Scale 3/4"=1'-0" ELEVATION SECTION

TRAYS & SHELVES

5'-11"

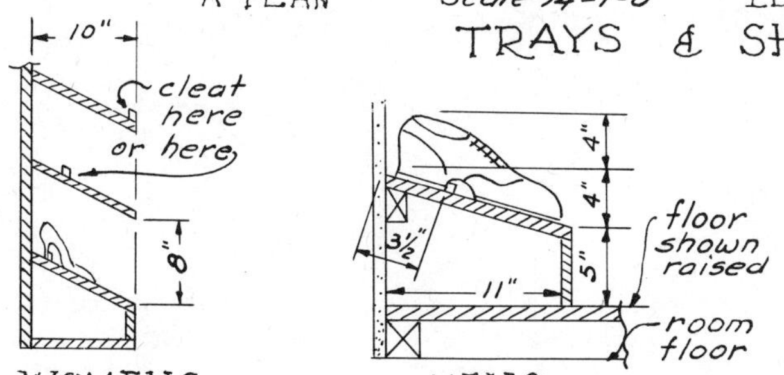
10"
cleat here or here
8"
4"
4"
3½"
5"
11"
floor shown raised
room floor

WOMENS MENS

SHOE RACKS Scale ½"=1'-0"

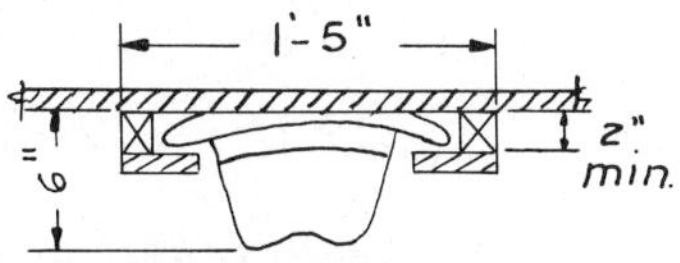
1'-5"
6"
2" min.

HAT RACK

all-shelf Closidor, other types available for bathroom, kitchen, buffet & wardrobe. All types made for standard doors & can be used for either right or left swing of door.

PERFORATED BOARD ACCESSORIES

PERFORATED BOARD ACCESSORIES

These sketches show some of the many fixtures and accessories available for use with perforated board. Although classified for a particular usage they may be used to suit the designers needs.

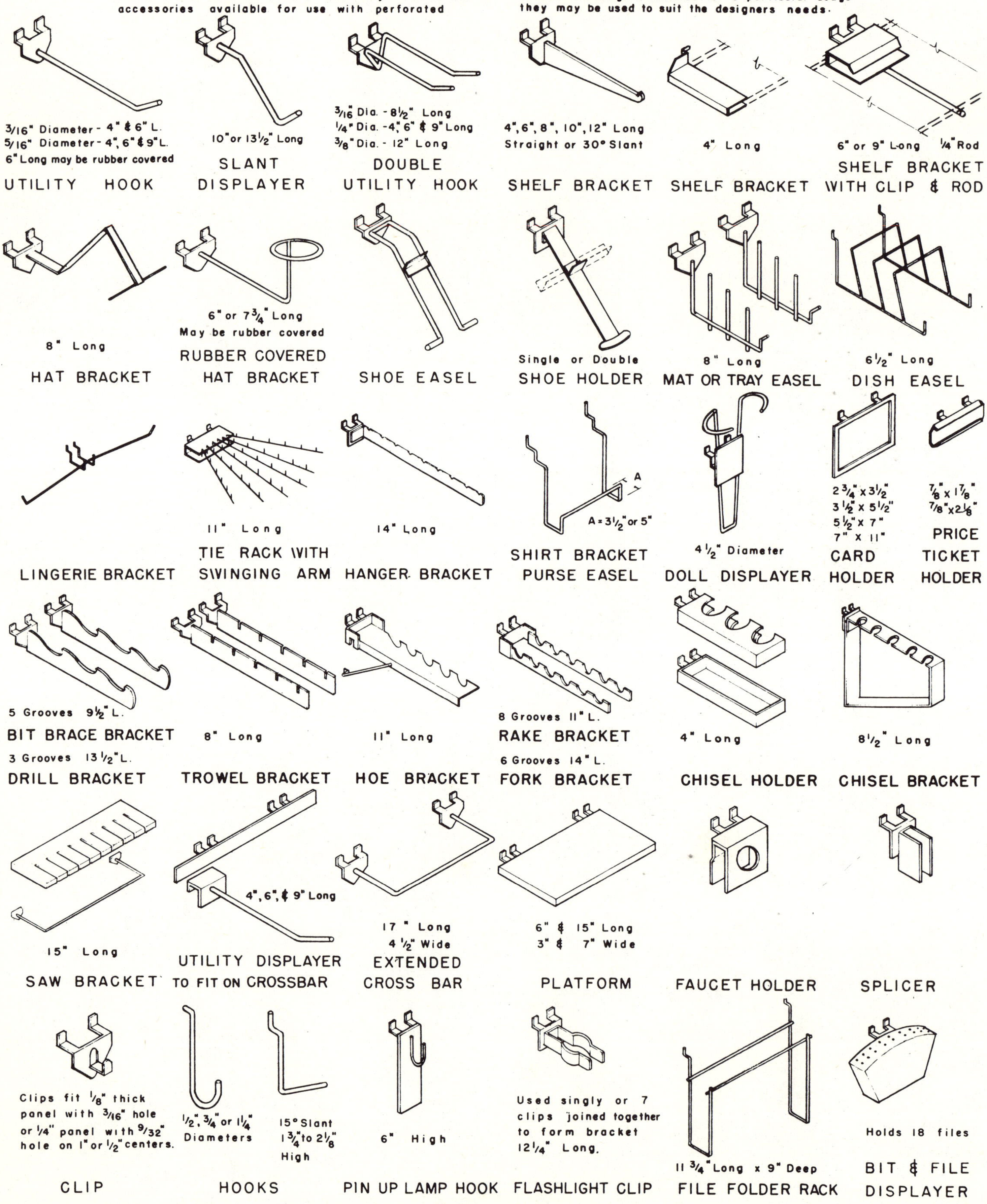
3/16" Diameter - 4" & 6" L.
5/16" Diameter - 4", 6" & 9" L.
6" Long may be rubber covered
UTILITY HOOK
10" or 13 1/2" Long
SLANT DISPLAYER
3/16" Dia. - 8 1/2" Long
1/4" Dia. - 4", 6" & 9" Long
3/8" Dia. - 12" Long
DOUBLE UTILITY HOOK
4", 6", 8", 10", 12" Long
Straight or 30° Slant
SHELF BRACKET
4" Long
SHELF BRACKET
6" or 9" Long
1/4" Rod
SHELF BRACKET WITH CLIP & ROD
8" Long
HAT BRACKET
6" or 7 3/4" Long
May be rubber covered
RUBBER COVERED HAT BRACKET
SHOE EASEL
Single or Double
SHOE HOLDER
8" Long
MAT OR TRAY EASEL
6 1/2" Long
DISH EASEL
LINGERIE BRACKET
11" Long
TIE RACK WITH SWINGING ARM
14" Long
HANGER BRACKET
A
A = 3 1/2" or 5"
SHIRT BRACKET
PURSE EASEL
4 1/2" Diameter
DOLL DISPLAYER
2 3/4" x 3 1/2"
3 1/2" x 5 1/2"
5 1/2" x 7"
7" x 11"
CARD HOLDER
7/8" x 1 7/8"
7/8" x 2 1/8"
PRICE TICKET HOLDER
5 Grooves 9 1/2" L.
BIT BRACE BRACKET
3 Grooves 13 1/2" L.
DRILL BRACKET
8" Long
TROWEL BRACKET
11" Long
HOE BRACKET
8 Grooves 11" L.
RAKE BRACKET
6 Grooves 14" L.
FORK BRACKET
4" Long
CHISEL HOLDER
8 1/2" Long
CHISEL BRACKET
15" Long
SAW BRACKET
4", 6", & 9" Long
UTILITY DISPLAYER TO FIT ON CROSSBAR
17" Long
4 1/2" Wide
EXTENDED CROSS BAR
6" & 15" Long
3" & 7" Wide
PLATFORM
FAUCET HOLDER
SPLICER
Clips fit 1/8" thick panel with 3/16" hole or 1/4" panel with 9/32" hole on 1" or 1/2" centers.
CLIP
1/2", 3/4" or 1 1/4" Diameters
15° Slant
1 3/4" to 2 1/8" High
HOOKS
6" High
PIN UP LAMP HOOK
Used singly or 7 clips joined together to form bracket 12 1/4" Long.
FLASHLIGHT CLIP
11 3/4" Long x 9" Deep
FILE FOLDER RACK
Holds 18 files
BIT & FILE DISPLAYER

CLOSET ACCESSORIES

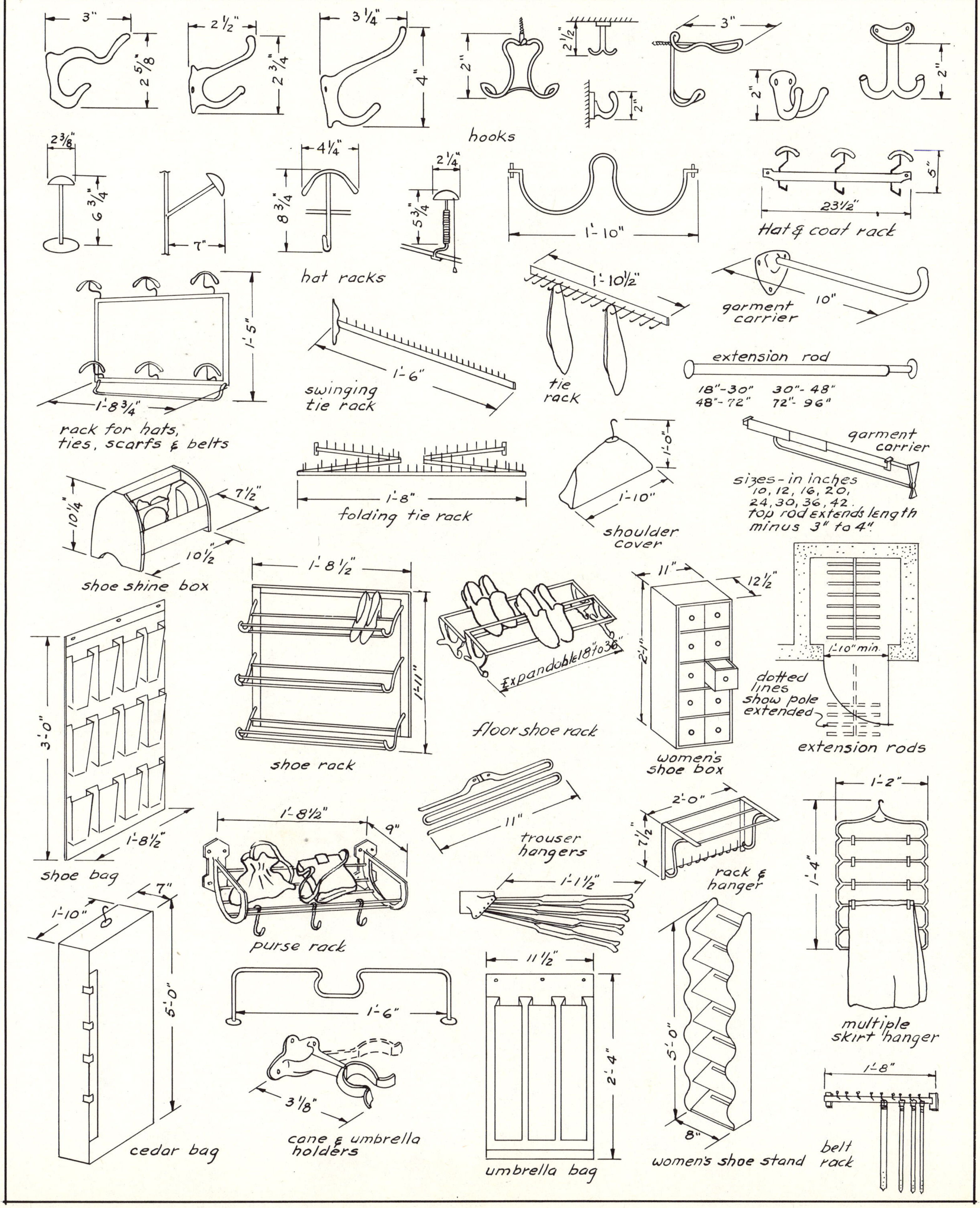

3"
2 5/8"
2 1/2"
2 3/4"
3 1/4"
4"
2"
2 1/2"
2"
3"
2"
2"
hooks
2 3/8"
6 3/4"
7"
4 1/4"
8 3/4"
2 1/4"
5 3/4"
hat racks
1'-10"
5"
23 1/2"
Hat & coat rack
1'-5"
1'-8 3/4"
rack for hats, ties, scarfs & belts
1'-6"
swinging tie rack
1'-10 1/2"
tie rack
10"
garment carrier
extension rod
18"-30" 30"-48"
48"-72" 72"-96"
1'-8"
folding tie rack
1'-0"
1'-10"
shoulder cover
garment carrier
sizes - in inches
10, 12, 16, 20,
24, 30, 36, 42.
top rod extends length
minus 3" to 4"
10 1/4"
7 1/2"
10 1/2"
shoe shine box
1'-8 1/2"
1'-11"
shoe rack
Expandable 18" to 36"
floor shoe rack
11"
12 1/2"
2'-1"
women's shoe box
1'-10" min.
dotted lines show pole extended
extension rods
3'-0"
1'-8 1/2"
shoe bag
1'-8 1/2"
9"
purse rack
11"
trouser hangers
2'-0"
7 1/2"
rack & hanger
1'-2"
1'-4"
multiple skirt hanger
1'-1 1/2"
1'-10"
7"
5'-0"
cedar bag
1'-6"
3 1/8"
cane & umbrella holders
11 1/2"
2'-4"
umbrella bag
5'-0"
8"
women's shoe stand
1'-8"
belt rack

GARAGE and CARPORT DETAILS

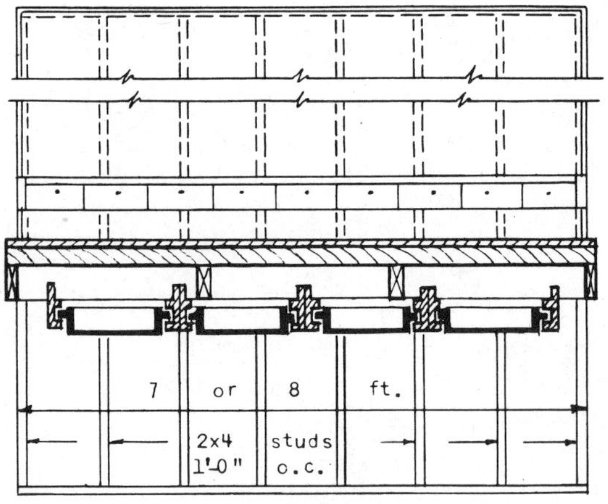
7
or
8
ft.
2x4
1'-0"
studs
o.c.

LONGITUDINAL SECTION

Scale: 3/8" = 1'-0"

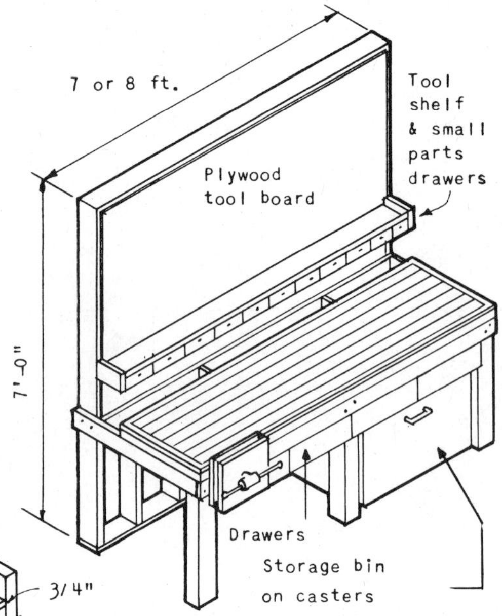
7 or 8 ft.
Tool shelf & small parts drawers
Plywood tool board
7'-0"
Drawers
Storage bin on casters

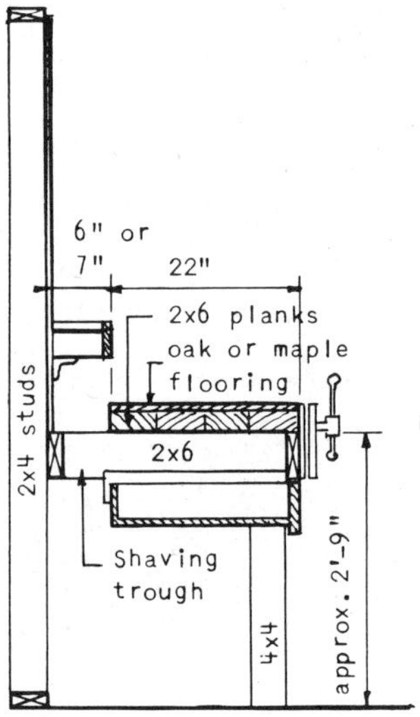
6" or 7"
22"
2x6 planks oak or maple flooring
2x4 studs
2x6
Shaving trough
4x4
approx. 2'-9"

VERTICAL SECTION

Scale: 3/8" = 1'-0"

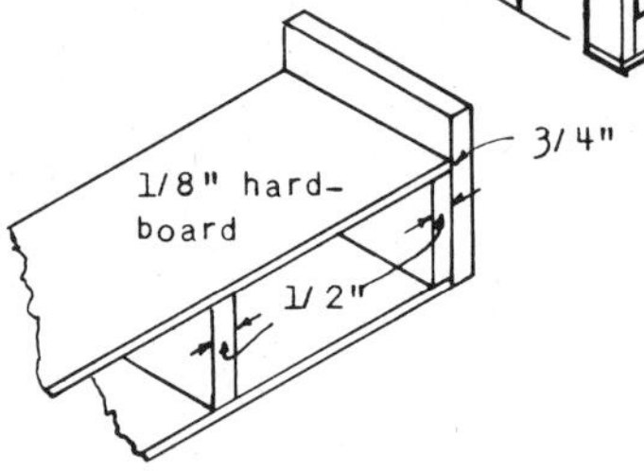
3/4"
1/8" hard-board
1/2"

TOOL SHELF

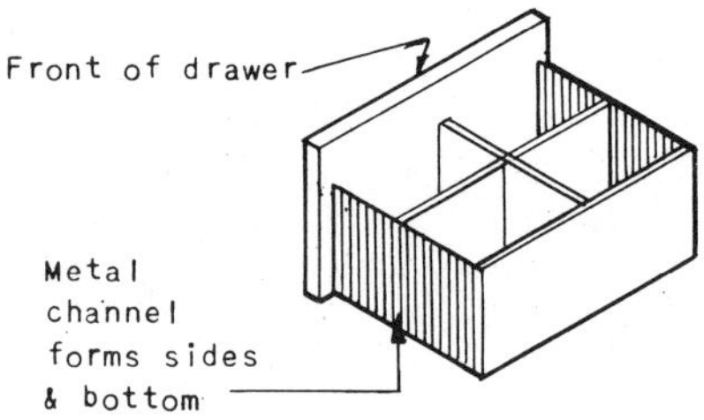
Front of drawer
Metal channel forms sides & bottom

SMALL PARTS DRAWERS

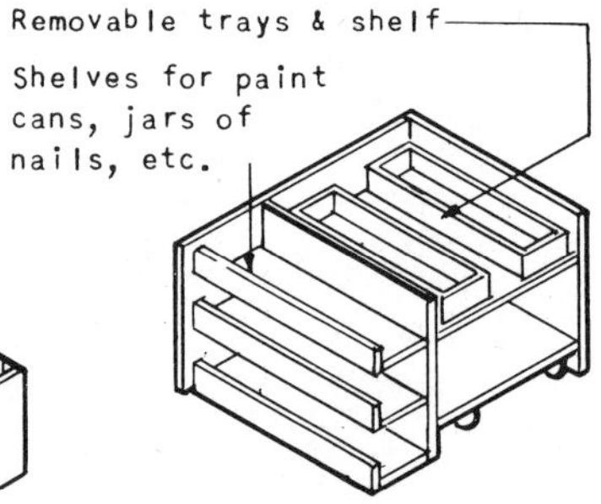
Removable trays & shelf
Shelves for paint cans, jars of nails, etc.

VIEW OF STORAGE BIN WITH FRONT REMOVED

WORKBENCH DETAILS

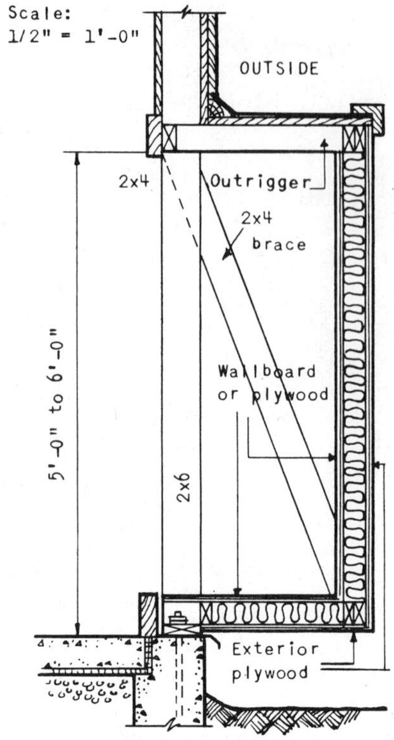
Scale: 1/2" = 1'-0"
OUTSIDE
2x4
Outrigger
2x4 brace
5'-0" to 6'-0"
Wallboard or plywood
2x6
Exterior plywood

CANTILEVERED STORAGE UNIT

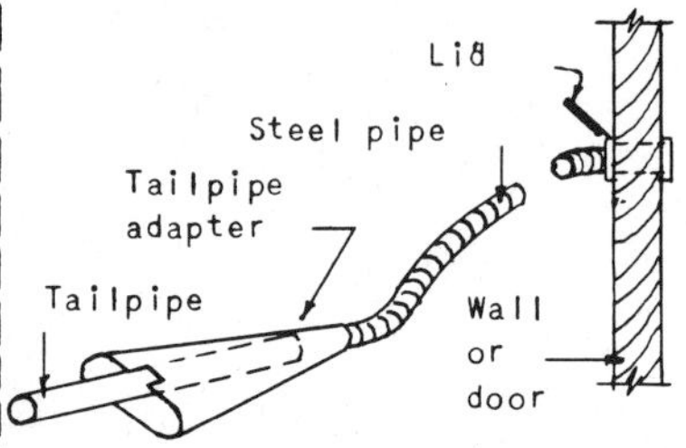
Lid
Steel pipe
Tailpipe adapter
Tailpipe
Wall or door

AUTOMOBILE EXHAUST

HEATING a greenhouse or planting bed may be done by extending the heating system of the main house or installing electric, oil or bottled gas space heaters. A central steam or hot water system can be extended to a greenhouse which is within 125 ft. of the main boiler. If artificial gas is used in a hot air system, the greenhouse should not be open to the furnace room.
Cool greenhouses are best for amateur use (smaller fuel bill, insects & diseases easier to control) - 40° to 50°
Warm greenhouses - 60°
ORIENTATION - Planting bed should face directly south.
VENTILATION - Ventilating a greenhouse is as important as heating it. Ventilators at sides and top provide flow of air.
1/4 to 1/3 of the glass area should be operable for proper ventilation.

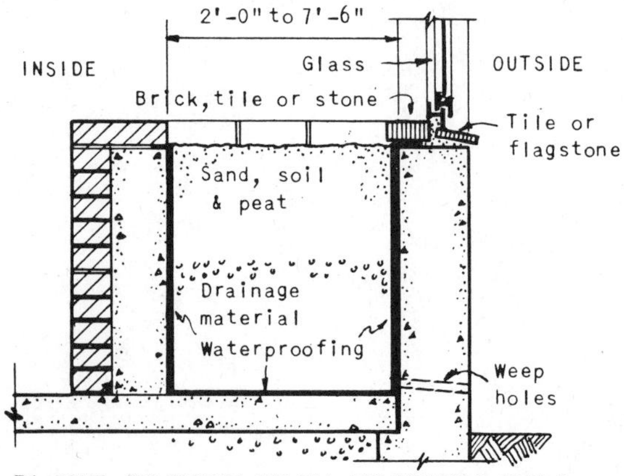
2'-0" to 7'-6"
INSIDE
Glass
OUTSIDE
Brick, tile or stone
Tile or flagstone
Sand, soil & peat
Drainage material
Waterproofing
Weep holes

PLANT POCKET WITH MASONRY WALL

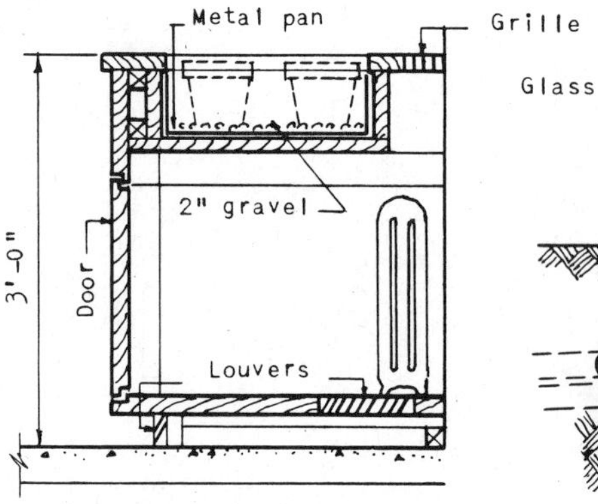
Metal pan
Grille
2" gravel
3'-0"
Door
Louvers

POTTING BENCH

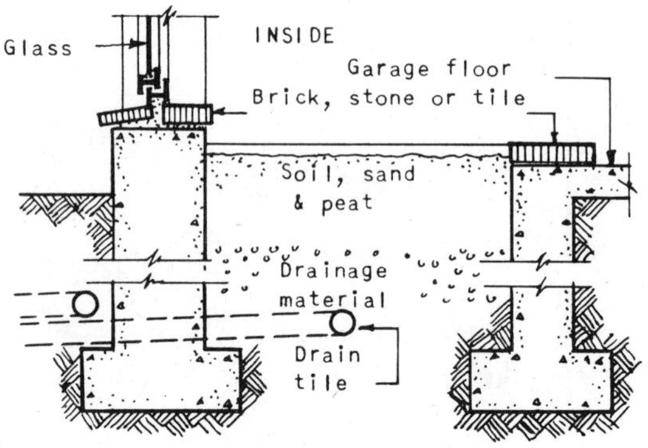
Glass
INSIDE
Garage floor
Brick, stone or tile
Soil, sand & peat
Drainage material
Drain tile

PLANT POCKET AT FLOOR LEVEL

Scale: 1/2" = 1'-0"

PLANTING BEDS IN GARAGES

HEIGHTS of SCHOOL FIXTURES

HEIGHTS OF FIXTURES AND EQUIPMENT

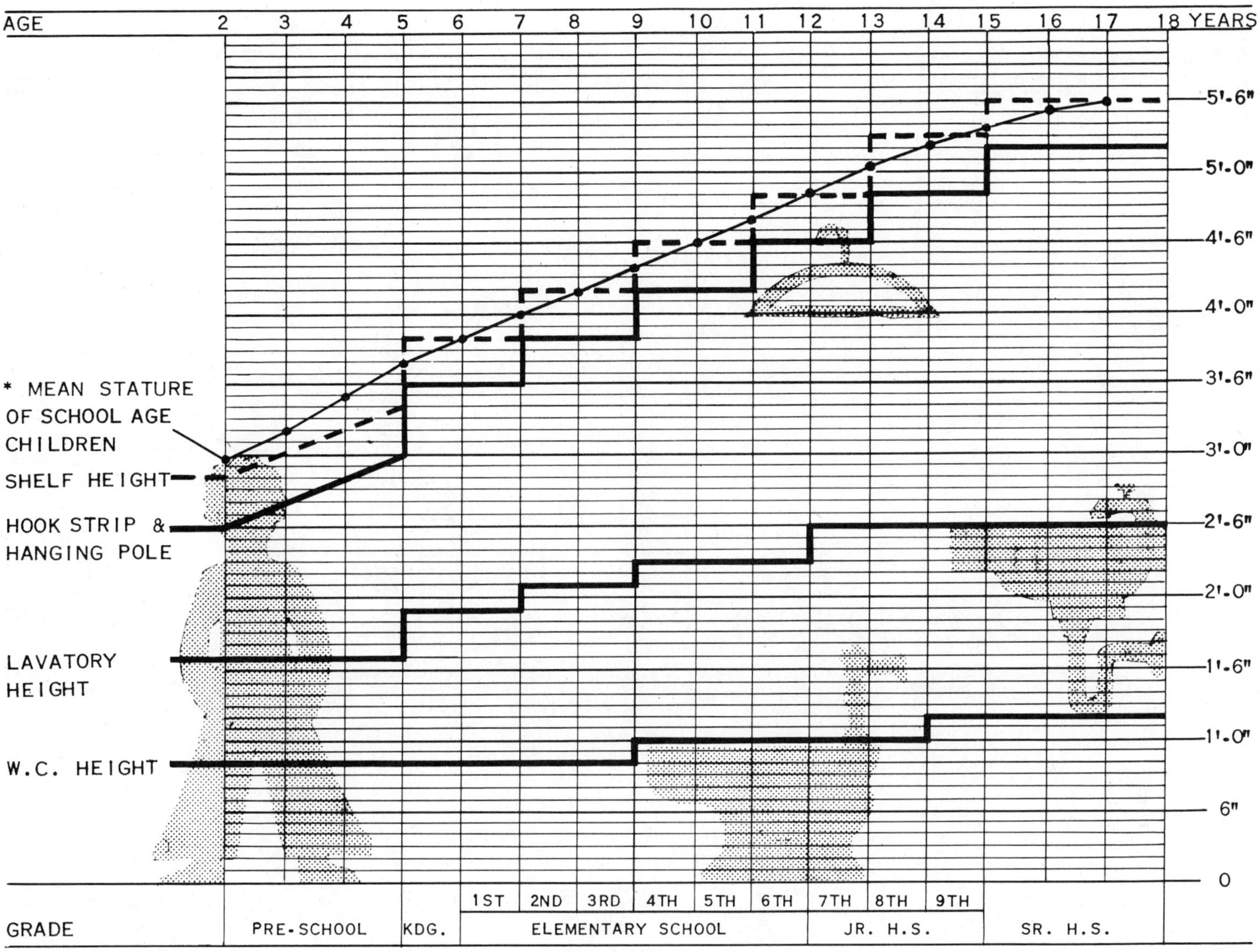
AGE
2 3 4 5 6 7 8 9 10 11 12 13 14 15 16 17 18 YEARS
5'-6"
5'-0"
4'-6"
4'-0"
3'-6"
3'-0"
2'-6"
2'-0"
1'-6"
1'-0"
6"
0
* MEAN STATURE OF SCHOOL AGE CHILDREN
SHELF HEIGHT
HOOK STRIP & HANGING POLE
LAVATORY HEIGHT
W.C. HEIGHT
GRADE
PRE-SCHOOL
KDG.
1ST 2ND 3RD 4TH 5TH 6TH 7TH 8TH 9TH
ELEMENTARY SCHOOL
JR. H.S.
SR. H.S.

* MEASUREMENTS BY U.S. DEPARTMENT OF HEALTH, EDUCATION, AND WELFARE

DESK AND SEAT SIZES BY GRADES

SEAT HEIGHTS	10"	11"	12"	13"	14"	15"	16"	17"	18"
DESK HEIGHTS	20"	20" 21"	21" 22"	22" 23"	24" 25"	25" 26"	26" 27"	27" 29"	28" 30"
% BY GRADES	%	%	%	%	%	%	%	%	%
KINDERGARTEN	20	60	20						
1ST GRADE		20	50	30					
2ND GRADE		10	40	50					
3RD GRADE			20	60	20				
4TH GRADE			10	40	50				
5TH GRADE				20	60	20			
6TH GRADE					30	40	30		
7TH GRADE					10	40	50		
8TH GRADE						20	40	40	
JUNIOR HIGH SCHOOL							40	50	10
SENIOR HIGH SCHOOL							30	50	20
ADULT							20	50	30

STATISTICS BY NORCOR MANUFACTURING COMPANY

CHILDREN'S FURNITURE, FIXTURES and EQUIPMENT

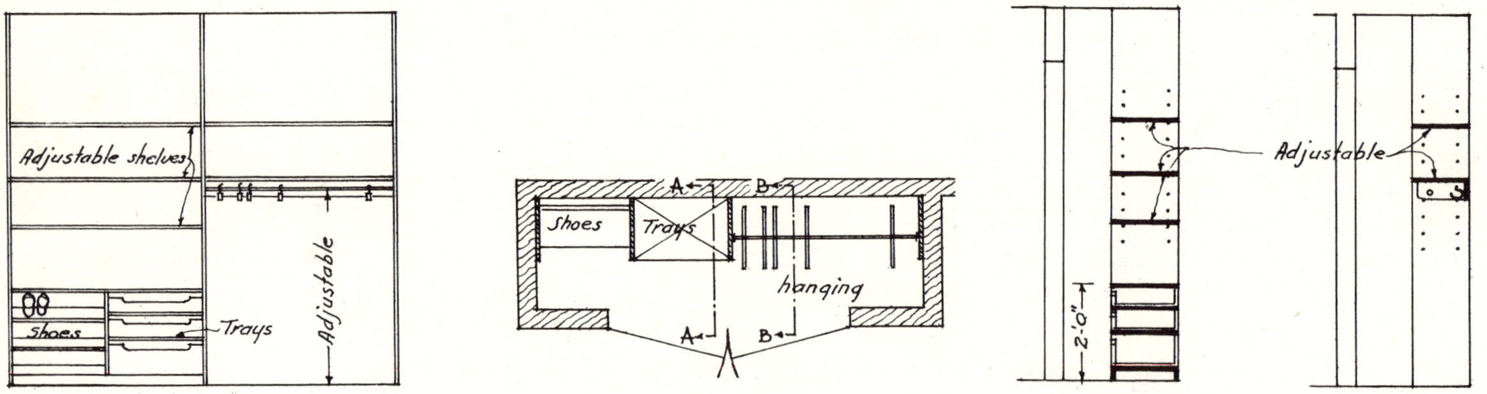

Adjustable shelves
Shoes
Trays
Adjustable
Shoes
Trays
hanging
A
B
2'-0"
Adjustable

ELEVATION PLAN SECTION A-A SECTION B-B

TYPICAL CLOTHES CLOSET
adjustable for any age
scale: ¼" = 1'-0"

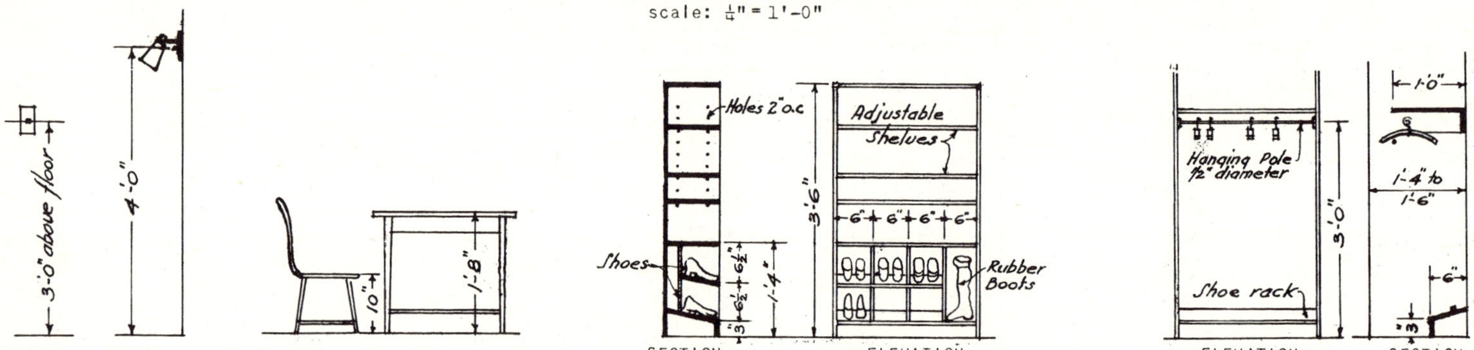

3'-0" above floor
4'-0"
10"
1'-8"
Holes 2" o.c.
Shoes
Adjustable Shelves
3'-6"
6" 6" 6" 6"
6½"
6½"
1'-4"
3"
Rubber Boots
Hanging Pole ½" diameter
Shoe rack
3'-0"
1'-0"
1'-4" to 1'-6"
6"
3"

SWITCH LIGHT CHAIR & TABLE

SECTION ELEVATION
BOOK SHELVES WITH SHOE & BOOT RACK UNDER

ELEVATION SECTION
HANGING CLOSET

SIZES FOR 1 YEAR TO 5 YEARS
scale: ⅜" = 1'-0"

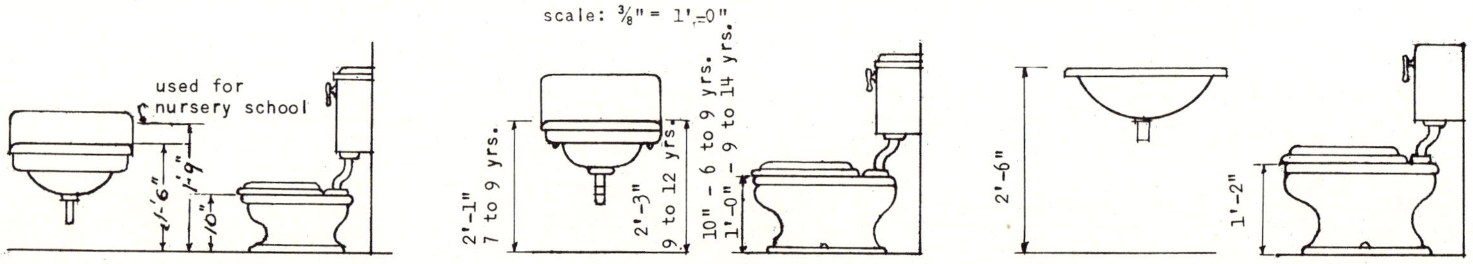

used for nursery school
1'-9"
1'-6"
10"
2'-1" 7 to 9 yrs.
2'-3" 9 to 12 yrs.
10" - 6 to 9 yrs.
1'-0" - 9 to 14 yrs.
2'-6"
1'-2"

to 6 years 6 to 12 years 12 years & over

PLUMBING FIXTURES
scale: ⅜" = 1'-0"

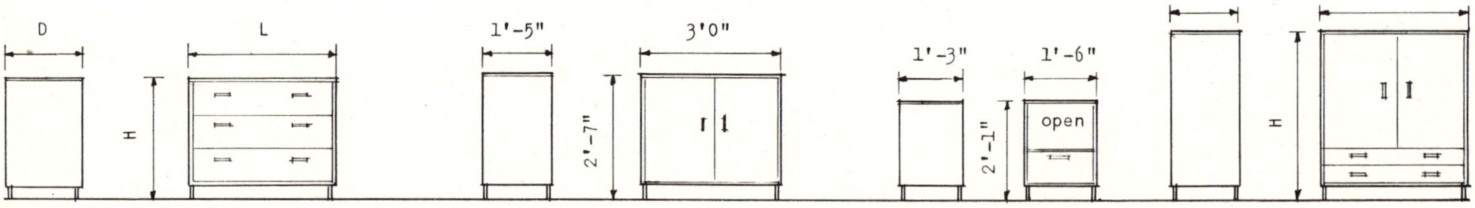

D
L
H
1'-5"
3'0"
2'-7"
1'-3"
1'-6"
open
2'-1"
D
L
H

CHEST	L	D	H
junior	1'-6"	1'-5"	2'-7"
3-drawer	3'-0"	1'-5"	2'-7"
5-drawer min:	2'-6½"	1'-4½"	3'-4"
max:	2'-10"	1'-6"	3'-11"

Bookcase same size as 3-drawer chest; top 2 shelves open, bottom shelf has hinged front.

CHESTS

Left half has 3 sliding drawers; right half is all wardrobe.

WARDROBE

scale: ¼" = 1'-0"

Top part open; 1 drawer in bottom

NIGHT TABLE

L = 2'-6½" to 3'-3"
H = 3'-7¾" to 4'-3"
D = 1'-4½" to 1'-5¾"

Arrangement and number of drawers and wardrobe sections vary.

CHIFFEROBE

Furniture data checked by Younger Set Interiors, Inc., N.Y.C., and Youthmart, Inc., N.Y.C.

CHILDREN'S FURNITURE, FIXTURES and EQUIPMENT

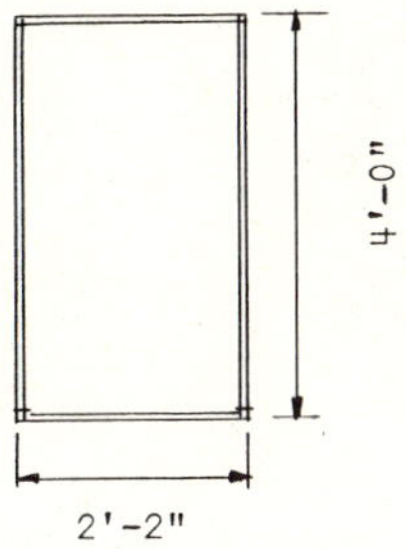
4'-0"
2'-2"

¾ SIZE CRIB

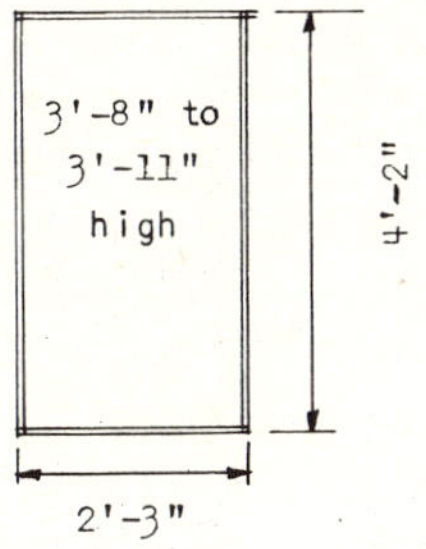
3'-8" to
3'-11"
high
4'-2"
2'-3"

CRIB

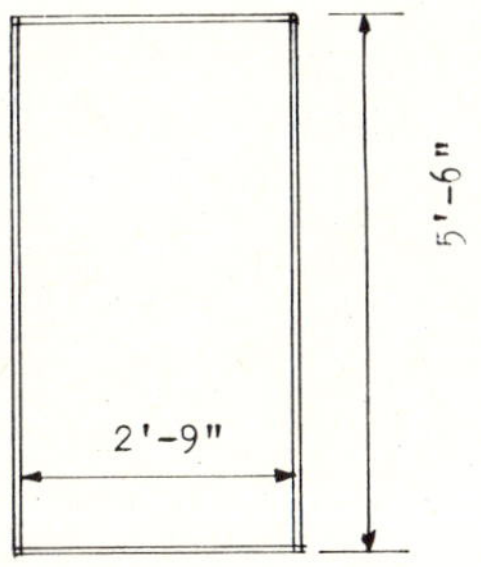
5'-6"
2'-9"

YOUTH BED

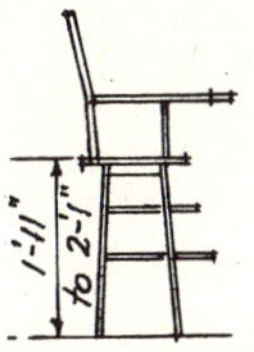
1'-11" to 2'-1"

HIGH CHAIR

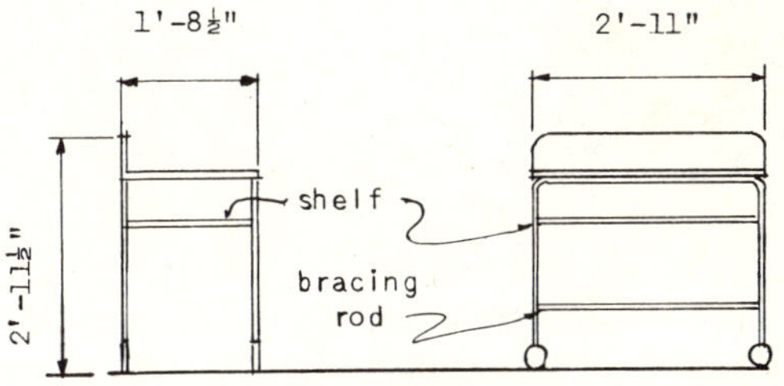
1'-8½"
2'-11"
shelf
bracing
rod
2'-11½"

BASSINET

Sizes given are mattress sizes.

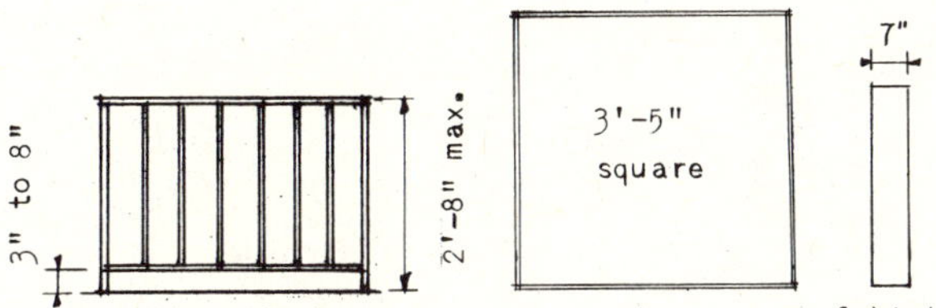
3" to 8"
2'-8" max.
3'-5"
square
7"

elevation plan folded

PLAY PEN

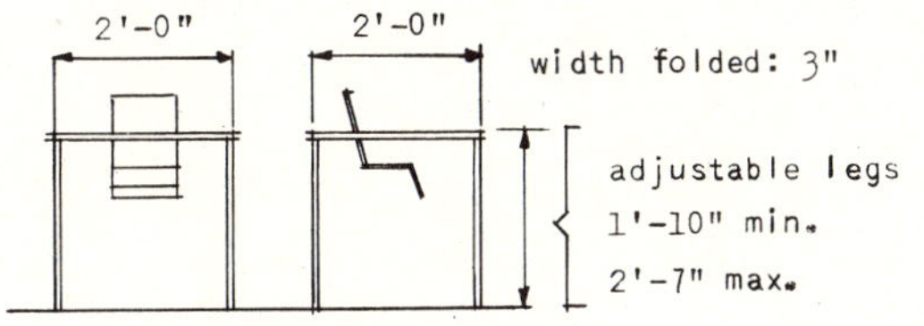
2'-0"
2'-0"
width folded: 3"
adjustable legs
1'-10" min.
2'-7" max.

FEEDING TABLE

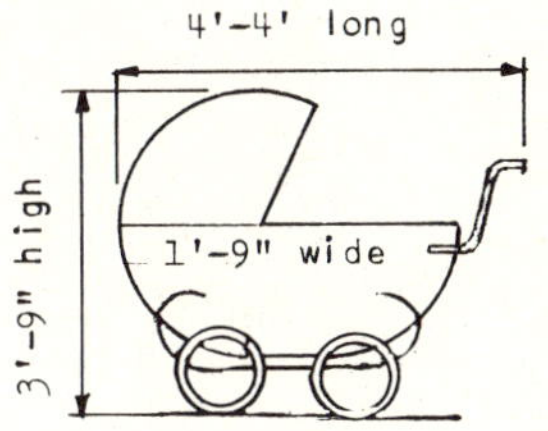
4'-4' long
3'-9" high
1'-9" wide

BABY CARRIAGE

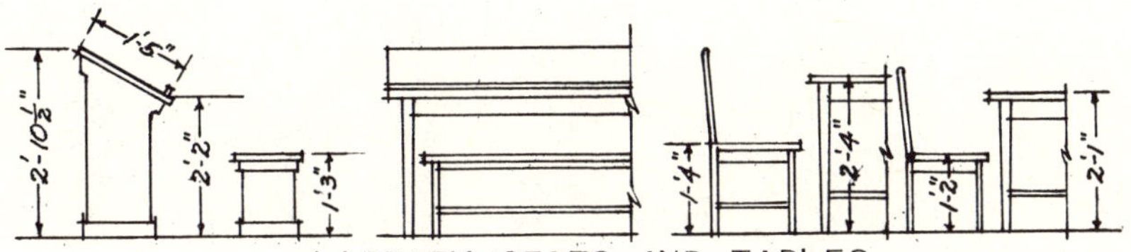
1'-5"
2'-10½"
2'-2"
1'-3"
1'-4"
2'-4"
1'-2"
2'-1"

LIBRARY SEATS AND TABLES

Height to seat:
Infants: 8½"
Juveniles: 11"-1'-1"
Youths: 1'-3"

ROCKERS

8" to 16" in
2" increments

CHAIR

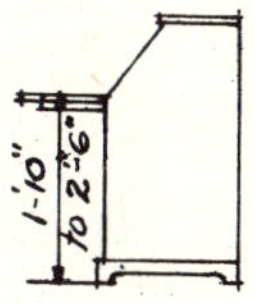
1'-10" to 2'-6"

DESK

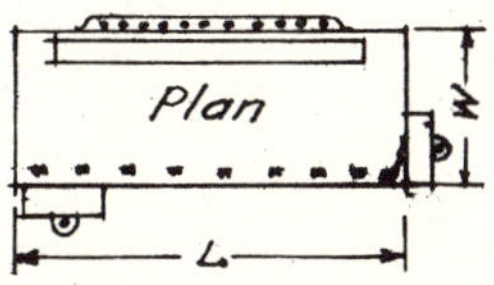
Plan
W
L

add 6" for overall.
*adult size.

L	W	H
*78"	24"	34"
51"	20"	33"
48"	18"	32"
42"	22"	32"
40"	16"	28"

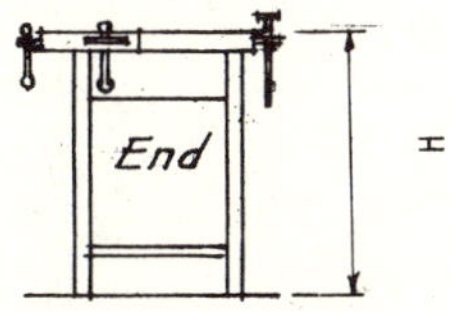
End
H

WORK BENCHES

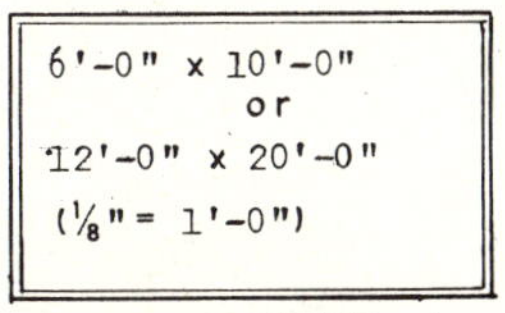
6'-0" x 10'-0"
or
12'-0" x 20'-0"
(⅛" = 1'-0")

NOTE: may be built at home to any size.

SAND BOX

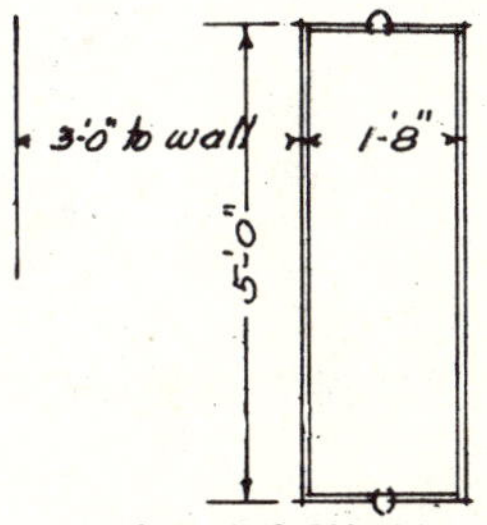
3'-0" to wall
1'-8"
5'-0"

TABLE HOCKEY

1'-10"
Max.
8"
8"
3'-3" max.
6'-0" Max.
"x"
1'-8" to 2'-4"

Frame size "x"
14" to 8 yrs.
16" to 12 yrs.
18" to 16 yrs.
20" & 22", adult

BICYCLES

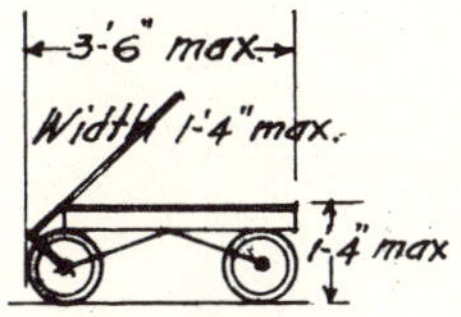
3'-6" max.
Width 1'-4" max.
1'-4" max

WAGON

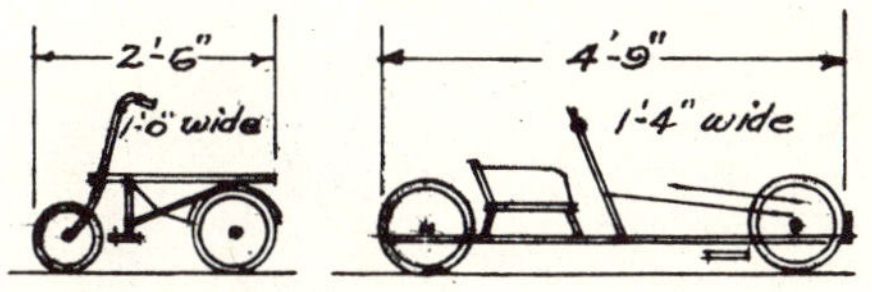
2'-6"
1'-0" wide
4'-9"
1'-4" wide

KIDDIE CAR

scale: ¼" = 1'-0"

9'-0" long, 20 bicycles
4'-6" long, 10 bicycles

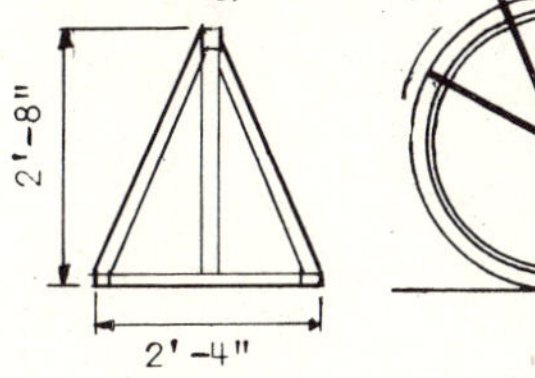
2'-8"
2'-4"

METAL RACK

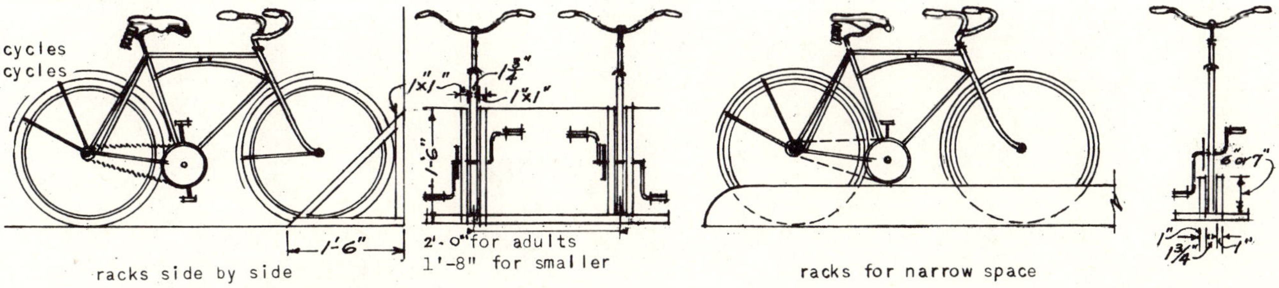
1"x1"
1¾"
1"x1"
1'-6"
1'-6"
2'-0" for adults
1'-8" for smaller
6" or 7"
1"
1¾"
1"

racks side by side

racks for narrow space

RACKS FOR BICYCLES

scale: ⅜" = 1'-0"

Furniture data checked by Younger Set Interiors, Inc., N.Y.C., and Youthmart, Inc., N.Y.C.

KITCHEN EQUIPMENT and UTENSILS

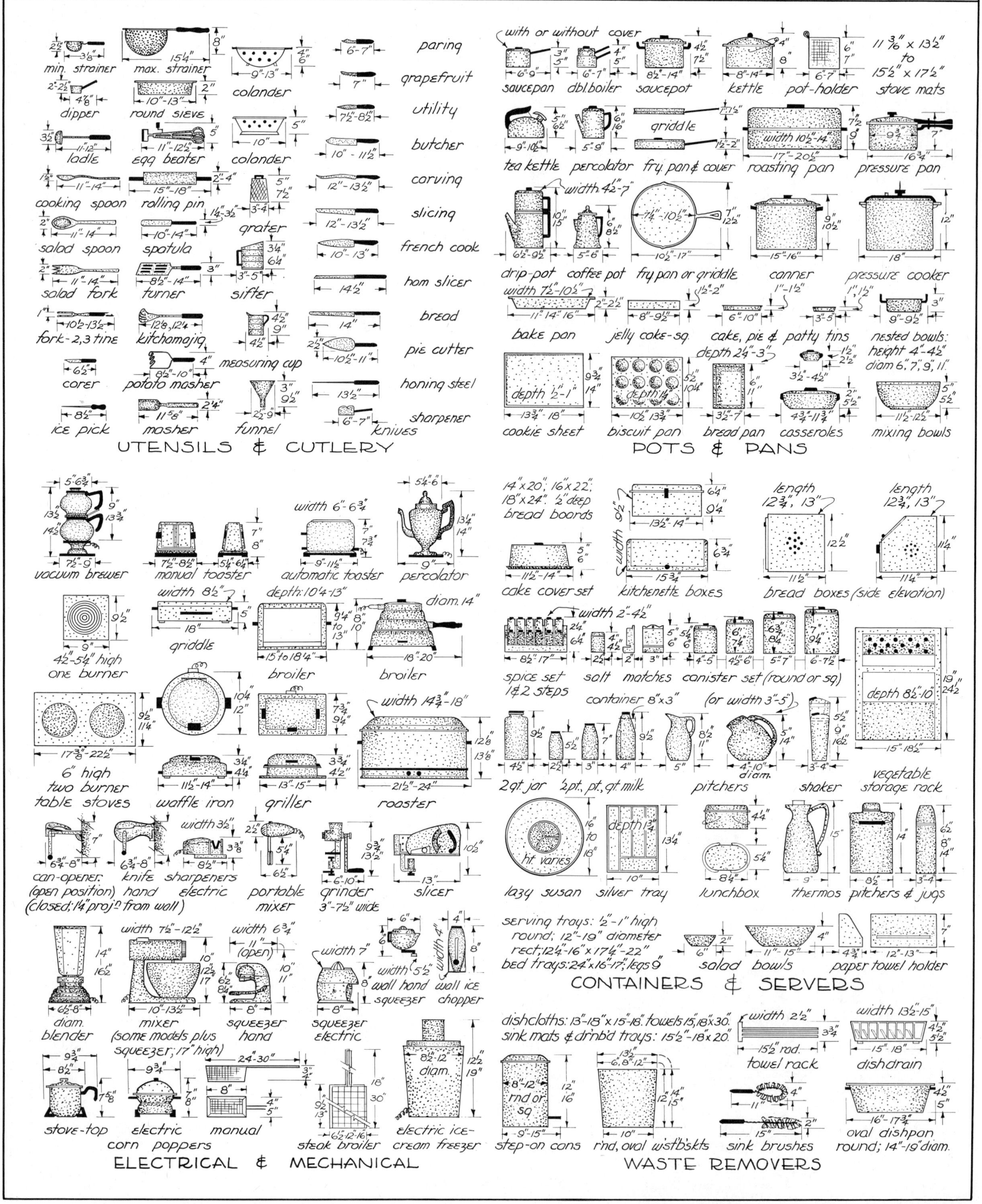
min. strainer
max. strainer
colander
paring
grapefruit
utility
butcher
carving
slicing
french cook
ham slicer
bread
pie cutter
honing steel
sharpener
knives
dipper
round sieve
ladle
egg beater
cooking spoon
rolling pin
grater
salad spoon
spatula
salad fork
turner
sifter
fork-2,3 tine
kitchamajig
measuring cup
corer
potato masher
ice pick
masher
funnel
UTENSILS & CUTLERY
with or without cover
saucepan
dbl. boiler
saucepot
kettle
pot-holder
11 3/16" x 13½" to 15½" x 17½" stove mats
tea kettle
percolator
griddle
fry pan & cover
roasting pan
pressure pan
drip-pot
coffee pot
fry pan or griddle
canner
pressure cooker
bake pan
jelly cake-sq.
cake, pie & patty tins
nested bowls: height 4"-4½" diam 6", 7", 9", 11"
cookie sheet
biscuit pan
bread pan
casseroles
mixing bowls
POTS & PANS
vacuum brewer
manual toaster
automatic toaster
percolator
4½"-5¼" high one burner
griddle
broiler
broiler
6" high two burner table stoves
waffle iron
griller
roaster
can-opener (open position) (closed; 1¼" projn from wall)
knife sharpeners hand electric
portable mixer
grinder 3"-7½" wide
slicer
blender
mixer (some models plus squeezer; 17" high)
squeezer hand
squeezer electric
wall hand squeezer
wall ice chopper
stove-top electric manual corn poppers
steak broiler
electric ice-cream freezer
ELECTRICAL & MECHANICAL
14"x20", 16"x22", 18"x24", ½" deep bread boards
cake cover set
kitchenette boxes
bread boxes (side elevation)
spice set 1&2 steps
salt
matches
canister set (round or sq.)
2 qt. jar
½ pt., pt., qt. milk
pitchers
shaker
vegetable storage rack
lazy susan
silver tray
lunchbox
thermos
pitchers & jugs
serving trays: ½"-1" high round; 12"-19" diameter rect; 12¼"-16" x 17¼"-22"
bed trays: 24" x 16"-17"; legs 9"
salad bowls
paper towel holder
CONTAINERS & SERVERS
dishcloths: 13"-18" x 15"-18". towels 15, 18" x 30".
sink mats & drnbd trays: 15½"-18" x 20".
towel rack
dishdrain
step-on cans
rnd, oval wstb'skts
sink brushes
oval dishpan round; 14"-19" diam.
WASTE REMOVERS

WOOD KITCHEN CABINETS and WORK HEIGHTS

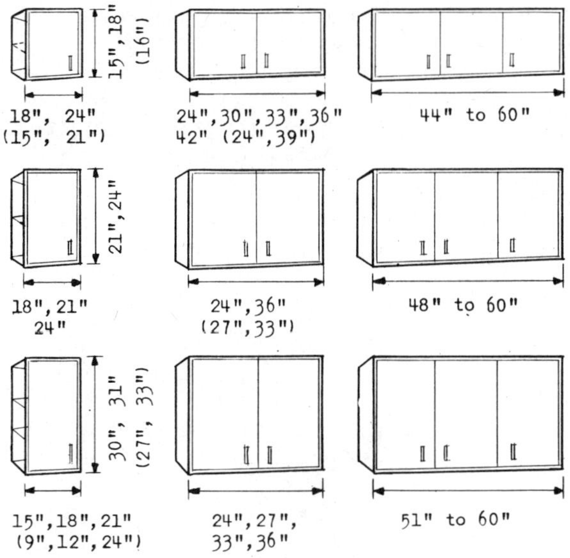
15", 18" (16")
18", 24" (15", 21")
24", 30", 33", 36" 42" (24", 39")
44" to 60"
21", 24"
18", 21" 24"
24", 36" (27", 33")
48" to 60"
30", 31" (27", 33")
15", 18", 21" (9", 12", 24")
24", 27", 33", 36"
51" to 60"

Depths: 12", 13", 14"
Available in 35", 36", 42" heights also.

TYPICAL WALL CABINETS

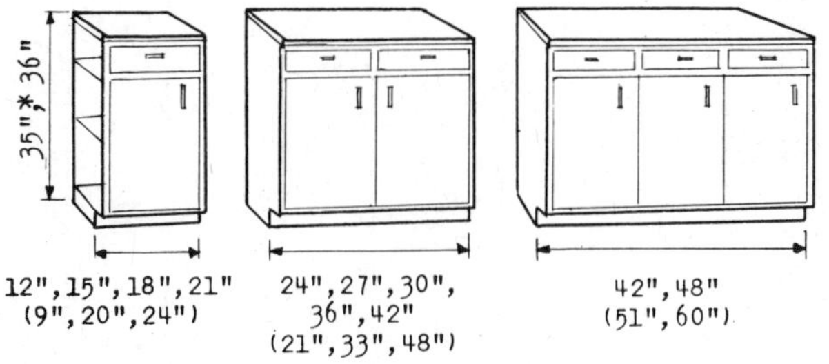
35"* 36"
12", 15", 18", 21" (9", 20", 24")
24", 27", 30", 36", 42" (21", 33", 48")
42", 48" (51", 60")

Depths: 22", 23", 25"
*35" height does not include counter top.
Units available without top drawer, with 3 or 4 drawers (no cupboard), and in many other combinations of drawers and cupboards. Also with special accessories: towel rack; sugar, vegetable, or flour bins; tray storage; pan rack, sliding table top; etc. See Accessories and Special Purpose Units on "Steel Kitchen Cabinets" page. Corner fillers and two-door models (with one door blinded) available for corner placement.

TYPICAL BASE CABINETS

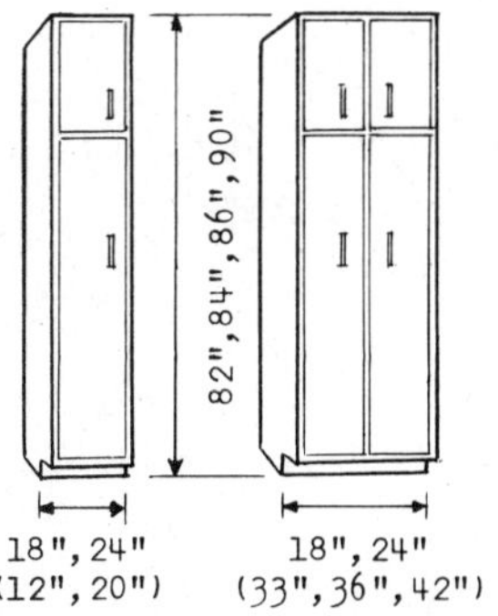
82", 84", 86", 90"
18", 24" (12", 20")
18", 24" (33", 36", 42")

Depths usually:
13", 14" 22", 24"
Available with 1, 2, or 3 shelves in top, with or without shelves in bottom, and in many other combinations such as ironing boards, desks, etc.

UTILITY CLOSETS

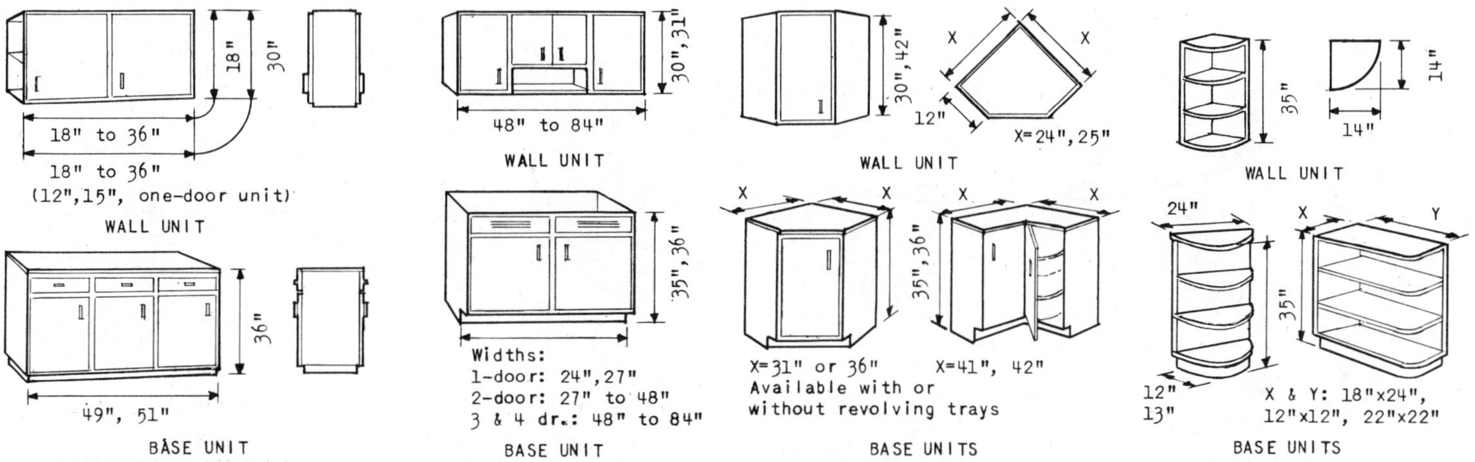
18"
30"
18" to 36"
18" to 36" (12", 15", one-door unit)
WALL UNIT
36"
49", 51"
BASE UNIT
30", 31"
48" to 84"
WALL UNIT
35", 36"
Widths:
1-door: 24", 27"
2-door: 27" to 48"
3 & 4 dr.: 48" to 84"
BASE UNIT
30", 42"
X
X
12"
X=24", 25"
WALL UNIT
X X X X
35", 36"
X=31" or 36"
X=41", 42"
Available with or without revolving trays
BASE UNITS
35"
14"
14"
WALL UNIT
24"
X
Y
35"
12"
13"
X & Y: 18"x24", 12"x12", 22"x22"
BASE UNITS

PENINSULA CABINETS — SINK CABINETS — CORNER CABINETS — END WHAT-NOTS

All dimensions given to nearest inch above fraction. Sizes vary among manufacturers. Dimensions given in parentheses ( ) are less common. Counter tops available in stainless steel, laminated plastic, linoleum, wood.

WOOD KITCHEN CABINETS

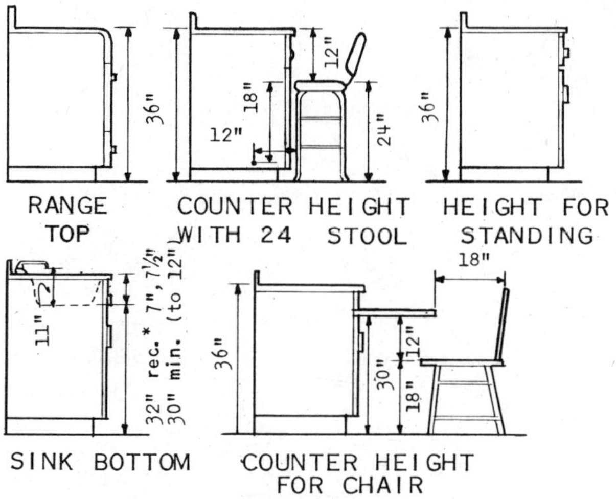
36"
RANGE TOP
12"
18"
12"
24"
36"
COUNTER HEIGHT WITH 24 STOOL
36"
HEIGHT FOR STANDING
11"
32" rec.* 7", 7½" 30" min. (to 12")
SINK BOTTOM
18"
36"
12"
30"
18"
COUNTER HEIGHT FOR CHAIR

*Not available in stock units.

IDEAL WORK HEIGHTS

Scale: 1/4"=1'-0"

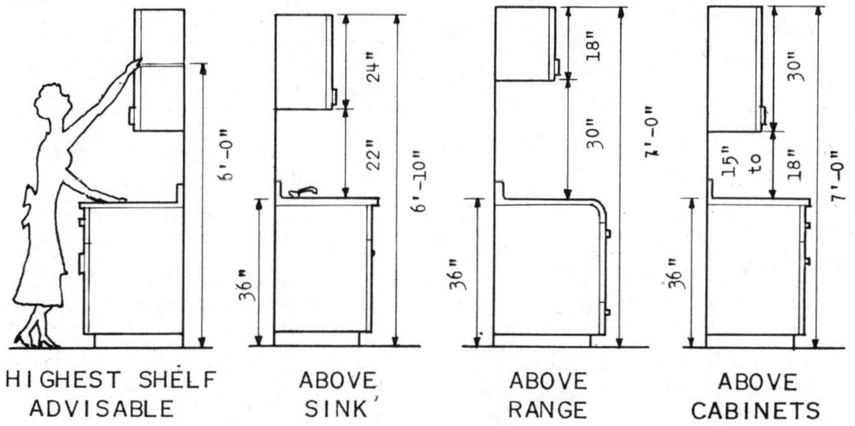
5'-0"
HIGHEST SHELF ADVISABLE
24"
22"
6'-10"
36"
ABOVE SINK
18"
30"
7'-0"
36"
ABOVE RANGE
30"
15" to 18"
7'-0"
36"
ABOVE CABINETS

For clearances above refrigerators see page on same.

WORK HEIGHTS FOR STOCK EQUIPMENT & IDEAL CLEARANCES ABOVE COUNTER

STEEL KITCHEN CABINETS and ACCESSORIES

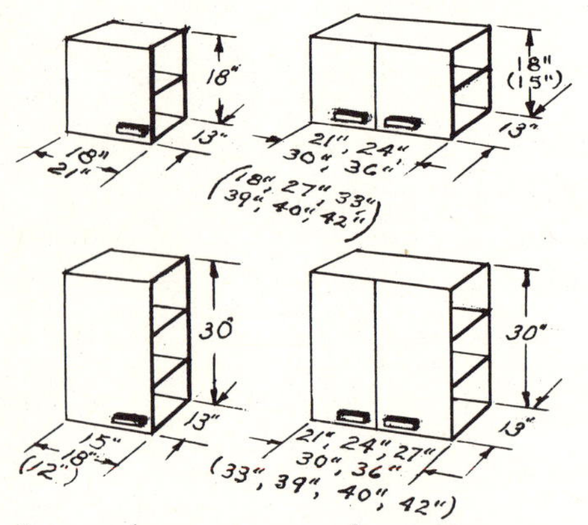
18"
13"
18"
21"
18"
(15")
13"
21", 24"
30", 36"
(18", 27", 33"
39", 40", 42")
30
13"
15"
18"
(12")
30"
13"
21", 24", 27"
30", 36"
(33", 39", 40", 42")

Sizes shown are most common. Others available are: h. 36", 42"; d. 13"; w. 12" thru 42".

WALL UNITS

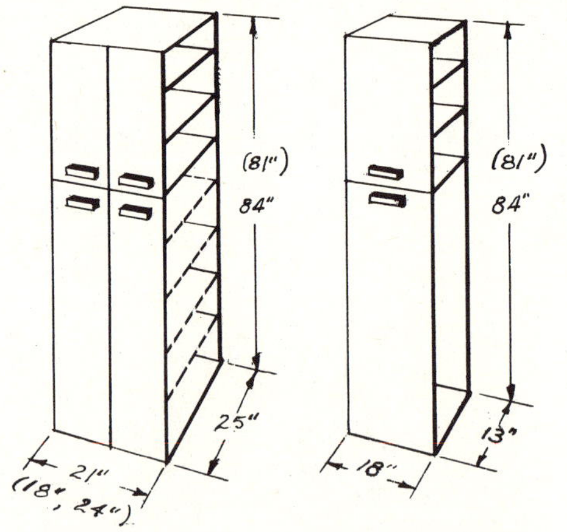
(81")
84"
25"
21"
(18", 24")
(81")
84"
13"
18"

Top compartment 1, 2 or 3 shelves. Bottom compartment 3 or 4 permanent or removable shelves, for brooms, linens.

UTILITY CLOSET

Other type units available are: (1) peninsula type. Wall unit: h. 30", 31"; d. 13", 30"; w. 24", 25". Base unit: h. 35"; d. 25"; w. 24". (2) sink base cabinets: h. 35"; d. 21", 25"; w. 15", 18" (1 door); 21" thru 36" (2 door); 42" thru 72" (3 & 4 door). (3) wall what-not: h. 30", 31"; d. 6", 9"; w. 13".

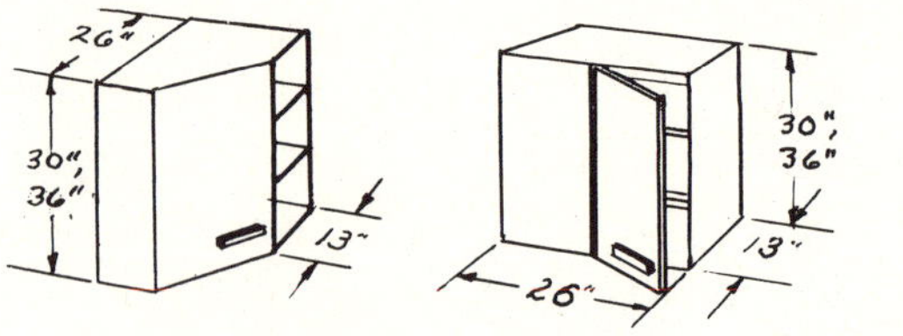
26"
30",
36"
13"
30",
36"
13"
26"

CORNER WALL UNITS

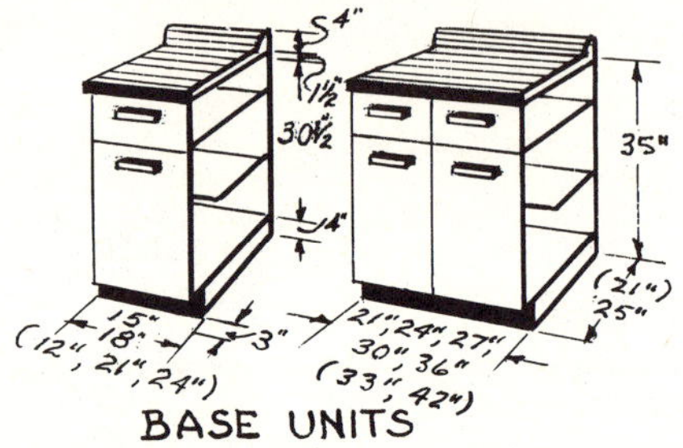
4"
1½
30½
1"
35"
15"
18"
(12", 21", 24")
3"
21", 24", 27"
30", 36"
(33", 42")
(21")
25"

BASE UNITS

Overall dimensions given to nearest inch above fraction. Dimensions in parentheses ( ) are less common.

Base units available without top drawer, or with several drawers; counter tops of stainless steel, wood, laminated plastic, linoleum.

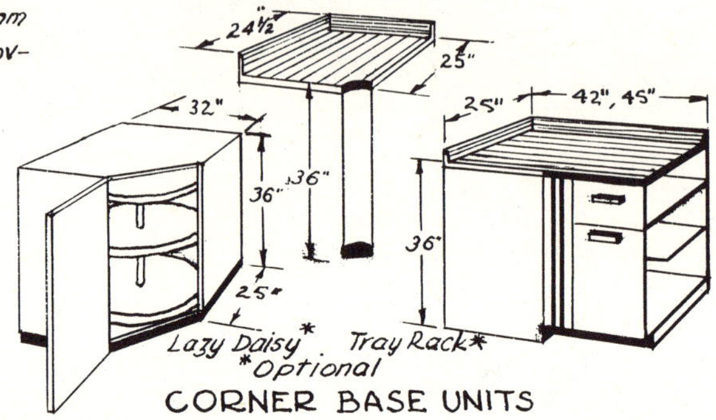
24½
25"
32"
36"
36"
25"
25"
42", 45"
36"

Lazy Daisy* Tray Rack*
*Optional

CORNER BASE UNITS

STEEL KITCHEN CABINETS

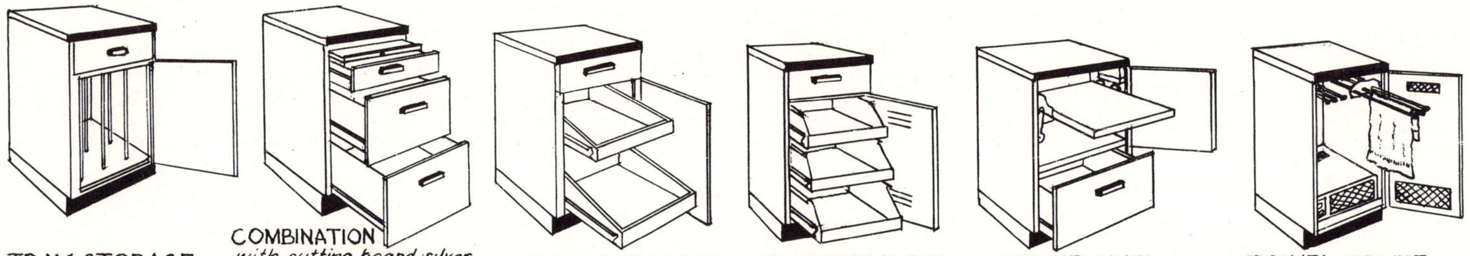

TRAY STORAGE

COMBINATION with cutting board, silver drawer, floor bin & lid file.

SLIDING SHELVES

VEGETABLE BIN

MIXER UNIT

TOWEL DRYER

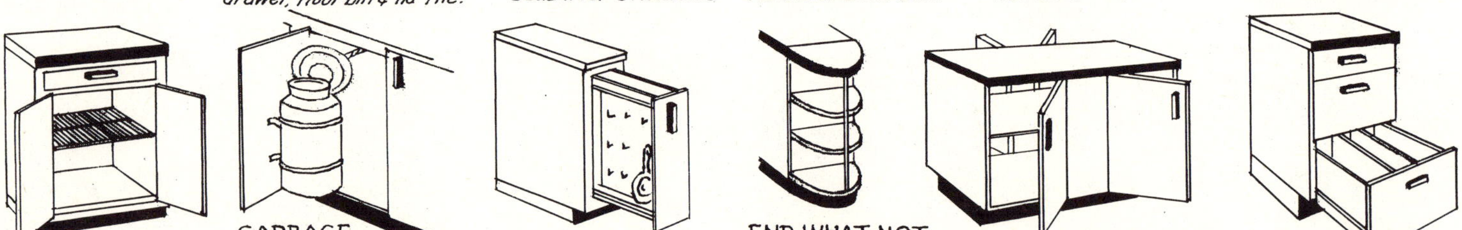

PLATE WARMER

GARBAGE CONTAINER

UTENSIL RACK

END WHAT-NOT OR SERVER

ISLAND STORAGE

LID & TIN FILE

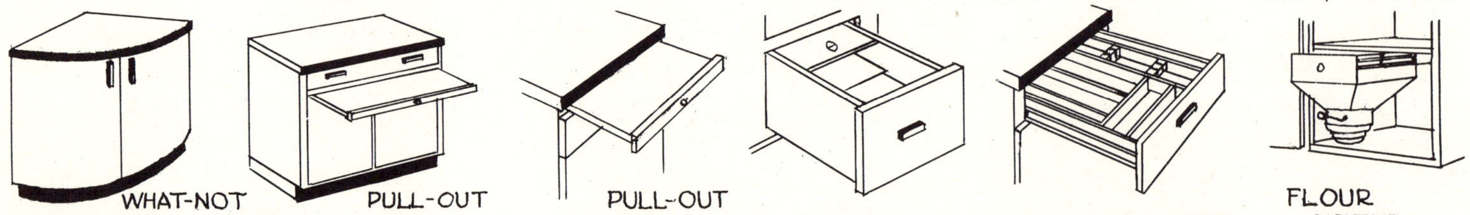

WHAT-NOT with DOORS for CORNER

PULL-OUT TABLE

PULL-OUT CUTTING BOARD

BREAD BOX

CUTLERY DRAWER

FLOUR SIFTER

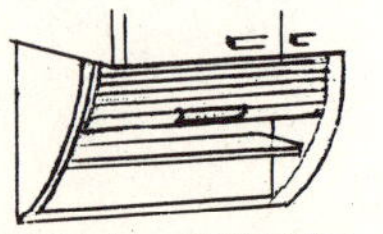

ROLL-DOWN CABINET

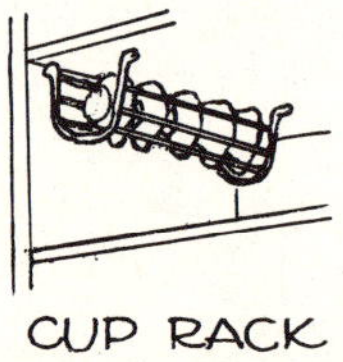

CUP RACK

ACCESSORIES & SPECIAL PURPOSE UNITS

COUNTER LIGHT (FLUORESCENT)

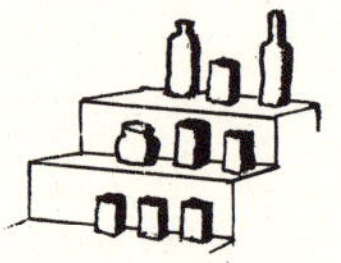

STEP-SHELF

RESIDENTIAL SINKS and DISHWASHERS

SINK TYPES AND SIZES*

FLAT-RIM AND LEDGE-TYPE SINKS							
PROFILE	MATERIAL	DBL. BOWL & DBL. DRAIN BD	DOUBLE BOWL	SINGLE BOWL, DBL. DRAIN BD	SINGLE BOWL & DRAINBOARD	SINGLE BOWL	BOWL & TRAY
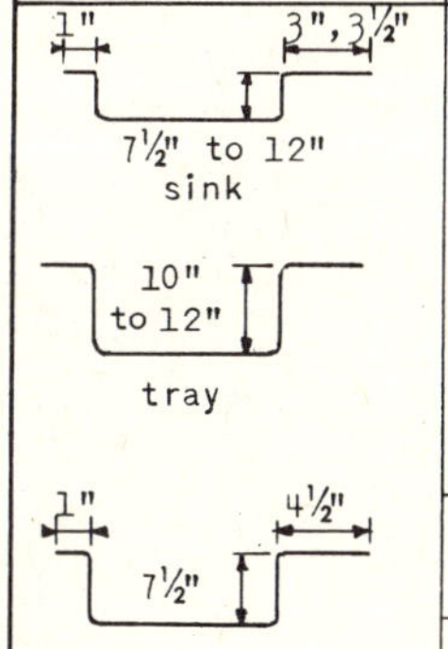 1" 3", 3½" 7½" to 12" sink 10" to 12" tray 1" 4½" 7½"	STAINLESS STEEL	60"x21" 72"x21"	32"x20", 21" 37¾"x17", 19" 28"x14", 18" 31", 36", 48"x 18" 36", 40", 44" & 54"x20" 28", 36"x17" 28", 32", 42"x 21"	54"x21" 60"x21"	42"x21"	14"x14" 18"x14", 15½" & 18" 20"x14", 18", 19" 14", 18"x17" 14", 16", 21", 24"&30"x21" 20"x14", 18" 24", 30"x18" 22", 27", 32"x 30"	32"x20", 21" 37¾"x17", 19" 32", 39", 42" x21"
	PORCELAIN ENAMELED STEEL		32"x18", 21"				
	ENAMELED CAST IRON**		30"x20", 21" 42"x20", 21" & 22"	54"x21"	42"x21"	12"x12" 24"x16", 18" 24", 30"x21" 30"x18" 24", 30"x20"	42"x20"
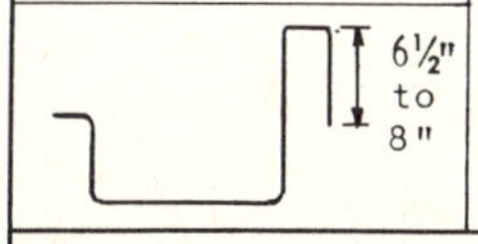 6½" to 8"						30"x20"	
ROLL OR SQUARE-RIM SINKS							
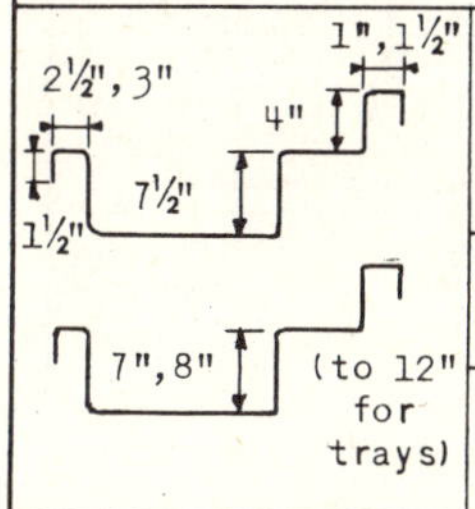 2½", 3" 1", 1½" 4" 7½" 1½" 7", 8" (to 12" for trays)	STAINLESS STEEL	60", 66", 72", 78", 84", 90" & 96"x25"	36"x25"	54", 60", 66" & 72"x25"			72", 84", 96" x25"
	PORCELAIN ENAMELED STEEL	66", 84"x25"	32"x18", 21" 42", 48"x25"	54"x25"	42", 48"x25"		42", 48"x25"
	ENAMELED CAST IRON**	60", 66", 72" x23½" to 25"	42"x23½" to 25"	54"x22", 23½" to 25"	42"x20", 22", 23½" to 25"		42", 48", 50" x24", 25"
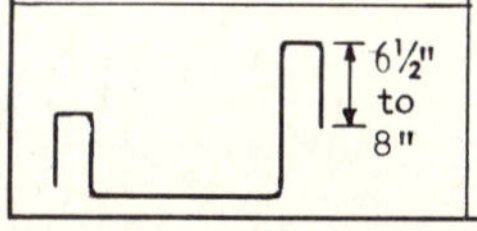 6½" to 8"						24"x18" 30"x20"	

*Sink heights: 32" fl. to bottom of sink rec.; 30" min. **From U. S. Commercial Standard CS 77-51

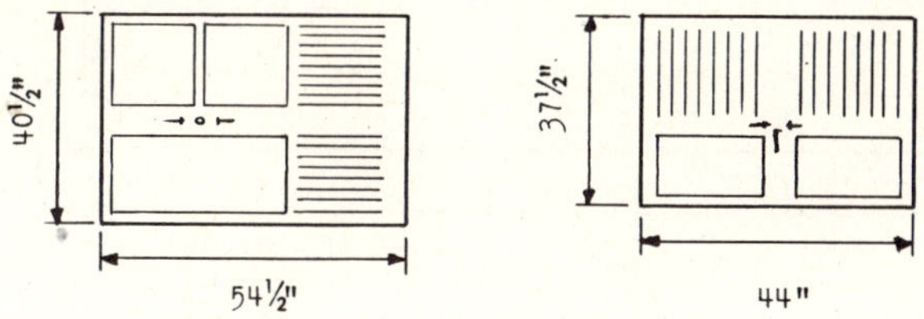
40½"
54½"
37½"
44"

PLANS

ISLAND OR PENINSULA SINKS

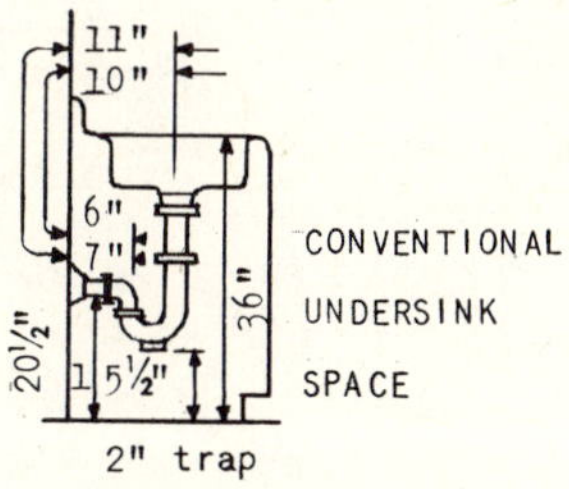
11"
10"
6"
7"
20½"
5½"
36"
CONVENTIONAL
UNDERSINK
SPACE
2" trap

TRAP & SINK DRAIN

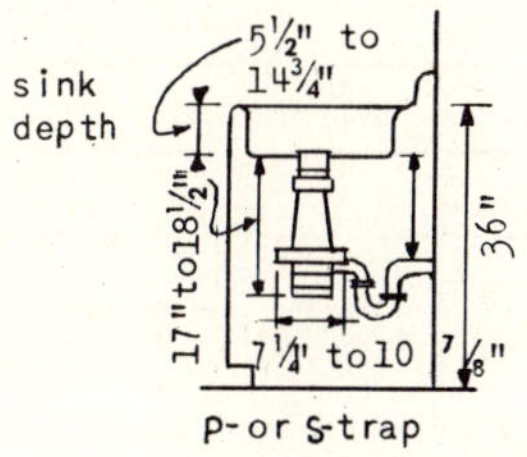
sink
depth
5½" to
14¾"
17" to 18½"
36"
7¼" to 10
7⅛"
P-or S-trap

Fits 3½" to 4¼" sink drain; 1½" conventional trap. Motor usually ¼" H.P. 115 volts.

TRAP & DISPOSAL UNIT

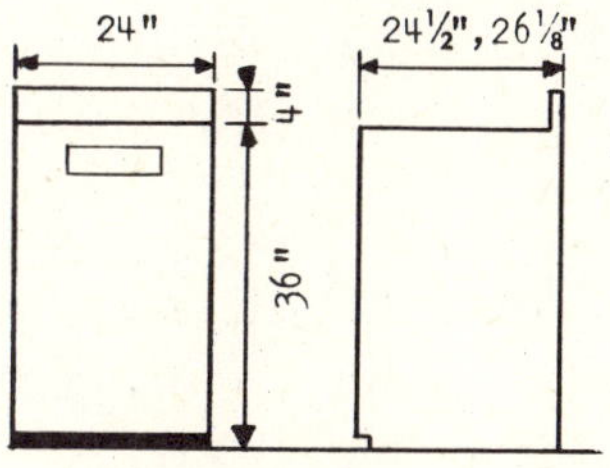
24"
24½", 26⅛"
4"
36"

CABINET *

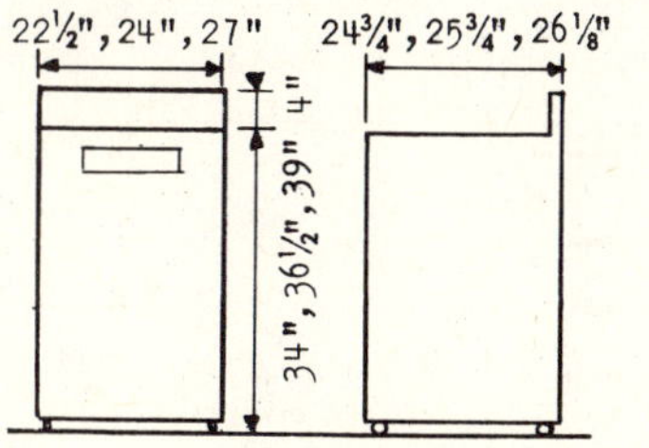
22½", 24", 27"
24¾", 25¾", 26⅛"
4"
34", 36½", 39"

PORTABLE *‡

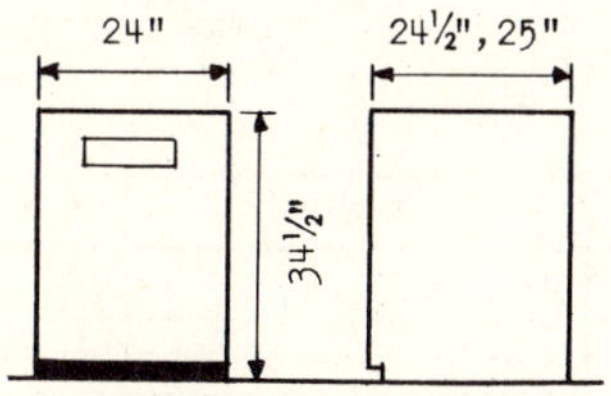
24"
24½", 25"
34½"

UNDERCOUNTER s

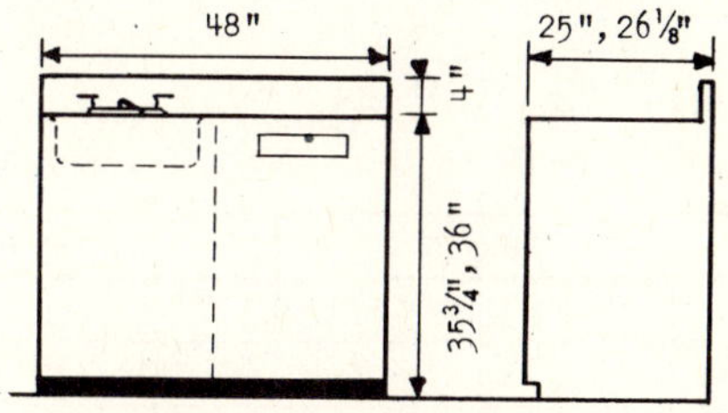
48"
25", 26⅛"
4"
35¾", 36"

WASHER-SINK COMBINATION s

* = top opening
‡ = front opening
s = entire unit slides out

DISHWASHERS

RESIDENTIAL RANGES

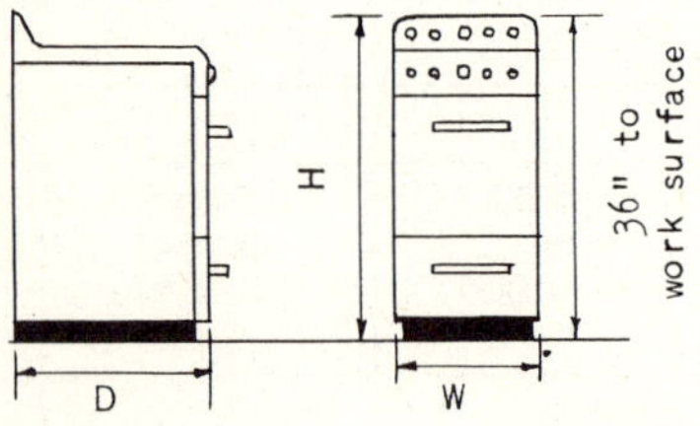
H
36" to work surface
D
W

NOTE: four burner (no counter) range shown. Others similar

NOTES

1. All dimensions are to nearest ¼"
2. Most conventional types are available in colored porcelain enamel. Most built-ins are in stainless steel.

SYMBOLS

O = oven W = warming oven
B = broiler S = storage
G = revolving grill
✕ = burner, gas or electric
⊗ = deep well or pressure cooker for electric, burner for gas
▭ = top griddle
[···] = controls.

NOTES AND SYMBOLS

CONVENTIONAL RANGE TYPES AND SIZES

				OTHERS *
THREE BURNER (electric only)	W	21"		
	H	40"		
	D	24½"		
FOUR BURNER (no counter)	W	MIN. 19"	MAX. 24"	
	H	45¾"	44¼"	39½" to 48"
	D	25"	25"	24½" to 27"
FOUR BURNER (small counter)	W	MIN. 30"	MAX. 36"	
	H	48¼"	46¼"	43" to 48"
	D	25¼"	28"	25½" to 27½"
FOUR BURNER (normal counter)	W	MIN. 39"	MAX. 41"	
	H	42¾"	53¼"	43" to 48"
	D	25"	28"	25¼" to 27½"
		NOTE: most range tops shown at right available with several combinations of ovens, storage, etc.		
SIX BURNER	W	38"		
	H	46¾"		
	D	25"		

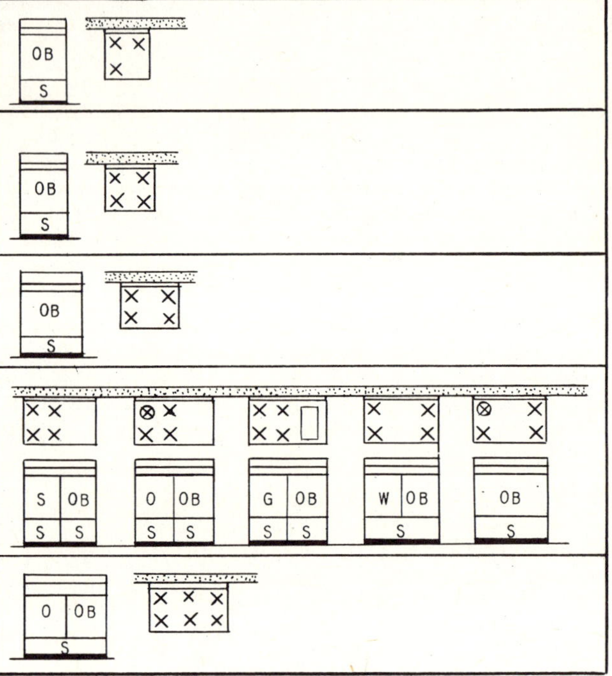

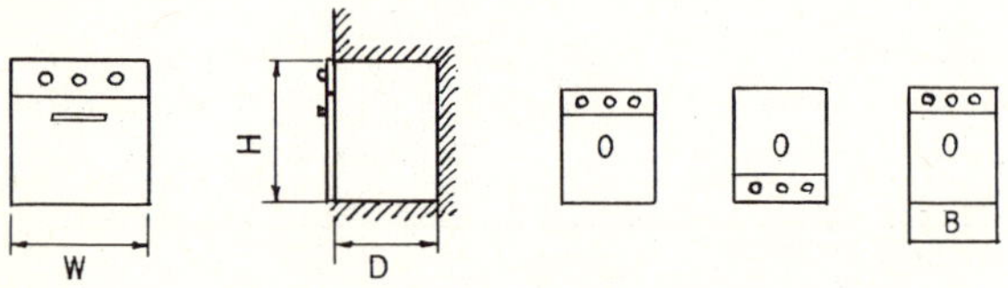
W
H
D
O
O
O
B

SIZES			OTHERS *
W	MIN. 20"	MAX. 30½"	
H	37½"	40"	23" to 28"
D	23"	22½"	21½" to 24¾"

BUILT-IN OVENS

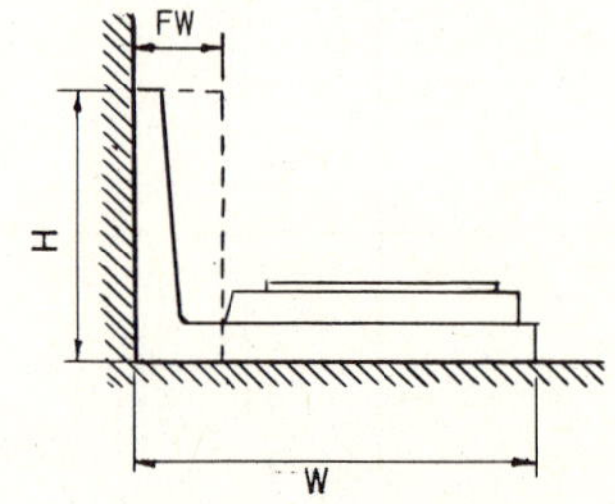
FW
H
W

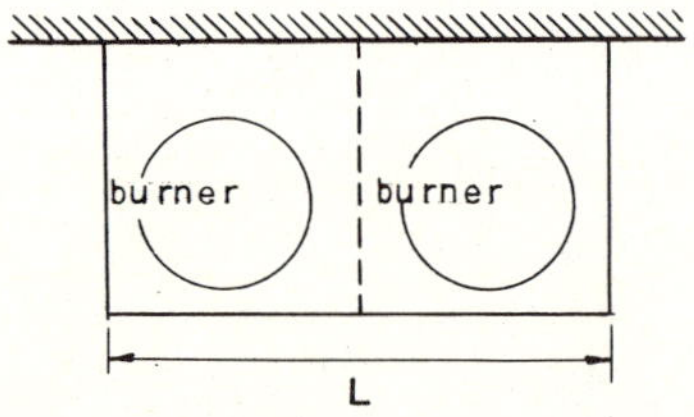
burner
burner
L

FW = size when folded up.

FW	W	H	L
3½"	14¼"	12"	19" (2 burners) 9½" (1 burner)
5¼"	19"	15"	30" (2 burners)

FOLD-UP UNITS

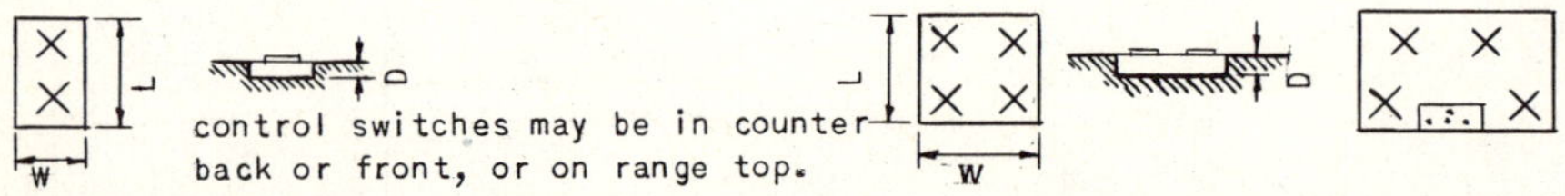
L
W
D
L
W
D

control switches may be in counter back or front, or on range top.

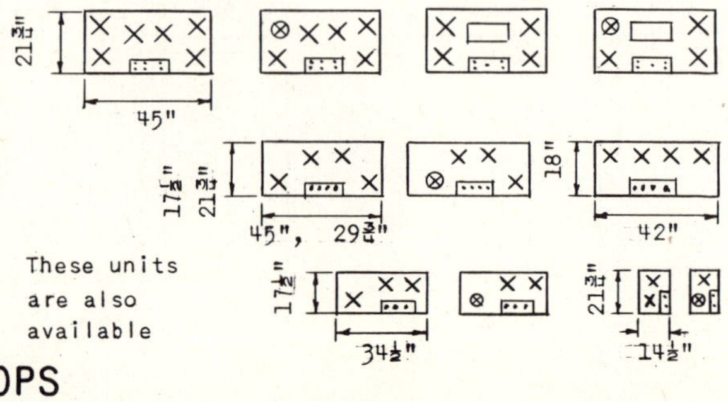
21¾"
45"
17½"
21¾"
45", 29¾"
18"
42"
17½"
34½"
21¾"
14½"

These units are also available

TWO BURNER			OTHERS *	FOUR BURNER		OTHERS *
W	MIN. 12¼"	MAX. 13½"		MIN. 24½"	MAX. 34"	
L	21½"	21¼"	21" to 21½"	21¾"	21"	20"
D	5½"	3¾"	5¼" to 5¾"	5½"	8"	5"

*These are the heights and depths available for ranges of other than minimum or maximum width.

BUILT-IN RANGE TOPS

REFRIGERATORS and FREEZERS

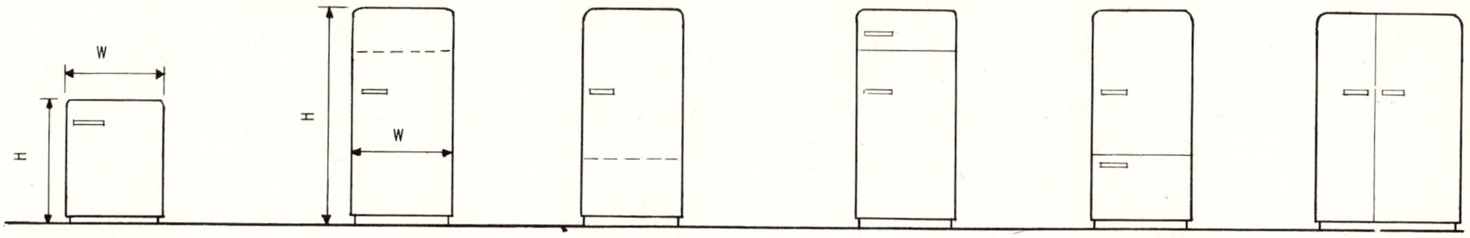
W
H
H
W

COUNTERHEIGHT (UNDERCOUNTER SIMILAR)

ONE DOOR: FREEZER AT TOP; FREEZER AT BOTTOM

TWO DOOR: FREEZER AT TOP; FREEZER AT BOTTOM; FREEZER IN LEFT HALF

Right-hand swing most common, but left-hand models available. Consult mfr.

ONE DOOR, FREEZER AT TOP												
	TO 7.0 CU. FT.			TO 8.0 CU. FT.			TO 10.0 CU. FT.			TO 12.0 CU. FT.		
	MIN. W.	MAX. W.	OTHERS	MIN. W.	MAX. W.	OTHERS	MIN. W.	MAX. W.	OTHERS	MIN. W.	MAX. W.	OTHERS
W	24"	24¾"	24¼"-24½"	24"	28¼"	24¼"-28"	24"	31"	24"-31"	24¼"	32"	28¼"-32"
D	28¼"	29¾"	27½"-29¾"	29"	29½"	28½"-29¾"	29¼"	31"	29"-31"	28¼"	29¾"	29¾"-32¼"
H	50"	54¾"	54¼"-55"	55½"	55½"	55½"-56½"	56½"	60"	55½"-60"	53½"	65½"	58"-66"
lbs	40	50	28-45	22	59	27-59	40	42	22-76	52	51	39-102
cu. ft.	6.0	6.6	6.0-7.0	7.7	7.8	7.5-8.0	8.1	10	8.1-9.5	10.5	12.2	10.7-12.6

	COUNTER-HEIGHT	UNDER-COUNTER	ONE DOOR FREEZER AT BOTTOM		TWO DOOR FREEZER AT TOP			TWO DOOR AT BOTTOM	TWO DOOR IN LEFT HALF
W	24½"	24"	MIN. 30½"	MAX. 31½"	MIN. 30½"	MAX. 32"	OTHERS: 31"	31"	47¾"
D	27"	27"	30"	32¼"	30¼"	29¾"	31"	31"	26½"
H	34½"	34½"	60"	61"	64"	65½"	65"-66"	70"	60"
lbs.	15.7	16	122	130	77	73	85	130	166
cu. ft.	4.4	4.0	7.9	9.0	10.0	11.5	12.1-12.9	13.7	11.0

CONVENTIONAL REFRIGERATORS

WITH FREEZERS

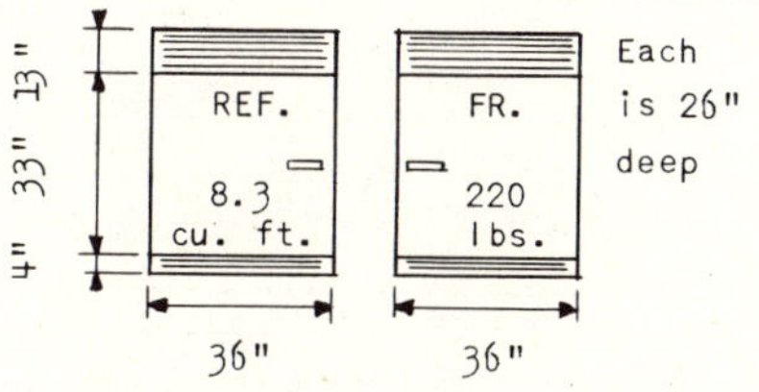
13"
33"
4"
REF.
8.3 cu. ft.
FR.
220 lbs.
36"
36"
Each is 26" deep

BUILT-IN

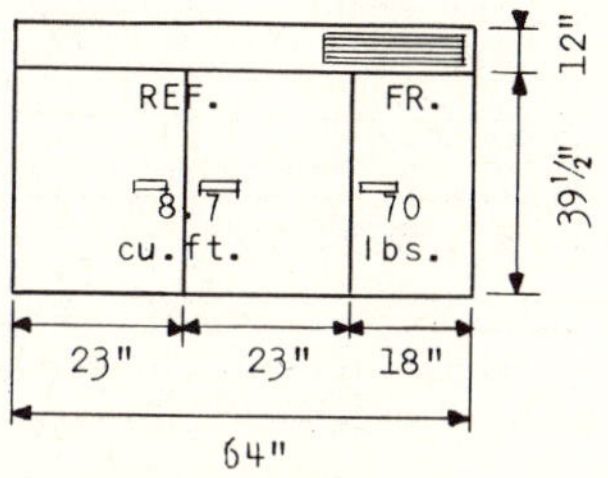
12"
39½"
REF.
8.7 cu. ft.
FR.
70 lbs.
23"
23"
18"
64"

WALL HUNG

WALL REFRIGERATORS - FREEZERS

Generally available in color and in chrome.

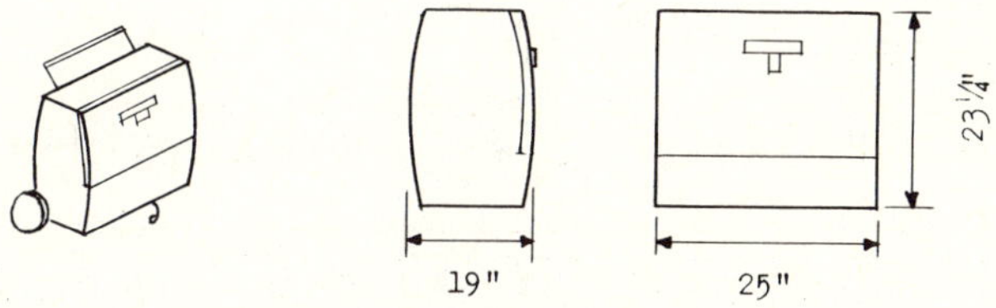
19"
25"
23¼"

Wheeled cart (shown) or legged base available.

PORTABLE REFRIGERATOR

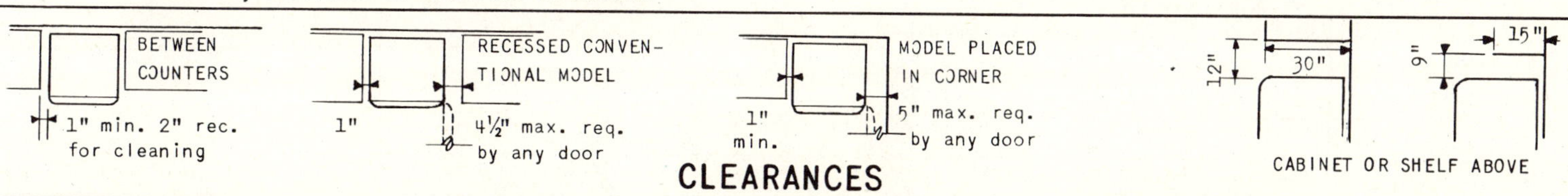
BETWEEN COUNTERS
1" min. 2" rec. for cleaning
RECESSED CONVENTIONAL MODEL
1"
4½" max. req. by any door
MODEL PLACED IN CORNER
1" min.
5" max. req. by any door
12"
30"
9"
15"
CABINET OR SHELF ABOVE

CLEARANCES

	MIN.W.	MAX.W.	OTHERS
W	28"	49"	28¼"-36"
D	30"	32½"	23" -35"
H	57½"	71"	58" -71"
lbs	294	875	402-665

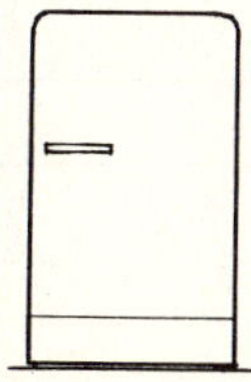

UPRIGHT TYPE

2 compartments: W. 80¾"-113¾"; D. 29"-31¾"; H, 38"-39½"; lbs. 878-1078

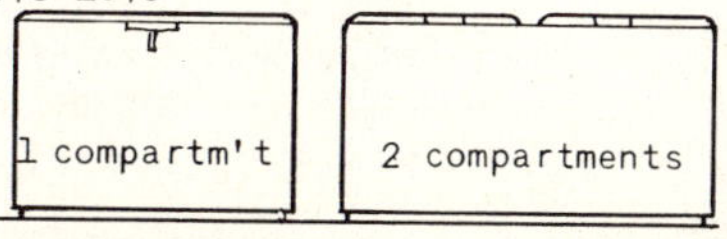
1 compartm't
2 compartments

	MIN.W.	MAX.W.	OTHERS
W	33"	85½"	37¼"-65"
D	29"	31¼"	25¼"-32½"
H	38"	39"	36" -39¾"
lbs	245	700	245-665

CHEST TYPE

FREEZERS

All refrigerator and freezer dimensions are to nearest ¼"

WASHING and DRYING MACHINES

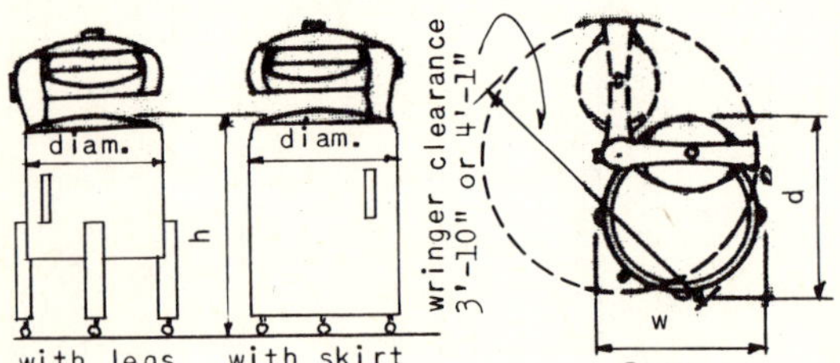
diam.
diam.
h
wringer clearance 3'-10" or 4'-1"
d
w

with legs TYPE A · with skirt TYPE B · PLAN

Wringer position varies with mfr.
Capacity: 7, 8, 9, 10 lbs. dry clothes.

TYPE	MFR.	AVER. DIMENSIONS			
		diam.	h	w	d
A	ABC	1'-11"	3'-2"	2'-0"	2'-0"
	Easy	2'-3⅛"	3'-1¼"	2'-2½"	2'-5¾"
	Maytag	1'-11"	2'-11½"	2'-3¼"	2'-2"
B	ABC	1'-11"	3'-2"	2'-2"	2'-2"
	Easy	1'-11⅛"	2'-9¾"	1'-11¼"	2'-2½"
	Norge	1'-11½"	3'-2¼"	2'-3"	2'-4"

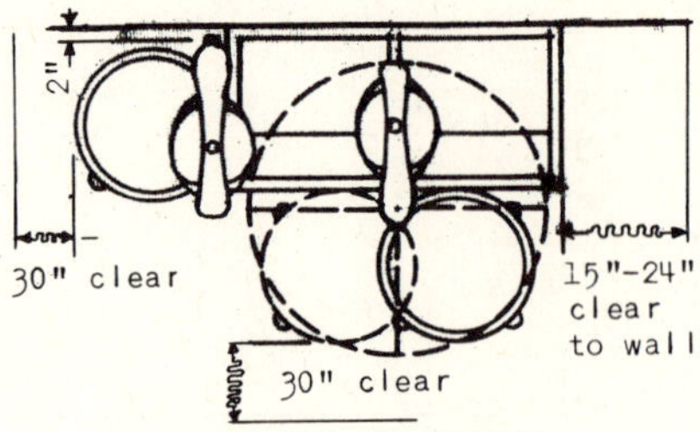
2"
30" clear
15"-24" clear to wall
30" clear

PLAN OF TUB AND WASHER WITH CLEARANCES

WRINGER WASHERS

MANUFACTURER	w	d	D	h	H	cap. lbs.	volts	NOTES
Bendix	3'-0"	2'-4⅜"	3'-6⅝"	3'-2½"	3'-2½"	8	230	outside vent'g not req'd
General Electric	2'-6"	2'-0½"	3'-6½"	2'-10½"	3'-0"	8	230	door hinged at right
					all data same for undercounter type.			
Westinghouse	2'-8"	2'-4¼"	3'-7¼"	3'-0⅝"	3'-4¼"	8	115/230	door hinged at bottom outside vent'g not req'd.

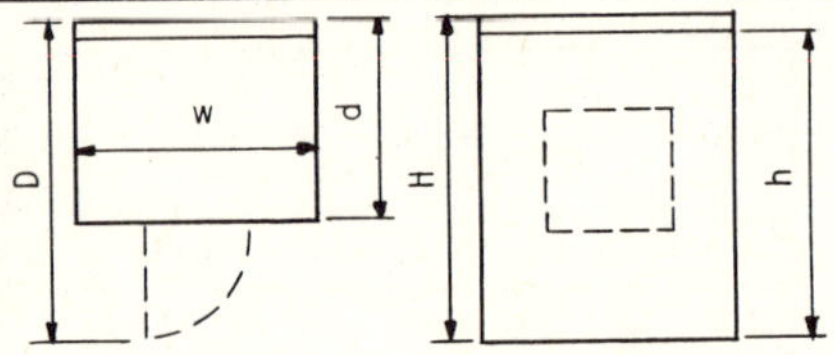
w
d
D
H
h

PLAN · ELEV.

AUTOMATIC WASHER-DRYER COMBINATIONS

MANUFACTURER	w	d	D	h	H	cap. lbs.	volts	NOTES
TYPE A								
Bendix	2'-6¼"	2'-2"	3'-5½"	3'-0"	–	9	115	
General Electric	2'-3"	2'-2½"	–	3'-0"	3'-4"	10-12	115	
Westinghouse	2'-7"	2'-4½"	3'-7⅝"	3'-0⅝"	3'-4"	9	115	door hinged at bottom
	2'-1"	2'-0½"	3'-3"	2'-11¾"	–	8	110/120	no backsplasher door hinged at bottom
TYPE B								
ABC	2'-2"	2'-4"	–	3'-0"	3'-6"	9	115	
Bendix	1'-11¾"	2'-3¼"	–	3'-0"	4'-9½"	8	115	full-opening top
Easy	2'-6"	2'-1⅝"	–	3'-0⅜"	4'-3⅛"	8	115	
Hotpoint	2'-1⅝"	2'-4⅞"	–	3'-0"	4'-4"	8	115	
Kelvinator	2'-1"	2'-4¼"	–	3'-0"	4'-5"	9	115	
Maytag	2'-1½"	2'-3¼"	–	3'-0"	4'-1"		115	
Norge	2'-1½"	2'-2¾"	–	3'-0"	4'-4"	9	110/120	

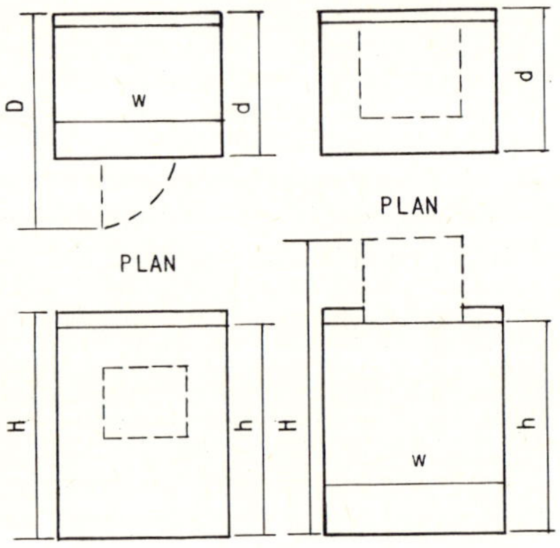
D
w
d
PLAN
PLAN
H
h
w

ELEV. TYPE A door in front · ELEV. TYPE B door in top

AUTOMATIC WASHERS

MANUFACTURER	w	d	D	h	H	cap. lbs.	volts	NOTES
ABC	2'-6"	2'-4"	3'-8"	3'-0"	3'-6"	9	115/230	
Bendix	2'-6"	2'-2"	3'-5½"	3'-0"	3'-0"	9	230	door hinged at left
Easy	2'-6"	2'-1⅝"	3'-5⅝"	3'-0⅝"	3'-3½"	9	115	
General Electric	2'-7"	2'-2½"	3'-9"	3'-0"	3'-4"	10	115/230	
Hotpoint	2'-7"	2'-4⅞"	4'-0½"	3'-0"	3'-3"	10	115/230	outside vent'g not req'd.
Kelvinator	2'-6"	2'-4¼"	3'-7½"	3'-0"	3'-8¼"	9	115/230	
Norge	2'-7"	2'-2¾"	–	3'-0"	3'-3⅝"	9	110/220	full width door hinged at bottom
Westinghouse	2'-7"	2'-4½"	3'-7⅝"	3'-0⅝"	3'-4"	9	115/230	door hinged at bottom
	2'-7"	2'-3½"	3'-6½"	3'-0½"	–	9	115/230	door hinged at bottom no backsplasher

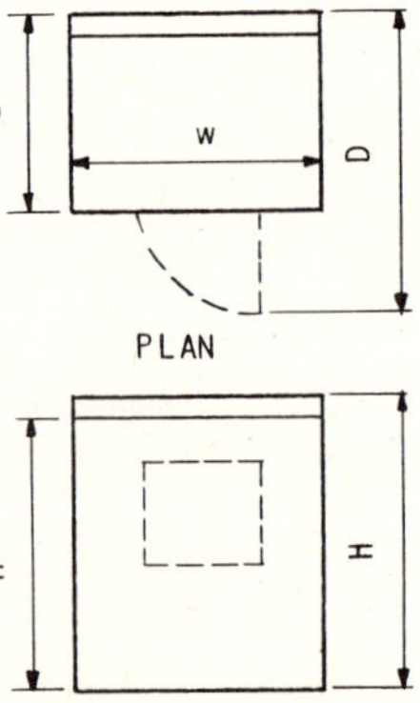
d
w
D
PLAN
h
H

ELEV.

AUTOMATIC DRYERS

NOTES ON AUTOMATIC WASHERS AND DRYERS

w = overall width
d = actual depth
D = depth with door open
h = top surface height
H = height to top of back-splasher or open door

1. Cap. lbs. = dry weight of clothes load.
2. All dimensions are to nearest ⅛".
3. Certain variations in body design may affect actual depths of models.
4. Certain models of both washers and dryers are available with gas. Consult "Reference Manual of Modern Gas Service."

Data checked by manufacturers listed.

LAUNDRY TRAYS - IRONING EQUIPMENT

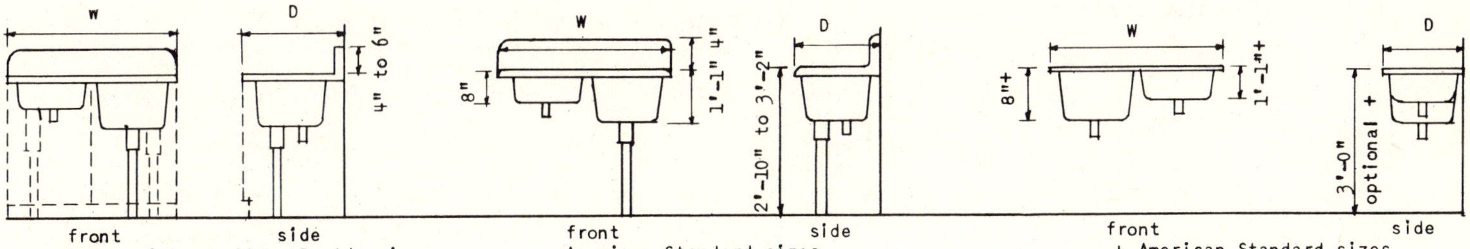
W
D
4" to 6"
front
side
W
8"
1'-1" 4"
2'-10" to 3'-2"
D
front
side
W
8"+
1'-1"+
D
3'-0"
optional +
front
side

U.S. Dept. of Comm. CS77-51 std. sizes.

W	D
3'-6"	2'-0"
4'-0"	or
4'-2"	2'-1"

RIM LEDGE WITH BACK

American-Standard sizes

W	D
3'-6"	2'-1"

ROLL RIM

+ American-Standard sizes

	W	D
Amer.-Std. & US CS77-51	3'-6"	1'-8"

FLAT RIM

ENAMELED CAST IRON

COMBINATION SINKS & LAUNDRY TRAYS

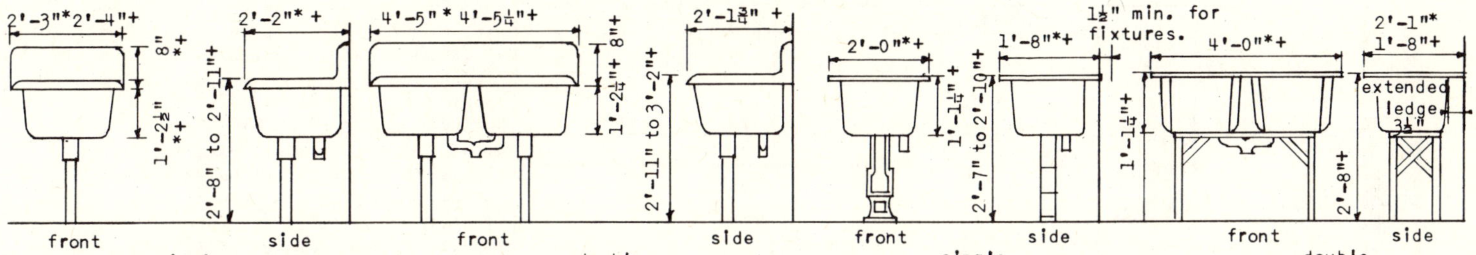
2'-3"*2'-4"+
8" *+
1'-2½" *+
2'-8" to 2'-11"+
2'-2"* +
front
side
single
4'-5"* 4'-5¼"+
8"+
1'-2¼"+
2'-11" to 3'-2"+
2'-1¾" +
front
side
double
2'-0"*+
1'-1¼" +
2'-7" to 2'-10"*+
1'-8"*+
1½" min. for fixtures.
front
side
single
4'-0"*+
1'-1¼"+
2'-8"+
2'-1"*
1'-8"+
extended ledge 3½"
front
side
double

ROLL RIM

FLAT RIM

* U.S. Dept of Comm. CS77-51 sizes.
\+ American-Standard sizes

ENAMELED CAST IRON

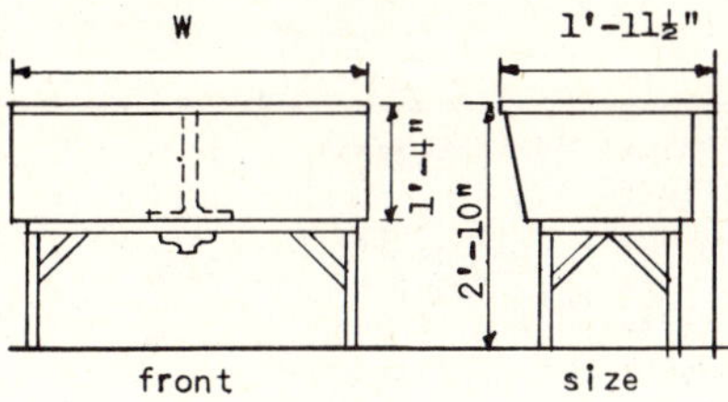
W
1'-11½"
1'-4"
2'-10"
front
size

	single	double	triple
W	2'-1"	4'-0"	6'-0"

FLAT RIM

CAST CEMENT

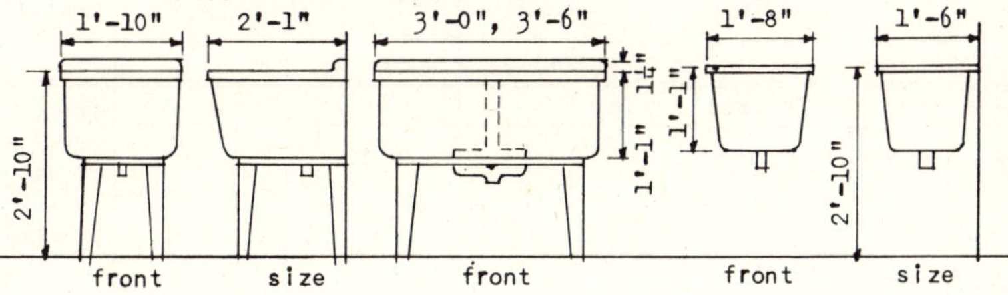
1'-10"
2'-1"
3'-0", 3'-6"
2'-10"
1¼"
1'-1"
1'-1"
1'-8"
1'-6"
2'-10"
front
size
front
front
size

single & double, with ledgeback
FLAT RIM (heavy)

single
FLAT RIM (regular)

VITREOUS CHINA

LAUNDRY TRAYS

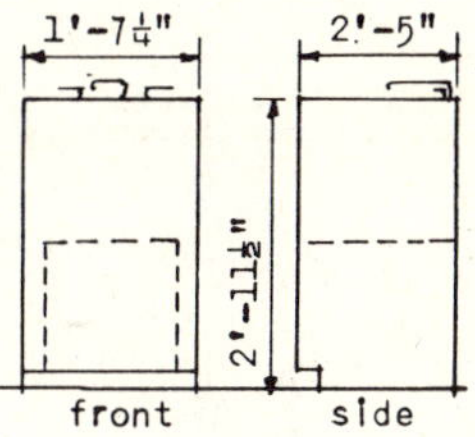
1'-7¼"
2'-5"
2'-11½"
front
side

storage cab. under
Mfr'd by Wessels Co.

FIBER GLASS

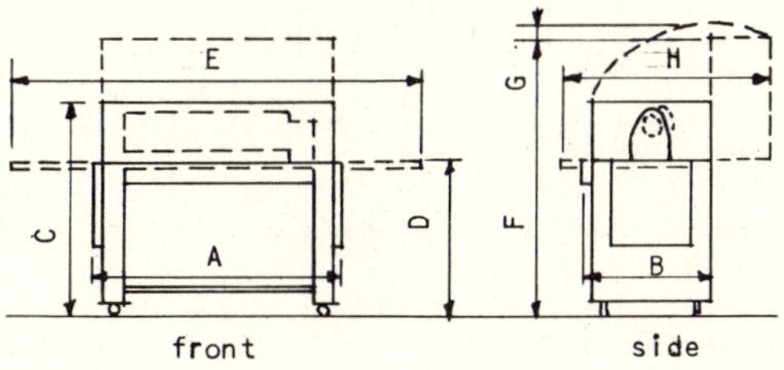
E
C
A
D
front
G
H
F
B
side

Sizes when closed				
mfr.	A	B	C	D
Ironrite Maytag	2'-6" 3'-1"	1'-8" 1'-5"	3'-0" 2'-11"	- 2'-0"

Sizes when open				
mfr.	E	F	G	H
Ironrite Maytag	4'-1" 5'-0"	3'-4" 3'-4½"	- 0'-3"	2'-10" 2'-9½"

ROTARY ELECTRIC IRONER

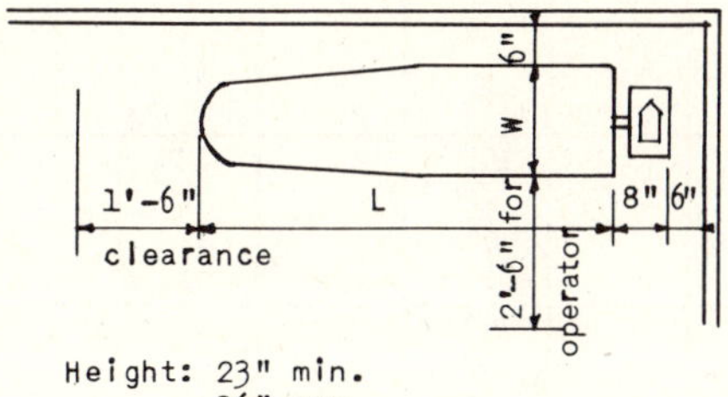
optional iron rest
6"
W
1'-6"
clearance
L
8"
6"
2'-6" for operator

Height: 23" min.
36" max.

(Metal boards are adjustable)

TYPE	L	W
wood	4'-0" 4'-6"	12" 15"
metal	4'-6"	15"

PORTABLE IRONING BOARD

Data checked by manutacturers listed.

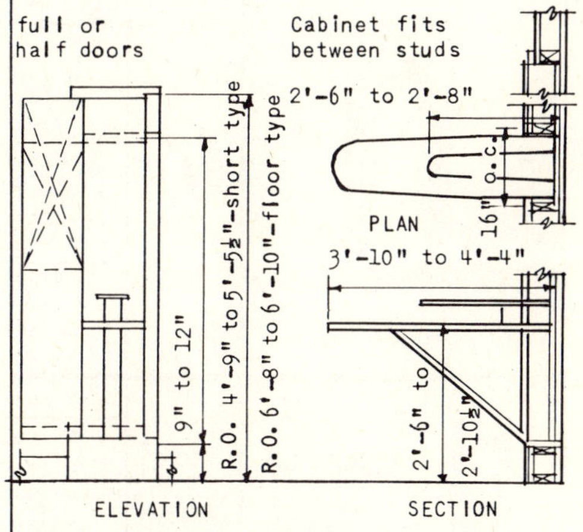
full or half doors
Cabinet fits between studs
2'-6" to 2'-8"
o.c.
16"
PLAN
3'-10" to 4'-4"
9" to 12"
R.O. 4'-9" to 5'-5½"-short type
R.O. 6'-8" to 6'-10"-floor type
2'-6" to 2'-10½"
ELEVATION
SECTION

(Surface type fin. cabinet sizes, 1½" to 1'-5¾" wide x 4'-9½" to 5'-4½" high & 2½" deep, set 8½" to 1'-11" from floor. For attaching to wall; similar to built-in type without sleeve board.)

BUILT-IN TYPE

CABINET IRONING BOARD

FIRE EXTINGUISHERS

FIRE CLASSIFICATION

CLASS A Incipient fires on which quenching and the cooling effect of water is prime importance. Fires of wood, paper, textiles and rubbish

CLASS B Incipient fires on which blanketing or smothering effect of extinguishing is prime importance. Fire of gasoline, oil, grease, and fat.

CLASS C Incipient fires in electrical equipment where the use of non conducting extinguishing agent is needed.

The number after the fire class (A_1, B_2, etc.), designates the number of extinguishers needed in each protection unit. Class I, light hazards (schools, offices, and public buildings), require one unit for each 5000 square feet of floor space. Class II, ordinary hazards (drygoods & warehouses) require a minimum of one unit for each 2500 square feet of floor space. Class III, extra hazardous (paint shops etc.) require a minimum of one unit for each 2500 square feet and must conform to local code.

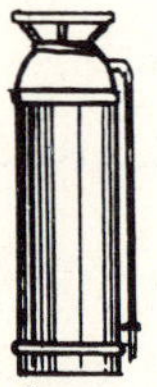
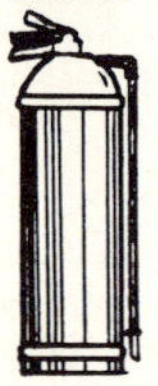

TYPE	CLASS	CAPACITY & SIZE (approximate size)					
WATER quenches cools	class **A** only	CAP. IN GALS.	2½	2½ & 5 PUMP		5 BACK PUMP	
		height	25"	26"	25"	15½"	
		diameter	7"	8"	10"	14"	
		weight(lbs)	36"	36	56	14"	
		class	A-1	A-1	A-1	A-1	
SODA-ACID quenches cools	class **A** only	CAP. IN GALS.			2½		
		height			25"		
		diameter			7"		
		weight(lbs)			34		
		class			A-1		
FOAM smothers cools	class **A & B** only	CAP. IN GALS.			2½		
		height			25"		
		diameter			7"		
		weight(lbs)			34		
		class			A1, B1		
LOADED STREAM Alka-metal salt quenches, cools and fireproofs	class **A & B** fires	CAP. IN GALS.	1	1¾	2½		
		height	17"	23"	25"		
		diameter	6"	6"	7"		
		weight(lbs)	21	30	34		
		class	A2-B4	A1-B2	A1-B1		

SERVICE SPECIFICATIONS

EFFECTIVE RANGE:
Water, Pump 30-40 ft. pressure 45-55 ft.
Soda-Acid 30-40 ft. foam 35-40 ft
Loaded Stream 35-40 ft.

RECHARGE: Soda-Acid & Foam - recharge after use; discharge & recharge yearly. Water - weigh use cylinder and check annually. In all cases, follow instructions on extinguisher label.

PRESSURE SOURCE:
Water - hand pump & gas cartridge.
Soda-Acid & Foam - chemical reaction
Loaded Stream - Pressure

TEMPERATURE EFFECT:
Soad-Acid, Foam & Water will freeze.
Loaded Stream - minus 40°F.

ELECTRICAL CONDUCTIVITY:
All water base extinguishing agents will conduct.

TYPE	CLASS	CAPACITY & SIZE					
CARBON DIOXIDE (Dimensions for 3 makes of extinguisher shown to show realitive sizes.)	class **B & C** fires	CAP. IN LBS.	2½	5	10	15	20
		height	17"	16"	27"	34"	37"
		diameter	8"	9"	11"	11"	11"
		weight	10	17	30	40	53
		class	B2	& C2	B2-C1	B1 &	C1
		height	17"	16"	26"	36"	36"
		diameter	4"	5"	7"	7"	8"
		weight	8	14	32	42	54
		class	B2	& C2	B2-C1	B1 &	C1
		height	17"	17"	28"	31"	33"
		diameter	8"	9"	11"	11"	12"
		weight	9	16	34	42	55
		class	B2	& C2	B2 & C1	B1 &	C1

EFFECTIVE RANGE: 3 to 8 feet
DISCHARGE TIME:
2½ lbs., 12 sec.; 5 lbs., 22 sec., 10 lbs., 23 sec.; 15 lbs., 26 sec.; 20 lbs., 25 sec.
RECHARGE: after use.
PRESSURE SOURCE: compressed gas.
TEMPERATURE EFFECT:
will operate at minus 40°F.
ELECTRICAL CONDUCTIVITY:
will not conduct.

TYPE	CLASS	CAPACITY & SIZE					
DRY CHEMICAL	class **B & C** only	CAP. IN LBS.	4	5	10	20	30
		height	18"		17"	20"	28"
		diameter	5"		12"	13"	13"
		weight(lbs)	12		27	37	51
		class	B2-C2		B2-C2	B-1 &	C-1
		height		15"		22"	29"
		diameter		4"		7"	7"
		weight(lbs)		10		37	50
		class		B2-C2		B1 &	C1
		height		19"	26"	27"	37"
		diameter		4"	6"	8"	8"
		weight(lbs)		14	28	41	58
		class		B2-C2	B1	&	C1

EFFECTIVE RANGE: 10 to 20 feet
DISCHARGE TIME:
4 & 5 lbs., 10 sec.; 10 lbs., 11 sec.; 20 lbs. 15 sec; 30 lbs., 24 sec.
RECHARGE: after use.
PRESSURE SOURCE: compressed gas.
TEMPERATURE EFFECT:
Will operate at minus 40°F.
ELECTRICAL CONDUCTIVITY:
will not conduct

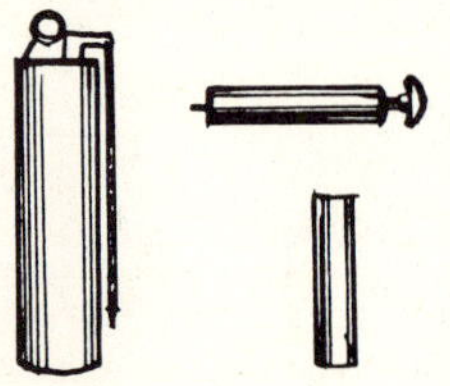

TYPE	CLASS	CAPACITY & SIZE					
VAPORIZING LIQUID	class **B & C** fires	HAND PUMP	1 QT.	1½ QT.	1 GAL.	2 GAL.	
		height	13"	17"	22"	27"	
		diameter	3"	3"	6"	8"	
		weight(lbs)	7	9	22	42	
		class	B2 &	C2	B2	& C1	
		PRESSURIZED	1 QT.	2 QT.	2½ QT.	1 GAL.	2 GAL.
		height	15"	19"	20"	23"	30"
		space used	5" x 8"	5" x 8"	5" x 10"	12" x 6"	14" x 7"
		weight	6	19	23	38	·63
		class	B-2	&	C-2	B-2 &	C-2

EFFECTIVE RANGE:
1 & 1½ qt. pump - 20-30 ft.
pressurized - 1 qt. 25-30 ft.; ½ gal. 25-30 ft.; 1 gal.& 2 gal., 30-35 ft.
RECHARGE: after use.
PRESSURE SOURCE: pump or pressurized.
TEMPERATURE EFFECT:
will operate at minus 40°F.
ELECTRICAL CONDUCTIVITY:
will not conduct.

FURNITURE

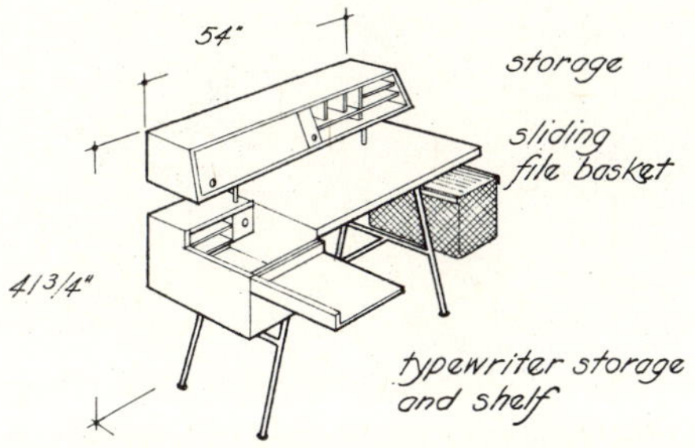
54"
storage
sliding file basket
41 3/4"
typewriter storage and shelf
28"
Desk - wood, plastic, or a leather top, metal legs

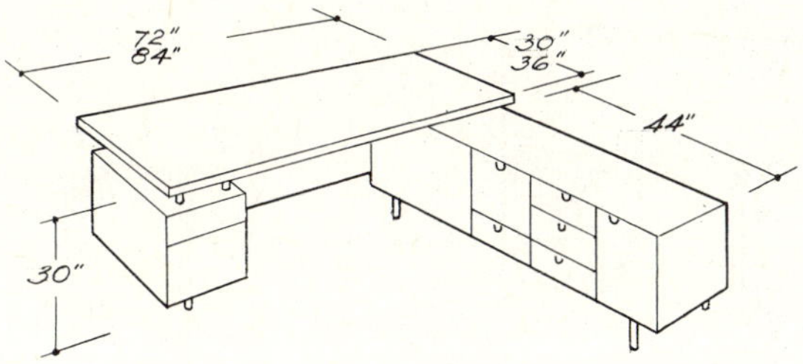
72"
84"
30"
36"
44"
30"
Desk with side storage unit - wood with metal legs.

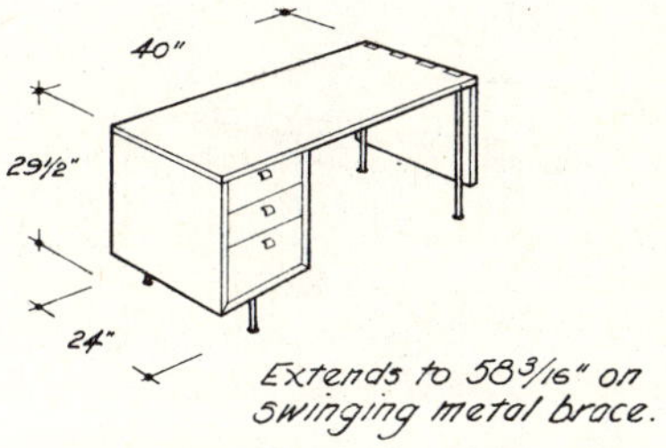
40"
29½"
24"
Extends to 58 3/16" on swinging metal brace.
small home desk, wood on tubular steel framework, drop leaf

HERMAN MILLER COLLECTION -

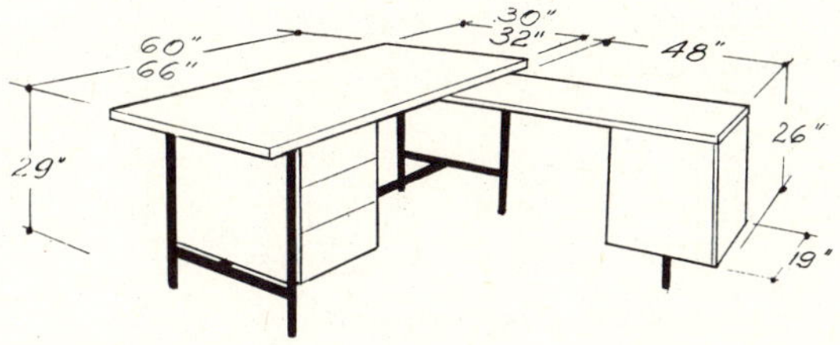
60"
66"
30"
32"
48"
29"
26"
19"
Executive secretarial desk

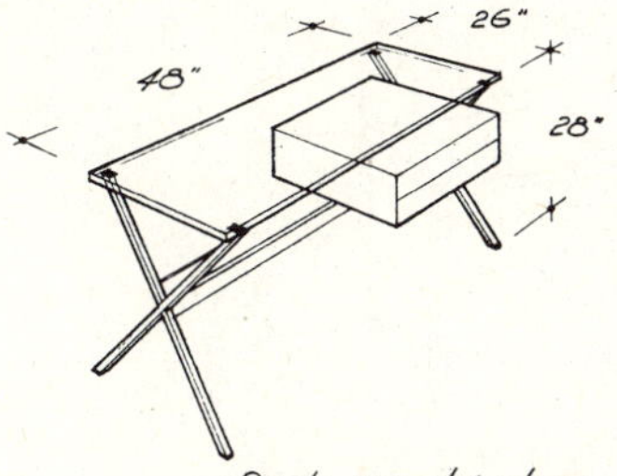
26"
48"
28"
Desk, wood & glass

- KNOLL ASSOCIATES -

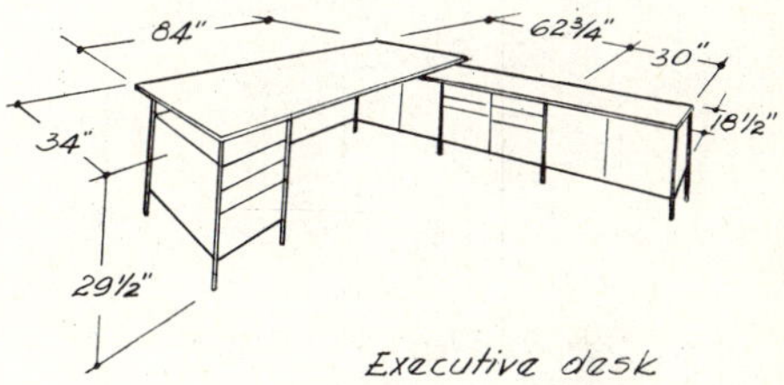
84"
62¾"
30"
18½"
34"
29½"
Executive desk
PAUL Mc COBB

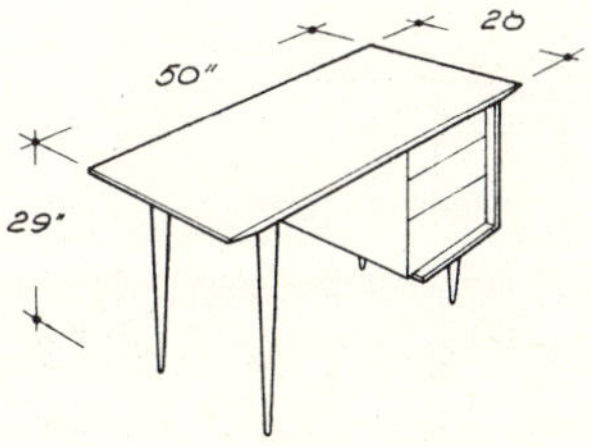
50"
26
29"
Desk, wood

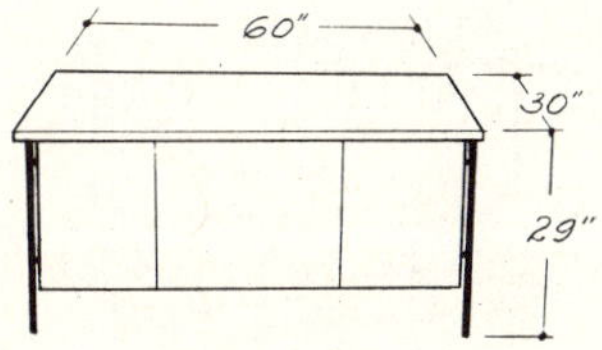
60"
30"
29"
Secretarial desk

KNOLL ASSOCIATES

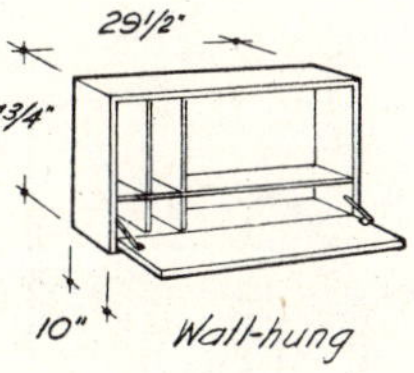
29½"
17¾"
10"
Wall-hung
Desk, wood

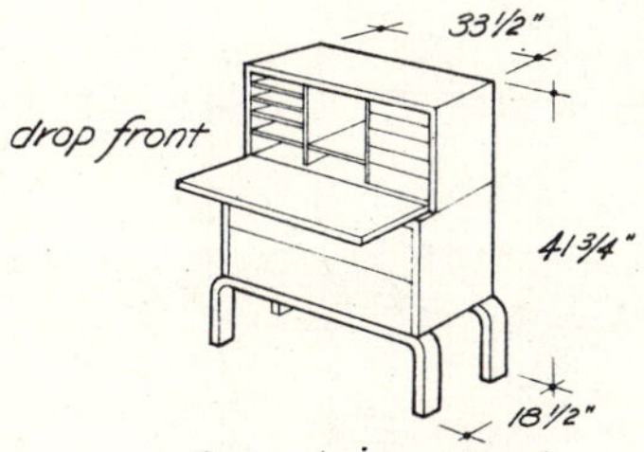
33½"
drop front
41¾"
18½"
Secretaire, wood

FINSVEN

DESKS

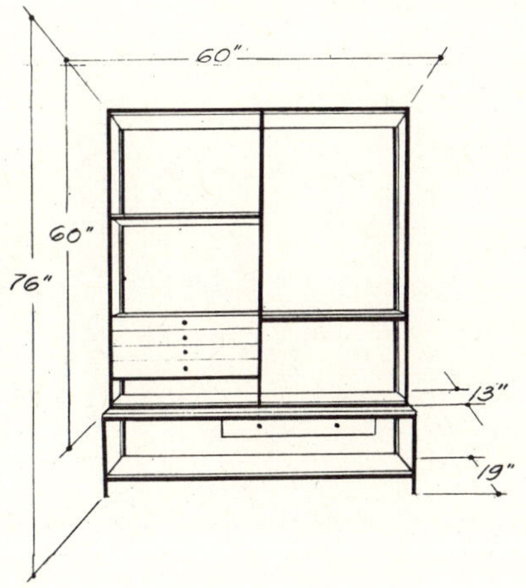
60"
60"
76"
13"
19"
Room divider
PAUL Mc COBB

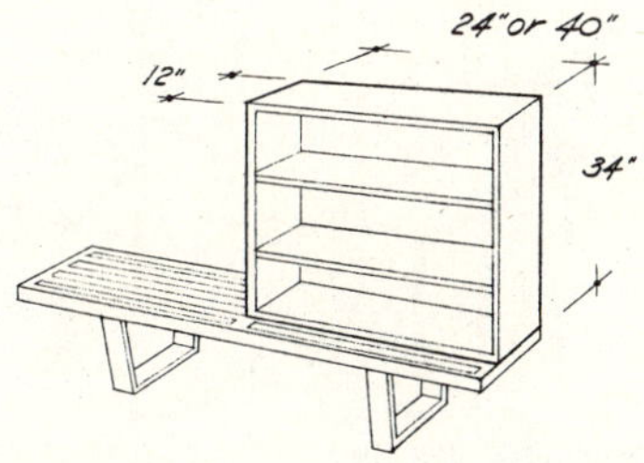
24" or 40"
12"
34"
Bookcase - may be wall-hung, on legs, or on benches (shown)

- HERMAN MILLER COLLECTION -

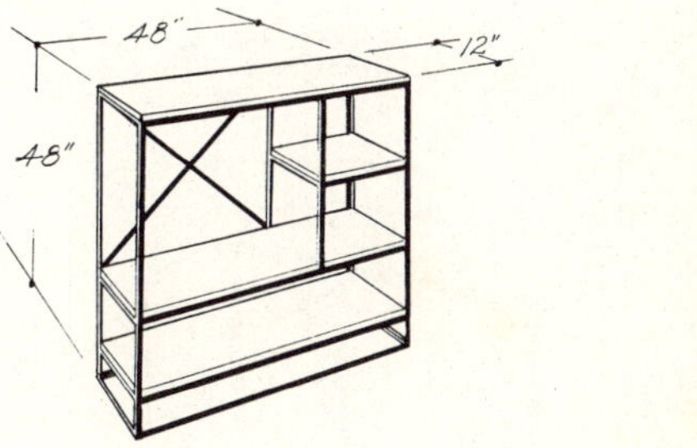
48"
12"
48"
Room divider
PAUL Mc COBB

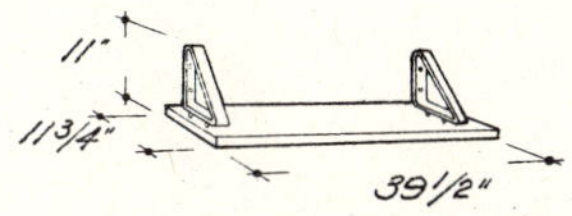
11"
11¾"
39½"
Bookshelf - wall-hung
- FINSVEN -

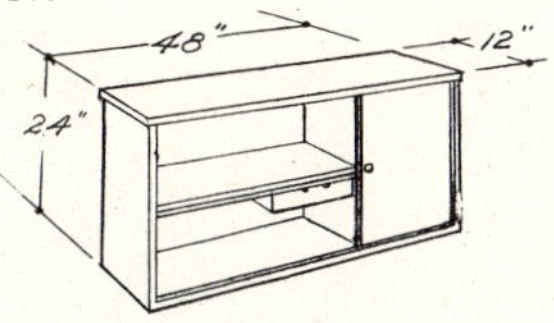
48"
12"
24"
Bookcase - wall-hung
PAUL Mc COBB

BOOK CASES

OFFICE FURNITURE

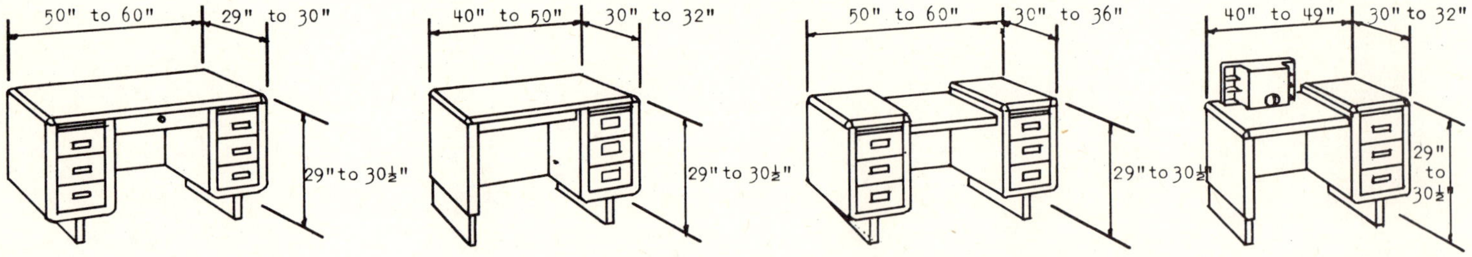
50" to 60"
29" to 30"
29" to 30½"
40" to 50"
30" to 32"
29" to 30½"
50" to 60"
30" to 36"
29" to 30½"
40" to 49"
30" to 32"
29" to 30½"

DOUBLE PEDESTAL SINGLE PEDESTAL DOUBLE PEDESTAL SINGLE PEDESTAL

FLAT TOP **FIXED PLATFORM**

Double pedestal desks are also available with dictating equipment installed in lower drawers.

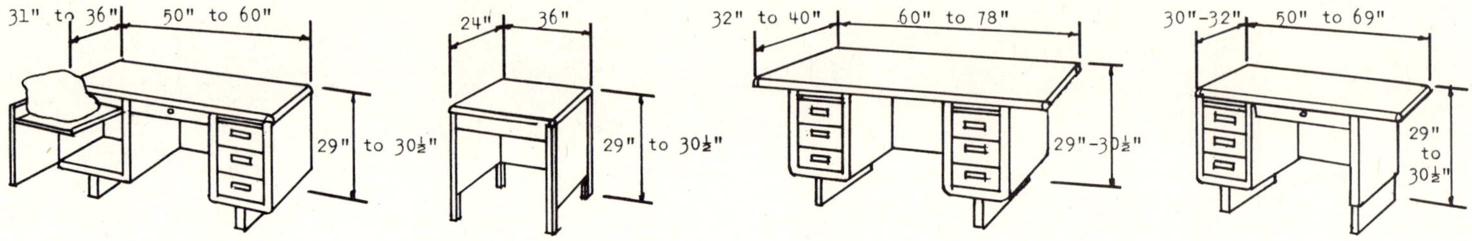
31" to 36"
50" to 60"
29" to 30½"
24"
36"
29" to 30½"
32" to 40"
60" to 78"
29"-30½"
30"-32"
50" to 69"
29" to 30½"

SECRETARIAL DESK SALESMAN'S DESK CONFERENCE DESK

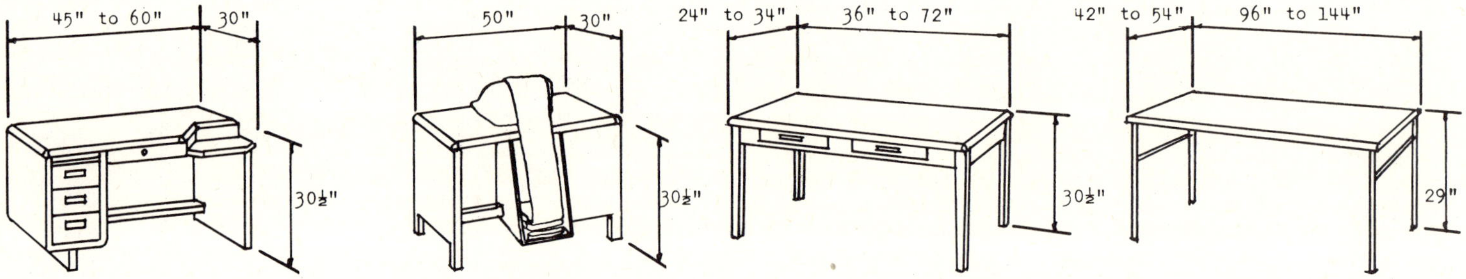
45" to 60"
30"
30½"
50"
30"
30½"
24" to 34"
36" to 72"
30½"
42" to 54"
96" to 144"
29"

CALCULATING MACHINE FANFOLD BILLING MACHINE OFFICE TABLE CONFERENCE DESK

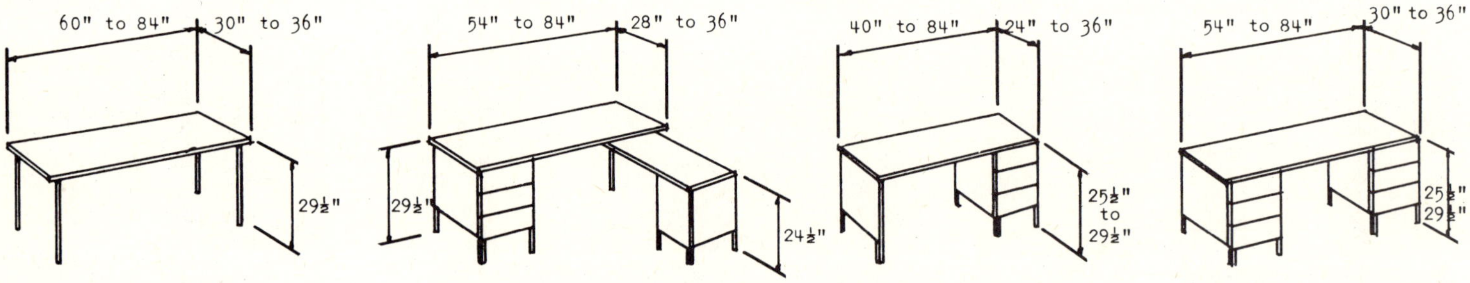
60" to 84"
30" to 36"
29½"
54" to 84"
28" to 36"
29½"
24½"
40" to 84"
24" to 36"
25½" to 29½"
54" to 84"
30" to 36"
25½"
29½"

TABLE-DESK WORK & TYPING DESK SINGLE PEDESTAL DOUBLE PEDESTAL

Separate units available as desks, tables, and Storage units. Maybe used in varying combinations. Usually of wood with wood or metal legs. Complete metal units also available.

DESK UNITS

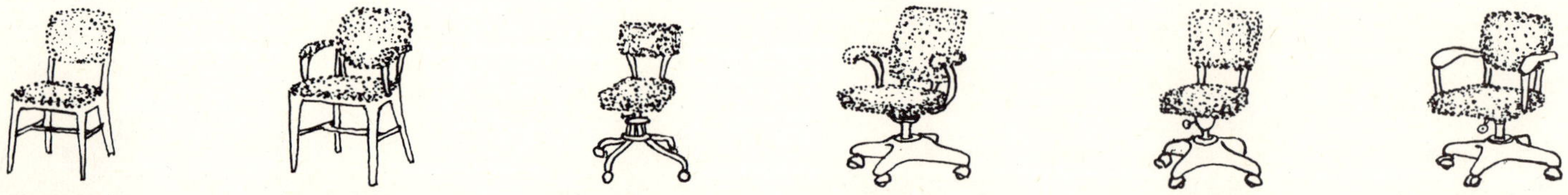

Width-17½" to 18" Depth-16" to 16½" Height-33" to 33½"	Width-20" to 21" Depth-17½" to 19½" Height-33½" to 34"	Width-18" to 19" Depth-18" to 19" Height-29" to 36"	Width-18" to 21" Depth-18" to 20" Height-30" to 33"	Width-17½" to 20" Depth-16" to 19" Height-32" to 33"	Width-22" to 28" Depth-18" to 23" Height-33" to 34"

SIDE CHAIRS POSTURE CHAIRS SWIVEL CHAIRS

OFFICE CHAIRS

OFFICE FURNITURE

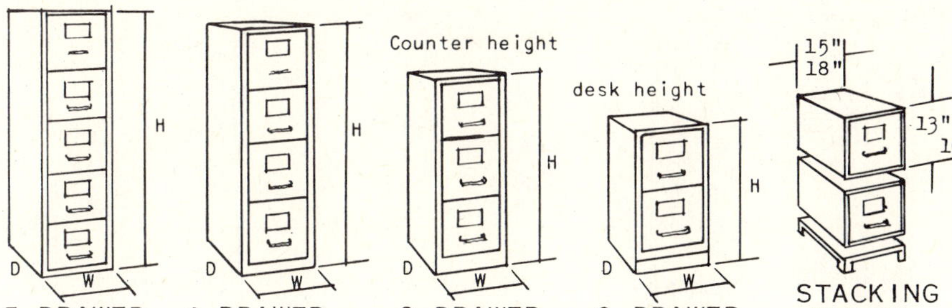

Counter height
desk height
H
D
W
15"
18"
13" to
16"

5 DRAWER 4 DRAWER 3 DRAWER 2 DRAWER STACKING UNITS

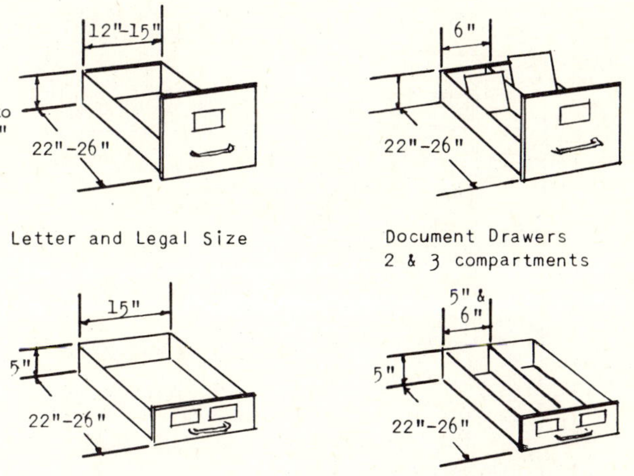

12"-15"
22"-26"
6"
22"-26"
15"
5"
22"-26"
5" &
6"
5"
22"-26"

Letter and Legal Size

Document Drawers
2 & 3 compartments

2 & 3 compartments

SUBSTITUTE DRAWER INSERTS

The above drawer inserts are available for use in the standard frame. Letter and legal size drawers maybe obtained in insulated fire file units.

STANDARD FILES

	Five drawer			Four drawer			Three drawer			Two drawer		
	W	H	D	W	H	D	W	H	D	W	H	D
Letter	15	57	25	14½	52	26	14	40	26	14½	30	26
		59½	28½	15		28½	15	42	28½	15		28½
Legal	17½	59½	26	13½	40	26	17½	40	26	17½	30	26
			28½	18	42	28½	18	42	28½	18		28½
Ledger							15	52	26½ 28½			
Bill	13	52	28½									

INSULATED FIRE FILES

Dimensions for fire files maybe approximated by the addition of 3" to all standard file dimensions.

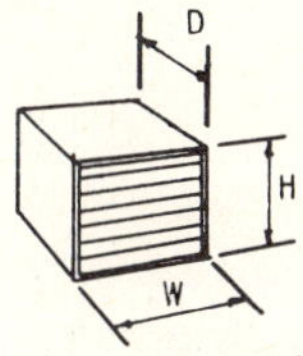

D
H
W

Drawer Type	W	H	D
Shallow	8-11½	12-18½	24½
Short	11½	23½	19
Deep	11½ 14½	11-26	24½

INDEX FILES

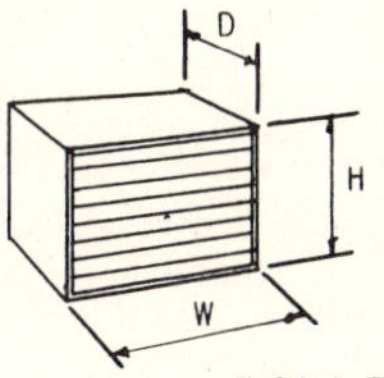

D
H
W

No. of Shelves	W	H	D
3 Shelves	36	12	19
4 Shelves	22-35	42-43	29-30
10 Shelves	22	52	29

ROLLER SHELF FILES

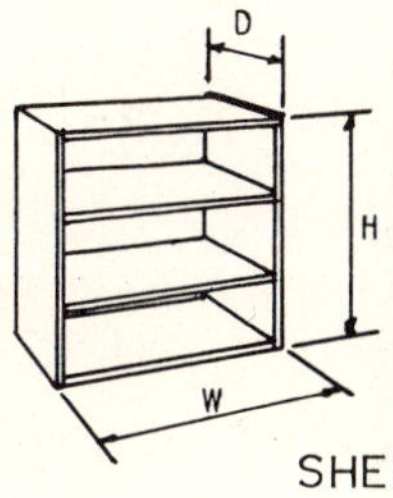

D
H
W

No. of Shelves	W	H	D
3 Shelves	30½	49	10
4 Shelves	36	87	18
5 Shelves	36	87	12

SHELVING UNITS

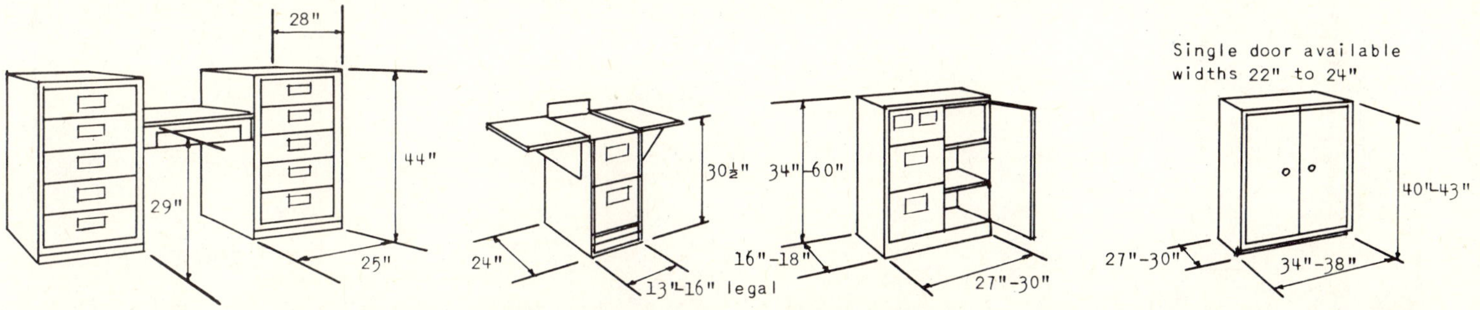

28"
44"
29"
25"
30½"
24"
13"-16" legal
34"-60"
16"-18"
27"-30"
Single door available
widths 22" to 24"
40"-43"
27"-30"
34"-38"

CARD RECORD CROSS FILES PORTABLE FILES CONCEALED VAULT CABINET COUNTER CUPBOARDS

OFFICE FILE & CABINET UNITS

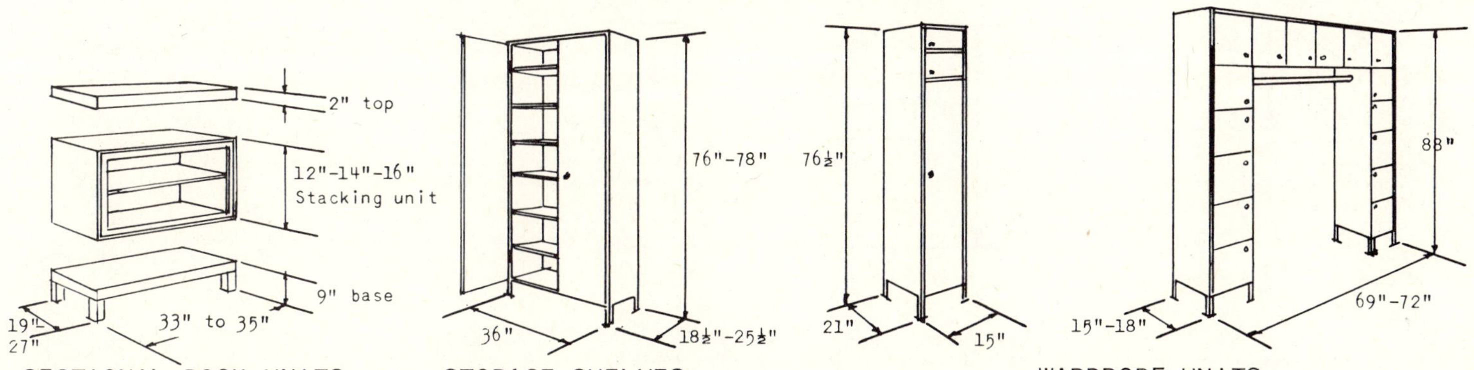

2" top
12"-14"-16"
Stacking unit
9" base
19"-
27"
33" to 35"
76"-78"
36"
18½"-25½"
76½"
21"
15"
88"
15"-18"
69"-72"

SECTIONAL BOOK UNITS STORAGE SHELVES WARDROBE UNITS

STORAGE & WARDROBE UNITS

FILING and REPRODUCTION EQUIPMENT for DRAFTING ROOMS

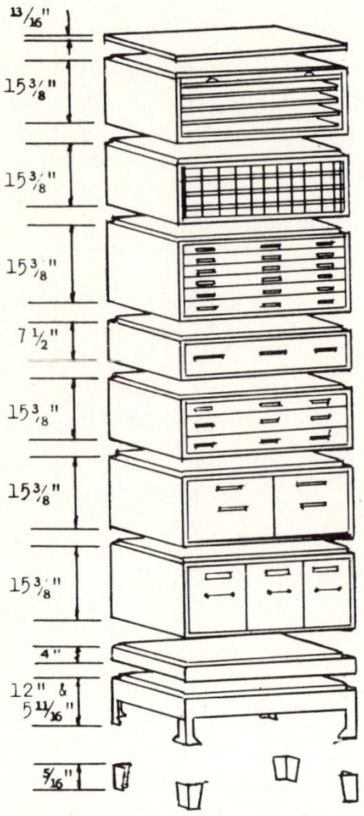
13/16"
Plan cap
15 3/8"
Shelf filing unit
15 3/8"
Roll tracing file
15 3/8"
5 drawer unit
7 1/2"
One drawer unit
15 3/8"
3 drawer unit
15 3/8"
Vertical filing unit. 2 drawer
15 3/8"
Vertical filing unit. 3 drawer
4"
Flush base
12" & 5 11/16"
Sanitary base
5/16"
6" Base legs

Depth - 28½" to 44½"   Width - 40 13/16" to 55 5/16"
Drawers extend from 26" to 42"
"PLAN-FILE"-Steel or wood

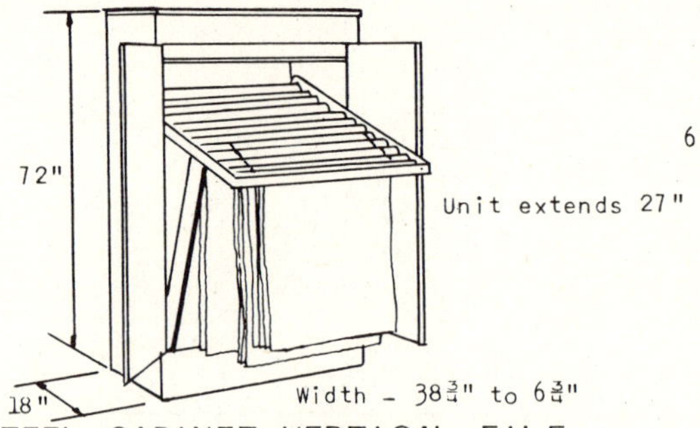
72"
Unit extends 27"
18"
Width - 38¾" to 6¾"

STEEL CABINET VERTICAL FILE

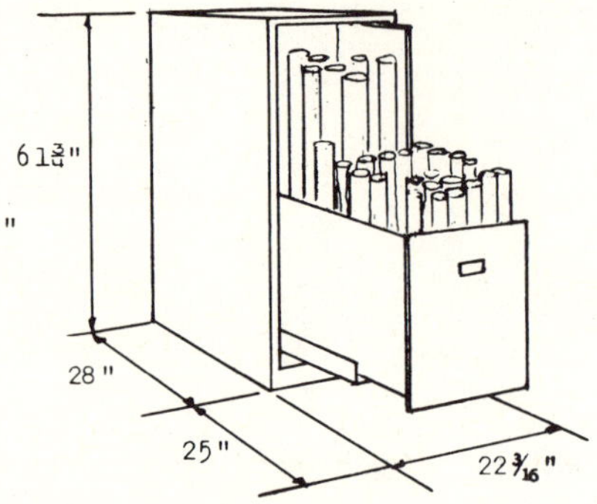
61¾"
28"
25"
22 3/16"

VERTICAL FILE

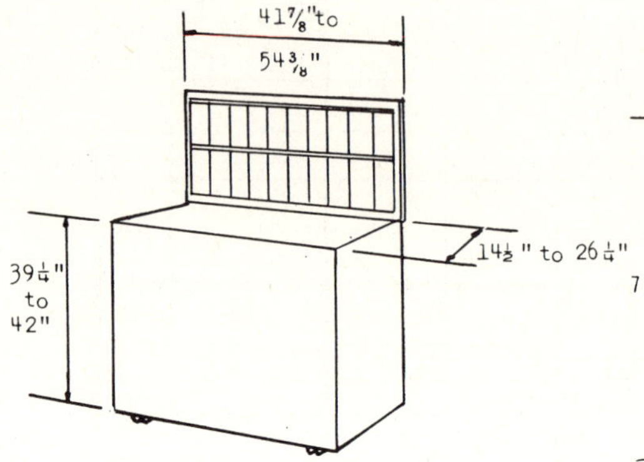
41 7/8" to
54 3/8"
39¼" to 42"
14½" to 26¼"

VERTICAL PLAN FILE
Steel

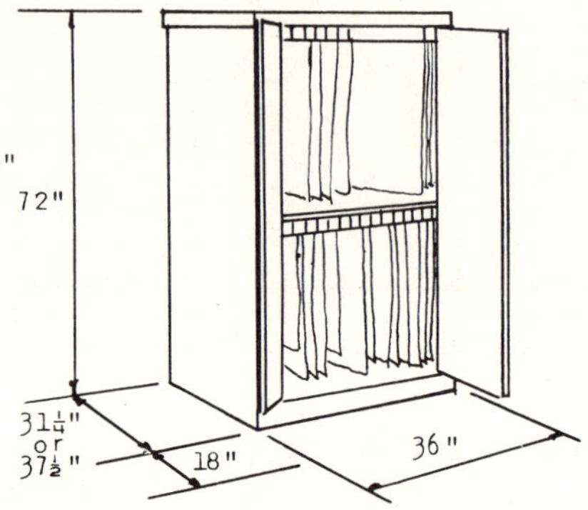
72"
31¼" or 37½"
18"
36"

CLIP FILE

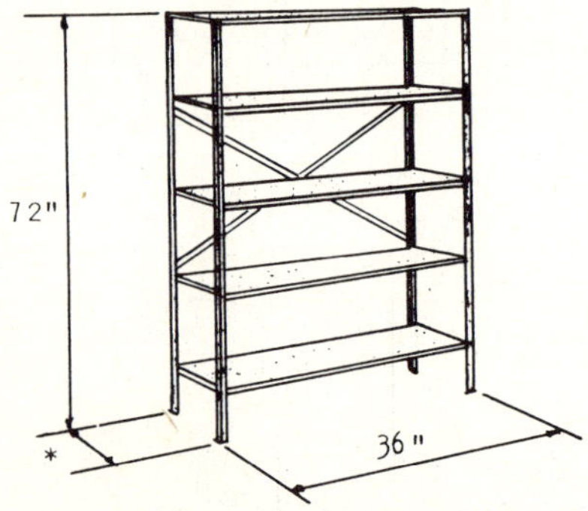
72"
*
36"

ADJUSTABLE STEEL SHELVING
*available in 11½" & 15" widths

TRANSPARENT PLASTIC STORAGE TUBE
2" dia , 13" to 55" long

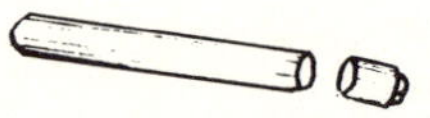

METAL STORAGE TUBE
2½" & 4" dia , 31" to 55" long

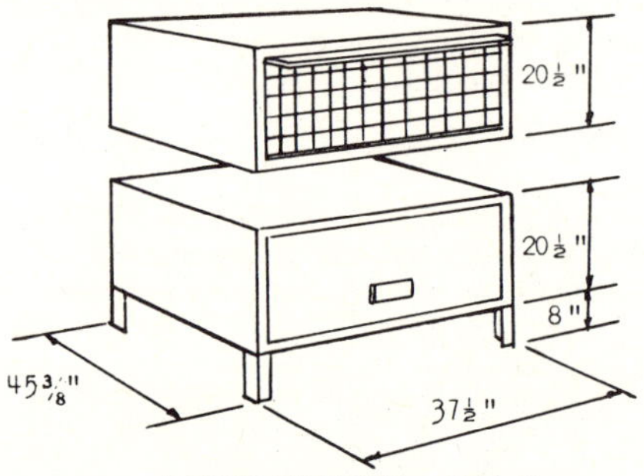
20½"
20½"
8"
45 3/8"
37½"

HORIZONTAL FILE

FILING AND STORAGE EQUIPMENT

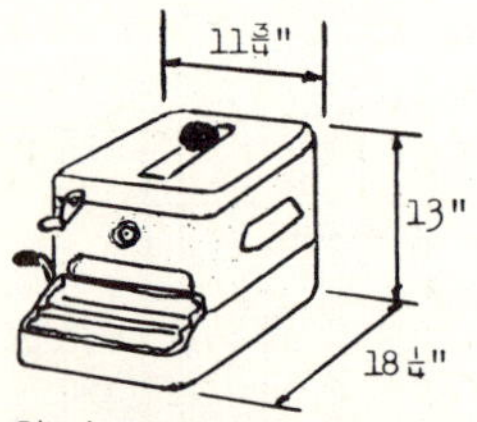
11¾"
13"
18¼"

Photocopy machines
(photographic method)

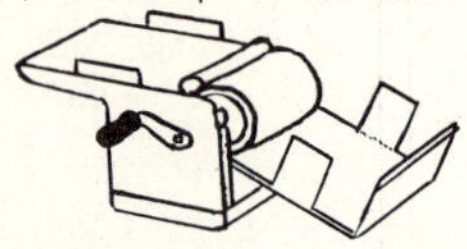

Spirit, gelatin, and photocopy duplicating machines are valuable for 8½"x 11" copy.

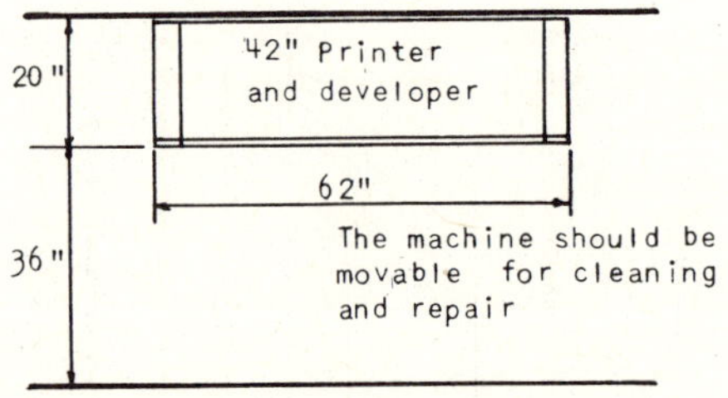
42" Printer
and developer
20"
62"
36"
The machine should be movable for cleaning and repair

The process used determines the requirements of space, light, plumbing, and ventilation.

For reproduction of tracings a printing and developing unit is necessary. The printer is located above the developing unit. With the two units and the proper chemicals and paper, blueprints, black and whites, bluelines, and other types of copy are possible.

When choosing equipment the individual requirements of the office determine the size and type of process chosen.

These machines should be ventilated for heat and chemical fumes. The 42" machine is the most used in medium sized offices today.

REPRODUCTION EQUIPMENT

DRAFTING ROOM FURNITURE and EQUIPMENT

32" to
42"
height

Adjustable

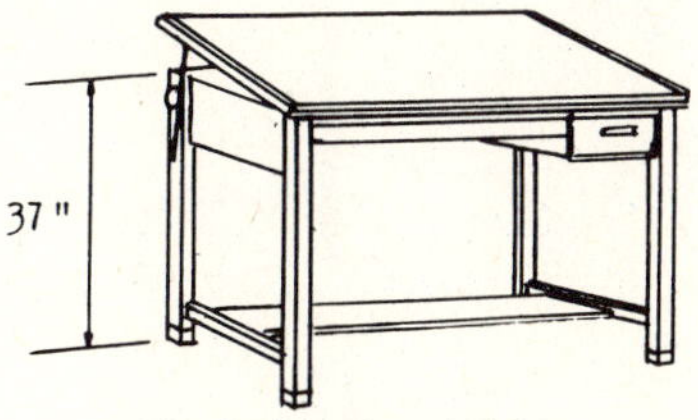
37"

Steel drawing table
with concealed raising
device, top & drawers wood

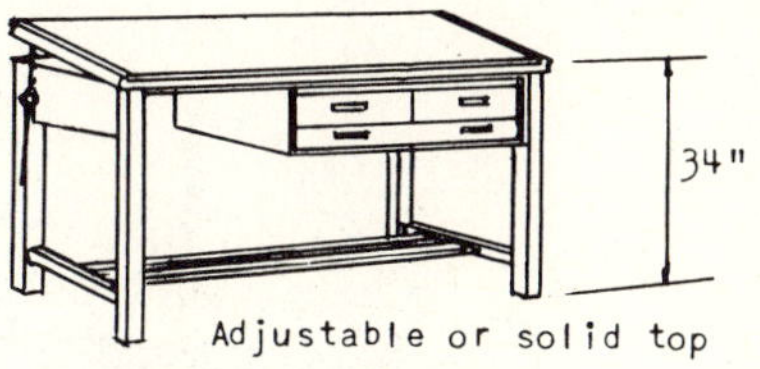
34"

Adjustable or solid top

Available 5 drawers, wood
Available 3 drawers, metal

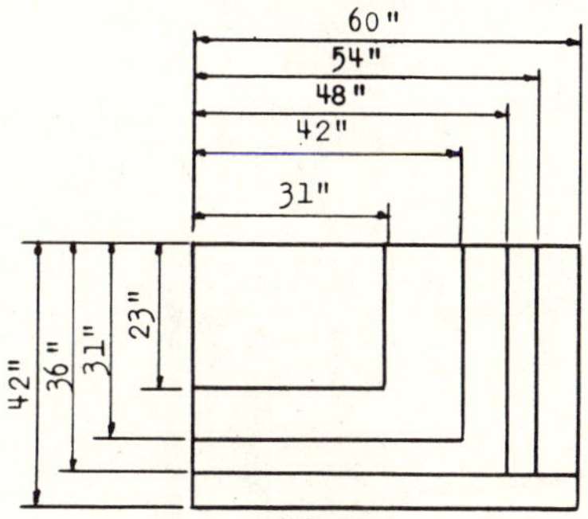
60"
54"
48"
42"
31"
42"
36"
31"
23"

PLAN
Basic table - metal or wood legs

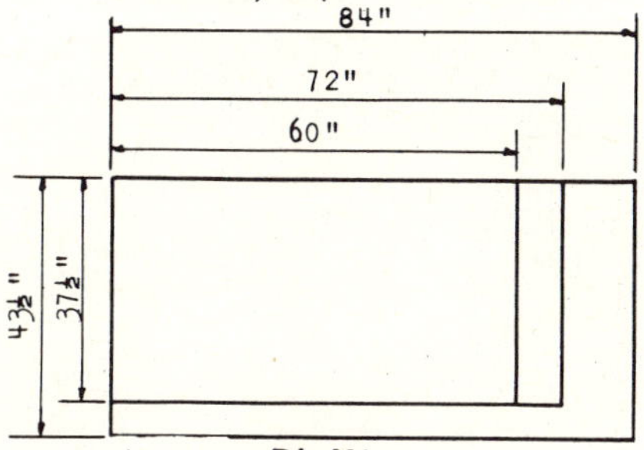
84"
72"
60"
43½"
37½"

PLAN
Engineering desk - tilting
metal base

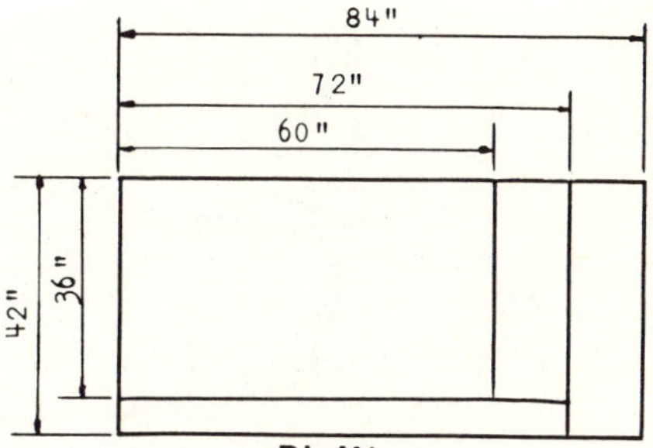
84"
72"
60"
42"
36"

PLAN
Table with wood or metal legs

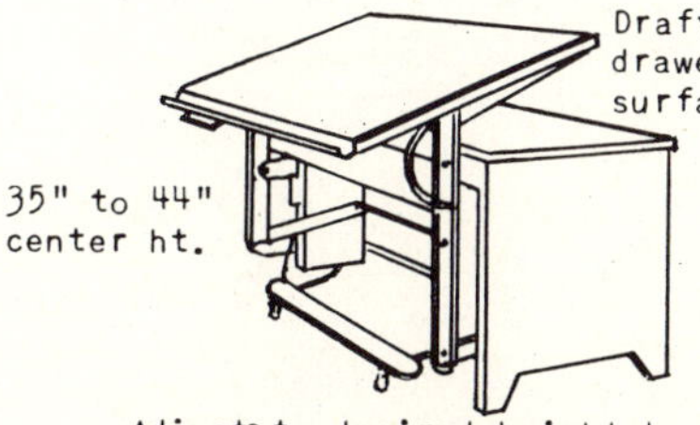
35" to 44"
center ht.

Draftsmen use the
drawers & reference
surface behind them.

Adjusts to desired height by foot
pedal and takes any stop, vertical, or
horizontal.

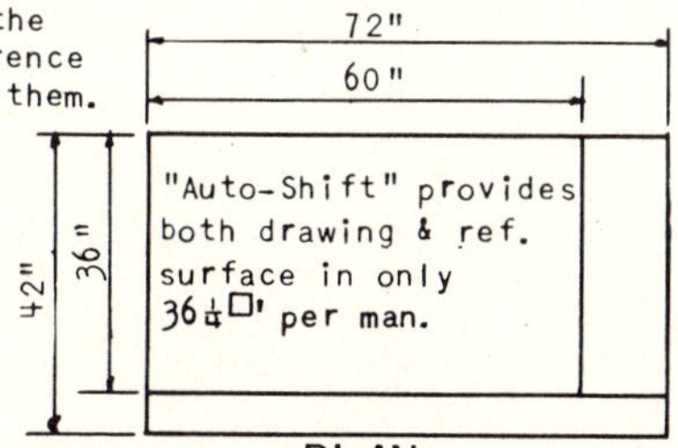
72"
60"
42"
36"
"Auto-Shift" provides
both drawing & ref.
surface in only
36¼□' per man.

PLAN
"Auto-shift" drawing table

Tracing tables
are obtainable
with 22"x 24" and
24"x 36" glass
tracing areas.
Portable tracing
boards in sizes
up to 24"x 36¾"
tracing areas.

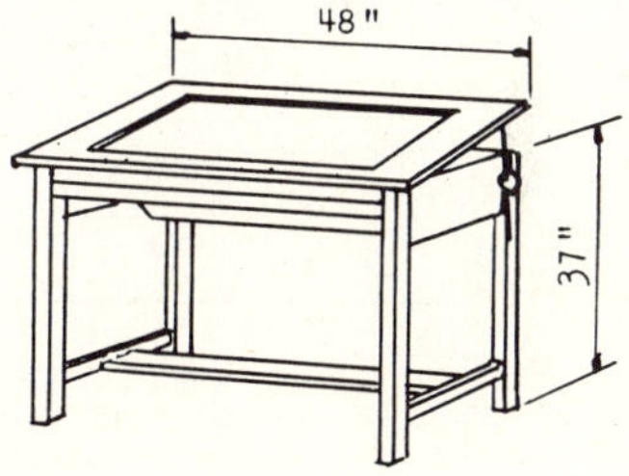
48"
37"

Reference tables shown on preceding
page are not stock items.

DRAFTING AND LIGHT TABLES

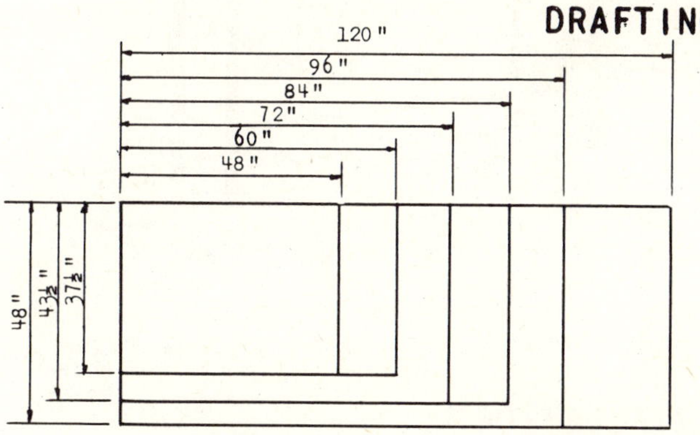
120"
96"
84"
72"
60"
48"
48"
43½"
37½"

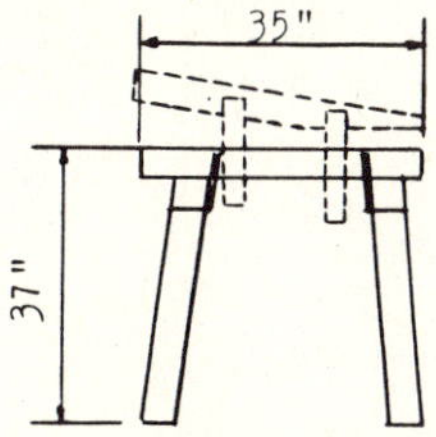
35"
37"

Adjustable trestles
or horses available;
adjust from 39" to 47"
in height

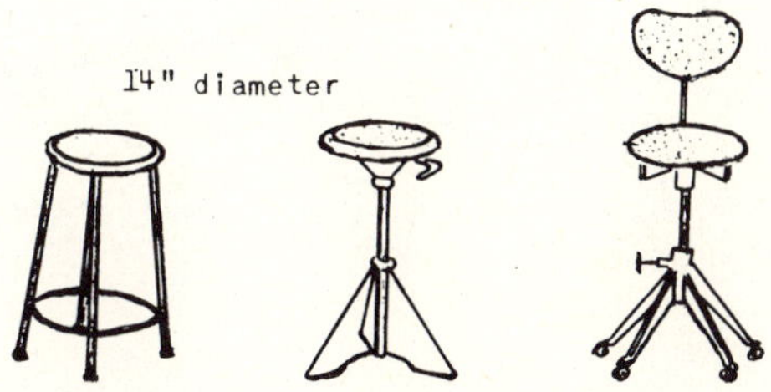
14" diameter

fixed height
28" & 30"

adjustable from
16½" to 24½"

TRESTLES, BOARDS, AND STOOLS

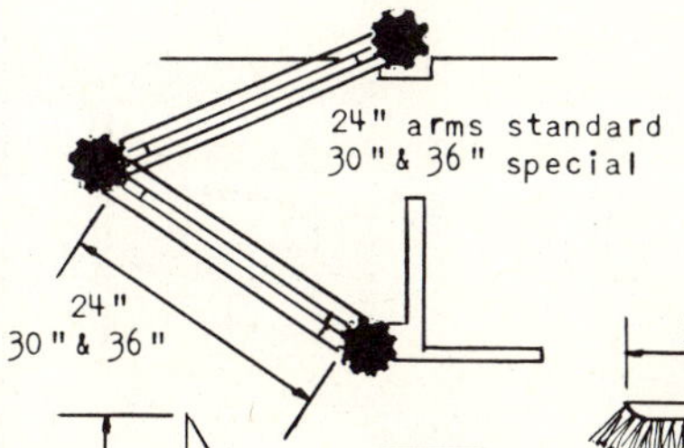
24" arms standard
30" & 36" special
24"
30" & 36"

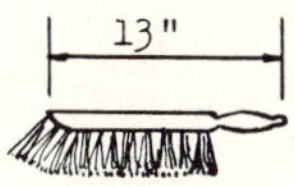
13"

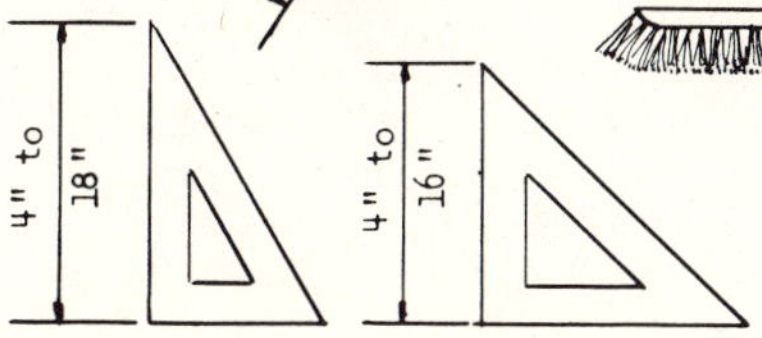
4" to
18"
4" to
16"

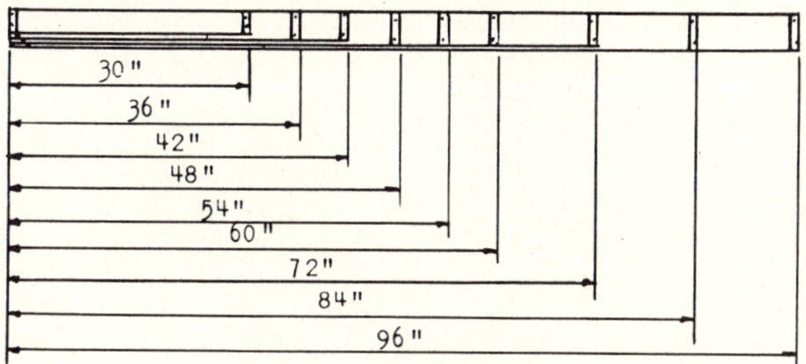
30"
36"
42"
48"
54"
60"
72"
84"
96"

Parallel straight edges

Sizes shown are obtainable from
leading manufactures and suppliers

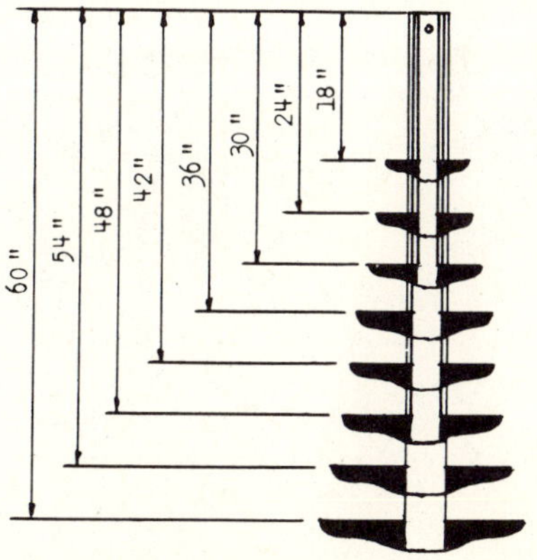
60"
54"
48"
42"
36"
30"
24"
18"

DRAFTING EQUIPMENT

SPECIAL DRAFTING TABLE INSTALLATIONS

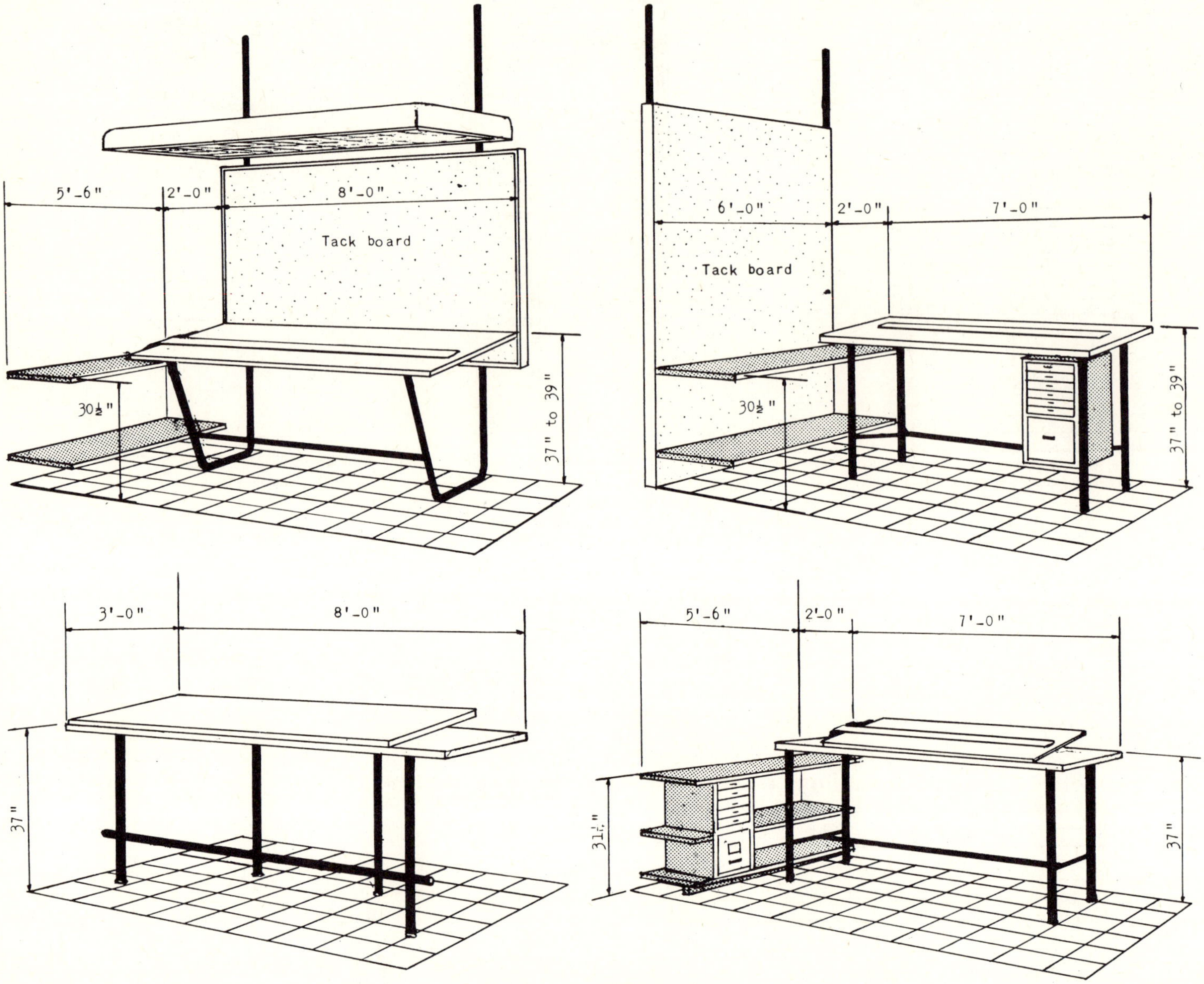
5'-6"
2'-0"
8'-0"
Tack board
30½"
37" to 39"
6'-0"
2'-0"
7'-0"
Tack board
30½"
37" to 39"
3'-0"
8'-0"
37"
5'-6"
2'-0"
7'-0"
31½"
37"

The above tables are constructed of
flush doors, built-up on pipe legs.
Stock steel file cabinets are used.

SPECIAL DRAFTING TABLE INSTALLATIONS

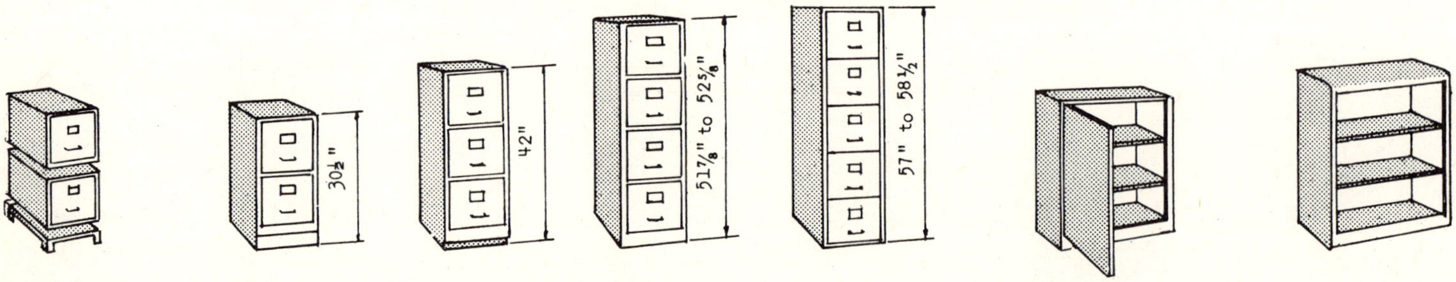
30½"
42"
51⅞" to 52⅝"
57" to 58½"

Upright files — Desk height — Counter height — Std. height — Extra height — Storage cabinet — Bookcase

Units + or − 1"
Letter–15"x 28"x 14" H
Legal –18"x 28"x 14" H
Ledger–15"x 28"x 16" H

Commercial files vary in size due to thickness of frame.
Letter files from 14⅜" W. 28⅝" D. to 15" W. 28" D.
Legal files from 17¼" W. 28⅝" D. to 18¼" W. 28" D.
Ledger files from 13¾" W. 28" D. to 14$\frac{15}{16}$" W. 28$\frac{7}{16}$" D.

18" W, 18" D, 30½" H, To
36" W, 24" D, 78" H.
Single or double doors.

37½" high
30½" wide
17" deep

FILING CABINETS AND BOOKCASES

VENDING MACHINES

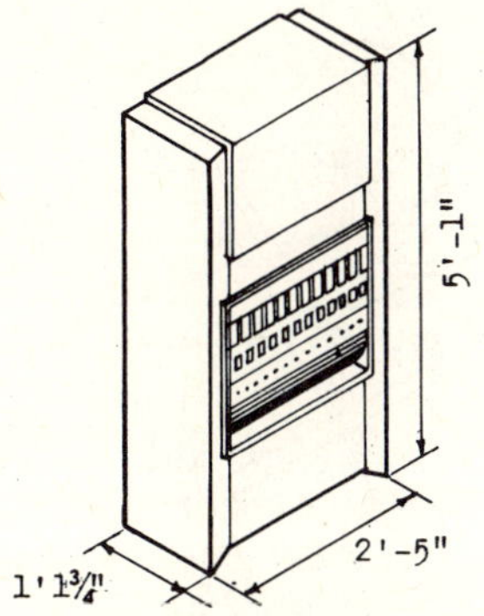
5'-1"
1'1¾"
2'-5"

CIGARETTES
(12 or 14 brands)

Same size vendors as shown at left also vend:
- Candy (8 brands)
- Sandwiches (4 kinds)
- Pastries (4 kinds)
- Cigars (4 kinds)

DATA BY ARTHUR H. DUGRENIER, INC.

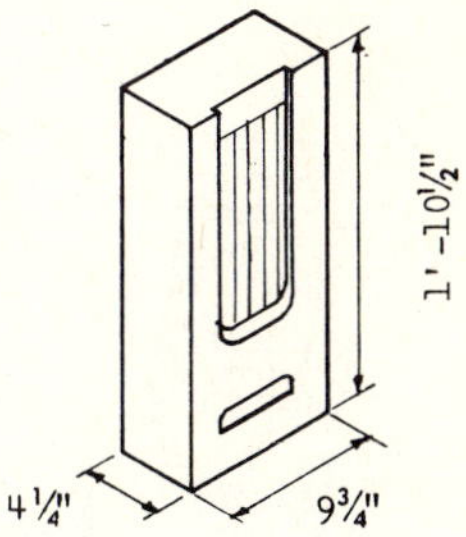
1'-10½"
4¼"
9¾"

CHEWING GUM
(290 pieces)

Scale: ½" = 1'-0"

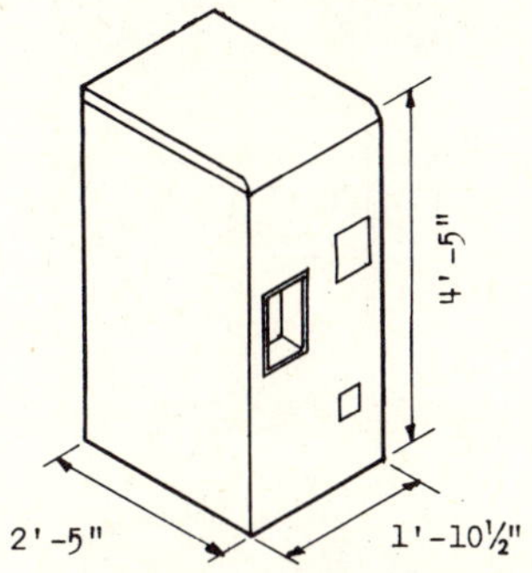
4'-5"
2'-5"
1'-10½"

Capacity: 150 cups orange juice
200 cups coffee
(110 volts)

COFFEE - ORANGE JUICE

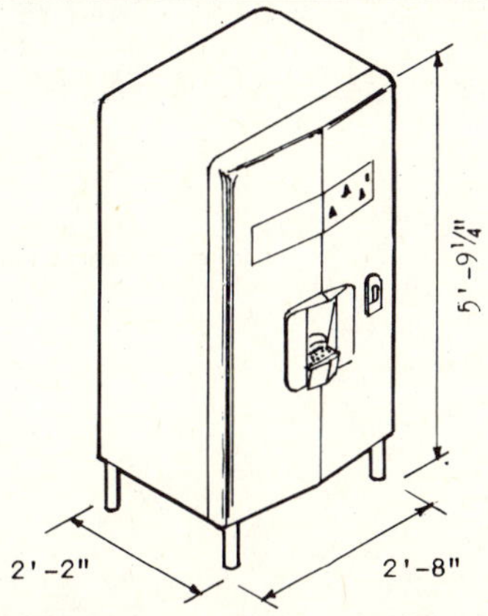
5'-9¼"
2'-2"
2'-8"

Capacity:
1000 cups

COFFEE - TEA - HOT CHOCOLATE

Capacity:
500 cups

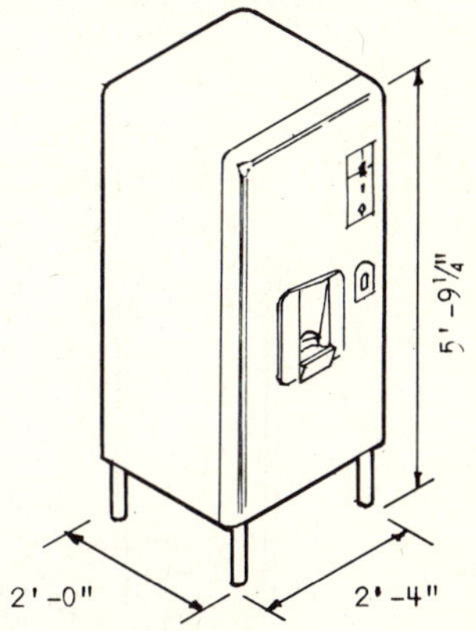
5'-9¼"
2'-0"
2'-4"

HOT & COLD CHOCOLATE

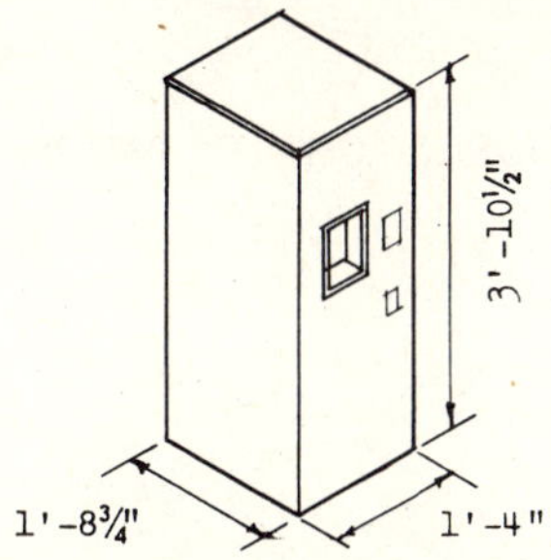
3'-10½"
1'-8¾"
1'-4"

Capacity: 150 cups
(115 volts)

COFFEE - HOT CHOCOLATE

DATA BY RUDD-MELIKIAN, INC.

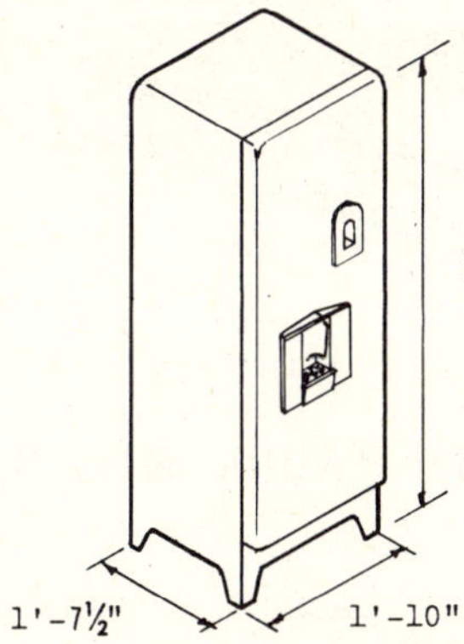
5'-9"
1'-7½"
1'-10"

Capacity:
200 cups

COFFEE - HOT CHOCOLATE

Capacity:
200 cups

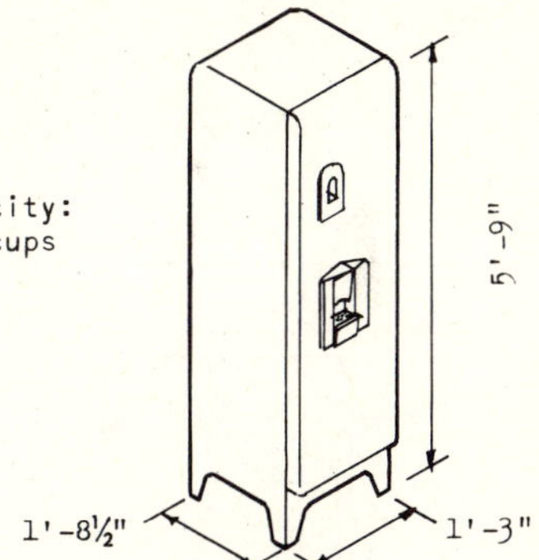
5'-9"
1'-8½"
1'-3"

SOUP OR
HOT CHOCOLATE

DATA BY THE BERT MILLS CORP.

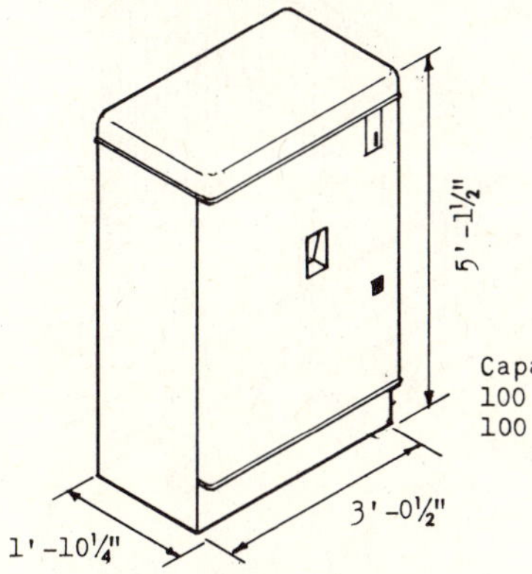
5'-1½"
1'-10¼"
3'-0½"

Capacity:
100 bars vending
100 bars storage

ICE CREAM BARS

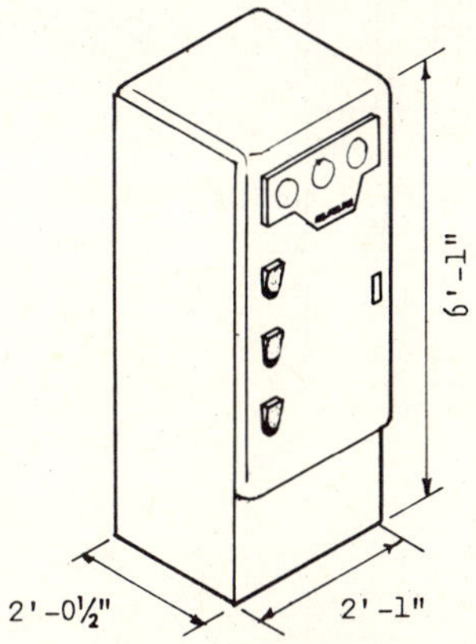
6'-1"
2'-0½"
2'-1"

Capacity:
37 bottles in
each compartment.
48 bottles in
pre-cool.
159 bottles total.

SOFT DRINKS

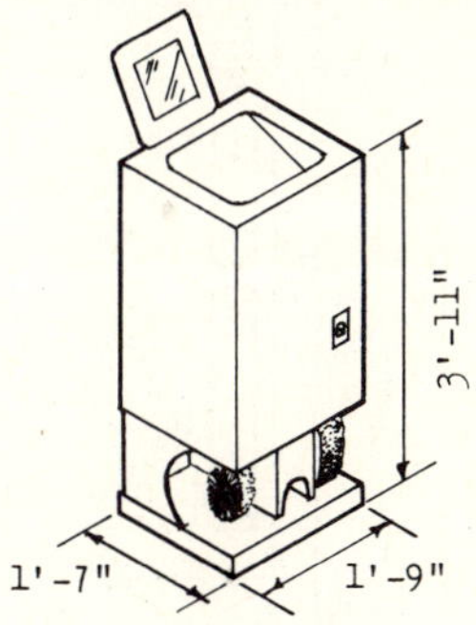
3'-11"
1'-7"
1'-9"

SHOE SHINES

All Atlas machines
shown are ¼ H.P.

DATA BY ATLAS TOOL AND MANUFACTURING CO.
Scales: ¼" = 1'-0" except as noted.

STORAGE of FOLDING CHAIRS

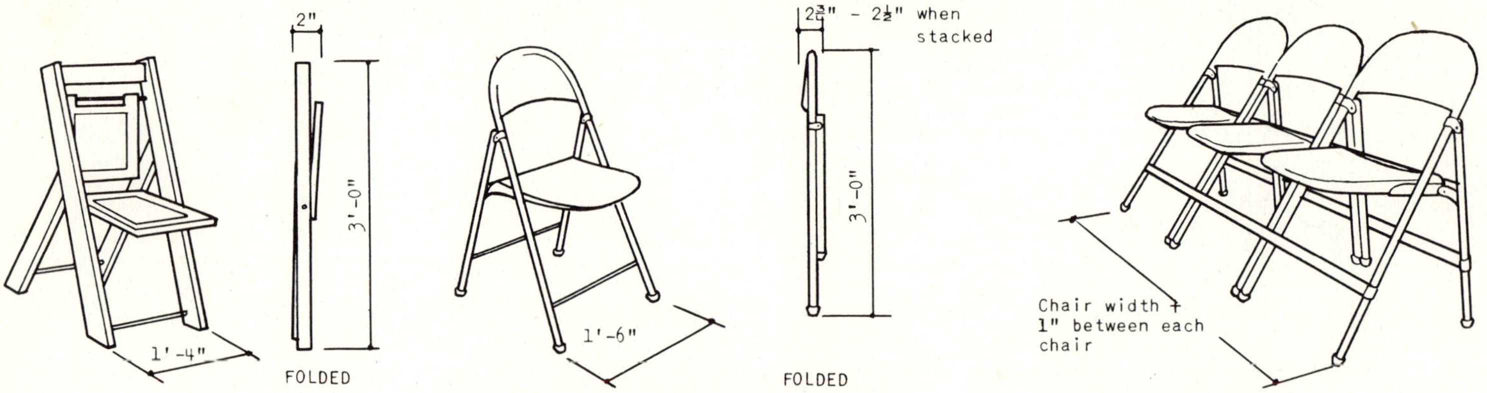
2"
3'-0"
1'-4"
FOLDED
2⅜" - 2½" when stacked
3'-0"
1'-6"
FOLDED
Chair width + 1" between each chair

WOOD FOLDING CHAIRS

TUBULAR STEEL FOLDING CHAIRS

TUBULAR STEEL CHAIRS CLAMPED IN SECTIONS

SIZES OF FOLDING CHAIRS

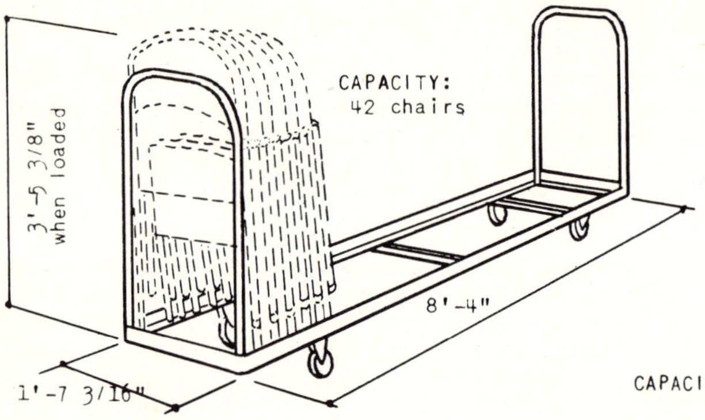
CAPACITY:
42 chairs
3'-5 3/8" when loaded
8'-4"
1'-7 3/16"

TRUCK FOR HANDLING UPRIGHT LOADS

Note: Doors to chair storage rooms must be wide enough for chair trucks to pass through

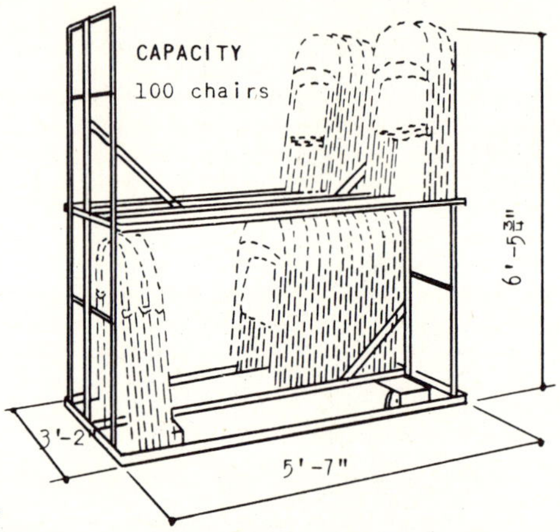
CAPACITY
100 chairs
6'-5¾"
3'-2"
5'-7"

DOUBLE CHAIR TRUCK

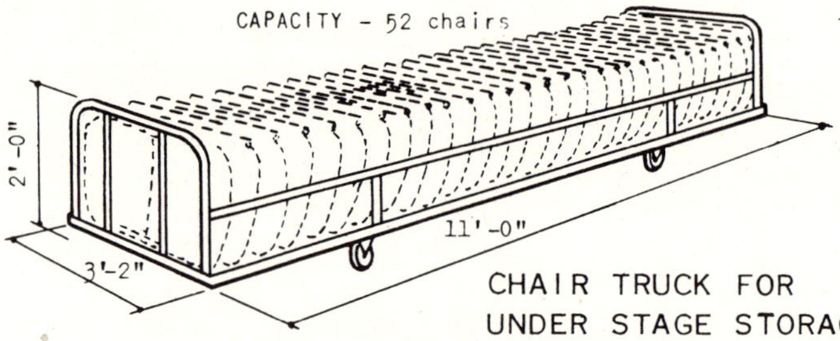
CAPACITY - 52 chairs
2'-0"
11'-0"
3'-2"

CHAIR TRUCK FOR UNDER STAGE STORAGE

CHAIR TRUCK SIZES

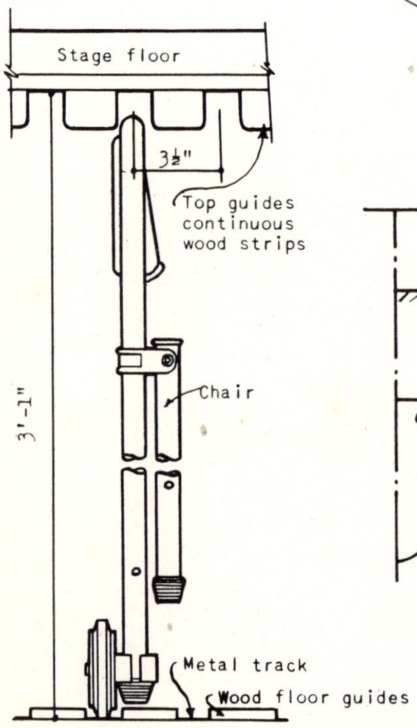
Stage floor
3½"
Top guides continuous wood strips
Chair
3'-1"
Metal track
Wood floor guides

ELEVATION

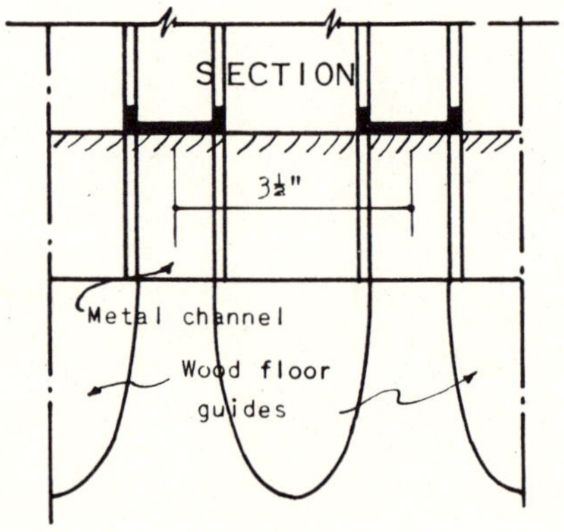
SECTION
3½"
Metal channel
Wood floor guides

PLAN

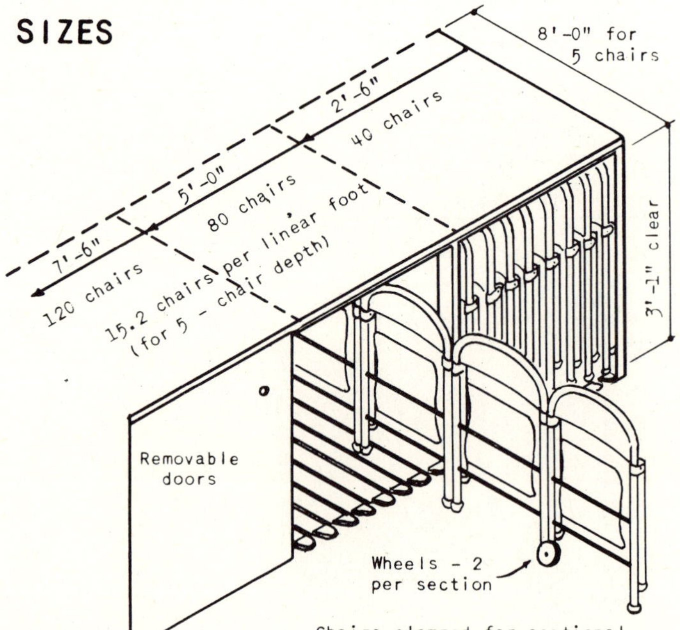
8'-0" for 5 chairs
2'-6"
40 chairs
5'-0"
80 chairs
7'-6"
120 chairs
15.2 chairs per linear foot (for 5 - chair depth)
3'-1" clear
Removable doors
Wheels - 2 per section

Chairs clamped for sectional grouping.

* Devised by Hornbostel & Bennett

TRACK DEVICE FOR STORING CHAIRS UNDER STAGES*

ELEMENTARY SCHOOL DESKS and SEATS

NOTE: Furniture on this page is shown to assist the architect with sizes in planning and to indicate the degree of design variation. Many other varieties of school desks and seats are available in addition to those here represented

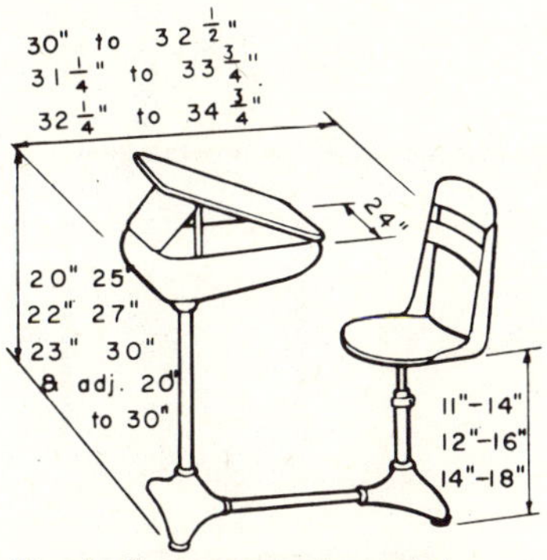
30" to 32 1/2"
31 1/4" to 33 3/4"
32 1/4" to 34 3/4"
24"
20" 25"
22" 27"
23" 30"
& adj. 20" to 30"
11"–14"
12"–16"
14"–18"

Wood & enameled metal
American Seating Company

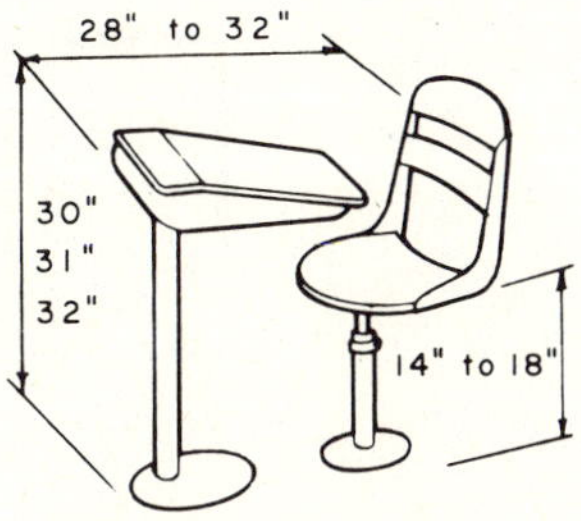
28" to 32"
30"
31"
32"
14" to 18"

Wood & enameled metal
American Seating Co.

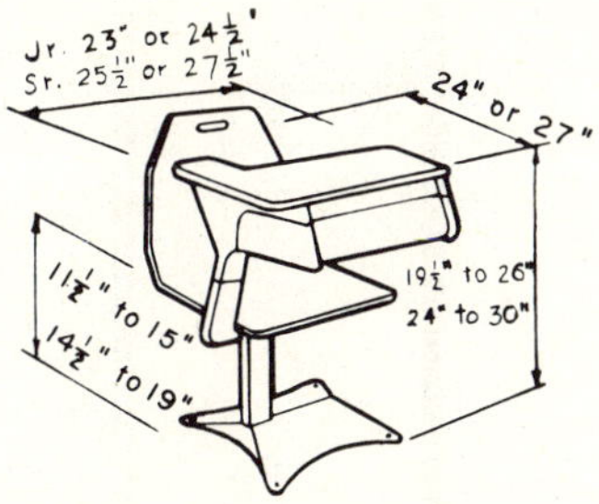
Jr. 23" or 24 1/2"
Sr. 25 1/2" or 27 1/2"
24" or 27"
11 1/2" to 15"
14 1/2" to 19"
19 1/2" to 26"
24" to 30"

Wood & enameled metal
General School Equipment Co.

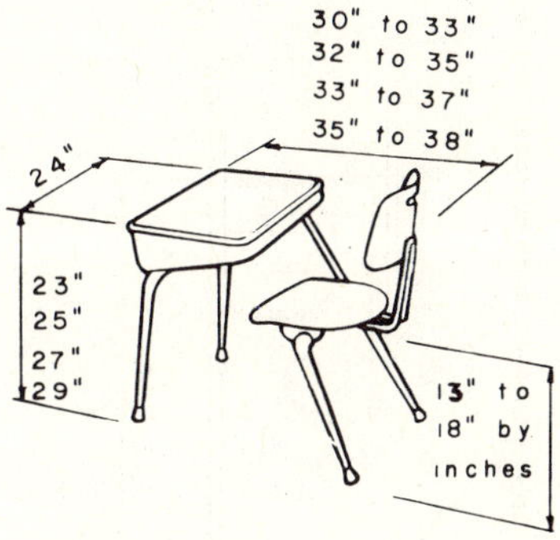
30" to 33"
32" to 35"
33" to 37"
35" to 38"
24"
23"
25"
27"
29"
13" to 18" by inches

Wood, or plastic, & metal
Brunswick-Balke-Collender Co.

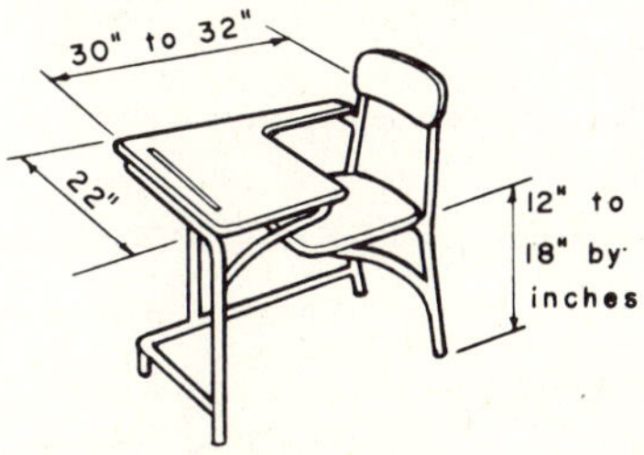
30" to 32"
22"
12" to 18" by inches

Steel tubing & wood
Heywood-Wakefield

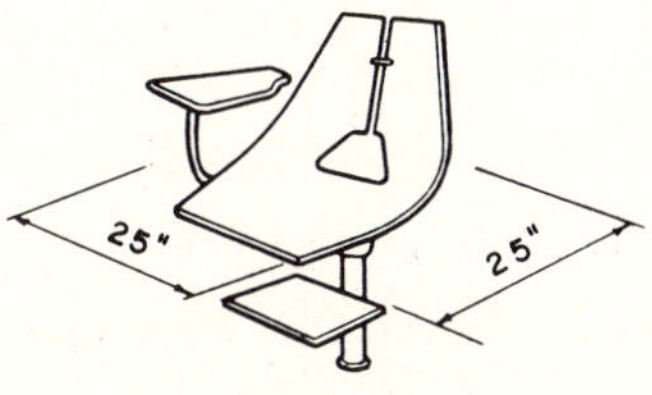
25"
25"

Molded plywood
J. G. Furniture Co.

Wood & enameled metal
Heywood - Wakefield

13"
15"
17"

Wood & enameled metal
Griggs Equipment Company

18" only

Wood & bent plywood
Thonet Industries, Inc.

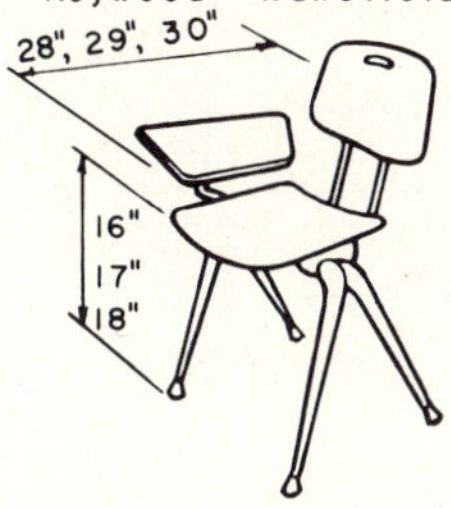
28", 29", 30"
16"
17"
18"

Wood or plastic, & metal
Brunswick-Balke-Collender

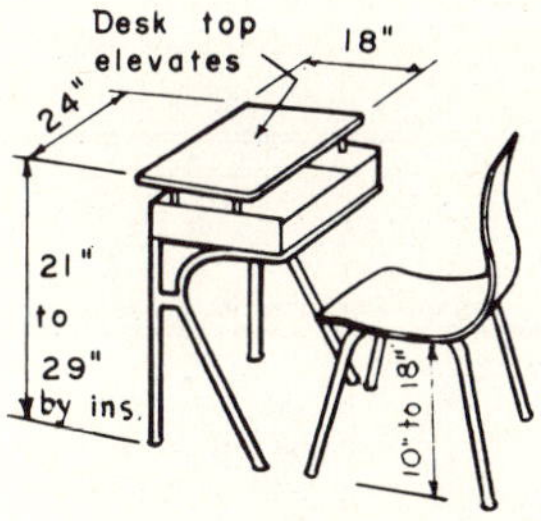
Desk top elevates
18"
24"
21" to 29" by ins.
10" to 18"

Wood & tubular steel
Gen'l School Equipment Co.

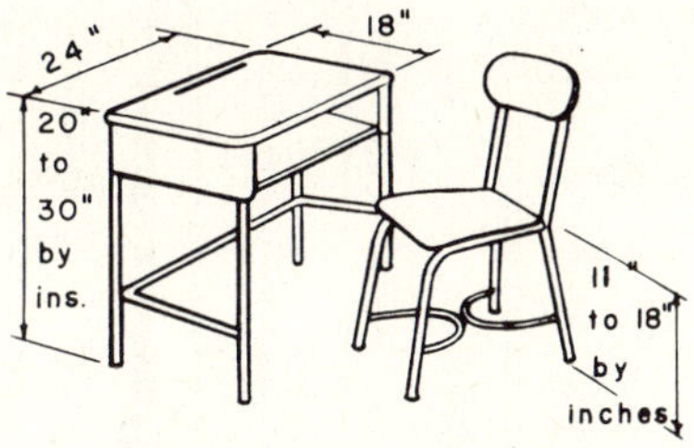
24"
18"
20 to 30 by ins.
11 to 18" by inches

Wood & enameled metal
Norcor Manufacturing Co.

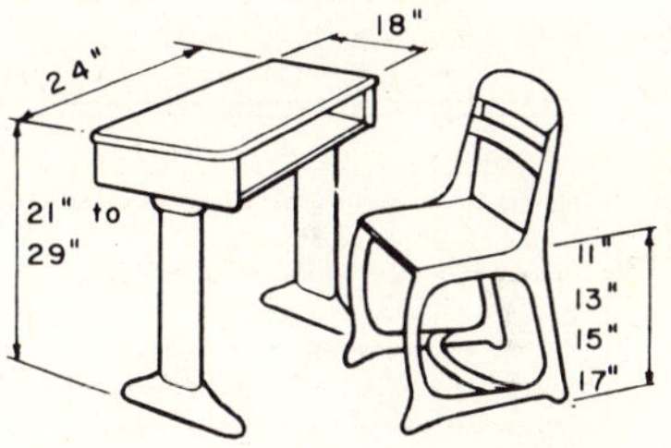
18"
24"
21" to 29"
11"
13"
15"
17"

Wood & enameled metal
American Seating Company

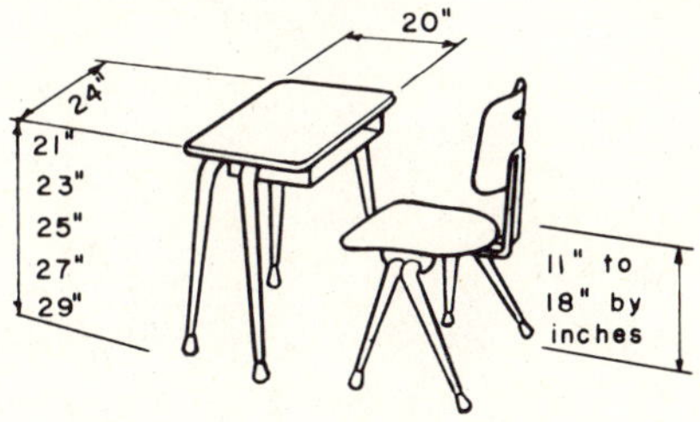
20"
24"
21"
23"
25"
27"
29"
11" to 18" by inches

Wood or plastic, & metal

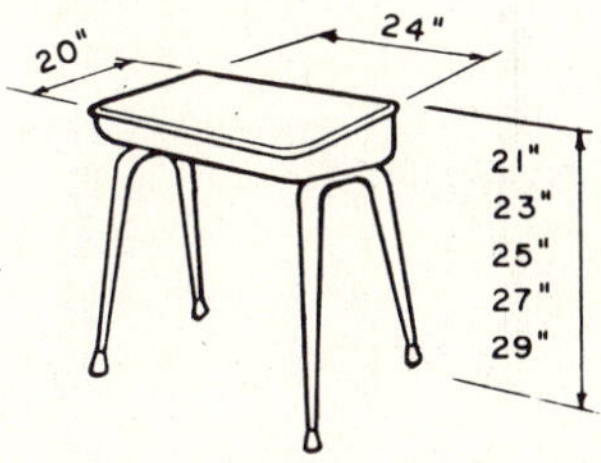
20"
24"
21"
23"
25"
27"
29"

Alternate desk

Brunswick – Balke – Collender Company

Wood & enameled metal
Griggs Equipment Co.

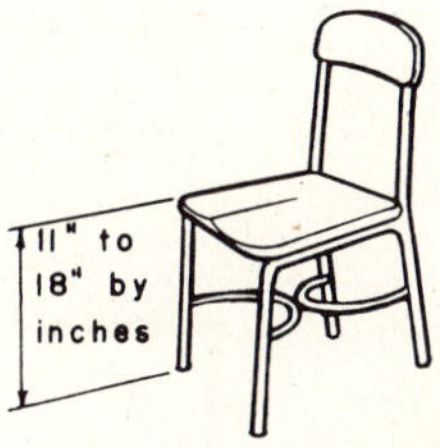
11" to 18" by inches

Wood & enameled metal
Heywood – Wakefield

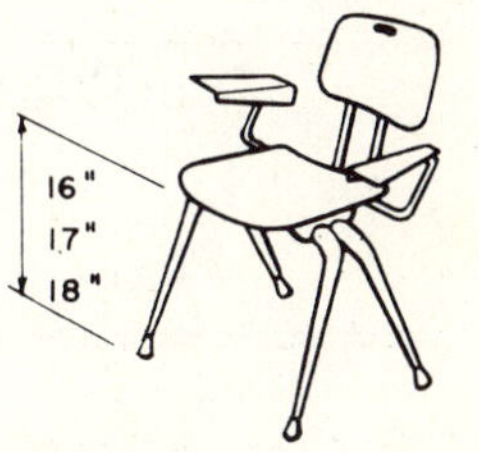
16"
17"
18"

Wood & metal
Brunswick-Balke-Collender

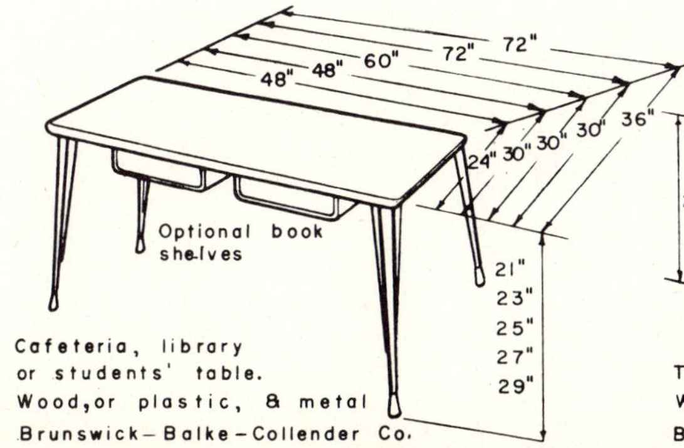
72"
72"
60"
48"
48"
24" 30" 30" 30" 36"
Optional book shelves
21"
23"
25"
27"
29"

Cafeteria, library
or students' table.
Wood, or plastic, & metal
Brunswick-Balke-Collender Co.

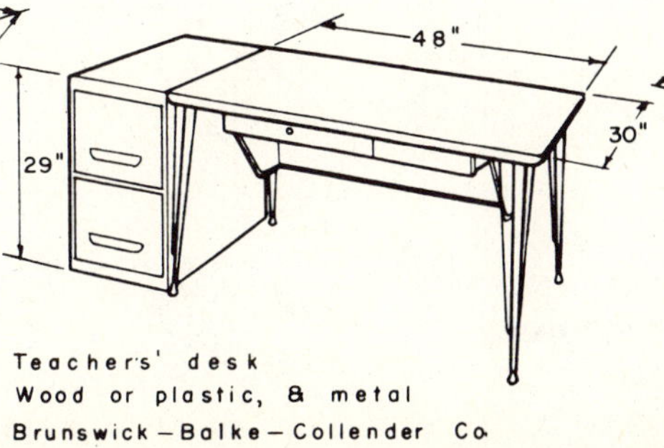
48"
30"
29"

Teachers' desk
Wood or plastic, & metal
Brunswick-Balke-Collender Co.

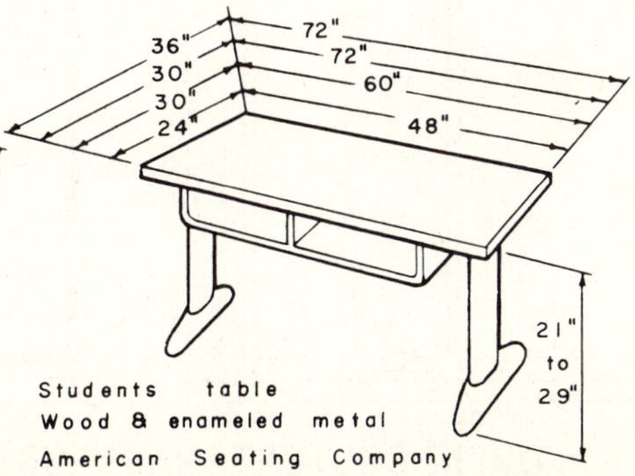
36"
30"
30"
24"
72"
72"
60"
48"
21" to 29"

Students table
Wood & enameled metal
American Seating Company

SCHOOL WARDROBE DETAILS

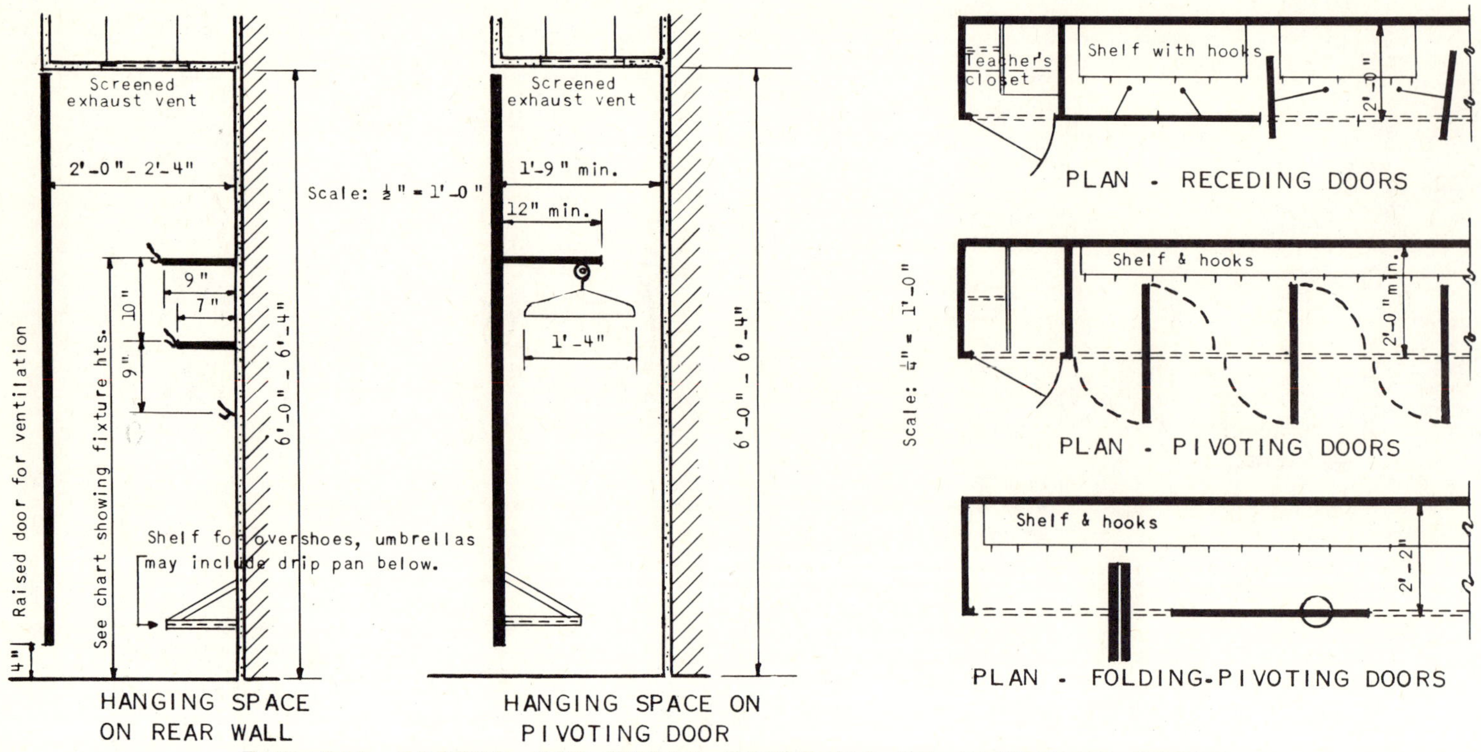
Screened
exhaust vent
2'-0" - 2'-4"
9"
7"
10"
9"
Raised door for ventilation
See chart showing fixture hts.
6'-0" - 6'-4"
Shelf for overshoes, umbrellas
may include drip pan below.
4"
HANGING SPACE
ON REAR WALL
Scale: ½" = 1'-0"
Screened
exhaust vent
1'-9" min.
12" min.
1'-4"
6'-0" - 6'-4"
HANGING SPACE ON
PIVOTING DOOR
Teacher's
closet
Shelf with hooks
2'-0"
PLAN - RECEDING DOORS
Scale: ¼" = 1'-0"
Shelf & hooks
2'-0" min.
PLAN - PIVOTING DOORS
Shelf & hooks
2'-2"
PLAN - FOLDING-PIVOTING DOORS

TYPICAL RECESS FOR STOCK RECEDING OR PIVOTING DOORS

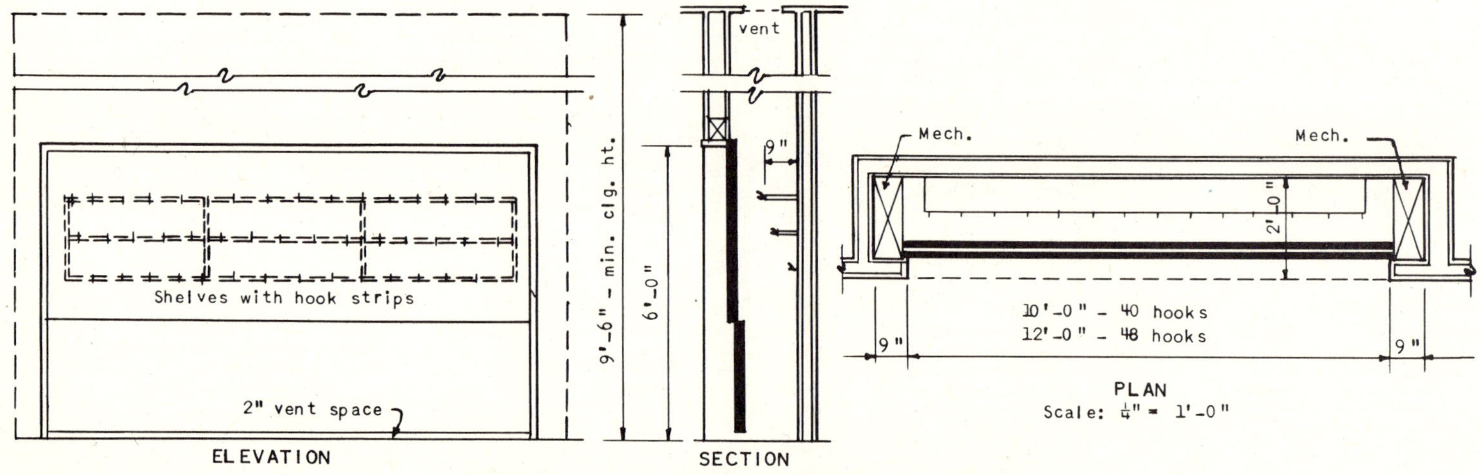
Shelves with hook strips
2" vent space
ELEVATION
9'-6" - min. clg. ht.
6'-0"
vent
9"
SECTION
Mech.
Mech.
2'-0"
10'-0" - 40 hooks
12'-0" - 48 hooks
9"
9"
PLAN
Scale: ¼" = 1'-0"

VERTICAL-SLIDING WARDROBE DOOR

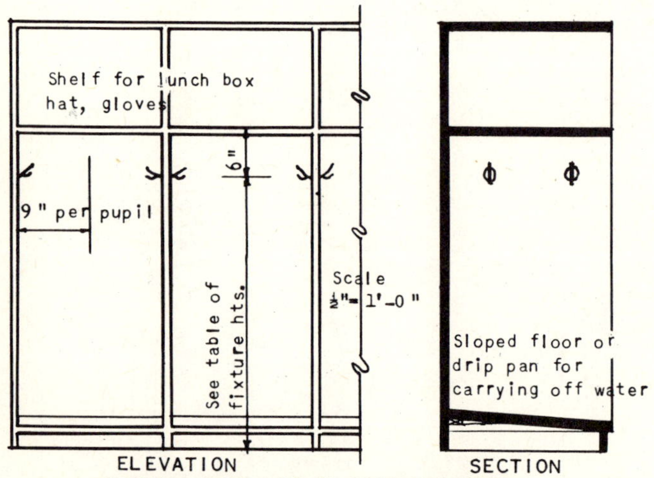
Shelf for lunch box
hat, gloves
6"
9" per pupil
See table of
fixture hts.
Scale
½" = 1'-0"
ELEVATION
Sloped floor or
drip pan for
carrying off water
SECTION

OPEN CUBICLE WARDROBE

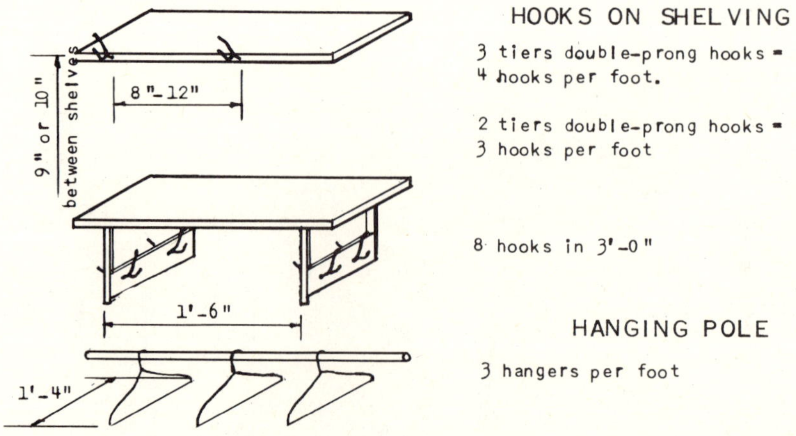
9" or 10"
between shelves
8"-12"
1'-6"
1'-4"
HOOKS ON SHELVING
3 tiers double-prong hooks =
4 hooks per foot.
2 tiers double-prong hooks =
3 hooks per foot
8 hooks in 3'-0"
HANGING POLE
3 hangers per foot

HANGING DEVICES

CHALKBOARD and TACKBOARD SIZES

RECOMMENDED HEIGHTS OF CHALKRAIL ABOVE FLOOR

GRADE	AUTHORITY MAKING RECOMMENDATION					
	Engelhardt, Engelhardt & Leggett	Nat'l Council on Schoolhouse Construction	Brown & Fields	Ray L. Hamon	N.Y. Code	California (Suggested by Dept of Education)
Kindergarten	20"			23"	24"	22" - 24"
1st grade	20" - 23"	24" - 28"	25.75"	24"	27"	24" - 26"
2nd grade	20" - 23"	24" - 28"	26.5"	25"	28"	24" - 26"
3rd grade	20" - 23"	26" - 30"	30.5"	26"	29"	27" - 28"
4th grade	28" - 30"	26" - 30"	32"	27"	30"	28"
5th grade	28" - 30"	28" - 32"	32.5"	28"	31"	30"
6th grade	28" - 30"	28" - 32"	32.5"	29"	32"	30"
Junior High School	34"	30" - 36"		31"		32"
Senior High School	36"	30" - 36"		33"		32" - 36"

TACKBOARD SIZES

COMPOSITION	TOTAL THICKNESS	MAXIMUM SIZE	COLORS AVAILABLE
1/8" CORK MOUNTED ON 1/4" WOOD FIBERBOARD	3/8"	4'-0" X 12'-0"	GREENS, TANS, GREYS, NATURAL
1/4" CORK MOUNTED ON 1/8" WOOD FIBERBOARD	3/8"	4'-0" X 12'-0"	GREENS, TANS, GREYS, NATURAL
1/4" CORK MOUNTED ON 1/4" WOOD FIBERBOARD	1/2"	4'-0" X 12'-0"	GREENS, TANS, GREYS, NATURAL
1/8" CORK MOUNTED ON 3/8" PRESSED WOOD PULP	1/2"	4'-0" X 12'-0"	GREENS, TANS, GREYS, NATURAL
UNMOUNTED CORK	1/4"	5'-0" & 6'-0" WIDE X 75'-0" OR 85'-0" LONG	GREENS, TANS, GREYS, NATURAL

CHALKBOARD SIZES

SURFACE	BASE COMPOSITION	THICKNESS	WIDTHS	LENGTHS	COLORS AVAILABLE
Vitreous enamel	Plate glass	1/4" ±	4" to 4'-0"	4" to 8'-0"	Green, ivory & black
	Aluminum alloy	3/16" +	3'-0", 3'-6", 4'-0"	3'-0" to 8'-0"	Green
	Steel & fiberboard	3/8"			Green, ivory & black
	Steel, backed with plywood & wood fiberboard	7/8"	3'-0", 3'-6", 4'-0"	4'-0" to 8'-0"	Green, ivory & black
Ceramic Porcelain on metal	Plywood on steel or aluminum	9/32" ±	3'-0", 3'-6", 4'-0"	6'-0", 7'-0", 8'-0", 9'-0", 10'-0"	2 greens, 2 greys chocolate brown
Solid acrylic plastic			3'-0", 3'-6", 4'-0"	5'-0" & 6'-0"	Green
Solid polyester-resin plastic		1/4"	3'-0", 3'-6", 4'-0"	up to 7'-0"	Green
Synthetic plastic	Cement asbestos board	3/16"	3'-6", 4'-0"	up to 8'-0"	Green, black
	Plastic & wood fiberboard		3'-0", 3'-6", 4'-0"	up to 12'-0"	Green, black
	Wood fiberboard		3'-0", 3'-6", 4'-0"	up to 12'-0"	Green, black
	Tempered wood fiberboard		3'-0", 3'-6", 4'-0"	up to 12'-0"	Green, black
Synthetic plastic & silicon carbide	Tempered wood fiberboard	1/4" & 1/2"	3'-0", 3'-6", 4'-0"	4'-0" to 12'-0"	Green, black
Carborundum	Cement asbestos board	3/16"	3'-6", 4'-0"	5'-0" to 8'-0"	Green, black
	Wood fiberboard	1/4"	3'-0", 3'-6", 4'-0"	up to 12'-0"	Green, black
	Hardboard	7/16"	3'-0", 3'-6", 4'-0"	up to 12'-0"	Green, black
	Laminated wood fiber	1/4"	3'-6", 4'-0"	up to 12'-0"	Green, black
Powdered slate	Wood fiberboard	1/4" to 7/16"	3'-6", 4'-0"	6'-0" to 12'-0"	Green, black
	Tempered wood fiberboard	1/4"	3'-0", 3'-6", 4'-0"	6'-0" to 12'-0"	Black, 2 greens
	Laminated wood pulp		3'-0", 3'-6", 4'-0"	up to 16'-0"	Black, 2 greens
Natural slate		1/4" to 3/8"	3'-0", 3'-6", 4'-0"	no standard	Black
Pulverized slate & carborundum	Laminated wood fiber	1/4"	3'-0", 3'-6", 4'-0"	up to 12'-0"	Green, black
	Wood fiberboard	1/4"	3'-6", 4'-0"	5'-0" to 12'-0"	Green, black
	Cement asbestos board	3/16"	3'-6", 4'-0"	5'-0" to 12'-0"	Green, black

CHALKBOARD DETAILS

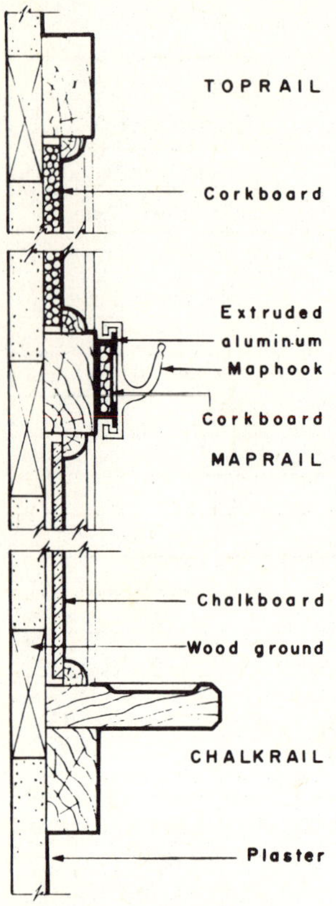
TOPRAIL
Corkboard
Extruded aluminum
Maphook
Corkboard
MAPRAIL
Chalkboard
Wood ground
CHALKRAIL
Plaster

CHALKBOARD WITH WOOD FRAMING

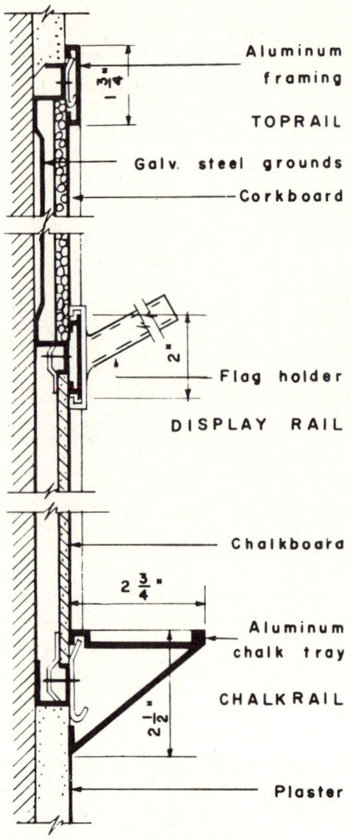
Aluminum framing
3/4"
TOPRAIL
Galv. steel grounds
Corkboard
2"
Flag holder
DISPLAY RAIL
Chalkboard
2 3/4"
Aluminum chalk tray
CHALKRAIL
2 1/2"
Plaster

CHALKBOARD WITH ALUMINUM FRAMING

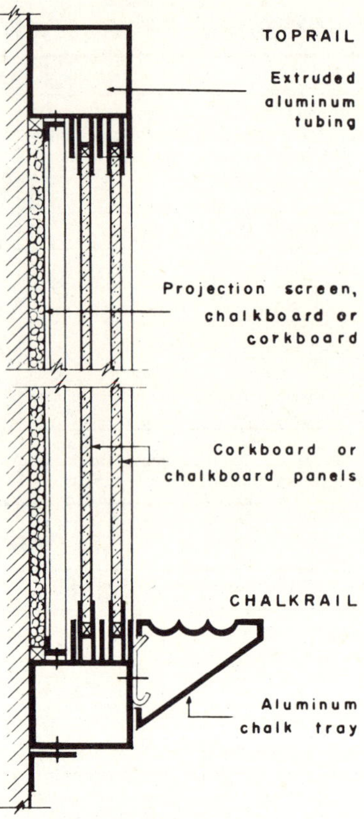
TOPRAIL
Extruded aluminum tubing
Projection screen, chalkboard or corkboard
Corkboard or chalkboard panels
CHALKRAIL
Aluminum chalk tray

HORIZONTAL-SLIDING CHALKBOARD

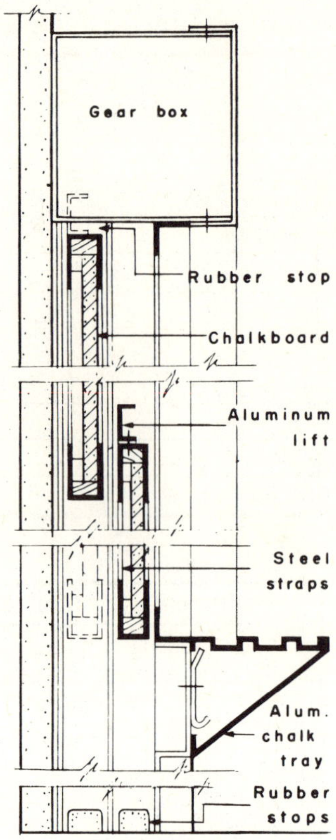
Gear box
Rubber stop
Chalkboard
Aluminum lift
Steel straps
Alum. chalk tray
Rubber stops

VERTICAL-SLIDING CHALKBOARD

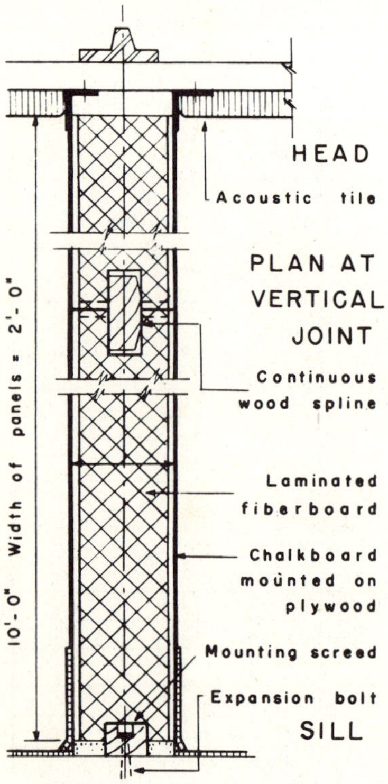
HEAD
Acoustic tile
PLAN AT VERTICAL JOINT
Continuous wood spline
10'-0" Width of panels = 2'-0"
Laminated fiberboard
Chalkboard mounted on plywood
Mounting screed
Expansion bolt
SILL

CHALKBOARD PARTITION

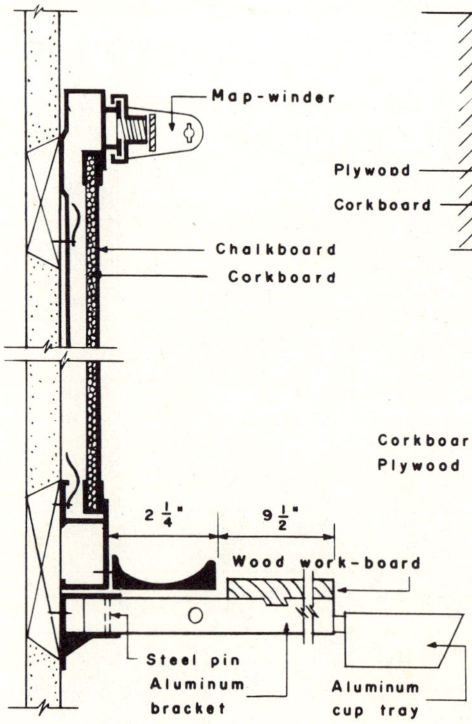
Map-winder
Chalkboard
Corkboard
2 1/4"
9 1/2"
Wood work-board
Steel pin
Aluminum bracket
Aluminum cup tray

REVERSIBLE EASEL BOARD

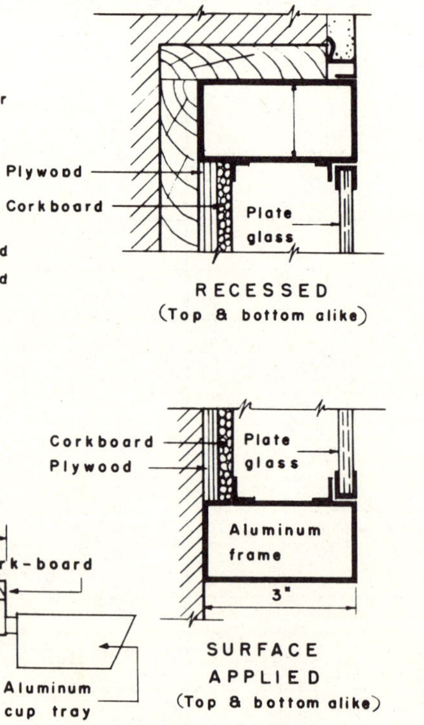
Plywood
Corkboard
Plate glass
RECESSED
(Top & bottom alike)
Corkboard
Plywood
Plate glass
Aluminum frame
3"
SURFACE APPLIED
(Top & bottom alike)

BULLETIN BOARD

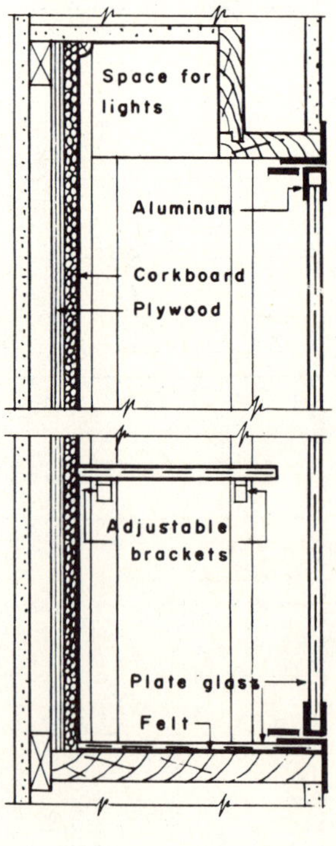
Space for lights
Aluminum
Corkboard
Plywood
Adjustable brackets
Plate glass
Felt

DISPLAY CASE

GLASS-ENCLOSED CASES

Scale: 3" = 1'-0"

LIBRARY EQUIPMENT

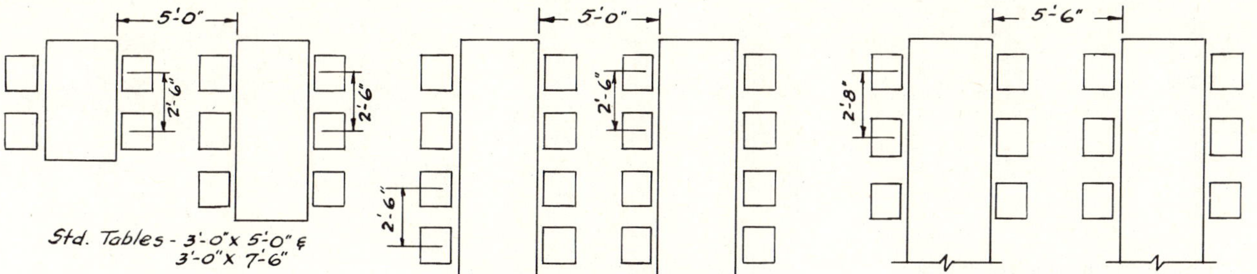
5'-0"
2'-6"
2'-6"
5'-0"
2'-6"
2'-6"
5'-6"
2'-8"

Std. Tables - 3'-0" x 5'-0" & 3'-0" x 7'-6"

Std. Tables 3'-4" x 10'-0"
Use 2'-6" seat spacing for magazines.

Tables used in college Libraries, etc. made to order 3'-6" wide & desired length.

Book Truck
Wood or Metal
Sizes

High	Wide	Long
3'-6 3/4	1'-2 1/8	3'-3 1/4
2'-11"	2'-2 5/8"	3'-0"
2'-11"	1'-3 1/4"	1'-11"

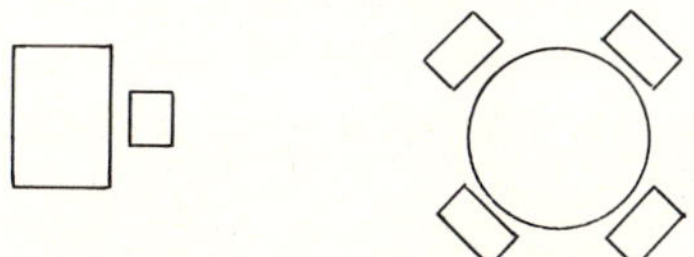

Occasional chairs in informal arrangements now widely used

Small Reading Tables
2'-0" x 3'-0" one chair
4'-0" dia.

SEATING & SPACING OF TABLES

Scale: 1/8" = 1'-0"

Wood ends available for stacks which have one end facing reading rooms.

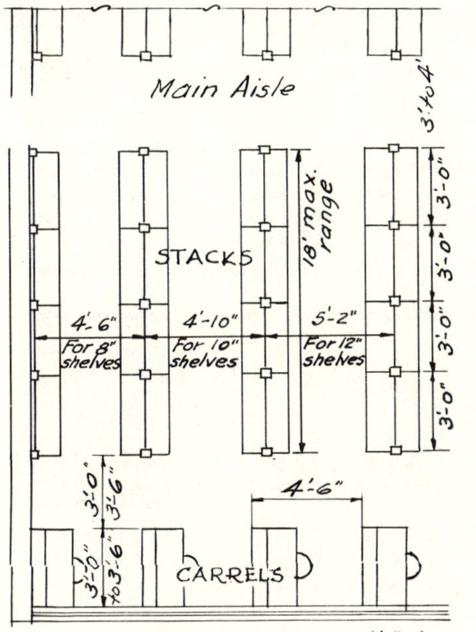
Main Aisle
3' to 4'
STACKS
18' max. range
4'-6"
For 8" shelves
4'-10"
For 10" shelves
5'-2"
For 12" shelves
3'-0"
3'-0"
3'-0"
3'-0"
3'-0"
3'-6"
4'-6"
3'-0"
to 3'-6"
CARRELS

TYPICAL PLAN 1/8" = 1'-0"
STACK RANGES & STUDY CARRELS

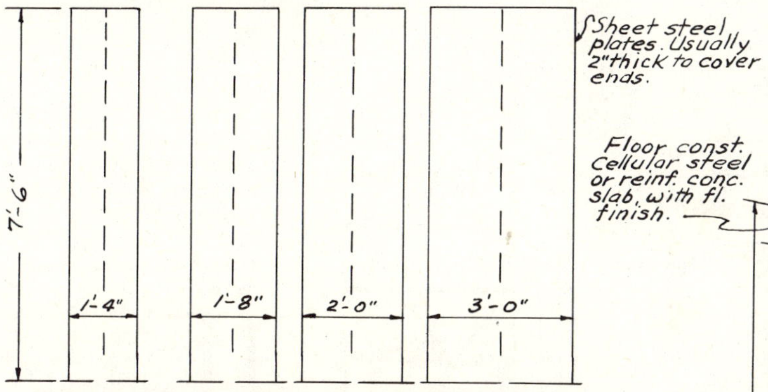
7'-6"
1'-4"
1'-8"
2'-0"
3'-0"
Sheet steel plates. Usually 2" thick to cover ends.

DOUBLE FACED RANGE-END ELEV.
SINGLE FACED RANGE - 8", 9", 10" 12"
Scale: 1/4" = 1'-0"
WIDTHS OF RANGES

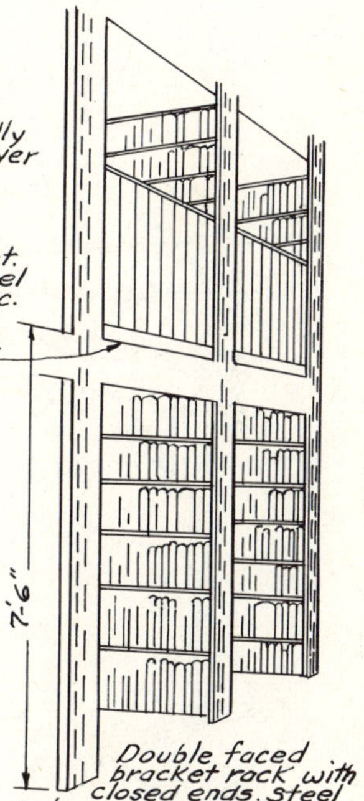
Floor const. Cellular steel or reinf. conc. slab, with fl. finish.
7'-6"

Double faced bracket rack with closed ends. Steel columns supporting deck floor above.

CARRELS: may be open or enclosed, movable or built-in. Steel partitions are recommended.

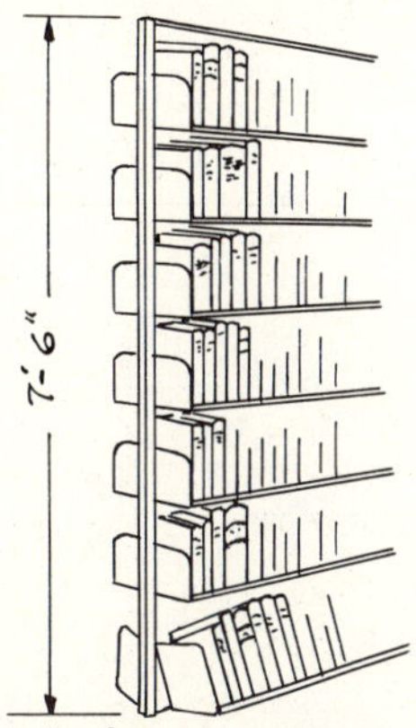
7'-6"

Double faced bracket stack with open ends. May be free standing or as support of concrete deck above. Bottom shelves may be tilted from front to back for clearer view of books.

6'-10"
3'-6"
5'-0 1/2
max. shelf depth: 10"
1'-0"
6'-1 1/2"

Wall magazine shelving

BOOK CAPACITY: No definite formula can be given for finding the number of books per gross stack room areas. Many variables must be considered: Size and kind of books (folios, bound periodicals, etc.); number & width of aisles; stairways; lifts, carrels, etc.; whether calculations are based on ultimate capacity or working capacity. Variance has been found to run from 13 1/2 - 19 books/sq. ft., according to local conditions. For rough rule of thumb, allow 16 books/sq. ft. of gross area.

SHELF CAPACITY & WIDTH

Type of Book	vols. per lin. ft.	shelf recom.
Circulating	7	8"
Fiction & Economics	7	8"
History & Gen. Lit.	7	8"
Reference	7	10"
Technical-Scientific	6	10"
Medical	5	8"
Law & Public documts	4 to 5	8"
Bound Periodicals	5	10" to 12"
U.S. Patent Spec.	2	8"
Cu. ft. of book range weighs 25#		

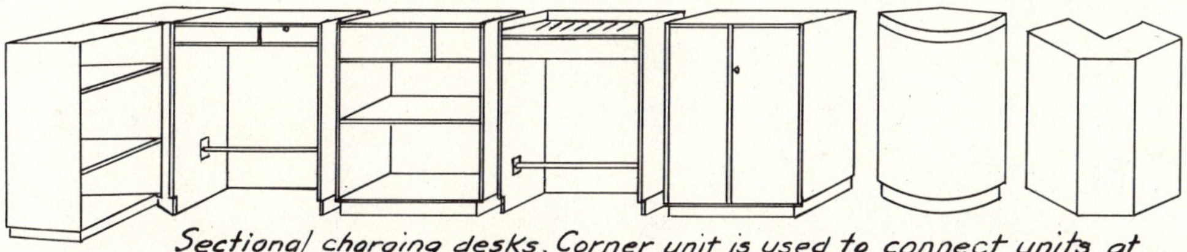

Sectional charging desks. Corner unit is used to connect units at right angles - may be round or squared, according to design. Units shown above are 2'-5 5/8" wide, 2'-1 13/16" deep & 3'-3" high. Made in sitting height - 2'-8 1/2" and standing height - 3'-3".

BOOK STACKS & STACKROOM EQUIPMENT - STEEL

Data checked by Library Bureau of Remington Rand, Inc.

CLOAK ROOMS and EQUIPMENT-OFFICE CLOSET EQUIPMENT

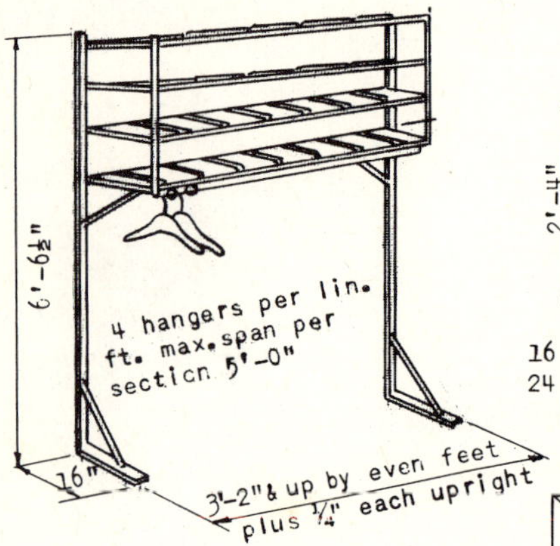
6'-6½"
4 hangers per lin. ft. max. span per section 5'-0"
16"
3'-2" & up by even feet plus ¼" each upright
SINGLE FACE COAT & HAT RACK

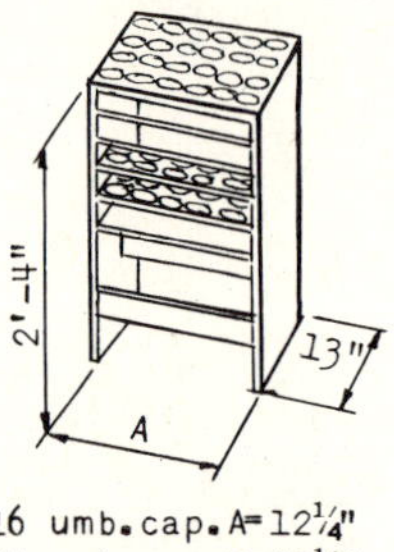
2'-4"
13"
A
16 umb. cap. A=12¼"
24 umb. cap. B=17¼"
UMBRELLA RACK

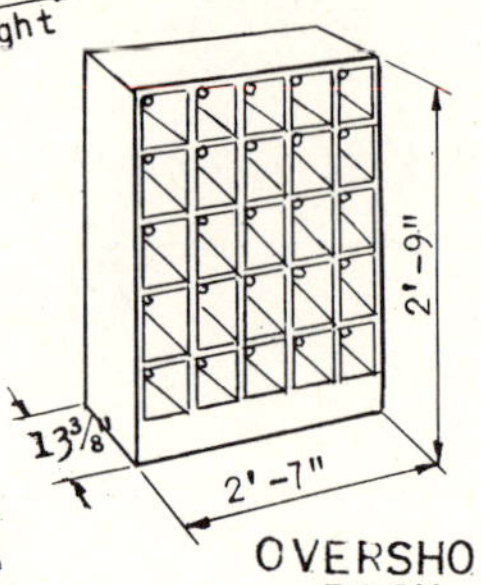
2'-9"
13⅜"
2'-7"
OVERSHOE RACK

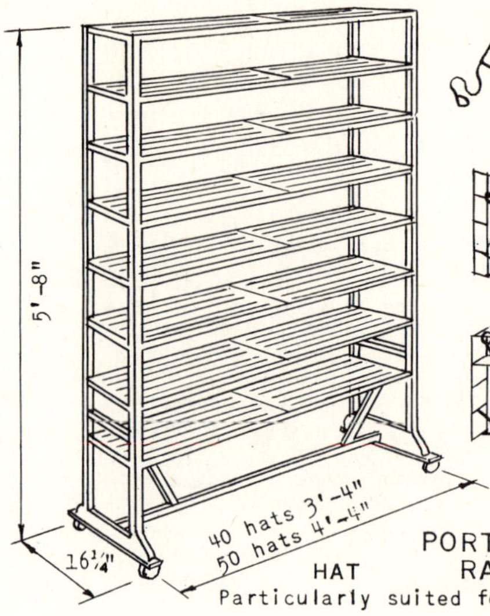
5'-8"
16¼"
40 hats 3'-4"
50 hats 4'-4"
HAT

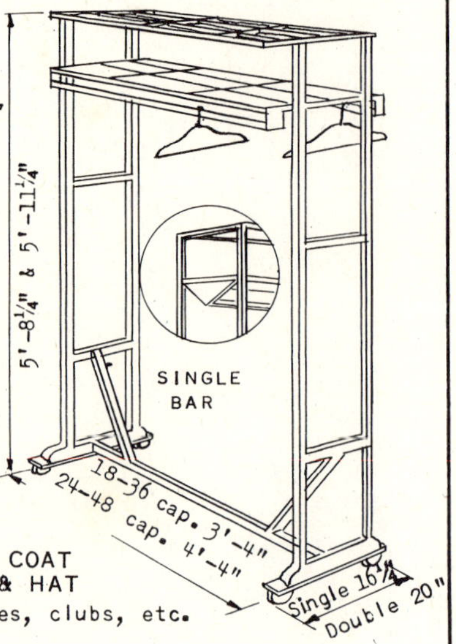
5'-8¼" & 5'-11¼"
SINGLE BAR
18-36 cap. 3'-4"
24-48 cap. 4'-4"
Single 16½"
Double 20"
COAT & HAT

PORTABLE RACKS

Particularly suited for churches, clubs, etc.

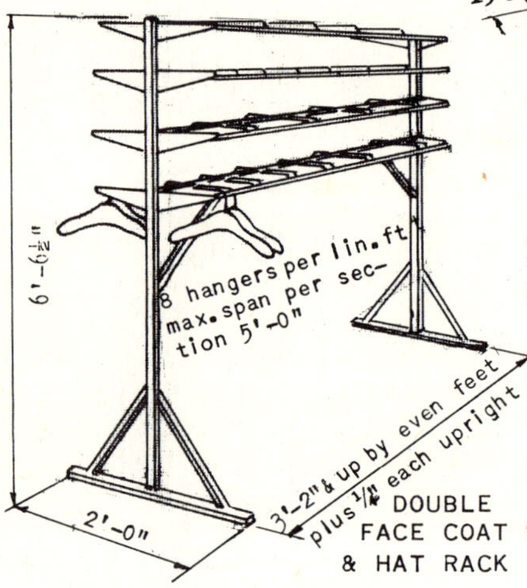
6'-6½"
8 hangers per lin. ft. max. span per section 5'-0"
2'-0"
3'-2" & up by even feet plus ¼" each upright
DOUBLE FACE COAT & HAT RACK

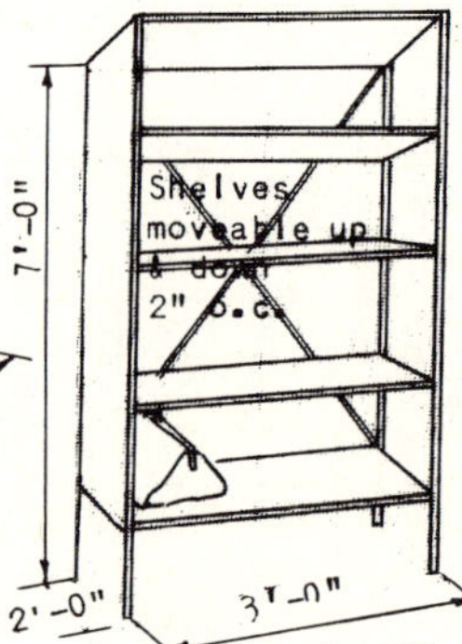
7'-0"
Shelves moveable up & down 2" o.c.
2'-0"
3'-0"
BAGGAGE RACK

CLOAK ROOM PLANNING

Allow 3/4 sq. ft. per hanger, which will include coat & hat, umbrella & overshoe requirements. Allow approx. 20% total hanger capacity each for overshoe & umbrella racks. Standard hanger spacing is 3" o.c. (4 per lin. ft.). Capacity may be increased 25% by spacing 2½" o.c. (5 per lin. ft.) & may be further increased on most models to max. 8 per ft. by substituting hooks for hangers.

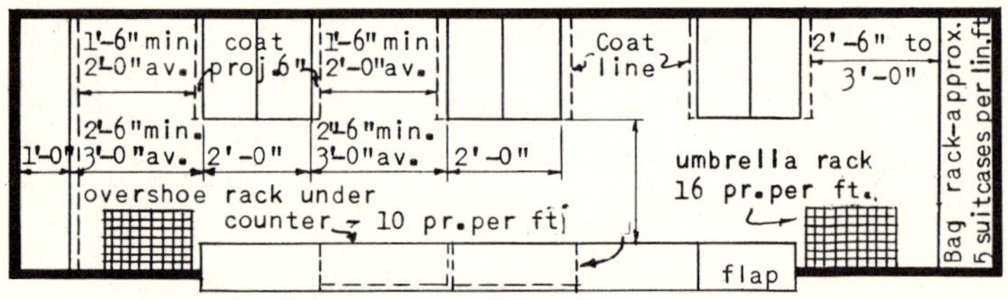
1'-6" min
2'-0" av.
coat proj. 6"
1'-6" min
2'-0" av.
Coat line
2'-6" to 3'-0"
2'-6" min.
3'-0" av.
2'-0"
2'-6" min.
3'-0" av.
2'-0"
1'-0"
overshoe rack under counter - 10 pr. per ft.
umbrella rack 16 pr. per ft.
flap
Bag rack-approx. 5 suitcases per lin. ft.
This is not a suggested coat room layout, but is arranged only to show req'd. spacing. Scale: 3/16" = 1'-0"

TYPICAL CLOAK ROOM LAYOUT

CLOAK ROOMS & EQUIPMENT

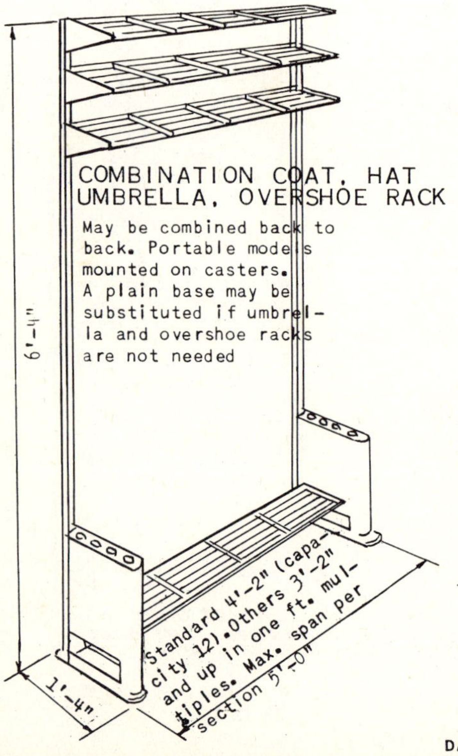
6'-4"
1'-4"
Standard 4'-2" (capacity 12). Others 3'-2" and up in one ft. multiples. Max. span per section 5'-0"
COMBINATION COAT, HAT UMBRELLA, OVERSHOE RACK

May be combined back to back. Portable models mounted on casters. A plain base may be substituted if umbrella and overshoe racks are not needed

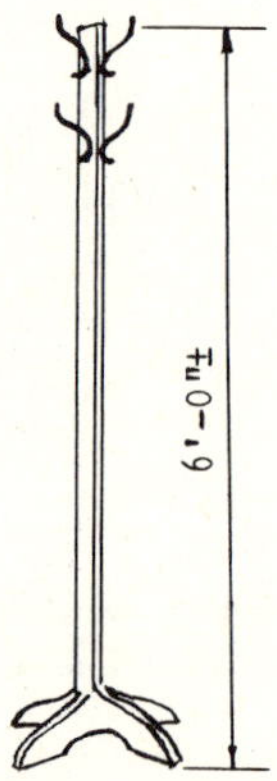
6'-0"±

5'-6" & 6'-6"
18"
3'-0"

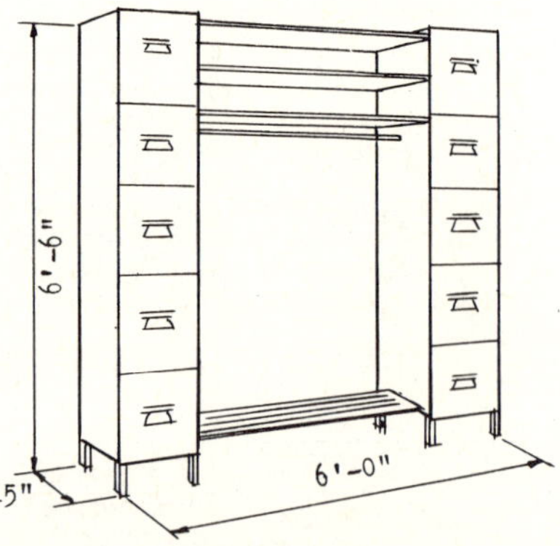
6'-6"
15"
6'-0"
COAT & LOCKER UNITS

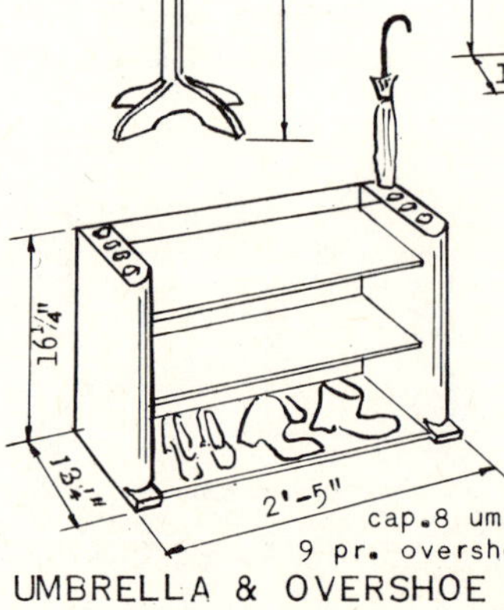
16¼"
13¼"
2'-5"
cap. 8 umb.
9 pr. overshoes

UMBRELLA & OVERSHOE STAND

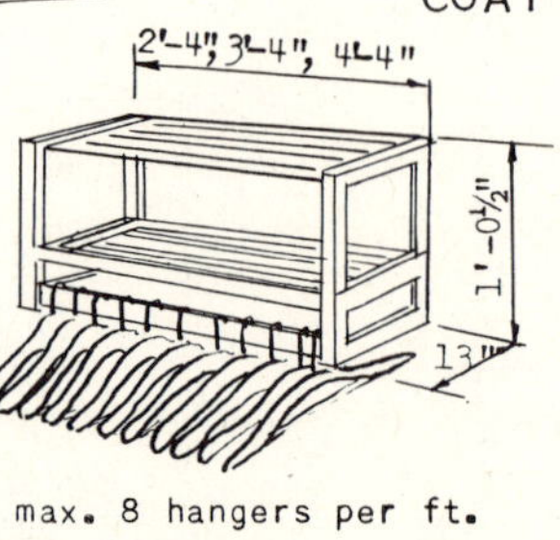
2'-4", 3'-4", 4'-4"
1'-0½"
13"
max. 8 hangers per ft.

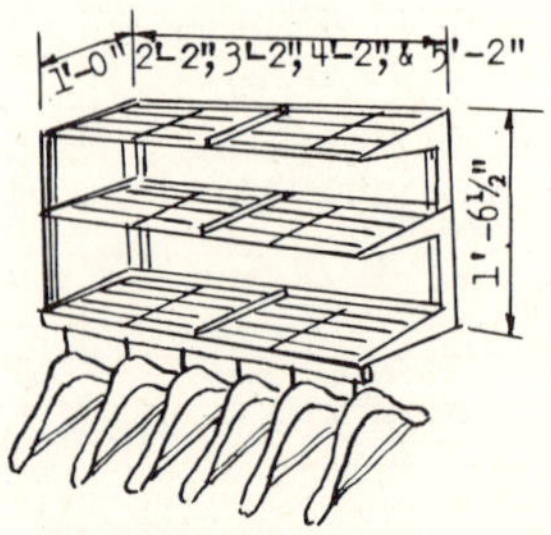
1'-0"
2'-2", 3'-2", 4'-2", & 5'-2"
1'-6½"
3 hangers per ft.

WALL RACKS

OFFICE CLOSET EQUIPMENT

DATA BY VOGEL-PETERSON CO. EXCEPT Ⓐ BY ANDREW WILSON CO.

CHECKING LOCKERS

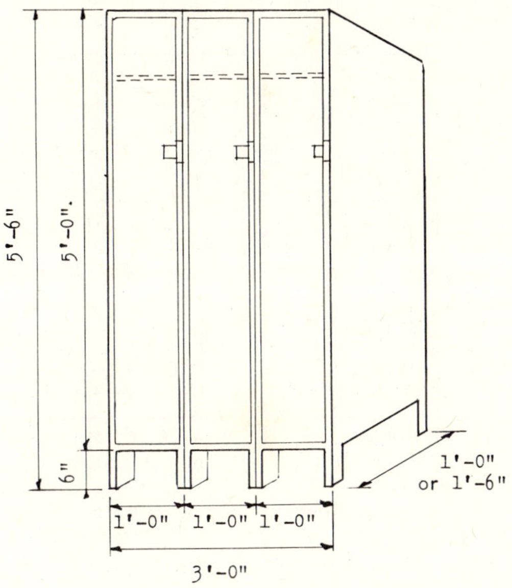
5'-6"
5'-0"
6"
1'-0"
1'-0"
1'-0"
3'-0"
1'-0"
or 1'-6"

SINGLE TIER

Light duty lockers are of baked-on enamel and thus are less costly than heavy duty lockers. They may be used in office buildings, department stores, bowling alleys, etc. They may have 5¢, 10¢ or 25¢ locks; multiple coin locks for collection of admission fees, as at a swimming pool; or coin return receptacles when free service is required, as in offices. A variety of models are available.

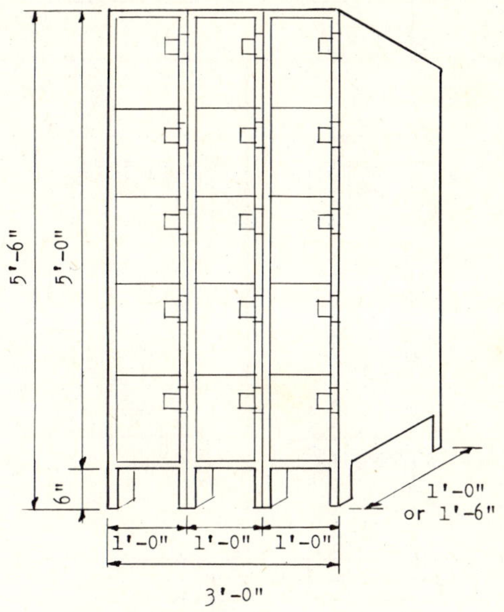
5'-6"
5'-0"
6"
1'-0"
1'-0"
1'-0"
3'-0"
1'-0"
or 1'-6"

MULTIPLE TIER

LIGHT DUTY LOCKERS

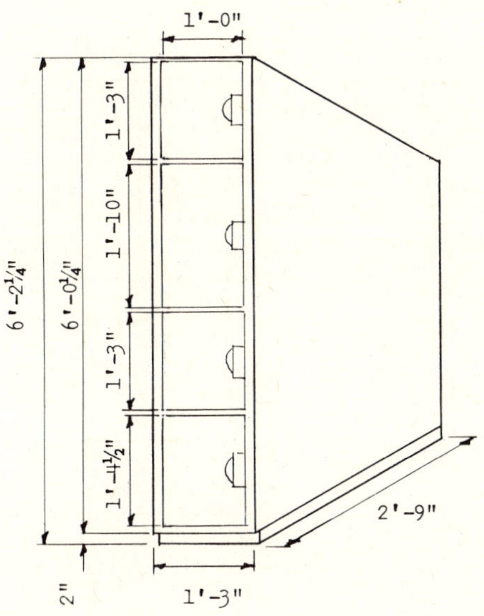
1'-0"
6'-2¼"
6'-0¾"
1'-3"
1'-10"
1'-3"
1'-4½"
2"
1'-3"
2'-9"

Heavy duty lockers are of stainless steel. They are primarily for transportation terminals and are available with 10¢ and 25¢ coin locks. The 2'-6" wide stack is also available with 6 drawers 1'-9"± high or with 8 drawers 1'-5⅛" high. The stacks may be grouped in a variety of combinations.

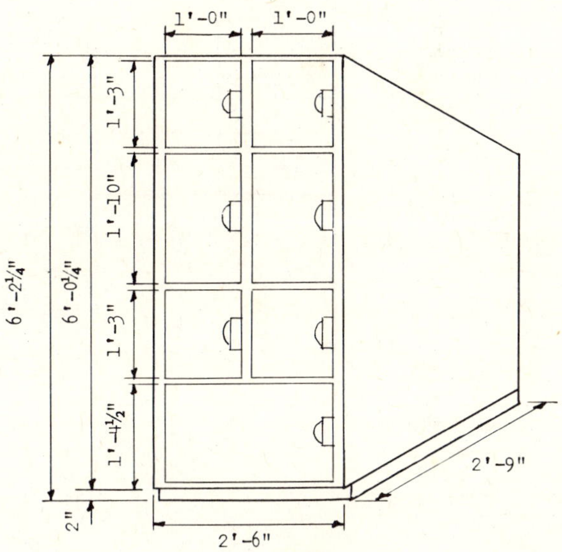
1'-0"
1'-0"
6'-2¼"
6'-0¾"
1'-3"
1'-10"
1'-3"
1'-4½"
2"
2'-6"
2'-9"

HEAVY DUTY LOCKERS

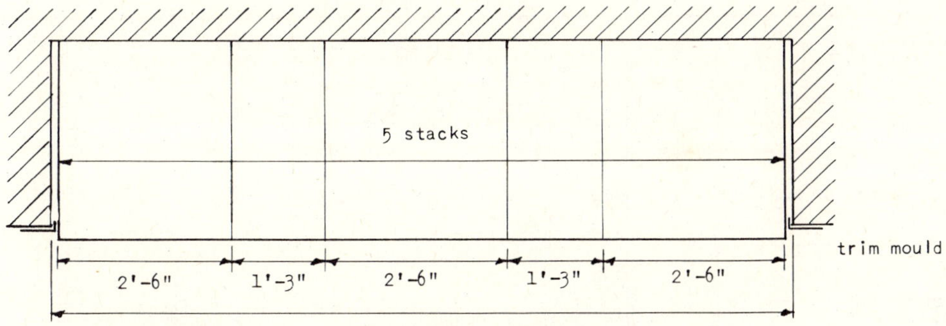
5 stacks
trim mould
2'-6"
1'-3"
2'-6"
1'-3"
2'-6"

Width = (width of each stack x number of stacks per each width) + (⅛" for each stack) + 2"

Example above:
Width = (2'-6"x3) + (1'-3"x2) + (⅛"x5) + 2"
= 10'-2⅝"

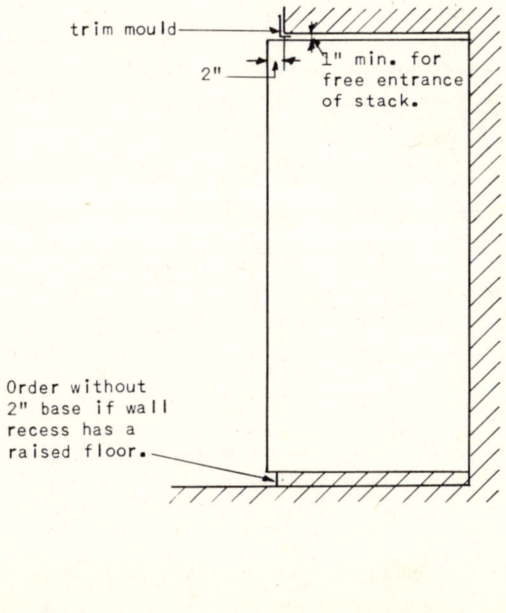
trim mould
2"
1" min. for free entrance of stack.
Order without 2" base if wall recess has a raised floor.

RECESSED LOCKERS

Data checked by: Flxible Locker Co.

STEEL LOCKERS, BASKETS and RACKS

TYPES AND SIZES OF STEEL LOCKERS

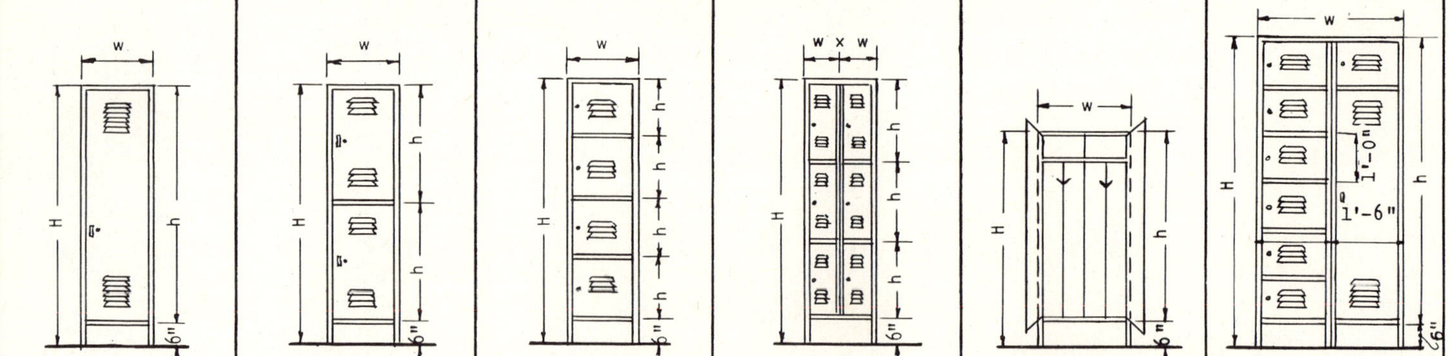
w
H
h
6"
w x w
1'-0"
1'-6"

SINGLE TIER | DOUBLE TIER | MULTIPLE TIER (Three to six tiers high.) | GYM STORAGE (Two to three tiers high.) | ELEMENTARY SCHOOL (4 compartments) or DUPLEX (2 compartments) | GROUP LOCKERS (7 person shown. 2 & 8 person lockers also mfrd.)

SINGLE TIER

w	d	h	*H
9" 1'-0"	1'-0"	5'-0"	5'-6"
1'-0" 1'-3"	1'-3"	5'-0"	5'-6"
1'-0" 1'-3"	1'-6"	5'-0"	5'-6"
9" 1'-0" 1'-3"	1'-0"	6'-0"	6'-6"
1'-0" 1'-3"	1'-3"	6'-0"	6'-6"
1'-0" 1'-3" 1'-6"	1'-6"	6'-0"	6'-6"
1'-6"	1'-9"	6'-0"	6'-6"

DOUBLE TIER

w	d	h	*H
1'-0"	1'-0"	2'-6"	5'-6"
1'-0"	1'-0"	3'-0"	6'-6"
1'-0" 1'-3"	1'-3"	3'-0"	6'-6"
1'-0"	1'-6"	3'-0"	6'-6"
1'-0"	1'-0"	3'-6"	7'-6"
1'-0" 1'-3"	1'-3"	3'-6"	7'-6"

MULTIPLE TIER

w	d	h	*H
Three Tiers			
9"	1'-0"	1'-8"	5'-6"
9" 1'-0"	1'-0"	2'-0"	6'-6"
Four Tiers			
1'-3"	1'-3"	1'-3"	5'-6"
Five Tiers			
1'-0"	1'-0"	1'-0"	5'-6"
1'-0" 1'-3"	1'-3"	1'-0"	5'-6"
Six Tiers			
1'-0"	1'-0"	1'-0"	6'-6"
1'-0" 1'-3"	1'-3"	1'-0"	6'-6"

GYM STORAGE

w	d	h	*H
Three Tiers			
9"	1'-0"	1'-8"	5'-6"
9" 1'-10"	1'-0"	2'-0"	6'-6"
Four Tiers			
9"	1'-0"	1'-6"	6'-6"

Provide hanging hooks in these lockers.

ELEMENTARY SCHOOL

w	d	h	*H
Four Compartments			
2'-0"	1'-0"	4'-6"	5'-0"
1'-10"	1'-0"	5'-0"	5'-6"
Duplex			
1'-10"	1'-3"	5'-0"	5'-6"
1'-3"	1'-3" 1'-6" 1'-9"	6'-0"	6'-6"

GROUP LOCKERS

w	d	h	*H
Seven Person			
3'-0"	1'-9"	6'-0"	6'-6"
Eight Person			
4'-6"	1'-9"	6'-0"	6'-6"
Two Person			
1'-3"	1'-3"	6'-0"	6'-6"

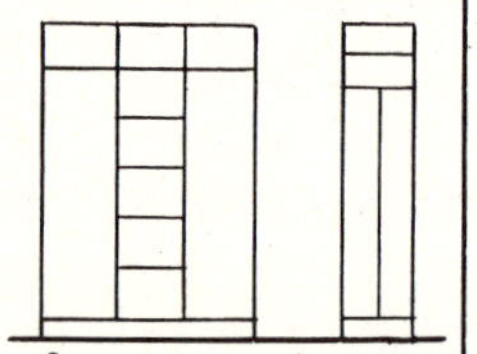

8 person   2 person

w = overall width
d = overall depth
h = locker height
H = overall height

*For overall height of lockers without legs, subtract 6" from H. Manufacturers will make any width, depth or height in multiples of 3". Sloped, dust-proof tops increase height by one-third of locker depth. Double doors may be installed in place of single doors on 2'-0" width only.

In fixed spaces, ¼" maximum allowance should be made for bolt heads at each end of each group of lockers.

Data checked by All-Steel Equipment Co., Berger Manufacturing Div. of Republic Steel Corp., Fred Medart Products, Inc., Lyon Metal Products, Inc. Also see U. S. Dept. of Commerce Simplified Practice Recommendation R35-44.

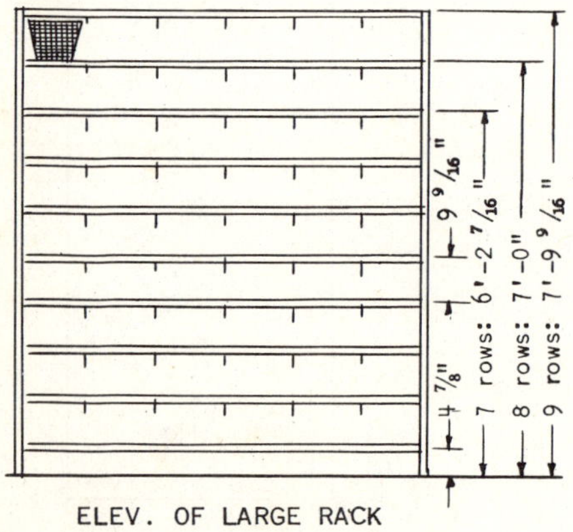
9 9/16"
4 7/8"
7 rows: 6'-2 7/16"
8 rows: 7'-0"
9 rows: 7'-9 9/16"

ELEV. OF LARGE RACK
(Heights of small rack same)

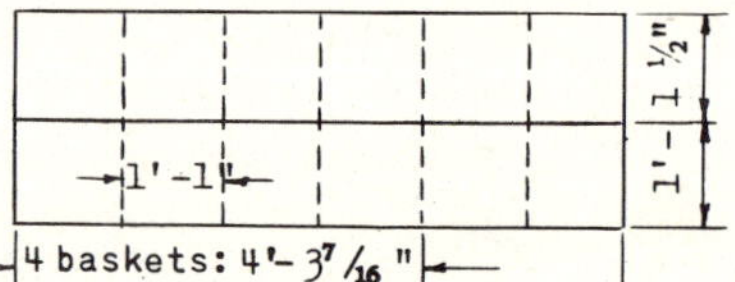
1'-1"
1'-1 1/2"
4 baskets: 4'-3 7/16"
6 baskets: 6'-4 3/16"

PLAN OF LARGE RACK

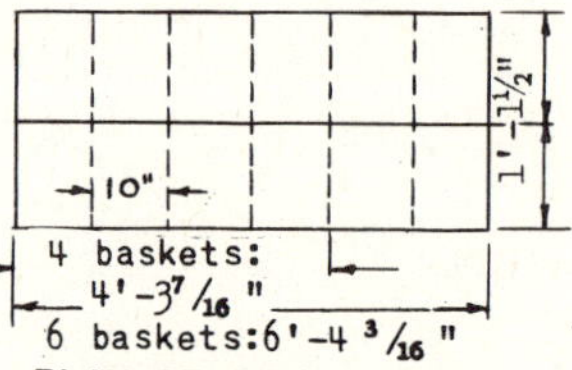
10"
1'-1 1/2"
4 baskets: 4'-3 7/16"
6 baskets: 6'-4 3/16"

PLAN OF SMALL RACK
(Elev. similar to Large Rack)

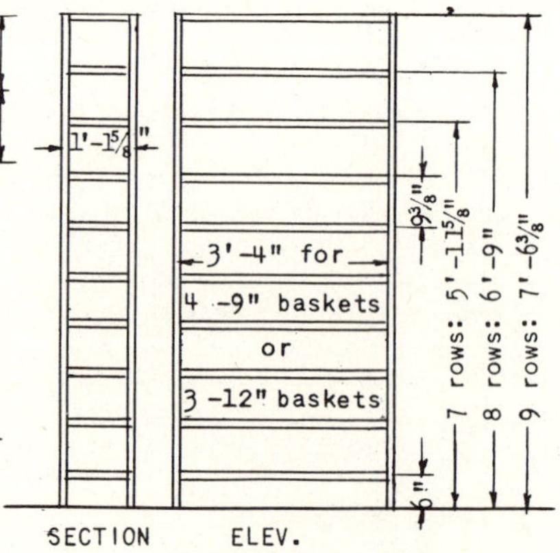
1'-1 5/8"
3'-4" for
4 -9" baskets
or
3 -12" baskets
9 3/8"
7 rows: 5'-11 5/8"
8 rows: 6'-9"
9 rows: 7'-6 3/8"
6"

SECTION   ELEV.
SINGLE DEPTH RACK

Baskets available in ¾" or 1" mesh.

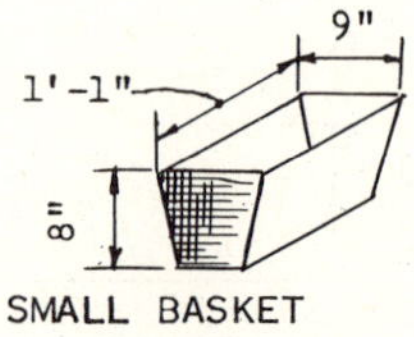
9"
1'-1"
8"

SMALL BASKET

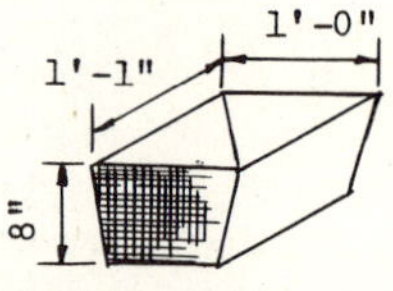
1'-0"
1'-1"
8"

LARGE BASKET
TOTE BOXES

BASKETS

Data checked by All-Steel Equipment Co.

RACKS

Data checked by Fred Medart Products, Inc.

LOCKER INSTALLATION

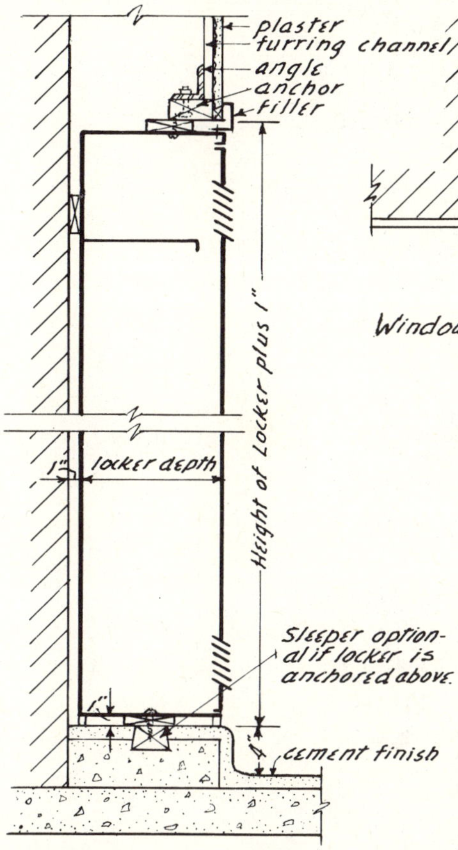
plaster
furring channel
angle
anchor
filler
Height of Locker plus 1"
1"
locker depth
Sleeper optional if locker is anchored above.
1"
4"
cement finish

SECTION through BUILT-IN LOCKERS
3/4" = 1'-0"

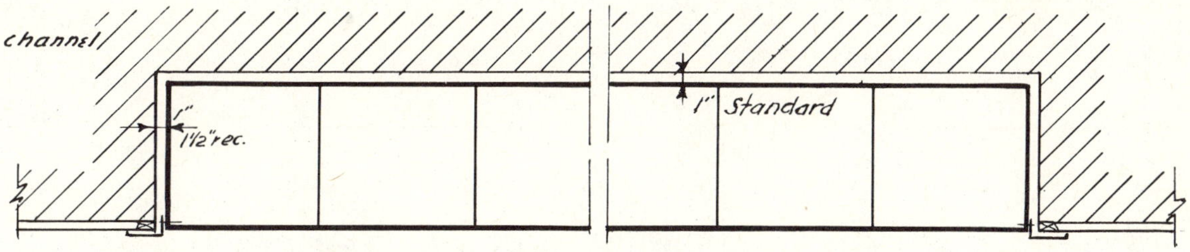
1"
1½" rec.
1" Standard

PLAN OF BUILT-IN LOCKERS
3/4" = 1'-0"

Windows 6'-0" above floor. Ceiling height 10'-0" recommended min. Radiators 6'-6" above floor.

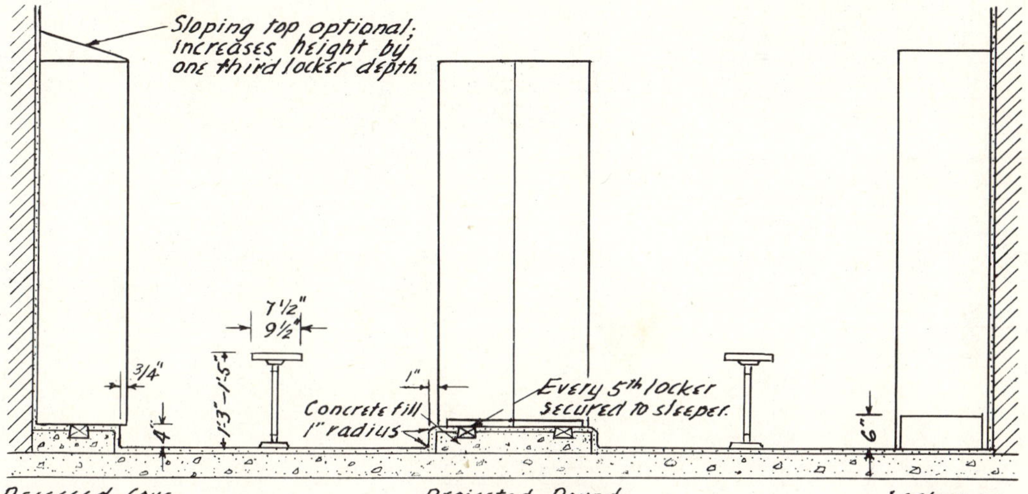
Sloping top optional; increases height by one third locker depth.
7½"
9½"
3/4"
1'3"-1'5"
4"
1"
Concrete fill 1" radius
Every 5th locker secured to sleeper.
6"
Recessed Cove Base
Projected Round-top Base
Locker on Legs

SECTION THROUGH LOCKER AISLES
3/8" = 1'-0"

LOCKER INSTALLATION DETAILS

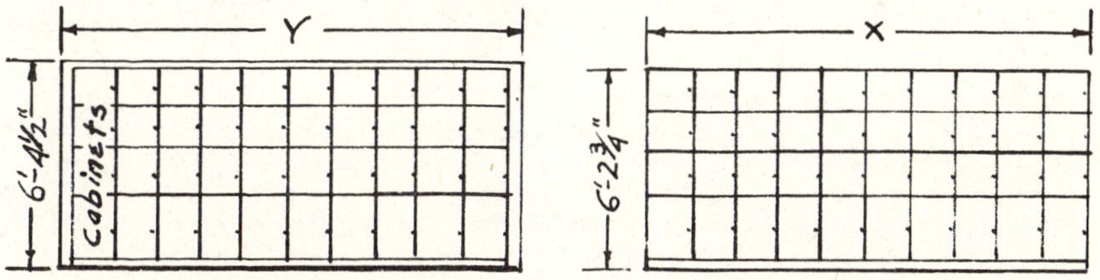
Y
6'-4½"
cabinets
X
6'-2¾"

Recessed
If lockers are recessed, depth = 2'-9"

Free standing

No. of Cabinets	1	2	3	4	5	6	7	8	9	10
Locker Dim. X	1'-4½"	2'-9"	4'-1½"	5'-6"	6'-10½"	8'-3"	9'-7½"	11'-0"	12'-4½"	13'-9"
Clear Openg Y		3'-0"	4'-5"	5'-10"	7'-2½"	8'-7"	10'-0"	11'-4½"	12'-9"	14'-2"

STANDARD PARCEL LOCKERS
Depth = 2'-4½" or 2'-6½"

No. of Cabinets	1	2	3	4	5	6	7	8	9	10
Locker Dim. X	1'-7"	3'-2"	4'-9"	6'-4"	7'-11"	9'-6"	11'-1"	12'-8"	14'-3"	15'-10"
Clear Openg Y		3'-5"	5'-0½"	6'-8"	8'-3"	9'-10"	11'-5½"	13'-0½"	14'-7½"	16'-3"

OVERSIZE PARCEL LOCKERS
Depth = 2'-8"

Note: Sizes subject to change, check with mfgr.

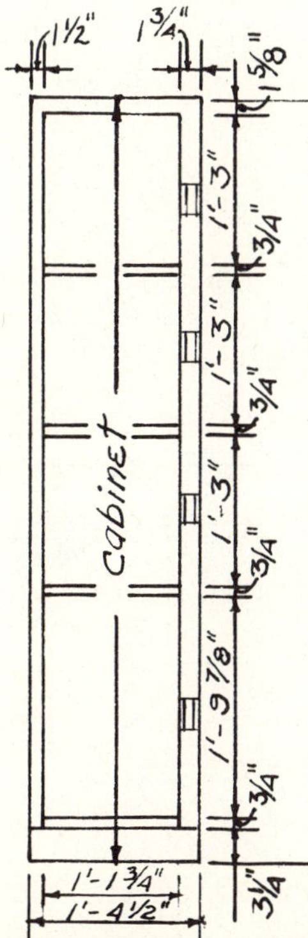
1½"
1¾"
1⅝
1'-3"
3/4
1'-3"
3/4
1'-3"
3/4
1'-9⅞"
3/4
3¼"
6'-2¾"
cabinet
1'-1¾"
1'-4½"

STANDARD LOCKER

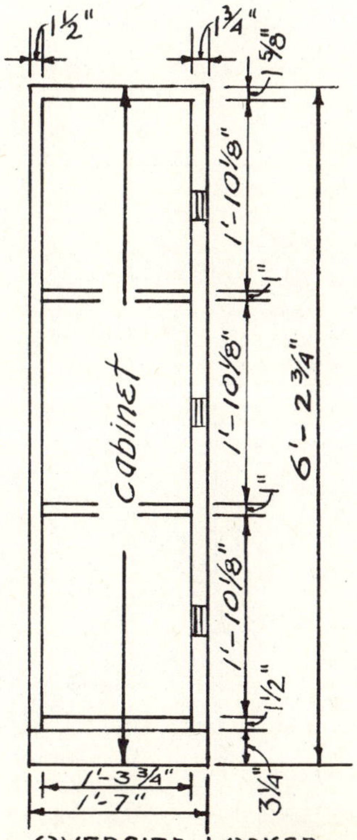
1½"
1¾"
1⅝
1'-10⅛"
1"
1'-10⅛"
1"
1'-10⅛"
1½"
3¼"
6'-2¾"
cabinet
1'-3¾"
1'-7"

OVERSIZE LOCKER

Data supplied by American Locker Company

COMMERCIAL KITCHEN EQUIPMENT

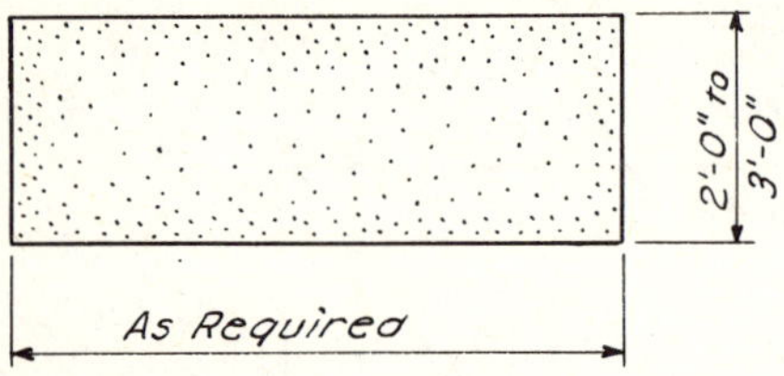
2'-0" to 3'-0"
As Required

WORK TABLE

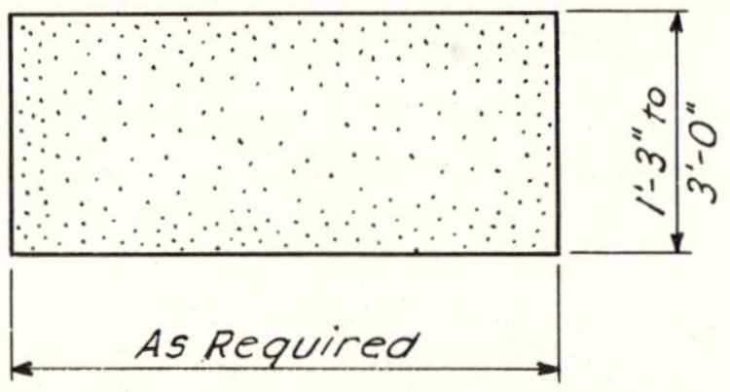
1'-3" to 3'-0"
As Required

PLATE WARMER

Can be freestanding or set into cook's tables or counters.

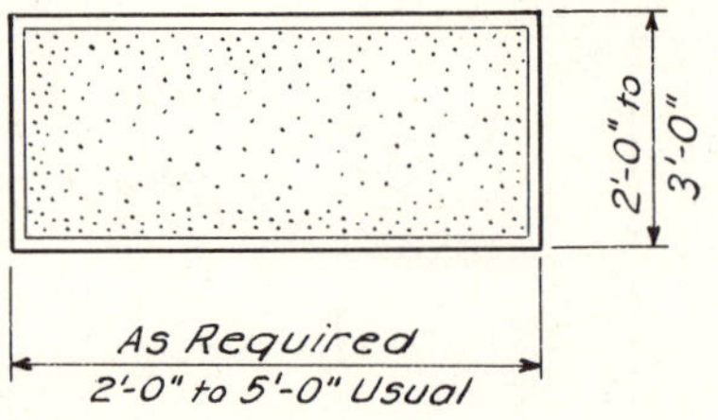
2'-0" to 3'-0"
As Required
2'-0" to 5'-0" Usual

BAIN MARIE

Can be freestanding or set into cook's tables or counters.

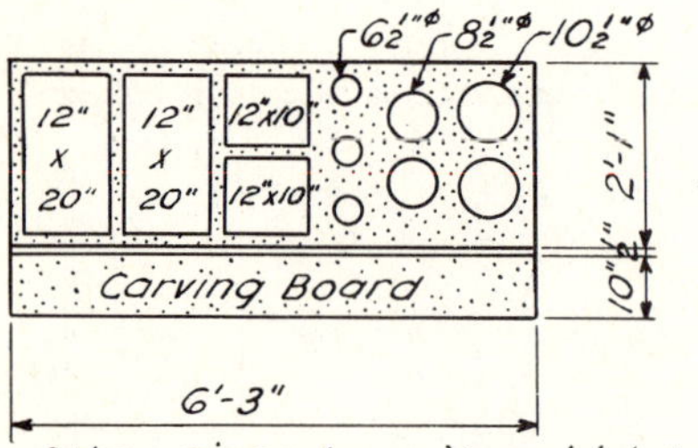
6½"φ
8½"φ
10½"φ
12" x 20"
12" x 20"
12"x10
12"x10
2'-1"
10½"
Carving Board
6'-3"

Other sizes to suit arrgmnt. at top and sizes of insets.

STEAM TABLE

NOTES: These units can be freestanding or fitted into cook's tables or counters. Many sizes and types available. Can be heated by steam, gas or electricity. Can have open stand or be fitted with warmer. Can have serving shelf above, on waiter's side.

ALL DRAWINGS NOT TO SCALE

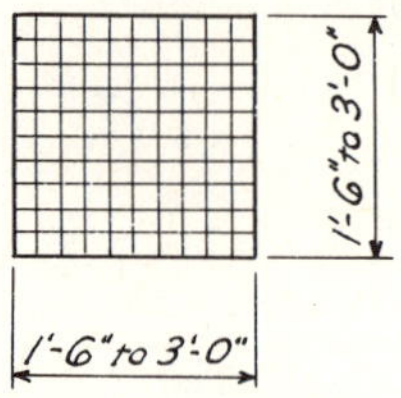
1'-6" to 3'-0"
1'-6" to 3'-0"

BUTCHER BLOCK

On legs

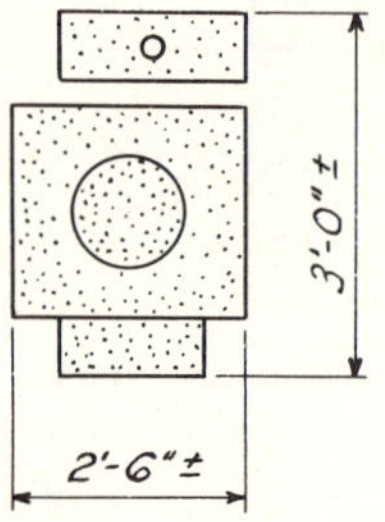
3'-0" ±
2'-6" ±

PARING MACHINE

Many types & sizes

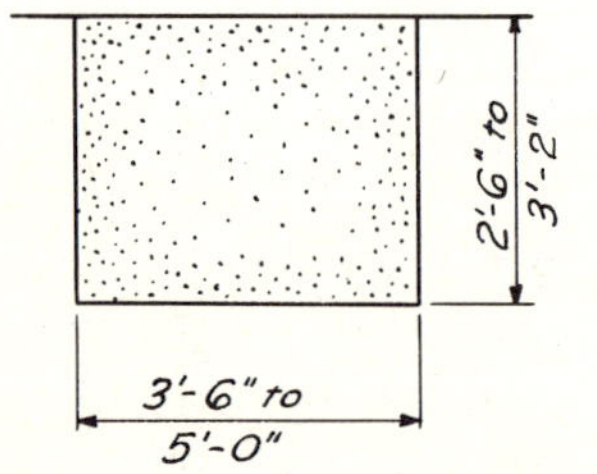
2'-6" to 3'-2"
3'-6" to 5'-0"

BAKE & ROAST OVEN

Gas & Electric
Many types & sizes

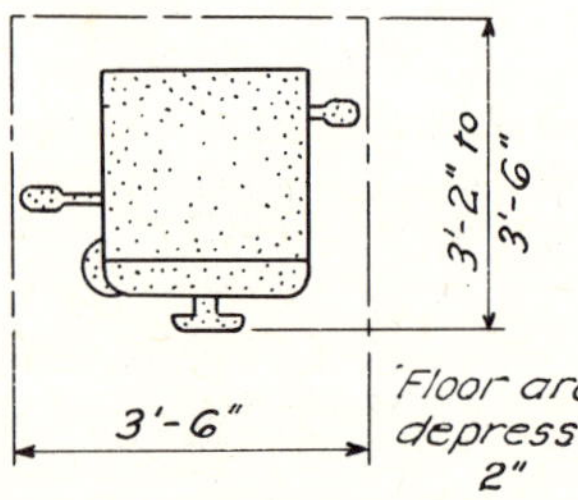
3'-2" to 3'-6"
3'-6"

Floor area depressed 2"

STEAMER

Steam, Gas & Electric

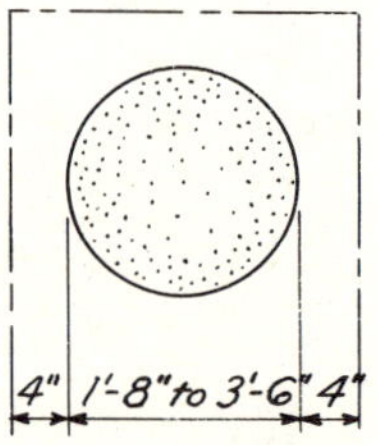
4"
1'-8" to 3'-6"
4"

STOCK KETTLE

Steam, Gas & Electric
Many types & sizes

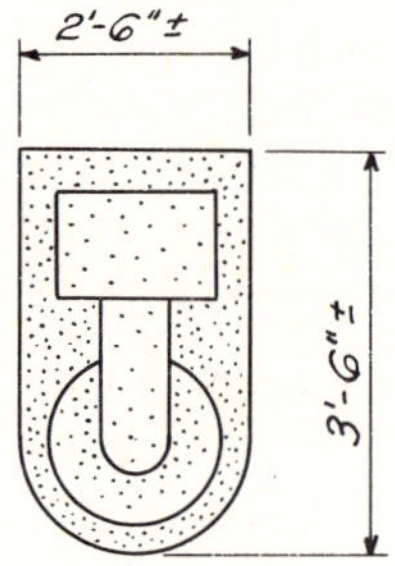
2'-6" ±
3'-6" ±

MIXING MACHINE

Many types & sizes

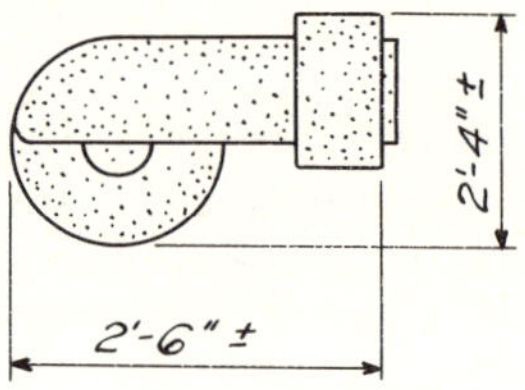
2'-4" ±
2'-6" ±

FOOD CUTTER

Many types & sizes

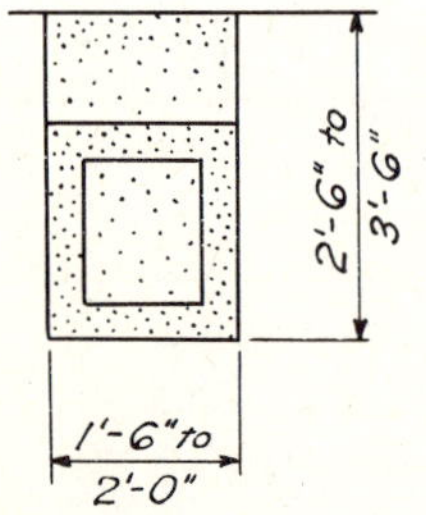
2'-6" to 3'-6"
1'-6" to 2'-0"

FRYER

Gas, Electric & Oil
Many types & sizes

NOTES: Bake and roast ovens, steamers, stock kettles, fryers and ranges should all have hoods with ductwork mechanically ventilated, or other approved type of ventilation. Ranges, fryers and ovens should have legs or set on masonry platforms. Steamers and kettles should set into depressed floor areas.

MISCELLANEOUS KITCHEN MACHINES:	
Meat saws	Glass washers
Meat grinders	Toasters
Meat slicers	Griddles
Bread slicers	Hot plates
Silver washers	Ice makers
Silver burnishers	Ice cream cabinets
Dish washers	& Others

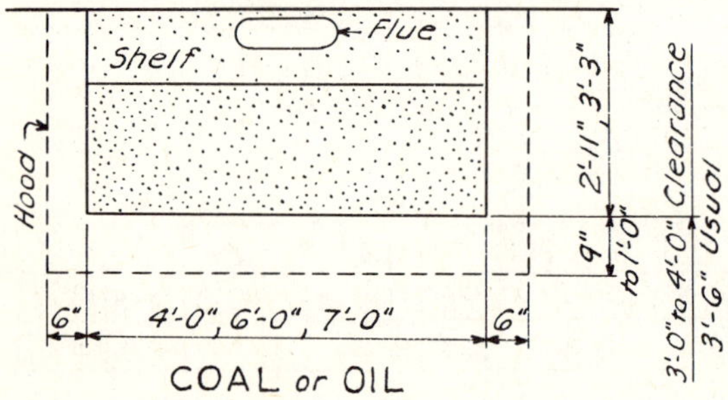
Shelf
Flue
Hood
2'-11", 3'-3"
9" to 1'-0"
6"
4'-0", 6'-0", 7'-0"
6"
3'-0" to 4'-0" Clearance
3'-6" Usual

COAL or OIL

Other sizes available.

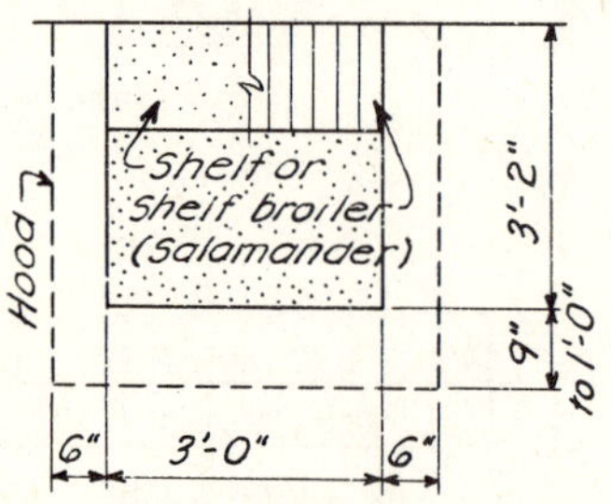
Hood
Shelf or Shelf broiler (Salamander)
3'-2"
9" to 1'-0"
6"
3'-0"
6"

ELECTRIC

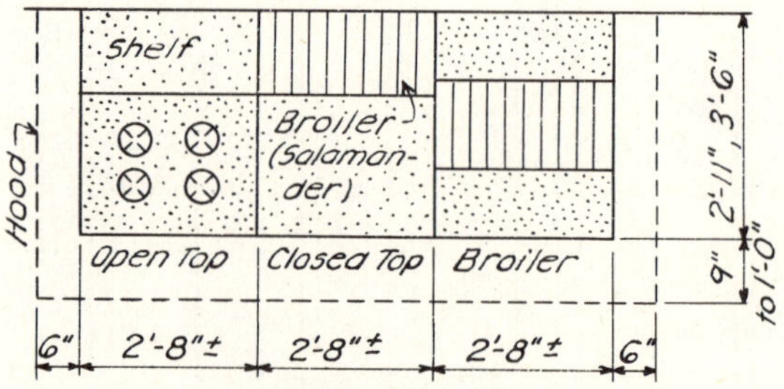
Shelf
Hood
Broiler (Salamander)
Open Top
Closed Top
Broiler
2'-11", 3'-6"
9" to 1'-0"
6"
2'-8" ±
2'-8" ±
2'-8" ±
6"

GAS

Many types and designs in Electric or Gas.

RANGES (Heavy Duty)

Data by A. J. Amendola, Food service equipment consultant

COMMERCIAL KITCHEN EQUIPMENT

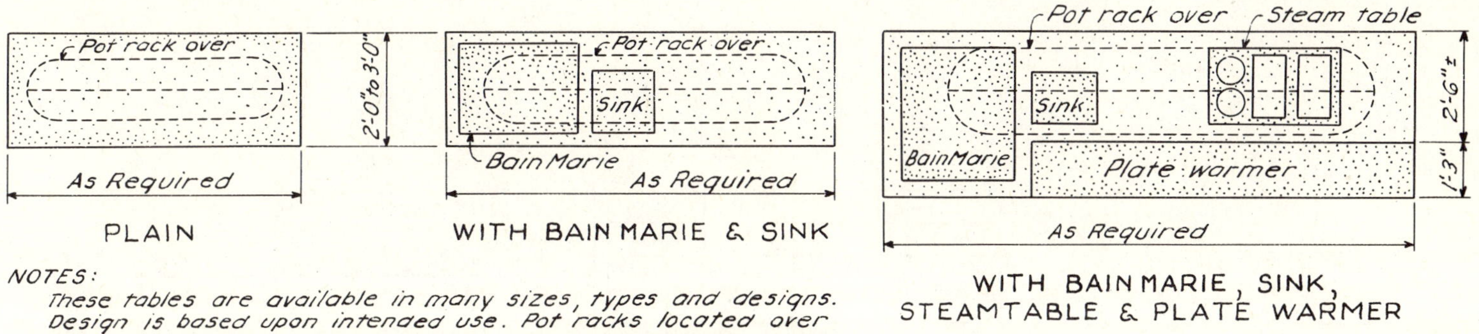
Pot rack over
2'-0" to 3'-0"
As Required
PLAIN
Pot rack over
Sink
Bain Marie
As Required
WITH BAIN MARIE & SINK
Pot rack over
Steam table
Sink
Bain Marie
Plate warmer
2'-6"±
1'-3"
As Required
WITH BAIN MARIE, SINK, STEAMTABLE & PLATE WARMER

NOTES:
These tables are available in many sizes, types and designs. Design is based upon intended use. Pot racks located over tables can be hung from ceiling or supported on standards. Space between tables and ranges is 3'-0" to 4'-0", usually 3'-6".

COOKS' TABLES

NOT TO SCALE

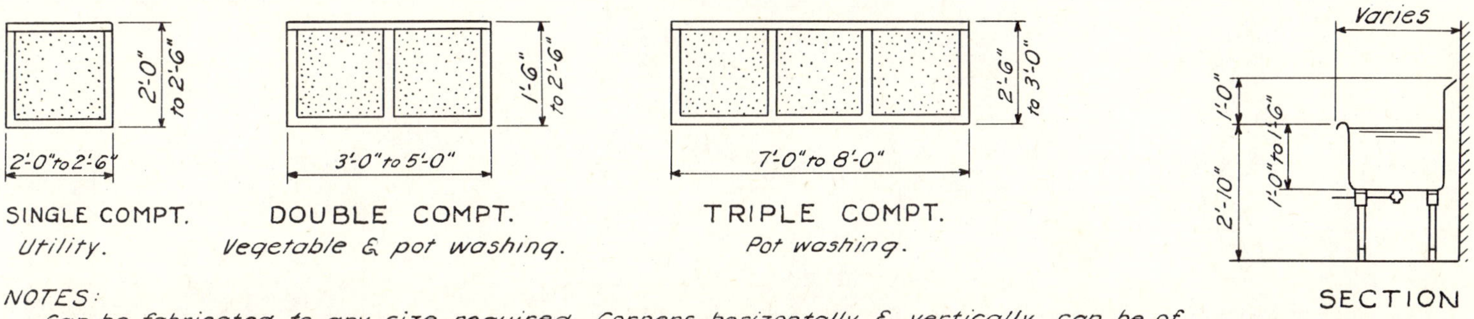
2'-0" to 2'-6"
2'-0" to 2'-6"
SINGLE COMPT.
Utility.
1'-6" to 2'-6"
3'-0" to 5'-0"
DOUBLE COMPT.
Vegetable & pot washing.
2'-6" to 3'-0"
7'-0" to 8'-0"
TRIPLE COMPT.
Pot washing.
Varies
1'-0"
1'-0" to 1'-6"
2'-10"
SECTION

NOTES:
Can be fabricated to any size required. Corners, horizontally & vertically, can be of square or rounded design. Usually furnished with drainboards at one or both ends. Drainboards can be any length; widths same as sink. Can be designed to set into tops of cook's table, counter, work table or dish table. Sinks can be supported on chair carriers embedded in wall, instead of legs.

SINKS

NOT TO SCALE

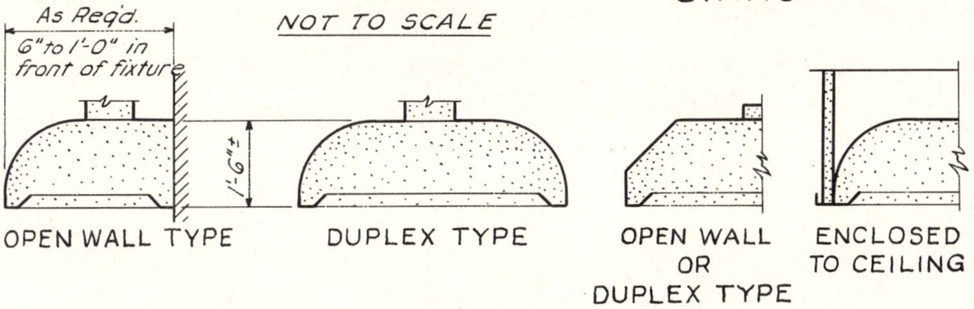
As Req'd.
6" to 1'-0" in front of fixture
1'-6"±
OPEN WALL TYPE
DUPLEX TYPE
OPEN WALL OR DUPLEX TYPE
ENCLOSED TO CEILING

HOODS

NOTES:
Many types and designs of hoods are possible. All can be made of galvanized iron or stainless steel; enclosed type can also be made of metal furring and plaster or tile, or metal sheets. Place hoods over ranges, kettles, steamers, ovens, hotplates, griddles, urns, dishwashers, glasswashers, etc. Connect to vent system and exhaust to outside air. Install grease filters over cooking areas using fat.

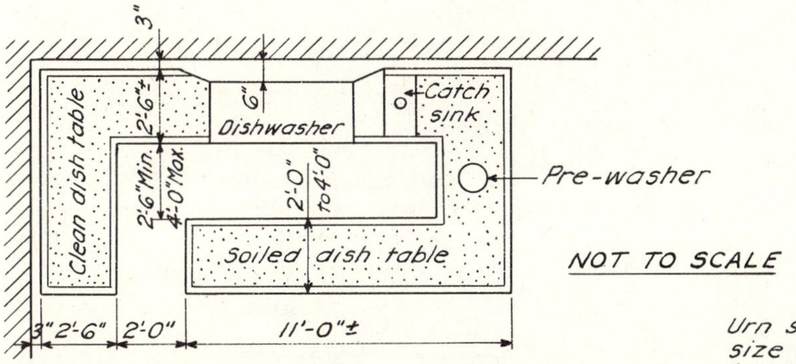
3"
2'-6"±
6"
Dishwasher
Catch sink
Clean dish table
2'-6" Min. 4'-0" Max.
2'-0" to 4'-0"
Pre-washer
Soiled dish table
NOT TO SCALE
3" 2'-6" 2'-0" 11'-0"±

TYPICAL DISHWASHING LAYOUT

Many designs can be adopted. Arrangement influenced by size of establishment and shape of space available. Arrangements for washing glasses, silver and trays are quite similar and may be designed within dishwashing area. Many types of machines are available for all types of operations.

2 PIECE SET				3 PIECE SET					URN SIZES		
CAP. (GALS.)		STAND SIZE		CAP. (GALS.)			STAND SIZE		CAP. (GALS.)		DIA. "
COF.	WAT.	LGTH.	WIDTH	COF.	WAT.	COF.	LGTH.	WIDTH	COF.	WAT.	
3	6	3'-0"	2'-0"	3	6	3	4'-2"	2'-0"	3	6	11
4	8	3'-0"	2'-0"	4	8	4	4'-6"	2'-0"	4	8	12
5	10	3'-0"	2'-0"	5	10	5	4'-9"	2'-0"	5	10	13
6	12	3'-6"	2'-0"	6	12	6	5'-0"	2'-0"	6	12	14
8	16	3'-6"	2'-3"	8	16	8	5'-3"	2'-2"	8	15	15
10	20	3'-8"	2'-3"	10	20	10	6'-0"	2'-4"	10	20	16

Urn stand is made to accom. size and no. of urns to set upon it. Urns are made in many designs and styles for coffee, tea, chocolate, water, fruit juices, etc. Can be heated by gas, steam or elec. "Combination" type urns available for holding coffee and water within one unit.

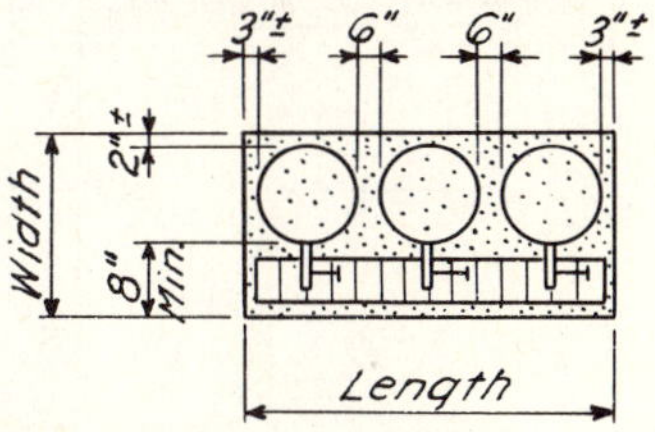
3"± 6" 6" 3"±
2"±
Width
8" Min.
Length

URNS & URN STANDS

Data by A.J. Amendolo, Food service equipment consultant.

LIQUOR SUPPLIES and EQUIPMENT

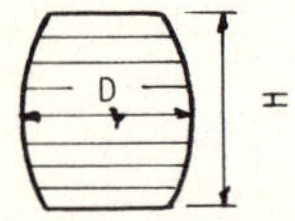

D
H

Kegs usually aluminum. Full keg holds 496 8 oz. glasses

KEG	D	H
full	23"	24¾"
1/2	17⅛"	25"
1/4	14½"	16½"

Beer keg & case data provided by Blatz Brewing Co.

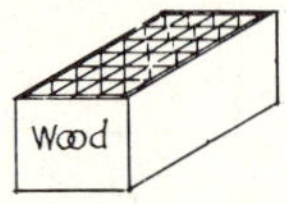

Wood

Cases usually of corrugated cardboard 24/12 oz. bottles: 16" to 18¾" long; 10¾" to 12½" wide: 8" to 10⅛" high.

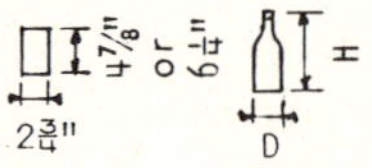

4⅞" or 6¼"
2⅝"
D
H

can bottle

Bottle	D	H
Small	3"	6½"
Aver.	2⅞"	9½"
Qt.*	3½"	9⅞"

*Refrig. qt. Now becoming common.

BEER

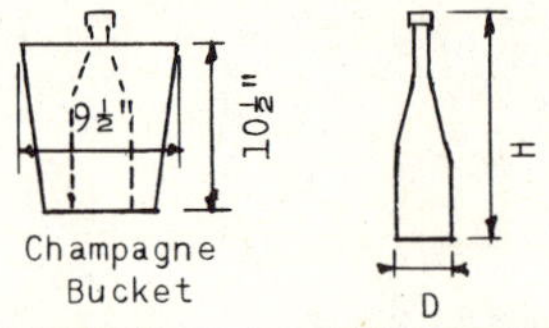

9½"
10½"
D
H

Champagne Bucket

LIQUOR	D	H
wine	2⅞"	14½"
whiskey	3½"	11½"
gin	3⅜"	11¾"
champagne fifth	3½"	12¾"
brandy	3"	12"
(fine champagne	3⅝"	10⅝")
vermouth – 30 oz.	3¼"	12½"
25-⅗ oz.	3"	12⅜"

Sizes given are for std. round bottles. Wine sizes vary with type of wine; size given is usual max.

LIQUOR

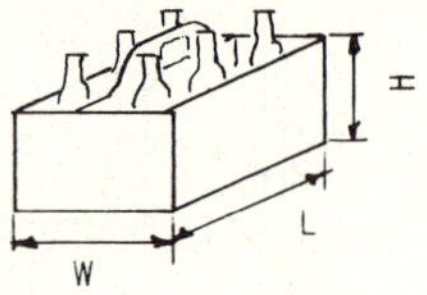

H
L
W

6 BOTTLE CONTAINERS			
KIND	L	W	H
Schweppes	7½"	5"	8¾"
Cola-Cola	7⅛"	4¾"	7¾"
Soda-12oz.	8"	5¼"	9¾"

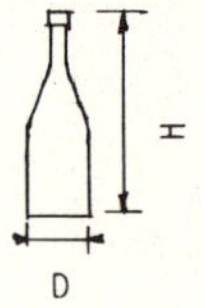

H
D

SINGLE BOTTLES		
KIND	H	D
quart	12"	3⅜"
pint-max.	9¾"	2½"
split	8⅛"	2¼"
12 oz. soda or soft drink	9¾"	2½"

MIXES AND SOFT DRINKS

CONTAINER SIZES

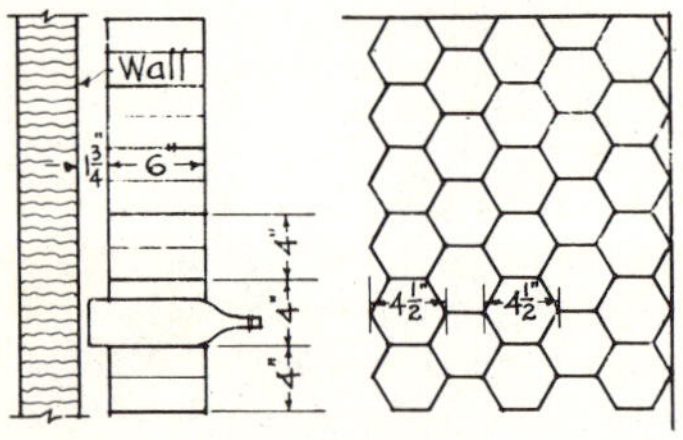

Wall
6"
4½"
4½"

Medium size for quarts.
Capacity 9½ bottles per sq. ft.

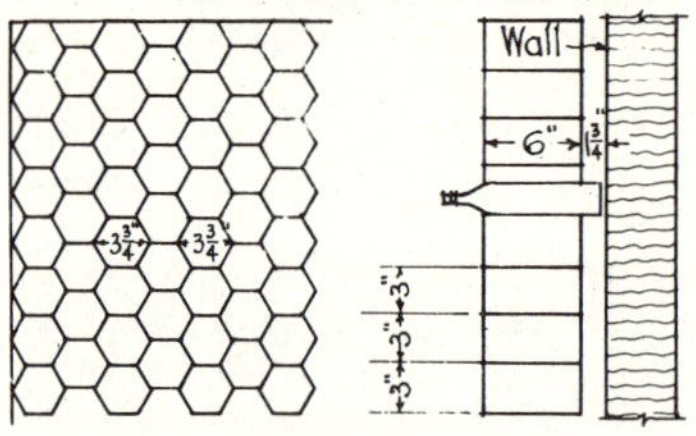

Wall
6"
3¾"
3¾"

Small size for pints.
Capacity 14 bottles per sq. ft.

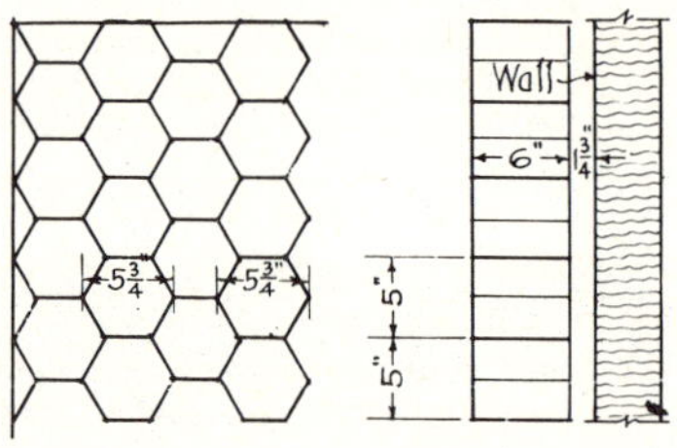

Wall
6"
5¾"
5¾"
5"

Large size for cordials.
Capacity 6½ bottles per sq. ft.

METAL HONEYCOMB BOTTLE STORAGE RACKS

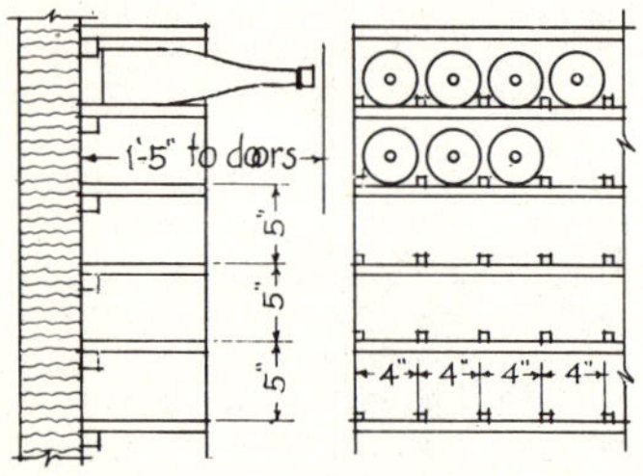

1'-5" to doors

Capacity 7 bottles per sq. ft. for qts.

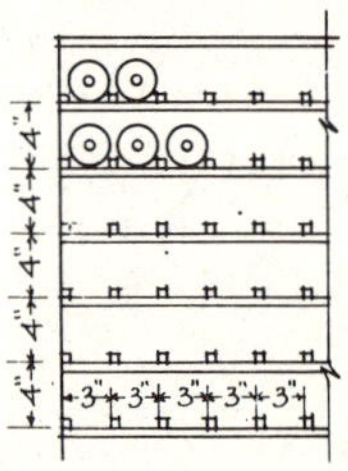

Capacity 12 bottles per sq. ft. for qts.

WOOD BOARD SHELVES

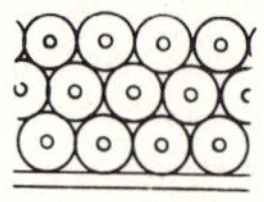

Bottle Size	Number per Sq. Ft
2½" dia	20
2¾" "	18
3" "	14
3½" "	9

These figures also for bottles standing.

STACKED

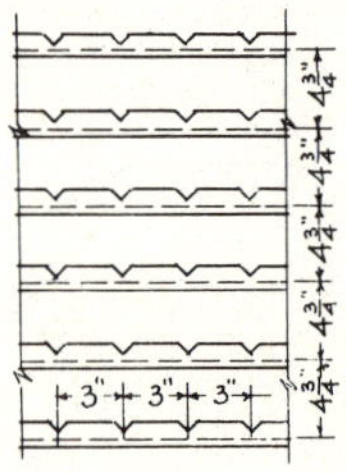

Capacity 11 bottles per sq. ft. for qts.

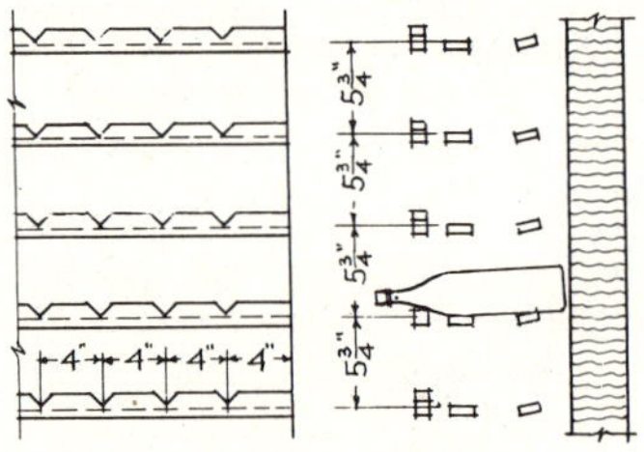

Capacity 6 bottles per sq. ft. for qts.

WOOD SLAT SHELVES

BOTTLE STORAGE

scale: ½" = 1'-0"

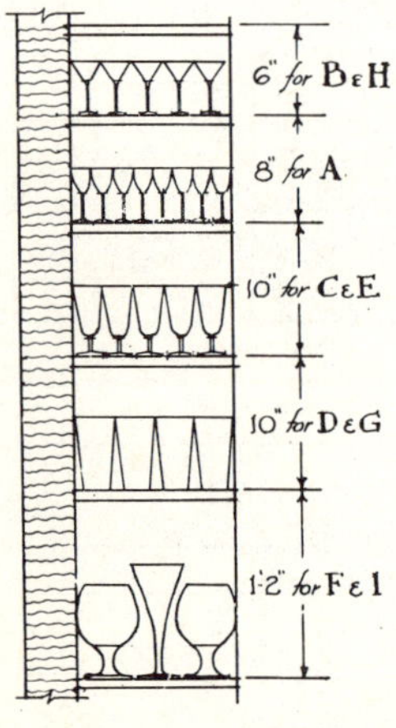

6" for B & H
8" for A
10" for C & E
10" for D & G
1'-2" for F & I

Lineal feet required for 1 doz. glasses on 1'-0" wide shelf				
	Type	Glass dia.	Glass Ht.	Lineal ft. of shelf
A	Cordial	½" to 2"	3½" - 4"	4" to 5"
B	Cocktail	2½" to 3"	2" to 4"	8" to 10"
C	Wine	2" to 2½"	5"	5" to 8"
D	Champagne	3½" to 4"	5" to 6"	1'-4" to 1'-7"
E	Beer	3½"	5"	1'-4"
F	Pilsener	3"	8½"	1'-0"
G	Highball	2¾"	5½"	9"
H	Old Fashion.	3"	3¼"	1'-0"
I	Brandy	4" to 5"	6" to 8"	1'-7" to 3'-0"

The above are average sizes and allowances. No exact standards exist

GLASS STORAGE

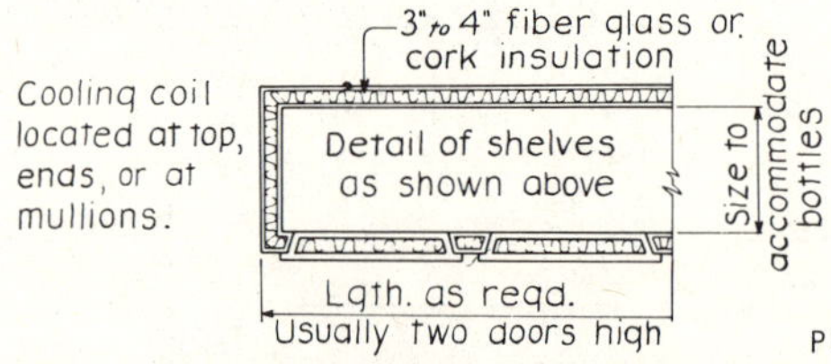

3" to 4" fiber glass or cork insulation
Cooling coil located at top, ends, or at mullions.
Detail of shelves as shown above
Size to accommodate bottles
Lgth. as reqd.
Usually two doors high

PLAN

WINE BOTTLE STORAGE REFRIGERATOR

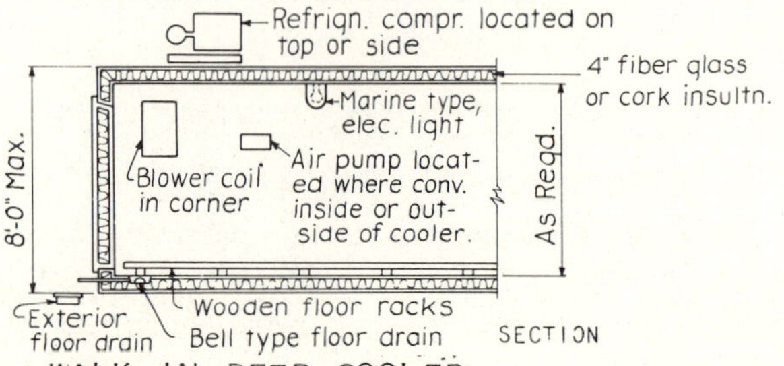

Refrign. compr. located on top or side
4" fiber glass or cork insultn.
Marine type, elec. light
Blower coil in corner
Air pump located where conv. inside or outside of cooler.
8'-0" Max.
As Reqd.
Exterior floor drain
Wooden floor racks
Bell type floor drain

SECTION

WALK-IN BEER COOLER

TOILET FIXTURES, ACCESSORIES and PARTITIONS

TABLE OF CONTENTS

LAVATORIES and WORK SINKS

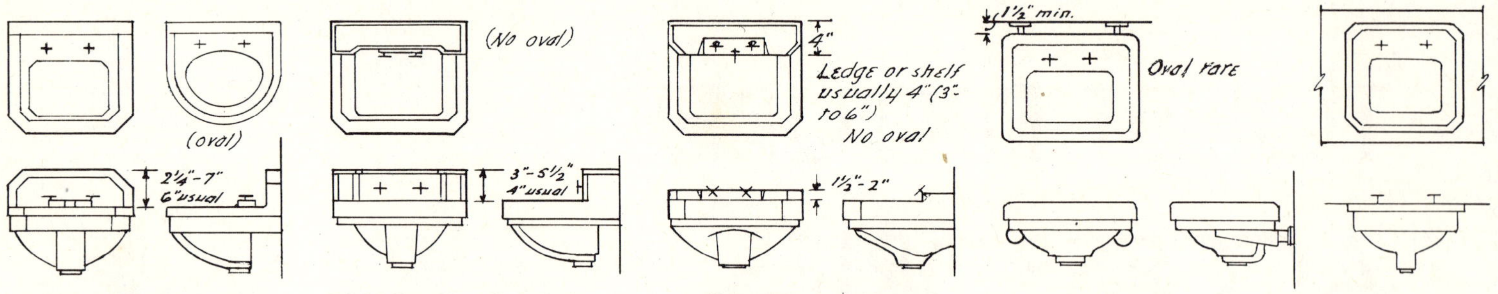
(oval)
(No oval)
4"
Ledge or shelf usually 4" (3"-to 6")
No oval
1½" min.
Oval rare
2¼"-7"
6" usual
3"-5½"
4" usual
1½"-2"

FLAT BACK — SHELF BACK — LEDGE BACK — SLAB — BUILT-IN

Lavatories shown with bevelled rectangular rims. Other models have rounded corners or D-shaped (oval) rims. Basins may be rectangular or oval, or in other shapes according to mfr. Flat back may have bevelled, rounded or D shaped corners.

Flat back

VIT. CH.	En. C.I.	En. Steel
Wall hung 12"×12"* 14"×14"† 18"×15"† 20"×19"* Wall hung or with legs 20"×18" p 24"×20" p† 24"×21" p†	Wall hung 15"×16"* 19"×17" 19"×19"* 20"×18"† L p 21"×18"† 22"×19"† L p	Wall hung, with legs or pedestal 24"×20" With legs (→ 27"×22"† L p, 26"×22" L)

Shelf back

VIT. CH.	En. C.I.	En. Steel
Wall hung or with legs 19"×16"* 19"×17"† 22"×18"† L p 22"×19"† L 24"×18"† 24"×20"† L 27"×22"† L p 26"×22" L	Wall hung 13"×13"† 18"×15" Wall hung or with legs 19"×17"† 22"×19"† 24"×18"†	Wall hung 19"×17" 20"×18"

Ledge back

VIT. CH.	En. Steel
Wall hung 18"×15" 20"×18" Wall or legs 22"×18" 24"×18"† 24"×20" 27"×22" Legs only 30"×22"	Wall hung or with legs 19"×17" p 24"×20 p 20"×18" Note: No ledge-back lavatories in En. C.I.

Slab

VIT. CH.	En. C.I.	En. Steel
Wall hung or with legs 20"×18"† L p 24"×20"† L p 24×21"† L p 27"×22" p With Legs 33"×22" c† 36"×22"†	Wall hung or with legs 20"×18"† p L 24"×20"† p L	Wall hung or with legs 24"×20" p

Built-in

VIT. CH.	En. Steel
20"×18"† 20"×19"† 24"×21"† 27"×20"† 24"×18"† 22"×18" EN. C.I. 20"×18"	19"×18½" 21"×17" PLASTIC 14"×13"

Vit Ch. = Vitreous China. En. C.I. = Enameled Cast Iron. En. Steel = Enameled Steel. p = May have vitreous china leg or pedestal in addition to wall brackets. * Made in oval rim only. L = May have 2 chrome legs & wall brackets. c = chair support. Sizes under "with legs" are supported by legs & brackets; they may not be used with bracket support alone. † = made in rectangular rim only. Height, finished floor to sink, 2'-6" to 2'-8" (Standard 2'-7")

Scale 3/8" = 1'-0"

LAVATORIES

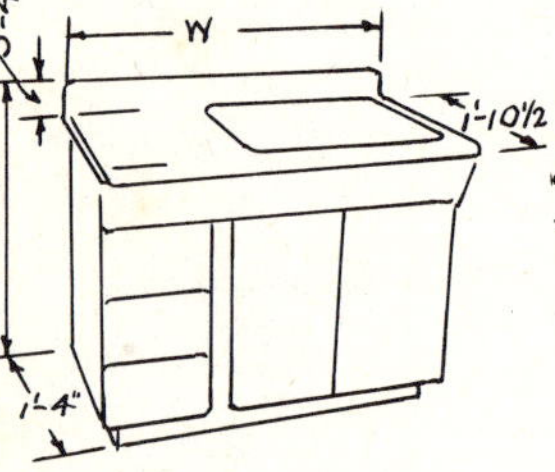
W
3'-4"
1'-10½
2'-7" to 2'-10"
1'-4"

W = 2', 2'-6", 3', 3'-6", 4', 4'-6", 5', 5'-6" & 6'
Two bowl units W = 5', 5'-6", & 6'. Units may have drawers, hampers or combinations.

CABINET

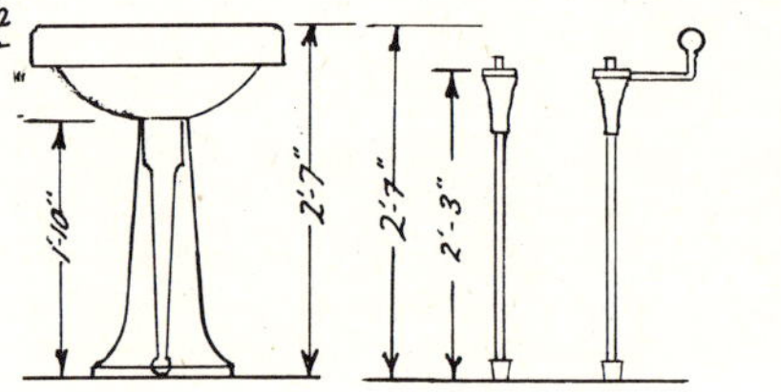
1'-10"
2'-7"
2'-7"
2'-3"

With wall bracket. Vitreous China.

LEG or PEDESTAL

Paired Legs with or without towel bars. – With wall bracket

CHROME LEGS

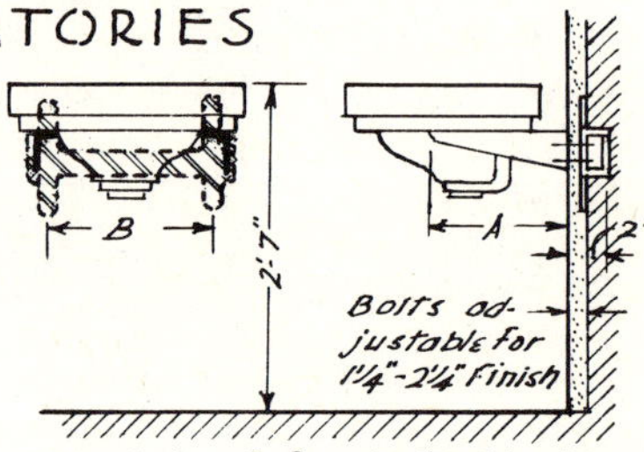
B
A
2"
2'-7"
Bolts adjustable for 1¼"-2¼" Finish

20"×18", A = 13", B = 16"; 24"×20", A = 13", B = 19"
Used on small sinks. Also used with legs or pedestal. 27"×22", A = 17", B = 23"; 30"×24": A = 17", B = 26"

BRACKET

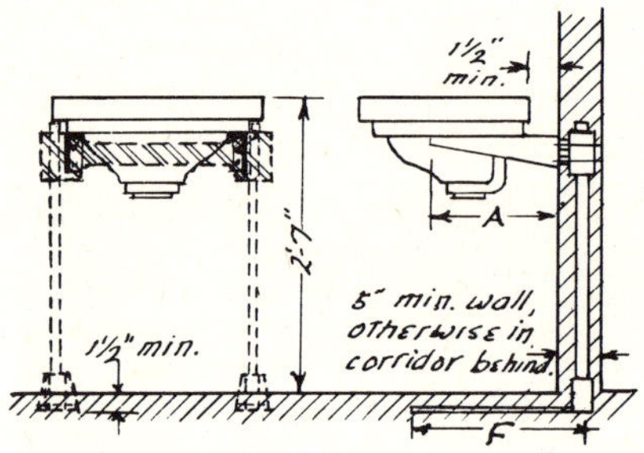
1½" min.
A
2'-7"
1½" min.
5" min. wall, otherwise in corridor behind
F

Used on larger sinks & where greater support is necessary. 20"×18", 24"×20": A = 13", F = 15", 27"×22", 30"×24" A = 17, F = 18"

CHAIR

• FLOOR-SUPPORTED • Scale 3/8" = 1'-0" • WALL-HUNG •

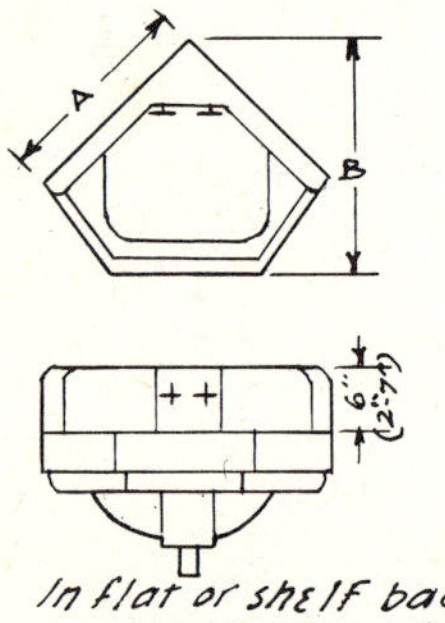
A
B
6" (2"-7")

A	B
Vitreous China:	
18"	21"
17"	20"
12½"	15"
14"	16"
Enam. C.I.	
16"	20½"
11"	16"
16½"	21"

In flat & shelf backs.

In flat or shelf backs; fixtures on panel or on rim of basin.

CORNER LAVATORY

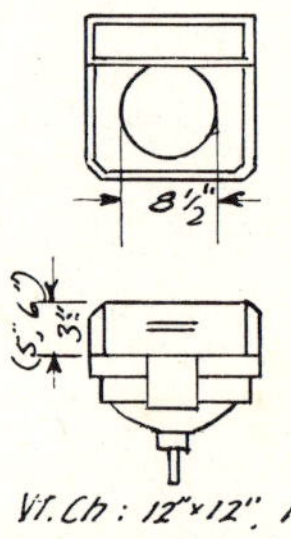
8½"
(5", 6")
3"

Vit. Ch: 12"×12", 13"×14", 14"×14"
Oval: 9"×9", 16"×16"

DENTAL

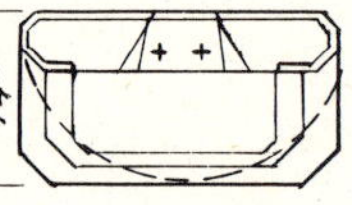
(13"-15½") 14"

Shelf back:
Vit. Ch.: 20", 22", 26" wide, 18"
En. C.I.: 16", 20", 24" wide, 19"
Ledge back:
Vit. Ch.: 20" wide
Flat back:
Vit. Ch. & En. C.I. - 20", 24", 26" wide

SPACE SAVER

BACK	NO BACK
VITREOUS CHINA	
20"×16"×10"+8"	20", 22"×18"
22"×19"×12"+10"	22", 24"×20"
24"×22"×12"+12"	
ENAMELED CAST IRON	
	16"×16"×10"
20"×16"×12"+12"	20"×14", 16"×12"
22"×18"/20"×12"+12"	22"/24"×18"/20"×12"
24"×26"×12"+12"	30", 36"×20"×12"
EARTHENWARE	
20"×18"×12"+8"	
22"×20"×12"+8"	

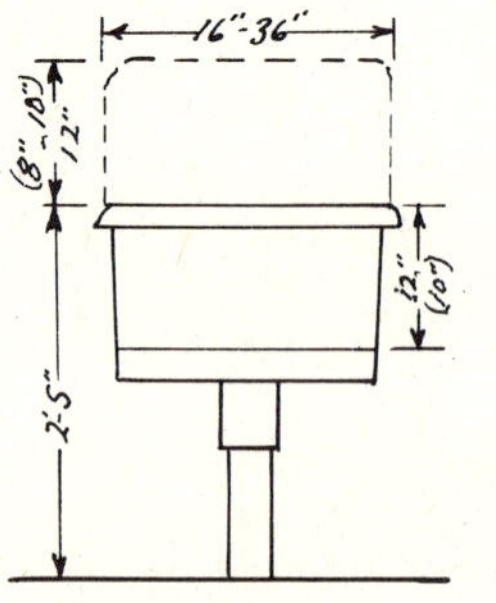
16"-36"
(8"-10") 12"
12" (10")
2'-5"

SERVICE SINK

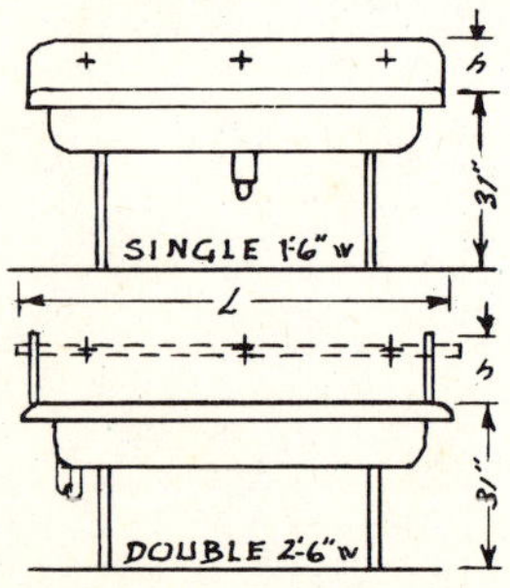
h
31"
SINGLE 1'-6" W
L
h
31"
DOUBLE 2'-6" W

L	Faucets Sgl.	Faucets Dbl.	h
4'-0"	2	4	8"
5'-0"	3	6	8"
6'-0"	3	6	8"
8'-0"	4	8	10"

Enameled C.I. only

WASH SINKS

A	SERVES
4'-6"	8 to 10
4'-0"*	8
3'-0"	5 to 6

*Cast iron only. Others in marble stone, stainless steel. Also semi-circular.

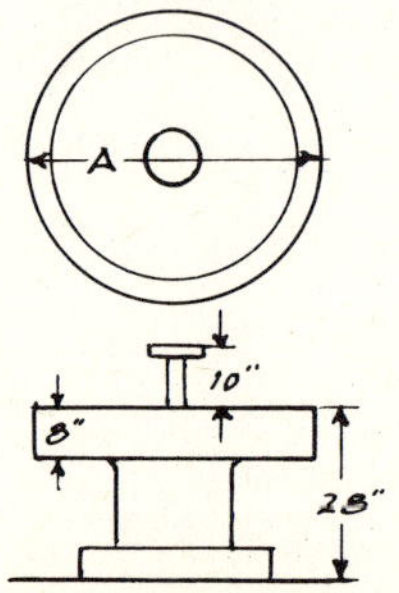
A
10"
8"
28"

WASH FOUNTAINS

	20"×18"	24"×20", 21"
	VIT. CH.	VIT. CH, EN. C.I.
A	5'-8" or 6'-2	6'-7" or 7'-2"
B	2'-0"	2'-4"
C	1'-8"	1'-10" to 2'-0"
D	3'-2" to 3'-4"	3'-6" to 3'-10"

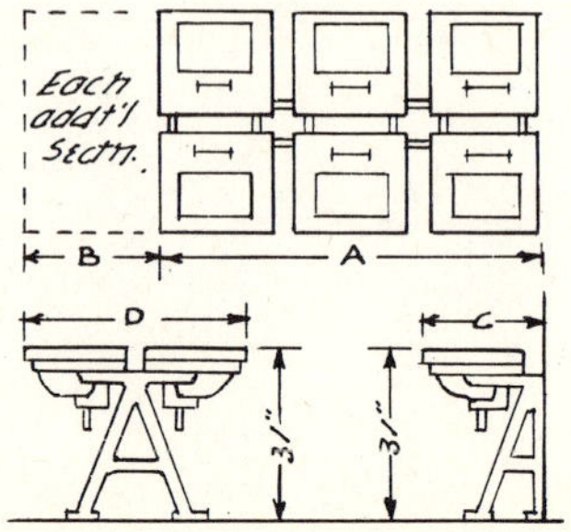
Each add'l Sect'n
B
A
D
C
31"
31"

BATTERY WASH SINKS

BATH TUBS and SHOWERS

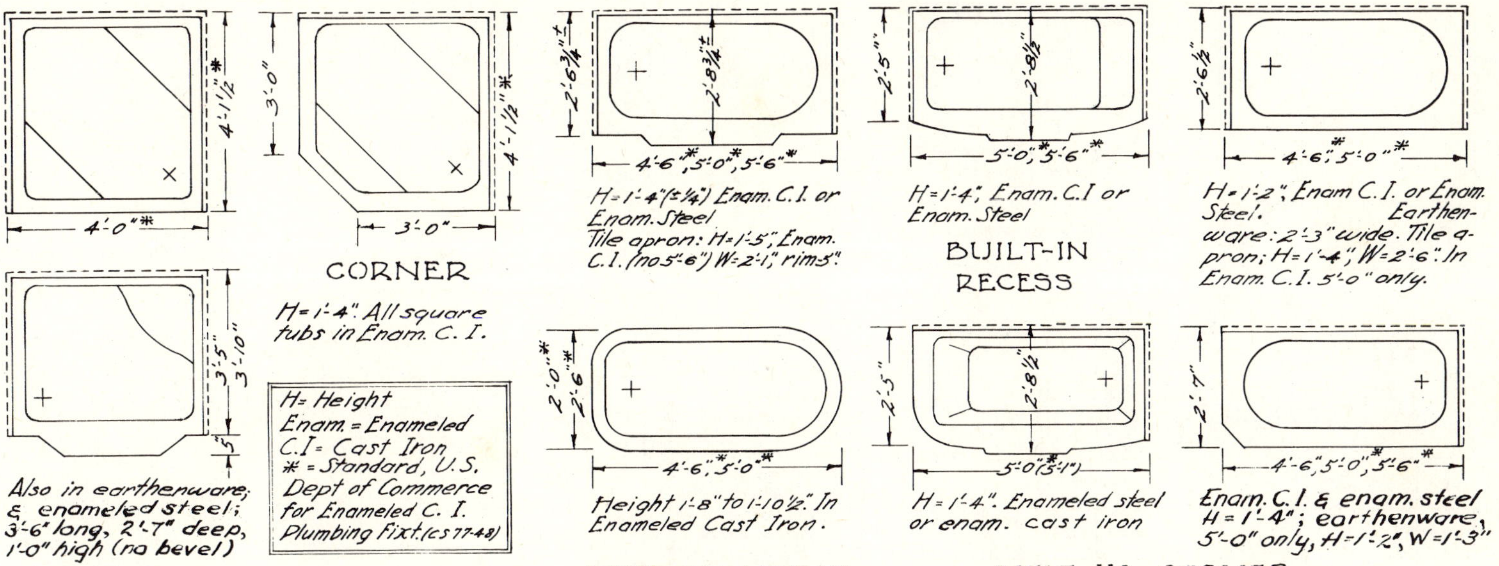
4'-1½"*
4'-0"*
3'-0"
4'-1½"*
3'-0"
CORNER
H=1'-4". All square tubs in Enam. C. I.
3'-5"
3'-10"
5"
Also in earthenware; & enameled steel; 3'-6" long, 2'-7" deep, 1'-0" high (no bevel)
H= Height
Enam.= Enameled
C.I= Cast Iron
* = Standard, U.S. Dept of Commerce for Enameled C. I. Plumbing Fixt. (CS 77-48)
2'-6¼"±
2'-8¼"±
4'-6"*, 5'-0"*, 5'-6"*
H=1'-4"(±¼") Enam. C.I. or Enam. Steel
Tile apron: H=1'-5", Enam. C.I. (no 5'-6") W=2'-1", rims".
2'-5"
2'-8½"
5'-0", 5'-6"*
H=1'-4", Enam. C.I or Enam. Steel
BUILT-IN RECESS
2'-6½"
4'-6", 5'-0"*
H=1'-2", Enam C.I. or Enam. Steel. Earthenware: 2'-3" wide. Tile apron; H=1'-4", W=2'-6". In Enam. C.I. 5'-0" only.
2'-0"*
2'-6"*
4'-6", 5'-0"*
Height 1'-8" to 1'-10½". In Enameled Cast Iron.
2'-5"
2'-8½"
5'-0"(5'-1")
H=1'-4". Enameled steel or enam. cast iron
2'-7"
4'-6", 5'-0", 5'-6"*
Enam. C.I. & enam. steel H=1'-4"; earthenware, 5'-0" only, H=1'-½", W=1'-3"

RECESS FREE-STANDING BUILT-IN CORNER

All dimensions are to rough. Allow 3/4" to 1" for finished wall; 1/2" for finished floor.

SQUARE & RECTANGULAR BATHTUBS

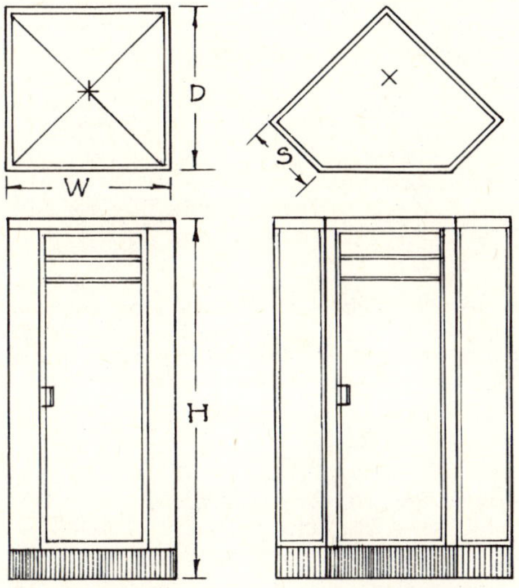
D
W
S
H

SQUARE				
W	D	H	Material-Walls	Mat'l-Receptors
2'-6"	2'-6"	6'-3"	Enameled Steel	Enameled Steel
2'-8"	2'-8"	6'-4"	Enam. Steel; Alum.	Enam. Steel, Terrazzo
		6'-8"	Enameled Steel	Terrazzo
3'-0"	3'-0"	6'-4"	Enam. Steel, Alum.	Enam. Steel, Terrazzo
		6'-8"	Enam. or stainless Steel	Terrazzo
		7'-0"†	Enameled Steel	Enameled Steel
3'-0"††	3'-6"	6'-5"	Enameled Steel	Terrazzo
3'-4"	3'-4"	6'-8"	Enameled Steel	Terrazzo
3'-6"	3'-6"	6'-5"	Enameled Steel	Terrazzo
†-Available to order 2'-6", 2'-8", 2'-10"; either dim. ††-Rare.				

Extended receptor for 3'-0" x 3'-0" cabinet; add 1'-0" to D.

CORNER						
W	D	H	S	Mat'l.-Walls	Mat'l.-Panels	Mat'l.-Receptor
3'-0"	3'-0"	6'-8"	1'-5"	Enam. Steel	Enam. Steel	Terrazzo
3'-4"	3'-4"	6'-8"	1'-7"	Enam. Steel	Glass	Terrazzo

SQUARE CORNER

FREE-STANDING SHOWER CABINETS

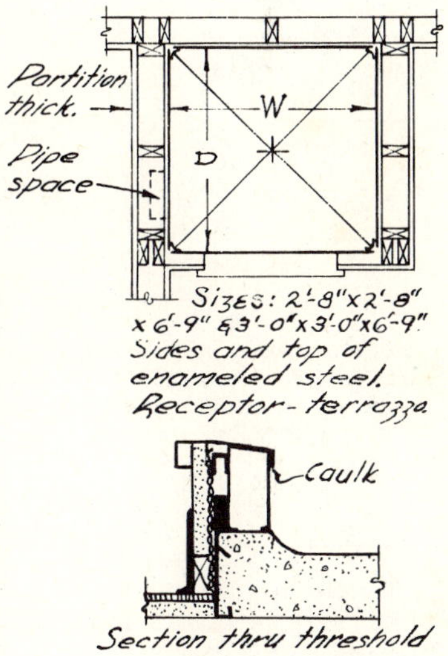
Partition thick.
W
Pipe space
D
Sizes: 2'-8" x 2'-8" x 6'-9" & 3'-0" x 3'-0" x 6'-9"
Sides and top of enameled steel.
Receptor - terrazzo
Caulk
Section thru threshold

BUILT-IN SHOWER CAB'T.

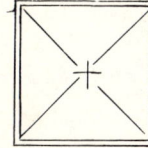

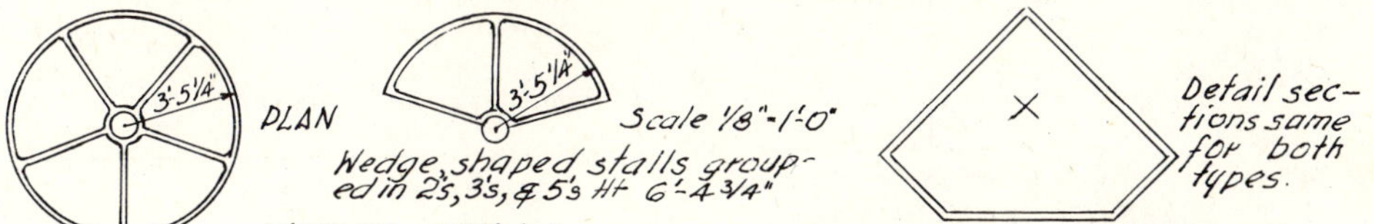
3'-5¼"
PLAN
3'-5¼"
Scale 1/8"-1'-0"
Wedge shaped stalls grouped in 2's, 3's, & 5's Ht 6'-4 3/4"
Detail sections same for both types.

MULTI STALL

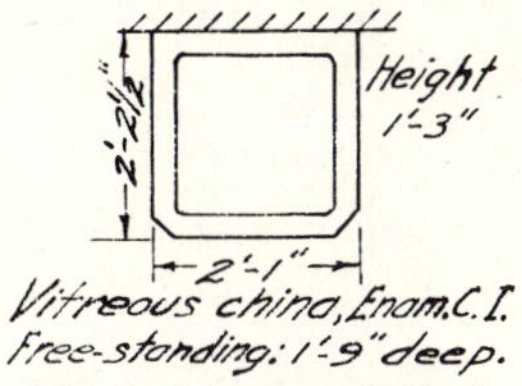
2'-2½"
Height 1'-3"
2'-1"
Vitreous china, Enam. C.I.
Free-standing: 1'-9" deep.

FOOT BATH

W	D	CORNER RECEPTORS
3'-0" 3'-4"	3'-0" 3'-4"	Flat, for tile, or with threshold for marble; both in terrazzo.
W	D	SQUARE RECEPTORS
2'-6"* 3'-0" 3'-4"	2'-6" 3'-0"* 3'-4"	Flat, for tile, in terrazzo, or enam. steel. With threshold for marble in terrazzo * Comm Standard CS.77-48 min.
3'-0"	3'-0"	Rabbetted, for marble, in terrazzo.
All receptors with 2" drain.		

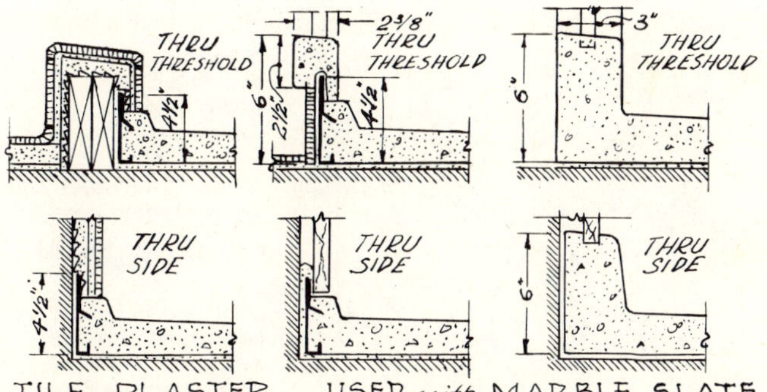
THRU THRESHOLD
4½"
2⅜"
THRU THRESHOLD
6"
2⅛"
4½"
3"
THRU THRESHOLD
6"
THRU SIDE
4½"
THRU SIDE
THRU SIDE
6"

TILE, PLASTER USED with MARBLE, SLATE

DOORS (1/4" plate glass): 2'-0" 2'-2" x 5'-5", 6'-0". & STRUCT. GLASS & STRUCT GLASS WALLS

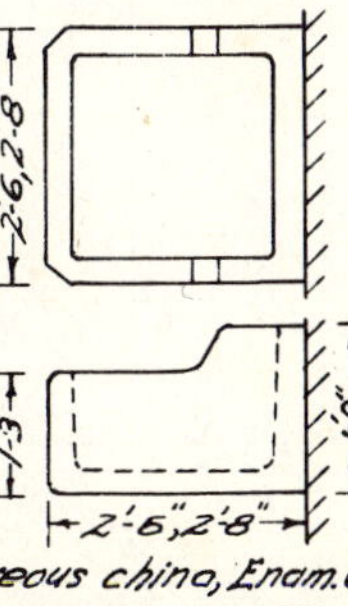
2'-6", 2'-8"
1'-3"
1'-9"
2'-6", 2'-8"
Vitreous china, Enam. C.I.

SHOWER RECEPTORS & DOORS for JOB ERECTED STALLS

SITZ BATH

Scale: 1/4" = 1'-0" except details

WATER CLOSETS & URINALS

Dimensions include seat. For closed-front seats, add 1" to B. With seat cover, add ¾" to height.

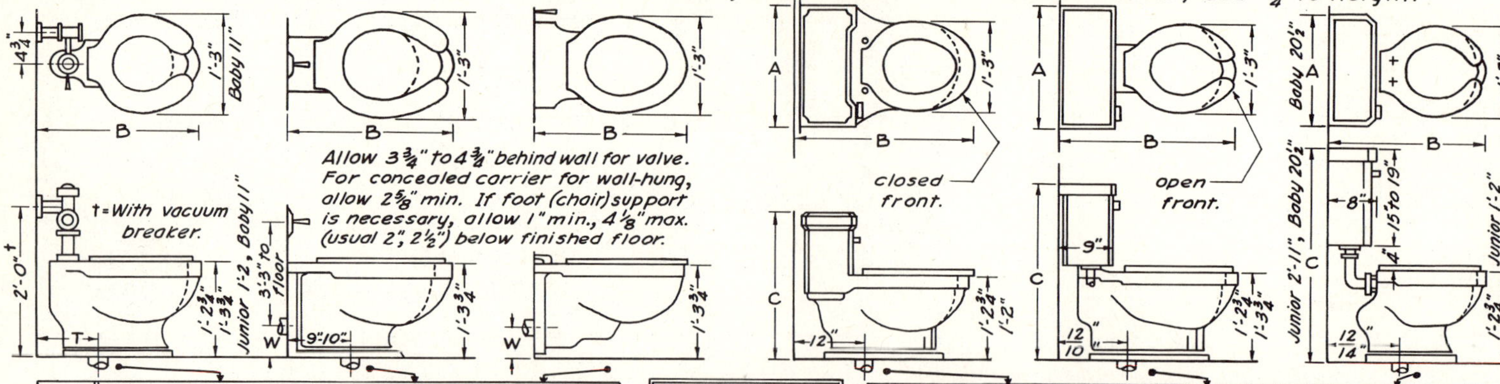
4¼"
1'-3"
Baby 11"
B
†=With vacuum breaker.
2'-0"†
T
1'-2¾"
1'-3¾"
Junior 1'-2, Baby 11"
3'-3" to floor
W
9"-10"
1'-3¾"
Allow 3¾" to 4¾" behind wall for valve. For concealed carrier for wall-hung, allow 2⅝" min. If foot (chair) support is necessary, allow 1" min., 4⅛" max. (usual 2", 2½") below finished floor.
A
C
closed front.
12"
1'-2¾"
1'-2"
open front.
9"
12
10
1'-2¾"
1'-3¾"
Baby 20½"
Baby 20½"
Junior 2'-1", Baby 20½"
8"
15" to 19"
4"
12
14
Junior 1'-2"
Baby 11"

		BOWLS for DIRECT-FLUSH VALVE							
		REGULAR				ANGLE		WALL-HUNG	
		S-J	R-T	WD	BO	S-J	BO	S-J	BO
T		10" 12"	10" 12"	5½" to 17½"	9"	10"	9" or 10"		
W						4½"	11"	4"* to 5½"	11"* to 12½" or 4½" to 5½"
B	Round	24" to 25½" 26* to 28* 25" 27"	25" 25½"*	22½" to 25½"	26"	None	20" to 26"		
B	Elong.	26" to 27½" 28* to 30* 27" 29"	27" 27½"*	None	24" to 28½"	25" to 27"	21½" to 28½"	24½" to 26"	20" 21½" to 26"

SUITABLE COMMERCIAL, INDUSTRIAL, INSTITUTIONAL

S-V = Siphon-Vortex
S-J = Siphon-Jet.
R-T = Reverse Trap.
WD = Washdown.
BO = Blowout.
Elong = Elongated bowl.
Round = Round bowl is shown dotted.
00 = most common.
* = Commercial Standard CS 20-56 for Vitreous China fixtures (All of Vitreous China except where noted)
All dimensions are given in inches.
Scale ⅜" = 1'-0"

		ONE-PIECE			CLOSE-COUPLED				LOW TANK		
		S-V	S-J	R-T	S-V	S-J	R-T	WD	S-J	R-T	WD
A		20½" to 22½	22"	22"	20½"	21" to 22½" 22"	20" to 21¾"	20½" to 21¾"	22¾" or 23½"	20½" or 22"	18" to 22"
B	Round	27"		27½"	27"	26½" to 28½ 28"	25" to 28 27"	26½" to 28½"	27"	27"	26" to 27"
B	Elong.	29"	29½"	29½"	29½"	29½" to 31" 30"	30"	None	29"	29"	None
C		24" or 18½"	28½"	28½" 18½"	29"	28" to 31½"	28" to 30"	28½" to 30"	36" to 40	30¾ to 35½"	30 to 35½"

SUITABLE RESIDENTIAL

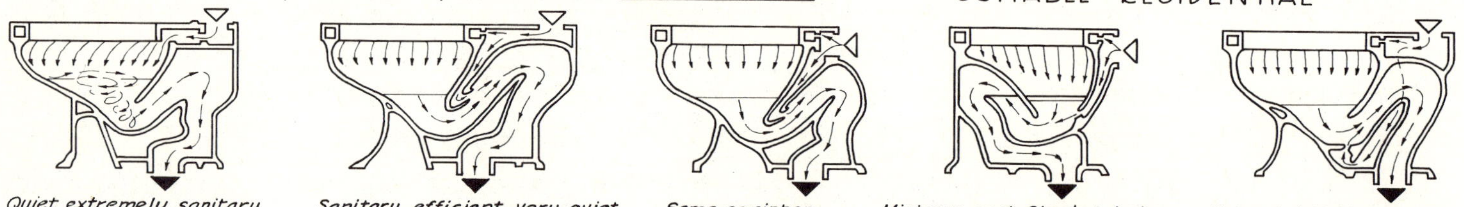

Quiet, extremely sanitary. Water directed thru rim to create vortex. Scours bowl. Folds over into jet; siphon.
SIPHON-VORTEX

Sanitary, efficient, very quiet. Water enters thru rim and thru jets in up-leg of trapway. Jet acts as siphon in down-leg.
SIPHON-JET

Same as siphon-jet, except that closet size is smaller.
REVERSE TRAP

Minimum cost. Simplest design. With round front bowl & front trapway only. Head formed in up-leg overflows, creating siphon.
WASHDOWN

Noisy, but highly efficient and water-saving. Strong jet into upleg forces contents out. Use with DFV only.
BLOWOUT

WATER CLOSETS

Allow 2⅝" min for concealed carrier for wall hung urinals. If foot (chair) support is used allow 1" min., 4⅛" max. (usual 2", 2½") below finished floor.

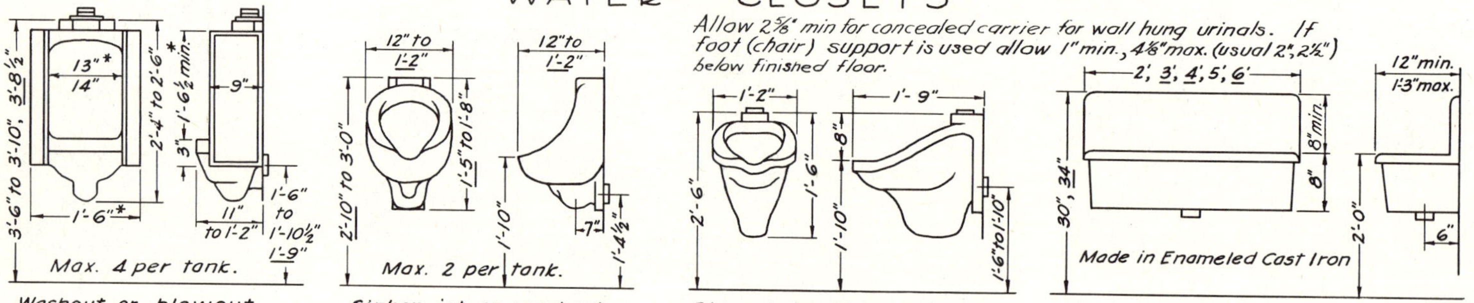
13"*
14"
3'-6" to 3'-10", 3'-8½"
2'-4" to 2'-6"*
1'-6½" min.
9"
3"
1'-6"*
11" to 1'-2"
1'-6" to 1'-10½"
1'-9"
Max. 4 per tank.
12" to 1'-2"
2'-10" to 3'-0"
1'-5" to 1'-8"
1'-10"
7"
1'-4½"
Max. 2 per tank.
1'-2"
1'-9"
2'-6"
1'-6"
1'-10"
8"
1'-6" to 1'-10"
2', 3', 4', 5', 6'
8" min.
8"
30", 34"
Made in Enameled Cast Iron
12" min.
1'-3" max.
2'-0"
6"

Washout or blowout

Siphon-jet or washout

Blowout for Direct Flush Valve

Trough type

WALL-HUNG URINALS

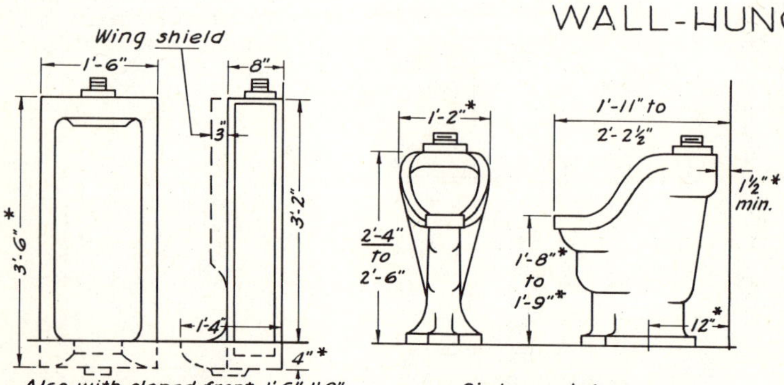
Wing shield
1'-6"
8"
3"
3'-6"*
3'-2"
1'-4"
4"*
1'-2"*
1'-11" to 2'-2½"
1½"* min.
2'-4" to 2'-6"
1'-8"* to 1'-9"*
12"*

Also with sloped front 1'-6", 1'-9" wide. Max. 4 per tank.
STALL URINAL

Siphon-jet. Maximum 1 per tank.
PEDESTAL URINAL

Height: top of tank to finished floor; 7'-8" to 7'-10".
Width from 15" to 2'-2½".
Depth from 7¼" to 14½".
Height from 10" to 14".
Made in vitreous china or enameled cast iron.
URINAL TANKS

Stall urinals available with seam covers for battery installation on 1'-9" or 2'-0" centers.
BATTERY STALLS

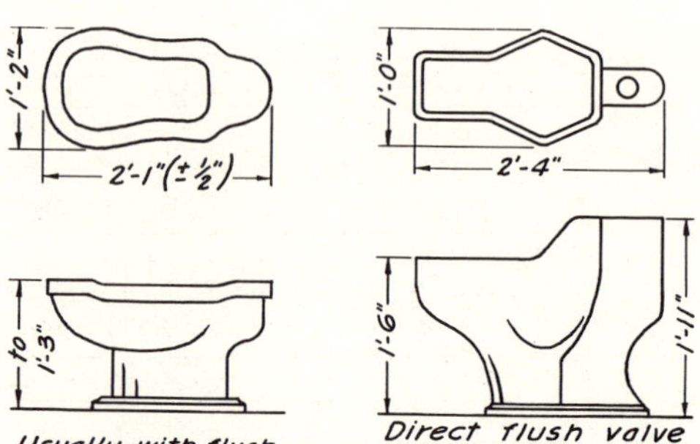
1'-2"
2'-1" (±½")
1'-2" to 1'-3"
1'-0"
2'-4"
1'-6"
1'-11"

Usually with flushing rim, douche; pop-up drain.
BIDET

Direct flush valve Siphon-vortex.
WOMEN'S URINAL

All urinals made for tank or flush valve.

Scale - ⅜" - 1'-0"

BATHROOM ACCESSORIES

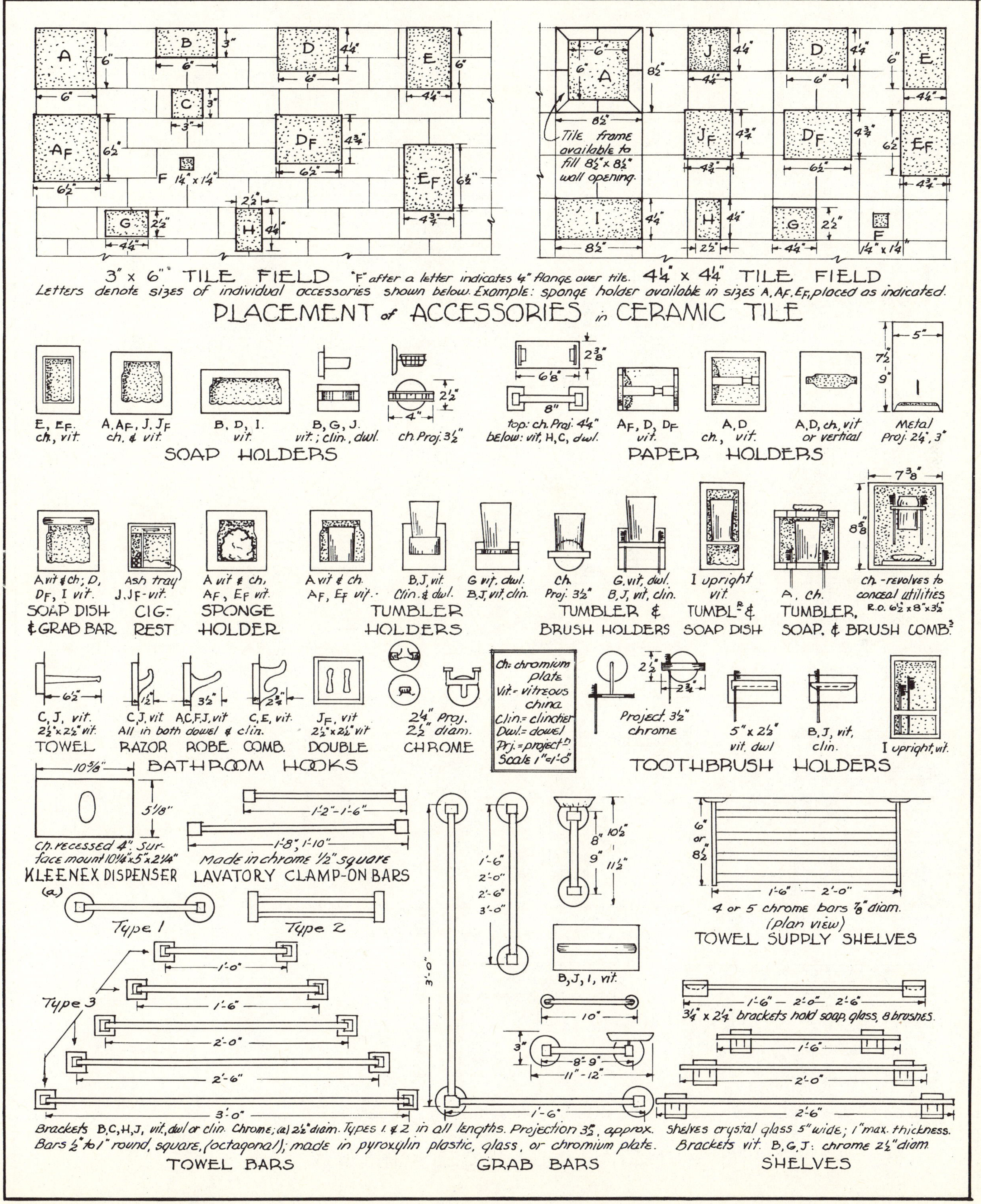
3" x 6" TILE FIELD
"F" after a letter indicates ¼" flange over tile.
4¼" x 4¼" TILE FIELD
Letters denote sizes of individual accessories shown below. Example: sponge holder available in sizes A, AF, EF, placed as indicated.
Tile frame available to fill 8½" x 8½" wall opening.
PLACEMENT of ACCESSORIES in CERAMIC TILE
E, EF. ch, vit.
A, AF, J, JF ch. & vit.
B, D, I. vit.
B, G, J. vit.; clin., dwl.
ch. Proj. 3½"
top: ch. Proj. 4¼" below: vit, H, C, dwl.
SOAP HOLDERS
AF, D, DF vit.
A, D ch., vit.
A, D, ch, vit or vertical
Metal Proj. 2¼", 3"
PAPER HOLDERS
A vit & ch; D, DF, I vit.
SOAP DISH & GRAB BAR
Ash tray J, JF-vit.
CIG-REST
A vit & ch, AF, EF vit.
SPONGE HOLDER
A vit & ch. AF, EF vit.
B, J, vit. Clin. & dwl.
G vit, dwl. B, J, vit, clin.
TUMBLER HOLDERS
Ch. Proj: 3½"
G, vit, dwl. B, J, vit, clin.
TUMBLER & BRUSH HOLDERS
I upright vit.
TUMBLR & SOAP DISH
A, ch.
Ch. - revolves to conceal utilities R.O. 6½" x 8" x 3½"
TUMBLER, SOAP, & BRUSH COMB.
C, J, vit. 2½" x 2½" vit.
TOWEL
C, J, vit All in both dowel & clin.
RAZOR
A, C, F, J, vit
ROBE
C, E, vit.
COMB.
JF, vit 2½" x 2½" vit
DOUBLE
2¼" Proj. 2½" diam.
CHROME
BATHROOM HOOKS
Ch = chromium plate
Vit. = vitreous china
Clin. = clincher
Dwl. = dowel
Prj. = projection
Scale 1" = 1'-0"
Project. 3½" chrome
5" x 2½" vit. dwl
B, J, vit, clin.
I upright, vit.
TOOTHBRUSH HOLDERS
Ch. recessed 4". Surface mount 10⅛" x 5" x 2¼"
KLEENEX DISPENSER (a)
Made in chrome ½" square
LAVATORY CLAMP-ON BARS
Type 1
Type 2
Type 3
4 or 5 chrome bars ⅞" diam. (plan view)
TOWEL SUPPLY SHELVES
B, J, I, vit.
3¼" x 2¼" brackets hold soap, glass, 8 brushes.
Brackets B, C, H, J, vit, dwl or clin. Chrome; (a) 2½" diam. Types 1 & 2 in all lengths. Projection 3⅜", approx.
Bars ½" to 1" round, square, (octagonal); made in pyroxylin plastic, glass, or chromium plate.
shelves crystal glass 5" wide; 1" max. thickness.
Brackets vit. B, G, J: chrome 2½" diam.
TOWEL BARS
GRAB BARS
SHELVES

BATHROOM CABINETS and ACCESSORIES

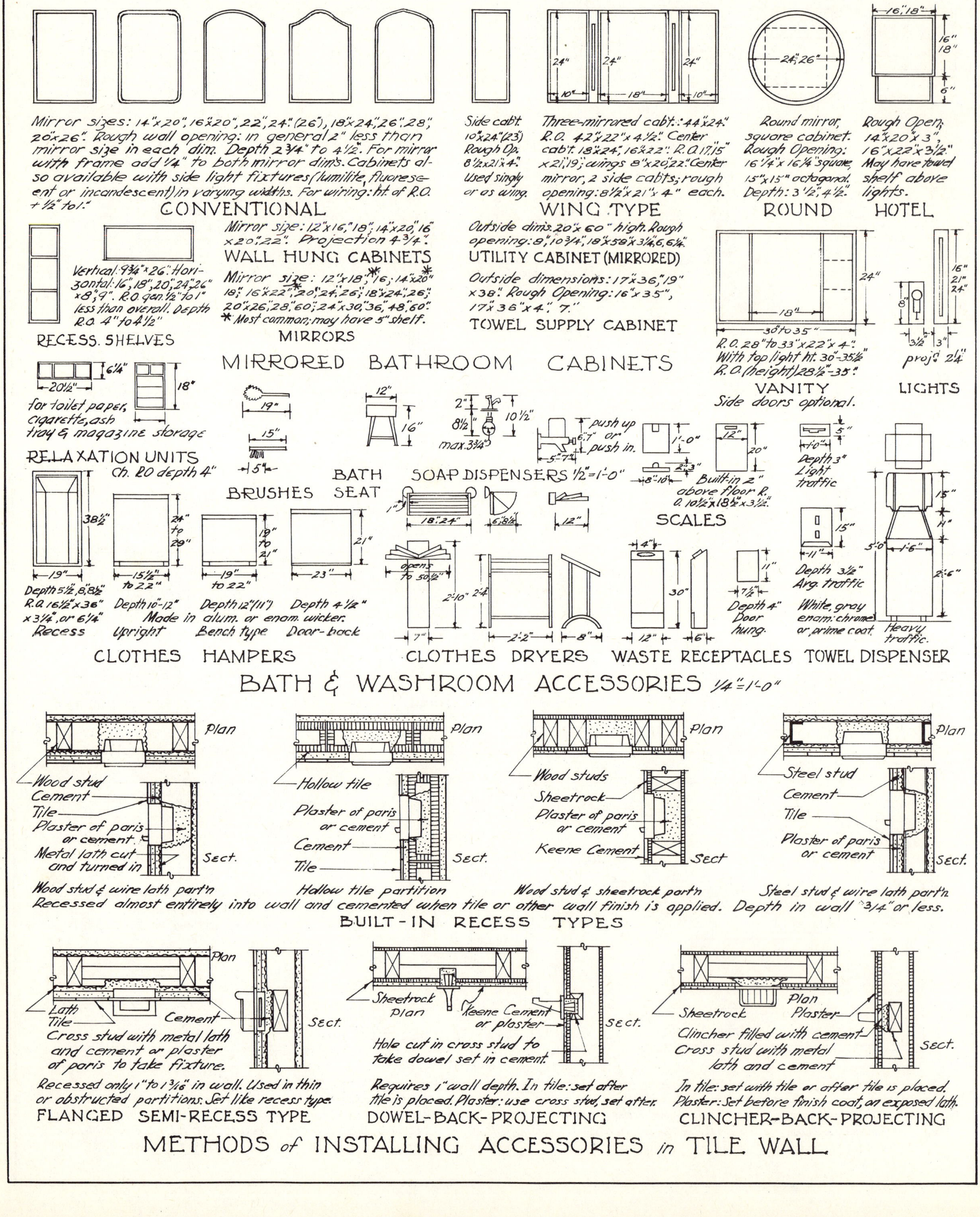

Mirror sizes: 14"x20", 16"x20", 22", 24" (26"), 18"x24", 26", 28", 20"x26". Rough wall opening: in general 2" less than mirror size in each dim. Depth 2 3/4" to 4 1/2". For mirror with frame add 1/4" to both mirror dim's. Cabinets also available with side light fixtures (lumilite, fluorescent or incandescent) in varying widths. For wiring: ht. of R.O. + 1/2" to 1'.
CONVENTIONAL
Side cab't. 10"x24" (23") Rough Op. 8 1/2"x21"x4". Used singly or as wing.
24" 24" 24" 10" 18" 10"
Three-mirrored cab't.: 44"x24". R.O. 42"x22"x4 1/2". Center cab't: 18"x24", 16"x22". R.O. 17,15" x 21,19"; wings 8"x20", 22". Center mirror, 2 side cab'ts.; rough opening: 8 1/2"x21"x 4" each.
WING TYPE
24", 26"
Round mirror, square cabinet. Rough Opening: 16 1/4"x16 1/4" square, 15"x15" octagonal. Depth: 3 1/2", 4 1/2".
ROUND
16", 18" 16" 18" 6"
Rough Open: 14"x20"x3", 16"x22"x3 1/2". May have towel shelf above lights.
HOTEL
Vertical: 9 3/4"x26". Horizontal: 16", 18", 20", 24", 26" x 8", 9". R.O. gen. 1/2" to 1" less than overall. Depth R.O. 4" to 4 1/2"
RECESS. SHELVES
Mirror size: 12"x16", 18"; 14"x20", 16" x 20", 22". Projection 4 3/4".
WALL HUNG CABINETS
Mirror size: 12"x18"*, 16; 14"x20"*, 18"; 16"x22", 20", 24", 26"; 18"x24", 26"; 20"x26", 28", 60"; 24"x30", 36", 48", 60".
* Most common; may have 5" shelf.
MIRRORS
Outside dims. 20"x 60" high. Rough opening: 8", 10 3/4", 18"x58"x3 1/4", 6, 6 1/4".
UTILITY CABINET (MIRRORED)
Outside dimensions: 17"x36", 19" x 38". Rough Opening: 16"x35", 17"x36"x4". 7".
TOWEL SUPPLY CABINET
24" 18" 30" to 35"
R.O. 28" to 33"x22"x4". With top light ht. 30"-35 1/2". R.O. (height) 28 1/2"-35".
VANITY
Side doors optional.
16" 21" 24" 8" 3 1/2" 3"
proj. 2 1/4"
LIGHTS
MIRRORED BATHROOM CABINETS
6 1/4" 20 1/2" 18"
for toilet paper, cigarette, ash tray & magazine storage
RELAXATION UNITS
Ch. 20 depth 4"
19" 15" 5"
BRUSHES
12" 16"
BATH SEAT
2" 8 1/2" 10 1/2" max. 3 3/4"
5"-7" 6"-7"
push up or push in.
SOAP DISPENSERS 1/2"=1'-0"
1'-0" 8"-10" 2"-3"
12" 20"
Built-in 2" above floor R.O. 10 1/2"x18 1/2"x3 1/2".
SCALES
5" 1'-0"
Depth 3" Light traffic
38 1/2" 19"
Depth 5 1/2, 8, 8 1/2". R.O. 16 1/2"x36" x 3 1/4", or 6 1/4"
Recess
24" to 29" 15 1/2" to 22"
Depth 10"-12"
Upright
19" to 21" 19" to 22"
Depth 12" (11")
Bench type
21" 23"
Depth 4 1/2"
Door-back
Made in alum. or enam. wicker.
CLOTHES HAMPERS
18"-24" 6", 8 1/2" 12"
opens to 50 1/2" 2'-10" 2'-4" 7" 2'-2" 8"
CLOTHES DRYERS
4" 30" 12" 6"
11" 7 1/2"
Depth 4" Door hung.
WASTE RECEPTACLES
15" 11"
Depth 3 1/2" Avg. traffic
White, gray enam.: chrome or prime coat.
15" 4" 5'-0" 1'-6" 2'-6"
Heavy traffic.
TOWEL DISPENSER
BATH & WASHROOM ACCESSORIES 1/4"=1'-0"
Plan
Wood stud
Cement
Tile
Plaster of paris or cement.
Metal lath cut and turned in
Sect.
Wood stud & wire lath part'n
Plan
Hollow tile
Plaster of paris or cement
Cement
Tile
Sect.
Hollow tile partition
Plan
Wood studs
Sheetrock
Plaster of paris or cement
Keene Cement
Sect
Wood stud & sheetrock part'n
Plan
Steel stud
Cement
Tile
Plaster of paris or cement
Sect.
Steel stud & wire lath part'n.
Recessed almost entirely into wall and cemented when tile or other wall finish is applied. Depth in wall 3/4" or less.
BUILT-IN RECESS TYPES
Plan
Lath
Tile
Cement
Sect.
Cross stud with metal lath and cement or plaster of paris to take fixture.
Recessed only 1" to 1 3/16" in wall. Used in thin or obstructed partitions. Set like recess type.
FLANGED SEMI-RECESS TYPE
Sheetrock
Plan
Keene Cement or plaster
Sect.
Hole cut in cross stud to take dowel set in cement.
Requires 1" wall depth. In tile: set after tile is placed. Plaster: use cross stud, set after.
DOWEL-BACK-PROJECTING
Sheetrock
Plan
Plaster
Clincher filled with cement
Cross stud with metal lath and cement
Sect.
In tile: set with tile or after tile is placed. Plaster: Set before finish coat, on exposed lath.
CLINCHER-BACK-PROJECTING
METHODS of INSTALLING ACCESSORIES in TILE WALL

LOCATION of BATHROOM ACCESSORIES

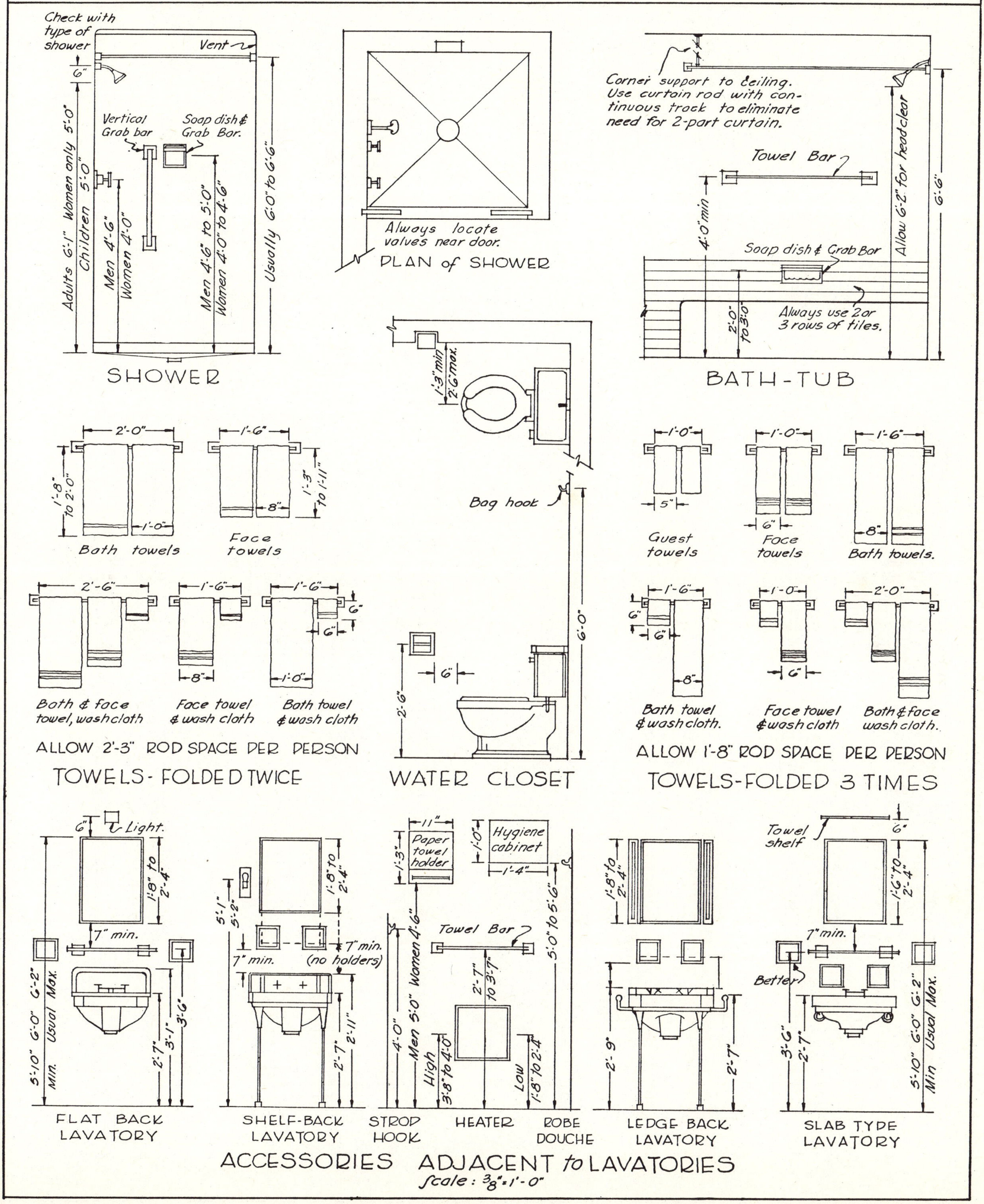

Check with type of shower
Vent
6"
Adults 6'-1" Women only 5'-0" Children 5'-0"
Vertical Grab bar
Soap dish & Grab Bar.
Men 4'-6" Women 4'-0"
Men 4'-6" to 5'-0" Women 4'-0" to 4'-6"
Usually 6'-0" to 6'-6"
SHOWER
Always locate valves near door.
PLAN of SHOWER
Corner support to ceiling. Use curtain rod with continuous track to eliminate need for 2-part curtain.
Towel Bar
4'-0" min
Allow 6'-2" for head clear
6'-6"
Soap dish & Grab Bar
2'-0" to 3'-0"
Always use 2 or 3 rows of tiles.
BATH-TUB
2'-0"
1'-8" to 2'-0"
1'-0"
Bath towels
1'-6"
8"
1'-3" to 1'-11"
Face towels
1'-3" min. 2'-6" max.
Bag hook
6'-0"
2'-6"
6"
1'-0"
5"
Guest towels
Face towels
1'-6"
8"
Bath towels.
2'-6"
Both & face towel, washcloth
1'-6"
8"
Face towel & wash cloth
1'-6"
6"
6"
1'-0"
Bath towel & wash cloth
ALLOW 2'-3" ROD SPACE PER PERSON
TOWELS - FOLDED TWICE
WATER CLOSET
1'-6"
6"
6"
8"
Bath towel & wash cloth.
1'-0"
6"
Face towel & wash cloth
2'-0"
Both & face wash cloth.
ALLOW 1'-8" ROD SPACE PER PERSON
TOWELS-FOLDED 3 TIMES
6"
Light.
1'-8" to 2'-4"
7" min.
5'-10" 6'-0" 6'-2"
Min. Usual Max.
2'-7"
3'-1"
3'-6"
FLAT BACK LAVATORY
5'-1" 5'-2"
1'-8" to 2'-4"
7" min.
7" min. (no holders)
2'-7"
2'-11"
SHELF-BACK LAVATORY
11"
Paper towel holder
1'-3"
1'-0"
Hygiene cabinet
1'-4"
4'-0"
Men 5'-0" Women 4'-6"
Towel Bar
2'-7" to 3'-7"
High 3'-8" to 4'-0"
Low 1'-8" to 2'-4"
5'-0" to 5'-6"
STROP HOOK
HEATER
ROBE DOUCHE
1'-8" to 2'-4"
2'-9"
2'-7"
LEDGE BACK LAVATORY
Towel shelf
6"
1'-6" to 2'-4"
7" min.
Better
3'-6"
2'-7"
5'-10" 6'-0" 6'-2"
Min Usual Max.
SLAB TYPE LAVATORY
ACCESSORIES ADJACENT to LAVATORIES
Scale: 3/8" = 1'-0"

STRUCTURAL GLASS TOILET STALLS

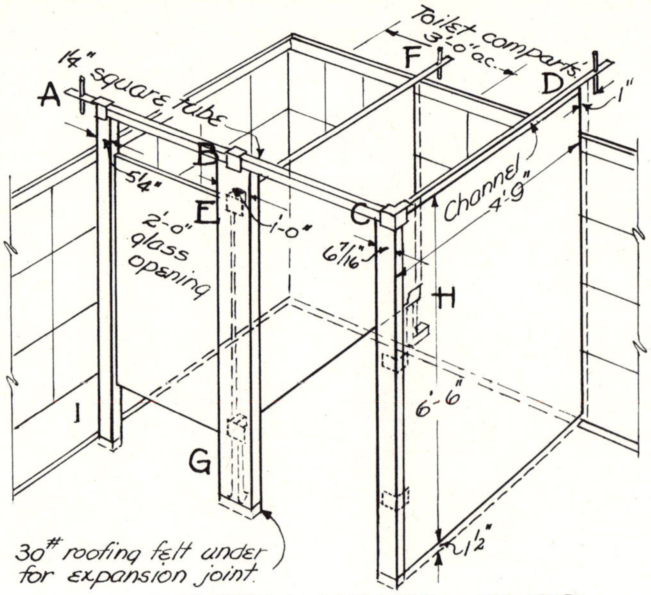

1¼" square tube
Toilet comparts. 3'-0" o.c.
A
B
C
D
E
F
G
H
I
1"
5¼"
2'-0" glass opening
1'-0"
6 7/16"
Channel 4'-9"
6'-6"
1½"
30# roofing felt under for expansion joint.

GOVERNMENT TYPE

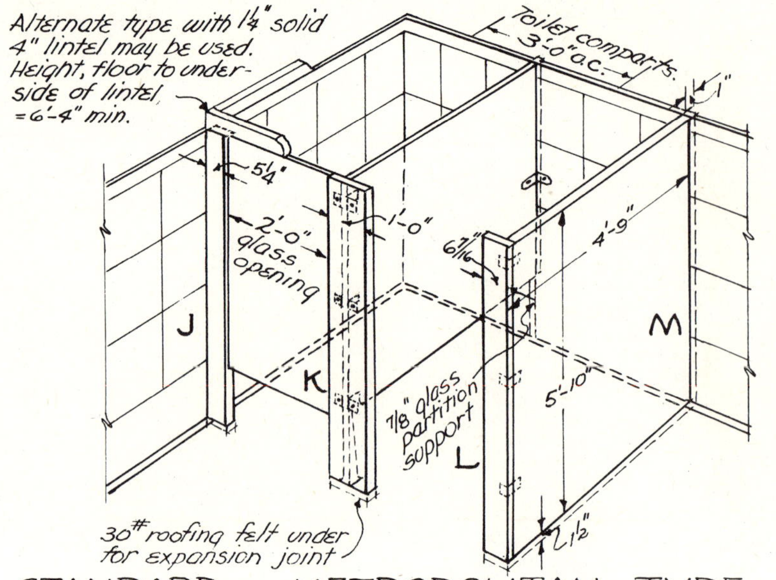

Alternate type with 1¼" solid 4" lintel may be used. Height, floor to underside of lintel, =6'-4" min.
Toilet comparts. 3'-0" o.c.
1"
5¼"
2'-0" glass opening
1'-0"
6 7/16"
4'-9"
5'-10"
7/8" glass partition support
J
K
L
M
1½"
30# roofing felt under for expansion joint

STANDARD or METROPOLITAN TYPE

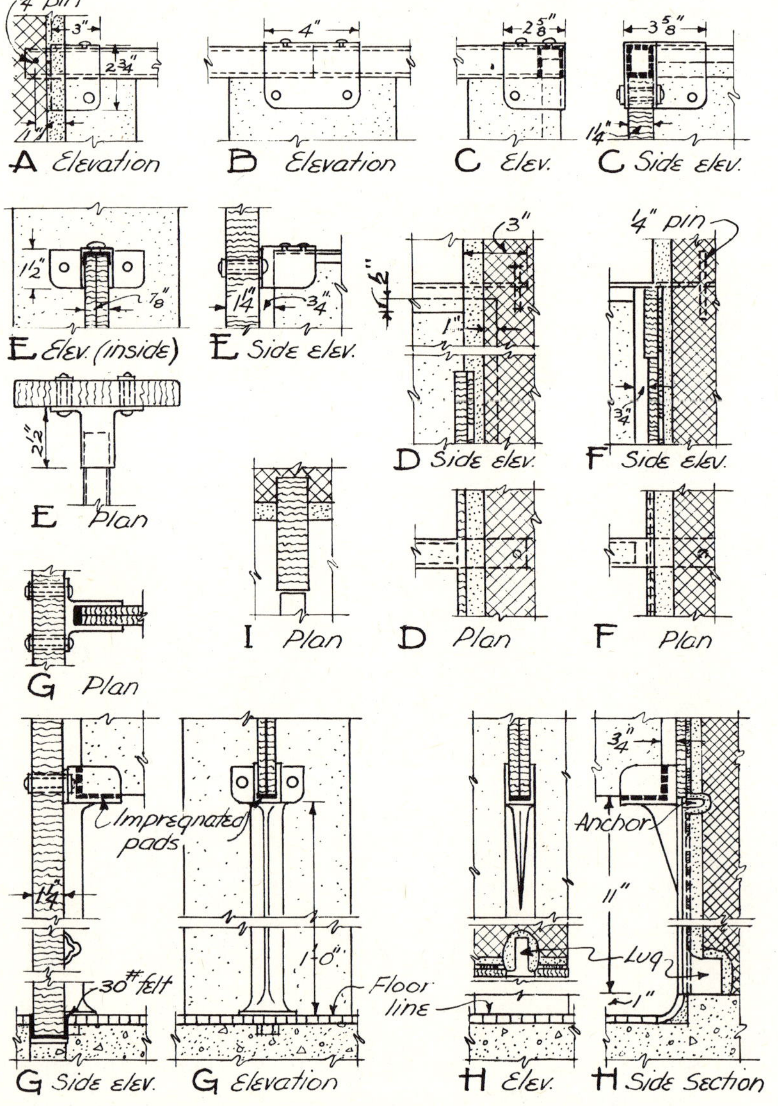

¼" pin
3"
2¾"
1"
A Elevation
4"
B Elevation
2 5/8"
C Elev.
3 5/8"
1¼"
C Side elev.
1½"
7/8"
E Elev. (inside)
1¼"
¾"
E Side elev.
2½"
E Plan
G Plan
I Plan
3"
1"
½"
D Side elev.
D Plan
¼" pin
¾"
F Side elev.
F Plan
Impregnated pads
1¼"
30# felt
G Side elev.
1'-0"
Floor line
G Elevation
H Elev.
¾"
Anchor
11"
Lug
1"
H Side Section

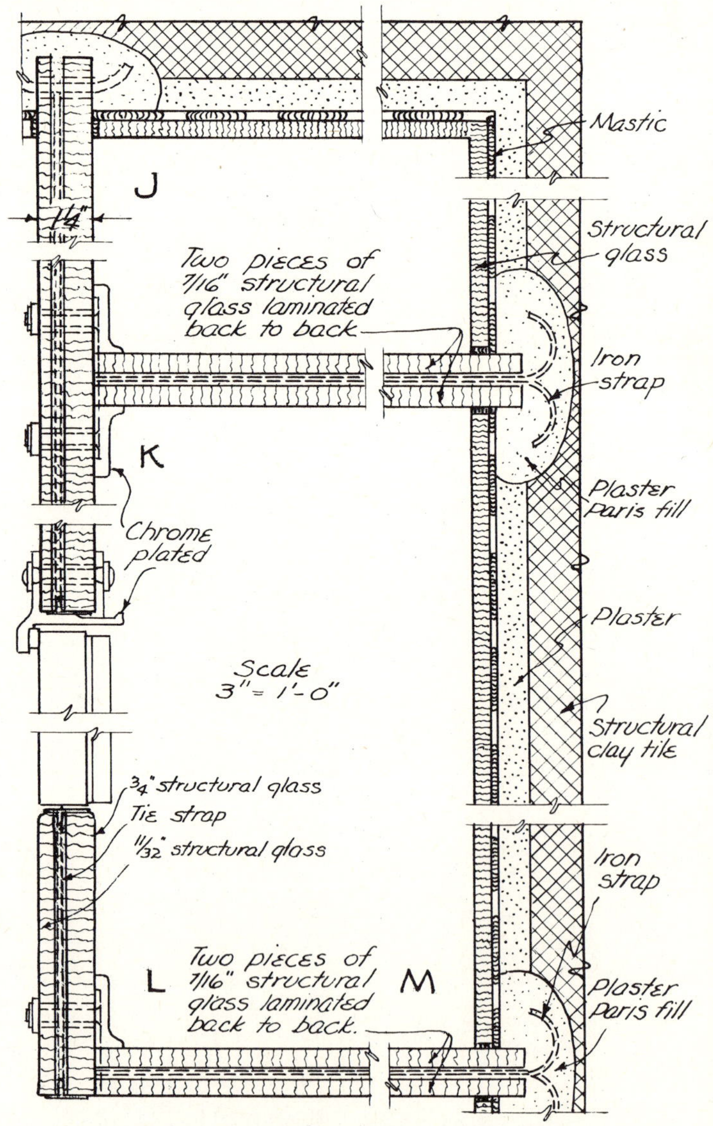

J
1¼"
Mastic
Structural glass
Two pieces of 7/16" structural glass laminated back to back
Iron strap
K
Plaster Paris fill
Chrome plated
Plaster
Scale 3" = 1'-0"
Structural clay tile
¾" structural glass
Tie strap
11/32" structural glass
Iron strap
L
Two pieces of 7/16" structural glass laminated back to back.
M
Plaster Paris fill

DETAILS - GOVERNMENT TYPE

Scale 1½" = 1'-0"
Details recommended by Pittsburgh Plate and Libbey - Owens - Ford.

DETAILS - STANDARD TYPE

Above details recommended by Libbey - Owens - Ford (Vitrolite). Similar type by Pittsburgh (Carrara) uses leg to support partition at stile, & omits straps in laminated partitions. Scale 3" = 1'-0".

METAL and STRUCTURAL GLASS TOILET STALLS

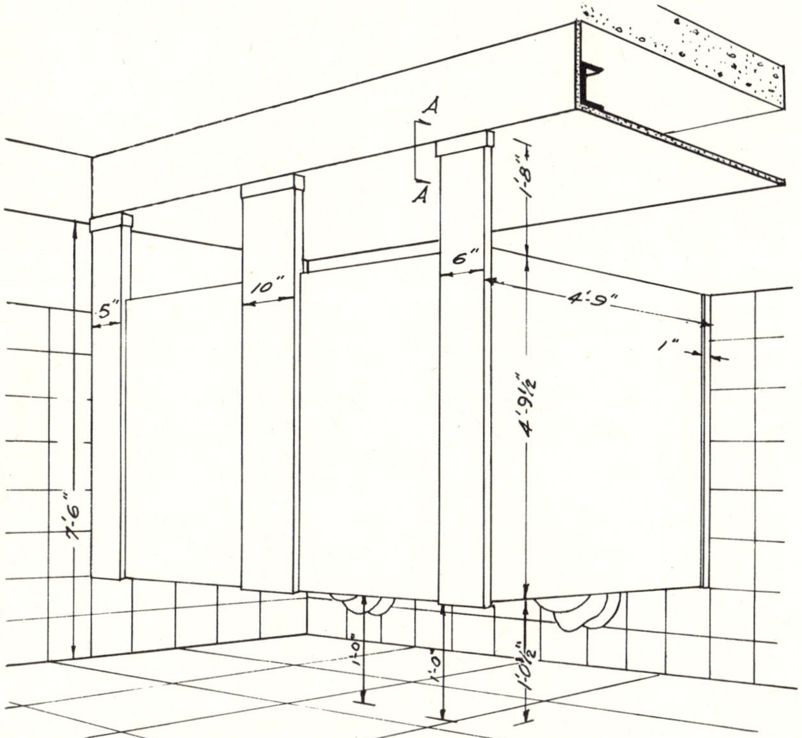
A
A
1'-8"
6"
10"
5"
4'-9"
1"
4'-9½"
7'-6"
1'-0"
1'-0"
1'-0½"

SUSPENDED TYPE — METAL

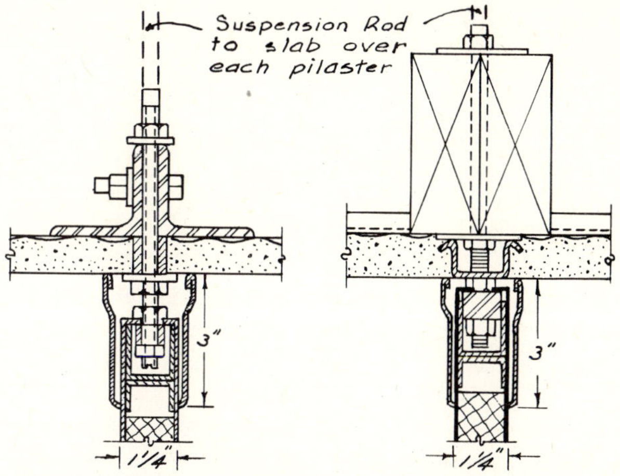
Suspension Rod to slab over each pilaster
3"
3"
1¼"
1¼"

A-A, STEEL ANGLES A-A, WOOD BEAM

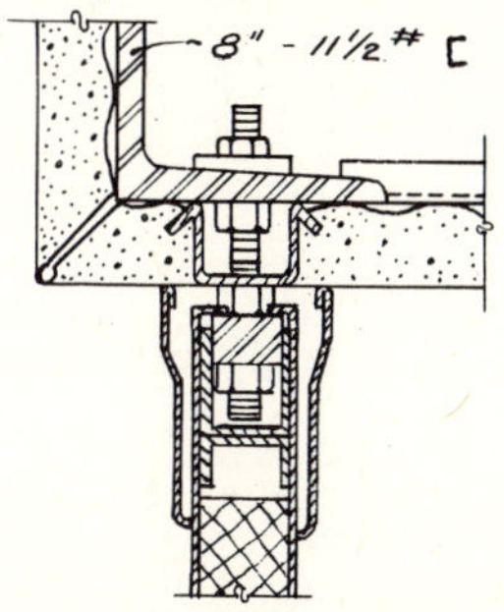
8" - 11½# [

A-A, STEEL CHANNEL
Ceiling furred down only over closet partitions.

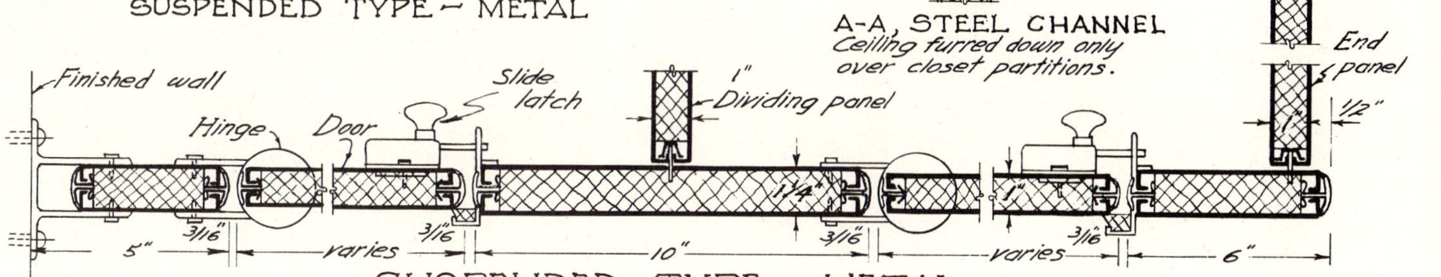
Finished wall
Hinge
Door
Slide latch
1"
Dividing panel
1¼"
1"
Finished wall
Sound Insulation
End panel
1"
½"
5"
3/16"
varies
3/16"
10"
3/16"
varies
3/16"
6"

SUSPENDED TYPE — METAL

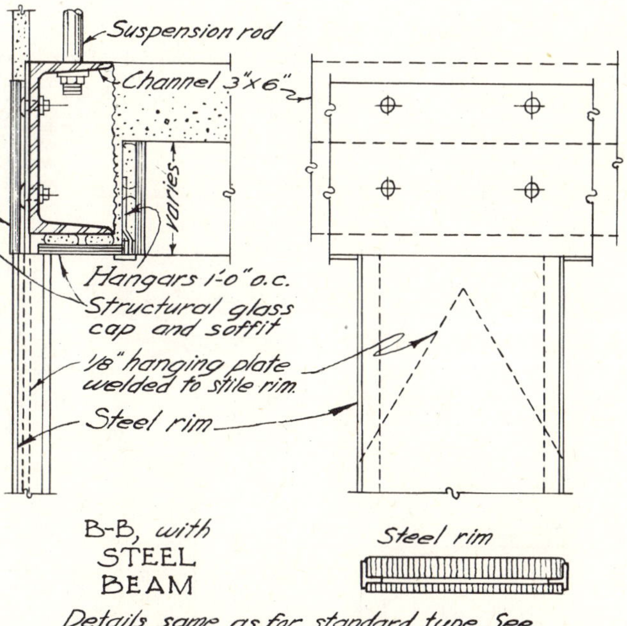
Suspension rod
Channel 3"x6"
Varies
Hangars 1'-0" o.c.
Structural glass cap and soffit
1/8" hanging plate welded to stile rim.
Steel rim
Steel rim

B-B, with STEEL BEAM

Details same as for standard type. See horizontal section on page of "Structural Glass Toilet Stalls".

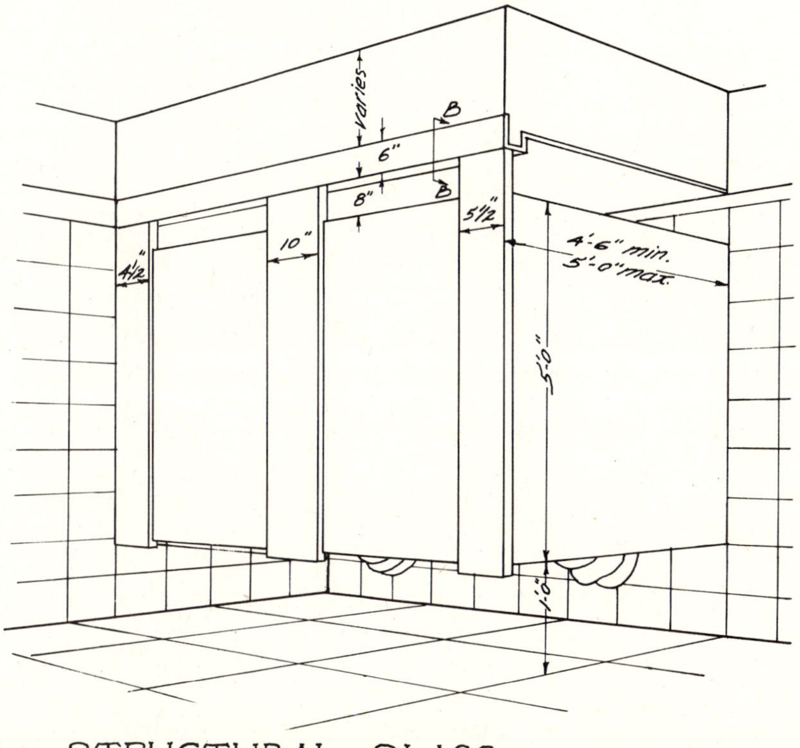
Varies
B
B
6"
8"
5½"
10"
4½"
4'-6" min.
5'-0" max.
5'-0"
1'-0"

SUSPENDED TYPE — STRUCTURAL GLASS

Data checked by Metal Compartments Association

MARBLE STALLS

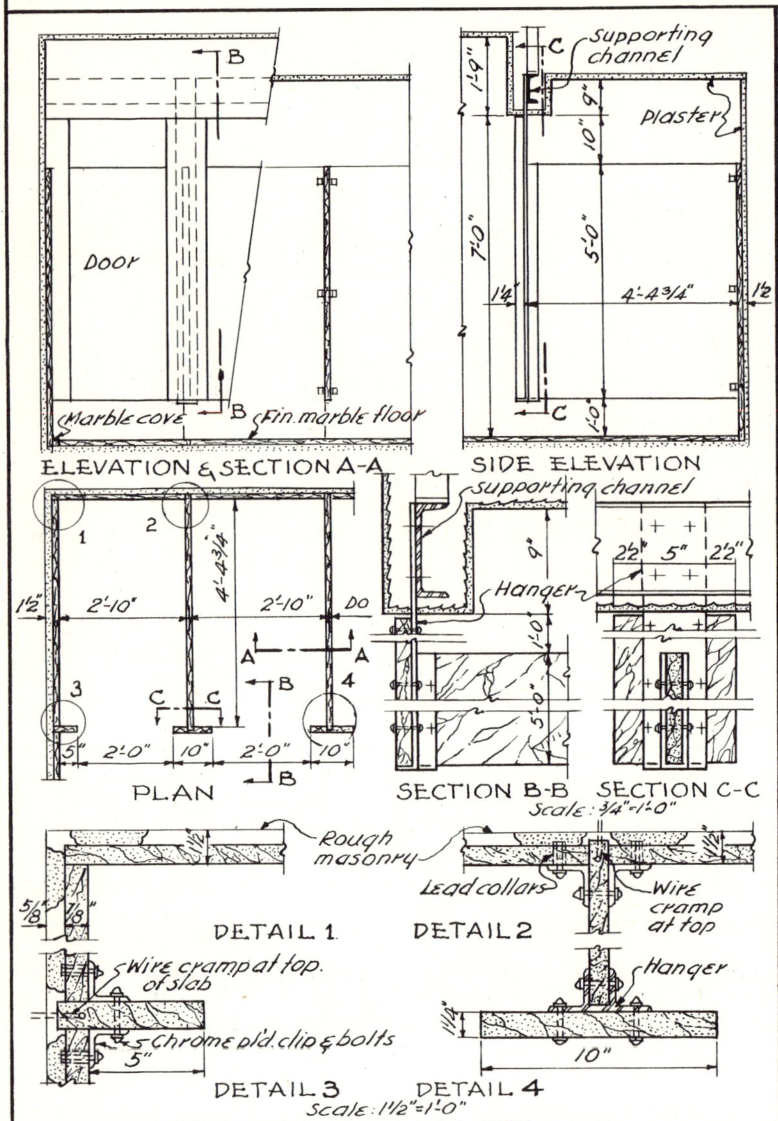
Supporting channel
Plaster
Door
Marble cove
Fin. marble floor
ELEVATION & SECTION A-A
SIDE ELEVATION
supporting channel
Hanger
PLAN
SECTION B-B
SECTION C-C
Scale: 3/4"=1'-0"
Rough masonry
Lead collars
Wire cramp at top
DETAIL 1
DETAIL 2
Wire cramp at top of slab
Chrome pl'd. clip & bolts
Hanger
DETAIL 3
DETAIL 4
Scale: 1 1/2"=1'-0"

SUSPENDED TOILET STALLS

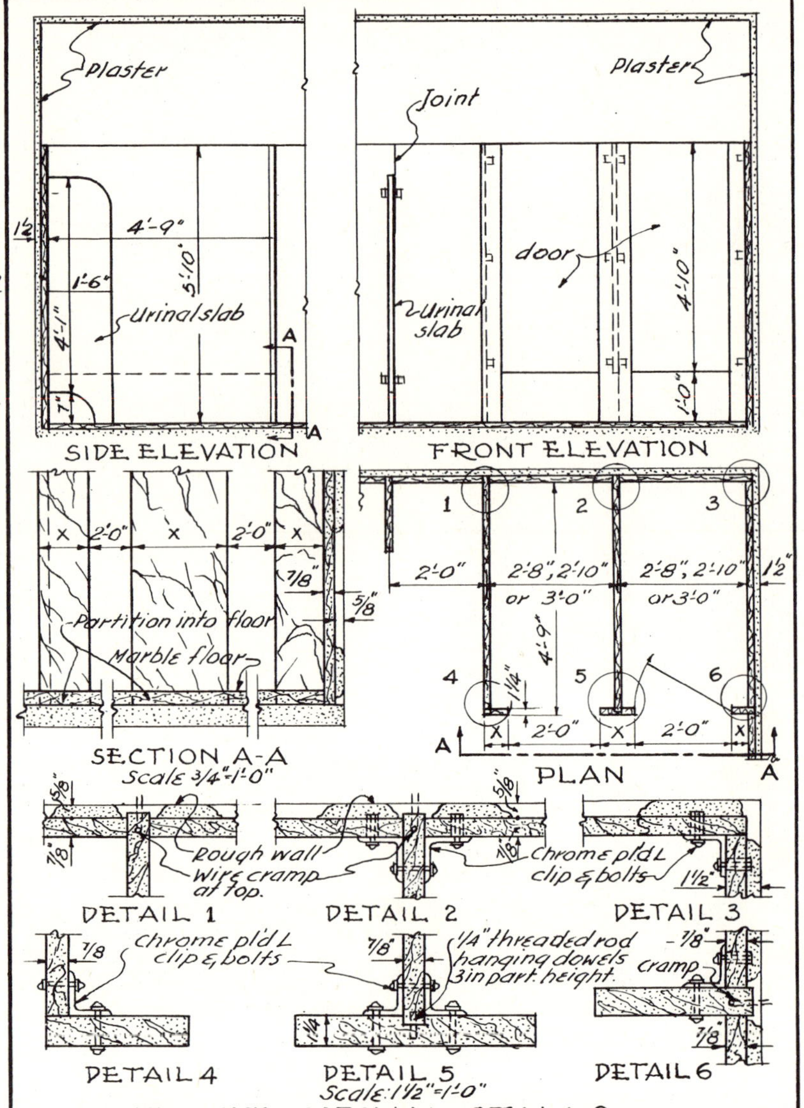
Plaster
Joint
Urinal slab
door
SIDE ELEVATION
FRONT ELEVATION
Partition into floor
Marble floor
SECTION A-A
Scale 3/4"=1'-0"
PLAN
Rough wall
Wire cramp at top.
Chrome pl'd L clip & bolts
DETAIL 1
DETAIL 2
DETAIL 3
1/4" threaded rod hanging dowels 3in part. height.
cramp
DETAIL 4
DETAIL 5
Scale: 1 1/2"=1'-0"
DETAIL 6

TOILET & URINAL STALLS

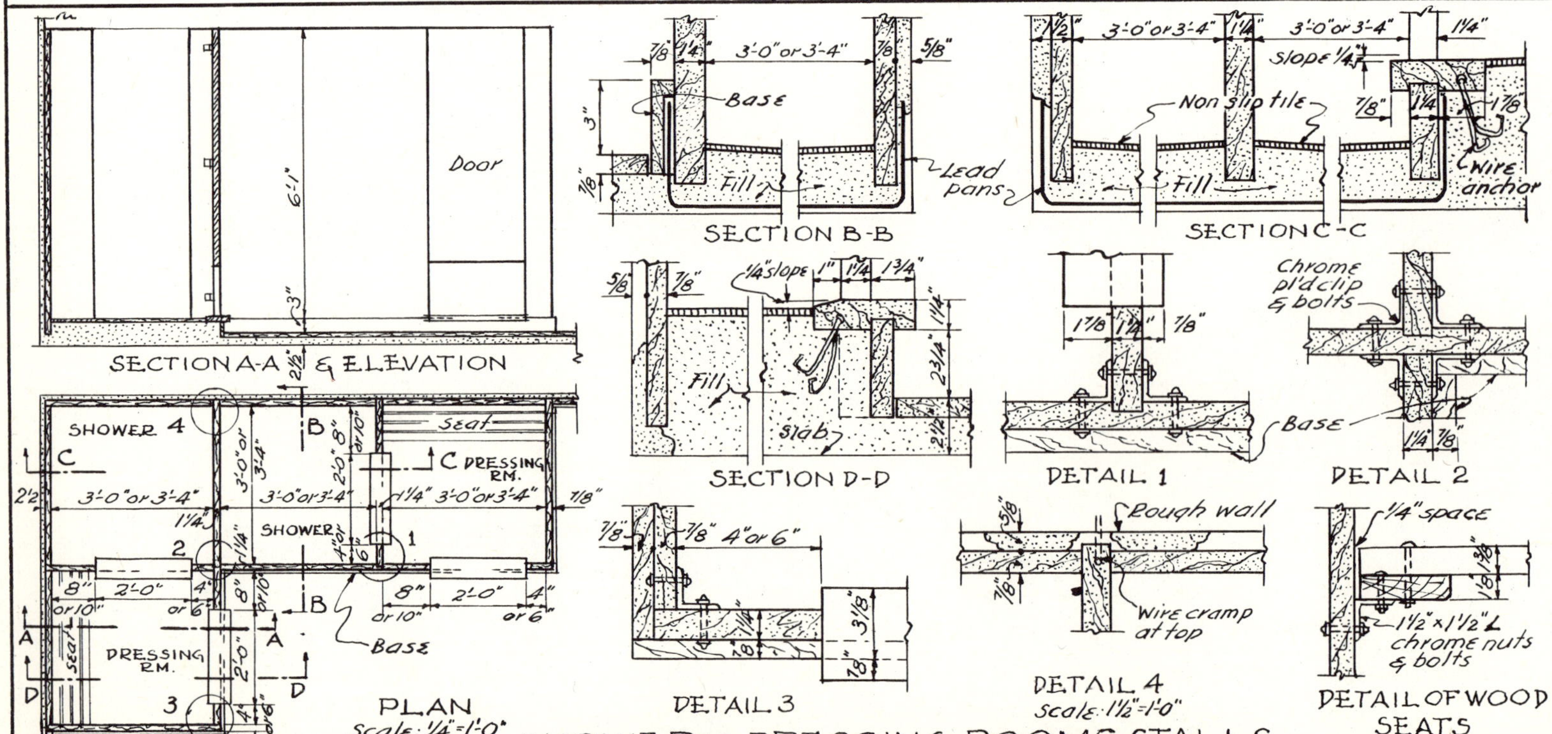
Door
SECTION A-A & ELEVATION
Base
Lead pans
Fill
SECTION B-B
Non slip tile
Slope 1/4"
Wire anchor
SECTION C-C
Chrome pl'd clip & bolts
Slab
SECTION D-D
DETAIL 1
DETAIL 2
SHOWER
Seat
DRESSING RM.
PLAN
Scale: 1/4"=1'-0"
DETAIL 3
Rough wall
Wire cramp at top
DETAIL 4
Scale: 1 1/2"=1'-0"
1/4" space
1 1/2"x1 1/2" L chrome nuts & bolts
DETAIL OF WOOD SEATS

SHOWER & DRESSING ROOMS STALLS

Data supplied by: Marble Institute of America Inc.

METAL TOILET ENCLOSURES

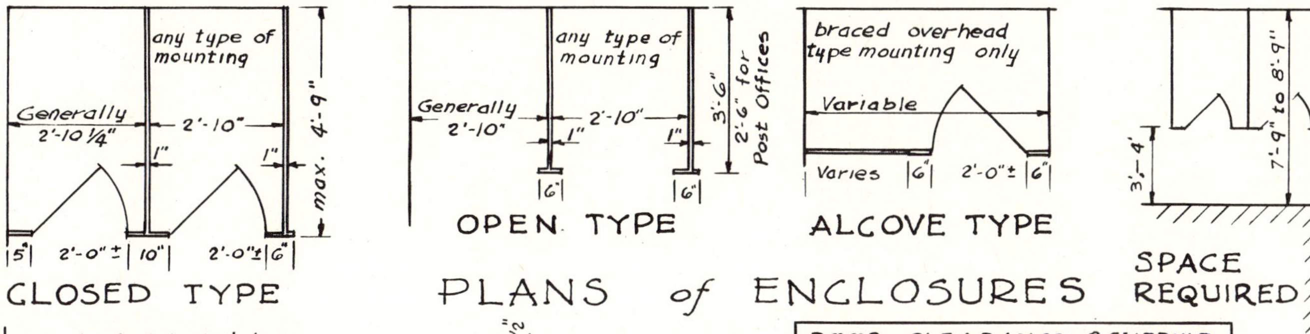
any type of mounting
Generally 2'-10 1/4"
2'-10"
1"
1"
max. 4'-9"
5"
2'-0"±
10"
2'-0"±
6"
any type of mounting
Generally 2'-10"
2'-10"
1"
1"
6"
6"
3'-6" 2'-6" for Post Offices
braced overhead type mounting only
Variable
Varies
6"
2'-0"±
6"
3'-4'
7'-9" to 8'-9"
12'-6" to 13'-6"

CLOSED TYPE — OPEN TYPE — ALCOVE TYPE — SPACE REQUIRED

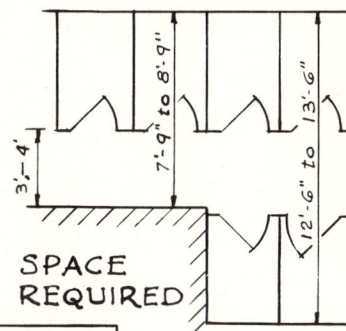

PLANS of ENCLOSURES

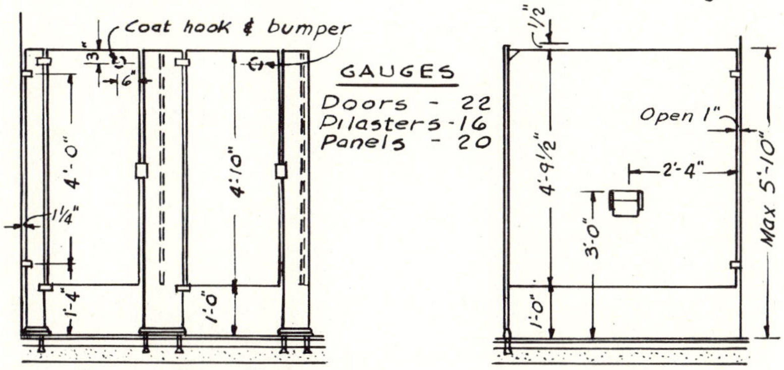
Coat hook & bumper
3"
6"
4'-0"
1 1/4"
1'-4"
4'-10"
1'-0"
GAUGES
Doors - 22
Pilasters - 16
Panels - 20
1 1/2"
Open 1"
2'-4"
4'-9 1/2"
3'-0"
1'-0"
Max 5'-10"

Front Elevation — Section

FLOOR SUPPORTED TYPE MOUNTING
bolts, directly into concrete slab

DOOR CLEARANCE SCHEDULE			
W*	D*	C*	REMARKS
2'-6"	1'-8" 2'-3"	11 1/2" 5 1/2"	All types + Braced o'head only
2'-8"	1'-8" 1'-10" 2'-0" 2'-5"	11 1/2" 10" 8 1/2" 4"	All types All types + Braced o'head only Braced o'head only
2'-10"	1'-8" 2'-0" 2'-2"	11 1/2" 8 1/2" 7"	All types All types + Braced o'head only
3'-0"	2'-0" 2'-2"	8 1/2" 7"	All types All types +

*W = Toilet enclosure width; "D" = door width; and "C" = door clearance + standard 10" stiles

Door clearance based on standard 4'-9" depth and longest fixture catalogued. Shorter fixtures and lesser enclosure depth available.
For colors consult mfrs. colors chart; special colors at a premium.

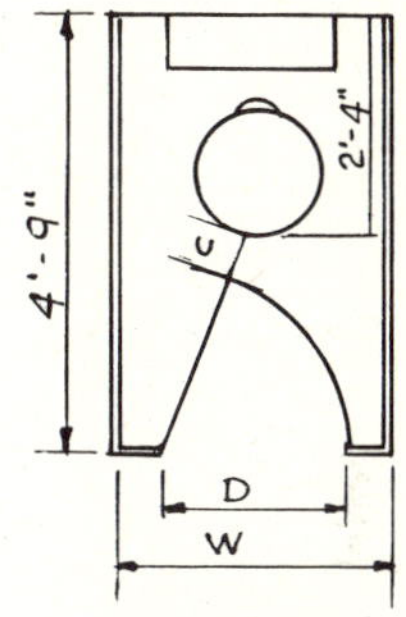
4'-9"
2'-4"
C
D
W

TOILET CLEARANCE of INSWINGING DOOR

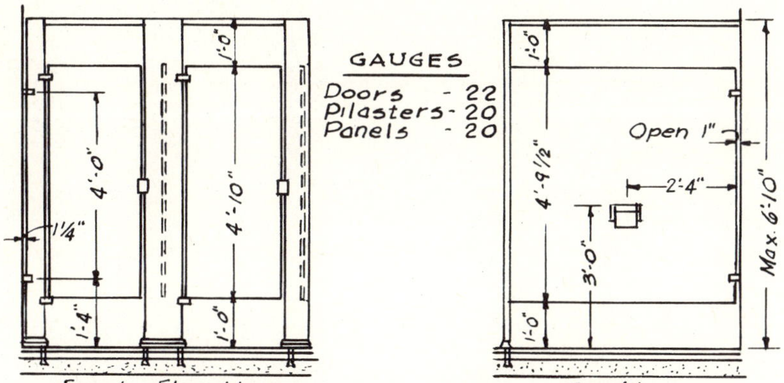
1'-0"
4'-0"
1 1/4"
1'-4"
4'-10"
1'-0"
GAUGES
Doors - 22
Pilasters - 20
Panels - 20
1'-0"
Open 1"
2'-4"
4'-9 1/2"
3'-0"
1'-0"
Max 6'-10"

Front Elevation — Section

BRACED OVERHEAD TYPE MOUNTING
bolts, into floor construction

FLUSH TYPE BAKED ENAMEL

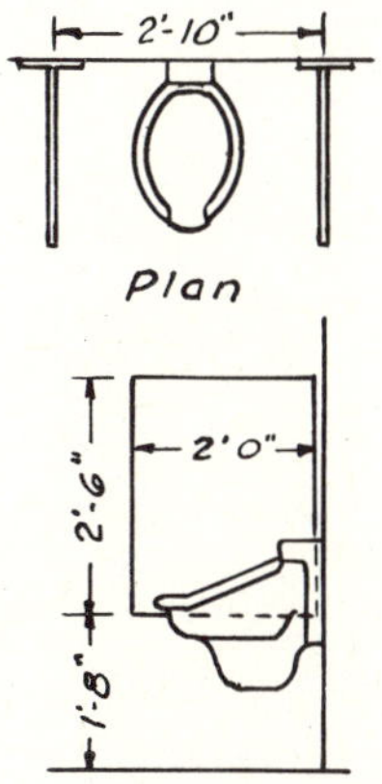
2'-10"
Plan
2'-0"
2'-6"
1'-8"
Section
WALL-HUNG

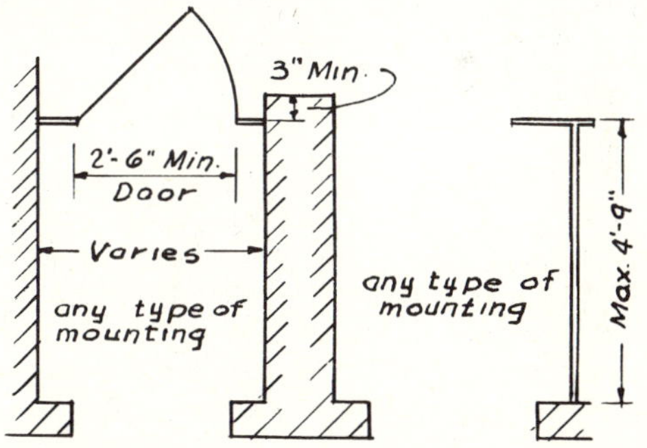
3" Min.
2'-6" Min.
Door
Varies
any type of mounting
any type of mounting
Max. 4'-9"
screen with door
screen without door

ROOM ENTRANCE PARTITIONS

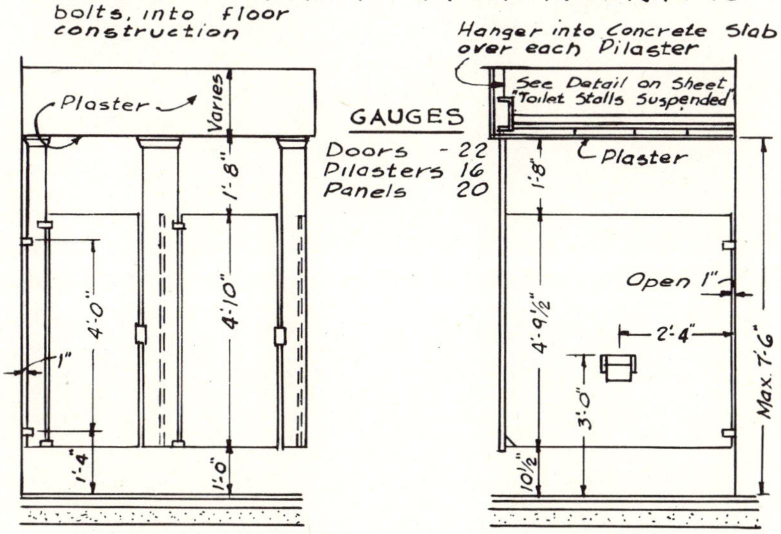
Hanger into Concrete Slab over each Pilaster
See Detail on Sheet "Toilet Stalls Suspended"
Plaster
Varies
GAUGES
Doors - 22
Pilasters 16
Panels 20
1'-8"
4'-0"
1"
1'-4"
4'-10"
1'-0"
Plaster
1'-8"
Open 1"
2'-4"
4'-9 1/2"
3'-0"
10 1/2"
Max. 7'-6"

Front Elevation — Section

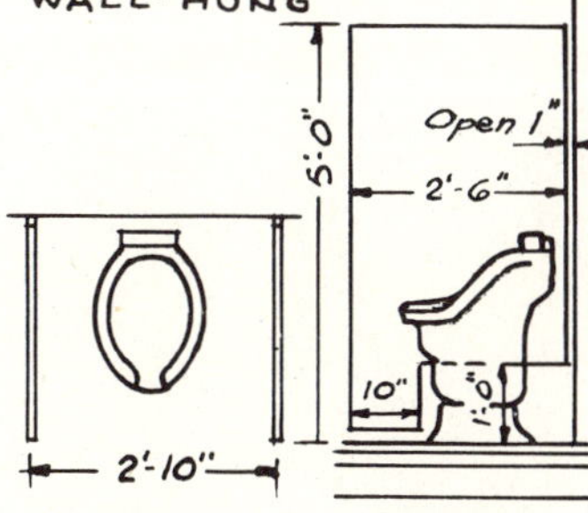
5'-0"
Open 1"
2'-6"
10"
1'-0"
2'-10"
Plan
Section

PEDESTAL

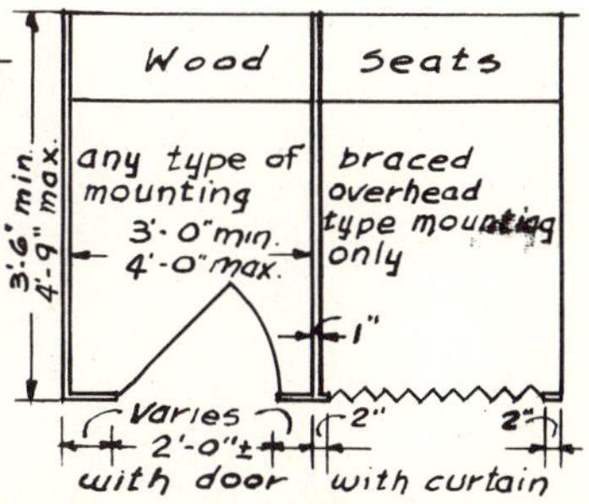
Wood
Seats
any type of mounting
3'-0" min.
4'-0" max.
braced overhead type mounting only
3'-6" min.
4'-9" max.
1"
Varies
2'-0"±
2"
2"
with door
with curtain

CEILING SUPPORTED TYPE MOUNTING — URINAL STALLS — DRESS. RM. ENCLOSURES

Data by Metal Compartments Association

MECHANICAL EQUIPMENT and RELATED TECHNICAL INFORMATION

TABLE OF CONTENTS

PIPING & HEATING & VENTILATING SYMBOLS

PIPING SYMBOLS

HEATING

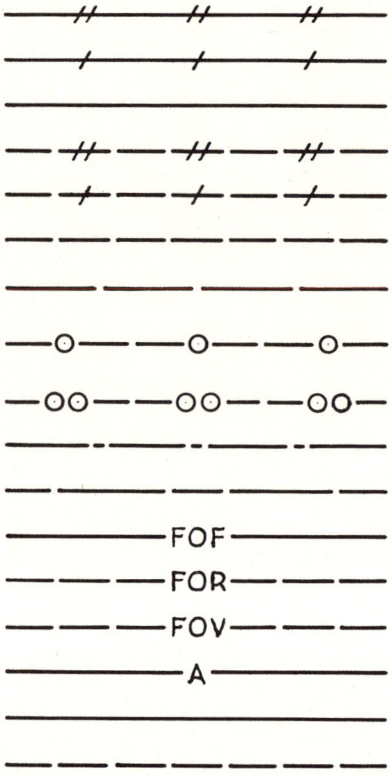
FOF
FOR
FOV
A

- High Pressure Steam
- Medium Pressure Steam
- Low Pressure Steam
- High Pressure Return
- Medium Pressure Return
- Low Pressure Return
- Boiler Blow Off
- Condensate or Vacuum Pump Discharge
- Feedwater Pump Discharge
- Make Up Water
- Air Relief Line
- Fuel Oil Flow
- Fuel Oil Return
- Fuel Oil Tank Vent
- Compressed Air
- Hot Water Heating Supply
- Hot Water Heating Return

AIR CONDITIONING

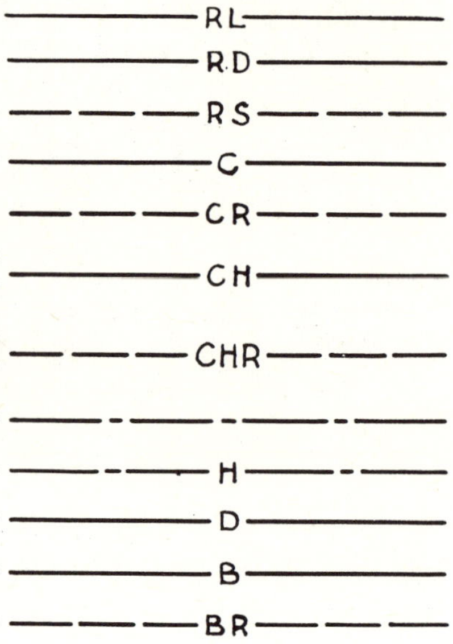
RL
RD
RS
C
CR
CH
CHR
H
D
B
BR

- Refrigerant Liquid
- Refrigerant Discharge
- Refrigerant Suction
- Condenser Water Flow
- Condenser Water Return
- Circulating Chilled or Hot Water Flow
- Circulating Chilled or Hot Water Return
- Make Up Water
- Humidification Line
- Drain
- Brine Supply
- Brine Return

All symbols approved as American Standard A.S.A. Z 32.23-1949 by American Standards Association

HEATING & VENTILATING SYMBOLS

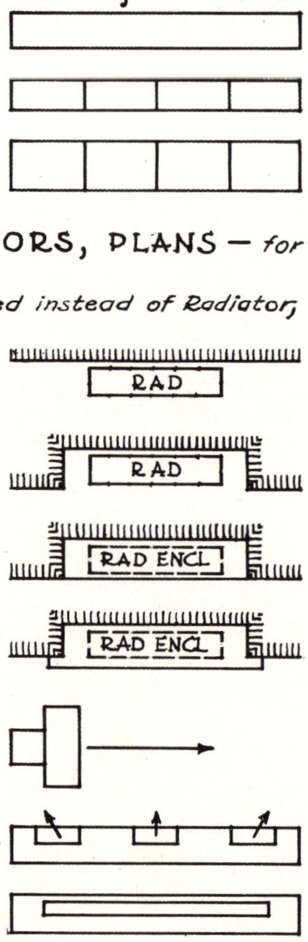
RAD
RAD
RAD ENCL
RAD ENCL

- Heat Transfer Surface, Plan
- * Wall Radiator, Plan
- * Wall Radiator on Ceiling, Plan

RADIATORS & CONVECTORS, PLANS — for Architectural Drawings.

For Radiator — If Convector is used instead of Radiator, substitute CONV. for RAD.

- *Exposed
- *Recessed
- *Enclosed, Flush
- *Enclosed, Projecting
- Unit Heater (Propeller), Plan
- Unit Heater (Centrifugal Fan), Plan
- Unit Ventilator, Plan

TRAPS

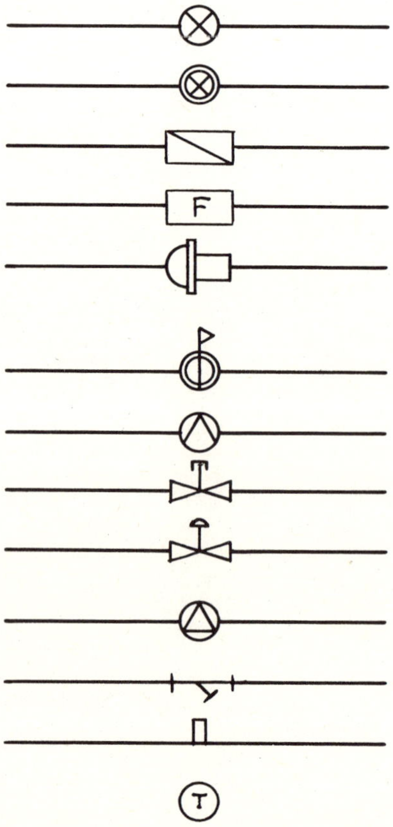
F
T

- Thermostatic
- Blast Thermostatic
- Float and Thermostatic
- Float
- Boiler Return

VALVES

- Reducing Pressure
- Air Line
- Lock and Shield
- Diaphragm
- Air Eliminator
- Strainer
- Thermometer
- Thermostat

*All Symbols, except those marked *, approved as American standard ASA Z 32.2.4-1949 by American Standards Association. (Reaffirmed-1953)*

DUCTWORK SYMBOLS

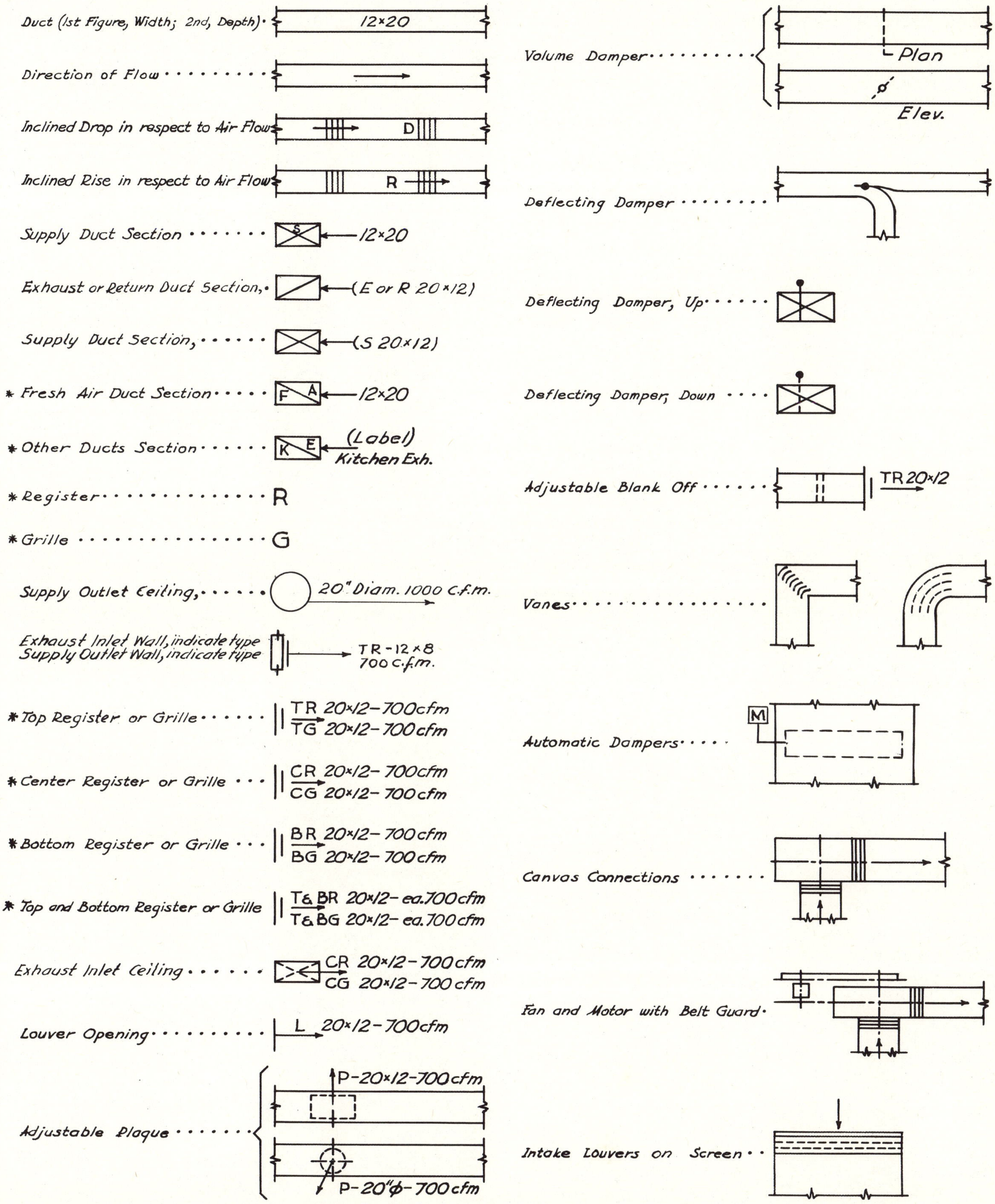
Duct (1st Figure, Width; 2nd, Depth)
12×20
Direction of Flow
Inclined Drop in respect to Air Flow
D
Inclined Rise in respect to Air Flow
R
Supply Duct Section
S
12×20
Exhaust or Return Duct Section,
(E or R 20×12)
Supply Duct Section,
(S 20×12)
* Fresh Air Duct Section
F
A
12×20
* Other Ducts Section
K
E
(Label)
Kitchen Exh.
* Register
R
* Grille
G
Supply Outlet Ceiling,
20" Diam. 1000 C.f.m.
Exhaust Inlet Wall, indicate type
Supply Outlet Wall, indicate type
TR-12×8
700 c.f.m.
* Top Register or Grille
TR 20×12-700cfm
TG 20×12-700cfm
* Center Register or Grille
CR 20×12-700cfm
CG 20×12-700cfm
* Bottom Register or Grille
BR 20×12-700cfm
BG 20×12-700cfm
* Top and Bottom Register or Grille
T&BR 20×12-ea.700cfm
T&BG 20×12-ea.700cfm
Exhaust Inlet Ceiling
CR 20×12-700cfm
CG 20×12-700cfm
Louver Opening
L
20×12-700cfm
Adjustable Plaque
P-20×12-700cfm
P-20"ϕ-700cfm
Volume Damper
Plan
Elev.
Deflecting Damper
Deflecting Damper, Up
Deflecting Damper, Down
Adjustable Blank Off
TR 20×12
Vanes
Automatic Dampers
M
Canvas Connections
Fan and Motor with Belt Guard
Intake Louvers on Screen

All Symbols, except those marked *, approved as American Standard, ASA Z 32.2.4-1949 American Standard Association (Reaffirmed 1953)

HEAT-POWER APPARATUS & REFRIGERATING SYMBOLS

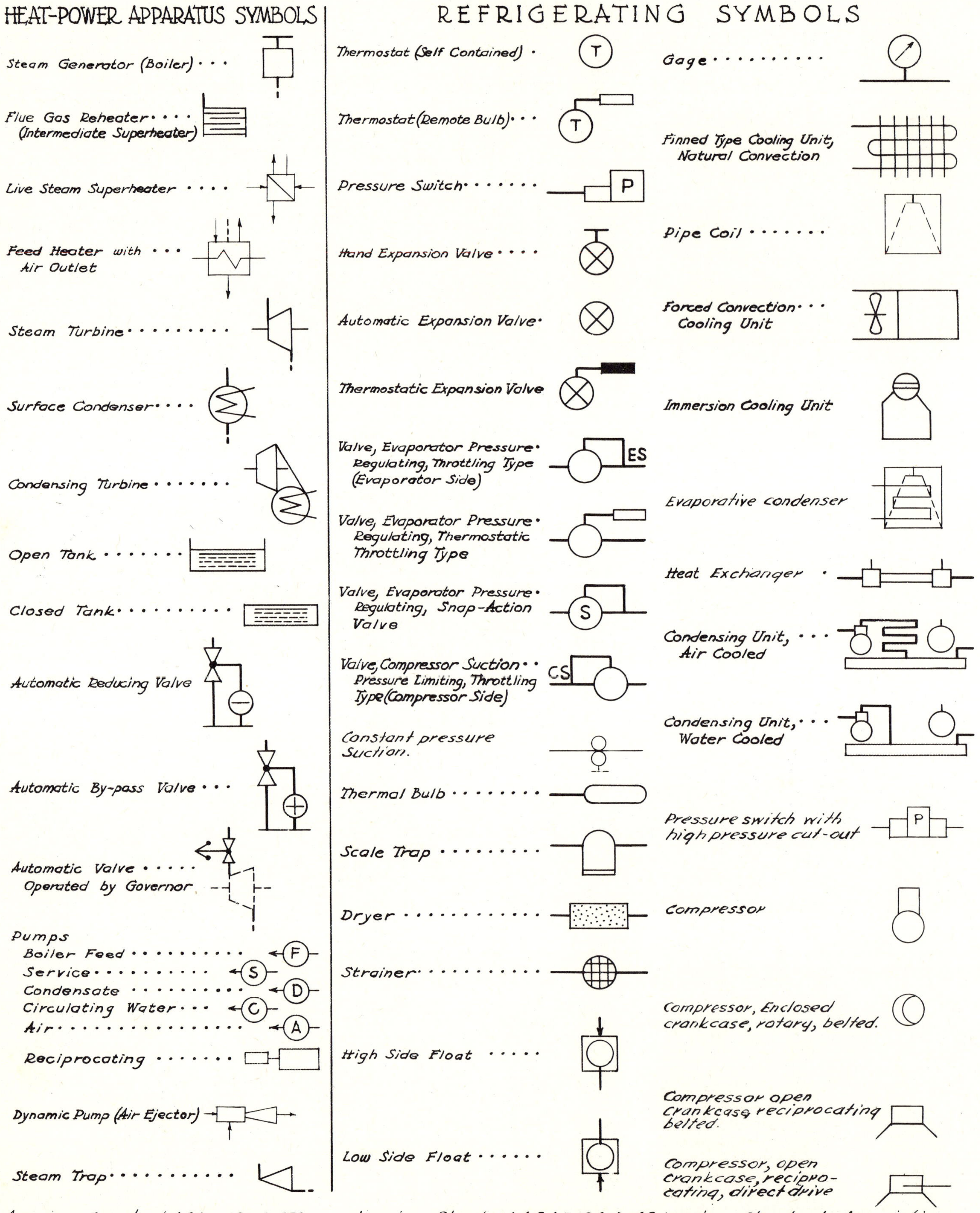
HEAT-POWER APPARATUS SYMBOLS
Steam Generator (Boiler)
Flue Gas Reheater (Intermediate Superheater)
Live Steam Superheater
Feed Heater with Air Outlet
Steam Turbine
Surface Condenser
Condensing Turbine
Open Tank
Closed Tank
Automatic Reducing Valve
Automatic By-pass Valve
Automatic Valve Operated by Governor
Pumps
Boiler Feed
F
Service
S
Condensate
D
Circulating Water
C
Air
A
Reciprocating
Dynamic Pump (Air Ejector)
Steam Trap
REFRIGERATING SYMBOLS
Thermostat (Self Contained)
T
Thermostat (Remote Bulb)
T
Pressure Switch
P
Hand Expansion Valve
Automatic Expansion Valve
Thermostatic Expansion Valve
Valve, Evaporator Pressure Regulating, Throttling Type (Evaporator Side)
ES
Valve, Evaporator Pressure Regulating, Thermostatic Throttling Type
Valve, Evaporator Pressure Regulating, Snap-Action Valve
S
Valve, Compressor Suction Pressure Limiting, Throttling Type (Compressor Side)
CS
Constant pressure Suction.
Thermal Bulb
Scale Trap
Dryer
Strainer
High Side Float
Low Side Float
Gage
Finned Type Cooling Unit, Natural Convection
Pipe Coil
Forced Convection Cooling Unit
Immersion Cooling Unit
Evaporative condenser
Heat Exchanger
Condensing Unit, Air Cooled
Condensing Unit, Water Cooled
Pressure switch with high pressure cut-out
P
Compressor
Compressor, Enclosed crankcase, rotary, belted.
Compressor open crankcase reciprocating belted.
Compressor, open crankcase, reciprocating, direct drive

American Standard A.S.A. Z 32.2.6-1950

American Standard, A.S.A Z 32.2.4.-49 American Standards Association Reffirmed-1953

RADIATORS-SLIM TUBE

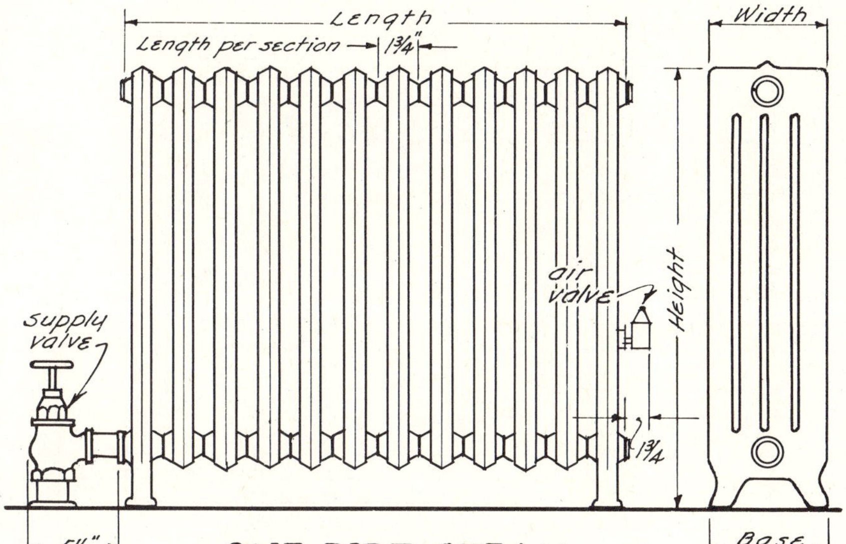
Length
Length per section → 1¾"
Width
air valve
Height
Supply valve
1¾
5½"
Base Width

ONE PIPE STEAM

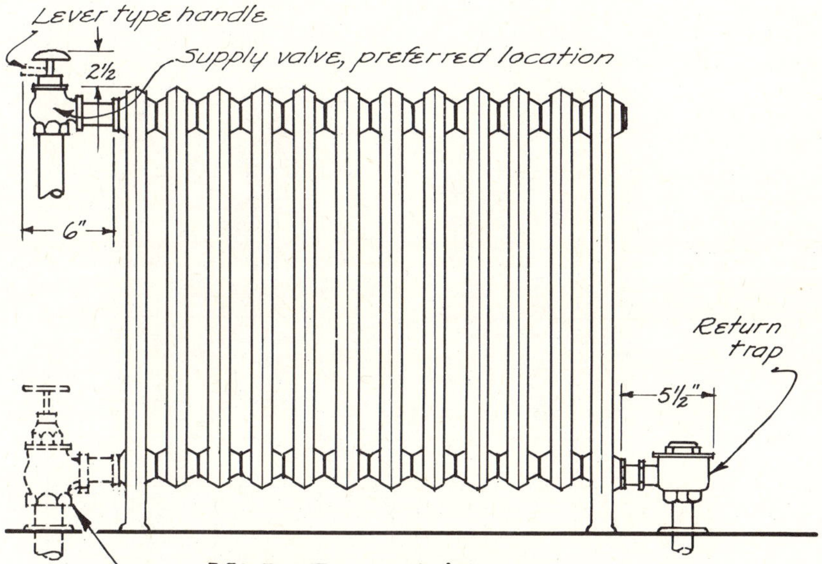
Lever type handle
2½
Supply valve, preferred location
6"
Return trap
5½"

VAPOR or VACUUM

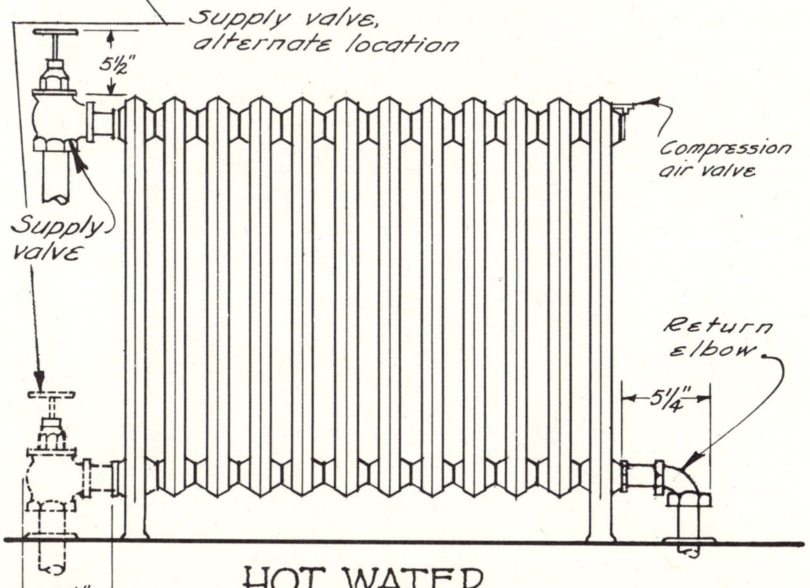
Supply valve, alternate location
5½"
Compression air valve
Supply valve
Return elbow
5¼"
5½"

HOT WATER

Compiled by the Office of Mongitore & Moesel, Consulting Engineers

DIMENSIONS							
NUMBER of TUBES →			3	4	5	6	MFR.
WIDTH			3½	4¾	6	7⅞	Amer.
			3⅜	4 9/16	5¾	7⅞	Natl.
			3¼	4 7/16	5⅝	7⅞	U.S.
			3½	4¾	6	7¼	Crane
			3¼	4 7/16	5 11/16	6 15/16	Burn.
BASE WIDTH			3½	4¾	6	7⅞	Amer.
			3⅜	4 9/16	5¾	7⅞	Natl.
			3¼	4 7/16	5⅝	7⅞	U.S.
			3½	4¾	6	7¼	Crane
			3¼	4 7/16	5 11/16	6 15/16	Burn.
HEIGHT			SQ. FT. PER SECTION				
WITH LEGS	LEGLESS△ 3, 4, 5	LEGLESS△ 6					
19"	17½	18		1.6		2.3	Amer.
	17⅝	17¾		1.6		2.3	Natl.
	17⅝	17 13/16		1.6		*2.3	U.S.
	17 9/16	17¾		1.6		2.3	Crane
	17½			1.6			Burn.
20"		17½				2.3	Burn.
22"	20½			1.8	2.1		Amer.
	20⅝			1.8	2.1		Natl.
	20⅝			1.8	2.1		U.S.
	20 9/16			1.8	2.1		Crane
	20½			1.8			Burn
23"	20½				2.1		Burn.
25"	23½	24	1.6	2.0	2.4	3.0	Amer
	23⅝	23¾	1.6	2.0	2.4	3.0	Natl.
	23⅝	24	1.6	2.0	2.4	3.0	U.S.
	23 9/16	23¾	1.6	2.0	2.4	3.0	Crane
	23½		1.6	2.0			Burn.
26"	23½	23½			2.4	3.0	Burn.
32"		31				3.7	Amer.
		30¾				3.7	Natl.
		31				3.7	U.S.
		30¾				3.7	Crane
33"		30½				3.7	Burn.

*Width is 6 13/16" △Indicates no. of tubes

Radiators supplied in even no. of sections - 2 sections being min.. All dimensions for valve, trap, etc., clearances are max. & vary with valve, trap, etc. sizes & mfr. Legs 2" higher than standard available. Some originally made with 1½" length per section & may still exist. Also called "thin tube" or "slenderized" rad.

MANUFACTURERS' NAMES IN FULL

American Radiator & Standard Sanitary Corp.
National Radiator Company
United States Radiator Corporation
Crane Company
Burnham Boiler Corporation

RADIATORS - CAST IRON TUBULAR

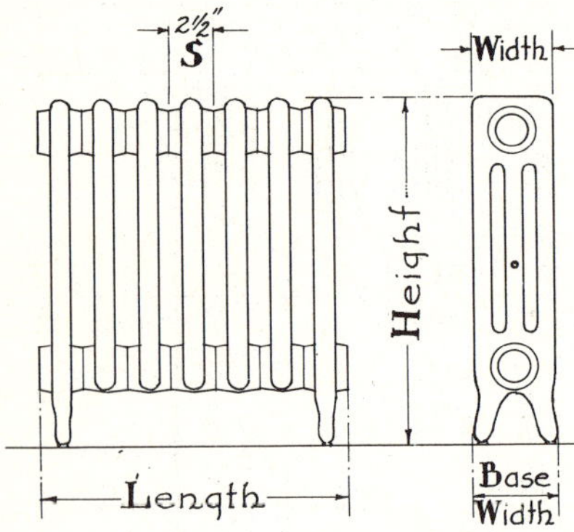

2 1/2"
S
Width
Height
Length
Base Width

KEY to TABLE

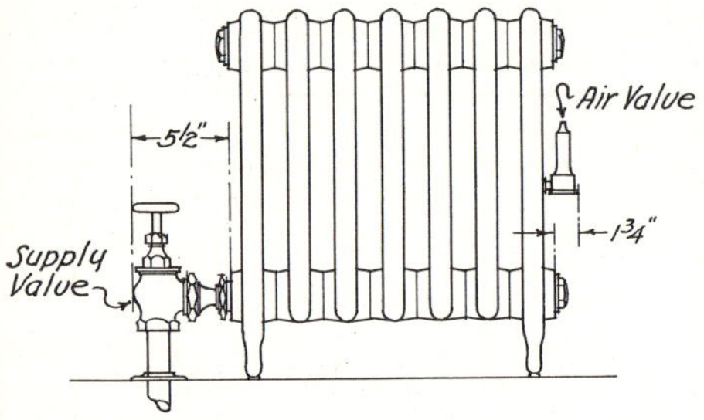

5 1/2"
Air Valve
1 3/4"
Supply Valve

ONE PIPE STEAM

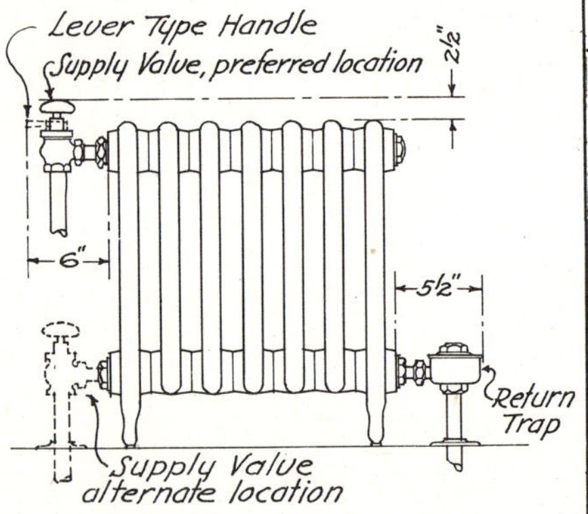

Lever Type Handle
Supply Valve, preferred location
2 1/2"
6"
5 1/2"
Return Trap
Supply Valve alternate location

VAPOR or VACUUM

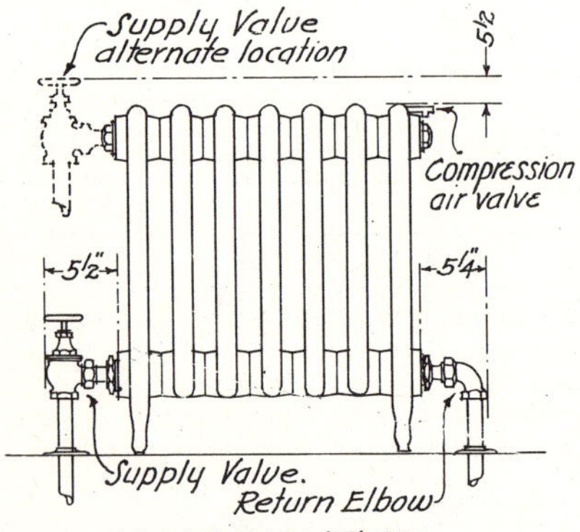

Supply Valve alternate location
5 1/2
Compression air valve
5 1/2"
5 1/4"
Supply Valve.
Return Elbow

HOT WATER

All dimensions for valve clearances etc. maximum. Dimensions vary with size and make of valve trap etc.

NO. OF TUBES		3	4	5	6	7
S = LENGTH PER SECTION		2 1/2"	2 1/2"	2 1/2"	2 1/2"	2 1/2"
Width	American					
	National	5 1/8"	6 13/16"	8 7/16"	9"	12"
	U.S.	4 15/16"	6 3/4"	8 9/16"	10 3/8"	12 3/16"
	Crane	4 5/8"	6 5/16"	8"	9 11/16"	11 3/8"
	Burnham		6 1/2"	8 1/2"	10 5/16"	12 1/8"
Base Width	American					
	National	5 1/8"	6 13/16"	8 7/16"	9"	12"
	U.S.	5 1/8"	6 15/16"	8 3/4"	10 9/16"	12 3/16"
	Crane	4 5/8"	6 5/16"	8"	9 11/16"	11 3/8"
	Burnham		6 5/8"	8 1/2"	10 5/16"	12 1/8"

NOTE

RADIATORS ON THIS PAGE ARE NO LONGER MADE AS OF 1949. DATA SHOWN IS FOR EXISTING RADIATORS.

*H = HEIGHT		SQ. FT. PER SECTION					HEIGHT - Legless Type				
		3	4	5	6	7	3	4	5	6	7
13"	U.S.					2 1/2					11 5/8
13 1/2"	National					2 1/2					12 3/4
14"	American					2 1/2					12 1/2
	Crane					2 1/2					11 3/4
	Burnham					2 2/3					12
16 1/2"	National					3					15 3/4
	U.S.					3					15 1/8
17"	American					3					15 1/2
	Crane					3					14 3/4
	Burnham					3 1/4					15
20"	American	1 3/4	2 1/4	2 2/3	3	3 2/3	17	17	17	17	18 1/2
	National	1 3/4	2.3	2.7	3	3.7	17 7/8	17 7/8	17 7/8	17 1/2	17 7/8
	U.S.	1 3/4	2 1/4	2.67	3	3.67	17 5/16	17 5/16	17 5/16	17 5/16	18 5/8
	Crane	1 3/4	2 1/4	2 2/3	3	3 2/3	16 1/4	16 1/4	16 1/4	16 1/4	17 3/4
	Burnham		2 1/4	2 2/3	3	3 2/3		16 1/2	16 1/2	16 1/2	18
23"	American	2	2 1/2	3			20	20	20		
	National	2	2 1/2	3			20 7/8	20 7/8	20 7/8		
	U.S.	2	2 1/2	3	3 1/2		20 1/8	20 1/8	20 1/8	20 1/8	
	Crane	2	2 1/2	3			19 1/4	19 1/4	19 1/4		
	Burnham		2 1/2	3				19 1/2	19 1/2		
26"	American	2 1/3	2 3/4	3 1/2	4		23	23	23	23	
	National	2 1/3	2.8	3 1/2	4	4.8	23 7/8	23 7/8	23 7/8	23 1/2	23 7/8
	U.S.	2 1/3	2 3/4	3 1/2	4		23 3/8	23 3/8	23 3/8	23 3/8	
	Crane	2 1/3	2 3/4	3 1/2	4		22 1/4	22 1/4	22 1/4	22 1/4	
	Burnham		2 3/4	3 1/2	4			22 1/2	22 1/2	22 1/2	
30"	National	3	3 1/2	4.4			27 7/8	27 7/8	27 7/8		
	U.S.	3					27 1/4				
32"	American	3	3 1/2	4 1/3			29	29	29		
	U.S.		3 1/2	4.33	5			29 1/8	29 1/8	29 1/8	
	Crane	3	3 1/2	4 1/3			28 1/4	28 1/4	28 1/4		
	Burnham		3 1/2	4 1/3				28 1/2	28 1/2		
36"	National	3	4.3	5			33 7/8	33 7/8	33 7/8		
	U.S.	3 1/2					32 3/4				
37"	U.S.		4 1/4	5	6			34 1/8	34 1/8	34 1/8	
38"	National				6					35 1/2	
	Crane	3 1/2	4 1/4	5	6		34 1/4	34 1/4	34 1/4	34 1/4	
	Burnham		4 1/4	5	6			35 1/2	35 1/2	35 1/2	
	American	3 1/2	4 1/4	5	6		35	35	35	35	

* The above radiators may exist with legs 1 1/2" higher than the standard type.

MANUFACTURERS' NAMES IN FULL	
	American Radiator & Standard Sanitary Corp.
	National Radiator Company
	United States Radiator Corporation
	Crane Company
	Burnham Boiler Corporation

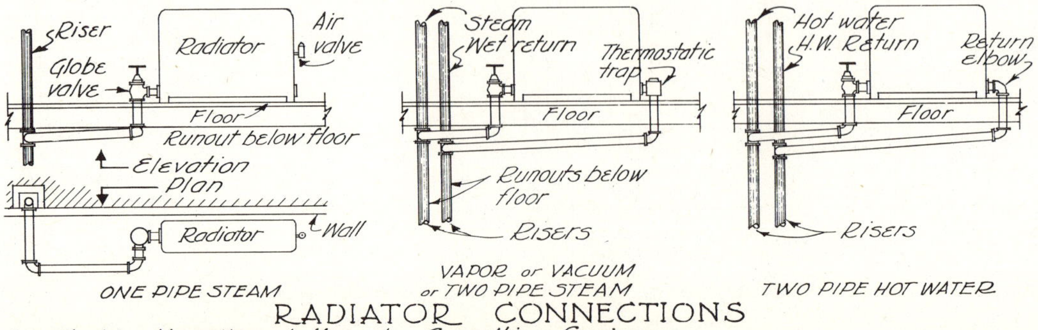

Riser
Globe valve
Radiator
Air valve
Floor
Runout below floor
Elevation
Plan
Radiator
Wall
ONE PIPE STEAM
Steam
Wet return
Thermostatic trap
Floor
Runouts below floor
Risers
VAPOR or VACUUM or TWO PIPE STEAM
Hot water
H.W. Return
Return elbow
Floor
Risers
TWO PIPE HOT WATER

RADIATOR CONNECTIONS

Compiled by Mongitore & Moesel, Consulting Engineers

RADIATOR ENCLOSURES

Figures with % below enclosures indicate efficiency of the enclosures in relation to an exposed radiator which is assumed at 100% efficiency

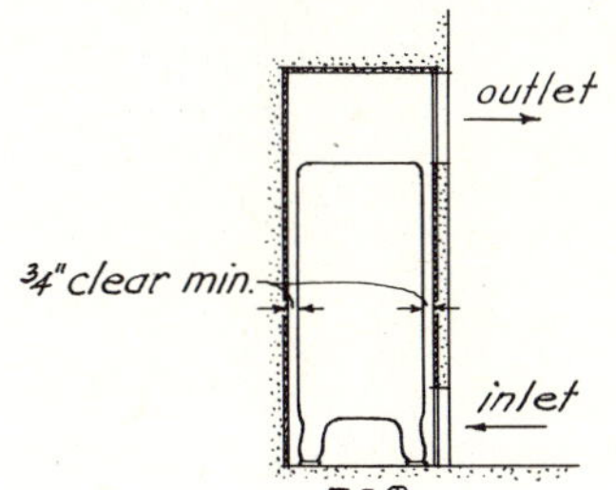
outlet
3/4" clear min.
inlet

75%

FRONT INLET & OUTLET

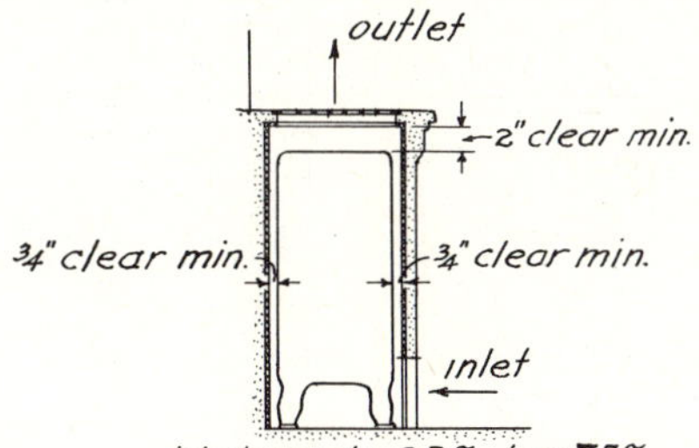
outlet
2" clear min.
3/4" clear min.
3/4" clear min.
inlet

high rads 85%, low 75%

FRONT INLET, TOP OUTLET

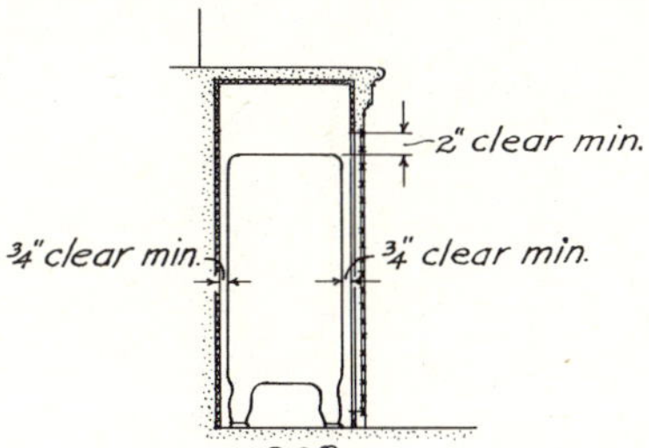
2" clear min.
3/4" clear min.
3/4" clear min.

80%

GRILLE FRONT

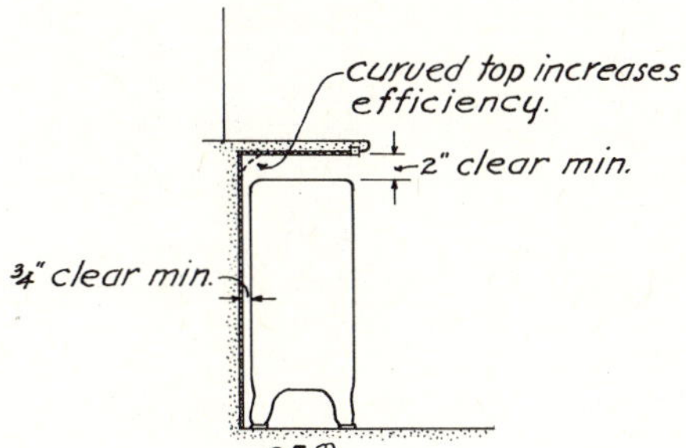
curved top increases efficiency.
2" clear min.
3/4" clear min.

95%

OPEN FRONT

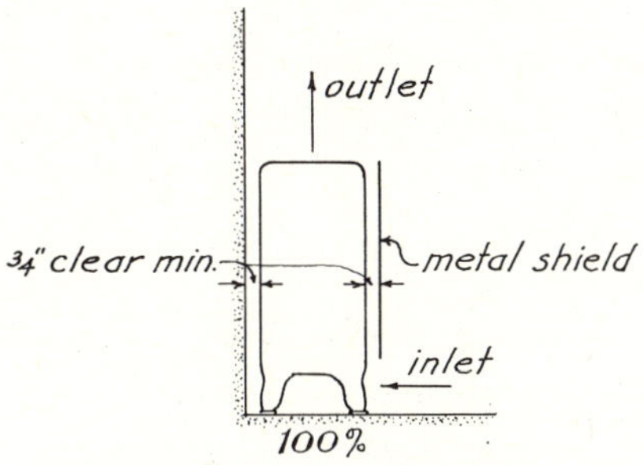
outlet
3/4" clear min.
metal shield
inlet

100%

SHIELDED FRONT

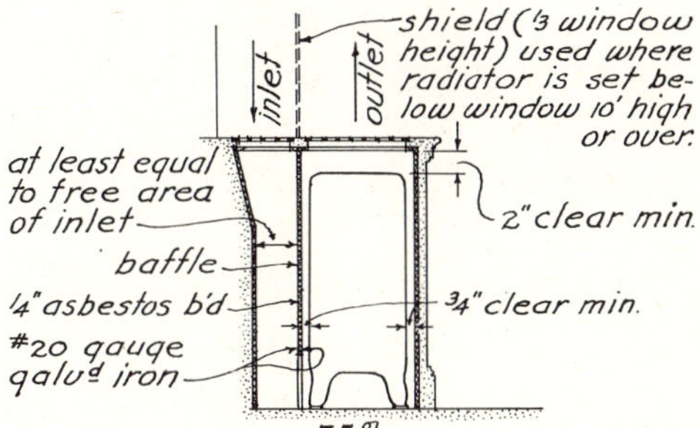
inlet
outlet
shield (1/3 window height) used where radiator is set below window 10' high or over.
at least equal to free area of inlet
2" clear min.
baffle
1/4" asbestos b'd
3/4" clear min.
#20 gauge galv'd iron

75%

TOP INLET & OUTLET

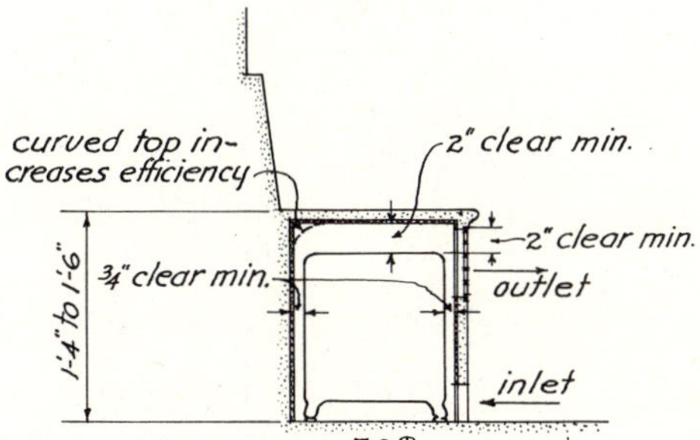
curved top increases efficiency
2" clear min.
2" clear min.
1'-4" to 1'-6"
3/4" clear min.
outlet
inlet

70%

FRONT INLET & OUTLET *under* SEAT.

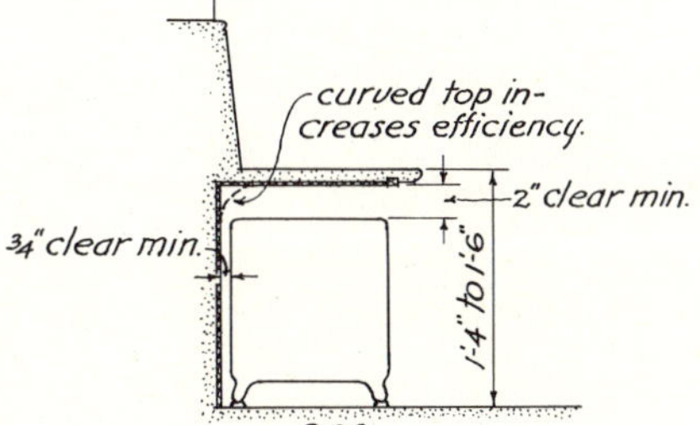
curved top increases efficiency.
2" clear min.
3/4" clear min.
1'-4" to 1'-6"

90%

OPEN FRONT *under* SEAT

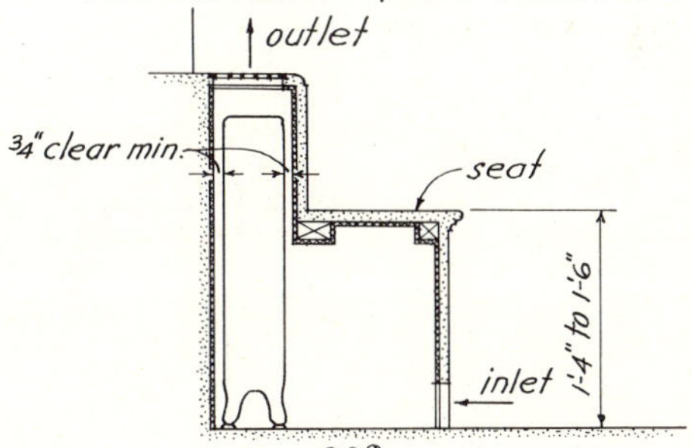
outlet
3/4" clear min.
seat
inlet
1'-4" to 1'-6"

90%

FRONT INLET TOP OUTLET *with* SEAT

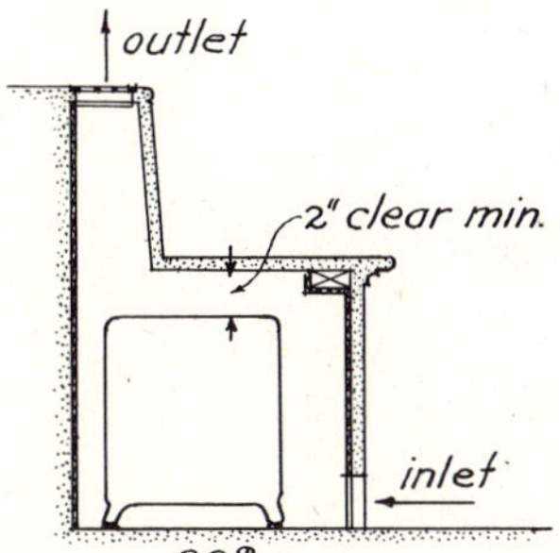
outlet
2" clear min.
inlet

90%

FRONT INLET TOP OUTLET *with* SEAT

Allow 6" clearance at each end of radiator except that for one pipe systems allow 6" on one end for valve and 3" on other end for air valve.
All enclosures lined with 1/4" asbestos board covered with #20 gauge galvanized iron.
Provide 6"×6" access door for valve control; or extension stem through top of enclosure.
Provide damper and control for outlet grilles or slots for quick control.
All grilles may be replaced by slots and slots replaced by grilles.
For same efficiency maintain same free area when changing from slot to grille and vice versa.
All efficiencies approximate; deeper radiators give lower efficiencies; narrower radiators higher efficiencies.
For same height radiator increasing height of enclosure increases efficiency, lowering enclosures lowers efficiency.

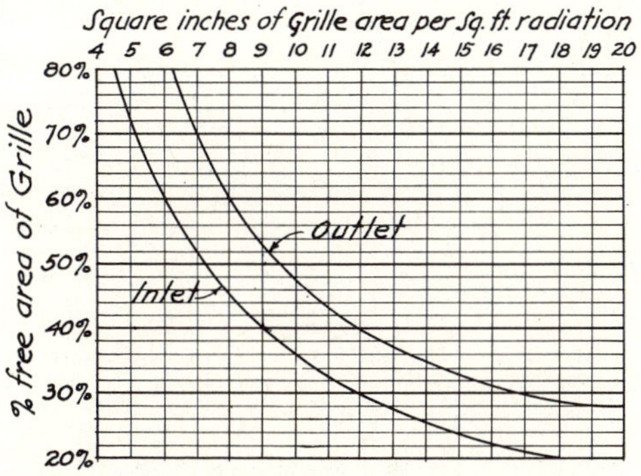
Square inches of Grille area per Sq. ft. radiation
4 5 6 7 8 9 10 11 12 13 14 15 16 17 18 19 20
80%
70%
60%
50%
40%
30%
20%
% free area of Grille
Outlet
Inlet

CURVE SHOWING GRILLE AREA REQUIRED *with* VARYING FREE AREA

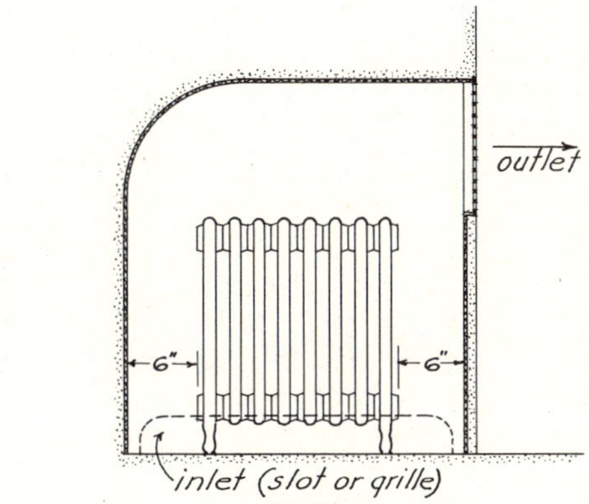
outlet
6"
6"
inlet (slot or grille)

70%

SECTION

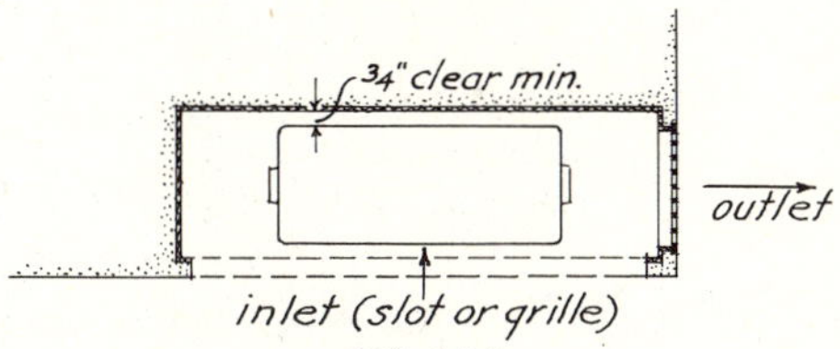
3/4" clear min.
outlet
inlet (slot or grille)

PLAN

FRONT INLET SIDE OUTLET

Compiled by Mongitore & Moesel, Consulting Engineers; N.Y.C.

RADIATOR ENCLOSURES

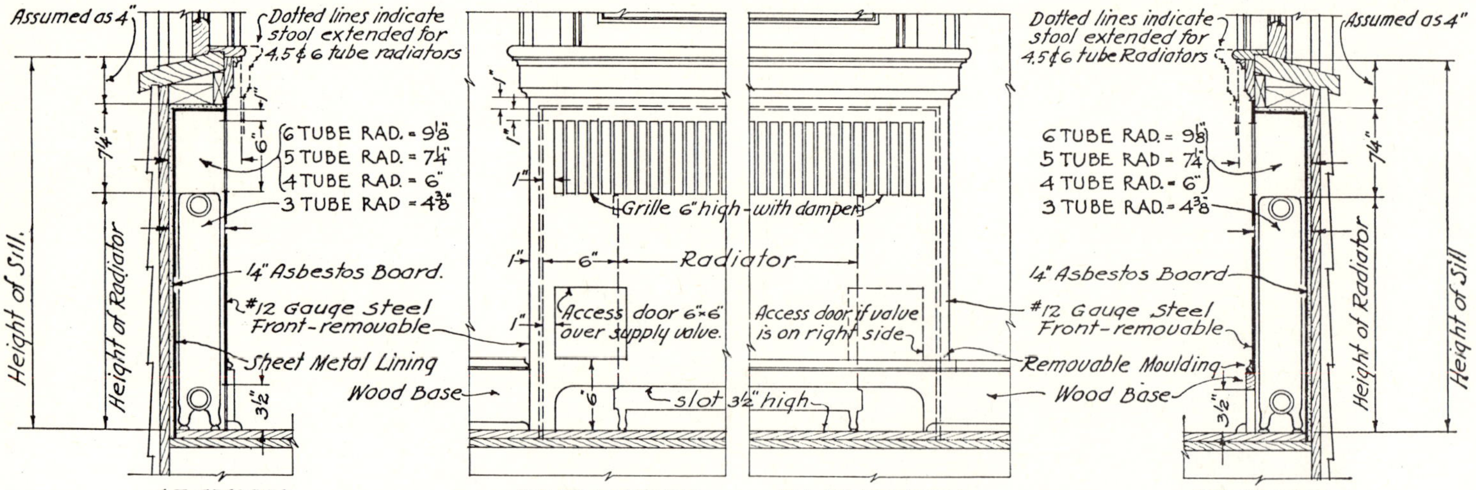

Assumed as 4"
Dotted lines indicate stool extended for 4,5 & 6 tube radiators
6 TUBE RAD. = 9⅝"
5 TUBE RAD. = 7¼"
4 TUBE RAD. = 6"
3 TUBE RAD = 4⅜"
Height of Sill.
Height of Radiator
¼" Asbestos Board.
#12 Gauge Steel Front-removable
Sheet Metal Lining
Wood Base
Grille 6" high-with damper
Radiator
Access door 6"×6" over supply valve.
Access door if valve is on right side
slot 3½" high
Removable Moulding

SECTION ELEVATION ELEVATION SECTION

INLET IN METAL FRONT CUT OUT INLET IN BASE

Grilles may be of any design. Reduction of free area reduces efficiency. Designs shown are 65% free area.

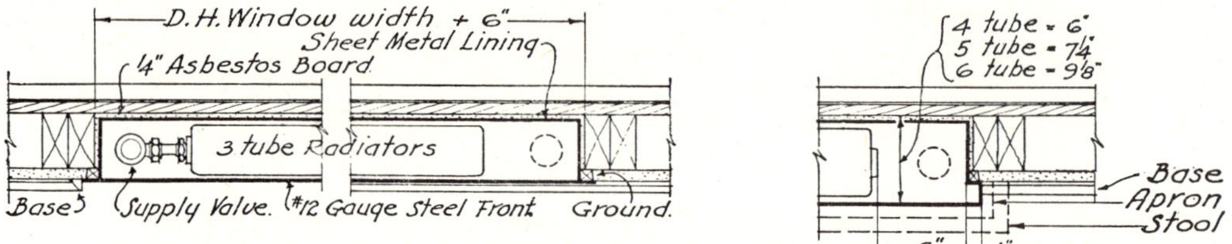

D.H. Window width + 6"
Sheet Metal Lining
¼" Asbestos Board
3 tube Radiators
Base
Supply Valve.
#12 Gauge Steel Front
Ground.
4 tube - 6"
5 tube - 7¼"
6 tube - 9⅝"
Base
Apron
Stool

PLAN PLAN PART PLAN - 4,5 & 6 TUBE RAD.

for THIN TUBE TYPE TUBULAR RADIATORS

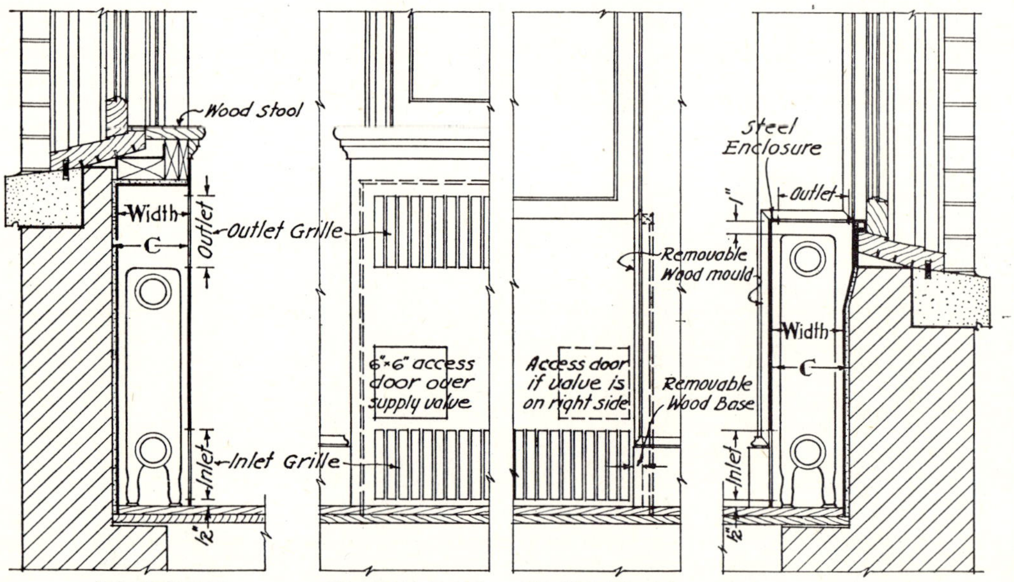

Wood Stool
Width
C
Outlet
Outlet Grille
Inlet
Inlet Grille
6"×6" access door over supply valve
Access door if valve is on right side
Removable Wood mould
Removable Wood Base
Steel Enclosure
Outlet

SECTION ELEVATION ELEVATION SECTION

FRONT OUTLET TOP OUTLET

Where supply valve is at top of radiator access door is to be set in outlet grille. Where top supply valve is used with sill grille provide valve with extended stem and plate or increase enclosure height to clear valve handle.

NO. OF TUBES	3		4		5		6		7	
Width	6¾"		8½"		10¼"		12¼"		13¾"	
C	7"		8¾"		10½"		12½"		14"	
Radiator Height	Inlet	Outlet	Inlet	Outlet	Inlet	Outlet	Inlet	Outlet	Inlet	Outlet
13"									5"	6"
13½"									5"	6"
14"									5"	6"
16½"									6"	8"
17"									6"	7"
20"	5"	5"	5"	6"	6"	7"	6"	7"	8"	10"
23"	5"	5"	5"	6"	6"	7"	7"	8"		
26"	5"	6"	5"	7"	7"	8"	8"	9"	9"	11"
30"	6"	7"	7"	8"	8"	10"			10"	13"
32"	6"	7"	7"	8"	8"	10"	9"	12"		
36"	7"	8"	8"	10"	9"	12"			13"	16"
37"			8"	10"	9"	12"	11"	14"		
38"	6"	7"	8"	10"	9"	12"	11"	14"		

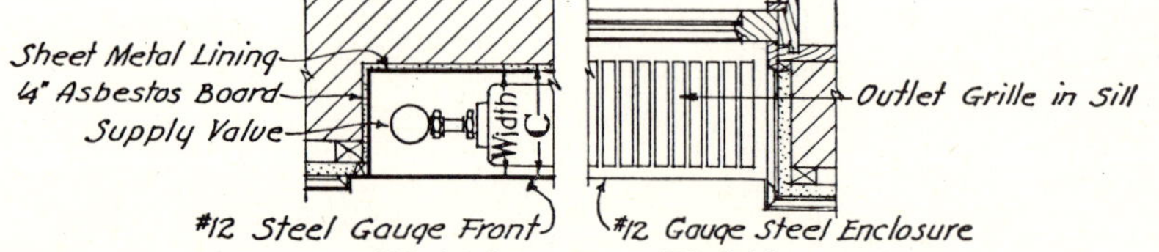

Sheet Metal Lining
¼" Asbestos Board
Supply Valve
Width
C
Outlet Grille in Sill
#12 Steel Gauge Front
#12 Gauge Steel Enclosure

PLAN PLAN

Where supply valve is at top of radiator access door is to be set in outlet grille. Where top supply valve is used with sill grille provide valve with extension stem and plate or increase enclosure height to clear valve handle.

no longer manufactured FOR STANDARD TYPE TUBULAR RADIATORS *no longer manufactured*

Compiled by Mongitore & Moesel, Consulting Engineers., N.Y.C.

FUEL DATA

BASEMENT OIL TANKS "OBROUND" TYPE

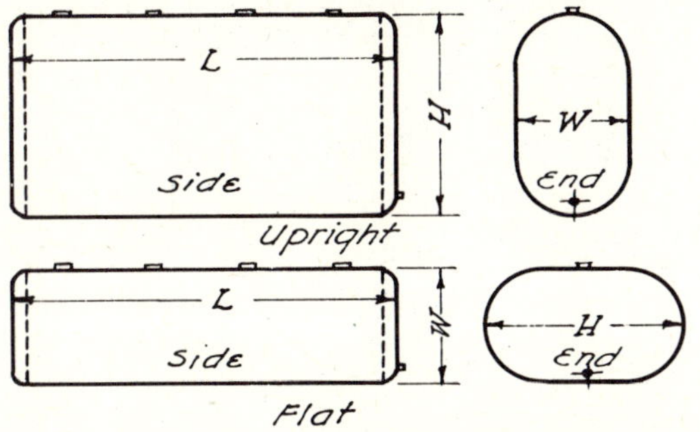
L
H
W
Side
End
Upright
L
W
H
Side
End
Flat

TYPE	GA.	CAPACITY (gallons)	WEIGHT (pounds)	DIMENSIONS (in inches) L	W	H	OPENINGS (dia. in inches) Top	Botm
Upright	14	275	220	66¼	26	42	4 - 2"	½
Flat	14	275	220	66¼	26	42	4 - 2"	½
Upright	12	275	300	66¼	26	42	4 - 2"	½
Flat	12	275	300	66¼	26	42	4 - 2"	½

QUANTITIES of VARIOUS FUELS REQUIRED TO GIVE EQUAL HEATING VALUE *

BUNKER "C" OIL #6	120 GALLONS
COAL	1 TON
LIGHT OIL #2 or #3	150 GALLONS
MANUFACTURED GAS	43,200 CU. FT.
NATURAL GAS	21,600 CU. FT.
ELECTRICITY	3200 KILOWATTS

* Based on comparative average seasonal operating efficiencies.

GRAPHIC COMPARATIVE FUEL COSTS

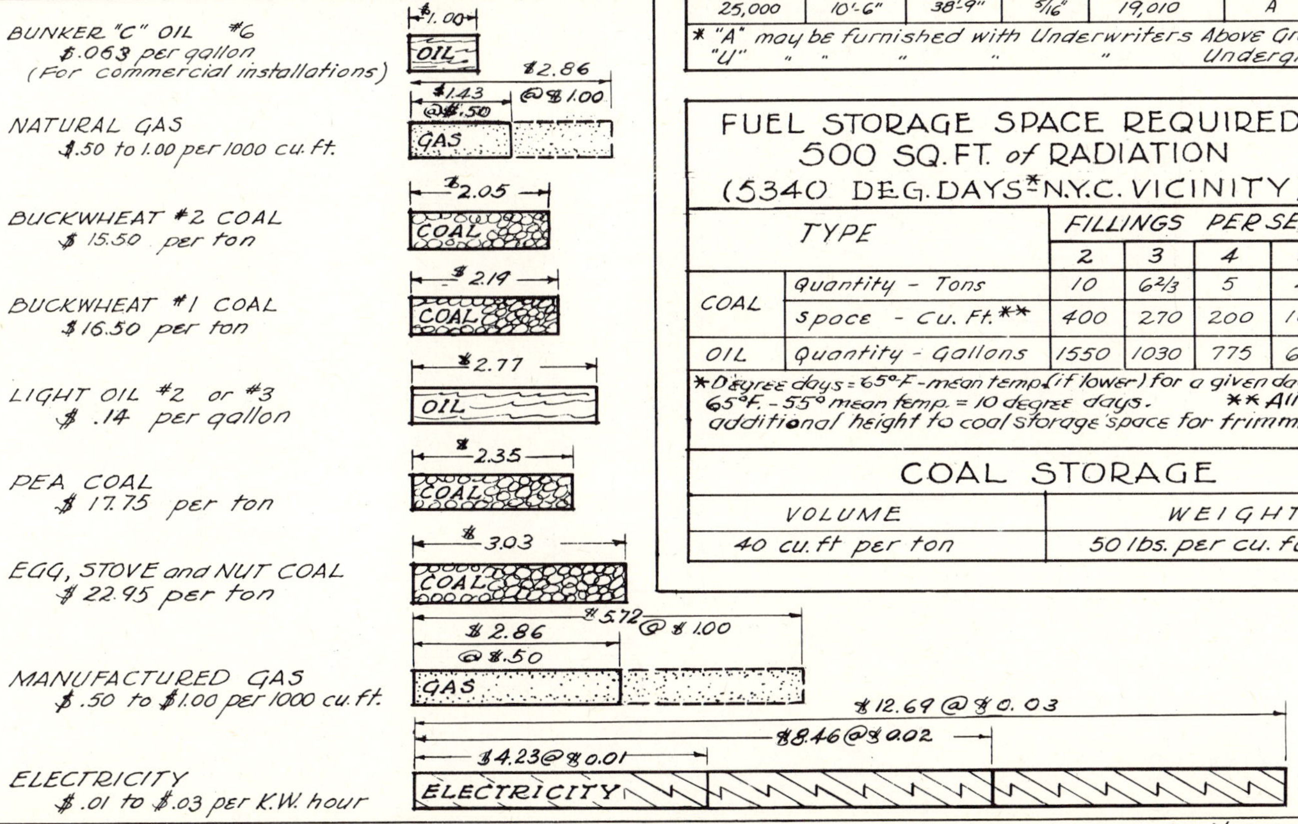
BUNKER "C" OIL #6
$.063 per gallon
(For commercial installations)
$1.00
OIL
NATURAL GAS
$.50 to 1.00 per 1000 cu. ft.
$1.43 @$.50
$2.86 @$1.00
GAS
BUCKWHEAT #2 COAL
$15.50 per ton
$2.05
COAL
BUCKWHEAT #1 COAL
$16.50 per ton
$2.19
COAL
LIGHT OIL #2 or #3
$ .14 per gallon
$2.77
OIL
PEA COAL
$17.75 per ton
$2.35
COAL
EGG, STOVE and NUT COAL
$22.95 per ton
$3.03
COAL
MANUFACTURED GAS
$.50 to $1.00 per 1000 cu. ft.
$2.86 @$.50
$5.72 @$1.00
GAS
ELECTRICITY
$.01 to $.03 per K.W. hour
$4.23 @$0.01
$8.46 @$0.02
$12.69 @$0.03
ELECTRICITY

Figures are ratios - with #6 Fuel Oil as unity. Based on costs as given April 4, 1955

FUEL OIL — STORAGE TANKS

NOMINAL CAPACITY (gallons)	DIMENSIONS DIA.	LENGTH	THICK.	WEIGHT (pounds)	*LABEL SERVICE	No. of SUPPORTS
280	3'-6"	4'-0"	3/16"	540	A or U	2
550	4'-0"	6'-0"	3/16"	800	A or U	2
1000	4'-0"	10'-8"	3/16"	1260	A or U	2
1000	5'-4"	6'-0"	3/16"	1160	A or U	2
1500	5'-4"	9'-0"	3/16"	1550	A or U	2
2000	5'-4"	12'-0"	3/16"	1950	A or U	2
3000	5'-4"	18'-0"	3/16"	2730	A or U	2
4000	5'-4"	24'-0"	3/16"	3510	A or U	2
5000	6'-0"	23'-9"	1/4"	5440	A or U	2
5000	7'-0"	17'-6"	1/4"	5130	A or U	2
6000	8'-0"	16'-1"	1/4"	5920	A or U	2
6000	8'-0"	16'-1"	5/16"	6720	A or U	2
8000	8'-0"	21'-4"	1/4"	7280	A or U	2
8000	8'-0"	21'-4"	5/16"	8330	A or U	2
10,000	8'-0"	26'-7"	1/4"	8680	A or U	3
10,000	8'-0"	26'-7"	5/16"	10,510	A or U	3
10,000	10'-0"	17'-2"	1/4"	8030	A or U	2
10,000	10'-0"	17'-2"	5/16"	9130	A or U	2
10,000	10'-6"	15'-8"	1/4"	8160	A or U	2
10,000	10'-6"	15'-8"	5/16"	9020	A or U	2
12,000	8'-0"	31'-11"	1/4"	10,550	A or U	3
12,000	8'-0"	31'-11"	5/16"	12,090	A or U	3
12,000	10'-0"	20'-6"	1/4"	8940	A or U	2
12,000	10'-0"	20'-6"	5/16"	10,700	A or U	2
15,000	8'-0"	39'-11"	1/4"	13,210	A	4
15,000	8'-0"	39'-11"	5/16"	14,620	A or U	4
15,000	10'-0"	25'-8"	1/4"	11,080	A	3
15,000	10'-0"	25'-4"	5/16"	12,580	A or U	3
15,000	10'-6"	23'-4"	1/4"	11,160	A	3
15,000	10'-6"	23'-4"	5/16"	12,390	A or U	3
20,000	10'-0"	34'-1"	1/4"	14,130	A	3
20,000	10'-0"	34'-1"	5/16"	16,330	A or U	3
20,000	10'-6"	31'-0"	1/4"	14,100	A	3
20,000	10'-6"	31'-0"	5/16"	15,700	A or U	3
25,000	10'-6"	38'-9"	1/4"	17,040	A	4
25,000	10'-6"	38'-9"	5/16"	19,010	A	4

* "A" may be furnished with Underwriters Above Ground Label.
"U" " " " " " Underground " .

FUEL STORAGE SPACE REQUIRED for 500 SQ. FT. of RADIATION (5340 DEG. DAYS* N.Y.C. VICINITY)

TYPE		FILLINGS PER SEASON 2	3	4	5	6
COAL	Quantity - Tons	10	6⅔	5	4	3⅓
	Space - Cu. Ft.**	400	270	200	160	135
OIL	Quantity - Gallons	1550	1030	775	620	515

*Degree days = 65°F - mean temp. (if lower) for a given day. Example: 65°F. - 55° mean temp. = 10 degree days. **Allow 2'-0" additional height to coal storage space for trimming.

COAL STORAGE

VOLUME	WEIGHT
40 cu. ft per ton	50 lbs. per cu. foot

Data compiled by the Office of Mangiore & Moesel, Consulting Engineers, N.Y.C.

ATTIC and CRAWL SPACE VENTILATION

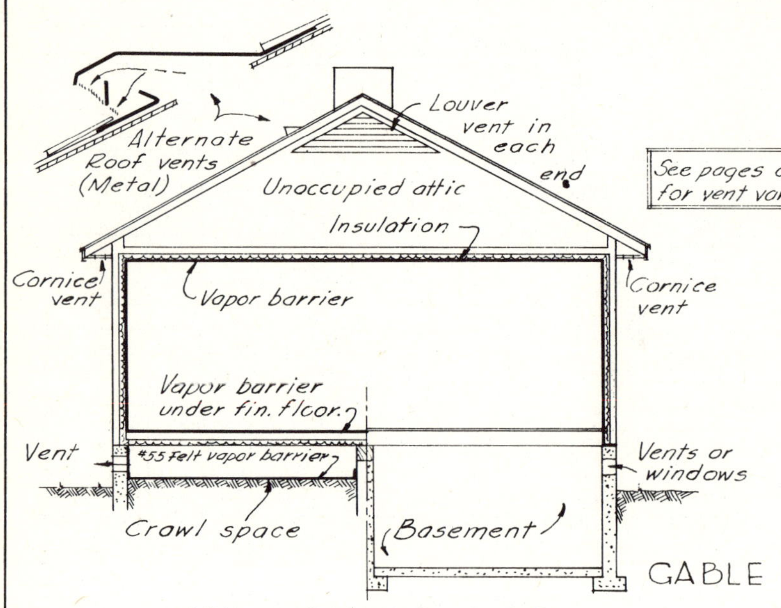
Alternate
Roof vents
(Metal)
Louver
vent in
each
end
Unoccupied attic
Insulation
Cornice
vent
Vapor barrier
Cornice
vent
Vapor barrier
under fin. floor.
Vent
#55 Felt vapor barrier
Vents or
windows
Crawl space
Basement

See pages on eaves for vent variations

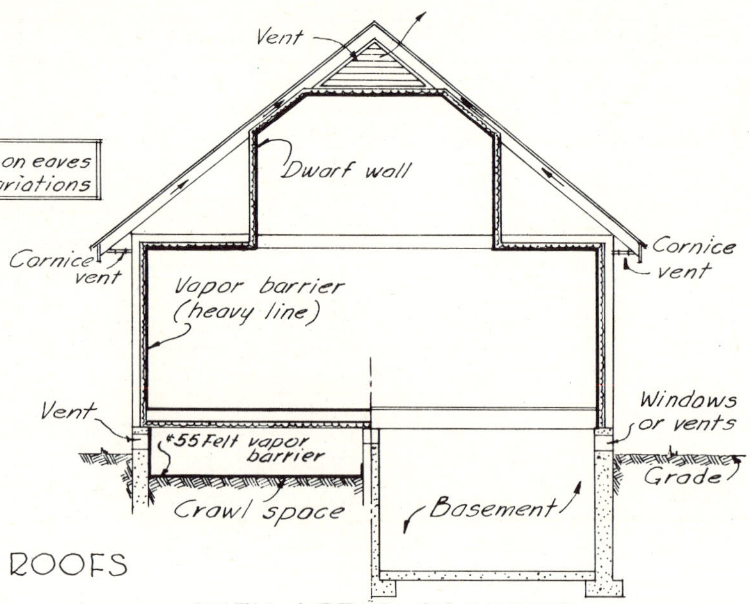
Vent
Dwarf wall
Cornice
vent
Cornice
vent
Vapor barrier
(heavy line)
Vent
#55 Felt vapor
barrier
Windows
or vents
Grade
Crawl space
Basement

GABLE ROOFS

WITH UNOCCUPIED ATTIC
Cornice vents not required if roof area is small.

WITH ATTIC OCCUPIED
Cornice vents nec. to create "stack effect" to ridge.

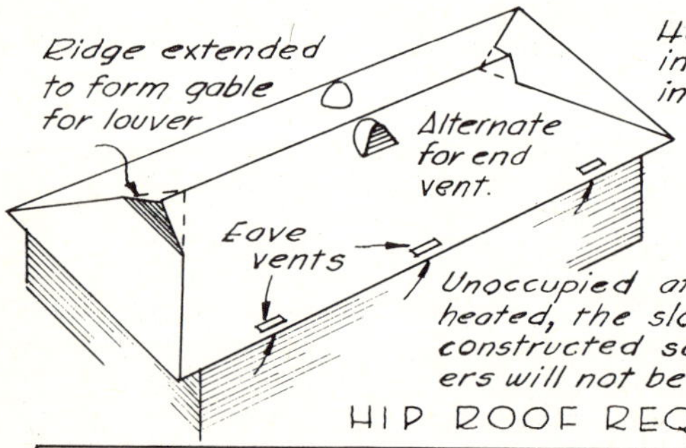
Ridge extended
to form gable
for louver
Alternate
for end
vent.
Eave
vents

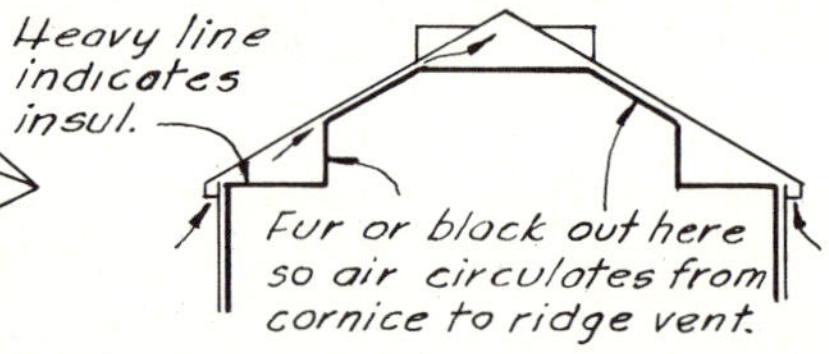
Heavy line
indicates
insul.
Fur or block out here
so air circulates from
cornice to ridge vent.

Unoccupied attic same as for gable roofs. If heated, the sloping part of attic wall must be constructed so that spaces between jack-rafters will not be closed off by the hip rafter.

HIP ROOF REQUIREMENTS

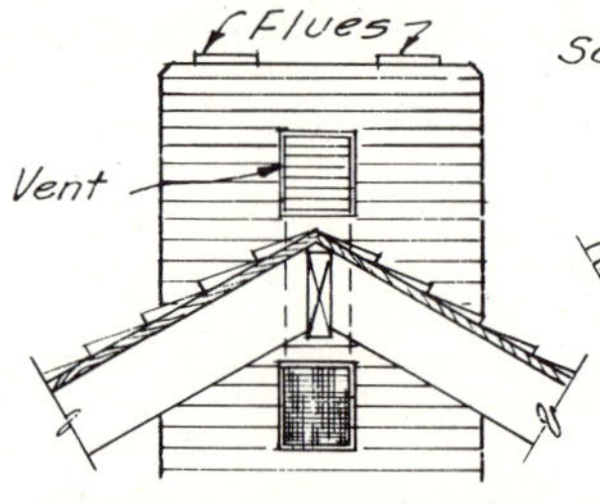
Flues
Vent

CHIMNEY VENT
Used when inside chimney ctr'd at ridge

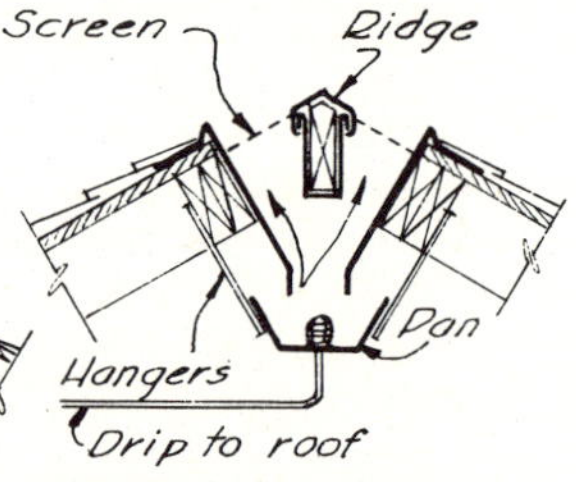
Screen
Ridge
Hangers
Pan
Drip to roof

RIDGE VENT

VENTILATION and VAPOR BARRIER REQUIREMENTS to PREVENT CONDENSATION*

CONDENSATION ZONES

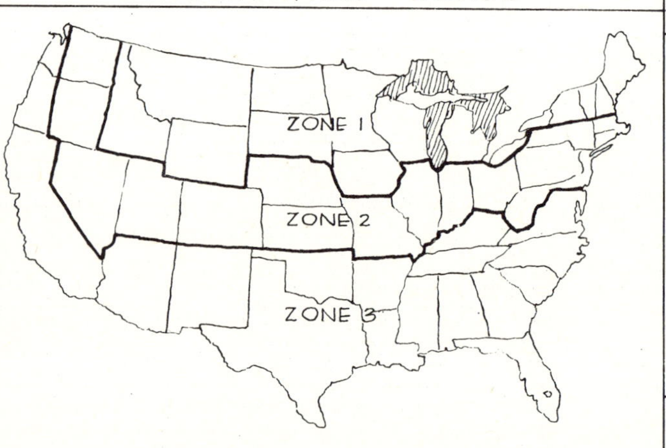
ZONE 1
ZONE 2
ZONE 3

Zone 1. roughly includes design temps. of -20°F & lower.
" 2. from 0°F to -10°.
" 3. areas warmer than 0°F.

Attic	TYPE of ROOF	TOTAL FREE AREA of VENTILATION*	VAPOR BARRIERS ZONE 1	ZONE 2	ZONE 3
Unheated	FLAT ROOF Slope less than 3/12	1/300 Uniformly distributed at eaves. Free circulation through all spaces required	Required on warm side in top story ceiling		
Unheated	GABLE ROOF Slope over 3/12	1/300 At least 2 louvers on opposite sides near ridge.	Required on warm side in top story ceil.	Considered unnecessary.	
Unheated	HIP ROOF	1/300 1/600 uniformly distributed at eaves & 1/600 at ridge with all spaces interconnected.	Recommended on warm side in top story ceiling	Considered unnecessary.	
Heated	GABLE or HIP ROOF		Recommended on warm side in top full story ceiling, dwarf walls sloping part of roof & attic story ceiling		Considered unnecessary if insulation is omitted.

* The figure given indicates that the clear opening of vents totaled should be 1/300 of the bldg. area at eave line. Only 10% of given figure necessary if bsmt. has slab, or crawl space earth covered with 55# felt lapped 2".

A
B
C
D
E
F

A: Conc. Block B: Hol. Clay tile C: Farm tile. D: Met. or wood louvers. E: Wire cloth F: Brick grille

CRAWL SPACE VENTS & REQUIREMENTS*

Total Free Ventilation Area should be 2 sq. ft. per 100 lineal ft. of bldg. perimeter plus .003% of crawl space ground area. A min. of 4 vents, one near each corner should be located as high as possible. Max. screen mesh = 1/4".

EFFECT of SCREENING and/or LOUVERS on VENTS*

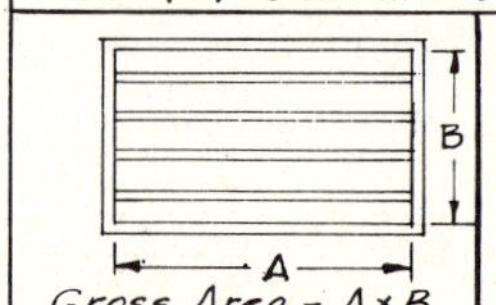
B
A

Gross Area = A×B
Max. screen openings for attic = 1/8".

The Gross Area must be increased:
1.00 x to use 1/4" mesh.
1.25 x " " 8 mesh.
2.00 x " " 16 mesh.
2.00 x if 1/4" mesh & louver.
2.25 x " 8 " "
3.00 x " 16 " "

* Housing & Home Finance Agency "Condensation Control in Dwelling Construction."

VENTILATION of RESIDENCES

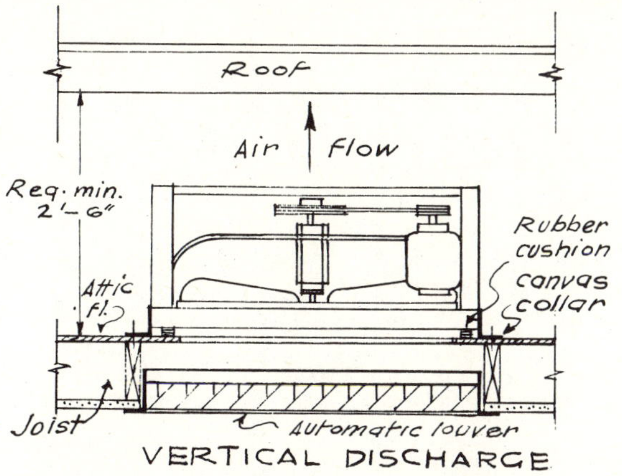

Roof
Air Flow
Req. min. 2'-6"
Rubber cushion
canvas collar
Attic Fl.
Joist
Automatic louver
VERTICAL DISCHARGE

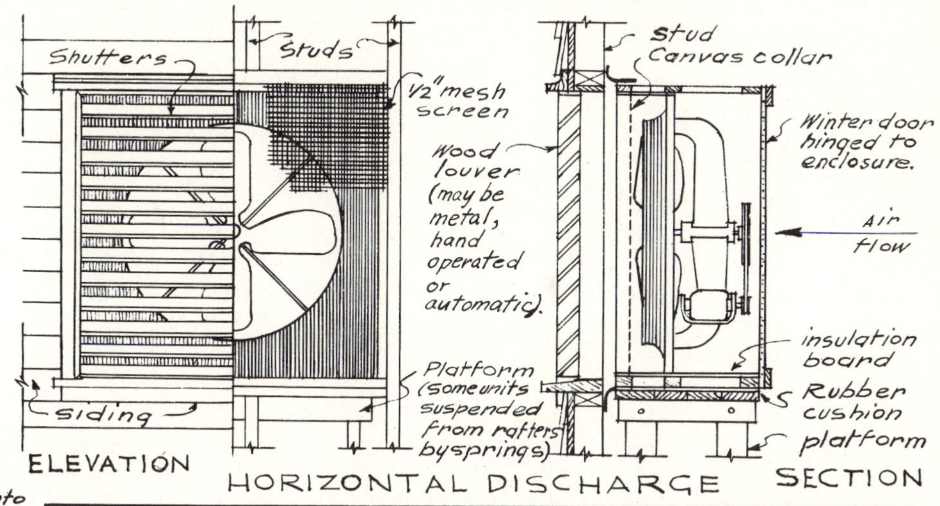

Shutters
Studs
1/2" mesh screen
Wood louver (may be metal, hand operated or automatic).
Platform (some units suspended from rafters by springs)
siding
ELEVATION
Stud
Canvas collar
Winter door hinged to enclosure.
Air flow
insulation board
Rubber cushion
platform
SECTION
HORIZONTAL DISCHARGE

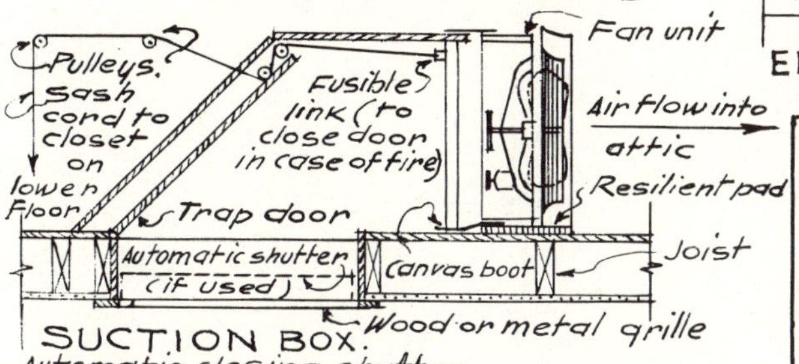

Pulleys. Sash cord to closet on lower floor
Fusible link (to close door in case of fire)
Fan unit
Air flow into attic
Resilient pad
Trap door
Automatic shutter (if used)
Canvas boot
Joist
Wood or metal grille

SUCTION BOX. Automatic closing shutter may be used instead.

Discharge of fans exhausting directly to outside should be with prevailing winds. Fans discharging into attic space should be centrally located over area to be ventilated. Horizontally discharging fans usually installed in outside wall if attic is finished, in a penthouse if bldg has flat roof, or on the attic floor with a plenum chamber (suction box) if attic is unfinished. Vertical discharge fans are installed in attic floor when attic is unfinshed or penthouse if roof is flat.

TYPICAL VENTILATING INSTALLATIONS

RECOMMENDED VENTILATION & SIZES of DISCHARGE OPENINGS

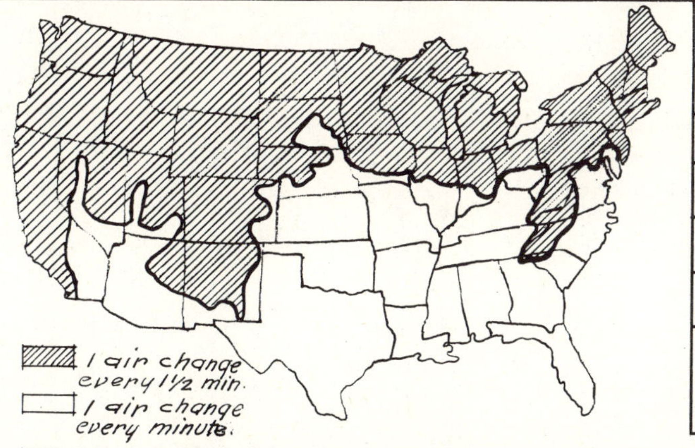

1 air change every 1 1/2 min.
1 air change every minute.

RECOMMENDED AIR CHANGE ZONES and CFM of FAN REQUIRED { Cubical contents of bldg ÷ 1 min. or { Cubical contents of bldg ÷ 1 1/2 min.

MINIMUM GROSS OUTLET AREAS for ATTIC FAN DISCHARGE OPENING

Type of Opening	Gross Area per 1000 CFM Free Air Fan Delivery
Wood louvers with 1/2" hardware cloth. 40% minimum free area.	2.27 sq. ft.
Metal louvers with 1/2" hardware cloth. 50% minimum free area.	1.82 sq. ft.
Plain opening covered with 1/2" hardware cloth 80% minimum free area.	1.14 sq. ft.
Automatic or manual shutters, 90% minimum free area.	1.01 sq. ft.

NOTE: If opening is covered with #16 mesh screen, double the gross area of opening or construct a box-like frame behind the opening or louver with a screen surface twice the area of the opening or louver.

TYPICAL AVERAGE FAN SIZES and SPECIFICATIONS

	CAPACITY CFM		MOTOR	FAN	FAN	DIMENSIONS	
	Free Air	0.1" SP	H.P.	SPEED	DIA	A	B
VERTICAL MOUNTING	5100	3800	1/6	580	24"	34"	14 3/8"
	7500	5500	1/4	430	30"	42 1/4"	15 3/4"
	11400	8300	1/3	375	36"	48 1/4"	16 1/4"
	16000	12000	1/2	355	42"	54 1/4"	19 3/4"
	20000	14200	1/2	295	48"	60 1/4"	19 3/4"
	22500	18400	3/4	330	48"	60 1/4"	19 3/4"
HORIZONTAL	5000	3700	1/6	580	24"	27	15"
	7000	5000	1/4	465	30"	36	15"
	10500	8000	1/3	375	36"	42	15"
	16000	12000	1/2	340	42"	48	21"

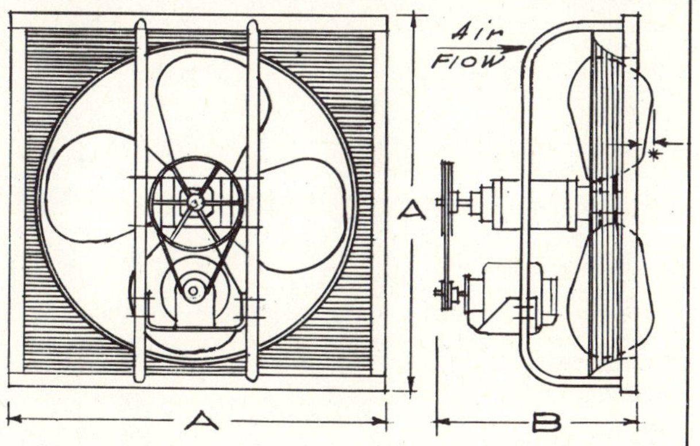

Air Flow
A
A
B

CFM ratings vary with mfrs. according to H.P. of motor, pulley sizes & design. DIA. of blades are considered standard up to 48". Dimensions vary and are approximate. Not all sizes made by all mfrs.

* Projection of blades varies from 0" to 1 3/4"

Data checked by Mongitore & Moesel

VENTS – WALL, PARTITION and DOOR

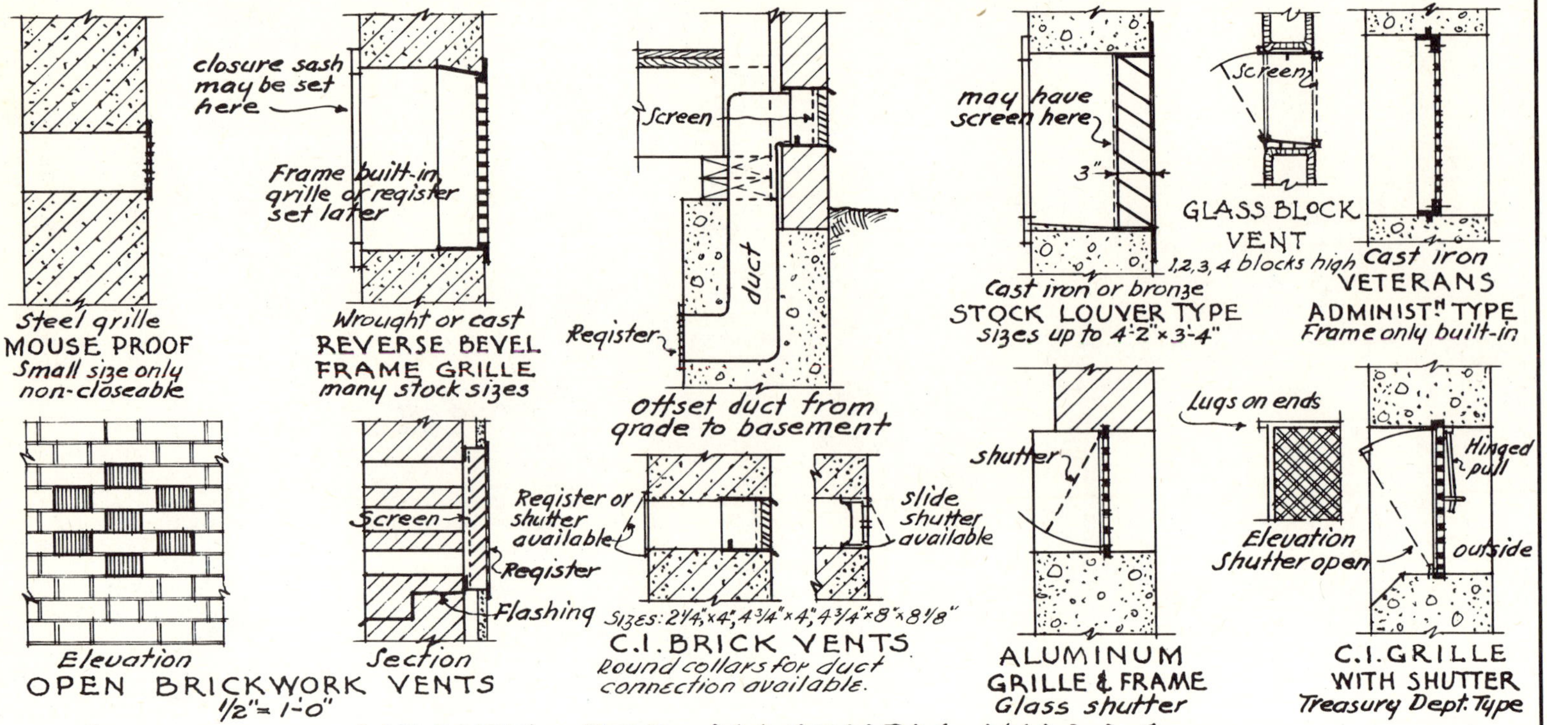
Steel grille
MOUSE PROOF
Small size only
non-closeable
closure sash may be set here
Frame built-in grille or register set later
Wrought or cast
REVERSE BEVEL
FRAME GRILLE
many stock sizes
Screen
duct
Register
offset duct from grade to basement
may have screen here
3"
Cast iron or bronze
STOCK LOUVER TYPE
sizes up to 4'-2" × 3'-4"
Screen
GLASS BLOCK VENT
1, 2, 3, 4 blocks high
Cast iron
VETERANS ADMINIST.N TYPE
Frame only built-in
Elevation
Screen
Register
Flashing
Section
OPEN BRICKWORK VENTS
1/2" = 1'-0"
Register or shutter available
slide shutter available
Sizes: 2 1/4" × 4", 4 3/4" × 4", 4 3/4" × 8" × 8 1/8"
C.I. BRICK VENTS
Round collars for duct connection available.
shutter
ALUMINUM GRILLE & FRAME
Glass shutter
Lugs on ends
Elevation
Shutter open
Hinged pull
outside
C.I. GRILLE WITH SHUTTER
Treasury Dept. Type

VENTS FOR MASONRY WALLS

Scale 3/4" = 1'-0" unless otherwise noted

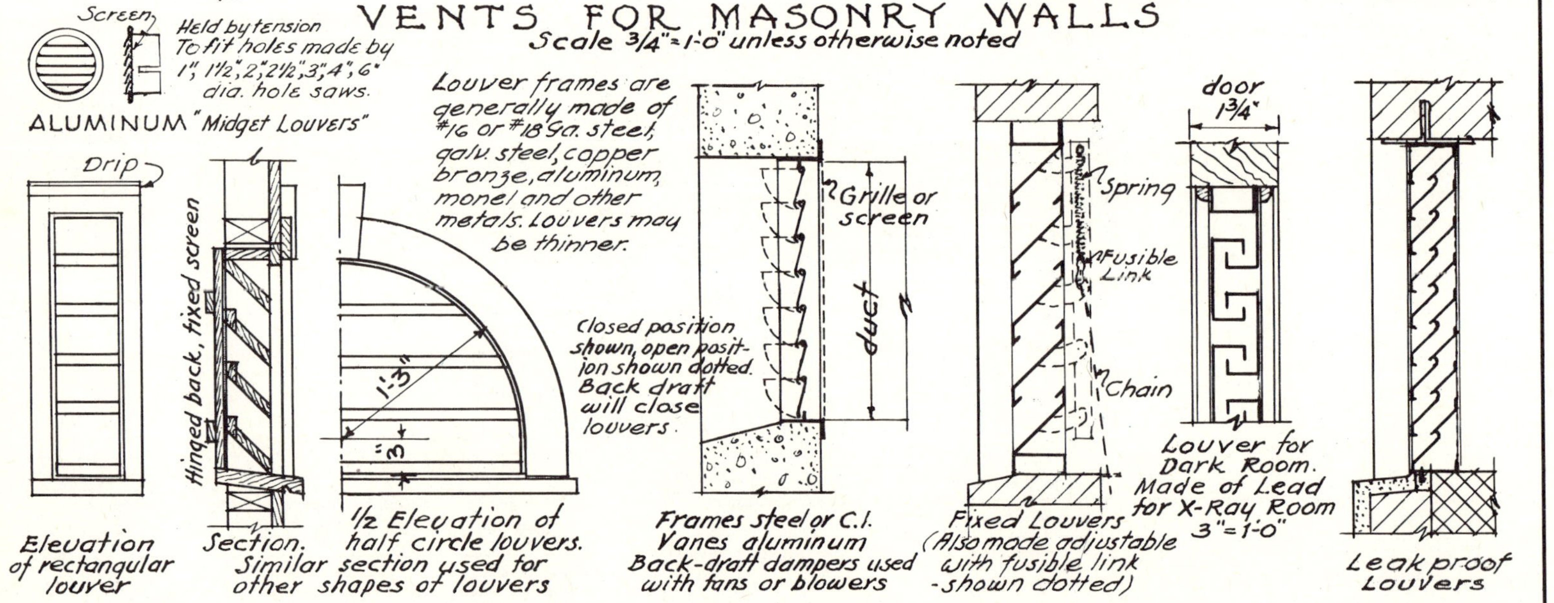
Screen
Held by tension
To fit holes made by 1", 1 1/2", 2", 2 1/2", 3", 4", 6" dia. hole saws.
ALUMINUM "Midget Louvers"
Louver frames are generally made of #16 or #18 ga. steel, galv. steel, copper bronze, aluminum, monel and other metals. Louvers may be thinner.
Drip
Hinged back, fixed screen
1'-3"
3"
Elevation of rectangular louver
Section.
1/2 Elevation of half circle louvers.
Similar section used for other shapes of louvers
Closed position shown, open position shown dotted. Back draft will close louvers.
Grille or screen
duct
Frames steel or C.I.
Vanes aluminum
Back-draft dampers used with fans or blowers
Spring
Fusible Link
Chain
Fixed Louvers
(Also made adjustable with fusible link - shown dotted)
door
1 3/4"
Louver for Dark Room.
Made of Lead for X-Ray Room
3" = 1'-0"
Leak proof Louvers

LOUVERS in FRAME WALLS. SHEET METAL LOUVERS – STEEL – COPPER ETC.

Scale – 3/4" = 1'-0"

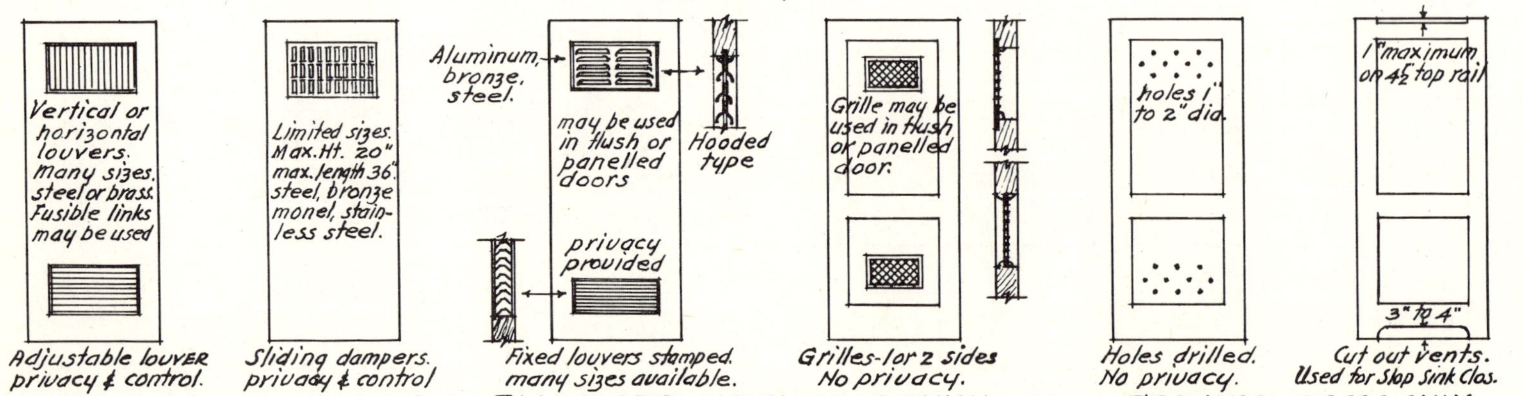
Vertical or horizontal louvers. Many sizes. steel or brass. Fusible links may be used
Adjustable louver privacy & control.
Limited sizes. Max. Ht. 20" max. length 36" steel, bronze monel, stainless steel.
Sliding dampers. privacy & control
Aluminum, bronze, steel.
may be used in flush or panelled doors
Hooded type
privacy provided
Fixed louvers stamped. many sizes available.
Grille may be used in flush or panelled door.
Grilles - 1 or 2 sides No privacy.
holes 1" to 2" dia.
Holes drilled. No privacy.
1" maximum on 4 1/2" top rail
3" to 4"
Cut out vents. Used for Slop Sink Clos.

MAY BE USED ON WOOD OR METAL DOORS, PANELLED OR FLUSH — FOR WOOD DOORS ONLY

Doors at 1/4" = 1'-0" — **DOOR VENTS** — Details at 3/4" = 1'-0"

INSULATING MATERIALS

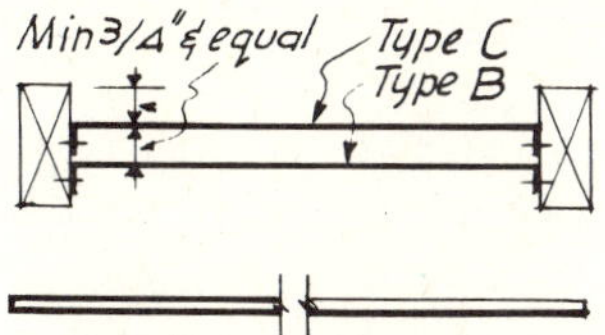
Min 3/4" & equal
Type C
Type B
Type B
Type C

Type B Aluminum is asphalt laminated to heavy kraft paper, one or both sides.
Widths: 25, 33, 36 inches, 250 sq. ft. per roll.
Type B used alone or with type C, space equally divided

METALLATION
Reynolds Metals Company

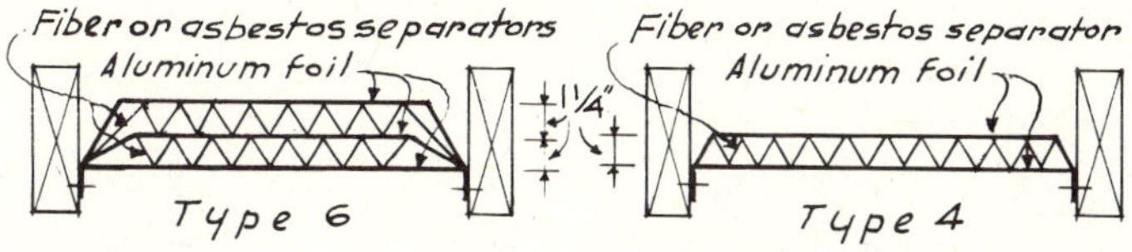
Fiber or asbestos separators
Aluminum foil
1¼"
Type 6
Fiber or asbestos separator
Aluminum Foil
Type 4

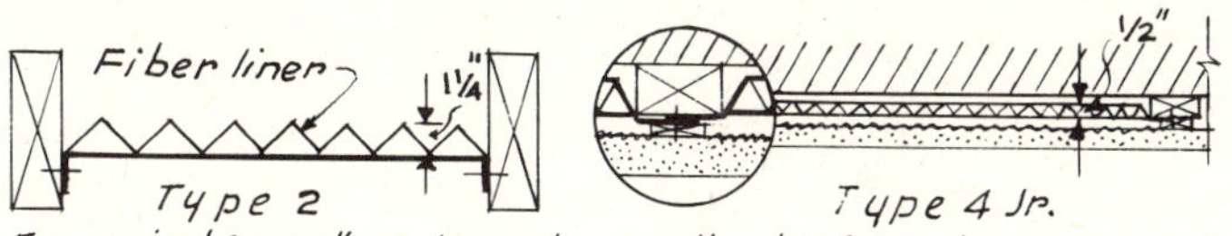
Fiber liner
1¼"
1/2"

Type 2
Economical for walls and crawl spaces. 16", 24", o.c. spacing

Type 4 Jr.
Used 1" furred masonry walls For 16" o.c. strip spacing

Types 6 & 4 std. 12", 16", 24" widths, heavy wt. foil in 16" & 24" widths

"INFRA" ACCORDION TYPE
Infra Insulation Incorporated

thin coat of alum. bonded 2 sides of "Sisal Kraft" bldg. paper

"SISALATION"
American Sisalkraft Co.

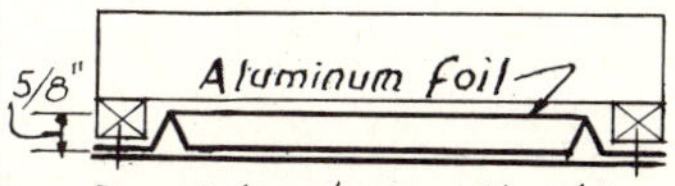
5/8"
Aluminum foil

Provides two reflective air spaces
Type 1A

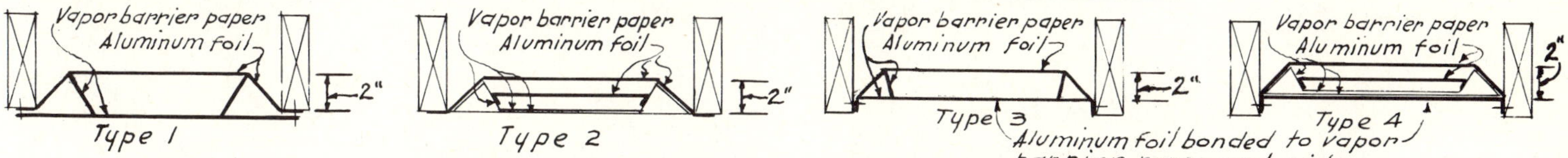
Vapor barrier paper
Aluminum foil
2"
Type 1
Vapor barrier paper
Aluminum foil
2"
Type 2
Vapor barrier paper
Aluminum foil
2"
Type 3
Vapor barrier paper
Aluminum foil
2"
Type 4
Aluminum foil bonded to vapor barrier paper on 1 side

Rolls of 500 sq. ft. in widths of 12, 16, 20 and 24 inches

"ALFOL" FOIL BLANKET – Reflectal Corporation

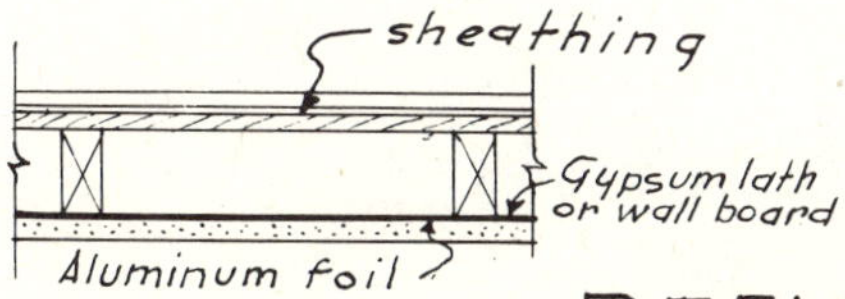
sheathing
Gypsum lath or wall board
Aluminum foil

Alum. foil laminated to one side, to face outside. Lath sizes: 16" × 48" × 3/8", 1/2" thick. Wallboard: 4'-0" × 7, 8, 10, 12 ft × 1/2", 3/8" thick; 4'-0" × 7, 9, 10, 12 ft × 1/4" thick

GYPSUM LATH & WALLBOARD with REFLECTIVE*

REFLECTIVE TYPE INSULATIONS

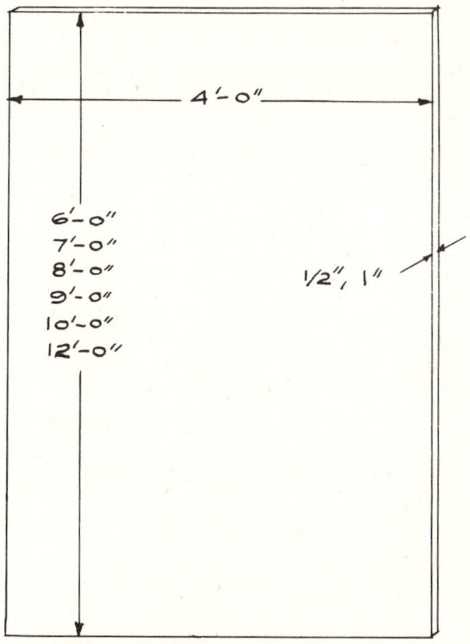
4'-0"
6'-0"
7'-0"
8'-0"
9'-0"
10'-0"
12'-0"
1/2", 1"

BUILDING BOARD
General-purpose use, natural finish
also **INTERIOR BOARDS** which are factory finished see page on "Fiber (Veg.) Boards for Interiors."

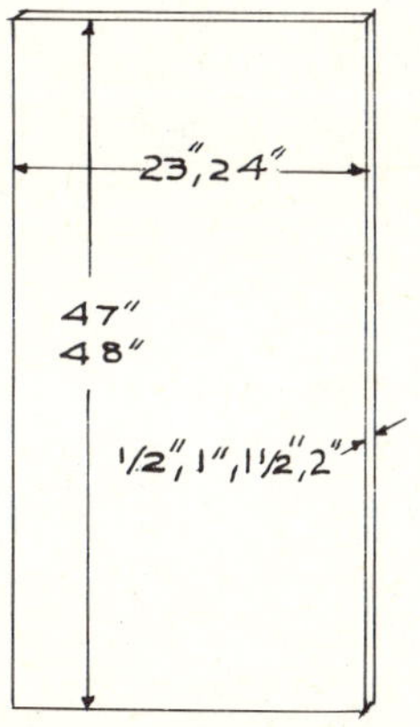
23", 24"
47"
48"
1/2", 1", 1½", 2"

ROOF INSULATION
Flat type

scale 1/2" = 1'-0"

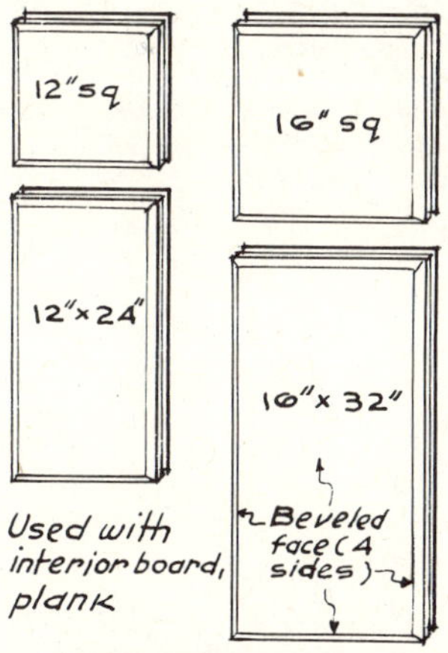
12" sq
16" sq
12" × 24"
16" × 32"
Beveled face (4 sides)
Used with interior board, plank

TILEBOARD (panels)
Generally tongued on 2 adjacent sides, grooved 2 adj. sides

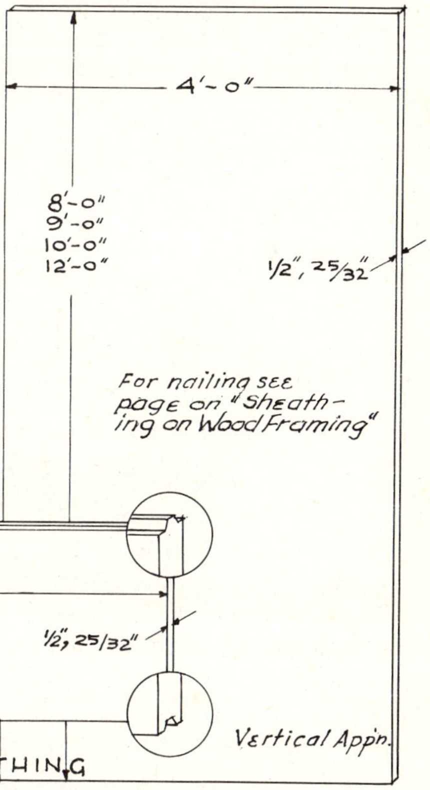
4'-0"
8'-0"
9'-0"
10'-0"
12'-0"
1/2", 25/32"
For nailing see page on "Sheathing on Wood Framing"
Vertical App'n.

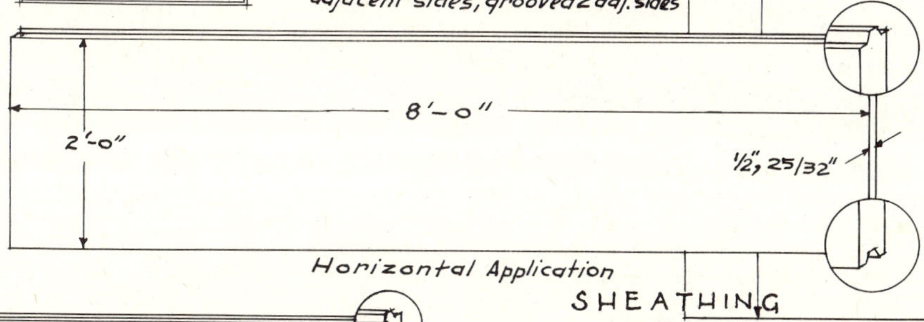
8'-0"
2'-0"
1/2", 25/32"
Horizontal Application

SHEATHING

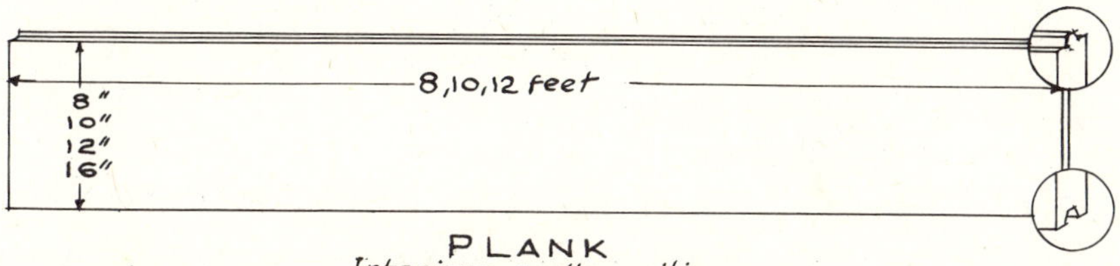
8, 10, 12 feet
8"
10"
12"
16"

PLANK
Interiors, walls, ceilings

Made of cane, wood or other vegetable fibers. Products used as interior finishes are often available in several designs (scoring, colors). Where edges are fabricated (other than square), they vary in type of joints with different mfrs.

INSULATING BOARD PRODUCTS*

* Not all sizes made by all or same mfrs.

INSULATING MATERIALS

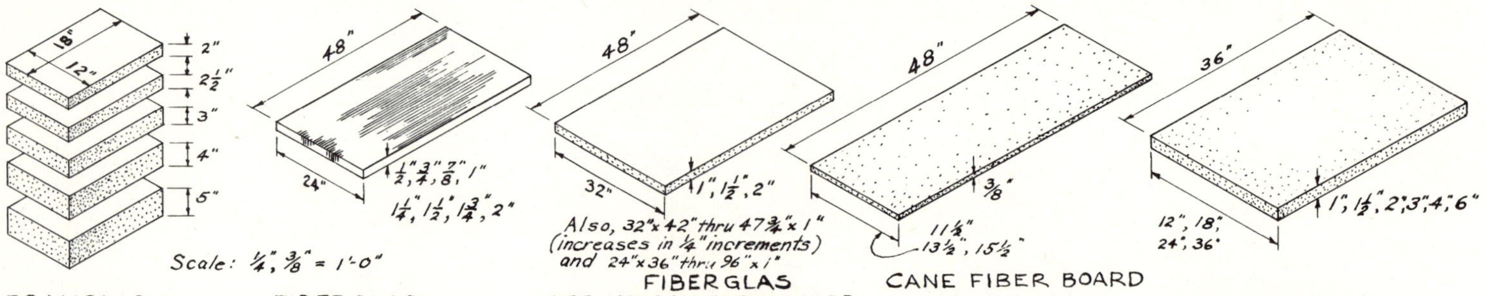
18"
12"
2"
2½"
3"
4"
5"
Scale: ¼", ⅜" = 1'-0"
48"
24"
½", ¾", ⅞", 1"
1¼", 1½", 1¾", 2"
48"
32"
1", 1½", 2"
Also, 32"x 42" thru 47¾" x 1"
(increases in ¼" increments)
and 24"x 36" thru 96" x 1"
48"
⅜"
11⅞"
13½", 15½"
36"
12", 18",
24", 36"
1", 1½", 2", 3", 4", 6"

FOAMGLAS
For flat roofs, masonry walls and basement slab floors

FIBERGLAS
Specifically for flat roofs under built-up roofing. For any type construction.

FIBERGLAS ACOUSTICAL FORM BOARD
Underlayment for poured-in-place gypsum decks. Underside may be used as a finished interior

CANE FIBER BOARD SHINGLE BACKER
Insulation and weather protection for outer wood shingles.

CORKBOARD
For flat roofs of commercial and industrial buildings. Also largely used for cold storage insulation.

TYPICAL SLAB, PANEL or BLOCK TYPE INSULATION

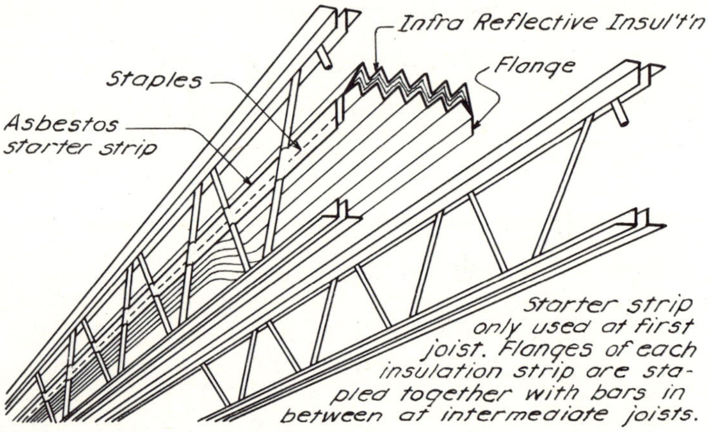
Infra Reflective Insul't'n
Flange
Staples
Asbestos starter strip
Starter strip only used at first joist. Flanges of each insulation strip are stapled together with bars in between at intermediate joists.

"INFRA" METHOD of FASTENING to STEEL JOISTS

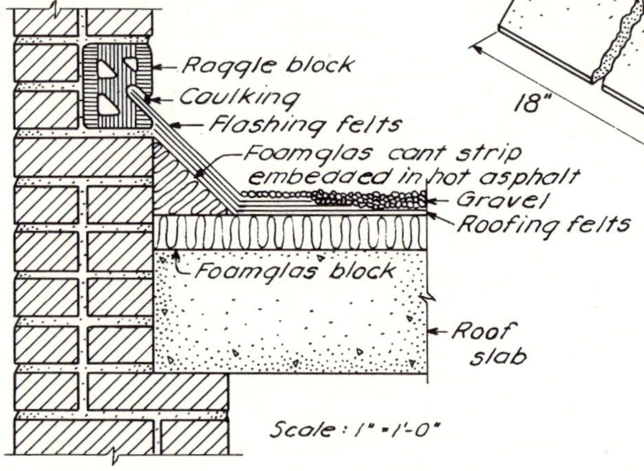
Raggle block
Caulking
Flashing felts
Foamglas cant strip embedded in hot asphalt
Gravel
Roofing felts
Foamglas block
Roof slab
Scale: 1" = 1'-0"

FOAMGLAS CANT STRIP

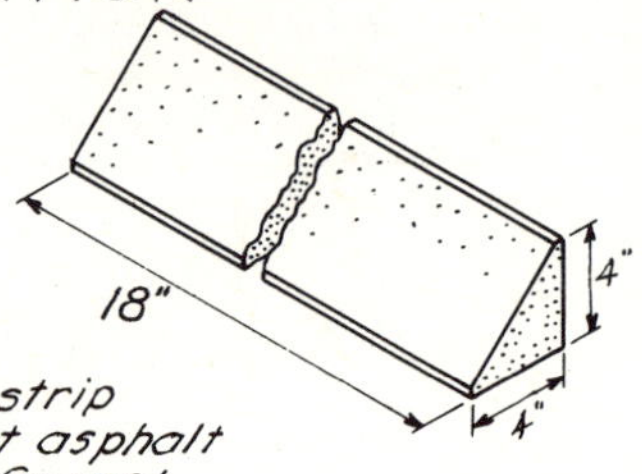
18"
4"
4"

CANT STRIP

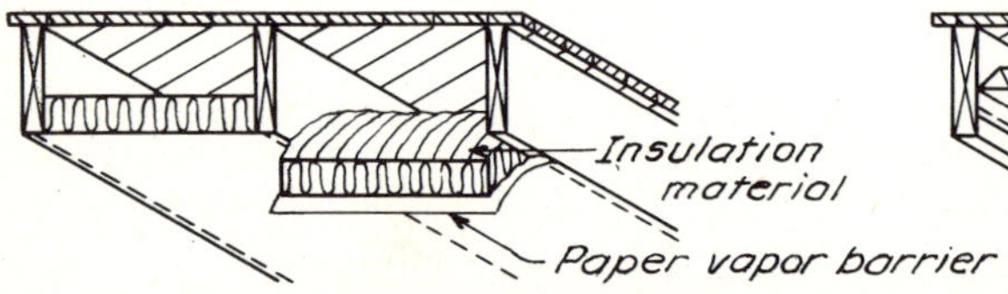
Insulation material
Paper vapor barrier

BATT or BLANKET in ROOF JOISTS
Similar in walls. If reflective backed or enclosed, install same as reflect. insul't'n.

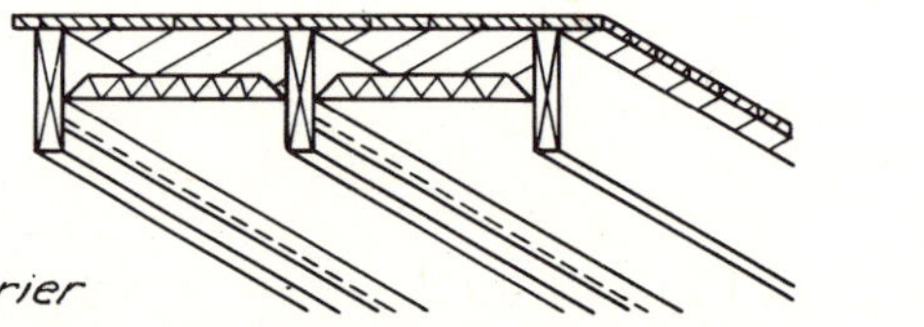

REFLECTIVE INSULATION
Allow for sag & 1" air space beneath. Similar in walls, air space both sides.

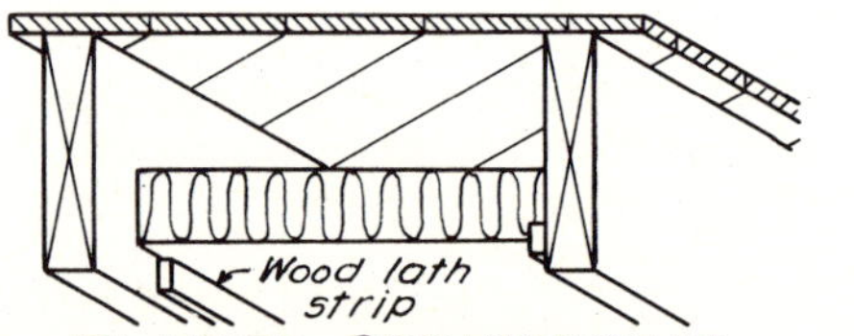
Wood lath strip

FLANGE REINFORCING
In cases where insulation is set back into joist or stud space, strips recmd.

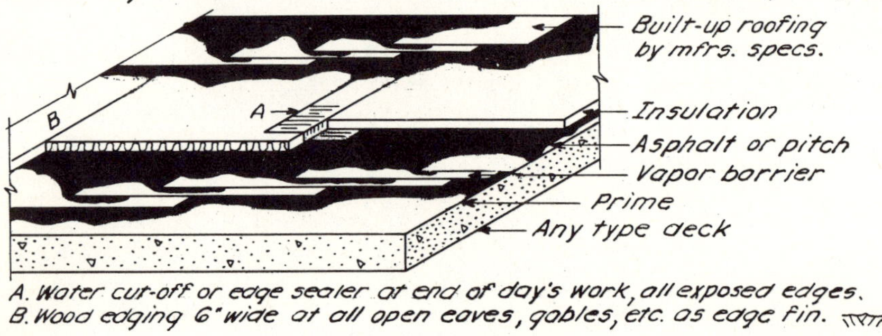
Built-up roofing by mfrs. specs.
Insulation
Asphalt or pitch
Vapor barrier
Prime
Any type deck
A
B
A. Water cut-off or edge sealer at end of day's work, all exposed edges.
B. Wood edging 6" wide at all open eaves, gables, etc. as edge fin.

BOARD or OTHER SLAB INSULATED DECKS

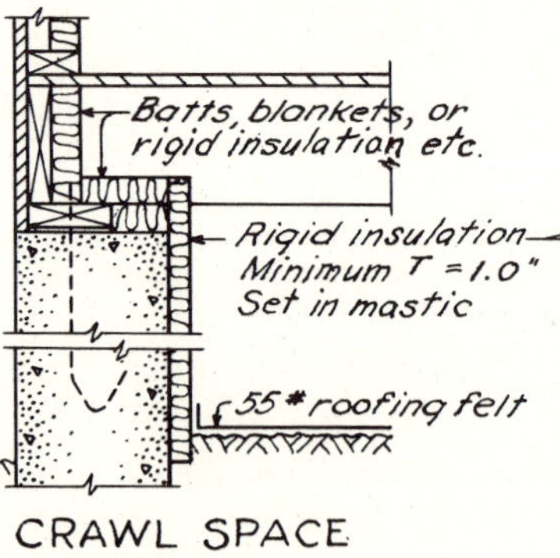
Batts, blankets, or rigid insulation etc.
Rigid insulation
Minimum T = 1.0"
Set in mastic
55# roofing felt

CRAWL SPACE

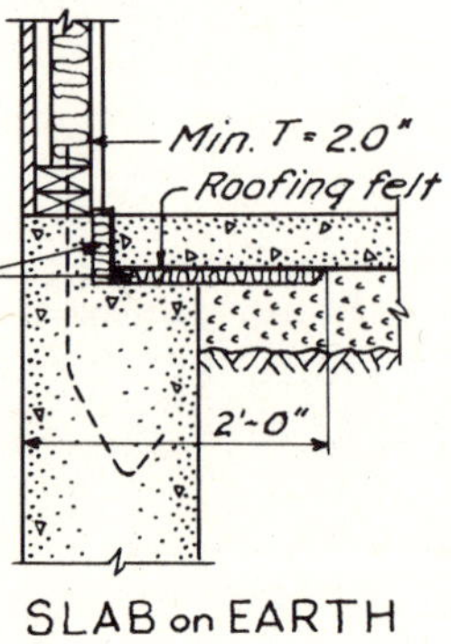
Min. T = 2.0"
Roofing felt
2'-0"

SLAB on EARTH

INSULATION APPLICATIONS

For further information see "Insulation"

Vermiculite and insulation materials which are produced in batt or blanket form are also available in granular form for hand pouring or pneumatic blowing.

LOOSE FILL

Aggregates of vermiculite, a mica-like mineral expanded under heat are used to produce insulating concrete & insulating plaster. Also available in a form for pouring between ceiling joists.

INSULATING CONCRETE & PLASTER

Scale: ½" = 1'-0" Unless Noted

INSULATING VALUES of EXTERIOR WALLS

EXPLANATORY NOTES

These notes pertain to all pages on insulating values of exterior walls.

1. U-factor is the overall heat-loss factor (BTU/hr./sq.ft./F° for total wall section).
2. For ¾" lath and plaster, ¾" metal lath and plaster was assumed.
3. For 1½" metal furring, (1) one air space was assumed. Where metal furring is shown, wood furring may be used with similar results.
4. Plaster was assumed to be three coats gypsum plaster (sand aggregate).
5. Concrete block was assumed to be made of sand and gravel aggregate.
6. Brick walls were assumed to be 4" face brick, the remainder common brick.
7. For all insulation except foamglas & reflective type insulation, the average value of K= 0.30 was used.
8. For wood frame walls, studs have been included in all cases.
9. Where stone is indicated, any stone or granite may be used with similar results.

NOTE: Vapor barriers are desirable in air-conditioned buildings to reduce latent heat load and in all heated buildings to control or prevent condensation. In all cases, place insulation on warm-in-winter side of wall, as near inside as possible.

NOTE: U-factor calculations are based on installation details shown on "Insulating Materials" page.

For U-factor = 0.25:
no insulation

For U-factor = 0.16:
thin coat aluminum "Sisalation"
½" Kimsul" blanket insulation

For U-factor = 0.14:
1½" batt or roll type insulation

For U-factor = 0.13:
1" "Kimsul" blanket insulation
Type 1 "Alfol" foil blanket
Type 1A "Alfol" foil blanket

For U-factor = 0.12:
Type 2 "Infra" accordion insulation

For U-factor = 0.11:
2" batt or roll type insulation
1" "Kimsul" blanket reflective insulation
2" layers of aluminum with air space. "Metallation."
Type 4 Jr. "Infra" accordion insulation.

For U-factor = 0.09:
3" batt or roll type insulation
2" "Kimsul" blanket insulation
2" "Kimsul" blanket reflective insulation
Type 4 "Infra" accordion insulation
Type 2 "Alfol" foil blanket
Type 3 "Alfol" foil blanket

For U-factor = 0.08:
Type 4 "Alfol" foil blanket
Type 6 "Infra" accordion insulation

(FRAMING: wood siding; 13/16" wood sheathing; 3⅝" wood studs; ¾" metal lath & plaster).

COMPARATIVE TYPES OF INSULATION IN WOOD STUD WALLS

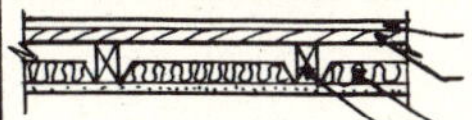

Siding or shingles
13/16" sheathing
2" insulation batts
3 ⅝" wood studs
FRAMING

For U-factor = 0.11
¾" plaster
⅜" gypsum wall board
½" gypsum wall board
⅜" gypsum lath & ½" plaster
2 layers of ⅜" gypsum wallboard
5/32" hardboard, pressed wood
⅜" asbestos cement board
¼" plywood strips & ¼" plywood
¾" plaster & ⅜" ceramic tile
¾" plaster & 3/32" vinyl tile
¾" plaster & ⅛" cork tile
¾" plaster & 3/16" cork tile
¾" plaster & metal tile

For U-factor = 0.10
¾" plywood

COMPARATIVE INTERIOR FINISHES ON WOOD FRAMING

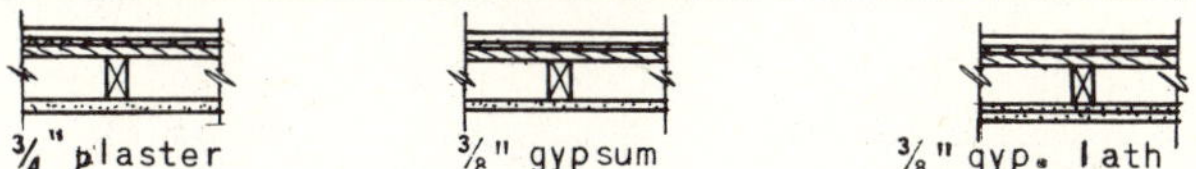

¾" plaster
⅜" gypsum wallboard
⅜" gyp. lath with alum. foil ½" plaster

	¾" plaster	⅜" gypsum wallboard	⅜" gyp. lath with alum. foil ½" plaster
U-factor:	0.19	0.19	0.15

(FRAMING: wood siding; ⅜" cane fiber shingle backer; 13/16" wood sheathing; 3⅝" stud.)

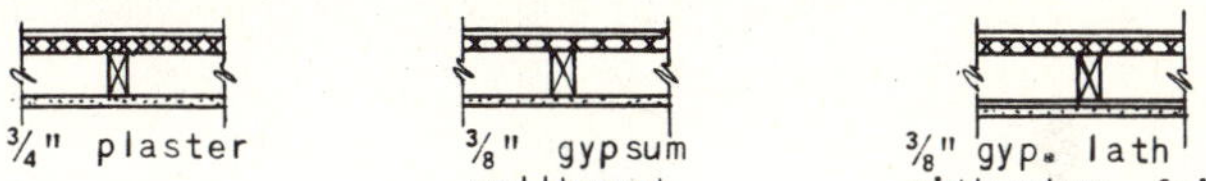

¾" plaster
⅜" gypsum wallboard
⅜" gyp. lath with alum. foil ½" plaster

	¾" plaster	⅜" gypsum wallboard	⅜" gyp. lath with alum. foil ½" plaster
U-factor:	0.20	0.19	0.15

(FRAMING: wood siding; 25/32" insulation sheathing; 3⅝" wood stud.)

COMPARATIVE SHEATHING INSULATION FOR WOOD STUD WALLS

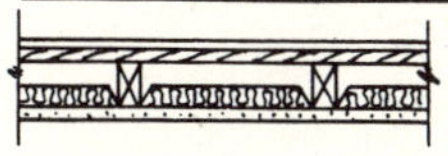

	U-factor
asbestos shingle	0.12
aluminum siding	0.12
wood siding	0.11
wood shingle	0.11
¾" vertical boards	0.11
2"x8" log siding	0.09

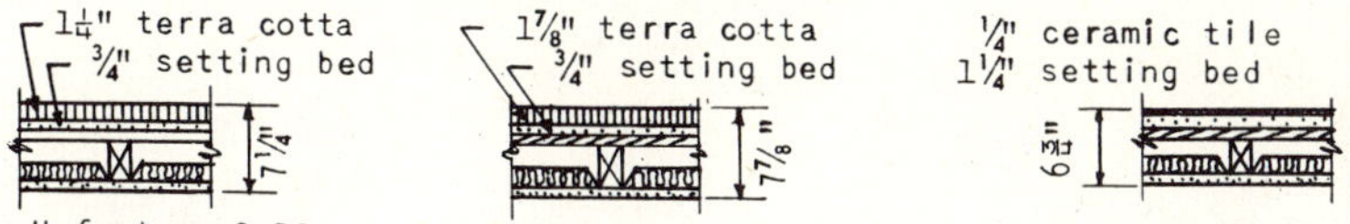

1¼" terra cotta
¾" setting bed
7¼"
1⅞" terra cotta
¾" setting bed
7⅞"
¼" ceramic tile
1¼" setting bed
6¾"

U-factor: 0.12 — terra cotta facing; 0.12; 0.12 — ceramic tile facing

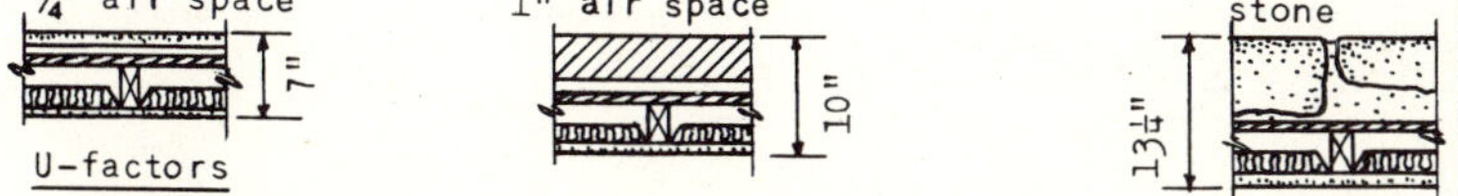

1" stucco
¾" air space
7"
3¾" brick
1" air space
10"
4" to 7" stone
13¼"

U-factors: 0.11 — cement stucco facing; 0.10 — brick veneer; 0.11 — stone veneer

(FRAMING: 13/16" wood sheathing; 3⅝" stud; 2" batt insulation; ¾" metal lath and plaster.)

COMPARATIVE EXTERIOR FINISHES ON WOOD FRAMING

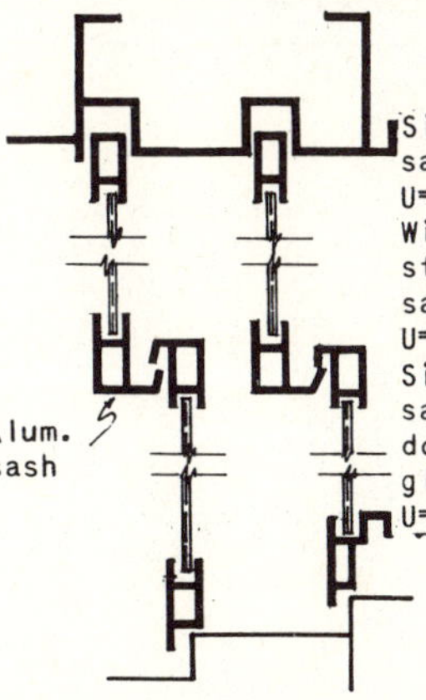

Single sash: U=1.13
With storm sash: U=0.58
Single sash with double glazing: U=0.72
Alum. sash

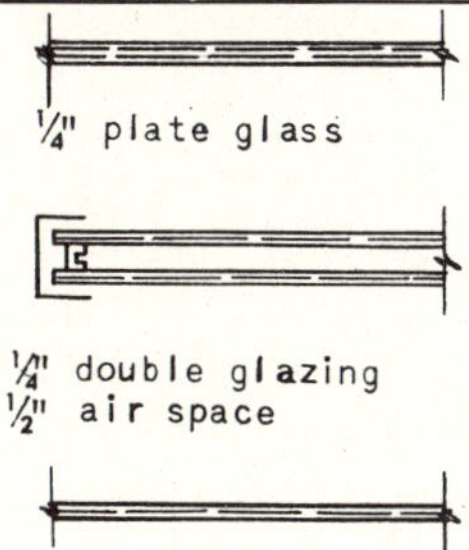

	U-factors
¼" plate glass	1.13
¼" double glazing ½" air space	0.55
⅛" glass	1.13

Above factors apply to glass sheet only.

WINDOWS AND GLASS

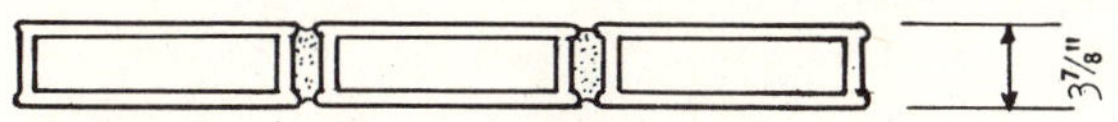

3⅞

			U-factor
15 ¾"	x	5 ¾"	= 0.60
7 ¾"	x	7 ¾"	= 0.56
11 ¾"	x	11 ¾	= 0.52

4" GLASS BLOCK

HEAT LOSS CALCULATIONS BY MONGITORE & MOESEL, CONSULTING ENGINEERS

INSULATING VALUES of EXTERIOR WALLS

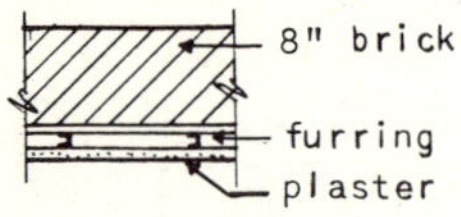
8" brick
furring
plaster

CONTACT TYPE

NOTE: For a fairly accurate U-factor of a wall having a type of furring different from furring shown in exterior wall examples: Find the difference in value between desired furring and furring shown in exterior wall to be used. Add or subtract this difference from U-factor for wall.

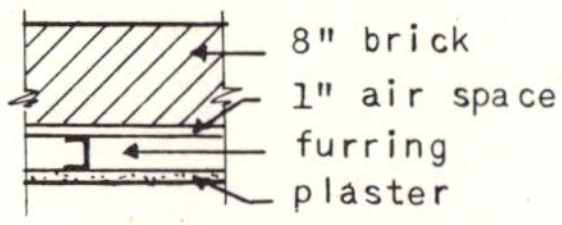
8" brick
1" air space
furring
plaster

FREE-STANDING TYPE

For U-factor = 0.44, use:
2" contact struc. facing tile & ⅝" plaster

For U-factor = 0.32, use:
¾" steel contact furring with ¾" cross-furring & ¾" plaster,
OR 1" x 2" wood contact furring with 1"x2" cross-furring & ¾" plaster,
OR 1"x2" wood contact furring & ¾" plaster,
OR 2"x3" wood contact furring & ¾" plaster,
OR 2"x4" wood contact furring & ¾" plaster

For U-factor = 0.31, use:
2" contact gyp. block & ½" plaster

For U-factor = 0.32, use:
3¼" free-standing metal studs & ¾" plaster,
OR 2"x3" free-standing wood studs & ¾" plaster,
OR 2"x4" free-standing wood studs & ¾" plaster

For U-factor = 0.26, use:
3" free-standing structural facing tile & ⅝" plaster,
OR 4" conc. block & ¾" plaster

For U-factor = 0.21, use:
3" free-standing gypsum block & ½" plaster

COMPARATIVE TYPES OF FURRING ON 8" BRICK

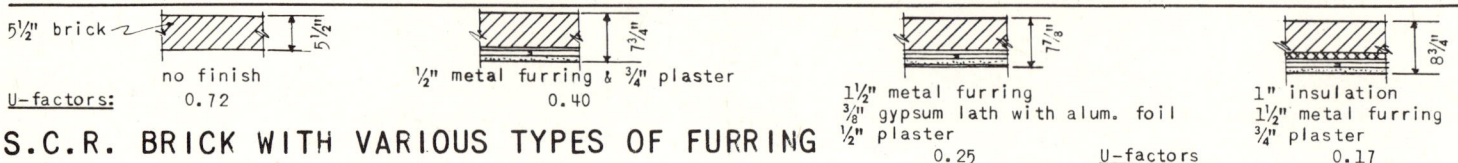

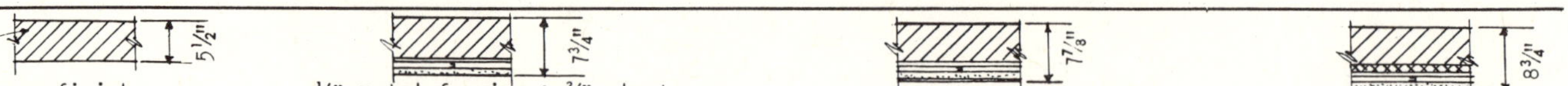
5½" brick
5½"
7¾"
7⅞"
8¾"

	no finish	½" metal furring & ¾" plaster	1½" metal furring, ⅜" gypsum lath with alum. foil, ½" plaster	1" insulation, 1½" metal furring, ¾" plaster
U-factors	0.72	0.40	0.25	0.17

S.C.R. BRICK WITH VARIOUS TYPES OF FURRING

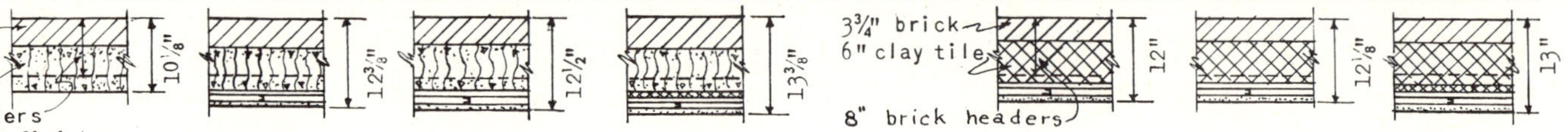
3¾" brick
6" (5⅝") conc. block
8" brick headers
10⅞"
12⅜"
12½"
13⅜"
3¾" brick
6" clay tile
8" brick headers
12"
12⅛"
13"

U-factors using:	no finish	1½" metal furring, ¾" lath & plaster	1½" metal furring, ⅜" gyp. lath with alum. foil, ½" plaster	1" insulation, 1½" metal furr'g, ¾" lath & plaster
6" (5⅝") block	0.48	0.31	0.21	0.15
8" (7⅝") block	0.44	0.29	0.20	0.15

U-factor using:	no finish	1½" metal furring, ¾" lath & plaster	1½" metal furring, ⅜" gyp. lath with alum. foil, ½" plaster	1" insulation, 1½" metal furring, ¾" lath & plaster
6" tile	0.26	0.19	0.14	
8" tile	0.24	0.18	0.13	

For 8" concrete block & 8" clay tile, add 2" to overall dimensions given above for each type of back-up.

4" BRICK FACING WITH VARIOUS TYPES OF FURRING

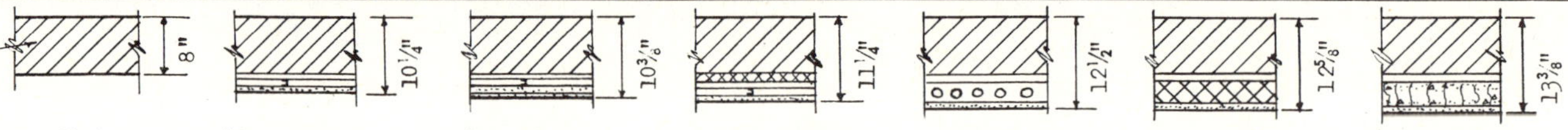
8" brick
8"
10¼"
10⅜"
11¼"
12½"
12⅝"
13⅜"

U-factors using:	no finish	1½" metal furring, ¾" lath & plaster	1½" metal furring, ⅜" gyp. lath with alum. foil, ½" plaster	1" insulation, 1½" metal furring, ¾" lath & plaster	1" air space, 3" gyp. block, ½" plaster	1" air space, 3" clay tile, ⅝" plaster	1" air space, 4" (3⅝") conc., ¾" plaster
8" brick	0.50	0.32	0.15	0.22	0.21	0.26	0.26
12" brick	0.36	0.25	0.14	0.19	0.18	0.21	0.22

For 12" brick wall, add 2½" to overall dimension given above

8" & 12" BRICK WALLS WITH VARIOUS TYPES OF FURRING

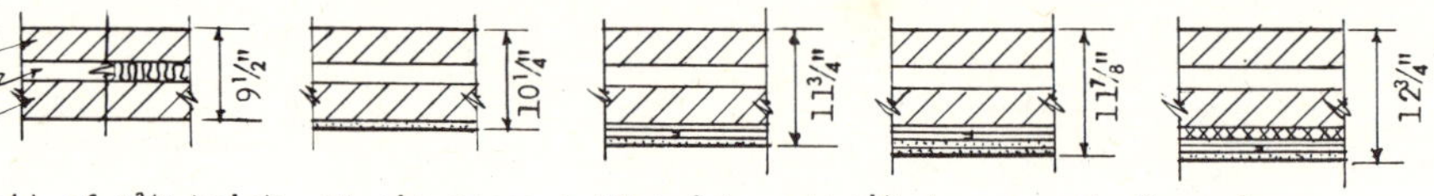
3¾" brick
2" air space
3¾" brick
9½"
10¼"
11¾"
11⅞"
12⅞"

For cavity wall of 3¾" brick, 2" air space & 8" brick, add 4½" to overall dimension.

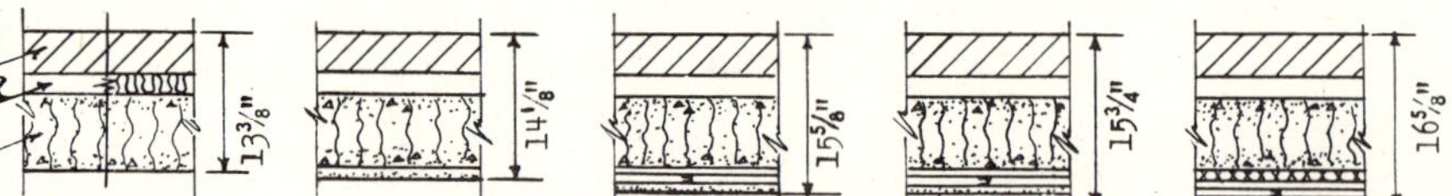
3¾" brick
2" air space
7⅝" conc. block
13⅜"
14⅛"
15⅝"
15¾"
16⅝"

U-factors using:	no finish, no insulation	no finish, insulation	¾" plaster	1½" metal furring, ¾" lath & plaster	1½" metal furring, ⅜" gyp. lath with alum. foil, ½" plaster	1" insulation, 1½" metal furring, ¾" lath & plaster
3¾" brick:	0.35	0.12	0.33	0.24	0.18	0.14
8" brick:	0.27	0.11	0.26	0.21	0.16	0.12
8" (7⅝") block:	0.31	0.11	0.30	0.23	0.17	0.13

10" & 14" CAVITY WALLS WITH VARIOUS TYPES OF FINISHES

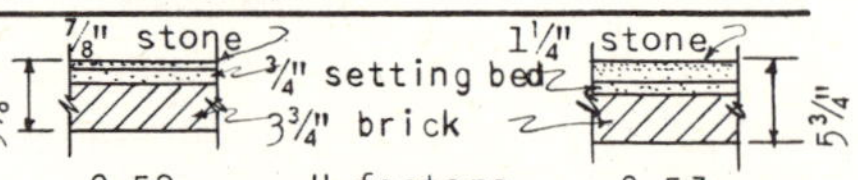
⅞" stone
¾" setting bed
3¾" brick
1¼" stone
5⅜"
5¾"

0.59 U-factors 0.57

ALBERENE STONE

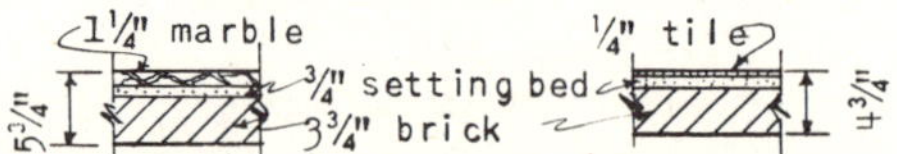
1¼" marble
¾" setting bed
3¾" brick
¼" tile
5¾"
4¾"

0.57 U-factors 0.59

MARBLE CERAMIC TILE

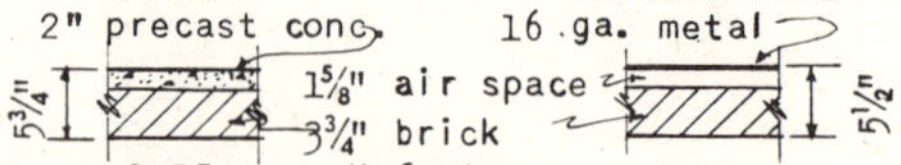
2" precast conc.
16 ga. metal
1⅝" air space
3¾" brick
5¾"
5½"

0.57 U-factors 0.41

PRECAST CONCRETE METAL FACING

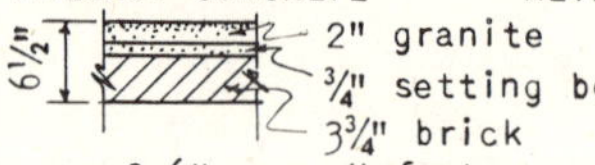
2" granite
¾" setting bed
3¾" brick
6½"

0.64 U-factor

PRECAST GRANITE

THIN SPANDREL VENEERS WITH 4" BACK-UP

HEAT LOSS CALCULATIONS BY MONGITORE & MOESEL, CONSULTING ENGINEERS

INSULATING VALUES of EXTERIOR WALLS

3⅝" block
2" air space
3⅝" block

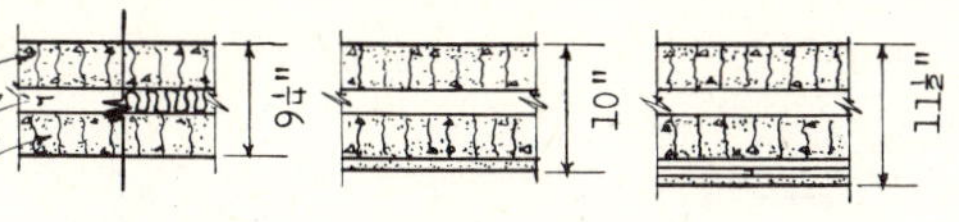
9¼"
10"
11½"

	no finish		¾" plaster	1½" metal furring ¾" lath & plaster
	no insulation	insulation		
U-factors:	0.32	0.12	0.31	0.24

10" CONCRETE BLOCK CAVITY WALLS

2" concrete
2" insulation
2" concrete

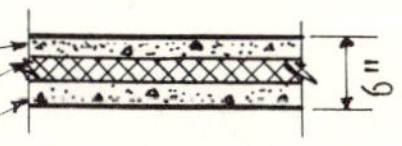
6"

U - factor is 0.13.

6" CONCRETE SANDWICH WALLS

1⅞" terra cotta
2½" setting bed
8" concrete

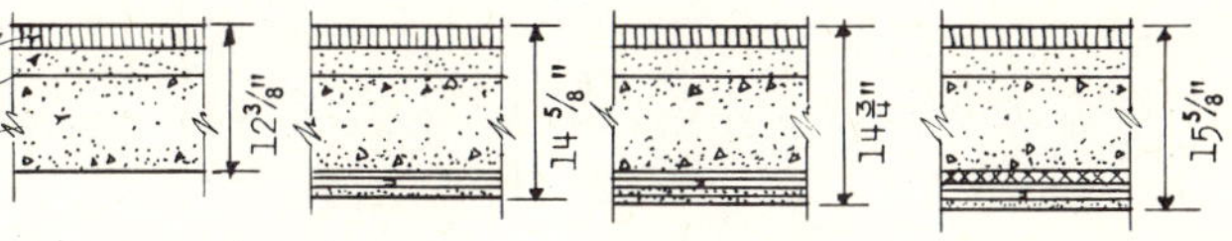
12⅜"
14⅝"
14¾"
15⅝"

	no finish	1½" metal furring ¾" lath & plaster	1½" metal furring ⅜" gyp. lath with alum. foil	1" insulation 1½" metal furring ¾" lath & plas.
U - factors:	0.51	0.32	0.22	0.16

1⅞" TERRA COTTA WITH VARIOUS TYPES OF BACKING

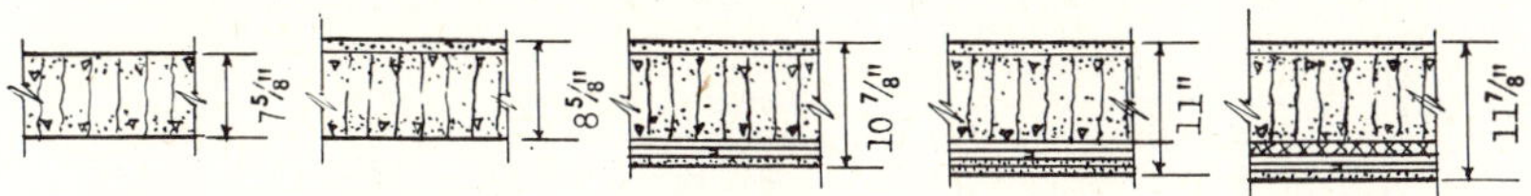
7⅝"
8⅝"
10⅞"
11"
11⅞"

U-factors using:	no finish	1" stucco on exterior no interior finish	1" stucco 1½" metal furring ¾" plaster	1" stucco 1½" metal furring ⅜" gyp. lath with alum. foil ½" plaster	1" stucco 1" insulation 1½" metal furring ¾" plaster
8" (7⅝") block:	0.53	0.51	0.32	0.22	0.16
10" (9⅝") block:	0.51	0.49	0.31	0.22	0.15
12" (11⅝") block:	0.49	0.48	0.31	0.21	0.15

Shown above is 8" concrete block. For 10" and 12" block, add 2" and 4" to overall dimension shown.

8", 10" & 12" CONCRETE BLOCK WITH VARIOUS FURRING

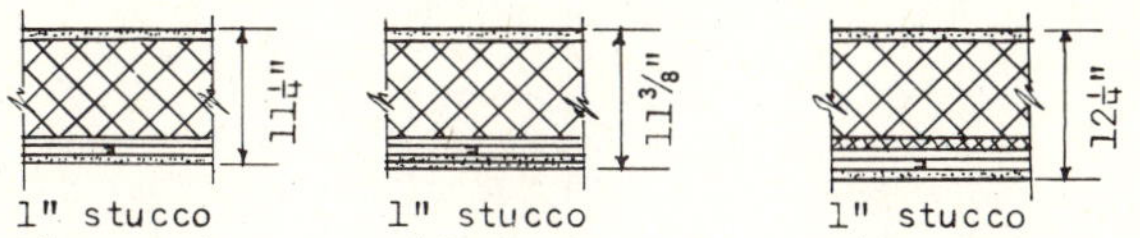
11¼"
11⅜"
12¼"

U-factors using:	1" stucco 1½" metal furring ¾" lath & plaster	1" stucco 1½" metal furring ⅜" gyp. lath with alum. foil ½" plaster	1" stucco 1½" metal furring ¾" plaster
8" tile:	0.26	0.19	0.14
10" tile:	0.24	0.18	0.13
12" tile:	0.22	0.17	0.13

Shown above is 8" tile. For 10" & 12" tile, add 2" & 4" to overall dimension shown.

STRUCTURAL CLAY TILE (VERTICAL UNITS)

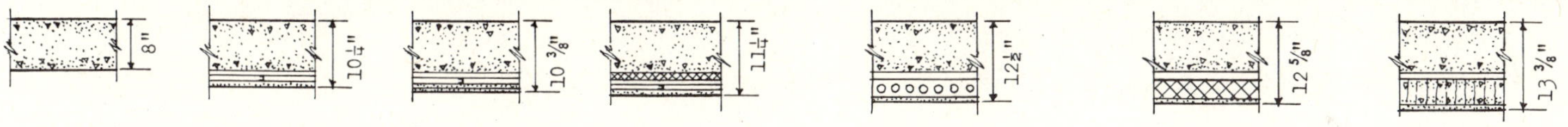
8"
10¼"
10⅜"
11¼"
12½"
12⅝"
13¾"

U-factors for:	no finish	1½" metal furring ¾" lath & plas.	1½" metal furring ⅜" gyp. lath with alum. foil ½" plaster	1" insulation 1½" metal furring ¾" lath & plas.	1" air space 3" gyp. block ½" plaster	1" air space 3" clay tile ⅝" plaster	1" air space 4" (3⅝") concrete block ¾" plaster
8" conc.	0.60	0.36	0.24	0.16	0.23	0.29	0.29
10" conc.	0.56	0.34	0.23	0.16	0.23	0.28	0.28
12" conc.	0.47	0.31	0.21	0.15	0.21	0.25	0.26

Shown above is 8" conc. wall. For 10" & 12" walls, add 2" & 4" to overall dimensions given above.

8" 10" & 12" CONCRETE WALLS

⅜" asbestos
8" (7⅝") conc. block

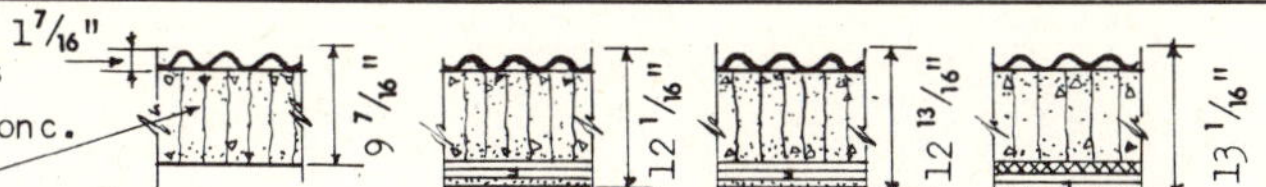
1 7/16"
9 7/16"
12 1/16"
12 13/16"
13 1/16"

U-factor using finishes given below: 0.41 | 0.28 | 0.20 | 0.15

⅜" asbestos
1½" furring
8" (7⅝") conc. block

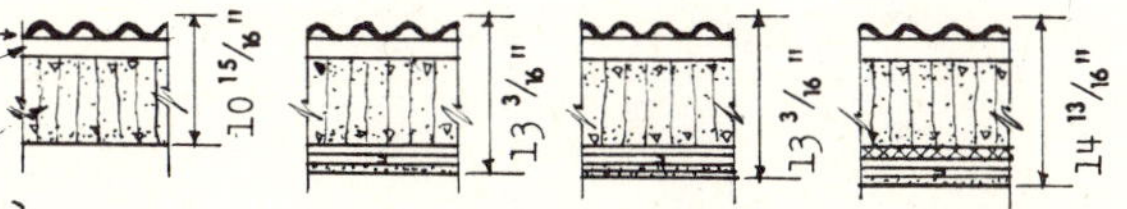
10 15/16"
13 3/16"
13 3/16"
14 13/16"

U-factor using finishes given below: 0.34 | 0.25 | 0.18 | 0.14

no finish	1½" metal furring ¾" plaster	1½" metal furring ⅜" gyp. lath with alum. foil ½" plaster	1" insulation 1½" metal furring ¾" plaster

CORRUGATED ASBESTOS SIDING WITH CONCRETE BLOCK BACK-UP

3¾" brick
1" air space
8" conc.

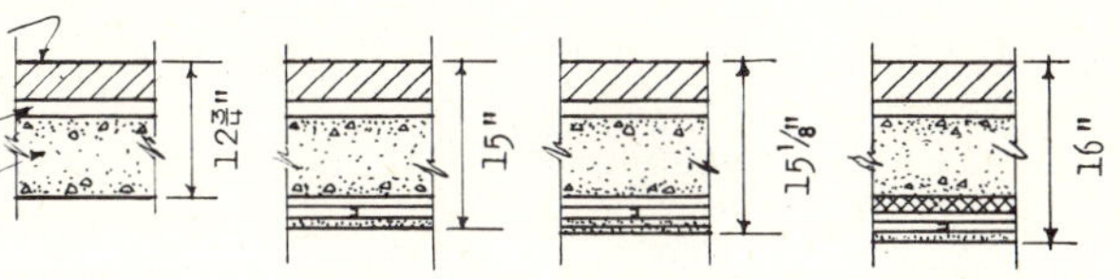
12¾"
15"
15⅛"
16"

	no finish	1½" metal furring ¾" lath & plaster	1½" metal furring ⅜" gyp. lath with alum. foil ½" plaster	1" insulation 1½" metal furring ¾" lath & plaster
U-factor:	0.33	0.24	0.18	0.13

4" BRICK VENEER ON CONCRETE

HEAT LOSS CALCULATIONS BY MONGITORE & MOESEL, CONSULTING ENGINEERS

INSULATING VALUES of EXTERIOR WALLS

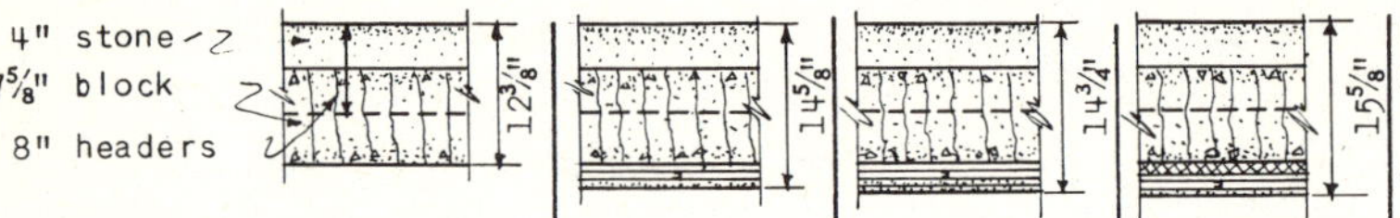
4" stone
7⅝" block
8" headers
12¾"
14⅝"
14¾"
15⅝"

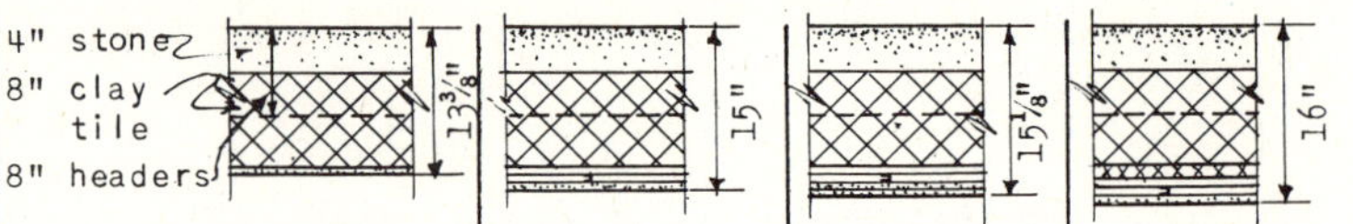
4" stone
8" clay tile
8" headers
12⅜"
15"
15⅛"
16"

U-factors using:					U-factors using:				
8" (7⅝") block	0.43	0.29	0.21	0.15	8" tile	0.32	0.23	0.17	0.13
10" (9⅝") block	0.42	0.28	0.20	0.15	10" tile	0.31	0.23	0.17	0.13
12" (11⅝") block	0.40	0.28	0.20	0.14	12" tile	0.30	0.22	0.17	0.13

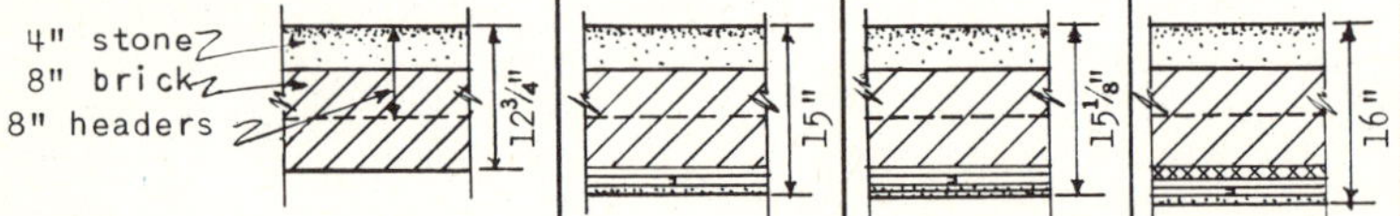
4" stone
8" brick
8" headers
12¾"
15"
15⅛"
16"

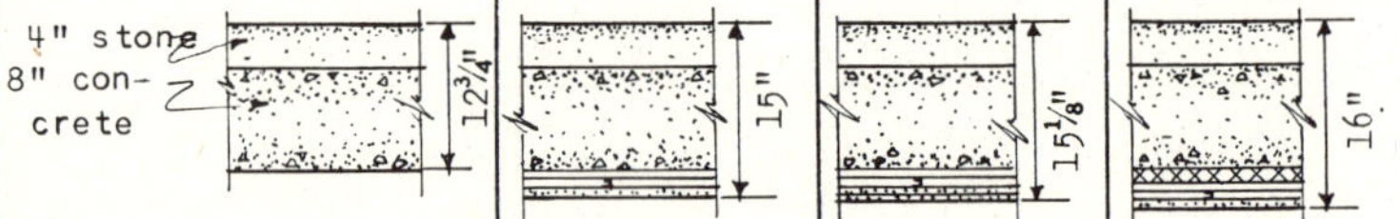
4" stone
8" concrete
12¾"
15"
15⅝"
16"

U-factors using:					U-factors using:				
8" brick	0.36	0.26	0.19	0.14	8" concrete	0.51	0.32	0.22	0.16
10" brick	0.35	0.25	0.18	0.14	10" concrete	0.48	0.31	0.21	0.15
12" brick	0.34	0.25	0.18	0.14	12" concrete	0.47	0.30	0.21	0.15
	no finish.	1½" metal furring ¾" plaster	1½" metal furring ⅜" gyp. lath with alum inum foil ½" plaster	1" insulation 1½" metal furring ¾" plaster	tile has ⅝" plaster concrete has no finish		1½" metal furring ¾" plaster	1½" metal furring ⅜" gyp. lath with aluminum foil ½" plaster	1" insulation 1½" metal furring ¾" plaster

For 10" and 12" backings, add 2" and 4" to overall dimensions shown.

4" STONE WITH VARIOUS TYPES OF BACKING

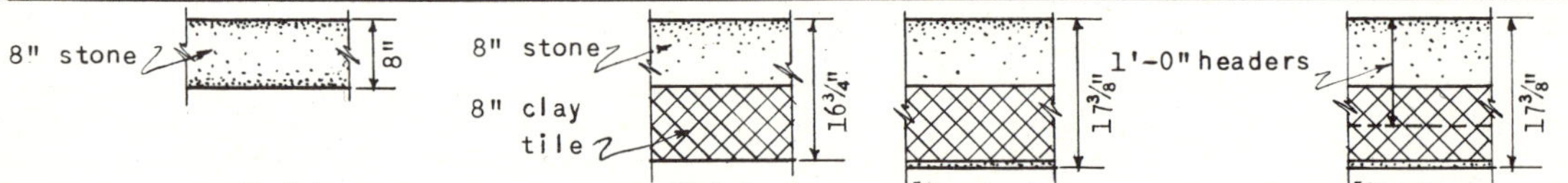
8" stone
8"
8" stone
8" clay tile
16¾"
17⅜"
1'-0" headers
17⅜"

	no finish	no finish	⅝" plaster	⅝" plaster
U-factor:	0.17	0.31	0.30	0.30

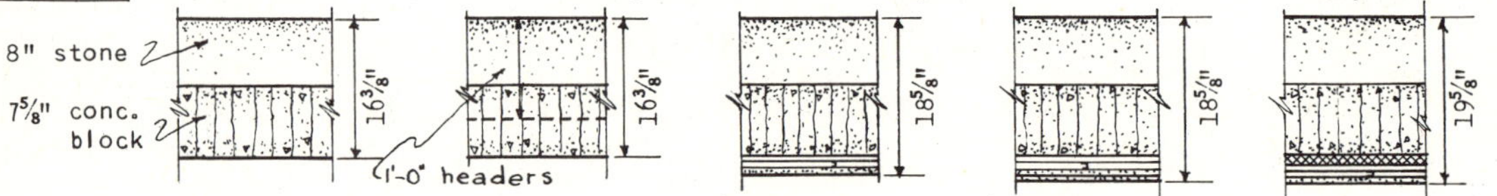
8" stone
7⅝" conc. block
16⅜"
1'-0" headers
16⅜"
18⅝"
18⅝"
19⅝"

	no finish	no finish	1½" metal furring ¾" plaster	1½" metal furring ⅜" gyp. lath with aluminum foil ½" plaster	1" insulation 1½" metal furring ¾" plaster
U-factors:	0.40	0.40	0.27	0.20	0.14

8" STONE WITH VARIOUS TYPES OF BACKING

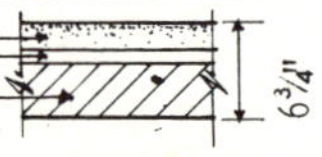
6¾"

2" stone
1" air space
3¾" brick
U-factor: 0.41
LIMESTONE FACING

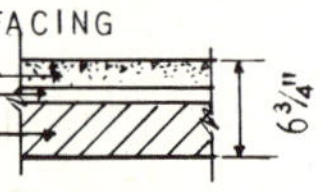
6¾"

2" pre-cast conc.
1" air space
3¾" brick
U-factor: 0.38
PRE-CAST CONCRETE FACING

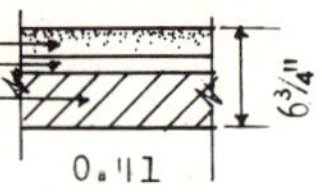
6¾"

2" stone
1" air space
3¾" brick
U-factor: 0.41
GRANITE FACING

7" STONE CAVITY SPANDREL

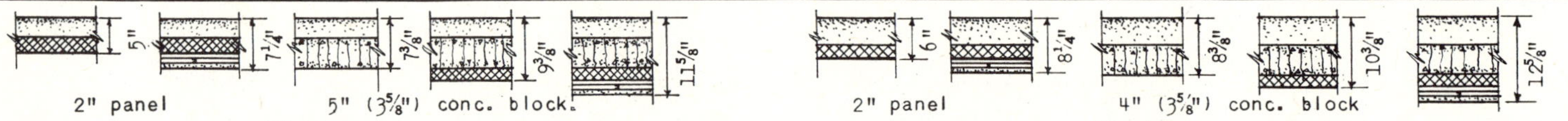
5"
7½"
7⅜"
9⅜"
11⅝"
6"
8¼"
8⅜"
10⅜"
12⅝"

	3" stone: 2" panel		3" stone: 5" (3⅝") conc. block			4" stone: 2" panel		4" stone: 4" (3⅝") conc. block		
	2" insulation 16 ga. steel	2" insulation 1½" metal furring ¾" plaster	concrete block	conc. block 2" insulation	conc. block 2" insulation 1½" metal furring ¾" plaster	2" insulation 16 ga. steel	2" insulation 1½" metal furring ¾" plaster	concrete block	conc. block 2" insulation	conc. block 2" insulation 1½" metal furring ¾" plaster
U-FACTORS:	0.13	0.11	0.55	0.12	0.10	0.13	0.11	0.53	0.18	0.10

3" & 4" STONE VENEER WITH VARIOUS TYPES OF BACKING

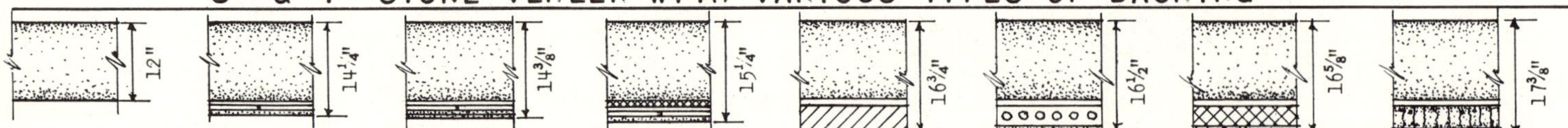
12"
14¼"
14⅜"
15¼"
16¾"
16½"
16⅝"
17⅜"

U-FACTORS	no finish	1½" metal furring ¾" plaster	1½" metal furring ⅜" gyp. lath with aluminum foil ½" plaster	1" insulation 1½" metal furring ¾" plaster	1" air space 3¾" brick	1" air space 3" gyp. block ½" plaster	1" air space 3" clay tile ⅝" plaster	1" air space 4" (3⅝") conc. block ¾" plaster
12" stone:	0.58	0.35	0.23	0.16	0.30	0.23	0.28	0.29
18" stone:	0.45	0.30	0.21	0.15	0.26	0.21	0.25	0.25

12" stone wall shown. For 18" stone wall, add 6" to overall dimension.

12" & 18" STONE WALLS WITH VARIOUS TYPES OF BACKING

HEAT LOSS CALCULATIONS BY MONGITORE & MOESEL, CONSULTING ENGINEERS.

INSULATING VALUES of EXTERIOR WALLS

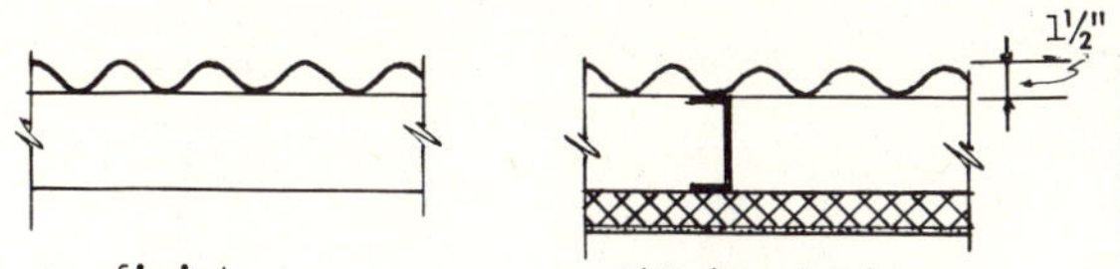
no finish
1½" insulation
3/8" asbestos sheets

	U-factor	
no finish	1.1	
1½" insulation, 3/8" asbestos sheets		0.15

CORRUGATED ASBESTOS ON 4" STEEL STUDS

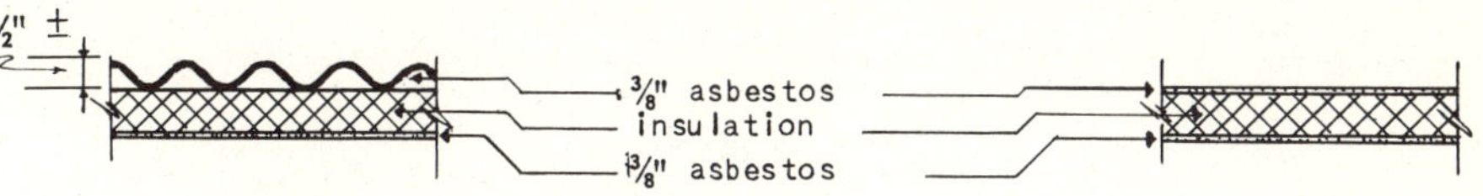
1½" ±
1½" ±
3/8" asbestos
insulation
3/8" asbestos

U-factor (corrugated)		U-factor (flat)
0.19	1" insulation	0.23
0.15	1½" insulation	0.17
0.12	2" insulation	0.13
0.10	2½" insulation	0.11
0.08	3" insulation	0.09

BOX TYPE ASBESTOS PANEL CURTAIN WALLS

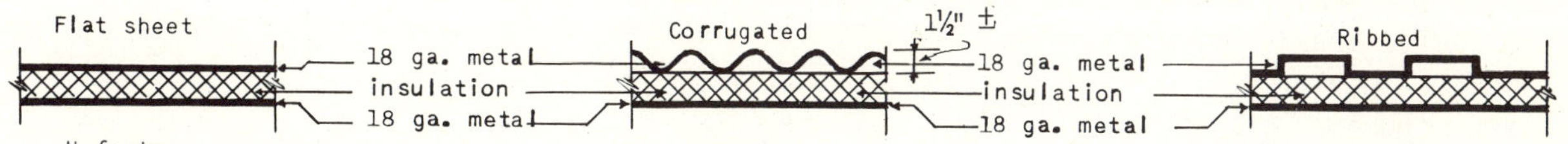
Flat sheet
Corrugated
1½" ±
Ribbed
18 ga. metal
insulation
18 ga. metal
18 ga. metal
insulation
18 ga. metal

	Flat sheet U-factor	Corrugated U-factor	Ribbed U-factor
1" insulation	0.24	0.21	0.22
1½" insulation	0.17	0.15	0.16
2" insulation	0.14	0.12	0.13
2½" insulation	0.11	0.10	0.11
3" insulation	0.09	0.09	0.09

BOX TYPE ALUMINUM, STAINLESS STEEL, OR PORCELAIN ENAMEL ON ALUMINUM OR STEEL PANEL CURTAIN WALLS

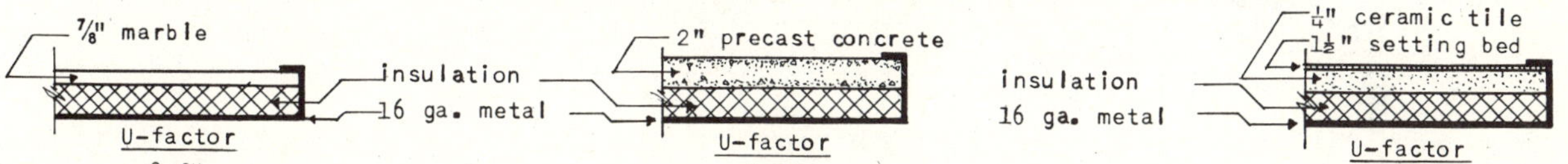
7/8" marble
insulation
16 ga. metal
2" precast concrete
¼" ceramic tile
1½" setting bed
insulation
16 ga. metal

	Marble U-factor	Precast concrete U-factor	Ceramic tile U-factor
1" insulation	0.24	0.23	0.23
1½" insulation	0.18	0.17	0.17
2" insulation	0.13	0.13	0.13
2½" insulation	0.11	0.11	0.11
3" insulation	0.09	0.09	0.09

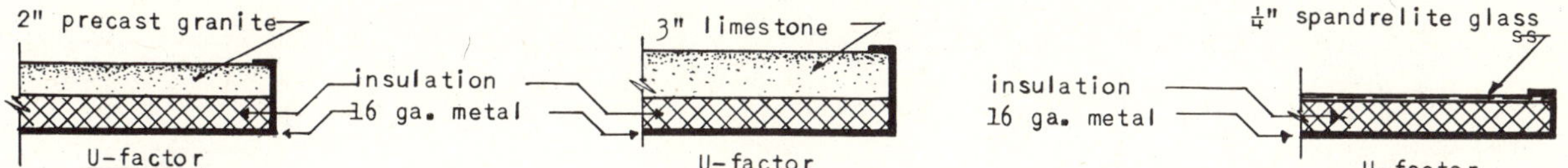
2" precast granite
insulation
16 ga. metal
3" limestone
¼" spandrelite glass
SS
insulation
16 ga. metal

	Precast granite U-factor	Limestone U-factor	Spandrelite glass U-factor
1" insulation	0.23	0.23	0.24
1½" insulation	0.17	0.17	0.17
2" insulation	0.13	0.13	0.13
2½" insulation	0.11	0.11	0.11
3" insulation	0.09	0.09	0.09

BOX TYPE OF CURTAIN WALLS

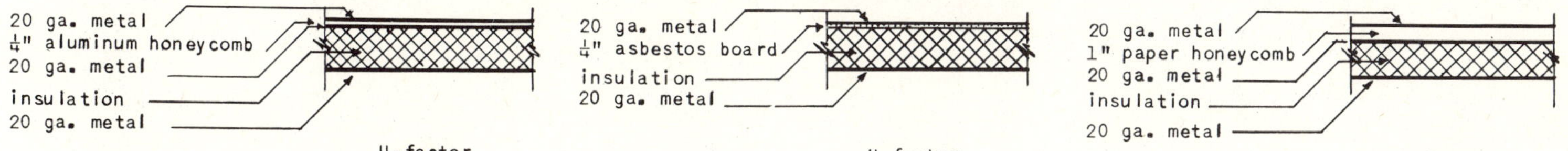
20 ga. metal
¼" aluminum honeycomb
20 ga. metal
insulation
20 ga. metal
20 ga. metal
¼" asbestos board
insulation
20 ga. metal
20 ga. metal
1" paper honeycomb
20 ga. metal
insulation
20 ga. metal

	Aluminum honeycomb U-factor	Asbestos board U-factor	Paper honeycomb U-factor
1" insulation	0.21	0.24	0.20
1½" insulation	0.16	0.17	0.15
2" insulation	0.12	0.13	0.12
2½" insulation	0.10	0.11	0.10
3" insulation	0.09	0.09	0.09

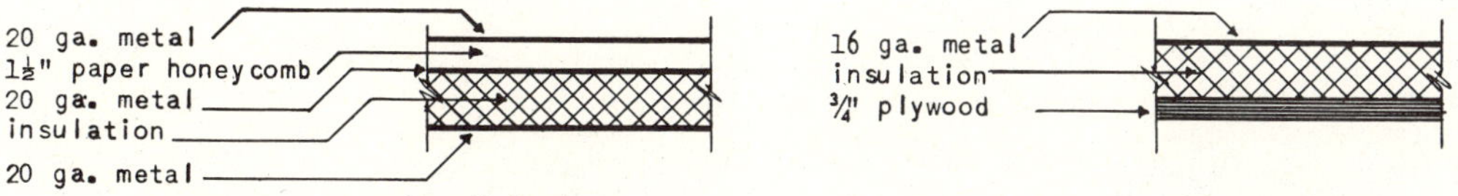
20 ga. metal
1½" paper honeycomb
20 ga. metal
insulation
20 ga. metal
16 ga. metal
insulation
¾" plywood

	Paper honeycomb U-factor	Plywood U-factor
1" insulation	0.20	0.20
1½" insulation	0.15	0.15
2" insulation	0.12	0.12
2½" insulation	0.10	0.10
3" insulation	0.09	0.09

NOTE: All heat loss factors given on this page are for the panel only - joints are not included.

SANDWICH TYPE OF CURTAIN WALLS.

HEAT LOSS CALCULATIONS BY MONGITORE & MOESEL, CONSULTING ENGINEERS

INSULATING MATERIALS & THEIR EFFECT ON OVERALL HEAT TRANSMISSION VALUES OF EXTERIOR WALLS

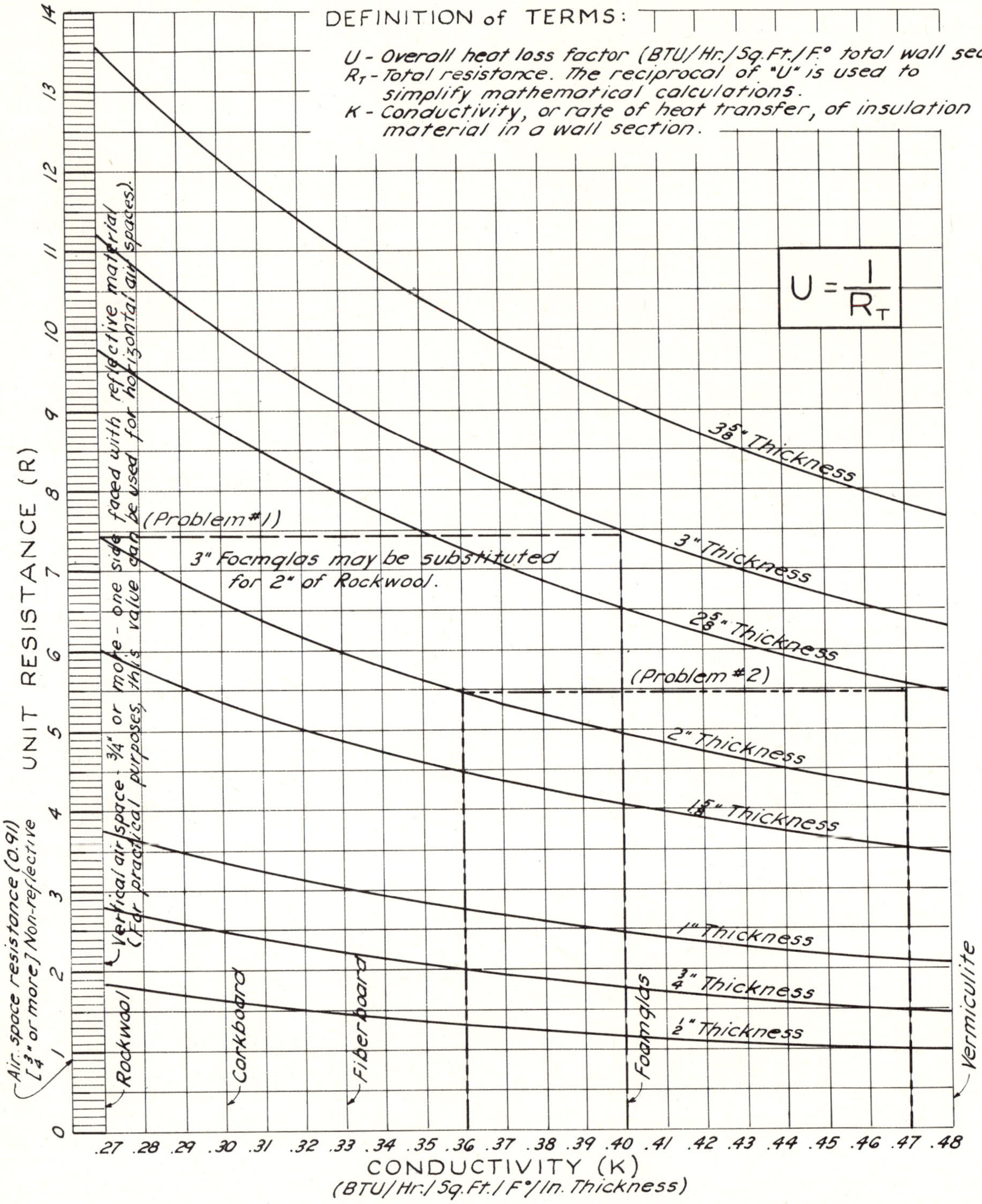
DEFINITION of TERMS:
U - Overall heat loss factor (BTU/Hr./Sq.Ft./F° total wall sect.)
R_T - Total resistance. The reciprocal of "U" is used to simplify mathematical calculations.
K - Conductivity, or rate of heat transfer, of insulation material in a wall section.
$U = \frac{1}{R_T}$
UNIT RESISTANCE (R)
0
1
2
3
4
5
6
7
8
9
10
11
12
13
14
Air space resistance (0.91) [3/4" or more] Non-reflective
Vertical air space: 3/4" or more - one side faced with reflective material (For practical purposes, this value can be used for horizontal air spaces).
(Problem #1)
3" Foamglas may be substituted for 2" of Rockwool.
(Problem #2)
3 5/8" Thickness
3" Thickness
2 5/8" Thickness
2" Thickness
1 5/8" Thickness
1" Thickness
3/4" Thickness
1/2" Thickness
Rockwool
Corkboard
Fiberboard
Foamglas
Vermiculite
.27 .28 .29 .30 .31 .32 .33 .34 .35 .36 .37 .38 .39 .40 .41 .42 .43 .44 .45 .46 .47 .48
CONDUCTIVITY (K)
(BTU/Hr./Sq.Ft./F°/In. Thickness)

RESISTANCE - CONDUCTIVITY GRAPH

OVERALL HEAT LOSS FACTOR U	TOTAL RESISTANCE R_T
.60	1.66
.59	1.69
.58	1.72
.57	1.76
.56	1.79
.55	1.82
.54	1.85
.53	1.89
.52	1.92
.51	1.96
.50	2.00
.49	2.04
.48	2.08
.47	2.13
.46	2.17
.45	2.22
.44	2.27
.43	2.33
.42	2.38
.41	2.44
.40	2.50
.39	2.56
.38	2.63
.37	2.70
.36	2.78
.35	2.86
.34	2.94
.33	3.03
.32	3.13
.31	3.23
.30	3.34
.29	3.45
.28	3.57
.27	3.70
.26	3.85
.25	4.00
.24	4.17
.23	4.35
.22	4.55
.21	4.76
.20	5.00
.19	5.26
.18	5.55
.17	5.88
.16	6.25
.15	6.67
.14	7.15
.13	7.69
.12	8.35
.11	9.09
.10	10.00
.09	11.11
.08	12.50
.07	14.29
.06	16.67
.05	20.00

USE of GRAPH to COMPARE INSULATION VALUES of DIFFERENT MATERIALS:

PROBLEM #1: ———————— (As indicated above)

What thickness of Foamglas may be substituted for 2" of Rockwool without lowering efficiency?

Step 1 - Follow the vertical line of Rockwool conductivity (K = .27) until it intercepts the 2" thickness curve.

2 - Extend a horizontal line to intersect the vertical line of Foamglas conductivity (K = .40).

3 - Read the thickness line which appears above the intersection; in this case 3" of Foamglas is sufficient.

PROBLEM #2: —-——-——-— (As indicated above)

Find the relative thicknesses of two insulating materials to obtain the same insulating values

Given: For one, K = 0.47; for other, K = 0.36 and material is 2" thick.

Step 1 - Follow the vertical line of K = 0.36 until it intercepts the 2" thickness curve.

2 - From the intersection found in Step 1, extend a horizontal line to vertical line K = 0.47.

3 - Read the thickness line at the intersection; 2 5/8" of K = 0.40 is needed to replace 2" of K = 0.36.

Data checked by Mangitore & Moesel, Consulting Engineers

INSULATING MATERIALS & THEIR EFFECT ON OVERALL HEAT TRANSMISSION VALUES OF EXTERIOR WALLS

USE of RESISTANCE-CONDUCTIVITY GRAPH for VARIOUS INSULATING VALUES of WALLS:
(Use in conjunction with page titled "Insulating Values of Exterior Walls" to add, remove or substitute insulation)

Step 1 - Select type of wall construction from page titled "Insulating Values of Exterior Walls" and note its "U", or Overall Heat Loss Factor.
2 - Find the corresponding resistance in the "U-R_T" table alongside the "U" value.
3 - To this resistance add or subtract, as the case may be, the resistance of the insulating material added or removed. (Include resistance of air space.)
4 - Find the new Heat Loss Factor (U) in the Table of U Reciprocals opposite the calculated value of the new total resistance.

EXAMPLES

PROBLEM	STEP 1	STEP 2	STEP 3	STEP 4
What effect will:	*Select wall type*	*Use "U-R_T" table*	*Calculation*	*New insulating value & Wall section*

① ADDITION of 1" of Foamglas to a 12" brick wall with ¾" plaster have on the insulating value of the wall?

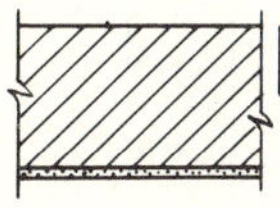

Step 1: .34

U	R_T
.34	2.94
.19	5.44

	2.94	
+R of 1" Foamglas	2.50	(From graph)
	5.44	= New R_T

Step 4: .19

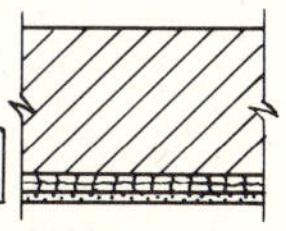

Note: Creation of an air space ¾" or more (R=0.91) may also be treated as an insulating material.

② REMOVAL of 1⅝" of rock wool have upon the insulating value of an 8" furred and plastered wall?

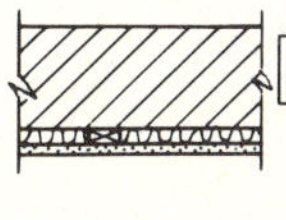

Step 1: .12

U	R_T
.12	8.35
.31	3.23

	8.35	
Less R of 1⅝" rock wool	6.03	(From graph)
	2.32	= Net R
+ R of created air space	0.91	(From graph)
	3.23	= New R_T

Step 4: .31

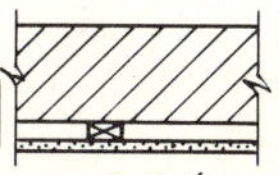

Note: Removal of insulation creates air space; its resistance must be added to Net R.

③ SUBSTITUTION of 3" of fiberboard for 1⅝" of rock wool have upon an 8" furred and plastered brick wall?

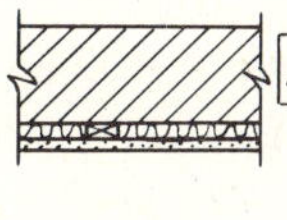

Step 1: .12

U	R_T
.12	8.35
.09	11.1

	8.35	
Less R of 1⅝" rock wool	6.03	(From graph)
	2.32	= Net R
+ R of 3" fiberboard	9.01	(From graph)
	11.33	= New R_T

Step 4: .09

Scale: ⅜" = 1'-0"

Note: In this case, substitution of insulation neither created nor eliminated an air space.

The above method of substituting materials applies only to those portions of the wall where substitution is being made - ie. in stud walls, the portion of wall with studs remains with original heat transmission.

Data checked by Mongitore & Moesel, Consulting Engineers

BATT-TYPE & BLANKET INSULATING MATERIALS

TYPE OF ENCLOSURE	INSULATING MATERIAL	SIZES OF BLANKETS	SIZES OF BATTS
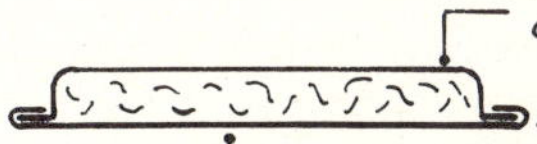 Reflective-coated cover; Reflective-coated backing combined with vapor barrier	Rock wool		2" thickness only. 15", 19" & 23" wide (some 15" only). Lengths 4'-0" & 8'-0" (some 2'-0").
	Wood fiber	1½" thickness available for 12", 16", 20", 24" & 33" stud spacing — 3" for 12", 16", 20" & 24" spacing	
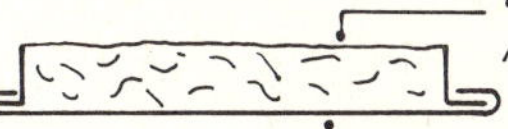 Vapor-permeable paper cover; Asphalt-coated or reflective-coated paper as vapor barrier.	Mineral wool (other than glass or rock).		1½", 2" & 3" thick. 15" & 19" wide (some 11" & 23"). 2'-0", 4'-0" & 8'-0" (1½" in 8'-0" only).
	Rock wool		1½", 2" (some 3") 15" wide (some 19" & 23"). 2'-0", 4'-0" & 8'-0" long.
	Glass wool	1½", 2" & 3" thick (some 2" & 3" only). 15", 19" & 23" wide. Rolls from 31'-0" to 80'-0"	2" & 3" (1½" in 15"×8'-0" only). 15" wide (23" in 4'-0" length). 2'-0", 4'-0" & 8'-0" long.
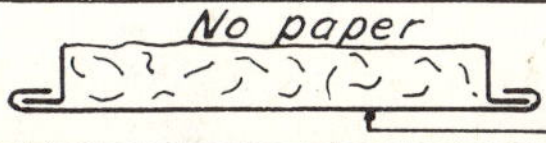 No paper; Asphalt-coated or reflective-coated paper	Glass wool	1½" thick 15", 19", 23" wide for 16", 20" & 24" stud spacing.	2" & 3" thick 15" × 2'-0"
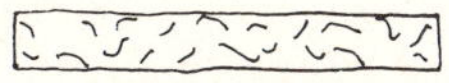 No paper backing or cover	Glass wool		2" thick 15" wide 4'-0" long

Rock wool, glass wool, other mineral wools & wood fiber available in loose form for pouring, spreading & pneumatic installation.

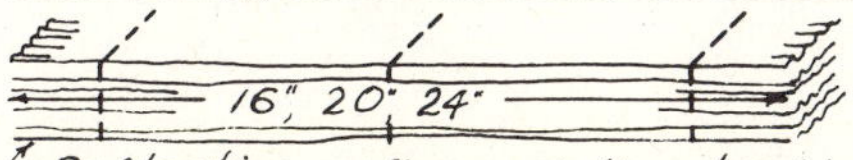

16", 20", 24"
Reflective or fire-resisting backing

Asphalt-treated cellulose plies, creped & stitched material. Accordion-like in application. ½", 1" & 2" thick, 16", 20", 24" & 48" widths. Reflective types made in 1" and 2" thicknesses. Thickness increases during application.

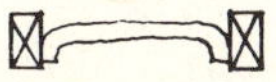

"KIMSUL" CREPED CELLULOSE PLIES with FIRE RESISTING BACKING

UNIVERSAL SUN CHART

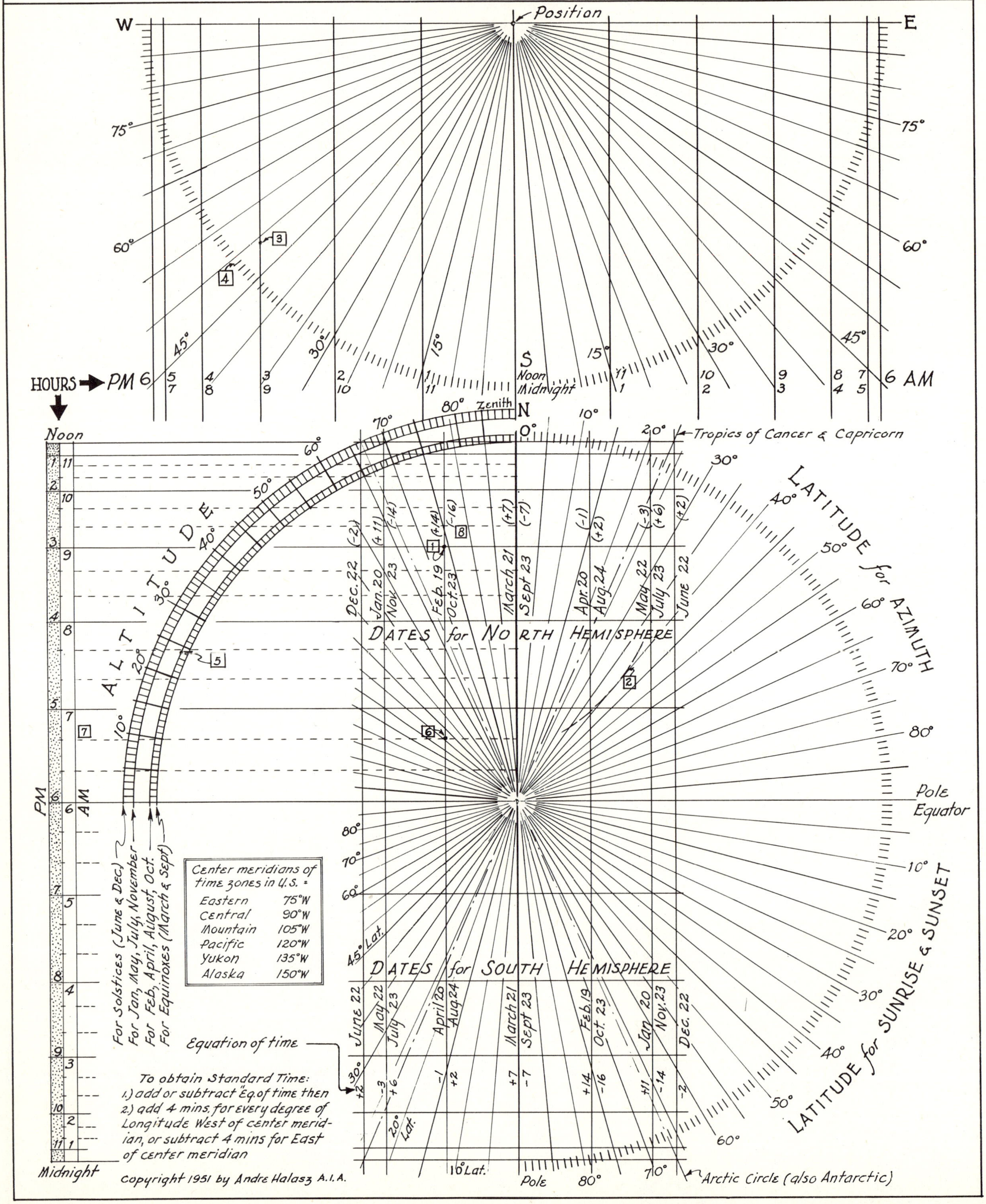
Position
W
E
S
N
Zenith
HOURS → PM
6 AM
Noon
Midnight
Tropics of Cancer & Capricorn
LATITUDE for AZIMUTH
ALTITUDE
DATES for NORTH HEMISPHERE
DATES for SOUTH HEMISPHERE
Dec. 22
Jan. 20
Nov. 23
Feb. 19
Oct. 23
March 21
Sept 23
Apr. 20
Aug. 24
May 22
July 23
June 22
Pole
Equator
LATITUDE for SUNRISE & SUNSET
Arctic Circle (also Antarctic)
Equation of time
PM
AM
For Solstices (June & Dec.)
For Jan, May, July, November
For Feb, April, August, Oct.
For Equinoxes (March & Sept)
Center meridians of time zones in U.S. =
Eastern 75°W
Central 90°W
Mountain 105°W
Pacific 120°W
Yukon 135°W
Alaska 150°W
To obtain Standard Time:
1.) add or subtract Eq. of time then
2.) add 4 mins. for every degree of Longitude West of center meridian, or subtract 4 mins for East of center meridian
45° Lat.
30° Lat.
20° Lat.
10° Lat.
Copyright 1951 by Andre Halasz A.I.A.

UNIVERSAL SUN CHART – APPLICATION

The UNIVERSAL SUN CHART is mathematically true for any hour of any day of the year, for any place on the globe. It may be interpolated by eye for any intermediate value, and is as accurate as the reading taken, i.e. better than 1°. To use, follow EXAMPLE.

EXAMPLE: Find the direction of the Sun's rays at Columbus, Ohio (Lat. 40°N, Long. 83°W) at 3 PM, February 19th. Start with lower chart. From intersection of vertical DATE line (North Hemisphere, Feb. 19) and Horizontal HOUR line (3 PM) [1] measure with dividers to inclined LATITUDE for AZIMUTH line (40°). For accuracy, swing dividers in tangent arc as shown [2]. Lay off this distance in <u>upper chart</u> along 3 PM vertical HOUR line, [3], starting at top, and read: [4] <u>azimuth = 49° West of South</u>. [Azimuth is angle of Sun's rays in plan.] Now measure distance from "azimuth point" [3] to POSITION and lay off in <u>lower chart</u>, horizontally to left of vertical ℄ until distance intersects ALTITUDE circle for February [5] (not along 3 PM hour line; move dividers up & down keeping distance horizontal; or lay off distance along any hour line and project vertically to February ALTITUDE circle). Read: <u>altitude = 24°</u> [Altitude is true angle of Sun's rays with the horizontal, see sketch below].*

For noon altitude, steps [3] & [4] may be omitted because noon azimuth = 0°. To find time of <u>Sunrise</u> & <u>Sunset</u>, find the intersection of vertical DATE line with inclined LATITUDE for SUNRISE & SUNSET [6] and read time by HOUR lines [7]: <u>Sunrise</u> = 6:40 AM. <u>Sunset</u> = 5:20 PM. To find azimuth of sunrise & sunset, repeat steps [2] & [3] from point [6]

Time shown is Sun Time. If desired to convert to Local Standard Time, 2 steps are necessary:
<u>Step 1</u> = add the small figure "equation of time" on DATE line [8]: 3 PM + 14 mins = 3:14 PM.
<u>Step 2</u>: add 4 mins for each degree West of Standard Time Meridian: 8 x 4 = 32; 3:14+32= <u>3:46</u> PM Standard Time. (This is a maximum case; more often the two corrections cancel out or are negligible.)

**When [2] is clockwise from [1] as in example, AZIMUTH is measured from the SOUTH; if counterclockwise, AZIMUTH is from the North (reverse for Southern Hemisphere).*

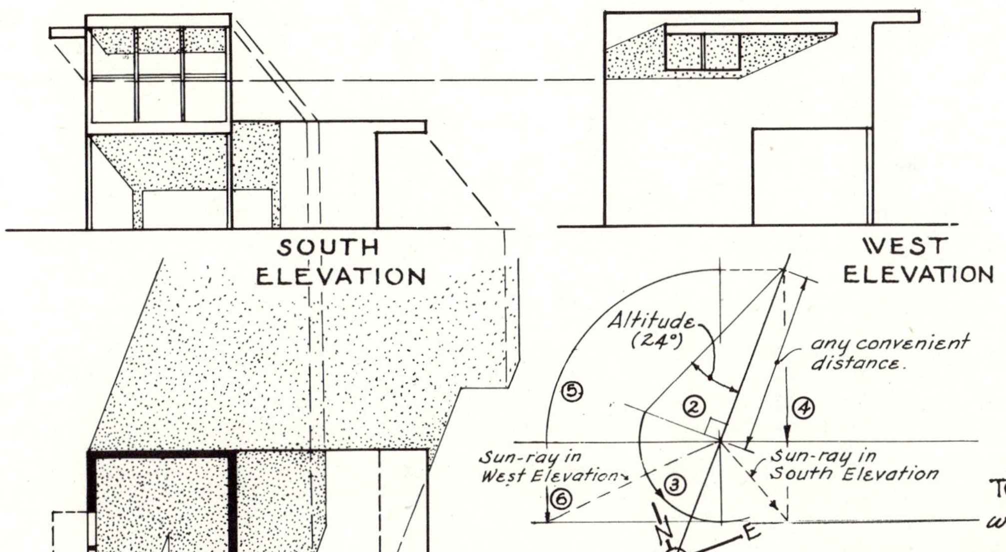

SOUTH ELEVATION
WEST ELEVATION
Altitude (24°)
any convenient distance.
Sun-ray in West Elevation
Sun-ray in South Elevation
N
E
W
S

TO CONSTRUCT SHADOWS with TRUE POSITION of SUN=

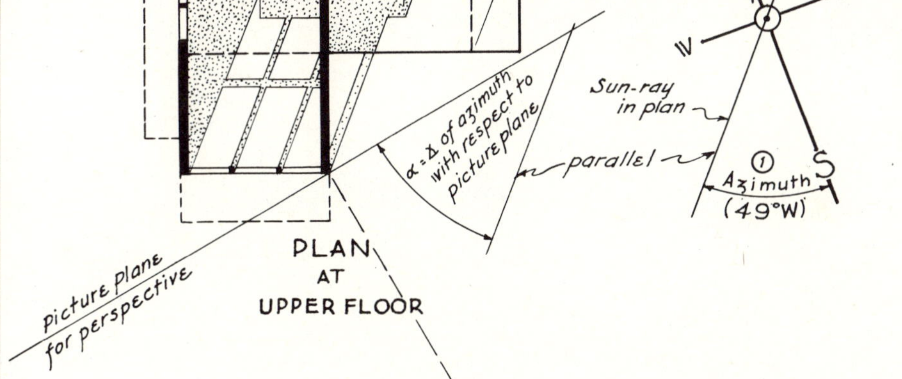

Sun-ray in plan
α = ∡ of azimuth with respect to picture plane
parallel
Azimuth (49°W)
PLAN AT UPPER FLOOR
picture plane for perspective

<u>For Plan & Elevations:</u>
(1) Lay out Azimuth in Plan with respect to Compass.
(2) Lay out Altitude upon Azimuth.
Follow steps 3, 4, 5, 6, to obtain Elevations of Sun-Ray. Proceed as in conventional Shades & Shadows.

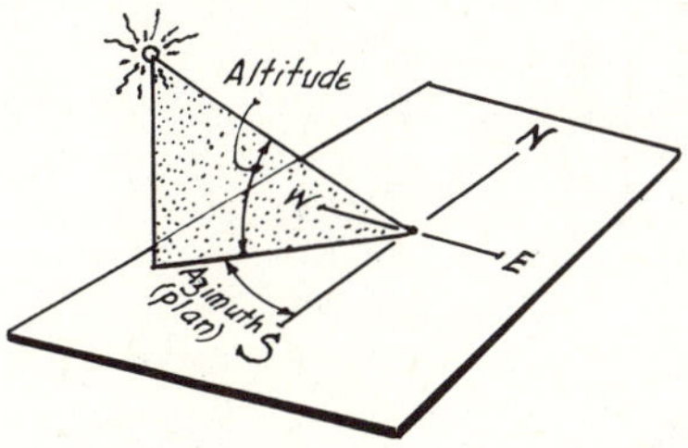

Altitude
N
W
E
Azimuth (plan)
S

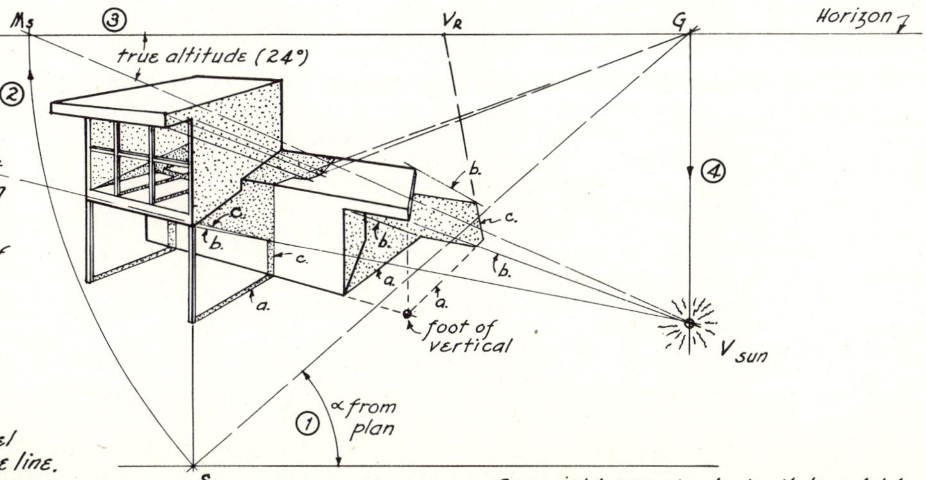

V_L
M_S
V_R
G
Horizon
true altitude (24°)
S_1
b.
c.
a.
foot of vertical
V_{sun}
α from plan

<u>For Perspective:</u>
Do not construct shadows in Plan & Elev. and plot into Perspective. Method is based on "Vanishing Points of Sloping Lines" (see "Perspective"). Find G, M_S & V_{sun} by steps (1) (2) (3) (4) Note: V_{sun} is below the horizon when sun is in back of observer as in example. If observer faces the sun, lay off Altitude upwards & obtain V_{sun} above horizon.

Construct shadows by Rules a, b, c.
<u>Rule a</u>: Shadow of vertical line upon horizontal plane goes from foot of vertical to G.
<u>Rule b</u>: Sun-rays go to V_{sun}
<u>Rule c</u>: Shadow of a line upon a surface parallel to it, goes to same vanishing point as the line.
Rules abc are illustrated in the diagram by a, b, c.

EXPLANATION of TABLES for SUN SHADES

EXPLANATION OF TABLES

The following 3 pages of tables give factors for shading of windows and depth that the sun will enter a room.
(a) By use of solid overhang. (b) By use of solid vertical shading device such as a fence, wall, or planting.
(c) Depth of penetration of sun through wall openings not covered by shading device.

EXPLANATION OF FACTORS

Numbers shown on tables are factors (F) in feet and 1/10 ths. of a foot. They are projections required to cast 1 foot of shade on a vertical plane, measured down from bottom of overhanging eave.

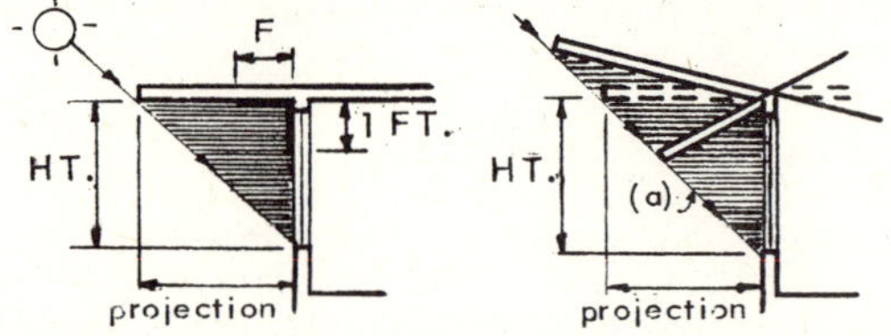

F
1 FT.
HT.
projection
HT.
(a)
projection

Note:
To find projection of horizontal overhang required to cast a specific shade below bottom of eave of overhang, multiply height required (HT. in feet) by factor F.
To find projection of sloping overhang required, solve as for a horizontal overhang. Take a section thru wall of your building and lay off calculated horizontal projection. Draw a line "a" through bottom of eave of overhang and bottom of shade. Where roof slope intersects this line, required overhang can be measured.

USE OF TABLES TO FIND FACTOR F

Step 1. Find the latitude of building site from the SUN SHADE MASTER MAP which follows tables.
(a) Select from TABLES OF SUN SHADE FACTORS the latitude nearest to site latitude.

Step 2. Directly under latitude select hours, A.M. to P.M. when shade is wanted. Hours & months when shade is wanted depend on the site, climate, use of building, if air conditioned, etc. Time shown is "Sun Time." at center of each hourly time zone. Find time zone of site from the SUN SHADE MASTER MAP which follows. To find Sun Time from Standard Time use the procedure outlined on the MASTER MAP.

Step 3. Select month or months when shade is wanted.

Step 4. Select from orientation diagrams below the one most similar to your building.

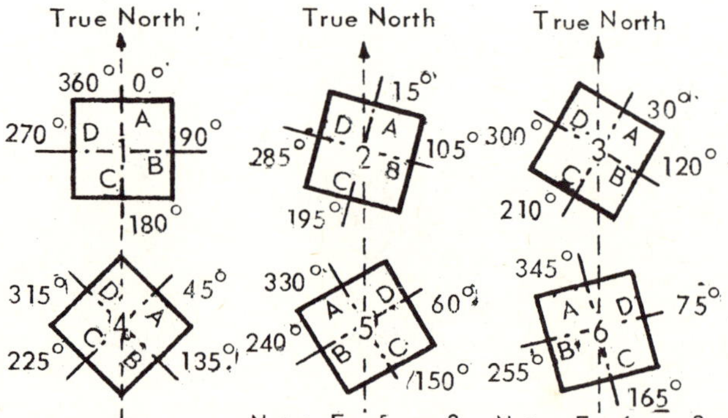

True North
True North
True North
360°
0°
15°
30°
270°
D
A
90°
1
C
B
180°
285°
2
105°
195°
300°
3
120°
210°
315°
45°
4
225°
135°
330°
60°
5
240°
150°
345°
75°
6
255°
165°

Note: For 5 use 3 Note: For 6 use 2

Angles shown read clockwise from True North 0° or 360°. East is 90°, South is 180°, West is 270°. Make correction from magnetic North for site deviation.
(a) Note that sides of diagram are labeled A, B, C, D. Decide which sides of your bldg. will require shade.
(b) Turn to table under month or months selected, find the orientation you selected – 1, 2, 3, or 4.
Note: (1) If your orientation is 5 use 3 in the chart. If your orientation is 6 use 2 in the chart.
(2) Also change times as follows: For times,

4 P. M.	of orientation 5 or 6 use time	8 A. M. of 3 or 2
3 P. M.	of orientation 5 or 6 use time	9 A. M. of 3 or 2
2 P. M.	of orientation 5 or 6 use time	10 A. M. of 3 or 2
10 A. M.	of orientation 5 or 6 use time	2 P. M. of 3 or 2
9 A. M.	of orientation 5 or 6 use time	3 P. M. of 3 or 2
8 A. M.	of orientation 5 or 6 use time	4 P. M. of 3 or 2

For noon do not substitute.

Step 5. Follow down under month & orientation number until the latitude and time rows previously selected are intersected. Here select sides (indicated as A, B, C, D) which you decided to shade and use factors following the letters.
(a) When a side (letter) does not appear it is because sun does not shine on it at that time.
(b) When selecting factors for several hours and for several months use the largest factor.

Step 6. Find projection of overhang required. (See note under EXPLANATION OF FACTORS).

Step 7. If length "x" is desired assume plane "a" perpendicular to end of window & calculate for its overhang.

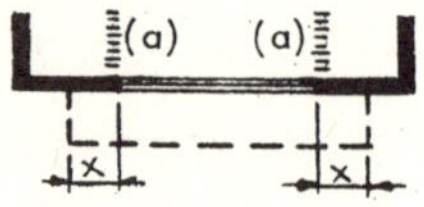

(a)
(a)
x
x

EXAMPLES

Problem "A":
1. Assume building is at Lat. 40° 16'. Use 40° Lat.
2. Shading wanted 9 A.M. to 3 P.M.
3. This shading wanted April 20th to Sept. 23rd.
4. Center of building is on an axis 61° East of North. Use Orientation No. 5. Bldg. on site 60° East of North.
5. On side C shade entire window to 5' below overhang eave. On side D shade entire window to 4' below overhang eave.

Solution
1. Interchange orientation No. 5 to orientation No. 3. For 3 P.M. of orientation No. 5 substitute 9 A.M. for No. 3 etc.
2. Largest factor for side C orientation No. 3, 40° Lat. between 9 A.M. & 3 P.M., April 20th to Sept 23rd, is factor 1.4' at 9 A.M. on Sept. 23rd (3 P.M. on table before conversion). Multiply 1.4' by 5' height = 7' projection.
3. Largest factor for side D is .69'. Multiply .69' by 4' height = 2.76' projection.

Problem B
1. To find height of vertical shading device. Known:
D – Distance from plane to be shaded to shading device.
H – Height from fl. to top of window or side to be shaded.
G – Height from floor to grade at shading device.
H' – Portion of shading device needed to shade H, (H'=H)

Unknown: Y height of vertical device above finished grade.

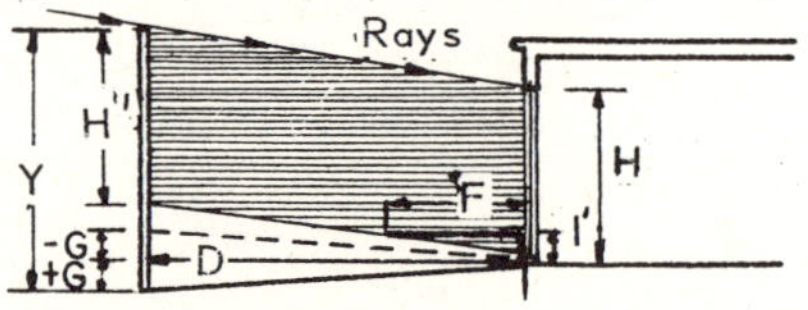

Rays
H'
Y
H
F
1'
-G
+G
D

Solution: Find factor F as in preceding problem.
1. Formula for Y = D/F + H ± G (in ft. and fractions of ft.),
2. If the height of the device is fixed and the distance D is sought the formula becomes D = F (Y - H ± G)

Note: If grade is below floor use - G { Differs from
If grade is above floor use + G { diagram

Problem C
1. To find depth of penetration of sun through wall opening. (Generally used to calculate penetration of winter sun).
Known: P – Projection of shading device.
Known: H – Height from bottom of eave of shading device to finished floor.
Unknown: X – Depth of sun penetration into room.

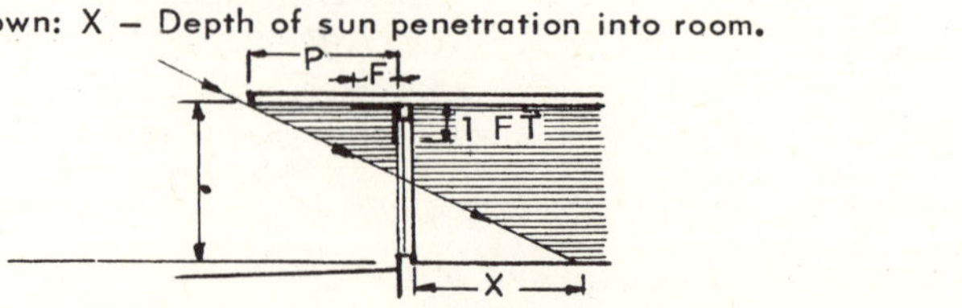

P
F
1 FT
X

Solution: Find factor F from table as in Problem A except select time & months you wish to know depth of sun penetration.
1. Formula for X = FH - P (in feet and fractions of feet.)

Sun Shade data prepared in consultation with Andre Halasz A.I.A.

TABLES for SUN SHADES

Date	Orientation	26° 8 AM	26° 9	26° 10	26° 12	26° 2 PM	26° 3	26° 4	30° 8 AM	30° 9	30° 10	30° 12	30° 2 PM	30° 3	30° 4	32° 8 AM	32° 9	32° 10	32° 12	32° 2 PM	32° 3	32° 4	34° 8 AM	34° 9	34° 10	34° 12	34° 2 PM	34° 3	34° 4
DEC. 22	1	B3.4	B1.6	B.85	C1.2	C1.3	C1.6	C2.4	B4.0	B1.7	B .9	C1.3	C1.5	C1.8	C2.9	B4.3	B1.8	B.96	C1.4	C1.6	C1.9	C3.2	B4.6	B1.9	B1.0	C1.5	C1.7	C2.1	C3.5
		C2.4	C1.6	C1.3	-	D.85	D1.6	D3.4	C2.9	C1.8	C1.5	-	D .9	D1.7	D4.0	C3.2	C1.9	C1.6	-	D.96	D1.8	D4.3	C3.5	C2.1	C1.7	-	D1.0	D1.9	D4.6
	2	B3.9	B1.9	B1.2	B .3	C1.5	C1.9	C3.2	B4.6	B2.1	B1.3	B.34	C1.7	C2.1	C3.8	B5.0	B2.2	B1.3	B .4	C1.8	C2.3	C4.2	B5.4	B2.4	B1.4	B .4	C1.9	C2.5	C4.6
		C1.5	C1.1	C1.1	C1.1	D.49	D1.1	D2.6	C1.8	C1.3	C1.2	C1.3	D .5	D1.2	D3.0	C2.0	C1.4	C1.3	C1.4	D.51	D1.3	D3.4	C2.2	C1.5	C1.4	C1.5	D.53	D1.3	D3.6
	3	B4.2	B2.1	B1.4	B.57	C1.6	C2.1	C3.8	B4.9	B2.4	B1.5	B.66	C1.7	C2.4	C4.5	B5.4	B2.5	B1.6	B.71	C1.9	C2.6	C5.0	B5.8	B2.7	B1.7	B .8	C2.0	C2.8	C5.3
		C .4	C.56	C.71	C1.	D.08	D.56	D1.1	C.53	C .7	C.84	C1.1	D.03	D.57	D2.0	C.61	C.75	C.90	C1.2	D.03	D .6	D2.2	C.68	C.85	C.98	C1.3	D .0	D.63	D2.3
	4	A.68	-	B1.5	B.81	B.32	C2.2	C4.1	A.74	B2.5	B1.7	B.94	B.41	B.06	C4.8	A.80	B2.6	B1.8	B1.0	B.45	B.08	C5.3	A.83	B2.9	B1.9	B1.1	B.50	B.11	C5.7
		B4.1	B2.2	C.32	C.81	C1.5		D.68	B4.8	C.06	C.41	C.94	C1.7	C2.5	D.74	B5.3	C.08	C.45	C1.0	C1.8	C2.6	D.80	B5.7	C.11	C.50	C1.1	C1.9	C2.9	D.83
JAN. 20 NOV. 23	1	B3.2	B1.5	B.81	C1.	C1.2	C1.4	C2.1	B3.7	B1.6	B.89	C1.2	C1.4	C1.6	C2.5	B4.3	B1.8	B.93	C1.3	C1.5	C1.7	C2.9	B4.7	B1.9	B.97	C1.4	C1.6	C1.9	C3.2
		C2.1	C1.4	C1.2	-	D.81	D1.5	D3.2	C2.5	C1.6	C1.4	-	D.89	D1.6	D3.7	C2.9	C1.7	C1.5	-	D.93	D1.8	D4.3	C3.2	C1.9	C1.6	-	D.97	D1.9	D4.7
	2	B3.6	B1.8	B1.1	B.27	C1.3	C1.7	C2.8	B4.3	B2.0	B1.2	B .3	C1.6	C2.0	C3.4	B4.9	B2.1	B1.3	B.33	C1.7	C2.1	C3.9	B5.4	B2.3	B1.3	B.35	C1.8	C2.3	C4.3
		C1.2	C.95	C.92	C1.	D.48	D1.1	D2.5	C1.5	C1.1	C1.1	C1.2	D .5	D1.2	D3.0	C1.7	C1.2	C1.2	C1.2	D.52	D1.2	D3.4	C1.9	C1.4	C1.3	C1.3	D.53	D1.3	D3.7
	3	B3.8	B2.0	B1.3	B.52	C1.4	C1.9	C3.4	B4.6	B2.2	B1.5	B.59	C1.6	C2.2	C4.0	B5.1	B2.4	B1.5	B.64	C1.7	C2.4	C4.6	B5.7	B2.6	B1.6	B.68	C1.8	C2.6	C5.1
		C.20	C.45	C.61	C .9	D.11	D.60	D1.7	C.31	C.56	C.73	C1.0	D.08	D.62	D2.0	C.38	C.63	C.80	C1.1	D.07	D.64	D2.2	C.45	C.70	C.86	C1.2	D.09	D.67	D2.4
	4	A.78	A.07	B1.4	B.73	B.25	C2.0	C3.7	A.93	A.03	B1.6	B.84	B.33	C2.3	C4.4	A.96	A 0	B1.7	B .9	B.37	C2.5	C5.1	A1.0	B2.7	B1.8	B.97	B.41	B.01	C5.6
		B3.7	B2.0	C.25	C.73	C1.4	D.07	D.78	B4.4	B2.3	C.33	C.84	C1.6	D.03	D.93	B5.1	B2.5	C.37	C .9	C1.7	D .0	D.96	B5.6	C.01	C.41	C.97	C1.8	C2.7	D1.0
FEB. 19 OCT. 23	1	B2.5	B1.3	B.72	C.75	C.81	C.91	C1.2	B2.8	B1.4	B.75	C.87	C.93	C1.0	C1.4	B2.9	B1.4	B.78	C.93	C1.0	C1.1	C1.5	B3.0	B1.5	B.81	C1.	C1.1	C1.2	C1.6
		C1.2	C.91	C.81	-	D.72	D1.3	D2.5	C1.4	C1.0	C.93	-	D.75	D1.4	D2.8	C1.5	C1.1	C1.0	-	D.78	D1.4	D2.9	C1.6	C1.2	C1.1	-	D.81	D1.5	D3.0
	2	B2.7	B1.5	B.90	B.19	C.97	C1.2	C1.8	B3.0	B1.6	B.97	B.22	C1.1	C1.4	C2.0	B3.2	B1.7	B1.0	B.24	C1.2	C1.5	C2.2	B3.3	B1.8	B1.1	B.25	C1.3	C1.6	C2.3
		C.48	C.54	C.60	C.75	D.48	D1.0	D2.1	C.62	C.65	C.70	C.84	D.48	D1.1	D2.3	C.69	C.72	C.77	C.90	D.50	D1.1	D2.4	C.77	C.77	C.83	C.95	D.50	D1.1	D2.5
	3	A.23	B1.6	B1.0	B.37	C1.1	C1.4	C2.3	A-.17	B1.7	B1.1	B.43	C1.2	C1.6	C2.6	A.15	B1.8	B1.2	B.46	C1.3	C1.7	C2.8	A.12	B1.9	B1.2	B .5	C1.3	C1.8	C2.9
		B2.7	C.14	C.34	C.65	D.21	D.66	D1.6	B3.1	C.21	C.43	C.75	D.18	D.67	D1.7	B3.3	C.26	C.48	C.80	D.17	D.68	D1.8	B3.4	C.29	C.52	C.86	D.16	D.69	D1.8
	4	A.93	A.26	B1.1	B.53	B.06	C1.6	C2.6	A.96	A.23	B1.2	B.62	B.12	C1.7	C2.9	A.99	A.21	B1.3	B.66	B.15	C1.8	C3.1	A1.0	A.20	B1.3	B .7	B.18	C1.9	C3.3
		B2.6	B1.6	C.06	C.53	C1.1	D.26	D.93	B2.9	B1.7	C.12	C.62	C1.2	D.23	D.96	B3.1	B1.8	C.15	C.66	C1.3	D.21	D.99	B3.3	B1.9	C.18	C .7	C1.3	D.20	D1.0
MAR. 21 SEPT. 23	1	B1.9	B1.1	B.63	C.49	C.49	C.50	C.50	B2.1	B1.1	B.65	C.57	C.58	C.58	C.60	B2.1	B1.2	B.67	C.61	C.62	C.63	C.65	B2.1	B1.2	B.68	C.67	C.67	C.67	C .7
		C.50	C.50	C.49	-	D.63	D1.1	D1.9	C.60	C.58	C.58	-	D.65	D1.1	D2.1	C.65	C.63	C.62	-	D.67	D1.2	D2.1	C .7	C.67	C.67	-	D.68	D1.2	D2.1
	2	A.01	B1.2	B.73	B.12	C.63	C.76	C1.0	B2.1	B1.3	B.78	B.14	C.73	C.86	C1.1	B2.2	B1.3	B.81	B.15	C.77	C.91	C1.2	B2.2	B1.3	B.83	B.17	C.82	C.96	C1.2
		B2.0	C.19	C.31	C.47	D.48	D.93	D1.8	C.05	C.27	C.39	C.55	D.48	D.94	D1.8	C.08	C.31	C.43	C.59	D.48	D.95	D1.9	C.12	C.34	C.47	C.64	D.48	D.97	D1.9
	3	A.54	A.12	B.79	B.24	C.76	C.98	C1.4	A.50	A.06	B.86	B.28	C.83	C1.1	C1.6	A.48	A.03	B.89	B .3	C.87	C1.1	C1.6	A.45	A 0	B.93	B.33	C.92	C1.2	C1.7
		B1.9	B1.2	C.11	C.42	D.30	D.70	D1.4	B2.1	B1.3	C.17	C.50	D.27	D.69	D1.5	B2.1	B1.3	C.20	C.53	D.26	D.68	D1.5	B2.2	B1.4	C.24	C.58	D.25	D.68	D1.5
	4	A1.0	A.42	A.09	B.34	C.79	C1.1	C1.7	A1.0	A.38	A.05	B .4	C.87	C1.2	C1.9	A1.0	A.37	A.03	B.43	B.03	C1.3	C1.9	A1.0	A.35	A 0	B.47	B 0	C1.3	C2.0
		B1.7	B1.1	B.79	C.34	D.09	D.42	D1.0	B1.9	B1.2	B.87	C .4	D.05	D.38	D1.0	B1.9	B1.3	B.91	C.43	C.91	D.37	D1.0	B2.0	B1.3	B.96	C.47	C.96	D.35	D1.0
APR. 20 AUG. 24	1	B1.7	B.98	B.57	C.26	C.23	C.18	C.07	B1.7	B1.0	B.58	C.33	C.31	C.25	C.15	B1.7	B1.0	B.59	C.37	C.35	C.29	C.19	B1.7	B1.0	B.60	C.42	C.39	C.33	C.23
		C.07	C.18	C.23	-	D.57	D.98	D1.7	C.15	C.25	C.31		D.58	D1.0	D1.7	C.19	C.29	C.35	-	D.59	D1.0	D1.7	C.23	C.33	C.39	-	D.60	D1.0	D1.7
	2	A.35	A.07	B.62	B.06	C.37	C.43	C.50	A.29	A 0	B.64	B.08	C.45	C.50	C.58	A.25	B1.1	B.66	B.09	C.49	C.54	C.62	A.21	B1.1	B.68	B.10	C.53	C.58	C.66
		B1.6	B.99	C.07	C.25	D.49	D.90	D1.6	B1.7	B1.0	C.15	C.32	D.48	D.90	D1.6	B1.6	C.02	C.18	C.36	D.48	D.90	D1.6	B1.7	C.05	C.22	C.40	D.48	D.89	D1.6
	3	A.76	A.33	A.08	B.13	C.49	C.64	C.89	A.71	A.27	A.03	B.16	C.56	C.72	C.97	A.68	A.25	B.69	B.18	C.60	C.76	C1.0	A.65	A.21	B.71	B.21	C.64	C.79	C1.1
		B1.5	B.94	B.61	C.22	D.38	D.76	D1.4	B1.5	B.99	B.66	C.28	D.36	D.73	D1.4	B1.6	B1.0	C 0	C.32	D.34	D.72	D1.4	B1.6	B1.0	C.03	C.36	D.32	D.71	D1.4
	4	A1.1	A.56	A.24	B.18	C.57	C.82	C1.2	A1.1	A.52	A.20	B.23	C.63	C.89	C1.3	A1.1	A.50	A.17	B.26	C.67	C.92	C1.3	A1.0	A.48	A.14	B.29	C.70	C.95	C1.4
		B1.2	B.82	B.57	C.18	D.24	D.56	D1.1	B1.3	B.89	B.63	C.23	D.20	D.52	D1.1	B1.3	B.92	B.67	C.26	D.17	D.50	D1.1	B1.4	B.95	B.70	C.29	D.14	D.48	D1.0
MAY 22 JULY 23	1	A.19	A.02	B.53	C.1	C.05	A.02	A.19	A.10	B .9	B.54	C.17	C.12	C.04	A.10	A.06	B.89	B.54	C.21	C.16	C.08	A.06	A.03	B.90	B.54	C.24	C.20	C.12	A.03
		B1.5	B.88	C.05	-	D.53	D.88	D1.5	B1.4	C.04	C.12		D.54	D .9	D1.4	B1.4	C.08	C.16	-	D.54	D.89	D1.4	B1.4	C.12	C.20	-	D.54	D.90	D1.4
	2	A.56	A.25	A.08	B.02	C.19	C .2	C.19	A.47	A.18	A.01	B.04	C.26	C.27	C.26	A.43	A.14	B.56	B.05	C.29	C.31	C.30	A.40	A.11	B.57	B.06	C.33	C.35	C.33
		B1.4	B.84	B.53	C .1	D .5	D.86	D1.5	B1.4	B.88	B.55	C.17	D.48	D.85	D1.4	B1.4	B.88	C.01	C.20	D.47	D.84	D1.4	B1.4	B.90	C.05	C.24	D.47	D.83	D1.4
	3	A.89	A.46	A.22	B.05	C.31	C.42	C.56	A.81	A.40	A.15	B.08	C.38	C.49	C.62	A.77	A.37	A.12	B.10	C.41	C.52	C.65	A.74	A.34	A.09	B.12	C.44	C.55	C.68
		B1.2	B.75	B.49	C.09	D.43	D.77	D1.4	B1.2	B .8	B.53	C.15	D.40	D.75	D1.3	B1.2	B.81	B.55	C.18	D.38	D.73	D1.3	B1.2	B.84	B.56	C.21	D.36	D.72	D1.3
	4	A1.2	A.64	A.34	B.07	C.42	C .6	C.89	A1.1	A.60	A.29	B.12	C.47	C.66	C.94	A1.1	A.57	A.26	B.15	C.49	C.69	C.96	A1.0	A.55	A.24	B.17	C.52	C.72	C.98
		B.89	B .6	B.42	C.07	D.34	D.64	D1.2	B.94	B.66	B.47	C.12	D.29	D.60	D1.1	B.96	B.69	B.49	C.15	D.26	D.57	D1.1	B.98	B.72	B.52	C.17	D.24	D.55	D1.0
JUNE 22	1	A.27	A.09	A 0	C.04	A 0	A.09	A.27	A.19	A.02	B.51	C.11	C.06	A.02	A.19	A.16	B.88	B.52	C.15	C.09	C.01	A.16	A.12	B.85	B.52	C.18	C.13	C.04	A.12
		B1.4	B.89	B.51	-	D.51	D.89	D1.4	B1.4	B.88	C.06	-	D.51	D.88	D1.4	B1.3	C.01	C.09	-	D.52	D.88	D1.3	B1.3	C.04	C.13	-	D.52	D.85	D1.3
	2	A.61	A.32	A.13	B.01	C.12	C.13	C.09	A.53	A.25	A.07	B.03	C.19	C.20	C.16	A .5	A.21	A.04	B.03	C.22	C.23	C.18	A.46	A.17	A 0	B.04	C.26	C.26	C.22
		B1.2	B.83	B.49	C.04	D.50	D.89	D1.4	B1.3	B.84	B.51	C.11	D.48	D.86	D1.4	B1.3	B.85	B.53	C.14	D.41	D.85	D1.3	B1.3	B.83	B.53	C.18	D.46	D.81	D1.3
	3	A.91	A.53	A.26	B.02	C.25	C.36	C.44	A.84	A.46	A.20	B.05	C.31	C.42	C.50	A.81	A.43	A.17	B.07	C.34	C.45	C.52	A.77	A.38	A.14	B.09	C.37	C.46	C.55
		B1.0	B.72	B.44	C.04	D.45	D.82	D1.3	B1.1	B.75	B.48	C.10	D.41	D.77	D1.3	B1.1	B.77	B.50	C.13	D.40	D.76	D1.2	B1.1	B.76	B.51	C.16	D.38	D.71	D1.2
	4	A1.2	A.70	A.36	B.03	C.36	C.56	C.77	A1.1	A.65	A.32	B.08	C.41	C.60	C.81	A1.1	A.61	A.30	B.10	C.43	C.63	C.83	A1.0	A.57	A.27	B.13	C.46	C.63	C.85
		B.77	B.56	B.36	C.03	D.36	D.70	D1.2	B.81	B.60	B.41	C.08	D.32	D.64	D1.1	B.83	B.63	B.43	C.10	D.30	D.61	D1.1	B.85	B.63	B.46	C.13	D.27	D.57	D1.0

TABLES for SUN SHADES

36° N. LATITUDE

Date	Orientation	8 AM	9	10	12	2 PM	3	4
DEC. 22	1	B5.1	B2.1	B1.1	C1.7	C1.8	C2.3	C3.8
		C3.8	C2.3	C1.8	-	D1.1	D2.1	D5.1
	2	B5.9	B2.6	B1.5	B.43	C2.0	C2.7	C5.0
		C2.4	C1.7	C1.5	C1.6	D.54	D1.4	D3.9
	3	B6.3	B2.9	B1.8	B.83	C2.1	C3.0	C5.8
		C.77	C.93	C1.1	C1.4		D.50	D2.5
	4	A.87	B3.1	B2.0	B1.2	B.54	B.14	C6.3
		B6.3	C.14	C.54	C1.2	C2.0	C3.1	D.87
JAN. 20 / NOV. 23	1	B5.2	B2.0	B1.0	C1.5	C1.7	C2.1	C3.6
		C3.6	C2.1	C1.7	-	D1.0	D2.0	D5.2
	2	B5.9	B2.5	B1.4	B.38	C1.9	C2.5	C4.8
		C2.2	C1.5	C1.4	C1.4	D.55	D1.4	D4.1
	3	B6.3	B2.8	B1.7	B.74	C1.9	C2.8	C5.7
		C.54	C.77	C.93	C1.3	D.04	D.70	D2.7
	4	A1.1	B2.9	B1.9	B1.	B.46	B.03	C6.2
		B6.2	C.03	C.46	C1.	C1.9	C2.9	D1.1
FEB. 19 / OCT. 23	1	B3.2	B1.5	B.84	C1.1	C1.2	C1.3	C1.7
		C1.7	C1.3	C1.2	-	D.84	D1.5	D3.2
	2	B3.5	B1.8	B1.1	B.27	C1.3	C1.6	C2.5
		C.83	C.84	C.89	C1.	D.51	D1.2	D2.0
	3	A.10	B2.0	B1.3	B.53	C1.4	C1.9	C3.1
		B3.6	C.34	C.57	C.92	D.15	D.69	D1.9
	4	A1.0	A.18	B1.4	B.75	B.22	C2.0	C3.5
		B3.5	B2.0	C.22	C.75	C1.4	D.18	D1.0
MAR. 21 / SEPT 23	1	B2.2	B1.2	B.7	C.71	C.72	C.73	C.75
		C.75	C.73	C.72	-	D.7	D1.2	D2.2
	2	B2.3	B1.4	B.87	B.18	C.88	C1.0	C1.3
		C.16	C.39	C.52	C.69	D.49	D.99	D1.9
	3	A.43	B1.4	B.97	B.35	C.98	C1.3	C1.7
		B2.3	C.02	C.27	C.62	D.24	D.69	D1.5
	4	A1.0	A.34	B1.0	B.5	B.01	C1.4	C2.1
		B2.1	B1.4	C.01	C.5	C1.0	D.34	D1.0
APR. 20 / AUG. 24	1	B1.7	B1.0	B.60	C.45	C.42	C.36	C.27
		C.27	C.36	C.42	-	D.60	D1.0	D1.7
	2	A.18	B1.1	B.69	B.11	C.56	C.61	C.70
		B1.7	C.09	C.25	C.44	D.47	D.89	D1.6
	3	A.62	A.19	B.73	B.22	C.67	C.82	C1.1
		B1.6	B1.1	C.06	C.39	D.31	D.70	D1.4
	4	A1.0	A.46	A.12	B.32	C.72	C.98	C1.4
		B1.4	B.98	B.72	C.32	D.12	D.46	D1.0
MAY 22 / JULY 23	1	B1.4	B.90	B.54	C.27	C.23	C.15	D1.4
		.	C.15	C.23	-	D.54	D.90	.
	2	A.36	A.08	B.58	B.07	C.36	C.38	C.36
		B1.4	B.91	C.08	C.26	D.46	D.83	D1.4
	3	A.70	A.31	A.07	B.13	C.47	C.58	C.70
		B1.2	B.86	B.59	C.24	D.35	D.70	D1.2
	4	A1.0	A.52	A.22	B.19	C.55	C.74	C1.0
		B1.0	B.74	B.55	C.19	D.22	D.52	D1.0
JUNE 22	1	A.08	B.85	B.52	C.22	C.16	C.08	A.08
		B1.3	C.08	C.16	-	D.52	D.85	D1.3
	2	A.42	A.14	B.54	B.05	C.29	C.29	C.26
		B1.3	B.84	C.02	C.21	D.46	D.80	D1.3
	3	A.74	A.35	A.11	B.11	C.40	C.49	C.59
		B1.1	B.77	B.53	C.19	D.36	D.69	D1.2
	4	A1.0	A.54	A.25	B.15	C.48	C.65	C.87
		B.87	B.65	B.48	C.15	D.25	D.54	D1.0

38° N. LATITUDE

Date	Orientation	8 AM	9	10	12	2 PM	3	4
DEC. 22	1	B6.0	B2.3	B1.1	C1.8	C2.0	C2.6	C4.6
		C4.6	C2.6	C2.0	-	D1.1	D2.3	D6.0
	2	B7.0	B2.9	B1.6	B.46	C2.3	C3.1	C6.0
		C2.9	C1.9	C1.7	C1.7	D.57	D1.5	D4.6
	3	B7.5	B3.3	B2.0	B.90	B.03	C3.4	C7.0
		C1.0	C1.1	C1.2	C1.6	C2.3	D.70	D2.9
	4	A1.0	B3.4	B2.2	B1.3	B.63	B.19	C7.5
		B7.5	C.19	C.63	C1.3	C2.2	C3.4	D1.0
JAN. 20 / NOV. 23	1	B6.2	B2.1	B1.1	C1.6	C1.8	C2.2	C4.4
		C4.4	C2.2	C1.8	-	D1.1	D2.1	D5.2
	2	B7.1	B2.6	B1.5	B.41	C2.1	C2.7	C5.8
		C2.6	C1.6	C1.5	C1.5	D.58	D1.5	D4.9
	3	B7.5	B3.0	B1.9	B.8	C2.1	C3.	C6.9
		C.67	C.86	C1.0	C1.4	D.03	D.73	D3.2
	4	A1.3	B3.1	B2.1	B1.1	B.51	B.06	C7.5
		B7.5	C.06	C.51	C1.1	C2.1	C3.1	D1.3
FEB. 19 / OCT. 23	1	B3.4	B1.6	B.89	C1.2	C1.3	C1.4	C1.9
		C1.9	C1.4	C1.3	-	D.89	D1.6	D3.4
	2	B3.7	B1.9	B1.2	B.29	C1.4	C1.8	C2.7
		C.92	C.92	C.97	C1.1	D.53	D1.2	D2.8
	3	A.07	B2.1	B1.4	B.57	C1.5	C2.0	C3.3
		B3.9	C.39	C.63	C.99	D.14	D.71	D2.
	4	A1.1	A.16	B1.5	B.81	B.25	C2.1	C3.7
		B3.7	B2.1	C.25	C.81	C1.5	D.16	D1.1
MAR. 21 / SEPT 23	1	B2.3	B1.3	B.72	C.77	C.77	C.79	C.82
		C.82	C.79	C.77	-	D.72	D1.3	D2.3
	2	B2.4	B1.4	B.90	B.20	C.93	C1.1	C1.4
		C.20	C.44	C.56	C.74	D.49	D1.0	D2.0
	3	A.42	B1.5	B1.0	B.38	C1.0	C1.3	C1.8
		B2.4	C.05	C.31	C.67	D.23	D.69	D1.6
	4	A1.0	A.33	B1.1	B.54	B.03	C1.5	C2.2
		B2.2	B1.5	C.03	C.54	C1.1	D.33	D1.0
APR. 20 / AUG. 24	1	B1.7	B1.0	B.61	C.49	C.46	C.41	C.31
		C.31	C.41	C.46	-	D.61	D1.0	D1.7
	2	A.14	B1.1	B.71	B.12	C.61	C.66	C.75
		B1.8	C.13	C.29	C.48	D.47	D.88	D1.6
	3	A.59	A.15	B.76	B.24	C.71	C.87	C1.1
		B1.7	B1.1	C.09	C.43	D.29	D.68	D1.3
	4	A1.0	A.43	A.10	B.35	C.76	C1.0	C1.5
		B1.5	B1.0	B.76	C.35	D.10	D.43	D1.0
MAY 22 / JULY 23	1	B1.4	B.90	B.55	C.31	C.27	C.19	C.03
		C.03	C.19	C.27	-	D.55	D.90	D1.4
	2	A.33	A.04	B.60	B.08	C.40	C.42	C.40
		B1.4	B.92	C.12	C.30	D.46	D.82	D1.4
	3	A.68	A.28	A.03	B.15	C.51	C.61	C.74
		B1.3	B.88	B.61	C.27	D.34	D.68	D1.2
	4	A.98	A.49	A.19	B.22	C.58	C.77	C1.0
		B1.0	B.77	B.58	C.22	D.19	D.49	D.98
JUNE 22	1	A.05	B.86	B.53	C.26	C.20	C.12	A.05
		B1.3	C.12	C.20	-	D.53	D.86	D1.3
	2	A.39	A.10	B.56	B.06	C.34	C.34	C.29
		B1.3	B.86	C.06	C.25	D.45	D.80	D1.3
	3	A.70	A.32	A.08	B.13	C.44	C.53	C.61
		B1.1	B.80	B.56	C.22	D.35	D.68	D1.2
	4	A.97	A.52	A.22	B.18	C.52	C.69	C.90
		B.90	B.69	B.52	C.18	D.22	D.52	D.97

40° N. LATITUDE

Date	Orientation	8 AM	9	10	12	2 PM	3	4
DEC. 22	1	B7.6	B2.4	B1.2	C1.9	C2.2	C2.7	C5.8
		C5.8	C2.7	C2.2	-	D1.2	D2.4	D7.6
	2	B8.8	B3.1	B1.8	B.49	C2.5	C3.3	C7.6
		C3.6	C2.0	C1.8	C1.9	D.60	D1.6	D5.8
	3	B9.4	B3.5	B2.2	B.95	B.05	C3.6	C8.8
		C1.2	C1.2	C1.3	C1.7	C2.5	D.72	D3.6
	4	A1.2	B3.6	B2.4	B1.4	B.70	B.22	C9.4
		B9.4	C.22	C.70	C1.4	C2.4	C3.6	D1.2
JAN. 20 / NOV. 23	1	B7.2	B2.2	B1.2	C1.7	C2.0	C2.4	C5.1
		C5.1	C2.4	C2.0	-	D1.2	D2.2	D7.2
	2	B8.2	B2.8	B1.6	B.44	C2.2	C2.9	C6.7
		C3.0	C1.7	C1.6	C1.7	D.6	D1.6	D5.6
	3	B8.7	B3.1	B2.0	B.86	C2.3	C3.2	C8.0
		C.80	C.93	C1.1	C1.5	D.02	D.75	D3.7
	4	A1.5	B3.3	B2.2	B1.2	B.57	B.09	C8.6
		B8.6	C.09	C.57	C1.2	C2.2	C3.3	D1.5
FEB. 19 / OCT. 23	1	B3.6	B1.7	B.93	C1.2	C1.3	C1.5	C2.0
		C2.0	C1.5	C1.3	-	D.93	D1.7	D3.6
	2	B4.0	B2.0	B1.2	B.31	C1.5	C1.9	C2.9
		C1.0	C.99	C1.1	C1.2	D.55	D1.3	D3.0
	3	A.05	B2.2	B1.5	B.61	C1.6	C2.1	C3.6
		B4.2	C.43	C.69	C1.1	D.14	D.72	D2.0
	4	A1.1	A.15	B1.6	B.87	B.28	C2.2	C4.0
		B4.0	B2.2	C.28	C.87	C1.6	D.15	D1.1
MAR. 21 / SEPT 23	1	B2.4	B1.3	B.74	C.83	C.83	C.85	C.90
		C.90	C.85	C.83	-	D.74	D1.3	D2.4
	2	B2.5	B1.5	B.92	B.21	C1.0	C1.2	C1.5
		C.26	C.49	C.61	C.8	D.5	D1.0	D2.0
	3	A.39	B1.6	B1.1	B.41	C1.1	C1.4	C2.0
		B2.5	C.09	C.35	C.72	D.22	D.69	D1.6
	4	A1.0	A.30	B1.1	B.58	B.06	C1.5	C2.3
		B2.3	B1.5	C.06	C.58	C1.1	D.30	D1.0
APR. 20 / AUG. 24	1	B1.8	B1.1	B.63	C.54	C.51	C.44	C.35
		C.35	C.44	C.51	-	D.63	D1.1	D1.8
	2	A.12	B1.1	B.74	B.14	C.65	C.71	C.79
		B1.8	C.16	C.33	C.52	D.47	D.90	D1.6
	3	A.58	A.13	B.80	B.27	C.75	C.92	C1.2
		B1.7	B1.1	C.12	C.47	D.29	D.68	D1.4
	4	A1.0	A.42	A.08	B.38	C.80	C1.1	C1.5
		B1.5	B1.1	B.80	C.38	D.08	D.42	D1.0
MAY 22 / JULY 23	1	B1.4	B.90	B.55	C.35	C.30	C.22	C.06
		C.06	C.22	C.30	-	D.55	D.90	D1.4
	2	A.30	A.01	B.61	B.09	C.43	C.45	C.43
		B1.4	B.93	C.15	C.34	D.45	D.81	D1.4
	3	A.65	A.25	A.01	B.17	C.54	C.64	C.77
		B1.3	B.89	B.63	C.31	D.32	D.67	D1.2
	4	A.96	A.48	A.17	B.25	C.60	C.80	C1.1
		B1.1	B.80	B.60	C.25	D.17	D.48	D.96
JUNE 22	1	A.01	B.85	B.53	C.29	C.24	C.15	A.01
		B1.3	C.15	C.24	-	D.53	D.85	D1.3
	2	A.35	A.07	B.57	B.07	C.37	C.36	C.32
		B1.3	B.86	C.09	C.28	D.44	D.78	D1.3
	3	A.67	A.29	A.05	B.14	C.47	C.55	C.64
		B1.1	B.81	B.58	C.25	D.33	D.66	D1.2
	4	A.94	A.49	A.20	B.20	C.54	C.71	C.92
		B.92	B.7[illegible]	B.54	C.20	D.20	D.49	D.94

41° N. LATITUDE

Date	Orientation	8 AM	9	10	12	2 PM	3	4
DEC. 22	1	B8.3	B2.6	B1.3	C2.0	C2.3	C2.9	C6.4
		C6.4	C2.9	C2.3	-	D1.3	D2.6	D8.3
	2	B9.6	B3.2	B1.9	B.52	C2.6	C3.5	C8.3
		C4.0	C2.2	C1.9	C2.0	D.63	D1.7	D6.3
	3	B10.	B3.7	B2.3	B1.0	B.05	C3.8	C9.6
		C1.4	C1.3	C1.4	C1.7	C2.7	D.77	D3.9
	4	A1.3	B3.9	B2.6	B1.4	B.74	B.25	C10.
		B10.	C.25	C.74	C1.4	C2.6	C3.9	D1.3
JAN. 20 / NOV. 23	1	B7.8	B2.3	B1.2	C1.8	C2.0	C2.5	C5.5
		C5.5	C2.5	C2.0	-	D1.2	D2.3	D7.8
	2	B8.9	B2.9	B1.7	B.46	C2.3	C3.0	C7.3
		C3.3	C1.8	C1.7	C1.7	D.62	D1.6	D5.8
	3	B9.5	B3.2	B2.0	B.9	C2.4	C3.3	C8.7
		C.88	C.98	C1.2	C1.6	D 0	D.76	D3.9
	4	A1.6	B3.4	B2.3	B1.3	B.60	B.11	C9.4
		B9.4	C.11	C.60	C1.3	C2.3	C3.4	D1.6
FEB. 19 / OCT. 23	1	B3.8	B1.7	B.94	C1.3	C1.4	C1.5	C2.1
		C2.1	C1.5	C1.4	-	D.94	D1.7	D3.8
	2	B4.2	B2.1	B1.3	B.33	C1.6	C1.9	C3.0
		C1.1	C1.0	C1.1	C1.2	D.55	D1.3	D3.1
	3	A.05	B2.3	B1.5	B.64	C1.7	C2.2	C3.7
		B4.3	C.45	C.71	C1.1	D.12	D.72	D2.2
	4	A1.2	A.14	B1.6	B.9	B.30	C2.3	C4.2
		B4.2	B2.3	C.30	C.9	C1.6	D.14	D1.2
MAR. 21 / SEPT 23	1	B2.4	B1.3	B.75	C.86	C.86	C.88	C.92
		C.92	C.88	C.86	-	D.75	D1.3	D2.4
	2	B2.5	B1.5	B.95	B.22	C1.0	C1.2	C1.5
		C.27	C.51	C.64	C.83	D.5	D1.0	D2.1
	3	A.38	B1.6	B1.1	B.43	C1.1	C1.4	C2.0
		B2.5	C.10	C.37	C.74	D.23	D.69	D1.6
	4	A1.0	A.30	B1.1	B.6	B.08	C1.6	C2.3
		B2.3	B1.6	C.08	C.6	C1.1	D.30	D1.0
APR. 20 / AUG. 24	1	B1.8	B1.1	B.63	C.56	C.53	C.47	C.37
		C.37	C.47	C.53	-	D.63	D1.1	D1.8
	2	A.10	B1.2	B.75	B.14	C.68	C.73	C.81
		B1.8	C.18	C.35	C.54	D.47	D.90	D1.6
	3	A.57	A.12	B.82	B.28	C.78	C.94	C1.2
		B1.7	B1.2	C.14	C.48	D.28	D.68	D1.4
	4	A1.0	A.41	A.07	B.39	C.82	C1.1	C1.5
		B1.5	B1.1	B.82	C.39	D.07	D.41	D1.0
MAY 22 / JULY 23	1	B1.4	B.91	B.55	C.38	C.32	C.24	C.08
		C.08	C.24	C.32	-	D.55	D.91	D1.4
	2	A.28	B.94	B.62	B.09	C.46	C.47	C.45
		B1.4	.	C.17	C.36	D.45	D.81	D1.4
	3	A.64	A.24	B.64	B.19	C.56	C.66	C.79
		B1.3	B.91	C 0	C.33	D.31	D.66	D1.2
	4	A.95	A.47	A.16	B.26	C.62	C.81	C1.1
		B1.1	B.81	B.62	C.26	D.16	D.47	D.95
JUNE 22	1	B1.3	B.86	B.53	C.31	C.26	C.17	C 0
		C 0	C.17	C.26	-	D.53	D.86	D1.3
	2	A.33	A.05	B.58	B.08	C.39	C.38	C.34
		B1.3	B.87	C.11	C.30	D.44	D.78	D1.3
	3	A.65	A.28	A.03	B.15	C.49	C.59	C.66
		B1.1	B.83	B.59	C.27	D.33	D.65	D1.1
	4	A.93	A.48	A.19	B.22	C.56	C.72	C.93
		B.93	B.72	B.56	C.22	D.19	D.48	D.93

TABLES for SUN SHADES

42° N. LATITUDE

Date	Orientation \ Time	8 AM	9	10	12	2 PM	3	4
DEC. 22	1	B9.5	B2.6	B1.3	C2.1	C2.4	C3.0	C7.4
		C7.4	C3.0	C2.4	-	D1.3	D2.6	D9.5
	2	B12.	B3.3	B1.9	B.54	C2.7	C3.6	C9.6
		C4.7	C2.2	C2.0	C2.0	D.64	D1.8	D7.3
	3	B12.	B3.8	B2.3	B1.0	B.06	C3.9	C11.
		C1.6	C1.3	C1.4	C1.8	C2.7	D.77	D4.6
	4	A1.5	B4.0	B2.6	B1.5	B.77	B.26	C12.
		B12.	C.26	C.77	C1.5	C2.6	C4.0	D1.5
JAN. 20 NOV. 23	1	B8.5	B2.4	B1.2	C1.9	C2.1	C2.6	C 6
		C 6	C2.6	C2.1		D1.2	D2.4	D8.5
	2	B9.8	B3.0	B1.8	B.48	C2.4	C3.1	C 8
		C3.6	C1.9	C1.8	C1.8	D.64	D1.7	D6.6
	3	B10.	B3.4	B2.1	B.93	C2.5	C3.5	C9.5
		C.97	C1.0	C1.2	C1.6	-	D.79	D4.3
	4	A1.7	B3.5	B2.4	B1.3	B.64	B.12	C10.
		B10.	C.12	C.64	C1.3	C2.4	C3.5	D1.7
FEB. 19 OCT. 23	1	B3.9	B1.8	B.95	C1.3	C1.4	C1.6	C2.2
		C2.2	C1.6	C1.4	-	D.95	D1.8	D3.9
	2	B4.4	B2.1	B1.3	B.34	C1.6	C2.0	C3.2
		C1.1	C1.1	C1.1	C1.3	D.55	D1.3	D3.2
	3	A.04	B2.3	B1.5	B.66	C1.7	C2.3	C3.9
		B4.5	C.49	C.75	C1.1	D.14	D.73	D2.3
	4	A1.2	A.12	B1.7	B.93	B.32	C2.4	C4.3
		B4.3	B2.4	C.32	C.93	C1.7	D.12	D1.2
MAR. 21 SEPT. 23	1	B2.4	B1.3	B.77	C.89	C.90	C.92	C.94
		C.94	C.92	C.90	-	D.77	D1.3	D2.4
	2	B2.6	B1.5	B.98	B.23	C1.1	C1.2	C1.5
		C.29	C.54	C.67	C.86	D.51	D1.1	D2.1
	3	A.37	B1.6	B1.1	B.44	C1.2	C1.5	C2.0
		B2.5	C.12	C.39	C.77	D.21	D.70	D1.6
	4	A1.0	A.29	B1.2	B.63	B.09	C1.6	C2.4
		A2.4	B1.6	C.09	C.63	C1.2	D.29	D1.0
APR. 20 AUG. 24	1	B1.8	B1.1	B.63	C.58	C.55	C.49	C.39
		C.39	C.49	C.55	-	D.63	D1.1	D1.8
	2	A.08	B1.2	B.76	B.15	C.70	C.75	C.84
		B1.8	C.20	C.37	C.56	D.47	D.90	D1.6
	3	A.55	A.10	B.83	B.29	C.80	C.96	C1.2
		B1.8	B1.2	C.16	C.50	D.27	D.68	D1.4
	4	A.99	A.40	A.05	B.41	C.84	C1.1	C1.6
		B1.6	B1.1	B.84	C.41	D.05	D.40	D.99
MAY 22 JULY 23	1	B1.4	B.91	B.56	C.40	C.35	C.26	C.10
		C.10	C.26	C.35	-	D.56	D.91	D1.4
	2	A.27	B.95	B.63	B.10	C.48	C.49	C.47
		B1.4	C.01	C.19	C.38	D.45	D.81	D1.4
	3	A.63	A.23	B.66	B.20	C.58	C.68	C.81
		B1.3	B.92	C.02	C.34	D.31	D.66	D1.2
	4	A.94	A.46	A.14	B.28	C.64	C.83	C1.1
		B1.1	B.83	B.64	C.28	D.14	D.46	D.94
JUNE 22	1	B1.3	B.86	B.53	C.33	C.28	C.19	C.02
		C.02	C.19	C.28	-	D.53	D.86	D1.3
	2	A.32	A.03	B.59	B.08	C.41	C.40	C.36
		B1.3	B.88	C.13	C.32	D.44	D.78	D1.3
	3	A.64	A.26	A.02	B.16	C.51	C.59	C.68
		B1.2	B.84	B.60	C.28	D.32	D.65	D1.1
	4	A.91	A.47	A.17	B.23	C.57	C.74	C.95
		B.95	B.74	B.57	C.23	D.17	D.47	D.91

43° N. LATITUDE

Date	Orientation \ Time	8 AM	9	10	12	2 PM	3	4
DEC. 22	1	B11.	B2.7	B1.4	C2.2	C2.5	C3.1	C8.3
		C8.3	C3.1	C2.5	-	D1.4	D2.7	D11.
	2	B12.	B3.5	B2.0	B.56	C2.8	C3.7	C11.
		C5.2	C2.3	C2.1	C2.1	D.66	D1.8	D8.1
	3	B13.	B3.9	B2.4	B1.1	B.07	C4.1	C13
		C1.8	C1.4	C1.5	C1.9	C2.9	D.85	D5.1
	4	A1.7	B4.2	B2.7	B1.5	B.81	B.28	C13
		B13.	C.28	C.81	C1.5	C2.7	C4.2	D1.7
JAN. 20 NOV. 23	1	B9.4	B2.6	B1.3	C1.9	C2.3	C2.8	C6.7
		C6.7	C2.8	C2.3	-	D1.3	D2.6	D9.4
	2	B11.	B3.3	B1.8	B.5	C2.5	C3.4	C8.9
		C4.0	C2.1	C1.8	C1.9	D.66	D1.8	D7.3
	3	B11.	B3.7	B2.3	B.97	B 0	C3.8	C11.
		C1.1	C1.1	C1.3	C1.7	C2.6	D.85	D4.8
	4	A1.9	B3.9	B2.5	B1.4	B.68	B.15	C11.
		B11.	C.15	C.68	C1.4	C2.5	C3.9	D1.9
FEB. 19 OCT. 23	1	B4.1	B1.8	B.99	C1.4	C1.5	C1.7	C2.3
		C2.3	C1.7	C1.5	-	D.99	D1.8	D4.1
	2	B4.5	B2.2	B1.3	B.35	C1.7	C2.1	C3.3
		C1.2	C1.1	C1.2	C1.3	D.57	D1.3	D3.3
	3	A.01	B2.4	B1.6	B.68	C1.8	C2.4	C4.1
		B4.7	C.51	C.78	C1.2	D.11	D.76	D2.4
	4	A1.2	A.12	B1.8	B.97	B.34	C2.5	C4.5
		B4.5	B2.5	C.34	C.97	C1.8	D.12	D1.2
MAR. 21 SEPT. 23	1	B2.4	B1.4	B.78	C.92	C.94	C.95	C.97
		C.97	C.95	C.94	-	D.78	D1.4	D2.4
	2	B2.6	B1.6	B1.0	B.23	C1.1	C1.3	C1.6
		C.32	C.56	C.70	C.89	D.51	D1.1	D2.1
	3	A.35	B1.7	B1.1	B.46	C1.2	C1.5	C2.1
		B2.6	C.14	C.42	C.80	D.20	D.70	D1.6
	4	A1.0	A.28	B1.2	B.65	B.11	C1.6	C2.4
		B2.4	B1.6	C.11	C.65	C1.2	D.28	D1.0
APR. 20 AUG. 24	1	B1.8	B1.1	B.64	C.61	C.58	C.51	C.41
		C.41	C.51	C.58	-	D.64	D1.1	D1.8
	2	A.06	B1.2	B.77	B.15	C.72	C.77	C.87
		B1.9	C.22	C.39	C.59	D.47	D.90	D1.6
	3	A.54	A.08	B.85	B.30	C.82	C.98	C1.3
		B1.8	B1.2	C.17	C:53	D.26	D.67	D1.4
	4	A.98	A.39	A.04	B.43	C.86	C1.1	C1.6
		B1.6	B1.1	B.86	C.43	D.04	D.39	D.98
MAY 22 JULY 23	1	B1.5	B.91	B.56	C.42	C.37	C.28	C.12
		C.12	C.28	C.37	-	D.56	D.91	D1.5
	2	A.25	B.96	B.64	B.10	C.50	C.51	C.49
		B1.4	C.03	C.21	C.40	D.45	D.81	D1.4
	3	A.61	A.21	B.67	B.21	C.60	C.70	C.83
		B1.3	B.93	C.03	C.36	D.30	'D.65	D1.2
	4	A.93	A.44	A.13	B.29	C.66	C.85	C1.1
		B1.1	B.85	B.66	C.29	D.13	D.44	D.93
JUNE 22	1	B1.3	B.86	B.53	C.35	C.30	C.20	C.04
		C.04	C.20	C.30	-	D.53	D.86	D1.3
	2	A.30	A.02	B.59	B.09	C.42	C.42	C.38
		B1.3	B.89	C.15	C.34	D.43	D.78	D1.3
	3	A.62	A.25	A 0	B.17	C.52	C.61	C.64
		B1.2	B.85	B.61	C.30	D.31	D.64	D1.1
	4	A.90	A.46	A.16	B.25	C.59	C.76	C.96
		B.96	B.76	B.59	C.25	D.16	D.46	D.90

44° N. LATITUDE

Date	Orientation \ Time	8 AM	9	10	12	2 PM	3	4
DEC. 22	1	B12.	B2.8	B1.4	C2.3	C2.7	C3.3	C9.3
		C9.3	C3.3	C2.7	-	D1.4	D2.8	D12.
	2	B14	B3.6	B2.1	B.58	C2.9	C3.9	C12.
		C5.9	C2.4	C2.2	C2.2	D.69	D1.9	D9.1
	3	B15.	B4.1	B2.6	B1.1	B.08	C4.3	C14.
		C2.1	C1.4	C1.6	C2.0	C3.0	D.90	D5.7
	4	A1.9	B4.3	B2.9	B1.6	B.86	B.30	C15
		B15	C.30	C.86	C1.6	C2.9	C4.3	D1.9
JAN. 20 NOV. 23	1	B10.	B2.7	B1.4	C 2.	C2.4	C3.0	C7.4
		C7.4	C 3.	C2.4	-	D1.4	D2.7	D10.
	2	B12.	B3.4	B1.9	B.52	C2.6	C3.6	C9.8
		C4.5	C2.2	C1.9	C 2.	D.69	D1.9	D8.0
	3	B13.	B3.8	B2.4	B1.0	B.01	C3.9	C12.
		C1.2	C1.2	C1.4	C1.8	C2.7	D.87	D5.2
	4	A2.1	B4.0	B2.6	B1.4	B.72	B.16	C13
		B13	C.16	C.72	C1.4	C2.6	C4.0	D2.1
FEB. 19 OCT. 23	1	B4.3	B1.9	B1.0	C1.4	C1.5	C1.7	C2.5
		C2.5	C1.7	C1.5	-	D1.0	D1.9	D4.3
	2	B4.8	B2.3	B1.4	B.37	C1.7	C2.1	C3.5
		C1.3	C1.2	C1.2	C1.4	D.58	D1.4	D3.5
	3	A 0	B2.5	B1.7	B.71	C1.8	C2.4	C4.3
		B4.9	C.54	C.81	C1.2	D.11	D.76	D2.5
	4	A1.3	A.11	B1.8	B1.	B.36	C2.5	C4.8
		B4.8	B2.5	C.36	C1.	C1.8	D.11	D1.3
MAR. 21 SEPT. 23	1	B2.5	B1.4	B.78	C.96	C.96	C.98	C1.0
		C1.0	C.98	C.96	-	D.78	D1.4	D2.5
	2	B2.7	B1.6	B1.0	B.24	C1.1	C1.3	C1.6
		C.34	C.59	C.72	C.92	D.51	D1.1	D2.1
	3	A.35	B1.7	B1.2	B.48	C1.2	C1.5	C2.1
		B2.6	C.15	C.44	C.83	D.20	D.70	D1.6
	4	A1.0	A.28	B1.2	B.67	B.12	C1.7	C2.5
		B2.5	B1.7	C.12	C.67	C1.2	D.28	D1.0
APR. 20 AUG. 24	1	B1.8	B1.1	B.65	C.63	C.59	C.54	C.43
		C.43	C.54	C.59	-	D.65	D1.1	D1.8
	2	A.05	B1.2	B.78	B.16	C.74	C.80	C.89
		B1.9	C.24	C.40	C.61	D.47	D.90	D1.7
	3	A.53	A.07	B.86	B.31	C.84	C1.0	C1.3
		B1.8	B1.2	C.19	C.55	D.26	D.66	D1.4
	4	A.98	A.38	A.03	B.45	C.88	C1.2	C1.6
		B1.6	B1.2	B.88	C.45	D.03	D.38	D.98
MAY 22 JULY 23	1	B1.5	B.93	B.56	C.44	C.39	C.30	C.15
		C.15	C.30	C.39	-	D.56	D.93	D1.5
	2	A.23	B.97	B.65	B.11	C.52	C.53	C.52
		B1.5	C.05	C.23	C.42	D.44	D.81	D1.4
	3	A.60	A.20	B.68	B.22	C.62	C.73	C.86
		B1.3	B.95	C.06	C.38	D.29	D.65	D1.2
	4	A.92	A.44	A.12	B.31	C.67	C.88	C1.1
		B1.1	B.88	B.67	C.31	D.12	D.44	D.92
JUNE 22	1	B1.3	B.87	B.54	C.37	C.32	C.22	C.05
		C.05	C.22	C.32	-	D.54	D.87	D1.3
	2	A.28	A 0	B.60	B.09	C.45	C.43	C.40
		B1.3	B.91	C.17	C.36	D.44	D.78	D1.3
	3	A.61	A.24	B.63	B.18	C.55	C.63	C.71
		B1.2	B.86	C 0	C.32	D.30	D.64	D1.1
	4	A.90	A.45	A.15	B.26	C.61	C.77	C.98
		B.98	B.77	B.61	C.26	D.15	D.45	D.90

46° N. LATITUDE

Date	Orientation \ Time	8 AM	9	10	12	2 PM	3	4
DEC. 22	1	B18.	B3.2	B1.6	C2.5	C3.0	C3.7	C14.
		C14.	C3.7	C3.0	-	D1.6	D3.2	D18.
	2	B21.	B4.1	B2.3	B.64	C3.3	C4.4	C18.
		C8.9	C2.8	C2.5	C2.4	D.76	D2.1	D14.
	3	B23.	B4.7	B2.9	B1.2	B.11	C4.8	C21.
		C3.2	C1.6	C1.8	C2.2	C3.4	D.91	D8.5
	4	A2.7	B4.9	B3.2	B1.8	B.98	B.37	C23.
		B23.	C.37	C.98	C1.8	C3.2	C4.9	D2.7
JAN. 20 NOV. 23	1	B12.	B2.9	B1.5	C2.2	C2.6	C3.2	C8.8
		C8.8	C3.2	C2.6	-	D1.5	D2.9	D12.
	2	B14.	B3.6	B2.1	B.56	C2.9	C3.8	C12.
		C5.4	C2.3	C2.1	C2.1	D.72	D2.0	D9.6
	3	B15.	B4.1	B2.5	B1.1	B.03	C4.2	C14.
		C1.5	C1.3	C1.5	C1.9	C2.9	D.93	D6.2
	4	A2.4	B4.3	B2.8	B1.6	B.79	B.19	C15.
		B15.	C.19	C.79	C1.6	C2.8	C4.3	D2.4
FEB. 19 OCT. 23	1	B4.7	B2.9	B1.1	C1.5	C1.6	C1.8	C2.7
		C2.7	C1.8	C1.6	-	D1.1	D2.0	D4.7
	2	B5.2	B2.4	B1.5	B.39	C1.9	C2.3	C3.8
		C1.4	C1.3	C1.3	C1.5	D.60	D1.4	D3.8
	3	B5.4	B2.6	B1.7	B.77	C2.0	C2.6	C4.7
		C.02	C.60	C.89	C1.3	D.10	D.82	D2.7
	4	A1.4	A.13	B1.9	B1.1	B.40	C2.7	C5.2
		B5.2	B2.7	C.40	C1.1	C1.9	D.13	D1.4
MAR. 21 SEPT. 23	1	B2.6	B1.4	B.81	C1.0	C1.0	C1.1	C1.1
		C1.1	C1.1	C1.0	-	D.81	D1.4	D2.6
	2	B2.8	B1.7	B1.1	B.26	C1.2	C1.4	C1.7
		C.39	C.64	C.78	C.99	D.51	D1.1	D2.2
	3	A.33	B1.8	B1.2	B.51	C1.3	C1.6	C2.3
		B2.8	C.19	C.48	C.88	D.18	D.71	D1.7
	4	A1.1	A.27	B1.3	B.72	B.15	C1.8	C2.6
		B2.6	B1.8	C.15	C.72	C1.3	D.27	D1.1
APR. 20 AUG. 24	1	B1.9	B1.1	B.66	C.68	C.65	C.58	C.47
		C.47	C.58	C.65	-	D.66	D1.1	D1.9
	2	A.01	B1.2	B.81	B.17	C.80	C.89	C.94
		B1.9	C.28	C.45	C.66	D.47	D.91	D1.7
	3	A.51	A.04	B.90	B.34	C.90	C1.1	C1.3
		B1.8	B1.2	C.23	C.59	D.25	D.66	D1.4
	4	A.97	A.36	A.01	B.48	C.93	C1.2	C1.7
		B1.7	B1.2	B.93	C.48	D.01	D.36	D.97
MAY 22 JULY 23	1	B1.5	B.94	B.57	C.48	C.43	C.34	C.18
		C.18	C.34	C.43	-	D.57	D.94	D1.5
	2	A.19	B.99	B.66	B.12	C.56	C.57	C.55
		B1.5	C.08	C.26	C.46	D.44	D.81	D1.4
	3	A.57	A.17	B.71	B.24	C.66	C.76	C.89
		B1.4	B.98	C.08	C.41	D.28	D.64	D1.2
	4	A.90	A.42	A.10	B.34	C.71	C.90	C1.2
		B1.2	B.90	B.71	C.34	D.10	D.42	D.90
JUNE 22	1	B1.3	B.87	B.54	C.42	C.36	C.26	C.09
		C.09	C.26	C.36	-	D.54	D.87	D1.3
	2	A.25	B.91	B.61	B.10	C.48	C.48	C.43
		B1.3	C.03	C.20	C.40	D.43	D.77	D1.3
	3	A.58	A.20	B.65	B.21	C.58	C.67	C.75
		B1.2	B.89	C.03	C.36	D.29	D.62	D1.1
	4	A.88	A.43	A.13	B.29	C.64	C.81	C1.0
		B1.0	B.81	B.64	C.29	D.13	D.43	D.88

MASTER MAP for SUN SHADES

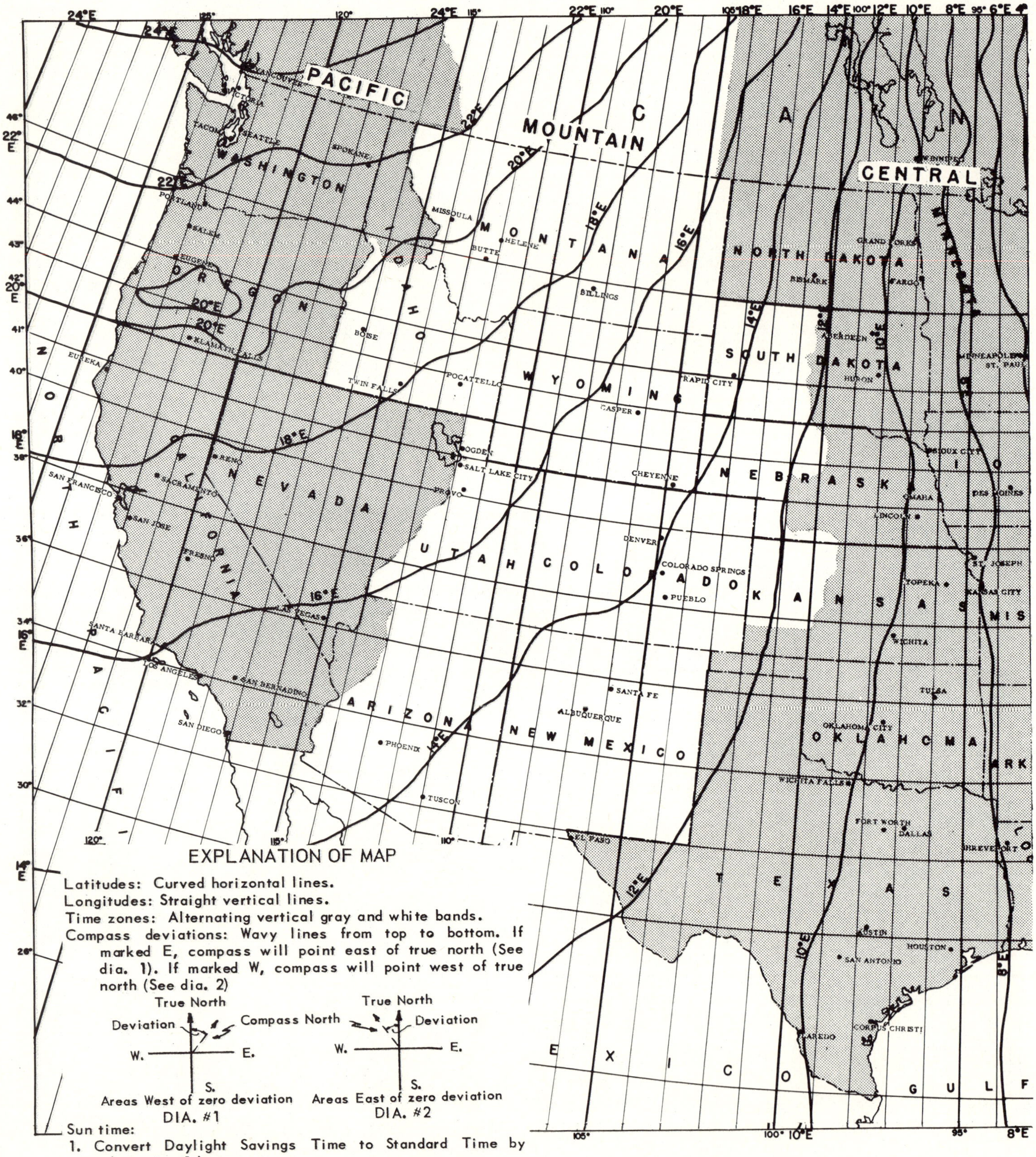
PACIFIC
MOUNTAIN
CENTRAL
CANADA
WASHINGTON
OREGON
IDAHO
MONTANA
WYOMING
NORTH DAKOTA
SOUTH DAKOTA
NEBRASKA
IOWA
MINNESOTA
NEVADA
UTAH
COLORADO
KANSAS
MIS
CALIFORNIA
ARIZONA
NEW MEXICO
OKLAHOMA
ARK
TEXAS
MEXICO
GULF
PACIFIC
VANCOUVER
VICTORIA
SEATTLE
TACOMA
SPOKANE
PORTLAND
SALEM
EUGENE
KLAMATH FALLS
EUREKA
MISSOULA
HELENA
BUTTE
BILLINGS
BOISE
TWIN FALLS
POCATELLO
CASPER
RAPID CITY
BISMARK
FARGO
GRAND FORKS
WINNIPEG
ABERDEEN
HURON
MINNEAPOLIS
ST. PAUL
SIOUX CITY
DES MOINES
OMAHA
LINCOLN
OGDEN
SALT LAKE CITY
PROVO
CHEYENNE
DENVER
COLORADO SPRINGS
PUEBLO
RENO
SACRAMENTO
SAN FRANCISCO
SAN JOSE
FRESNO
LAS VEGAS
SANTA BARBARA
LOS ANGELES
SAN BERNADINO
SAN DIEGO
PHOENIX
TUSCON
SANTA FE
ALBUQUERQUE
EL PASO
TOPEKA
ST. JOSEPH
KANSAS CITY
WICHITA
TULSA
OKLAHOMA CITY
WICHITA FALLS
FORT WORTH
DALLAS
SHREVEPORT
AUSTIN
SAN ANTONIO
HOUSTON
LAREDO
CORPUS CHRISTI
24°E
22°E
20°E
18°E
16°E
14°E
12°E
10°E
8°E
6°E
4°E
125°
120°
115°
110°
105°
100°
95°
46°
44°
43°
42°
41°
40°
38°
36°
34°
32°
30°
28°

EXPLANATION OF MAP

Latitudes: Curved horizontal lines.
Longitudes: Straight vertical lines.
Time zones: Alternating vertical gray and white bands.
Compass deviations: Wavy lines from top to bottom. If marked E, compass will point east of true north (See dia. 1). If marked W, compass will point west of true north (See dia. 2)

True North, Deviation, Compass North, W., E., S.
Areas West of zero deviation
DIA. #1

True North, Deviation, W., E., S.
Areas East of zero deviation
DIA. #2

Sun time:

1. Convert Daylight Savings Time to Standard Time by subtracting 1 hour.
2. Correct Standard Time for site location: Subtract 4 minutes for every degree of longitude that site is west of central longitude or add 4 mins. for every degree of longitude site is east of central longitude. Central longitudes of Time zones are:

Eastern Time Zone 75°	Mountain Time Zone 105°
Central Time Zone 90°	Pacific Time Zone 120°

3. Correct for time variations for day and month: Add or subtract minutes as follows:

Jan. 20	−11 min.	May 22	+3 min.	Sept. 23	+ 7 min.
Feb. 19	+14 min.	June 22	−2 min.	Oct. 23	+16 min.
Mar. 21	− 7 min.	July 23	−6 min.	Nov. 23	+14 min.
Apr. 20	+ 1 min.	Aug. 24	−2 min.	Dec. 22	+ 2 min.

MASTER MAP *for* SUN SHADES

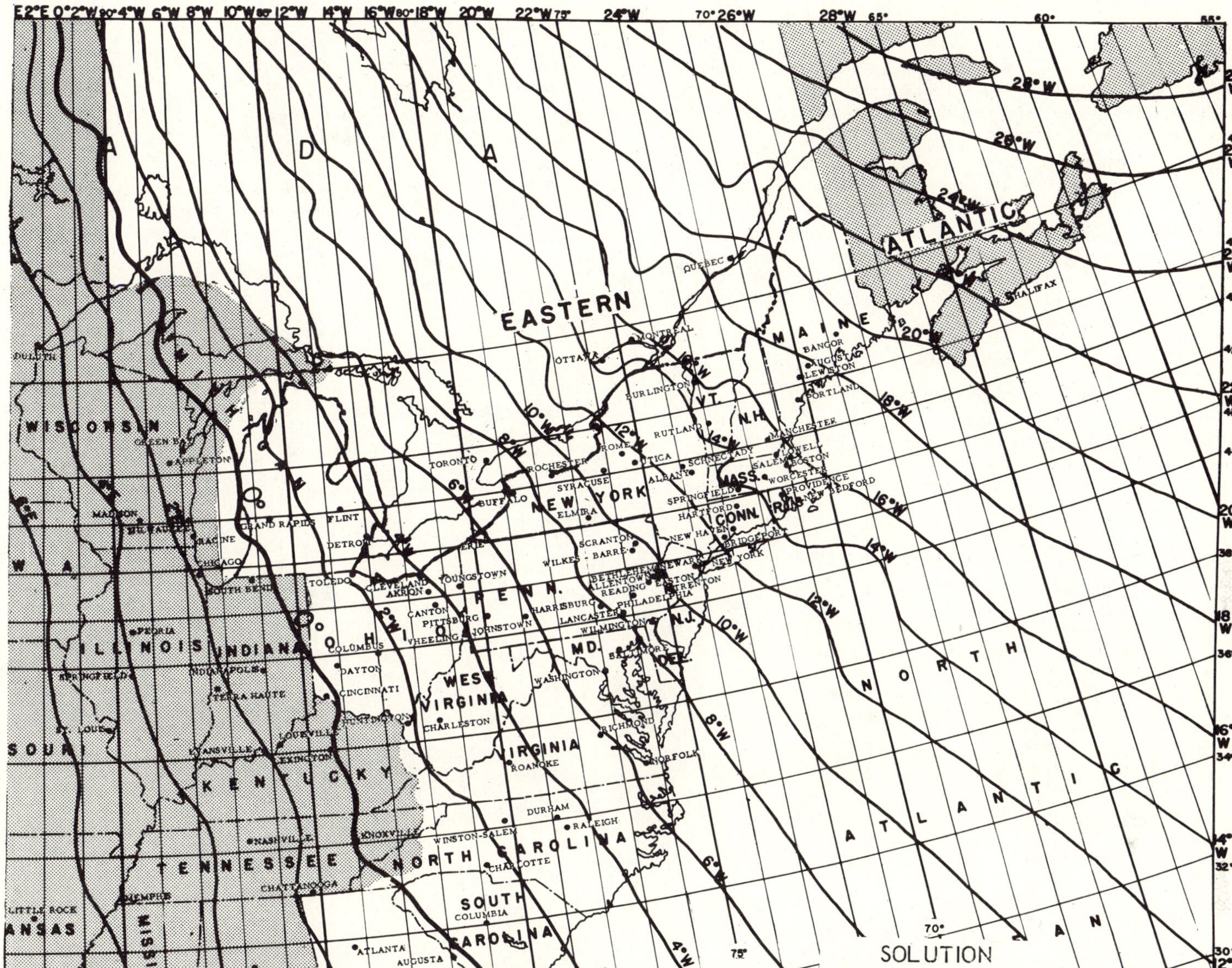
EASTERN
ATLANTIC
NORTH ATLANTIC OCEAN
OF MEXICO
WISCONSIN
ILLINOIS
INDIANA
OHIO
PENN.
NEW YORK
MAINE
VT.
N.H.
MASS.
CONN.
N.J.
DEL.
MD.
WEST VIRGINIA
VIRGINIA
KENTUCKY
TENNESSEE
NORTH CAROLINA
SOUTH CAROLINA
GEORGIA
ALABAMA
MISSISSIPPI
FLORIDA
10°W
12°W
14°W
16°W
18°W
20°W
22°W
24°W
26°W
28°W
8°W
6°W
4°W
2°W
0°
2°E
4°E
6°E

SOLUTION

Step 1. Locate Wichita on map. Nearest latitude is 38° and nearest longitude is 97°.

Step 2. Nearest compass deviation is the 10° E. line. From dia. 4 below it is seen that True North is 10° West of the compass North reading.

Step 3. 12:00 Daylight Savings Time is 11:00 Standard Time. Wichita is in Central Time Zone and central longitude of zone is 90 degrees. Wichita is 7 degrees west of central longitude. Therefore subtract 4 minutes for each degree or 7 x 4 minutes or 28 minutes from 11:00 o'clock, changing time to 10:32 o'clock. Correct for day & month August 24, subtract 2 minutes from 10:32 changing time to 10:30.

Step 4. Correction of orientation diagram.

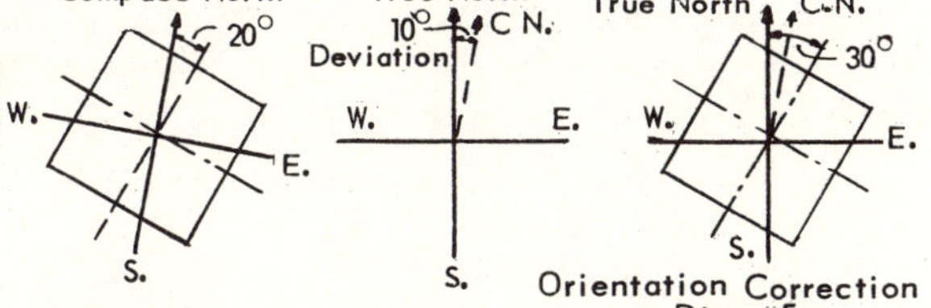
Compass North
20°
W.
E.
S.
True North
10°
C N.
Deviation
W.
E.
S.
True North
C. N.
30°
W.
E.
S.

Compass Orientation Dia. #3

Compass Deviation Dia. #4

Orientation Correction Dia. #5

To be used for Step 4. "Use of Tables to find factor (F)" of Sun Shades

PROBLEM

Known: Compass North of a site in Wichita, Kansas

To Find:
1. Latitude and Longitude of site.
2. True North of site
3. Sun time at site for 12 noon Daylight Savings Time on August 24th.

LOUVER SPACING for SUN SHADING OVERHANGS

LOUVER SPACING FOR OVERHANGS

The preceding sheets on sunshades show how to calculate the width of a solid overhang. The following shows a method for calculating the spacing or height of vertical and sloping louvers that run parallel to the building, to provide complete shade.

Step 1. Find the width of the projection as in steps one through six on sun shade pages. This width was based on the lowest angle of the sun.

Step 2. The calculations for the spacing of the louvers, however, are determined from the highest angle of the sun. Thus we must now use the smallest "F" factor found in step one to solve the problem of spacing.

PROBLEM

Known. "F" smallest factor obtained in step one. This is a pure number, related to one unit.

"H" height in inches (assumed vertical height of louver; for sloping louvers the desired angle of the louver and the width of board to be used should be laid out on paper and "H" measured vertically between highest and lowest corners.

Unknown. "D" distance between louvers in inches.

Vertical louvers: horizontal distance between inside faces of Louvers.
Sloping louvers: horizontal distance from top inside corner of one louver to bottom inside corner of second.

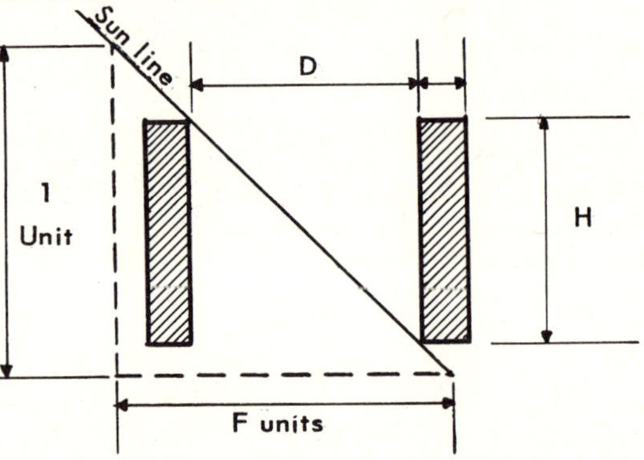

Sun line
D
1
Unit
H
F units

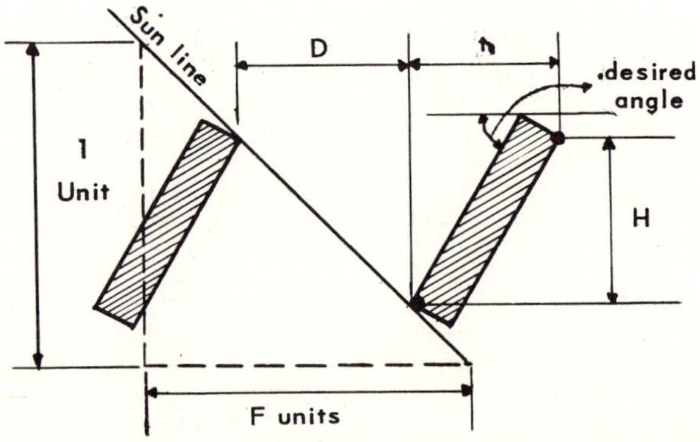

Sun line
D
desired
angle
1
Unit
H
F units

Solution. Substitute in the following formula the various dimensions obtained and solve to find the distance between louvers, "D"

$$D = \frac{FH}{I} \text{ (D \& H in inches)}$$

or

$$H = \frac{D}{F} \text{ (D \& H in inches)}$$

Unknown. "D" horizontal distance in inches for vertical or sloping louvers on a pitched roof.

Solution. Lay out to scale the triangle "I" to "F" to determine sun line. Then superimpose the roof pitch across sun line.

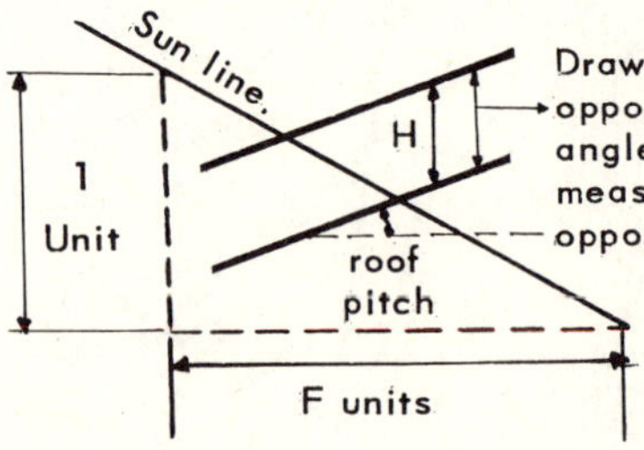

Sun line.
H
1
Unit
roof
pitch
F units

Draw narrowest pair of lines across opposite corners of louver at the angle of roof pitch. "H" is now measured between these lines of opposite corners.

At points of intersection of roof pitch and sun line lay out the desired vertical or sloping louvers with the "points of opposite corners touching these intersections. Then measure "D" for distance required.

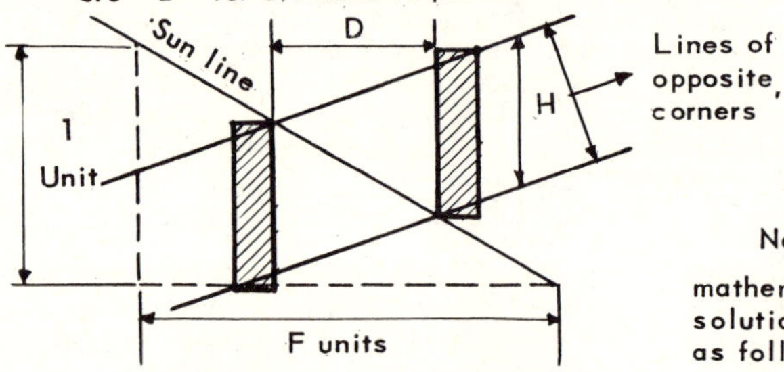

Sun line
D
H
Lines of
opposite
corners
1
Unit
F units

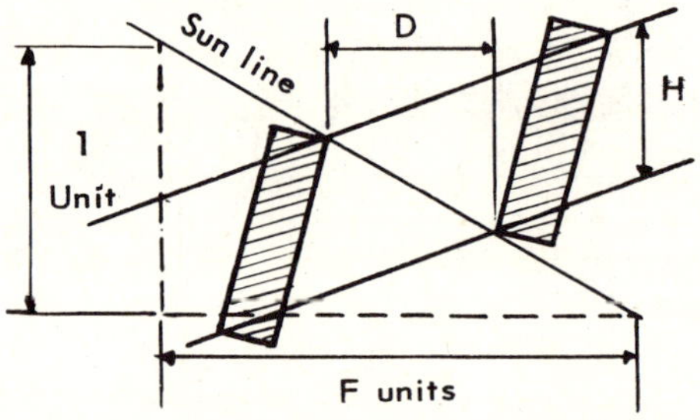

Sun line
D
H
1
Unit
F units

Note

mathematical solution is as follows:

the formula is

$$D = \frac{F\,H}{1+F2}$$

where "r" is the pitch ratio of the roof, i. e. 6 to 12 = 0.5

CORNER INTERSECTION

If it is desired to shade two walls by the use of louvered overhangs, the procedure to find the overhangs is the same for both walls as outlined above. The corner joining of the two may be made in either of the following ways:

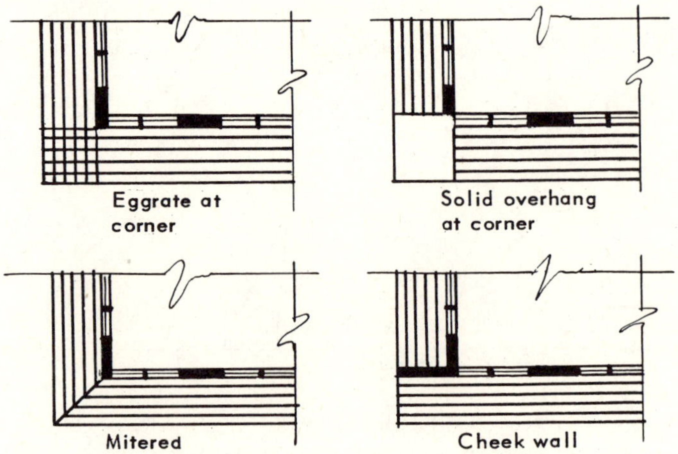

Eggrate at corner — Solid overhang at corner — Mitered corner intersection — Cheek wall on either side of corner

PLAN AT CORNER — LOOKING UP

data prepared in consultation with Andre Halasz A.I.A.

SUN-SHADING DEVICES

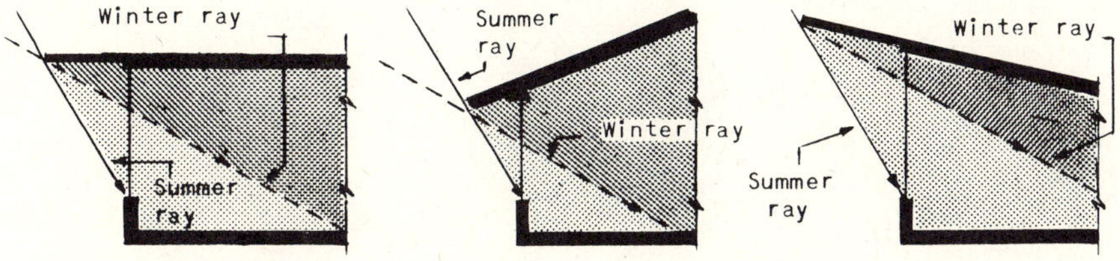
Winter ray
Summer ray
Summer ray
Winter ray
Winter ray
Summer ray

SOLID ROOF OVERHANG - FLAT AND PITCHED: effective primarily on South wall. Length of overhang can be calculated to eliminate summer sun's rays completely and to allow desirable winter rays to enter. Prevents free air movement. Darkens room on overcast days.

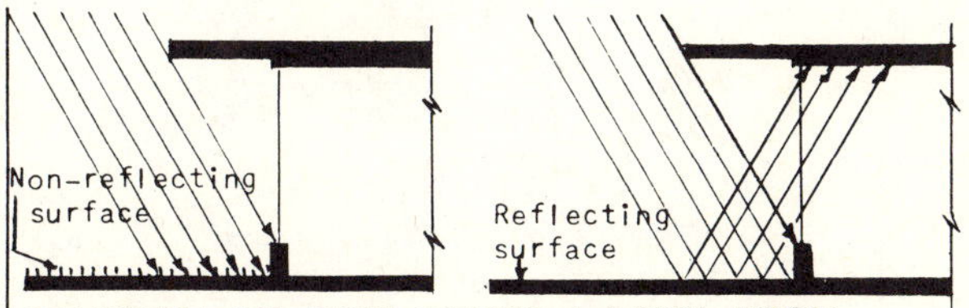
Non-reflecting surface
Reflecting surface

CONTROL OF REFLECTED LIGHT FROM GROUND ADJACENT TO GLASS AREA: light-colored concrete, cement, gravel or tile negate use of overhang by reflecting sun's rays into room. Grass, flagging or dark paving absorb or diffuse light.

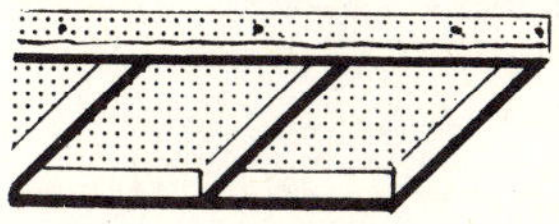

OVERHANGING BEAMS WITH REMOVABLE FABRIC: eliminates summer sun's rays. Removable to allow entry of winter rays. Hinders free air movement.

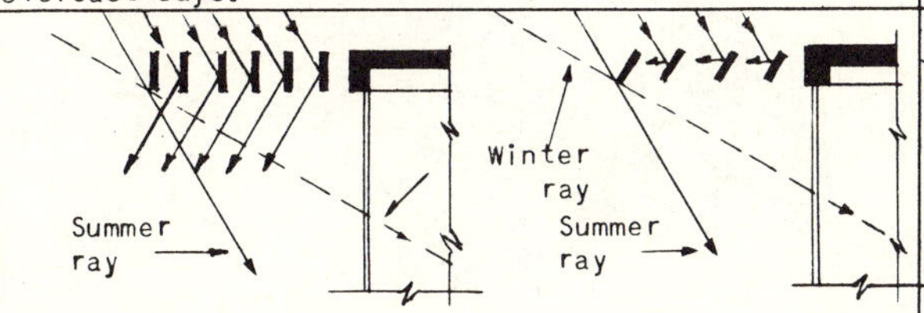
Summer ray
Winter ray
Summer ray

LOUVERED OVERHANG: eliminates direct rays of sun. Spacing of louvers and projection of overhang should be calculated if louvers are fixed. Permits free air movement and entry of diffused light.

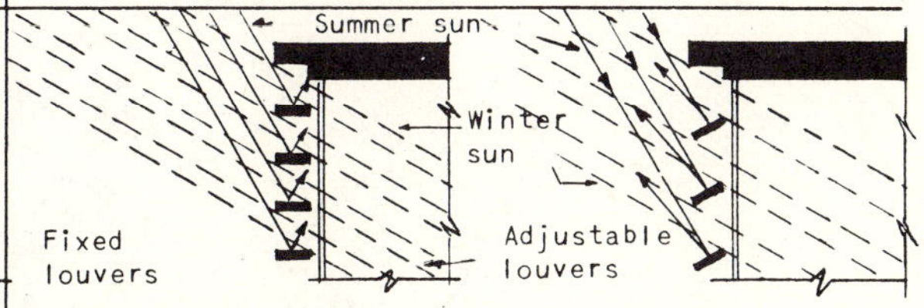
Summer sun
Winter sun
Fixed louvers
Adjustable louvers

ADJUSTABLE HORIZONTAL LOUVERS: adjustable to control direct sun's rays and glare. View is broken by horizontal lines. Operation is questionable in northern climate.

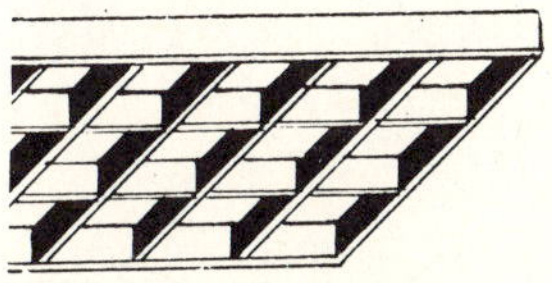

EGGCRATE OVERHANG: more effective than louvers as it eliminates oblique rays of sun. Permits free air movement and entry of diffused light. Expensive.

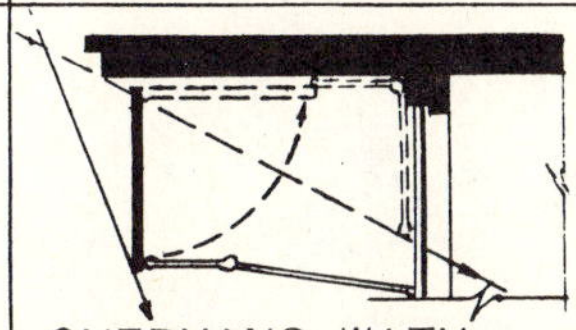

OVERHANG WITH HINGED SHADES: adjustable to eliminate summer sun's rays and to permit entry of winter rays. Interferes with view and free air movement.

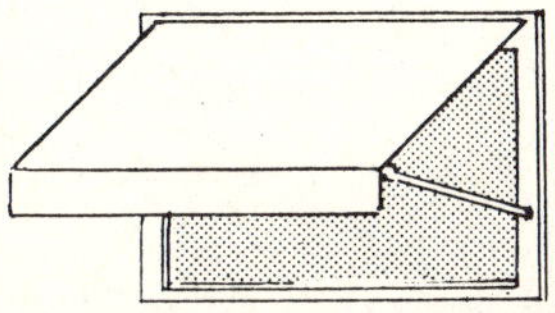

AWNING: adjustable to eliminate summer rays and to permit entry of winter rays. Interferes with view and free air movement. Expensive upkeep.

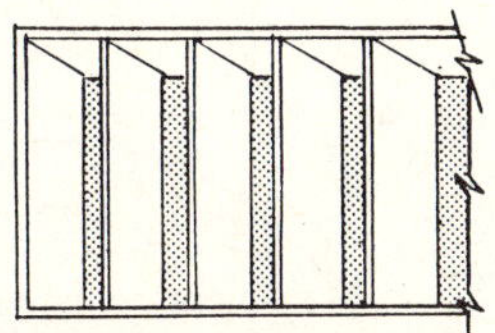

VERTICAL LOUVERS: On South, eliminates low rays. Use with overhang to eliminate all sun. Interferes with view. For Southern use.

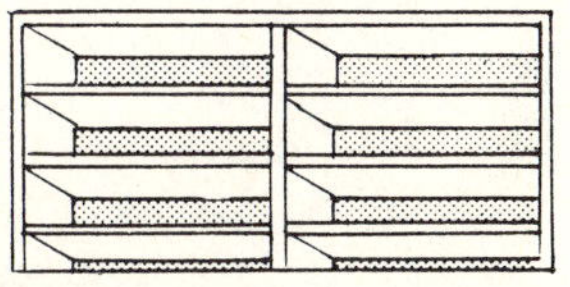

HORIZONTAL VERTICAL LOUVERS: On South, eliminates all sun's rays and glare. Interferes with view. For Southern Use.

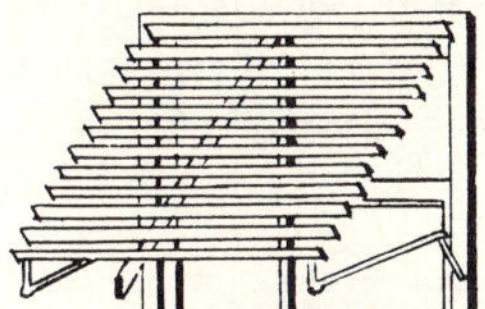

ADJUSTABLE METAL LOUVERED AWNING: controls sun at any angle. Operation doubtful in cold climate.

LOUVERED WINDOW UNIT OR JALOUSIE: adjustable to control direct sun's rays and glare. View is broken by horizontal louvers.

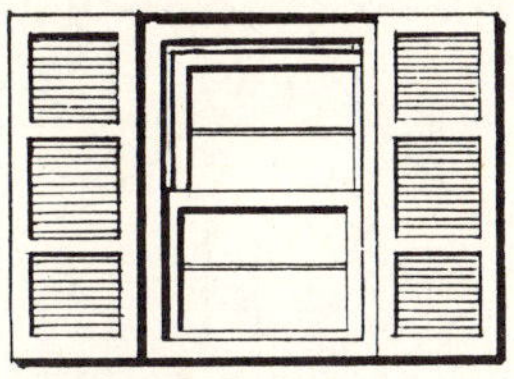

OPERATING SHUTTERS: eliminates sun's rays when closed. Interferes with view.

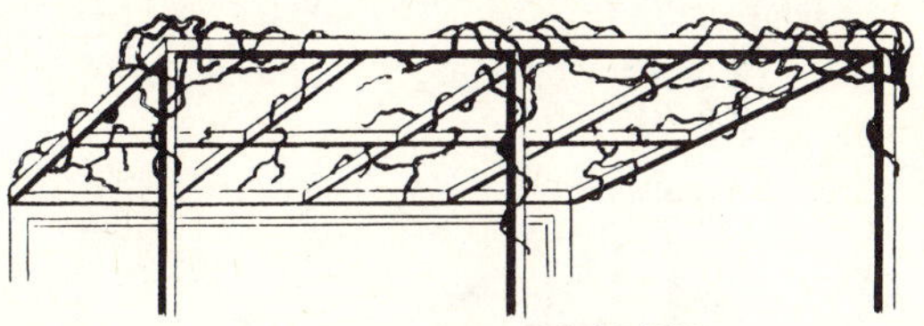

TRELLIS WITH NATIVE GROWTH: a thick growth eliminates sun's rays; some diffused light will penetrate. Allows sun penetration through bare vines in winter. Air moves freely around leaves.

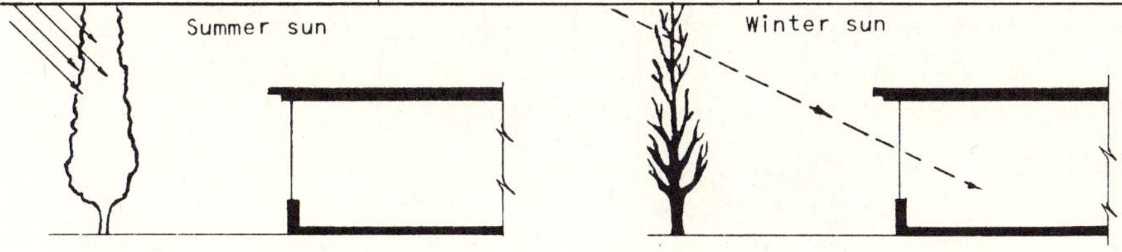
Summer sun
Winter sun

DECIDUOUS TREES (adjacent to South wall): eliminate or diffuse sun's rays in summer, allow sun penetration through bare branches in winter.

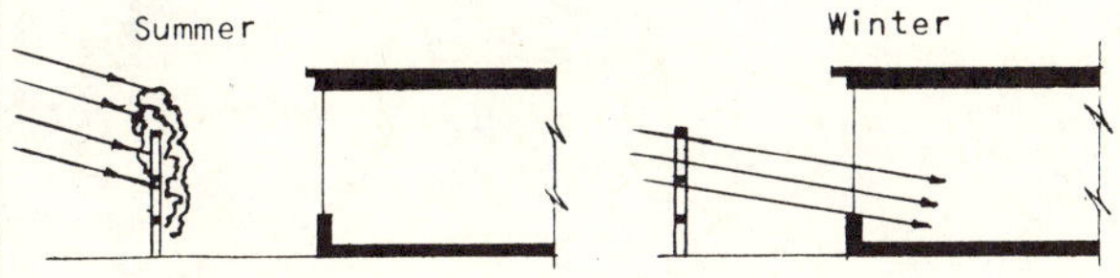
Summer
Winter

FENCE, HEDGE, WALL OR GROWTH ON LATTICE: eliminates low East and West rays of sun during summer. If growth is used, it allows sun penetration through bare vines in winter.

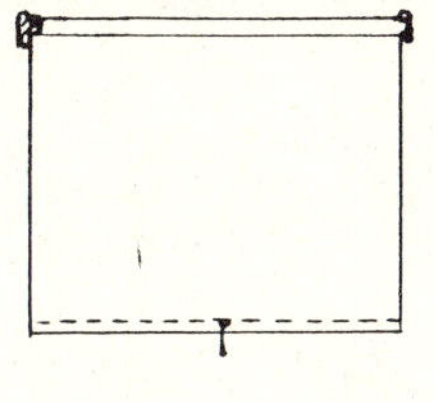

Fabric shades

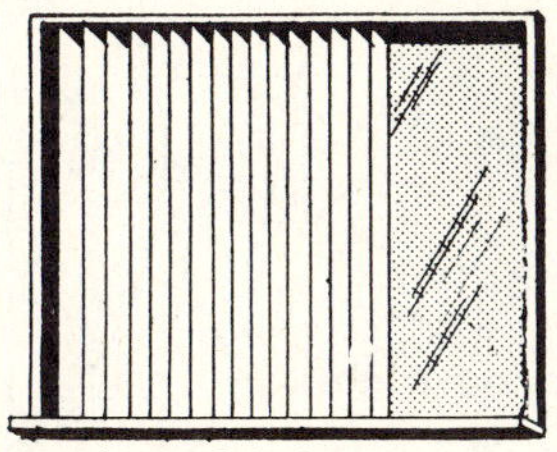

Vertical fabric or wood blinds

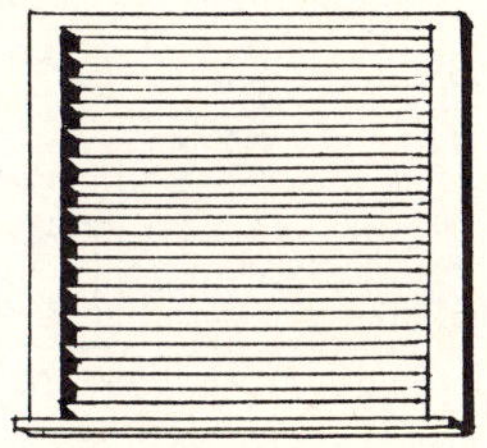

Venetian blinds

INTERIOR DEVICES: easily installed and economical. Eliminate direct rays. However, heat gain through glass is high.

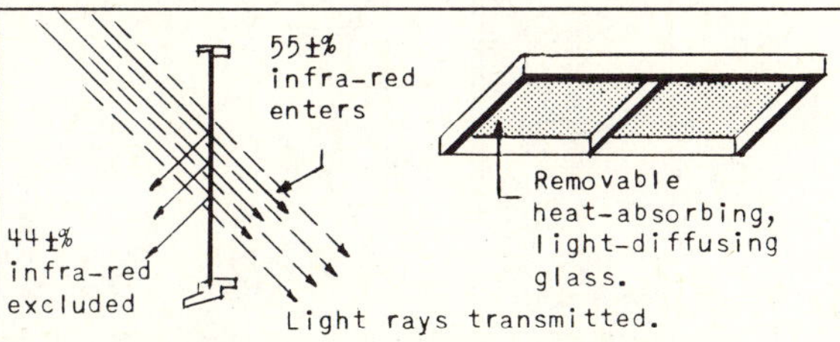
55±% infra-red enters
44±% infra-red excluded
Removable heat-absorbing, light-diffusing glass.
Light rays transmitted.

HEAT-ABSORBING GLASS: reduces amount of solar heat which enters room. Almost 1/2 of the sun's infra-red rays are excluded.

OVERHANG DETAILS *for* SUN SHADING

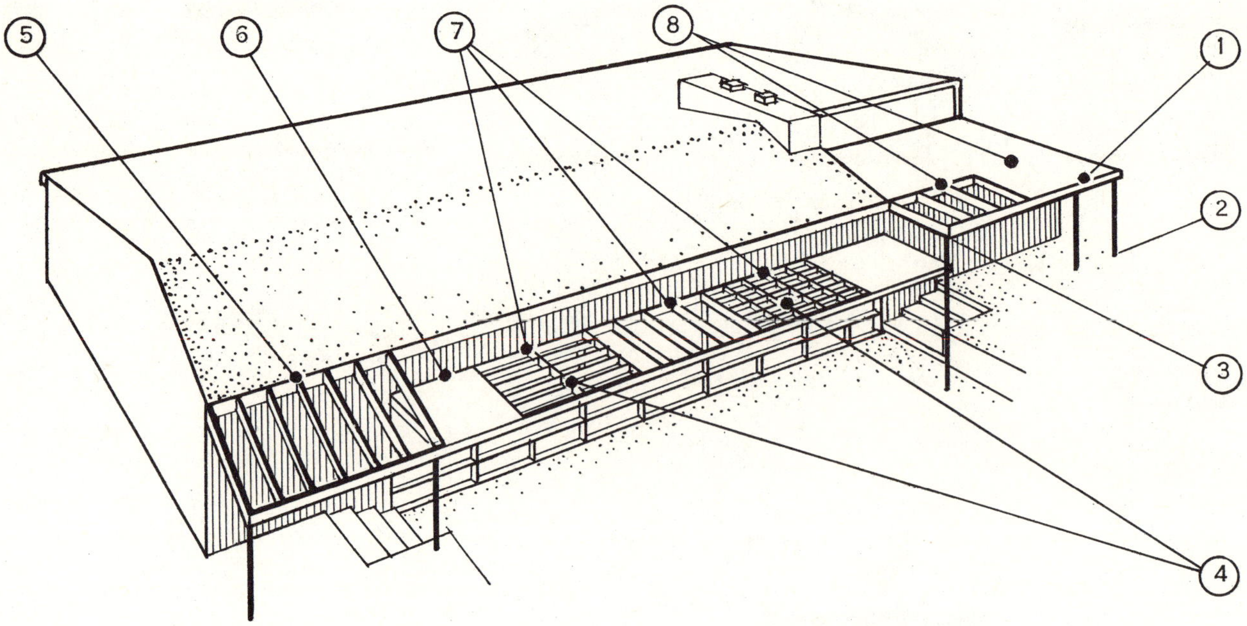
5
6
7
8
1
2
3
4

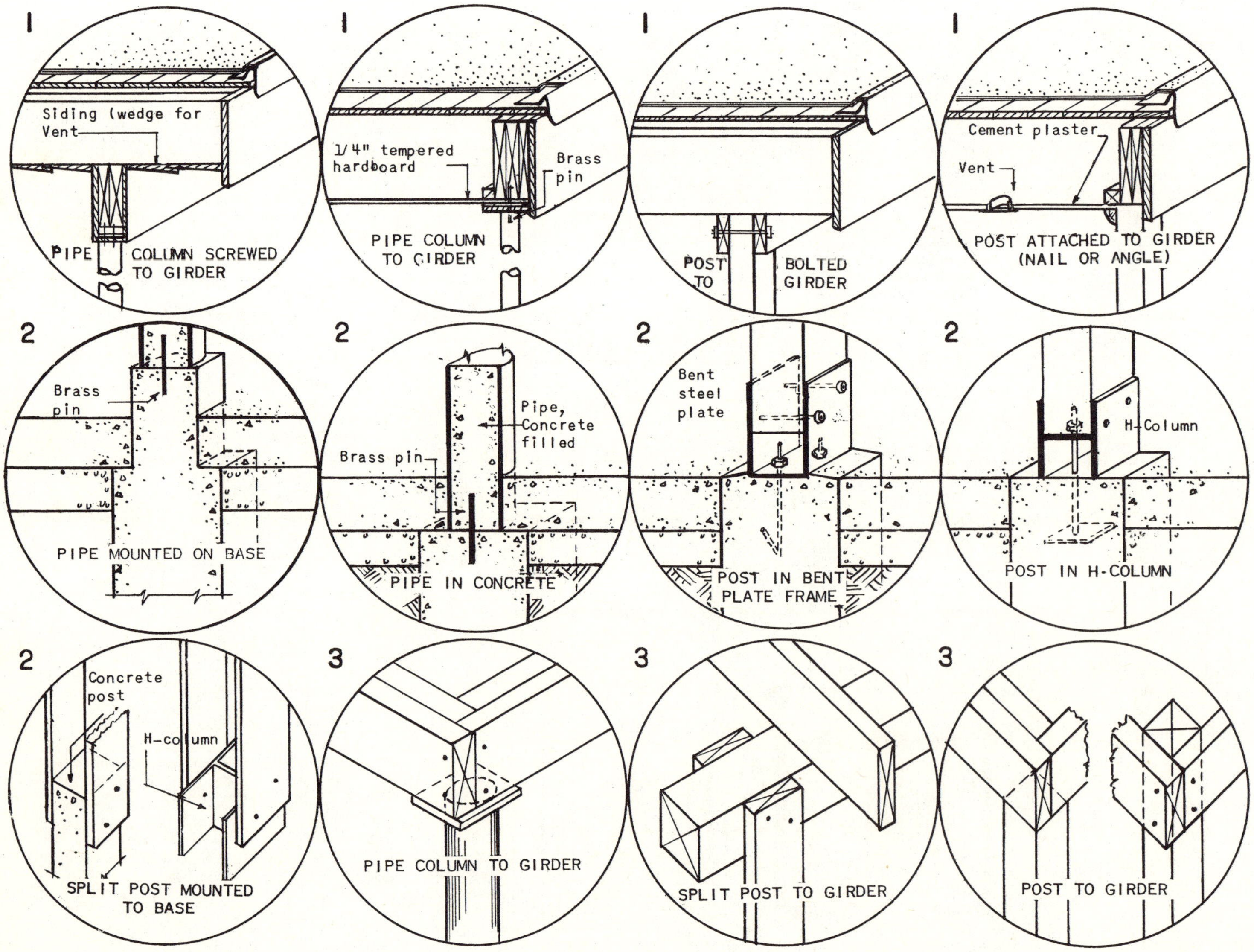
1
Siding (wedge for Vent
PIPE COLUMN SCREWED TO GIRDER
1
1/4" tempered hardboard
Brass pin
PIPE COLUMN TO GIRDER
1
POST TO BOLTED GIRDER
1
Cement plaster
Vent
POST ATTACHED TO GIRDER (NAIL OR ANGLE)
2
Brass pin
PIPE MOUNTED ON BASE
2
Pipe, Concrete filled
Brass pin
PIPE IN CONCRETE
2
Bent steel plate
POST IN BENT PLATE FRAME
2
H-Column
POST IN H-COLUMN
2
Concrete post
H-column
SPLIT POST MOUNTED TO BASE
3
PIPE COLUMN TO GIRDER
3
SPLIT POST TO GIRDER
3
POST TO GIRDER

OVERHANG DETAILS for SUN SHADING

4

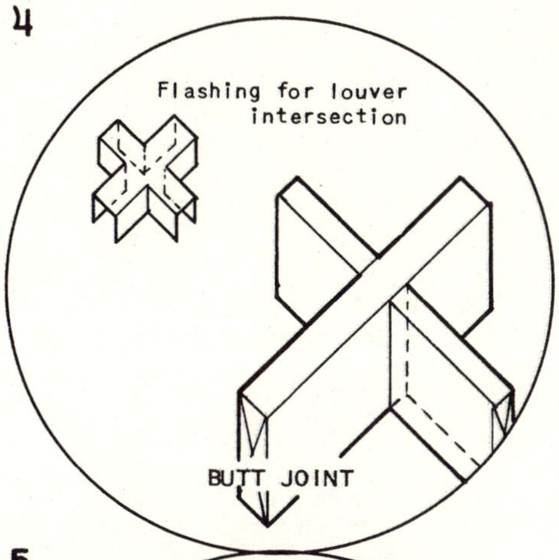
Flashing for louver intersection

BUTT JOINT

4

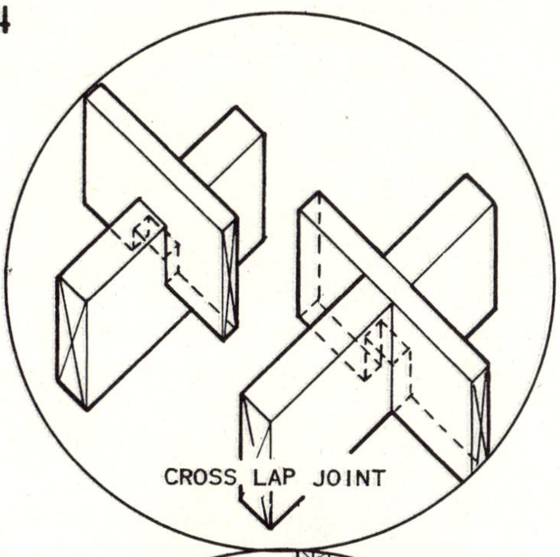

CROSS LAP JOINT

4

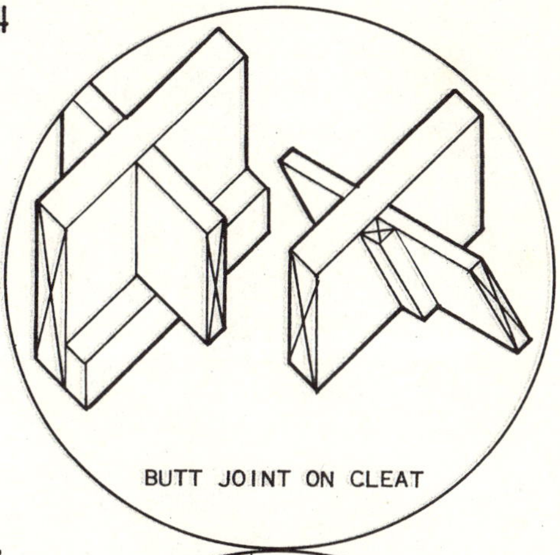

BUTT JOINT ON CLEAT

5

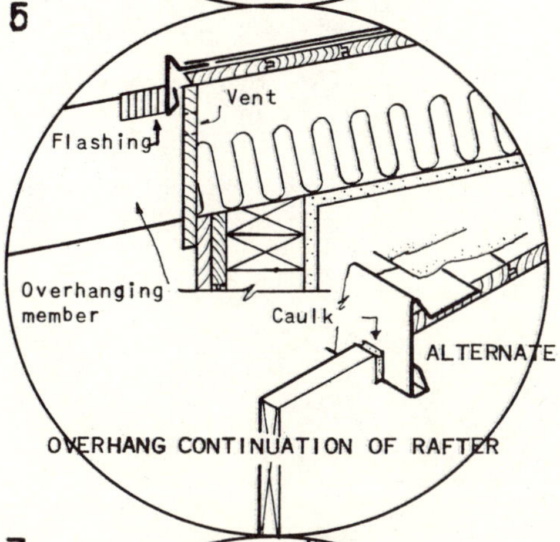
Vent
Flashing
Overhanging member
Caulk
ALTERNATE

OVERHANG CONTINUATION OF RAFTER

6

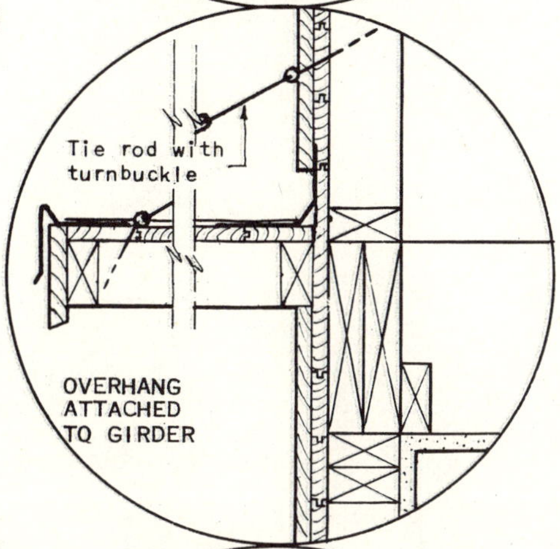
Tie rod with turnbuckle

OVERHANG ATTACHED TO GIRDER

7

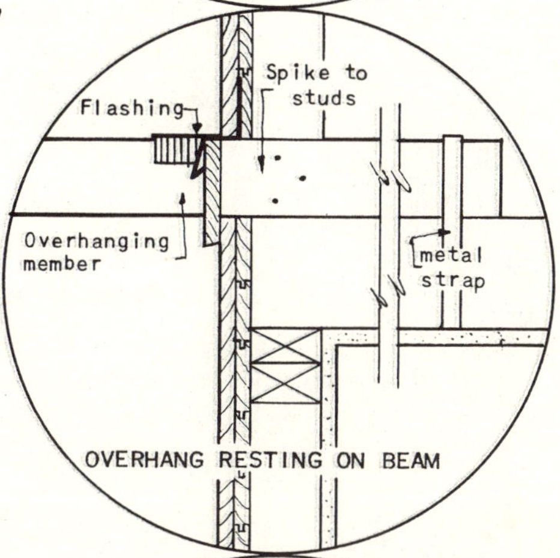
Spike to studs
Flashing
Overhanging member
metal strap

OVERHANG RESTING ON BEAM

7

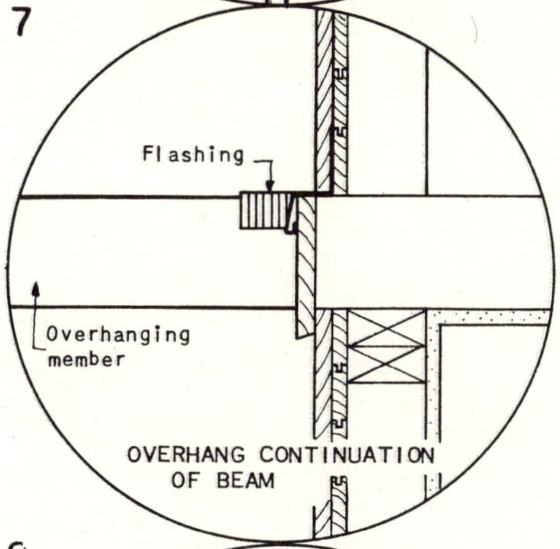
Flashing
Overhanging member

OVERHANG CONTINUATION OF BEAM

7

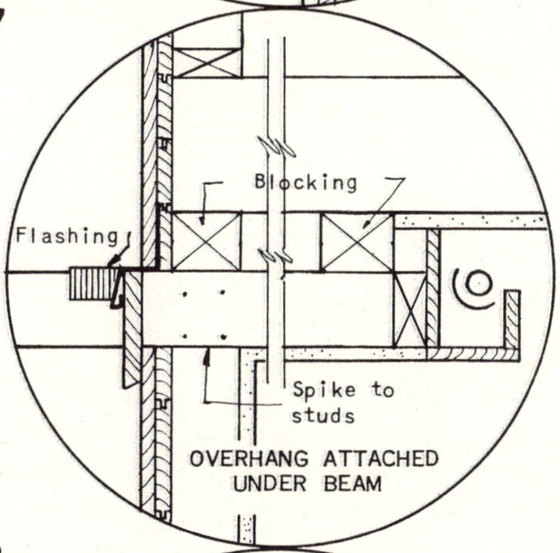
Blocking
Flashing
Spike to studs

OVERHANG ATTACHED UNDER BEAM

8

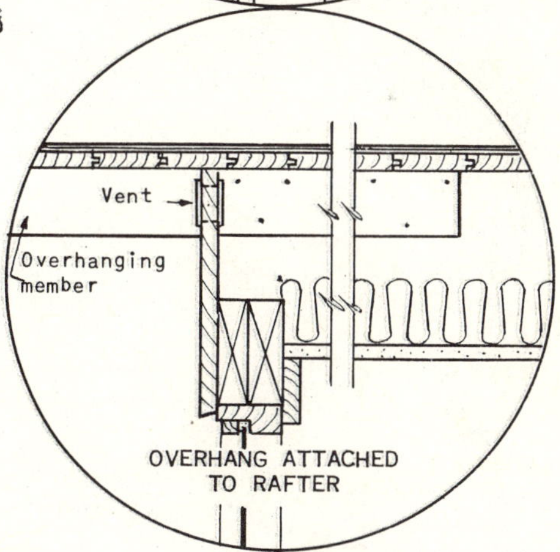
Vent
Overhanging member

OVERHANG ATTACHED TO RAFTER

8

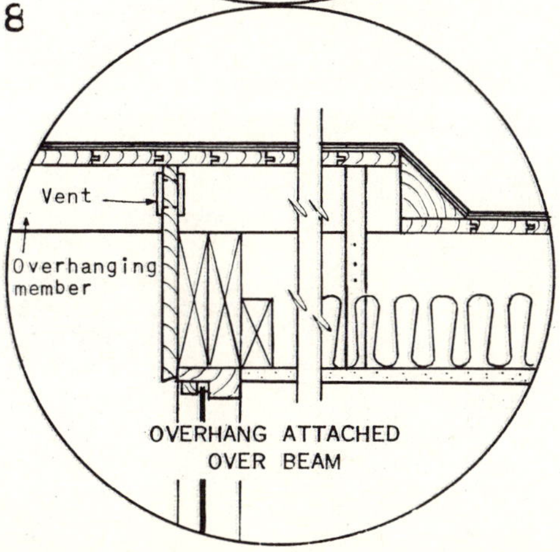
Vent
Overhanging member

OVERHANG ATTACHED OVER BEAM

8

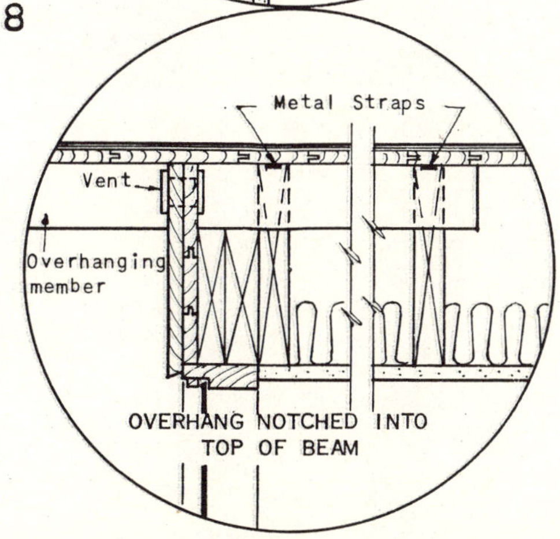
Metal Straps
Vent
Overhanging member

OVERHANG NOTCHED INTO TOP OF BEAM

8

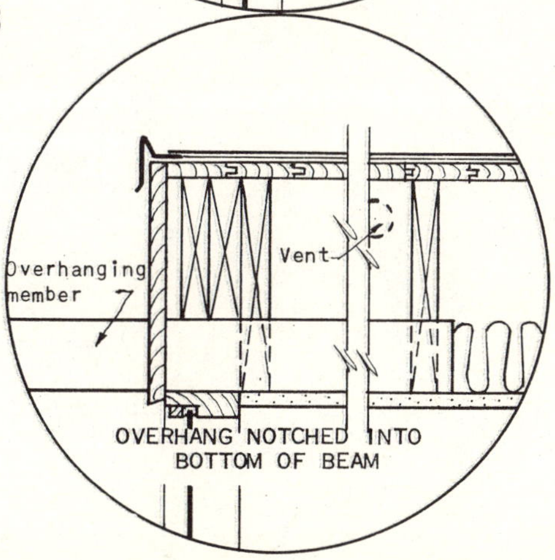
Overhanging member
Vent

OVERHANG NOTCHED INTO BOTTOM OF BEAM

CANOPIES and AWNINGS

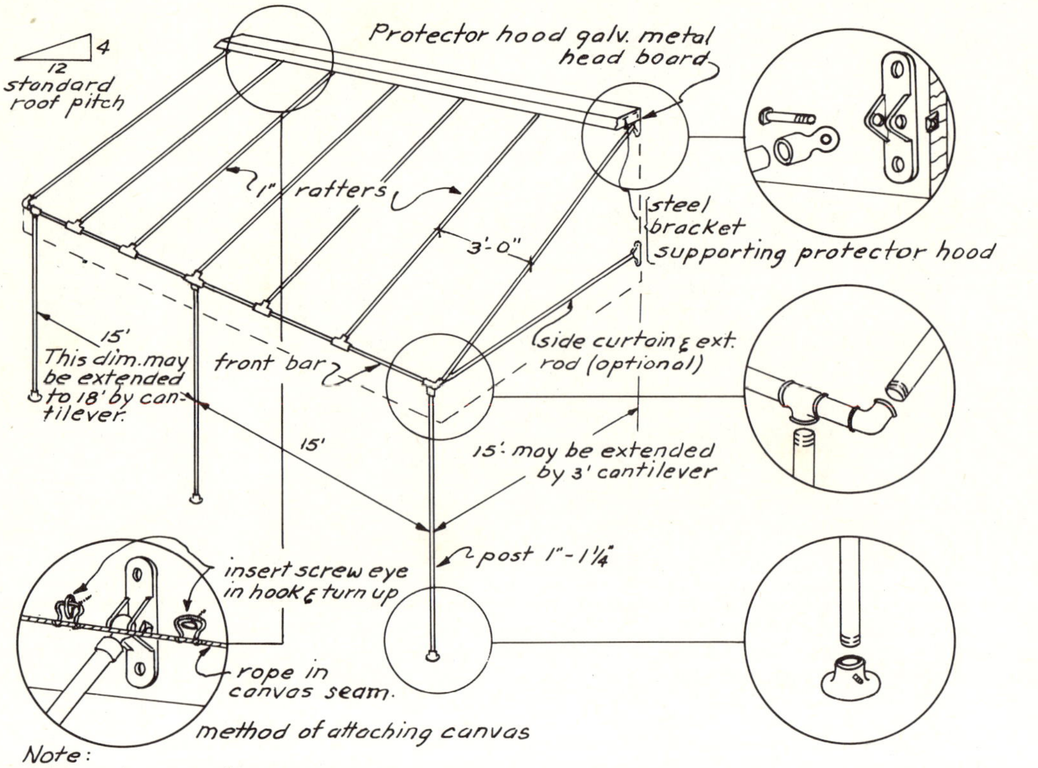
4
12
standard roof pitch
Protector hood galv. metal head board
1" rafters
3'-0"
steel bracket supporting protector hood
15'
This dim. may be extended to 18' by cantilever.
front bar
side curtain & ext. rod (optional)
15'
15' may be extended by 3' cantilever
post 1"-1¼"
insert screw eye in hook & turn up
rope in canvas seam.
method of attaching canvas

Note:
To provide complete sun shade protection the overall length of the awning bar should extend 3 inches past glass line on both sides.
For proper sun shade protection - awnings should project at least as far forward from face of the window as the bottom of the window is below awning front bar.

The "wall measurement" of an awning is the distance down the face of the building from the point where the awning attaches to the face of the building (or from the center of the roller in the case of the roller type awning)
The "projection" of an awning is the distance from the face of the building to the front bar of the awning in its correct projected position.

Right and left of an awning are your right and left facing the awning looking into the building.

Framework - galvanized steel pipe, non-rattling fittings. Awning is lace-on type with rope reinforced eave. Protector hood is galvanized. Sheet metal: bronze, copper, aluminum.

Note:
Awning laced to frame around perimeter & every other rafter

TERRACE OR ROOF AWNINGS

Note: Roller type awnings may also be used - see sheet "Awnings"

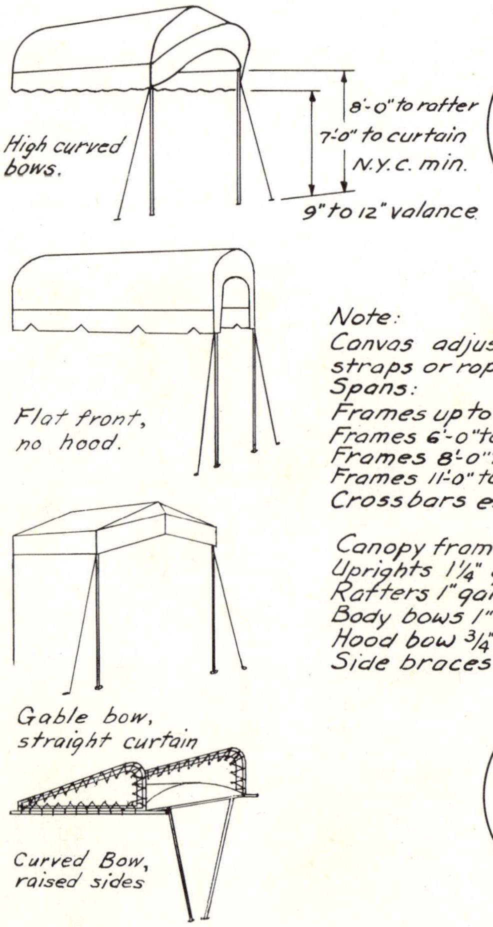
High curved bows.
8'-0" to rafter
7'-0" to curtain
N.Y.C. min.
9" to 12" valance
Flat front, no hood.
Gable bow, straight curtain
Curved Bow, raised sides

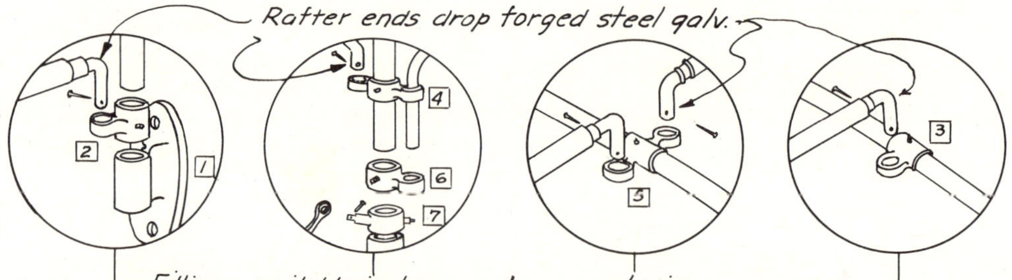
Rafter ends drop forged steel galv.
1
2
3
4
5
6
7

Fittings available in bronze, chrome & aluminum & other plated & polished finishes as required.

Note:
Canvas adjusted to frame with leather straps or rope reinforced lashing eave.
Spans:
Frames up to 6'-0" width take 5 rafters
Frames 6'-0" to 8'-0" take 7 rafters
Frames 8'-0" to 11'-0" take 9 rafters
Frames 11'-0" to 15'-0" take 11 rafters
Crossbars exceeding 8'-0" trussed.

Canopy frame specifications:
Uprights 1¼" galvanized pipes
Rafters 1" galv. pipe to 15'-0" length
Body bows 1" galvanized pipe
Hood bow ¾" galvanized pipe
Side braces ⅝" steel or brass.

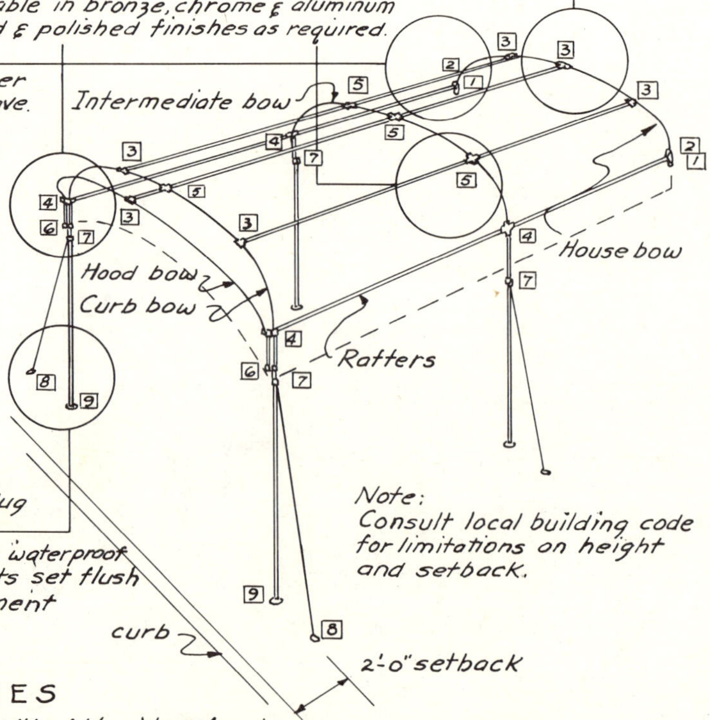
Intermediate bow
House bow
Hood bow
Curb bow
Ratters
curb
2'-0" setback

Note:
Consult local building code for limitations on height and setback.

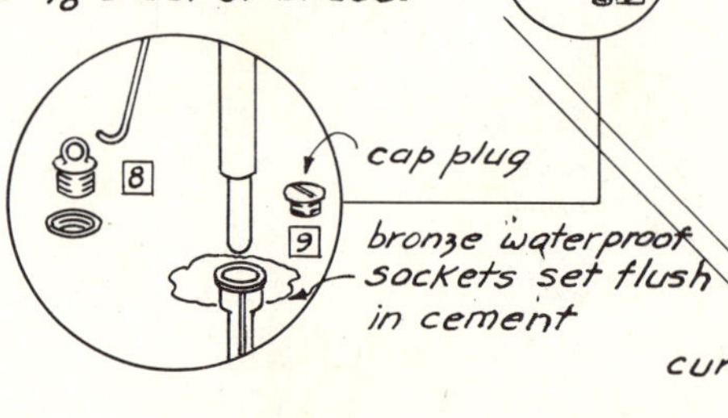
8
9
cap plug
bronze waterproof sockets set flush in cement

CANOPIES

Data supplied by Mr. L. A. Repetti of New York Awning Co.

AWNINGS

AWNING BOX CLEARANCES:

RECESSED BOX SIZES	"H"	"A"	"B"	"C"	"D"
A. LATERAL ARM TYPE	9'6" to 11'0"	10"	10½"	10"	12½"
	9'6" to 12'0"	10½"	12"	10"	12½"
	9'6" to 14'0"	11"	13½"	10"	12½"
B. OUTRIGGER ARM TYPE	varies	6½"	6½"	6½"	

NOTE: The box dimensions above are based on use of Fabric for awning. If a metal type awning is used add 2" to each box dimension.

The awning should be as wide as the window and may be up to 20'-0" wide supported on two arms. If wider than 20'-0" add an arm for each 10'-0" of additional width.

The awning box should be 12" wider than the awning extended 6" on either side of the window. (For housing awning mechanism.)

The awning box for the lateral arm installation should be supported by the equivalent of a 4" x 12" wood beam. For the outrigger type, support by the equivalent of a 2" x 12".

AWNING MATERIALS:

1. Canvas
2. Interlocking metal slats
   a. Aluminum (see below)
   b. Bronze
   c. Stainless Steel
3. Fiberglas

AWNING OPERATORS:

1. Detachable handle control
2. Gear Box & Shaft (Concealed or Exposed) with removable handle inside or outside of building.
3. Electrically driven control.

Detail of Interlocking construction of Aluminum awning slat.

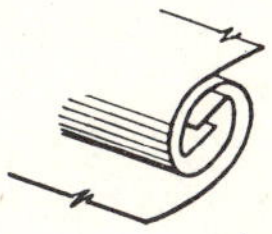

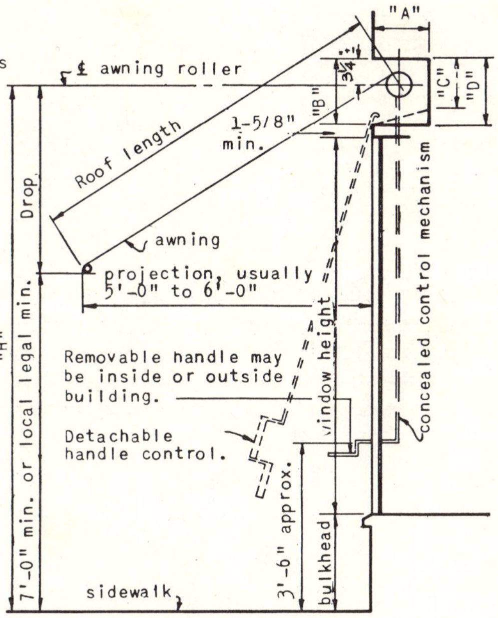
"A"
℄ awning roller
"B"
"C"
"D"
Roof length
1-5/8" min.
Drop
awning
projection, usually 5'-0" to 6'-0"
"H"
7'-0" min. or local legal min.
Removable handle may be inside or outside building.
Detachable handle control.
window height
concealed control mechanism
3'-6" approx.
bulkhead
sidewalk

DIAGRAMMATIC SECTION
RECESSED BOX INSTALLATION

TYPES OF ARM OPERATORS:

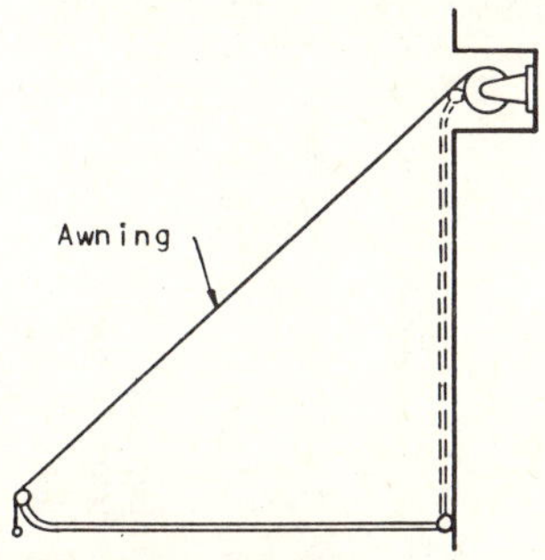
Awning

THE PIPE ARM

The simplest and most economical: but is limited for use only where ℄ of roller is a minimum of 12'-0" above sidewalk. The Pipe Arm must be hinged at least 7'-0" above sidewalk.

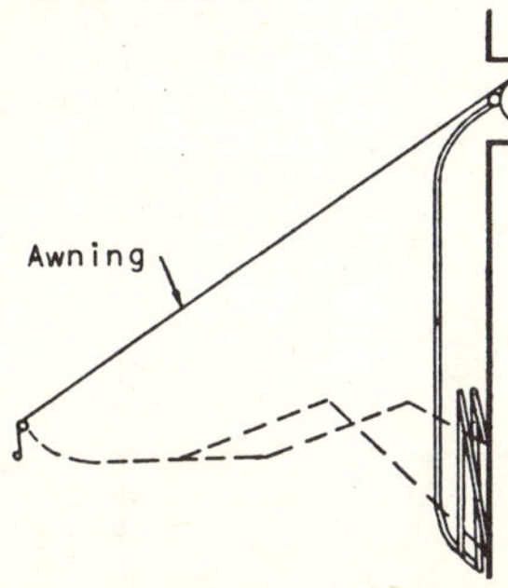
Awning

THE OUTRIGGER ARM

The scissors acting arms of this installation permit the awning to be projected the desired distance while allowing the ℄ of the roller to be located as low as 9'-6" from the sidewalk. The arms may be concealed in the jamb recesses at either side of the window.

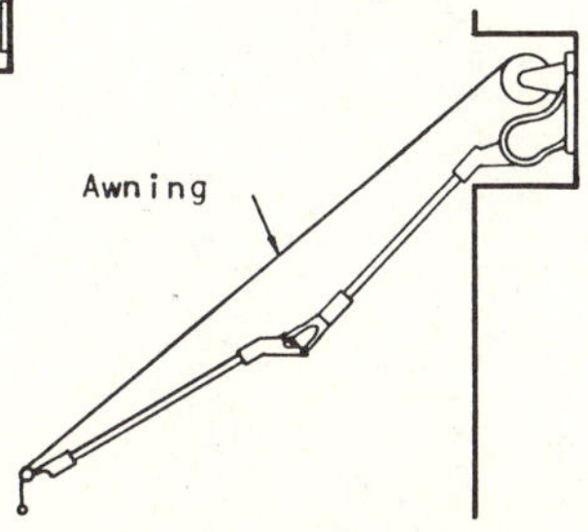
Awning

THE LATERAL ARM

The neatest installation. The lateral acting arms follow the line of and are immediately under the awning when open. When closed, the arms fold into the recessed box entirely out of sight. This type permits the advantage of having continuous awnings as long as 60'-0" without any support other than that of the awning box.

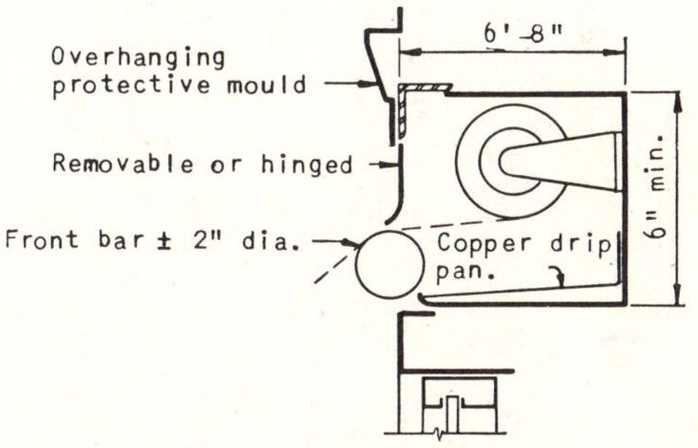
6'-8"
Overhanging protective mould
Removable or hinged
Front bar ± 2" dia.
Copper drip pan.
6" min.

RECESSED POCKET
PARTLY EXPOSED FRONT BAR
used with pipe or outrigger type awning arms. Cannot be used with lateral arm. Side arm brackets may be concealed.

NOTE:

a. The arm operators above show the awning roller in a recessed box; the mechanism may be concealed by a lid either hinged or pivoted. A separate gear raises the lid allowing the awning to be lowered. A second type is the open face installation; the mechanism is mounted on face of building and protected by a hood. A third type is the soffit installation; box is recessed in soffit of store entry to allow for continuity of facing material.
b. Mouldings are diagrammatic only.

Details (1) and (2) below show mechanism housed in steel box (±1/8" thick, non-structural.)
Detail (3) below shows knock-down type where mechanism is housed in pocket and assembled at site.

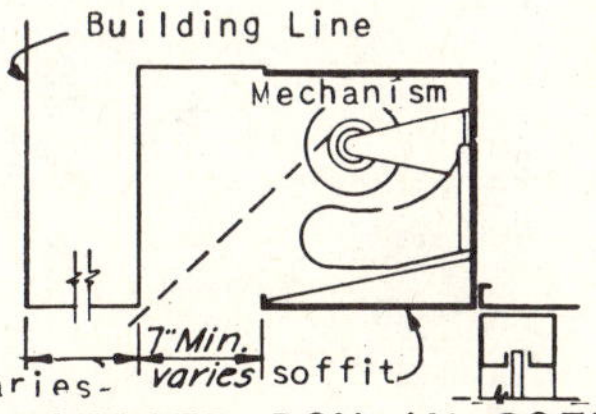
Building Line
Mechanism
7" Min. varies
varies
soffit

RECESSED BOX IN SOFFIT
Lateral Arm installation shown. Consult manufacturer for use of stock mechanism.

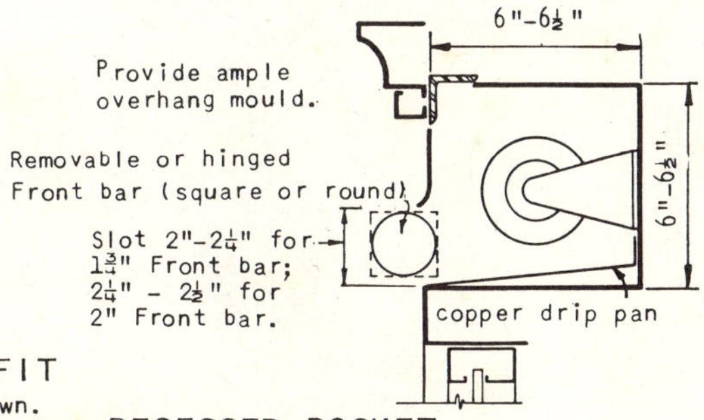
6"-6½"
Provide ample overhang mould.
Removable or hinged
Front bar (square or round)
Slot 2"-2¼" for 1¾" Front bar; 2¼" - 2½" for 2" Front bar.
copper drip pan
6"-6½"

RECESSED POCKET
EXPOSED FRONT BAR
SIDE ARMS EXPOSED
Used when box may not be brought forward.

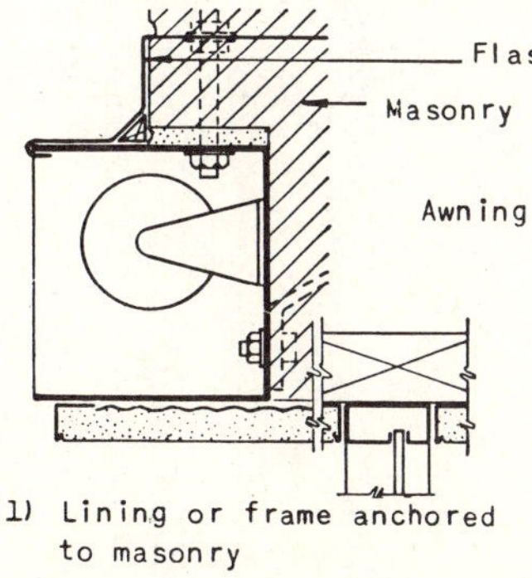
Flashing
Masonry
Awning Roller

(1) Lining or frame anchored to masonry

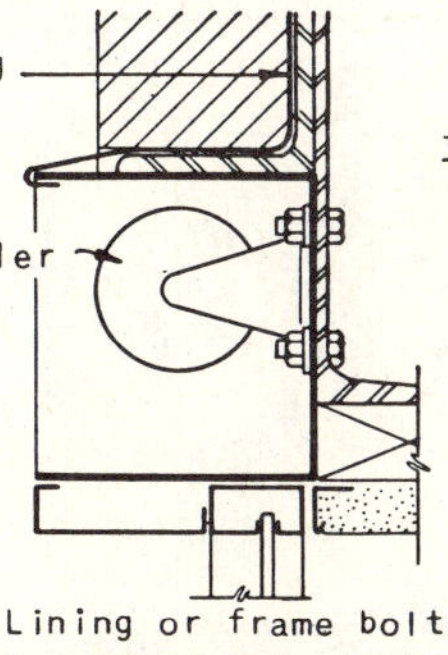

(2) Lining or frame bolted to structural steel.

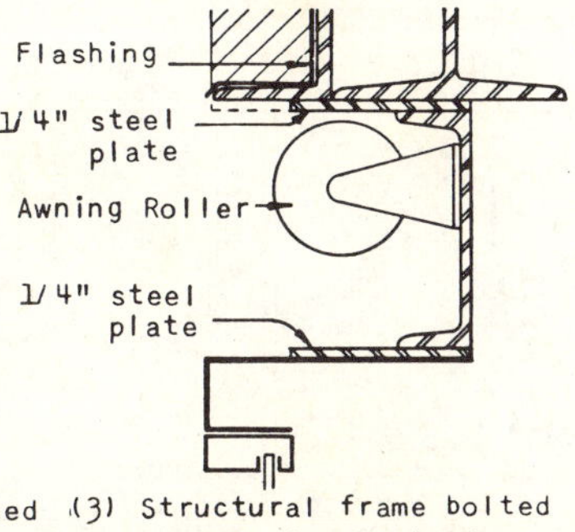
Flashing
1/4" steel plate
Awning Roller
1/4" steel plate

(3) Structural frame bolted to structural steel.

Scale: 1½" = 1'-0"

TYPICAL CONSTRUCTION DETAILS

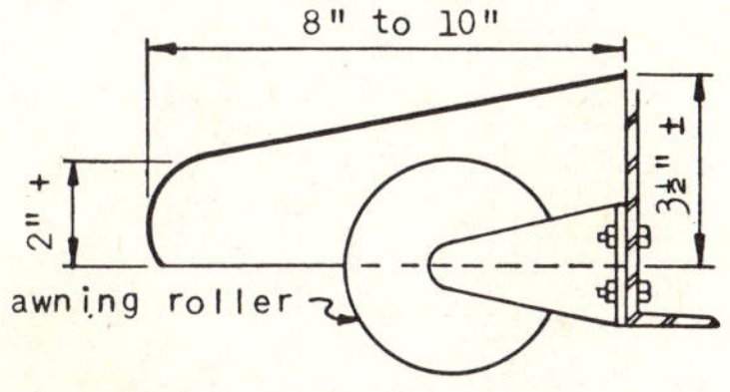
8" to 10"
2" ±
3½" ±
awning roller

HOOD FOR AWNING ROLLER
EXPOSED MECHANISM AND ARMS

Awning mechanism fastened to face of building. The pipe, outrigger, or lateral arm may be used with this installation.

DATA PREPARED BY DANIEL SCHWARTZMAN, ARCHITECT

ORIENTATION

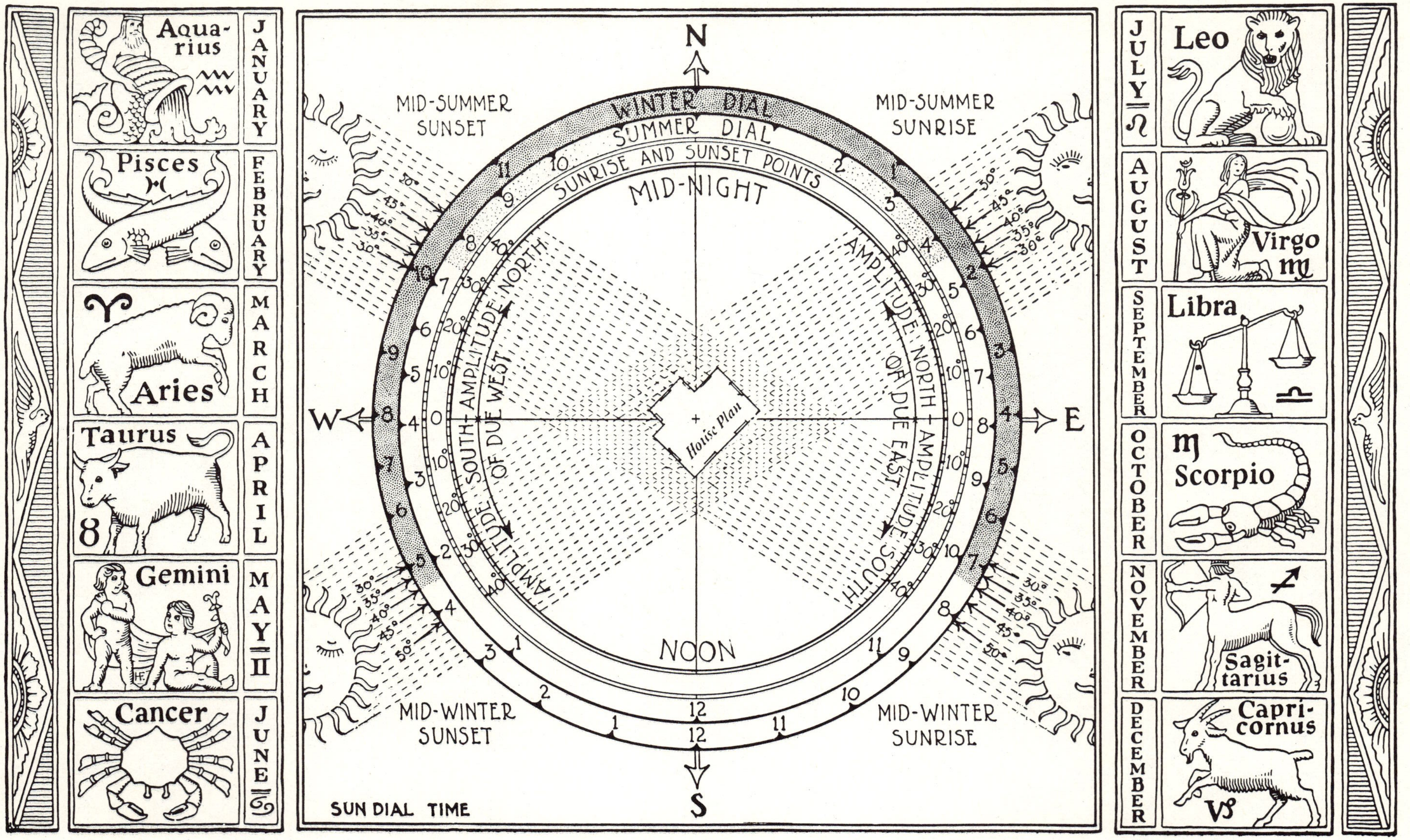
N
S
E
W
MID-SUMMER SUNSET
MID-SUMMER SUNRISE
MID-WINTER SUNSET
MID-WINTER SUNRISE
WINTER DIAL
SUMMER DIAL
SUNRISE AND SUNSET POINTS
MID-NIGHT
NOON
AMPLITUDE NORTH – AMPLITUDE SOUTH OF DUE EAST
SOUTH – AMPLITUDE NORTH AMPLITUDE OF DUE WEST
House Plan
SUN DIAL TIME
Aquarius
JANUARY
Pisces
FEBRUARY
Aries
MARCH
Taurus
APRIL
Gemini
MAY
Cancer
JUNE
Leo
JULY
Virgo
AUGUST
Libra
SEPTEMBER
Scorpio
OCTOBER
Sagittarius
NOVEMBER
Capricornus
DECEMBER

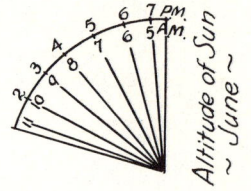

Orientation Chart

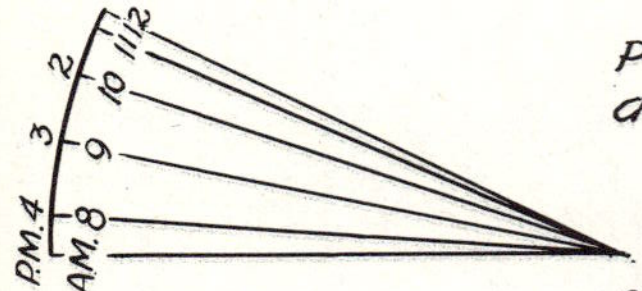
P.M.4 3 2
AM.8 9 10 11 12

Altitude of Sun
~ December ~

Directions for use

Pin cut-out of small scale plan at center and revolve same until sun strikes at desired angles.

Outer dial indicates Midwinter and black indicates darkness.

Second dial indicates Summer and grey indicates darkness.

Third dial shows degrees North and South of due East and West, for locating rising and setting sun.

Degree markings at end of arrows pointing to outer perimeter indicate corrections for latitudes other than 40° of North latitude for which chart is made; this is line through Philadelphia, Denver and Reno.

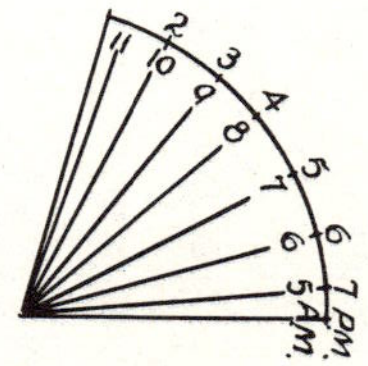
2 3 4 5 6 7 P.M.
11 10 9 8 7 6 5 A.M.

Altitude of Sun
~ June ~

Courtesy of House Beautiful and American Face Brick Association.

PLUMBING SYMBOLS

PLUMBING FIXTURE SYMBOLS

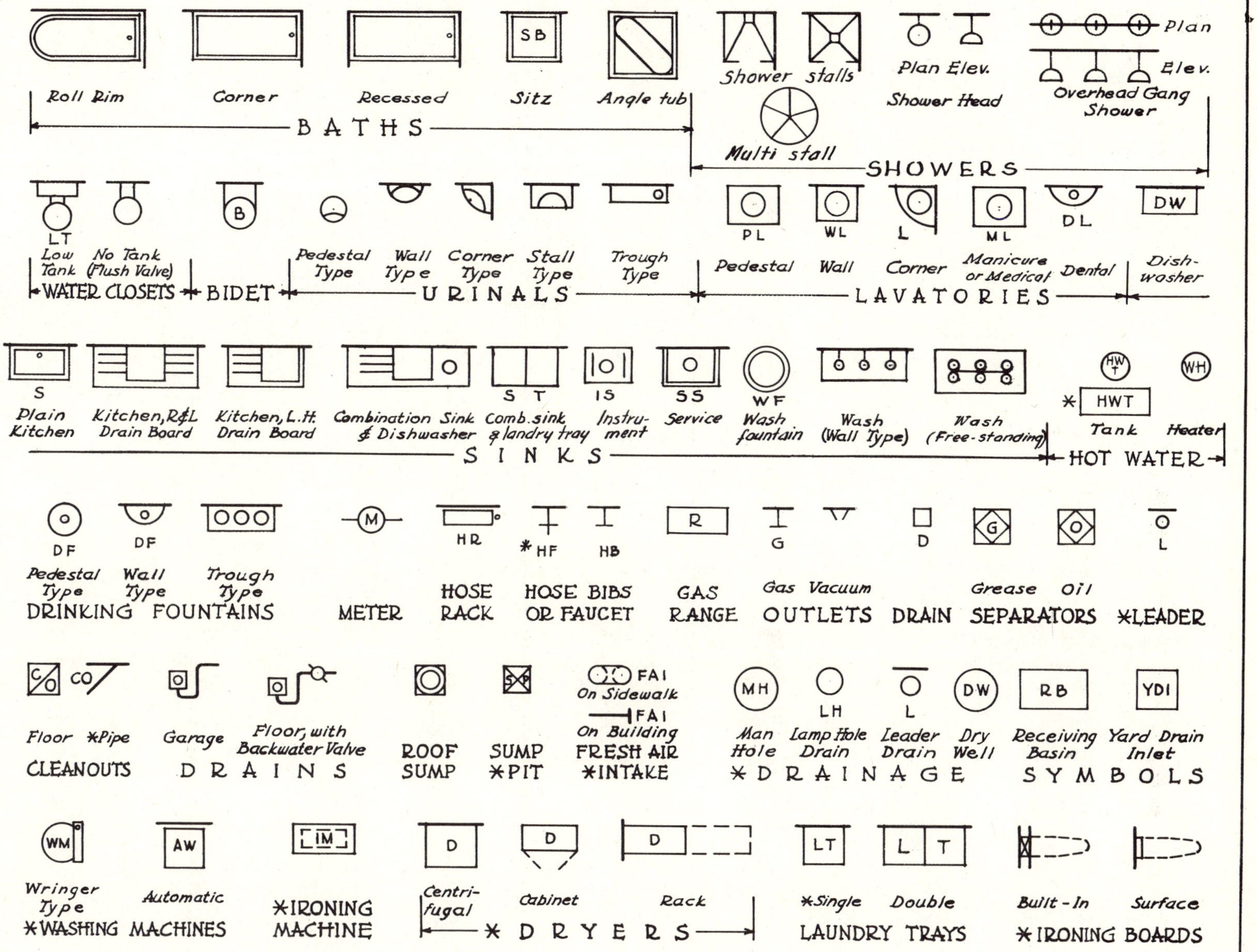
Roll Rim
Corner
Recessed
SB
Sitz
Angle tub
BATHS
Shower stalls
Multi stall
Plan Elev.
Shower Head
Plan
Elev.
Overhead Gang Shower
SHOWERS
LT
Low Tank
No Tank (Flush Valve)
WATER CLOSETS
B
BIDET
Pedestal Type
Wall Type
Corner Type
Stall Type
Trough Type
URINALS
PL
Pedestal
WL
Wall
L
Corner
ML
Manicure or Medical
DL
Dental
DW
Dish-washer
LAVATORIES
S
Plain Kitchen
Kitchen, R&L Drain Board
Kitchen, L.H. Drain Board
Combination Sink & Dishwasher
S T
Comb. sink & landry tray
IS
Instru-ment
SS
Service
WF
Wash fountain
Wash (Wall Type)
Wash (Free-standing)
SINKS
HWT
*
Tank
WH
Heater
HOT WATER
DF
Pedestal Type
DF
Wall Type
Trough Type
DRINKING FOUNTAINS
M
METER
HR
HOSE RACK
*HF
HB
HOSE BIBS OR FAUCET
R
GAS RANGE
G
Gas
Vacuum
OUTLETS
D
DRAIN
G
Grease
O
Oil
SEPARATORS
L
*LEADER
CO
Floor
*Pipe
CLEANOUTS
Garage
Floor, with Backwater Valve
DRAINS
ROOF SUMP
SUMP *PIT
FAI
On Sidewalk
FAI
On Building
FRESH AIR *INTAKE
MH
Man Hole
LH
Lamp Hole Drain
L
Leader Drain
DW
Dry Well
RB
Receiving Basin
YDI
Yard Drain Inlet
*DRAINAGE SYMBOLS
WM
Wringer Type
AW
Automatic
*WASHING MACHINES
IM
*IRONING MACHINE
D
Centri-fugal
D
Cabinet
D
Rack
*DRYERS
LT
*Single
L T
Double
LAUNDRY TRAYS
Built-In
Surface
*IRONING BOARDS

PIPING SYMBOLS

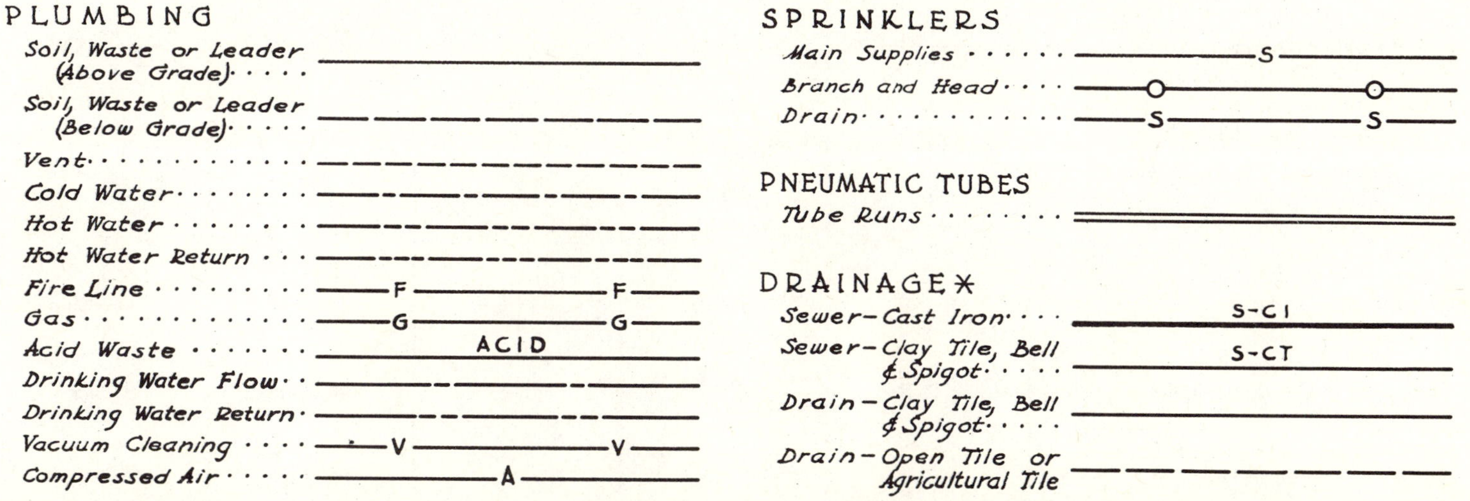
PLUMBING
Soil, Waste or Leader (Above Grade)
Soil, Waste or Leader (Below Grade)
Vent
Cold Water
Hot Water
Hot Water Return
Fire Line
F
F
Gas
G
G
Acid Waste
ACID
Drinking Water Flow
Drinking Water Return
Vacuum Cleaning
V
V
Compressed Air
A
SPRINKLERS
Main Supplies
S
Branch and Head
Drain
S
S
PNEUMATIC TUBES
Tube Runs
DRAINAGE*
Sewer—Cast Iron
S-CI
Sewer—Clay Tile, Bell & Spigot
S-CT
Drain—Clay Tile, Bell & Spigot
Drain—Open Tile or Agricultural Tile

All Symbols, except those marked *, approved as American Standard, ASA Z32.2.3-'49 by American Standards Association. (Reaffirmed 1953)

SYMBOLS for PIPE FITTINGS & VALVES

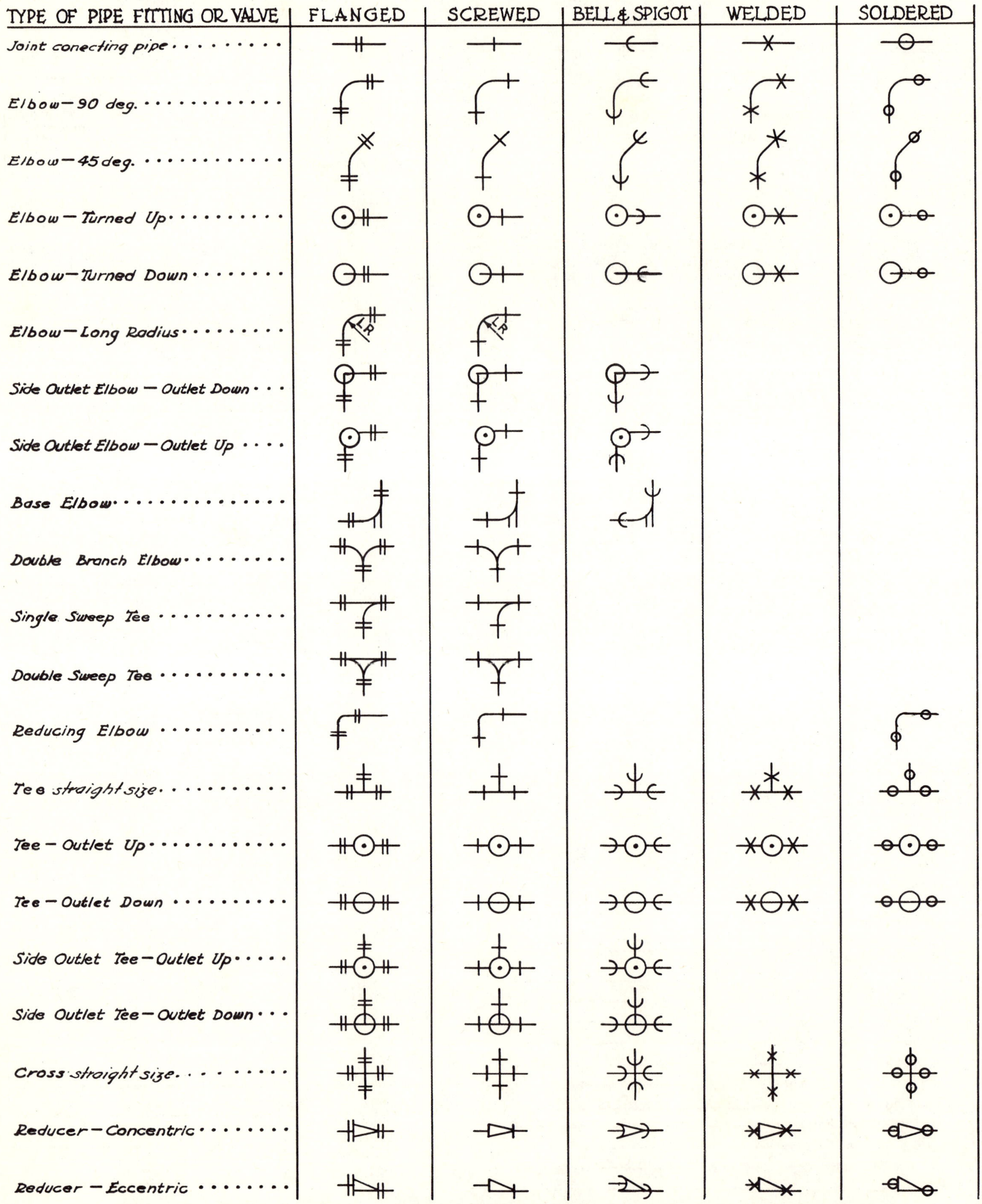
TYPE OF PIPE FITTING OR VALVE
FLANGED
SCREWED
BELL & SPIGOT
WELDED
SOLDERED
Joint conecting pipe
Elbow—90 deg.
Elbow—45 deg.
Elbow—Turned Up
Elbow—Turned Down
Elbow—Long Radius
LR
Side Outlet Elbow—Outlet Down
Side Outlet Elbow—Outlet Up
Base Elbow
Double Branch Elbow
Single Sweep Tee
Double Sweep Tee
Reducing Elbow
Tee straight size
Tee—Outlet Up
Tee—Outlet Down
Side Outlet Tee—Outlet Up
Side Outlet Tee—Outlet Down
Cross straight size
Reducer—Concentric
Reducer—Eccentric

All Symbols approved as American Standard ASA Z32.2.3-'49 by American Standards Association.
(Reaffirmed-1953)

SYMBOLS for PIPE FITTINGS & VALVES

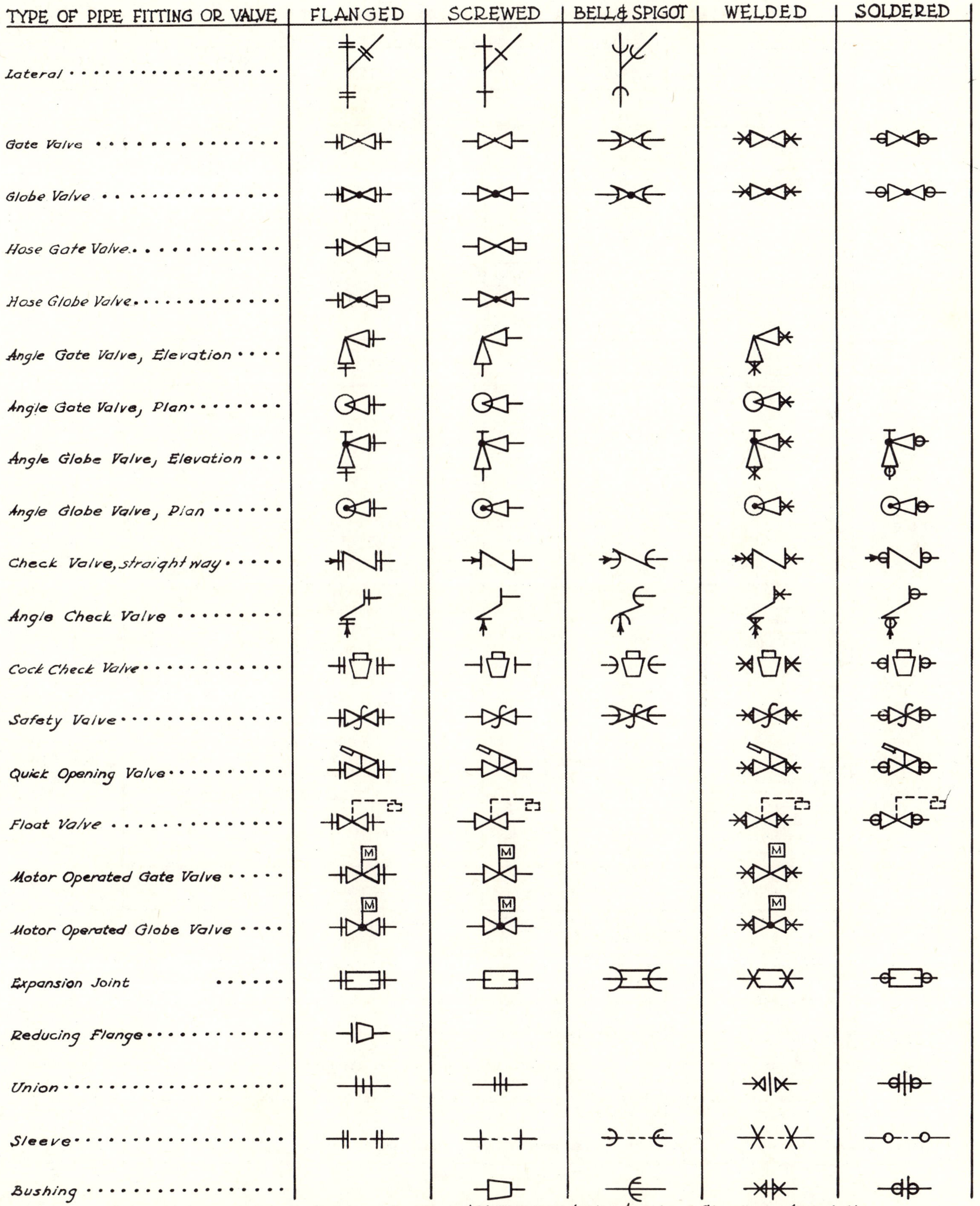
TYPE OF PIPE FITTING OR VALVE
FLANGED
SCREWED
BELL & SPIGOT
WELDED
SOLDERED
Lateral
Gate Valve
Globe Valve
Hose Gate Valve
Hose Globe Valve
Angle Gate Valve, Elevation
Angle Gate Valve, Plan
Angle Globe Valve, Elevation
Angle Globe Valve, Plan
Check Valve, straight way
Angle Check Valve
Cock Check Valve
Safety Valve
Quick Opening Valve
Float Valve
Motor Operated Gate Valve
Motor Operated Globe Valve
Expansion Joint
Reducing Flange
Union
Sleeve
Bushing

All Symbols approved as American Standard, ASA Z32.2.3–49 by American Standards Association. (Reaffirmed 1953)

PLUMBING FIXTURE REQUIREMENTS

MINIMUM NUMBER OF FIXTURES REQUIRED[7]

The figures shown are based on one fixture being the minimum required for the number of persons indicated or any fraction thereof.

TYPE OF BUILDING[1]	WATER CLOSETS			URINALS[5]		LAVATORIES[5]		BATH TUBS OR SHOWERS	DRINKING FOUNTAINS[6]
	NO. OF PERSONS	CLOSETS MALE	CLOSETS FEMALE	NO. OF PERSONS	URINALS	NO. OF PERSONS	LAVATORIES		
SCHOOLS	Up to 15	1	1	Up to 15	1	Up to 15	1		One for each 75 persons
	16 to 30	1	2	16 to 30	1	16 to 55	2		
	31 to 55	2	3	31 to 55	1	56 to 100	3		
	56 to 80	3	4	56 to 80	2	Over 100 add 1 (one) lavatory for each additional 50 persons.			
	81 to110	4	5	81 to 110	2				
	111to150	5	6	111 to 150	2				
	151to190	6	7	151 to 190	3				
	Over 190 add one (1) closet for each additional 30 persons			Over 190 add one (1) urinal for each additional 60 males.					
GYMNASIUMS — HIGH SCHOOL	One for each 50 males One for each 30 females			One for each 25 males		One for each 20 persons		One for each 2.5 males One for each 3.3 females	
GYMNASIUMS — COLLEGES	One for each 25 males One for each 25 females			One for each 12 males		One for each 25 persons		One for each 4 males One for each 3 females	
OFFICE OR PUBLIC BUILDINGS	NO. OF PERSONS	CLOSETS		Whenever urinals are provided for men one water closet less than the number specified herein may be provided for each urinal, except that the number of water closets in such cases shall not be reduced to less than 2/3 the number specified herein.		NO. OF PERSONS	LAVATORIES		One for each 75 persons
	Up to 15	1				Up to 15	1		
	16 to 35	2				16 to 35	2		
	36 to 55	3				36 to 60	3		
	56 to 80	4				61 to 90	4		
	81 to 110	5				91 to 125	5		
	111 to 150	6				Over 125 add one (1) lavatory for each additional 45 persons.			
	151 to 190	7							
	Over 190 add one (1) closet for each additional 30 persons.								
MANUFACTURING, WAREHOUSE WORKSHOP & LOFT BUILDINGS, MINES, FOUNDRIES, ETC.[2]	NO. OF PERSONS	CLOSETS		Same as for Office and Public Buildings		NO. OF PERSONS	LAVATORIES[3]	One for each 15 persons who may be exposed to excessive heat or to skin contamination with poisonous, infectious or irritating material	One for each 75 persons
	Up to 9	1				Up to 100	One for each 10 persons		
	10 to 24	2							
	25 to 49	3							
	50 to 100	5				Over 100 add one (1) Lavatory for each additional 15 persons. (4)			
	Over 100 add one (1) closet for each additional 30 persons.								
DWELLINGS OR APARTMENT HOUSES	One for each apartment or dwelling unit					One for each apartment or dwelling unit		One for each apartment or dwelling unit	
	Laundry Tubs - One single compartment tub for each apartment or dwelling unit or a multiple compartment tub for each 10 apartments. Kitchen Sinks - One for each apartment or dwelling.								

1-Hospitals, sanitoriums, hotels and lodging houses, etc. are not included and must be considered individually
2-As required by the American Standard Safety Code for Industrial Sanitation in manufacturing Establishments, (A.S.A. Z4.1 1935)
3-Where there is exposure to skin contamination with poisonous, infectious, or irritating materials, provide one lavatory for each five persons.
4-Twenty four (24) linear inches of wash sink, or eighteen (18) inches of circular basin, when provided with water outlets for such space, shall be considered equivalent to one lavatory.
5-Special requirements applicable to water closets, urinals, and lavatories over and above those listed, should be made by the administrative authority for spaces where food or drink is prepared or served.
6-Drinking fountains shall not be installed in toilet rooms.
7-Consult local codes and follow same if their requirements exceed these recommendations.

Continued on next page.

Source of information: "Plumbing Code" A.S.A. A40.7-1949, The American Society of Mechanical Engineers
Compiled by the Office of Mongitore & Moesel - Consulting Engineers, N.Y.C.

PLUMBING FIXTURE and HOT WATER REQUIREMENTS

MINIMUM NUMBER OF FIXTURES REQUIRED (7)

The figures shown are based on one fixture being the minimum required for the number of persons indicated or any fraction thereof.

TYPE OF BUILDING (1)	WATER CLOSETS			URINALS (5)		LAVATORIES (5)			BATH TUB OR SHOWERS		DRINKING FOUNTAINS (6)
	NO. OF PERSONS	CLOSETS MALE	CLOSETS FEMALE	NO. OF PERSONS	URINALS	NO. OF PERSONS	LAVATORIES MALE	LAVATORIES FEMALE	NO. OF PERSONS	BATHTUBS OR SHOWERS	
DORMITORIES	Up to 15	1	1	Up to 30	1	Up to 15	1	2	Up to 7	1	One for each 75 persons
	16 to 30	2	2	31 to 60	2	16 to 30	2	3	8 to 15	2	
	31 to 50	3	4	61 to 100	3	31 to 50	3	4	16 to 25	3	
	51 to 75	4	6	101 to 150	4	51 to 75	4	5	26 to 35	4	
	76 to 100	6	8	Over 150 add one (1) for each additional 50 males		76 to 100	6	7	36 to 45	5	
	101 to 150	8	10			101 to 125	7	9	46 to 55	6	
	Over 150 add one (1) additional closet for each 25 males and each 20 females additional.					Over 125 add one (1) lavatory for each 20 additional males and 15 additional females.			Over 55 and not over 200 add 1 tub or shower for each 10 persons. Over 200 add one tub or shower for each 20 persons.		

TYPE OF BUILDING	NO. OF PERSONS	CLOSETS MALE	CLOSETS FEMALE	NO. OF PERSONS	URINALS	NO. OF PERSONS	LAVATORIES		DRINKING FOUNTAINS
THEATERS & PLACES OF PUBLIC ASSEMBLY	Up to 100	1	1	Up to 200	1	Up to 200	1		One for each 100 persons
	101 to 200	2	2	200 to 400	2	201 to 400	2		
	201 to 400	3	3	401 to 600	3	401 to 750	3		
	Over 400 add one (1) closet for each 500 additional males and one (1) for each 300 females.			Over 600 add one (1) urinal for each 300 additional males.		Over 750 add one (1) lavatory for each additional 500 persons.			

See preceding page for footnotes.

HOT WATER HEATING REQUIREMENTS

Figures given are in gallons of water per hour per fixture and are based on a final temperature of 150°F

FIXTURE	APT. HOUSE	CLUB	GYM	HOSPITAL	HOTEL	INDUST'L PLANT	LAUNDRY	OFFICE BLD'G	PUBLIC BATH	PRIVATE RES.	SCHOOL	Y.M.C.A.
PRIVATE LAVATORY	3	3	3	3	3	3	3	3	3	3	3	3
PUBLIC LAVATORY	5	8	10	8	10	15	10	8	15	--	18	10
BATH TUBS	15	15	30	15	15	30	--	--	45	15	--	30
FOOT BASINS	3	3	12	3	3	12	--	--	--	3	3	12
KITCHEN SINK	10	20	--	20	20	20	--	--	--	10	10	20
DISH WASHER	15	30	--	30	30	30	--	--	--	15	30	30
AUTOMATIC CLOTHES WASHER	75	75	--	100	150	--	100-150	--	100	75	--	100
WRINGER CLOTHES WASHER	25	35	--	35	35	--	42	--	--	25	--	35
PANTRY SINK	10	20	--	20	20	--	--	--	--	10	20	20
SHOWER	50	200	200	50	50	200	--	--	200	50	200	200
SLOP SINK	20	20	--	20	30	20	10	15	15	15	20	20
DISH WASHING MACHINES	300 gallons per hour at 180°F. for serving capacity of 500 people.											
Percent of total water likely to be drawn at one time.												
	20%	50%	80%	60%	50%	90%	100%	15%	100%	50%	25%	75%
Storage Capacity in percent of Maximum Heating Capacity												
	100%	75%	50%	50%	25%	50%	25%	100%	50%	100%	50%	50%

Source of Information "The Ideal Fitter" American Radiator Co.
Compiled by the Office of Mongitore & Moesel Consulting Engineers, N.Y.C.

WATER COOLERS

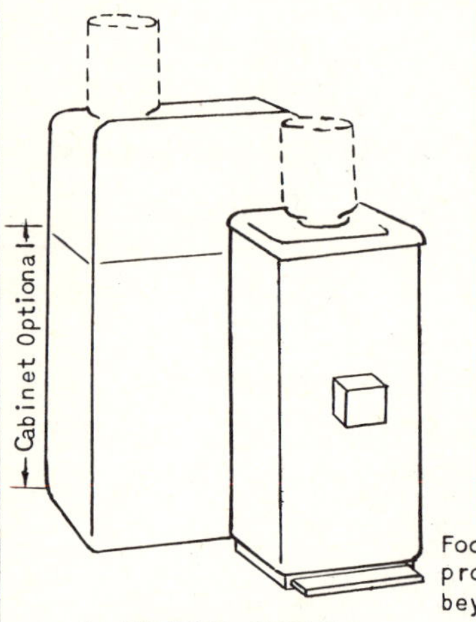
Cabinet Optional

BOTTLE TYPES

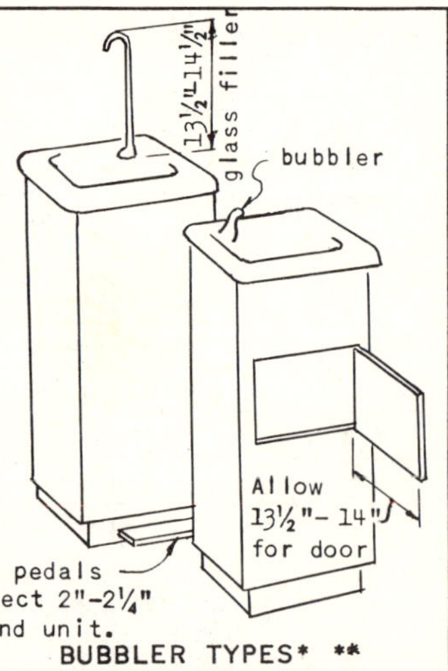
13½"-14½"
glass filler
bubbler
Allow 13½"-14" for door
Foot pedals project 2"-2¼" beyond unit.

BUBBLER TYPES* **

Glass shelf optional
Fountain may be added here for schools

CAFETERIA TYPES* •†

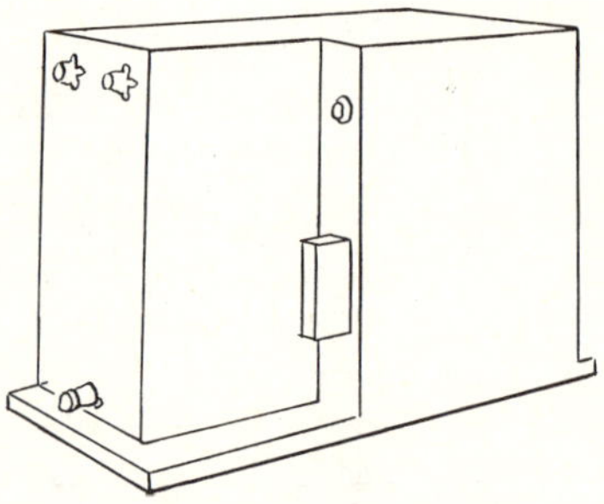

For use with multiple fountains shown below. Small units for 1-2 fountains may be concealed in wall, behind wall or may be wall hung.

REMOTE TYPE*†

BOTTLE TYPES				BUBBLER TYPES* **				CAFETERIA TYPES* •†				REMOTE TYPE*†			
HEIGHT	HT. WITH BOTTLE	WIDTH	DEPTH	HEIGHT	WIDTH	DEPTH	G.P.H.‡	HEIGHT	WIDTH	DEPTH	G.P.H.‡	HEIGHT	WIDTH	DEPTH	G.P.H.‡
39"	56"	16"	16"	39"	16"	16"	3-12	34"	57"	24"	50	15¼"	23½" & 30¼"	11¾"	3-5
40"	57"	15¾"	19¾"	39⅞"	15¼"	15½"	5	36"	16"	24"	12	16"	34"	13⅞"	10
41"	59"	16"	16"	40"	24"	20"	9-11	36"	36"	23"	15	18 & 24"	23"	6¾"	5-10
41 3/16"	59"	14 3/16"	14 3/16"	40 5/16"	14 3/16"	14 3/16"	7-22	39¼"	14¾"	14¾"	11	24"	23"	8¼"	5-10
41 9/16"	59½"	12⅞"	14½"	41"	12⅞"	14½"	15	48"	45"	22"	10	26"	40"	21"	10
41⅝"	59"	16¼"	16¼"	43⅝"	15¼"	15½"	5-15	52"	55"	28"	53-72	26"	48"	22"	10
				44½"	22⅝"	20⅞"	21					34"	57"	22"	38
												57"	60 & 66"	25"	52-75
												64"	83"	30"	101-175
												70"	110"	36"	239-311
												72"	86 & 96"	82"	478-622

*Air cooled condensers are used for normal room temperatures; water cooled for high room temperature – 110° and above. Certain models are available in explosion proof construction. **Additional fountains can be attached low on the side for use in elementary schools. Some models are available in 31" height for primary grades. •Bubbler fixtures can replace glass fillers on cafeteria models for use in schools. †Max. water storage for cafeteria types is 40 gals.; for remote types, 300 gals. ‡Cooling capacity is based on 90° room temperature and 80° inlet water temperature. Power: 110, 115, 230 volts; 50 to 60 cycles, single phase A.C., otherwise transformer is used.

DRINKING WATER REQUIREMENTS

TYPE OF SERVICE	G.P.H. PER PERSON		PERSON PER G.P.H.	
	CUP	BUBBLER	CUP	BUBBLER
Offices, Schools, Cafeterias, Hotels (per room) Hospitals (per bed & per attendant)	0.033	0.083	30	12
Restaurants	0.04	0.1	25	10
Light manufacturing	0.0573	0.143	17.5	7
Heavy manufacturing	0.08	0.20	12.5	5
Hot, heavy mfrg.	0.10	0.25	10	4
Theaters per 100 seats	0.4 gph/ 100 seats	1.0 gph/ 100 seats	250 seats/ gph	100 seats/ gph
Department stores, lobbies for hotel & office bldgs.	1.6-2.0 gph/fount.	4-5 gph/ fount.	0.5-0.625 fount./gph	0.2-0.25 fount./gph

TYPE COOLER	RECOMMENDED CAPACITY IN G.P.H.						
	2	3	5	10	15	20	30
	MINIMUM CAPACITY IN G.P.H.						
Bottle	1.5	2.7	–	–	–	–	–
PRESSURE BUBBLER							
*Air cooled condenser	–	2.7	4.5	9	13.5	18	–
*Water cooled cond.	–	–	–	9	13.5	18	27
GLASS FILLER							
*Air cooled condenser	–	–	–	9	–	18	27
*Water cooled cond.	–	–	–	9	–	18	27

Adapted from CS 127-45

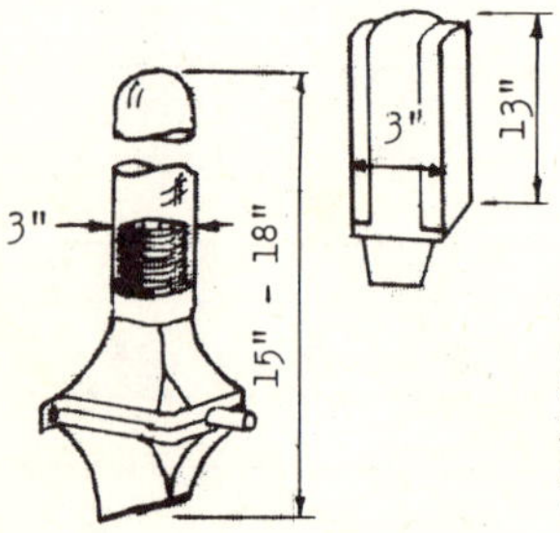
3"
13"
3"
15" - 18"

CUP DISPENSERS
4'-0"± from base to floor

Circular bowl 9½" dia., 2½"h. Oval 2½"-4"h., 10½"-14"W., 5"-10½"d. All Pedestal fountains 30"&36" high.

PEDESTAL

Oval: 3½"-4" h., 14"W., 8" 10"d. Rectangular: 3½"-11½" h, 11"-14" W., 11¾"-13¼" d.

WALL-HUNG

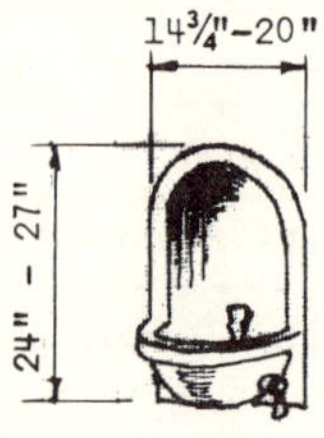
14¾"-20"
24" - 27"

Recess 4½"

SEMI-RECESSED

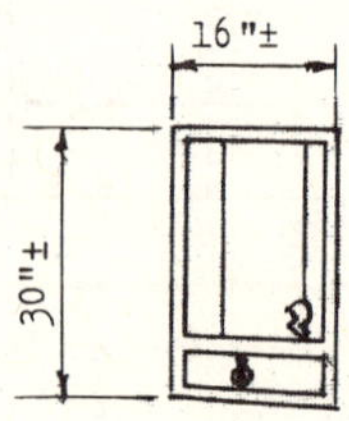
16"±
30"±

Recess 10"±

RECESSED

FOUNTAINS
For use with remote storage coolers

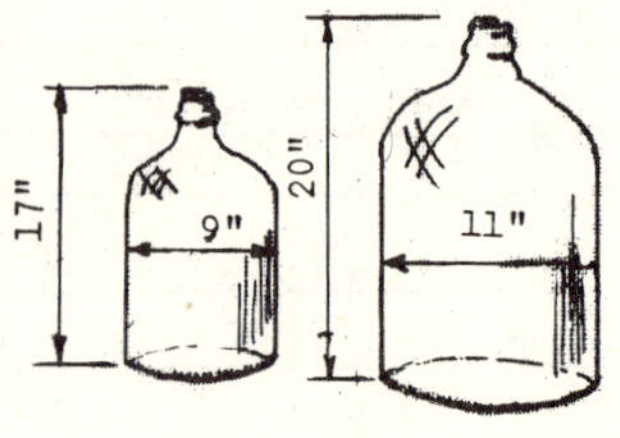
17"
9"
20"
11"

BOTTLES

ACCESSORIES

WATER SOFTENERS

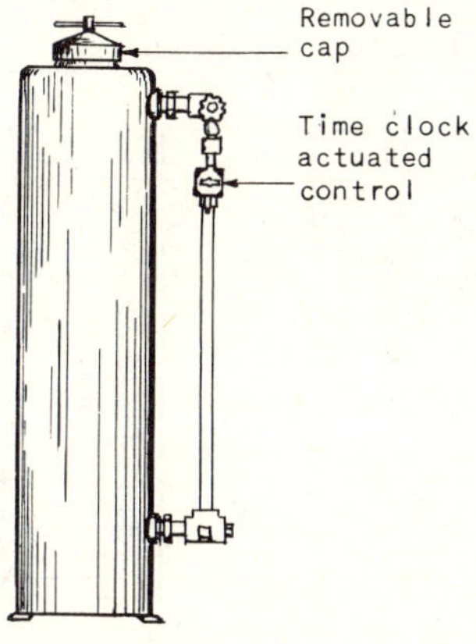
Removable cap
Time clock actuated control

DSQ SERIES**

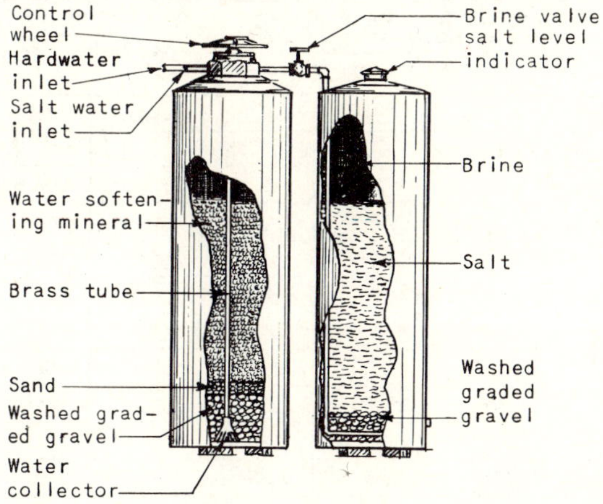
Control wheel
Hardwater inlet
Salt water inlet
Brine valve salt level indicator
Water softening mineral
Brine
Brass tube
Salt
Sand
Washed graded gravel
Washed graded gravel
Water collector

OSQ SERIES

NOTES

Hardness varies with different localities, but it is always present in some degree unless removed. For convenience hardness is quoted in grains per gallon. Some typical waters are: New York City, 1½-3 grains; Midwestern cities, 20 grains; private wells, 10-30 grains.

To select the proper sized softener multiply the number of people in the house by 50, if there are one or two bathrooms; by 75, if there are more than two bathrooms. Assume weekly regeneration.

For example: If there are four people in a house with two bathrooms multiply 4 x 50 x 7 which equals 1400 gallons of water per week. Assuming that the water is 10 grains in hardness, model DSQ-25, which furnishes 2500 gallons between regenerations, is ample.

SPECIFICATIONS

CHARACTERISTICS	EXPRESSED IN	MODEL *			
		DSQ 25	DSQ 50	OSQ 20	OSQ 28
Capacity	Grains	25,000	50,000	120,000	228,000
Flow Rate	gpm	6	8	26	50
Wash Rate	gpm	2	35	11.2	22.0
Pipe Size	Inches	3/4	3/4	1 1/4	1 1/4
Height	Inches	41 1/2	47	61	64
Floor Space	Inches	12x17	15x20	21x43	30x59
Shipping weight	Pounds	110	260	972	1692
Operating weight	Pounds	140	340	1700	3100
Softener Tank Diameter	Inches	9	17	20	28
Area of Bed	Sq. ft.	0.44	0.78	2.18	4.28
Softener Mineral	Cu. ft.	0.9	1.8	5.0	9.5
Sand	Pounds			38	75
Softener Gravel (fine)	Pounds			58	75
Softener Gravel (medium)	Pounds				75
Softener Gravel (coarse)	Pounds				178
Salt Tank Dia.	Inches			20	28
Salt Tank Refill	Pounds			270	528
Regenerations per Salt Refill	Units			6	6
Salt Tank Gravel	Pounds			67	94
Salt per Regeneration	Pounds	15**	30**	45	88

Where water contains moderate amounts of suspended matter and softener will also act as a filter use following ratings:

Flow rate	gpm	5.25	10.0	17.5	34
Wash rate	gpm	4	7.5	13	26

GALLONS OF SOFTENED WATER DELIVERED BETWEEN REGENERATIONS

HARDNESS OF WATER IN GRAINS PER U.S. GALLON

HARDNESS	DSQ 25	DSQ 50	OSQ 20	OSQ 28	HARDNESS	DSQ 25	DSQ 50	OSQ 20	OSQ 28
2	12,500	25,000	60,000	114,000	46	544	1,088	2,608	4,956
3	8,333	16,666	40,000	76,000	48	521	1,042	2,500	4,750
4	6,250	12,500	30,000	57,000	50	500	1,000	2,400	4,560
5	5,000	10,000	24,000	45,600	52	481	962	2,307	4,384
6	4,166	8,333	20,000	38,000	54	463	926	2,222	4,222
7	3,571	7,142	17,142	32,571	56	447	894	2,142	4,071
8	3,125	6,250	15,000	28,500	58	431	862	2,068	3,931
9	2,777	5,554	13,333	25,333	60	417	834	2,000	3,800
10	2,500	5,000	12,000	22,800	62	403	806	1,936	3,678
11	2,273	4,546	10,909	20,727	64	391	782	1,875	3,562
12	2,084	4,168	10,000	19,000	66	379	758	1,818	3,455
13	1,923	3,846	9,230	17,538	68	368	736	1,765	3,353
14	1,786	3,571	8,571	16,285	70		714	1,714	3,257
15	1,666	3,332	8,800	15,200	72		695	1,667	3,167
16	1,563	3,126	7,500	14,250	74		676	1,622	3,090
18	1,389	2,778	6,666	12,666	76		658	1,579	3,000
20	1,250	2,500	6,000	11,400	78		641	1,539	2,924
22	1,136	2,272	5,454	10,363	80		625	1,500	2,850
24	1,042	2,084	5,000	9,500	82		609	1,464	2,781
26	962	1,924	4,615	8,769	84		595	1,429	2,715
28	893	1,786	4,285	8,142	86		582	1,396	2,652
30	833	1,666	4,000	7,600	88		568	1,364	2,591
32	781	1,562	3,750	7,125	90		555	1,333	2,533
34	735	1,470	3,529	6,705	92		544	1,305	2,479
36	695	1,390	3,333	6,333	94		533	1,278	2,428
38	658	1,316	3,157	6,000	96		522	1,250	2,375
40	625	1,250	3,000	5,700	98		511	1,225	2,327
42	595	1,190	2,857	5,428	100		500	1,200	2,280
44	568	1,136	2,727	5,181					

* DSQ25, DSQ50, OSQ20, OSQ28 are models manufactured by the Permutit Company, New York City. The DSQ series operates between 20-100# per sq. in. pressure; the OSO series between 25-100# per sq. in. pressure.

** Regenerated by adding dry pellet type salt directly into softener.

COMPILED BY THE OFFICE OF MONGITORE & MOESEL, CONSULTING ENGINEERS, N.Y.C.

WATER TANK CAPACITIES

CAPACITY of CYLINDRICAL WATER TANKS - TOTAL GALLONS

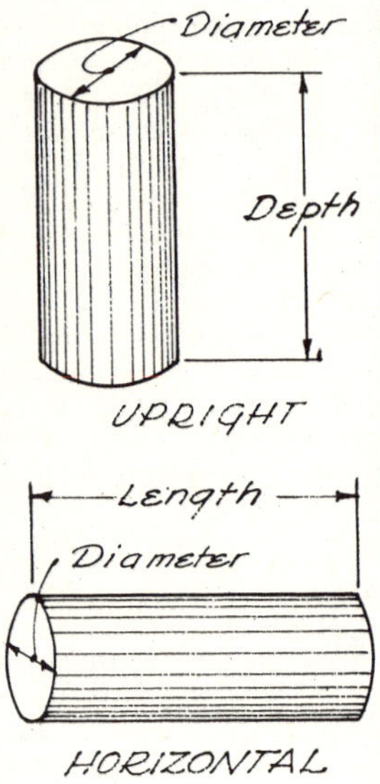
Diameter
Depth
UPRIGHT
Length
Diameter
HORIZONTAL

DEPTH or LENGTH	DIAMETER 12"	18"	24"	30"	36"	42"	48"	54"	60"	66"	72"
1"	.49	1.10	1.96	3.06	4.41	5.99	7.83	9.91	12.24	14.81	17.63
1'-0"	5.88	13.22	23.50	36.72	52.88	71.97	94.00	118.97	146.88	177.72	211.51
1'-6"	9	20	35	55.08	79.	108	141	179	220	267	317
2'-0"	12	26	47	73.	106.	144	188	238	294	356	423
2'-6"	15	33	59	92.	132	180	235	297	367	444	529
3'-0"	18	40	71	110.	159	216	282	357	441	533	635
3'-6"	21	46	82	129	185	252	329	416	514	622	740
4'-0"	24	53	94.	147	212	288	376	476	588	711	846
4'-6"	27	60	106.	165	238	324	423	535	661	800	952
5'-0"	29	66.	118	184	264	360	470	595	734	889	1058
5'-6"	32	73.	129	202	291	396	517	654	808	978	1163
6'-0"	35	79.	141	220	317	432	564	714	881	1066	1269
7'-0"	41	93	165	257	370	504	658	833	1028	1244	1481
8'-0"	47	106	188	294	423	576	752	952	1175	1422	1692
9'-0"	53	119	212	331	476	648	846	1071	1322	1600	1904
10'-0"	59	132	235	367	529	720	940	1190	1469	1777	2115
12'-0"	71	159	282	441	635	864	1128	1428	1763	2133	2538
14'-0"	82	185	329	514	740	1008	1316	1666	2056	2488	2961
16'-0"	94	212	376	588	846	1152	1504	1904	2350	2844	3384
18'-0"	106	238	423	661	952	1296	1692	2142	2644	3199	3807
20'-0"	118	264	470	734	1058	1439	1880	.2380	2938	3555	4230

CAPACITY of RECTANGULAR WATER TANKS - GALLONS per ft. of Height

WIDTH of TANK	LENGTH OF TANK 2'-0"	2'-6"	3'-0"	3'-6"	4'-0"	4'-6"	5'-0"	5'-6"	6'-0"	6'-6"	7'-0"	7'-6"	8'-0"	8'-6"	9'-0"	9'-6"	10'-0"	10'-6"	11'-0"	11'-6"	12'-0"
2'-0"	29.92	37.40	44.88	52.36	59.84	67.32	74.81	82.29	89.77	97.25	104.73	112.21	119.69	127.17	134.65	142.13	149.61	157.09	164.57	172.05	179.53
2'-6"		46.75	56.10	65.45	74.80	84.16	93.51	102.86	112.21	121.56	130.91	140.26	149.61	158.96	168.31	177.66	187.01	196.36	205.71	215.06	224.41
3'-0"			67.32	78.54	89.77	100.99	112.21	123.43	134.65	145.87	157.09	168.31	179.53	190.75	201.97	213.19	224.41	235.63	246.86	258.07	269.30
3'-6"				91.64	104.73	117.82	130.91	144.0	157.09	170.18	183.27	196.36	209.45	222.54	235.63	248.73	261.82	274.90	288.00	301.09	314.18
4'-0"					119.69	134.65	149.61	164.57	179.53	194.49	209.45	224.41	239.37	254.34	269.30	284.26	299.22	314.18	329.14	344.10	359.06
4'-6"						151.48	168.31	185.14	201.97	218.80	235.63	252.47	269.30	286.13	302.96	319.79	336.62	353.45	370.28	387.11	403.94
5'-0"							187.01	205.71	224.41	243.11	261.82	280.52	299.22	317.92	336.62	355.32	374.03	392.72	411.43	430.13	448.83
5'-6"								226.28	246.86	267.43	288.00	308.57	329.14	349.71	370.28	390.85	411.43	432.00	452.57	473.14	493.71
6'-0"									269.30	291.74	314.18	336.62	359.06	381.50	403.94	426.39	448.83	471.27	493.71	516.15	538.59
6'-6"										316.05	340.36	364.67	388.98	413.30	437.60	461.92	486.23	510.54	534.85	559.16	583.47
7'-0"											366.54	392.72	418.91	445.09	471.27	497.45	523.64	549.81	575.99	602.18	628.36
7'-6"												420.78	448.83	476.88	504.93	532.98	561.04	589.08	617.14	645.19	673.24
8'-0"													478.75	508.67	538.59	568.51	598.44	628.36	658.28	688.20	718.12
8'-6"														540.46	572.25	604.05	635.84	667.63	699.42	731.21	763.00
9'-0"															605.92	639.58	673.25	706.90	740.56	774.23	807.89
9'-6"																675.11	710.65	746.17	781.71	817.24	852.77
10'-0"																	748.05	785.45	822.86	860.26	897.66
10'-6"																		824.73	864.00	903.26	942.56
11'-0"																			905.14	946.27	987.43
11'-6"																				989.29	1032.3
12'-0"																					1077.2

EXAMPLE

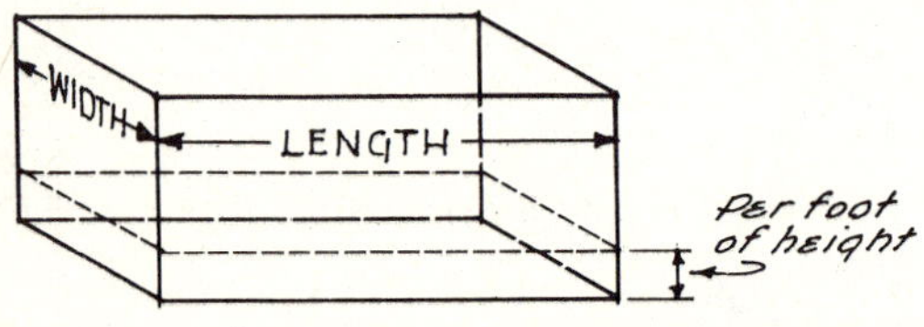
WIDTH
LENGTH
Per foot of height

Select a tank of approx. 5000 gals. capacity which must not exceed 8'-0" in width. No limit as to height or length.

8'-0" wide x 12'-0" long = 718 gals per ft. of height.

$\frac{5000}{718}$ = 7 ft. high - tank required.

Compiled by the Office of Mongitore & Moesel, Consulting Engineers, N.Y.C.

FERROUS WATER TANK SIZES

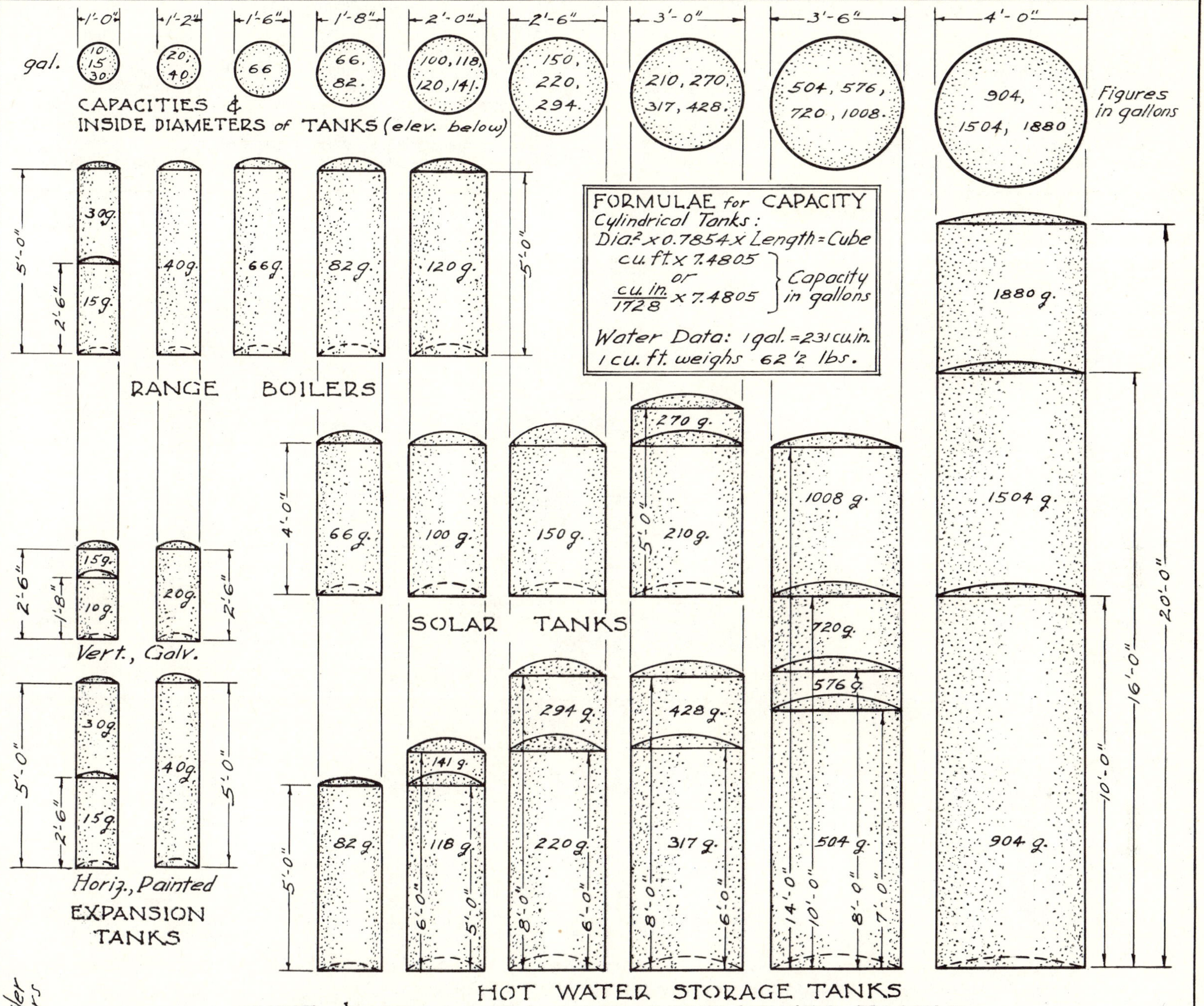
1'-0"
1'-2"
1'-6"
1'-8"
2'-0"
2'-6"
3'-0"
3'-6"
4'-0"
gal.
10, 15, 30
20, 40
66
66, 82
100, 118, 120, 141
150, 220, 294
210, 270, 317, 428
504, 576, 720, 1008
904, 1504, 1880
Figures in gallons
CAPACITIES & INSIDE DIAMETERS of TANKS (elev. below)
FORMULAE for CAPACITY
Cylindrical Tanks:
Dia.² x 0.7854 x Length = Cube
cu.ft. x 7.4805 or cu.in./1728 x 7.4805 } Capacity in gallons
Water Data: 1 gal. = 231 cu.in.
1 cu. ft. weighs 62½ lbs.
30 g.
15 g.
40 g.
66 g.
82 g.
120 g.
5'-0"
2'-6"
RANGE BOILERS
15 g.
10 g.
20 g.
2'-6"
1'-8"
Vert., Galv.
30 g.
15 g.
40 g.
Horiz., Painted
EXPANSION TANKS
66 g.
100 g.
150 g.
270 g.
210 g.
4'-0"
SOLAR TANKS
1008 g.
720 g.
576 g.
504 g.
1880 g.
1504 g.
904 g.
20'-0"
16'-0"
10'-0"
82 g.
141 g.
118 g.
294 g.
220 g.
428 g.
317 g.
6'-0"
8'-0"
14'-0"
7'-0"
HOT WATER STORAGE TANKS

SIZE & CAPACITY of FERROUS WATER TANKS

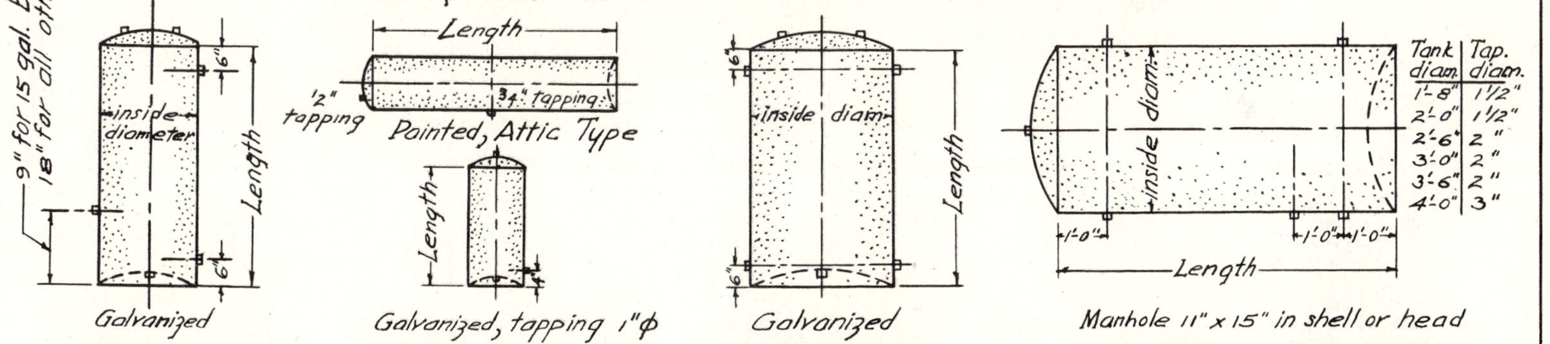
9" for 15 gal. boiler
18" for all others
inside diameter
Length
6"
Galvanized
Length
½" tapping
¾" tapping
Painted, Attic Type
Length
Galvanized, tapping 1"φ
inside diam.
Length
6"
Galvanized
inside diam.
1'-0"
Length
Manhole 11" x 15" in shell or head
Tank diam. | Tap. diam.
1'-8" | 1½"
2'-0" | 1½"
2'-6" | 2"
3'-0" | 2"
3'-6" | 2"
4'-0" | 3"

RANGE BOILER
Standard press. = 85#/□"
Extra Heavy " = 150#/□"
Double Extra Hvy. = 150#/□"
2'-0" diameter tank-tapping is 1½", others 1".

EXPANSION TANKS
Max. pressure = 30#/□".
Max. no. of tappings shown.

SOLAR TANK
Double Extra Hvy. = 120#/□"
Used vertically only. 1'-8" diam. tank, 1" tapping;
All others 1½" tapping.

HOT WATER STORAGE TANK
Standard pressure = 65#/□"
Extra Heavy " = 100#/□"
Tanks used vert. or horiz.
6 tappings in each tank as shown.

Figures on plans & elevations are U.S. Standard Gallons. Length is length of sheets.

TYPES of TANKS, LOCATIONS of TAPS, and GENERAL DATA

Hot Water Storage Tanks are Dept. of Commerce Simplified Practice Recommendation #25, others are # R8-47.

Scale ¼" = 1'-0"

Data checked by the Office of Mongitore & Moesel, Consulting Engineers, N.Y.C.

HOSE RACKS, REELS and CABINETS

Hose installed for use with building standpipes should not exceed 1½" in diameter and 75 feet in length. A larger hose used by amateurs is likely to tangle and cause excessive water damage.

In addition a connection for 2½" hose should be available to each station for the use of fireman. Many codes require 2½" outlets at all standpipes. By using a reducing coupling 1½" hose can be attached. When 2½" stream is required the coupling may be removed. Industrial installations use 2½" hoses and train personnel in the use of the heavier equipment.

Unlined woven linen hose is recommended for use on stand pipe installations. Cotton rubber lined hose is the standard fire department and heavy equipment hose.

Valves may be located 5'6" above floor (check local code)

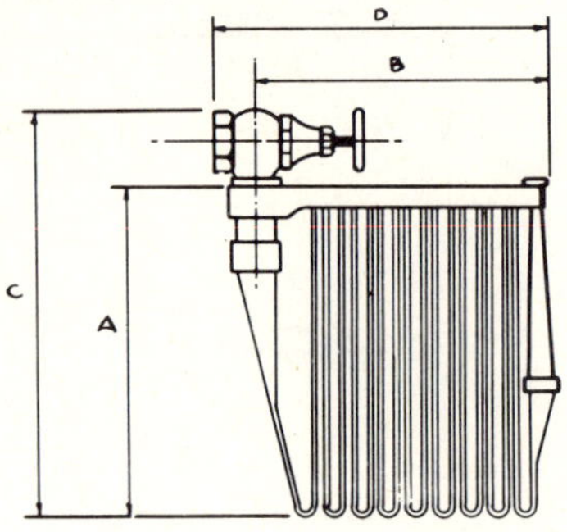
D
B
C
A

SWING RACK - SEMI-AUTOMATIC
1½" LINEN HOSE

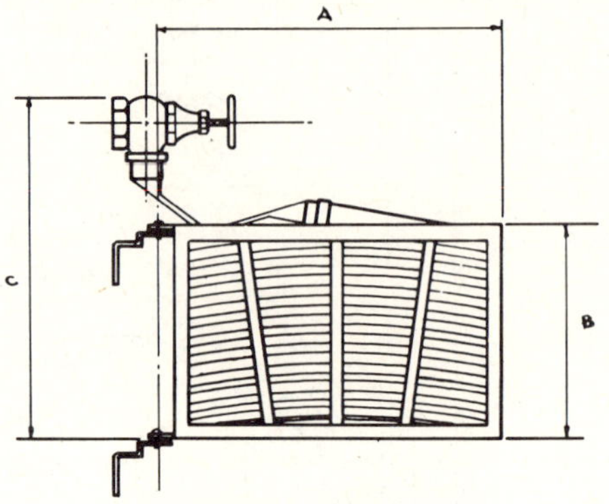
A
C
B

HUMP BACK - SWING RACK
1½" & 2½" LINEN HOSE

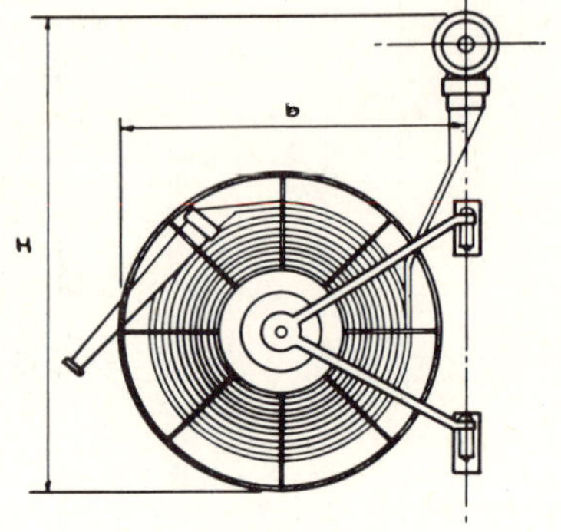
b
H

SWING REEL
1½" & 2½" HOSE

HOSE CAPACITY	25	50	75	100
A	10"	20"	24"	29"
B	15"	15"	19"	19"
C	14"	23"	26"	33"
D	17"	17"	21"	22"

HOSE CAPACITY	50	100	150	200
A	30"	30"	34"	40"
B	17"	21"	28"	39"
C	30"	33"	40"	50"
WIDTH	4"	4"	4"	4"

HOSE CAPACITY	50	100	150
diameter	15"	21"	26"
height	38"	38"	36"
width	29"	29"	14"

FIRE HOSE RACKS & REELS

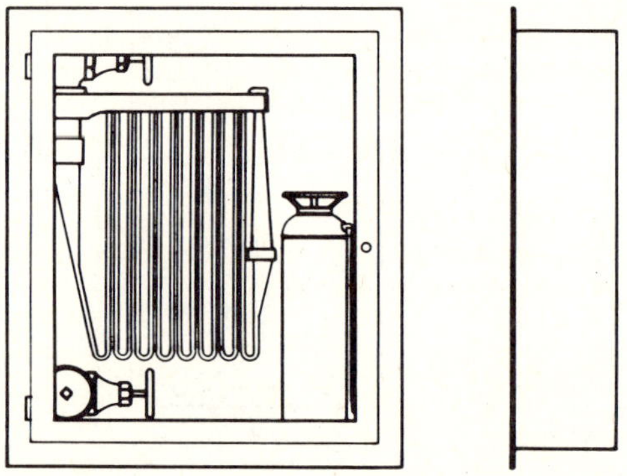

CONTENTS - 75 FT. 1½" LINEN HOSE & RACK
1½" & 2½" ANGLE VALVE, 2½ GAL. EXTINGUISHER
33" x 40" x 8½" TO 32" x 40" x 9"

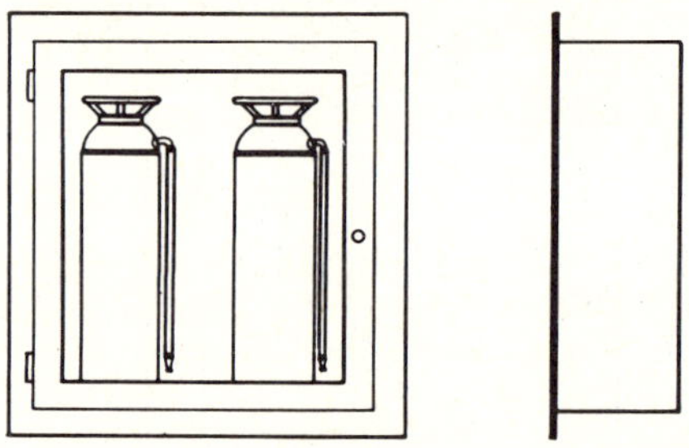

CONTENTS - TWO 2½ GAL. EXTINGUISHERS.
20" x 29½" x 7" TO 21" x 30" x 8"

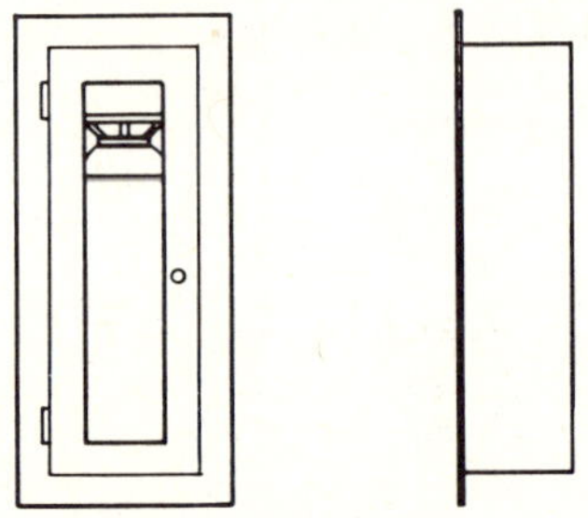

CONTENTS - ONE 2½ GAL. EXTINGUISHER, 10"x28" x8½" TO 13"x28"x8"

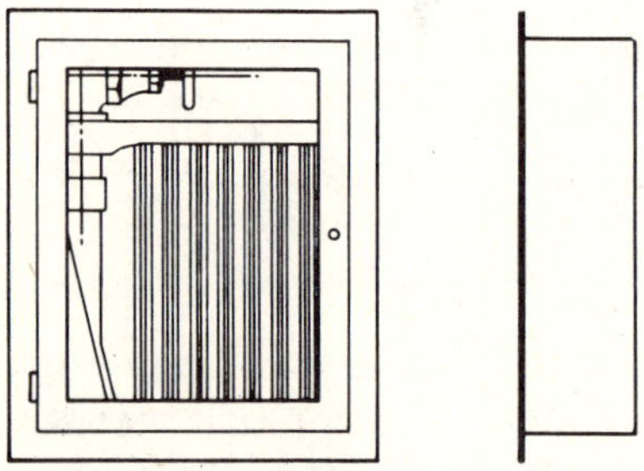

CONTENTS - 75 FT. 1½" LINEN HOSE
RACK & ANGLE VALVE
22" x 32" x 6" TO 24" x 33" x 8"

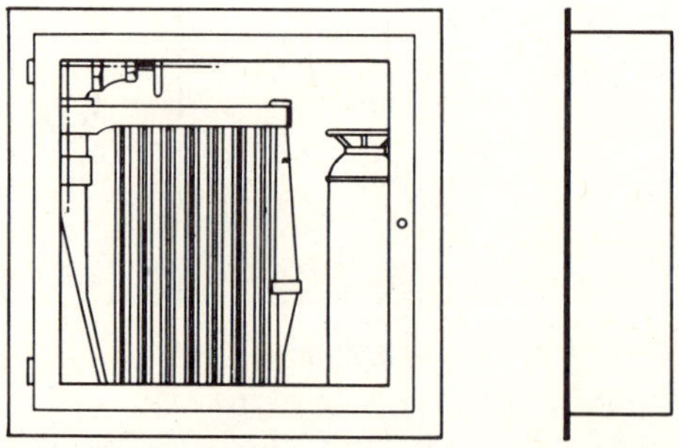

CONTENTS - 75 FT. 1½" LINEN HOSE, RACK
& ANGLE VALVE, 2½ GAL. EXTINGUISHER
33" x 33" x 8½" TO 33" x 34" x 9"

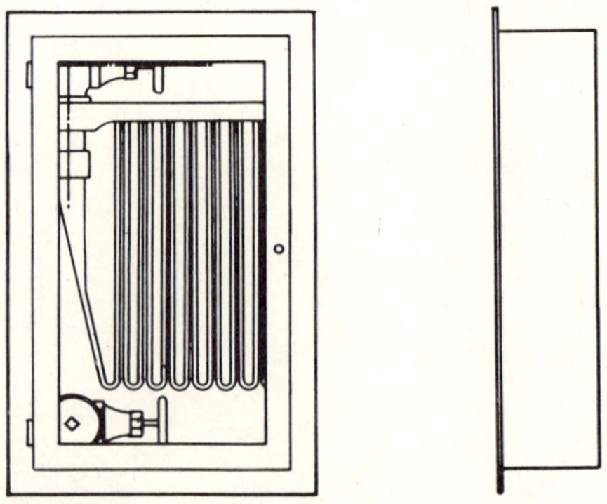

CONTENTS - 75 FT. 1½" LINEN
HOSE,RACK, 1½" & 2½"ANGLE VALVE.
23"x 40" x 8½" TO 26"x 40" x 9"

Cabinets are obtainable for 25, 50, 75, & 100 foot hose racks. Rough dimensions are shown.

FIRE HOSE & EXTINGUISHER CABINETS

DRAINAGE RISERS-OFFICE BUILDINGS

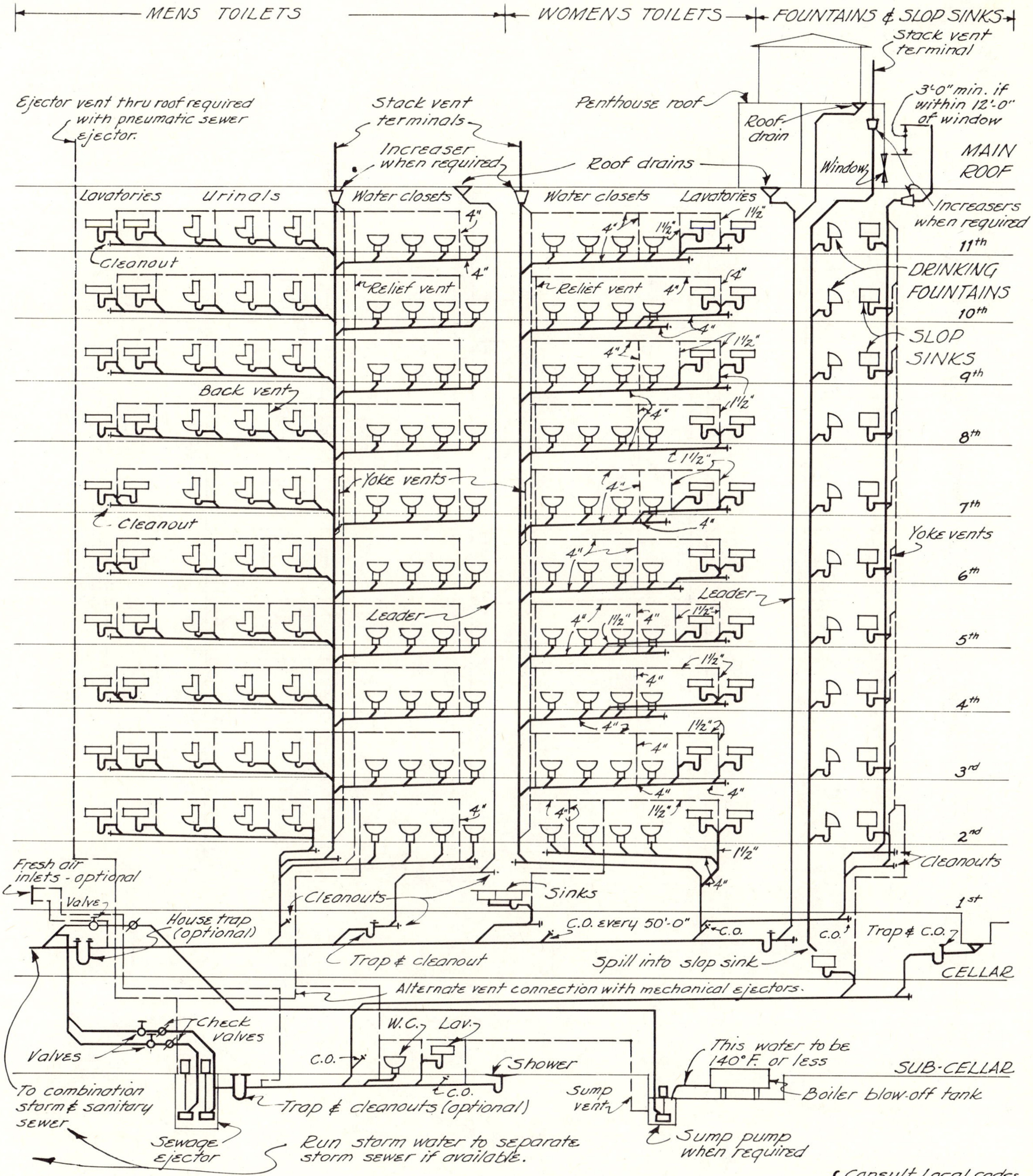
MENS TOILETS
WOMENS TOILETS
FOUNTAINS & SLOP SINKS
Stack vent terminal
Ejector vent thru roof required with pneumatic sewer ejector.
Stack vent terminals
Increaser when required
Penthouse roof
Roof drain
3'-0" min. if within 12'-0" of window
Roof drains
Window
MAIN ROOF
Lavatories
Urinals
Water closets
Water closets
Lavatories
Increasers when required
Cleanout
Relief vent
Relief vent
DRINKING FOUNTAINS
SLOP SINKS
Back vent
Yoke vents
Cleanout
Yoke vents
Leader
Leader
11th
10th
9th
8th
7th
6th
5th
4th
3rd
2nd
1st
CELLAR
SUB-CELLAR
4"
1½"
Fresh air inlets - optional
Valve
House trap (optional)
Cleanouts
Sinks
Cleanouts
C.O. every 50'-0"
C.O.
Trap & C.O.
Trap & cleanout
Spill into slop sink
Alternate vent connection with mechanical ejectors.
Check valves
Valves
W.C.
Lav.
C.O.
Shower
This water to be 140°F. or less
Boiler blow-off tank
Sump vent
To combination storm & sanitary sewer
Trap & cleanouts (optional)
Sewage ejector
Run storm water to separate storm sewer if available.
Sump pump when required

Note: This diagram was prepared to conform to the ASME Plumbing Code, 1949. {Consult Local codes for differences, sizes, etc.

TYPICAL DRAINAGE RISER DIAGRAM for MULTI-STORY OFFICE BUILDINGS

Compiled by the Office of Mongitore & Moesel, Consulting Engineers, N.Y.C.

DRAINAGE RISERS-APARTMENT BUILDINGS

Increasers are required when there is a possibility of frost formation sufficient to restrict ventilation.

SYMBOLS

C.O. — Cleanout
WC — Water Closet
BT — Bath tub
LAV — Lavatory
S&T — Sink & Tray
S.S. — Slop Sink

Extend all stack vents 1'-0" above roof, except where roof is used for human activity, in which case, the extension should be 6'-0".

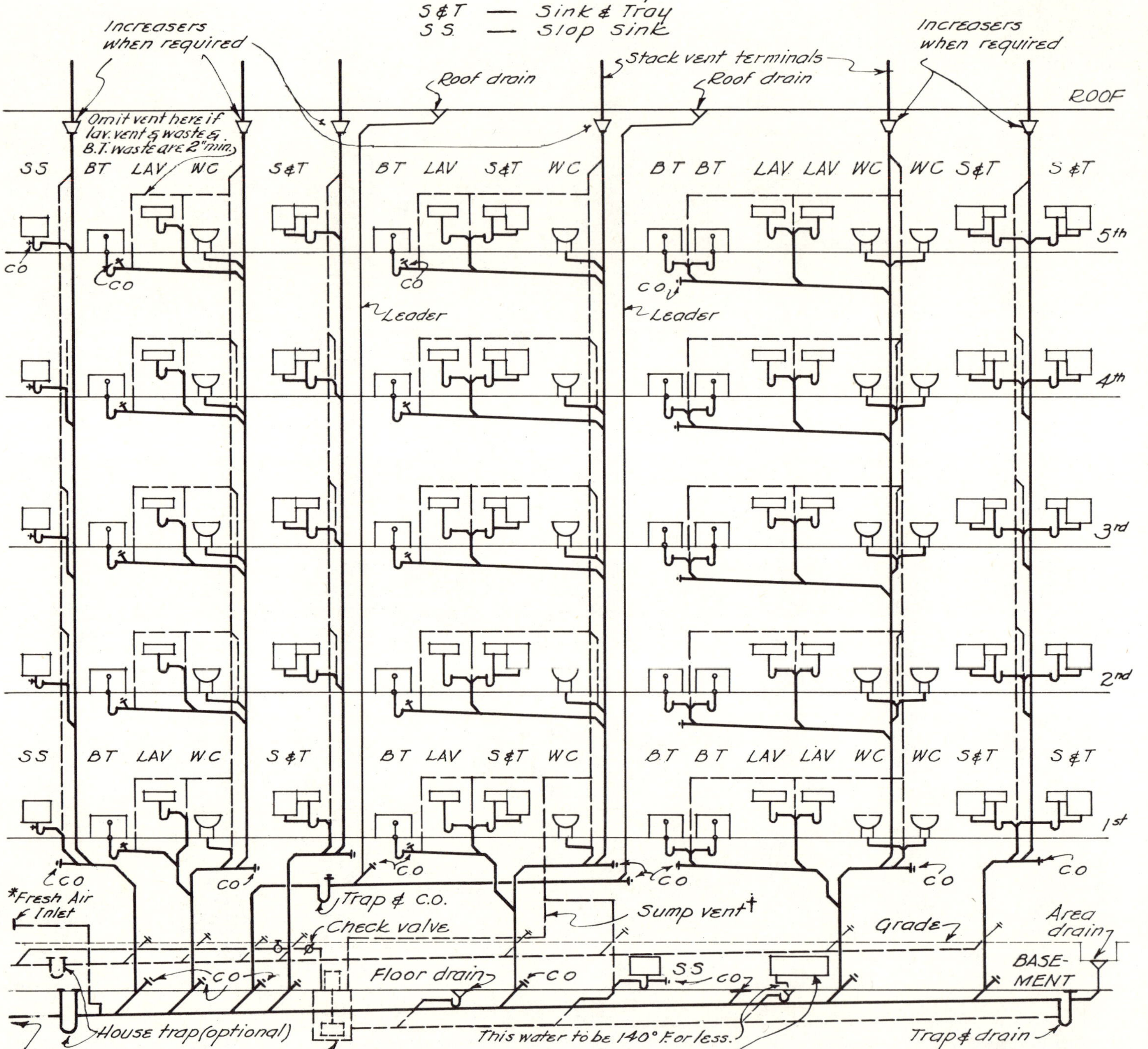

Increasers when required
Omit vent here if lav. vent & waste & B.T. waste are 2" min.
Roof drain
Stack vent terminals
Roof drain
Increasers when required
ROOF
SS
BT
LAV
WC
S&T
BT
LAV
S&T
WC
BT
BT
LAV
LAV
WC
WC
S&T
S&T
5th
4th
3rd
2nd
1st
CO
Leader
Leader
CO
CO
Trap & C.O.
*Fresh Air Inlet
Sump vent†
Check valve
Grade
Area drain
BASE-MENT
Floor drain
SS
House trap (optional)
This water to be 140° F. or less.
Trap & drain

To combination storm & sanitary sewer. Run storm water to storm sewer if separate sewers are available.

Sump pump or sewage ejector as required.

Boiler blow-off tank.

Sub-drain into sump pit or sewage ejector when street sewer is above lowest fixtures.

† *Run sump vent thru roof if pneumatic sewage ejector is used.*

* *Optional*

NOTE: This diagram was prepared to conform to the A.S.M.E. Plumbing Code 1949. { *Consult Local codes for differences, sizes, etc.*

TYPICAL DRAINAGE RISER DIAGRAM *for* MULTI-STORY APARTMENT BUILDINGS

Compiled by the Office of Mongitore & Moesel, Consulting Engineers, N.Y.C.

RESIDENTIAL DRAINAGE and WATER PIPING DIAGRAMS

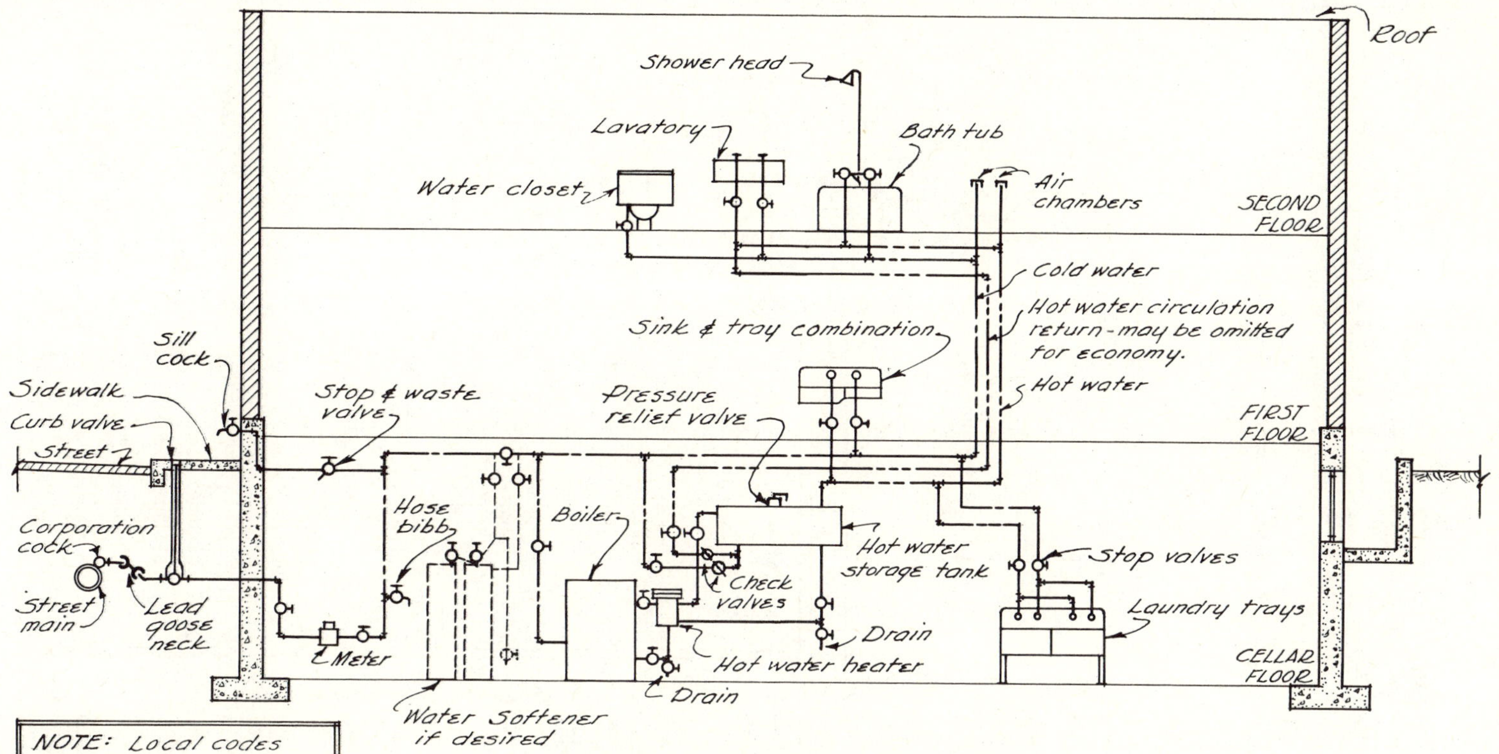
Roof
Shower head
Lavatory
Bath tub
Water closet
Air chambers
SECOND FLOOR
Cold water
Hot water circulation return-may be omitted for economy.
Sink & tray combination
Hot water
Sill cock
Sidewalk
Curb valve
Street
Stop & waste valve
Pressure relief valve
FIRST FLOOR
Corporation cock
Street main
Lead goose neck
Hose bibb
Boiler
Hot water storage tank
Check valves
Stop valves
Laundry trays
Drain
Meter
Hot water heater
Drain
CELLAR FLOOR
Water Softener if desired

NOTE: Local codes should be consulted for pipe sizes & other requirements in plumbing systems.

WATER PIPING DIAGRAM

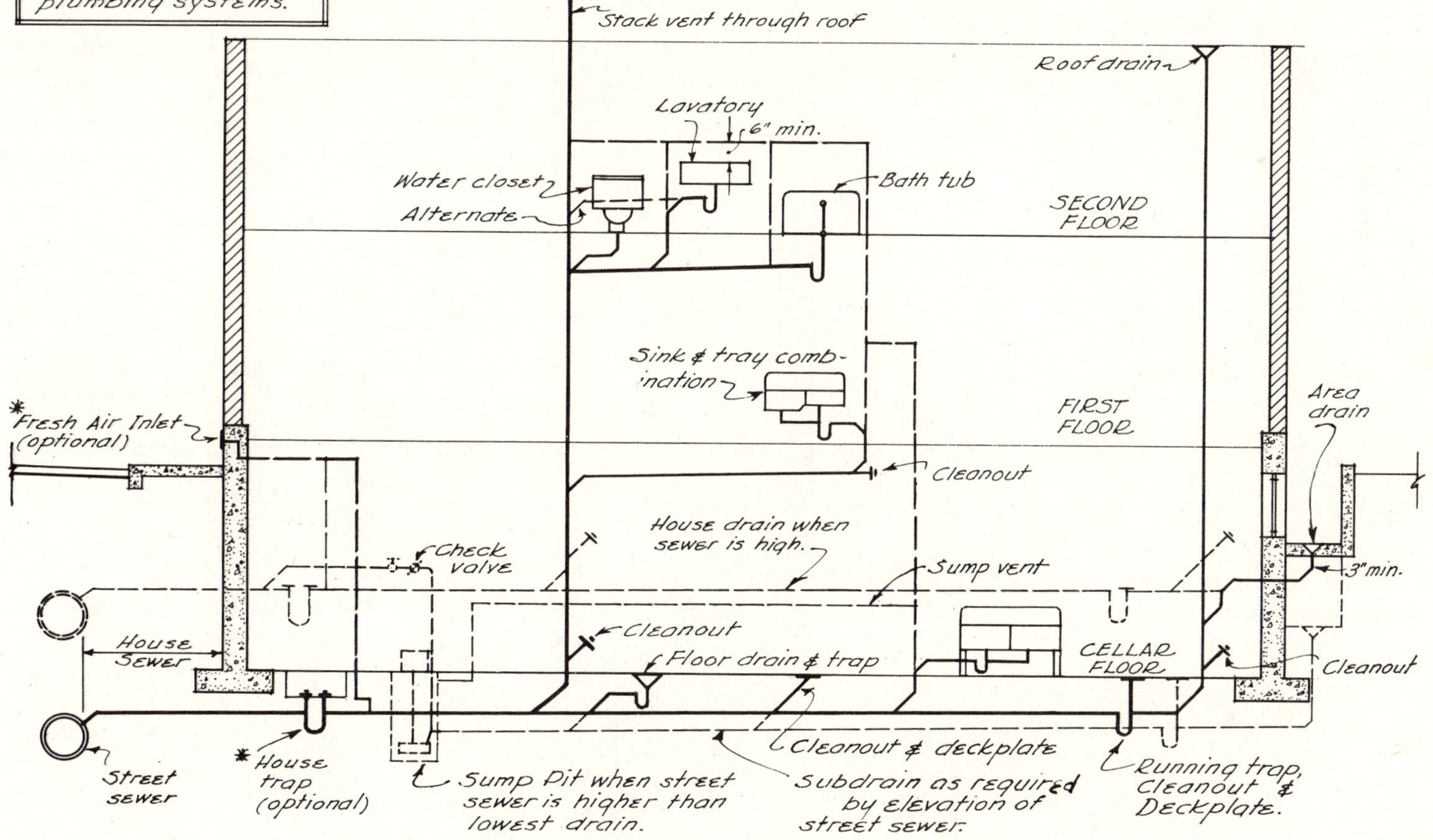
Stack vent through roof
Roof drain
Lavatory
6" min.
Water closet
Alternate
Bath tub
SECOND FLOOR
Sink & tray combination
FIRST FLOOR
Area drain
*Fresh Air Inlet (optional)
Cleanout
Check valve
House drain when sewer is high.
Sump vent
3" min.
Cleanout
House Sewer
Floor drain & trap
CELLAR FLOOR
Cleanout
Street sewer
* House trap (optional)
Cleanout & deckplate
Sump Pit when street sewer is higher than lowest drain.
Subdrain as required by elevation of street sewer.
Running trap, Cleanout & Deckplate.

DRAINAGE PIPING DIAGRAM

* Required by some local codes. Not considered necessary by U.S. Dept. of Commerce," Recommended Minimum Requirements for Plumbing" BH 13

Compiled by the Office of Mongitore & Moesel, Consulting Engineers, N.Y.C.

EXTRA HEAVY CAST IRON SOIL PIPE and FITTINGS

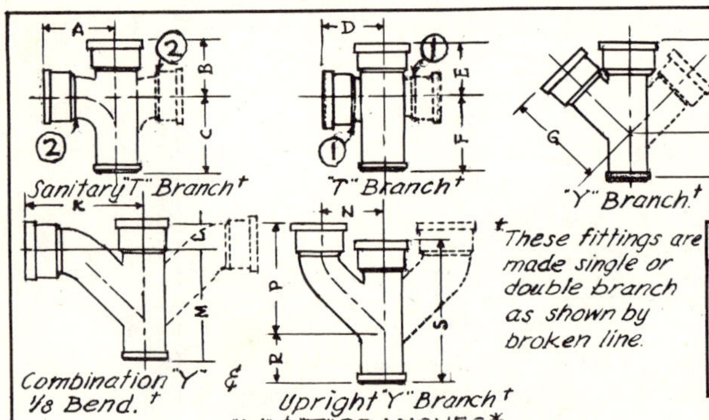

Sanitary "T" Branch†
"T" Branch†
"Y" Branch†
Combination "Y" & 1/8 Bend.†
Upright "Y" Branch†

†These fittings are made single or double branch as shown by broken line.

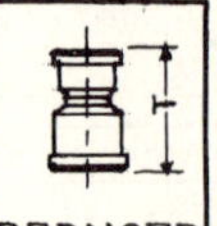

REDUCER

"Y" & "T" BRANCHES*

SIZE	SANITARY "T" BRANCH			"T" BRANCH			"Y" BRANCH			COMBINATION "Y" & 1/8 BEND			UPRIGHT "Y" BRANCH				REDUCER
	A	B	C	D	E	F	G	H	J	K	L	M	N	P	R	S	T
2"	5 1/4	4 1/4	6 1/4	4 1/4	4 1/4	6 1/4	6 1/2	6 1/2	4	7 3/8	3 1/8	7 3/8	4 1/2	8 1/2	4	10 1/2	
3"	6 3/4	5 1/4	7 1/2	5 1/4	5 1/4	7 1/2	8 1/4	8 1/4	5	9 3/4	3 3/16	10 1/16	5 1/2	10 3/16	5	13 1/4	
4"	7 1/2	6	8	6	6	8	9 3/4	9 3/4	5 1/4	12	2 15/16	12 1/16	6 1/2	11 11/16	5 1/4	15	
5"	8	6 1/2	8 1/2	6 1/2	6 1/2	8 1/2	11	11	5 1/2	14	2 3/8	14 1/8	7 1/2	12 7/8	5 1/2	16 1/2	
6"	8 1/2	7	9	7	7	9	12 1/4	12 1/4	5 3/4	15 7/8	1 15/16	16 1/16	8 1/2	14 1/16	5 3/4	18	
8"	10 1/8	8 3/4	11 3/4	8 3/4	8 3/4	11 3/4	15 5/16	15 5/16	7 11/16								
10"	11 1/8	9 3/4	12 3/4	9 3/4	9 3/4	12 3/4	18	18	8								
12"	13	11 3/4	15	11 3/4	11 3/4	15	21 1/8	21 1/8	10 1/8								
15"	14 1/2	13 1/4	16 1/2	13 1/4	13 1/4	16 1/2	25	25	10 3/4								
3"×2"	6 1/2	4 3/4	7	5	4 3/4	7	7 1/2	7 9/16	4 3/16	8 1/4	3 9/16	8 3/16	5	9 1/4	4 3/16	11 3/4	7 1/4
4"×2"	7	5	7	5 1/2	5	7	8 1/4	8 3/8	3 5/8	8 3/4	3 13/16	8 3/16	5 1/2	9 3/4	3 11/16	12	7 1/2
4"×3"	7 1/4	5 1/2	7 1/2	5 3/4	5 1/2	7 1/2	9	9 1/16	4 7/16	10 1/4	3 7/16	10 1/16	6	10 11/16	4 1/2	13 1/2	7 3/4
5"×2"	7 1/2	5	7	6	5	7	9	8 7/8	3 1/8	9 1/4	3 5/8	8 3/8	6	10 1/4	3 3/8	12	7 1/2
5"×3"	7 3/4	5 1/2	7 1/2	6 1/4	5 1/2	7 1/2	9 3/4	9 5/8	3 7/8	10 3/4	3 7/16	10 11/16	6 1/2	11 3/16	4	13 1/2	7 3/4
5"×4"	8	6	8	6 1/2	6	8	10 1/2	10 5/16	4 11/16	12 1/2	2 15/16	12 1/16	7	12 3/16	4 3/4	15	8
6"×2"	8	5	7	6 1/2	5	7	9 3/4	9 7/16	2 9/16	9 3/4	3 13/16	8 3/16	6 1/2	10 3/4	2 11/16	12	7 1/2
6"×3"	8 1/4	5 1/2	7 1/2	6 3/4	5 1/2	7 1/2	10 1/2	10 1/8	3 3/8	11 1/4	3 7/16	10 1/16	7	11 11/16	3 1/2	13 1/2	7 3/4
6"×4"	8 1/2	6	8	7	6	8	11 1/4	10 13/16	4 3/16	13	2 15/16	12 1/16	7 1/2	12 11/16	4 1/4	15	8
6"×5"	8 1/2	6 1/2	8 1/2	7	6 1/2	8 1/2	11 3/4	11 9/16	4 15/16	14 1/2	2 5/16	14 3/16	8	13 3/8	5 1/16	16 1/2	8
8"×2"	9	5 3/4	8 3/4	7 3/4	5 3/4	8 3/4	11	10 7/8	3 1/8								8 1/2
8"×3"	9 1/4	6 1/4	9 1/4	8	6 1/4	9 1/4	11 3/4	11 9/16	3 15/16								8 3/4
8"×4"	9 1/2	6 3/4	9 3/4	8 1/4	6 3/4	9 3/4	12 1/2	12 1/4	4 3/4								9
8"×5"	9 1/2	7 1/4	10 1/4	8 1/4	7 1/4	10 1/4	13	13	5 1/2								9
8"×6"	9 1/2	7 3/4	10 3/4	8 1/4	7 3/4	10 3/4	13 1/2	13 11/16	6 5/16								9
10"×4"	10 1/2	6 3/4	9 3/4	9 1/4	6 3/4	9 3/4	14 1/8	13 7/16	3 9/16								9
10"×5"	10 1/2	7 1/4	10 1/4	9 1/4	7 1/4	10 1/4	14 5/8	14 3/16	4 5/16								9
10"×6"	10 1/2	7 3/4	10 3/4	9 1/4	7 3/4	10 3/4	15 1/8	14 7/8	5 1/8								9
10"×8"	11 1/8	8 3/4	11 3/4	9 3/4	8 3/4	11 3/4	16 15/16	16 1/2	6 1/2								9 1/2
12"×4"	11 1/2	7 3/4	11	10 1/4	7 1/2	11 1/4	15 7/16	15 1/8	4 1/8								9 1/2
12"×5"	11 1/2	8 1/4	11 1/2	10 1/4	8	11 3/4	15 15/16	15 7/8	4 7/8								9 1/2
12"×6"	11 1/2	8 3/4	12	10 1/4	8 1/2	12 1/4	16 7/16	16 9/16	5 11/16								9 1/2
12"×8"	12 1/8	9 3/4	13	10 3/4	9 3/4	13	18 1/4	18 3/16	7 1/16								10
12"×10"	12 1/8	10 3/4	14	10 3/4	10 3/4	14	19 5/16	19 11/16	8 9/16								10
15"×6"	13	8 3/4	12	10 3/4	8 1/2	12 1/4	18 3/4	18 1/4	4								9 1/2
15"×8"	13 5/8	9 3/4	13	12 1/4	9 3/4	13	20 9/16	19 7/8	5 3/8								10
15"×10"	13 5/8	10 3/4	14	12 1/4	10 3/4	14	21 5/8	21 3/8	6 7/8								10
15"×12"	14 1/2	11 3/4	15	13 1/4	11 3/4	15	23 7/16	22 13/16	8 7/16								10 3/4

*T Branches and Sanitary T Branches in the following sizes: 2"×2", 3"×2", 4"×2", 5"×2" & 6"×2" are available tapped for pipe thread. T-Branches may be tapped for 1 1/4" to 2" pipe thread located at (1). Sanitary T Branches may be tapped for 1 1/4" to 2" pipe THD. at (2).

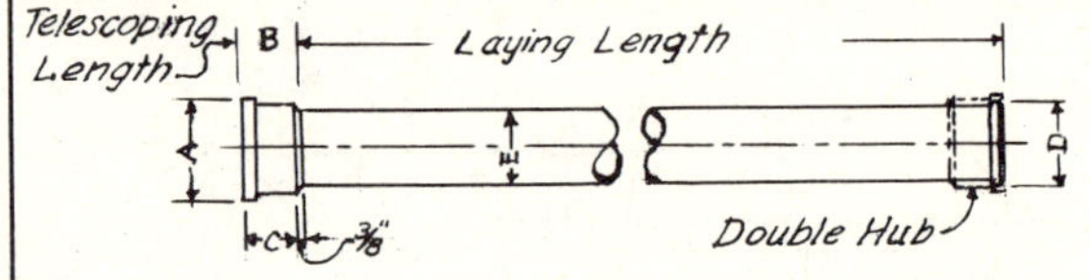

Telescoping Length
B
Laying Length
A
E
D
C
3/8"
Double Hub

EXTRA HEAVY CAST IRON SOIL PIPE

SIZE	A	B	C	D	E	SIZE	A	B	C	D	E
2"	3 15/16	2 1/2	2 3/8	2 3/4	2 3/8	8"	10 7/8	3 1/2	3 9/16	9	8 5/8
3"	5 3/16	2 3/4	2 11/16	3 7/8	3 1/2	10"	13 1/8	3 1/2	3 9/16	11 1/8	10 3/4
4"	6 3/16	3	2 15/16	4 7/8	4 1/2	12"	15 1/4	4 1/4	4 3/8	13 1/8	12 3/4
5"	7 3/16	3	2 15/16	5 7/8	5 1/2	15"	18 5/8	4 1/4	4 3/8	16 1/4	15 7/8
6"	8 3/16	3	2 15/16	6 7/8	6 1/2						

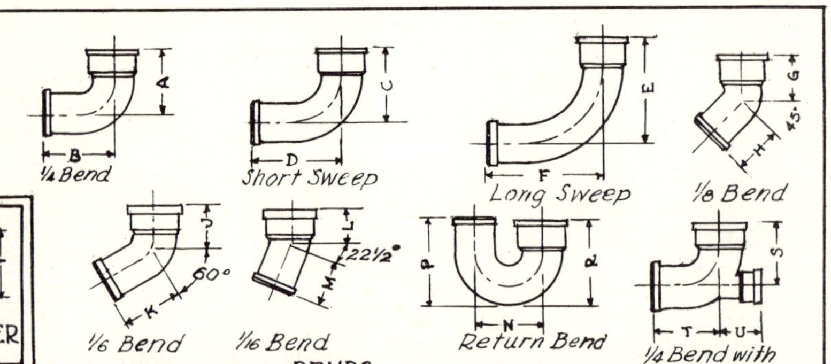

1/4 Bend
Short Sweep
Long Sweep
1/8 Bend
1/6 Bend
1/16 Bend
Return Bend
1/4 Bend with Heel Inlet

BENDS

SIZE	1/4 BEND		SHORT SWEEP		LONG SWEEP		1/8 BEND		1/6 BEND		1/16 BEND		RETURN BEND			1/4 BEND WITH HEEL INLET			
	A	B	C	D	E	F	G	H	J	K	L	M	N	P	R	SIZE	S	T	U
2"	5 3/4	6	7 3/4	8	10 3/4	11	4	4 1/4	4 1/2	4 3/4	3 3/8	3 5/8	6	7 3/16	6 15/16	3×2	6 3/4	7	4 1/2
3"	6 3/4	7	8 3/4	9	11 3/4	12	4 11/16	4 15/16	5 1/4	5 1/2	3 15/16	4 3/16	7	8 3/4	8 1/2	4×2	7 1/2	8	5
4"	7 1/2	8	9 1/2	10	12 1/2	13	5 3/16	5 11/16	5 13/16	6 5/16	4 5/16	4 13/16	8	10 1/4	9 3/4	4×3	7 1/2	8	5 1/4
5"	8	8 1/2	10	10 1/2	13	13 1/2	5 3/8	5 7/8	6 1/8	6 5/8	4 3/8	4 7/8	9	11 1/4	10 3/4	5×2	8	8 1/2	5 3/4
6"	8 1/2	9	10 1/2	11	13 1/2	14	5 9/16	6 1/16	6 3/8	6 7/8	4 1/2	5	10	12 1/4	11 3/4	5×3	8	8 1/2	6
8"	10 1/8	11 1/2	12 1/8	13 1/2	15 1/8	16 1/2	6 5/8	8	7 5/8	9	5 5/16	6 11/16	12	15 13/16	14 7/16	5×4	8	8 1/2	6 1/4
10"	11 1/8	12 1/2	13 1/8	14 1/2	16 1/8	17 1/2	7	8 3/8	8 3/16	9 9/16	5 1/2	6 7/8				6×2	8 1/2	9	6
12"	13	15	15	17	18	20	8 5/16	10 5/16	9 5/8	11 5/8	6 5/8	8 5/8				6×3	8 1/2	9	6 1/4
15"	14 1/2	16 1/2	16 1/2	18 1/2	19 1/2	21 1/2	8 15/16	10 15/16	10 1/2	12 1/2	6 7/8	8 7/8				6×4	8 1/2	9	6 1/2

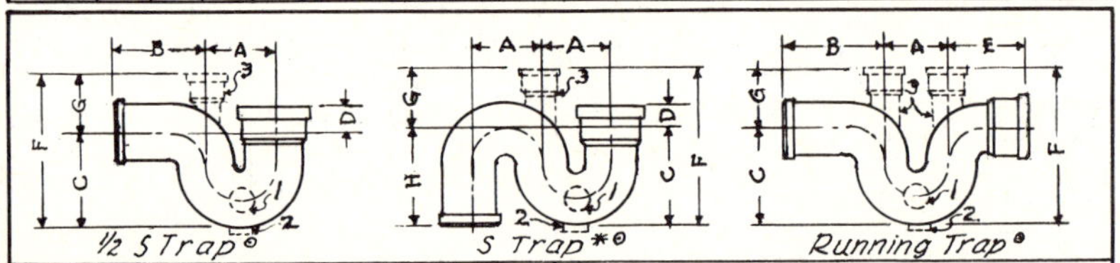

1/2 S Trap °
S Trap *°
Running Trap °

*Standard "S" Traps are made in sizes 2×2 through 6×6 only.
°Traps are made with or without the following tappings: 2" trap - 1 1/2" tapping at 3, 1 1/4" tapping at 1 or 2; 3" trap - 2 1/2" tapping at 3; 1 1/2" tapping at 1 or 2; 4" trap 3 1/2" tapping at 3, 3" tapping at 1 or 2; 5" & 6" trap - 4" tapping at 3, 3" tapping at 1 or 2; 8", 10", 12" & 15" trap - 3" tapping at 1 or 2. All traps are made single or double branch as shown by broken line.

TRAPS

SIZE	A	B	C	D	E	F	G	H
*2×2	4	5 1/2	5 3/16	1	5	9 11/16	4 1/2	5 1/2
*3×2	5	7	7 1/4	1 1/2	5 3/4	12 1/4	5	7
*3×3	5	7	7 1/4	1 1/2	5 3/4	12 1/2	5 1/4	7
*4×2	6	8	8 3/4	2	6 1/2	14 1/4	5 1/2	8 1/2
*4×3	6	8	8 3/4	2	6 1/2	14 1/2	5 3/4	8 1/2
*4×4	6	8	8 3/4	2	6 1/2	14 3/4	6	8 1/2
*5×4	7	8 1/2	10 1/4	2 1/2	7	16 3/4	6 1/2	10
*5×5	7	8 1/2	10 1/4	2 1/2	7	16 3/4	6 1/2	10
*6×4	8	9	11 3/4	3	7 1/2	18 3/4	7	11 1/2
*6×6	8	9	11 3/4	3	7 1/2	18 3/4	7	11 1/2
8×4	10	12	15 5/16	4	9 1/8	23 13/16	8 1/4	
8×6	10	12	15 5/16	4	9 1/8	23 13/16	8 1/4	
10×6	12	13	18 3/8	5	10 1/8	27 5/8	9 1/4	
12×6	15	15 1/2	21 3/8	6	12 1/2	31 5/8	10 1/4	
12×8	15	15 1/2	21 3/8	6	12 1/2	32 1/8	10 1/4	
15×8	18 1/2	17 1/4	26 7/16	7 1/2	14 1/4	38 11/16	12 1/4	

1/8 BEND

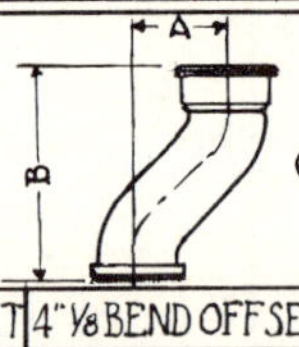

A
B

OFFSET

2" 1/8 BEND OFFSET			3" 1/8 BEND OFFSET			4" 1/8 BEND OFFSET			5" 1/8 BEND OFFSET			6" 1/8 BEND OFFSET		
SIZE	A	B	SIZE	A	B	SIZE	A	B	SIZE	A	B	SIZE	A	B
2×2	2	9 3/4	3×2	2	11 1/4	4×2	2	12	5×2	2	12 1/2	6×2	2	13
2×4	4	11 3/4	3×4	4	13 1/4	4×4	4	14	5×4	4	14 1/2	6×4	4	15
2×6	6	13 3/4	3×6	6	15 1/4	4×6	6	16	5×6	6	16 1/2	6×6	6	17
2×8	8	15 3/4	3×8	8	17 1/4	4×8	8	18	5×8	8	18 1/2	6×8	8	19
2×10	10	17 3/4	3×10	10	19 1/4	4×10	10	20	5×10	10	20 1/2	8×10	10	21
2×12	12	19 3/4	3×12	12	21 1/4	4×12	12	22	5×12	12	22 1/2	6×12	12	23
2×14	14	21 3/4	3×14	14	23 1/4	4×14	14	24	5×14	14	24 1/2	6×14	14	25
2×16	16	23 3/4	3×16	16	25 1/4	4×16	16	26	5×16	16	26 1/2	6×16	16	27
2×18	18	25 3/4	3×18	18	27 1/4	4×18	18	28	5×18	18	28 1/2	6×18	18	29
2×20	20	27 3/4	3×20	20	29 1/4	4×20	20	30	5×20	20	30 1/2	6×20	20	31
2×22	22	29 3/4	3×22	22	31 1/4	4×22	22	32	5×22	22	32 1/2	6×22	22	33
2×24	24	31 3/4	3×24	24	33 1/4	4×24	24	34	5×24	24	34 1/2	6×24	24	35

The above fittings include those most commonly used; for other fittings refer to manufacturers' catalogs.
All dimensions in the above tables are given in inches, and are American Standard. Sizes are nominal.
Compiled by the Office of Mongitore & Moesel, Consulting Engineers — N.Y.C.

STANDARD MALLEABLE IRON and CAST IRON FITTINGS

STANDARD MALLEABLE IRON PATTERN

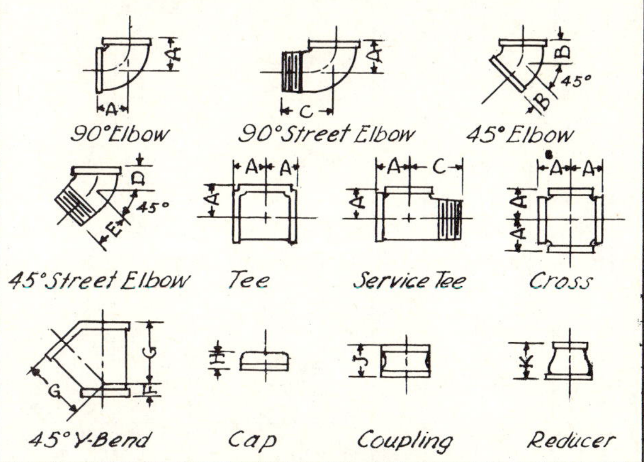

90° Elbow
90° Street Elbow
45° Elbow
45° Street Elbow
Tee
Service Tee
Cross
45° Y-Bend
Cap
Coupling
Reducer

FITTING DIMENSIONS

SIZE	A	B	C	D	E	F	G	H	J	K
1/8	11/16	1/2	*1	11/16	13/16			9/16	15/16	
1/4	13/16	3/4	1 3/16	3/4"	15/16			5/8	1 1/16	1
3/8	15/16	13/16	1 7/16	11/16	1 1/16	11/16	1 7/16	3/4	1 3/16	1 1/8
1/2	1 1/8	7/8	1 5/8	13/16	1 3/16	3/4	1 11/16	7/8	1 5/16	1 1/4
3/4	1 5/16	1	1 7/8	15/16	1 5/16	3/4	2 1/16	1 15/16	1 1/2	1 7/16
1	1 1/2	1 1/8	2 1/8	1 1/8	1 1/2	15/16	2 7/16	1 3/16	1 11/16	1 11/16
1 1/4	1 3/4	1 5/16	2 7/16	1 1/4	1 11/16	1 1/8	2 15/16	1 1/4	1 15/16	2 1/16
1 1/2	1 15/16	1 7/16	2 11/16	1 3/8	1 7/8	1 3/16	3 5/16	1 5/16	2 1/8	2 5/16
2	2 1/4	1 11/16	3 1/4	1 11/16	2 1/4	1 7/16	4	1 7/16	2 1/2	2 13/16
2 1/2	2 11/16	1 15/16	*3 13/16	1 7/8	2 9/16	1 9/16	4 11/16	1 5/8	2 7/8	3 1/4
3	3 1/8	2 3/16	*4 1/2	2 1/8	3	1 11/16	5 9/16	1 3/4	3 3/16	3 11/16
3 1/2	3 7/16	2 3/8	5 1/8	2 3/8	3 3/8			1 15/16	3 7/16	4
4	3 3/4	2 5/8	5 11/16	2 5/8	3 3/4	1 15/16	6 15/16	2 1/16	3 11/16	4 3/8
5	4 1/2	3 1/16	*6 7/8					2 5/16	4 1/4	3 7/8
6	5 1/8	3 7/16	*8					2 9/16	4 3/4	4 3/8

* Applies to street elbows only.

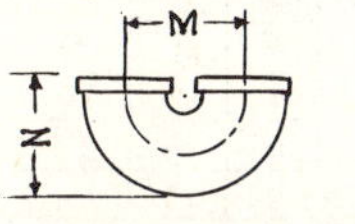

M
N

Return Bend

RETURN BEND DIMENSIONS

Close pattern Size	M	N	Open pattern Size	M	N
1/2"	1	1 3/4"	1/2"	1 1/2"	1 7/8"
3/4"	1 1/4"	2 3/16"	3/4"	2"	2 1/4"
1"	1 1/2"	2 1/2"	1"	2 1/2"	2 5/8"
1 1/4"	1 3/4"	2 13/16"	1 1/4"	3"	3 3/16"
1 1/2"	2 3/16"	3 3/16"	1 1/2"	3 1/2"	3 5/8"
2"	2 5/8"	3 7/8"	2"	4"	4 3/8"
Medium Pattern.			2 1/2"	4 1/2"	4 15/16"
1/2"	1 1/4"	1 5/8"	3"	5	5 9/16
3/4"	1 1/2	1 15/16	4	6	6 11/16
1"	1 7/8	2 1/4			
1 1/4	2 1/4	2 13/16			
1 1/2	2 1/2	3 3/16			
2	3	3 7/8			

Sizes are nominal; all dimensions are in inches.

For reducing tees, crosses, etc. consult manufacturers' catalogs.

AVAILABLE REDUCERS & REDUCING ELBOWS

SIZE	M. I. Reducing Elbows	M. I. Reducers	C. I. Reducing Elbows	C. I. Reducers	C. I. Eccentric Reducers
1/4 × 1/8	●	●			
3/8 × 1/4	●	●			
3/8 × 1/8	●	●			
1/2 × 3/8	●	●	●		
1/2 × 1/8	●	●			
1/2 × 1/4	●	●			
3/4 × 1/2	●	●	●	●	
3/4 × 3/8	●	●			
3/4 × 1/4	●	●			
1 × 3/4	●	●	●	●	
1 × 1/2	●	●	●	●	
1 × 1/4		●			
1 × 3/8	●	●			
1 1/4 × 1	●	●	●	●	●
1 1/4 × 3/4	●	●	●		●
1 1/4 × 1/2	●	●	●		
1 1/2 × 1 1/4	●	●	●	●	●
1 1/2 × 1	●	●	●		●
1 1/2 × 3/4	●	●	●		●
1 1/2 × 1/2		●	●		
2 × 1 1/2	●	●	●	●	●
2 × 1 1/4	●	●	●	●	●
2 × 1	●	●	●	●	●
2 × 3/4	●	●	●		●
2 × 1/2		●	●		
2 1/2 × 2	●	●	●	●	●
2 1/2 × 1 1/2	●	●	●		●
2 1/2 × 1 1/4		●	●	●	●
2 1/2 × 1		●	●		●
3 × 2 1/2	●	●	●	●	●
3 × 2	●	●	●	●	●
3 × 1 1/2		●	●	●	●
3 × 1 1/4		●	●	●	●
3 × 1		●			●
3 1/2 × 3		●	●		●
3 1/2 × 2 1/2		●			●
3 1/2 × 2		●			●
3 1/2 × 1 1/2					●
3 1/2 × 1 1/4					●
3 1/2 × 1					●
4 × 3 1/2		●	●	●	●
4 × 3	●	●	●	●	●
4 × 2 1/2		●	●	●	●
4 × 2		●	●	●	
4 × 1 1/2		●			●
4 × 1 1/4					●
4 × 1					●
5 × 4		●	●	●	●
5 × 3 1/2					●
5 × 3			●		●
5 × 2 1/2			●		●
5 × 2					●
6 × 5		●	●	●	●
6 × 4		●	●	●	●
6 × 3 1/2					●
6 × 3			●		●
6 × 2 1/2					●
6 × 2					●
8 × 6			●	●	●
8 × 4					
8 × 5					●

STANDARD CAST IRON PATTERN

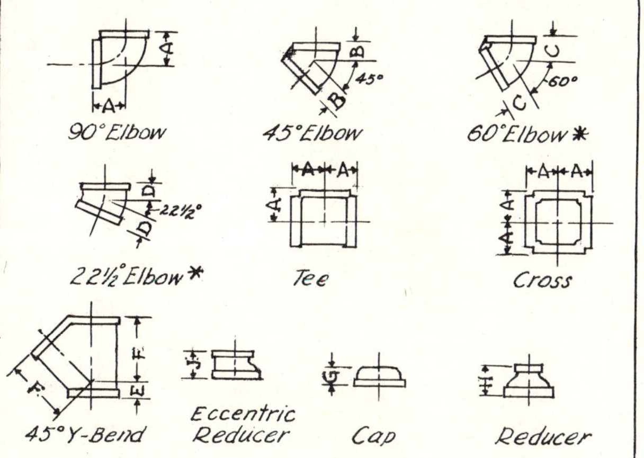

90° Elbow
45° Elbow
60° Elbow *
22 1/2° Elbow *
Tee
Cross
45° Y-Bend
Eccentric Reducer
Cap
Reducer

* 60° and 22 1/2° elbows are made by some manufacturers but are not standard.

FITTING DIMENSIONS

Size	A	B	C	D	E	F	G	H	J
1/4	13/16	3/4							
3/8	15/16	13/16							
1/2	1 1/8	7/8	1	3/4				1 3/8	
3/4	1 5/16	1	1 1/16	7/8	3/4	2 1/4		1 1/2	
1	1 1/2	1 1/8	1 1/4	1	3/4	2 3/4		1 11/16	
1 1/4	1 3/4	1 5/16	1 7/16	1 1/8	1	3 1/4		2 1/8	2 1/8
1 1/2	1 15/16	1 7/16	1 5/8	1 1/4	1 1/16	3 13/16		2 1/4	2 1/4
2	2 1/4	1 11/16	1 7/8	1 7/16	1 1/4	4 1/2		2 7/16	2 7/16
2 1/2	2 11/16	1 15/16	2 3/16	1 9/16	1 9/16	5 3/16	1 13/16	2 5/8	2 11/16
3	3 1/8	2 3/16	2 1/2	1 3/4	1 3/4	6 1/8	1 15/16	2 7/8	2 15/16
3 1/2	3 7/16	2 3/8					2 1/16	3 1/8	3 1/8
4	3 3/4	2 5/8	3	2 1/16	2 1/8	7 5/8	2 3/16	3 3/8	3 3/8
5	4 1/2	3 1/16	3 1/2	2 1/4			2 3/8	3 7/8	3 7/8
6	5 1/8	3 7/16	4 1/16	2 7/16			2 5/8	3 13/16	4 3/8
8	6 9/16	4 1/4					2 7/8	5 1/4	5 1/4
10	*8 1/16	5 3/16					3 1/2		
12	*9 1/2	6					3 7/8		

* This dimension applies to elbows and tees only.

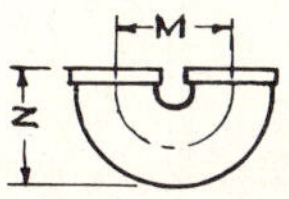

M
N

Return Bend

RETURN BEND DIMENSIONS

Close pattern Size	M	N	Open pattern Size	M	N	Wide pattern Size	M	N
1/2	1 1/4	1 23/32	1/2	1 3/4	1 15/16	1	3	3
3/4	1 1/2	2 1/32	3/4	1 7/8	2 7/32	1	4	3 1/2
1	1 3/4	2 3/8	1	2 1/2	2 11/16	1 1/4	4	3 3/4
1 1/4	2 1/4	2 29/32	1 1/4	3	3 9/32	1 1/4	6	4 3/4
1 1/2	2 1/2	3 1/4	1 1/2	3 1/2	3 3/4	1 1/2	6	5
2	3 1/4	3 3/32	2	4 1/2	4 19/32	2	6	5 5/16
2 1/2	3 3/4	4 9/16	2 1/2	5 1/2	5 7/16			
3	4 1/2	5 3/16	3	6 1/2	6 5/16			
4	6	6 13/16	4	7 1/2	7 9/16			

Compiled by the Office of Mongitore & Moesel, Consulting Engineers, N.Y.C.

SCREWED CAST IRON DRAINAGE PIPE and FITTINGS

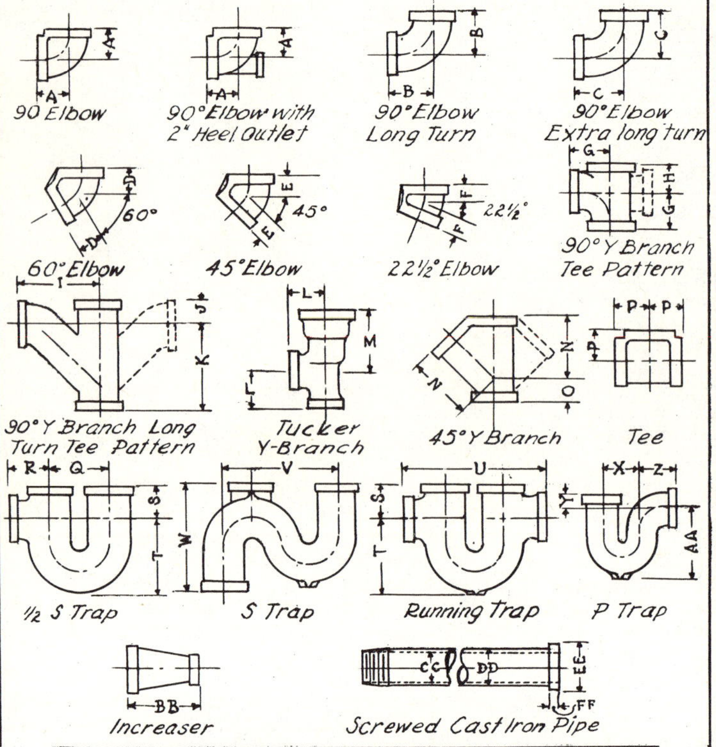
90 Elbow
90° Elbow with 2" Heel Outlet
90° Elbow Long Turn
90° Elbow Extra long turn
60° Elbow
45° Elbow
22 1/2° Elbow
90° Y Branch Tee Pattern
90° Y Branch Long Turn Tee Pattern
Tucker Y-Branch
45° Y Branch
Tee
1/2 S Trap
S Trap
Running Trap
P Trap
Increaser
Screwed Cast Iron Pipe

PIPE & FITTING DIMENSIONS

FITTING	SIZE	1 1/4"	1 1/2"	2"	2 1/2"	3"	4"	5"	6"	8"	10"	12"
90° Elbow	A	1 3/4	1 15/16	2 1/4	2 11/16	3 1/16	3 13/16	4 1/2	5 1/8	6 9/16	7 3/4	
90° Elbow (Long turn)	B	2 1/4	2 1/2	3 1/16	3 11/16	4 1/4	5 3/16	6 1/8	7 1/8	8 3/4	10 7/8	13
90° Elbow Extra Long Turn	C	3	3 1/2	4	4 1/2	5 1/4	6 1/4					
60° Elbow	D	1 9/16	1 3/4	2 1/16	2 1/2	2 7/8	3 3/8	3 7/8	4 1/4	5 3/8		
45° Elbow (short)	E	1 5/16	1 7/16	1 11/16	1 15/16	2 3/16	2 5/8	3 1/16	3 7/16	4 1/4	5 3/16	5 1/4
22 1/2° Elbow	F	1 1/8	1 1/4	1 7/16	1 3/4	2	2 5/16	2 5/8	2 15/16	3 9/16		
90° Y-Branch Tee Pattern	G	2 1/4	2 1/2	3 1/16	3 11/16	4 1/4	5 3/16	6 1/8	7 1/8	9 1/4	12 1/8	13 7/8
	H	1 1/2	1 3/4	2 1/8	2 5/8	3	3 9/16	4 3/16	4 13/16	6 1/4	7	8 3/16
90° Y Branch Long Turn Tee Pattern	I	3 5/8	4 1/8	5 1/4	6 1/4	7 1/2	9 7/8	12 1/4	14 5/8	14 1/8	16 3/8	21 3/4
	J	1 1/8	1 1/4	1 3/4	2	2 3/8	3 1/8	3 1/2	4 1/8	3 3/4	7 3/8	4 3/8
	K	3 5/8	4 1/8	5 1/4	6 1/4	7 1/2	9 7/8	12 1/4	14 1/8	13 1/4	15 3/8	21 5/8
Tucker Y-Branch	L	2 1/4	2 1/2	3 1/16		4 1/4						
	M	3 15/16	4 1/4	4 11/16		5 3/8						
45° Y Branch	N	3 1/4	3 5/8	4 7/8	5 3/8	6 3/16	7 11/16	9 3/16	10 3/4	13 9/16	16 1/2	19 5/8
	O	1 3/4	1 7/8	2 1/8	2 1/2	2 13/16	3 3/16	3 3/4	4 1/8	5 1/4	6 1/2	4 5/8
Tee	P	1 3/4	1 15/16	2 1/4	2 11/16	3 1/16	3 13/16	4 1/2	5 1/8	6 1/2	8 1/16	9 1/2
1/2 S Trap	Q	3 1/8	3 3/8	4	4 3/4	5 3/8	7	8 3/8	10 1/8	12 3/8	14 3/4	
	R	2 5/16	2 1/2	3 1/16	3 5/8	4 1/8	5 1/8	6 1/16	6 9/16	8 15/16	10 3/4	
Running Trap	S	2	2 1/4	2 9/16	3 1/4	3 1/2	4 3/16	4 3/4	5 7/16	6 3/4	8 1/4	
	T	4 1/2	4 15/16	5 11/16		7 3/8	9 3/8	11 3/8	13 1/2	17 1/4	20 3/4	
	U	7 3/4	8 3/8	10 1/8		13 3/4	17 1/4	20 1/2	23 1/4	30 1/4	36 3/4	
S Trap	V	7 3/4	6 13/16	8		11 3/4	13 1/2					
	W	2	7 1/4	8 3/4		11 1/4	13 7/8					
P Trap	X	2	2 1/4	2 3/4		3 3/4	5					
	Y	3/4	7/8	7/8		1 3/16	1 1/2					
	Z	1 15/16	2 1/8	2 9/16		3 3/8	4 1/4					
	AA	4 1/2	5	5 11/16		7 3/4	9 3/16					
Increaser	BB			9	9	9	9	9	9	9	9	9
Screwed Cast Iron Pipe	CC	1 15/64	1 29/64	1 57/64	2 21/64	2 29/32	3 53/64	4 13/16	5 49/64	7 5/8		
	DD	1 21/32	1 29/32	2 3/8	2 7/8	3 1/2	4 1/2	5 9/16	6 5/8	8 5/8		
	EE	2 25/64	2 11/16	3 9/32	3 55/64	4 5/8	5 51/64	7 3/64	8 9/32	10 5/8		
	FF	45/64	23/32	49/64	1 9/64	1 13/64	1 19/64	1 13/32	1 33/64	1 45/64		

AVAILABLE REDUCING FITTINGS

NOMINAL SIZES — Available where marked ●

a	b	90° Elbow	Double 90° Y Branch Tee Pat.	Double 90° Y Branch (lg. tn.) Tee Pat.	Double 45° Y Branch	Increaser
1 1/2	1 1/4	●	●	●	●	
2	1 1/2	●	●	●	●	●
2	1 1/4	●	●	●		
2 1/2	2		●	●	●	
2 1/2	1 1/2		●	●	●	
3	2 1/2				●	
3	2		●	●	●	●
3	1 1/2		●	●	●	
3 1/2	3					
4	3	●	●	●	●	●
4	2		●	●	●	●
4	1 1/2		●	●	●	
5	4	●	●	●	●	●
5	3		●	●	●	
5	2		●	●	●	●
5	1 1/2					
6	5		●	●	●	●
6	4		●	●	●	●
6	3		●	●	●	●
6	2		●	●	●	
8	6		●	●	●	●
8	4		●	●	●	
8	3		●	●	●	
10	8		●		●	●
10	6		●		●	●
10	4		●		●	
8	5		●		●	●
10	5				●	
12	10					●
12	6					●

NOMINAL SIZES — Available where marked ●

a	b	c	90° Y-Branch Tee Pattern	90° Y Branch Longturn Tee Pat.	45° Y Branch	Tee
1 1/2	1 1/2	1 1/4	●	●	●	●
1 1/2	1 1/4	1 1/4	●			
2	2	1 1/2	●	●	●	●
2	2	1 1/4	●	●	●	●
2	1 1/2	2	●	●		
2	1 1/2	1 1/2	●		●	
2 1/2	2 1/2	2	●	●	●	●
2 1/2	2 1/2	1 1/2		●	●	●
3	3	2 1/2	●	●	●	
3	3	2	●	●	●	●
3	3	1 1/2	●	●	●	●
3	3	1 1/4	●			
4	4	3	●	●	●	●
4	4	2 1/2	●			
4	4	2	●	●	●	●
4	4	1 1/2	●	●	●	
5	5	4	●	●	●	●
5	5	3	●	●	●	●
5	5	2 1/2				
5	5	2	●	●	●	●
5	5	1 1/2	●	●	●	
5	5	1 1/4			●	
6	6	5	●	●	●	●
6	6	4	●	●	●	●
6	6	3	●	●	●	●
6	6	2	●	●	●	●
6	6	1 1/2	●		●	
8	8	6	●	●	●	●
8	8	5	●		●	●
8	8	4	●	●	●	●
8	8	3	●	●	●	
10	10	8	●		●	●
10	10	6	●	●	●	●
10	10	5			●	●
10	10	4	●		●	●
12	12	10			●	
12	12	8		●	●	●
12	12	6			●	
12	12	4	●			

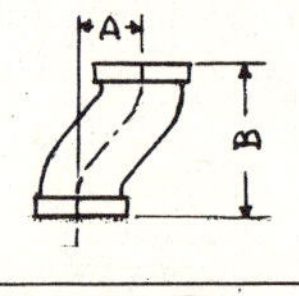

OFFSETS

SIZE	A	B	SIZE	A	B
2"	4	7 1/2	4"	10	15 3/4
2"	6	9 1/2	4"	12	17 3/4
2"	8	11 1/2	5"	6	12 5/8
2"	10	13 1/2	5"	8	14 5/8
3"	4	8 3/4	5"	10	16 5/8
3"	6	10 3/4	5"	12	18 5/8
3"	8	12 3/4	6"	6	13 5/8
3"	10	14 3/4	6"	8	15 5/8
4"	4	9 3/4	6"	10	17 5/8
4"	6	11 3/4	6"	12	19 5/8
4"	8	13 3/4			

Sizes are nominal, all dimensions are in inches.

Compiled by the Office of Mongitore & Moesel, Consulting Engineers, N.Y.C.

PLUMBING

DIMENSIONS of STANDARD IRON SCREW PIPE (ASA Schedule 40)

Nominal Internal Diameter	1/8"	1/4"	3/8"	1/2"	3/4"	1"	1 1/4"	1 1/2"	2"	2 1/2"	3"	3 1/2"	4"	5"	6"	8"	10"	12"
Actual Internal Diameter	.269	.364	.493	.622	.824	1.049	1.38	1.61	2.067	2.469	3.068	3.548	4.026	5.047	6.065	7.981	10.02	12.00
Actual External Diameter	.405	.540	.675	.840	1.05	1.315	1.66	1.90	2.375	2.875	3.50	4.00	4.50	5.563	6.625	8.625	10.75	12.75
Internal Area	.057	.104	.191	.304	.533	.864	1.496	2.036	3.355	4.788	7.393	9.886	12.73	20.00	28.89	50.02	78.85	113.09

DIAMETERS of FITTINGS-ACROSS FACE OUTSIDE

Nominal Size	1/8"	1/4"	3/8"	1/2"	3/4"	1"	1 1/4"	1 1/2"	2"	2 1/2"	3"	3 1/2"	4"	5"	6"	8"	10"	12"
Malleable 150#SWP*	11/16	7/8"	1"	1 1/4	1 1/2"	1 13/16"	2 3/16"	2 7/16"	3"	3 9/16"	4 5/16"	4 7/8"	5 7/16"	6 5/8"	7 13/16"			
Malleable 300#SWP**		15/16"	1 1/8"	1 3/8"	1 5/8"	1 15/16"	2 3/8"	2 11/16"	3 5/16"	3 7/8"	4 5/8"	5 1/4"	5 13/16"	7 1/16	8 5/16"			
Cast Iron Screw 125# SWP***		15/16"	1 1/8"	1 3/8"	1 5/8"	1 15/16"	2 3/8"	2 11/16	3 5/16"	3 7/8"	4 5/8"	5 1/4"	5 13/16"	7 1/16"	8 5/16"	10 5/8"	13 1/8"	15 1/2"
Cast Iron Screw Drainage							2 3/8"	2 11/16"	3 5/16"	3 7/8"	4 5/8"		5 13/16"	7 1/16"	8 5/16"	10 5/8"		
External Diameter of soil Pipe X H.									2 3/8"		3 1/2"		4 1/2"	5 1/2"	6 1/2"	8 5/8"	10 3/4"	12 3/4"
Ext. Dia. of Bell on Soil Pipe & Fittings X H.									3 15/16"		5 3/16"		6 3/16"	7 3/16"	8 3/16"	10 7/8"	13 1/8"	15 1/4"

Standard lengths of iron soil pipes = 5'-0" laying lengths
* 150 #SWP malleable fittings are used on water and vent piping.
** 300 #SWP malleable fittings are used for severe service
*** 125 #SWP cast iron screw fittings are used for sprinkler and steam piping.

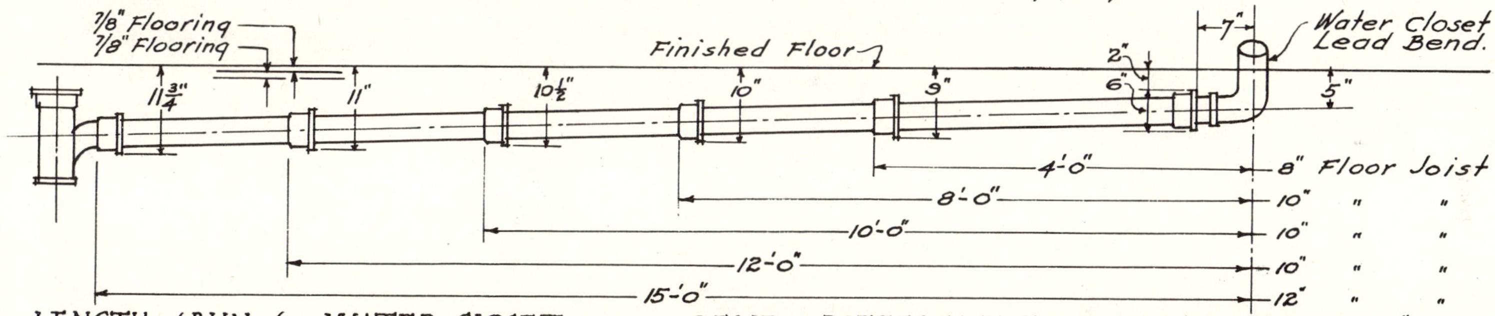

7/8" Flooring
7/8" Flooring
Finished Floor
11 3/4"
11"
10 1/2"
10"
9"
2"
6"
7"
Water Closet Lead Bend.
5"
4'-0"
8'-0"
10'-0"
12'-0"
15'-0"
8" Floor Joist
10" " "
10" " "
10" " "
12" " "

LENGTH of RUN from WATER CLOSET including BEND in DIFFERENT FLOOR THICKNESSES. C.I. 4" SOIL

DIMENSIONS of INTERSECTIONS for SOIL & VENT or WASTE LINE

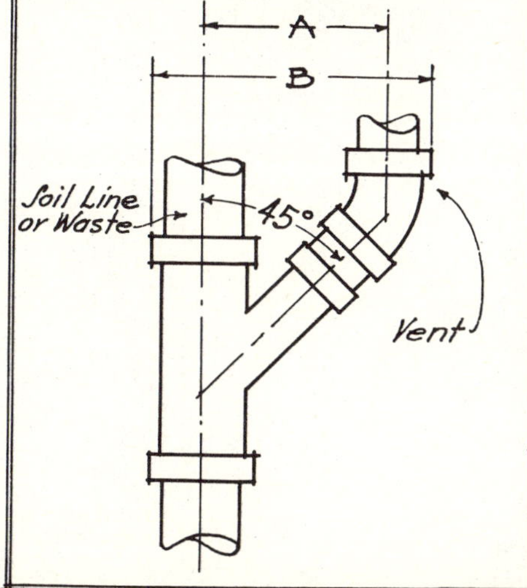

A
B
Soil Line or Waste
45°
Vent

Vents (Nominal Pipe Sizes)		Soil or Waste 1 1/2"	2"	3"	4"	5"	6"
1 1/2"	A	4 1/8"	4 7/16"	5 1/8"	5 13/16"		
	B	6 13/16"	7 7/16"	8 3/4"	10 1/16		
2"	A		5 3/16"	5 7/8"	6 1/2"	7 1/4"	7 13/16"
	B		8 7/16	9 13/16"	11 1/16"	12 1/2"	13 9/16"
3"	A			6 3/4"	7 7/16"	7 15/16"	8 9/16
	B			11 5/16"	12 5/8"	13 3/4"	15 15/16"
4"	A				8 5/8"	9 3/16"	9 13/16"
	B				14 7/16"	15 5/8"	16 7/8"
5"	A					10 3/16"	10 3/4"
	B					17 1/4"	18 7/16"

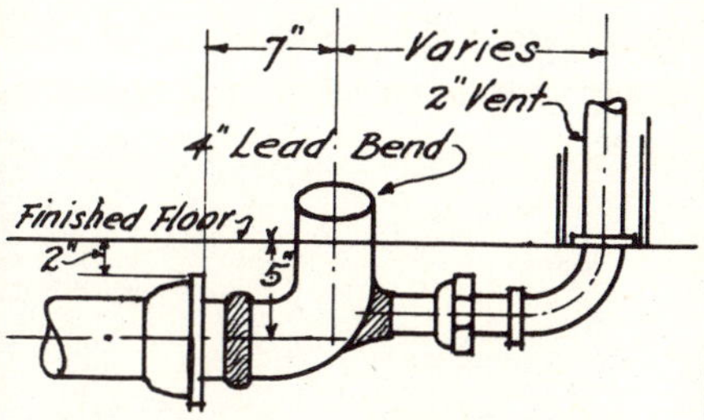

7"
Varies
2" Vent
4" Lead Bend
Finished Floor
2"
5"

DETAIL OF LEAD BEND WITH VENT CONNECTION.

Data checked by: Mongitore & Moesel, Consulting Engineers N.Y.C.

PIPING in CHASES and PARTITIONS

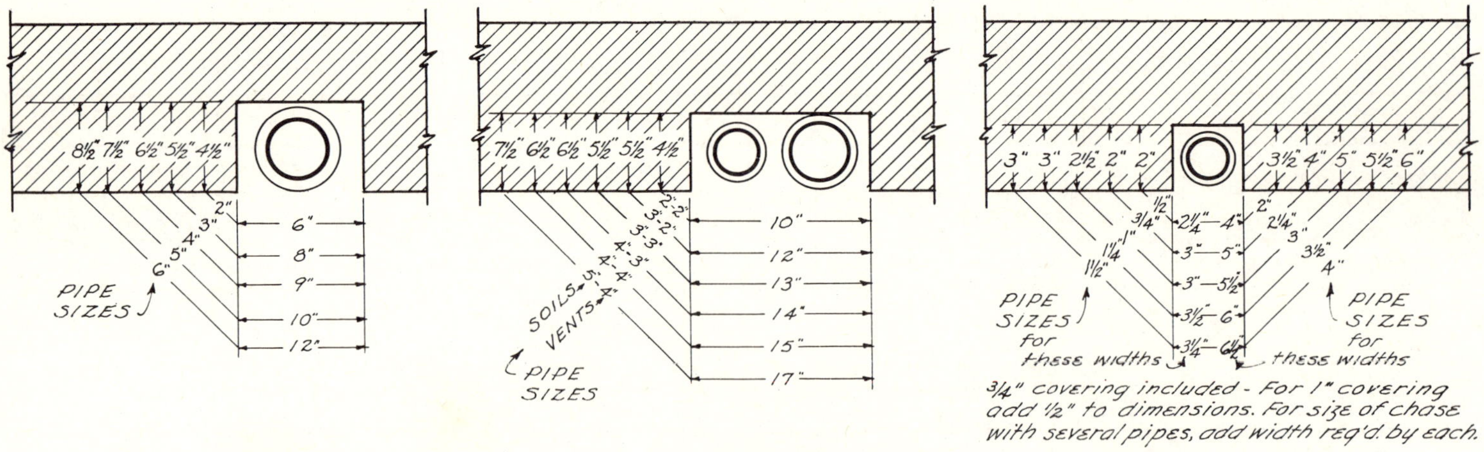

8½" 7½" 6½" 5½" 4½"
2" 3" 4" 5" 6"
6" 8" 9" 10" 12"
PIPE SIZES
7½" 6½" 6½" 5½" 5½" 4½"
2"-2" 3"-3" 3"-3" 4"-3" 5"-4" 4"-4"
SOILS VENTS
10" 12" 13" 14" 15" 17"
PIPE SIZES
3" 3" 2½" 2" 2"
3½" 4" 5" 5½" 6"
½" ¾" 1" 1¼" 1½"
2" 2¼" 3" 3½" 4"
2¼" 4" 3" 5" 3" 5½" 3½" 6" 3¾" 6¼"
PIPE SIZES for these widths
PIPE SIZES for these widths
¾" covering included - For 1" covering add ½" to dimensions. For size of chase with several pipes, add width req'd. by each.

ONE SOIL, WASTE or VENT — TWO SOILS, WASTES or VENTS — WATER PIPES

HOW PIPE SIZES AFFECT WALL CHASES

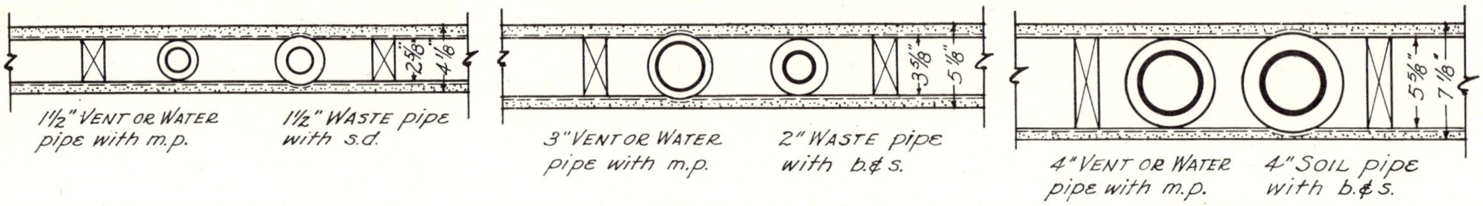

2⅝" 4⅛"
1½" VENT OR WATER pipe with m.p.
1½" WASTE pipe with s.d.
3⅝" 5⅛"
3" VENT OR WATER pipe with m.p.
2" WASTE pipe with b.& s.
5⅝" 7⅛"
4" VENT OR WATER pipe with m.p.
4" SOIL pipe with b.& s.

3" STUD — 4" STUD — 6" STUD

IN WOOD PARTITIONS with ¾" METAL LATH & PLASTER

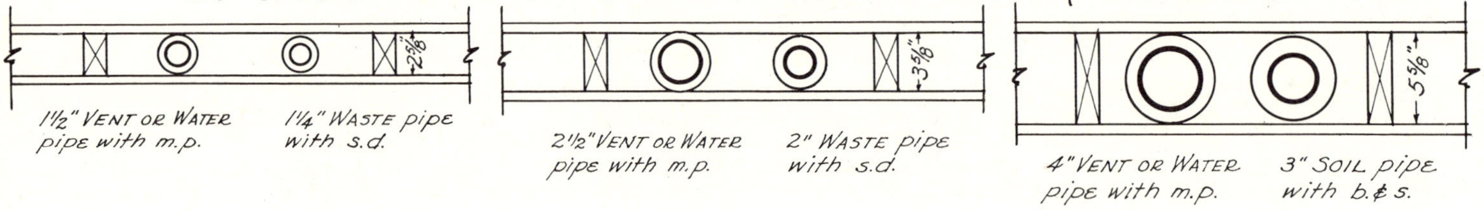

2⅝"
1½" VENT OR WATER pipe with m.p.
1¼" WASTE pipe with s.d.
3⅝"
2½" VENT OR WATER pipe with m.p.
2" WASTE pipe with s.d.
5⅝"
4" VENT OR WATER pipe with m.p.
3" SOIL pipe with b.& s.

3" STUD — 4" STUD — 6" STUD

IN WOOD PARTITIONS with RIGID BOARD or RIGID LATH

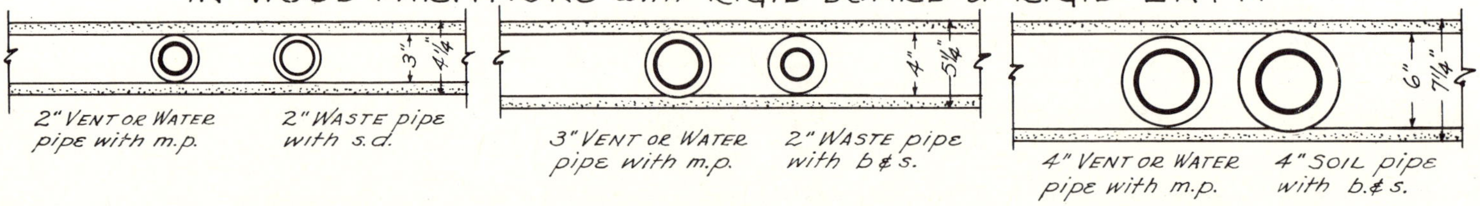

3" 4¼"
2" VENT OR WATER pipe with m.p.
2" WASTE pipe with s.d.
4" 5¼"
3" VENT OR WATER pipe with m.p.
2" WASTE pipe with b& s.
6" 7¼"
4" VENT OR WATER pipe with m.p.
4" SOIL pipe with b.& s.

3" BLOCK or TILE — 4" BLOCK or TILE — 6" BLOCK or TILE

IN MASONRY PARTITIONS with ⅝" PLASTER

MAXIMUM PIPE SIZES for VARIOUS PARTITIONS

Partitions with ¾" lath & plaster are shown with certain max. pipes encroaching on the lath & plaster. When rigid board such as gypsum or plaster board is used, the extreme dimen. of the bead or bell of the pipe fitting should come within the actual dimen. of studs. See "Diameters of Fittings-Across Face Outside."

FITTING ABBREVIATIONS: **m.p.** = malleable pattern. **s.d.** = cast iron screw drainage. **b.& s.** = extra heavy cast iron bell & spigot.

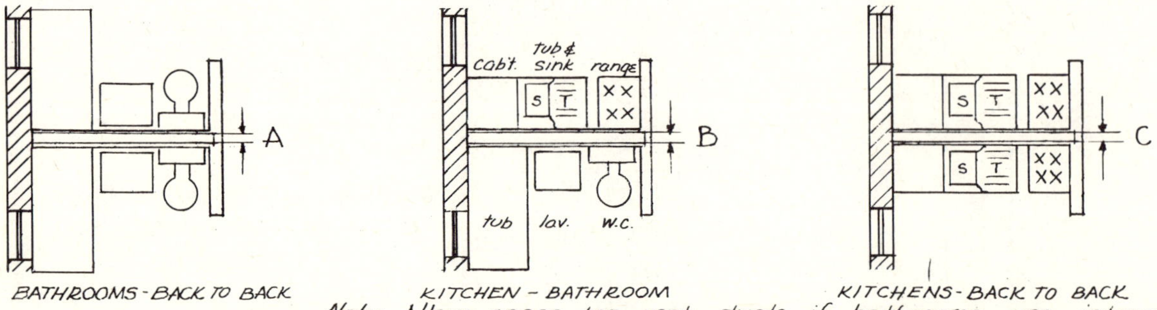

A
Cab't. tub & sink range
S T
B
tub lav. w.c.
C
S T

BATHROOMS - BACK TO BACK — KITCHEN - BATHROOM — KITCHENS - BACK TO BACK

shaft width	13 STORY	7 STORY	3 STORY
A	10"	9"	8"
B	10"	9"	8"
C	8"	7"	7"

TABLE

Note: Allow space for vent ducts if bathrooms are interior.

TYPICAL CLEAR SPACE for PIPES THROUGH FLOORS

Compiled by the Office of Mongitore & Moesel, Consulting Engineers, New York City

SEWAGE DISPOSAL

HOUSE SEWER

LENGTH= *Make 50'-0" to 100'-0" long, run as directly as possible; If over 300'-0" long place Manhole at center. Longer runs are desirable.*

MATERIAL= *Salt glazed clay bell and spigot tile pipe or cement bell & spigot (cast iron is excellent but expensive). If near well or any water supply use cast iron.*
Where trees or shrubs may cause root stoppage in clay pipe use cast iron.
Use 5'-0" to 6'-0" of Cast Iron pipe where leaving building.
Use cement joints for clay pipe, lead for cast iron.

SIZE= *4" for small installation, but 6" is better in all cases.*

GRADE= *In Northern latitudes start sewer approximately 1'-6" below grade. In Southern latitudes start may be just below grade.*

PITCH= *Pitch 4" sewer 1/5" per foot minimum (equivalent to 2" in 10'-0"). Pitch 6" sewer 1/10" per foot minimum. (equivalent to 1" in 10'-0").*

SEPTIC TANK

EFFLUENT SEWER

LENGTH= *10'-0" for small system, for large systems allow 40'-0" to 50'-0" min.*

MATERIAL= *Same as for house sewer.*

SIZE= *4" unless very large system.*

PITCH= *1/20" to the foot minimum. (equivalent to 1/2" in 10'-0").*
Pitch should be uniform.

DISTRIBUTION FIELD

(Absorption field) for disposal of Effluent or filtering of Effluent.

Pitch for closed joints 5" per 100 lin. ft.

Pitch for open joints 3" to 4" per 100 lin. ft.

DISPOSAL METHODS
3 POSSIBLE TYPES. A. B. C.

For details see {Details 4. 5. 6 / Tables A. B. C.

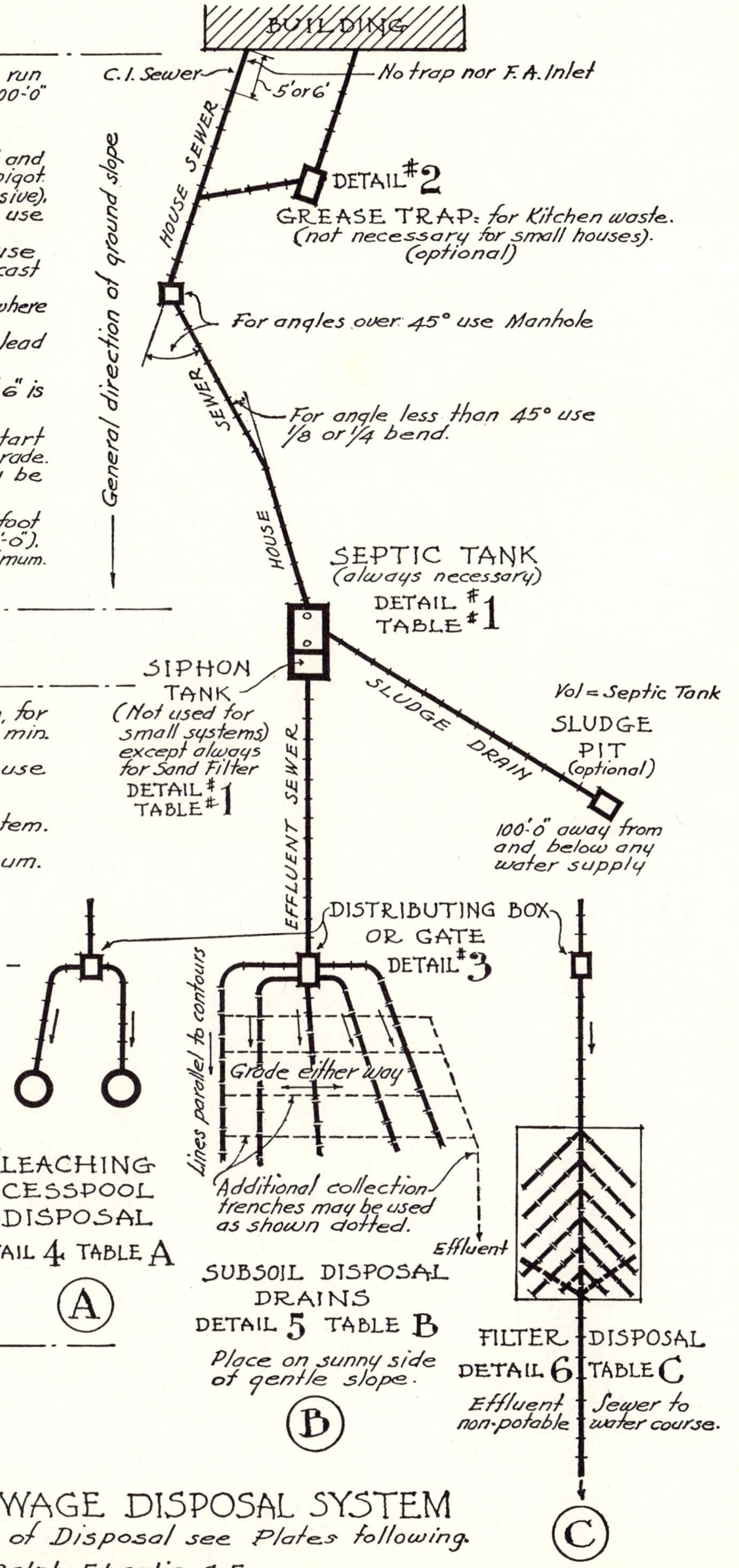
BUILDING
C. I. Sewer
No trap nor F. A. Inlet
5' or 6'
HOUSE SEWER
DETAIL #2
GREASE TRAP: for Kitchen waste. (not necessary for small houses). (optional)
General direction of ground slope
For angles over 45° use Manhole
For angle less than 45° use 1/8 or 1/4 bend.
SEPTIC TANK (always necessary)
DETAIL #1
TABLE #1
SIPHON TANK
(Not used for small systems) except always for Sand Filter
DETAIL #1
TABLE #1
SLUDGE DRAIN
Vol = Septic Tank
SLUDGE PIT (optional)
100'-0" away from and below any water supply
EFFLUENT SEWER
DISTRIBUTING BOX OR GATE
DETAIL #3
Lines parallel to contours
Grade either way
Additional collection trenches may be used as shown dotted.
Effluent
LEACHING CESSPOOL DISPOSAL
DETAIL 4 TABLE A
A
SUBSOIL DISPOSAL DRAINS
DETAIL 5 TABLE B
Place on sunny side of gentle slope.
B
FILTER DISPOSAL
DETAIL 6 TABLE C
Effluent non-potable
Sewer to water course.
C

KEY DIAGRAM *of* SEWAGE DISPOSAL SYSTEM

For selection of System of Disposal see Plates following.

Checked by Ralph Eberlin, C.E.

SEWAGE DISPOSAL

CRITERIA for SELECTION of TYPE of DISTRIBUTION of the EFFLUENT

	A· LEACHING CESSPOOL (one or more may be used as needed).	B· SUBSOIL DISPOSAL DRAINS Type 5.1 includes, in addition, collection tile under the distributing tile.	C· SAND FILTER Rectangular, circular or narrow trench types. Open or closed type.
TERRAIN SLOPE OR GRADE	Applicable to any slope.	For level or slight slope.	Applicable to any slope, except filter area to be approximately level.
POROSITY OF SOIL	Soil adjacent to cesspools must be fairly porous below intake. Above may be impervious.	Top 1'-6" to 2'-0" must be fairly porous unless type 5.1 is used, and this may be used with impervious soil.	Soil may be impervious.
GROUND WATER	Water level must be at least 8' below grade at cesspools. Never less than 2'-0" below bottom of cesspools.	Water level 2'-6" under grade at field. For type 5.1 4'-0".	Water level approximately 4'-0" below grade at filter.
ORIENTATION AND LOCATION	Not important. Small area required, not less than 15'-0" from building.	If possible place field on southern slope; drains run parallel to contours. Requires large area.	Open type requires placing to leeward and away from buildings; on sunny site. Closed type requires more area than open. Small area required.
FINAL DISPOSAL OF EFFLUENT	No provision necessary.	No provision necessary, except for type 5.1 it is desirable.	Means for final disposal necessary in water course that will not pollute any potable water supply.
MAINTENANCE	Cleaned approximately every 2 years.	Cleaned only when absorption ceases, may be years if septic tank is kept in condition.	When filtering ceases remove and replace top 2".
INITIAL COST	Usually lowest cost.	More expensive than cesspools but type 5.1 is more expensive.	Most expensive. Only used where other types are not possible. Open type cheaper than closed.

DESIGN of SEWAGE DISPOSAL SYSTEMS

EXPLANATION of TABLES BELOW

"No. of persons served" in 1st. column below refers to "Residential Work". To use tables for other types of buildings multiply this "No. of persons served" by the conversion factor in the last column to the right and select data on the same line and to the right of the resulting "No. of persons served.

TYPE of BUILDING	GAL'S of SEWAGE per PERSON	CONVERSION FACTORS
Residential	50	1. (unity)
Camps	25	.5
Summer Cottages, small farms	40	.8
Day Schools, factories without kitchens or showers	15 to 25	.3 to .25
" " " with " and "	30 to 50	.6 to .5
Institutions except hospitals	100	2.
Hospitals	150 to 250	3. to 5.

TABLE 1 — SEPTIC & SIPHON TANKS

NO. OF PERSONS SERVED	SEPTIC TANK: Gals. working capacity	length	width	air space	liquid depth	SIPHON TANK (*Not essential for these sizes): length	width	depth	SIPHON: size	drawing depth	CONCRETE THICKNESS: walls	top	bottom
1-4	325	5'-0"	2'-6"	1'-0"	3'-6"								
5-9	450	6'-0"	2'-6"	1'-0"	4'-0"	*3'-0"	*2'-6"	*3'-0"	3"	1'-6"	6"	4"	5"
10-14	720	7'-0"	3'-6"	1'-0"	4'-0"	*3'-6"	*3'-6"	*3'-0"	3"	1'-6"	6"	4"	6"
15-20	1000	8'-0"	4'-0"	1'-0"	4'-0"	4'-0"	4'-0"	3'-0"	4"	1'-8"	6"	4"	6"
21-25	1250	9'-0"	4'-6"	1'-0"	4'-3"	4'-6"	4'-6"	3'-0"	4"	1'-8"	7"	5"	6"
26-30	1480	9'-6"	4'-8"	1'-3"	4'-6"	4'-8"	4'-8"	3'-6"	4"	2'-2"	8"	5"	6"
31-35	1720	10'-0"	5'-0"	1'-3"	4'-8"	5'-0"	5'-0"	3'-6"	4"	2'-2"	8"	5"	6"
36-40	1950	10'-6"	5'-3"	1'-3"	4'-9"	5'-3"	5'-3"	3'-6"	4"	2'-2"	9"	5"	6"
41-45	2175	11'-0"	5'-6"	1'-3"	4'-10"	5'-6"	5'-6"	3'-6"	5"	2'-2"	9"	5"	6"
46-50	2400	11'-6"	5'-9"	1'-3"	5'-0"	5'-9"	5'-9"	3'-6"	5"	2'-2"	9"	5"	6"

TABLE A — LEACHING CESSPOOL DISPOSAL

NO. OF PERSONS SERVED	•FOR RAPID ABSORPTION: no. of cesspools	dia.	depth	absorptive area per person	•FOR MEDIUM ABSORPTION: no. of cesspools	dia.	depth	absorptive area per person	•FOR SLOW ABSORPTION: no. of cesspools	dia.	depth	absorptive area per person
1-4	1	5'-0"	5'-0"	24.5 □'	1	6'-0"	6'-0"	35. □'	2	5'-0"	5'-0"	49 □'
5-9	1	6'-0"	6'-0"	15.7 □'	2	6'-0"	6'-0"	31.3 □'	2	8'-0"	7'-0"	48 □'
10-14	1	8'-0"	6'-0"	14.4 □'	2	8'-0"	6'-0"	28.7 □'	2	10'-0"	8'-0"	46.7 □'
15-20	2	6'-0"	6'-0"	14.1 □'	2	9'-0"	7'-0"	26.14 □'	3	10'-0"	8'-0"	49.5 □'
21-25	2	7'-0"	6'-0"	13.6 □'	2	10'-0"	8'-0"	27.1 □'	4	9'-0"	8'-0"	46.4 □'
26-30	2	8'-0"	6'-0"	13.4 □'	3	9'-0"	7'-0"	26.14 □'	4	10'-0"	8'-0"	43.6 □'
31-35	1 1	8'-0" 9'-0" }	7'-0"	13.6 □'	1 2	9'-0" 10'-0"	7'-0" 8'-0"	26.1 □'	5	10'-0"	8'-0"	46.7 □'
36-40	1 1	9'-0" 9'-0"	7'-0" 8'-0" }	13.7 □'	4	9'-0"	7'-0"	26.1 □'	4	12'-0"	10'-0"	48.9 □'
41-45	3	8'-0"	6'-0"	13.4 □'	4	9'-0"	8'-0"	25.7 □'	5	12'-0"	10'-0"	54.3 □'
46-50	2	10'-0"	8'-0"	13.0 □'	4	10'-0"	8'-0"	26.1 □'	5	12'-0"	10'-0"	48.9 □'

TABLE B — SUBSOIL DISPOSAL DRAINS-4" / TABLE C — SAND FILTERS

NO. OF PERSONS SERVED	TABLE B LINEAL FEET: •rapid absorp.	•med. absorp.	•slow absorp.	TABLE C area required in square ft.: open	closed
1-4	100	150	250	100	200
5-9	200	350	700	450	900
10-14	340	500	1000	700	1400
15-20	475	650	1250	1000	2000
21-25	600	800	1500	1250	2500
26-30	725	1025	1800	1500	3000
31-35	850	1150	2100	1750	3500
36-40	975	1300	2400	2000	4000
41-45	1100	1450	2700	2250	4500
46-50	1200	1600	3000	2500	5000

Capacity of above septic tanks is based on 50 gallons flow of sewage per person for 24 hours, and is for residential work. To design tanks of other sizes use the following formulae.

Number of persons served × gallons of sewage per person = gallons capacity (of liquid).

$$\frac{\text{gallons capacity}}{7.5} = \text{cu. ft. capacity (of liquid).}$$

1 Cu. ft = 7.48 gallons. 1 gallon = .13+ cu. ft.

Length of tanks should be approximately twice width. Minimum liquid depth 3'-6".

When purchasing a pre-fabricated septic tank, require Manufacturer's guarantee that the tank will treat the gals. capacity as above calculated within a 24 hour period.

Recommend min. septic tank of 500 gal. working capacity. If garbage destructor is used & discharges into septic tank, increase tank capacity for additional sludge, up to 50%.

***Some codes require 100 gals. for residences; 25 to 30 gals. for factory, offices, & commercial.**

Capacity of above cesspools based on 50 gallons flow of sewage per person per 24 hours, and is for residential work; to design other sizes use the following formulae. Select absorptive area per person from above.

Absorptive area per person × number of persons = Total absorptive area.

Total absorptive area = area of walls (below inlet) + area of bottom. N.Y. State allows bottom area only.

Total absorptive area = $2\pi R \times \text{height} + \pi R^2$

Absorptive areas for given sizes in square feet:–

5' dia. × 5' depth = 99	8' dia. × 6' depth = 201	9' dia. × 8' depth = 293
6' " × 6' " = 142	8' " × 7' " 216	10' " × 8' " 330
7' " × 6' " = 170	9' " × 7' " 262	12' " × 10' " 489

Assuming 1' wide absorption trench bottom. These lengths are based on lineal ft. per person:– Rapid absorp.ⁿ = 24, Med. absorp.ⁿ = 34, Slow absorp.ⁿ = 60. Reduce lin. ft. for wider trenches.

These areas are based on 1 gallon per sq. foot per day for closed and 2 gallons per sq. foot per day for open filters.

•METHOD of RELATIVE ABSORPTION DETERMINATION (to select proper table above)

Dig test pit 12" square × 1'-6" deep on disposal site. For cesspool locate pit ½ distance between inlet and bottom. For drains locate this at grade. Fill pit twice with 6" of water & time SECOND disappearance. Divide time in minutes by 6. Result is time required for water to drop 1."

MINUTES REQUIRED FOR WATER TO DROP 1 INCH	RELATIVE ABSORPTION	TYPE OF SOIL	DISPOSAL METHOD RECOMMENDED
0 to 3	Rapid absorption	Coarse sand or gravel.	Cesspool or drains.
3 to 5	Medium "	Fine sand, sandy loam.	" " "
5 to 30	Slow "	Clay with sand or loam.	" " "
30 to 60	Semi-impervious	Dense clay.	Dr'ns, collect'r. dr'ns, filters.
60 & over	Impervious	Hard pan, rock.	Filters.

Checked by Ralph Eberlin, C.E.

SEWAGE DISPOSAL

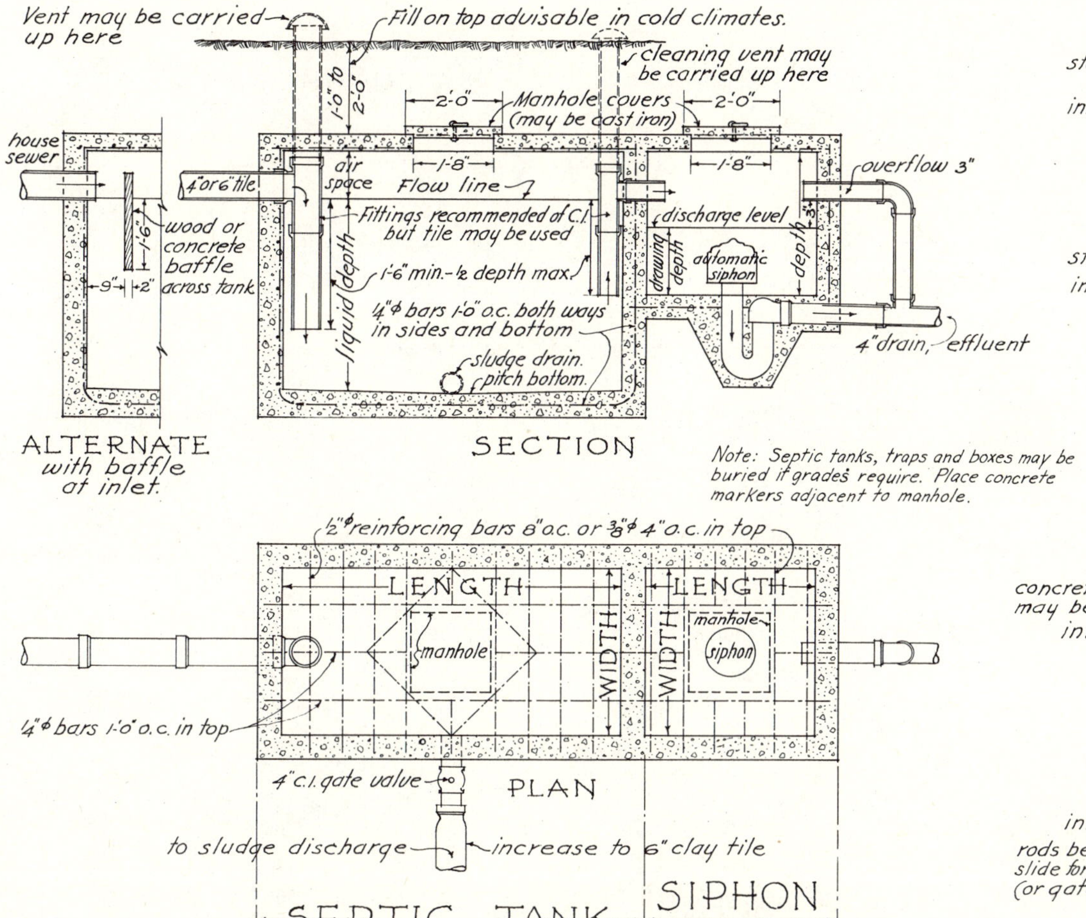
Vent may be carried up here
Fill on top advisable in cold climates.
cleaning vent may be carried up here
1'-0" to 2'-0"
2'-0"
Manhole covers (may be cast iron)
2'-0"
house sewer
1'-8"
1'-8"
overflow 3"
4" or 6" tile
air space
Flow line
Fittings recommended of C.I. but tile may be used
discharge level
wood or concrete baffle across tank
1'-6"
9"
2"
liquid depth
1'-6" min.-½ depth max.
drawing depth
automatic siphon
depth
4"ϕ bars 1'-0" o.c. both ways in sides and bottom
4" drain, effluent
sludge drain. pitch bottom.
ALTERNATE with baffle at inlet.
SECTION
Note: Septic tanks, traps and boxes may be buried if grades require. Place concrete markers adjacent to manhole.
½"ϕ reinforcing bars 8" o.c. or ⅜"ϕ 4" o.c. in top
LENGTH
LENGTH
manhole
manhole
siphon
WIDTH
WIDTH
¼"ϕ bars 1'-0" o.c. in top
4" c.i. gate value
PLAN
to sludge discharge
increase to 6" clay tile

SEPTIC TANK — used for all systems

SIPHON TANK — may be omitted on small installations.

①

Cylindrical Brick tanks of 4" or 8" walls, parged on inside & outside, corbelled dome, with adjoining siphon tank of similar shape and construction are commonly used, other features follow above septic tank.

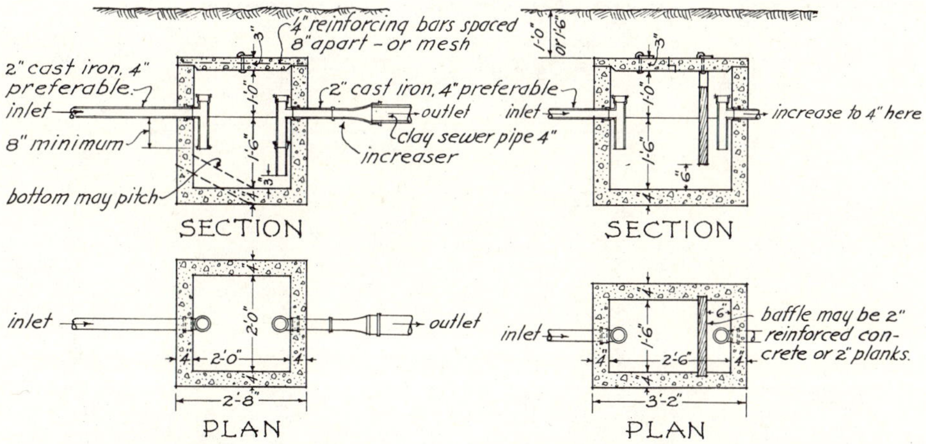
2" cast iron, 4" preferable.
¼" reinforcing bars spaced 8" apart - or mesh
3"
1'-0" or 1'-6"
3"
inlet
1'-0"
2" cast iron, 4" preferable
outlet
inlet
1'-0"
increase to 4" here
8" minimum
1'-6"
clay sewer pipe 4"
increaser
1'-6"
6"
bottom may pitch
3"
SECTION
SECTION
inlet
2'-0"
outlet
inlet
1'-6"
6"
baffle may be 2" reinforced concrete or 2" planks.
2'-0"
2'-6"
4"
2'-8"
3'-2"
PLAN
PLAN

SQUARE TYPE WITHOUT BAFFLE — Vol. = 6 cu. ft.

RECTANGULAR TYPE WITH BAFFLE — Vol. = 5.625 cu. ft.

Cast Iron connections shown but these may be clay tile for economy. May have 8" brick walls

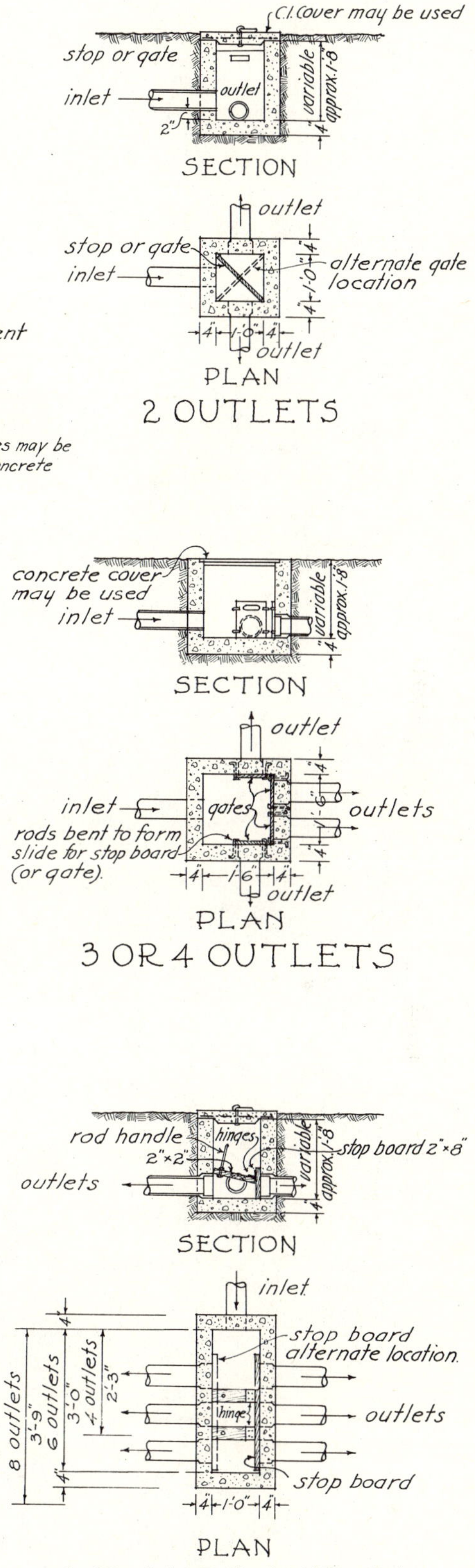
C.I. Cover may be used
stop or gate
inlet
outlet
2"
variable approx. 1'-8"
SECTION
outlet
stop or gate
inlet
alternate gate location
1'-0"
4
4
outlet
PLAN
2 OUTLETS
concrete cover may be used
inlet
variable approx. 1'-8"
SECTION
outlet
inlet
gates
outlets
rods bent to form slide for stop board (or gate).
1'-6"
outlet
PLAN
3 OR 4 OUTLETS
rod handle
hinges
2"×2"
stop board 2"×8"
outlets
variable approx. 1'-8"
SECTION
inlet
stop board alternate location.
8 outlets 3'-9"
6 outlets 3'-0"
4 outlets 2'-3"
hinge
outlets
stop board
1'-0"
PLAN
4 OR MORE OUTLETS

③

② Scale-¼" = 1 Foot

DISTRIBUTING BOXES

All outlets must be set exactly level. Stop boards are used to provide a rest period for a part of the disposal field. Always used for filter beds and recommended for all but very small installations of all types.

GREASE TRAPS

May be omitted in small systems

Checked by Ralph Eberlin, C.E.

SEWAGE DISPOSAL

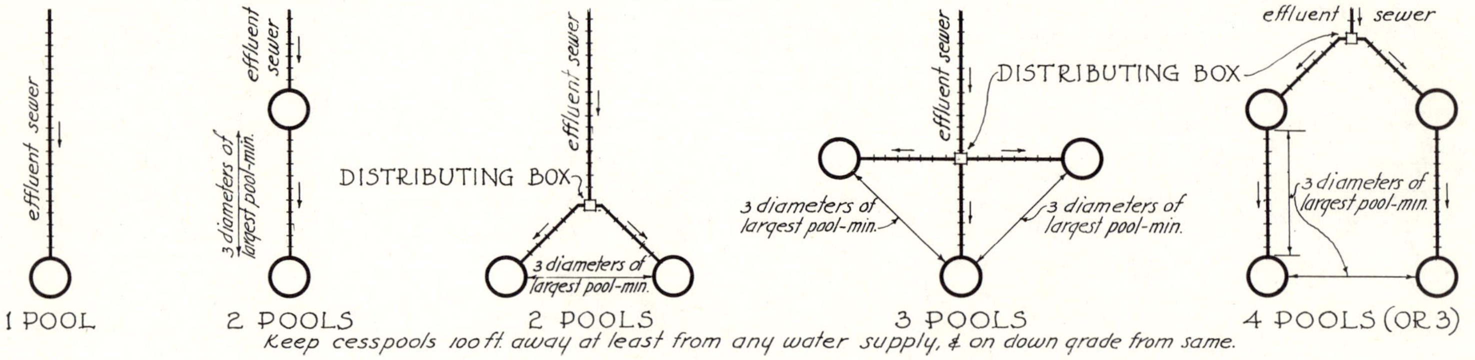
effluent sewer
1 POOL
effluent sewer
3 diameters of largest pool-min.
2 POOLS
effluent sewer
DISTRIBUTING BOX
3 diameters of largest pool-min.
2 POOLS
effluent sewer
DISTRIBUTING BOX
3 diameters of largest pool-min.
3 diameters of largest pool-min.
3 POOLS
effluent
sewer
DISTRIBUTING BOX
3 diameters of largest pool-min.
4 POOLS (OR 3)

Keep cesspools 100 ft. away at least from any water supply, & on down grade from same.

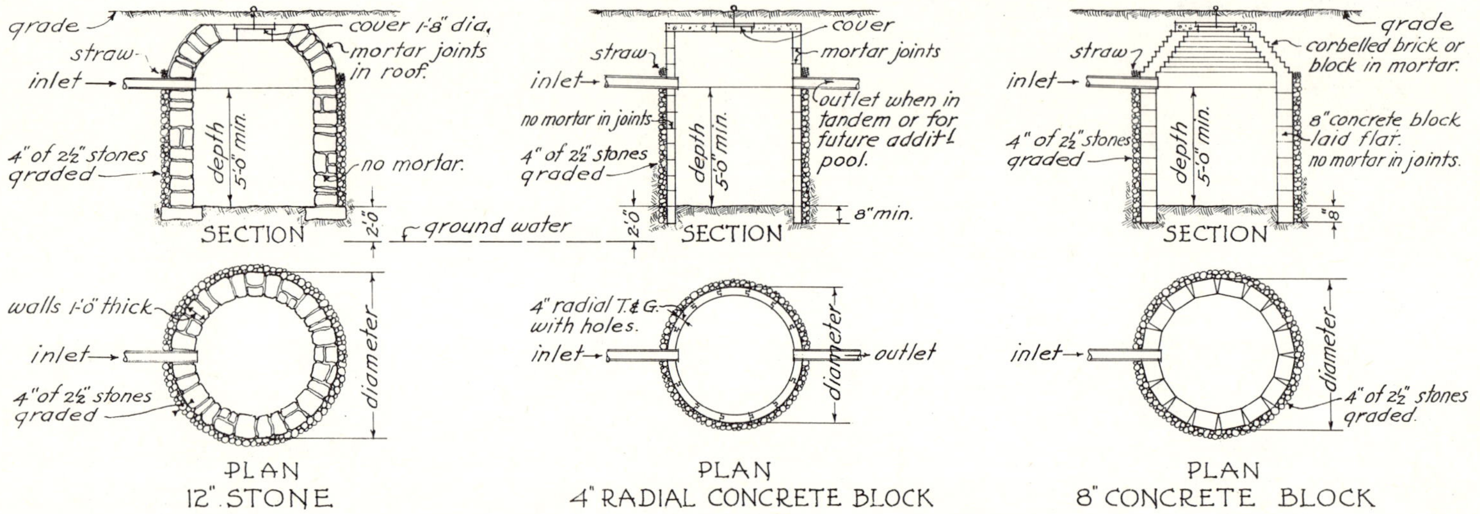
grade
straw
inlet
cover 1'-8" dia.
mortar joints in roof.
4" of 2½" stones graded
depth 5'-0" min.
no mortar.
SECTION
2'-0"
ground water
walls 1'-0" thick
inlet
4" of 2½" stones graded
diameter
PLAN
12" STONE
straw
inlet
cover
mortar joints
outlet when in tandem or for future addit'l pool.
no mortar in joints
4" of 2½" stones graded
depth 5'-0" min.
2'-0"
SECTION
8" min.
4" radial T. & G. with holes.
inlet
diameter
outlet
PLAN
4" RADIAL CONCRETE BLOCK
grade
straw
inlet
corbelled brick or block in mortar.
4" of 2½" stones graded
depth 5'-0" min.
8" concrete block laid flat. no mortar in joints.
8"
SECTION
inlet
diameter
4" of 2½" stones graded.
PLAN
8" CONCRETE BLOCK

Cesspool tops are interchangeable

DETAILS of LEACHING CESSPOOLS

LEACHING CESSPOOL DISPOSAL

(4)

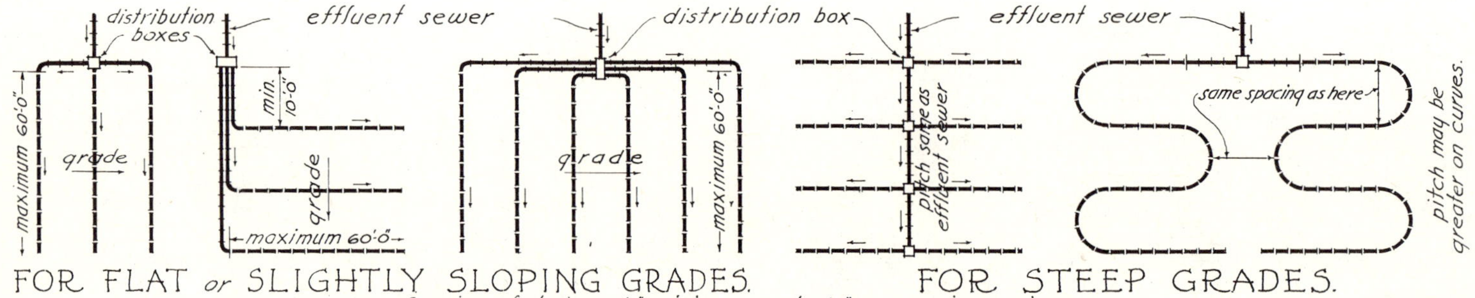
distribution boxes
effluent sewer
maximum 60'-0"
grade
min. 10'-0"
grade
maximum 60'-0"
distribution box
grade
maximum 60'-0"
effluent sewer
pitch same as effluent sewer
same spacing as here
pitch may be greater on curves.

FOR FLAT or SLIGHTLY SLOPING GRADES. FOR STEEP GRADES.

Spacing of drains - 5'-0" minimum and 10'-0" economic maximum

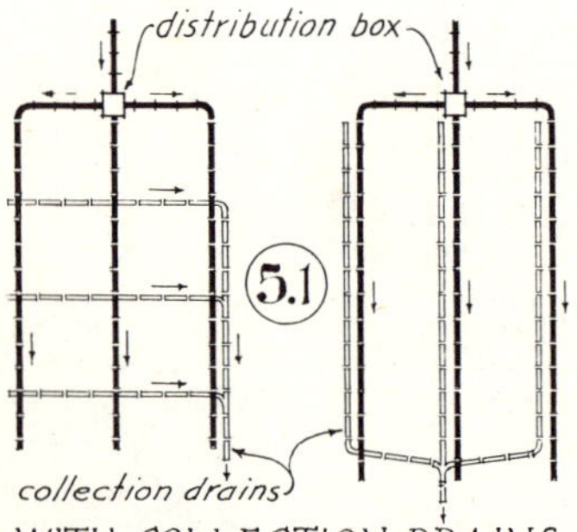
distribution box
5.1
collection drains

WITH COLLECTION DRAINS

=Bell & Spigot Sewer Pipe.
=Open tile drains.

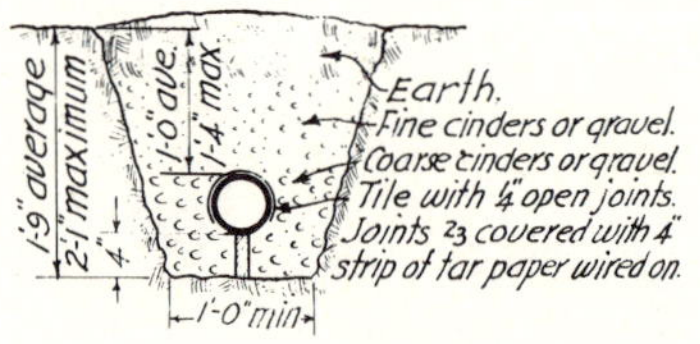
1'-9" average
2'-1" maximum
1'-0" ave.
1'-4" max.
4"
Earth.
Fine cinders or gravel.
Coarse cinders or gravel.
Tile with ¼" open joints.
Joints ⅔ covered with 4" strip of tar paper wired on.
1'-0" min.

DRAIN TILE TRENCH

Scale of Details ⅜" = 1'-0"

(5)

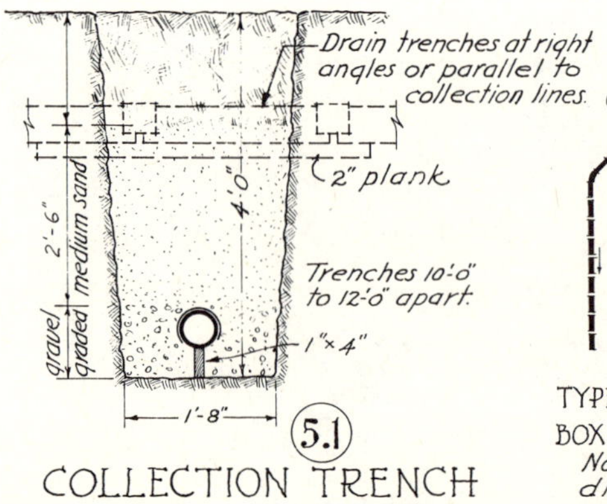
Drain trenches at right angles or parallel to collection lines.
2" plank
2'-6"
medium sand
graded gravel
4'-0"
Trenches 10'-0" to 12'-0" apart.
1" × 4"
1'-8"
5.1

COLLECTION TRENCH

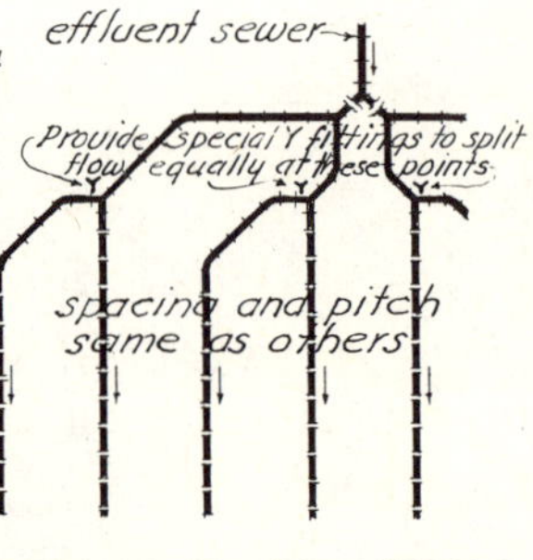
effluent sewer
Provide special Y fittings to split flow equally at these points
spacing and pitch same as others

TYPE WITHOUT DISTRIBUTION BOX - USING SPECIAL Y TILE
Not as satisfactory as distribution box type.

Important; Pitch lines uniformly. Pitch 0.5 % without dosing siphon; 0.3 % when dosing siphon is used.

TYPES OF SUB-SOIL DISPOSAL FIELD DRAINS.

Checked by Ralph Eberlin, C.E.

SEWAGE DISPOSAL and CISTERNS

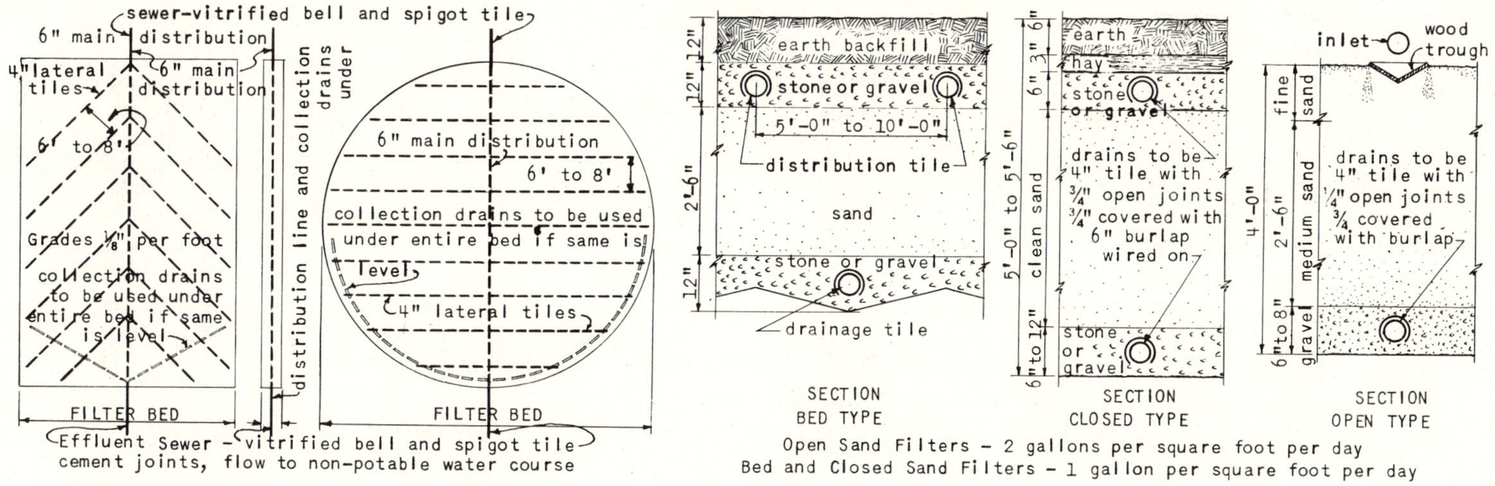
sewer-vitrified bell and spigot tile
6" main distribution
4" lateral tiles
6" main distribution
6' to 8'
Grades 1/8" per foot
collection drains to be used under entire bed if same is level
distribution line and collection drains under
FILTER BED
Effluent Sewer - vitrified bell and spigot tile
cement joints, flow to non-potable water course
6" main distribution
6' to 8'
collection drains to be used under entire bed if same is level
4" lateral tiles
FILTER BED
earth backfill
stone or gravel
5'-0" to 10'-0"
distribution tile
sand
stone or gravel
drainage tile
12" 12" 2'-6" 12"
SECTION
BED TYPE
earth
hay
stone or gravel
drains to be 4" tile with 3/4" open joints 3/4" covered with 6" burlap wired on
clean sand
stone or gravel
3" 6" 5'-0" to 5'-6" 6" to 12"
SECTION
CLOSED TYPE
inlet
wood trough
fine sand
medium sand
gravel
drains to be 4" tile with 1/4" open joints 3/4 covered with burlap
4'-0" 2'-6" 6" to 8"
SECTION
OPEN TYPE
Open Sand Filters - 2 gallons per square foot per day
Bed and Closed Sand Filters - 1 gallon per square foot per day

RECTANGULAR LONG — ROUND — DETAILS

SAND FILTERS

Data checked by Ralph Eberlin C.E.

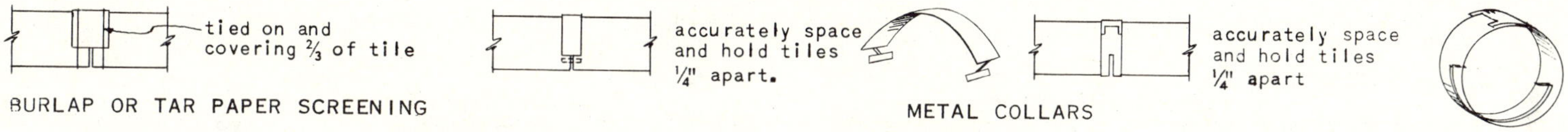
tied on and covering 2/3 of tile
BURLAP OR TAR PAPER SCREENING
accurately space and hold tiles 1/4" apart.
accurately space and hold tiles 1/4" apart
METAL COLLARS

DRAINAGE TILE JOINTS - CONNECTORS AND COLLARS

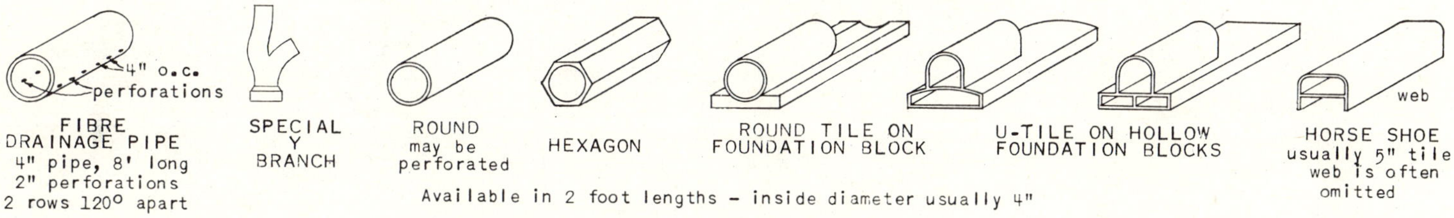
4" o.c. perforations
FIBRE DRAINAGE PIPE
4" pipe, 8' long
2" perforations
2 rows 120° apart
SPECIAL Y BRANCH
ROUND
may be perforated
HEXAGON
ROUND TILE ON FOUNDATION BLOCK
U-TILE ON HOLLOW FOUNDATION BLOCKS
web
HORSE SHOE
usually 5" tile
web is often omitted
Available in 2 foot lengths - inside diameter usually 4"

DRAINAGE TILES

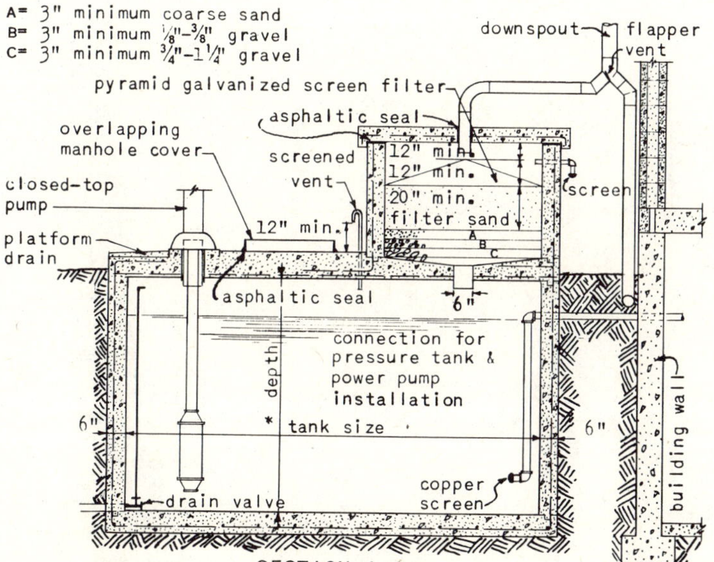
A= 3" minimum coarse sand
B= 3" minimum 1/8"-3/8" gravel
C= 3" minimum 3/4"-1 1/4" gravel
downspout
flapper vent
pyramid galvanized screen filter
asphaltic seal
overlapping manhole cover
screened vent
closed-top pump
platform drain
12" min.
12" min.
12" min.
20" min. filter sand
A
B
C
screen
asphaltic seal
6"
connection for pressure tank & power pump installation
depth
* tank size
6"
6"
copper screen
drain valve
building wall

SECTION A-A

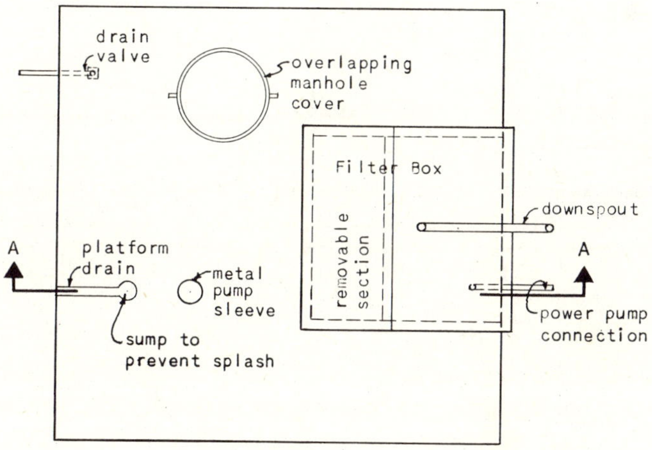
drain valve
overlapping manhole cover
Filter Box
removable section
downspout
A
platform drain
metal pump sleeve
sump to prevent splash
A
power pump connection

PLAN

AVERAGE DAILY HUMAN CONSUMPTION OF WATER:
50 to 100 gallons per day per person.

AVERAGE DAILY LIVESTOCK CONSUMPTION OF WATER:

Each milk cow	35 gal.	Each hog	4 gal.
Each steer or dry cow	12 gal.	Each sheep	2 gal.
Each horse	12 gal.	Each 100 chickens	4 gal.

* TANK AND CISTERN CAPACITIES IN GALLONS

DEPTH Feet	SQUARE TANKS			ROUND TANKS			
	8'□	10'□	12'□	8'φ	10'φ	12'φ	14'φ
4	1,920	3,000	4,320	1,500	2,350	3,380	4,610
6	2,880	4,500	6,480	2,250	3,520	5,070	6,920
8	3,840	6,000	8,640	3,000	4,700	6,760	9,220
10	....	7,500	10,800	3,760	5,870	8,460	11,520
12	....	....	12,960	4,510	7,040	10,150	13,830

CISTERN FOR RAINWATER STORAGE

DRAINAGE ~ MANHOLES

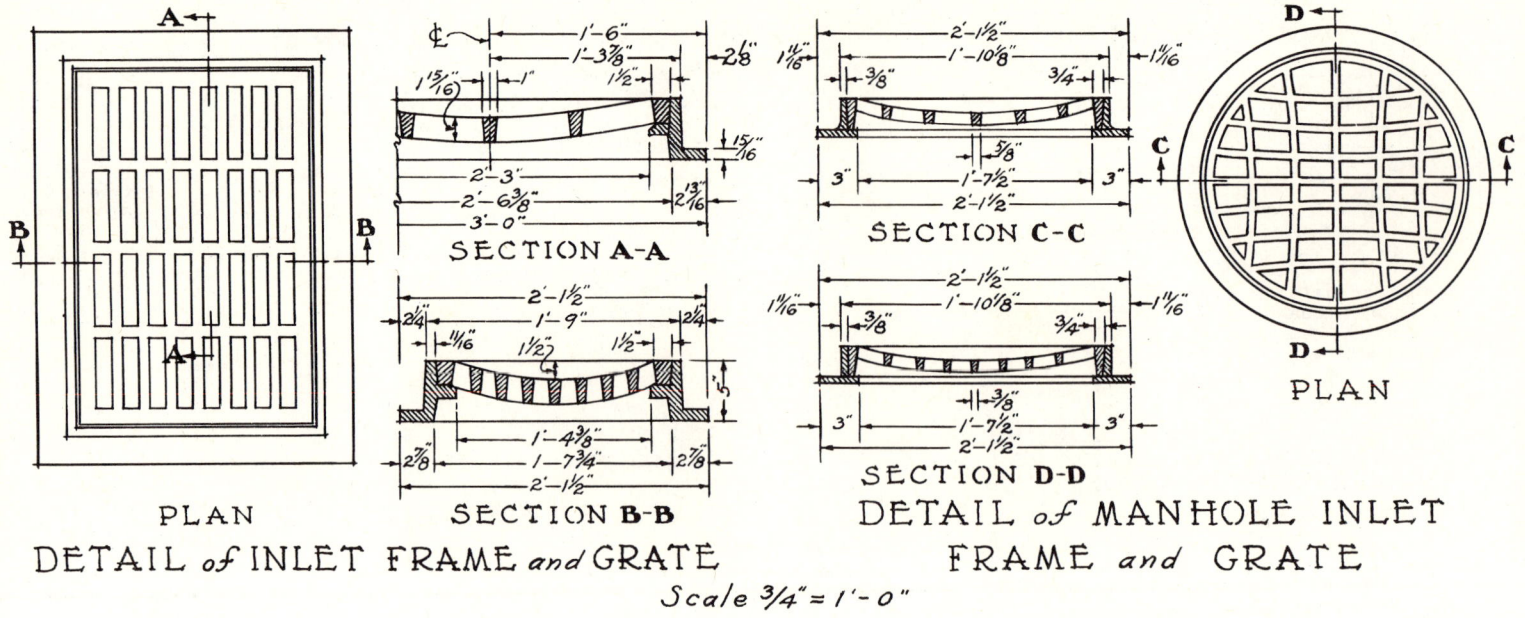

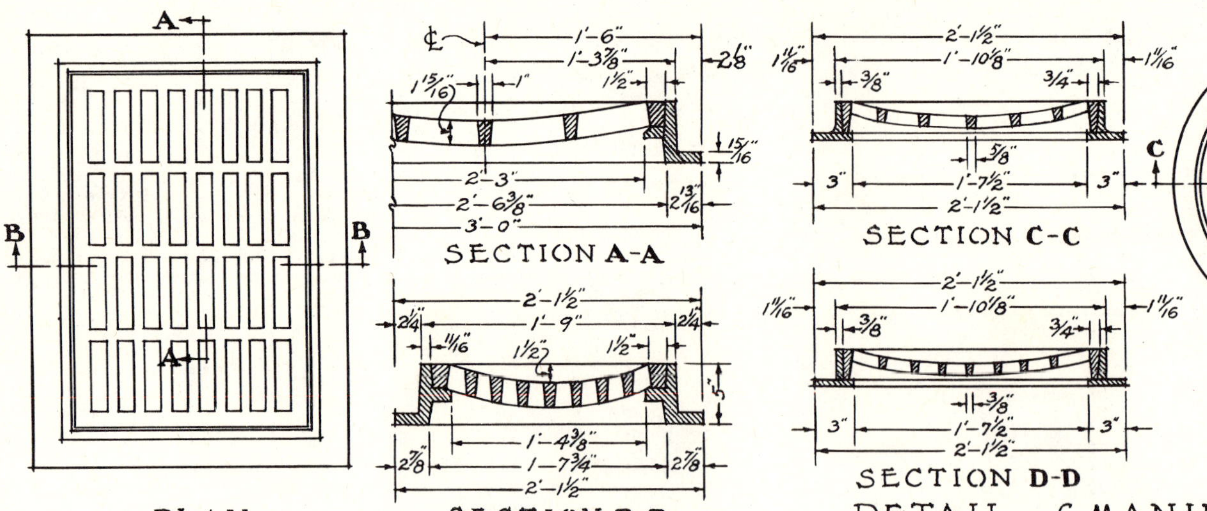
SECTION A-A
SECTION C-C
SECTION D-D
PLAN
SECTION B-B
PLAN

DETAIL of INLET FRAME and GRATE

DETAIL of MANHOLE INLET FRAME and GRATE

Scale 3/4" = 1'-0"

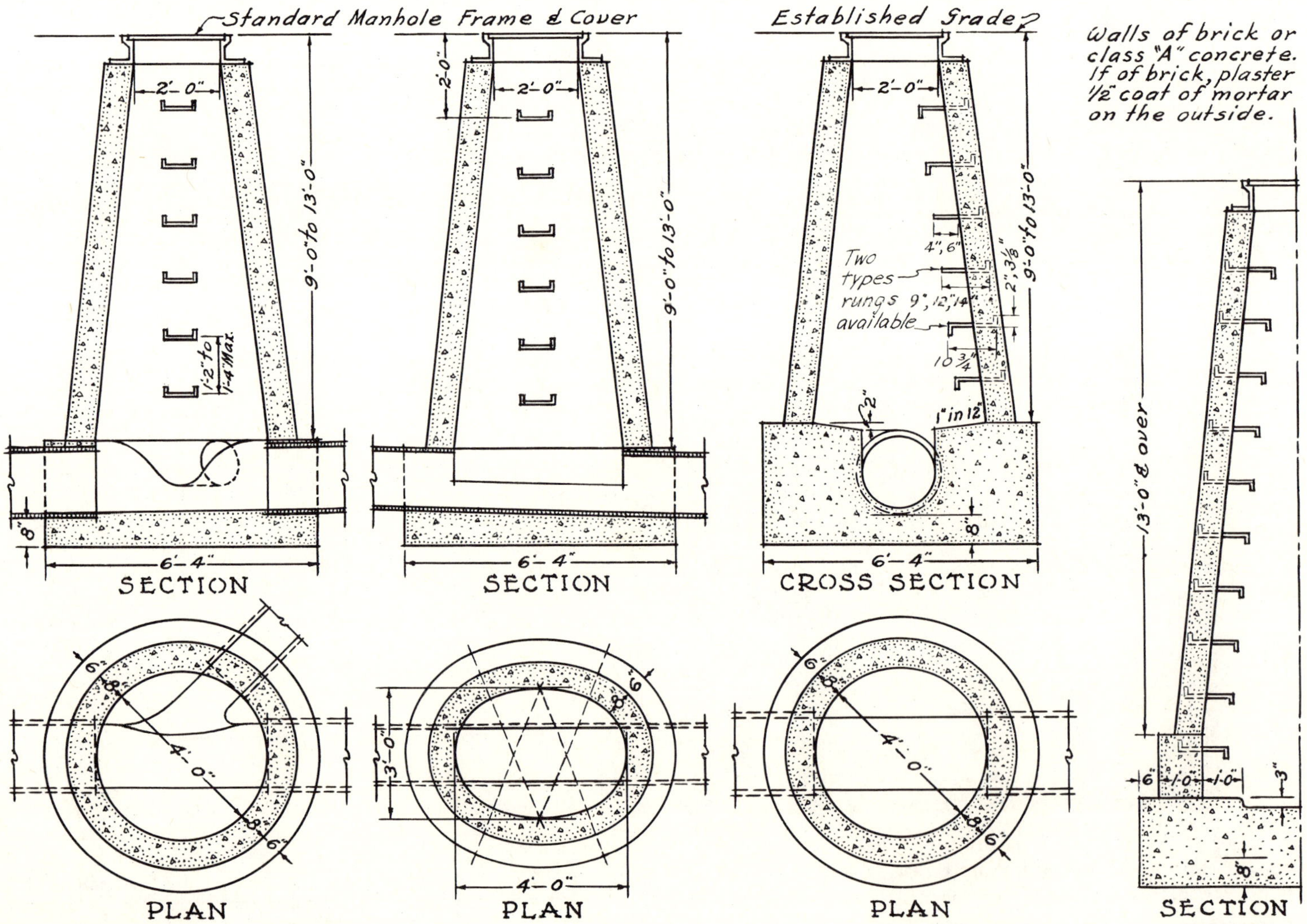
Standard Manhole Frame & Cover
Established Grade
Walls of brick or class "A" concrete. If of brick, plaster 1/2" coat of mortar on the outside.
Two types rungs 9", 12", 14" available
1" in 12"
9'-0" to 13'-0"
13'-0" & over
6'-4"
4'-0"
SECTION
SECTION
CROSS SECTION
PLAN
PLAN
PLAN
SECTION

INTERSECTING MANHOLE 8" TO 24" DIAMETER PIPES

8", 12" & 15" DIA. PIPES

18" TO 24" DIAMETER PIPES

Scale 1/4" = 1'-0"

DEEP MANHOLE

STANDARD MANHOLES FOR SANITARY & STORM SEWERS

Scale 1/4" = 1'-0"

Compiled with the aid of Ralph Eberlin, C.E.

DRAINAGE – EXTERIOR DETAILS

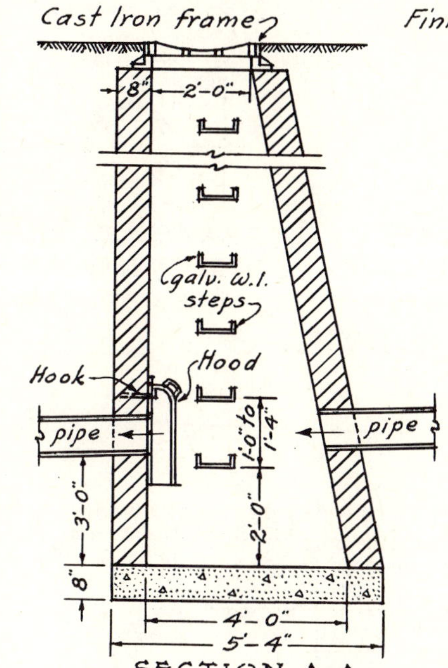
Cast Iron frame
8"
2'-0"
galv. W.I. steps
Hook
Hood
pipe
pipe
1'-0" to 1'-4"
3'-0"
2'-0"
8"
4'-0"
5'-4"

SECTION A-A

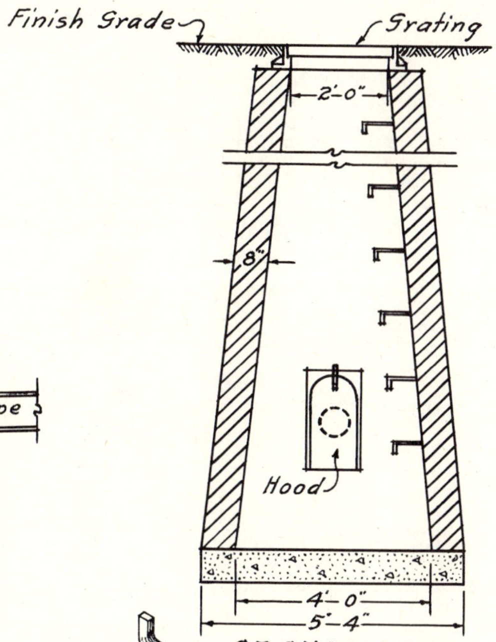
Finish Grade
Grating
2'-0"
8"
Hood
4'-0"
5'-4"

SECTION B-B

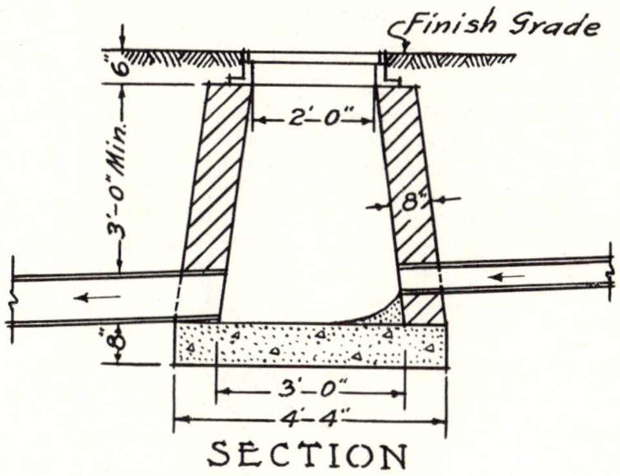
Finish Grade
6"
3'-0" Min.
2'-0"
8"
8"
3'-0"
4'-4"

SECTION

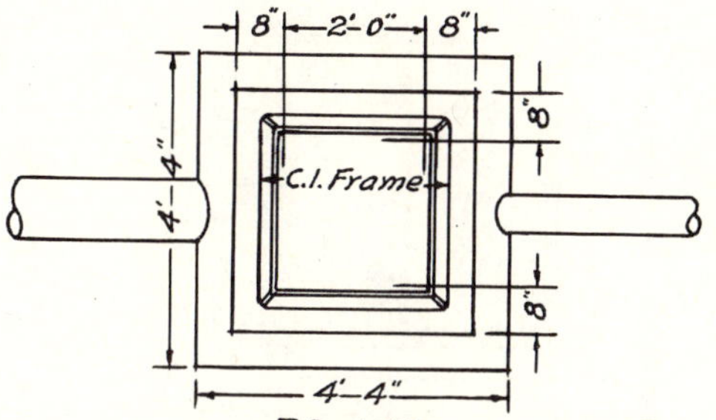
8"
2'-0"
8"
4'-4"
8"
C.I. Frame
8"
4'-4"

PLAN

YARD DRAINAGE INLET

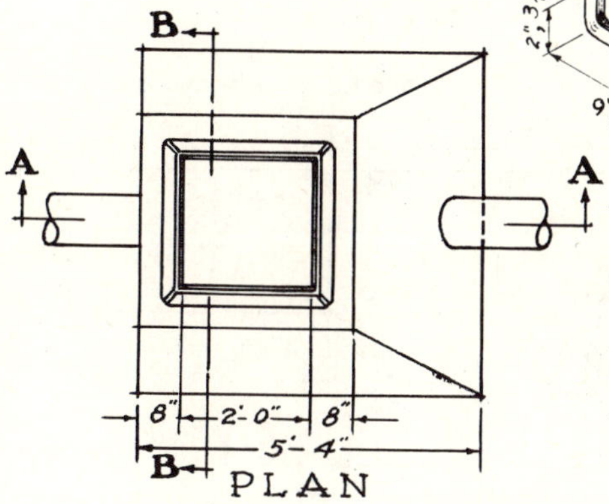
B
A
A
8"
2'-0"
8"
5'-4"
B

PLAN

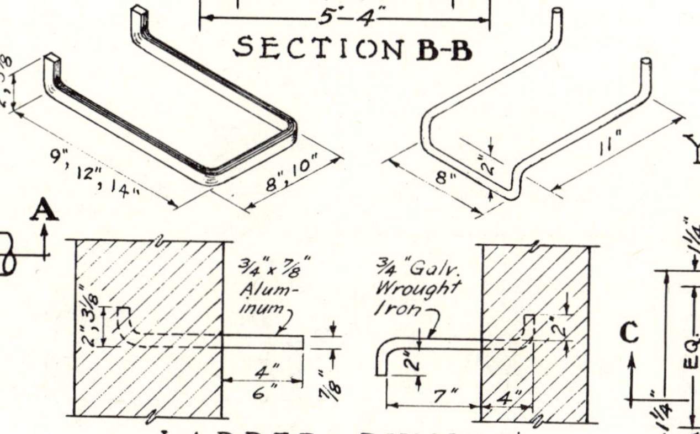
2", 3 1/8"
9", 12", 14"
8", 10"
2"
8"
11"
3/4" x 7/8" Aluminum
2", 3 1/8"
4"
6"
7/8"
3/4" Galv. Wrought Iron
2"
2"
7"
4"

LADDER RUNGS & MANHOLE STEPS

YARD DRAINAGE BASIN

1/4" = 1'-0"

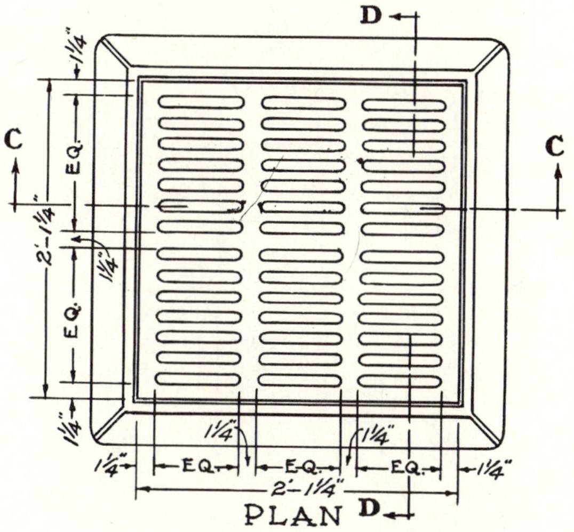
D
C
C
1 1/4"
E.Q.
2'-1 1/4"
1 1/4"
E.Q.
1 1/4"
1 1/4"
1 1/4"
1 1/4"
E.Q.
E.Q.
E.Q.
1 1/4"
2'-1 1/4"
D

PLAN

PLAN of COVER

	R	X	Y	H	W	D
6" & 8" outlet	5"	13 1/2"	23 1/2"	20 1/2"	11 1/2"	5 1/2"
10" outlet	6"	15 1/4"	26 1/2"	23 1/2"	13 1/2"	6 1/2"
12" outlet	7"	17 3/4"	29"	26"	15 3/4"	7 1/2"
15" outlet	8 1/2"	20"	30"	27"	18"	9"
18" outlet	10"	23"	33"	30"	21"	11"
20" outlet	11"	25 1/2"	35"	32"	23 1/2"	11"

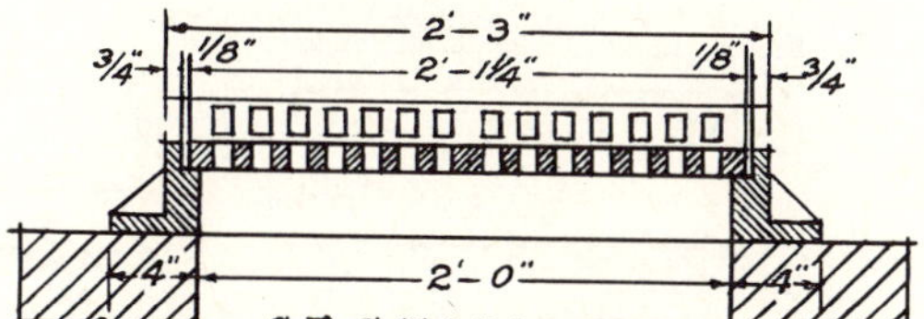
2'-3"
3/4"
1/8"
2'-1 1/4"
1/8"
3/4"
4"
2'-0"
4"

SECTION D-D

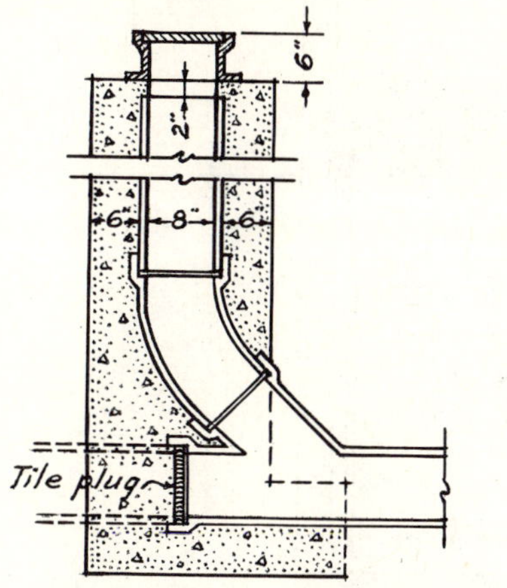
6"
2"
6"
8"
6"
Tile plug

DETAIL OF INSPECTION BOX AND CLEAN-OUT (LAMP HOLE)

3/8" = 1'-0"

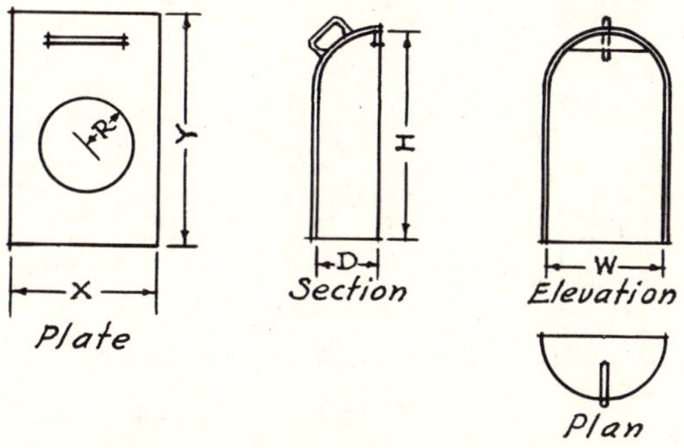
R
Y
X
Plate
H
D
Section
W
Elevation
Plan

CAST IRON HOOD

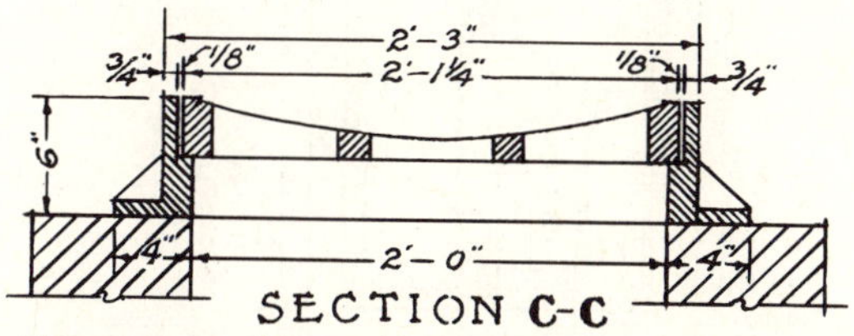
2'-3"
3/4"
1/8"
2'-1 1/4"
1/8"
3/4"
6"
4"
2'-0"
4"

SECTION C-C

FRAME & GRATING FOR YARD DRAINAGE INLETS & BASINS

3/4" = 1'-0"

Compiled with the aid of Ralph Eberlin, C.E.

DRAINAGE - EXTERIOR DETAILS

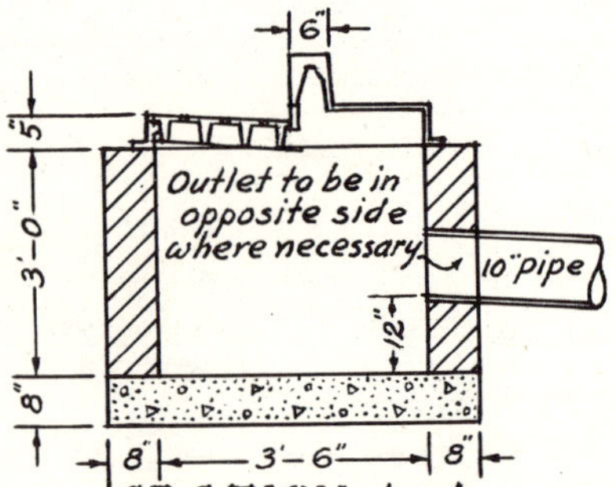
6"
5"
3'-0"
Outlet to be in opposite side where necessary
10" pipe
12"
8"
8" 3'-6" 8"

SECTION A-A

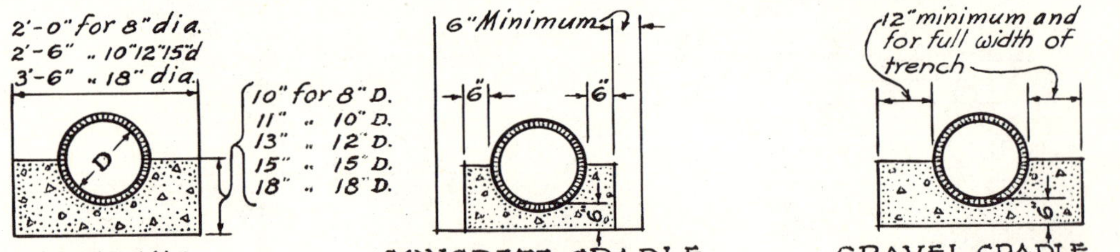
2'-0" for 8" dia.
2'-6" " 10" 12" 15" d
3'-6" " 18" dia.
D
10" for 8" D.
11" " 10" D.
13" " 12" D.
15" " 15" D.
18" " 18" D.
6" Minimum
6" 6"
6"
12" minimum and for full width of trench
6"

CONCRETE CRADLE IN EARTH

CONCRETE CRADLE IN ROCK FOR GRADIENTS OVER 5%

GRAVEL CRADLE IN ROCK FOR GRADIENTS of 5% or LESS

CRADLES FOR PIPE SEWERS

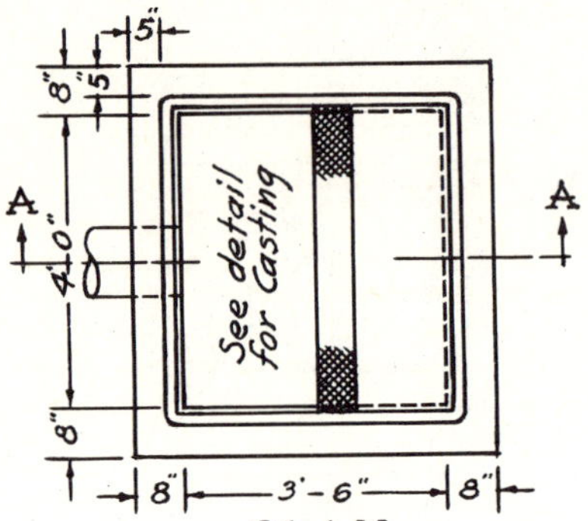
5"
8"
5"
A
A
4'-0"
See detail for Casting
8"
8" 3'-6" 8"

PLAN

DETAIL of INLET

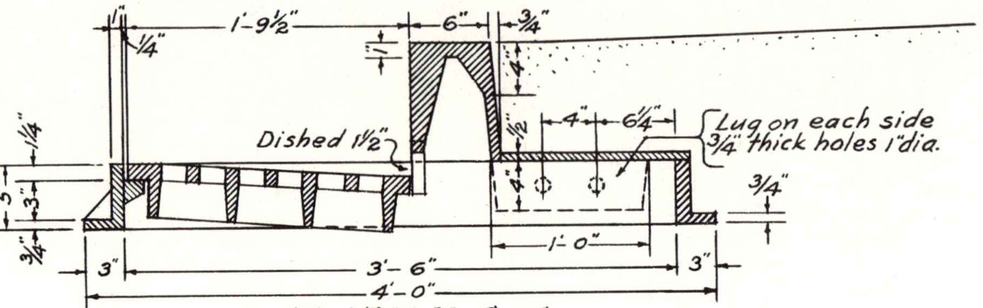
1" 1'-9½" 6" ¾"
¼"
1"
4"
1¼"
Dished 1½"
½"
4" 6¼"
Lug on each side ¾" thick holes 1" dia.
5"
3"
4"
¾"
¾"
1'-0"
3" 3'-6" 3"
4'-0"

SECTION C-C

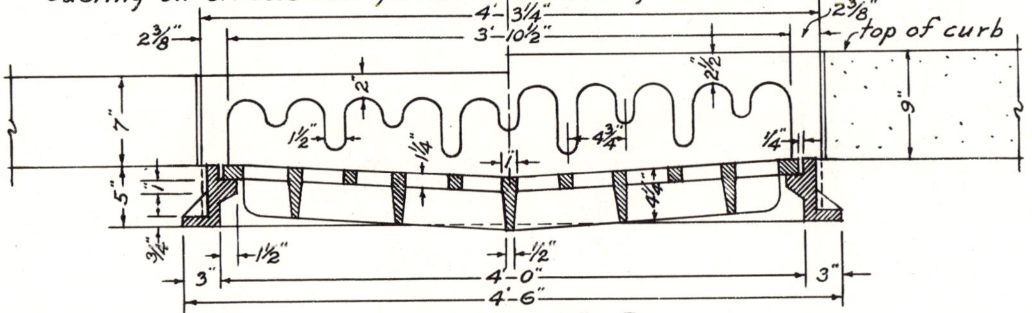
Casting on streets with gutters
Casting on streets with curbs
4'-3¼"
3'-10½"
2⅜"
2⅜"
top of curb
2"
2½"
7"
9"
1½"
1¼"
4¾"
¼"
1"
5"
1"
1¼"
¾"
1½"
½"
3" 4'-0" 3"
4'-6"

SECTION D-D

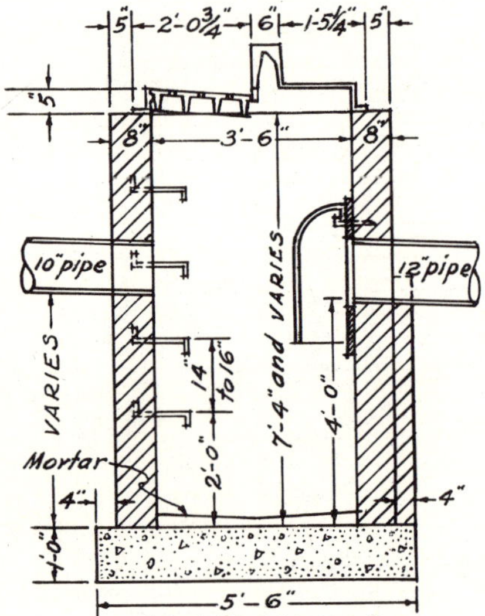
5" 2'-0¾" 6" 1'-5¼" 5"
5"
8" 3'-6" 8"
10" pipe
12" pipe
VARIES
7'-4" and VARIES
4'-0"
14" to 16"
2'-0"
Mortar
4"
4"
1'-0"
5'-6"

SECTION B-B

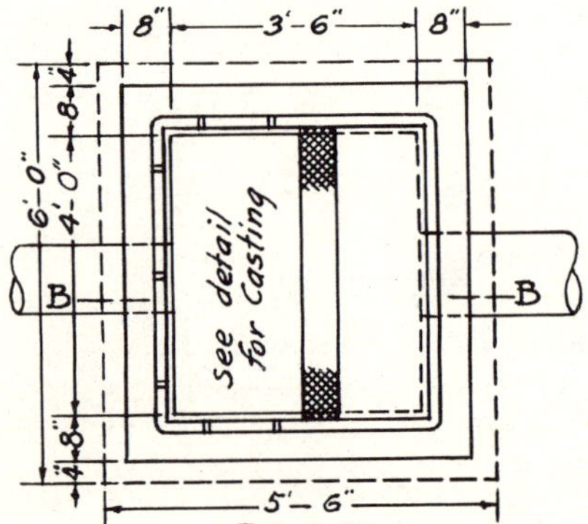
8" 3'-6" 8"
8
4
6'-0"
4'-0"
B
B
See detail for Casting
4
8
5'-6"

PLAN

RECEIVING BASIN

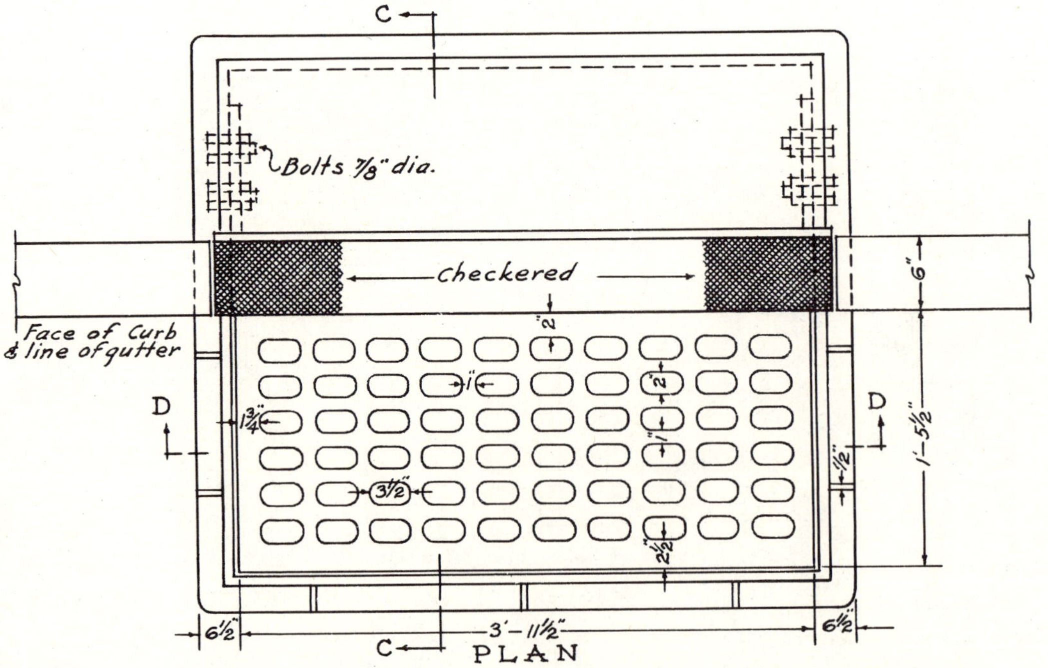
C
Bolts ⅞" dia.
Checkered
6"
Face of Curb & line of gutter
2"
1"
2"
1¾"
D
D
1"
3½"
1½"
1'-5½"
2½"
6½" 3'-11½" 6½"
C

PLAN

DETAIL of STANDARD CASTING FOR INLET AND RECEIVING BASINS ¾" = 1'-0"

Scale ¼" = 1'-0"

Compiled with the aid of Ralph Eberlin, C.E.

VITRIFIED CLAY SEWER PIPE and FITTINGS

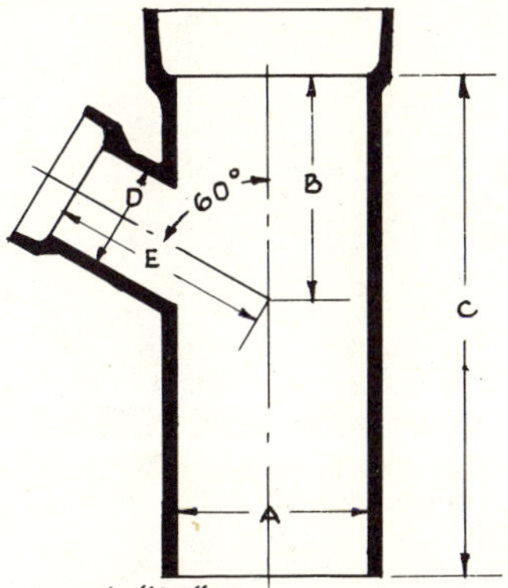
60°
B
C
D
E
A

* "Y" Branch

A	B	C	D	E
4"	8"	1'-0"	4"	6 3/4"
6"	8 3/4"	1'-6"	4"	7 1/2"
6"	9 3/4"	1'-6"	6"	8 3/4"
8"	9 1/4"	2' & 3'	4"	8 3/4"
8"	11 1/4"	"	6"	9 3/4"
8"	1'-0 1/4"	"	8"	11"
10"	11"	"	4"	10 3/4"
10"	1'-1"	"	6"	11 1/4"
10"	1'-2"	"	8"	1'-0"
10"	1'-3"	"	10"	1'-1"
1'-0"	11 1/4"	"	4"	1'-0 1/4"
1'-0"	1'-0 1/4"	"	6"	1'-0 3/4"
1'-0"	1'-2 1/4"	"	8"	1'-1 1/2"
1'-0"	1'-3 1/4"	"	10"	1'-2 1/4"
1'-0"	1'-5 1/4"	"	1'-0"	1'-3"

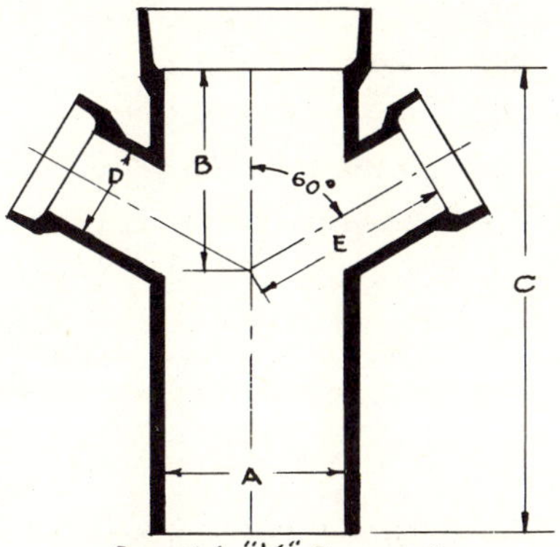
B
60°
D
E
C
A

Double "Y" Branch

A	B	C	D	E
4"	8	1'-0"	4"	6 3/4"
6"	8 3/4"	1'-6"	4"	7 1/2
6"	9 3/4"	1'-6"	6"	8 3/4"
8"	11 1/4"	2'-3"	6"	9 3/4"

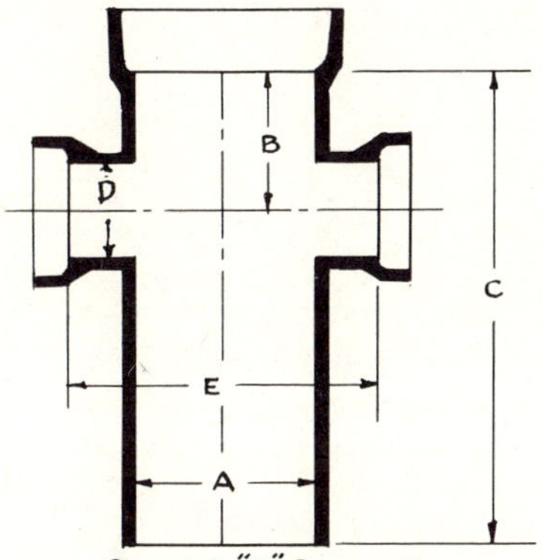
B
D
C
E
A

Double "T" Branch

A	B	C	D	E
4"	5"	1'-0"	4"	8 1/2"
6"	5 1/4"	1'-6"	4"	11"
6"	6 1/4"	1'-6"	6"	11"
8"	6 1/2"	2'-3"	6"	1'-1 1/2"

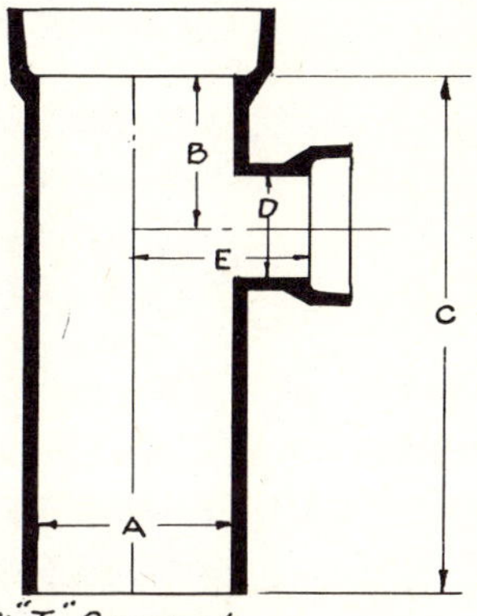
B
D
E
C
A

* "T" Branch

A	B	C	D	E
4"	5	1'-0"	4"	4 1/4"
6"	5 1/4"	1'-6"	4"	5 1/2"
6"	6 1/4"	1'-6"	6"	5 1/2"
8"	5 1/2"	2, & 3,	4"	6 1/2"
8"	6 1/2"	"	6"	6 3/4"
8"	7 3/4"	"	8"	7"
10"	6"	"	4"	7"
10"	6 3/4"	"	6"	7 3/4"
10"	7 3/4"	"	8"	8 1/4"
10"	9"	"	10"	8 1/2"
1'-0"	6 1/4"	"	4"	8 3/4"
1'-0"	6 3/4"	"	6"	9"
1'-0"	8"	"	8"	9 1/2"
1'-0"	9 1/4"	"	10"	9 3/4"
1'-0"	10 1/2"	"	1'-0"	10"

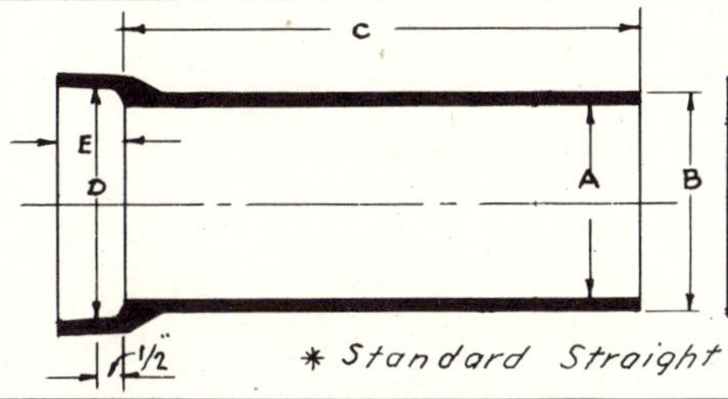
C
E
D
A
B
1/2"

* Standard Straight Pipe

A	B	C	D	E
4"	5 1/8"	2, 2 1/2, 3	6 1/8"	1 3/4"
6"	7 7/16"	"	8 5/8"	2 1/4"
8"	9 3/4"	"	11"	2 1/2"
10"	1'-0"	"	1'-1 1/4"	2 5/8"
1'-0"	1'-2 5/16"	"	1'-3 3/4"	2 3/4"

* Diameters in varying increments up to 3'-0" available

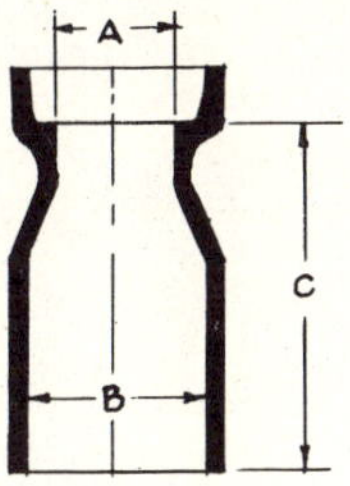
A
C
B

Increasers

A	B	C
4"	6"	1'-0"
6"	8"	1'-0"
6"	10"	1'-0"
8"	10"	1'-0"
10"	1'-0"	1'-0"
1'-0"	1'-3"	1'-0"
1'-3"	1'-6"	1'-0"

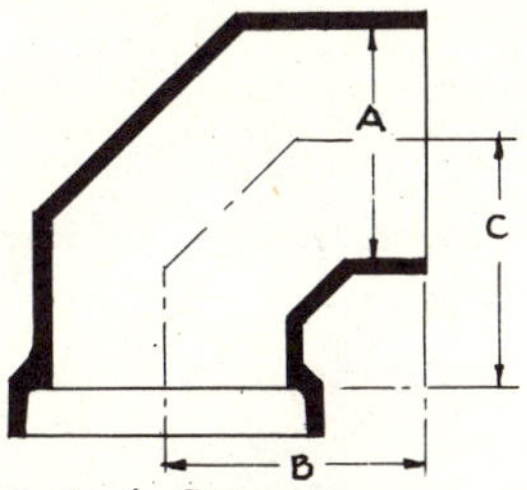
A
C
B

* Cut Elbows

A	B	C
8"	8"	8"
10"	9 1/2"	9"
1'-0"	10 3/4"	10 3/4"

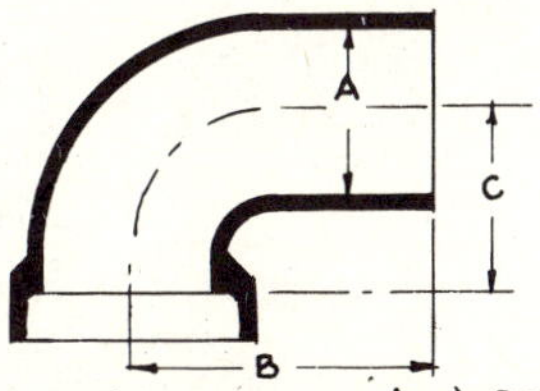
A
C
B

Elbow (Short Radius) 90°

A	B	C
4"	7"	4 3/4"
6"	11"	6 1/2"
8"	1'-2"	8"

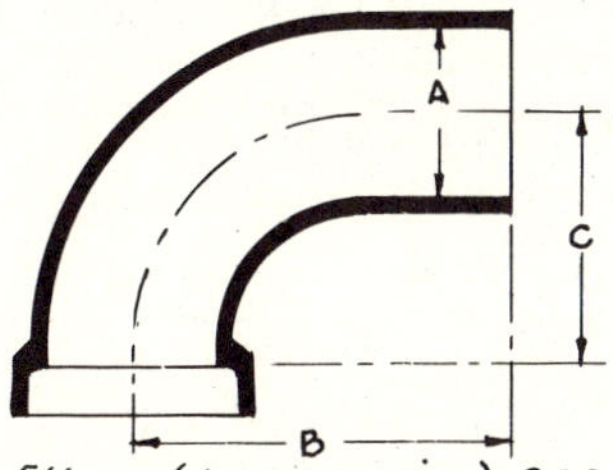
A
C
B

Elbow (Long Radius) 90°

A	B	C
4"	9 3/4"	10"
6"	10"	1'-2 1/2"
8"	1'-0"	1'-5"

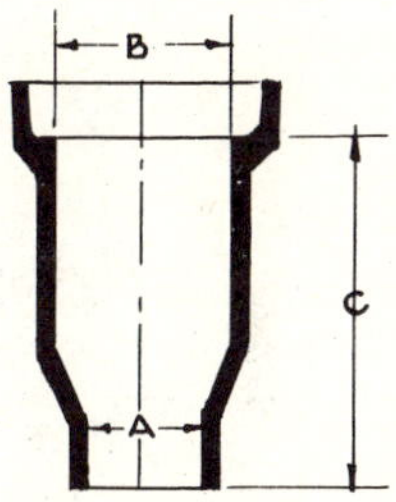
B
C
A

Reducers

A	B	C
4"	6"	1'-0"
6"	8"	1'-0"
8"	10"	1'-0"
10"	1'-0"	1'-0"

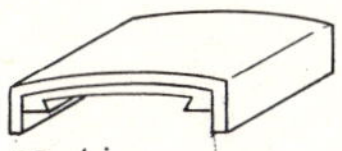

Robinson

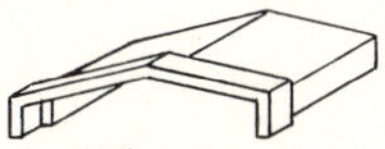

Double - Slant

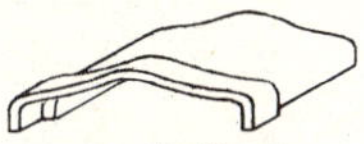

Camel Back

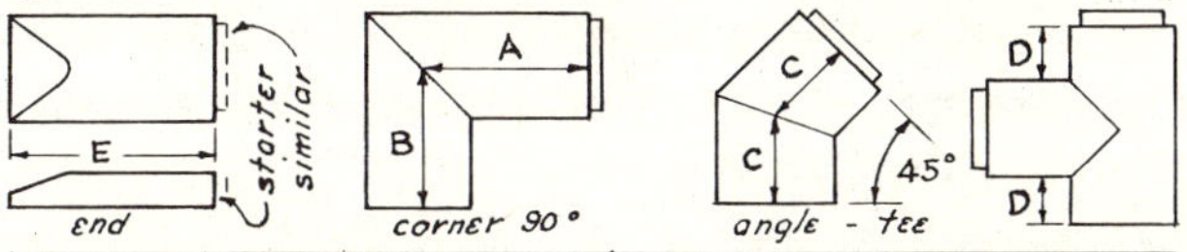
E
starter similar
end
A
B
corner 90°
C
C
45°
angle - tee
D
D

WALL WIDTH	A	B	C	D	E	Straight Coping
9"	9"	9"	6 1/4"	6 3/4"	12"	9", 12", 24"
13"	11"	11"	7"	4 7/8"	12"	9", 12", 24"
18"	14"	14"	8 1/4"	2"	18"	9", 12", 24"

Robinson (above)

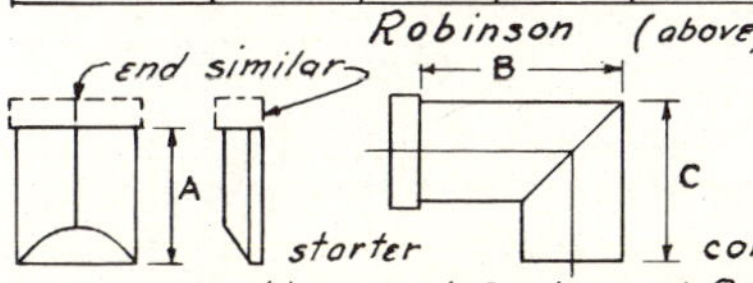
end similar
A
starter
B
C
corner

WALL	A	B	C	Straight Coping
9"	12"	16 1/4"	17 1/2"	24"
13"	12"	17 3/8"	18 1/8"	24"
18"	18"	22 1/4"	23"	24"

Double - Slant Coping and Camel Back Coping

Wall Copings

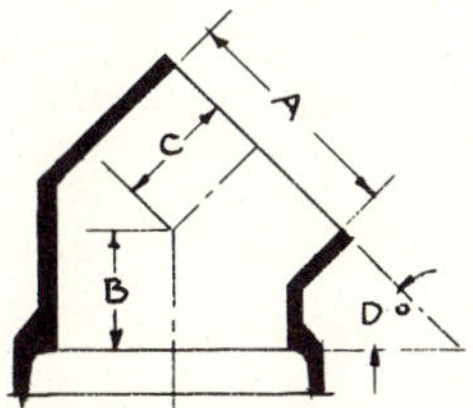
A
C
B
D°

Cut Curves

A	B	C	D°
8	4 1/2"	4 5/8"	30°, 45°
10"	5 1/8"	5 1/2"	"
1'-0"	5 7/8"	5 7/8"	"

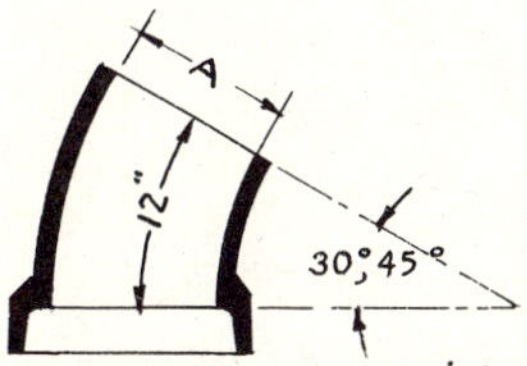
A
12"
30°, 45°

Curve (Short Radius)

A	4"	6"

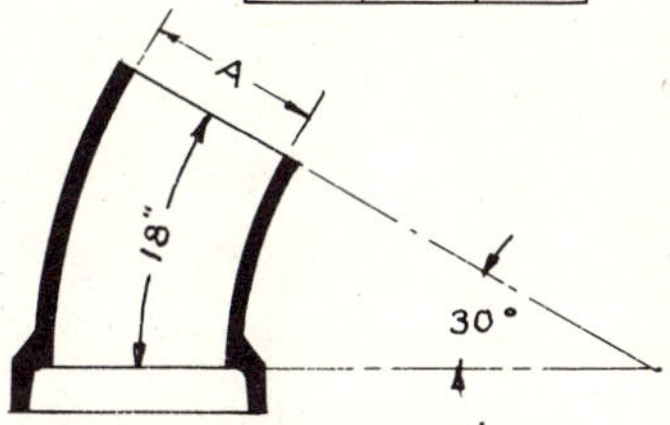
A
18"
30°

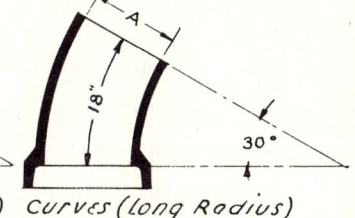

Curves (Long Radius)

A	4"	6"

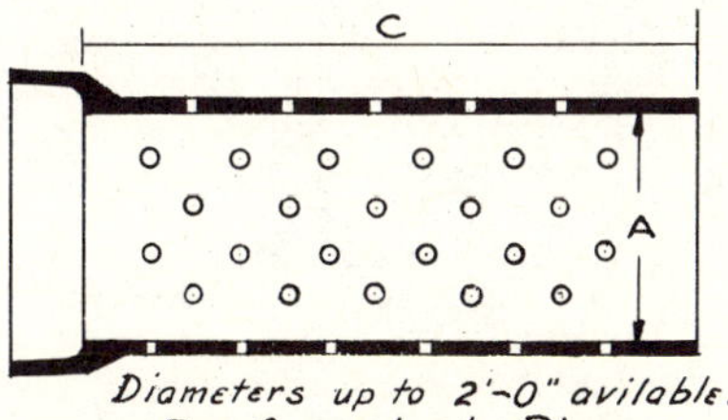
C
A

A	C
4"	2'-0"
6"	2'-0"
8"	2'-0"
10"	2'-0"
1'-0"	2'-0"

Diameters up to 2'-0" avilable.

Perforated Pipe

Data from "Clay Pipe Engineering Manual", by Clay Sewer Pipe Association, Inc.

ELECTRICAL SYMBOLS

GENERAL OUTLETS

CEILING WALL

O	—O	Outlet
B	—B	Blanked Outlet
D		Drop Cord
E	—E	Electrical Outlet; for use only when circle used alone might be confused with columns, plumbing symbols, etc.
F	—F	Fan Outlet
J	—J	Junction Box
L	—L	Lamp Holder
L_PS	—L_PS	Lamp Holder with Pull Switch
S	—S	Pull Switch
V	—V	Outlet for vapor Discharge Lamp
X	—X	Exit Light Outlet
C	—C	Clock Outlet (Specify Voltage)

CONVENIENCE OUTLETS

Duplex Convenience Outlet

Convenience Outlet other than Duplex 1 = Single, 3 = Triplex, etc.

WP Weatherproof Convenience Outlet

R Range Outlet

S Switch and Convenience Outlet

R Radio and Convenience Outlet

Special Purpose Outlet (Describe in Spec.)

Floor Outlet

SWITCH OUTLETS

S	Single Pole Switch
S_2	Double Pole Switch
S_3	Three Way Switch
S_4	Four Way Switch
S_D	Automatic Door Switch
S_E	Electrolier Switch
S_K	Key Operated Switch
S_P	Switch and Pilot Lamp
S_CB	Circuit Breaker
S_WCB	Weatherproof Circuit Breaker
S_MC	Momentary Contact Switch
S_RC	Remote Control Switch
S_WP	Weatherproof Switch
S_F	Fused Switch
S_WF	Weatherproof Fused Switch

SPECIAL OUTLETS

O a,b,c etc.

a,b,c etc.

S a,b,c etc.

Any Standard Symbol as given above with the addition of a lower case subscript letter may be used to designate some special variation of Standard Equipment of particular interest in a specific set of Architectural Plans.

When used they must be listed in the key of Symbols on each drawing and if necessary further described in the Specifications.

PANELS, CIRCUITS & MISCELLANEOUS

Lighting Panel

Power Panel

—— Branch Circuit; Concealed in ceiling or wall

—·— Branch Circuit—Concealed in floor

---- Branch Circuit; Exposed

→ Home Run to Panel Board. Indicate number of Circuits by number of arrows. Note: Any circuit without further designation indicates a two-wire circuit. For a greater number of wires indicate as follows: —⧸⧸⧸— (3 wires) —⧸⧸⧸⧸— (4 wires), etc.

— Feeders. Note: Use heavy lines and designate by number corresponding to listing in Feeder Schedule.

Under floor Duct and Junction Box. Triple System. Note: For double or single Systems eliminate one or two lines. This symbol is equally adaptable to auxiliary system layouts.

G	Generator
M	Motor
I	Instrument
T	Power Transformer. (Or draw to scale)
⊠	Controller
	Isolating Switch

AUXILIARY SYSTEMS

⊡	Push Button
	Buzzer
	Bell
◇	Annunciator
	Outside Telephone
	Interconnecting Telephone
	Telephone Switchboard
T	Bell Ringing Transformer
D	Electric Door Opener
F	Fire Alarm Bell
F	Fire Alarm Station
⊠	City Fire Alarm Station
FA	Fire Alarm Central Station
FS	Automatic Fire Alarm Device
W	Watchman's Station
W	Watchman's Central Station
H	Horn
N	Nurse's Signal Plug
M	Maid's Signal Plug
R	Radio Outlet
SC	Signal Central Station
	Interconnection Box
⦀	Battery

—·—·— Auxiliary System Circuits Note: Any line without further designation indicates two-wire system. For a greater number of wires designate with numerals in manner similar to —·—·—12-No. 18 W—¾" C. Designate by number corresponding to listing in Schedule.

☐ a,b,c, etc. Special Auxiliary Outlets Subscript letters refer to notes on plans or detailed description in Specifications.

Note: for other symbols not A.S.A. see page "Electrical Wiring Devices."

American Standard Graphical Electrical Symbols for Architectural Plans, Y 32.9-1943

RESIDENTIAL ELECTRIC WIRING

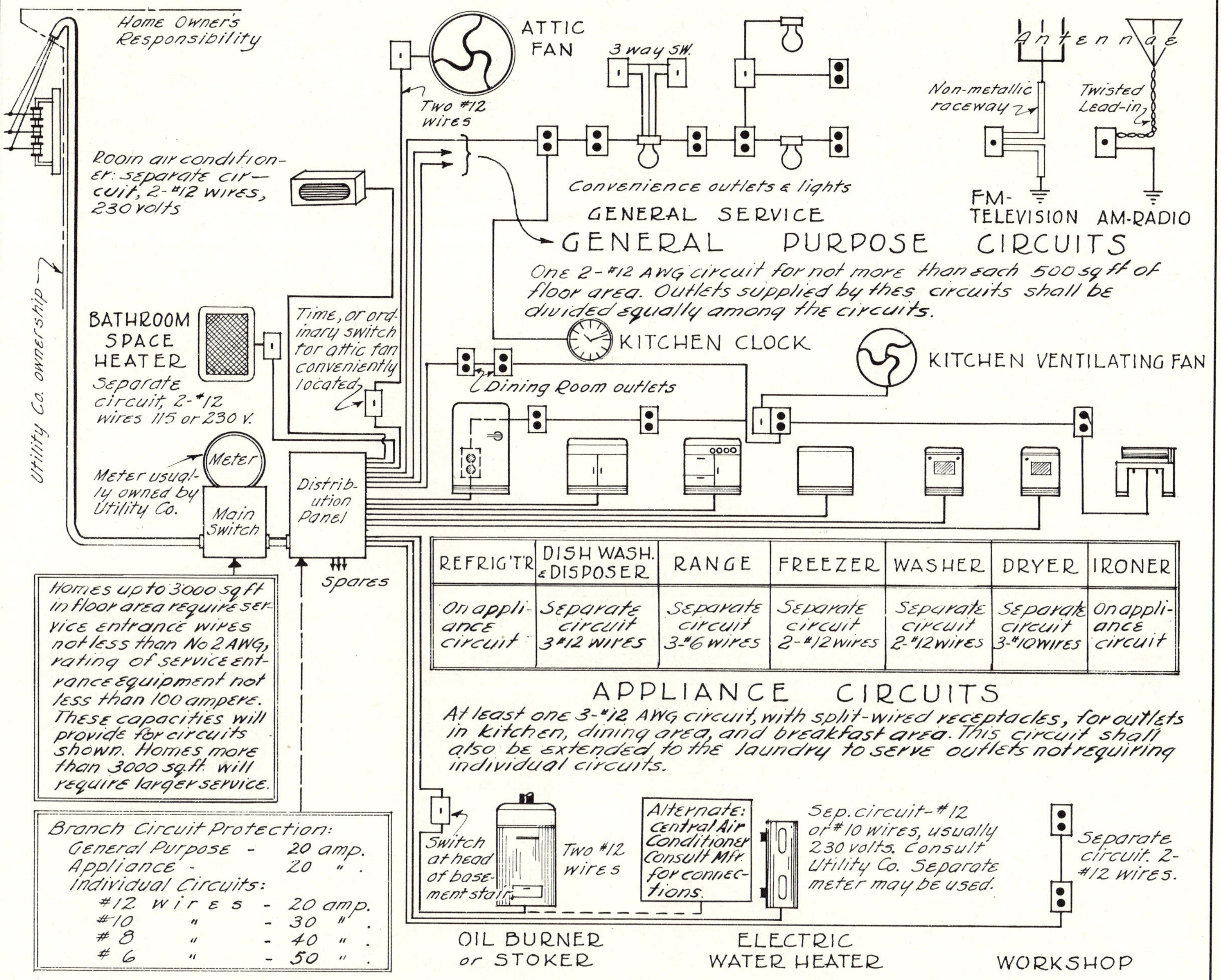
Home Owner's Responsibility
Utility Co. ownership
ATTIC FAN
Two #12 wires
3 way SW.
Room air conditioner: separate circuit, 2-#12 wires, 230 volts
Convenience outlets & lights
GENERAL SERVICE
GENERAL PURPOSE CIRCUITS
One 2-#12 AWG circuit for not more than each 500 sq ft of floor area. Outlets supplied by thes circuits shall be divided equally among the circuits.
Antennae
Non-metallic raceway
Twisted Lead-in
FM-TELEVISION
AM-RADIO
BATHROOM SPACE HEATER
Separate circuit, 2-#12 wires 115 or 230 V.
Time, or ordinary switch for attic fan conveniently located
KITCHEN CLOCK
KITCHEN VENTILATING FAN
Dining Room outlets
Meter
Meter usually owned by Utility Co.
Main Switch
Distribution Panel
Spares
Homes up to 3000 sq ft in floor area require service entrance wires not less than No 2 AWG, rating of service entrance equipment not less than 100 ampere. These capacities will provide for circuits shown. Homes more than 3000 sq.ft. will require larger service.
APPLIANCE CIRCUITS
At least one 3-#12 AWG circuit, with split-wired receptacles, for outlets in kitchen, dining area, and breakfast area. This circuit shall also be extended to the laundry to serve outlets not requiring individual circuits.
Switch at head of basement stair
Two #12 wires
Alternate: central Air Conditioner Consult Mfr. for connections.
Sep. circuit-#12 or #10 wires, usually 230 volts. Consult Utility Co. Separate meter may be used.
Separate circuit. 2-#12 wires.
OIL BURNER or STOKER
ELECTRIC WATER HEATER
WORKSHOP

REFRIG'T'R	DISH WASH. & DISPOSER	RANGE	FREEZER	WASHER	DRYER	IRONER
On appliance circuit	Separate circuit 3-#12 wires	Separate circuit 3-#6 wires	Separate circuit 2-#12 wires	Separate circuit 2-#12 wires	Separate circuit 3-#10 wires	On appliance circuit

Branch Circuit Protection:

General Purpose	-	20 amp.
Appliance	-	20 " .
Individual Circuits:		
#12 wires	-	20 amp.
#10 "	-	30 " .
# 8 "	-	40 " .
# 6 "	-	50 " .

Recommendations of the National Adequate Wiring Bureau

WATTAGE* OF ELECTRICAL OUTLETS for RESIDENTIAL WORK

TYPE	WATTS	TYPE	WATTS	TYPE	WATTS
Air Conditioner	850-1200, 3100	Home Freezer	300-670	Refrigerator	200-670
Attic Fan	500-1500	Hot Plate	600-1000	Roaster	1150-1650
Chafing Dish	660	Infra-red Lamp	500	Stoker	400-1250
Clothes Dryer	up to 4500	Iron, Hand	660-1000	Sunlamp	250
Dishwasher	530-1000	Ironer, Home	1275-1620	Television	200-400
Disposer	380-530	Juice Extractor	60-100	Toaster	600-1350
Egg Cooker	660	Mixer	125-150	Towel Dryer	100-500
Electric Fan	50-300	Motor, 1/4 H.P.	530	Vacuum Cleaner	300
Furnace Blower	380-670	Oil Burner	300-550	Waffle Iron	660-1000
Grill	1000	Percolater	400-600	Washing Machines:	
Hair Dryer	250	Radio	50-200	Automatic	350-900
Heater	1000-1650	Range	7000-14000	Wringer Type	375-450
Heating Pad	65	Razor Sharpener	50	Water Heater	750-3000

*average Data checked by: Mongitore & Moesel, Consulting Engineers, N.Y.C.

ELECTRIC WIRING DEVICES

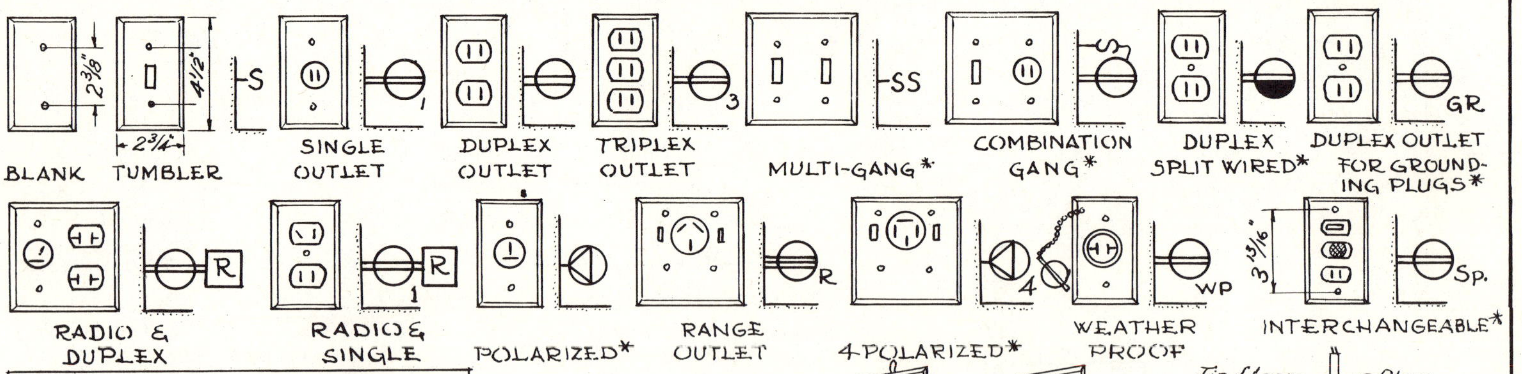
2 3/8
4 1/2
2 1/4
S
1
3
SS
GR
BLANK
TUMBLER
SINGLE OUTLET
DUPLEX OUTLET
TRIPLEX OUTLET
MULTI-GANG*
COMBINATION GANG*
DUPLEX SPLIT WIRED*
DUPLEX OUTLET FOR GROUNDING PLUGS*
R
1
4
WP
Sp.
3 13/16"
RADIO & DUPLEX
RADIO & SINGLE
POLARIZED*
RANGE OUTLET
4 POLARIZED*
WEATHER PROOF
INTERCHANGEABLE*

GANG SIZE				
	HORIZONTAL		VERTICAL	
Gang	Height	Width	Height	Width
2	4 1/2"	4 9/16"	8 1/8"	2 3/4"
3	"	6 3/8"	11 3/4"	"
4	"	8 3/16"	15 3/8"	"
5	"	10"	19"	"
6	"	11 13/16"	22 5/8"	"
Note	Add 1 13/16" ea. added gang. Screws 1 13/16" o.c.		Add 3 5/8" ea. added gang.	

Plates made in plastic; brass 0.04, 0.06 in. thick; stainless steel 0.04"

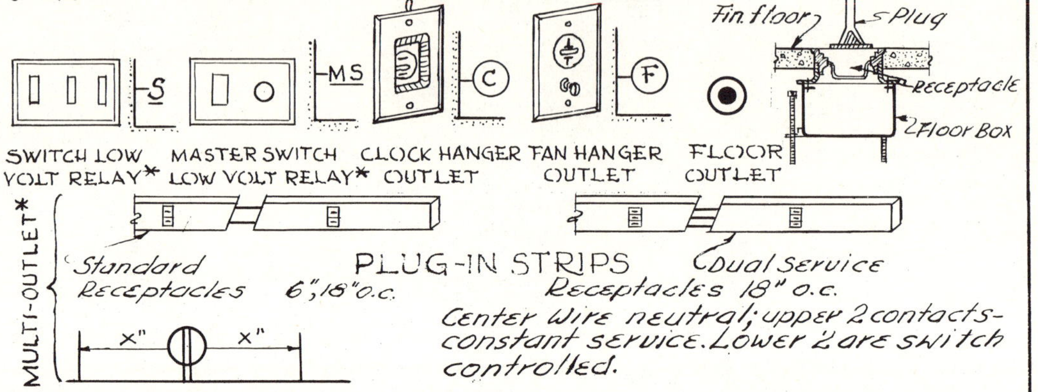
S
MS
C
F
Fin. floor
Plug
Receptacle
Floor Box
SWITCH LOW VOLT RELAY*
MASTER SWITCH LOW VOLT RELAY*
CLOCK HANGER OUTLET
FAN HANGER OUTLET
FLOOR OUTLET
MULTI-OUTLET*
Standard Receptacles 6", 18" o.c.
PLUG-IN STRIPS
Dual Service Receptacles 18" o.c.
Center wire neutral; upper 2 contacts-constant service. Lower 2 are switch controlled.
x"
x"

Outlets & switches shown are most generally used. Number of gangs behind one wall plate depends on types of devices used. Symbols used are ASA standard (except those marked *). See page on "Electric Symbols." + Interchangeable devices (Despard) available in various combinations using any 1, 2 or 3 of the following: switch, convenience outlet, radio outlet, pilot light, bell button, in one gang. Combined gangs made.

TYPES and SIZES of OUTLETS

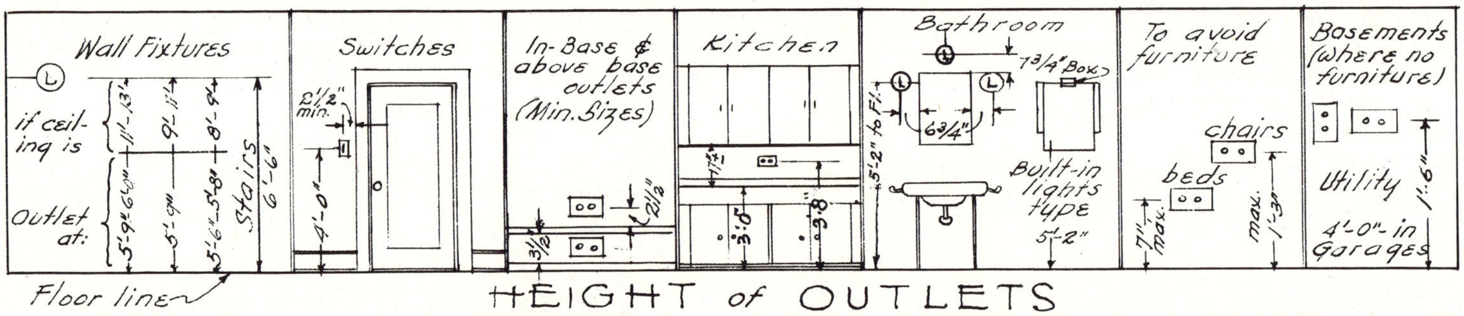
Wall Fixtures
L
if ceiling is
11'-13'
9'-11'
8'-9'
Outlet at:
5'-9"-6'-0"
5'-9"
5'-6"-5'-8"
Stairs 6'-6"
Floor line
Switches
2 1/2" min.
4'-0"
In-Base & above base outlets (Min. Sizes)
2 1/2
3 1/2
Kitchen
1 1/2
3'-8"
3'-8"
Bathroom
7 3/4" Box
6 3/4"
5'-2" to Fl.
Built-in lights type 5'-2"
To avoid furniture
chairs
beds
7" max.
max. 1'-3"
Basements (where no furniture)
Utility
1'-6"
4'-0" in Garages

HEIGHT of OUTLETS

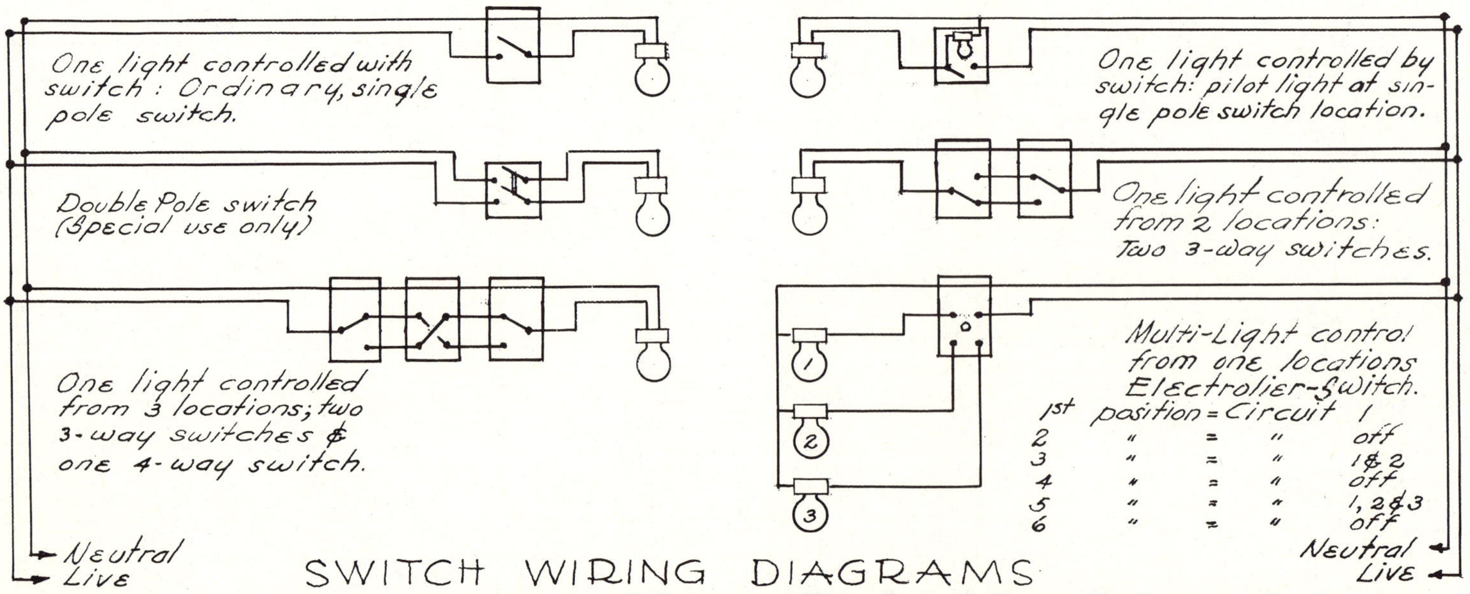
One light controlled with switch: Ordinary, single pole switch.
One light controlled by switch: pilot light at single pole switch location.
Double Pole switch (Special use only)
One light controlled from 2 locations: Two 3-way switches.
One light controlled from 3 locations; two 3-way switches & one 4-way switch.
Multi-Light control from one locations Electrolier-Switch.
1st position = Circuit 1
2 " = " off
3 " = " 1 & 2
4 " = " off
5 " = " 1, 2 & 3
6 " = " off
1
2
3
Neutral
Live
Neutral
Live

SWITCH WIRING DIAGRAMS

Data by Mongitore & Moesel, Consulting Engineers, N.Y.C.

ELECTRIC WIRING MATERIAL

CABLES, CONDUITS and TUBING

STANDARD NOMINAL SIZES in inches

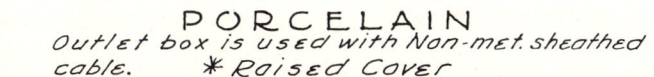

Conduit
Coupling
Bushing
Locknut

1/2, 3/4, 1, 1 1/4, 1 1/2, 2, 2 1/2, 3, 3 1/2, 4, 4 1/2, 5, 6.

RIGID CONDUIT

For fireproof construction

See page on "Conduits" for graphic sizes & weights.

Tubing
Coupling
Connector

1/2, 3/4, 1, 1 1/4, 1 1/2, 2

ELECTRICAL METALLIC TUBING

For fireproof construction. Some use as Rigid Conduit above. Walls are thinner, therefore economical.

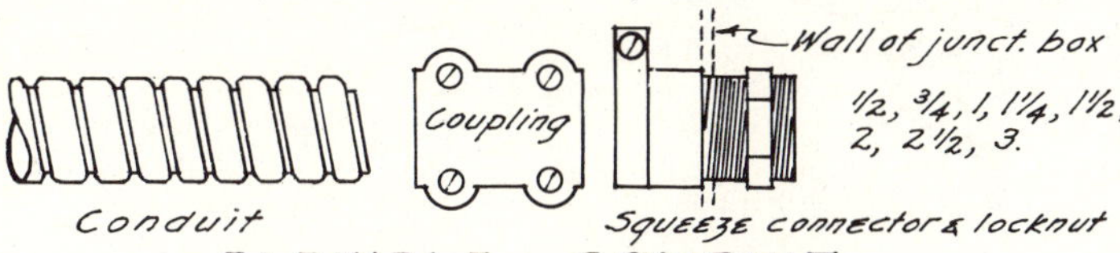
Wall of junct. box
Coupling
Conduit
Squeeze connector & locknut

1/2, 3/4, 1, 1 1/4, 1 1/2, 2, 2 1/2, 3.

FLEXIBLE CONDUIT

For fireproof construction

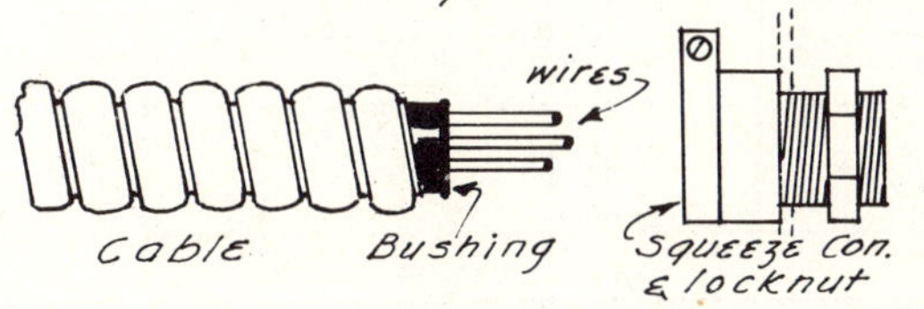
wires
Cable
Bushing
Squeeze Con. & locknut

2 & 3 Conductor: #14, 12, 10, 8, 6, 4, 2.
4 Conductor: #14, 12, 10, 8, 6, 4.
Lead covered – 2 cond. in #14, 12, 10, 8 & 6; 3 cond. in #14, 12, 10, 8, 6 & 4.

ARMORED CABLE (BX)

For frame construct. Lead covered for wet locations.

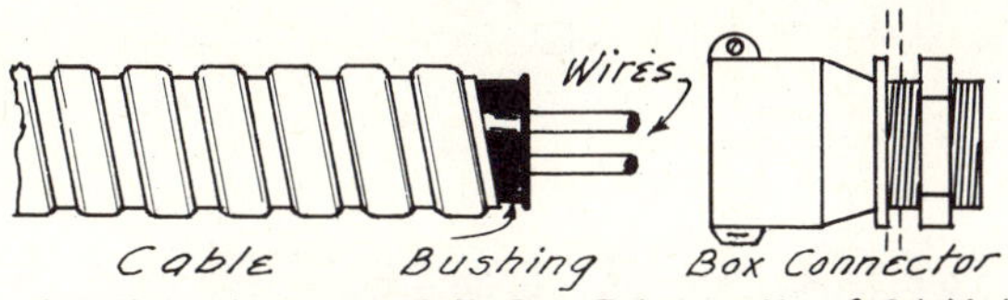
Wires
Cable
Bushing
Box Connector

2 Conductor: #14, 12, 10
3 Conductor: #14, 12

FLAT ARMORED CABLE (OVALFLEX)

For plaster extensions

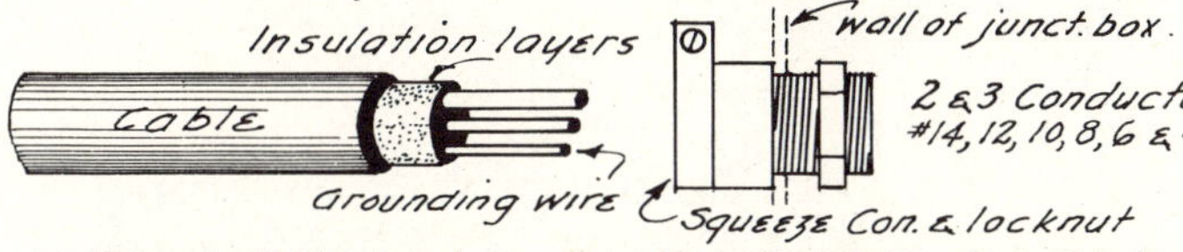
Insulation layers
Wall of junct. box
Cable
Grounding wire
Squeeze Con. & locknut

2 & 3 Conductor: #14, 12, 10, 8, 6 & 4

NON-METALLIC SHEATHED CABLE

For frame construct. (except N.Y.C.), is cheapest.

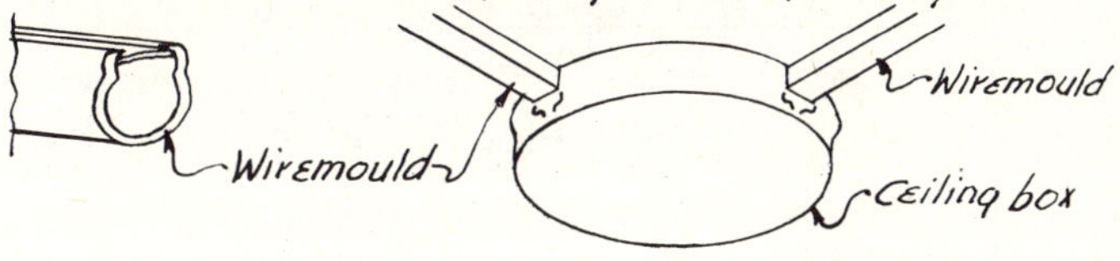
Wiremould
Wiremould
Ceiling box

MOULDED METALLIC CONDUIT

OUTLET and JUNCTION BOXES

SIZES in inches

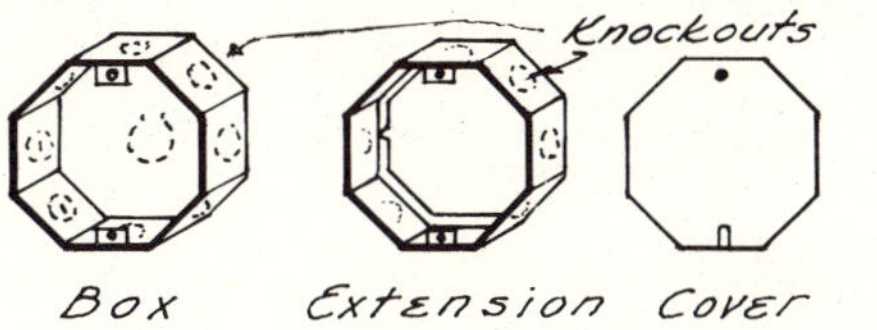
Knockouts
Box
Extension
Cover

Width	x	Depth
3 1/4	x	1 1/2
3 1/2	x	1 1/2
4	x	1 1/2
4	x	2 1/8

OCTAGONAL

Used in ceilings and walls

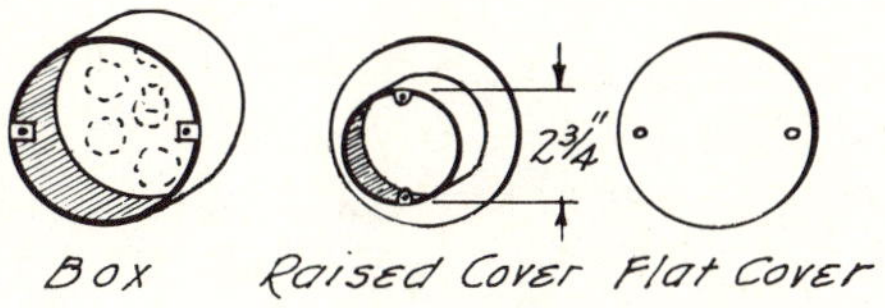
2 3/4"
Box
Raised Cover
Flat Cover

Width	x	Depth
3 1/4	x	3/4, 1 1/2
3 1/2	x	1/2, 1 1/2
4	x	1/2
*4	x	5/8

ROUND

Used in ceilings

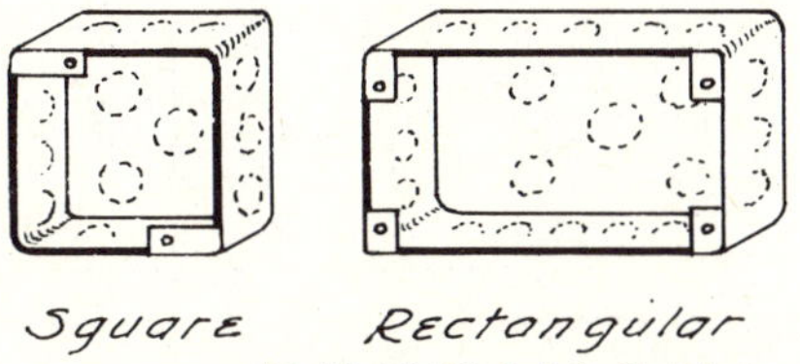
Square
Rectangular

Width x Depth
Square box:
4 x 1 1/2, 2 1/8
4 11/16 x 1 1/2, 2 1/8
2 Gang box:
4 1/2 x 1 3/4 x 6 13/16 long (size varies)

RECTANGULAR

Used in ceilings and walls

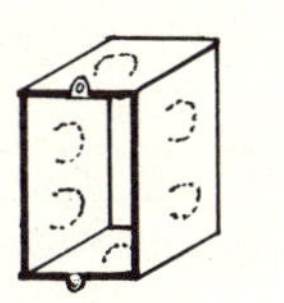

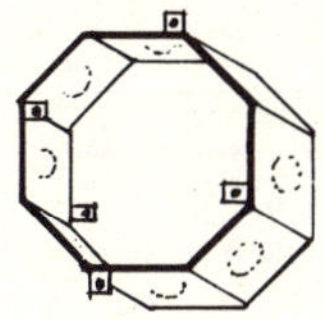

Tapping hole

GEM for switch or receptacle in narrow locat. 2" wide x 3" long x 2" or 2 1/2" deep

4" Octagonal for concrete 1 1/2, 2, 2 1/2; 3, 3 1/2, 4, 5, 6 deep

Flush Floor Box for masonry Sizes vary

IN MASONRY

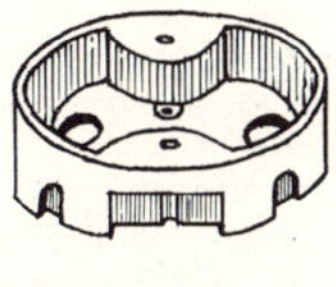

Outlet Box 3 1/4" & 4" dia. 1 1/2" deep (becoming obsolete)

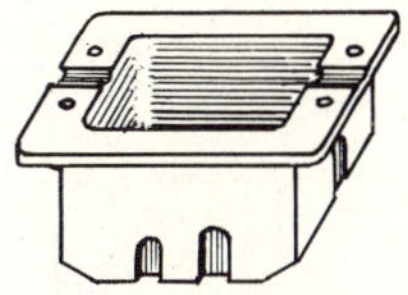

Switch Box Standard Size

PORCELAIN

Outlet box is used with Non-met. sheathed cable. * Raised Cover

CONDULETS (FOR EXPOSED WORK)

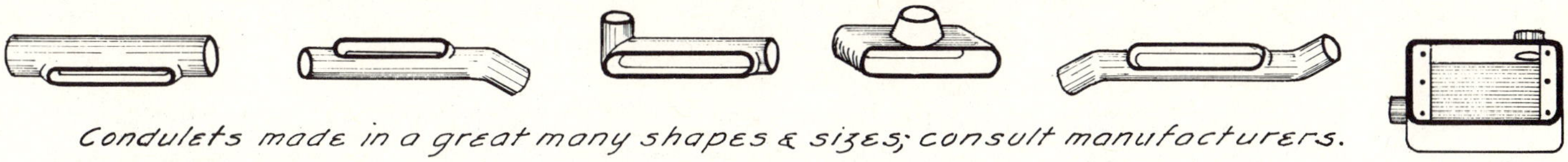

Condulets made in a great many shapes & sizes; consult manufacturers.

All box sizes are inside dimensions.

Data checked by Mongitore & Moesel, Consulting Engineers, NYC

PANELBOARDS and FUSES

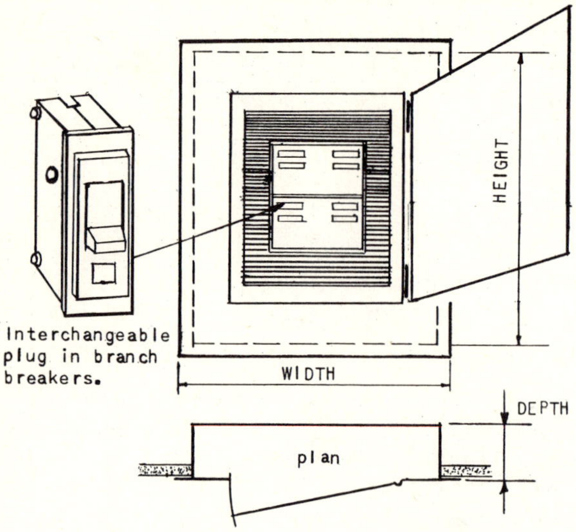

HEIGHT
WIDTH
DEPTH
plan
Interchangeable plug in branch breakers.

MANUFACTURER	MAX. NO. OF CIRCUITS	BOX SIZES IN INCHES		
		WIDTH	HEIGHT	DEPTH
BULL DOG	12	10-3/4	20	3-3/4
	18	10-3/4	24	3-3/4
SQUARE D	12	9	16	3-3/4
	20	9	20-1/2	↓
	32	12	32	↓
GEN. ELEC. CO. (TRUMBULL)	12	14	18	4
	20	↓	22	↓
	30	↓	33	↓
	42	↓	39	↓
WESTINGHOUSE	12	15	20	4-5/8
	20	↓	24	↓
	30	↓	30	↓
	40	↓	34	↓

Other manufacturers' panels available in similar sizes.

CIRCUIT BREAKER LIGHTING PANELS

for better residential & lower cost commercial work.
Automatic circuit breaker– an adjustable time – setting device designed to open a circuit upon any desired degree of overload current.

WIDTH = 20", DEPTH = 5-3/4"
For box height see table below.

MAX. NO. OF CK'T'S	BOX HEIGHT
8	19
16	22
20	24-1/4
24	27-1/2
32	30
36	33
42	35-1/2

Individual circuit breakers may have trip sizes; 15, 20, 30, 40, & 50 amps.

CIRCUIT BREAKER LIGHTING PANEL, FOR BEST QUALITY WORK.

WIDTH = 20" DEPTH = 5-3/4
For box height see table below.

MAX. NO. OF CK'T'S	BOX HEIGHT
8	22
12	24-1/2
16	27
20	32
24	33
28	35-1/2
32	36
36	41
40	44

FUSIBLE SWITCH LIGHTING PANELS
Cartridge type fuse used.

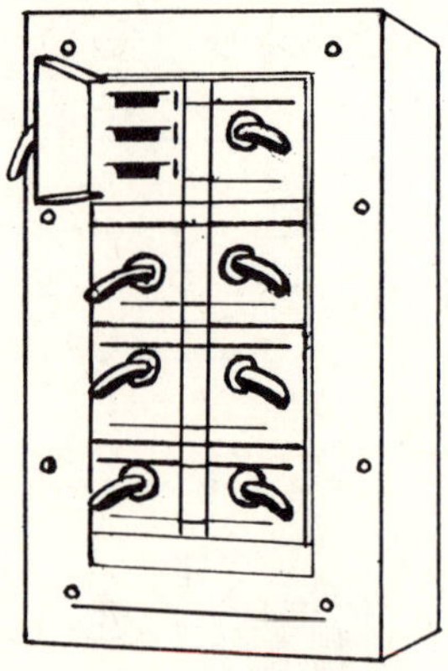

Note: Circuit breaker power panels or fusible switches power panels vary in size according to number of circuits & size of individual breakers or switches.

FUSIBLE SWITCH POWER PANELS

Cartridge fuse used.

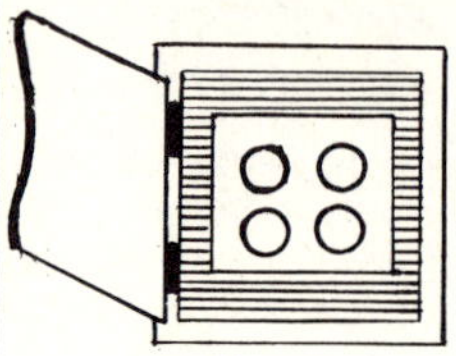

Box dimensions below. For outside dimension add 1-1/4" to height & width.

PLUG FUSE

BRANCHES	HEIGHT	WIDTH	DEPTH
2	6-5/8	6-5/8	2-3/4
4	6-5/8	6-5/8	2-3/4
6	11-1/8	7-3/8	3-1/8
8	14-1/8	7-3/8	3-1/8
Up to 12 branches, same as 8 branches			

For apartments & small houses

PLUG FUSE CABINET

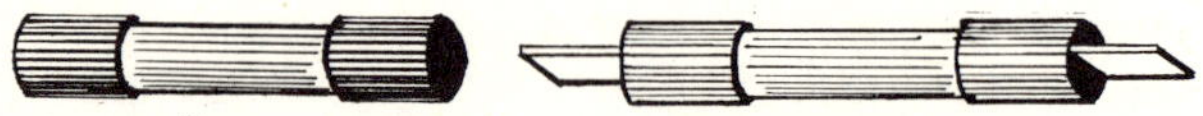

Ferrule contact 1 to 60 amps.

Knife blade contact 70 to 600 amps.

CARTRIDGE FUSES

Ferrule type non-renewable.
Knife blade type non-renewable & renewable link.

STANDARD FUSE SIZES	
Plug Fuse:	1, 3, 5, 6, 8, 10, 15, 20, 25, and 30 amperes.
Cartridge:	1, 3, 6, 10, 15, 20, 25, 30, 35, 40, 50, 60, 70, 80, 90, 100, 110, 125, 150, 175, 200, 225, 250, 275, 300, 325, 350, 400, 450, 500 & 600 amperes.

Standard Knife switches are rated at 30, 60, 100, 200, 400 & 600 amps and take cartridge fuses up to and including their rating.

Circuit breakers at 50 (trip at 15, 20, 30, 40, 50); 100 (trip at 15, 20, 30, 40, 50, 70, 100); 225 (70-225, increment 25); 600 (125-350 incre. 25 & 400, 500, 600 amp).

Data Checked by Mongitore & Moesel

ELECTRICAL WIRING DETAILS

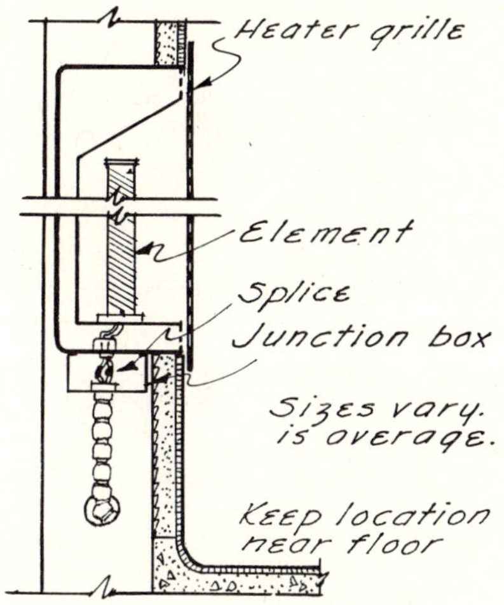
Heater grille
Element
Splice
Junction box
Sizes vary. 10" x 13" x 3½" is average.
Keep location near floor

AUXILIARY HEATER
1½" = 1'-0"

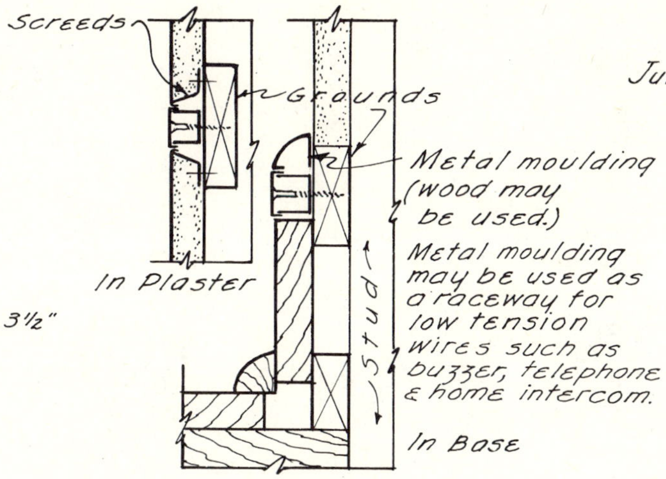
Screeds
Grounds
In Plaster
Metal moulding (wood may be used.)
Metal moulding may be used as a raceway for low tension wires such as buzzer, telephone & home intercom.
Stud
In Base

"PLUG-IN" STRIP
3" = 1'-0"

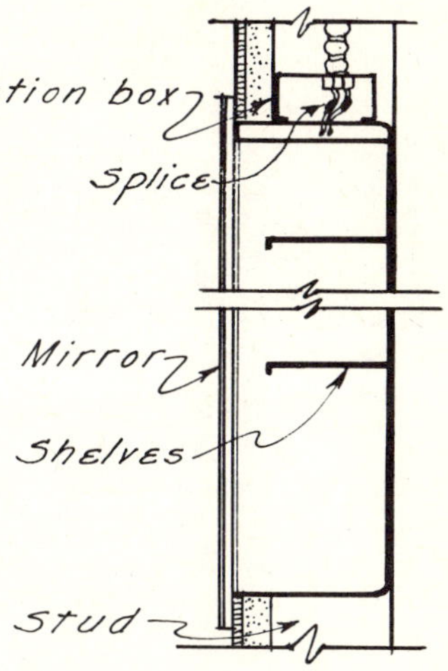
Junction box
Splice
Mirror
Shelves
Stud

MEDICINE CABINET
1½" = 1'-0"

ELECTRICAL WORK IN BUILT-IN EQUIPMENT

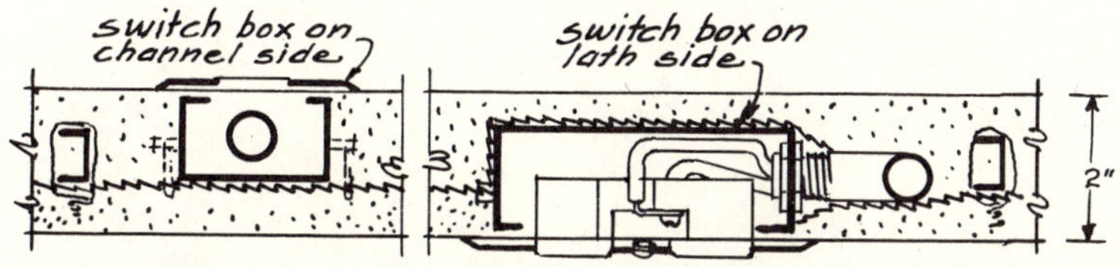
switch box on channel side
switch box on lath side
2"

PLAN OF SWITCH BOX
Box may be set vertically or horizontally.

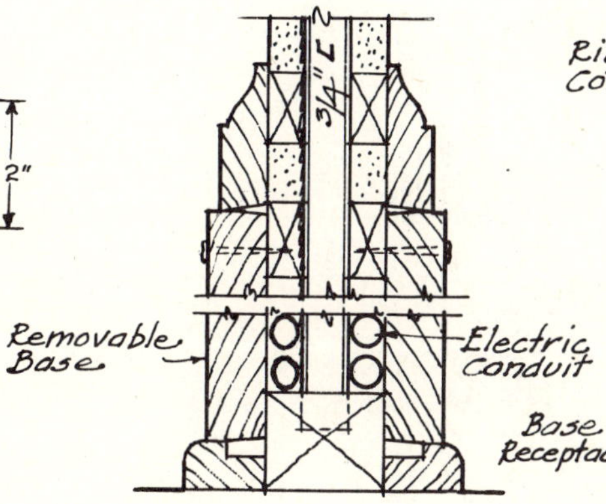
3/4" L
Removable Base
Electric Conduit

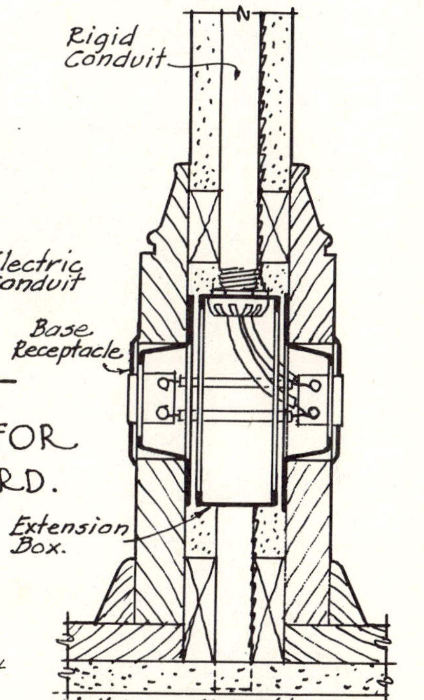
Rigid Conduit
Base Receptacle
Extension Box.

Wall Box with Double Opening.
Scale 3" = 1'-0"

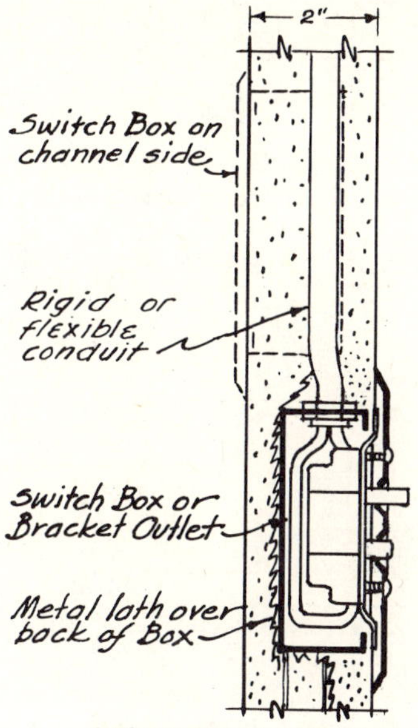
2"
Switch Box on channel side
Rigid or flexible conduit
Switch Box or Bracket Outlet
Metal lath over back of Box

SECTION OF BOX.

Note: These shallow devices are now stocked by Local Dealers - specify them for best results.

SWITCHES OR WALL BRACKETS

RACEWAY WIRING FOR WOOD BASE BOARD.
Scale 3" = 1'-0"

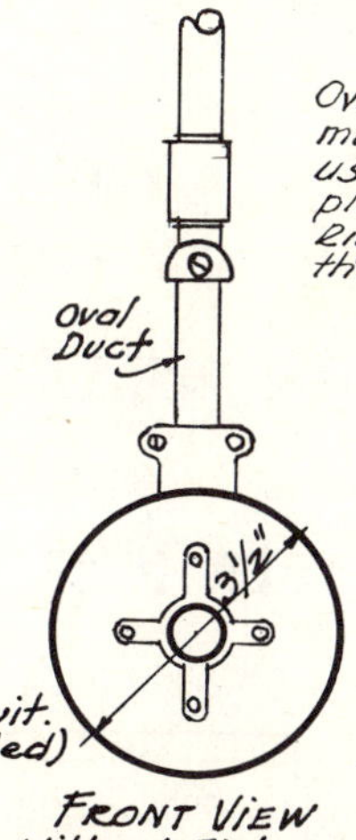
Oval Duct
3½

FRONT VIEW Without Fixture and Plaster.

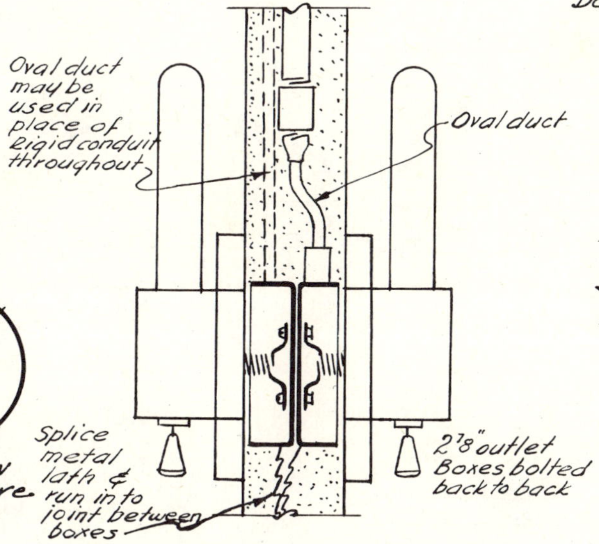
Oval duct may be used in place of rigid conduit throughout
Oval duct
Splice metal lath & run in to joint between boxes
2⅞" outlet Boxes bolted back to back

SECTION & ELEV. OF WALL BRACKET.
Scale 3" = 1'-0"

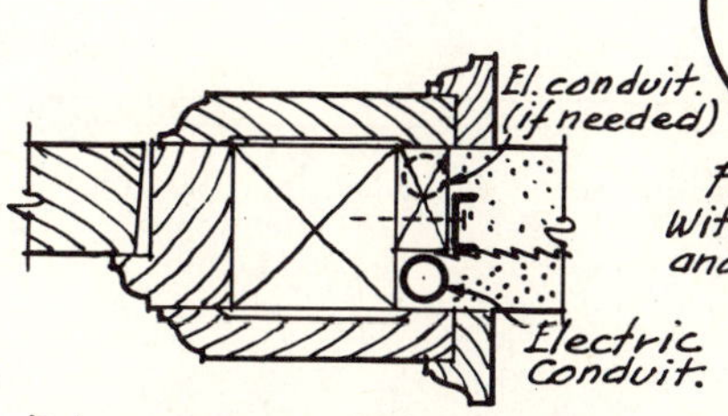
El. conduit. (if needed)
Electric Conduit.

RACEWAY AROUND DOORS
Scale 3" = 1'-0"

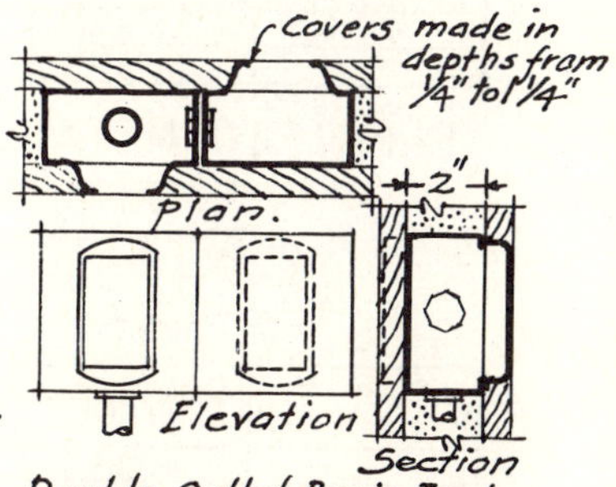
Covers made in depths from ¼" to 1¼"
Plan.
2"
Elevation
Section

Double Outlet Box in Tandem.
Sq. or Octagon Boxes (Std.)
Scale 1½" = 1'-0"

BASE BOARD BOXES

ELECTRICAL WORK IN 2" SOLID LATH & PLASTER PARTITIONS

Data checked by Mangitore & Moesel, Consulting Engineers.

RACEWAYS, CONDUITS and UNDER FLOOR DUCTS

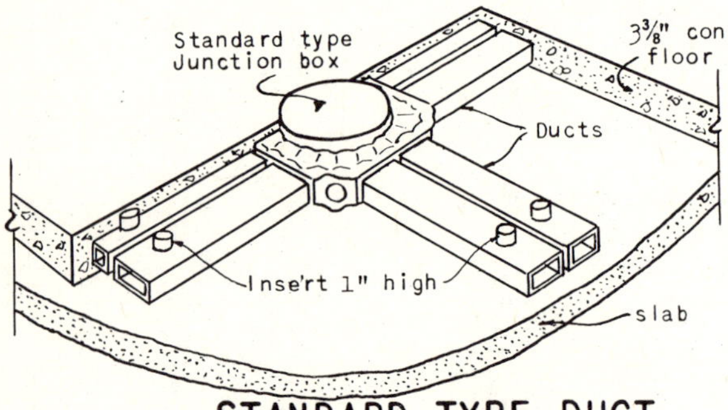
Standard type
Junction box
3⅜" concrete
floor fill min.
Ducts
Insert 1" high
slab

STANDARD TYPE DUCT

Placed on top of structural slab
Duct supports are required if the duct is not placed on top of slab.
Junction boxes are available in the following sizes 3", 2½", flush box & standard heights.

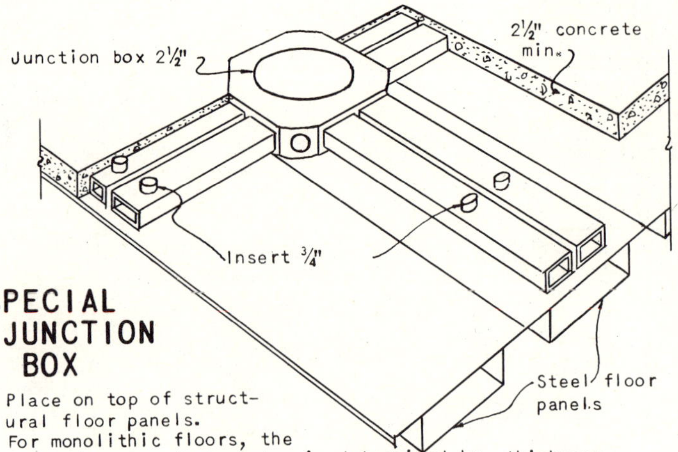
Junction box 2½"
2½" concrete
min.
Insert ¾"
Steel floor
panels

SPECIAL JUNCTION BOX

Place on top of structural floor panels.
For monolithic floors, the type of proper duct system is determined by thickness of slab, the supporting steel or beam structure & the location of reinforcing.

Data supplied by Walker Bros.

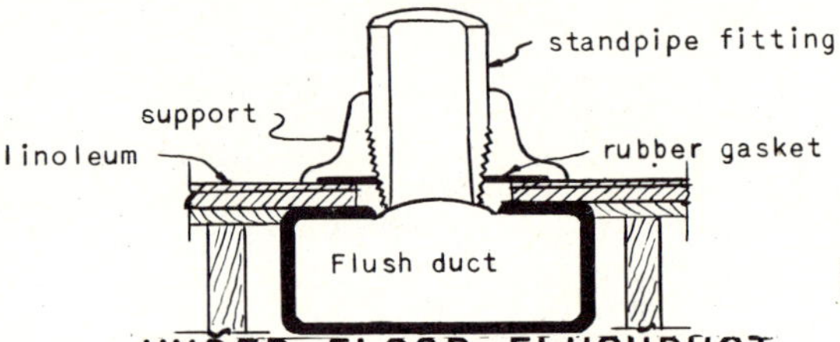
standpipe fitting
support
linoleum
rubber gasket
Flush duct

UNDER FLOOR FLUSHDUCT

Data supplied by Walker Bros.

STEEL UNDER FLOOR DUCTS

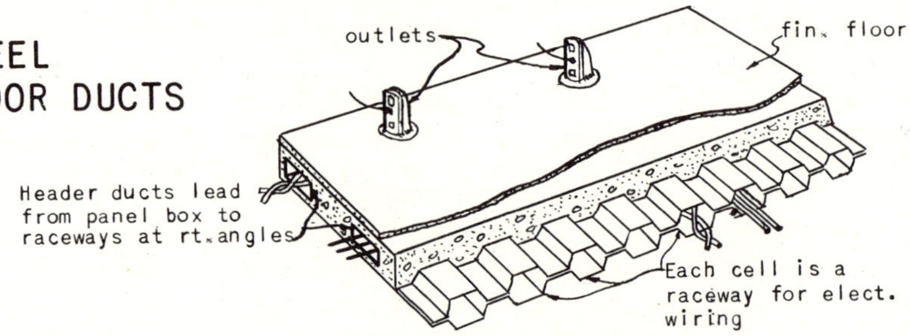
outlets
fin. floor
Header ducts lead
from panel box to
raceways at rt. angles
Each cell is a
raceway for elect.
wiring

Data supplied by H.H. Robertson Co.
"Q FLOOR"

Nom.	O.D.
1"	1.315
2"	2.375
3"	3.50
4"	4.50

STANDARD ELEC. CONDUITS

Preset insert

Fiber duct installed in concrete slab & available with or without factory set inserts.
Single duct junction boxes, 9⅛" sq. & 2⁹⁄₁₆" high.

Sizes in inches	Diameter internal	Diameter external	Wall thickness
⅜"	0.493	0.577	0.042
½"	0.622	0.706	0.042
¾"	0.824	0.922	0.049
1"	1.049	1.163	0.057
1¼"	1.380	1.510	0.065
1½"	1.610	1.740	0.065
2"	2.067	2.197	0.065

ELECTRIC METALLIC TUBING

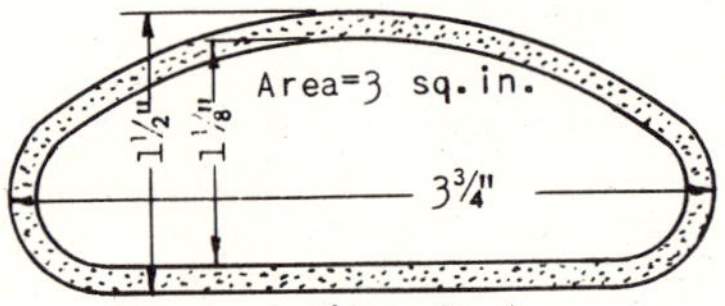
Area=3 sq. in.
1½"
1⅛"
3¾"

Standard Fiber Duct

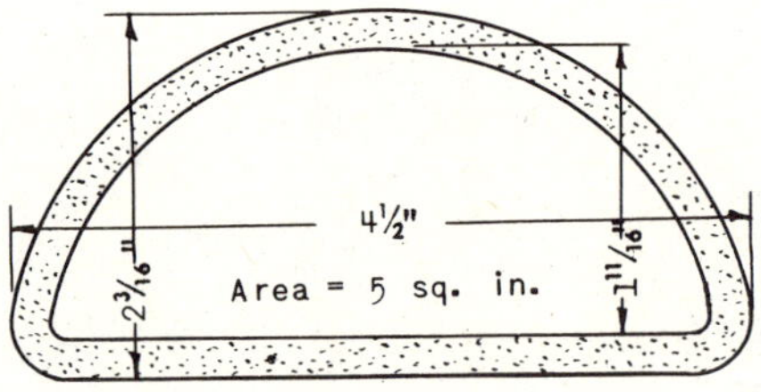
4½"
Area = 5 sq. in.
2³⁄₁₆"
1¹¹⁄₁₆"

Large Fiber Duct

Both fiber ducts made by General Electric Co. & Orangeburg Manufacturing Co. Inc.

FIBER DUCT

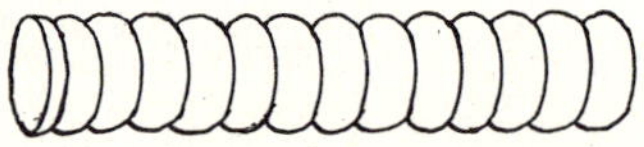

Sizes in inches	approx. diameter inside	outside	thickness of steel strip
⅜	0.383	0.610	0.034
½	0.638	0.910	0.040
¾	0.829	1.090	0.040
1	1.020	1.370	0.055
1¼	1.275	1.600	0.055
1½	1.530	1.940	0.060
2	2.040	2.420	0.060
2½	2.550	3.000	0.060
3	3.060	3.350	0.060

FLEXIBLE CONDUITS

STEEL DUCTS

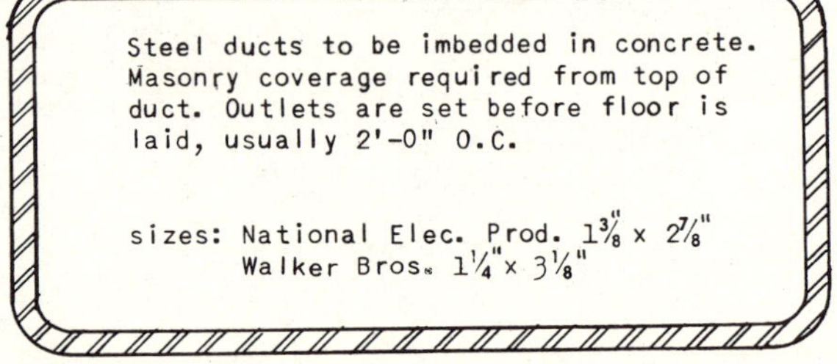

Steel ducts to be imbedded in concrete. Masonry coverage required from top of duct. Outlets are set before floor is laid, usually 2'-0" O.C.

sizes: National Elec. Prod. 1⅜ x 2⅞"
Walker Bros. 1¼" x 3⅛"

Data checked by Mongitore & Moesel

ELECTRIC LIGHT BULBS

A TYPE - General Lighting

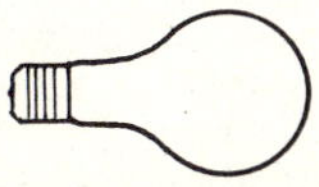

15 - 150 watts
Standard shape

WATTS	DIA.	LENGTH	BASE	BULB
15	1 7/8	3 1/2	Med.	A-15
25	2 3/8	3 15/16	Med.	A-19
40	2 3/8	4 1/4	Med.	A-19
50	2 3/8	4 7/16	Med.	A-19
60	2 3/8	4 7/16	Med.	A-19
60*	2 3/8	4 7/16	Med.	A-19
75	2 3/8	4 7/16	Med.	A-19
100	2 5/8	5 5/16	Med.	A-21
100*	2 7/8	6 1/16	Med.	A-23
150	2 7/8	6 5/16	Med.	A-23

*Daylight type

PS TYPE - General Lighting

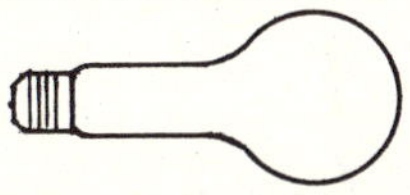

150-1500 Watts
Pear shape

WATTS	DIA.	LENGTH	BASE	BULB
150	3 1/8	6 15/16	Med.	PS-25
200	3 3/4	8 1/16	Med.	PS-30
300	3 3/4	8 1/16	Med.	PS-30
300	4 3/8	9 3/8	Mog.	PS-35
300	4 3/8	9 7/8	Med.Skt.	PS-35
500	5	9 3/4	Mog.	PS-40
750	6 1/2	13 1/16	Mog.	PS-52
1000	6 1/2	13 1/16	Mog.	PS-52
1500	6 1/2	13 1/16	Mog.	PS-52

REFLECTORS & PROJECTORS

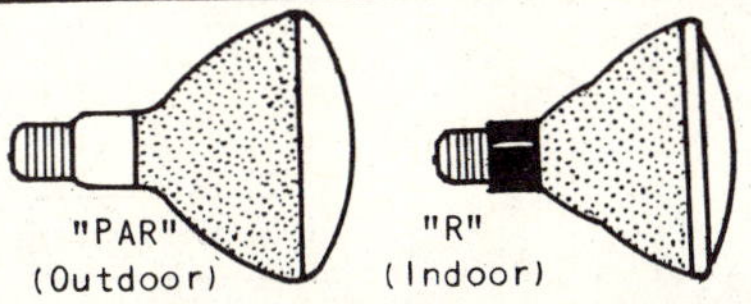
"PAR"
(Outdoor)
"R"
(Indoor)

WATTS	DIA.	LGTH	BASE	BULB	TYPE
75	3 3/4	5 3/16	Med.	R-30	Spot
75	3 3/4	5 3/16	Med.	R-30	Flood
150	5	6 1/2	Med.	R-40	Spot
150	5	6 1/2	Med.	R-40	Flood
150*	4 3/4	5 5/16	Med.Skt	PAR-38	Spot
150*	4 3/4	5 5/16	Med.Skt	PAR-38	Flood
300	5	6 1/2	Med.	R-40	Spot
300	5	6 1/2	Med.	R-40	Flood
500*	5	7 1/4	Mog.	R-40	Spot
500*	5	7 1/4	Mog.	R-40	Flood

*Outdoor

SCREW BASES

B

Skirted type base

TYPE	SIZE "B"
Candelabra	1/2
Intermediate	5/8
Medium	1
Mogul	1 1/2

FLUORESCENT

STANDARD PREHEAT

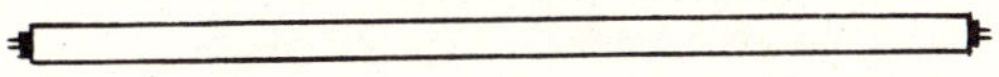

Daylight white | Soft white, Std. cool white, Std. Warm white | Deluxe cool white, Deluxe warm white

WATTS	LENGTH	DIA.	BASE	BULB
4	6	5/8	Min. Bipin	T-5
6	9	5/8	Min. Bipin	T-5
8	12	5/8	Min. Bipin	T-5
13	21	5/8	Min. Bipin	T-5
14	15	1 1/2	Med. Bipin	T-12
15	18	1	Med. Bipin	T-8
15	18	1 1/2	Med. Bipin	T-12
20	24	1 1/2	Med. Bipin	T-12
25	33	1 1/2	Med. Bipin	T-12
30	36	1	Med. Bipin	T-8
40	48	1 1/2	Med. Bipin	T-12
40*	60	2 1/8	Mog. Bipin	T-17
90	60	2 1/8	Mog. Bipin	T-17
100	60	2 1/8	Mog. Bipin	T-17
100**	96	1 1/2	Recessed D.C.	T-12

* Also available in rapid start.
** High output rapid start.
Note: All above lamps 30 watts and under when equipped with "trigger-start" ballasts use no starters and have rapid starting characteristics.

SLIMLINE - Instant Starting

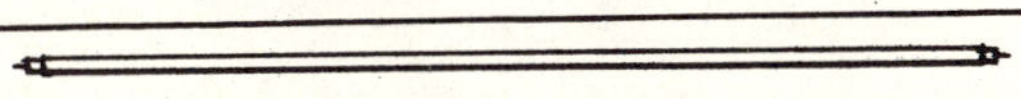

Daylight White | Soft White, Std. Cool White, Std. Warm White | Deluxe cool white, Deluxe warm white

WATTS*	LENGTH	DIA.	BASE	BULB
17.5 / 25.0 / 32.5	42	3/4	Single Pin	T-6
25.5 / 37 / 48	64	3/4	Single Pin	T-6
24.5 / 36.5 / 48.5	72	3/4	Single Pin	T-6
32 / 49 / 65	96	3/4	Single Pin	T-6
38	48	1 1/2	Single Pin	T-12
55	72	1 1/2	Single Pin	T-12
74	96	1 1/2	Single Pin	T-12

*Where more than one wattage is given, lower is for 120 MA operation, middle is for 200 MA operation and highest is for 300 MA operation. Where single wattage is shown lamp operates at 430 MA.

CIRCLINE

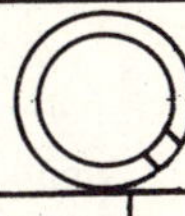

Std. Cool White, Std. Warm White, Daylight* | Deluxe Cool White, Deluxe Warm White

WATTS	BULB DIA.	DIA.	BASE	BULB
22	1 1/8	8 1/4	4-Pin	T-9
32	1 1/4	12	4-Pin	T-10
40	1 1/4	16	4-Pin	T-10

*Available in 32 watt only.

DECORATIVE & SPECIAL

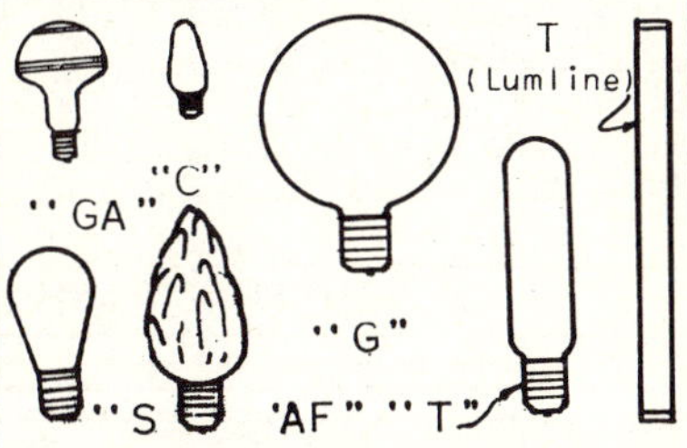
T
(Lumline)
"GA"
"C"
"G"
"S
'AF"
"T"

WATTS	DIA.	LENGTH	BASE	BULB
6	1 3/4	3 1/2	Med.	S-14
7	7/8	2 1/8	Cand.	C-7
7 1/2	1 3/8	2 1/4	Med.	S-11
10	1 3/8	2 5/16	Inter.	S-11
10	1 3/4	3 1/2	Med.	S-14
15	1 1/4	3 1/16	Cand.	F-10
15	1 1/4	3 1/8	Inter.	F-10
25	1 7/8	4 1/2	Med.	F-15
25	2 1/16	3	Cand.	G-16 1/2
25	3 1/8	4 7/16	Med.	G-25
25	1 1/4	5 5/8	Med.	T-10
25	13/16	5 1/2	Inter.	T-6 1/2
30	1	17 3/4	Disc.	T-8
40	1 7/8	4 1/2	Med.	F-15
40	3 1/8	4 7/16	Med.	G-25
40	1	11 3/4	Disc.	T-8
40	1	11 7/8	Med.	T-8
40	1 1/4	5 5/8	Med.	T-10
50	2 1/8	4 7/16	Med.	GA-25
60	1	17 3/4	Disc.	T-8
100	3 3/4	66 3/16	Med.	GA-30

THREE-WAY LAMPS

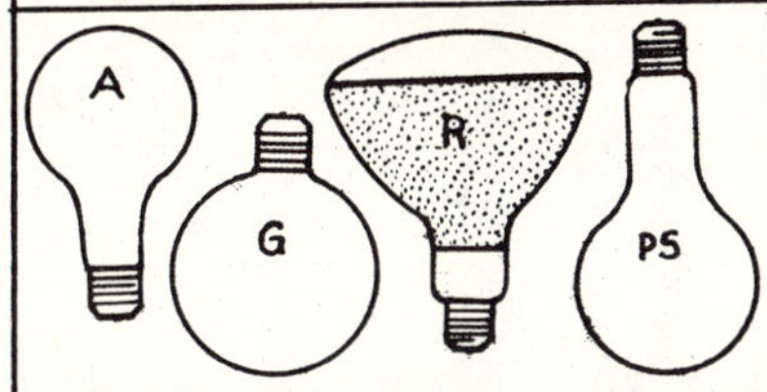
A
G
R
PS

WATTS	DIA.	LENGTH	3-WAY BASE	BULB
30-70-100	2 5/8	5 5/16	Med.	A-21
50-100-150	3 1/8	5 15/16	Med.	PS-25
50-100-150	3 1/8	6 13/16	Mog.	PS-25
50-100-150	5	6 1/8	Med.	R-40
100-200-300	3 3/4	6 3/4	Mog.	G-30

GENERAL NOTES

Sizes given are nominal, in inches. Length = maximum overall length in inches. Number after lamp shape symbol = number of eighths of an inch in diameter (PS-30). Standard voltage of 115 to 125 is assumed.

All fluorescent lamps require auxiliary equipment. Wattages of slimline lamps vary with different manufacturers.

DATA PREPARED BY:
MONGITORE & MOESEL,
CONSULTING ENGINEERS, N.Y.C.

COLD CATHODE TUBE LIGHTING

Cold cathode lamps are fluorescent lamps with iron cathodes that require no preheating. They are particularly applicable to outdoor use because their operation is not affected by low temperatures or high humidity as are other types of fluorescent lamps. Longevity of these lamps is in excess of 10,000 hrs., a feature making them useful in high or luminous ceilings or in difficult to service locations. Lamps should be changed by prearrangement when 10,000 burning hours are passed. At end of this economic life, lamps do not burn out, but light output is reduced by 32%. Initial costs of cold cathode installations are not necessarily higher than regular fluorescent lamps. Cold cathode lighting may be used in residential work, but series installations generally require prior approval by the National Board of Fire Underwriters, whose recommendations are almost universally incorporated in local building codes throughout the United States.

STANDARD LAMPS

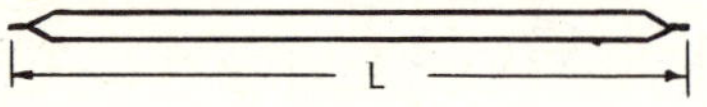
L

COLORS AVAILABLE:

Warmtone	Soft White	Pink
Warm White	Daylight	Gold
3500° White	Blue	Red
	Green	

F.L.A. LAMP TYPE*	LENGTH "L" IN INCHES**	DIAM. IN INCHES	MAX. OP. CURRENT-M.A.†
2045	45	3/4	150
2545	45	1	200
3545	45	1½	240
2069	69	3/4	150
2569	69	1	200
3569	69	1¼	240
2093	93	3/4	150
2593	93	1	200
3593	93	1½	240

*Standard lamps also available in 52", 64" 72" and 84" lengths with above diameters and operating currents.

**Nominal lengths with sockets for these lamps are 48", 72" and 96".

†Operating currents are controlled by ballast or transformer used. Standards are from 50 MA to values listed.

ILLUMINATION DATA

CURRENT M. A.	LUMENS PER FOOT	LAMP WATTS PER FOOT
50	163	3.15
120	310	5.25
150	370	6.38
200	425	7.50
240	456	8.25

Above data based on 96° warmtone lamps.

SPECIAL LAMPS ‡

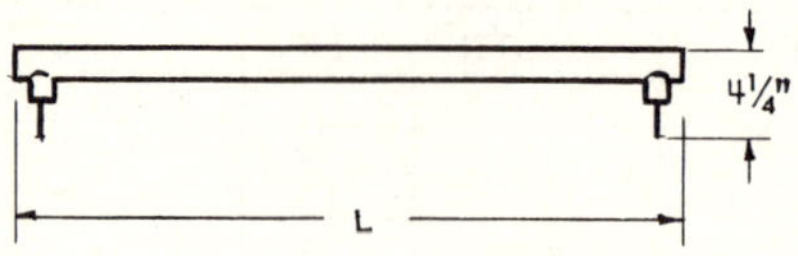
4¼"
L

1. Available in all standard colors
2. Length "L" available in any dimension up to max. 96"
3. Diameters of lamps available are ¾", 1" and 1½".

CUSTOM RIGHT ANGLE LAMP

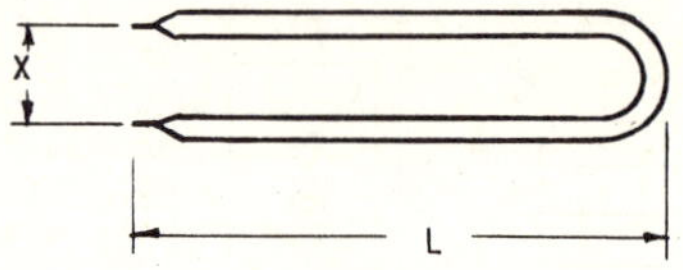
X
L

1. Available in all standard colors
2. Length "L" available in any dimension up to max. 45"
3. Normal electrode spacing "x" is 6". Other spacings available.
4. Diameters of lamps available are ¾", 1" and 1½".

HAIR PIN LAMP

‡All special shapes available in standard lamp diameters and colors.

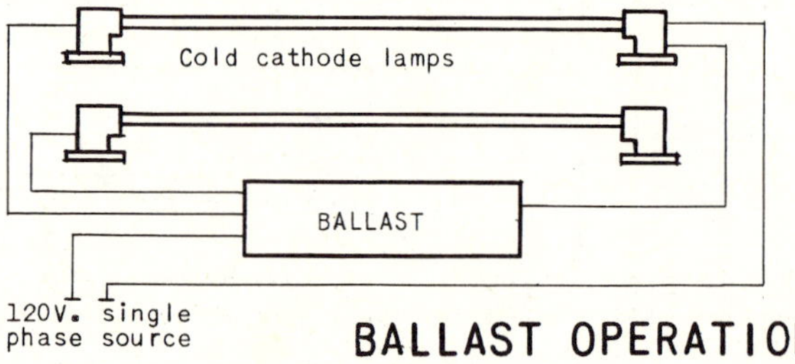
Cold cathode lamps
BALLAST
120V. single phase source

NOTE
Maximum ballast size is 14" long, 3⅛" wide, 2⅝" high.

BALLAST OPERATION

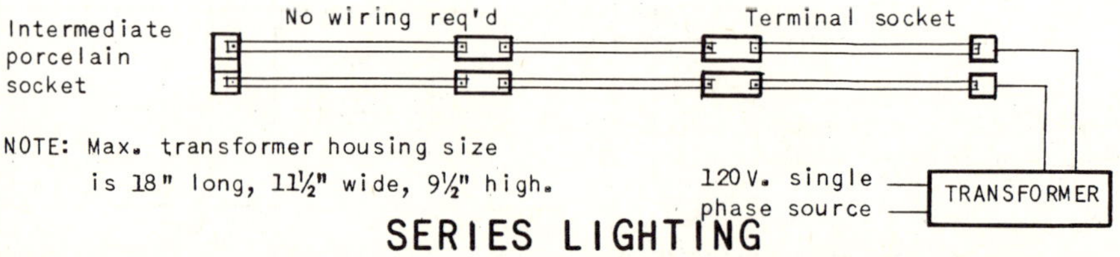
Intermediate porcelain socket
No wiring req'd
Terminal socket
120V. single phase source
TRANSFORMER

NOTE: Max. transformer housing size is 18" long, 11½" wide, 9½" high.

SERIES LIGHTING

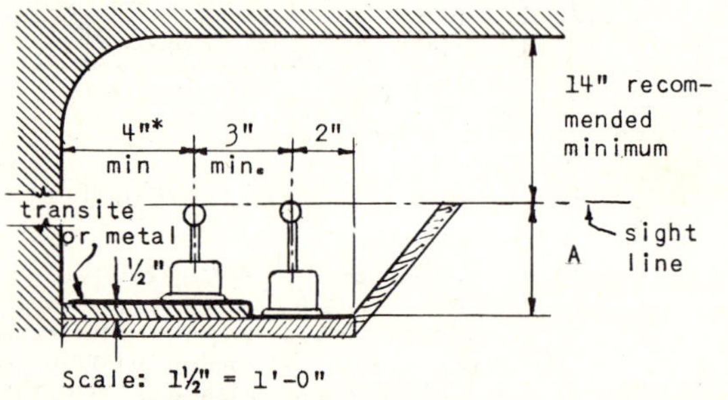
4"*
min
3"
min.
2"
14" recommended minimum
transite or metal
½"
A
sight line
Scale: 1½" = 1'-0"

NOTE

① "A" dimension for straight electrodes = 3¾" for 1½" diameter lamps; 3½" for 1" diameter lamps; 3⅜" for ¾" diameter lamps

② "A" dimension for custom right angle electrodes = 5½" for 1½" diameter lamps; 5¼" for 1" diameter lamps; 5⅛" for ¾" diameter lamps

③ Dimension marked * should not be reduced

COVE DETAIL

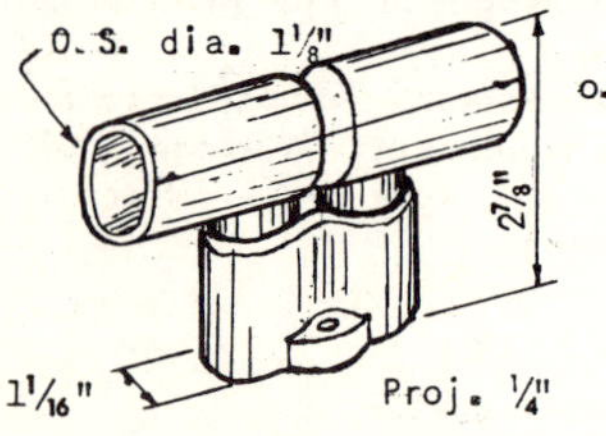
O.S. dia. 1⅛"
2⅞"
1¹⁄₁₆"
Proj. ¼"

JACK TYPE
(for straight lamps)

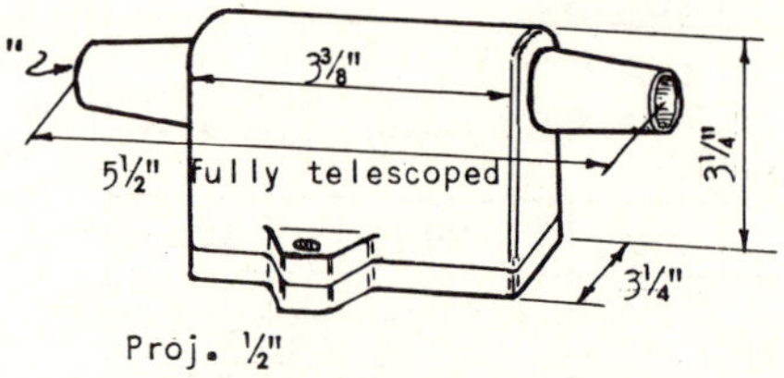
o.s.dia. 1"
3⅜"
5½" fully telescoped
3¼"
3¼"
Proj. ½"

TELESCOPING TYPE
(for straight lamps)

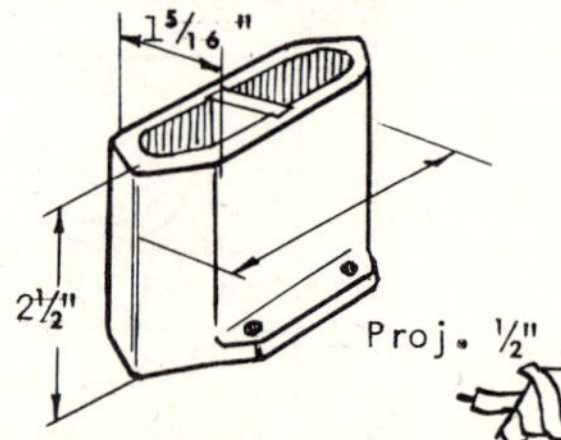
1⁵⁄₁₆"
2½"
Proj. ½"

CUSTOM TYPE
(for right angle lamps)

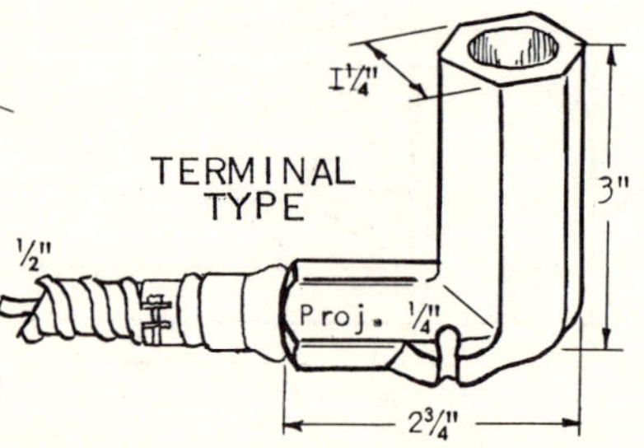
1¼"
3"
Proj. ¼"
2¾"

TERMINAL TYPE

TYPICAL SOCKETS

DATA FURNISHED BY COLD CATHODE LIGHTING CORP.; CHECKED BY MONGITORE & MOESEL, CONSULTING ENGINEERS, N.Y.C.

APARTMENT HOUSE MAIL BOXES

FINISHES

Sprayed brass is stock and standard. Other sprayed polished, and plated finishes to order are extra.

POST OFFICE REGULATIONS

Max. ht. from floor to center of gov't master lock (supplied by P.O. Dept. after boxes are installed) = 66". Arrange gauge so that min. no. of gov't locks are used. Supply alphabetical directory of all persons receiving mail in installations of 25 receptacles or more.

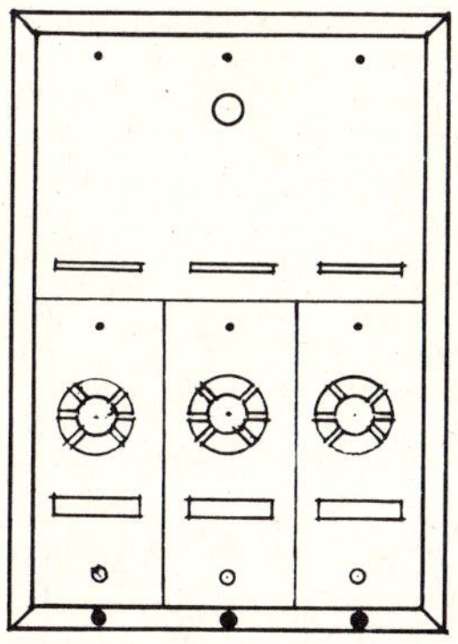

Plain or with bell buttons on mail box trim.

PLAIN OR BELL BUTTON

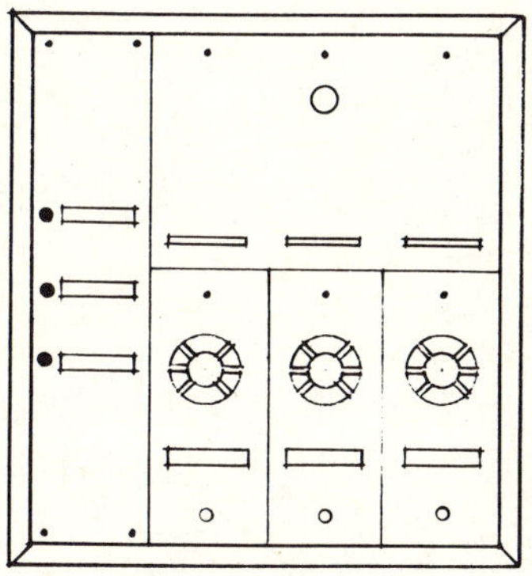

Bell buttons placed in separate compartment. 1 compartment/20 buttons.

SIDE DIRECTORY

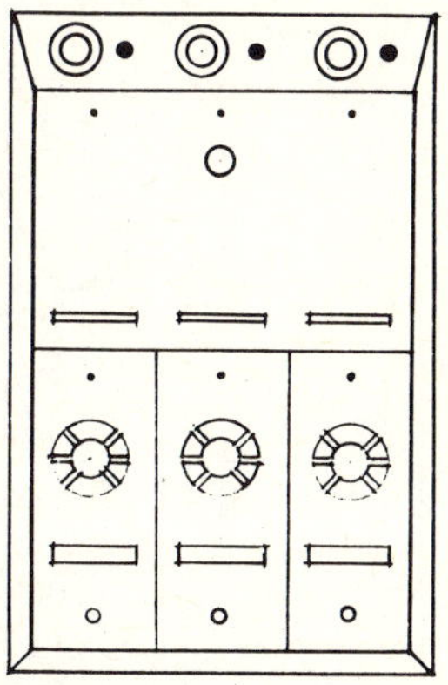

Bell buttons and speaking tubes above upper trim.

TOP SPEAKING TUBE.

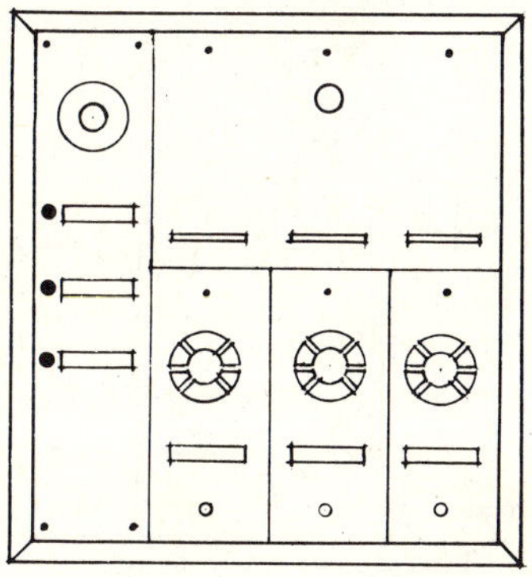

Bell buttons & common speaking tube in separate compartment.

SIDE PHONE SYSTEM

Gov't approved mail boxes are made in 3-12 units inclusive to a gang, each gang provide with mounting for a gov't master lock. Where push buttons are located in separate compartment, it is in a space which would have been used by a tenant box. Additional equip. (teleph., spk'g tube, etc.) usually requires 2 tenants space for up to 32 buttons & 1 additional space for the next 20 buttons or fraction thereof. Single Row mounting indicates gangs are placed in a line beside one another. In Double Row mounting, gangs are one above another. If 25 or more receptacles are used (see Post Office Regulations) push buttons may be integrated with alphabetical directory instead of with mail-boxes. Various call systems are grouped to occupy 2 tenant boxes. In specifications mail boxes are usually placed under Electrical Work if bell buttons or signal systems are incorporated.

NARROWEST M'F'R'D	11½"	14¾"	18"	21¼"	24½"	27¾"	31 1/16"	34 5/16"	37½"	40¾"
UNITS PER GANG	3	4	5	6	7	8	9	10	11	12
WIDEST M'F'R'D	12⅝"	16"	19½"	23"	26½"	30"	33½"	37"	40½"	44"

height 16½" min. 17⅛" max.

Most manufacturers make mail-boxes closer in dimensions to the max. shown above. When row mounting, either single or double, to determine space requirement, add the overall dim. given of gang sizes used.

TYPES AND SPACE REQUIREMENTS

Sections

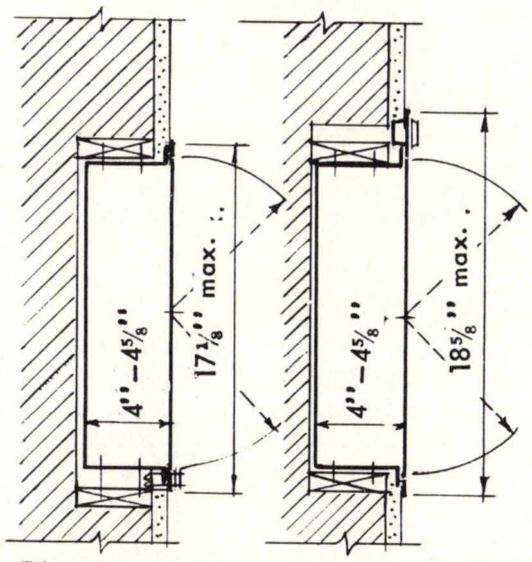

4"–4⅝"
17⅛" max.
4"–4⅝"
18⅝" max.

Plain or with bell-buttons

Speaking tube mouth piece.

SINGLE ROW

Single row mounting only for speak tube type is usual, check local code. For allowable depth of wall cut-out.

Section

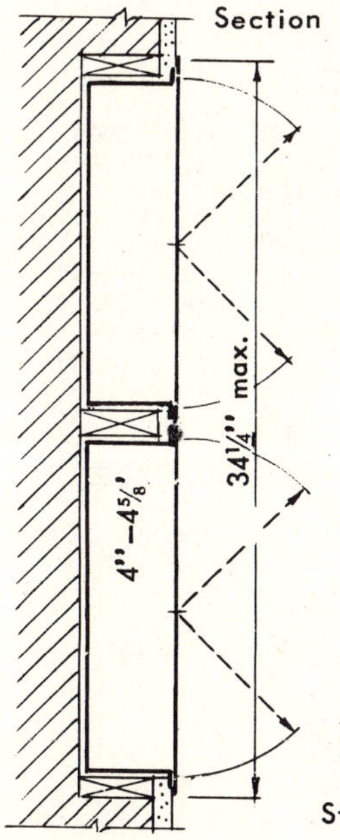

4"–4⅝"
34¼" max.

Plain

DOUBLE ROW

FLUSH MOUNTED MAIL BOXES

Scale 1" = 1'-0"

For specific sizes and wall cutout req'd see cat's of signaling system; metal specialties mfrs.

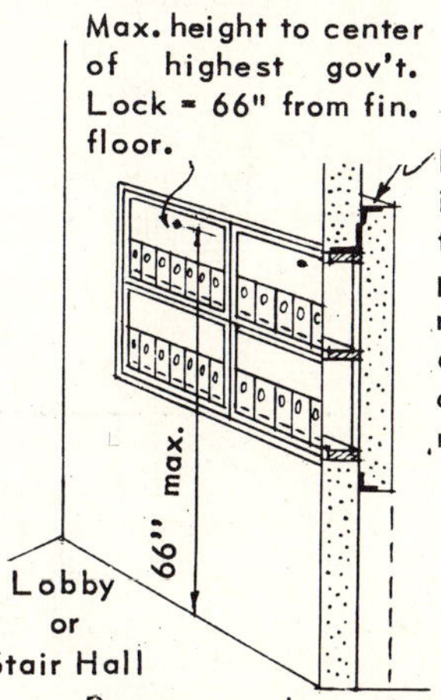

Max. height to center of highest gov't. Lock = 66" from fin. floor.
Fire-proofing wall (same thickness as partition) when req'd by bldg. code. Maybe cont'd. to fl. if nec.
66" max.
Lobby or Stair Hall

Boxes may be projected out to decrease back projection.

THIN PARTITIONS

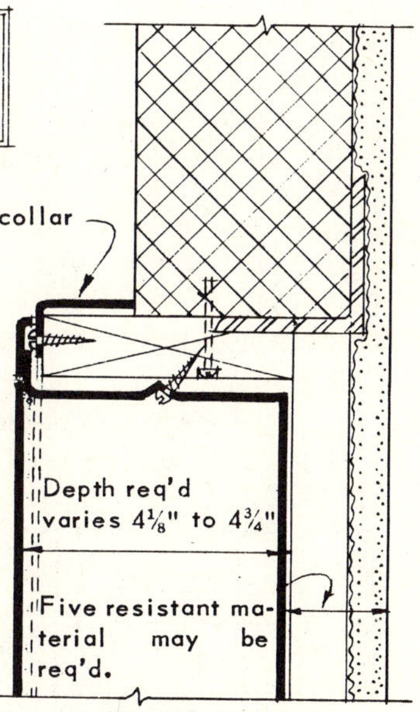

Brass collar
Depth req'd varies 4⅛" to 4¾"
Five resistant material may be req'd.

Fire proofing of this type may be allowed by some code.

PROJECTING BOXES

Scale 3" = 1'-0"

TELEPHONES

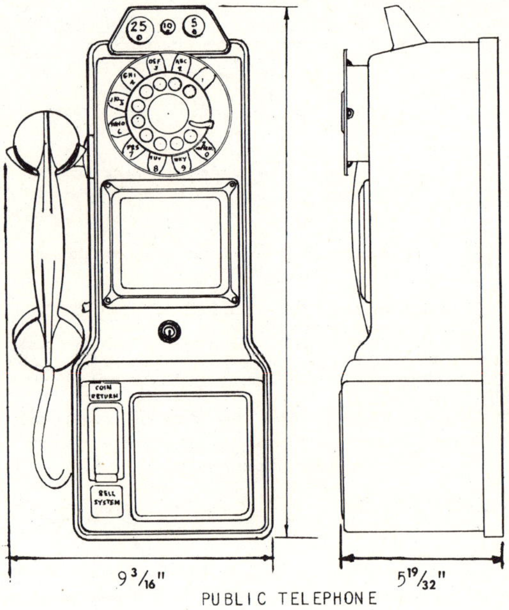
9 3/16"
5 19/32"

PUBLIC TELEPHONE

5"
7 1/2"

Hand Telephone Set

5 1/2"
9"

Six Button

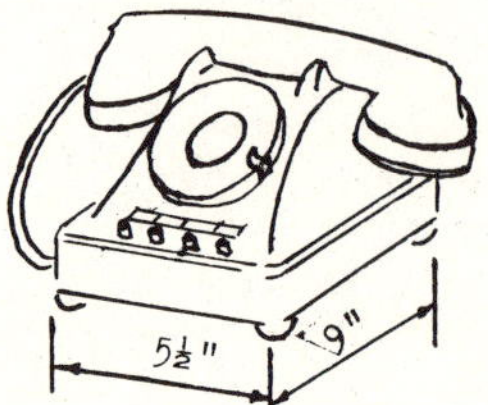
5 1/2"
9"

Four Button

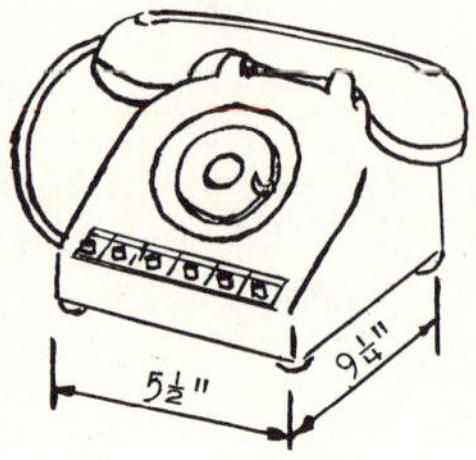
5 1/2"
9 1/4"

Six Button

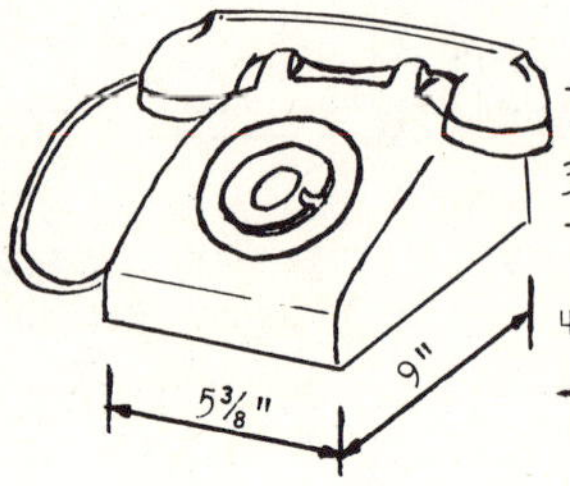
5 3/8"
9"

Combined Set

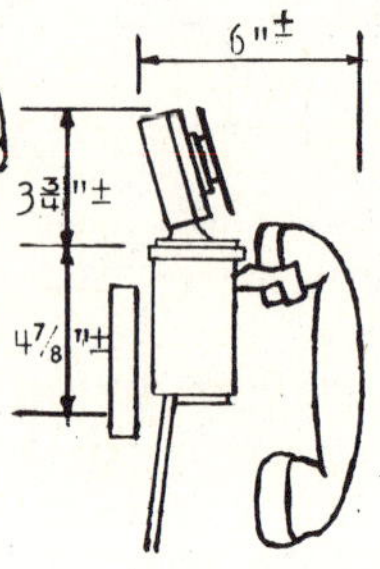
6"±
3 3/4"±
4 7/8"±

HANGING TYPE

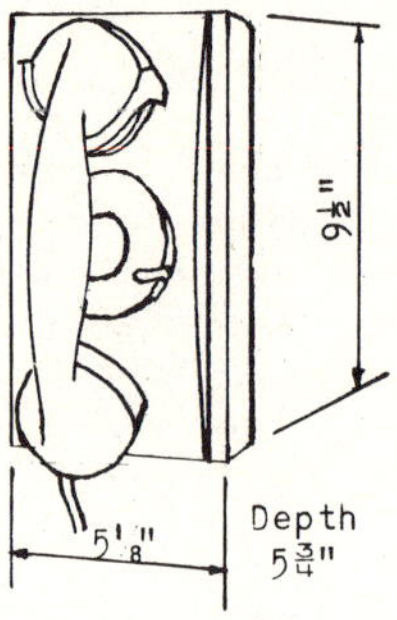
9 1/2"
5 1/8"
Depth
5 3/4"

WALL TYPE

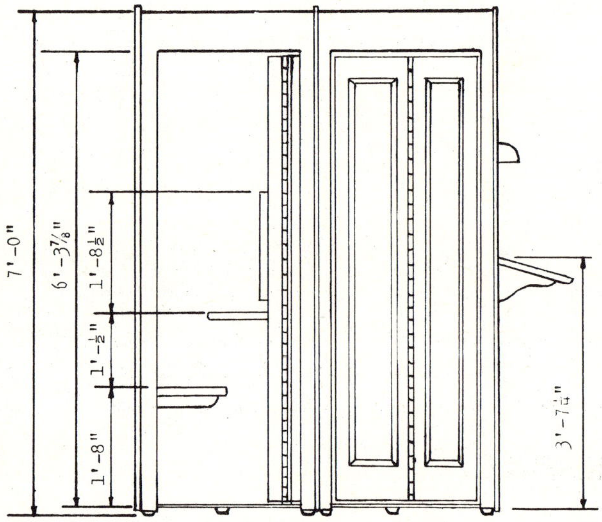
7'-0"
6'-3 7/8"
1'-8 1/2"
1'-1/2"
1'-8"
3'-7 1/4"

open closed
TELEPHONE BOOTHS

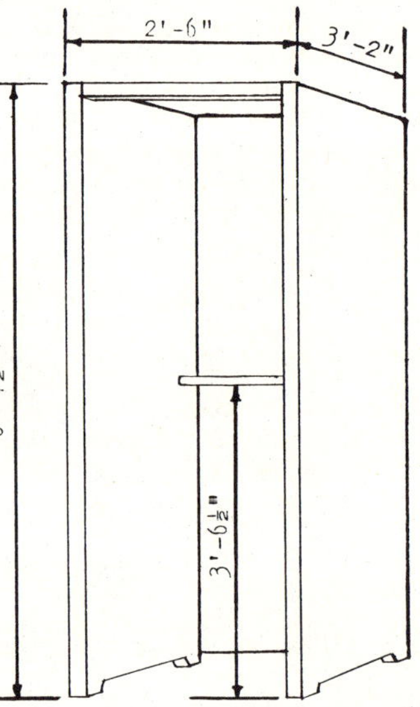
2'-6"
3'-2"
6'-7 1/2"
3'-6 1/2"

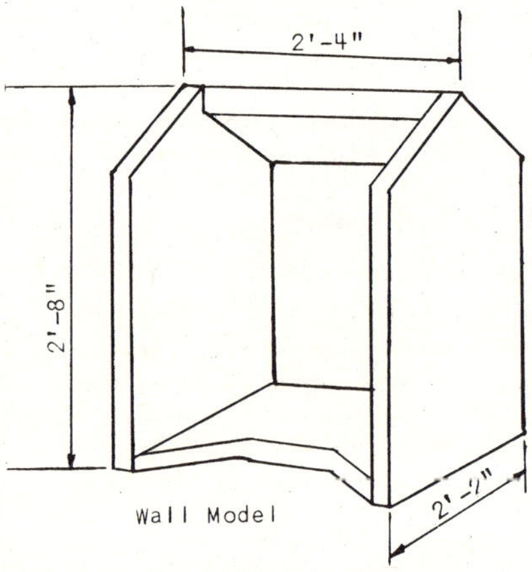
2'-4"
2'-8"
2'-4"

Wall Model

Floor & wall models made in wood & steel

Interior surfaces perforated

ACOUSTICAL TELEPHONE BOOTHS
Data supplied by Burgess-Manning Co.

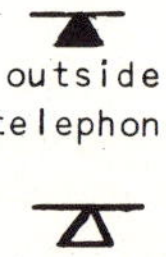

outside telephone

interconnecting telephone

CONVENTIONS

6 1/8"x 9 1/4" & 9"x11"

TELEPHONE BOOK SIZES

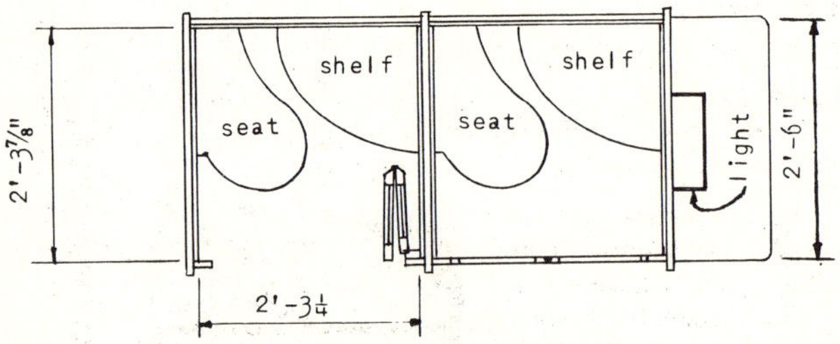
shelf
shelf
seat
seat
light
2'-3 7/8"
2'-6"
2'-3 1/4

PLAN OF TELEPHONE BOOTHS

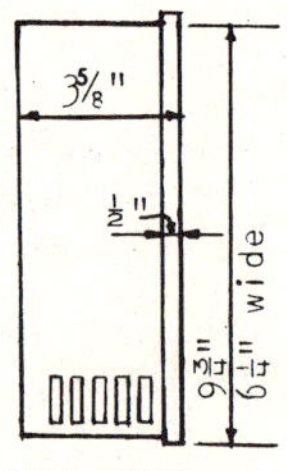
3 5/8"
1/2"
9 3/4"
6 1/4"
wide

BELL BOX

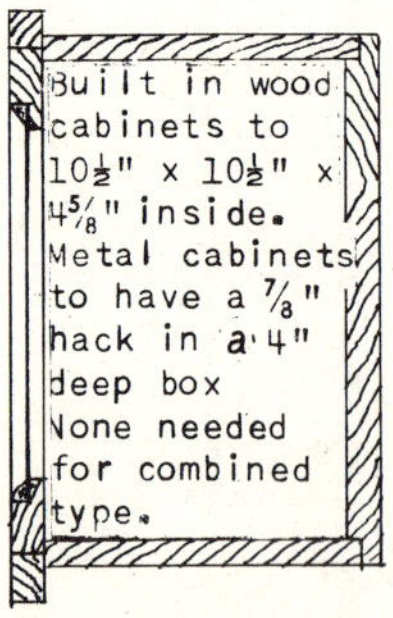
Built in wood
cabinets to
10 1/2" x 10 1/2" x
4 5/8" inside.
Metal cabinets
to have a 7/8"
hack in a 4"
deep box
None needed
for combined
type.

BELL BOX CABINET

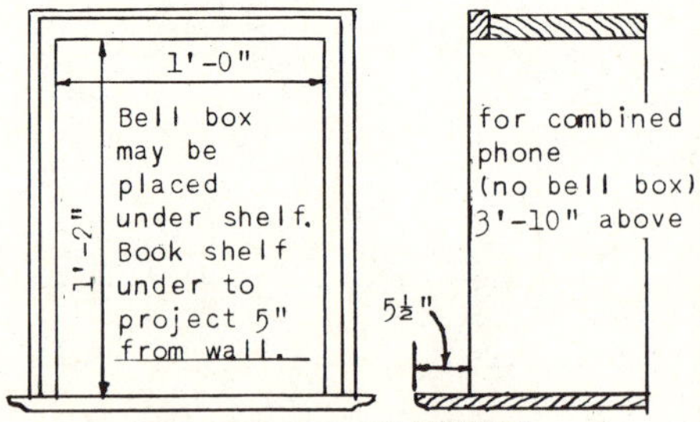
1'-0"
1'-2"
Bell box
may be
placed
under shelf.
Book shelf
under to
project 5"
from wall.
for combined
phone
(no bell box)
3'-10" above
5 1/2"

CABINETS FOR TELEPHONES

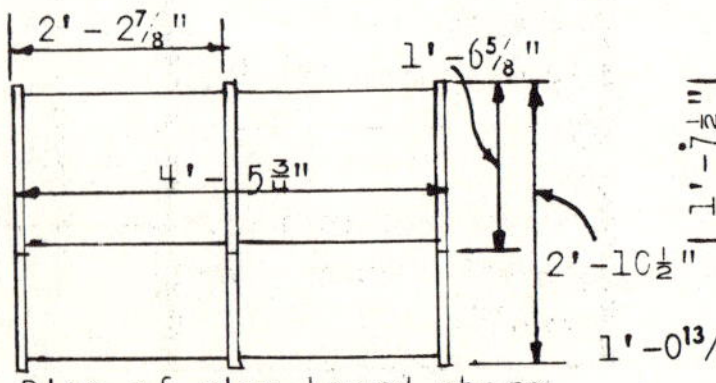
2'-2 7/8"
1'-6 5/8"
4'-5 3/4"
2'-10 1/2"
1'-0 13/16"

Plan of plug board where more than one is required.

Data checked by American Telephone & Telegraph Co.

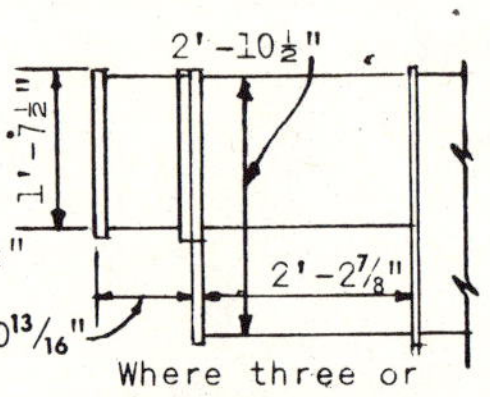
2'-10 1/2"
1'-7 1/2"
2'-2 7/8"

Where three or more boards are together a distribution frame is required.

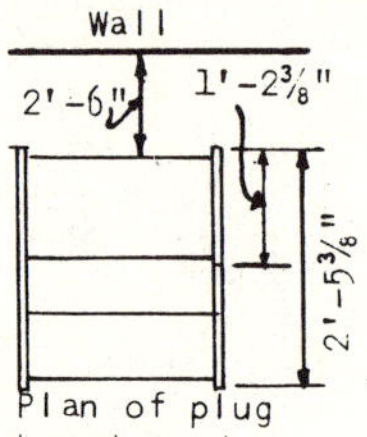
Wall
2'-6"
1'-2 3/8"
2'-5 3/8"

Plan of plug board used singly.

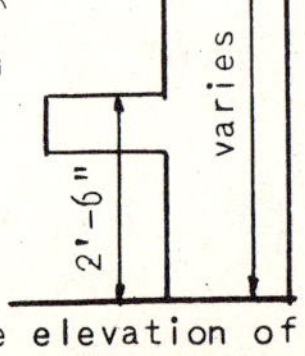
varies
2'-6"

Side elevation of plug switch board

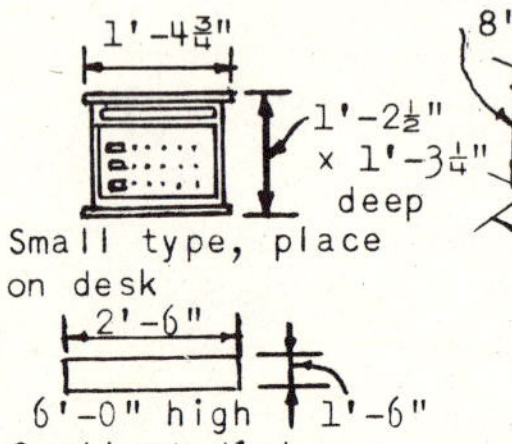
1'-4 3/4"
1'-2 1/2"
x 1'-3 1/4"
deep
2'-6"
1'-6"

Small type, place on desk

6'-0" high
Smallest dial branch exch.

8"
19"
13 1/4"
&
19 1/4"

Cordless private branch exchange switchboard

TELEVISION RECEIVERS, VIEWING ANGLES, ANTENNA

T-V RECEIVERS - NOMINAL SIZES

TUBE SIZE	HEIGHT	WIDTH	DEPTH
TABLE MODEL			
17"	15"-20½"	18⅛"-22⅝"	17¾"-20½"
21"	19¼"-24½"	22¾"-27"	20¾"-23"
24"	25⅞"	25⅞"	23⅜"
CONSOLETTE			
21"	35"-38⅝"	22¾"-26¾"	20¾"-22¼"
24"	39½"	25⅞"	23⅜"
CONSOLE			
21"	35⅛"-39¼"	26¾"-36⅝"	22"-24½"
24"	38½"-41"	30"-36¼"	22⅞"-26⅝"
30"	47½"	49¾"	27¼"
COLOR CONSOLETTE			
21"	37½"-37⅞"	32⅝"	27"-27¾"

Note: There are other black and white tube size receivers on the market but the 17", 21" and 24" sets are most popular. The 30" console is the largest comm. mfrd.

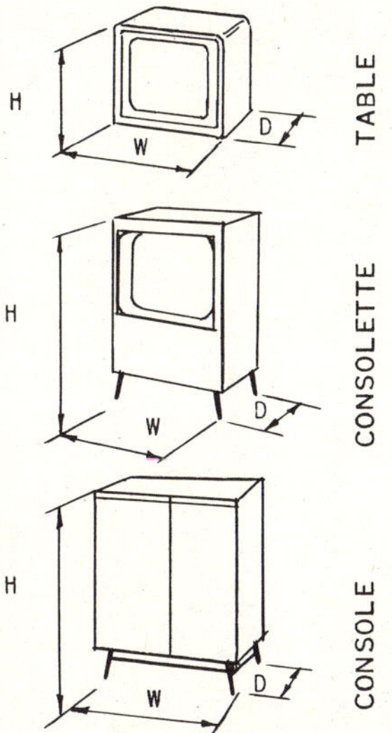
H
W
D
TABLE
CONSOLETTE
CONSOLE

Note: some sets have a 3" to 5" proj. behind cabinet housing small end of pic. tube.

T-V RECEIVER

APPROX. VIEWING DISTANCE TO RECEIVER*

TUBE SIZE	HT. OF PICTURE	MIN. DISTANCE	OPTIMUM DISTANCE	MAX. DISTANCE
17"	11½"	3'-10"	5'-9"	9'-7"
21"	13½"	4'-6"	6'-9"	11'-3"
24"	17"	5'-8"	8'-6"	14'-2"

* Distance approx. since ht. of picture varies with mfr. Also viewer preferences vary. For other size tubes min. = 4 times, optimum 6 times & max. 10 times picture ht. Color T-V increases max. to 12 times ht. of picture.

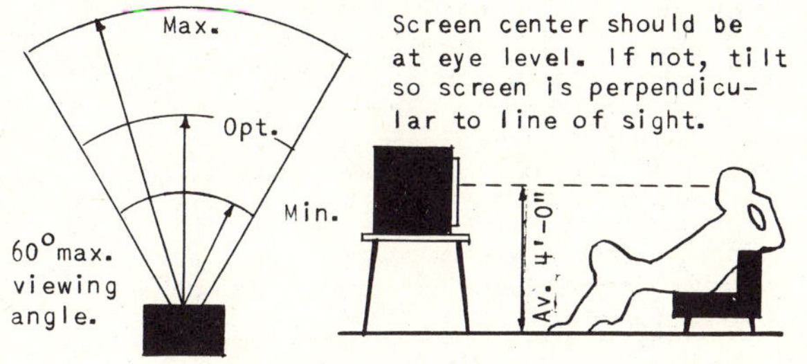
Max.
Opt.
Min.
60° max. viewing angle.
Screen center should be at eye level. If not, tilt so screen is perpendicular to line of sight.
Av. 4'-0"

VIEWING COMFORT

RECOMMENDATIONS ON LIGHTING: Television should be viewed in a dimmed room. Total darkness increases intensity of screen and is tiring. Recessed lighting above set and directed on ceiling is best. Direct lighting should be kept out of viewing area; if not, it may reflect light from the screen.

Note: The following data is supplied for architectural guidance. Selection of antenna and related equipment, its location and installation should be left to mfrs.' service company or its authorized dealer. Some of the factors which must be considered for good set reception are quality of the set, strength of the sending station, distance of the set from the station, topographical or other obstructions between the antenna and the station, the presence of electrical interference.

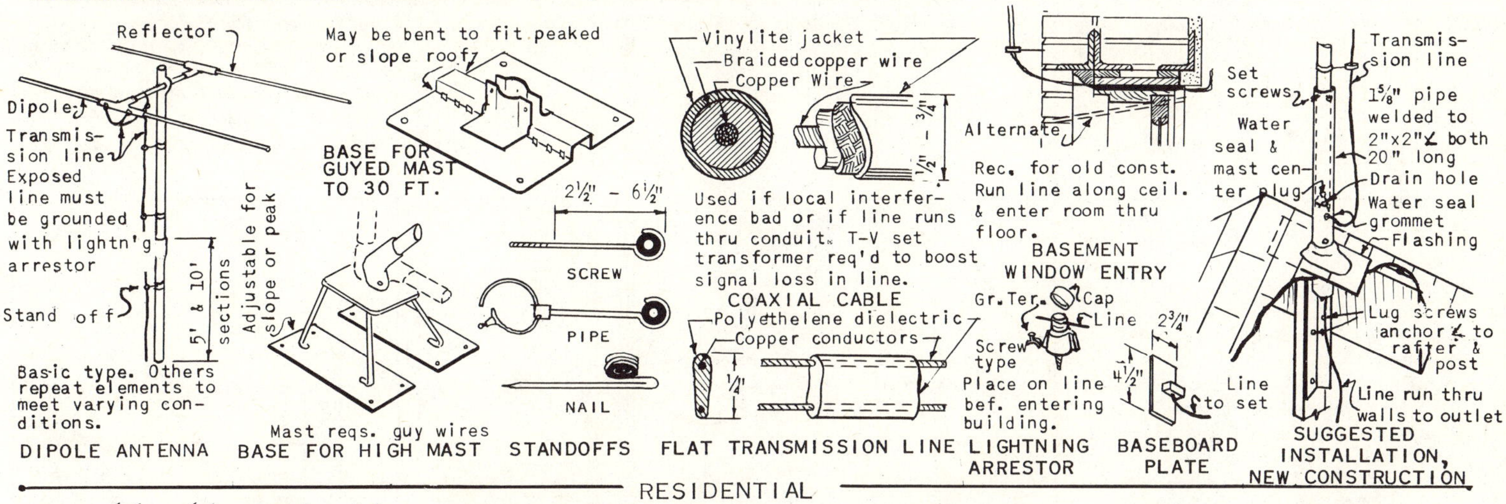
Reflector
Dipole
Transmission line
Exposed line must be grounded with lightn'g arrestor
Stand off
5' & 10' sections
Adjustable for slope or peak
Basic type. Others repeat elements to meet varying conditions.
DIPOLE ANTENNA
May be bent to fit peaked or slope roof
BASE FOR GUYED MAST TO 30 FT.
Mast reqs. guy wires
BASE FOR HIGH MAST
2½" - 6½"
SCREW
PIPE
NAIL
STANDOFFS
Vinylite jacket
Braided copper wire
Copper Wire
3/4"
1/2"
Used if local interference bad or if line runs thru conduit. T-V set transformer req'd to boost signal loss in line.
COAXIAL CABLE
Polyethelene dielectric
Copper conductors
1/4"
FLAT TRANSMISSION LINE
Alternate
Rec. for old const. Run line along ceil. & enter room thru floor.
BASEMENT WINDOW ENTRY
Gr. Ter.
Cap
Line
Screw type
Place on line bef. entering building.
LIGHTNING ARRESTOR
2¾"
4½"
Line to set
BASEBOARD PLATE
Transmission line
Set screws
Water seal & mast center plug
1⅝" pipe welded to 2"x2"∠ both 20" long
Drain hole
Water seal grommet
Flashing
Lug screws anchor ∠ to rafter & post
Line run thru walls to outlet
SUGGESTED INSTALLATION, NEW CONSTRUCTION

RESIDENTIAL

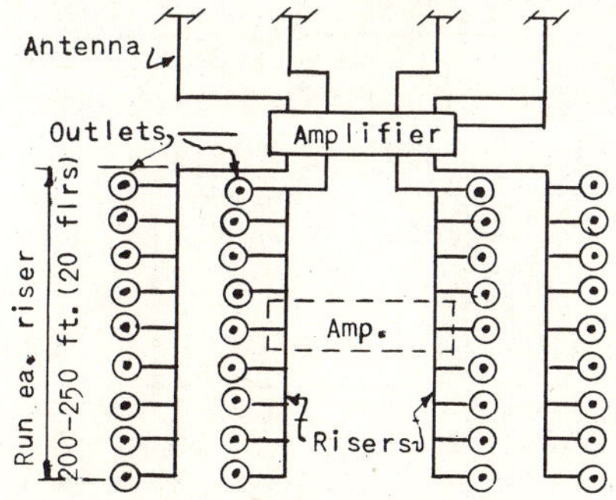
Antenna
Outlets
Amplifier
Amp.
Run ea. riser 200-250 ft. (20 flrs)
Risers

Depending on local conditions place amp. as close as possible to antenna or centrally in riser field.

BUILDINGS TO 20 STORIES

ANTENNA: Number req'd depends on number of stations in area. Each antenna directed to 1-2 stations.
AMPLIFIERS: House inside, in stairwell or if electrical interference not too great, in elevator penthouse. Amplifiers have outlets for 1, 4, 7, 16 or 64 risers. Sizes: from approx. 4" x 5" x 4" to 4' x 2' x 10"
RISERS: Coaxial cable, each handing up to 20 receiver outlets. Run in conduits thru walls of rooms where outlets to be located, generally living rooms.

Drawings are diagrammatic. All outlets not shown.

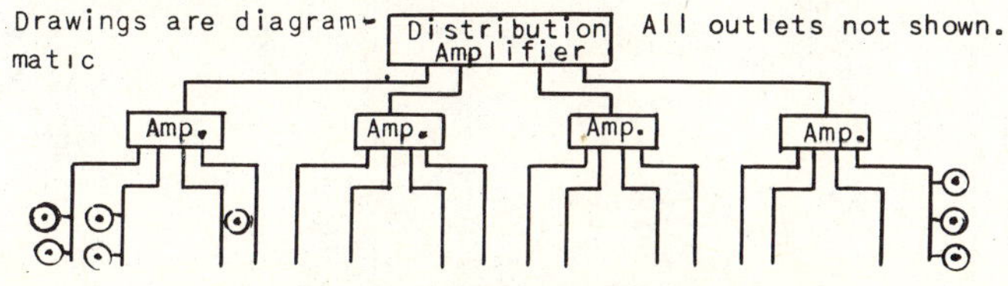
Distribution Amplifier
Amp.

HORIZONTAL BUILDINGS

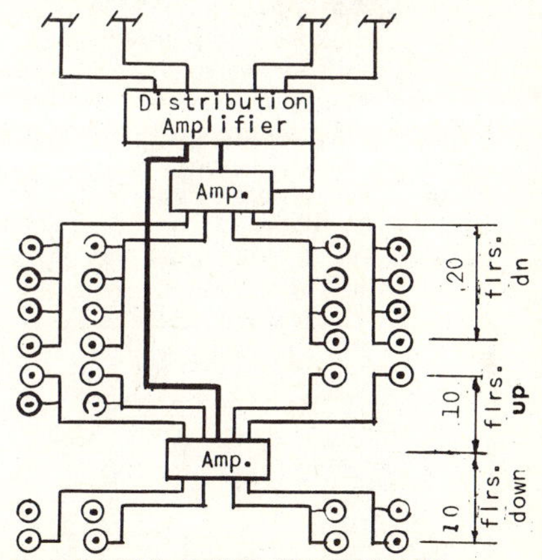
Distribution Amplifier
Amp.
20 flrs. dn
10 flrs. up
10 flrs. down

BUILDINGS OVER 20 STORIES

MULTI-DWELLING INSTALLATIONS

ANTENNA INSTALLATION

Data checked by R.C.A.

NOMENCLATURE and DATA for ELEVATORS

ELEVATOR: a hoisting or lowering mechanism which moves in guides in a vertical direction.
CONTROL PANEL: registers calls and governs response of elevator(s) to them.
STARTER & GENERATOR: supplies direct current to motor. Used with generator-field control.
GENERATOR-FIELD CONTROL: uses an individual generator for each elevator, in which the voltage applied to the hoisting motor is adjusted by varying the strength of the generator-field. Allows wide range of speed, including high speeds, and permits smooth acceleration and retardation of car.
MACHINE BEAMS: structural support for elevator machine.
GUIDE RAILS: with guide shoes, serve to guide car in vertical direction and prevent sideways or twisting motion.

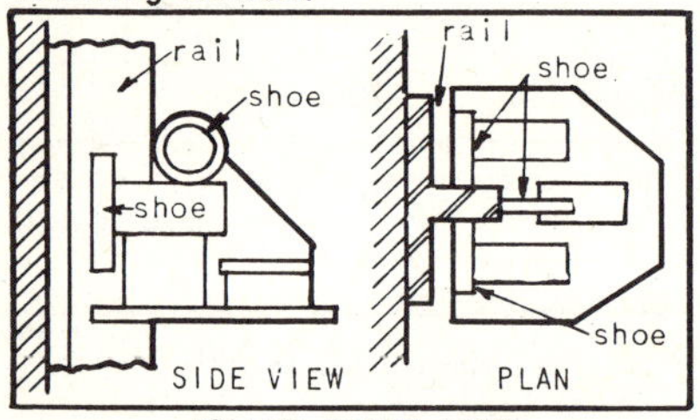
rail
shoe
shoe
rail
shoe
shoe
SIDE VIEW
PLAN

ROLLER GUIDE SHOE

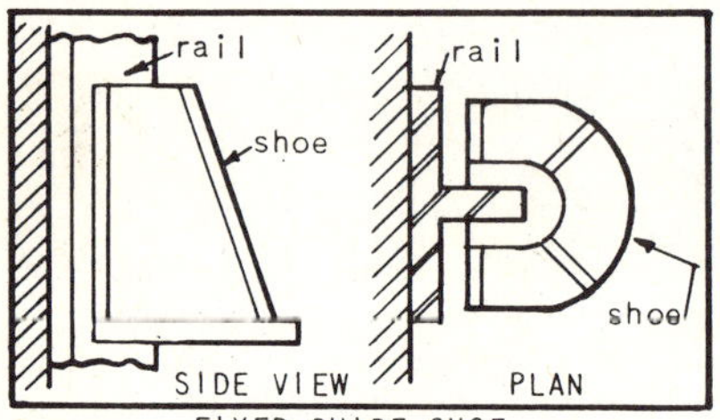
rail
shoe
rail
shoe
SIDE VIEW
PLAN

FIXED GUIDE SHOE

GUIDE SHOES: fastened to car frame and counterweight at top and bottom. They fit guide rails.
TRAVEL: the vertical distance between the bottom and top terminal landings.
COMPENSATION CABLES: cables hung from the bottom of the car and counterweight, for weight of hoisting cables. Used when travel exceeds 100 feet, the chains may be used to 400 feet.
PIT: that portion of a hoistway extending below the level of the bottom landing to provide for over travel and clearance and parts which require space below the bottom limit of car travel.
BUFFER: a device to absorb impact of car or counterweight at the lower limits of travel.

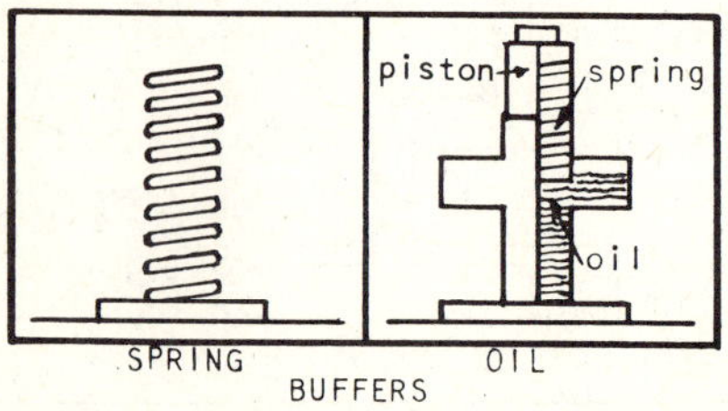
piston
spring
oil
SPRING
OIL

BUFFERS

TYPICAL INSTALLATION OF AN ELECTRIC ELEVATOR

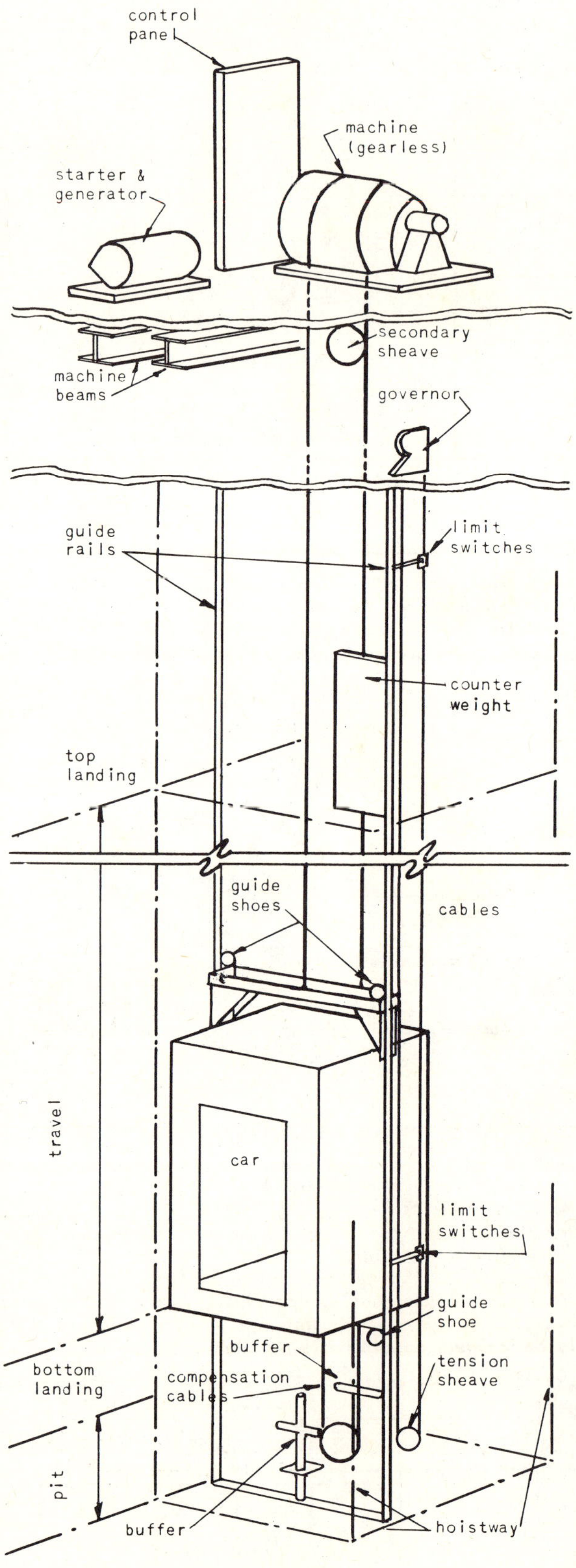
control panel
machine (gearless)
starter & generator
secondary sheave
machine beams
governor
guide rails
limit switches
counter weight
top landing
guide shoes
cables
travel
car
limit switches
guide shoe
buffer
tension sheave
bottom landing
compensation cables
pit
buffer
hoistway

GEARLESS MACHINE: one in which power is transmitted directly to the driving sheave without intermediate gears or mechanism.

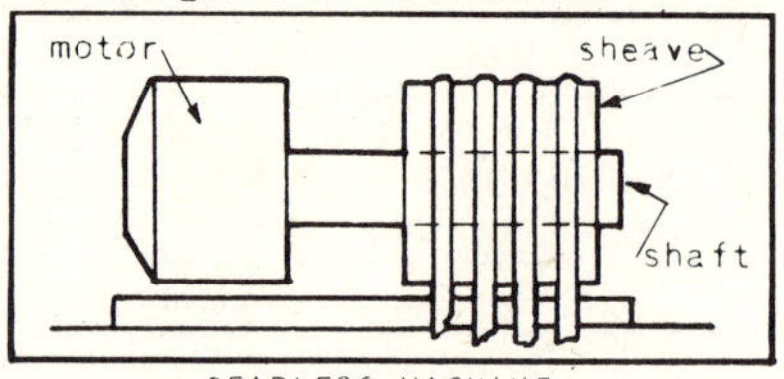
motor
sheave
shaft

GEARLESS MACHINE

SECONDARY SHEAVE: acts as guide for counterweight and provides double wrap for traction.
GOVERNOR: stops car and (if required) counterweight in case of emergency by actuating the safety.
SAFETY: a device incorporated in the bottom beam of the car frame and counterweight. Exerts retarding force in case of overspeed, free fall or slack cables.
LIMIT SWITCHES: an automatic device for stopping the car within the overtravel independently of the operating device.
OPERATING DEVICE: the car switch, push button, wheel, lever, etc. which enables the operator to actuate the control.
CABLES: strand steel "ropes" attached to and supporting car and counterweight.
TENSION SHEAVE: gives stability to governor's ropes.
HOISTWAY: any vertical opening or space in which an elevator or dumbwaiter is designed to operate.
CAR: the load-carrying unit, including its platform, frame and enclosure.

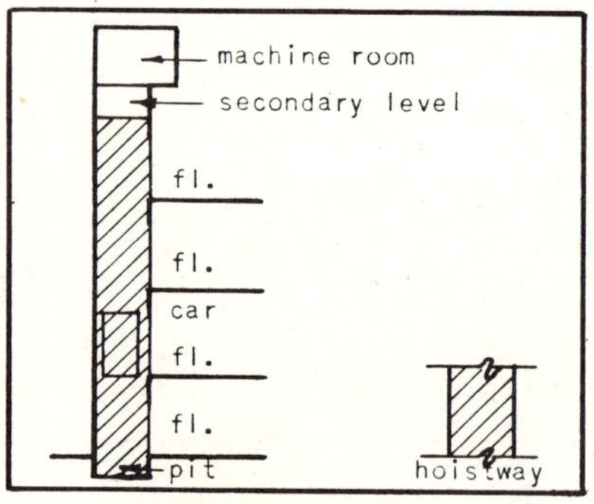
machine room
secondary level
fl.
fl.
car
fl.
fl.
pit
hoistway

HOISTWAY DIAGRAM

COUNTERWEIGHT: balances weight of car. Usually equals weight of car plus 40% of car capacity.

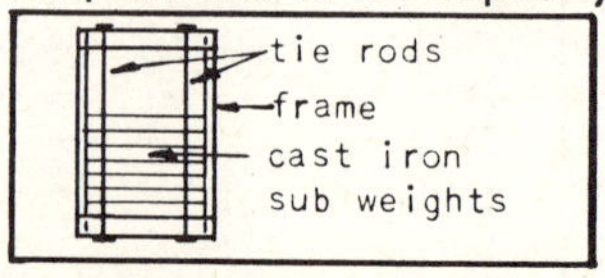
tie rods
frame
cast iron
sub weights

COUNTERWEIGHT DIAGRAM

CAR-LEVELLING DEVICE: any mechanism or control which will move the car within a limited zone to, and stop it at, the landing.
LANDING ZONE: 18 inches above or below a landing is the zone for an automatic type elevator car. Zone for a manual car switch control with automatic landing may be greater.

NOMENCLATURE and SELECTION of PASSENGER ELEVATORS

CAR FRAME: the supporting frame to which the platform, upper and lower set of guide shoes and the hoisting cables are usually attached.

CAR PLATFORM: the structure which supports the floor of the car and directly supports the load.

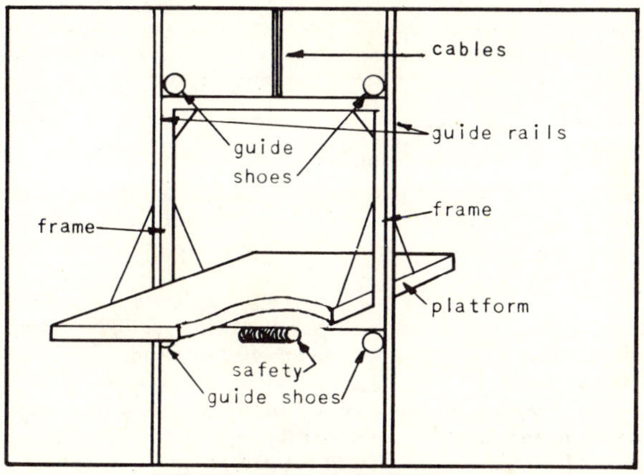
cables
guide rails
guide
shoes
frame
frame
platform
safety
guide shoes

TYPICAL FRAME & PLATFORM

CONTRACT SPEED: the speed given in the contract specifications or in application for permit, to be attained in up and down directions with contract load.

CONTRACT LOAD: capacity given in the specifications for purchase of elevator. Depends on net inside square foot area of platform as allowed by governing code.

GEARED MACHINE: one in which power is transmitted to the driving sheave or drum thru worm or spur gearing. Uses rheostatic as well as generator-field control.

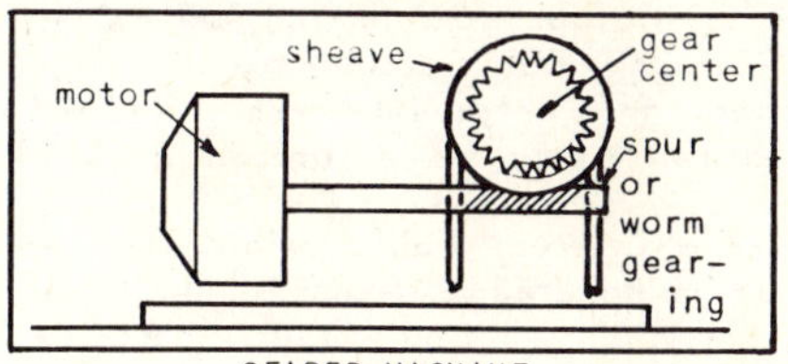
sheave
motor
gear
center
spur
or
worm
gear-
ing

GEARED MACHINE

WINDING DRUM MACHINE: one in which the cables are fastened to and wound on a drum. No counterweight required.

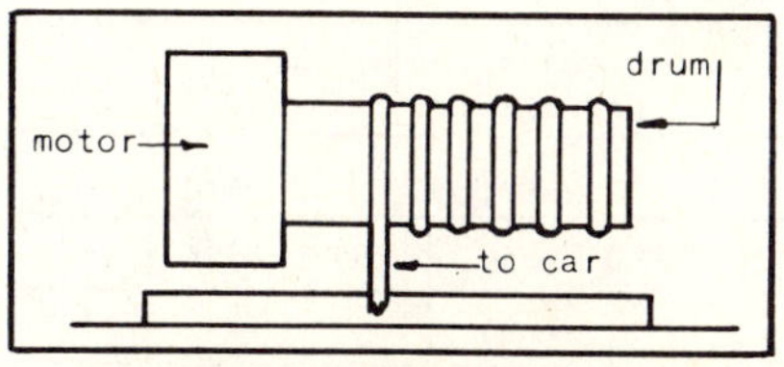
drum
motor
to car

WINDING DRUM MACHINE

TRACTION MACHINE: one in which the motion of the car is obtained by means of friction between the traction sheave and the hoisting cables.

Least wear & traction
HALF-ROUND &
DOUBLE WRAP
Highest wear
& traction
UNDERCUT-V
High wear & traction
UNDERCUT
HALF-ROUND

TRACTION SHEAVES

RHEOSTATIC CONTROL: a direct current system of control by varying resistance and reactance in the field circuit of the hoisting motor. Alternating current motors start across the line.

HYDRAULIC ELEVATOR: one in which the motion of the car is obtained from a liquid under pressure. (May use water; short rise plunger lifts generally use oil. Plunger must extend below basement level a minimum distance equal to travel.) Used where travel is short, required speed is low, and where overhead machine room is not desired.

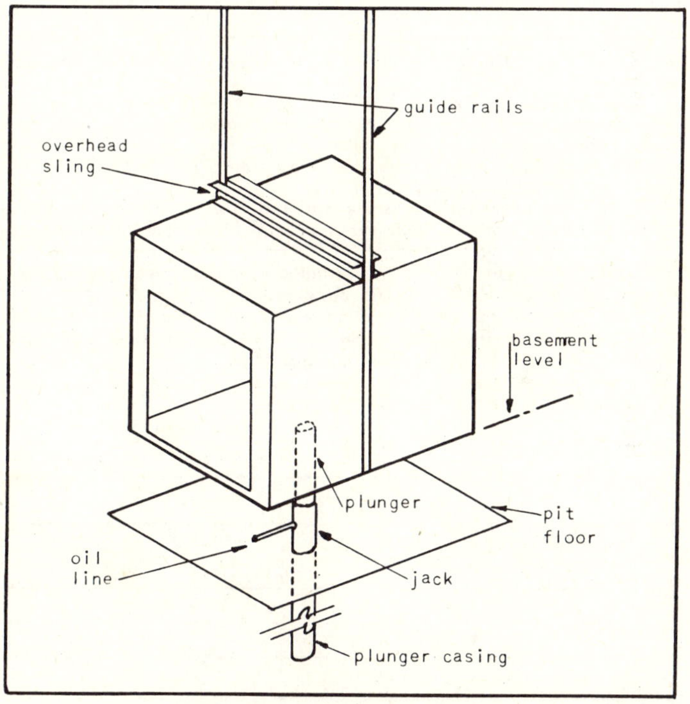
guide rails
overhead
sling
basement
level
plunger
pit
floor
oil
line
jack
plunger casing

OIL LIFT HYDRAULIC ELEVATOR

PASSENGER ELEVATORS: PRELIMINARY SELECTION

The data given on this and the following pages is to assist in the selection of passenger elevators for office buildings, industrial buildings, hotels, department stores, apartment houses, and hospitals. The results of the calculations will give general information on the economical number, characteristics, and groupings (local or express) of elevator installations. The cost of various installations must also be considered. A competent elevator engineer should be consulted before any decision is made.

The selection of elevators will depend on factual information concerning the particular building, and certain other determinations, as follows:

A. Factual information
   1. building characteristics
      a. number of floors
      b. floor-to-floor heights
      c. travel
      d. location
   2. population characteristics (the tempo of the traffic)

B. Determinations
   1. average round-trip time
   2. interval
   3. passenger-carrying capacity of the system.

The round-trip time depends on various times involved in the operation of an elevator, such as running time, number of stops, time required in passenger loading and unloading, and so on. Calculations of the times governing round-trip time are expressed in the Round-Trip Time graphs given on a following page.

The interval is the average time a passenger must wait for an elevator. Minimum intervals are given below. The desirable interval depends on the type and location of the building. In large cities the maximum interval is 30 seconds. For small buildings, 40 seconds is usually satisfactory. Intervals longer than 40 seconds are permissible only in hospitals, apartment houses, or buildings where one or two elevators will provide more than adequate passenger-carrying capacity.

SELECTION of PASSENGER ELEVATORS

The passenger-carrying capacity of an elevator is expressed as the percentage of the building population that can be carried one way in a period of time, usually five minutes. Exception: the passenger-carrying capacity of department store elevators is generally expressed as the number of people that can be carried in one hour. Elevator capacities are given below.

EXAMPLE OF PRELIMINARY SELECTION

Given: type of building: office
number of floors: 20 (above ground floor)
floor-to-floor height: 12 feet
total population: 2000 (see Speed and Travel Table, a following page).
maximum interval: 30 seconds

1. Find the total travel (equals the number of floors above ground floor times the floor-to-floor height) = 20 x 12 = 240 feet.
2. Find the required passenger-carrying capacity. This equals the maximum number of people expected to arrive or depart in any five minute period. Where this figure is not known, the following assumptions may be made:

Type of traffic	Percent of Population
light	12
average	13
heavy	14 for first 30 floors, 12 in any tower section. (Requirements for a single - occupancy building may vary.)

Assume light traffic. Use 13% of 2000 population, or, 260 people.
3. Use Speed and Travel Table to select an elevator capacity. The table for Office Buildings indicates that the minimum speed for a travel of 240 feet is 700 feet per minute. This speed is available with any capacity from 2500 to 4000 pounds. Select the 3000 capacity for trial.
4. Using the selected capacity and the number of floors (above ground floor), find from the Round-Trip Time graphs the round-trip time in seconds. Graph "C", for a 3000-pound capacity, indicates that the round-trip time for a 700 feet per minute elevator, for 20 floors, is 148 seconds.
5. Find the number of passengers per trip, normal peak, from Elevator Capacities Table below. For 3000-pound capacity, the normal peak is 16 passengers per trip.
6. Find the number of passengers one car can carry in five minutes by using the following formula:

$$\text{passenger cap. per car, 5 min.} = \frac{60 \times 5 \times \text{number passengers per trip}}{\text{round-trip time (seconds)}}$$

$$= \frac{60 \times 5 \times 16}{148} = 32.5 \text{ people for 5 min.}$$

7. Find the number of cars required in the bank elevators: divide the required passenger-carrying capacity by the number of passengers one car can carry in 5 minutes: $\frac{260}{32.5} = 8$ cars
8. Check the result by finding the interval. The determined interval should be equal to or more than the minimum given in the Minimum Interval Table below, and should not exceed the given maximum interval.

$$\text{interval} = \frac{\text{round-trip time}}{\text{number of cars in bank}} = \frac{148}{8} = 18.5 \text{ seconds}$$

The minimum interval for a 3000-pound capacity elevator is 18 seconds; the given maximum interval was 30 seconds. Therefore eight 3000-pound, 700 feet per minute elevators is one acceptable solution.
9. Another trial may be made with a larger selected capacity to determine if fewer cars can be used. Using a 4000-pound capacity, the solution would be seven 4000-pound, 700 feet per minute elevators.

It may be determined if the use of local and express cars would result in a better solution by figuring separately the required number of elevators for the local floors and the express floors.

In all cases, the cost of the various types of installations will affect a final decision.

10. When population of the building is unknown, a different approach must be used. From "Office Buildings, etc." on the Speed and Travel Table page, find the appropriate square-foot area per person. For example, use 90 sq. ft. per person.
11. The area on which calculations are based is the net usable area. This is roughly 75% of the total floor area and does not include such items as partitions, mechanical equipment rooms, etc. Assume total floor area is 240,000 sq. ft. Then net usable area = 0.75 x 240,000 = 180,000 sq. ft.
12. With 90 sq. ft. per person and a net usable area of 180,000 sq. ft., the population density may be estimated at 2000 persons.
13. Refer to the Capacity and Interval Table below. Assume 14% of the population must be handled in five minutes. Read down under 14% to the figure 2000. To find required car size, read left to car capacity — in this case, 4000 lbs.
14. With this information, return to step 4 to complete the preliminary selection.

ELEVATOR CAPACITIES

WEIGHT CAP., POUNDS	PASSENGER CAPACITY	PASSENGERS PER TRIP, NORMAL PEAK
1200	7	6
2000	14	10
2500	16	13
3000	19	16
3500	22	18
4000	26	21

MAXIMUM CAPACITY, ONE BANK OF ELEVATORS

CAR CAPACITY	AVER. PASS./TRIP	MIN. INT.	PERCENTAGE OF TOTAL POP. HANDLED IN 5 MINUTES					
			12.5	13	13.5	14	14.5	15
2000	10	12	2000	1920	1850	1785	1725	1670
2500	13	15	2080	2000	1935	1855	1800	1735
3000	16	18	2130	2050	1965	1900	1830	1775
3500	18	20	2160	2080	2000	1930	1865	1800
4000	21	23	2220	2140	2065	2000	1940	1885
5000	26	28	2260	2180	2090	2020	1950	1895

RECOMMENDED SPEEDS

TYPE OF BLDG.	FEET/MIN.
Office or Hotel (to 12 floors)	100 to 350
Office or Hotel (over 12 floors)	350 to 500
Store or Hospital (to 4 floors)	100 to 350
Store or Hospital (over 4 floors)	350 to 500
Apartment	100 to 350
Residence	35 to 100

Passenger capacity is generally found by dividing the rated capacity of the elevator by 150 and subtracting one for the elevator operator.

Passengers per trip, average, is assumed to be 80 percent of the elevator passenger capacity.

Data by courtesy of Westinghouse Elevator Division, Westinghouse Electric Corporation.

SELECTION of PASSENGER ELEVATORS

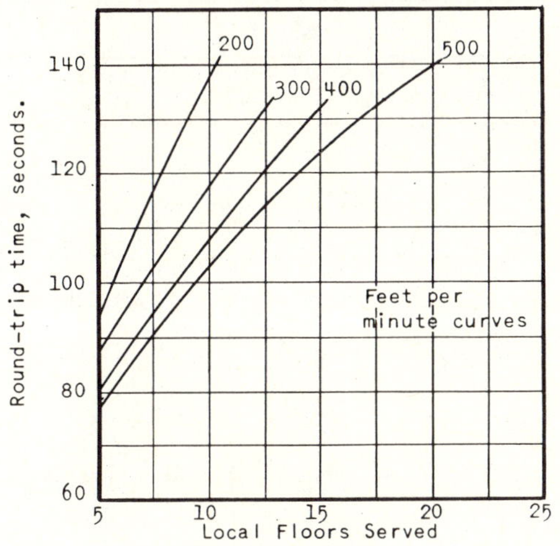
Round-trip time, seconds.
140
120
100
80
60
200
300
400
500
Feet per minute curves
5
10
15
20
25
Local Floors Served

GRAPH A: 2000 lbs. cap.

TYPE "A" CONTROL

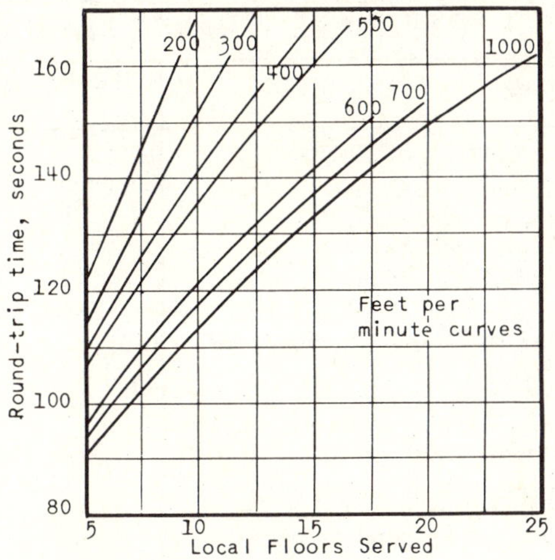
Round-trip time, seconds
160
140
120
100
80
200
300
400
500
600
700
1000
Feet per minute curves
5
10
15
20
25
Local Floors Served

GRAPH B: 2500 lbs. cap.

TYPE "A" CONTROL

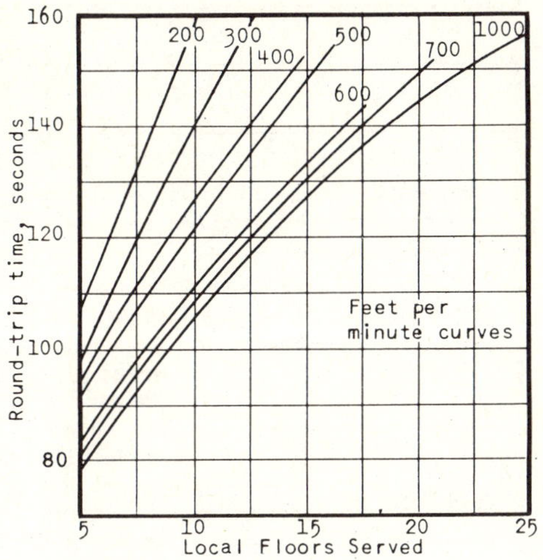
Round-trip time, seconds
160
140
120
100
80
200
300
400
500
600
700
1000
Feet per minute curves
5
10
15
20
25
Local Floors Served

GRAPH C: 3000 lbs. cap.

TYPE "A" CONTROL

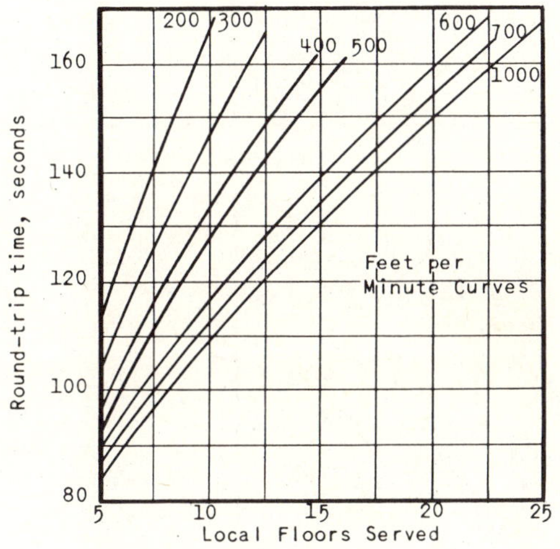
Round-trip time, seconds
160
140
120
100
80
200
300
400
500
600
700
1000
Feet per Minute Curves
5
10
15
20
25
Local Floors Served

GRAPH D: 3500 lbs. cap.

TYPE "A" CONTROL

Basically Type "A" and Type "B" control systems are very much alike, differing in the use for which they were intended. Type "A", having a supervisory system with six traffic patterns, is chiefly for use in an office buildings, hotel, etc., where traffic tends to be heavy. Type "B" is essentially for apartment houses or office buildings of light, moderate traffic.

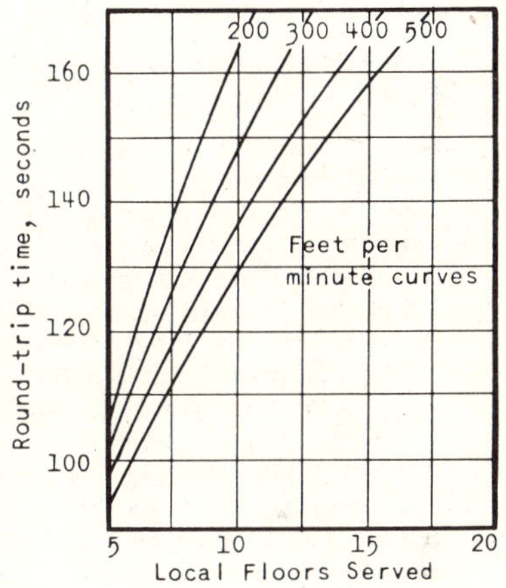
Round-trip time, seconds
160
140
120
100
200
300
400
500
Feet per minute curves
5
10
15
20
Local Floors Served

GRAPH G: 2000 lbs. cap.

TYPE "B" CONTROL

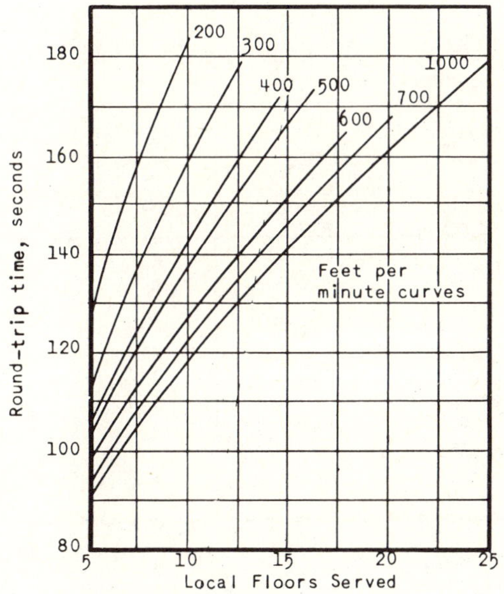
Round-trip time, seconds
180
160
140
120
100
80
200
300
400
500
600
700
1000
Feet per minute curves
5
10
15
20
25
Local Floors Served

GRAPH E: 4000 lbs. cap.

TYPE "A" CONTROL

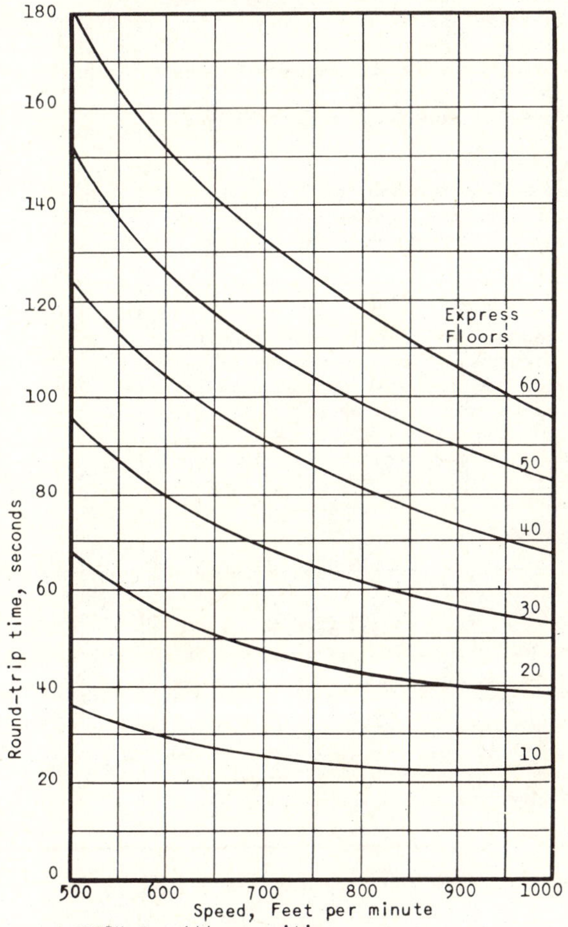
Round-trip time, seconds
180
160
140
120
100
80
60
40
20
0
Express Floors
60
50
40
30
20
10
500
600
700
800
900
1000
Speed, Feet per minute

GRAPH F: All capacities

TYPE "A" OR "B" CONTROLS

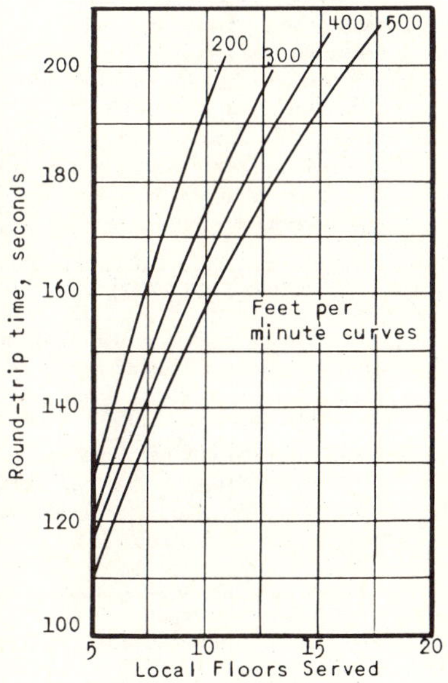
Round-trip time, seconds
200
180
160
140
120
100
200
300
400
500
Feet per minute curves
5
10
15
20
Local Floors Served

GRAPH H: 2500 lbs. cap.

TYPE "B" CONTROL

ROUND-TRIP TIME GRAPHS

Based on an assumed floor-to-floor height of 12 feet

Data by courtesy of Westinghouse Elevator Division, Westinghouse Electric Corporation

SELECTION of PASSENGER ELEVATORS

SPEED AND TRAVEL TABLE

TYPE OF BUILDING	CAPACITY (pounds)	SPEED [1] (feet per minute)	TRAVEL (feet)
OFFICE BUILDINGS, HOTELS AND INDUSTRIAL BUILDINGS Where expected population or density per floor is unknown, assume one person for each given square-foot area, as follows: Square-foot Area — Governing Conditions 80 (for one person) — for lower floors, single occupancy buildings 90 (for one person) — for lower floors, buildings in congested areas (heavy traffic) 100 (for one person) — for lower floors, buildings in business sections of average cities (average traffic) 110 (for one person) — for lower floors, buildings in business sections of small cities or outlying districts of larger cities (light traffic) *10 (for one person) — for buildings of over 20 floors, or where upper floors have smaller areas *25 (for one person) — for buildings of over 30 floors, in any tower section. *Add to base figure of Square-foot Area for lower floors.	2000 [2] 2500 3000 3500 4000 All given speeds are available with any given capacity	200 250 350 500 700 800 1000	up to 100 up to 125 [3] up to 150 [3] up to 175 up to 250 up to 350 over 350
APARTMENT HOUSES Elevator selection may be based on the number of bedrooms or on traffic studies. The traffic depends on the class of tenant and location of the building in relation to the business center and schools. The heaviest traffic peak may be: 1. the morning downpeak (approximately 50 percent of the population must be handled in 1½ to 2 hours). 2. the after-school peak (where the number of school children in the building is large). 3. the evening peak (to local amusements). A passenger-carrying capacity (for five minutes) of 7 percent of the population is satisfactory due to the smaller and more extended peak in an apartment house. For low-cost housing, percent of population varies from 3.6 to 6.2.	1200 2000 2500 All given speeds are available with any given capacity	100 200 250 350 400 500 700	up to 70 up to 100 up to 125 [3] up to 150 [3] up to 175 up to 250 up to 350
HOSPITALS In large hospitals a bank of passenger elevators may be installed separately from the service elevators. If so, select passenger elevators as for office buildings. For selection of elevators for combined passenger and vehicle use, see notes on the "Hospital Elevators" *in Building Planning and Design Stcndards by H.R. Sleeper* Intervals should not be longer than one minute. An automatic control system is recommended. It should have an optional feature allowing attendant operation. At least one elevator should be on the emergency electric power system.	3500 4000 All given speeds are available with either given capacity	100 200 250 350 400 500 700	up to 70 up to 100 up to 125 [3] up to 150 [3] up to 175 up to 250 up to 350
DEPARTMENT STORES Each department store presents a traffic problem because of the use of electric stairways and the distribution of merchandise. Therefore, round-trip time must be separately calculated for each installation. Electric stairways handle the majority of traffic. Only ten to twenty percent of the population should usually be considered in planning the elevator installation. For approximation figure one person per 25 square feet of merchandising area, above first floor.	3000 4000 5000 All given speeds are available with any given capacity	200 350 400 500 700	up to 100 up to 125 [3] up to 175 up to 250 up to 350

[1] Speeds are recommended minimums for indicated travel.

[2] The highest recommended speed for this capacity is 500 feet per minute.

[3] Gearless elevators, with speeds beginning at 400 to 500 feet per minute, are recommended for this and higher travels.

Data by courtesy of Weetinghouse Elevator Division, Westinghouse Electric Corporation.

PASSENGER ELEVATORS - 2:1 ROPING

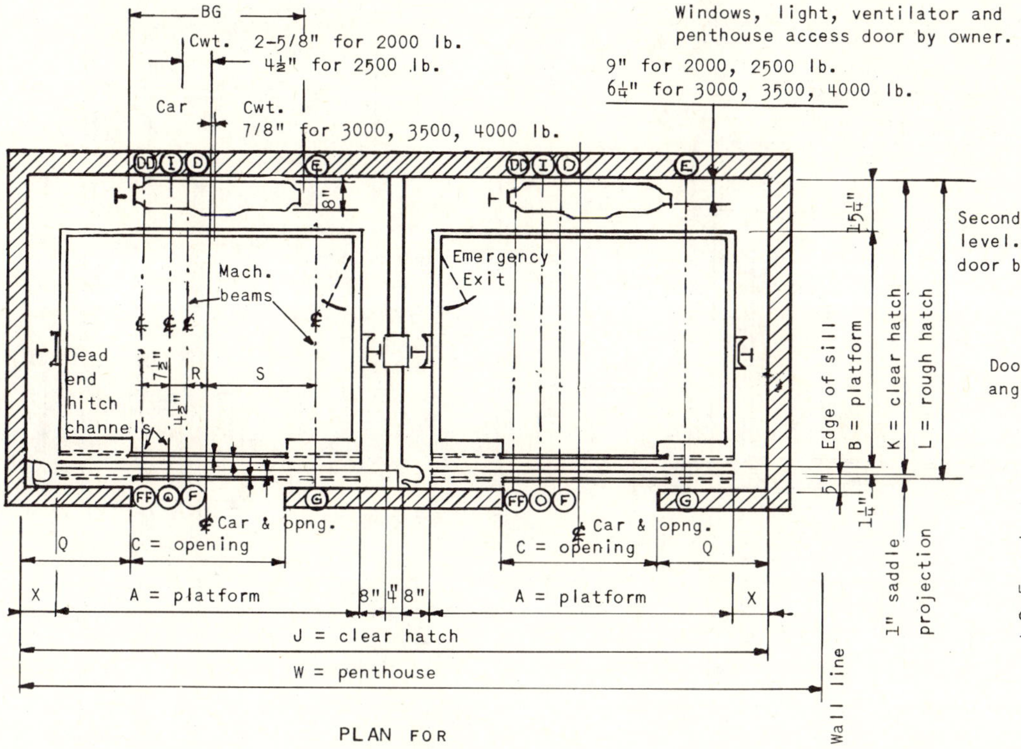

BG
Cwt. 2-5/8" for 2000 lb.
4½" for 2500 lb.
Car
Cwt.
7/8" for 3000, 3500, 4000 lb.
Windows, light, ventilator and
penthouse access door by owner.
9" for 2000, 2500 lb.
6¼" for 3000, 3500, 4000 lb.
DD
I
D
E
8"
Mach.
beams
Emergency
Exit
Dead
end
hitch
channels
R
S
FF
O
F
G
Car & opng.
C = opening
Q
X
A = platform
8"
4"
8"
J = clear hatch
W = penthouse
Wall line
15¼"
Edge of sill
B = platform
K = clear hatch
L = rough hatch
5"
1¼"
1" saddle
projection

PLAN FOR
TWO-CAR BANK

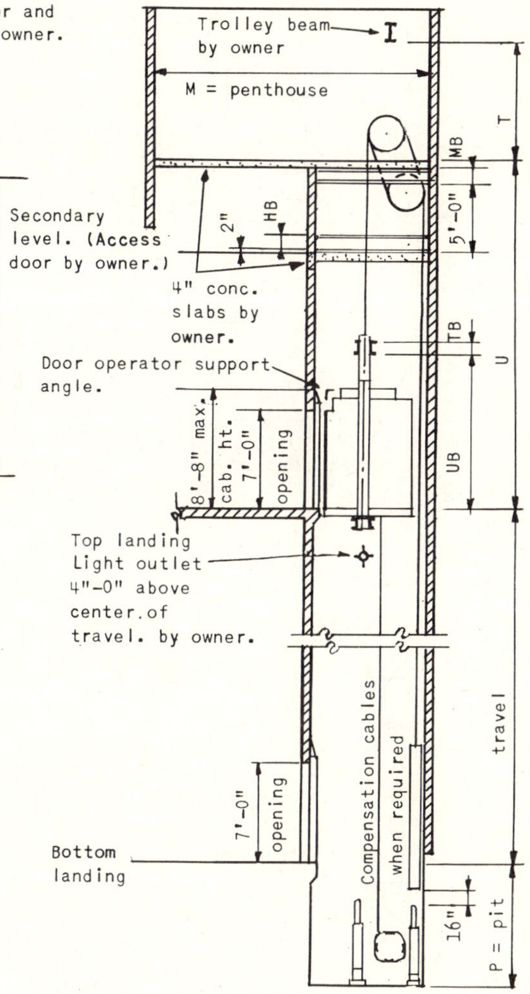

Trolley beam
by owner
M = penthouse
T
MB
Secondary
level. (Access
door by owner.)
2"
HB
5'-0"
4" conc.
slabs by
owner.
TB
U
Door operator support
angle.
8'-8" max.
cab. ht.
7'-0"
opening
UB
Top landing
Light outlet
4"-0" above
center of
travel. by owner.
Compensation cables
when required
travel
7'-0"
opening
Bottom
landing
16"
P = pit

HOISTWAY SECTION

Penthouse, pit depth and top clearance shown may be increased if required by local code. Do not decrease.

Reactions include allowance for impact

CAPACITY pounds	SPEED ft/min.	DIMENSIONS					TRAVEL feet	OVERHEAD LOAD IN LBS.							
		BG	UB	TB	MB	HB		D	E	F	G	I	O	DD	FF
2000	400 500	42"	11'-9"	9"	10"	10"	200 250	8800 9000	7900 8100	6100 6300	3800 3900	4800 5100	4100 4300	3200 3300	700 700
2500	500	42"	11'-9"	10"	12"	12"	250	10300	9000	7300	3800	5000	3800	3600	700
3000	500	42"	11'-0"	12"	12"	10"	200	7700	8600	5400	6100	5900	3400	5900	3400
3500	500	42"	11'-0"	12"	12"	12"	350	8500	10000	6300	7400	7500	4100	7500	4100
4000	500	42"	11'-0"	12"	12"	12"	220	8700	9800	6400	7100	7400	4100	7400	4100

CAPACITY pounds	SPEED ft/min.	DIMENSIONS													
		A	B	C	J	K	L	M	P	Q	R	S	T	U	W	X
2000	400 500	6'-4"	4'-5"	3'-0"	15'-8"	5'-9½"	5'-10½"	14'-6"	7'-9" 8'-9"	2'-4"	3¼"	2'-11"	8'-6"	24'-7" 26'-1"	15'-7¾"	8"
2500	500	7'-0"	5'-0"	3'-6"	17'-0"	6'-4½"	6'-5½"	23'-0"	10'-3"	2'-5"	5-1/8"	1'-9-1/8"	8'-6"	26'-1"	21'-6"	8"
3000	500	7'-0"	5'-6"	3'-6"	17'-0"	6'-10½"	6'-11½"	23'-0"	10'-3"	2'-6"	6-5/16"	2'-4-15/16"	8'-6"	26'-1"	21'-6"	8"
3500	500	7'-0"	6'-2"	3'-6"	17'-0"	7'-6½"	7'-7½"	23'-0"	10'-3"	2'-6"	6-5/16"	2'-4-15/16"	8'-6"	26'-1"	22'-3"	8"
4000	500	7'-6"	6'-6"	3'-10"	18'-4"	7'-10½"	7'-11½"	23'-0"	10'-3"	2'-8"	6-5/16"	2'-4-15/16"	9'-0"	26'-1"	23'-0"	10"

Data by courtesy of Westinghouse Elevator Division, Westinghouse Electric Corporation.

PASSENGER ELEVATORS - 1:1 ROPING

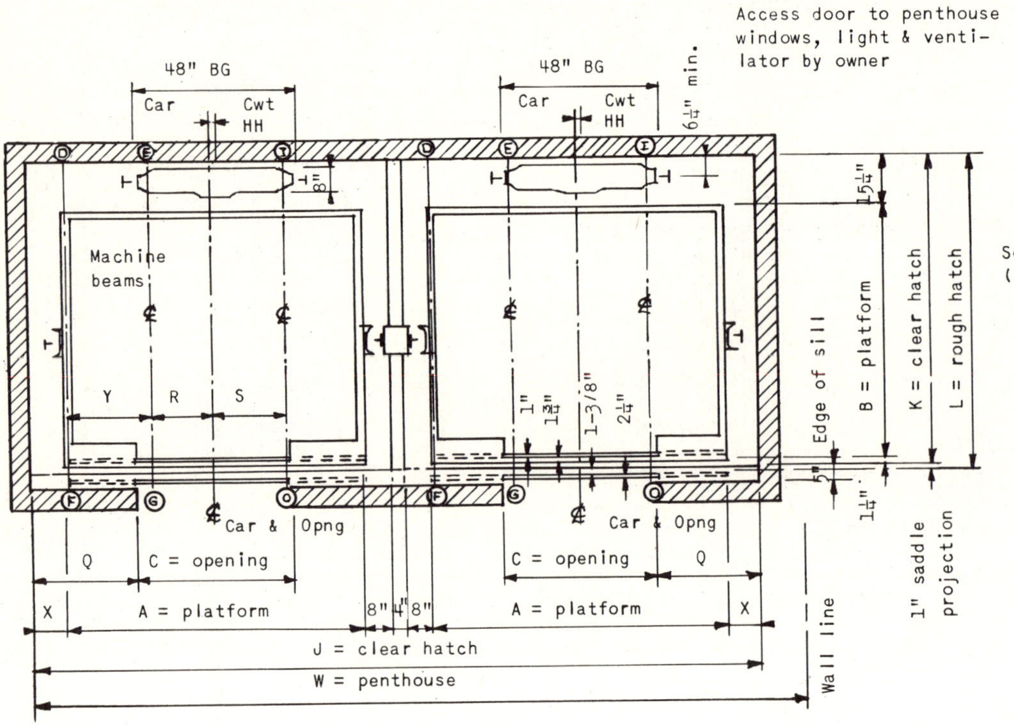
Access door to penthouse windows, light & ventilator by owner
48" BG
Car
Cwt HH
6¼" min.
8"
15¼"
Machine beams
Y
R
S
1"
1¾"
1-3/8"
2¼"
B = platform
K = clear hatch
L = rough hatch
Edge of sill
5"
1¼"
Car & Opng
C = opening
Q
X
A = platform
8" 4" 8"
J = clear hatch
W = penthouse
Wall line
1" saddle projection

PLAN FOR TWO-CAR BANK

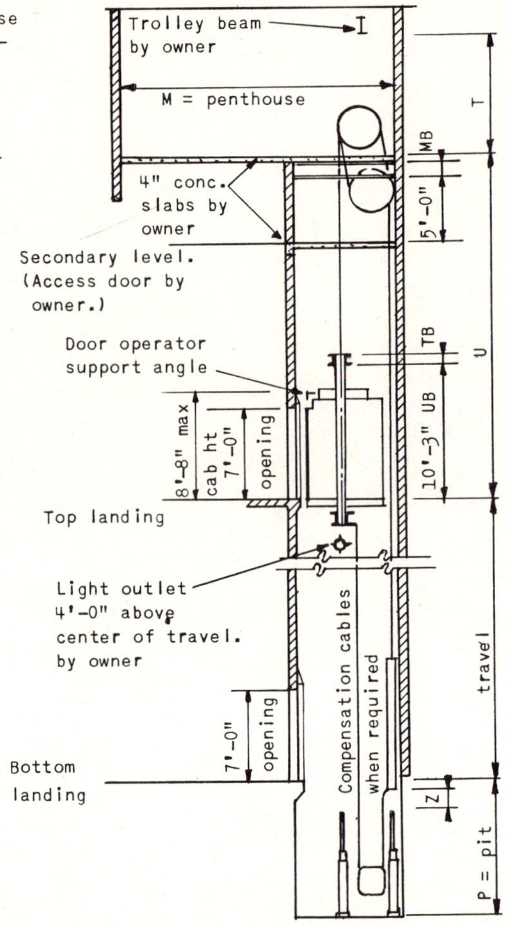
Trolley beam by owner
M = penthouse
4" conc. slabs by owner
Secondary level. (Access door by owner.)
Door operator support angle
8'-8" max
cab ht 7'-0"
opening
Top landing
Light outlet 4'-0" above center of travel. by owner
Compensation cables when required
7'-0"
opening
Bottom landing
T
MB
5'-0"
TB
U
10'-3" UB
travel
Z
P = pit

HOISTWAY SECTION

Penthouse, pit depth and top clearance shown may be increased if required by local code. Do not decrease.

Reactions at D, E, F, G, I & O include allowance for impact.

CAPACITY pounds	SPEED ft/min	DIMENSIONS X	Y	Z	TB	MB	HH	TRAVEL feet	OVERHEAD LOAD IN LBS. D	E	F	G	I	O
2500	700 800	9"		20"	10"	15"	1-1/16"	350 300		13500 13700		9000 8800	17000 17400	16300 11200
3000	700 800 1000	9"	2'-4½" 2'-4½"	20" 20" 22"	10" 12" 12"	15" 14" 14"	1-1/16" 1-1/8" 1-1/8"	275 400 600	8200 8600	14600 10300 10800	5000 5600	9000 6200 7000	18300 21300 23300	11200 13000 15000
3500	700 800 1000	9"	2'-4½"	39" 32" 35"	12"	14" 14" 16"	1-1/8"	550 450 490	8800 9100 9200	11300 11500 11550	5200 5300 5300	6400 6700 6700	23800 24800 25950	14100 14500 14550
4000	700 800 1000	10"	2'-4½"	32" 30" 60"	12"	16"	1-1/8"	450 420 850	8900 8800 11600	11250 11000 13100	5800 5900 8000	7350 7400 9000	24600 24700 28900	15900 16100 19850

CAPACITY pounds	SPEED ft/min	DIMENSIONS A	B	C	J	K	L	M	P	Q	R	S	T	U	W
2500	700 800	7'-0"	5'-0"	3'-6"	17'-2"	6'-4½"	6'-5½"	23'-0"	12'-6"	2'-6"	2'-0-3/16"	1'-1-3/16"	9'-6" 10'-6"	27'-6" 29'-10"	21'-6"
3000	700 800 1000	7'-0"	5'-6"	3'-6"	17'-2"	6'-10½"	6'-11½"	23'-0"	12'-6"	2'-6"	2'-0-3/16" 1'-3-1/8" 1'-3-1/8"	1'-1-3/16" 1'-4-5/8" 1'-4-5/8"	9'-6" 10'-6" 10'-6"	27'-6" 29'-10" 29'-10"	21'-6"
3500	700 800 1000	7'-0"	6'-2"	3'-6"	17'-2"	7'-6½"	7'-7½"	23'-0" 24'-0" 24'-0"	13'-0"	2'-6"	1'-3-1/8"	1'-4-5/8"	10'-6"	27'-6" 29'-10" 29'-10"	22'-3"
4000	700 800 1000	7'-6"	6'-6"	3'-10"	18'-4"	7'-10½"	7'-11½"	23'-0" 24'-0" 24'-0"	13'-0"	2'-8"	1'-3-1/8"	1'-4-5/8"	10'-6"	27'-6" 29'-10" 29'-10"	23'-0"

Data by courtesy of Westinghouse Elevator Division, Westinghouse Electric Corporation.

PASSENGER ELEVATORS - GEARED

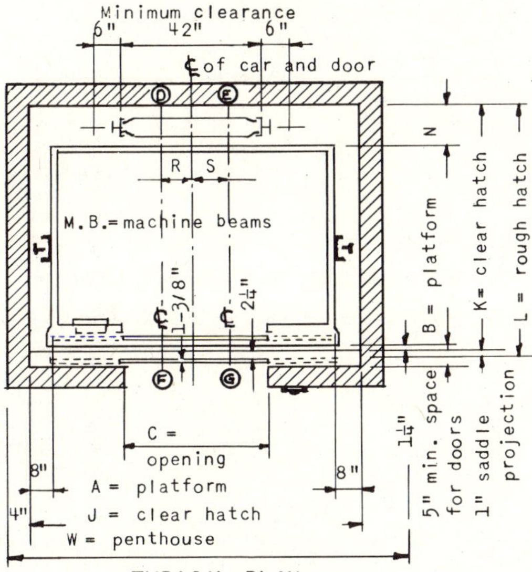
Minimum clearance
6"
42"
6"
℄ of car and door
D
E
R
S
M.B.=machine beams
1-3/8"
2¼"
F
G
N
B = platform
K = clear hatch
L = rough hatch
1¼"
5" min. space for doors
1" saddle projection
C = opening
8"
8"
4"
A = platform
J = clear hatch
W = penthouse

TYPICAL PLAN

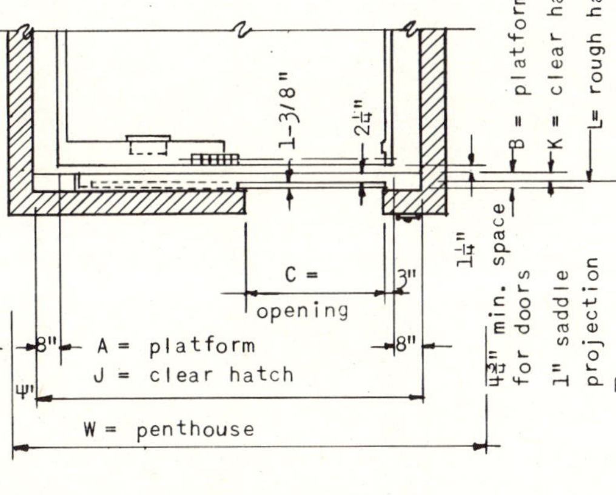
1-3/8"
2¼"
C = opening
3"
8"
8"
A = platform
J = clear hatch
4"
W = penthouse
1¼"
4½" min. space for doors
1" saddle projection
B = platform
K = clear hatch
L = rough hatch

Has single or center-opening doors.

PLAN FOR 2000# CAPACITY ONLY

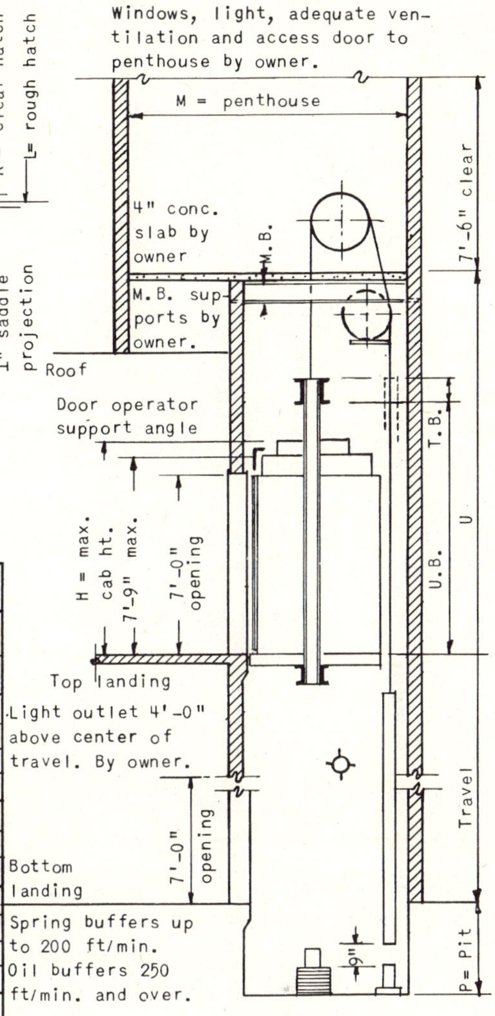
Windows, light, adequate ventilation and access door to penthouse by owner.
M = penthouse
7'-6" clear
4" conc. slab by owner
M.B.
M.B. supports by owner.
Roof
Door operator support angle
T.B.
H = max. cab ht.
7'-9" max.
7'-0" opening
U.B.
U
Top landing
Light outlet 4'-0" above center of travel. By owner.
Travel
7'-0" opening
Bottom landing
Spring buffers up to 200 ft/min.
Oil buffers 250 ft/min. and over.
9"
P = Pit

SECTION

Pit depth and top clearance shown may be increased if required by local code. Reactions at D, E, F and G include allowance for impact. Wt. of concrete slab not included. Abbreviations:
T.B.= top beam; U.B.= under beam

GEARED GENERAL PURPOSE ELEVATORS		FOR OFFICES, HOTELS, STORES AND INDUSTRIAL BUILDINGS.						
CAPACITY pounds	SPEED ft/min.	DIMENSIONS			OVERHEAD LOAD IN POUNDS			
		MP	TB	UB	D	E	F	G
2000	*100	10"	8"	9'-6"	7,500	7,000	3,800	3,600
	200				8,700	7,900	4,500	4,200
	250				9,000	8,200	4,600	4,300
	300				9,200	8,500	4,800	4,400
2500	*100	10"	8"	9'-6"	8,000	7,300	5,500	5,000
	200	12"	9"	10'-3"	9,000	8,200	6,200	5,700
	350				10,700	9,800	6,500	5,800
3000	*100	12"	9"	10'-3"	8,700	7,900	6,000	5,600
	200				10,400	9,500	6,600	6,000
	300				11,100	10,100	7,000	6,300
	350				11,300	10,300	7,100	6,400
3500	*100	12"	10"	10'-3"	9,500	8,800	6,900	6,400
	250				11,700	10,700	7,600	7,000
	300				12,300	10,900	8,100	7,200
	350				13,300	12,600	7,600	7,200
4000	*100	12"	12"	10'-3"	11,900	11,100	7,900	7,400
	200				12,600	11,600	8,400	7,700
	250				13,000	11,900	8,700	8,000
	350	15"			15,000	14,000	8,900	8,200

CAPACITY pounds	SPEED ft/min.	DIMENSIONS													
		A	B	C	H	J	K	L	M	N	P	R	S	U	W
2000	*100	6'-4"	4'-5"	3'-0"	8'-2"	7'-8"	5'-7¼"	5'-8¼"	11'-0"	13"	4'-6"	8¾"		16'-9"	11'-0"
	200								11'-6"		4'-10"	10¾"		17'-0"	
	250										6'-8"	10¾"		17'-6"	
	300											13-3/8"			
2500	*100	7'-0"	5'-0"	3'-6"	8'-2"	8'-4"	6'-2¼"	6'-3¼"	11'-0"	13"	4'-7"	10¾"		16'-9"	11'-0"
	200				8'-8"				11'-6"		5'-2"	10-5/8"		17'-0"	
	350										7'-8"	10¼"		18'-3"	
3000	*100	7'-0"	5'-6"	3'-6"	8'-2"	8'-4"	6'-8¼"	6'-9¼"	11'-0"	13"	4'-9"	10-5/8"		16'-9"	11'-0"
	200				8'-8"				12'-0"		5'-2"	13¼"		17'-0"	
	300										6'-8"			17'-6"	
	350										7'-8"			18'-3"	
3500	*100	7'-0"	6'-2"	3'-6"	8'-8"	8'-4"	7'-4¼"	7'-5¼"	11'-6"	13"	4'-9"	10-5/8"		16'-9"	12'-0"
	250								12'-0"		6'-9"	13¼"		17'-6"	
	300								13'-6"						
	350										7'-8"	15½"	14½"	18'-3"	
4000	*100	7'-6"	6'-6"	3'-10"	8'-8"	8'-10"	7'-8"	7'-9"	11'-6"	13"	4'-6"	13¼"		17'-3"	12'-0"
	200								12'-0"		5'-4"			17'-6"	
	250								13'-6"					19'-6"	
	350								14'-0"		6'-4"	15¼"	14¾"		

*Rheostatic A-C control

Data by courtesy of Westinghouse Elevator Division, Westinghouse Electric Corporation.

APARTMENT HOUSE ELEVATORS

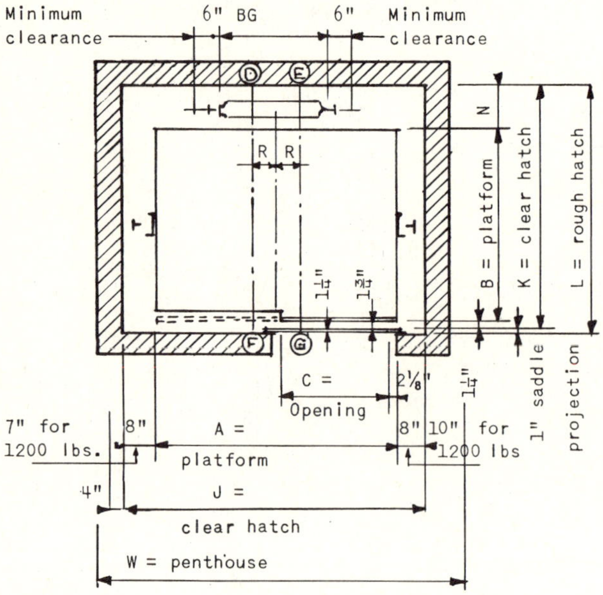
Minimum clearance
6" BG
6"
Minimum clearance
R R
B = platform
K = clear hatch
L = rough hatch
C = Opening
7" for 1200 lbs.
8"
A = platform
8"
10" for 1200 lbs
1" saddle projection
4"
J = clear hatch
W = penthouse

SINGLE SPEED CAR DOOR - SWING HATCH DOOR
1200 LB. AND 2000 LB. CAPACITY ONLY

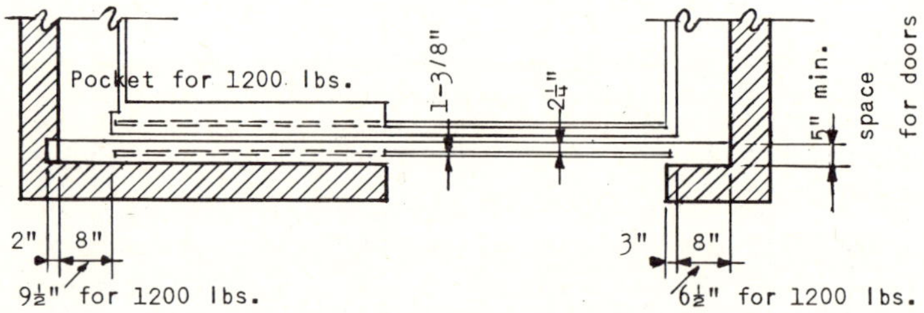
Pocket for 1200 lbs.
1-3/8"
$2\frac{1}{4}$"
5" min. space for doors
2"
8"
$9\frac{1}{2}$" for 1200 lbs.
3"
8"
$6\frac{1}{2}$" for 1200 lbs.

SINGLE SPEED CAR DOOR - SWING HATCH DOOR
1200, 2000 AND 2500 LB. CAPACITY

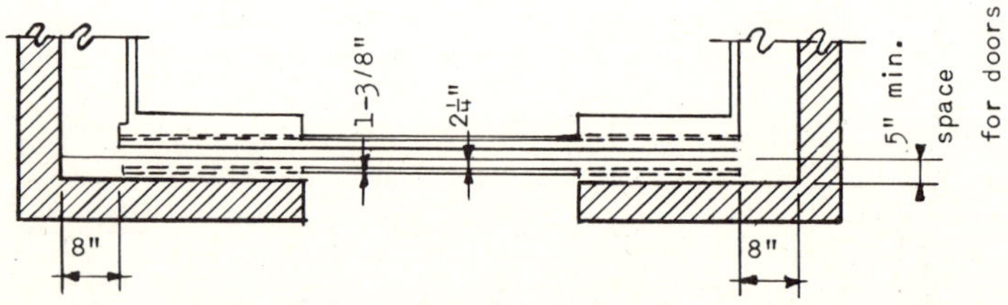
1-3/8"
$2\frac{1}{4}$"
5" min. space for doors
8"
8"

CENTER OPENING CAR AND HATCH DOORS, 2500 LB. CAPACITY ONLY

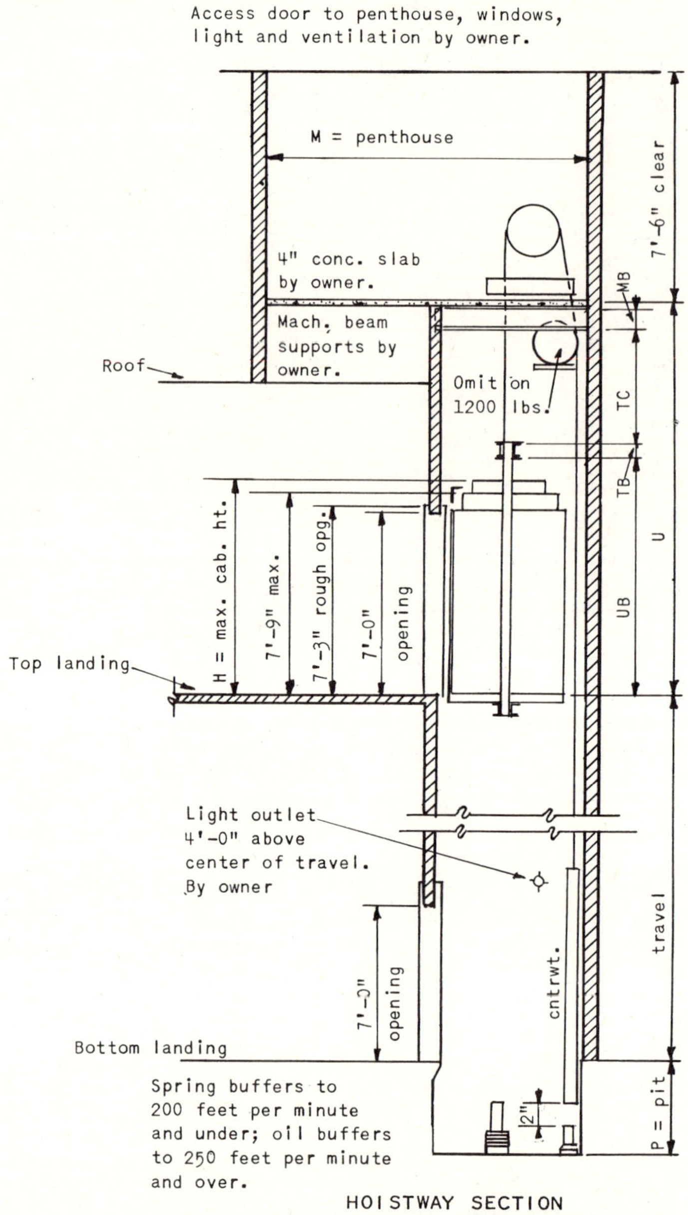
Access door to penthouse, windows, light and ventilation by owner.
M = penthouse
7'-6" clear
4" conc. slab by owner.
MB
Mach. beam supports by owner.
Roof
Omit on 1200 lbs.
TC
TB
U
UB
H = max. cab. ht.
7'-9" max.
7'-3" rough opg.
7'-0" opening
Top landing
Light outlet 4'-0" above center of travel. By owner
travel
cntrwt.
7'-0" opening
Bottom landing
Spring buffers to 200 feet per minute and under; oil buffers to 250 feet per minute and over.
12"
P = pit

HOISTWAY SECTION

Rough opening to be filled in around door frame after it is in place.

Pit depth and TC (top clearance) may be increased if required by local code.

Reactions at D, E, F and G include allowance for impact. Weight of concrete slab is not included.

CAPACITY pounds	SPEED ft/min.	DIMENSIONS					OVERHEAD LOAD IN POUNDS			
		BG	MB	TB	TC	UB	D	E	F	G
1200	*100	36"	8"	7"	5'-8"	9'-6"	6200	5800	3200	3100
2000	*100 250	42"	10"	8"	5'-5" 6'-2"	9'-6"	7500 9000	7000 8200	3800 4600	3600 4300
2500	200 350	42"	12"	9"	4'-8" 5'-11"	10'-3"	9000 10700	8200 9800	6200 6500	5700 5800

CAPACITY pounds	SPEED ft/min.	DIMENSIONS													
		A	B	C	H	J	K	L	M	N	P	R	U	W	Z
1200	*100	5'-0"	4'-0"	3'-0"**	8'-2"	6'-4"	5'-$2\frac{1}{4}$"	5'-4"	9'-6"	13"	4'-6"	9"	16'-9"	7'-0"	18"
2000	*100 250	6'-4"	4'-5"	3'-0"	8'-2"	7'-8"	5'-$7\frac{1}{4}$"	5'-$8\frac{1}{4}$"	11'-0" 11'-6"	13"	4'-6" 6'-8"	$8\frac{3}{4}$" $10\frac{3}{4}$"	16'-9" 17'-6"	11'-0"	18" 22"
2500	200 350	7'-0"	5'-0"	3'-6"	8'-8"	8'-4"	6'-$2\frac{1}{4}$"	6'-$3\frac{1}{4}$"	11'-6"	13"	5'-2" 7'-8"	10-5/8" $3\frac{1}{4}$"	17'-0" 18'-3"	11-0"	20" 26"

*A-C Control

** Swing doors on hatch 2'-8"

Data by courtesy of Westinghouse Elevator Division, Westinghouse Electric Corporation.

DUMBWAITERS and RESIDENTIAL ELEVATORS

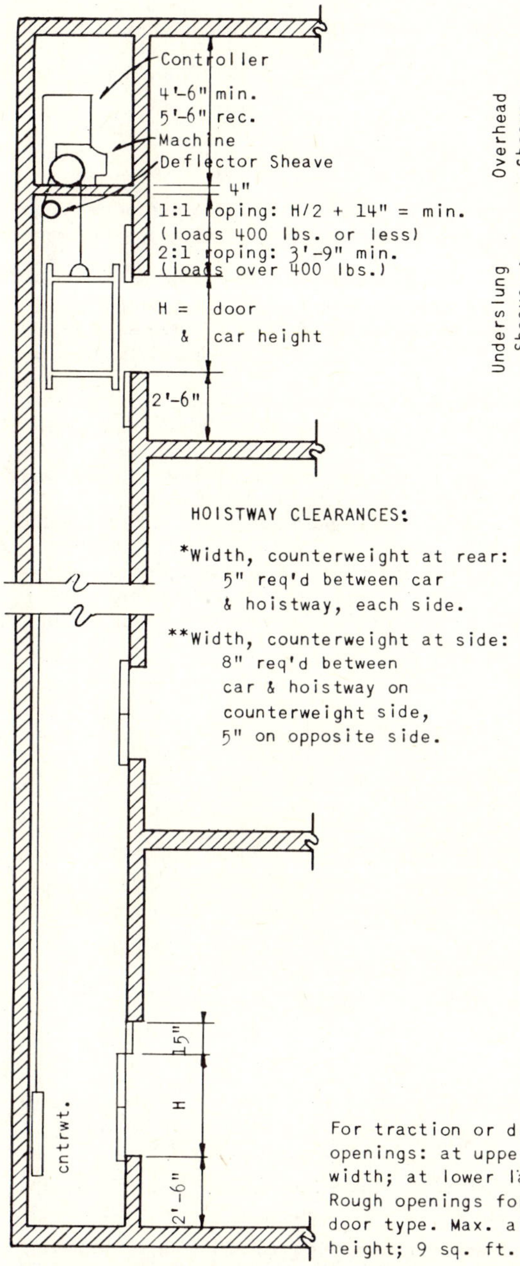
Controller
4'-6" min.
5'-6" rec.
Machine
Deflector Sheave
4"
1:1 roping: H/2 + 14" = min.
(loads 400 lbs. or less)
2:1 roping: 3'-9" min.
(loads over 400 lbs.)
H = door
& car height
2'-6"
HOISTWAY CLEARANCES:
*Width, counterweight at rear:
5" req'd between car
& hoistway, each side.
**Width, counterweight at side:
8" req'd between
car & hoistway on
counterweight side,
5" on opposite side.
15"
H
2'-6"
cntrwt.

TRACTION TYPE (SECTION)

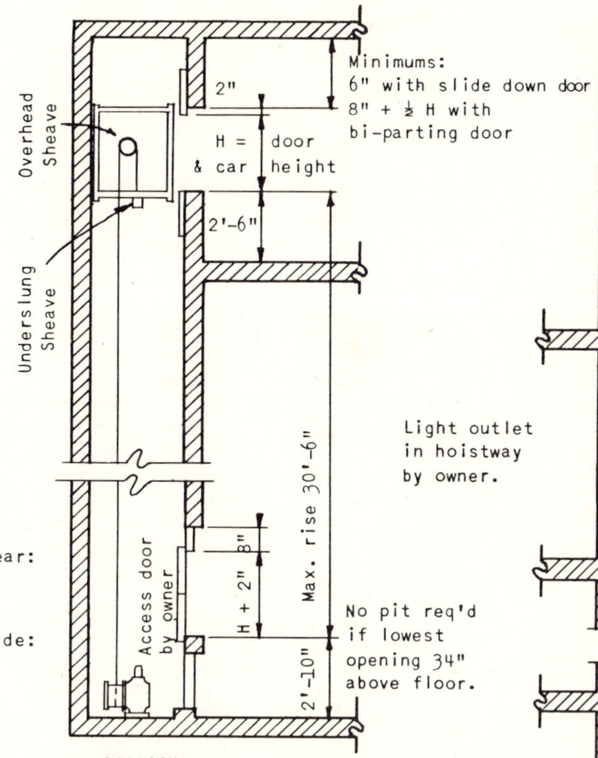
Overhead Sheave
2"
Minimums:
6" with slide down door
8" + ½ H with
bi-parting door
H = door
& car height
2'-6"
Underslung Sheave
Max. rise 30'-6"
Access door by owner
3"
H + 2"
2'-10"
No pit req'd
if lowest
opening 34"
above floor.

SECTION

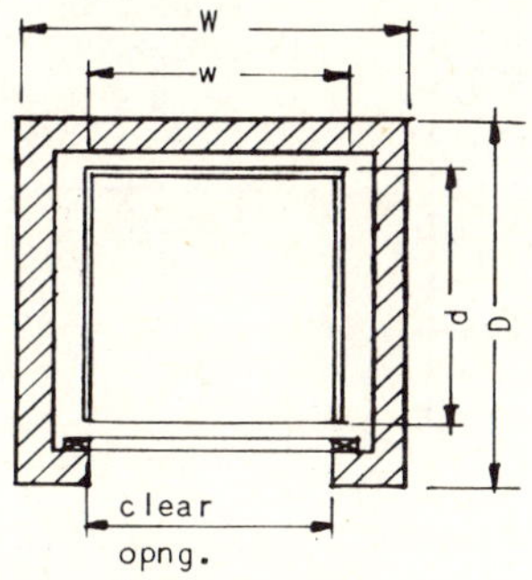
W
w
d
D
clear
opng.

PLAN

For traction or drum type dumbwaiter. Clear openings: at upper landing, same as car width; at lower landing, car width + 4". Rough openings for door framings vary with door type. Max. allowable size for dumbwaiters: 48" height; 9 sq. ft. area.

DRUM TYPE

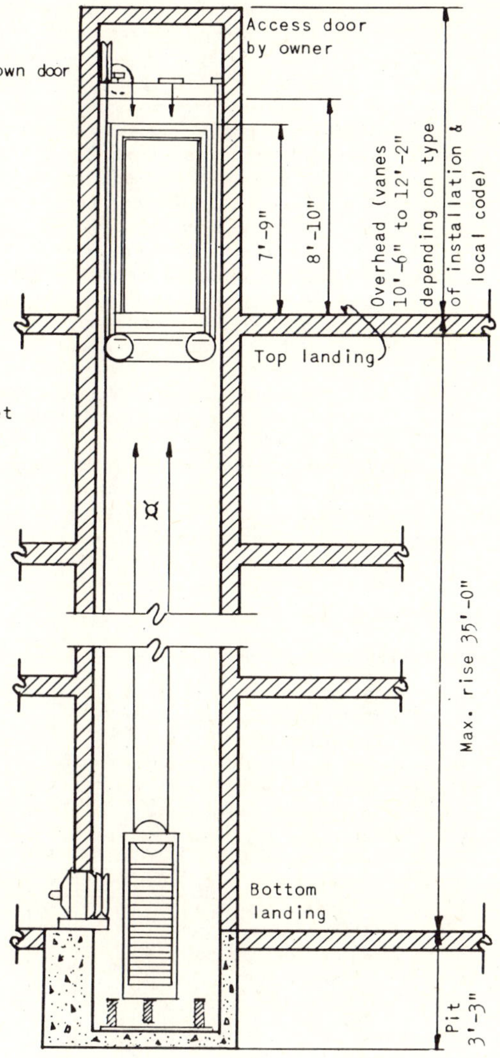
Access door
by owner
7'-9"
8'-10"
Overhead (vanes 10'-6" to 12'-2" depending on type of installation & local code)
Top landing
Light outlet
in hoistway
by owner.
Max. rise 35'-0"
Bottom
landing
Pit
3'-3"

SECTION

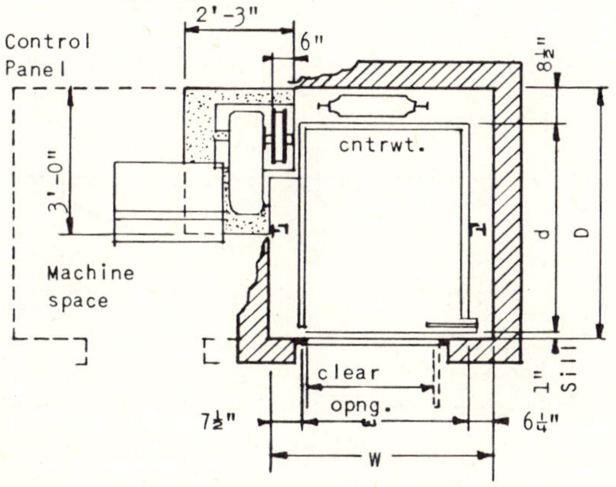
2'-3"
6"
8½"
Control
Panel
cntrwt.
3'-0"
Machine
space
d
D
1"
Sill
clear
opng.
7½"
6¼"
W

DUMBWAITERS								
CAR		HOISTWAY (approx.)						
width x depth		Traction Type				Drum Type		
		cntrwt. at rear		cntrwt. at side		W	D	
		W-Width *	D-Depth	W-Width**	D-Depth	Width*	Depth	
2'-0"	2'-0"	–	–	–	–	2'-10"	2'-5"	
	2'-6"	2'-10"	3'-5"	3'-1"	2'-11"	2'-10"	2'-11"	
	3'-0"	2'-10"	3'-11"	3'-1"	3'-5"	2'-10"	3'-5"	
2'-6"	2'-0"	–	–	–	–	3'-4"	2'-5"	
	2'-6"	3'-4"	3'-5"	3'-7"	2'-11"	3'-4"	2'-11"	
	3'-0"	3'-4"	3'-11"	3'-7"	3'-5"	3'-4"	3'-5"	
	3'-6"	3'-4"	4'-5"	3'-7"	3'-11"	–	–	
3'-0"	2'-0"	–	–	–	–	3'-10"	2'-5"	
	2'-6"	3'-10"	3'-5"	4'-1"	2'-11"	3'-10"	2'-11"	
	3'-0"	3'-10"	3'-11"	4'-1"	3'-5"	3'-10"	3'-5"	
3'-6"	2'-6"	4'-4"	3'-5"	4'-7"	2'-11"	–	–	
Car heights		3'-0", 3'-6", & 4'-0"				2'-6", 3'-0", 4'-0"		
Under-counter car heights						2'-6", 3'-0"		
Hoistway dimensions		based on use of bi-parting doors.				vary slightly with type of door		

* & ** see Hoistway Clearances.

RESIDENCE ELEVATOR (Speed 35 ft./min.)					
Rated Passenger Capacity	Platform		Hoistway		Hoistway door
	w width	d depth	W Width	D Depth	clear opng.
Two	3'-0"	3'-0"	4'-2"	3'-11"	2'-0"
Four or Wheel-chair & Attend't	3'-4"	4'-4"	4'-6"	5'-2½"	2'-8"

Platform sizes available from 2'-3" wide x 2'-7"* deep to 3'-5" wide x 4'-4" deep. Std. door 7'-0" high. (*contingent upon type of safety.)

Data by courtesy of Otis Elevator Co.

SELECTION of FREIGHT ELEVATORS

The following explanations and examples are to serve as guides in choosing a freight elevator and its carrying capacity for various conditions.

The carrying capacity per hour is determined by the normal load of the elevator and the time required per round trip. The round trip time is made up of the following four elements, as shown below on the Time Curve:

(All time is in seconds.)

1. Running Time: equals the distance travelled divided by the car speed chosen. May be read directly from the Time Curve.
2. Accelerating and Retarding Time: the additional time required to accelerate and the car for each stop.
3. Door Time: the time required to operate car gate and hoistway doors for each stop.
4. Loading Time: the time required to load and unload the car. Varies greatly with the type of material handled and the method of handling used.

NOTE: It is recommended that whenever practical a study be made of the loading and unloading operations of a similar elevator. If local studies on a similar elevator determine more closely the loading time, such figures should be used in preference to those given in the Time Curve.

It is advisable to add 20% to the calculated round trip time.

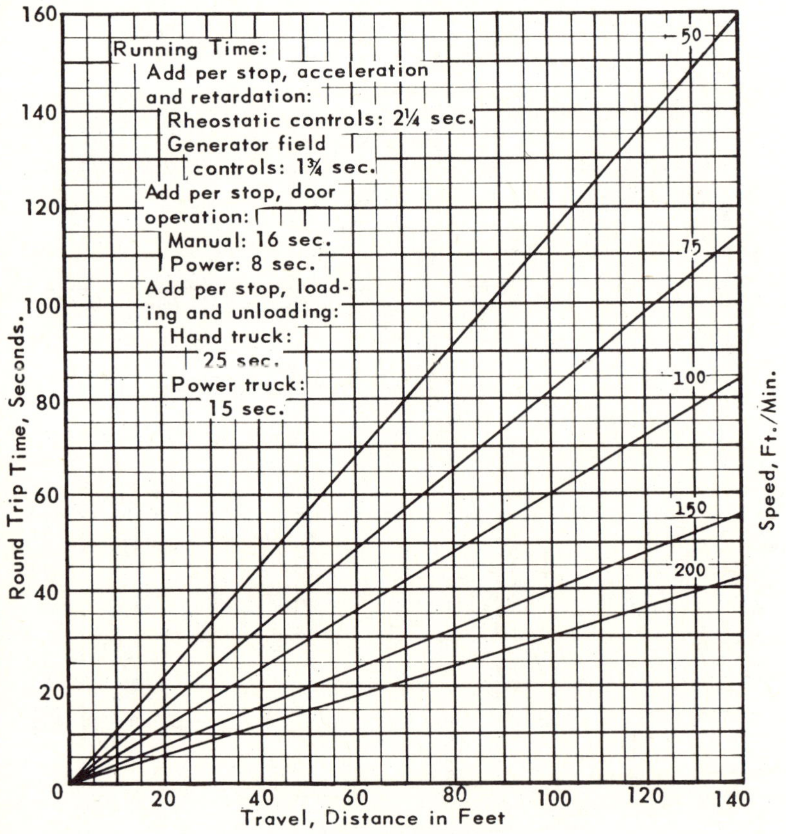

Running Time:
Add per stop, acceleration and retardation:
Rheostatic controls: 2¼ sec.
Generator field controls: 1¾ sec.
Add per stop, door operation:
Manual: 16 sec.
Power: 8 sec.
Add per stop, loading and unloading:
Hand truck: 25 sec.
Power truck: 15 sec.
50
75
100
150
200
160
140
120
100
80
60
40
20
0
20
40
60
80
100
120
140
Round Trip Time, Seconds.
Speed, Ft./Min.
Travel, Distance in Feet

TIME CURVE

EXAMPLE ONE

Given: a 5-story building.

Floor	Height
1 to 2	18 feet
2 to 3	16 "
3 to 4	16 "
4 to 5	16 "

Total travel distances: 66 feet

material to be handled:

1. 225,000 pounds in pallets between 1st and 4th floors on power trucks. A power truck is 6'-0" long, 4'-0" wide, and weighs 3500 pounds empty, 6500 pounds loaded.
2. 75,000 pounds in and out between various floors by hand truck and package.

Total: 300,000 pounds in and out of building per day.

CALCULATIONS:

Capacity and size. The capacity of the elevator depends on the weight of the loaded power truck. A 6000 pound rating could be used if the truck remains on the floor but it provides no reserve. From the General Data table on the following page, the 8'-4" x 10'-0" platform size 8000 pound rating would be selected. (It is not necessary, with a 6'-0" x 4'-0" power truck, to go to the 8'-4" x 12'-0" platform size, which also has an 8000 pound rating.)

Type of equipment. Leveling equipment is desirable to assure accurate landing at the floors to facilitate moving the power truck on and off the car. The weight of material to be moved per day will cause this elevator to be quite active, and thus generator field equipment should be considered.

Door operation. Power operated doors are desirable where elevator is quite active.

Speed selection. See General Data Table, on a following page. The recommended speed for 5 floors (66 feet travel), with generator field controls, is 150 feet per minute.

Calculation of time. For 3/4 service between first and fourth floors:

with loaded power truck on elevator

Running Time	20	sec.
Acceleration and Retardation	1¾	"
Door Operation	8	"
Loading and Unloading	15	"
Total time one way	44¾	sec. Use: 45 sec.

Round trip time = 2 x 45 = 90 sec. plus 20% = 108 sec.

$\frac{225,000 \text{ lbs.}}{3,000 \text{ lbs/trip}}$ = 75 trips. 75 trips x 108 sec. = 2 hours 15 minutes.

with power truck remaining on floor (assume 2 pallets per trip)

Running Time	20	sec.
Acceleration and Retardation	1¾	"
Door Operation	8	"
Loading and Unloading	90	" (varies widely)
Total time one way	119¾	Use: 120 sec.

Round trip time = 2 x 120 = 240 sec. plus 20% = 288 sec.

$\frac{225,000 \text{ lbs.}}{6,000 \text{ lbs./trip}}$ = 38 trips. 38 trips x 288 sec. = 3 hours 3 minutes.

The balance of the service is moving 75,000 pounds between first and various floors by hand truck and package. Assume an average load of 1500 pounds; average travel first to third floor, 34 feet; and an average of 3 stops per round trip.

Running Time	14	sec.
Acceleration and Retardation (average)	2-5/8	"
Door Operation (average)	12	"
Loading and Unloading (2 hand trucks)	50	"
Total time one way	78-5/8	sec. Use 80 sec.

Round trip time = 2 x 80 = 160 sec. plus 20% = 192 sec.

$\frac{75,000 \text{ lbs. (1st to 3rd fl.)}}{15,000 \text{ lbs./trip}}$ = 50 trips. 50 trips x 192 sec. = 2 hours 40 minutes

Total time to move 300,000 pounds in and out of building is:

a. If power truck remains on elevator with load:
2 hrs. 15 min. plus 2 hrs. 40 mins. = 4 hrs. 55 mins.

b. If power truck remains on floor:
3 hrs. 3 mins. plus 2 hrs. 40 mins. = 5 hrs. 43 mins.

Data by courtesy of Westinghouse Elevator Division, Westinghouse Electric Corporation

SELECTION of FREIGHT ELEVATORS

EXAMPLE TWO

Given: a 3-story building

Floor	Feet
1 to 2	18
2 to 3	16
Total Travel distance . . .	34 feet

material to be handled:

1. miscellaneous freight, some to be moved in hand trucks and some in package form
2. hand truck size is 4'-6" long, 2'-6" wide; truck weight 250 lbs., load weight 750 lbs.

total: 20,000 lbs. in and out of building per day (8 hrs.)

CALCULATIONS:

Capacity and size. From the General Date Table, the 6'-4" x 8'-0" car would be chosen, to accommodate two hand trucks per trip or 45 square feet for loads of miscellaneous packages. The 3000 pound capacity elevator would be preferable for possible greater loads in the future.

Type of equipment. It is evident that this elevator will not be very active so rheostatic controls will be considered.

Door operation. Because this elevator will not be very active, manually operated doors will be chosen.

Speed selection. See General Data Table. The recommended speed for 3 floors (34 feet travel) with rheostatic control is 75 feet per minute.

Calculation of time. For service from first to third floor without an intermediate stop. Refer to Time Curve on preceding page.

Running Time	27	sec.
Acceleration and Retardation	2¼	sec.
Door Operation	16	sec.
Loading and Unloading	50	sec.
Total time one way	95¼	sec. Use 95 sec.

Round trip time = 2 × 95 = 190 sec. plus 20% = 228 sec.

$\frac{20{,}000 \text{ lbs./day}}{15{,}000 \text{ lbs./trip}}$ = 13 trips. 13 trips × 228 sec. = 50 minutes.

If most of the material is carried in package loads, the two types of handling should be figured separately, and the total used. Package loading time will increase the trip times, and will vary greatly.

GEARED FREIGHT ELEVATORS. Capacity 4000 to 10000 lbs. Speed 50 to 200 feet per minute. 2:1 roping

CAPACITY pounds	SPEED ft/min.	DIMENSIONS A	B	C	J	K = Plan 1. Q = 5"	K = Plan 1. Q = 6¾"	K = Plan 2. Q = 5"	K = Plan 2. Q = 6¾"	K = Plan 2. Q = φ	L	S	N	P	R	R'	T	V	Z
4000	75	6'-4"	8'-0"	6'-0"	8'-5"	8'-7¼"	8'-9"	8'-10"	9'-1½"	8'-11¾"	12"	17"	8"	4'-6"	10⅝"		13⅜"	10"	6¾"
	100	8'-4"	10'-0"	8'-0"	10'-5"	10'-7¼"	10'-9"	10'-10"	11'-1½"	10'-11¾"	12⅝"						9½"		
5000	75	8'-4"	10'-0"	8'-0"	10'-5"	10'-7¼"	10'-9"	10'-10"	11'-1½"	10'-11¾"	12⅜"	18"	8"	4'-9"	10⅝"		9½"	10"	7¾"
	100		12'-0"			12'-7¼"	12'-9"	12'-10"	13'-1½"	12'-11¾"									
	200		10'-0" 12'-0"			10'-7¼" 12'-7¼"	10'-9" 12'-9"	10'-10" 12'-10"	11'-1½" 13'-1½"	10'-11¾" 12'-11¾"	18¾"			5'-3"	13¼"			11"	
6000	50	8'-4"	10'-0" 12'-0"	8'-0"	10'-5"	10'-7¼" 12'-7¼"	10'-9" 12'-9"	10'-10" 12'-10"	11'-1½" 13'-1½"	10'-11¾" 12'-11¾"	12⅜"	18"	8"	4'-9"	10⅝"		9½"	10"	7¾"
	75		10'-0"			10'-7¼"	10'-9"	10'-10"	11'-1½"	10'-11¾"	17¾"				13¼"		10½"	11"	
	100		12'-0"			12'-7¼"	12'-9"	12'-10"	13'-1½"	12'-11¾"									
	200		10'-0" 12'-0"			10'-7¼" 12'-7¼"	10'-9" 12'-9"	10'-10" 12'-10"	11'-1½" 13'-1½"	10'-11¾" 12'-11¾"				5'-3"					
8000	50	8'-4"	10'-0"	8'-0"	10'-10"	10'-7¼"	10'-9"	10'-10"	11'-1½"	10'-11¾"	14⅞"	20"	10"	5'-6"	13"		12½"	12"	8¾"
	100		12'-0"			12'-7¼"	12'-9"	12'-10"	13'-1½"	12'-11¾"	14½"								8½"
	200		10'-0" 12'-0"			10'-7¼" 12'-7¼"	10'-9" 12'-9"	10'-10" 12'-10"	11'-1½" 13'-1½"	10'-11¾" 12'-11¾"	21" 20¾"				14¾"	15¼"	14"	15"	8¾" 8½"
10000	75	8'-4" 10'-4"	12'-0" 14'-0"	8'-0" 10'-0"	10'-11" 12'-11"	12'-7¼" 14'-7¼"	12'-9" 14'-9"	12'-10" 14'-10"	13'-1½" 15'-1½"	12'-11¾" 14'-11¾"	12½"	21"	10"	5'-6"	13"		14½"	12"	9"
	100	8'-4" 10'-4"	12'-0" 14'-0"	8'-0" 10'-0"	10'-11" 12'-11"	12'-7¼" 14'-7¼"	12'-9" 14'-9"	12'-10" 14'-10"	13'-1½" 15'-1½"	12'-11¾" 14'-11¾"	20" 17⅞"			6'-0"	14¾"	15¼"		15"	

CAPACITY pounds	SPEED ft/min.	DIMENSIONS U	M	W	BG	MB	TB	Minimum O.T.	Minimum T.C.	SHEAVES CAR	SHEAVES CWT	OVERHEAD LOAD IN POUNDS D	E	F	G	H	X	Y
4000	75	16'-0"	13'-9"	11'-1"	30"	10"	9"	2'-1"	4'-0"	24"	24"	8650	5400	4500	3900	3150	5500	6200
	100		10'-3"	12'-3"	36"				4'-2"			10250	6500	4050	3900	4300	6100	6150
5000	75	16'-1"	13'-9"	11'-1"	36"	12"	10"	2'-1"	4'-2"	24"	24"	11000	6600	4800	4900	4850	6700	7050
	100											11350	6900	5500	5100	5050	6950	7550
	200	16'-4"	15'-4"	14'-0"			12"	2'-5"	4'-3"			14250 14400	7400 7700	5300 11500	6250 6400	5250 0	7300 7300	8000 9100
6000	50	15'-10"	13'-9"	11'-1"	36"	12"	10"	2'-11"	3'-11"	24"	24"	11550 11650	7000 7250	5100 5700	5150 5400	5250 5400	7100 7150	7500 7600
	75	16'-1"							4'-2"			12900	6750	10400	5700	0	6650	7300
	100	16'-3"						2'-4"				13150.	7050	10600	5900	0	6700	8300
	200	16'-4"	15'-4"	14'-0"			12"	2'-5"	4'-3"			14700 15050	7850 8100	5650 11950	6450 6700	5600 0	7850 7800	8350 9400
8000	50	16'-6"	13'-9"	11'-4"	36"	15"	12"	2'-1"	3'-11"	27"	24"	14650	8050	7450	7250	7300	7300	8650
	100				42"			2'-4"	4'-2"		30"	15200	8350	7700	7500	7500	7500	9000
	200	16'-8"	15'-4"	14'-0"	36"			2'-5"	4'-3"		24" 30"	19450 20150	9900 10200	16400 17000	8200 8500	0 0	8400 8700	7750 8000
10000	75	16'-10"	15'-4"	14'-3"	42"	15"	12"	2'-4"	4'-2"	27"	30"	15310 17350	10200 11400	8900 9200	7800 8000	8350 9400	9760 10850	11000 11200
	100	17'-1"			42" 48"		15"					20950 21000	10600 12500	17700 11900	8800 11050	0 11500	9050 12400	8300 12500

Data by courtesy of Westinghouse Elevator Division, Westinghouse Electric Corporation.

GENERAL DATA for TYPICAL FREIGHT ELEVATORS

GENERAL DATA

TYPES AND USES

Type of Traffic	Method of Loading	Capacity (pounds)	Max. Rise (No. of floors)	Type of Elevator
Very Light	Manual *	2500	3 (or 30') to sidewalk Level	Sidewalk
		2500	3 (or 35') inside bldg.	Self supporting
Light		2500 to 3500	6, 7 or more	General Purpose
Medium	Manual * or Auto-mobile**	3500 to 8000	Any no. of floors	
Heavy		8000 to 10,000		
	Industrial or Auto Truck	8000 to 20,000 & more		Truck

*Includes uses of hand trucks and small, slow speed electric pallet trucks
**Includes passenger cars and light trucks.

CONTROL SYSTEM

Generator Field (floors)	Rheostatic (floors)	ELEVATOR SPEED ft/min.
	2	50
2 or 3 (10,000 pound cap.)	3 or 4	75
2 or 3	5 to 8	100
4 or 5		150
6 to 10		200

1. If one of the floors exceeds 20 feet in height, the next higher speed is desirable.
2. Higher speeds available if needed.

STANDARD CAR SIZES

Figures given as Width X Depth.

Inside Dimensions	Platform Dimensions	Standard opening size	Net Area (sq.ft.)	Standard Capacity Rating in thousands of pounds	
5'-0" x 6'-6"	5'-4" x 7'-0"	5'-0" x 8'-0"	32.5	2.5, 3	(3)*
6'-0" x 7'-6"	6'-4" x 8'-0"	6'-0" x 8'-0"	45.0	2.5, 3, 4	(5)*
8'-0" x 9'-6"	8'-4" x 10'-0"	8'-0" x 8'-0"	76.0	4, 5, 6, 8	(8)*
8'-0" x 11'-6"	8'-4" x 12'-0"	8'-0" x 8'-0"	92.0	5, 6, 8, 10	(10)*
10'-0" x 13'-6"	10'-4" x 14'-0"	10'-0" x 8'-0"	135.0	10	(16)*
10'-0" x 15'-6"	10'-4" x 16'-0"	Usually determined by load characteristics.		12	
10'-0" x 19'-6"	10'-4" x 20'-0"			14	
12'-0" x 15'-6"	12'-4" x 16'-0"			16, 18, 20	
Special	Usually determined by load characteristics.			24, 30	*Recommended, if also used for passengers.

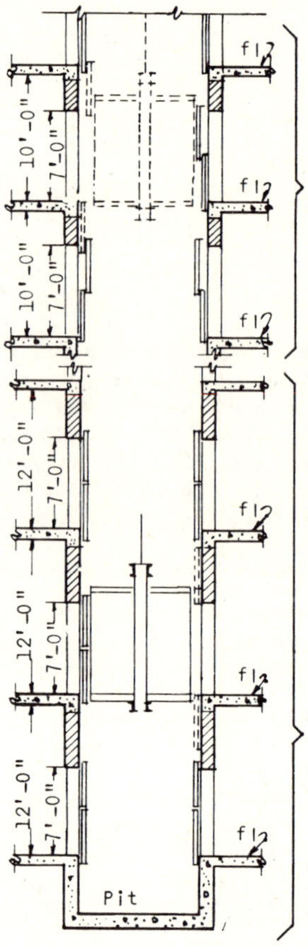

fl
10'-0"
7'-0"
12'-0"
Pit

Q = 6¾" (See plan #1) for pass type counter-balanced doors.

NOTE:
Pass type doors are required when floor heights are less than 11'-0" for a 7'-0" high opening or less than 12'-6" for an 8'-0" high opening.

Q = 5" for a regular type counter-balanced door.

Q = ℄ when one pass type & one regular type door are required

FREIGHT HOISTWAY DOOR TYPES

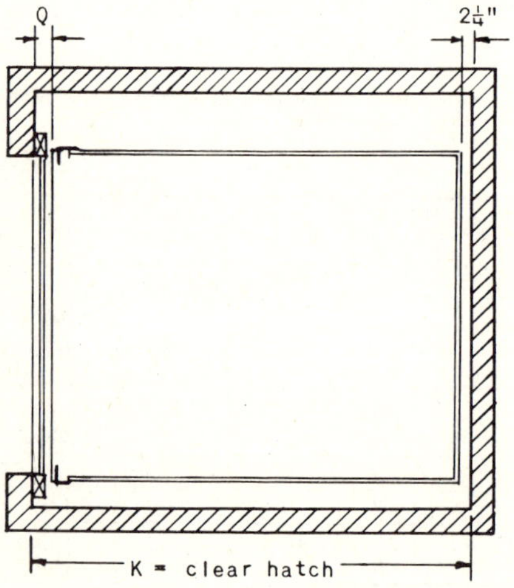

Q
2¼"
K = clear hatch

Dimension indications same as Plan #2.

PLAN #1: FRONT OPENING

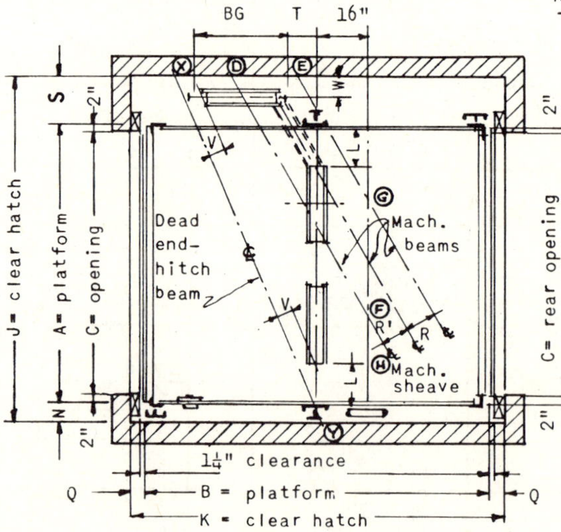

BG
T
16"
S
2"
W
Dead end-hitch beam
Mach. beams
Mach. sheave
J = clear hatch
A = platform
C = opening
C = rear opening
N
1¼" clearance
B = platform
K = clear hatch
Q

PLAN #2: FRONT AND REAR OPENING

Windows, light, adequate ventilation and access door to penthouse by owner.

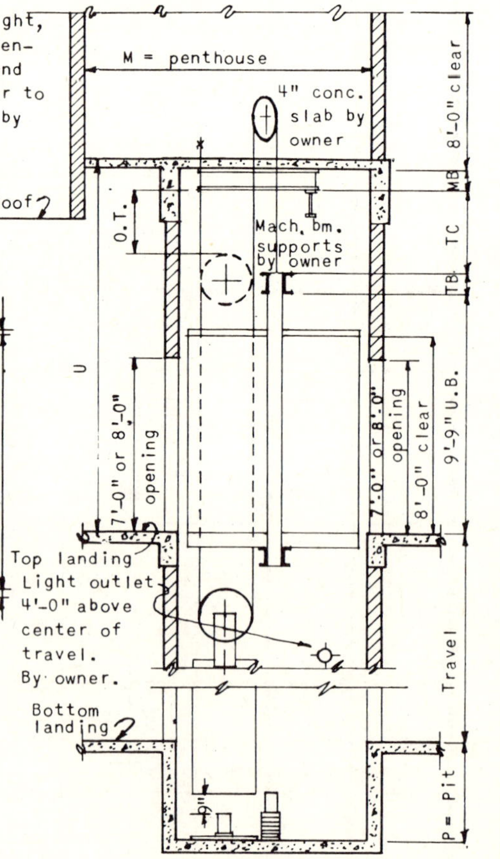

M = penthouse
4" conc. slab by owner
8'-0" clear
Roof
MB
O.T.
TC
Mach. bm. supports by owner
TB
U
7'-0" or 8'-0" opening
8'-0" clear
9'-9" U.B.
Top landing
Light outlet 4'-0" above center of travel. By owner.
Travel
Bottom landing
P = Pit

SECTION

Reactions at D, E, F, G, X and Y include allowance for impact. See Plans.
Weight of concrete slab not included. Increase pit depth and top clearance if required by local code.
NOTE: Dimensions and reactions may be found on "Selection of Freight Elevators" pages.

GEARED FREIGHT ELEVATORS: 2 to 1 roping, 4,000 to 10,000 lb. capacity, 50 to 200 ft. per minute.

Data by courtesy of Westinghouse Elevator Division, Westinghouse Electric Corporation.

GEARED FREIGHT and SIDEWALK ELEVATORS

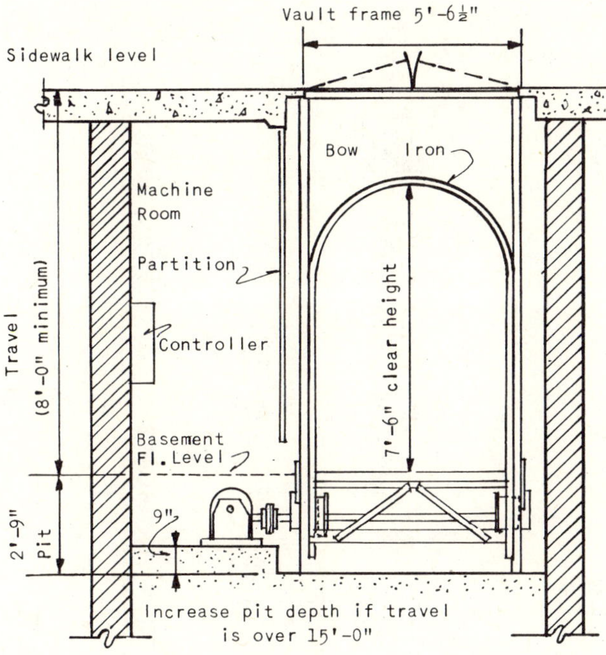

Vault frame 5'-6½"
Sidewalk level
Bow Iron
Machine Room
Partition
Controller
Travel (8'-0" minimum)
7'-6" clear height
Basement Fl. Level
9"
2'-9" Pit
Increase pit depth if travel is over 15'-0"

SECTION

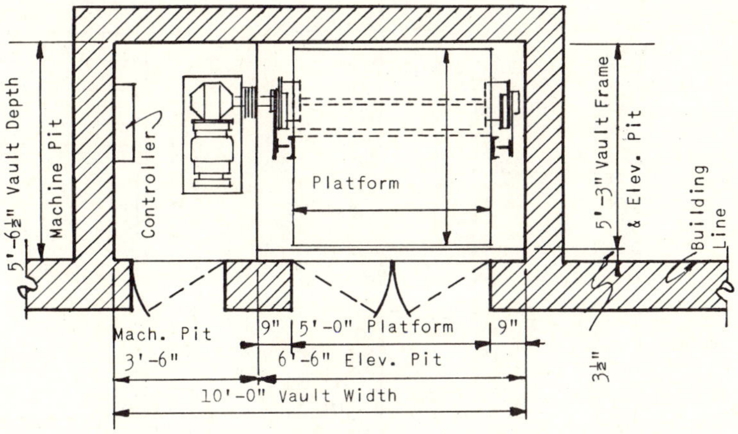

5'-6½" Vault Depth
Machine Pit
Controller
Platform
5'-3" Vault Frame & Elev. Pit
Building Line
Mach. Pit 3'-6"
9" 5'-0" Platform 9"
6'-6" Elev. Pit
10'-0" Vault Width
3½"

PLAN

Layout is for 15'-0" travel, between sidewalk and basement levels. Standard capacity is usually 2000 lbs. Control is of continuous pressure push button type with Up-Down buttons in each car. Maximum standard platforms are 5'-0" x 5'-0" or equivalent, with minimum front-to-back dimension 4'-0". Where local codes or special conditions of travel and capacity govern, special car sizes and capacities can be provided.

SIDEWALK ELEVATORS

Data by courtesy of Sedgwick Machine Works, N.Y., N.Y.

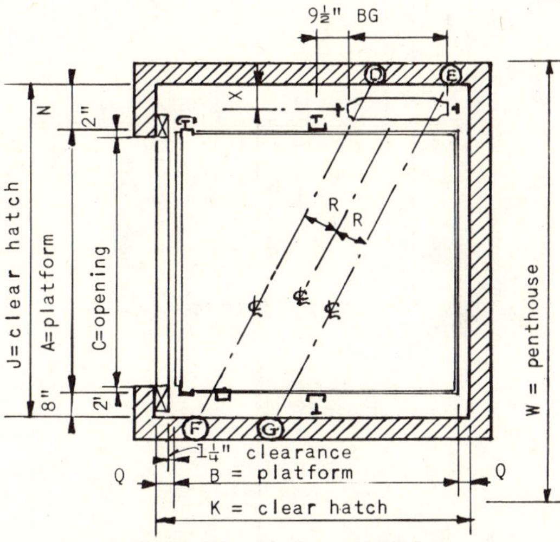

9½" BG
X
N
2"
R
R
J=clear hatch
A=platform
C=opening
W = penthouse
8"
2'
1¼" clearance
B = platform
K = clear hatch
Q
Q

PLAN #1 - Front Opening

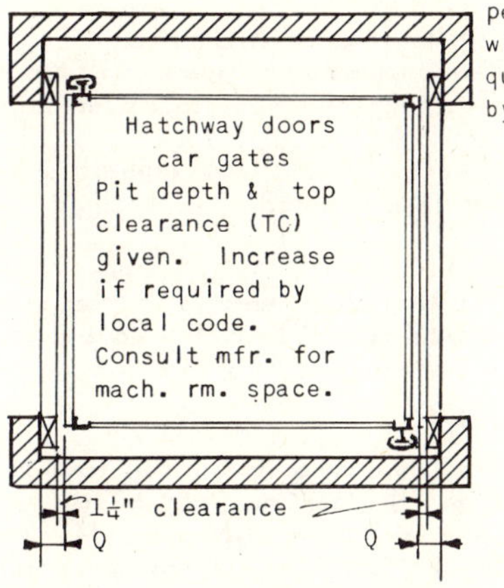

Hatchway doors
car gates
Pit depth & top
clearance (TC)
given. Increase
if required by
local code.
Consult mfr. for
mach. rm. space.
1¼" clearance
Q
Q

PLAN #2 - Front & Rear Opening

Max. distance between guide rail supports = 14'-0". Decrease if required by local code. Requirements for Q given on page "Geared Freight Elevators, 2:1 roping, etc."

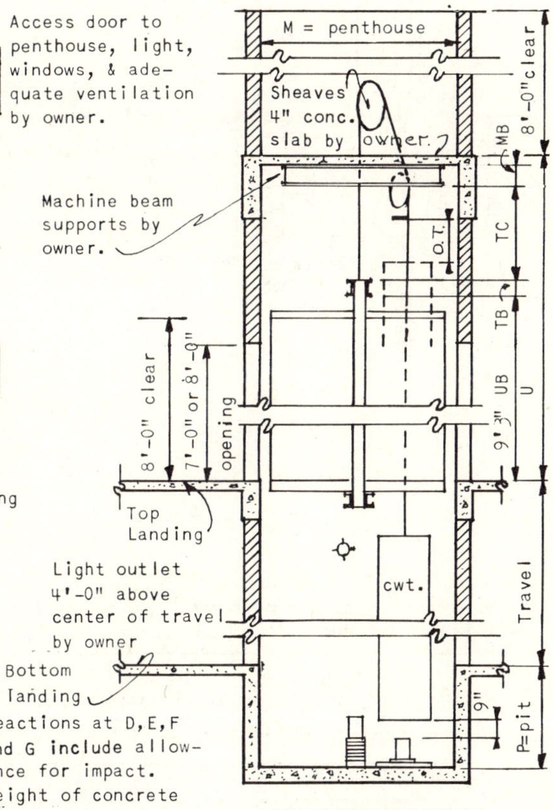

Access door to penthouse, light, windows, & adequate ventilation by owner.
M = penthouse
8'-0" clear
Sheaves
4" conc. slab by owner.
MB
Machine beam supports by owner.
O.T.
TC
TB
8'-0" clear
7'-0" or 8'-0" opening
UB
U
9'-3"
Top Landing
Light outlet 4'-0" above center of travel by owner
cwt.
Travel
Bottom landing
9"
P=pit

HOISTWAY SECTION

Reactions at D, E, F and G include allowance for impact. Weight of concrete slab not included.

GEARED FREIGHT ELEVATORS. 1:1 roping

Capacity 3000 and 4000 lbs. Speed 50 to 200 ft. per min.

CAPACITY pounds	SPEED ft/min.	DIMENSIONS							
		BG	MB	TB	K - Plan 1		K - Plan 2		
					Q = 5"	Q=6¾"	Q = 5"	Q= 6¾"	Q = φ
3000	50 100	27"	12"	8"	7-7¼" 8'-7¼"	7'-9" 8'-9"	7'-10" 8'-10"	8'-1½" 9'-1½"	7'-11¾" 8'-11¾"
4000	200	30" 33"	15"	9" 12"	8'-7¼" 10'-7¼"	8'-9" 10'-9"	8'-10" 10'-10"	9'-1½" 11'-1½"	8'-11¾" 10-11¾"

CAPACITY pounds	SPEED ft/min.	DIMENSIONS												OVERHEAD LOAD IN LBS.			
		A	B	C	J	N	P	R	U	X	M	W	Minimum O.T.	Minimum T.C.	D	E	F	G
3000	50 100	5'-4" 6'-4"	7'-0" 8'-0"	5'-0" 6'-0"	7'-3" 8'-3"	15"	4'-6"	10 5/8"	15'-6" 16'-0"	6"	9'-9" 10'-3"	10'-2" 11'-0"	2'-1" 2'-4"	3'-1" 3'-11"	8900 9200	6650 7300	4900 5450	5900 6100
4000	200	6'-4" 8'-4"	8'-0" 10'-0"	6'-0" 8'-0"	8'-5" 10'-5"	17"	5'-3"	13¼"	16'-4"	6½"	9'-6"	13'-0"	2'-5"	4'-3"	14150 15150	10850 12500	7800 9300	9450 10350

Data by courtesy of Westinghouse Elevator Division, Westinghouse Electric Corporation.

OIL-LIFT HYDRAULIC FREIGHT ELEVATORS

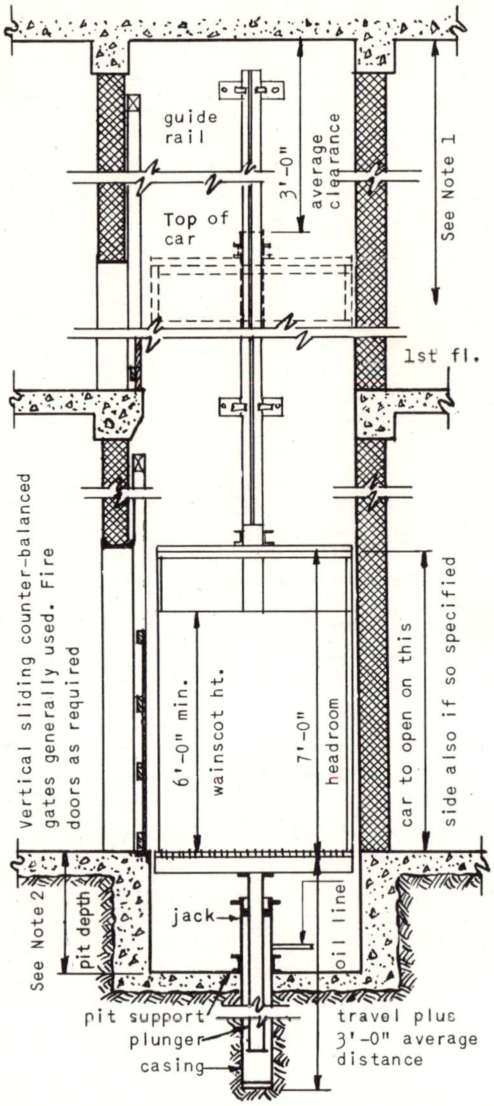
guide rail
3'-0"
average clearance
See Note 1
Top of car
1st fl.
Vertical sliding counter-balanced gates generally used. Fire doors as required
6'-0" min.
wainscot ht.
7'-0"
headroom
car to open on this side also if so specified
See Note 2
pit depth
jack
oil line
pit support
plunger
casing
travel plus 3'-0" average distance

SECTION
HATCHWAY GATES

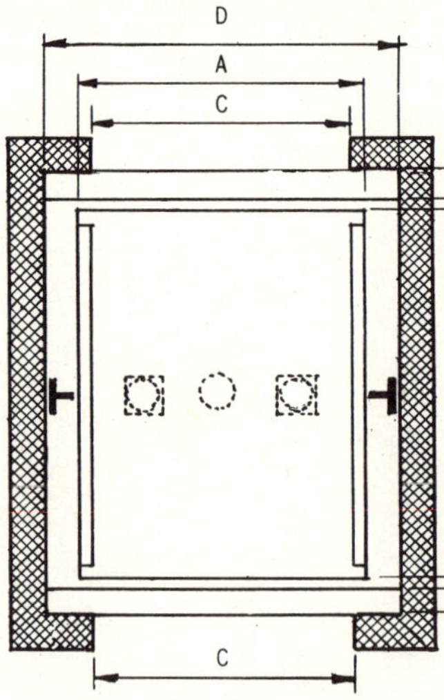
D
A
C
B
C
C

PLAN

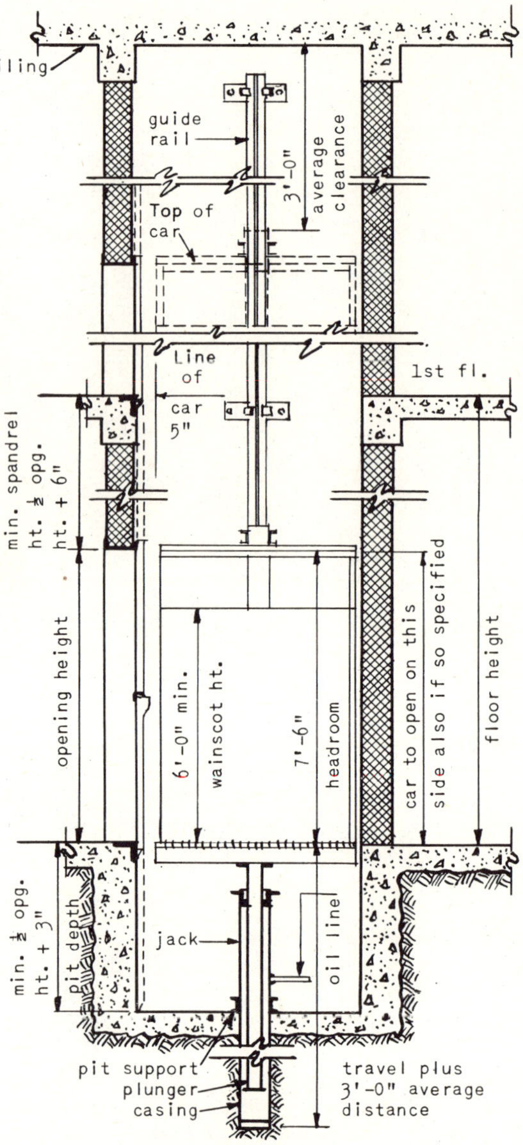
ceiling
guide rail
3'-0"
average clearance
Top of car
Line of car 5"
1st fl.
min. spandrel ht. ½ opg. ht. + 6"
opening height
6'-0" min.
wainscot ht.
7'-6"
headroom
car to open on this side also if so specified
floor height
min. ½ opg. ht. + 3"
pit depth
jack
oil line
pit support
plunger
casing
travel plus 3'-0" average distance

SECTION
HATCHWAY DOORS

HATCHWAY DOORS:
Dimensions shown on section cover regular bi-parting hatchway doors. Where floor heights are less than 11'-9" (for 7'-6" opening height) "pass" type doors are used. These require a minimum spandrel height of 10" and clearance of 6¾" is needed instead of 5".

BUILDING STRUCTURE:
To support only guide rail bracket loadings. Vertical loads supported through hydraulic jack to pit floor. Penthouse and load-supporting columns eliminated.

NOTE 1:
Ceiling clearance: 13'-6" for single blade gates; 11'-0" for double-blade gates or 11'-6" for fire doors.

NOTE 2:
Pit depth: for bi-parting fire doors use ½ door opening height plus 3". For manually operated gates, 3'-0" minimum, or to meet local codes.

RD = Regular duty elevators. Equipment built to handle maximum unit load of one-half total capacity on the axle, with total net reasonably distributed over platform area.

HD = Heavy duty elevators. Will handle fork trucks and other power-operated vehicles, with 80% of total capacity concentrated on one axle.

CAPACITY, pounds	Recom. Aver. Speed, ft. per min.* Landings			Platform Dimensions		Opening Width	Manual Gates	Manual Doors	Motorized Doors	Manual Gates	Bi-Parting Doors	Pass-Type Doors
	2	3	4	A	B	C	D	D	D	E	E	E
2000 RD	45	65	85	4'-0"	6'-0"	3'-9"	4'-10½"	5'-3"	5'-9"	7'-1½"	6'-10"	7'-1½"
4000 RD	40	55	80	5'-0"	7'-0"	4'-9"	6'-1"	6'-3"	6'-9"	8'-1½"	7'-10"	8'-1½"
5000 R&HD	40	65	80	6'-0"	8'-0"	5'-9"	7'-1"	7'-3"	7'-9"	9'-1½"	8'-10"	9'-1½"
7500 R&HD	25	45	65	8'-0"	10'-0"	7'-9"	9'-6"	9'-6"	9'-9"	11'-1½"	10'-10"	11'-1½"
10000 RD	30	40	60	10'-0"	12'-0"	9'-9"	11'-6"	11'-6"	11'-9"	13'-1½"	12'-10"	13'-1½"
10000 HD	30	40	60	10'-0"	12'-0"	9'-9"	12'-0"	12'-0"	12'-0"	13'-1½"	12'-10"	13'-1½"
15000 HD	20	35	45	10'-0"	15'-0"	9'-9"	12'-6"	12'-6"	12'-6"	16'-1½"	15'-10"	16'-1½"
20000 HD	20	30	30	10'-0"	20'-0"	9'-9"	13'-0"	13'-0"	13'-0"	21'-1½"	20'-10"	21'-1½"

*EXAMPLE: 60 ft. per min. up, 70 ft. per min. down = 65 ft. per min. average
Data by courtesy of Burwak Elevator Co., N.Y., N.Y.

ESCALATORS

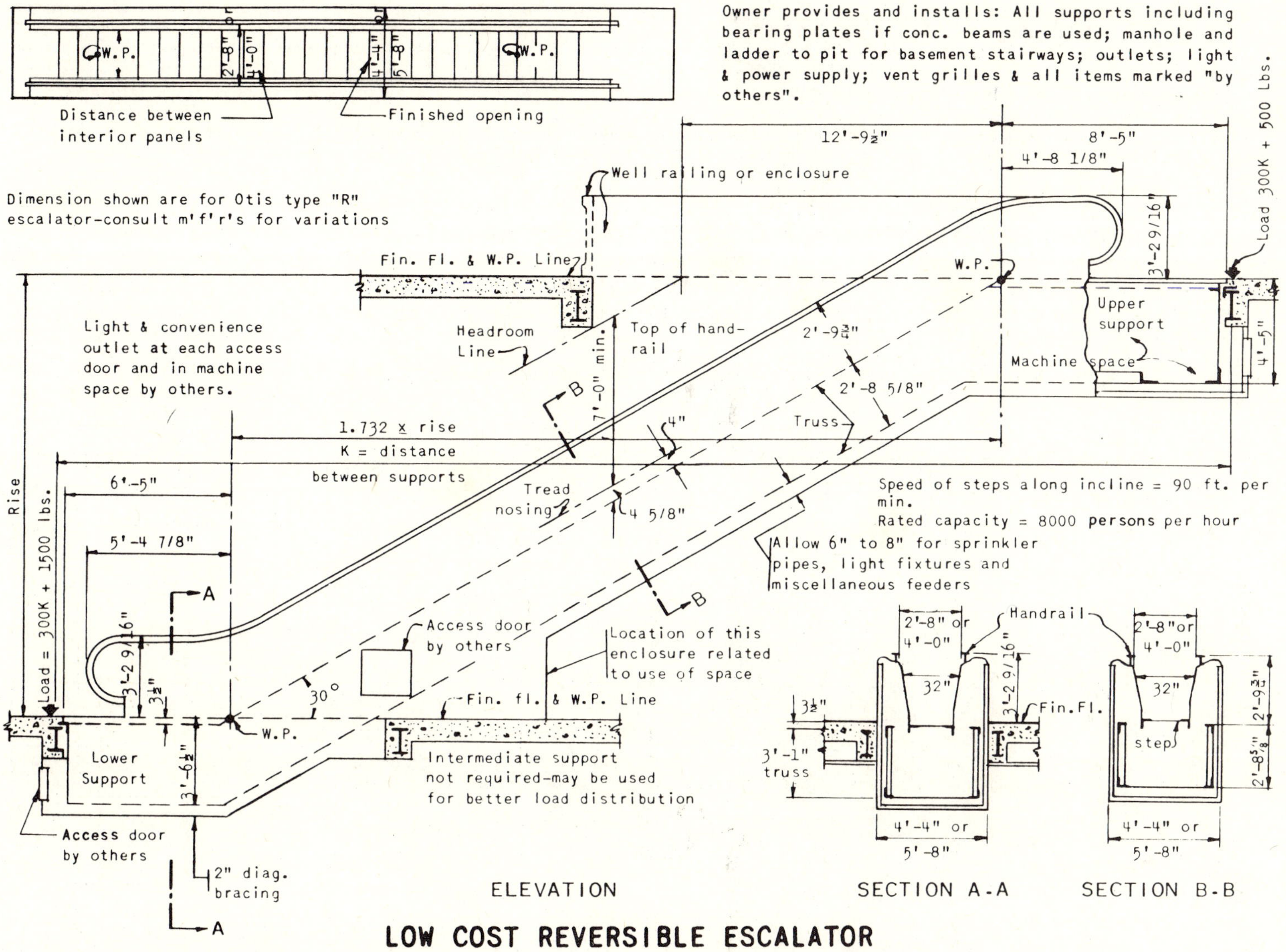
W.P.
2'-8"
4'-0"
4'-4"
5'-8"
W.P.
Distance between interior panels
Finished opening
Owner provides and installs: All supports including bearing plates if conc. beams are used; manhole and ladder to pit for basement stairways; outlets; light & power supply; vent grilles & all items marked "by others".
12'-9½"
8'-5"
4'-8 1/8"
Load 300K + 500 Lbs.
Well railing or enclosure
Dimension shown are for Otis type "R" escalator-consult m'f'r's for variations
3'-2 9/16"
Fin. Fl. & W.P. Line
W.P.
Light & convenience outlet at each access door and in machine space by others.
Headroom Line
7'-0" min.
Top of handrail
2'-9¾"
Upper support
Machine space
4'-5"
2'-8 5/8"
Truss
1.732 x rise
K = distance between supports
4"
Rise
6'-5"
Tread nosing
4 5/8"
Speed of steps along incline = 90 ft. per min.
Rated capacity = 8000 persons per hour
Allow 6" to 8" for sprinkler pipes, light fixtures and miscellaneous feeders
5'-4 7/8"
Load = 300K + 1500 lbs.
A
B
B
3'-2 9/16"
Access door by others
Location of this enclosure related to use of space
30°
3½"
Fin. fl. & W.P. Line
W.P.
Lower Support
3'-6½"
Intermediate support not required-may be used for better load distribution
Access door by others
2" diag. bracing
A
2'-8" or 4'-0"
Handrail
3'-2 9/16"
32"
3½"
Fin. Fl.
3'-1" truss
4'-4" or 5'-8"
2'-8" or 4'-0"
32"
2'-9¾"
step
2'-8⅝"
4'-4" or 5'-8"
ELEVATION
SECTION A-A
SECTION B-B

LOW COST REVERSIBLE ESCALATOR

A further step in the development of horizontal and vertical transportation in the extension of the principal lanes of circulation or transportation is the continuous moving passenger conveyor or belt. The conveyor for public use operates without attendant at a speed of between 152 to 180 feet per minute on a recommended maximum incline of 10 degrees.

Moving passenger conveyors will be found most useful in buildings where large groups of people must move long distances horizontally & go up or down a short rise-such as in air or other transportation terminals connections between terminals, stadiums, arenas.

Max. incline: 10 degrees
3'-4" for 2 persons width

MOVING PASSENGER CONVEYORS

Data supplied by Otis Elevator Co.-checked by Mongitore & Moesel, Consulting Engineers.

PNEUMATIC TUBES

Pneumatic tube systems provide very rapid Transmission of small articles, paper and liquids in "carriers" to and from predetermined stations. Also any office paper which can be folded to a 5½" x 2⅜" size (see dwg. below) may act as its own carrier. One end of the folded paper is turned up, acting as a sail, and the air in the system carries the paper to its destination. The power may be either vacuum or pressure.

Tube size may be selected from 1½" to 3" x 12" and the system used will vary with the articles to be carried and the service demanded

Pneumatic tube systems have proved useful not only in long accepted uses such as in department stores, post offices, mills and hospitals, but in many industries, especially in product control, and in building types as listed below.

CARRIER

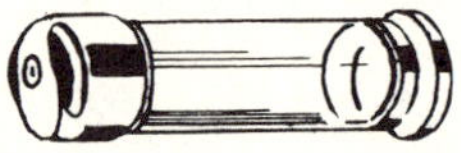

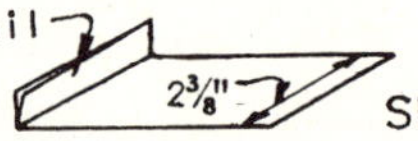
sail
2⅜"

SELF CARRIER PAPER

INSTALLATION

Installation may be exposed in furred space, in floor slabs, outside of the building or underground.

Exposed lines and lines through refrigerated space must be protected to prevent condensation on the interior of the tube.

Underground tube should be placed below frost line in conduit and the interior of conduit and space around tubes filled with tar.

The minimum radius of the tubes as indicated on the following table must be considered in determining the location where tubes will be run as their minimum radii vary from 18" to 5'-0".

SELECTION OF SIZES

BUILDING TYPE	CARRIER INSIDE			TUBE	
	DIA., SIZE	LENGTH	CU.IN.	SIZE	RADII
Office	1 3/8"	6"	8.9	2¼"	18"
	1 7/16"	6½" 8½"			24" 36"
	1 3/8"	9" 10"	13.36 14.85		42" 48"
	7 15/16"	10" 12"	29.5 35.38	3"	48"
	1¾" x 4½"	12"		3" x 6"	48"
	10 11/16" x 2 11/16"	15"	430.83	3" x 12"	60"
Dept. Stores & Banks	1 3/8"	6" 9" 10"	8.9 13.36 14.85	2¼"	18" 42" 48"
	5 9/16" x 2 9/16"	12"	154.14	4" x 7"	48"
Railroad Yard install.	7 15/16"	12"	35.38	3"	48"
	2 11/16"	12"	68.0	4"	48"
	5 9/16" x 2 9/16"	12" 14"	154.14 179.83	4" x 7"	48" 60

BUILDING TYPE	CARRIER INSIDE			TUBE	
	DIA., SIZE	LENGTH	CU.IN.	SIZE	RADII
Telegraph & Post Office	1 3/8"	6"	8.9	2¼"	42"
	5 9/16" x 2 9/16"	12" 14"	154.14 179.83	4" x 7"	48" 60"
Mills	1 15/16"	10" 12"	29.5 35.38	3"	48" 48"
	2½"	5½"		4"	48"
M.F.G. Co.	10 11/16" x 2 11/16"	15"	430.83	3" x 12"	60"
Product Contr.	2 3/16"	7½"		4"	38"
Laboratory	1 15/16"	10" 12"	29.5 35.38	3"	48" 48"
	2 11/16"	12" 14"	68.0 69.0	4"	48" 60"
Hospitals	2 11/16"	12" 14"	68.0 69.0	4"	48" 60"
	5 9/16" x 2 9/16"	14"	179.83	4" x 7"	60"
Blue print	1 7/8"	24"		3"	60"

The table indicates that offices may use a variety of carrier sizes and the specific size selected will depend on the article to be transported. This applies also to mills and laboratories to a lesser degree, when the carrier size is determined the tube size is indicated as well as the minimum radius of a bend of the tube.

Data supplied by: Standard Conveyor Co. and Lamson Co.

3" x ½" tube for self carrier paper form is well adapted in Hospitals, Banks, Stock markets, Offices, Restaurants, Telegraph Exchange. The radius of the tube is 12" (flat bend) or 30" (edge bend)

Data supplied by: International Standard Trading Corporation

POWER UNITS TO PROVIDE AIR POWER (for vacuum or pressure type)

The air power to transmit the carriers may be generated by:

1. Turbo blower and exhauster (centritugal type power units).
2. Positiverotary type.

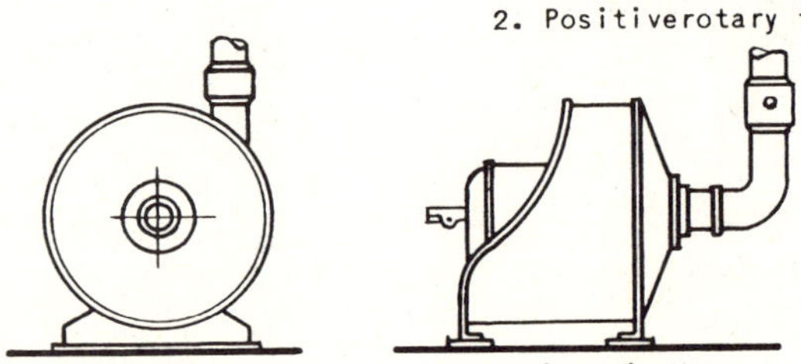

Front view   Side view

1 - CENTRIFUGAL TYPE POWER UNIT

The centrifugal type power units are quiet, may be set in almost any location inside or outside and operates on suction or combination of suction and pressure. Are recommended generally except where extremely long lines are to be used.

Side view

2 - POSITIVE TYPE POWER UNIT

The positive rotary type power unit operates equally well on pressure or suction or combinations of the two. This unit is recommended for use where long lines are to be used and reversible action is desirable. The unit may be located any place inside or outside.

Data supplied by: The Spencer Turbine Co.

PNEUMATIC TUBES

TYPES OF SYSTEMS

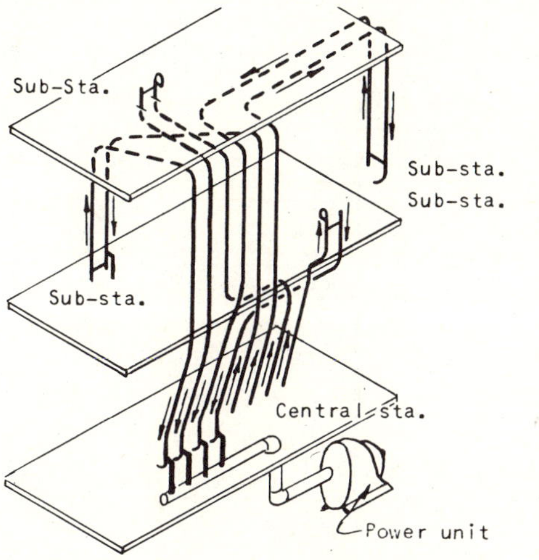
Sub-Sta.
Sub-sta.
Sub-sta.
Sub-sta.
Central sta.
Power unit

This system is the finest and most efficient. It permits dispatching of carriers from all stations simultaneously and can handle an almost unlimited, continuous flow of transactions. It may have any number of stations and consists of independent lines to and from all stations. The system is low in maintenance cost and is quietest system.

VACUUM TYPE INDEPENDENT TWIN LINE

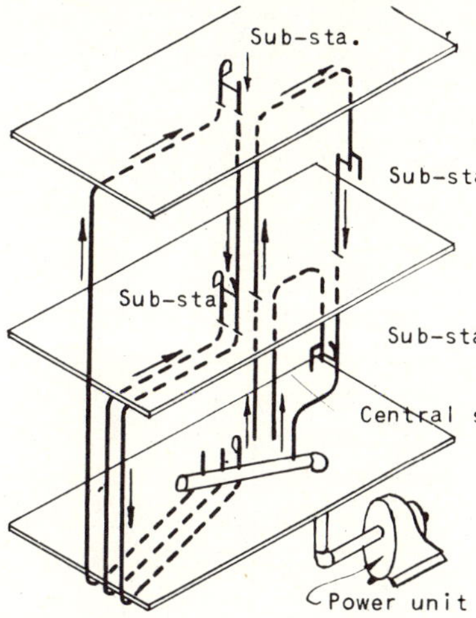
Sub-sta.
Sub-sta.
Sub-sta
Sub-sta.
Central sta.
Power unit

This system may dispatch carriers from the central station to all sub-stations via separate lines, but return lines are common. Where intermittent service is satisfactory, such as in mail order houses and industrial plants, this system may be used to advantage.

VACUUM TYPE COMBINATION LINE

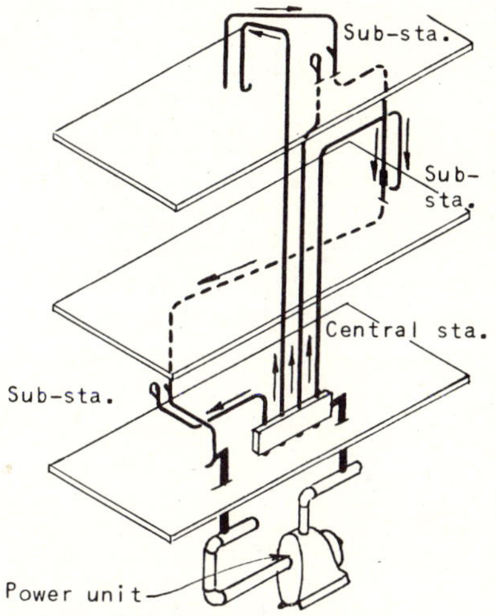
Sub-sta.
Sub-sta.
Central sta.
Sub-sta.
Power unit

This system utilizes both vacuum and pressure. It is economical of power and of length of return lines. It is necessary that the number of open ends be the same for the vacuum as for the pressure lines. Provides quick service. Its use is restricted to mercantile houses, drug, grocery and meat packing plants and similar types of buildings.

VACUUM-PRESSURE TYPE COMBINATION LINE

Station

In this system a single line for transmission in both directions. A line can carry only one carrier at a time. It is noisy while carrier is in transmit. It is restricted in its use to railway yards, factories, and other industrial buildings where fast but limited service is required.

PRESSURE TYPE

Data supplied by: Standard Conveyor Co.

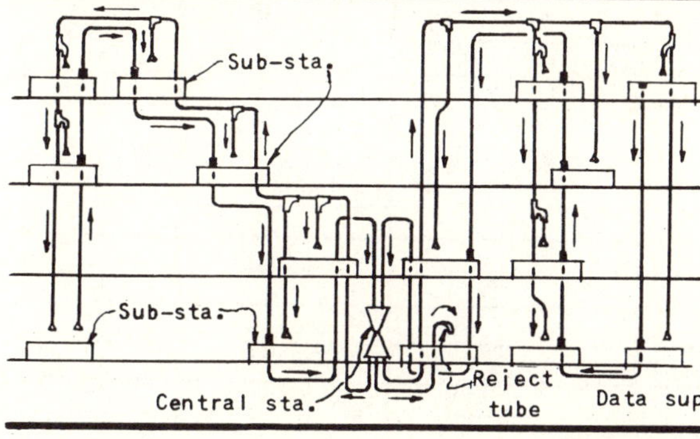
Sub-sta.
Sub-sta.
Central sta.
Reject tube

This system operates automatically once the carrier's adjustable ring is set for the proper destination. Within seconds electromechanical switching carries the carrier to the correct station. First, the carrier travels by vacuum to the central station where it is automatically tested to determine the correct line and station. This is done by relays & selectors which establishes the path the carrier is to follow to reach its destination. If the carrier is set by mistake for a non existent station, it will be discharged into a "reject" tube at the central station. A signal light and bell will indicate an error. This system provides for quicker delivery with less chance of error. It yields economy of length of line. Typical buildings which might find this type suitable are: hotels, airline, terminals, railroad stations, hospitals, industry.

AUTOMATIC SELECTIVE SYSTEM

Data supplied by: International Standard Trading Corp.

TYPES OF INTAKES & DISCHARGES

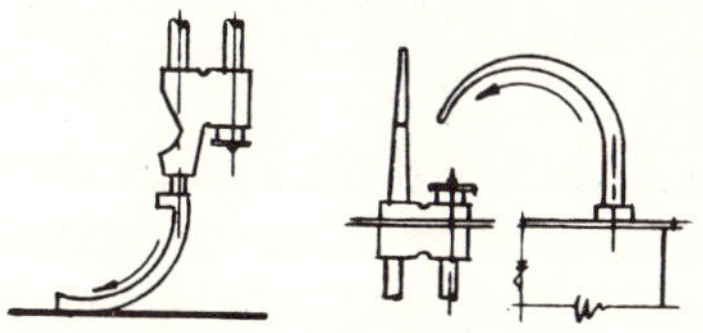

CEILING FLOOR

DISCHARGE SINGLE VALVE

Single valve discharge is recommended for department store or industrial plant installations where quietness is not important factor.

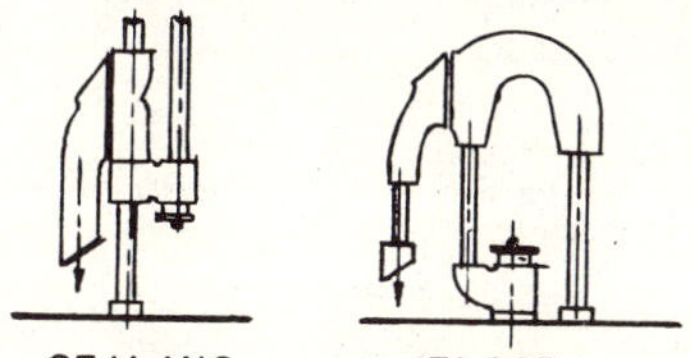

CEILING FLOOR

DISCHARGE (VACUUM) DOUBLE VALVE

Double valve discharge should be used where smooth delivery and quiet operation is desired. On system having long lines or heavy traffic requiring a higher vacuum, this type is recommended.

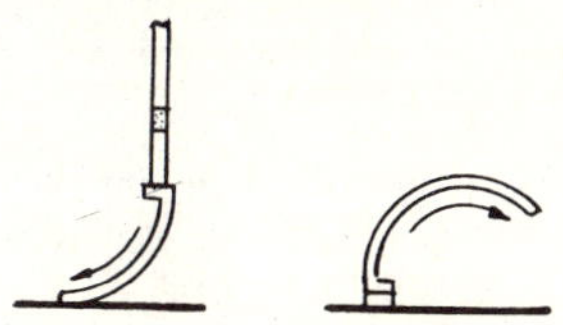

CEILING FLOOR

DISCHARGE PRESSURE

Pressure discharge used on pressure type system line.

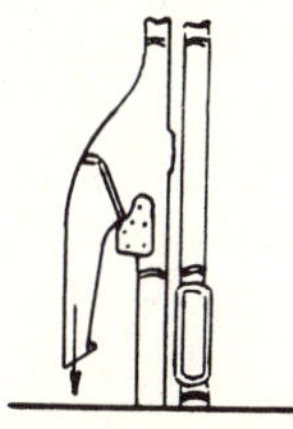

AUTOMATIC DISCHARGE

Automatic discharge is automatically actuated from central station or for longer lines, by contact ahead of the sub station. Arrival of the carrier is signal by light

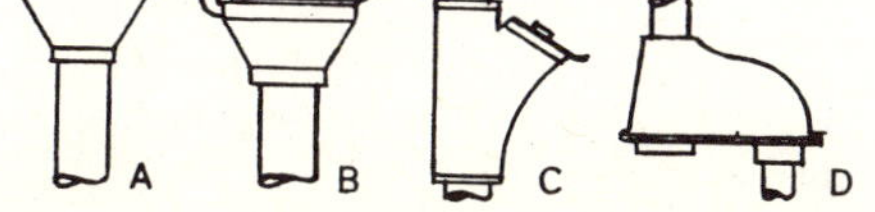
A
B
C
D

A: Bellmouth intake (vacuum type) is used on all vacuum type systems. Two or three way intakes allow the insertion of carrier through only one intake at a time and are used on vacuum types combination lines. B: Claper intake or C: Y intake (vacuum type) are used where its design suits station condition. D: Pressure type (pressure type).

Data supplied by: Standard Conveyor Co. and International Standard Trading Corp.

PNEUMATIC TUBES

CARRIER SIZES

SYSTEM SIZE & DESCRIPTION		MAT.	INSIDE DIA. & SIZE	INSIDE LENGTH	CUBIC SIZE (CU. IN)	RADII OF TUBE BEND	COMPANY
2¼"		R T	1 3/8"	6",9",10"	8.9,13.36,14.85		L
		R	1 3/8"	4 5/8",10"	5.9,14.8	14",18",24",42"	A
	Ticket & Tags	T F R	1 3/8"	4",9"		13",18"	G, S
	Documents	T F	1 7/16"	As required	—	—	S
		F	1 7/16"	4 5/8",10"	7.5,16.2	14",18",24",42"	A
	Charge & Sales	T	1 1/2"	4 1/8"		13"	G
		*	1 1/2"	8 11/16"		48"	I
		T A	1 1/2"	4 5/8",10"	8.1,17.5	14",18",24",42"	A
	Cash & Messages	S	1 5/8"	4¼",7½"		13",42"	G
		R	1 3/4"	2½",3½"		14"	S
		R	1 5/8"	2½",3"	5.2,6.2	14"	A
3"		R	1 3/4"	11 1/8"			L
	Blue prints	A	1 7/8"	24"			G & S
		T	1 15/16"	9",10",12"	29.5 & 35.38		L
		F R	2"	6" to 10"	18.8,31.4	24",42"	A
		T F	2"	As required	—	—	S
	Documents	T	2"	9" to 12"		38" & 48"	G
		T	2 1/16"	9" to 12"	30.6,40.4	24",42"	A
		*	2 1/8"	9 1/8"		48"	I
		A	2 1/8"	9" to 12"	32.0,42.5	24",42"	A
	Cash	S	2 3/16"	7½"		38"	G
4"	Blue prints	A	1 7/8"	24"		60"	G
	2" ϕ Bottles	F	2"	10"	2" ϕ Bottle		S
	Blue prints	A	2 3/8"	28"		120"	G
	Test pieces	S	2 1/2"	5½"		48"	G
		*	2 1/2"	13 1/8"		48"	I
	Glass Test Tubes and Bottles	T	2 11/16"	10",12",14"	56.7,67.0,79.4		L
		T F	2 3/4"	As required	—	—	S
		T	2 3/4"	10",12"		48"	G,S
		T L	2 3/4"	10" to 14"	59.0,83.0	48"	A
		A	2 7/8"	10" to 14"	65.0,91.0	48"	A
		F	2 7/8"	12 3/8"			S
		*	2 7/8"	12 3/8"	80.38		L
	I.B.M. Cards	A	3 1/4"	7 3/8"		48"	G
		F	3 1/4"	8 1/8"			L
5½"	Documents	A	4"	16¼"		96"	G
		L	4 1/8"	16"			L
3" x 6"		T F	1 5/8" x 4 1/2"	As required	—	—	S
3" x 12"	Documents	A	2 11/16" x 10 11/16"	15"	430.83		L
4" x 7"		T	2 9/16" x 5 9/16"	12",14"		60"	G,L,S
		*	2 9/16" x 5 9/16"	12",14"			G
4" x 12"	Papers	A	2 11/16" x 10 3/8"	15"		60"	G
6" x 12"	Documents	A	4" x 11"	16"	690	48"	A

A = Aluminum B = Brass F = Fiber L = Leather R = Rubber S = Steel T = Tenite (Transparent)
* = Automatic Selective Carrier

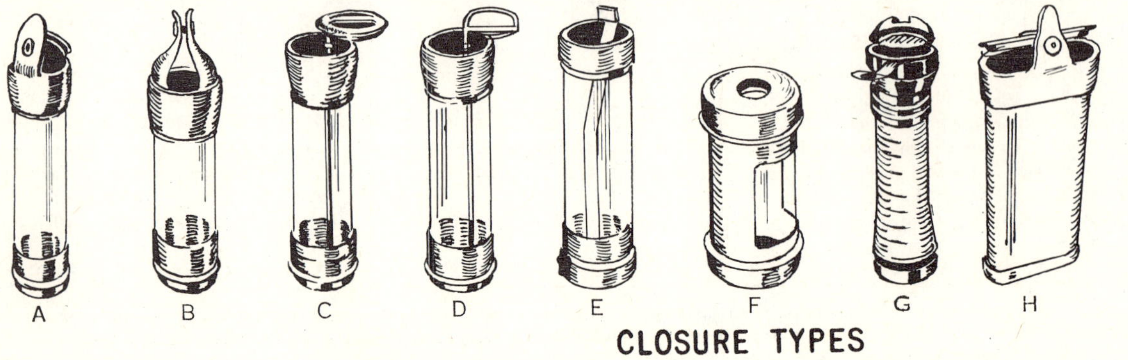
A
B
C
D
E
F
G
H

A = Fiber & Transparent Cover
B = Strap Closure
C = Spiral Spring with Cover
D = Spiral Spring only
E = Spring Clip
F = Screw Cap
G = Automatic Dial Carrier with Flap
H = Snap Flap

CLOSURE TYPES

Data supplied by: S = Standard Conveyor Co. L = Lamson Corp. G = Grover Co.
I = International Standard Trading Corp. A = Airmatic System Inc.

PNEUMATIC TUBES

TUBE SIZE AND RADII OF BENDS

RADII "R"	MATERIAL	GAUGE NO.	LENGTH L	LENGTH L'	STRAIGHT LENGTH TUBE REQUIRED 90°	STRAIGHT LENGTH TUBE REQUIRED 45°	CAST BEND DEGREE	H	MAX. INSIDE LENGTH CARRIER	COMPANY
1½" DIA.										
18"	Brass, Steel	20	22"	5"	3'-4"	2'-4"			3¼"	A, S
2¼" DIA.										
4½"	C.I.-C.B.						180°	8"	Cash	S
7½"	C.I.-C.B. Brass	20		5½"			90°	10¼" 8" 13"	Cash	A, S
12"	Brass	20		6½"	2'-8"				Cash	S
13"	Brass, Steel	20	19'	6"	2'-8"				5½"	G
14"			19"						5" & Cash	A, L
18"	Brass, Steel	20	22" 24"	5" 6"	3'-6" 3'-4"	2'-4" 2'-4"	90°	18"	5" & Cash 5 5/8", 6", 6¾"	S L, A, G
24"	Brass, Steel	20	29"	5"	4'-3"	2'-8"			6½", 7", 7¾"	S, A, G
36"	Brass, Steel	20		6"	5'-10"	3'-6"			8½"	S
42"	Brass, Steel	20	46" 50"	4" 6"	7'-9" 6'-9"	 3'-10"			10¾" 9", 10", 10"	G S, L, A
48"	Brass, Steel	20		6"	7'-8"	4'-3"			10"	S
3" DIA.										
7½"	C.I.						90°		11"	S
24"	Brass, Steel, C.A	19	32¼"	9"	4'-5"	2'-11"	90°	26½"	9", 12"	A
36"	Brass, Steel	19		6"	5'-10"	3'-6"			9"	S
38"	Brass, Steel	19	28"	6"	6'-4"				10½"	G
42"	Brass, Steel	19		6"	6'-9"	3'-10"			9½", 10", 12"	S, S, A
44"	Brass, Steel	19	51						11"	L
48"	Brass, Steel	19	 48	6" 7"	7'-8" 8'-0"	4'-3"			11" 12"	S G
4" DIA.										
18", 24"	C.I.						90°	22"	12", 14"	S, A
48"	Brass, Steel Brass, Steel Brass, St, Alum.	16 16 16	 54" 48"	6½" 6½" 8"	7'-9" 7'-9" 8'-0"	4'-4" 4'-4"			12", 14" 13¼" 12"	S, A L G
60"	Brass, Steel Steel, Alum.	16 16	 60"	12" 9"	8'-6" 10'-0"				12" 14"	S, A G
120"	Steel	16	132"	12"		8'-10"			28"	G
5½" DIA.										
60"	Aluminum	.090	73"	13"	10'-0"				14"	G
3"x6" SIZE										
48"	Brass, Steel	16"		12"	8'-6"				12"	S, A
3"x 12" SIZE										
48"	Brass, Steel								15" approx.	L
4"x7" SIZE										
48"	Alum., Brass	16	64	12½"	9'-0"	5'-7½"			14"	A
60"	Steel	16	73"	13"	10'-0"				14"	G
4"x 12" SIZE										
60"	Steel	16								G
3" x ½" SIZE Tube for self carrier paper - Bend as shown below										I

Expanded bends - Must not be used where travel is upward

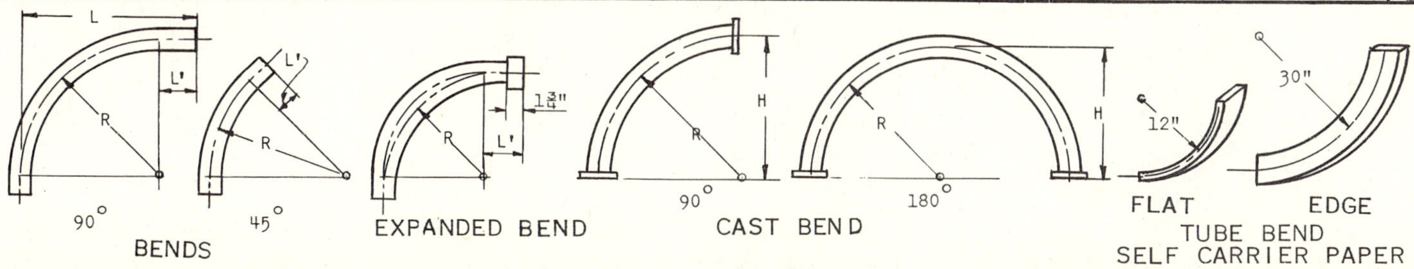
L
L'
R
90°
L'
R
45°
BENDS
1¾"
L'
R
EXPANDED BEND
H
R
90°
H
R
180°
CAST BEND
12"
30"
FLAT
EDGE
TUBE BEND
SELF CARRIER PAPER

Data supplied by: L = Lamson Corp. G = Grover Co. S = Standard Conveyor Co. I = International Standard Trading Corp. A = Airmatic System Inc.

PNEUMATIC TUBES

TYPE	TUBE SIZE	A	B	C	D
①	1½"	21"	14"	2¼"	
	2¼"	22½"	14½"	3¼"	
②	2¼"	36"	7"	3¼"	4½"
	3"	43"	8"	4¼"	6¼"
③	4"	62"	20"	6"	10"
		58"	30"	9"	18"

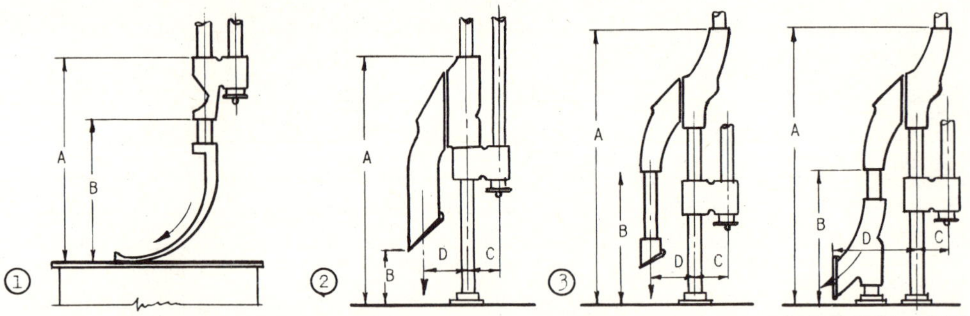

① 1½", 2¼" SINGLE VALVE ② 2¼", 3" DOUBLE VALVE ③ VERTICAL HEAD HORIZONTAL HEAD 4" DOUBLE VALVE

VACUUM TYPE CEILING DISCHARGE

TYPE	TUBE SIZE	A	B	C	D
①	2¼"		14½"	3¼"	
	3"	16"	17"	4¼"	
②	4"	50"	20"	35½"	10"
③	2¼"	25⅝"	15⅝"	5"	
	3"	28½"	17½"	6½"	
④	2¼"	17¾"	11¾"	3¼"	
⑤	2¼"	18"	21"	7½"	
	3"	18"	21"	7½"	
	4"	18"	26½"	11½"	
⑥	2¼"	15¼"	12"	10"	5"

Type B with vertical or horizontal head available
Type C intake also available on opposite end
Type F made for either floor or ceiling discharge

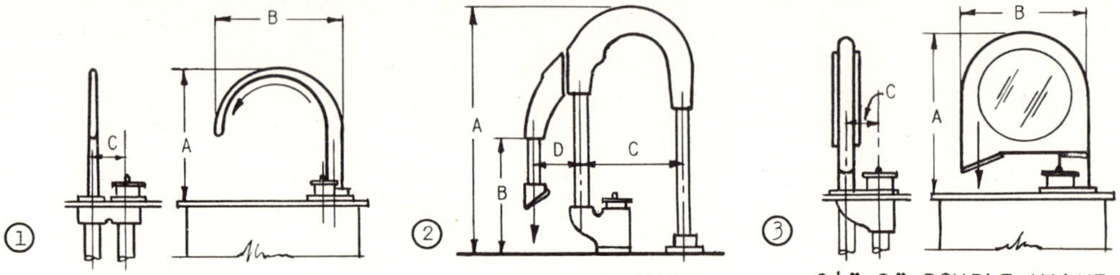

① 2¼", 3" SINGLE VALVE ② 4" DOUBLE VALVE ③ 2¼", 3" DOUBLE VALVE OVERSHOT

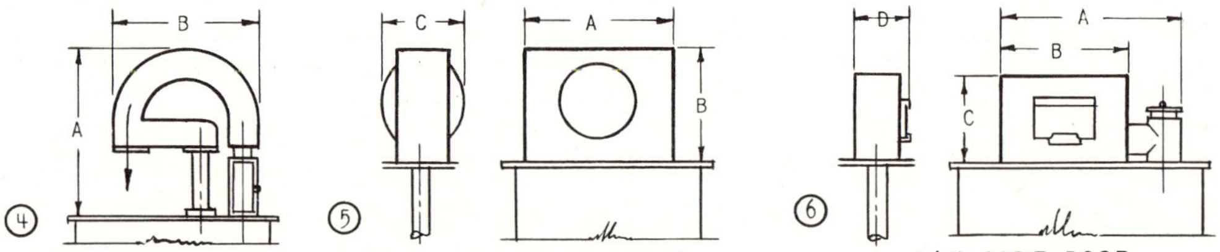

④ 2¼" SINGLE VALVE OVERSHOT ⑤ 2¼", 3", 4" END DOOR (MESSAGE) ⑥ 2¼" SIDE DOOR (CASH)

VACUUM TYPE FLOOR DISCHARGE

Data supplied by Standard Conveyor Co. and Lamson Co.

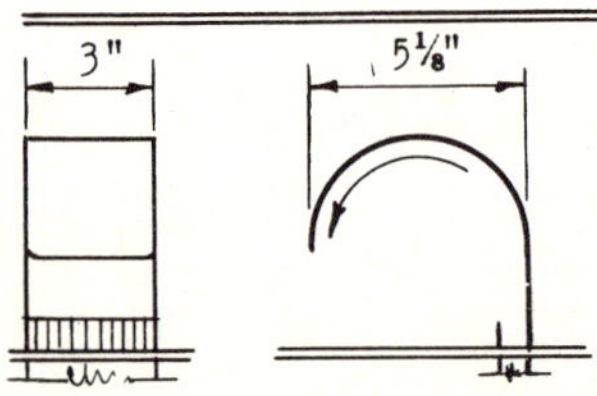

3"
5⅛"

PRESSURE DISCHARGE

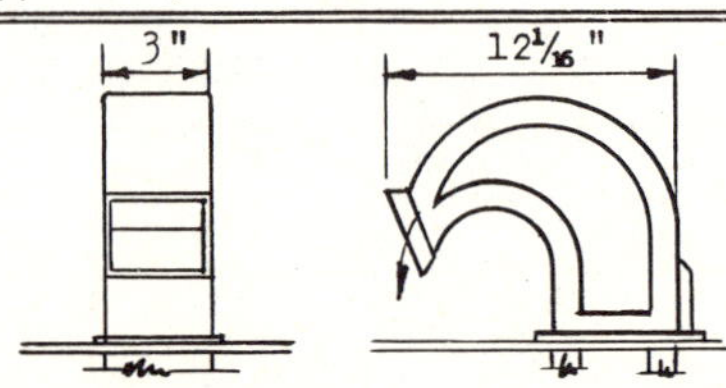

3"
12¹⁄₁₆"

VACUUM DISCHARGE

2¼", 3", 4" DISCHARGE

3" X ½" SELF CARRIER PAPER SYSTEM

AUTOMATIC SELECTIVE SYSTEM

Data supplied by: International Standard Trading Co.

TYPE	TUBE SIZE	A	B	C	D
①	2¼"	43"	29"	4⅝"	16"
②	2¼" 3"	42"	18"	32"	36"
③	2¼"	53"	36"	12"	21"
	3"	53"	36"	12"	21"
	4"	62"*	36"	24"	40"
	4"x7"	62"*	36"	24"	40"

*For floor discharge A=62"
Steel construction. Tropic Tan finish with carrier storage compartment.

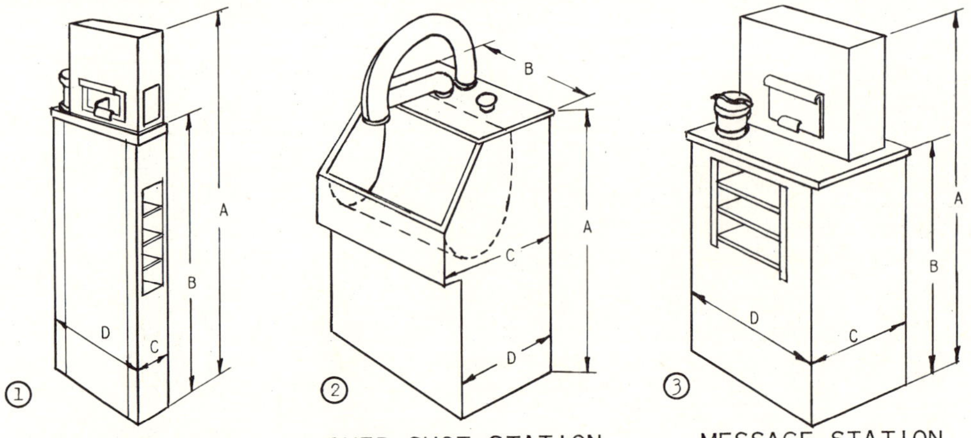

① CASH STATION ② OVER SHOT STATION ③ MESSAGE STATION

VACUUM TYPE PEDESTAL

Data supplied by: Lamson Company

PNEUMATIC TUBES

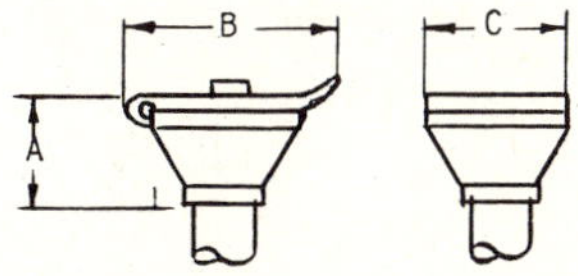
B
C
A

CLAPPER INTAKE

TUBE DIA.	A	B	C
2¼"	1½"	3¾"	3⅜"
3"	2⅝"	5½"	3⅝"
4"	5"	9⅝"	5½"

TUBE DIA.	A	B
2¼"	1⅞"	2⅝"
3"	2¼"	3½"
4"	2¾"	4⅝"

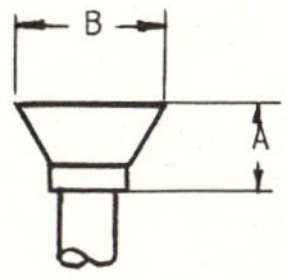
B
A

BELMOUTH INTAKE

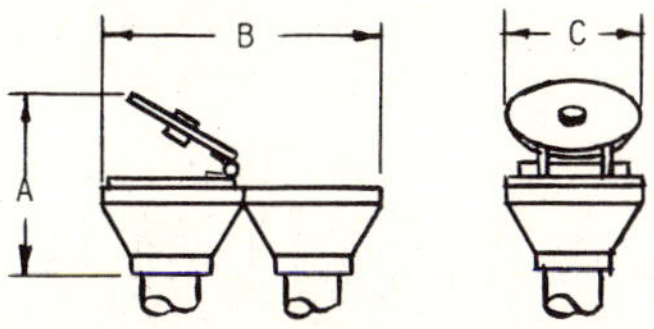
B
C
A

TWO-LINE COMBINATION INTAKE

TUBE DIA.	A	B	C
2¼"	4"	5⅝"	2⅝"
3"	5"	7¾"	3⅜"
4"	9¾"	11½"	5½"

TUBE DIA.	A	B	C
2¼"	3¾"	8⅝"	2⅝"
3"	5"	12"	3⅜"
4"	9½"	18¾"	5⅝"

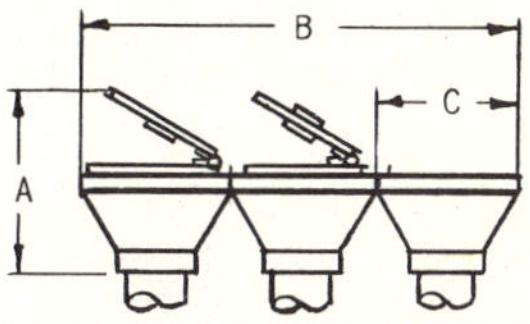
B
C
A

THREE-LINE COMBINATION LINE

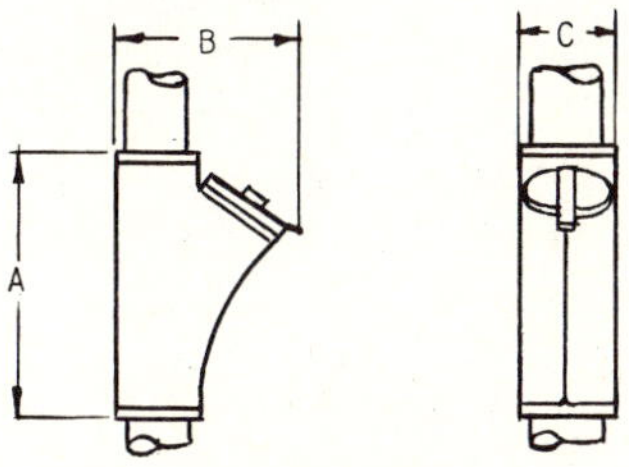
B
C
A

"Y" INTAKE

TUBE SIZE	A	B	C
2¼" cash	8 9/16"	6⅛"	3⅜"
2¼" mess.	12¾"	5½"	3⅜"
3" mess.	13¾"	7⅞"	3⅝"
4" mess.	26"	13¼"	5½"

TUBE SIZE	A	B	C
2¼" cash	8"	4¾"	3⅜"
2¼" mess.	13 7/16"	4¾"	3¼"
3" mess.	15"	6¼"	5¾"
4" mess.	19⅝"	7¾"	6⅛"

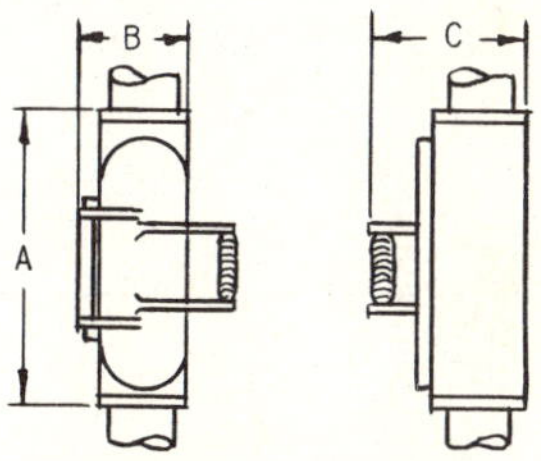
B
C
A

SENDING BOX

VACUUM TYPE FLOOR & CEILING INTAKE

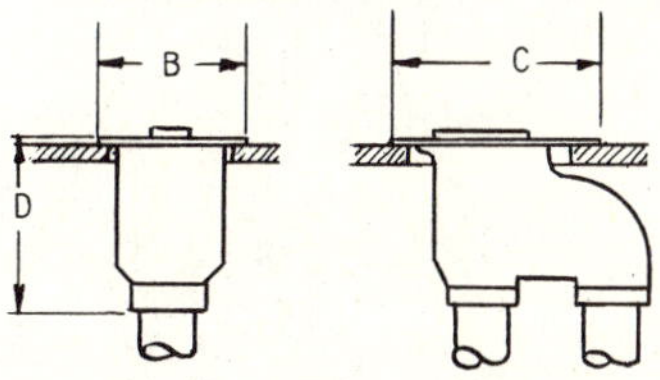
B
C
D

SINGLE FLOOR INTAKE

TUBE SIZE	A	B	C	D	E	F
1½"	2¼"			3⅝"	4½"	2⅛"
2¼"	4½"	3¼"	6½"	5⅛"	6¾"	3 1/16"
3"	6"	4¼"	8⅝"	5⅞"	8¾"	4"

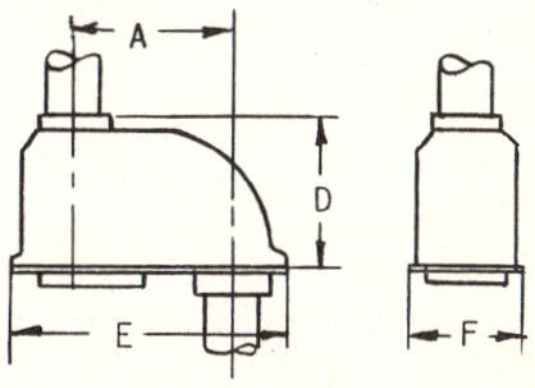
A
D
E
F

SINGLE CEILING INTAKE

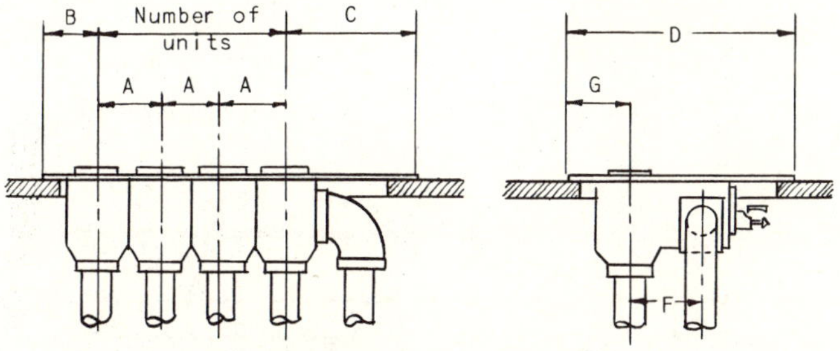
B
Number of units
C
A
A
A
D
G
F

FLOOR INTAKE

TUBE SIZE	A	B	C	D	E	F	G
2¼"	3¼"	2¼"	4½"	12"	5¼"	3 15/16"	2 15/16"
3"	4¼"	3"	7"	14"	6 5/16"	4⅞"	3⅜"

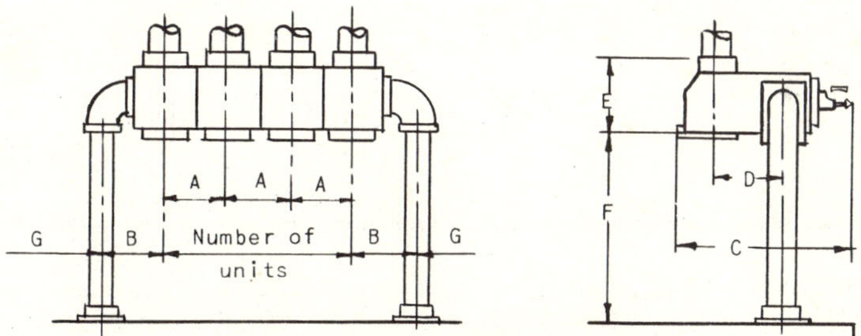
A
A
A
G
B
Number of units
B
G
E
D
F
C

CEILING INTAKE

TUBE SIZE	A	B	C	D	E	F	G
2¼"	3¼"	3⅝"	10½"	3 15/16"	5¼"	17"	1 5/16"
3"	4¼"	4⅝"	12⅜"	4⅞"	6 5/16"	17"	1 11/16"

PRESSURE TYPE FLOOR & CEILING INTAKE

Data supplied by Standard Conveyor Co.

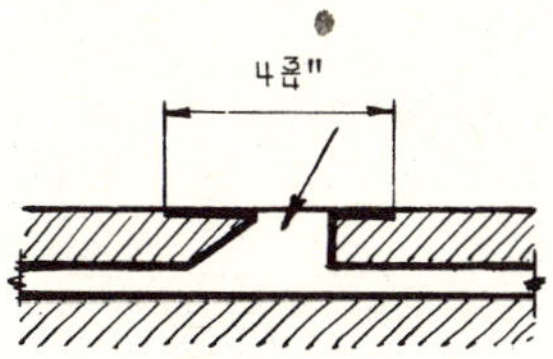
4¾"

VACUUM INTAKE

PRESSURE INTAKE

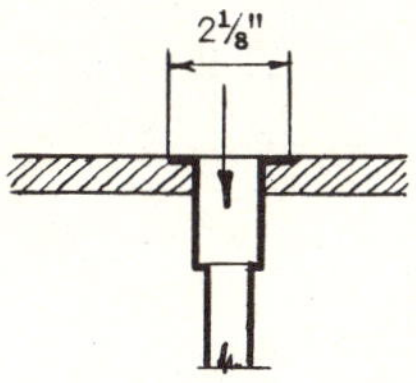
2⅛"

SELF CARRIER PAPER SYSTEM

Data supplied by International Standard Trading Corp.

PNEUMATIC TUBES

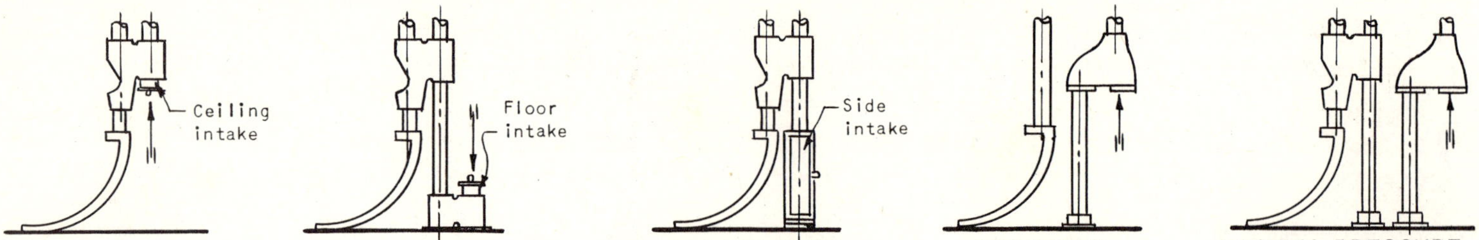
Ceiling intake
Floor intake
Side intake

VACUUM TYPE | VACUUM TYPE | VACUUM TYPE | PRESSURE | VACUUM-PRESSURE

SUB-STATIONS

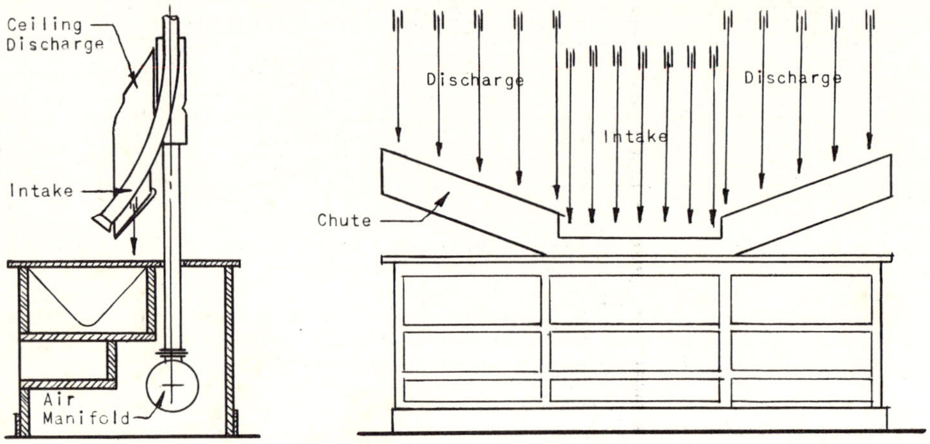
Ceiling Discharge
Intake
Air Manifold
Chute
Discharge
Intake
Discharge

Section

Front View

VACUUM CHUTE

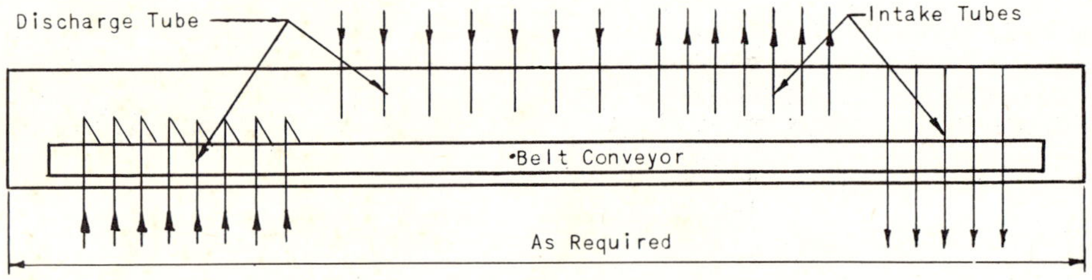
Discharge Tube
Intake Tubes
Belt Conveyor
As Required

BELT CONVEYOR

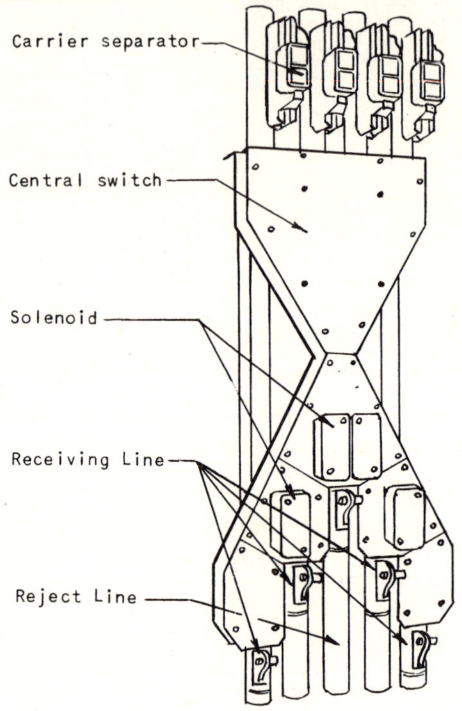
Carrier separator
Central switch
Solenoid
Receiving Line
Reject Line

AUTOMATIC FOR 4 LOOP LINES

CENTRAL STATIONS

Data supplied by Standard Conveyor Co. and International Standard Trading Corp.

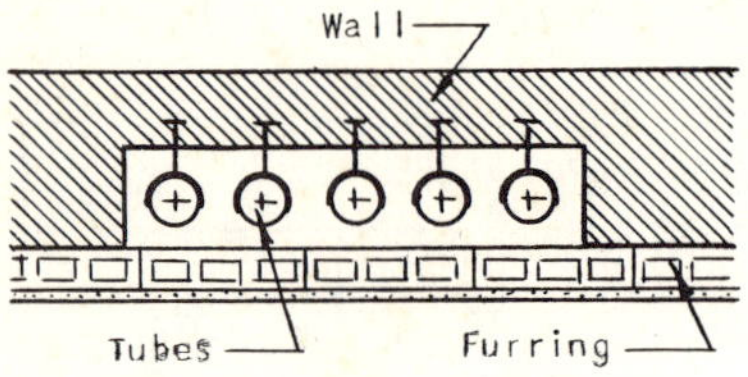
Wall
Tubes
Furring

TUBE INSIDE WALL INSTALLATION

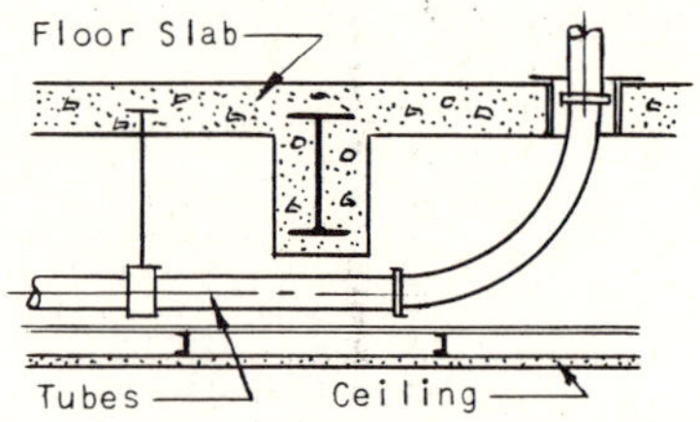
Floor Slab
Tubes
Ceiling

TUBE UNDER & THROUGH FLOOR INSTALLATION

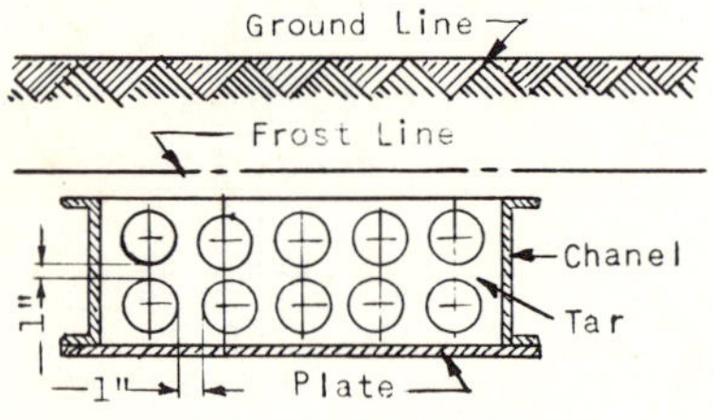
Ground Line
Frost Line
Chanel
Tar
1"
1"
Plate

STEEL CONDUIT

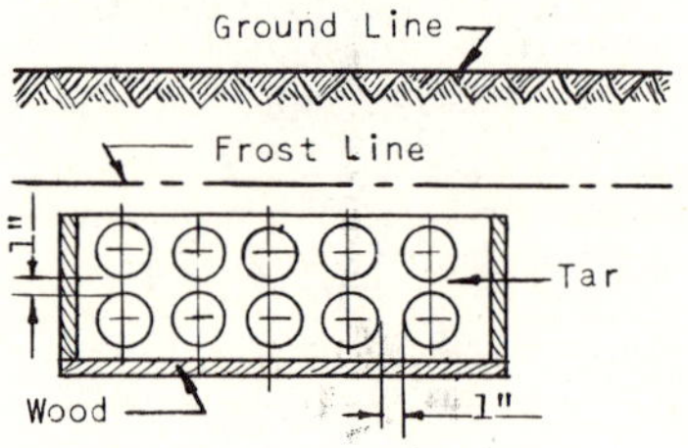
Ground Line
Frost Line
1"
Tar
Wood
1"

WOOD CONDUIT

TUBE INSTALLATION-UNDER GROUND

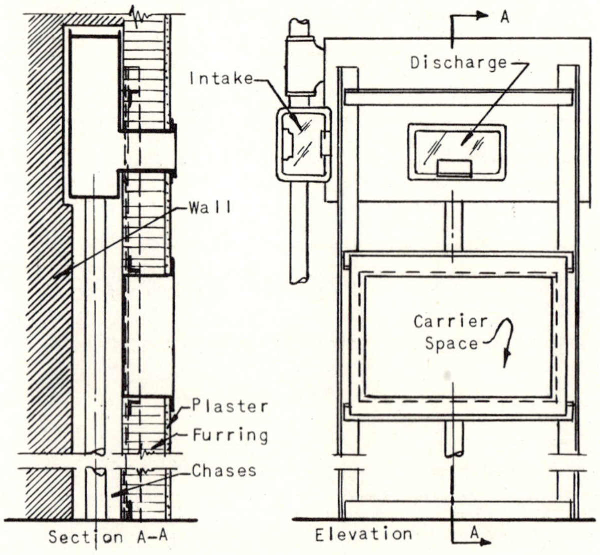
Intake
Wall
Plaster
Furring
Chases
Section A-A
A
Discharge
Carrier Space
Elevation
A

SUB-STATION FLUSH WALL INSTALLATION

DETAILS - METHODS OF INSTALLATION

Data supplied by Standard Conveyor Co.

LIGHTNING PROTECTION

Following are based on: "Code for Protection against Lightning", Parts I & II - U.S. Department of Commerce National Bureau of Standards Handbook H 4b, approved as A.S.A. Standard C-5.2-1953. also the same as National Fire Codes for Bldg. Const. & Equipment published by National Fire Protection Association 1944. If Underwriters Laboratories Master Label is required, include; "Install complete lightning protection system as required by the Underwriters Laboratories in accord with the 'Installation Requirements for a Master Label Lightning Protection System'. Upon completion attach a Master's Label to Building."

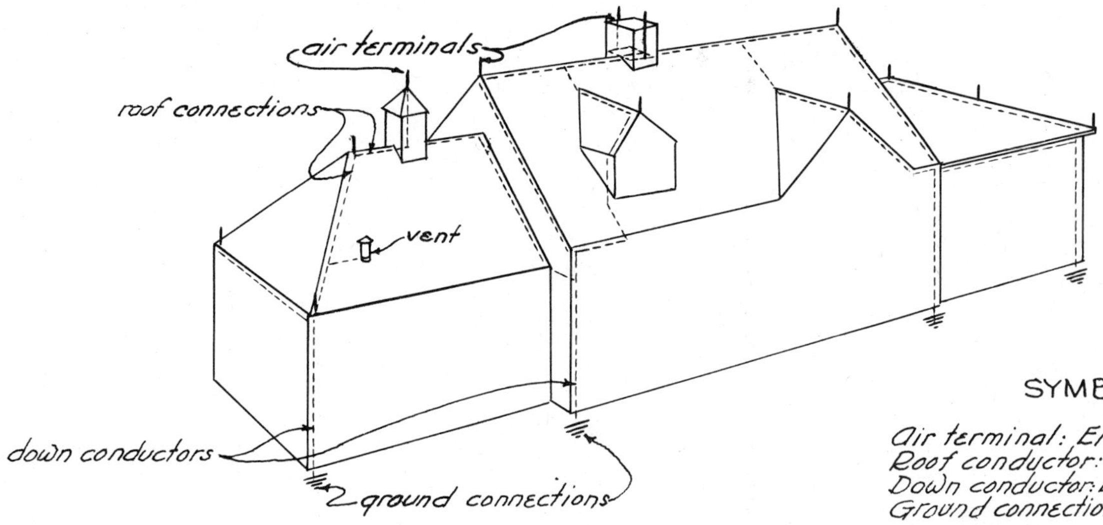
air terminals
roof connections
vent
down conductors
2 ground connections

SYMBOLS

Air terminal: Elevation | Plan ●
Roof conductor: - - - - - - - - - - -
Down conductor: Elev. - - - - - Plan ⊙
Ground connection ⏚

GENERAL LAYOUT *for* RESIDENTIAL BUILDING

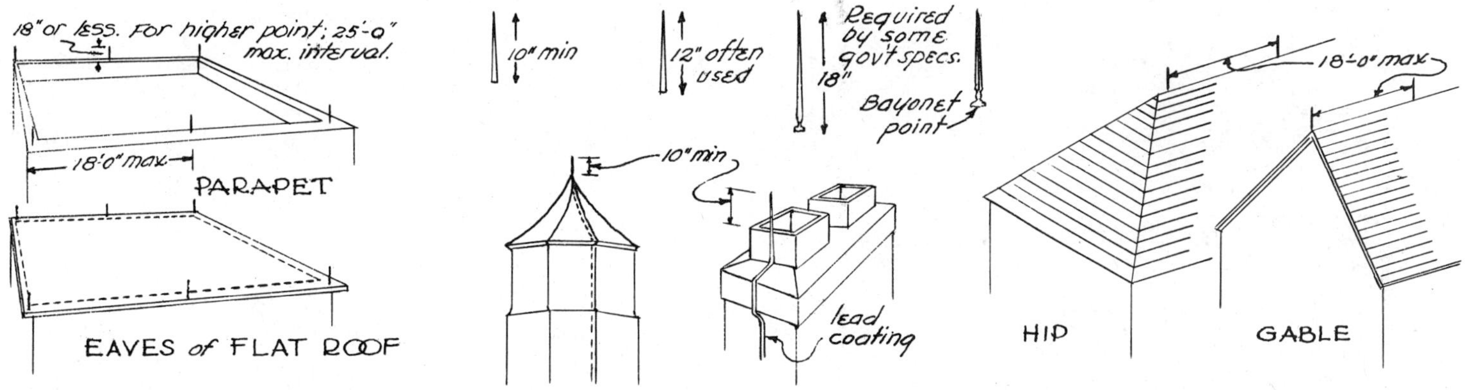
18" or less. For higher point; 25'-0" max. interval.
18'-0" max.
PARAPET
EAVES of FLAT ROOF
10" min
12" often used
Required by some govt specs.
18"
Bayonet point
10" min
lead coating
18'-0" max.
HIP
GABLE

Height of air terminal above top of structure min. 10" to max. 5'-0" for flat roofs. Air terminals required on decks, sky-lights, dormers, chimneys, vents, flagpoles, spires, steeples, towers, silos. Terminal must be within 2'-0" of object or corner. No terminals required for metal projections such as ventilator, stacks; but they shall be bonded to conductors.

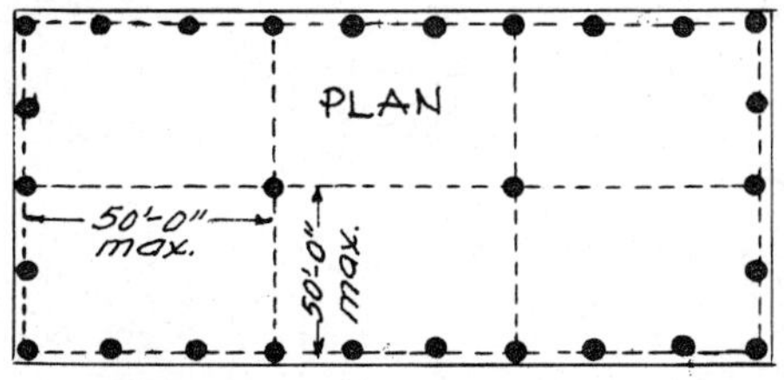
PLAN
50'-0" max.
50'-0" max.

LARGE FLAT *or* SLIGHTLY SLOPING ROOFS
Divide surface into rectangles not exceeding 50'-0" in length or width.

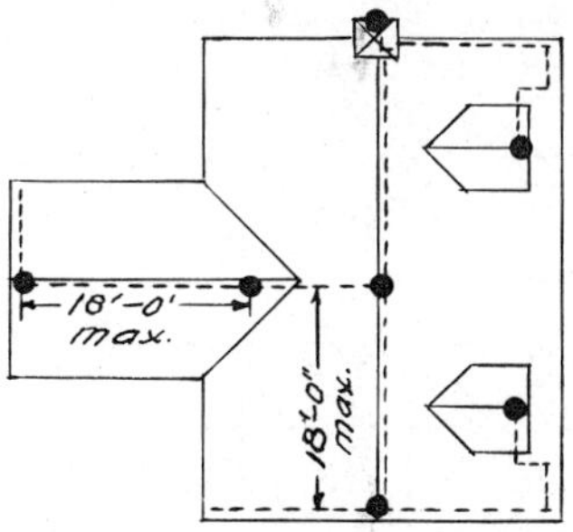
18'-0" max.
18'-0" max.

GABLE *or* HIP ROOF *with* DORMERS *and* CHIMNEY

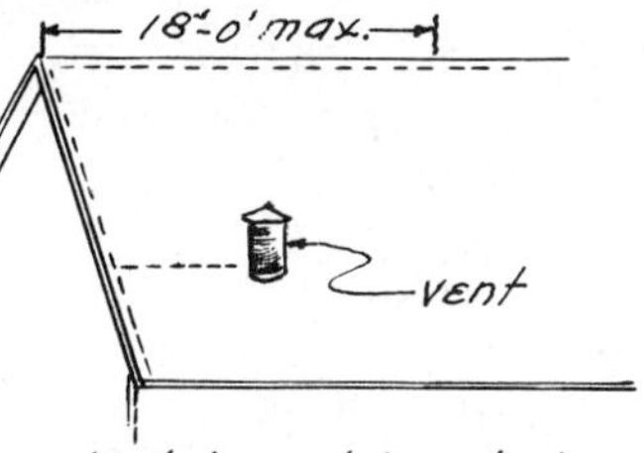
18'-0" max.
vent

Metal vent bonded to conductor. No terminal required.

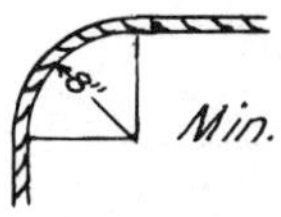
8"

Min. bend of conductor.

Roof conductors to form an enclosing network to join each air terminal to all the rest in system.
For ground connections see following pages

AIR TERMINALS & ROOF CONDUCTORS

LIGHTNING PROTECTION

Symbol for down conductor ●

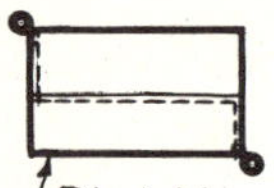
PLAN
perimeter 110'-0" or less.

Plan 110'-0" or less in perimeter; minimum of 2 down conductors. If over 110'-0" in perimeter, add 1 for each additional 50'-0" or fraction thereof.

Plan 300'-0" or less in perimeter; minimum of 2 down conductors. If over 300'-0" in perimeter add 1 for each additional 100'-0" or fraction thereof.

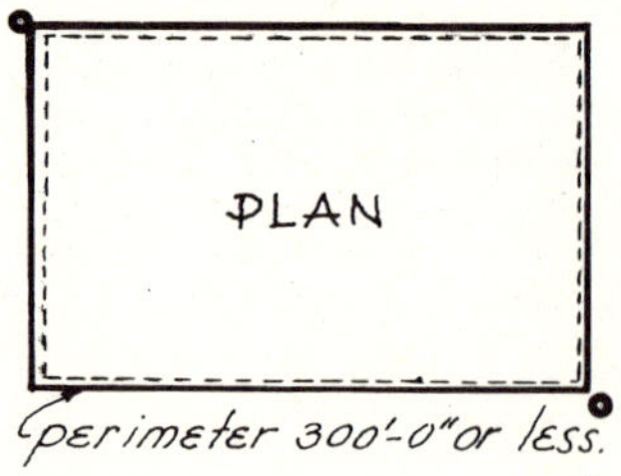
PLAN
perimeter 300'-0" or less.

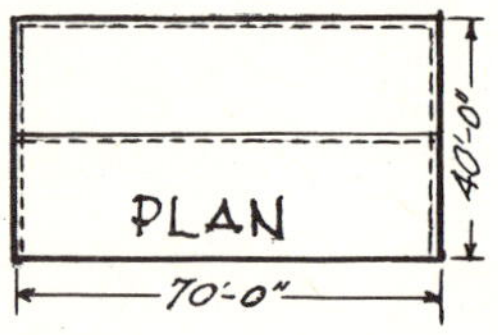
PLAN
40'-0"
70'-0"

EXAMPLE
Perimeter 220'-0"
110'-0" perimeter; Two ●
220'-0" - 110'-0" = 110'-0"
110/50 = 2+1 = Three ●
Total = Five ●

GABLE, GAMBREL, or HIPPED ROOFS

Scale: 1/64" = 1'-0"

EXAMPLE
Perimeter 410'-0"
300'-0" perimeter; Two ●
410'-0" - 300'-0" = 110'-0"
110/100 = 1+1 = Two ●
Total = Four ●

FLAT, FRENCH or SAWTOOTH ROOFS

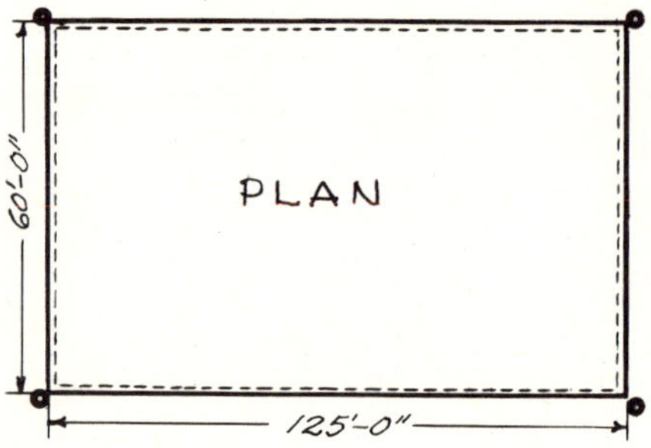
PLAN
60'-0"
125'-0"

DOWN CONDUCTORS REQUIRED for SQUARE or RECTANGULAR SHAPED STRUCTURES

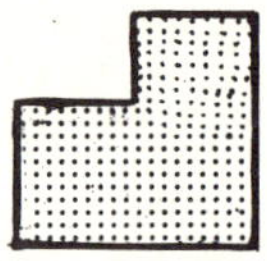
ELL SHAPE
Add one ●

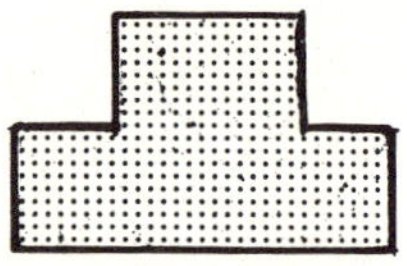
T SHAPE
Add one ●

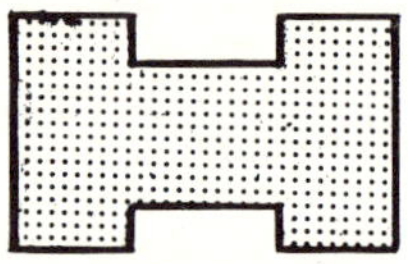
H SHAPE
Add two ●

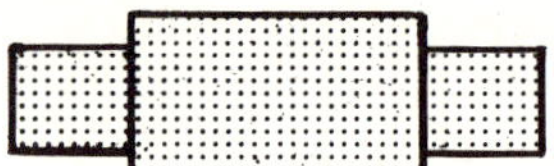
WING TYPE
Add one ● per wing

In addition to the above requirements: On irregular shaped structures, the total number of down conductors shall be sufficient to make the average distance between them along the perimeter not greater than 100'-0".

EXTRA DOWN CONDUCTORS REQUIRED for IRREGULAR SHAPED STRUCTURES

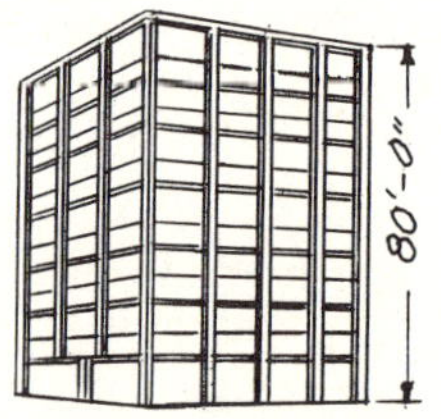
80'-0"
PERSPECTIVE

If structure is over 60'-0" high; add one down conductor for each additional 60'-0" or fraction thereof, but not so as to cause down conductors placed about perimeter at intervals of less than 50'-0".

EXAMPLE
Flat roof; perimeter 340'-0"
By plan: 3 down conductors required. By elevation: 1 extra required because of height.
By plan: Three ●
By elevation: One ●
Total Four ●

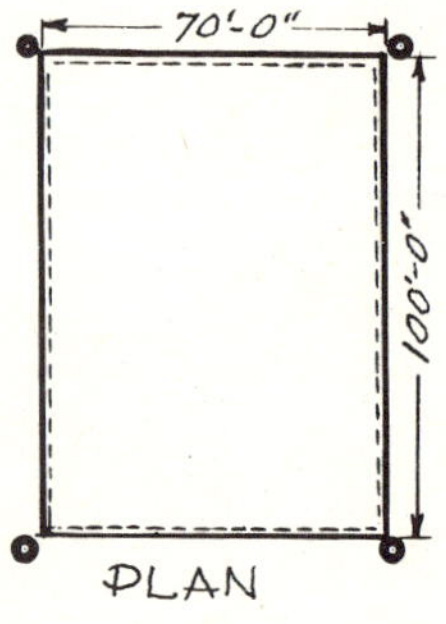
70'-0"
100'-0"
PLAN

Extra down conductors are not required if distance between is less than 50'-0". This plan does not have conductors at less than 50'-0" intervals, so none can be omitted.

EXTRA DOWN CONDUCTORS REQUIRED for STRUCTURES OVER 60'-0" HIGH

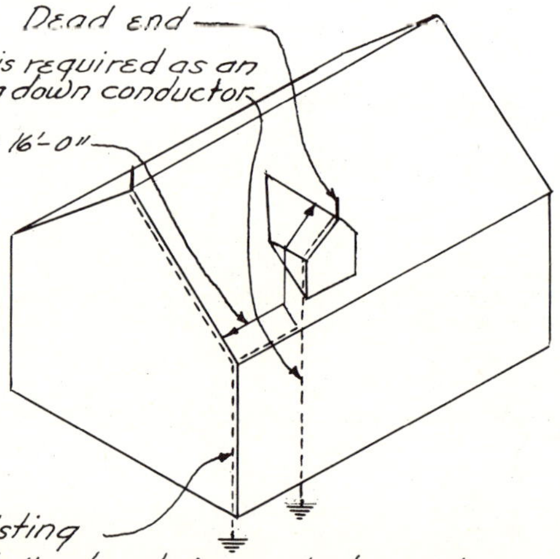
Dead end
This is required as an extra down conductor
Over 16'-0"
Existing

Install extra down conductors wherever it becomes necessary to avoid dead ends, or branch conductors ending at air terminals, which exceed 16'-0" in length, except that single down conductors descending flagpoles, spires & similar structures which are adjuncts of buildings shall not be regarded as dead ends, but shall be treated as air terminals.

DEAD ENDS

Requirements for metal roofed or clad buildings, if sections are insulated from one another, are same as for buildings composed of non-conductive materials. When metal is continuous, terminals and conductors, if used, shall be bonded to it and grounded. Structures of steel frame or reinforced concrete construction need no protection if steel is connected and grounded.

LIGHTNING PROTECTION

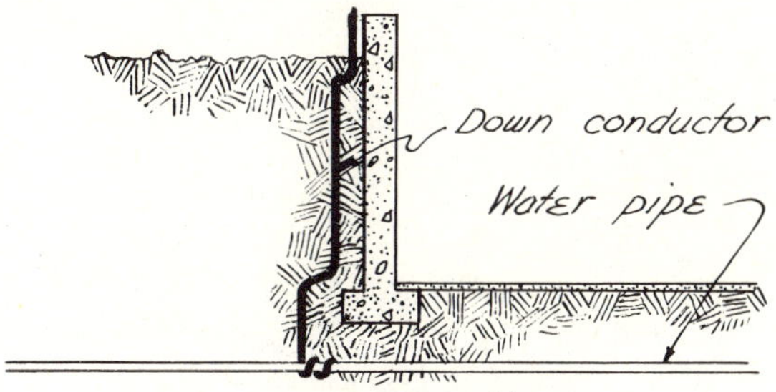
Down conductor
Water pipe

Ground connection to metal water pipe.

GROUNDING to PIPE

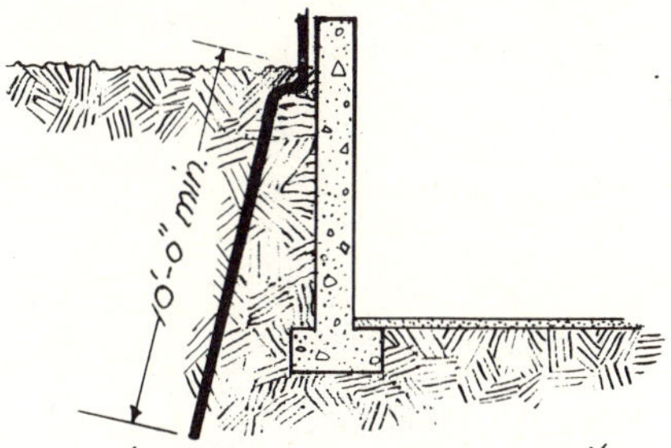
10'-0" min.

In moist clay or other soil of similar character as to electrical resistivity, extend rod into soil not less than 10'-0".

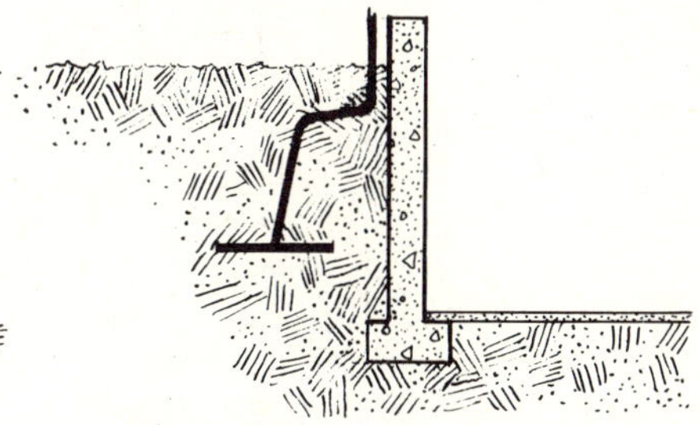

When soil is largely sand, gravel, or stones, enlarge electrodes by addition of rods, strips, or plates.

GROUNDING to DEEP SOIL

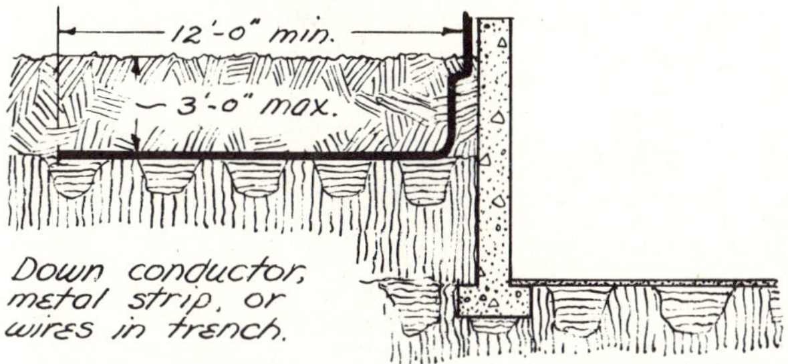
12'-0" min.
3'-0" max.

Down conductor, metal strip, or wires in trench.

Detail sections 1/8" = 1'-0".

Rock at least 1'-0" under grade. Maximum required trench depth 3'-0". Minimum 1'-0". If trench cannot be dug over 1'-0" in depth (because of rock), encircle building with a buried conductor and connect to all down conductors.

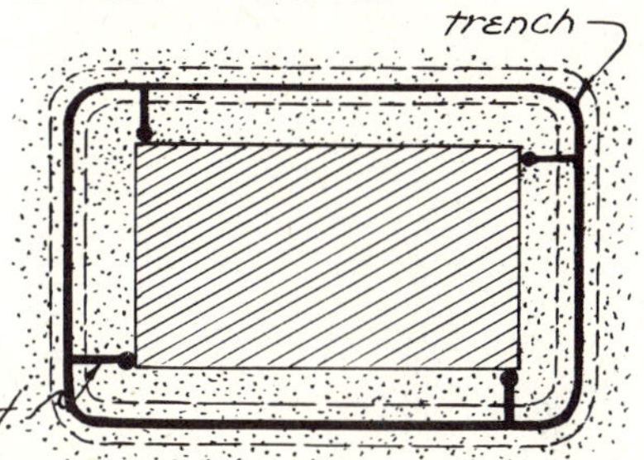
trench
Connection to down conduct.

Plan 1/32" = 1'-0".

GROUNDING to SHALLOW SOIL

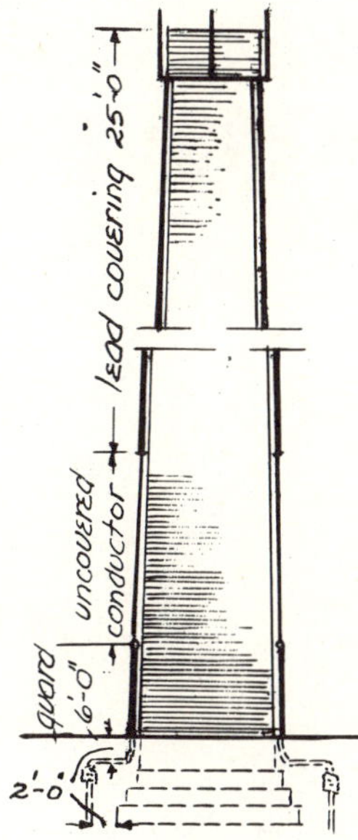
lead covering 25'-0"
uncovered conductor
guard 6'-0"
2'-0"

SMOKE STACK

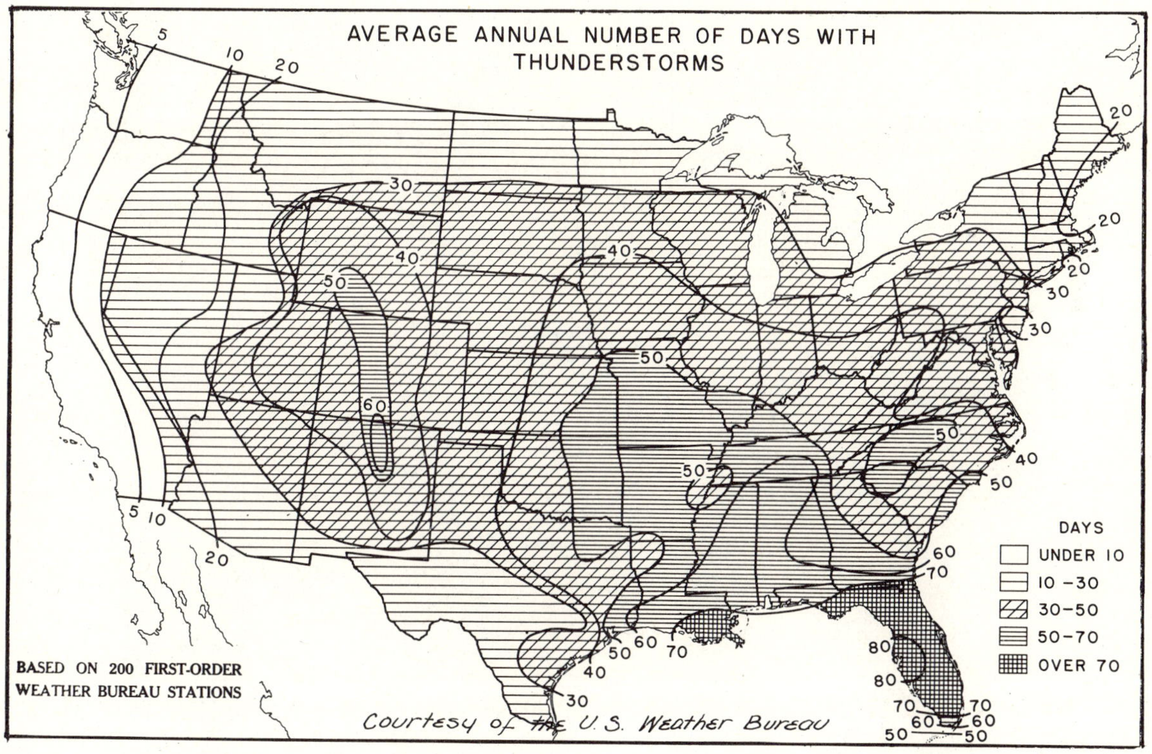
AVERAGE ANNUAL NUMBER OF DAYS WITH THUNDERSTORMS
DAYS
UNDER 10
10 –30
30–50
50–70
OVER 70
BASED ON 200 FIRST-ORDER WEATHER BUREAU STATIONS

Courtesy of the U.S. Weather Bureau

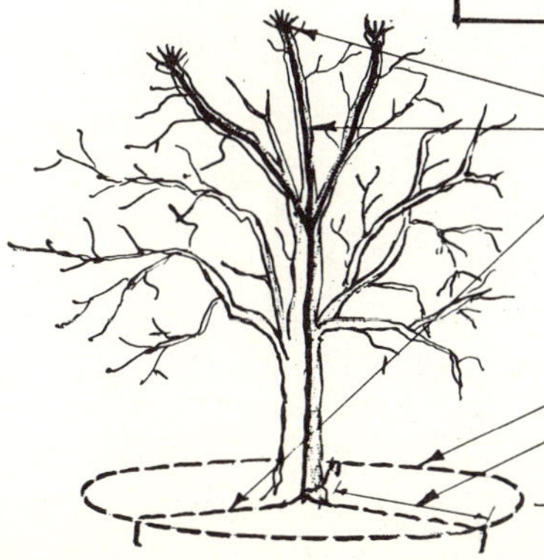

Terminals on highest parts.
Main conductor down trunk.

Radial conductor in trench 1'-0" deep. Required: 3 for every main conductor. Need shallow network to prevent damage to roots.

Encircling conductor. Average 10'-0" to 25'-0".

TREE PROTECTION

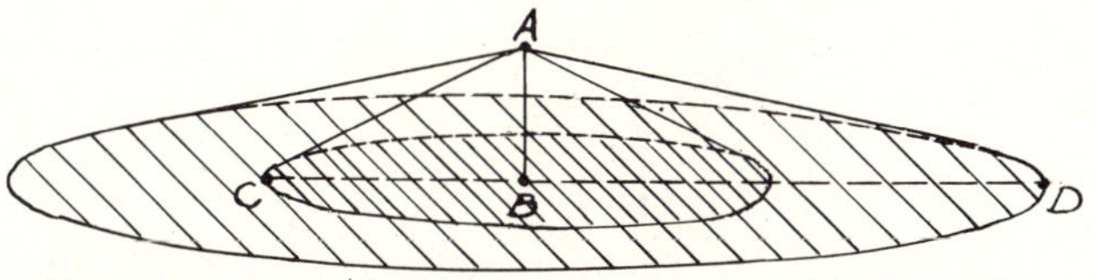
A
B
C
D

Maximum protection; cone ABC. Minimum; ABD. Vertical conductor assumed to divert strikes which might fall in conical space. Cone of influence is not a zone of complete protection.

CONE of INFLUENCE

LIGHTNING PROTECTION

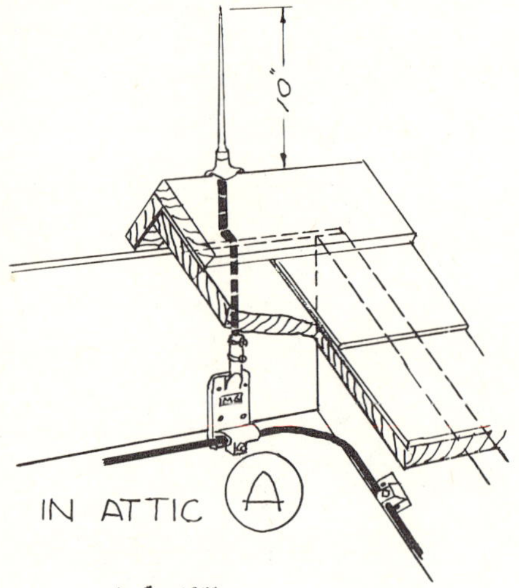
10"
IN ATTIC
A

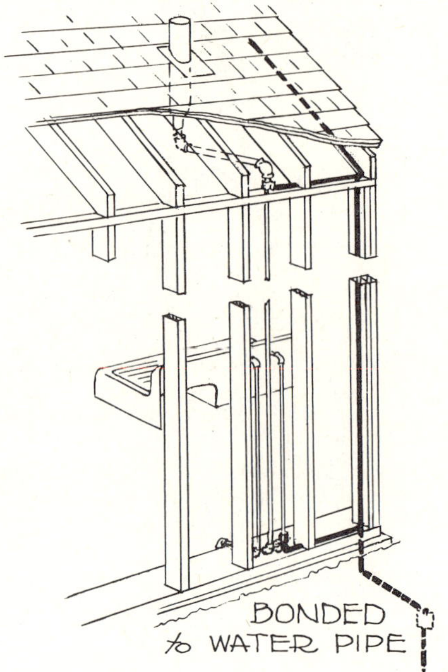
BONDED
to WATER PIPE

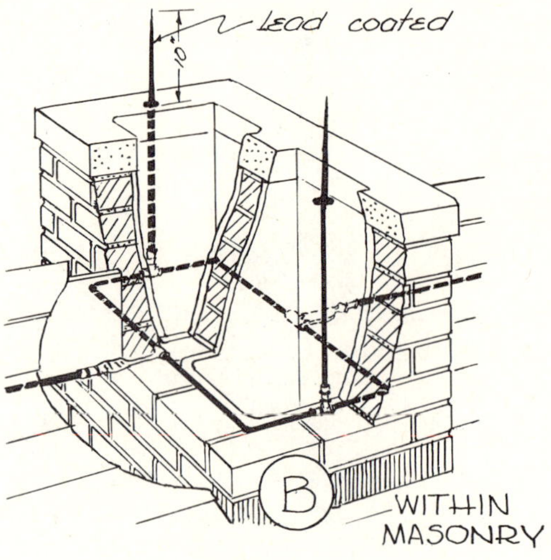
Lead coated
10"
B
WITHIN
MASONRY

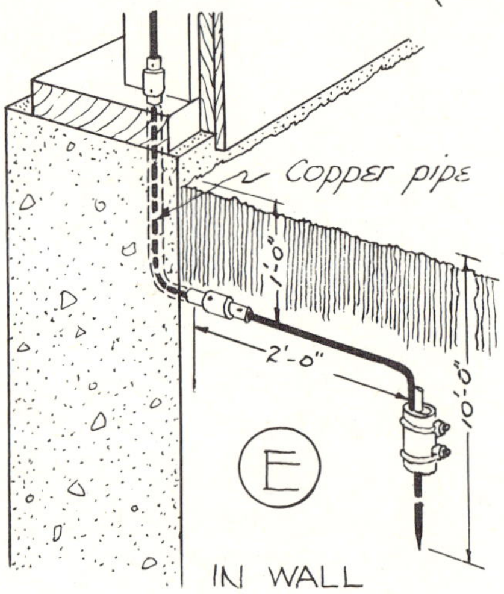
Copper pipe
1'-0"
2'-0"
10'-0"
E
IN WALL

CONCEALED TYPE

This type installed during construction.

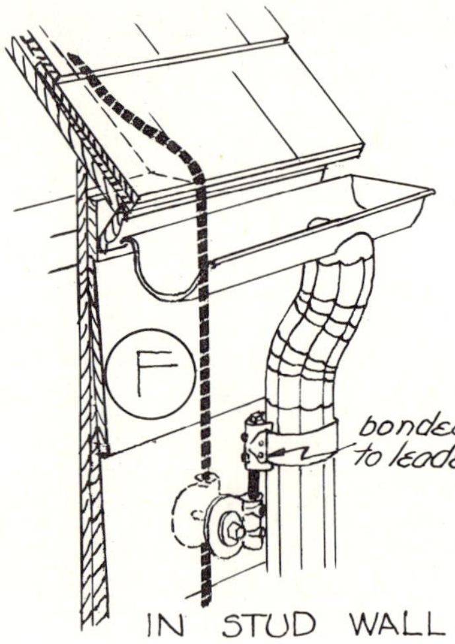
F
bonded
to leader
IN STUD WALL

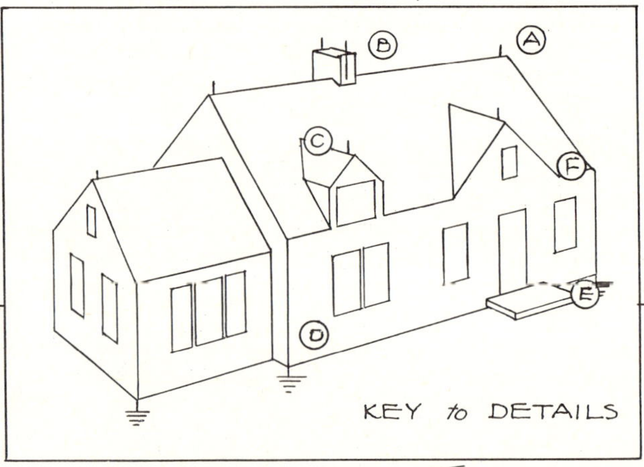
B
A
C
F
E
D
KEY to DETAILS

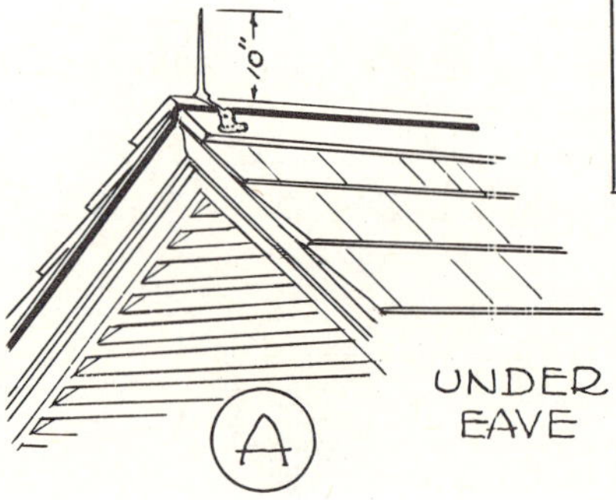
10"
A
UNDER
EAVE

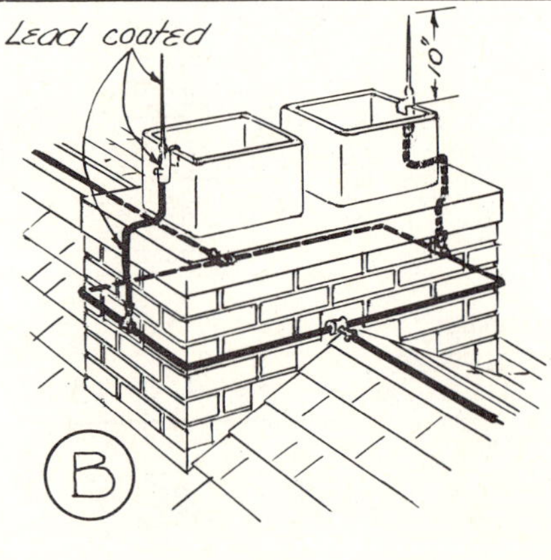
Lead coated
10"
B

UNDER
EAVE
C

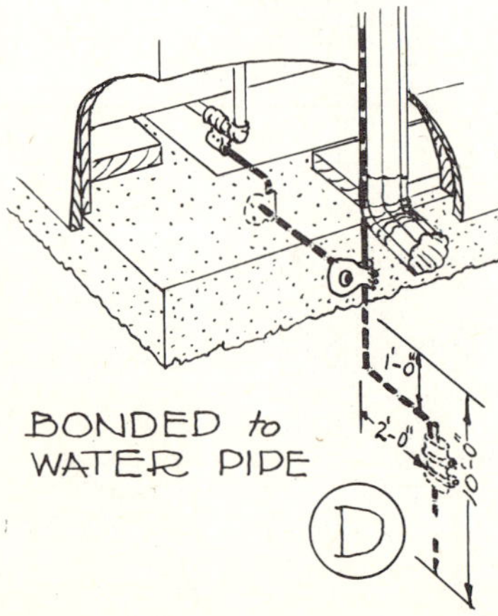
BONDED to
WATER PIPE
1'-0"
2'-0"
10'-0"
D

SEMI-CONCEALED TYPE

All details on this sheet are applicable to residential buildings. Heavy solid lines indicate lightning conductors exposed to view. Heavy dotted lines indicate lightning conductors hidden from view.

Courtesy of West Dodd Lightning Conductor Corp.

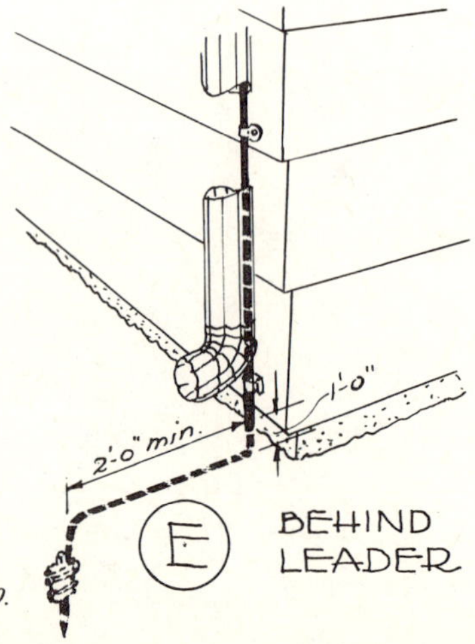
1'-0"
2'-0" min.
E
BEHIND
LEADER

LIGHTNING PROTECTION

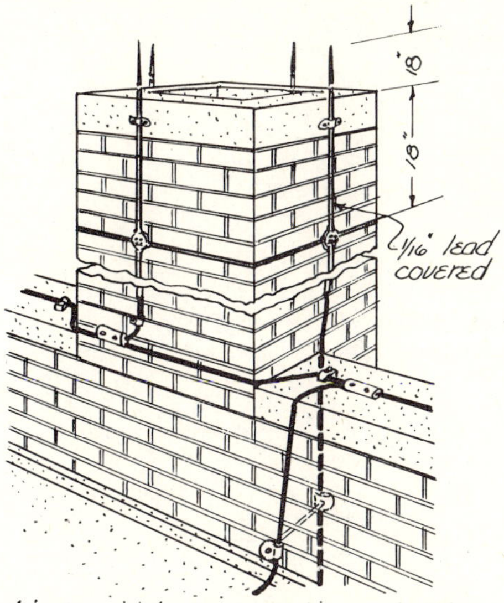
18"
18"
1/16" lead covered

Air terminals & connections to the top of coping conductor. Terminals must be within 2'-0" of each corner.
LARGE CHIMNEY

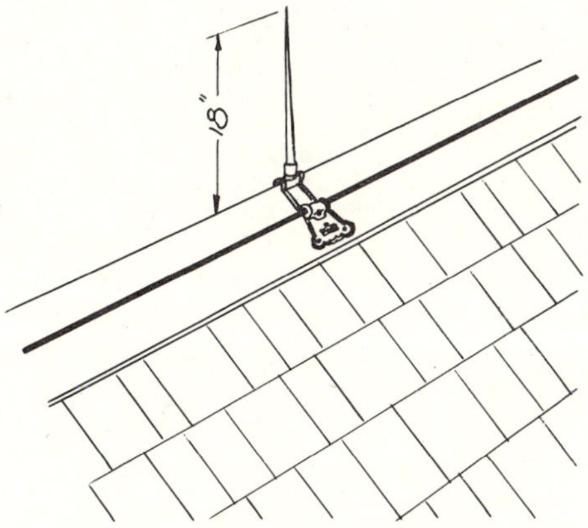
18"

Air terminal and ridge conductor.
ROOF RIDGE

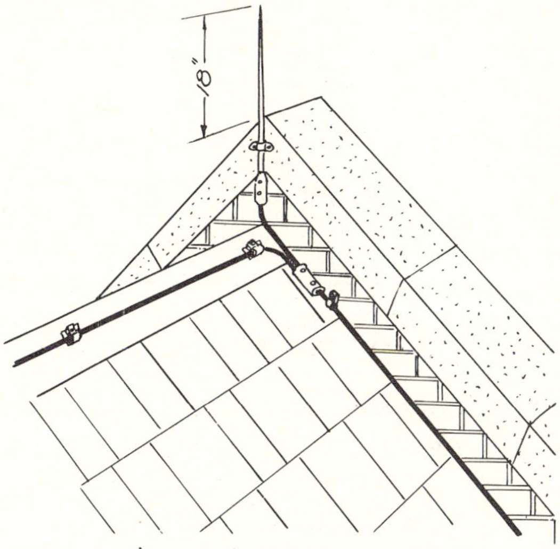
18"

Air terminal & connections to the roof conductor.
STONE GABLE

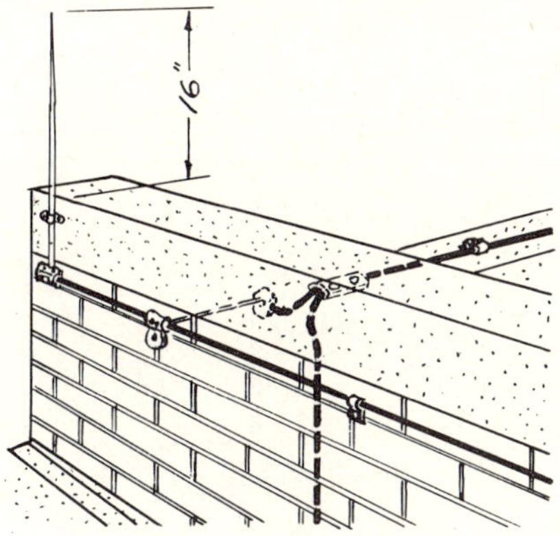
16"

conductor from air terminal.
BELOW COPING

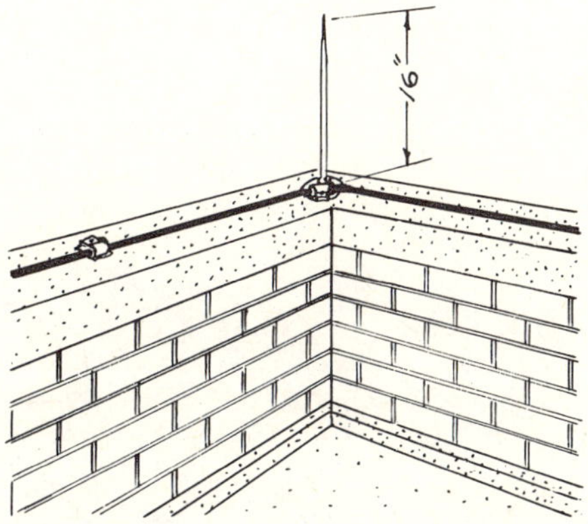
16"

Conductor with corner air terminal. Terminals must be within 2'-0" of corner.
TOP *of* COPING

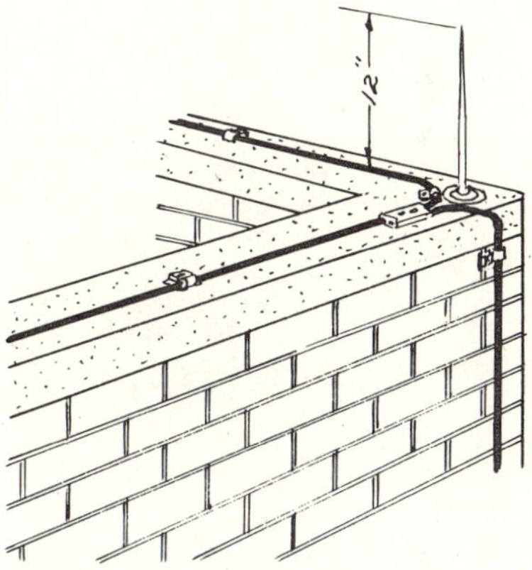
12"

Conductor with corner air terminal & down conductor.
TOP *of* COPING

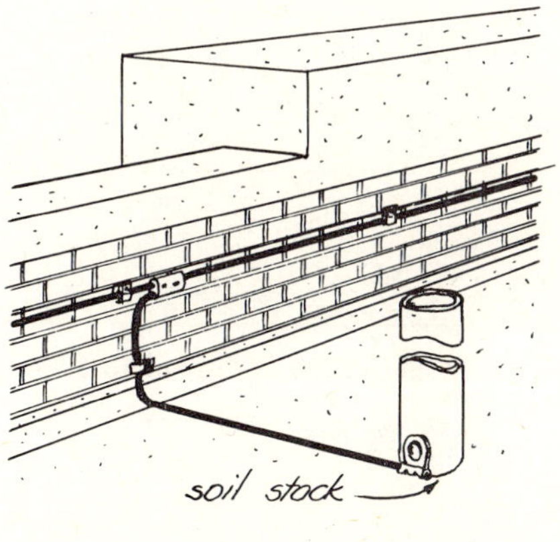
soil stack

Parapet & conductor to soil stack.
BOND *from* INSIDE

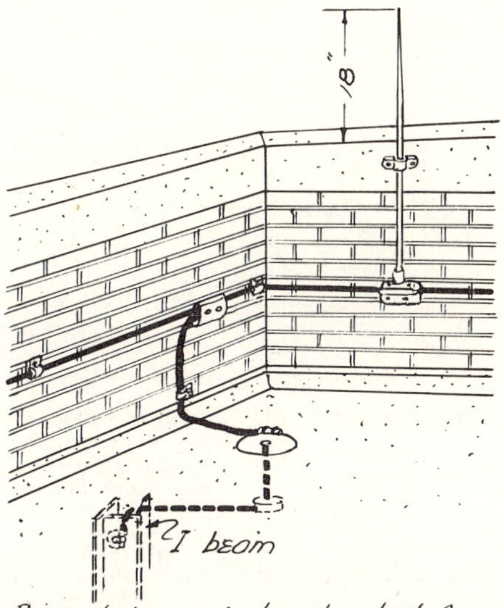
18"
I beam

Parapet & conductor to steel frame.
BOND *from* INSIDE

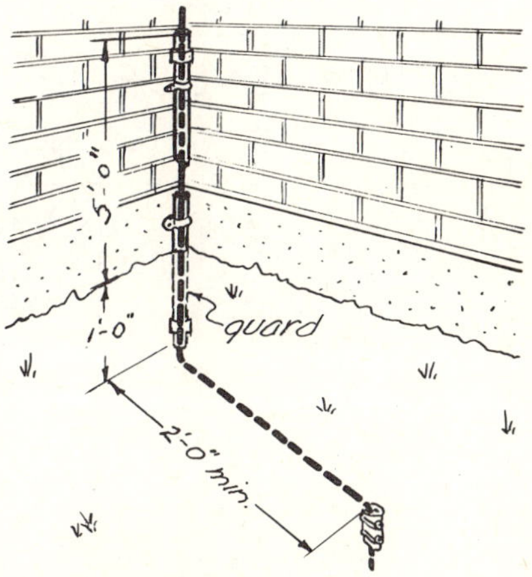
5'-0"
1'-0"
guard
2'-0" min.

GROUND CONNECTION

EXPOSED TYPE

Details on this sheet are mainly applicable to commercial bldgs. Heavy solid lines indicate lightning conductors exposed to view. Heavy dotted lines indicate lightning conductors hidden from view.

Courtesy of West Dodd Lightning Conductor Corp.

NOISE REDUCTION

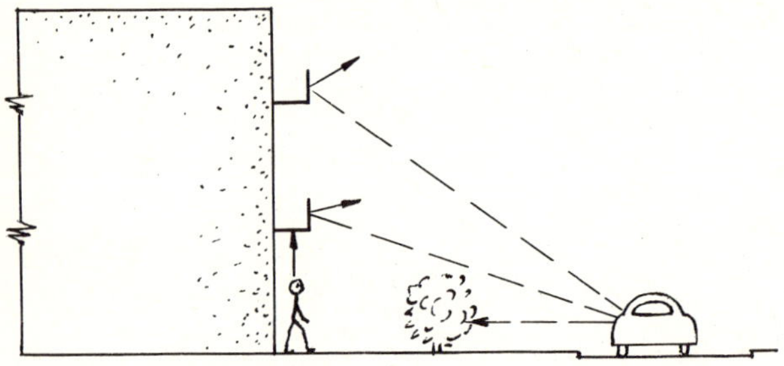

BALCONIES & PLANTS AS AIDS
Not to scale

REDUCTION *of* EXTERIOR NOISES

By Planning

- Select quiet site.
- Orient bedrooms on quietest exposure.
- Set house back from noisy streets or neighbors.
- Avoid small or deep courts and yards.
- Use balconies as baffles.
- Plant out noise sources.
- Use fixed windows on noisy exposures

By Insulation

- Use weatherstrips for openings.
- Use double glazing or storm sash.

EXTERIOR NOISES

REDUCTION *of* INTERIOR NOISES

Impact & Conducted Noises

- Select soft floor finishes.
- Insulate vibratory noises (e.g., machines) at source.
- Use quiet switches.
- Use water hammer eliminators.
- Wrap drainage pipes.
- Select quiet toilets.
- Insulate ducts.

Airborne Noises

- Space windows of adjoining apartments maximum distance apart.
- Place noisy areas - back-to-back.
- Place closets between noisy and quiet areas.
- Use weather strips on interior doors.
- Use heavy doors for residential work.

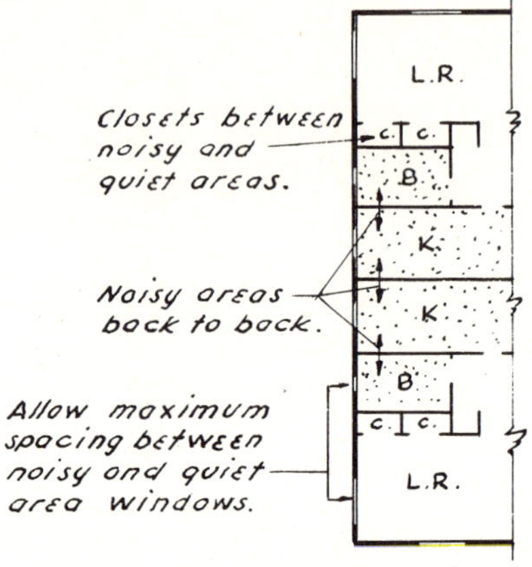
L.R.
Closets between noisy and quiet areas.
C
C
B
K
Noisy areas back to back.
K
B
C
C
Allow maximum spacing between noisy and quiet area windows.
L.R.

PLANNING FOR NOISE REDUCTION
Not to scale

INTERIOR NOISES

Scale 3" = 1'0"

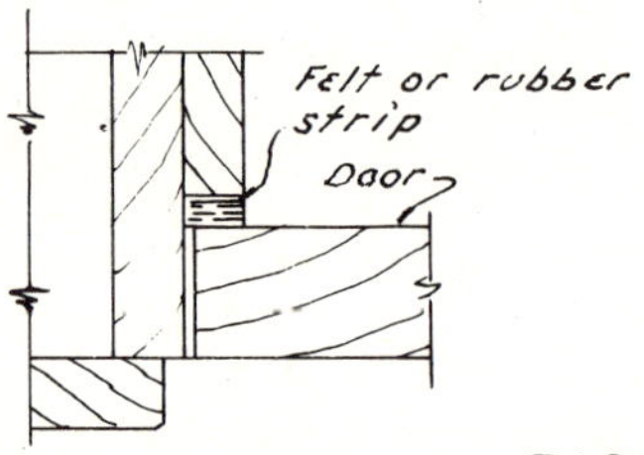
Felt or rubber strip
Door

JAMB

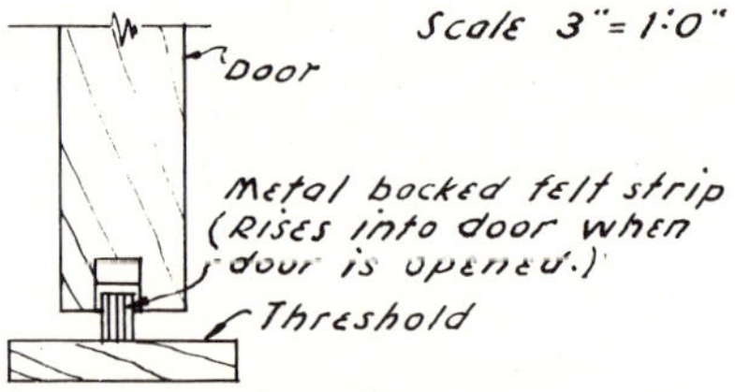
Door
Metal backed felt strip (Rises into door when door is opened.)
Threshold

RISING WEATHERSTRIP AT DOOR BOTTOM

DOOR SEALING *(For other seals and insulation, see door weather stripping).*

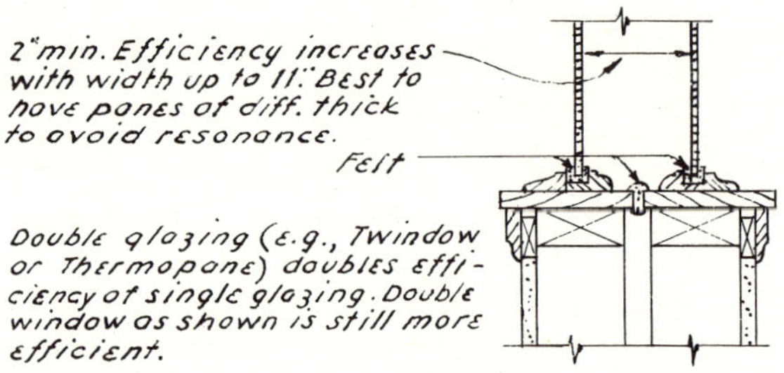
2" min. Efficiency increases with width up to 11." Best to have panes of diff. thick to avoid resonance.
Felt
Double glazing (e.g., Twindow or Thermopane) doubles efficiency of single glazing. Double window as shown is still more efficient.

DOUBLE WINDOW

GUIDE TABLE *for* ESTABLISHING TRANSMISSION LOSS (AIRBORNE) *of* CONSTRUCTION WHICH YOU INTEND *to* USE

TYPE *of* HOUSING *Select a, b, or c*	"ASSUMED TOLERANCE" is decibels of sound you assume will not be objectionable within space.		CONSTRUCTION SHOULD PROVIDE FOLLOWING TRANSMISSION LOSS			
	ASSUMED TOLERANCE		If noise in neighboring apartments is 65 decibels (average), use these colums.		If noise in neighboring apartments is 75 decibels (exceptional), use these colums.	
	LIV. RM., DIN. RM. & KITCHEN	BED RM. & QUIET RMS.				
			LIVING RM.	BED RM.	LIVING RM	BED RM.
a. Low Cost	30	20 (Avg whisper 4' away).	35 to 40	46 to 50	46 to 50	56 to 60
b. Medium Cost	25	15	41 to 45	51 to 55	51 to 55	61 to 65
c. High Cost	20	10 (Quiet whisper 5' away).	46 to 50	56 to 60	56 to 60	66 to 70

See following pages for construction which meets the LOSS selected

SOUND TRANSMISSION LOSS—FLOORS, PARTITIONS & WALLS

Sound Transmission Loss Data on the following sheets has been taken from "Building Material and Structures Report 144, Sound Insulation of Wall & Floor Constructions" February 25, 1955. U.S. Department of Commerce, National Bureau of Standards. Supersedes BMS 17, and its supplements 1 and 2. Data published with permission.

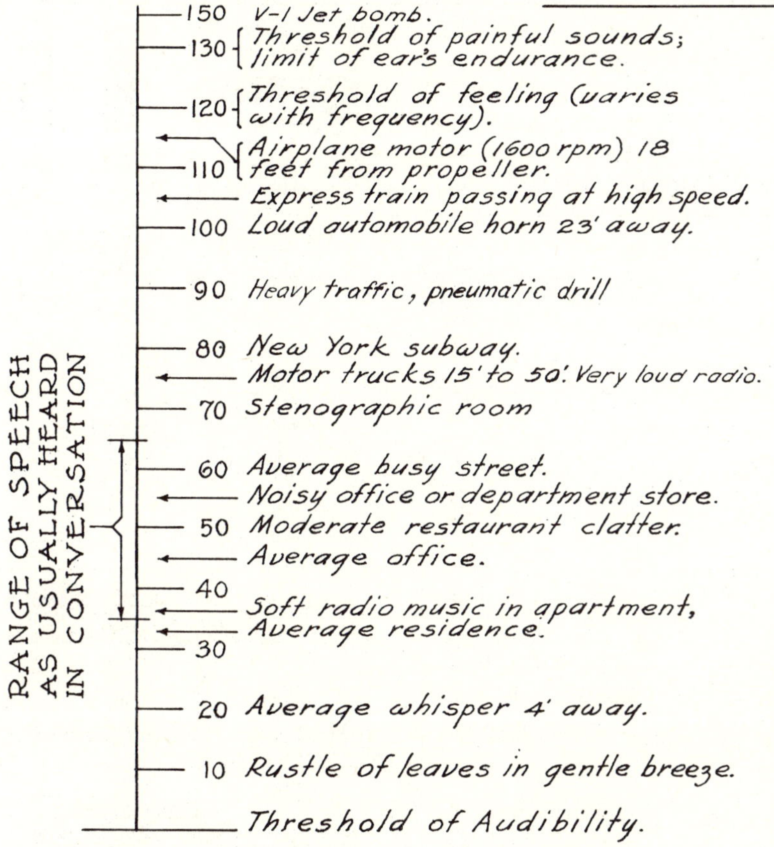
150 V-1 Jet bomb.
130 Threshold of painful sounds; limit of ear's endurance.
120 Threshold of feeling (varies with frequency).
Airplane motor (1600 rpm) 18 feet from propeller.
110
Express train passing at high speed.
100 Loud automobile horn 23' away.
90 Heavy traffic, pneumatic drill
80 New York subway.
Motor trucks 15' to 50'. Very loud radio.
70 Stenographic room
60 Average busy street.
Noisy office or department store.
50 Moderate restaurant clatter.
Average office.
40
Soft radio music in apartment,
Average residence.
30
20 Average whisper 4' away.
10 Rustle of leaves in gentle breeze.
Threshold of Audibility.
RANGE OF SPEECH AS USUALLY HEARD IN CONVERSATION

DECIBEL SCALE OF SOUND INTENSITIES

The decibel unit represents the smallest change in energy that the human ear can hear.

SOUND TRANSMISSION LOSSES GIVEN ON THE FOLLOWING SHEETS REPRESENT THE LOSS, IN DECIBELS, WHICH OCCURS WHEN A SOUND PASSES THRU A GIVEN TYPE OF CONSTRUCTION.

THE LOSSES ARE THE AVERAGE OF 6 FREQUENCIES IN COLUMN 256-1024 AND FOR 9 FREQUENCIES IN COLUMN 128-4096

Threshold of audibility may be raised by general local noise level, and should be considered in selection of structures, i.e. partition satisfactory for business district would not give same satisfaction in country house.

Sound recording studios	6 to 8
Radio broadcasting studios	8 to 10
Hospitals	8 to 12
Music studios	10 to 15
Apartments, hotels and homes	10 to 20
Theaters, churches, auditoriums, class rooms, libraries	12 to 24
Talking picture theaters	15 to 25
Private office, etc.	20 to 30
Public offices, banking rooms, etc.	25 to 40

MAXIMUM NOISE LEVELS WHICH SHOULD BE TOLERATED.

The above optimum are seldom found (Knudsen).

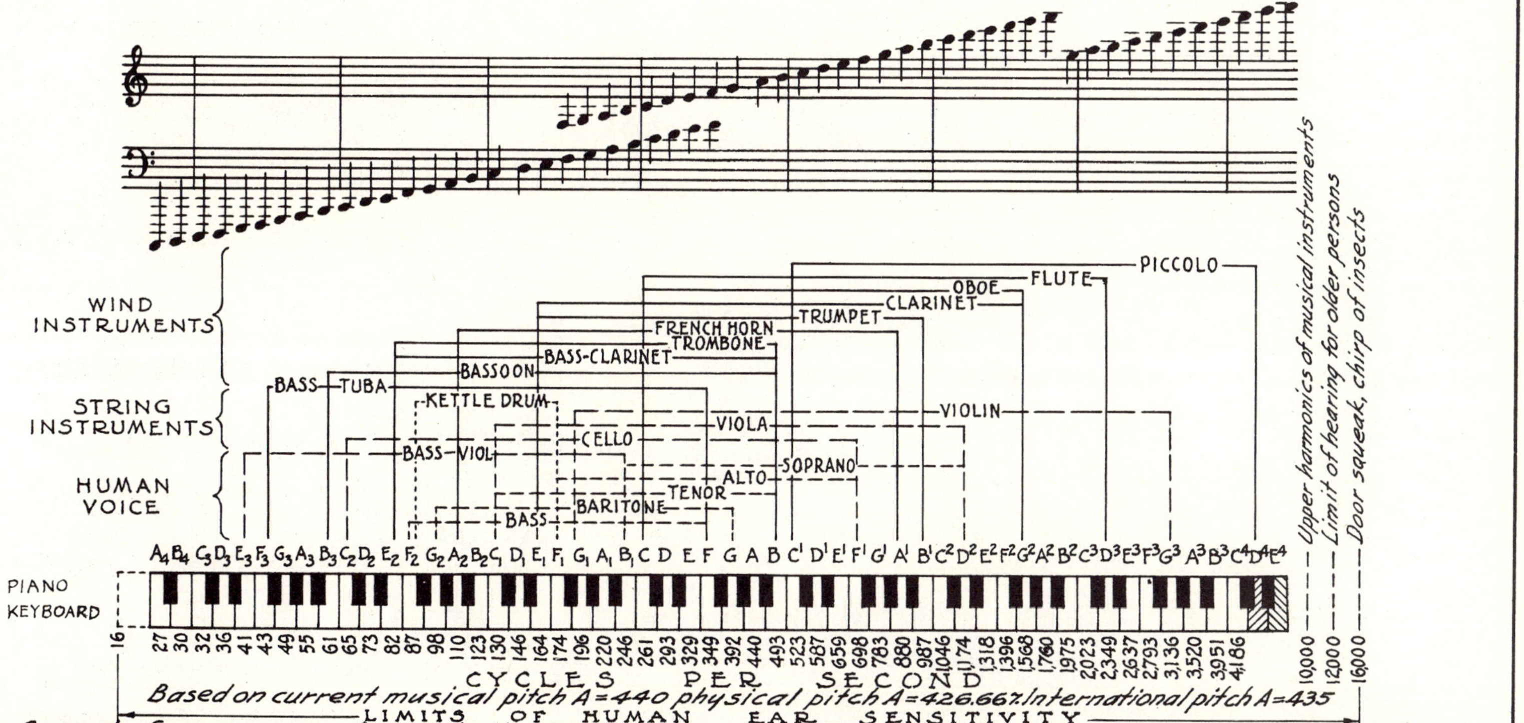
WIND INSTRUMENTS
STRING INSTRUMENTS
HUMAN VOICE
PICCOLO
FLUTE
OBOE
CLARINET
TRUMPET
FRENCH HORN
TROMBONE
BASS-CLARINET
BASSOON
BASS
TUBA
KETTLE DRUM
VIOLIN
VIOLA
CELLO
BASS-VIOL
SOPRANO
ALTO
TENOR
BARITONE
BASS
PIANO KEYBOARD
16 27 30 32 36 41 43 49 55 61 65 73 82 87 98 110 123 130 146 164 174 196 220 246 261 293 329 349 392 440 493 523 587 659 698 783 880 987 1046 1174 1318 1396 1568 1760 1975 2023 2349 2637 2793 3136 3520 3951 4186
10,000 12,000 16,000
Upper harmonics of musical instruments
Limit of hearing for older persons
Door squeak, chirp of insects
CYCLES PER SECOND
Based on current musical pitch A=440 physical pitch A=426.667. International pitch A=435
LIMITS OF HUMAN EAR SENSITIVITY

Sound-frequency characteristics, as graphically represented in a chart copyrighted by Electronics, through the courtesy of whose editors it is here reproduced.

SOUND TRANSMISSION LOSS – FLOOR STRUCTURES

TYPE of FLOOR STRUCTURES SIZES	CEILING CONSTN AND FINISH	FLOOR CONSTRUCTION AND FINISH-INSULATION	AVERAGE TRANSMISSION LOSS IN DECIBELS AT FREQUENCIES (CYCLES PER SECOND) 256-1024	TAPPING	SECTIONS – 3/4" = 1'-0"
DOORS					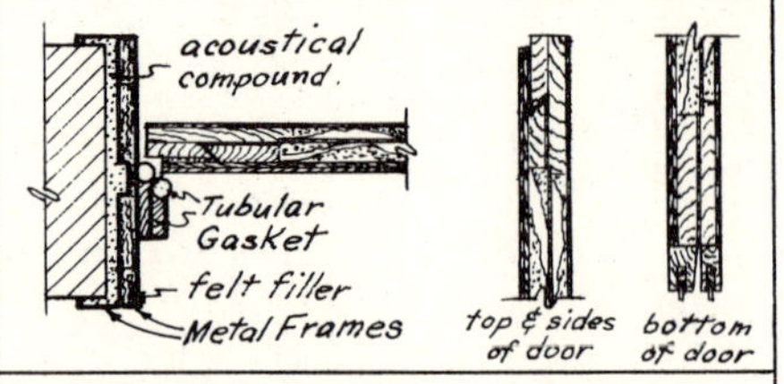acoustical compound Tubular Gasket felt filler Metal Frames top & sides of door bottom of door
Heavy Wooden door, approximately 2½" thick; special hardware; rubber gasket around sides and top; drop felt at bottom of door.			*28 30	—	
Wooden door 2⅝" thick; 3'-0" x 7'-0", with double frames insulated from each other with hair felt; door formed of ¼" hardwood panels; door hung in split frame with felt insert; frame mounted in 12" brick wall; Two tubular gaskets form a double seal around both sides and at the top of the door, with two drop felts at the bottom of the door.			*35 40	—	
FLOOR STRUCTURES					
Wood Joists 2"x8", 16" o.c.	7/8" gypsum plaster on expanded metal lath.	13/16" subfloor and 13/16" oak finished floor	33	11	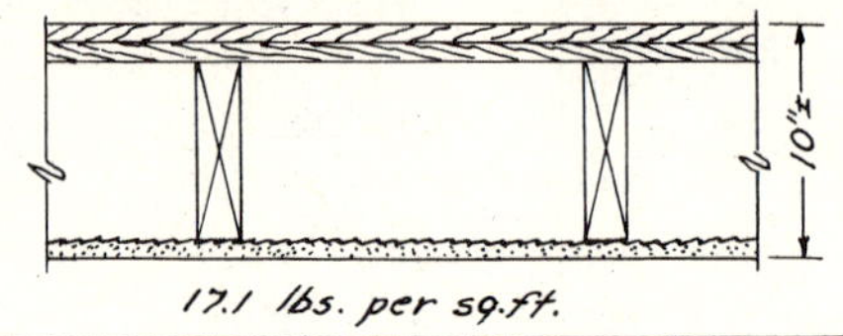10"± 17.1 lbs. per sq.ft.
ditto.	7/8" gypsum plaster on wood lath.	A Subfloor, 3/8" finished wood floor	A 45.9	A 14	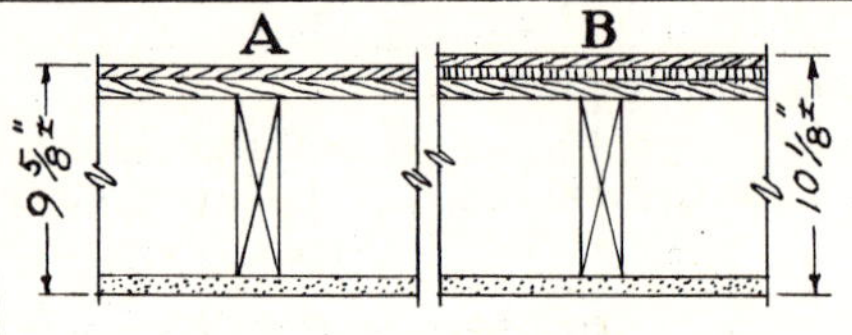A B 9⅝"± 10⅛"±
		B ditto, with ½" fiberboard between floorings	B 46.4	B 14	
ditto.	ditto.	A Subfloor, ½" fiberboard, 1"x3" nailing strips, rough and finished wood floors.	A 58.2	A 22	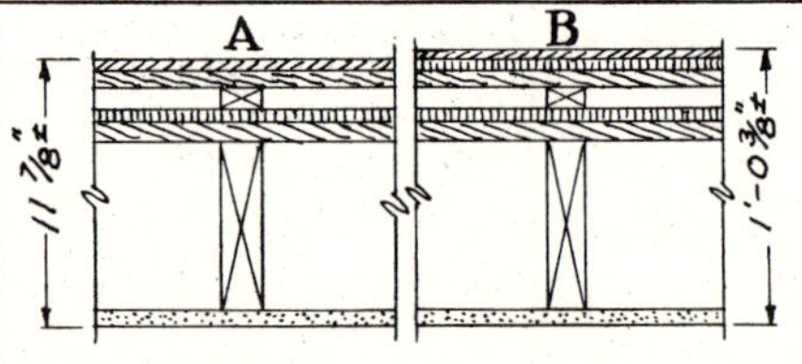A B 11⅞"± 1'-0⅜"±
		B ditto, with ½" fiberboard between rough and finished wood floors.	B 58.8	B 22	
Wood Joists Independent floor and ceiling joists with common bearing	½" Insulite plaster ½" fiberboard	A Rough and finished floors	A 52.6	A 22	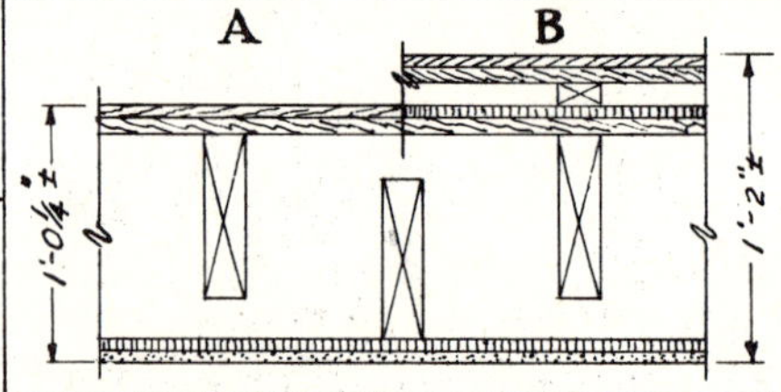A B 1'-0¼"± 1'-2"±
		B Rough floor, ½" fiberboard, Floating floor of 1"x2" nailing strips, rough floor and 3/8" hardwood finished floor.	B 63.8	B 30	
Wood Floor Joists 2"x8", 16" o.c. Ceiling Joists 2"x4", 16" o.c.	½" fiberboard ½" gypsum plaster	1" pine subfloor ½" fiberboard 1"x3" furring strips, 16" o.c. 1" pine finished floor	*54	25	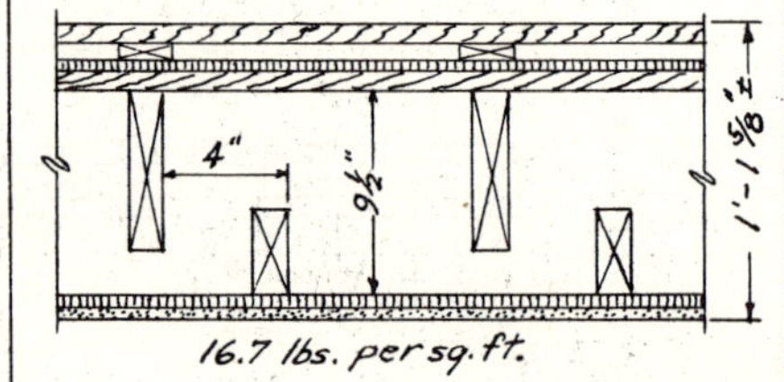4" 9½" 1'-1⅝"± 16.7 lbs. per sq. ft.
Wood Joists 2"x6", 16" o.c.	¾" gypsum plaster on expanded metal lath	A Subfloor, 2"x2" sleepers 16" o.c., hardwood finished floor.	A *38	A 10	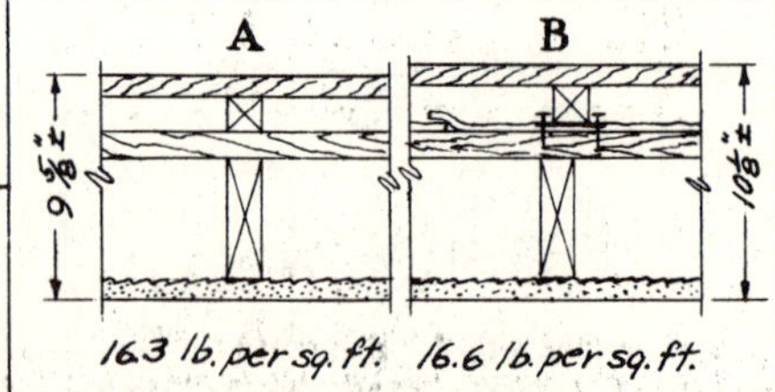A B 9⅝"± 10⅝"± 16.3 lb. per sq. ft. 16.6 lb. per sq. ft.
		B ditto, with ½" wood fiber wool blanket on subfloor, sleepers attached with special clips.	B *50	B 16	
Wood Joists 2"x8", 16" o.c.	A ¾" fiberboard	1" pine subfloor and 1" pine finished floor.	A *40	A 6	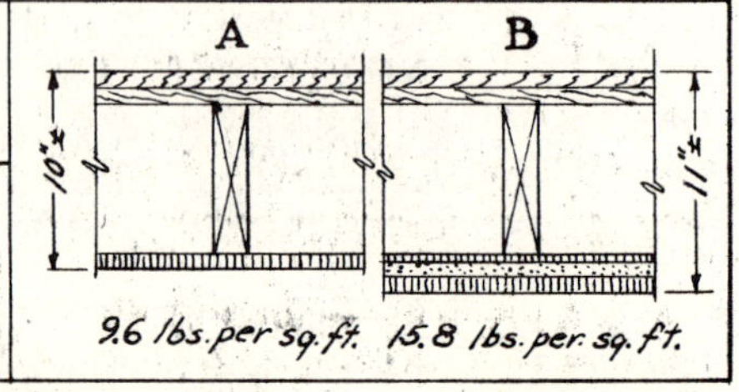A B 10"± 11"± 9.6 lbs. per sq. ft. 15.8 lbs. per sq. ft.
	B ½" fiberboard ½" gypsum plaster brown coat. ¾" fiberboard face		B *42	B 11	

* Averages obtained for frequencies 128-4096 c.p.s.

SOUND TRANSMISSION LOSS - FLOOR STRUCTURES

TYPE of FLOOR STRUCTURES SIZES	CEILING CONSTN AND FINISH	FLOOR CONSTRUCTION AND FINISH-INSULATION	AVERAGE TRANSMISSION LOSS IN DECIBELS AT FREQUENCIES (CYCLES PER SECOND) 128-4,096	TAP-PING	SECTIONS — 1/4" = 1'-0"
Wood joists 2"x8", 16" o.c.	1/2" gypsum plaster on 1/2" fiber board	A 1" pine subfloor and 1" pine finished floor B 1" pine subfloor, 1/2" fiber board, 1"x3" sleepers 16" o.c. 1" pine finished floor.	A 45 B 50	A 11 B 12	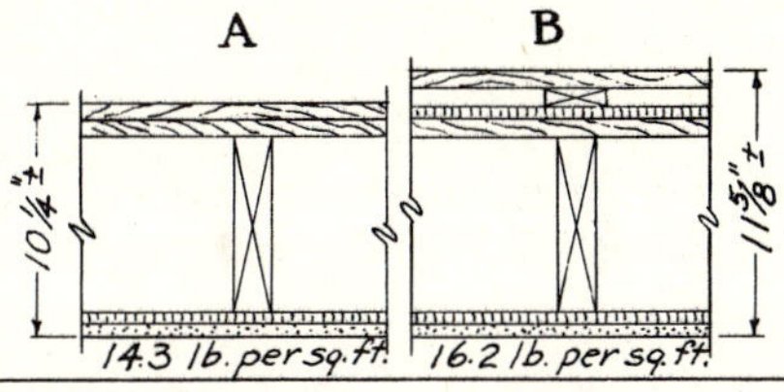 A: 10 1/4" ±, 14.3 lb. per sq. ft.; B: 11 5/8" ±, 16.2 lb. per sq. ft.
ditto	A 1/2" gyp. plaster on 1/2" fiber brd. 1"x3" fur. strip 16" o.c., ceiling repeats. B Same as "A", except omit top plaster.	1" pine subfloor and 1" pine finished floor.	A 45 B 47	A 10 B 14	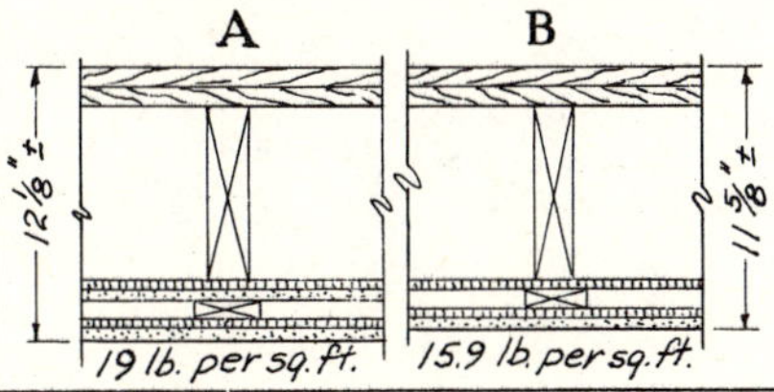 A: 12 1/8" ±, 19 lb. per sq. ft.; B: 11 5/8" ±, 15.9 lb. per sq. ft.
Wood joists 2"x8" and 2"x2" suspended joists, 16" o.c.	1/2" plaster on 1/2" fiberboard; addition. plaster & fiberboard suspended by screw eyes & wire loops 36" o.c., 4" below upper ceiling; 5"x5"x2" fiberbrd. block pads at fastening	1" pine subfloor and 1" pine finished floor.	56	26	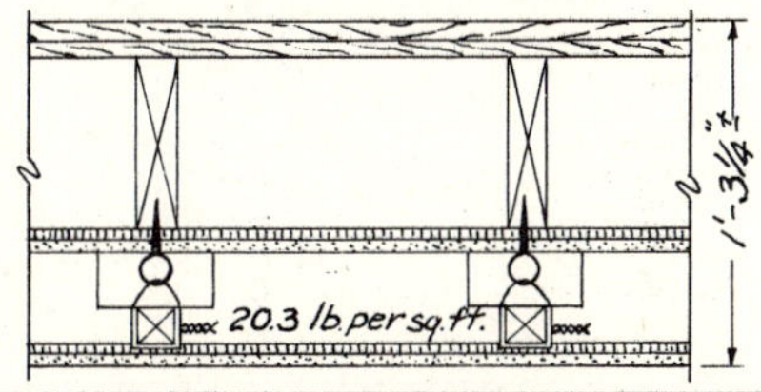 1'-3 1/4" ±, 20.3 lb. per sq. ft.
Wood joists 2"x10", 16" o.c.	A 1/2" plaster on 3/8" gypsum lath attached with U.S.G. clips R1 and R2 B 3/4" plaster on metal lath, held by 1/4" metal rods, attached with spring clips.	1" pine subfloor, building paper, and 13/16" pine finished floor.	A 49 B 51	A 19 B 22	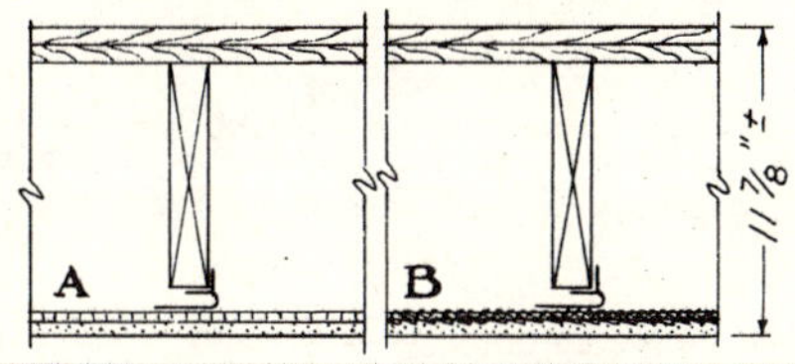 11 7/8" ±
Reinforced Concrete flat slab, 4" thick	None.	A None. B 1 1/8" asphaltic concrete	A 47 B 51	A 2 B 8	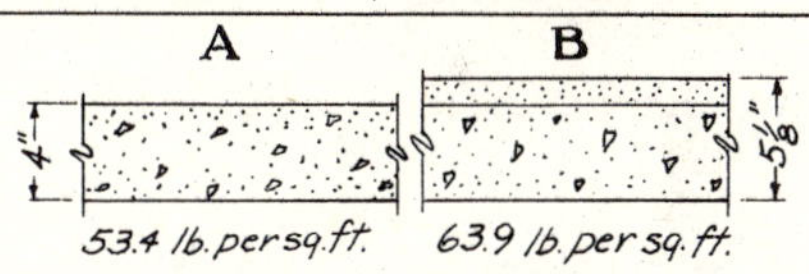 A: 4", 53.4 lb. per sq. ft.; B: 5 1/8", 63.9 lb. per sq. ft.
ditto.	3/4" furring strips 14 1/2" o.c., expanded metal lath & 7/8" gyp. plaster.	A 3/4" parquet floor set in 3/32" mastic. B Same as "A" but with 1/2" fiberboard set in mastic.	A 49 B 48	A 8 B 17	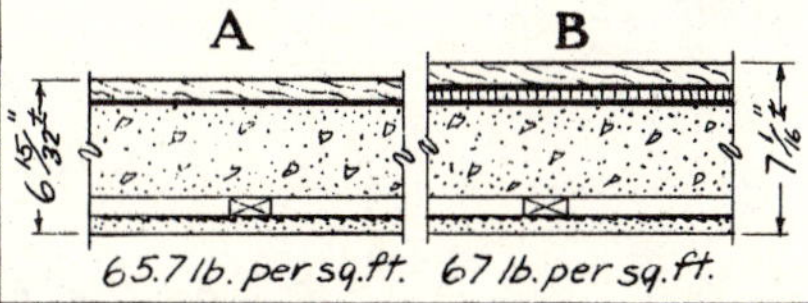 A: 6 15/32" ±, 65.7 lb. per sq. ft.; B: 7 1/16" ±, 67 lb. per sq. ft.
Concrete flat slab 4" thick reinforced with No. 3 ø rods 9" o.c.	13/16"x2" furring strips 16" o.c., 1/2" wood fiber board, 1/2" gyp. plaster.	No finish	*57	1	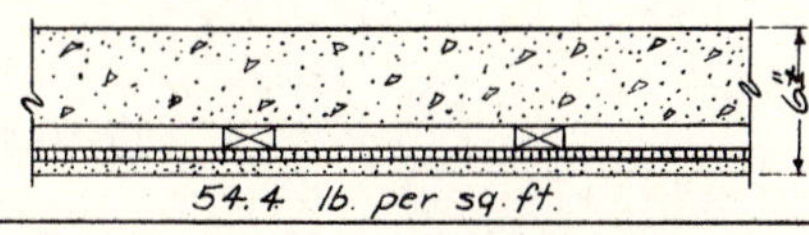 6" ±, 54.4 lb. per sq. ft.
ditto.	ditto	Floating floor of 1"x2" nailing strips, 3/4" subfloor and 3/8" oak finished floor.	*60	30	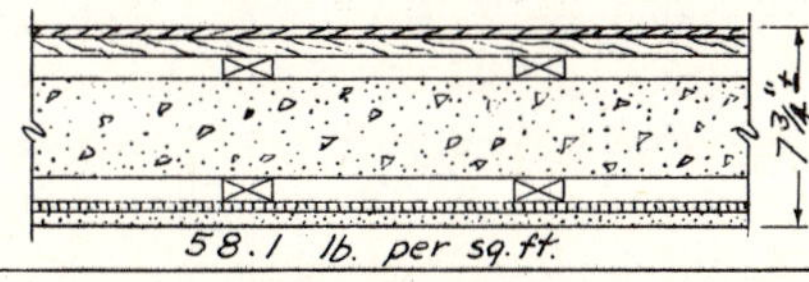 7 3/4" ±, 58.1 lb. per sq. ft.
ditto.	ditto.	ditto - with addition of 1/2" Insulite between slab and strips	*60	33	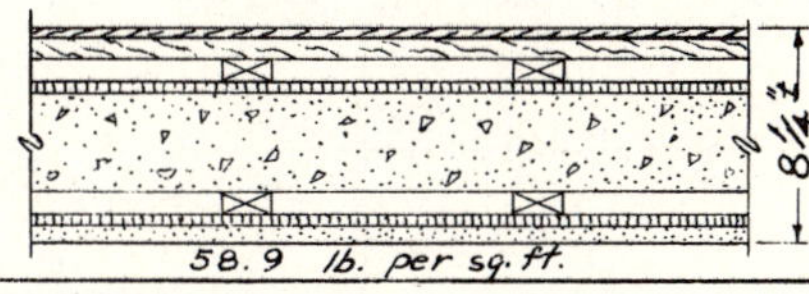 8 1/4" ±, 58.9 lb. per sq. ft.
Concrete Slab 4" thick	Construction beneath slab. Special coiled spring stirrup hangers 24"x 34" o.c., 1 1/2" furring channels 34" o.c., 3/4" channel cross furring 16" o.c., 3/8" gyp. lath, 1/4" gypsum brown coat and 1/2" acoustical plaster (trowel finish). Insulation above lath varies.	Above lath: 3" ground cork 4" mineral wool 3" ground scraps gyp. lath & wall brd.	54 55 55	11 12 12	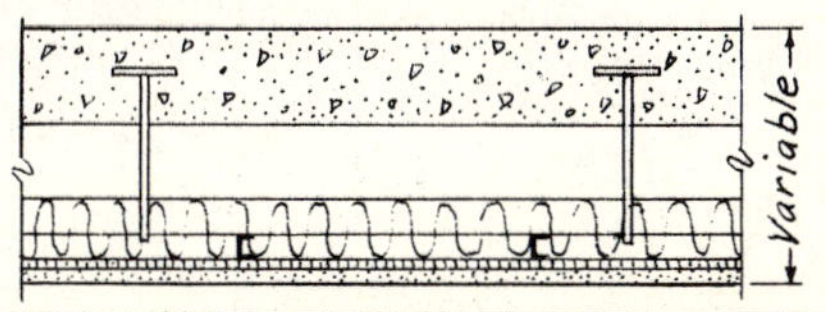 Variable

* Averages obtained for frequencies 256 - 1,024 c.p.s.

SOUND TRANSMISSION LOSS – FLOOR STRUCTURES

TYPE of FLOOR STRUCTURES SIZES	CEILING CONST^N AND FINISH	FLOOR CONSTRUCTION AND FINISH	AVERAGE TRANSMISSION LOSS IN DECIBELS AT FREQUENCIES – (CYCLES PER SECOND): 256-1,024	TAPPING	SECTIONS – 3/4" = 1'-0"
Combination Floor, 6"x12"x12" clay tile 18" o.c. & 2" concrete slab above tile.	5/8" Brown coat and hard white plaster	A No finish	A 49	—	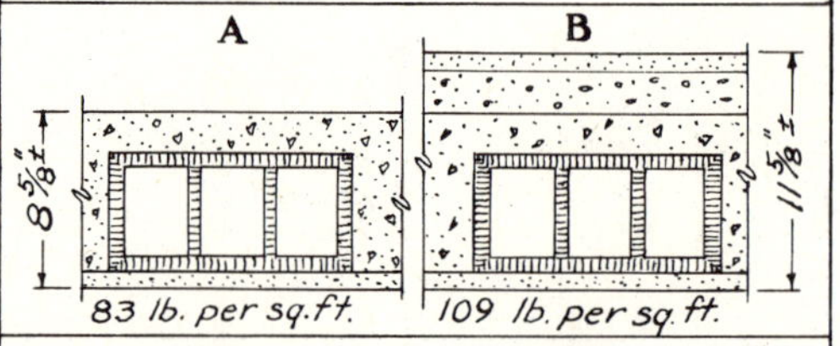A B 8 5/8"± 11 5/8"± 83 lb. per sq. ft. 109 lb. per sq. ft.
		B 2" Cinder concrete 1" Cement Finish	B 50	—	
Combination Floor, 4"x12"x12" clay tile 17" o.c. & 2 1/2" concrete slab above tile.	2"x13/16" Furring strips 16" o.c., 1/2" wood fiber board and 1/2" gypsum brown coat and hard white plaster.	A No finish	A 57	A 5	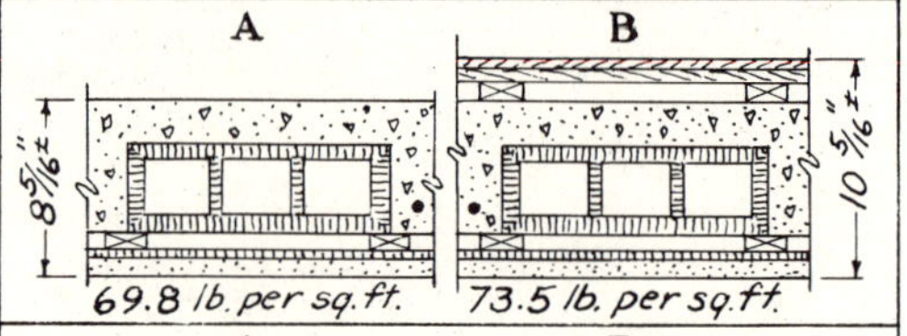A B 8 5/16"± 10 5/16"± 69.8 lb. per sq. ft. 73.5 lb. per sq. ft.
		B 1"x2" Nailing strips 16" o.c., 3/4" rough flooring and 3/8" oak finish floor.	B 63	B 34	
ditto.	A ditto.	Ditto, plus 1/2" wood fiber board between concrete slab and nailing strips.	A 66	A 35	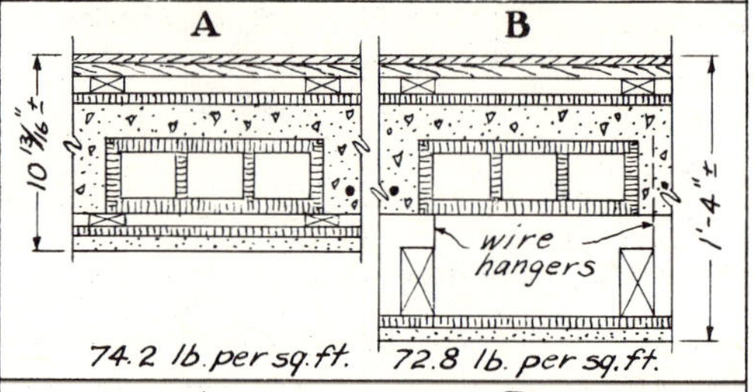A B 10 13/16"± 1'-4"± wire hangers 74.2 lb. per sq. ft. 72.8 lb. per sq. ft.
	B Suspended 2"x4" wood furring, 16" o.c., 1/2" fiberboard and 1/2" gypsum brown coat & hard white plaster.		B 69	B 51	
Combination Floor, 4"x12"x12" clay tile 18" o.c. & 2" concrete slab above tile.	1/2" gypsum brown coat & hard white plaster.	A 2"x2" nailing strips, 16" o.c., 13/16" oak finish floor.	A 41	A 23	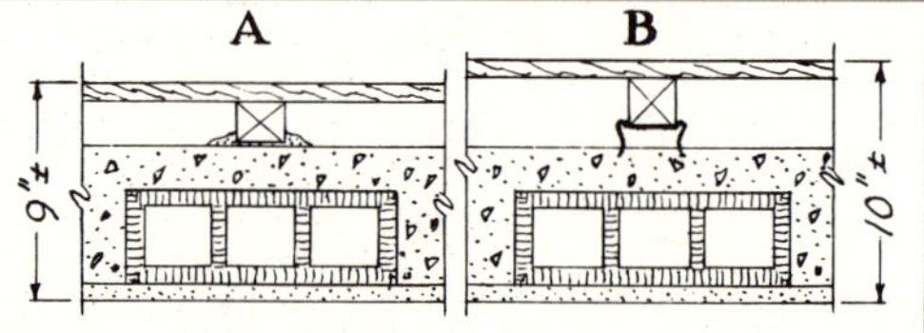A B 9"± 10"±
		B Ditto, except nailing strips rest on U.S. Gypsum resilient steel clips.	B 58	B 33	

TYPE of FLOOR STRUCTURES SIZES	CEILING CONST^N AND FINISH	FLOOR CONSTRUCTION AND FINISH	256-1,024	128-4,096	TAPPING	SECTIONS
8" Steel, Bar Joists 20" o.c.	3/4" High-rib metal lath and 3 coats gypsum plaster	Standard 3/4" rib lath 2 1/2" Concrete slab 1/4" Linoleum	55.6	55	13	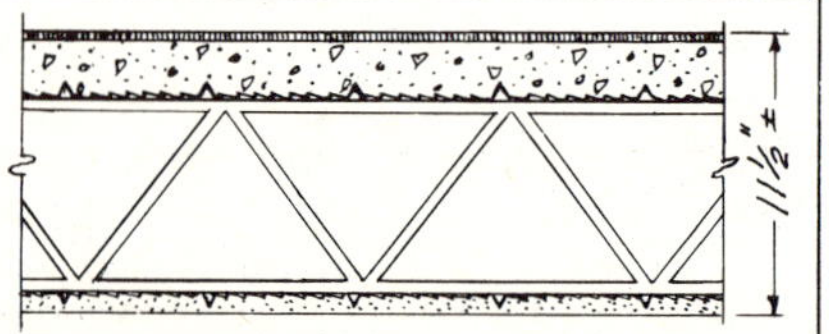11 1/2"±
ditto.	1" wood fiberboard, and 1/2" gypsum brown coat and hard white plaster.	ditto	52.4	54	14	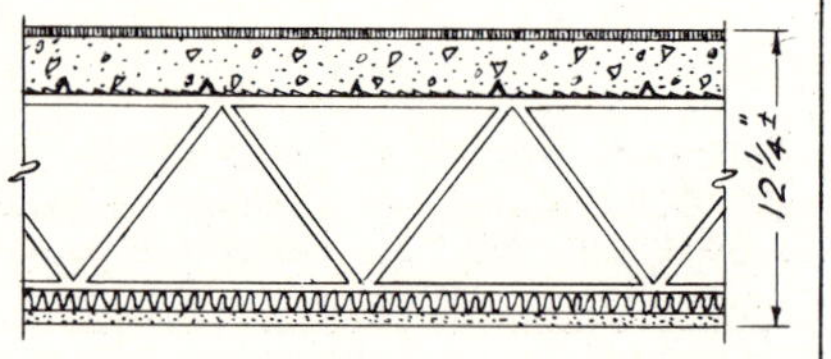12 1/4"±
ditto.	ditto.	3" wood fiberboard, 1/2" Cement and 1/4" Linoleum.	50.2	53	12	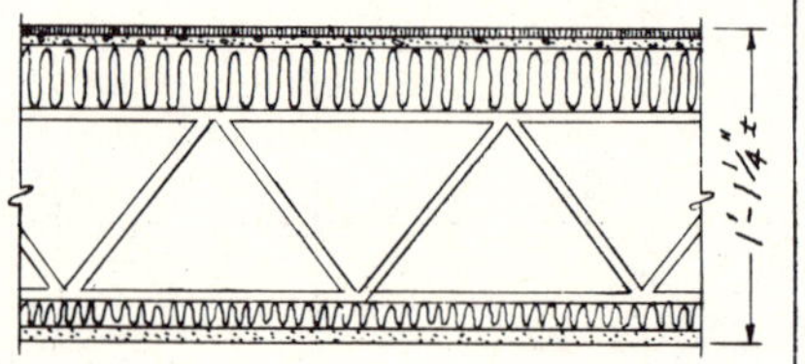1'-1 1/4"±
Steel cellular floor section with flat top.	Suspended metal lath and 7/8" plaster, 4" between steel and plaster.	A 2" Concrete slab	A 52.4	A 53	A 6	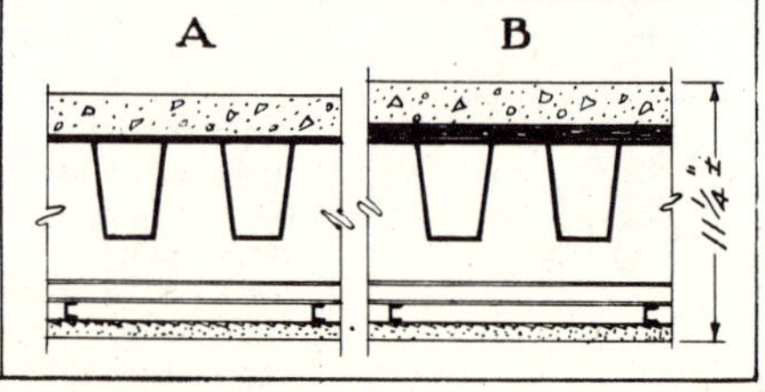A B 11 1/4"±
		B 1/2" Emulsified asphalt 2" Concrete slab.	B 59.8	B 61	B 21	

SOUND TRANSMISSION LOSS-PARTITIONS and WALLS

2"x4" WOOD STUDS 16" on centers (unless otherwise noted)

TYPE OF LATH AND FURRING	TYPE OF FINISH Unless otherwise noted, finish is the same on both sides of the partition	AVERAGE TRANSMISSION LOSS IN DECIBELS AT FREQUENCIES - (CYCLE PER SECOND) WEIGHT lbs/ft.^{2}	256-1,024	128-4,096	PLANS - 3/4" = 1'-0"
Wood Lath	7/8" sanded lime plaster, 3 coats	15.6	41.8	42	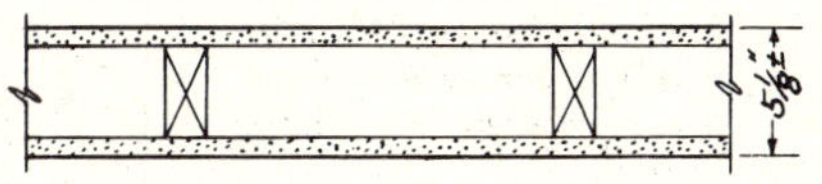
	7/8" sanded gypsum plaster, 3 coats	15.1	32.4	35.7	
Expanded Metal Lath	7/8" sanded lime plaster, 3 coats	19.8	45.2	44.4	
	7/8" sanded gypsum plaster, 3 coats	20	38.2	39.3	
1/2" Wood Fiberboard	1/2" sanded gypsum plaster, 2 coats	13.3	48	51.8	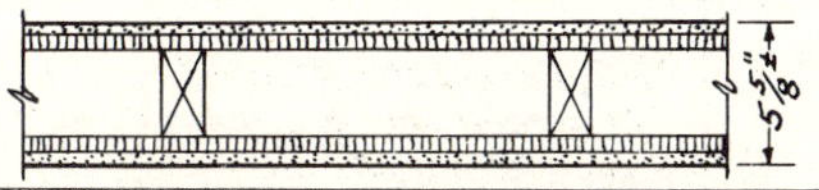
1/2" Wood Fiberboard	Joints filled - No plaster	5.1	29.7	36	
Gypsum lath nailed to studs at 6" o.c. intervals.	1/2" sanded gypsum plaster, 2 coats	15.2	39	41.2	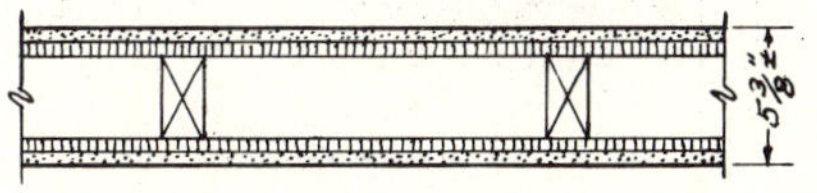
Gypsum lath nailed to studs between joints with special large head nails.		15.7	45.8	47.7	
1/2" Wood Fiberboard on staggered studs	Joints filled - No plaster	4.9	33.3	42.1	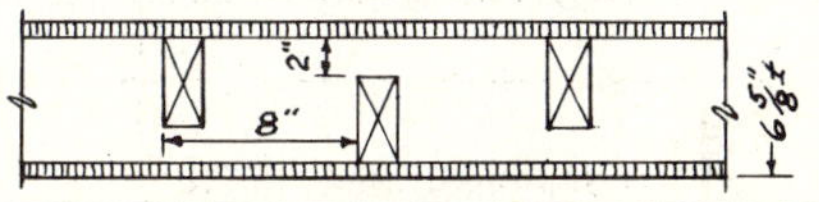
1/2" Wood Fiberboard on staggered studs	1/2" sanded gypsum plaster, 2 coats	13.1	53.7	54.1	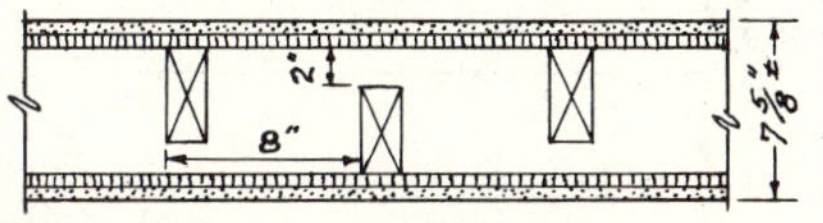
3"x4" Wood Studs with 3/8" gypsum lath attached by spring clips.	1/2" sanded gypsum plaster, 2 coats	—	51.6	51.7	
2"x4" Wood Studs with 3/8" perforated gypsum lath attached by spring clips.		15.7	49.6	51.8	
ditto. and space between studs filled with glass wool packed to a density of 1.5 pounds per square foot.	1/2" sanded gypsum plaster, 2 coats	16.9	53.8	54.8	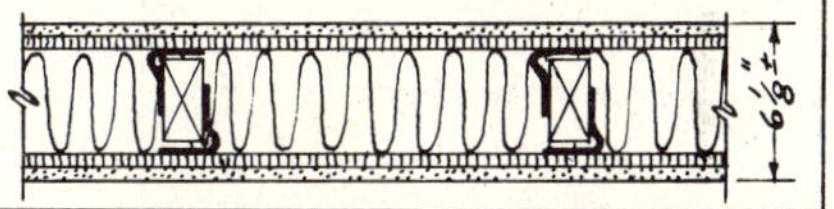
Paper-backed Expanded metal lath	3/4" sanded gypsum plaster, 3 coats	12.6	33	35	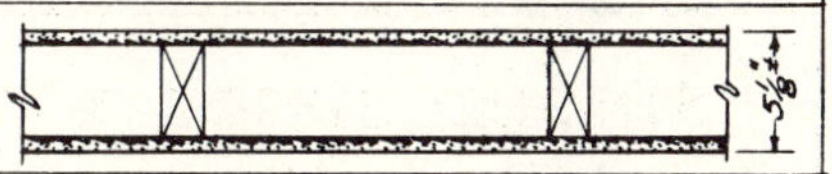
Expanded metal lath on staggered studs	3/4" sanded gypsum plaster, 3 coats	19.8	48.4	49.8	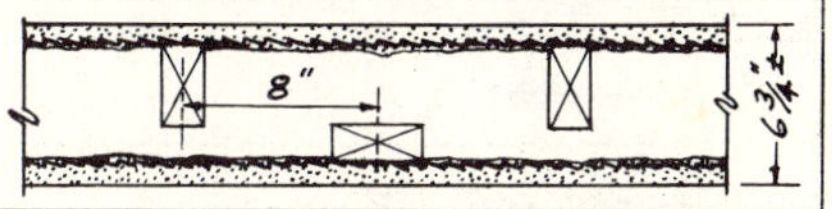
3/8" gypsum lath held by metal clip, nailed through clip to hold lath and clip firm on stud.	1/2" sanded gypsum plaster, 2 coats	A 14.4	A 35.6	A 35.9	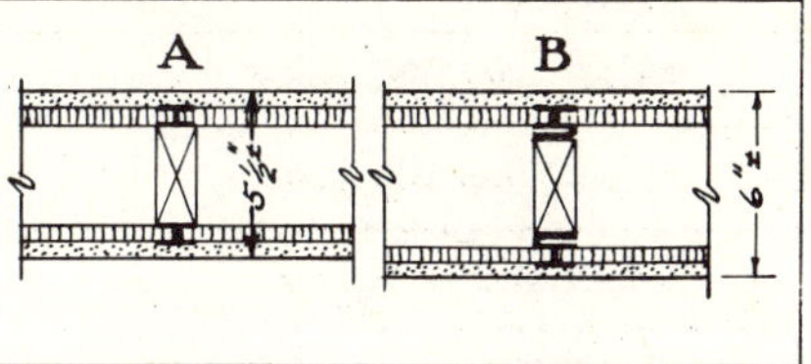
Perforated gypsum lath held by metal clip, nailed through back of clip, against stud allowing lath small movement.		B 14.9	B 45	B 45.8	
3/8" Plywood	Light cotton fabric glued on one side and Heavy cotton duck glued on the other, no plaster	A 4.6	A 32.4	A 31.1	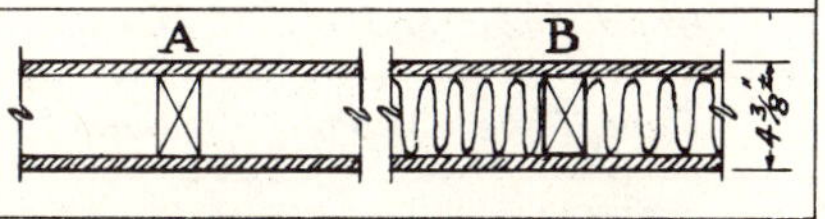
	ditto, with 4" cotton bat placed between studs	B 4.8	B 37	B 35.1	
3/8" gypsum lath	1/2" sanded gypsum plaster, 2 coats	A 15	A 31.2	A 34.9	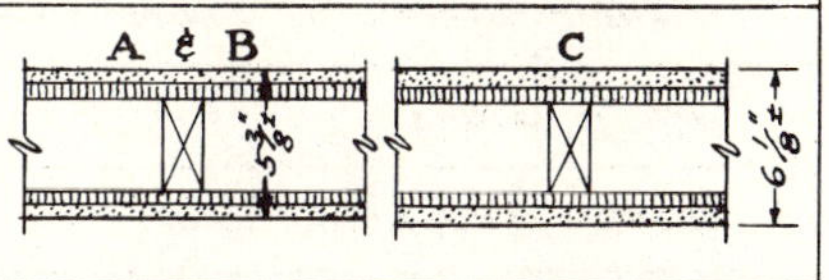
	1/2" Vermiculite gypsum plaster, 2 coats	B 9.6	B 30	B 32.7	
3/8" Perforated gypsum lath	7/8" Vermiculite gypsum plaster, 3 coats	C 12.9	C 32.6	C 36.8	
1/2" dense wood fiberboard	Joints at studs - No plaster	3.8	30.6	32.2	

SOUND TRANSMISSION LOSS-PARTITIONS and WALLS

TYPE OF LATH AND FURRING		TYPE OF FINISH *Unless otherwise noted, finish is the same on both sides of the partition*	AVERAGE TRANSMISSION LOSS IN DECIBELS AT FREQUENCIES - (CYCLE PER SECOND) WEIGHT lbs/ft.²	256-1,024	128-4,096	PLANS - 3/4" = 1'-0"
2" x 4" WOOD STUDS 16" o.c. (unless otherwise noted)	*Expanded metal lath attached with spring clips and No. 2 (Pencil) rods.*	*5/8" Gypsum Plaster, 2 coats*	19.1	51.8	52	
	3/8" Gypsum Lath attached with special spring clips, of intermediate stiffness.	*1/2" Gypsum Plaster, 2 coats*	13.1	53.8	52	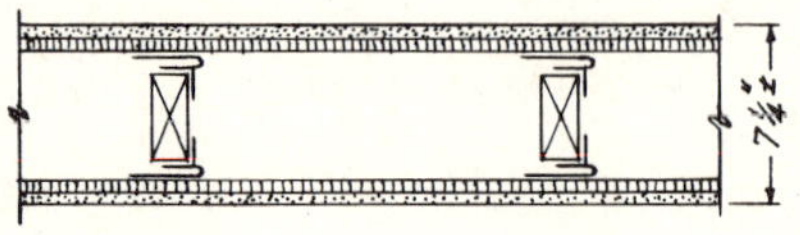
	3/8" Perforated Gypsum Lath attached with special spring clips	*1/2" Perlite Plaster, 2 coats*	11.9	52.6	50.7	
	1" x 3" Wood Studs, 16" o.c.	*1/4" Plywood glued to studs*	2.5	23.8	24.6	
	1" x 3" Wood Studs, 16" o.c.	*1/4" Plywood glued to staggered studs.*	2.9	26.8	26.1	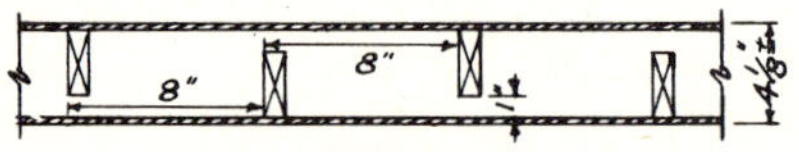
	None	*1/2" Gypsum wallboard with joints filled and covered with paper tape.*	5.6	35.6	34.2	
	None	*Two layers 3/8" gypsum wallboard cemented together with joints filled and covered with paper tape.*	8.2	38.8	36.9	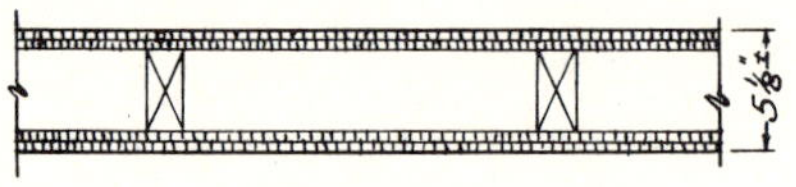
	Expanded Metal Lath	*3/4" Gypsum Plaster, 2 coats*	18.1	38.4	38.6	

SINGLE SHEET MATERIALS	THICKNESS	WEIGHT Pounds per Square Foot	256-1,024 Cycles per Second	128-4,096 Cycles per Second
Aluminum	0.025"	.35	16.3	19.4
Galvanized Iron	0.030"	1.2	24.7	28.2
Three-ply Plywood	1/8"	.52	19.7	22.4
Three-ply Plywood	1/4"	.73	22.7	23.2
Glass Fiberboard	2"	5.3	27.6	30
Wood Fiberboard (Example: Insulite, etc.)	1/2"	.75	22	22.8
Cane Fiberboard (Example: Celotex, etc.)	7/16"	.66	20.7	22.8
Double-strength Window Glass	1/8"	1.6	28	29.2
Plate Glass	1/4"	3.5	32.7	32.8
Heavy Wrapping Paper	—	.016	1.7	2.4
Lead	1/16"	3.9	32.3	32.2
Lead	1/8"	8.2	32	34.6

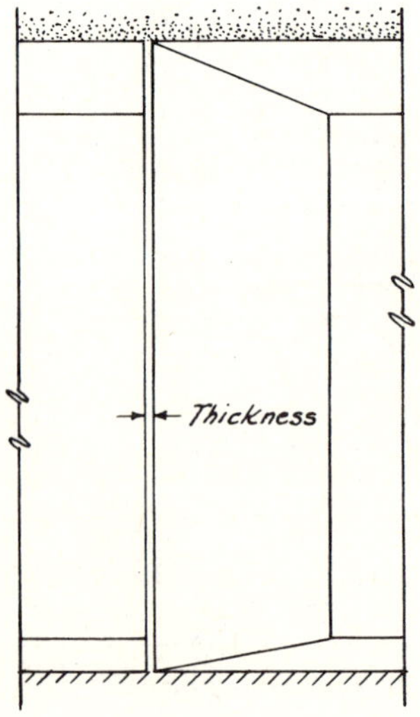
Thickness

SOUND TRANSMISSION LOSS-PARTITIONS *and* WALLS

TYPE OF WALL OR PARTITION	TYPE OF FINISH *Unless otherwise noted, finish is the same on both sides of the partition*	AVERAGE TRANSMISSION LOSS IN DECIBELS AT FREQUENCIES – (CYCLES PER SECOND) WEIGHT lbs/ft.²	256-1,024	128-4,096	PLANS – ¾" = 1'-0"
A *Hollow Gypsum Block 3" x 12" x 30"*	*½" Gypsum Plaster, 2 coats*	A 21.8	A 37.8	A 39.3	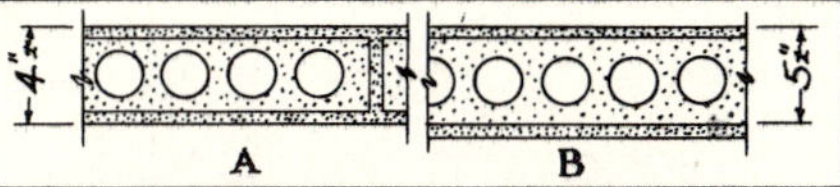
B *Hollow Gypsum Block 4" x 12" x 30"*		B 23.4	B 41.6	B 40.6	
Hollow Gypsum Block 3" x 12" x 30"	*½" Gypsum Plaster, 2 coats on one side; ⅞" gypsum plaster, 3 coats on expanded metal lath on the other side held by spring clips.*	—	52.7	57.5	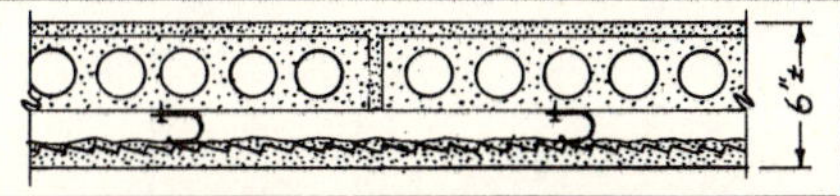
Hollow Clay Tile three-cell 3" x 12" x 12"	A *⅝" Gypsum Plaster, 2 coats*	A 28	A 40 42.3	A 44.4 45.4	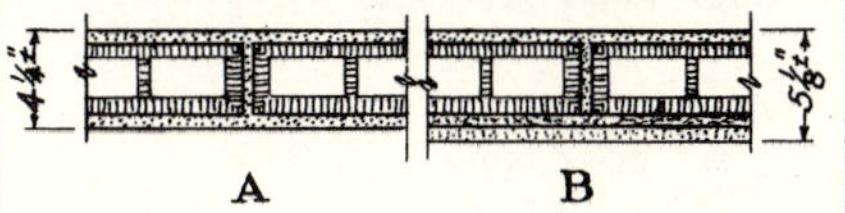
	B *⅝" Sprayed fibrous acoustic material on one side; ¾" gypsum plaster, 2 coats on both sides.*	B 29.6	B 36	B 41.3	
A *Hollow Clay Tile 4" x 12" x 12"*	*⅝" Gypsum Plaster, 2 coats*	A 33.4	A 40.3	A 44.2	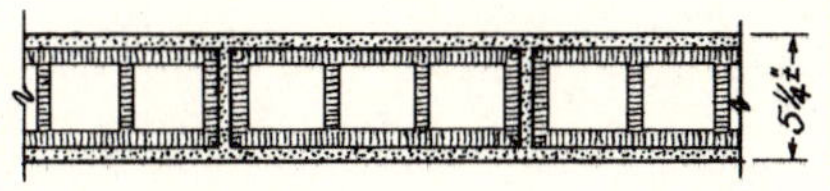
B *ditto, three-cell*		B 29	B 41	B 44	
C *ditto, porous tile*		C 27.5	C 38	C 42.2	
D *ditto, with 1" shells*		D 37.5	D 43.7	D 47	
E *ditto.*	*⅝" Gypsum Vermiculite Plaster, 2 coats*	E 25.2	E 36.8	E 38.4	
A *Hollow Clay Tile, three-cell 6" x 12" x 12", Medium Burned*	*⅝" Gypsum Plaster, 2 coats*	A 37	A 41	A 45.6	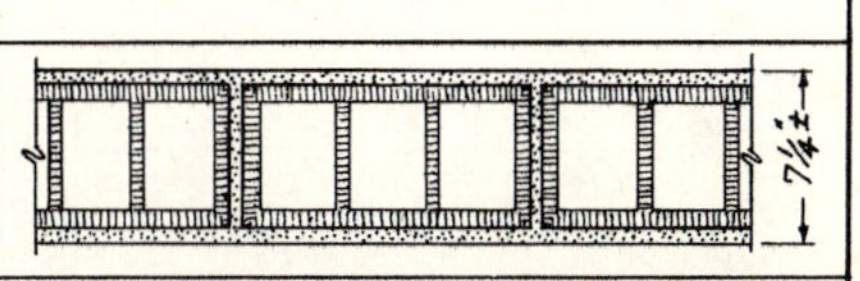
B *Hollow Clay Tile, three-cell 6" x 12" x 12", Soft*		B 37	B 42.3	B 44.6	
Hollow Clay Tile, six-cell 6" x 12" x 12", Load Bearing	*⅝" Gypsum Plaster, 2 coats*	39	42.7	47.4	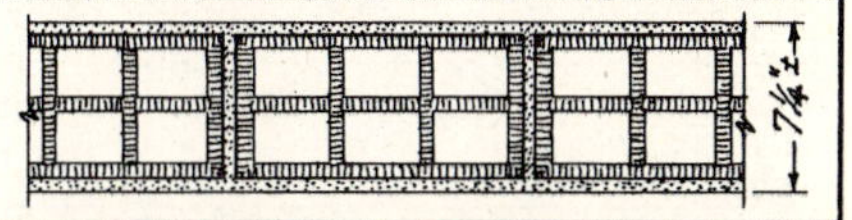
Hollow Clay Tile, six-cell 8" x 12" x 12", Load Bearing	*⅝" Gypsum Plaster, 2 coats*	48	45.7	49.6	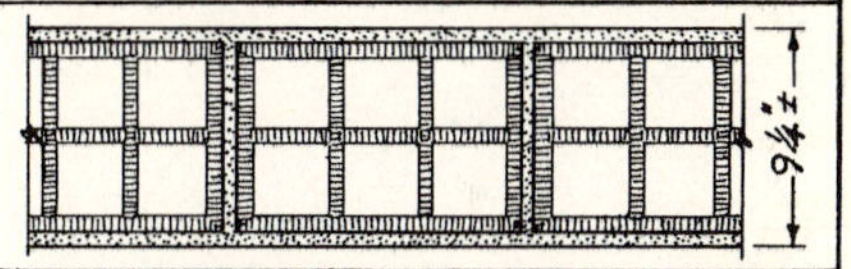
A *Hollow Clay Tile, 3¾" x 12" x 12" and 8" x 12" x 12" End Construction*	*⅝" Gypsum Plaster, 2 coats*	A 65	A 42	A 47	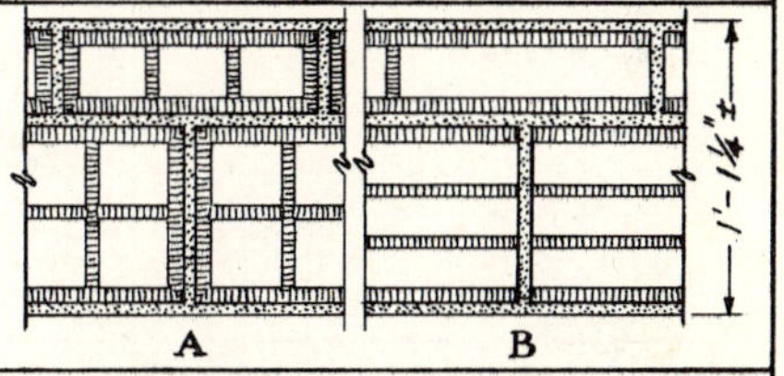
B *Hollow Clay Tile, 3¾" x 5" x 12" and 8" x 5" x 12" End Construction*		B 66	B 48	B 49.8	
Hollow Clay Tile, three-cell 4" x 12" x 12"	A *1¼" furring strips 12" o.c., tar paper backed expanded metal lath and ⅞" Gypsum Plaster, 3 coats.*	A 34	A 55.3	A 57.6	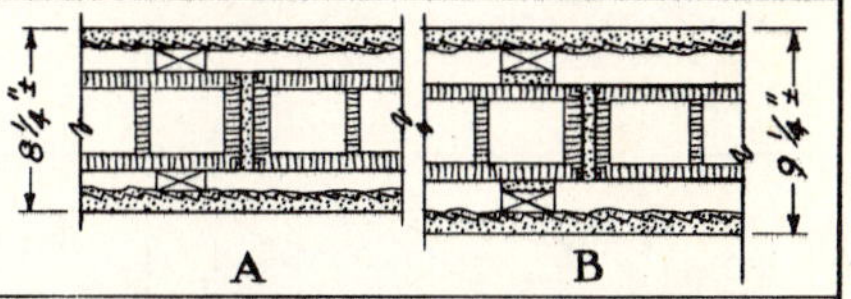
	B *ditto, with ½" flax felt pads between wall and ¾" furring strips.*	B 34	B 53.7	B 58.2	
Hollow Clay Tile, three-cell 4" x 12" x 12"	A *1¼" furring strips 12" o.c., dense wood fiberboard, ⅜" Gypsum Plaster, 2 coats*	A 28	A 55	A 60.8	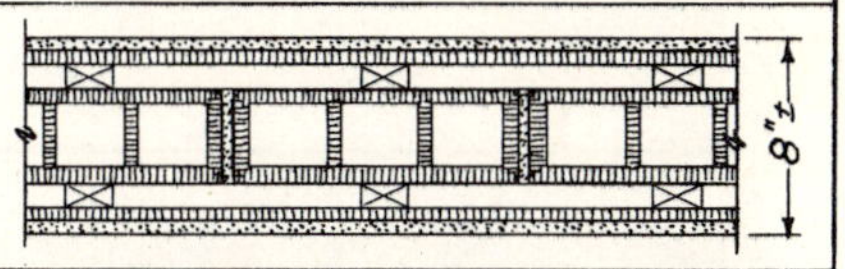
	B *13/16" furring strips 16" o.c., ½" wood fiberboard, ½" Gypsum Plaster, 2 coats*	B 34	B 55	B 57.3	
Hollow Clay Tile Double Partition of 3" x 12" x 12"	*1¾" cavity space between walls and 1" flax fiberboard butted tight, placed within cavity.*	50	52.3	59.2	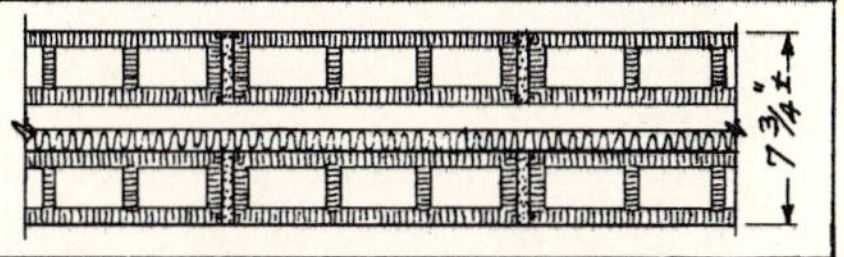
A *Hollow Cinder Block 4" x 8" x 18"*	*⅝" Gypsum Plaster, 2 coats*	A 29.7	A 38.7	A 43	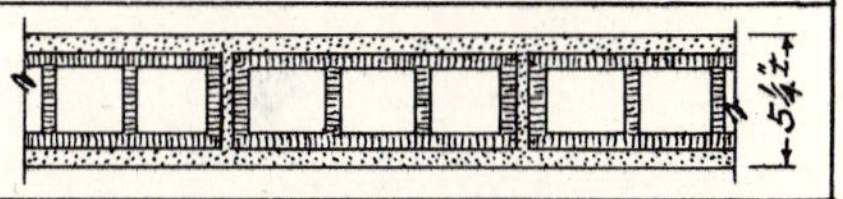
B *Ditto, 4" x 8" x 16"*		B 35.8	B 44	B 47.1	
Hollow Cinder Block 3" x 8" x 16"	*⅝" Gypsum Plaster, 2 coats*	32.2	42.8	45	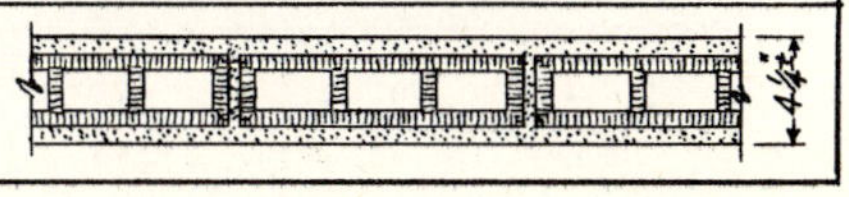

SOUND TRANSMISSION LOSS-PARTITIONS *and* WALLS

	TYPE OF WALL OR PARTITION LATH AND FURRING	TYPE OF FINISH *Unless otherwise noted, finish is the same on both sides of the partition*	AVERAGE TRANSMISSION LOSS IN DECIBELS AT FREQUENCIES - (CYCLE PER SECOND) WEIGHT lbs/ft.²	256-1,024	128-4,096	PLANS - 3/4" = 1'-0"
	4" Brick Wall	5/8" sanded lime plaster, 2 coats	—	45	50	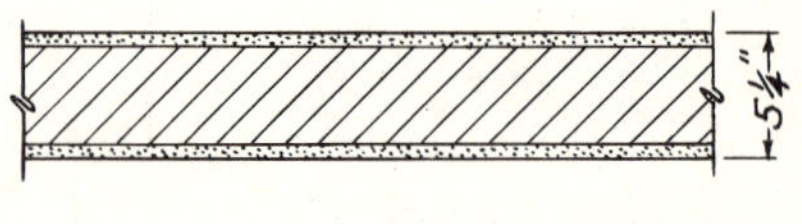5¼"
	4" Brick Wall	5/8" sanded gypsum plaster, 2 coats	—	47.5	53.5	
	8" Brick Wall Poor Workmanship	5/8" sanded gypsum plaster, 2 coats	92	50.7	53.6	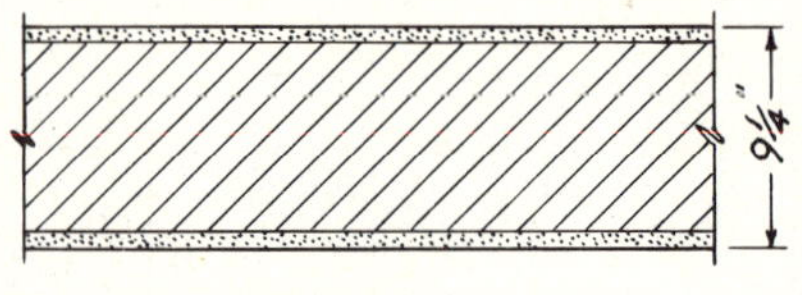9¼"
	8" Brick Wall Good Workmanship	5/8" sanded gypsum plaster, 2 coats	97	51.3	56.6	
			87	51.3	57.4	
	12" Brick Wall	None	121	52.4	53	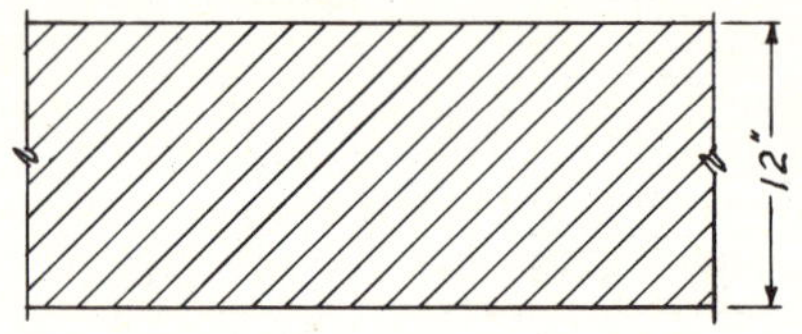12"
	Brick laid Rowlock (on edge)	5/8" sanded gypsum plaster, 2 coats	31.6	42	48.8	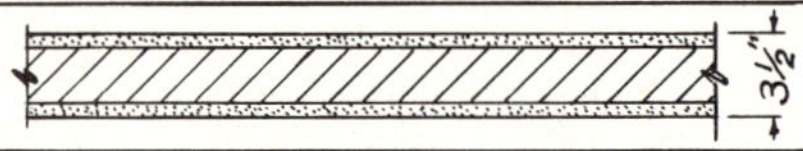3½"
	Brick laid Rowlock (on edge)	13/16" x 2" furring strips wired to brick surface 16" o.c., 3/8" gypsum lath and 1/2" sanded gypsum plaster, 2 coats	36.5	51.7	53.4	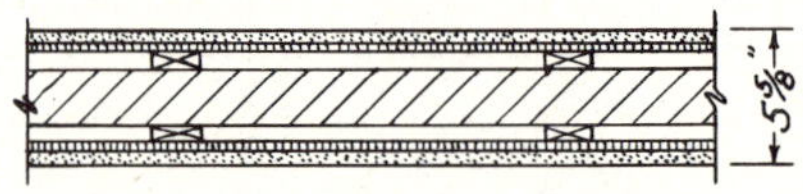5⅝"
	Brick laid Rowlock (on edge)	Ditto, except furring is nailed to plugs in the brick	38.2	48.3	55	
	Brick laid Rowlock (on edge)	Ditto, except 1/2" wood fiberboard is in the place of 3/8" gypsum lath	33.3	53	54.6	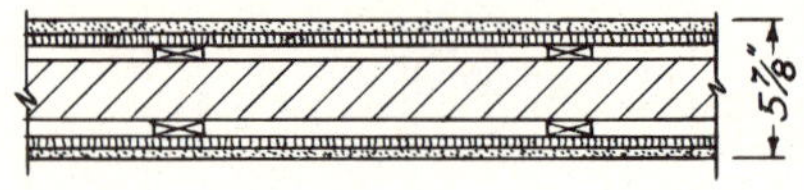5⅞"
	Glass Brick 3¾" x 4⅞" x 8"	None	—	41.6	40.7	3¾"
	Porous Pumice and portland cement hollow tile, two-cell, 4" x 8" x 16"	A 1/2" sanded gypsum plaster, 2 coats	A 25.3	A 35.8	A 37.4	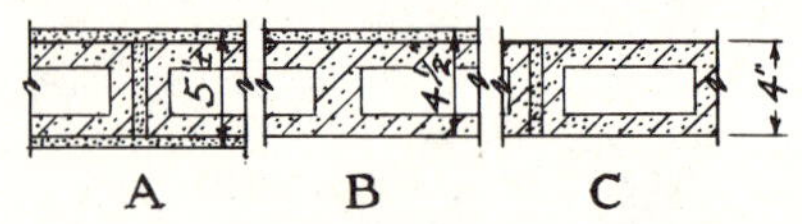5" 4" A B C
		B Ditto, but plastered one side only	B 20.4	B 33.4	B 34.7	
		C None	C 15.5	C 9.4	C 10.9	
	3" Wood fiberboard laid in sanded gypsum plaster mortar	1/2" sanded gypsum plaster, 2 coats	—	32.8	34.8	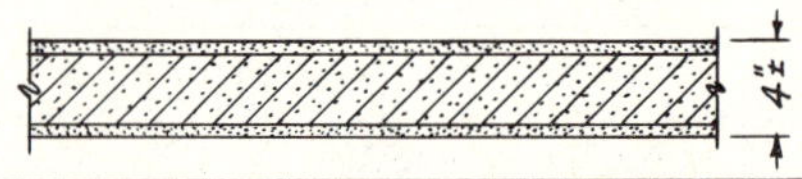4"
STUDLESS	3/8" Gypsum Lath	13/16" sanded gypsum plaster, 2 coats	16.1	31	36	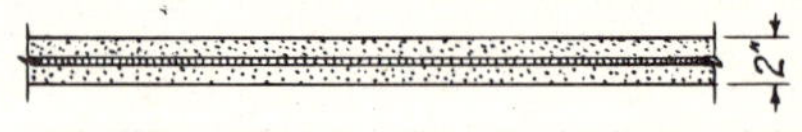2"
STUDLESS	3/8" Gypsum Lath	1 1/16" sanded gypsum plaster, 2 coats	20.2	37.6	39.9	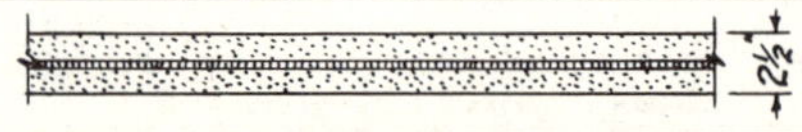2½"
STUDLESS	3/8" Gypsum Lath	1 5/16" sanded gypsum plaster, 2 coats	25.4	36.6	39.9	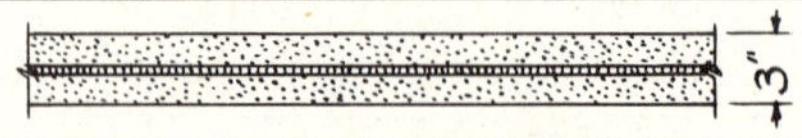3"
STUDLESS	3/8" Gypsum Lath	3/4" sanded gypsum plaster on one side, 7/8" on the other side.	16.8	32.4	36.7	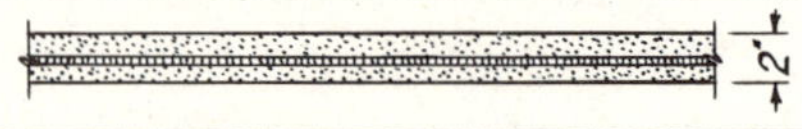2"
STUDLESS	1/2" fiberboard is held between 1/2" and 3/8" gypsum lath by special wire clips setting a 1/4" air space on both sides of the fiberboard	1/2" sanded gypsum plaster, 2 coats	15.9	45.8	46.8	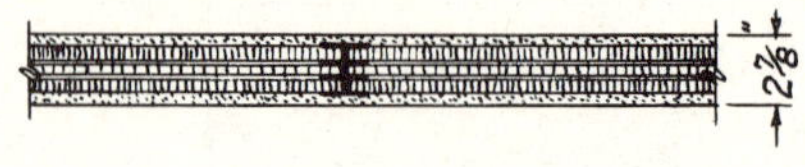2⅜"
STUDLESS	3/8" Gypsum Lath	A 13/16" sanded gypsum plaster, 2 coats	A 16.8	A 32.4	A 37.3	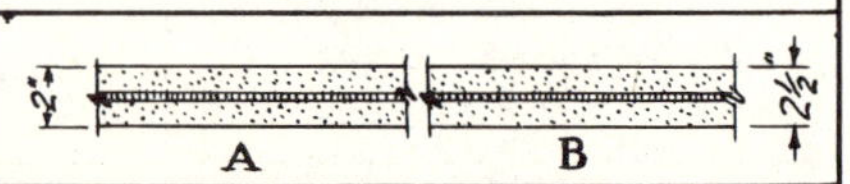2" 2½" A B
STUDLESS		B 1 1/16" sanded gypsum plaster, 2 coats	B 19.7	B 34.8	B 38.7	

SOUND TRANSMISSION LOSS-PARTITIONS *and* WALLS

	TYPE OF LATH AND FURRING	TYPE OF FINISH *Unless otherwise noted, finish is the same on both sides of the partition*	AVERAGE TRANSMISSION LOSS IN DECIBELS AT FREQUENCIES – (CYCLE PER SECOND) WEIGHT lbs/ft.²	256-1,024	128-4,096	PLANS – 3/4" = 1'-0"
STUDLESS	*Expanded metal lath*	A 2" panel, gypsum perlite plaster	A 8.8	A 27.6	A 32.9	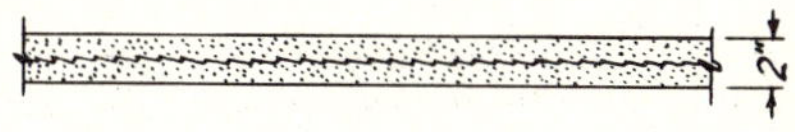2"
		B 2" panel, sanded gypsum plaster	B 18.1 18.4	B 35 33.6	B 38.4 38.2	
	½" and ⅜" gypsum lath held together at vertical joints by special wire clips with ¼" air space between laths.	⅝" sanded gypsum plaster, 2 coats	12.9	37.4	40.2	2⅜"
	Ditto, but ⅜" gypsum lath is replaced by ½" gypsum lath.	½" sanded gypsum plaster on one side, 11/16" on the other side.	13.6	39.4	41.8	2¼"
	2 sheets ⅜" gypsum lath separated by ⅛" felt pad spacers.	13/16" sanded gypsum plaster, 2 coats	17.9	38.2	41.7	2½"
	Ditto.	½" sanded gypsum plaster on one side, 1⅛" on the other side.	19.2	40	41.9	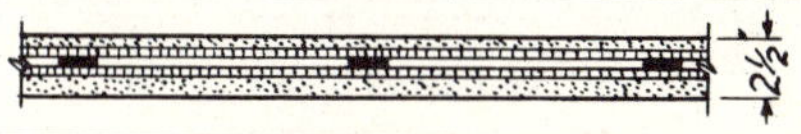2½"
	2 sheets ½" long-length gypsum lath held by special double clips setting a ¼" air space between the lath.	¾" sanded gypsum plaster, 2 coats	18.9	43.4	46.7	2¾"
	Ditto, except ¼" air space is ⅛"	¾" sanded gypsum plaster, 2 coats	17.1	42.4	44.1	2⅝"
STEEL CHANNEL STUDS	*Paper backed expanded metal lath on ¾" steel channels, 16" o.c.*	2" panel, sanded gypsum plaster	—	36	39.9	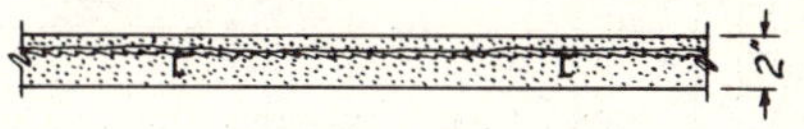2"
	Perforated gypsum Lath on ¾" steel channels, 16" o.c.	2" panel, sanded gypsum plaster	19.4	34	36.6	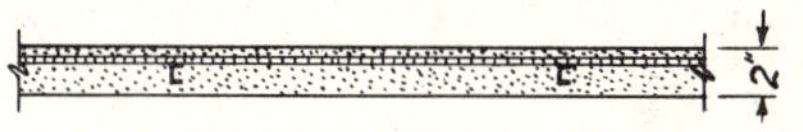2"
	Expanded metal lath on ¾" steel channels, 12" o.c.	2" panel, sanded gypsum plaster	16.4 17.7 18.1 18.8	34.2 31.4 32 30.8	37.8 35.1 37.4 36	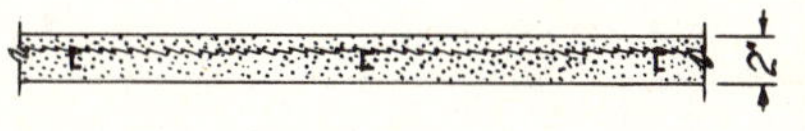2"
	Ditto.	2½" panel, sanded gypsum plaster	22.4	37	39.1	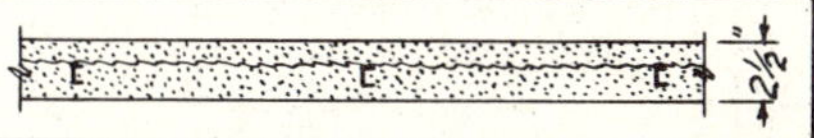2½"
	Expanded metal lath on ¾" steel channels, 16" o.c.	2" panel, vermiculite gypsum plaster	8.8	30.6	34.3	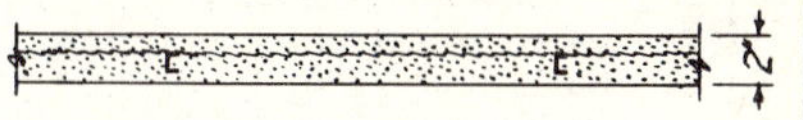2"
	Ditto.	2" panel, sanded gypsum plaster	17.9	35.4	39.3	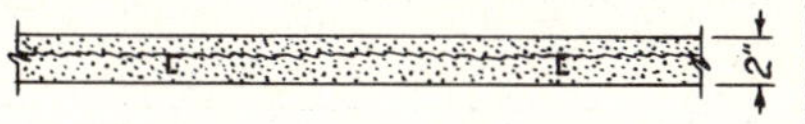2"
	Expanded metal lath on ¾" steel channel studs, approximately 11" o.c.	2" panel, sanded gypsum plaster	18.7	34.6	39	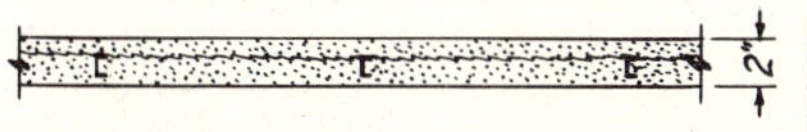2"
	Ditto.	2" panel, gypsum perlite plaster	9.6	29.2	33.8	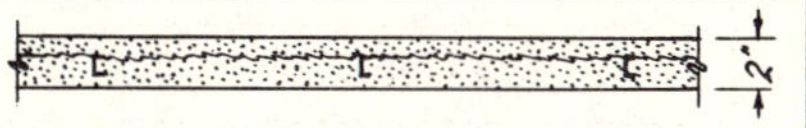2"
	Expanded metal lath on ¾" steel channels, 22" o.c.	1½" panel, gypsum perlite plaster	7.4	30.3	32.7	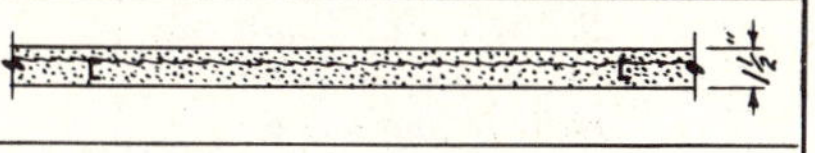1½"
	1½" cold rolled steel channel studs, 16" o.c.	A ⅞" Gypsum plaster, 3 coats on expanded metal lath	A 17.6	A 30.3	A 34.3	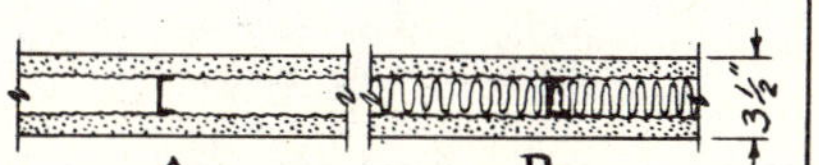3½" A B
		B Ditto, with mineral wool packed in the space between the lath and studs.	B —	B 36	B 42.2	

SOUND TRANSMISSION LOSS-PARTITIONS and WALLS

	TYPE OF WALL OR PARTITION	TYPE OF FINISH (Unless otherwise noted, finish is the same on both sides of the partition)	AVERAGE TRANSMISSION LOSS IN DECIBELS AT FREQUENCIES - (CYCLE PER SECOND): WEIGHT lbs/ft.^{2}	256-1,024	128-4,096	PLANS - 3/4" = 1'-0"
STEEL TRUSS STUDS AND PREFABRICATED STEEL STUDS	3¼" Steel Studs Prefabricated, 16" o.c.	A 7/8" Gypsum Plaster, 3 coats on Expanded Metal Lath	A 19.6	A 35.6	A 36.8	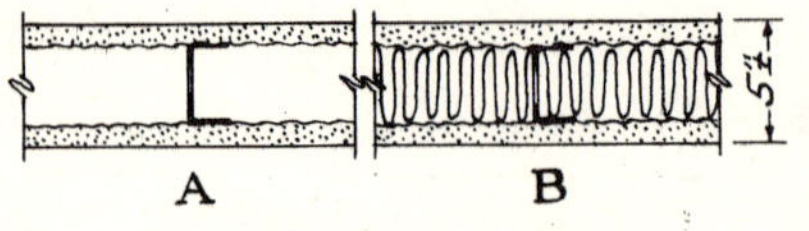 5½" A B
		B ditto, with mineral wool bats packed to a density of 5.2 pounds per cubic foot in the space between the lath and studs.	B 21.1	B 36.4	B 38.1	
	3¼" Steel Trusses used as studs, 16" o.c.	¾" Gypsum Plaster, 3 coats, on Expanded Metal Lath	19.1	37.8	40.4	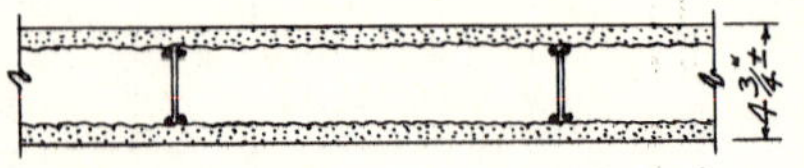 4¾"
	1½" horizontal steel channels 28¼" o.c. wire tied to both sides of 1½" vertical channels approximately 33" o.c.	¾" Gypsum Plaster, 2 coats, on ½" Long Length Gypsum Lath wire tied to channels.	17.3	45.2	47.4	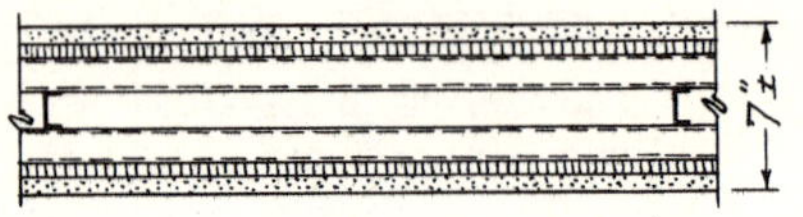 7"
	¾" horizontal steel channels 12" o.c. wire tied to both sides of ¾" vertical channels approximately 33" o.c.	ditto.	17.4	49	51.3	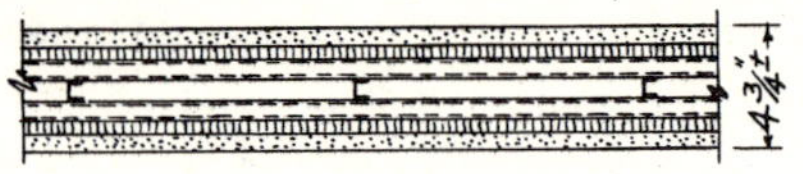 4¾"
	3¼" Steel Trusses used as studs, 24" o.c.	A ½" Gypsum Plaster, 2 coats, on 3/8" perforated gypsum lath held to studs by special spring and wire clips.	A 15.7	A 46.4	A 46.3	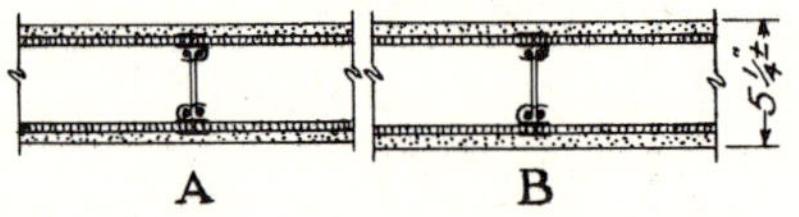 5¼" A B
		B ditto, except 5/8" Perlite Gypsum Plaster	B 11.7	B 40.8	B 38.8	
	3¼" Steel Trusses used as studs, 16" o.c.	¾" Gypsum Plaster, 3 coats on Expanded Metal Lath tied to No. 2 rods tied to spring clips attached to studs 16" o.c.	19	55.6	54.7	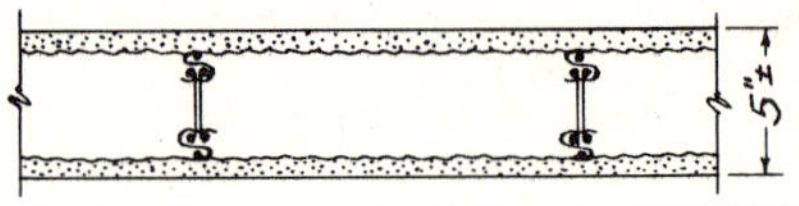 5"
	¾" Cold Rolled Steel Channel Studs 12" o.c. stiffened by 1" Channels horizontally halfway up the panel.	¾" Gypsum Plaster, 3 coats on Expanded Metal Lath, one side only.	8.1	33.2	33.3	 2¼"

	TYPE OF WALL OR PARTITION	TYPE OF FINISH	WEIGHT lbs/ft.^{2}	256-1,024	128-4,096	W
DOUBLE STEEL CHANNEL STUDS	¾" Cold Rolled Steel Channel Studs 12" o.c. stiffened halfway up the panel by horizontal 1" Channels, & 2 such panels placed back to back and resting on 1" Cork base	¾" Gypsum Plaster, 3 coats on Expanded Metal Lath	17.2	53	55.2	W = 10"
			17.2	52.4	54.7	W = 8½"
			17.2	51.6	54	W = 7"
			17.2	50.8	53.3	W = 5½"
			17.2	49.4	52.9	W = 4½"
			17.2	47.4	51	* W = 4 3/8"
	Ditto, except 1" cork base is 1½"	¾" Heat Insulating Plaster, 3 coats on Expanded Metal Lath	9.1	47.4	46.1	W = 5"
	Ditto, except 1½" cork base is replaced by a 1" board.	¾" Gypsum Plaster, 3 coats on Expanded Metal Lath	17.2	48	51.4	W = 4½"
	Ditto, except partition rests on concrete without any base.	ditto.	17.2	46.4	48.1	W = 4½"
	Ditto, except the two panels with ¾" channel shoes tied 36" o.c.	ditto.	17.2	44.8	45.7	W = 4½"

SECTION
¾" = 1'-0"

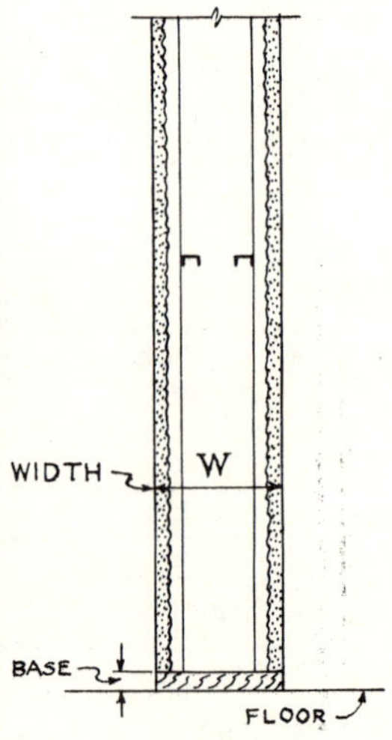
WIDTH
W
BASE
FLOOR

* Braces at corners are in contact with each other.

ACOUSTICAL CORRECTION

Rule of Thumb NOISE REDUCTION COEFFICIENTS*

	N.R.C.
RESIDENTIAL - Apartments, Residences & Clubs	
Living, dining & bed rooms; library, study, etc.	.40 - .50
Kitchens, recreation & bath rooms	.60 - .70
Assume normal ceiling heights in both categories.	
CORRIDORS in PUBLIC BUILDINGS - Apartment,	
Dormitory, Hospital, School & similar	.60 - .70
Assume ceiling height 9'-0" maximum.	
BUSINESS OFFICES:	
Sparse desk spacing, no noisy machines, 10'-14' ceil'g	.60 - .70
Dense desk spacing, no noisy machines, 10'-14' ceil'g	.70 - .80
Noisy machines (tabulators, elect. typewriters, etc.) ceil'g height 12'-0" maximum; part of wall may require acoustical treatment in addition to ceiling	.75 - .85
COMMERCIAL SPACES:	
Barber shops, beauty parlors; normal ceiling heights	.60 - .85
Cafeterias, Restaurants, Bars	.65 - .75
Diet kitchens, Food service spaces	.75 - .85
Retail stores & shops; 12'-0" max. ceiling height	.50 - .70
Gymnasiums, swimming pools, exercise rooms	.60 - .80
Shooting Ranges (Partial wall treatment may be necessary; consider as special, secure experts advice	.75 - .85
Bowling alley: At pin end .70 - .85 rest of ceiling	.50 - .65
Note: In the best type of installations, a drop hung partition, acoustically treated on both sides, is installed 10'-6" from the back of the alleys for the entire width of the room & extending down to within 4'-2" of floor. If a curtain is used in lieu of a partition, treat entire ceiling at	.50 - .60

*Assume that at least 90% of ceiling area is to be treated.

ACOUSTICAL TREATMENT CONSIDERATIONS

HIGH CEILINGS require material with a higher noise reduction coefficient than given above or treating upper wall surfaces with given reduction coefficient

NARROW, HIGH CEILING SPACES where ceiling area is small, compared to wall area, will usually require treatment of a wall or part of several walls.

PANELING CEILINGS or partial treatment with high coefficient materials is not as desirable as treating the entire ceiling (except beams, where effect of treatment would be negligible) with a low coefficient material. If required, partial treatment can be very effective.

NOTE:

For each type of space in the Rule of Thumb table a low and high noise reduction coefficient is given, the choice of which is determined by the characteristics of the space to be treated: –

CONSIDER:

1. Types of floor covering
2. Type & extent of hangings, draperies, etc.
3. Intensity, type & number of noise sources.
4. Quantity and type of furniture
5. Use of space
6. Cost of acoustical material (those with a higher noise reduction coefficient generally cost more.)
7. Table cloths, rugs etc. tend to lessen noise besides acting as sound absorbents

ACOUSTICAL MATERIALS

Types & designations are according to "Sound Absorption Coefficients of Architectural Acoustical Materials", Bulletin XVI, 1956, of the Acoustical Materials Association.

TYPE	DESIGNATION
I	Regularly perforated cellulose fiber tile.
II	Random perforated cellulose fiber tile.
III	Slotted cellulose fiber tile.
IV	Textured or fissured cellulose tile.
V	Perforated mineral fiber tile.
VI	Fissured mineral fiber tile.
VII	Textured or smooth mineral fiber tile or board.
VIII	Membrane-faced mineral fiber tile or board.
IX	Perforated metal pans with mineral fiber pads.
X	Perforated asbestos board panels with mineral fiber pads.

SIZES

Acoustic tile: most common is 12" x 12". Other available sizes are 12" x 24", 24" x 24", and 24" x 48".
Acoustic board: 24" x 48", 32" x 36", and 48" x 48".
Metal pan units: most common is 12" x 24". Also available: 24" x 24" and 24" x 48".

See page on "Noise Reduction Coefficients of Acoustic Materials" for listing of type number of materials given by manufacturers' trade names.

NOISE REDUCTION COEFFICIENT (N.R.C.) –
To obtain a figure to use as an index of the noise reducing efficiency of a material, average the coefficients from 250 thru 2000 cycles, and call this the Noise Reducing Coefficient (NRC). The NRC is expressed to the nearest multiple of 0.05.

Opinion of the Acoustical Materials Association is that because of the empirical basis of calculations, minor differences in NRC values should not be overemphasized. However, NRC values on individual materials may be calculated from Producers Tables in Bulletin XVI of the Acoustical Materials Association.

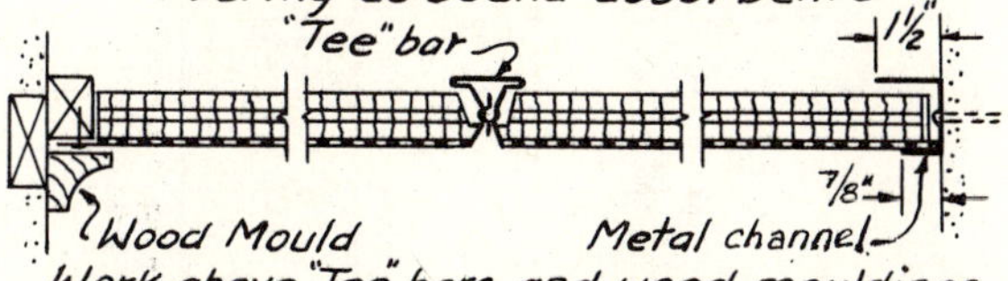
"Tee" bar
1½"
7/8"
Wood Mould
Metal channel

Work above "Tee" bars and wood mouldings usually not included in acoustical specs.

in METAL SUSPENSION SYSTEMS

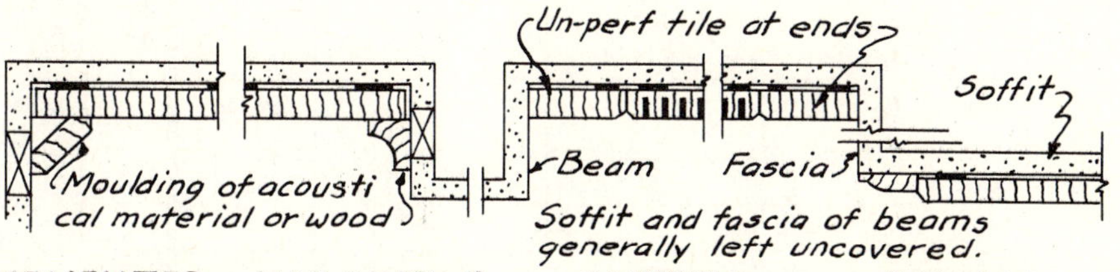
Un-perf tile at ends
Soffit
Beam
Fascia
Moulding of acoustical material or wood

Soffit and fascia of beams generally left uncovered.

CEMENTED or NAILED TILE on SOFFITS and BEAMS

EDGE and WALL CLOSING DETAILS 1½" = 1'-0"

NOISE REDUCTION COEFFICIENTS of ACOUSTICAL MATERIALS

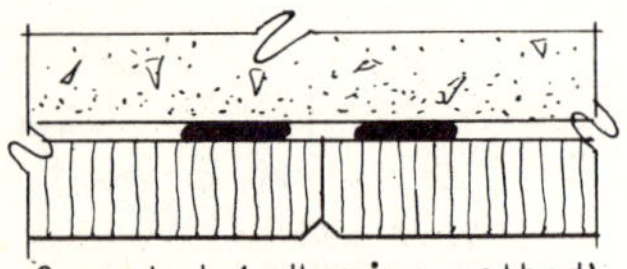

Cemented (adhesive method) to plaster board with 1/8" air space. Considered equivalent to cementing to plaster or concrete ceiling.

TYPE 1

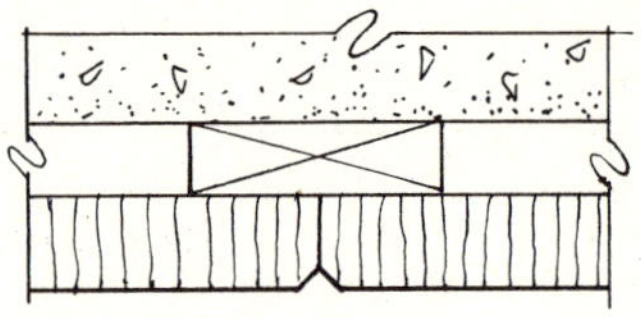

Nailed to 1" to 3" wood furring, 12" O.C.

TYPE 2

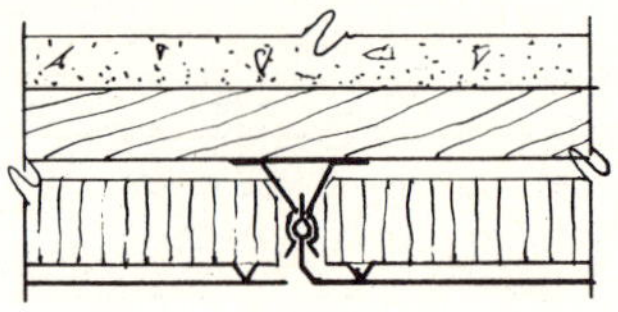

Attached to metal supports applied to 1" x 3" wood furring.

TYPE 3

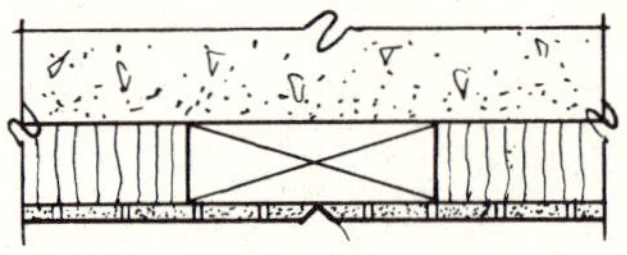

Furred 1", furring 24" o.c. 1" mineral wool between furring.

TYPE 5

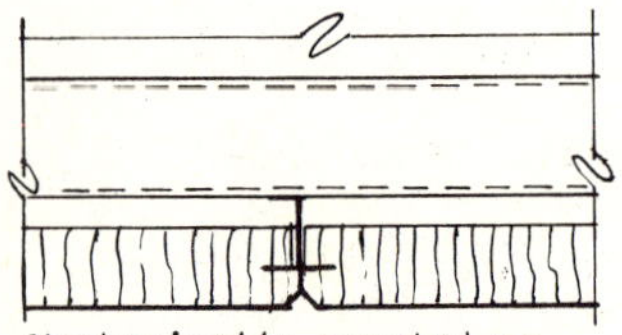

Mechanically mounted on special metal supports (suspension systems). For specific systems consult mfrs. See also A.G.S. pages on "Acoustical suspended Ceilings.

TYPE 7

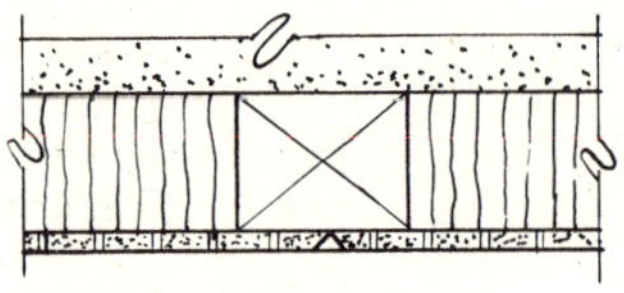

Furred 2" furring 24" o.c. 2" mineral wool between furring.

TYPE 8

For designations of types of acoustical materials, and determination of N.R.C., see Acoustical Materials columns on page "Acoustical Correction".

Data is from "Sound Absorption Coefficients of Architectural Materials", Bull. XVI, 1956, Acoustical Materials Association.

TYPES OF MOUNTING

(used in conducting sound absorption tests)

NRC	MATERIAL	TYPE	MOUNTING	THICKNESS
0.40-0.50	Fiberglas Acoustical Tile Type TXW	VII	1	1/2"
0.45-0.55	Corkoustic	IV	7	1-1/4"
0.50-0.60	Acousti -Celotex Type CR-1 Acoustifibre Random Pattern Auditone Random Perforat'd Cushiontone Full Random Fibretone Variety Drilled Flintkote Ac. Tile Type MS Simpson Ac. Tile Type S-1-S	II	1	1/2"
	Econacoustic	IV	1	1/2"
	Fiberglas Ac. Tile Type PRW Minatone	V	1	1/2"
	Fiberglas Ac. Tile Type TXW	VII	2	1/2"
0.55-0.65	Acousti-Celotex Type C-1 Acoustifibre Auditone Perforated Cushiontone Fibretone Fir-Tex Perforated Flintkote Ac. Tile Type RS Simpson Ac. Tile Type S-1	I	1	1/2"
	Cushiontone Full Random Fibretone Variety Drilled Simpson Ac. Tile Type S-1-S	II	2	1/2"
	Acousti-Celotex Type CR-2 Acoustifibre Random Pattern Flintkote Ac. Tile Type MS Simpson Ac. Tile Type S-2-S	II	1	5/8"
	Simpson Forestone	IV	1,2	9/16"
			7	3/4"
	Celotone	VI	7	11/16"
	Crestone (Striated)	VII	1,7	5/8"
	Acoustimetal, 50-50 Pattern Sanacoustic, Type KK, 50-50 Pattern	IX	3	2-1/2"

NRC	MATERIAL	TYPE	MOUNTING	THICKNESS
0.60-0.70	Acousti-Celotex Type C-1 Auditone Perforated Cushiontone Fibretone Simpson Ac. Tile Type S-1	I	2	1/2"
	Acousti-Celotex Type C-2 Simpson Ac. Tile Type S-2	I	1	5/8"
	Acoustifibre Fir-Tex Perforated Flintkote Ac. Tile Type RS	I	1 OR 2	1/2" 5/8"
	Simpson Ac. Tile Type S-2-S	II	2	5/8"
	Auditone Random Perforat'd Fibretone Variety Drilled Flintkote Ac. Tile Type MS	II	1	3/4"
	Acousti-Celotex CR-9 Acoustifibre Random Pattern Cushiontone Full Random Simpson Ac. Tile Type S-3-S	II	1,7	3/4"
	Auditone Slotted	III	1	3/4", 1"
	Simpson Forestone	IV	1	3/4"
	Fiberglas Ac. Tile Type PRW Minatone	V	2	1/2"
	Acousti-Celotex Type M-1 Fiberglas Ac. Tile Type PRW " " " " PRWR Minatone	V	1	5/8"
	Fiberglas Ac. Tile Type PRW	V	1	3/4"
	Celotone	VI	1,7	11/16"
	Acoustone Simpson Fissured Min'l Tile Travacoustic Travertone	VI	1	11/16"
	Motif'd Acoustone (Striated) Pattern #19	VII	1	11/16"
	Fiberglas Ac. Tile, Stria	VII	1	3/4"

NOISE REDUCTION COEFFICIENTS of ACOUSTICAL MATERIALS

NRC	MATERIAL	TYPE	MOUNT-ING	THICK-NESS
0.60–0.70, cont.	Fiberglas Ac. Tile Type TXW	VII	1	3/4"
	Fiberglas Sono-Faced Ac. Tile, Center Units	VIII	1	3/4"
	Steelacoustic	IX	7	1-1/4"
	Acoustipanel	IX	7	1-3/8"
0.65–0.75	Acoustifibre Flintkote Ac. Tile Type RS Simpson Ac. Tile Type S-2	I	2	5/8"
	Acousti-Celotex Type C-2 Fir-Tex Perforated	I	2,7	5/8"
	Auditone Perforated Fibretone Flintkote Ac. Tile Type RS	I	1	3/4"
	Acousti-Celotex Type C-9 Acoustifibre Cushiontone Fir-Tex Perforated Simpson Ac. Tile Type S-3	I	1,7	3/4"
	Acousti-Celotex Type CR-9 Acoustifibre Random Pattern Cushiontone Full Random Fibretone Variety Drilled Simpson Ac. Tile Type S-3-S	II	2	3/4"
	Acousti-Celotex Type CR-8	II	2	1"
	Cushiontone Full Random	II	2,7	1"
	Auditone Slotted	III	2	3/4", 1"
	Simpson Forestone	IV	2	3/4"
	Minatone	V	2,7	5/8"
	Acousti-Celotex Type M-1 Fiberglas Ac. Tile Type PRW	V	7	5/8"
	Fiberglas Ac. Tile Type PRW	V	2,7	3/4"
	Minatone	V	1	7/8"
	Acousti-Celotex Type M-2	V	1	1"
	Acoustone F Celotone Travacoustic Travertone	VI	7	11/16"
	Permacoustic	VI	1	3/4"
	Celotone Simpson Fissur'd Mineral Tile Travacoustic Travertone	VI	1	13/16"
	Acoustone F Permacoustic	VI	1	7/8"
	Celotone	VI	1	15/16"
	Fiberglas Ac. Tile, Stria " " " Type, TXW " " " " TXE	VII	2	3/4"
	Motif'd Acoustone (Stri-ated) Pattern #19	VII	1	7/8"
	Fiberglas Ac. Tile Type TXW	VII	1	1"
	Perforated Asbestos Bd. Panel Transite Acoustical Panels	X	5	1-3/16"
0.70–0.80	Acousti-Celotex Type C-9 Acoustifibre Auditone Perforated Cushiontone Fibretone Fir-Tex Perforated Flintkote Ac. Tile Type RS Simpson Ac. Tile Type S-3	I	2	3/4"
0.70–0.80, cont.	Acousti-Celotex Type C-8 Auditone Perforated Fibretone Flintkote Ac. Tile Type RS Simpson Ac. Tile Type S-5	I	1	1"
	Cushiontone Fir-Tex Perforated	I	1,7	1"
	Acousti-Celotex Type C-7	I	7	1"
	Acousti-Celotex Type CR-8 Cushiontone Full Random Flintkote Ac. Tile Type MS	II	1	1"
	Acousti-Celotex Type M-7	V	7	13/16"
	Celotone Simpson Fissur'd Mineral Tile Travertone	VI	7	13/16"
	Acoustone F Permacoustic Travacoustic	VI	7	7/8"
	Celotone	VI	7	15/16"
	Motif'd Acoustone (Stri-ated) Pattern #19	VII	7	7/8"
	Fiberglas Sono-Faced Ac. Tile Center Units Fiberglas Sono-Faced Ceiling Board-Center Tile	VIII	7	3/4"
	Acoustipanel	IX	7	1-5/8"
0.75–0.85	Acousti-Celotex Type C-8 Auditone Perforated Cushiontone Fibretone Fir-Tex Perforated Flintkote Ac. Tile Type RS	I	2	1"
	Fiberglas Ac. Tile Type PRWR	V	7	5/8"
	Permacoustic	VI	7	3/4"
	Celotone	VI	7	15/16"
	Fiberglas Ac. Tile Type TXW " Ceiling Board	VII	7	3/4"
	Fiberglas Ac. Tile Type TXW	VII	7	1"
	Asbestos Board Panel Perforated Asbestos Bd. Panel	X	8	2-3/16"
0.80–0.90	Minatone	V	7	7/8"
	Acousteel Acoustimetal Arrestone D & R Acoustical Metal Pan Flintkote Perf'd Metal Ac. Tile Sanacoustic, Type KK Sanacoustic, Spincoustic Pads Simpson Metal Ac. Units	IX	3	2-1/2"
	Acoustipanel	IX	7	2-5/8"
	Transite Acoustical Panels	X	8	2-3/16"
0.85–0.95	Fiberglas Ac. Tile, Stria " " " Type TXE	VII	7	3/4"
	Fiberglas Ceiling Board	VII	7	1"
	Corrutone	IX	7	2"

Data is from "Sound Absorption Coefficients of Architectural Materials", Bull. XVI, 1956, Acoustical Materials Association.

LANDSCAPING and SITE WORK

TABLE OF CONTENTS

TREES and SHRUBS

DECIDUOUS TREES – SCALE 1" = 80'

Silhouettes indicate specimens of typical form, height & spread, grown in ideal open conditions. Spacing is distance o.c. for usual row planting & may be varied for conditions. Hedge & screen spacing should be considerably less, depending on size of plant used. Arranged alphabetically. (with exceptions).

Silhouette	Tree	Height Mature	Dia. Trunk	Spread	Spaced O.C.
	AILANTHUS *Ailanthus glandulosa*	50'-75'	2'-3'	40'-60'	30'-40'
	APPLE *Malus pumila*	20'-40'	1'-2'	20'-40'	25'
	ASH, WHITE *Fraxinus americana*	70'-80'	2'-3'	35'-50'	40'-50'
	BEECH, AMERICAN *Fagus americana*	50'-75'	1½'-4'	40'-50'	30'-40'
	BEECH, EUROPEAN *Fagus sylvatica*	50'-75'	3'-4'	50'-70'	50'-60'
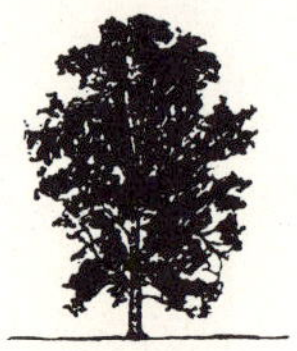	BIRCH, WHITE (European) *Betula pubescens* — See small trees for Grey Birch.	50'-75'	1'-3'	30-50	30'-40'
	CATALPA, NORTHERN *Catalpa speciosa*	80'-100'	3'-4'	50'-60'	50'-60'
	GINKGO BILOBA *Maidenhair tree*	60'-80'	2'-3'	50'-60'	50'-60'
	ELM, AMERICAN *Ulmus americana*	80'-100'	4'-8'	70'-80'	60'-70'
	ELM, ENGLISH *Ulmus procera*	75'-100'	3'-4'	50'-60'	50'-60'
	HORSECHESTNUT *Aesculus hippocastanum*	60'-70'	2'-3'	40'-50'	40'-50'
	LOCUST, BLACK *Robinia pseudoacacia*	40'-70'	2'-4'	30'-40'	30'-40'
	LOCUST, HONEY *Gleditsia triacanthos*	40'-60'	2'-3'	20'-30'	30'-40'
	LINDEN *Tilia (species)*	70'-90'	2'-4'	50'-60'	40'-50'
	MAGNOLIA (Cucumber tree) *Magnolia acuminata*	70'-90'	3'-4'	60'-70'	50'-60'
	MAPLE, NORWAY *Acer platanoides*	60'-80'	2'-3'	60'-70'	50'-60'
	MAPLE, RED *Acer rubrum*	50'-75'	2'-3'	40'-50'	40'-50'
	MAPLE, SUGAR *Acer saccharum*	70'-100'	2'-4'	50'-60'	50'-60'
	OAK, PIN *Quercus palustris*	60'-80'	3'-4'	40'-50'	40'-50'
	OAK, NORTHERN RED *Quercus borealis*	60'-80'	2'-6'	60'-70'	50'-60'
	OAK, WHITE *Quercus alba*	80'-100'	3'-6'	80'-100'	100'
	PLANE TREE (ORIENTAL) (Sycamore, Buttonwood) *Platanus orientalis*	70'-80'	3'-4'	50'-60'	50'-60'

Prepared with the assistance of Leo A. Novick, Landscape Architect

Drawings by Alice Recknagel.

TREES and SHRUBS

DECIDUOUS TREES (Continued) - SCALE 1" = 80'

See notes on previous page

POPLAR, CAROLINA
Populus canadensis eugenei

HEIGHT MATURE	DIA. TRUNK	SPREAD	SPACED O.C.
75'-100'	3'-5'	40'-50'	30'-40'

POPLAR, LOMBARDY
Populus nigra theresting, Lombardy

HEIGHT MATURE	DIA. TRUNK	SPREAD	SPACED O.C.
75'-100'	2'-6'	20'-30'	20'-30'

SWEET GUM
Liquidambar styraciflua

HEIGHT MATURE	DIA. TRUNK	SPREAD	SPACED O.C.
80'-120'	3'-5'	40'-50'	40'-50'

TULIP TREE
Liriodendron tulipifera

HEIGHT MATURE	DIA. TRUNK	SPREAD	SPACED O.C.
100'-120'	3'-4'	50'-60'	50'-60'

WALNUT, BLACK
Juglans nigra

HEIGHT MATURE	DIA. TRUNK	SPREAD	SPACED O.C.
75'-150'	3'-5'	50'-75'	50'-60'

WEEPING WILLOW
Salix babylonica

HEIGHT MATURE	DIA. TRUNK	SPREAD	SPACED O.C.
30'-40'	1'-2'	30'-40'	30'-40'

SMALL DECIDUOUS TREES - SCALE 1" = 40'

For large deciduous trees see previous sheet

COMMON NAME	GREY BIRCH	CRABAPPLE, FLOWERING	DOGWOOD, FLOWERING	HAWTHORNE	MAGNOLIA, SAUCER	COMMON NAME
Botanical name	*Betula populifolia*	*Malus (species)*	*Cornus florida*	*Crataegus (species)*	*Magnolia soulangeana*	*Botanical name*
Height	20' - 35'	15' - 20'	20' - 25'	15' - 30'	20' - 25'	*Height*
Dia. Trunk	clumps, stems, under 1'	Less than 1'-0"	Less than 1'-0"	6" to 1'-0"	9" to 1'-0"	*Dia. Trunk*
Spread	15' - 20'	20' - 25'	25' - 35'	20' - 40'	20' - 25'	*Spread*
Spacing O.C.	10' - 20'	20' - 30'	20' - 30'	20' - 30'	20' - 30'	*Spacing O.C.*

For large deciduous trees see previous sheet

SMALL EVERGREEN TREES - SCALE 1" = 40'

For larger Evergreen trees see following sheet

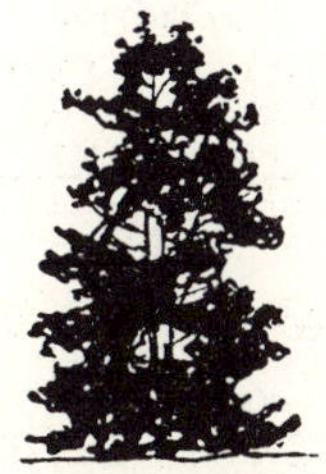

COMMON NAME	ARBOR VITAE	BOX TREE	HOLLY, AMERICAN	JUNIPER (Red Cedar)	COMMON NAME
Botanical name	*Thuja occidentalis*	*Buxus sempervirens*	*Ilex opaca*	*Juniperus virginiana*	*Botanical name*
Height	25' - 50'	20' - 30'	40' - 50'	25' - 50'	*Height*
Dia. Trunk	1' - 2'	1' - 2'	1' - 2'	1' - 2'	*Dia. Trunk*
Spread	10' - 20'	25' - 30'	25' - 35'	10' - 15'	*Spread*
Spacing O.C.	10' - 20'	20' - 25'	30' - 40'	20' - 30'	*Spacing O.C.*

Spacing for hedges may be much closer than that below

PLAN INDICATIONS

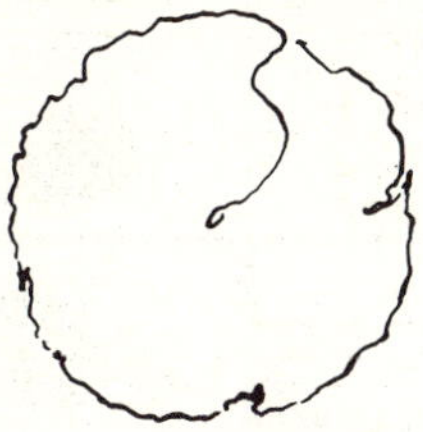

TREE
1" = 40'

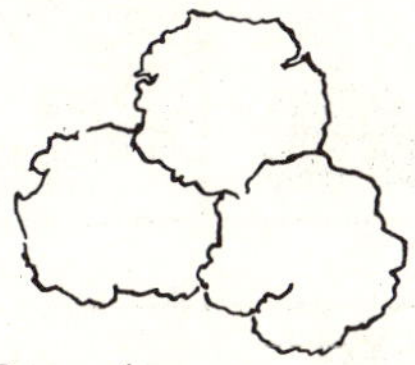

Deciduous

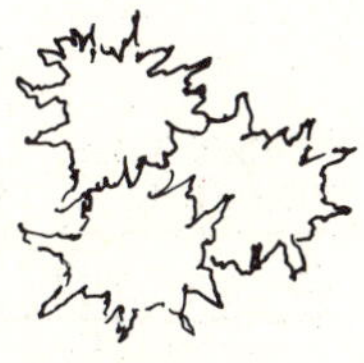

Evergreen

SHRUBS
1" = 20'

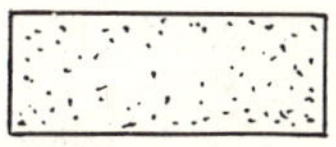

GRASS

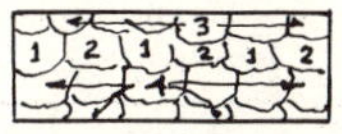

1
2
3

Numbers indicate specified variety.

PLANTING BED

HEDGES

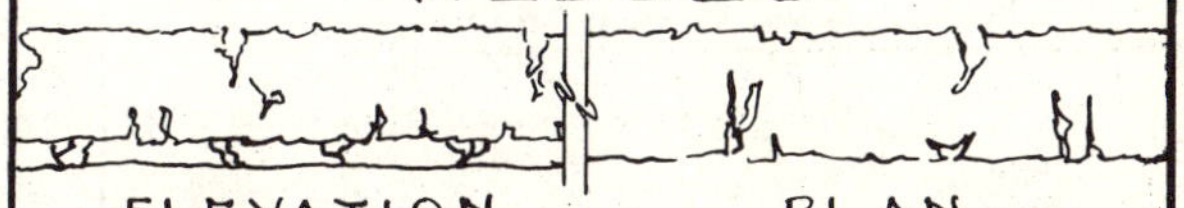

ELEVATION PLAN

SPACING FOR HEDGES

Type of Hedge	Height	Single row	Staggered double row
Barberry	1'-6"	1'-0"	1'-3"
Privet (Amurense)	3'	1'-6"	2'-0"
Yew (Hicksi)	2'	1'-0"	1'-3"

Prepared with the assistance of Leo A. Novick, Landscape Architect

Drawings by Alice Recknagel

TREES and SHRUBS

H = HEIGHT
D = TRUNK DIA.
S = SPREAD
O.C. = SPACING

EVERGREEN TREES – SCALE 1" = 80'

See notes at top of Deciduous Tree sheet

Tree	H	D	S	O.C.
BALD CYPRESS, *Taxodium distichum* (Mature tree; Young tree)	100'-150'	3'-5'	50'-100'	60'-70'
DOUGLAS FIR, *Pseudotsuga taxifolia* (Mature tree; Young tree)	100'-200	10'-12'	50'-60'	50'-60'
YEW, IRISH, *Taxus baccata fastigiata*	50'-60'	4'-6'	30'-40'	30'-40'
CYPRESS, SAWARA, *Chamaecyparis pisifera (varieties)*	20'-40'	9"-15"	15'-20'	20'-30'
FIR, WHITE, *Abies concolor*	100'-150'	3'-4'	50'-60'	50'-60'
HEMLOCK, CANADA, *Tsuga Canadensis*	60'-100'	2'-4'	40'-60'	40'-50'
LARCH, EUROPEAN, *Larix decidua*	50'-60'	1'-3'	30'-40'	40'-50'
MAGNOLIA, SOUTHERN, *Magnolia Grandiflora*	70'-80'	2'-3'	50'-60'	50'-60'
LIVE OAK, *Quercus Virginiana*	50'-60'	4'-6'	60'-70'	60'-70'
PINE, AUSTRIAN, *Pinus nigra*	60'-80'	2'-3'	30'-40'	40'-50'
PINE, MONTEREY, *Pinus radiata*	50'-60'	4'-6'	50'-60'	50'-60'
PINE, RED (NORWAY), *Pinus resinosa*	60'-80'	2'-3'	30'-40'	40'-50'
PINE, WHITE, *Pinus strobus*	80'-100'	4'-5'	60'-80'	50'-60'
SPRUCE, COLORADO, *Picea pungens*	70'-90	1½'-3'	30'-40'	40'-50'
SPRUCE, NORWAY, *Picea abies*	50'-100'	2'-3'	40'-50'	40'-50'

DECIDUOUS SHRUBS

	H	S
MYRTLE, CRAPE, *Lagerstroemia indica*	15'-20	15'-25'
LILAC, COMMON, *Syringa vulgaris*	12'-15'	10'-12
WHITE FRINGE TREE, *Chionanthus virginicus*	10'-15'	10'-15'
MOCK-ORANGE, *Philadelphus (species)*	8'-10'	6'-8'
ROSE OF SHARON, *Hibiscus (varieties)*	10'-12'	8'-10'
ARROW-WOOD, *Viburnum dentatum*	10'-12'	10'-12'
PRIVET, REGELS, *Ligustrum obtusifolium regelianum*	5'-6'	4'-5'
HONEYSUCKLE, *Lonicera (species)*	6'-12'	6'-12'
FORSYTHIA, DROOPING, *Forsythia suspensa*	6'-8'	8'-10'
SPIREA, VAN HOUTTE, *Spirea van houttei*	5'-6'	5'-6'
SNOWBALL, JAPANESE, *Viburnum tomentosum sterile*	6'-8'	6'-8'
BLUEBERRY, HIGHBUSH, *Vaccinium corymbosum*	6'-8'	6'-8'
COTONEASTER, *Cotoneaster horizontalis*	2'-3'	6'-9'
HYDRANGEA, SNOW HILL, *Hydrangea arborescens grandiflora*	4'-5'	5'-6'
BARBERRY, *Berberis thunbergi*	4'-5'	4'-6'

EVERGREEN SHRUBS

	H	S	O.C.
HOLLY, JAPANESE, *Ilex crenata*	15'-20'	10'-15'	8'-10'
BOX, DWARF, *Buxus suffruticosa*	10'-12'	10'-15'	variable
YEW, JAPANESE, *Taxus cuspidata*	12'-15'	12'-15'	variable
PITTOSPORUM TOBIRA	6'-10'	6'-10'	4'-6'
RHODODENDRON, *Rhododendron (species)*	6'-30'	6'-15'	5'-15'
OLEANDER, *Nerium oleander*	7'-15'	7'-12'	6'-10'
PINE, MUGHO, *Pinus mugho mughus*	6'-8'	8'-12'	10'-15'
MOUNTAIN LAUREL, *Kalma latifolia*	4'-10'	4'-8'	4'-8'
JUNIPER, PFITZERS, *Juniperus chinensis pfitzeriana*	6'-8'	6'-8'	5'-10'

PALMS

	H	D	S	O.C.
DATE PALM, *Phoenix canariensis*	80'-100'	3'-5'	50'-60'	50'-60'
COCONUT PALM, *Cocos nucifera*	40'-100'	12"-18"	40'-50'	40'-50
WASHINGTON PALM, *Washingtonia robusta*	60'-90'	3'-4'	25'-35'	20'-40'
ROYAL PALM, *Roystonea regia*	100'	1½'-2'	30'-40'	40'-50'

Prepared with the assistance of Leo A. Novick, Landscape Architect   *Drawings by Alice Recknagel.*

GREENHOUSE DETAILS

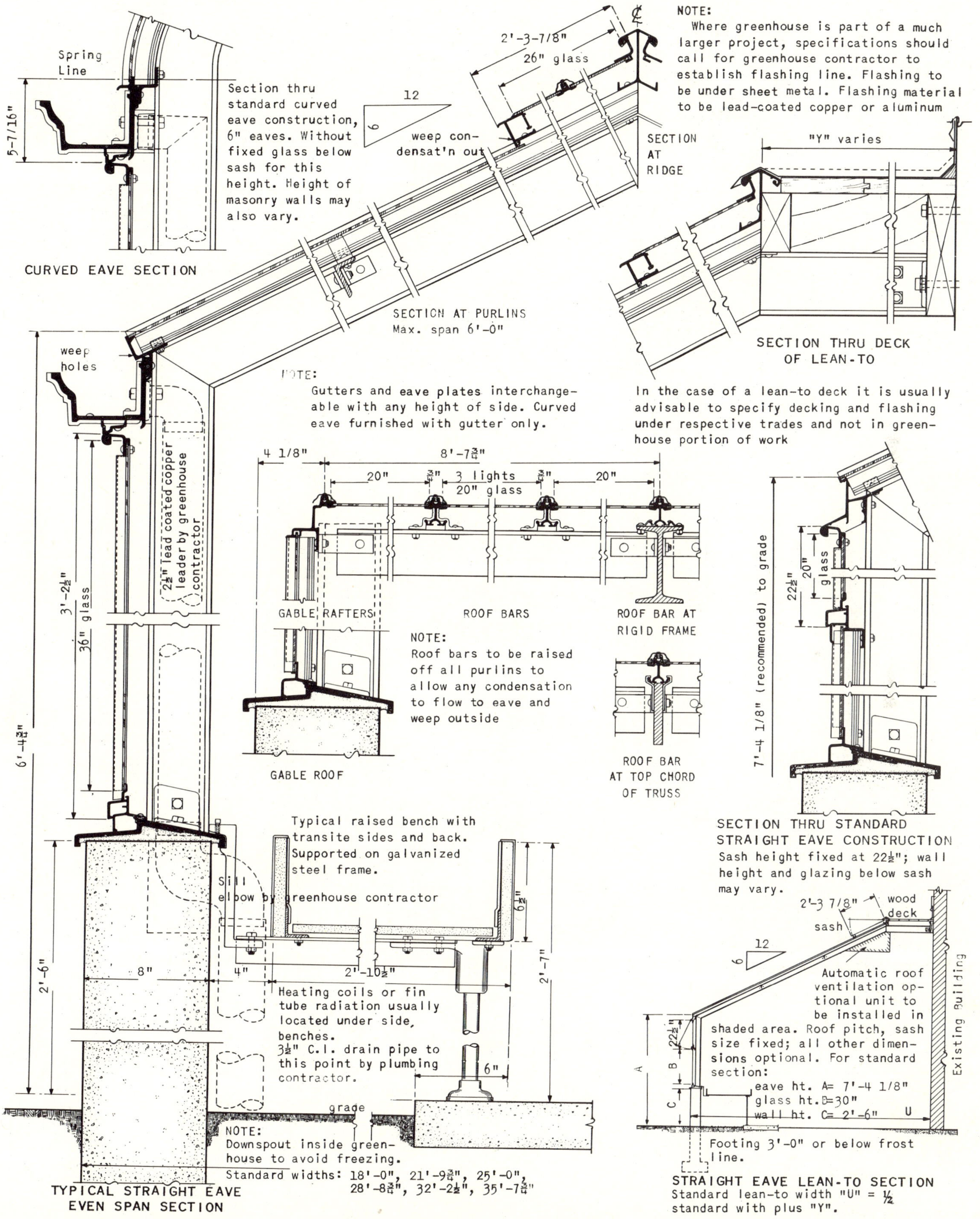
Spring Line
5-7/16"
Section thru standard curved eave construction, 6" eaves. Without fixed glass below sash for this height. Height of masonry walls may also vary.
CURVED EAVE SECTION
12
6
weep condensat'n out
2'-3-7/8"
26" glass
℄
SECTION AT RIDGE
NOTE:
Where greenhouse is part of a much larger project, specifications should call for greenhouse contractor to establish flashing line. Flashing to be under sheet metal. Flashing material to be lead-coated copper or aluminum
"Y" varies
SECTION AT PURLINS
Max. span 6'-0"
SECTION THRU DECK OF LEAN-TO
weep holes
NOTE:
Gutters and eave plates interchangeable with any height of side. Curved eave furnished with gutter only.
In the case of a lean-to deck it is usually advisable to specify decking and flashing under respective trades and not in greenhouse portion of work
6'-4¾"
3'-2½"
36" glass
2½" lead coated copper leader by greenhouse contractor
4 1/8"
8'-7¾"
20"
¾"
3 lights
20" glass
GABLE RAFTERS
ROOF BARS
ROOF BAR AT RIGID FRAME
NOTE:
Roof bars to be raised off all purlins to allow any condensation to flow to eave and weep outside
GABLE ROOF
ROOF BAR AT TOP CHORD OF TRUSS
7'-4 1/8" (recommended) to grade
22½"
20" glass
SECTION THRU STANDARD STRAIGHT EAVE CONSTRUCTION
Sash height fixed at 22½"; wall height and glazing below sash may vary.
Typical raised bench with transite sides and back. Supported on galvanized steel frame.
Sill elbow by greenhouse contractor
6½"
2'-7"
2'-6"
8"
4"
2'-10½"
Heating coils or fin tube radiation usually located under side benches.
3½" C.I. drain pipe to this point by plumbing contractor.
6"
grade
NOTE:
Downspout inside greenhouse to avoid freezing.
Standard widths: 18'-0", 21'-9¾", 25'-0", 28'-8¾", 32'-2½", 35'-7¾"
TYPICAL STRAIGHT EAVE EVEN SPAN SECTION
2'-3 7/8"
sash
wood deck
12
6
Automatic roof ventilation optional unit to be installed in shaded area. Roof pitch, sash size fixed; all other dimensions optional. For standard section:
eave ht. A= 7'-4 1/8"
glass ht. B=30"
wall ht. C= 2'-6"
A
B
C
22½"
U
Existing Building
Footing 3'-0" or below frost line.
STRAIGHT EAVE LEAN-TO SECTION
Standard lean-to width "U" = ½ standard with plus "Y".

Data by Lord & Burnham, Irvington, N.Y. and Des Plaines, Ill.

GARDEN EQUIPMENT

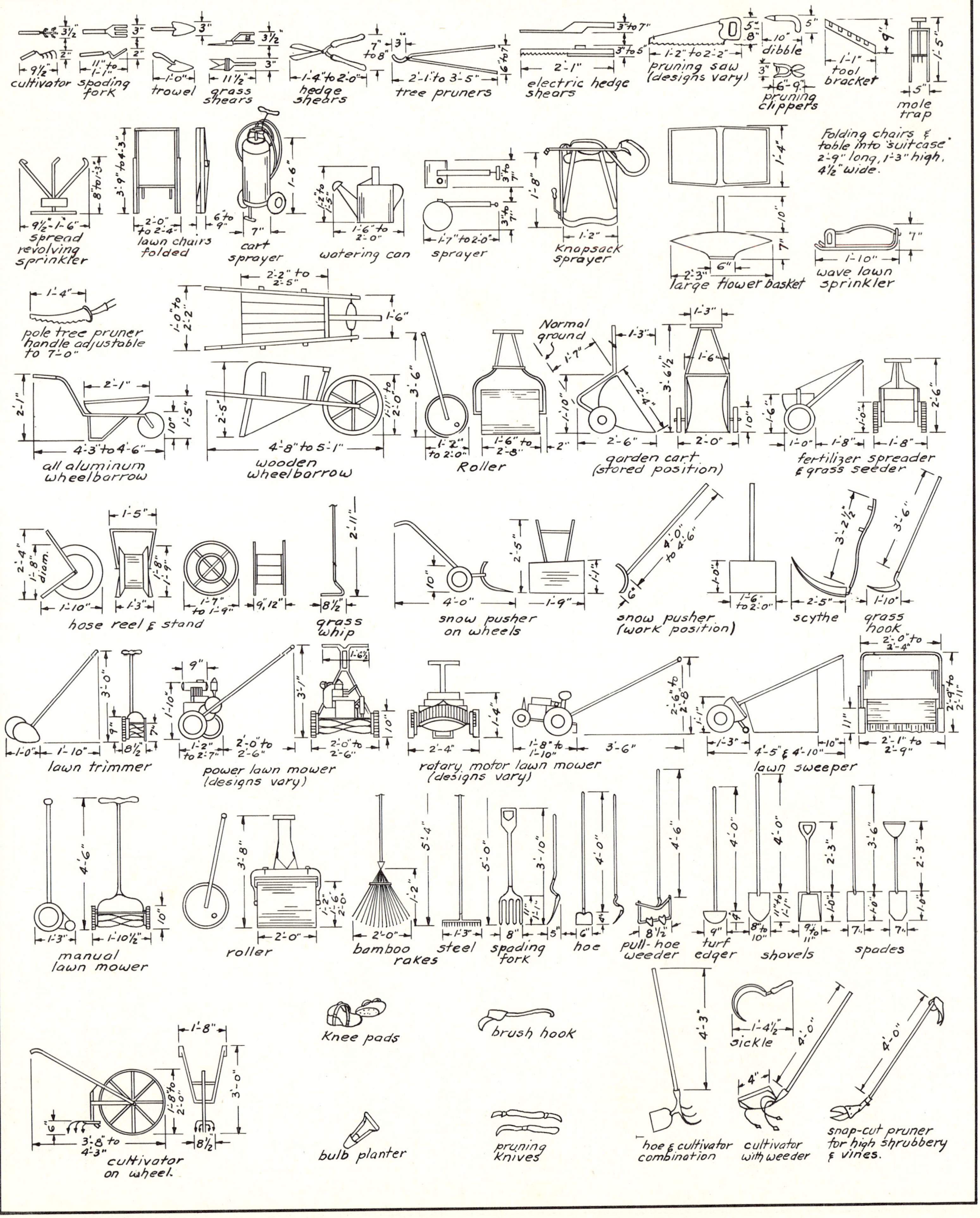
cultivator
spading fork
trowel
grass shears
hedge shears
tree pruners
electric hedge shears
pruning saw (designs vary)
dibble
pruning clippers
tool bracket
mole trap
spread revolving sprinkler
lawn chairs folded
cart sprayer
watering can
sprayer
Knapsack sprayer
Folding chairs & table into "suitcase" 2'-9" long, 1'-3" high, 4½" wide.
large flower basket
wave lawn sprinkler
pole tree pruner handle adjustable to 7'-0"
all aluminum wheelbarrow
wooden wheelbarrow
Roller
Normal ground
garden cart (stored position)
fertilizer spreader & grass seeder
hose reel & stand
grass whip
snow pusher on wheels
snow pusher (work position)
scythe
grass hook
lawn trimmer
power lawn mower (designs vary)
rotary motor lawn mower (designs vary)
lawn sweeper
manual lawn mower
roller
bamboo rakes
steel
spading fork
hoe
pull-hoe weeder
turf edger
shovels
spades
Knee pads
brush hook
sickle
cultivator on wheel.
bulb planter
pruning knives
hoe & cultivator combination
cultivator with weeder
snap-cut pruner for high shrubbery & vines.

BRICK PAVING

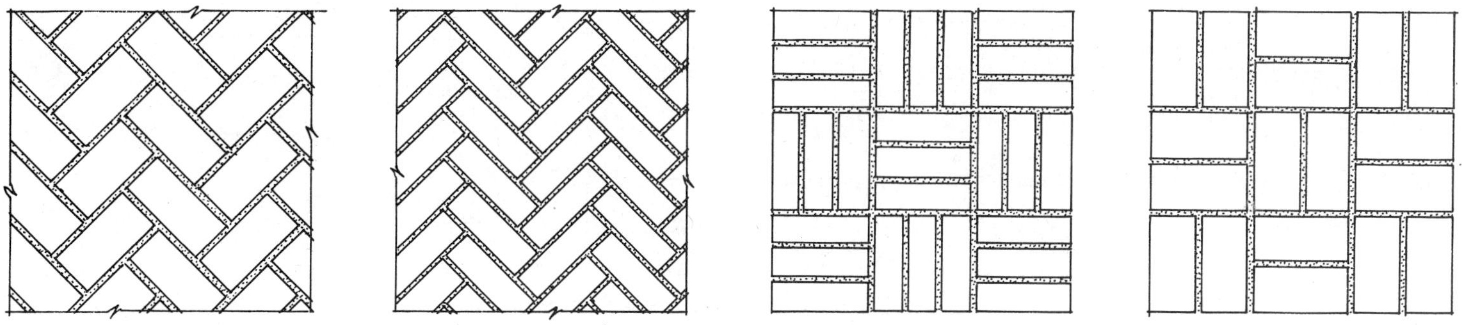

FLAT | ON EDGE | ON EDGE | FLAT

HERRING - BONE | BASKET WEAVE

PAVING PATTERNS - WALKS - TERRACES - PORCHES

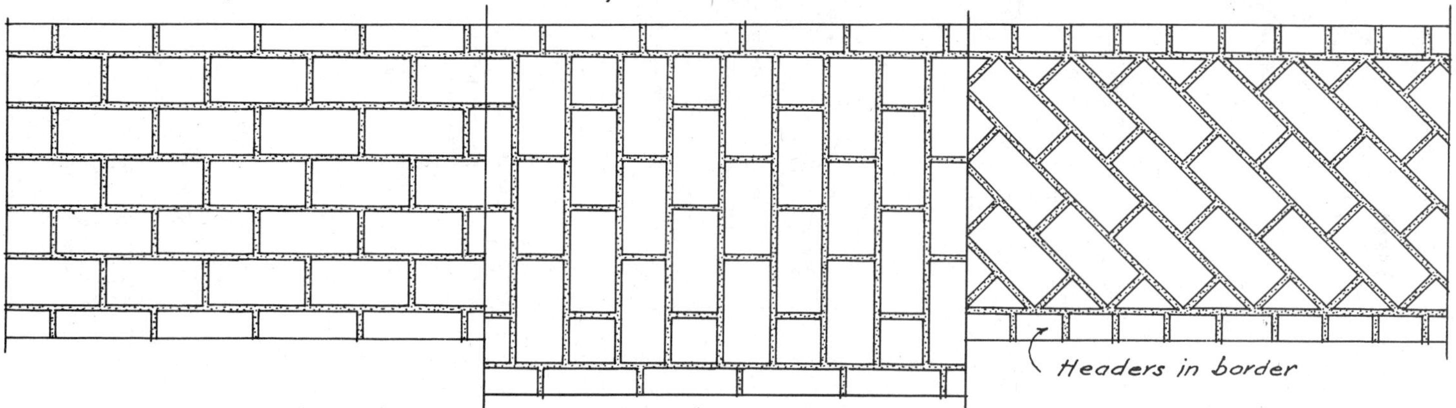
Headers in border

RUNNING - FLAT | CROSS - FLAT | DIAGONAL - FLAT

PATTERNS USUALLY USED FOR WALKS

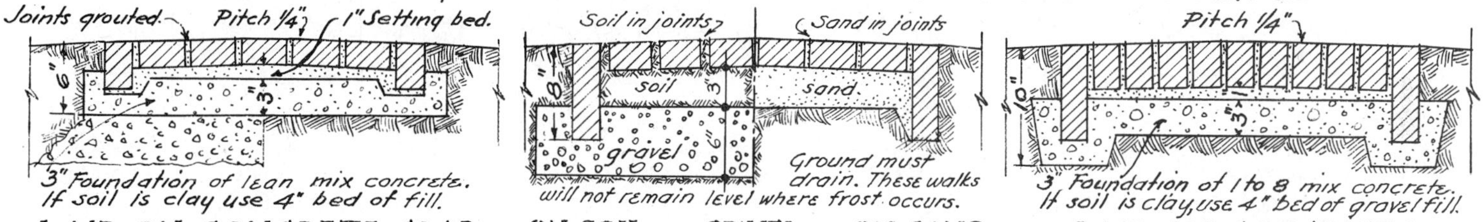
Joints grouted.
Pitch 1/4"
1" Setting bed.
6"
3"
3" Foundation of lean mix concrete.
If soil is clay use 4" bed of fill.
Soil in joints
Sand in joints
3"
soil
sand
6"
gravel
Ground must drain. These walks will not remain level where frost occurs.
Pitch 1/4"
10"
3"
3" Foundation of 1 to 8 mix concrete.
If soil is clay, use 4" bed of gravel fill.

LAID ON CONCRETE SLAB | ON SOIL over GRAVEL | ON SAND | LAID ON CONCRETE

SECTIONS of TYPICAL WALKS or TERRACES.

3/4" = 1'-0"

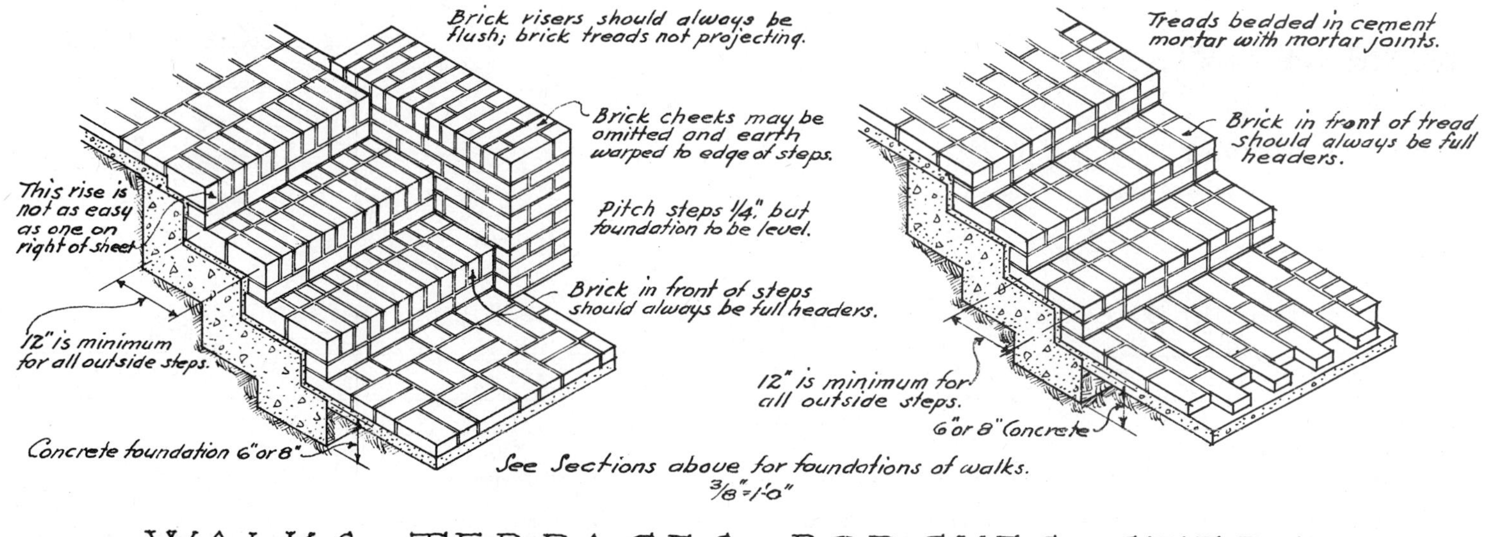
Brick risers should always be flush; brick treads not projecting.
Brick cheeks may be omitted and earth warped to edge of steps.
This rise is not as easy as one on right of sheet
Pitch steps 1/4" but foundation to be level.
Brick in front of steps should always be full headers.
12" is minimum for all outside steps.
Concrete foundation 6" or 8"
Treads bedded in cement mortar with mortar joints.
Brick in front of tread should always be full headers.
12" is minimum for all outside steps.
6" or 8" Concrete

See Sections above for foundations of walks.

3/8" = 1'-0"

WALKS - TERRACES - PORCHES - STEPS.

Recommendations of the Common Brick Manufacturers Association of America.

PAVING - WALKS, PATHS, TERRACES ETC.

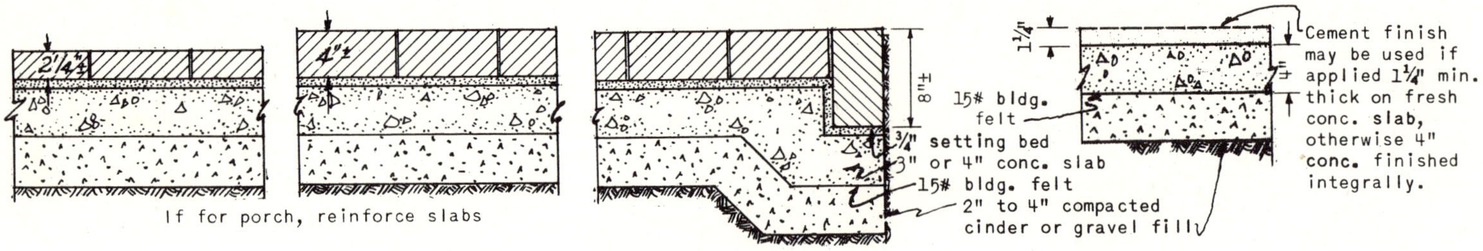
2¼"±
4"±
8"±
If for porch, reinforce slabs
15# bldg. felt
¾" setting bed
3" or 4" conc. slab
15# bldg. felt
2" to 4" compacted cinder or gravel fill
1¼"
Cement finish may be used if applied 1¼" min. thick on fresh conc. slab, otherwise 4" conc. finished integrally.

FLAT — ON EDGE — BORDER BRICK ON EDGE

BRICK ON CONCRETE SLAB — CONCRETE SLAB

SECTIONS THRU PAVING

Scale: ¾" = 1'-0"

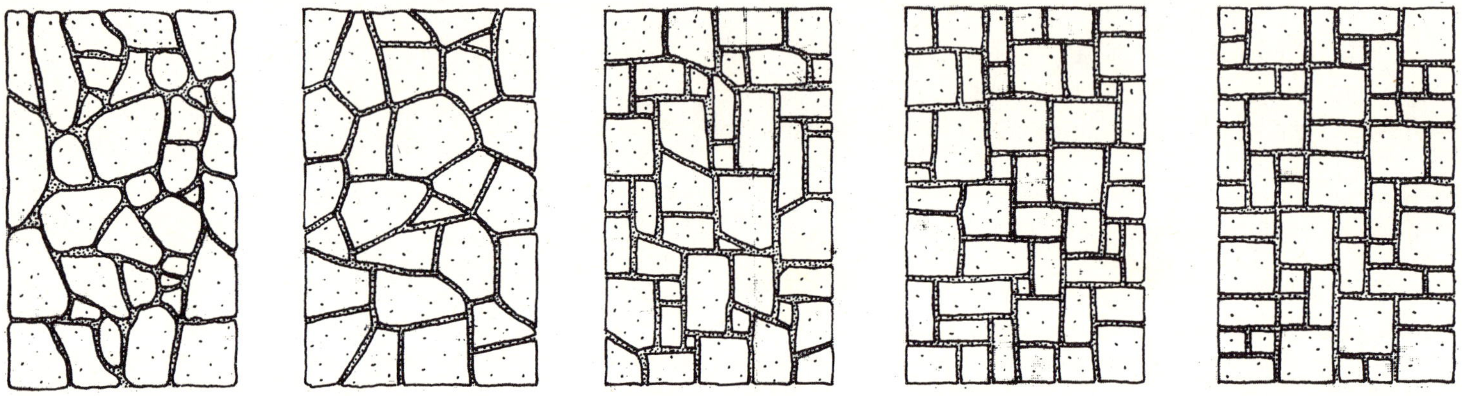

Irregular (not fitted). — Irregular (fitted) — Semi-irregular — Random Rectangular — Rectangular (limited sizes)

These are usually specified run of quarry but may be limited by specifying maximum and minimum sizes. These are average size but may vary considerably according to the quarry.

FLAGSTONE PATTERNS

Scale: ⅛" = 1'-0"

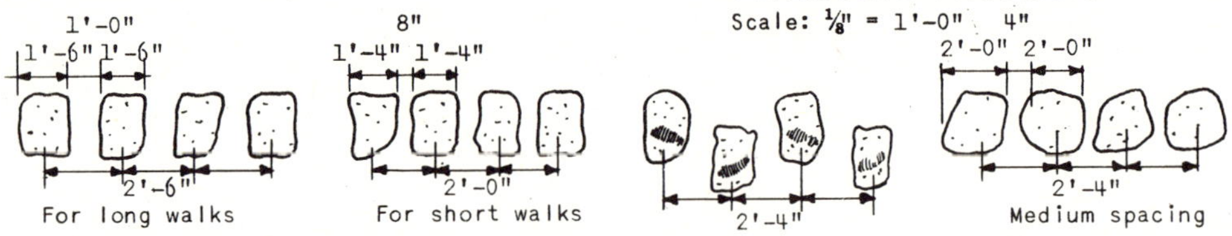
1'-0"
1'-6" 1'-6"
2'-6"
For long walks
8"
1'-4" 1'-4"
2'-0"
For short walks
2'-4"
4"
2'-0" 2'-0"
2'-4"
Medium spacing

Walks may be from 1'-4" to 2'-4" wide. Spacing for short walks 2'-0" and for longer walks 2'-4" to 2'-6". Stones usually 1'-4" to 1'-6" average length

STEPPING STONES

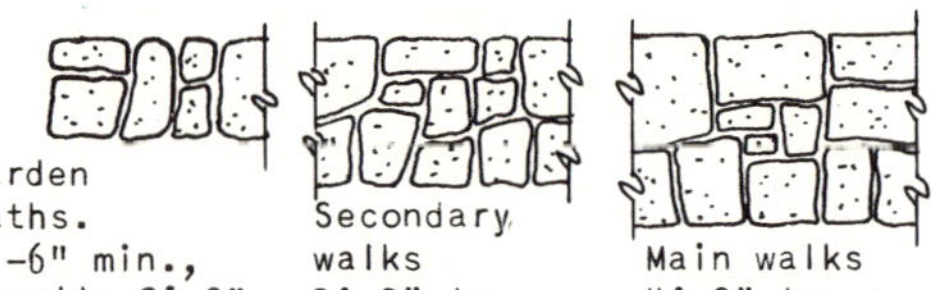
Garden paths. 1'-6" min., usually 2'-0" to 2'-6"
Secondary walks 3'-0" to 4'-0" wide
Main walks 4'-0" to 5'-0" wide.

WALKS AND PATHS

Scale: ⅛" = 1'-0"

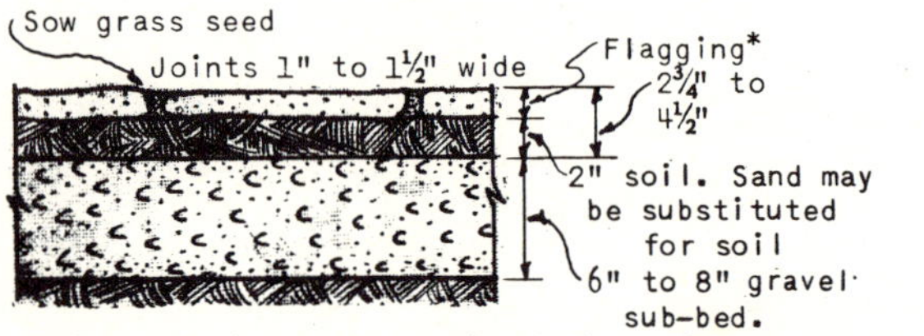
Sow grass seed
Joints 1" to 1½" wide
Flagging*
2¾" to 4½"
2" soil. Sand may be substituted for soil
6" to 8" gravel sub-bed.

This type will not stay level where frost occurs.

*Slate ¾" to 1"
Quartzite 1¼" to 2½"
Sandstone 1½"

STONE DIRECTLY ON EARTH

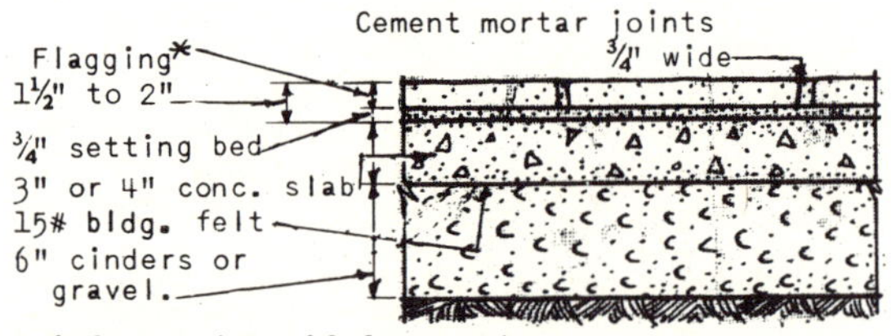
Cement mortar joints ¾" wide
Flagging*
1½" to 2"
¾" setting bed
3" or 4" conc. slab
15# bldg. felt
6" cinders or gravel.

Reinforce slabs if for porches.

*Slate ¾" to 1"
Quartzite ¾" to 1"
Sandstone 1"

STONE ON CONCRETE SLAB

Scale: ¾" = 1'-0"

MATERIAL	SURFACE FINISH	EDGE FINISH
Slate	Natural split (quarry cleft)	Sawed or hand trimmed
Quartzite	Natural split (quarry cleft)	Snapped finish
Sandstone	Natural split (quarry cleft), rubbed, sawed or planed	Flag cut, quarry cut, sawed or rubbed.

Note: Bluestone is a type of sandstone available in blue, grey red, pink and greenish colors .

ROADS, PATHS and PAVING BLOCKS

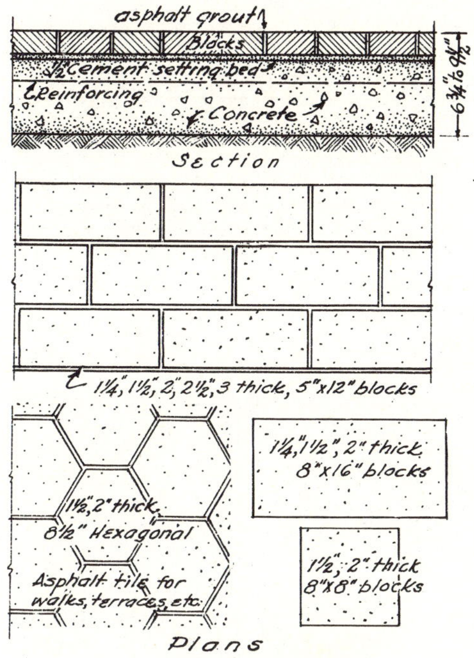
asphalt grout
Blocks
1/2" Cement setting bed
Reinforcing
Concrete
6 3/4" to 9 1/2"
Section
1 1/4, 1 1/2, 2, 2 1/2, 3 thick, 5"x12" blocks
1 1/2, 2" thick, 8 1/2" Hexagonal
Asphalt tile for walks, terraces, etc.
1 1/4, 1 1/2, 2" thick, 8"x16" blocks
1 1/2, 2" thick 8"x8" blocks
Plans

Pitch 1/8" to 1'-0"
ASPHALT PAVING BLOCKS AND TILES

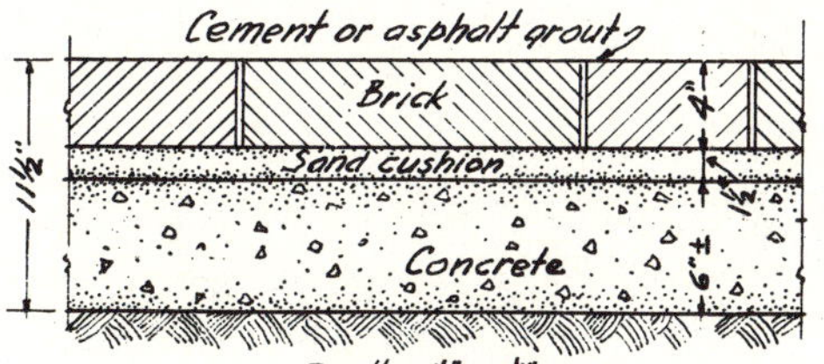
Cement or asphalt grout
Brick
Sand cushion
Concrete
11 1/2"
4"
1 1/2"
6"±

Depths 2 1/2, 3, 3 1/2, 4"
Widths 3 1/2" and 4"
Lengths - 8 1/2"
See U.S. Dept. of Commerce Simplified Practice Recommendation R1 - 1940 for sizes

VITRIFIED PAVING BRICK
Pitch 1/8" to 1'-0"

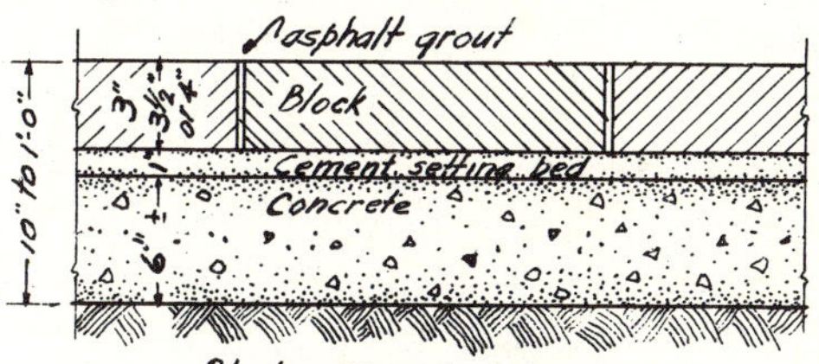
asphalt grout
Block
Cement setting bed
Concrete
10" to 1'-0"
3" - 3 1/2" or 4"
1"
6"±

Blocks 5" to 10" long, average 8"
3 1/2" to 4" wide
Depths 4" for heavy traffic
3 1/2" for medium "
3" for light "

WOOD PAVING BLOCK
Pitch 1/6" to 1'-0"

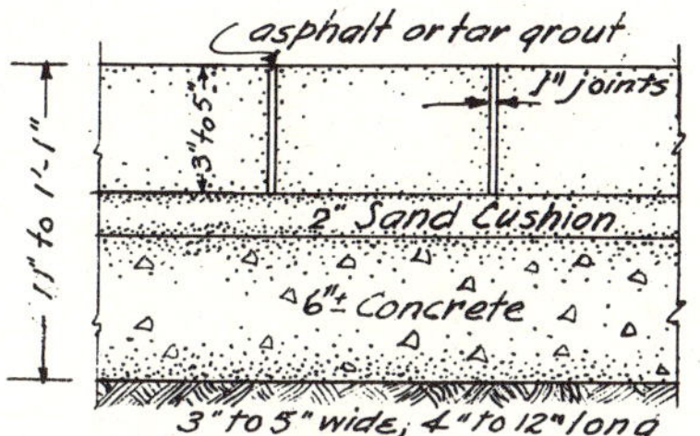
asphalt or tar grout
1" joints
3" to 5"
2" Sand Cushion
6"± Concrete
11" to 1'-1"

3" to 5" wide, 4" to 12" long
If on earth, use earth joints
Section
Granite, pitch 1/8" to 1'-0"
RUBBLE PAVEMENT STONE BLOCKS

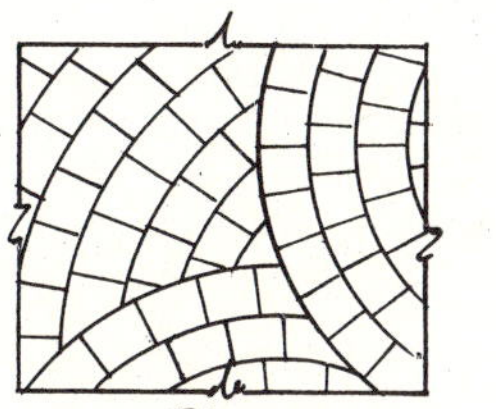

Plan
Roughly cubed 2 3/4" to 3 1/2" granite blocks on edge. 1/2" joints. Usually laid in concentric circles.
DURAX BLOCKS

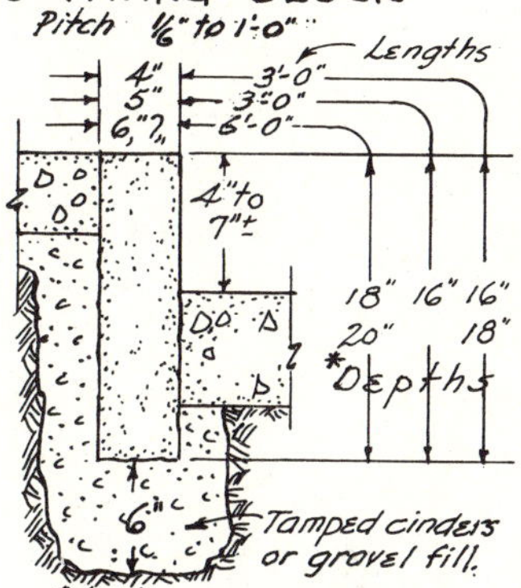
4"
5"
6", 7"
3'-0"
3'-0"
6'-0"
Lengths
4" to 7"±
18" 16" 16"
20" 18"
*Depths
6"±
Tamped cinders or gravel fill.

*Nominal, may vary 1"±. End joints usually set in mortar.
GRANITE CURBS
For city, congested areas.

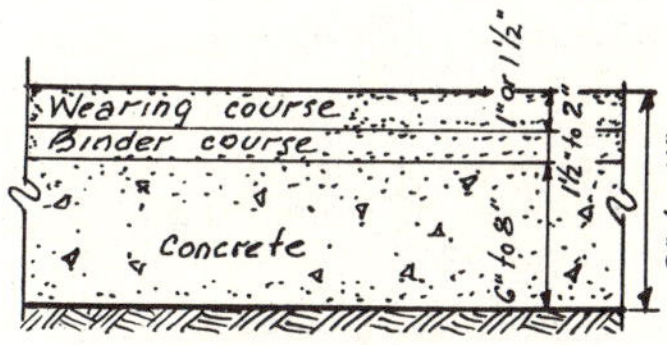
Wearing course
Binder course
Concrete
1" or 1 1/2"
1 1/2" to 2"
6" to 8"
9" to 11"

Type used in cities.
Pitch 1/8" to 1/4" per foot.
SHEET ASPHALT ON CONCRETE

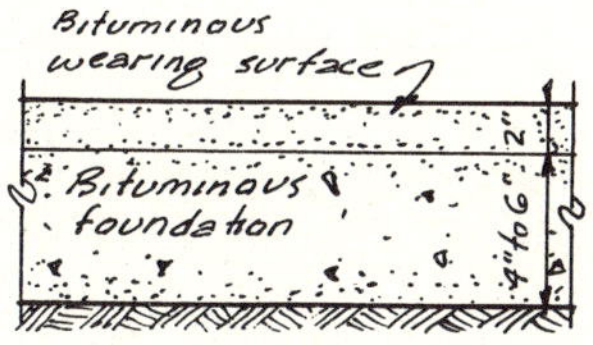
Bituminous wearing surface
Bituminous foundation
2"
4" to 6"

Pitch 1/4" to 1/2" per foot
BITUMINOUS CEMENT

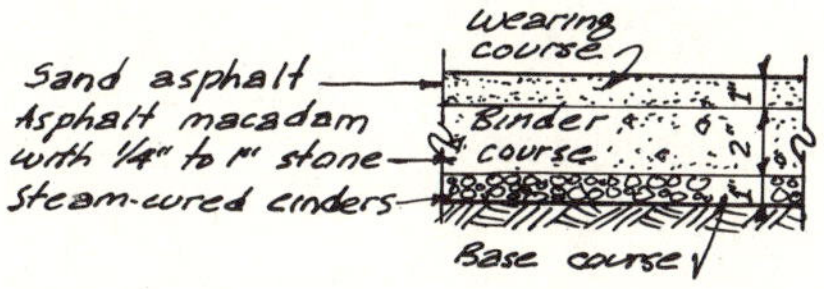
Wearing course
Sand asphalt
Asphalt macadam with 1/4" to 1" stone
Binder course
Steam-cured cinders
Base course

PLAY AREAS & PATHS
BLACK TOP

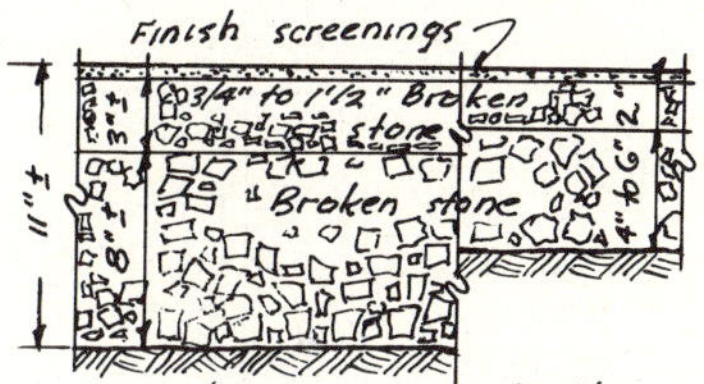
Finish screenings
3/4" to 1 1/2" Broken stone
Broken stone
11"±
8"±
4" to 6"

Heavy Light
Pitch 1/2" to 3/4" per foot.
BROKEN STONE

MISCELLANEOUS PAVEMENTS

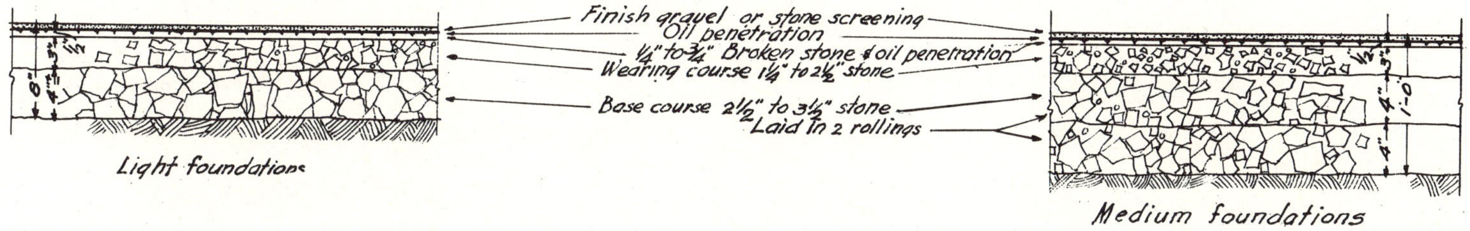
Finish gravel or stone screening
Oil penetration
1/4" to 3/4" Broken stone & oil penetration
Wearing course 1 1/4" to 2 1/2" stone
Base course 2 1/2" to 3 1/2" stone
Laid in 2 rollings
8"
3"
1/2"
4"
1'-0"

Light foundations
Medium foundations

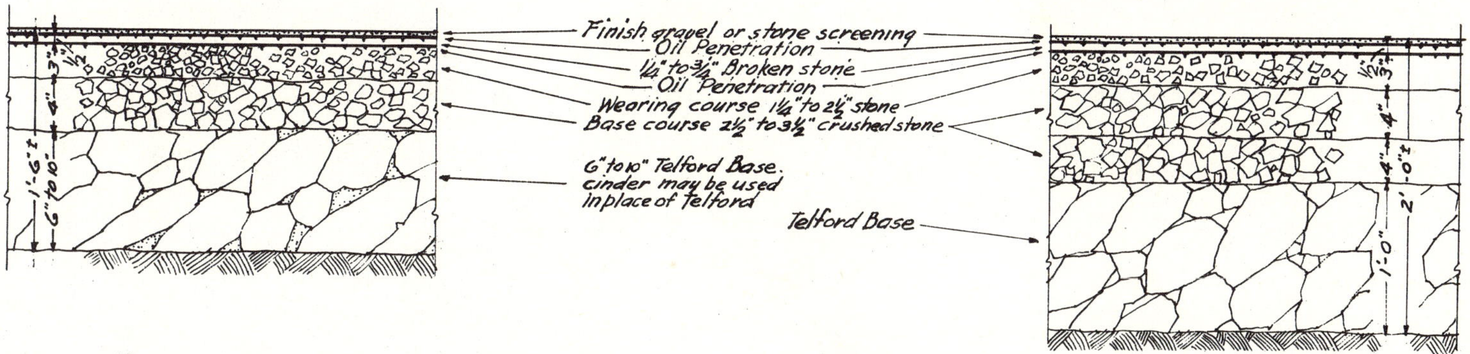
Finish gravel or stone screening
Oil Penetration
1/4" to 3/4" Broken stone
Oil Penetration
Wearing course 1 1/4" to 2 1/2" stone
Base course 2 1/2" to 3 1/2" crushed stone
6" to 10" Telford Base. cinder may be used in place of Telford
Telford Base
1'-6"±
6" to 10"
2'-0"±
1'-0"

Heavy foundations
Extra heavy foundations

BITUMINOUS MACADAM ROADS

RESIDENTIAL ROADS and SIDEWALKS

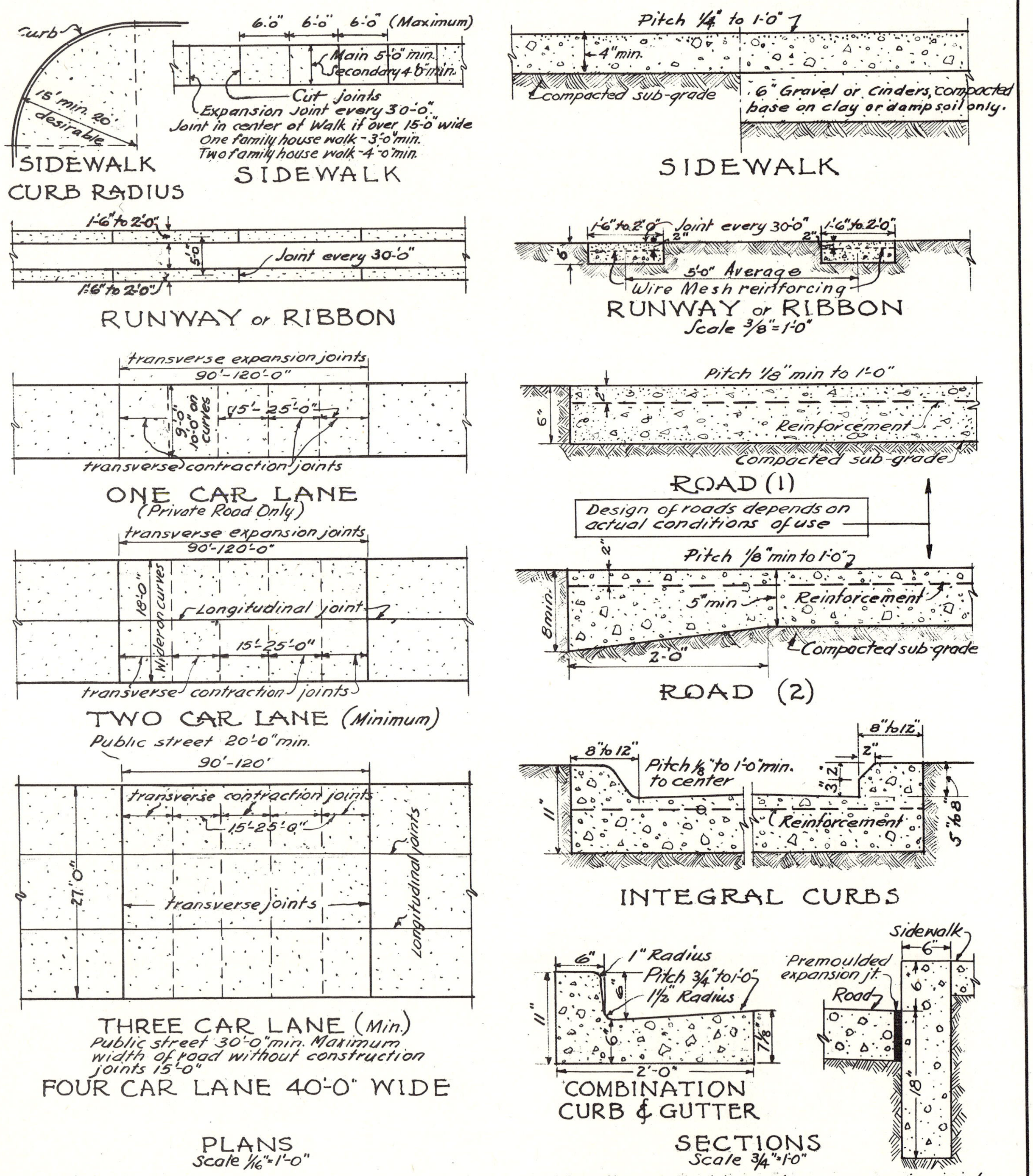
Curb
15' min. 20' desirable
SIDEWALK CURB RADIUS
6'-0" 6'-0" 6'-0" (Maximum)
Main 5'-0" min.
Secondary 4'-0" min.
Cut joints
Expansion joint every 30'-0".
Joint in center of walk if over 15'-0" wide
One family house walk - 3'-0" min.
Two family house walk - 4'-0" min.
SIDEWALK
Pitch 1/4" to 1'-0"
4" min.
Compacted sub-grade
6" Gravel or cinders, compacted base on clay or damp soil only.
SIDEWALK
1'-6" to 2'-0"
5'-0"
Joint every 30'-0"
1'-6" to 2'-0"
RUNWAY or RIBBON
1'-6" to 2'-0" Joint every 30'-0" 1'-6" to 2'-0"
2" 2"
6"
5'-0" Average
Wire Mesh reinforcing
RUNWAY or RIBBON
Scale 3/8"=1'-0"
transverse expansion joints
90'-120'-0"
9'-0" 10'-0" on curves
15'-25'-0"
transverse contraction joints
ONE CAR LANE
(Private Road Only)
Pitch 1/8" min to 1'-0"
2"
6"
Reinforcement
Compacted sub-grade
ROAD (1)
Design of roads depends on actual conditions of use
transverse expansion joints
90'-120'-0"
18'-0" wider on curves
Longitudinal joint
15'-25'-0"
transverse contraction joints
TWO CAR LANE (Minimum)
Public street 20'-0" min.
2"
Pitch 1/8" min to 1'-0"
8" min.
5" min
Reinforcement
Compacted sub-grade
2'-0"
ROAD (2)
90'-120'
transverse contraction joints
15'-25'-0"
27'-0"
transverse joints
Longitudinal joints
8" to 12"
Pitch 1/8" to 1'-0" min. to center
8" to 12"
2"
3 1/2"
11"
Reinforcement
5" to 8"
INTEGRAL CURBS
THREE CAR LANE (Min.)
Public street 30'-0" min. Maximum width of road without construction joints 15'-0"
FOUR CAR LANE 40'-0" WIDE
6"
1" Radius
Pitch 3/4" to 1'-0"
1 1/2" Radius
11"
6"
6"
7/8"
2'-0"
COMBINATION CURB & GUTTER
Sidewalk
6"
Premoulded expansion jt.
Road
6"
18"
PLANS
Scale 1/16"=1'-0"
SECTIONS
Scale 3/4"=1'-0"

Data checked by Rolph Eberlin C.E.

Sidewalk paralled to curb: no expansion joint necessary at junction.
Sidewalk perpendicular to (and terminating at) curb: Provide premoulded expansion joint.

PRIVATE ROADS & TURNS

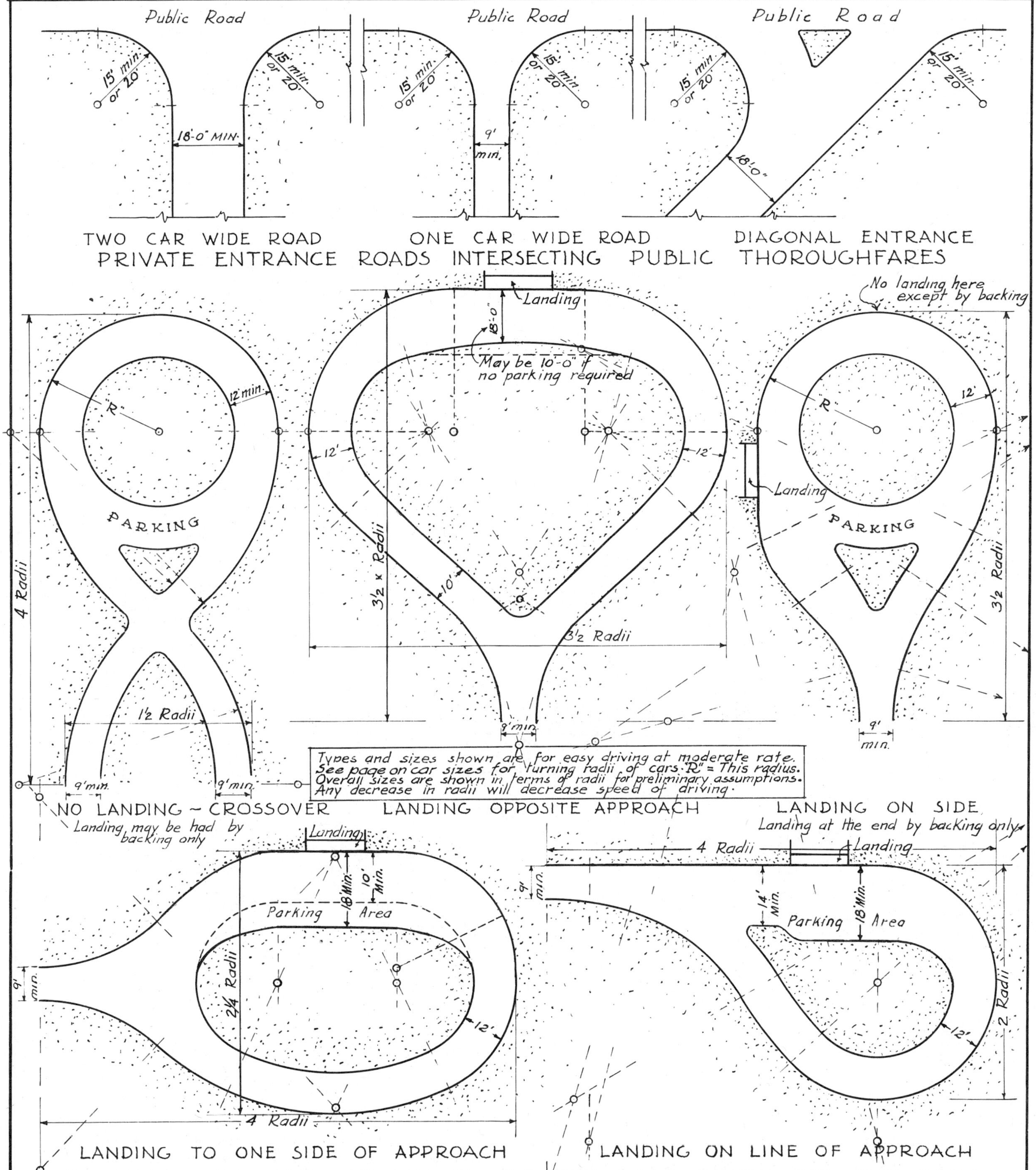
Public Road
Public Road
Public Road
15' min. or 20'
18'-0" MIN.
9' min.
18'-0"
TWO CAR WIDE ROAD
ONE CAR WIDE ROAD
DIAGONAL ENTRANCE
PRIVATE ENTRANCE ROADS INTERSECTING PUBLIC THOROUGHFARES
Landing
No landing here except by backing
8'-0"
May be 10'-0" if no parking required
"R"
12' min.
12'
PARKING
4 Radii
3½ x Radii
3½ Radii
1½ Radii
10'
9' min.
Types and sizes shown are for easy driving at moderate rate.
See page on car sizes for turning radii of cars. "R" = This radius.
Overall sizes are shown in terms of radii for preliminary assumptions.
Any decrease in radii will decrease speed of driving.
NO LANDING ~ CROSSOVER
Landing may be had by backing only
LANDING OPPOSITE APPROACH
LANDING ON SIDE
Landing at the end by backing only
4 Radii
18' Min.
10' Min.
14' Min.
Parking Area
2¼ Radii
2 Radii
12'
LANDING TO ONE SIDE OF APPROACH
LANDING ON LINE OF APPROACH

TURNAROUNDS - ONE CAR WIDTH - DOUBLE ROAD WIDTH FOR TWO CARS

PRIVATE ROADS, DRIVES & TURNAROUNDS

Scale: 1" = 30'

Checked by Ralph Eberlin, C.E.

GARAGE ROADS & TURNS

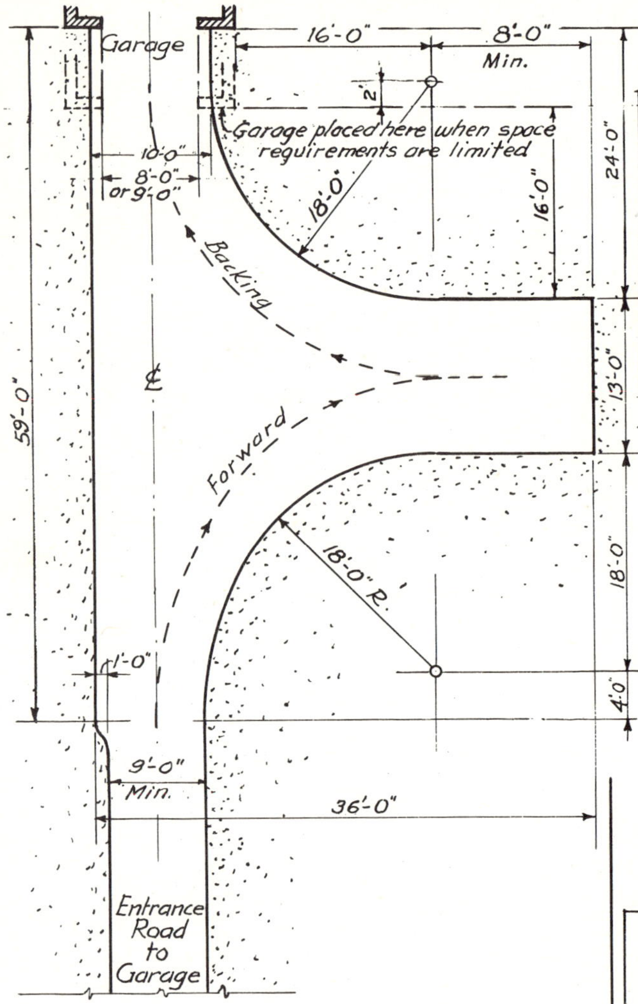
Garage
16'-0"
8'-0"
Min.
2'
Garage placed here when space requirements are limited
10'-0"
8'-0" or 9'-0"
18'-0"
16'-0"
24'-0"
Backing
℄
13'-0"
59'-0"
Forward
18'-0" R.
18'-0"
1'-0"
4'-0"
9'-0" Min.
36'-0"
Entrance Road to Garage

"Y" TURN FOR BACKING IN
Dotted line shows route going in
Scale: 1/16" = 1'-0"

Note:
All turns require 1'-6" clearance beyond road line shown.— These turns are for easy driving with average size car.— Larger radii will permit faster & easier driving. Smaller radii should be used for small cars only.

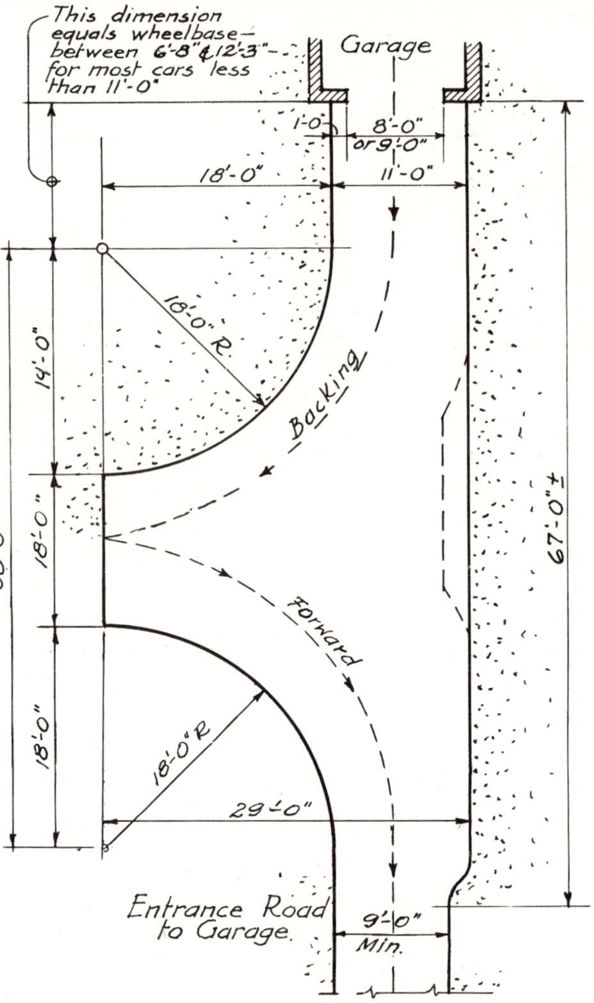
This dimension equals wheelbase— between 6'-8" & 12'-3"— for most cars less than 11'-0"
Garage
1'-0"
8'-0" or 9'-0"
18'-0"
11'-0"
16'-0" R
14'-0"
Backing
50'-0"
18'-0"
Forward
67'-0" ±
18'-0"
18'-0" R
29'-0"
Entrance Road to Garage
9'-0" Min.

"Y" TURN FOR BACKING OUT
Dotted line shows route going out
Scale: 1/16" = 1'-0"

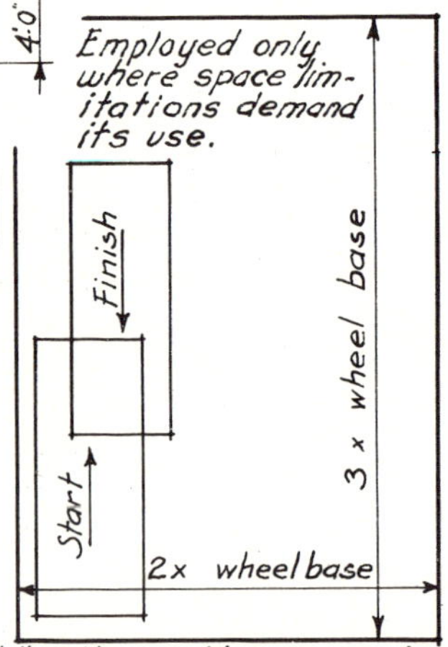
Employed only where space limitations demand its use.
Finish
Start
3 x wheel base
2x wheelbase

Wheelbase Minimum 6'-8"
do. Maximum 12'-6"
normally under 11'-0"

MINIMUM TURNING SPACE-BACKING THREE TIMES

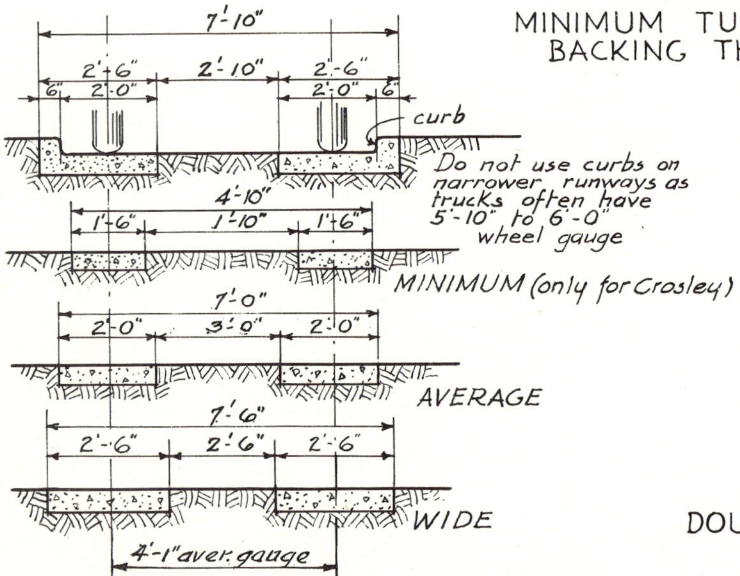
7'-10"
2'-6"
2'-10"
2'-6"
6"
2'-0"
2'-0"
6"
curb
Do not use curbs on narrower runways as trucks often have 5'-10" to 6'-0" wheel gauge
4'-10"
1'-6"
1'-10"
1'-6"
MINIMUM (only for Crosley)
7'-0"
2'-0"
3'-0"
2'-0"
AVERAGE
7'-6"
2'-6"
2'-6"
2'-6"
WIDE
4'-1" aver. gauge

CONCRETE RUNWAYS TO GARAGES
Widen for all turns

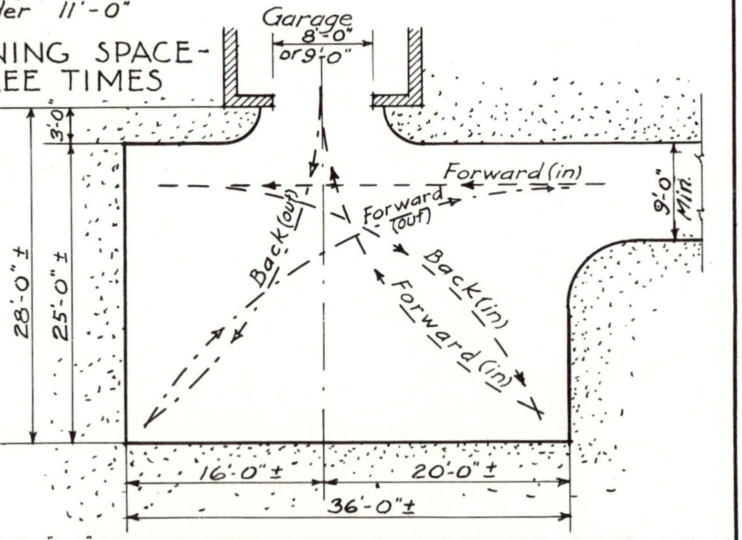
Garage
8'-0" or 9'-0"
3'-0"
Forward (in)
9'-0" Min.
Back (out)
Forward (out)
Back (in)
Forward (in)
28'-0" ±
25'-0" ±
16'-0" ±
20'-0" ±
36'-0" ±

DOUBLE "Y" TURN REQUIRING BACKING BOTH WAYS
Exact size depends on car. This is for average car
Employed only where space limitations demand its use.

Data checked by Ralph Eberlin, C.E.

ROADS AND TURNS FOR PRIVATE GARAGES

GARAGE and LOT PARKING

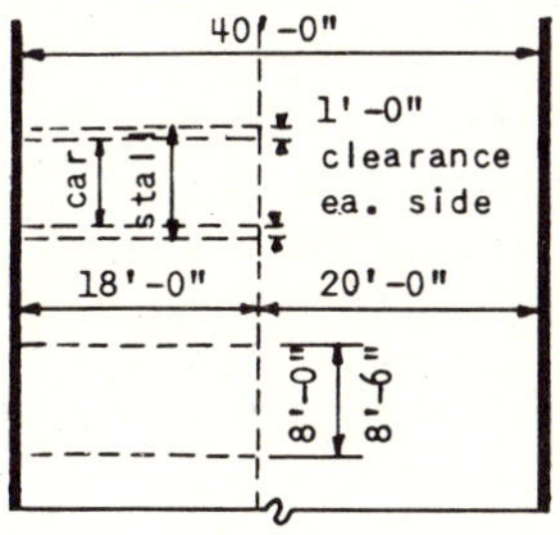
40'-0"
1'-0"
clearance
ea. side
car
stall
18'-0"
20'-0"
8'-0"
8'-6"

ONE ROW

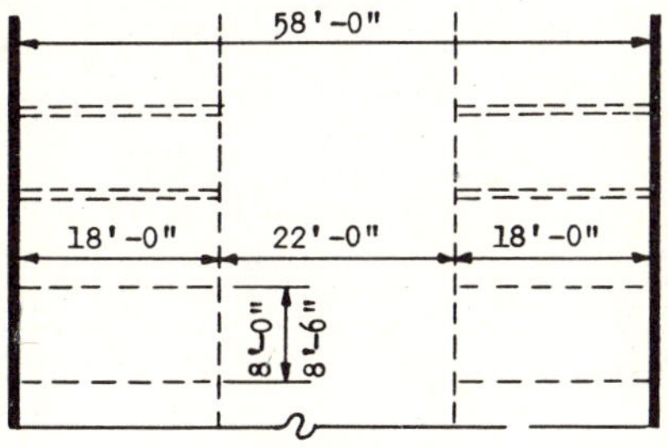
58'-0"
18'-0"
22'-0"
18'-0"
8'-0"
8'-6"

TWO ROWS

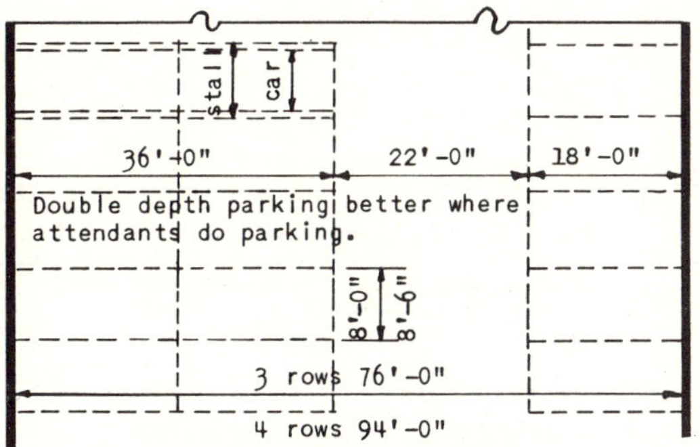
stall
car
36'-0"
22'-0"
18'-0"
Double depth parking better where attendants do parking.
8'-0"
8'-6"
3 rows 76'-0"
4 rows 94'-0"

THREE AND FOUR ROWS

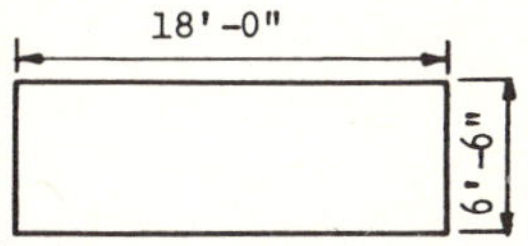
18'-0"
6'-6"

Assumed average size. Larger cars may protrude into aisle; will have less space for door swing.

AVERAGE CAR

No allowance has been made for columns on this page. Allow 1'-0"±

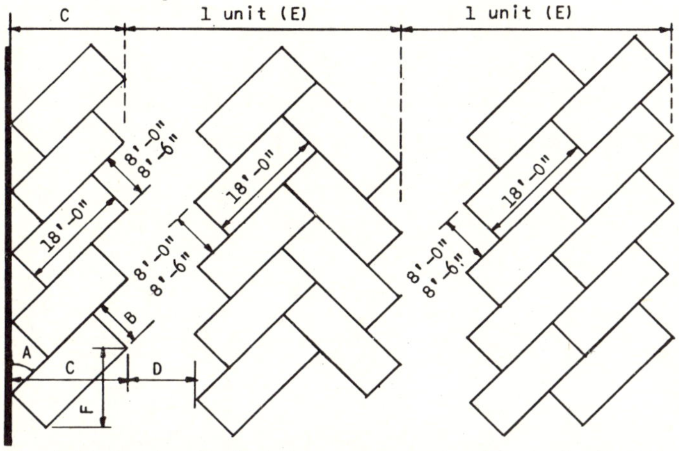
C
1 unit (E)
1 unit (E)
8'-0"
8'-6"
18'-0"
18'-0"
18'-0"
18'-0"
8'-0"
8'-6"
8'-0"
8'-6"
B
A
C
D
F

E = Unit Parking Depth (clear span construction). Angle-parking not feasible indoors; should be used only where space does not permit an integral number of 90° unit Parking Depths.

ANGLE-PARKING*

RECOMMENDED STALL & AISLE DIMENSIONS

A	Direction of parking	B	C	D	E	No. of stalls in length X	Area per car sq. ft.
90°	back-in	8'-0"	18'-0"	22'-0"	58'-0"	X/8	232
60°	back-in	8'-0"	18'-10"	17'-4"	55'-0"	(X-11)/9.25	254
45°	drive-in	8'-0"	17'-2"	12'-8"	47'-0"	(X-17)/11.3	266
90°	back-in	8'-6"	18'-0"	22'-0"	58'-0"	X/8.5	247
60°	back-in	8'-6"	18'-10"	18'-4"	56'-0"	(X-11)/9.8	270
45°	drive-in	8'-6"	17'-2"	12'-8"	47'-0"	(X-17)/12	282

Use 8'-0" for attendant parking; 8'-6" for customer parking.

maximum
15%
12%
preferred

PITCH OF RAMPS*

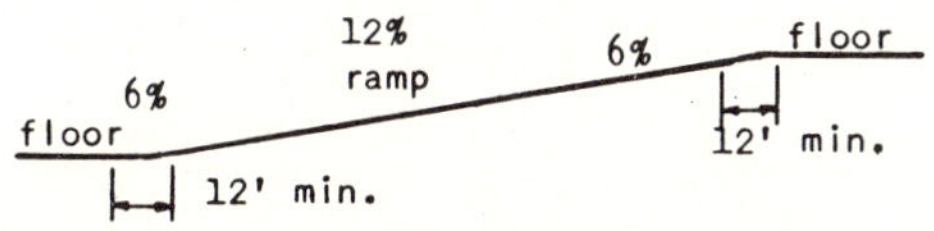
12%
ramp
6%
6%
floor
floor
12' min.
12' min.

BLENDING RAMP & FLOOR GRADES*

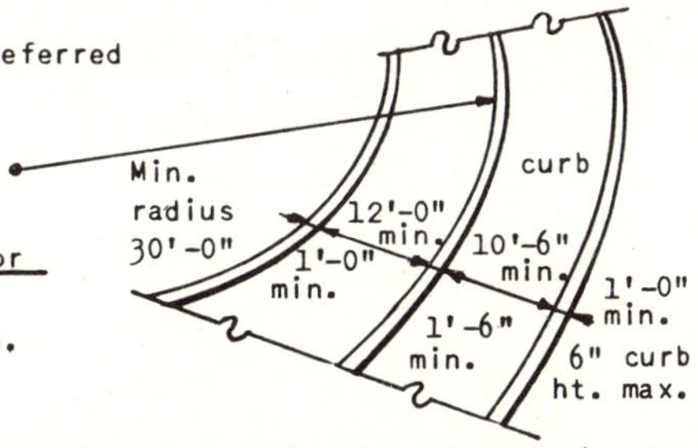
curb
Min.
radius
30'-0"
12'-0" min.
1'-0" min.
10'-6" min.
1'-0" min.
1'-6" min.
6" curb ht. max.

CURVED RAMP*

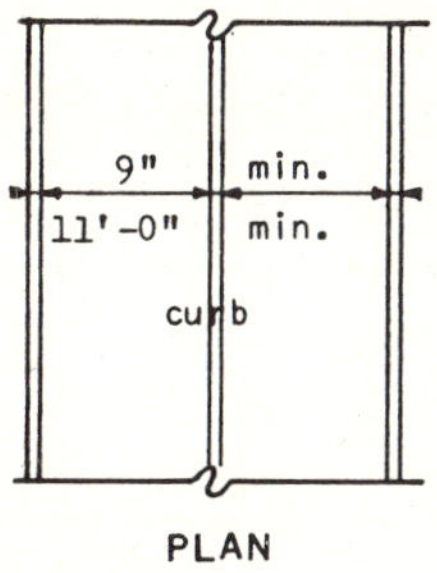
9"
min.
11'-0"
min.
curb
PLAN

STRAIGHT RAMP*

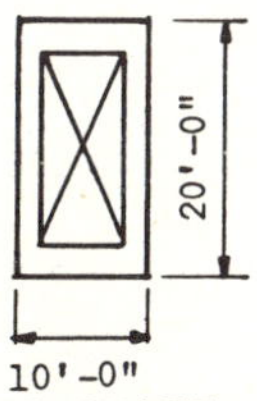
20'-0"
10'-0"

ELEVATOR SHAFT

Usually allow 1 elevator to 100 to 150 cars. Allow 1 minute for delivery.

DATA FOR COMMERCIAL GARAGES

*Data from "The Traffic Design of Parking Garages" by E. R. Ricker, published by the Eno Foundation. When clear span (see "E" in table above) is not available, use 25'-6" between column faces. Clear ceiling height 7'-6". Floor-to-floor height 8'-6" to 10'-0". Super elevation of curved ramps 0.1 to 0.15 foot per foot.

Provide extra width for walks along side of parking bay to compensate for bumper overhang.

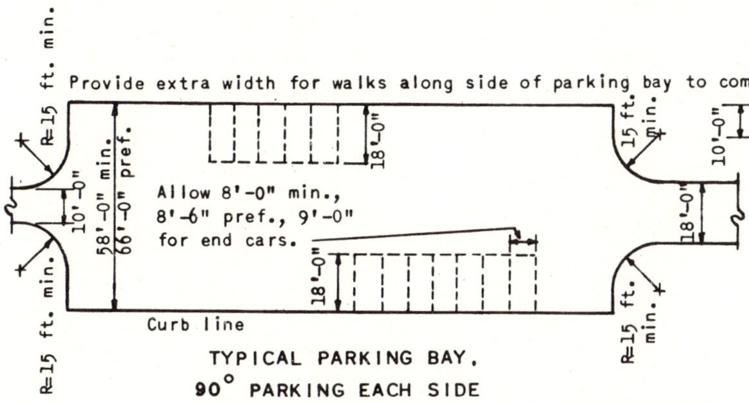
R=15 ft. min.
18'-0"
10'-0"
58'-0" min.
66'-0" pref.
Allow 8'-0" min., 8'-6" pref., 9'-0" for end cars.
18'-0"
15 ft. min.
18'-0"
R=15 ft. min.
R=15 ft. min.
Curb line

TYPICAL PARKING BAY, 90° PARKING EACH SIDE

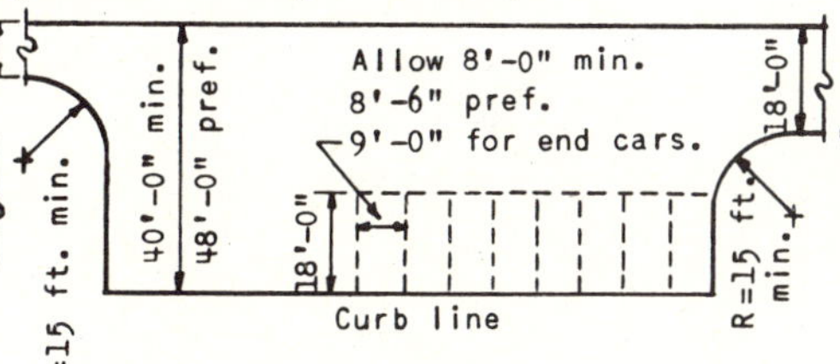
10'-0"
R=15 ft. min.
40'-0" min.
48'-0" pref.
Allow 8'-0" min.
8'-6" pref.
9'-0" for end cars.
18'-0"
18'-0"
R=15 ft. min.
Curb line

TYPICAL PARKING BAY, 90° PARKING ONE SIDE

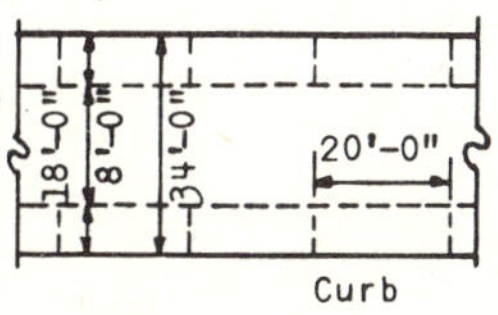
Curb
18'-0"
8'-0"
34'-0"
20'-0"
Curb

TYPICAL 2-LANE DRIVE, PARALLEL PARKING EACH SIDE

Allow 9'-0" for each additional lane in road or drive

OFF-STREET PARKING

Data supplied by Ralph Eberlin, C.E.

TRUCK and TRAILER SIZES

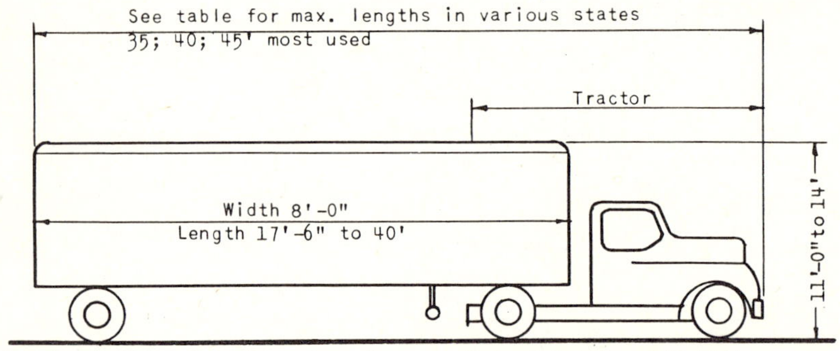
See table for max. lengths in various states
35; 40; 45' most used
Tractor
Width 8'-0"
Length 17'-6" to 40'
11'-0" to 14'

Turning radius of trailer depends on radius of tractor (24'-43')

Max. Length	States
45'	Ala. Conn. Ga. Ill. Iowa. Ky. Me. Mass. Minn. Miss. Mo. N.D. N.H. N.J. Ohio Tenn. Tex. Va. W.Va.
48'	N.C.
50'	Ark.D.C. Del.Fla.Ind.Kans.La.Nebr. N.Y. Okla. Ore. R.I. S.C. S.D. Vt. Wisc.
55'	Md. Mich.
60'	Calif.Colo. Idaho Mont.Utah.Wash.Wyo.
65'	Ariz. N.M. Nevada (no restriction)

SEMI-TRAILER & TRUCK TRACTOR

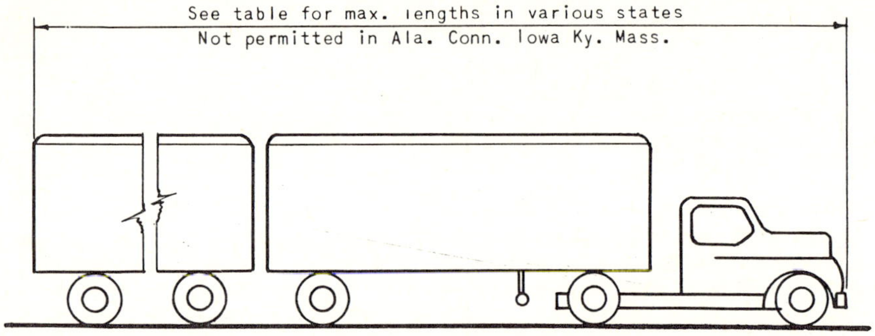
See table for max. lengths in various states
Not permitted in Ala. Conn. Iowa Ky. Mass.

In many western states combinations of truck & full trailer and tractor semi-trailer & full trailer are used to full legal length.

Max. Length	States
45'	Ga.Ill.Me.Minn.Miss.Mo.N.D. N.H. Tenn. Tex. Va. W.Va.
48'	N.C.
50'	Ark.D.C. Fla.Ind.Kans.Nebr. N.J. N.Y. Okla.Pa.R.I. S.C. S.D. Oreg.Vt.Wisc.
55'	Md. Mich.
60'	Calif. Colo. Del. La. Mont. Ohio. Wash. Wyo. Utah.
65'	Ariz.Idaho N.M. Nevada (no restriction)

FULL TRAILER SEMI-TRAILER & TRUCK TRACTOR

DATA CHECKED BY OPERATIONS COUNCIL, AMERICAN TRUCKING ASSOCIATIONS INC.

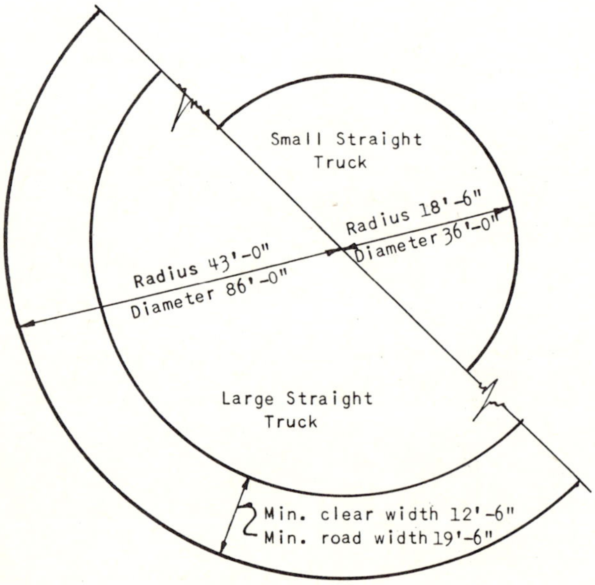
Small Straight Truck
Radius 18'-6"
Diameter 36'-0"
Radius 43'-0"
Diameter 86'-0"
Large Straight Truck
Min. clear width 12'-6"
Min. road width 19'-6"

MOTOR TRUCK
TURNING RADII

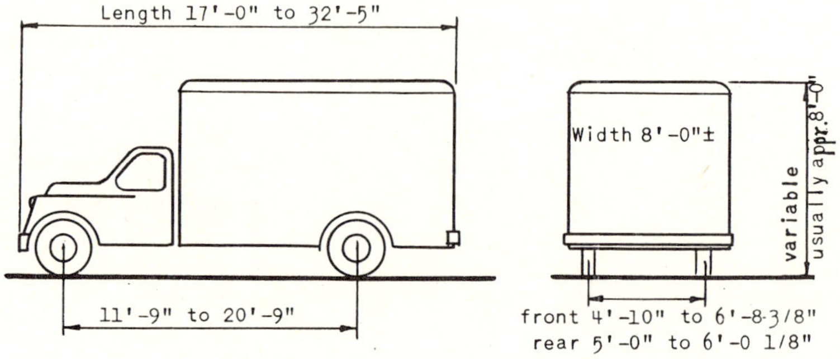
Length 17'-0" to 32'-5"
11'-9" to 20'-9"
Width 8'-0"±
variable
usually appr. 8'-0"
front 4'-10" to 6'-8 3/8"
rear 5'-0" to 6'-0 1/8"

VAN TYPE TRUCK

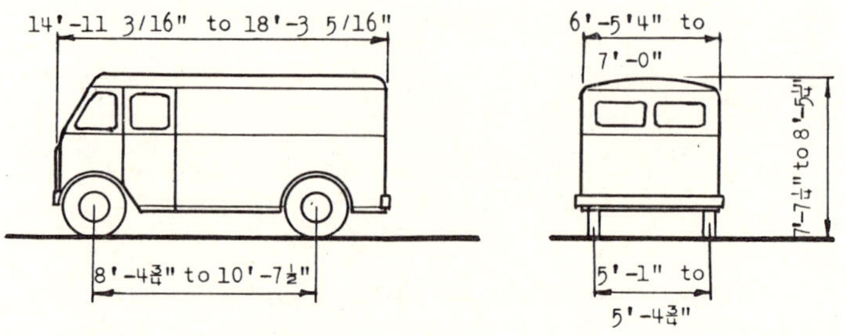
14'-11 3/16" to 18'-3 5/16"
8'-4 3/8" to 10'-7 1/2"
6'-5 1/4" to
7'-0"
7'-7 1/4" to 8'-5 1/4"
5'-1" to
5'-4 3/8"

DELIVERY TRUCK

DIMENSIONS OF MOTOR VEHICLES

TRUCKING DOCKS

Outside Single Doors:

Space between end of building and first door opening where there are stairs inside at dock 3'. No stairs a min. of 1'.

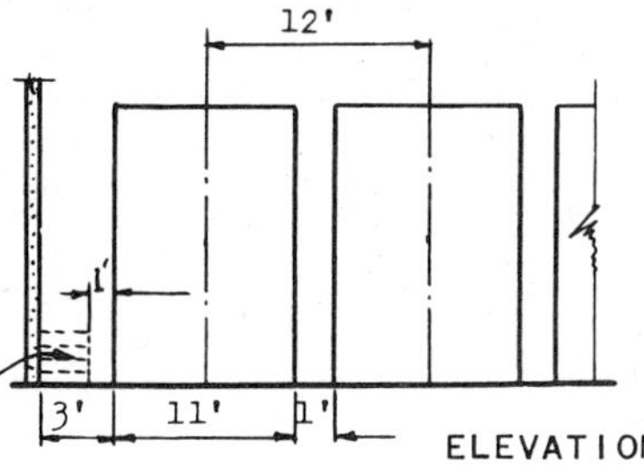
12'
1'
24" to 36" stairs inside at dock
3'
11'
1'
ELEVATION

Size of Vehicle	A clearance outside of bldg. includ. street	B clearance inside bldg.
50'	50'	55'
30'	30'	35'
25'	25'	30'

Double Doors

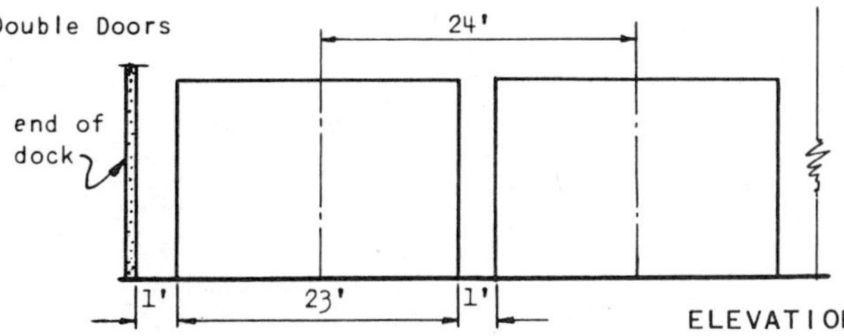
24'
end of dock
1'
23'
1'
ELEVATION

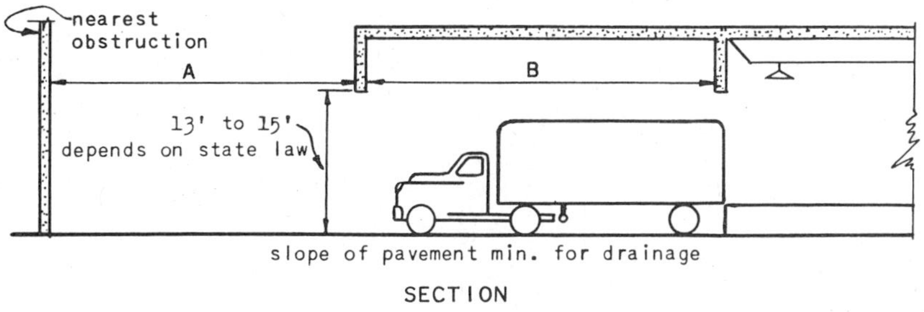
nearest obstruction
A
B
13' to 15' depends on state law
slope of pavement min. for drainage
SECTION

NOTE: All doors electrically operated. Width of doors depends on construction material of piers

CLOSED MOTOR CARRIER DOCK

Doors at Dock: Single Doors:

Space between end of bldg. & first door opening where there are no stairs min. 1'.

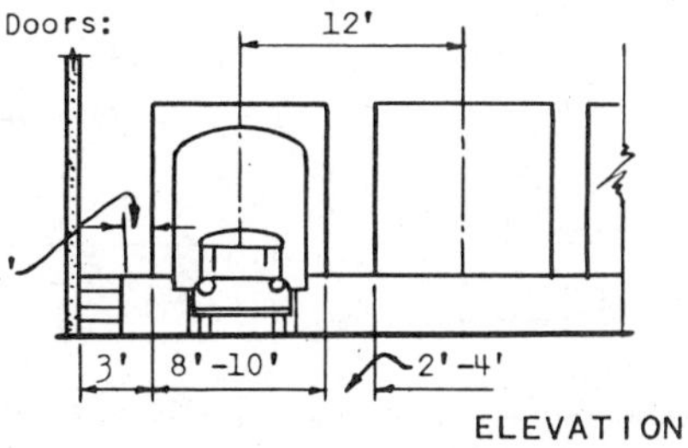
12'
min. 1'
3'
8'-10'
2'-4'
ELEVATION

Size of vehicle	A clearance from dock to nearest obstruction
50'	100'
30'	60'
25'	50'

Double Doors:

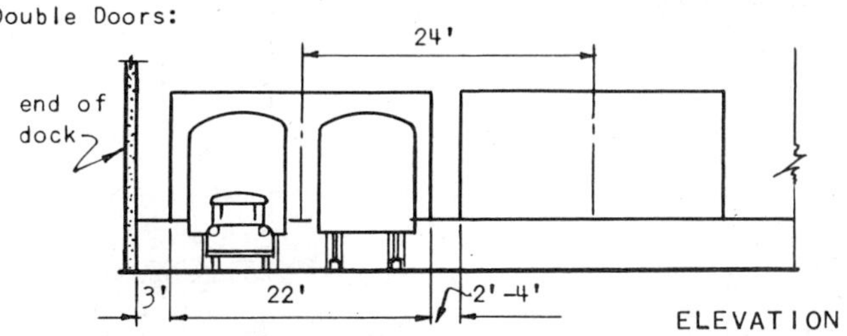
24'
end of dock
3'
22'
2'-4'
ELEVATION

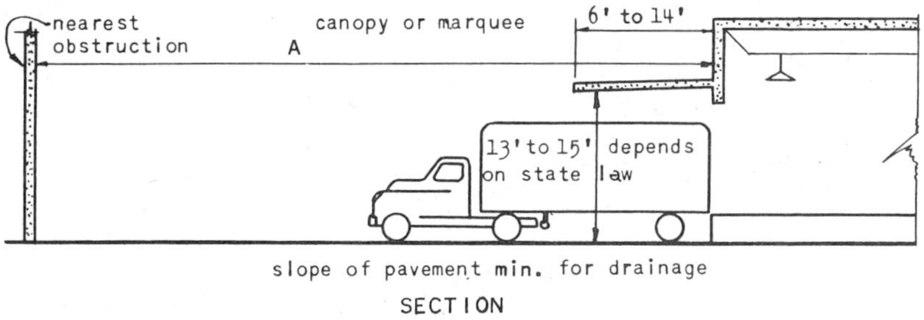
nearest obstruction
canopy or marquee
6' to 14'
A
13' to 15' depends on state law
slope of pavement min. for drainage
SECTION

NOTE: Width of doors depends on construction material of dock piers.

OPEN MOTOR CARRIER DOCK

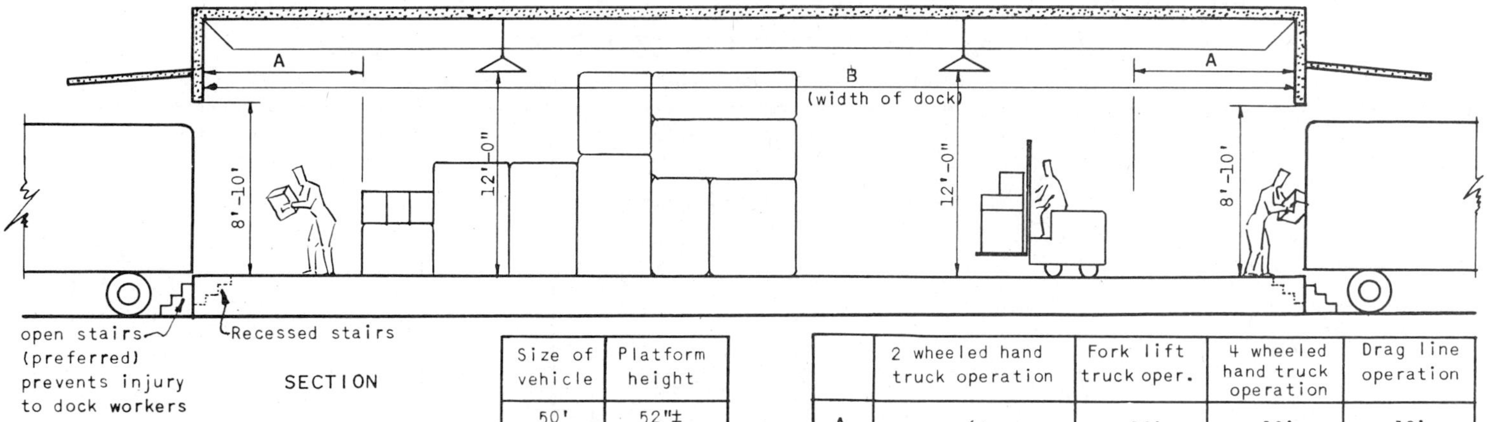
A
B
(width of dock)
A
8'-10'
12'-0"
12'-0"
8'-10'
open stairs (preferred) prevents injury to dock workers
Recessed stairs
SECTION

Size of vehicle	Platform height
50'	52"±
30'	48"±
25'	44"±

	2 wheeled hand truck operation	Fork lift truck oper.	4 wheeled hand truck operation	Drag line operation
A	6'	10'	10'	10'
B	50'	60'	70'	80'

NOTE: These dimensions same for all types of Motor Carrier Docks

MOTOR CARRIER DOCK CLEARANCES

DATA SUPPLIED BY OPERATIONS COUNCIL, AMERICAN TRUCKING ASSOCIATIONS INC.

TRUCKING-CLEARANCES and DETAILS

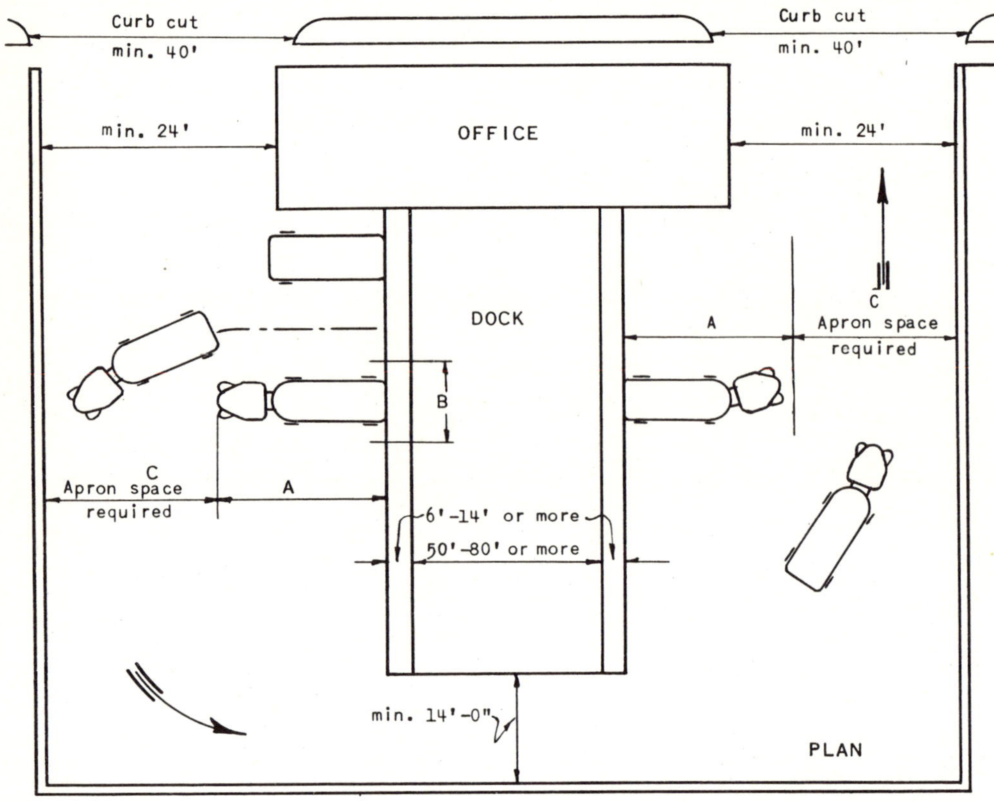
Curb cut
min. 40'
Curb cut
min. 40'
OFFICE
min. 24'
min. 24'
DOCK
A
C
Apron space
required
B
C
Apron space
required
A
6'-14' or more
50'-80' or more
min. 14'-0"
PLAN

Curb cut: used to prevent accident on swing into yard or gate.

Traffic flow #1
Counter clockwise around dock, preferred since it permits backing from left (driver's side)

APRON SPACE required for maneuver into or out of position for tractor trailer

A	B	C
Tractor trailer length	Width of position	Apron space required
35'	10' 12' 14'	46' 43' 39'
40'	10' 12' 14'	48' 44' 42'
45'	10' 12' 14'	57' 49' 48'

LOADING OF MOTOR VEHICLES

DATA SUPPLIED BY OPERATIONS COUNCIL, AMERICAN TRUCKING ASSOCIATIONS INC.

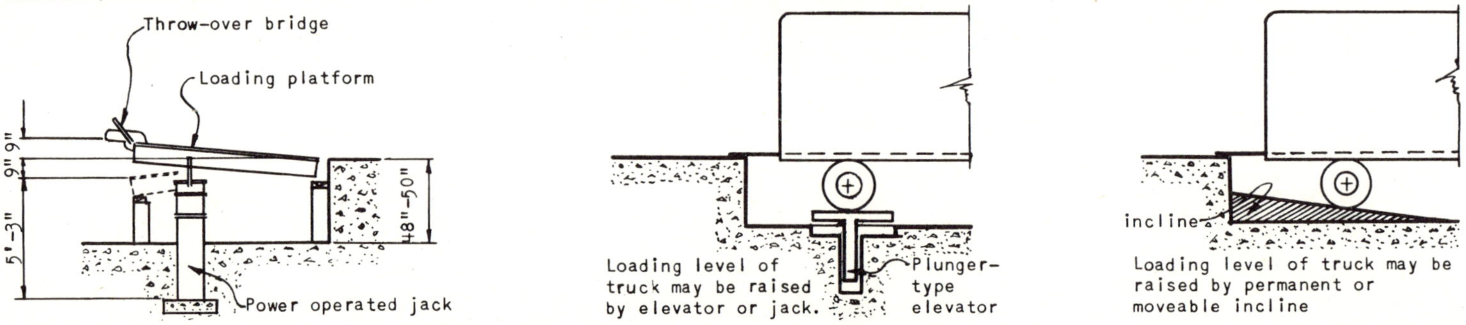
Throw-over bridge
Loading platform
9"
9"
5'-3"
48"-50"
Power operated jack
Loading level of truck may be raised by elevator or jack.
Plunger-type elevator
incline
Loading level of truck may be raised by permanent or moveable incline

Loading levels of trailer ("L") variable from 44" to 50" (48" to 54" for heavy-duty units). For van-type trucks 42" to 46" (44" to 46" average). For delivery trucks 25" to 31".

LOADING DOCK LEVELING DEVICES SECTIONS

DATA CHECKED BY OPERATIONS COUNCIL AMERICAN TRUCKING ASSOCIATIONS INC.

Used for protection of door jams, walls, and corners. May be combined with corners & col. guards.

Usually made of cast iron, ½" min. thickness. For heavy traffic, thicker metal is required.

Other patterns available. Sizes given are made by most manufacturers, though given pattern may vary.

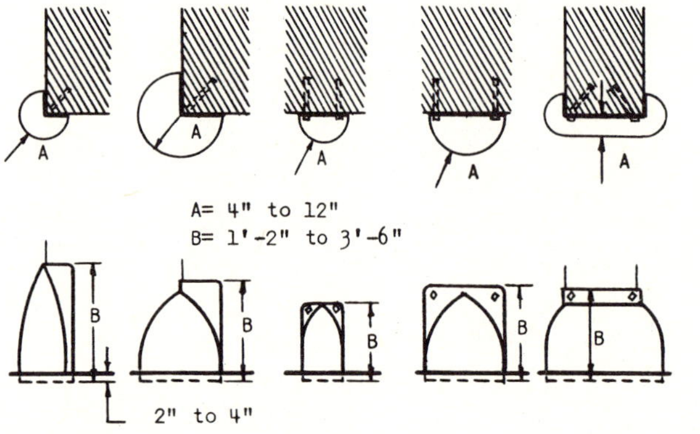
A
A
A
A
A
A= 4" to 12"
B= 1'-2" to 3'-6"
B
B
B
B
B
2" to 4"

WHEEL GUARDS

DATA FROM "ARCHITECTURAL METAL HANDBOOK" BY PERMISSION OF THE NATIONAL ASSOCIATION ARCHITECTURAL METAL MFRS.

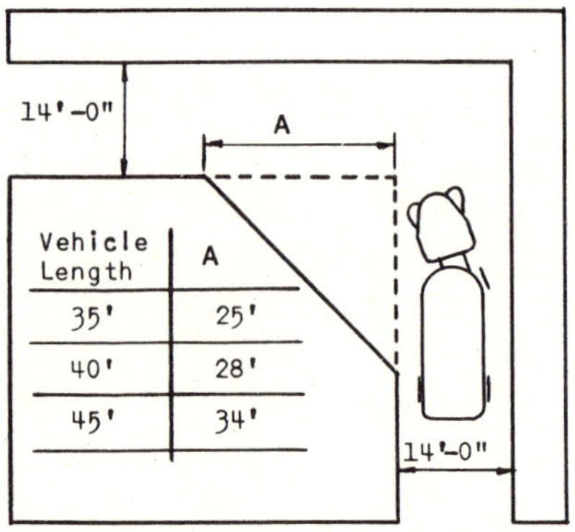
14'-0"
A
14'-0"

Vehicle Length	A
35'	25'
40'	28'
45'	34'

TURNING CLEARANCE FOR INSIDE DRIVEWAY

1953-54 CAR SIZES

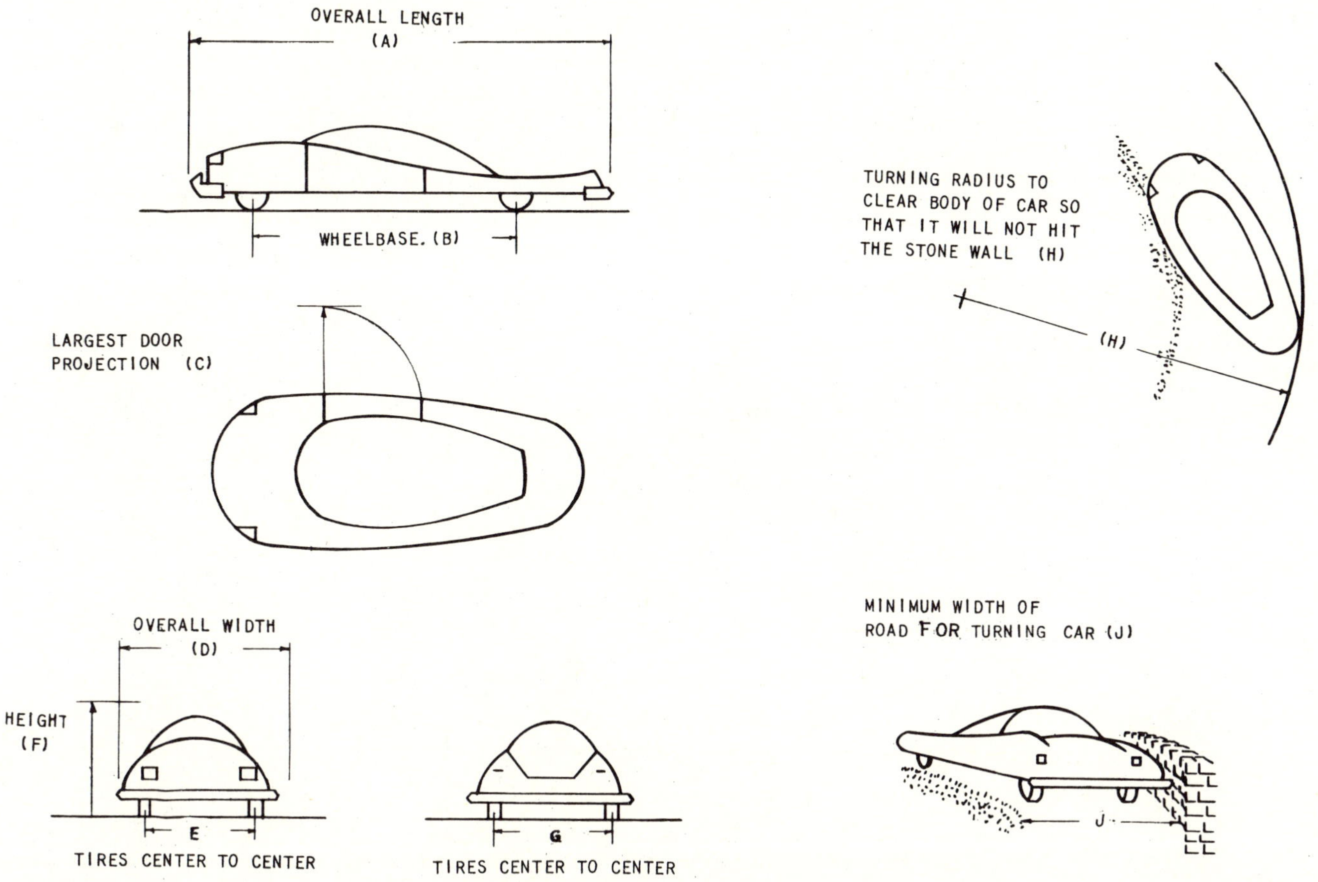
OVERALL LENGTH
(A)
WHEELBASE. (B)
TURNING RADIUS TO
CLEAR BODY OF CAR SO
THAT IT WILL NOT HIT
THE STONE WALL (H)
(H)
LARGEST DOOR
PROJECTION (C)
MINIMUM WIDTH OF
ROAD FOR TURNING CAR (J)
OVERALL WIDTH
(D)
HEIGHT
(F)
E
TIRES CENTER TO CENTER
G
TIRES CENTER TO CENTER
J

MAKE	MODEL	YEAR	A	B	C	D	E	F	G	H	J	K
BUICK	40	1953	17' 2"	10' 2"	2' 9"	6' 4"	5'	5' 4"	4' 11"	19' 9"		*
	50 & 70	1953	17' 4"	10' 2"	2' 8"	6' 8"	5'	5' 2"	5' 3"	19' 9"		2D
	50 & 70	1953	17' 8"	10' 5"	2' 8"	6' 8"	5'	5' 3"	5' 3"	20' 9"		4D
	SPECIAL 40	1954	17' 3"	10' 2"	2' 11"	6' 5"	4' 11"	5' 1"	4' 11"	20' 10"		*
	CENTURY 60	1954	17' 3"	10' 2"	2' 11"	6' 5"	4' 11"	5' 1"	4' 11"	20' 10"		4D
	CENTURY 60	1954	17' 3"	10' 2"	2' 11"	6' 5"	4' 11"	5' 0"	4' 11"	20' 10"		2D
	SUPER 50	1954	18' 1"	10' 7"	2' 10"	6' 8"	4' 11"	5' 3"	5' 3"	21' 6"		4D
	SUPER 50	1954	18' 1"	10' 7"	2' 10"	6' 8"	4' 11"	5' 0"	5' 3"	21' 6"		2D
	ROADMASTER 70	1954	18' 1"	10' 7"	2' 10"	6' 8"	4' 11"	5' 3"	5' 3"	21' 6"		4D
	ROADMASTER 70	1954	18' 1"	10' 7"	2' 10"	6' 8"	4' 11"	5' 1"	5' 3"	21' 6"		2D
CADILLAC	6237 6237D 6267	1953	18' 5"	10' 6"	2' 9"	6' 8"	4' 11"	5' 1"	5' 3"	21' 7"		2D
	6267S	1953	18' 5"	10' 6"	2' 9"	6' 8"	4' 11"	4' 10"	5' 3"	21' 7"		2D
	6219	1953	18'	10' 6"	2' 4"	6' 8"	4' 11"	5' 3"	5' 3"	21' 7"		4D
	6019	1953	18' 9"	10' 10"	2' 4"	6' 8"	4' 11"	5' 3"	5' 3"	22' 1"		4D
	75	1953	19' 9"	12' 3"	2' 4"	6' 8"	4' 11"	5' 4"	5' 3"	24' 1"		4D
	6237 6237D	1954	18' 7"	10' 9"	2' 7"	6' 8"	5'	5'	5' 3"	23' 8"		2D
	6267 6267S	1954	18' 7"	10' 9"	2' 7"	6' 8"	5'	5' 1"	5' 3"	23' 8"		2D
	6219	1954	18'	10' 9"	2' 4"	6' 8"	5'	5' 2"	5' 3"	23' 8"		4D
	6019	1954	18' 11"	11' 1"	2' 4"	6' 8"	5'	5' 2"	5' 3"	24' 4"		4D
	75	1954	19' 9"	12' 6"	2' 4"	6' 8"	5'	5' 4"	5' 3"	27' 1"		4D
CHEVROLET	1502 2102 2402 1504 1524 2124	1953	16' 4"	9' 7"		6' 3"	4' 9"	5' 5"	4' 11"	19'		2D
	2134 2434 2154 2454	1953	16' 4"	9' 7"		6' 3"	4' 9"	5' 4"	4' 11"	19'		2D
	1508	1953	16' 4"	9' 7"		6' 3"	4' 9"	5' 8"	4' 11"	19'		2D
	1503 2103 2403	1953	16' 4"	9' 7"		6' 3"	4' 9"	5' 5"	4' 11"	19'		4D
	1509 2109 2119	1953	16' 6"	9' 7"		6' 3"	4' 9"	5' 9"	4' 11"	19'		4D
	1502 1512 2102 2124 2402	1954	16' 5"	9' 7"		6' 3"	4' 9"	5' 5"	4' 11"	19'		2D
	2434 2454	1954	16' 5"	9' 7"		6' 3"	4' 9"	5' 4"	4' 11"	19'		2D
	1508	1954	16' 5"	9' 7"		6' 3"	4' 9"	5' 8"	4' 11"	19'		2D
	1503 2103 2403	1954	16' 5"	9' 7"		6' 3"	4' 9"	5' 5"	4' 11"	19'		4D
	1509 2109 2419	1954	16' 7"	9' 7"		6' 3"	4' 9"	5' 9"	4' 11"	19'		4D

* Dimensions identical for two & four door models

NOTE: Dimensions shown are to nearest inch above actual size.

1953-54 CAR SIZES

MAKE	MODEL	YEAR	A	B	C	D	E	F	G	H	J	K
AUSTIN	SEDAN A30	†	11' 5"	6' 8"		4' 8"	3' 9"	4' 11"	3' 9"	17' 6"		2D
	CONV A40	†	13' 4"	7' 9"		5' 3"	4' 1"	5' 2"	4' 2"	18' 6"		2D
	SEDAN A40	†	13' 4"	7' 9"		5' 3"	4' 1"	5' 4"	4' 2"	18' 6"		4D
	HEALY	†	12' 2"	7' 6"			4' 1"	3' 1"	4' 2"	17' 6"		2D
CHRYSLER	C60-1 C60-2 C56-1 C56-2	1953	17' 7"	10' 6"	3'	6' 5"	4' 9"	5' 3"	5'	22'		*
	C58	1953	18' 3"	11' 2"	3'	6' 5"	4' 10"	5' 3"	5' 1"			4D
	C59	1953	18' 2"	12' 2"	3'	6' 10"	4' 10"	5' 9"	5' 6"			4D
	WINSOR DELUXE C62 NEW YORKER C63-1 } NEW YORKER DELUXE C63-2	1954	18'	10' 6"	2' 11"	6' 6"	4' 9"	5' 3"	5'	22' 3"	10'	*
	CUSTOM IMPERIAL C64	1954	18' 8"	11' 2"	2' 11"	6' 6"	4' 10"	5' 3"	5' 1"	23' 7"	10' 2"	4D
	CUSTOM IMPERIAL NEWPORT	1954	18' 6"	11'	2' 11"	6' 6"	4' 10"	5' 3"	5' 1"	23' 2"	10' 2"	2D
DE SOTO	S18 S16	1953	17' 10"	10' 6"	2' 11"	6' 6"	4' 9"	5' 3"	5'	21'		*
	FIREDOME S19 POWERMASTER S20	1954	17' 11"	10' 6"	2' 11"	6' 6"	4' 9"	5' 3"	5'	22'	9' 9"	*
DODGE	D46 D46 SPECIAL	1953	16' 10"	9' 11"	2' 11"	6' 2"	4' 9"	5' 2"	5'	20' 9"		*
	D44	1953	16' 10"	9' 11"	2' 11"	6' 2"	4' 8"	5' 2"	4' 11"	20' 8"		*
	D47	1953	15' 10"	9' 6"	3' 6"	6' 2"	4' 9"	5' 3"	5'	20' 8"		2D
	D48	1953	16'	9' 6"	3' 5"	6' 2"	4' 8"	5' 1"	4' 11"	19' 10"		2D
	D51-1	1954	17' 2"	9' 11"	2' 11"	6' 2"	4' 9"	5' 2"	5'	21' 4"	9' 4"	*
	D51-2	1954	17' 2"	9' 11"	2' 11"	6' 2"	4' 8"	5' 2"	4' 11"	21' 4"	9' 4"	*
	D52	1954	16' 4"	9' 11"	3' 6"	6' 2"	4' 9"	5' 3"	5'	20' 6"	9' 3"	4D
	D52	1954	15' 11"	9' 6"	3' 6"	6' 2"	4' 9"	5' 3"	5'	20' 6"	9' 3"	2D
	D50-3	1954	17' 2"	9' 11"	2' 10"	6' 3"	4' 8"	5' 2"	4' 11"	20'	9' 4"	*
	D52-2	1954	16' 4"	9' 6"	3' 5"	6' 2"	4' 8"	5' 1"	4' 11"	20' 3"	9' 3"	*
	D53-3	1954	16' 4"	9' 6"	3' 5"	6' 2"	4' 8"	5' 1"	4' 11"	20' 3"	9' 3"	2D
	D50-1 D50-2	1954	17' 2"	9' 11"	2' 11"	6' 2"	4' 8"	5' 2"	4' 11"	20'	9' 4"	*
FORD INTERNATIONAL	ANGLIA	†	12' 7"	7' 3"	2' 6"	5'	4'	4' 11"	3' 11"	16' 6"	7'	2D
	PREFECT	†	12' 7"	7' 3"	2' 6"	5'	4'	4' 11"	3' 11"	16' 6"	7'	4D
	CONSUL	†	13' 8"	8' 4"	2' 8"	5' 4"	4' 2"	5' 1"	4' 1"	20'	8'	4D
	ZEPHYR	†	14' 4"	8' 8"	2' 8"	5' 4"	4' 2"	5' 1"	4' 1"	21'	8'	4D
FORD	60A 60B 76B	1953	16' 6"	9' 7"	3' 6"	6' 3"	4' 10"	5' 3"	4' 8"	21' 8"	9' 5"	2D
	70A 70B 72B	1953	16' 6"	9' 7"	3' 6"	6' 3"	4' 10"	5' 4"	4' 8"	21' 8"	9' 5"	2D
	72G	1953	16' 6"	9' 7"	3' 7"	6' 2"	4' 10"	5' 4"	4' 8"	21' 8"	9' 5"	2D
	59A	1953	16' 6"	9' 7"	3' 7"	6' 2"	4' 10"	5' 6"	4' 8"	21' 8"	9' 5"	2D
	73A 73B	1953	16' 6"	9' 7"	3'	6' 3"	4' 10"	5' 5"	4' 8"	21' 8"	9' 5"	4D
	79B	1953	16' 6"	9' 7"	3'	6' 3"	4' 10"	5' 6"	4' 8"	21' 8"	9' 5"	4D
	78A	1953	16' 6"	9' 7"	3' 7"	6' 2"	4' 10"	5' 6"	4' 8"	21' 8"	9' 5"	4D
	60A 60B 60F 76B	1954	16' 7"	9' 8"	3' 6"	6' 3"	4' 10"	5' 3"	4' 8"			2D
	70B 72B 72C	1954	16' 7"	9' 8"	3' 6"	6' 3"	4' 10"	5' 4"	4' 8"			2D
	73B	1954	16' 7"	9' 8"	3'	6' 3"	4' 10"	5' 5"	4' 8"			4D
	59A	1954	16' 7"	9' 8"	3' 6"	6' 3"	4' 10"	5' 6"	4' 8"			2D
	79B	1954	16' 7"	9' 8"	3'	6' 3"	4' 10"	5' 6"	4' 8"			4D
	78A	1954	16' 7"	9' 8"	3' 6"	6' 3"	4' 10"	5' 7"	4' 8"			2D
HILLMAN	SEDAN	†	13' 4"	7' 9"		5' 4"	4' 1"	5'	4' 1"	16' 6"		4D
	CONV COUPE & HARDTOP	†	13' 4"	7' 9"		5' 4"	4' 1"	4' 11"	4' 1"	16' 6"		2D
	ESTATE CAR	†	13' 8"	7' 9"		5' 4"	4' 1"	5' 6"	4' 1"	16' 6"		2D
HUDSON	JET 1C SUPER JET 2C IN '54 1D 2D 3D	†	15' 1"	8' 9"	3'	5' 8"	4' 6"	5' 1"	4' 4"	21' 6"		*
	WASP DELUXE 4C IN '54 4D	†	16' 10"	10'	2' 11"	6' 6"	4' 11"	5' 1"	4' 8"	22' 3"		4D
	WASP DELUXE 4C IN '54 4D	†	16' 10"	10'		6' 6"	4' 11"	5' 1"	4' 8"	22' 3"		2D
	WASP SUPER 5C IN '54 5D	†	16' 11"	10'	2' 11"	6' 6"	4' 11"	5' 1"	4' 8"	22' 3"		4D
	WASP SUPER 5C IN '54 5D	†	16' 11"	10'		6' 6"	4' 11"	5' 1"	4' 8"	22' 3"		2D
	HORNET 7C IN '54 7D	†	17' 5"	10' 4"	2' 11"	6' 6"	4' 11"	5' 1"	4' 8"	23' 5"		4D
	HORNET 7C IN '54 7D	†	17' 5"	10' 4"		6' 6"	4' 11"	5' 1"	4' 8"	23' 5"		2D
HUMBER	HAWK SEDAN	†	15' 1"	8' 10"		5' 10"	4' 8"	5' 5"	4' 9"	18' 6"		4D
	SUPER SNIPE SEDAN	†	16' 5"	9' 8"		6' 2"	4' 10"	5' 6"	4' 9"	20'		4D
KAISER	MANHATTAN & DELUXE	†	17' 8"	9' 11"	3' 3"	6' 3"	4' 10"	5' 2"	4' 11"	20' 9"	10'	2D
	MANHATTAN DELUXE	†	17' 8"	9' 11"	2' 5"	6' 3"	4' 10"	5' 2"	4' 11"	20' 9"	10'	4D
LINCOLN	60A 60B 76A	1953	17' 11"	10' 3"	3' 1"	6' 6"	4' 11"	5' 3"	4' 11"	24' 1"	9' 8"	2D
	73A 73B	1953	17' 11"	10' 3"	3'	6' 6"	4' 11"	5' 3"	4' 11"	24' 1"	9' 8"	4D
	60A 60C 76A	1954	17' 11"	10' 3"	3' 7"	6' 6"	4' 11"	5' 3"	4' 11"			2D
	73B	1954	17' 11"	10' 3"	3'	6' 6"	4' 11"	5' 5"	4' 11"			4D

* Dimensions identical for two & four door models.

† Dimensions & models similar for 1953 & 1954

NOTE: Dimensions shown are to nearest inch above actual size.

1953-54 CAR SIZES

MAKE	MODEL	YEAR	A	B	C	D	E	F	G	H	J	K
MERCURY	60B 60E 76B	1953	16' 11"	9' 10"	3' 6"	6' 2"	4' 10"	5' 3"	4' 8"	22' 6"	9' 4"	2D
	70A 70B 70D	1953	16' 11"	9' 10"	3' 6"	6' 2"	4' 10"	5' 5"	4' 8"	22' 6"	9' 4"	2D
	73B 73C	1953	16' 11"	9' 10"	3' 1"	6' 2"	4' 10"	5' 5"	4' 8"	22' 6"	9' 4"	4D
	79B 79D	1953	16' 11"	9' 10"	3' 1"	6' 2"	4' 10"	5' 6"	4' 8"	22' 6"	9' 4"	4D
	60B 60E 76B	1954	17'	9' 10"	3' 6"	6' 3"	4' 10"	5' 3"	4' 8"			2D
	70B 70D	1954	17'	9' 10"	3' 6"	6' 3"	4' 10"	5' 5"	4' 8"			2D
	73C	1954	17'	9' 10"	3' 6"	6' 3"	4' 10"	5' 5"	4' 8"			4D
	79B 79D	1954	17'	9' 10"	3' 6"	6' 3"	4' 10"	5' 6"	4' 8"			4D
NASH	5340	1953	16' 11"	9' 7"	3'	6' 6"	4' 8"	5' 2"	5'	22' 10"		4D
	5340	1953	16' 11"	9' 7"	3' 6"	6' 6"	4' 8"	5' 2"	5'	22' 10"		2D
	5360	1953	17' 6"	10' 2"	3'	6' 6"	4' 8"	5' 3"	5' 1"	23' 11"		4D
	5360	1953	17' 6"	10' 2"	3' 6"	6' 6"	4' 8"	5' 3"	5' 1"	23' 11"		2D
	5440	1954	16' 11"	9' 7"	3'	6' 6"	4' 8"	5' 2"	5'	23' 3"	10'	4D
	5440	1954	16' 11"	9' 7"	3' 6"	6' 6"	4' 8"	5' 2"	5'	23' 3"	10'	2D
	5460	1954	17' 6"	10' 2"	3'	6' 6"	4' 8"	5' 3"	5' 1"	24'	10'	4D
	5460	1954	17' 6"	10' 2"	3' 6"	6' 6"	4' 8"	5' 3"	5' 1"	24'	10'	2D
	5450	1954	17' 9"	9' 7"	3'	6' 6"	4' 8"	5' 2"	5'	23' 3"	10'	4D
	5450	1954	17' 9"	9' 7"	3' 6"	6' 6"	4' 8"	5' 2"	5'	23' 3"	10'	2D
	5470	1954	18' 4"	10' 2"	3'	6' 6"	4' 8"	5' 3"	5' 1"	24'	10'	4D
	5470	1954	18' 4"	10' 2"	3' 6"	6' 6"	4' 8"	5' 3"	5' 1"	24'	10'	2D
OLDSMOBILE	DELUXE & SUPER 88	1953	17' 2"	10'	2' 9"	6' 5"	4' 11"	5' 4"	4' 11"	23' 3"	9' 8"	*
	98	1953	17' 10"	10' 4"	2' 9"	6' 5"	4' 11"	5' 4"	4' 11"	23' 4"	10' 4"	*
	88 & SUPER 88	1954	17' 2"	10' 2"	2' 6"	6' 7"	4' 11"	5' 1"	4' 10"	22' 7"	9' 8"	4D
	98	1954	17' 11"	10' 6"	2' 6"	6' 7"	4' 11"	5' 1"	4' 10"	23' 2"	10' 4"	4D
	88 & SUPER 88	1954	17' 2"	10' 2"	3' 5"	6' 7"	4' 11"	5' 1"	4' 10"	22' 7"	9' 8"	2D
	98	1954	17' 11"	10' 6"	3' 5"	6' 7"	4' 11"	5' 1"	4' 10"	23' 2"	10' 4"	2D
PACKARD	2601 2611	1953	17' 10"	10' 2"	4' 1"	6' 6"	5'	5' 3"	5' 1"	21' 6"		2D
	2601 2611	1953	17' 10"	10' 2"	3' 5"	6' 6"	5'	5' 3"	5' 1"	21' 6"		4D
	2631	1953	17' 10"	10' 2"	3' 9"	6' 6"	5'	5' 2"	5' 2"	21' 6"		2D
	CARIBBEAN	1953	18' 6"	10' 2"	3' 9"	6' 6"	5'	5' 2"	5' 2"	21' 6"		2D
	2602 2606	1953	18' 3"	10' 7"	3' 9"	6' 6"	5'	5' 3"	5' 2"	22' 6"		4D
	5400	1954	18'	10' 2"	3' 9"	6' 6"	5'	5' 3"	5'	21' 6"		2D
	5431	1954	17' 8"	10' 2"	3' 9"	6' 6"	5'	5' 3"	5' 1"	21' 6"		2D
	5401 5411	1954	18'	10' 2"	4' 1"	6' 6"	5'	5' 3"	5'	21' 6"		2D
	5402 5406	1954	18' 1"	10' 7"	3' 9"	6' 6"	5'	5' 3"	5' 1"	22' 6"		4D
	CARIBBEAN	1954	18' 6"	10' 2"	3' 9"	6' 6"	5'	5' 2"	5' 1"	21' 6"		2D
	5401 5411	1954	18'	10' 2"	3' 5"	6' 6"	5'	5' 3"	5'	21' 6"		4D
PLYMOUTH	P24-1 P24-2	1953	15' 10"	9' 6"	2' 10"	6' 2"	4' 8"	5' 2"	4' 11"	20' 6"	9' 2"	*
	P25-1	1954	16' 2"	9' 6"	2' 10"	6' 2"	4' 8"	5' 2"	4' 11"	20' 6"	9' 2"	*
	P25-2 P25-3	1954	16' 2"	9' 6"	2' 10"	6' 3"	4' 8"	5' 2"	4' 11"	20' 6"	9' 2"	*
PONTIAC	25 & 27	1953	16' 11"	10' 2"	3' 2"	6' 5"	4' 11"	5' 4"	5'	20' 2"		2D
	25 & 27	1953	16' 11"	10' 2"	2' 9"	6' 5"	4' 11"	5' 4"	5'	20' 2"		4D
	25 27	1954	16' 11"	10' 2"	3' 2"	6' 5"	4' 11"	5' 4"	5'	20' 7"		2D
	25 27	1954	16' 11"	10' 2"	2' 9"	6' 5"	4' 11"	5' 4"	5'	20' 7"		4D
	28	1954	17' 10"	10' 4"	3' 2"	6' 5"	4' 11"	5' 4"	5'	21' 5"		2D
	28	1954	17' 10"	10' 4"	2' 9"	6' 5"	4' 11"	5' 4"	5'	21' 5"		4D
ROVER	SEDAN 75 SEDAN 90	1954	14' 11"	9' 3"		5' 6"	4' 4"	5' 4"	4' 4"	18' 6"		4D
STUDEBAKER	CHAMP. & COMDR.	1953	16' 7"	9' 9"	2' 10"	5' 10"	4' 9"	5' 1"	4' 8"	21'		4D
	CHAMP. & COMDR.	1953	16' 7"	9' 9"	3' 3"	5' 10"	4' 9"	5' 1"	4' 8"	21'		2D
	COUPE & HARDTOP	1953	16' 10"	10' 1"	3' 5"	5' 11"	4' 9"	4' 9"	4' 8"	21' 9"		*
	LAND CRUISER	1953	16' 11"	10' 1"	2' 10"	5' 10"	4' 9"	5' 1"	4' 8"	21' 9"		4D
	CHAMP. & COMM.	1954	16' 7"	9' 9"	2' 10"	5' 10"	4' 9"	5'	4' 8"	21'		4D
	CHAMP.& COMM. COUPE & HARDTOP	1954	16' 11"	10' 1"		5' 11"	4' 9"	4' 9"	4' 8"	21' 9"		*
	CHAMP. & COMM. STATIONWAGON	1954	16' 4"	9' 9"		5' 10"	4' 9"	5' 3"	4' 8"	21'		*
	LAND CRUISER	1954	16' 11"	10' 1"	2' 10"	5' 10"	4' 9"	5'	4' 8"	21' 9"		4D
SUNBEAM	SEDAN	†	14'	8' 2"		5' 3"	4'	5' 1"	4' 3"	18' 6"		4D
	CONV. COUPE	†	14'	8' 2"		5' 3"	4'	4' 11"	4' 3"	18' 6"		2D
	ALPINE	†	14' 1"	8' 2"		5' 3"	4'	4' 8"	4' 3"	18' 6"		2D
WILLYS	ACE	†	15' 3"	9'	3' 4"	6'	4' 10"	5' 2"	4' 9"	21' 6"	8' 8"	2D
	ACE	†	15' 3"	9'	2' 10"	6'	4' 10"	5' 2"	4' 9"	21' 6"	8' 8"	4D

* Dimensions identical for two & four door models

† Dimensions & models similar for 1953 & 1954

NOTE: Dimensions shown are to nearest inch above actual size.

1955 CAR SIZES

MAKE	MODEL	YEAR	A	B	C	D	E	F	G	H	J	K
AUSTIN	ALL MODELS	1955	Same as 1954									
BUICK	SPECIAL 40 ROADMASTER 70	1955 1955	17'3" 18'	10'2" 10'7"	NA NA	6'5" 6'8"	4'11" 4'11"	5'1" 5'3"	4'11" 5'3"	20'9" 21'6"		
CADILLAC	6219 7523, 7533	1955 1955	18'1" 19'10"	10'9" 12'6"	3'-1" 3'	6'8" 6'8"	5' 5'	5'5" 5'7"	5'4" 5'4"	22'11" 27'1"		4D 4D
CHEVROLET	1502,1512,2102,2124,2402 1503,2103,2403,2434,2154,2454 1529,2129,2109,2409,1508,2429	1955 1955	16'4" 16'6"	9'7" 9'7"	2'8" to 3'4"	6'2" 6'2"	4'10" 4'10"	5'1" to 5'3"	4'11" 4'11"	20'6" 20'6"		* *
CHRYSLER	C67-C68	1955	18'2"	10'6"	3'2"	6'7"	5'0"	5'2"	5'	21'10"	8'6"	*
DE SOTO	S21-S22	1955	18'2"	10'6"	3'8"	6'7"	5'1"	5'1"	5'	23'2"	9'10"	*
DODGE	D55,D56 Exc. Suburban D55 Suburban	1955 1955	17'8" 17'11"	10' 10'	3'2" 3'10"	6'2" 6'2"	4'11" 4'11"	5' 5'1"	4'11" 4'11"	21'2" 21'5"	9' 9'3"	* *
FORD INTER-NATIONAL	All Models	1955	Same as 1954									
FORD	Tudor Sedan 70 A.B.C. Fordor 73 Crown Victoria 64 A.B. conv. 76B Victoria 60B	1955	16'7"	9'8"	NA	6'4"	4'10"	5'3" 5'1" 5'2"	4'8"	20'8"	NA	* * *
	Station wagon 59A,B,79B,C.	1955	16'6"	9'8"	NA	6'4"	4'10"	5'4"	4'8"	20'8"	NA	*
HILLMAN	Husky Mark VIII	1955 1955	12'2" 13'7"	7'0" 7'9"	NA NA	5'4" 5'4"	4'1" 4'1"	5'1" 5'1"	4'1" 4'1"	15'6" 16'6"	NA NA	2D *
HUDSON	Rambler 5510 Hornet 8	1955 1955	14'11" 18'4"	8'4" 10'2"	3'3" 3'0"	6'2" 6'6"	4'7" 5'	5' 5'3"	4'5" 5'1"	19' 22'7"		2D 4D
HUMBER	Hawk Mk VI Super Snipe Mk IV B	1955 1955	15'1" 16'5"	8'10" 9'8"	NA NA	6'0" 6'2"	4'8" 4'10"	5'5" 5'6"	4'9" 4'9"	18'6" 22'	NA NA	4D 4D
IMPERIAL	C69 C70	1955 1955	18'8" 20'4"	10'10" 12'6"	3'6" 3'2"	6'7" 6'7"	5'2" 5'2"	5'2" 5'3"	5'0" 5'1"	22'7" 25'11"	8'11" 10'2"	4D 4D
KAISER	All Models	1955	Same as 1954									
LINCOLN	60A, 60C, 76A 73A, 73B	1955 1955	18' 18'	10'3" 10'3"	3'7" 3'	6'6" 6'6"	4'11" 4'11"	5'2" 5'3"	5' 5'	22'11" 22'11"		
MERCURY	79 BC 60B,E,64A,B,70B,73B,C,58A,76B	1955 1955	16'10" 17'2"	9'10" 9'11"	3'1"	6'5" 6'5"	4'10" 4'1"	5'3" 5'	4'9" 4'11"	21'6" 21'6"		*
METROPOLITAN		1955	12'6"	7'1"	3'1"	5'2"	3'10"	4'6"	3'9"	19'		2D
NASH	Ambassador 8	1955	18'4"	10'2"	3'-0"	6'6"	5'-0"	5'-3"	5'-1"	23'-6"		4D
OLDSMOBILE	88-Sedan & Holiday Coupe 98-Holiday Coupe & Starfire	1955 1955	17'0" 17'9"	10'2" 10'6"	2'6" 3'5"	6'6" 6'6"	4'11" 4'11"	5'1" 5'	4'10" 4'10"	21' 21'6"	9'8" 10'4"	4D 2D
PACKARD	5540,5560 5580	1955 1955	17'11" 18'3"	10'2" 10'7"	2'11" 2'11"	6'6" 6'6"	5' 5'	5'2" 5'3"	5'1" 5'1"	21'6" 22'6"	NA NA	* *
PLYMOUTH	4 Door Sedan Suburban P27	1955 1955	17' 17'5"	9'7" 9'7"	3'2" 3'10"	6'2" 6'2"	4'11" 4'11"	5'2" 5'2"	4'11" 4'11"	20'6" 20'6"	10'10" 10'10"	4D 2D
PONTIAC	27 Series 28 Series	1955 1955	17'1" 17'8"	10'2" 10'4"	3'4" 3'4"	6'4" 6'4"	4'11" 4'11"	5'1" 5'1"	5' 5'	21'2" 21'6"	NA NA	* *
ROVER	90	1955	14'11"	9'3"	NA	5'6"	4'8"	5'4"	4'8"	18'6"	NA	
STUDEBAKER	Champ, & Comdr. Station Wagons President 4 Door Sedan	1955 1955	16'6" 17'3"	9'9" 10'1"	3'3" 2'10"	5'11" 5'11"	4'9" 4'9"	5'2" 5'1"	4'8" 4'8"	20'6" 19'9"	NA NA	
SUNBEAM	MK III	1955	14'	8'2"	NA	5'3"	4'	5'1"	4'3"	18'3"		
WILLYS	CJ 3B Jeep	1955	10'10"	6'8"	NA	5'9"	4'1"	5'7"	4'1"	19'11"	NA	

* Dimension identical for two and four door models. NOTE: Dimensions shown are to nearest inch above actual size. Only the smallest and largest models of each mfg. are shown. NA-Dimensions not available

PARK EQUIPMENT

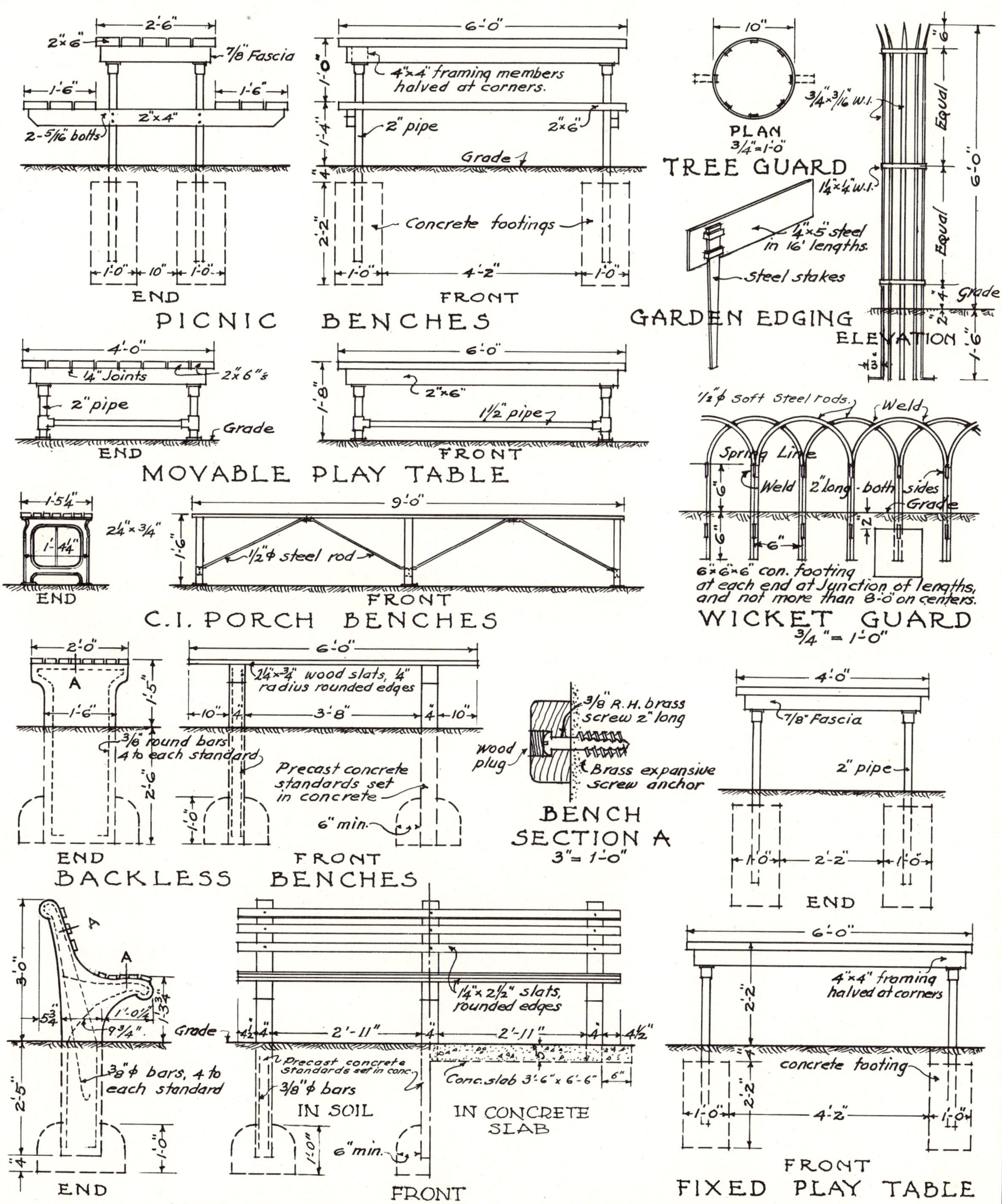

2'-6"
2"×6"
7/8" Fascia
1'-6"
1'-6"
2"×4"
2-5/16" bolts
1'-0"
10"
1'-0"
END
6'-0"
4"×4" framing members halved at corners.
1'-0"
1'-4"
2" pipe
2"×6"
Grade
4"
2'-2"
Concrete footings
1'-0"
4'-2"
1'-0"
FRONT
PICNIC BENCHES
10"
PLAN
3/4"=1'-0"
TREE GUARD
3/4"×3/16" W.I.
1/4"×1/4" W.I.
Equal
Equal
6'-0"
6"
Grade
4"
2"
1'-6"
3"
ELEVATION
1/4"×5" steel in 16' lengths.
Steel stakes
GARDEN EDGING
4'-0"
1/4" Joints
2"×6"s
2" pipe
Grade
END
6'-0"
1'-8"
2"×6"
1 1/2" pipe
FRONT
MOVABLE PLAY TABLE
1'-5 1/4"
2 1/4"×3/4"
1'-4 1/4"
END
9'-0"
1'-6"
1/2"ϕ steel rod
FRONT
C.I. PORCH BENCHES
1/2"ϕ soft steel rods.
Weld
Spring Line
Weld 2" long - both sides
Grade
6"
6"
6"
2"
6"×6"×6" con. footing at each end at junction of lengths, and not more than 8'-0" on centers.
WICKET GUARD
3/4" = 1'-0"
2'-0"
A
1'-6"
1'-5"
3/8" round bars 4 to each standard
2'-6"
1'-0"
END
6'-0"
2 1/4"×3/4" wood slats, 1/4" radius rounded edges
10"
4"
3'-8"
4"
10"
Precast concrete standards set in concrete
6" min.
FRONT
BACKLESS BENCHES
3/8" R.H. brass screw 2" long
Wood plug
Brass expansive screw anchor
BENCH SECTION A
3" = 1'-0"
4'-0"
7/8" Fascia
2" pipe
1'-0"
2'-2"
1'-0"
END
A
A
3'-0"
1'-3 3/4"
5 3/4"
1'-0 1/4"
9 3/4"
Grade
3/8"ϕ bars, 4 to each standard
2'-5"
1'-0"
4"
END
1 1/4"×2 1/2" slats, rounded edges
4 1/2"
4"
2'-11"
4"
2'-11"
4"
4 1/2"
Precast concrete standards set in conc.
3/8"ϕ bars
Conc. slab 3'-6" × 6'-6"
6"
IN SOIL
IN CONCRETE SLAB
1'-0"
6" min.
FRONT
FIXED BENCHES
6'-0"
4"×4" framing halved at corners
2'-2"
4"
2'-2"
concrete footing
1'-0"
4'-2"
1'-0"
FRONT
FIXED PLAY TABLE

Scale 3/8" = 1'-0" except as noted

WOOD FENCES

Materials: Several makes imported from France made of treated Chestnut. Made in this country of cedar or cypress. Fastened with 12 gauge copper bond wire doubled, or galv. wire. Gates are 3'-6" & 10' wide. These fences are flexible & are delivered in 5'-0" panels for tightly woven fences & 10'-0" rolls for cleft woven. Half round cedar.

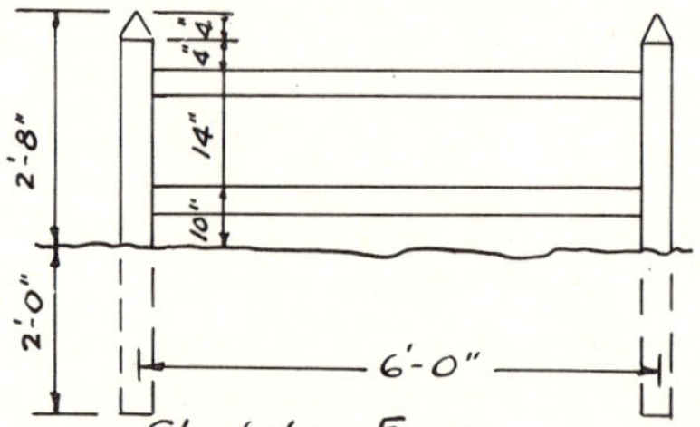

2'-8"
4"
14"
10"
2'-0"
6'-0"

Stretcher Fence

Std. Stretcher fence. Posts 4 x 4 Rails 2 x 4. Rails may be fitted between posts with large finishing nails - toe nailed. This type of fence often used for straight run of over 100 ft. for appearance & economy.

Scale : 1/4" = 1'-0"

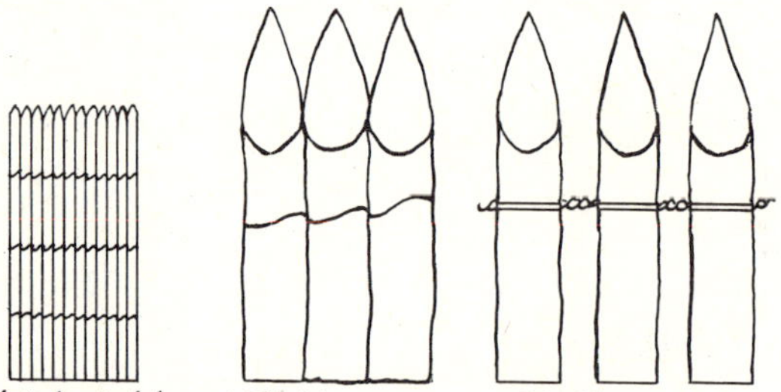

Std. heights: 1'-6", 3'-10", 4'-11", 6'-6", 8'-0" & 10'-0"

Tight woven Posts usually 2" dia.

Cleft woven 1/4 & 3/4 apart

WOVEN WOOD FENCING

Rails 2 x 4 or equal
Posts depend on height
Fencing nailed to rails
Scale : 1/8" = 1'-0"

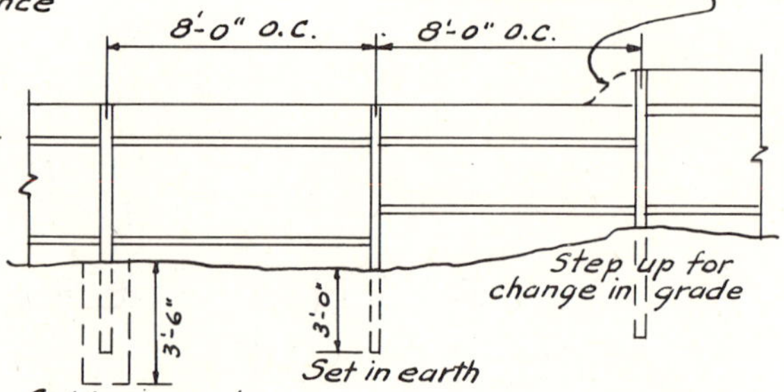

Alternate method
8'-0" o.c.
8'-0" o.c.
3'-6"
3'-0"
Step up for change in grade
Set in concrete
Set in earth

Method of erecting woven wood fence

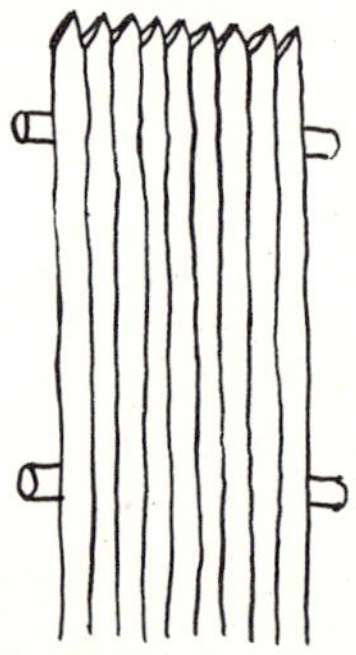

Cedar poles. May be peeled or unpeeled halved or whole round, nailed closely together on cedar rails.

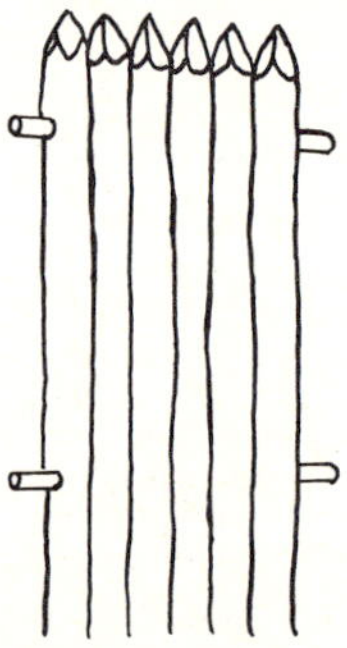

Tight fence - Cedar poles. Pickets held together with galv. pipe running thru them.

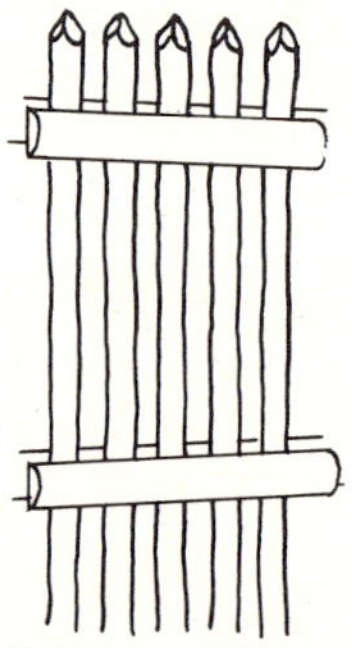

Half or whole round cedar poles nailed to halved cedar rails 2" pickets with 2" spacing

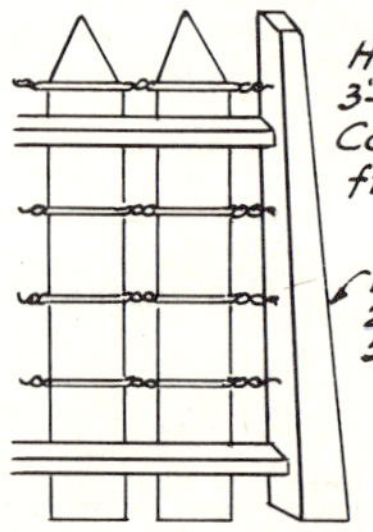

Heights - 1'-6", 3'-0", 3'-6", 4'-0", 5'-0", 6'-0" Comes in 50 & 100 ft. rolls.

Posts - 2 1/2" x 5" at top 5" x 5" at bottom.

Interwoven picket fence. Galv. wire. Red-wood post.

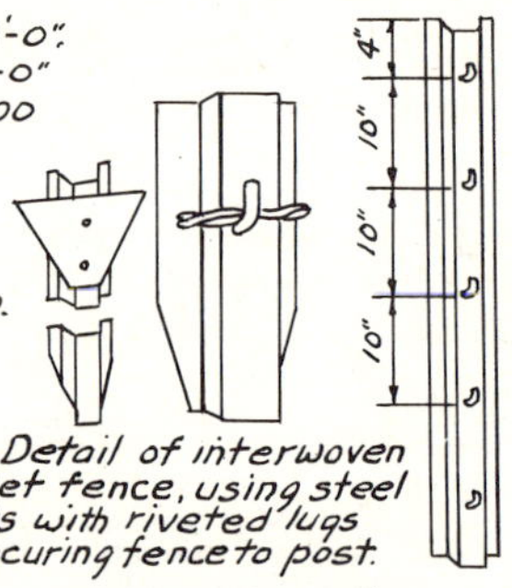

4"
10"
10"
10"

Detail of interwoven picket fence, using steel posts with riveted lugs for securing fence to post.

For use as a snow fence or to prevent soil erosion, steel posts are recommended. Std. type pickets are 2" x 7/16 spaced 2 1/4" apart & 1 1/2" x 1/2" spaced 2" apart.

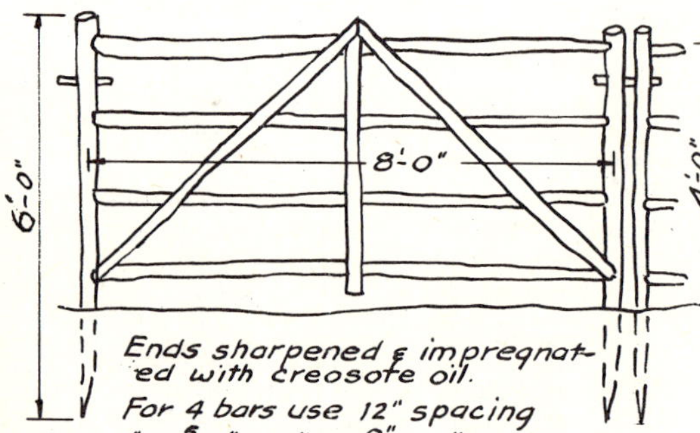

6'-0"
8'-0"
4'-0"

Ends sharpened & impregnated with creosote oil.
For 4 bars use 12" spacing
" 5 " " 9" "
" 6 " " 7" "
Braced on both sides. Gates, 4' & 10'

HURDLE FENCE

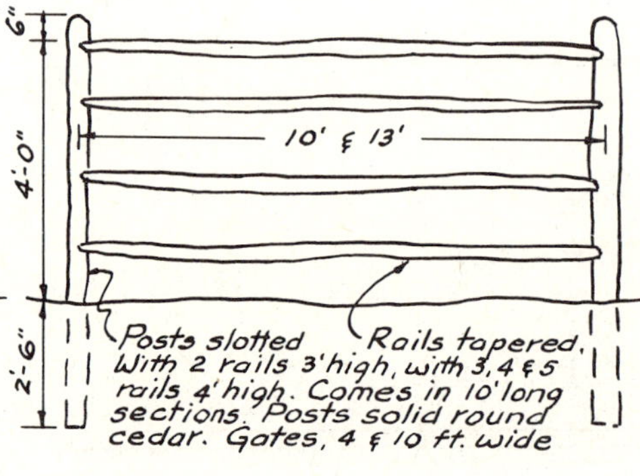

6"
4'-0"
2'-6"
10' & 13'

Posts slotted With 2 rails 3' high, with 3, 4 & 5 rails 4' high. Comes in 10' long sections. Posts solid round cedar. Gates, 4 & 10 ft. wide

Rails tapered.

POST & RAIL FENCE

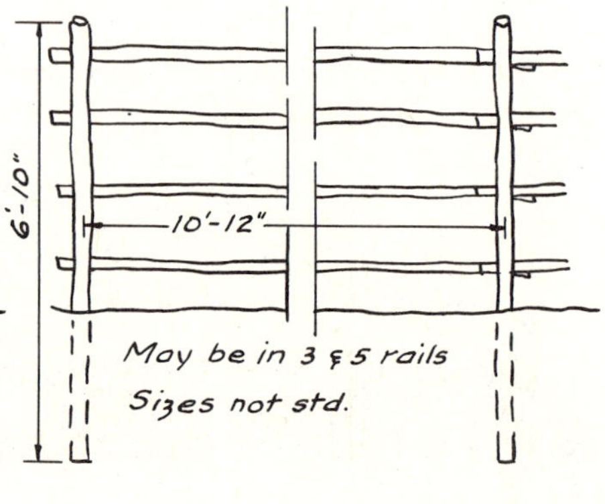

6'-10"
10'-12"

May be in 3 & 5 rails

Sizes not std.

SPLIT RAIL FENCE

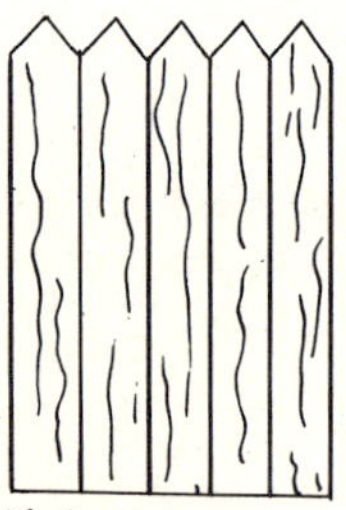

Natural wood Stained fence as a screen.

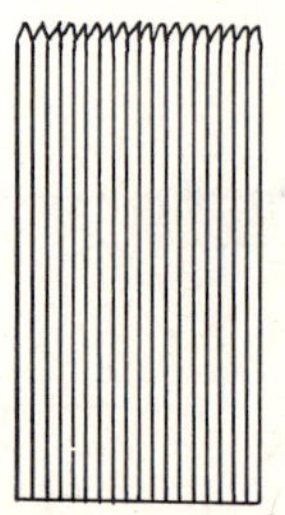

Cedar picket fence Halved cedar poles nailed close together Gates, 3'-6" & 10 feet Heights - 4 5 6 8 & 10 ft. Also called Stockade

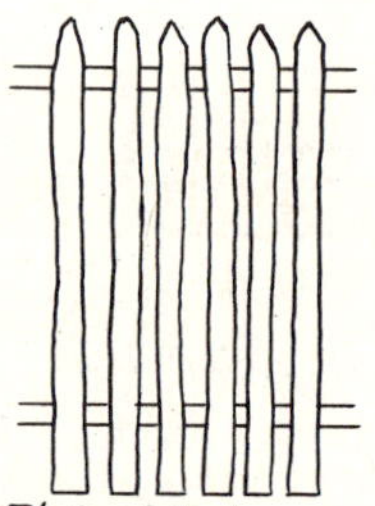

Flat pickets, rough sawed, 1" thick. Pickets average 3 1/2" wide, 2" spacing. Cedar, 3, 4, 5, 6 8 ft. high

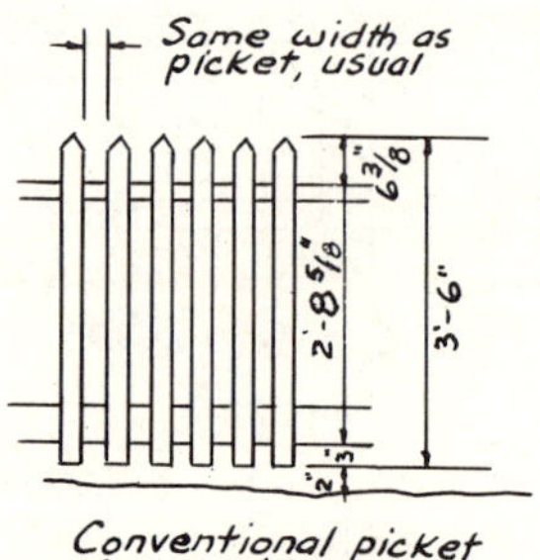

Same width as picket, usual
3 1/8
6 5/8
2'-8 5/8"
3'-6"
2 1/2
3

Conventional picket fence. 4' to 5' high Pickets made from 1 x 2 or 1 x 3. Stringers usually 2 x 4

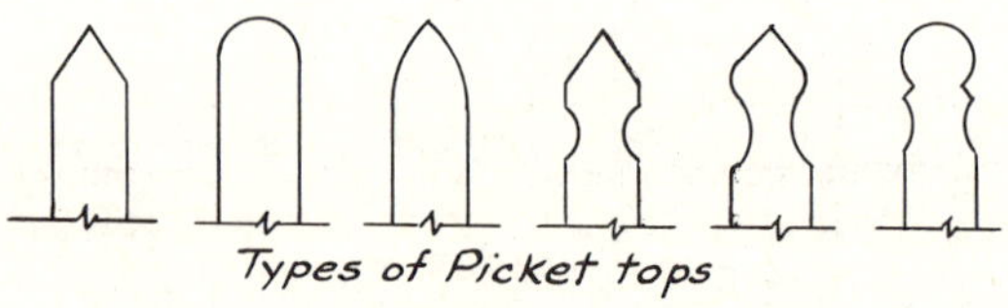

Types of Picket tops

There is a wide variety of styles & designs in picket fences. Ready cut pickets are available in several std. lengths & widths & in four or five different patterns. Pickets may be round, flat, square & dowel.

PICKET FENCES

Data checked by, Habitant Fence Co., Lincraft Incorporated, Western Pine Association

SPORTS and GAMES

TABLE OF CONTENTS

PLAYGROUND EQUIPMENT

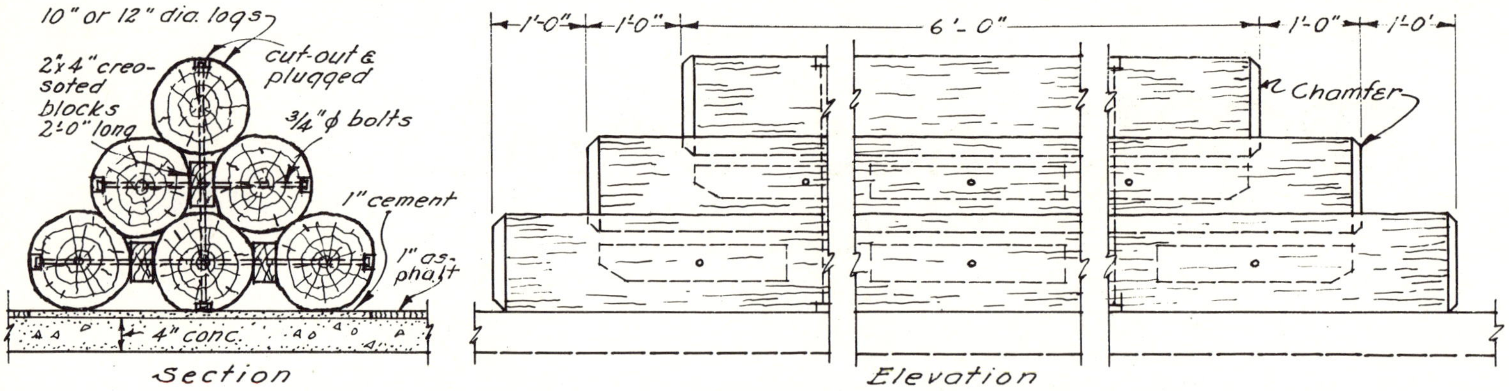
10" or 12" dia. logs
cut-out & plugged
2"x 4" creosoted blocks 2'-0" long
3/4" ϕ bolts
1" cement
1" asphalt
4" conc.
Section
1'-0"
1'-0"
6'-0"
1'-0"
1'-0"
Chamfer
Elevation

PLAY LOG PILE

1/2" = 1'-0"

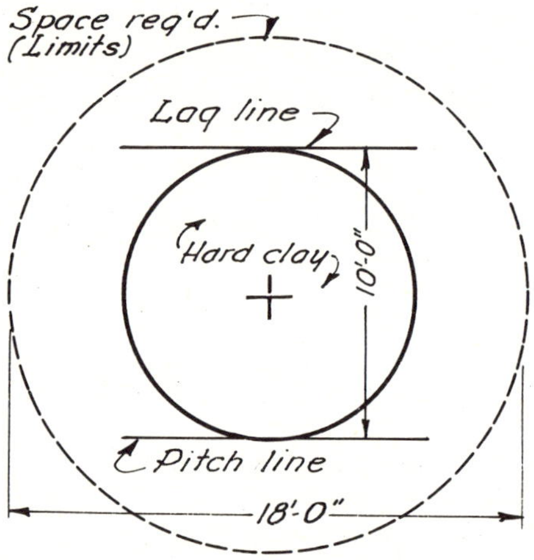
Space req'd. (Limits)
Lag line
Hard clay
10'-0"
Pitch line
18'-0"

MARBLES RING

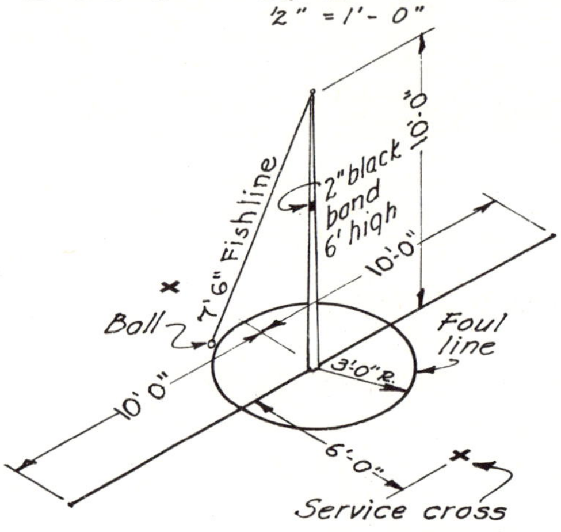
10'-0"
2" black band 6' high
7'6" Fishline
Ball
10'-0"
Foul line
3'-0" R.
10'-0"
6'-0"
Service cross

TETHER TENNIS

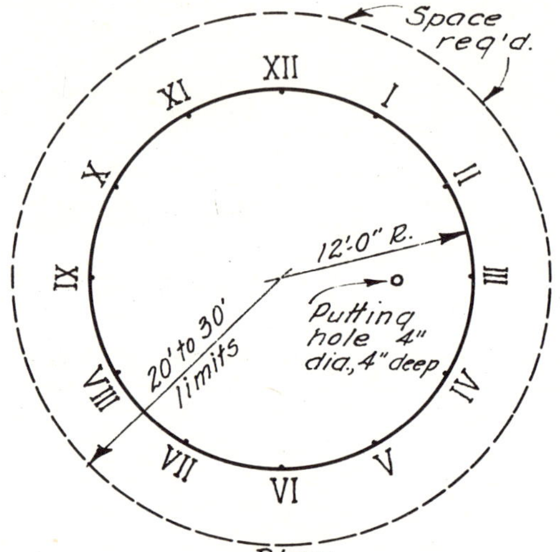
Space req'd.
XII
I
II
III
IV
V
VI
VII
VIII
IX
X
XI
12'-0" R.
Putting hole 4" dia., 4" deep
20' to 30' limits

Plan

CLOCK GOLF

1" = 16'

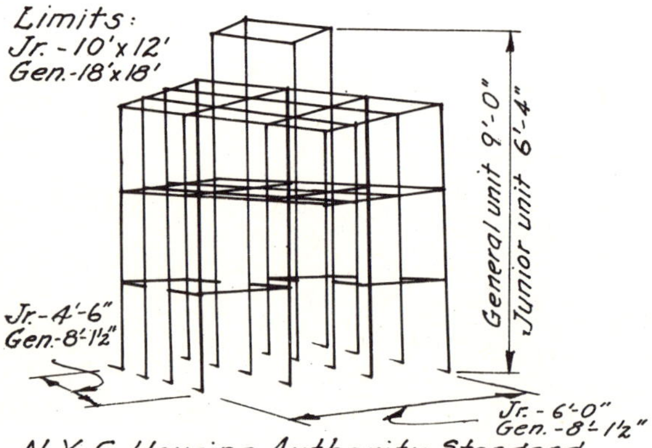
Limits:
Jr. - 10' x 12'
Gen. - 18' x 18'
General unit 9'-0"
Junior unit 6'-4"
Jr. - 4'-6"
Gen. - 8'-1½"
Jr. - 6'-0"
Gen. - 8'-1½"

N. Y. C. Housing Authority Standard

CLIMBING APPARATUS

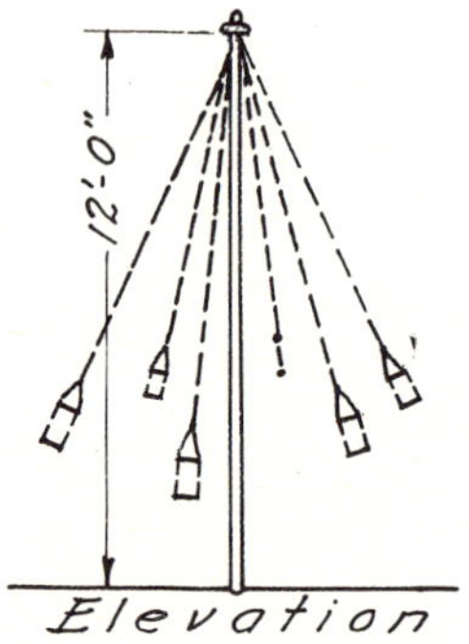
12'-0"

Elevation

Space required = 30'-0" dia.

GIANT STRIDE

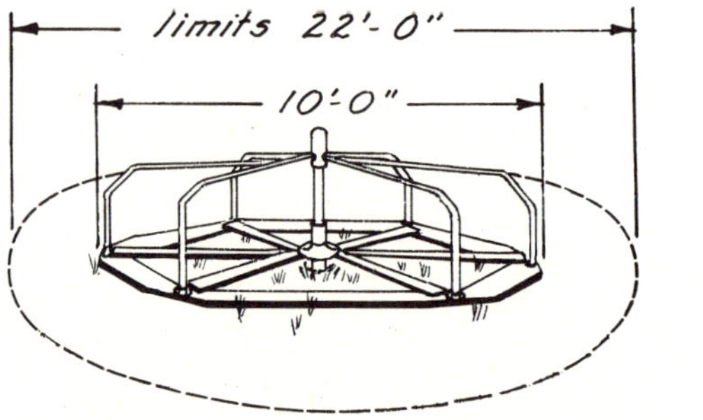
limits 22'-0"
10'-0"

10 ft. diameter is considered standard. Other diameters = 12', 14' & 16'. Limits 24', 26' & 28' ϕ.

MERRY-GO-ROUND

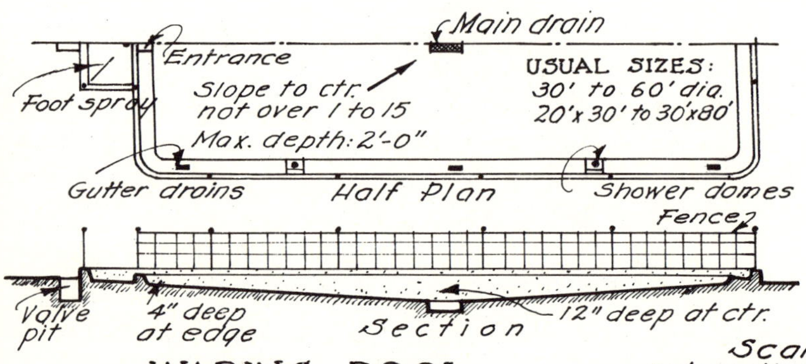
Main drain
Entrance
Foot spray
Slope to ctr. not over 1 to 15
Max. depth: 2'-0"
USUAL SIZES:
30' to 60' dia.
20' x 30' to 30' x 80'
Gutter drains
Half Plan
Shower domes
Fence
Valve pit
4" deep at edge
Section
12" deep at ctr.

WADING POOL

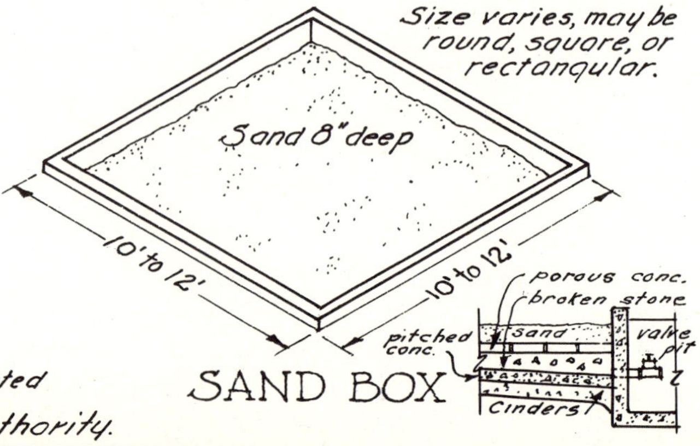
Size varies, may be round, square, or rectangular.
Sand 8" deep
10' to 12'
10' to 12'
porous conc.
broken stone
sand
pitched conc.
valve pit
cinders

SAND BOX

Scale unless otherwise noted 1/8" = 1'-0"

Data checked by N.Y.C. Housing Authority.

PLAYGROUND EQUIPMENT

Adjacent slides: 7'-6" (chutes c. to c.) Others 10'-0" o.c.

NOTE
Enclosure limits indicated by broken lines.

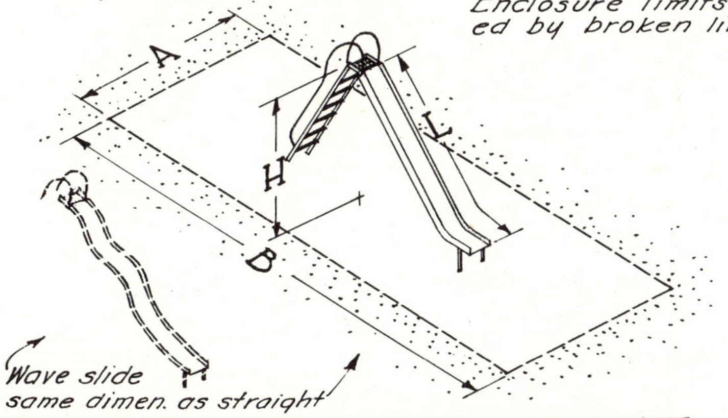
A
H
L
B
Wave slide
same dimen. as straight

Seats & chairs generally 1'-6" from ground.

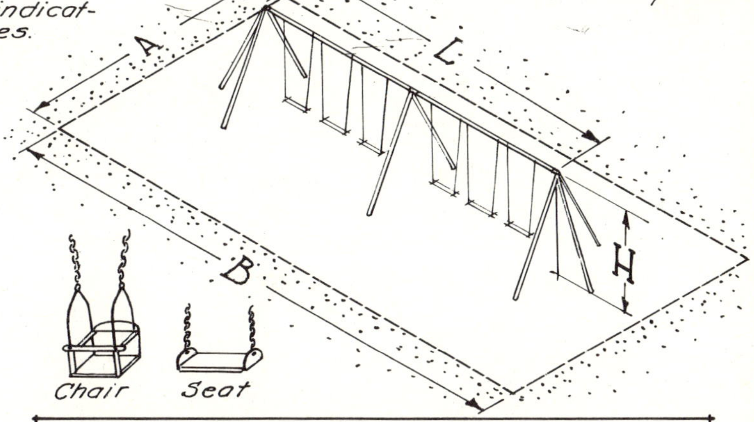
A
L
B
H
Chair
Seat

SLIDES

H	L	Nursery		Straight		Racer	
		A	B	A	B	A	B
5	10	8	20	·	·	·	·
6	12	8	22	·	·	·	·
7	14	8	24	·	·	·	·
8	16	·	·	12	30	20	30
10	20	·	·	12	35	20	35
12	24	·	·	15	40	25	40
13½	30	·	·	15	45	25	45

SWINGS

Number of Swings	Chair Type			Seat Type						
	L	A	B	L	A	B	A	B	A	B
2	8	17	24	9	17	25	21	25	25	25
3	10	17	26	15	17	31	21	31	25	31
4	16	17	32	18	17	34	21	34	25	34
6	20, 24	17	38	27, 30	17	46	21	46	25	46
8	·	·	·	36	17	52	21	52	25	52
9	·	·	·	45	17	61	21	61	25	61
Height	8'			8', 10', 12'	8'		10'		12'	

COMBINATION UNITS

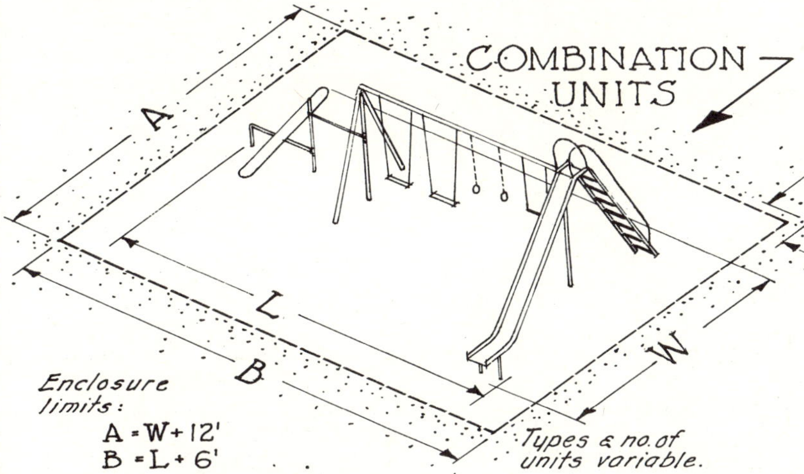
A
L
B
W

Enclosure limits:
A = W + 12'
B = L + 6'

Types & no. of units variable.

Height of ctr. pipe 1'-0" to 3'-0" above ground.

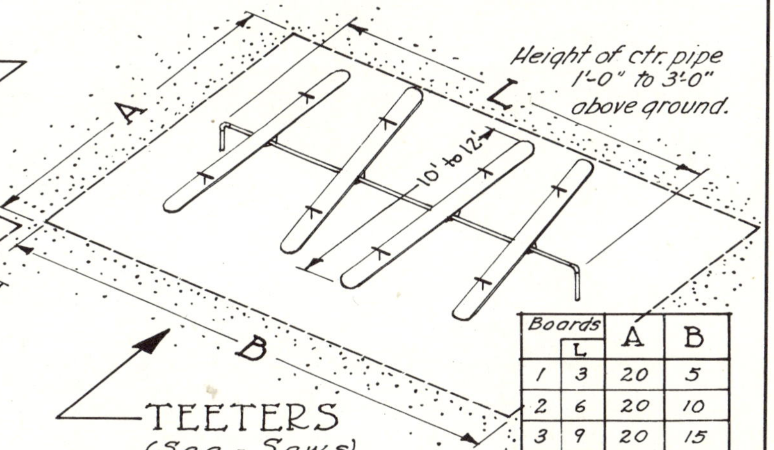
A
L
10' to 12'
B

Boards	L	A	B
1	3	20	5
2	6	20	10
3	9	20	15
4	12	20	20
6	18	20	25

TEETERS
(See-Saws)

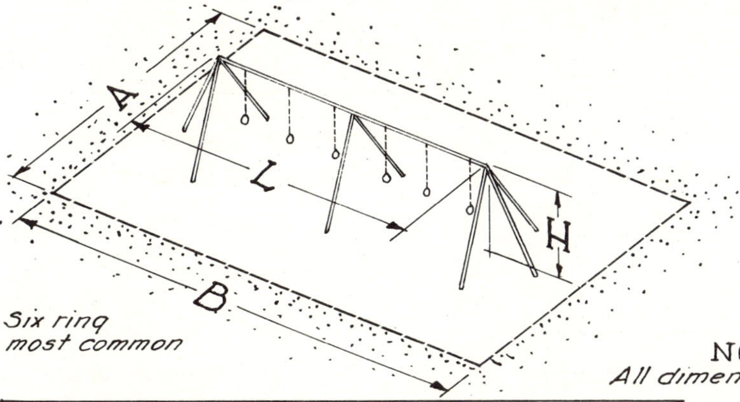
A
L
H
B

Six ring most common

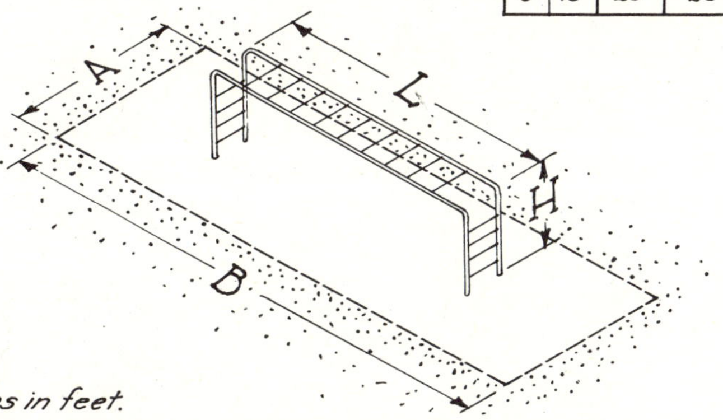
A
L
H
B

NOTE
All dimensions in feet.

TRAVELING RINGS

Height	Length	A	B
10	36	20	60
12	36	20	60

HORIZONTAL LADDER

Height	Length	A	B
6	12	8	25
7½	16	8	30

Data checked by N.Y.C. Housing Authority

PLAYGROUND EQUIPMENT

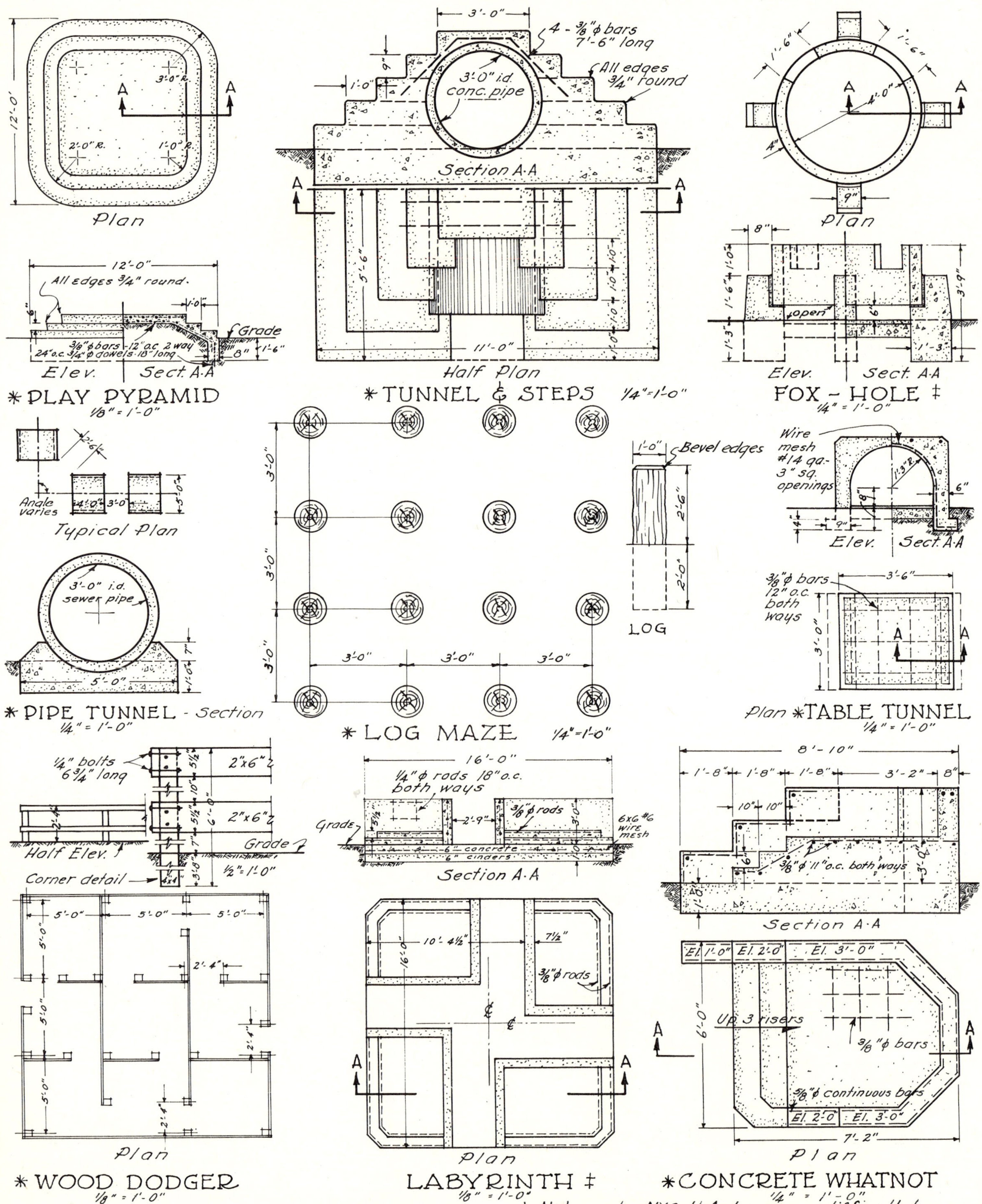

12'-0"
3'-0" R.
2'-0" R.
1'-0" R.
Plan
12'-0"
All edges 3/4" round.
3/8"φ bars-12" o.c. 2 way
24" o.c. 3/4"φ dowels 18" long
Grade
Elev.
Sect. A-A
* PLAY PYRAMID
1/8" = 1'-0"
3'-0"
4 - 3/8"φ bars 7'-6" long
3'-0" i.d. conc. pipe
All edges 3/4" round
Section A-A
11'-0"
Half Plan
* TUNNEL & STEPS
1/4" = 1'-0"
1'-6"
4'-0"
9"
Plan
8"
open
3'-9"
1'-3"
Elev.
Sect. A-A
FOX - HOLE ‡
1/4" = 1'-0"
Typical Plan
Angle varies
3'-0" i.d. sewer pipe
5'-0"
* PIPE TUNNEL - Section
1/4" = 1'-0"
3'-0"
Bevel edges
LOG
* LOG MAZE
1/4" = 1'-0"
Wire mesh #14 ga. 3" sq. openings
1'-3" R.
Elev.
Sect. A-A
3/8"φ bars 12" o.c. both ways
3'-6"
Plan
* TABLE TUNNEL
1/4" = 1'-0"
1/4" bolts 6 3/4" long
2"x6"
Half Elev.
Grade
Corner detail
4x4
1/2" = 1'-0"
16'-0"
1/4"φ rods 18" o.c. both ways
3/8"φ rods
Grade
6x6 #6 wire mesh
6" concrete
6" cinders
Section A-A
8'-10"
3/8"φ 11" o.c. both ways
Section A-A
5'-0"
2'-4"
Plan
* WOOD DODGER
1/8" = 1'-0"
10'-4 1/2"
7 1/2"
3/8"φ rods
Plan
LABYRINTH ‡
1/8" = 1'-0"
El. 1'-0"
El. 2'-0"
El. 3'-0"
Up 3 risers
3/8"φ bars
5/8"φ continuous bars
7'-2"
Plan
* CONCRETE WHATNOT
1/4" = 1'-0"

* Standards adopted by the NYC Housing Authority.

‡ Not rec. by NYC. H.A. because difficult to maintain in sanitary condition.

SPORTS and GAMES

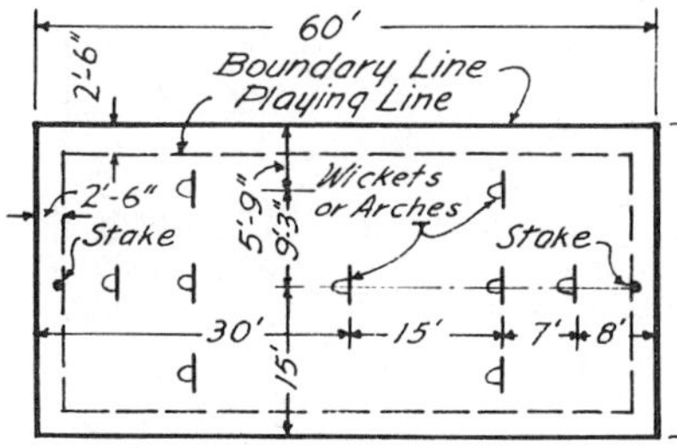
60'
2'-6"
Boundary Line
Playing Line
2'-6"
Wickets or Arches
5'-9"
9'-3"
Stake
Stake
30'
15'
7'
8'
15'
30'

AMERICAN CROQUET
1" = 32'

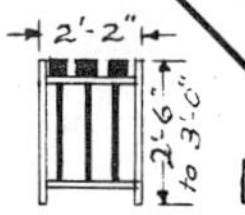
2'-2"
2'-6" to 3'-0"

1'-0" deep 8" = 1'

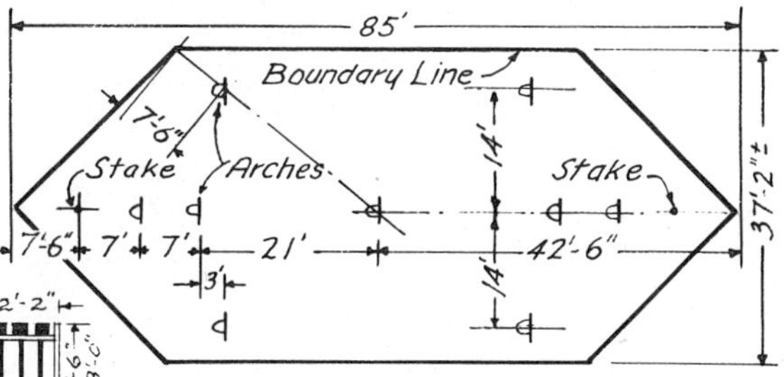
85'
Boundary Line
7'-6"
Stake
Arches
Stake
14'
7'-6"
7'
7'
21'
42'-6"
3'
14'
37'-2" ±

MODERN CROQUET
1" = 32'

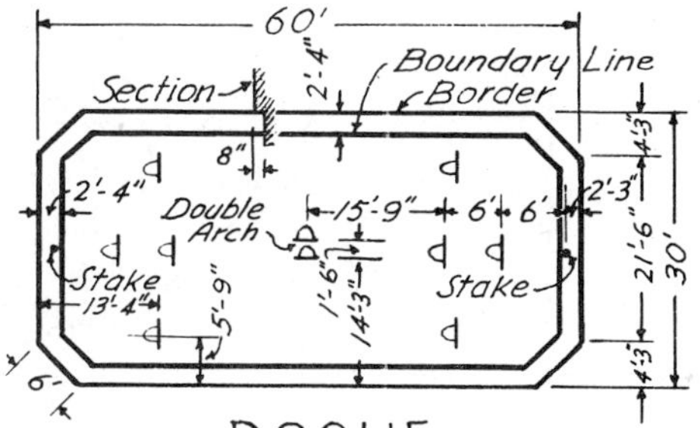
60'
Section
2'-4"
Boundary Line
Border
8"
2'-4"
Double Arch
15'-9"
6'
6'
2'-3"
Stake
13'-4"
5'-9"
1'-6"
14'-3"
Stake
4'-3"
21'-6"
30'
4'-3"
6'

ROQUE
1" = 32'

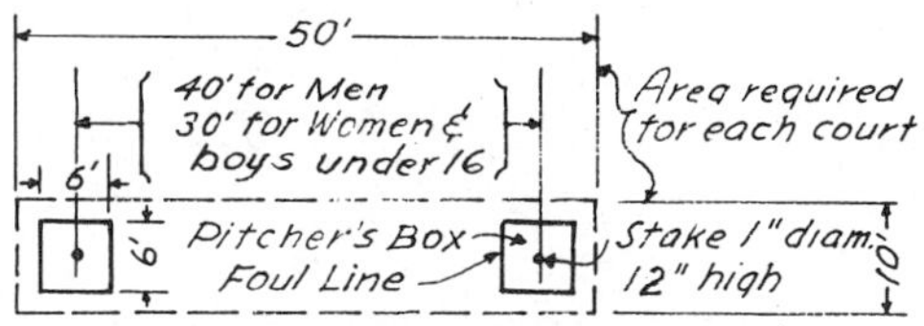
50'
40' for Men
30' for Women & boys under 16
Area required for each court
6'
6'
Pitcher's Box
Foul Line
Stake 1" diam. 12" high
10'

HORSESHOES
1" = 32'

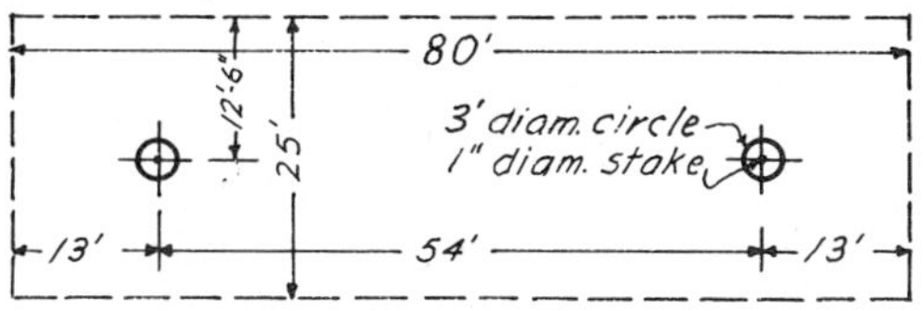
80'
12'-6"
25'
3' diam. circle
1" diam. stake
13'
54'
13'

QUOITS
1" = 32'

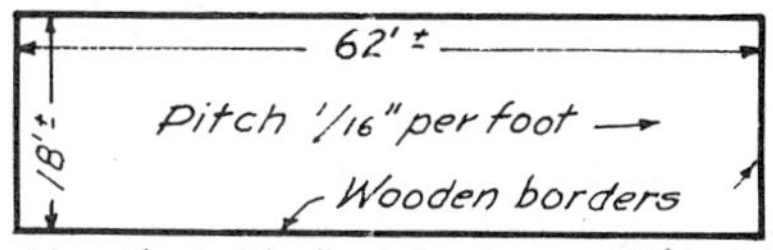
62' ±
18' ±
Pitch 1/16" per foot
Wooden borders

New York City Park Dept. uses 72' to 84' long by 12' wide

BOCCIE
1" = 32'

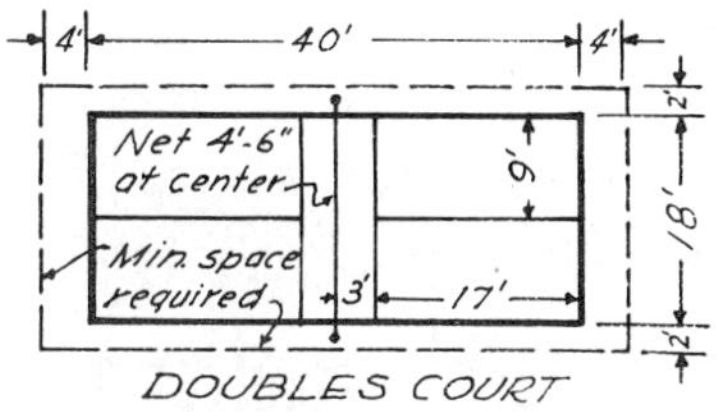
4'
40'
4'
2'
Net 4'-6" at center
9'
18'
Min. space required
3'
17'
2'

DOUBLES COURT

NOTE: Doubles Court may be marked for singles also.

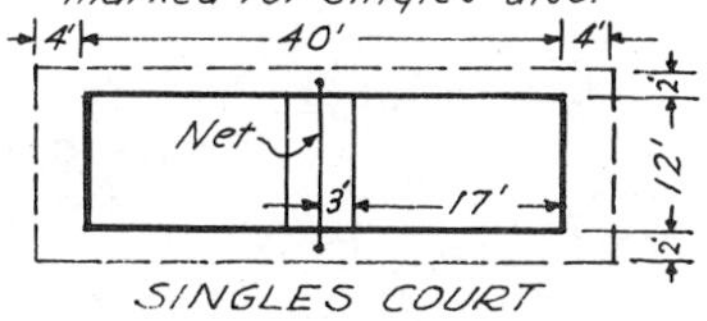
4'
40'
4'
2'
Net
12'
3'
17'
2'

SINGLES COURT

DECK TENNIS
1" = 32'

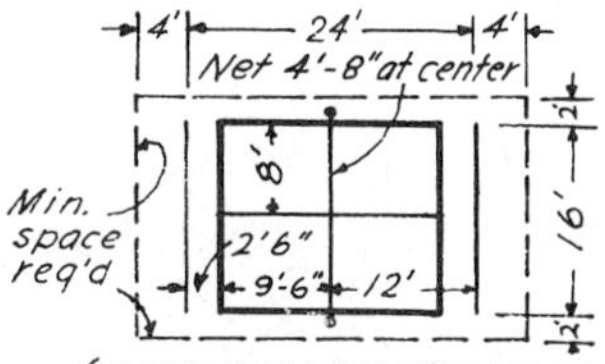
4'
24'
4'
Net 4'-8" at center
2'
8'
16'
Min. space req'd
2'6"
9'-6"
12'
2'

(ALSO CALLED TENIQUOIT)

QUOITENNIS
1" = 32

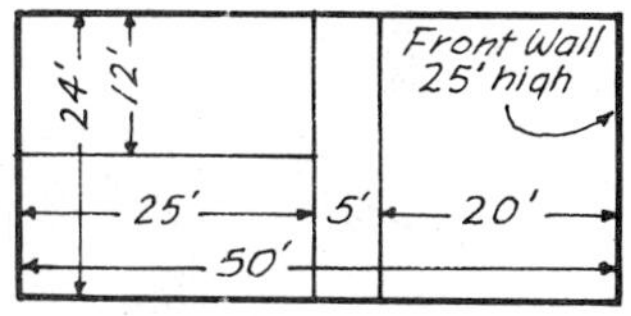
24'
12'
Front Wall 25' high
25'
5'
20'
50'

SQUASH HANDBALL
1" = 32'

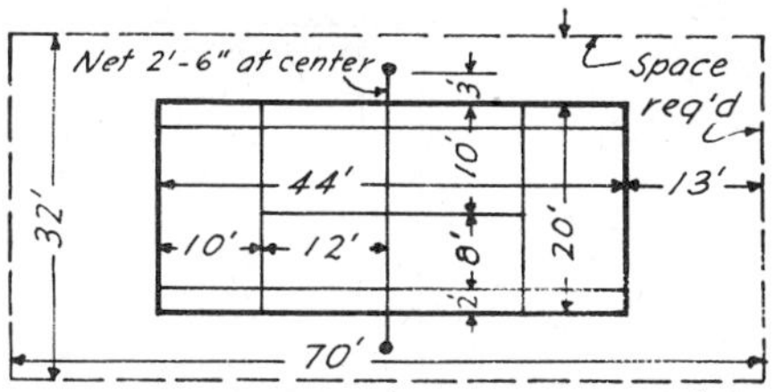
Net 2'-6" at center
Space req'd
3'
10'
44'
13'
20'
32'
10'
12'
8'
2'
70'

SENIOR COURT (OFFICIAL PLAY)

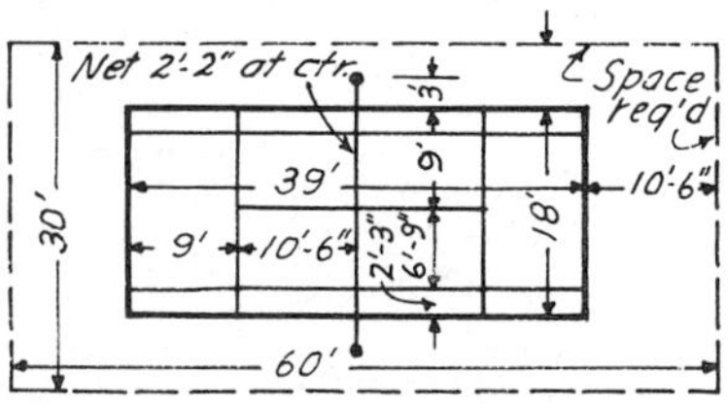
Net 2'-2" at ctr.
Space req'd
3'
9'
39'
10'-6"
30'
18'
9'
10'-6"
2'-3"
6'-9"
60'

JUNIOR COURT

PADDLE TENNIS
1" = 32'

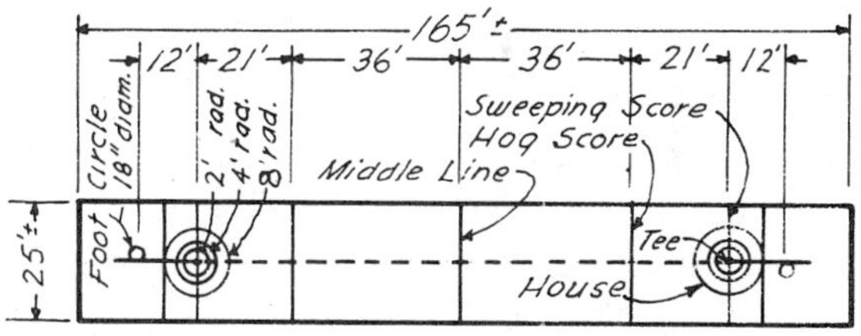
165' ±
12'
21'
36'
36'
21'
12'
Circle 18" diam.
2' rad.
4' rad.
8' rad.
Sweeping Score
Hog Score
Middle Line
25' ±
Foot
Tee
House

CURLING
1" = 64'

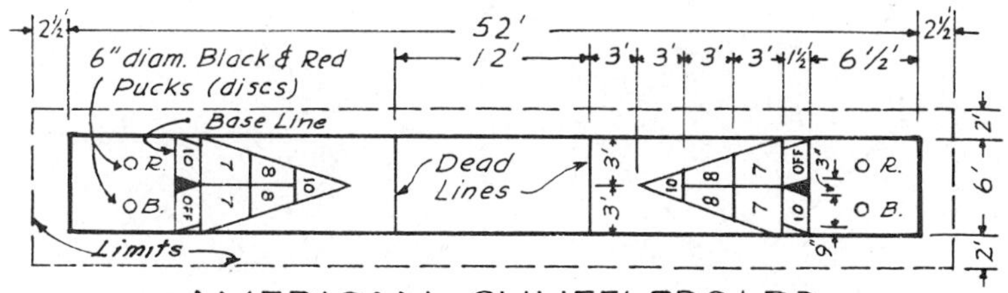
2½
52'
2½
6" diam. Black & Red Pucks (discs)
12'
3'
3'
3'
3'
1½
6½'
Base Line
2'
O R.
O B.
OFF
Dead Lines
3'
6'
O R.
O B.
Limits
2'

AMERICAN SHUFFLEBOARD
1" = 16'

Tables 2'-6" high
Net 6" high
Headroom 7'-0" Min.

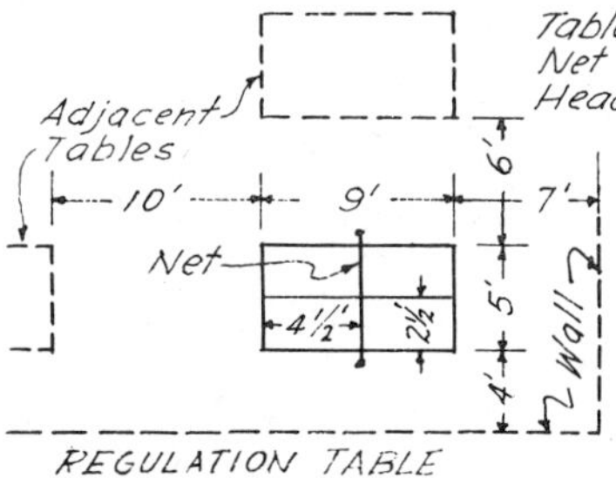
Adjacent Tables
6'
10'
9'
7'
Net
4½'
2½'
5'
4'
Wall

REGULATION TABLE

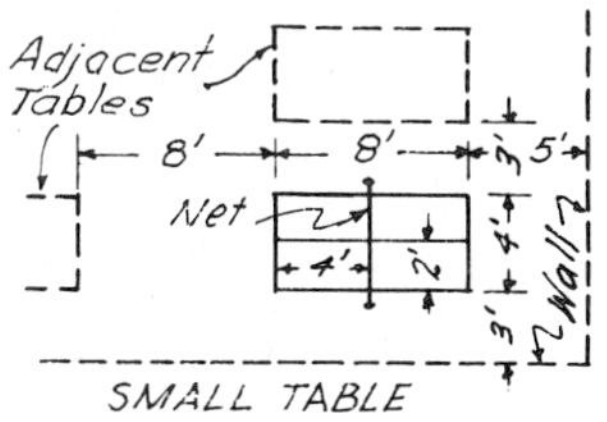
Adjacent Tables
8'
8'
3'
5'
Net
4'
2'
4'
3'
Wall

SMALL TABLE

TABLE TENNIS
1" = 16'

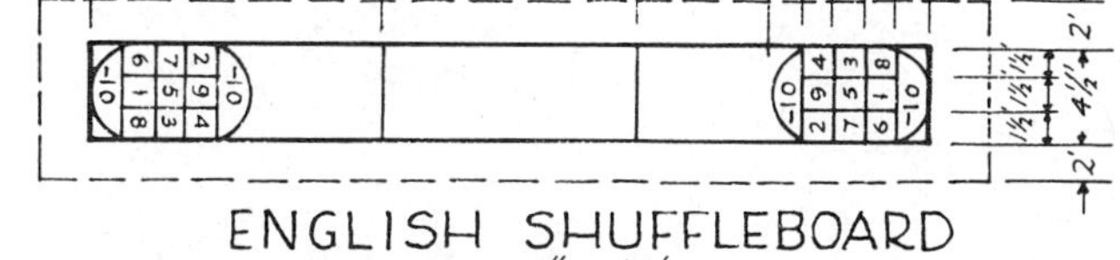
2½
40'
2½
14'
12'
6½'
1½
2'
4½'
2'
10
10

ENGLISH SHUFFLEBOARD
1" = 16'

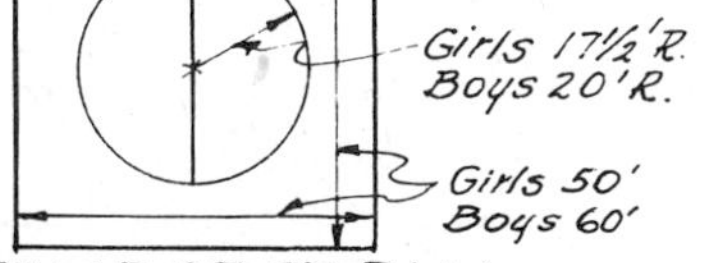
Girls 17½' R.
Boys 20' R.
Girls 50'
Boys 60'

TEAM DODGE BALL
1" = 64'

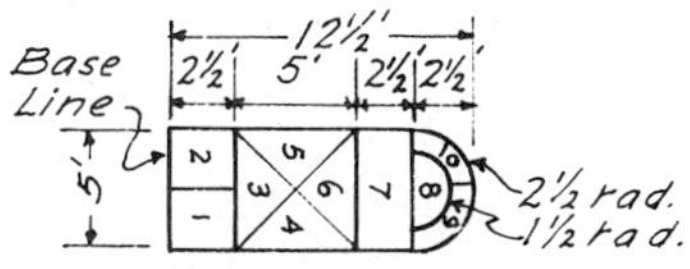
12½'
2½'
5'
2½'
2½'
Base Line
5'
1
2
3
4
5
6
7
8
9
10
2½ rad.
1½ rad.

HOPSCOTCH
1" = 16'

BASEBALL and SOFTBALL

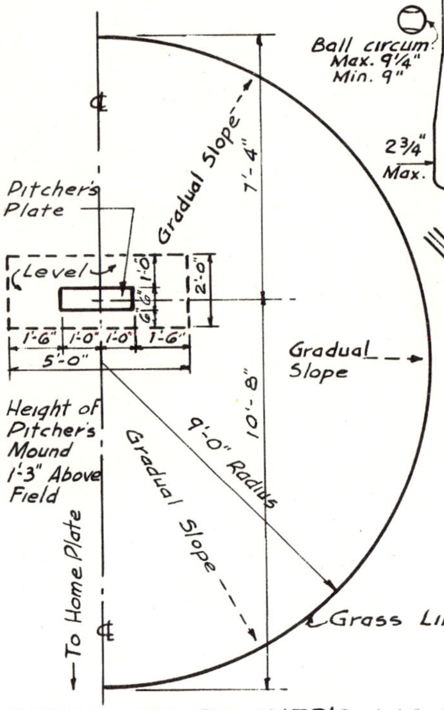

Pitcher's Plate
Level
Gradual Slope
7'-4"
Gradual Slope
Height of Pitcher's Mound 1'-3" Above Field
9'-0" Radius
10'-8"
Gradual Slope
Grass Line
To Home Plate
1'-6" 1'-0" 1'-0" 1'-6"
5'-0"
2'-0"

DETAIL OF PITCHER'S MOUND
Scale: 3/16" = 1'-0"

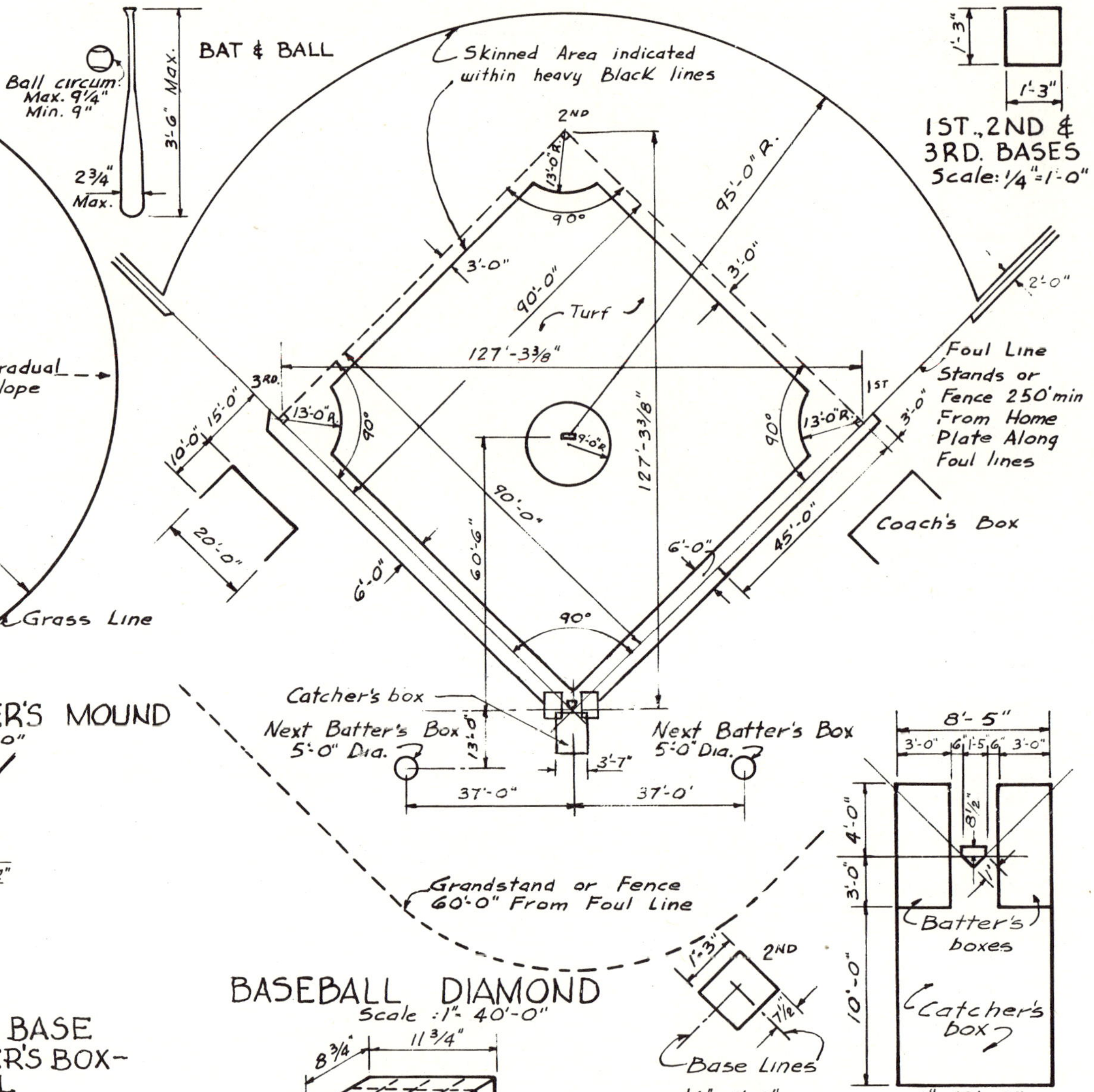

BAT & BALL
Ball circum. Max. 9¼" Min. 9"
3'-6" Max.
2¾" Max.
1'-3"
1'-3"
1ST., 2ND & 3RD. BASES
Scale: ¼"=1'-0"
Skinned Area indicated within heavy Black lines
2ND
13'-0"R.
90°
95'-0" R.
3'-0"
3'-0"
90'-0"
Turf
127'-3⅜"
3RD.
1ST
13'-0"R.
90°
9'-0"R.
127'-3⅜
Foul Line
Stands or Fence 250' min From Home Plate Along Foul lines
2'-0"
10'-0" 15'-0"
20'-0"
60'-6"
90'-0"
6'-0"
45'-0"
Coach's Box
90°
Catcher's box
Next Batter's Box 5'-0" Dia.
Next Batter's Box 5'-0" Dia.
13'-0"
3'-7"
37'-0"
37'-0"
Grandstand or Fence 60'-0" From Foul Line
8'-5"
3'-0" 6" 1'-5" 6" 3'-0"
4'-0"
8½"
3'-0"
Batter's boxes
10'-0"
Catcher's box
1'-3"
2ND
1½"
Base Lines

BASEBALL DIAMOND
Scale: 1" 40'-0"

¼" = 1'-0"
1" = 10'-0"

DETAILS OF HOME BASE
& SECOND - SOFTBALL

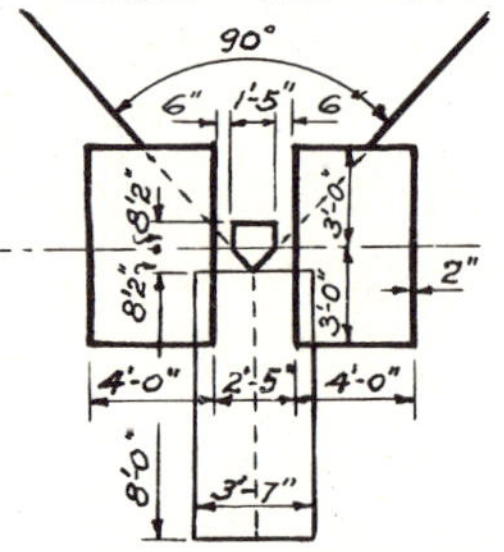

90°
6" 1'-5" 6"
8½"
3'-0"
2"
4'-0" 2'-5" 4'-0"
8'-0"
3'-7"

DETAIL OF HOME BASE
BATTER'S & CATCHER'S BOX-
BASEBALL

ORIENTATION:
No standard - Consider time of day for games; months when played; location of field, surrounding bldgs., & stands. Possible choices: Home plate in S.W., N.W., N., S., or S.S.W.

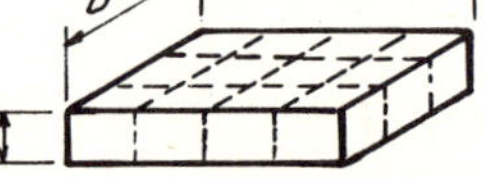

11¾"
8¾"
2⅞"

BOX OF 12 BASEBALLS
Contains 12 individ'l. boxes

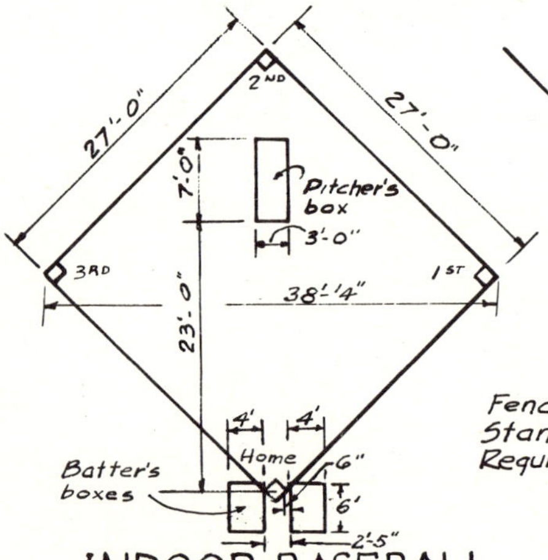

27'-0"
27'-0"
2ND
7'-0"
Pitcher's box
3'-0"
3RD
1ST
38'-4"
23'-0"
4' 4'
Home
6"
6'
2'-5"
Batter's boxes

INDOOR BASEBALL
Scale 1" = 20'-0"

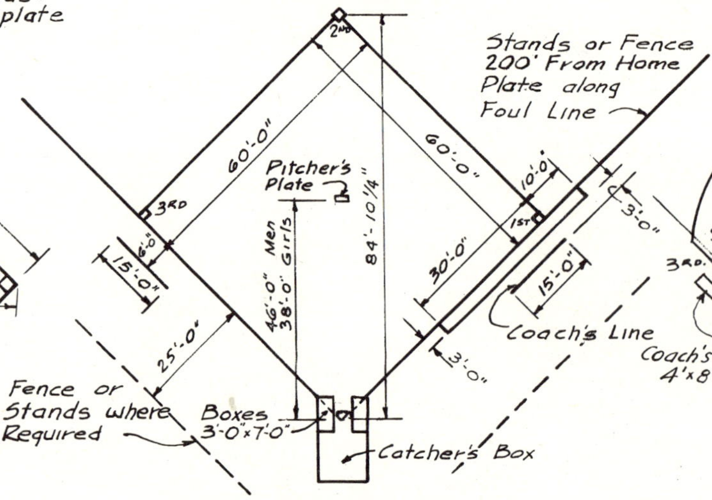

2ND
Stands or Fence 200' From Home Plate along Foul Line
60'-0"
60'-0"
Pitcher's Plate
3RD
1ST
10'-0"
3'-0"
15'-0"
15'-0"
46'-0" Men
38'-0" Girls
84'-10¼"
30'-0"
25'-0"
Coach's Line
3'-0"
Fence or Stands where Required
Boxes 3'-0"x7'-0"
Catcher's Box

SOFTBALL DIAMOND
Scale 1" = 40'-0"

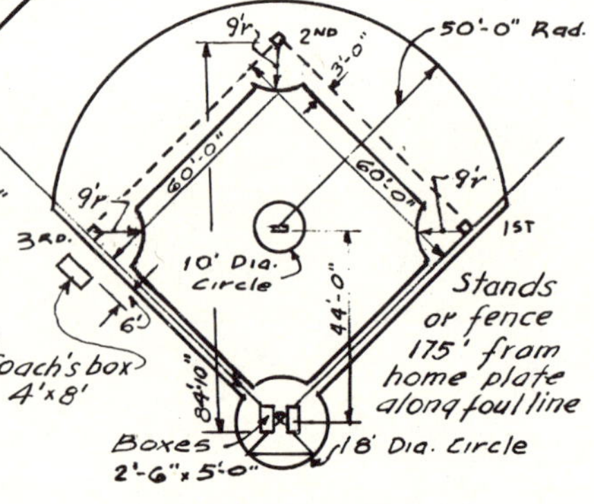

9'r.
2ND
50'-0" Rad.
3'-0"
60'-0"
60'-0"
9'r.
9'r.
3RD.
1ST
10' Dia. Circle
44'-0"
6'
Coach's box 4'x8'
Stands or fence 175' from home plate along foul line
84'-10"
Boxes 2'-6"x5'-0"
18' Dia. Circle

LITTLE LEAGUE BASEBALL
Scale: 1" = 60'-0"

TENNIS COURTS

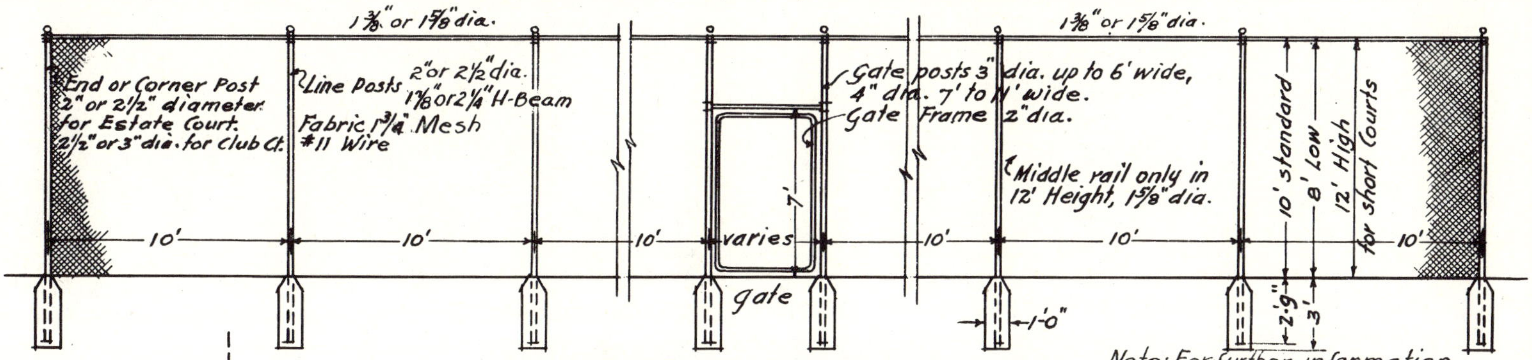

1⅜" or 1⅝" dia.
1⅜" or 1⅝" dia.
End or Corner Post 2" or 2½" diameter for Estate Court. 2½" or 3" dia. for Club Ct.
Line Posts 2" or 2½" dia. 1⅞" or 2¼" H-Beam
Fabric 1¾" Mesh #11 Wire
Gate posts 3" dia. up to 6' wide, 4" dia. 7' to 11' wide.
Gate Frame 2" dia.
Middle rail only in 12' Height, 1⅝" dia.
10' standard
8' Low
12' High for short courts
10'
10'
10'
varies
7'
10'
10'
10'
gate
1'-0"
2'-9"
3'

ELEVATION of ENCLOSURE

1" = 8'

Note: For further information check page on "Chain Link Fences"

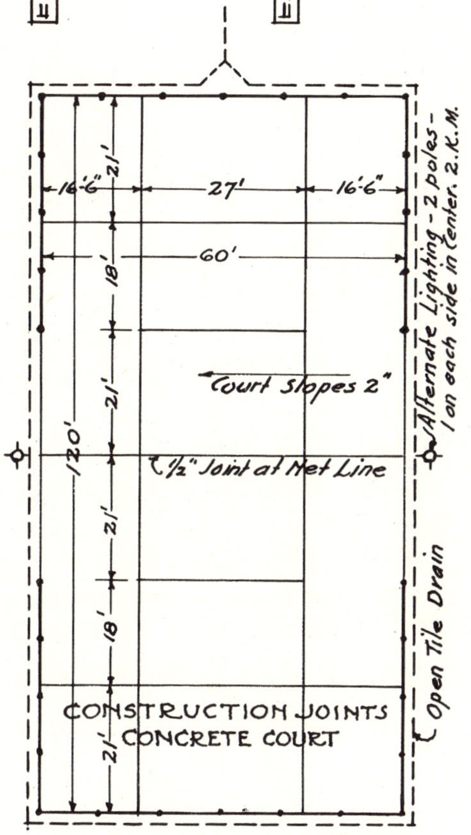

16'-6"
27'
16'-6"
60'
21'
18'
21'
21'
18'
21'
120'
Court slopes 2"
½" Joint at Net Line
CONSTRUCTION JOINTS CONCRETE COURT
Alternate Lighting - 2 poles - 1 on each side in Center. 2. K.M.
Open Tile Drain

HALF ENCLOSURE

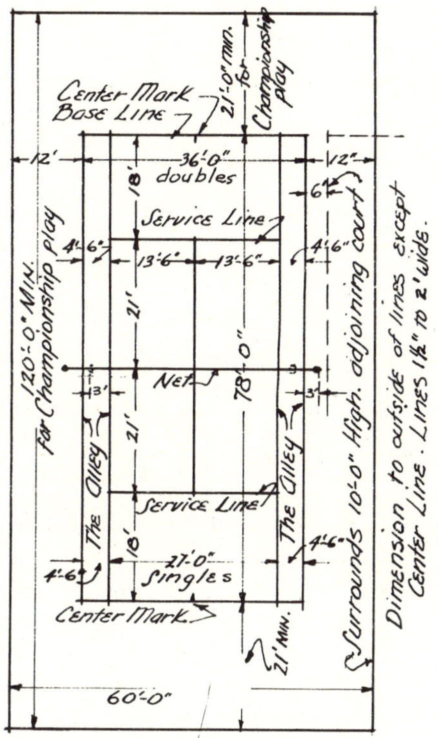

21'-0" min. for Championship play
Center Mark Base Line
12'
36'-0" doubles
12'
18'
6'
Service Line
4'-6"
13'-6"
13'-6"
4'-6"
120'-0" MIN. For Championship play
21'
Net
78'-0"
3'
3'
The Alley
The Alley
Service Line
18'
4'-6"
27'-0" Singles
4'-6"
Center Mark
21' MIN.
60'-0"
Surrounds 10'-0" High, adjoining court
Dimension to outside of lines except Center Line. Lines 1½" to 2" wide.

COURT SIZES

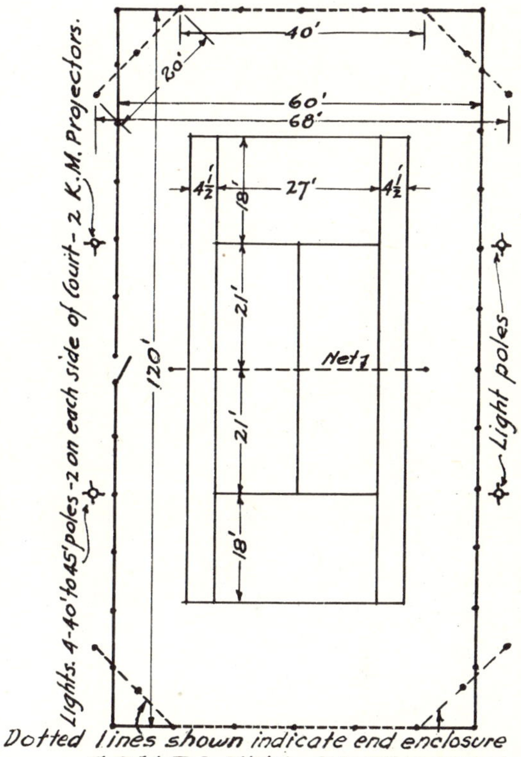

40'
20'
60'
68'
4½'
27'
4½'
18'
21'
120'
Net
21'
18'
Lights. 4-40' to 45' poles - 2 on each side of court - 2 K.M. Projectors.
Light poles
Dotted lines shown indicate end enclosure

COMPLETE ENCLOSURE

ENCLOSURES ETC:

1" = 32'

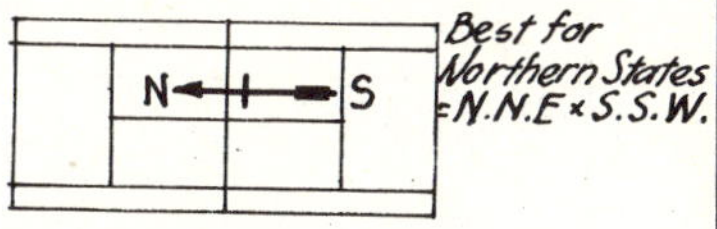

N
S
Best for Northern States = N.N.E. × S.S.W.

ORIENTATION

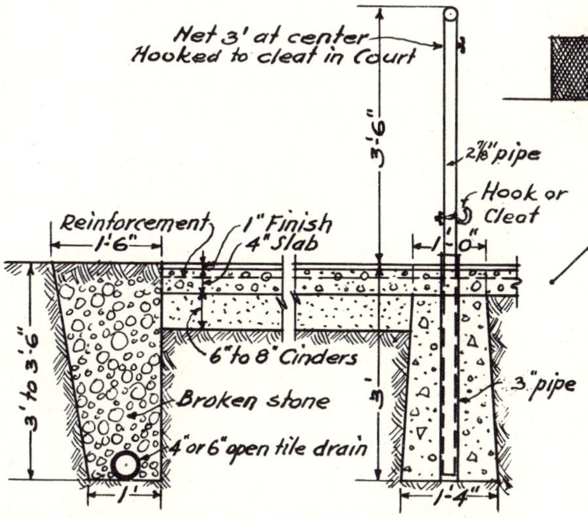

Net 3' at center Hooked to cleat in Court
3'-6"
2⅞" pipe
Hook or Cleat
Reinforcement
1'-6"
1" Finish
4" Slab
1'-0"
3' to 3'-6"
6" to 8" Cinders
Broken stone
3'
3" pipe
4" or 6" open tile drain
1'
1'-4"

DETAIL of CONCRETE COURT

3/8" = 1'

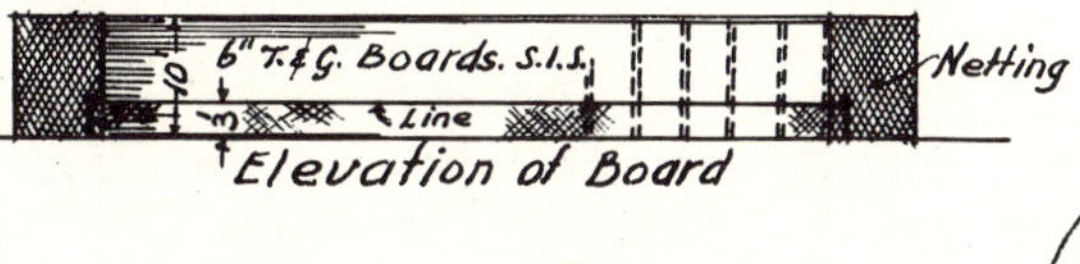

6" T.&G. Boards. S.I.S.
10'
3'
Line
Netting
Elevation of Board

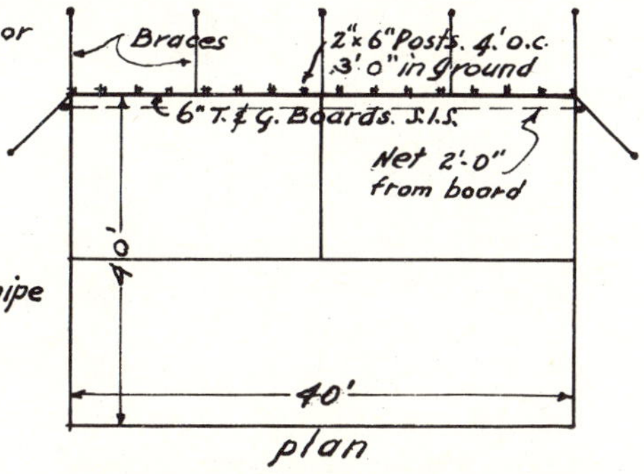

Braces
2" × 6" Posts. 4' o.c. 3'0" in ground
6" T.&G. Boards. S.I.S.
Net 2'-0" from board
40'
40'
plan

PRACTICE COURT

1" = 32'

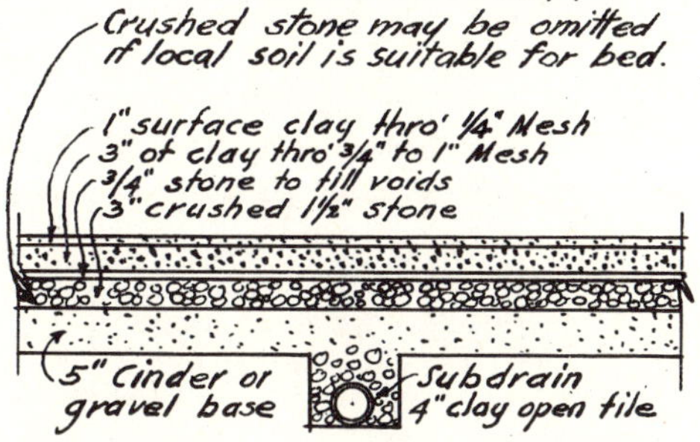

Crushed stone may be omitted if local soil is suitable for bed.
1" surface clay thro' ¼" Mesh
3" of clay thro' ¾" to 1" Mesh
¾" stone to fill voids
3" crushed 1½" stone
5" Cinder or gravel base
Subdrain 4" clay open tile

DETAIL of CLAY COURT

3/8" = 1'

Note: Preferred layout of batteries of courts is side by side, primarily for saving space; also in end to end layouts, players facing adjoining court play against background of moving players.

TENNIS COURT DETAILS

Data checked by Tennis Courts Inc.

TENNIS COURTS

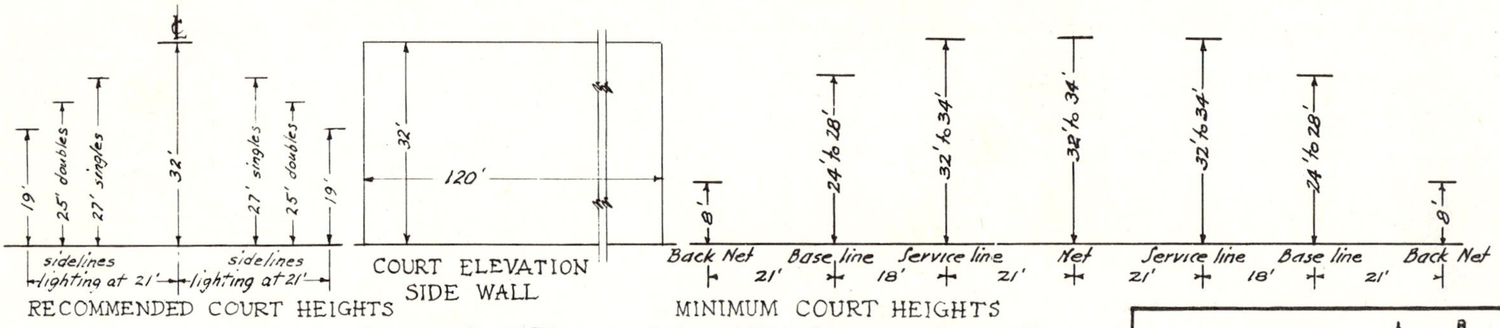
19'
25' doubles
27' singles
32'
27' singles
25' doubles
19'
sidelines lighting at 21'
sidelines lighting at 21'
RECOMMENDED COURT HEIGHTS
32'
120'
COURT ELEVATION SIDE WALL
8'
24' to 28'
32' to 34'
32' to 34'
32' to 34'
24' to 28'
8'
Back Net
Base line
Service line
Net
Service line
Base line
Back Net
21'
18'
21'
21'
18'
21'
MINIMUM COURT HEIGHTS

INDOOR TENNIS HEIGHT REQUIREMENTS

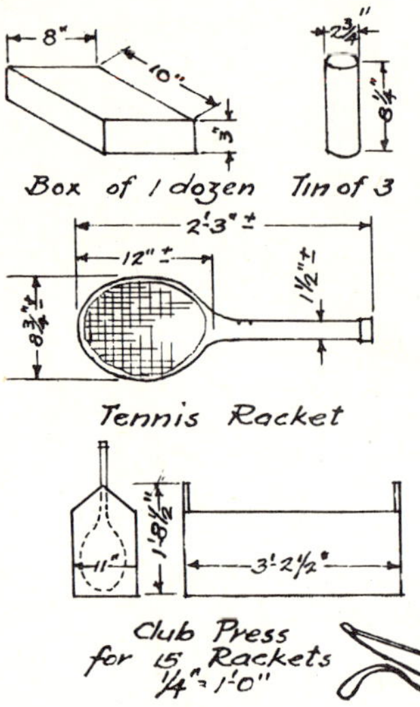
8"
10"
3"
Box of 1 dozen
2¾"
8¼"
Tin of 3
2'3" ±
12" ±
8¾" ±
1½" ±
Tennis Racket
11"
1'8½"
3'-2½"
Club Press for 15 Rackets
¼" = 1'-0"

TENNIS ACCESSORIES

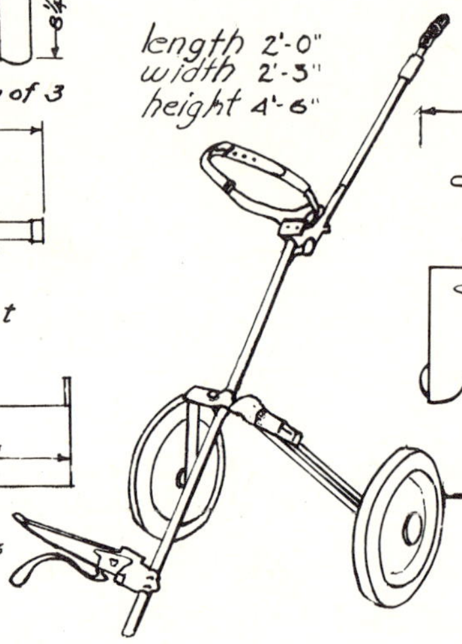
length 2'-0"
width 2'-3"
height 4'-6"

GOLF CART

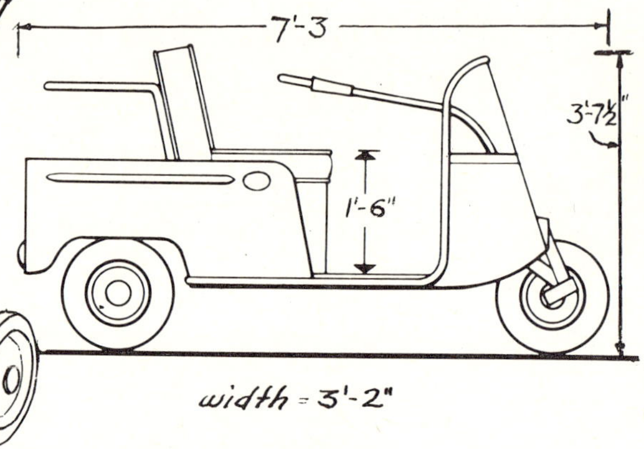
7'-3
3'-7½"
1'-6"
width = 3'-2"

GOLFMOBILE

Data supplied by Autoette, N.Y.C.

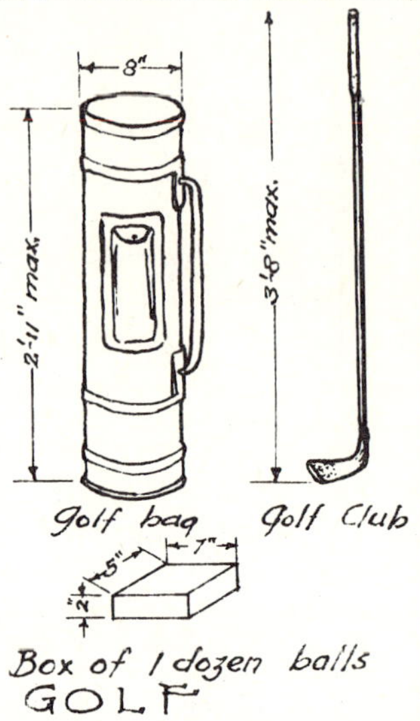
8"
2'-11" max.
3'-8" max.
Golf bag
Golf Club
7"
5"
2"
Box of 1 dozen balls

GOLF ACCESSORIES

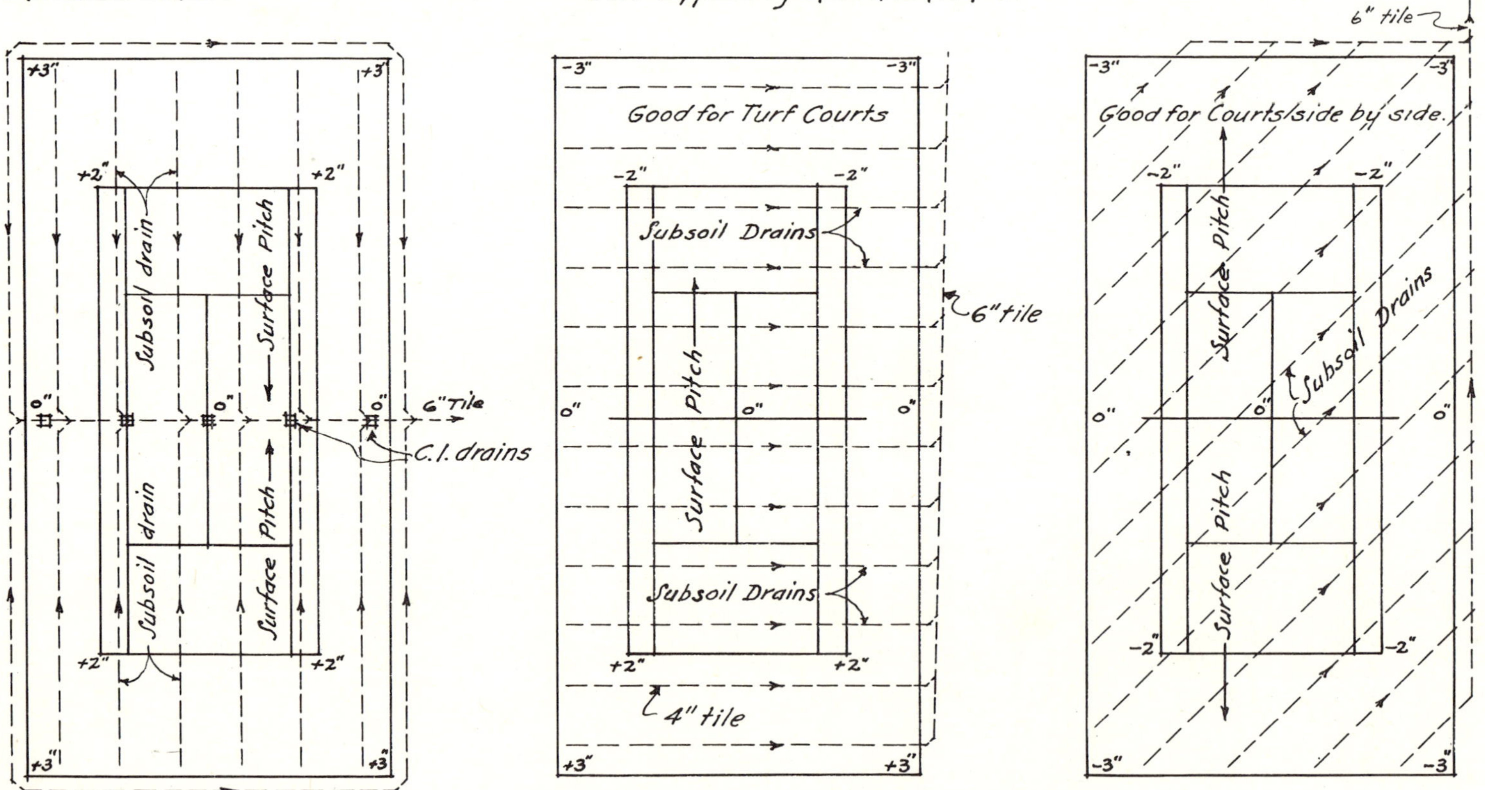
+3"
+3"
+2"
+2"
Subsoil drain
Surface Pitch
0"
0"
0"
0"
6" Tile
C.I. drains
Subsoil drain
Surface Pitch
+2"
+2"
+3"
+3"
-3"
-3"
Good for Turf Courts
-2"
-2"
Subsoil Drains
6" tile
0"
Pitch
0"
Surface
0"
Subsoil Drains
+2"
+2"
4" tile
+3"
+3"
6" tile
-3"
-3"
Good for Courts side by side.
-2"
-2"
Surface Pitch
Subsoil Drains
0"
0"
0"
Surface Pitch
-2"
-2"
-3"
-3"

②DRAINING TO NET ①BATTERY of COURTS ③DRAINING FROM NET

Surface drainage preference = from ① best to ③ poorest. Subsoil drains 10' to 15' apart. Pitch ⅛" to ¼" per lin. ft. Whether drainage is necessary & how much is dependent on soil conditions. Amounts shown are maximums.

TENNIS COURT DRAINAGE PLANS

1" = 32'.

Data checked by: Tennis Courts Inc.

SPORTS and GAMES

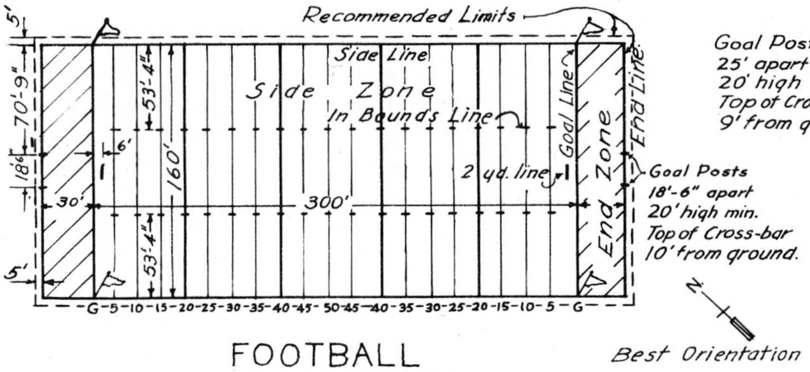
Recommended Limits
Side Line
Side Zone
In Bounds Line
Goal Line
End Line
End Zone
2 yd. line
5'
70'-9"
18'6"
6'
53'-4"
160'
30'
300'
53'-4"
5'
G-5-10-15-20-25-30-35-40-45-50-45-40-35-30-25-20-15-10-5-G
Goal Posts
18'-6" apart
20' high min.
Top of Cross-bar
10' from ground.
Best Orientation

FOOTBALL

* NCAA Rules - 1954

1" = 120'

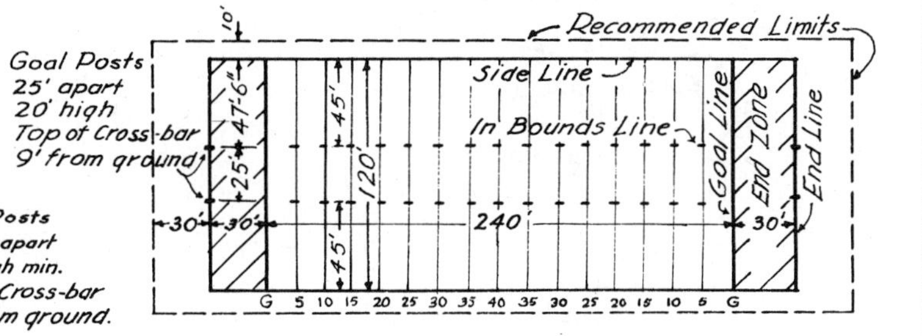
Recommended Limits
Goal Posts
25' apart
20' high
Top of Cross-bar
9' from ground
10'
25'
47'-6"
45'
120'
45'
30'
30'
240'
30'
Side Line
In Bounds Line
Goal Line
End Zone
End Line
G 5 10 15 20 25 30 35 40 35 30 25 20 15 10 5 G

SIX-MAN FOOTBALL

Nat'l Federation of State High School Athletic Assoc. - Rules-'48

1" = 120'

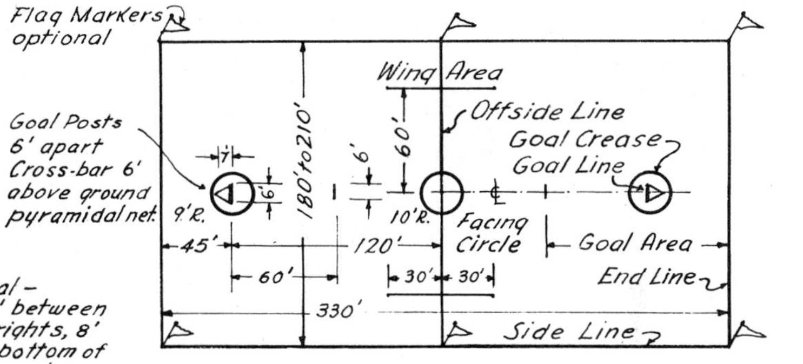
Flag Markers
optional
Wing Area
Offside Line
Goal Crease
Goal Line
Goal Posts
6' apart
Cross-bar 6'
above ground
pyramidal net
180' to 210'
60'
6'
7'
6'
9' R.
10' R.
Facing Circle
Goal Area
End Line
45'
120'
60'
30'
30'
330'
Side Line

LACROSSE

1" = 120' * NCAA Rules - 1954

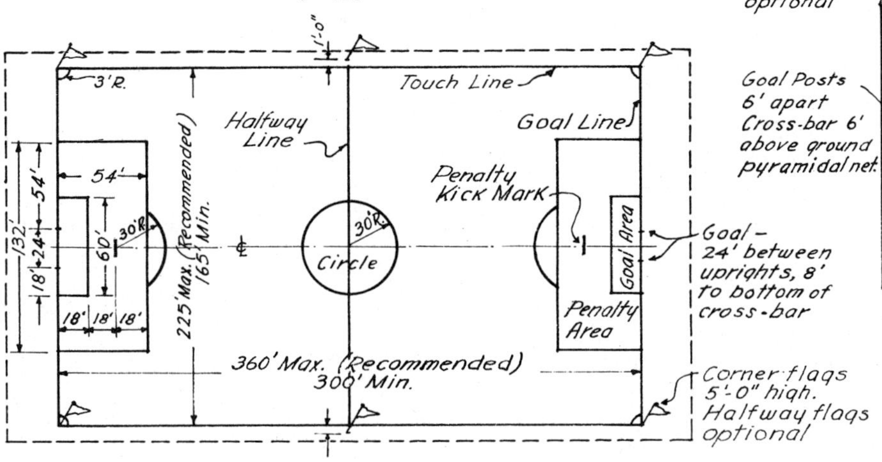
1'-0"
3' R.
Touch Line
Halfway Line
Goal Line
Penalty Kick Mark
54'
132'
54'
24'
18'
60'
30' R.
18'
18'
18'
225' Max. (Recommended)
165' Min.
30' R.
Circle
Goal Area
Penalty Area
Goal -
24' between
uprights, 8'
to bottom of
cross-bar
360' Max. (Recommended)
300' Min.
Corner flags
5'-0" high.
Halfway flags
optional

SOCCER

* NCAA Rules - 1954

1" = 120'

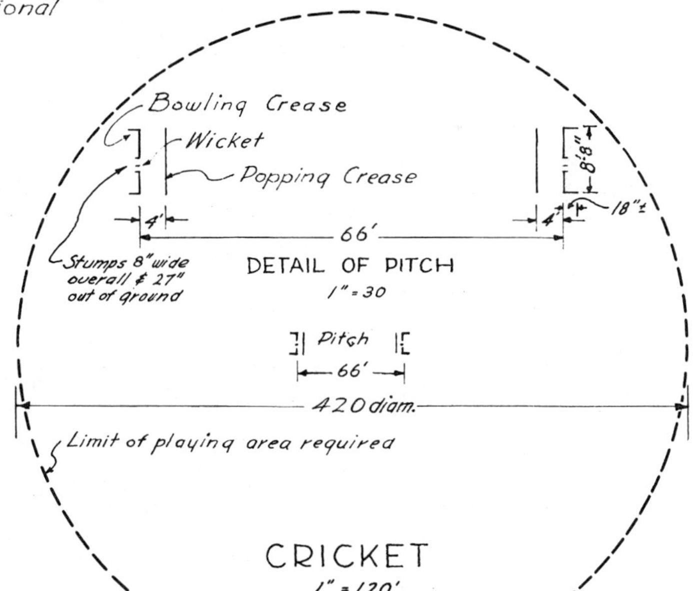
Bowling Crease
Wicket
Popping Crease
8'8"
4'
66'
4'
18" ±
Stumps 8" wide
overall & 27"
out of ground
DETAIL OF PITCH
1" = 30
Pitch
66'
420 diam.
Limit of playing area required

CRICKET

1" = 120'

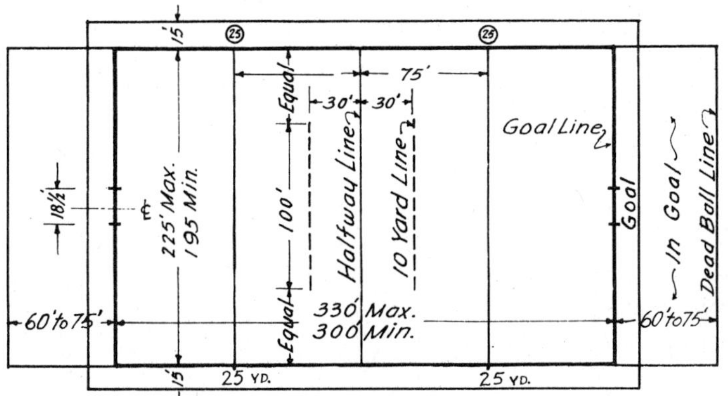
15'
25
25
75'
30'
30'
Equal
Equal
Goal Line
18½'
225' Max.
195 Min.
100'
Halfway Line
10 Yard Line
Goal
In Goal
Dead Ball Line
60' to 75'
330' Max.
300' Min.
60' to 75'
15'
25 YD.
25 YD.

RUGBY

1" = 120'

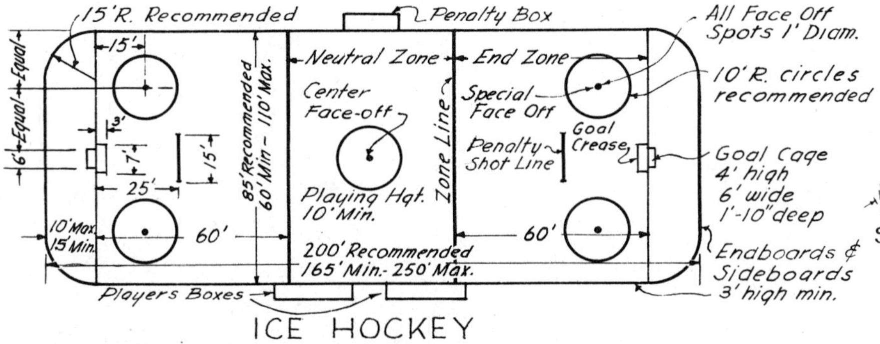
15' R. Recommended
Penalty Box
All Face Off
Spots 1' Diam.
15'
Equal
Equal
6'
3'
7'
15'
25'
85' Recommended
60' Min - 110' Max.
Neutral Zone
End Zone
Center
Face-off
Special
Face Off
Zone Line
Penalty
Shot Line
Goal
Crease
10' R. circles
recommended
Goal Cage
4' high
6' wide
1'-10" deep
Playing Hgt.
10' Min.
10' Max.
15' Min.
60'
60'
200' Recommended
165' Min. - 250' Max.
Endboards &
Sideboards
3' high min.
Players Boxes

ICE HOCKEY

* NCAA Rules - 1955 1" = 60'

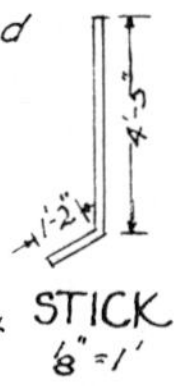
4'-3"
1'-2"

STICK

1/8" = 1'

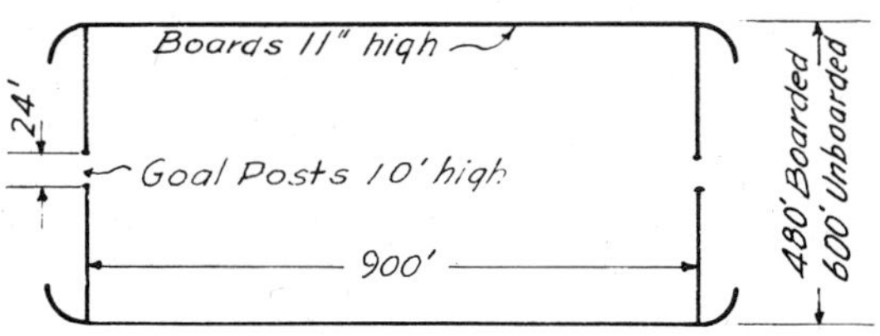
Boards 11" high
24'
Goal Posts 10' high
900'
480' Boarded
600' Unboarded

POLO

1" = 500'

Data checked by:
U.S. Polo Assn - 1954

* Data checked by: Nat'l. Collegiate Athletic Assn.

SPORTS and GAMES

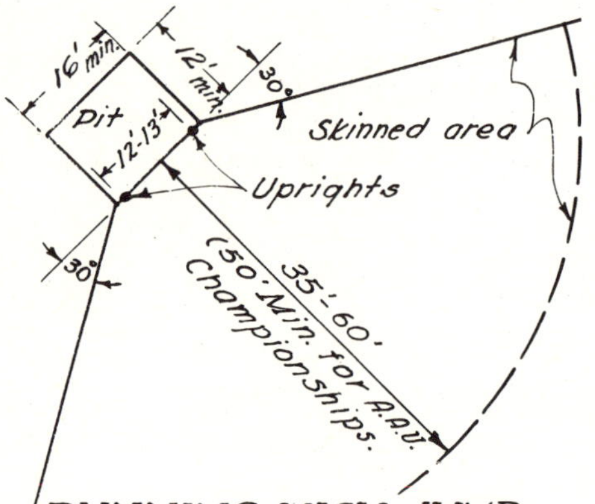
16' min.
12' min.
30°
Pit
12'-13'4"
Skinned area
Uprights
35'-60'
(50' Min. for A.A.U. Championships.
30°

* RUNNING HIGH JUMP
1" = 30'

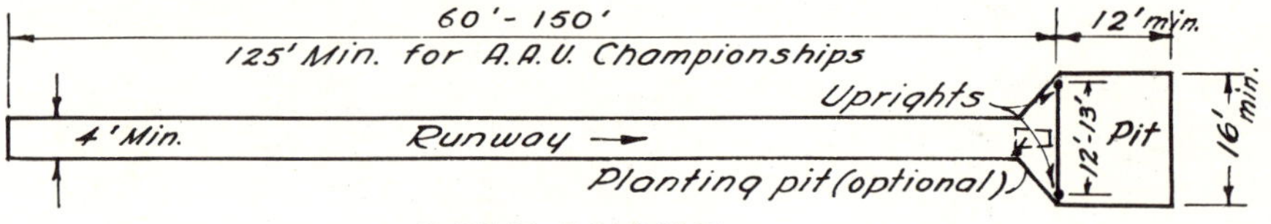
60'-150'
125' Min. for A.A.U. Championships
12' min.
Uprights
4' Min.
Runway →
Pit
12'-13'4"
16' min.
Planting pit (optional)

* POLE VAULT
1" = 30'

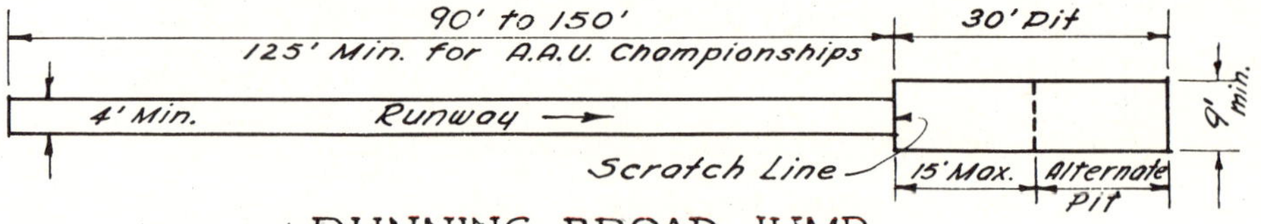
90' to 150'
125' Min. for A.A.U. Championships
30' Pit
9' min.
4' Min.
Runway →
Scratch Line
15' Max.
Alternate Pit

* RUNNING BROAD JUMP
1" = 30'

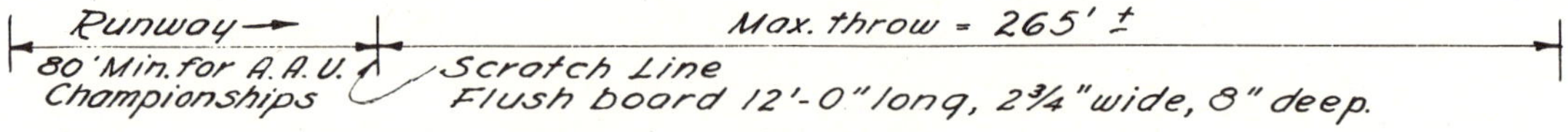
Runway →
Max. throw = 265' ±
80' Min. for A.A.U. Championships
Scratch Line
Flush board 12'-0" long, 2¾" wide, 8" deep.

JAVELIN THROW
1" = 60'

* N.C.A.A. Track & Field Guide, 1955

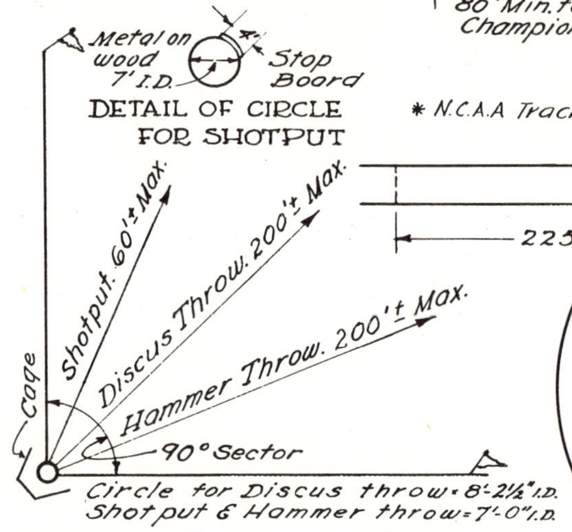
Metal on wood 7' I.D.
4"
Stop Board
DETAIL OF CIRCLE FOR SHOTPUT
Shotput. 60'± Max.
Discus Throw. 200'± Max.
Hammer Throw. 200'± Max.
Cage
90° Sector
Circle for Discus throw = 8'-2½" I.D.
Shot put & Hammer throw = 7'-0" I.D.

NOTE: For Women & Juniors a 10'-0" x 2" Throwing Line may be used instead of a circle.

SHOTPUT, DISCUS THROW & HAMMER THROW
No scale

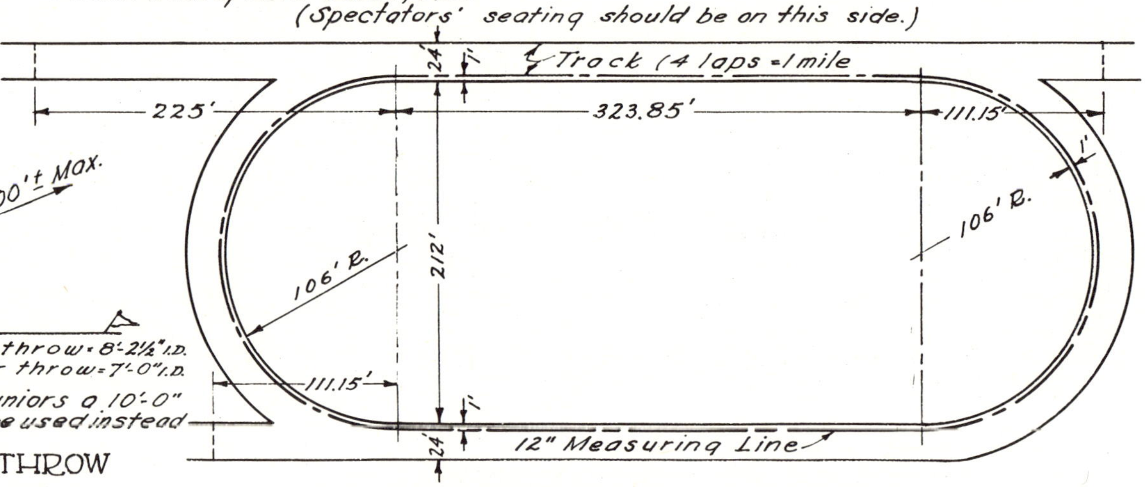
(Spectators' seating should be on this side.)
24'
1'
Track (4 laps = 1 mile
225'
323.85'
111.15'
1'
106' R.
106' R.
212'
111.15'
1'
24'
12" Measuring Line

QUARTER MILE RUNNING TRACK
1" = 120'

TRACK & FIELD

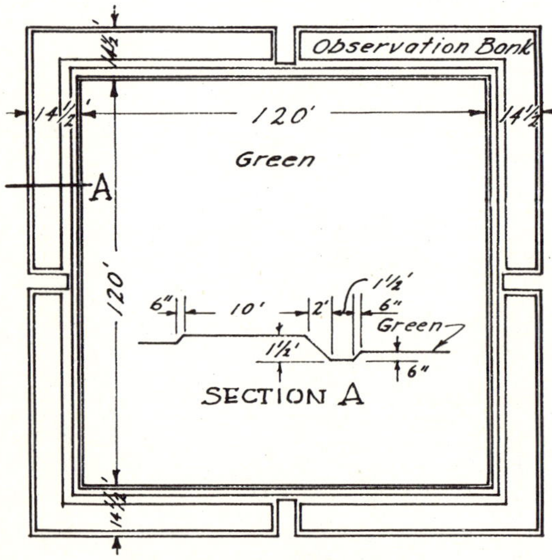
14½'
Observation Bank
14½'
120'
14½'
Green
A
120'
6"
10'
2'
1½'
6"
Green
1½'
6"
SECTION A
14½'
A

PUBLIC GREEN

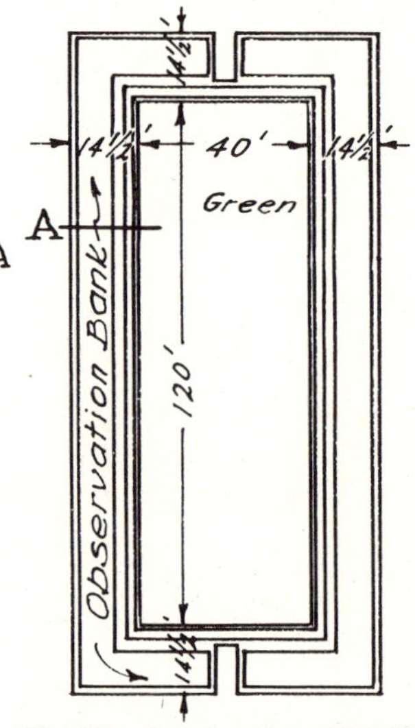
14½'
A
14½'
40'
14½'
Green
Observation Bank
120'
14½'

TWO ALLEY GREEN

BOWLING GREENS
1" = 60'

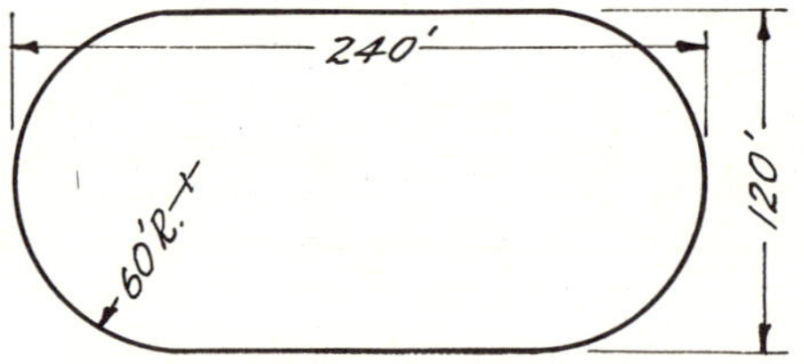
240'
120'
60' R. ±

OUTDOORS

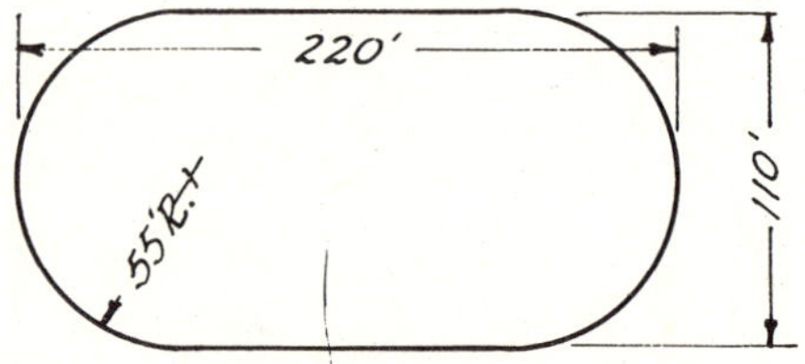
220'
110'
55' R. ±

INDOORS

Sizes recommended by the National Horse Show Assoc.

HORSE SHOW RINGS
1" = 120'

Data checked by Nat'l. Collegiate Athletic Assn

SPORTS and GAMES

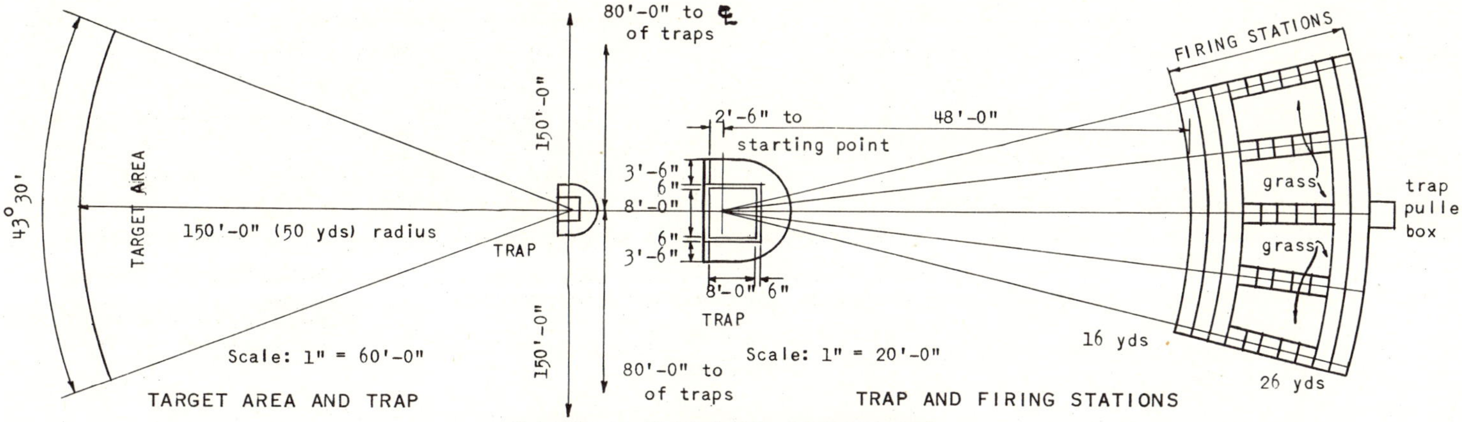
43° 30'
TARGET AREA
150'-0" (50 yds) radius
TRAP
Scale: 1" = 60'-0"
150'-0"
150'-0"
80'-0" to ℄ of traps
80'-0" to of traps
2'-6" to starting point
48'-0"
3'-6"
6"
8'-0"
6"
3'-6"
8'-0"
6"
TRAP
Scale: 1" = 20'-0"
FIRING STATIONS
grass
grass
trap puller box
16 yds
26 yds

TARGET AREA AND TRAP

TRAP AND FIRING STATIONS

SINGLE TARGET SHOOTING

Trapshooting data checked by Amateur Trapshooting Assn.

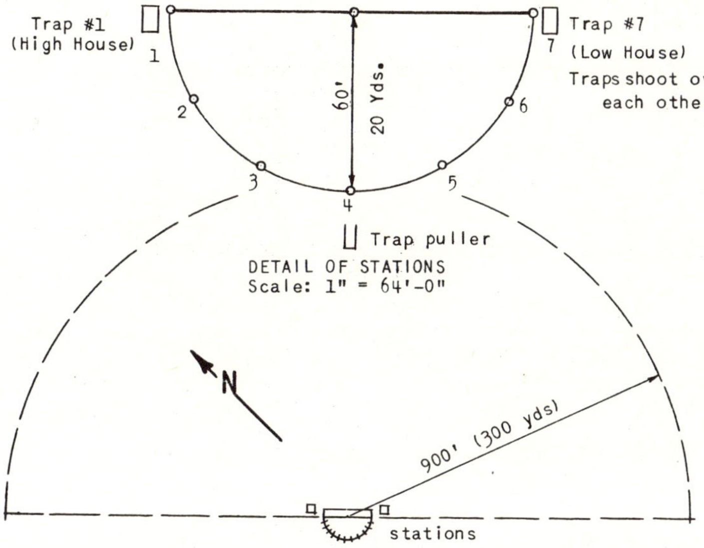
Trap #1 (High House)
1
2
3
4
5
6
7
Trap #7 (Low House)
Traps shoot over each other
60'
20 Yds.
Trap puller
DETAIL OF STATIONS
Scale: 1" = 64'-0"
N
900' (300 yds)
stations

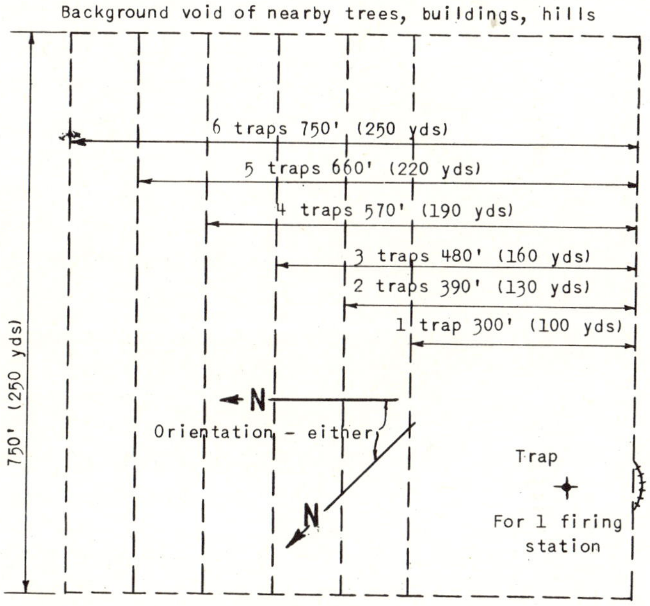
Background void of nearby trees, buildings, hills
6 traps 750' (250 yds)
5 traps 660' (220 yds)
4 traps 570' (190 yds)
3 traps 480' (160 yds)
2 traps 390' (130 yds)
1 trap 300' (100 yds)
750' (250 yds)
N
Orientation – either
N
Trap
For 1 firing station

SKEET SHOOTING

TARGET SHOOTING

AREA REQUIREMENTS

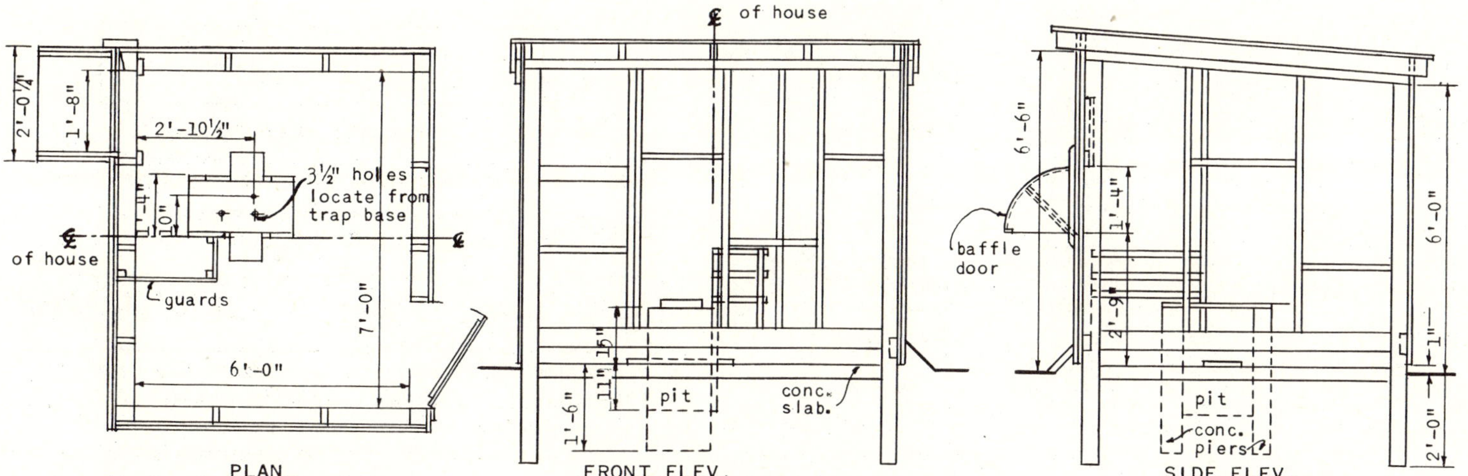
2'-0¼"
1'-8"
2'-10½"
3½" holes locate from trap base
1'-4"
10"
℄ of house
℄
guards
7'-0"
6'-0"
℄ of house
15"
11"
1'-6"
pit
conc. slab.
6'-6"
baffle door
1'-4"
2'-9"
6'-0"
1"
2'-0"
pit
conc. piers

PLAN

Consult mfr. for details of trap house shown, and high or combination trap houses.

FRONT ELEV. (Sheathing removed)

SIDE ELEV. (Sheathing removed)

Scale: ¼" = 1'-0"

#7 STATION TRAP HOUSE (LOW)

Skeet shooting data supplied by National Skeet Shooting Association.

SPORTS and GAMES

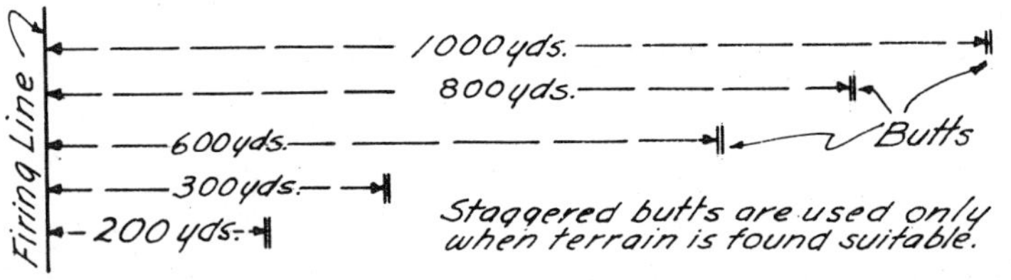
Firing Line
1000 yds.
800 yds.
600 yds.
300 yds.
200 yds.
Butts
Staggered butts are used only when terrain is found suitable.

STAGGERED BUTT RIFLE RANGE

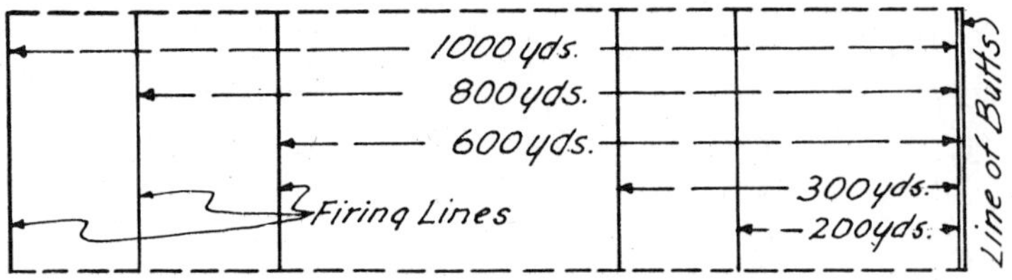
1000 yds.
800 yds.
600 yds.
300 yds.
200 yds.
Firing Lines
Line of Butts

BUTT-IN-LINE RIFLE RANGE

Orientation: - Face northward for general shooting, westward for morning shooting and eastward for afternoon shooting.

Small Bore Ranges: - 50 yards, 100 yards, and 50 meters.
Pistol Ranges: - 25 yards, 50 yards, and 25 meters.

SPACING OF TARGETS

Pistol	4'-0" o.c.
Small bore rifle	5'-0" "
High power "	12'-0" "

OUTDOOR RIFLE & PISTOL RANGES

No scale

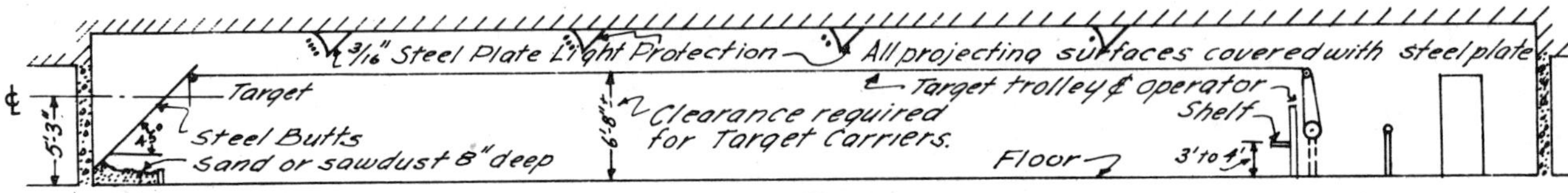
3/16" Steel Plate Light Protection
All projecting surfaces covered with steel plate
Target
Steel Butts
Sand or sawdust 8" deep
5'-3"
6'-8"
Clearance required for Target Carriers.
Target trolley & operator
Shelf
Floor
3' to 4'

SECTION

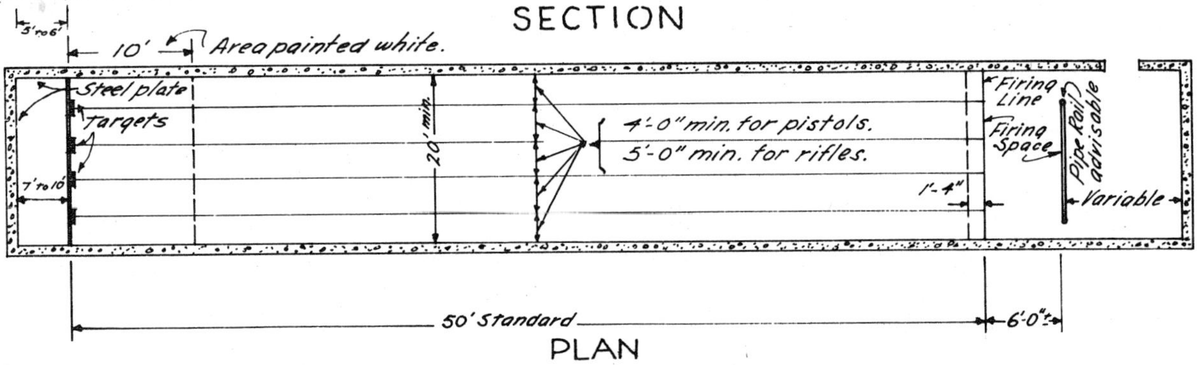
3' to 6'
10'
Area painted white.
Steel plate
Targets
7' to 10'
20' min.
4'-0" min. for pistols.
5'-0" min. for rifles.
1'-4"
Firing Line
Firing Space
Pipe Rail advisable
Variable
50' Standard
6'-0"±

PLAN

Rifle and Pistol ranges 50' standard for indoor ranges.

INDOOR REGULATION RIFLE & PISTOL RANGE

Data by National Rifle Association

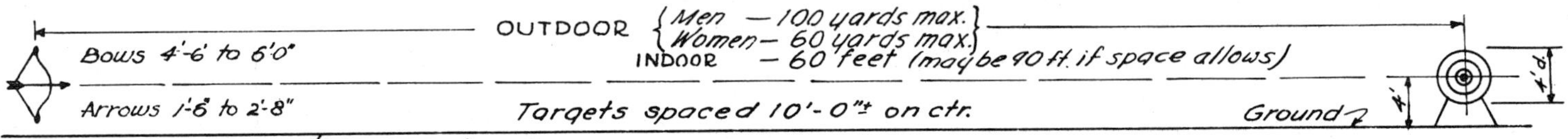
OUTDOOR { Men — 100 yards max. / Women — 60 yards max. }
INDOOR — 60 feet (may be 90 ft. if space allows)
Bows 4'-6' to 6'0"
Arrows 1'-6" to 2'-8"
Targets spaced 10'-0"± on ctr.
Ground
4'
4' d.

Data checked by Nat'l Archery Assn.

ARCHERY

No scale

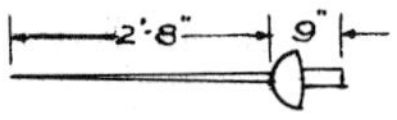
2'-8"
9"

FOIL 1/4" = 1'

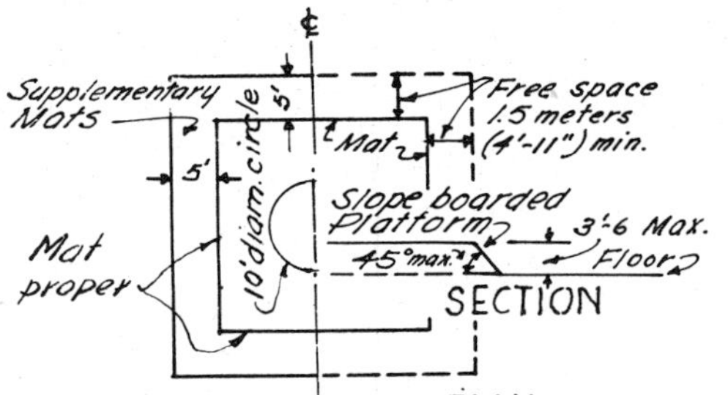
Supplementary Mats
5'
5'
Mat proper
10' diam. circle
Free space 1.5 meters (4'-11") min.
Mat
Slope boarded Platform
45° max.
3'-6 Max.
Floor
SECTION

PLAN   PLAN

Rope and raised platform illegal

MAT SIZE:
Intercollegiate competition: - 24' x 24' min. & standard

NCAA RULES

Ropes illegal. Raised platform legal but not recommended.

MAT SIZES:
Internat'l compet'n 6 m. x 6 m. (19'-8 1/4") min.
Olympic compet'n - 8 m. x 8 m. (26'-3") min.

AAU RULES

WRESTLING

1/32" = 1'

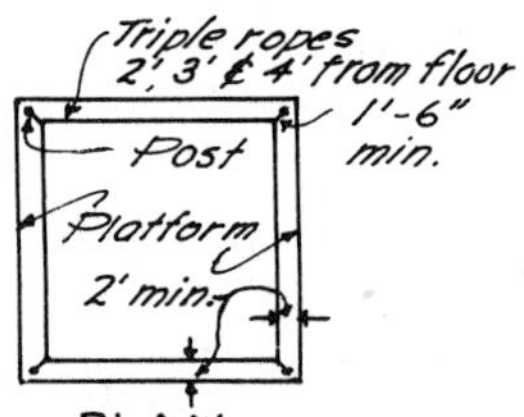
Triple ropes 2', 3' & 4' from floor
1'-6" min.
Post
Platform
2' min.

PLAN

If ring is on floor, extend pads 3' min. beyond ropes.

RING SIZES: (inside ropes)
NCAA - 18' x 18' min.
AAU - 16' x 16' min. / 20' x 20 max.

A room for 2 rings requires 2600 sq. ft

BOXING

1/32" = 1'

Data checked by Nat'l Collegiate Athletic Assn.

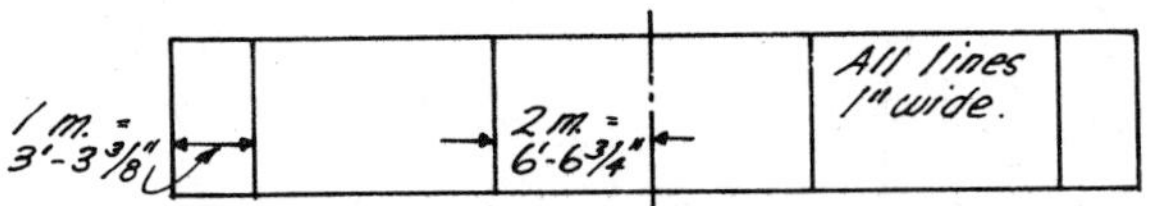
1 m. = 3'-3 3/8"
2 m. = 6'-6 3/4"
All lines 1" wide.

ALTERNATE MARKINGS

According to rules of Féderacion International d'Escrime. Permitted in AFLA competitions, but not Intercollegiate.

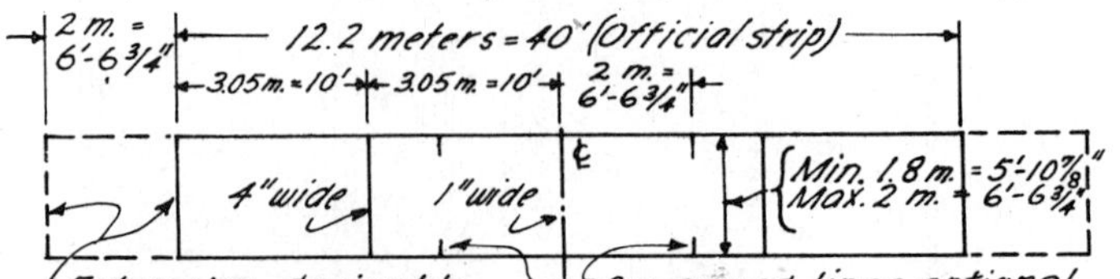
2 m. = 6'-6 3/4"
12.2 meters = 40' (Official strip)
3.05 m. = 10'
3.05 m. = 10'
2 m. = 6'-6 3/4"
4" wide
1" wide
Min. 1.8 m. = 5'-10 7/8"
Max. 2 m. = 6'-6 3/4"
Extension desirable
On guard lines optional

OFFICIAL STRIP for CHAMPIONSHIP EVENTS

Amateur Fencers League of America & NCAA

For non-championship events the min. size strip is 3' x 30'

FENCING

1/16" = 1'

Data checked by Amateur Fencers League of America

WOMEN'S SPORTS

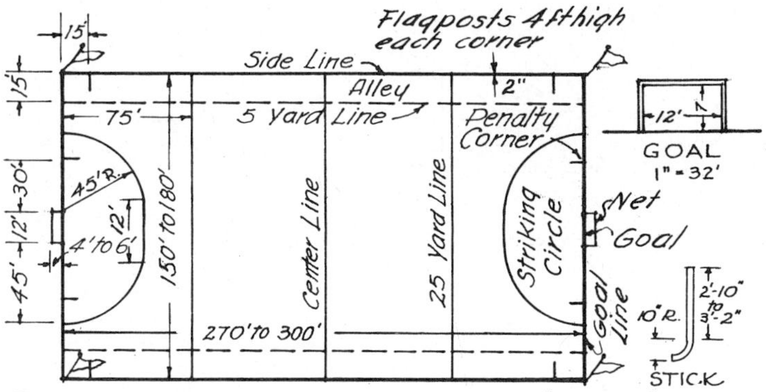

Flagposts 4 ft high each corner
15'
Side Line
Alley
2"
15'
75'
5 Yard Line
Penalty Corner
30'
45'R.
12'
4' to 6'
45'
150' to 180'
Center Line
25 Yard Line
Striking Circle
Net
Goal
Goal Line
270' to 300'
12'
7'
GOAL
1" = 32'
10"R.
2'-10" to 3'-2"
STICK

For young girls the Min. size is 135' x 255'

FIELD HOCKEY
1" = 120'

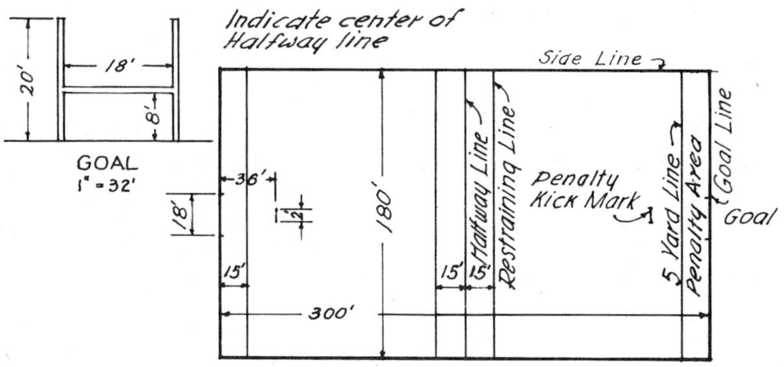

20'
18'
8'
GOAL
1" = 32'
Indicate center of Halfway line
Side Line
36'
18'
180'
Halfway Line
Restraining Line
Penalty Kick Mark
5 Yard Line
Penalty Area
Goal Line
Goal
15'
15'
15'
300'

For High School girls the field may be 120' x 240'

SPEEDBALL
1" = 120'

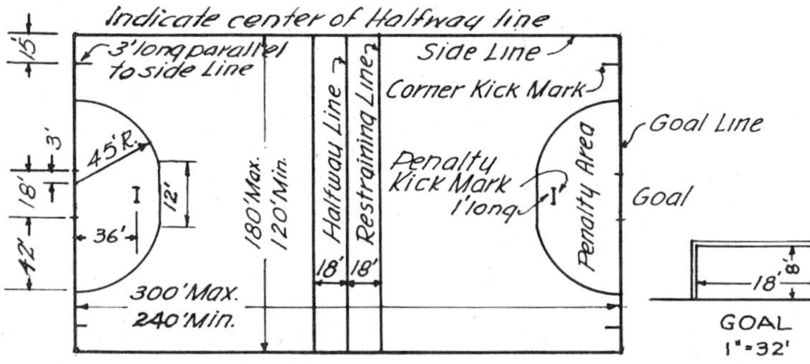

Indicate center of Halfway line
15'
3' long parallel to side Line
Side Line
Corner Kick Mark
Goal Line
3'
45'R.
18'
12'
36'
42'
180' Max.
120' Min.
Halfway Line
Restraining Line
Penalty Kick Mark 1' long
Penalty Area
Goal
18'
18'
300' Max.
240' Min.
18'
8'
GOAL
1" = 32'

SOCCER
1" = 120'

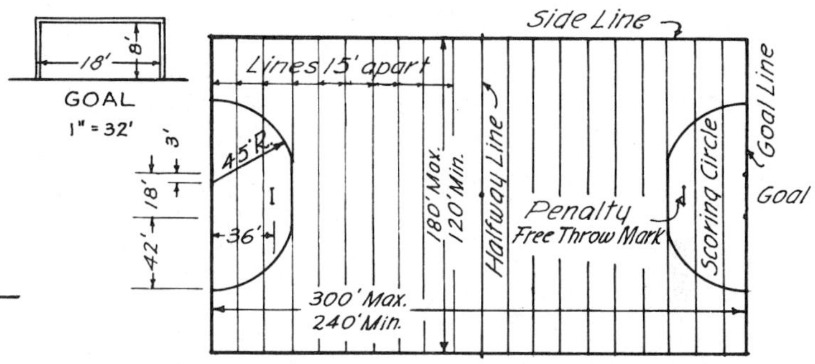

18'
8'
GOAL
1" = 32'
Side Line
Lines 15' apart
3'
45'R.
18'
36'
42'
180' Max.
120' Min.
Halfway Line
Penalty Free Throw Mark
Scoring Circle
Goal Line
Goal
300' Max.
240' Min.

FIELD BALL
1" = 120'

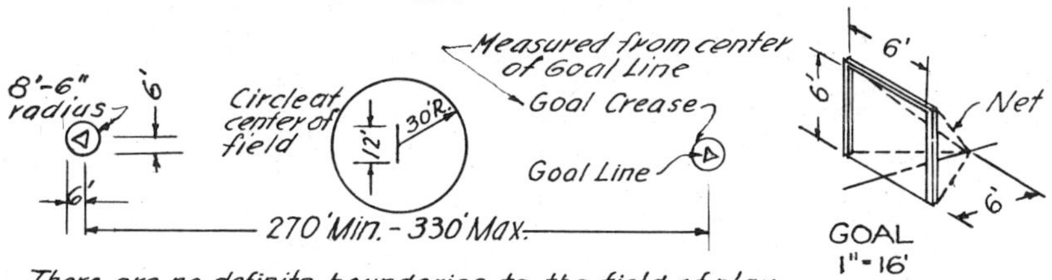

8'-6" radius
6'
6'
Circle at center of field
12'
30'R.
Measured from center of Goal Line
Goal Crease
Goal Line
270' Min. - 330' Max.
6'
6'
Net
6'
GOAL
1" = 16'

There are no definite boundaries to the field of play

LACROSSE
1" = 120'

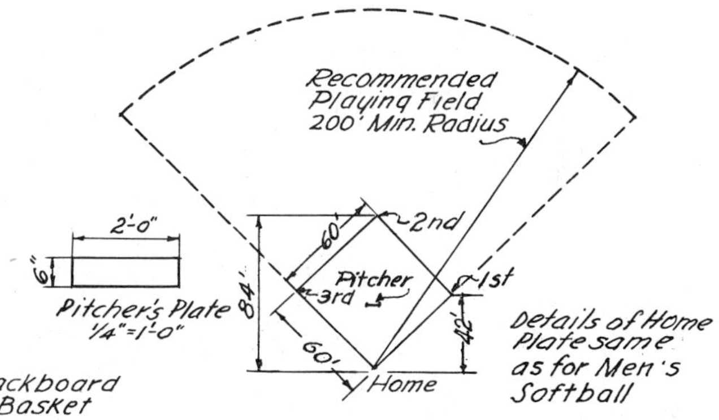

Recommended Playing Field 200' Min. Radius
2'-0"
6"
Pitcher's Plate
1/4" = 1'-0"
84'
60'
2nd
Pitcher
3rd
1st
42'
60'
Home
Details of Home Plate same as for Men's Softball

SOFTBALL
1" = 120'

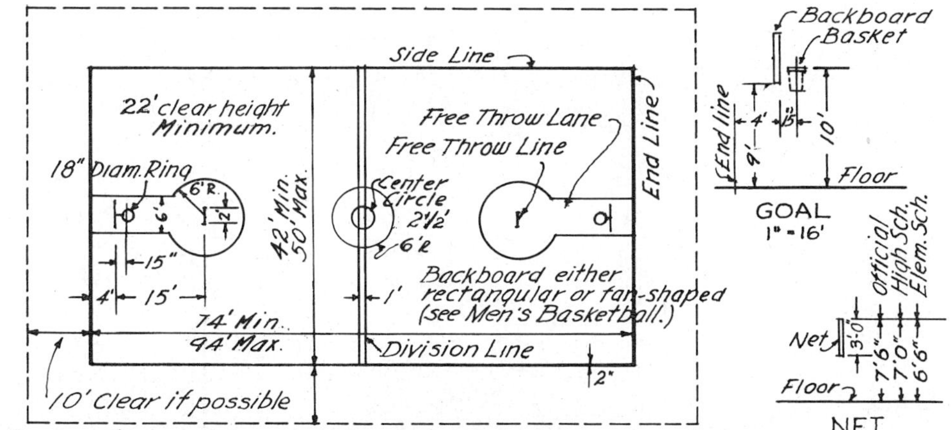

Side Line
22' clear height Minimum.
18" Diam. Ring
6'R.
6'
12'
15"
4'
15'
42' Min.
50' Max.
Center Circle
2'
6'R.
Free Throw Lane
Free Throw Line
End Line
1'
Backboard either rectangular or fan-shaped (see Men's Basketball.)
74' Min.
94' Max.
Division Line
2"
10' Clear if possible
Backboard
Basket
End line
4'
6"
9'
10'
Floor
GOAL
1" = 16'

The Canadian court is 50' x 94' divided into 3 equal parts instead of 2.

BASKETBALL
1" = 32'

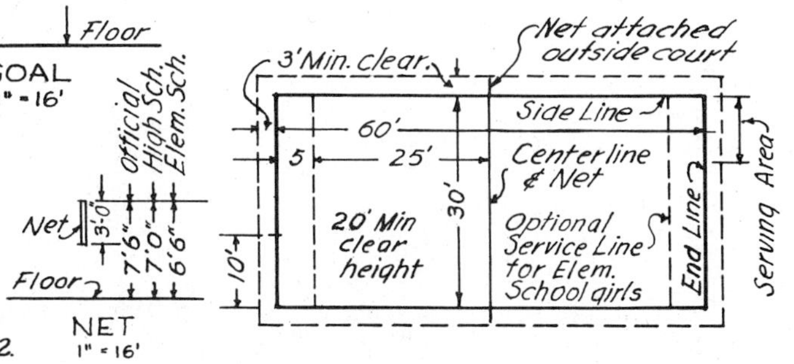

Official
High Sch.
Elem. Sch.
Net
3'-0"
7'-6"
7'-0"
6'-6"
Floor
NET
1" = 16'
3' Min. clear
Net attached outside court
Side Line
60'
5
25'
30'
Centerline & Net
20' Min clear height
Optional Service Line for Elem. School girls
End Line
10'
Serving Area

VOLLEY BALL
1" = 32'

Source: Official Rules - Nat'l Section on Women's Athletics of the Amer. Assoc. for Health, Phys. Ed. & Rec.-1955.

SPORTS and GAMES

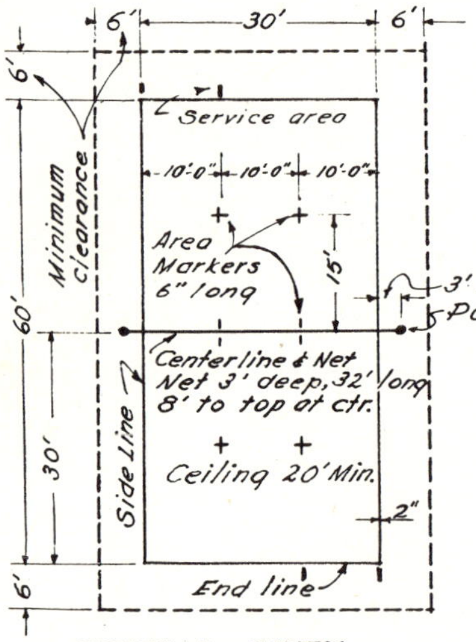
6'
30'
6'
Minimum clearance
Service area
10'-0"
10'-0"
10'-0"
Area Markers 6" long
15'
3' Min.
Post
60'
Centerline & Net
Net 3' deep, 32' long
8' to top at ctr.
30'
Side Line
Ceiling 20' Min.
2"
End line
6'

OFFICIAL COURT

United States Volley Ball Association
1" = 32

For Unofficial games, court may be varied to suit players & space. Min. clearance 3'-0". See sheet on Women's Sports.
Outdoor court - 40' x 80' Max.

VOLLEY BALL

Data checked by: U.S. Volley Ball Assn.

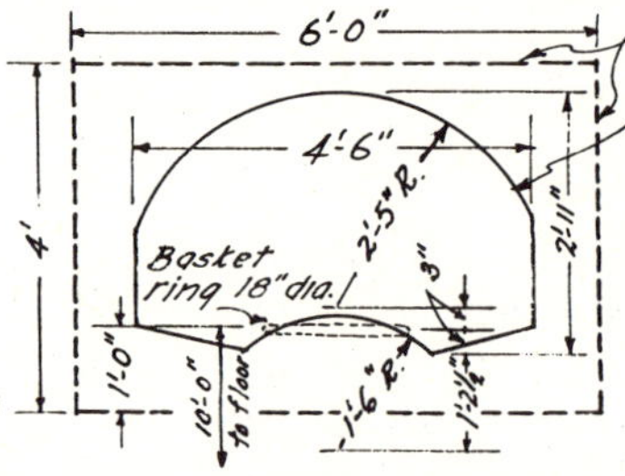
6'-0"
Rectangular Backboard (shown dotted).
Modified Backboard (shown solid).
4'-6"
2'-5" R.
4'
2'-11"
Basket ring 18" dia.
8"
1'-0"
10'-0" to floor
1'-6" R.
1'-2½"

Both types legal for College & High School games. For new H.S. courts, use the modified type.

BACKBOARD DETAIL
¼" = 1'-0"

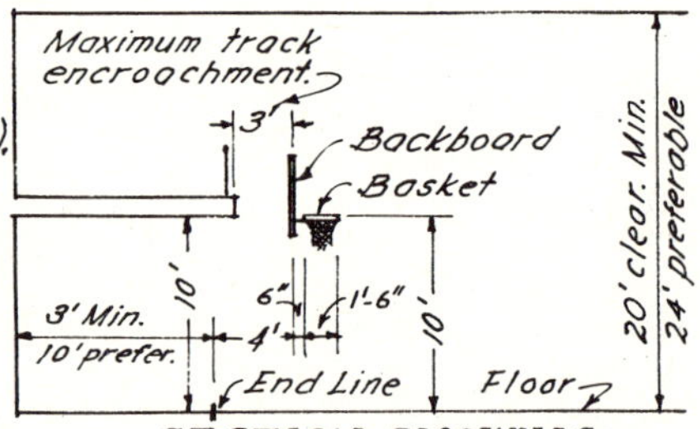
Maximum track encroachment.
3'
Backboard
Basket
10'
6"
1'-6"
3' Min.
10' prefer.
4'
10'
End Line
Floor
20' clear. Min.
24' preferable

SECTION SHOWING BASKET & ENCROACHMENTS
1" = 16'

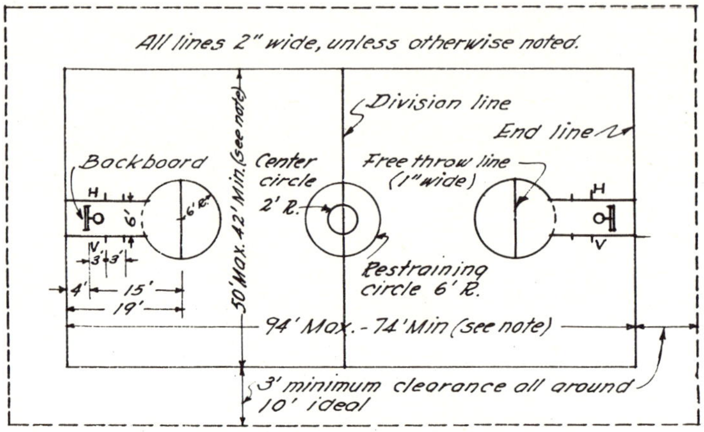
All lines 2" wide, unless otherwise noted.
Division line
End line
Backboard
Center circle
2' R.
Free throw line (1" wide)
H
V
6'
6' R.
3'
3'
50' Max. 42' Min. (See note)
Restraining circle 6' R.
4'
15'
19'
94' Max. - 74' Min (see note)
3' minimum clearance all around
10' ideal

STANDARD COURT FOR MEN
1" = 32'

IDEAL COURT SIZES MEN & BOYS

College Age	50'x94'
High School	50'x84'
Junior H.S.	42'x74'

Max. size for Women's courts 50'x 94'

For marking of Women's courts, see sheet on Women's Sports.

Data checked by: Nat'l Fed. of State H.S. Athletic Association.

BASKETBALL

See "Women's Sports" for Women's Basketball.

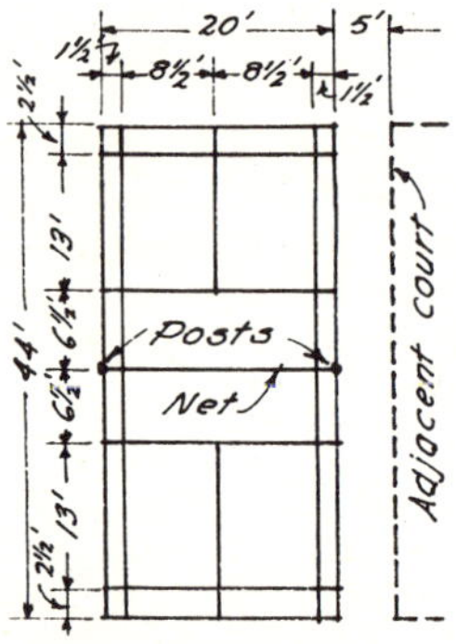
20'
5'
1½'
8½'
8½'
1½'
2½'
13'
44'
6½'
6½'
Posts
Net
13'
2½'
Adjacent court

STANDARD COURT

Lined for both doubles and singles.
All lines 1½" wide.

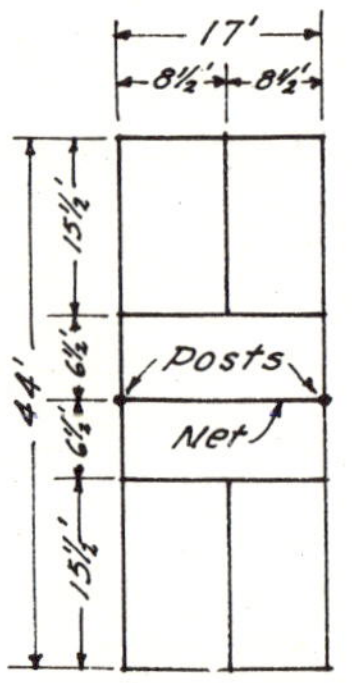
17'
8½'
8½'
15½'
44'
6½'
6½'
Posts
Net
15½'

SINGLES COURT

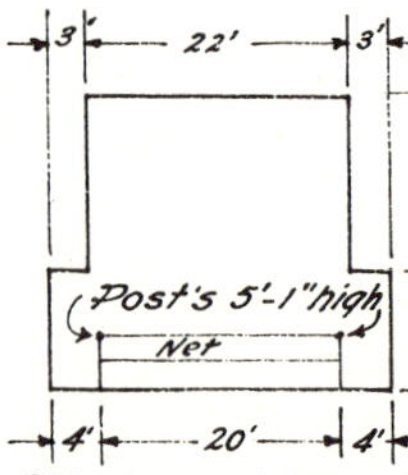
3'
22'
3'
25'
10'
Posts 5'-1" high
Net
4'
20'
4'

CROSS-SECTION

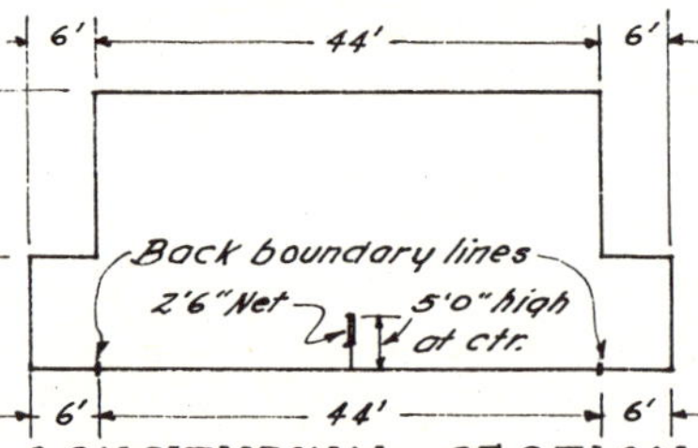
6'
44'
6'
Back boundary lines
2'6" Net
5'0" high at ctr.
6'
44'
6'

LONGITUDINAL SECTION

ENCROACHMENTS

BADMINTON ~ MEN & WOMEN

1" = 32'

Data checked by: American Badminton Assn.

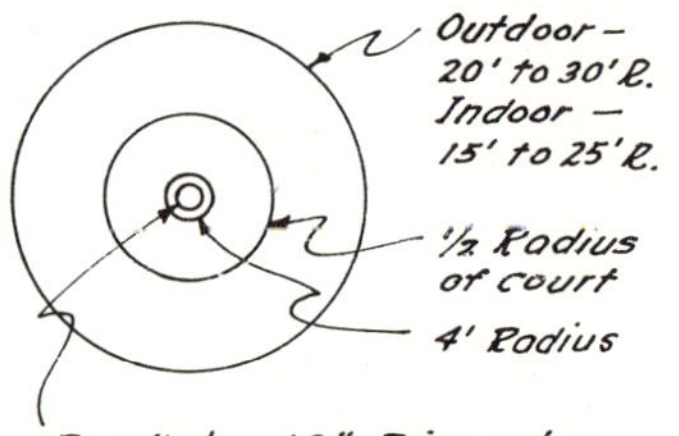
Outdoor - 20' to 30' R.
Indoor - 15' to 25' R.
½ Radius of court
4' Radius

Basket - 18" Diameter
8' height - Element. Sch. use.
9' " - Junior H.S. "
10' " - H.S. & College.

GOAL-HI COURT
1" = 32'

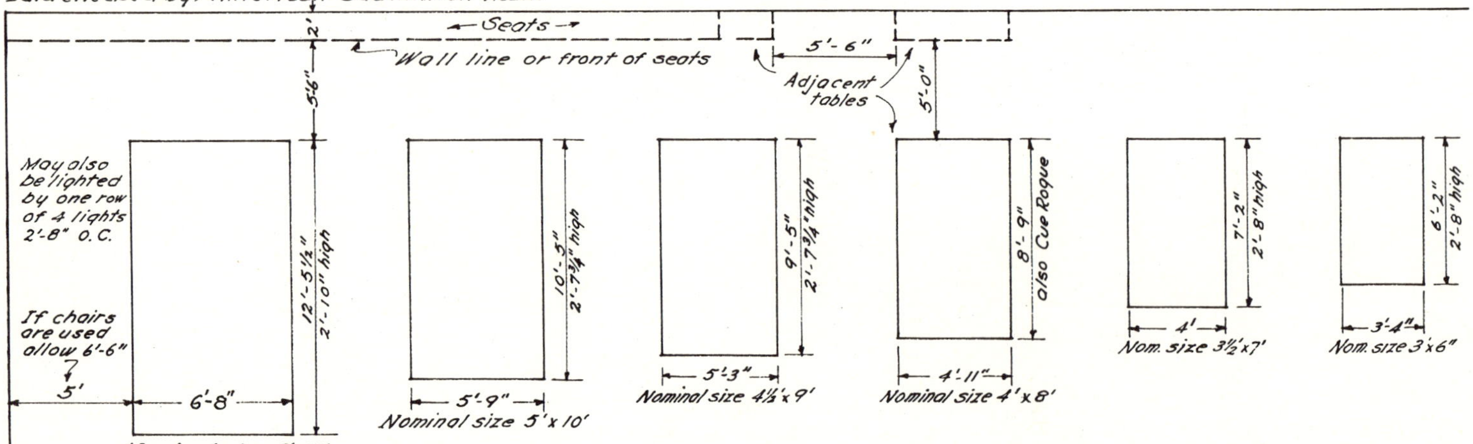
Seats
2'
Wall line or front of seats
5'-6"
Adjacent tables
5'-0"
5'-6"
May also be lighted by one row of 4 lights 2'-8" O.C.
If chairs are used allow 6'-6"
5'
6'-8"
12'-5½"
2'-10" high
Nominal size 6'x12'
10'-5"
2'-7¾" high
5'-9"
Nominal size 5'x10'
9'-5"
2'-7¾" high
5'-3"
Nominal size 4½'x9'
8'-9"
also Cue Rogue
4'-11"
Nominal size 4'x8'
7'-2"
2'-8" high
4'
Nom. size 3½'x7'
6'-2"
2'-8" high
3'-4"
Nom. size 3'x6'

ENGLISH TABLE | STANDARD TABLES (Cues 57" long) | JUNIOR TABLES

POOL and BILLIARDS

Data checked by Brunswick-Balke-Collender

HANDBALL COURTS

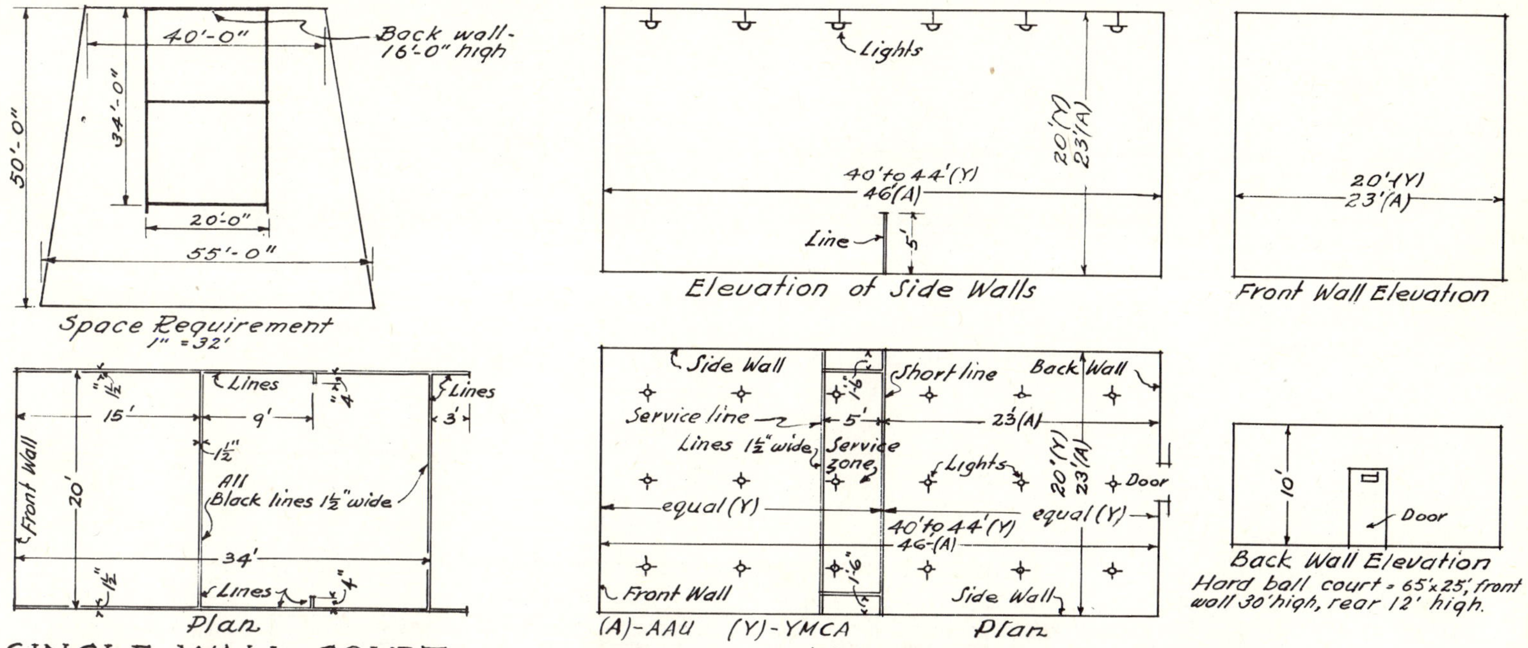
Back wall-
16'-0" high
40'-0"
34'-0"
50'-0"
20'-0"
55'-0"
Space Requirement
1" = 32'
Lights
20'(Y)
23'(A)
40' to 44'(Y)
46'(A)
Line
5'
Elevation of Side Walls
20'(Y)
23'(A)
Front Wall Elevation
Lines
Lines
15'
9'
3'
Front Wall
20'
1½"
All
Black lines 1½" wide
34'
Lines
Plan
Side Wall
Short line
Back Wall
Service line
5'
23'(A)
Lines 1½" wide
Service zone
Lights
20'(Y)
23'(A)
Door
equal (Y)
40' to 44'(Y)
equal (Y)
46'(A)
Front Wall
Side Wall
(A)-AAU (Y)-YMCA
Plan
10'
Door
Back Wall Elevation
Hard ball court = 65'x25', front wall 30' high, rear 12' high.

SINGLE WALL COURT

1/16" = 1'

FOUR WALL COURT

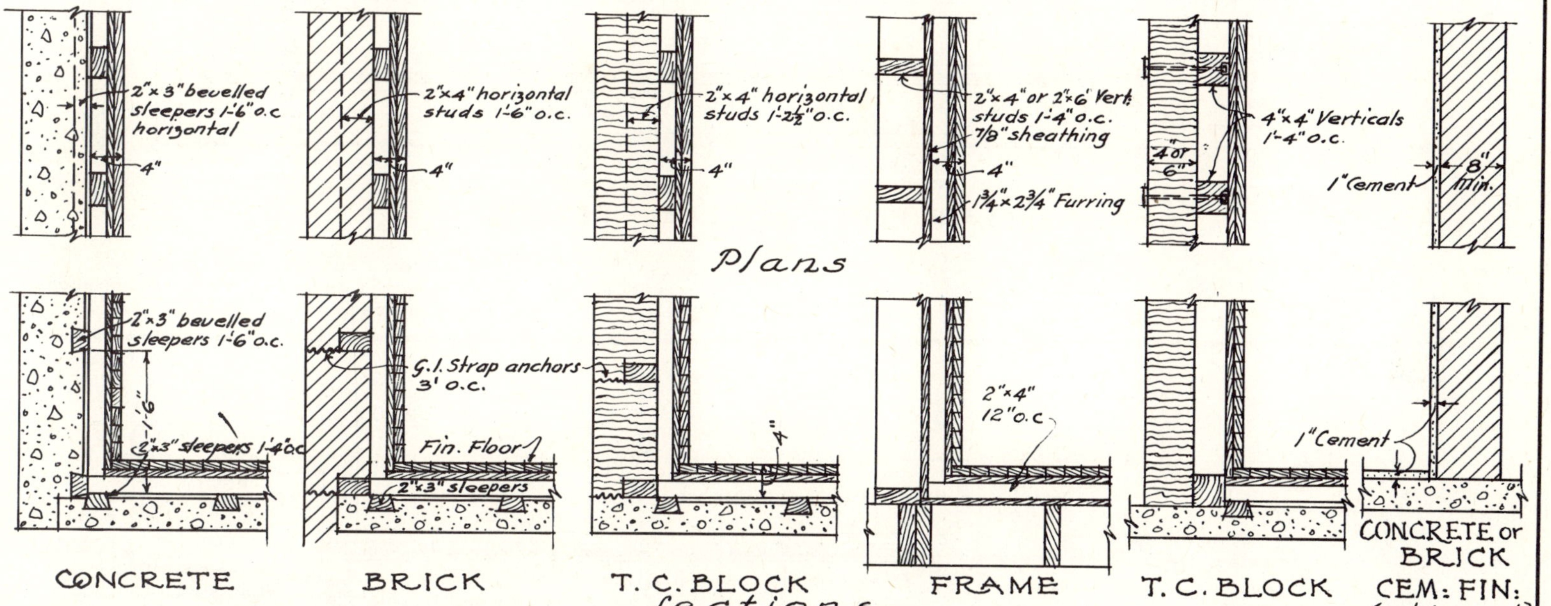
2"x3" bevelled sleepers 1'-6" o.c. horizontal
4"
2"x4" horizontal studs 1'-6" o.c.
4"
2"x4" horizontal studs 1'-2½" o.c.
4"
2"x4" or 2"x6" Vert. studs 1'-4" o.c.
7/8" sheathing
4"
1¾"x2¾" Furring
4"x4" Verticals 1'-4" o.c.
4" or 6"
8" Min.
1" Cement
Plans
2"x3" bevelled sleepers 1'-6" o.c.
1'-6"
2"x3" sleepers 1'-4" o.c.
G.I. Strap anchors 3' o.c.
Fin. Floor
2"x3" sleepers
4"
2"x4"
12" o.c.
1" Cement
CONCRETE
BRICK
T. C. BLOCK
FRAME
T. C. BLOCK
CONCRETE or BRICK
CEM. FIN.
(out-doors only)

Sections

All Finish Floors and Walls (except Cement Finish) to be 1⅛"×2¼" tongued and grooved Rock Maple laid on 1"×6"-7/8" diagonal sheathing

INDOOR COURTS

1/2" = 1'

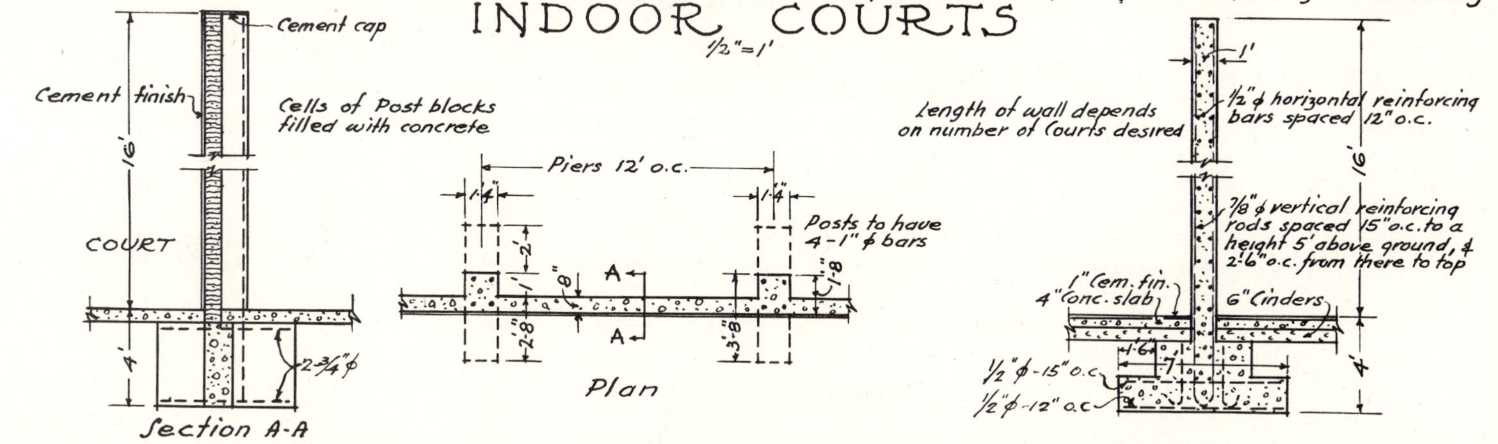
Cement cap
Cement finish
Cells of Post blocks filled with concrete
16'
COURT
4'
2-¾"⌀
Section A-A
Piers 12' o.c.
1'-4"
1'-4"
Posts to have 4-1" ⌀ bars
2'
8"
1'-8"
A
A
2'-8"
3'-8"
Plan
1'
Length of wall depends on number of Courts desired
½"⌀ horizontal reinforcing bars spaced 12" o.c.
16'
7/8"⌀ vertical reinforcing rods spaced 15" o.c. to a height 5' above ground, & 2'-6" o.c. from there to top
1" Cem. fin.
4" Conc. slab
6" Cinders
1'-6"
4'
½"⌀-15" o.c.
½"⌀-12" o.c.

SINGLE-FACE CONCRETE BLOCK WALL, CEM. FINISH

DOUBLE-FACE CONCRETE WALL

OUTDOOR SINGLE WALL COURTS

1/8" = 1'

BOWLING ALLEYS

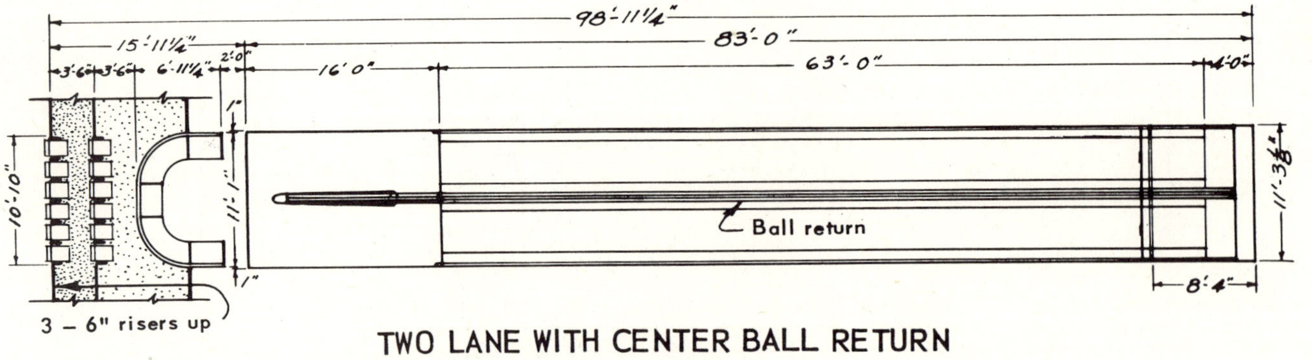
98'-11¼"
15'-11¼"
83'-0"
3'-6"
3'-6"
6'-11¼"
2'-0"
16'-0"
63'-0"
4'-0"
10'-10"
11'-1"
1"
1"
11'-3⅝"
Ball return
8'-4"
3 – 6" risers up

TWO LANE WITH CENTER BALL RETURN

SCALE: 1/16" = 1'0"

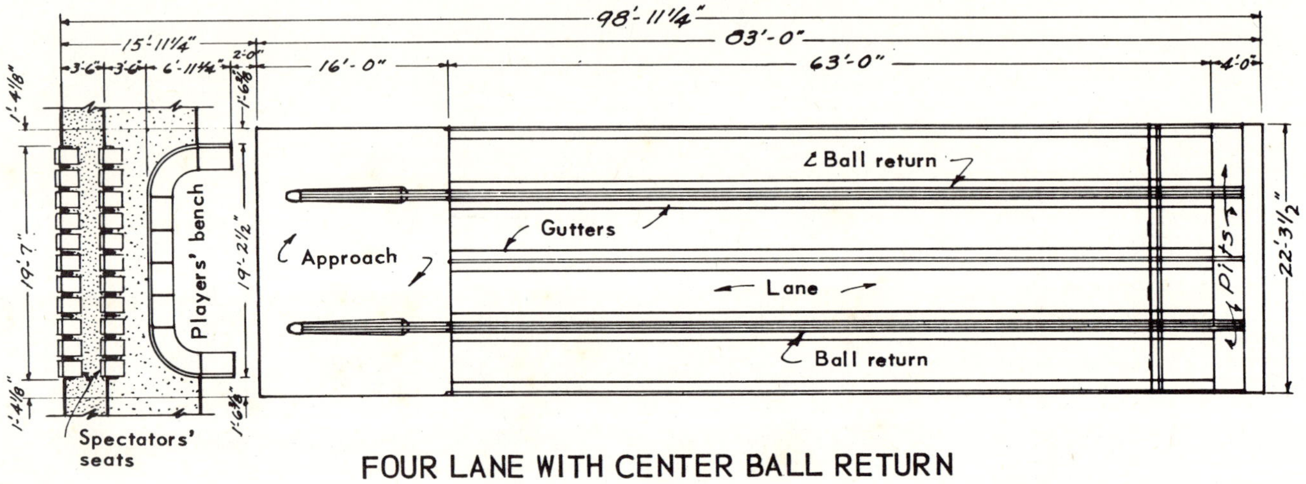
98'-11¼"
15'-11¼"
83'-0"
3'-6"
3'-6"
6'-11¼"
2'-0"
16'-0"
63'-0"
4'-0"
1'-4⅛"
19'-7"
1'-4⅛"
Players' bench
19'-2½"
Ball return
Gutters
Approach
Lane
Ball return
Pits
22'-3½"
Spectators' seats

FOUR LANE WITH CENTER BALL RETURN

SCALE: 1/16" = 1'0"

Note: Four lane with center ball return is used, but is not recommended practice.

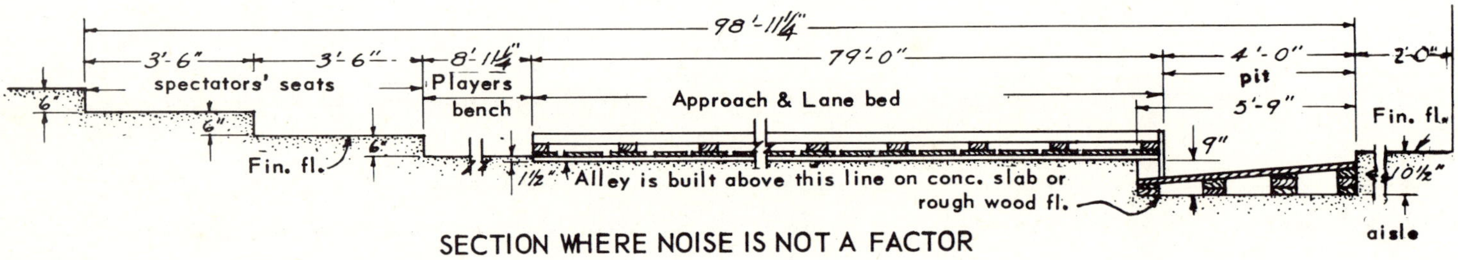
98'-11¼"
3'-6"
3'-6"
spectators' seats
8'-11¼"
Players bench
79'-0"
Approach & Lane bed
4'-0"
pit
5'-9"
2'-0"
6"
6"
6"
Fin. fl.
1½"
Alley is built above this line on conc. slab or rough wood fl.
9"
Fin. fl.
10½"
aisle

SECTION WHERE NOISE IS NOT A FACTOR

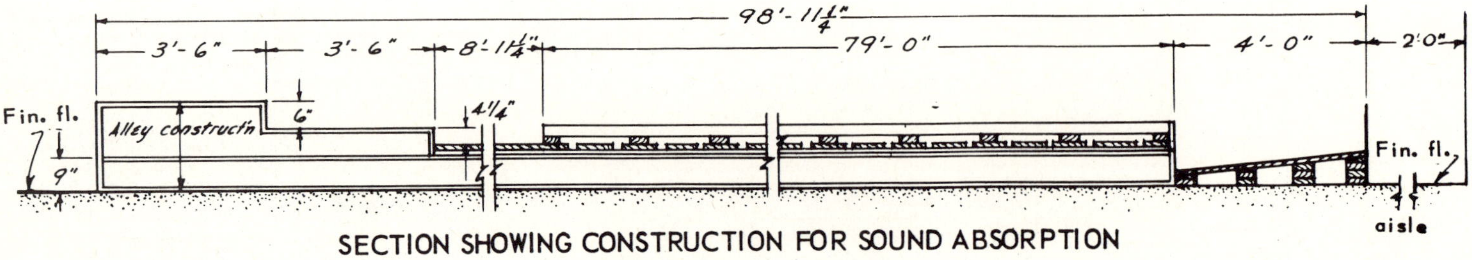
98'-11¼"
3'-6"
3'-6"
8'-11¼"
79'-0"
4'-0"
2'-0"
Fin. fl.
Alley constructn
6"
4¼"
9"
Fin. fl.
aisle

SECTION SHOWING CONSTRUCTION FOR SOUND ABSORPTION

LONGITUDINAL SECTIONS

SCALE: ¼" = 1'0"

DATA BY BRUNSWICK-BALKE-COLLENDER CO.

BOWLING ALLEYS

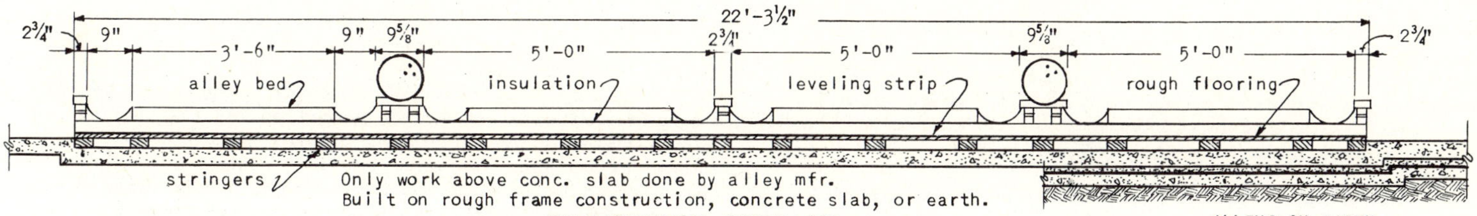
22'-3½"
2¾"
9"
3'-6"
9"
9⅝"
5'-0"
2¾"
5'-0"
9⅝"
5'-0"
2¾"
alley bed
insulation
leveling strip
rough flooring
stringers
Only work above conc. slab done by alley mfr.
Built on rough frame construction, concrete slab, or earth.
ALLEYS ON EARTH

TRANSVERSE SECTION

FOUR LANE - CENTER RETURN

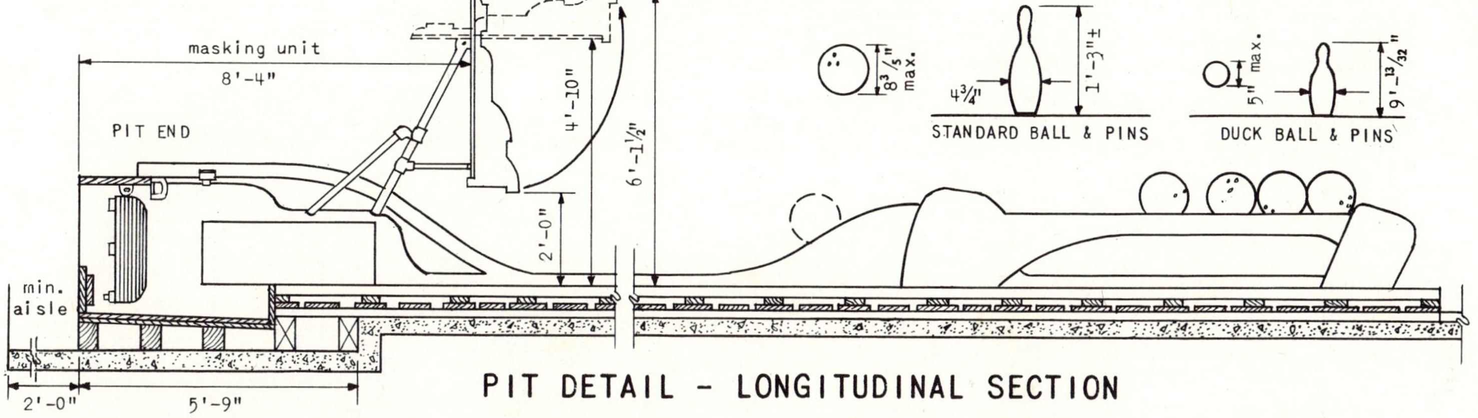
8 3/5" max.
4¾"
1'-3"±
STANDARD BALL & PINS
5" max.
9'-13/32"
DUCK BALL & PINS
masking unit
8'-4"
PIT END
4'-10"
6'-1½"
2'-0"
min. aisle
2'-0"
5'-9"

PIT DETAIL - LONGITUDINAL SECTION

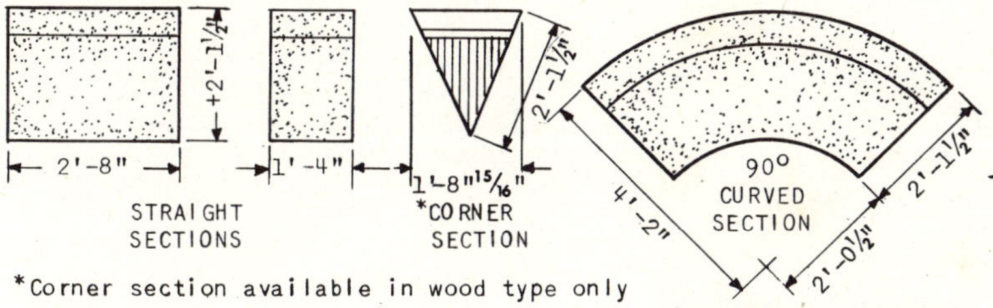
+2'-1½"
2'-8"
1'-4"
STRAIGHT SECTIONS
2'-1½"
1'-8 15/16"
*CORNER SECTION
4'-2"
90°
CURVED SECTION
2'-1½"
2'-0½"
*Corner section available in wood type only

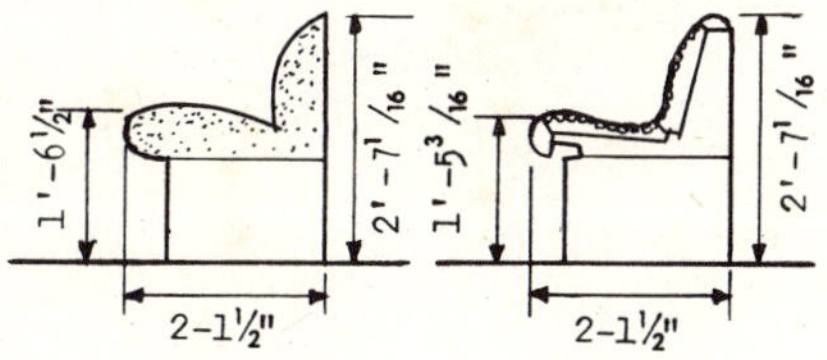
1'-6½"
2'-7 1/16"
2-1½"
UPHOLSTERED
1'-5 3/16"
2'-7 1/16"
2-1½"
WOOD SLATS

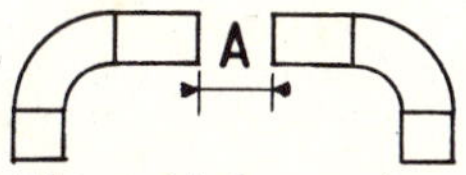
A

A=width req'd for center aisle if side access is limited.
A=2'-8½" min; 3'-1⅞" max.

PLAN

PLAYERS' BENCH

SETTEE DETAILS

End panels for wood seats ¾"; for upholstered, 1¼". Use of 1'-4" wide seats recommended only where space is a limiting factor. The 2'-0" aisle between alley approach and players' bench may be 1'-0" if necessary.

NOTE: (1) Outside ball return may be used but is not recommended. (2) Installation of stringers and rough flooring by alley manufacturers is recommended. (3) Alleys usually sold in pairs or even numbers, rarely in odd numbers.

Data by the Brunswick-Balke-Collender Co.

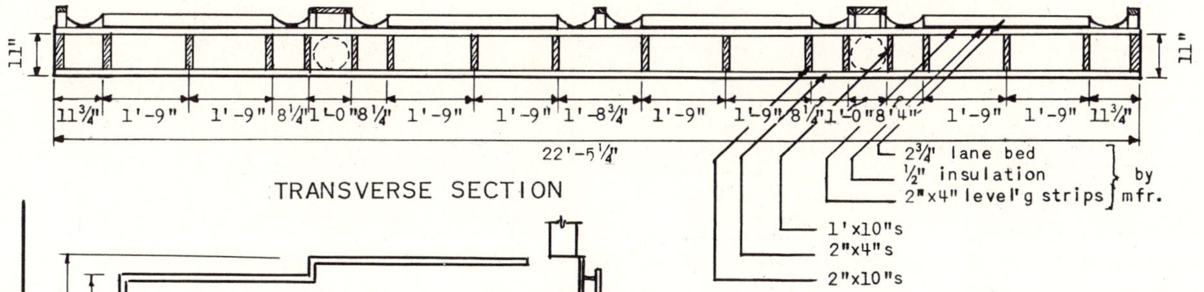
11"
11"
11¾"
1'-9"
1'-9"
8¼"
1'-0"
8¼"
1'-9"
1'-9"
1'-8¾"
1'-9"
1'-9"
8¼"
1'-0"
8'4"
1'-9"
1'-9"
11¾"
22'-5¼"
2¾" lane bed
½" insulation
2"x4" level'g strips
by mfr.
1'x10"s
2"x4"s
2"x10"s

TRANSVERSE SECTION

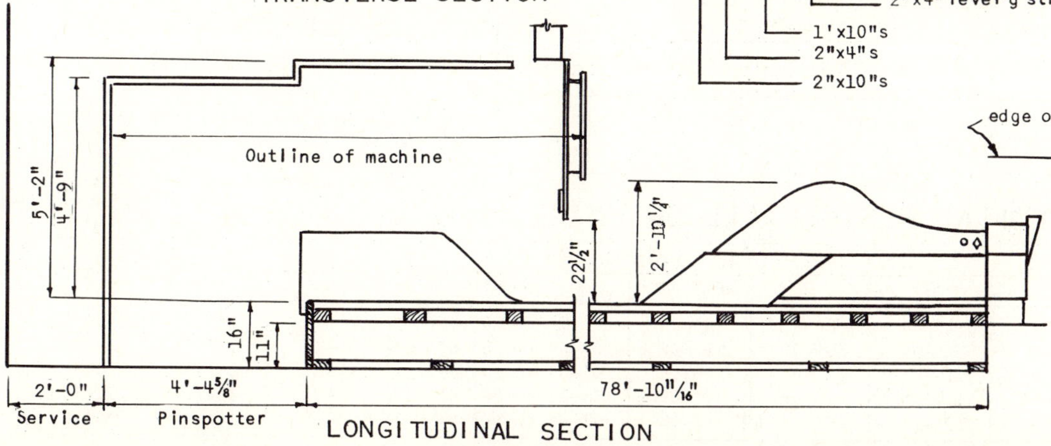
Outline of machine
5'-2"
4'-9"
16"
11"
22½"
2'-10¼"
2'-0"
Service
4'-4⅝"
Pinspotter
78'-10 11/16"

LONGITUDINAL SECTION

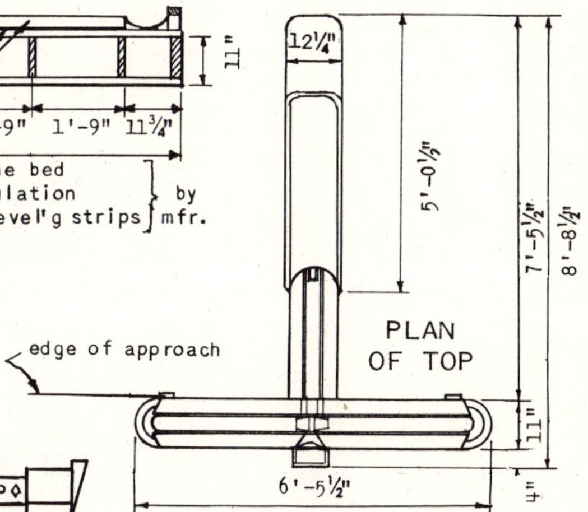
12¼"
5'-0½"
7'-5½"
8'-8½"
PLAN OF TOP
edge of approach
11"
4"
6'-5½"

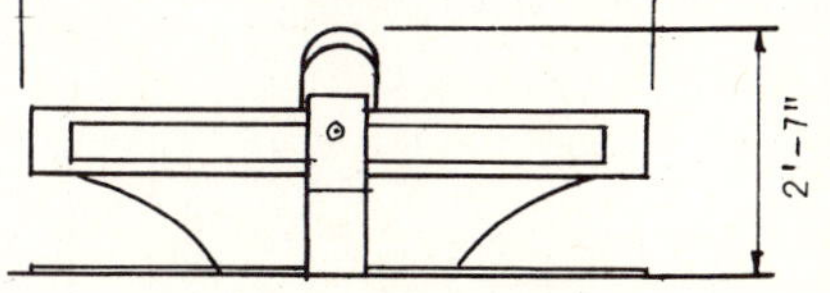
2'-7"

REAR ELEVATION

UNDERLANE SINGLE-T-BALL RETURN

Data by AMF Pinspotters Inc.

Scale: ¼"-1'-0"

RESIDENTIAL SWIMMING POOLS

PERMITS & RESTRICTIONS: Required in most areas from the Departments of Building, Plumbing, Electricity, and Zoning Board. Check for setback restrictions and easements covering power and telephone lines, sewers, and storm drains.

SITE CONSIDERATIONS: Check site for the following conditions, any of which will increase costs considerably:

1. Fill more than 3'–0" below the proposed pool deck;
2. Hard rock which will require drilling and blasting;
3. The presence of underground water or springs necessitating pumping;
4. Accessibility of the site for mechanical equipment, minimum entry 8'–0" wide, 7' to 8' high with a grade easy enough for a truck to reach the site; and
5. The slope of the site which should be as near level as possible; a steep slope requires retaining walls for the pool.

POOL CONSTRUCTION & SHAPES: Pools may be made of reinforced concrete, either poured on the job, precast, or gunite sprayed; concrete block, steel, or plastic with or without block backup. Concrete and steel pools are available in any size and, except for precast concrete, in any shape—rectangular, square, oval, kidney shaped, or free form. Complete plastic installations and plastic pool liners with block back-up are available only in manufacturers' standard shapes and sizes. For practical purposes a rectangular pool is most satisfactory, giving the longest swimming distance.

NOTE: Locate pool where it will get the most sun during the swimming season and where it can be seen from the most lived-in rooms. Place deep end, if possible, so a person diving dives away from, not into, the afternoon sun. Avoid overhanging branches near the pool.

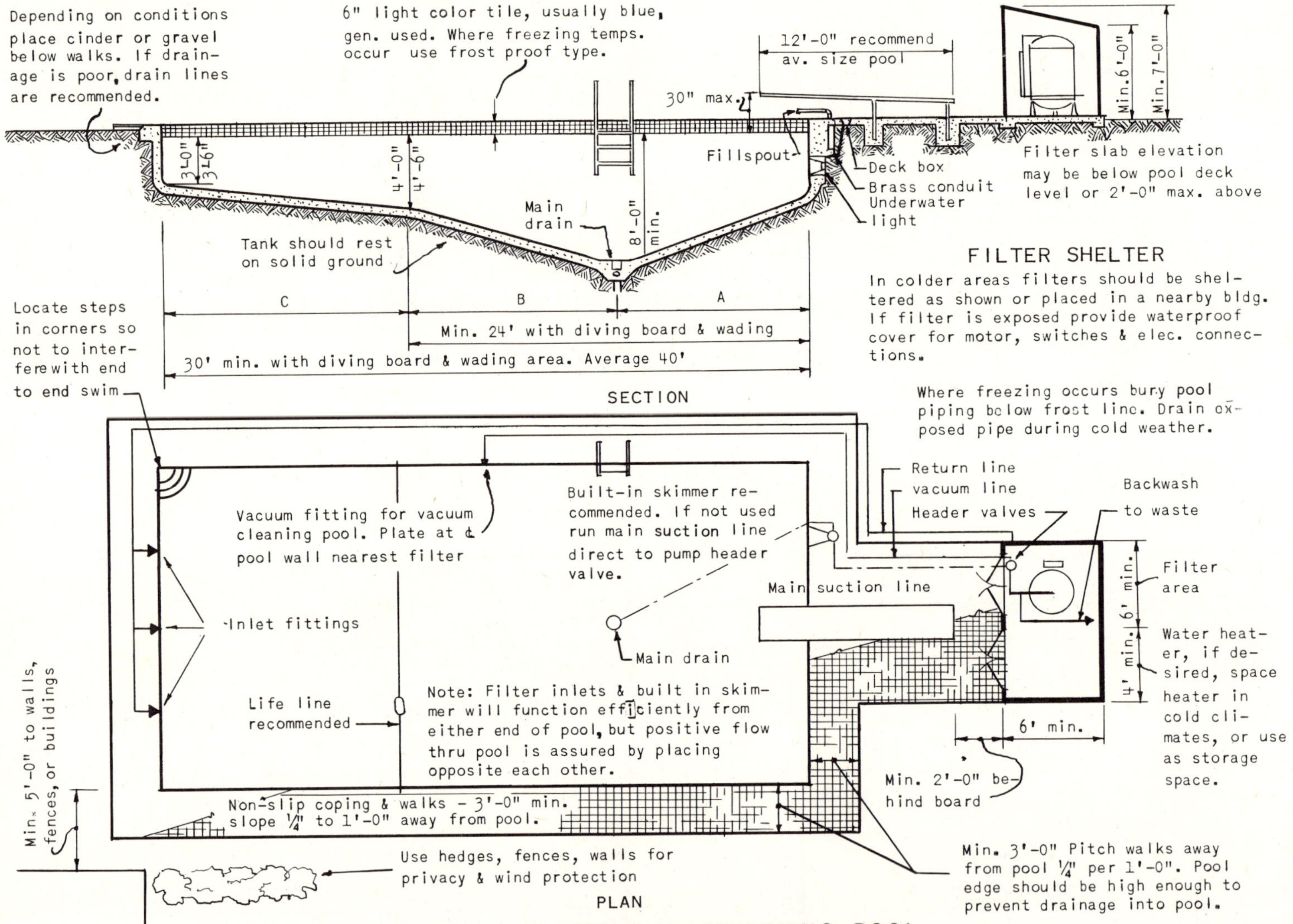
Depending on conditions place cinder or gravel below walks. If drainage is poor, drain lines are recommended.
6" light color tile, usually blue, gen. used. Where freezing temps. occur use frost proof type.
12'-0" recommend av. size pool
30" max.
Min. 6'-0"
Min. 7'-0"
3'-0"
3'-6"
4'-0"
4'-6"
Fillspout
Deck box
Brass conduit
Underwater light
Filter slab elevation may be below pool deck level or 2'-0" max. above
Main drain
8'-0" min.
Tank should rest on solid ground
FILTER SHELTER
In colder areas filters should be sheltered as shown or placed in a nearby bldg. If filter is exposed provide waterproof cover for motor, switches & elec. connections.
C
B
A
Min. 24' with diving board & wading
30' min. with diving board & wading area. Average 40'
Locate steps in corners so not to interfere with end to end swim
SECTION
Where freezing occurs bury pool piping below frost line. Drain exposed pipe during cold weather.
Return line
vacuum line
Header valves
Backwash to waste
Vacuum fitting for vacuum cleaning pool. Plate at ℄ pool wall nearest filter
Built-in skimmer recommended. If not used run main suction line direct to pump header valve.
Filter area
Min. 6' min.
Main suction line
Inlet fittings
Main drain
Water heater, if desired, space heater in cold climates, or use as storage space.
4' min.
Life line recommended
Note: Filter inlets & built in skimmer will function efficiently from either end of pool, but positive flow thru pool is assured by placing opposite each other.
6' min.
Min. 2'-0" behind board
Min. 5'-0" to walls, fences, or buildings
Non-slip coping & walks - 3'-0" min. slope 1/4" to 1'-0" away from pool.
Use hedges, fences, walls for privacy & wind protection
PLAN
Min. 3'-0" Pitch walks away from pool 1/4" per 1'-0". Pool edge should be high enough to prevent drainage into pool.

TYPICAL RESIDENTIAL SWIMMING POOL

RESIDENTIAL POOL SIZE CHART

LENGTH	WIDTH	A	B	C	LENGTH	WIDTH	A	B	C
30'-0"	15'-0" to 17'-0"	11'-0"	11'-0"	8'-0"	40'-0"	17'-0" to 20'-0"	12'-0"	13'-0"	15'-0"
32'-0"	15'-0" to 17'-0"	11'-0"	11'-0"	10'-0"	42'-0"	17'-0" to 20'-0"	12'-0"	13'-0"	17'-0"
34'-0"	15'-0" to 17'-0"	11'-0"	11'-0"	12'-0"	45'-0"	18'-0" to 20'-0"	13'-0"	13'-0"	19'-0"
36'-0"	15'-0" to 18'-0"	12'-0"	12'-0"	12'-0"	48'-0"	18'-0" to 20'-0"	13'-0"	13'-0"	22'-0"
38'-0"	16'-0" to 18'-0"	12'-0"	12'-0"	14'-0"	50'-0"	18'-0" to 20'-0"	13'-0"	13'-0"	24'-0"

Note: If no springboard is to be installed now or in the future, A & B may be from 7' to 9' each.

POOL CAPACITY: As a rule of thumb allow 36 sq. ft. each swimmer, 100 sq. ft. each diver. A 20' x 40' pool will accommodate 14 people at one time, but since not every one will be in the water at the same time this size pool and its surroundings is adequate for 30-40 people.

DATA BY LANDON, INC., N. HOLLYWOOD, CALIF.

PUBLIC SWIMMING POOLS - SHAPES

GENERAL: Public pools are usually considered as those belonging to municipalities, schools, country clubs, hotels, motels, apartments and resorts. Permits for their construction are required in most areas from local and state Boards of Health, as well as the Departments of Building, Plumbing and Electricity.

Community pools should be integrated with existing and projected recreational facilities, such as picnic areas and parks, for maximum usage. Transportation should be good and there should be ample parking space. In a hot climate enough shade areas should be provided, particularly in the lounging areas, so located that they can be easily converted to spectator space by the erection of bleachers.

POOL DESIGN: Formerly most public pools were designed to meet competitive swimming requirements. The trend today is to de-emphasize iron-clad competitive dimensions and to design for all-around use. The following should be considered:

1. Ratio of shallow water to deep water. Formerly 60% pool area 5' deep and less was considered adequate. Now 80% is considered more realistic.
2. Ratio of loungers to bathers. Generally no more than one-third of people attending a public pool are in the water at one time. Consequently the 6' to 8' walks formerly surrounding pools and used for lounging have been enlarged so that lounging area now approximates pool size.

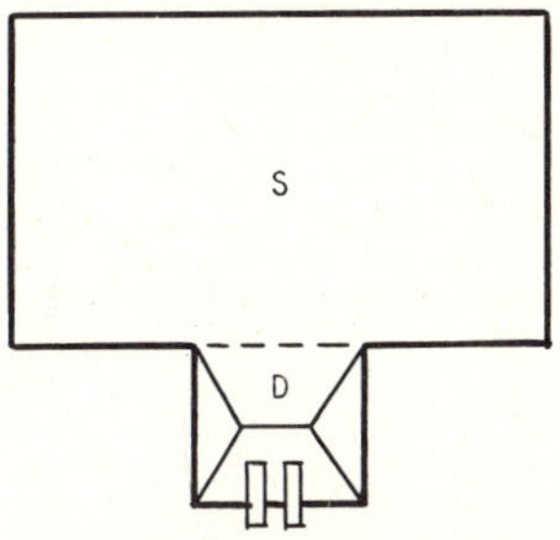
S
D

Provides large shallow area. Diving area off to one side. Water in large part of pool from 3'-3" to 4'-6" deep, adequate for regular competitive events.

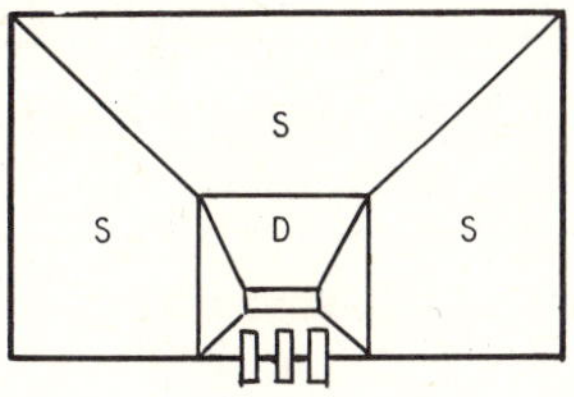
S
S
D
S

Variation of Tee, more economical to build. Difficult to separate deep and shallow areas by float lines.

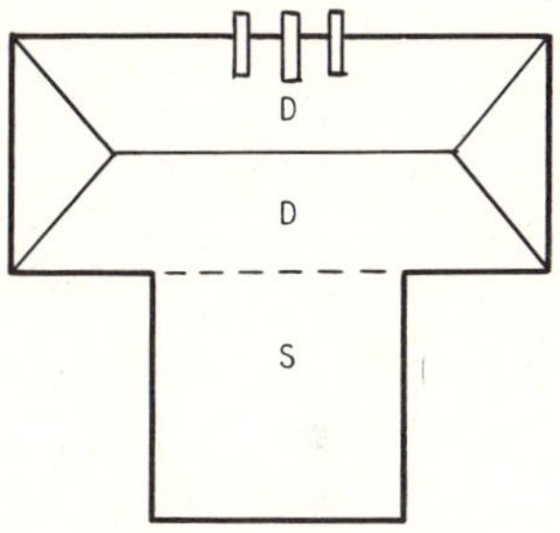
D
D
S

Enlarged deep area provides for large number of divers-swimmers separated from non-swimmers. Costly.

TEE SHAPED POOLS

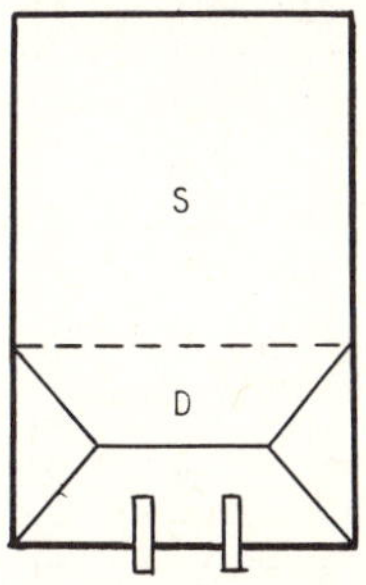
S
D

Standard design. Good for competitive swimming & indoor pool design. Shallow area often inadequate.

RECTANGULAR

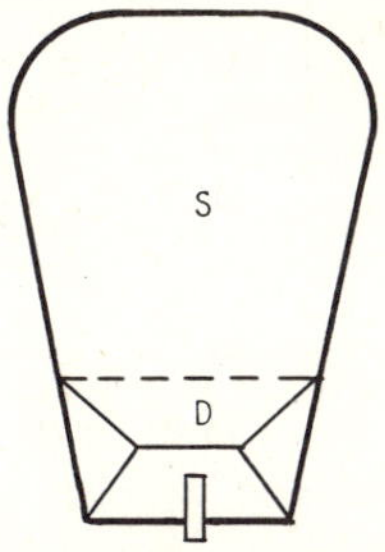
S
D

S = shallow
D = deep

Very successful where high percentage of children. Largest area for shallow depth. Deep area can be roped off easily.

FAN SHAPE

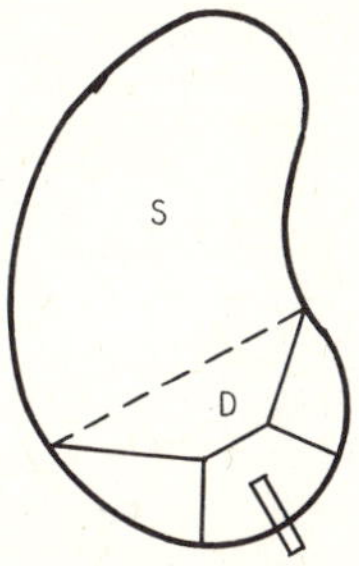
S
D

Kidney and oval shapes are most common free forms. Shapes generally determined by terrain and architect's judgment.

FREE FORM

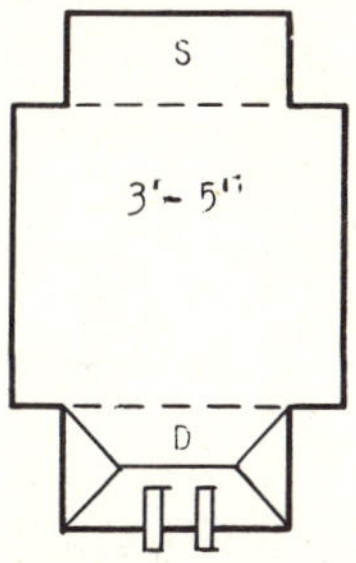
S
3'- 5'
D

Provides three areas which can be separated by float lines: shallow wading area, 3' to 5' area, and diving area.

CROSS SHAPE

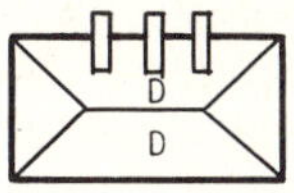
D
D

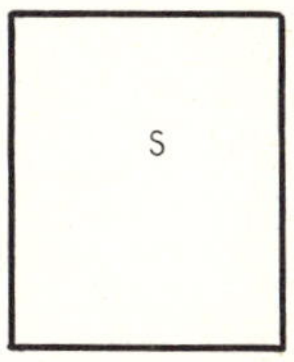
S

WADING POOLS

Generally provided in connection with community pools. Placed away from swimming area to avoid congestion. If near swimming pool, wading area should be fenced off for children's protection. To add play appeal provide spray fittings, small fountains in pool, sand beaches near pool. Also provide seats and benches for adults who accompany children to pool.

MULTIPLE POOLS

Separate pools for beginners and swimmers. Ultimate in desirability especially if pool is intended for large numbers of people. Variation at right shows single pool with causeway over it with advantage that swimmers are kept out of area reserved for beginners. Both designs may use a common filtration system.

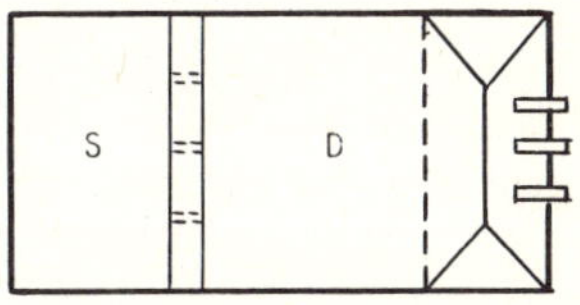
S
D

PLAN

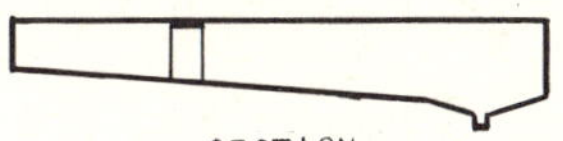

SECTION

PUBLIC POOL SHAPES

CODE REQUIREMENTS: Most local codes require that public pools have (1) multiple unit filters; (2) mechanical chlorination; (3) a prescribed floor slope; (4) scum gutters in very large pools.

DATA FROM "TRENDS IN SWIMMING POOL DESIGN", ISSUED BY SWIMMING POOL DEPT., ELGIN SOFTENER CORP., ELGIN, ILLINOIS

PUBLIC SWIMMING POOLS - DATA

	A	B	C	D	E	F	G
Low board (18"-30")	12' min.	12' min.	12' min.	5' max.	8' to 9'	3' to 3'-6"	12' max.
1-meter board	15' min.	15' to 20'	15' to 20'	5' max.	9' to 10'	4' to 4'-6"	14'-16'
3-meter board	25' min.	20' to 25'	15' to 20'	5' min.	9' to 12'	4'-6" to 5'	14' to 16'
Pools should be 42' long for a diving board, definitely not less than 36'							

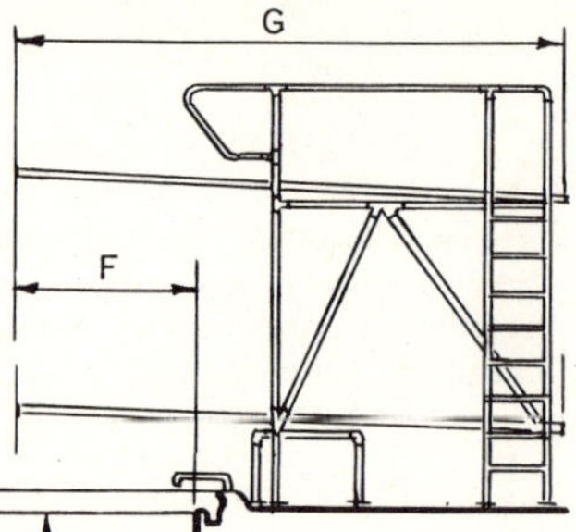
G
F

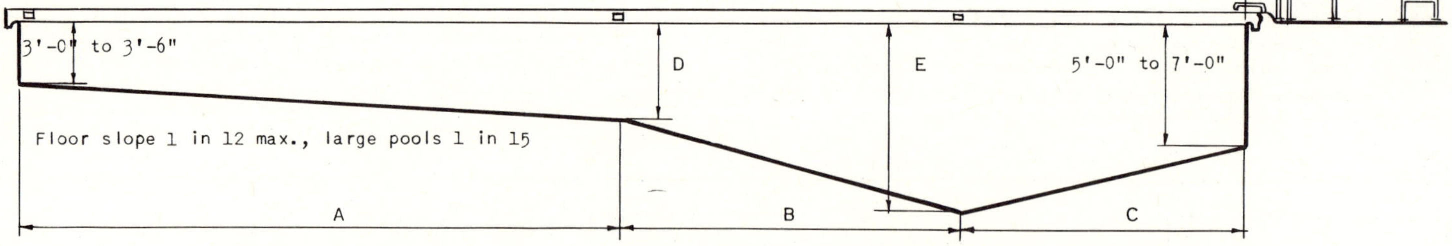
3'-0" to 3'-6"
D
E
5'-0" to 7'-0"
Floor slope 1 in 12 max., large pools 1 in 15
A
B
C

PUBLIC POOL WITH DIVING BOARD: RECOMMENDED DIMENSIONS

DATA BY LANDON INC.

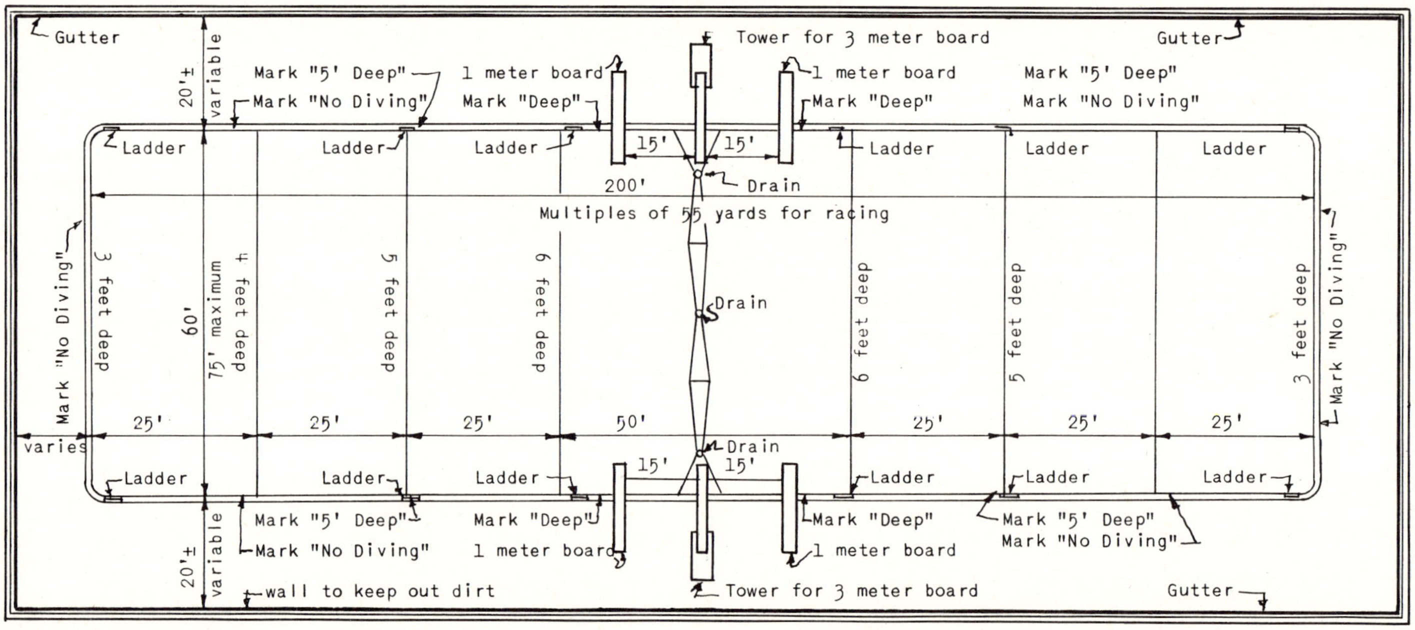
Gutter
Tower for 3 meter board
Gutter
20'±
variable
Mark "5' Deep"
Mark "No Diving"
1 meter board
Mark "Deep"
1 meter board
Mark "Deep"
Mark "5' Deep"
Mark "No Diving"
Ladder
Ladder
Ladder
15'
15'
Drain
Ladder
Ladder
Ladder
200'
Multiples of 55 yards for racing
Mark "No Diving"
3 feet deep
60'
75' maximum
4 feet deep
5 feet deep
6 feet deep
Drain
6 feet deep
5 feet deep
3 feet deep
Mark "No Diving"
25'
25'
25'
50'
25'
25'
25'
varies
Drain
15'
15'
Ladder
Ladder
Ladder
Ladder
Ladder
Ladder
Mark "5' Deep"
Mark "No Diving"
Mark "Deep"
1 meter board
Mark "Deep"
1 meter board
Mark "5' Deep"
Mark "No Diving"
20'±
variable
wall to keep out dirt
Tower for 3 meter board
Gutter

PLAN

Not for championship races unless turning boards are provided at proper distance

On outdoor pools provide expansion joints and under-tile drain. Provide pipe tunnel around pool.

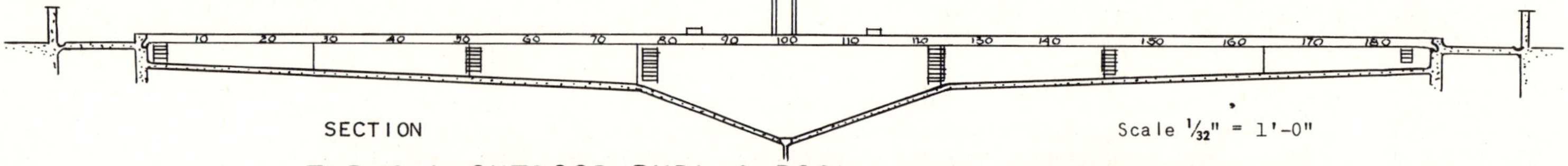
10
20
30
40
50
60
70
80
90
100
110
120
130
140
150
160
170
180

SECTION

Scale $\frac{1}{32}$" = 1'-0"

TYPICAL OUTDOOR PUBLIC POOL: DEEP CENTER TYPE

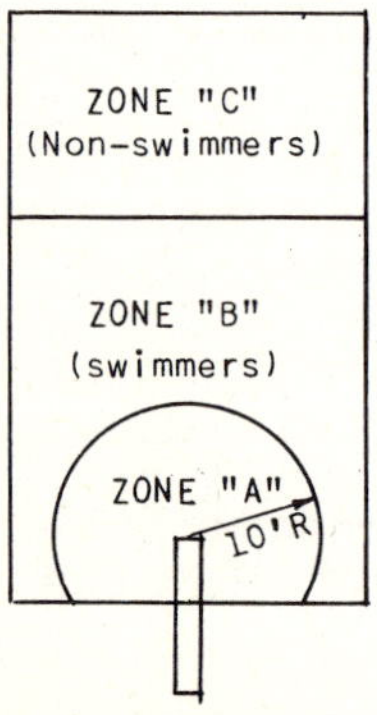
ZONE "C"
(Non-swimmers)
ZONE "B"
(swimmers)
ZONE "A"
10'R

Swimming pool capacity requirements vary from one locality to another. Check local regulations. The following is suggested by The American Public Health Association.

FORMULA DERIVATION:

ZONE "A" Diving area defined by 10' radius from diving board or platform. 12 divers per board; 2-3 in water, the rest on shore.

ZONE "B" Swimming area; 27 sq.ft. per swimmer. Based on volume displaced each swimmer (4/5 square of average ht.) and adjusted by number swimmers using pool at one time (2/3 total swimmers).

ZONE "C" Non-swimmer area, 10 sq.ft. per person. Based on volume displaced per person (1/2 area allowed per swimmer) and adjusted by number not using water - 50%. (In some pools with a large number non-swimmers this can be upped as high as 75%).

FORMULA:

$$\text{Max. pool capacity} = 12 \times \text{No. diving boards or platforms} + \frac{\text{Area Zone "B"}}{27} + \frac{\text{Area Zone "C"}}{10}$$

PUBLIC SWIMMING POOL CAPACITY

COMPETITIVE SWIMMING POOLS

LENGTH OF POOLS

60 ft. pools meet national championship requirements.

75 ft. is the minimum pool length for world's records and to meet interscholastic & intercollegiate requirements (should actually be a fraction of an inch longer than 75'-0'').

WIDTH OF POOLS

All drawings show 7' lanes. 6 ft. lanes (with pool width a multiple of 6'-0'') also meet all championship requirements. Strictly competitive pools should have 7' lanes.

Minimum width of 75 ft. pools (AAU standard) is 36 ft. or 42 ft. depending on lane width.

Gutters at sides of pool only if used for swimming meets or water polo.

Scale: 1/16" = 1'-0"

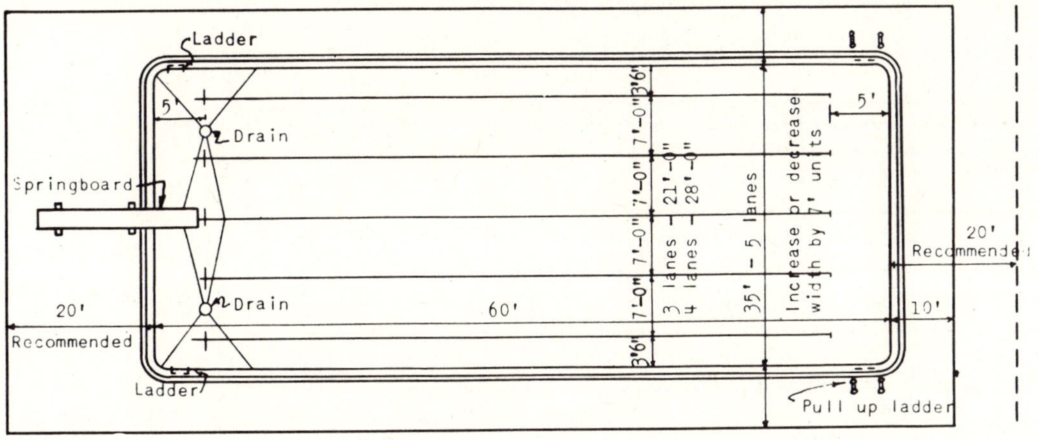
Ladder
Drain
Springboard
Drain
20'
Recommended
60'
Ladder
3'6"
7'-0"
3 lanes - 21'-0"
4 lanes - 28'-0"
35' - 5 lanes
Increase or decrease width by 7' units
5'
20'
Recommended
10'
Pull up ladder

PLAN

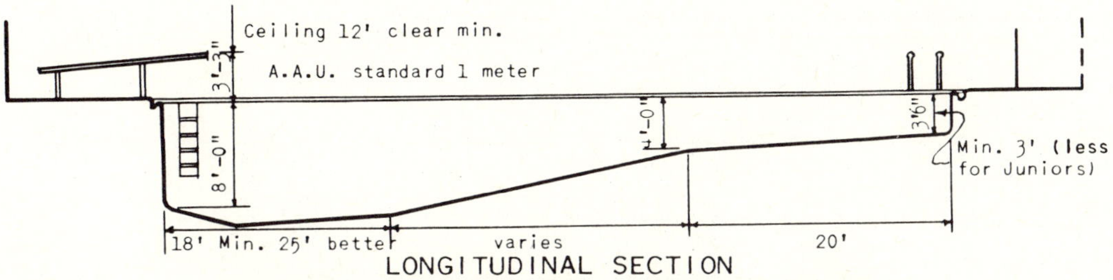
Ceiling 12' clear min.
A.A.U. standard 1 meter
3'-3"
8'-0"
1'-0"
3'6"
Min. 3' (less for Juniors)
18' Min. 25' better
varies
20'

LONGITUDINAL SECTION

MINIMUM DIMENSIONS FOR 60' POOL

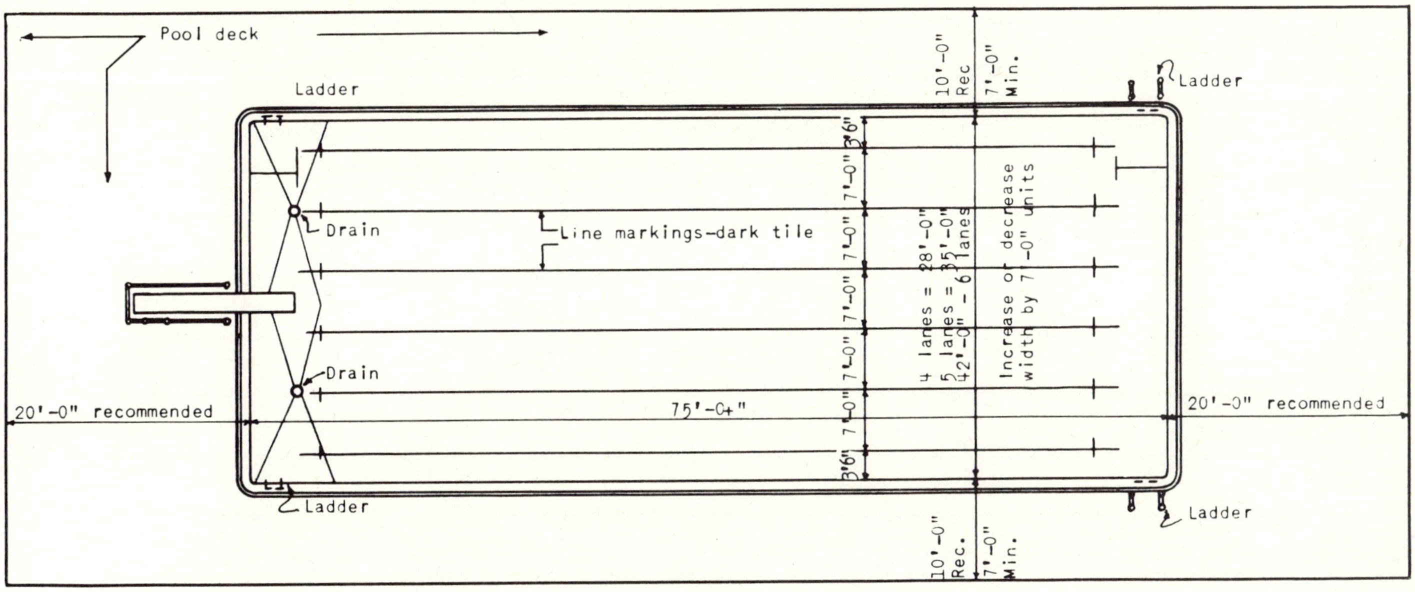
Pool deck
Ladder
Drain
Line markings-dark tile
Drain
20'-0" recommended
75'-0+"
Ladder
3'6"
7'-0"
4 lanes = 28'-0"
5 lanes = 35'-0"
42'-0" - 6 lanes
Increase or decrease width by 7'-0" units
10'-0" Rec
7'-0" Min.
Ladder
20'-0" recommended
Ladder
10'-0" Rec.
7'-0" Min.

PLAN

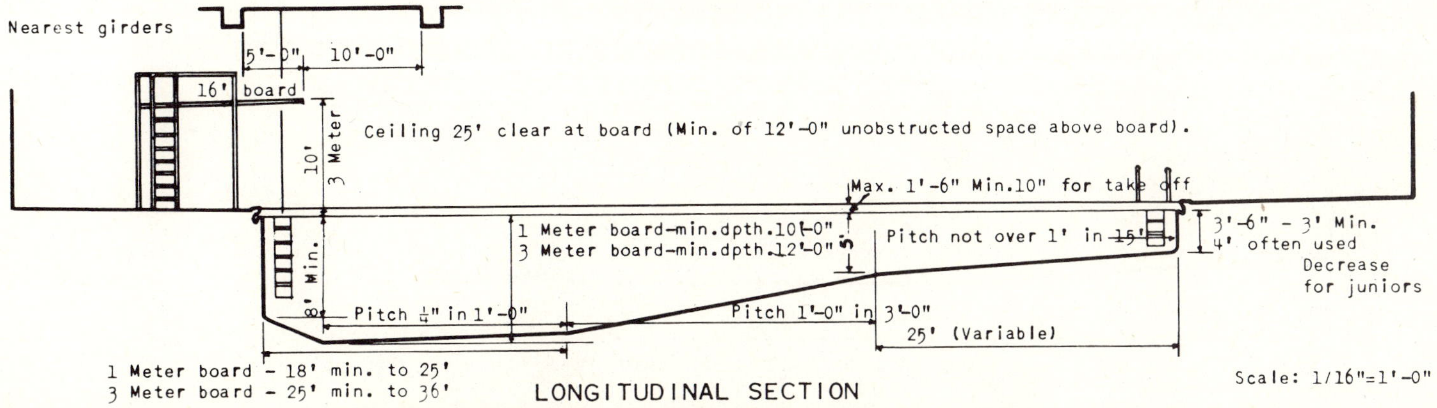
Nearest girders
5'-0"
10'-0"
16' board
10'
3 Meter
Ceiling 25' clear at board (Min. of 12'-0" unobstructed space above board).
Max. 1'-6" Min.10" for take off
1 Meter board-min.dpth.10'-0"
3 Meter board-min.dpth.12'-0"
5'
Pitch not over 1' in 15'
3'-6" - 3' Min.
4' often used
Decrease for juniors
8' Min.
Pitch ¼" in 1'-0"
Pitch 1'-0" in 3'-0"
25' (Variable)
1 Meter board - 18' min. to 25'
3 Meter board - 25' min. to 36'

LONGITUDINAL SECTION

Scale: 1/16"=1'-0"

RECOMMENDED DIMENSIONS FOR 75' POOL

COMPETITIVE SWIMMING POOLS; IDEAL A.A.U. METRIC

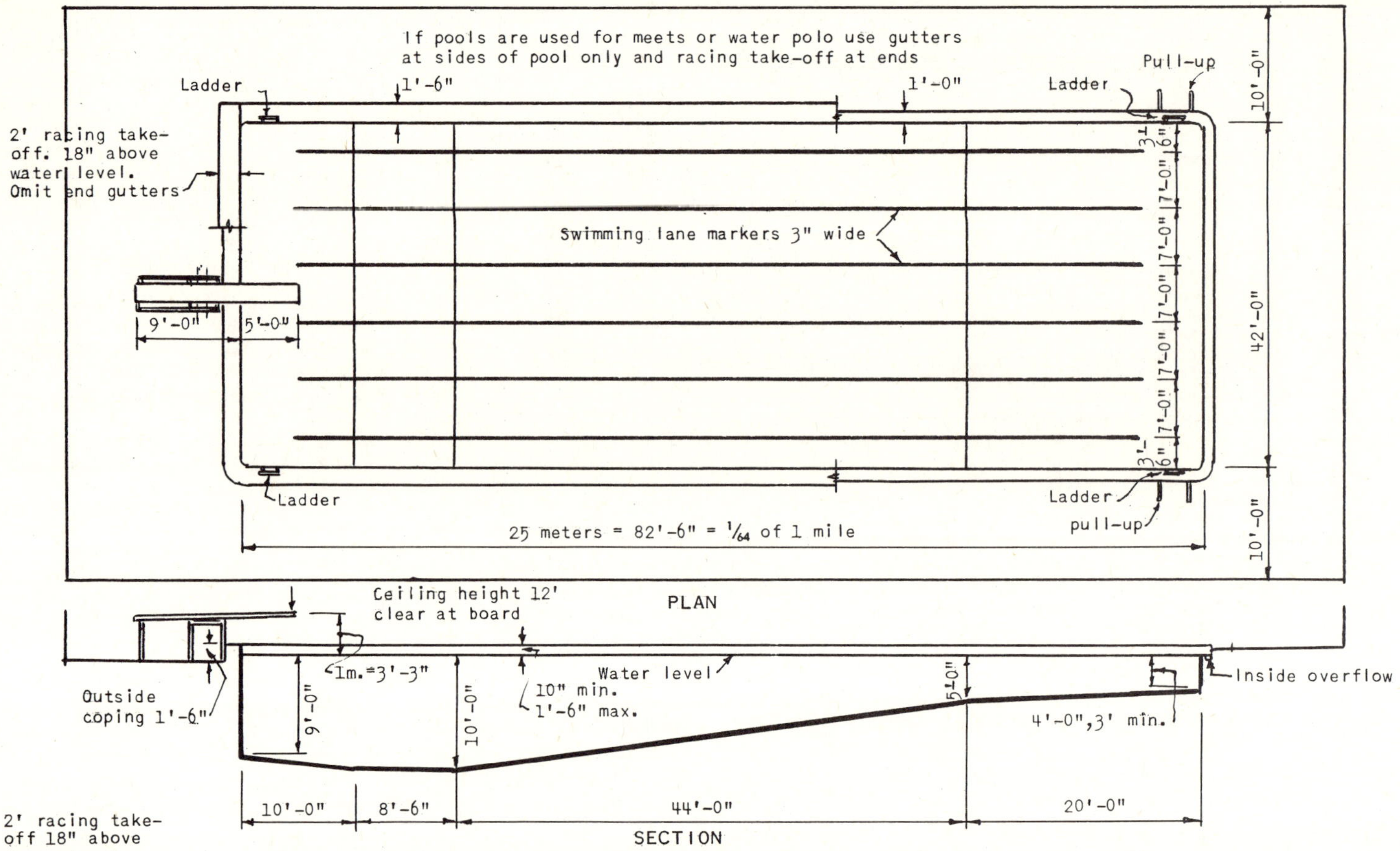
If pools are used for meets or water polo use gutters at sides of pool only and racing take-off at ends
Ladder
1'-6"
1'-0"
Ladder
Pull-up
10'-0"
2' racing take-off. 18" above water level. Omit end gutters
Swimming lane markers 3" wide
3'-6"
7'-0"
7'-0"
7'-0"
7'-0"
7'-0"
7'-0"
3'-6"
42'-0"
9'-0"
5'-0"
Ladder
Ladder
pull-up
10'-0"
25 meters = 82'-6" = 1/64 of 1 mile
PLAN
Ceiling height 12' clear at board
1m.=3'-3"
Water level
10" min.
1'-6" max.
Outside coping 1'-6"
9'-0"
10'-0"
5'-0"
Inside overflow
4'-0",3' min.
10'-0"
8'-6"
44'-0"
20'-0"
SECTION

25 METER POOL

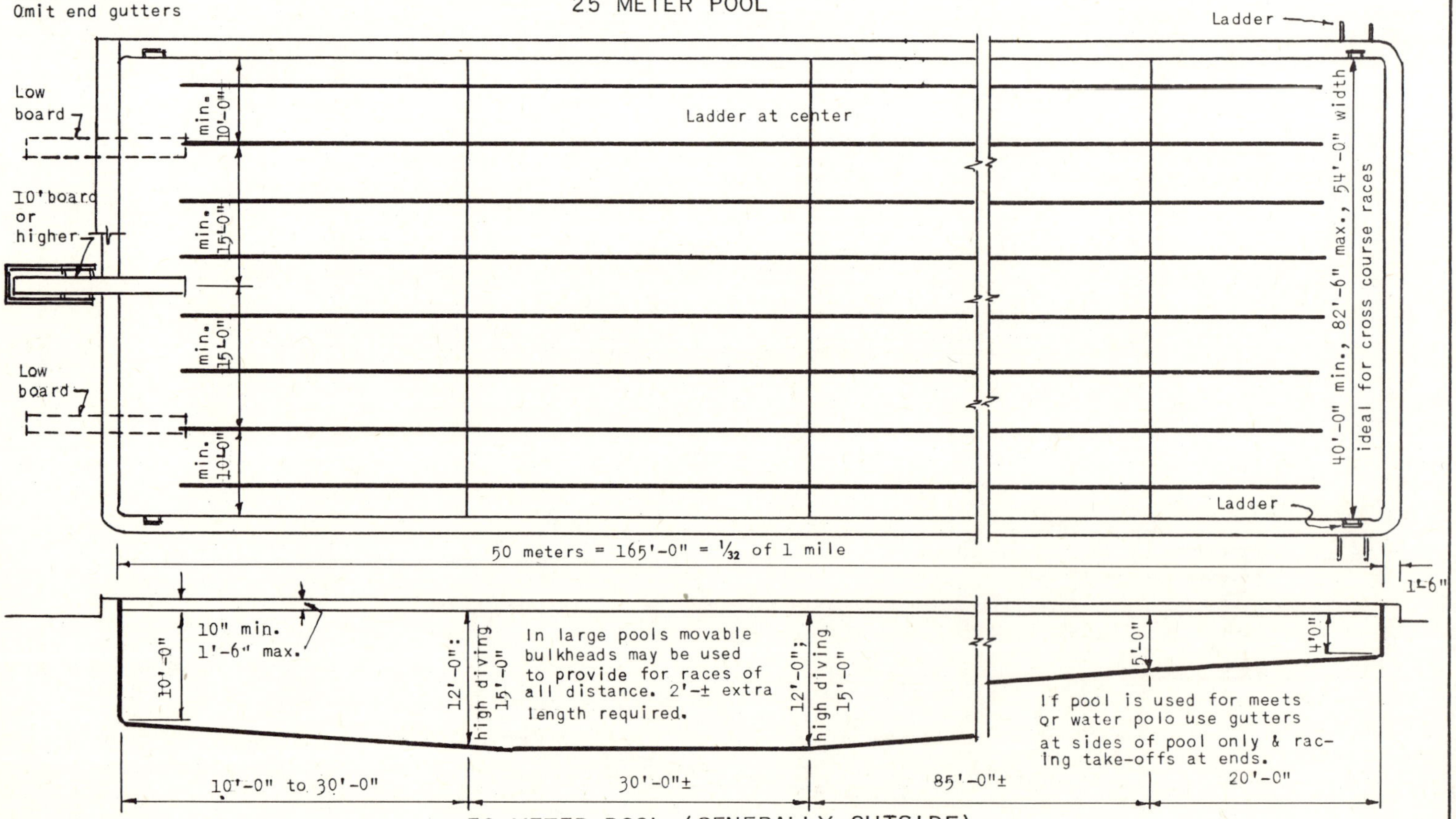
2' racing take-off 18" above water level. Omit end gutters
Ladder
Low board
min. 10'-0"
Ladder at center
10' board or higher
min. 15'-0"
min. 15'-0"
Low board
min. 10'-0"
40'-0" min., 82'-6" max., 54'-0" width
ideal for cross course races
Ladder
50 meters = 165'-0" = 1/32 of 1 mile
1'-6"
10'-0"
10" min.
1'-6" max.
12'-0"; high diving 15'-0"
In large pools movable bulkheads may be used to provide for races of all distance. 2'-± extra length required.
12'-0"; high diving 15'-0"
5'-0"
4'-0"
If pool is used for meets or water polo use gutters at sides of pool only & racing take-offs at ends.
10'-0" to 30'-0"
30'-0"±
85'-0"±
20'-0"

50 METER POOL (GENERALLY OUTSIDE)

DATA CHECKED BY AMATEUR ATHLETIC UNION

STANDARD Y.M.C.A. SWIMMING POOLS

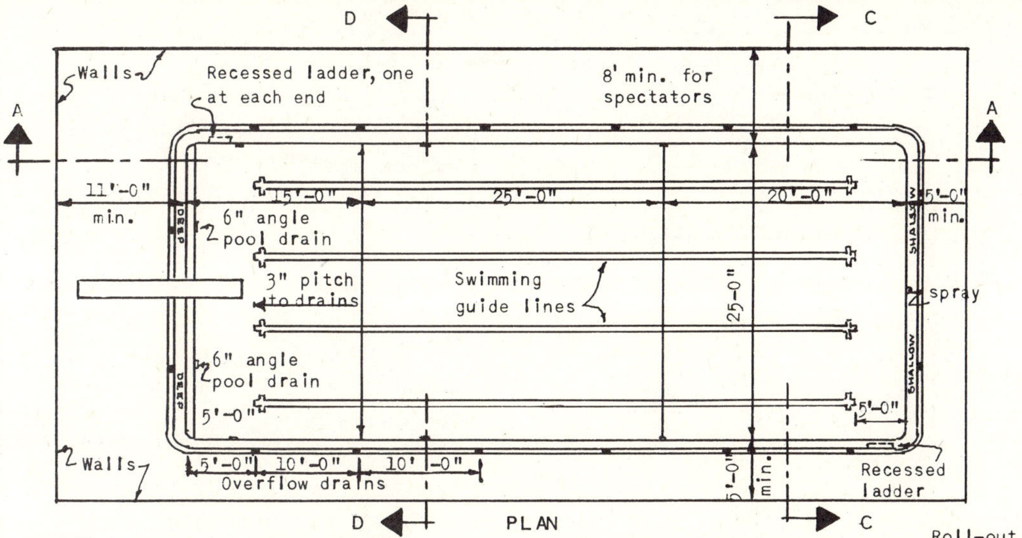
D
C
A
Walls
Recessed ladder, one at each end
8' min. for spectators
11'-0" min.
15'-0"
25'-0"
20'-0"
5'-0" min.
6" angle pool drain
3" pitch to drains
Swimming guide lines
25'-0"
spray
6" angle pool drain
5'-0"
5'-0"
Walls
5'-0"
10'-0"
10'-0"
Overflow drains
5'-0" min.
Recessed ladder
PLAN

Y.M.C.A. pools are generally used for instruction and informal swimming and consequently their requirements differ from competitive pools.

LANES: 4 @ 6'-0" for pools 25' wide, 5 @ 6'-0" for pools 30' wide. Lane markings are 12" bands of black tile.

GUTTERS: Roll-out and semi-projected types. For details see page on "Tile Swimming Pools."

DISTANCE AND DEPTH MARKS: See page on "Tile Application in Swimming Pools."

WALK DRAINS: No separate drains except in states requiring walk drains at walls. 2" pitch for walkways to overflow drains.

DIVING BOARDS: See page on 1-meter boards. Roll-out gutter pools require board stands with extra step to raise board to req'd. ht. above water.

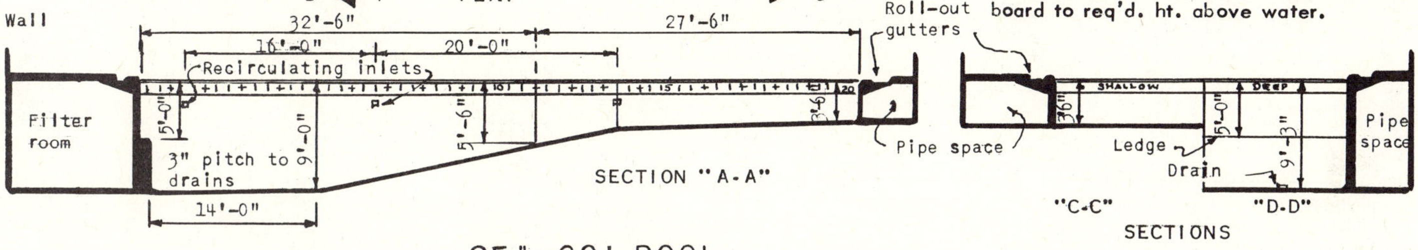
Wall
32'-6"
27'-6"
16'-0"
20'-0"
Recirculating inlets
Roll-out gutters
Filter room
5'-0"
9'-0"
5'-6"
3'-6"
3" pitch to drains
14'-0"
Pipe space
SECTION "A-A"
SHALLOW
DEEP
3'6"
5'-0"
9'-3"
Pipe space
Ledge
Drain
"C-C"
"D-D"
SECTIONS

25"x60' POOL

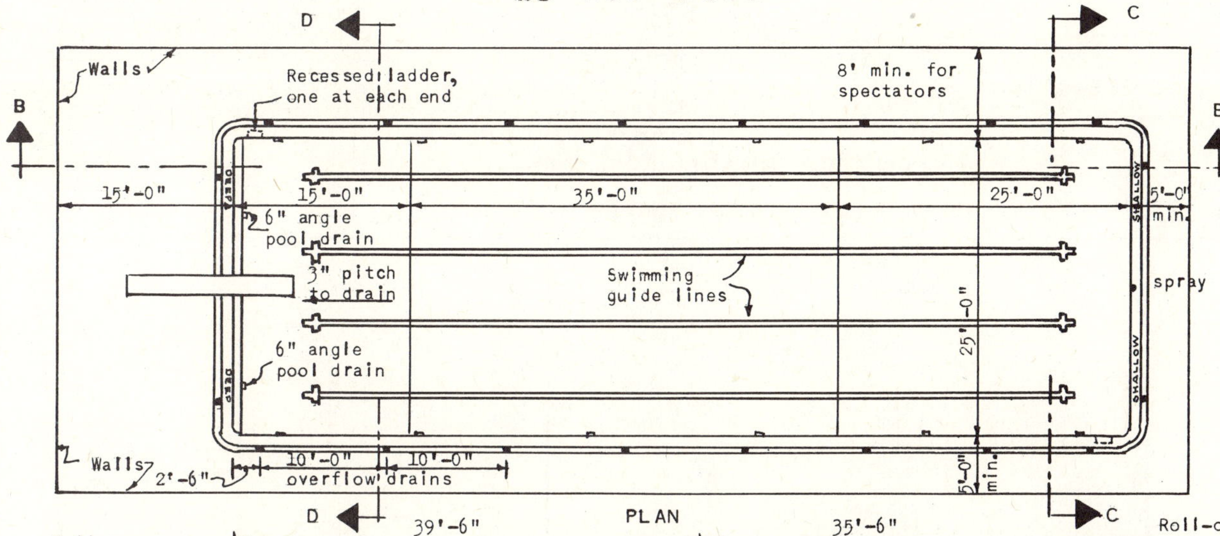
D
C
B
Walls
Recessed ladder, one at each end
8' min. for spectators
15'-0"
15'-0"
35'-0"
25'-0"
5'-0" min.
6" angle pool drain
3" pitch to drain
Swimming guide lines
spray
25'-0"
6" angle pool drain
Walls
2'-6"
10'-0"
10'-0"
overflow drains
5'-0" min.
PLAN

SURFACE TREATMENT: Pool lining-¾" & 1" sqs. white impervious porcelain tile; decks-semi-vitreous nat. clay cushion edge tile; walls—vitreous porcelain or semi-vitreous nat. clay tile. All bottom and vertical corners have 5" radius as shown on page on "Tile Swimming Pools."

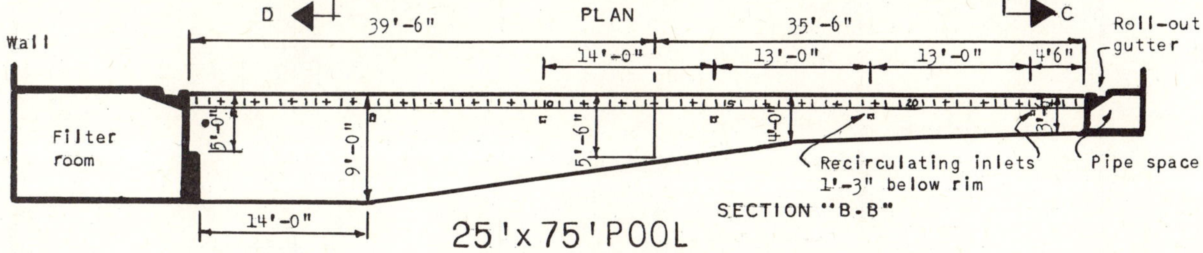
Wall
39'-6"
35'-6"
14'-0"
13'-0"
13'-0"
4'6"
Roll-out gutter
Filter room
5'-0"
9'-0"
5'-6"
4'-0"
3'
Recirculating inlets 1'-3" below rim
Pipe space
14'-0"
SECTION "B-B"

25'x75'POOL

INDOOR POOL CAPACITY

SIZE	TYPE	AREA	WATER CU. FT.	WATER GAL.	WATER LBS. AT 75°F.	INDOOR POOL SWIMMER CAP.*
25' x 60'	Standard	1500 □'	9,278	69,399	577,657	72
25' x 75'	Standard	1875 □'	11,371	85,068	708,032	92

$$\text{* Indoor swimmer capacity} = \frac{\text{Area of water less than } 5\tfrac{1}{2} \text{ ft. deep}}{15} + \frac{\text{Area water over } 5\tfrac{1}{2} \text{ ft. deep}}{30}$$

Outdoor pool capacity is obtained by multiplying the above by 1.35. This formula is taken from "Swimming Pool Operation" Circular No. 125 issued by State of Illinois Department of Public Health. Check local regulations for variations.

DATA BY Y.M.C.A. BUILDING AND FURNISHING SERVICE., N.Y.C.

I-METER DIVING BOARD - REQUIRED DEPTHS

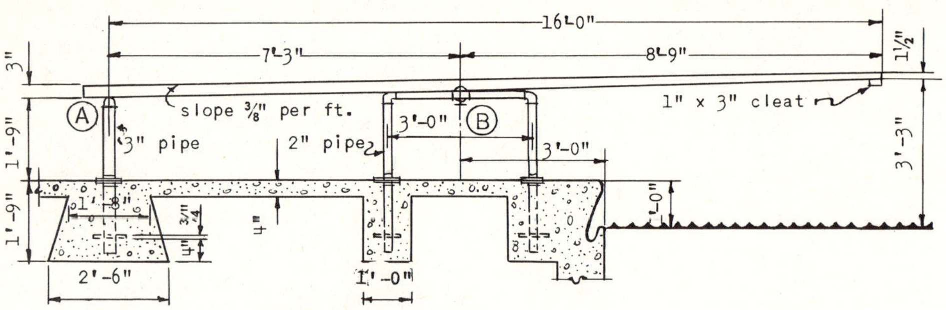
16'-0"
7'-3"
8'-9"
1½"
3"
slope ⅜" per ft.
1" x 3" cleat
A
B
3" pipe
2" pipe
3'-0"
3'-0"
3'-3"
1'-9"
1'-9"
1'-8"
4"
¾"
4"
1'-0"
2'-6"
1'-0"

SIDE ELEVATION

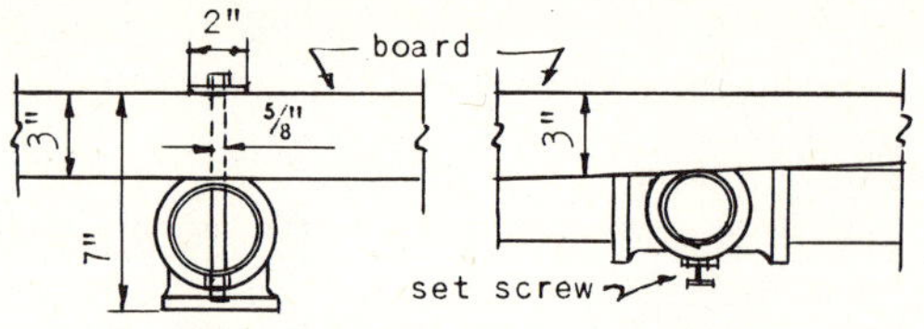
2"
board
3"
⅝"
7"
3"
set screw

DETAIL "A" DETAIL "B"

Both 1-meter and 3-meter boards are required for amateur, collegiate and international meets.

All boards shall be painted or oiled and covered with cocoa matting or similar material.

All lower flanges which are set in concrete shall be of brass.

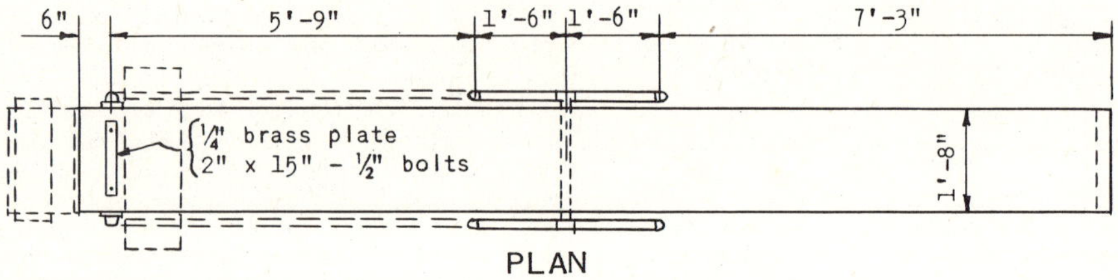
6"
5'-9"
1'-6"
1'-6"
7'-3"
¼" brass plate
2" x 15" - ½" bolts
1'-8"

PLAN

Dotted line indicates alternate board mount construction. For pools using roll-out gutter.

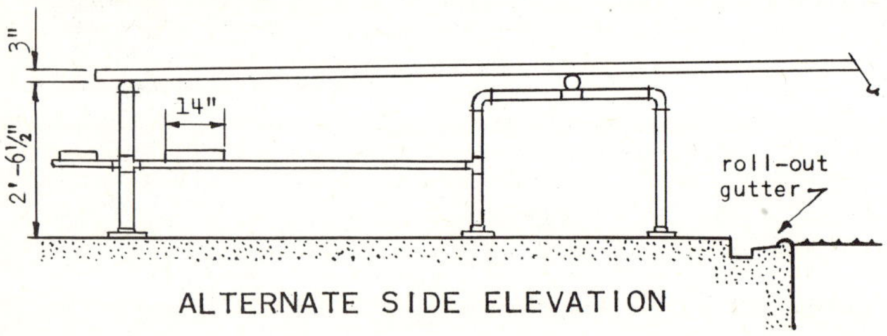
3"
2'-6½"
14"
roll-out
gutter

ALTERNATE SIDE ELEVATION

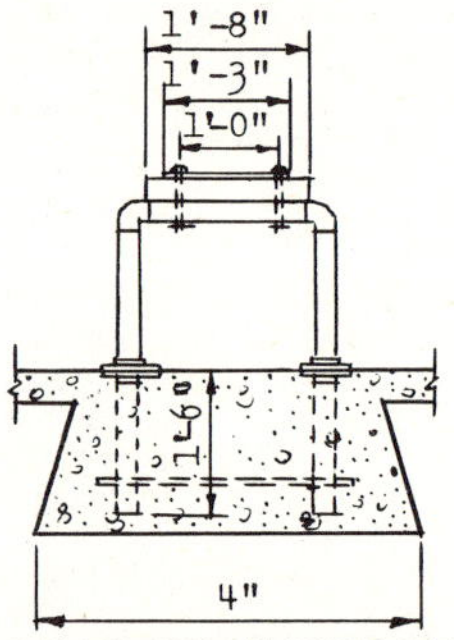
1'-8"
1'-3"
1'-0"
1'-6"
4"

REAR ELEVATION

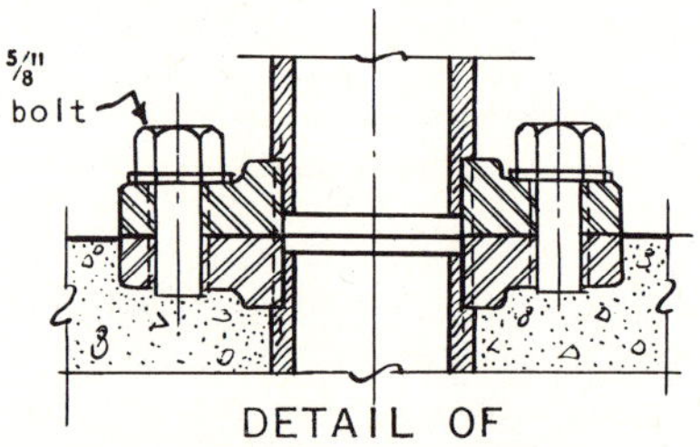
⅝"
bolt

DETAIL OF FLOOR FLANGE

I-METER BOARD (3'-3")

Data by National Collegiate Athletic Association

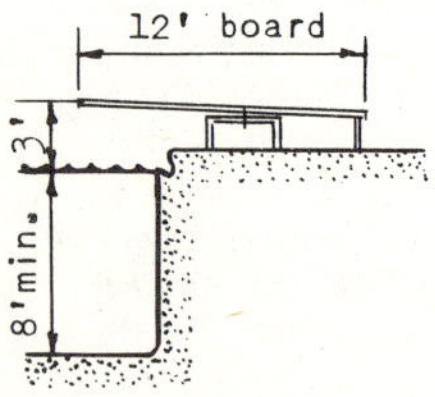
12' board
3'
8' min.

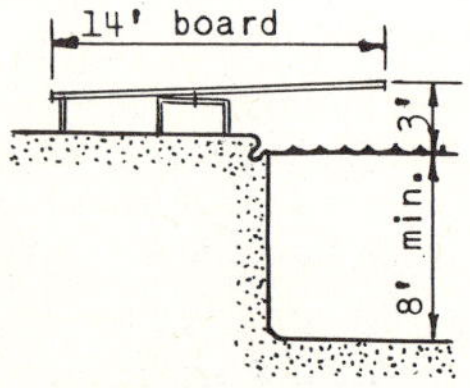
14' board
3'
8' min.

Used generally. Boards should be painted or oiled & covered with cocoa matting or similar material.

UNOFFICIAL BOARDS

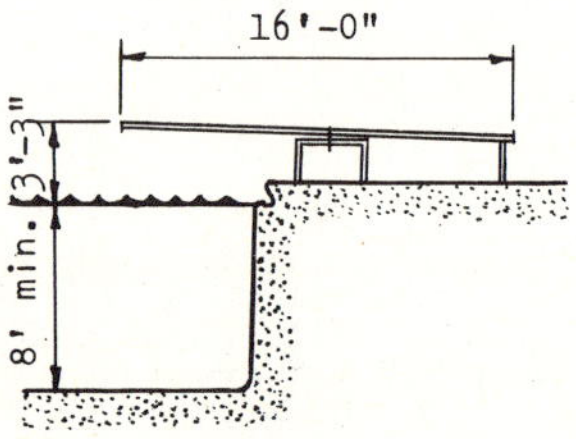
16'-0"
3'-3"
8' min.

STANDARD 1-METER BOARD

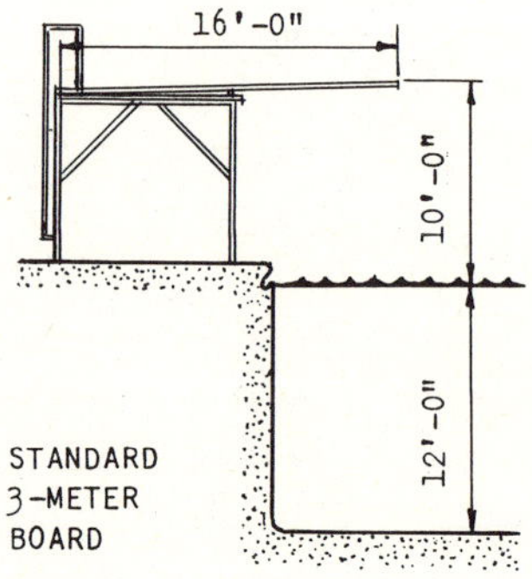
16'-0"
10'-0"
12'-0"

STANDARD 3-METER BOARD

OFFICIAL BOARDS

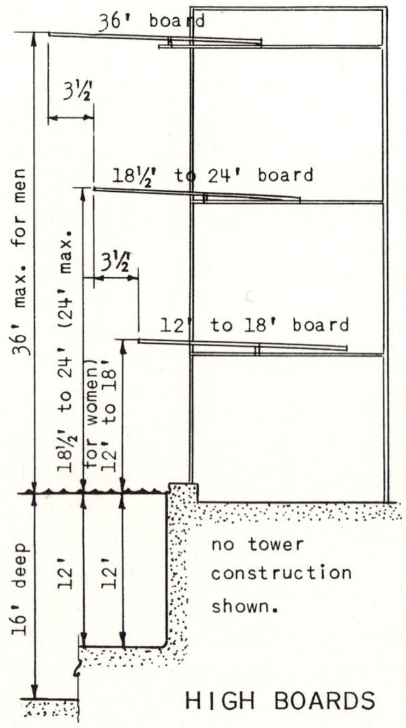
36' board
3½'
18½' to 24' board
3½'
12' to 18' board
36' max. for men
18½' to 24' (24' max. for women)
12' to 18'
16' deep
12'
12'
no tower construction shown.

HIGH BOARDS

Boards placed side-by-side should be 15'-0" apart & a min. of 10'-0" from side of pool.

HEIGHTS OF BOARDS AND WATER DEPTHS REQUIRED

3-METER DIVING BOARD

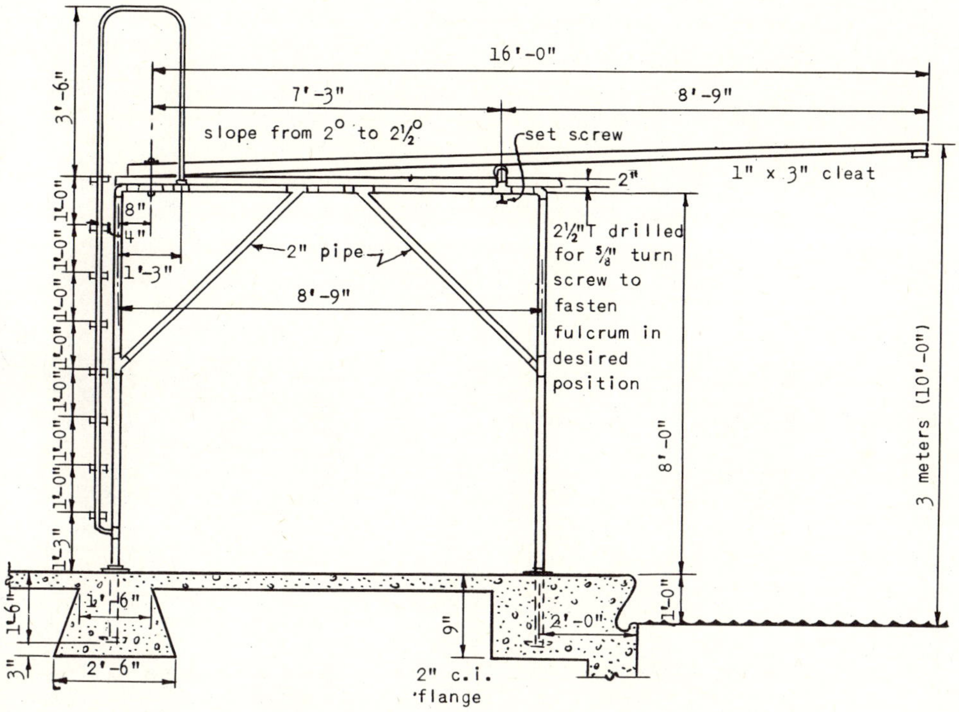
16'-0"
7'-3"
8'-9"
slope from 2° to 2½°
set screw
1" x 3" cleat
2"
8"
4"
1'-3"
2" pipe
8'-9"
2½"T drilled for ⅝" turn screw to fasten fulcrum in desired position
8'-0"
3 meters (10'-0")
3'-6"
1'-0" 1'-0" 1'-0" 1'-0" 1'-0" 1'-0" 1'-0" 1'-0"
1'-3"
1'-6"
1'-6"
2'-0"
1'-0"
9"
3"
2'-6"
2" c.i. flange

SIDE ELEVATION

adjusting wheel

Brandsten Automatic adjustable fulcrum springboard Available for 1 meter and 10'-0" uses.

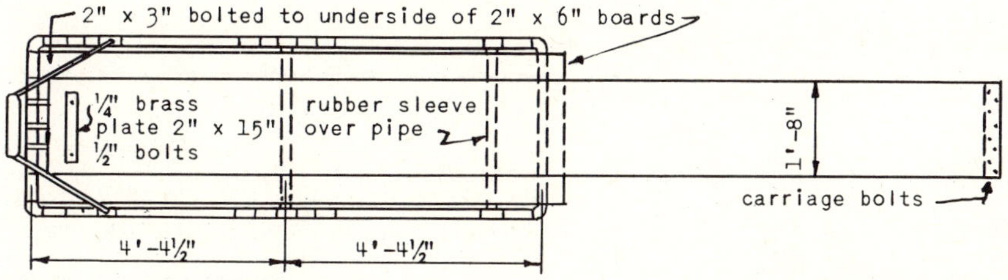
2" x 3" bolted to underside of 2" x 6" boards
¼" brass plate 2" x 15" ½" bolts
rubber sleeve over pipe
1'-8"
carriage bolts
4'-4½"
4'-4½"

PLAN

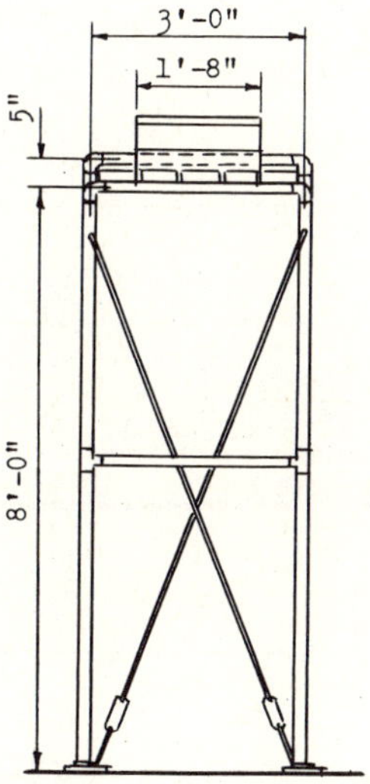
3'-0"
1'-8"
5"
8'-0"

FRONT OF STAND

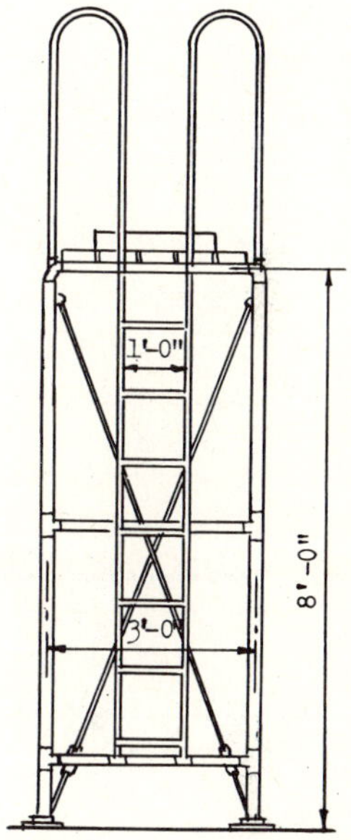
1'-0"
3'-0"
8'-0"

REAR OF STAND

NOTES

Both 1-meter and 3-meter boards are required for amateur, collegiate, and international competition.

Boards to pitch ⅜" per foot. All boards shall be painted or oiled and covered with cocoa matting or similar material.

Steps to be 1½" x 3" solid oak covered with non-slip material and set on 1½" pipe rungs. If pool has roll-out gutter an additional step is required to bring the board to the required height above the water.

All lower flanges set in concrete shall be of brass.

Entire structure to be free of all exposed bolts, nuts, screws, nails, and splinters.

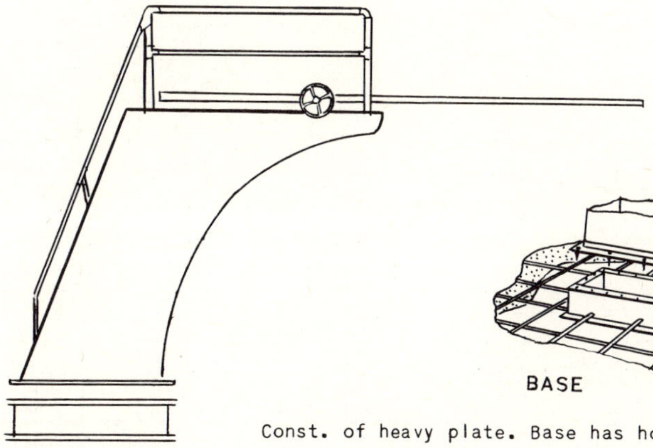

SIDE ELEVATION

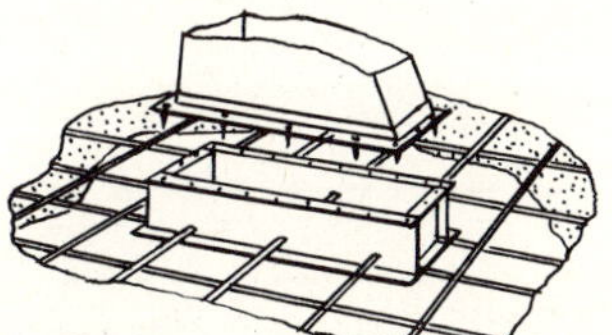

BASE

Const. of heavy plate. Base has holes for reinforcing bars in floor slab. After deck has set, ¾" bolts attach superstructure to base flange.

Data by Lifetime Metal Products Co.

STEEL CANTILEVER 3-METER BOARD

3 METER BOARD (10'-0")

Data by National Collegiate Athletic Association

WATER POLO; SWIMMING POOL LIGHTING

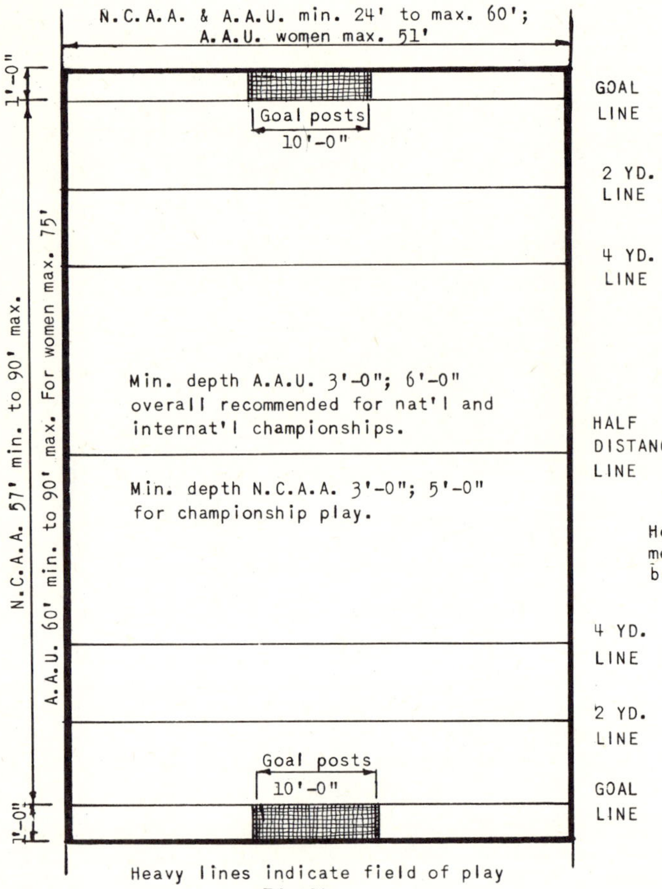
N.C.A.A. & A.A.U. min. 24' to max. 60';
A.A.U. women max. 51'
1'-0"
Goal posts
10'-0"
GOAL LINE
2 YD. LINE
4 YD. LINE
N.C.A.A. 57' min. to 90' max.
A.A.U. 60' min. to 90' max. For women max. 75'
Min. depth A.A.U. 3'-0"; 6'-0" overall recommended for nat'l and internat'l championships.
Min. depth N.C.A.A. 3'-0"; 5'-0" for championship play.
HALF DISTANCE LINE
4 YD. LINE
2 YD. LINE
Goal posts
10'-0"
GOAL LINE
1'-0"

Heavy lines indicate field of play

PLAN

(No scale)

Distinctive marks must be provided on both sides of field of play indicating goal line, 2 & 4 yd. lines & half distance between goal lines. These must be clearly visible from any position within the field of play. Allow sufficient space on walkways so referees may move freely from end to end of field of play. Provide space at goal lines for goal judges.

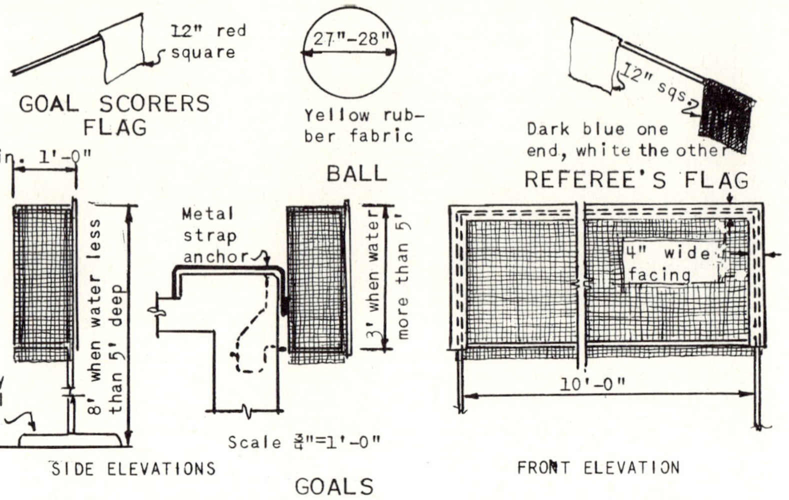
12" red square
GOAL SCORERS FLAG
27"-28"
Yellow rubber fabric
BALL
12" sqs.
Dark blue one end, white the other
REFEREE'S FLAG
min. 1'-0"
8' when water less than 5' deep
Heavy metal base
Metal strap anchor
3' when water more than 5'
Scale 3/4"=1'-0"
SIDE ELEVATIONS
4" wide facing
10'-0"
FRONT ELEVATION

GOALS

GOAL REQUIREMENTS: Posts and crossbar, rigid & perpendicular. AAU, wood or metal, 3" sq., painted single distinct color; NCAA, metal, 1½" dia. painted yellow or orange. Nets to hang loosely on frame.

Frames are custom made with bracing placed where necessary. It is recommended that they be collapsible for easy storage. Anchorage methods depend on the pool with those above commonly used, or brass couplings may be placed in pool walls to which frame may be attached. If pool is longer than req'd. playing length, one of goals may be floated & anchored with guy wires.

WATER POLO

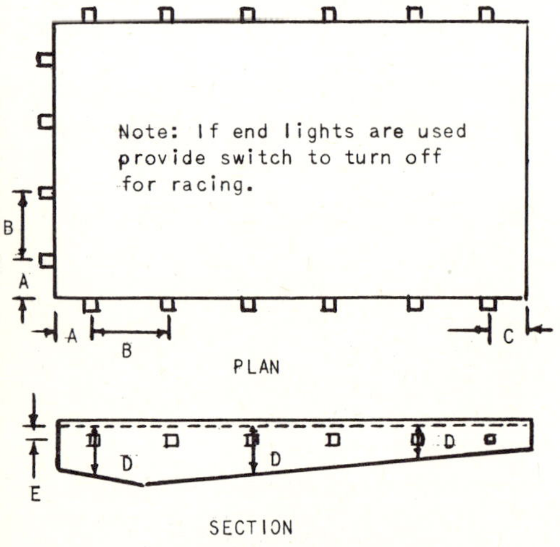
Note: If end lights are used provide switch to turn off for racing.
B
A
A
B
C
PLAN
D
D
D
E
SECTION

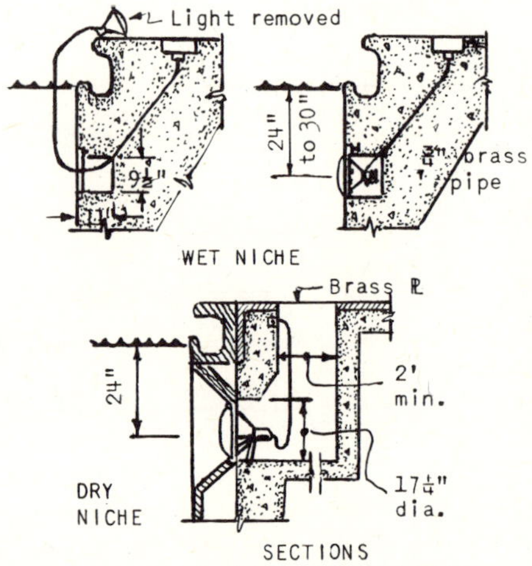
Light removed
9½"
24" to 30"
brass pipe
WET NICHE
Brass
24"
2' min.
DRY NICHE
17¼" dia.
SECTIONS

TYPICAL UNDERWATER LIGHTS

LAMP RATINGS (WATTS)	EQUIPMENT SPACING					
	A (ft.)	B ℄ to ℄ max. (ft.)		C (ft.)	E to ℄ (inches)	
		D > 5 ft.	D < 5 ft.		Min.	Max.
250 400	4	8	10	5	12	15
500 1000 1500	6	12	15	7½	18	24

UNDERWATER

INDOOR

5 watts per sq. ft. is considered good practice; 3 watts per sq. ft. minimum. The AAU requires a minimum of 30-foot-candles 3 ft. above surface of water for championship meets.

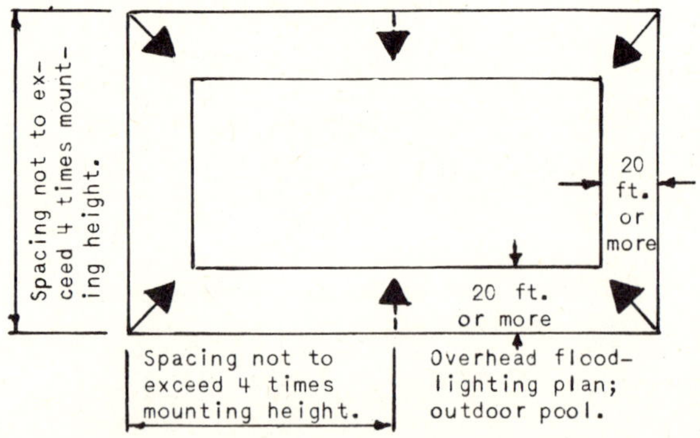
Spacing not to exceed 4 times mounting height.
20 ft. or more
20 ft. or more
Spacing not to exceed 4 times mounting height.

Overhead floodlighting plan; outdoor pool.

Floodlights are mounted at least 20 ft. above water. Select lamps to allow 1.75 watts per sq. ft. for type 5 GP floodlights or 2.5 watts per sq. ft. for type 6 O floodlights. AAU rules for championship meets require a min. of 30-foot-candles 3 ft. above surface of water.

OUTDOOR

ABOVE WATER

SWIMMING POOL LIGHTING

Data from I.E.S. Lighting Handbook

TYPICAL SWIMMING POOL PLUMBING DIAGRAM

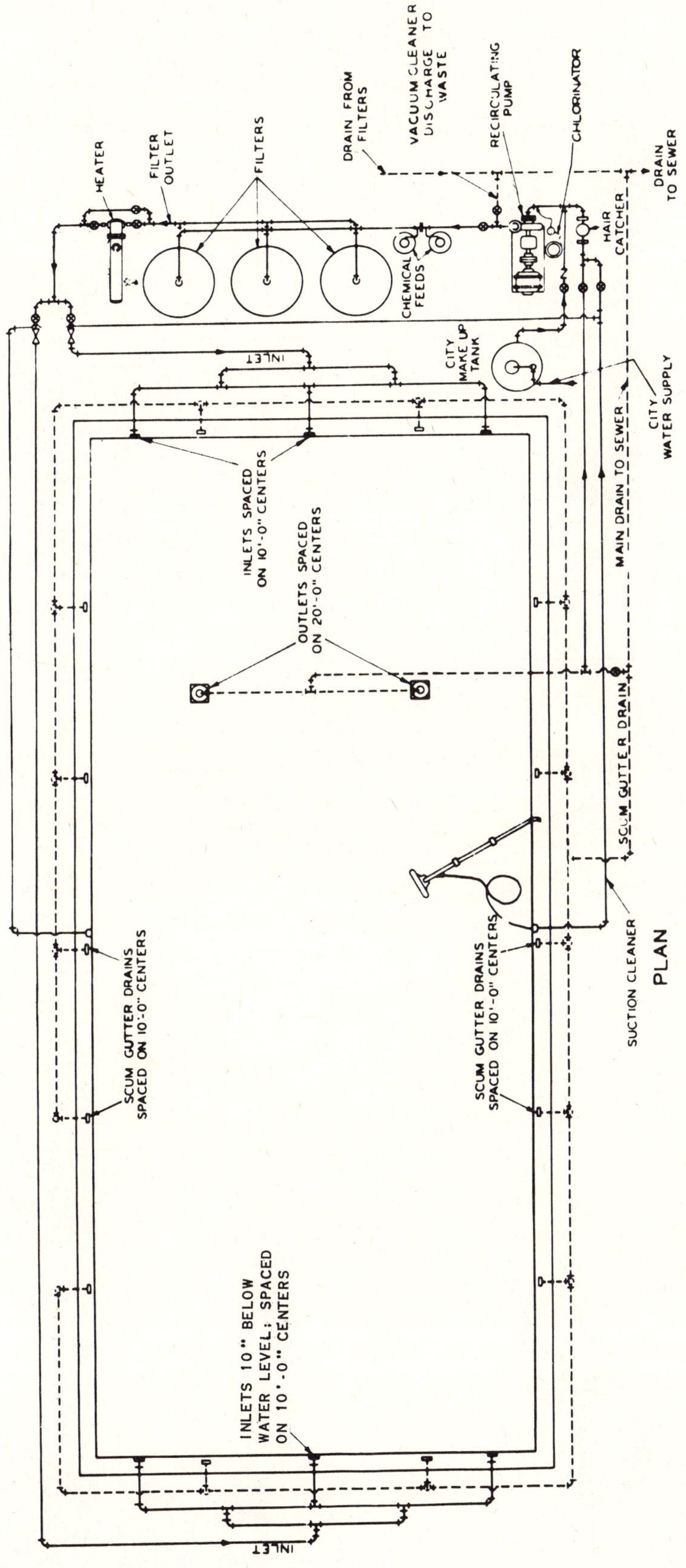
HEATER
FILTER OUTLET
FILTERS
DRAIN FROM FILTERS
VACUUM CLEANER DISCHARGE TO WASTE
RECIRCULATING PUMP
CHLORINATOR
DRAIN TO SEWER
HAIR CATCHER
CHEMICAL FEEDS
CITY MAKE UP TANK
CITY WATER SUPPLY
INLET
INLETS SPACED ON 10'-0" CENTERS
OUTLETS SPACED ON 20'-0" CENTERS
MAIN DRAIN TO SEWER
SCUM GUTTER DRAIN
SUCTION CLEANER
SCUM GUTTER DRAINS SPACED ON 10'-0" CENTERS
SCUM GUTTER DRAINS SPACED ON 10'-0" CENTERS
INLETS 10" BELOW WATER LEVEL; SPACED ON 10'-0" CENTERS
INLET

PLAN

Location of inlets and outlets depends on size and shape of pool. They should be placed to avoid dead spots in water circulation. Floor inlets are also available.

In large pools pipe trench should run around pool.

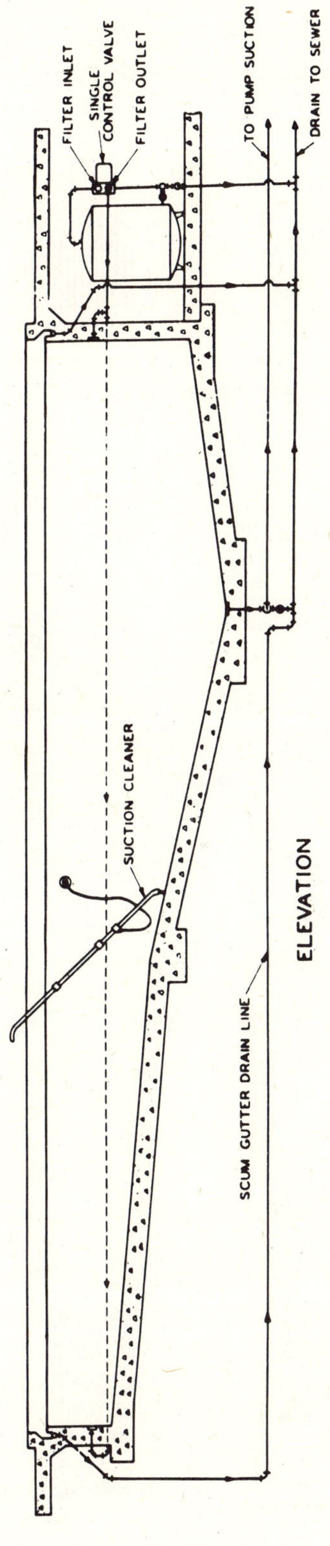
FILTER INLET
SINGLE CONTROL VALVE
FILTER OUTLET
TO PUMP SUCTION
DRAIN TO SEWER
SUCTION CLEANER
SCUM GUTTER DRAIN LINE

ELEVATION

Filter room may also be located above grade.

Pool drains should be adequate to empty pool in 4 hours. Orifice size to be twice size of pipe.

Note: Floor drains may be set at pool edge, as shown, in the center of walkways, or along indoor pool wall (consult local codes). Pitch deck ⅛"/ft. to drains.

DATA BY THE PERMUTIT COMPANY

SWIMMING POOL FIXTURES, FITTINGS and ACCESSORIES

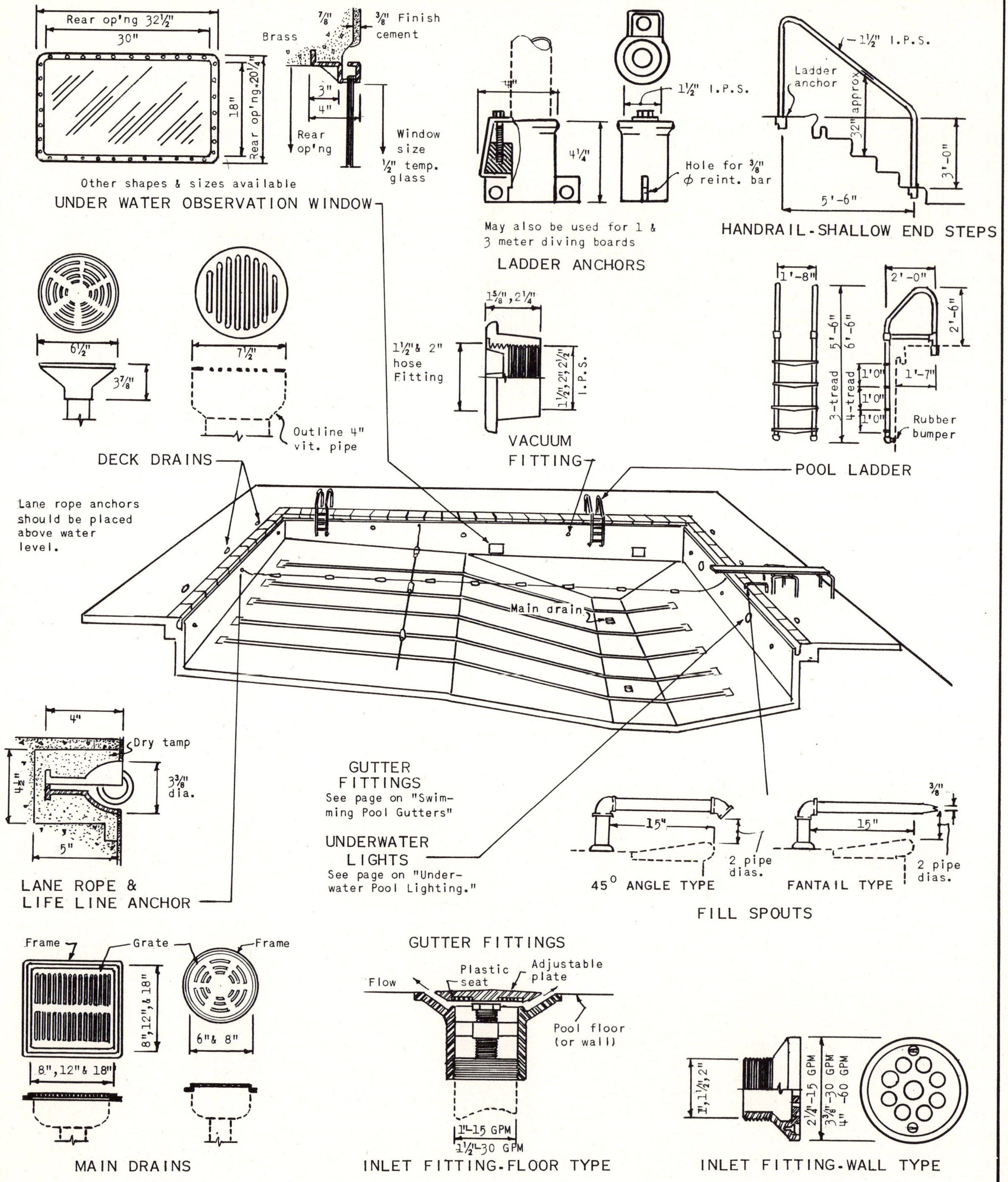
Rear op'ng 32½"
30"
18"
Rear op'ng 20¼"
Other shapes & sizes available
UNDER WATER OBSERVATION WINDOW
⅞"
Brass
⅜" Finish cement
3"
4"
Rear op'ng
Window size
½" temp. glass
4"
4¼"
1½" I.P.S.
Hole for ⅜" ϕ reint. bar
May also be used for 1 & 3 meter diving boards
LADDER ANCHORS
1½" I.P.S.
Ladder anchor
32" approx
3'-0"
5'-6"
HANDRAIL-SHALLOW END STEPS
6½"
3⅞"
7½"
Outline 4" vit. pipe
DECK DRAINS
1⅝", 2¼"
1½" & 2" hose Fitting
1½", 2", 2½" I.P.S.
VACUUM FITTING
1'-8"
2'-0"
3-tread 5'-6"
4-tread 6'-6"
2'-6"
1'0"
1'0"
1'0"
1'-7"
Rubber bumper
POOL LADDER
Lane rope anchors should be placed above water level.
Main drain
4"
Dry tamp
4½"
3⅜" dia.
5"
LANE ROPE & LIFE LINE ANCHOR
GUTTER FITTINGS
See page on "Swimming Pool Gutters"
UNDERWATER LIGHTS
See page on "Underwater Pool Lighting."
15"
2 pipe dias.
45° ANGLE TYPE
⅜"
15"
2 pipe dias.
FANTAIL TYPE
FILL SPOUTS
Frame
Grate
Frame
8", 12", & 18"
8", 12" & 18"
6" & 8"
MAIN DRAINS
GUTTER FITTINGS
Flow
Plastic seat
Adjustable plate
Pool floor (or wall)
1"-15 GPM
1½"-30 GPM
INLET FITTING-FLOOR TYPE
1", 1½", 2"
2¼"-15 GPM
3⅜"-30 GPM
4"-60 GPM
INLET FITTING-WALL TYPE

DATA BY LANDON, INC.

No scale

SWIMMING POOL GUTTERS = PROFILES, FITTINGS, PLUMBING, SECTIONS

Swimming pool gutters serve three purposes: draining off surface debris; acting as an overflow, there by keeping water level even; and providing exit from the pool. Water entering gutters should flow away quickly, sloping to outlets at 1-1/4" every 10 ft.

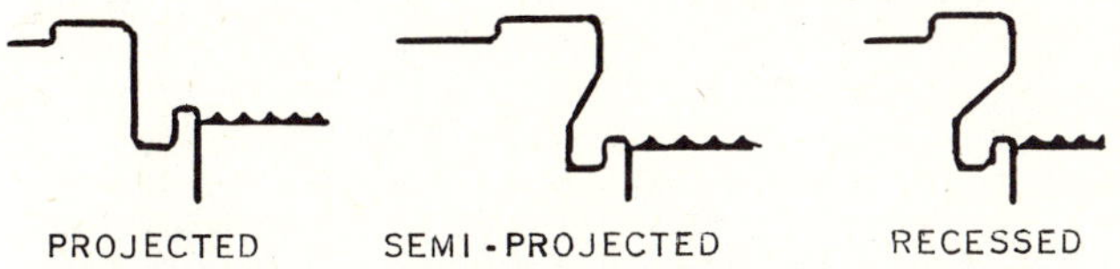

PROJECTED
SEMI-PROJECTED
RECESSED

Traditional types. Difficult exit from pool as swimmer must raise himself 12" to 15" vs. 2" to 3" for roll-out types. Almost all Boards of Health disapprove of fully recessed type as being hard to clean and dangerous to bathers who may catch an arm or foot in gutter.

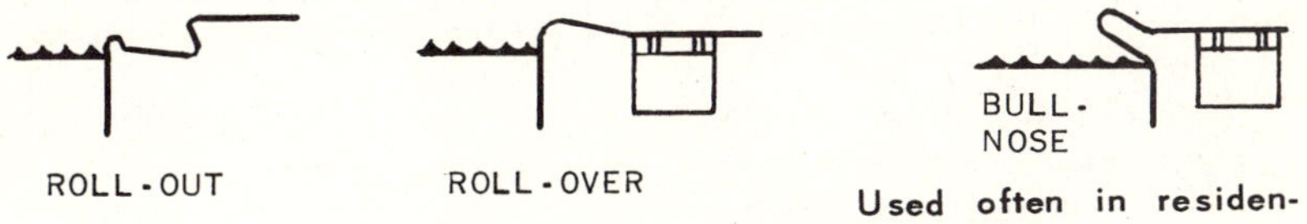

ROLL-OUT
ROLL-OVER
BULL-NOSE

Used often in residential work.

Combines gutter & walk drains, eliminating piping. Not accepted by all Boards of Health.

Provide easy exit. Pools can be overflowed readily to carry off floating debris. If pools used for race meets platform req'd at deep end to raise starting level to min. 18" above water.

BASIC SWIMMING POOL GUTTER PROFILES

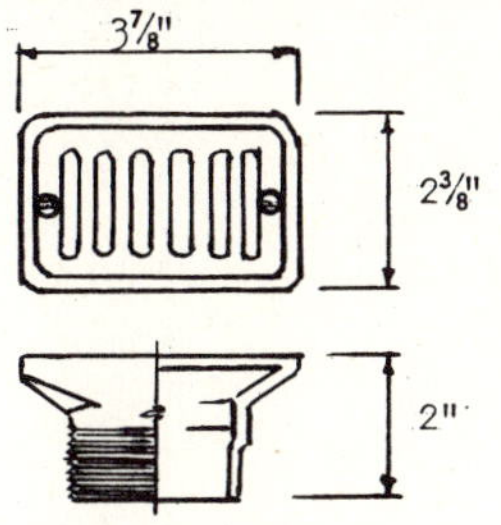

3⅞"
2⅜"
2"

FLAT TYPE

Both types shown are designed to fit standard 3" wide gutter bottom

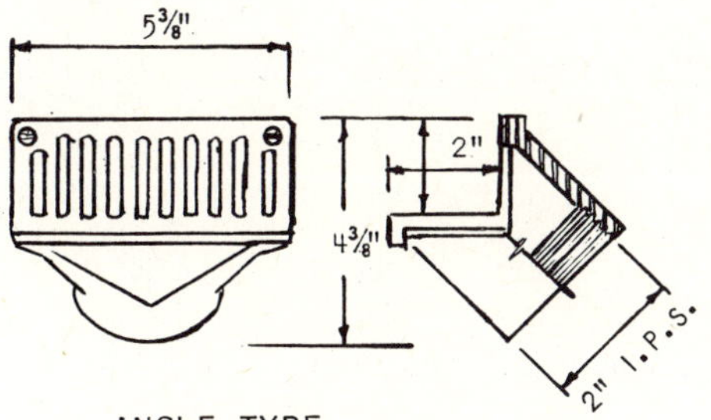

5⅜"
2"
4⅜"
2" I.P.S.

ANGLE TYPE

GUTTER FITTINGS

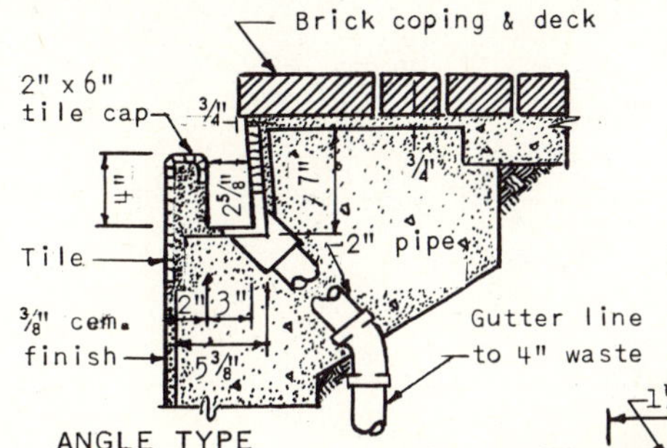

Brick coping & deck
2" x 6" tile cap
¾"
4"
2⅝"
7"
¾"
Tile
2" pipe
2" 3"
⅜" cem. finish
5⅜"
Gutter line to 4" waste

ANGLE TYPE FITTING

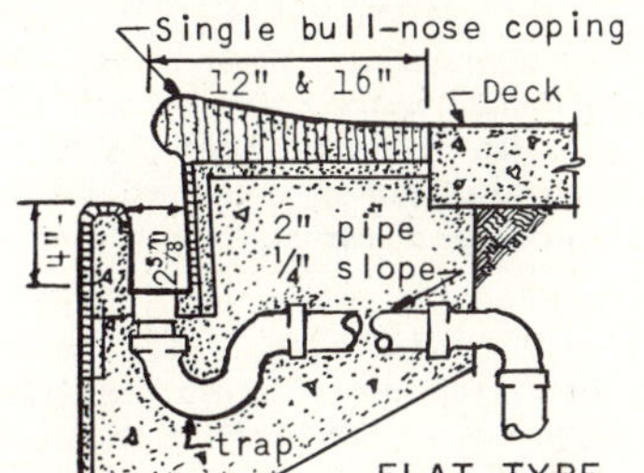

Single bull-nose coping
12" & 16"
Deck
4"
2⅝"
2" pipe
¼" slope
trap

FLAT TYPE WITH TRAP

Check local codes to see if traps req'd.

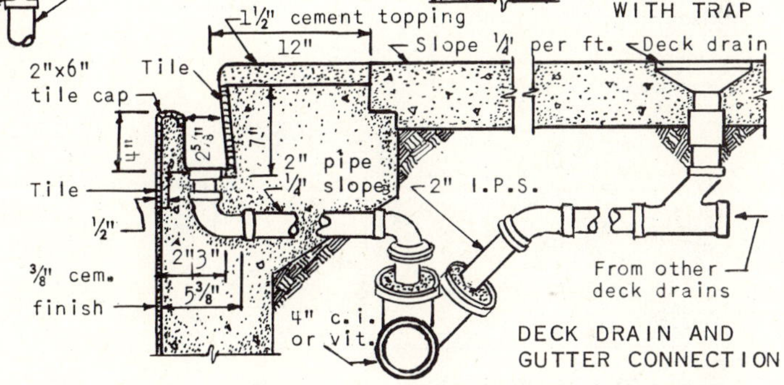

1½" cement topping
12"
Slope ¼" per ft.
Deck drain
Tile
2"x6" tile cap
4"
2⅝"
7"
2" pipe
¼" slope
2" I.P.S.
Tile
½"
2" 3"
⅜" cem. finish
5⅜"
4" c.i. or vit.
From other deck drains

DECK DRAIN AND GUTTER CONNECTION

TYPICAL GUTTERS WITH DRAIN FITTINGS & PIPING

Scale 1½" = 1'-0"

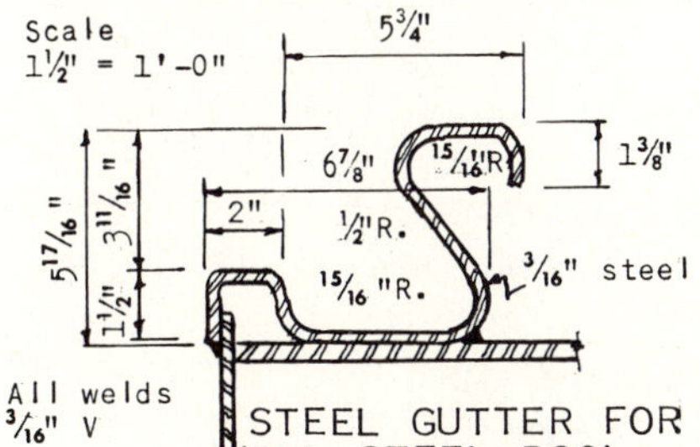

5¾"
6⅞"
15/16"R
1⅜"
2"
½"R.
15/16 "R.
3/16" steel
5 17/16"
3 11/16"
1½"
All welds 3/16" V

STEEL GUTTER FOR ALL STEEL POOL

Data by Koven Steel Swimming Pools, Inc.

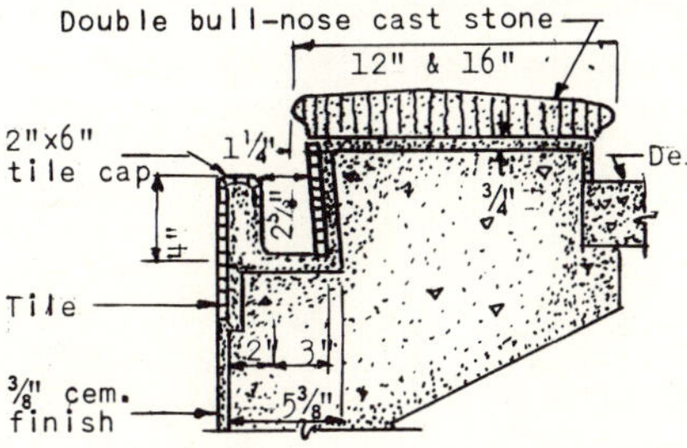

Double bull-nose cast stone
12" & 16"
Deck
2"x6" tile cap
1¼"
4"
2⅝"
¾"
Tile
2" 3"
⅜" cem. finish
5⅜"

Note: No reinf. shown. Trim tile gen. 4½"x4¼" or 6"x6", frostproof for outdoor pools in colder climates.

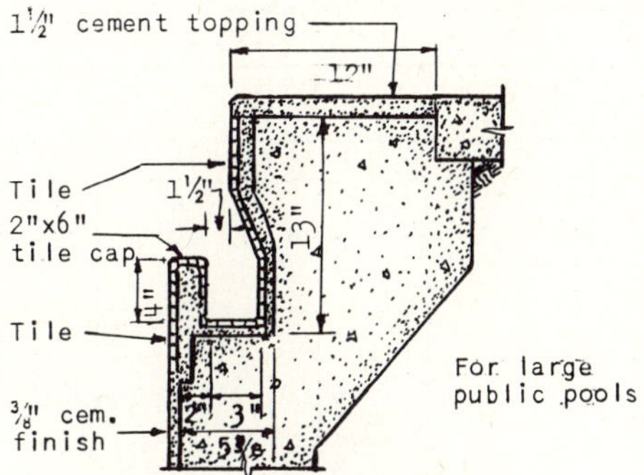

1½" cement topping
12"
Tile
1½"
2"x6" tile cap
13"
4"
Tile
⅜" cem. finish
2" 3"
5⅜"

For large public pools

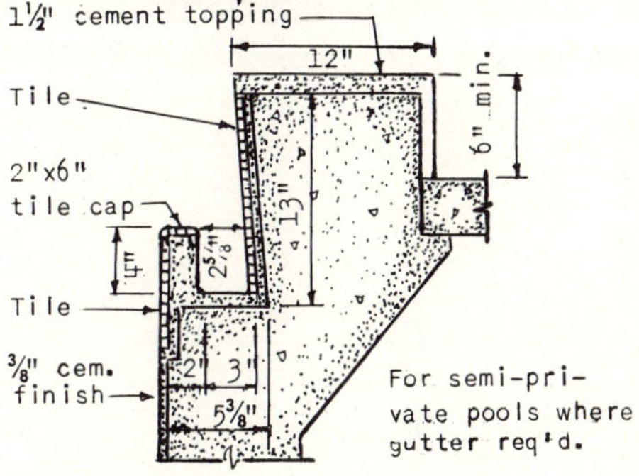

1½" cement topping
12"
6" min.
Tile
2"x6" tile cap
13"
4"
2⅝"
Tile
⅜" cem. finish
2" 3"
5⅜"

For semi-private pools where gutter req'd.

TYPICAL GUTTER SECTIONS

Data by Landon, Inc. except as otherwise noted

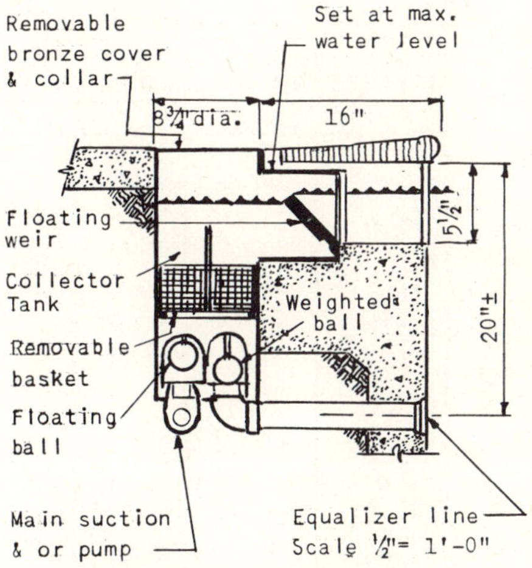

Removable bronze cover & collar
Set at max. water level
3¾" dia.
16"
5½"
Floating weir
Collector Tank
Weighted ball
20"±
Removable basket
Floating ball
Main suction & or pump
Equalizer line Scale ½"= 1'-0"

Used with or in place of gutter drains. Utilizes suction from filter pumps to pull debris from pool surface. Floating weir adjusts to water level. Removable basket prevents debris from entering suction line. Not approved by all Boards of Health.

SURFACE SKIMMER

Scale ¾" = 1'-0" except as otherwise noted

SWIMMING POOL WATER PURIFICATION; SAND and GRAVEL FILTERS

GENERAL: Size filter depends on (1) pool size and (2) recirculation rate. Private pools gen. require 2 turnovers per day; semi-private, 2, preferably 3; public, 3 to 4. Besides sand and gravel as the filtering medium graded charcoal may be substituted if water supplied has unpleasant taste or smell. Calcium carbonate may also be used for filtering and to restore alkalinity to water thus eliminating alkali feed, shown below. Horizontal sand gravel and gravity filters are available but are little used. The following data concern larger pools using 3 and 4 filter units. Small residential pools require only 1 or 2 units as shown on page concerning residential pools.

ALKALI FEED
Replaces alkali in water removed by alum coagulants. Sal soda or soda ash used as agents.

ALUM FEED
Provides crystal potash or amonium alum or sulfate of alumina to coagulate finely divided matter into particles more easily removed by filters.

RECIRCULATING PUMP
Motor driven centrifugal pump best suited for swimming pools. Where 3 or more filters used pump should have capacity to deliver req'd backwash for each filter.

CHLORINATOR
For sterilization of water. There are several types, utilizing either chlorine gas or sodium hypochlorite.

HAIR CATCHER
Removes hair, lint, and large particles before they reach pump or filters. Equipped with removable basket. Located on suction side of recirculating pump.

MAKEUP TANK
Used for introducing additional city water into system, replacing that lost by evaporation and backwashing.

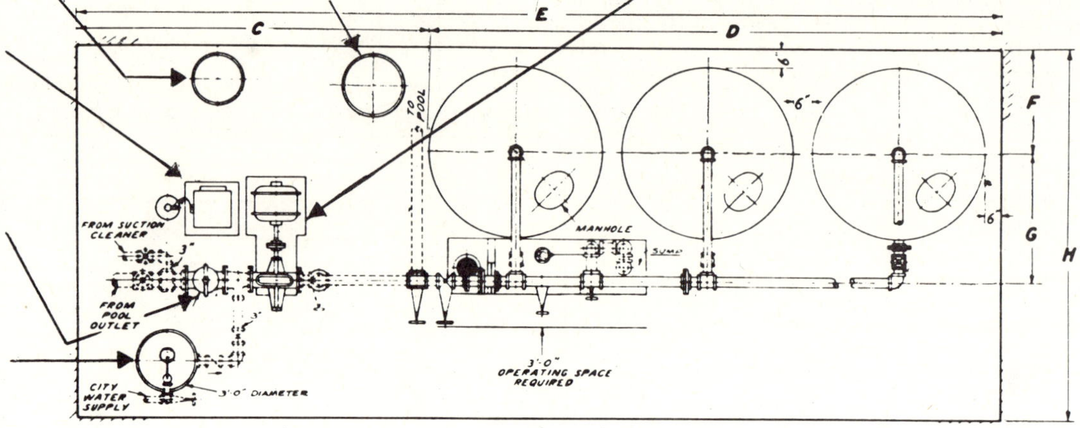
C
E
D
TO POOL
FROM SUCTION CLEANER
3"
MANHOLE
SUMP
FROM POOL OUTLET
CITY WATER SUPPLY
3'-0" DIAMETER
3'-0" OPERATING SPACE REQUIRED
6"
F
G
H

PLAN

No Scale

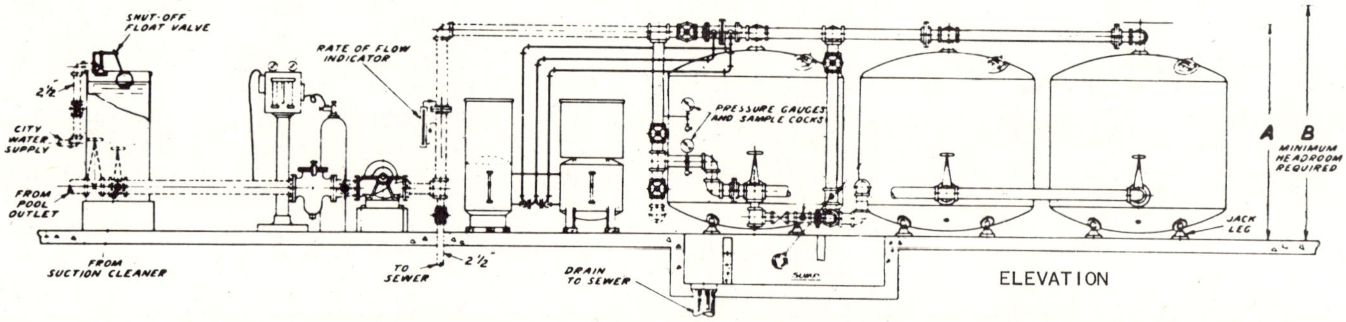
SHUT-OFF FLOAT VALVE
2½"
CITY WATER SUPPLY
FROM POOL OUTLET
FROM SUCTION CLEANER
RATE OF FLOW INDICATOR
TO SEWER
2½"
DRAIN TO SEWER
PRESSURE GAUGES AND SAMPLE COCKS
SUMP
JACK LEG
A B
MINIMUM HEADROOM REQUIRED

ELEVATION

SAND & GRAVEL FILTERS & ACCESSORIES – APPROX. SPACE REQUIREMENTS*

8 HR. TURNOVER – READ TO RIGHT | 12 HR. TURNOVER – READ TO LEFT

POOL SIZE-FT.	CAP. IN GAL.	FILTER DIA.	FILLED WT. EA. FILTER	PUMP GPM	PUMP HP	A	B	C	D	E	F	G	H	POOL SIZE-FT	CAP. IN GAL.
THREE-UNIT															
15x45	30,000	3'-0"	5,200#	65	1½	6'-10"	7'-6"	10'-6"	10'-6"	21'-0"	2'-0"	2'-7"	9'-0"	20x50	45,000
20x45	36,000	3'-6"	7,000	75	2	7'-8"	8'-1"	10'-6"	12'-0"	22'-6"	2'-3"	2'-10"	9'-6"	20x60	55,000
20x60	55,000	4'-0"	8,900	115	2	8'-0"	8'-3"	10'-6"	13'-6"	24'-0"	2'-6"	3'-4"	10'-6"	25x75 / 30x60	80,000
25x60	68,000	4'-6"	11,300	145	3	8'-1"	8'-5"	11'-0"	15'-0"	26'-0"	2'-9"	3'-8"	11'-0"	25x90	102,000
25x75 / 30x60	80,000	5'-0"	14,000	170	3	8'-5"	8'-7"	11'-0"	16'-6"	27'-6"	3'-0"	4'-0"	11'-6"	30x90	120,000
25x90	102,000	5'-6"	17,400	210	5	8'-7"	8'-8"	11'-0"	18'-0"	29'-0"	3'-3"	4'-4"	12'-6"	35x105	155,000
30x90	120,000	6'-0"	20,800	250	5	8'-9"	8'-10"	11'-0"	19'-6"	30'-6"	3'-6"	4'-7"	13'-0"	40x105 / 45x90	180,000
35x90	140,000	6'-6"	24,500	300	7½	8'-11"	9'-0"	11'-0"	21'-0"	32'-0"	3'-9"	5'-1"	13'-6"	40x120	207,000
35x105 / 40x90	155,000	7'-0"	28,700	340	7½	9'-1"	9'-5"	11'-6"	22'-6"	34'-0"	4'-0"	5'-4"	14'-6"	55x120 / 50x135	248,000
40x105 / 45x90	180,000	7'-6"	33,100	390	7½	9'-4"	9'-10"	12'-0"	24'-0"	36'-0"	4'-3"	5'-7"	15'-0"	55x120 / 50x135	280,000
40x120	207,000	8'-0"	37,700	450	10	9'-6"	10'-3"	12'-0"	25'-6"	37'-6"	4'-6"	5'-10"	15'-6"	50x150	310,000
50x120 / 45x135	248,000	8'-6"	43,000	510	10	9'-8"	10'-9"	12'-6"	27'-0"	39'-6"	4'-9"	6'-1"	16'-0"	60x150	372,000
55x120 / 50x135	280,000	9'-0"	48,500	570	10	9'-11"	11'-2"	13'-6"	28'-6"	42'-0"	5'-0"	6'-5"	17'-0"	75x135 / 60x180	420,000
50x150	310,000	10'-0"	58,500	650	15	10'-2"	12'-1"	13'-6"	31'-6"	45'-0"	5'-6"	6'-11"	18'-0"	75x150 / 70x180	465,000
FOUR-UNIT															
50x150	310,000	8'-6"	43,000	650	15	9'-5"	10'-2"	13'-6"	36'-0"	49'-6"	4'-9"	6'-0"	16'-0"	75x150 / 70x180	465,000
60x150 / 60x180	370,000	9'-0"	48,500	770	15	9'-8"	10'-7"	13'-6"	38'-0"	51'-6"	5'-0"	6'-6"	17'-0"	70x220	558,000
75x135	420,000	10'-0"	58,500	880	15	9'-11"	11'-6"	13'-6"	42'-0"	55'-6"	5'-6"	7'-0"	18'-0"	90x180 / 100x150	630,000

*Note: If pool water to be heated, place heater in filter room. Allow approx. 3 sq. ft.

DATA BY THE PERMUTIT CO.

SWIMMING POOL WATER PURIFICATION: DIATOMITE FILTERS

GENERAL: The diatomite filter uses diatomaceous silica as its filtering medium, which because of its microscopic size, produces a brilliantly clear water. This type filter, because of its compactness, requires 1/10 to 1/5 the floor space needed by conventional filtering units.

In operation, diatomaceous silica is either introduced directly or in the form of a slurry into the filtering tank where it is deposited as a coating on a strainer type septa, either of porous stone or metal. Because of finer filtration the diatomite filter requires more frequent backwashing and cleaning than sand and gravel units.

In diatomite filters, alum, as a coagulant, need not be used, thus eliminating both the alum and alkali feeds, standard equipment with sand and gravel filters.

Note: The following data is for approximate overall sizes of diatomite filter rooms in new construction. There are many other arrangements possible to meet existing conditions and manufacturers should be consulted in these cases. Size filter, number required, etc. depend on pool gallonage and use and these should be left to qualified judgement. Ceiling height, shown in column "G" is important as headroom must be maintained in order to remove filter elements from tank.

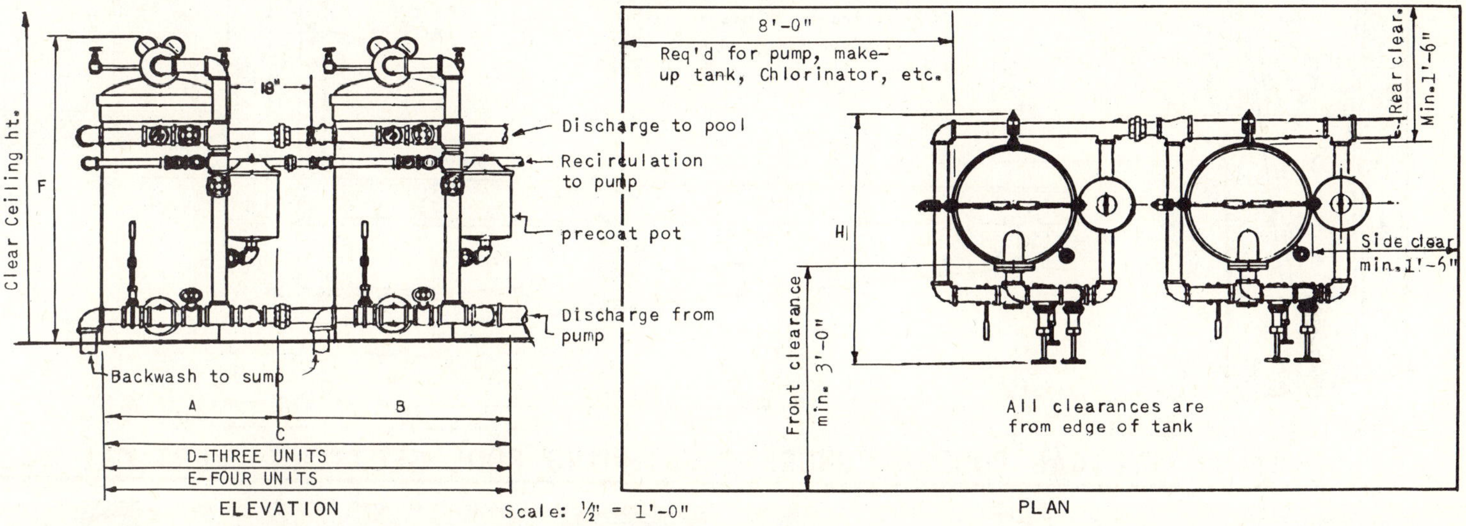
G
Clear Ceiling ht.
F
18"
Discharge to pool
Recirculation to pump
precoat pot
Discharge from pump
Backwash to sump
A
B
C
D-THREE UNITS
E-FOUR UNITS
ELEVATION
Scale: ½" = 1'-0"
8'-0"
Req'd for pump, make-up tank, Chlorinator, etc.
Rear clear. Min. 1'-6"
H
Side clear min. 1'-6"
Front clearance min. 3'-0"
All clearances are from edge of tank
PLAN

*The 8 ft. side clearance provides for other equipment needed in a filter room. Approx. sizes of this equipment are: pump, 1'-6" x 3'-0"; hair strainer, 2□; chlorinator, 2'-0" x 1'-6"; make-up tank, 3' & 5' diameter x 5' high; slurry feeder (optional) 1' diameter x 3'-7" high. If water heater is to be used provide additional 3□.

APPROX. SPACE REQUIREMENTS: DIATOMITE FILTERS*

APPROX. POOL SIZE	POOL CAPACITY GALS.	NO. FILTERS REC'D**	FILTER SIZE SQ. FT.	FILTER DIA.	FLOW RATE GPM***	PIPE SIZE	A	B	C	D	E	F	G	H
Small private pools	10,000	2	7	8"	30	1¼"	1'-3"	1'-9"	3'-0"			3'-7¼"	7'-0"	2'-0"
	13,000	1	18	12½"	36	1½" 2"	2'-7¼"					4'-11¼"	7'-11"	3'-1¼" 3'-1½"
20x45	35,000	1	42	1'-6½"	84	2" 3"	3'-5¾"					5'-7½"	8'-0"	3'-8¾" 4'-1½"
20x60	60,000	2	42	1'-6½"	170	2" 3"	3'-5¾"	3'-5½" 4'-0"	6'-11¼" 7'-5¾"			5'-7½"	8'-0"	3'-8¾" 4'-1½"
25x75 30x60	90,000	3	42	1'-6½"	250	2" 3"	3'-5¾"	3'-5½" 4'-0"	6'-11¼" 7'-5¾"	10'-4¾" 11'-5¾"		5'-7½"	8'-0"	3'-8¾" 4'-1½"
30x90	115,000	2	79	2'-2½"	320	3" 4"	4'-1¾"	4'-4" 4'-10"	8'-5¾" 8'-11¾"			6'-0¾"	9'-0"	4'-9¾" 5'-6"
40x105 45x90	170,000	3	79	2'-2½"	475	3" 4"	4'-1¾"	4'-4" 4'-10"	8'-5¾" 8'-11¾"	12'-9¾" 13'-9¾"		6'-0¾"	9'-0"	4'-9¾" 5'-6"
40x120	225,000	3	104	2'-2½"	600	3" 4"	4'-1¾"	4'-4" 4'-10"	8'-5¾" 8'-11¾"	12'-9¾" 13'-9¾"		7'-0¾"	10'-0"	4'-9¾" 5'-6"
60x180 75x135	430,000	3	200	3'-0½"	1200	4" 6"	5'-4"	5'-3¼" 6'-8¼"	10'-7¼" 12'-0¼"	15'-10½" 18'-8½"		7'-3"	10'-0"	6'-4½" 7'-9½"
Large outdoor pool	720,000	4	248	3'-0½"	2000	4" 6"	5'-4"	5'-3¼" 6'-8¼"	10'-7¼" 12'-0¼"	15'-10½" 18'-8½"	21'-1¾" 25'-4¾"	7'-3"	10'-0"	6'-4½" 7'-9½"

* Dimensions are to nearest ¼" above fraction.

** Filters should be installed in banks of two or more to provide uninterrupted service while cleaning. For example, in an installation requiring 200□ filter area it is better to use two 104□ units than one unit of 200□.

*** Combined flow rate for total recommend. filters, based on filtration rate 2 gals./min./sq.ft. filter area & a circulation period of 6-hrs.

DATA BY BOWSER, INC.

CONCRETE and GUNITE SWIMMING POOL CONSTRUCTION

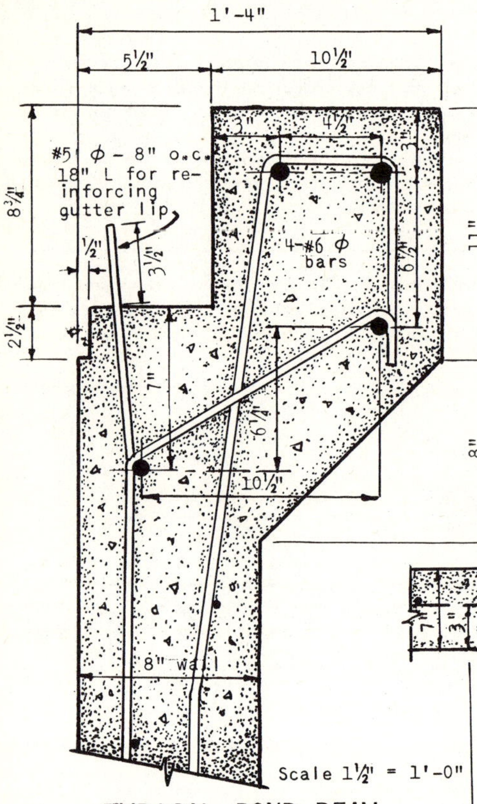
1'-4"
5½"
10½"
3"
4½"
#5 ϕ - 8" o.c.
18" L for reinforcing gutter lip
8¾"
½"
3½"
4-#6 ϕ bars
6½"
11"
2½"
7"
6¼"
10½"
8"
8" wall
Scale 1½" = 1'-0"

TYPICAL BOND BEAM DETAIL

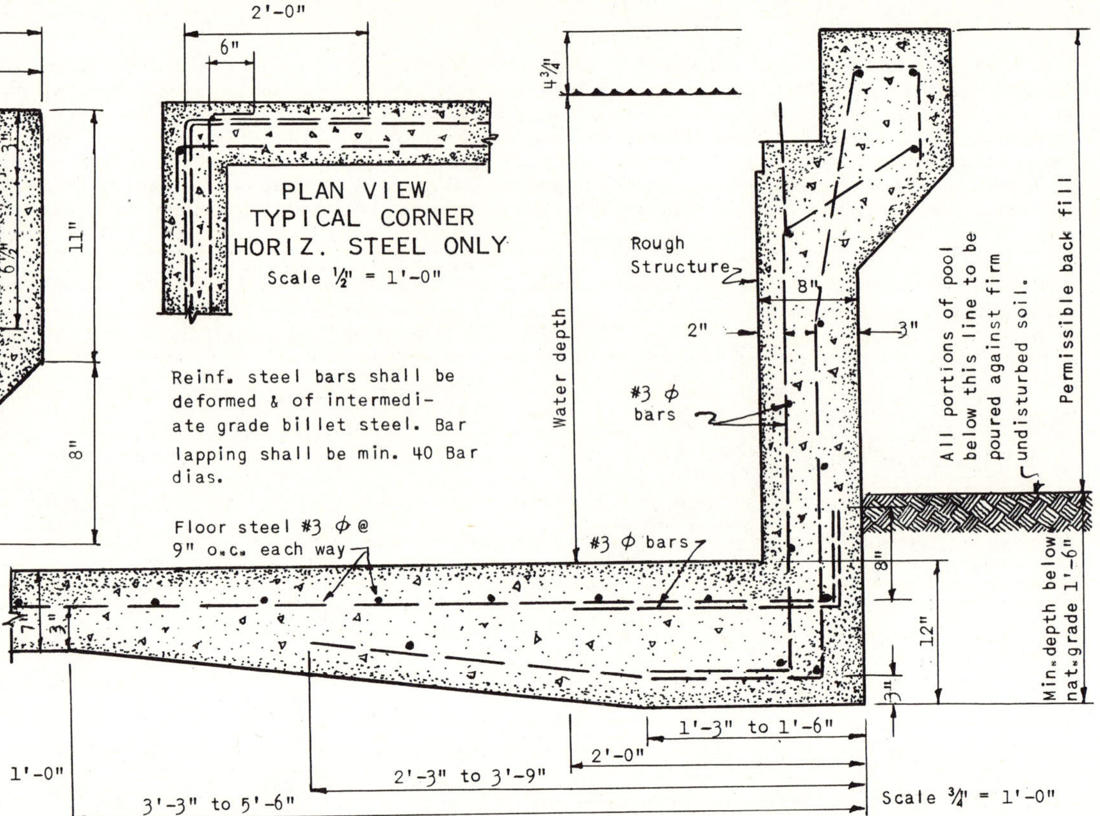
2'-0"
6"
PLAN VIEW
TYPICAL CORNER
HORIZ. STEEL ONLY
Scale ½" = 1'-0"
Reinf. steel bars shall be deformed & of intermediate grade billet steel. Bar lapping shall be min. 40 Bar dias.
Floor steel #3 ϕ @ 9" o.c. each way
4¾"
Water depth
Rough Structure
8"
2"
3"
#3 ϕ bars
#3 ϕ bars
All portions of pool below this line to be poured against firm undisturbed soil.
Permissible back fill
8"
12"
3"
Min. depth below nat. grade 1'-6"
7"
3"
1'-3" to 1'-6"
2'-0"
2'-3" to 3'-9"
3'-3" to 5'-6"
Scale ¾" = 1'-0"

TYPICAL POURED CONCRETE SWIMMING POOL SECTION - VERTICAL WALLS

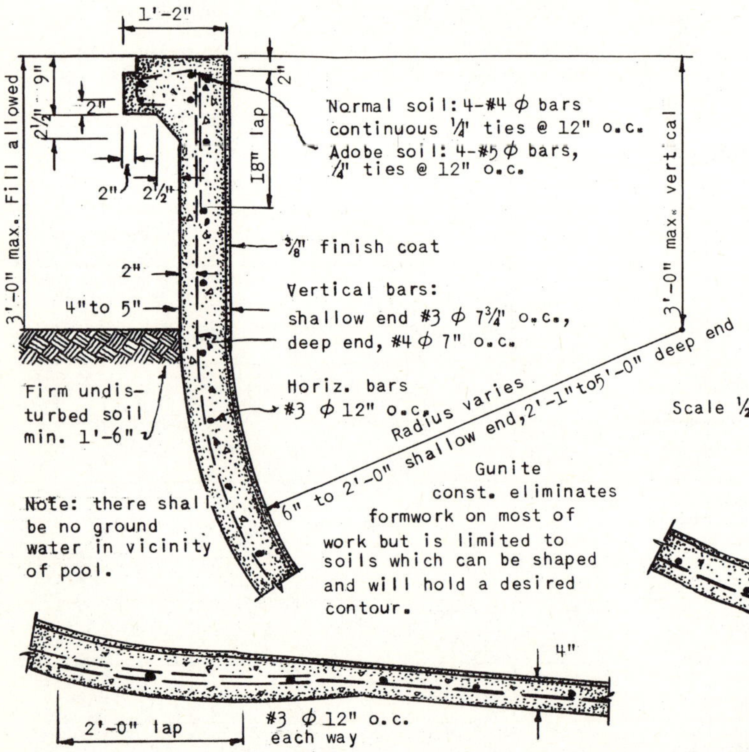
1'-2"
9"
2"
2½"
2"
2"
2½"
3'-0" max. Fill allowed
18" lap
Normal soil: 4-#4 ϕ bars continuous ¼" ties @ 12" o.c.
Adobe soil: 4-#5 ϕ bars, ¼" ties @ 12" o.c.
3'-0" max. vertical
2"
4" to 5"
⅜" finish coat
Vertical bars:
shallow end #3 ϕ 7¾" o.c.,
deep end, #4 ϕ 7" o.c.
Horiz. bars
#3 ϕ 12" o.c.
Radius varies
6" to 2'-0" shallow end, 2'-1" to 5'-0" deep end
Firm undisturbed soil min. 1'-6"
Note: there shall be no ground water in vicinity of pool.
Gunite const. eliminates formwork on most of work but is limited to soils which can be shaped and will hold a desired contour.
4"
2'-0" lap
#3 ϕ 12" o.c. each way

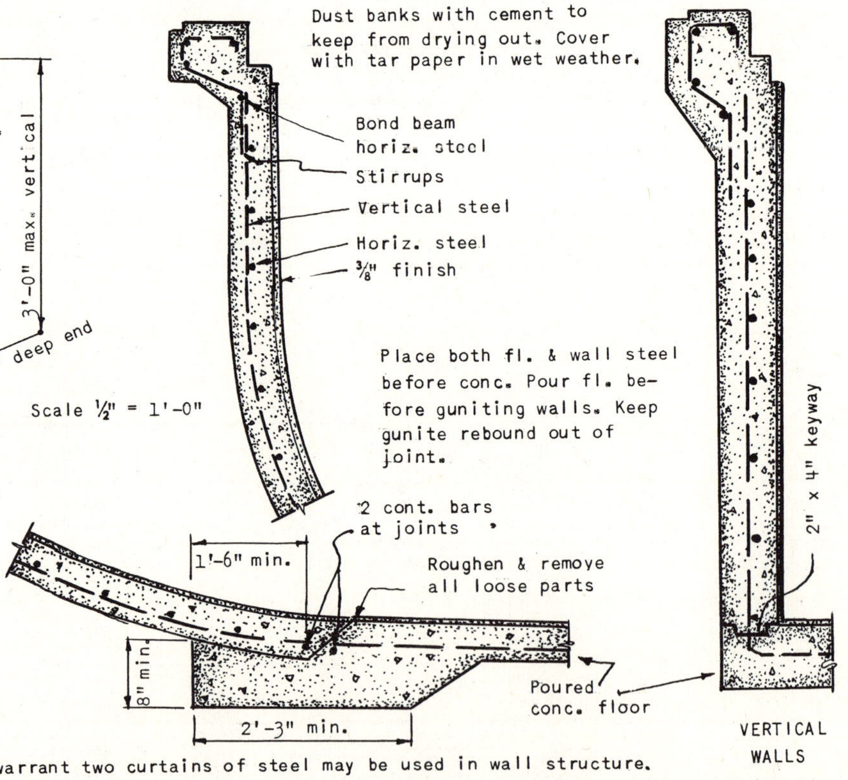
Dust banks with cement to keep from drying out. Cover with tar paper in wet weather.
Bond beam horiz. steel
Stirrups
Vertical steel
Horiz. steel
⅜" finish
Scale ½" = 1'-0"
Place both fl. & wall steel before conc. Pour fl. before guniting walls. Keep gunite rebound out of joint.
2" x 4" keyway
2 cont. bars at joints
1'-6" min.
Roughen & remove all loose parts
8" min.
2'-3" min.
Poured conc. floor
VERTICAL WALLS

Note: Where soil or climate conditions warrant two curtains of steel may be used in wall structure.

TYPICAL SECTION-ALL GUNITE CONST. TYPICAL SECTIONS -POURED FLOORS, GUNITE WALLS

Note: Pool sides & bottom should be smooth to prevent scraping & collection of algae. 3/8" finish coat is hand troweled white cement of white silica sand or marble chips. This finish, although commonly referred to as plaster, should not contain lime. Final coat may be left white, giving water a sparkling bluish cast. Color may be added by painting. Light green or blue on sides with darker shade on bottom creates illusion of deep clear pool. Most Boards of Health require public pools to be white or a light color. See also page on tile surfacing for swimming pools.

DATA BY LANDON, INC.

STEEL SWIMMING POOL CONSTN - PLASTIC POOLS & POOL LINERS

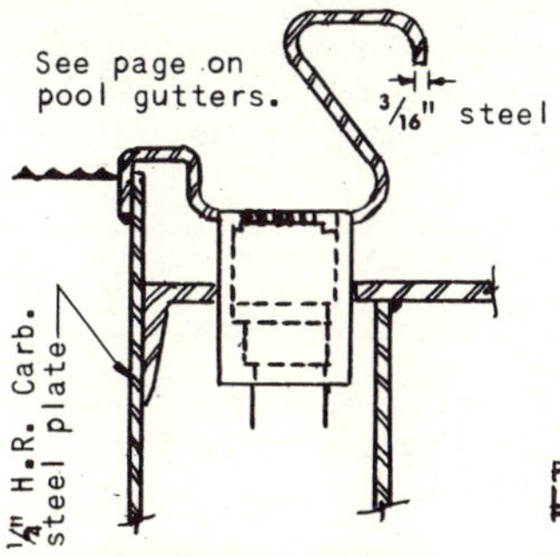
See page on pool gutters.
3/16" steel
1/4" H.R. Carb. steel plate

SECTION THRU ALL STEEL TANK

Size members varies with design. Sm. pool takes 10" x 5.3#[for verticals and diagonals; 15" x 33.9 #[for bottom members on which pool rests.

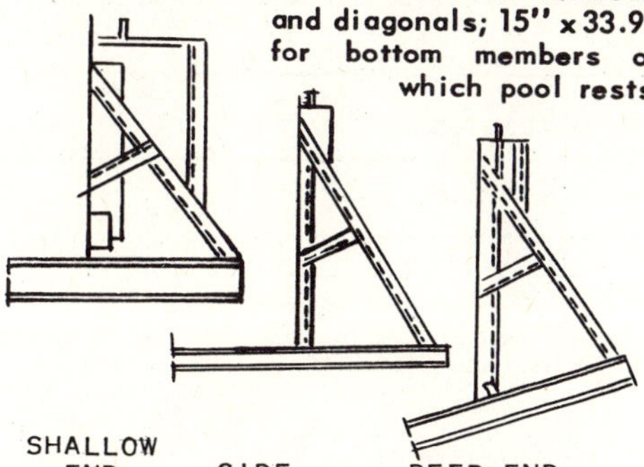
SHALLOW END
SIDE
DEEP END

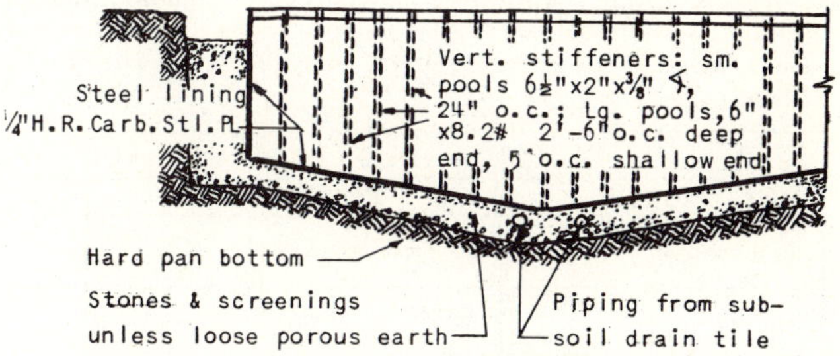
Steel lining
1/4"H.R. Carb. Stl. PL
Vert. stiffeners: sm. pools 6½"x2"x3/8" ∠, 24" o.c.; Lg. pools, 6" x8.2# 2'-6"o.c. deep end, 5' o.c. shallow end
Hard pan bottom
Stones & screenings unless loose porous earth
Piping from sub-soil drain tile

Small pools require 4" pitched layer of 1" coarse stone topped with 2" layer coarse screening. Large pools, 6" to 7" layer 1" crushed stone covered with coarse sand. Roll to form firm foundation.

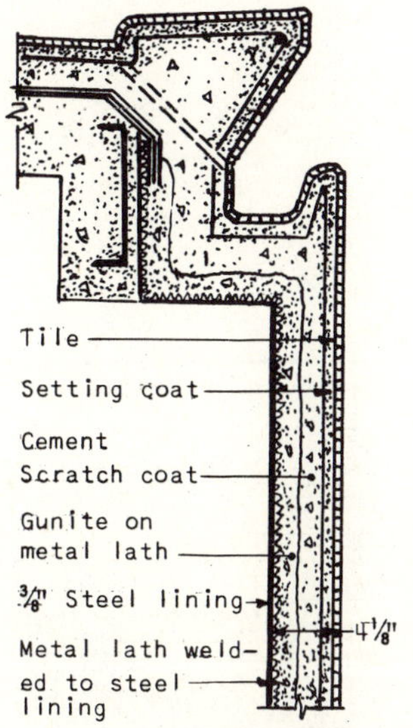
Tile
Setting coat
Cement Scratch coat
Gunite on metal lath
3/8" Steel lining
4 1/8"
Metal lath welded to steel lining

SECTION THRU STEEL LINED CONC. TANK

Side buttresses are welded in place to form base & wall framework to which side & bottom PL's are welded. Pools 50' long req. two sets side buttresses; pools less than 50' req. only one. Pools less than 30' wide do not req. end buttresses.

BUTTRESSES

WELDING

Bottom PL's bonded by 1" lap welds with long fillets. Side PL's butt welded together & to bottom PL's. All joints ground smooth.

SURFACE TREATMENT

Exterior, black asphaltum; interior, sandblasted to remove mill scale, 3 coats primary, 2 coats finish waterproof enamel.

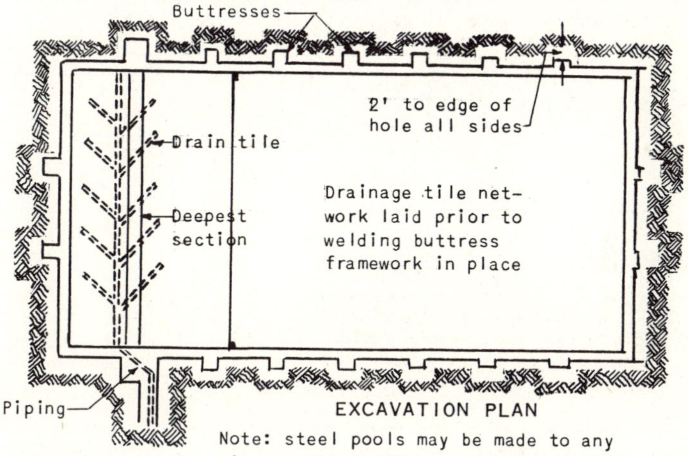
Buttresses
2' to edge of hole all sides
Drain tile
Deepest section
Drainage tile network laid prior to welding buttress framework in place
Piping

EXCAVATION PLAN

Note: steel pools may be made to any size or shape. Std. sm. pools are 16' x 30' & 40' & 20' x 40' & 50'

ALL STEEL SWIMMING POOLS

DATA BY KOVEN STEEL SWIMMING POOLS, INC.

No scale

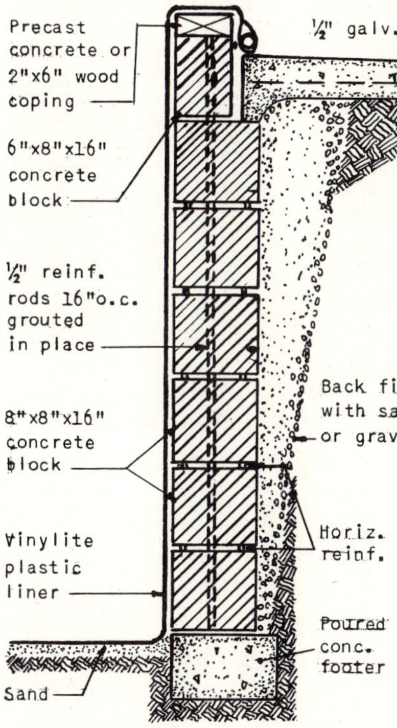
Precast concrete or 2"x6" wood coping
1/2" galv. pipe
Conc. walk 66 10/10 wire reinforcing
Pitch 1" in 3'-0" for walkway runoff
6"x8"x16" concrete block
1/2" reinf. rods 16"o.c. grouted in place
Back fill with sand or gravel
8"x8"x16" concrete block
Horiz. reinf.
Vinylite plastic liner
Poured conc. footer
Sand

SECTION
Scale: 3/4" = 1'-0"

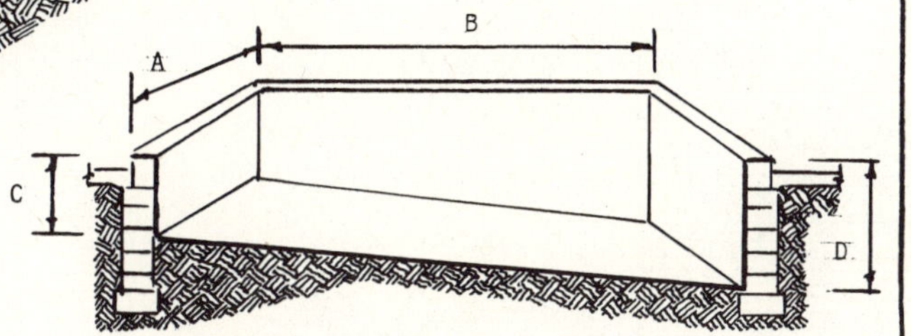
A
B
C
D

Excavation leveled at max. depth & walls built at this ht. allowing conc. base to be poured w/o wood forms and eliminating staggered block construction. Pool deck backfilled to correct slope & covered with sand.

Liner is 20 ga. Krene vinylite. Stan. plumb. drains may be fitted to liner. Filter may be used. If underwater lights desired liner may be ordered with clear plastic windows.

STANDARD SIZES

A	B	C	D
12'	27'	3'	5'
16'	32'	3'	7'
20'	40'	3'	8'

CONCRETE BLOCK POOL WITH PLASTIC LINER

DATA BY LIN-O-PLAST CORP.

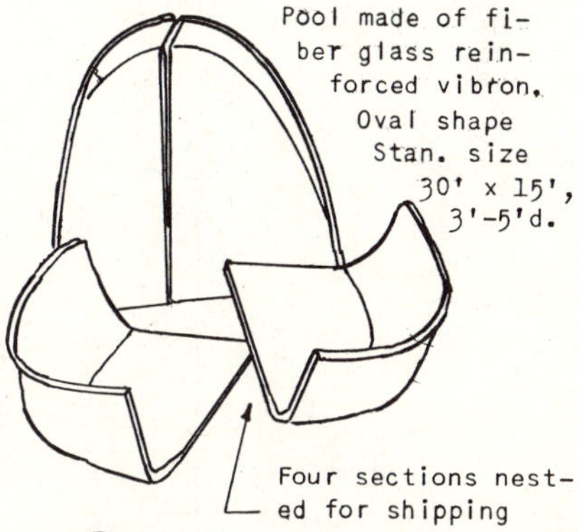
Pool made of fiber glass reinforced vibron. Oval shape Stan. size 30' x 15', 3'-5'd.
Four sections nested for shipping

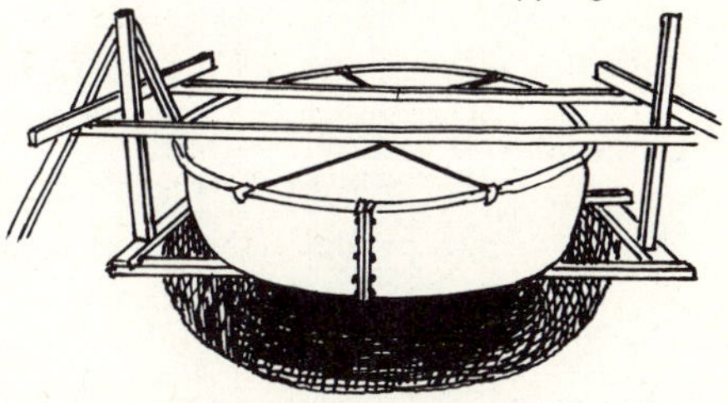

Hole excavated to fit pool contours, drain lines installed. Pool sections assembled in frame over excavation. After plastic pipe connections made pool is lowered into hole.

ALL PLASTIC POOL

DATA BY PADDOCK POOL EQUIPMENT CO.

TILE SWIMMING POOLS

Tile is an ideal finishing material for swimming pools. It is durable, waterproof, and sanitary and is available in a variety of sizes and colors. A light color tile, preferably white, should be used under water, with patterns and color above water and around pool. All lines under water should be dark to contrast with pool floor and walls. Frost-proof tile should always be used in outdoor pools in freezing climates.

RECOMMENDED TILE USE FOR SWIMMING POOLS		
AREA	TYPE TILE	SIZES
POOL LINING	Ceramic mosaics	$\frac{3}{4}$"*, $1\frac{1}{16}$" & $1\frac{19}{16}$" sqs. & $1\frac{9}{16}$" × $\frac{3}{4}$", all $\frac{1}{4}$" th.
GUTTERS	Ceramic mosaics	3/4" sq.* 1/4" th.
	Formed faience	See drawing below.
DECK, TAKE-OFF & ADJACENT FLOORS USED BY SWIMMERS	Unglazed nat. clay tile	$1\frac{1}{16}$" & $2\frac{3}{16}$" sqs. $2\frac{3}{16}$" × $1\frac{1}{16}$",
	Quarry.	4"&6" sqs., $\frac{1}{2}$" th.; 8" sq. $\frac{3}{4}$" th.
	Ceramic mosaics with abrasive content**	$\frac{3}{4}$" sq. $\frac{1}{4}$" th.
NATATORIUM FLOORS USED BY LOUNGERS	Unglazed nat. clay tile	See "Decks, take-offs" above
	Ceramic mosaics	See "Pool lining" above.
NATATORIUM WALLS; WALLS OF ADJACENT AREAS SUCH AS TOILETS, SHOWERS, DRESSING ROOMS, ETC.	Glazed wall tile, matt-fin	$4\frac{1}{4}$" & 6" sqs., 6"x3", 6"x$4\frac{1}{4}$", all
	Bright glaze wall tile.	$\frac{3}{8}$" th.; 9"x6", $\frac{1}{2}$" th.
	Unglazed nat. clay tile	See "Decks, take-offs" above
	ceramic mosaics	See "Pool lining" above.

* $\frac{3}{4}$" tile is very popular as it will fit small radius concave or convex curves and 15 tiles with stan. joints = 1'-0" making it an easy unit to work with.

** Also used to 3 ft. below water level at ends of competitive pools to facilitate turning.

TILE CHARACTERISTICS

CERAMIC MOSAICS: porcelain type (impervious) dust pressed, unglazed, square edge.

UNGLAZED NATURAL CLAY TILE: vitreous, dust pressed, unglazed, color mottled, native non-slip texture, cushion or square edge.

GLAZED WALL TILE, MATT FINISH: Dull finish, not weatherproof.

BRIGHT GLAZE WALL TILE: Enamel finish, not weatherproof.

QUARRY: natural clay type, vitreous or non-vitreous, unglazed, very durable.

FAIENCE: vitreous body, hard glaze; hand crafted appearance, for special effects, Sizes: 1" & 2" sqs. 2"x1" 1/4" th.; $1\frac{1}{2}$", 2", 3", $4\frac{1}{4}$" & 6" sqs., $4\frac{1}{4}$"x2", 6"x3", 6" octagon, $4\frac{1}{4}$" pentagon, $\frac{1}{2}$" th.; 9" sq., 9"x6", 6"x12", 8" octagon, 5/8" th.

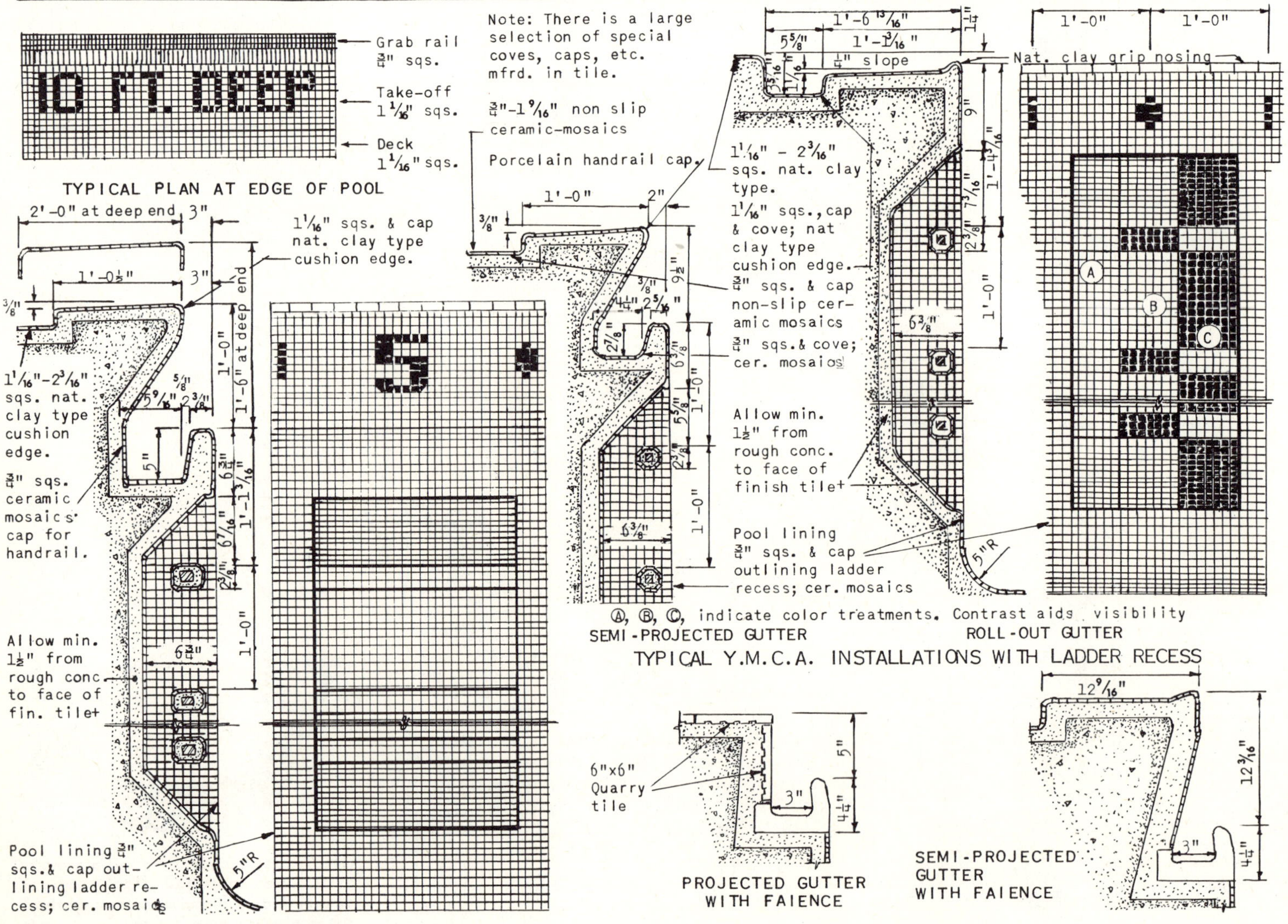

Grab rail $\frac{3}{4}$" sqs.
10 FT. DEEP
Take-off $1\frac{1}{16}$" sqs.
Deck $1\frac{1}{16}$" sqs.
TYPICAL PLAN AT EDGE OF POOL
Note: There is a large selection of special coves, caps, etc. mfrd. in tile.
$\frac{3}{4}$"-$1\frac{9}{16}$" non slip ceramic-mosaics
Porcelain handrail cap.
$1\frac{1}{16}$" sqs. & cap nat. clay type cushion edge.
$1\frac{1}{16}$"-$2\frac{3}{16}$" sqs. nat. clay type cushion edge.
$\frac{3}{4}$" sqs. ceramic mosaics cap for handrail.
Allow min. $1\frac{1}{2}$" from rough conc to face of fin. tile+
Pool lining $\frac{3}{4}$" sqs.& cap outlining ladder recess; cer. mosaics
$1\frac{1}{16}$" - $2\frac{3}{16}$" sqs. nat. clay type.
$1\frac{1}{16}$" sqs., cap & cove; nat clay type cushion edge.
$\frac{3}{4}$" sqs. & cap non-slip ceramic mosaics
$\frac{3}{4}$" sqs.& cove; cer. mosaics
Allow min. $1\frac{1}{2}$" from rough conc. to face of finish tile+
Pool lining $\frac{3}{4}$" sqs. & cap outlining ladder recess; cer. mosaics
$\frac{1}{4}$" slope
Nat. clay grip nosing
Ⓐ, Ⓑ, Ⓒ, indicate color treatments. Contrast aids visibility
6"x6" Quarry tile

SEMI-PROJECTED GUTTER & LADDER RECESS COMPETITIVE POOLS

SEMI-PROJECTED GUTTER — ROLL-OUT GUTTER

TYPICAL Y.M.C.A. INSTALLATIONS WITH LADDER RECESS

PROJECTED GUTTER WITH FAIENCE

SEMI-PROJECTED GUTTER WITH FAIENCE

\+ This dimension is important as it increases rough construction length & width min. 3", depth, min. $1\frac{1}{2}$".

Scale $\frac{3}{4}$"=1'0"

TYPICAL TILE APPLICATIONS IN SWIMMING POOLS

Scale $\frac{3}{4}$"=1'-0"

DATA BY AMERICAN OLEAN TILE CO. AND THE MOSAIC TILE CO.

SWIMMING POOLS

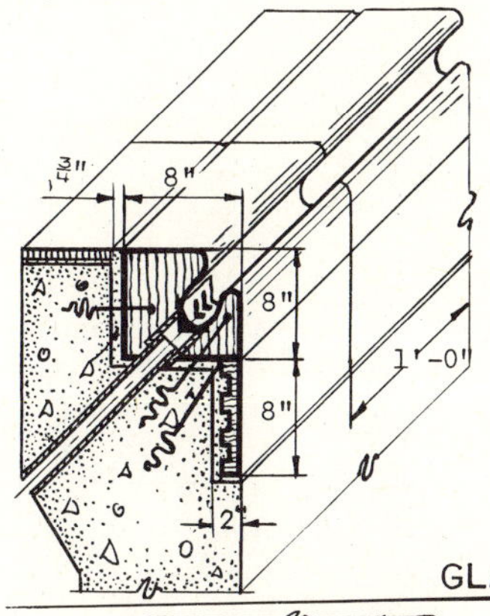
8"
8"
8"
1'-0"
2"

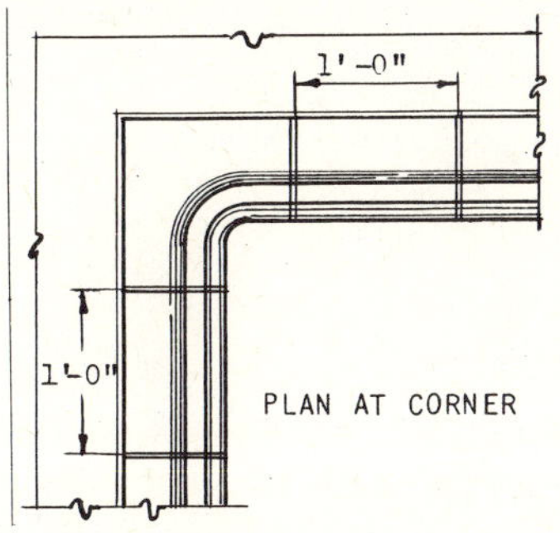
1'-0"
1'-0"
PLAN AT CORNER

GOOSE NECK TYPE

GLAZED OVERFLOW RIM 8"x 8"

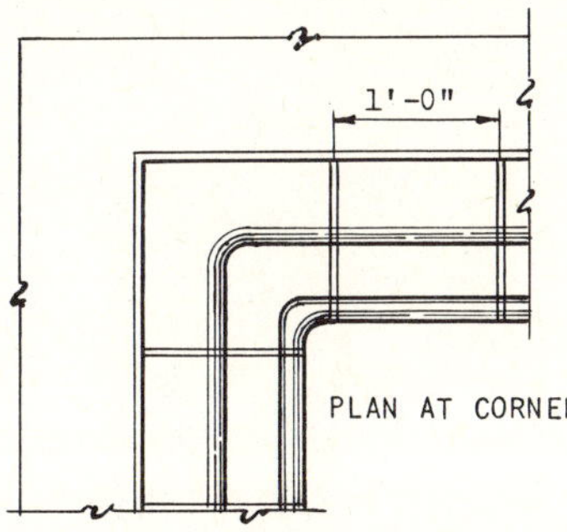
1'-0"
PLAN AT CORNER

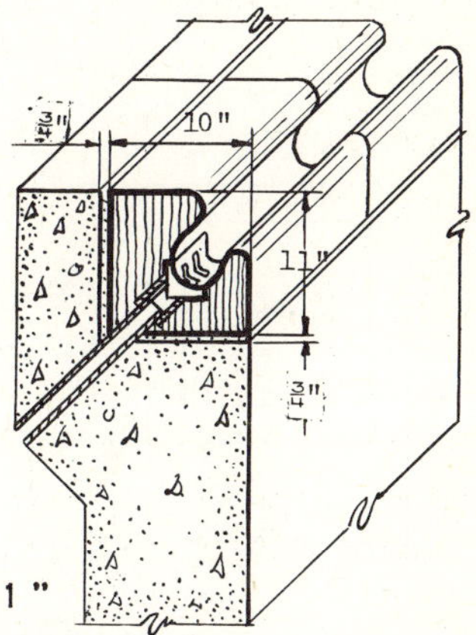
10"
11"

GOOSE NECK TYPE

GLAZED OVERFLOW RIM 10"x 11"

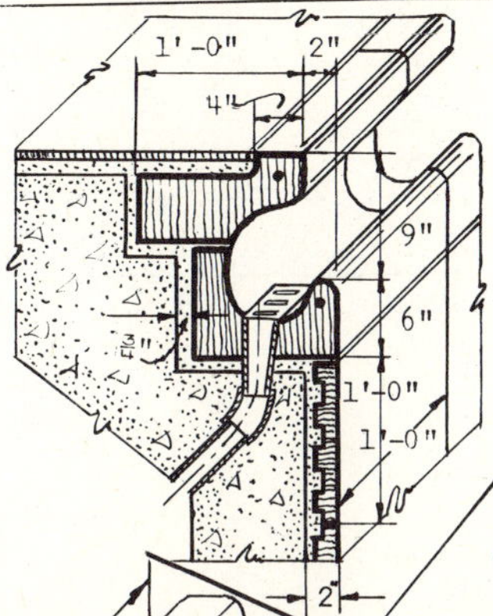
1'-0"
2"
4"
9"
6"
1'-0"
1'-0"
2"

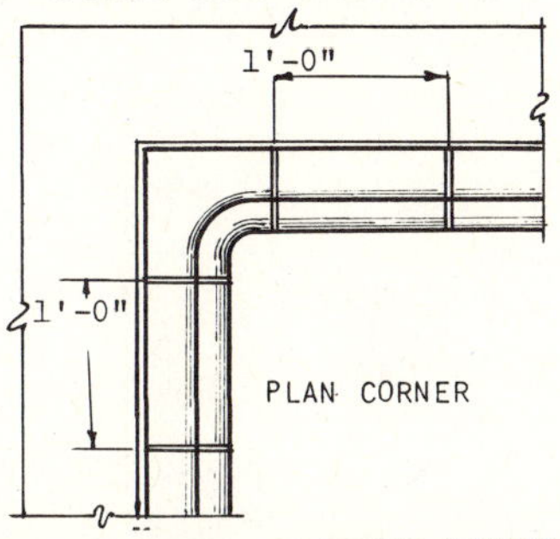
1'-0"
1'-0"
PLAN CORNER

TWO-SECTION GOOSE NECK

GLAZED OVERFLOW RIM 14"x15

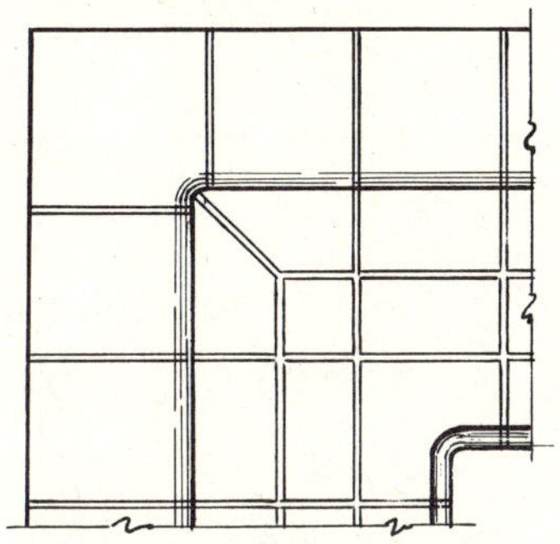

Plan at corner

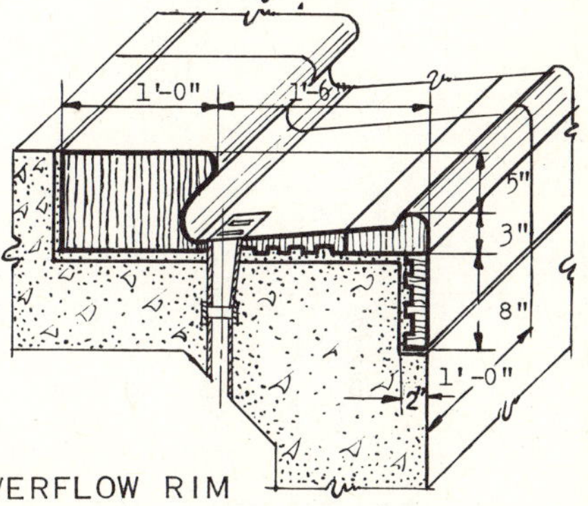
1'-0"
1'-6"
5"
3"
8"
1'-0"
2"

SEAT TYPE GLAZED OVERFLOW RIM

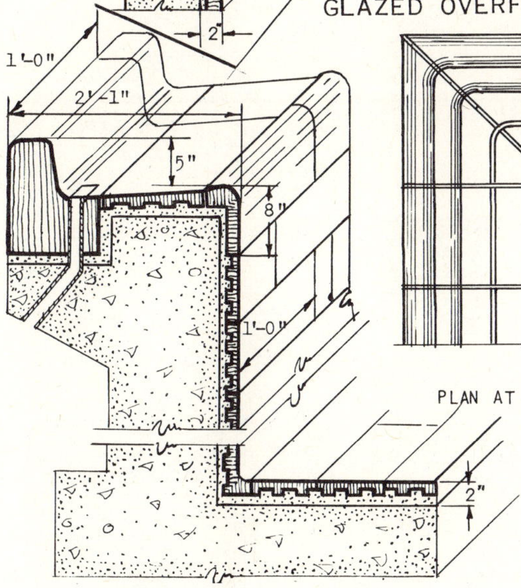
1'-0"
2'-1"
5"
8"
1'-0"
2"

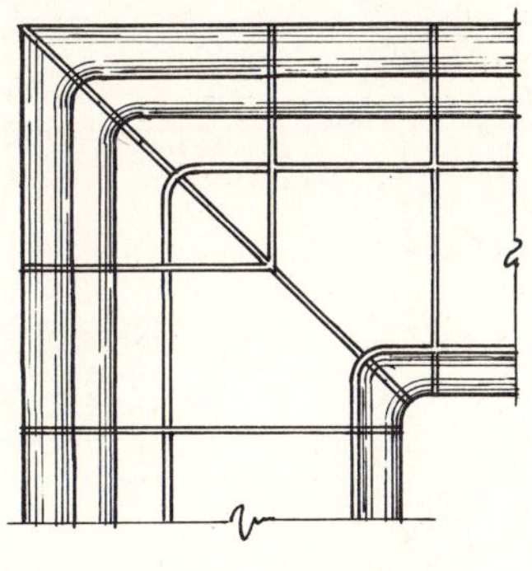

PLAN AT CORNER

SEAT TYPE GLAZED OVERFLOW RIM

WALLS & FLOORS

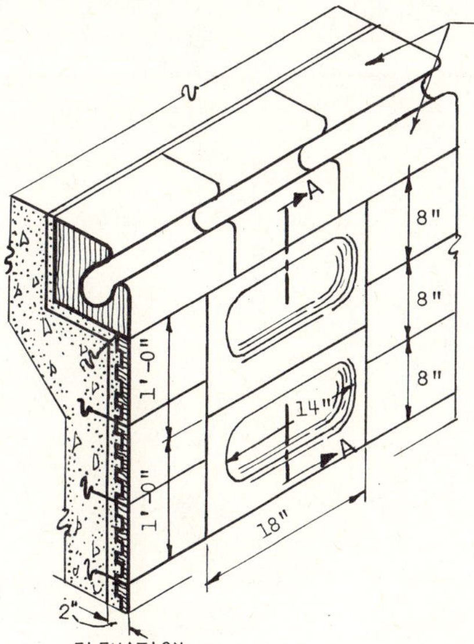
Sanded glazed slip -- resisting surface
A
8"
8"
8"
1'-0"
1'-0"
14"
A
18"
2"
ELEVATION

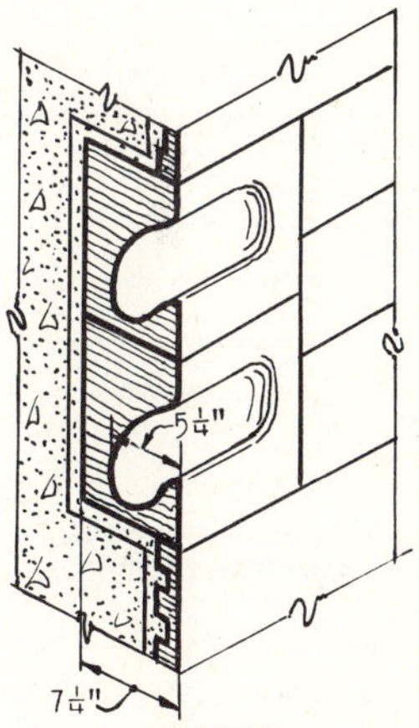
5¼"
7¼"
SECTION

STEPS

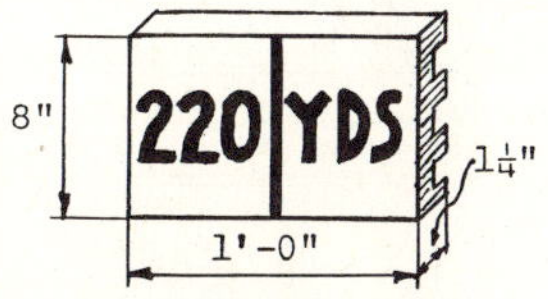
8"
220 YDS
1¼"
1'-0"

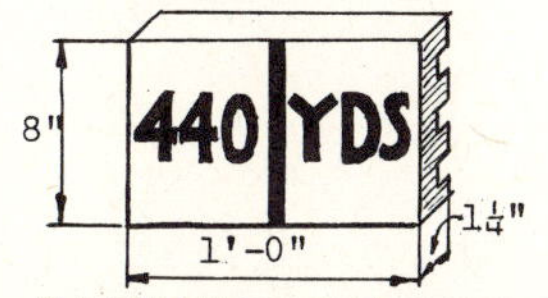
8"
440 YDS
1¼"
1'-0"

DISTANCE MARKERS

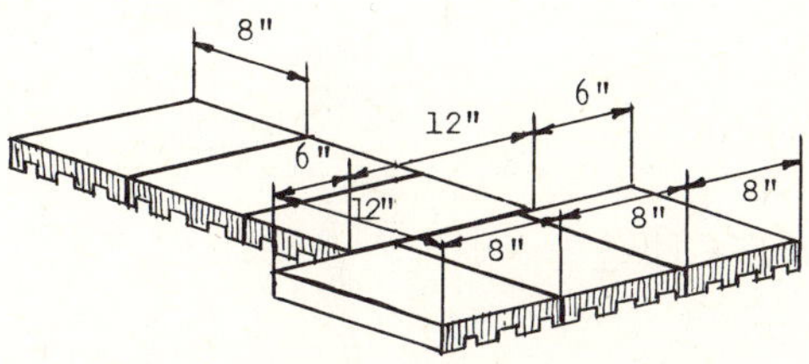
8"
12"
6"
6"
12"
8"
8"
8"

END VIEW OF SWIMMING LINE

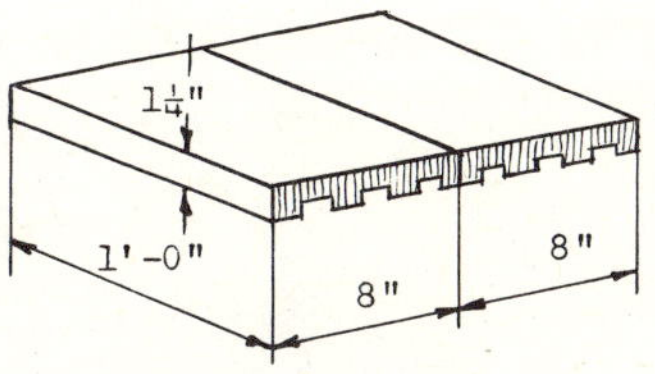
1¼"
1'-0"
8"
8"

LANE MARKERS

8"
DEPTH
3 FEET
1¼"
1'-0"
1'-0"

DEPTH MARKERS

8"
10 FEET
1¼"
1'-0"

DISTANCE MARKERS

TERRA COTTA LINING, GUTTERS, AND MARKERS

Overflow rims are all manufactured of clays specially blended to properly function under exterior weather conditions. A wide selection of high-fire glazed colors is available. Inscriptions and lane markers are usually black or dark blue glazed. Overflow rim outlets spaced approximately 20'-0" c. to c. Expansion joints (mastic) spaced approximately 20'-0" c. to c. Terra cotta overflow rim to have no pitch to outlet.

Data supplied by: Federal Seaboard Terra Cotta Corporation

BEACH EQUIPMENT

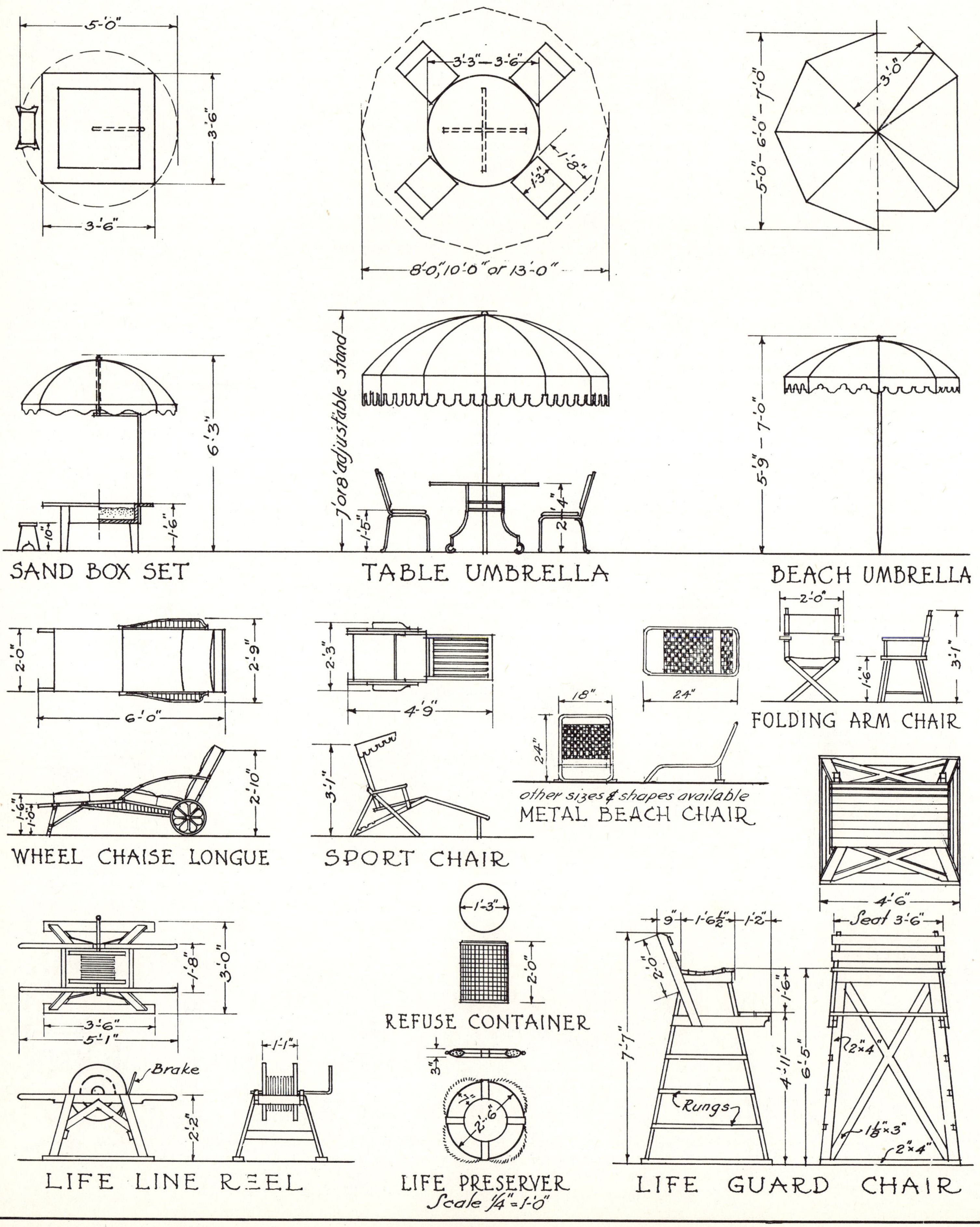
5'-0"
3'-6"
3'-6"
3'-3" — 3'-6"
1'-8"
1'-3"
8'-0", 10'-0" or 13'-0"
3'-0"
5'-0" – 6'-0" – 7'-0"
6'-3"
1'-6"
10"
SAND BOX SET
7' or 8' adjustable stand
1'-5"
2'-4"
TABLE UMBRELLA
5'-9" – 7'-0"
BEACH UMBRELLA
2'-0"
2'-9"
6'-0"
2'-10"
1'-6"
1'-0"
WHEEL CHAISE LONGUE
2'-3"
4'-9"
3'-1"
SPORT CHAIR
18"
24"
24"
other sizes & shapes available
METAL BEACH CHAIR
2'-0"
1'-6"
3'-1"
FOLDING ARM CHAIR
4'-6"
Seat 3'-6"
9" 1'-6½" 1'-2"
2'-0"
1'-6"
7'-7"
4'-11"
6'-5"
2"×4"
Rungs
1⅝"×3"
2"×4"
LIFE GUARD CHAIR
1'-3"
2'-0"
REFUSE CONTAINER
3"
2'-6"
7"
LIFE PRESERVER
Scale ¼" = 1'-0"
1'-8"
3'-0"
3'-6"
5'-1"
Brake
1'-1"
2'-2"
LIFE LINE REEL

BOATS & CANOES

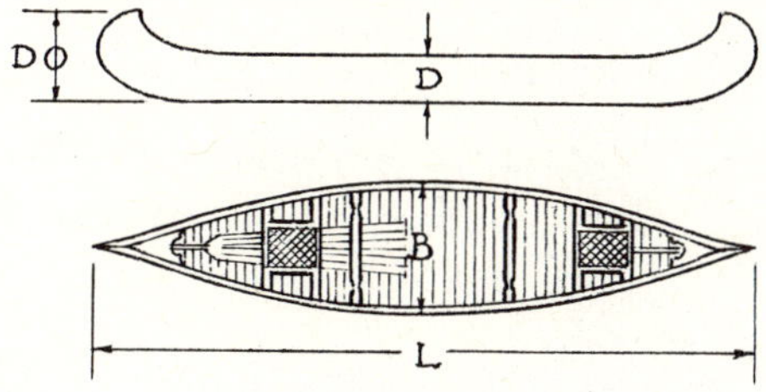
DO
D
B
L

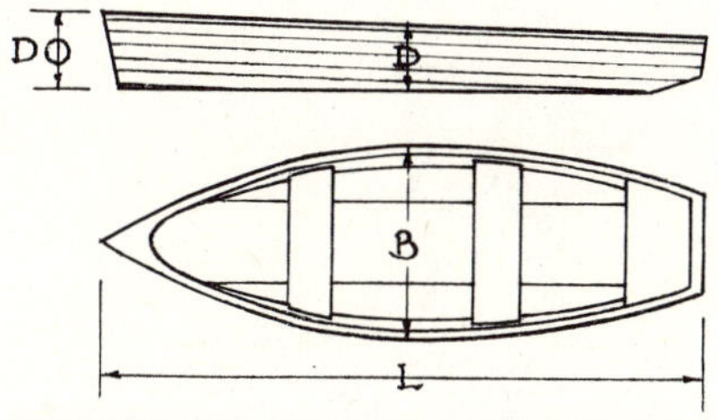
DO
D
B
L

1/8" = 1'-0"

TYPES	L	B (Beam)	D	DO
One man	9' to 15'	2'-10½" to 3'-0"	11" to 12½"	24" to 28"
Standard	16' to 18'	2'-9" to 3'-1"	12" to 13"	
Safety	16' to 18'	3'-5" to 3'-7"	12" to 13"	
Guides	18' to 20'	3'-0" to 3'-3"	13" to 13½"	
War Canoes				
11 Paddles	25'	3'-5"	14½"	
21 ,,	34'	3'-8"	15"	

CANOES

TYPES	L	B (Beam)	D	DO
Many Types and designs	8'-0" to 16'-0"	3'-8" to 4'-7"	1'-2" to 1'-8"	2'-0" ±
Skiffs are of similar design and sizes; are flat bottomed.				

ROW-BOATS

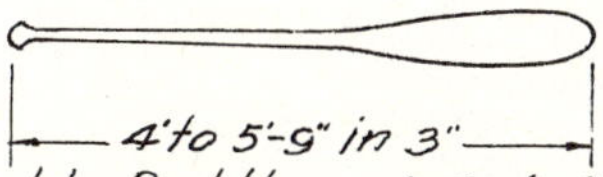
4' to 5'-9" in 3"
Double Paddles 8'-6", 9'-0", 9'-6"

PADDLES
1/4" = 1'-0"

STORAGE REQUIREMENTS FOR SAILBOAT EQUIPMENT.
Mast spars, sheets, sails (usually in heated space), halyards, buoys, anchor, pump, oars, life preservers, cushions.

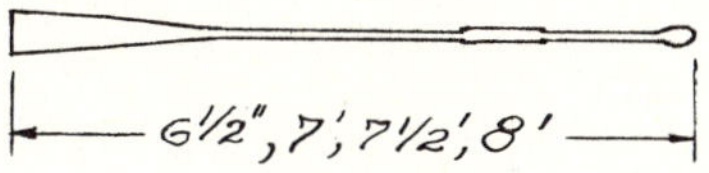
6½", 7', 7½', 8'

OARS
1/4" = 1'-0"

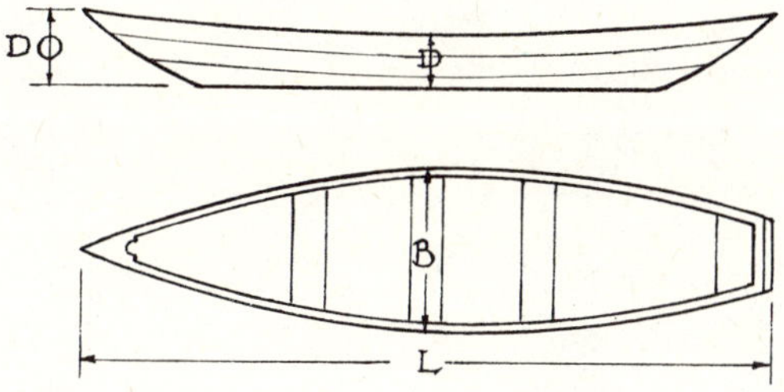
DO
D
B
L

1/8" = 1'-0"

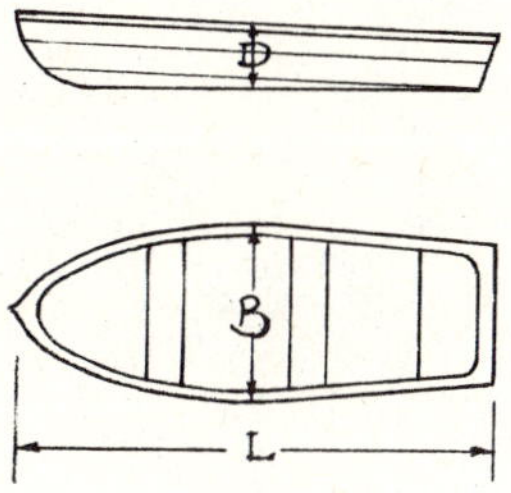
D
B
L

TYPE	L	B (Beam)	D	DO
Life Saving	18'-0"	4'-6"	20"	23"±
Fisherman's	14'-0"	4'-1"		
Average sizes shown				

DORY

L	B (Beam)	D
7'-6" to 14'-0"	42" to 54"	18" to 20"
Wood plastic or canvas covered		

DINGHY or TENDER

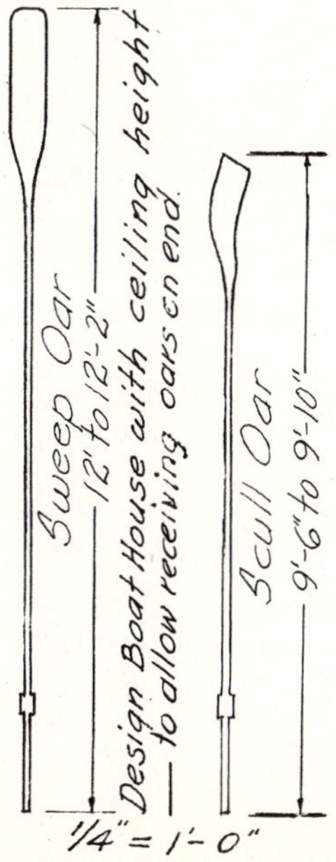
Sweep Oar
12' to 12'-2"
Design Boat House with ceiling height to allow receiving oars on end.
Scull Oar
9'-6" to 9'-10"

1/4" = 1'-0"

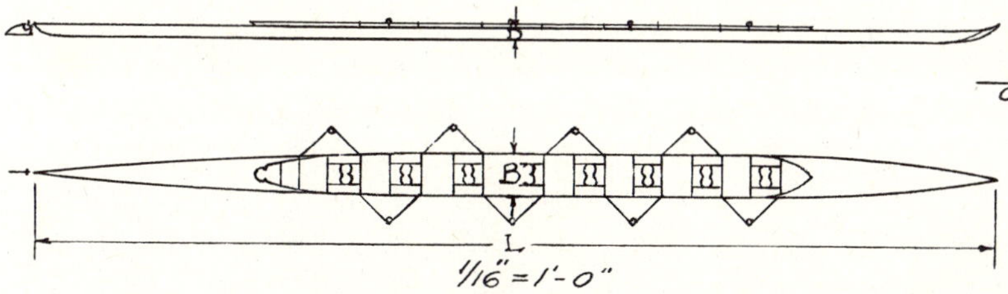
B
L

1/16" = 1'-0"

TYPE	L	B (Beam)	D	WEIGHT
Single Racing	25' to 27'	12"	6½"	30#
Double ,,	31' to 35'	16"	7"	60#
Four-Oared	38' to 47'	21"	8½"	120#
8-Oared Shell	56' to 63'	24"	10"	270#
Practice Gigs	Gigs in all classes, same depth but shorter and wider than shells.			

RACING SHELL & GIG ~ ROWING
Data checked by Sparkman & Stephens, N.Y.C.

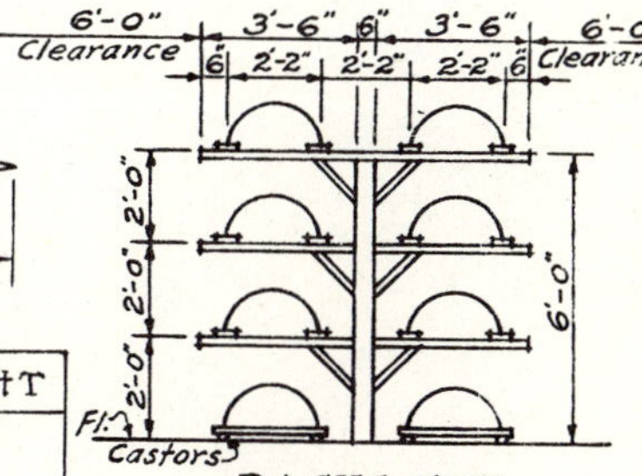
6'-0" Clearance
3'-6"
6"
3'-6"
6'-0" Clearance
6
2'-2"
2'-2"
2'-2"
6
2'-0"
2'-0"
2'-0"
6'-0"
Fl.
Castors

RACKS FOR EIGHTS & FOURS
1/8" = 1'-0"

Notes:
All dimensions minimum
Racks 15'-0" apart
3 for an eight

GENERAL INFORMATION

TABLE OF CONTENTS

ARCHITECTURAL SYMBOLS

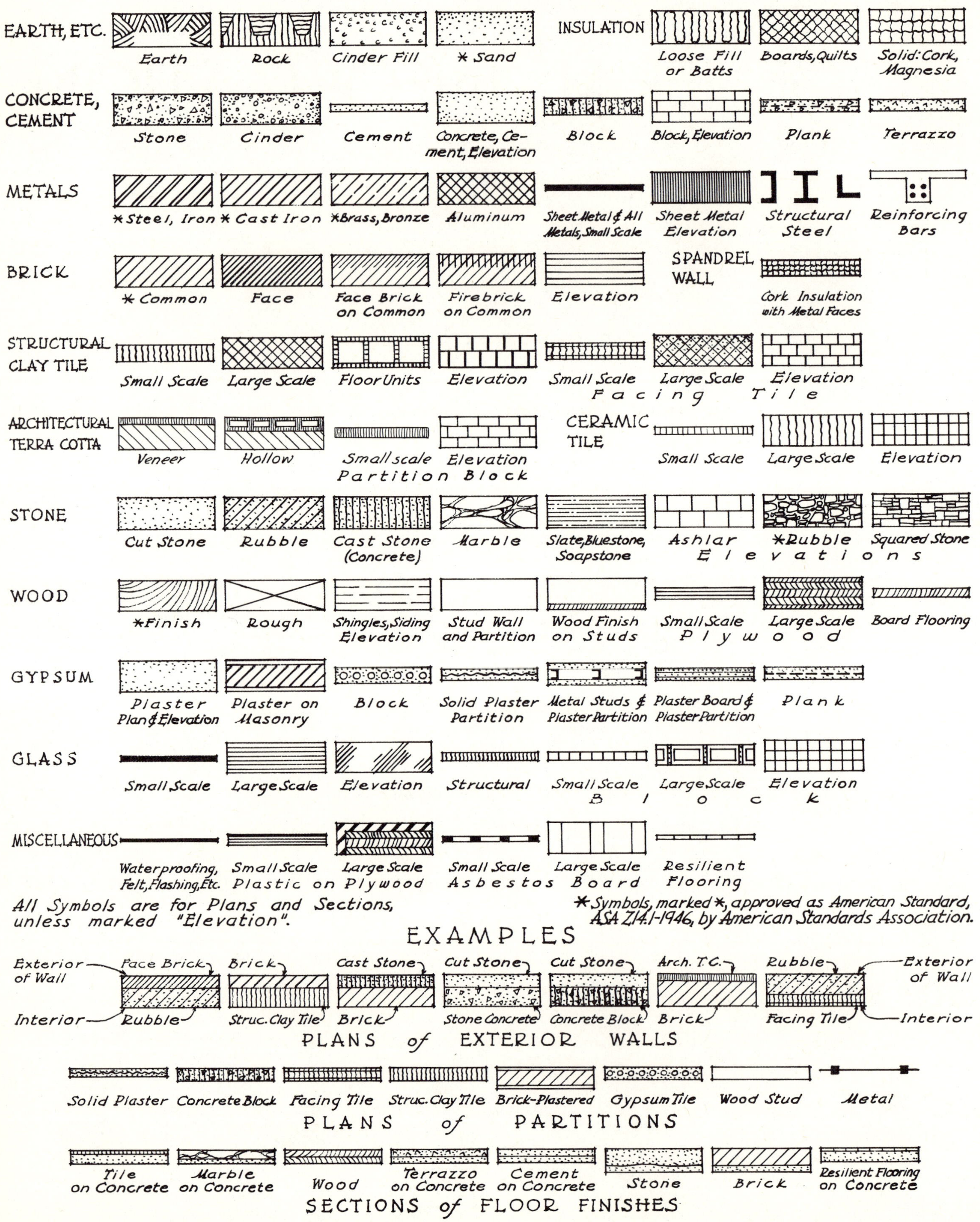
EARTH, ETC.
Earth
Rock
Cinder Fill
* Sand
INSULATION
Loose Fill or Batts
Boards, Quilts
Solid: Cork, Magnesia
CONCRETE, CEMENT
Stone
Cinder
Cement
Concrete, Cement, Elevation
Block
Block, Elevation
Plank
Terrazzo
METALS
* Steel, Iron
* Cast Iron
* Brass, Bronze
Aluminum
Sheet Metal & All Metals, Small Scale
Sheet Metal Elevation
Structural Steel
Reinforcing Bars
BRICK
* Common
Face
Face Brick on Common
Firebrick on Common
Elevation
SPANDREL WALL
Cork Insulation with Metal Faces
STRUCTURAL CLAY TILE
Small Scale
Large Scale
Floor Units
Elevation
Small Scale
Large Scale
Elevation
Facing Tile
ARCHITECTURAL TERRA COTTA
Veneer
Hollow
Small scale
Elevation
Partition Block
CERAMIC TILE
Small Scale
Large Scale
Elevation
STONE
Cut Stone
Rubble
Cast Stone (Concrete)
Marble
Slate, Bluestone, Soapstone
Ashlar
* Rubble
Squared Stone
Elevations
WOOD
* Finish
Rough
Shingles, Siding Elevation
Stud Wall and Partition
Wood Finish on Studs
Small Scale
Large Scale
Plywood
Board Flooring
GYPSUM
Plaster Plan & Elevation
Plaster on Masonry
Block
Solid Plaster Partition
Metal Studs & Plaster Partition
Plaster Board & Plaster Partition
Plank
GLASS
Small Scale
Large Scale
Elevation
Structural
Small Scale
Large Scale
Elevation
Block
MISCELLANEOUS
Waterproofing, Felt, Flashing, Etc.
Small Scale
Large Scale
Plastic on Plywood
Small Scale
Large Scale
Asbestos Board
Resilient Flooring
All Symbols are for Plans and Sections, unless marked "Elevation".
* Symbols, marked *, approved as American Standard, ASA Z14.1-1946, by American Standards Association.
EXAMPLES
Exterior of Wall
Interior
Face Brick
Rubble
Brick
Struc. Clay Tile
Cast Stone
Brick
Cut Stone
Stone Concrete
Cut Stone
Concrete Block
Arch. T.C.
Brick
Rubble
Facing Tile
Exterior of Wall
Interior
PLANS of EXTERIOR WALLS
Solid Plaster
Concrete Block
Facing Tile
Struc. Clay Tile
Brick-Plastered
Gypsum Tile
Wood Stud
Metal
PLANS of PARTITIONS
Tile on Concrete
Marble on Concrete
Wood
Terrazzo on Concrete
Cement on Concrete
Stone
Brick
Resilient Flooring on Concrete
SECTIONS of FLOOR FINISHES

CONVENTIONS

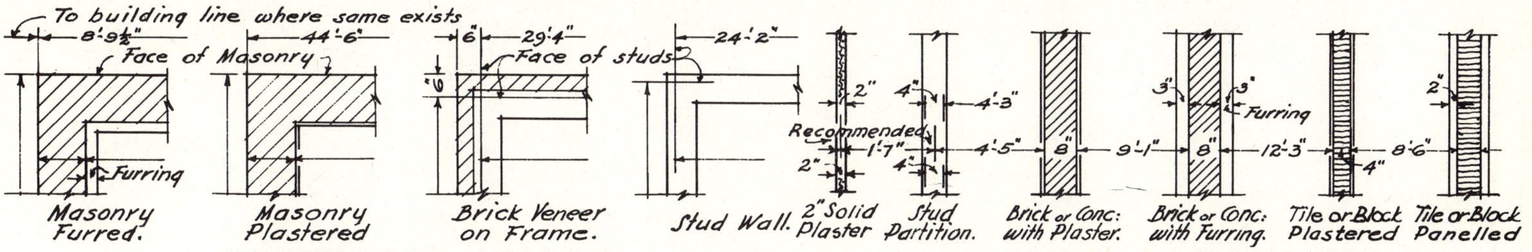
To building line where same exists
8'-9½"
44'-6"
Face of Masonry
6"
29'-4"
Face of studs
6"
24'-2"
Furring
Masonry Furred.
Masonry Plastered
Brick Veneer on Frame.
Stud Wall.
2"
Recommended
1'-7"
2"
2" Solid Plaster
4"
4"
4'-3"
4'-5"
Stud Partition.
8"
Brick or Conc: with Plaster.
9'-1"
3"
3"
Furring
8"
Brick or Conc: with Furring.
12'-3"
4"
Tile or Block Plastered
8'-6"
2"
Tile or Block Panelled

EXTERIOR WALLS

INTERIOR PARTITIONS

RECOMMENDED METHODS for DIMENSIONING WALLS and PARTITIONS

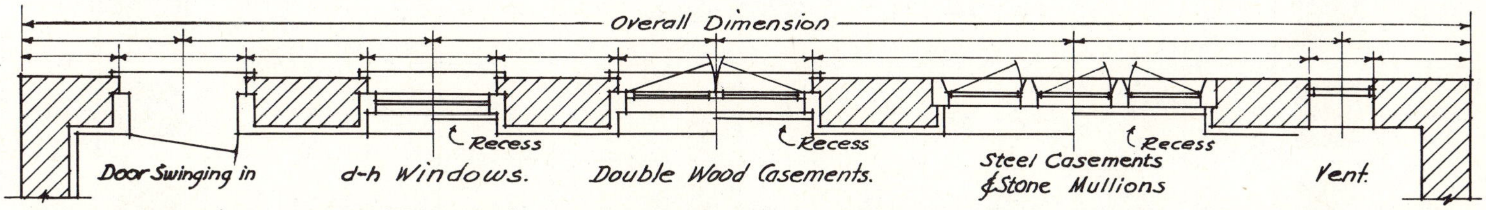
Overall Dimension
Recess
Recess
Recess
Door Swinging in
d-h Windows.
Double Wood Casements.
Steel Casements & Stone Mullions
Vent.

DIMENSIONS & INDICATIONS of WINDOWS & DOORS in EXTERIOR MASONRY WALLS

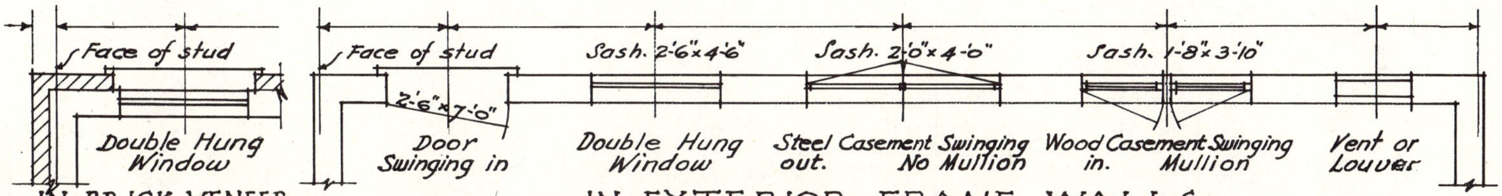
Face of stud
Double Hung Window
Face of stud
2'-6"x7'-0"
Sash. 2'-6"x4'-6"
Sash. 2'-0"x4'-0"
Sash. 1'-8"x3'-10"
Door Swinging in
Double Hung Window
Steel Casement Swinging out.
No Mullion
Wood Casement Swinging in.
Mullion
Vent or Louver

IN BRICK VENEER.

IN EXTERIOR FRAME WALLS.

DIMENSIONS & INDICATIONS OF WINDOWS & DOORS

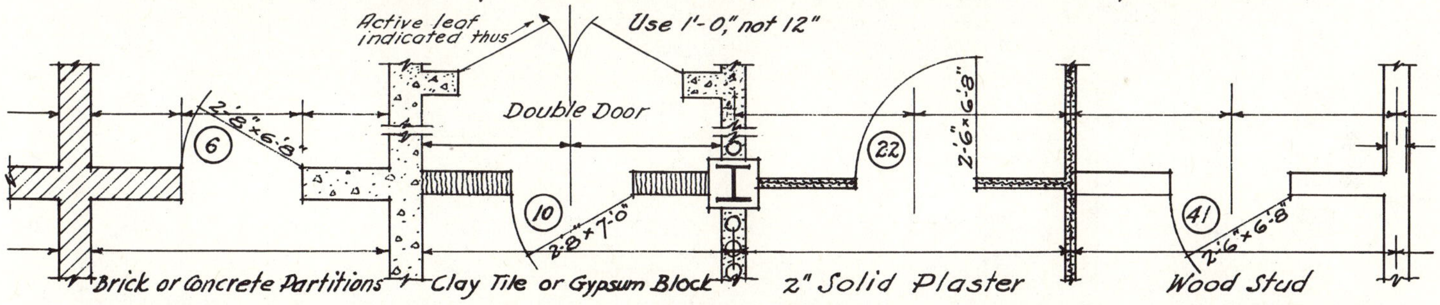
Active leaf indicated thus
Use 1'-0," not 12"
Double Door
2'-8"x6'-8"
6
10
2'-8"x7'-0"
22
2'-6"x6'-8"
41
2'-6"x6'-8"
Brick or Concrete Partitions
Clay Tile or Gypsum Block
2" Solid Plaster
Wood Stud

DIMENSIONS & INDICATIONS of DOORS in INTERIOR PARTITIONS

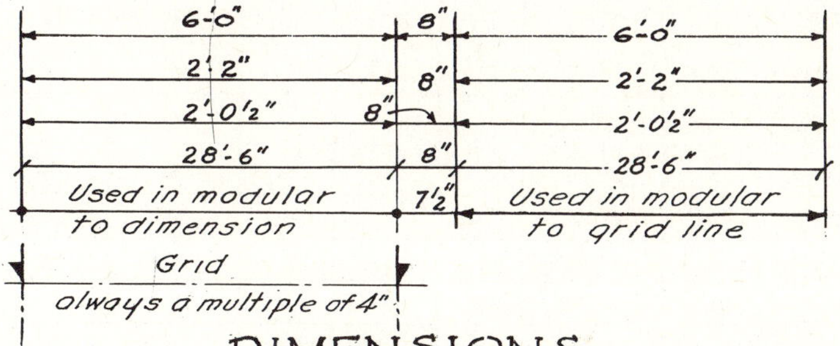
6'-0"
8"
6'-0"
2'-2"
8"
2'-2"
2'-0½"
8"
2'-0½"
28'-6"
8"
28'-6"
Used in modular to dimension
7½"
Used in modular to grid line
Grid
always a multiple of 4"

DIMENSIONS

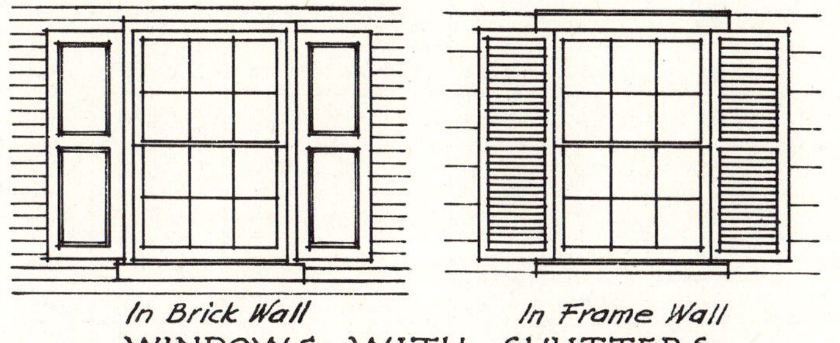
In Brick Wall
In Frame Wall

WINDOWS WITH SHUTTERS

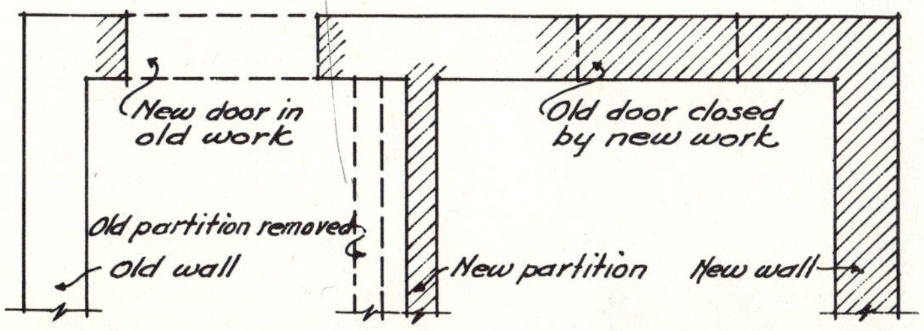
New door in old work
Old door closed by new work
Old partition removed
Old wall
New partition
New wall

INDICATIONS for ALTERATIONS

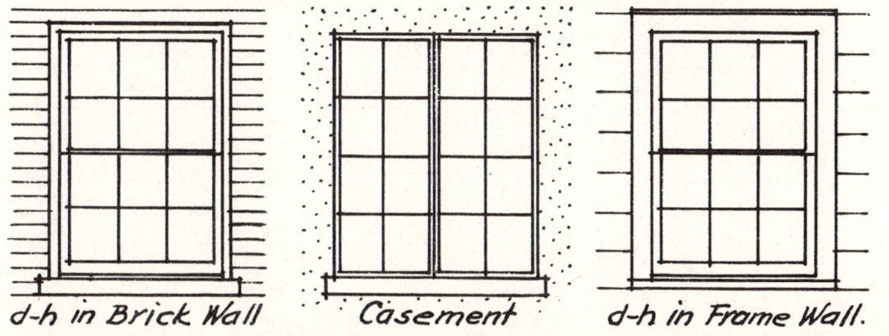
d-h in Brick Wall
Casement
d-h in Frame Wall.

WINDOW INDICATIONS in ELEVATION

¼" = 1'-0"

COMPARATIVE GAUGES

GAUGE NO. These run from #0,000,000 to #40	GRAPHIC SIZES Based on U S Std gauge	U S STD REVISED (Manufact'rs thickness weight ga.) For hot and cold rolled steel sheets.		UNITED STATES STANDARD (USS) For stainless steel & monel metal sheets		AMERICAN STEEL WIRE or WASHBURN & MOEN (W&M) For iron and steel wire.		BROWN AND SHARP (B&S) or AMERICAN WIRE (AW) For aluminum, copper, brass, bronze & nickel silver strip & wire and small sizes copper & brass tubing.		BIRMINGHAM WIRE (BWG) or STUBS IRON WIRE for hot and cold rolled steel strip. Flat steel wire. Steel, aluminum, bronze, monel, stainless steel tubing & larger size copper and brass tubing.		MACHINE AND WOOD SCREWS For ferrous & non-ferrous metals.		For lead weights & Zinc ga. see pages on those materials. GRAPHIC SIZES Based on B&S gauge	GAUGE NO. These run from #0,000,000 to #40
		Decimal	Fract^n	Decimal	Fract^n	Decimal	Fract^n	Decimal	Fract^n	Decimal	Fract^n	Decimal	Fract^n		
000	■	.3750"	3/8"	.3750"	3/8"	.3625"	23/64"	.4096"	13/32"+	.425"	27/64"+	Graphic sizes do not apply to this column		●	000
00	■	.3437"	11/32"	.3437"	11/32"	.3310"	21/64"+	.3648"	23/64"+	.380"	3/8"+			●	00
0	■	.3125"	5/16"	.3125"	5/16"	.3065"	5/16"-	.3249"	21/64"-	.340"	11/32"-	.060"	1/16"	●	0
1	■	.2812"	9/32"	.2812"	9/32"	.2830"	9/32"+	.2893	19/64"-	.300"	19/64"+	.073"	5/64"-	●	1
2	■	.2656"	17/64"	.2656"	17/64"	.2625"	17/64"-	.2576"	1/4"+	.284"	9/32"+	.086"	3/32"-	●	2
3	■	.2391"	15/64"+	.2500"	1/4"	.2437"	1/4"-	.2294"	15/64"-	.259"	17/64"-	.099"	3/32"+	●	3
4	■	.2242"	7/32"+	.2344"	15/64"	.2253"	7/32"+	.2043"	13/64"+	.238"	15/64"+	.112"	7/64"+	●	4
5	■	.2092"	13/64"+	.2187"	7/32"	.2070"	13/64"+	.1819"	3/16"-	.220"	7/32"+	.125"	1/8"	●	5
6	■	.1943"	3/16"+	.2031"	13/64"	.1920"	3/16"+	.1620	5/32"+	.203"	13/64"	.138"	9/64"-	●	6
7	■	.1793"	11/64"+	.1875"	3/16"	.1770"	11/64"+	.1443"	9/64"+	.180"	3/16"-	.151"	5/32"-	●	7
8	■	.1644"	11/64"-	.1719"	11/64"	.1620"	5/32"+	.1285"	1/8"+	.165"	11/64"-	.164"	11/64"-	●	8
9	■	.1495"	5/32"-	.1562"	5/32"	.1483"	9/64"+	.1144"	7/64"+	.148"	9/64"+	.177"	11/64"+	●	9
10	■	.1345"	9/64"-	.1406"	9/64"	.1350"	9/64"-	.1019"	7/64"-	.134"	9/64"-	.190"	3/16"+	●	10
11	■	.1196"	1/8"-	.1250"	1/8"	.1205"	1/8"-	.0907"	3/32"-	.120"	1/8"-	.203"	13/64"	●	11
12	■	.1046"	7/64"-	.1094"	7/64"	.1055"	7/64"-	.0808"	5/64"+	.109"	7/64"	.216"	7/32"-	●	12
13	■	.0897"	3/32"-	.0938"	3/32"	.0915"	3/32"-	.0719"	5/64"-	.095"	3/32"+	–	–	●	13
14	■	.0747"	5/64"-	.0781"	5/64"	.0800"	5/64"+	.0641"	1/16"+	.083"	5/64"+	.242"	1/4"-	●	14
15	■	.0673"	1/16"+	.0703"	5/64"-	.0720"	5/64"-	.0571"	1/16"-	.072"	5/64"-	–	–	●	15
16	■	.0598"	1/16"-	.0625"	1/16"	.0625"	1/16"	.0508"	3/64"+	.065"	1/16"+	.268"	17/64"+	●	16
17	■	.0538"	3/64"+	.0562"	1/16"-	.0540"	3/64"+	.0453"	3/64"-	.058"	1/16"-	–	–	●	17
18	■	.0478"	3/64"+	.0500"	3/64"+	.0475"	3/64"+	.0403"	3/64"-	.049"	3/64"+	.294"	19/64"-	●	18
19	■	.0418"	3/64"-	.0437"	3/64"-	.0410"	3/64"-	.0359"	1/32"+	.042"	3/64"-	–	–	●	19
20	■	.0359"	1/32"+	.0375"	1/32"+	.0348"	1/32"+	.0320"	1/32"+	.035"	1/32"+	.320"	5/16"+	●	20
21	■	.0329"	1/32"+	.0344"	1/32"+	.0318"	1/32"+	.0285"	1/32"-	.032"	1/32"+	–	–	●	21
22	■	.0299"	1/32"-	.0312"	1/32"	.0286"	1/32"-	.0253"	1/32"-	.028"	1/32"-	–	–	●	22
23	■	.0269"	1/32"-	.0281"	1/32"-	.0258"	1/32"-	.0226"	1/64"+	.025"	1/32"-	–	–	●	23
24	■	.0239"	1/32"-	.0250"	1/32"-	.0230"	1/64"+	.0201"	1/64"+	.022"	1/64"+	.372"	3/8"-	●	24
25	■	.0209"	1/64"+	.0219"	1/64"+	.0204"	1/64"+	.0179"	1/64"+	.020"	1/64"+	–	–	●	25
26	■	.0179"	1/64"+	.0187"	1/64"+	.0181"	1/64"+	.0159"	1/64"+	.018"	1/64"+	–	–	●	26
27	■	.0164"	1/64"+	.0172"	1/64"+	.0173"	1/64"+	.0142"	1/64"-	.016"	1/64"+	–	–	●	27
28	■	.0149"	1/64"-	.0156"	1/64"	.0162"	1/64"+	.0126"	1/64"-	.014"	1/64"-	–	–	●	28
29	■	.0135"	1/64"-	.0141"	1/64"-	.0150"	1/64"-	.0113"	1/64"-	.013"	1/64"-	–	–	●	29
30	■	.0120"	1/64"-	.0125"	1/64"-	.0140"	1/64"-	.0100	1/64"-	.012"	1/64"-	.450"	29/64"	●	30

ABBREVIATIONS

Standardized abbreviations are marked with reference numbers 1 TO 8 incl. and these refer to the following:

1 American Standard ABBREVIATIONS FOR SCIENTIFIC & ENGINEERING TERMS, ASA Z10.1-1941
2 Lumber Standards Simplified Practice Recommendation 16-53
3 American Standard GRAPHICAL SYMBOLS FOR FITTINGS, VALVES, AND PIPING A.S.A. Z32.2.3-1949 (reaffirmed 1953) Abbreviations used with symbols.
4 American Standard GRAPHIC ELECTRICAL SYMBOLS FOR ARCHITECTURAL PLANS, Y32.9-1943 (abbreviations used with symbols).
5 Hardware. Approved by the American Society of Hardware Consultants & National Contract Hardware Association 1949.
6 American Standard ABBREVIATIONS FOR USE ON DRAWINGS, ASA Z32.13-1950
7 American Standards GRAPHICAL SYMBOLS FOR PLUMBING A.S.A. Z32.2.2-1949
8 American Standards GRAPHICAL SYMBOLS FOR HEATING, VENTILATING AND AIR CONDITIONING A.S.A. Z32.2.4-1949 (reaffirmed 1953).

The non-standardized abbreviations are generally based on the following:
- (a) Same abbreviation for singular and plural.
- (b) Periods used only to avoid misinterpretation.
- (c) Spaces between letters used for clarity only.
- (d) Capitals used generally in view of the fact that most of these abbreviations are for use on drawings.

Recommendations

Where two or more standardized abbreviations are shown for the same item: for drawings use reference numbers 3, 4, 6 or 7, and for text use reference numbers 1, 2, or 5.

Include an abbreviation list on each set of drawings.

Abbreviations for Texts: It is usual to capitalize only when the letter stands for a proper noun. Signs such as " # * are not recommended.

abbreviation................ABBREV
access area....................AA
access door....................AD[8]
access panel....................AP[6]
acoustic....................ACST[6]
acoustical plaster.......ACST PLAS
acoustical tile....................AT
acre............ACRE[1] (spell out)
actual....................ACT.[6]
addendum....................ADD.[6]
addition....................ADD.[6]
adhesive....................ADH[6]
aggregate....................AGGR[6]
air conditioning.........AIR COND[6]
alarm....................ALM[6]
alcove....................A
alternating current....a-c[1] or AC[6]
altitude....................ALT[6]
aluminum....................AL[6]
American Concrete Institute ...ACI
American Gas Association.......AGA
American Institute of Architects...............A.I.A.
American Institute of Electrical Engineers........AIEE
American Institute of Steel Construction....AISC or A.I.S.C.
American Society of Civil Engineers............ASCE
American Society of Heating & Ventilating Engineers A.S.H.V.E.
American Society of Mechanical Engineers....A.S.M.E.
American Society of Refrigerating Engineers.....ASRE
American Society for Testing Materials.......A.S.T.M.
American Standard.........AMER STD
American Standards Association..................ASA
American Water Works Association................AWWA
American Welding Society.......AWS
American Wire Gauge...........AWG[6]
amount....................AMT[6]
ampere................amp or AMP[6]
anchor bolt....................AB[6]
angle....................∠
annunciator....................ANN[6]
apartment....................APT.[6]
approved....................APPD[6]
approximate...............APPROX[6]
architect....................ARCH
architectural....................ARCH
architectural terra cotta......ATC
area....................A[6]
area drain....................AD
article....................ART
asbestos....................ASB[6]
asbestos board....................AB
asbestos millboard............AMB
asbestos roof shingles........ARS
asphalt....................ASPH[6]
asphalt tile....................AT
asphalt tile base.............ATB
assemble....................ASSEM[6]
assembly....................ASSY[6]
associate....................ASSOC[6]
Associate Royal Institute of British Architects.A.R.I.B.A.
association.........ASSN[6] or ASSOC
Association of American Railroads....................AAR
at....................@
atmospheric pressure.....ATM PRESS
automatic....................AUTO[6]
automatic washing machine......AWM
avenue....................AVE[6]
average........avg[1] or av[2] or AVG[6]
axis....................AX
back feed....................BF[6]
backset....................BS[5]
back water valve..............BWV[6]
bag....................BG
barrel...............bbl[1] or BBL[6]
basement....................BSMT
bathroom....................B
bath tub....................BT
beaded one side..............BIS[2]
beam....................BM[6]
bedroom....................BR
bell and flange..............B&F[6]
bell and spigot..............B&S[6]
benchboard...............BNCHBD[6]
bench mark....................BM[6]

ABBREVIATIONS

bending moment..........M[6]
better..........BTR or Btr[2]
between..........BET.[6]
beveled..........Bev[2]
bidet..........B[3]
block..........BLK[6]
blocking..........BLKG
blower..........BLO[6]
blow-off..........BO[6]
blueprint..........BP[6]
bluestone..........BS
board..........bd[2] or BD[6]
board foot..........fbm[1] or bd ft[2]
board measure..........b.m.[2]
boiler..........BLR[6]
boiler feed..........BF[6]
boiler house..........BH[6]
boiler room..........BR
bolts..........BT
book shelves..........BK SH
borrowed light..........BLT[6]
bottom..........BOT[6]
boulevard..........BLVD
boundary..........BDY[6]
bracket..........brkt
brass..........BRS[6]
brass steeple tips..........BST[5]
brazing..........BRZG[6]
breadth..........B[6]
brick..........BRK[6]
brine return(pipe)..........BR[3]
brine supply(pipe)..........B[3]
British thermal
  units..........B[1] or BTU[6] or Btu
bronze..........BRZ[6]
broom closet..........BC
Brown and Sharpe
  gauge..........B&S[6] or B&S ga
building..........BLDG[6]
building line..........BL[6]
built-in..........BLT-IN
bulb angle..........BA
bulkhead..........BHD[6]
bullet tips..........BLT[5]
bulletin board..........BB
bundle..........bdl[2] or BDL[6]
Bureau of Standards..........BU STN[6]
burglar alarm..........BA
button..........BUT.[6]
buzzer..........BUZ[6]
by (as 6' x8')..........X
by-pass..........BP[6]
cabinet..........CAB.[6]
cadmium..........Cd[6]
cadmium plate..........CD PL[6]
calcimine..........C
calking..........CLKG[6]
candlepower..........CP[6]
carpenter..........CARP.
casing..........CSG
cast (used with other materials)C[6]
cast box strike..........CBX[5]
cast brass..........CB
cast concrete..........C CONC
cast iron..........CI[6]
cast iron pipe..........CIP[6]
cast steel..........CS[6]
cast stone..........CS
casting..........CSTG[6]
catch basin..........CB[6]
ceiling..........Clg[2] or CLG[6]
cellar..........CEL
cement..........CEM[6]
cement asbestos..........CEM A[6]
cement asbestos board..........CEM AB
cement floor..........CEM FL[6]
cement mortar..........CEM MORT
cement plaster..........CEM PLAS[6]
cement water paint..........CEM P
cent..........c or ¢
center..........CTR
center line..........℄ or CL[6]
center matched..........CM[2]
centers on..........OC
center to center...c to c[1] or C to C
ceramic..........CER[6]
cesspool..........CP[6]
chalk board..........Ch B
chamfer..........CHAM[6]
change..........CHG[6]
channel..........CHAN[6] or [or]
channel iron frame..........CIF[5]
check valve..........CV[6]
china cabinet..........CH CAB
chromium plate..........Cr PL[6]
cinder block..........CIN BL
circle..........CIR[6]
circuit..........CKT[6]
circuit breaker..........CIR BKR
circular..........cir[1] or CIR[6]
circular mils.....cir mils[1] or CM[6]
circulating chilled or
  hot water flow..........CH[3]
circulating chilled or
  hot water return..........CHR[3]
circulating water pump..........CWP[6]
circumference..........CIRC[6]
class..........CL[6]
cleanout..........CO[6,7]
cleanout and deck plate....CO & DP
cleanout door..........COD
clear..........Clr[2] or CLR[6]
clearance..........CL[6]
clear glass..........CL GL
clear wire glass..........CL W GL
clock outlet..........C[4]
closet..........C or CL or CLO[6]
clothes line hook..........CLH
clothes pole..........CP
coal bin..........CB
coat closet..........CC
coat hook..........CH[6]
coated..........CTD[6]
coefficient..........COEF[6] or C
cold rolled steel..........CRS[6]
cold water..........CW[6]
column..........COL[6]
combination..........COMB.[6]
commercial projected window...CPW
Commercial Standard..........CS
common..........Com[2] or COM[6]
company..........CO[6]
compartment..........COMPT[6]
compressed air line..........A[3]
concrete..........CONC[6]
concrete block..........CONC B[6]
concrete ceiling..........CONC CLG[6]
concrete floor..........CONC FL[6]
condenser water flow..........C[3]
condenser water return..........CR[3]
conductance, thermal..........C
conductivity, thermal..........k
conductor..........COND[6]
conduit..........CND[6]
cone tips..........CT[5]
connection..........CONN
construction..........CONST[6]
continuous or continue..........CONT
contract..........CONT[6]
contractor..........CONTR
convector..........CONV
convector enclosure..........CONV ENCL
copper..........COP
copper covered..........COP COV
cork tile..........CT
corner..........COR[6]
corner guards..........CG
counter..........CTR[6]
counter flashing..........CFLG[6]
countersink..........CSK[6]
countersunk screw..........CS
countersunk wood screw..........CWS
courses..........C[6]
cover..........COV[6]
cover plate..........COV PL
cross section..........X-SECT[6]
cubic..........cu[1] or CU[6]
cubic foot.....cu ft[1,2] or CU FT[6]
cubic feet per minute..cfm[1] or CFM[6]
cubic inch.....cu in.[1] or CU IN.[6]
cubic yard.......cu yd[1] or CU YD[6]
current..........CUR[6]
curtain rod..........C R
cut out..........CO[6]
cycle..........CY[6]
cycles per minute..........CPM[6]
cycles per second..........CPS[6]
cylinder..........cyl[1] or CYL[6]
cylinder lock..........CYL L[6]
damper..........DMPR[6]
dampproofing..........DP
decibel..........db[1] or DB[6]
degree..........(°)[1,6] or DEG[6]
degree centigrade..........C[1]
degree Fahrenheit..........F[1]
department..........DEPT[6]
detail..........DET[6]
diagram..........DIAG[6]
diameter.......diam[1] or DIA[6] or ϕ
dimension..........dim[2] or DIM[6]
dinette..........Dt
dining alcove..........D A
dining room..........D R
direct current.......d-c[1] or DC[6]
disconnect..........DISC[6]

ABBREVIATIONS

dishwasher........DW[7]
distance........DIST[6]
distributed........DIST
ditto........" or DO.[6]
division........DIV[6]
double acting........DA
double glass........DG[6]
double hung window........DHW
dovetail........DVTL[6]
dowel........DWL[6]
down........DN[6] or D
downspout........DS[6]
dozen........doz[1] or DOZ[6]
drain........D[3,7] or DR[6]
drain board........DB
drawing........DWG[6]
dressed (lumber)........DRS[6]
dressed and matched........D&M[2]
dressing table........DR T
drinking fountain........DF[6,7]
drop cord (outlet)........D[4]
dryer........D
dry well........DW
duct section, exhaust........E[8]
duct section, fresh air........FA
duct section, recirculation........R[8]
duct section, supply........S[8]
dumbwaiter........DW[6]
duplex........DX[6]
duplicate........DUP[6]
each........EA[6]
each face........EF[6]
east........E[6]
east northeast........ENE
east by north........EbN
edge........E[2]
edge grain........E G[2]
elbow........ELL[6]
electric........elec[1] or ELEC[6]
electric panel........EP
elevation........el[1] or EL[6]
elevator........Elev
emergency........EMER[6]
enamel........E
enclose........ENCL[6]
enclosure........ENCL
end to end........E to E[6]
engineer........ENGR[6]
entrance........ENT[6]
equipment........EQUIP[6]
equivalent square feet........E□'
equivalent direct radiation........EDR[6]
escutcheon........ESC[6]
estimate........EST[6]
excavate........EXC[6]
executive........EXEC[6]
exhaust duct section........E[3]
existing........EXIST.[6]
exit light outlet........X[4]
expansion bolt........EXP BT
expansion joint........EXP JT[6]
extension........EXT[6]
exterior........EXT[6]
external........EXT[6]
extinguisher, fire........F EXT
extra heavy........X HVY[6] or XH
extrude........EXTR[6]
fabricate........FAB[6]
face to face........F to F[6]
facing tile........FT
factory........FCTY
Fahrenheit........F[6]
fan (outlet)........F[4]
federal........FED.[6]
federal specifications........FS[6]
feeder........FDR[6]
feed water........FW[6]
feet........(')[6] or FT[6]
feet board measure........FBM[6] or ft b m[2]
feet per minute........FPM[6]
feet per second........FPS[6]
feet surface measure........FTSM
Fellow American Institute of Architects........F.A.I.A.
Fellow Royal Institute of British Architects........F.R.I.B.A.
figure........FIG.[6]
fillet........FIL[6]
finish........FIN.[6]
finished floor........Fin Fl
firebrick........FBRK
Fire Department Connection........FDC[6]
fire door........F DR[6]
fire extinguisher........F EXT
fire hose........FH[6]
fire hose cabinet........FHC[6]
fire hose rack........FHR[6]
fire hydrant........FHY[6]
fire line........F[3]
fire main........FM[6]
fire place........FP[6]
fireproof........FPRF
fireproof self closing........FPSC
fire standpipe........FSP
fitting........FTG[6]
fixture........FIX.[6]
flame proof........FP[6]
flange........FLG[6]
flashing........FL[6]
flat finish........F
flat grain........F G[2]
flat head........FH[6]
flat headed screw........FHS
flat headed wood screw........FHWS
floor........FL[6]
floor cabinet........FL CAB
floor drain........FD[6]
flooring........Flg[2] or FLG[6]
fluorescent........FLUOR[6]
flush........FL[6]
flush metal saddle........FMS
flush metal threshold........FMT
flush threshold........FT
foot........ft[1,2] or (')[2,6] or FT[6]
foot bath........FB[3,7]
foot-candle........FT-C or ft-c[1]
foot-Lambert........FT-L or ft-L[1]
foot pound........ft lb[1] or FT LB[6]
footing........FTG[6]
foundation........FDN
frame........FR[6]
framework........FRWK[6]
framing........Frm[2]
free-on-board........fob[1]
freezing point........fp[1] or FP[6]
frequency........FREQ[6]
fresh air duct section........FA
fresh air intake (or inlet)........FAI
front........FR[6]
fuel oil........FO[6]
fuel oil flow (pipe)........FOF[3]
fuel oil return (pipe)........FOR[3]
fuel oil tank vent (pipe)........FOV[3]
full size........FS
furnish........FURN[6]
furred ceiling, fur........FC
gallery........GALL[6]
gallon........gal[1] or GAL[6]
gallons per acre per day........GPAD[6]
gallons per hour........GPH[6]
gallons per minute........gpm[1] or GPM[6]
gallons per second........gps[1] or GPS[6]
galvanized........GALV[6]
galvanized iron........GI[6]
galvanized steel........GS[6] or galv S
games room........GR
gas range........G[7]
gas line or outlet........G[3,7]
gate valve........GTV[6]
gauge........GA[6]
general contract........GEN CONT
general contractor........GEN CONT
generator........G[4] or GEN[6]
glass........GL[6]
glass block........GL BL
glaze........GL[6]
government........GOVT[6]
grade........GR[6]
grade line........GL[6]
grand master keyed........GMK[5]
granite........G
grating........GRTG[6]
gravity........G[6]
grease trap........GT[6]
grease separator........G[7]
green........GRN[6]
grid (modular)........G[6]
grille........G
grille, bottom........BG
grille, ceiling........CR
grille, center........CG
grille, top........TG
grille, top & bottom........T&BG
guard........GD[6]
gypsum........GYP[6]
half-round........H RD[6]
handhole........HH[6]
hanging closet........H CL
hardware........HDW[6]
hardwood........HDWD or Hdwd[2]
head........HD[6]
heartwood........hrtwd[2]
heater........HTR
heater, water........WH[3,6]
heater room........HR
height........HGT[6] H or HT

ABBREVIATIONS

hexagonal....HEX[6]
high point....H PT[6]
high-pressure....HP[6]
hollow metal....HM
hollow metal door....HMD[5]
hollow metal frame....HMF[5]
horizon....H
horizontal....HOR[6]
horsepower....hp[1] or HP[6]
hose bibb....HB[7]
hose cabinet....H CAB
hose faucet....HF or HB
hose rack....HR [7]
hospital....HOSP[6]
hot rolled steel....HRS[6]
hot water....HW[6]
hot water, circulating....HW C[6]
hot water heater....HWH or WH[7]
hot water tank....HWT [7]
hour....hr[1] or HR[6]
house....HSE[6]
humidification line....H[3]
hundred....C
I beam....I
Illuminating Engineering
Society....IES
inch....(")[1,2,6] or in[1,2] or IN[6]
include....INCL[6]
incorporated....INC[6]
indicated horsepower....IHP[6]
information....INFO[6]
inlet....IN[6]
inlet manhole....IMH[6]
inside diameter....ID[1,6]
inside pipe size....IPS
instantaneous....INST[6]
insulate....INS[6]
insulation....INS
interior....INT[6]
intermediate....INTER[6]
internal....int[1] or INT[6]
invert....INV[6]
iron....I[6]
ironing machine....IM
iron-pipe size....IPS[6]
jamb-template machine screws.JTMS[5]
janitor's closet....J CL
joint....JT[6]
junction box (outlet)....J[4]
kalamein....KAL
kalamein door....KD[5]
kalamein frame....KF[5]
kalsomine....K
keyed alike....KA[5]
keyed alike & master keyed...KAMK[5]
keyed alike & grand
master keyed....KAGMK[5]
kick plate....KP[6]
kiln-dried....KD[2,6]
kilo....K[6]
kilocycle....KC[6]
kilogram....KG[6]
kilometer....km[1] or KM[6]
kilowatt....kw[1] or KW[6]
kilowatthour.... KWH[6] kwhr[1]
kip (1000 lb)....K[6]

kitchen....K
kitchen sink....KS or S[7]
knocked down....k.d.[2] or KD[6]
laboratory....LAB[6]
ladder....LAD.[6]
lamphole....LH
landing....LDG[6]
lateral....LAT
lath....lth[2] or LTH
latitude....LAT° or φ
laundry....LAU[6]
laundry chute....LC
laundry trays....LT [7]
lavatory.... or LAV[6] or L[7]
lavatory, dental....DL[7]
lavatory, medical....ML[7]
lavatory, pedestal....PL[7]
lavatory, wall....WL [7]
lead and oil....LO
lead covered....LC[6]
leader....L
leader drain....LD
left....L[6]
left hand....LH[5]
left hand reverse....LHR[5]
length....lgth[2] or LG[6] or L
length overall....LOA[6]
level....LEV
library....LIB
light....LT[8]
light weight concrete....LWC
light weight insulating
concrete....LWIC
limestone....LS
line....L[6]
linear feet....lin ft[1,2]
linen chute....L CH
linen closet....L CL
lining....Lng[2] or LN
linoleum....Lino
linoleum base....LB
linoleum floor....LF
liveload....LL
living room....LR
locker....LKR°
locker room....LKR R
long....LG[6]
louver....LV
louver opening....LVO or L[8]
louvered door....LVD
low frequency....LF
low point....LP
low pressure....LP
low tension....LT
lumber....lbr[2] or LBR[6]
lumen....L[6]
machine....MACH[6]
machine room....MACH R
magnesia block....MB
mail chute....MC
main....MN[6]
malleable iron....MI[6]
malleable iron pipe....MIP
manhole....MH[6]
manufacture....MFR[6]
manufactured[6]....MFD[6]
manufacturer....MFR
marble....MR[6]

mark....MK[6]
masonry opening....MO
master keyed....MK[5]
material....MATL[6]
maximum....max[1] or MAX[6]
mean high tide....MHT[6]
mean sea level....MSL[6]
measurement....MST
mechanic....MEC
mechanical....MECH[6]
medical lavatory....ML[7]
medicine cabinet....MC
medium....MED
membrane....MEMB[6]
men's rest room....MRR
men's toilet....MT
men's wash room....MWR
merchantable....Merch
metal....MET.[6] or M
metal base....MB
metal covered wood....MCW
meter (instrument of measure)M [6,7]
meter (measure)....m[1]
mezzanine....MEZZ[6]
millimeter....mm[1]
minimum....min[1] or MIN[6]
minute.... MIN[6] min[1]
minute (angular measure)....(')[1]
miscellaneous....MISC[6]
model....MOD[6]
modern tips....MT[5]
modular....MOD
modulus of elasticity....E
monitor....MON[6]
monument....MON[6]
moment, bending....M
motor....M[4]
motor generator....MG[6]
moulding....Mldg[2] or MLDG
mounting....MTG[6]
movable partition....M PART
nail....N
national....NATL[6]
National Board of
Fire Underwriters....NBFU
National Bureau of
Standards....NBS
National Electric Code....NEC[1]
National Electrical
Manufacturers Assoc....NEMA
National Fire Protection
Association....NFPA
National Lumber Manufacturers
Association....NLMA
nickel....NI[6]
nickel-silver....NI-SIL[6]
nipple....NIP[6]
nominal....NOM[6]
non-corrosive....NC
non-removable pin
(set screw in barrel)....NRP
non-slip....NS
normal....NOR[6]
north....N[6]
north-northwest....NNW
Not in Contract....NIC
number....No[2] or NO.[6] or #

ABBREVIATIONS

oak ... O
octagon ... OCT[6]
octagonal ... OCT
office ... OFF[6]
on center ... OC[6]
one thousand feet board measure ... MBM
opening ... OPNG[6]
opposite ... OPP[6]
ornament ... ORN[6]
ounce ... oz[1] or OZ[6]
out to out ... O to O[6]
outlet ... OUT[6]
outside diameter ... OD[1,6]
oval headed screw ... OHS
oval headed wood screw ... OHWS
overall ... OA[6]
overflow ... OVFL[6]
overhead ... OVHD[6]
overload ... OVLD[6]
page ... P[6]
painted ... PTD
pair ... PR[6]
panel ... PNL[6]
pantry ... PAN.[6]
parallel ... PAR[6]
parkway ... PKWY[6]
part ... PT[6]
partition ... PTN[6]
parts per million ... ppm
passage ... PASS.[6]
passenger ... PASS.[6]
pedestal ... PED[6]
pedestal lavatory ... PL
penny (nail size) ... d[1,6]
per ... /
percent ... % or p c
perpendicular ... PERP[6]
pet cock ... P C
phase ... PH[6]
pi (ratio of circ. to dia. of a circle) ... π
piece ... PC[6]
pint ... pt[1]
pipe shaft ... P S
pipe sleeve ... P SL[6]
place ... PL
plain sawed ... Pln[2]
plaster ... PLAS[6] or PL
plastic ... PLSTC[6]
plate (steel) ... PL[6] or ₽
plate glass ... PL GL
platform ... PLAT
plumbing ... PLMB[6]
plumbing stack ... ST
point ... PT[6]
point of tangent ... PT
polish ... POL[6]
polished plate glass ... PPGL
polished wire glass ... PWGL
porch ... P
portable ... PORT.[6]
position ... POS
pound ... # or lb[1] or LB[6]
pounds per cubic foot ... PCF[6]
. lb per cu ft[1] or LB/CU FT or LBS/FT
pounds per square foot ... PSF[6] or #/□' or LB/FT^2
pounds per square inch ... PSI[6] or #/□" or LB/SQ IN
powder room ... PR
power ... PWR[6]
power house ... PH[6]
precast ... PRCST[6]
prefabricated ... PREFAB[6]
premolded ... PRMLD[6]
pressure reducing valve ... PRV[6]
property ... Prop
proposed ... PROP
protected cast box strike ... PCBX[5]
protected strike ... PX[5]
protected wrought box strike ... PWBX[5]
pull chain ... P or PC
push button ... PB[6]
quantity ... QTY[6]
quarry ... QRY[6]
quarry tile base ... QTB[6]
quarry tile floor ... QTF
quarry tile roof ... QTR
quart ... qt[1] or QT[6]
quartered ... Qtd
radial ... RAD[6]
radiator (exposed & recessed) ... RAD[6]
radiator enclosed ... RAD ENCL
radiator recess ... RAD REC
radio ... R[4]
radius ... r or R[6]
random ... rdm[2]
range ... R
range, gas ... R[7]
receiving basin ... RB
receptacle ... RECP[6]
recirculate ... RECIRC[6]
recirculation duct section ... R[3]
rectangle ... RECT[6]
reducer ... RED[6]
reflective ... REFL
reflector ... REFL[6]
refrigerator ... REF
refrigerant discharge (pipe) ... RD[3]
refrigerator suction ... RS[3]
register ... REG[6]
register, bottom ... BR
register, ceiling ... CR
register, center ... CR
register, top ... TR
register, top & bottom ... T&BR
regulator ... REG[6]
reinforce or reinforcing ... REINF
relative humidity ... RH[6]
relief valve ... RV
remote control ... RC[6]
remove ... REM[6]
repair ... REP[6]
required ... REQD[6]
resin emulsion ... RE
return ... RET[6]
revision ... REV
revolutions per minute ... rpm[1] or RPM[6]
revolutions per second ... rps[1] or RPS[6]
right ... R[6]
right hand ... RH[6]
right hand reverse ... RHR[5]
riser ... R
rivet ... RIV[6]
road ... RD[6]
roof ... RF[6]
roof drain ... RD
roofing ... Rfg[2] or RFG
room ... RM[6] or R
rough ... RGH[6]
rough wire glass ... RWGL
round ... rnd[2] or RD[6]
roundheaded screw ... RHS
Royal Architectural Institute of Canada ... R.A.I.C.
rubber ... RUB[6]
saddle ... SDL[6] or S
safe working pressure ... SWP[6]
safety ... SAF[6]
safety valve ... SV[6]
sapwood ... Sap[2]
scale ... SC
schedule ... SCH[6]
screw ... SCR[6]
screwed (piping) ... scd
scupper ... SCUP[6]
scuttle ... S[6]
seamless ... SMLS[6]
second ... SEC[6] or sec[1]
second (angular measure) ... (")[1]
section ... SECT[6]
select ... Sel[2] or SEL[6]
self-closing ... SC
service ... SERV[6]
set screw ... SS[6]
sewer ... SEW.[6]
sewer, cast iron pipe ... S-CI
sewer, clay tile ... S-CT
sheathing ... SHTHG[6]
sheet ... SH[6]
shelves (as 2 shelves) ... 2 SH
shiplap ... Shlp[2]
shower ... SH[6]
shut off valve ... SOV[6]
siding ... Sdg[2] or SDG[6]
sill-cock ... S-C
Simplified Practice Recommendations ... SPR
sink ... SK[6] or S[7]
sink and laundry tray ... S & T[3]
sink, service ... SS[7]
sitz bath ... SB[7]
slate ... SL[6]
sleeve ... SLV[6]
slop sink or service sink ... SS
socket ... SOC[6]
soil pipe ... SP[6]
solder ... SLD[6]
south ... S[6]
south by west ... SbW
southwest ... SW
speaker ... SPKR[6]
specifications ... SPEC[6]
sprinkler ... SPR[6]
square ... Sq[2] or SQ[6] or □
square edge ... Sq E[2]

ABBREVIATIONS

square foot ... sq ft[1] or □'
square inch ... sq in[1] or □"
stained ... stnd[2] or STN
staggered ... stag
stained-waxed ... SW
stainless steel ... SST
stairs ... ST
stairway ... STWY[6]
stanchion ... STAN[6]
standard ... std[1] or Std[2] or STD[6]
standard wire gauge ... S.W.G.
standpipe ... SP[6]
static pressure ... SP[6]
station ... STA[6]
steam working pressure ... ST WP[6]
steel ... STL[6]
steel partition ... ST PART
steel saddle ... ST S
steel steeple tips ... SST[5]
sterilizer ... STER[6]
stiffener ... STIFF[6]
stirrup ... STIR.[6]
stock ... stk or STK[6]
stone ... STN[6]
storage ... STG[6]
storage closet ... ST CL
storm water ... ST W[6]
street ... ST[6]
strike only-template
  machine screws ... STMS[5]
string ... STR
structural ... STR[6]
Structural Clay Research "SCRbrick"
substitute ... SUB[6]
sump pit ... SP
superintendent ... SUPT[6]
supersede ... SUPSD[6]
supplement ... SUPP[6]
supplementary ... SUPPY
supply ... SUP[6]
supply duct section ... S[8]
support ... SUP[6]
surface ... SUR[6]
surface area ... A or S
surface foot ... SF
surfaced and matched ... S&M
surfaced four sides ... S4S
surfaced one side and
  one edge ... SISIE
surface measure ... SM
suspend ... SUSP[6]
suspended ceiling ... SUSP CEIL
switch ... SW[6] or S[4]
switch, automatic door ... SD[4]
switchboard ... SWBD[6]
switch, key operated ... SK[4]
symbol ... SYM[6]
system ... SYS[6]
tangent ... tan[1] or TAN[6]
technical ... TECH[6]
tee ... T[6]
telegraph ... TLG[6]
telephone ... TEL[6]
telephone booth ... TB
temperature ... temp[1] or TEMP[6]
template ... TEMP[6]
template-machine screws ... TMS[5]
tensile strength ... TS[6]
terminal ... TERM.[6]
terrazzo ... TER[6]
terra cotta ... TC[6]
thermal conductance ... C
thermal conductivity ... k
thermometer ... THERM[6]
thermostat ... THERMO[6]
thick or thickness ... THK[6] or T
thousand ... M[2,6]
thousand pounds ... kip[1] or KIP[6]
thread ... THD[6]
threaded ... THR
toenail ... TN
toilet ... T
tongue and groove ... T&G[2,6]
top, bottom and sides ... TB&S[2]
transformer, power ... T[4] or TRANS[6]
transom ... T
tray ... T
tread ... T or TR
trimmed opening ... TO
trough urinal ... TU[7]
turnbuckle ... TRNBKL[6]
typewriter ... TYPW
typical ... TYP[6]
ultimate ... ULT[6]
Underwriters Laboratories ... UL
unfinished ... UNFIN
United States Standard ... USS[6]
U.S. Standard Gauge ... USSG
unit heater ... UH[6]
up ... U
urinal ... UR[6]
urinal, trough type ... TU[7]
utility room ... UR
vacuum ... VAC[6]
vacuum cleaning line ... V[7]
valve box ... VB[6]
vanishing point ... VP
vapor proof ... VAP PRF[6]
variable ... VAR[6]
varnish ... VARN[6]
velocity ... V[6]
vent ... V
vent duct ... VD
vent pipe ... VP[6]
vent shaft ... VS
vent stack ... VS[6]
ventilate ... VENT.[6]
ventilation ... VENT
ventilator ... V
vertical ... VERT[6]
vertical grain ... VG
vestibule ... VEST.
vitreous ... VIT[6]
volt ... V[6] or v[1]
volume ... VOL[6] or V
wall ... W[6]
wall cabinet ... W CAB
wall lavatory ... WL[7]
wall paint flat ... WF
wall paint gloss ... WG
wall paint semi gloss ... WSG
wall vent ... WV
warehouse ... WHSE[6]
Washburn and Moen gauge ... W&M GA
washing machine ... WM
washroom ... WR
water ... W[6]
watercloset ... WC[6]
water cooler ... WCR[6]
water heater ... WH[6]
water line ... WL[6]
waterproof or
  waterproofing ... WP
watertight ... WT[6]
watt ... W[6] or w[1]
watthour ... WHR[6]
waxed ... W
weather stripping ... WS[6]
weatherproof ... WP[6]
weephole ... WH
weight ... wt[1,2] or WT[6]
west ... W[6]
wide flange (steel) ... WF
width ... Wth[2] or W[6]
window ... WDW
wire ... W[6]
wire glass ... W GL
with ... W/
with (hardware) ... X
without ... W/O
women's rest room ... WRR
women's toilet ... WT
wood ... WD[6]
wood door ... WD[5]
wood frame ... WF[5]
working pressure ... WP[6]
wringer-washing machine ... WWM
wrought ... WRT[6]
wrought iron ... WI[6]
yard ... yd[1] or YD[6]
yard drain inlet ... YDI
year ... yr[1] or YR[6]
yellow ... YEL[6]
zinc ... Z[6]

For reference numbers see first page of abbreviations.

DIMENSIONS of THE HUMAN FIGURE

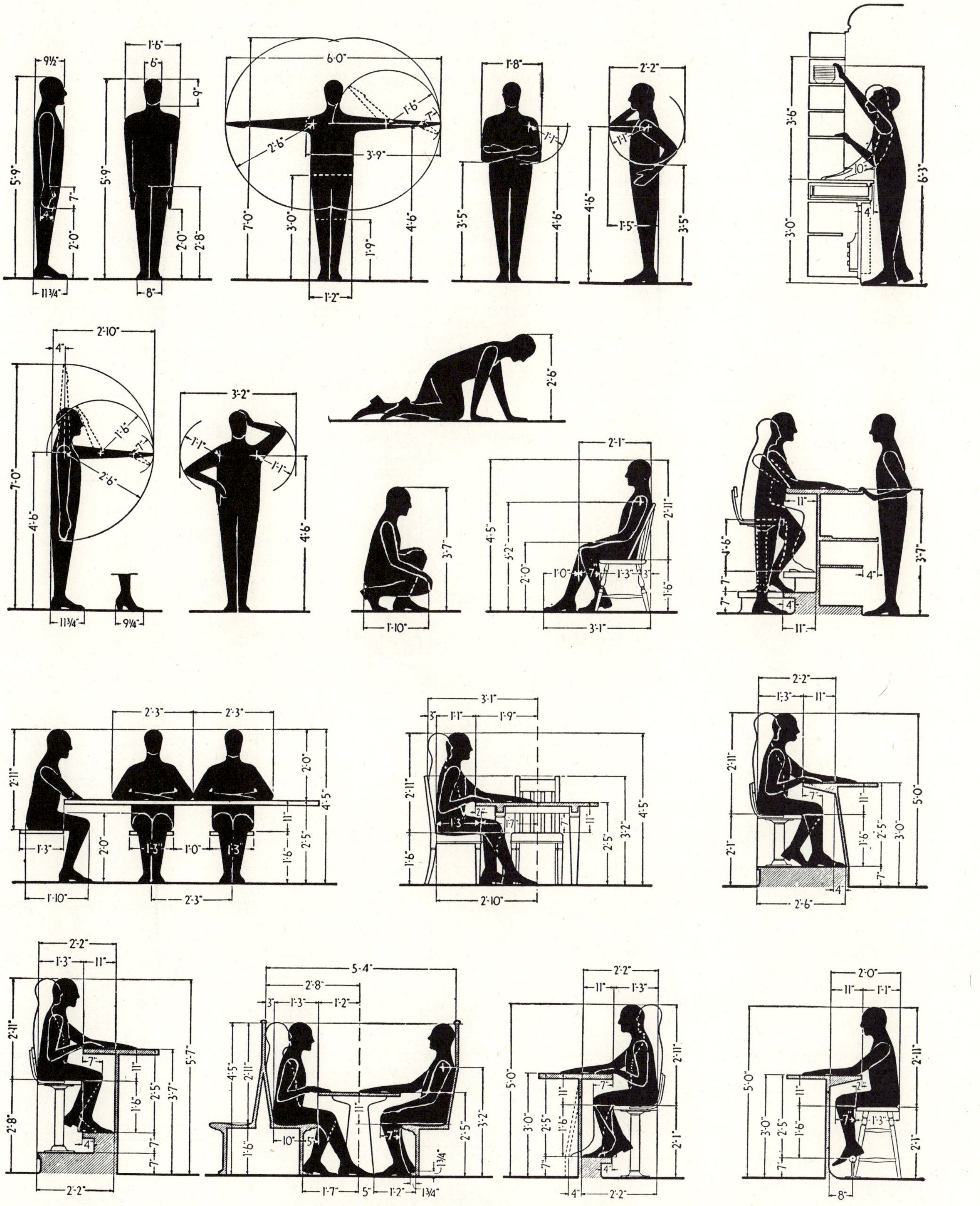

Scale of Human Figure 1/4" = 1'-0"

These dimensions are based on the average or normal adult. As clearances are minimum they should be increased when conditions will allow.

Table, desk, and other sitting work-top heights are shown 2'-5"; however some authorities prefer 2'-6" or 2'-6 1/2". See sheets on children's furniture for their sizes and furniture.

Drawings by Ernest Irving Freese

MODULAR COORDINATION

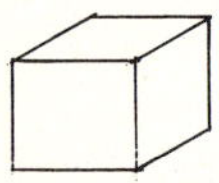

"Modular Coordination" applies specifically to Project A62 of the American Standards Association with the primary objective of promoting basic economies in building. Sponsored by The American Institute of Architects, The Producers Council Inc. & *NAHB, it is organized so that experts from all of the branches of the construction industry can cooperate to establish American Standard Coordinated Sizes (Modular Sizes) for building materials and equipment; together with practical methods for their application.

The determination of coordinated sizes, details for their assembly, and building dimensions that will produce the required harmony and proper fitting together of the various parts, is accomplished by means of a Standard Grid.

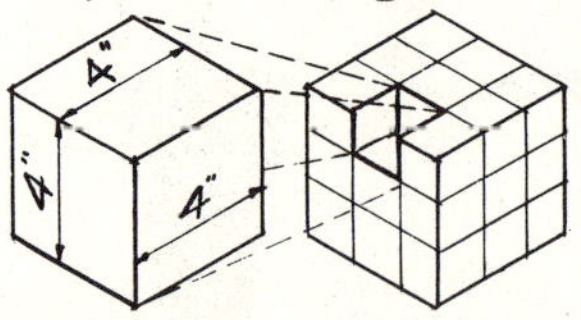

4"
4"
4"

The Standard Grid is three dimensional and therefore, appears in each of the principal planes of buildings & building parts as a grid of 4" squares. Grid lines are not drawn on small scale drawings but are on detail drawings.

All plans, elevations, sections and details are drawn on the Standard Grid. This enables the lines of the grid to be used as a constant and uniform series of reference or witness points. Because it is impractical to show the grid on small-scale drawings, dimensional symbols are used. Arrows on dimensions indicate grid lines and dots, non-grid points.

To grid line
Non-grid

* NAHB - National Assoc. Home Builders.

SMALL SCALE PLANS DIMENSIONED AS BELOW

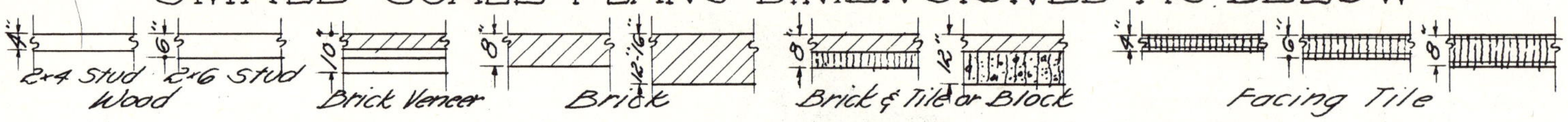

4"
6"
2×4 Stud
2×6 Stud
Wood
10"
8"
12" 16"
Brick Veneer
Brick
8"
12"
Brick & Tile or Block
4"
6"
8"
Facing Tile

MODULAR WALL THICKNESSES FOR SMALL SCALE DRAWINGS

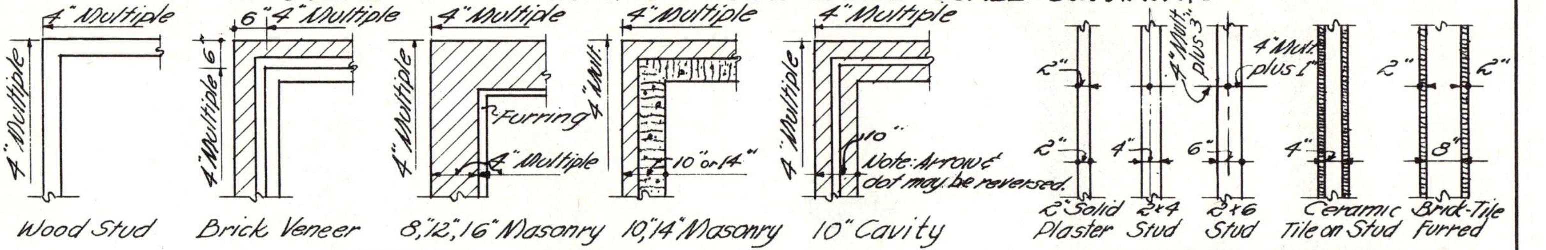

4" Multiple
4" Multiple
Wood Stud
6" 4" Multiple
6"
4" Multiple
Brick Veneer
4" Multiple
4" Multiple
Furring
4" Multiple
8", 12", 16" Masonry
4" Multiple
4" Mult.
10" or 14"
10", 14" Masonry
4" Multiple
4" Multiple
10"
Note: Arrow & dot may be reversed.
10" Cavity
EXTERIOR WALLS
2"
2"
2" Solid Plaster
4" Mult. plus 3"
4"
2×4 Stud
4" Mult. plus 1"
6"
2×6 Stud
4"
Ceramic Tile on Stud
2"
2"
8"
Brick-Tile Furred
INTERIOR PARTITIONS

WALLS AND PARTITIONS

Scale: 1/4" = 1'-0"

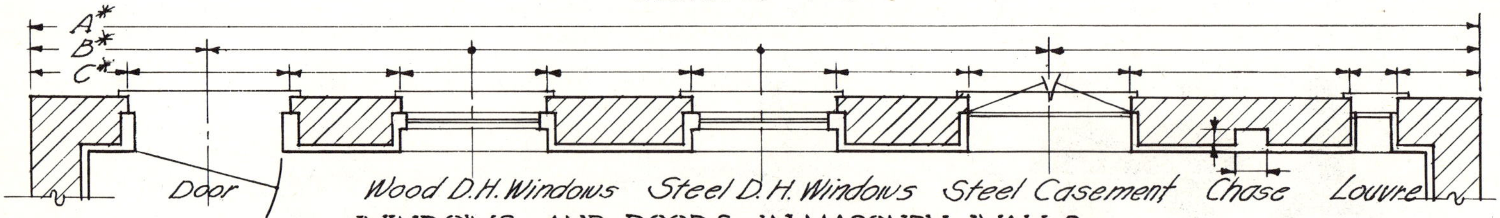

A*
B*
C*
Door
Wood D.H. Windows
Steel D.H. Windows
Steel Casement
Chase
Louvre

WINDOWS AND DOORS IN MASONRY WALLS

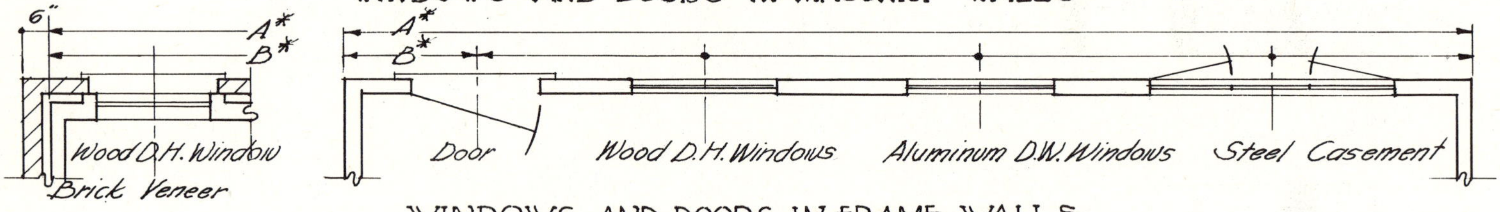

6"
A*
B*
Wood D.H. Window
Brick Veneer
A*
B*
Door
Wood D.H. Windows
Aluminum D.W. Windows
Steel Casement

WINDOWS AND DOORS IN FRAME WALLS

Scale: 1/4" = 1'-0"

*Overall dimensions A should equal a multiple of 4". Center-line dimensions B should equal a multiple of 4" for doors and windows which are an <u>even</u> 4" multiple in width - e.g. 3'-4", 4'-0", etc., and a multiple of 4 in. plus 2" for windows and doors which are an <u>odd</u> multiple of 4" in width - e.g. 3'-0", 3'-8", etc. except when two occur together. Masonry dimensions C should equal a multiple of 4 inches.

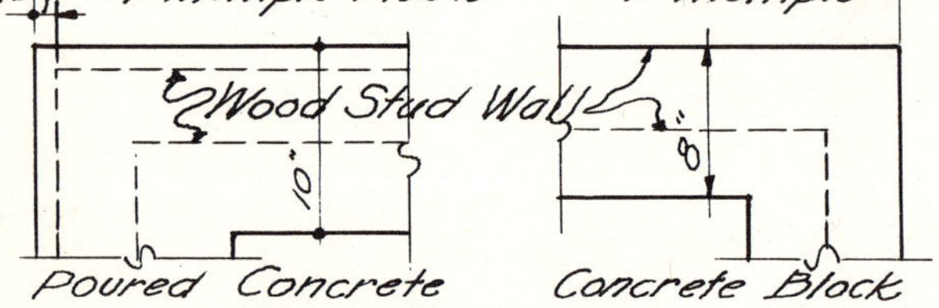

1"
4" Multiple Plus 2"
Wood Stud Wall
10"
Poured Concrete
4" Multiple
8"
Concrete Block

FOUNDATIONS

Scale: 3/4" = 1'-0"

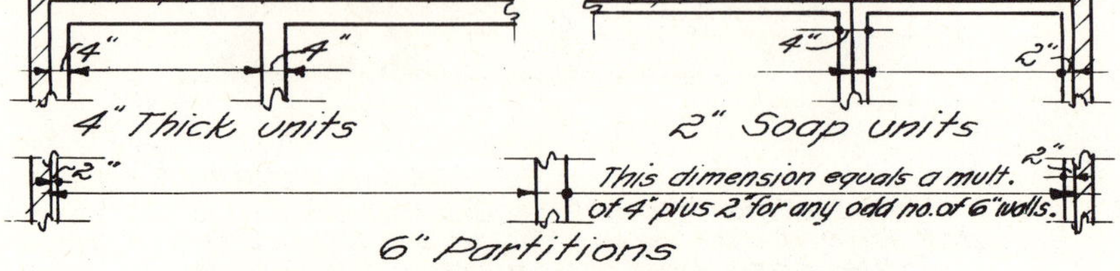

4"
4"
4" Thick units
4"
2"
2" Soap units
2"
This dimension equals a mult. of 4" plus 2" for any odd no. of 6" walls.
2"
6" Partitions

FACING TILE PARTITIONS

Scale: 1/4" = 1'-0"

Note: "Modular measure" may be used instead of "modular coordination"

Prepared by: Prentice Bradley, A.I.A.

MODULAR COORDINATION

SMALL SCALE PLAN DIMENSIONING (cont.)

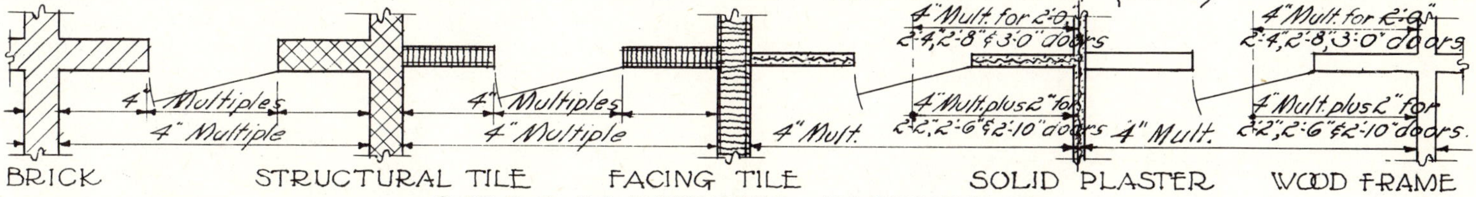

Grid line
Non-grid line
4" Multiples
4" Multiple
4" Multiples
4" Multiple
4" Mult.
4" Mult. for 2'-0", 2'-4", 2'-8" & 3'-0" doors
4" Mult. plus 2" for 2'-2", 2'-6" & 2'-10" doors
4" Mult.
4" Mult. for 2'-0", 2'-4", 2'-8", 3'-0" doors
4" Mult. plus 2" for 2'-2", 2'-6" & 2'-10" doors
BRICK
STRUCTURAL TILE
FACING TILE
SOLID PLASTER
WOOD FRAME

DOORS IN INTERIOR PARTITIONS

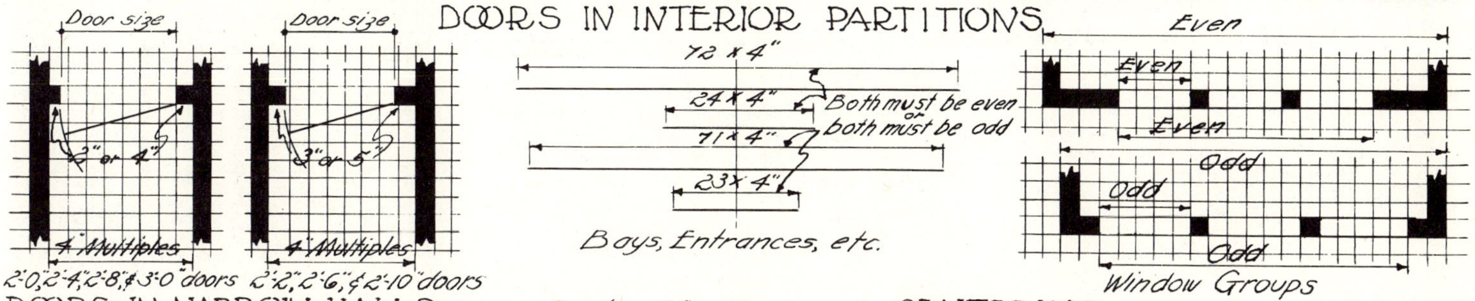

Door size
2" or 4"
4" Multiples
2'-0", 2'-4", 2'-8", & 3'-0" doors
Door size
3" or 5"
4" Multiples
2'-2", 2'-6", & 2'-10" doors
72 x 4"
24 x 4"
71 x 4"
23 x 4"
Both must be even or both must be odd
Bays, Entrances, etc.
Even
Even
Even
Odd
Odd
Odd
Window Groups

DOORS IN NARROW HALLS

Scale: 1/4" = 1'-0"

CENTERING

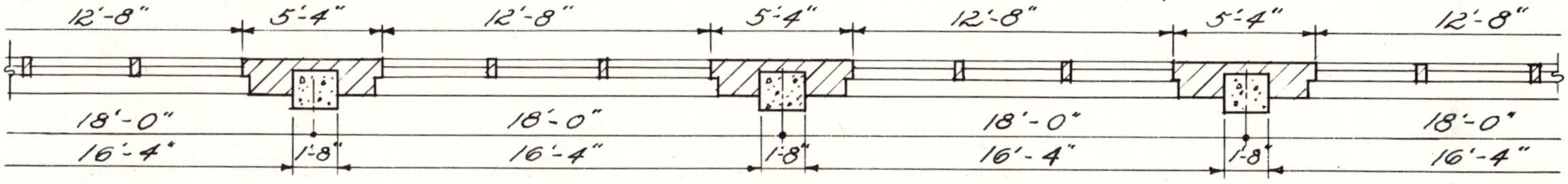

12'-8"
5'-4"
12'-8"
5'-4"
12'-8"
5'-4"
12'-8"
18'-0"
16'-4"
1'-8"
18'-0"
16'-4"
1'-8"
18'-0"
16'-4"
1'-8"
18'-0"
16'-4"

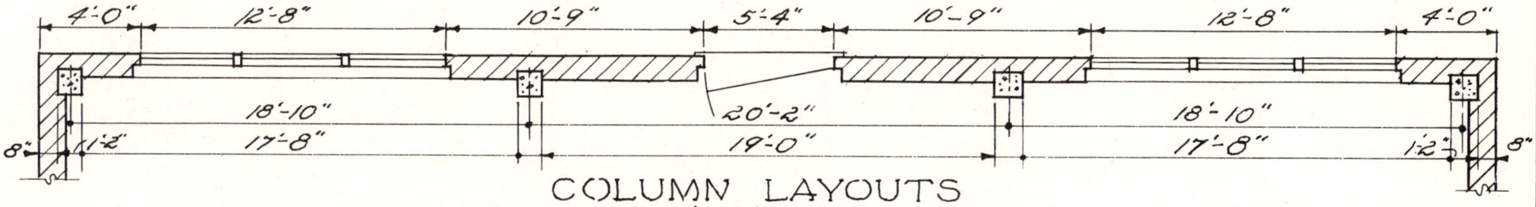

4'-0"
12'-8"
10'-9"
5'-4"
10'-9"
12'-8"
4'-0"
18'-10"
20'-2"
18'-10"
8"
1'-2"
17'-8"
19'-0"
17'-8"
1'-2"
8"

COLUMN LAYOUTS

Scale: 1/8" = 1'-0"

Column sizes for small scale are shown equal to a 4" multiple, or 4" multiple plus 2", so as to coordinate with the masonry. Other multiples of 4" may be substituted for the dimensions that are consistent with modular window width.

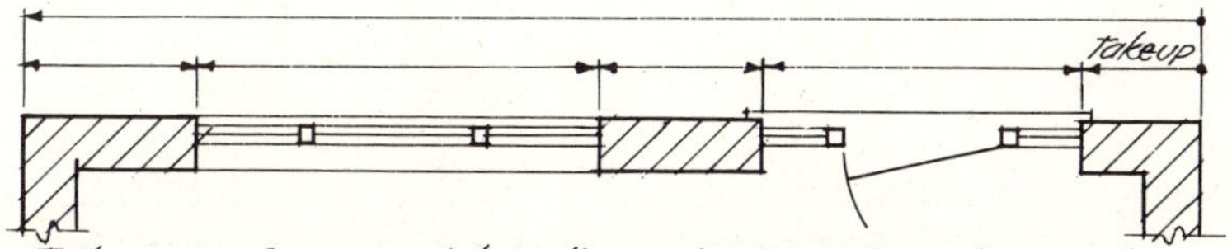

Take-up

Take-up of non-modular dimensions may be at one side, or if it is a symmetrical design, it may be at both sides.

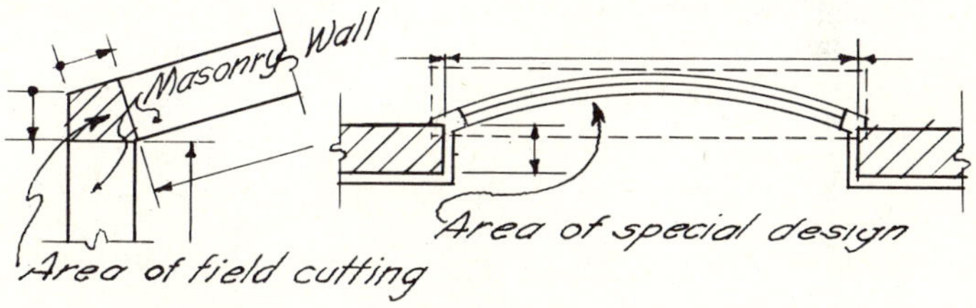

Masonry Wall
Area of field cutting
Area of special design

ODD LOT & PARTY WALL CONDITIONS

NON-RECTANGULAR CONDITIONS

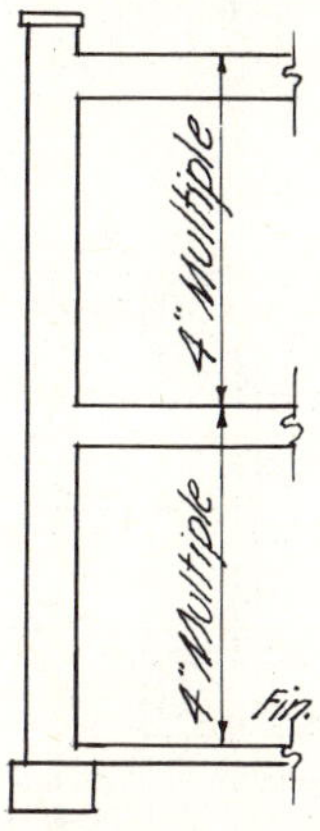

4" Multiple
4" Multiple
Fin. fl.

FLOOR H'GTS.

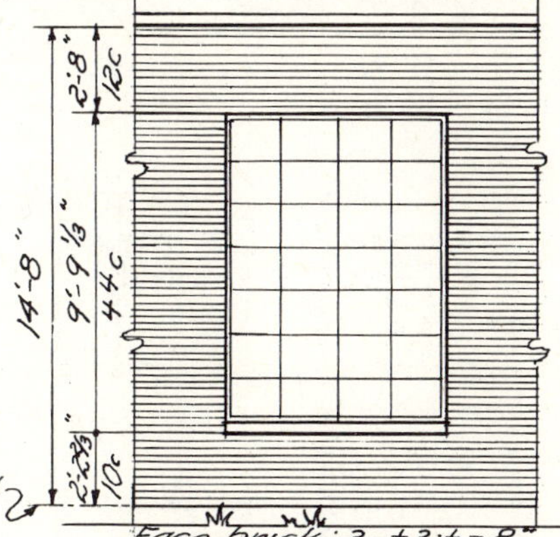

2'-8"
12c
9'-9 1/3"
44c
14'-8"
2'-2 2/3"
10c

Face brick: 3c + 3jt = 8"
Back-up block: 1c + 1jt = 8"

BRICK WALL with Steel Sash

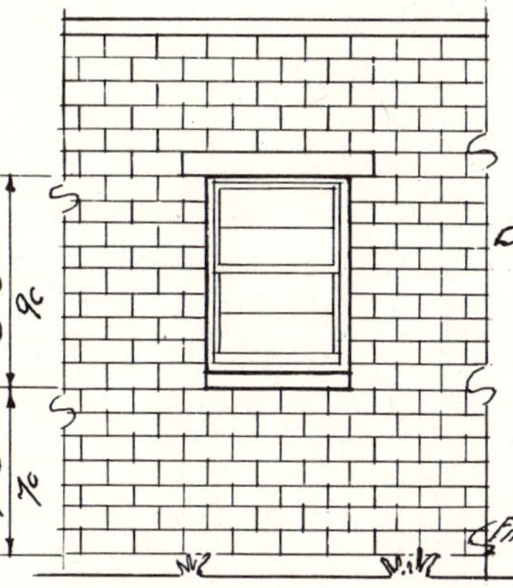

6'-0"
9c
4'-8"
7c

Conc. block: 1c + 1jt = 8"

CONC. BLOCK WALL with D.H. Wind.

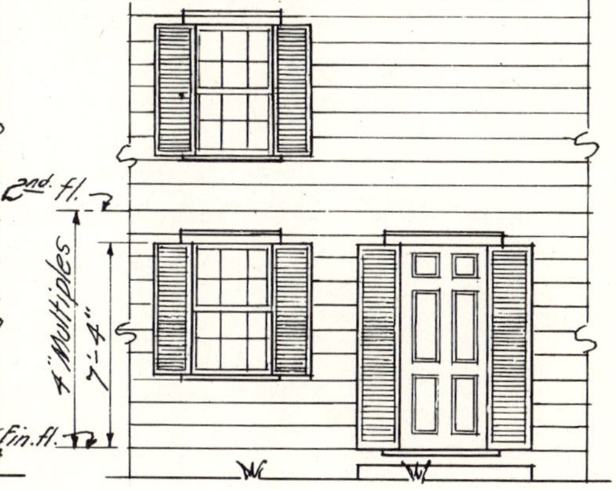

2nd. fl.
4" Multiples
7'-4"
Fin. fl.

WOOD STUD WALL with Door & Wind.

ELEVATIONS

Scale: 1/8" = 1'-0"

Floor to floor heights always equal a multiple of 4". Course heights are taken to center-lines of joints. For masonry course heights, see pages following. Otherwise, dimensioning elevations & sections is similar to conventional practice.

Note: "Modular measure" may be used instead of "modular coordination"

Prepared by: Prentice Bradley, A.I.A.

MODULAR COORDINATION

DETAILING

Grid line — Non-grid line

Grid and non-grid dimensions of small scale drawings are determined by modular details, e.g.-drawings referenced to the Standard 4" Grid. The following details illustrate the Grid Positions of the various building parts comprising the walls, partitions, windows, doors, etc. shown on the preceding two pages.

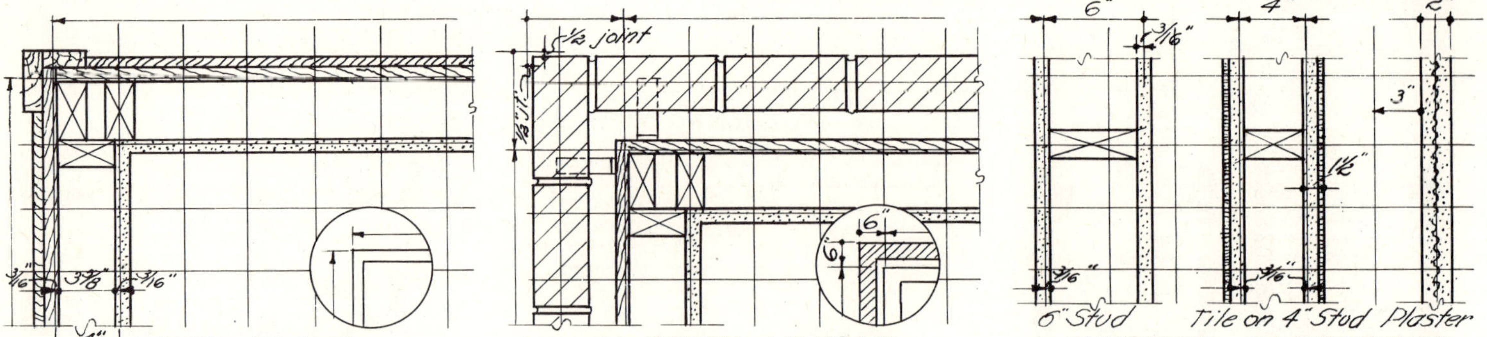

3/16"
3 5/8"
3/16"
4"
1/2 joint
1/2" jt.
16"
6"
6"
3/16"
4"
2"
3"
1 1/2"
3/16"
6" Stud
Tile on 4" Stud
Plaster

WOOD FRAME — BRICK VENEER — INTERIOR PARTITIONS

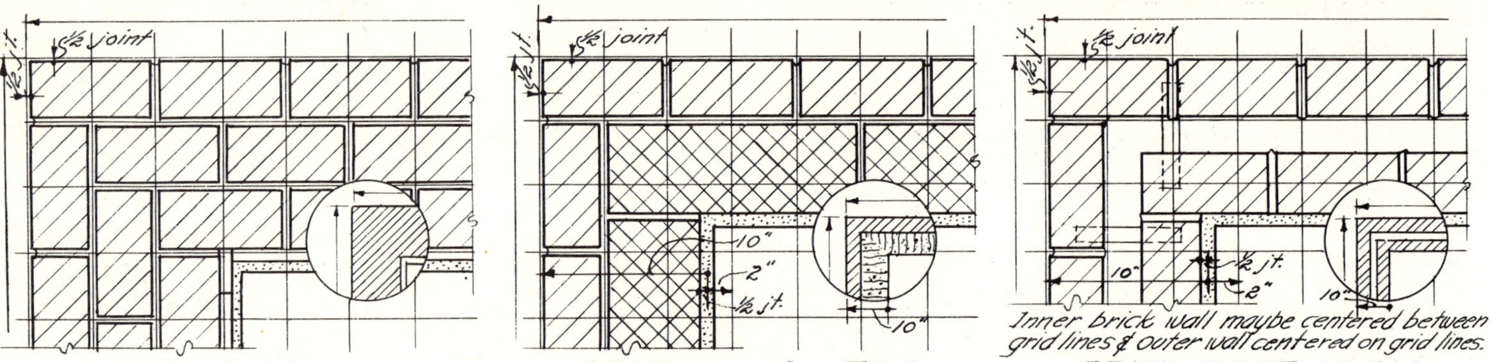

1/2 joint
1/2 jt.
10"
2"
1/2 jt.
10"
1/2 jt.
2"
10"
Inner brick wall maybe centered between grid lines & outer wall centered on grid lines.

SOLID BRICK — BRICK with 6" or 10" TILE — BRICK CAVITY WALL

Note: Inserts show same details at smaller scale of 1/4" = 1'-0"

Scale: 1" = 1'-0"

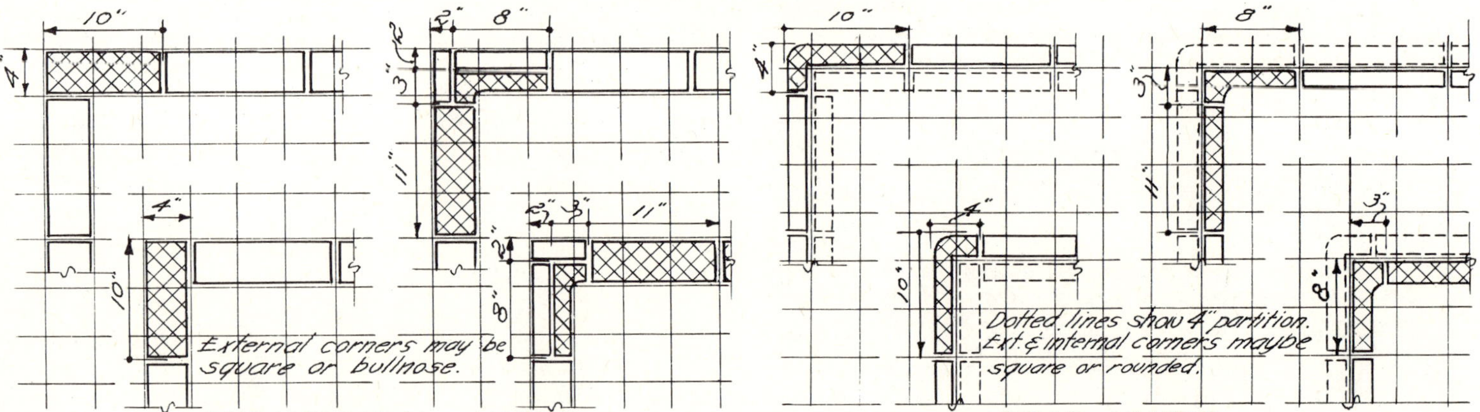

10"
4"
4"
10"
External corners may be square or bullnose.
2"
8"
2"
3"
11"
2"
3"
11"
2"
8"
10"
4"
4"
10"
Dotted lines show 4" partition. Ext. & internal corners maybe square or rounded.
8"
3"
11"
3"
8"

STRUCTURAL UNITS — SOAP UNITS

PLANS

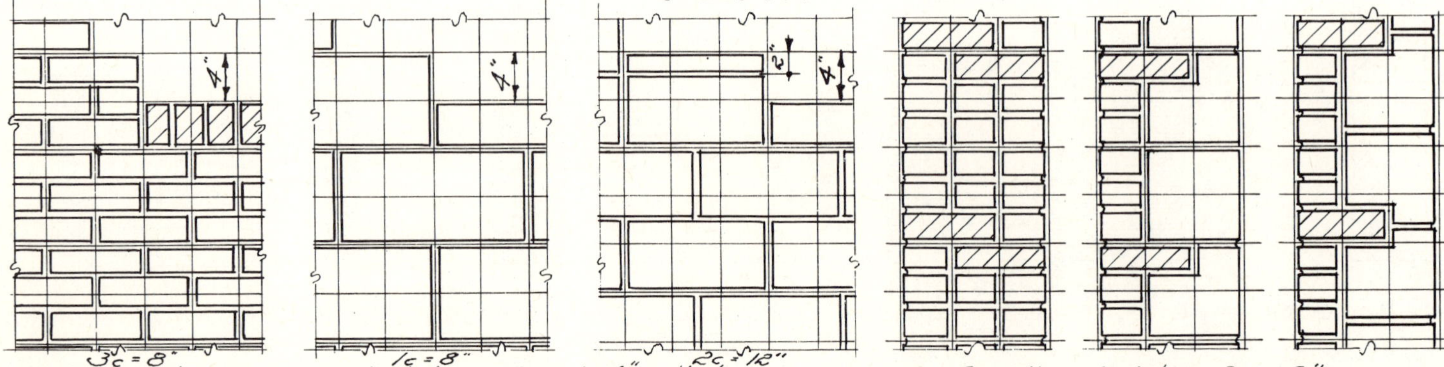

4"
4"
2"
4"
3c = 8"
1c = 8"
2c = 12"

Take-up units to meet vertical dimensions in 4" multiples. — Bonding-brick @ 3c = 8"

WALL ELEVATIONS — Scale: 3/4" = 1'-0" — WALL SECTIONS

Note: "Modular measure" may be used instead of "modular coordination."

Prepared by Prentice Bradley, A.I.A.

MODULAR COORDINATION

DETAILING (Cont.)

Grid lines — Non-Grid lines

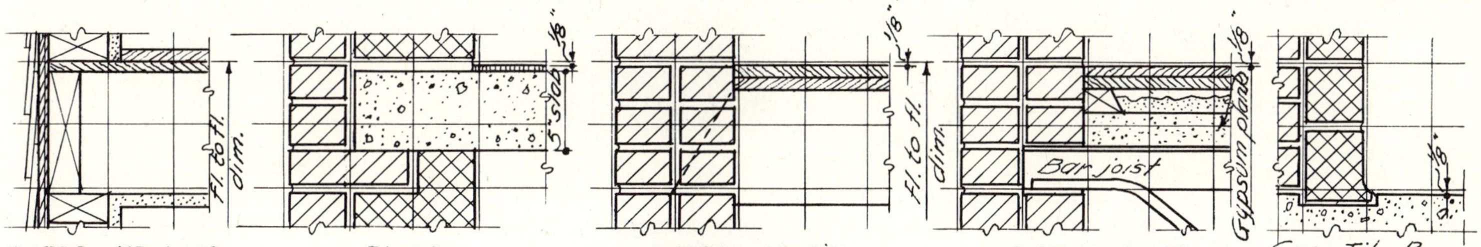
Fl. to fl. dim.
5" slab
1/8"
Fl. to fl. dim.
1/8"
Bar joist
Gypsum plank
1/8"
1/8"

WOOD FRAME — Top of subfloor coincides with grid line.

SLAB — WOOD JOIST — BAR JOIST — Cove Tile Base

For all types of construction except wood frame the finished floor is 1/8" below the grid line.

FLOOR CONSTRUCTION

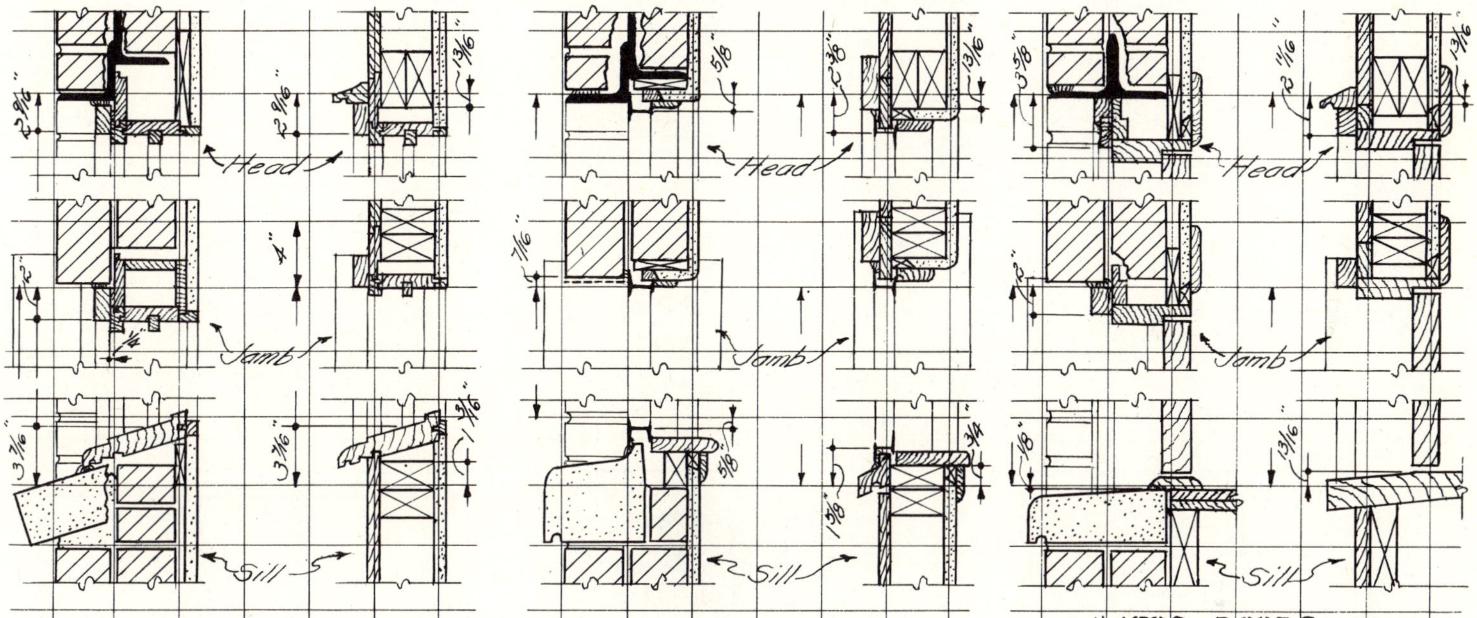
Head
Jamb
Sill
Head
Jamb
Sill
Head
Jamb
Sill

WOOD DOUBLE-HUNG WINDOWS
Sash width equal to multiples of 4 in.
Sash heights equal to 4 multiples, plus 2".

STEEL CASEMENT WINDOWS
Bar center widths equal to 4 in. multiples.
" " height equal to 4 in. multiples.

WOOD DOORS
Door hgts. (fl. to head) equal 4" Mult. plus 1/2"
Note: details above show 4" Mult. door width.
If 4" mult. + 2" dr. width used then masonry jamb dim. is 3" & frame jamb dim. is 1".

WINDOW AND DOOR DETAILS Scale: 1"=1'-0"

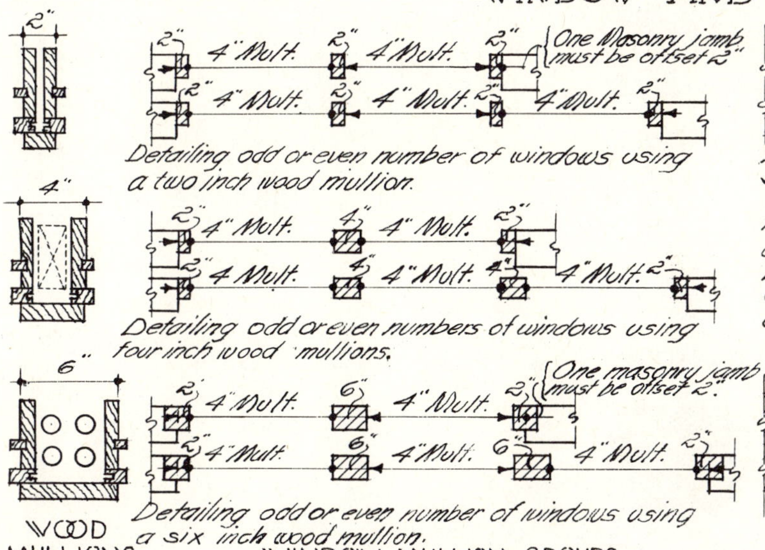
2"
4"
6"
4" Mult.
One Masonry jamb must be offset 2"
Detailing odd or even number of windows using a two inch wood mullion.
Detailing odd or even numbers of windows using four inch wood mullions.
One masonry jamb must be offset 2".
Detailing odd or even number of windows using a six inch wood mullion.

WOOD MULLIONS — WINDOW MULLION GROUPS Scale: 3/8" = 1'-0"

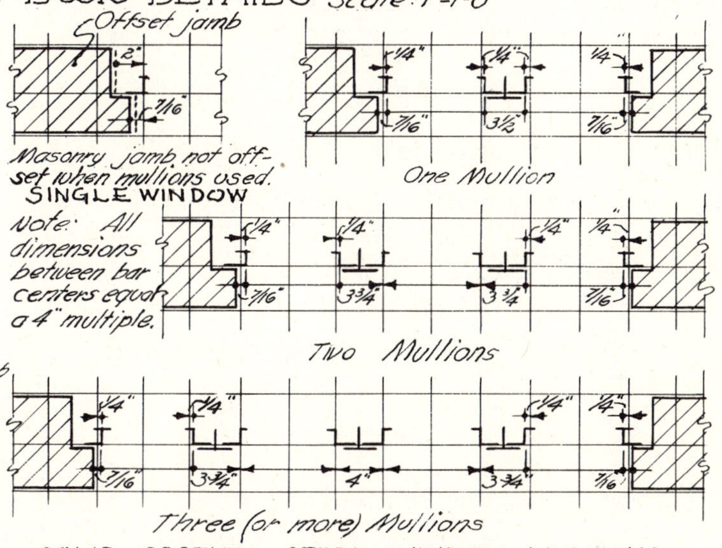
Offset jamb
Masonry jamb not offset when mullions used.
SINGLE WINDOW
One Mullion
Note: All dimensions between bar centers equal a 4" multiple.
Two Mullions
Three (or more) Mullions

SOLID SECTION STEEL WINDOW MULLIONS Scale: 3/4" = 1'-0"

For further information & data refer to "Concrete Masonry Cost Details" by National Concrete Masonry Assoc. "Technical Notes on Modular Measure" by Structural Clay Products Inst., "The New Measure for all Masonry" by Stark Ceramics, Inc., "Building Better from Modular Drwgs," by H.H.F.A. & other data sheets which are located elsewhere in this volume - see index.

NOTE: "Modular measure" may be used instead of "modular coordination."

Prepared by Prentice Bradley, A.I.A.

ROMAN ORDERS of ARCHITECTURE

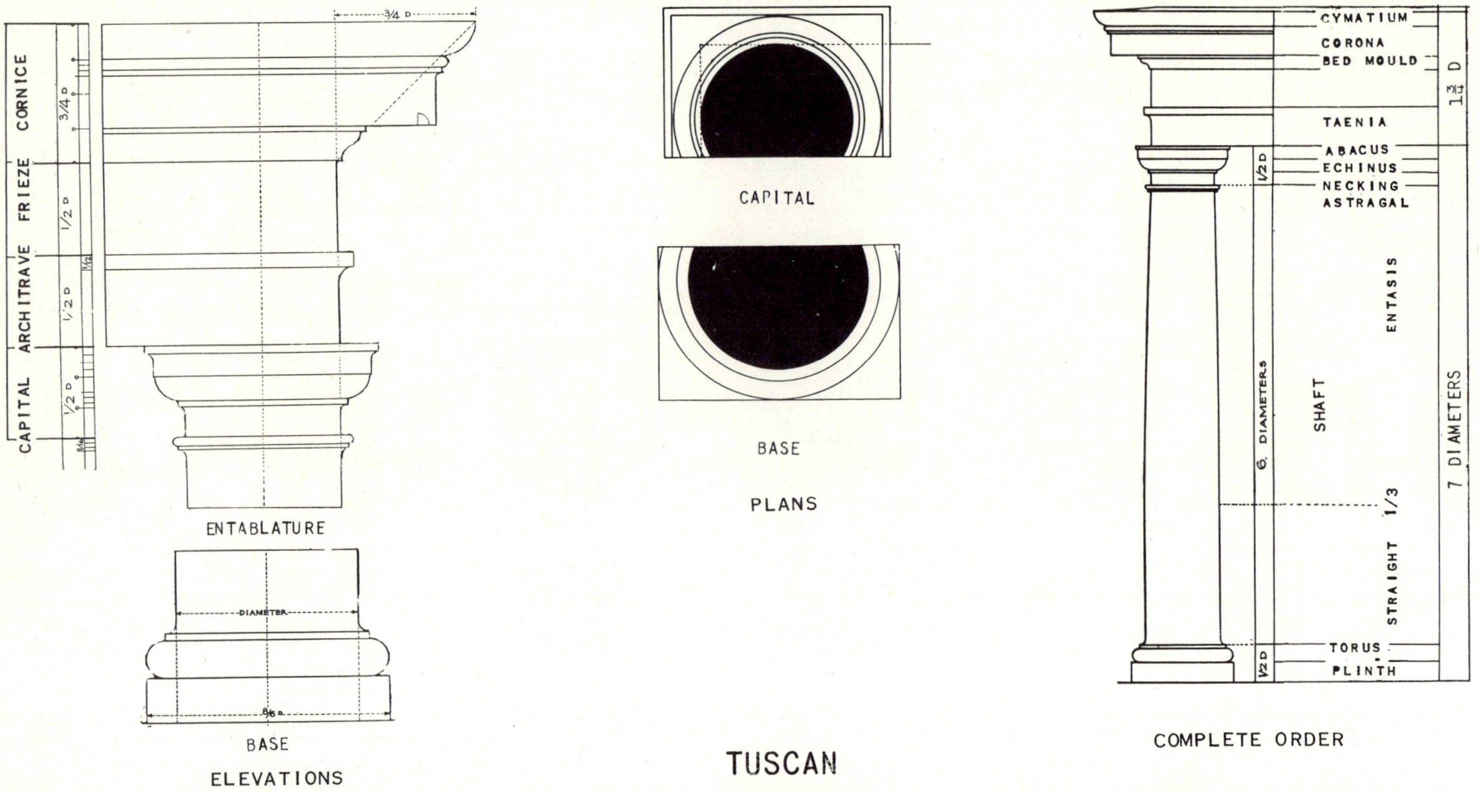

CORNICE
FRIEZE
ARCHITRAVE
CAPITAL
3/4 D
1/2 D
1/2 D
1/2 D
3/4 D
ENTABLATURE
DIAMETER
BASE
ELEVATIONS
CAPITAL
BASE
PLANS
TUSCAN
CYMATIUM
CORONA
BED MOULD
TAENIA
ABACUS
ECHINUS
NECKING
ASTRAGAL
ENTASIS
SHAFT
6 DIAMETERS
1/3
STRAIGHT
7 DIAMETERS
TORUS
PLINTH
1/2 D
COMPLETE ORDER

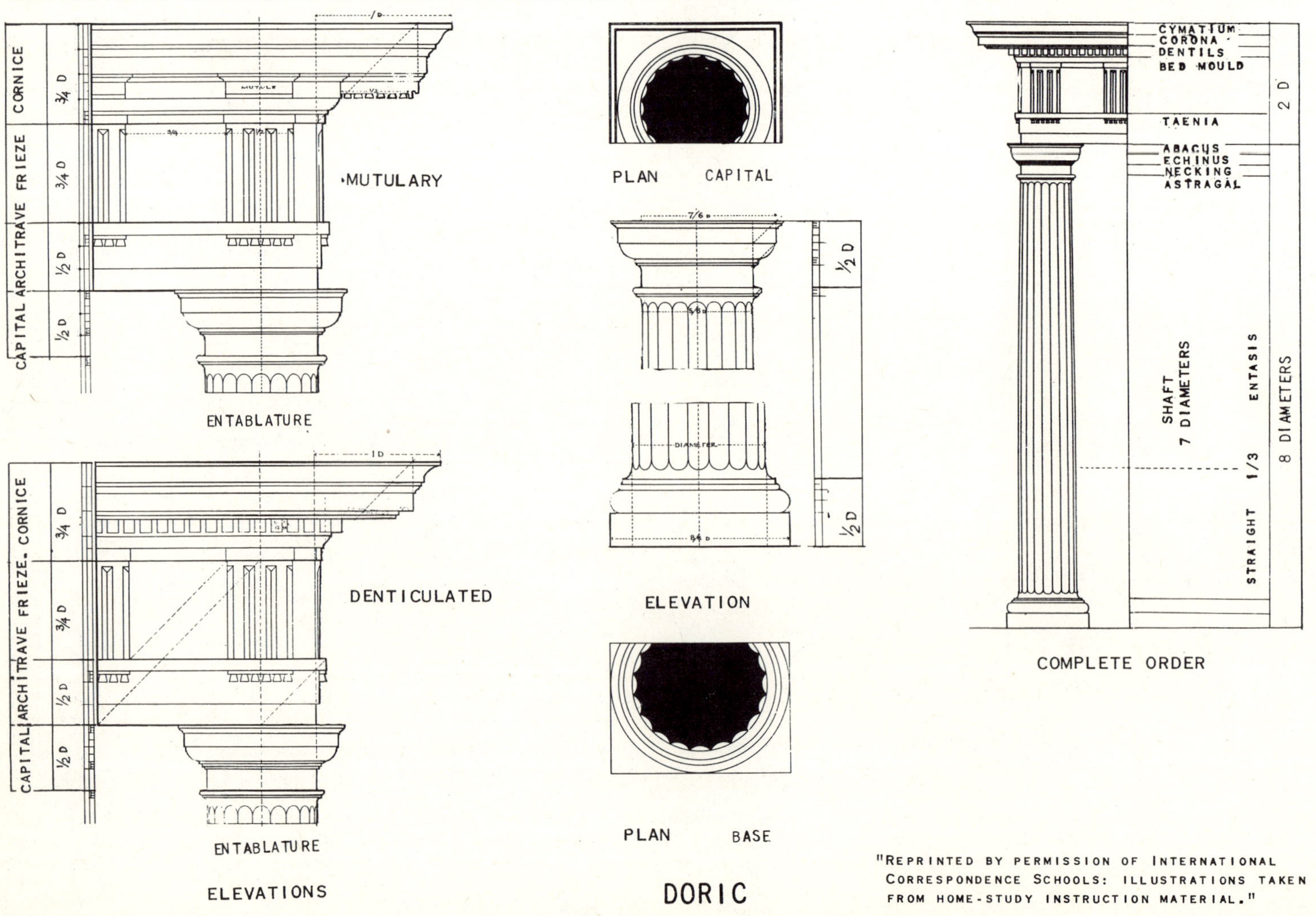

CORNICE
FRIEZE
ARCHITRAVE
CAPITAL
3/4 D
3/4 D
1/2 D
1/2 D
MUTULE
MUTULARY
ENTABLATURE
DENTICULATED
ENTABLATURE
ELEVATIONS
PLAN
CAPITAL
7/6 D
1/2 D
DIAMETER
1/2 D
ELEVATION
PLAN
BASE
DORIC
CYMATIUM
CORONA
DENTILS
BED MOULD
TAENIA
2 D
ABACUS
ECHINUS
NECKING
ASTRAGAL
SHAFT
7 DIAMETERS
ENTASIS
1/3
STRAIGHT
8 DIAMETERS
COMPLETE ORDER

"Reprinted by permission of International Correspondence Schools: illustrations taken from home-study instruction material."

ROMAN ORDERS of ARCHITECTURE

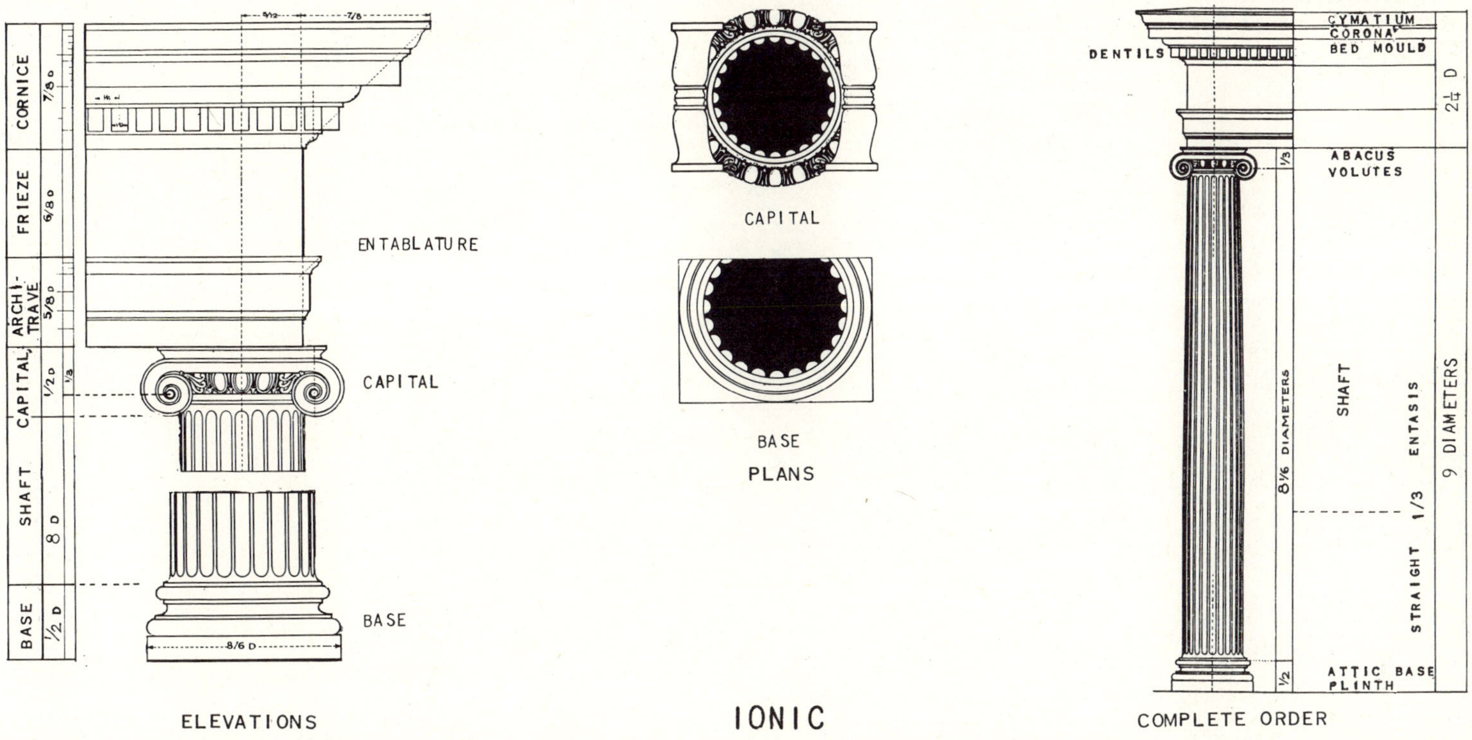
CORNICE 7/8 D
FRIEZE 6/8 D
ARCHITRAVE 5/8 D
CAPITAL 1/2 D
SHAFT 8 D
BASE 1/2 D
ENTABLATURE
CAPITAL
BASE
8/6 D
ELEVATIONS
CAPITAL
BASE
PLANS
CYMATIUM
CORONA
BED MOULD
DENTILS
2 1/4 D
ABACUS
VOLUTES
SHAFT
8 1/6 DIAMETERS
STRAIGHT 1/3 ENTASIS
9 DIAMETERS
ATTIC BASE
PLINTH
COMPLETE ORDER

IONIC

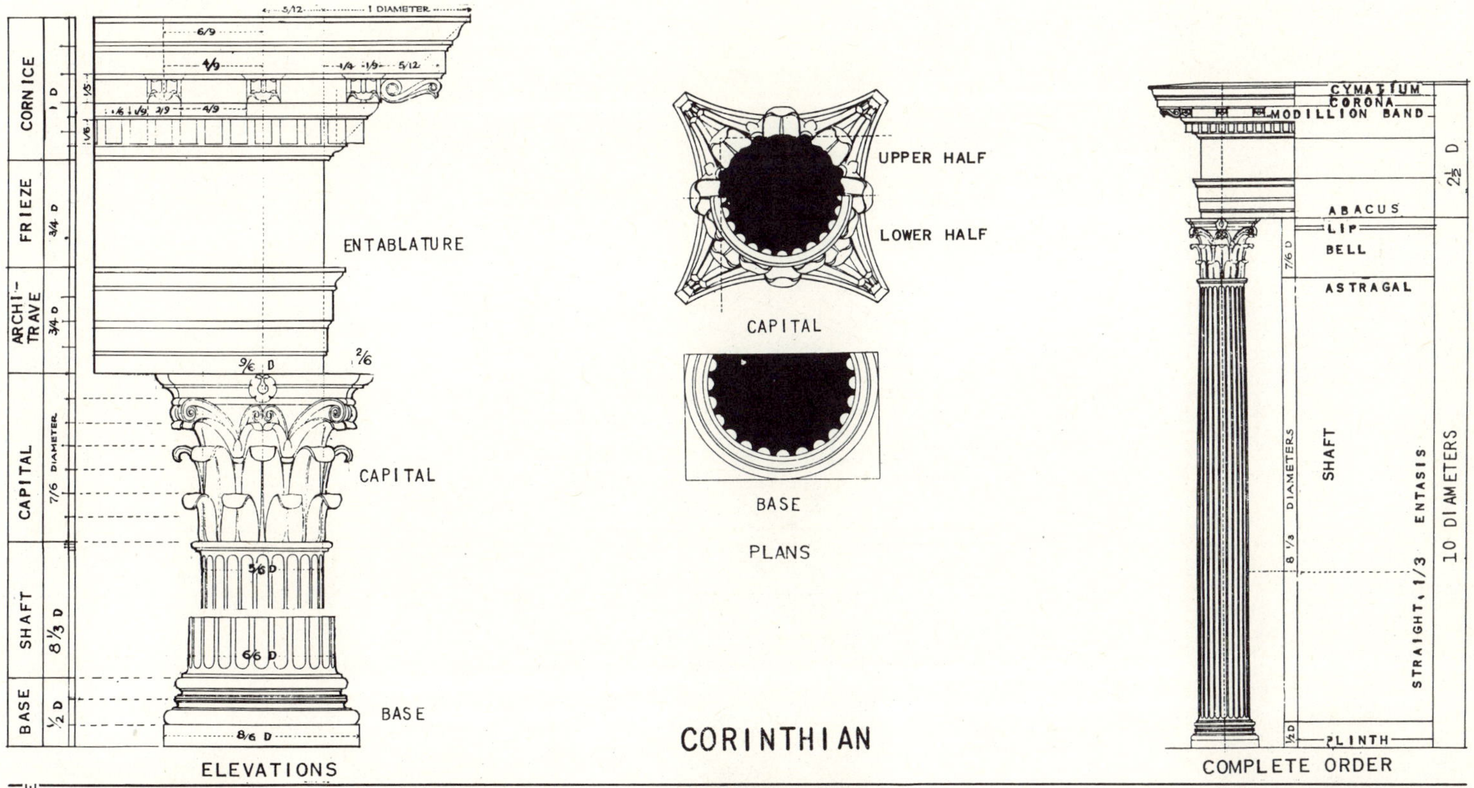
CORNICE 1 D
FRIEZE 3/4 D
ARCHITRAVE 3/4 D
CAPITAL 7/6 DIAMETER
SHAFT 8 1/3 D
BASE 1/2 D
1 DIAMETER
ENTABLATURE
CAPITAL
BASE
ELEVATIONS
UPPER HALF
LOWER HALF
CAPITAL
BASE
PLANS
CYMATIUM
CORONA
MODILLION BAND
2 1/2 D
ABACUS
LIP
BELL
ASTRAGAL
SHAFT
8 1/3 DIAMETERS
STRAIGHT, 1/3 ENTASIS
10 DIAMETERS
PLINTH
COMPLETE ORDER

CORINTHIAN

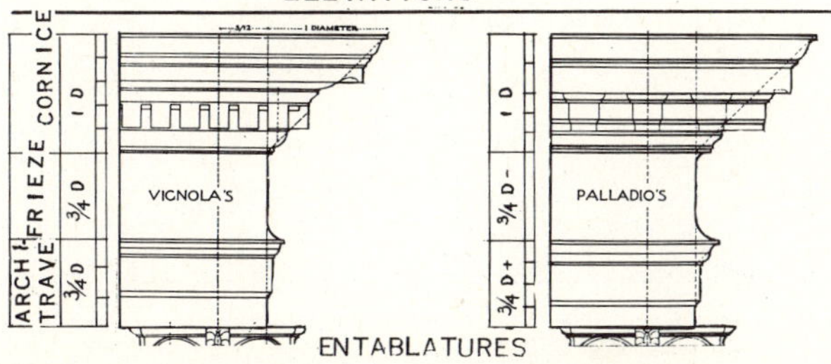
CORNICE 1 D
FRIEZE 3/4 D
ARCHITRAVE 3/4 D
VIGNOLA'S
PALLADIO'S
ENTABLATURES

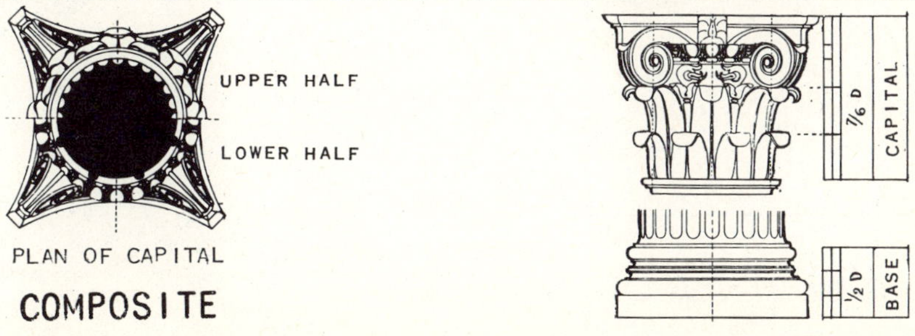
UPPER HALF
LOWER HALF
PLAN OF CAPITAL
CAPITAL 7/6 D
BASE 1/2 D

COMPOSITE

"Reprinted by permission of International Correspondence Schools; illustrations taken from home-study instruction material."

ENTASIS, VOLUTE, RAKE MOULDS and POLYGONS

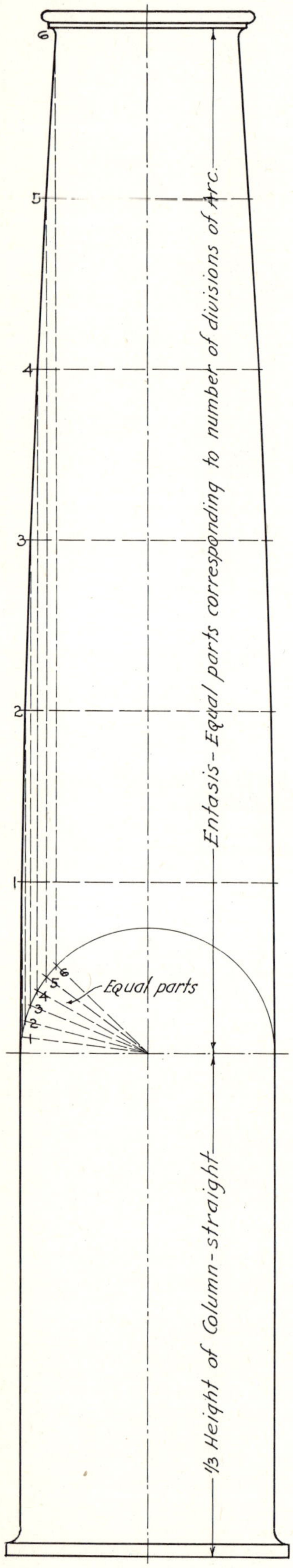

6
5
4
3
2
1
Equal parts
Entasis–Equal parts corresponding to number of divisions of Arc.
1/3 Height of Column–straight

ENTASIS

Divide height into 8 parts and describe circle between 4th and 5th parts as eye of volute; inscribe square in eye as shown; through the center, and parallel to sides of square, draw lines bisecting the latter and divide each line, from center to side of square, into 3 equal parts. These points are the centers of arcs required and are taken in order of succession starting at No.1 shown on enlarged drawing of eye. The limits of each separate arc are obtained by producing the straight line joining two successive central points, starting with Arc No.1

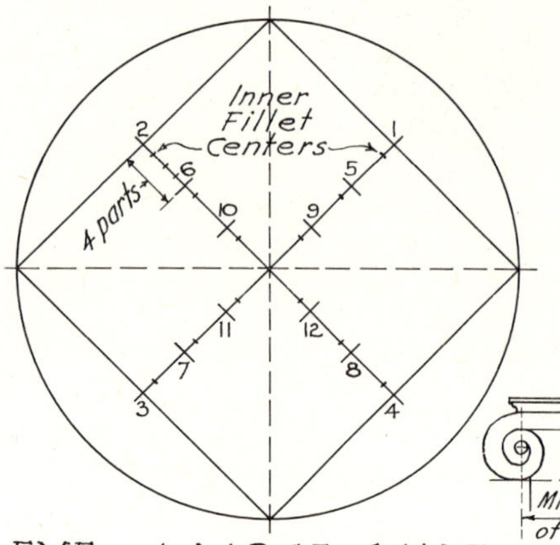

Inner Fillet Centers
4 parts

EYE at LARGE SCALE

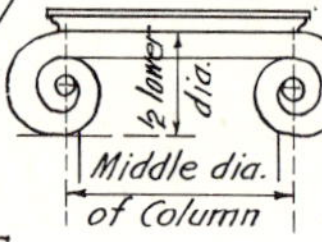

½ lower dia.
Middle dia. of Column

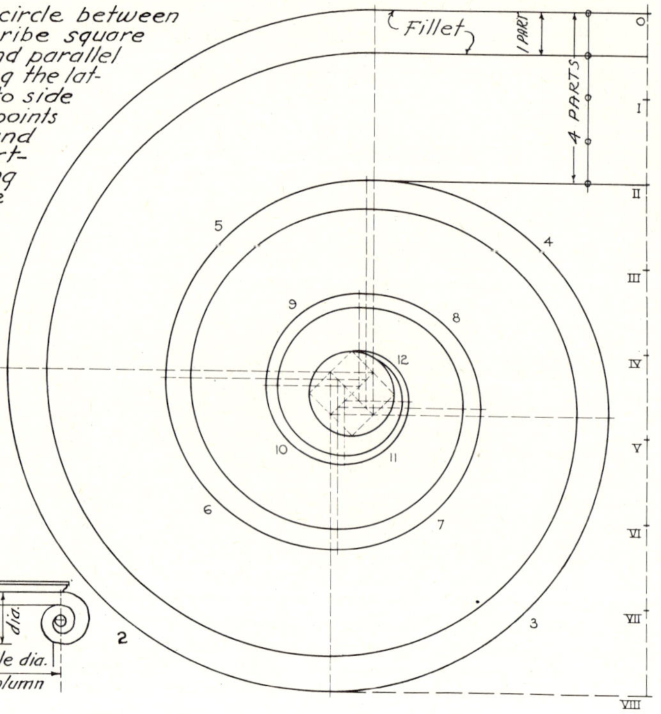

Fillet
1 PART
4 PARTS
I
II
III
IV
V
VI
VII
VIII

METHOD of DRAWING a VOLUTE

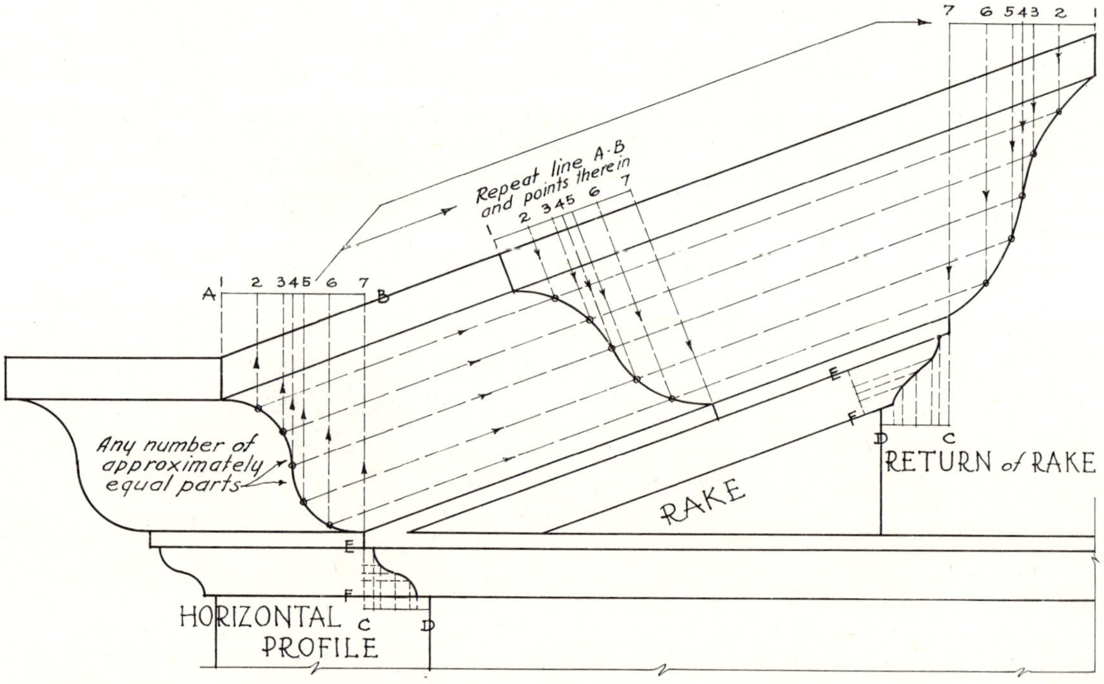

Repeat line A-B and points therein
A
B
Any number of approximately equal parts
RAKE
RETURN of RAKE
HORIZONTAL PROFILE

RAKING MOULDINGS

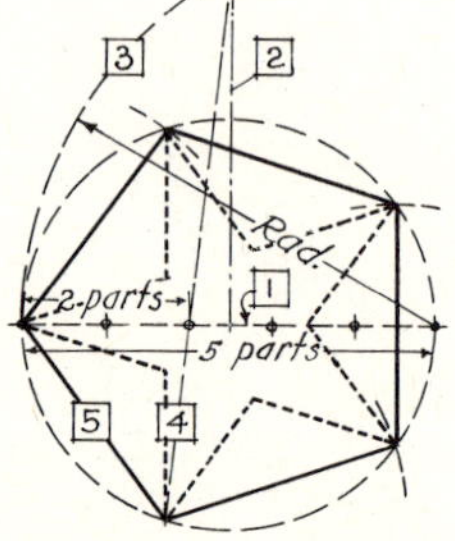

Rad.
2 parts
5 parts

PENTAGON
(in given circle)

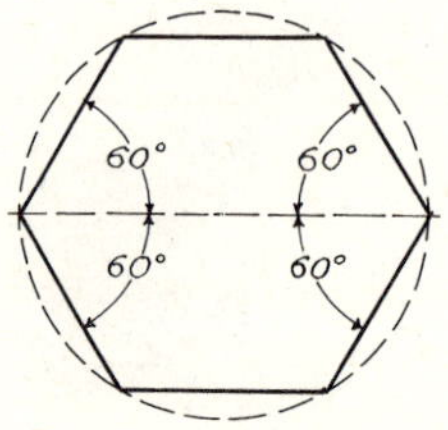

60°

HEXAGON
(in given circle)

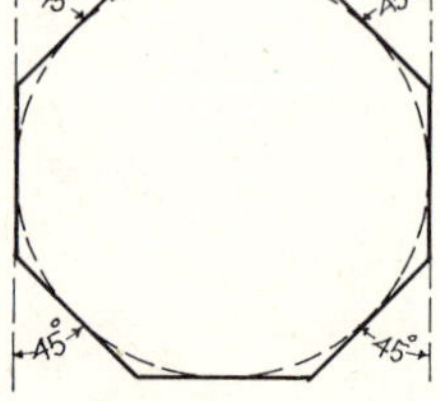

45°

OCTAGON
(around given circle)

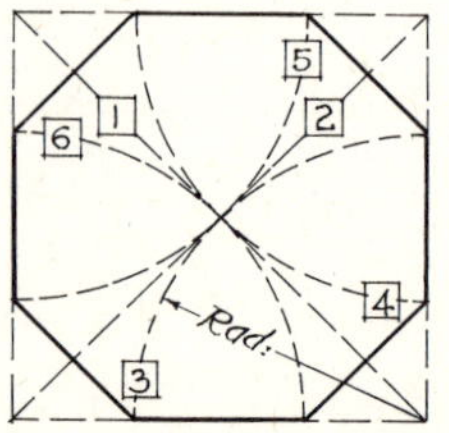

Rad.

OCTAGON
(in given square)

PERSPECTIVE

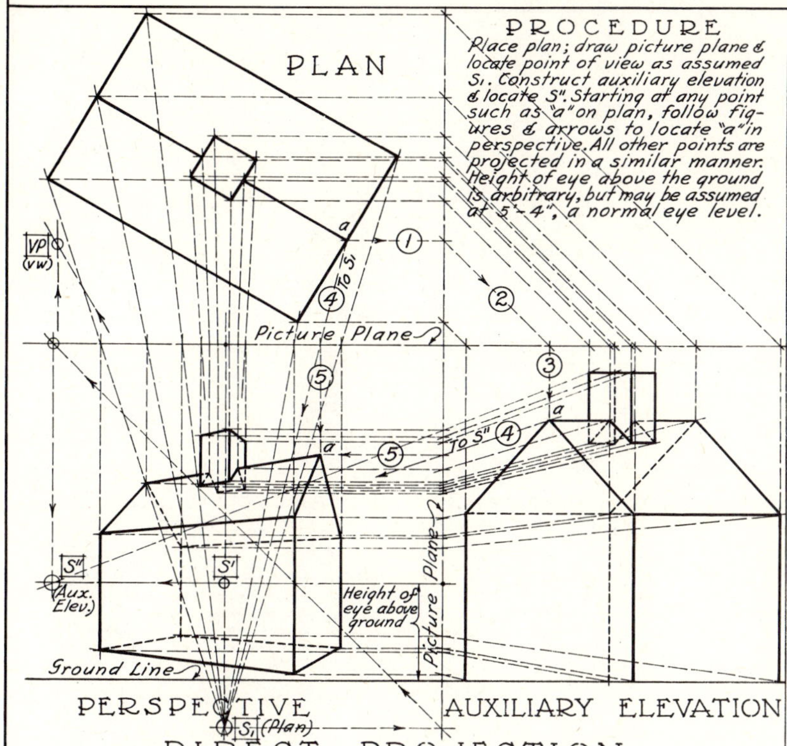
PLAN
Picture Plane
To S₁
To S''
Ground Line
Height of eye above ground
Picture Plane
Aux. Elev.
S₁ (Plan)
PERSPECTIVE
AUXILIARY ELEVATION

PROCEDURE

Place plan; draw picture plane & locate point of view as assumed S_1. Construct auxiliary elevation & locate S''. Starting at any point such as "a" on plan, follow figures & arrows to locate "a" in perspective. All other points are projected in a similar manner. Height of eye above the ground is arbitrary, but may be assumed at 5'-4", a normal eye level.

DIRECT PROJECTION

PROCEDURE

Draw A.B.C.D., section cut by P.P. at any desired scale, and locate S' (point of view in elevation) on line of sight from S_1. Locate the 45° vanishing points V_L & V_R either side of S' and as distant as S_1 is from the picture plane. All lines parallel to P.P. will remain parallel and all plane figures parallel to P.P. will show their true shape. Vertical lines will be vertical in perspective. Horizontal lines parallel to P.P. will be horizontal. Horizontal lines perpendicular to P.P. will vanish at S'. Horizontal lines at 45° to P.P. (used to measure distances ⊥ to P.P.) will vanish at 45° VPs.

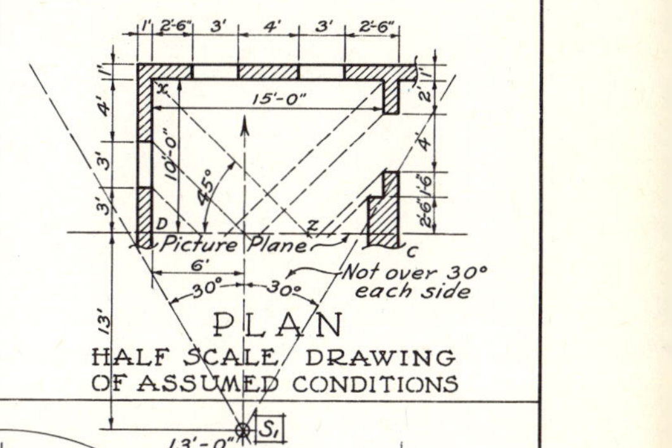
15'-0"
10'-0"
Picture Plane
Not over 30° each side
30°
30°
PLAN
HALF SCALE DRAWING
OF ASSUMED CONDITIONS

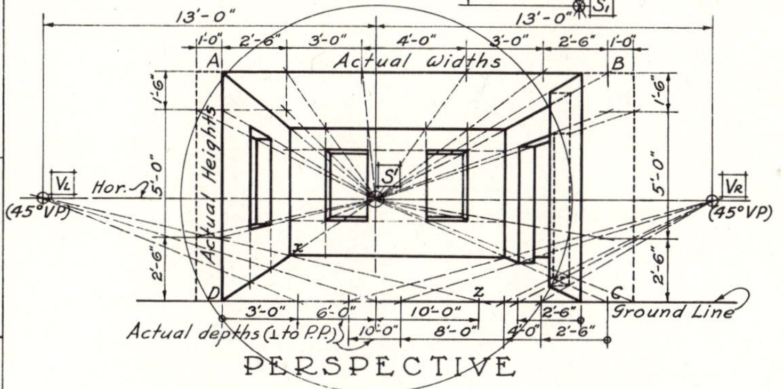
13'-0"
13'-0"
Actual Widths
Actual Heights
Hor.
(45°VP)
(45°VP)
Ground Line
Actual depths (⊥ to P.P.)
PERSPECTIVE

"ONE-POINT" or PARALLEL PERSPECTIVE

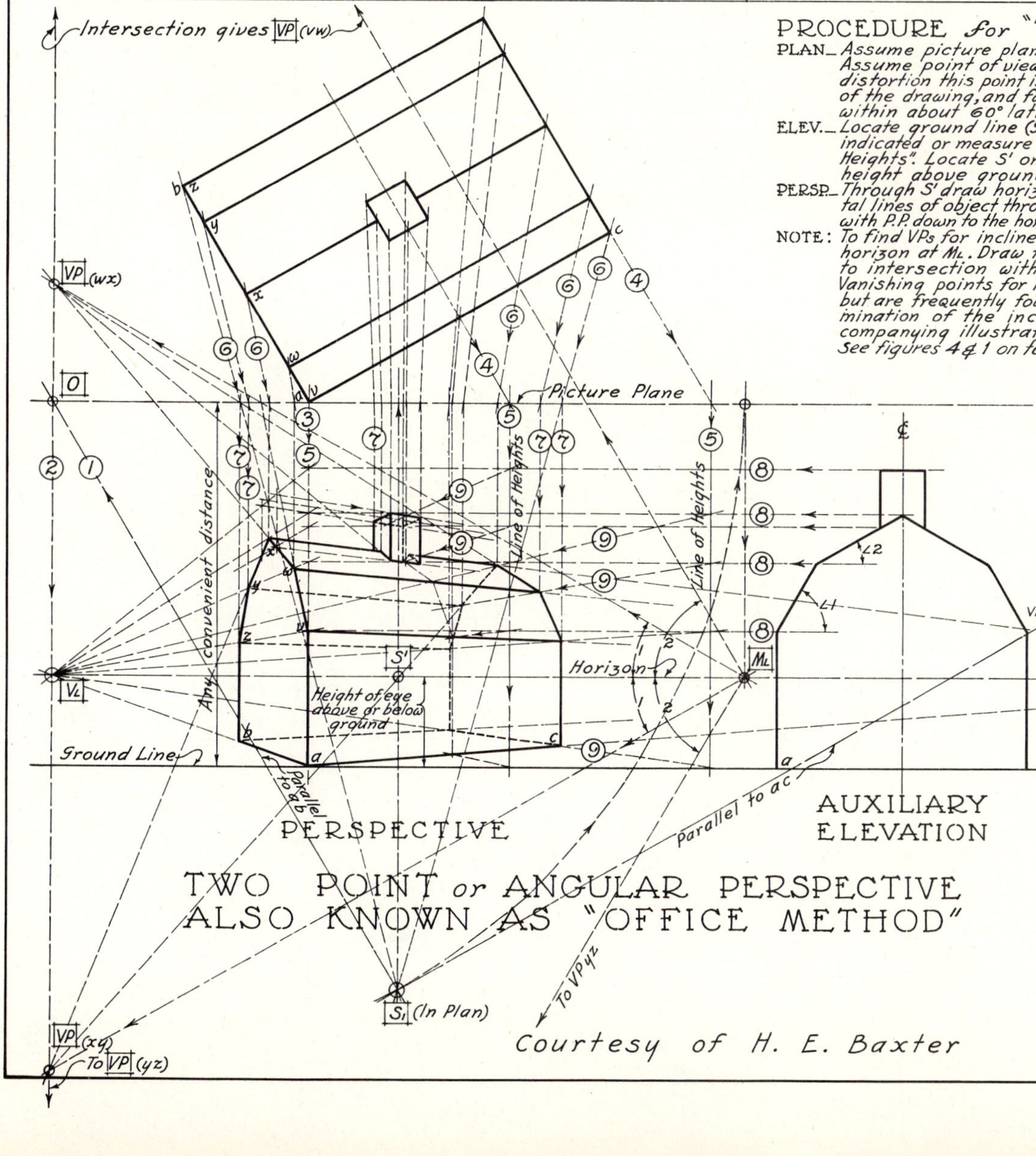
Intersection gives VP (vw)
VP (wx)
Picture Plane
Line of Heights
Line of Heights
Any convenient distance
Horizon
Height of eye above or below ground
Ground Line
Parallel to ab
Parallel to ac
To VP yz
S₁ (In Plan)
VP (xy)
To VP (yz)
AUXILIARY ELEVATION
PERSPECTIVE

PROCEDURE for "TWO POINT" PERSPECTIVE

PLAN_ Assume picture plane (P.P.) and locate plan of object as desired. Assume point of view or station point S_1. To minimize apparent distortion this point is commonly taken about opposite the center of the drawing, and far enough away to keep the field of view within about 60° latitude.

ELEV._ Locate ground line (G.L.) where convenient. Place elevation as indicated or measure heights directly on any vertical "Line of Heights". Locate S' on vertical through S_1 and at assumed height above ground line.

PERSP._ Through S' draw horizon (Hor.). Draw parallels to principal horizontal lines of object through S_1 (in plan), and project intersections with P.P. down to the horizon, giving principal vanishing points V_L & V_R.

NOTE: To find VPs for inclined lines swing S_1 about O into P.P. & project to horizon at M_L. Draw through M_L parallel to actual slopes (∠s 1&2) to intersection with vertically projected line through V_L. Vanishing points for inclined lines are not absolutely essential, but are frequently found very useful as is shown in the determination of the inclined lines of the "Gambrel" roof in the accompanying illustration. Follow arrows and numbered lines. See figures 4 & 1 on following page.

NOTES ON MANIPULATION WHEN VANISHING POINTS ARE OFF BOARD

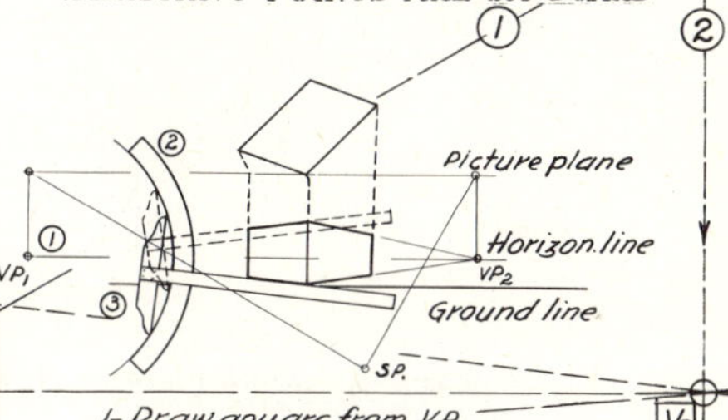
Picture plane
Horizon line
Ground line
VP₁
VP₂
S.P.

1- Draw any arc from V.P.
2- Place a cardboard cut-out against curve of circle
3- Place head of t-square against cut-out, making sure both ends of head are always touching cut-out before drawing lines

NOMENCLATURE for PERSPECTIVES	
S, S_1	Station Point (in plan)
S', S''	Station Point (in elevation)
VP	Vanishing Point
V_L, V_R, V_V	Left, right, & vertical van. points
P.P.	Picture Plane
G.L.	Ground Line
Hor.	Horizon
M_R	Point for plotting distance to right
M_L	Point for plotting distance to left
M_V	Point for plotting heights
$V45°$	45° Vanishing Point

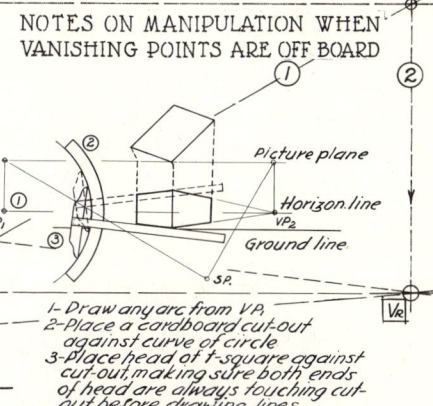

TWO POINT or ANGULAR PERSPECTIVE ALSO KNOWN AS "OFFICE METHOD"

Courtesy of H. E. Baxter

PERSPECTIVE ~ PLAN METHOD

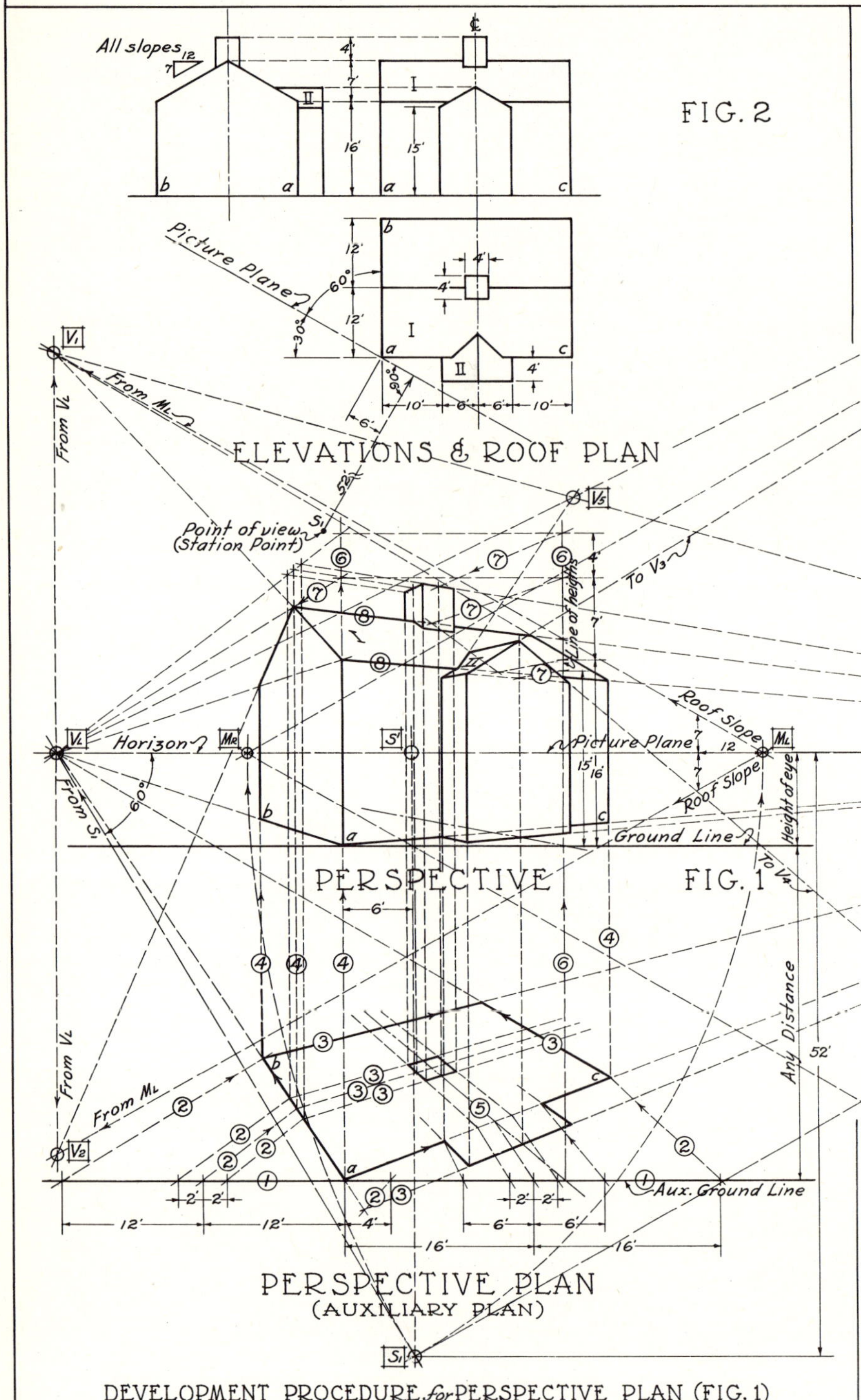
All slopes
12
7
℄
4'
7'
I
II
16'
15'
b
a
a
c
Picture Plane
60°
30°
12'
12'
4'
4'
4'
90°
6'
10'
6'
6'
10'
V1
From VL
From ML
52'
S1
V3
Point of view (Station Point)
To V3
Line of heights
Roof Slope
Roof Slope
VL
Horizon
MR
S1
Picture Plane
ML
12
7
7
15'
16'
Height of eye
60°
From S1
Ground Line
To V4
6'
Any Distance
52'
From VL
From ML
V2
Aux. Ground Line
12'
12'
4'
6'
6'
16'
16'
S1

FIG. 2

ELEVATIONS & ROOF PLAN

PERSPECTIVE

FIG. 1

PERSPECTIVE PLAN
(AUXILIARY PLAN)

FIG. 3

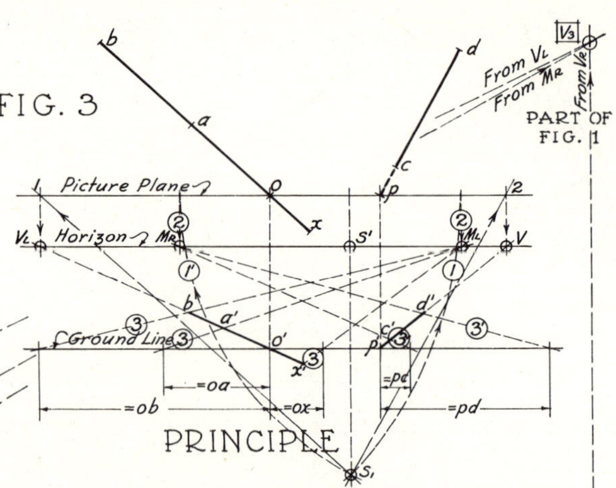
b
a
d
c
Picture Plane
o
p
x
V3
From VL
From MR
From VR
Horizon
MR
S'
ML
V
Ground Line
a'
o'
x'
c'
d'
p'
=oa
=ob
=ox
=pc
=pd
S1

PART OF FIG. 1

PRINCIPLE

MEASUREMENT *of* DISTANCES ON LINES LYING IN GROUND PLANE *and* RECEDING FROM PICTURE PLANE.

Find vanishing point and draw perspective of line as usual, as for x–b above. With point 1 as center, swing S_1 into P.P. and project onto Horizon, locating M_L, the "measuring point" for x–b. From O' measure actual distances along ground, to the left or right, for points behind or in front of picture plane respectively. Draw lines 3 to M_L. Intersections of these "measuring lines" with perspective of line itself will be the perspective of the required points. Procedure for line cd is similar, using its measuring point, M_R. Follow numbers and arrows from 1 to 3 & 1' to 3' consecutively.

From V_L — V_R — 30° — From S_1

NOTE: FIGS. 3 & 4 ARE FOR GENERAL USE, BUT SHOWN ON THIS SHEET IN ORDER TO CLARIFY IMPORTANT STEPS IN THE CONSTRUCTION *of* FIG. 1

FIG. 4

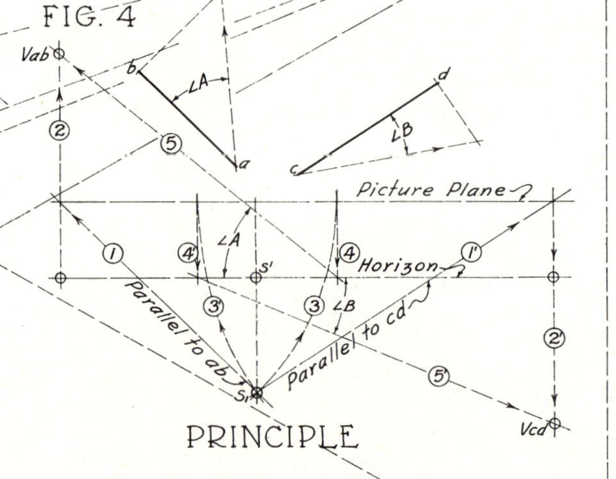
Vab
b
∠A
a
d
∠B
c
Picture Plane
∠A
S'
Horizon
∠B
Parallel to ab
Parallel to cd
S1
Vcd

PRINCIPLE

From V_R — From M_R — V_4

PART OF FIG. 1

DEVELOPMENT PROCEDURE *for* PERSPECTIVE PLAN (FIG. 1)

NOTE: *Small scale elevations and roof plan are used for data only. In order to eliminate waste space and unnecessary drawing, same line is used for both picture plane (plan) and Horizon (perspective) Fig. 1.*

Locate S_1 and draw S_1V_L and S_1V_R at angles made with P.P. by principal horizontal lines of building, thus locating the vanishing points V_L and V_R.

Locate M_L and M_R as shown in Fig. 3 or by laying off the distances $V_L M_L = V_L S_1$ and $V_R M_R = V_R S_1$.

Locate Vanishing points for roof lines V_1, V_2, V_3, V_4 as in Fig. 4.

Draw $V_1 V_2$, the "vanishing trace" of main roof plane I and $V_3 V_4$ correspondingly for secondary roof plane II. The intersection of these lines, V_5, is the vanishing point for the line of intersection of the roof planes (the valley line).

Starting with point a, draw perspectives of ab & ac. Measure the distances along these lines as described in Fig. 3. (The auxiliary or "sunken" plan gives better intersections and keeps the drawing cleaner).

Complete the plan in perspective by carrying lines to proper vanishing points. Verticals are drawn and heights are measured as usual. (See Two Point or Angular Perspective, known as "Office Method.")

Follow numbers and arrows consecutively from 1 to 8 inclusive.

VANISHING POINTS *of* SLOPING LINES

NOTE:

It is frequently very useful to have available the vanishing point for a series of inclined parallel lines; the diagram above shows a procedure for directly locating any such points.

Two cases are illustrated.

The line ab slopes upward from a to b at the angle "A". Starting at S_1, follow arrows & numbers 1 to 5 inclusive locating Vab, which is the vanishing point for ab & all the lines parallel to it.

Line cd slopes downward from c to d at the angle "B". Proceed as above, using numbers 1' to 5' inclusive. Vcd is the required vanishing point. Note that line 5 is drawn upward while 5' is downward.

Courtesy of H. E. Baxter

PERSPECTIVE ~ THREE POINT

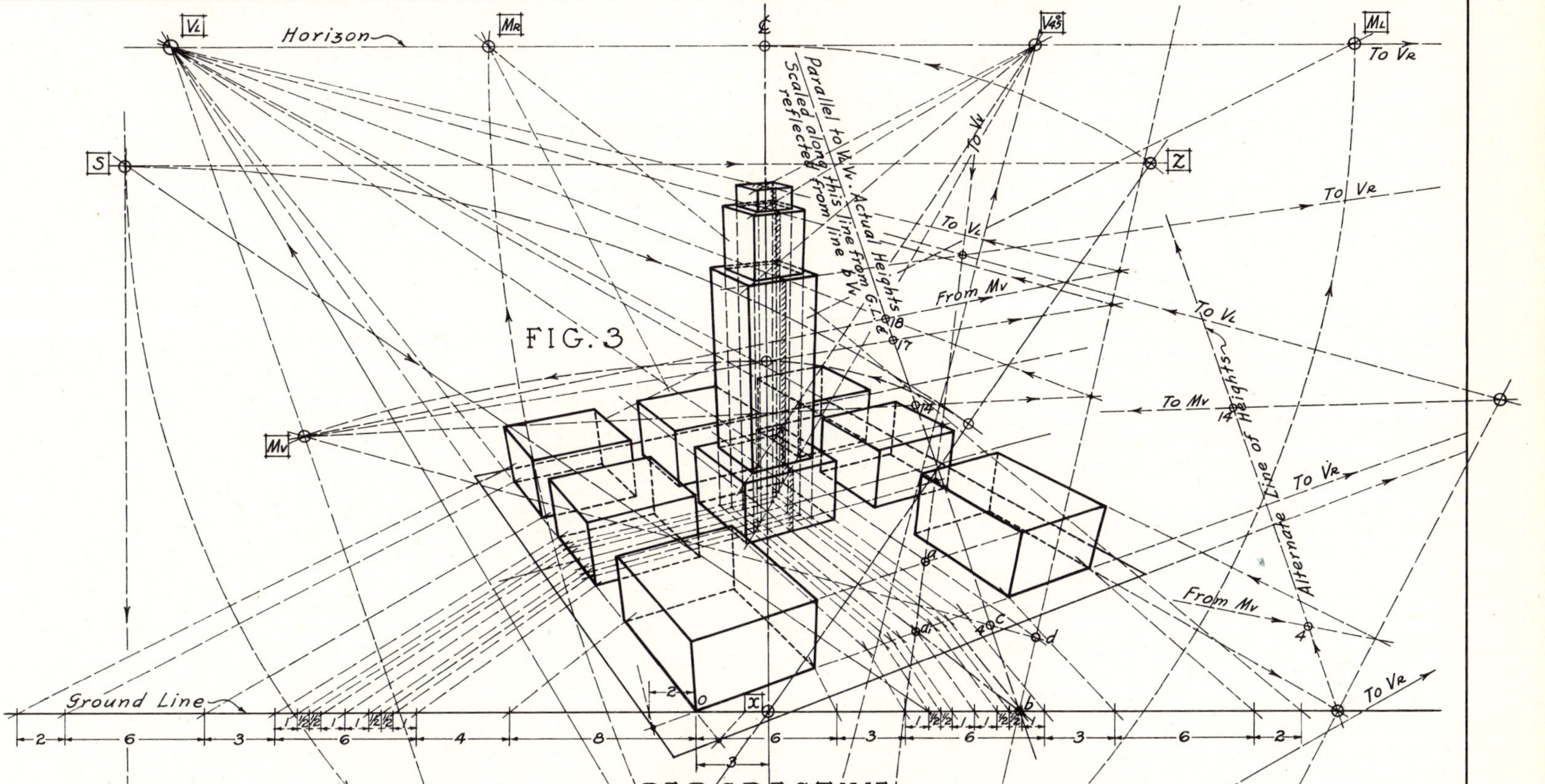

VL
MR
℄
V45°
ML
Horizon
To VR
S
Z
Parallel to VL VV Actual Heights
Scaled along this line from G.L.
reflected from line b VL
To VV
To VR
To VL
From MV
18
17
To VL
To MV
14
Line of Heights
Alternate
MV
To VR
From MV
4
c
d
a1
a
Ground Line
x
b
To VR
2
6
3
4
8
6
3
6
3
6
2
1
1/2

FIG. 3

PERSPECTIVE

DEVELOPMENT PROCEDURE *for* ILLUSTRATION ABOVE

Assume ground line and center line where convenient. Locate V_V & M_V as shown in Fig. 2. Horizontal lines and measurements, and hence the plan, are handled exactly as in the "Perspective Plan" method. Vertical lines pass through the corresponding points in plan and converge at V_V. To get any point such as "a" in perspective, draw through "a_1" (plan of "a") to V_L and continue to intersection with ground line at "b". Through "b" draw one line, (bc) parallel to $V_L V_V$ and another through V_V ($b V_V$). Scale off actual heights above (or below) ground along bc. Draw cM_V to "d" and draw dV_L. Where dV_L intersects $V_V a_1$ is the perspective point of "a".

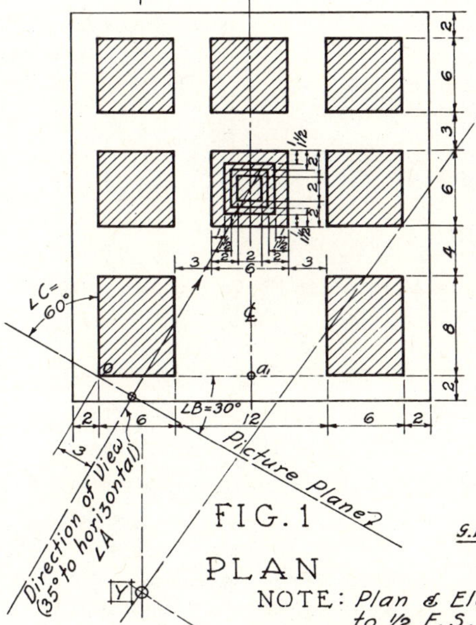

∠C = 60°
∠B = 30°
℄
a1
b
Picture Plane
Direction of View (35° to horizontal) ∠A
Y
2
6
3
6
4
8
2
12

FIG. 1

PLAN

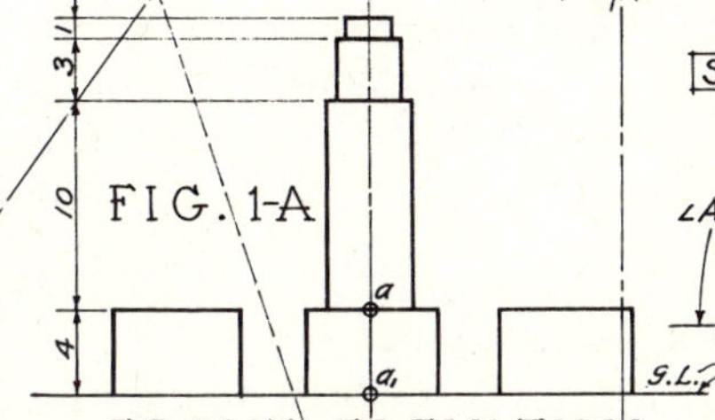

a
a1
G.L.
3
10
4

FIG. 1-A

FRONT ELEVATION

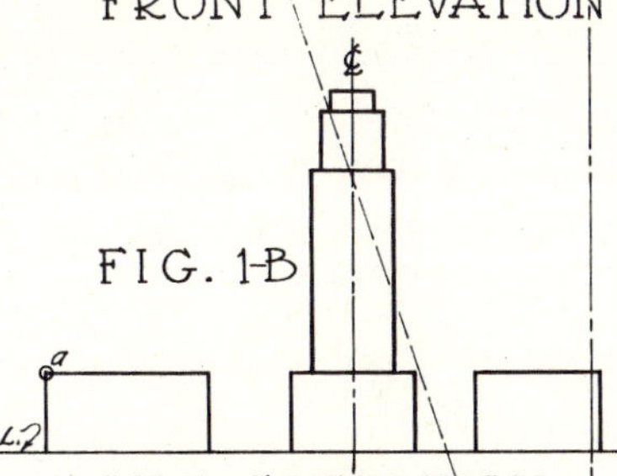

℄
a
G.L.

FIG. 1-B

SIDE ELEVATION

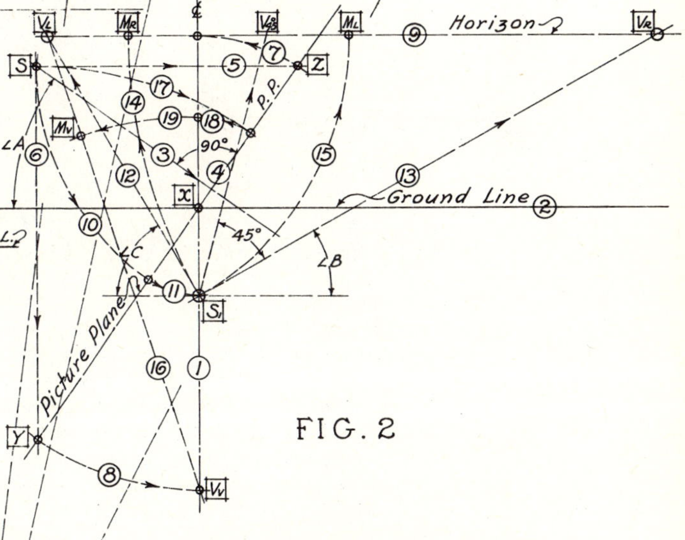

S1
VL
MR
℄
V45°
ML
VR
Horizon
S
Z
P.P.
MV
90°
∠A
x
Ground Line
45°
∠C
∠B
Picture Plane
Y
VV

FIG. 2

DEVELOPMENT PROCEDURE

Small Scale layout diagram showing method (1/4 F.S.)

NOTE: *Plan & Elevations are drawn to 1/2 F.S. Used for data only.*

DEVELOPMENT PROCEDURE NOTES *for* EVOLUTION *of* PERSPECTIVE

(Note: See Fig. 2 above). Draw center line (1) and ground line (2) at will. Using these as vertical and horizontal planes as seen in profile, assume station point [S] as desired. Draw line of sight (3) from [S] toward "center of interest" of the object, and through [X] draw P.P. (4) at right angle to (3). Follow arrows and numbers through (9). Swing [S] about [Z] into P.P. & then about [X] into ℄ locating [S_1]. Draw (12) and (13) through [S_1] at angles plan makes with ground line (∠s B and C), locate V_L and V_R, and from these find M_L and M_R. Draw V_L and V_V and on it locate M_V, by following numbers or by making $V_V M_V = SY$.

Courtesy of H. E. Baxter

BUILDING AREA CALCULATION

SUGGESTED STANDARDS FOR AREA CALCULATIONS

To calculate floor areas, include the full square foot area of spaces on all floors enclosed within the face of exterior wall surfaces of the building with the addition of dormers, bays and chimneys.

INCLUDE THE FOLLOWING AREAS PARTIALLY

Garage	2/3 of area	
Carport	1/2 of area	
Unenclosed porch	1/2 of area	
Enclosed porch	2/3 of area	
Unfinished basement	1/2 of area	(finished basement, full area)
Covered walkways	1/3 of area	
Open area under building	1/3 of area	(building on stilts).
Overhangs	1/4 of area	
Two story living room	1-1/4 of area	
Penthouse	1/2 of area	

EXCLUDE THE FOLLOWING:

Unfinished attics (finished attics are included where headroom is 5'-0" or over), crawl spaces and terraces.

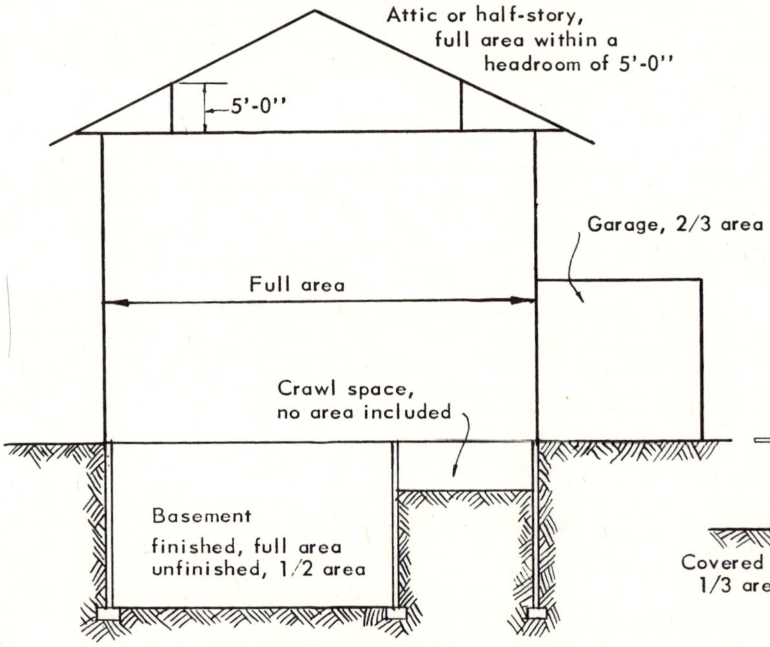
Attic or half-story, full area within a headroom of 5'-0"
5'-0"
Garage, 2/3 area
Full area
Crawl space, no area included
Basement
finished, full area
unfinished, 1/2 area

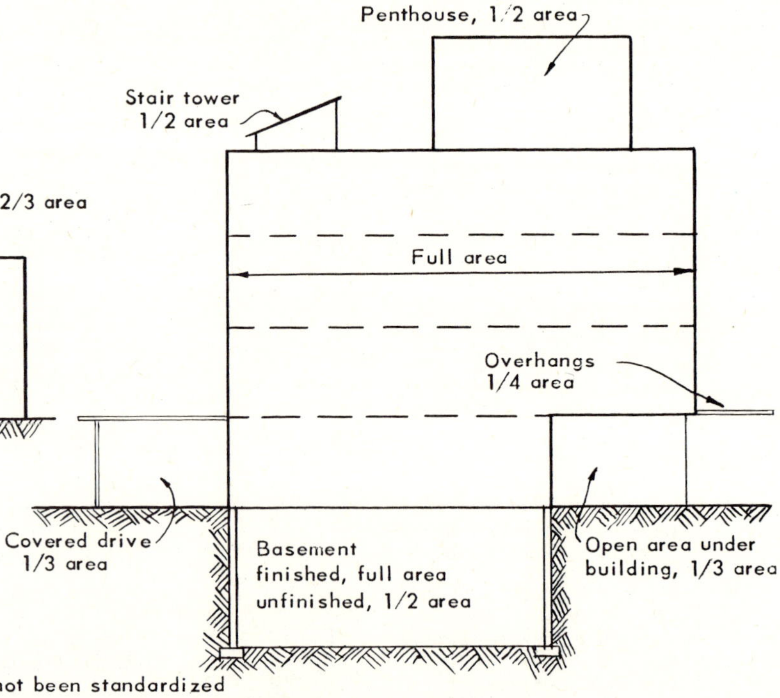
Penthouse, 1/2 area
Stair tower 1/2 area
Full area
Overhangs 1/4 area
Covered drive 1/3 area
Basement
finished, full area
unfinished, 1/2 area
Open area under building, 1/3 area

The above has not been standardized

STANDARD OF THE FEDERAL HOUSING ADMINISTRATION

Include areas of floors above basement, measured from outside surfaces of exterior walls; include bays, dormers, utility rooms, vestibules, hall & closets.

Do not include garage or finished attic spaces.

In a half story measure from outside surfaces of exterior walls or partitions enclosing the areas, except do not include areas where ceiling height is less than 5'-0".

Do not deduct for stairwells, interior light shafts, chimneys, fireplaces, thickness of partitions, or thickness of enclosing walls.

Porches, attached terraces, balconies and projecting fireplaces or chimneys, outside the exterior walls, are not included.

DEFINITIONS:

Half story: If finished as living area, must be 50% or greater than 50% of the calculated area of floor below.

Full story: Completely finished for living area, enclosed by exterior walls with a ceiling height 5'-0" min. at exterior walls.

Attic: Unfinished or partially finished as living area when the calculated area is less than 50% of floor below.

BUILDING CUBE

The definition of Standard Cubic Contents requires the cube of dormers, pent houses, vaults, pits, enclosed porches, and other enclosed appendages to be included as a part of the cube of building. It does not include the cube of courts or light shafts, open at the top, or the cube of outside steps, cornices, parapets, or open porches or loggias.

The following items shall be listed separately:
(a) Cube of enclosed courts or light shafts, open at top, measured from outside face of enclosing walls and from six inches below the finished floor or paving to top of enclosing walls.
(b) Cube of open porches measured from outside face of wall, outside face of columns, finished floor, and finished roof.
It is recommended that the following items also be listed separately:
(a) Square foot area of all stoops, balconies, and terraces.
(b) Memoranda, or brief description of caissons, piling, special foundations or features, if any.

The above is similar to the A.I.A. Documen. #239-1953.

CUBAGE *includes the following volumes taken in full:*
Bays, oriels, dormers, chimneys, pent house, tanks, vaults, pits, trenches (if of masonry), enclosed porches in full, and the cubic content of the actual space enclosed within the outer surfaces of the outside walls and contained between the outside of roof and bottom of basement floor slab.
This includes the following volumes in part:
a. Non-enclosed porches:- If built within house proper and having no screens or sash ________ 2/3 volume
If built as extension to house and having no screens or sash ________ 1/2 volume
If built as extension to house and having screens and sash ________ Full volume
b. Areaways: ________ 1/2 Volume
The cubage does not include the following volumes: Outside steps, terraces, light shafts, cornices, parapets, footings, piles, caissons, deep foundations, exterior garden walls; Special foundations, etc., should be allowed for in $

CUBIC FOOT COST *equals net cost ÷ the above total cubage.*

NET COST *includes the following according to usual practice:*
Building construction, mechanical trades, hardware, lighting fixtures, elevators, sprinklers, signal systems.
The following items are usually excluded from net costs:-
Furnishings, and equipment such as ranges, laundry and kitchen equipment, clocks, organs, lockers, files, hangings, shades, awnings, Venetian blinds, furniture not built in. Also roads, walks, exterior walls, terraces, steps, landscape work, sewage disposal system, power plant, wells, water supply, services to building, etc. Also Architect's and Engineer's fee.

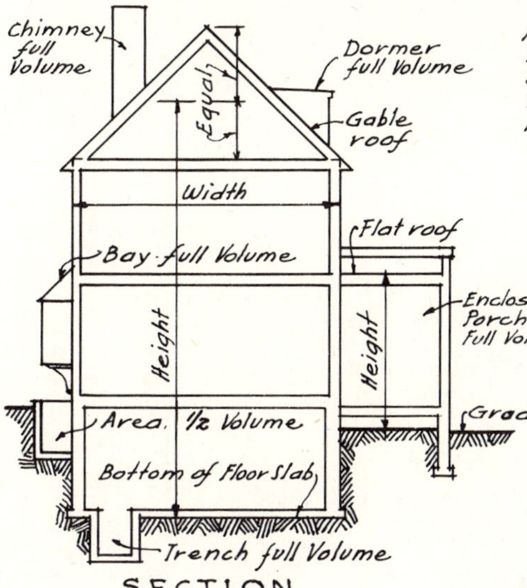
Chimney full Volume
Dormer full Volume
Equal
Gable roof
Width
Flat roof
Bay full Volume
Height
Height
Enclosed Porch Full Volume
Grade
Area. 1/2 Volume
Bottom of Floor Slab
Trench full Volume

SECTION

Note: For high bldgs. with set backs take cube by horizontal planes.

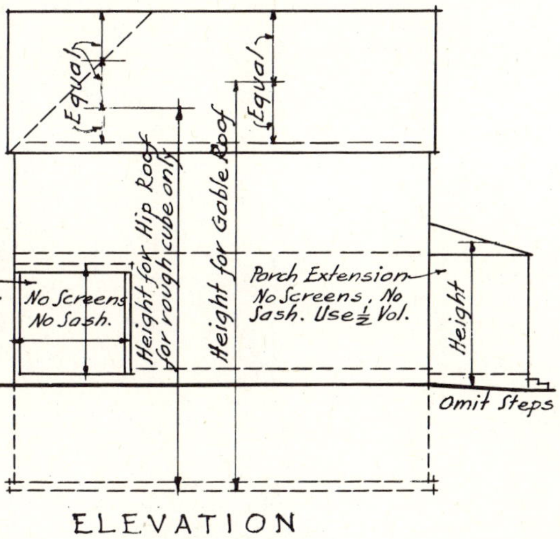
Equal
Equal
Height for Hip Roof for rough cube only
Height for Gable Roof
Open Porch Within House Use 2/3 Vol.
No Screens No Sash.
Porch Extension No Screens, No Sash. Use 1/2 Vol.
Height
Omit Steps

ELEVATION

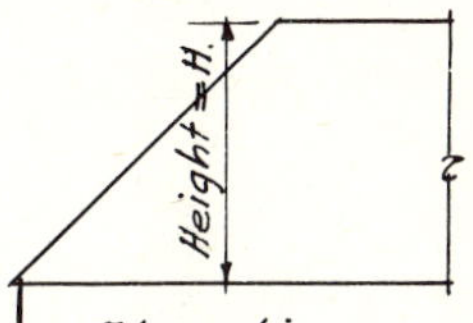
Height = H.

Elevation

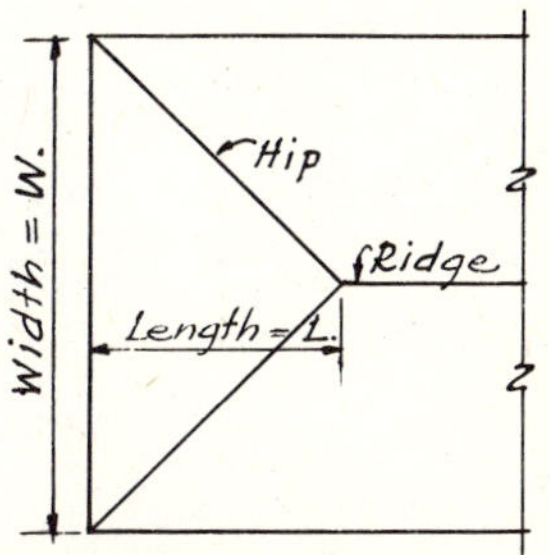
Hip
Ridge
Length = L.
Width = W.

Plan of Roof

Deduct from cube for gable roof:
for 1 Hip End $- \frac{1}{6} \times W \times L \times H$.
for 2 Hip Ends $- \frac{1}{3} \times W \times L \times H$.

CUBE DEDUCTIONS FOR HIP ROOFS

Note:- Add to usual cube the volume for connecting roofs.
$Vol. = \frac{1}{6}\ W \times L \times H$
See diagrams at right →

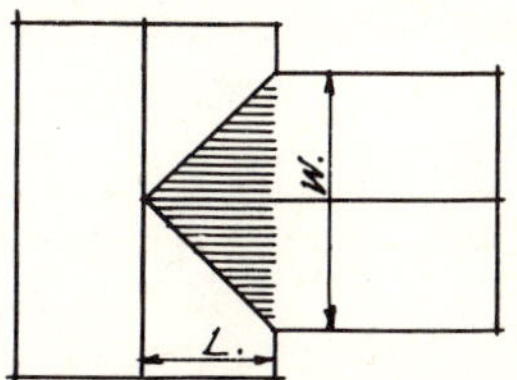
W.
L.

ROOF PLAN

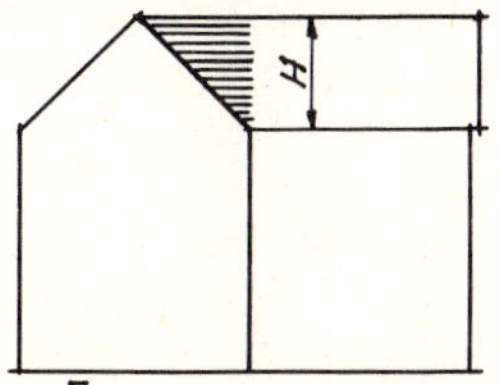
H

ELEVATION

Unit	Length	Width	Height	Area	Factor	Cube	@¢ per CU. FT.	Cost $	Total Cost	(Diagram here):
A	20	16	32	320		10,240	1.00	10,240		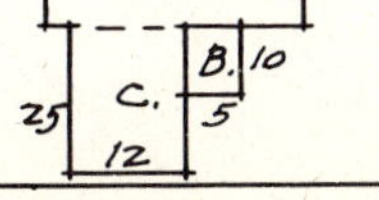 20 A. 16 B. 10 C. 5 25 12
B	10	5	10	50	1/2	250	1.00	250		
C	25	12	30	300		9,000	1.00	9,000		
									$19,490	

AREA & CUBE NOMOGRAPH

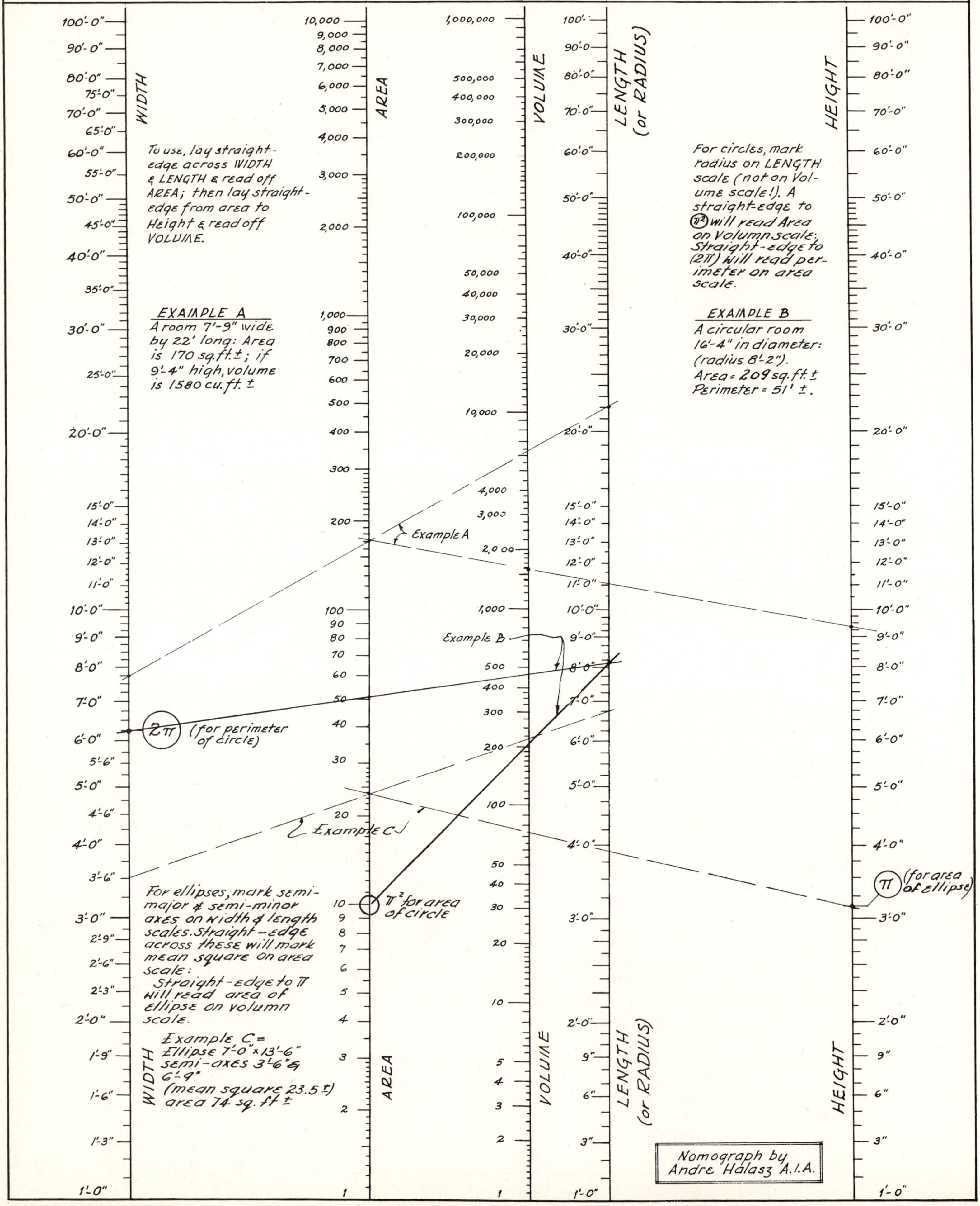
WIDTH
AREA
VOLUME
LENGTH (or RADIUS)
HEIGHT
To use, lay straight-edge across WIDTH & LENGTH & read off AREA; then lay straight-edge from area to Height & read off VOLUME.
EXAMPLE A
A room 7'-9" wide by 22' long: Area is 170 sq.ft.±; if 9'-4" high, volume is 1580 cu.ft.±
For circles, mark radius on LENGTH scale (not on Volume scale!). A straight-edge to (π²) will read Area on Volumn scale; Straight-edge to (2π) will read perimeter on area scale.
EXAMPLE B
A circular room 16'-4" in diameter: (radius 8'-2").
Area = 209 sq.ft.±
Perimeter = 51' ±.
Example A
Example B
Example C
2π (for perimeter of circle)
π² for area of circle
π (for area of ellipse)
For ellipses, mark semi-major & semi-minor axes on width & length scales. Straight-edge across these will mark mean square on area scale:
Straight-edge to π will read area of ellipse on volumn scale.
Example C = Ellipse 7'-0" x 13'-6" semi-axes 3'-6" & 6'-9" (mean square 23.5±) area 74 sq. ft ±
Nomograph by Andre Halasz A.I.A.

DECIMAL EQUIVALENTS

DECIMALS OF A FOOT						DECIMALS OF AN INCH	
FRACTION	DECIMAL	FRACTION	DECIMAL	FRACTION	DECIMAL	FRACTION	DECIMAL
1/16	0.0052	4-1/16	0.3385	8-1/16	0.6719	1/64	0.015625
1/8	0.0104	4-1/8	0.3438	8-1/8	0.6771	1/32	0.03125
3/16	0.0156	4-3/16	0.3490	8-3/16	0.6823	3/64	0.046875
1/4	0.0208	4-1/4	0.3542	8-1/4	0.6875	1/16	0.0625
5/16	0.0260	4-5/16	0.3594	8-5/16	0.6927	5/64	0.078125
3/8	0.0313	4-3/8	0.3646	8-3/8	0.6979	3/32	0.09375
7/16	0.0365	4-7/16	0.3698	8-7/16	0.7031	7/64	0.109375
1/2	0.0417	4-1/2	0.3750	8-1/2	0.7083	1/8	0.125
9/16	0.0469	4-9/16	0.3802	8-9/16	0.7135	9/64	0.140625
5/8	0.0521	4-5/8	0.3854	8-5/8	0.7188	5/32	0.15625
11/16	0.0573	4-11/16	0.3906	8-11/16	0.7240	11/64	0.171875
3/4	0.0625	4-3/4	0.3958	8-3/4	0.7292	3/16	0.1875
13/16	0.0677	4-13/16	0.4010	8-13/16	0.7344	13/64	0.203125
7/8	0.0729	4-7/8	0.4063	8-7/8	0.7396	7/32	0.21875
15/16	0.0781	4-15/16	0.4115	8-1/16	0.7448	15/64	0.234375
1-	0.0833	5-	0.4167	9-	0.7500	1/4	0.250
1-1/16	0.0885	5-1/16	0.4219	9-1/16	0.7552	17/64	0.265625
1-1/8	0.0938	5-1/8	0.4271	9-1/8	0.7604	9/32	0.28125
1-3/16	0.0990	5-3/16	0.4323	9-3/16	0.7656	19/64	0.296875
1-1/4	0.1042	5-1/4	0.4375	9-1/4	0.7708	5/16	0.3125
1-5/16	0.1094	5-5/16	0.4427	9-5/16	0.7760	21/64	0.328125
1-3/8	0.1146	5-3/8	0.4479	9-3/8	0.7813	11/32	0.34375
1-7/16	0.1198	5-7/16	0.4531	9-7/16	0.7865	23/64	0.359375
1-1/2	0.1250	5-1/2	0.4583	9-1/2	0.7917	3/8	0.375
1-9/16	0.1302	5-9/16	0.4635	9-9/16	0.7969	25/64	0.390625
1-5/8	0.1354	5-5/8	0.4688	9-5/8	0.8021	13/32	0.40625
1-11/16	0.1406	5-11/16	0.4740	9-11/16	0.8073	27/64	0.421875
1-3/4	0.1458	5-3/4	0.4792	9-3/4	0.8125	7/16	0.4375
1-13/16	0.1510	5-13/16	0.4844	9-13/16	0.8177	29/64	0.453125
1-7/8	0.1563	5-7/8	0.4896	9-7/8	0.8229	15/32	0.46875
1-15/16	0.1615	5-15/16	0.4948	9-15/16	0.8281	31/64	0.484375
2-	0.1667	6-	0.5000	10-	0.8333	1/2	0.500
2-1/16	0.1719	6-1/16	0.5052	10-1/16	0.8385	33/64	0.515625
2-1/8	0.1771	6-1/8	0.5104	10-1/8	0.8438	17/32	0.53125
2-3/16	0.1823	6-3/16	0.5156	10-3/16	0.8490	35/64	0.546875
2-1/4	0.1875	6-1/4	0.5208	10-1/4	0.8542	9/16	0.5625
2-5/16	0.1927	6-5/16	0.5260	10-5/16	0.8594	37/64	0.578125
2-3/8	0.1979	6-3/8	0.5313	10-3/8	0.8646	19/32	0.59375
2-7/16	0.2031	6-7/16	0.5365	10-7/16	0.8698	39/64	0.609375
2-1/2	0.2083	6-1/2	0.5417	10-1/2	0.8750	5/8	0.625
2-9/16	0.2135	6-9/16	0.5469	10-9/16	0.8802	41/64	0.640625
2-5/8	0.2188	6-5/8	0.5521	10-5/8	0.8854	21/32	0.65625
2-11/16	0.2240	6-11/16	0.5573	10-11/16	0.8906	43/64	0.671875
2-3/4	0.2292	6-3/4	0.5625	10-3/4	0.8958	11/16	0.6875
2-13/16	0.2344	6-13/16	0.5677	10-13/16	0.9010	45/64	0.703125
2-7/8	0.2396	6-7/8	0.5729	10-7/8	0.9063	23/32	0.71875
2-15/16	0.2448	6-15/16	0.5781	10-15/16	0.9115	47/64	0.734375
3-	0.2500	7-	0.5833	11-	0.9167	3/4	0.750
3-1/16	0.2552	7-1/16	0.5885	11-1/16	0.9219	49/64	0.765625
3-1/8	0.2604	7-1/8	0.5938	11-1/8	0.9271	25/32	0.78125
3-3/16	0.2656	7-3/16	0.5990	11-3/16	0.9323	51/64	0.796875
3-1/4	0.2708	7-1/4	0.6042	11-1/4	0.9375	13/16	0.8125
3-5/16	0.2760	7-5/16	0.6094	11-5/16	0.9427	53/64	0.828125
3-3/8	0.2813	7-3/8	0.6146	11-3/8	0.9479	27/32	0.84375
3-7/16	0.2865	7-7/16	0.6198	11-7/16	0.9531	55/64	0.859375
3-1/2	0.2917	7-1/2	0.6250	11-1/2	0.9583	7/8	0.875
3-9/16	0.2969	7-9/16	0.6302	11-9/16	0.9635	57/64	0.890625
3-5/8	0.3021	7-5/8	0.6354	11-5/8	0.9688	29/32	0.90625
3-11/16	0.3073	7-11/16	0.6406	11-11/16	0.9740	59/64	0.921875
3-3/4	0.3125	7-3/4	0.6458	11-3/4	0.9792	15/16	0.9375
3-13/16	0.3177	7-13/16	0.6510	11-13/16	0.9844	61/64	0.953125
3-7/8	0.3229	7-7/8	0.6563	11-7/8	0.9896	31/32	0.96875
3-15/16	0.3281	7-15/16	0.6615	11-15/16	0.9948	63/64	0.984375
4-	0.3333	8-	0.6667	12-	1.0000	1"	1.000

Reprinted from "Wood Structural Design Data," Vol. 1, courtesy of the National Lumber Manufacturers Assoc.

MATHEMATICS: AREAS, VOLUMES, SURFACES

AREAS of PLANE FIGURES

FORM	NAME	AREA	FORM	NAME	AREA (Note: $\pi = 3.1416$)
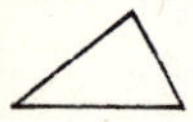	TRIANGLE	Either side × 1/2 altitude (Altitude perpendicular distance to opposite vertex or corner)	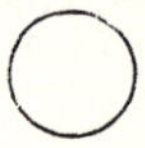	CIRCLE	πr^2 $0.7854 \times \text{diam.}^2$ $0.0796 \times \text{circumference}^2$
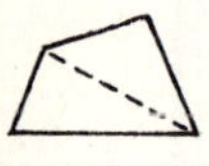	TRAPEZIUM (irregular quadrilateral)	Divide by a diagonal into two triangles and proceed as above	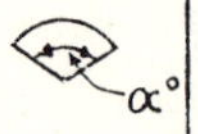	SECTOR of circle	$\frac{\alpha^\circ}{360^\circ} \times \pi r^2$ Or: Length of arc × 1/2 radius
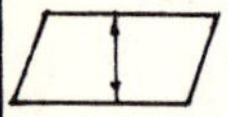	PARALLELOGRAM	Either side × altitude (Altitude = perpendicular distance to opposite side)	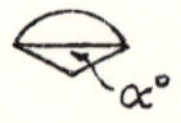	SEGMENT of circle	$\frac{r^2}{2}\left(\frac{\alpha^\circ}{180^\circ} - \sin\alpha\right)$ Or: Subtract triangle from sector
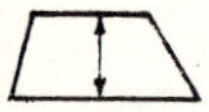	TRAPEZOID	1/2 sum of parallel sides × altitude. In European nomenclature a trapezoid is called a Trapezium.	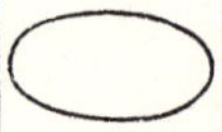	ELLIPSE	Major axis × minor axis × 0.7854
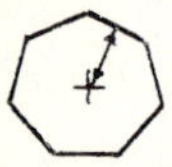	REGULAR POLYGON	1/2 sum of all sides × inside radius	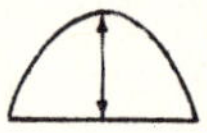	PARABOLA	Base × 2/3 altitude

VOLUMES of TYPICAL SOLIDS

ANY PRISM OR CYLINDER RIGHT OR OBLIQUE REGULAR OR NOT

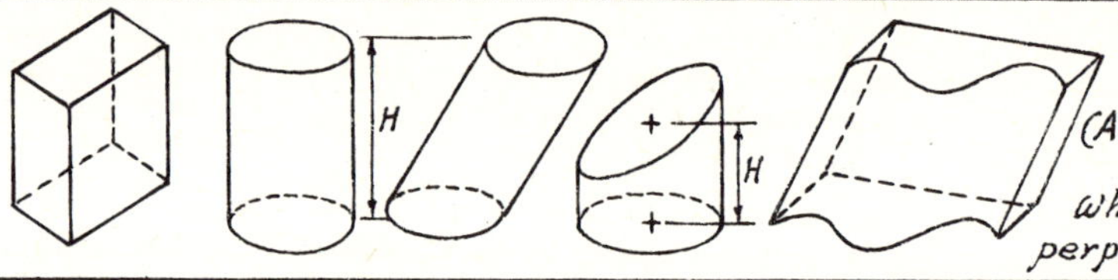

H
H

VOLUME = AREA of BASE × ALTITUDE (Altitude = distance between parallel bases, measured perpendicular to the bases. When bases are not parallel: Altitude = perp. distance from one base to center of other).

ANY PYRAMID OR CONE RIGHT OR OBLIQUE REGULAR OR NOT

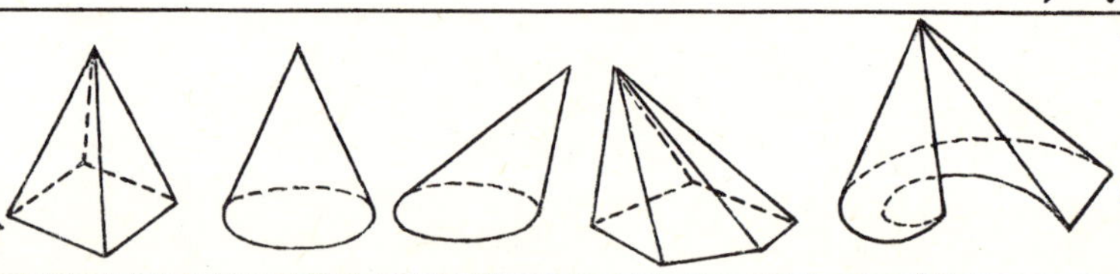

VOLUME = AREA of BASE × 1/3 ALTITUDE (Altitude = distance from base to apex, measured perpendicular to base).

ANY FRUSTUM OR TRUNCATED PORTION OF THE ABOVE SOLIDS

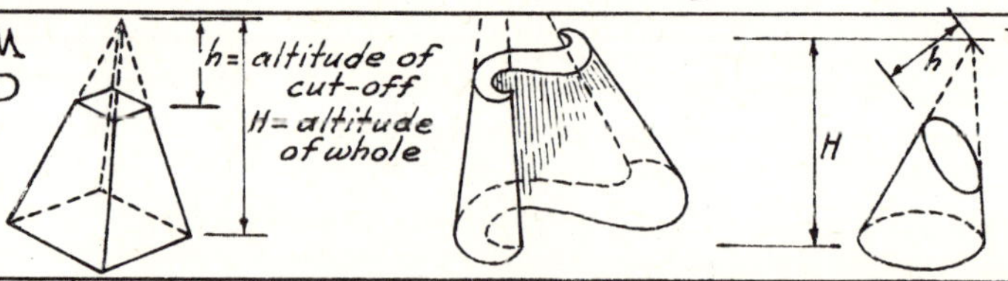

h = altitude of cut-off
H = altitude of whole
H
h

VOLUME = From the volume of the whole solid if complete, subtract the volume of the portion cut off. Note: The altitude of the cut-off part must be measured perpendicular to its own base.

SURFACES OF THE ABOVE SOLIDS

The area of the surface is best found by adding together the areas of all the faces. The area of a right cylindrical surface = perimeter of base × length of elements (average length if other base is oblique). The area of a right conical surface = perimeter of base × 1/2 length of elements. There is no simple rule for the area of an oblique conical surface, or for a cylindrical one where neither base is perpendicular to the elements. Best method is to construct a development, as if for making a paper model, and measure its area by method given on next page.

VOLUMES and SURFACES of DOUBLE-CURVED SOLIDS

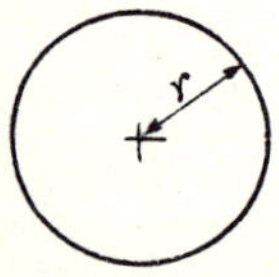

r

SPHERE

VOLUME = $\frac{4}{3}\pi r^3 = 0.5236\, d^3$

SURFACE = $4\pi r^2 = 3.14159265\, d^2$

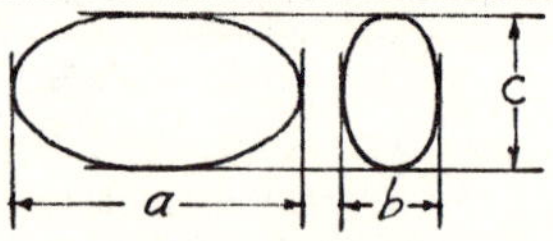

c
a
b

ELLIPSOID

VOLUME = $\frac{1}{6}\pi abc$

No simple rule for the surface.

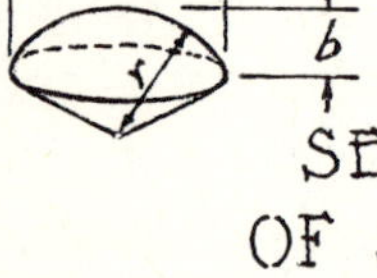

c
b
r

SECTOR OF SPHERE

VOLUME = $\frac{2}{3}\pi r^2 b$

SURFACE = $\frac{1}{2}\pi r(4b + c)$ (or: Segment + Cone).

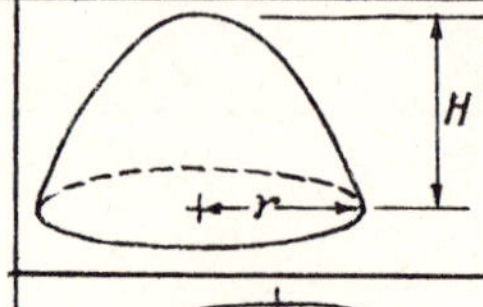

H
r

PARABOLOID of REVOLUTION

VOLUME = Area of circular base × 1/2 altitude

No simple rule for the surface

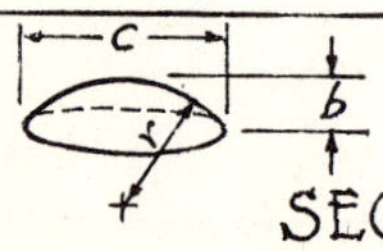

c
b
r

SEGMENT OF SPHERE

VOLUME = $\frac{1}{3}\pi b^2(3r - b)$ (or: Sector − Cone)

SURFACE = $2\pi rb$ (not including the circle)

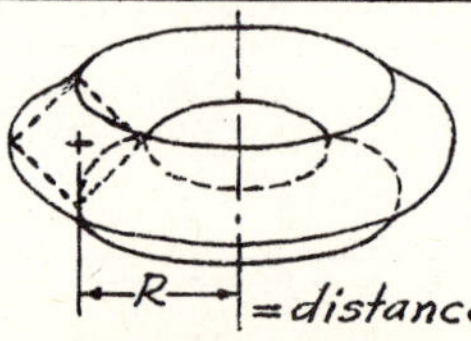

R

VOLUME = Area of section × $2\pi R$

SURFACE = Perimeter of section × $2\pi R$

Note: consider the section on one side of axis only.

R = distance from axis of ring to true center of section.

CIRCULAR RING OF ANY SECTION

Compiled by Prof. Andre Halasz A.I.A.

MATHEMATICS: IRREGULAR AREAS & VOLUMES

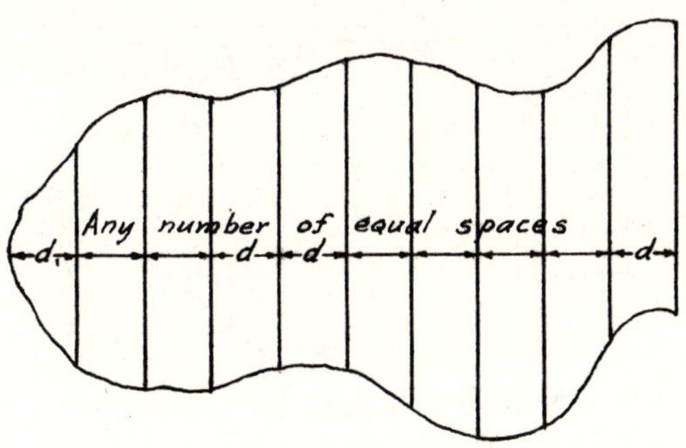
Any number of equal spaces
d
d
d
d

1. *Divide the figure into parallel strips by equally spaced parallel lines.*
2. *Measure the length of each of the parallel lines.*
3. *Obtain a summation of the unit areas by one of the three "rules" given:*

   a. "*Trapezoid Rule*". *Add together the lengths of the parallels, taking the first and last at 1/2 value, and mutiply by the interval "d".*

   b. "*Simpson's Rule*". *Add the parallels, taking the first & last at full value; the second, fourth, sixth, etc., from each end, at 4 × full value; and the third, 5th etc. from each end, at 2 × full value; multiply by 1/3 d.*
   Note: Simpson's works only with an even number of intervals.

   c. "*Durand's Rule*". *Add the parallels, taking the first & last at 5/12 value; the second from each end at 13/12 value; & all others at full value; multiply by d.*

a. *is sufficiently accurate for estimating & other ordinary purposes.*
b. *is very accurate for areas bounded by smooth curves, but note limitations.*
c. *is most accurate for very irregular shapes.*

AREAS OF IRREGULAR PLANE FIGURES

Note: A Planimeter is a simple instrument with which irregular areas can be directly read off.

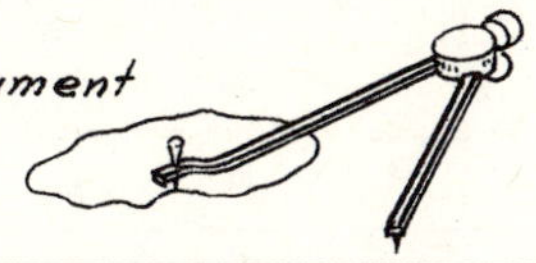

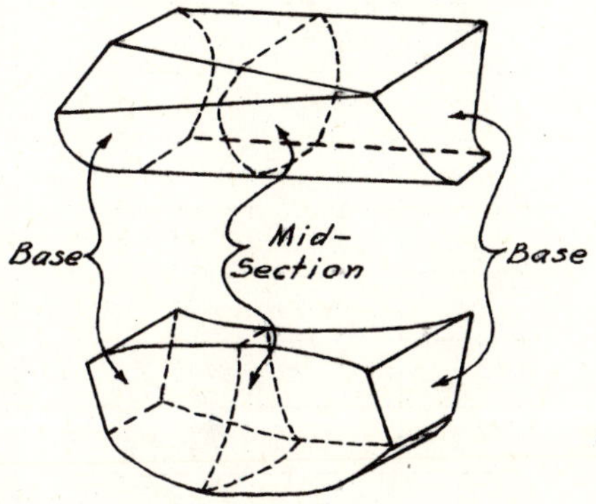
Base
Mid-Section
Base

This formula is quite accurate for any solid with two parallel bases, connected by a surface of straight line elements (upper figure), or smooth simple curves (lower figure). Construct a section midway between the bases; then

VOLUME = *Areas of two bases + 4 × area of mid-section; multiply the sum by 1/6 perp. distance between bases.*

THE PRISMATOID FORMULA *for* IRREGULAR SOLIDS

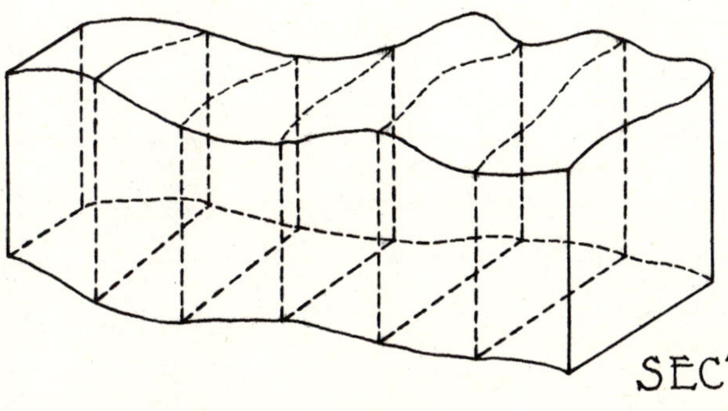

This method in general use for estimating quantities of earth work, etc.

1. *Construct a series of equally spaced sections ("profiles").*
2. *Determine the area of each section by methods given above (preferably with a planimeter).*
3. *Apply any of the three summation "rules" given above, to determine total volume.*

SECTIONING METHOD *for* VERY IRREGULAR VOLUMES

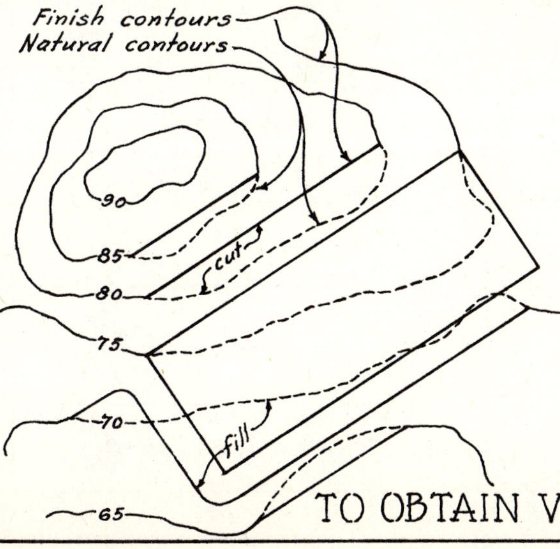
Finish contours
Natural contours
90
85
80
75
70
65
cut
fill

This method more rapid than the sectioning method, and is sufficiently accurate for estimating purposes, and for balancing cut and fill.

1. *Draw "natural" and "finish" contours on same contour map.*
2. *Measure the differential areas between new and old contours, at each contour; enter in parallel columns according to whether cut or fill.*
3. *Where a cut or fill ends right on a contour level, use 1/2 value.*

EXAMPLE

Contour	Cut	Fill
85	300	
80	960	
75	2,460÷2=1,230	3,800÷2=1,900
70	20	2,200
Totals	9,200	6,800
	×5=46,000 cu.ft.	34,000 cu.ft.

4. *Add up each column & multiply by the contour interval, to get volume in cu.ft.*

The closer the contour interval, the greater the accuracy.

TO OBTAIN VOLUME *of* CUT & FILL DIRECT *from* CONTOUR PLAN

Compiled by Prof. Andre Halasz A.I.A.

TRIANGLES, ARCS & CHORDS

OBLIQUE TRIANGLES

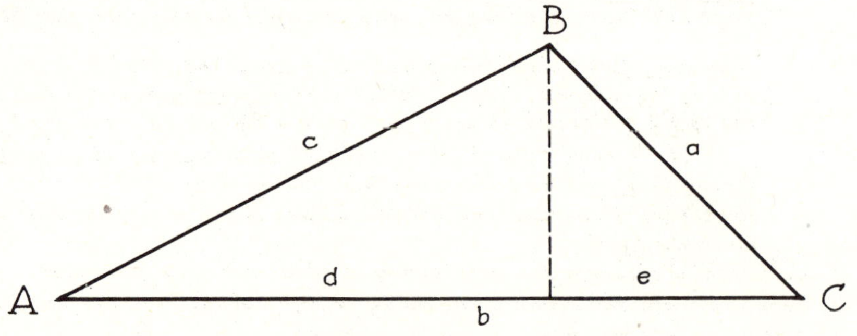
B
c
a
A
d
e
C
b

FIND	GIVEN	SOLUTION	FIND	GIVEN	SOLUTION
a	ABb	$b \sin A \div \sin B$	A	abcs	$\sin \frac{1}{2} A = \sqrt{(s-b)(s-c) \div bc}$
	ABc	$c \sin A \div \sin(A+B)$			$\cos \frac{1}{2} A = \sqrt{s(s-a) \div bc}$
	ACb	$b \sin A \div \sin(A+C)$			$\tan \frac{1}{2} A = \sqrt{(s-b)(s-c) \div s(s-a)}$
	ACc	$c \sin A \div \sin C$		Bab	$\sin A = a \sin B \div b$
	BCb	$b \sin(B+C) \div \sin B$		Bac	$\frac{1}{2}(A+C) + \frac{1}{2}(A-C)$
	BCc	$c \sin(B+C) \div \sin C$		Cab	$\frac{1}{2}(A+B) + \frac{1}{2}(A-B)$
	Abc	$\sqrt{b^2+c^2-2bc.\cos A}$		Cac	$\sin A = a \sin C \div c$
b	ABa	$a \sin B \div \sin A$	B	abcs	$\sin \frac{1}{2} B = \sqrt{(s-a)(s-c) \div s(s-a)}$
	ABc	$c \sin B \div \sin(A+B)$			$\cos \frac{1}{2} B = \sqrt{s(s-b) \div ac}$
	ACa	$a \sin(A+C) \div \sin A$			$\tan \frac{1}{2} B = \sqrt{(s-a)(s-c) \div s(s-b)}$
	ACc	$c \sin(A+C) \div \sin C$		Aab	$\sin B = b \sin A \div a$
	BCa	$a \sin B \div \sin(B+C)$		Abc	$\frac{1}{2}(B+C) + \frac{1}{2}(B-C)$
	BCc	$c \sin B \div \sin C$		Cab	$\frac{1}{2}(A+B) - \frac{1}{2}(A-B)$
	Bac	$\sqrt{a^2+c^2-2ac.\cos B}$		Cac	$\sin B = b \sin C \div c$
c	ABa	$a \sin(A+B) \div \sin A$	C	abcs	$\sin \frac{1}{2} C = \sqrt{(s-a)(s-b) \div ab}$
	ABb	$b \sin(A+B) \div \sin B$			$\cos \frac{1}{2} C = \sqrt{s(s-c) \div ab}$
	ACa	$a \sin C \div \sin A$			$\tan \frac{1}{2} C = \sqrt{(s-a)(s-b) \div s(s-c)}$
	ACb	$b \sin C \div \sin(A+C)$		Aac	$\sin C = c \sin A \div a$
	BCa	$a \sin C \div \sin(B+C)$		Abc	$\frac{1}{2}(B+C) - \frac{1}{2}(B-C)$
	BCb	$b \sin C \div \sin B$		Bac	$\frac{1}{2}(A+C) - \frac{1}{2}(A-C)$
	Cab	$\sqrt{a^2+b^2-2ab.\cos C}$		Bbc	$\sin C = c \sin B \div b$
$\frac{1}{2}(B+C)$	Abc	$90° - \frac{1}{2} A$	Area	abc	$\sqrt{s(s-a)(s-b)(s-c)}$
$\frac{1}{2}(B-C)$		$\tan = [(b-c)\tan(90° - \frac{1}{2} A)] \div (b+c)$		Cab	$\frac{1}{2} ab \sin C$
$\frac{1}{2}(A+C)$	Bac	$90° - \frac{1}{2} B$	s	abc	$a+b+c \div 2$
$\frac{1}{2}(A-C)$		$\tan = [(a-c)\tan(90° - \frac{1}{2} B)] \div (a+c)$	d	abcs	$(b^2+c^2-a^2) \div 2b$
$\frac{1}{2}(A+B)$	Cab	$90° - \frac{1}{2} C$	e	abcs	$(a^2+b^2-c^2) \div 2b$
$\frac{1}{2}(A-B)$		$\tan = [(a-b)\tan(90° - \frac{1}{2} C) \div (a+b)$			

RIGHT TRIANGLES

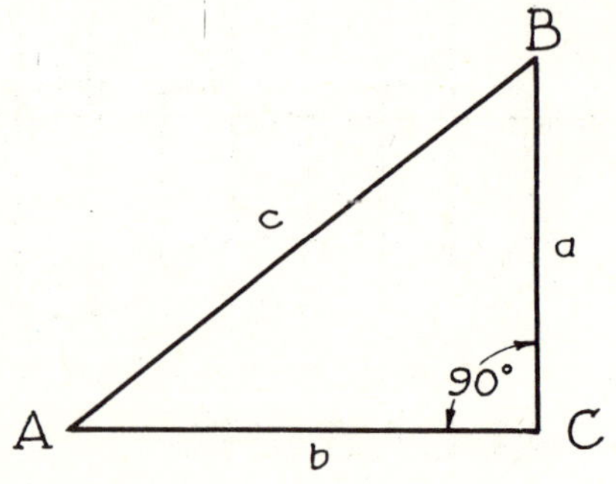
B
c
a
90°
A
C
b

FIND	GIVEN	SOLUTION
A	ab	$\tan A = a \div b$
	ac	$\sin A = a \div c$
	bc	$\cos A = b \div c$
B	ab	$\tan B = b \div a$
	ac	$\cos B = a \div c$
	bc	$\sin B = b \div c$
a	Ab	$b \tan A$
	Ac	$c \sin A$
b	Aa	$a \div \tan A$
	Ac	$c \cos A$
c	Aa	$a \div \sin A$
	Ab	$b \div \cos A$
Area	ab	$ab \div 2$

ARC

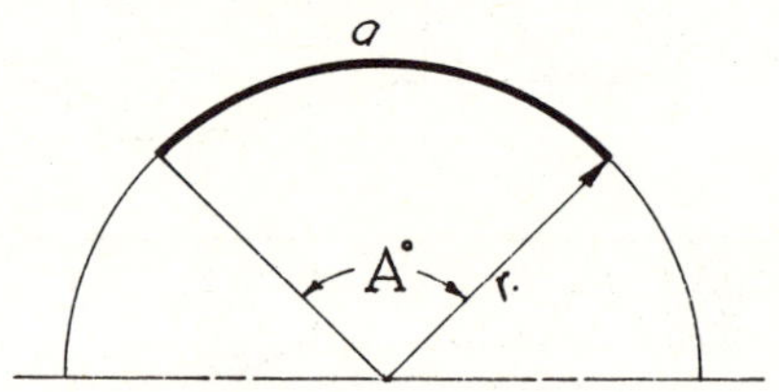
a
A°
r.

$$\text{Arc } a = \frac{\pi r A°}{180°}$$

CHORD

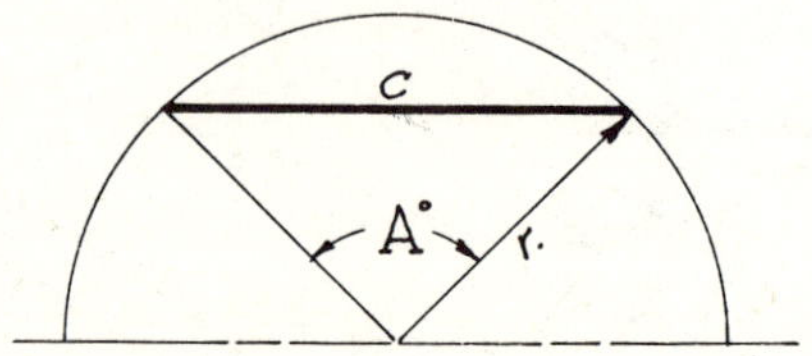
c
A°
r.

$$\text{Chord } c = 2 r \sin \frac{A}{2}$$

Formulae checked by Ralph Eberlin C.E.

ELLIPSES

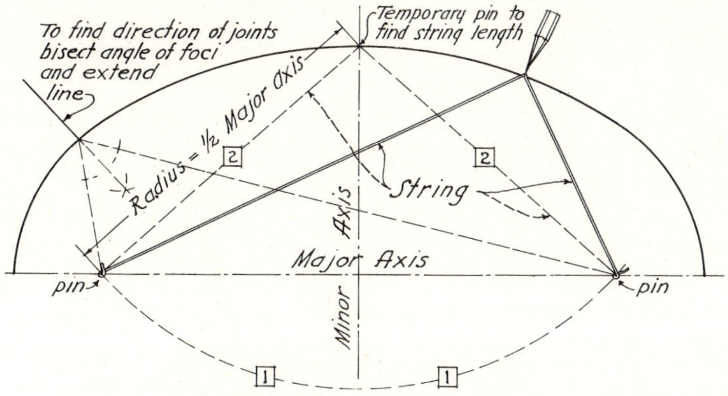
To find direction of joints bisect angle of foci and extend line
Temporary pin to find string length
Radius = ½ Major axis
String
Axis
Major Axis
Minor
pin
pin
2
2
1
1

STRING METHOD

For large scale and full size

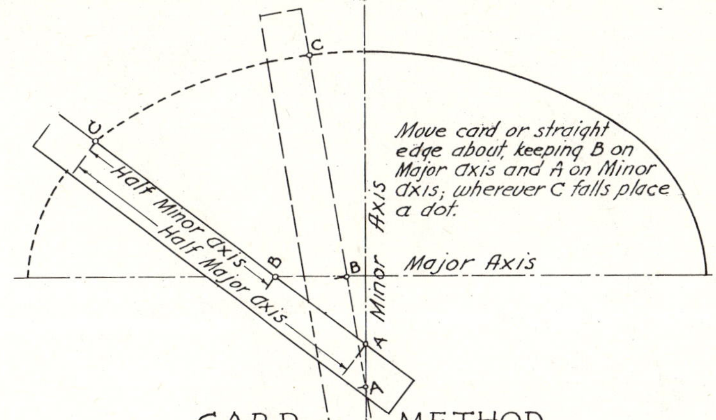
Move card or straight edge about, keeping B on Major axis and A on Minor axis; wherever C falls place a dot.
C
C
Half Minor axis
Half Major axis
B
B
A
A
Axis
Major Axis
Minor

CARD METHOD

For small scale

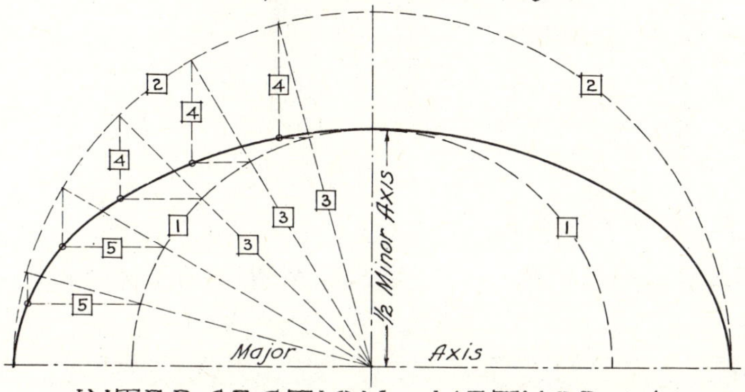
½ Minor Axis
Major
Axis
1
2
3
4
5

INTERSECTION METHOD-A

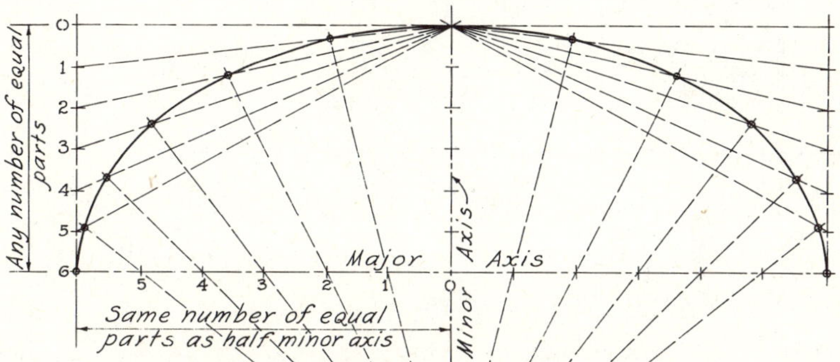
Any number of equal parts
0
1
2
3
4
5
6
Major
Axis
Axis
Minor
Same number of equal parts as half minor axis

INTERSECTION METHOD - B

Note: Accuracy of int. methods A & B depends on № of intersections

This method can also be used when the given axes are at an angle (conjugate axes) i.e.: to inscribe an ellipse in a parallelogram — see below

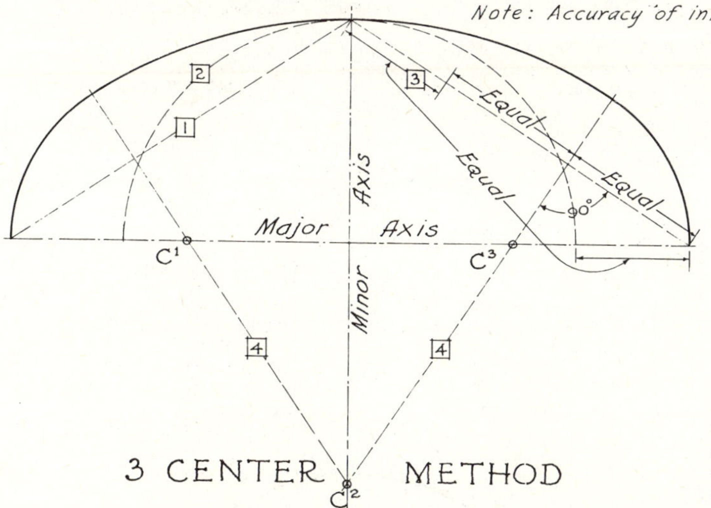
Equal
Equal
Equal
90°
Major
Axis
Axis
Minor
C¹
C³
C²
1
2
3
4

3 CENTER METHOD

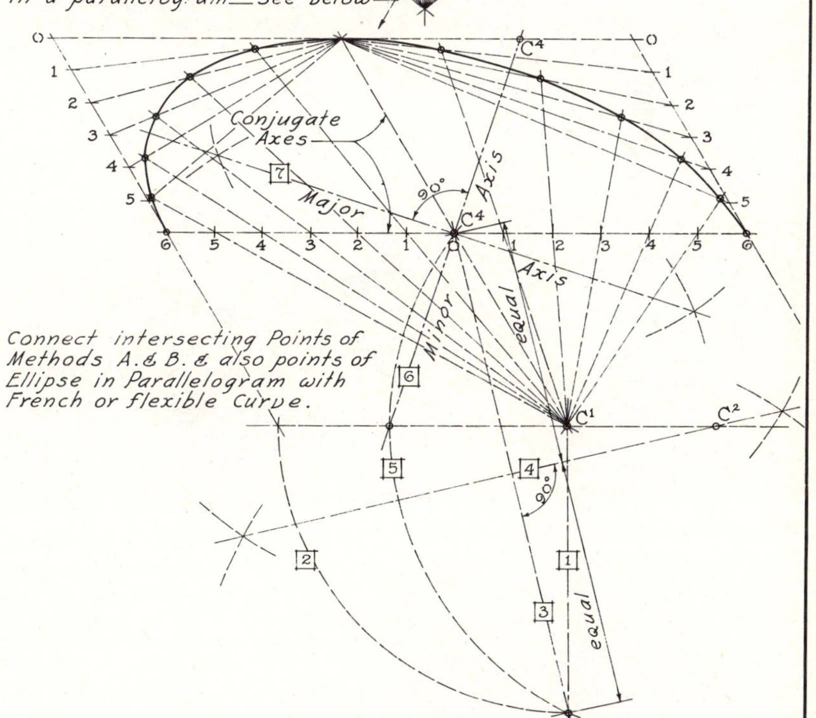
Conjugate Axes
Major
Axis
Axis
Minor
equal
90°
C⁴
C⁴
C¹
C²
0
1
2
3
4
5
6
7

Connect intersecting Points of Methods A. & B. & also points of Ellipse in Parallelogram with French or flexible Curve.

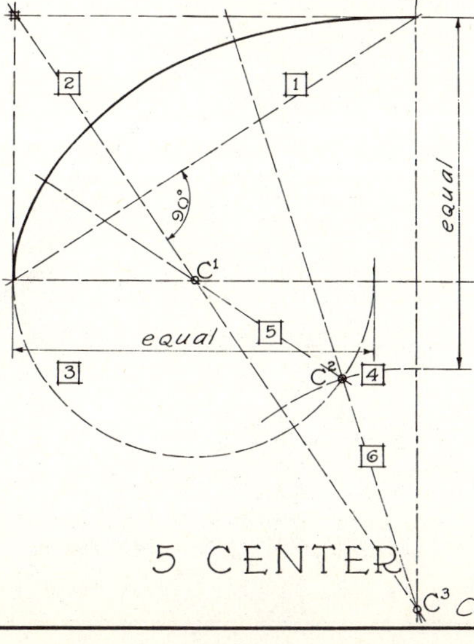
equal
equal
90°
C¹
C²
C³
1
2
3
4
5
6

3 & 5 center methods are not true ellipses but only approximations.

3 & 5 Center methods are useful for making small scale ink drawings of ellipses.

5 CENTER METHOD

TO FIND TRUE MAJOR AND MINOR AXES OF AN ELLIPSE INSCRIBED IN A PARALLELOGRAM

For procedure in laying out ellipses, follow numbers consecutively from № [1]. For compass methods use centers C^1 & C^2 as compass Center points.

Compiled by Prof. Andre Halasz A.I.A.

PARABOLA & ENTASIS

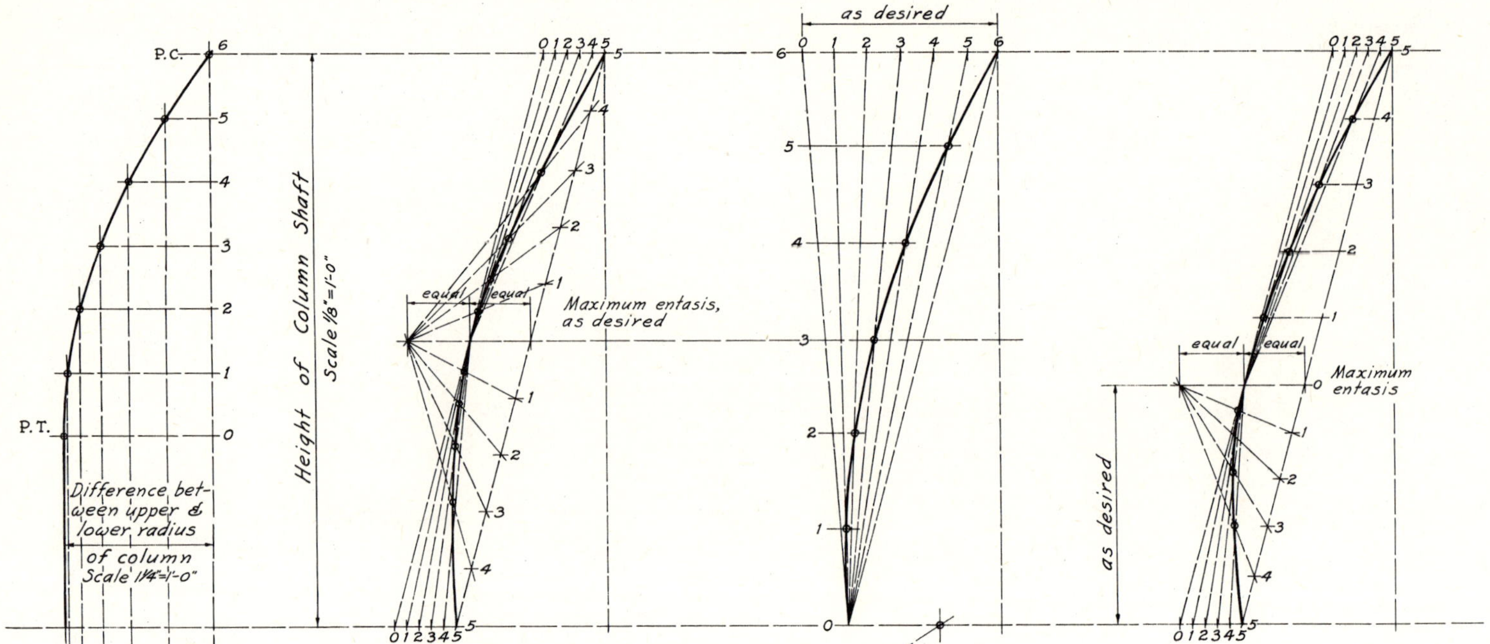
as desired
P.C.
P.T.
Height of Column Shaft
Scale 1/8"=1'-0"
Difference between upper & lower radius of column
Scale 1/4"=1'-0"
equal
equal
Maximum entasis, as desired
Maximum entasis
as desired
Radius

COMPARATIVE ENTASES

VIGNOLAS' ENTASIS

This is the same entasis shown on following page with the vertical scale reduced about 10 times in order to emphasize the full shape of the curve.

Objections: Too sharply sloping at top. Straight lower portion.

HYPERBOLA

Sharpest Curvature near maximum entasis straightening at top and bottom. Maximum entasis as desired.

PARABOLA

Curvature sharpest near bottom straightening toward the top. Maximum entasis as desired.

COMBINATION

Hyperbolic Curve in lower portion, Parabolic curve in upper portion of illustration. Maximum entasis where desired.

These entases were generally used by the Greeks. The above illustrations will enable the designer to determine to best advantage the amount of "Bulge" and its relative position and also the change of curvature.
(After G.P. Stevens)

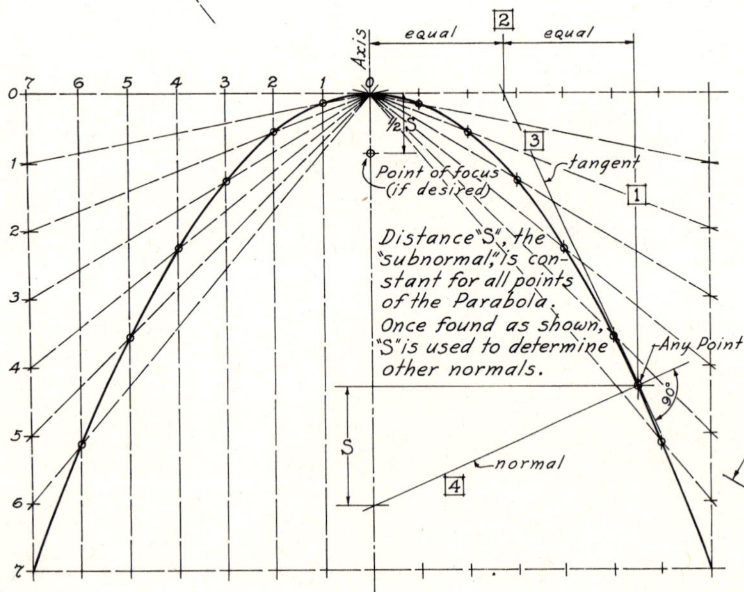
Axis
equal
equal
2
3
1
tangent
1/2 S
Point of focus (if desired)
Distance "S", the "subnormal," is constant for all points of the Parabola. Once found as shown, "S" is used to determine other normals.
Any Point
90°
S
4
normal

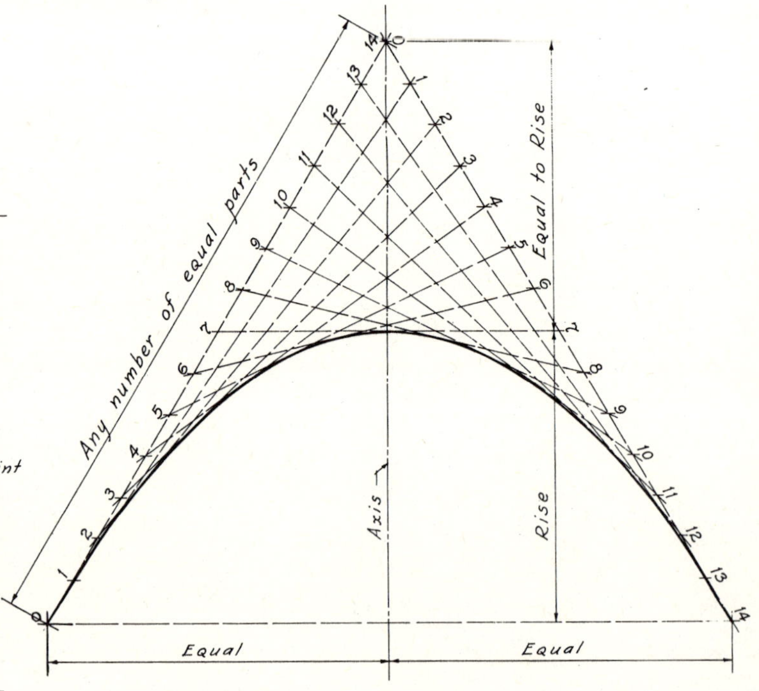
Any number of equal parts
Equal to Rise
Axis
Rise
Equal
Equal

GEOMETRY OF THE PARABOLA

INTERSECTION METHOD ~ TANGENT & NORMAL

This is comparable to the intersection method for the ellipse shown on previous page, & is equally good for inscribing a parabola in a parallelogram.

ENVELOPE METHOD

This method does not give points on the curve, but a series of tangents which outline the parabola directly.

Compiled by Prof. Andre Halasz A. I. A.

MISCELLANEOUS DATA

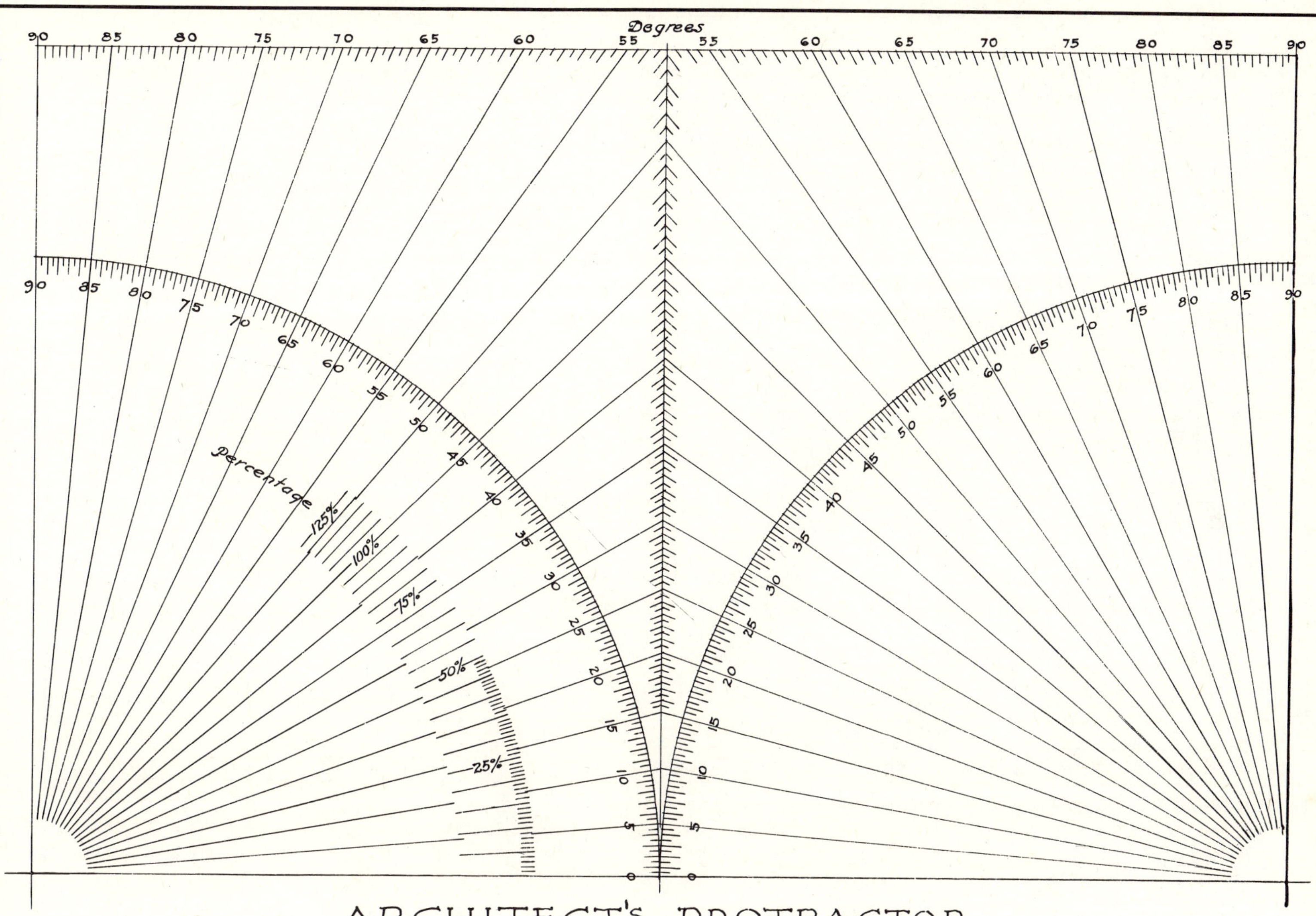
Degrees
Percentage
125%
100%
75%
50%
25%

ARCHITECT'S PROTRACTOR

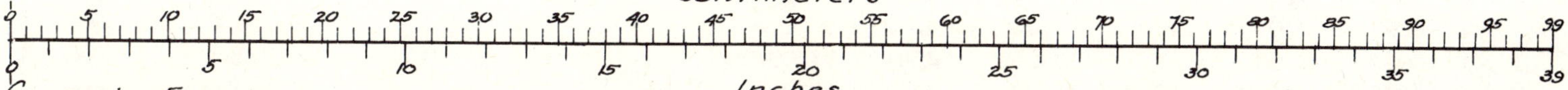
Centimeters
Inches

Conversion Formula
1 c. = 0.3937 inches

CENTIMETERS to INCHES

Conversion Formula
1 Inch = 2.540c.

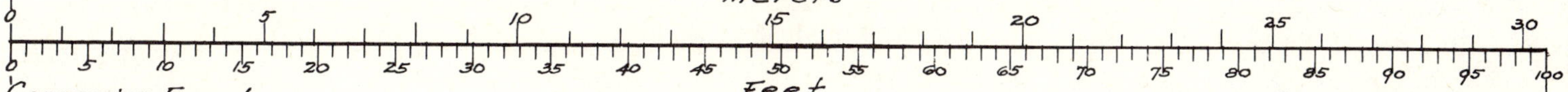
Meters
Feet

Conversion Formula
1 m. = 3.281 ft.

METERS to FEET

Conversion Formula
1 ft. = 0.3048 m.

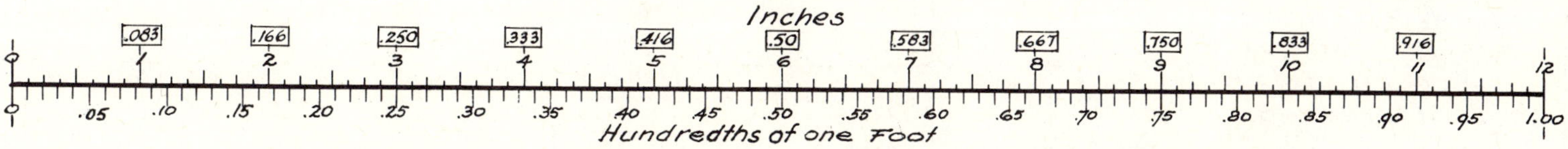
Inches
Hundredths of one Foot

DECIMAL EQUIVALENTS of ONE FOOT

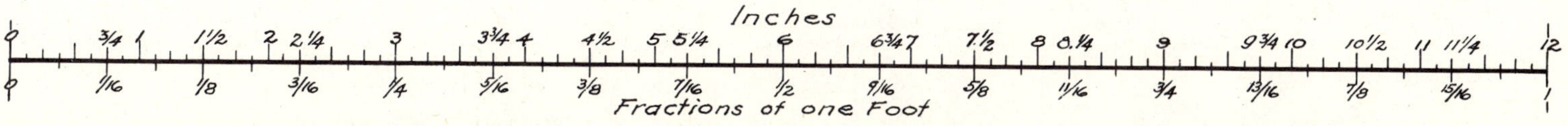
Inches
Fractions of one Foot

FRACTIONAL EQUIVALENTS of ONE FOOT

LAND MEASUREMENT

When estimating area available for lots on large scale site developments it is safe to assume that 20% of entire area will be in streets.
To estimate number lots of a given size which a site will yield, using the above percentage for streets, use the following formula.
Note: 80% of 1 acre = 34,848 sq. ft.

$$\text{No. of lots} = \frac{\text{Total site area, (acres)} \times 34{,}848}{\text{Width of lots} \times \text{Depth of lots}}$$

Example: Site 50 acres
Lots are 60 ft. x 120 ft.

$$\text{or} = \frac{50 \text{ acres} \times 34{,}848}{60 \text{ ft.} \times 120 \text{ ft.}} = 242 \text{ lots}$$

USUAL LOT SIZES

a = acres; □' = sq. ft.

DEPTH OF LOT		FRONT OR WIDTH OF LOT 20'	40'	50'	60'	75'	80'	100'
100'	□'	2,000	4,000	5,000	6,000	7,500	8,000	10,000
	a	.0459	.0718	.1148	.1377	.1722	.1837	.2296
110'	□'	2,200	4,400	5,500	6,600	8,250	8,800	11,000
	a	.0505	.1010	.1263	.1515	.1894	.2021	.2525
120'	□'	2,400	4,800	6,000	7,200	9,000	9,600	12,000
	a	.0551	.1102	.1377	.1653	.2066	.2204	.2755
130'	□'	2,600	5,200	6,500	7,800	9,750	10,400	13,000
	a	.0597	.1194	.1492	.1791	.2238	.2388	.2984
140'	□'	2,800	5,600	7,000	8,400	10,500	11,200	14,000
	a	.0643	.1286	.1607	.1929	.2411	.2571	.3214
150'	□'	3,000	6,000	7,500	9,000	11,250	12,000	15,000
	a	.0689	.1377	.1722	.2066	.2582	.2755	.3444

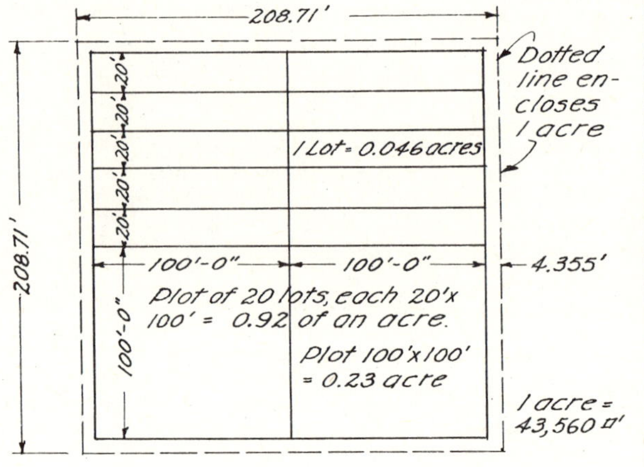
208.71'
Dotted line encloses 1 acre
20'
20'
20'
20'
20'
1 Lot = 0.046 acres
208.71'
100'-0"
100'-0"
4.355'
Plot of 20 lots, each 20'x 100' = 0.92 of an acre.
100'-0"
Plot 100'x100' = 0.23 acre
1 acre = 43,560 □'

PLOT OF 20 LOTS, *each* 20'x100' *in* RELATION *to* ONE ACRE

CONVERSION TABLE - SQ.FT. TO ACRES

SQ.FT.	ACRES	SQ.FT.	ACRES	SQ.FT.	ACRES	SQ.FT.	ACRES	SQ.FT.	ACRES	SQ.FT.	ACRES
10 =	.0002	600 =	.0138	11,000 =	.2525	25,000 =	.5739	39,000 =	.8953	435,600 =	10.0000
20 =	.0005	700 =	.0161	12,000 =	.2755	26,000 =	.5969	40,000 =	.9183	479,160 =	11.0000
30 =	.0007	800 =	.0184	13,000 =	.2984	27,000 =	.6198	41,000 =	.9412	522,720 =	12.0000
40 =	.0009	900 =	.0207	14,000 =	.3214	28,000 =	.6428	42,000 =	.9642	566,280 =	13.0000
50 =	.0011	1,000 =	.0230	15,000 =	.3444	29,000 =	.6657	43,000 =	.9871	609,840 =	14.0000
60 =	.0014	2,000 =	.0459	16,000 =	.3673	30,000 =	.6887	43,560 =	1.0000	653,400 =	15.0000
70 =	.0016	3,000 =	.0689	17,000 =	.3903	31,000 =	.7117	87,120 =	2.0000	696,960 =	16.0000
80 =	.0018	4,000 =	.0918	18,000 =	.4132	32,000 =	.7346	130,680 =	3.0000	740,520 =	17.0000
90 =	.0021	5,000 =	.1148	19,000 =	.4362	33,000 =	.7576	174,240 =	4.0000	784,080 =	18.0000
100 =	.0023	6,000 =	.1377	20,000 =	.4591	34,000 =	.7805	217,800 =	5.0000	827,640 =	19.0000
200 =	.0046	7,000 =	.1607	21,000 =	.4821	35,000 =	.8035	261,360 =	6.0000	871,200 =	20.0000
300 =	.0069	8,000 =	.1837	22,000 =	.5051	36,000 =	.8264	304,920 =	7.0000	914,760 =	21.0000
400 =	.0092	9,000 =	.2066	23,000 =	.5280	37,000 =	.8494	348,480 =	8.0000	958,320 =	22.0000
500 =	.0115	10,000 =	.2296	24,000 =	.5510	38,000 =	.8724	392,040 =	9.0000	1,001,880 =	23.0000

AREA EQUIVALENTS

NOTE

Subscripts after any figure, 0_4, 0_5, etc. mean that that figure is to be repeated the indicated number of times.

EXAMPLE:

$0{,}0_4 2551 = 0{,}00002551$

SQUARE METERS	SQUARE INCHES	SQUARE FEET	SQUARE YARDS	SQUARE RODS	SQUARE CHAINS	RODS	ACRES	SQ.MILES OR SECTIONS
1	1550	10.76	1.196	0.0395	0.002471	$0.0_3 9884$	$0.0_3 2471$	$0.0_6 3861$
$0.0_3 6452$	1	0.006944	$0{,}0_3 7716$	$0.0_4 2551$	$0.0_5 1594$	$0.0_6 6377$	$0.0_6 1594$	$0.0_9 2491$
0.09290	144	1	0.1111	0.003673	$0.0_3 2296$	$0.0_4 9184$	$0.0_4 2296$	$0.0_7 3587$
0.8361	1296	9	1	0.03306	0.002066	$0.0_3 8264$	$0.0_3 2066$	$0.0_6 3228$
25.29	39204	272.25	30.25	1	0.0625	0.02500	0.00625	$0.0_5 9766$
404.7	627264	4356	484	16	1	0.4	0.1	$0.0_3 1562$
1012	1568160	10890	1210	40	2.5	1	0.25	$0.0_3 3096$
4047	6272640	43560	4840	160	10	4	1	0.001562
$2589_3 8$	....	27878400	3097600	102400	6400	2560	640	1

OTHER AREA MEASURES:

1 are = a square 10 meters x 10 meters = 100 sq. meters.

1 hectare = 100 ares = 10,000 centiares

1 section of Gov't. surveyed land = 1 sq. mile = 640 acres

1 acre (Texas) = 5645 sq. varas

1 square (Architects' measure) = 100 sq. ft.

compiled by Ralph Eberlin, C.E.

WEIGHTS & MEASURES

VOLUME

MEASURES

VOLUME
1 cord of wood = 128 cu. ft.
1 perch of masonry = 16½ " ". (In most localities). Standard is 24¾ cubic feet.

LIQUID
4 gills = 1 pint = 16 fluid oz.
2 pints = 1 quart = 32 " ".
4 quarts = 1 gallon = 128 fl. oz.

APOTHECARY
1 fluid oz. = 8 drams = 480 minims = 2 tablespoons = 6 teaspoons = 1.805 cu. in. = 29.58 cu. cm. = 1/128th gallon.

DRY
2 pints = 1 quart = 67.2 cu. in.
4 quarts = 8 pints = 268.8 " ".
1 peck = 16 pints = 537.6 " ".
4 pecks = 1 bushel = 2150.42 " ".
1 standard barrel (for fruit

DRY (continued)
& veg.) = 7056 cu. in. = 105 dry quarts. "Struck barrel" is 20" dia., 28½" high.

BOARD
1 board foot = 144 sq. in. = a volume of board 1 ft. sq. & 1" thick. No. of board feet in a log = $\frac{1}{4}(d''-4)^2L$, where d = smaller dia. of log; L = length of log in feet; 4 = deduction allowance for slab.

MISCELLANEOUS
1 ton round timber = 40 cu. ft.
1 ton hewn timber = 50 " ".
All dressed stock is measured as "Strip Count." i.e., the full size of rough material in manufacture.

EQUIVALENTS

Cubic inches	Cubic feet	Cubic yards	U.S. Apothecary ounces	U.S. Quarts Liquid	U.S. Quarts Dry	U.S. Gallons Liquid	U.S. Gallons Dry	U.S. Bushels	Liters
1	$0.0_3 5787$	$0.0_4 2143$	0.5541	0.01732	0.01488	$0.0_2 4329$	$0.0_2 3720$	$0.0_3 4650$	0.01639
1728	1	0.03704	957.5	29.92	25.71	7.4805	6.429	0.8036	28.32
46656	27	1	25853	807.9	694.3	202.0	173.6	21.70	764.6
1.805	0.001044	$0.0_4 3868$	1	0.03125	0.02686	0.007813	0.006714	$0.0_3 8392$	0.02957
57.75	0.03342	0.001238	32	1	0.8594	0.25	0.2148	0.02686	0.9464
67.20	0.03889	0.001440	37.24	1.164	1	0.2909	0.25	0.03125	1.101
231	0.1337	0.004951	128	4	3.437	1	0.8594	0.1074	3.785
268.8	0.1556	0.005761	148.9	4.655	4	1.164	1	0.125	4.405
2150	1.244	0.04609	1192	37.24	32	9.309	8	1	35.25
61.02	0.03531	0.001308	33.81	1.057	0.9081	0.2642	0.2270	0.02838	1

WEIGHT

MEASURES

NOTE: *Unit of grain is same in all.*

AVOIRDUPOIS
16 drams = 437.5 grains = 1 ounce.
16 ounces = 7000 grains = 1 pound.
100 lbs. = 1 hundredweight = 1 cental.
2000 lbs. = 20 " = 1 short ton.
28 lbs. = 2 stones = 1 quarter
4 quarters (long unit) = 112 lbs.
2240 lbs. = 20 hundredwt. = 1 long ton
1 standard lime bbl. small = 180# net.
1 " " " large = 280# ".
1 standard bag lime = 80# net.
1 " " cement = 94# ".

TROY
24 grains = 1 pennyweight (dwt.)
20 dwts. = 480 grains = 1 ounce
1 assay ton = 29,167 milligrams
1 carat (for weighing diamonds) = 3.086 grains = 200 grams.

APOTHECARY
20 grains = 1 scruple ℈
3 scruples = 60 grains = 1 dram ʒ
8 drams (drachms) = 1 ounce ℥

METRIC
10 milligrams = 1 centigram
10 centigrams = 1 decigram
10 decigrams = 1 gram
10 grams = 1 decagram
10 decagrams = 1 hectogram
10 hectograms = 1 kilogram

IRON & LEAD
14 pounds = 1 stone
21½ stones = 1 pig
8 pigs = 1 fother

EQUIVALENTS

Kilograms	Grains	Ounces Troy & Apoth'y	Ounces Avoirdupois	Pounds Troy & Apoth'y	Pounds Avoirdupois	Tons Short	Tons Long	Tons Metric
1	15,432	32.15	35.27	2.6792	2.205	$0.0_2 1102$	$0.0_3 9842$	0.001
$0.0_4 6480$	1	$0.0_2 2083$	$0.0_2 2286$	$0.0_3 1736$	$0.0_3 1429$	$0.0_7 7143$	$0.0_7 6378$	$0.0_7 6480$
0.03110	480	1	1.09714	0.08333	0.06857	$0.0_4 3429$	$0.0_4 3061$	$0.0_4 3110$
0.02835	437.5	0.9115	1	0.07595	0.0625	$0.0_4 3125$	$0.0_4 2790$	$0.0_4 2835$
0.3732	5,760	12	13.17	1	0.8229	$0.0_3 4114$	$0.0_3 3673$	$0.0_3 3732$
0.4536	7,000	14.58	16	1.215	1	0.0005	$0.0_3 4464$	$0.0_3 4536$
907.2	140_6	29,167	320_3	2,431	2,000	1	0.8929	0.9072
1,016	15680_4	32,667	35,840	2,722	2,240	1.12	1	1.016
1,000	15,432,356	32,151	35,274	2,679	2,205	1.102	0.9842	1

LINEAR

MEASURES

LENGTH
4 inches = 1 hand
9 inches = 1 span
12 inches = 1 foot
3 feet = 1 yard
5½ yds = 16½ feet = 1 rod = 1 pole = 1 perch.
40 poles = 220 yds. = 1 furlong
8 furlongs = 1,760 yds. = 5,280 feet = 1 mile.
3 miles (U.S. Naut.) = 1 league

NAUTICAL
6,080.27 feet = 1 nautical mile
1.15156 statute mi. = " "
1 nautical mi. per hr. = 1 knot
6 feet = 1 fathom
120 fathoms = 1 cable length

SURVEYOR OR GUNTHER
7.92 inches = 1 link
100 links = 66 ft. = 4 rods = 1 chain
80 chains = 1 mile
1 vara (Texas) = 33⅓ in. = 2¾ ft.

EQUIVALENTS

Centimeters	Inches	Feet	Yards	Meters	Chains	Kilometers	Miles
1	0.3937	0.03281	0.01094	0.01	$0.0_3 4971$	$0.0_4 1$	$0.0_5 6214$
2.540	1	0.0833	0.02778	0.0254	0.001263	$0.0_4 254$	$0.0_4 1578$
30.48	12	1	0.3333	0.3048	0.01515	$0.0_3 3048$	$0.0_3 1894$
91.44	36	3	1	0.9144	0.04545	$0.0_3 9144$	$0.0_3 5682$
100	39.37	3.281	1.0936	1	0.04971	0.001	$0.0_3 6214$
2012	792	66	22	20.12	1	0.02012	0.0125
100,000	39,370	3,281	1,093.6	1,000	49.71	1	0.6214
160,935	63,360	5,280	1,760	1,609	80	1.609	1

Subscripts after any figure, 0_2, 0_3 etc., mean that that figure is to be repeated the indicated number of times, i.e., $0.0_3 27$ = 0.00027

LUMBER ~ SIZES & WEIGHTS

Nominal Size inches	Dressed Size inches	Area of Section sq. in.	Weight per ft. lbs.	Wt. of Beams or Studs 16" o.c. (lbs/sq.')	Nominal Size inches	Dressed Size inches	Area of Section sq. in.	Weight per ft. lbs.
2 x 4	1⅝ x 3⅝	5.89	1.64	1.23	4 x 8	3⅝ x 7½	27.2	7.55
2 x 6	1⅝ x 5⅝	9.14	2.54	1.91	4 x 10	3⅝ x 9½	34.4	9.57
2 x 8	1⅝ x 7½	12.2	3.39	2.54	4 x 12	3⅝ x 11½	41.7	11.6
2 x 10	1⅝ x 9½	15.4	4.29	3.22	4 x 14	3⅝ x 13½	48.9	13.6
2 x 12	1⅝ x 11½	18.7	5.19	3.89	6 x 6	5½ x 5½	30.3	8.4
3 x 4	2⅝ x 3⅝	9.52	2.64	1.98	6 x 8	5½ x 7½	41.3	11.4
3 x 6	2⅝ x 5⅝	14.8	4.10	3.08	6 x 10	5½ x 9½	52.3	14.5
3 x 8	2⅝ x 7½	19.7	5.47	4.10	6 x 12	5½ x 11½	63.3	17.5
3 x 10	2⅝ x 9½	24.9	6.93	5.31	8 x 8	7½ x 7½	56.3	15.6
3 x 12	2⅝ x 11½	30.2	8.39	6.29	8 x 10	7½ x 9½	71.3	19.8
4 x 4	3⅝ x 3⅝	13.1	3.65	2.74	8 x 12	7½ x 11½	86.3	23.9
4 x 6	3⅝ x 5⅝	20.4	5.66	4.25	8 x 14	7½ x 13½	101.3	28.0

Weights based on 40 lbs. per cu. foot.

HYDROSTATICS for PLUMBING

1 cu. ft. water weighs 62.5 lbs.
1 cu. in. " " .03617 lbs.
1 gallon " " 8.338 lbs.
1 cu. in. water = .003617 gals.
Gallons x 0.16 = cubic ft.

To find water pressure: Head (ft.) x 0.434 = Pressure (#/□").
Example: 125' x 0.434 = 54.25 #/□"

To find water head: $\frac{\text{Pressure (\#/□")}}{0.434}$ = Head (feet)
Example: $\frac{54.25\text{ \#/□"}}{0.434}$ = 125'

WEIGHTS of MATERIALS

WEIGHTS OF MATERIAL

WEIGHTS GIVEN ARE AVERAGE

SOILS, MASONRY & CONCRETE MATERIALS	LBS. per CU. FT.
Cement, dry	94
Cinders or ashes	40-45
Clay, damp & plastic	110
Clay, dry	63
Clay & gravel, dry	100
Earth, dry & loose	76
Earth, dry & packed	95
Earth, moist & loose	78
Earth, moist & packed	96
Earth, mud, packed	115
Granite, without mortar	158-168
Limestone, marble, without mortar	150-165
Sand or gravel, dry & loose	90-105
Sand or gravel, dry & packed	100-120
Sand or gravel, dry & wet	118-120
Sandstone, bluestone, with mortar	147
Slate	175

METALS

Aluminum, cast	165
Brass, red	546
Brass, yellow, extruded bronze	528
Bronze, commercial	552
Bronze, statuary	509
Copper, cast or rolled	556
Iron, cast gray	450
Iron, wrought	485
Lead	710
Monel metal	552-556
Nickel	555-565
Stainless steel, rolled	492-510
Steel, rolled	490
Zinc, rolled or cast	440

FUELS & LIQUIDS

Coal, piled, anthracite	47-58
Coal, piled, bituminous	40-54
Gasoline	75
Water, at 4° C	62.43

WOOD (12% MOISTURE CONTENT)

	LBS. per CU. FT.
Birch, red oak	44
Cedar, northern white	22
Cedar, western red	23
Cypress, southern	32
Douglas fir, (coast region)	34
Fir, commercial white; idaho white pine	27
Hemlock	28-29
Maple, hard (black & sugar)	42
Oak, white	47
Pine, long-leaf southern	29
Pine; northern white sugar	25
Pine, ponderosa; spruce; eastern & sitka	28
Pine, short leaf, southern	36
Poplar, yellow; redwood	28
Walnut, black	38

CONCRETE (See Floor Materials, Flooring & Roof Slabs)

Cinder, concrete fill	60
Cinder, reinforced	100-115
Slag, plain	130
Stone, plain	144
Stone, reinforced	150

BRICK MASONRY (INCLUDING MORTAR)

Cell type	115
Common	120
Pressed	140
Soft	100

STONE ASHLAR MASONRY (INCLUDING MORTAR)

Granite	155-162
Limestone, marble	150
Sandstone, bluestone	130

For rubble masonry deduct 10 lbs. from the above

MORTAR & PLASTER

Cement, portland	144
Mortar, masonry	116
Plaster	96

EXTERIOR WALLS & WALL MATERIALS

Masonry (Incl. mortar; no plaster unless noted)	LBS. per SQ. FT.
2" Solid architectural T. C.	16
4" Solid architectural T. C.	32
4" brickwork	35
8" brickwork	74
12" brickwork	115
4" brick veneer on wood, with sheathing & plaster	45
4" brick with 6" concrete block backup	75-88
4" brick with 8" concrete block backup	90-100
4" brick with 6" hollow clay tile backup	70-74
4" brick with 8" hollow clay tile backup	74-82
Cavity wall 4" brick & 4" brick	70

(Brick assumed at 4.5 lbs. each laid with 1/2" joints. Weight of brick varies from 4 lbs. to 6 lbs. each.)

	LBS. per SQ. FT.
8" concrete, reinforced stone or gravel	100
10" concrete, reinforced stone or gravel	125
12" concrete, reinforced stone or gravel	150
4" concrete block, stone or gravel	27-33
6" concrete block, stone or gravel	35-43
8" concrete block, stone or gravel	50-60
12" concrete block, stone or gravel	74-85
2" granite with 1/2" parging	29-30
4" granite with 1/2" parging	58-60
4" glass block	20
4" hollow clay tile (load bearing)	21-24
6" hollow clay tile (load bearing)	30-34
8" hollow clay tile (load bearing)	34-42
12" hollow clay tile (load bearing)	49-66
4" limestone facing, 1/2" parging	55
4" limestone, 8" brick backing	134
4" limestone, 8" hollow concrete block backing	105-115
4" limestone, 8" hollow clay tile backing	89-97
4" sandstone or bluestone facing, 1/2" parging	49
1" mortar	10-12

Wood Frame

Normal standard dead load for wood frame house, lbs. per sq. ft. per tier. For wood joists, bridging, flooring, and underflooring, lath & plaster on walls and ceilings-17

4" wood studs, wood sheathing, lath & plaster	10
1" wood sheathing, 1/4" asbestos board	2.5
1/2" gypsum sheathing or gypsum board	2.2
1/2" wood fiber sheathing or insulation board	0.8
Wood siding, asphalt siding	2
Asbestos cement siding	1.8
Plaster	4-5
2" wood furring, lath & plaster	7.5

Miscellaneous

#20 gauge corrugated iron siding	2
Corrugated asbestos siding	3.5-4
Corrugated glass, 2 1/2" O.C.	6.5
Fenestra type "C" insulated panel aluminum	3
Fenestra type "C" insulated panel steel	6.5
Precast Bldg. Sections (Atterbury) 8" stone concrete	50
(Atterbury) 8" light weight concrete	33

WEIGHTS of MATERIALS (cont'd)

LBS. per CU. FT.

FLOOR MATERIAL & FLOORING & ROOF SLABS

Concrete, Aerocrete----------50-80
Concrete, cinder fill----------60
Concrete, Haydite----------85-100
Concrete, Nailcode----------75
Concrete, Perlite----------35-50
Concrete, Porete, light weight----------25-80
Concrete, pumice----------60-90
Concrete, Vermiculite----------25-60
For other Concrete - See "Concrete"

LBS. per SQ. FT.

Cement finish, 1" thick----------12
Fenestra bldg. systems, variable for depth (1 1/2"-7 1/2") & gauges----------4-11
Fill, cinder concrete, per 1" thickness----------8
Flexicore, 6" precast light weight concrete----------30
Flexicore, 6" precast stone concrete----------40
Flooring, hardwood, 25/32"----------4
Flooring or underflooring, soft wood----------2.5-3
Flooring, wood block, 3"----------15
Joist, floor, 2" x 8", 16" o.c. with subflooring----------6
Joist, floor, 2" x 10", 16" o.c. with subflooring----------6.5
Joist, floor, 2" x 12", 16" o.c. with subflooring----------7
Marble & setting bed----------25-30
Plywood, 1/2" subflooring----------1.5
Pyrofill, per 1" thickness----------5
Terrazzo, 2", 3"----------25-38
Tile, ceramic & setting bed--15-23

FLOORING MATERIAL & FLOORING & ROOF SLABS
Metal tile & joists 20" wide pans & 5" joists

4" deep plus 2 1/2" topping----------45
6" " " " " "----------50
8" " " " " "----------56
10" " " " " "----------64
12" " " " " "----------69

One way clay tile - 16" wide tile & 4" joists

4" deep with 2" topping----------51
5" " " " "----------57
6" " " " "----------63
7" " " " "----------67
8" " " " "----------73
9" " " " "----------79
10" " " " "----------84

Two way slag block - 16" x 16" blocks & 4" JOISTS

4 1/2" deep with no topping----------39
6" " " " "----------49

LBS. per SQ. FT.

7" deep with no topping----------54
8" " " " "----------59
9" " " " "----------67
10" " " " "----------74
10" " " 1" "----------86

Two way clay tile & joist - 16" x 16" Blocks & 4" Joists

4" deep with no topping----------31
$4\frac{1}{2}$" deep with no topping----------35
5" deep with 2" topping----------67
6" deep with 2" topping----------73
7" deep with 2" topping----------80
8" deep with 2" topping----------89
9" deep with 2" topping----------97
10" deep with 2" topping----------104

ROOFING & ROOFING MATERIALS

Acoustical Tile (without supports) per 1/2"----------.5-.8
Built up----------5-6.5
Cemesto roof deck, 1 9/16"----------4.8
Copper----------1.5-2.5
Corrugated asbestos----------3.5-4
Corrugated glass----------6.3
Corrugated iron----------1.27-1.75
Deck, steel roof, without finish or insulation----------2.25-3.6
Galvanized iron----------1.25-1.75
Gypsum tile, roof, 3"----------17
Hung ceiling----------8-10
Kalo insulating tile, roofing2.6-5
Lead, 1/8"----------6-8
Monel metal----------1.25-1.5
Plank, cinder concrete, 2"----------15
Plank, Durisol roof, 3 1/4" & 4-1/4"----------14, 17
Plank, gypsum, 2"----------12
Plank, Porex, 3 1/4"----------14
Shingles, asbestos cement--2.5-2.8
Shingles, asphalt----------1.7-2.8
Shingles, wood----------2-3
Skylights, glass & frame----------10-12
Slab, Porex per 1"----------2.4
Slab, precast concrete, light weight channel, 3 1/2"----------12-14
Slate, 3/16" to 1/4"----------7-9.5
Slate, 3/8" & 1/2"----------14, 18
Stainless steel----------2.5
Tile, cement flat----------13.0
Tile, cement ribbed----------16
Tile, clay flat with setting bed 15-20
Tile, clay mission----------13.5
Tile, clay shingle type----------8-16

FOR CONCRETE & COMBINATION ROOF SLABS SEE FLOORING SLABS

PARTITIONS

Building board, wall board (wood fibre) 1/2" thick----------.8
4" Concrete partition block, light weight, plaster 2S----------34

LBS. per SQ. FT.

6" Concrete partition block, light weight, plaster 2S---32-45
3" Gypsum block, plaster 2S----------21
4" Gypsum block, plaster 2S----------25
6" Gypsum block, plaster 2S----------31
Gypsum board, 1/2" thick----------2.1
Johns-Manville, Universal & Imperial Partitions----------4,11
Kalo partitions, 1" & 1 3/4" 2.2,3.75
Lath & plaster, 2" x 4" wood studs----------14-16
Movable, steel (office type)---4-8
Plaster----------4-5
Plywood, 1/2" thick----------1.5
2" Solid plaster partition----------18
3" Solid plaster partition----------27
2" Facing tile, structural---16-17
4" Facing tile, structural---27-30
6" Facing tile, structural----------41
3" Hollow clay tile, with plaster 2S----------24
4" Hollow clay tile, with plaster 2S----------25
6" Hollow clay tile, with plaster 2S----------32
4" Hollow metal studs, lath and plaster 2S---18

INSULATION

Bats, blankets, per 1" thickness .1-.4
Boards, vegetable fibre----------1.5-2
Cork board---------- 75
Fiber glass----------1.3
Foam glass----------1.

MISCELLANEOUS

C. I. 4" extra heavy soil pipe (per lin. ft.)----------13
C.I. radiator, per sq. ft. of radiation----------7
Glass: double strength & single strength----------1.6, 1.2
Glass, single strength----------1.2
Glass, 1/4" plate----------3.27
Plastics, 1/4" acrylic----------1.5
Suspended metal lath and plaster ceiling----10

LIVE LOADS

In general. See building codes for specific requirements.
Dwellings, apts. hotels, clubs, hospitals, prisons----------40
Factories & workshops, etc., variable, see Bldg. Code
Office buildings: office space--50
corridors & public space----------100
Schools: class rooms---40,50 or 60
corridors----------100
Sidewalks----------250 & 300
Theater lobbies, gyms, grandstands, stages, places of assembly with no fixed seats----------100
Theaters, auditoriums with fixed seats----------50-100
Stairs & fire escapes, except private residences----------100
Roofs, flat----------20-40

REFERENCES AND ACKNOWLEDGEMENTS

STRUCTURAL CLAY TILE: "TILE ENGINEERING, HANDBOOK OF DESIGN" BY HARRY C. PLUMMER & E. F. WANNER. BRICKWORK: "BRICK ENGINEERING, HANDBOOK OF DESIGN" BY HARRY C. PLUMMER & LESLIE J. REARDON. STEEL & OTHER METAL: "MANUAL OF THE AMERICAN INSTITUTE OF STEEL CONSTRUCTION", "ARCHITECTURAL METAL HANDBOOK" - NATL. ASSOC. OF ARCH. METAL MFGRS. SOLID PLASTER PARTITIONS: "THE PARTITION HANDBOOK" BY ERDWIN M. LURIE, METAL LATH MFGRS. ASSOC. FLOORING & ROOFING SYSTEMS& SLAB WEIGHTS: "DESIGN, DATA BOOK FOR CIVIL ENGINEERS" BY ELWYN E. SEELYE. CONCRETE BLOCK: PORTLAND CEMENT ASSOCIATION

ENGINEERING LETTERING

VERTICAL LETTERING

TYPE 1

ABCDEFGHIJKLMNOP
QRSTUVWXYZ& 1234567890 $\frac{1}{2}$ $\frac{3}{4}$ $\frac{5}{8}$
TITLES & DRAWING NUMBERS

TYPE 2

FOR SUB-TITLES OR MAIN TITLES (on small drawings)

TYPE 3

ABCDEFGHIJKLMNOPQRSTUVWXYZ& 1234567890 $\frac{1}{2}$ $\frac{3}{4}$ $\frac{5}{8}$ $\frac{9}{32}$
FOR HEADINGS AND PROMINENT NOTES

TYPE 4 ABCDEFGHIJKLMNOPQRSTUVWXYZ& 1234567890 $\frac{1}{2}$ $\frac{3}{4}$ $\frac{5}{8}$ $\frac{23}{64}$
FOR DIMENSIONS & GENERAL NOTES

TYPE 5 OPTIONAL TYPE SAME AS TYPE 4 BUT USING TYPE 3 FOR FIRST LETTER OF PRINCIPAL WORDS.

TYPE 6 abcdefghijklmnopqrstuvwxyz

INCLINED LETTERING (Slope 2 in 5)

TYPE 1

ABCDEFGHIJKLMNOP
QRSTUVWXYZ& 1234567890 $\frac{1}{2}$ $\frac{3}{4}$ $\frac{5}{8}$ $\frac{7}{16}$
MAIN TITLES & DRAWING NUMBERS

TYPE 2

ABCDEFGHIJKLMNOPQRSTUVWXYZ&
1234567890 $\frac{13}{64}$ $\frac{5}{8}$ $\frac{1}{2}$ *FOR SUB-TITLES*

TYPE 3

ABCDEFGHIJKLMNOPQRSTUVWXYZ& *1234567890* $\frac{1}{2}$ $\frac{3}{4}$ $\frac{5}{8}$ $\frac{7}{16}$
FOR HEADINGS AND PROMINENT NOTES

TYPE 4 *ABCDEFGHIJKLMNOPQRSTUVWXYZ&* *1234567890* $\frac{1}{2}$ $\frac{1}{4}$ $\frac{3}{8}$ $\frac{5}{16}$ $\frac{7}{32}$ $\frac{1}{8}$
FOR DIMENSIONS & GENERAL NOTES

TYPE 5 *OPTIONAL TYPE SAME AS TYPE 4 BUT USING TYPE 3 FOR FIRST LETTER OF PRINCIPAL WORDS.*

TYPE 6

abcdefghijklmnopqrstuvwxyz *Type 6 may be used in place of Type 4*

Lettering approved as American Standard, ASA Z14.1-1946, by American Standards Association.

LETTERING

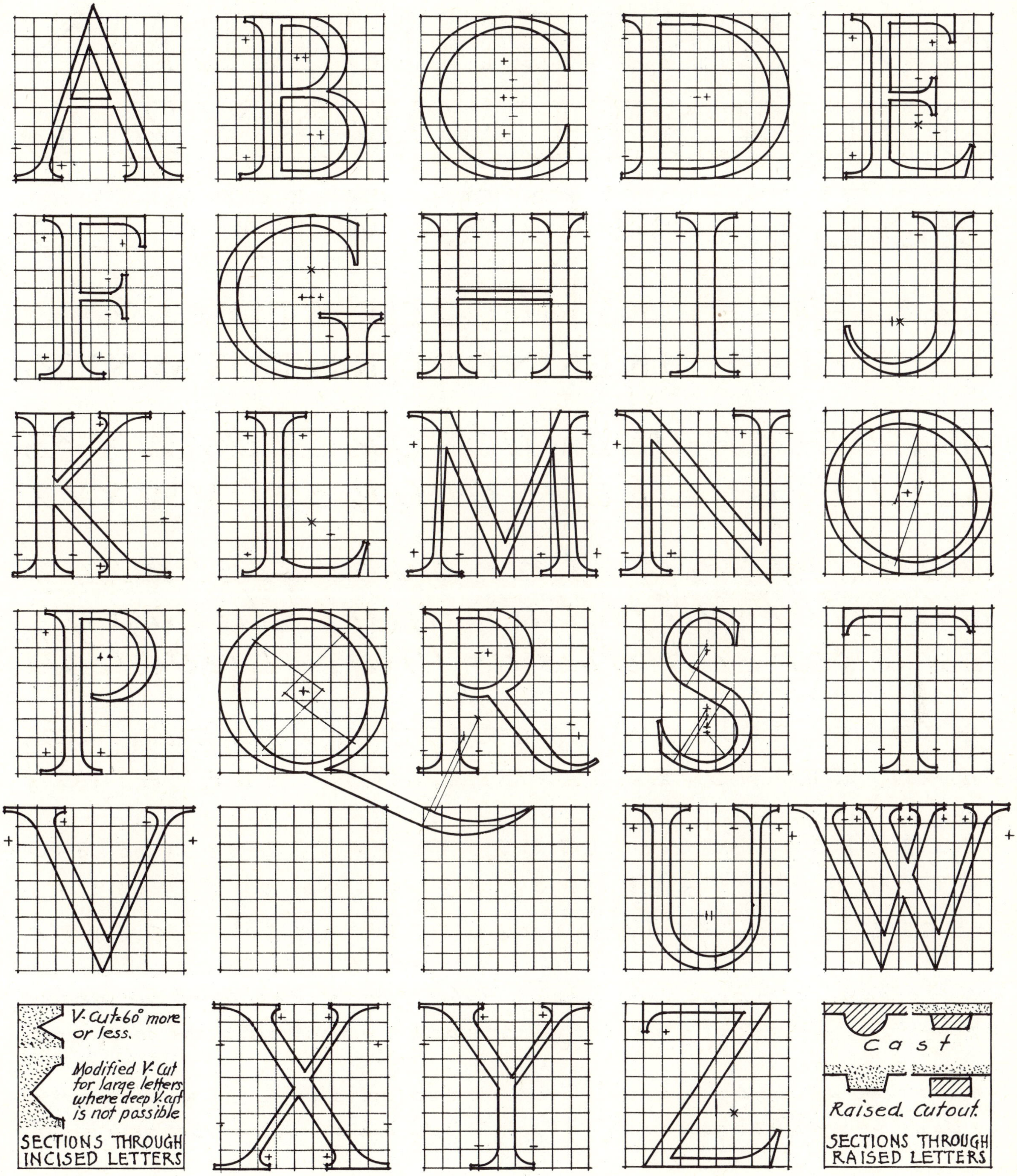
V-Cut=60° more or less.
Modified V-Cut for large letters where deep V-cut is not possible
SECTIONS THROUGH INCISED LETTERS
Cast
Raised. Cutout.
SECTIONS THROUGH RAISED LETTERS

LETTERING

ABCDEFGHIJKLMN
OPQRSTUVWXYZ &
USED FOR TITLES

ABCDEFGHIJKLMNOPQRSTUVWXYZ
ABCDEFGHIJKLMNOPQRSTUVWXYZ

ABCDEFGHIJKLMNOPQRSTUVWXYZ
ABCDEFGHIJKLMNOPQRSTUVWXYZ

abcdefghijklmnopqrstuvwxyz
abcdefghijklmnopqrstuvwxyz
used for subtitles as Plan · Elevation

ABCDEFGHIJKLMNOPQRSTUVWXYZ - PLAN - POOL
PLAN TRANSVERSE SECTION ELEVATION

ABCDEFGHIJKLMNOPQRSTUVWXYZ~1234567890
THIS·IS·ANOTHER·TYPE·USED·FOR·SUB-TITLES
ABCDEFGHIJKLMNOPQRSTUVWXYZ - SLOPING

abcdefgghijklmnopqrstuvwxyz This type is often used for notes
abcdefghijklmnopqrstuuwxyz an upright variation of the foregoing

ABCDEFGHIJKLMNOPQRSTUVWXYZ - NOTES OR SMALL SCALE TITLES
ABCDEFGHIJKLMNOPQRSTUVWXYZ - A SLOPING VARIATION OF ABOVE

abcdefghijklmnopqrstuvwxyz an upright type of lettering which may be used for notes
abcdefghijklmnopqrstuvwxyz Type of lettering used frequently for notes in this book

LEROY® LETTERING

60C-000	FOR DIMENSIONS AND GENERAL NOTES ABCDEFGHIJ 1234
80C-000	FOR DIMENSIONS AND GENERAL NOTES 56789
100C-00	FOR HEADINGS AND PROMINENT NOTES.
120C-0	SCHEDULE HEADINGS AND LARGE NOTES
140C-1	ROOM CAPTIONS AND SUB-HEADINGS
175C-2	SMALL TITLES
200C-3	**HEADINGS & SUBTITLES**
240C-3	FOR TITLES
290C-4	**FOR TITLES**
350C-4	LARGE TITLE
425C-5	DISPLAY T
500C-6	DISPLAY

DISPLAY	700C-9
DISPL	1000C-10
DIS	1350C-12
DS	2000C-14

Above are examples of lettering done with LEROY *Lettering Equipment, made by Keuffel & Esser Co., showing template sizes used and pen width recommended for each size. Either vertical or slanting letters can be produced from the same template.*

WRICO LETTERING

GUIDE NO.	POINT NO.	
G 80 CN	13	ABCDEFGHIJKLMNO1234567890
G 90 CN	13	PQRSTUVWXYZ & 1234567890
G100CN	17	ABCDEFGHIJKLM 1234567890
G120CN	17	NOPQRSTUV&123456789
G140CN	21	WXYZABCD123456789
G175CN	26	EFGHIJKL23456789
G200CN	26	MNOPQR234567
G240C	35	STUVWXYZ&A
G240N	35	1234567890°.″
G290C	35	BCDEFGHIJK
G290N	35	1234567890
G350C	43	LMNOPQR
G350N	43	123456789
G425C	55	STUVWX
G425N	55	1234567
G500C	67	YZABC
G500N	67	89023
G625C	83	DEFG
G625N	83	4567

GUIDE NO.	BRUSH PEN	
AC 75	C	AB
AC100	C	CD
AC 125	D	EF
AC 150	D	G
AC 185	E	H
DC 250	E	K

SPELLING & ROMAN NUMERALS

ROMAN NUMERALS

ARABIC	=	1	5	10	50	100	500	1000	50,000
ROMAN	=	I	V	X	L	C	D	M	$\bar{L}$

RULES:

1. *If no letter precedes a letter of greater value, add the number represented by the letters.*
   Example: XXX represents 30, VI represents 6
2. *If a letter precedes a letter of greater value, subtract the smaller from the greater, add the remainder or the remainders thus obtained to the numbers represented by the other letters.*
   Example: IV represents 4; XL represents 40; CXLV represents 145
3. *A bar placed over a letter multiplies value by 1000.*

OTHER ILLUSTRATIONS	=	9	13	14	42	55	96	1601	4240
		IX	XIII	XIV	XLII	LV	XCVI	MDCI	$\overline{IV}$CCXL

SPELLING

(See Index for spelling of other words.)

Where two spellings are given, the first is preferred.

abbreviations
abutment, abutted, abutting
baluster, balustrade
bat or batt
bathroom (one word)
bathtub (one word)
bedroom (one word)
bevel, beveled or bevelled, beveling or bevelling
brickwork
bridging
bulletin
calk, caulk
cantilever
car-port (or two words)
center, centre (latter usually in England)
colonnade
cupola
dampproofing
datum (singular), data (plural, but may be used as singular)
dining room (two words)
downstairs
drafting, draughting, (latter seldom used)
draftsman, draughtsman (latter seldom used)
enclose, inclose (latter preferable for land)
enclosure, inclosure (latter preferable for land)
entasis
equivalent
escalator
escutcheon
Fahrenheit
faience (tile)
fascia
flagstone (one word)
focus (singular), foci or focuses (plural)
games room (two words)
gauge or gage
grill (to cook on)
grille or grill (grating)
gymnasium (singular), gymnasiums or gymnasia (plural)
hanger (a hanging device)
hangar (a garage for planes)
integral
kalamein
kalsomine or calcimine
lanai (a Hawaiian veranda)
lean-to-roof
level, leveled or levelled, leveling or levelling
lien (mechanics)
living room
louver (Louvre is a building in Paris)
mantel, mantle (latter is also a cloak)
marquee
mat (finish, Matt is a name)
miter, or mitre, mitered or mitred
modillion
mould or mold
mortgage
movable
oriel (oriole is a bird)
paneled or panelled, paneling or panelling
parallel
permanent, permanency
permeable
plaster-work
playroom (one word)
practice (practice of Architecture)
precede, preceding
program or programme
rabbet (pronounced like the animal) or rebate (commonly pronounced like rabbet but may be pronounced as spelled) rabbetted
raggle or reglet (a groove in masonry. The Dictionary defines "reglet" as a narrow flat moulding)
receptacle
remove, removable
sheet metal
spackle or sparkle (usually pronounced like latter. Several other spellings used but none in dictionaries)
stile (of a door. Style of Architecture)
supersede (not supercede)
template or templet
terrazzo
theater (in England often theatre)
through or thru (latter not in some dictionaries)
transept
upstairs
wainscot
wallboard (one word)
waterproofing
weephole (one word)
underpinning

SPACES, SIZES and HEIGHTS for VARIOUS USES

Figures are in square feet	L.R.	D.R.	DINING ALCOVE, DINETTE	KITCHEN	BEDROOMS
minimum	150	100	25 (4 persons)	* 50	80 - limited to 1 bed - crowded
very small	175	120	36 (6 persons)	70	110 - limited to 1 bed
small	220	135	50	90	120 - dble. bed may be used - crowded
medium (aver.)	260	155	60	110	140 - twin beds may be used - crowded
above medium	280	175	70	135	170 - twin beds may be used
large	300	195	80	165	190 - twin beds may be used
very large	320	215	90	180	220 - twin beds may be used

*Kitchens under 50 sq. ft. are termed kitchenettes; common to apartments.

Where living room and dining room or dining room and kitchen are combined, the area may be slightly less than the total of the two areas in separate rooms.

Room sizes are often determined by door and window locations, arrangement, amount and size of furniture, arrangement of plan for traffic, number of occupants of room, and size of family.

Living and dining room sizes are especially dependent on number of persons in family; bedrooms, on number of occupants and type of beds.

Bathrooms today are seldom made much larger than the minimum of 35 sq. ft. (5' x 7')

SIZE OF ROOMS FOR SMALL HOUSES AND APARTMENTS

Heights given are for use for preliminary assumptions until these conditions are fully investigated: (1) local codes, (2) framing systems, (3) ducts for vent. and air-conditioning, (4) pipes and conduits, (5) economy, (6) appearance, (7) use, (8) wall treatment.

Residential ceiling heights based on appearance which is assumed related to room widths. However, ceiling height of 8'-0" is being used as standard in dry wall, prefabricated construction.

RESIDENTIAL CEILING HEIGHTS - ACCEPTABLE MINIMUMS

L.R., D.R., STUDY, ETC. WIDTH	HEIGHT	BEDROOM	KITCHEN
10'-12'	7'-8" - 7'-10"	small - 7'-6"	min. 7'-4" takes standard cabinets but is bad for ventilation. 7'-6" to 8'-0" good, but requires more furring over cabinets. Usually depends on height of other 1st floor spaces.
12'-14'	8'-0" - 8'-2"	medium - 7'-8" - 8'-0"	
14'-16'	8'-4" - 8'-6"	med. large-8'-0"-8'-2"	
16'-18'	8'-8" - 9'-0"	very large-8'-2"-8'-4"	
18'-20'	9'-2" - 9'-6"	customary to use 7'-6" on 2nd floor of small houses.	
20'-22'	9'-8" - 10'-0"		

HOTELS - Bedroom ceiling heights ± 8'-0". 1st to 2nd fl. heights, 17'-6" to 18'-0" possible. This allows for mechanical trade offsets and mezzanine.

SCHOOL CLASS ROOMS - Often governed by state codes. These often require 11' to 12' clear ceiling heights. Also consider room sizes, window heights, type of construction. 10'-0" to 12'-0" quite generally used. Height at exterior walls varies from 9'-0" to 13'-0" in contemporary buildings.

OFFICE BUILDINGS - 1st fl. ceiling height, 12'-0" min., 24'-0" with mezzanine. Typical floor to floor height, considering air-conditioning, using corridor for ducts, 11'-3" to 12'0", resulting in following ceiling heights: (1) corridor, 8'-0" to 8'-6"; (2) unfurred outer bays, 10'-8" to 11'-0"; (3) spaces with hung ceilings, 8'-10" to 9'-6".

LOFT BUILDINGS - Consider use. Generally 12'-0" to 12'-6".

LIBRARY STACKS - Floor to floor, 7'-6". Ceiling heights, 7'-2½" to 7'-3½".

SPECIALTY SHOPS - 1st fl. ceiling heights, 12'-0" min., except 8'-0" to mezzanine.

DEPARTMENT STORES - 1st fl. ceiling heights, 13'-0" for open area of 50,000 sq. ft. and under. Typical floors, 11'-0" clear ceiling heights.

CEILING AND STORY HEIGHTS

NOTE: local codes will govern.

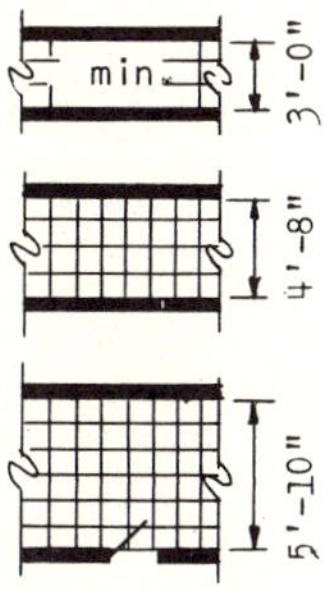
min.
3'-0"
4'-8"
5'-10"

widths depend on traffic load, door swings.

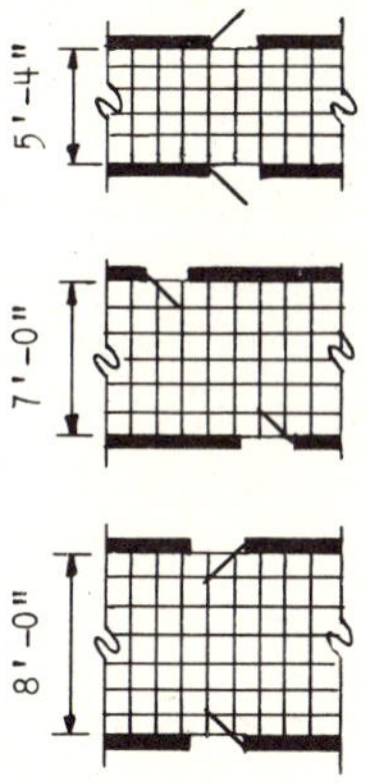
5'-4"
7'-0"
8'-0"

OFFICE BLDG. CORRIDORS

ELEVATOR LOBBIES

Elevator one side-6'-0" min.
9'-0" ample

Elevator two sides-10'-0" min.
12'-0" ample.

RESIDENTIAL BUILDINGS

Front hall (stairs)- 7'-8"
Front hall (no stairs)-5'-0" to 7'-0"

Bedroom halls- 3'-0" to 5'-0"
Service halls (min.) - 3'-0"
Dormitories- 5'-0" to 7'-0"

*Nat'l Building Code requirements.

STAIR WIDTHS:

Service or access:
1 person: 2'-0" to 2'-6"
2 persons: 3'-6" to 4'-0"

Residences: 3'-0" min., 3'-4" to 3'-6" rec.
Residential folding stairs: 2'-0", 2'-4", 2'-6"
Req'd exit stairs: 3'-8" min., except for single tenant, 40 person max. occupancy: 3'-0" min.*

Unit of exit width: 22"*

TYPE OF OCCUPANCY	# OF PERSONS/UNIT OF EXIT WIDTH
Places of assembly, street or ground floor..............	100
Public, Business or Storage......................	60
Residential or Institutional....	30

CORRIDORS, LOBBIES, HALLS AND STAIRS.

AREA REQUIREMENTS for PLANNING

TABLE OF CONTENTS

HOUSE BATHROOMS; BEDROOMS and CLOTHES STORAGE

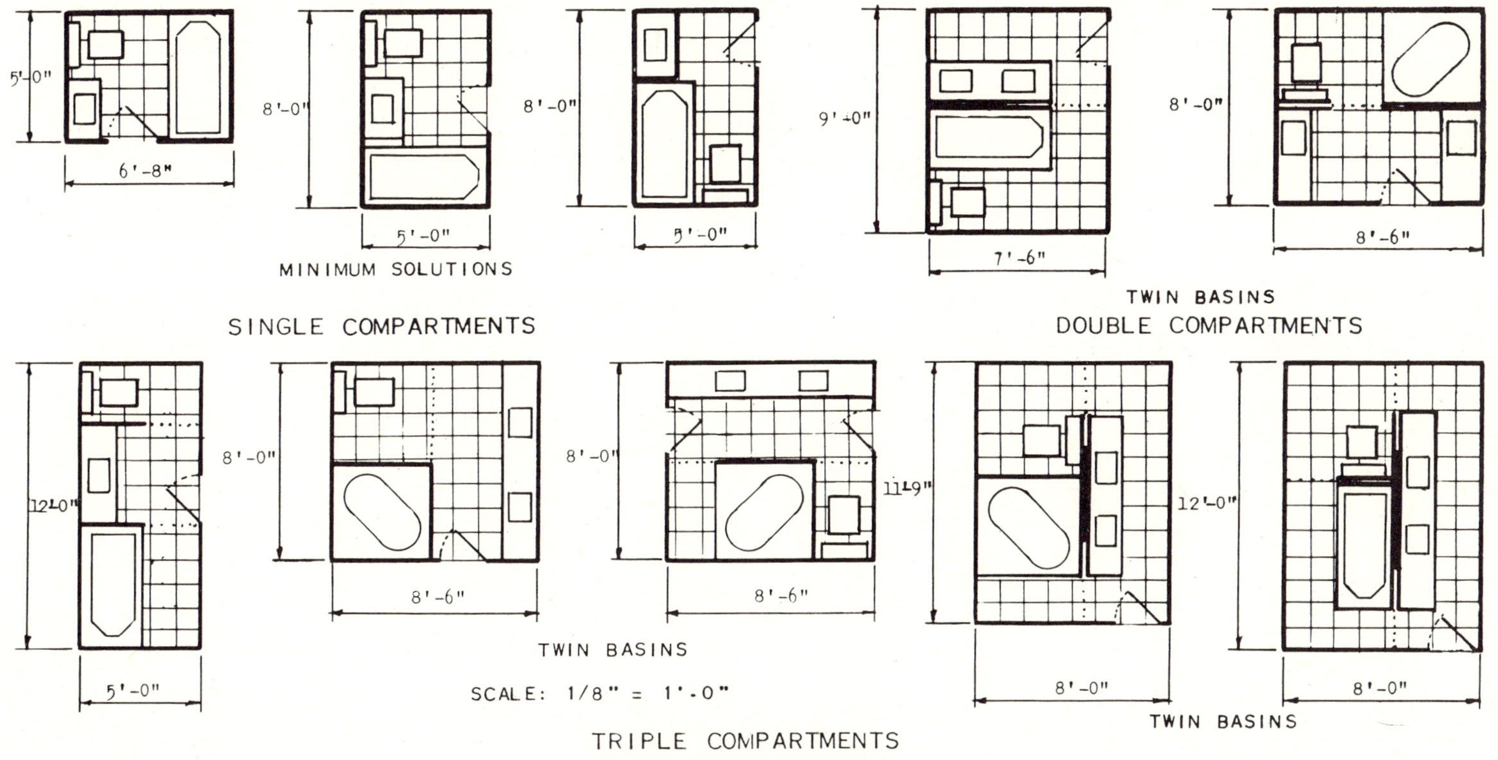
5'-0"
6'-8"
8'-0"
5'-0"
8'-0"
5'-0"
MINIMUM SOLUTIONS
SINGLE COMPARTMENTS
9'-0"
7'-6"
8'-0"
8'-6"
TWIN BASINS
DOUBLE COMPARTMENTS
12'-0"
5'-0"
8'-0"
8'-6"
8'-0"
8'-6"
TWIN BASINS
SCALE: 1/8" = 1'-0"
11'-9"
8'-0"
12'-0"
8'-0"
TWIN BASINS
TRIPLE COMPARTMENTS

BATHROOM SIZES

The average person requires eight linear feet of drawer space for clothing. Clearances required for the pulling out of drawers and for closet access and entry into room must be taken into consideration. The bedroom clearances shown are recommended for passage and are desirable for bedmaking.

The diagrams below show a relationship of square foot areas required when planning bedrooms with clothes storage. Sitting, writing, and make-up areas are not included. These must be added if required.

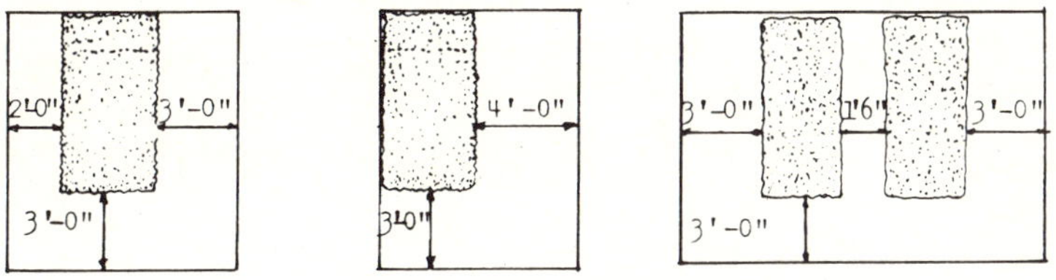
2'-0"
3'-0"
3'-0"
4'-0"
3'-0"
3'-0"
1'-6"
3'-0"
3'-0"

BEDROOM CLEARANCES

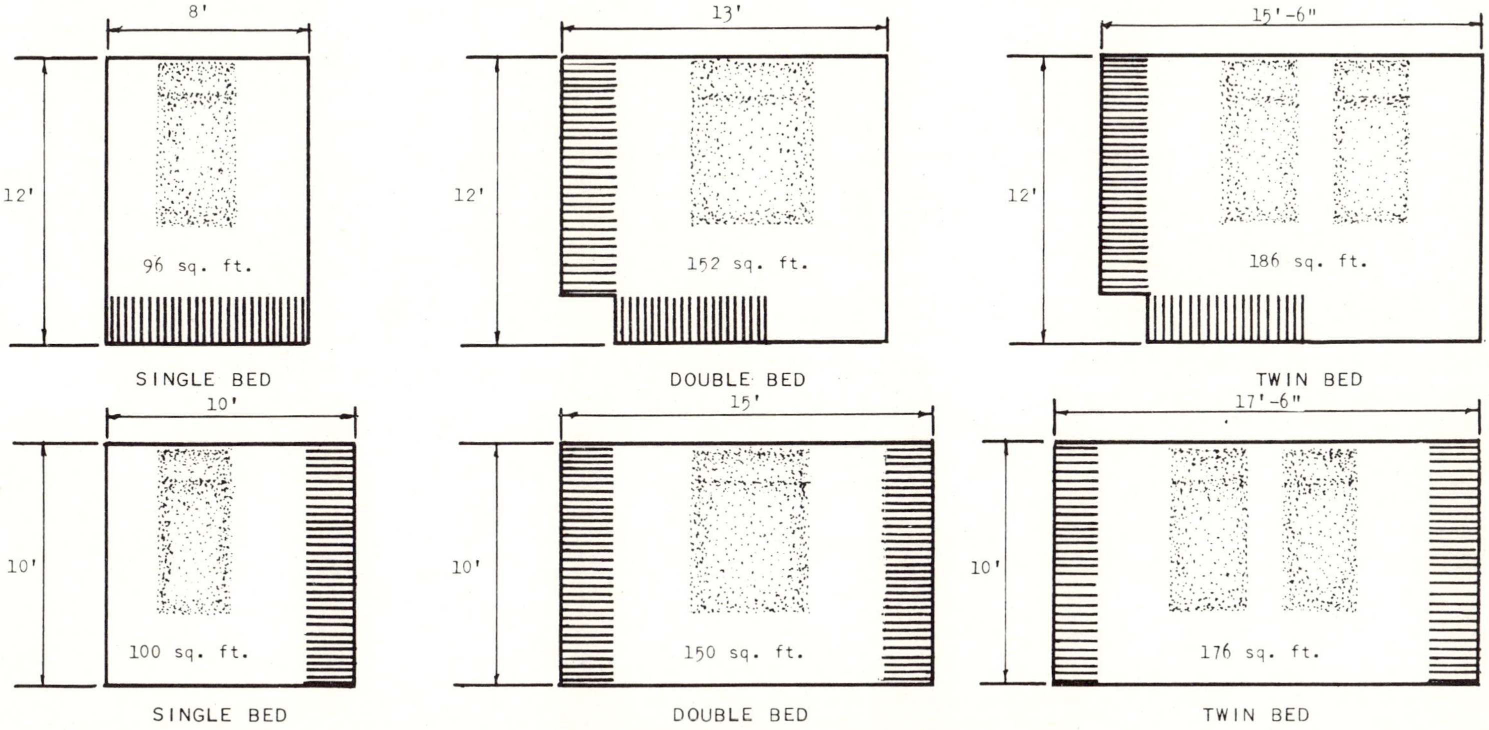
8'
12'
96 sq. ft.
SINGLE BED
13'
12'
152 sq. ft.
DOUBLE BED
15'-6"
12'
186 sq. ft.
TWIN BED
10'
10'
100 sq. ft.
SINGLE BED
15'
10'
150 sq. ft.
DOUBLE BED
17'-6"
10'
176 sq. ft.
TWIN BED

BEDROOMS AND CLOTHES STORAGE

FURNITURE - SPACE REQUIREMENTS

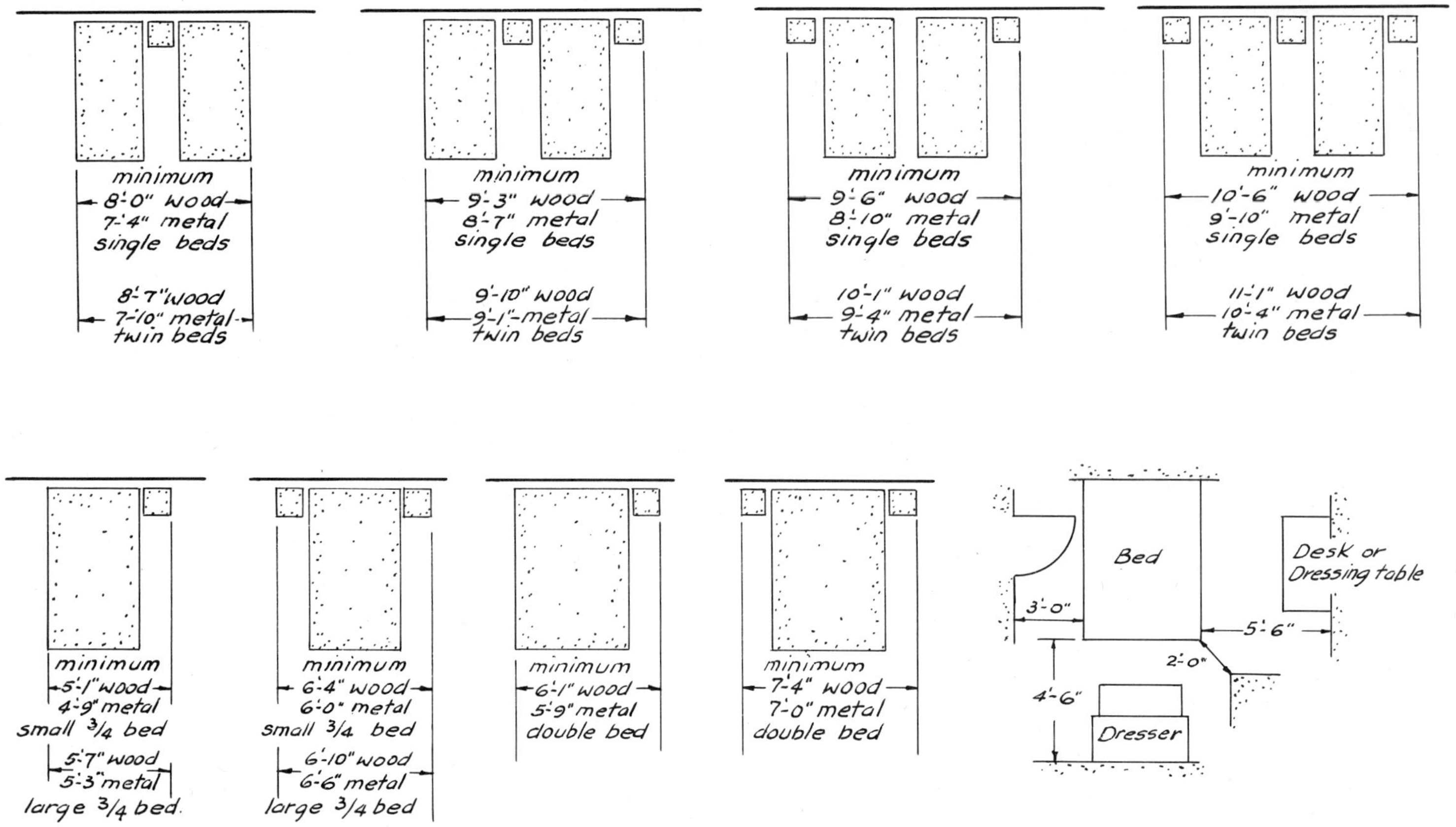
minimum
8'-0" wood
7'-4" metal
single beds
8'-7" wood
7'-10" metal
twin beds
minimum
9'-3" wood
8'-7" metal
single beds
9'-10" wood
9'-1" metal
twin beds
minimum
9'-6" wood
8'-10" metal
single beds
10'-1" wood
9'-4" metal
twin beds
minimum
10'-6" wood
9'-10" metal
single beds
11'-1" wood
10'-4" metal
twin beds
minimum
5'-1" wood
4'-9" metal
small 3/4 bed
5'-7" wood
5'-3" metal
large 3/4 bed
minimum
6'-4" wood
6'-0" metal
small 3/4 bed
6'-10" wood
6'-6" metal
large 3/4 bed
minimum
6'-1" wood
5'-9" metal
double bed
minimum
7'-4" wood
7'-0" metal
double bed
Bed
Desk or
Dressing table
3'-0"
5'-6"
2'-0"
4'-6"
Dresser

WALL SPACE REQUIREMENTS FOR BED & NIGHT TABLE ARRANGEMENTS

(For bed sizes see page showing beds)
Scale 1/8" = 1'-0"

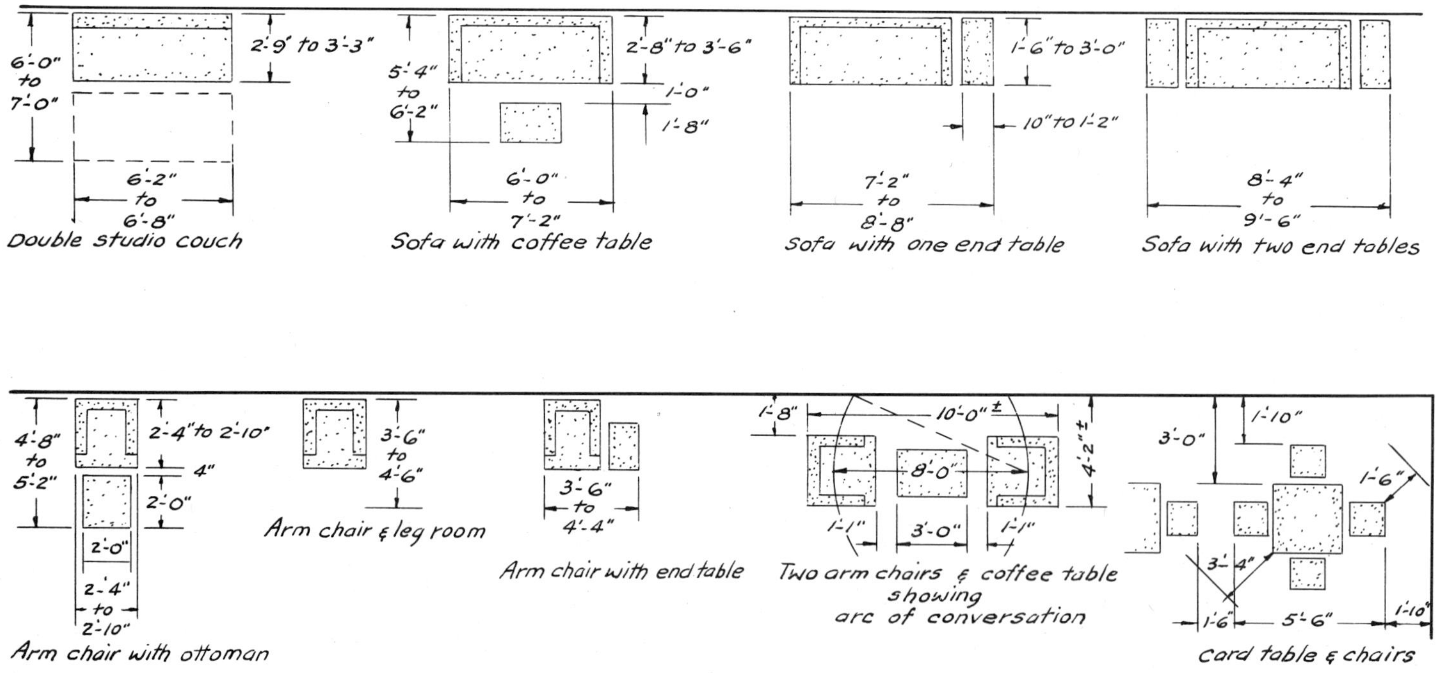
6'-0"
to
7'-0"
2'-9" to 3'-3"
6'-2"
to
6'-8"
Double studio couch
5'-4"
to
6'-2"
2'-8" to 3'-6"
1'-0"
1'-8"
6'-0"
to
7'-2"
Sofa with coffee table
1'-6" to 3'-0"
10" to 1'-2"
7'-2"
to
8'-8"
Sofa with one end table
8'-4"
to
9'-6"
Sofa with two end tables
4'-8"
to
5'-2"
2'-4" to 2'-10"
4"
2'-0"
2'-0"
2'-4"
to
2'-10"
Arm chair with ottoman
3'-6"
to
4'-6"
Arm chair & leg room
3'-6"
to
4'-4"
Arm chair with end table
1'-8"
10'-0" ±
4'-2" ±
8'-0"
1'-1"
3'-0"
1'-1"
Two arm chairs & coffee table
showing
arc of conversation
3'-0"
1'-10"
1'-6"
3'-4"
1'-6"
5'-6"
1'-10"
Card table & chairs

LIVING ROOM SPACE REQUIREMENTS

(See other furniture sheets for other sizes)
Scale 1/8" = 1'-0"

BATHROOMS - MISCELLANEOUS

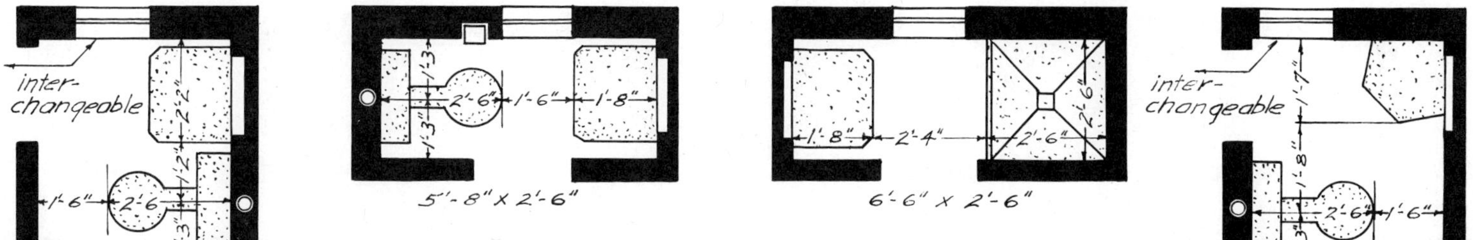
inter-
changeable
4'-0" x 4'-7"
5'-8" x 2'-6"
6'-6" x 2'-6"
inter-
changeable
4'-0" x 4'-6"

TWO FIXTURE LAVATORIES

For fixture sizes used, see notes on preceding bathroom pages

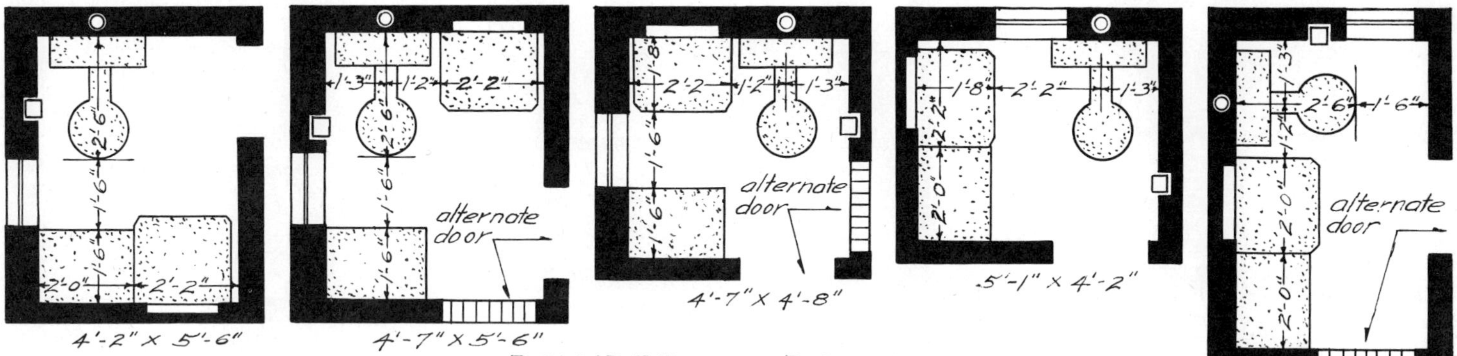
4'-2" x 5'-6"
alternate
door
4'-7" x 5'-6"
alternate
door
4'-7" x 4'-8"
5'-1" x 4'-2"
alternate
door
4'-0" x 6'-5"

POWDER ROOMS

Scale: 1/4" = 1'-0"

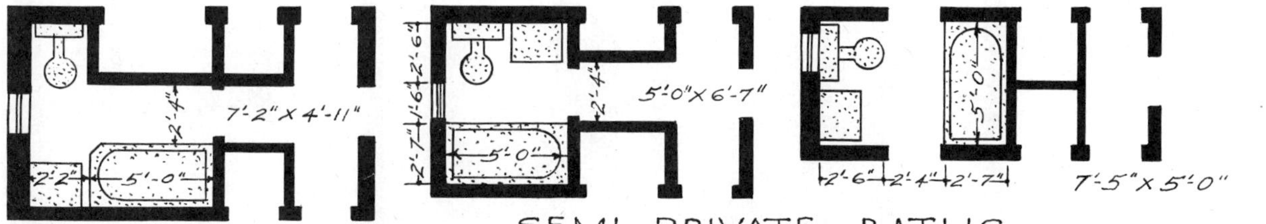
7'-2" x 4'-11"
5'-0" x 6'-7"
7'-5" x 5'-0"

SEMI-PRIVATE BATHS

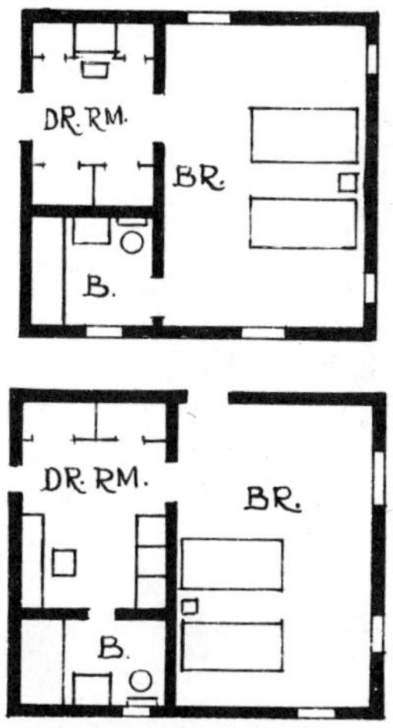
DR. RM.
BR.
B.
DR. RM.
BR.
B.

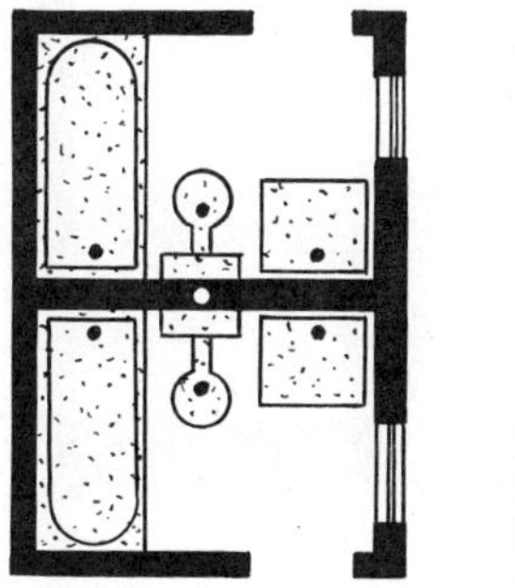

ECONOMICAL GROUPING of BATHS — BACK to BACK

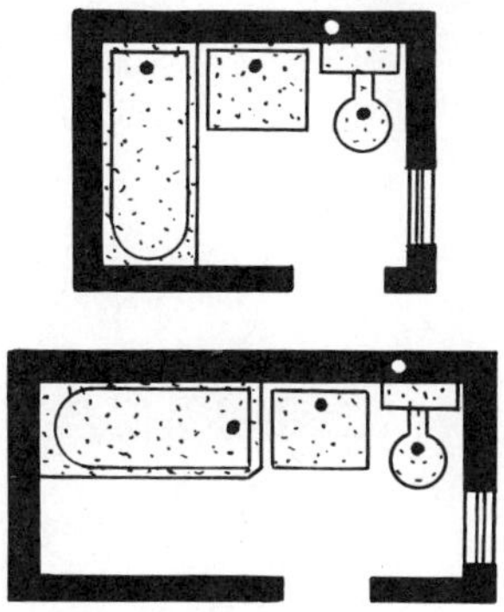

ECONOMICAL

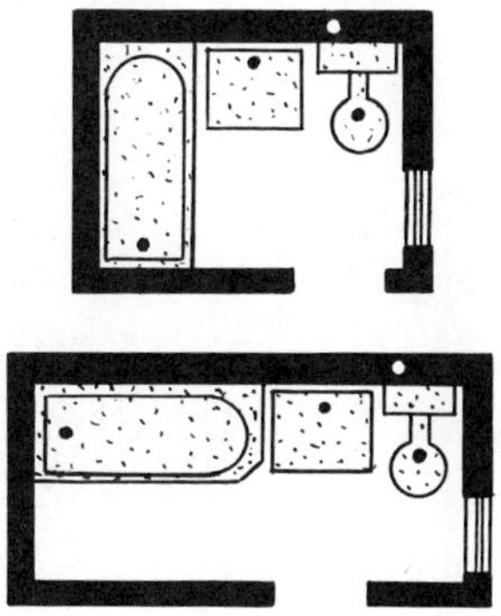

UNECONOMICAL

ECONOMICAL
Bath at left has shorter run of waste. Bath at right will require either special floor framing or hung ceiling below.

UNECONOMICAL
Bath at left has shorter run of waste. Bath at right may require hung ceiling below if joists are shallow.

Total area of bedroom plus dressing room is about the same as conventional bedroom with closets

BEDROOM DRESSING ROOM & BATH

LOCATION of FIXTURE OUTLETS for PIPING ECONOMY

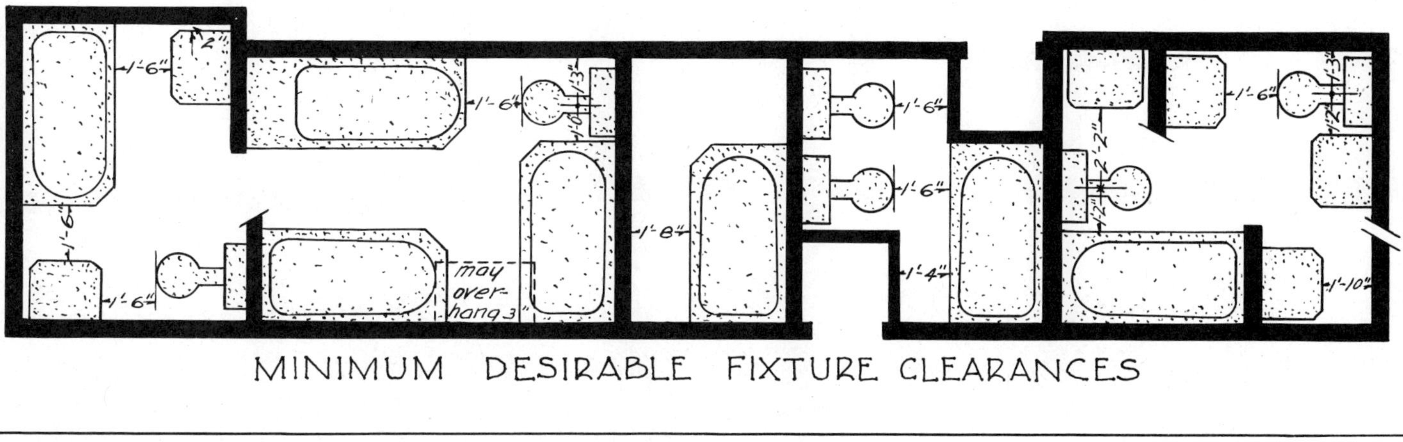
may
over-
hang 3"

MINIMUM DESIRABLE FIXTURE CLEARANCES

BATHROOMS - COMPARTMENTED

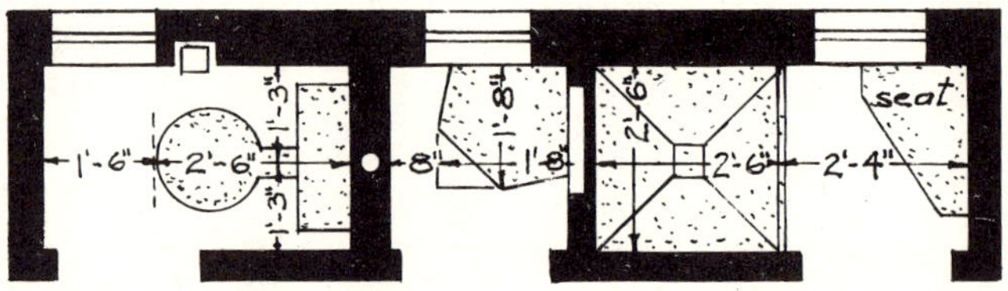
seat

12'-2" x 2'-6"

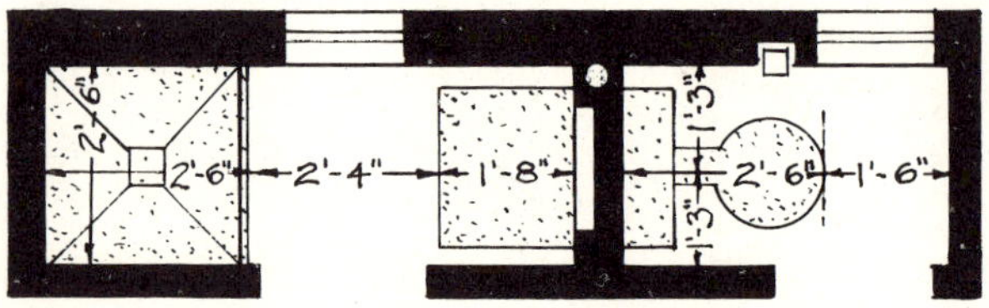

11'-1" x 2'-6"

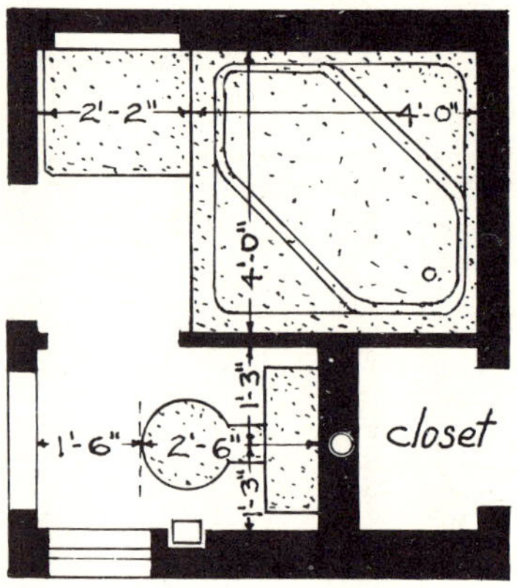
closet

6'-2" x 6' 9"

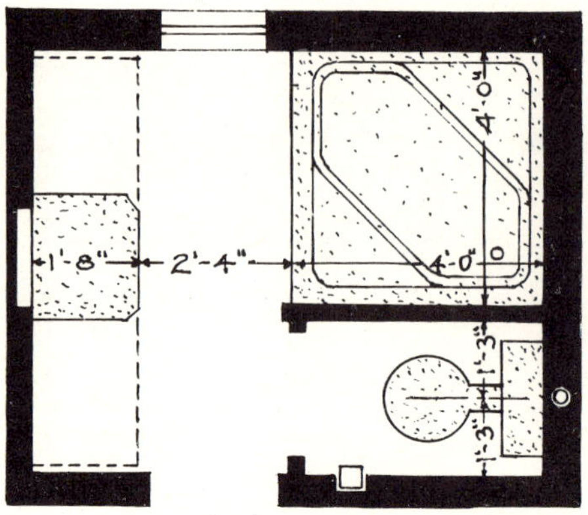

8'-0" x 6'-9"

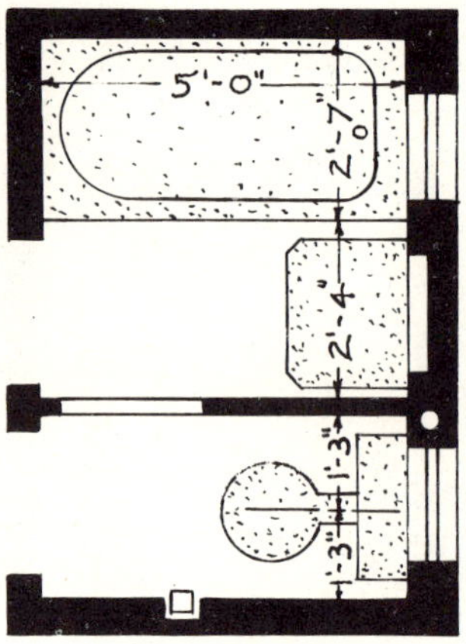

5'-0" x 7'-8"

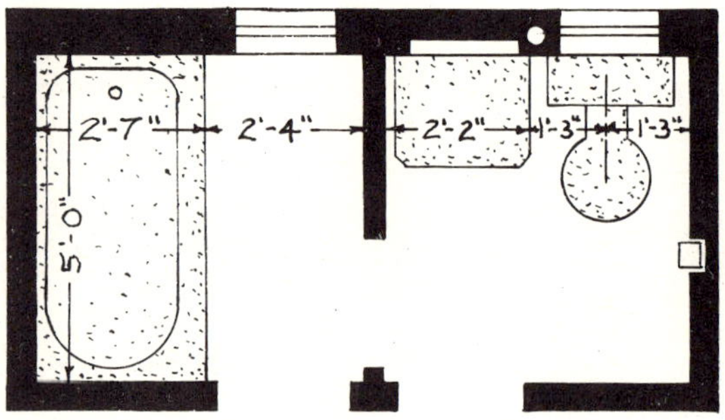

9'-10" x 5'-0"

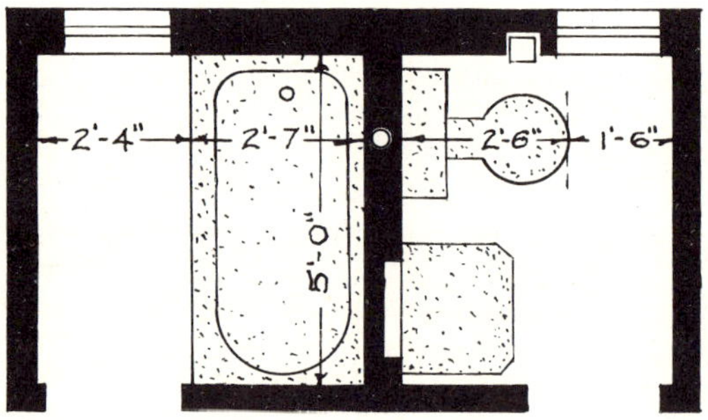

9'-6" x 5'-0"

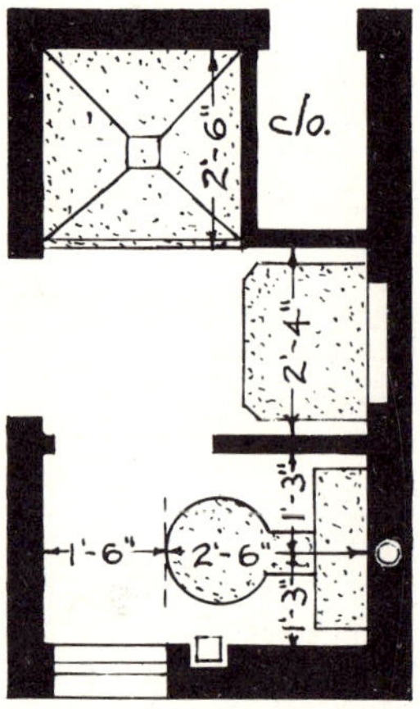
clo.

4'-0" x 7'-7"

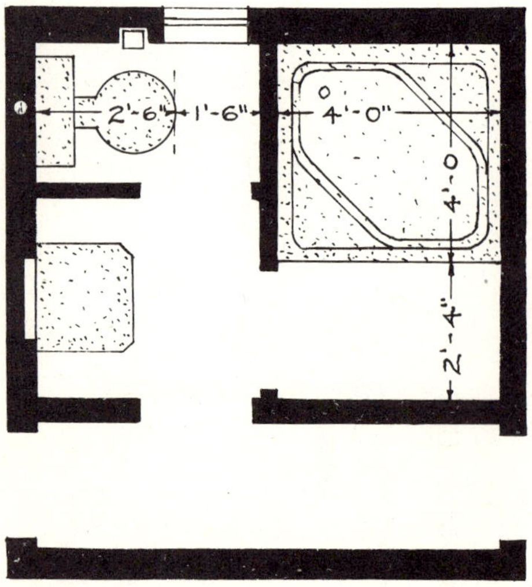

8'-3" x 6'-4"

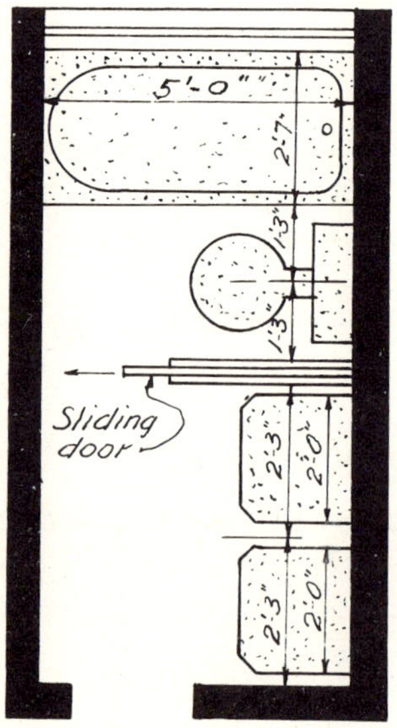
Sliding door

5'-0" x 10'-0"

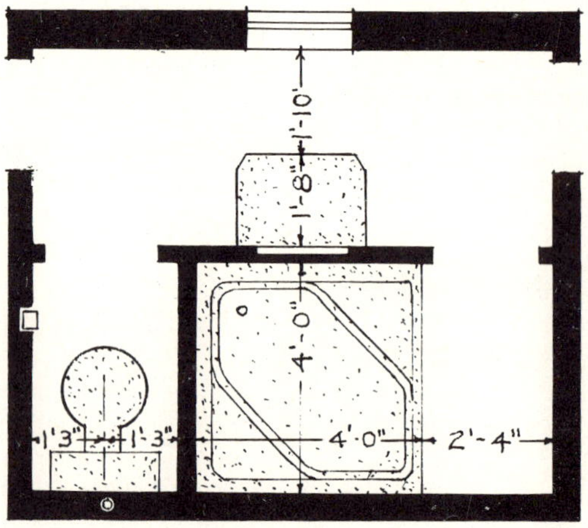

9'-1" x 7'-9"

Note: Fixture areas and space allowances used in plans are: tub, square, 4'-0" x 4'-0", rectangular, 5'-0" x 2'-7" (Dimensions are to rough plaster. Deduct 3/4-1" wherever tub butts wall to allow for finish coat); shower 2'-6" x 2'-6"; lavatory 2'-0" x 1'-8"; corner lavatory 1'-8" x 1'-8", 1'-9" from corner to front; water closet, 1'-10½" x 2'-6"; doors; 2'-0". Windows and doors are in optimum locations. If different fixture sizes are used change room sizes accordingly. Cumulative dimensions include partitions. Refer to pages on fixtures & clearances

Scale: 1/4 = 1'-0"

BATHROOMS - THREE and FOUR FIXTURES

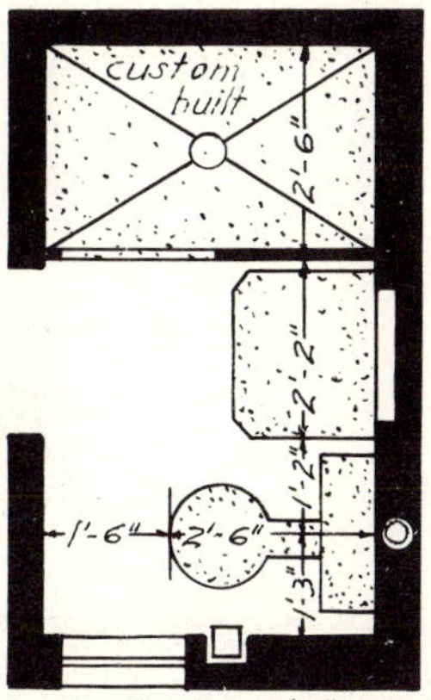
custom built
2'-6"
2'-2"
1'-2"
1'-6"
2'-6"
1'-3"
4'-0" x 7'-1"

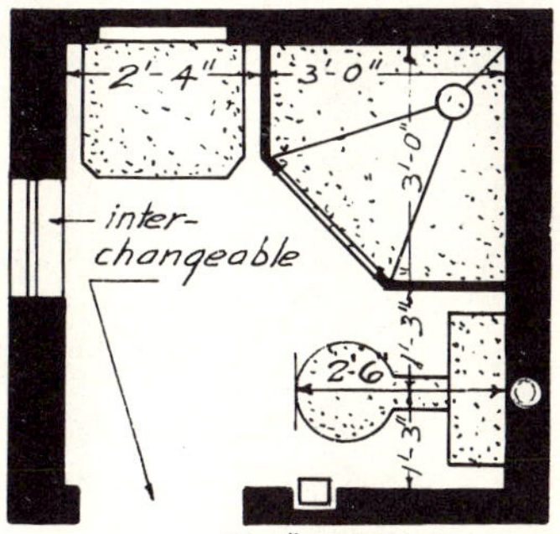
2'-4"
3'-0"
3'-0"
inter-changeable
1'-3"
2'-6"
1'-3"
5'-4" x 5'-6"

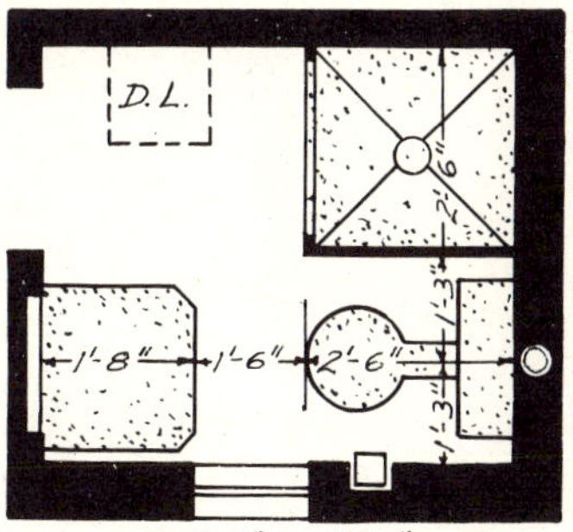
D.L.
2'-6"
1'-3"
1'-8"
1'-6"
2'-6"
1'-3"
5'-8" x 5'-0"

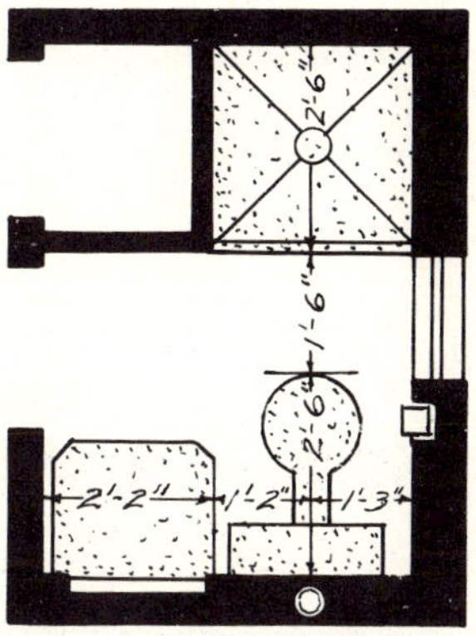
2'-6"
1'-6"
2'-6"
2'-2"
1'-2"
1'-3"
4'-7" x 6'-6"

THREE FIXTURE BATHROOM with SHOWER

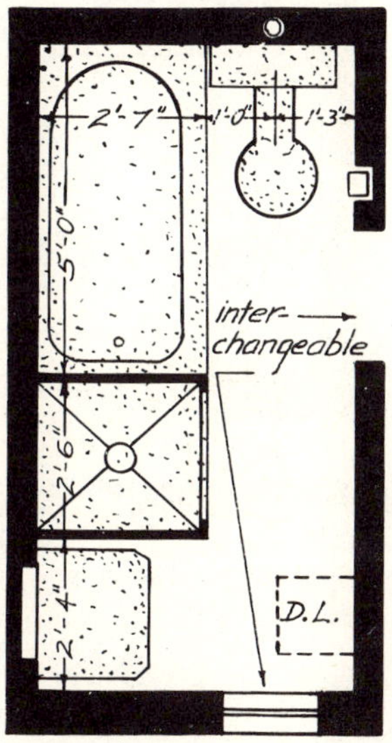
2'-7"
1'-0"
1'-3"
5'-0"
inter-changeable
2'-6"
2'-4"
D.L.
4'-10" x 9'-10"

Note: Fixture areas and space allowances are: Tubs rectangular 5'-0" x 2'-7" to rough plaster (deduct 3/4"-1" where tub butts wall); showers, square 2'-6" x 2'-6", bevel corner 3'0" (bevel 2'-3"), shower door swing 2'-2"; lavatory 1'-8" x 2'-0"; dental lavatory 1'-2" x 1'-2"; water closet 1'-10 1/2" x 2'-6". If different fixture sizes are used, change room sizes accordingly. Windows and doors (2'-0") are in optimum positions. Cumulative dimensions include partitions. Refer to pages on fixtures and clearances.

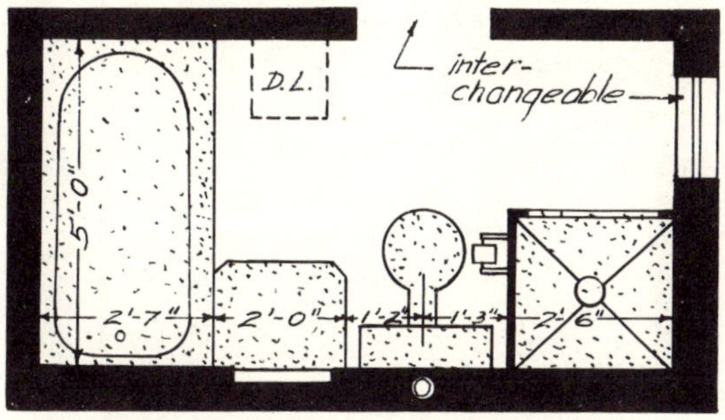
D.L.
inter-changeable
5'-0"
2'-7"
2'-0"
1'-2"
1'-3"
2'-6"
9'-6" x 5'-0"

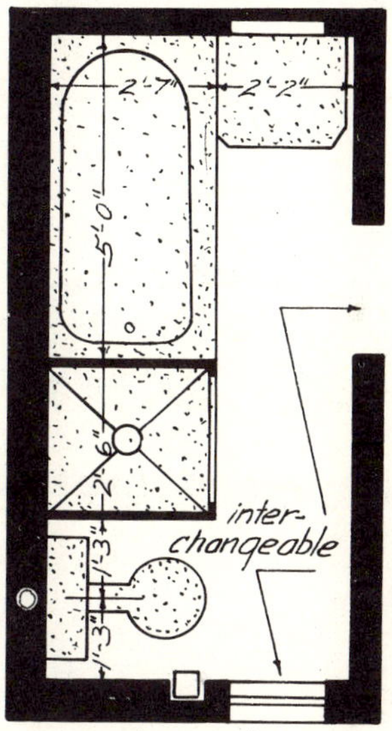
2'-7"
2'-2"
5'-0"
2'-6"
inter-changeable
1'-3"
1'-3"
4'-9 x 10'-0"

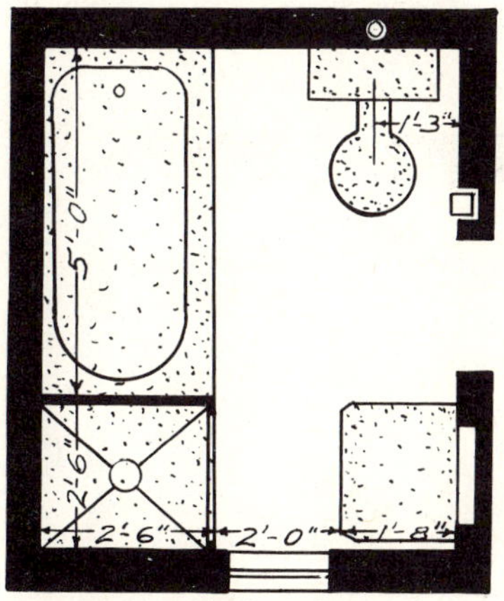
1'-3"
5'-0"
2'-6"
2'-6"
2'-0"
1'-8"
6'-2" x 7'-6"

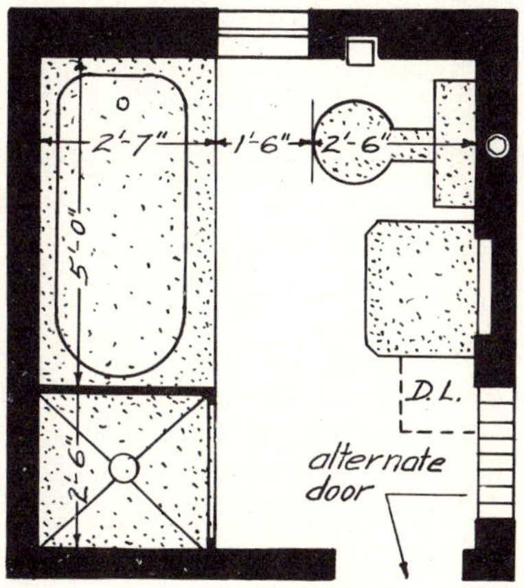
2'-7"
1'-6"
2'-6"
5'-0"
D.L.
2'-6"
alternate door
6'-7" x 7'-6"

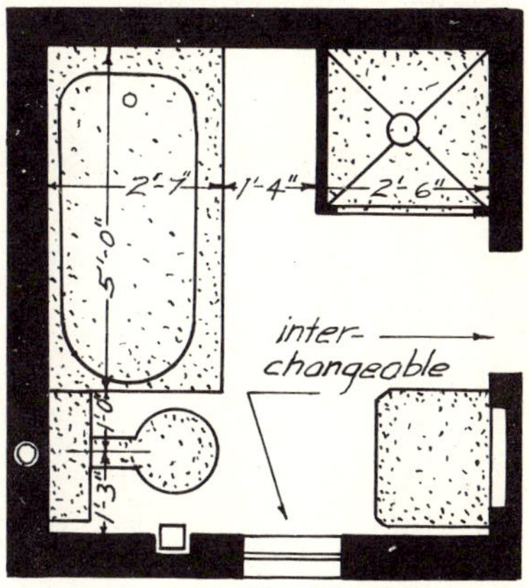
2'-7"
1'-4"
2'-6"
5'-0"
inter-changeable
1'-0"
1'-3"
6'-5" x 7'-3"

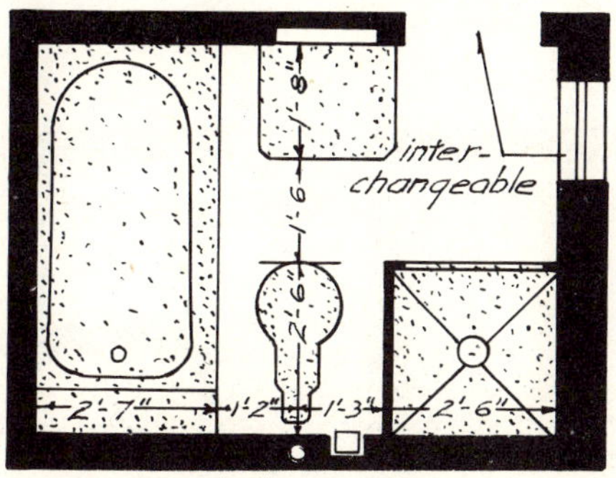
1'-8"
inter-changeable
1'-6"
2'-6"
2'-7"
1'-2"
1'-3"
2'-6"
7'-6" x 5'-8"

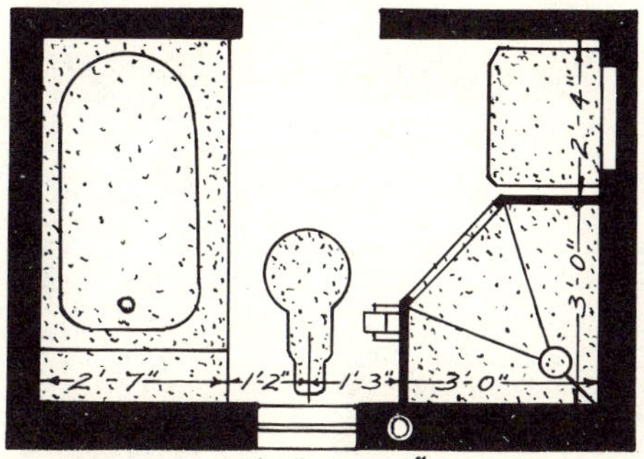
2'-4"
3'-0"
2'-7"
1'-2"
1'-3"
3'-0"
8'-0" x 5'-4"

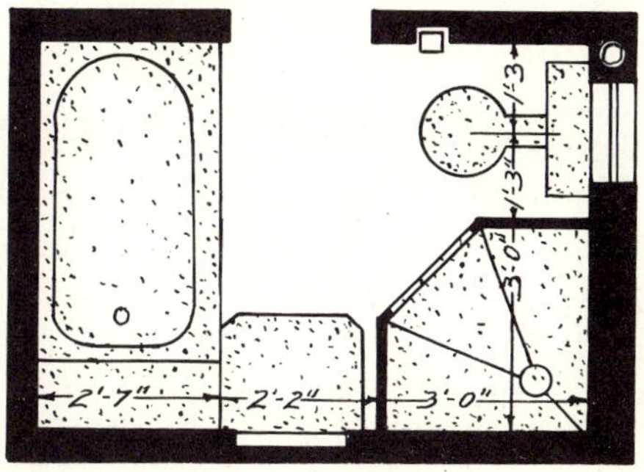
1'-3"
1'-3"
3'-0"
2'-7"
2'-2"
3'-0"
7'-9" x 5'-6"

Scale. 1/4" = 1'-0"

FOUR FIXTURE BATHROOM

BATHROOMS - THREE FIXTURES

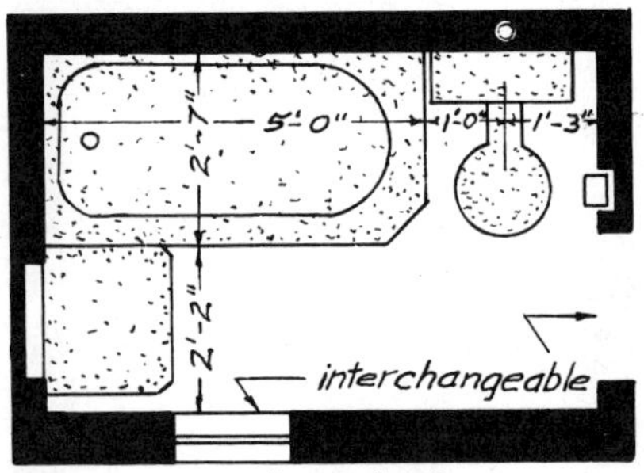
5'-0"
2'-7"
1'-0"
1'-3"
2'-2"
interchangeable

7'-3" x 4'-9"

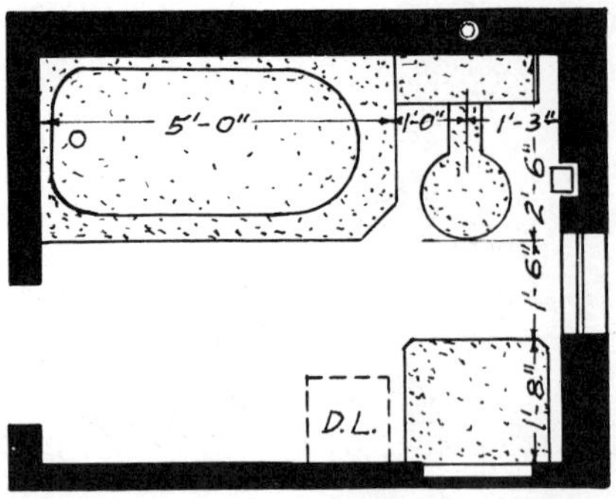
5'-0"
1'-0"
1'-3"
2'-6"
1'-6"
1'-8"
D.L.

7'-3" x 5'-8"

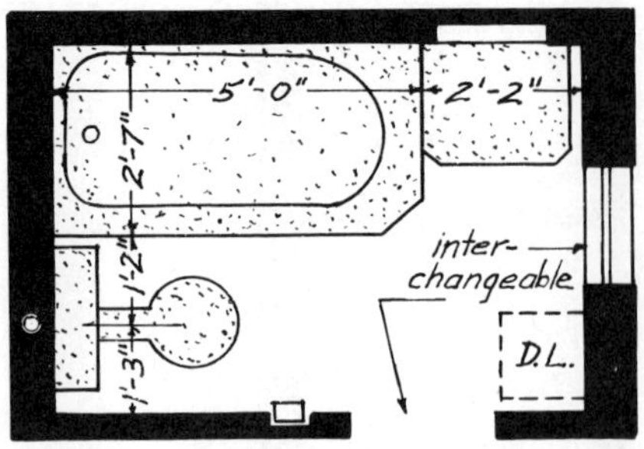
5'-0"
2'-2"
2'-7"
1'-2"
1'-3"
inter-
changeable
D.L.

7'-2" x 5'-0"

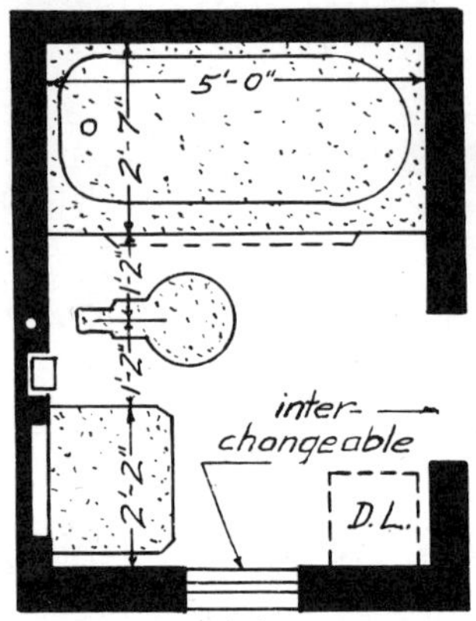
5'-0"
2'-7"
1'-2"
1'-2"
2'-2"
inter-
changeable
D.L.

5'-0" x 7'-1"

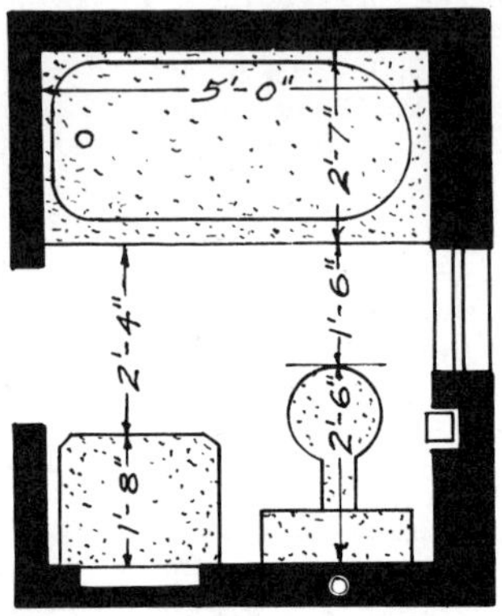
5'-0"
2'-7"
2'-4"
1'-6"
2'-6"
1'-8"

5'-0" x 6'-7"

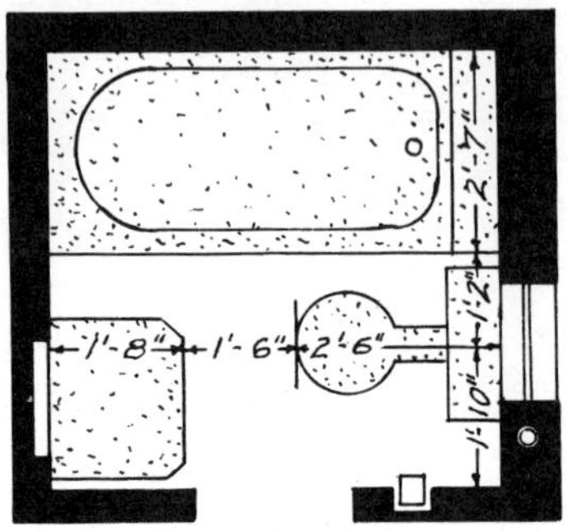
2'-7"
1'-8"
1'-6"
2'-6"
1'-2"
1'-10"

5'-8" x 5'-7"

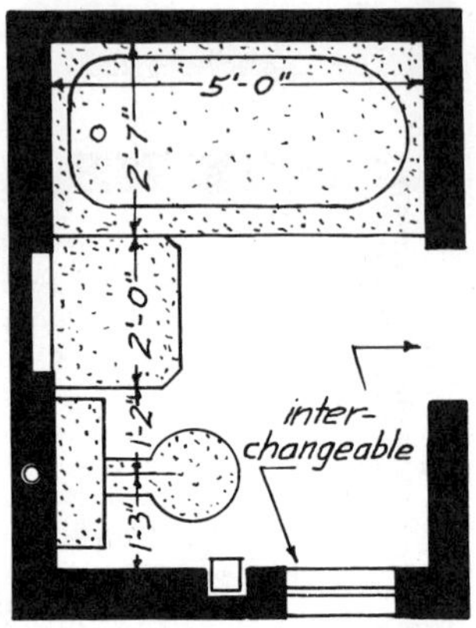
5'-0"
2'-7"
2'-0"
1'-2"
1'-3"
inter-
changeable

5'-0" x 7'-0

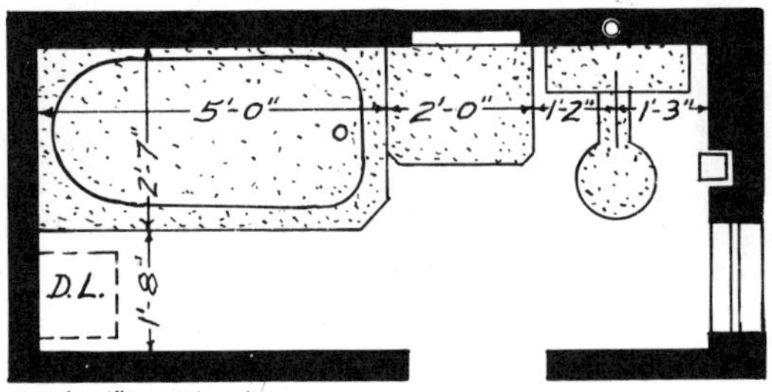
5'-0"
2'-0"
1'-2"
1'-3"
2'-7"
1'-8"
D.L.

9'-5" x 4'-3"

Note: Fixture areas & space allowances used in plans are: tub square, 4'-0", rect. 5'-0" x 2'-7" (Sizes are to rough plaster. Deduct ¾"-1" where tub butts wall for finish coat.) lav. 1'-8" x 1'-8", dental lav. 1'-2" x 1'-2"; W.C. 1'-10½" x 2'-6". For other size fixtures change room size accordingly. Doors (2'-0") and windows are in optimum locations. Alternate location ▭ See pages on clearances & fixtures

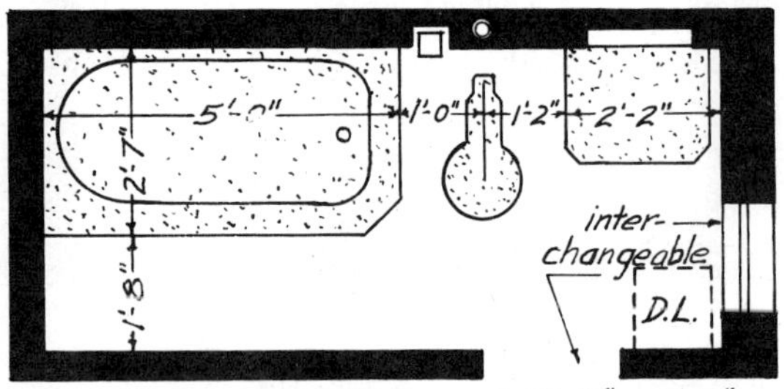
5'-0"
1'-0"
1'-2"
2'-2"
2'-7"
1'-8"
inter-
changeable
D.L.

9'-4" x 4'-3"

THREE FIXTURE BATHROOMS with RECTANGULAR TUB

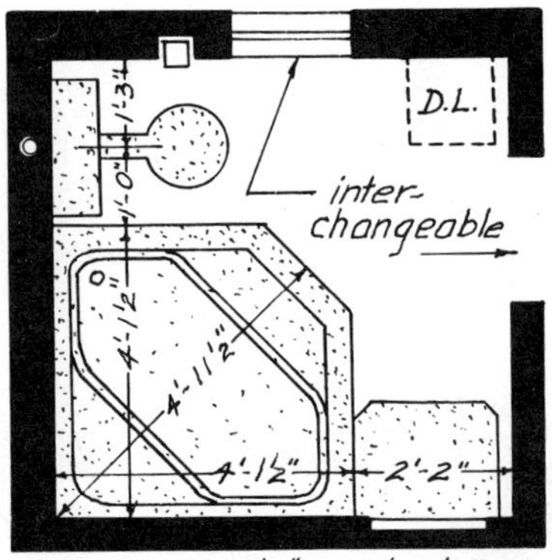
1'-3"
1'-0"
D.L.
inter-
changeable
4'-1½"
4'-11½"
4'-1½"
2'-2"

6'-3½" x 6'-4½"

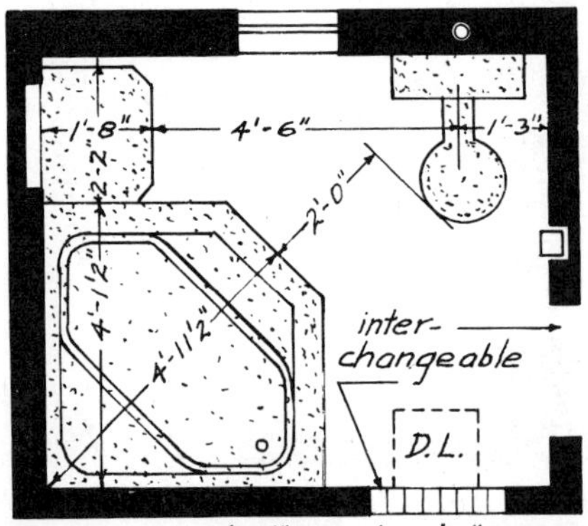
1'-8"
4'-6"
1'-3"
2'-2"
2'-0"
4'-1½"
4'-11½"
inter-
changeable
D.L.

7'-5" x 6'-3½"

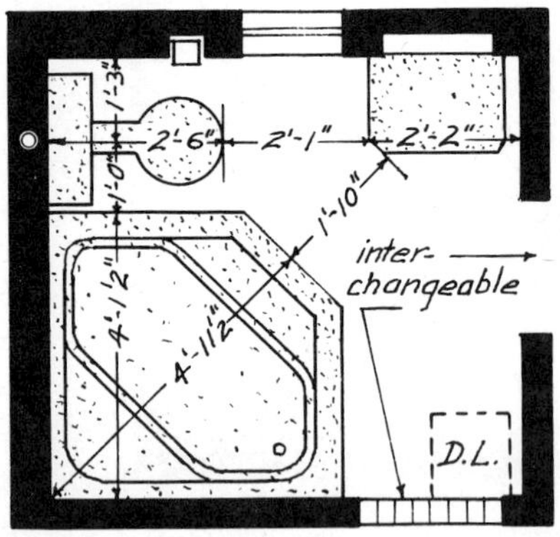
1'-3"
2'-6"
2'-1"
2'-2"
1'-0"
1'-10"
4'-1½"
4'-11½"
inter-
changeable
D.L.

6'-9" x 6'-4½"

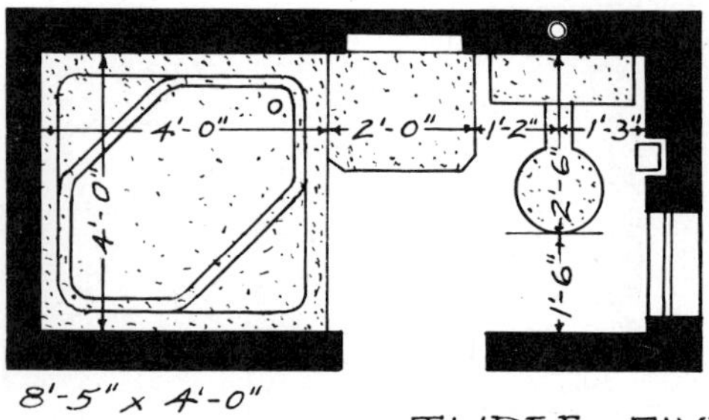
4'-0"
2'-0"
1'-2"
1'-3"
4'-0"
2'-6"
1'-6"

8'-5" x 4'-0"

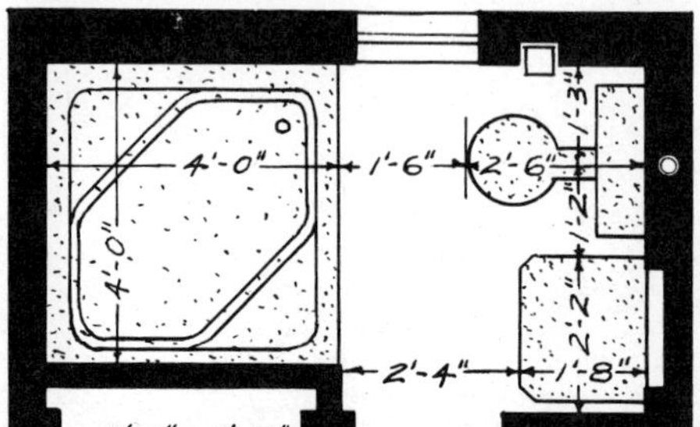
4'-0"
1'-6"
2'-6"
1'-3"
1'-2"
4'-0"
2'-2"
2'-4"
1'-8"

8'-0" x 4'-7"

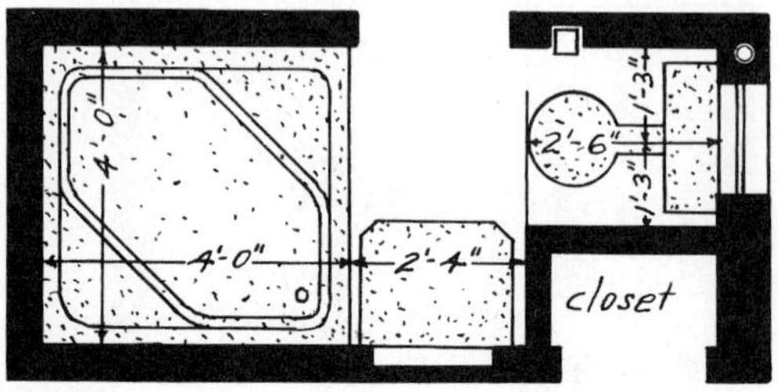
4'-0"
4'-0"
2'-4"
2'-6"
1'-3"
1'-3"
closet

8'-10" x 4'-0"

THREE FIXTURE BATHROOMS with SQUARE TUB

Scale: ¼" = 1'-0"

KITCHEN SPACE PLANNING *for* RESIDENCES

Areas suggested are a result of a study of furniture, appliances, storage, and clearances required for the medium priced home.

Furniture and appliances should be located on plans or at early sketch stages to check clearances and flow rather than to depend on square foot area to determine room size.

Kitchens are calculated for storage, work, and floor area desired for efficient spacing, but location of appliance areas and their order or service should be studied for individual preference.

To simplify a comparison of room types, basic sizes of furniture and clearances are assumed as equal. Base and wall storage units are equal in width but vary in length in relation to the type of layout.

The graph below gives approximate storage space required. For a complete table service for 12 including china, glass, linen and silver, without duplications or reserve space, allow 6 feet of wall space fitted with (a) upper cabinets with 3 shelves 12" wide, totaling 18 linear feet, and (b) lower cabinets with 2 shelves, 20" wide, totaling 12 linear feet.

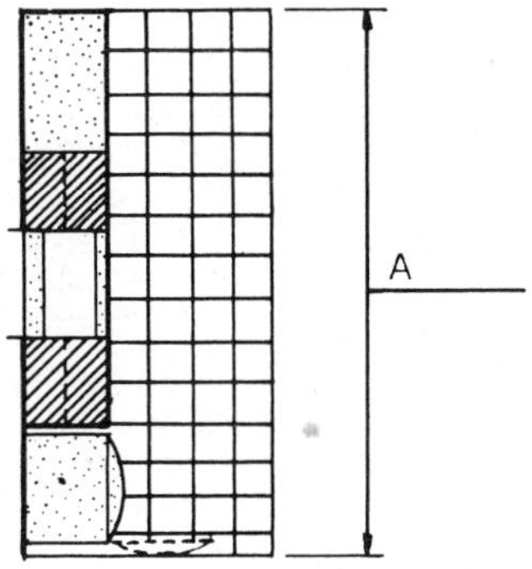
A

STORAGE SPACE FOR:	LENGTH "A"	KITCHEN AREA
3 persons	15'-6"	93□'
4 persons	16'-6"	99□'
5 persons	17'-6"	109□'
6 persons	18'-6"	111□'

"I" TYPE

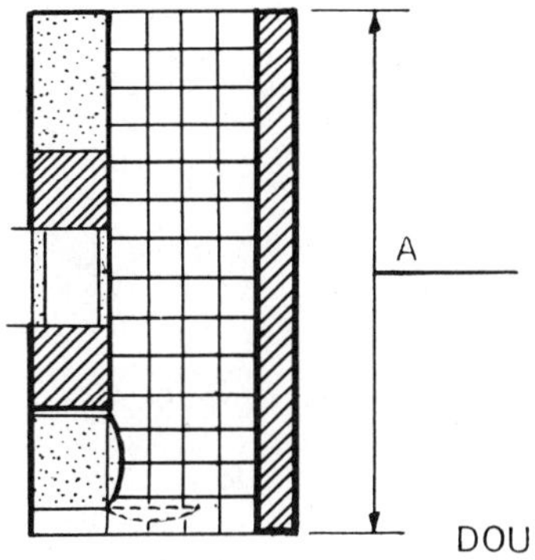
A

STORAGE SPACE FOR:	LENGTH "A"	KITCHEN AREA
8 persons	13'-6"	88□'

DOUBLE "I"

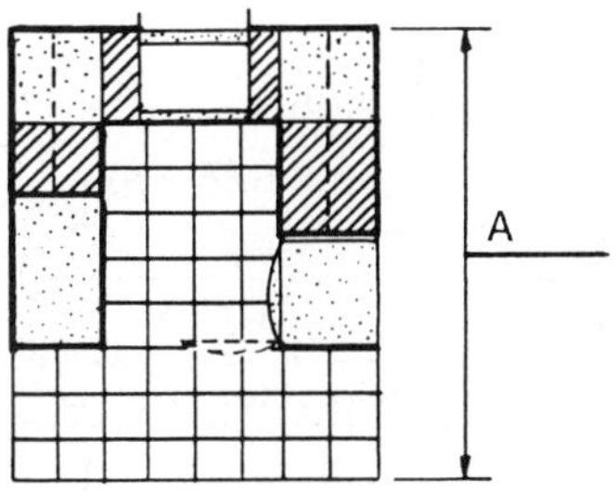
A

STORAGE SPACE FOR:	LENGTH "A"	KITCHEN AREA
3 persons	10'-0"	80□'
4 persons	10'-6"	84□'
5 persons	11'-0"	88□'
6 persons	11'-6"	92□'

"U" TYPE

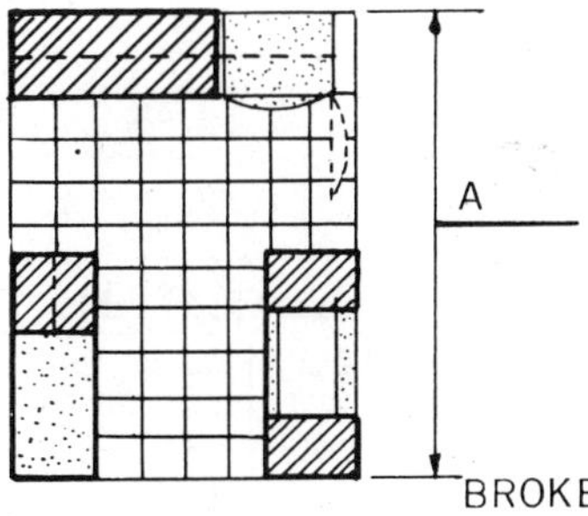
A

STORAGE SPACE FOR:	LENGTH "A"	KITCHEN AREA
5 persons	11'-0"	88□'
6 persons	11'-6"	92□'
7 persons	12'-0"	96□'

BROKEN "U"

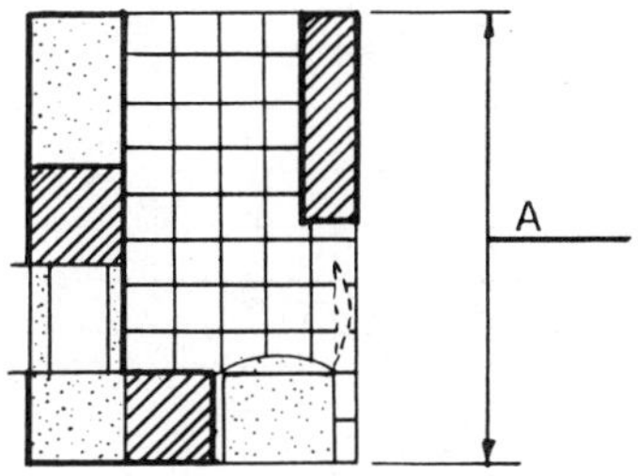
A

STORAGE SPACE FOR:	LENGTH "A"	KITCHEN AREA
4 persons	10'-0"	70□'
5 persons	10'-9"	75¼□'
6 persons	11'-6"	80½□'
7 persons	12'-3"	85¾□'

"L" TYPE

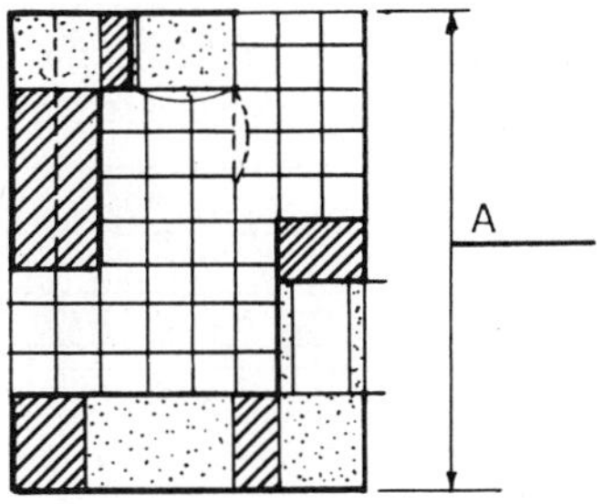
A

STORAGE SPACE FOR:	LENGTH "A"	KITCHEN AREA
6 persons	11'-0"	88□'
7 persons	11'-6"	92□'

BROKEN "L"

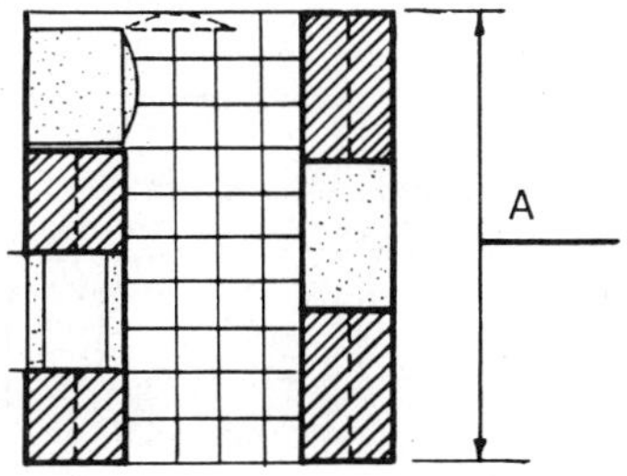
A

STORAGE SPACE FOR:	LENGTH "A"	KITCHEN AREA
3 persons	8'-6"	68□'
4 persons	9'-3"	74□'
5 persons	10'-0"	80□'
6 persons	10'-9"	86□'

SPLIT SERVICE - DOUBLE "I"

Kitchen storage graph is based on an eighteen square foot minimum for general storage with six square feet for each person usually served.

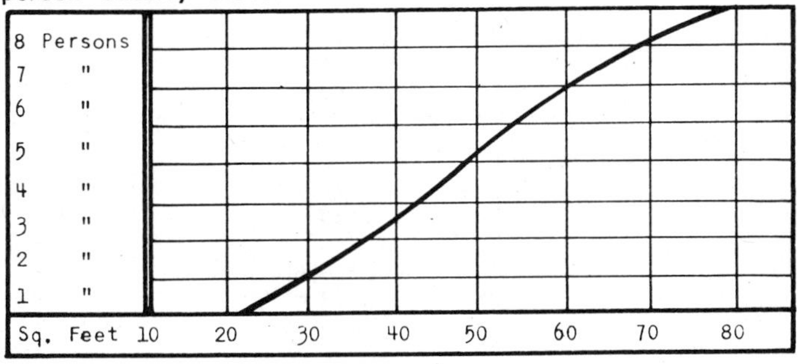
8 Persons
7 "
6 "
5 "
4 "
3 "
2 "
1 "
Sq. Feet 10 20 30 40 50 60 70 80

STORAGE AREA GRAPH

SCALE: 1/8" = 1'-0"

KITCHEN SPACE PLANNING

KITCHEN WORK CENTERS; DINING ROOMS

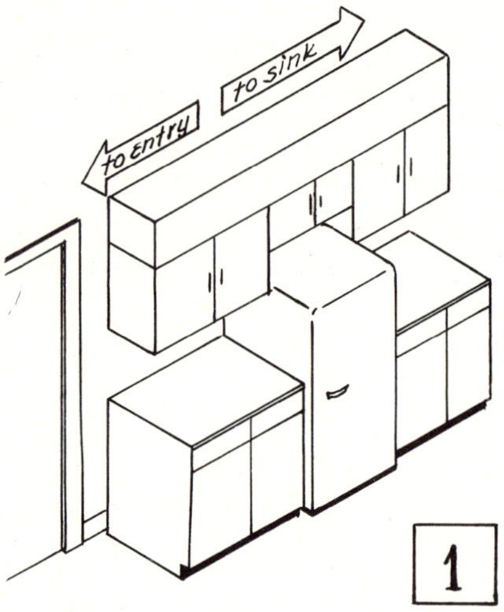

to entry
to sink
1

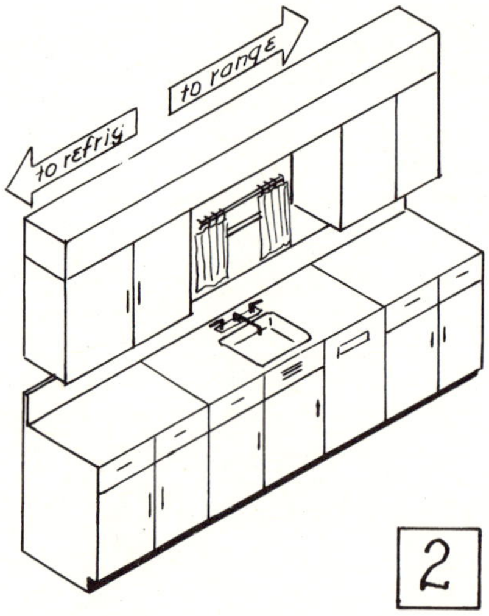

to refrig
to range
2

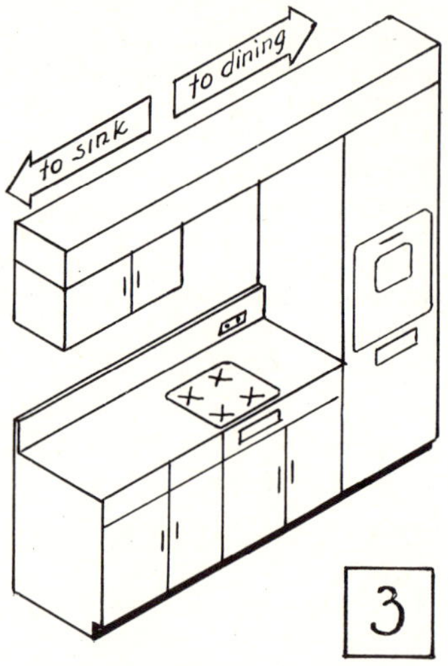

to sink
to dining
3

Mixing bowls, utensils, mixer, sifter, grater, salad molds, cake & pie tins, canned goods, staples, condiments, receiving & work counters, extra storage, occasional dishes. (Also brooms)

RECEIVING and MIXING

REFRIGERATOR CENTER

Everyday dishes, glassware, pots, silver, cutlery, pitchers, cocktail shaker, cleaning materials & utensils, garbage can or disposal, wastebasket, towel rack, dryer, linen drawer, dishdrain, vegetable bins

CLEANING

SINK CENTER

Pots, casseroles, frying pans, roaster, potholders, cooking utensils, canned goods, seasoning, grease container, plate warmer, serving dishes, platters, trays, bread bin & board, toaster, etc.

COOKING and SERVING

RANGE CENTER

KITCHEN WORK CENTER

REQUIRED STORAGE AREA FOR TABLEWARE

TABLEWARE	LINEAR FEET of SHELF SPACE		TABLEWARE	LINEAR FEET of SHELF SPACE	
China	In Wall Cabinets Shelves 12" wide	In Floor Cabinets Shelves 20" wide	Glassware	In Wall Cabinets Shelves 12" wide	In Floor Cabinets Shelves 20" wide
12 Service Plates	1'-0"		12 Tumblers 2¾" to 3" diameter	10" to 12"	
Dinner Service for 12. - Four sizes of plates. Demi-tasse service and all related china.	6'-0"	1'-6" for platters	12 Grapefruit Bowls 5" diameter	1'-6"	
			12 Sherbert or Champagne Glasses 3½" ø	1'-4"	
Luncheon Set for 12 - Plates, cream, soup plates, and related china.	1'-4"	1'-6" if platters not part of dinner set.	12 Cocktail or Wine Glasses 2¼" ø	8"	
			12 Cordial Glasses 1¾" diameter	4"	
Breakfast Set for 12 - Coffee, eggs, cereal, cream and sugar, etc.	2'-6"	See note for trays	12 Finger Bowls - stacked	6"	
			12 Celery - Olive Comports	8" or more	
Tea Set for 12.	3'-0"	See note for trays	1 Punch Bowl 3¾ gallon		1'-6"
Salad service, Glass or China, for 12.	8"	1'-0" for bowl	1 Pitcher, Decanter, etc.	6" each	

Note - Cups in above sets are assumed to be stored in stacks of 4 saucers and 4 cups nested on top.

STORAGE for TRAYS

Small Trays - Provide in upper cabinet or between counter and upper units a series of thin vertical partitions 2" apart to receive small trays.

Large trays - Provide in lower cabinet a series of thin vertical partitions 2" or 3" on centers to receive large trays. Wire racks may be used to form partitions.

DRAWER HEIGHTS

For Flat Silver = 2" to 3" high, fitted with silver racks or with division strips front to rear 2" and 3" on centers. Lined.

For Doilies = 2" to 3"; for mats, runners, etc., 3" to 3½"; for napkins, tablecloths, etc., 6" to 8½"; for table pads 8" to 10.

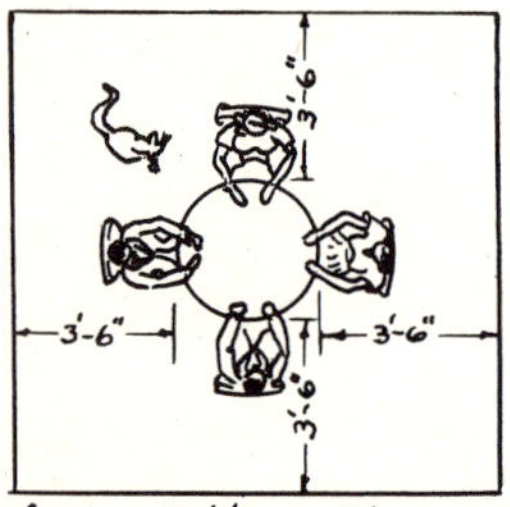

3'-6"
3'-6"
3'-6"
3'-6"

Seats	Table	Clear Space
4	3'-0" diam.	10'-0" sq.
6	4'-0" "	11'-0" sq.
8	5'-6" "	12'-6" sq.

AT ROUND TABLE

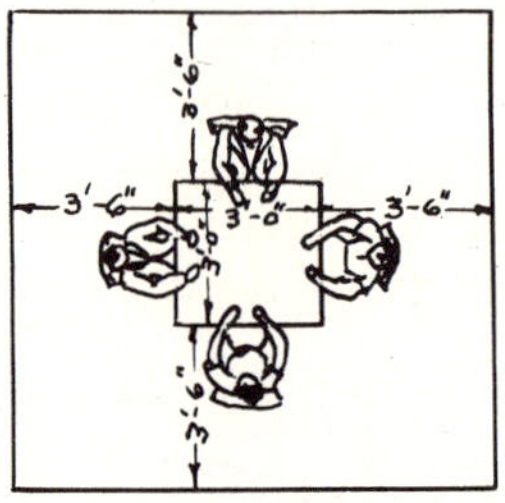

3'-6"
3'-6"
3'-6"
3'-0"
3'-0"
3'-6"

10'-0" x 10'-0"

DINING for 4

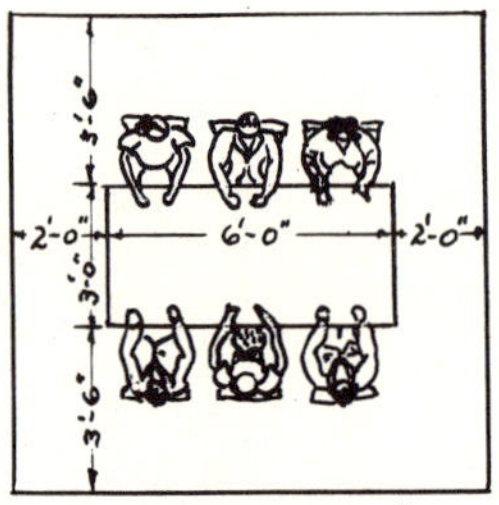

3'-6"
2'-0"
6'-0"
2'-0"
3'-0"
3'-6"

10'-0" x 10'-0"

DINING for 6

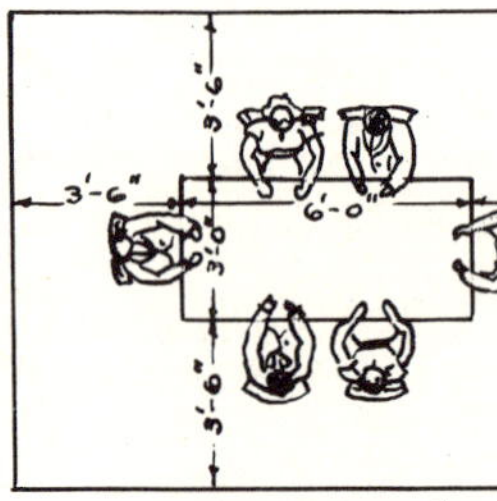

3'-6"
3'-6"
6'-0"
3'-6"
3'-6"

10'-0" x 13'-0"

DINING for 6

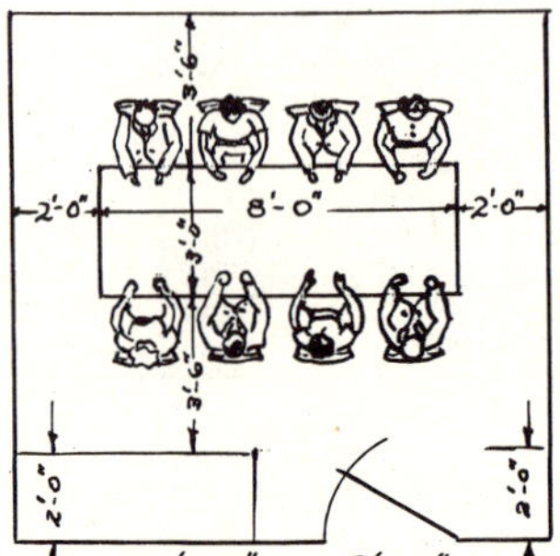

3'-6"
2'-0"
8'-0"
2'-0"
3'-6"
3'-6"
2'-0"
2'-0"

10'-0" x 12'-0"

SEE NOTE

DINING for 8

Allow 2'-0" additional for furniture, door swing, or serving passage between wall and chair.

DINING SPACE

KITCHENETTES - PANTRIES - DINING SPACES

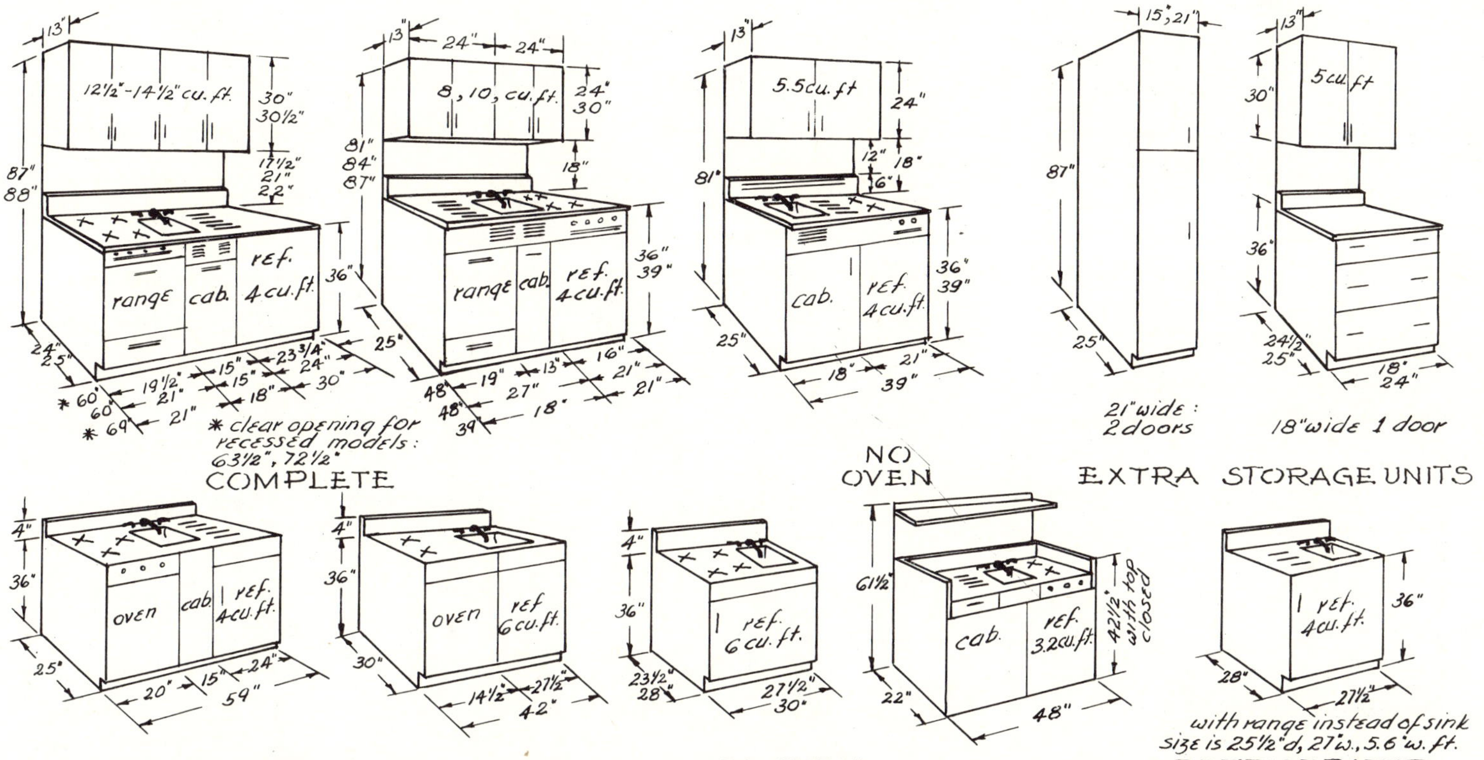
12½"-14½" cu. ft.
30" 30½"
17½" 21" 22"
87" 88"
36"
range
cab.
ref. 4 cu. ft.
* clear opening for recessed models: 63½", 72½"
COMPLETE
8, 10, cu. ft.
24" 30"
81" 84" 87"
18"
range
cab.
ref. 4 cu. ft.
36" 39"
5.5 cu. ft
24"
12" 18"
6"
81"
cab.
ref. 4 cu. ft.
36" 39"
NO OVEN
87"
21" wide: 2 doors
5 cu. ft
30"
36"
18" wide 1 door
EXTRA STORAGE UNITS
oven
cab
ref. 4 cu. ft.
COMPLETE
oven
ref 6 cu. ft.
ref. 6 cu. ft.
61½"
cab.
ref. 3.2 cu. ft.
42½" with top closed
NO OVEN
ref. 4 cu. ft.
with range instead of sink size is 25½" d, 27" w., 5.6 cu. ft.
REFRIGERATOR WITH SINK

PACKAGED KITCHENETTES

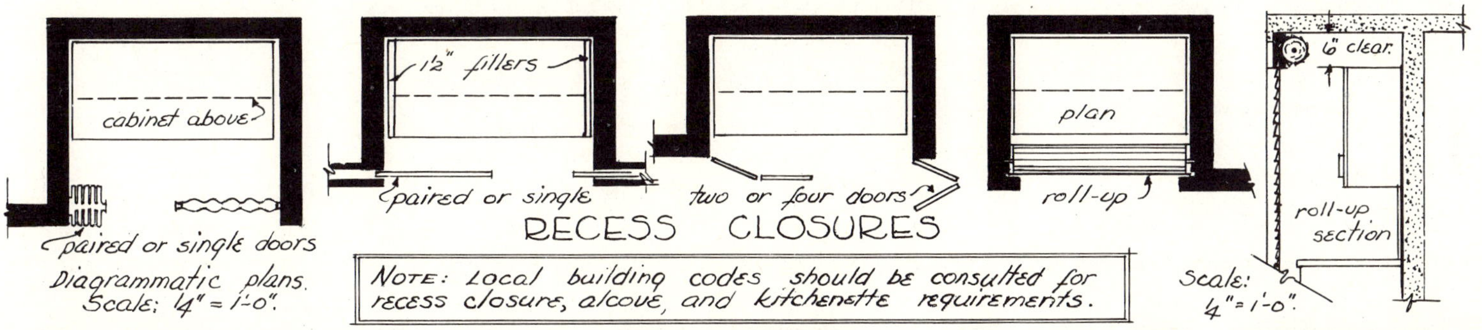
cabinet above
paired or single doors
Diagrammatic plans.
Scale: ¼" = 1'-0".
1½" fillers
paired or single
two or four doors
plan
roll-up
6" clear.
roll-up section
Scale: ¼" = 1'-0".

RECESS CLOSURES

NOTE: Local building codes should be consulted for recess closure, alcove, and kitchenette requirements.

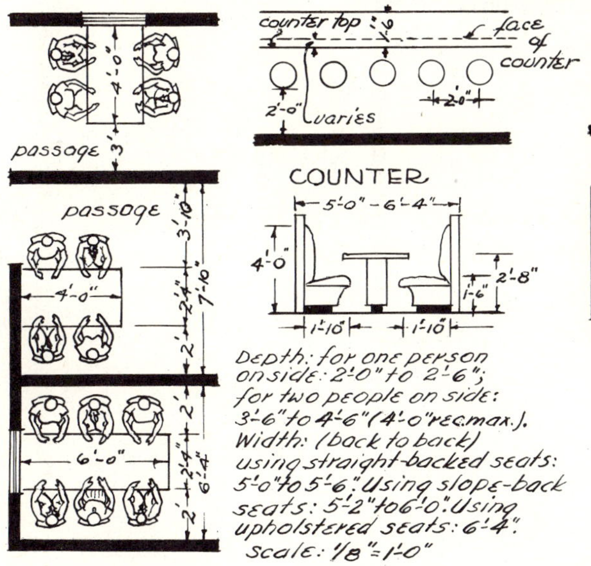
passage
passage
4'-0"
6'-0"
counter top
face of counter
2'-0"
varies
COUNTER
5'-0" - 6'-4"
4'-0"
2'-8"
1'-6"
1'-10"
Depth: for one person on side: 2'-0" to 2'-6"; for two people on side: 3'-6" to 4'-6" (4'-0" rec. max.). Width: (back to back) using straight-backed seats: 5'-0" to 5'-6". Using slope-back seats: 5'-2" to 6'-0". Using upholstered seats: 6'-4".
scale: ⅛" = 1'-0"
ALCOVE
BOOTH

CLEARANCES - DINING SPACE

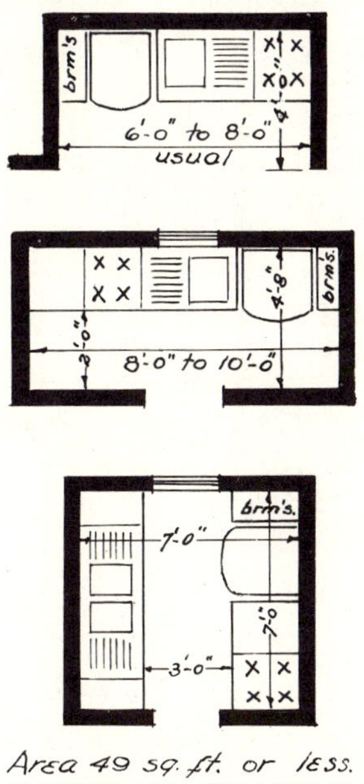
brm's
6'-0" to 8'-0" usual
8'-0" to 10'-0"
brm's
7'-0"
3'-0"
Area 49 sq. ft. or less.

KITCHENETTES

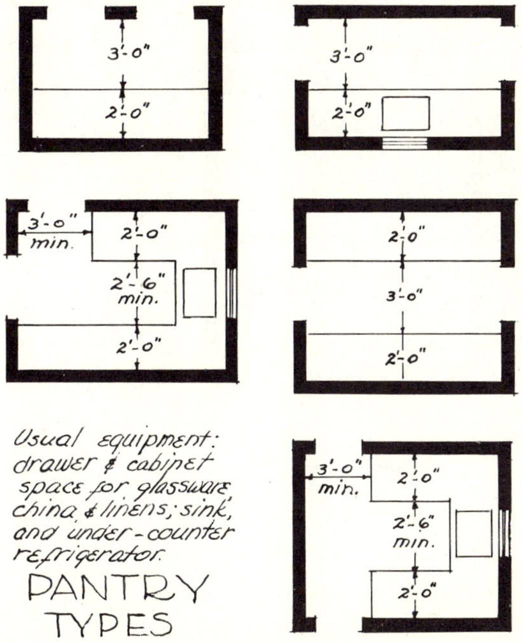
3'-0"
2'-0"
3'-0" min.
2'-6" min.
Usual equipment: drawer & cabinet space for glassware, china, & linens; sink, and under-counter refrigerator.

PANTRY TYPES

LAUNDRY PLANNING

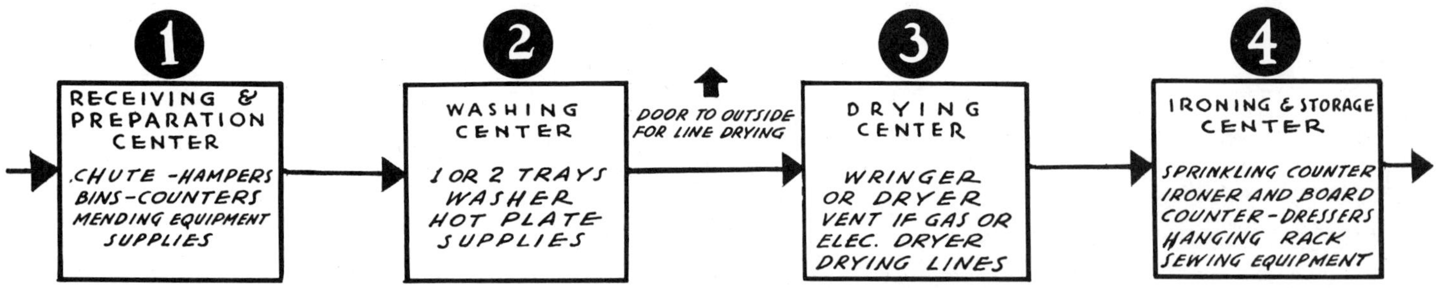
1
RECEIVING & PREPARATION CENTER
CHUTE - HAMPERS
BINS - COUNTERS
MENDING EQUIPMENT
SUPPLIES
2
WASHING CENTER
1 OR 2 TRAYS
WASHER
HOT PLATE
SUPPLIES
DOOR TO OUTSIDE FOR LINE DRYING
3
DRYING CENTER
WRINGER OR DRYER
VENT IF GAS OR ELEC. DRYER
DRYING LINES
4
IRONING & STORAGE CENTER
SPRINKLING COUNTER
IRONER AND BOARD
COUNTER - DRESSERS
HANGING RACK
SEWING EQUIPMENT

IDEAL SEQUENCE FOR MAXIMUM EFFICIENCY

MAY BE REVERSED FROM RIGHT TO LEFT

SPACE REQUIRED FOR LAUNDRIES

VERY SMALL	7'-0" x 10'-0"	70 SQ. FT.
SMALL	9'-0" x 10'-0"	90 SQ. FT.
MEDIUM	10'-0" x 10'-0"	100 SQ. FT.
LARGE	10'-0" x 12'-0"	120 SQ. FT.

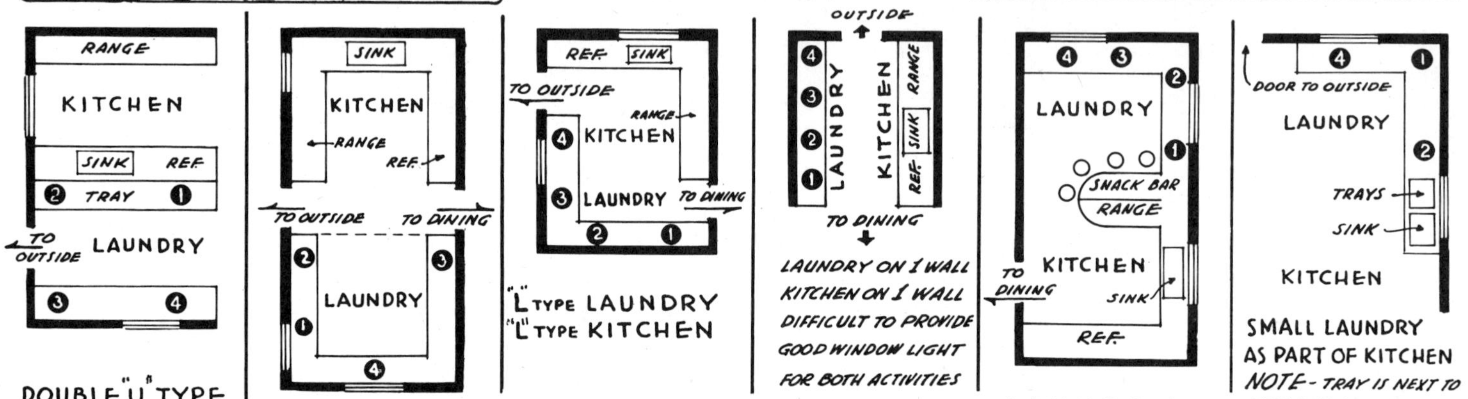
RANGE
KITCHEN
SINK
REF.
TRAY
TO OUTSIDE
LAUNDRY
SINK
KITCHEN
RANGE
REF.
TO OUTSIDE
TO DINING
LAUNDRY
REF.
SINK
TO OUTSIDE
RANGE
KITCHEN
LAUNDRY
TO DINING
OUTSIDE
LAUNDRY
KITCHEN
RANGE
SINK
REF.
TO DINING
LAUNDRY
SNACK BAR
RANGE
TO DINING
KITCHEN
SINK
REF.
DOOR TO OUTSIDE
LAUNDRY
TRAYS
SINK
KITCHEN

DOUBLE "U" TYPE

EACH IN SEPARATE "U"
GATE AT BROKEN LINE WOULD TURN LAUNDRY INTO PLAY SPACE

"L" TYPE LAUNDRY
"L" TYPE KITCHEN

LAUNDRY ON 1 WALL
KITCHEN ON 1 WALL
DIFFICULT TO PROVIDE GOOD WINDOW LIGHT FOR BOTH ACTIVITIES

LAUNDRY, KITCHEN, AND SNACK BAR

SMALL LAUNDRY AS PART OF KITCHEN
NOTE - TRAY IS NEXT TO SINK FOR ECONOMY. THIS IS AN EXCEPTION FROM BEST SEQUENCE

ABOVE PLANS SHOW LAUNDRY & KITCHEN IN SAME AREA

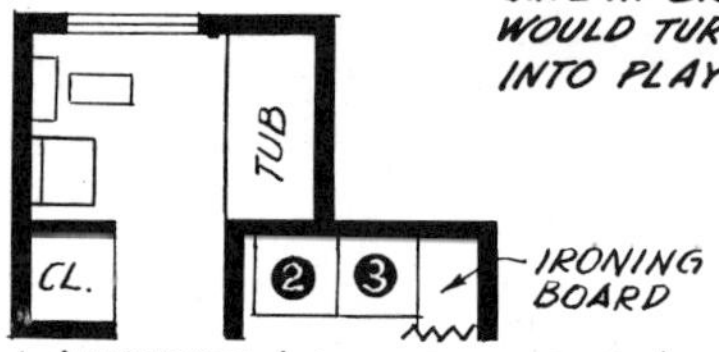
TUB
CL.
IRONING BOARD

LAUNDRY (WASHER & DRYER) NEAR BATH (USE OF COMBINATION WASHER-DRYER WILL SAVE SPACE.)

THE DIAGRAMMATIC PLANS IN THIS SECTION ILLUSTRATE POSSIBLE LAYOUTS OF LAUNDRIES IN COMBINATION WITH OTHER ROOMS. USE OF AUTOMATIC DRYER MAKES FEASIBLE OMISSION OF OUTSIDE DRYING YARD.
NOTE: MOST AUTOMATIC DRYERS REQUIRE VENTING TO OUTSIDE.

SCALE: 3/32" = 1'-0"

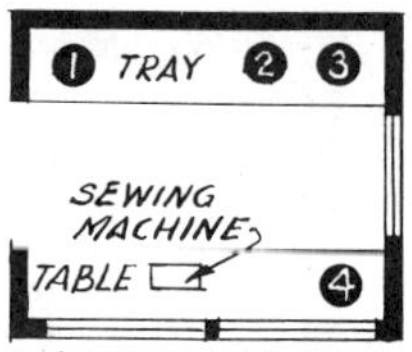
TRAY
SEWING MACHINE
TABLE

LAUNDRY AND SEWING CENTER

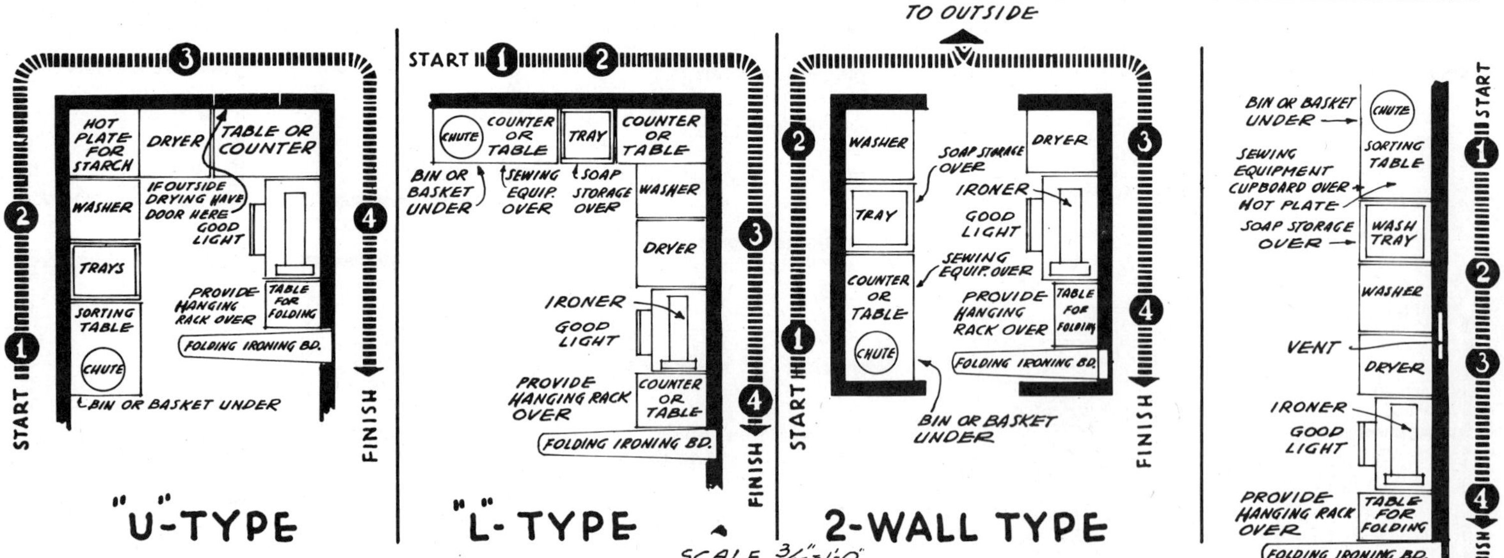
START
HOT PLATE FOR STARCH
DRYER
TABLE OR COUNTER
WASHER
IF OUTSIDE DRYING HAVE DOOR HERE
GOOD LIGHT
TRAYS
SORTING TABLE
PROVIDE HANGING RACK OVER
TABLE FOR FOLDING
CHUTE
FOLDING IRONING BD.
BIN OR BASKET UNDER
FINISH
START
CHUTE
COUNTER OR TABLE
TRAY
COUNTER OR TABLE
BIN OR BASKET UNDER
SEWING EQUIP. OVER
SOAP STORAGE OVER
WASHER
DRYER
IRONER
GOOD LIGHT
PROVIDE HANGING RACK OVER
COUNTER OR TABLE
FOLDING IRONING BD.
FINISH
TO OUTSIDE
WASHER
SOAP STORAGE OVER
DRYER
IRONER
TRAY
GOOD LIGHT
SEWING EQUIP. OVER
COUNTER OR TABLE
PROVIDE HANGING RACK OVER
TABLE FOR FOLDING
CHUTE
FOLDING IRONING BD.
BIN OR BASKET UNDER
START
FINISH
BIN OR BASKET UNDER
CHUTE
SORTING TABLE
SEWING EQUIPMENT CUPBOARD OVER
HOT PLATE
SOAP STORAGE OVER
WASH TRAY
WASHER
VENT
DRYER
IRONER
GOOD LIGHT
PROVIDE HANGING RACK OVER
TABLE FOR FOLDING
FOLDING IRONING BD.
START
FINISH

"U"-TYPE

"L"-TYPE

2-WALL TYPE

1-WALL TYPE

SCALE 3/16" = 1'-0"

TYPES OF LAUNDRIES

NUMBERS IN CIRCLES INDICATE THE DIFFERENT CENTERS AS SHOWN AT TOP OF PAGE

INFORMATION FROM "THE HOUSE FOR YOU" BY CATHARINE & HAROLD SLEEPER

GARAGES, TRAILERS and MOTORCYCLES

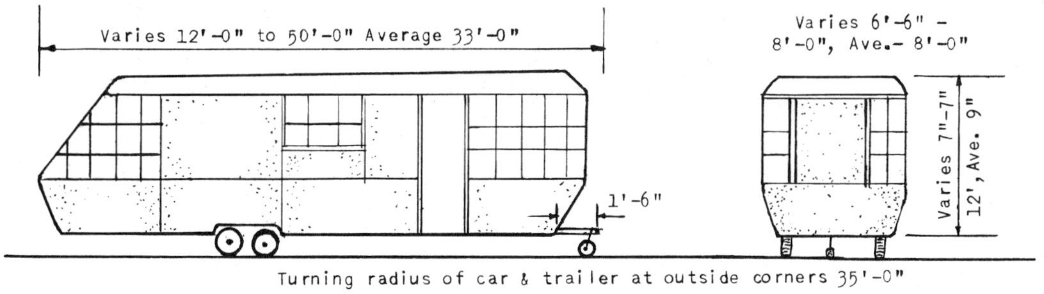
Varies 12'-0" to 50'-0" Average 33'-0"
Varies 6'-6" - 8'-0", Ave.- 8'-0"
1'-6"
Varies 7"-7" 12', Ave. 9"
Turning radius of car & trailer at outside corners 35'-0"

TOURING TRAILERS

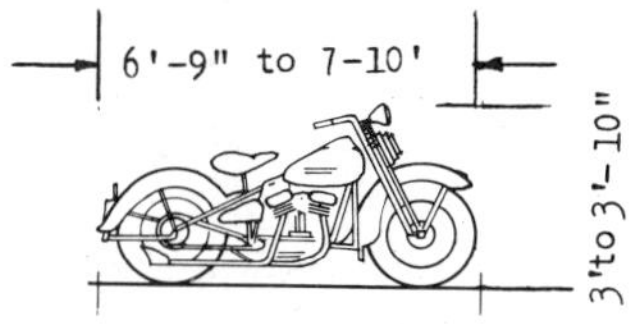
6'-9" to 7-10'
3'to 3'-10"

Width of motorcycle handle bars, 2'-4" to 3'-0"
When parked on jiffy stand, motorcycle leans approx. 10°

Width of motorcycle with sidecar, 6'-0"

MOTORCYCLES

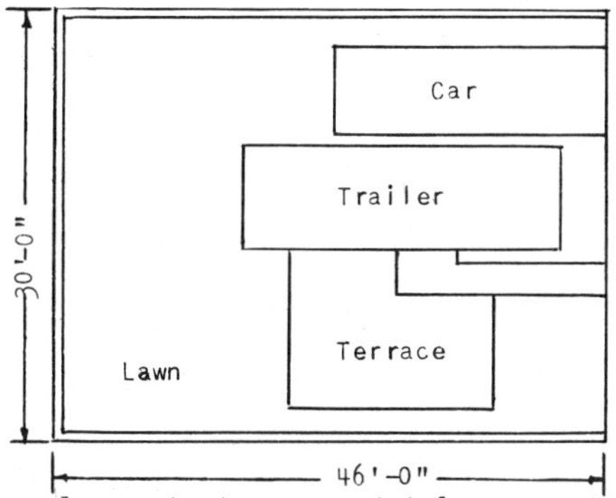
Car
Trailer
Terrace
Lawn
30'-0"
46'-0"
3'-0" sidewalk

1 acre land recommended for every 25 trailer coaches

Max.* Length	STATES
45'-0"	Ga., Ill., Iowa, Me., Miss., N.H., Pa., Tenn., Va., W. Va., N.D. (47'-3"), Ala. & N.C. 48'-0"
50'-0"	Ark., Conn., D.C., Fla., Ind., Kans., La., Mich., Neb., N.J., N.Y., Okla., Ore., R.I., S.C., S.D., Vt.
55'-0"	Md., Minn., Tex.
60'-0"	Calif., Colo., Del., Idaho, Mo., Mont., Ohio, Utah, Wash., Wisc., Wy.,
65'-0"	Ariz., N.M.
No restriction, Ky., Mass., Nev.	
*length of car included.	

TRAILER PARK LOT *MAX. STATE LIMITS FOR CAR & TRAILER

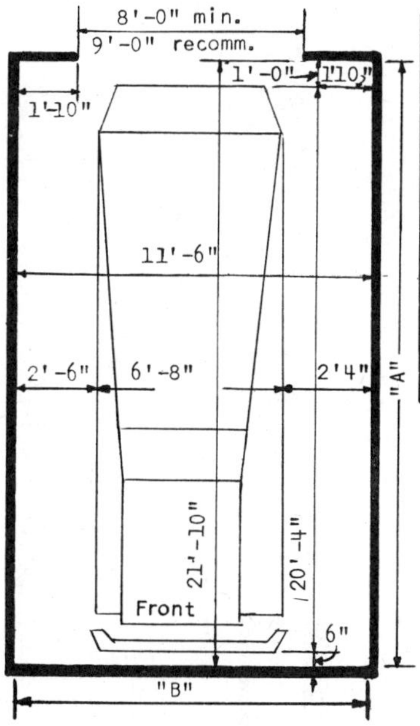
8'-0" min.
9'-0" recomm.
1'-0"
1'10"
1'-10"
11'-6"
2'-6"
6'-8"
2'4"
"A"
21'-10"
20'-4"
Front
6"
"B"

RECOMMENDED INSIDE DIMENSIONS FOR ONE-CAR GARAGE		
Car Size	length "A"	Width "B"
Largest	21'-10"	11'-6"
Medium	19'-7"	11'-6"
Small	18'-11"	11'-2"
Midget	15'-6"	10'-1"

ONE-CAR GARAGE
FOR ANY CAR

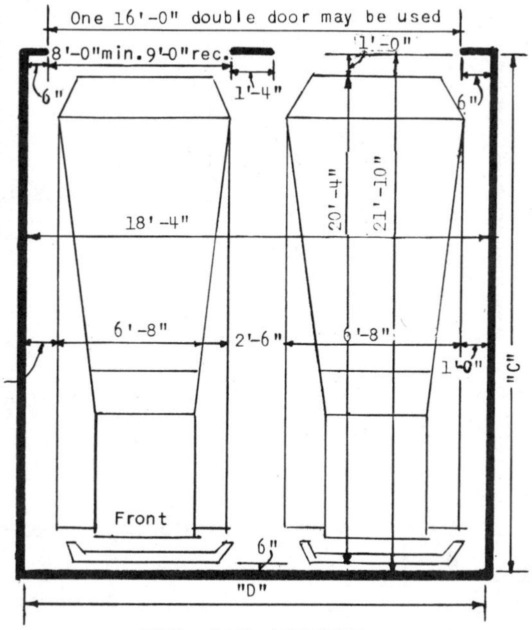
One 16'-0" double door may be used
8'-0"min. 9'-0"rec.
1'-0"
6"
1'-4"
6"
18'-4"
20'-4"
21'-10"
6'-8"
2'-6"
6'-8"
1'-2"
1'-0"
"C"
Front
6"
"D"

RECOMMENDED INSIDE DIMENSIONS FOR TWO-CAR GARAGES		
Car Size	length "C"	width "D"
2 Large	21'-10"	18'-0"
2 Medium	19'-7"	18'-0"
2 Small	18'-11"	17'-4"
2 Midget	15'-6"	15'-2"
1 Large & 1 Medium	21'-10"	18'-0"
1 Large & 1 Small	21'-10"	17'-8"
1 Large & 1 Midget	21'-10"	16'-7"
1 Medium & 1 Small	19'-7"	17'-8"
1 Medium 1 Midget	19'-7"	16'-7"
1 Small & 1 Midget	18'-11"	16'-3"

TWO-CAR GARAGE
FOR ANY TWO CARS

For multiple garage, spacing of 10'-0" per car will allow room to work around cars. For economy, 9'-0" spacing.

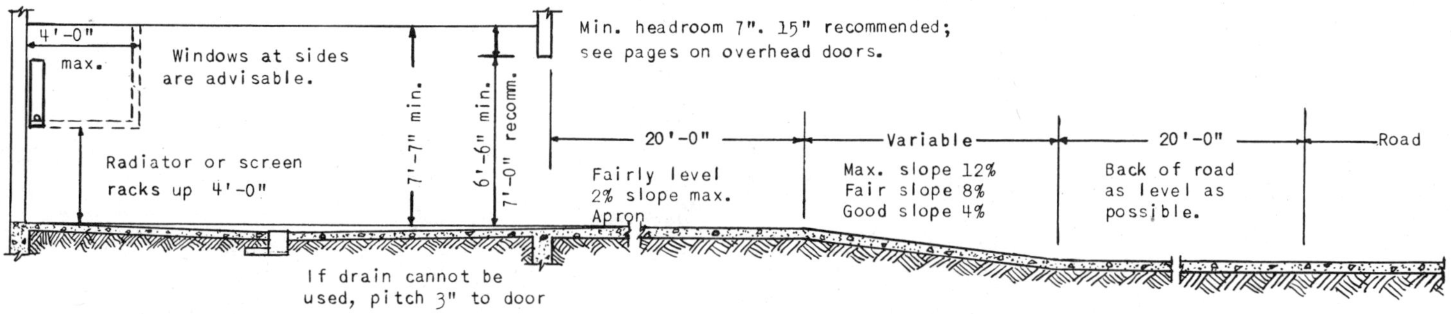
4'-0" max.
Windows at sides are advisable.
Radiator or screen racks up 4'-0"
7'-7" min.
6'-6" min.
7'-0" recomm.
Min. headroom 7". 15" recommended; see pages on overhead doors.
20'-0"
Variable
20'-0"
Road
Fairly level 2% slope max. Apron
Max. slope 12% Fair slope 8% Good slope 4%
Back of road as level as possible.
If drain cannot be used, pitch 3" to door

SECTION THRU GARAGE

RECOMMENDED SLOPES GARAGE TO ROAD

MULTIPLE-USE GARAGES and CARPORTS

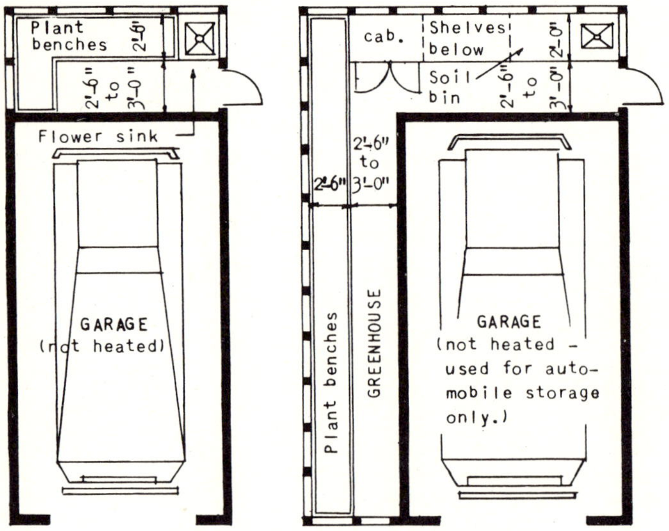
Plant benches
2'-6"
2'-6" to 3'-0"
Flower sink
GARAGE (not heated)
cab.
Shelves below
Soil bin
2'-6" to 3'-0"
2'-0"
2'-6" to 3'-0"
2'-6"
Plant benches
GREENHOUSE
GARAGE (not heated - used for automobile storage only.)

GREENHOUSES ATTACHED TO GARAGE

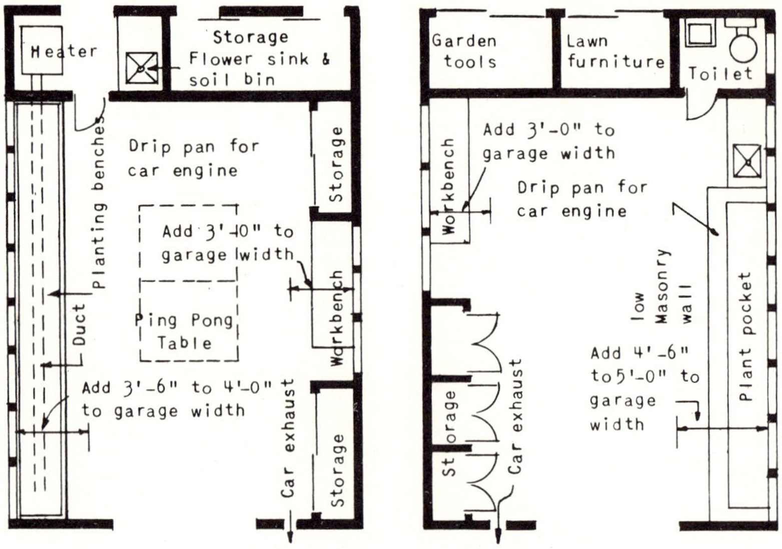
Heater
Storage
Flower sink & soil bin
Planting benches
Drip pan for car engine
Storage
Add 3'-0" to garage width
Ping Pong Table
Workbench
Duct
Add 3'-6" to 4'-0" to garage width
Car exhaust
Storage
Garden tools
Lawn furniture
Toilet
Add 3'-0" to garage width
Workbench
Drip pan for car engine
low Masonry wall
Plant pocket
Storage
Car exhaust
Add 4'-6" to 5'-0" to garage width

ACTIVITY GARAGES WITH PLANTING AREAS

Scale of all drawings:
3/32" = 1'-0"

GREENHOUSE GARAGES

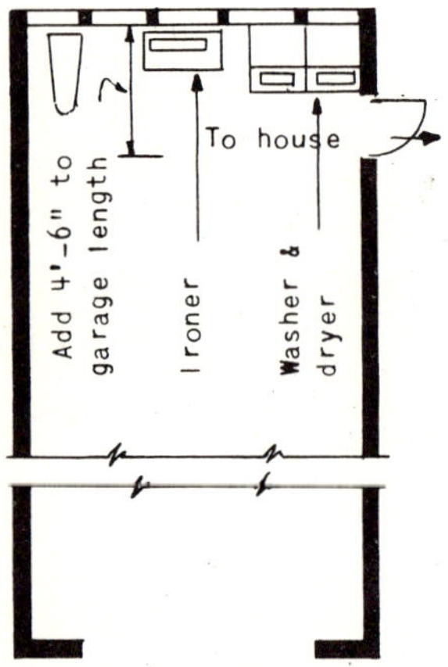
To house
Add 4'-6" to garage length
Ironer
Washer & dryer

LAUNDRY ONLY

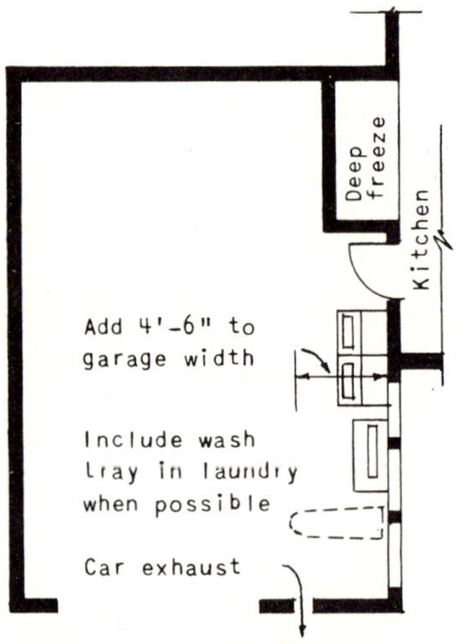
Deep freeze
Kitchen
Add 4'-6" to garage width
Include wash tray in laundry when possible
Car exhaust

WITH DEEP FREEZE

LAUNDRY IN ENLARGED GARAGE

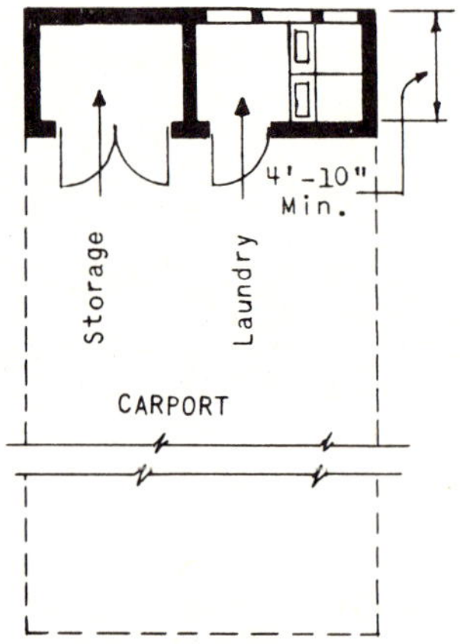
4'-10" Min.
Storage
Laundry
CARPORT

LAUNDRY-STORAGE UNIT FOR CARPORT

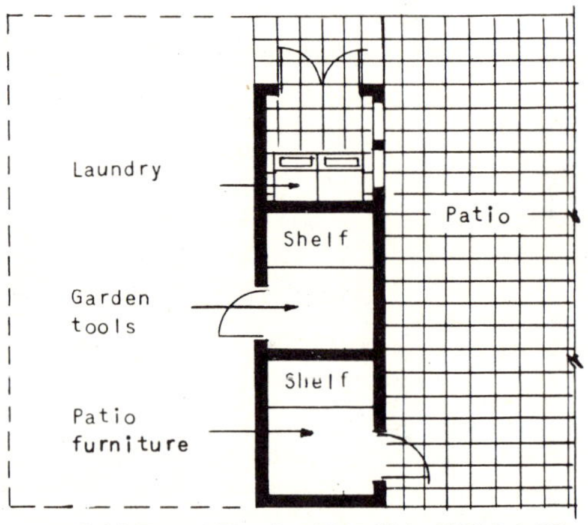
Laundry
Patio
Shelf
Garden tools
Shelf
Patio furniture

CARPORT WITH LAUNDRY-STORAGE UNIT USED TO CREATE OUTDOOR LIVING SPACE

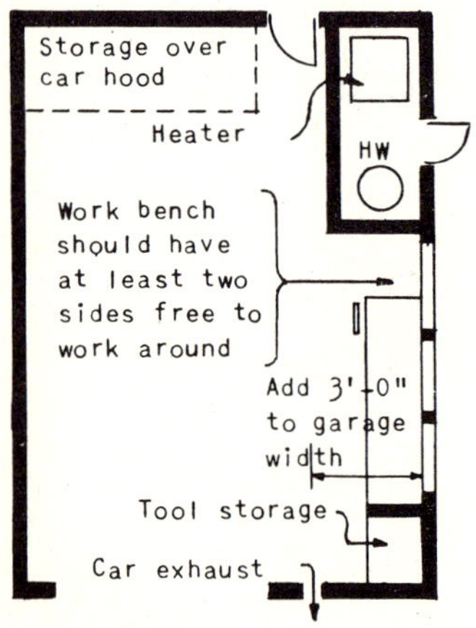
Storage over car hood
Heater
HW
Work bench should have at least two sides free to work around
Add 3'-0" to garage width
Tool storage
Car exhaust

HEATER & WORKSHOP IN GARAGE

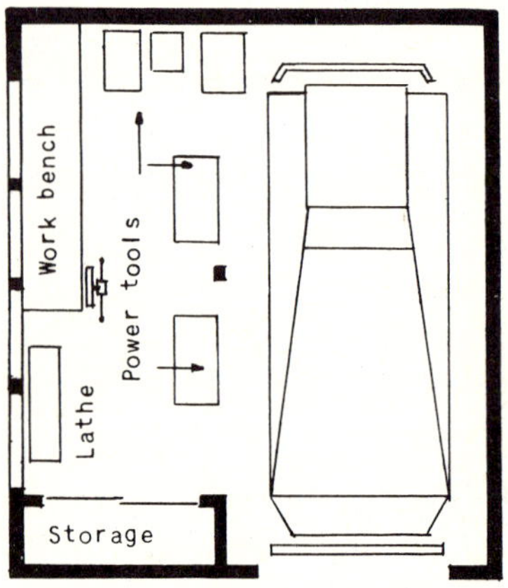
Work bench
Power tools
Lathe
Storage

TWO-CAR-SIZE GARAGE WITH COMPLETE WORKSHOP

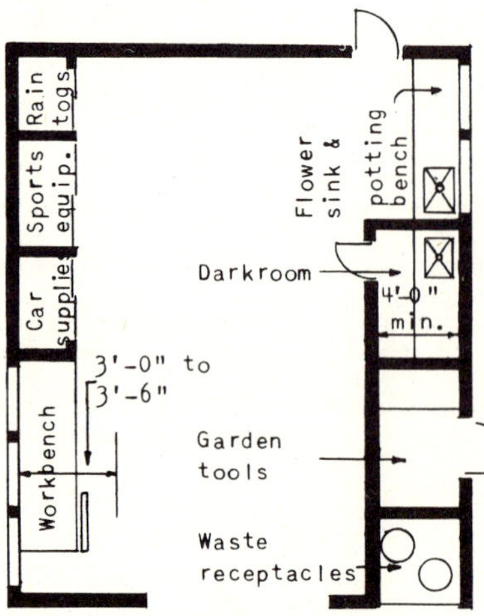
Rain togs
Sports equip.
Car supplies
Flower sink &
potting bench
Darkroom
4'-0" min.
3'-0" to 3'-6"
Workbench
Garden tools
Waste receptacles

TWO CAR SIZE ACTIVITY GARAGE

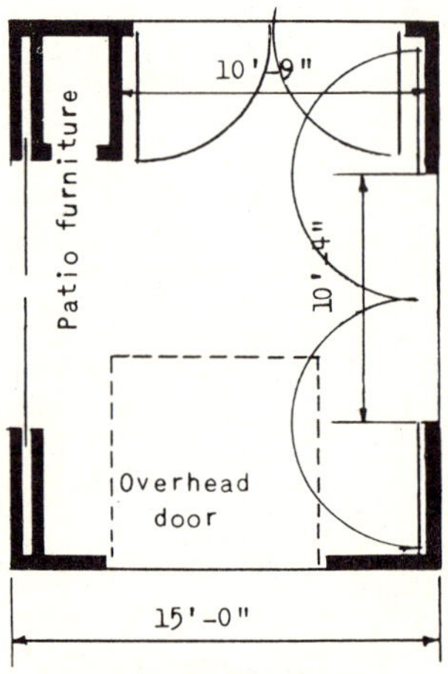
10'-9"
Patio furniture
10'-4"
Overhead door
15'-0"

CONVERSION OF GARAGE TO OUTDOOR COVERED AREA

GARAGE and CARPORT STORAGE

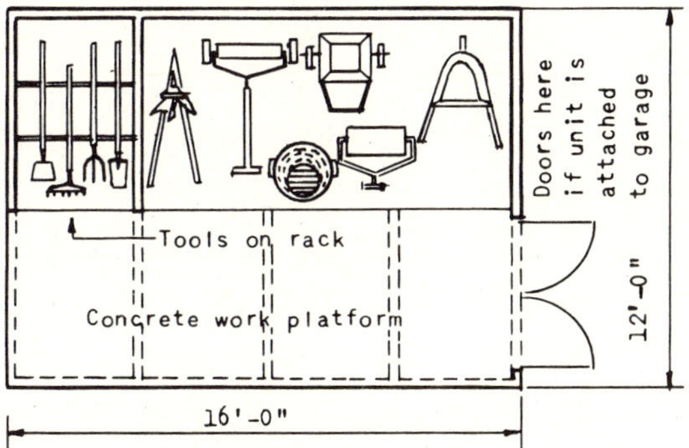
Tools on rack
Concrete work platform
Doors here if unit is attached to garage
12'-0"
16'-0"

PLAN
Scale: 1/8" = 1'-0"

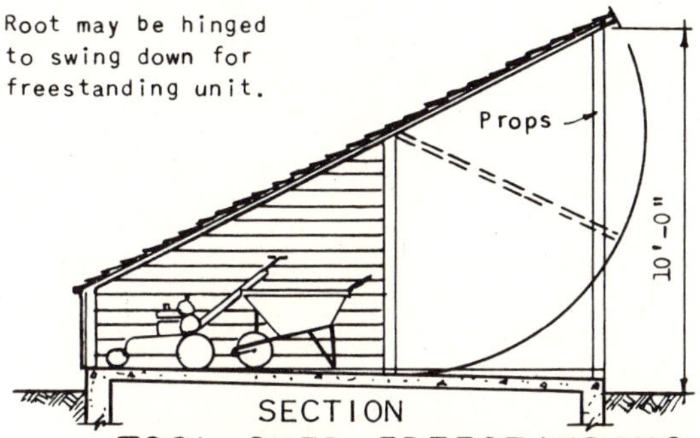
Roof may be hinged to swing down for freestanding unit.
Props
10'-0"

SECTION

TOOL SHED-FREESTANDING OR ATTACHED TO GARAGE

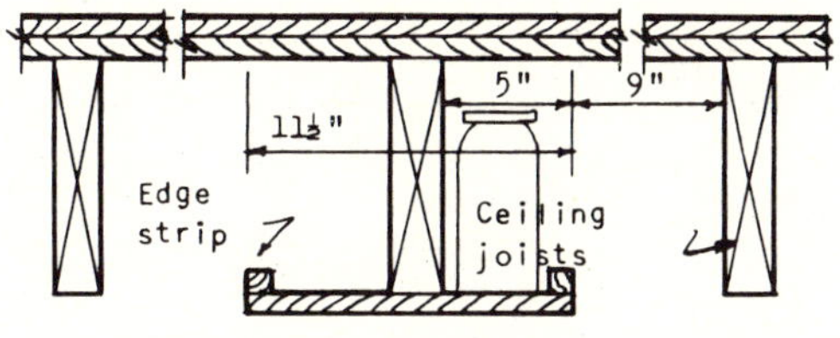
11½"
5"
9"
Edge strip
Ceiling joists

SHELVING ATTACHED TO EXPOSED JOISTS SECTION

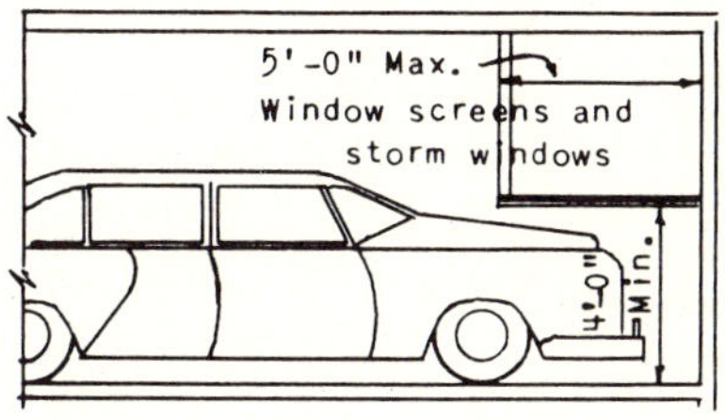
5'-0" Max.
Window screens and storm windows
4'-0" Min.

STORAGE ABOVE CAR HOOD

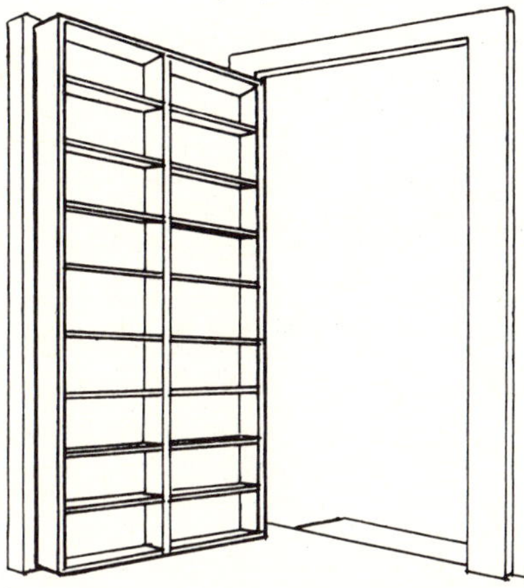

SHALLOW SHELVES ON DOOR

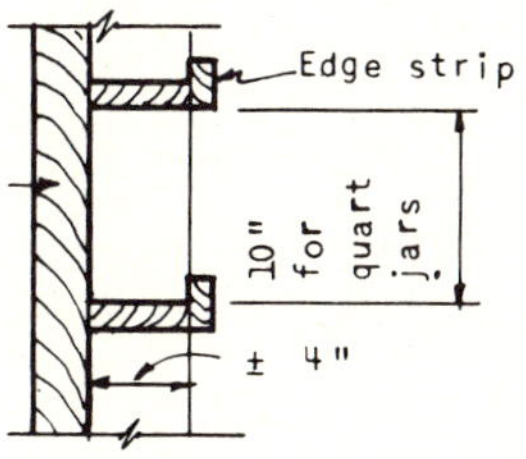
Edge strip
Door
10" for quart jars
± 4"

VERTICAL SECTION

Scale: 3/4" = 1'-0"

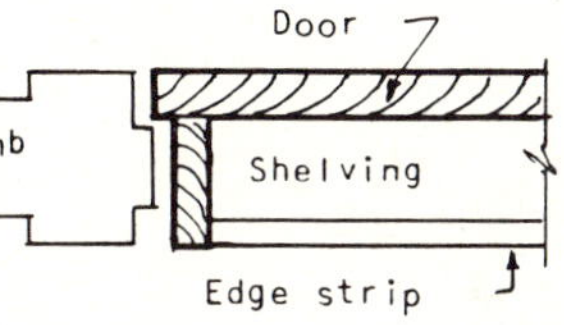
Door
Jamb
Shelving
Edge strip

PLAN

STORAGE IN MINIMUM SIZE GARAGE

ITEMS WHICH MUST BE PROTECTED FROM DAMPNESS IF STORED IN GARAGE

Sports equipment - tennis rackets, football, baseball & basket ball equipment, boxing gloves, etc.
Clothes - Rain togs & work clothes
Wheeled toys & conveyances - bicycles, tricycles, baby carriages, wagons
Canned food & deep freeze
Car supplies - oils, greases, parts, tools
Paint supplies - Varnishes, paints, brushes, solvents
Window screens & storm windows
Tools & supplies for house & furniture repair
Miscellaneous - Bicycle pumps, trunks, luggage, firewood, newspapers & magazines

ITEMS WHICH WILL NOT BE HARMED BY DAMPNESS - May have outside access doors

Garden tools - Wheel barrow, lawn mowers & rollers, hose, hoe, forks, spades, shovels, rakes, carts, flower pots, small garden tools
Garden chairs & tables
Containers - jars, bottles, buckets, waste cans.
Canned food in glass jars
Spare tires

Scale: 1/8" = 1'-0"

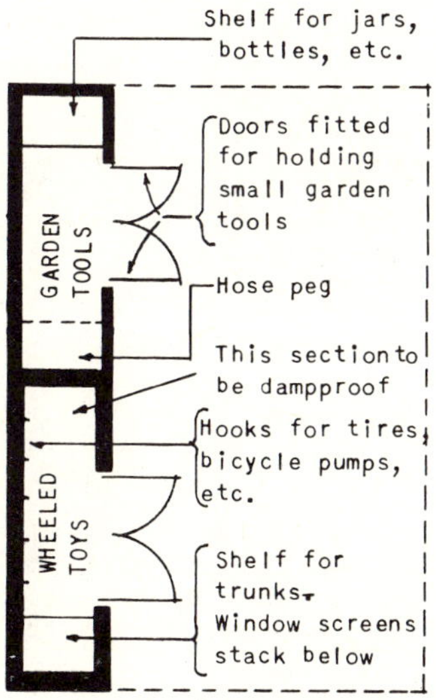
Shelf for jars, bottles, etc.
Doors fitted for holding small garden tools
GARDEN TOOLS
Hose peg
This section to be dampproof
Hooks for tires, bicycle pumps, etc.
WHEELED TOYS
Shelf for trunks. Window screens stack below

CARPORT STORAGE WALL

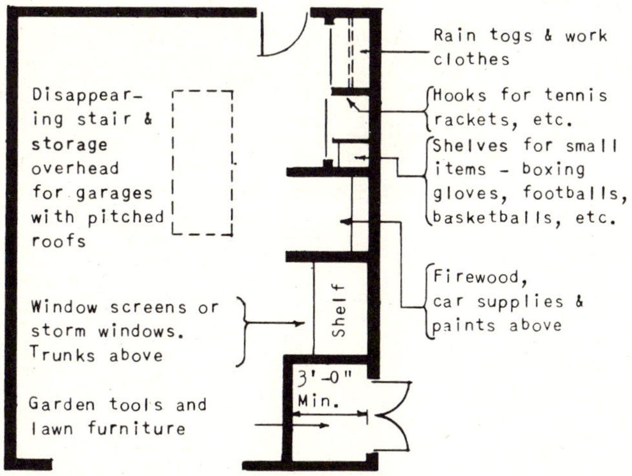
Disappearing stair & storage overhead for garages with pitched roofs
Window screens or storm windows. Trunks above
Garden tools and lawn furniture
Rain togs & work clothes
Hooks for tennis rackets, etc.
Shelves for small items - boxing gloves, footballs, basketballs, etc.
Firewood, car supplies & paints above
Shelf
3'-0" Min.

STORAGE FACILITIES IN GARAGE

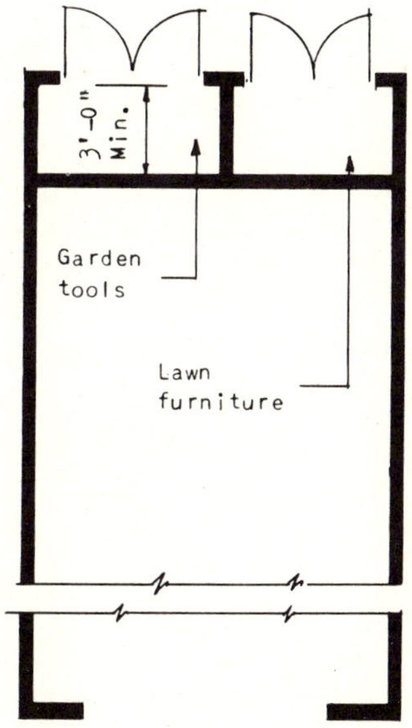
3'-0" Min.
Garden tools
Lawn furniture

ATTACHED STORAGE UNIT

ENLARGED GARAGES

DRAFTING ROOM LAYOUTS

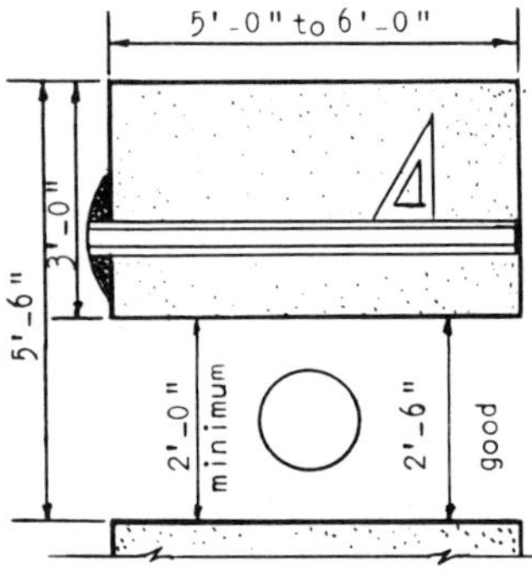
5'-0" to 6'-0"
3'-0"
5'-6"
2'-0" minimum
2'-6" good

MINIMUM AREA

□' per man	5' board	6' board
work	15 sq.ft.	18 sq.ft.
reference	--	--
total	27½ sq.ft.	33 sq.ft.

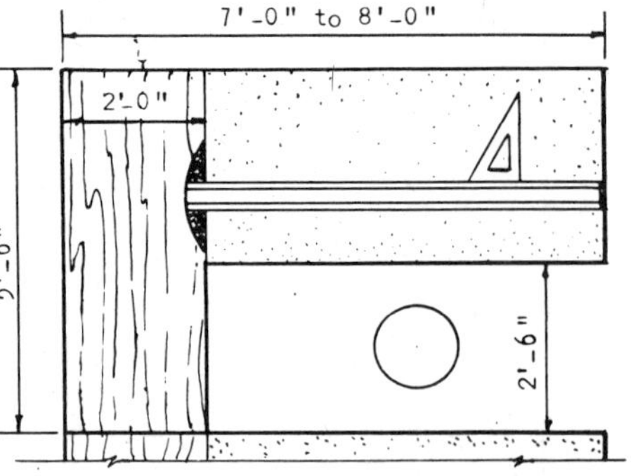
7'-0" to 8'-0"
2'-0"
5'-6"
2'-6"

SIDE REFERENCE AREA

□' per man	5' board	6' board
work	15 sq.ft.	18 sq.ft.
reference	11 sq.ft.	11 sq.ft.
total	38½ sq.ft.	44 sq.ft.

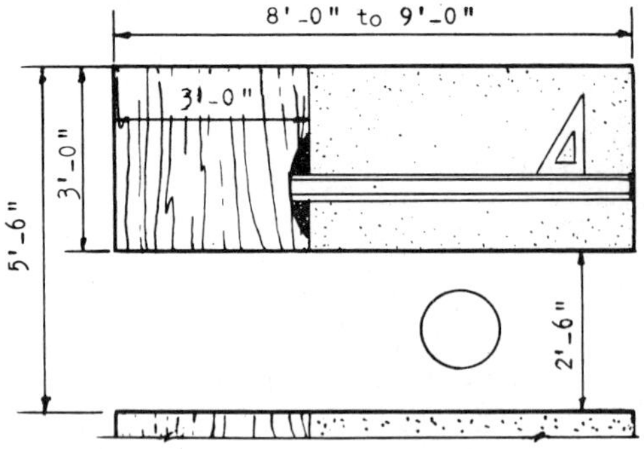
8'-0" to 9'-0"
3'-0"
3'-0"
5'-6"
2'-6"

END REFERENCE AREA

□' per man	5' board	6' board
work	15 sq.ft.	18 sq.ft.
reference	9 sq.ft.	9 sq.ft.
total	44 sq.ft.	49½ sq.ft.

Scale: 1/4" = 1'-0"

DRAFTING UNITS

Unit includes table, reference, and sitting areas

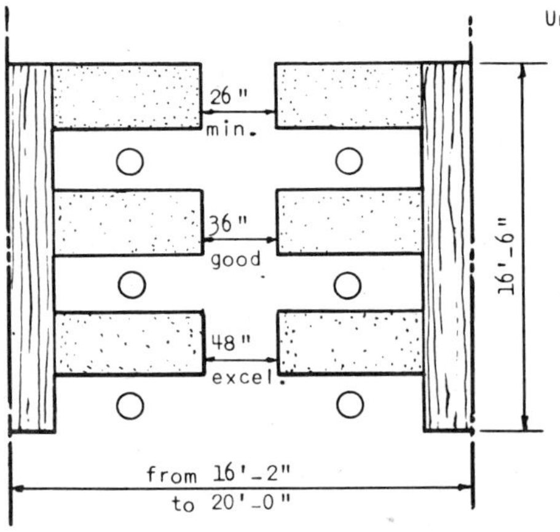
26" min.
36" good
48" excel.
16'-6"
from 16'-2"
to 20'-0"

CENTER AISLE SIDE REFERENCE

□' per man	5' board	6' board
minimum	44¼ sq.ft.	49¾ sq.ft.
good	46¾ sq.ft.	52¼ sq.ft.
excellent	49½ sq.ft.	55 sq.ft.

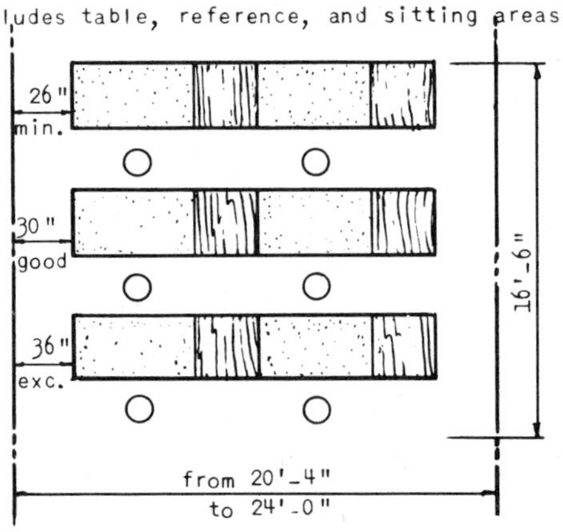
26" min.
30" good
36" exc.
16'-6"
from 20'-4"
to 24'-0"

SIDE AISLES

□' per man	5' board	6' board
minimum	56 sq.ft.	61½ sq.ft
good	57¾ sq.ft.	63½ sq.ft
excellent	60½ sq.ft.	66 sq.ft

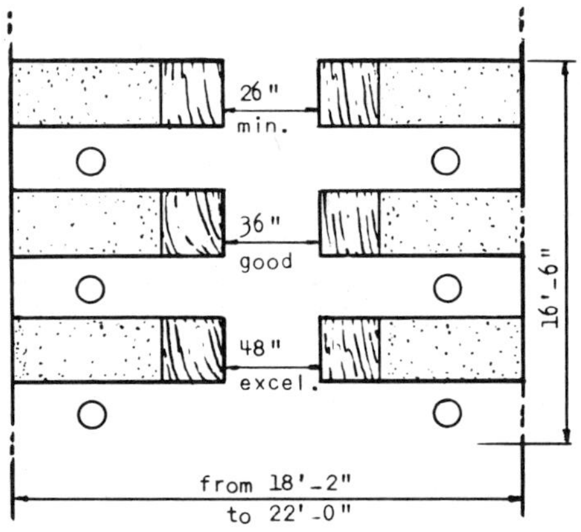
26" min.
36" good
48" excel.
16'-6"
from 18'-2"
to 22'-0"

CENTER AISLE END REFERENCE

□' per man	5' board	6' board
minimum	55 sq.ft.	61 sq.ft.
good	57½ sq.ft	63¼ sq.ft.
excellent	60½ sq.ft.	66 sq.ft.

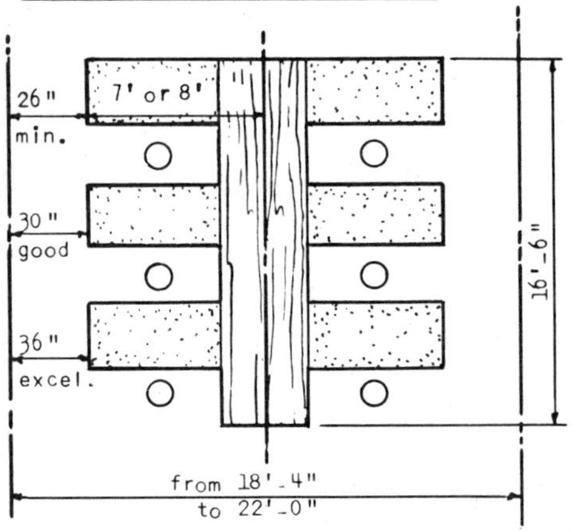
26" min.
7' or 8'
30" good
36" excel.
16'-6"
from 18'-4"
to 22'-0"

SIDE AISLE
CENTRAL REFERENCE

□' per man	5' board	6' board
minimum	50¼ sq.ft.	55¾ sq.ft.
good	52¼ sq.ft.	57¾ sq.ft.
excellent	55 sq.ft.	60½ sq.ft.

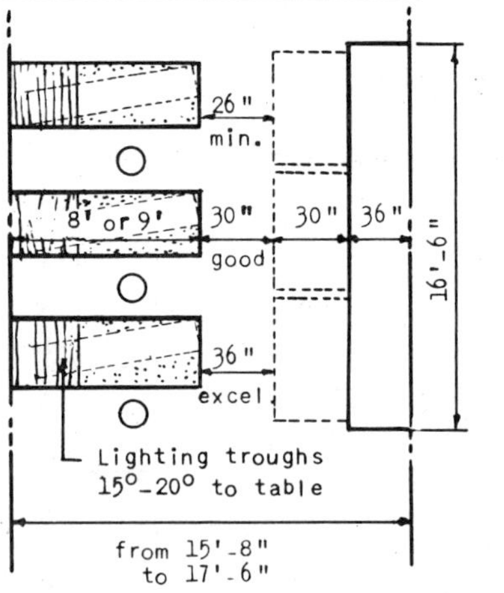
26" min.
8' or 9'
30" good
30"
36"
36" excel.
16'-6"
Lighting troughs
15°-20° to table
from 15'-8"
to 17'-6"

SIDE AISLE WITH STORAGE AREA

□' per man	5' board	6' board
minimum	86¼ sq.ft.	91¾ sq.ft.
good	88 sq.ft.	93½ sq.ft.
excellent	90¾ sq.ft.	96¾ sq.ft.

Scale: 3/32" = 1'-0"

COMPARATIVE DRAFTING AREAS

Areas include units plus aisle

Dimensions shown are based on the use of 3'x 5' and 3'x 6' drafting tables. If larger tables are used they will replace reference areas and the total areas will not increase. Provide one large table for detailing, reference, and wrapping.

The draftsman requires 80 to 100 foot-candles of light on his board or approximately 6 watts per square foot. Avoid sharp contrasts of light in drafting room. The board illumination should never be more than seven times as bright as the surroundings. Fluorescent trough fixtures are most practical when hung diagonally to tables.

For the medium-sized architectural drafting office 100 square feet per man is ideal. This includes areas for drafting, reference, plan storage, aisle and supply. Reception, office, conference, and wash rooms are not included

GYMNASIUM SHOWERS and DRESSING ROOMS

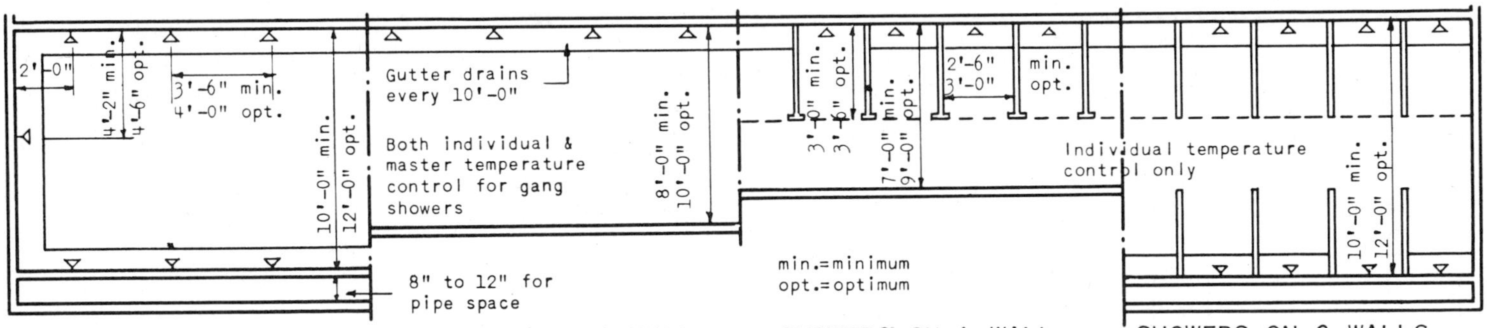
2'-0"
4'-2" min.
4'-6" opt.
3'-6" min.
4'-0" opt.
10'-0" min.
12'-0" opt.
Gutter drains every 10'-0"
Both individual & master temperature control for gang showers
8'-0" min.
10'-0" opt.
8" to 12" for pipe space
3'-0" min.
3'-6" opt.
7'-0" min.
9'-0" opt.
2'-6"
3'-0"
min.
opt.
Individual temperature control only
min.=minimum
opt.=optimum
10'-0" min.
12'-0" opt.

SHOWERS ON 2 WALLS SHOWERS ON 1 WALL

GANG SHOWERS

SHOWERS ON 1 WALL SHOWERS ON 2 WALLS

INDIVIDUAL SHOWERS

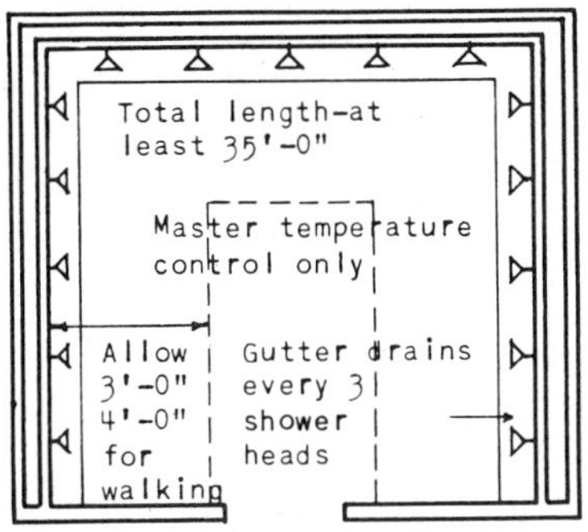
Total length-at least 35'-0"
Master temperature control only
Allow 3'-0" 4'-0" for walking
Gutter drains every 3 shower heads

BOYS' WALK-AROUND SHOWER

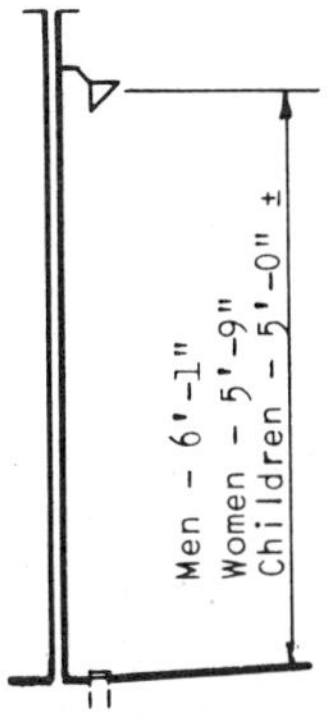
Men - 6'-1"
Women - 5'-9"
Children - 5'-0" ±

HEIGHT OF SHOWER HEAD

RECOMMENDATIONS FOR SHOWERING FACILITIES		
BLDG. TYPE	NUMBER OF SHOWERS	TYPE
School gymnasiums	Girls - 40% of peak period load + 1 to 3 individual showers Boys - 30% of peak period load. Can be reduced by 1/3 for walk-around type	Gang & individual Gang & walk-around
Bathhouses	Women-1 shower for each 250 women using pool. Men-1 shower for each 250 men using pool	Individual Gang
Community recreation buildings	Minimum for women-6 gang + 4 individual Minimum of 12 for men	Gang & individual Gang

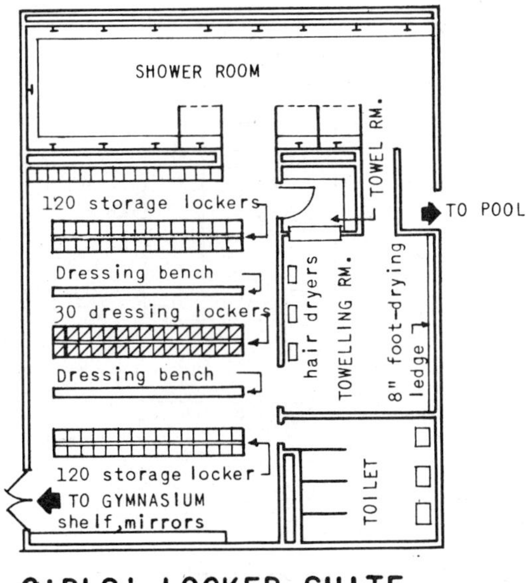
SHOWER ROOM
TOWEL RM.
TO POOL
120 storage lockers
Dressing bench
30 dressing lockers
Dressing bench
hair dryers
TOWELLING RM.
8" foot-drying ledge
120 storage locker
TO GYMNASIUM
shelf, mirrors
TOILET

GIRLS' LOCKER SUITE
(Serves peak period load of 30)

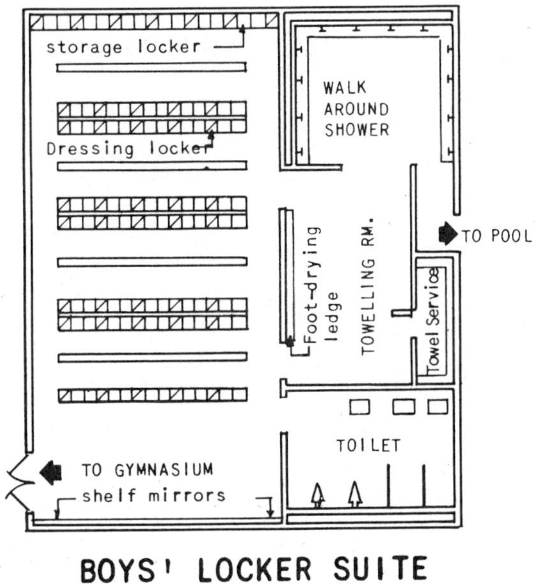
storage locker
WALK AROUND SHOWER
Dressing locker
TO POOL
Foot-drying ledge
TOWELLING RM.
Towel Service
TOILET
TO GYMNASIUM
shelf mirrors

BOYS' LOCKER SUITE
(Serves peak period load of 40)

Scale: 1/16" = 1'-0"

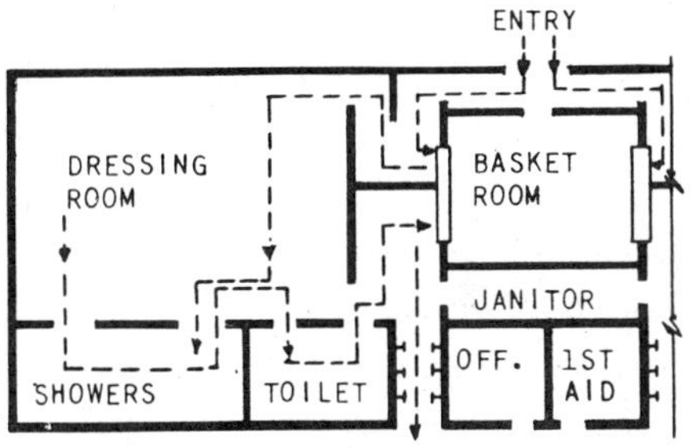
ENTRY
DRESSING ROOM
BASKET ROOM
JANITOR
SHOWERS
TOILET
OFF.
1ST AID

DRESSING UNIT FOR POOL

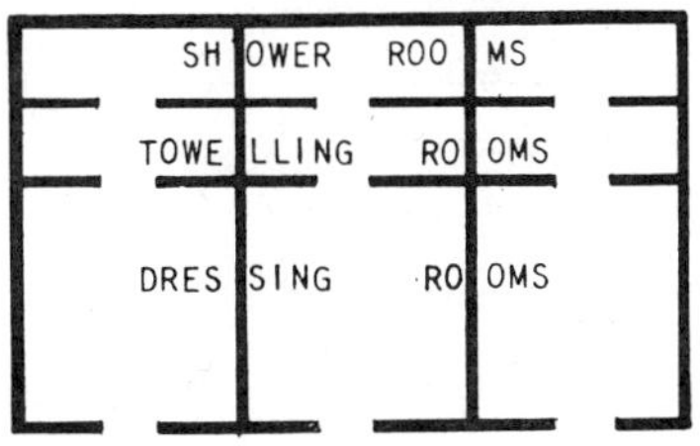
SHOWER ROOMS
TOWELLING ROOMS
DRESSING ROOMS

DRESSING UNITS FOR COMMUNITY USE

RECOMMENDED TOILET FIXTURES FOR GYM LOCKER SUITES		
FIXTURE	NO. OF FIXTURES-BY PROPORTION	MINIMUM
Toilets	Girls - 1 to 30	3
	Boys - 1 to 50	2
Urinals	1 to 25	2
Lavatories	Girls - 1 to 20	3
	Boys - 1 to 20	3

AUXILIARY ROOMS FOR GYM LOCKER SUITES	
TOWELLING ROOM	Equal to shower room in area
Towel service room	Area varies with material to be stored (Room may also be used to distribute uniforms)
Equipment drying room	Depends on drying time & no. of uniforms. This room requires special heating and ventilating.

GYMNASIUM LOCKERS and DRESSING ROOMS

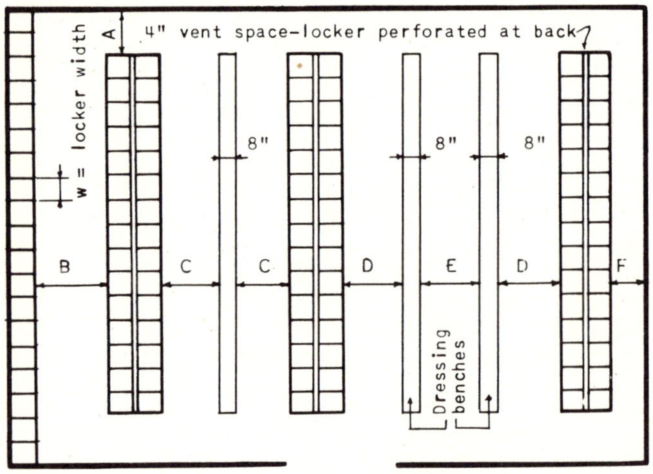
4" vent space-locker perforated at back
A
w = locker width
8"
8"
8"
B
C
C
D
E
D
F
Dressing benches

MINIMUM AISLE SPACE FOR DRESSING ROOMS

	SCHOOLS	AVERAGE TRAFFIC
A	2'-0"	2'-0"
B	2W + 12"	2W + 12"
C	2'-6"	W + 6"
D	2'-6"	W + 6"
E	2'-6"	1'-8"
F	2'-6"	W + 12"

Rule of thumb area for locker rooms (school gymnasiums & community recreation buildings) 14 sq. ft. per person (peak period load) exclusive of locker space.

LOCKER ROOM FACILITIES

Stationary benches
Mirrors for both boys & girls.
Shelves below mirrors for girls
Full-length mirror for girls.
Drinking fountain
Bulletin board
Lighting located so that aisles and passages are well illuminated.
Windows located with regard to height and arrangement of lockers.
Adequate ventilation for all storage lockers.

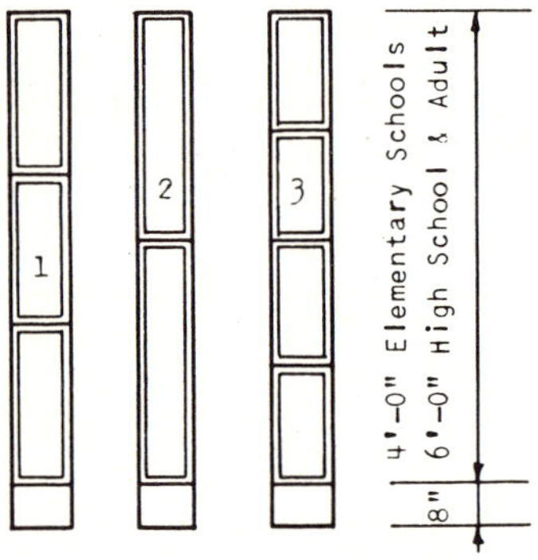
1
2
3
4'-0" Elementary Schools
6'-0" High School & Adult
8"

RECOMMENDED LOCKERS FOR GYMNASIUM CLOTHING STORAGE:

1. 7½" wide x 12" deep x 24" high
2. 6" wide x 12" deep x 36" high
3. 7½" wide x 12" deep x 18" high.

STORAGE LOCKERS

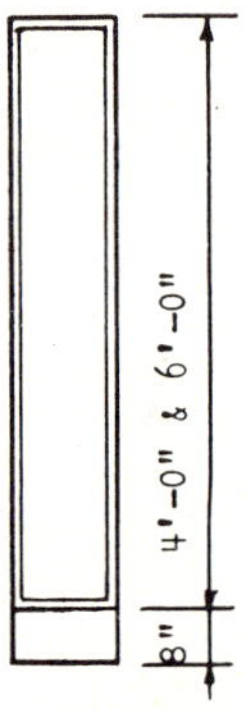
4'-0" & 6'-0"
8"

RECOMMENDED DRESSING LOCKER SIZES:

12" wide x 12" deep x 48" high

12" wide x 12" deep x 72" high

DRESSING LOCKERS

NO. OF LOCKERS REQUIRED FOR SCHOOL GYMNASIUMS:

1 Dressing locker per student (peak period load)+ 10% to allow for variation in class sizes & scheduling.

1 Storage locker per student enrolled + 10% to allow for expansion.

GYMNASIUM DRESSING ROOMS & LOCKERS

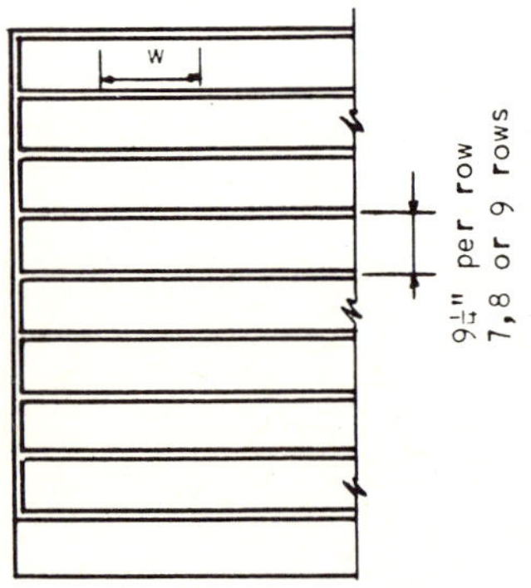
w
9¼" per row
7,8 or 9 rows

w = 1'-1" for large baskets, 10" for small baskets.

Depth of baskets = 1'-1½"

BASKET RACK

NOTE: Basket type lockers are not recommended for schools because:

① They do not allow for hygienic care of dressing equipment.

② They are subject to hard wear and must be replaced often.

③ An **attendant** is required for proper administration

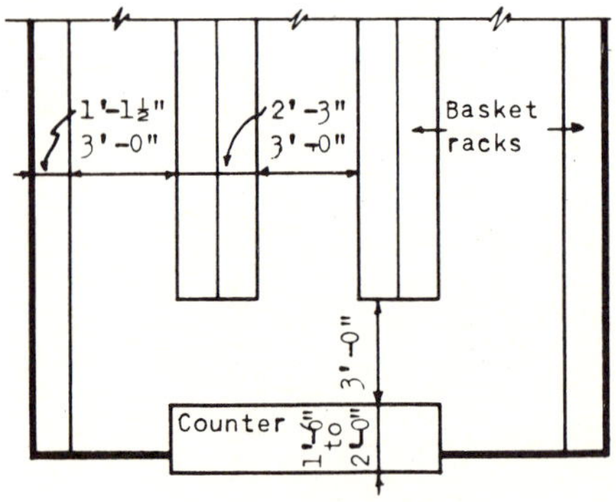
1'-1½"
3'-0"
2'-3"
3'-0"
Basket racks
3'-0"
Counter
1'-6" to 2'-0"

BASKET ROOM

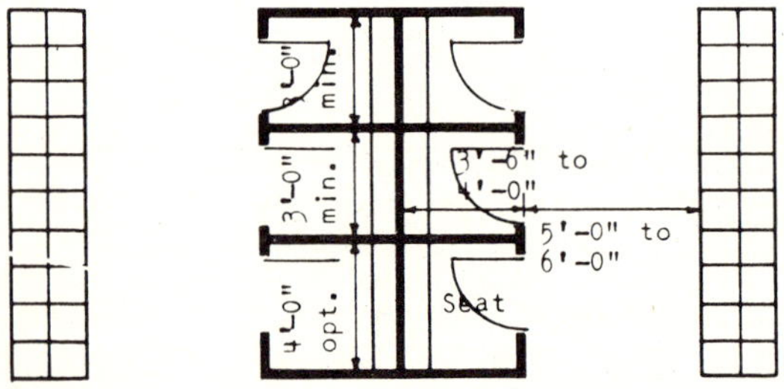
3'-0" min.
3'-0" min.
4'-0" opt.
3'-6" to 4'-0"
5'-0" to 6'-0"
Seat

DRESSING ROOMS WITH LOCKERS

NO. OF DRESSING CUBICLES FOR SWIMMING POOLS.

1 to 12 baskets
1 to 6 **lockers.**

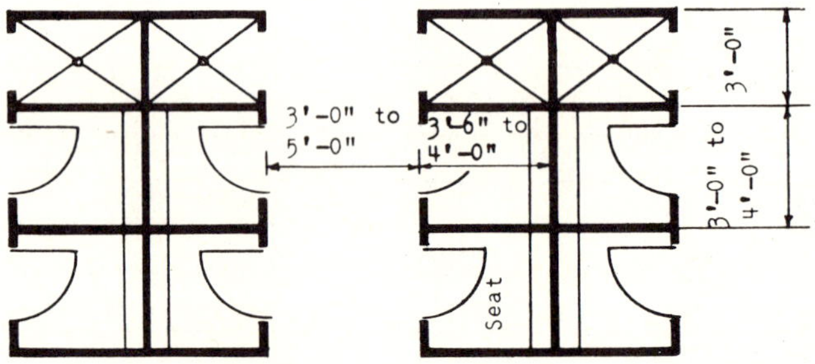
3'-0" to 5'-0"
3'-6" to 4'-0"
3'-0"
3'-0" to 4'-0"
Seat

DRESSING ROOMS WITH SHOWERS

SWIMMING POOL DRESSING ROOMS & LOCKERS

SHOWERS, DRESSING ROOMS, CABANAS

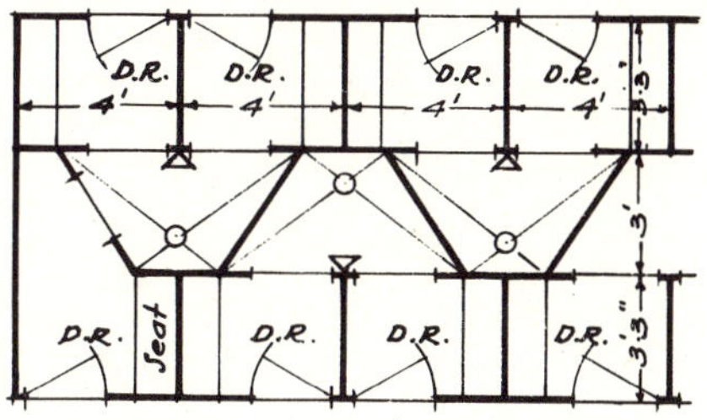
D.R.
4'
Seat
3'-3"
3'

2 Dressing Rooms to each Shower.

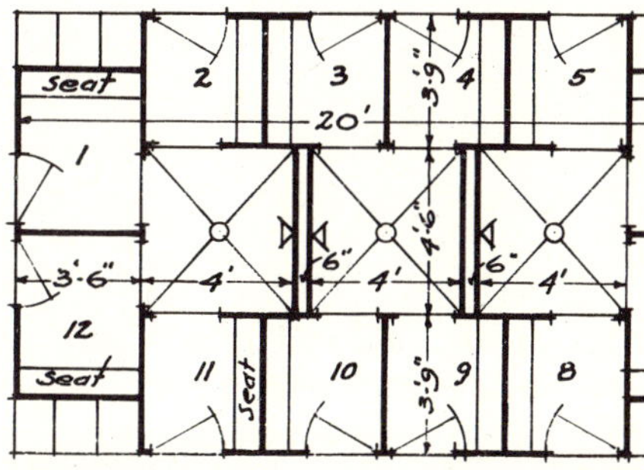
Seat
20'
3'-6"
4'
6"
4'-6"
3'-9"
12'

12 Dressing Rms. 3 Showers. 12 Lockers.
planning allowance = 20ϕ per Dressing Rm.
Total Area = 240 Sq. Feet.

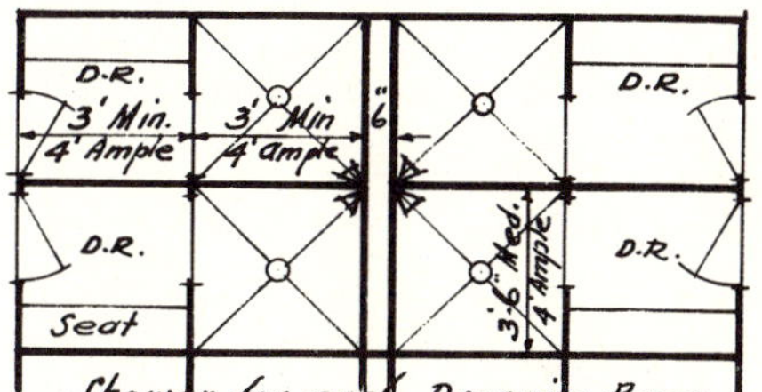
D.R.
3' Min.
4' Ample
6"
Seat
3'-6" Med.
4' Ample

Shower for each Dressing Room
planning allowance 22ϕ to 32ϕ.

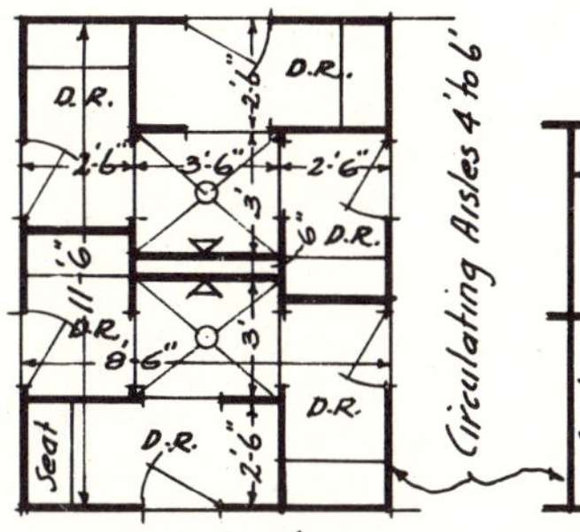
D.R.
Seat
Circulating Aisles 4' to 6'

6 Dr. Rms. 2 Showers
Allow 16ϕ per Dr. Rm.
Total Area = 96ϕ

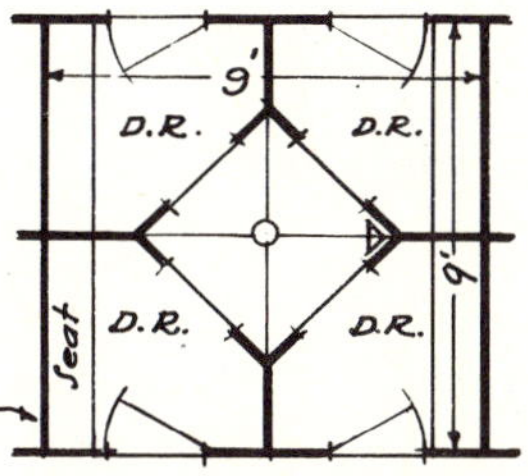
D.R.
9'
Seat

4 Dr. Rms. 1 Shower
Allow 20ϕ per Dr. Rm.
Total Area 81ϕ

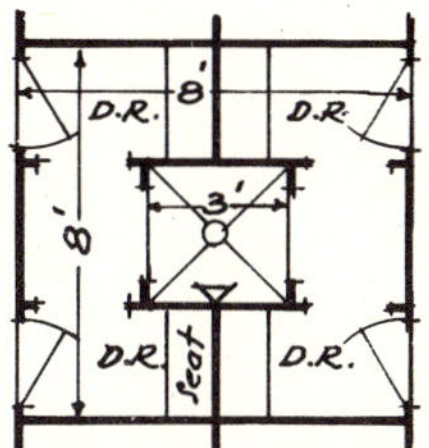
D.R.
8'
3'
Seat

4 Dr. Rms. 1 Shower
Allow 16ϕ per Dr. Rm.
Total Area = 64ϕ

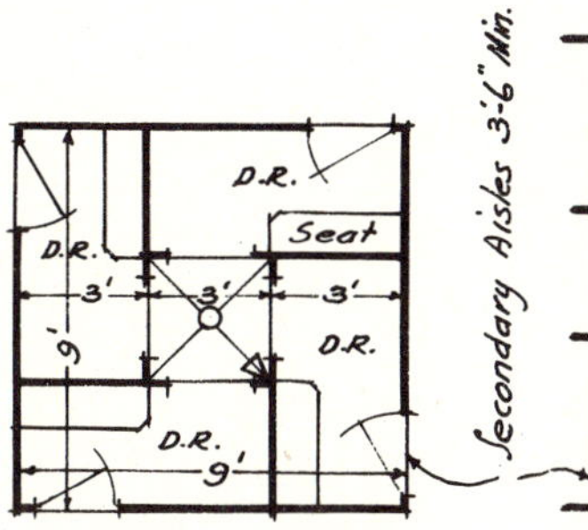
D.R.
Seat
3'
9'
Secondary Aisles 3'-6" Min.

4 Dr. Rms. 1 Shower
Allow 20ϕ per Dr. Rm.
Total Area 81ϕ

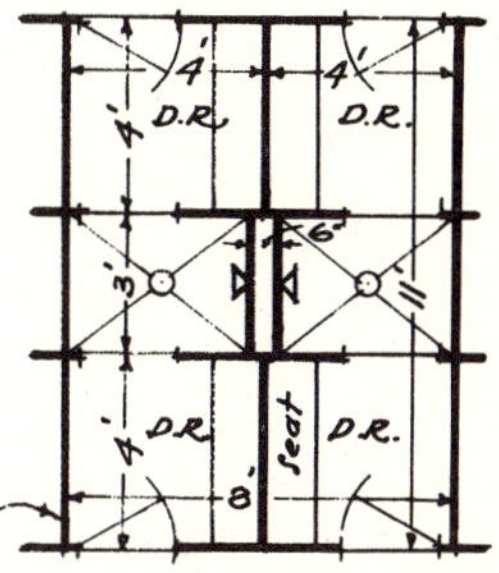
D.R.
4'
3'
6"
8'
Seat

4 Dr. Rms. 2 Showers
Allow 22ϕ per Dr. Rm.
Total Area = 88ϕ

COMBINATION SHOWERS and DRESSING ROOMS

Usually used for Women and girls.

1/8" = 1'

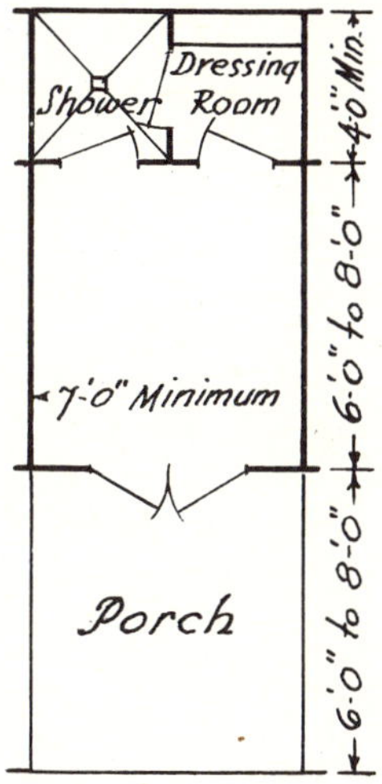
Shower
Dressing Room
4'-0" Min.
7'-0" Minimum
6'-0" to 8'-0"
Porch

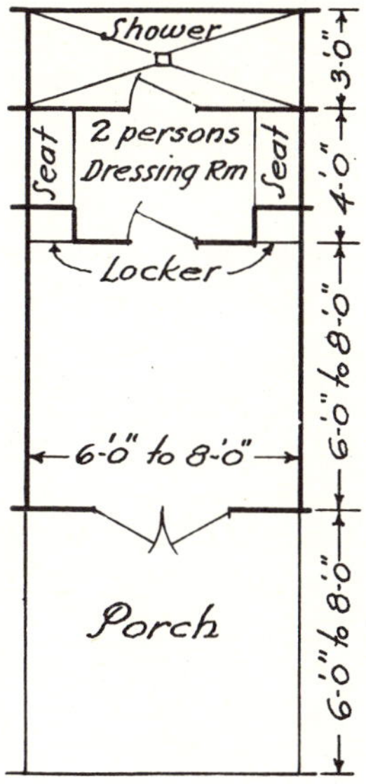
Shower
3'-0"
Seat
2 persons Dressing Rm
4'-0"
Locker
6'-0" to 8'-0"
Porch

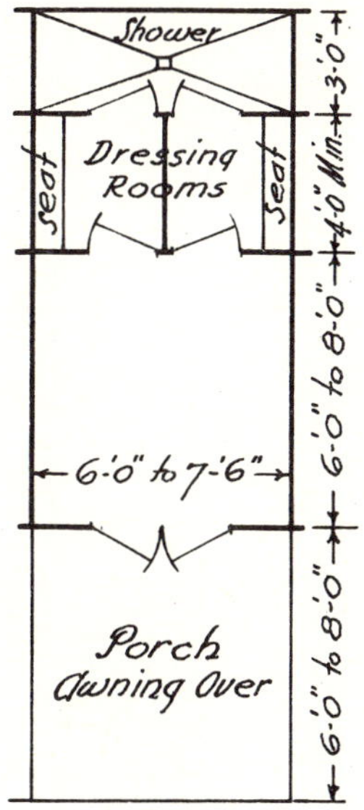
Shower
3'-0"
Seat
Dressing Rooms
4'-0" Min.
6'-0" to 7'-6"
6'-0" to 8'-0"
Porch
Awning Over

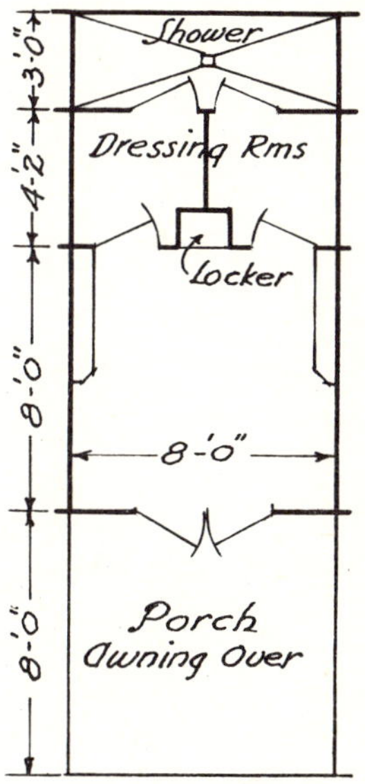
Shower
3'-0"
Dressing Rms
4'-2"
Locker
8'-0"
Porch
Awning Over

ONE DRESSING ROOM

TWO DRESSING ROOMS

CABANAS

3'-6"
3'-0"
3'-6"
3'-6"
4'-0"
3'-0"
4'-0"
3'-6"

Small Medium Large Very Large

SIZE of SHOWER STALLS

Bath House Stalls are usually larger than those in other buildings. For Beach & Outdoor Pools allow 1 shower for 250 people.

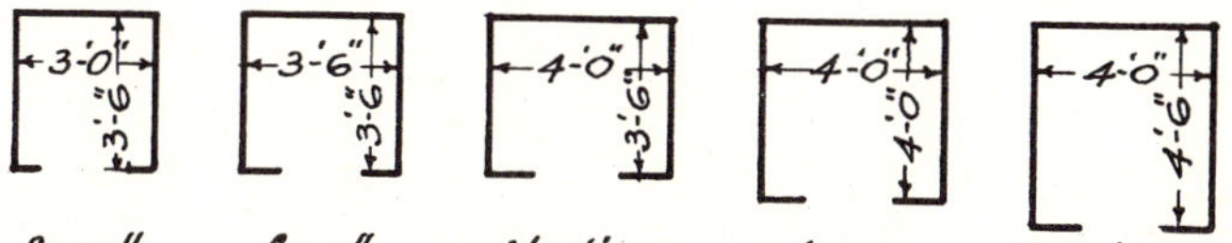
3'-0"
3'-6"
3'-6"
3'-6"
4'-0"
3'-6"
4'-0"
4'-0"
4'-0"
4'-6"

Small Small Medium Large Very Large

SIZE of DRESSING ROOMS

Also termed "Stalls," Compartments" and "Cubicles". Seats 1'-0" to 1'-3" wide.

COMMERCIAL KITCHEN EQUIPMENT LAYOUTS

This and the following page show schematic drawings of various kitchen areas. The drawings are intended to show efficient functional relationships of the main equipment and do not attempt to present design solutions to kitchen equipment layout.

Type, quantity and layout of equipment will vary with anticipated patronage and menu. For example, large kitchens may need more items, such as ranges and kettles, than are shown under "Cooking Sections". Small kitchens may combine in a cooking area functions shown separately below, such as cooking and baking.

Work aisles:

If no thru-traffic, minimum width is 3'-0". With 2 parallel work tables, minimum aisle width is 3'-6", preferably 4'-0" to 4'-6".

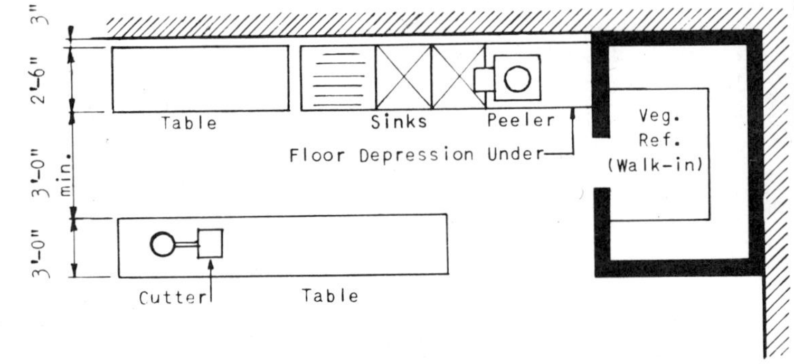
3"
2'-6"
3'-0" min.
3'-0"
Table
Sinks
Peeler
Floor Depression Under
Veg. Ref. (Walk-in)
Cutter
Table

VEGETABLE AND SALAD PREPARATION

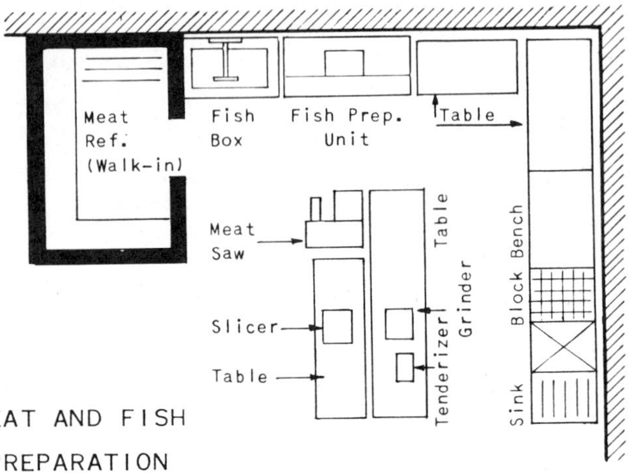
Meat Ref. (Walk-in)
Fish Box
Fish Prep. Unit
Table
Meat Saw
Slicer
Table
Table
Tenderizer
Grinder
Block Bench
Sink

MEAT AND FISH PREPARATION

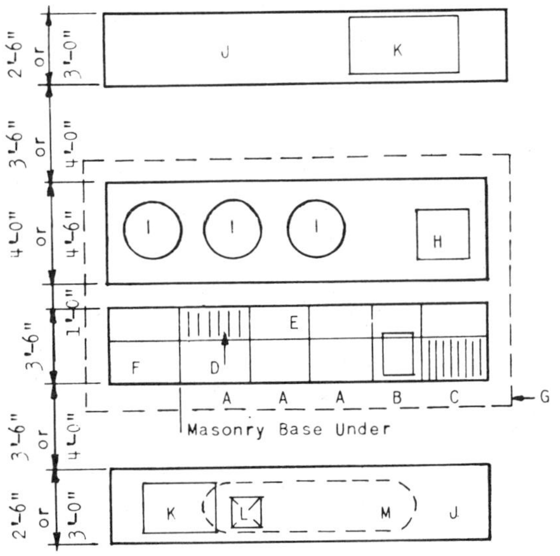
2'-6" or 3'-0"
3'-6" or 4'-0"
4'-0" or 4'-6"
1'-0"
3'-6"
3'-6" or 4'-0"
2'-6" or 3'-0"
J
K
I
I
I
H
E
F
D
A
A
A
B
C
G
Masonry Base Under
K
L
M
J

ISLAND-TYPE SECTION

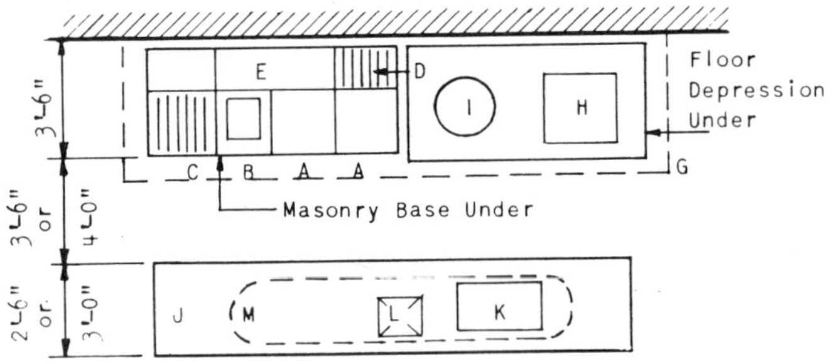
3'-6"
3'-6" or 4'-0"
2'-6" or 3'-0"
E
D
I
H
Floor Depression Under
C
B
A
A
G
Masonry Base Under
J
M
L
K

SECTION AGAINST WALL

KEY TO EQUIPMENT

A. Ranges
B. Fryers
C. Broilers
D. Salamanders
E. Shelves
F. Roasters
G. Hood (over)
H. Steamer
I. Kettle
J. Cook's Table
K. Bain Marie
L. Sink
M. Pot Rack (over)
N. Short Order Ref.
O. Steam Table
P. Plate Warmer
Q. Mixer

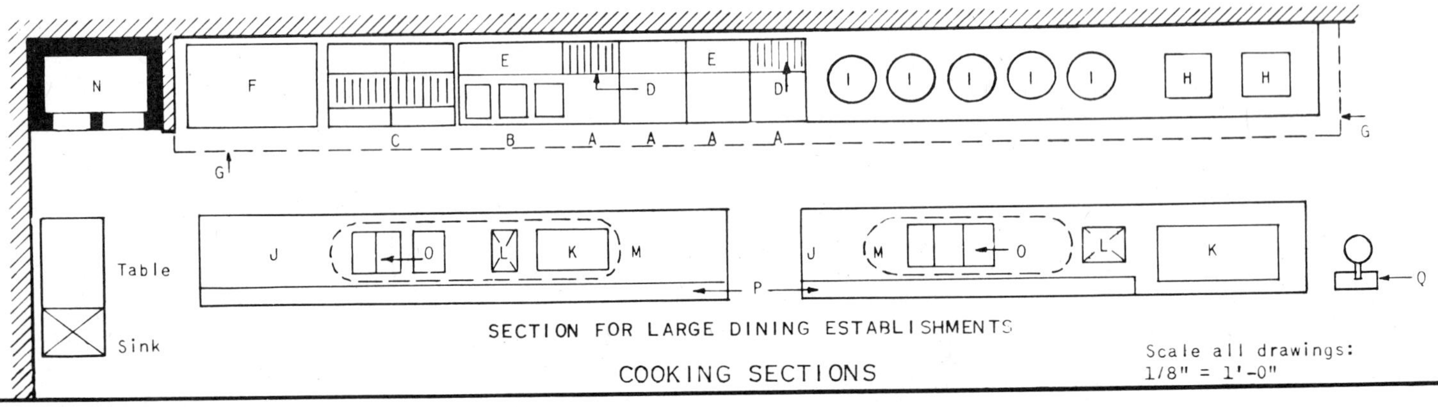
N
F
E
E
D
D
I
I
I
I
I
H
H
C
B
A
A
A
A
G
G
Table
Sink
J
O
L
K
M
P
J
M
O
L
K
Q

SECTION FOR LARGE DINING ESTABLISHMENTS

Scale all drawings: 1/8" = 1'-0"

COOKING SECTIONS

Data by Anthony J. Amendola, Food Service Equipment Consultant

COMMERCIAL KITCHEN EQUIPMENT LAYOUTS

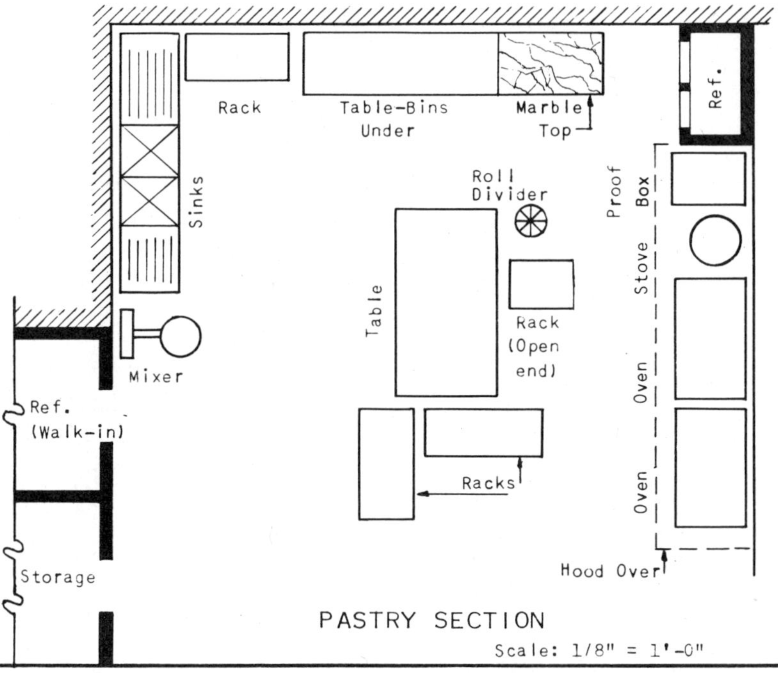
Rack
Table-Bins
Under
Marble
Top
Ref.
Sinks
Roll
Divider
Proof
Box
Stove
Table
Rack
(Open
end)
Mixer
Oven
Ref.
(Walk-in)
Racks
Oven
Storage
Hood Over

PASTRY SECTION

Scale: 1/8" = 1'-0"

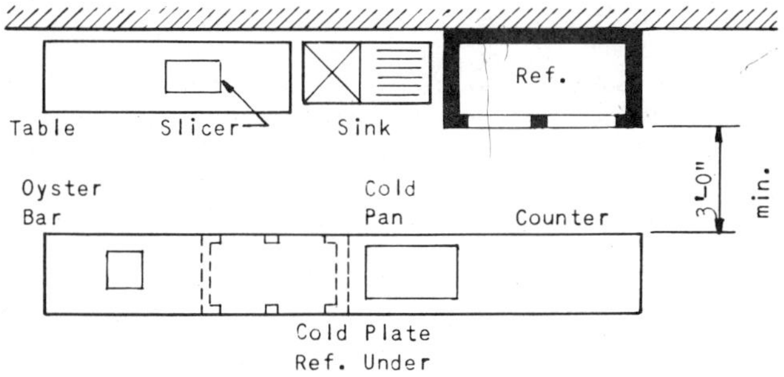
Ref.
Table
Slicer
Sink
Oyster
Bar
Cold
Pan
Counter
3'-0"
min.
Cold Plate
Ref. Under

COLD FOODS

Scale: 1/8" = 1'-0"

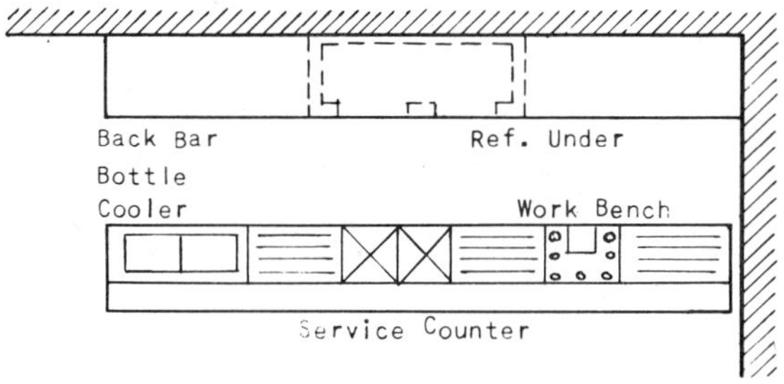
Back Bar
Ref. Under
Bottle
Cooler
Work Bench
Service Counter

SERVICE BAR

Scale: 1/8" = 1'-0"

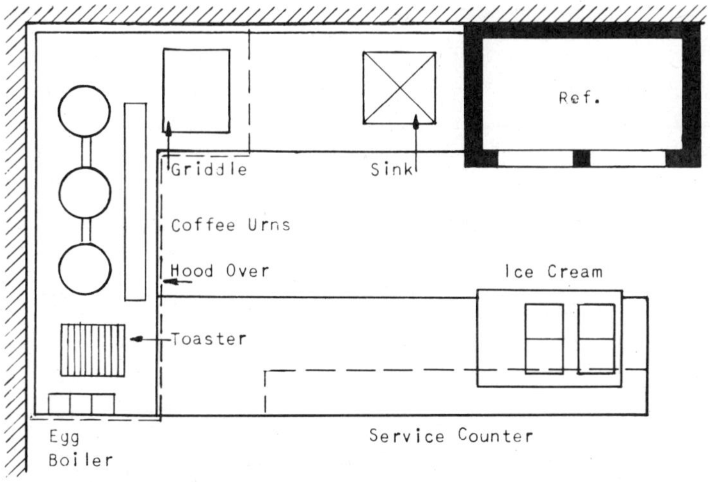
Ref.
Griddle
Sink
Coffee Urns
Hood Over
Ice Cream
Toaster
Egg
Boiler
Service Counter

PANTRY

Scale: 1/4" = 1'-0"

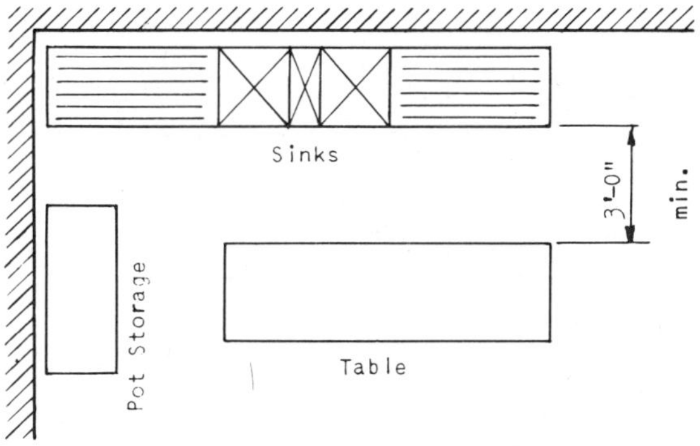
Sinks
3'-0"
min.
Pot Storage
Table

POT WASHING

Scale: 1/8" = 1'-0"

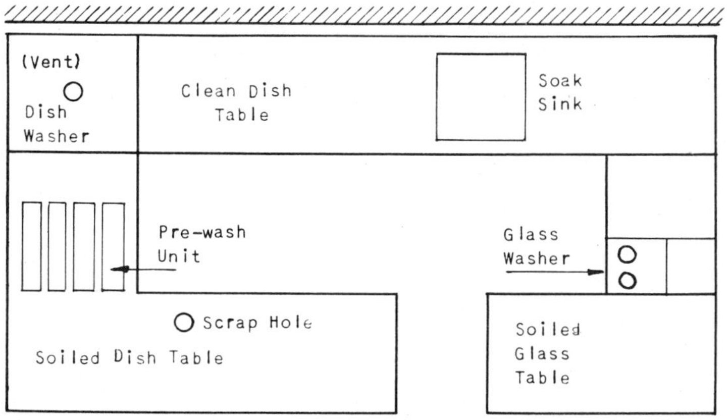
(Vent)
Dish
Washer
Clean Dish
Table
Soak
Sink
Pre-wash
Unit
Glass
Washer
Scrap Hole
Soiled Dish Table
Soiled
Glass
Table

Many types of dish and glass washers are available. Work tables may be of various shapes and designs, depending on requirements.

Provide shelving, movable racks, soiled silverware basket, etc., as required.

Silver washers, dryers, and burnishers are sometimes incorporated in this area.

Check local codes for use of garbage grinder under scrap hole on soiled dish table.

DISH, GLASS, SILVER AND TRAY WASHING

Scale: 1/4" = 1'-0"

Data by Anthony J. Amendola, Food Service Equipment Consultant

FAST FOOD SERVICE INSTALLATIONS

Fast food service is that type provided by luncheonettes, soda fountains, and dinettes (serving simple meals), which provide counter service, and by short-order sections of main kitchens. Counter service operations may have a separate kitchen with food preparation, cooking, and dishwashing areas.

The basic installations for counter service are:

1. back-bar
2. front counter
3. island
4. combinations of the above

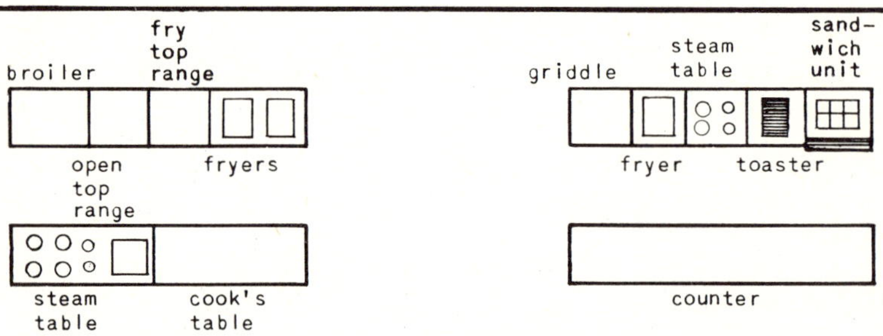

broiler
fry top range
open top range
fryers
steam table
cook's table
griddle
steam table
sand-wich unit
fryer
toaster
counter

A short-order section in a main kitchen does the same type of cooking as behind-the-counter installations, but usually has heavy equipment larger than that used in counters. Unit at right provides a more simple service than that at left.

SHORT-ORDER KITCHEN

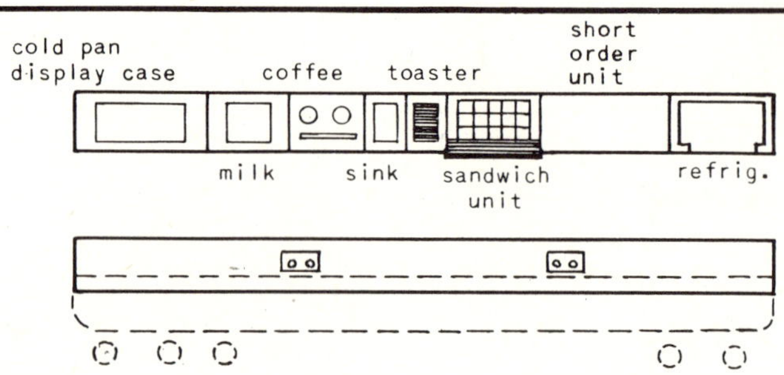

cold pan display case
coffee
toaster
short order unit
milk
sink
sandwich unit
refrig.

Usually for a small operation, with minimum menu and rapid customer turn-over. Has short counter; therefore usually uses straight counter rather than bay.

BACK-BAR INSTALLATION (SMALL)

May have entire cooking unit in back-bar installation. Lengthy counter requires duplication of coffee-making facilities. Bay counter seating may be used also.

BACK-BAR INSTALLATION (LARGE)

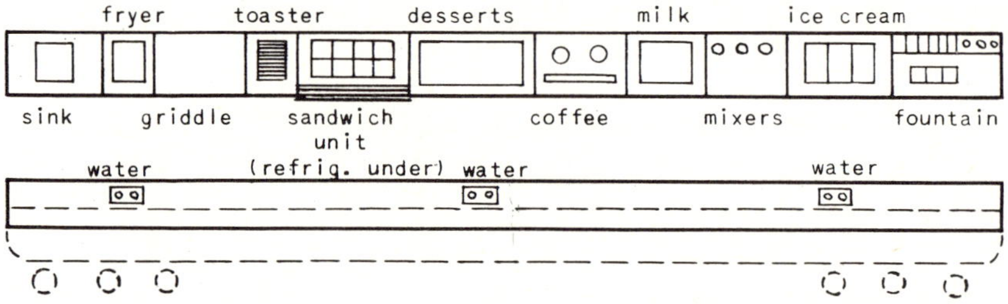

fryer
toaster
desserts
milk
ice cream
sink
griddle
sandwich unit (refrig. under)
coffee
mixers
fountain
water
water
water

sandwich unit (refrig. under)
ice cream
coffee
toaster
sink

May have refrigerators and shelving along back wall. Front-counter installations are generally used where there are space limitations from rear wall to front of serving counter; allows a saving of 8'' to 14''. May have more elaborate cooking equipment in separate kitchen, located at one end of counter.

FRONT-COUNTER INSTALLATION

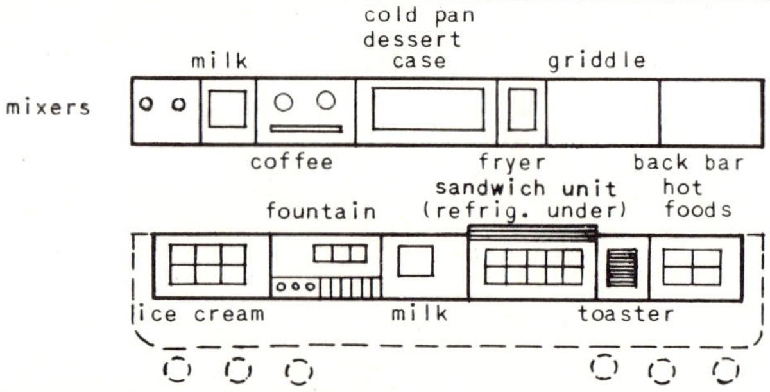

mixers
milk
cold pan dessert case
griddle
coffee
fryer
back bar hot foods
fountain
sandwich unit (refrig. under)
ice cream
milk
toaster

Usually for operations with limited area and staff, and a larger menu. May serve booths from waitress stand at end of counter.

COMBINED FRONT-COUNTER AND BACK-BAR INSTALLATION

May have straight or bay counter seating; also allows for direct booth service by counter waiters.

ISLAND INSTALLATION

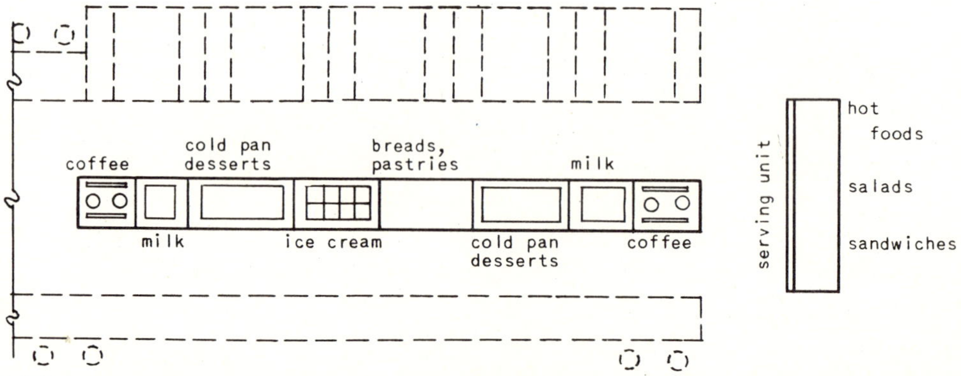

coffee
cold pan desserts
breads, pastries
milk
milk
ice cream
cold pan desserts
coffee
serving unit
hot foods
salads
sandwiches

Data by Anthony J. Amendola, Food Service Equipment Consultant

Drawings not to scale

COUNTER ARRANGEMENTS for FOOD SERVICE

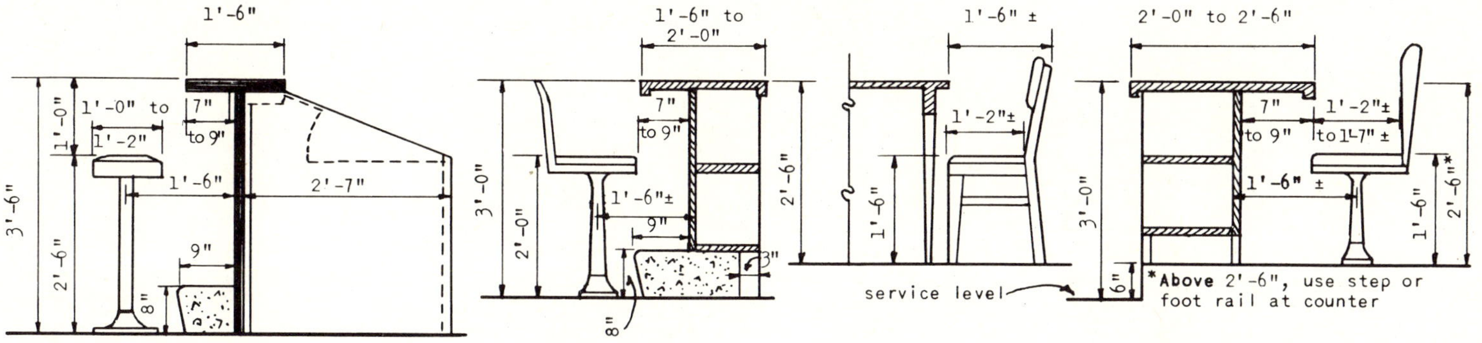
1'-6"
1'-0" to
1'-2"
7"
to 9"
1'-6"
2'-7"
9"
8"
1'-0"
2'-6"
3'-6"
1'-6" to
2'-0"
7"
to 9"
1'-6"±
9"
3"
8"
3'-0"
2'-0"
2'-6"
1'-6" ±
1'-2"±
1'-6"
service level
2'-0" to 2'-6"
7"
to 9"
1'-2"±
to 1'-7" ±
1'-6" ±
3'-0"
1'-6"
2'-6"*
6"
*Above 2'-6", use step or foot rail at counter

SODA FOUNTAIN

For standing or sitting at counter

LUNCH COUNTER

CHAIR AT TABLE

DINING COUNTER

For chair height stool

SECTION THROUGH COUNTERS AND SEAT

Scale: 3/8" = 1'-0"

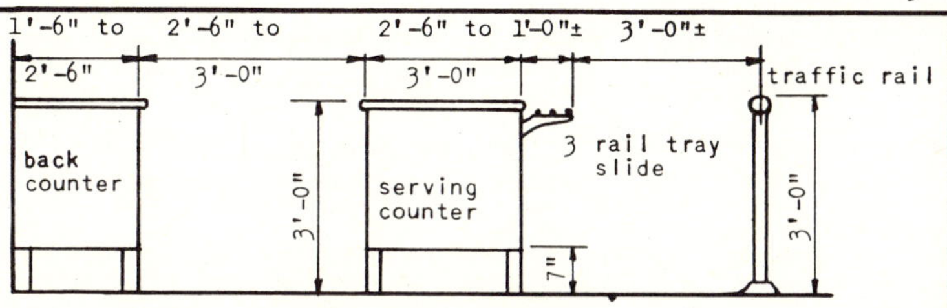
1'-6" to
2'-6"
2'-6" to
3'-0"
2'-6" to
3'-0"
1'-0"±
3'-0"±
traffic rail
back
counter
serving
counter
3 rail tray
slide
3'-0"
7"
3'-0"

CAFETERIA COUNTERS

Scale: 1/4" = 1'-0"

KEY TO DIMENSIONS

A With one waitress, the minimum width of work aisles is 2'-6". With two or more waitresses working in one area, increase work aisle width to 3'-0"

B Increase bay work aisle width as the length of the bay is increased. Average width is 2'-6" to 3'-0".

C All seats are 2'-0" o.c.

D Minimum width is 2'-3". Recommended width is 3'-0".

E Back-bar width depends on the **type of equipment** used. With only small counter appliances, 1'-6" to 1'-8" may be adequate. With reach-in refrigerator or heavy equipment, 2'-0" to 2'-9" will be required.

F Distance from counter to counter, with multiple bays, is 5'-0" to 5'-6".

Scale: 3/32" = 1'-0"

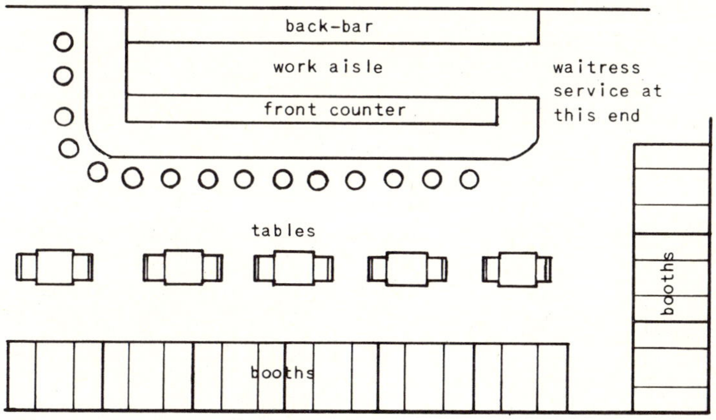
back-bar
work aisle
front counter
waitress
service at
this end
tables
booths
booths

COMBINED COUNTERS AND TABLES

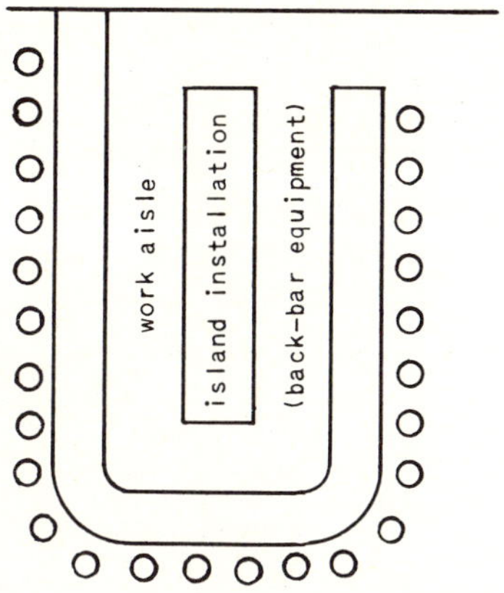
work aisle
island installation
(back-bar equipment)

SINGLE BAY

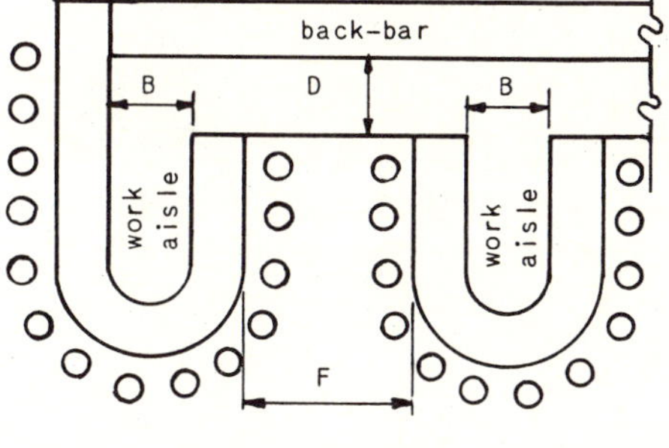
back-bar
B
D
B
work
aisle
work
aisle
F

MULTIPLE BAY

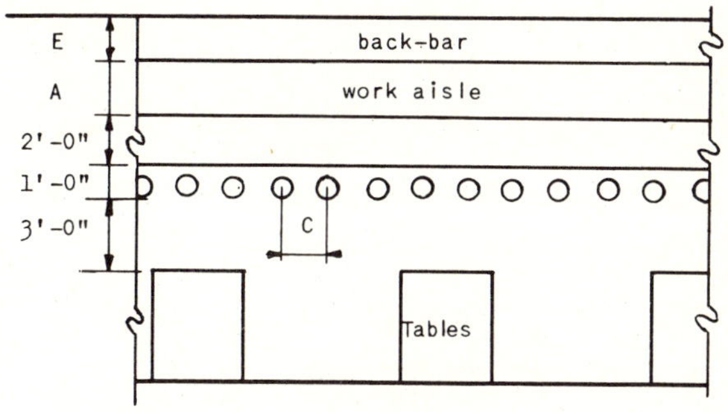
E
back-bar
A
work aisle
2'-0"
1'-0"
3'-0"
C
Tables

STRAIGHT

Dimensions of work aisles, seat spacing, etc., do not vary with different types of counter arrangements.

TYPICAL COUNTER ARRANGEMENTS

Data by Anthony J. Amendola, Food Service Equipment Consultant

BARS, SEATS, BOOTHS and TABLES

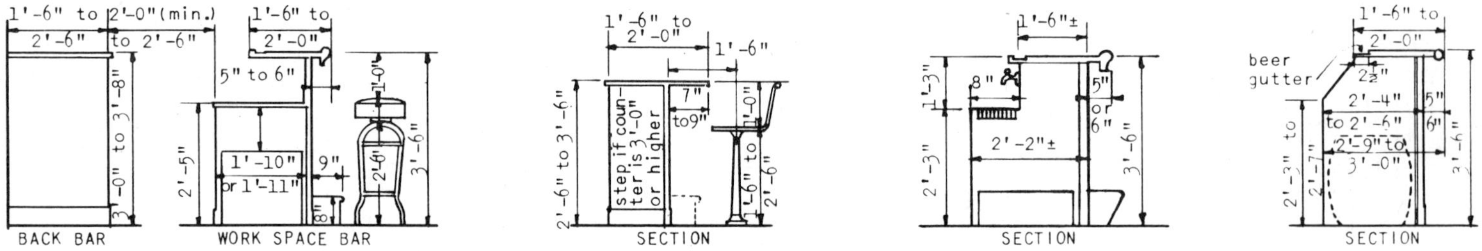
1'-6" to 2'-6"
2'-0" (min.) to 2'-6"
1'-6" to 2'-0"
5" to 6"
3'-0" to 3'-8"
2'-5"
1'-10" or 1'-11"
9"
8"
1'-0"
2'-6"
3'-6"
BACK BAR
WORK SPACE BAR
1'-6" to 2'-0"
1'-6"
7" to 9"
step if counter is 3'-0" or higher
2'-6" to 3'-6"
1'-6" to 2'-6"
1'-0"
SECTION
1'-6"±
8"
5" or 6"
1'-3"
2'-2"±
2'-3"
3'-6"
SECTION
beer gutter
1'-6" to 2'-0"
2½"
2'-4"
5"
to 2'-6"
6"
2'-9" to 3'-0"
2'-2" to 2'-7"
3'-6"
SECTION

COMPLETE BAR-END ELEVATION — FOOD COUNTER — BEER DISPENSER — SELF-CONTAINED BEER DISPENSING UNIT

Stock units shown below fit under these bars in various combinations. Bar heights are standard. Other dimensions vary slightly.

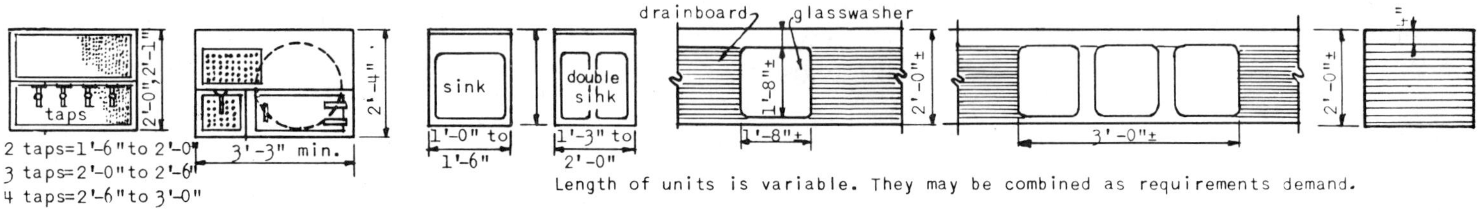
taps
2'-0", 2'-1"
3'-3" min.
2'-4"
sink
double sink
1'-0" to 1'-6"
1'-3" to 2'-0"
drainboard
glasswasher
1'-8"±
1'-8"±
2'-0"±
3'-0"±
2'-0"±

2 taps=1'-6" to 2'-0"
3 taps=2'-0" to 2'-6"
4 taps=2'-6" to 3'-0"

Length of units is variable. They may be combined as requirements demand.

BEER DISPENSER — SELF-CONTAINED BEER DISPENSING UNIT — UNITS OF SINKS AND WORKBOARDS — WORKBOARDS

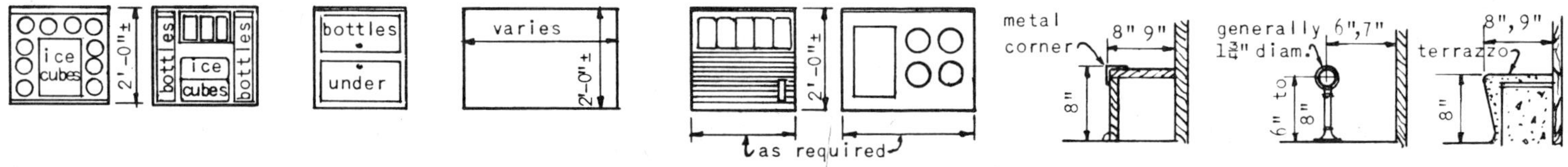
ice cubes
2'-0"±
bottles
ice cubes
bottles
bottles
under
varies
2'-0"±
2'-0"±
as required
metal corner
8" 9"
8"
generally 6", 7"
1½" diam.
6" to 8"
8", 9"
terrazzo
8"

SET-UP AND BOTTLE RACKS — STORAGE — COCKTAIL WAGON — SANDWICH BOARD — STEAM TABLE — FOOT RAILS

BAR AND RESTAURANT EQUIPMENT

chair rail heights are determined by dimension D

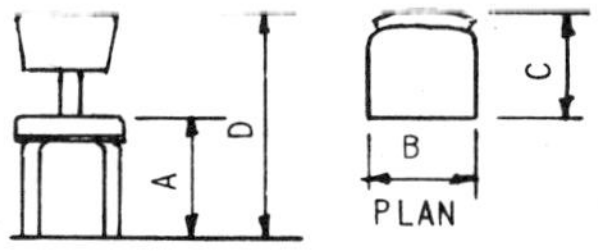
A
D
B
C
PLAN

VARIOUS DESIGNS

CHAIRS

CHAIR DIMENSIONS				
TYPE	A	B	C	D
Straight	1'-5" to 1'-6½"	1'-2" to 1'-4"	1'-2" to 1'-4"	2'-8" to 3'-0"
Windsor	1'-5", 1'-6"	1'-3" to 1'-7"	1'-3" to 1'-6"	3'-0"
Arm	1'-5", 1'-6"	1'-7" to 2'-0"	1'-3" to 2'-0"	2'-10" to 3'-6"
Dining Rm.	1'-6"	1'-6" to 1'-9"	1'-6" to 1'-10"	2'-10" to 3'-3"
Tavern	1'-5"	1'-5" to 1'-8"	1'-3" to 1'-6"	2'-4" to 2'-6"
Metal	1'-6"	1'-3" to 1'-7"	1'-2" to 1'-6"	2'-6"
Mold'd Plywood	1'-6"	1'-3" to 1'-6"	1'-3" to 1'-6"	2'-8", 2'-9"
Mold'd Plywd. with arms	1'-6"	1'-6" to 1'-10"	1'-3" to 1'-7"	2'-7" to 2'-9"

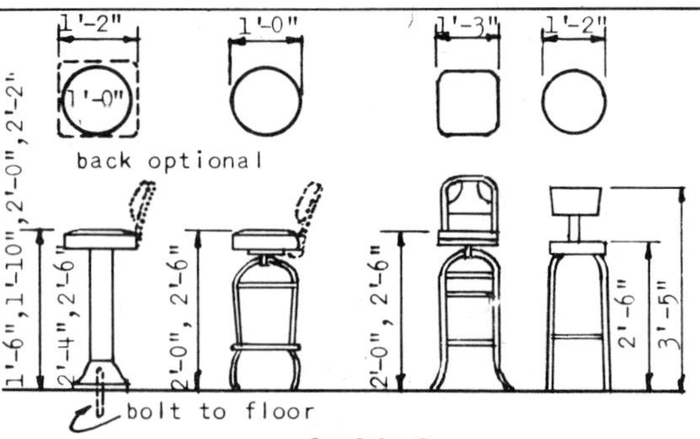
1'-2"
1'-0"
1'-0"
1'-3"
1'-2"
back optional
1'-6", 1'-10", 2'-0", 2'-2"
2'-4", 2'-6"
2'-0", 2'-6"
2'-0", 2'-6"
2'-6"
3'-5"
bolt to floor

STOOLS

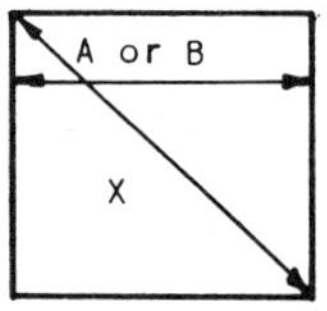
A or B
X

SQUARE

PERSONS	A or B	X
2	2'-0" or 2'-6"	2'-10" or 3'-6"
4	2'-6" or 3'-0"	3'-6" or 4'-3"

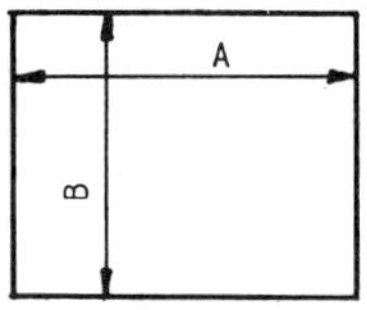
A
B

RECTANGULAR

PERSONS	A	B
2 seats on 1 side	4'-0"	1'-6"
2	2'-0" to 2'-6"	2'-6"
4	3'-6" to 4'-0"	2'-3" 2'-6"
6	5'-0" to 6'-0"	2'-9"
6 to 8	7'-0" to 8'-0"	3'-0"

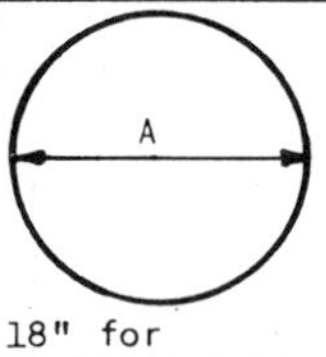
A

18" for cocktail table

PERSONS	A
2	2'-0"
3	2'-6"
4	3'-0"
5 to 6	3'-6" to 4'-0"
6 to 8	4'-0" to 4'-6"
10 to 12	5'-0" to 6'-0"
14 to 16	7'-0" to 8'-0"

Minimum sizes are satisfactory for drink service. Use larger for food service. All tables wider than 2'-6" will seat 2 extra at ends. Table heights are usually 2'-6". Four-legged tables increase cleaning difficulties. On a carpet, use heavy bases with a wide spread.

TABLES

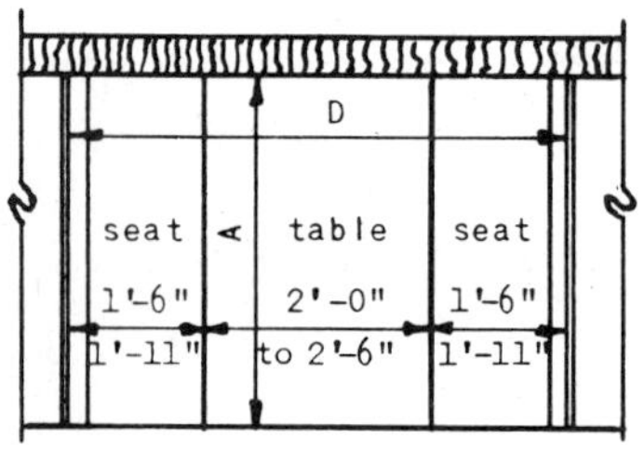
D
seat
A
table
seat
1'-6"
2'-0"
1'-6"
1'-11"
to 2'-6"
1'-11"

PLAN

A: One person per side: 2'-0" to 2'-6"
A: Two persons per side: 3'-6" to 4'-6" (4'-0" is the recommended maximum for serving, cleaning)
D: without sloping seat back: 5'-0" to 5'-6"
D: with sloping seat back: 5'-2" to 6'-0"
D: with upholstered seat back: 6'-4"± c. to. c.

Local regulations limit height of booth partitions.
Tables are often 2" shorter than seats; have corners rounded.
Circular booths have overall diameter of 6'-4"±

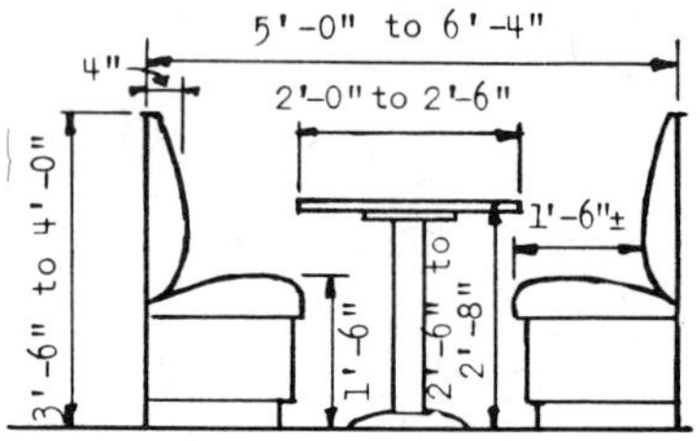
5'-0" to 6'-4"
4"
2'-0" to 2'-6"
1'-6"±
3'-6" to 4'-0"
1'-6"
2'-6" to 2'-8"
pedestal type table

ELEVATION

BOOTHS

Drawings not to scale. Data by Anthony J. Amendola, Food Service Equipment Consultant

SEATING for RESTAURANTS and BARS

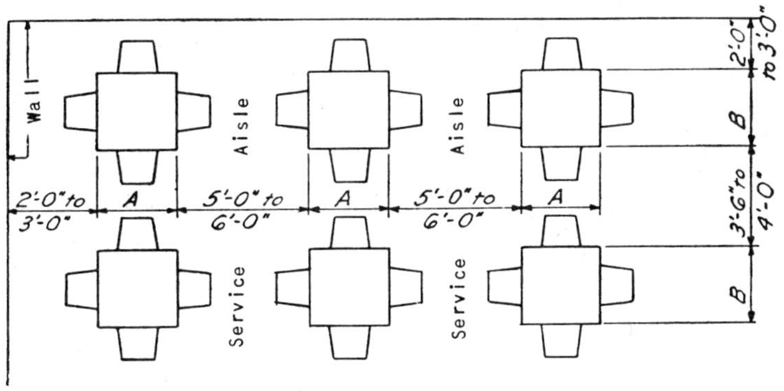
Wall
Aisle
Aisle
Service
Service
2'-0" to 3'-0"
A
5'-0" to 6'-0"
A
5'-0" to 6'-0"
A
2'-0" to 3'-0"
B
3'-6" to 4'-0"
B

SQUARE SPACING

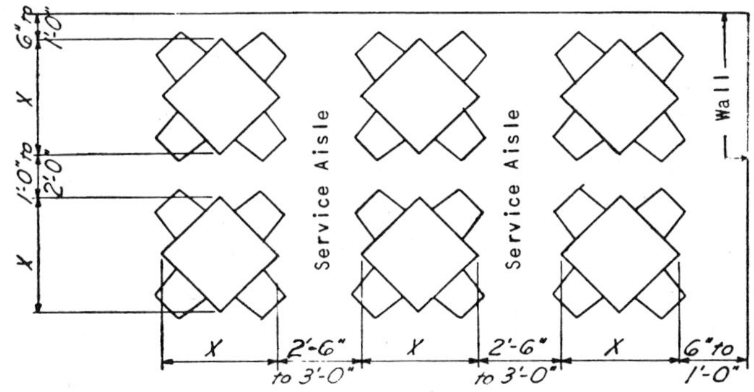
6" to 1'-0"
X
1'-0" to 2'-0"
X
Service Aisle
Service Aisle
Wall
X
2'-6" to 3'-0"
X
2'-6" to 3'-0"
X
6" to 1'-0"

DIAGONAL SPACING

SEATING ALLOWANCES may be approximated only, until seating layout is made, by use of following (non-standardized) rule-of-thumb for square feet-per-person. Use maximum figures for large spaces and minimum for small spaces.								
Type of Room	Normal	Emergency	Type of Room	Normal	Emergency	Type of Room	Normal	Emergency
Banquet & Large D.R.	10-11	7	Dining Room/Restaurant	14-15	10-12	Lunchrms: counter & chair-table types. Incl. counters, chairs, tables.	20	16
Tea Room	12-14	10	Cafeteria	15	12			

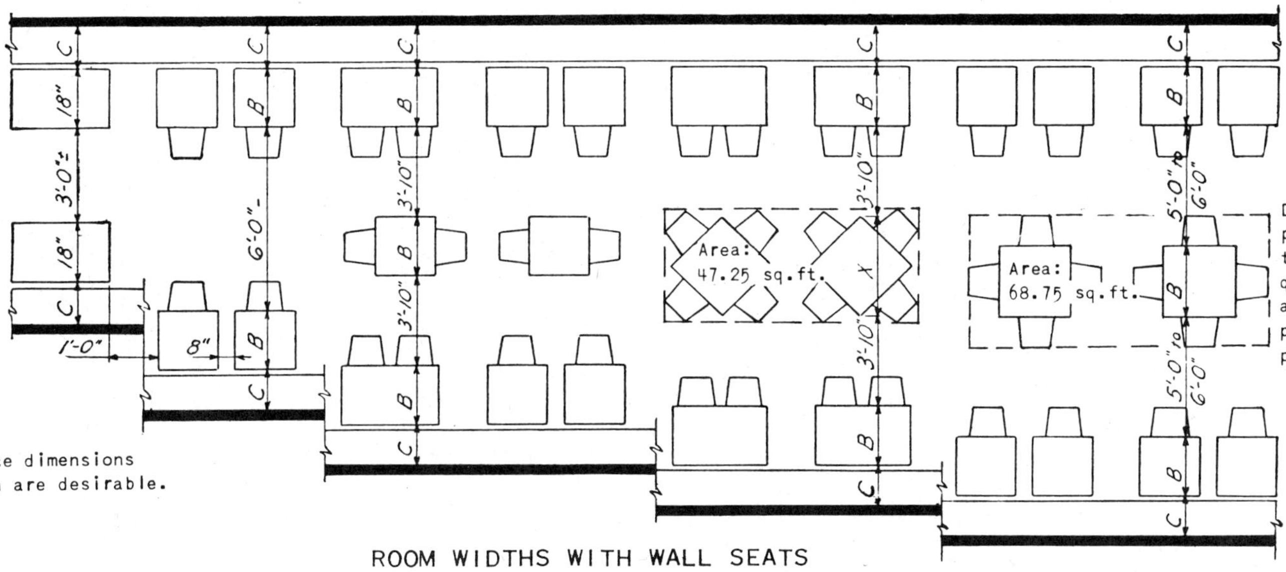
C
18"
3'-0"±
18"
C
1'-0"
8"
B
6'-0"–
C
B
3'-10"
B
3'-10"
B
C
Area:
47.25 sq.ft.
X
3'-10"
3'-10"
B
C
Area:
68.75 sq.ft.
5'-0" to 6'-0"
B
5'-0" to 6'-0"
B
C
Diagonal placement of tables requires less area than parallel placement.
Clearance dimensions as shown are desirable.

ROOM WIDTHS WITH WALL SEATS

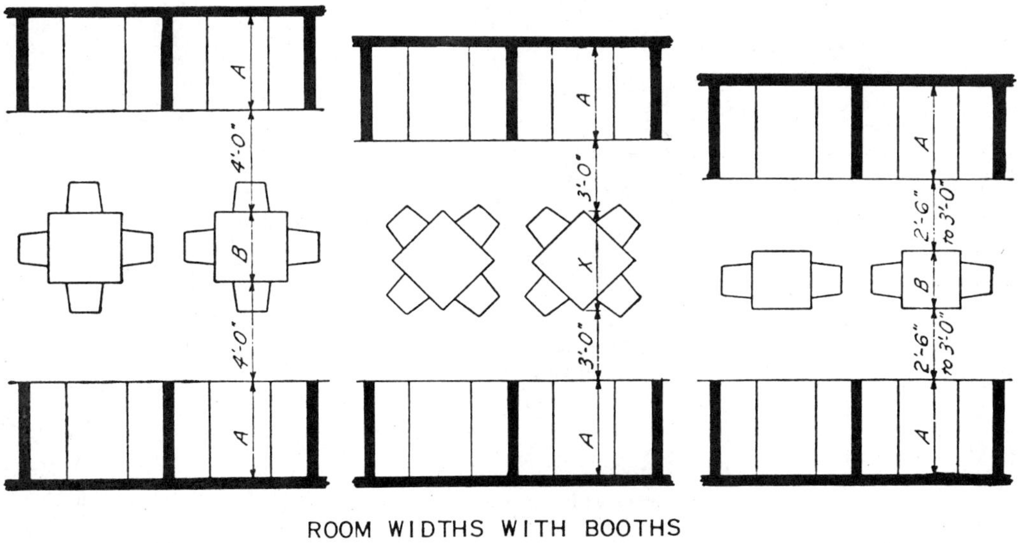
A
4'-0"
B
4'-0"
A
A
3'-0"
X
3'-0"
A
A
2'-6" to 3'-0"
B
2'-6" to 3'-0"
A

ROOM WIDTHS WITH BOOTHS

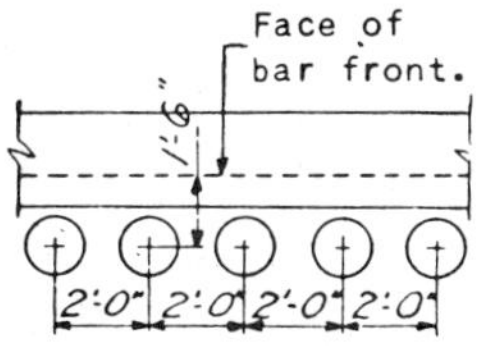
Face of bar front.
1'-6"
2'-0"
2'-0"
2'-0"
2'-0"

SEATS AT BAR

Two small tables allow a more versatile layout than one large table.

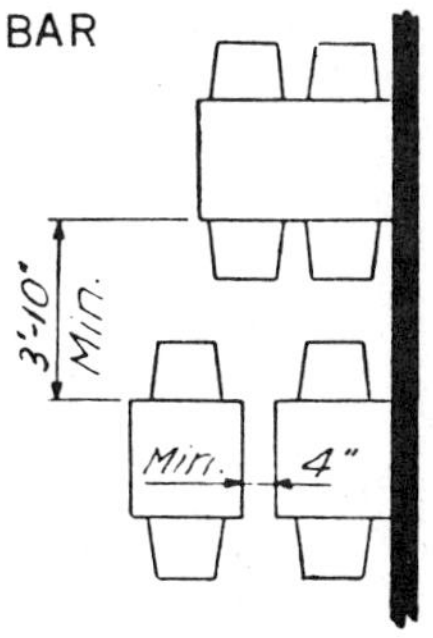
3'-10" Min.
Min.
4"

WALL TABLES

For dimensions A, B, C, and X see preceding page.

Scale: 1/8" = 1'-0"

Data by Anthony J. Amendola, Food Service Equipment Consultant.

SEATS and SEAT SPACING for THEATERS and AUDITORIUMS

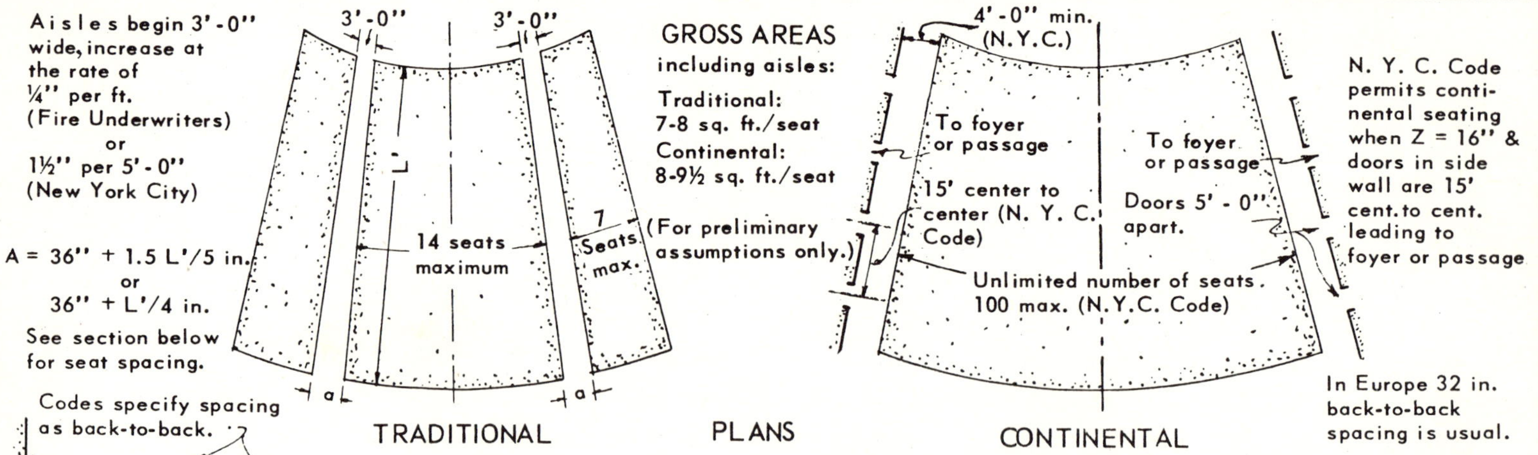
Aisles begin 3'-0" wide, increase at the rate of ¼" per ft. (Fire Underwriters) or 1½" per 5'-0" (New York City)
A = 36" + 1.5 L'/5 in. or 36" + L'/4 in.
See section below for seat spacing.
3'-0"
3'-0"
L'
14 seats maximum
7 Seats max.
a
a
TRADITIONAL
GROSS AREAS including aisles:
Traditional: 7-8 sq. ft./seat
Continental: 8-9½ sq. ft./seat
(For preliminary assumptions only.)
PLANS
4'-0" min. (N.Y.C.)
To foyer or passage
15' center to center (N. Y. C. Code)
To foyer or passage
Doors 5'-0" apart.
Unlimited number of seats. 100 max. (N.Y.C. Code)
N. Y. C. Code permits continental seating when Z = 16" & doors in side wall are 15' cent. to cent. leading to foyer or passage
CONTINENTAL
In Europe 32 in. back-to-back spacing is usual.

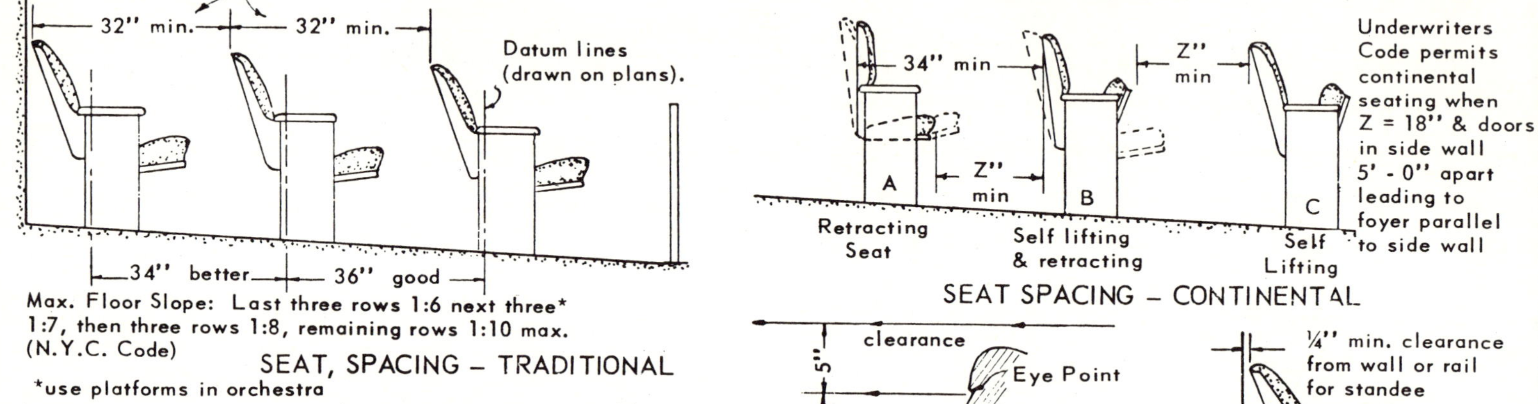
Codes specify spacing as back-to-back.
32" min.
32" min.
Datum lines (drawn on plans).
34" better
36" good
Max. Floor Slope: Last three rows 1:6 next three* 1:7, then three rows 1:8, remaining rows 1:10 max. (N.Y.C. Code)
*use platforms in orchestra
34" min
Z" min
Z" min
A
B
C
Retracting Seat
Self lifting & retracting
Self Lifting
Underwriters Code permits continental seating when Z = 18" & doors in side wall 5'-0" apart leading to foyer parallel to side wall

SEAT, SPACING – TRADITIONAL

SEAT SPACING – CONTINENTAL

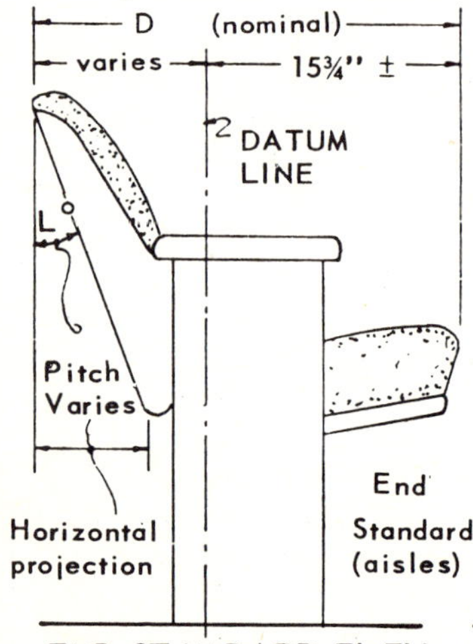
D (nominal)
varies
15¾" ±
DATUM LINE
L°
Pitch Varies
Horizontal projection
End Standard (aisles)

END STANDARD ELEV.

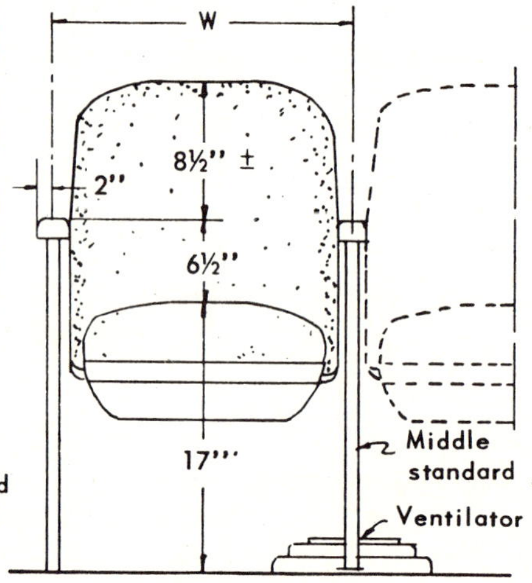
W
2"
8½" ±
6½"
17"
Middle standard
Ventilator

FRONT ELEV.

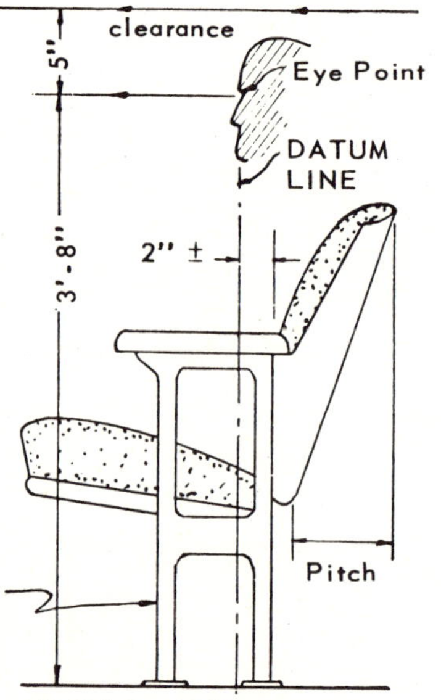
clearance
5"
Eye Point
DATUM LINE
3'-8"
2" ±
Pitch

MIDDLE ST'D. ELEV.

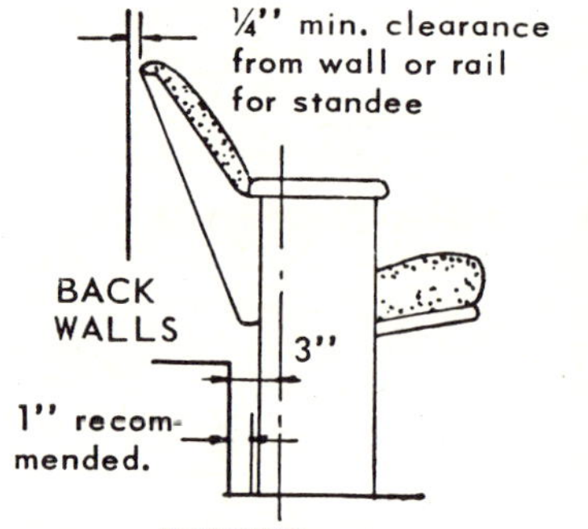
¼" min. clearance from wall or rail for standee
BACK WALLS
3"
1" recommended.

RISERS

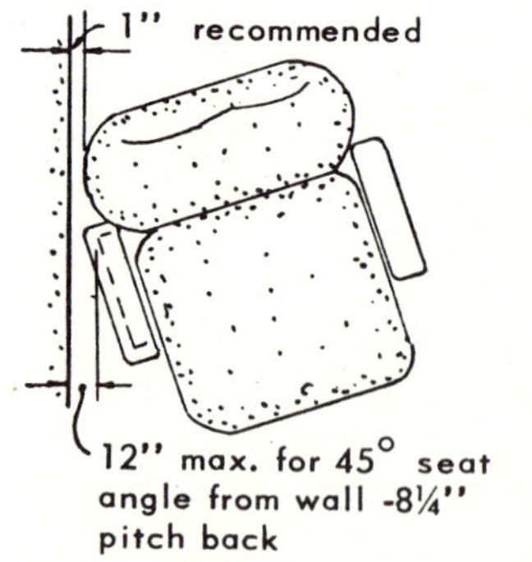
1" recommended
12" max. for 45° seat angle from wall -8¼" pitch back

SIDEWALLS

SIZES	
W	D
18" *	26 7/8"
19" †	27¼"
20"	27 5/8"
21"	28"
22"	28 3/8"
23"	28 3/4"
24"	29 1/8"

* Not recommended

† For ends of rows only.

20" to 22" usual for all locations

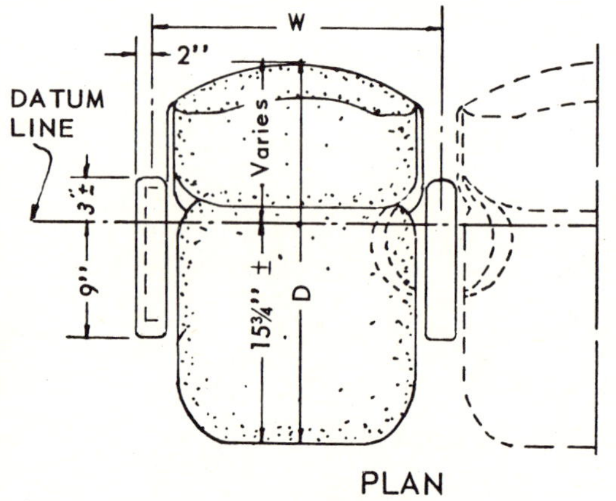
W
2"
DATUM LINE
3±
9"
Varies
15¾" ±
D

PLAN

TYPICAL SEAT DIMENSIONS

Eye point is assumed as 3'-8" above floor, with 5" for top-of-head clearance. These distances are used to calculate floor slope.

PITCH: Measured by angle of horizontal projection 5¼" usual min; 8¼" usual max; 6¾", 7½" standard; 3", 4" special.

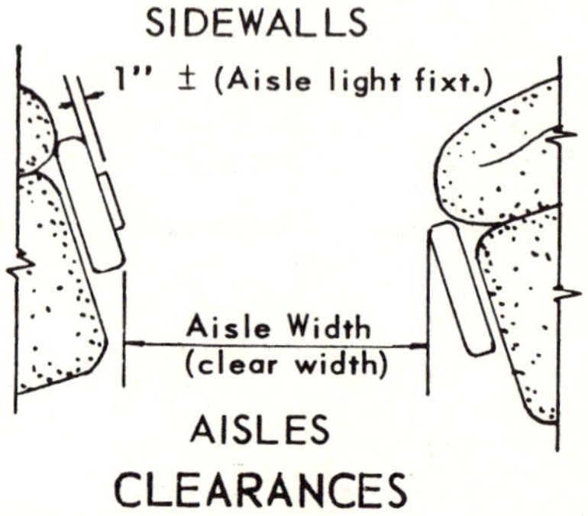
1" ± (Aisle light fixt.)
Aisle Width (clear width)

AISLES

CLEARANCES

Compiled by Andre Halasz A. I. A.

PEW and SEAT DETAILS

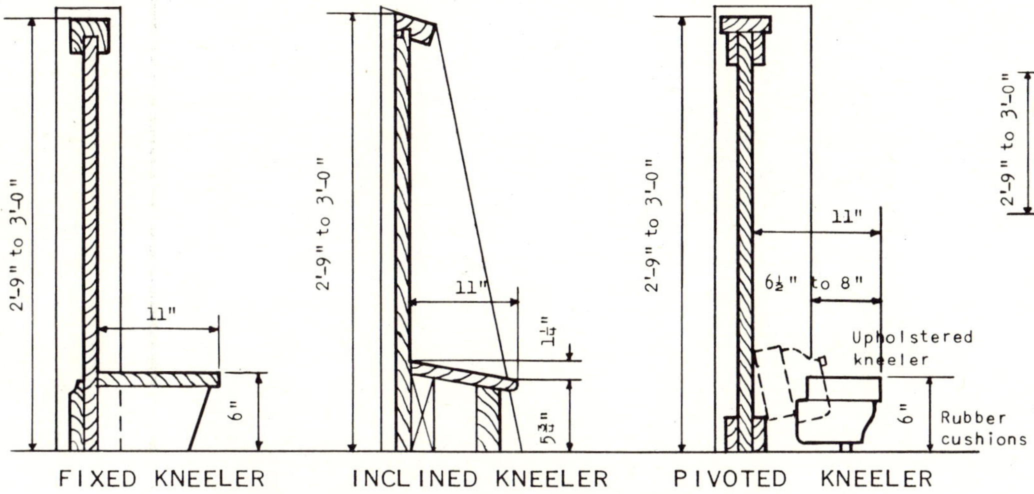
2'-9" to 3'-0"
11"
6"
FIXED KNEELER
2'-9" to 3'-0"
11"
1¼"
5¾"
INCLINED KNEELER
2'-9" to 3'-0"
11"
6½" to 8"
Upholstered kneeler
6"
Rubber cushions
PIVOTED KNEELER

FRONT RAILS WITH KNEELERS

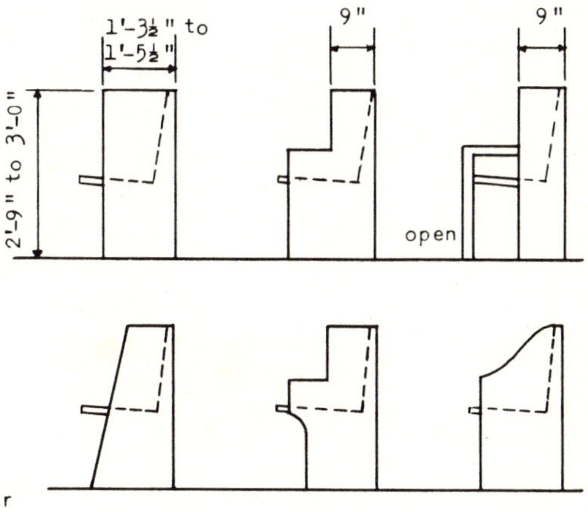
1'-3½" to
1'-5½"
9"
9"
2'-9" to 3'-0"
open

BASIC PEW END FORMS

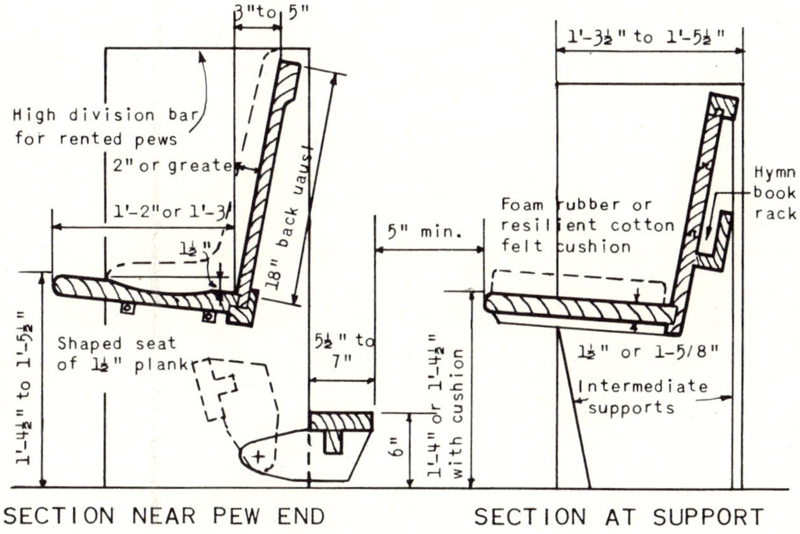
3"to 5"
High division bar for rented pews
2" or greater
1'-2" or 1'-3"
1½"
18" back
Shaped seat of 1½" plank
5½" to 7"
6"
1'-4½" to 1'-5½"
5" min.
1'-3½" to 1'-5½"
Foam rubber or resilient cotton felt cushion
Hymn book rack
1½" or 1-5/8"
Intermediate supports
1'-4" or 1'-4½" with cushion
SECTION NEAR PEW END
SECTION AT SUPPORT

TWO-PIECE BACK AND SEAT

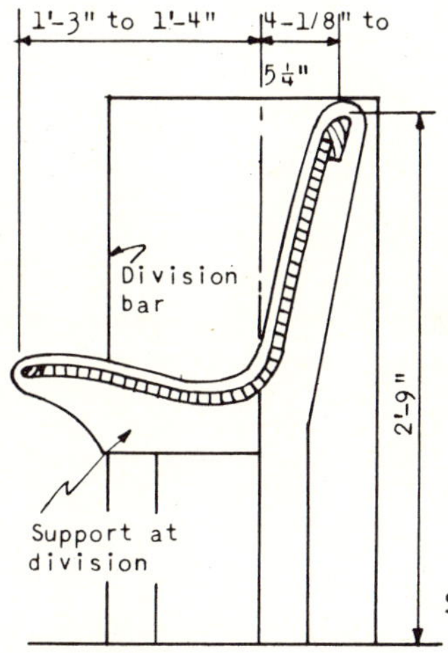
1'-3" to 1'-4"
4-1/8" to 5¼"
Division bar
Support at division
2'-9"

MOLDED PLYWOOD BACK AND SEAT

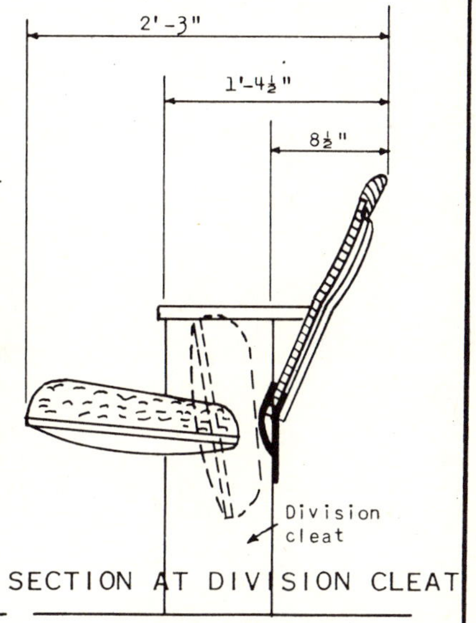
2'-3"
1'-4½"
8½"
Division cleat
SECTION AT DIVISION CLEAT

COMBINATION SEATING

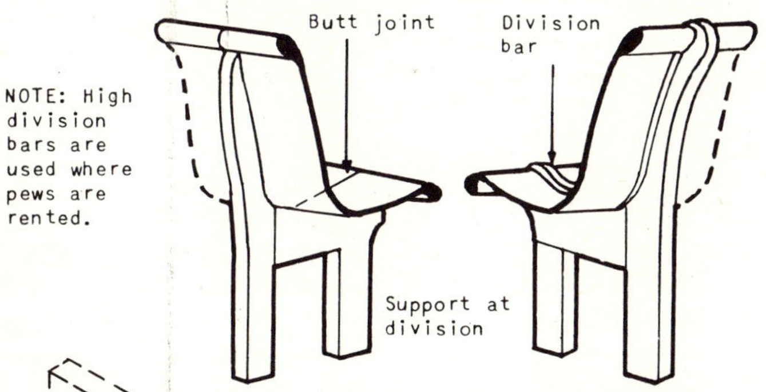
NOTE: High division bars are used where pews are rented.
Butt joint
Division bar
Support at division

JOINING OF PEW SECTIONS

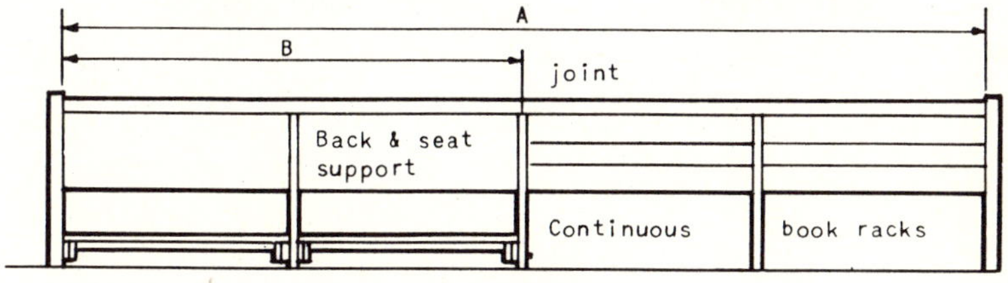
A
B
joint
Back & seat support
Continuous
book racks

PEW REAR

A–Maximum pew length (14 persons–22" seat width) = 25'-8"
B–Maximum length without joint = 12'-0" for molded plywood

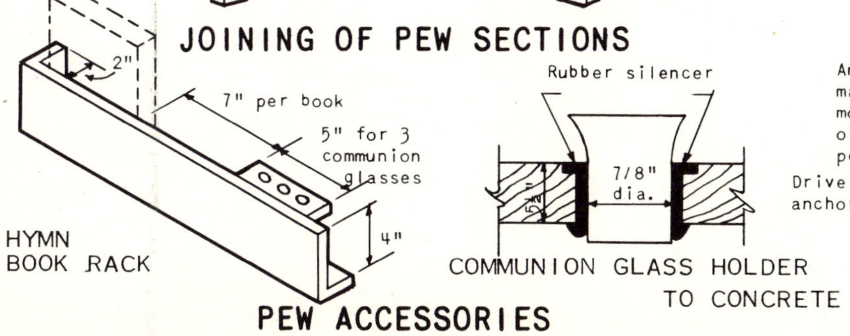
2"
7" per book
5" for 3 communion glasses
4"
HYMN BOOK RACK
Rubber silencer
7/8" dia.
5/8"
COMMUNION GLASS HOLDER

PEW ACCESSORIES

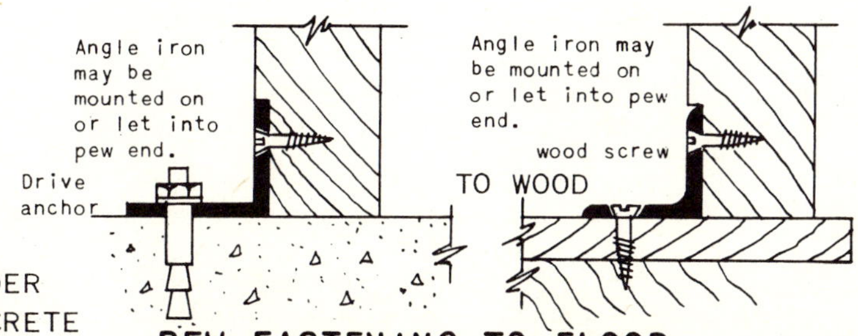
Angle iron may be mounted on or let into pew end.
Drive anchor
TO CONCRETE
Angle iron may be mounted on or let into pew end.
wood screw
TO WOOD

PEW FASTENING TO FLOOR

INDEX